Petersen's

BIG BOOK of AUTO REPAIR

ACKNOWLEDGMENTS

In the compilation of this book, the editors acknowledge with appreciation the helpful sources of information provided by the following automotive manufacturers and their divisions: General Motors Corporation (Chevrolet, Pontiac, Oldsmobile, Buick and Cadillac Divisions), and Chevrolet Transmission Product Assurance Group, Hydra-Matic Division, and Rochester Products Division; Ford Motor Company (Ford and Lincoln-Mercury Divisions), and Service Technical Communications Division; Chrysler Corporation (Dodge and Chrysler-Plymouth Divisions), and Service & Parts Sales Division; and American Motors Corporation.

In addition, thanks are due the following parts/equipment suppliers, and the individuals named, for their cooperative support: Holley Carburetor Division, Colt Industries; Champion Spark Plug Company; Fram Corporation (Autolite Spark Plugs); Michael Goldman, Southern California Regional Occupational Center, Torrance, California (transmission overhaul); and Charles Marinos, Galpin Motors, Sepulveda, California.

Illustrations from factory service manuals and technical training materials relating to specific corporate systems and components are held in copyright by the respective manufacturers, and are reproduced with permission.

BIG BOOK OF AUTO REPAIR

Editorial Director/Spence Murray
Editor/Kalton C. Lahue
Managing Editor/Jim Norris
Technical Editor/Jay Storer
Art Director/Dick Fischer
Layout/Production Coordinator/Dana Sephton
Graphics Designer/George Fukuda
Production Artists/Wanda Acevedo, Bea Hackler, Vera Carmignini, Don Schnabel, Gary Schuster
Editorial Assistant/Angie Ullrich
Cover Designer/Al Isaacs
Cover Illustrator/Chuck Ren

SPECIALTY PUBLICATIONS DIVISION

Erwin M. Rosen/Executive Editor
Spencer Murray/Senior Editor
Al Hall/Editor
Dick Fischer/Art Director
Jim Norris/Managing Editor
Chriss Ohliger Jay/Managing Editor
Jay Storer/Feature Editor
Eric Rickman/Photo Editor
George Fukuda/Assistant Art Director
Angie Ullrich/Editorial Assistant

Library of Congress Catalog Card No. 76-18639

ISBN 0-8227-5046-5

PETERSEN PUBLISHING COMPANY

R.E. Petersen/Chairman of the Board
F.R. Waingrow/President
Robert E. Brown/Sr. Vice President
Dick Day/Sr. Vice President
Jim P. Walsh/Sr. Vice President, National Advertising Director
Robert MacLeod/V.P., Publisher
Thomas J. Siatos/V.P., Group Publisher
Philip E. Trimbach/V.P. Finance
William Porter/V.P., Circulation Director
James J. Krenek/V.P. Manufacturing

Jack Thompson/Assistant Director, Circulation
Nigel P. Heaton/Director, Circulation Administration & Systems
Louis Abbott/Director, Production
Don McGlathery/Director, Research
Al Isaacs/Director, Graphics
Bob D'Olivo/Director, Photography
Carol Johnson/Director, Advertising Administration
Maria Cox/Director, Data Processing

INTRODUCTION

For years the editors of Petersen's automotive magazines and books have been producing publications whose prime purpose has been to enlighten and instruct readers in the fundamental (and some of the finer) points of automotive appreciation and participation. Through clear-cut explanation, coupled with show-it-all pictorial presentation, the basics of design/operation/servicing of automobile systems and components have been made easier to understand. As a result, many hundreds of thousands of car drivers have been informed and guided in better car care.

Now, with the *Big Book of Auto Repair* (more than 750,000 copies in use with this fourth edition), Petersen presents another significant achievement in how-to-do-it publishing that helps readers extend their do-it-yourself involvement. Family car owners, auto shop students, freshman mechanics—all can profit from a copy of this handy service manual kept next to their toolbox.

Despite the seeming complexity of the modern automobile, the properly informed owner-enthusiast can do a considerable share of his own family car maintenance and repair. The mechanical challenge can be successfully met—and this book is specifically designed to help.

The *Big Book* reader turns to the section that applies to his make and year of car in any of the appropriate subject chapters—and then just follows the words and pictures. Logical explanations of how to diagnose the problem are followed by 1-2-3- directions on how to

remove, repair, re-install or replace the troublesome component. In the typical Petersen approach to know-how via show-how, the *Big Book* has scores of photo-caption "how-to's" that break down the most complex repair job into a simple, illustrated step-by-step sequence. It's like having a factory-trained mechanic whispering instructions in your ear while he guides your hands at work.

Each chapter has an index (with page references) to all key sections of the text: description of system operation, troubleshooting diagnosis, test steps, repair procedures, etc. Detailed drawings and photographs of systems and components have been carefully selected to complement the text, and are number-keyed in boldface at points where reference to the illustration will be most helpful. Special attention has been paid to easy-to-read type and clean, organized layouts which invite pre-work reading and facilitate on-the-job reference. And as a final considerate thought, the standard binding is in a smudge-resistant flexible cover which permits the book to fit the contour of a fender during a repair job, or to adapt itself more readily to crowded workbench conditions.

Now that you've been introduced to the *Big Book of Auto Repair,* consider it as a ready, willing and able friend—standing by to lend a helping hand whenever you want to roll up your sleeves and dig into that car repair job you may have been putting off until this moment.

—Erwin M. Rosen

For those readers who may not be fully familiar with the Petersen family of technical automotive books—and who may wish to acquire further specific backgrounding in the theory, design and operation of their car's basic systems and components—here is a list of current titles that can make do-it-yourselfing easier . . . and can help save many dollars in costly labor charges.

Basic Carburetion & Fuel Systems
Basic Ignition & Electrical Systems
Basic Cams, Valves & Exhaust Systems
Basic Clutches & Transmissions
Basic Chassis, Suspension & Brakes
Basic Bodywork & Painting

Basic Automotive Tools
Basic Tune-Up & Test Equipment
Basic Automotive Measuring Tools
Basic Automotive Troubleshooting
Basic Auto Repair Manual
How to Tune Your Car

Petersen Publishing Co., Book Division, 6725 Sunset Blvd., Los Angeles, CA 90028

HOW TO USE THIS BOOK

(and make it pay for itself the first time)

It can probably be safely assumed that most of you holding this book have some knowledge of automotive mechanics, and more than likely, some "hands-on" experience in do-it-yourself car fixing. Some of you may have used an in-depth auto repair manual before; others may be picking up one for the first time. Since this volume is a little different, it may be helpful to all readers to review some basic approaches to using it to save time, trouble and money in working on your auto.

Know your car. To use the particular information that applies to your vehicle, you need to know which specific features your year/model car has—engine displacement, carburetor make, transmission model, auxiliary units, etc. Some systems and components are fairly standard across a given car maker's product line (such as starter, steering system, suspension, driveline, charging system, brakes, etc.). Others may vary with year, model, place of sale, running production changes, parts substitution, etc.

If you bought your car new (and can't quite recall what features you ordered), check your owner's manual or verify with your original dealer's sales records. If your car was acquired used and you're not certain of its parts ancestry, check the item identification listings in the respective chapters of this book, and compare your car's components with those described and illustrated herein. In any event, you must know what exact items your car contains before you can assess what and where the problems may be, and how to fix them.

In addition to knowing what elements make up your automobile, you should try to become consciously familiar with its normal performance level, and what it feels and sounds like when it's in good tune and running trouble-free. Read the various diagnostic charts to be alerted to any symptom of impending trouble—so it can be analyzed and corrected before it reaches the danger (and expensive) point. Whether you're going to tackle a simple or a challenging fix-it job yourself—or take it to a specialist for diagnosis and/or repair—it can be important to your safety and to your pocketbook to have some idea of what's involved.

Study the text and illustrations. When you have determined that your automobile has an operating problem, and you would like to undertake the repair yourself, first carefully read (and re-read) the pertinent text—concentrating also on the accompanying keyed illustrations—until you become familiar with the part's design and operation, what its pieces look like and what they're called, and how it comes apart and goes back together. This familiarity will not only increase your self-confidence, but it will also save you time and trouble in effecting the repairs. Before undertaking any repair job, you should carefully read the "general description" at the beginning of the applicable chapter. This will put the chapter subject into overall perspective, and add to your understanding of the repair procedures involved.

Check your tools. After ascertaining what tools, gauges and test instruments are required or recommended, double-check your toolbox (and, if necessary, those of friends, relatives, or neighbors) to make sure that you can have the proper tools at hand at the moment of need. Make-do application of improper tools or equipment can result in skinned knuckles and damaged parts—as well as a car that you may not be able to put back together.

Where the test or repair procedure calls for a tool that you don't have—and infrequent use may not justify a purchase investment—try to borrow it, or perhaps rent it from the increasing number of automotive tool rental outfits. If you have several cars in your family on which you might be working—or if you can get a neighbor or friend to share the cost and use of a special tool—then buying it may become more practical.

If it's a factory-designed tool that's required, you may have to look a little harder to find the one for a particular job—or this may be that part of the job which should best be turned over to a professional with the specialized equipment. Even if it gets to this—and you should try to determine beforehand if it will become necessary or advisable—you can still save a major portion of the usual hourly labor charges by doing the component removal and reinstallation yourself, plus as many of the various outlined test procedures as you can perform.

It's amazing how many jobs can be handled with the average, fairly complete car owner's tool chest, but bear in mind that certain jobs may require a specialized piece of equipment. If you have determined this ahead of time, you can be properly prepared for the necessary course of action.

Plan the job. This includes more than knowing your car, pre-studying the text and illustrations, and checking over your tools. It also means being realistic about the jobs you're mechanically able to tackle at present, about the time you may have to allow to complete the job(s), and about the cost—and available sources—of replacement parts or special machining that may be needed. Try to run through the entire job in your mind—envisioning all the steps and possible problems involved—before you dive in.

Follow the book. The instructions in this book are based on the recommendations of experienced and factory-trained mechanics. Procedures are given in appropriate detail and in prescribed sequential order. Where deemed necessary, safety precautions are spelled out—and where a procedure may be judged to be beyond the capability of the average do-it-yourselfer, a recommendation is made to consult an expert. We want you to be able to do as much of your own work as you progressively can, but we don't want you to get in over your head in the beginning.

Even though at this point you may feel quite humble in your estimate of your car-mechanic skills, you can probably do more than you think you can—if you go about it prudently. (And don't be afraid to ask a more knowledgeable person—he may even offer to give you a hand.)

Following these guidelines to using this book should help you repair your car more easily, more quickly and more satisfyingly. If you haven't handled a detailed repair manual before, at first glance some of the pages may seem a bit formidable, but after a brief study of some of the text and the keyed illustrations—particularly the photographic how-to sequences—you'll sense a growing self-assurance that will become the prime tool in your do-it-yourself kit.

To avoid duplicating descriptive and repair information when more than one division of a corporate car maker uses the same mechanical systems and components, the material in this book is basically organized first into company and then into division product lines, grouped by year(s). Separate subsections and charts cover distinguishing differences in applications such as engines, transmissions, auxiliary units, specifications, etc.

Listed below are the auto manufacturers and their respective car families treated in this volume. Included in the given name groups are the various models offered under that series nameplate since 1970. The specific information applicable to a given car by year(s) will be found under the appropriate identifying section heading.

AMERICAN MOTORS CORPORATION

Ambassador	Gremlin	Pacer
AMX	Hornet	Rebel
Concord	Javelin	Spirit
	Matador	Wagons

CHRYSLER CORPORATION

CHRYSLER-IMPERIAL

Cordoba	New Yorker	Town & Country
Le Baron	300	Wagons
Newport	St. Regis	Imperial

DODGE

Aspen	Dart	Monaco
Challenger	Demon	Omni
Charger	Diplomat	Polaro
Coronet	Magnum	Swinger
		Wagons

PLYMOUTH

Barracuda	GTX	Scamp
Belvedere	Horizon	Sport Fury
'Cuda	Road Runner	Valiant
Duster	Satellite	Volaré
Fury		Wagons

FORD MOTOR COMPANY

FORD

Custom	Granada	Pinto
Elite	LTD	Ranchero
Fairlane	LTD II	Thunderbird
Fairmont	Maverick	Torino
Falcon	Mustang	Wagons
Galaxie	Mustang II	

LINCOLN-MERCURY

Lincoln Continental	Cougar	Montego
Lincoln Continental	Cyclone	Monterey
Mark III–V	Marauder	Versailles
Bobcat	Marquis	Wagons
Capri	Monarch	Zephyr
Comet		

GENERAL MOTORS CORPORATION

BUICK

Apollo	Gran Sport	Skyhawk
Centurion	Le Sabre	Skylark
Century	Regal	Wildcat
Electra	Riviera	Wagons

CADILLAC

Cadillac	Eldcrado	Seville

CHEVROLET

Bel Air	Chevette	Monte Carlo
Biscayne	Corvette	Monza
Camaro	El Camino	Nova
Caprice	Impala	Vega and
Chevelle	Malibu	Cosworth Vega
		Wagons

OLDSMOBILE

Cutlass	4-4-2	Starfire
Delta 88	Ninety-Eight	Toronado
F-85	Omega	Wagons

PONTIAC

Astre	Grand Am	Phoenix
Bonneville	Grand Prix	Sunbird
Catalina	Grand Ville	Tempest
Executive	GTO	Ventura
Firebird	Le Mans	Wagons

CONTENTS

INDEX

STARTING SYSTEMS

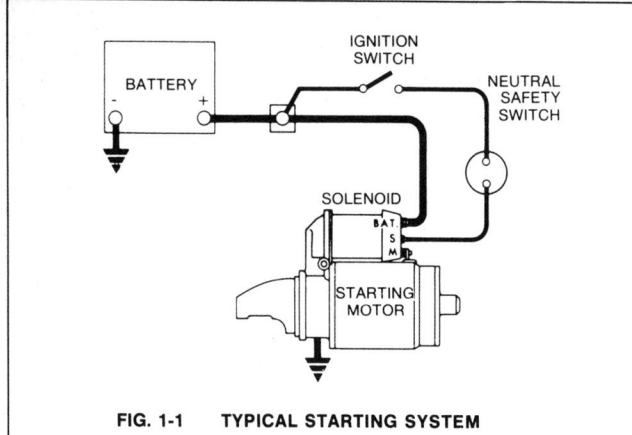

FIG. 1-1 **TYPICAL STARTING SYSTEM**

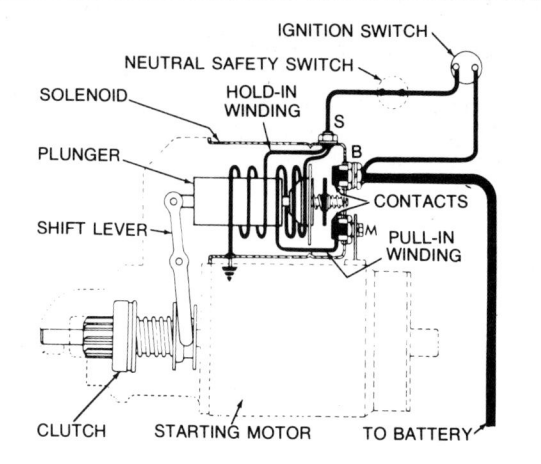

FIG. 1-2 **DELCO-REMY STARTING MOTOR DESIGN**

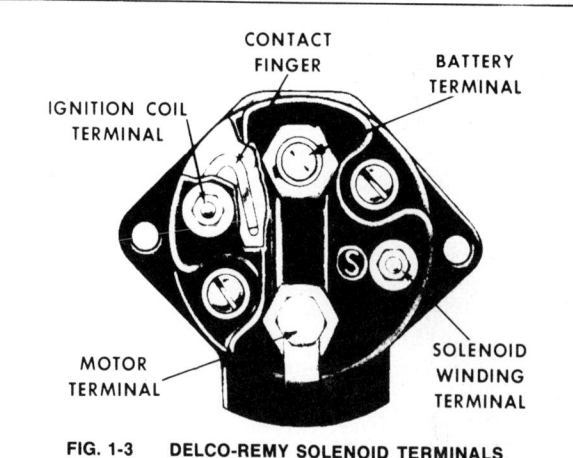

FIG. 1-3 **DELCO-REMY SOLENOID TERMINALS**

STARTING CIRCUITS

Each make of car has its own typical layout for the starting system circuit. This is usually determined by the type of starter motor and drive used. However, the choice of transmission and optional accessories offered may also be influential. Yet, all automotive starting systems are basically similar in their design and function **(Fig. 1-1)** and consist of the following components:

1. Battery—The automotive storage battery supplies the energy required to crank the engine and provides the necessary power for the ignition system. It also supplies current (for a limited time) to meet electrical system requirements when the total system demand is greater than the alternator output.

2. Ignition Switch—A key-operated switch located in the steering column which controls current flow in the primary ignition circuit and energizes the starting circuit to crank the engine.

3. Neutral Safety Switch—Prevents the starting motor from cranking the engine unless the automatic transmission is in PARK or NEUTRAL. It may be located either on the transmission, where it grounds the solenoid, or on the steering column, where it can contact the shift linkage, and is usually combined with the back-up lamp switch in a single unit. The 1971-79 Fords and 1974-79 Cadillacs with a column mounted shift lever rely upon an ignition lock cylinder-to-shift lever interlock instead of a neutral safety switch to prevent starting of the engine in any gear other than PARK or NEUTRAL. Some manual transmission cars use a clutch linkage mounted safety switch to prevent the starting motor from operating until the clutch pedal is depressed.

4. Starter Solenoid—A switch whose primary function is to make contact for the starting motor. When mounted directly on or in the starting motor, it also acts to mesh the starter drive clutch with the engine flywheel.

5. Starting Motor—This special type of motor is designed for intermittent use only. It converts electrical energy drawn from the battery into mechanical energy or cranking output. As such, it should not be operated for periods of more than 15-20 seconds without a pause to let it cool.

6. Wiring Circuit—The connecting cables which transmit electricity as required from one component to another.

GENERAL MOTORS DESCRIPTION

Since General Motors has used the same basic Delco starter design for many years, the system now in use shows few if any changes from one model year to the next **(Fig. 1-2)**. The solenoid is mounted directly on the top of Delco starting motors and engages the starter drive with the engine flywheel, as well as closing the internal contacts to make the final connection between the positive battery terminal and the starter windings.

There are three terminals located on the end of the solenoid cover **(Fig. 1-3)**, the largest of which is connected directly to the battery by a heavy cable. One of the two smaller terminals is connected to the ignition switch and actuates the starter when the switch is turned to the START position. Resistance wiring used as ballast in the ignition system connects the ignition switch and the coil, with a spliced wire running to the other small solenoid terminal. When the starter is actuated, the solenoid contacts pick up current directly from the larger cable connecting the starting motor to the battery and send full battery voltage to the coil by way of the spliced wire.

Once the engine has started, the solenoid disengages the starter drive, cutting off current flow from the battery. Current for the ignition system now flows from the ignition switch by way of the resistance wire. Connections between the resistance wire and the plain wire have been handled differently over the years. Some GM cars run two wires to the coil—one, the resistance wire from the ignition switch, and the other, the plain wire from the starter solenoid. In other models, a simplified wire loom construction is used—the resistance wire ends at or near the starting motor and the plain wire runs from that point to the coil.

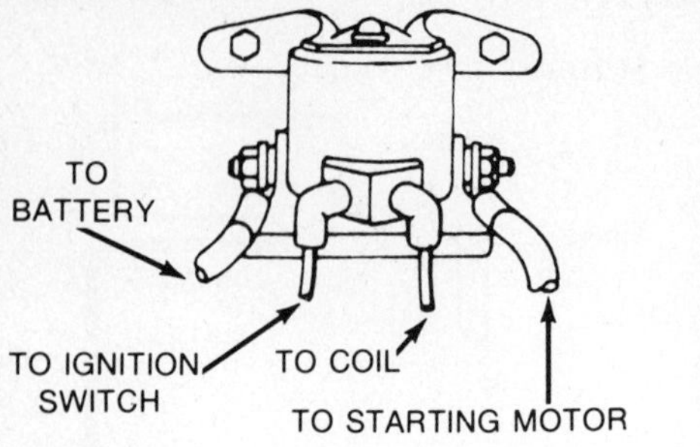

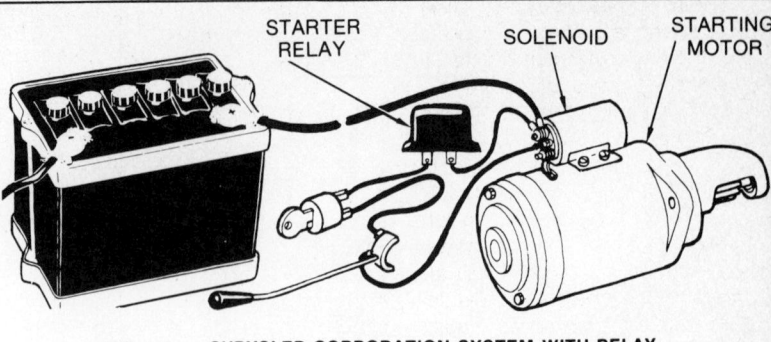

FIG. 1-4   FORD MOTOR COMPANY STARTER RELAY

TO BATTERY

TO IGNITION SWITCH   TO COIL

TO STARTING MOTOR

FIG. 1-5   CHRYSLER CORPORATION SYSTEM WITH RELAY

STARTER RELAY   SOLENOID   STARTING MOTOR

Current GM cars use two cables connected to the positive battery terminal. The larger one serves the starter only, and the smaller cable supplies the rest of the car's electrical system. This small cable usually passes to the horn relay first, with wires radiating from that point to provide electricity to other parts of the car.

FORD MOTOR COMPANY DESCRIPTION

With the exception of some 429- and all 460-cu.-in. engines, all Ford Motor Company cars use a positive-engagement, or Bendix-drive, starting motor. With this design, there is no need to mount the starter solenoid or relay on the starting motor itself; thus, on Ford, Mercury and Lincoln cars, it is a separate sealed unit **(Fig. 1-4),** usually mounted on the firewall or fender housing inside the engine compartment. A single heavy cable between the relay and the positive battery terminal supplies both the starting motor and the rest of the electrical system with current.

This starter relay has two large terminals and two small ones. The cable from the positive battery terminal is connected to one of the large terminals, and a similar cable from the other terminal connects the relay to the starting motor. One of the small terminals is connected to the ignition switch and, when the key is turned to the START position, current is directed to the relay, causing it to close the main circuit between the battery and the starting motor. Current to the ignition switch, as well as to the rest of the car's electrical system, is drawn from a wire attached to the large terminal on the relay to which the battery cable is connected. The other small terminal on the relay supplies full unballasted battery current to the ignition coil during starting.

CHRYSLER CORPORATION DESCRIPTION

Chrysler Corporation cars use a solenoid in or on the starter and incorporate a relay **(Fig. 1-5)** in the wiring circuit. When the ignition key is turned to the START position, this starter relay bypasses the ignition ballast and energizes the solenoid on the starting motor. Current for the entire electrical system is drawn from a terminal on the starter relay which has its own connection with the positive battery terminal. The solenoid at the starting motor simply couples the starting motor to the heavy cable that leads to the positive battery terminal. Once the engine has started and the ignition key is returned to the ON position, the ignition system is no longer supplied by the relay. The ignition system now receives its power through the ballast resistor, which takes its electrical energy from the ignition terminal on the alternator regulator.

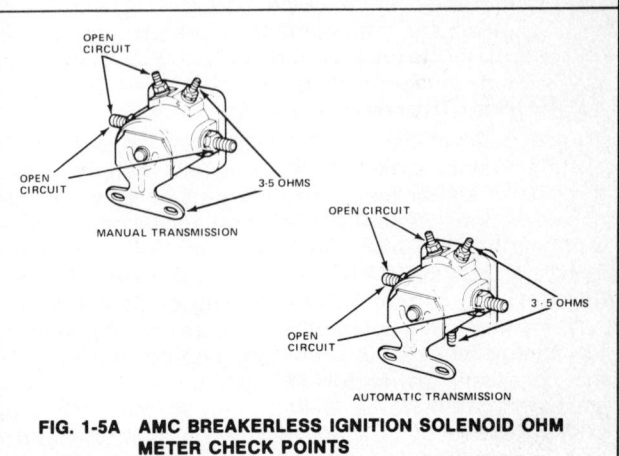

OPEN CIRCUIT

OPEN CIRCUIT   3-5 OHMS

MANUAL TRANSMISSION

OPEN CIRCUIT

OPEN CIRCUIT   3-5 OHMS

AUTOMATIC TRANSMISSION

FIG. 1-5A   AMC BREAKERLESS IGNITION SOLENOID OHM METER CHECK POINTS

AMERICAN MOTORS DESCRIPTION

American Motors cars referred to in this volume use the Autolite-Motorcraft positive-engagement starting motor and separate sealed relay unit discussed under "Ford Motor Company Description." All testing and overhaul procedures specified for this starting motor apply to AMC-built cars. Specifications are provided as given by the AMC factory.

There are, however, some differences in configuration of the system and components used. For this reason, do not try to substitute Ford parts for AMC components. A revised starting motor design was introduced as a running change during the 1977 model year. This design incorporates a simplified brush guide/spring assembly, a revised drive yoke clamp, and relocation of the input terminal on the end plate at the brush end. Different sized starting motors are used according to engine size. The cross-sectioned area of the field coils determines the performance level of the starting motor.

Two different starter solenoids are used with AMC engines equipped with breakerless ignitions **(Fig. 1-5A).** They differ in the method of grounding the solenoid pull-in coil. On manual transmission cars, the ground circuit is completed through the solenoid mounting bracket. The pull-in coil is grounded on automatic transmission cars by using an extra terminal on the solenoid. This terminal is connected to the NEUTRAL safety switch on the transmission and ground is completed only when the transmission is in NEUTRAL or PARK. These solenoids are very similar in appearance to those used with breaker-point ignitions, but differ internally. Use of the wrong solenoid can damage the NEUTRAL safety switch. *Do not loosen the retaining nuts on the blade terminal studs—this can cause a loss of internal connection and require replacement of the solenoid.*

THE AUTOMOTIVE BATTERY

Automotive batteries **(Fig. 1-6)** consist of six individual cells, each a battery in itself producing approximately 2 volts, depending upon its state of charge. The cells contain a number of positive and negative plates of lead which react chemically with battery electrolyte in such a way that there is a flow of electrons set up between the plates. Cells are connected in series—the negative terminal of one cell is joined to the positive terminal of the next, and so on. This produces a voltage output for the entire battery equal to the sum of that produced by the individual cells. The positive pole of the first cell and the negative pole of the last provide the terminals to which the car's battery cables are attached. Each cell is separated from the others so that there is no mixing of electrolyte from cell to cell.

As battery current is used, the sponge lead of the negative plates is partially converted into crystalline normal lead sulphate, while the lead dioxide of the positive plates is converted to lead sulphate. When all the available electrolyte acid has been absorbed into the chemical structure of the plates, the battery becomes fully discharged. But directing current into the battery cells reverses the chemical reaction by driving sulphuric acid from the plates and increasing the acid content of the electrolyte. Once this is accomplished, the battery is ready to start producing current once again.

In actual practice, the electrolyte is kept at a steady state of acidity by the current delivered to it by the car's alternator. After running the starting motor, the amount of acid in the electrolyte is low, because the heavy demand for current has caused it to be absorbed into the plates. Because the voltage of the battery is now low, current will flow from the alternator into the battery.

FIG. 1-6   BATTERY CONSTRUCTION

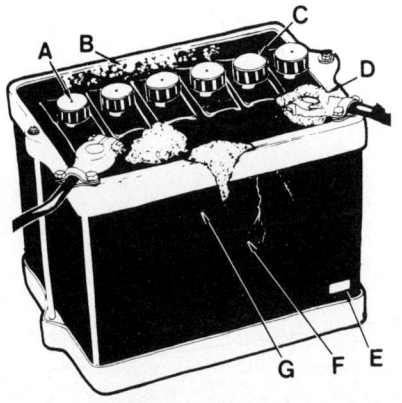

FIG. 1-7   VISUAL BATTERY INSPECTION

BATTERY SERVICE PROCEDURES

VISUAL INSPECTION

Before undertaking any testing procedures, make a careful visual inspection of the battery to check for defects shown in **Fig. 1-7.** What you see can be very useful as well as important when analyzing test readings. Follow the inspection procedure outlined below:

1. Make sure that the filler/vent cap holes (A) are not plugged.

2. Check the battery case top (B) for dirt and electrolyte; this will cause excessive self-discharge and should be removed.

3. Look for raised cell covers (C) or a warped battery case. Either of these indicates the battery has been overheated or overcharged.

4. Check battery terminals, clamps and cables (D) for loose connections, corrosion, etc.

5. Locate the "ampere-hour rating" if it is stamped on the battery case (E) and compare it to the manufacturer's specifications. The battery rating should equal or exceed the specifications for normal starting system operation.

6. Inspect the battery case (F) for cracks and leaks.

7. Remove filler/vent caps and check electrolyte level (G). If it is below the top of the plates, add water. If it is low, but not below the plate level, test cells with a hydrometer before adding water.

MEASURING SPECIFIC GRAVITY

A battery hydrometer is used to measure the specific gravity of the electrolyte. This instrument indicates how much unused sulphuric acid remains in the electrolyte and thus determines the battery's state of charge. The hydrometer used should be graduated in 0.005 intervals of specific gravity from 1.160 to 1.320; markings should be accurate to within 0.002 specific gravity. To test specific gravity with a hydrometer:

1. Remove the filler/vent cap from each battery cell.

2. Insert the tube at the bottom of the tester into each cell in turn.

3. Hold the hydrometer vertically and squeeze the rubber bulb gently, then release it. This will draw sufficient electrolyte into the tester barrel to float the test gauge freely.

4. Withdraw the hydrometer from the cell and hold in a vertical position at eye level so that the float stands free of the barrel sides.

5. Read the float scale at the point where the surface of the liquid meets it. With some hydrometer designs, surface tension can cause a curvature of the liquid against the float—disregard any curvature or the reading will be incorrect **(Fig. 1-8).**

6. Compare the specific gravity reading obtained with **Fig. 1-9.**

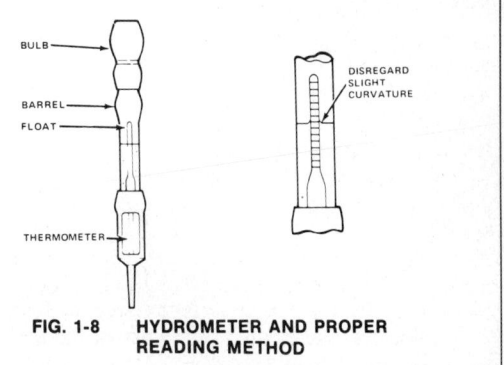

FIG. 1-8   HYDROMETER AND PROPER
READING METHOD

INTERPRETING HYDROMETER TEST RESULTS

Any reading below 1.220 indicates a poor charge condition. Below 1.150 means that, for all practical purposes, the cell is dead. If the reading of any one cell is lower than the others by 0.50 or more, that particular cell is shorted and the battery will have to be replaced.

When all cells test in the 1.220 or below range, the battery should be recharged with a charging unit, leaving the filler/vent caps loose or completely off. The cells can be tested during charging to determine when the process is complete. When the specific gravity remains the same in three successive readings taken an hour apart, and all cells are expelling gas (or the electrolyte is bubbling), the battery has accepted as much of a charge as it can hold. The expelled gas (hydrogen) is highly explosive; do not smoke, create sparks or bring an open flame near the battery.

To determine the actual specific gravity at this point, it is necessary to let the battery sit, off-charge, for an hour before taking another hydrometer reading. If charging does not bring the battery cells up to at least a 50% charge, the battery will have to be replaced.

TEMPERATURE CORRECTION

As ambient temperature increases, the battery electrolyte expands, reducing the specific gravity; as temperature decreases, the electrolyte contracts and the specific gravity increases. Battery hydrometer readings are considered as correct when the electrolyte temperature is 80°F. For each 10° above 80°F, you must add 0.004 (also known as four points of gravity) to the original reading; for each 10° below 80°, you must subtract 0.004 from the reading **(Fig. 1-10).**

Unless these variations in specific gravity and temperature are taken into consideration, the hydrometer reading will provide only an approximate indication of the amount of acid in the electrolyte when its temperature is other than 80°F. Temperature correction can be made by taking the temperature of the electrolyte with a battery immersion thermometer before taking the specific gravity reading or by using a hydrometer equipped with a thermometer.

BATTERY CAPACITY TEST

Also referred to as a "load test," this check of a battery's ability to provide current and maintain the minimum required voltage determines its overall condition. Satisfactory capacity tests can only be made when the battery has a specific gravity of at least 1.220. Battery electrolyte should be at room temperature (70°F ± 10°F) before performing this following test:

1. Connect a battery/starter tester as shown in **Fig. 1-11.**

2. With the load control knob in the OFF position, set the voltmeter selector switch to the range closest to 12 volts.

3. Adjust the load control knob clockwise until the ammeter reads three times the battery's ampere-hour rating.

4. Hold the load constant for 15 seconds, read the voltmeter scale and reduce the load by turning the knob to the OFF position.

5. A voltmeter reading of not less than 9.5 volts for a 12-volt battery indicates that the battery's output capacity is good and the battery can be placed back in service.

STATE OF CHARGE	SPECIFIC GRAVITY AS USED IN COLD AND TEMPERATE CLIMATES
Fully Charged	1.265
75% Charged	1.225
50% Charged	1.190
25% Charged	1.155
Discharged	1.120

FIG. 1-9   SPECIFIC GRAVITY CHART

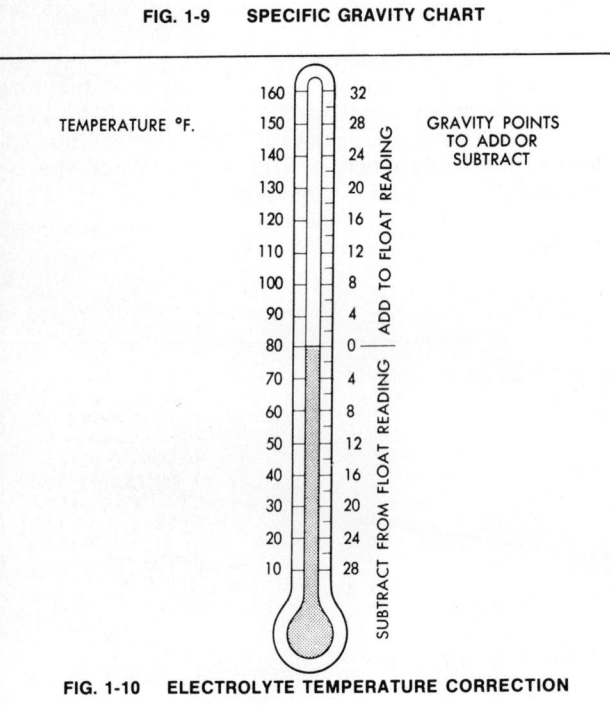

FIG. 1-10   ELECTROLYTE TEMPERATURE CORRECTION

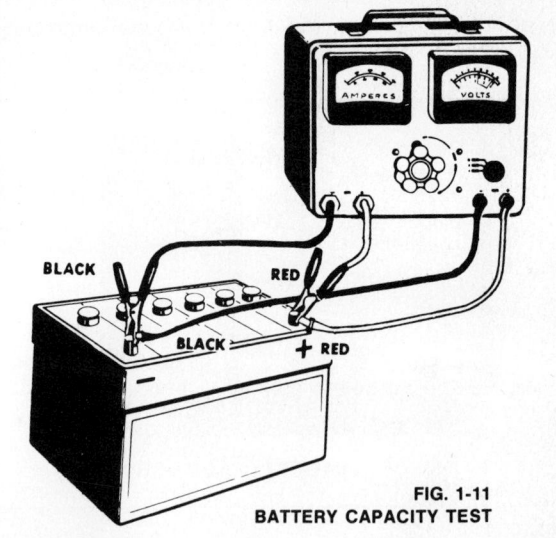

FIG. 1-11
BATTERY CAPACITY TEST

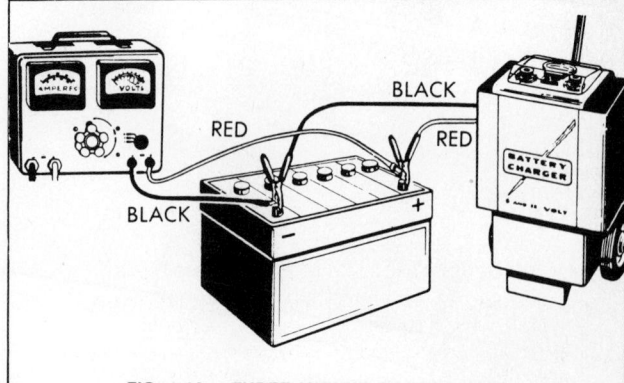

FIG. 1-12   THREE-MINUTE CHARGE TEST

6. If the reading is below 9.5 volts for a 12-volt battery, a possible defective condition is indicated and the three-minute charge test should be used to determine whether the battery is defective or simply discharged.

THREE-MINUTE CHARGE TEST

This test should not be performed on the battery unless it has already failed the capacity test. Battery electrolyte temperature should *not* be below 60°F.

1. Connect the battery charger and battery/starter tester to battery as shown in **Fig. 1-12.**

2. Turn on the battery charger, adjusting it to produce a 40-amp fast-charge rate for 12-volt battery.

3. Wait three minutes and, with the battery still on fast charge, read the voltmeter scale.

4. If total voltage during the fast charge *exceeds* 15.5 volts, the battery is sulphated or worn out. While it

is sometimes possible to rejuvenate a sulphated battery by slow charging, it is usually better to replace it.

BATTERY LEAKAGE TEST

When the top of a battery is covered with dirt and/or electrolyte, the contamination can result in a continuous battery discharge, because it produces a path which battery current can follow. To check for leakage:

1. Connect a battery/starter tester to the battery as shown in **Fig. 1-13.**

2. Adjust the voltage selector switch to the 4-volt position.

3. Move a screwdriver, with the voltmeter lead attached to it, around the top surface of the battery, using care not to touch the positive battery terminal.

4. Watch the voltmeter needle as the screwdriver probe is moved; if the needle does not deflect, there is

---

STARTING SYSTEM DIAGNOSIS

CONDITION		CORRECTION		CONDITION		CORRECTION

STARTER WILL NOT OPERATE

(a)	Battery discharged or defective.	**(a)**	Check headlight operation; if dim or will not glow, charge battery. If battery cannot pass light-load test after charging, replace.
(b)	Poor cable wire connections.	**(b)**	Check connections at battery, solenoid, cowl connector, and ignition switch.
(c)	Neutral start switch out of adjustment or defective.	**(c)**	Move shift lever through all ranges with foot brake set and key in start position. If starter cranks in R and D, position shift lever in N with key off, remove neutral start switch, reinstall and try starting in N and P. If starter cranks in L2 and L1, replace switch.
(d)	Fusible link burned out.	**(d)**	Inspect condition of fusible link. If burned, replace and recheck starting.
(e)	Ignition switch defective.	**(e)**	Shift lever in neutral and turn ignition switch ON to see if wipers and turn signals operate. If not, check for disconnected cowl and/or ignition switch connector or burned fusible link. If all are OK, replace ignition switch.
(f)	Solenoid defective.	**(f)**	Connect voltmeter to solenoid ''S'' terminal and starter frame. Take reading when trying to start engine; if reading is 9 volts or more, replace solenoid.
(g)	Seat belts not fastened.	**(g)**	Fasten seat belts.

STARTER CLICKS BUT WILL NOT CRANK

(a)	Poor connections at battery and/or starter.	**(a)**	Check and retighten connections.
(b)	Solenoid or starter motor defective.	**(b)**	Remove starter motor, check solenoid and/or starter and repair or replace.

STARTER CRANKS ENGINE SLOWLY

(a)	Battery discharged or defective.	**(a)**	Check headlight operation
(b)	Poor connections at battery and/or starter.	**(b)**	Check and retighten connections.
(c)	Wrong starter motor on car.	**(c)**	Check part numbers to insure that starter is correct for car; replace if incorrect.
(d)	Starter is defective.	**(d)**	Remove starter motor, inspect bushings and repair as necessary.
(e)	Cranking voltage is low.	**(e)**	Check cranking voltage at positive terminal of ignition coil; it should be at least 9.5 volts. If less, check condition of battery, cables and starter connections. If over 9.5 volts, low temperature or too heavy oil may be causing excessive drag.

STARTER SPINS BUT WILL NOT CRANK ENGINE

(a)	Armature shaft dirty or corroded.	**(a)**	Clean shaft and lubricate with lithium soap grease.
(b)	Starter drive clutch defective.	**(b)**	Check drive clutch. Replace if necessary.
(c)	Missing teeth on flywheel ring gear.	**(c)**	Replace flywheel ring gear and inspect teeth on drive pinion gear. Replace starter drive if necessary.

STARTER CRANKS ENGINE BUT IS EXCESSIVELY NOISY

(a)	Drive pinion to ring gear clearance incorrect.	**(a)**	Measure distance between tip of pinion tooth and root of two ring gear teeth with round feeler gauge at three locations around ring gear. Distance should be within .025 to .060-in. If distance is less than .025-in., shim starter away from engine block at both attaching bolts. If distance is greater than .060-in., shim to maximum of .30-in. at outboard attaching bolt. Recheck for correct clearance.
(b)	Starter drive or ring gear is defective.	**(b)**	Check drive and ring gear; replace if necessary.
(c)	Starter bushing worn.	**(c)**	Replace.

no loss of energy. If the needle moves, it indicates a continuous battery discharge, and the battery should be removed from the car and its top thoroughly cleaned with a solution of baking soda and ammonia or water. Dry thoroughly before returning the battery to the car.

SERVICE-FREE ENERGIZERS (BATTERIES)

The charging current from the alternator is hot. This heat is transmitted through the plate grids and causes evaporation of the water in the electrolyte. The result is a low cell fluid level and a battery which appears to have "lost" water. By substituting calcium alloy plate grids for the traditional antimony grids, internal heat is sharply reduced in a bettery, as less charging current is required. This change in battery construction has resulted in the so-called "Lifetime" or "Maintenance-Free" battery.

Such batteries have sealed tops with no vent caps. Venting to relieve internal pressure is usually accomplished by two small slits on the battery case sides at the top. In addition to requiring no water during its useful life, the maintenance-free battery reduces terminal corrosion, which is nothing more than condensation of normal battery gassing.

Delco Freedom—and some Chrysler batteries—use a charge indicator eye, much like that found in older Delco Energizers. This indicator is really a built-in temperature-corrected hydrometer. Testing maintenance-free batteries requires a somewhat different procedure from that used with older battery designs.

TESTING DELCO & OTHER MAINTENANCE-FREE BATTERIES

(Steps 1 & 2 apply only to Delco Batteries)

1. Clean the charge indicator eye before inspecting it **(Fig. 1-14.)** If necessary use a light to determine the color of the eye. If the indicator is dark, the energizer has sufficient electrolyte. If it is light, the electrolyte level is too low and the energizer must be replaced.

2. If a green dot is visible in the middle of the eye, the energizer can be tested; if no green dot can be seen, the energizer must be charged until the dot appears before it is tested. Should the indicator appear clear or light yellow, the battery is serviceable, but must not be tested, charged, or jump-started. If starting problems persist, replace the energizer with a new one.

3. Disconnect the High Energy Ignition wire harness

at the distributor and crank the engine for 15 seconds to remove any surface charge.

4. Connect a voltmeter across the battery terminals and apply the following load according to battery type: 85-5, 170 amps; 85-4, 130 amps; 87-5, 210 amps.

5. Read the voltmeter after 15 seconds and remove the load.

6. Estimate the ambient battery temperature and refer to **Fig. 1-15.** If the voltmeter reading is less than the minimum specified at the estimated temperature, replace the energizer.

STARTING SYSTEM TESTS

The following starting system tests can be performed with the starting motor on the car. On Ford Motor Company cars, the vacuum line to the Thermactor bypass valve should be disconnected before any cranking tests are performed. After testing is completed, run the engine three minutes before reconnecting the vacuum line. Always check the battery before attempting any of the tests, since a battery in less than satisfactory condition will adversely affect the results, leading to incorrect conclusions.

CRANKING VOLTAGE TEST

1. Connect a voltmeter as shown in **Fig. 1-16.**

2. Disconnect the distributor primary lead, or electronic distributor wire harness, to prevent the engine from starting when cranked.

ELECTROLYTE TEMPERATURE F	MINIMUM VOLTAGES*
Down to 80°	9.6
70°	9.6
60°	9.5
50°	9.4
40°	9.3
30°	9.1
20°	8.9
10°	8.7
0	8.5

*Voltage must not drop below minimum listed at given temperature when battery is subjected to the proper load for 15 seconds and is 1.200 specific gravity @ 80° F or more.

FIG. 1-15   VOLTAGE AND TEMPERATURE CHART

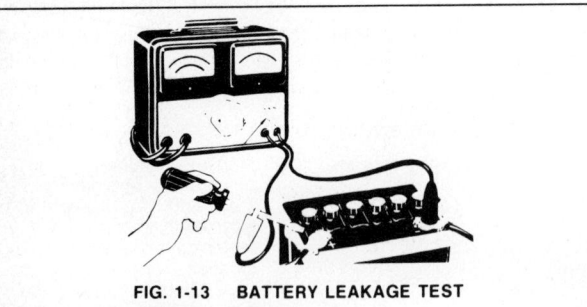

FIG. 1-13   BATTERY LEAKAGE TEST

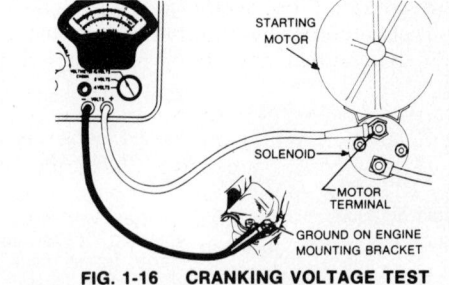

FIG. 1-16   CRANKING VOLTAGE TEST

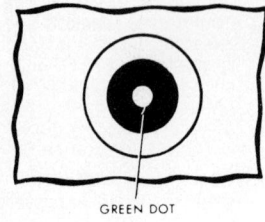

GREEN DOT

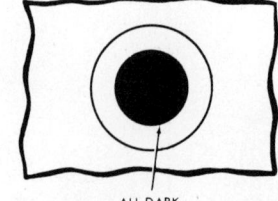

ALL DARK

FIG. 1-14   ENERGIZER CHARGE INDICATOR

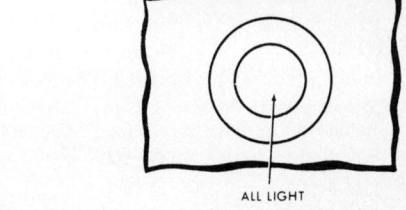

ALL LIGHT

3. Crank the engine while reading the voltmeter scale and listening to the starting-motor cranking speed.

4. Starting motor should crank the engine uniformly at a good rate of speed, and the voltmeter scale should read 9.6 volts or more.

5. If the starting motor sounds sluggish, perform the starting circuit resistance (voltage drop) tests described later.

6. If the cranking voltage is below 9.6 volts, test battery capacity, starting-motor current draw and starting-circuit voltage drop.

CURRENT DRAW (AMPERAGE) TEST

1. Set the voltage selector switch on battery/starter tester at the range closest to 12 volts and connect as shown in **Fig. 1-17.**

2. Disconnect the distributor primary lead, or electronic distributor wire harness, to prevent the engine from starting when cranked.

3. Crank the engine for 15 seconds and read the voltmeter scale.

4. Adjust the load control knob on battery/starter tester until the voltmeter reading is identical to that obtained while the engine was cranking.

5. Ammeter needle now indicates the current drawn by the starting motor while cranking the engine. Reduce the load to zero.

INTERPRETING CURRENT DRAW RESULTS

With the engine at normal operating temperature, current draw for engines under 200 cu. ins. should range from 90 to 125 amps; 200 to 351 cu. ins. from 125 to 165 amps; 360 to 455 cu. ins., 165 to 200 amps.

A normal current draw accompanied by a low cranking speed indicates excessive resistance in the starting circuit. Run a complete resistance check of the insulated and ground circuits as the following sections indicate. If resistance is not excessive in the circuits, the starting motor must be removed and bench-checked for poor brush or commutator conditions, and/or loose or high-resistance connections in the armature and field circuits.

A low starting-motor current draw, coupled with low cranking speed or none at all (a total failure to crank the engine), requires the same troubleshooting procedure. A high starting-motor current draw indicates trouble in the starting circuit, but can also occasionally be due to an overheated or overly tight engine. If the engine has been recently overhauled, or if it runs hot, let it cool for 30 minutes and then repeat the current draw test.

If current draw is still above specifications, there may be either a mechanical drag in the starting motor or the engine, or a short or excessive resistance in the starting circuit wiring. Check for shorts or excessive wiring resistance first. If neither is present, remove the starting motor for a free-running or "no-load" test to find out whether it or the engine is at fault.

VOLTAGE DROP—BATTERY SIDE (INSULATED CIRCUIT RESISTANCE TEST)

1. Connect a voltmeter as shown in **Fig. 1-18.**

2. Disconnect the distributor primary lead, or electronic distributor wire harness, to prevent the engine from starting when cranked.

3. Crank the engine and read the voltmeter. A reading of 0.5-volt or less indicates that voltage drop is normal.

4. If voltage drop exceeds 0.5-volt, remove the lead connected to the starter field terminal, connect it to the

solenoid battery terminal and crank the engine. Voltmeter reading should not exceed 0.1-volt.

5. Connect the lead to the solenoid starting-motor terminal and crank engine. Voltmeter reading should not exceed 0.3-volt.

VOLTAGE DROP—GROUND SIDE (GROUND CIRCUIT RESISTANCE TEST)

1. Connect a voltmeter as shown in **Fig. 1-19.**

2. Disconnect the distributor primary lead, or electronic distributor wire harness, to prevent the engine from starting when cranked.

3. Crank the engine and read the voltmeter. A reading of 0.2-volt or less indicates a normal voltage drop.

4. If voltage drop exceeds 0.2-volt, trace the exact point of excessive resistance by removing the voltmeter leads and touching across each connection and cable in the battery ground circuit, reading the voltmeter scale while cranking the engine. Readings across each connection should be zero; on ground cables less than 24 ins. long, 0.1-volt or less; on ground cables longer than 24 ins., 0.2-volt or less.

ALL GENERAL MOTORS ENGINES
Delco-Remy Starting Motor
STARTING MOTOR DESCRIPTION

All Delco-Remy starting motors are 12-volt extruded frame units incorporating an external solenoid, enclosed shift lever and overrunning clutch. Because this starter design has been used by all divisions of General Motors for a considerable number of years, there are various versions in existence, depending upon engine application. The primary difference between the different versions is one of electrical circuitry—that is, how the field coils are wound and wired. Regardless of this, the mechanical operation and overhaul procedures remain unchanged, despite engine application. Since the High Energy Ignition (HEI) appeared as an option in 1974 and as standard equipment in 1975, one change has been made in solenoid design. On cars with the HEI system installed, the solenoid "R" terminal has been removed, since there is no requirement for an electrical lead from the starter solenoid to the ignition coil. The first design change in many years appeared on some 1978 GM engines with the introduction of a different starting motor. The new 5MT model has field coils and pole shoes which are bonded permanently to the motor frame. This means that the frame and field coils must be serviced as an assembly. Motor testing and overhaul procedures are essentially the same as for previous 10MT models.

Mating spiral splines on the armature shaft and drive clutch help to mesh gears and prevent cranking power from being transmitted until the drive pinion gear is fully engaged with the flywheel ring gear. Positioned between the armature end and the clutch drive collar,

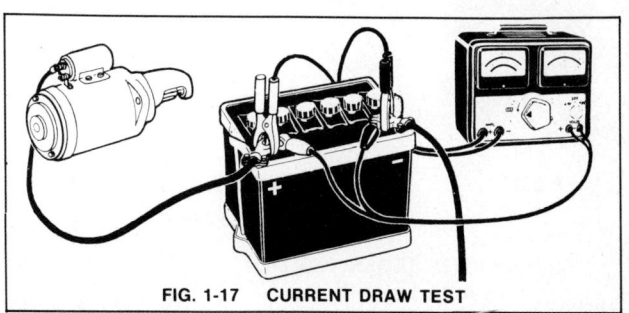

FIG. 1-17   CURRENT DRAW TEST

a special assist spring helps the solenoid to overcome return spring force as the clutch begins to move along the armature shaft. End thrust is taken by a pinion stop composed of a snap ring, retainer and thrust collar on the armature shaft.

When the ignition switch is turned to the START position, the solenoid is energized and pulls the plunger in, causing the shift lever to move the pinion drive gear forward. When the switch is turned from START to the ON position, the return spring withdraws the plunger from the solenoid, moving the shift lever back and withdrawing the drive pinion gear from mesh with the engine flywheel ring gear **(Fig. 1-20)**.

STARTING CIRCUIT AND TEST SEQUENCE

The starting circuit includes the following components:

1. Interlock system.
2. Neutral safety switch (automatic transmission).
3. Clutch start switch (manual transmission).
4. Starter solenoid.
5. Connecting wiring.

Test procedures follow for each component in the control circuit, and should be performed in the order specified below. Disconnect the distributor primary lead or the electronic distributor wire harness to prevent the engine from starting before proceeding with the test.

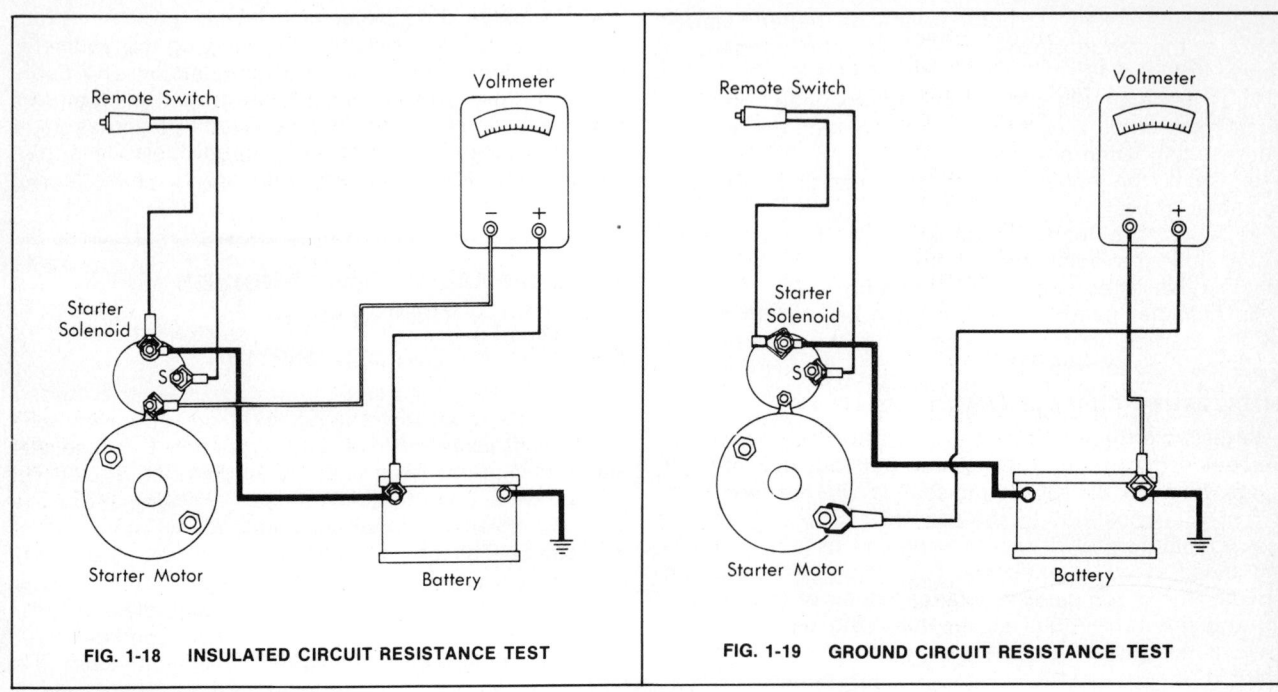

FIG. 1-18   INSULATED CIRCUIT RESISTANCE TEST

FIG. 1-19   GROUND CIRCUIT RESISTANCE TEST

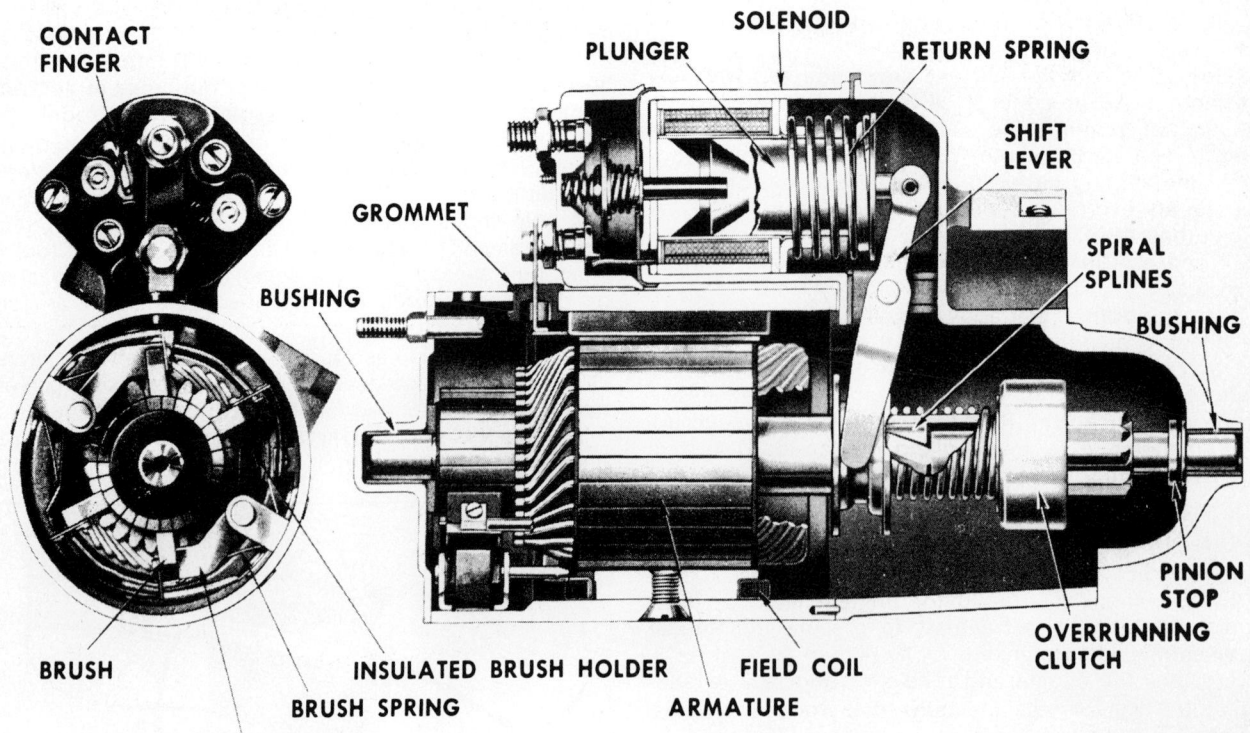

FIG. 1-20   DELCO-REMY STARTING MOTOR

INTERLOCK SYSTEM

The interlock system was used on 1974-75 models and controls current flow to the starter solenoid, which in turn activates the starting motor. **Fig. 1-21** shows a typical GM installation. While the interlock relay is positioned in various places, depending upon the body style and GM division involved, it can be easily traced from the fusebox.

1. If the starter solenoid does not click and the starting motor does not operate when the ignition switch is turned to the START position, press and release the override relay located under the hood (generally on the engine cowl). Turn the ignition switch to the START position again.

2. If the engine cranks, check the neutral safety or clutch safety switch terminals with a test probe. If both are carrying current, the safety switch is good, but if neither terminal has current, replace the switch.

3. If the engine did not crank during Step 1, set the parking brake, place the automatic transmission selector in the PARK position and turn the ignition switch from outside the car with the seat belts unfastened. If the car is equipped with a manual transmission, the shift lever must be in NEUTRAL with the clutch depressed, which requires an additional person to help you.

4. If the starter does not crank, disconnect the three-wire connector leading out of the fusebox **(Fig. 1-22)** and turn the ignition switch to START again. If the starter cranks, the problem is in the seat belt system; if it does not crank, go to the interlock relay.

5. Turn off the ignition, disconnect the interlock relay assembly and check each wire by connecting a test lamp between the wire and ground. Test lamp should light each time. If it does not light on a given wire, look for a break in the circuit.

6. If the wiring all checks out, but the starting motor still does not crank, apply 12 volts to the purple wire **(Fig. 1-23)** and turn the ignition switch to START. If the starter cranks, replace the interlock module.

7. If the starter does not crank, check the engine firewall where the instrument panel harness and engine harness connect. Look for either a break in the purple wire or a connector whose pins are bent or not making proper contact.

STARTER SOLENOID SWITCH TEST

1. Connect a voltmeter to the solenoid as shown in **Fig. 1-24.** Set the voltmeter to high scale.

2. Turn the ignition switch to the START position and crank the engine. Switch the voltmeter from the high to low scale and take a reading as fast as possible, then switch the voltmeter back to the high scale and shut the engine off.

3. If the voltmeter reads in excess of 0.2–volt, the solenoid contacts are defective and the unit should be repaired or replaced.

STARTER REMOVAL/INSTALLATION

TO REMOVE

Starting motor removal varies considerably according to the model year and engine application. The following procedure is thus a general guide for all General Motors cars and may vary somewhat depending upon

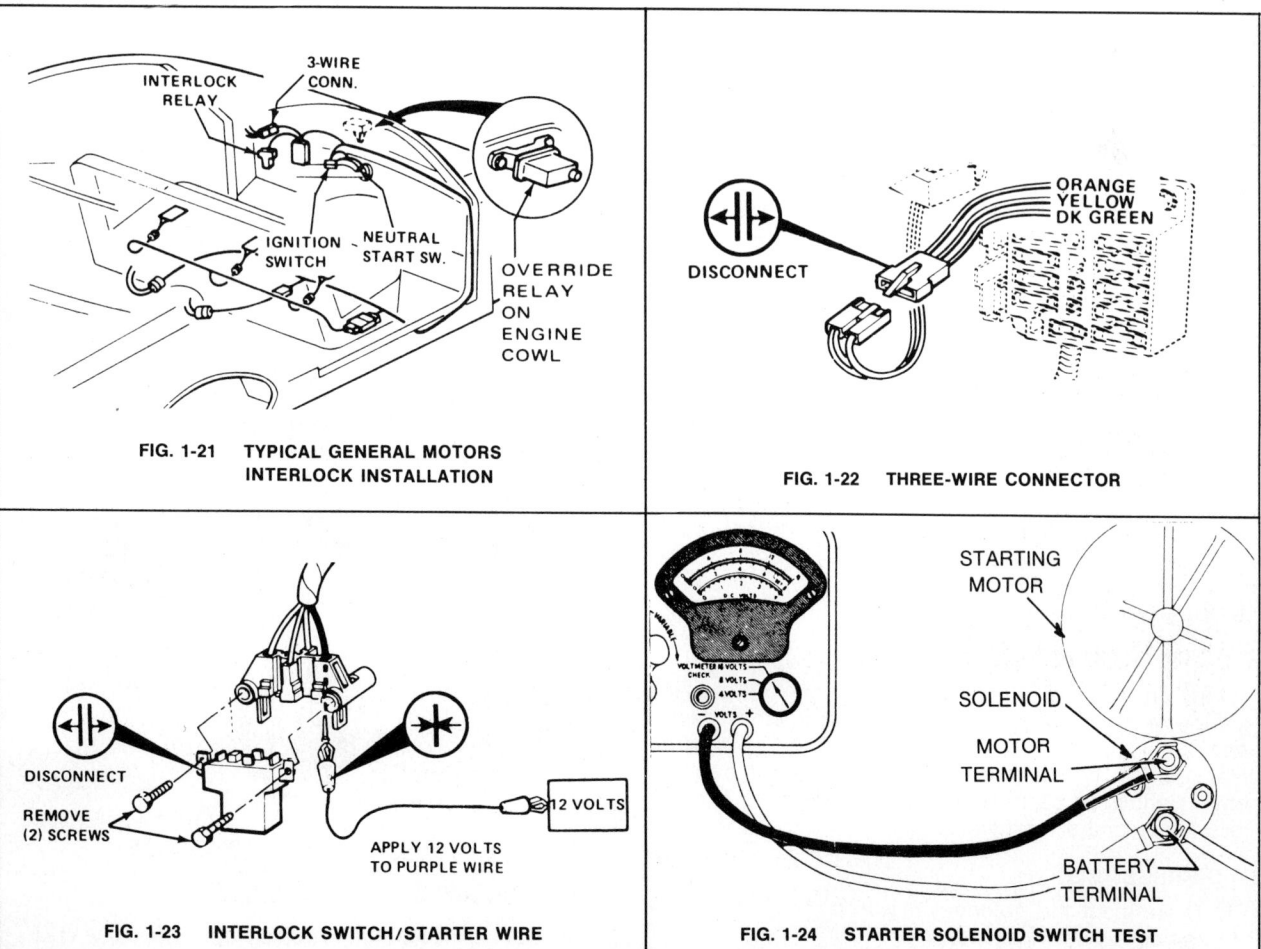

FIG. 1-21 TYPICAL GENERAL MOTORS INTERLOCK INSTALLATION

FIG. 1-22 THREE-WIRE CONNECTOR

FIG. 1-23 INTERLOCK SWITCH/STARTER WIRE

FIG. 1-24 STARTER SOLENOID SWITCH TEST

GM division, car series, engine and model year involved.

1. Disconnect the battery ground cable.

2. On Eldorado and Toronado only, disconnect the starter harness connector at the rear of the engine and slip it out of the guide clips.

3. Disconnect all wires at the solenoid terminals, replacing each nut as the wire is removed. Since nut thread differs, this will prevent mixing them up and inadvertently stripping their threads by incorrect replacement.

4. Loosen the bolt in the support bracket at the front of the starting motor and remove the other mount bolts. Some V-8 engines after 1973 incorporate a heat shield around the solenoid. If so, remove the support-bracket upper bolt and disconnect the heat shield.

5. Remove the support bracket nut or bolt and turn the bracket to one side, pulling the starting motor forward until the drive pinion gear clears the flywheel ring gear.

6. Hold the starting motor against the bellhousing and remove according to the available working space—this may mean rolling it end-over-end, lifting up and over the steering linkage, etc.

TO INSTALL

1. Work the starting motor back in its proper position and locate it in the flywheel housing.

2. Replace mounting bolts and torque to 45 ft.-lbs.

3. Swing the front support bracket into place, replacing the heat shield if removed, and install the support bracket bolt or nut as required.

4. Reinstall all wires to the solenoid terminals and tighten the nuts securely.

5. On Eldorado and Toronado only, replace the starter harness connector at the rear of the engine and fit it into the guide clips.

6. Reconnect the battery ground cable.

FREE-RUNNING STARTER CURRENT DRAW TEST

1. Secure the starting motor in a bench vise and connect a battery/starter tester as shown in **Fig. 1-25.**

2. Read the voltmeter scale with the starter running at ''no-load.''

3. Disconnect the starting motor from the battery and adjust the load control knob until the voltmeter reading is identical to that obtained with the starter connected.

4. Read ''no-load'' current draw on the ammeter scale and compare to specifications.

If current draw is greater than that specified, the starting motor may have shorted circuits, a rubbing armature, a bent armature shaft or tight bushings. A low or zero reading indicates excessive internal resistance. Check for loose or high resistance connections in the field or armature circuits, or for poor brush or commutator condition.

STARTING MOTOR OVERHAUL

Work on a clean bench with clean tools. Clean the exterior of the starting motor with a soft cloth dampened in solvent and wipe dry before beginning disassembly—*do not* use solvent on interior components. Handle all parts **(Fig. 1-26)** carefully to prevent nicks, burrs and scratches.

TO DISASSEMBLE

1. Disconnect the solenoid motor terminal from the field coil connector.

2. Remove screws and lockwashers holding the solenoid unit to the starter drive housing.

3. Rotate the solenoid counterclockwise, to release the flange from the center frame, and remove solenoid.

4. Remove the through-bolts, commutator end frame and braking washer.

5. Separate the field frame from the drive housing and remove the snap ring holding the shift-lever pivot pin in place.

6. Remove the pivot pin, plunger, shift-lever assembly and armature from the drive end housing.

7. Slide the thrust collar from the end of the armature shaft **(Fig. 1-27).**

8. Fit a ⅝-in.-deep socket over the armature shaft and tap it with a hammer to drive the retainer off the snap ring.

9. Remove the snap ring. If retainer removal causes snap ring distortion, use a new one for reassembly.

10. Remove the retainer and clutch assembly from the armature shaft.

11. Clean all parts thoroughly with a brush and clean dry cloth.

12. Check the brush condition. Brushes that are oil-soaked or worn more than one-half their original length should be replaced.

BRUSH REPLACEMENT

Brushes cannot be inspected or serviced unless starting-motor disassembly is according to the above procedure. Brush holding parts should not be changed unless damaged. If brush replacement is required, do so in the following manner:

1. Remove the brush-holder pivot pin and brush spring.

2. Remove the brush attaching screw.

3. Install the new brush, with tradename visible, and tighten the attaching screw.

4. Insert the brush spring in the center frame slot.

5. Install one insulated and one ground brush in the brush holder and fasten in place with the pivot pin.

TO TEST ARMATURE

FOR SHORT CIRCUIT

1. With the armature positioned in a growler **(Fig. 1-28),** hold a hacksaw blade parallel to the core.

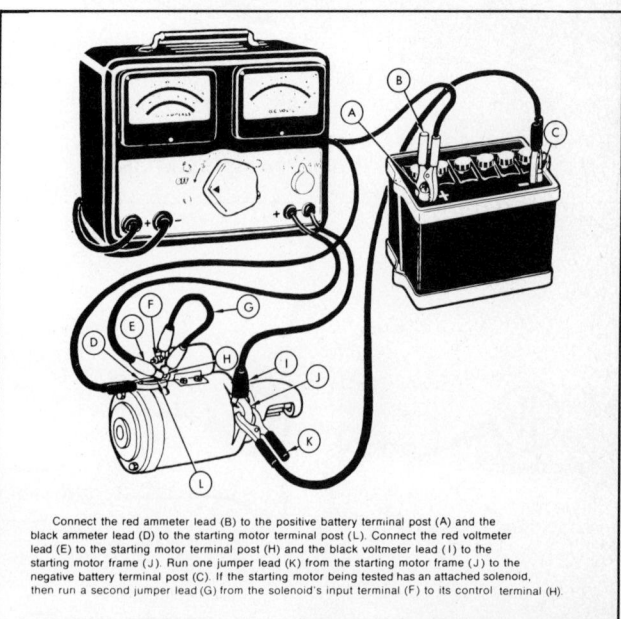

Connect the red ammeter lead (B) to the positive battery terminal post (A) and the black ammeter lead (D) to the starting motor terminal post (L). Connect the red voltmeter lead (E) to the starting motor terminal post (H) and the black voltmeter lead (I) to the starting motor frame (J). Run one jumper lead (K) from the starting motor frame (J) to the negative battery terminal post (C). If the starting motor being tested has an attached solenoid, then run a second jumper lead (G) from the solenoid's input terminal (F) to its control terminal (H).

FIG. 1-25   FREE-RUNNING STARTER CURRENT DRAW TEST

2. Slowly rotate the armature in the growler. If the blade vibrates and is attracted to the core, the armature is shorted and must be replaced.

FOR GROUND

1. Touch the armature shaft and each commutator riser bar with test lamp probes.

2. If the lamp lights, the armature is grounded and must be replaced.

FOR COMMUTATOR RUNOUT

1. With the armature in a pair of ''V'' blocks, measure the runout with a dial indicator as in **Fig. 1-29.** If the armature is out of round, reface.

2. Should the commutator require refacing, secure it in a lathe and make very light cuts across its face until the commutator is once again round and concentric with the shaft in its center. Frequent checking with the dial indicator is recommended.

TO TEST FRAME AND FIELD COILS

1. Place one probe of a 110-volt test lamp on each end of the field coils connected in series **(Fig. 1-30).** If the lamp does not light, the field coils are open and must be replaced.

2. Disconnect the shunt coil ground and place a 110-volt test lamp probe on the connector strap and the other lead on the field frame **(Fig. 1-31).** If the lamp lights, field coils are grounded and must be replaced.

3. With the shunt coil still disconnected, place one 110-volt test lamp probe on each end of the shunt coil **(Fig. 1-32).** If the lamp does not light, the shunt coil is open and must be replaced.

TO ASSEMBLE

1. Lubricate the armature shaft and replace the clutch drive. Pinion gear must face toward shaft end.

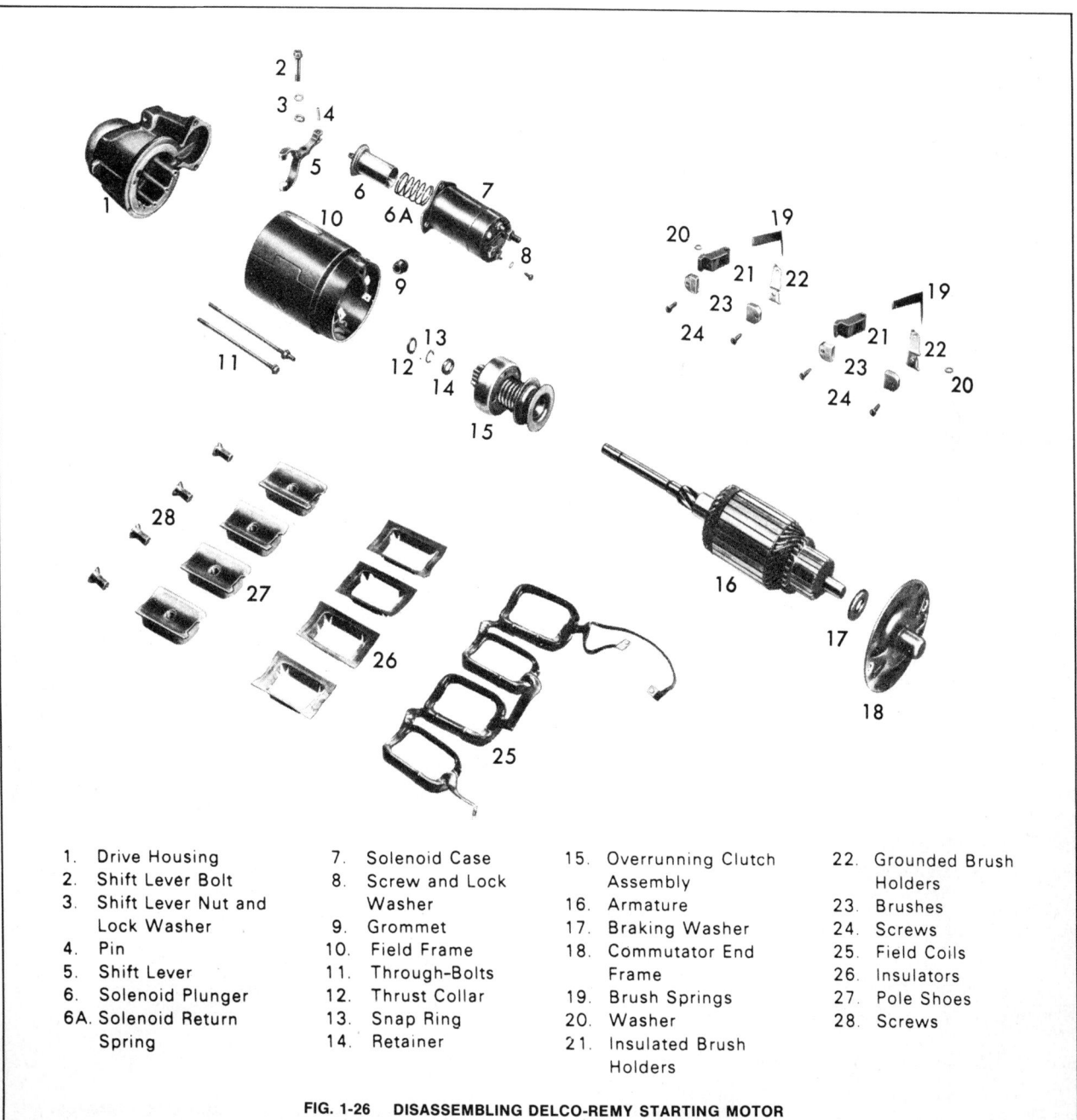

1.	Drive Housing	7.	Solenoid Case
2.	Shift Lever Bolt	8.	Screw and Lock Washer
3.	Shift Lever Nut and Lock Washer	9.	Grommet
4.	Pin	10.	Field Frame
5.	Shift Lever	11.	Through-Bolts
6.	Solenoid Plunger	12.	Thrust Collar
6A.	Solenoid Return Spring	13.	Snap Ring
		14.	Retainer

15.	Overrunning Clutch Assembly	22.	Grounded Brush Holders
16.	Armature	23.	Brushes
17.	Braking Washer	24.	Screws
18.	Commutator End Frame	25.	Field Coils
19.	Brush Springs	26.	Insulators
20.	Washer	27.	Pole Shoes
21.	Insulated Brush Holders	28.	Screws

FIG. 1-26   DISASSEMBLING DELCO-REMY STARTING MOTOR

2. With the cupped side facing the shaft end, slide the retainer on the armature shaft.

3. With the armature shaft standing upright (commutator down) on a block of soft wood, place the snap ring on the upper end of the shaft. Fit a 7/16-in. socket over it and tap lightly with a hammer to force the snap ring into position on the second groove.

4. Fit the thrust collar on the armature shaft, with its shoulder facing the snap ring.

5. Grip the retainer and snap ring with two pairs of pliers and squeeze together to force the snap ring into the retainer **(Fig. 1-33)**.

6. Put a small amount of grease in the drive-housing grease retainer.

7. Fit the shift-lever assembly legs into the clutch grooves.

8. With the thrust washer in place on the shaft end, install armature and clutch drive in the drive housing.

9. Replace the shift-lever pivot pin in the housing recess and fasten with the snap ring.

10. Position the solenoid return spring and solenoid in place, and replace the attaching screws and lockwashers.

11. Apply a quantity of non-hardening sealing compound to the point of contact between the solenoid flange and the frame assembly.

12. Fit the frame assembly over the armature and install the drive housing. Spread the brush holders apart to engage the commutator. Index the dowel pin to the dowel pin hole.

13. Put a small amount of grease on the commutator end-frame bushing and replace the braking washer on the armature shaft.

14. Slide the end frame on the shaft and replace the through-bolts.

15. Reconnect the field-coil terminal connection to the solenoid motor terminal and fasten with self-tapping screw and washer.

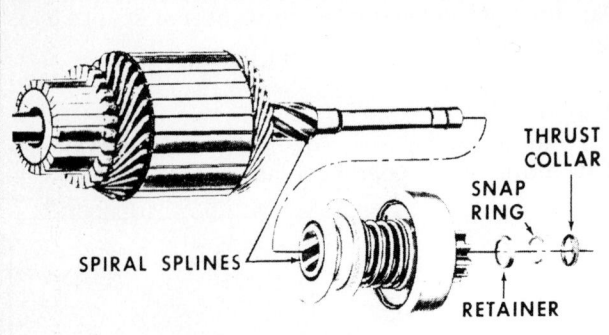

FIG. 1-27 ARMATURE AND OVERRUNNING CLUTCH ASSEMBLY

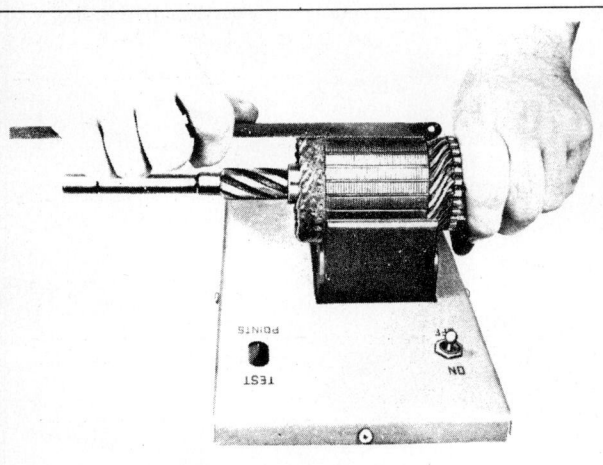

FIG. 1-28 ARMATURE SHORT TEST

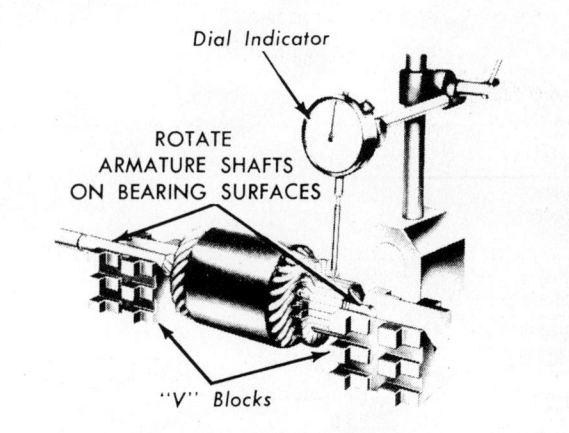

FIG. 1-29 COMMUTATOR RUNOUT

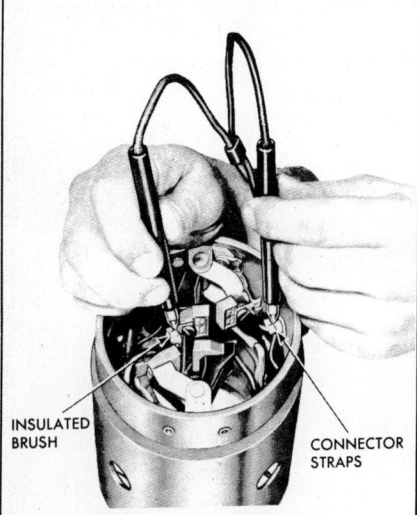

FIG. 1-30 FIELD COIL OPEN TEST

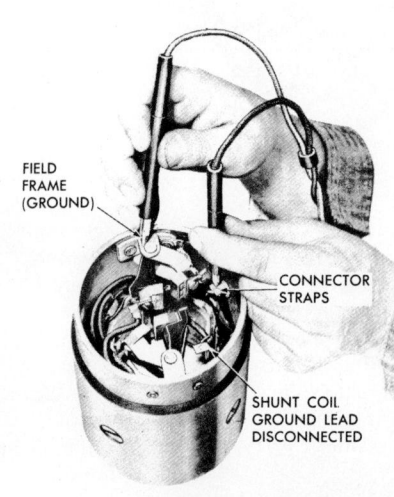

FIG. 1-31 FIELD COIL GROUND TEST

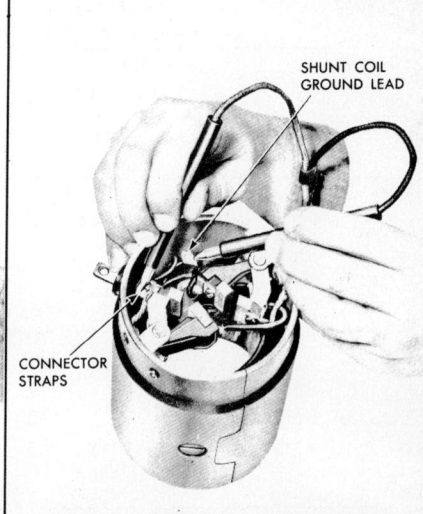

FIG. 1-32 SHUNT COIL OPEN TEST

CHECKING PINION CLEARANCE

Whenever the starting motor is disassembled and reassembled, pinion clearance should be checked. Since clearance is nonadjustable, it is important that it be correct. Too little clearance prevents the solenoid from properly closing, while too much causes incorrect engagement with the flywheel ring gear. Improper pinion clearance is caused by excessive internal wear or improper reassembly. To check clearance:

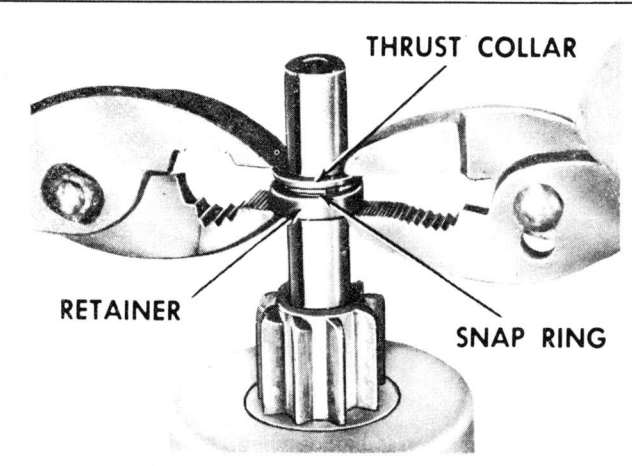

FIG. 1-33 POSITIONING RETAINER OVER SNAP RING

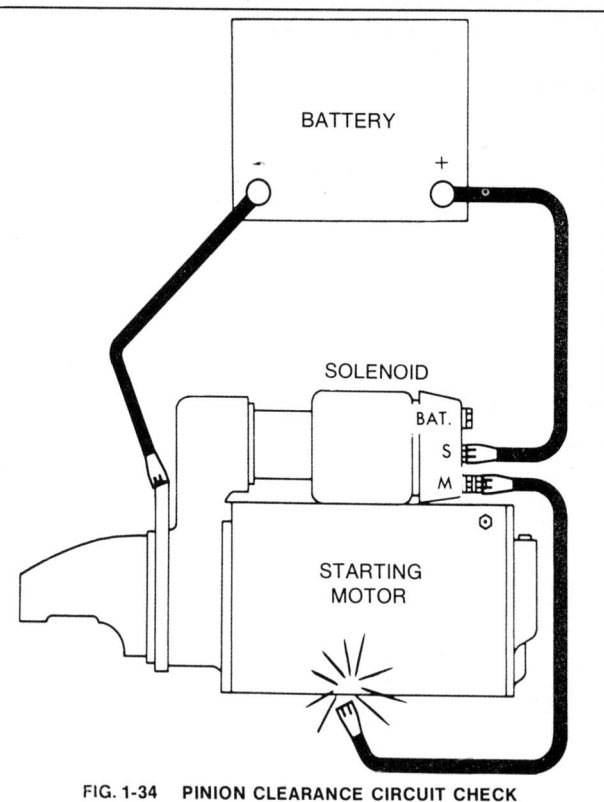

FIG. 1-34 PINION CLEARANCE CIRCUIT CHECK

GENERAL MOTORS STARTER SPECIFICATIONS

MODEL NO.	APPLICATION	SPEC. NO.	RING GEAR DIA. (ins.)	Volts	FREE SPEED Amperes	RPM
1108365 1108774**	250-cu.-in. I-6 Engine 230-cu.-in. I-6 Engine 153-cu.-in. I-4 Engine	3573	12-3/4	9	50-80*	5500-10,500
1108418 1108775**	350- & 454-cu.-in. V-8 Engines w/Man. trans.	3563	14	9	65-95*	7500-10,500
1108430 1108776**	350, 400 & 454-cu.-in. V-8 Engines w/Auto. Trans.	3563	14	9	65-95*	7500-10,500
1108512 1108790**	4.3-Litre V-8 Engine	2438	14	9	55-80*	3500-6000
1108400	Corvette 454 V-8, w/Man. Trans.	3563 (Ultra High)	14	9	65-95*	7500-10,500
1108429	Corvette 454 V-8, w/Auto. Trans.	3563 (Ultra High)	14	9	65-95*	7500-10,500
1108367	Monte Carlo, Chevelle, Camaro & Nova 307 V-8 w/3-spd., 4-spd., P.G., or M-38	3573 (Low)	12-3/4	9	50-80*	5500-10,500
1108427	Chevrolet, Chevelle & Nova 350 V-8 w/PG, or M-38 Corvette 350 V-8 (4-bbl.) w/M-40	2438 (Intermediate)	12-3/4	9	55-80*	3500-6000
1108338	Chevrolet, Chevelle & Nova 350 V-8 w/3-spd. & 4-spd. Corvette 350 V-8 (4-bbl.) w/3-spd., or 4-spd.	2438 (Intermediate)	14	9	55-80*	3500-6000

*Includes solenoid.
** Has "R" terminal removed.

1. Disconnect the motor field-coil connector and connect a 12-volt battery between the solenoid "S" terminal and ground. This energizes the solenoid.

2. Quickly touch a jumper lead from the solenoid "M" terminal to the grounded housing **(Fig. 1-34)**. This shifts the pinion into cranking position, where it will remain as long as the battery is connected.

3. Eliminate slack movement by pushing the pinion back toward the commutator.

4. Use a feeler gauge to measure the gap between the pinion and pinion stop. Clearance should be 0.010- to 0.140-in. If not, disassemble and check for worn parts or improper assembly.

ALL FORD MOTOR COMPANY ENGINES (Except 429 and 460 cu. ins.); ALL AMERICAN MOTORS ENGINES

Autolite-Motorcraft Positive-Engagement Starting Motor

STARTING MOTOR DESCRIPTION

Turning the ignition switch to the START position actuates the starter relay through the control circuit. The starter relay acts to connect the starting motor to the battery, sending battery current through the grounded field coil to operate a moving pole shoe. As the pole shoe is connected to the starter-drive plunger lever, it forces the drive to engage the engine flywheel ring gear. Once the moving pole shoe is fully seated, it opens the field-coil ground contacts and the starting motor is in operation. A holding coil keeps the moving pole shoe in its fully seated position while the starting motor turns the engine.

STARTING CIRCUIT AND TEST SEQUENCE

The starting system circuit includes the following components:

1. Remote-control starter switch (part of the ignition switch).
2. Neutral start switch (automatic transmission with floor console only).
3. Ignition switch—transmission interlock (automatic transmission with column shift; Ford and Mercury divisions only).
4. Starter relay.
5. Interlock system.
6. Circuit wiring.

TEST PROCEDURE

If the starting motor does not operate when the ignition switch is turned to the START position, the malfunction may be in any one of the control circuit components, the starting motor or the battery. Test the battery specific gravity first, then check the remote-control starter part of the ignition switch by placing a jumper lead across its terminals and trying to crank the engine. If the engine *does* crank, the starter switch is defective and should be replaced.

STARTER RELAY TEST

1. Use a heavy jumper lead to connect the starter relay ignition and battery terminals. Engine will crank if the starter relay is good.
2. If engine does not crank, inspect the wiring and connections from the relay to the starting motor for loose or corroded connections and repeat Step 1.
3. If the engine still fails to crank, the starting motor must be removed for repair.

STARTER RELAY TEST—AUTOMATIC TRANSMISSION

1. Set the transmission selector lever in NEUTRAL or PARK position.
2. Connect a jumper lead between the battery and ignition terminals on the starter relay. If engine cranks, the starter relay is good.
3. If the engine does not crank, connect a second jumper lead between the starter-relay ground terminal and a good ground. Repeat Step 2.
4. If the engine cranks, the starter relay is good, but the neutral safety switch is defective. If the engine does not crank, the starter relay is defective.

INTERLOCK SYSTEM

The interlock system was used on 1974-75 models and controls current flow to the starter relay, which in turn activates the starting motor. Test the interlock device as follows:

1. Connect a lead from a probe-type test lamp to a good ground and touch the probe to the ignition terminal "I" on the starter relay.
2. A second person is required to sit in the driver's seat with the seat belt fastened properly and to turn the ignition switch to the START position.
3. The test lamp will light if the interlock is operating properly.
4. If the lamp does not light, remove the interlock connectors and use a jumper lead to connect the battery and starter relay wires briefly while cranking the engine.
5. If the engine cranks over, the interlock unit is defective and must be replaced. If the engine will not crank, use the test lamp to check for voltage between the battery wire and starter relay wire. If no voltage is present, there is an open circuit in the wiring.
6. If there is voltage, check the starter relay wire for an open circuit.

STARTER REMOVAL/INSTALLATION (All Models Except Pinto, Bobcat and Mustang II)

TO REMOVE

1. Disconnect the battery ground cable and unhook the starting motor cable at the starting motor terminal.
2. Remove the attaching bolts holding the starting motor assembly in place and angle the starting motor to the left or right as required to remove it from its mount.

TO INSTALL

1. Fit the starting motor to the engine flywheel housing and replace the attaching bolts loosely.
2. Hold the starting motor flat against its mounting surface and be sure it is inserted completely in the pilot hole as the bolts are torqued to 15-20 ft.-lbs.
3. Reconnect the starting motor cable and the battery ground cable.

STARTER REMOVAL/INSTALLATION (Pinto, Bobcat and Mustang II)

TO REMOVE

1. Disconnect the battery ground cable.
2. Remove the crossmember retaining bolts from under the bellhousing.
3. Disconnect the steering-input-shaft flexible coupling and remove the steering gearbox from the crossmember.
4. Unhook the starting motor cable from its terminal.

5. Remove the attaching bolts holding the starting motor in place, and remove starting motor.

TO INSTALL

1. Fit the starting motor to the engine flywheel housing and replace the attaching bolts. Torque to 15-20 ft.-lbs.

2. Connect the starting motor cable to the motor terminal.

3. Align the steering-gearbox input shaft and the flexible coupling with the steering column shaft. Fit the steering gearbox to its position on the crossmember and install the mounting bolts and nuts. Torque to 15-20 ft.-lbs.

4. Replace the flexible-coupling clamping screw.

5. Replace the crossmember and install the retaining bolts.

6. Connect the battery ground cables.

FREE-RUNNING STARTER CURRENT DRAW TEST

1. Secure the starting motor in a bench vise and connect a battery/starter tester as shown in **Fig. 1-44.**

2. Read the voltmeter scale with the starter running at "no-load."

3. Disconnect the starting motor from the battery and adjust the load control knob until the voltmeter reading is the same as that obtained with the starter connected.

4. Read "no-load" current draw on the ammeter scale and compare to specifications.

If current draw is greater than that specified, the starting motor may have shorted circuits, a rubbing armature, a bent armature shaft or tight bushings. A low or zero reading indicates excessive internal resistance. Check for loose or high resistance connections in the field or armature circuits, or for poor brush or commutator condition.

STARTING MOTOR OVERHAUL

Work on a clean bench with clean tools. Clean the exterior of the starting motor with a soft cloth dampened in solvent and wipe dry before beginning disassembly—*do not* use solvent on interior components. Handle all parts **(Figs. 1-35 and 1-36)** carefully to prevent nicks, burrs and scratches.

TO DISASSEMBLE

1. Remove the brush-cover-band retaining screw, cover band and starter-drive plunger-lever cover.

2. Note the brush position for ease in reassembly and remove the commutator brushes from the brush holders.

3. Remove the two through-bolts and lightly tap the starter-drive end housing to break the seal.

4. Remove the starter-drive, plunger-lever return spring, and tap out the plunger-lever pivot pin with a hammer and appropriate punch.

5. Remove the plunger lever and withdraw the armature from the starter frame.

6. Remove the stop ring retainer and stop ring from the front of the starter drive. Discard the stop ring; reuse retainer.

7. Pull the starter drive assembly off the armature shaft.

8. Disconnect the brush end plate and remove the screws holding the ground brushes to the starter frame.

9. Locate the field coil that operates the starter-drive actuating lever. It has a tab on the retaining sleeve. Bend the tab up and remove the sleeve.

10. Remove the three coil retaining screws and use a 300-watt soldering iron to unsolder the field coil leads from the terminal screw. Extract the pole shoes and field coils from the starter frame. (If field coils are to be tested for ground, perform the test *before* carrying out this disassembly test.)

11. Unsolder or cut the insulated brush leads as close as possible to the field connection point, and remove the brushes.

12. Clean all parts thoroughly with a clean dry cloth—*do not* use solvent.

13. Check brush condition. Brushes that are oil-soaked or worn to ¼-in. or less should be replaced before reassembly.

14. Inspect the starter-drive, pinion-teeth wear pattern. If pinion teeth do not penetrate to a depth at least one-half that of the flywheel ring-gear teeth, premature ring gear and/or starter drive failure will occur.

15. Replace the starter drive or ring gear if engagement teeth are milled, pitted, broken or excessively worn **(Fig. 1-37).**

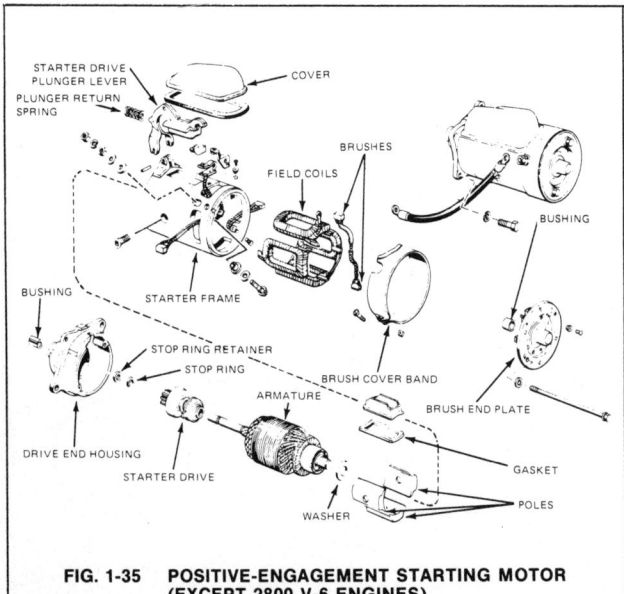

FIG. 1-35 POSITIVE-ENGAGEMENT STARTING MOTOR (EXCEPT 2800 V-6 ENGINES)

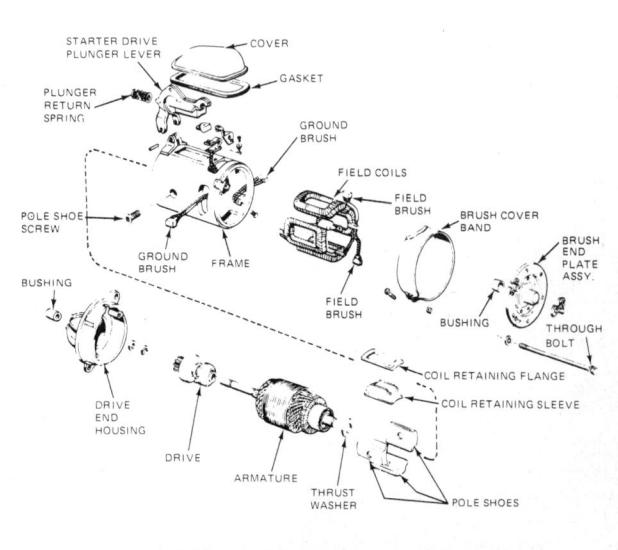

FIG. 1-36 POSITIVE-ENGAGEMENT STARTING MOTOR (2800 V-6 ENGINES ONLY)

TO TEST ARMATURE

FOR SHORT CIRCUIT

1. With the armature positioned in a growler, hold a hacksaw blade parallel to and just above the core **(Fig. 1-38)**.

2. Slowly rotate the armature in the growler. If the blade vibrates and is attracted to the core, the armature is shorted and must be replaced.

FOR GROUND

1. Connect a voltmeter and jumper lead to a battery as shown in **Fig. 1-39**.

2. Touch the voltmeter positive lead to each commutator riser bar, and the jumper lead to the armature.

3. If the voltmeter indicates any voltage reading, the armature is grounded and must be replaced.

FOR COMMUTATOR RUNOUT

1. With the armature in a pair of "V" blocks, measure the runout with a dial indicator as in **Fig. 1-29**. If runout exceeds 0.005-in., reface.

2. Should the commutator require refacing, secure it in a lathe and make very light cuts across its face until the commutator is once again round and concentric with the shaft in its center. Frequent checking with the dial indicator is recommended.

TO TEST FIELD COILS FOR GROUND

1. Connect a voltmeter and jumper lead to a battery as shown in **Fig. 1-40**.

2. Disconnect the holding coil ground lead, insert an insulator between the contacts, and fold the field brushes and holding-coil ground lead over the frame so that they do not make contact with each other or the frame.

3. Clip the jumper lead to the starter frame and the voltmeter positive lead to the starter terminal.

4. If the voltmeter indicates any voltage reading, the field windings are grounded and must be replaced.

TO ASSEMBLE

1. Use a 300-watt soldering iron to reconnect the field coils and solenoid wire to the starter terminal.

2. Place the starter-brush end plate on the starter frame with its boss in the frame slot.

3. Replace the starter drive on the armature shaft and install a new stop ring.

4. Insert the armature and starter-drive assembly in the starter frame and install the plunger lever and pivot pin. Plunger lever must engage the starter-drive assembly properly.

5. Replace the stop ring retainer and fill the drive-end housing bore approximately one-quarter full of grease.

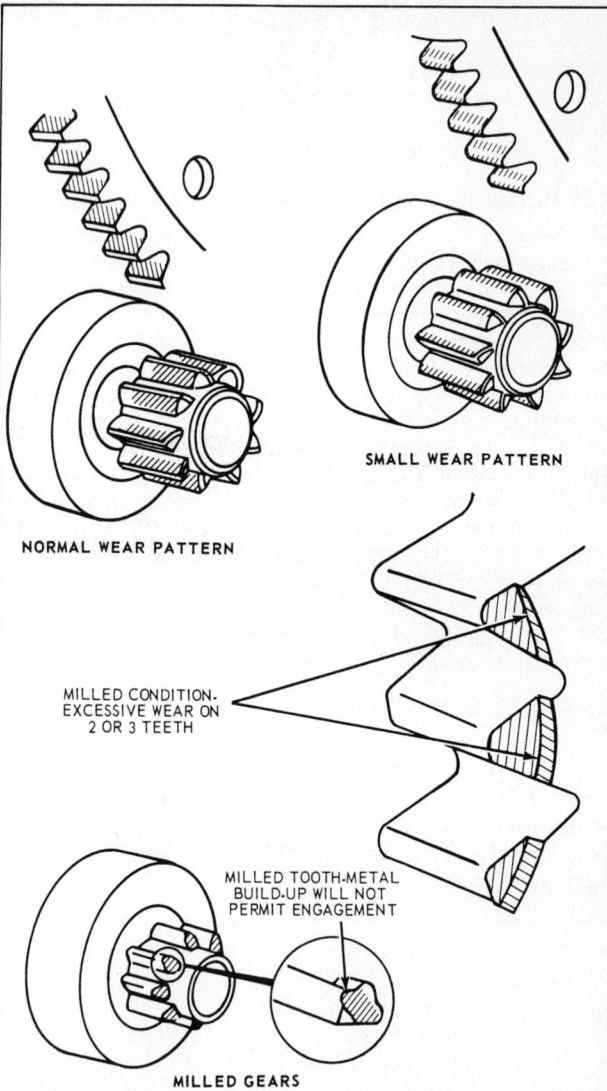

FIG. 1-37   STARTER PINION AND RING GEAR WEAR PATTERNS

AMERICAN MOTORS SPECIFICATIONS (Positive Engagement Starter)	
BRUSH LENGTH	0.5 in.
WEAR LIMIT	0.25 in.
BRUSH SPRING TENSION	40 oz.
VOLTS	12.0
AMPERES @ RPM	65 @ 9250; 67 @ 9356; 69 @ 6709; 77 @ 9600
LOCK TEST STALL TORQUE	13 ft.-lbs. minimum @ 600 amps and approximately 3.4 volts.

FORD MOTOR COMPANY SPECIFICATIONS
(Positive Engagement Starter)

	POSITIVE ENGAGEMENT STARTER MOTOR					STARTER BRUSHES			BOLT TORQUE	
Dia. (ins.)	Current Draw Under Normal Load (amps)	Normal Engine Cranking Speed (rpm)	Min. Stall Torque @5 Volts (ft.-lbs.)	Max. Load (amps)	No Load (amps)	Mfg. Length (ins.)	Wear Limit (ins.)	Spring Tension (oz.)	Through-Bolt Torque (in.-lbs.)	Mounting Bolt Torque (ft.-lbs.)
4	150-200	180-250	9.0	460	70	0.50	0.25	40	55-75	15-20
4-1/2	150-180	150-290	15.5	670	70*	0.50	0.25	40*	55-75	15-20

Maximum commutator runout is 0.005 inch. Maximum starting circuit voltage drop (battery positive terminal to starter terminal) at normal engine temperature is 0.5 volt.

* 80 from 1974 on.

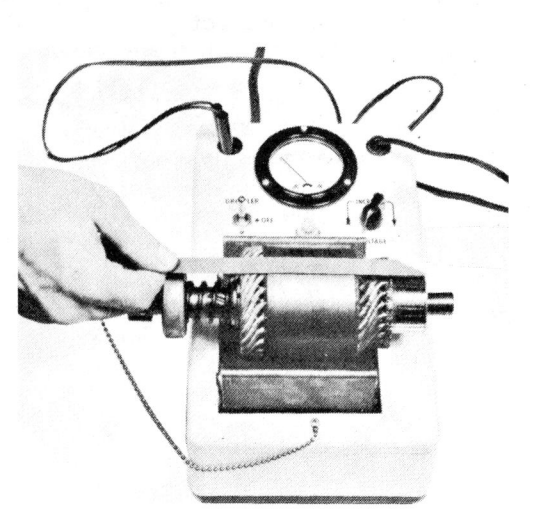

FIG. 1-38   ARMATURE SHORT TEST

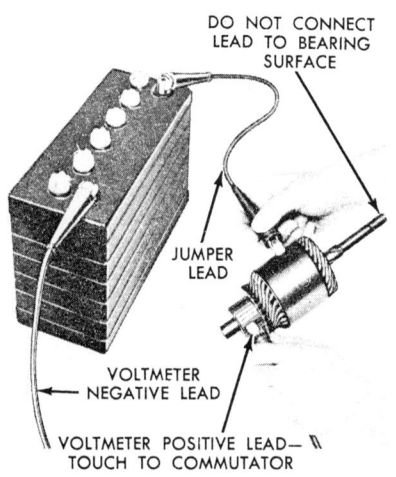

DO NOT CONNECT
LEAD TO BEARING
SURFACE

JUMPER
LEAD

VOLTMETER
NEGATIVE LEAD

VOLTMETER POSITIVE LEAD—
TOUCH TO COMMUTATOR

FIG. 1-39   ARMATURE GROUNDED TEST

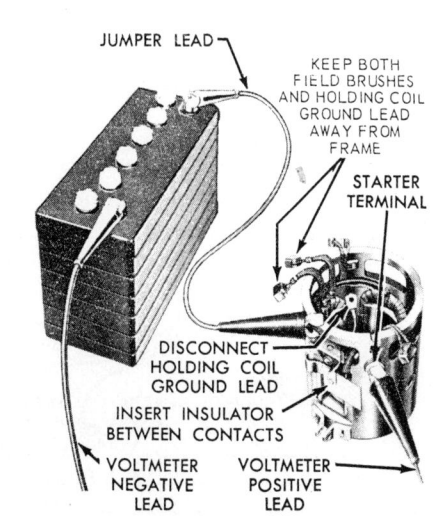

JUMPER LEAD

KEEP BOTH
FIELD BRUSHES
AND HOLDING COIL
GROUND LEAD
AWAY FROM
FRAME

STARTER
TERMINAL

DISCONNECT
HOLDING COIL
GROUND LEAD

INSERT INSULATOR
BETWEEN CONTACTS

VOLTMETER
NEGATIVE
LEAD

VOLTMETER
POSITIVE
LEAD

FIG. 1-40   FIELD GROUNDED CIRCUIT TEST

6. Fit the plunger-lever return spring in place and secure the drive end housing to the starter frame. Check to make sure the stop ring retainer is fully seated and that the brush leads are not pinched, then torque the through-bolts to 55-75 in.-lbs.

7. Replace the insulated brushes in the brush holder and center the brush springs on the brushes.

8. Install the plunger lever cover, and replace the brush band cover with a new gasket. Tighten the band retaining screw.

FORD MOTOR COMPANY
(429- and 460-cu.-in. Engines)

Autolite-Motorcraft
Solenoid-Actuated Starting Motor

STARTING MOTOR DESCRIPTION

An overrunning clutch design **(Fig. 1-41)**, this Autolite-Motorcraft starting motor uses an external solenoid mounted to a flange on the starter-drive housing, but the shift lever and solenoid plunger are fully enclosed in the drive housing to prevent exposure to road splash and dirt. Beginning in the 1973 model year, a metal heat shield was installed to protect the solenoid from excessive manifold/exhaust-pipe heat, because the solenoid contains plastic components that could otherwise be damaged by the high temperatures involved. This heat shield is thus an important part of starting motor operation and should always be reinstalled when removed, or replaced when damaged.

Turning the ignition switch to the START position energizes the solenoid, which shifts the starting-motor pinion gear into mesh with the engine flywheel ring gear by means of a shift fork. At the same time, solenoid electrical contacts close to direct battery current to the starting motor, causing the armature to rotate. When the ignition switch is moved back to the ON position, the solenoid circuit opens. This causes the solenoid return spring to restore the shift fork to its normal position and disengages the starter drive from the ring gear. The overrunning clutch allows the starter drive gear to rotate at a faster rate than the armature as the engine starts, and prevents the armature from being driven by the engine.

While the function of the starter relay used with the Autolite-Motorcraft positive-engagement starting motor is handled by the solenoid in this design, the starter relay is installed on all cars on the production line regardless of the type of starting motor to be used. When the solenoid-actuated starting motor is installed, it is necessary to also install a special connector link on the solenoid to connect the battery terminal with the solenoid operating windings **(Fig. 1-42)**. When the ignition switch is turned to its START position, the starter relay sends battery current to the starter solenoid through this link. Whenever starting motor or solenoid replacement is required, it is also necessary to replace the link properly or the car cannot be started.

STARTING CIRCUIT AND TEST SEQUENCE

The starting system circuit includes the following components:

1. Remote-control starter switch (part of the ignition switch).

2. Neutral start switch (automatic transmission with floor console only).

3. Ignition switch—transmission interlock (automatic transmission with column shift only).

4. Starter relay/starter solenoid.
5. Interlock system.
6. Circuit wiring.

TEST PROCEDURE

If the starting motor does not operate when the ignition switch is turned to the START position, the malfunction may be in any one of the control circuit components—the starting motor or the battery. Test the battery specific gravity first, then check the remote-control starter part of the ignition switch by placing a jumper lead across its terminals and trying to crank the engine. If the engine does crank, the starter switch is defective and should be replaced.

STARTER RELAY TEST

1. Use a heavy jumper lead to connect the starter relay ignition and battery terminals. Engine will crank if the starter relay is good.
2. If the engine does not crank, inspect the wiring and connections from the relay to the starting motor for loose or corroded connections and repeat Step 1.
3. If the engine still fails to crank, the starting motor must be removed for repair.

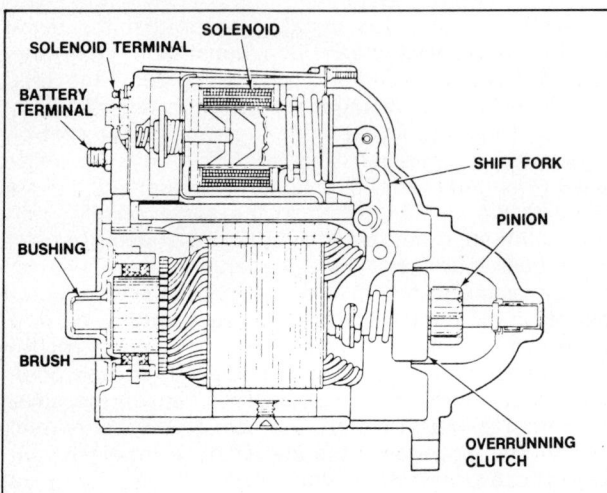

FIG. 1-41   AUTOLITE-MOTORCRAFT SOLENOID-ACTUATED STARTING MOTOR

STARTER RELAY TEST—AUTOMATIC TRANSMISSION

1. Set the transmission selector lever in NEUTRAL or PARK position.
2. Connect a jumper lead between the battery and ignition terminals on the starter relay. If engine cranks, the starter relay is good.
3. If the engine does not crank, connect a second jumper lead between the starter relay ground terminal and a good ground. Repeat Step 2.
4. If the engine cranks, the starter relay is good, but the neutral safety switch is defective. If the engine does not crank, the starter relay is defective.

INTERLOCK SYSTEM

The interlock system was used on 1974-75 models and controls current flow to the starter relay, which in turn activates the starting motor. Test the interlock device as follows:
1. Connect a probe-type test lamp lead to a good ground and touch the probe to the ignition terminal "I" on the starter relay.
2. A second person is required to sit in the driver's seat with the seat belt fastened properly and to turn the ignition switch to the START position.
3. The test lamp will light if the interlock is operating properly.
4. If the lamp does not light, remove the interlock connectors and use a jumper lead to connect the battery and starter relay wires briefly while cranking the engine.
5. If the engine cranks over, the interlock unit is defective and must be replaced. If the engine will not crank, use the test lamp to check for voltage between the battery wire and starter relay wire. If no voltage is present, there is an open circuit in the wiring.
6. If there is voltage, check the starter relay wire for an open circuit.

STARTER SOLENOID TEST

1. Connect a voltmeter between the starter-solenoid switch terminal and ground.
2. Turn the ignition key to START and read the voltmeter scale.
3. If the reading is in excess of 9.5 volts, replace the solenoid.

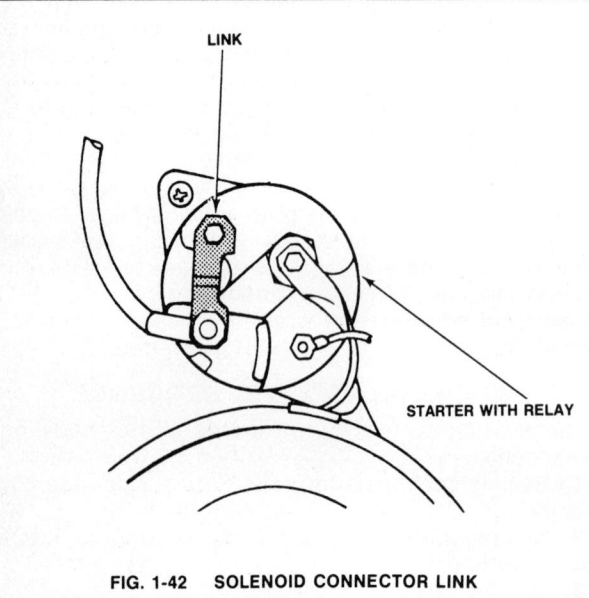

FIG. 1-42   SOLENOID CONNECTOR LINK

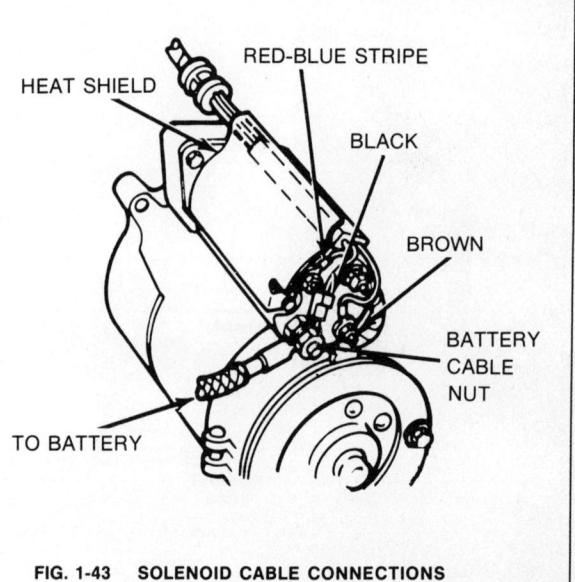

FIG. 1-43   SOLENOID CABLE CONNECTIONS

STARTER REMOVAL/INSTALLATION

TO REMOVE

1. Disconnect the battery ground cable and remove the cable and wires from the solenoid.

2. With Thunderbird and Lincoln Continental Mark IV models, loosen the front-brace attaching bolts, remove the other brace bolts and let the brace hang.

3. Turn the front wheels all the way to the right and remove the steering idler arm from the frame.

4. Unbolt and remove the starting motor assembly.

TO INSTALL

1. Fit the starting motor to the mounting plate and loosely install the mounting bolts.

2. Holding the starting motor flat against its mounting plate, tighten the mounting bolts to 15-20 ft.-lbs.

3. Reconnect the cable and wires to the solenoid terminal and torque the battery cable nut to 45-95 in.-lbs. **(Fig. 1-43)**.

4. Reposition the front brace on Thunderbird and Mark IV models. Tighten front brace bolts and install, then tighten the remainder.

5. Fit the steering idler arm to the frame and replace the attaching bolts, torquing to 28-35 ft.-lbs.

6. Reconnect the battery ground cable.

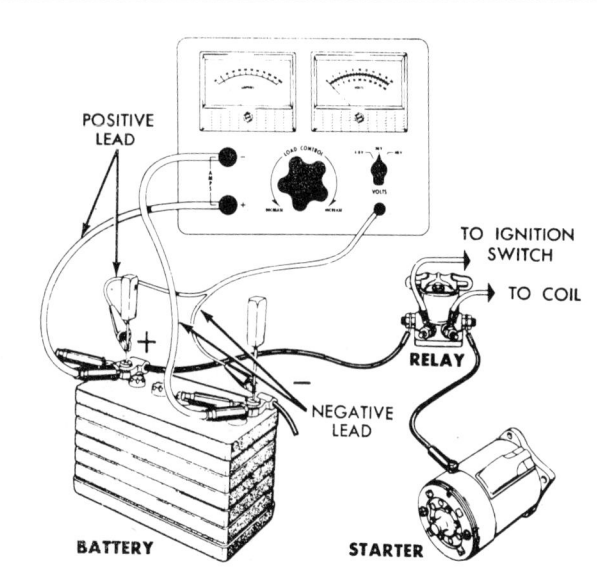

FIG. 1-44   FREE-RUNNING STARTER CURRENT DRAW TEST

FREE-RUNNING STARTER CURRENT DRAW TEST

1. Secure the starting motor in a bench vise and connect a battery/starter tester as shown in **Fig. 1-44.**

2. Read the voltmeter scale with the starter running at "no-load."

3. Disconnect the starting motor from the battery and adjust the load control knob until the voltmeter reading is the same as that obtained with the starter connected.

4. Read "no-load" current draw on the ammeter scale and compare to specifications.

If current draw is greater than that specified, the starting motor may have shorted circuits, a rubbing armature, a bent armature shaft or tight bushings. A low or zero reading indicates excessive internal resistance. Check for loose or high resistance connections in the field or armature circuits, or for poor brush or commutator condition.

STARTING MOTOR OVERHAUL

Work on a clean bench with clean tools. Clean the exterior of the starting motor with a soft cloth dampened in solvent and wipe dry before beginning disassembly—*do not* use solvent on interior components. Handle all parts **(Fig. 1-45)** carefully to prevent nicks, burrs and scratches.

TO DISASSEMBLE

1. Unhook the copper strap from the solenoid starter terminal.

2. Remove the solenoid retaining screws and lift the solenoid unit from the drive housing.

3. Loosen the brush-cover-band retaining screw and slide the band back on the starter frame to provide access to the brushes.

4. Remove the commutator brushes from their holders. Use a small hook to pull the brush spring back and slide the brush free of its holder.

5. Remove the two through-bolts and tap the starter drive housing lightly with a plastic hammer. Separate the drive housing, starter frame and end plate assemblies.

6. Remove the shift fork and solenoid plunger assembly. Separate, if necessary for replacement, by driving out the connecting roll pin with a hammer and punch.

7. Lift the armature and drive gear from the starter frame. Slide the drive away from the armature after removing the drive stop ring.

FORD MOTOR COMPANY SPECIFICATIONS
(Solenoid-Actuated Starter)

	SOLENOID-ACTUATED STARTING MOTOR				STARTER BRUSHES			BOLT TORQUE	
Dia. (ins.)	Current Draw Under Normal Load (amps)	Normal Engine Cranking Speed @70° F (rpm)	No Load (amps)	Mfg. Length (ins.)	Wear Limit (ins.)	Spring Tension (oz.)	Through-Bolt Torque (in.-lbs.)	5/16-in. Bolt Three Hole Mtg. (ft.-lbs.)
4½	180-210	140-170	70*	0.50	0.25	40**	45-85	15-20

Maximum commutator runout is 0.005-in at normal engine temperature is 0.5-volt.   Maximum starting circuit voltage drop (battery positive terminal to starter terminal)

* 90 amps, in 1974 models only.
** 80 oz. in 1974 models only.

8. Remove the drive stop retainer from the drive housing and discard.

9. Clean all parts thoroughly with a brush and a clean dry cloth—*do not* use solvent.

10. Check the brush condition. Brushes that are oil-soaked or worn to ¼-in. or less should be replaced before reassembly.

11. Inspect the starter-drive, pinion-teeth wear pattern. If pinion teeth do not penetrate to a depth at least one-half that of the flywheel ring gear teeth, premature ring gear and/or starter-drive failure will occur.

12. Replace the starter drive or ring gear if engagement teeth are milled, pitted, broken or excessively worn **(Fig. 1-37)**.

TO TEST ARMATURE

FOR SHORT CIRCUIT

1. With the armature positioned in a growler, hold a hacksaw blade parallel to and just above the core **(Fig. 1-38)**.

2. Slowly rotate the armature in the growler. If the blade vibrates and is attracted to the core, the armature is shorted and must be replaced.

FOR GROUND

1. Connect a voltmeter and jumper lead to a battery as shown in **Fig. 1-39**.

2. Touch the voltmeter positive lead to each commutator riser bar, and the jumper lead to the armature.

3. If the voltmeter indicates any voltage reading, the armature is grounded and must be replaced.

FOR COMMUTATOR RUNOUT

1. With the armature in a pair of "V" blocks, measure the runout with a dial indicator as in **Fig. 1-46**. If runout exceeds 0.005-in., reface.

2. Should the commutator require refacing, secure it in a lathe and make very light cuts across its face until the commutator is once again round and concentric with the shaft in its center. Frequent checking with the dial indicator is recommended.

TO TEST FIELD COILS FOR GROUND

1. Connect a voltmeter and jumper lead to a battery as shown in **Fig. 1-47**.

2. Disconnect the holding-coil ground lead, insert an insulator between the contacts, and fold the field brushes and holding-coil ground lead over the frame so they do not make contact with each other or the frame.

3. Clip the jumper lead to the starter frame and the voltmeter positive lead to the starter terminal.

4. If the voltmeter indicates any voltage reading, the field windings are grounded and must be replaced.

TO ASSEMBLE

1. Lubricate the armature-shaft splines, slide the drive gear in place and install a new stop ring.

2. Grease the shift-fork pivot pin and place the solenoid-plunger/shift-fork assembly in position in the starter drive housing.

3. Fit a new stop ring retainer in the drive housing, grease the drive end of the armature shaft and install it in the drive housing, engaging the shift fork tangs in the drive assembly correctly.

4. Grease the commutator end of the armature shaft and fit the drive housing to the starter frame. Frame must index correctly to the drive housing.

5. Index and install the brush end plate on the starter frame. Replace the through-bolts and torque to 45-85 in.-lbs.

6. Install the brushes in their holders by pulling

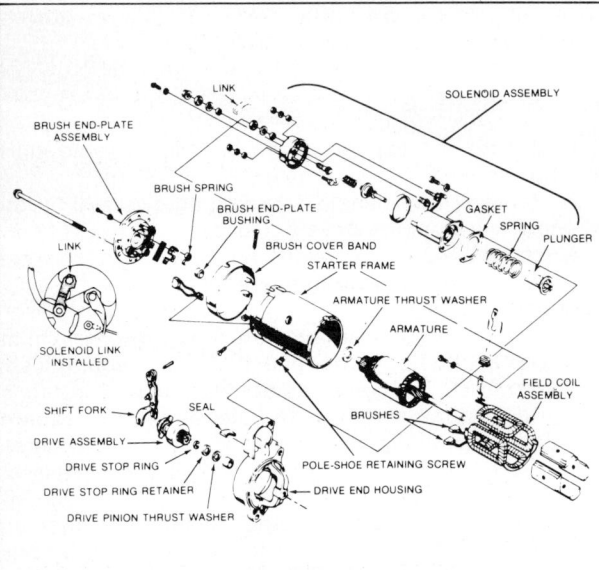

FIG. 1-45   DISASSEMBLING SOLENOID-ACTUATED STARTING MOTOR

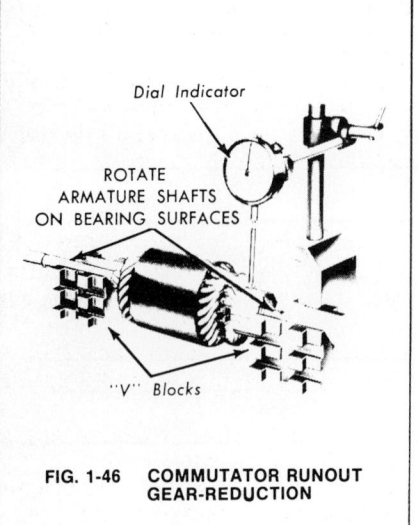

FIG. 1-46   COMMUTATOR RUNOUT GEAR-REDUCTION

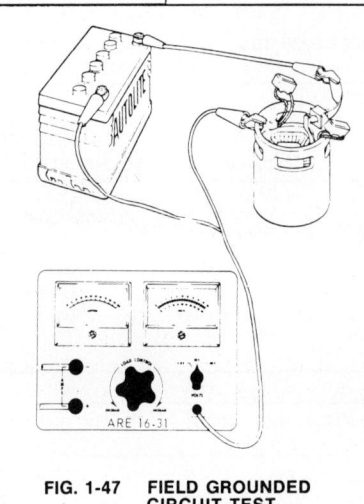

FIG. 1-47   FIELD GROUNDED CIRCUIT TEST

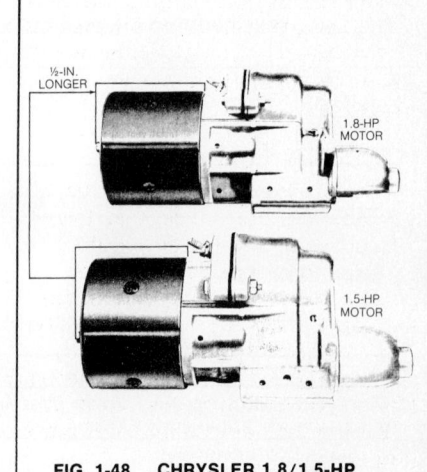

FIG. 1-48   CHRYSLER 1.8/1.5-HP STARTING MOTORS

each spring back with a small hook. Center brush spring on the brush and press the commutator leads away from other components to avoid the possibility of shorting.

7. Fit the rubber gasket between the solenoid motor and frame. Replace the solenoid and install the attaching screws.

8. Reconnect the solenoid starter terminal and copper strap.

9. Slide the cover band back into position and tighten the retaining screws.

ALL CHRYSLER CORPORATION ENGINES (Except Omni/Horizon & 1971-72 225-cu.-in.)
Chrysler Reduction-Gear Starting Motor

STARTING MOTOR DESCRIPTION

Enclosed in the starting motor housing, the solenoid is energized through the ignition switch. When the switch is turned to the START position, the solenoid engages the starter drive gear by means of a shift fork. As the solenoid plunger reaches the end of its travel, it closes a switch which revolves the drive. An overrunning clutch protects against damage if the ignition switch is held in the START position after the engine starts.

Through 1974, a 1.5-hp, 3.5:1-reduction-gear starting motor was used; in 1975, a 1.8-hp, 2:1-reduction-gear model was added and fitted to the 360, 400 and 440-cu.-in. engines. Although the two starting motors look identical **(Fig. 1-48),** they are not the same internally. The field frame assembly, armature and shifter fork used in the 1.8-hp motor are larger than those in the 1.5-hp motor. Testing procedures are the same, but parts are *not* interchangeable. The 1.8-hp model is also equipped with a shock-absorber clutch drive unit to absorb initial cranking shock and protect the clutch unit if the engine should backfire during cranking.

STARTING CIRCUIT AND TEST SEQUENCE

The starting system circuit includes the following components:
1. Interlock system.
2. Starter solenoid and starter relay.
3. Neutral safety switch (automatic transmission).
4. Clutch start switch (manual transmission).
5. Connecting wiring.

Test procedures follow for each component in the control circuit and should be performed in the order specified below. Disconnect the distributor primary lead or the electronic distributor wire harness to prevent engine from starting *before* proceeding with the test sequence.

INTERLOCK SYSTEM

The interlock system was used on 1974-75 models and controls current flow to the starter relay, which in turn activates the starting motor.

1. Connect one lead of a probe-type test lamp to a good ground and touch the probe to the ignition terminal ''I'' on the starter relay **(Fig. 1-49).**

2. A second person is required to sit in the driver's seat with the seat belt fastened properly and to turn the ignition switch to the START position.

3. The test lamp will light if the interlock is operating properly.

4. If the lamp does not light, remove the interlock connectors and use a jumper lead to connect the red wire to the yellow wire briefly while cranking engine.

5. Replace the interlock unit if the engine cranks.

6. If the engine will not crank, use the test lamp to check for voltage between the red wire and ground (red wire goes to the battery). If no voltage is present, there is an open circuit in the wiring.

7. If there is voltage, check the yellow wire (to starter relay) for an open circuit.

STARTER SOLENOID TEST

1. Use a heavy jumper lead to connect the starter relay's battery and solenoid terminals **(Fig. 1-49).** Engine will crank if the starter solenoid is good.

2. If the engine does not crank, inspect the wiring and connections from the relay to the starting motor for loose or corroded connections and repeat Step 1.

3. If the engine still fails to crank, the starter must be removed for repair.

STARTER RELAY TEST—AUTOMATIC TRANSMISSION

1. Set the transmission selector lever in NEUTRAL or PARK position.

2. Connect a jumper wire between the battery and ignition terminals on the starter relay. If the engine cranks, the starter relay is good.

3. If the engine does not crank, connect a second jumper lead between the starter relay ground terminal ''G'' and a good ground. Repeat Step 2.

4. If the engine cranks, the starter relay is good, but the neutral safety switch is defective. If the engine does not crank, the starter relay is defective.

STARTER RELAY TEST—MANUAL TRANSMISSION

1. Have a second person depress the clutch pedal.

2. Connect a jumper lead between the battery and ignition terminals on the starter relay. If the engine cranks, the starter relay is good.

3. If the engine does not crank, connect a second jumper lead between the starter-relay ground terminal and a good ground. Repeat Step 2.

4. If the engine cranks, the starter relay is good, but the clutch start switch is defective or out of adjustment. If engine does not crank, the starter relay is defective.

STARTER REMOVAL/INSTALLATION

TO REMOVE

1. Disconnect battery ground cable at the battery.

2. Unhook the cable at the starter terminal.

3. Remove the solenoid lead wires from the solenoid terminals.

4. Remove the bolt and stud nut holding the starting motor to the flywheel housing.

5. If the car is equipped with an automatic transmission, slide the oil-cooler tube bracket from the stud.

6. Remove the starting motor, taking care not to damage the flywheel housing seal.

TO INSTALL

1. Clean the starting-motor and flywheel-housing mounting surfaces to provide a good electrical contact.

2. Fit the starting motor to the flywheel housing seal.

3. Replace the starting motor, washer and bolt. Fit the oil-cooler tube bracket (if equipped) and install the washer and nut.

4. Hold the starting motor away from the engine while tightening the bolt to 50 ft.-lbs.

5. Reconnect the solenoid lead wire to the solenoid switch terminal and the cable to the starter terminal.

6. Connect the battery ground cable and check for proper engine cranking.

FREE-RUNNING STARTER CURRENT DRAW TEST

1. Secure the starting motor in a bench vise and connect a battery/starter tester as shown in **Fig. 1-44.**

2. Read the voltmeter scale with the starter running at "no load."

3. Disconnect the starting motor from the battery and adjust the load control knob until the voltmeter reading is the same as that obtained with the starter connected.

4. Read "no-load" current draw on the ammeter scale and compare to specifications.

If current draw is greater than that specified, the starting motor may have shorted circuits, a rubbing armature, a bent armature shaft or tight bushings. A low or zero reading indicates excessive internal resistance. Check for loose or high resistance connections in the field or armature circuits, or for poor brush or commutator condition.

STARTING MOTOR OVERHAUL

Work on a clean bench with clean tools. Clean the exterior of the starting motor with a soft cloth dampened in solvent and wipe dry before beginning disassembly—*do not* use solvent on interior components. Handle all parts **(Fig. 1-50)** carefully to prevent nicks, burrs and scratches.

TO DISASSEMBLE

1. Remove the two through-bolts and end head assembly. It may be necessary to tap the end head lightly with a plastic hammer to free it from the housing.

2. Pull the armature outward from the gear housing and the field frame assembly.

3. Separate the field frame assembly from the housing sufficiently to expose the terminal screw.

4. Place finger under the brush terminal screw for support and remove it. On some models, it may be necessary to unsolder the shunt field-coil lead from the brush terminal.

5. Remove the field frame assembly.

6. Remove the solenoid and brush-plate attaching nuts holding the assembly to the gear housing, then remove the assembly.

7. Remove the nut, washer and insulator washer shown in **Fig. 1-51** from the solenoid terminal.

8. Unwind the solenoid lead wire from the brush terminal and remove the solenoid attaching screws holding it to the brush plate.

9. Remove the solenoid battery-terminal nut and terminal from the brush plate.

10. Pull the solenoid contact and plunger assembly from the solenoid, then remove the return spring from the solenoid moving core.

11. Pry off the dust cover from the gear housing.

12. Release the snap ring which positions the gear on the pinion shaft **(Fig. 1-52)**. Since the snap ring is under tension, cup your hand over it to prevent it from flying away as it is removed.

13. Remove the "C" clip from the other end of the pinion shaft.

14. Use a blunt punch to push the pinion shaft toward the rear of the housing. Remove the thrust washers, retaining ring, clutch and pin assembly and the two nylon shift-fork actuators.

15. Pulling the shift fork forward, remove the solenoid moving core.

16. Pull out the shift-fork retaining pin and remove the shift fork **(Fig. 1-53)**.

17. Clean all parts thoroughly. Wipe all parts with a clean dry cloth only. Clean the terminal contacts and contactor with crocus cloth.

18. Check brush condition. Brushes that are oil-soaked or worn more than one-half their original length should be replaced.

19. Inspect the shift fork for side movement. Since the fork is formed from two spring-steel plates riveted together, there should be about 1/16-in. side play to assure proper pinion gear movement.

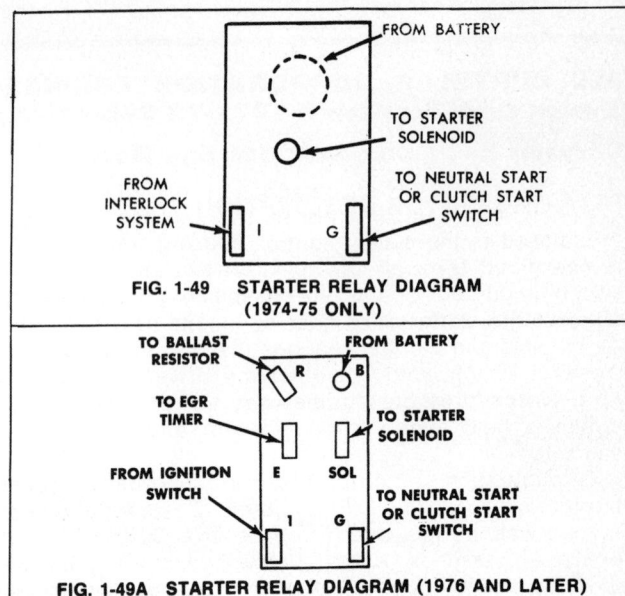

FIG. 1-49   STARTER RELAY DIAGRAM (1974-75 ONLY)

FIG. 1-49A   STARTER RELAY DIAGRAM (1976 AND LATER)

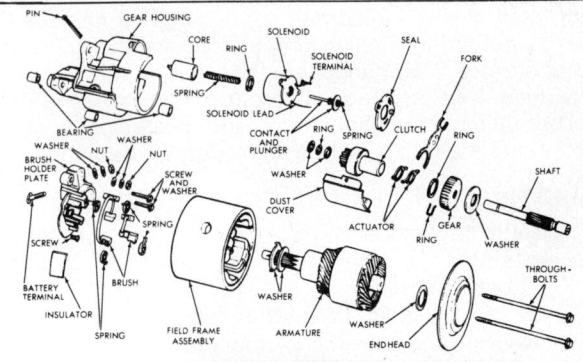

FIG. 1-50   DISASSEMBLING GEAR-REDUCTION STARTING MOTOR

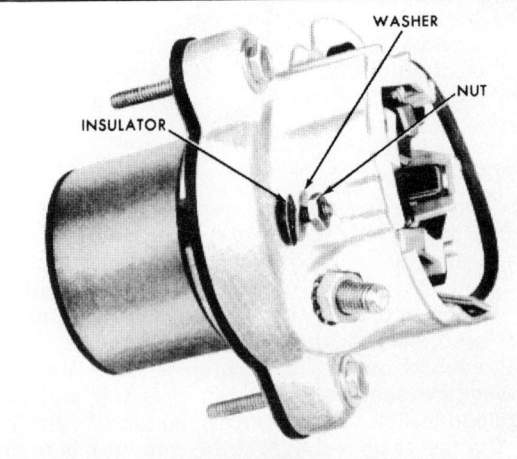

FIG. 1-51   SOLENOID TERMINAL NUT, WASHER, INSULATOR SEQUENCE

TO TEST ARMATURE
FOR SHORT CIRCUIT

1. With the armature positioned in a growler, hold a hacksaw blade parallel to and just above the core **(Fig. 1-54)**.

2. Slowly rotate the armature in the growler. If the blade vibrates and is attracted to the core, the armature is shorted and must be replaced.

FOR GROUND

1. Touch the armature shaft and each commutator riser bar with test lamp probes.

2. If the lamp lights, the armature is grounded and must be replaced.

FOR COMMUTATOR RUNOUT

1. With the armature in a pair of "V" blocks, measure the runout with a dial indicator as in **Fig. 1-55**. If runout exceeds 0.004-in., reface.

2. Should the commutator require refacing, secure it in a lathe and make very light cuts across its face until the commutator is once again round and concentric with the shaft in its center. Frequent checking with the dial indicator is recommended.

TO TEST FIELD COILS FOR GROUND

1. Remove the field frame assembly from the hous-

ing and drill out the rivet holding the field-coil ground leads to the field frame.

2. Insulate the field-coil leads from the field frame.

3. Touch one probe of a 110-volt test lamp to the field-coil lead and the other to the field frame. If the lamp lights, the field coils are grounded and the field frame must be replaced as a unit; coils are not serviced separately.

TO SERVICE STARTER CLUTCH UNIT

1. Rotate the pinion. Gear should turn smoothly in one direction, but not in the other.

2. If the clutch unit does not function properly, or if the pinion is worn or damaged, replace the entire unit **(Fig. 1-56)**.

TO ASSEMBLE

1. Fit the shift fork in the drive housing and replace the shift-fork retaining pin. Bend one tip of the pin at a 15° angle away from the housing, and check both the fork and pin for free operation.

2. Replace the solenoid moving core and engage the shift fork.

3. Install the pinion shaft in the drive housing and replace the friction washer and drive gear.

4. Replace the clutch/pinion assembly, thrust washer, retaining ring and thrust washer, engaging the shift

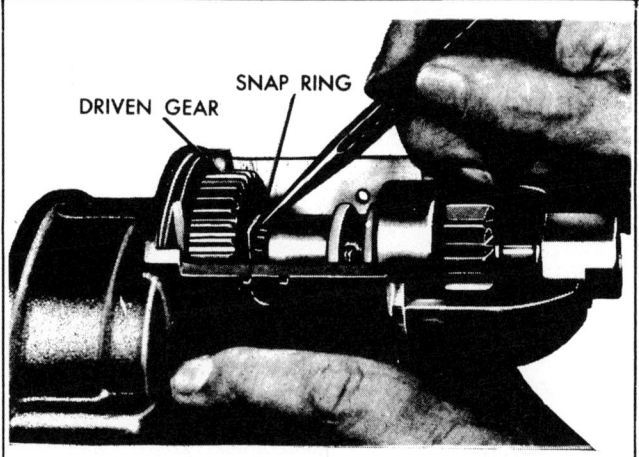

FIG. 1-52   REMOVING DRIVEN-GEAR SNAP RING

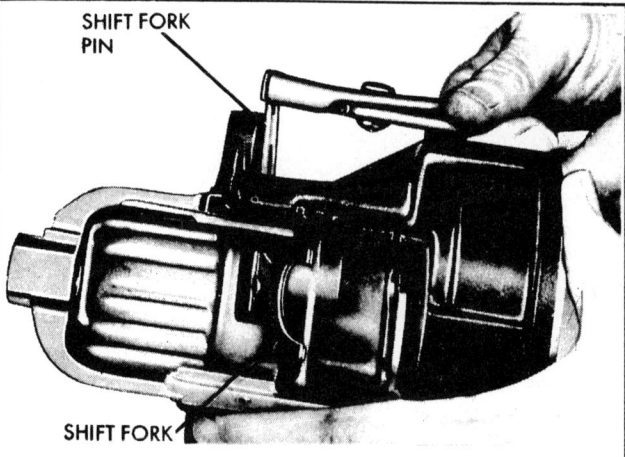

FIG. 1-53   REMOVING SHIFT FORK PIN

FIG. 1-54   ARMATURE SHORT TEST

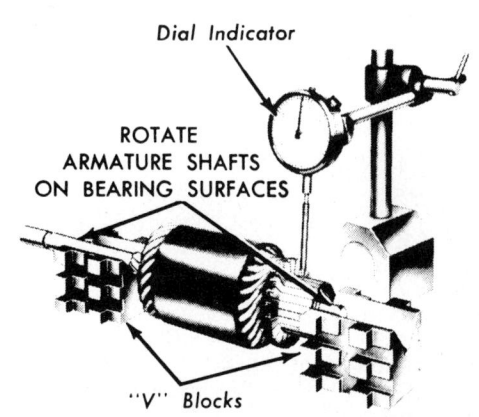

FIG. 1-55   COMMUTATOR RUNOUT TEST

fork with the clutch actuators. Make sure the friction washer is positioned on the pinion shaft splines before positioning the driven gear.

5. Install the driven-gear snap ring and pinion-shaft "C" clip to secure the pinion shaft in place.

6. Replace the solenoid return spring in the moving core and install the contact plunger in the solenoid. If the contact washer is burned from arcing, disassemble and reverse the washer before installing.

7. Assemble the battery terminal stud in the brush holder and place the seal on the brush holder plate.

8. Fit the solenoid lead wire through the brush holder hole and replace the stud, washers and nut.

9. Wrap the lead wire around the brush terminal post tightly. Solder with a high-temperature, resin-core solder and resin flux for a low-resistance connection.

10. Fit the brush holder to the solenoid attaching screws.

11. Carefully install the coil and brush plate assembly into the gear housing. Position the brush plate assembly and install the housing nuts.

12. Use the armature thrust washers to hold the brushes in position and install the brush terminal screw.

13. Locate the field frame to the housing and insert the armature. Engage the shaft splines with the reduction gear by rotating the armature slightly.

14. Replace the thrust washer on the armature shaft.

15. Fit the end head assembly in place, replace the through-bolts and tighten securely.

OMNI/HORIZON & 1971-72 CHRYSLER CORPORATION
(225-cu.-in. Engine)

Chrysler, Bosch & Nippondenso Direct-Drive Starting Motor

STARTING MOTOR DESCRIPTION

The direct-drive starting motor is an overrunning clutch design with an externally mounted solenoid energized through the ignition switch. When the switch is turned to the START position, the solenoid engages the starter drive gear by means of a shift fork. As the solenoid plunger reaches the end of its travel, it closes a switch which revolves the drive. An overrunning clutch protects against damage if the ignition switch is

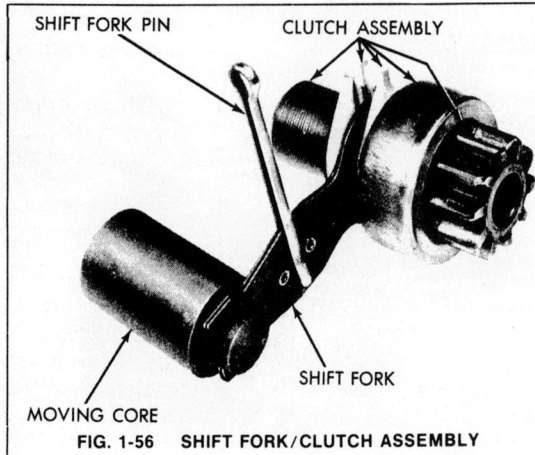

FIG. 1-56 **SHIFT FORK/CLUTCH ASSEMBLY**

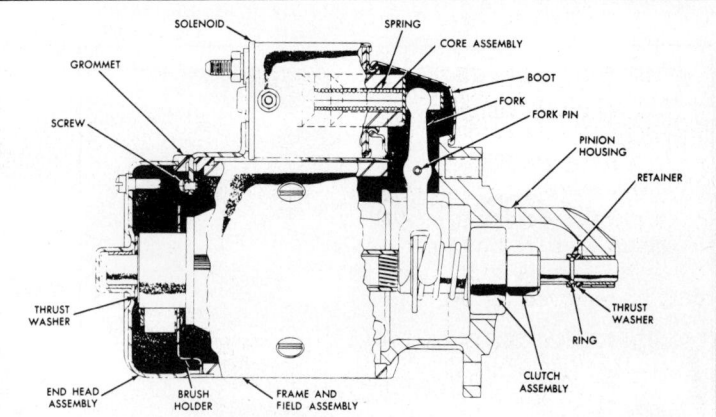

FIG. 1-57 **CHRYSLER CORPORATION DIRECT-DRIVE STARTING MOTOR**

CHRYSLER CORPORATION SPECIFICATIONS
(Reduction Gear Starter)

Starting motor model	1.5 hp—3755900 1.8 hp—3755250	2875560	3656575
Make	Chrysler built	Chrysler built	Chrysler built
Voltage	12	12	12
Number of fields	4 series parallel	4 (3 series, 1 shunt)	4 series parallel
Number of poles	4	4	4
Brushes	4	4	4
Spring tension	32 to 36 oz.	32 to 36 oz.	32 to 36 oz.
Drive	Solenoid shift overrunning clutch	Solenoid shift overrunning clutch	Solenoid shift overrunning clutch
End play	.010 in.–.045 in.	.010 in.–.045 in.	.010 in.–.045 in.
*Cranking amperage draw	165 to 180 amps. 225, 318 cu. ins. 180 to 200 amps. 360, 400, 440 cu. ins.	155 to 170 amps. 198 cu. ins. 165 to 180 amps. 225, 318, 340 cu. ins. 180 to 200 amps. 360, 400, 440 cu. ins.	180 to 200 amps. 360, 400, 440 cu. ins
FREE-RUNNING TEST			
Voltage	11	11	11
Amperage draw	90	90	90
Minimum speed rpm	1.5 hp—3700 1.8 hp—5700	1925 to 2600	4300
LOCKED RESISTANCE TEST			
Voltage	4	4	4
Amperage draw	475 to 550	400 to 450	475 to 550
SOLENOID SWITCH			
Pull-in coil	13 to 15 amps @ 6 volts @ 77°F	13.3 to 14.9 amps @ 6.0 volts @ 77°F	14.4 to 16.0 amps @ 6 volts @ 77°F
Hold-in coil	8 to 9 amps @ 6 volts @ 77°F	8.0 to 9.0 amps @ 6.0 volts @ 77°F	11.5 to 12.6 amps @ 6 volts @ 77°F

*Engine should be at operating temperature.

held in the START position after the engine starts.

Fig. 1-57 shows the Chrysler version used on the 1971-72 Chrysler 225-cu.-in. engine; the two Bosch and two Nippondenso direct-drive starting motors used on the Omni/Horizon are essentially similar to each other and to the larger Chrysler design. The test and overhaul procedures which follow can be applied to any of these starting motors; however, there are slight differences between the models used for manual and those used for automatic transmission applications. If something does not come apart exactly as described during an overhaul procedure, do not force pieces apart. Simply rethink the situation and apply common sense.

STARTING CIRCUIT AND TEST SEQUENCE

The starting system circuit includes the following components:
1. Starter solenoid.
2. Starter relay.
3. Neutral safety switch (automatic transmission).
4. Connecting wiring.

Test procedures for each component in the control circuit follow and should be performed in the order specified below. Disconnect the distributor primary lead or the electronic distributor wire harness to prevent the engine from starting *before* proceeding with the test sequence.

STARTER SOLENOID TEST

1. Use a heavy jumper lead to connect the starter relay battery and solenoid terminals **(Fig. 1-49)**. Engine will crank if the starter solenoid is good.
2. If the engine does not crank, inspect the wiring and connections from the relay to the starting motor for loose or corroded connections and repeat Step 1.
3. If the engine still does not crank, the starter should be removed for overhaul.

STARTER RELAY TEST—AUTOMATIC TRANSMISSION

1. Set the transmission selector lever in NEUTRAL or PARK position.
2. Connect a jumper lead between the battery and ignition terminals on the starter relay. If the engine cranks, the starter relay is good.

3. If the engine does not crank, connect a second jumper lead between the starter-relay ground terminal and a good ground. Repeat Step 2.
4. If engine now cranks, the starter relay is good, but the neutral safety switch is defective. If the engine does not crank, the starter relay is defective.

STARTER RELAY TEST—MANUAL TRANSMISSION

1. Place the transmission in NEUTRAL with the parking brake set.
2. Connect a jumper lead between the battery and ignition terminals on the starter relay. If the engine cranks, the starter relay is good.
3. If the engine does not crank, connect a second jumper lead between the starter-relay ground terminal and a good ground. Repeat Step 2.
4. If the engine still does not crank, the starter relay is defective.

STARTER REMOVAL/INSTALLATION

TO REMOVE

1. Disconnect battery ground cable at the battery.
2. Unhook the cable at the starter terminal.
3. Remove the solenoid lead wires from the solenoid terminals.
4. Remove the bolt and stud nut holding the starting motor to the flywheel housing.
5. If the engine is equipped with an automatic transmission, slide the oil-cooler tube bracket from the stud.
6. Remove the starting motor, taking care not to damage the flywheel housing seal.

TO INSTALL

1. Clean the starting-motor and flywheel-housing mounting surfaces to provide a good electrical contact.
2. Fit starting motor to the flywheel housing seal.
3. Position the starting motor, washer and bolt on the mounting surface. Fit the oil-cooler tube bracket (if removed) and install the washer and nut.
4. Hold the starting motor away from the engine while tightening the bolt to 50 ft.-lbs.
5. Reconnect the solenoid lead wire to the solenoid switch terminal and the cable to the starter terminal.
6. Connect the battery ground cable and check for proper engine cranking.

FREE-RUNNING STARTER CURRENT DRAW TEST

1. Secure the starting motor in a bench vise and connect a battery/starter tester as shown in **Fig. 1-58.**
2. Read the voltmeter scale with the starter running at ''no load.''
3. Disconnect the starting motor from the battery and adjust the load control knob until the voltmeter reading is the same as that obtained with the starter connected.
4. Read the ammeter scale; ''no-load'' current draw should be 78 amps maximum at 3800 minimum revolutions.

If current draw is greater than that specified, the starting motor may have shorted circuits, a rubbing armature, a bent armature shaft or tight bushings. A low or zero reading indicates excessive internal resistance. Check for loose or high resistance connections in the field or armature circuits, or for poor brush or commutator condition.

STARTING MOTOR OVERHAUL

Work on a clean bench with clean tools. Clean the

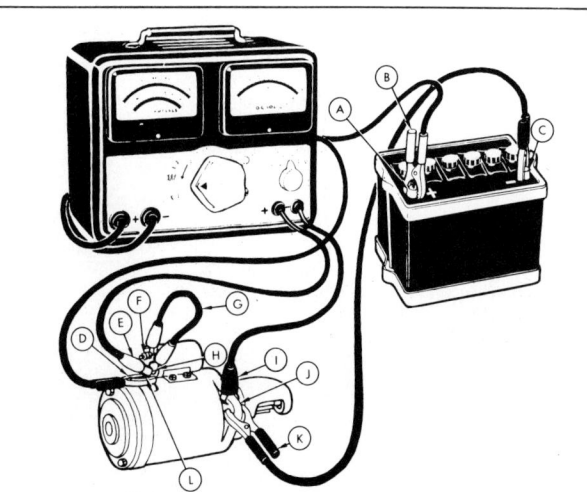

Connect the red ammeter lead (B) to the positive battery terminal post (A) and the black ammeter lead (D) to the starting motor terminal post (L). Connect the red voltmeter lead (E) to the starting motor terminal post (H) and the black voltmeter lead (I) to the starting motor frame (J). Run one jumper lead (K) from the starting motor frame (J) to the negative battery terminal post (C). If the starting motor being tested has an attached solenoid, then run a second jumper lead (G) from solenoid's input terminal (F) to its control terminal (H).

FIG. 1-58 FREE-RUNNING STARTER CURRENT DRAW TEST

exterior of the starting motor with a soft cloth dampened in solvent and wipe dry before beginning disassembly—*do not* use solvent on interior components. Handle all parts carefully to prevent nicks, burrs and scratches **(Fig. 1-59)**.

TO DISASSEMBLE

1. Remove the two through-bolts and end head assembly. It may be necessary to tap the end head lightly with a plastic hammer to free it from the housing.

2. Remove the thrust washers from the armature shaft and lift the brush holder springs to remove the brushes, then remove the brush plate **(Fig. 1-60)**.

3. When disconnecting the field coil leads from the solenoid connector, remove the screws holding the solenoid to the housing and slide the solenoid and boot off the shift fork.

4. With a hammer and appropriate punch, drive the clutch shift-fork pivot pin from the housing.

5. Remove the pinion-housing drive end and spacer washer. Some starting motors may be fitted with a rubber seal; if so equipped and the seal is damaged, replace the pinion housing assembly.

6. Remove the shift fork from the starter drive.

7. Sliding the clutch pinion gear to the rear, drive the stop retainer toward the pinion gear until a snap ring is exposed. Remove the snap ring.

8. Slide the clutch drive from the armature shaft.

9. Clean all parts thoroughly. Wipe all parts with a clean dry cloth only.

10. Check brush condition. Brushes that are oil-soaked or worn more than one-half their original length should be replaced.

11. Brush sets are removed and replaced as a screw-on assembly. Attach the insulated set to the series field terminal and the ground set to the field frame.

TO TEST ARMATURE

The armature is tested for shorts, grounds and commutator runout by the same procedures described under the "Chrysler Reduction-Gear Starting Motor." Commutator runout should not exceed 0.003-in., or refacing is necessary.

TO TEST FIELD COILS FOR GROUND

1. Touch one probe of a 110-volt test lamp to the series field coil lead and the other to the field frame. If the lamp lights, the series field coils are grounded.

DIRECT-DRIVE STARTER MOTOR

Part Number		
Automatic Transmission	5206260	5206270
Standard Transmission	5206255	5206265
Make Model	Bosch	Nippondenso
Voltage	12	12
No. of Fields	4 (Series Parallel)	4 (Series Parallel)
No. of Poles	4	4
Brushes	4	4
Drive	Solenoid Shift Overrunning Clutch	Solenoid Shift Overrunning Clutch
Cranking Amperage Draw Test*	120-160 Amps	120-160 Amps
Free-Running Test		
Voltage	11	11
Amperage Draw	47 Amps	47 Amps
Minimum Speed RPM	6600 RPM	6600 RPM
Solenoid Closing Voltage	7.5 Volts	7.5 Volts

*Engine should be up to operating temperature. Extremely heavy oil or tight engine will increase starter amperage draw.

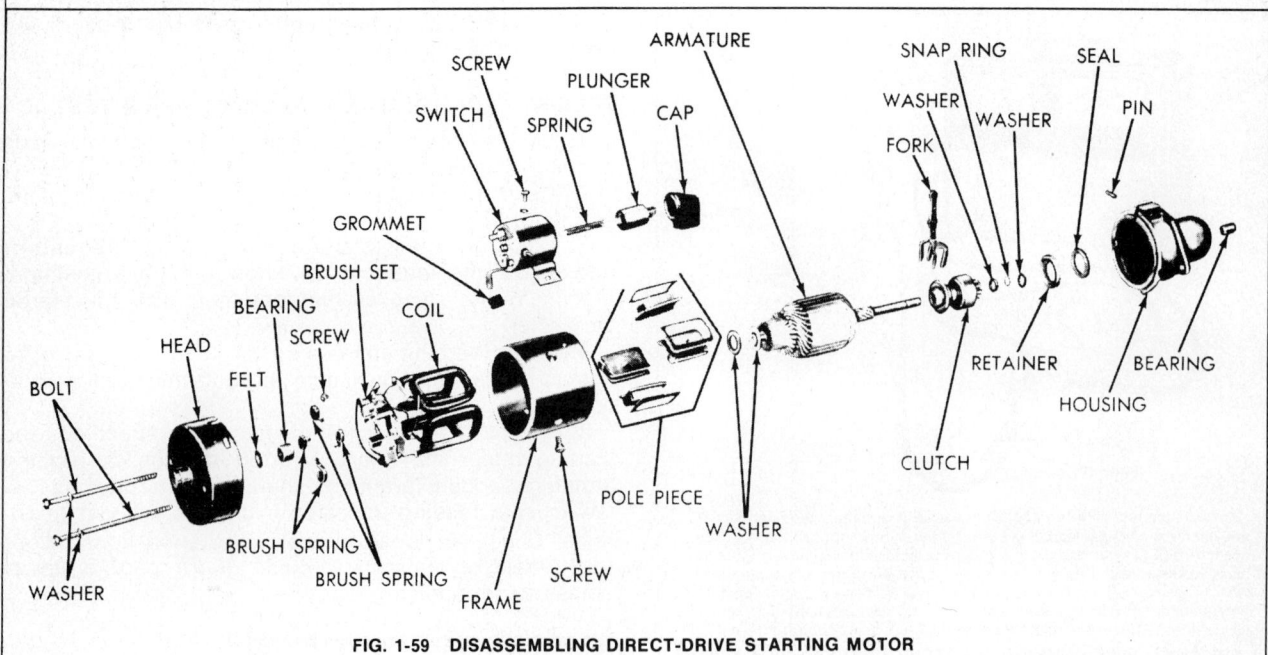

FIG. 1-59 DISASSEMBLING DIRECT-DRIVE STARTING MOTOR

2. Touch one test probe to the shunt field-coil lead and the other to the field frame. If the lamp lights, the shunt field coil is grounded.

3. If either the series or shunt field coils are grounded, unsolder the connector wires and test each one separately to isolate faulty coil. Replace with new coil.

TO TEST BRUSH HOLDERS FOR GROUND

1. Holding one test probe against the brush ring, touch the other probe to each brush holder in turn. Two of the holders directly opposite each other are intentionally grounded and should cause the test lamp to light. The other two holders are insulated, and lamp should not light.

2. Should one or both of the insulated holders cause the test lamp to light, they are grounded on the brush ring and the entire brush ring assembly must be replaced **(Fig. 1-61)**.

TO SERVICE STARTER DRIVE UNIT

1. Rotate the pinion. Gear should turn smoothly in one direction, but not in the other.

2. If the clutch unit does not function properly, or if the pinion is worn or damaged, replace the entire unit.

TO ASSEMBLE

1. Lubricate the armature shaft and splines using SAE 10W or SAE 30W oil.

2. Fit the starter clutch drive, retaining collar, snap ring and spacer washer on the armature shaft.

3. Position the shift fork over the retaining collar, with the narrow legs facing to the rear (toward the armature). If the fork is incorrectly installed, its travel will be limited and cause a lockup in the clutch drive **(Fig. 1-62)**.

4. Replace the pinion housing on the armature shaft and index the shift fork with the housing slot. Secure the fork with the pivot pin.

5. When sliding the armature into the field frame housing, index the pinion housing with the frame housing slot.

6. Replace the solenoid and boot assembly, torquing screws to 60-70 in.-lbs.

7. Hook the field coil leads to the solenoid connector, making sure the terminals do not touch the field frame.

8. Index the brush-holder-plate tang in the field frame hole and replace the plate.

9. Install the brushes in their respective holders. Leads must rest behind the brush holder ring and not interfere with brush operation.

10. Replace the thrust washers on the commutator end of the armature shaft. A 0.010-in. minimum end play is necessary here.

11. Replace the end head and install the through-bolts, tightening each to 40-50 in.-lbs.

12. Insert a wedge between the solenoid and starter frame. Depress the solenoid plunger with a screwdriver until it bottoms and insert a feeler gauge to check pinion clearance.

13. Clearance should be ⅛-in. If adjustment is required to bring it into specifications, loosen the solenoid attaching screws, move the solenoid until the required clearance is obtained and retighten the screws to specifications.

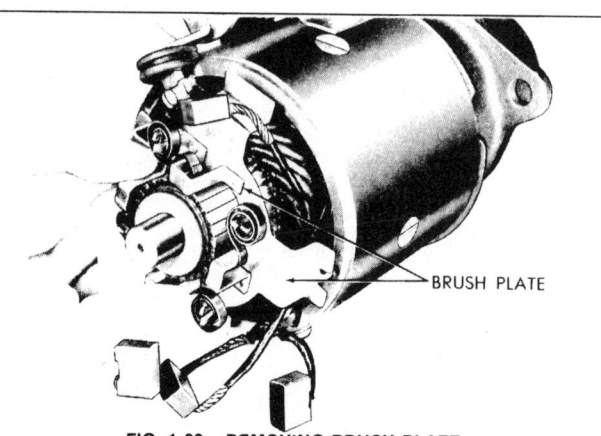

FIG. 1-60   REMOVING BRUSH PLATE

FIG. 1-61   BRUSH HOLDER GROUND TEST

CHRYSLER CORPORATION SPECIFICATIONS
Direct Drive Starter

STARTING MOTOR MODEL	1889100
MAKE	Chrysler
VOLTAGE	12
NUMBER OF FIELDS	4 (3 series, 1 shunt)
NUMBER OF POLES	4
BRUSHES	4
SPRING TENSION	32 to 36 oz.
DRIVE	Solenoid shift overrunning clutch
END PLAY	0.005-in. minimum
*CRANKING AMPERAGE DRAW	165 to 185 amps
FREE-RUNNING TEST	
Voltage	11
Amperage Draw	78 amps maximum
Minimum Speed RPM	3800
LOCKED RESISTANCE TEST	
Voltage	4
Amperage Draw	310 to 445 amps
SOLENOID SWITCH	
Pull-In Coil	22.4 to 24.0 amps @ 6 volts @ 77°F
Hold-In Coil	8.3 to 9.3 amps @ 6 volts @ 77°F

*Engine should be at operating temperature.

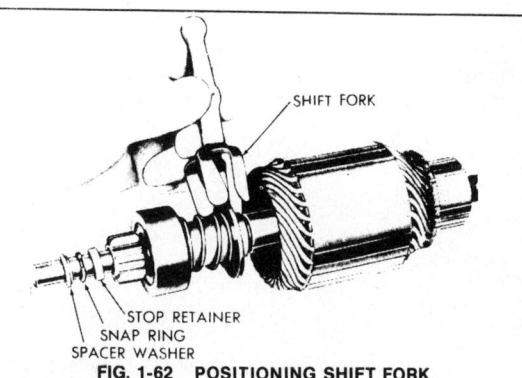

FIG. 1-62   POSITIONING SHIFT FORK

HOW TO: Delco-Remy Starter Overhaul

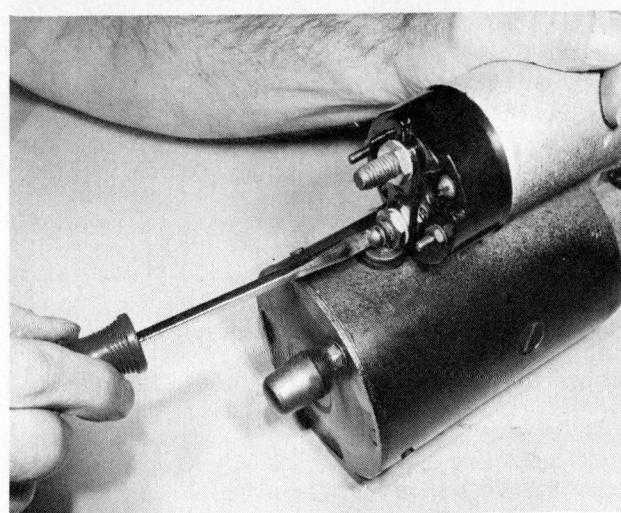

1. Begin disassembly by removing the screw which connects the solenoid motor terminal to the field coil connector. This particular starting motor fits a 1974 Chevrolet Vega.

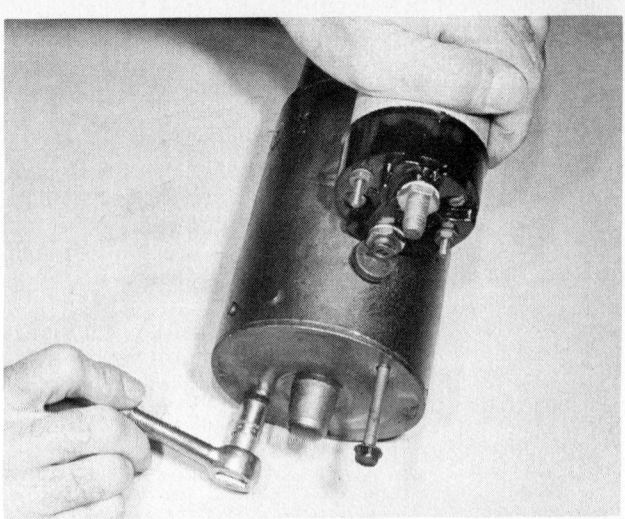

2. Various versions of the Delco-Remy starting motor exist with only slight internal differences between them. Loosen and remove the two through-bolts from the end plate.

3. The end plate will now slip off easily. Note the leather washer on the end of the armature shaft. Inspect the bushing in the end plate for wear or damage.

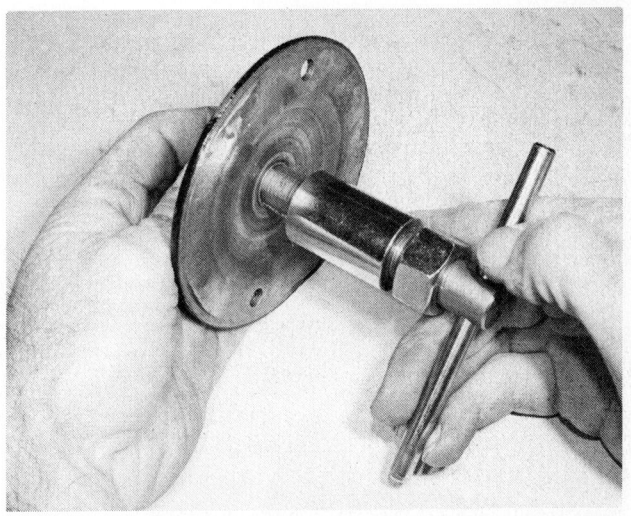

4. Do not try to pry the old bushing out or you'll deform the end plate. Bushing removal is made easy and safe with this Speed Puller from Wesley Manufacturing Company.

5. Twist slightly and remove the commutator end frame, the field frame and the armature assembly from the drive housing. Do not remove the solenoid before this step.

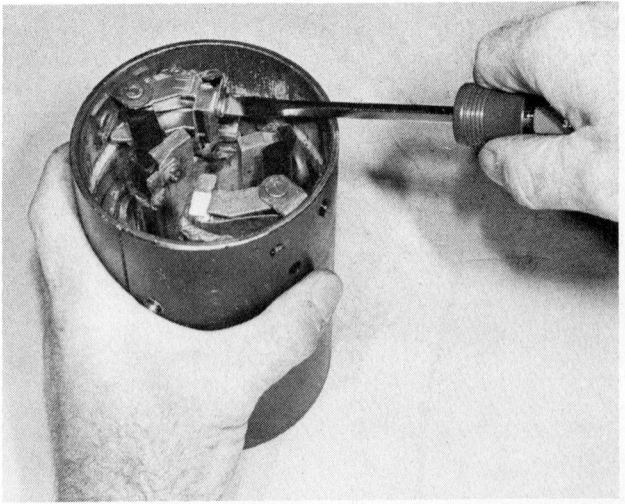

6. The commutator brushes are held in the brush holder by screws. If the brushes are pitted or worn more than one-half their original length, they should be replaced.

7. Don't mistakenly pull the brush-holder pivot pin out to remove the brushes, or you'll end up with a mess like this. Everything falls out once the pivot pin is removed.

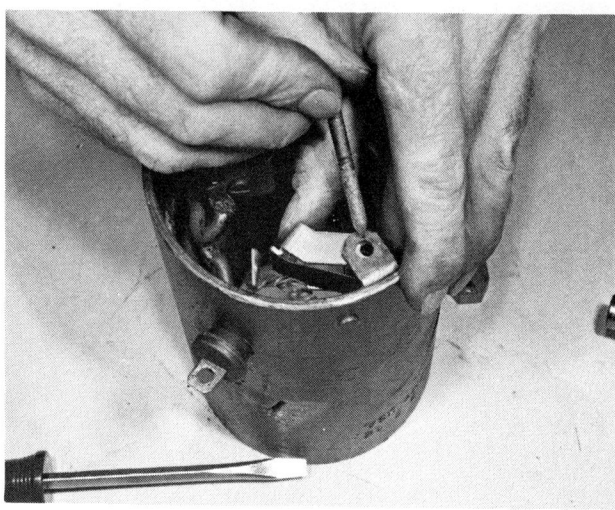

8. If you should make the mistake of pulling the pivot pin, use the other brush holder assembly as a guide in helping you to position the pieces correctly while reinstalling pivot pin.

9. Remove the solenoid attaching screws with caution, because the plunger spring exerts a good deal of pressure and may send the solenoid unit flying across the room.

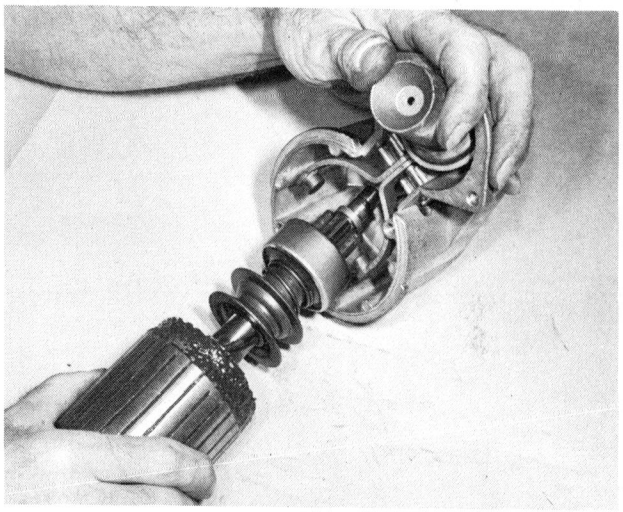

10. If the shift fork is not to be removed, angle the armature shaft to disengage the drive gear pulley from the fork legs, and remove the armature shaft from the drive housing.

11. On many of the Delco-Remy starting motors, the shift-fork pivot pin is simply driven out for removal, but this Vega model uses a snap ring (arrow) to hold the pivot pin in place.

12. The retaining ring over the snap ring must be driven back toward the drive mechanism to uncover the snap ring for removal. Use a socket and mallet, as shown, and tap gently.

HOW TO: Delco-Remy Starter Overhaul

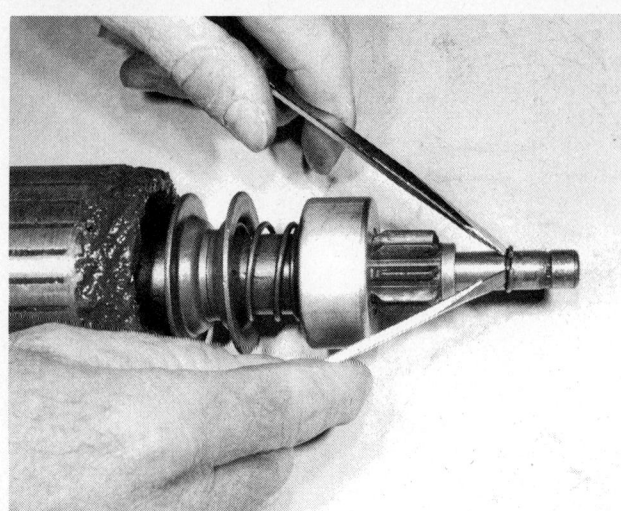

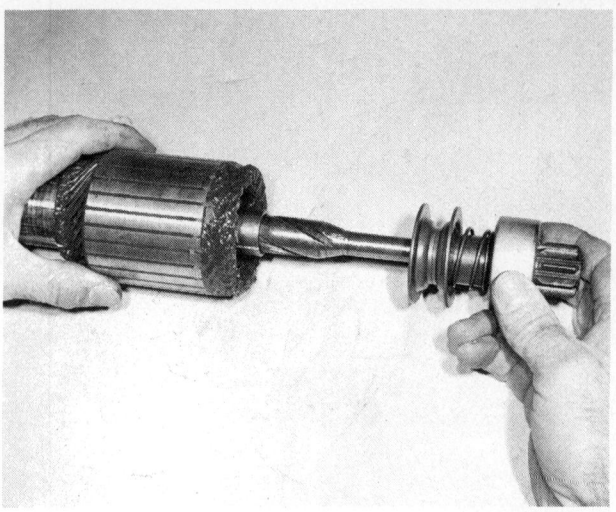

13. With the retainer pushed back off the snap ring, two screwdrivers must be used to pry the snap ring from the shaft groove. Snap ring pliers will not do the job in this case.

14. With the snap ring removed, the drive mechanism can be pulled from the armature shaft. Check the splines on the armature shaft for wear or damage, inspect drive mechanism.

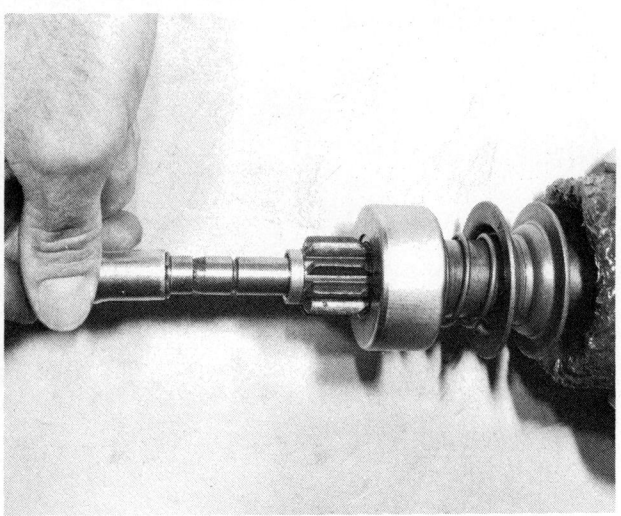

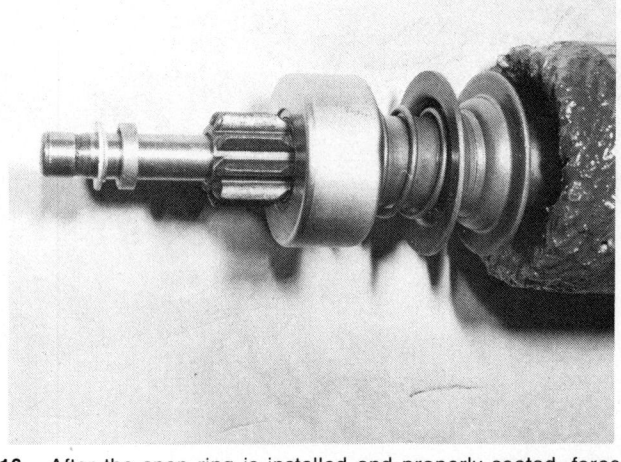

15. A new snap ring must be installed when replacing the drive mechanism on the armature shaft. Fit the snap ring to the end of the shaft, and use a socket to force it into place.

16. After the snap ring is installed and properly seated, force the retainer over it. Don't forget to reinstall the thrust collar on the shaft end before inserting it in the drive housing.

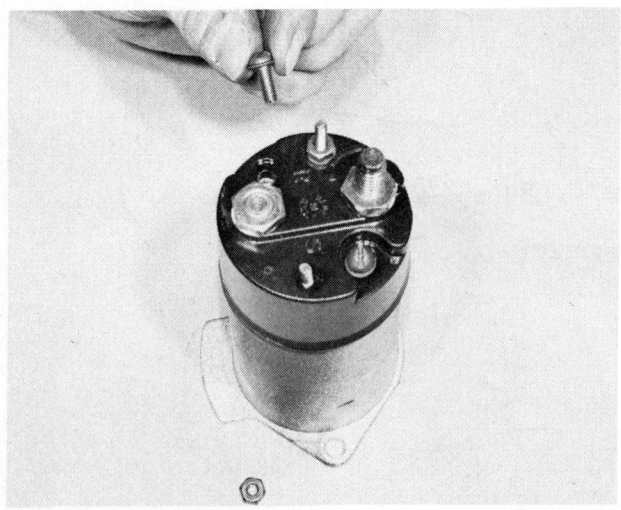

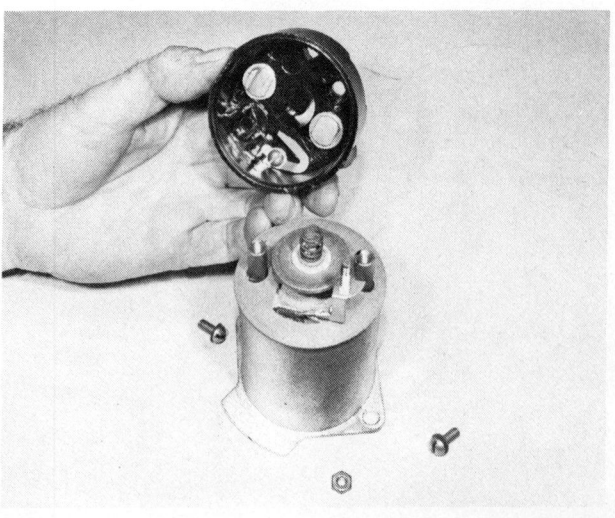

17. If the starter solenoid is not operating properly, it can be easily disassembled and the Delco contact washer replaced. Remove the holding screws and take the nuts off the terminals.

18. Lift off the solenoid cover. This solenoid, you will notice, differs considerably in design from the other Delco-Remy units—the motor connector strap terminal is not soldered.

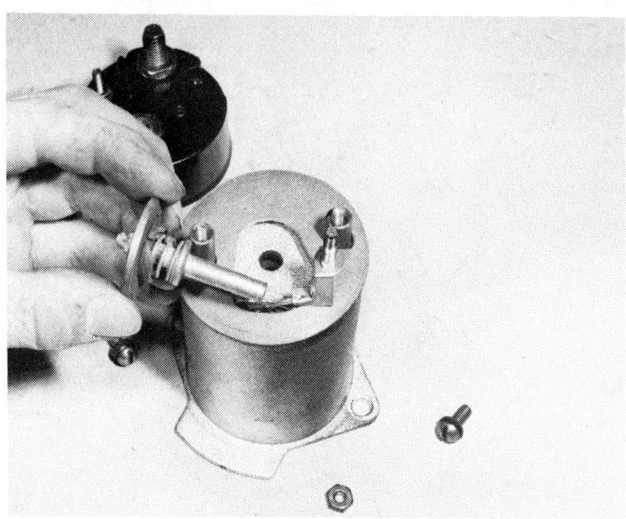

19. The plunger assembly can be disassembled and a worn contact ring can be reversed on some other solenoid models, but this one is constructed to be replaced as a unit.

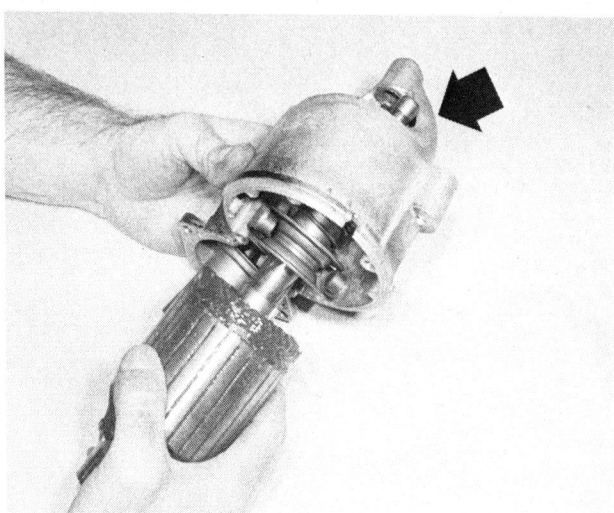

20. To reinstall the starter drive in the housing without removing the shift fork, angle the shaft (arrow) so that it bypasses the housing bushing, and connect fork to the pulley.

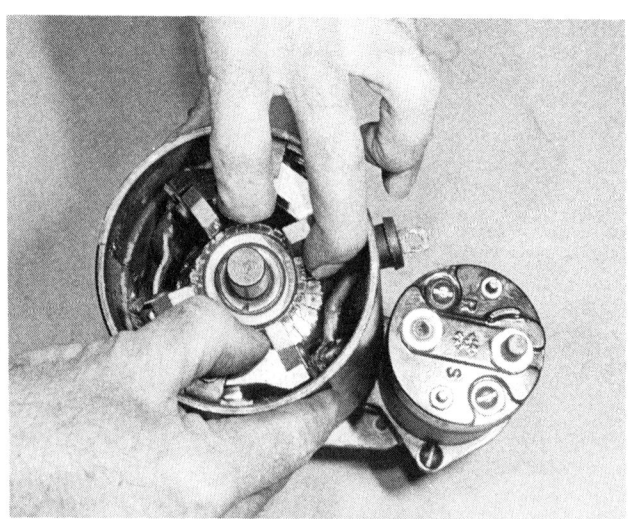

21. You must hold all four brushes against the field frame with your fingers, as shown, to install the armature. Work slowly and do not try to force armature in place.

22. If you remove and replace the commutator brushes, their contour must match that of the armature. The arrows point to incorrectly installed brushes; unscrew and reverse them.

23. To replace the field frame and the drive housing, line up the dowel pin that is protruding from the field frame with a corresponding pin hole (circle) in the drive housing.

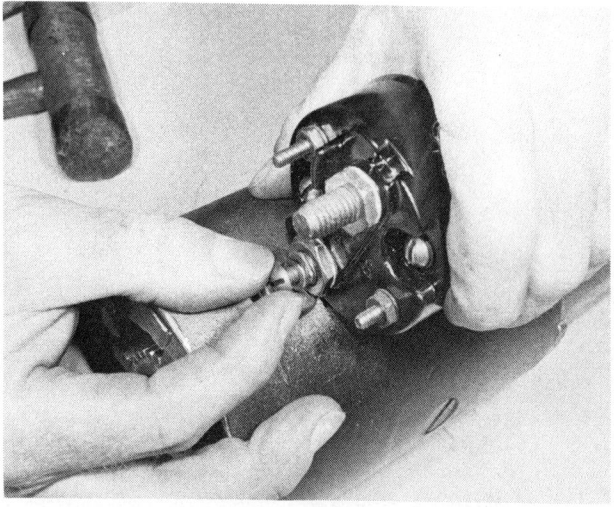

24. Fit the drive housing and field frame together, then reconnect the field coil and solenoid motor terminal. Replace the end frame and install the through-bolts. Overhaul is completed.

HOW TO: Autolite-Motorcraft Positive-Engagement Starter Overhaul

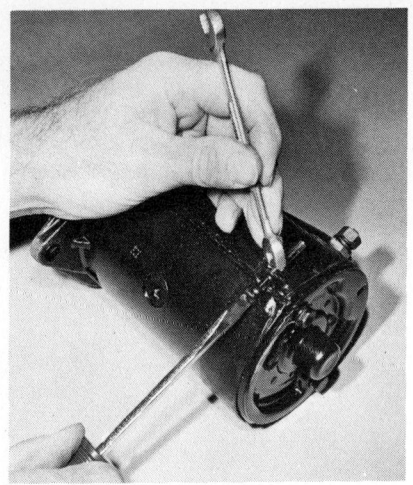

1. The positive-engagement starter differs slightly internally according to model year and application. This one fits a '74 Pinto. Loosen band retainer first.

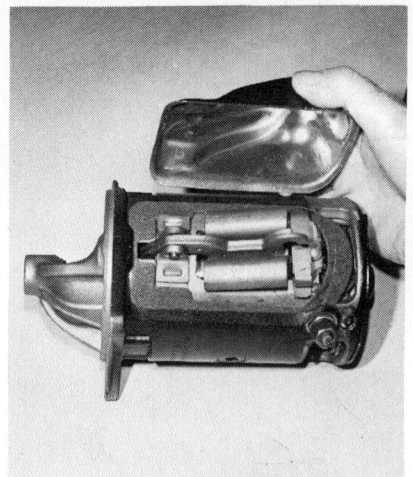

2. Slide band off housing and lift off drive-gear plunger-lever cover and gasket. This is held in place by brush band at one end and housing lip at the other.

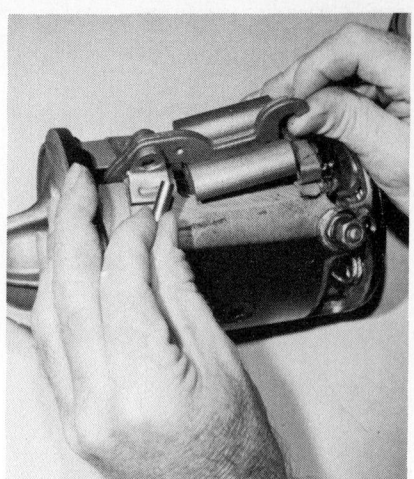

3. Remove pivot pin holding drive gear plunger in place. If unit has not been recently overhauled, you may have to drive pin out with a punch and hammer.

4. Brushes must be removed from holders before brush end plate can be removed. Use two small hooks to bend brush spring back, lift brush from holder.

5. With brush end plate and through-bolts removed, tap the armature shaft gently with a soft-faced hammer to separate the drive housing from field frame.

6. When drive housing comes free, a small spring falls out. This happens so fast you may not notice where it came from. Arrows show correct location.

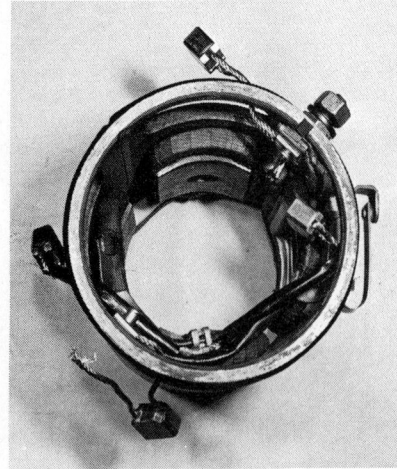

7. Here's the problem—broken ground brush lead. Ground brushes can be replaced easily since they are secured by a screw; insulated brushes are soldered.

8. Twin grooves on this armature indicate that it was rubbing on the pole pieces. Shaft should be checked for straightness and the armature refaced.

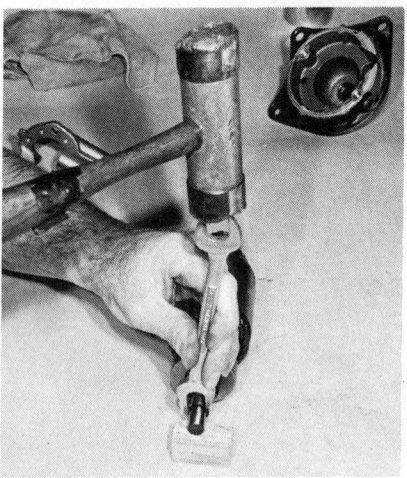

9. To remove drive gear from armature shaft, use a wrench and mallet as shown to drive the snap ring off shaft groove. Tap lightly and it pops right off.

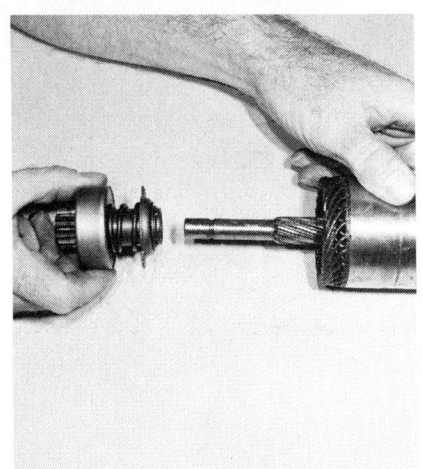

10. Inspect armature shaft splines for wear or damage. Some drive gears can be disassembled, but this particular one must be replaced as an entire unit.

11. Replace drive gear on armature shaft and reinstall snap ring by tapping gently with brass hammer. Be sure to support end of shaft with wooden block.

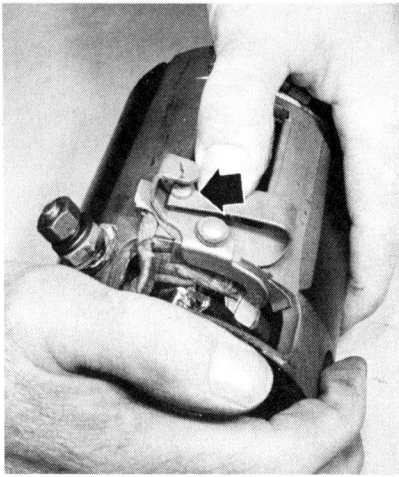

12. Check these contact points on the field frame. If burned or pitted, you can resurface them with an igniton file. If badly burned or pitted, replace them.

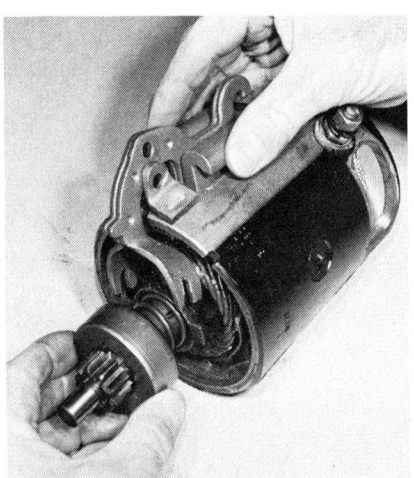

13. Insert armature into field frame and reposition drive gear so that tooth in the shift fork engages lips one each side of the drive gear retainer.

14. Place field frame on its end and install the small spring on the shift fork tangs. Fit drive end housing in place so that spring engages hole in housing.

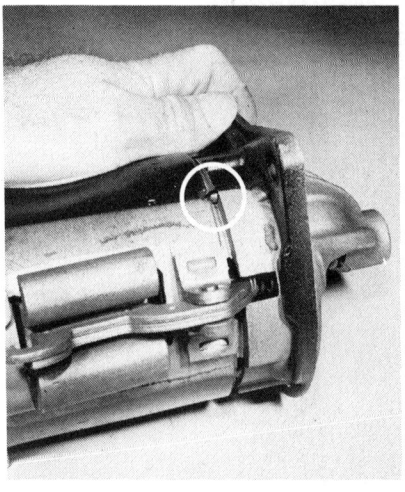

15. Replace pivot pin in shift fork and align the small dowel on the drive end housing with the cutout in the field frame to fit the two together correctly.

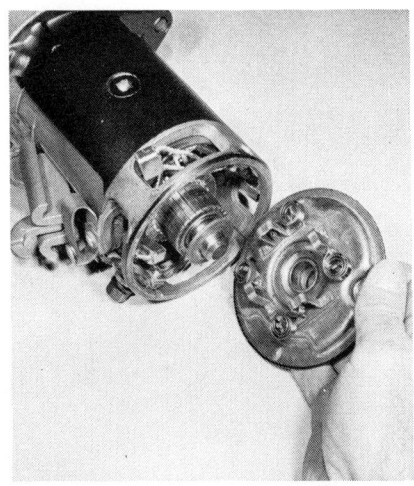

16. Inspect and replace brush end plate bushing if necessary, then fit the end plate back to the field frame and install the through-bolts, tightening loosely.

17. Pull back the brush springs with the small hook and reinstall each brush in its holder. Make sure that spring rests in small cutout on top of the brush.

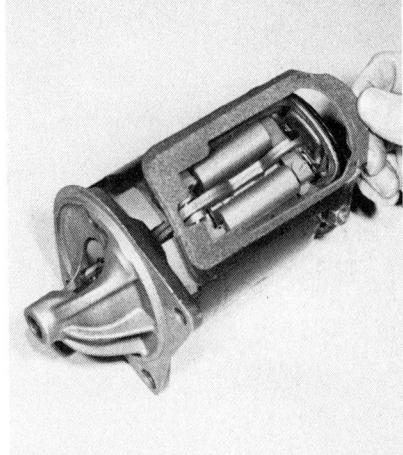

18. Tighten through-bolts securely, replace drive plunger cover gasket and cover, then slide brush band over field frame and tighten. Overhaul is done.

HOW TO: Chrysler Starter/Reduction Gear Overhaul

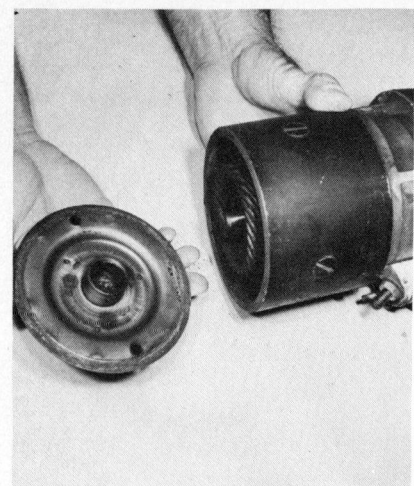

1. Chrysler has used reduction gear starter motor for years. Brush holder differs on some models. Remove through-bolts and part end head from field frame.

2. Inspect end head bearing. If replacement is necessary, you'll need a special bearing removal tool to cut old interference bearing out of frame. Press fit.

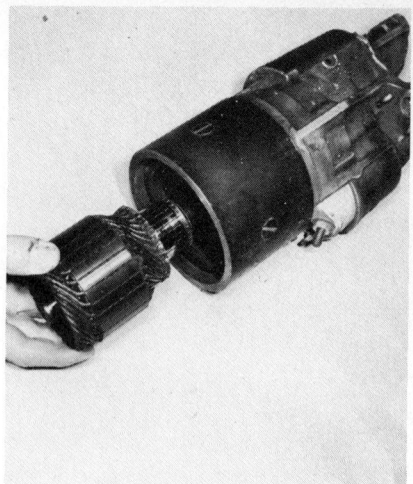

3. Remove armature carefully by pulling from field frame/gear housing assembly. Note that thrust washers are used on both ends of armature shaft.

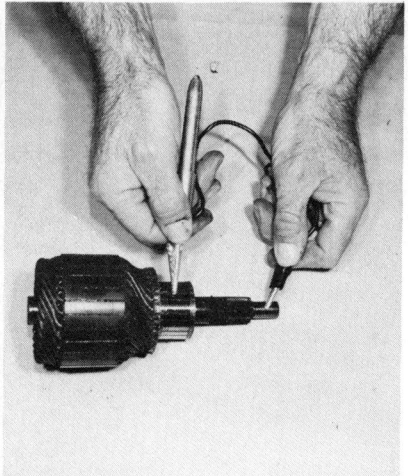

4. Check armature for ground with self-powered test light. Touch shaft with one probe and commutator riser bars with other probe. Replace if lamp lights.

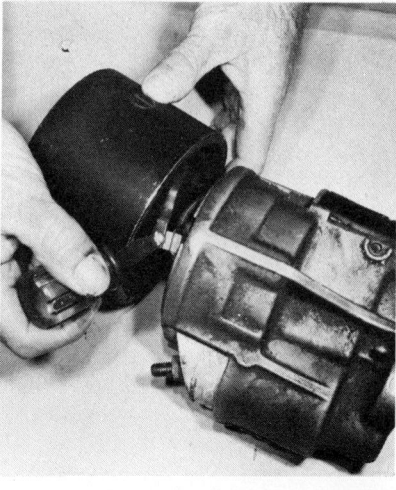

5. Carefully separate field frame from gear housing assembly sufficiently to expose terminal screw. Screw must be removed before field frame can be removed.

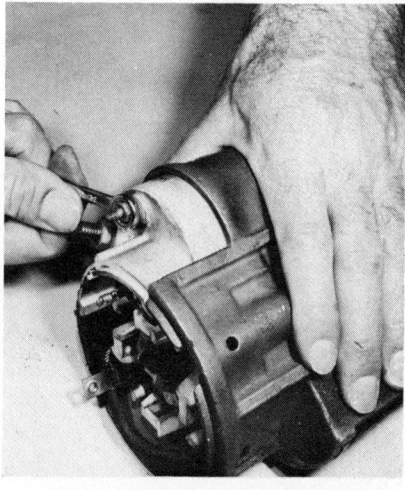

6. Remove nut, steel washer and insulating washer from solenoid terminal. Configuration of brush holder plate will differ according to starter motor model use.

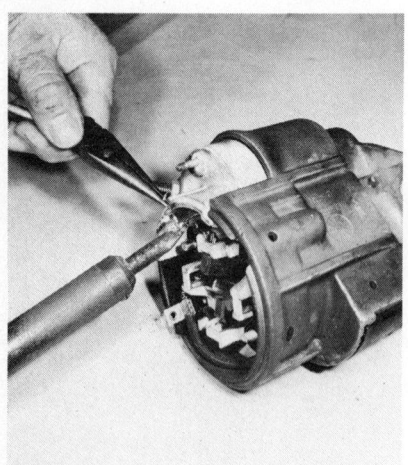

7. Use a low-heat iron and a pair of pliers to unsolder solenoid lead wire from brush terminal, then unwind wire carefully. Remove brush plate from housing.

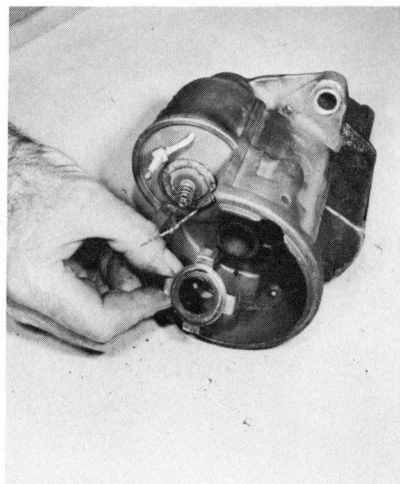

8. Check gear housing assembly carefully for this tanged washer if it was not on armature shaft with flat thrust washer when armature was removed.

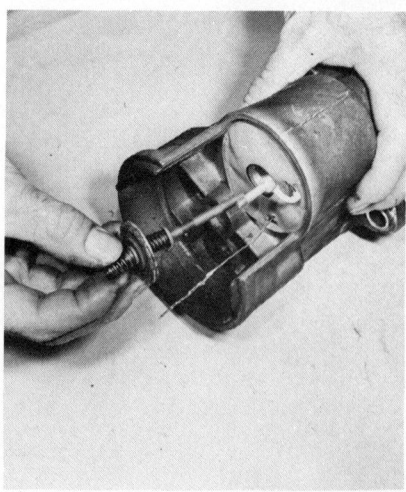

9. Remove solenoid plunger shaft and contact assembly from solenoid. Face of contact should show arcing; if excessive, contact can be removed and reversed.

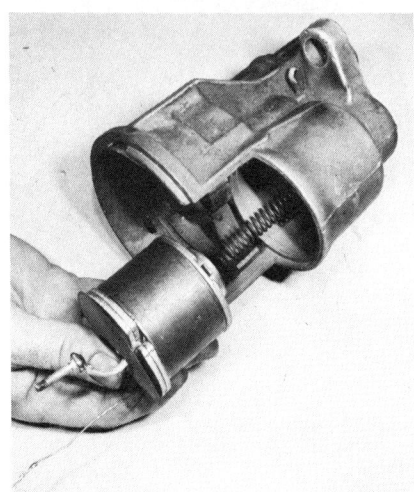

10. Withdraw solenoid winding and return spring from gear housing. Plunger core will remain in housing with shift fork. On some, solenoid/brush plate are as one.

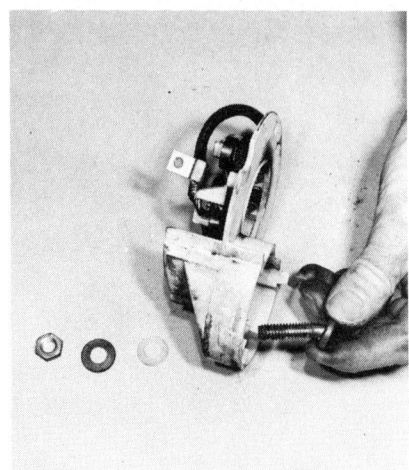

11. Remove nut and washers from battery terminal and withdraw terminal frum brush holder plate. Replace battery terminal if head is worn excessively.

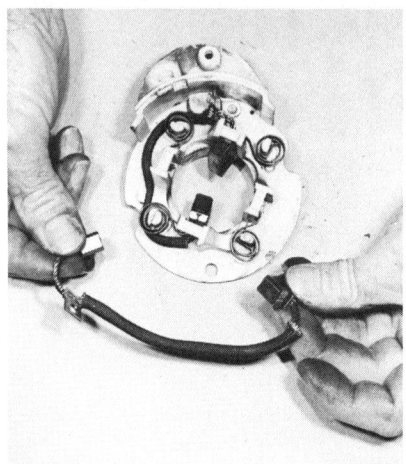

12. Remove brushes and leads from brush holder plate and inspect carefully for damaged leads. Replace brushes if oil-soaked, or if one-half of new length.

13. Use small screwdriver to pry dust cover from gear housing. Remove snap ring holding driven gear to pinion shaft with punch/screwdriver (will pop off).

14. Use snap ring pliers to remove snap ring between pinion and end of drive housing (arrow). Do not expand snap ring more than necessary to move it out.

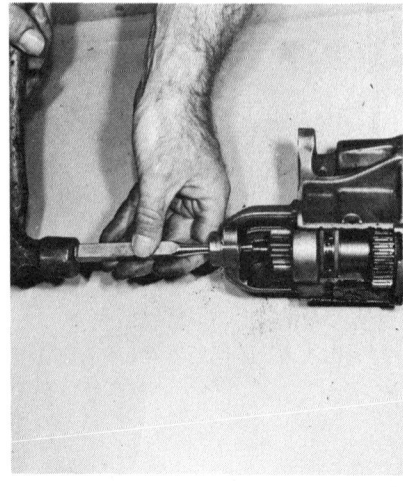

15. Once both snap rings are removed, drive pinion gear toward driven gear using a punch and hammer until shaft clears nose of gear housing and comes free.

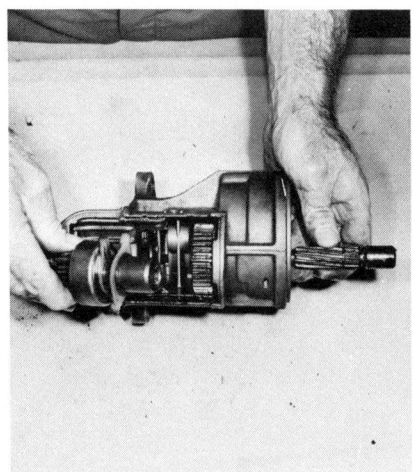

16. Withdraw shaft from open end of gear housing. Remove clutch and pinion assembly, retainer ring and thrust washers, and two shift fork actuators.

17. Remove driven gear and friction washer from gear housing. Inspect driven and pinion gears carefully for signs of wear, or burring, etc. Replace washer.

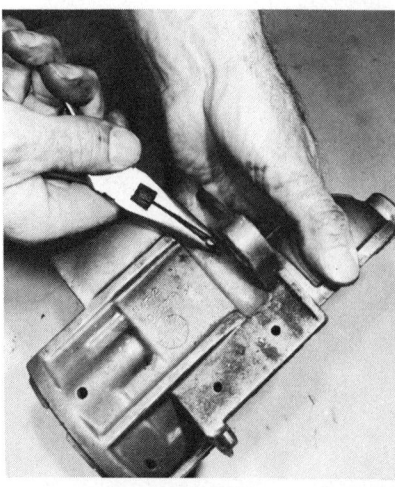

18. Pull shifter fork forward and remove solenoid moving core, then pull shift fork retaining pin from housing and remove shift fork assembly. Wipe all parts clean.

HOW TO: Chrysler Starter/Reduction Gear Overhaul

19. To begin reassembly, position shift fork in drive housing. Shift fork retaining pin is like giant cotter pin; install over shift fork and through housing.

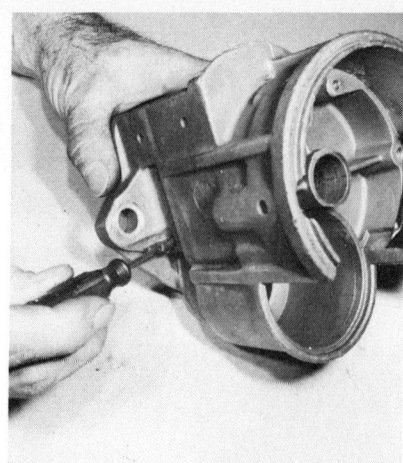

20. Hold head of retaining pin with one hand and bend one tip of pin about 15° away from gear housing (not other tip). Install solenoid moving core to lock fork.

21. Position friction washer on driven gear. Insert gear and washer into front of housing and replace shaft through rear of housig, engaging driven gear/washer.

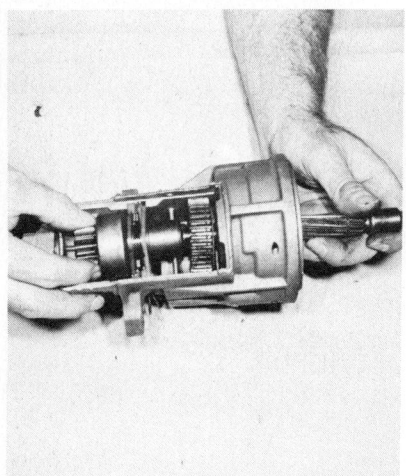

22. Now install pinion/clutch assembly from front of housing. Engage shift fork with actuators and revolve shaft through pinion/clutch assembly.

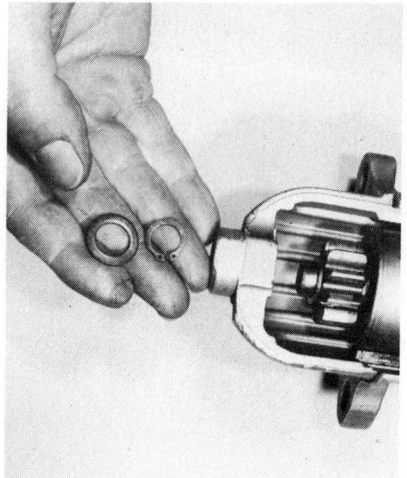

23. Position thrust washer and snap ring in front of shaft. Slide shaft forward to engage front of gear housing. Expand snap ring sufficiently to seat in shaft groove.

24. Make sure friction washer is seated on shoulder of shaft spines before securing driven gear to shaft with snap ring. Tap shaft gently into drive end bushing.

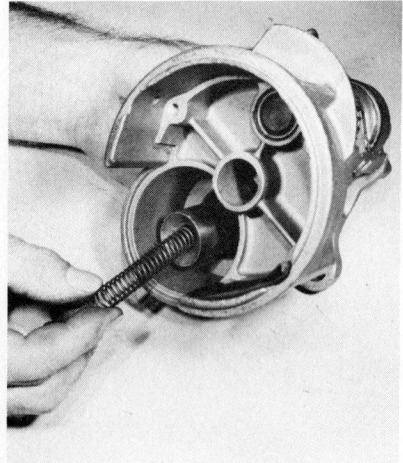

25. Check operation of shift fork and pinion/clutch assembly. It should move freely, without binding. Install return spring in solenoid plunger core.

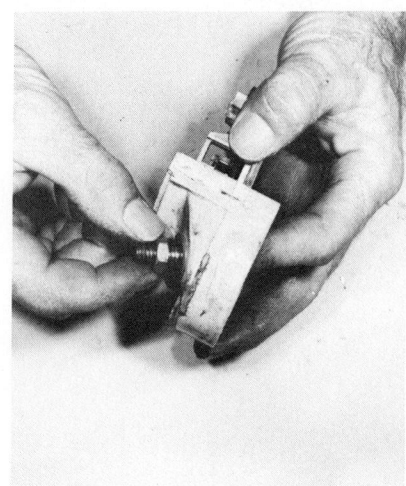

26. Fit battery terminal stud through brush plate holder and install insulating washer, steel washer and nut. Tighten nut snugly. Terminal head must fit holder recess.

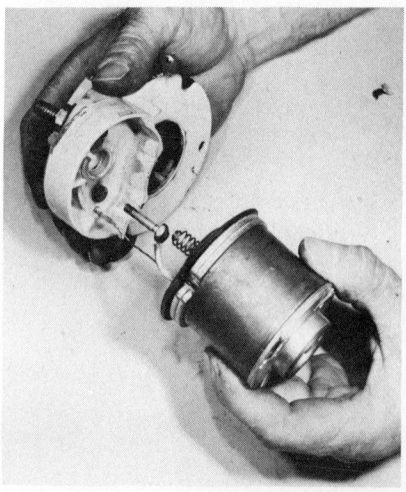

27. Replace contact plunger in solenoid. Thread solenoid terminal and lead wire through brush plate holder and seat solenoid to holder.

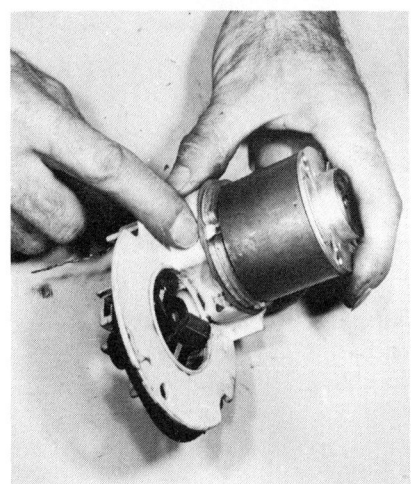

28. Be sure that this seal is used between brush plate holder and solenoid. Install insulating washer on solenoid stud, then replace flat washer and nut.

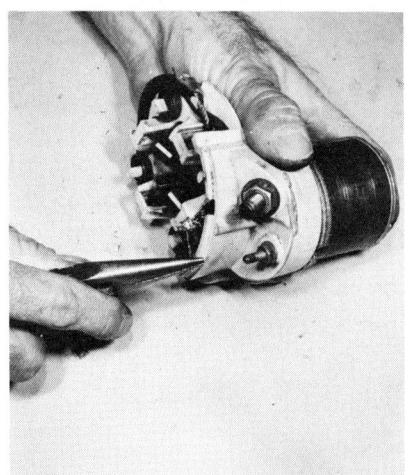

29. Wind solenoid lead wire tightly around brush terminal post. Solder terminal post/ wire-connection with high-temperature resin core solder and resin flux.

30. Install brush plate holder/solenoid assembly to gear housing with return spring engaging solenoid. Other models use screws to attach the two components.

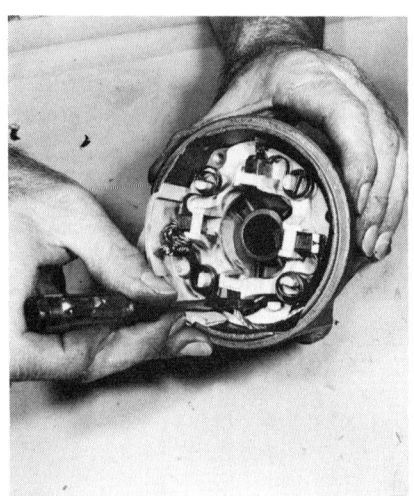

31. Replace brushes in their respective slots in the brush plate holder. Using a screwdriver, position brush springs away from brushes as shown.

32. Install armature thrust washer with tangs resting against brushes. (Now replace springs on brushes and washer will hold brushes from commutator.)

33. To reassemble field frame to gear housing, align field frame with housing and connect field lead to brush terminal with screw, then seat frame securely.

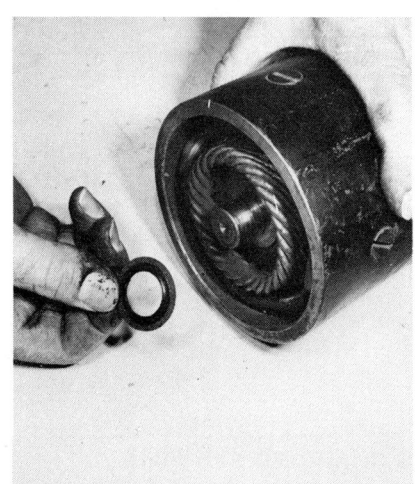

34. Install thrust washer on front of armature shaft and insert into assembly, rotating slightly to engage shaft splines with reduction gear. Add 2nd thrust washer.

35. Replace and seat end head on field frame. Install through bolts and tighten snugly. Do not overtighten bolts, as this can cause problems in starter operation.

36. Snap dust cover into place over drive gear housing and reduction gear starter overhaul is complete. Starter is ready to reinstall on car.

INDEX

CHARGING SYSTEMS

CHARGING CIRCUITS

Charging systems and circuits vary in output and the manner in which the output is regulated, but all are basically similar in design and function, and consist of the following components **(Fig. 2-1):**

1. Battery—The automotive battery supplies the energy required to crank the engine and provides the necessary power for the ignition system. It also supplies current (for a limited time) to meet electrical system requirements when the total system demand is greater than the alternator output.

2. Alternator—An electro-mechanical device which converts mechanical energy into alternating current. This AC current is changed internally to DC current by rectifier diodes and then supplied to the car's electrical systems and battery as required.

3. Regulator—An electronic or electro-mechanical switching device which controls the voltage allowed into the system at all times, protects the battery from an overcharge and keeps battery current from flowing into the alternator stator during periods of low output. In some charging systems, the regulator is an internal part of the alternator; in others, it is a separate device.

4. Indicator lamp—Typically, current is supplied from the ignition switch through either the indicator bulb or a resistor in the alternator regulator and flows to the alternator regulator terminal, which is connected in turn to the field (rotor) winding of the alternator. This current causes the indicator bulb to light when the ignition switch is turned ON and stays lit until alternator output voltage develops at the regulator terminal. When alternator voltage exceeds battery voltage, the light goes out. Should trouble develop in the charging sys-

tem, and alternator voltage drops below that of the battery, the light goes back on as a warning signal.

5. Wiring circuit—The connecting cables which transmit electricity as required from one component to another. Many wiring circuits also include one or more fusible links.

6. Drive belt—The V-belt connecting the alternator pulley with the engine crankshaft pulley provides the mechanical motion to turn the alternator rotor.

THE BATTERY

Battery construction, operation and testing is covered in detail in Chapter 1. The battery is charged by current supplied directly from the alternator output terminal to the positive battery terminal. The alternator is grounded to complete the return circuit to the negative battery terminal. The amount of charge received depends upon the battery's state of charge and internal condition, proper operation of the voltage regulator and the amount of current consumed by other electrical requirements such as the heater, lights, etc.

Since battery charging is a function of the charging system, methods of recharging the battery are discussed in this chapter. The three common methods of recharging a battery differ primarily in the length of time and rate at which current is supplied. Before recharging a battery by any of the following methods, check and adjust the electrolyte level according to battery requirements.

PREPARATION FOR CHARGING

A highly explosive gas mixture (hydrogen) forms in each cell during charging. Be certain to use precau-

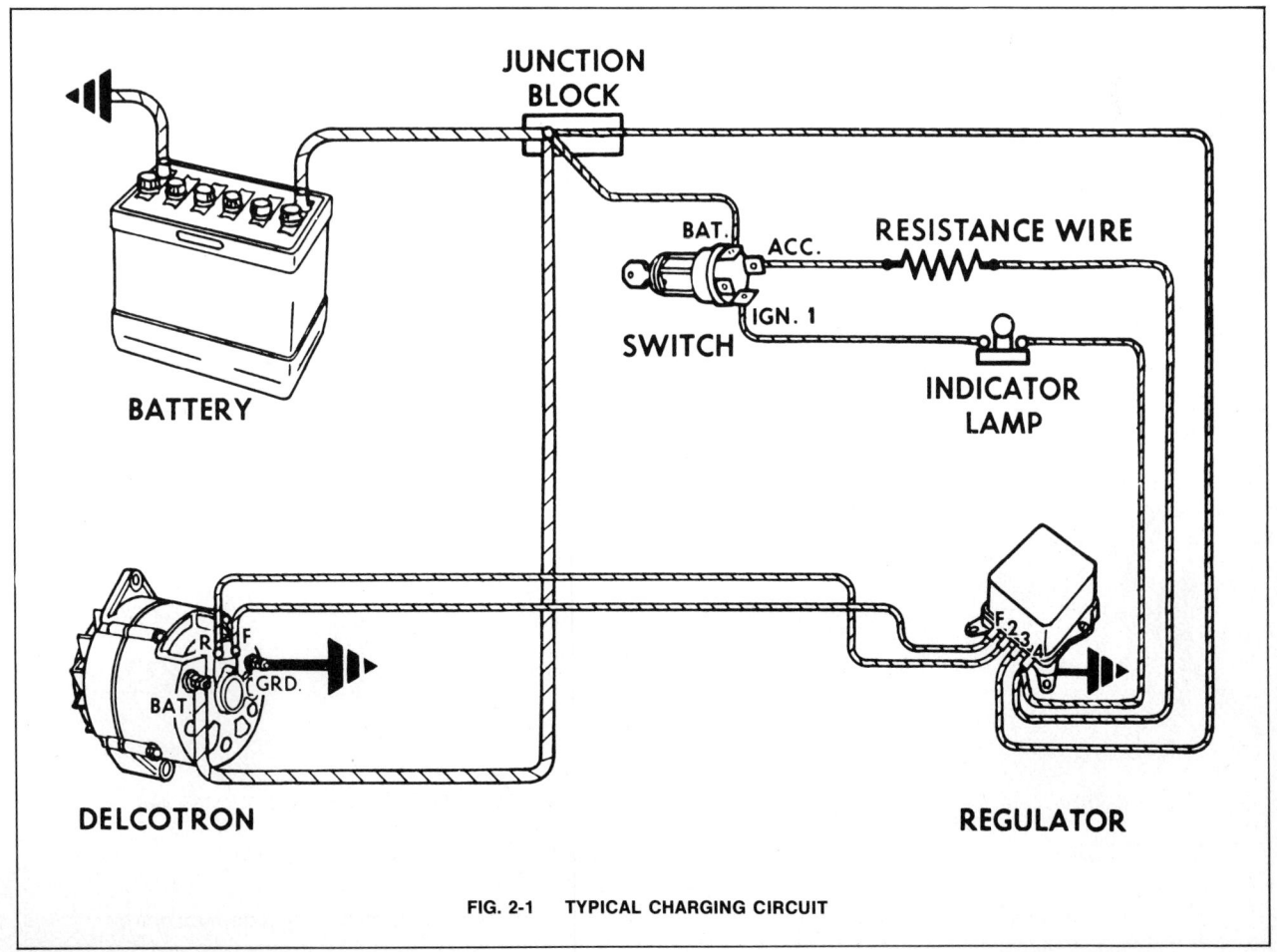

FIG. 2-1   TYPICAL CHARGING CIRCUIT

tions when working around a battery that is under charge. Do not smoke, create sparks or bring an open flame near the battery. To prevent an electrical arc that could cause an explosion, always connect the AC power cord to a line outlet *after* the charger leads are connected, and disconnect the power cord *before* disconnecting the leads. Before hooking up the charger, do the following:

1. Loosen or remove the filler/vent caps.
2. Check, clean and tighten both battery cables.
3. Replace worn or defective cables.
4. If battery is to be charged with its cables removed, clean the terminal posts thoroughly with a terminal post cleaning tool **(Fig. 2-2)**.

CONNECTING THE BATTERY CHARGER

The charger unit should always be connected to the battery before it is plugged into an AC outlet. Disconnect the battery cables before connecting the charger. This will prevent accidental damage to electronic components from reverse polarity.

1. Remove the positive battery terminal cable first, then the negative or ground cable **(Fig. 2-3)**.
2. Connect the charger positive lead to the positive battery terminal, and the negative charger lead to the negative battery terminal **(Fig. 2-4)**.
3. Rock the charger leads back and forth to assure a good connection.
4. If sparking takes place when clamping the leads to the battery terminal posts, they are incorrect and must be reversed.

EMERGENCY BOOST CHARGE

If the battery is not sufficiently charged to crank the engine, an emergency boost charge may be used. Charge at a 40- to 50-ampere rate for 30 minutes. An emergency boost will not restore the battery sufficiently for continuous service and must be followed by either a slow or fast charge.

SLOW CHARGE

To slow charge a battery, charge at a 4-ampere rate for 24 hours or more, as required. When the cells gas freely and three temperature-corrected specific gravity readings can be taken at hourly intervals with no increase between them, a full charge condition has been reached.

Many discharged batteries, especially those that are sulphated, can be brought back to good condition by a slow charge. Sulphating is a battery condition that takes place when large areas of the plates become covered with heavy deposits of lead sulphate caused by inadequate charging or old age. The chemical reaction between the lead plates and electrolyte acid changes some of the material into lead sulphate. If the battery is not charged enough to convert the compound back into usable materials, sulphating gradually takes place. As sulphated areas tend to harden permanently, their chemical convertibility can be lost. A long, slow charge is the only means of completely displacing the acid from the sulphated areas and restoring the battery to its full capacity. A lesser charge will not remove the sulphate, but it can return the battery to service temporarily.

FAST CHARGE

To fast charge a battery, charge at a 40- to 50-ampere rate for 1½ hours. Should the electrolyte temperature reach 125° F before the recommended time interval is up, remove the battery from charge temporarily, or reduce the charging rate to avoid battery damage.

CHARGING SYSTEM DESCRIPTION
THE ALTERNATOR

The basic components of an alternator are the housing end frames, rotor, stator, rectifier diodes, shields and pulley.

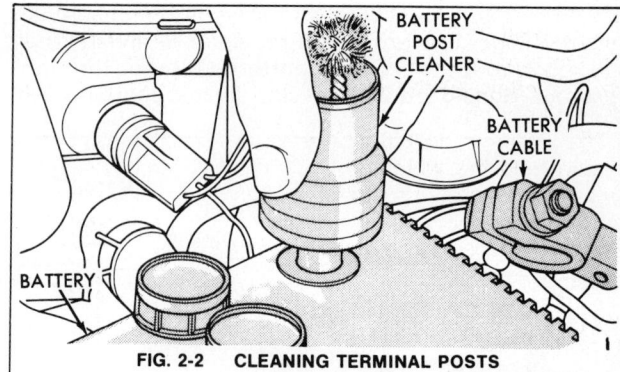

FIG. 2-2   CLEANING TERMINAL POSTS

FIG. 2-4   BATTERY CHARGER CONNECTIONS

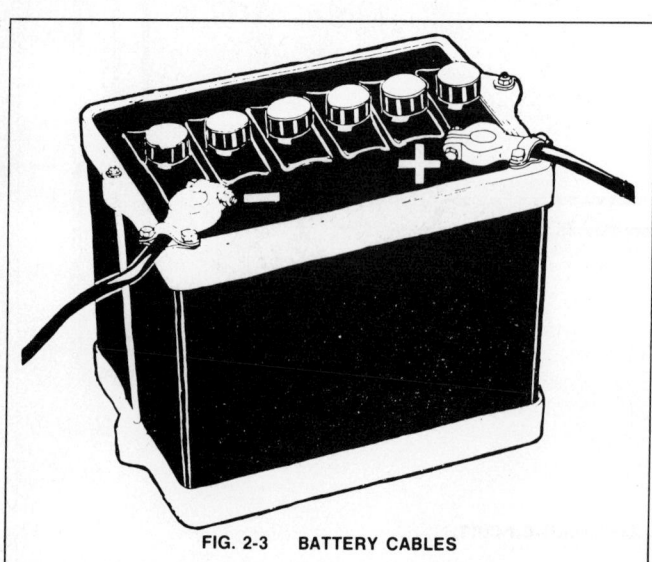

FIG. 2-3   BATTERY CABLES

The housing serves primarily to hold the stator in place, supply bearing support for the rotor and provide a mounting point for the unit **(Fig. 2-5)**. Openings allow for the passage of cooling air, and a fan is incorporated into the rotor and shaft assembly to improve its circulation. The bearings which support the rotor shaft are permanently lubricated ball-bearing type, although plain or needle bearings prepacked with lubricant have been used on smaller units at the brush end. The alternator is thus virtually service-free.

Rotor construction is simple—its field poles are like two star-shaped pieces of mild steel with their points bent inward to interlock. These produce a series of magnetic poles of alternating polarity all around the rotor's circumference. One field winding serves to magnetize both poles. This is coiled in a simple manner around an insulated spool which slips over the iron core on the rotor shaft to separate the two pole pieces. Each end of the rotor's coil attaches to individual slip rings, both of which are insulated from the rotor shaft.

Small carbon brushes ride against the slip rings to provide current to the rotor's field coil. In many units the brushes can be removed for replacement and inspection without disassembling the alternator. Even those which must be taken apart for access to the brushes have them mounted in a separate holder for ease in servicing. One brush is connected to the regulator and tied to the hot side of the battery. The other is placed in contact with ground, often by being wired to the alternator housing. The field relay in the regulator automatically shuts off current to the rotor when the ignition switch is turned off. In some designs, there is no field relay, so the ignition switch must then control the field current.

The stator is built up from many laminations, which in turn hold the windings in place. Although the windings in the stator may appear to be complex, they are really only simple coils overlapping one another in multiples of three, such as 12, 18, 24, etc. These are linked together into three basic, interconnected circuits which feed current from their juncture points to three pairs of rectifier diodes.

Simple transistors having the unique property of allowing electrical current to flow through in only one direction, these positive-negative diodes change the alternating current (AC) output into direct current (DC). The six rectifying diodes in the alternator are supplied with alternating current from the stator windings—three diodes permit passage of negative-polarity current and the other three allow only positive current to pass. Three of the diodes feed current to the battery and electrical parts of the car, while the remaining three diodes are grounded in the alternator and act as a return path for the electricity that has done its work at the battery, lights and accessories.

The windings of the stator overlap, and the voltage peaks produced by the three pairs of diodes overlap. But their output is fed into a common wire and the end result is either positive or negative current of relatively uniform voltage. Diodes are highly susceptible to heat and reverse polarity.

THE REGULATOR

Electro-mechanical regulators used with alternator systems employ double-contact, voltage-limiting relays. This type of regulator is protected by a cover **(Fig. 2-6)** and is usually located on the firewall or fenderwell.

Chrysler Corporation and Ford relay armatures each have a double-faced contact, with stationary contacts mounted above and below, so that the contact on the movable armature may touch either stationary contact, depending upon the armature's position **(Fig. 2-7)**. When the upper contacts are closed, full voltage is supplied to the field windings, and the alternator is permitted to produce its maximum output. When the lower contacts are closed, excess voltage goes to ground.

Delco voltage regulator relays, however, are constructed with double points on the armature and a sin-

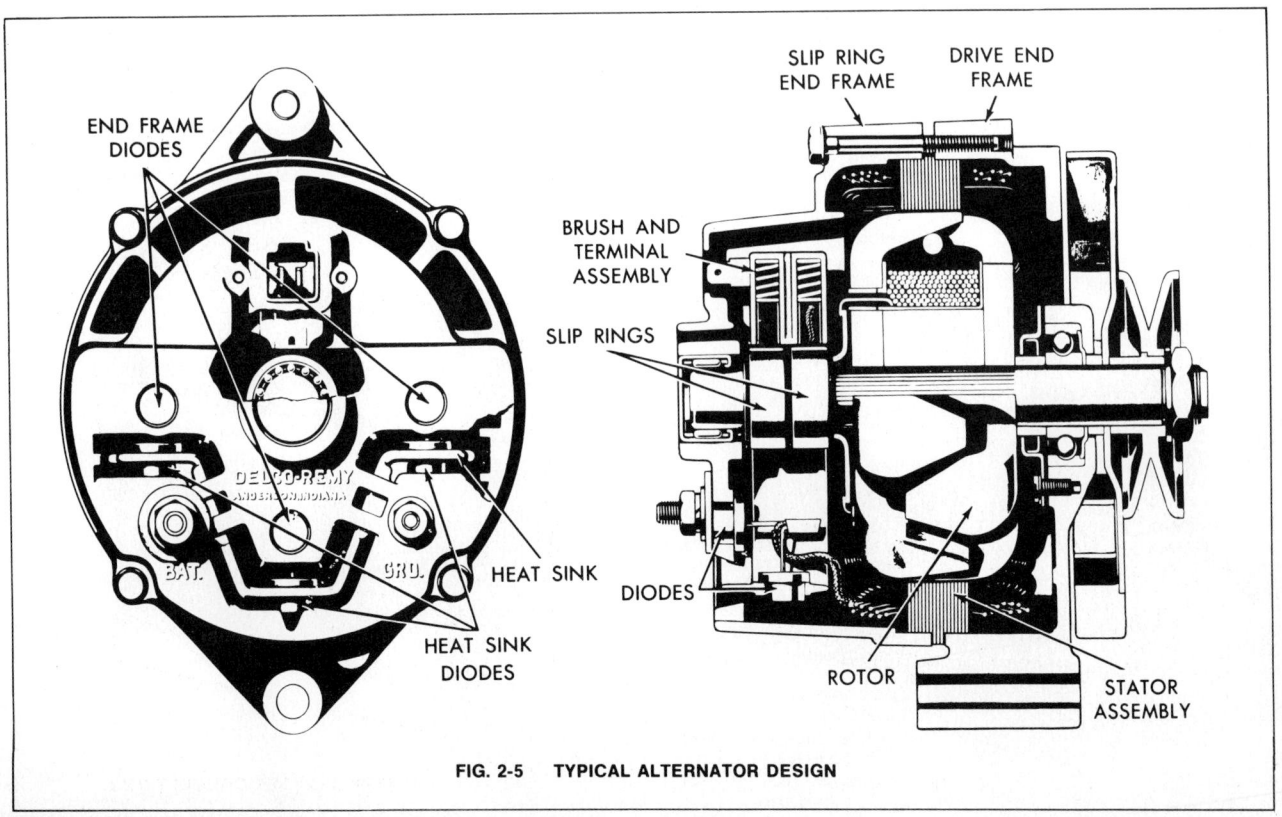

FIG. 2-5   TYPICAL ALTERNATOR DESIGN

gle, double-faced point that is stationary. The result is that the resistor contact (to charge) is the lower and the shorting contact (to ground) is the upper, but the effect on alternator output is identical with the Chrysler and Ford designs.

The circuits between a transistorized regulator **(Fig. 2-8)** and the alternator are exactly the same as those associated with conventional, relay-controlled regulator units. Transistors, however, control the field current. These are generally triodes, which vary electrical flow through two connections in proportion to the strength of the current fed into the third connection. The precision of their operation and their inherent, long service life, compared to that of the mechanical contact-point type, give them obvious features of superiority. In those units having a screw permitting adjustments to the charging rate, it is a mistake to assume that you are "adjusting a transistor." *Transistors are not adjustable.* The adjustment actually controls the variable resistance (rheostat) that determines voltage delivered to triodes.

Electronic regulators have no moving parts, require no adjustments after being set at the factory and can be serviced only by replacement **(Fig. 2-9)**. Whether mounted inside the alternator or externally, the electronic regulator contains semiconductors, transistors, diodes, resistors and a capacitor. This reliance on electronic components not only reduces the size of the unit, but produces a control circuit able to vary the regulated-system voltage according to temperature.

CHARGING SYSTEM TESTING

Various system testers and individual test units can be used to perform the alternator/regulator tests described in the following sections of this chapter. Identical results will be obtained regardless of the type used. If your equipment is different from that specified, follow the manufacturer's instructions.

1979 GENERAL MOTORS ENGINES
Delco-Remy 15-SI Series Delcotron

SYSTEM DESCRIPTION

Introduced on some GM engines during the latter part of the 1979 model year, the 15-SI Delcotron is essentially similar in design, service and diagnosis to the 10-SI. There are five primary differences between the two units; the 15-SI:

1. Is physically larger.

2. Produces 50 amps at idle and 70 amps at full speed.

3. Uses different drive-end and slip-ring end bearings.

4. Has a stator with delta windings. The windings cannot be checked for opens.

5. Capacitor lead connects to the rectifier bridge with a push-on clip rather than a screw.

CHARGING SYSTEM DIAGNOSIS

CONDITION		CORRECTION	CONDITION		CORRECTION
ALTERNATOR LIGHT STAYS ON WITH ENGINE RUNNING			(b)	Belt is loose or broken.	(b) Replace belt if necessary; tighten belt to specs.
(a)	Belt is loose or broken.	(a) Replace belt if necessary; tighten belt tension to specs.	(c)	Low alternator output.	(c) Connect voltmeter across battery and record voltage reading. Set carburetor on high step of fast idle cam, start engine, and turn on all continuous use accessories. If voltage across battery reads lower than open circuit voltage just recorded, alternator current output is low. Remove unit and repair.
(b)	No alternator output.	(b) Connect test lamp to alternator No. 1 terminal. If lamp lights dimly, alternator receives initial field current but has no output. Ground alternator field. If light does not brighten, remove and repair alternator. If light does brighten, the alternator is OK and voltage regulator is defective.			
			(d)	Low voltage regulator setting.	(d) Set up test as in (c) above but turn off all accessories. When engine is at operating temperature any reading between 13.5 and 15.0 volts indicates regulator is OK.
ALTERNATOR LIGHT ON WITH IGNITION OFF					
(a)	Positive diode shorted.	(a) Replace diode bridge.	(e)	High resistance in starting circuit or ignition resistor bypass.	(e) Connect jumper from negative terminal of coil to ground to prevent starting engine. Connect voltmeter to positive coil terminal and ground. Crank engine. Any reading below 9.0 volts requires a further test. Check voltage across battery posts during cranking. If voltage reading is within 0.5-volt of that at coil, circuits are OK but battery is too low.
ALTERNATOR LIGHT OFF WITH IGNITION ON BUT ENGINE NOT RUNNING					
(a)	Indicator bulb burned out.	(a) Replace bulb and socket assembly.			
(b)	Blown fuse.	(b) Replace fuse controlling indicator lights if all are off. If indicator lights do not come on with new fuse, check for an open in indicator light feed wire.			
(c)	Open between bulb and ground in alternator.	(c) Ground No. 1 terminal wire. If bulb lights, remove alternator for repair. If bulb still does not light, check further for an open circuit between bulb	**BATTERY OVERCHARGED**		
			(a)	Shorted battery cell.	(a) Perform battery load test to determine if battery cell is at fault.
UNDERCHARGED BATTERY			(b)	Voltage regulator setting too high.	(b) See Undercharged Battery (c) above. Set up test as in (c) and perform as in (d). If voltage is over 15.0 volts, replace regulator.
(a)	Continuous small drain on battery.	(a) Disconnect positive cable from battery. Connect test light between cable and battery post. If test lamp lights, trace and correct source of drain.			

FIG. 2-6   ELECTRO-MECHANICAL REGULATOR

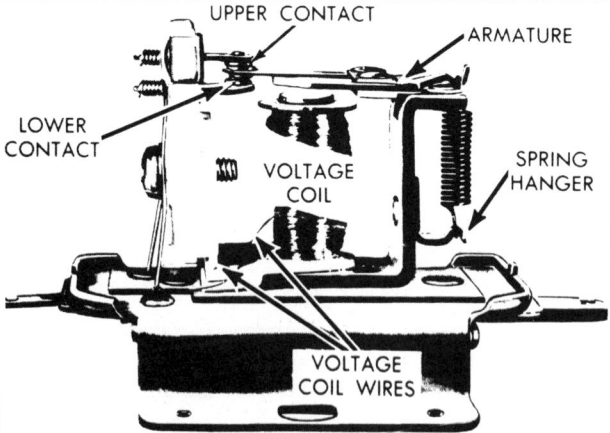

FIG. 2-7   CHRYSLER CORPORATION ELECTRO-MECHANICAL REGULATOR

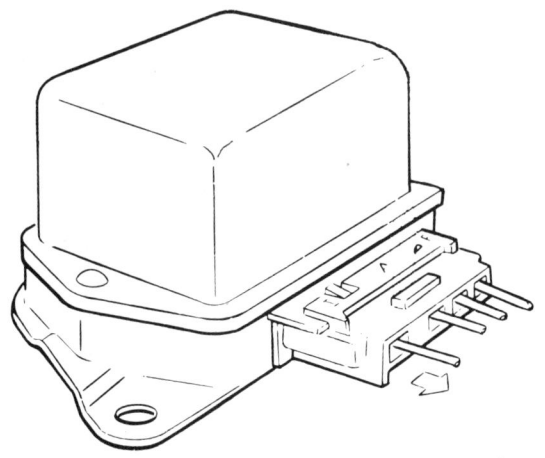

FIG. 2-8   TRANSISTORIZED REGULATOR

FIG. 2-9   GENERAL MOTORS INTEGRAL REGULATOR

1970-79 GENERAL MOTORS ENGINES: 1975-79 AMERICAN MOTORS ENGINES (4- and 6-cylinder)
Delco-Remy 10-SI Series Delcotron
SYSTEM DESCRIPTION

The 10-SI series Delcotron uses a solid-state voltage regulator with integrated circuit built into the end frame. Basic operation, test and overhaul procedures are the same for all versions, regardless of the rated output. No periodic adjustment or maintenance is required on the Delcotron. Prelubricated bearings support the rotor assembly: a ball bearing in the drive end frame and a roller bearing in the slip–ring (rear) end frame. A capacitor or condenser mounted in the end frame serves to protect the rectifier bridge and diode from high voltages, and suppresses radio noise.

FUSIBLE LINK CIRCUIT PROTECTION

All 10-SI Delcotron charging systems are protected by fusible links against a short to ground in the wiring harness or a heavy current flow such as that created by incorrectly connecting the booster equipment. Fusible link location for GM cars is detailed in **Fig. 2-10**; fusible link locations for AMC cars equipped with the 10-SI Delcotron are shown in **Fig. 2-11**. Always inspect the fusible link as a first step in any troubleshooting procedure involving a no-charge condition, and replace if open or burned.

BUICK..............Battery terminal on starter solenoid at lower end of main supply wires.

CADILLAC.......Battery terminal on starter solenoid to main wire harness.

CHEVROLET...Molded splice at solenoid battery terminal.
Molded splice at horn relay.
Molded splice in voltage regulator circuit wire.
Molded splices on both sides of ammeter in ammeter circuit.

OLDSMOBILE..At horn-relay jet block (except Omega).
Twin links at horn relay jet block (Omega only).
At starter solenoid battery terminal (Omega only).

PONTIAC........Positive battery cable pigtail lead (requires entire cable replacement).
At horn relay.
Molded splice in circuit at jet block and horn relay (some single and some twin).

FIG. 2-10   GENERAL MOTORS FUSIBLE LINK LOCATOR

1. **a)** Battery terminal of starter relay to main wire harness.
   b) Battery terminal of horn relay to main wire harness.
   c) Accessory terminal of ignition switch to wire harness.

2. **a)** Battery terminal of starter relay to heated rear window relay.
   b) B-3 terminal of ignition switch to circuit breaker.
   c) 1-3 terminal of ignition* switch to circuit breaker.

3. **a)** 1-3 terminal of ignition* switch (single wire at the switch splits into two feed wires).
   b) Engine compartment harness at AV terminal of dash connector.
   c) SOL terminal of ignition switch to wire harness.

*Only one of these links is used on any one vehicle.

FIG. 2-11   AMERICAN MOTORS FUSIBLE LINK LOCATOR

IN-CAR TEST PROCEDURES

In checking the charging system operation to determine the exact area of malfunction, a voltmeter, ammeter, ohmmeter, carbon pile and 10-ohm resistor are required. The following steps should be taken before beginning any test procedure:

1. Disconnect the continuous blower on those cars so equipped.

2. Make sure the battery is at full charge. If it is not, either charge it or replace with one that is fully charged for the duration of the test procedure.

3. Inspect all charging circuit wiring for defects, and all circuit connections for looseness.

4. Check drive belt tension, readjust if necessary.

Engine Run-On—1976-77 AMC Engines

Electrical feedback from the alternator can cause engine dieseling on certain 1976-77 AMC 6-cylinder engines. To cure this problem, install a special jumper wire (AMC P/N 8128393) between the No. 1 alternator terminal and the lead wire presently connected to it.

LOW CHARGE RATE TEST (Fig. 2-12)

1. Turn ignition switch on and connect a voltmeter from:
   a) Delcotron BAT terminal to ground. Read voltmeter.
   b) Delcotron No. 1 terminal to ground. Read voltmeter.
   c) Delcotron No. 2 terminal to ground. Read voltmeter.

2. If voltmeter reads zero when connected to any one of the three terminals, there is an open circuit between that terminal and the battery.
   a) An open No. 2 lead will cause uncontrolled voltage which can damage the battery and accessories. The 10-SI Delcotron circuitry prevents the unit from turning on if an open circuit exists in the wiring harness which connects with the No. 2 terminal. Check for the open circuit between the terminals, at the crimp between the terminal and harness wire or in the wire itself.

3. Disconnect the battery ground cable and connect test equipment as shown in **Fig. 2-13**.

4. Turn on all accessories to their highest setting.

5. Start the engine and run at 1500-2000 rpm. Adjust carbon pile to get the maximum current output possible.

6. If ammeter reading is not within 10% of Delcotron rated output, ground the field winding by inserting a screwdriver blade in the test hole **(Fig. 2-14)** until it touches the small metal tab positioned about ¾-in. inside the casting. Ground is complete when the screwdriver tip touches the tab and the side of the blade touches the end frame.

7. With the engine running at 1500-2000 rpm, adjust carbon pile to get maximum current output possible.

8. If ammeter reads within 10% of the rated output for the unit under test, the regulator is defective. It must be replaced and the field winding checked.

9. If ammeter does not read within 10% of the rated output, the Delcotron should be removed and disassembled, and the field winding, diode trio, rectifier bridge and stator tested.

HIGH CHARGE RATE TEST (Fig. 2-12)

1. Connect a voltmeter from Delcotron No. 2 terminal to ground.

2. If voltmeter reads zero, there is an open circuit between the No. 2 terminal and the battery.
   a) An open No. 2 lead will cause uncontrolled voltage which can damage the battery and accessories. The 10-SI Delcotron circuitry prevents the unit from turning on if an open circuit exists in the wiring harness which connects with the No. 2 terminal. Check for the open circuit between the terminals, at the crimp between the terminal and harness wire or in the wire itself.

3. If voltmeter does not indicate the presence of an open circuit the Delcotron must be disassembled for further testing.

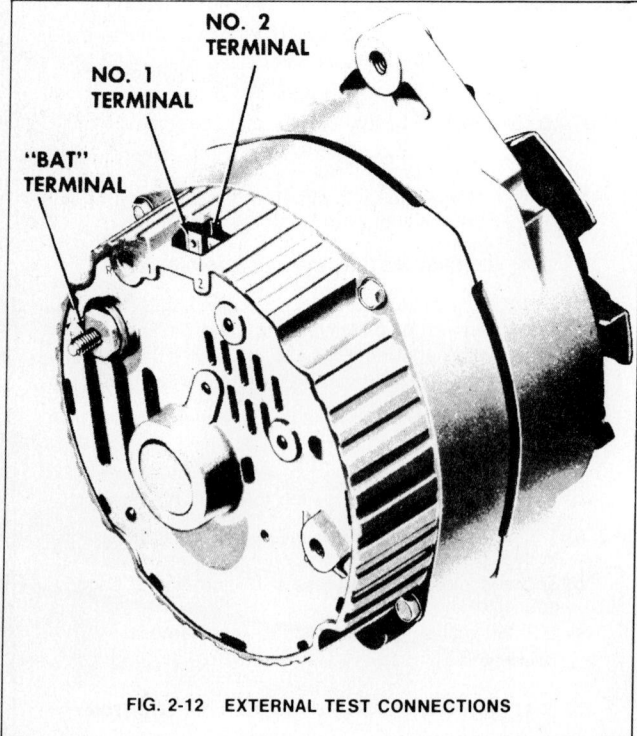

FIG. 2-12 EXTERNAL TEST CONNECTIONS

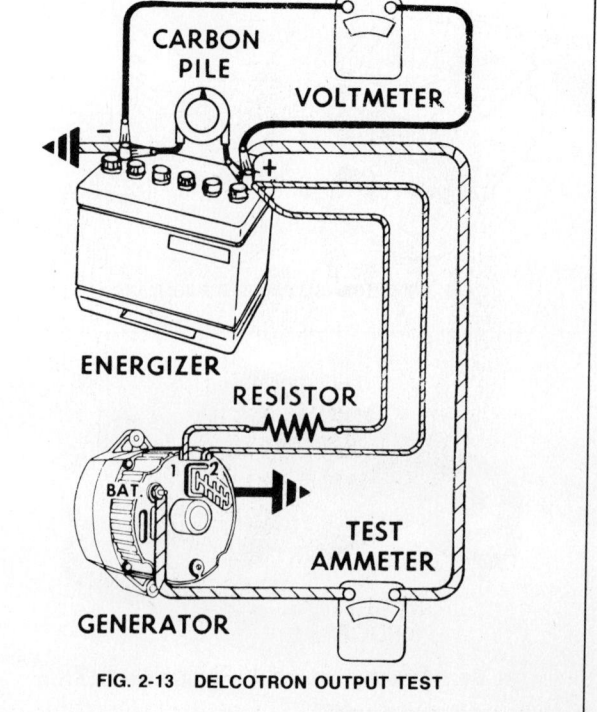

FIG. 2-13 DELCOTRON OUTPUT TEST

4. Follow disassembly procedure outlined just after this section and separate the end frames.

5. Adjust ohmmeter to lowest range scale and connect the leads from the brush lead clip to the end frame as shown in "Ohmmeter #1" **(Fig. 2-15)**.

6. Read ohmmeter and reverse the lead connections. Read ohmmeter again.

7. If both readings are zero, either the regulator is defective or the brush lead clip is grounded.

8. If the regulator is good, check the insulating washers **(Fig. 2-15)**. Remove the screws and inspect the insulating sleeves. If sleeves and washers check out satisfactorily, retest the regulator.

ALTERNATOR REMOVAL/INSTALLATION

TO REMOVE

1. Disconnect the positive battery cable from the battery terminal.

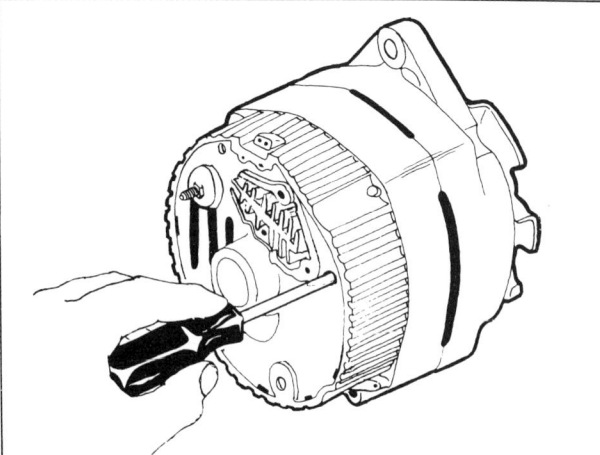

FIG. 2-14   GROUNDING DELCOTRON FIELD

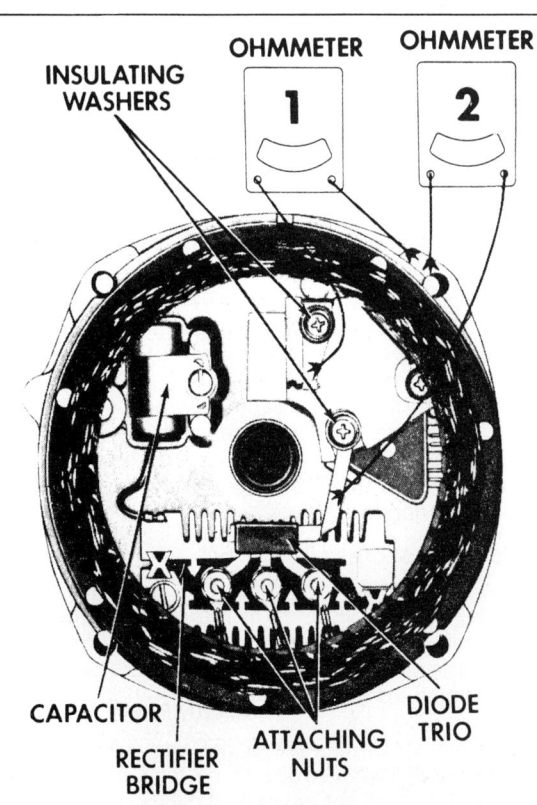

FIG. 2-15   SLIP RING END FRAME

2. Disconnect the battery lead and the two-terminal plug from rear of Delcotron.

3. Loosen adjusting bolts.

4. Slip the V-belt off drive pulley.

5. Remove the through-bolt holding Delcotron and remove unit from the car.

TO INSTALL

1. Replace Delcotron on the mounting bracket with bolts, washers and nuts. Replace through-bolt. *Do not* tighten.

2. Slip the V-belt over drive pulley.

3. Adjust the unit for specified belt tension and tighten the through-bolt to 30 ft.-lbs., adjusting the bracket bolt to 20 ft.-lbs.

4. Replace the battery lead and two-terminal plug to rear of Delcotron.

5. Reconnect the positive battery cable to battery terminal.

ALTERNATOR DISASSEMBLY/TESTING (Fig. 2-16)

TO DISASSEMBLE:

1. Position the Delcotron in a vise, with its mounting flange lengthwise, and clamp securely.

2. Make a chalk mark across the end frames as an alignment guide for reassembly, and then remove the end frame through-bolts.

3. Pry the slip-ring end frame (or housing) and stator assembly from the drive end and rotor assembly with a screwdriver.

4. Tape the slip-ring end-frame bearing and shaft to prevent bearing contamination.

5. Separate the stator from the end frame by removing the stator-lead attaching nuts. Test procedures

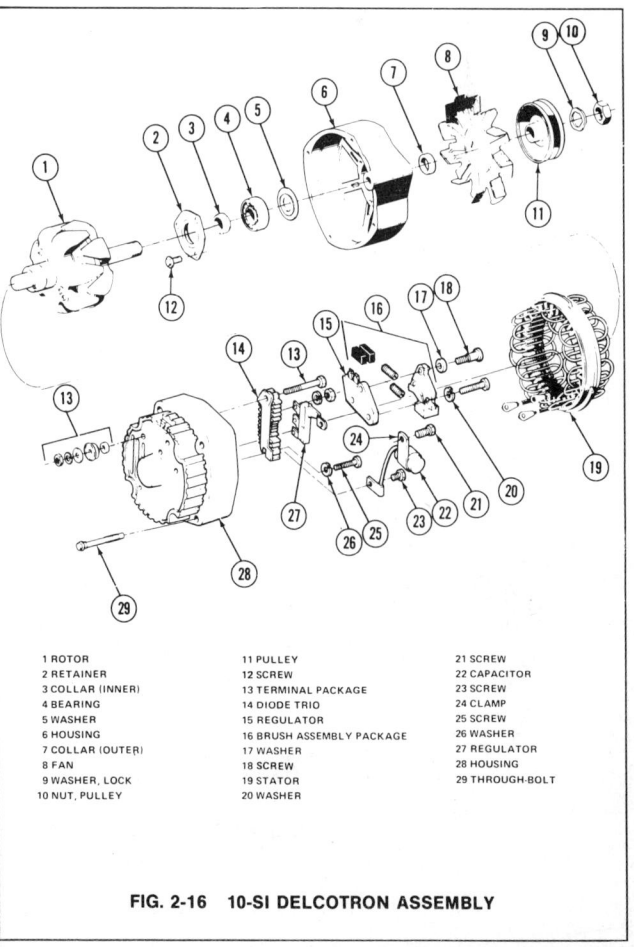

1 ROTOR	11 PULLEY	21 SCREW
2 RETAINER	12 SCREW	22 CAPACITOR
3 COLLAR (INNER)	13 TERMINAL PACKAGE	23 SCREW
4 BEARING	14 DIODE TRIO	24 CLAMP
5 WASHER	15 REGULATOR	25 SCREW
6 HOUSING	16 BRUSH ASSEMBLY PACKAGE	26 WASHER
7 COLLAR (OUTER)	17 WASHER	27 REGULATOR
8 FAN	18 SCREW	28 HOUSING
9 WASHER, LOCK	19 STATOR	29 THROUGH-BOLT
10 NUT, PULLEY	20 WASHER	

FIG. 2-16   10-SI DELCOTRON ASSEMBLY

which follow completion of this disassembly sequence can be performed at this point. Continue further disassembly *only* if necessary to replace components.

6. Remove the screw holding the diode trio to the brush holder assembly and lift diode trio from end frame.

7. To remove the rectifier bridge from the end frame, remove the attaching screw, the BAT terminal screw and disconnect the capacitor lead.

8. Remove the brush holder and regulator assembly. Brush retaining clips have insulators on their tops; attaching screws have special insulating sleeves. If brushes have dropped onto the rotor shaft during disassembly, they are contaminated with bearing grease and should be cleaned or replaced.

9. Remove the capacitor from end frame.

10. If the slip-ring end-frame bearing is to be replaced because of wear or lack of lubricant, press out from the outside of the housing, using a suitable piece of pipe or a socket on the outer race. Always discard the bearing if it is removed and replace it with a new one—*do not* attempt to relubricate the bearing and reinstall.

11. Fit a 15/16-in. box wrench on the retaining nut and insert a 5/16-in. Allen wrench into the drive-shaft end hole to keep the shaft from moving while the pulley retaining nut is loosened **(Fig. 2-17).** If Delcotron is equipped with a double-groove pulley, use a 15/16-in. socket, placed over the nut with its wrench flats closest to the drive end, and turn with a 15/16-in. box wrench.

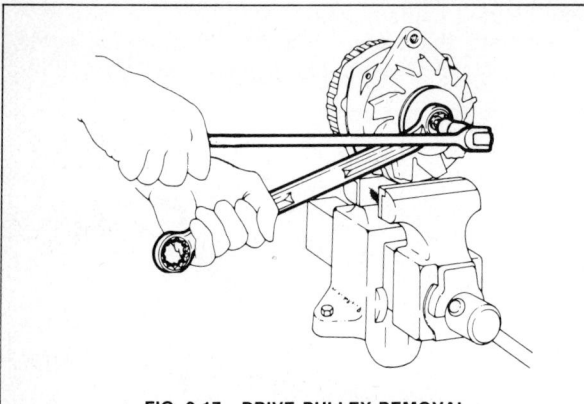

FIG. 2-17 DRIVE PULLEY REMOVAL

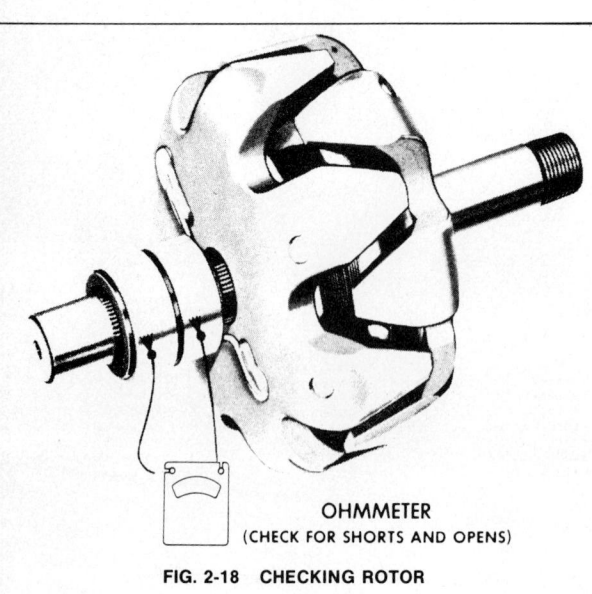

OHMMETER
(CHECK FOR SHORTS AND OPENS)

FIG. 2-18 CHECKING ROTOR

12. Remove the rotor and spacer from the drive end frame.

13. If the front bearing is to be replaced, remove the bearing retainer plate from the end frame.

14. Press out the old bearing, using a suitable piece of pipe or a socket on the outer race.

TEST PROCEDURES

ROTOR FIELD WINDING CHECK

1. See **Fig. 2-18.**

2. Ground Check—Connect ohmmeter from either slip ring to rotor or rotor poles. If ohmmeter reading is low, the field winding is grounded.

3. Open Check—Connect ohmmeter to each slip ring. If meter reading is infinite, field winding is open.

4. Short Circuit Check—Connect a 12-volt battery and ammeter in series with the slip rings. Note ammeter reading and compare to specifications for Delcotron under test. If field amperage draw is higher than that specified, the windings are shorted.

5. Replace rotor if it fails the above test sequence.

STATOR CHECK

1. See **Fig. 2-19.**

2. Disconnect stator leads and separate stator from end frame.

3. Ground Check—Connect ohmmeter to one stator lead and to frame. If ohmmeter reading is low, the stator is grounded.

4. Open Check—Connect ohmmeter successively between the stator leads. If ohmmeter reading is high, there is an open circuit in the stator.

5. Short Circuit Check—Low winding resistance makes it difficult to locate a short. If all other electrical tests prove satisfactory and the Delcotron still fails to supply its rated output, a short in the stator winding is logical.

6. Replace stator if it fails the above test sequence.

DIODE TRIO TEST

There are two different-appearing diode trio units in use, but they are both tested in the same manner and are completely interchangeable **(Fig. 2-20).**

1. Connect an ohmmeter containing a 1½-volt battery to the single connector on the diode trio and to one of the three stator lead connectors. Use of a high-voltage test device, such as a 110-volt test lamp, will damage the diode trio.

2. Note ohmmeter reading (lowest range scale) and reverse the leads to the same two connectors.

3. Repeat Steps 1-2 with each of the other two stator-lead connectors.

4. If any or all give a reading when reversing connections which are the same, replace the trio. A good diode gives one low and one high reading, and when diodes are used in units, all high readings should be in the opposite direction.

RECTIFIER BRIDGE TEST

All diodes located in the heat sink and slip ring end of the Delcotron are situated in the rectifier bridge **(Fig. 2-21).** If one diode proves to be defective, the entire bridge is replaced as a unit. Make sure that the rectifier bridge is completely insulated before performing this test.

1. Connect an ohmmeter to the grounded heat sink and to the base of one of the three terminals inside the heat sink.

2. Read the ohmmeter scale and then reverse the connections and read ohmmeter scale again.

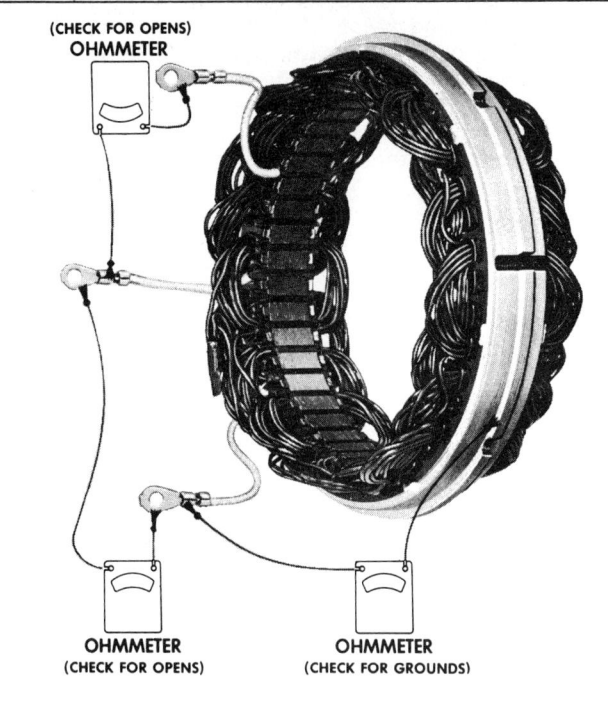

FIG. 2-19 CHECKING STATOR

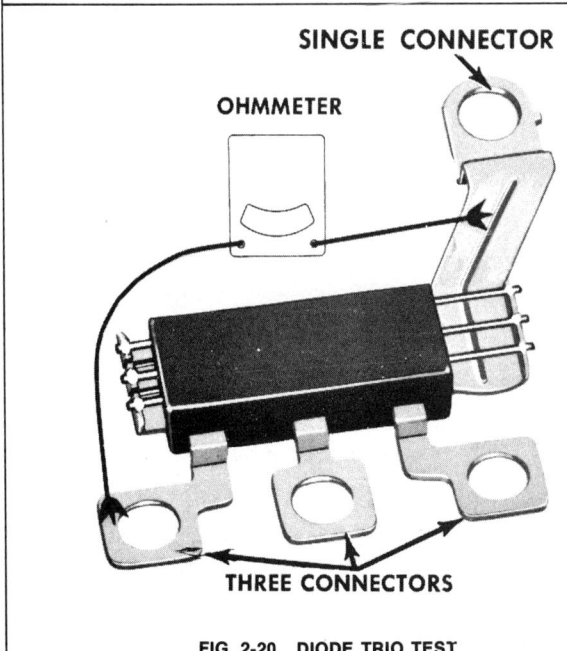

FIG. 2-20 DIODE TRIO TEST

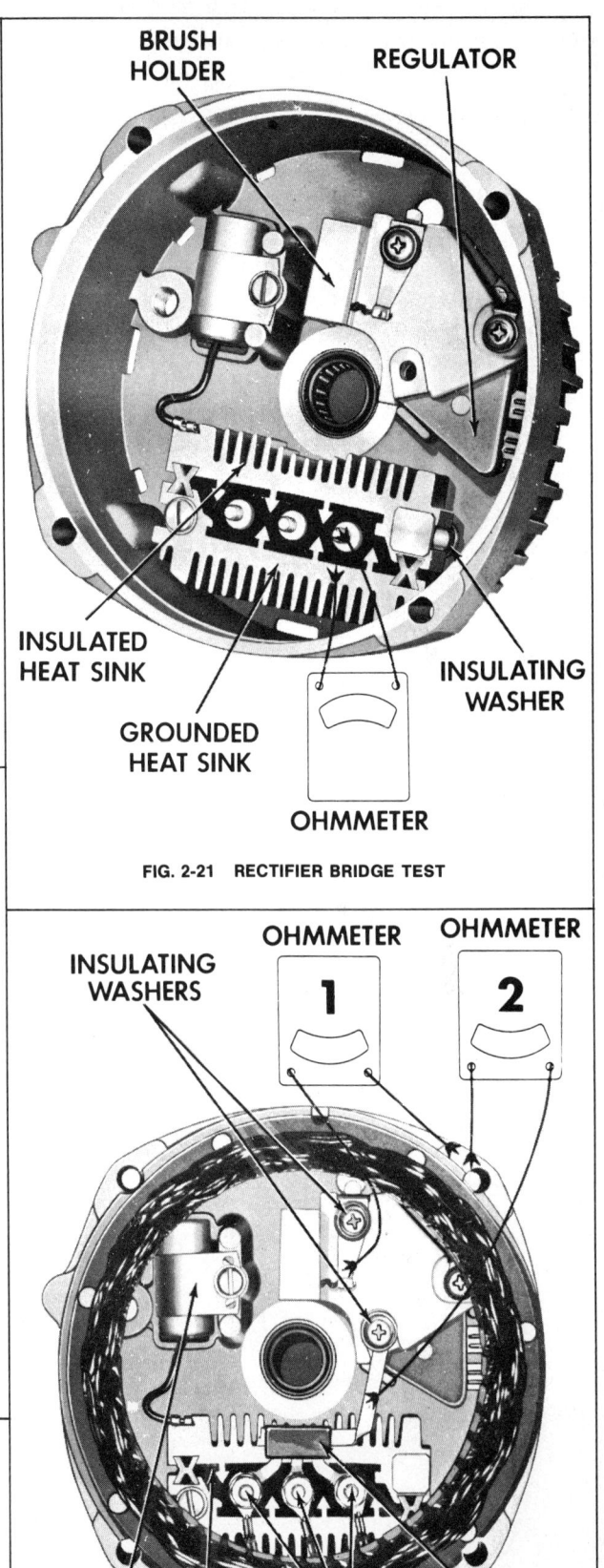

FIG. 2-21 RECTIFIER BRIDGE TEST

FIG. 2-22 BRUSH LEAD CLIP TESTS

3. Repeat Steps 1-2 above with each of the other two terminals. All diodes should give one high and one low reading in the same direction.

4. Repeat entire test sequence with the ohmmeter connected to the insulated heat sink and the three terminals. All diodes should read high in the same direction and low in the opposite direction. If one pair of readings is the same, replace rectifier bridge as a unit.

BRUSHES AND/OR VOLTAGE REGULATOR TEST

1. Connect an ohmmeter from the end frame to the brush lead clip as in "Ohmmeter #1" **Fig. 2-22.**

2. Reverse ohmmeter leads and read ohmmeter scale.

3. If both readings are zero, either the brush lead clip is grounded or the voltage regulator is defective.

4. Inspect the brush holder assembly **(Fig. 2-23)** as follows:

a) Inspect the brush holder screws for cracked or worn insulation. The screw nearest the regulator terminal does not have an insulated washer—it may or may not have an insulating sleeve.

b) Inspect the brushes and springs for wear, damage or corrosion.

c) The entire brush holder is serviced as a unit and must be replaced if any of its component parts are defective.

TO REASSEMBLE

1. If drive end frame bearing was removed, press a new one in place using a suitable piece of pipe or a socket to apply pressure *only* on the outer race. Install bearing retainer.

2. If the slip-ring end-frame bearing was removed, press a new one in place using technique in Step 1.

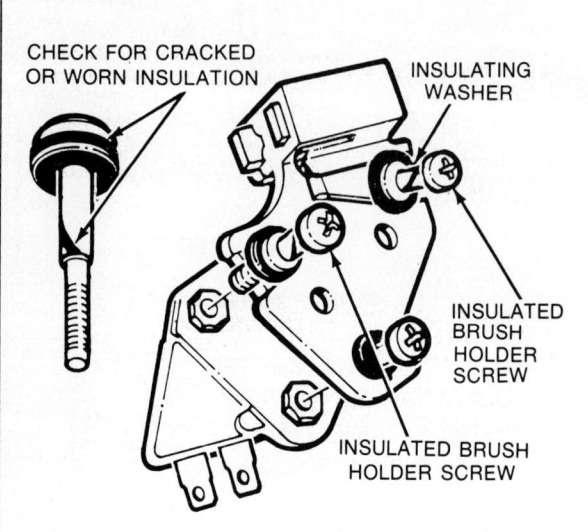

FIG. 2-23 BRUSH HOLDER ASSEMBLY

CHECK FOR CRACKED OR WORN INSULATION

INSULATING WASHER

INSULATED BRUSH HOLDER SCREW

INSULATED BRUSH HOLDER SCREW

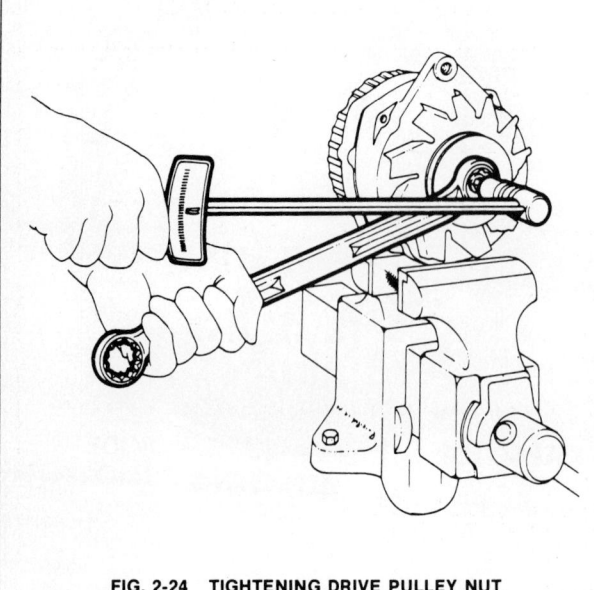

FIG. 2-24 TIGHTENING DRIVE PULLEY NUT

3. Reinstall the capacitor and position the rectifier bridge in the end frame. Secure the capacitor, but install rectifier bridge screw and washer loosely.

4. Fit insulating washer on BAT terminal and install the terminal through the housing and rectifier bridge. Replace the flat washer and nut on screw.

5. Tighten the rectifier bridge screw and BAT terminal nut. Torque nut to 3 ft.-lbs.

6. Replace the capacitor-lead attaching screw.

7. Locate voltage regulator in the end frame.

8. Fit the brushes and spring in the brush holder assembly. Hold in place with a toothpick or short wire inserted through the brush holder hole.

9. Locate the brush holder on the voltage regulator with brush retaining wire or toothpick sticking out of the hole in the end frame.

10. Replace the brush-holder retaining screw *with* insulator in the hole with the exposed brush terminal strap, but *do not* tighten.

11. Replace the brush-holder retaining screw *without* insulating washer into the hole nearest the two regulator terminals, but *do not* tighten.

12. Locate the diode trio on the rectifier bridge.

13. Install the brush-holder retaining screw *with* insulating washer and tighten all brush-holder retaining screws alternately and tightly.

14. Replace the stator, with stator lead wires over the rectifier bridge terminal. Stator notches should line up with the through-bolt holes.

15. Replace flat washers and attaching nuts on the rectifier bridge stud and tighten.

16. Align chalk marks on the two end frames and fit them together.

17. Replace and tighten all through-bolts, then remove the wire or pick holding the brushes.

18. Attach spacer, fan, drive pulley, washer and retaining nut on the drive shaft.

19. With the Delcotron secured in a vise by its mounting flange, fit a 15/16-in. box wrench over the retaining nut and insert a 5/16-in. Allen wrench into the drive-shaft end hole. Torque nut to 40-50 ft.-lbs. **(Fig. 2-24).**

20. Spin fan and drive pulley to check for binding.

1970-73 GENERAL MOTORS ENGINES
Delco-Remy Series 1D (5.5-ins.) Delcotron
SYSTEM DESCRIPTION

Series 1D Delcotron units use an external voltage regulator and, although similar in general appearance to the 10-SI Delcotron, can be identified by the horizontal placement of the relay and field terminals **(Fig. 2-25)**. Stator and rotor design is essentially the same as the 10-SI, and basic operation, test and overhaul procedures are identical for all Series 1D versions, regardless of the rated output.

A double-contact regulator assembly **(Fig. 2-26)** limits voltage to a preset value by controlling field current. The regulator unit also contains an internal field relay which permits the indicator lamp to light up when the ignition is on without the engine running. Once the engine is started, and the alternator output rises, the light goes out to indicate normal system operation.

FUSIBLE LINK CIRCUIT PROTECTION

All Series 1D Delcotron charging systems are protected by fusible links against a short to ground in the wiring harness or a heavy current flow such as that created by incorrectly connecting booster equipment.

Fusible link locations for GM cars are detailed in **Fig. 2-10.** Always inspect the fusible link as a first step in any troubleshooting procedure involving a no-charge condition, and replace if open or burned.

IN-CAR TEST PROCEDURES

In checking the charging system operation to determine the exact area of malfuntion, a voltmeter, ammeter, ohmmeter, carbon pile and ¼-ohm/25-watt resistor are required. The following steps should be taken before beginning any test procedure:

1. Make sure the battery is at full charge. If it is not, either charge it or replace with one that is fully charged for the duration of the test procedure.

2. Inspect all charging circuit wiring for defects, and all circuit connections for looseness **(Fig. 2-27).**

3. Check drive belt tension, readjust if necessary.

CHARGING SYSTEM CONDITION TEST (Fig. 2-28)

On standard models, the indicator lamp circuit produces initial field priming which causes the lamp to light. As the Delcotron output rises, the field relay closes, applying battery voltage to both sides of the lamp, and it goes out. On cars equipped with an ammeter instead of an indicator lamp, the control circuits are the same, except that the lamp is not included.

1. Connect a voltmeter from the junction block relay to ground at the regulator base and hook a tachometer to the engine.

2. Indicator lamp—Turn the ignition switch to ON position and check the indicator lamp. Lamp should light.

Ammeter—Turn ignition switch to ACC position, turn on the heater blower and read ammeter. Ammeter should read "Discharge."

Horizontal   Vertical

Viewing alternator from the side, plug-in terminals on GM vehicles are either horizontal or vertical. Horizontal plug-in denotes separate external voltage regulator. Vertical plug-in denotes a built-in voltage regulator.

FIG. 2-25 DELCOTRON PLUG-IN TERMINAL ARRANGEMENT

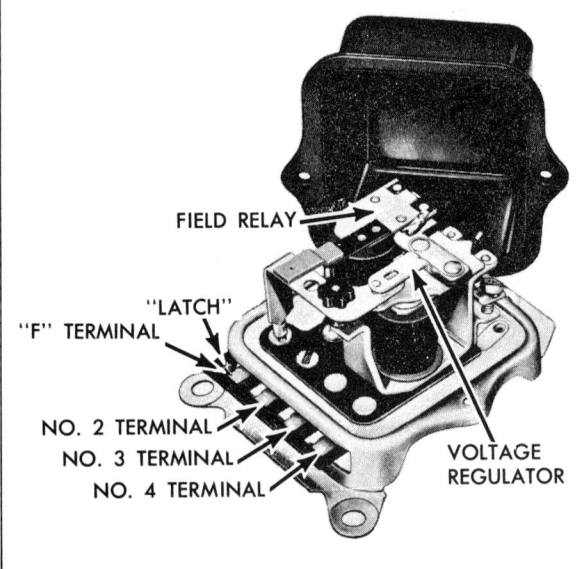

FIG. 2-26 DOUBLE-CONTACT VOLTAGE REGULATOR

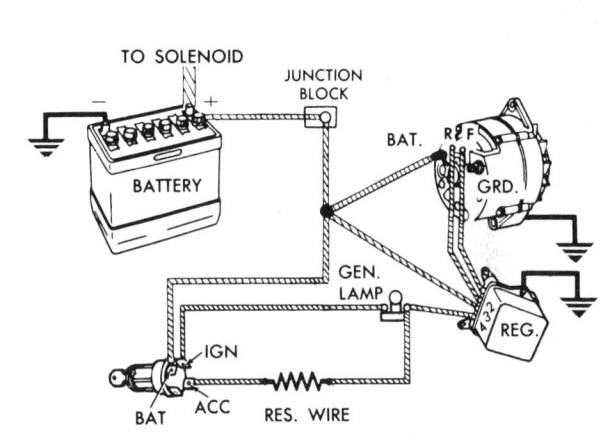

FIG. 2-27 CHARGING CIRCUIT WIRING

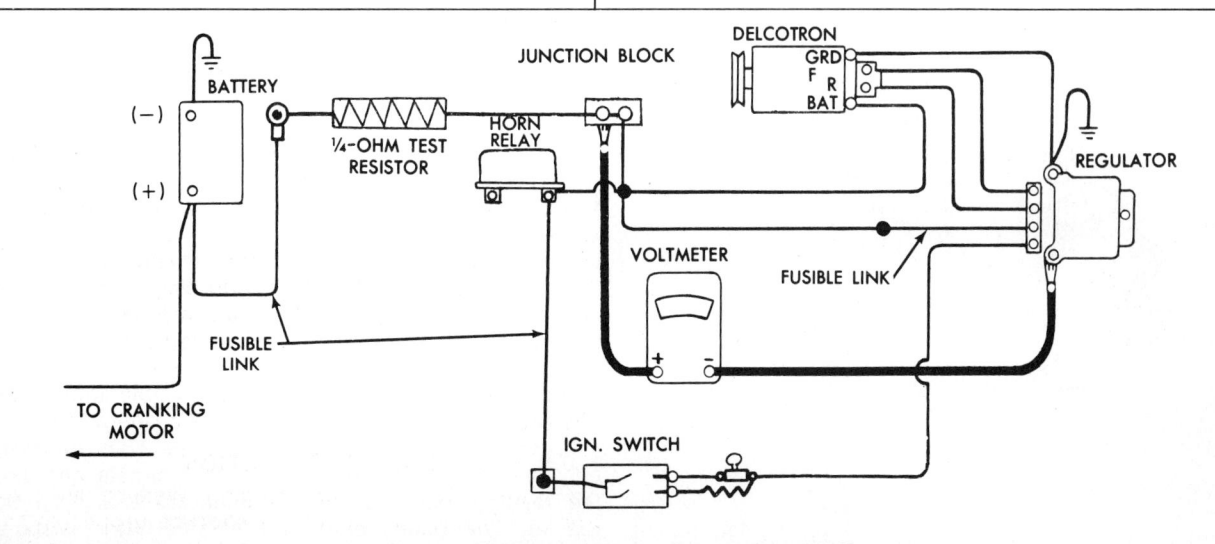

FIG. 2-28 CHARGING SYSTEM TEST CONNECTIONS

3. Indicator lamp—Start engine and run at 1500 rpm. Lamp should go out.

Ammeter—Start engine and run at 1500 rpm. Meter should move up scale to "Charge" from its original position.

If the indicator-lamp/ammeter operate correctly in Steps 2 and 3, continue test procedure below. If lamp/ammeter do not function properly, stop the test procedure at this point and perform an "Initial Field Excitation Circuit Test," explained later.

4. With the engine running at 1500 rpm, turn the headlamps on high beam and the blower motor to high speed. Read voltmeter.

5. If the voltmeter reading is 12½ volts or more, turn off the electrical load and engine. Charging system is good. If the reading is under 12½ volts, perform an "Output Test" with an ammeter.

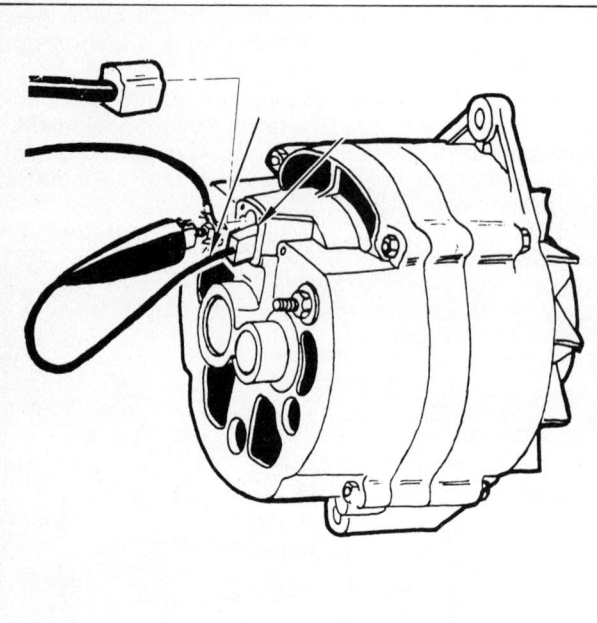

FIG. 2-29 BYPASSING THE VOLTAGE REGULATOR

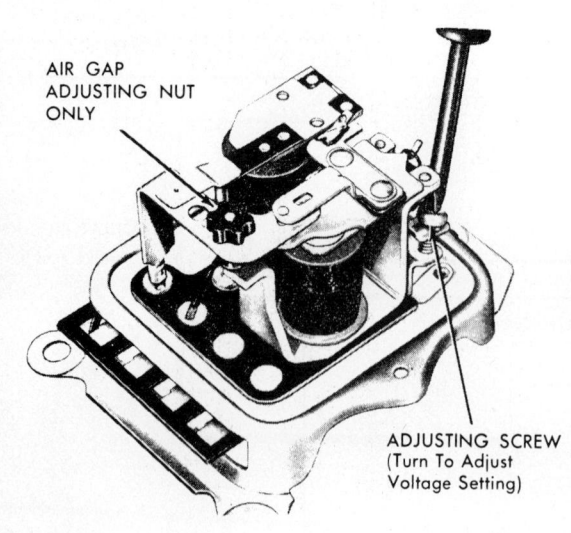

AIR GAP
ADJUSTING NUT
ONLY

ADJUSTING SCREW
(Turn To Adjust
Voltage Setting)

FIG. 2-30 VOLTAGE REGULATOR SETTING ADJUSTMENT

OUTPUT TEST

1. Disconnect the battery ground cable at the battery terminal.

2. Disconnect the wire from the Delcotron BAT terminal and connect an ammeter in series between the terminal and wire.

3. Connect a voltmeter from the battery terminal to a ground on the Delcotron unit.

4. Disconnect Delcotron F-R terminal connector and connect a jumper lead between the F and BAT terminals as shown in **Fig. 2-29.**

5. Connect the battery ground cable and hook an adjustable carbon pile across the battery terminals.

6. Start the engine and slowly bring speed up to 1500 rpm, adjusting the carbon pile at the same time to hold the voltage at 14 volts.

7. Read the amperage and compare to specifications.

a) If output is not within test specifications, remove the Delcotron and bench-test.

b) If output is within test specifications, disconnect the regulator connector, remove the regulator cover and reinstall the connector. *Connector must be disconnected when removing or reinstalling regulator cover to prevent against regulator damage by short circuits.*

8. With engine running at 1500 rpm, turn the headlamps on high beam and the blower motor to high speed. Read voltmeter.

9. Turn the voltage adjusting screw **(Fig. 2-30)** until voltmeter reads 12½ volts. If this setting cannot be obtained, replace the regulator.

10. Shut off the engine and the electrical load, and connect the ¼-ohm/25-watt resistor into the charging circuit as shown in **Fig. 2-28.**

11. Start the engine and run at 1500 rpm for 15 minutes to warm the regulator to normal operating temperature.

12. Disconnect and reconnect the regulator connector to cycle regulator voltage control.

13. If voltage is between 13.5 and 15.2, the regulator is good. If voltage is less than 13.5 volts, disconnect the regulator connector and remove regulator cover.

14. Reconnect the regulator connector and turn the voltage adjusting screw until voltage reads 14.2 to 14.6 volts.

15. Disconnect the regulator connector, replace the cover and reconnect regulator connector.

16. Run engine for 5-10 minutes longer to reestablish internal regulator temperature.

17. Cycle the regulator as in Step 12 and read the voltage. If regulator reads between 13.5 and 15.2, it is good. If reading is less than 13.5, replace the regulator.

DIODE AND FIELD TEST

This test sequence in the car will indicate the presence of a good, shorted or open field, or a shorted diode, but will *not* indicate a failed open diode. If Delcotron output is low, but it passes this test, it should be disassembled and bench tested to locate the exact reason for the low output.

1. Disconnect the battery ground cable at the battery terminal.

2. To test the positive diodes: Connect an ohmmeter between the Delcotron R and BAT terminals and note the reading. Reverse the connections and note this reading. The ohmmeter should indicate high resistance in one direction and low resistance in the other. Similar readings in both directions indicate a defective diode.

3. To test the negative diodes: Connect an ohmmeter between the Delcotron R and GRD terminals and note the reading. Reverse the connections and note this reading. The ohmmeter should indicate high resistance in one direction and low resistance in the other. Similar readings in both directions indicate a defective diode.

4. To test for an open field or a grounded stator: Connect the ohmmeter from the Delcotron F to GRD terminal stud. Meter should read between 7 and 20 ohms. If it reads more or less than this range, the Delcotron is malfunctioning and must be disassembled and bench tested to determine the exact cause.

INITIAL FIELD EXCITATION CIRCUIT TEST

1. Disconnect the regulator connector and turn the ignition switch on. Connect a test lamp from the connector terminal 4 to ground **(Step 1, Fig. 2-31).**

a) If the test lamp does not light, look for a defective indicator bulb, socket or an open circuit between the regulator connector and ignition switch.

2. Connect the test lamp between connector F and 4 terminal **(Step 2, Fig. 2-31).**

a) If the lamp does not light, the malfunction is either in the wire between the two F terminals or in the Delcotron field windings.

b) If the test lamp does light, the malfunction is in the regulator.

3. Connect the test lamp between the Delcotron F and connector 4 terminals **(Step 3, Fig. 2-31).**

a) If the test lamp does not light, the Delcotron field has an open circuit.

b) If the test lamp does light, there is an open circuit in the wire between the F terminals.

FIELD CIRCUIT RESISTANCE WIRE TEST

Although the resistance wire is an integral component in the ignition harness, it cannot be soldered. As such, it must be spliced with a crimp-type connector. To check for an open resistor or field excitation wire, proceed as follows:

1. Connect a test lamp as shown in Step 1, **Fig. 2-31.**

2. Turn the ignition switch on. If the test lamp lights, resistance is satisfactory. If the lamp does not light, the resistor is open. Confirm this by checking the dash lamp. It should not light during the test, because series resistance of the two bulbs causes very low amperage.

FIELD RELAY TEST

1. Connect a voltmeter as shown in **Fig. 2-32.**

2. If the voltmeter reads zero voltage at the regulator, the problem is between the No. 2 regulator terminal and the Delcotron R terminal.

3. Start the engine and run at 1500 rpm. If the voltmeter exceeds closing voltage specifications and the test lamp remains lighted, the regulator field relay is not operating correctly and a closing voltage adjustment is required.

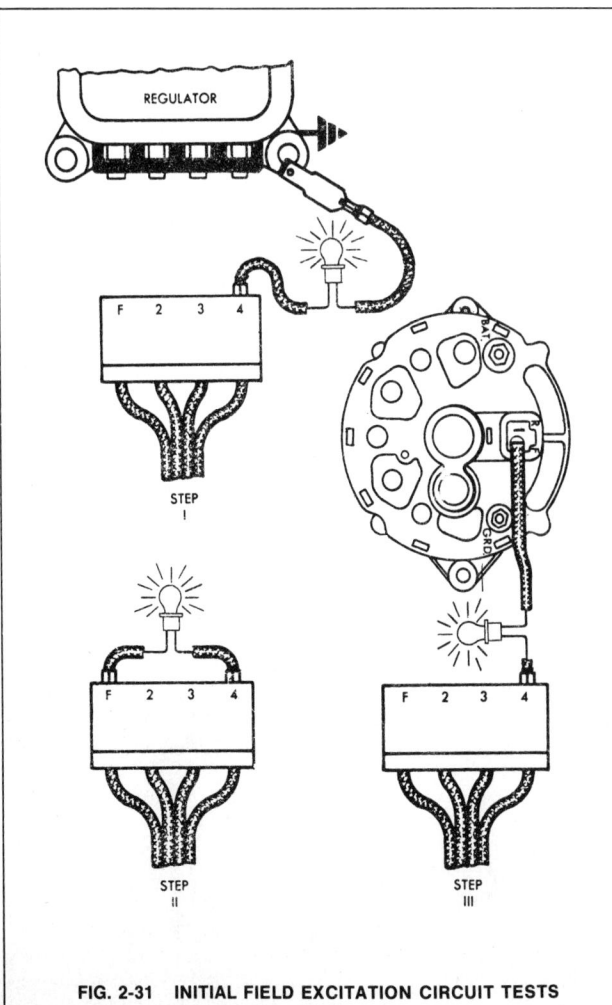

FIG. 2-31   INITIAL FIELD EXCITATION CIRCUIT TESTS

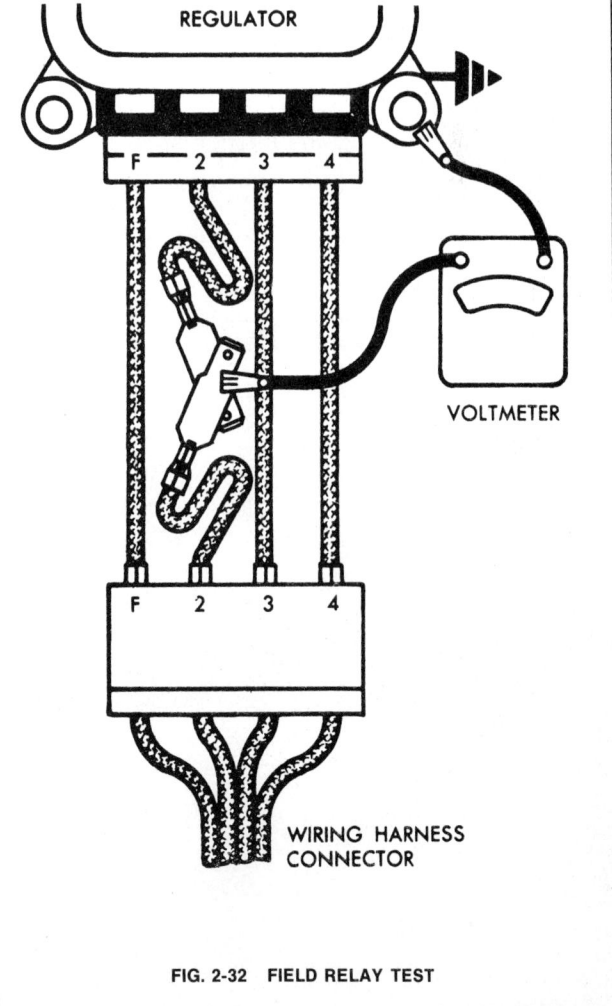

FIG. 2-32   FIELD RELAY TEST

CLOSING VOLTAGE ADJUSTMENT

1. Connect a voltmeter and 50-ohm variable resistor as shown in **Fig. 2-33.**

2. Turn the resistor to open position and the ignition switch to OFF.

3. Decrease resistance slowly and note the relay closing voltage. Adjust by bending the heel iron as shown in **Fig. 2-34.**

OFF-CAR REGULATOR ADJUSTMENTS

Most regulator adjustments are made on the car, but the unit can be removed for field relay point and air gap adjustments. *Never clean the voltage regulator contacts as abrasive material will destroy them.*

1. Field relay point opening is checked with a feeler gauge as shown in **Fig. 2-35.** If adjustment is required, bend the armature stop carefully.

2. Air gap does not normally require adjusting. When opening and closing voltages are within specifications, the relay will open correctly, even if the air gap is not within specifications. If adjustment is necessary, bend the flat contact spring after checking with a feeler gauge **(Fig. 2-36).**

ALTERNATOR REMOVAL/INSTALLATION

TO REMOVE

1. Disconnect the positive battery cable from the battery terminal.

2. Disconnect the wiring leads from the rear of the Delcotron.

3. Remove the alternator brace bolt and slip the V-belt off the drive pulley.

4. Remove the through-bolt holding the Delcotron to the mounting bracket and remove unit from the car.

TO INSTALL

1. Position the Delcotron on the mounting bracket and replace the adjusting and through-bolts, but *do not* tighten.

2. Slip the V-belt over the drive pulley.

3. Adjust the unit for specified belt tension and tighten the through-bolt to 30 ft.-lbs, adjusting bracket bolt to 20 ft.-lbs.

4. Replace the wiring leads at rear of Delcotron.

5. Reconnect the positive battery cable to the battery terminal.

ALTERNATOR DISASSEMBLY AND TESTING

TO DISASSEMBLE

1. Position the Delcotron in a vise with its mounting flange lengthwise and clamp it securely.

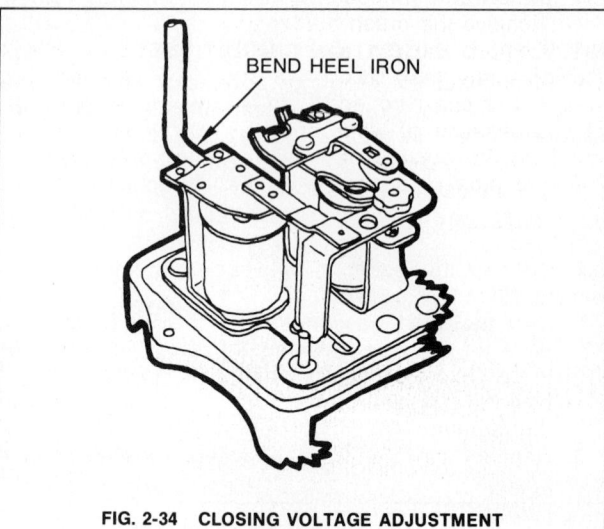

FIG. 2-34   CLOSING VOLTAGE ADJUSTMENT

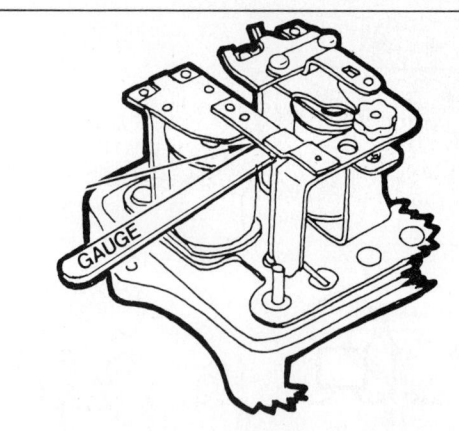

FIG. 2-35   FIELD RELAY OPENING CHECK

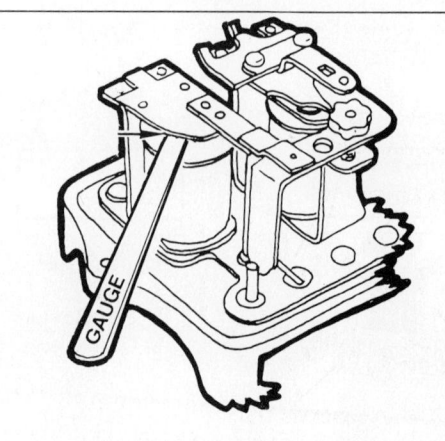

FIG. 2-36   AIR GAP CHECK

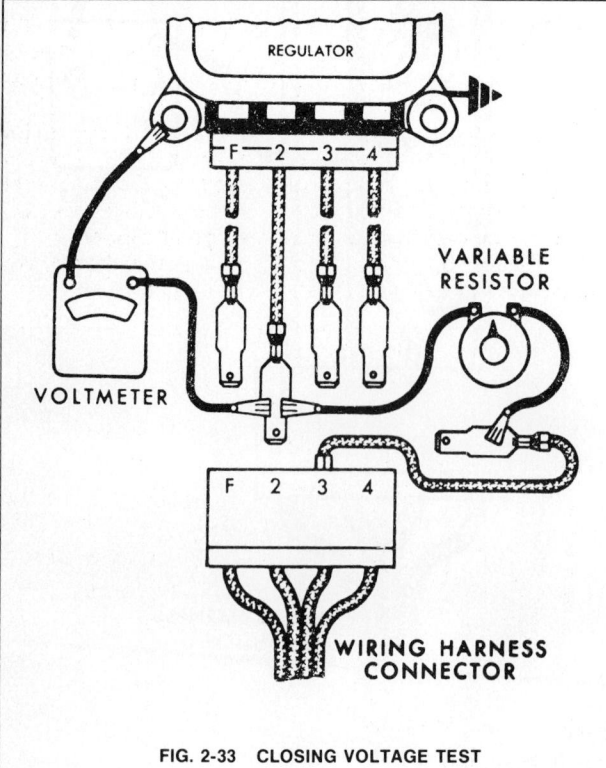

FIG. 2-33   CLOSING VOLTAGE TEST

2. Make a chalk mark across the end frames as an alignment guide for reassembly, and then remove the end frame through-bolts.

3. Pry the slip-ring end frame and stator assembly from the drive end and rotor assembly with a screwdriver.

4. Tape the slip-ring end-frame bearing and shaft to prevent bearing contamination.

5. Separate the stator from the end frame by removing the stator-lead attaching nuts. Test procedures which follow completion of this disassembly sequence can be performed at this point. Continue further disassembly *only* if necessary to replace components.

6. Remove the brush holder assembly.

7. Remove the BAT and GRD terminals and one attaching screw, then lift out the end-frame heat sink.

8. If the slip-ring end-frame bearing is to be replaced because of wear or lack of lubricant, press it out from the outside of the housing, using a suitable piece of pipe or a socket on the outer race. Always

discard the bearing if it is removed and replace it with a new one—*do not* attempt to relubricate the bearing and reinstall.

9. Fit a 15/16-in. box wrench on the retaining nut and insert a 5/16-in. Allen wrench into the drive shaft end hole to keep the shaft from moving while the pulley retaining nut is loosened **(Fig. 2-17)**. If the Delcotron is equipped with a double-groove pulley, use a 15/16-in. socket placed over the nut, with its wrench flats closest to the drive end, and turn it with a 15/16-in. box wrench.

10. Remove the spacers and rotor from the drive end frame.

11. If the front bearing is to be replaced, remove the bearing retainer plate from the end frame.

12. Press out the old bearing, using a suitable piece of pipe or a socket on the outer race.

TEST PROCEDURES

The equipment and procedures for testing the rotor field winding and stator are identical with those for the 10-SI Delcotron. See page 2-9.

HEAT SINK DIODE TEST (Fig. 2-37)

1. Disconnect the stator leads from the heat sink. Connect one lead of a 12-volt test lamp to the heat sink and the other test lead to a diode.

2. Reverse the test leads to the same connections. Test lamp should light in only one direction. If it lights in both directions, or fails to light, diode is defective.

3. Repeat Steps 1-2 with each remaining diode.

END FRAME DIODE TEST (Fig. 2-37)

1. Connect one lead of a 12-volt test lamp to the end frame and the other test lead to the diode lead.

2. Reverse the test leads to the same connections. Test lamp should light in only one direction. If it lights in both directions, or fails to light, diode is defective.

3. Repeat Steps 1-2 with each remaining diode.

HEAT SINK DIODE REPLACEMENT (Fig. 2-38)

1. Remove the heat-sink attaching screws and the heat sink from the end frame. Note the sequence in which parts are removed so that GRD and BAT terminals can be properly reassembled.

2. Press out the defective diode(s) and press in the new replacement diode(s) of the correct color. Positive diodes are red, negative diodes black. *Do not* strike the diode or attempt to punch out the defective one, because shock can damage the other good diodes.

3. Reassemble the heat sink to the end frame, following the parts sequence shown in **Fig. 2-38**.

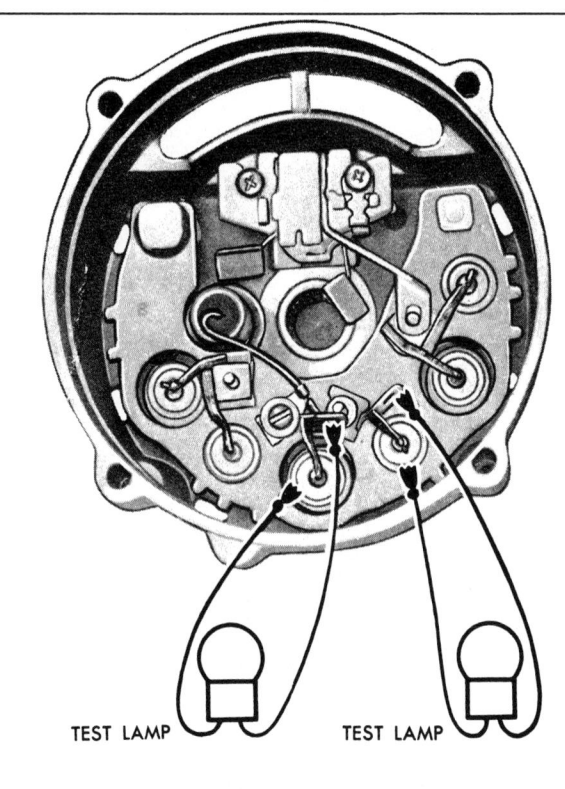

TEST LAMP   TEST LAMP

FIG. 2-37   DIODE TESTS

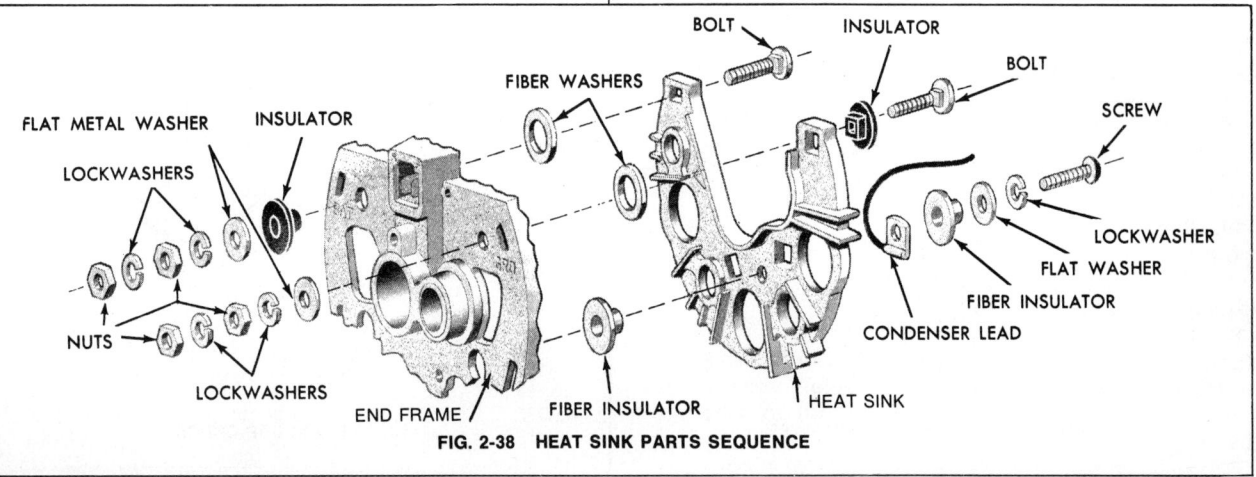

FIG. 2-38   HEAT SINK PARTS SEQUENCE

END FRAME DIODE REPLACEMENT

1. Press out the defective diode(s) and press in the new replacement diode(s) of the correct color. Positive diodes are red, negative diodes black. *Do not* strike the diode or attempt to punch out the defective one, because shock can damage the other good diodes.

BRUSH HOLDER REPLACEMENT (Fig. 2-39)

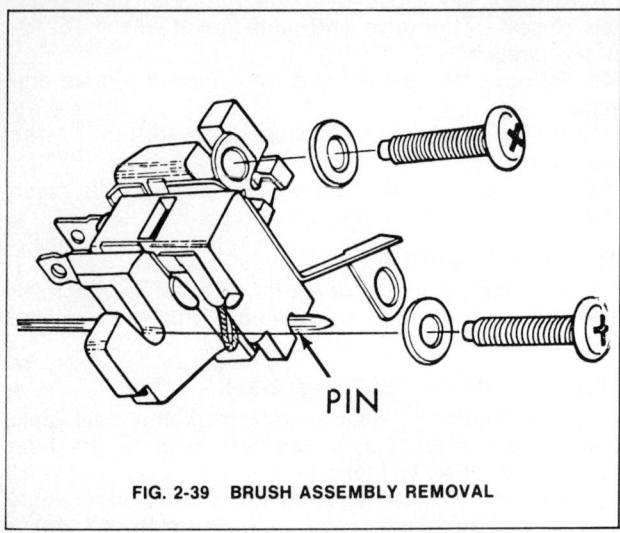

PIN

FIG. 2-39   BRUSH ASSEMBLY REMOVAL

1. Remove the stator nut holding the relay terminal connector.

2. Remove the brush-holder mounting screws.

3. Install the new brush holder assembly and replace the retaining screws.

4. Connect the relay-terminal wire lead and install the stator lead nut. Individual brush replacement is shown on page 2-17.

TO ASSEMBLE

1. If drive end-frame bearing was removed, press a new one in place, using a suitable piece of pipe or a socket to apply pressure *only* on the outer race. Install the bearing retainer.

2. If the slip-ring end-frame bearing was removed, press a new one in place, using technique in Step 1.

3. Install the stator in the slip-ring end frame and place the diode connectors over the relay, diode and stator leads. Tighten the terminal nuts.

4. Replace the rotor in the drive end frame.

5. Fit the brushes and spring in the brush holder assembly. Hold it in place with a toothpick or a short wire inserted through the brush holder hole.

6. Locate the brush holder on the end frame, with brush retaining wire or toothpick sticking out of the hole in the end frame.

7. Replace the brush-holder retaining screws.

8. Replace the stator. Notches should line up with the through-bolt holes.

9. Align the chalk marks on the two end frames and fit them together.

10. Replace and tighten the through-bolts, then remove the wire or pick holding the brushes.

11. Attach spacer, fan, drive pulley, washer and retaining nut on the drive shaft.

12. With the Delcotron secured in a vise by its mounting flange, fit a 15/16-in. box wrench over the retaining nut and insert a 5/16-in. Allen wrench into the drive-shaft end hole. Torque the nut to 40-50 ft.-lbs. **(Fig. 2-24).**

13. Spin fan and drive pulley to check for binding.

1970-72 VOLTAGE REGULATOR SPECIFICATIONS—Series 1D Delcotron Only

REGULATOR MODEL	1119515	119519
Application	Base	Service Only
Field Relay: Air Gap	.015	.015
Point Opening	.030	.030
Closing Voltage	1.5-3.2	1.5-3.2
Voltage Regulator: Air Gap	.067	.067
Point Opening	.014	.014
Voltage Setting	13.8-14.8 @ 85°F	13.8-14.8 @ 85°F

OLDSMOBILE ALTERNATOR SPECIFICATIONS

MODEL NO.	RATED HOT OUTPUT (Amps)	COLD OUTPUT (Amps @ Engine rpm)	FIELD CURRENT (Amps @ 80° F @ 12 Volts)
1102449	37	29 @ 1500	2.2-2.6
1100905	37	29 @ 1500	2.2-2.6
1100888	37	29 @ 1500	2.2-2.6
1100761	37	29 @ 1500	2.2-2.6
1100947	37	32 @ 5000	4.0-4.5
1102443	42	32 @ 1500	2.2-2.6
1100943	42	32 @ 1500	2.2-2.6
1100691	42	32 @ 1500	2.2-2.6
1100926	42	40 @ 5000	4.0-4.5
1102448	55	44 @ 1500	2.2-2.6
1102442	55	44 @ 1500	2.2-2.6
1100931	55	44 @ 1500	2.2-2.6
1100924	55	44 @ 1500	2.2-2.6
1100892	55	44 @ 1500	2.2-2.6
1100774	55	44 @ 1500	2.2-2.6
1100946	55	50 @ 5000	4.0-4.5
1102450	61	47 @ 1500	2.2-2.6
1100932	61	47 @ 1500	2.2-2.6
1100860	61	47 @ 1500	2.2-2.6
1100948	61	55 @ 5000	4.0-4.5
1102447	63	51 @ 1500	2.8-3.2
1100933	63	51 @ 1500	2.8-3.2
1100925	63	58 @ 5000	4.0-4.5
1101018	80	74 @ 5000	4.0-4.5

OLDSMOBILE REGULATOR SPECIFICATIONS

VOLTAGE REGULATOR APPLICATION		#1119515 #1119519
Field Relay	Air Gap	0.015
	Point Opening	0.030
	Closing Voltage	2.3-3.7
Voltage Regulator	Air Gap	0.067
	Point Opening	0.014
	Voltage Setting	13.8-14.8 @ 85°F

PONTIAC ALTERNATOR SPECIFICATIONS

MODEL NO.	RATED HOT OUTPUT (Amps)	COLD OUTPUT (Amps @ Engine rpm)	FIELD CURRENT (Amps @ 80° F @ 12 Volts)
1100704	37	35 @ 1825	2.2-2.6
1100888	37	35 @ 1750	2.2-2.6
1100905	37	35 @ 1750	2.2-2.6
1100550	37	32 @ 5000	4.0-4.5
1100927	37	32 @ 5000	4.0-4.5
1100497	37	36 @ 7000	4.0-4.9
1100700	55	50 @ 1660	2.2-2.6
1100891	55	50 @ 1750	2.2-2.6
1100892	55	50 @ 1750	2.2-2.6
1100920	55	50 @ 5000	4.0-4.5
1100928	55	50 @ 5000	4.0-4.5
1100906	55	50 @ 1750	2.2-2.6
1100895	61	58 @ 1660	2.2-2.6
1117765	62	55 @ 2400	4.1-4.6
1101015	80	74 @ 5000	4.0-4.5

BUICK ALTERNATOR/REGULATOR SPECIFICATIONS

Make and Type... Delco-Remy, Delcotron
Drive and Rotation.. Fan Belt, Clockwise
Voltage Regulator:
Make and Type... Delco-Remy Integral
Regulator Number... 1116384
Setting @ 2000 Engine RPM
(After 15-min. Warmup at 1500 Engine RPM).................... 14 ± 0.5 Volts

1975-77 APPLICATIONS:

Ampere Rating	37 Amps	42 Amps	55 Amps	61 Amps	63 Amps	80 Amps
Alternator Number	1102384	1102389	1102495	1102391	1102392	1101024
	1102388	1102400	1102840	1102460	1102461	1101031
	1102483	1102861	1102390	1102862	1102467	1101016
	1102491		1102494			
	1102399		1102560			
	1102388		1102478			
			1102488			
			1102457			

Field Current Draw—Rotor Removed (Amps @ 80° F and 12 volts)	4-4.5	4.4-5	4-4.5	4-4.5	4-4.5	4-4.9
Bench Test @ 14 Volts and 80°F (Amps @ Alternator RPM)	37 @ 5500	42 @ 5500	55 @ 5500	61 @ 5500	63 @ 5500	80 @ 5500

1972-74 APPLICATIONS:

Ampere Rating	37 Amps	37 Amps	42 Amps	55 Amps	61 Amps	63 Amps
Alternator Number	1100947	1100497	1100926	1100946	1100948	1100925
Field Current Draw (Amps) at 80°F and 12 Volts	4-4.5 Amps	4-4.5 Amps	4-4.5 Amps	4-4.5 Amps	4-4.5 Amps	4-4.5 Amps
Bench Test @ 14 Volts and 80° F (Amps @ Alternator RPM)	32 @ 5000	37 @ 5000	37 @ 5000	50 @ 5000	55 @ 5000	58 @ 5000

1970-71 APPLICATIONS:

Ampere Rating	37 Amps	42 Amps	55 Amps	61 Amps	63 Amps
Alternator Number	1100905	1100943	1100931	1100932	1100933
	1100888	1100691	1100892	1100860	
	1100761		1100774		
Field Current Draw (Amps) @ 80°F and 12 Volts	2.2-2.6	2.2-2.6	2.2-2.6	2.2-2.6	2.8-3.2
Bench test @ 14 Volts & 80°F (Amps at Alternator RPM)	37 @ 6500	42 @ 6500	55 @ 6500	61 @ 6500	63 @ 6500
Min. Current Output @ 500 Engine RPM	7 Amps	9 Amps	9 Amps	12 Amps	13 Amps
Min. Current Output @ 1500 Engine RPM	29 Amps	32 Amps	44 Amps	47 Amps	51 Amps

(1970-71)

Make and Type..Delco-Remy, Double Contact
Regulator Number (All Except 63-Amp)...1119515
Regulator Number (63-Amp)...1119519
Field Relay Closing Voltage...1.5-3.2
Field Relay Air Gap...0.015-in.
Field Relay Point Opening...0.030-in.
Voltage Regulator Air Gap, Lower Points Just Touching...0.067-in.
Voltage Regulator Upper Contact-Point Opening...0.014-in.
Voltage Regulator Upper Contact Setting @ 2000 Engine RPM
(After 15-Min. Warmup at 1500 Engine RPM)...14 ± 0.5 Volts
Voltage Regulator Lower Contact Setting (Step Voltage)...0.1-0.3 Below Upper Setting

1970-79 CHEVROLET DELCOTRON SPECIFICATIONS

MODEL NO.	APPLICATION	DELCO REMY SPEC NO.	FIELD CURRENT Amps (80°F @ 12 Volts)	COLD OUTPUT* (Amps @ 5000 rpm)	RATED HOT OUTPUT** (Amps)
1100497	All I-6 (Base)	4519	4-4.5	33	37
1100544	Corvette with K76 or C60	4522	4-4.5	55 [1]	61
1100560	Nova I-6 with K77 or C60	4520	4-4.5	50 [2]	55
1100575	Nova V-8 with K77 or C60	4520	4-4.5	50 [2]	55
1100597	All (Exc. Corvette & Nova) V-8 with K76 or C60	4522	4-4.5	55 [1]	61
1100950	Corvette (Base)	4521	4-4.5	38	42
1102347	All (Exc. Nova) I-6 with K76 or C60	4522	4-4.5	55 [1]	61
1102397	Camaro Z28 (Base)	4519	4-4.5	33	37
1102483	All (Exc. Camaro Z28 & Corvette) V-8 (Base)	4519	4-4.5	33	37
1102493	Chevrolet with B02 or B07	4521	4-4.5	38	42
1100545	All I-4 (Base)	4531	4-4.5	31	32
1100546	All I-4 with C49 RPO L11—with C60	4520	4-4.5	50	55
1100559	All I-4 with N41 (less C49 or C60)	4531	4-4.5	31	32
1102500	RPO L11 with C49 + NB2 or C60 + NB2; RPO L13 with C60	4520	4-4.5	50	55
1102854	All V-8 (Base)	4533	4-4.5	60	63
1102856	All I-4 with NB2 (less C49 or C60)	4519	4-4.5	33	37
1102857	All V-8 with C49 + C60	4533	4-4.5	60	63
1102353	Corvette with LS-4 & with N40	4521	4-4.5	37	42
1100934	All V-8's exc. Corvette, B02 & B07	4519	4-4.5	32	37
1100497	All I-6 exc. B02 & B07 & L25	4519	4-4.5	36@ 7000 rpm	37
1100573	All V-8 with B02 & B07	4521	4-4.5	37	42
1100597	Camaro, Chevrolet, Chevelle with K76, C60 & LT4	4522	4-4.5	55	61
1100950	Corvette, with LS4, L48 or L82 & RPO LT1	4521	4-4.5	37	42
1102354	I-6 with K85	4533	4-4.5	58	63
1100542	Chevrolet, Monte Carlo & Chevelle with C60	4533	4-4.5	58	63
1102346	I-6 with B02 & B07	4521	4-4.5	37	42
1100543	Corvette—with RPO LS5, LS6	4521	4-4.5	37	42
1100566	All with 307, 350, 400 & 454 V-8's. All with base I-6. Not used RPO B02, B07, Z28 or LS6	3395	2.2-2.6	35	37
1100836	All I-6 with N-40	3395	2.2-2.6	35	37
1100837	All with RPO Z28 & LS6	3395	2.2-2.6	35	37
1100843	Chevelle, Camaro & Nova with C60	4500	2.2-2.6	58	61
1100917	Chevrolet with C60, Chevrolet & Chevelle with RPO K85	3398	2.8-3.2	59	63
1100567	RPO B02 & B07	3396	2.2-2.6	40	42
1100897	Nova I-6 with AC & N-40 or A.I.R.		2.2-2.6	61	14
1100846	All RPO K-85 with AC or without AC Mandatory with RPO C49		2.2-2.6	63	14
1100896	RPO B02 I-6 without AC		2.2-2.6	61	14
1100857	Corvette 350 V-8 without AC or K-66		2.2-2.6	42	14
1100839	307, 350, 400 & 454 V-8's with RPO K-79, I-6 base engine		2.2-2.6	42	14
1100841	K-79 I-6 with N-40		2.2-2.6	42	14
1100825	Corvette 350 & 427 V-8 with AC and with K-66		2.2-2.6	61	14
1100833	Corvette 427 V-8 without AC or K-66		2.2-2.6	42	14
1100834	All with 307, 350, 400 & 454 V-8's. All with base I-6.		2.2-2.6	37	14

*Alternator temperature approximately 80°F.
**Ambient temperature 80°F.
[1] 1978—57 amps
[2] 1978—51 amps

1971-79 VEGA/MONZA DELCOTRON SPECIFICATIONS

MODEL NO.	APPLICATION	DELCO REMY SPEC. NO.	FIELD CURRENT AMPS (80°F @ 12 Volts)	COLD OUTPUT* (Amps @ 5000 Rpm)	RATED HOT OUTPUT** (Amps)
1100545	All I-4 (Base)	4531	4-4.5	31	32
1102858	All I-4 (Base)	4519	4-4.5	33	37
1100546	All I-4 with C49, RPO L11 with C60	4520	4-4.5	50	55
1102851	All I-4 with C49 or C60	4520	4-4.5	51	55
1100559	All I-4 with N41 (less C49 or C60)	4531	4-4.5	31	32
1100560	All I-4 with N41 (plus C49 or C60) V-8 with C49 or C60	4520	4-4.5	50	55
1102891	All I-4 with C60 + K19	4520	4-4.5	51	55
1102893	All I-4 with C49 + C60	4533	4-4.5	60	63
1102500	RPO L11 with C49 + NB2 or C60 + NB2; RPO L13 with C60	4520	4-4.5	50	55
1102394	All V-8 (Base)	4519	4-4.5	33	37
1102856	All I-4 with NB2 (less C49 or C60)	4519	4-4.5	33	37
1102479	All V-8 with C49	4520	4-4.5	51	55
1102857/ 1102854	All V-8 with C60 or C60 + C49	4533	4-4.5	60	63

*Alternator temperature approximately 80°F.   **Ambient temperature 80°F.

CADILLAC ALTERNATOR SPECIFICATIONS

MODEL YEAR	RATED OUTPUT (@14 Volts)	FIELD CURRENT DRAW (@12 Volts & 80°F)
1970-73 Without Integral Regulator	42	2.2-2.6
	55	2.2-2.6
	63	2.8-3.2
1973-79 With Integral Regulator	42	4.0-4.5
	63	4.0-4.5
	80	4.0-4.5

CADILLAC REGULATOR SPECIFICATIONS

MODEL YEAR	NORMAL OPERATING RANGE (@ 125°F)	LOWER CONTACT POINT SETTING (Lower than upper point setting)
1970-73 Without Integral Charging System	13.5-14.4 Volts	0.1-0.3 Volt

FORD, MERCURY, LINCOLN; 1976-78 AMERICAN MOTORS I-4 & V-8 ENGINES
Autolite-Ford-Motorcraft Alternator

SYSTEM DESCRIPTION

The Autolite-Ford alternator design has been used in a variety of ampere ratings, but all are essentially similar in operation. Before attempting any diagnosis or testing, identify the unit by model year and output or stamp color on the alternator to make certain you are following the correct specifications. Autolite-Ford charging systems may use one of four regulator types: an externally mounted electro-mechanical, electronic, or transistorized, or an integral regulator mounted to the rear of the alternator. A correct determination of the regulator used is necessary when working on a Ford charging system.

Beginning in 1974, Continental Mark IV's and Thunderbirds equipped with a heated windshield and rear window are fitted with a second high-voltage alternator whose wiring circuit is completely separate and isolated from the car's primary charging system. Warning tags will be located on all connections of this system.

CHARGING SYSTEM FUSIBLE LINKS

Since 1972, a fusible (or fuse) link has been inserted in Ford Motor Company charging systems to protect the alternator against a short to ground in the wiring harness, or a heavy current flow such as that involved in incorrectly connecting booster equipment. All such fusible links have a molded flag on the wire or on the terminal insulator, and are color-coded as follows: blue—20 gauge wire; red—18 gauge wire; yellow—17 gauge wire; orange—16 gauge wire; green—14 gauge wire. Fusible link locations shown in **Fig. 2-40** have remained unchanged since 1972; those shown in **Fig. 2-40A** are new for 1979. Always inspect the fusible link as the first step in any troubleshooting procedure involving a no-charge condition, and replace if open or burned.

IN-CAR TEST PROCEDURES (EXTERNAL REGULATOR ALTERNATOR)

In checking the charging system operation to determine the area of malfunction, a voltmeter, ammeter and ohmmeter are required.

1. Connect the voltmeter negative lead to the negative battery terminal and the positive voltmeter lead to the positive battery terminal. Note the battery voltage reading on voltmeter scale.

2. Connect a tachometer, start the engine and run at 1500 rpm. With no electrical load, the voltmeter reading should increase between 1 and 2 volts.

3. Now turn on all accessories to maximum power draw and increase engine speed to 2000 rpm. Voltmeter reading should remain at least 0.5-volt greater than the battery voltage reading.

TEST RESULTS

VOLTMETER READS MORE THAN 2 VOLTS ABOVE BATTERY VOLTAGE

1. Shut the engine off. Clean and tighten regulator-to-alternator and regulator-to-engine ground condition.

2. Repeat the voltmeter test. Voltmeter should now read battery voltage. If it does not, unhook the regulator from the system.

3. Repeat the voltmeter test. If the voltmeter now reads battery voltage, replace the regulator. If it does not, locate and correct a short in the alternator-to-regulator wiring.

4. Replace the regulator and connect it to the wiring harness. Repeat the voltmeter test. Voltmeter should read battery voltage.

VOLTMETER READS LESS THAN 0.5-VOLT

1. Check regulator Plug ''I'' for battery voltage as shown in **Fig. 2-41.** Then move the jumper lead and check regulator plug ''A'' for battery voltage. if none is present, repair the wiring and repeat the voltmeter test.

2. If voltage still does not increase 0.5-volt above battery voltage, check the regulator plug-to-alternator (field circuit). Disconnect the regulator wiring plug and connect an ohmmeter between its field plug ''F'' and ground **(Fig. 2-42).** Ohmmeter reading should indicate

between 4 and 250 ohms.

3. Connect the ohmmeter between the regulator ''I'' and ''F'' terminals **(Fig. 2-43).** Ohm reading should be zero; if 10 ohms or more, the regulator connector wire inside is open.

4. If the field circuit is normal (Step 2), unhook the wiring plug at the regulator and connect a jumper lead between the ''A'' and ''F'' terminals **(Fig. 2-44).** Repeat the voltmeter test.

5. If an under-voltage condition still occurs, remove

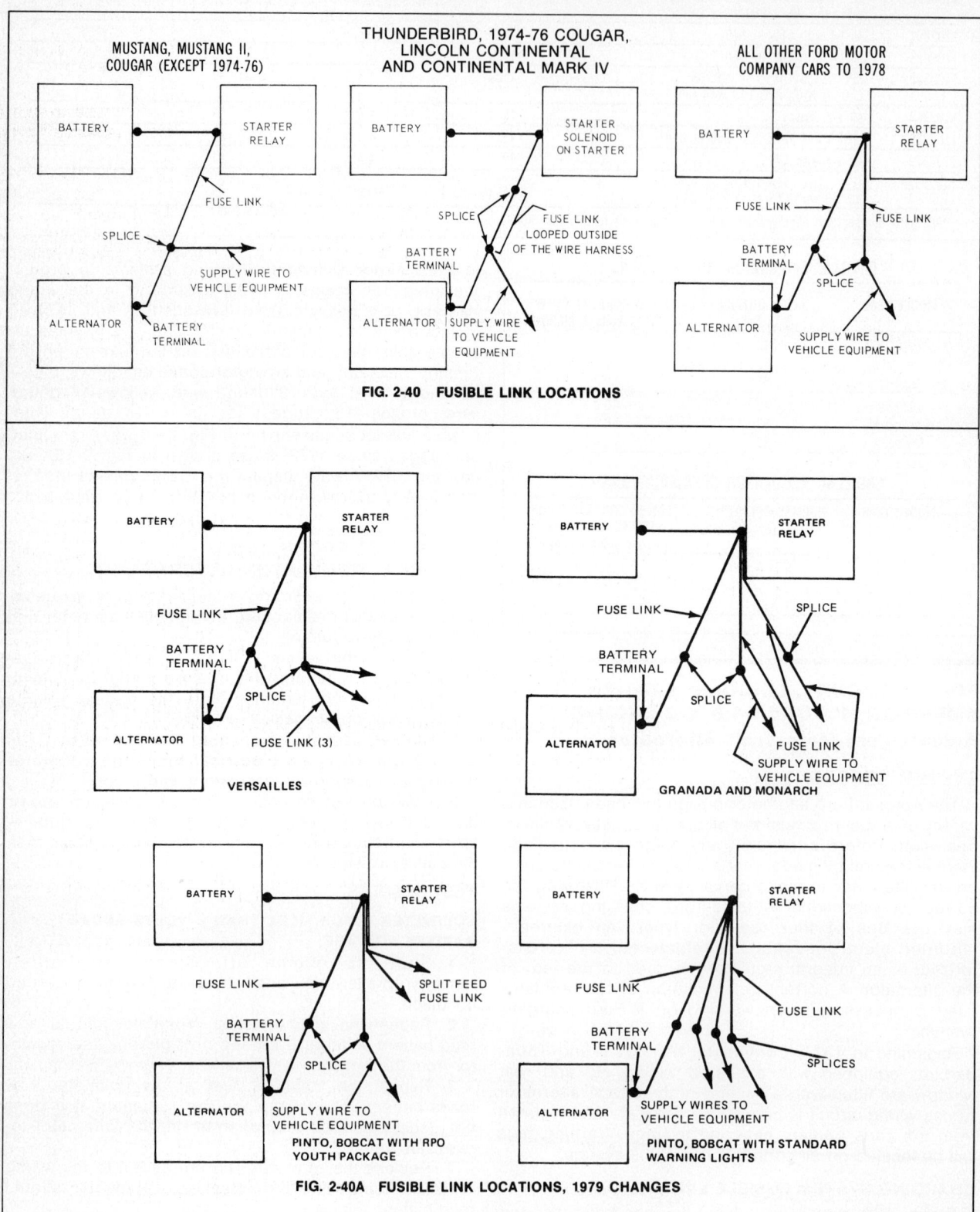

FIG. 2-40 FUSIBLE LINK LOCATIONS

FIG. 2-40A FUSIBLE LINK LOCATIONS, 1979 CHANGES

the jumper lead from the "A" and "F" terminals and connect it to the alternator FLD and BAT terminals **(Fig. 2-45)**. Repeat the voltmeter test.

6. If voltage is now normal, the wiring harness from the alternator to regulator must be replaced or repaired. If the voltage reading is still below normal, remove and replace the alternator.

DIODE TEST

1. Disconnect the electric choke and voltage regulator wiring plug.

2. Hook the jumper lead between "A" and "F" terminals of the wiring plug **(Fig. 2-44)**.

3. Connect a voltmeter to the battery terminals.

4. Start the engine and run at idle. Note voltmeter reading.

5. Switch the positive voltmeter lead to the alternator "S" terminal. Note voltmeter reading.

TEST RESULTS

1. If the voltmeter reads one-half battery voltage, the diodes are good.

2. A voltmeter reading of about 1.5 volts indicates a shorted negative diode or a grounded stator winding.

3. A voltmeter reading of about 1.5 volts *below* battery voltage indicates a shorted positive diode.

4. A voltmeter reading of about 1.0 to 1.5 volts *greater than one-half battery voltage* indicates an open

negative diode.

5. A voltmeter reading of about 1.0 to 1.5 volts *less than one-half battery voltage* indicates an open positive diode.

IN-CAR TEST PROCEDURE (INTEGRAL REGULATOR ALTERNATOR)

Care *must* be exercised in connecting test equipment into the charging circuit, because the alternator output terminal is connected at all times to the battery, and connecting the regulator BAT terminal to the regulator FLD terminal will destroy the regulator.

1. Connect an alternator/generator/regulator tester to the alternator as shown in **Fig. 2-46**. Bypass the regulator by connecting the regulator FLD terminal to ground with a jumper lead.

2. Close the battery adapter switch, start the engine and open the switch.

3. Increase engine speed to 2000 rpm and, with all accessories off, turn the load control until the voltmeter reads 15 volts. Ammeter reading should range between 50-57 amps.

4. If the alternator tests within specifications, the regulator is malfunctioning and should be replaced. If the alternator output is not within specifications (regulator is bypassed), the alternator should be removed for bench-testing to determine exactly what is wrong.

a) An output of 2-8 amps below specifications

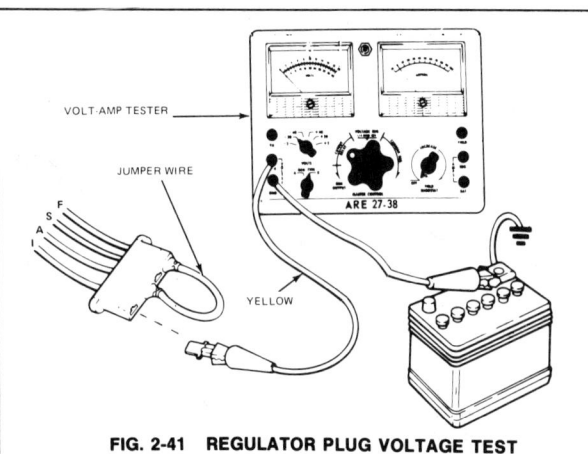
FIG. 2-41 REGULATOR PLUG VOLTAGE TEST

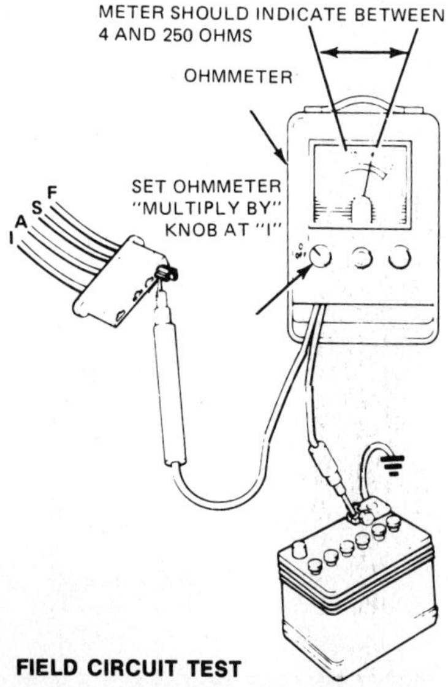

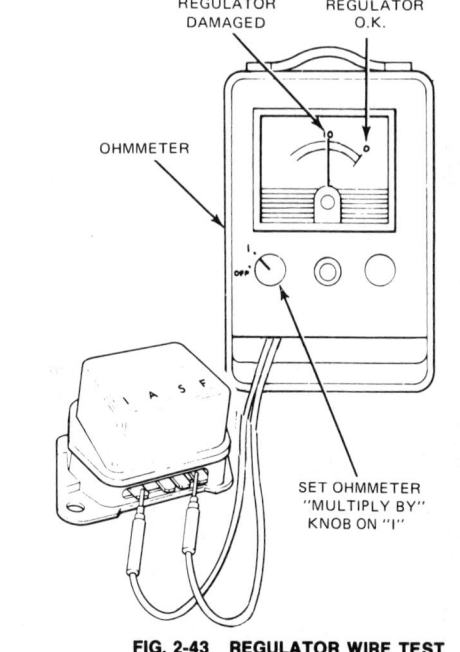
FIG. 2-43 REGULATOR WIRE TEST

FIG. 2-42 FIELD CIRCUIT TEST

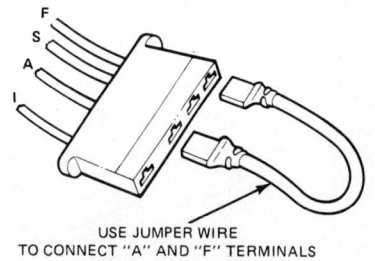
FIG. 2-44 REGULATOR-PLUG JUMPER LEAD CONNECTIONS

usually indicates an open diode.
b) An output of 10-15 amps below specifications usually indicates a shorted diode (listen for idle speed whine).

VOLTAGE REGULATOR TEST PROCEDURES
ELECTRO-MECHANICAL, ELECTRONIC, INTEGRAL REGULATORS

These regulators are factory-calibrated, sealed and nonadjustable. When one does not operate within specified limits, it must be replaced. Never substitute an electro-mechanical type for the 1978 electronic regulator.

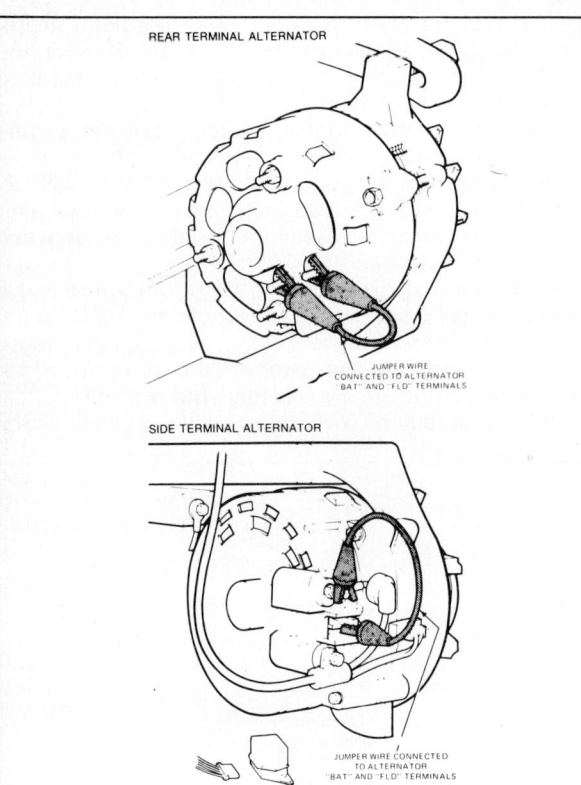

FIG. 2-45 ALTERNATOR JUMPER LEAD CONNECTIONS

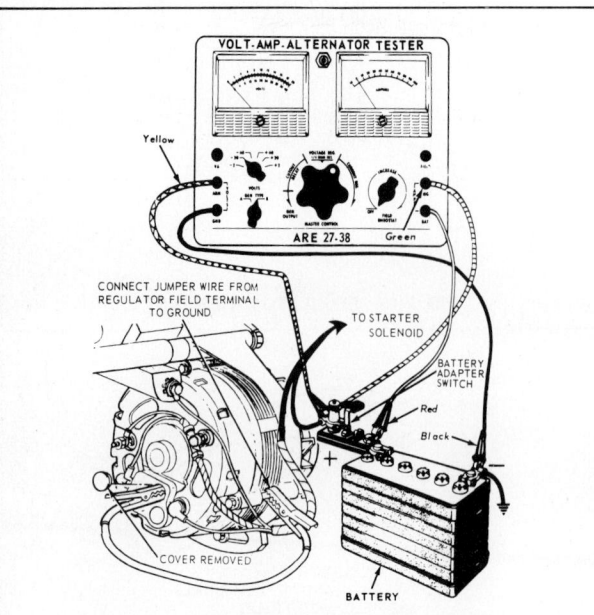

FIG. 2-46 ALTERNATOR OUTPUT TEST—INTEGRAL REGULATOR CONNECTIONS

Systems for 1978 using a warning light have a 500-ohm resistor on the back of the instrument cluster instead of the 15-ohm resistance wire previously used.

To test:
1. Connect a voltmeter to the battery and note the reading (Fig. 2-47).
2. Connect a tachometer and start the engine, increasing its rpm to 1800-2200 for 3-4 minutes.
3. Note the voltmeter reading, which should be 1 to 2 volts higher than the initial reading (for integral regulators, see Step 6).
4. If the voltmeter reading is less than 1 volt or more than 2½ volts, replace the regulator.
5. If the voltmeter reading is between 1 and 2 volts, turn on the headlamps and heater/air-conditioner blower. If voltage decreased more than 0.5-volt from the reading in Step 3, replace the regulator.
6. If the voltage reading does not rise above battery voltage with an integral regulator, connect a 12-volt test lamp between the regulator supply lead and ground.
7. Test lamp should glow when the ignition switch is turned on. If it does not, the supply circuit is faulty and the regulator must be replaced.

TRANSISTORIZED REGULATOR

The transistorized regulator operates in a manner similar to other regulators, but uses transistors and diodes rather than a vibrating armature and relay. A voltage limit adjustment is possible with this regulator (Fig. 2-48).
1. With the regulator at normal operating temperature, remove the cover.
2. Turn the adjusting screw clockwise to increase the voltage setting or counterclockwise to decrease the voltage setting. Use a fiber rod as a screwdriver.
3. Replace the cover.

ALTERNATOR REMOVAL/INSTALLATION
TO REMOVE
1. Disconnect the battery ground cable.
2. Loosen the alternator mounting bolts, remove the

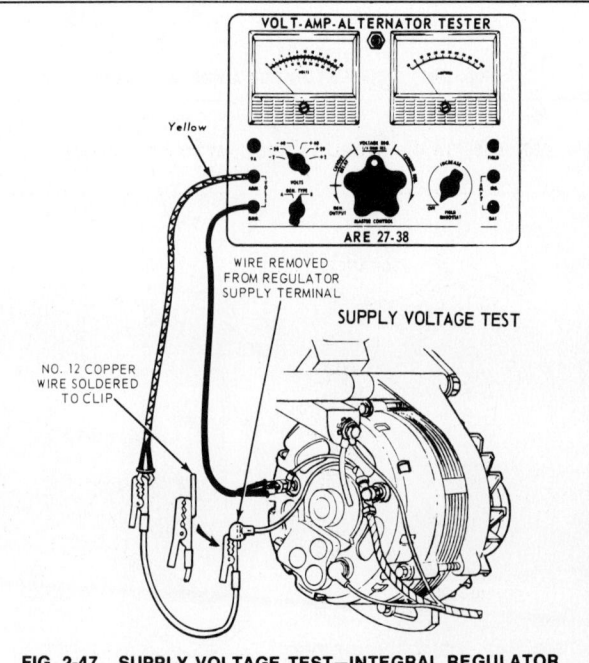

FIG. 2-47 SUPPLY VOLTAGE TEST—INTEGRAL REGULATOR

adjustment arm and slip the V-belt off the pulley.

3. Disconnect electrical connections. Push-on stator and field connectors are used on the rear-terminal alternator and should be pulled straight off to prevent terminal stud damage. Side-terminal alternators use a push-on blade with a lock tab which engages the alternator housing. Depress the tab before pulling connections off the terminals.

4. Remove the mounting bolt and alternator.

TO INSTALL

1. Fit the alternator to the engine and install attaching bolt and spacer (if used). Tighten the bolt snugly.

2. Replace the adjustment-arm-to-alternator attaching bolt.

3. Fit V-belt on the alternator pulley, adjust belt tension and tighten the alternator mounting and attachment arm bolts.

4. Replace electrical connections tightly **(Fig. 2-49)** and connect the battery ground cable.

BENCH TESTS

RECTIFIER SHORT OR GROUNDED; STATOR GROUNDED TEST

1. Calibrate ohmmeter and connect one probe to

the alternator BAT terminal and the other to the rear blade STA terminal. Note ohmmeter reading.

2. Reverse probes and repeat test, noting reading.

3. A reading of approximately 60 ohms should be obtained in one direction, with no reading in the other. A reading in both directions indicates a defective negative diode, a grounded positive diode plate or a grounded BAT terminal.

4. Repeat Steps 1 and 2, using the probes on the STA and GRD terminals. If a reading is obtained in both directions, look for a defective negative diode, a grounded positive diode plate or grounded BAT terminal.

5. If no needle movement takes place in all four test positions, the STA terminal lead connection inside the alternator is open.

FIELD OPEN; SHORT CIRCUIT TEST

1. Connect ohmmeter probes to the alternator FLD terminal and GRD terminal. For alternators with an integral regulator, connect as shown in **Fig. 2-50**.

2. Spin the alternator pulley by hand and note the ohmmeter scale.

3. No ohmmeter reading indicates an open brush lead, worn or stuck brushes, or a defective rotor assembly.

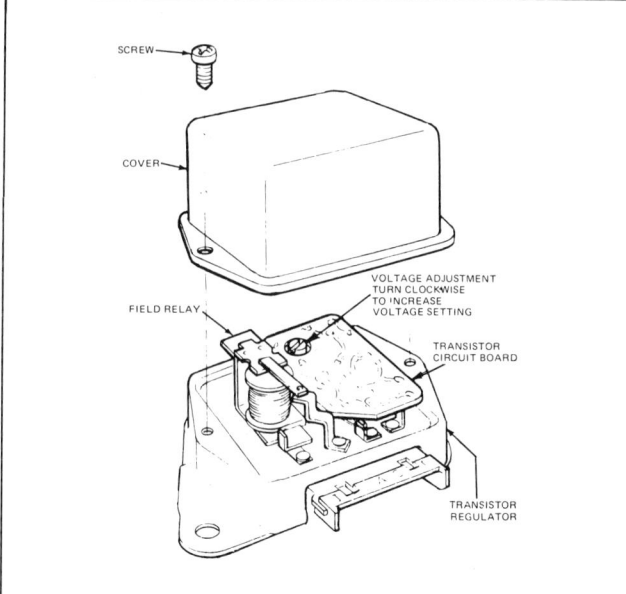

FIG. 2-48 TRANSISTORIZED REGULATOR ADJUSTMENT

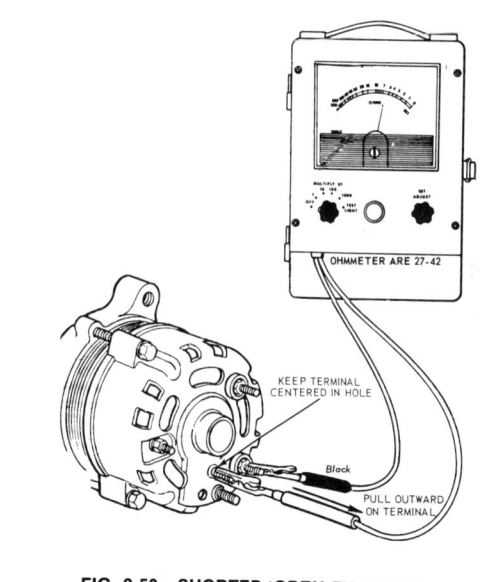

FIG. 2-50 SHORTED/OPEN FIELD TEST— INTEGRAL REGULATOR

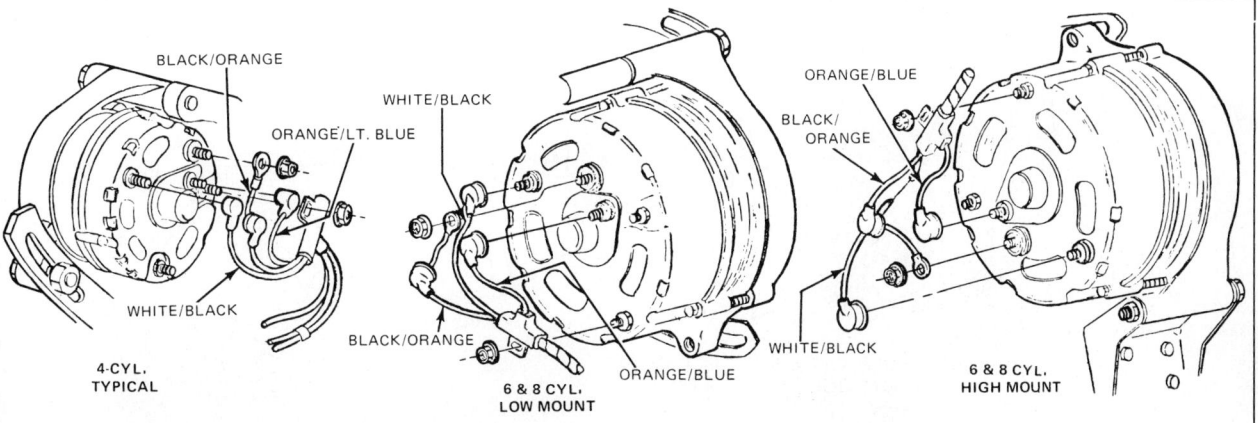

FIG. 2-49 TYPICAL FORD ALTERNATOR ELECTRICAL CONNECTIONS

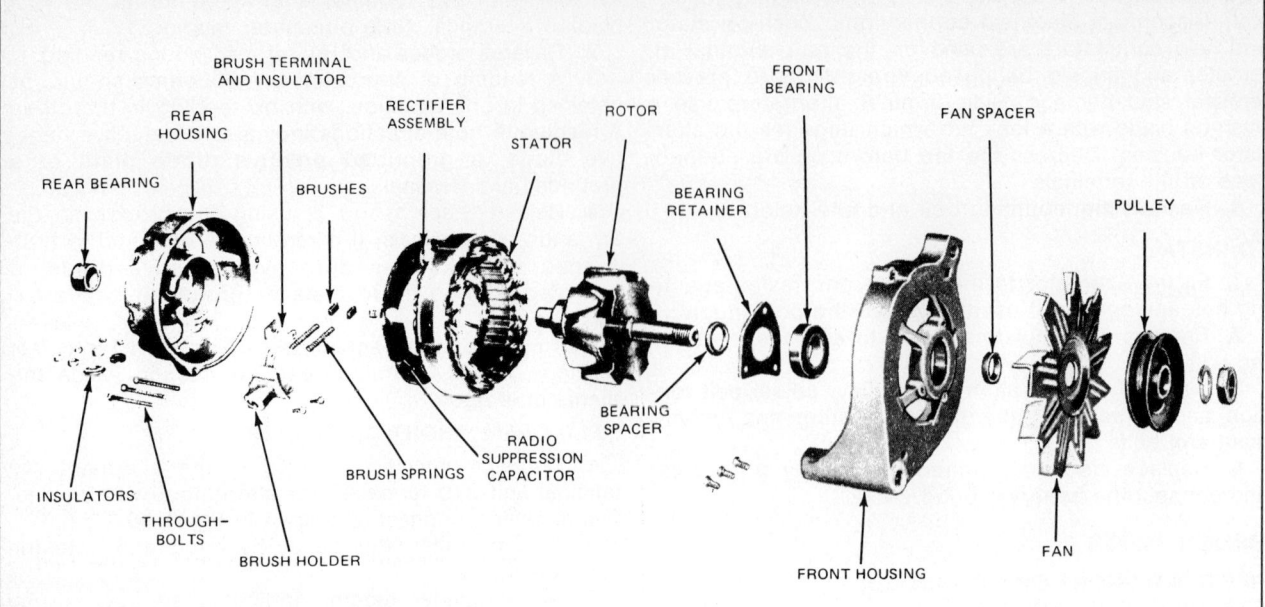

FIG. 2-51 REAR TERMINAL ALTERNATOR DISASSEMBLY

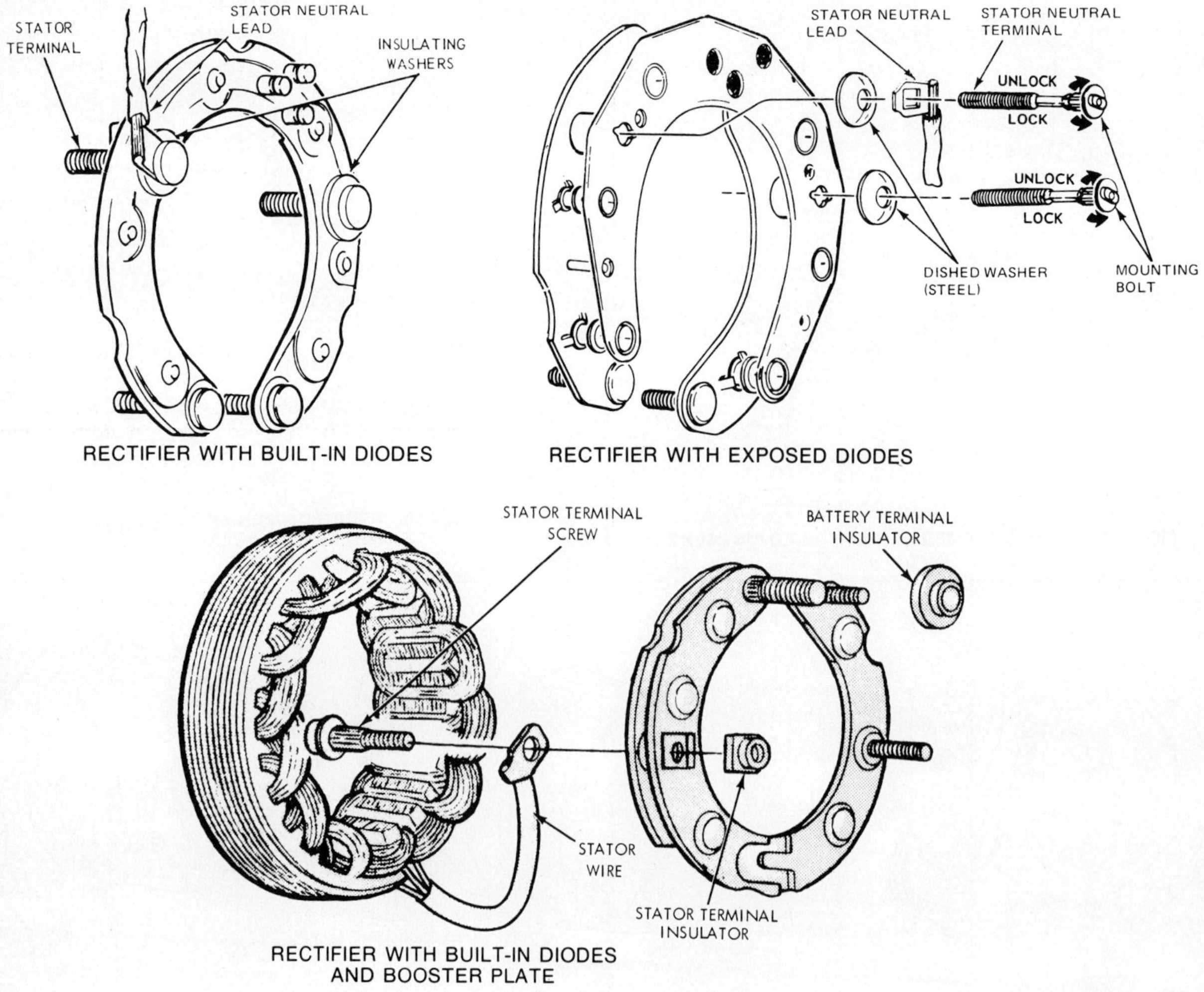

RECTIFIER WITH BUILT-IN DIODES

RECTIFIER WITH EXPOSED DIODES

RECTIFIER WITH BUILT-IN DIODES
AND BOOSTER PLATE

FIG. 2-52 RECTIFIER CIRCUIT BOARDS

4. An ohmmeter reading less than 3.5 ohms (4 ohms for integral regulator models) indicates a grounded brush assembly or field terminal, or a defective rotor.

5. A fluctuating ohmmeter reading between 3.5 and 250 ohms (4 to 150 ohms for integral regulator models) indicates that the alternator field is good.

DIODE TEST

1. Remove the rectifier assembly following the disassembly procedure.

2. Touch one ohmmeter probe to the diode plate and the other to each of the stator lead terminals in turn.

3. Reverse the probes and repeat Step 2. Test each of the six diodes (eight diodes in the 61-amp model).

4. All diodes should give approximately a 60-ohm reading in one direction and no reading in the opposite direction.

STATOR COIL OPEN OR GROUNDED TEST

1. Remove the stator from the alternator following the disassembly procedure below.

2. Connect one ohmmeter probe to the stator laminated core and the other to one stator lead.

3. Repeat for each stator lead. Touching the metal probes or stator leads with your hands during the test will give an incorrect reading.

4. The meter needle should not move. If it does, the stator winding is shorted to the core and must be replaced.

ROTOR OPEN OR SHORT TEST

1. Disassemble housing and rotor according to "Alternator Disassembly" following this section.

2. Connect each ohmmeter probe to a rotor slip ring. The meter should read 3.5 to 4.5 ohms.

3. A higher reading indicates a damaged slip-ring solder connection or a broken wire. Replace the rotor.

4. A lower reading indicates a shorted wire or slip ring. Replace the rotor.

5. Touch one probe to a slip ring and the other to the rotor shaft. If the meter needle moves, the rotor is shorted and must be replaced.

ALTERNATOR DISASSEMBLY AND ASSEMBLY

TO DISASSEMBLE REAR-TERMINAL ALTERNATOR (Fig. 2-51)

1. Make a chalk mark across the alternator housing and stator as an alignment guide for reassembly, and then remove housing through-bolts.

2. Separate the front housing and rotor from the rear housing and stator.

3. Disassemble nuts and insulators from the rear housing and separate the housing from the stator and rectifier assembly.

4. Unscrew the brush-holder attaching screws and remove the holder, brushes, brush springs, insulator and terminal.

5. If the rear bearing requires replacement, press from the rear housing. Support the housing close to the bearing boss to prevent damage.

6. If the rectifier assembly requires testing or replacement, unsolder the stator leads from the printed circuit board terminals with a low-heat soldering iron.

7. Rectifier assembly circuit boards will be one of three types **(Fig. 2-52):**

  a) Single circuit board with built-in diodes. Push the stator terminal screw straight out.

  b) Circuit board spaced from diode plate, exposing the diodes. Rotate the bolt head one-quarter turn clockwise to unlock and remove.

  c) Circuit board with built-in diodes and diode booster plate with additional two diodes (61-amp alternator only). Press the stator terminal screw from the circuit board 1/4-in., remove the nut and lift the screw from the circuit board.

8. Fit a 15/16-in. socket over the rotor shaft. Then, in a vise, secure an Allen head wrench which will fit the pulley-shaft end opening. Place the pulley-shaft end over the Allen head wrench and use a 3/4-in. open end wrench to remove the drive pulley nut.

9. Remove the lockwasher, pulley, fan and spacer, front housing and rotor stop from the rotor shaft.

10. Remove the front end-bearing retainer screws and retainer.

11. If the bearing requires replacement, press out as in Step 5.

12. Run the diode and field tests outlined earlier.

13. Wipe the rotor, stator and bearing with a clean cloth—*do not* use solvent.

TO ASSEMBLE REAR-TERMINAL ALTERNATOR (Fig. 2-51)

1. If the front bearing was removed, press a new bearing in place and replace the retainer.

2. Fit a new stop ring on the rotor drive shaft. Push the ring on the shaft and into the groove. Spreading the stop ring with pliers will damage it.

3. Locate the rotor stop on the drive shaft, with the recessed side against the stop ring.

4. Replace the front housing, fan spacer and fan, pulley and lockwasher on the drive shaft, and install retaining nut, using the same tools and setup as in Step 8 of the preceding disassembly procedure.

5. If the rear bearing was replaced, press a new bearing in flush with the outer end surface.

6. Replace brushes, brush springs, terminal and terminal insulator in the brush holder and insert a small drill bit through the terminal hole and holder to keep them in place.

7. Attach the brush holder in the rear housing with screws and position leads.

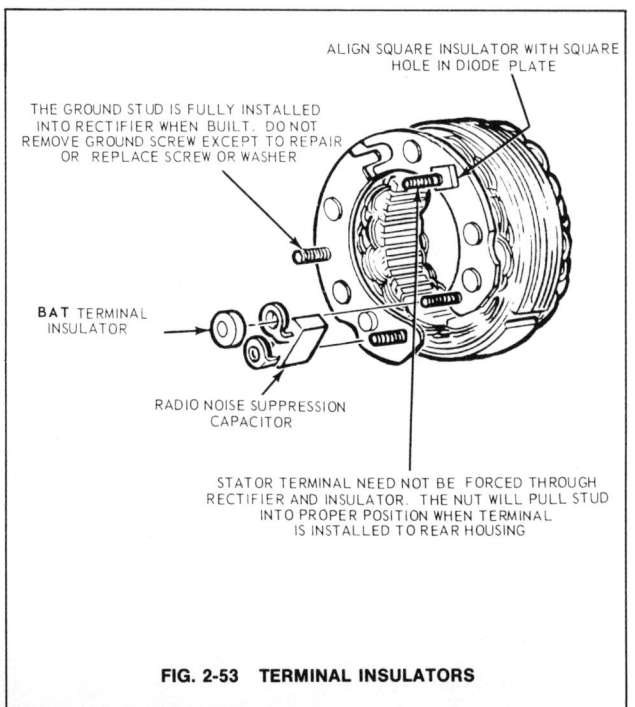

ALIGN SQUARE INSULATOR WITH SQUARE HOLE IN DIODE PLATE

THE GROUND STUD IS FULLY INSTALLED INTO RECTIFIER WHEN BUILT. DO NOT REMOVE GROUND SCREW EXCEPT TO REPAIR OR REPLACE SCREW OR WASHER

BAT TERMINAL INSULATOR

RADIO NOISE SUPPRESSION CAPACITOR

STATOR TERMINAL NEED NOT BE FORCED THROUGH RECTIFIER AND INSULATOR. THE NUT WILL PULL STUD INTO PROPER POSITION WHEN TERMINAL IS INSTALLED TO REAR HOUSING

FIG. 2-53 TERMINAL INSULATORS

8. Wrap the stator winding leads around the circuit board terminals and solder with a low-heat iron.

9. Fit the stator neutral-lead eyelet on the stator terminal screw and install the screw through the rectifier assembly **(Fig. 2-53).**

10. Replace the stator terminal in the circuit board as shown in **Fig. 2-52.**

11. Locate the radio noise-suppression capacitor on the rectifier terminal and install the terminal insulators.

12. Place the stator and rectifier assembly in the rear housing with all terminal insulators properly seated in their recesses. Replace the remaining terminal insulators on the terminal and screw the retaining nuts in place.

13. Fit the housings and stator together, using the chalk alignment mark as a guide, and reinstall the through-bolts.

14. Remove the drill bit holding the brushes in place and use a small amount of waterproof cement over the hole to seal it.

15. Spin the fan and pulley to check for binding.

TO DISASSEMBLE SIDE-TERMINAL ALTERNATOR (Fig. 2-54)

1. Make a chalk mark across the alternator housing and stator as an alignment guide for reassembly, and then remove the housing through-bolts.

2. Separate the front housing and rotor from the rear housing and stator. Use the slots provided in the front housing if pressure must be applied.

3. Remove drive pulley nut as in Step 8 of rear-terminal alternator disassembly.

4. Remove lockwasher, pulley, fan and fan spacer.

5. Withdraw the rotor and shaft from the front housing and remove the rotor shaft spacer.

6. Remove the front bearing retainer. If the bearing requires replacement, press it out while supporting the housing close to the bearing boss.

7. Use a medium-heat soldering iron to disconnect the stator-to-rectifier leads, and lift the stator from the rear housing.

8. Unsolder and disconnect the brush holder lead from the rectifier.

9. Remove the capacitor lead-to-rectifier screw.

10. Unscrew the rectifier assembly from the rear housing, remove the terminal nuts and insulator from the outside of the housing, then lift the rectifier assembly out.

11. Remove the brush holder from the housing, and separate the brushes from the holder.

12. Unscrew the capacitor from the rear housing.

13. If the rear bearing requires replacement, press from rear housing. Support the housing close to the bearing boss to prevent damage.

FORD ALTERNATOR SPECIFICATIONS

1970-74 FORD AUTOLITE ALTERNATOR (G.P.D. Rear Terminal)

SUPPLIER	STAMP COLOR	RATING Amperes @ 15V	RATING Watts @ 15V	FIELD CURRENT (Amps @ 12V)	CUT-IN SPEED (rpm)	RATED OUTPUT SPEED (Engine rpm) Cold	Hot	SLIP-RING TURNING (Ins.) Min. Dia.	Max. Runout	BRUSH LENGTH (Ins.) New	Wear-Limit	PULLEY NUT TORQUE (ft.-lbs.)	BELT[1] TENSION (lbs.)
Ford	Purple	38	570	2.4	400	2000	2900	1.22	0.0005	1/2	5/16	60-100	70-100
Ford	Orange	42	630	2.9	400	2000	2900	1.22	0.0005	1/2	5/16	60-100	70-110
Ford	Red	55	825	2.9	400	2000	2900	1.22	0.0005	1/2	5/16	60-100	70-110
Ford	Green	61	915	2.9	400	2000	2900	1.22	0.0005	1/2	5/16	60-100	70-110
Ford[2]	Black	65	975	2.9	360	1640	—	1.22	0.0005	5/8	3/8	60-100	70-110

[1] Used Belt. New Belt 140. A used belt is one that has been in operation more than 10 minutes. If belt tension is out of specification or belt has been removed, reset to 110 lbs.
[2] 1970-73 only.

1975-79 FORD AUTOLITE ALTERNATOR (G.P.D. Rear Terminal)

SUPPLIER	STAMP COLOR	RATING Amperes @ 15V	RATING Watts @ 15V	FIELD CURRENT (Amps @ 12V)	CUT-IN SPEED (rpm)	RATED OUTPUT SPEED (Engine rpm) Cold	Hot	SLIP-RING TURNING (Ins.) Min. Dia.	Max. Runout	BRUSH LENGTH (Ins.) New	Wear-Limit	PULLEY NUT TORQUE (ft.-lbs.)	BELT[1] TENSION (lbs.)
Ford	Orange	40	600	2.9	400	2000	2900	1.22	0.0005	1/2	5/16	60-100	90-110
Ford	Green	60	900	2.9[2]	400	2000	2900	1.22	0.0005	1/2	5/16	60-100	90-110
Ford[2]	Black	65	975	2.9	360	1640		1.22	0.0005	1/2	3/16	60-100	90-110

[1] Used Belt. New Belt 140. A used belt is one that has been in operation more than 10 minutes. If belt tension is out of specification or belt has been removed, reset to 110 lbs. [2] A field current of 4 amps is used with solid-state alternator; 1978 and later.

1972-79 FORD ALTERNATOR (G.P.D. Side Terminal)

RATING Amperes @ 15V	RATING Watts @ 15V	FIELD CURRENT (Amps @ 12V)	CUT-IN SPEED (Engine rpm)	RATED OUTPUT SPEED (Engine rpm)	SLIP-RING TURNING (Ins.) Min. Dia.	Max. Runout	BRUSH LENGTH (Ins.) New	Wear-Limit	PULLEY NUT TORQUE (ft.-lbs.)	BELT[1] TENSION (lbs.)
70	1050	2.9	725	5000	1.22	0.0005	1/2	5/16	60-100	70-110[3]
90	1350	2.9[4]	875	5000	1.22	0.0005	1/2	5/16	60-100	70-110[3]
100	1350	4.0	875	5000	1.22	0.0005	1/2	5/16	50-100	90-110

[1] Used Belt. New Belt 140. A used belt is one that has been in operation more than 10 minutes. If belt tension is out of specification, or belt has been removed, reset to 110 lbs.
[2] A field current of 4 amps is used with solid-state alternator; 1978 and later.
[3] 1978 on, 90-110
[4] A field current of 4 amps is used with solid-state alternator; 1978 and later.

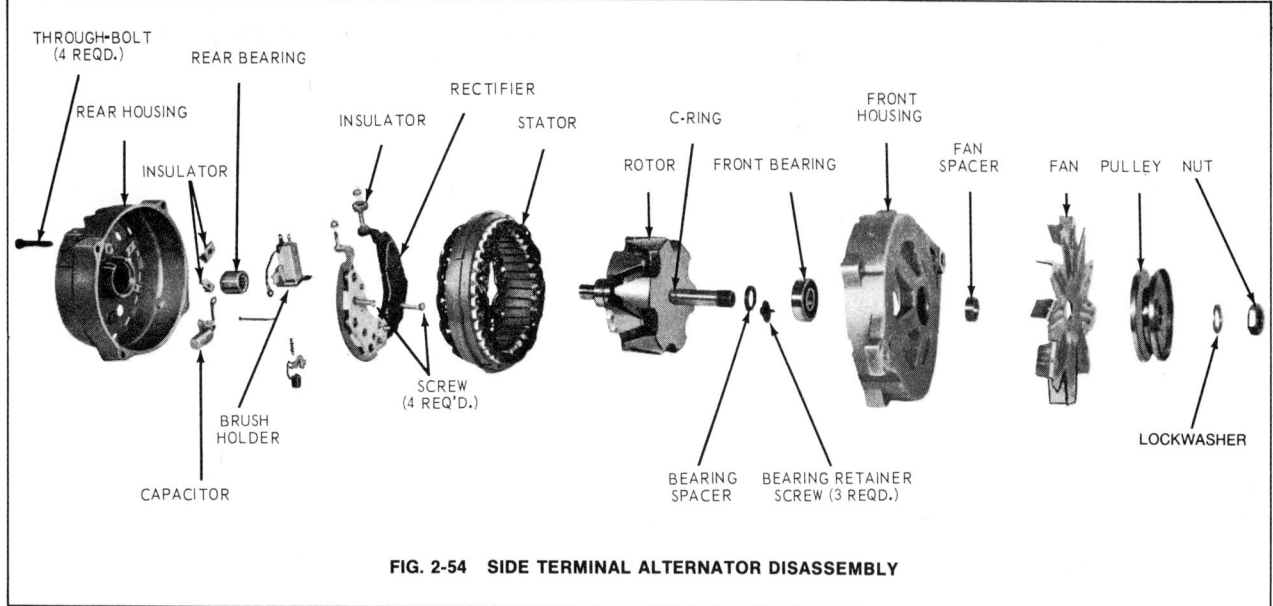

FIG. 2-54 SIDE TERMINAL ALTERNATOR DISASSEMBLY

14. Run diode and field tests outlined earlier.

15. Wipe the rotor, stator and bearing with a clean cloth—*do not* use solvent.

TO ASSEMBLE SIDE TERMINAL ALTERNATOR (Fig. 2-54)

1. If the front bearing was removed, press a new bearing in place and replace the retainer.

2. With the inner spacer replaced on the rotor shaft, insert the shaft into the front housing and bearing.

3. Replace fan spacer, fan, pulley, lockwasher and nut, using the same tools and setup earlier described in Step 8 of rear-terminal alternator disassembly.

4. If the rear bearing was removed, press a new bearing in place until it is flush with the outer surface of the boss.

5. Replace the brushes, brush springs and terminals in the brush holder, inserting a small drill bit through the holder to keep the assembly in place.

6. Attach the brush holder in the rear housing with screws. Push the holder in the direction of the rotor-shaft opening and tighten the screws.

7. Install the capacitor to the rear housing.

8. Fit the two rectifier insulators on the bosses inside the housing **(Fig. 2-55).**

9. Fit the insulator on the large BAT terminal of the rectifier and place the rectifier in the rear housing. Install the outside insulator on the BAT terminal and replace the nuts finger-tight on both outside terminals.

10. Replace the rectifier attaching screws loosely.

11. Now tighten the outside terminal nuts and then the rectifier attaching screws.

12. Fit the capacitor lead to the rectifier and secure with the screw.

13. Solder the brush holder lead to the rectifier pin.

14. Align the stator in the rear housing according to the chalk mark. Solder the stator leads to the rectifier pins.

15. Fit the rotor and front housing into the stator and rear housing. Align by chalk mark and install the through-bolts, tightening two opposing bolts first and the two remaining bolts after.

16. Remove the drill bit holding the brushes in place, and use a small amount of waterproof cement over the hole to seal it.

17. Spin the fan and pulley to check for binding.

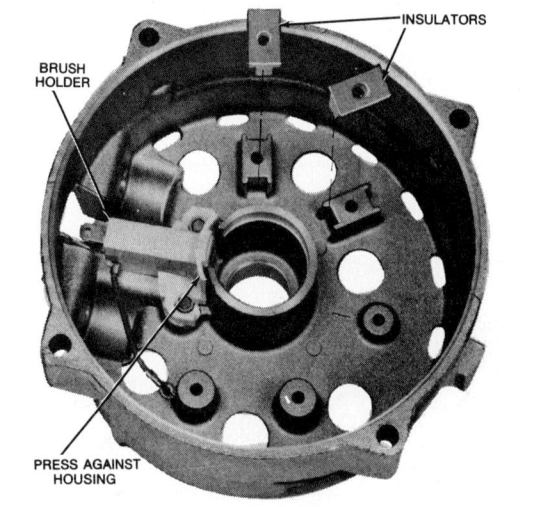

FIG. 2-55 BRUSH HOLDER/RECTIFIER INSULATOR INSTALLATION

1970-72 FORD, MERCURY
Leece-Neville Alternator and Regulator
SYSTEM DESCRIPTION

The general design and operation of the 65-amp Leece-Neville alternator is the same as that of the Autolite-Ford-Motorcraft, but the field brushes are mounted in a sealed holder on the brush housing, and two shielded and sealed ball bearings are used as support for the rotor in each end housing.

The regulator used with the Leece-Neville alternator contains dual control units in a single housing—a double-contact voltage limiter and a field relay. The field relay connects the battery to the alternator field through the upper contacts and is controlled by the ignition switch. The voltage limiter controls the amount of current supplied to the rotating field and is temperature-compensated.

VOLTAGE REGULATOR LIMITER TEST

Voltage limiter calibration must be done with the regulator on the car, and with battery and ignition loads only.

1. Make the test connections as shown in **Fig. 2-56**.

2. Check that all accessories are off.

3. Close the battery adapter switch, start the engine and open the switch.

4. Place a voltage regulator thermometer (or any air-temperature thermometer) on the regulator cover.

5. Run the engine at 2000 rpm for 15 minutes to bring the regulator to proper operating temperature.

6. Ammeter should indicate less than 10 amps with the master control set at ¼-ohm position.

7. Cycle the regulator as follows:
   a) Turn the ignition switch to OFF.
   b) Close the adapter switch.
   c) Start the engine.
   d) Open the adapter switch.

8. Wait one minute, then read the voltmeter scale and thermometer. Compare readings to the following chart.

AMBIENT AIR TEMPERATURE °F	VOLTAGE LIMITER SETTING (VOLTS)
50	14.1-15.1
75	13.9-14.9
100	13.7-14.7
125	13.6-14.6

9. If the voltage setting is not within specifications, remove the regulator and adjust the voltage limiter.

FIELD RELAY TEST

1. Remove the regulator from the car and make the test connections shown in **Fig. 2-57**.

2. Turn the field rheostat clockwise *(slowly)* from a full counterclockwise position.

3. Read the voltmeter when the field relay contact closes—this is the closing relay voltage.

4. If the closing voltage is not to specifications, adjust the relay.

REGULATOR GAP ADJUSTMENT (Fig. 2-58)

TO ADJUST VOLTAGE LIMITER

1. Remove the regulator from the car and remove the regulator cover.

2. Loosen the adjusting-arm lock screw and adjust the contact gap to specifications. Tighten the lock screw.

3. Loosen the voltage-limiter core-gap lock screw and move the contact insulator until the gap between the coil core and the armature is to specifications. Tighten the lock screw.

TO ADJUST FIELD RELAY

1. Loosen the field-relay core-gap lock screw and move the contact insulator until the gap between the coil core and the armature is to specifications. Tighten the lock screw.

2. Bend the field-relay adjusting arm with a small screwdriver blade to set the specified contact gap.

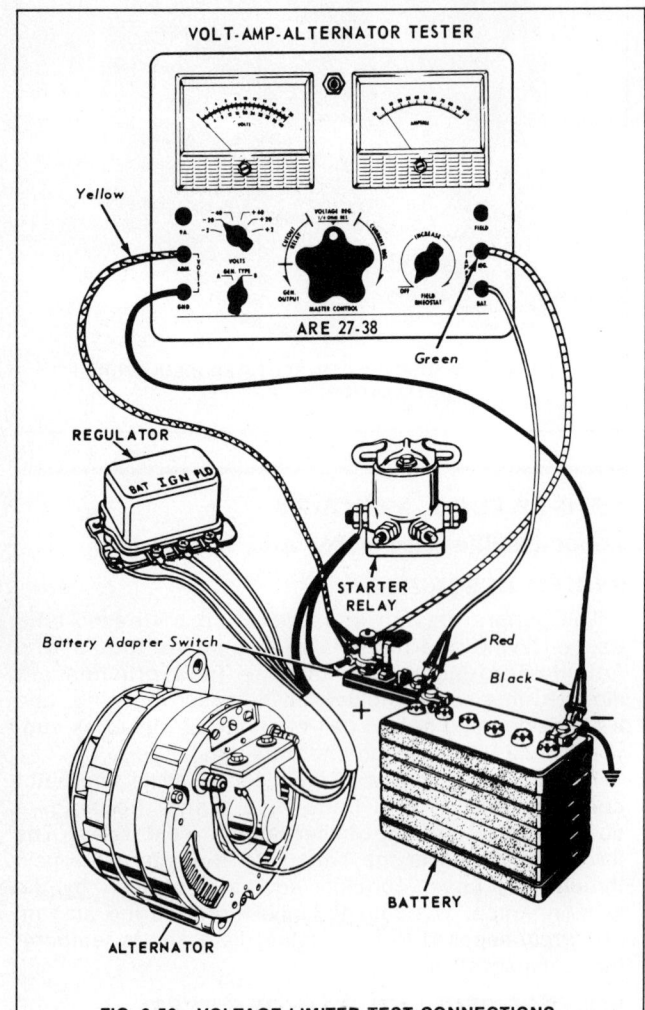

FIG. 2-56 VOLTAGE LIMITER TEST CONNECTIONS

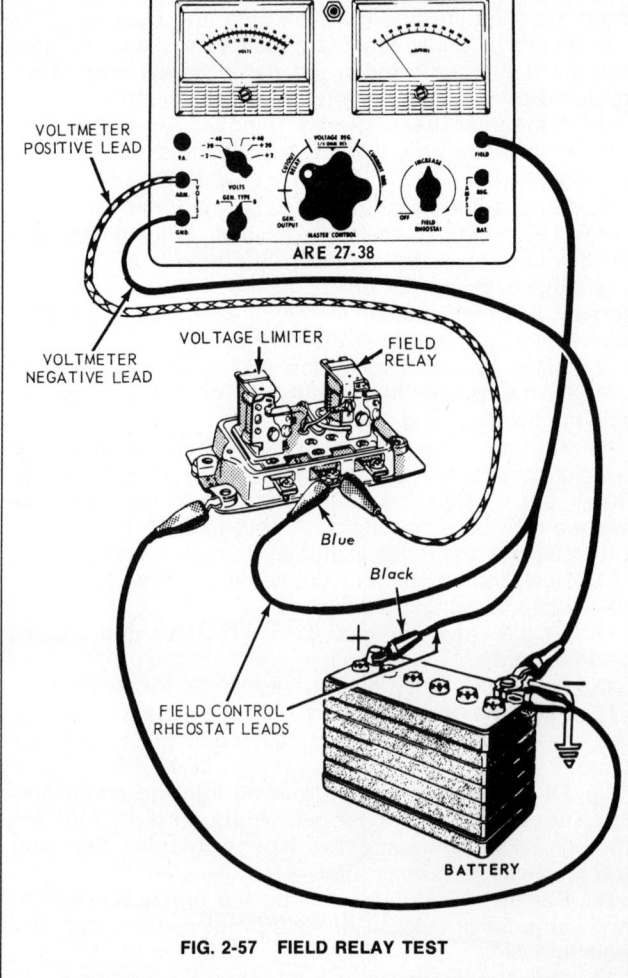

FIG. 2-57 FIELD RELAY TEST

REGULATOR VOLTAGE ADJUSTMENT (Fig. 2-59)

TO ADJUST VOLTAGE LIMITER

1. Cycle the regulator before making adjustments by reducing alternator speed to zero and turning the ignition switch off momentarily.

2. Remove the regulator from the car and remove the regulator cover.

3. Bend the adjusting arm down to increase voltage setting.

4. Bend the adjusting arm up to decrease voltage setting.

TO ADJUST FIELD RELAY

1. Bend the adjusting arm down to increase cut-in voltage.

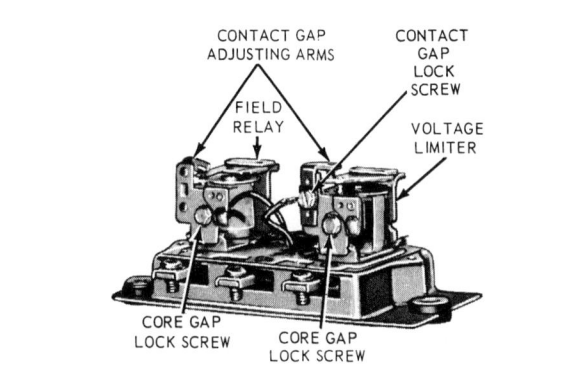

FIG. 2-58 REGULATOR GAP ADJUSTMENTS

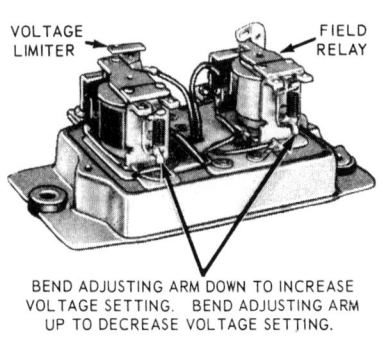

BEND ADJUSTING ARM DOWN TO INCREASE VOLTAGE SETTING. BEND ADJUSTING ARM UP TO DECREASE VOLTAGE SETTING.

FIG. 2-59 REGULATOR ADJUSTMENTS

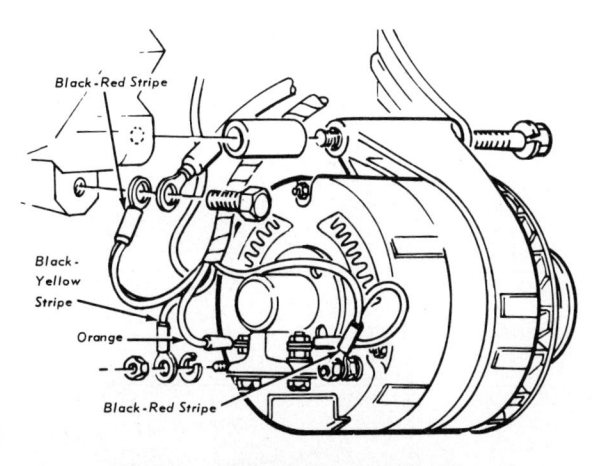

FIG. 2-60 ALTERNATOR MOUNTING AND CONNECTION SEQUENCE

2. Bend the adjusting arm up to decrease cut-in voltage.

ALTERNATOR REMOVAL/INSTALLATION

TO REMOVE

1. Disconnect the battery ground cable.

2. Loosen the alternator mounting bolts, remove the adjustment arm and slip the V-belt off the drive pulley.

3. Disconnect the alternator wires and remove the alternator.

TO INSTALL

1. Fit the alternator to the engine and install the attaching bolt and spacer (if used). Tighten the bolt securely.

2. Replace the adjustment-arm-to-alternator attaching bolt.

3. Fit the V-belt on the alternator pulley, adjust belt tension and tighten the alternator mounting and attachment arm bolts.

4. Replace electrical connections as shown in **Fig. 2-60**, and connect the battery ground cable.

BENCH TESTS

FIELD OPEN OR SHORT CIRCUIT TEST

1. Connect test equipment as shown in **Fig. 2-61**.

2. Spin the alternator pulley by hand and note the ammeter scale. Current draw should be to specifications.

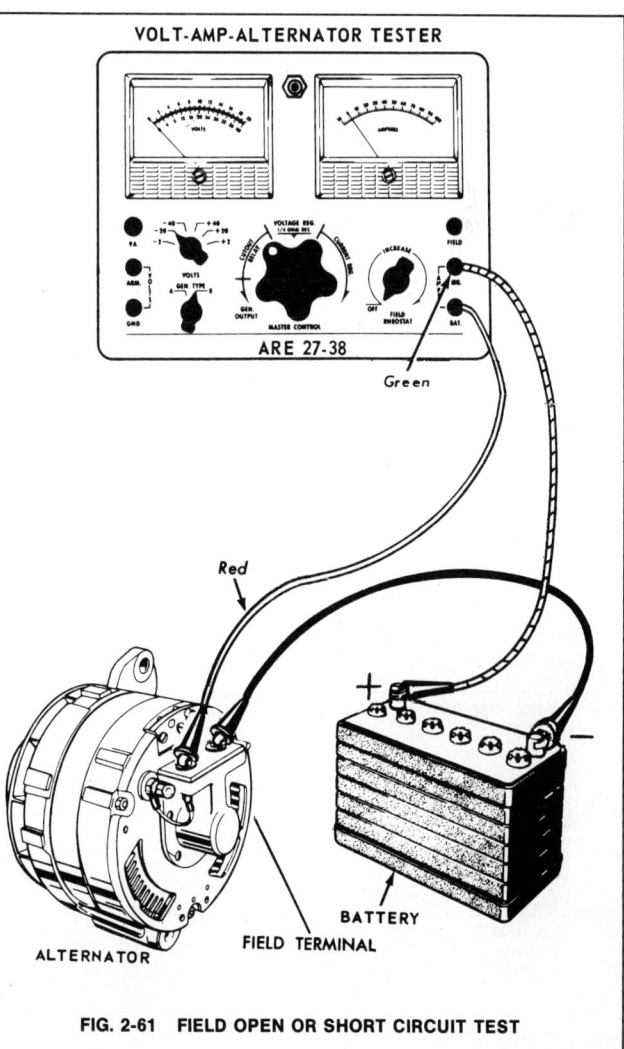

FIG. 2-61 FIELD OPEN OR SHORT CIRCUIT TEST

3. Little or no current flow indicates that field or brushes are open or have a high resistance.

4. A higher than specified current flow indicates shorted or grounded field terminals or brush leads touching.

5. Output at low rpm and none at high rpm indicates that the rotor windings may be shorting to ground. Run the alternator at high speed on a test-stand and repeat Steps 1-4.

DIODE TEST

1. Remove the rectifier assembly according to the

disassembly procedure, which follows these tests.

2. Touch one ohmmeter probe to the diode plate and the other to each of the stator lead terminals in turn.

3. Reverse the probes and repeat Step 2. Test each of the six diodes in turn.

4. All diodes should give a reading of approximately 60 ohms in one direction and no reading in the opposite direction.

OPEN/GROUNDED STATOR COIL TEST

1. Remove the stator from the alternator and con-

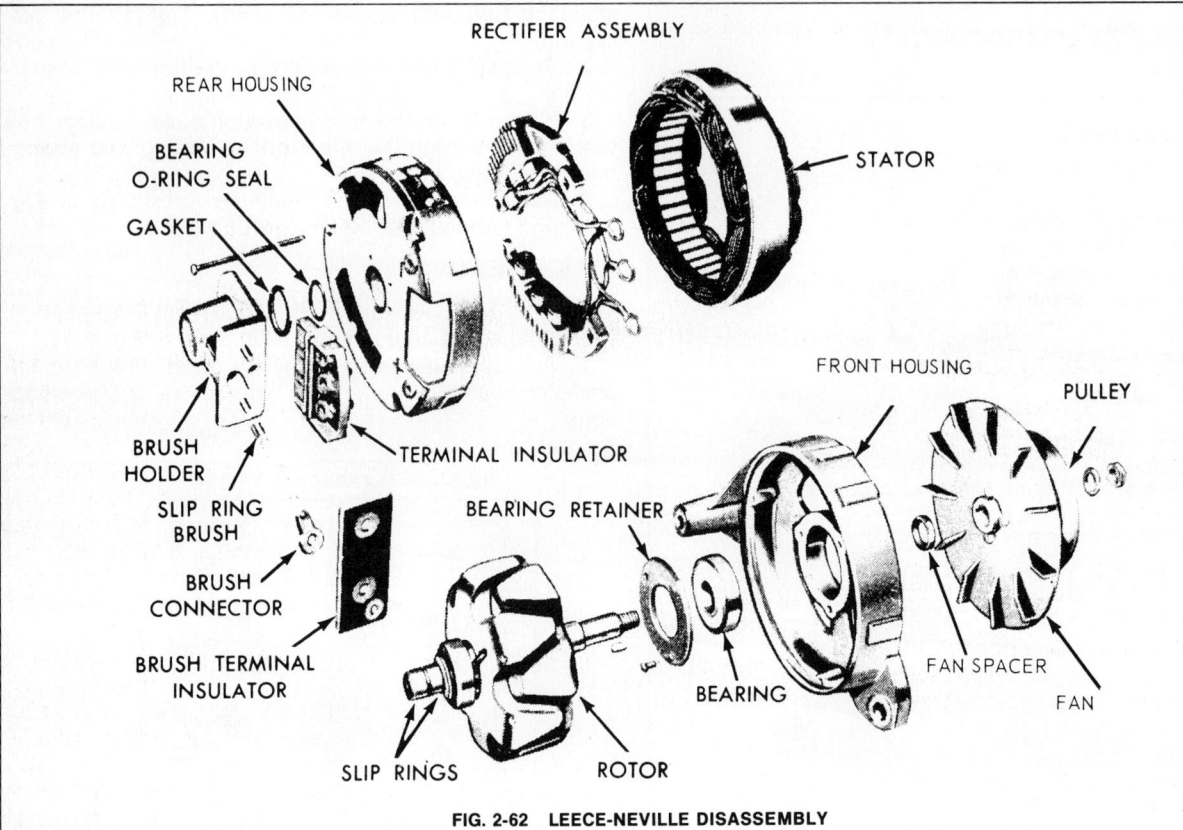

FIG. 2-62 LEECE-NEVILLE DISASSEMBLY

1970-72 LEECE-NEVILLE ALTERNATOR SPECIFICATIONS

SUPPLIER	RATING Amperes @ 15V	RATING Watts @ 15V	FIELD CURRENT (Amps @ 12V)	CUT-IN SPEED (Engine rpm)	RATED OUTPUT SPEED (Engine rpm) Cold	RATED OUTPUT SPEED (Engine rpm) Hot	SLIP-RING TURNING (Ins.) Min. Dia.	SLIP-RING TURNING (Ins.) Max. Runout	BRUSH LENGTH (Ins.) New	BRUSH LENGTH (Ins.) Wear Limit	PULLEY NUT TORQUE (ft-lbs.)	BELT₁ TENSION (lbs.)
Leece-Neville	65	975	2.9	400	1600	2000	Light Cut	0.002	1/2	9/32	40-50	70-110

₁ Used Belt. New Belt 140. A used belt is one that has been in operation more than 10 minutes. If belt tension is out of specification, or belt has been removed, reset to 110 lbs.

FORD MOTOR COMPANY REGULATOR SPECIFICATIONS

REGULATOR	CURRENT RATING	VOLTAGE REGULATION (Volts) Temp °F	VOLTAGE REGULATION (Volts) Setting	VOLTAGE LIMITER Contact Gap (Ins.)	VOLTAGE LIMITER Core Air Gap (Ins.)	FIELD RELAY Contact Gap (Ins.)	FIELD RELAY Core Air Gap (Ins.)	Closing Volts
Leece-Neville Ammeter Circuit	Used with 65-Ampere Leece-Neville Alternator	50	14.1-15.1	0.018-0.020 (with lower contacts closed)	0.042-0.052 (with lower contacts closed)	0.024-0.026	0.011-0.013 With contacts touching	6.2-7.2
		75	13.9-14.9					
		100	13.7-14.7					
		125	13.6-14.6					

nect the ohmmeter probes between each pair of stator leads.

2. Ohmmeter should show equal reading between each pair. If not, the stator is open and must be replaced.

GROUNDED STATOR TEST

1. Connect the ohmmeter probes between one stator lead and the stator core.

2. Make sure that electrical connection is good and note the ohmmeter scale.

3. If the ohmmeter shows *any* reading, the stator winding is grounded, and the stator must be replaced.

ALTERNATOR DISASSEMBLY AND ASSEMBLY (Fig. 2-62)

TO DISASSEMBLE

1. Unscrew and remove the drive pulley nut and washer.

2. Remove the drive pulley with a gear puller, then remove the shaft key and spacer.

3. Disconnect the brushes and terminal insulator, and remove the brush holder from the brush housing.

4. Remove the through-bolts, and separate the rear housing and stator from the rotor and front housing.

5. Remove the three AC terminal nuts and separate the stator from the rear housing.

6. Rotor should be removed from the front housing *only* if the bearing requires replacement. Use a gear puller or arbor press for rotor removal.

7. If the slip ring bearing must be removed, unsolder the field leads from the slip rings. Use a gear puller to remove the slip rings and bearing from the slip ring end of the rotor shaft.

8. Remove the front-housing bearing retainer and press out the old bearing.

9. Remove the rectifier-assembly mounting bolts, terminals and insulators to separate the rectifier assemblies from the housing.

10. Remove the stator terminal insulator.

11. Wipe the rotor, stator and bearing with a clean cloth—*do not* use solvent.

12. Run the bench tests outlined earlier.

TO ASSEMBLE

1. If the slip ring bearing was removed, press a new one in place. Heat the slip rings to prevent the insulation from cracking, and press the slip rings on the shaft, soldering the field wires to the rings.

2. If the front housing bearing was removed, press a new one into the housing and install bearing retainer.

3. Fit the slip ring end of shaft on a flat plate in an arbor press and position the front housing and bearing on the drive end of the shaft, using a piece of pipe or socket to direct pressure *only* on the bearing's inner race.

4. Replace the stator insulator and position the rectifier insulators.

5. Locate the rectifier assemblies in the housing and install the mounting screws and terminals. Rectifier assemblies must be insulated from the end frame.

6. Position the rectifier terminals to the terminal studs and position the wires *beneath* the tabs which extend from each heat sink. This will prevent interference with the rotor's operation.

7. Install the stator and line up the housing through-bolt holes to match those in the stator, then locate the stator terminal over the rectifier terminals and replace the terminal nuts.

8. Fit the rear housing and stator assembly over the rotor. Line up the housing, install and tighten the through-bolts.

9. Replace the brush holder, with 0-ring seal and gasket between the brush holder and frame.

10. Fit the brushes and springs in the brush holder so that the extruded part of the brush connectors rests against the terminal screw shoulders.

11. Use a steel ruler to hold the brush connectors in place until the terminal insulator can be installed, then withdraw the scale.

12. Replace the fan spacer, shaft key, fan, pulley, lockwasher and nut. Torque the nut to 40 ft.-lbs.

13. Spin fan and drive pulley to check for binding.

14. Replace the alternator on the car.

ALL CHRYSLER CORPORATION CARS
Chrysler Isolated-Field Alternator

SYSTEM DESCRIPTION

The Chrysler isolated-field alternator uses an electronic regulator, which replaced the older grounded-brush design beginning with the 1970 model year. Through 1971, the rectifiers (diodes) were mounted directly into the stator rather than a separate subframe and could be replaced individually. From 1972 on, rectifiers have been mounted in negative and positive heat-sink units, and the entire assembly must be replaced if one or more rectifiers are bad. Although this may seem to be wasteful, it greatly simplifies their replacement. In the event of a total electrical system failure, check the single fusible link installed between the starter relay and junction box.

The charging-system wiring circuit was redesigned in 1975 on all models, except Valiant/Dart, by the insertion of an ignition-switch-operated, field-loads relay **(Fig. 2-63)** between the battery and the voltage regulator. In conjunction with this, the voltage regulator temperature-response characteristics were changed to increase charging rate at low temperatures and reduce it at high temperatures. If regulator replacement is required, be certain the replacement unit has the same characteristics as that provided by the factory. Specifications and parts numbers are provided at the end of this section and should be adhered to. Test procedures are the same for all versions of the Chrysler isolated-field alternator, except the 100-amp model.

IN-CAR TEST PROCEDURES
CHARGING CIRCUIT RESISTANCE TEST

Under some conditions, the alternator will work properly but the battery's charging rate remains insufficient. This is due to excessive voltage loss in the circuit, and the following test will determine the amount of voltage drop between the alternator-output terminal wire and the battery. Chrysler test procedure calls for a DC ammeter, voltmeter and carbon pile rheostat, and circuit diagrams are included for that equipment. An alternator/generator/regulator tester can also be used, and should be connected according to the test equipment manufacturer's instructions.

To perform the test:

1. Disconnect the battery ground cable.

2. Disconnect the lead marked BAT at the alternator output terminal.

3. Connect a DC ammeter (0 to 100-amp scale) in series between the disconnected BAT lead wire and the alternator battery terminal **(Figs. 2-64, 2-65, 2-65A)**.

4. Connect the voltmeter positive lead to the disconnected BAT lead wire and the negative voltmeter lead to the battery positive terminal.

5. Disconnect the regulator (green) field lead wire from the alternator and connect a jumper lead from ground to the alternator field terminal.

6. Hook up a tachometer and reconnect the battery ground cable.

7. With its control in the OFF or OPEN position, connect a variable carbon-pile rheostat to the battery terminals.

8. Start the engine and reduce rpm to idle speed.

9. Adjust carbon pile and engine rpm to get and maintain 20 amps in the circuit. Voltmeter scale should not exceed 0.7-volt.

10. If the voltmeter reading exceeds 0.7-volt, you should inspect, clean and tighten each circuit connection. Repeat the test at each connection until you locate the source of excessive resistance.

CURRENT OUTPUT TEST

Maximum output from the alternator is necessary to run this test, which will determine if the alternator is capable of delivering its rated current output.

1. Disconnect the battery ground cable.

2. Disconnect the lead marked BAT at the alternator output terminal.

3. Connect a DC ammeter (0 to 100-amp scale) in series between the disconnected BAT lead wire and the alternator battery terminal **(Figs. 2-66, 2-67, 2-67A)**.

4. Connect the voltmeter positive lead to the battery terminal of the alternator.

5. Connect the voltmeter negative lead to ground.

6. Disconnect the green field wire to the voltage regulator at the alternator.

7. Connect a jumper lead from the alternator field terminal to ground.

8. Connect a tachometer and reconnect the battery ground cable.

9. With its control in the OFF or OPEN position, connect a variable carbon-pile rheostat to the battery terminals.

10. Start the engine and reduce rpm to idle speed.

11. Adjust carbon pile and engine rpm to 1250 rpm (900 rpm for 100-amp unit) and voltage reading of 15 volts (13 volts for 100-amp unit).

12. Ammeter reading should be within that specified

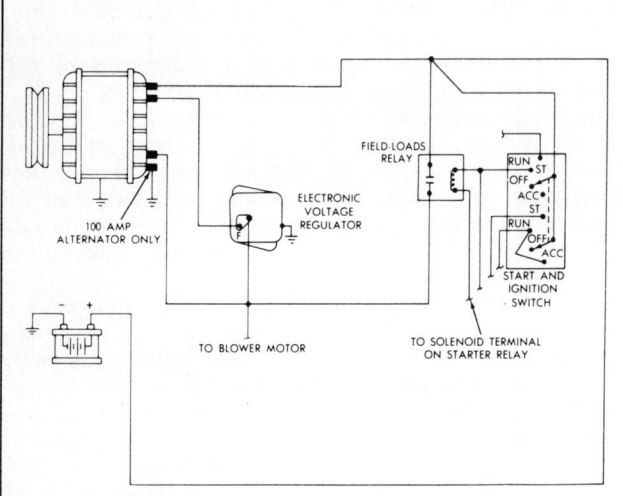

FIG. 2-63 FIELD-LOADS RELAY SYSTEM

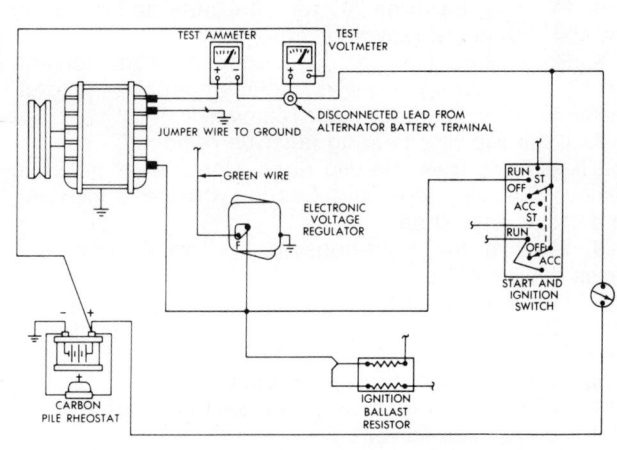

FIG. 2-64 CHARGING CIRCUIT RESISTANCE HOOKUP, ALL 1970-74 CARS AND 1975-76 VALIANT/DART

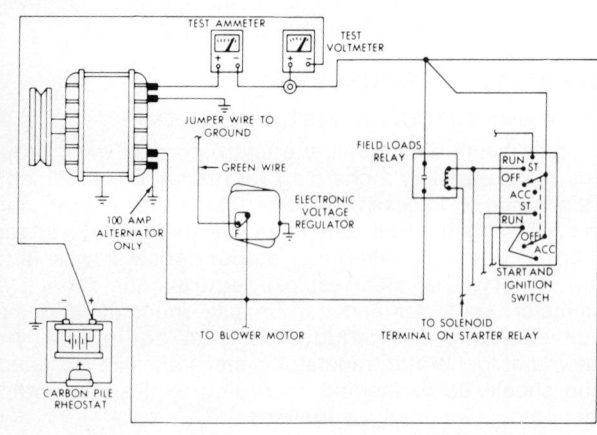

FIG. 2-65 CHARGING CIRCUIT RESISTANCE HOOKUP, ALL 1975-76 CARS (EXCEPT VALIANT/DART)

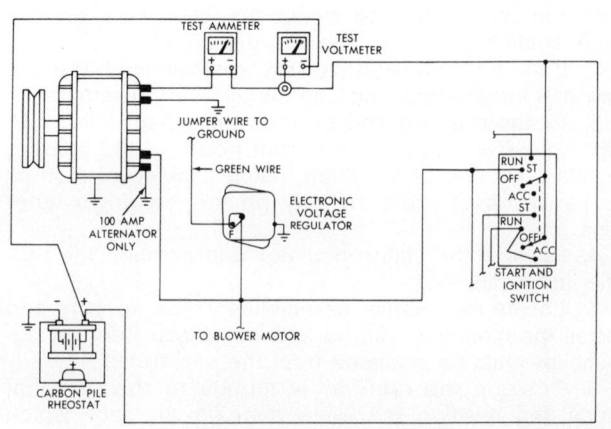

FIG. 2-65A CHARGING CIRCUIT RESISTANCE HOOKUP, ALL 1977-79 MODELS

for the size alternator under test. If the ammeter reading is less than that specified, remove the alternator from the car for further testing. On 1975-76 circuits with the field-load relay installed, check for its proper operation before removing the alternator.

VOLTAGE REGULATOR TEST

1. Clean the battery terminals and check the specific gravity. If specific gravity is less than 1.200, charge or substitute another battery for the test, removing the undercharged battery from the circuit.

2. On all 1970-74 Chrysler Corporation cars and 1975-76 Valiant/Dart circuits, connect the voltmeter positive lead to the ballast resistor terminal with a blue or blue/black wire connected, but do not remove the connector from the ballast resistor terminal **(Fig. 2-68).**

3. On 1975-78 circuits (except Valiant/Dart), connect the voltmeter positive lead to the positive battery terminal **(Fig. 2-69 and 2-69A).**

4. Connect the voltmeter negative lead to a ground on the car body.

5. Start the engine and advance speed to 1250 rpm (all lights and accessories off). Read the voltmeter scale. If the regulator is working properly, the reading should agree with the following chart:

AMBIENT TEMPERATURE BESIDE VOLTAGE REGULATOR	1970-74 VOLTAGE	1975-79 VOLTAGE
-20° F	14.3-15.3	14.9-15.9
80° F	13.8-14.4	13.9-14.6
140° F	13.3-14.0	13.3-13.9
Above 140° F	Less Than 13.8	Less than 13.6

Ammeter will show an immediate charge and then gradually return to its normal position.

6. If voltage fluctuates or is below that specified above:

a) Check the regulator ground for an open circuit.

b) Disconnect the voltage regulator connector and check the terminals. Repeated plugging/ unplugging may cause them to spread and cause an open circuit or intermittent condition.

c) With the ignition switch off, remove the wiring harness from the regulator. Turn the ignition switch on and check for battery voltage at the terminals with blue and green leads.

d) If Steps a, b and c test satisfactory, replace the voltage regulator and retest. On all 1975-78 circuits (except Valiant/Dart), check the field-loads relay first. If it tests good, replace the regulator and retest.

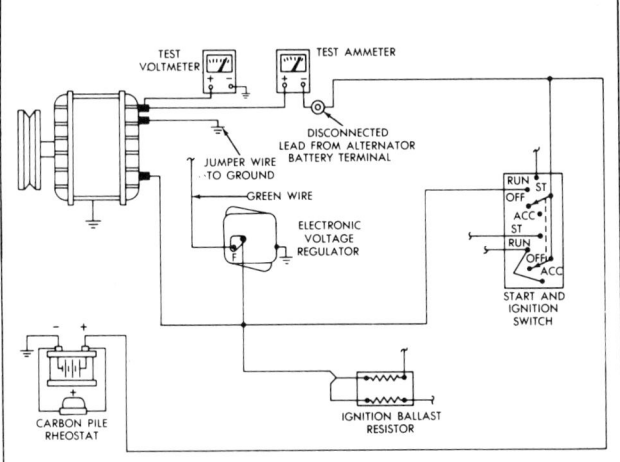

FIG. 2-66 CURRENT OUTPUT HOOKUP, ALL 1970-74 CARS AND 1975-76 VALIANT/DART

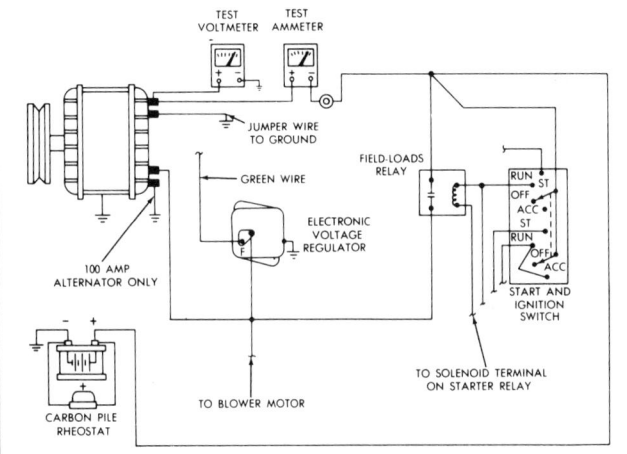

FIG. 2-67 CURRENT OUTPUT HOOKUP, ALL 1975-76 CARS (EXCEPT VALIANT/DART)

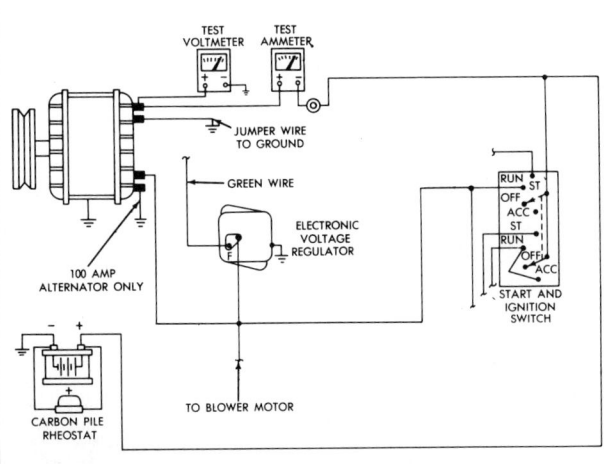

FIG. 2-67A CURRENT OUTPUT HOOKUP, ALL 1977-79 MODELS

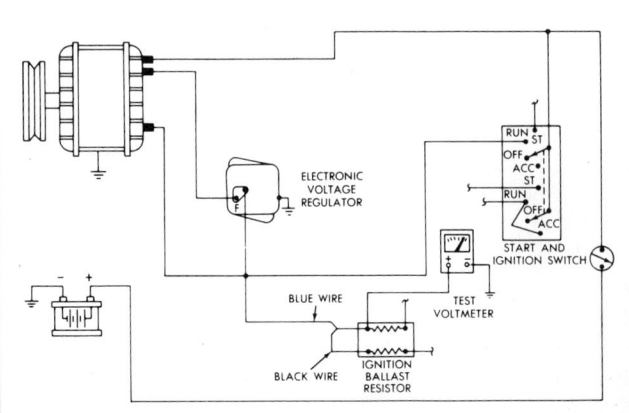

FIG. 2-68 VOLTAGE REGULATOR TEST, ALL 1970-74 CARS AND 1975-76 VALIANT/DART

7. If voltage reads above that specified:

a) Turn the ignition switch off and check the voltage regulator connector for spread terminals.

b) Turn the ignition switch on and check for battery voltage at the wiring harness terminal. Both leads (blue and green) should read battery voltage.

c) If Steps a and b test satisfactory, replace the voltage regulator and retest. On all 1975-78 circuits (except Valiant/Dart), check the field-loads relay first. If it tests good, replace the regulator and retest.

FIELD-LOADS RELAY TEST

1. Disconnect the voltage-regulator wiring-harness connector.

2. Connect a voltmeter negative lead to ground on the car and turn the ignition switch on, but *do not* start the engine.

3. Touch the positive voltmeter lead to terminals of the wiring harness connector.

4. If the voltage reading equals battery voltage, the field-loads relay is working properly. If the reading does not equal battery voltage, check all wiring and connectors in the circuit for opens, shorts or high resistance. If these test satisfactory, replace the field-loads relay.

ALTERNATOR REMOVAL/INSTALLATION
TO REMOVE

1. Disconnect the battery ground cable from the battery terminal.

2. Disconnect the alternator output BAT, FLD and GRD leads.

3. Remove the alternator mounting bolts and remove the alternator unit from the mounting bracket. On some installations, it may be necessary to loosen or remove the smog pump, power steering pump or air conditioning compressor to provide sufficient access for alternator removal.

TO INSTALL

1. Replace the alternator on the mounting bracket and install the mounting bolts loosely.

2. Fit the drive belt over the alternator pulley and adjust tension, then tighten alternator mounting bolts.

3. Reconnect the alternator output BAT, FLD and GRD leads.

4. Reconnect the battery ground cable.

BENCH TEST PROCEDURE
ROTOR FIELD COIL CURRENT DRAW

1. Connect a jumper lead between one alternator

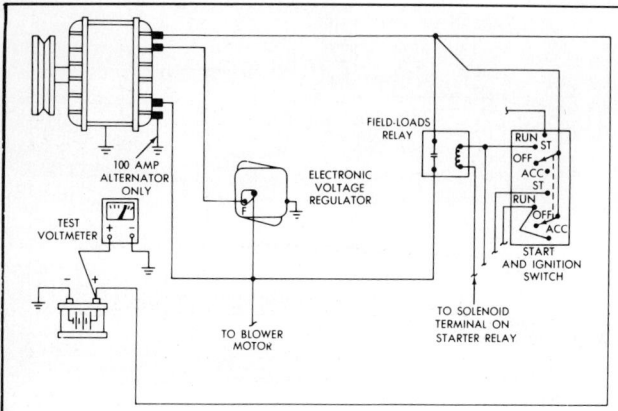

FIG. 2-69   VOLTAGE REGULATOR TEST, ALL 1975-76 CARS (EXCEPT VALIANT/DART)

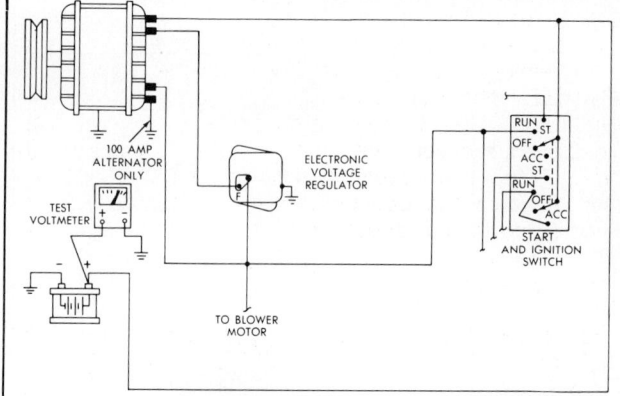

FIG. 2-69A   VOLTAGE REGULATOR TEST, ALL 1977-79 MODELS

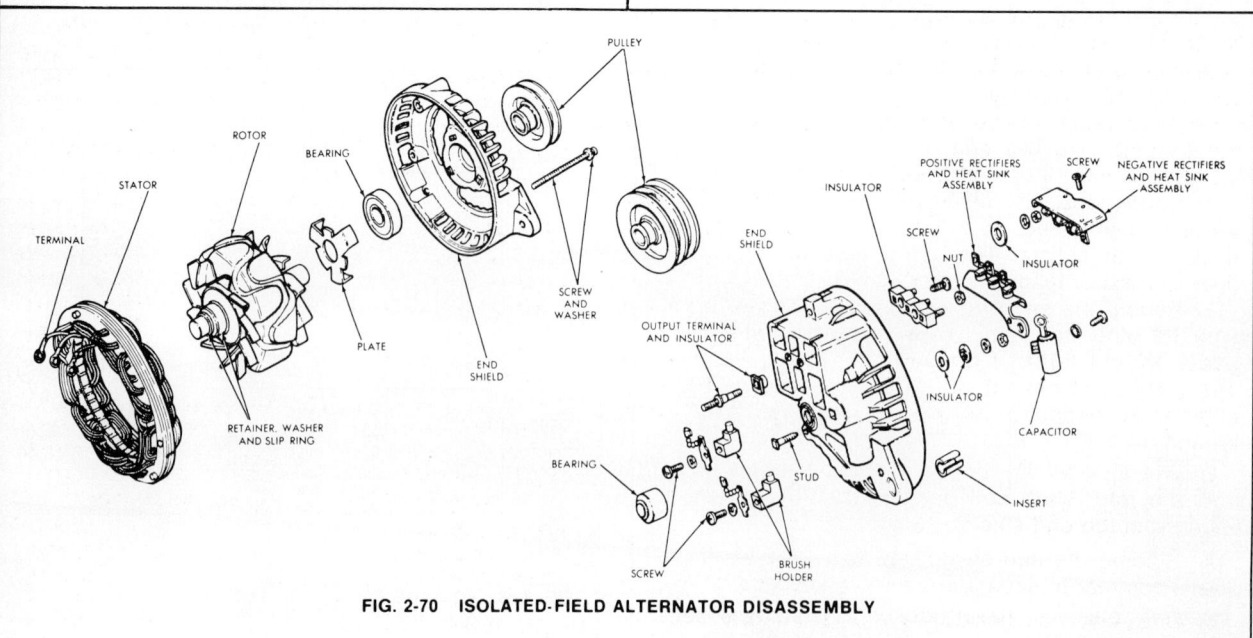

FIG. 2-70   ISOLATED-FIELD ALTERNATOR DISASSEMBLY

field terminal and the positive terminal of a fully charged battery.

2. Connect the positive ammeter lead to the other alternator field terminal and negative battery terminal.

3. Rotate the alternator rotor by hand slowly and read the ammeter scale.

4. Check the reading against specifications. A low reading indicates high resistance in the field coil circuit. A high reading indicates a grounded rotor or shorted rotor coil. No reading indicates defective brushes or an open rotor.

ALTERNATOR DISASSEMBLY/TEST PROCEDURE
(Fig. 2-70)

1. Brush assemblies should be removed before separating the end shields. The field brushes are located in plastic units which hold them against the rotor slip rings. Because the stator is of laminated construction, do not burr stator or end shields during disassembly.

2. Removing the attaching screw and insulator, lift the brush assembly from the end shield.

3. Chalk the end frames for easy alignment during reassembly and remove the through-bolts.

4. Pry between the stator and drive end shield with a screwdriver blade, carefully separating the drive end from the rotor and rectifier end shield.

5. Unscrew the three terminal-block stud nuts holding the stator windings and rectifier straps.

6. Remove the stator winding terminals and pry the stator assembly from the end shield carefully.

7. Use a 12-volt test lamp to test the rectifiers. Touch the rectifier heat sink with one probe and the strap on top of the rectifier with the other.

8. Reverse the position of the probes. If the test lamp lights in one direction only, the rectifier is good. When the lamp lights in both directions, the rectifier is shorted; if it does not light in either direction, the rectifier is open.

9. Repeat Steps 7 and 8 for each of the remaining rectifiers in both negative and positive assemblies. The lamp should light in the same direction for all rectifiers in one assembly. If not, change the rectifier/heat-sink assembly as follows.

10. Positive rectifiers—Remove the two nuts and washers holding the assembly to the insulated end shield terminal. Remove the screw which grounds the capacitor to the case and lift out the capacitor, rectifier and heat sink assembly.

Negative rectifiers—Loosen the four screws holding the assembly to the end shield. Remove the outer screws and lift the assembly out of the end shield.

11. Touch one test probe to any pin on the stator frame and the other to each of the stator lead terminals, one at a time. Test lamp should not light; if it does, the stator lead is grounded.

12. Touch one test probe on one stator lead terminal and the other to each of the remaining stator leads. Lamp should light. If it does not, stator winding is open. This test cannot be performed on the 100-amp alternator, because its stator windings are Delta Wound.

13. Use a puller to remove the interference fit pulley from the rotor shaft and pry the drive-end bearing retainer from the end shield.

14. Holding the end shield, tap the rotor shaft with a plastic hammer to separate the rotor and end shield.

15. Drive-end ball bearing is also an interference fit and must be removed with a puller.

1970-71 CHRYSLER ALTERNATOR SPECIFICATIONS

Rotation	Clockwise at Drive End
Voltage	12 Volt System
Current Output	Design Controlled
Voltage Output	Limited by Voltage Regulator
Brushes (Field)	2
Condenser Capacity	0.50 Microfarad ± 20%

Field Current Draw

Rotating Rotor by Hand @ 12 Volts	2.38 to 2.75 Maximum Amp.

Current Output—

Std. with 198 & 225 Cu.-In. Eng.	26 ± 3 Amp.*
Std. (All Other Models)	34.5 ± 3 Amp.*
Special Equipment,	
Heavy Duty and/or Air Conditioning	44.5 ± 3 Amp.*
Special Equipment (Fleets)	51 ± 3 Amp.*

*Plus or minus three ampere tolerance is provided to allow for temperature variation. Current output is measured at 1250 engine rpm and 15 volts at the alternator. If measured at the battery, current output will be approximately 5 amperes lower than above values. Voltage is controlled by variable load (carbon pile) across the battery.

1972-73 CHRYSLER ALTERNATOR SPECIFICATIONS

Rotation	Clockwise at Drive End
Voltage	12 Volt System
Current Output	Design Controlled
Voltage Output	Limited by Voltage Regulator
Brushes (Field)	2
Condenser Capacity	0.50 Microfarad plus or minus 20%

Field Current Draw

Rotating by Hand	2.5 to 3.1 Amp.

Current Rating	Current Output
34 Amp.—Std.	39 ± 3 Amp.
41 Amp.—Std.	41 ± 3 Amp.
50 Amp.—Spec. Equip.	50 ± 3 Amp.
60 Amp.—Spec. Equip.	60 ± 3 Amp.

* Plus or minus three ampere tolerance is provided to allow for temperature variation. Current output is measured at 1250 engine rpm and 15 volts at the alternator. If measured at the battery, current output will be approximately 5 amperes lower than above value. Voltage is controlled by variable load (carbon pile) across the battery.

1974-79 CHRYSLER ALTERNATOR SPECIFICATIONS

1974-76	1977-79	
Yellow Tag		34 Amp.
Red Tag	Bronze/Violet	41 Amp.
Green Tag	Natural	50 Amp.
Blue Tag	Yellow	60 Amp.
Natural Tag		60 Amp.
Black Tag	Brown	65 Amp.
Yellow Tag	Yellow	100 Amp.

Rotation	Clockwise at Drive End
Voltage	12 Volt System
Current Output	Design Controlled
Voltage Output	Limited by Voltage Regulator
Brushes (Field)	2
Condenser Capacity	0.50 Microfarad plus or minus 20%
Field Current Draw Rotating by Hand	2.5 to 3.7 Amperes @ 12V[2]
	except 100 Amp. 4.75 to 6.0 @ 12V

Current Rating	Current Output
34 Amp.	36 Amp. Minimum
41 Amp.	40 Amp. Minimum
50 Amp.	47 Amp. Minimum
60 Amp.	57 Amp. Minimum
65 Amp.	62 Amp. Minimum
100 Amp.	84 Amp. Minimum[3]

Current output is measured at 1250 engine rpm and 15 volts at the alternator, 900 rpm and 13 volts for 100 amp. alternator. If measured at the battery, current output will be approximately 5 amp. lower than above. Voltage is controlled by variable load (carbon pile) across the battery.

CHRYSLER ELECTRONIC VOLTAGE REGULATOR

1970-74 Part Number	3438150[1]
1975-77 Part Number	3755960
	3755850

[1] Some early 1975 production Valiant/Dart.
[2] 1977 and later; 4.5 to 6.5 amps @ 12V.
[3] 1977 and later; 72 amps minimum.

16. Unless rectifier end-shield bearing requires replacement, do not remove. If removal is necessary, it should be pressed out carefully.

17. Test the rotor assembly as follows:
   a) For grounded field coil—Connect the ohmmeter from each slip ring to the rotor shaft. A reading of zero or higher indicates a ground.
   b) For an open field coil—Connect the ohmmeter to the slip rings. A reading higher than 6 ohms indicates high resistance (1.7 to 2.1 ohms with 100-amp alternator).
   c) For a shorted field coil—Connect the ohmmeter to the two slip rings. A reading below 3 ohms indicates the field coil is shorted. If testing the 100-amp alternator, the reading should be 1.7 ohms.

ALTERNATOR ASSEMBLY PROCEDURE
(Fig. 2-70)

1. Fit the grease retainer on the rotor shaft and press in place.

2. If bearings are being replaced, press them into place. New bearings are prelubricated. Press the bearing end shield in place.

3. Install the pulley on the rotor shaft until pulley touches the inner race of the drive end bearing.

4. Replace the negative rectifier assembly in the end shield. Fit the straps over the terminal studs and tighten the attaching screws securely.

5. Install the positive rectifier assembly in the end shield. Fit the straps over the terminal studs and replace the capacitor terminal on the capacitor end stud.

6. Replace the capacitor shoulder insulator and ground bracket to the end shield. Replace and tighten the positive rectifier lockwashers and nuts.

7. Place the stator over the rectifier end shield and fit the winding terminal on the terminal block, pressing the stator pins into the end shield.

8. Replace and tighten the winding terminal nuts, routing the lead to prevent contact with the rotor or negative heat sink.

9. Place the rotor and drive end-shield assembly over the stator and rectifier end shield. Use the chalk mark made during disassembly for alignment.

10. Press both end shields in toward the stator and replace the through-bolts. Torque them evenly to 20-30 in.-lbs. for 1970-74 alternators; 40-60 in.-lbs. for 1975-76 units.

11. Replace the field brushes in their holders and position them correctly in the rectifier end shield.

12. Install the insulating washer on each field brush terminal, then replace and tighten the lockwashers and attaching screws.

13. Rotate the pulley by hand slowly to make sure the rotor blades do not hit the stator winding leads.

14. Replace the alternator on car and test current output.

1979 American Motors V-8 Engines
Bosch Type K1 Alternator
SYSTEM DESCRIPTION

The Bosch charging system replaced the Autolite-Ford system on all 1979 AMC V-8 engines. Two alternator ratings are offered: 45 & 55 ampere. A solid-state

voltage regulator contains an integral brush holder/brush assembly, and is attached to the rear of the alternator. This arrangement permits brush replacement without alternator disassembly. Current from the alternator output terminal is routed to the battery by way of the starter solenoid.

IN-CAR TEST PROCEDURES

The indicator lamp on the instrument panel remains lighted only when a no-charge condition exists. To determine whether the alternator or regulator is at fault, check the charging system operation as follows. A voltmeter and tachometer are required.

1. Check alternator belt tension and adjust to 90-115 lbs. if necessary.

2. Connect the voltmeter negative lead to the negative battery terminal and the positive voltmeter lead to the positive battery terminal. Start the engine and note the voltmeter reading.

3. Connect a tachometer and run the engine at fast idle.

4. Insert a screwdriver blade between the alternator housing and the metal sleeve of the voltage regulator. Note the voltmeter reading and compare with that obtained in Step 2.

5. If the voltage reading in Step 4 exceeds that of Step 2, replace the voltage regulator. If the reading in Step 4 is the same or lower than that of Step 2, remove and overhaul the alternator.

ALTERNATOR LEAKAGE

A bulb socket (No. 158 bulb) with jumper leads attached is necessary to determine if the alternator is discharging the battery due to excess leakage.

1. Disconnect the negative battery cable at the battery and the positive battery cable at the starter solenoid junction.

2. Connect the bulb in series between the battery lead and the alternator output terminal. If the bulb lights (even dimly), replace the diode plate assembly.

3. If the bulb does not light, disconnect the "R" terminal connector at the rear of the alternator and connect the bulb in series between the alternator "R" terminal and the positive battery post. If the bulb lights (even dimly), test the diode plate assembly. Replace the diode plate if defective; if it is not, replace the voltage regulator.

ALTERNATOR REMOVAL/INSTALLATION
TO REMOVE

1. Disconnect the battery ground cable.

2. Raise the vehicle front and support with safety stands.

3. Unhook the battery lead and 2-terminal plug at the rear of the alternator.

4. Remove the mounting/adjusting bolts with washers.

5. Slip the alternator drivebelt from its pulley and remove.

6. Lift the alternator from the mounting bracket. Removal on Pacers with air conditioning and sway bar is somewhat complicated as the unit must be angled properly to fit between the sway bar and steering gear.

TO INSTALL

1. Replace the alternator on the mounting bracket and install the bolts and washers finger-tight. Make the electrical connections at this time on Pacers.

2. Install the drivebelt and tighten to proper tension.

3. Torque the bolt in the sliding slot bracket to 20 ft.-lbs. and all others to 30 ft.-lbs.

4. Make the electrical connections to the alternator.

5. Remove the safety stands, lower the vehicle and reconnect the battery ground cable.

BENCH TESTS

ROTOR SHORT-TO-GROUND TEST

1. Separate the rotor/front housing from the stator/rear housing.

2. Set the ohmmeter to its 1000 scale and calibrate. A 110-volt test lamp can also be used for this test.

3. Touch one test lead to the rotor shaft and the other to each slip ring, as shown in **Fig. 2-70A.** If the ohmmeter needle moves or the test lamp lights, a short-to-ground exists.

ROTOR OPEN TEST

1. Separate the rotor/front housing from the stator/rear housing.

2. Set the ohmmeter to its "1" scale and calibrate. A 110-volt test lamp can also be used for this test.

3. Touch one test lead to each slip ring **(Fig. 2-70B).** The ohmmeter should read between 3.0 and 3.7 ohms or the test lamp should light. If the ohmmeter reading is infinite or the test lamp does not light, the rotor winding is open.

ROTOR INTERNAL SHORT TEST

1. Separate the rotor/front housing from the stator/rear housing.

2. Connect a 12-volt battery and an ammeter in series with the slip rings **(Fig. 2-70C).** Field current at 80° F temperature should be between 3.5 and 5.0 amps. A reading greater than 5.0 amps indicates shorted windings.

STATOR SHORT-TO-GROUND TEST

1. Separate the rotor/front housing from the stator/rear housing.

2. Separate the stator leads from the rectifier terminals.

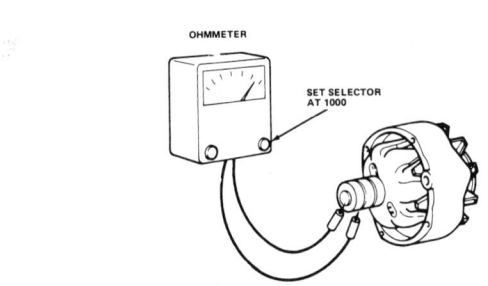

FIG. 2-70A   ROTOR SHORT-TO-GROUND TEST

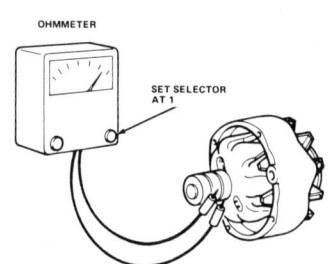

FIG. 2-70B   ROTOR OPEN TEST

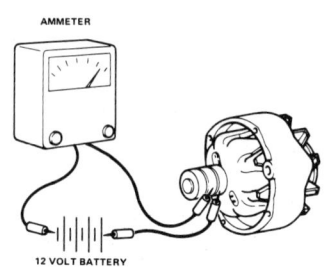

FIG. 2-70C   ROTOR INTERNAL SHORT TEST

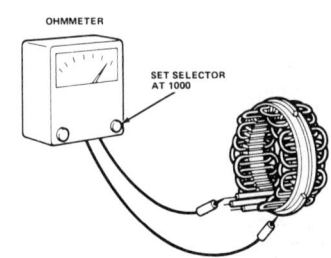

FIG. 2-70D   STATOR SHORT-TO-GROUND TEST

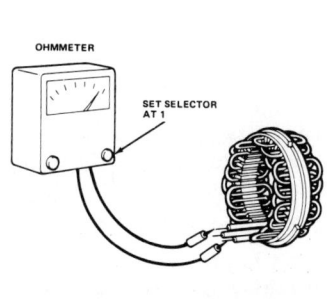

FIG. 2-70E   STATOR CONTINUITY TEST

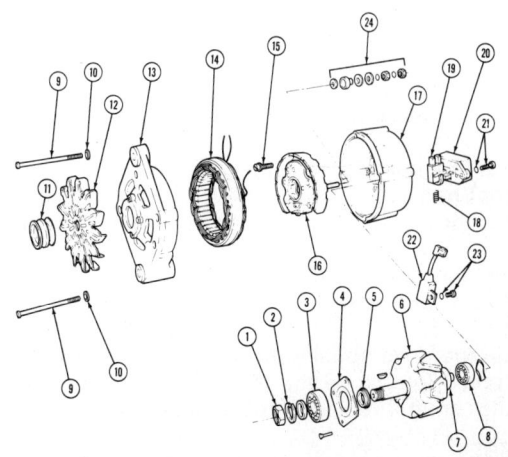

FIG. 2-70F   EXPLODED VIEW OF BOSCH K1 ALTERNATOR

3. Set the ohmmeter to its 1000 scale and calibrate. A 110-volt test lamp can also be used.

4. Touch one test lead to the stator core (bare metal surface) and the other test lead to the end of one stator lead (**Fig. 2-70D**). Since all three stator leads are soldered together, only one lead need be tested. If the ohmmeter reads other than infinity or the test lamp lights, replace the stator.

STATOR CONTINUITY TEST

1. Separate the rotor/front housing from the stator/rear housing.

2. Set the ohmmeter to its 1 scale and calibrate.

3. Touch the ohmmeter leads to two stator leads and note the reading (**Fig. 2-70E**). Test each pair of stator leads in combination—each pair should give the same reading. If the ohmmeter needle does not move, an open winding is indicated. A reading in excess of 1 ohm indicates a poor solder joint. Check and resolder the neutral junction splice, then retest.

DIODE TEST

1. Unsolder the stator windings at their junctions.

2. Set the ohmmeter to its 1 scale and calibrate.

3. Touch ohmmeter test leads to the heat sink and diode junctions individually. Each terminal combination should give one high and one low reading. If any one reading does not agree with the others, replace the diode plate assembly.

ALTERNATOR DISASSEMBLY AND ASSEMBLY

TO DISASSEMBLE

(Fig. 2-70F)

1. Scribe a chalk mark across the front and rear housing as an alignment guide for reassembly.

2. Remove the screws holding the regulator/brush assembly to the alternator, then tilt and lift the assembly from the rear housing.

3. Disconnect the condenser lead and remove the condenser assembly.

4. Remove the housing through-bolts and separate the halves.

5. Remove the wave washer from the rear housing and place a piece of masking tape over the rear housing bearing and slip ring end of the rotor shaft. The tape will prevent dirt and other contaminants from entering.

6. Remove the nuts and washers from the battery terminal stud. For correct reassembly sequence, refer to **Fig. 2-70F** or label each with masking tape and number.

7. Place the rotor in a soft-jaw vise and tighten only enough to allow loosening of the shaft nut. Excessive tightening may distort the rotor.

8. Loosen and remove shaft nut, lockwasher, pulley, key and fan.

9. Remove the bearing retainer and rotor assembly from the front housing.

10. Remove the stator/diode assembly from the rear housing.

11. Unsolder the stator leads from the diode plate assembly. Avoid bending the phase lead-out wires excessively.

12. Separate the drive housing from the rotor shaft.

13. Use a press to remove the front and rear bearings from the rotor shaft if replacement is necessary.

TO ASSEMBLE

(Fig. 2-70F)

1. Use bearing grease (Bosch lubricant No. Ftlv34 or

equivalent) to fill retaining plate-bearing cavity one-quarter full (an excessive amount can cause overheating of the bearing).

2. Install the front and rear bearings on the rotor shaft, if removed.

3. Fit the rotor into the front housing.

4. Resolder the stator leads to the diode plate assembly and install the stator to the rear housing.

5. Remove the protective masking tape from the rotor shaft and rear bearing, then assemble the halves after aligning the scribe marks.

6. Replace and tighten the through-bolts.

7. Install the shaft key, fan, pulley and washer on the rotor shaft, then replace the drive pulley nut.

8. Place the rotor in a soft-jaw vise and tighten the vise sufficiently to permit tightening of the pulley nut. Excessive tightening can distort the shaft.

9. Replace the washer and nuts on the battery terminal stud in their correct order. Refer to **Fig. 2-70F** if necessary.

10. Replace the condenser at the rear of the housing and plug the condenser lead wire in place.

11. Replace the voltage regulator/brush assembly to the rear of the housing.

Output Voltage Specifications

Ambient Temperature in Degrees Fahrenheit	Acceptable Voltage Range
0-50	14.5-15.1
50-100	14.1-14.7
100-150	13.4-14.4
150-200	13.2-14.0

1970-75 AMERICAN MOTORS ENGINES
Motorola Alternator

SYSTEM DESCRIPTION

The Motorola alternator passes all DC current through an isolation diode(s) mounted outside the unit in an aluminum heat sink. Because of its design, a small amount of current is required to excite or prime the field before current is generated. This "priming" current is made available by an 82-ohm resistor located inside the voltage regulator, and is one of the initial checkpoints to examine before carrying out extensive testing and troubleshooting procedures.

The alternator voltage regulator is a sealed electronic type and non-adjustable. If it malfunctions, the unit must be replaced. Some Motorola alternators used with engines having 4-bbl. carburetors are fitted with an additional terminal on the rear housing which delivers approximately 7 volts of current to the carburetor choke-cover heating element. This terminal is located in the negative diode assembly.

The nameplate containing voltage, type of ground, serial number, amperage rating and model number identification is riveted to the rear housing and should be consulted before buying replacement components.

CHARGING SYSTEM FUSIBLE LINKS

System protection is provided by a fusible link located near the horn-relay battery terminal. All electrical system functions will stop if this link fails. On 1975 and later charging systems, two fusible links are used for system protection. One is located between the starter solenoid and ignition switch, and the other between the voltage regulator and ignition switch (**Fig. 2-71**).

IN-CAR TEST PROCEDURES

ALTERNATOR OUTPUT TEST (REGULATOR IN CIRCUIT)

1. Connect a voltmeter to the battery and start the engine.

2. Turn the headlamps on low beam and run the engine at 1000 rpm for approximately 2 minutes.

3. Read the voltmeter scale. Voltage should remain above 13 volts. If not, conduct an amperage test.

AMPERAGE (FIELD DRAW) TEST

1. Disconnect the voltage regulator from the charging circuit.

2. Connect an ammeter between the wire leading to the alternator insulated-brush terminal and the positive battery terminal.

3. Turn the alternator rotor slowly and read the ammeter scale. Reading should range between 1½ and 3 amperes.

4. If amperage is excessive, remove the brush assembly and test.

5. If the brush assembly tests out good and amperage remains excessive, the alternator rotor field winding should be tested.

ALTERNATOR OUTPUT TEST (REGULATOR BYPASSED)

If the alternator fails the output and amperage tests, bypass the regulator and retest the output to determine whether malfunction is in the alternator or regulator.

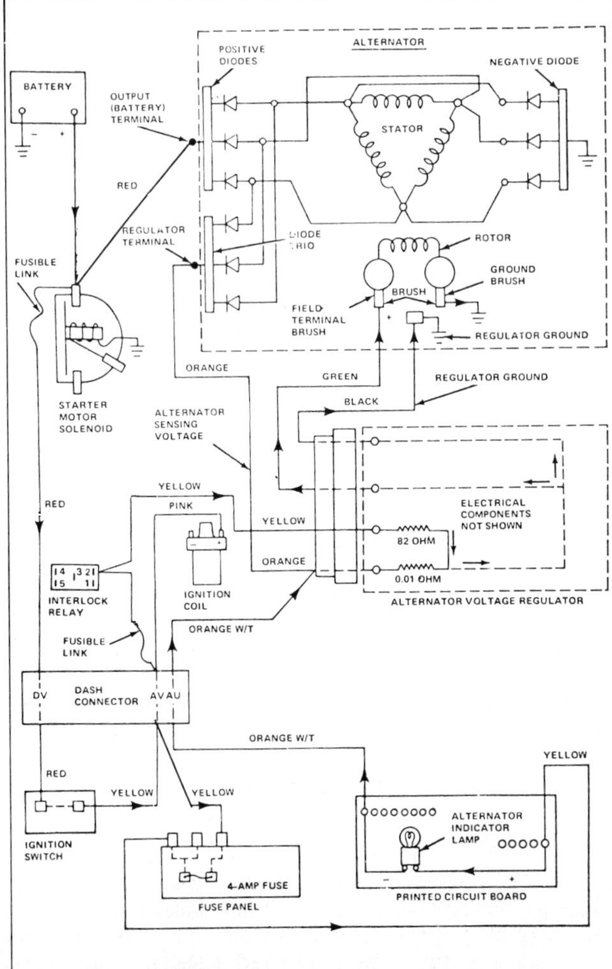

1. Disconnect the voltage regulator from the charging circuit and connect a voltmeter to the battery.

2. Start the engine and run at idle.

3. Connect an ammeter between the wire leading to the alternator insulated-brush terminal and the positive battery terminal.

4. Slowly increase engine rpm and note the voltmeter reading. If the reading approaches 16 volts, the regulator is defective. Do not exceed 16 volts in this test, because it can damage the electrical components.

DIODE TRIO TEST

If one or more diodes in a trio are open or shorted, the alternator output will be reduced. A quick check for marginal defects follows, but the alternator must pass the output test first, or the diode trio test results will not be accurate.

1. Start the engine and run at idle.

2. Connect the voltmeter positive lead to the alternator output terminal and the negative lead to the alternator regulator terminal.

3. Turn the headlamps on and set the blower switch on high speed. Wait approximately 2 minutes and turn the accessories off.

4. Voltmeter scale should read from zero to 0.2-volt if trio is good. If the reading ranges between 0.2- and 0.5-volt, the diode trio is beginning to break down under heat. If the voltage drop is 0.6 or greater, the diode trio must be replaced.

5. If the diode trio reading is 0.6-volt, but the alternator previously passed the output test, or if the meter scale needle pulsates, the soldered joints may be at fault rather than the trio. Remove the diode trio for bench-testing.

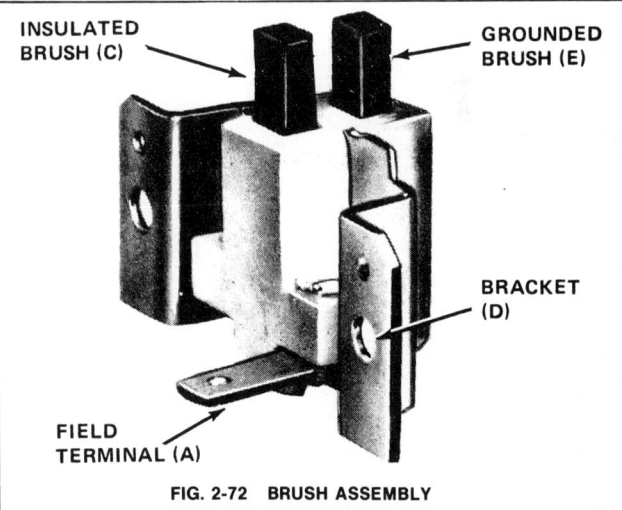

FIG. 2-72 BRUSH ASSEMBLY

FIG. 2-71 AMERICAN MOTORS FUSIBLE LINK LOCATION

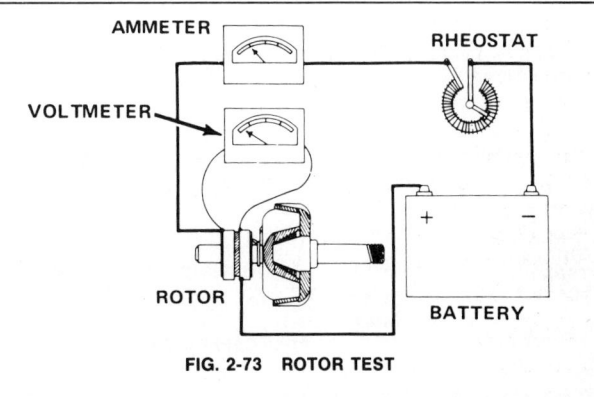

FIG. 2-73 ROTOR TEST

POSITIVE DIODE LEAK TEST

1. Disconnect the positive battery cable and remove the battery lead wire from alternator output terminal.
2. Connect an ammeter to the alternator output terminal and the positive battery terminal.
3. Any reading other than zero indicates the possibility of a shorted diode. Remove the alternator from the car for disassembly and further testing.

VOLTAGE REGULATOR TEST PROCEDURE

1. Connect a voltmeter to the battery and turn the headlamps on low beam.
2. Start the engine and run at idle for 15 minutes to bring voltage regulator to operating temperature.
3. Increase engine speed to 1000 rpm and note the voltage reading. If not within specification for the regulator temperature, replace the regulator.

ALTERNATOR REMOVAL/INSTALLATION

TO REMOVE

1. Disconnect the negative battery cable at battery.
2. Remove the battery lead and terminal connectors from rear of the alternator. Some AMC installations make it necessary to continue removal from beneath the engine.
3. Remove the adjusting bolts and washers, and slip the V-belt from the drive pulley.
4. Lift the alternator from the mounting bracket.

TO INSTALL

1. Position the alternator on the mounting bracket and install washers and bolts finger-tight.
2. Replace the V-belt on the drive pulley and adjust belt tension. On 6-cyl. engines, pry against the front housing, using the air conditioning bracket (where equipped) as a pivot point. On V-8 engines without air conditioning, an adjusting hole is provided in the bracket for prying. If air conditioning is installed, insert a ½-in. drive tool in the square hole provided in the bracket and apply leverage.

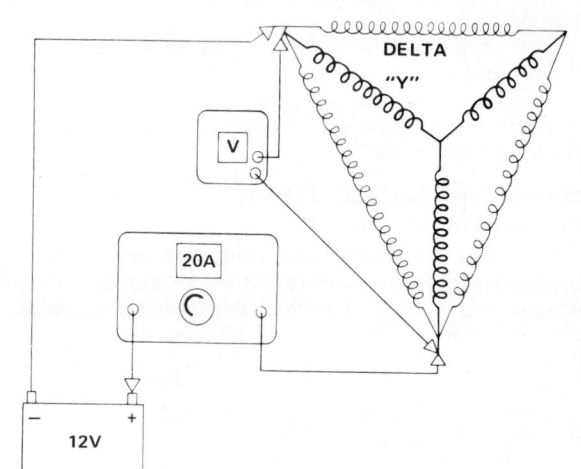

ALTERNATOR	LOAD	MAXIMUM VOLTAGE DROP	MAXIMUM VARIANCE BETWEEN WINDINGS
37	20A	7.2 – 8.2	.7
51	20A	5.5 – 6.5	.6
62	20A	6.7 – 7.2	.5

FIG. 2-75 STATOR LEAD TEST

FIG. 2-74 DIODE TRIO BENCH TEST

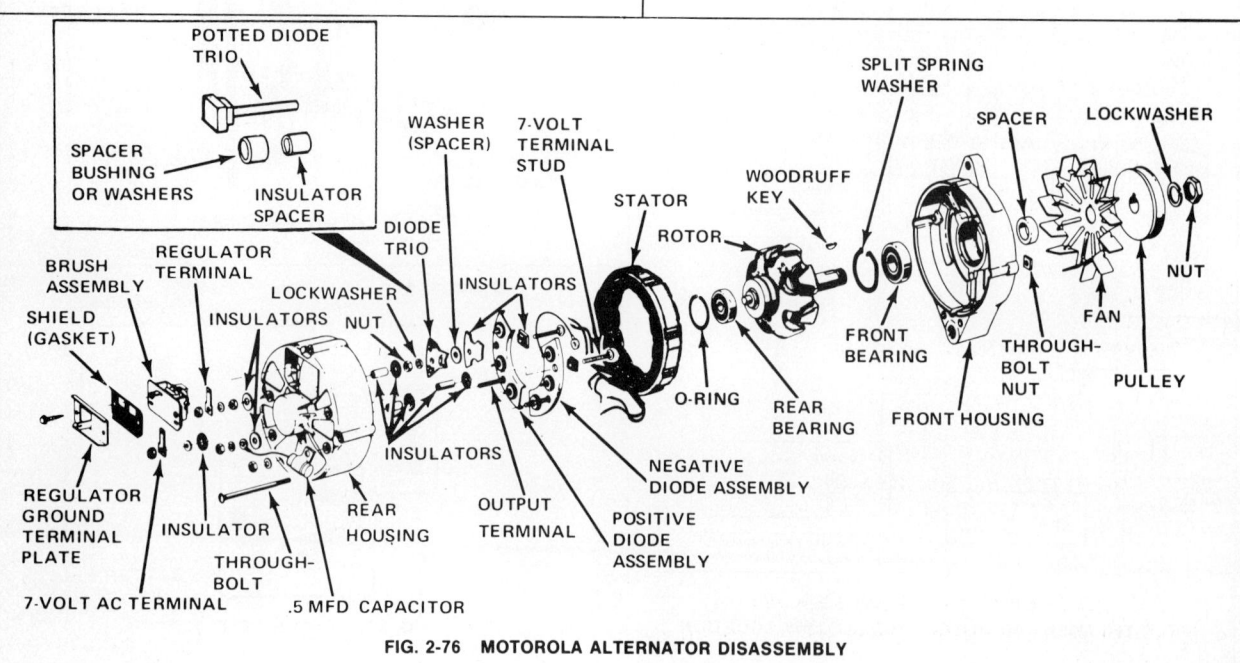

FIG. 2-76 MOTOROLA ALTERNATOR DISASSEMBLY

3. Torque the mounting bolts to 30 ft.-lbs.—bolt at sliding slot bracket is torqued to 20 ft.-lbs.

4. Replace the terminal connectors and battery lead on rear of the alternator.

5. Connect the negative battery cable to the battery.

BENCH TESTS
BRUSH ASSEMBLY INSULATION TEST

1. Connect an ohmmeter to the field terminal (A) and bracket (D) shown in **Fig. 2-72.**

2. Resistance reading should be zero; if not, the brush assembly is shorted and must be replaced.

CONTINUITY TEST

1. Connect the ohmmeter to the field terminal (A) and insulated brush (C) shown in **Fig. 2-72.**

2. Resistance reading should be zero.

3. Rock the brush and brush lead wire back and forth to make certain the lead wire connections are not intermittent—reading should not vary as a result.

4. Connect the ohmmeter to bracket (D) and ground brush (E).

5. Resistance reading should be zero.

DIODE TRIO AND RECTIFIER DIODE

Do not use a self-powered test lamp for checking diodes, because it does not produce a load sufficient to test for diode breakdown due to heat. Use a test lamp capable of producing a 1-amp load on the trio and a 15-amp load on the rectifier diode.

1. Connect the test load to one diode so that the test lamp lights. Leave load on the diode 1-2 minutes to check for a heat failure.

2. Repeat the same connection on the other diodes. Lamp should also light.

3. Reverse the test load connections and repeat Steps 1-2. Lamp should not light this time. If it does, replace the trio or rectifier assembly.

STATOR TEST

1. Connect a DC test lamp lead to a diode terminal and ground the other lead.

2. Reverse the leads. Lamp should light in only one direction.

    a) If lamp does not light in either direction, all three rectifiers in the negative diode assembly are open.

    b) If the lamp lights in both directions, one of the negative rectifier diodes is shorted or the stator winding is shorted to the stator. Retest the stator after unsoldering the diode assemblies (see following test procedure).

ROTOR (FIELD COIL) TEST

1. Place one probe of a 110-volt test lamp on a slip ring and the other probe on the rotor core. If the lamp lights, the rotor winding is grounded.

2. Connect an ammeter, a voltmeter and a rheostat to the rotor as shown in **Fig. 2-73.**

3. Reduce the rheostat resistance to zero slowly. This applies full battery voltage to the field coil.

4. Field current should fall within the range specified for the unit under test—see specifications.

5. Too great a current draw means the field winding turns are shorted; too little means the windings are open.

DIODE TRIO TEST—REAR HOUSING REMOVED

1. Unsolder the wires at the diode trio and connect a test lamp capable of drawing a 1-amp load (at 12V) to a good 12-volt battery.

2. Connect the negative tester clip to the threaded stud **(Fig. 2-74)** of the diode trio.

3. Connect the positive tester clip to one of the diode trio terminals **(Fig. 2-74).**

4. Test lamp should light. Hold the load on the diode for 3 minutes. If the light flickers or dies, the diode is breaking down under heat.

5. After 3 minutes under load, immediately reverse the test leads. Test lamp should not light. If it does, the diode is defective.

6. Test the remaining two diodes in the same way.

RECTIFIER DIODE TEST—REAR HOUSING REMOVED

1. Place a heat absorber between the diode and diode-wire solder joints, and unsolder each wire from the diodes.

2. Connect a test lamp capable of drawing a 15-amp load to a good 12-volt battery.

3. Attach one test lead to the diode heat sink.

4. Attach the other test lead to the diode lead. Connect the leads so that the test lamp will light.

5. Hold the load constant on the diode for 3 minutes. If light flickers or dies, diode is defective.

6. After 3 minutes under load, immediately reverse the test leads. Test lamp should not light. If it does, the diode is defective.

7. Test the remaining two diodes in the same way.

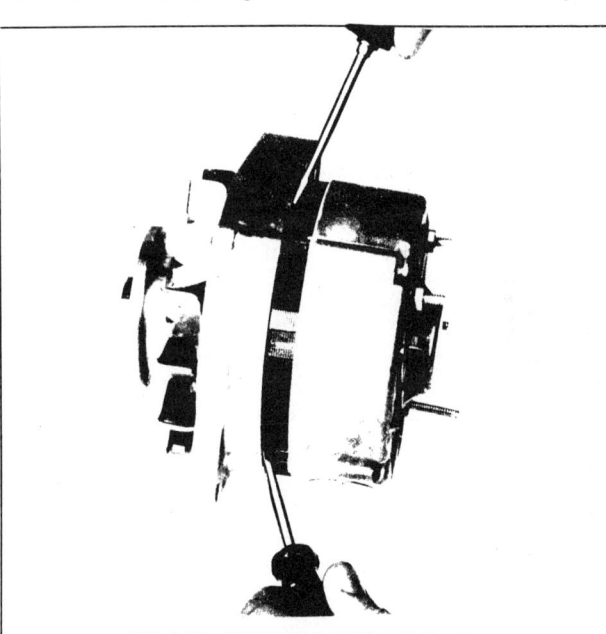

FIG. 2-77 REMOVING REAR HOUSING

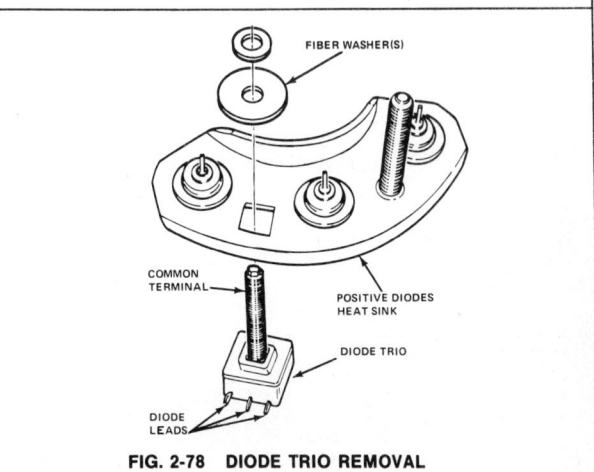

FIG. 2-78 DIODE TRIO REMOVAL

STATOR TEST—REMOVED FROM DIODE ASSEMBLY

1. Connect a 12-volt battery negative lead to any of the three stator winding leads represented in **Fig. 2-75** as ''Y'' points of the delta.

2. Connect the battery positive lead to a variable load control.

3. Connect the other side of the load control to either of the remaining stator leads.

4. Connect the voltmeter to the same two stator leads and set the load control to draw 20 amps.

5. Let the stator windings heat for 15 seconds, note the voltmeter reading, and reduce the load to zero.

6. Repeat Steps 3-5 on the other untested stator lead.

7. Compare the voltmeter readings. The amount of variance between each winding should be within the limits specified in **Fig. 2-75**.

ALTERNATOR DISASSEMBLY AND ASSEMBLY (Fig. 2-76)

TO DISASSEMBLE

1. Make a chalk mark across the alternator housing and stator as an alignment guide for reassembly, and then remove the housing through-bolts.

2. Remove the brush assembly and carefully separate the rear housing and stator from the front housing. Use two screwdrivers to pry the stator from the front housing at the two through-bolt slots opposite each other. Work with care to avoid inserting the blades **(Fig. 2-77)** more than 1/16-in. or the stator windings will be damaged.

3. Remove the locknuts and insulating washers, then separate the stator from the rear housing.

4. Remove the stator and diodes as one assembly—*do not* unsolder the stator-to-diode junction and *do not* bend the stator wires when removing the diode assemblies from the housing.

5. Unsolder the diode trio leads and remove the trio **(Fig. 2-78)**.

6. If the alternator is equipped with the AC terminal (4-bbl. carburetor usage only), remove the terminal attaching nut and drop the terminal stud through the heat sink to remove it from the housing.

7. Remove the rotor from the front housing *only* if the field coil is defective or if the front bearing must be

replaced. To separate the rotor, use a double-jaw puller to remove the drive pulley.

8. Unseat the Woodruff key and remove the spacer.

9. The split ring washer between the rotor and front bearing must be removed. Use a snap ring tool inserted through the front housing opening and compress the ring while applying pressure toward the rotor.

10. Tap the rotor shaft lightly with a plastic hammer and remove the rotor, washer and front bearing as an assembly.

11. Carefully press front and rear bearings from the rotor shaft.

TO ASSEMBLE

1. If the front bearing was removed, clean inside of the bearing hub and install a new bearing, applying pressure only to the outside race while supporting the housing boss. A 1⅛-in. socket can be used as a seating tool.

2. Replace the split ring washer in the front housing hub and seat it in the hub groove. Double-check this step, because it is one of those often overlooked.

3. Lubricate the rotor shaft lightly and install it in the front housing. Apply sufficient pressure to just seat the bearing against the rotor shaft shoulder.

4. Insert the Woodruff key on the rotor shaft and replace the spacer, fan and pulley.

5. Install the lockwasher and retaining nut.

6. If the rear bearing was removed, install a new bearing using a 7/16-in. socket and seating the bearing against the shoulder of the rotor shaft.

7. If the alternator is equipped with the AC terminal (4-bbl. carburetor usage only), install the terminal through the heat sink.

8. Use a pair of needlenose pliers inserted between the positive diode and its solder point as a heat sink; then solder the wires to the diode assembly. Make sure that solder connections face toward the outside of the alternator.

9. Replace the stator/diode assembly in the rear housing and fit the flat fiber washers on the positive-diode attaching studs. Those alternators with a 7-volt AC terminal should have a plastic sleeve installed on the AC stud, followed by a fiber washer.

10. Place plastic sleeves on all insulated terminals, and fit a flat fiber washer, a flat metal washer and locknut in that order.

11. Install the two terminal blades and tighten.

12. Line up the chalk mark previously made on the housing and stator.

13. Make certain that insulating washers are fitted to the regulator and battery post terminals, then install the through-bolts and tighten.

14. Spin fan and drive pulley to check for binding.

15. Tip the brush holder assembly toward the housing, line up with the locating pins and fit it in place.

16. Replace the shield and ground terminal plate, and fasten securely with self-tapping screws.

1970 AMERICAN MOTORS
360 and 390 Engines
Prestolite Alternator

SYSTEM DESCRIPTION

The Prestolite charging system, including the AM alternator and electronic voltage regulator, is practically identical in operation to the Motorola system used by American Motors. One major difference is in the positioning of the isolation diode as a component part of the internal positive heat sink. Test procedures as

SPECIFICATIONS MOTOROLA ALTERNATOR		
RATING (Amps)	FIELD CURRENT (Amps)	ROTATION
35	2.0—2.6	Clockwise at drive end
37	1.8—2.5	Clockwise at drive end
51	1.8—2.5	Clockwise at drive end
55	1.8—2.4	Clockwise at drive end
62	1.8—2.5	Clockwise at drive end

MOTOROLA VOLTAGE REGULATOR		
Model	8RD-2001	8RH-2003
Type	Solid State	Solid State
Adjustment	None	None
Voltage Range @ Regulator Temp	0°...14.65-15.4	0° to 50°...15.3-14.2
	20°...14.4 -15.0	50° to 100°...14.8-13.7
	40°...14.2 -14.7	100° to 150°...14.3-13.1
	60°...13.95-14.4	150° to 200°...13.8-12.7
	80°...13.75-14.2	
	100°...13.6 -14.05	
	120°...13.45-13.95	
	140°...13.3 -13.85	
	160°...13.1 -13.75	

specified for the Motorola alternator also apply to the Prestolite, and are not repeated here—refer to the Motorola section beginning on page 2-39. Disassembly and assembly procedures vary, as the following section shows.

ALTERNATOR DISASSEMBLY AND ASSEMBLY (Fig. 2-79)

TO DISASSEMBLE

1. Unscrew the brush assembly cover and tip the brush holder away from the alternator to remove.

2. Make a chalk mark across the alternator housing and stator as an alignment guide for reassembly, and then remove the housing through-bolts.

3. Tap the stator and rear housing lightly with a plastic hammer to separate from the front drive end housing.

4. Remove locknuts and insulating washers, then separate the stator from the rear housing.

5. Remove the stator and diodes as an assembly— *do not* unsolder the stator leads unless either diode or stator replacement is required.

6. Remove the rotor from the front housing *only* if the field coil is defective or if the front bearing must be replaced. To separate the rotor, use a double-jaw puller to remove the drive pulley.

7. Remove the fan, unseat the Woodruff key and remove the spacer.

8. The split ring washer between the rotor and front bearing must be removed. Use a snap ring tool inserted through the front housing opening and compress the ring while applying pressure toward the rotor.

9. Tap the rotor shaft lightly with a plastic hammer and remove the rotor.

10. Remove the front bearing retainer and press out the bearing.

11. If the rectifier diodes or isolation diode need replacement, protect the diode-wire solder joints from excessive heat and unsolder the connections.

12. With the stator removed, unscrew the mounting nuts from AUX and OUTPUT terminals.

13. Remove the positive-diode heat sink. Negative diodes are mounted in the rear housing. If diode replacement is necessary, remove and install diodes with a diode remover/installer tool. Do not drive diodes in or out, because this will damage them.

14. If installing new diodes, be sure the positive diodes are installed in the heat sink and the negative diodes are installed in the rear housing.

15. Solder stator leads in place. Each stator lead is paired to one negative and one positive diode.

TO ASSEMBLE

1. If the front housing bearing was removed, press a new bearing in place. The dust seal must face the rotor.

2. Install the bearing-retainer snap ring.

3. Replace the spacer, Woodruff key, fan, pulley, lockwasher and retaining nut—tighten nut securely.

4. Replace the diode heat sink and solder all stator-to-diode connections which were disconnected.

5. Align the chalk mark previously made on the housing halves and stator. Fit the front and rear housings together and install the through-bolts.

6. Replace the brush holder assembly, taking care that stator leads and brush holder assembly do not rub on the rotor.

7. Spin the fan and the drive pulley to check for any binding.

SPECIFICATIONS PRESTOLITE (AM) ALTERNATOR		
RATING (Amps)	FIELD CURRENT (Amps)	ROTATION
35	2.4–2.5	Clockwise at drive end

VOLTAGE REGULATOR	
MOTOROLA 8RD-2001, SOLID STATE, NON-ADJUSTABLE VOLTAGE RANGE	
AT REGULATOR TEMP...... 0°	14.65–15.4
20°	14.4 –15.0
40°	14.2 –14.7
60°	13.95–14.4
80°	13.75–14.2
100°	13.6 –14.05
120°	13.45–13.95
140°	13.3 –13.85
160°	13.1 –13.75

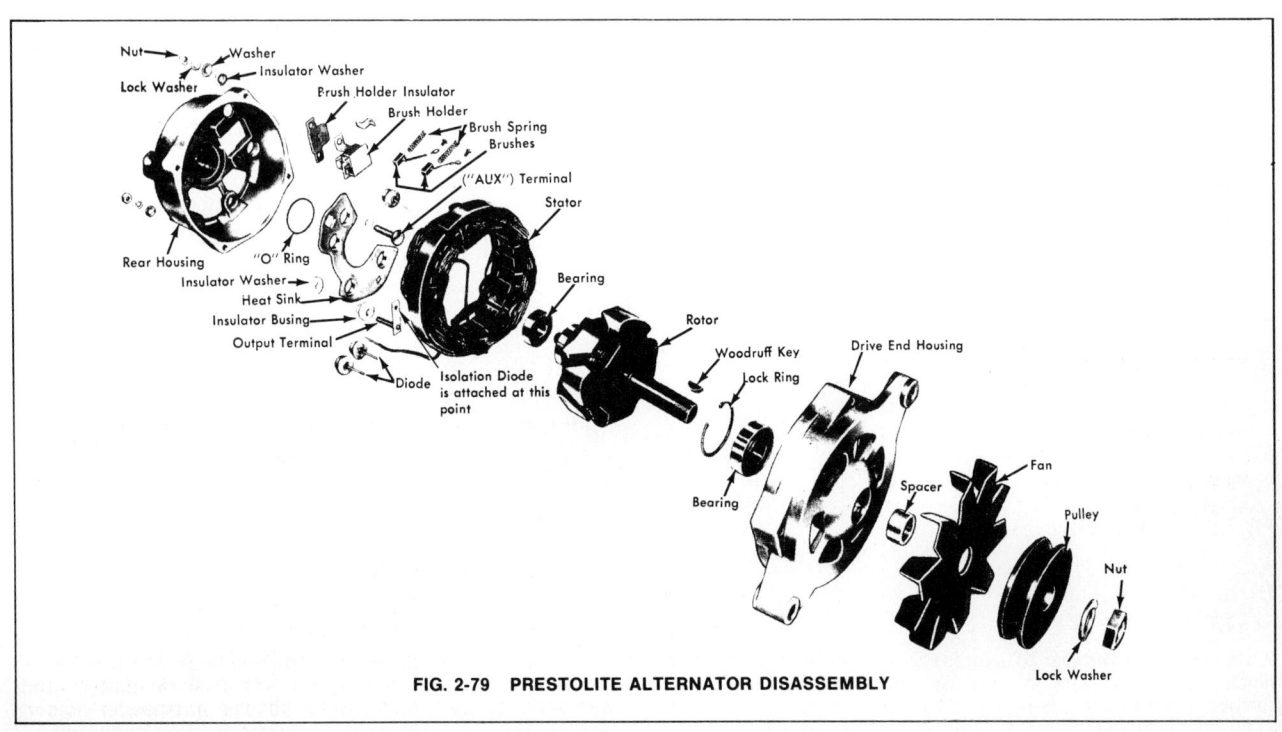

FIG. 2-79 PRESTOLITE ALTERNATOR DISASSEMBLY

HOW TO: Delcotron 1D Removal & Overhaul

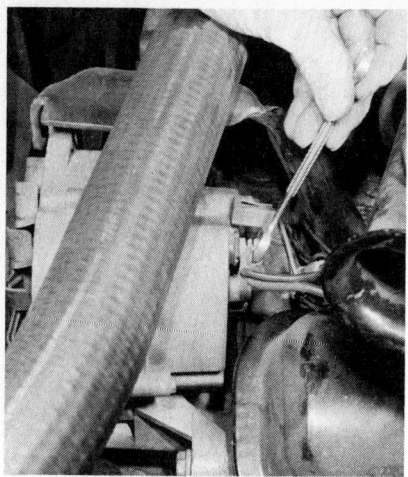

1. When working on the charging system, always disconnect battery first, then disconnect leads at back of Delcotron and remove terminal plug-in lead.

2. Loosen the adjusting bolt and the through-bolt (arrow). To remove the through-bolt on power steering installations, you'll have to loosen pump too.

3. With power steering pump loosened and moved to one side, through-bolt will now clear pump pulley and can be withdrawn from the mount. Remove unit.

4. Scribe chalk line across end frames. Drive end frame and rotor should now pull apart from slip-ring end frame and stator with a gentle twisting motion.

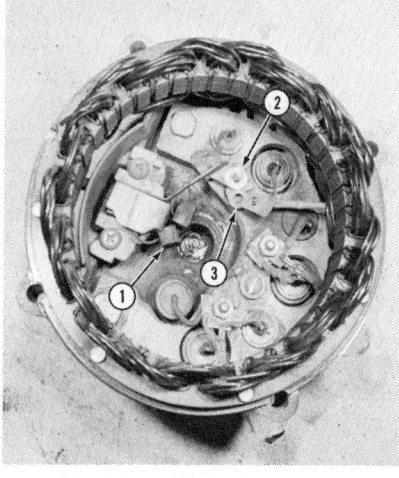

5. Low output appears to have caused brush wear (1). To remove brush holder, first remove nut from stud (2), lift off diode/stator connection (3).

6. Loosen brush-holder attaching screws and carefully lift entire unit up and out of end frame. Blow out accumulated brush deposits with low-pressure air.

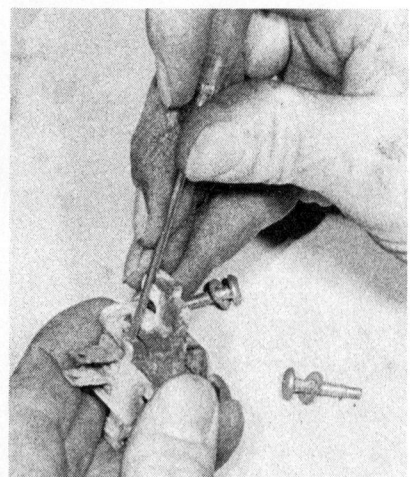

7. Use small screwdriver to depress tang holding one brush terminal in place, and remove; other terminal is removed by lifting it off the holder.

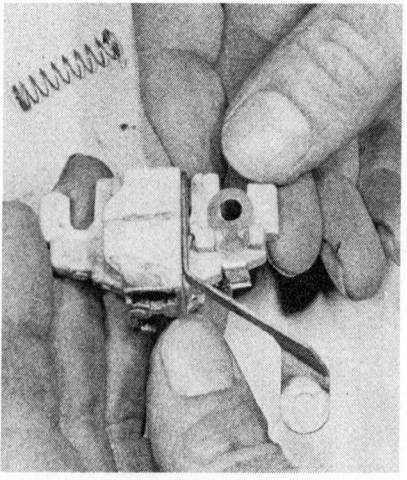

8. Replace push-in terminal first. Other terminal is inserted in its slot until it seats. If tang interferes with seating, depress with screwdriver, push in place.

9. Replace brush springs and brushes in brush holder and position unit in end frame while holding brushes in holder. Insert small drill bit through end frame.

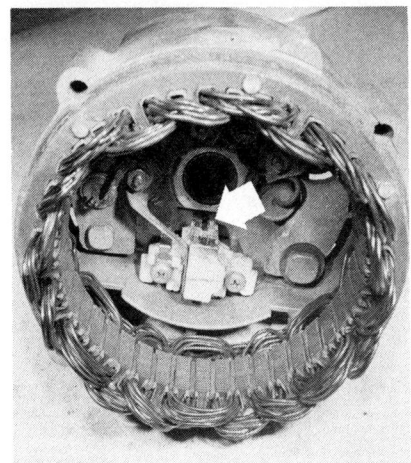

10. Drill passes through brush holder (arrow) and keeps the brushes in place when rotor shaft and slip rings are installed. Reconnect diode/stator leads.

11. Drive pulley, fan must be removed with box wrench and Allen wrench. Remove retaining nut. Don't mix sequence of spacers around pulley and fan.

12. Remove drive-end retainer and gasket to inspect bearing. Bearing grease here has almost solidified; bearing must be regreased or replaced.

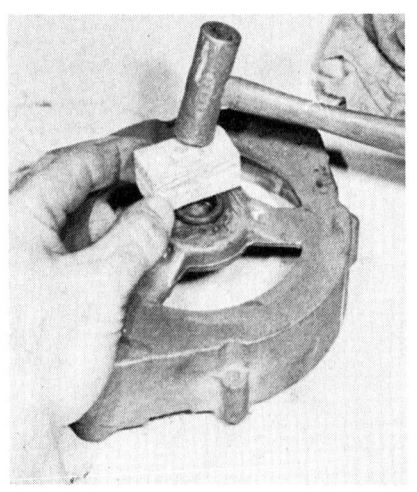

13. If you do not have a press, remove the old bearing by using one of the spacers under a wood block. Tap wood block until spacer forces bearing out.

14. Fill bearing only half-full of grease. Too much bearing grease will melt and run due to high heat. Replace new bearing carefully as shown.

15. Once the bearing is properly seated in the bore, install a new gasket and replace the bearing retainer cap. Tighten the screws securely.

16. Replace end frame on rotor shaft, taking care to reinstall the spacers exactly as they were removed. Replace fan and pulley, and tighten retaining nut.

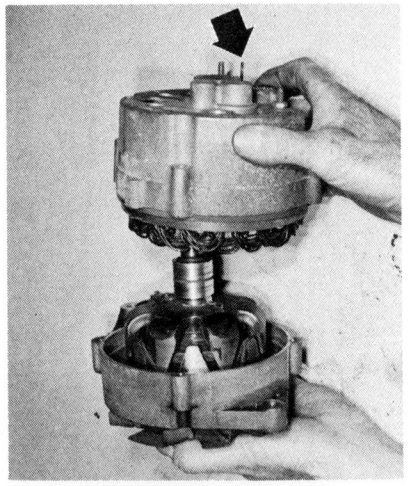

17. Align end frames according to the chalk mark made earlier and slip stator end frame over rotor slip rings. Note drill (arrow) still holding brushes.

18. Replace through-bolts and tighten securely. Be sure to remove the drill so that brushes will seat on slip rings. Now reinstall Delcotron in the car.

HOW TO: Delcotron 10-SI Overhaul

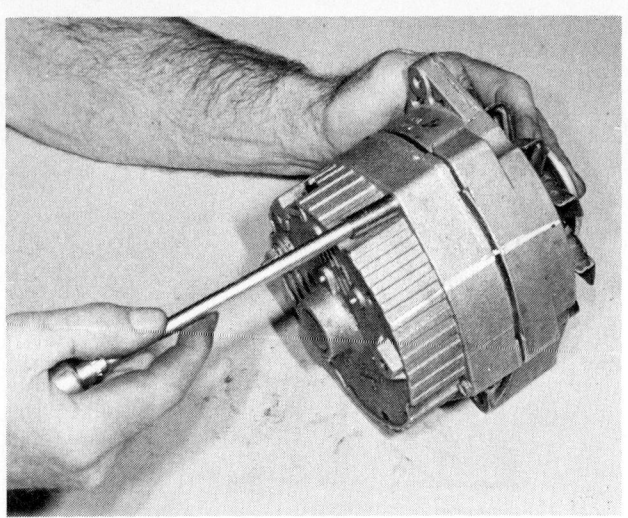

1. This Delcotron has proven to be very dependable, and is used on GM cars since 1970. Begin overhaul by scribing reference mark across end frames, and remove through-bolts.

2. The slip-ring end frame and stator should separate easily from the rotor end frame. If it does not, pry apart carefully, using a screwdriver at each side of the stator slot provided.

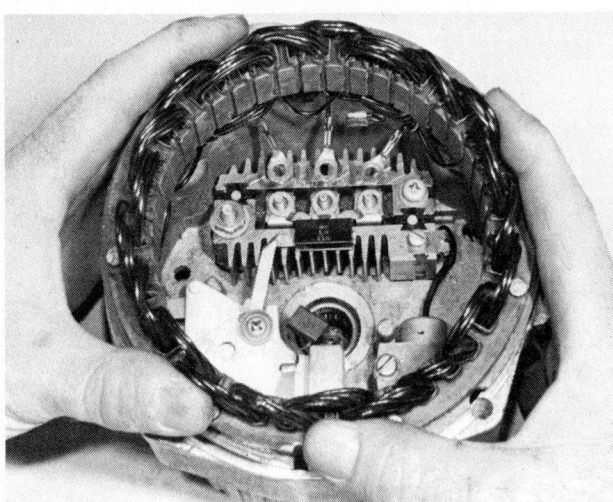

3. Remove three nuts holding stator leads to heat sink, and remove stator from the end frame. While this unit looks complicated, it's one of the easiest alternators to work on.

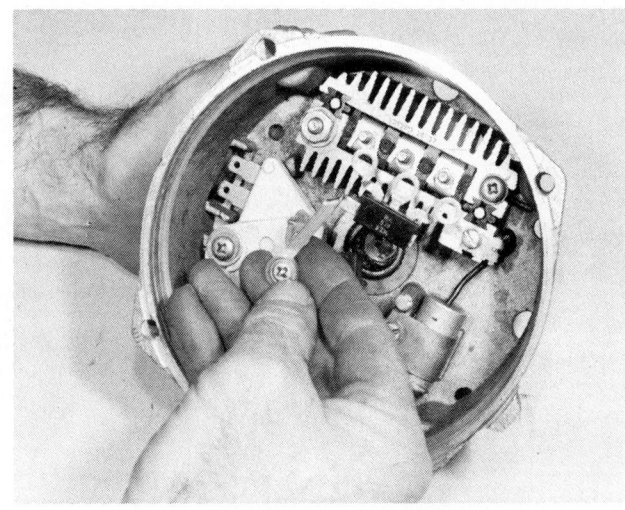

4. Remove screw which holds the diode trio to brush holder assembly, and remove trio from the end frame. Diode trio can be checked for grounded brush-lead clip at this point.

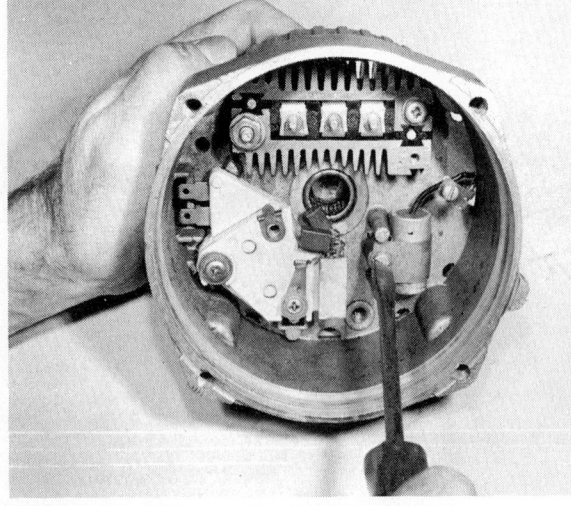

5. Disconnect the capacitor lead from the heat sink and then unscrew and remove the capacitor. The capacitor should be tested before reinstalling it in the end frame.

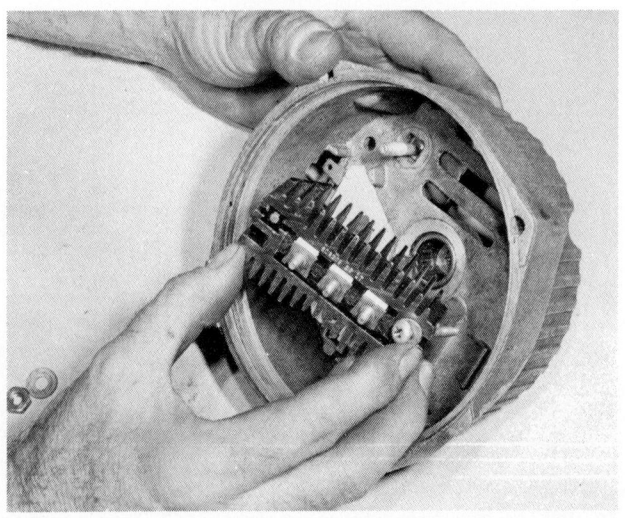

6. Now remove rectifier-bridge attaching screw and the BAT terminal screw and lift rectifier bridge from end frame. Be sure to keep track of different screws as you remove them.

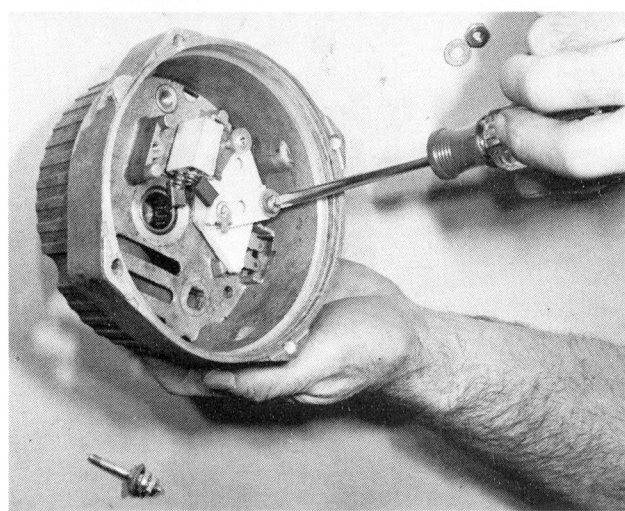

7. Remove two attaching screws holding brush holder and integral voltage regulator assembly. Two insulators are assembled over top of brush retaining clips; screws have sleeves.

8. Separate voltage regulator from brush holder. Remove brush springs and set aside. Inspect brushes for excessive wear and replace if necessary. Always replace in pairs.

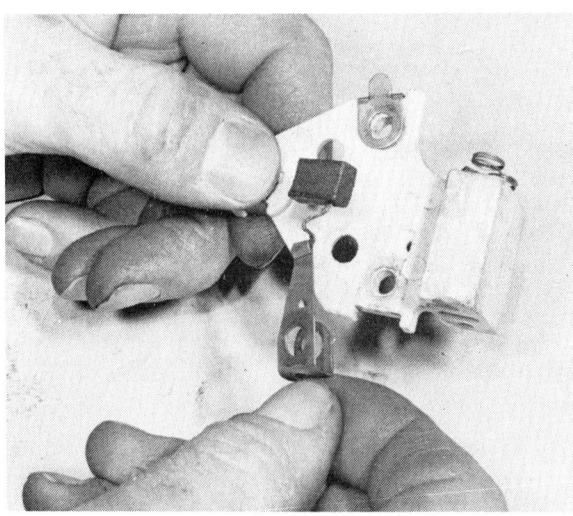

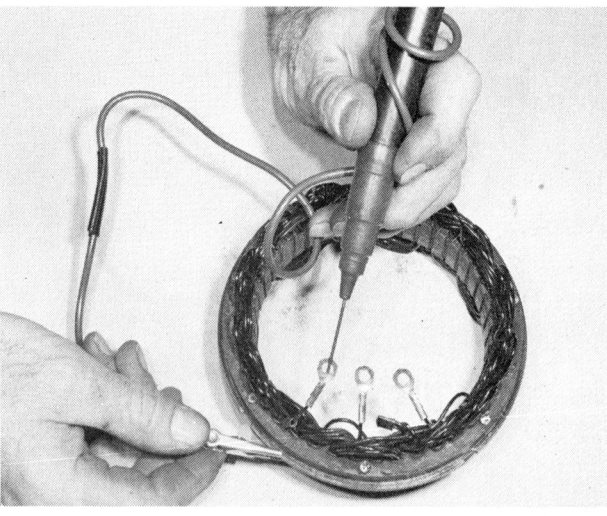

9. Both brush assemblies are identical and simply slip off the holder. Brush leads are connected to the brush assemblies and the entire unit is replaced by slipping a new one in its place.

10. Test stator for ground by touching one lead of test lamp or ohmmeter to stator frame and other lead to a stator lead. If lamp lights or ohmmeter reads low, windings are grounded.

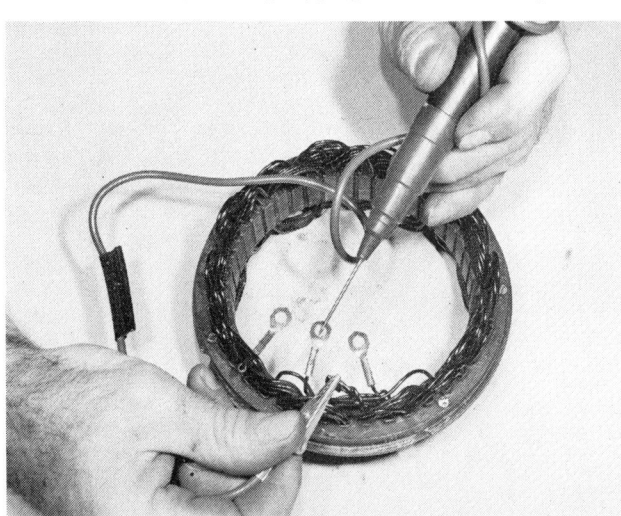

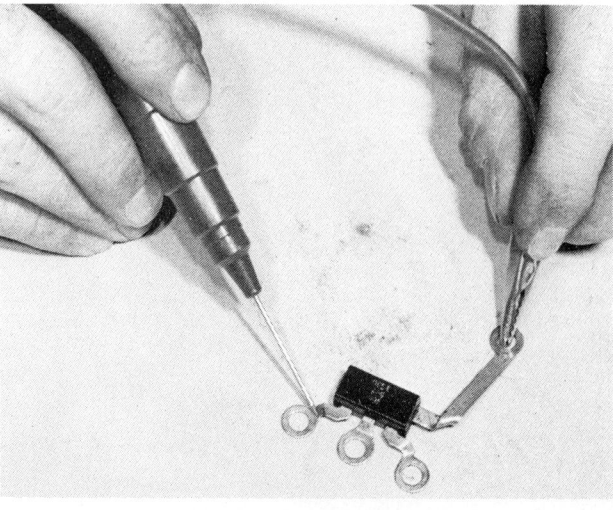

11. Test stator for opens; lamp should light or ohmmeter should read low. Because of low resistance of windings, locating a short in the stator windings requires special equipment.

12. To test the diode trio, connect one test lamp lead to the single connector and the other lead to any one of the three connectors, and note whether or not the lamp lights.

HOW TO: Delcotron 10-SI Overhaul

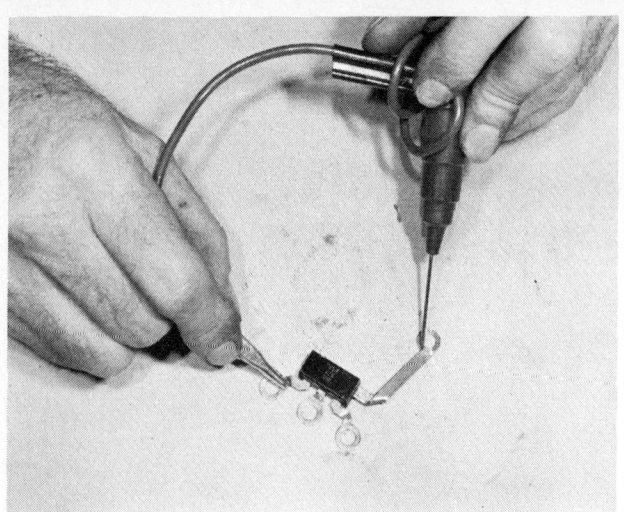

13. Reverse test leads on same connectors, and note lamp reaction. Test lamp should light in one direction only, if diode trio is good; if it lights in both or does not light, replace trio.

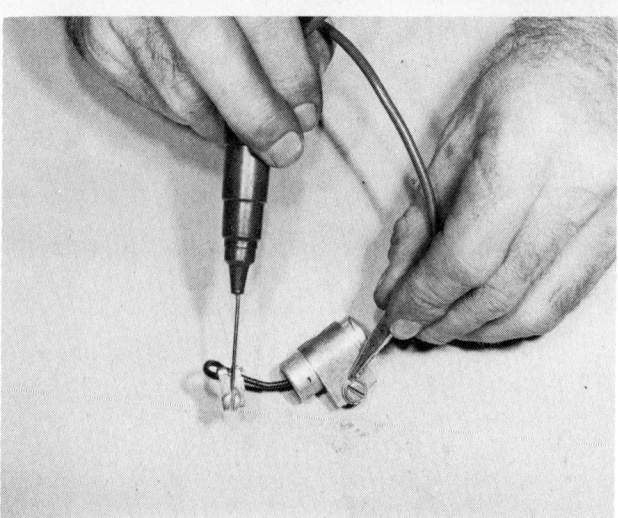

14. The capacitor can also be tested with the same powered test lamp. It should not light if the unit is satisfactory; if it does light, the capacitor is shorted.

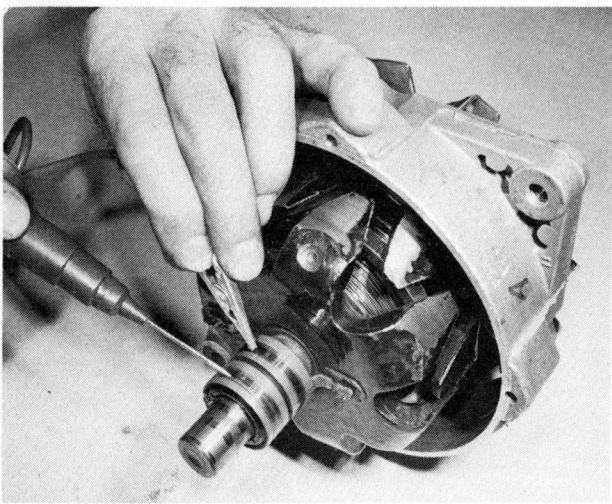

15. Check rotor for an open by touching each test lead to slip rings as shown. Test lamp will light if windings are okay. Ohmmeter can be used; should give a high reading.

16. To test the rotor for grounds, connect the test lamp leads as shown. If rotor slip rings require cleaning, use a 400-grain polishing cloth and blow dry to remove the residue.

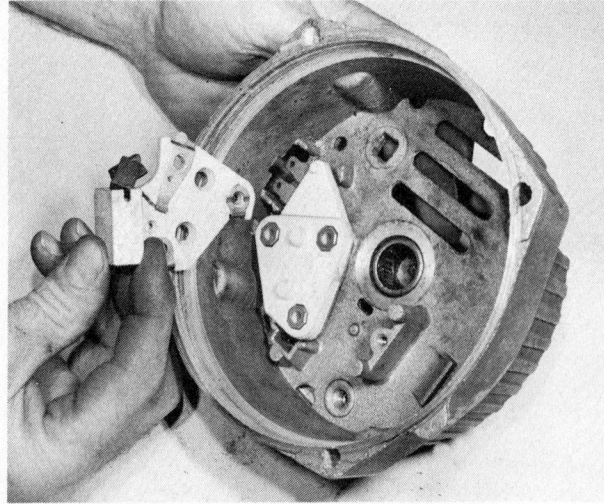

17. Begin Delcotron reassembly by reinstalling voltage regulator and brush holder. Regulator slips into position in end frame holder; two holes in brush holder fit over regulator studs.

18. Before replacing brush-holder attaching screws, check insulating sleeve on each; be sure it's not cracked or damaged. Screw shown here may or may not have insulating washer.

19. Brush springs are installed and brushes fitted in holder, then a small drill bit or piece of stiff wire is inserted through a hole in end frame (arrow) to keep brushes in place.

20. Before replacing rectifier bridge, install BAT terminal from rear. Insulated insert must be in position and properly seated in hole, or problems will develop when connecting battery.

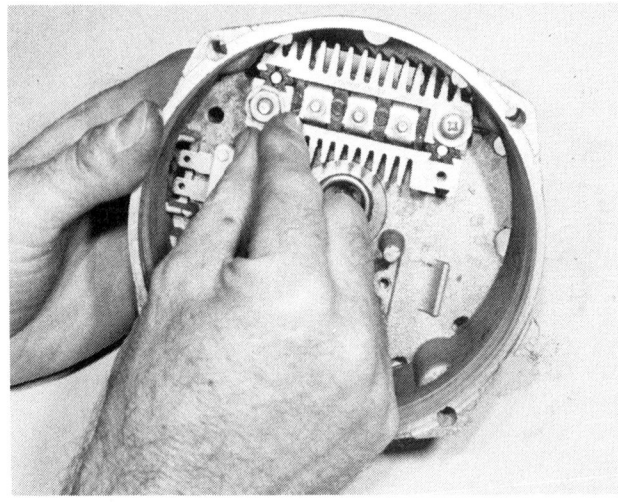

21. Fit rectifier bridge over BAT terminal, install retaining screw with insulator at its upper right, then replace nut on battery terminal, which secures left side of bridge.

22. Replace capacitor; connect its lead to rectifier bridge, then replace diode trio. Trio attaching screw must have insulating sleeve. Trio leads fit over terminals on rectifier bridge.

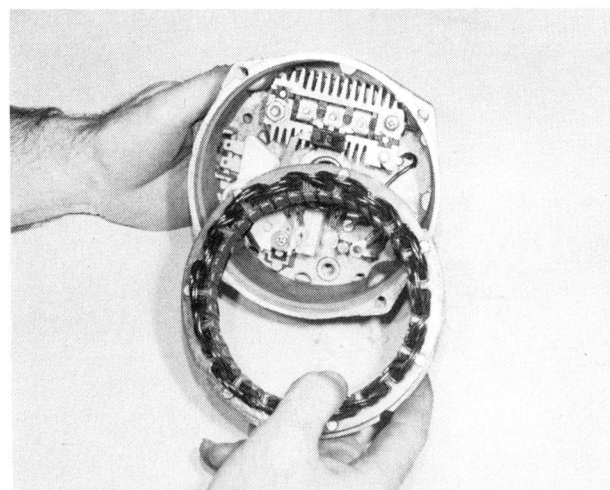

23. The stator is the final part of the assembly to be replaced. Fit the stator leads over the rectifier bridge terminals and seat stator, then replace the attaching nuts to the terminals.

24. Align end frames according to scribed chalk mark, fit together and install four through-bolts. Remove drill or wire to allow brushes to contact slip rings. Overhaul is complete.

HOW TO: Autolite Rear-Terminal Alternator Overhaul

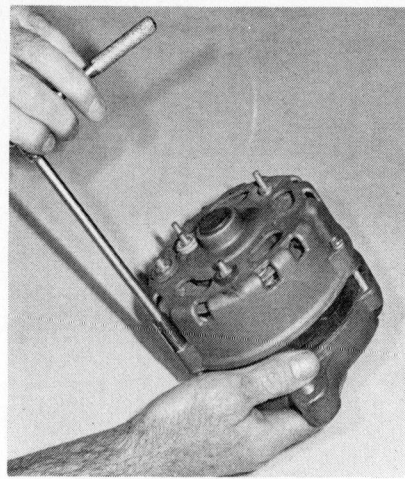

1. Disassembly is similar to older Autolite unit. Scribe alignment mark and remove through-bolts. It may be necessary to gently tap end frames apart.

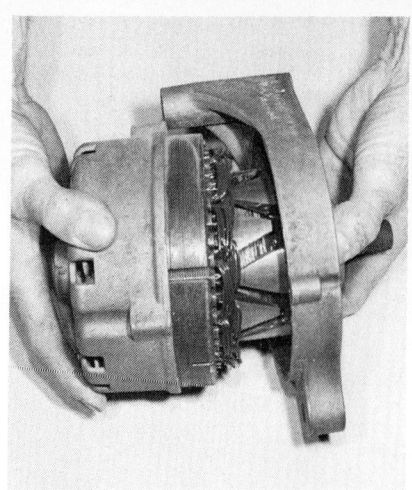

2. Once seal is broken between stator and rotor end frames, separate. Rotor is removed with one end frame, and stator is removed with other end frame.

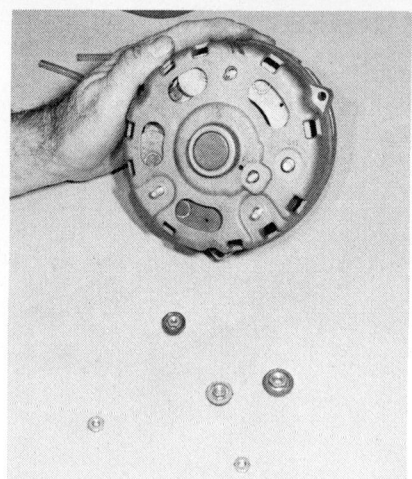

3. Remove nuts, lockwashers, washers and grommets from end frame. If integral regulator included, remove that first. Each terminal nut has different threads.

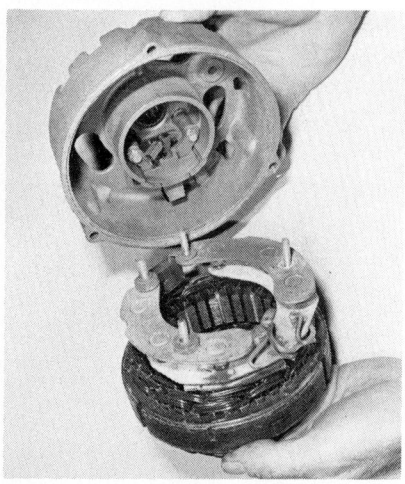

4. With terminal nuts removed, stator and rectifier assembly can be pulled from end frame. Brushes and brush springs will pop out of brush holder.

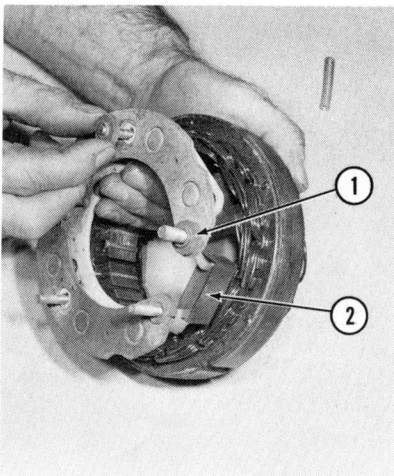

5. Remove stator terminal insulator, battery terminal insulator (1) and radio suppression capacitor (2). Integral regulator model has no battery terminal insulator.

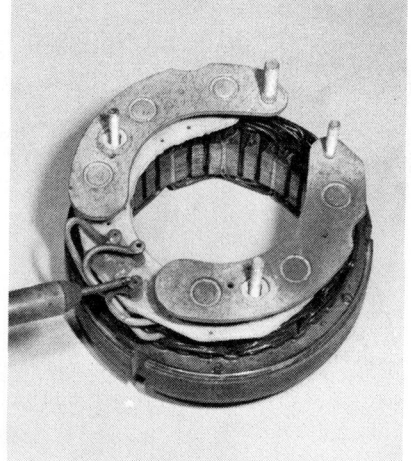

6. To replace rectifier assembly, unsolder stator leads from printed-circuit-board terminals with low-heat soldering iron (100 watts); resolder new assembly.

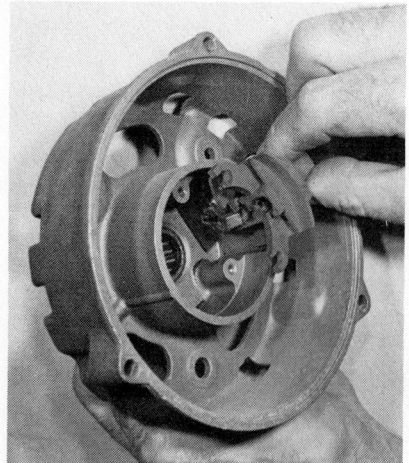

7. Brush holder, with brushes, is lifted from stator end frame. Inspect brushes for excessive wear, replace if necessary. If stator end frame cracked, replace.

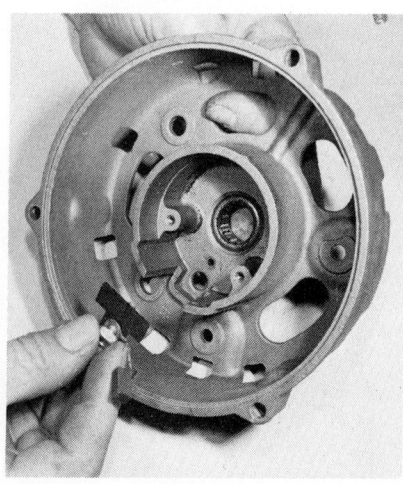

8. Withdraw brush terminal insulator, with brush attached to the field terminal. Don't forget to reinstall this insulator when reassembling alternator.

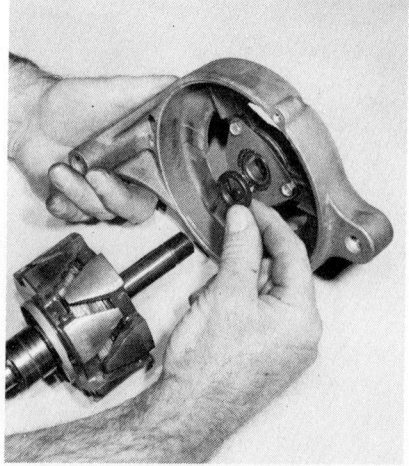

9. Remove rotor from end frame to inspect front bearing. Bearing spacer may stick to bearing retainer; should be removed and installed on rotor shaft.

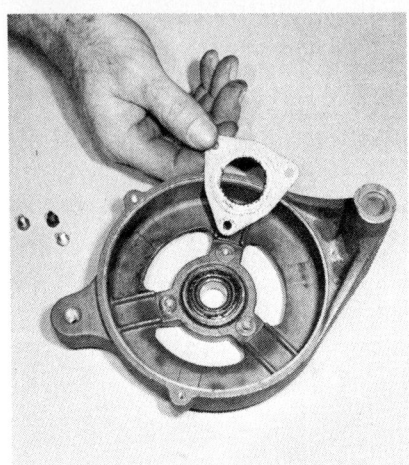

10. Remove three screws holding front bearing retainer in place; lift retainer off. Bearing should be removed only if defective or if it has lost lubricant.

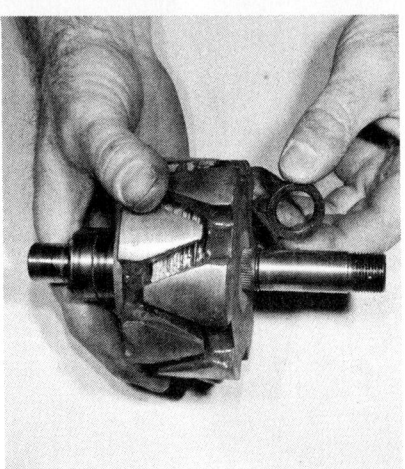

11. Bearing spacer has chamfered side designed to fit into groove on rotor shaft next to the rotor. Be sure to replace spacer correctly during reassembly.

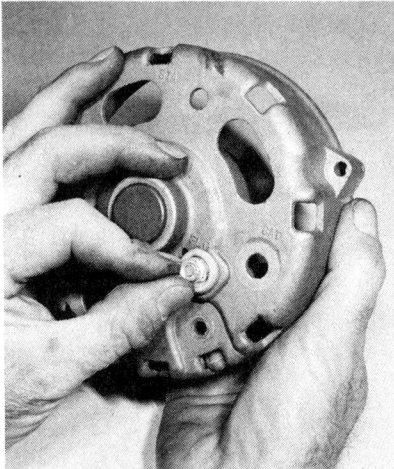

12. Before reinstalling brush holder, the field terminal—with insulator and brush attached—should be replaced, with terminal insulator, washer and nut.

13. Always check field terminal and brush after securing nut. Installation shown is incorrect—terminal head is not aligned, brush lead is touching frame.

14. Replace brush springs and brushes, holding them in place while inserting small drill bit or stiff wire through endframe hole to keep brushes in place.

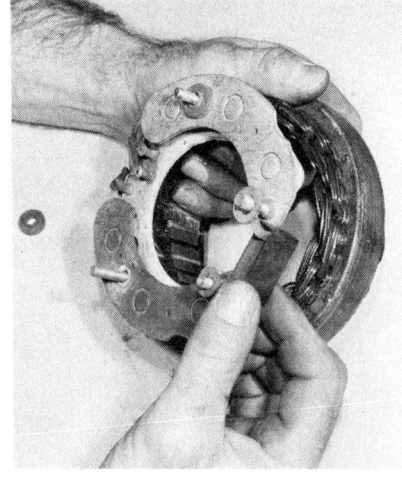

15. Reinstall stator neutral lead terminal, stator terminal insulator. Replace radio suppression capacitor over rectifier terminals. Fit battery terminal insulator.

16. Fit stator and rectifier assembly into stator end frame, making sure all terminal insulators are properly seated in their respective recesses.

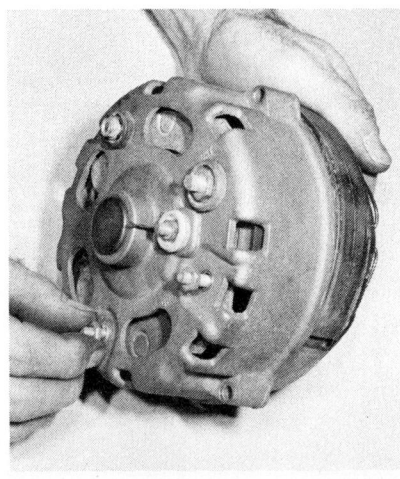

17. If you've set terminal attachments aside in the same configuration they were removed, line up alternator terminals with the nuts, and reinstall them.

18. Align chalk mark scribed as reference for reassembling end frames. Replace and tighten through-bolts, withdraw drill holding brushes in place.

HOW TO: Motorola Diode Replacement

1. If in-car alternator tests indicate there is a defective diode, remove and mount the alternator in a vise by its housing flange as shown. Loosen the terminal plate screws.

2. Remove the terminal plate screws and the plate, exposing the brush assembly, shown above. Pry out the insulator and lift the brush assembly out of the alternator end frame.

3. Loosen and remove the through-bolts after marking end frames and stator with a piece of chalk to help realign end frames during reassembly. Remove the terminal nuts.

4. Lift the end frame off the alternator. If the unit has not been recently overhauled, it may be necessary to free the end frame by tapping it gently with a mallet.

5. Once the end frame is removed from the alternator, lift out the positive diode plate. Underneath the diode plate, shown above, is the new diode trio used on 1974 models.

6. Unsolder the diode plate/trio from the stator leads to remove and replace the diode trio. Be sure to protect the diode from excessive heat whenever soldering or unsoldering.

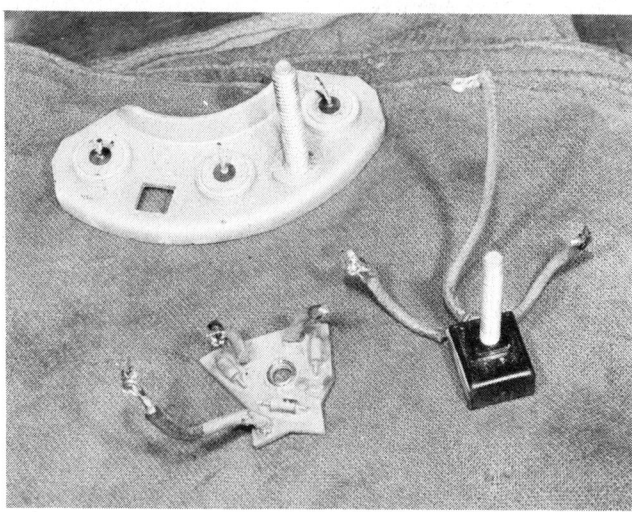

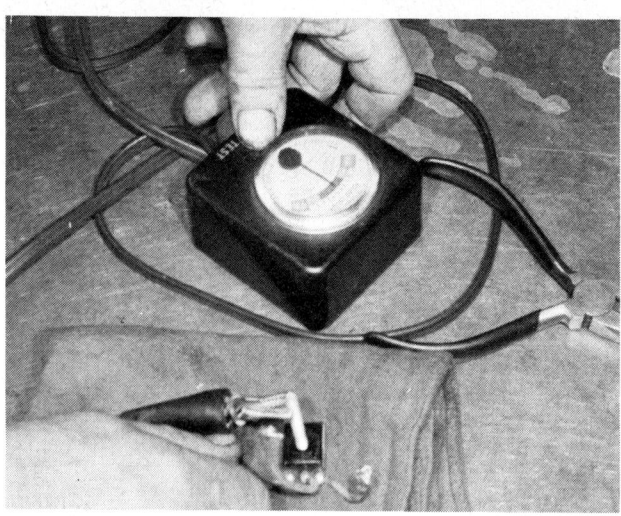

7. The field diode at left was used until late 1973; the new trio at right came into use in late 1973. The newer integral terminal is insulated from the plate by fiber washer.

8. Use a diode tester to run the diode check, touching each of the three wire connections, one at a time, with the tester lead. This particular diode is a defective one.

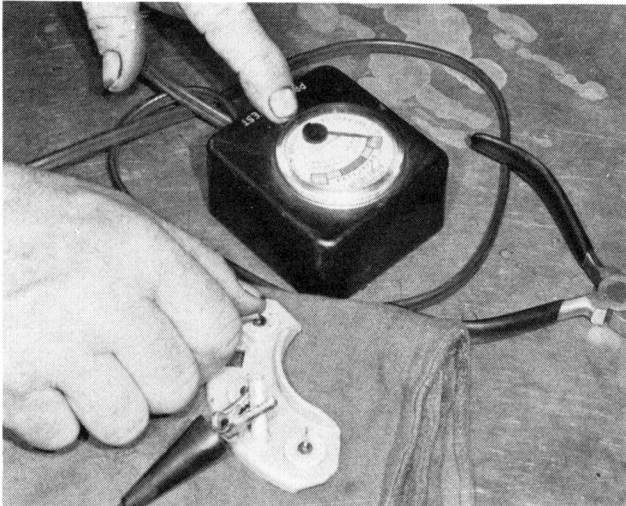

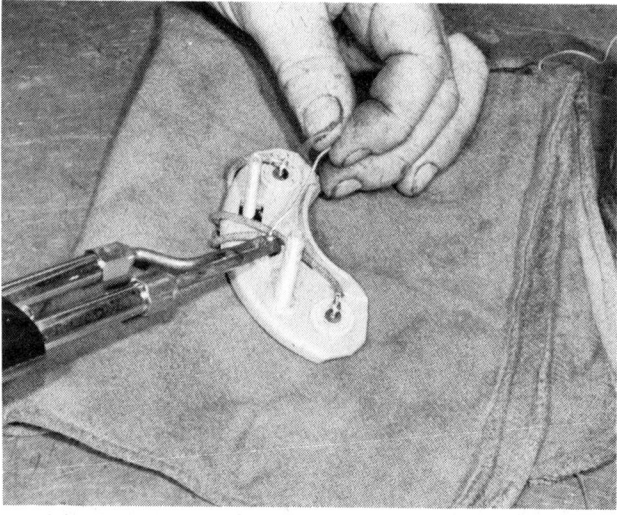

9. Test the diode plate to be sure that the trouble is confined to the trio itself. Touch each diode lead separately, with the diode tester connected to the diode plate terminal.

10. Locate the new diode trio beneath the positive diode plate. Then reconnect the leads by soldering them with resin-core solder. Heat the wire and touch the solder to it.

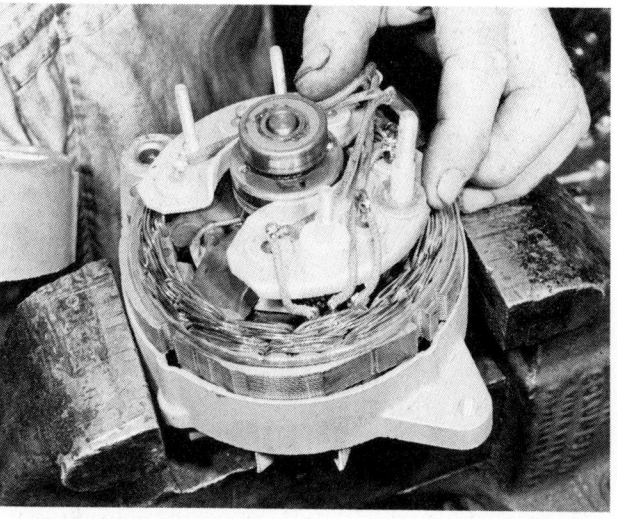

11. Install the positive diode plate and reconnect the stator leads. Hold them in place on the diode lead with pliers and heat the connections. Do not use excessive solder.

12. Reassemble the insulators on the positive diode assembly as shown here. The end frame will not seat properly if the spacers are reversed. Replace the through-bolts.

HOW TO: Chrysler Alternator Overhaul

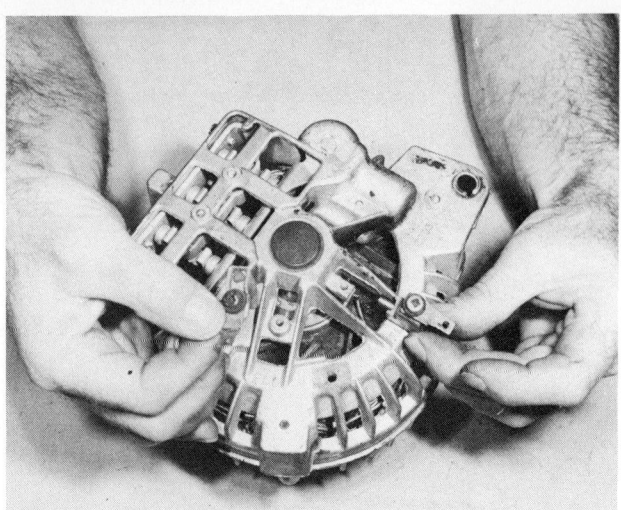

1. Except for diode placement inside alternator, Chrysler design has remained unchanged for over a decade. Remove brush holders from rear end shield frame to begin disassembly.

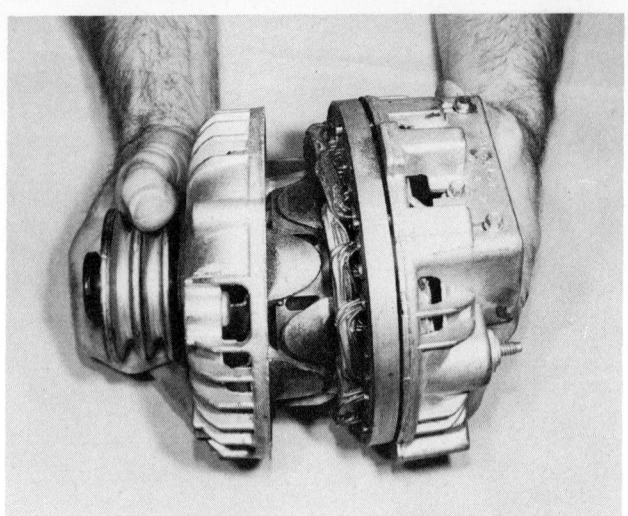

2. Scribe a chalk mark across front and rear end frames to assist in realignment when reassembling. Remove three through-bolts, separate end frames; tap with rubber mallet.

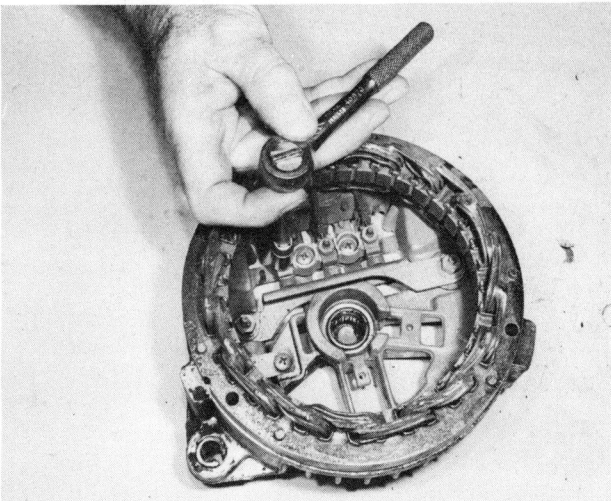

3. To separate stator from rear end frame, remove three nuts which hold stator leads to rectifier assembly. Remove stator from end frame. Tap stator with rubber mallet if necessary.

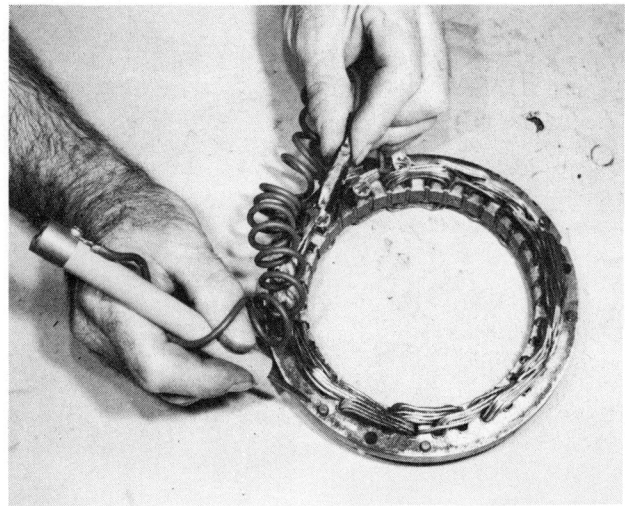

4. Use a self-powered test lamp to test stator for ground. Press one test probe on stator frame pin and other probe to each of three lead terminals, one at a time. Lamp should light.

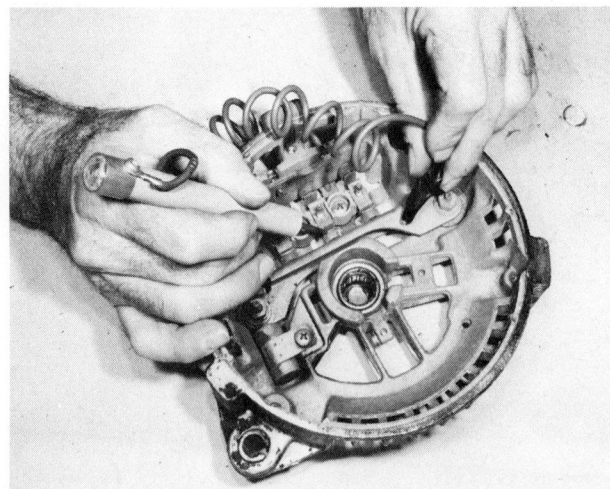

5. Use self-powered test lamp to test positive rectifier. Press one test probe to rectifier heat sink and other test probe to strap at base of each diode, one at a time.

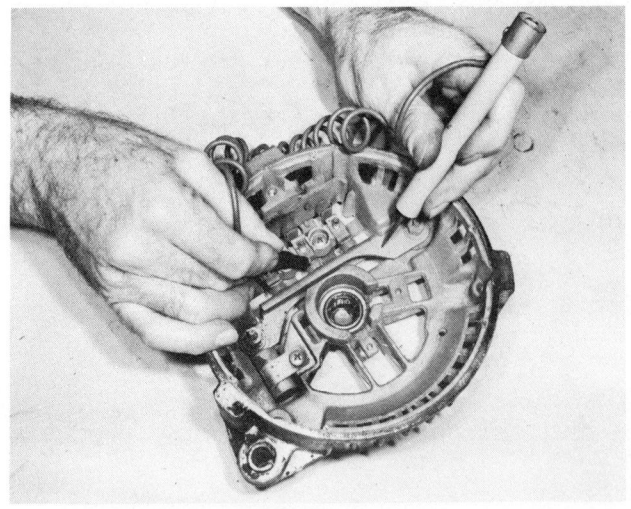

6. Reverse probes and repeat Step 5. Test lamp should light in one direction for each diode, but not in the other. If lamp does not light in one direction, or lights in both, replace rectifier.

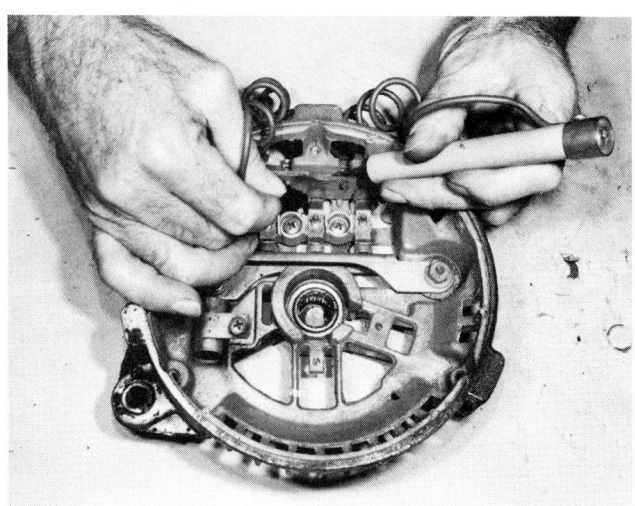

7. Test negative rectifier in same manner. Press one test probe to rectifier heat sink and other probe to strap at base of diode, one at a time.

8. Reverse probes and repeat Step 7. Test lamp should light in one direction for each diode, but not in the other. If lamp does not light in one direction, or lights in both, replace rectifier.

9. Remove screw which grounds capacitor to end frame and nut on heat sink stud. Lift capacitor from end frame. Some capacitors are held in place only by ground screw.

10. Remove nuts and screws which hold positive/negative rectifier assemblies in end frame and lift rectifiers out. Positive rectifier is removed first, then negative rectifier.

11. Check rear bearing; if replacement is necessary, press or drive bearing from end frame carefully. Install new bearing as shown from outside of end frame and seat completely.

12. To replace rectifiers, reinstall BAT terminal and insulator at rear of end frame. Be sure to replace insulating washer between end frame and rectifier assembly inside end frame.

HOW TO: Chrysler Alternator Overhaul

13. Install positive rectifier assembly first. Be sure to replace insulating washer on other mounting stud before replacing rectifier, then tighten screws/nuts securely.

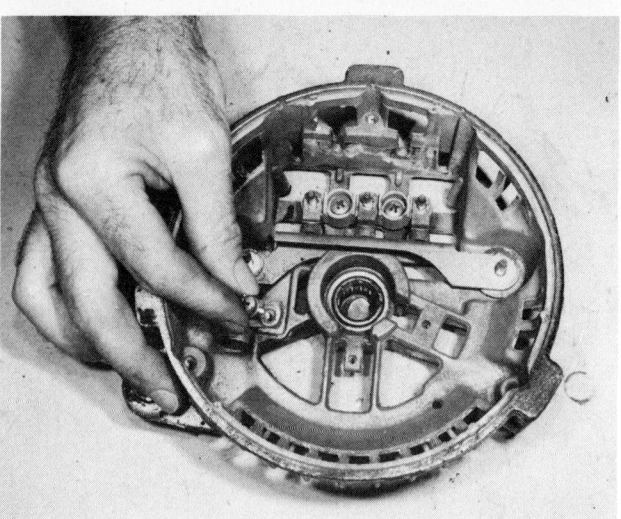

14. Test capacitor for opens and shorts, then reinstall in end frame. Replace ground screw and insulated stud nut (if used). Tighten screw/nut securely.

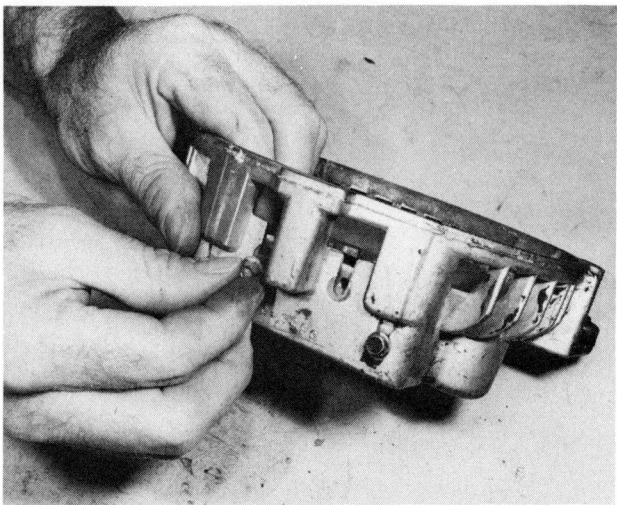

15. Replace negative rectifier assembly in end frame and install retaining cap nuts through top of end frame as shown. Tighten cap nuts securely.

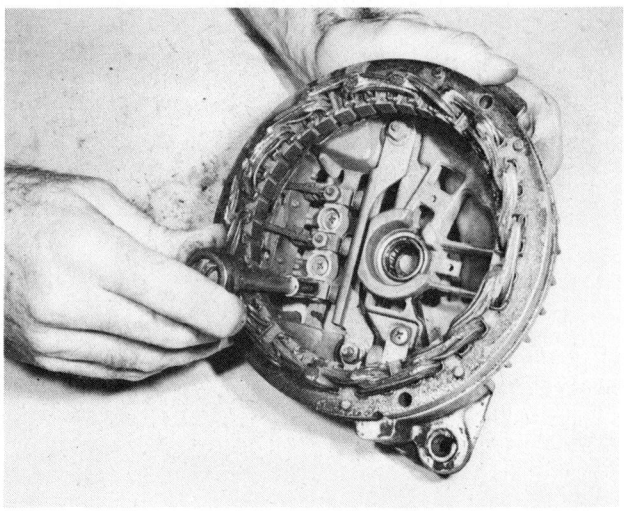

16. Install stator to end frame and align stator pins with holes in end frame. Seat stator against end frame and replace leads on rectifier terminals, tightening nuts securely.

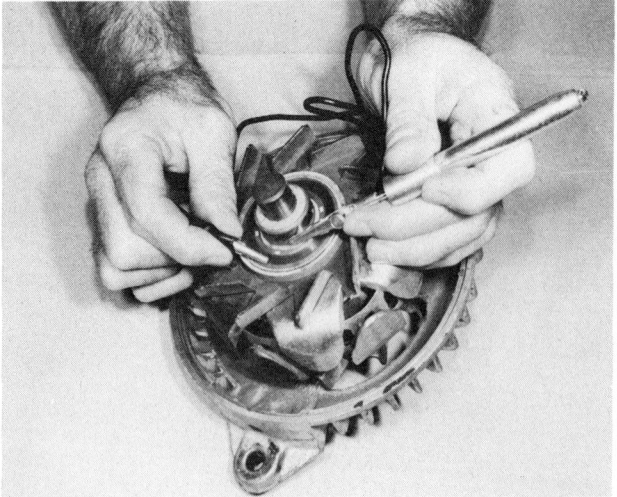

17. Check rotor for open or grounded field coils with self-powered test lamp. Ground test is shown; place both probes on slip rings to check for an open coil.

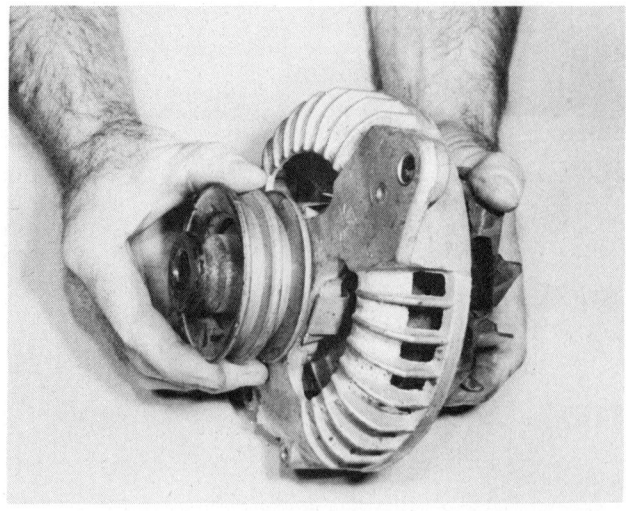

18. To replace rotor or front bearing, you'll need a special puller (Chrysler tool C-4068) to remove pulley from rotor shaft, as it's an interference fit. Substitute pullers won't work.

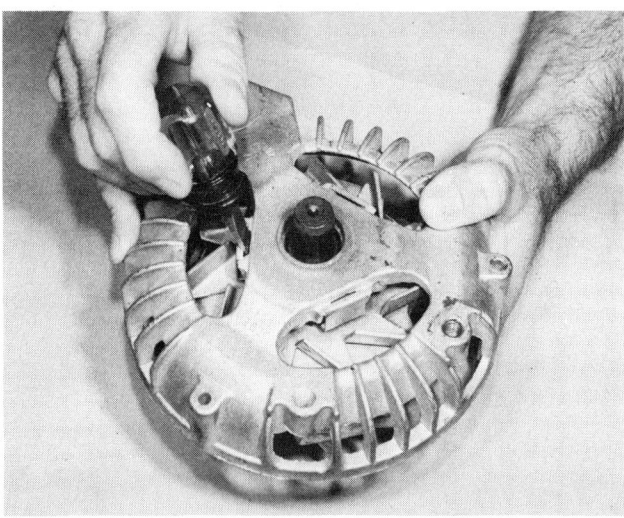

19. After removing pulley, disengage three bearing retainer clips from end frame by prying with screwdriver blade. Tap rotor shaft gently to separate rotor from end frame.

20. If you do not have a press, use a large socket to support end frame and a bearing removal tool (or appropriate size socket and punch) to remove end frame bearing.

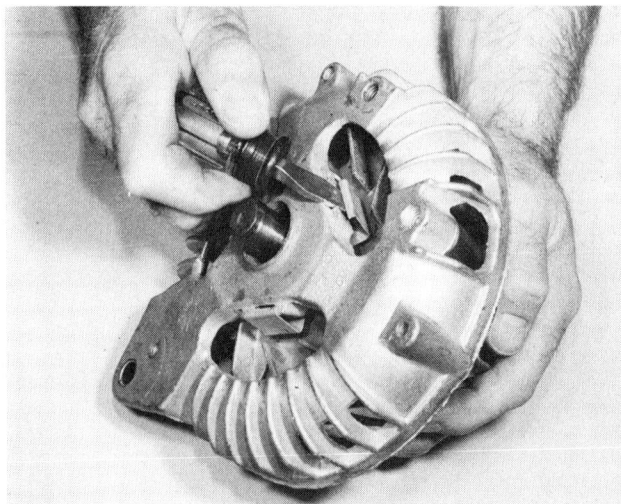

21. Install new bearing in end frame with press or socket. To replace bearing on rotor shaft drive end, use same puller as in Step 18 and press on new bearing. Install rotor and clips.

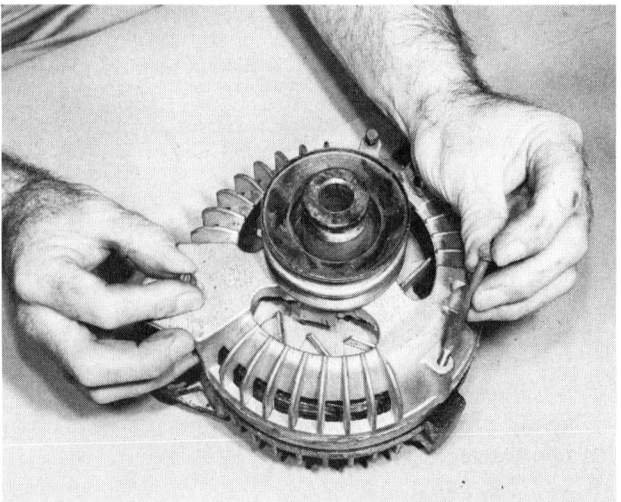

22. Press pulley onto rotor shaft, then align both end frames according to chalk mark and install through-bolts. Draw end frames together and torque bolts to 40-60 ft.-lbs.

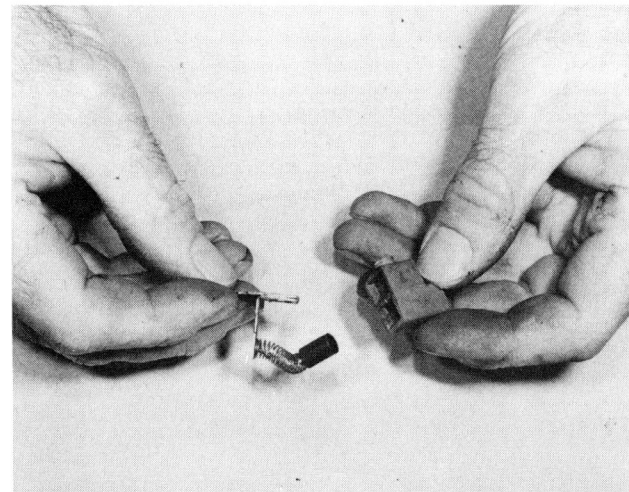

23. Remove field brushes from insulated holders and inspect for wear. It's a good idea to install new brushes whenever alternator is overhauled. Fit brushes back into holders.

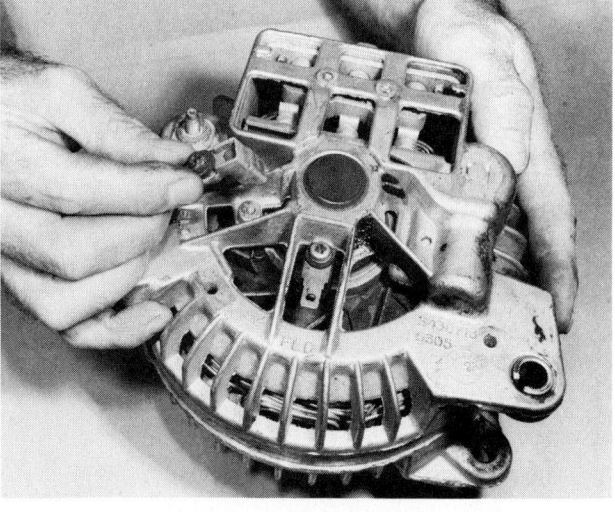

24. Replace vertical/horizontal field brushes in their proper location in rear end frame. Be sure to install insulating washer on each brush terminal before replacing washers/screws.

INDEX

CONVENTIONAL IGNITION SYSTEMS

IGNITION SYSTEM DESCRIPTION

The automotive ignition system has two basic functions: 1) It steps up the relatively low battery voltage sufficiently to overcome the resistance offered by the spark plug gap and to fire the plug; 2) it delivers the spark and controls the timing of the firing to suit varying engine speeds and load requirements.

Automotive ignition systems have two electrical circuits—the primary (low voltage) and secondary (high voltage). See **Fig. 3-1.** The primary circuit operates on battery current controlled by the ignition switch and the breaker points. The secondary circuit carries high voltage induced in the coil, and consists of a high-tension cable between the distributor and coil, the distributor rotor and cap, the spark plug cables and the spark plugs.

When the ignition switch is turned on, current flows from the battery through the ignition switch to the coil primary windings, then to the distributor points which are connected to ground. Whenever the distributor points are closed, there is a continuous flow of current from the battery, through the ignition switch, through the coil primary and through the points. This current flow through the coil primary creates a magnetic field which remains as long as current flows and the points stay closed.

As the engine rotates, the distributor cam pushes the points apart. This breaks the primary circuit and stops the flow of current. When the current flow stops, the magnetic field in the coil collapses and, as this happens, induction pulls the current from the primary to the secondary windings. Since there are many more turns of wire in the secondary windings, the voltage from the primary is multiplied many times—to as much as 25,000 or 30,000 volts.

The secondary windings are connected to the spark plugs. This high voltage is necessary to jump the spark plug gap, which in turn fires the air/fuel mixture and makes the engine run. The distributor cam is timed to the engine so that it will open the points at exactly the right moment when the combustion chamber is full with a fresh charge of air/fuel mixture.

THE COIL

An automotive coil is simply an induction transformer which takes the 12 volts available from the battery and steps it up sufficiently to a voltage high enough to jump the preset gap at the spark plug **(Fig. 3-2).** Every modern coil has three terminals—two small, threaded posts for the primary wire and a large center tower which is the connection for the secondary.

Inside the coil is an iron core, with the primary and secondary windings around it. The ratio of turns between the primary and secondary windings determines how great the step-up in voltage will be. Because the step-up is from comparatively low battery voltage (12 volts) to very high spark plug voltage (25-30 KV), the primary has relatively few turns and the secondary has many.

Current flow in the secondary is created in the coil and flows out along the secondary lead to the distribu-

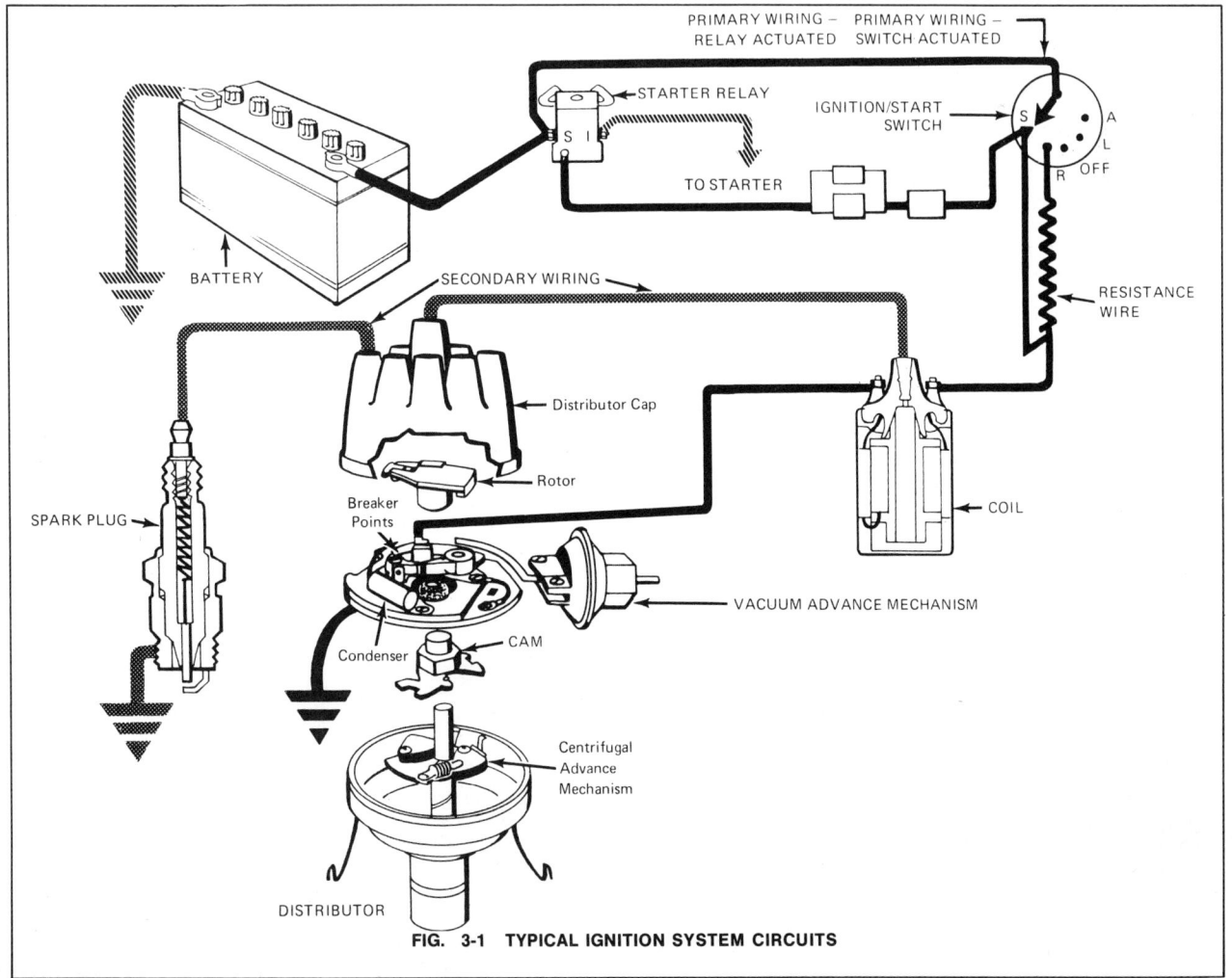

FIG. 3-1 TYPICAL IGNITION SYSTEM CIRCUITS

tor and then to the spark plugs. Primary wiring connections to the coil must observe proper polarity. These connections are marked either positive (+) and negative (-), or BAT (battery) and DIST (distributor). Replacement coils must match the rating and polarity of the system. Reversing polarity or installing the improper voltage-rated coil will result in poor voltage output to the spark plugs and lead to plug misfiring.

THE CONDENSER

A condenser is attached across the breaker points of the distributor. The condenser may be installed inside the distributor housing or mounted externally; in either case, it has only one lead wire. The outer case or mounting bracket is ground. The wire lead is connected to the coil primary, usually at the same place as the wire from the coil to the distributor points. A very important part of the point switching system, the condenser is in the circuit to speed up collapse of the magnetic field within the coil and acts as a small storage tank whose capacity is balanced to the circuit.

Condensers may develop internal leaks which disturb this balance. The effects of unbalance appear in the form of metal transfer on the breaker points. Even a new condenser in perfect condition will cause this metal transfer if it is not of the proper capacity rating. Condensers are rated in microfarads (mfds.), which can be measured using a condenser tester. Capacity usually runs from 0.21 to 0.25 mfds.

THE BREAKER POINTS

As pointed out earlier, the breaker points installed in the distributor are basically a switching device operated by the distributor cam as it revolves. As long as they are closed, the coil remains magnetized, with current flowing through it and through the points to ground.

When the points open, the primary current is suddenly switched off and the magnetic field collapses, causing high voltage current to be induced in the secondary windings.

Proper breaker-point operation is interdependent upon the condenser. An examination of the points will indicate whether or not the condenser capacity is correct by applying the "minus-minus-minus" rule: *If the minus (negative) point is minus metal (pitted), the condenser is minus capacity.* This condition is corrected by increasing the condenser capacity. If the pit is on the positive point, then the condenser has too much capacity and should be replaced with one having less capacity. Allowable contact-point metal transfer is 0.020-in. **(Fig. 3-3).**

While it's easier to install a new condenser than to test the old one, many apparent cases of low-capacity condenser damage result from poor ground contact between the condenser case and the distributor. A new condenser will not help, unless the mounting area is kept clean and bright to provide a satisfactory contact.

Delco introduced a one-piece breaker-point/condenser unit for service on some 1972 General Motors cars. Mounted on the points, the condenser is connected to the insulated point arm by two thin ribbons of metal, which flex each time the points open and close. With no wire lead connecting the points and condenser, radio interference is greatly reduced and the metal suppression shield used over the points is not necessary. This Uni-Set was used only a short time—governmental objections to the cost of the replacement points/condenser unit caused its removal from the market, but it was later approved and reintroduced in 1974. Separate points and condenser can be mounted in the Uni-Set distributor, but since there was no mounting hole for the separate condenser in 1972 distributors, a GM conversion kit was required.

SECONDARY WIRING

Secondary or high-voltage wiring differs considerably in construction from the primary wiring used to carry current from the battery to the coil.

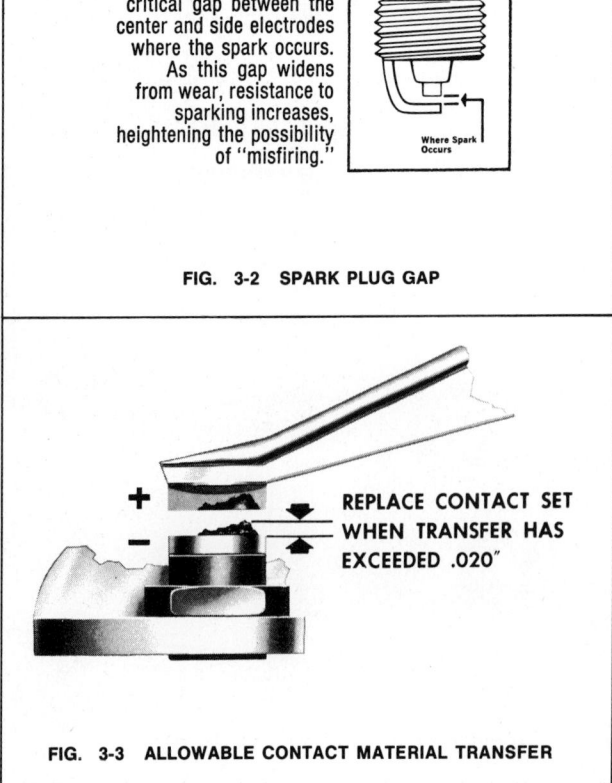

Firing-end showing the critical gap between the center and side electrodes where the spark occurs. As this gap widens from wear, resistance to sparking increases, heightening the possibility of "misfiring."

Where Spark Occurs

FIG. 3-2 SPARK PLUG GAP

REPLACE CONTACT SET WHEN TRANSFER HAS EXCEEDED .020"

FIG. 3-3 ALLOWABLE CONTACT MATERIAL TRANSFER

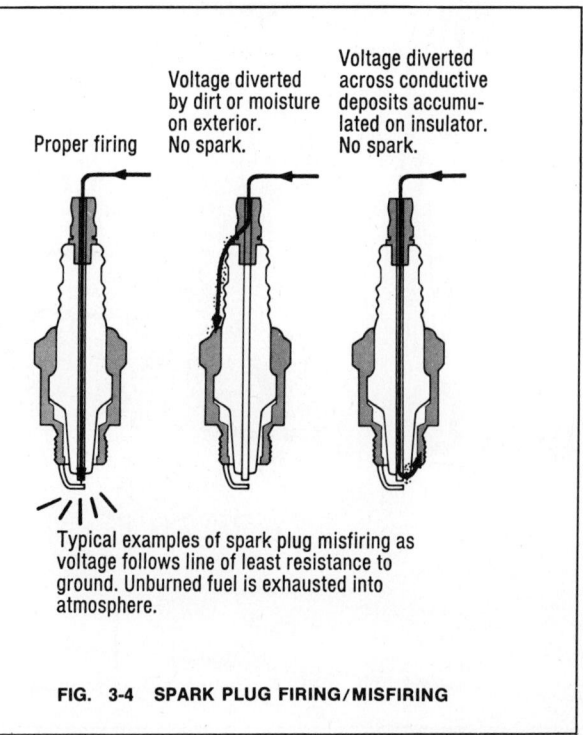

Proper firing

Voltage diverted by dirt or moisture on exterior. No spark.

Voltage diverted across conductive deposits accumulated on insulator. No spark.

Typical examples of spark plug misfiring as voltage follows line of least resistance to ground. Unburned fuel is exhausted into atmosphere.

FIG. 3-4 SPARK PLUG FIRING/MISFIRING

Unlike primary wiring, the cable used in the secondary circuit must be heavily insulated to contain the high voltage it carries. Most cables are sheathed with Hypalon insulation. This has good resistance to oil contamination and is better able to withstand the higher, underhood temperatures in the engine compartment than the neoprene insulation used in the past. A silicone rubber insulation, which will operate at temperatures up to 450°F, is used on cables designed for maximum heat resistance, and is found with increasing frequency on V-8 engines from 1975 on.

THE BALLAST RESISTOR

This is a means of controlling the spark and lengthening the life of the coil by reducing current flow when it is not actually necessary. Ballast resistors may be built into the coil, mounted on the firewall or built into the primary wiring itself, between the ignition switch and the coil. Removing the resistor permits greater voltage to the plugs, but it also results in rapid burning of the breaker points.

SPARK PLUGS

The spark plugs have one main function—to fire properly under all normal, engine operating conditions. Sharp edges on the plug electrodes tend to concentrate ionization and lower the voltage requirement, but at the same time, spark plug electrodes begin to erode away with use, rounding the electrodes and widening the gap at the average rate of 0.001-in. every 1000-2000 miles. Both changes increase the plug's voltage requirement, and when the voltage required to produce a spark finally exceeds the output of the ignition system, the plug will no longer fire. Voltage also tends to follow the path of least resistance to ground,

and if it is diverted for any reason, the plug does not fire and the unburned fuel in that cylinder is exhausted into the air **(Fig. 3-4)**.

Spark plugs differ in reach, heat range and gap style.

1. Reach—This refers to the length of the threaded part of the plug shell. Always check the reach of the new plugs against that of the old ones removed. Installing a plug with a ¾-in. reach in an engine designed for use with ⅜-in. reach spark plugs can bend the valves or knock holes in the pistons. Installing a short reach plug in a deep hole will not cause mechanical damage, but it will mean a definite power loss and very quick fouling or burning of the spark plugs.

2. Heat range—Control of heat dissipation requires that engineers design a specific plug to best suit the operating characteristics of a given engine. Lengthening the insulator creates a longer and slower escape path for the heat, or a "hotter" plug; shortening the insulator creates a faster escape path, or a "colder" plug **(Fig. 3-5)**. Each spark plug thus has a rated "heat range."

GAP BRIDGED
IDENTIFIED BY DEPOSIT BUILD-UP CLOSING GAP BETWEEN ELECTRODES. CAUSED BY OIL OR CARBON FOULING. IF DEPOSITS ARE NOT EXCESSIVE, THE PLUG CAN BE CLEANED.

OIL FOULED
IDENTIFIED BY WET BLACK DEPOSITS ON THE INSULATOR SHELL BORE ELECTRODES CAUSED BY EXCESSIVE OIL ENTERING COMBUSTION CHAMBER THROUGH WORN RINGS AND PISTONS, EXCESSIVE CLEARANCE BETWEEN VALVE GUIDES AND STEMS, OR WORN OR LOOSE BEARINGS. CAN BE CLEANED IF ENGINE IS NOT REPAIRED, USE A HOTTER PLUG.

CARBON FOULED
IDENTIFIED BY BLACK, DRY FLUFFY CARBON DEPOSITS ON INSULATOR TIPS, EXPOSED SHELL SURFACES AND ELECTRODES. CAUSED BY TOO COLD A PLUG, WEAK IGNITION, DIRTY AIR CLEANER, DEFECTIVE FUEL PUMP, TOO RICH A FUEL MIXTURE, IMPROPERLY OPERATING HEAT RISER OR EXCESSIVE IDLING. CAN BE CLEANED.

WORN
IDENTIFIED BY SEVERELY ERODED OR WORN ELECTRODES. CAUSED BY NORMAL WEAR. SHOULD BE REPLACED

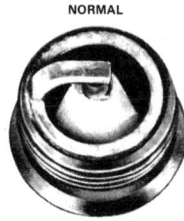
NORMAL
IDENTIFIED BY LIGHT TAN OR GRAY DEPOSITS ON THE FIRING TIP. CAN BE CLEANED.

LEAD FOULED
IDENTIFIED BY DARK GRAY, BLACK, YELLOW OR TAN DEPOSITS OR A FUSED GLAZED COATING ON THE INSULATOR TIP. CAUSED BY HIGHLY LEADED GASOLINE. CAN BE CLEANED.

PRE-IGNITION
IDENTIFIED BY MELTED ELECTRODES AND POSSIBLY BLISTERED INSULATOR. METALLIC DEPOSITS ON INSULATOR INDICATE ENGINE DAMAGE. CAUSED BY WRONG TYPE OF FUEL, INCORRECT IGNITION TIMING OR ADVANCE, TOO HOT A PLUG, BURNT VALVES OR ENGINE OVERHEATING. REPLACE THE PLUG.

OVERHEATING
IDENTIFIED BY A WHITE OR LIGHT GRAY INSULATOR WITH SMALL BLACK OR GRAY BROWN SPOTS AND WITH BLUISH-BURNT APPEARANCE OF ELECTRODES, CAUSED BY ENGINE OVERHEATING. WRONG TYPE OF FUEL, LOOSE SPARK PLUGS, TOO HOT A PLUG, LOW FUEL PUMP PRESSURE OR INCORRECT IGNITION TIMING. REPLACE THE PLUG.

FUSED SPOT DEPOSIT
IDENTIFIED BY MELTED OR SPOTTY DEPOSITS RESEMBLING BUBBLES OR BLISTERS. CAUSED BY SUDDEN ACCELERATION. CAN BE CLEANED.

FIG. 3-6 SPARK PLUG INSPECTION

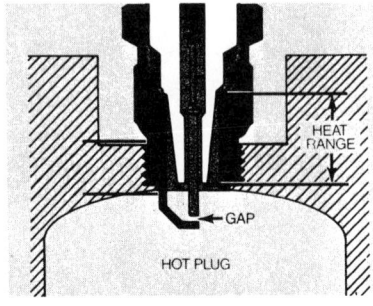

(TOP)
Heat flows slowly when much of the insulator is exposed. This means a longer heat path from tip to shell.

HEAT RANGE
GAP
HOT PLUG

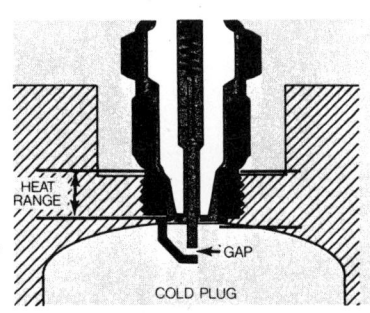

(BOTTOM)
Heat flows faster when less of the insulator is exposed. This means a shorter heat path from tip to shell.

HEAT RANGE
GAP
COLD PLUG

FIG. 3-5 SPARK PLUG HEAT RANGE

3. Gap Style—There are two popular types used in cars: standard gap and projected nose. The standard gap is the traditional plug design, with its ceramic insulator nose wholly contained within the plug shell. The projected nose insulator extends beyond the end of the threaded portion of the plug shell. Both standard-gap and projected-nose spark plugs may be listed as alternatives in a spark plug manufacturer's chart. Where possible, the projected nose type should be used, because it gives better fouling resistance and increases power in most engines. In some cases, however, it may be necessary to retard the spark a few degrees to eliminate excessive "pinging." Projected nose plugs should not be used in engines for which they are not specifically recommended, because there is a chance the valves or piston crown may strike the plug nose, with resulting damage.

Resistor plugs of 5000 ohms are standard equipment on General Motors cars, which also use resistor wires. Before resistor wires and plugs were used together, the resistance value of the plugs was 10,000 ohms. Champion manufactures both values: the 10,000-ohm plug with an R prefix, and the 5000-ohm plug with an X prefix.

SPARK PLUG TESTING, CLEANING AND REUSE

The air-pressure "plug tester" used in many garages is simply a way to keep customers who ask for a plug test happy. There is no way to test spark plugs outside an engine. Plug testers do not test plugs, because the plugs are at room temperature. Spark plugs normally function in the engine combustion chamber at a temperature of several thousand degrees. A visual inspection of spark plugs **(Fig. 3-6 and Page 3-27)** will reveal far more than any tester. The inner porcelain should be clean, and the center electrode should be square and sharp, with the proper gap setting.

Used plugs, which have been operating at the proper heat range and whose electrodes are not badly eroded or burned, can be filed and regapped after cleaning, and will give added satisfactory mileage with conventional ignition systems. The spark will jump from a sharp edge on the center electrode far more easily than from a rounded, worn electrode. With the spark plug shell secured in a vise, bend the ground electrode out of the way and file the center electrode flat and sharp with a small file. Blow out all the filings and set the gap with a round wire gauge. Do not use a flat feeler gauge, because it *will not* give you a correct indication of the true gap **(Fig. 3-7)**.

Whenever plugs are installed, certain precautions should be observed. Make certain the cylinder-head plug holes are cleaned and free from dirt and/or carbon particles, both at the gasket seat and inside the threads. Plug threads should also be clean, undamaged and lubricated. Plugs should be screwed in finger-tight against the gasket, then tightened an additional quarter turn with a plug wrench. The quarter turn recommendation is sufficient for plugs which use gaskets, but for tapered plugs (those without gaskets), a one-sixteenth turn is the recommended limit—no more **(Fig. 3-8)**.

THE DISTRIBUTOR

The distributor **(Fig. 3-9)** is an electro-mechanical

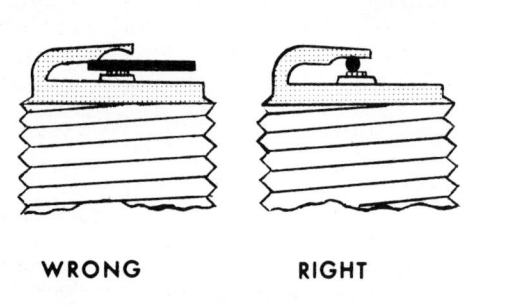

WRONG   RIGHT

FIG. 3-7 MEASURING PLUG GAP

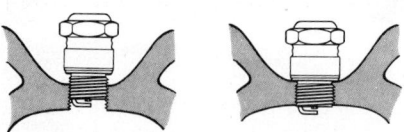

Spark plugs with gaskets should be tightened about ¼-turn past finger-tight to effect a gas-tight seal. Champion's attached gaskets do not fall off during installation and can be reused if the plug is reinstalled.

Spark plugs without gaskets (taper-seat design) should be tightened only firmly enough to assure a gas-tight seal, about 1/16 turn past finger-tight. No more!

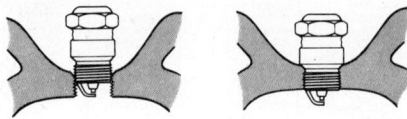

FIG. 3-8 PLUG TIGHTENING RECOMMENDATIONS

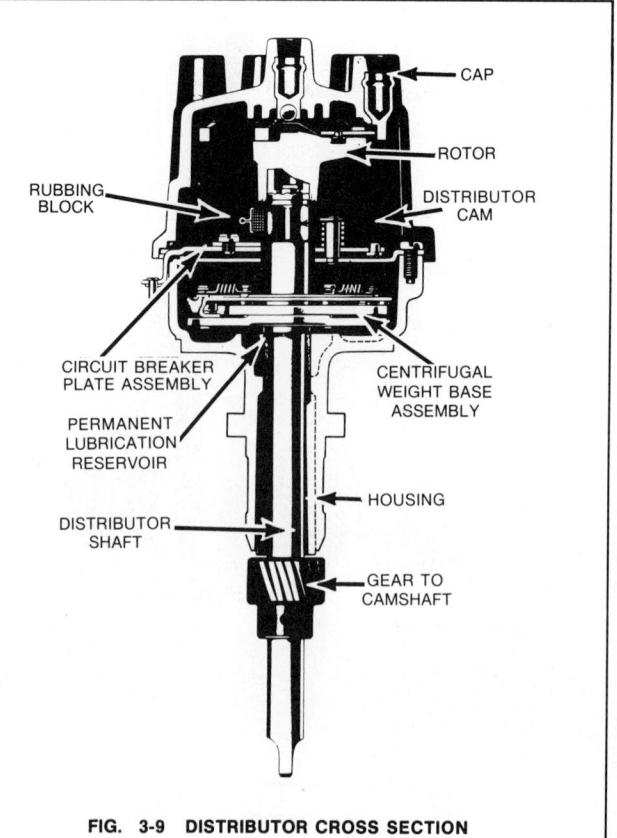

FIG. 3-9 DISTRIBUTOR CROSS SECTION

switching device whose function is: 1) to switch the current supplying the coil's primary windings on and off and 2) to distribute the high-voltage secondary output of the coil to the individual spark plugs according to the firing order of the engine. The distributor is driven off the camshaft by a pair of helical spiral gears—one on the distributor shaft and one on the camshaft. The ratio of these gears is 1:1, so that the distributor shaft, like the camshaft, turns at one-half engine crankshaft speed.

Since the gearing of the distributor shaft is in time with the engine, the distributor must be replaced correctly whenever it is removed from the engine. The switching of the primary circuit is accomplished by the breaker points. These are operated by a multi-lobed cam on the distributor shaft. The distributor cam has an equal number of lobes and flat spots corresponding with the number of cylinders in the engine. The points have a nylon or phenolic block attached to them, which rides against the cam. As each lobe of the cam passes under and makes contact with this rubbing block, the points are opened. The lobe is followed immediately by a flat spot on the cam, which permits the points to close by not contacting the rubbing block. During this time, the points are kept closed by a

spring, whose tension is very important to proper ignition operation. A weak spring will allow the points to "bounce" at high rpm and cause the timing to become erratic. A spring with too much tension will cause rapid wear of the rubbing block and thus decrease the point gap with operation, bringing about a marked fall-off in engine performance as well as a rough idle and hard starting.

Ignition breaker points are made of very hard tungsten alloys, but are still subject to wear and spark erosion, so they require periodic replacement. Because they control both low-voltage saturation of the coil when closed and the release of high voltage when open, they should mate as perfectly as possible for total contact **(Fig. 3-10)**.

The time the points remain closed is called dwell or cam angle **(Fig. 3-11)** and is measured in degrees. Dwell will vary according to the point gap, or distance between the points when opened. Wide point gaps open slowly, cause excessive arcing and burning, and result in a too-short dwell. This causes insufficient coil saturation and a missed spark. If the gap is too close, the points are snapped open and have a tendency to bounce. A close gap gives more dwell, but the points do not separate sufficiently to produce a clean collapse of the primary, and the result is a misfire.

The distributors used on some cars are equipped with two sets of breaker points (dual points) connected to allow the primary current to flow when either set is closed. The points are staggered so that one set opens before the other, with the spark taking place when the second set opens. Due to their staggered position, the first set closes before the second set, increasing the dwell for greater spark intensity at high rpm.

The timing of the spark to the stroke of the pistons must be varied relative to engine speed and load demands. Timing is adjusted automatically by the distributor's internal spark advance system. Most distributors employ two forms of spark advance—1) a centrifugal mechanism which advances or retards the distributor cam relative to the distributor drive shaft and 2) a vacuum diaphragm which advances or retards the position of the breaker points relative to the distributor cam.

The centrifugal advance mechanism consists of two weights anchored by springs and the cam assembly. As engine speed increases, the weights swing outward against spring tension, turning the cam assembly to advance the breaker cam relative to the distributor drive shaft. The higher the engine speed, the more the weights move out and the farther the breaker plate is advanced. As engine speed decreases, the spring tension pulls the weights back toward the cam assembly, moving the breaker cam back in the direction of its original position **(Fig. 3-12)**.

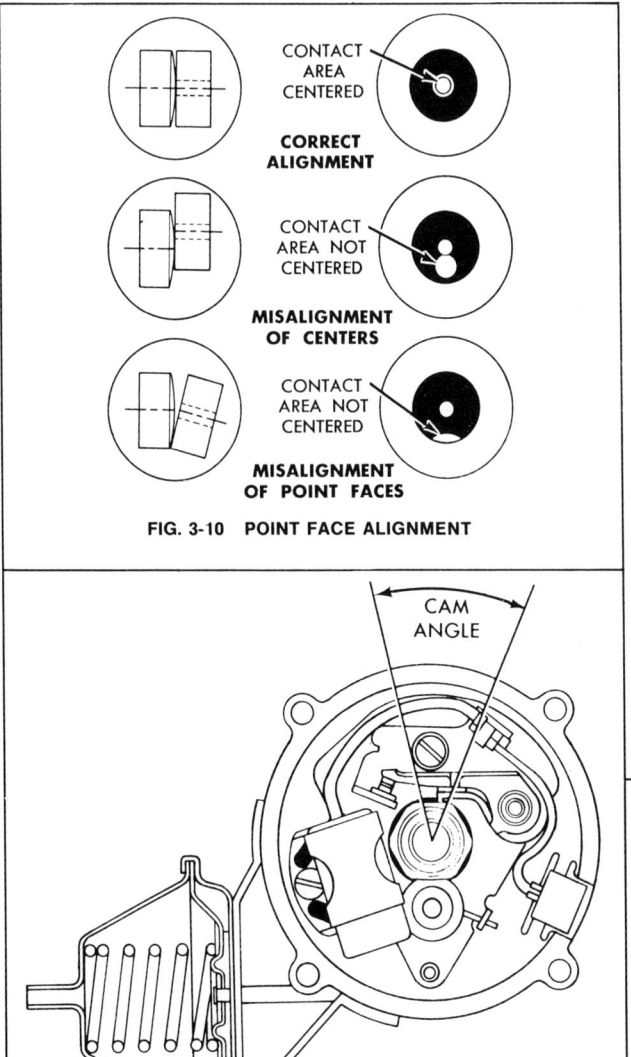

CONTACT AREA CENTERED

CORRECT ALIGNMENT

CONTACT AREA NOT CENTERED

MISALIGNMENT OF CENTERS

CONTACT AREA NOT CENTERED

MISALIGNMENT OF POINT FACES

FIG. 3-10   POINT FACE ALIGNMENT

CAM ANGLE

FIG. 3-11   CAM ANGLE

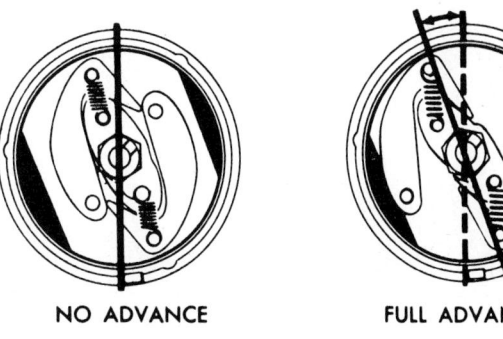

NO ADVANCE   FULL ADVANCE

FIG. 3-12   CENTRIFUGAL ADVANCE OPERATION

A high vacuum develops in the intake manifold under part-throttle operation, so less air and gas enter the cylinder. Under such conditions, additional advance above that provided by the centrifugal mechanism will produce better fuel economy. This extra advance is provided by a spring-loaded diaphragm connected by linkage to the distributor breaker plate **(Fig. 3-13)**. During part-throttle operation, the vacuum diaphragm movement is transmitted by the linkage to the breaker plate, which rotates to carry the breaker points around the breaker cam to an advance point. Vacuum advance is really a device for increasing fuel economy when properly used; driving at wide-open throttle in any gear will not produce this additional advance.

Some distributors are equipped with dual-chamber vacuum advance units to reduce exhaust emissions at low rpm. These are identified by the twin vacuum lines leading to the diaphragm chamber on the distributor. Chrysler has also used an electric solenoid to retard the spark at idle and/or during certain types of low-speed driving. This unit can be identified by the small plastic ''box'' and solenoid lead located on the side of the distributor **(Fig. 3-14)**.

Attempting to adjust either advance mechanism without the use of a distributor tester can result in permanent damage to the engine from an incorrect spark-advance curve. Advance curves are specified by the manufacturer for both distributor advance functions, according to their engine application, and are provided at the end of this chapter for use by those with test-bench facilities for checking and adjusting distributor advance to manufacturer's specifications.

IGNITION SYSTEM TESTING

Ignition system problems are caused by a failure in either the primary or secondary circuit, incorrect ignition timing or incorrect distributor advance. When the trouble can be traced to a circuit failure, look for:
1. Shorts.
2. Corroded or dirty terminals.
3. Loose connections.
4. Defective wiring insulation.
5. A cracked distributor cap or rotor.
6. Fouled spark plugs.
7. Defective distributor breaker points.
8. Incorrect dwell or cam angle.

When difficulty in starting or operating an engine is caused by the ignition system, you can determine whether the problem is in the primary or secondary circuits with the following test procedure.

SPARK INTENSITY TEST

1. Connect a remote start switch into the starting circuit.
2. Disconnect the coil high-tension lead from the distributor cap.
3. Turn the ignition switch on.
4. Hold the high tension lead about 3/16-in. from the cylinder head or other good ground, and crank the engine.
5. If the spark is good, the problem is in the secondary circuit.
6. If there is only a weak spark, or none at all, the problem is in the primary circuit, the coil-to-distributor high-tension lead or the coil.

PRIMARY CIRCUIT TEST

To isolate a primary circuit problem, use a voltmeter and perform the following three test procedures:

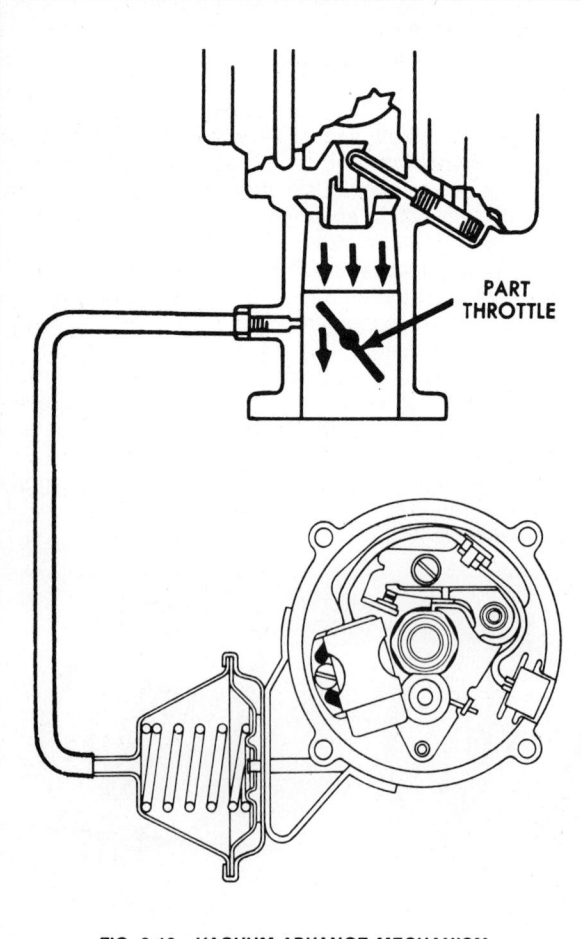

FIG. 3-13   VACUUM ADVANCE MECHANISM

PART THROTTLE

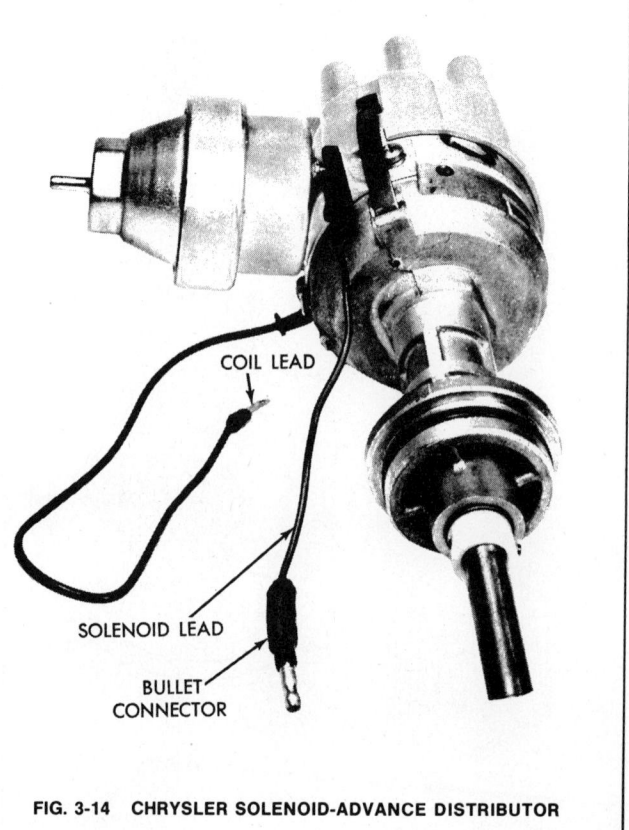

COIL LEAD

SOLENOID LEAD

BULLET CONNECTOR

FIG. 3-14   CHRYSLER SOLENOID-ADVANCE DISTRIBUTOR

BATTERY TO COIL TEST

1. Connect a voltmeter as shown in **Fig. 3-15.**

2. Connect a jumper lead from the coil DIST terminal to a good ground.

3. Turn off all lights and accessories, and turn the ignition switch on.

4. Voltmeter should read between 4.5 and 6.9 volts if the battery-to-coil circuit is good.

5. If the voltmeter reads *more* than 6.9 volts, check:
  a) The battery and cables for loose connections or corrosion.
  b) The primary wiring for loose/corroded terminals, broken strands or worn/damaged insulation.

6. If voltmeter reads *less* than 4.5 volts, replace the ignition resistance wire.

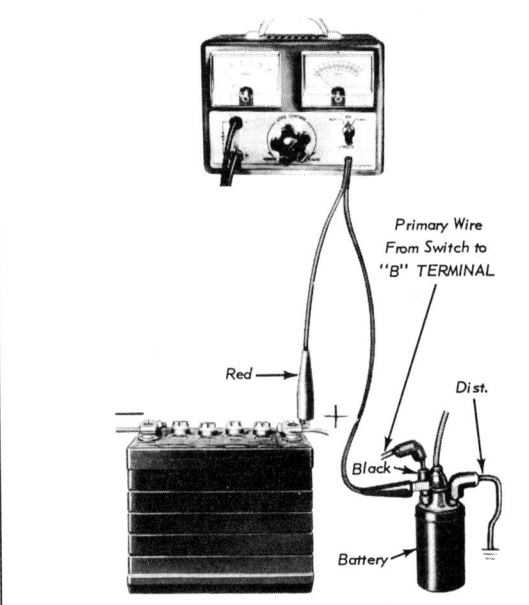

FIG. 3-15 PRIMARY CIRCUIT TEST

Primary Wire From Switch to "B" TERMINAL

Red

Dist.

Black

Battery

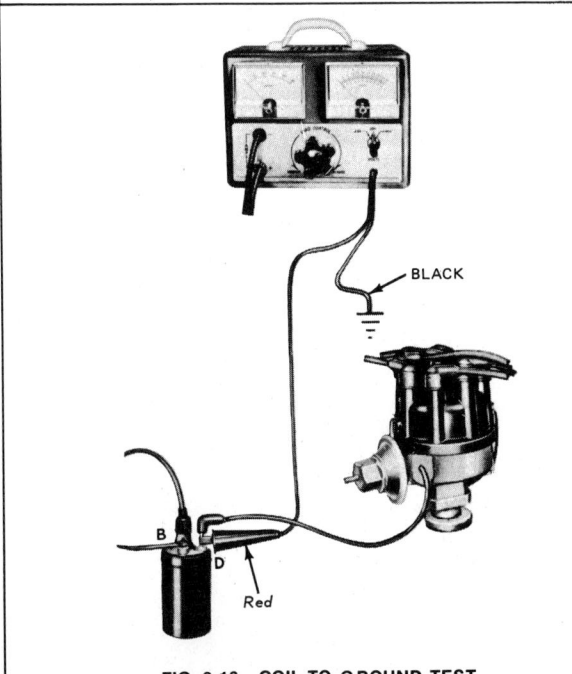

FIG. 3-16 COIL-TO-GROUND TEST

BLACK

B

D

Red

STARTING IGNITION CIRCUIT TEST

1. Connect a voltmeter as shown in **Fig. 3-15.**

2. Disconnect and ground the coil-to-distributor high-tension lead at the distributor.

3. Crank the engine with the ignition switch off and read the voltage drop.

4. If voltage drop is 0.4-volt or *less,* the starting ignition circuit is good.

5. If voltage drop is *greater* than 0.4-volt, clean and tighten all terminals in the circuit, or replace the wiring if necessary.

COIL TO GROUND TEST

1. Connect a voltmeter as shown in **Fig. 3-16.**

2. Rotate the distributor shaft to close the points.

3. Turn off all lights and accessories, and turn the ignition switch on.

4. Voltmeter should read 0.20- to 0.25-volt or *less* if the primary circuit from coil to ground is good; if voltmeter reading *exceeds* 0.20- to 0.25-volt, check the voltage drop between each of the following:
  a) Coil and breaker-plate connection of the coil-to-distributor primary wire, as shown in **Fig. 3-17.**
  b) Breaker plate and movable breaker point, as shown in **Fig. 3-18.**
  c) Breaker plate to distributor housing, as shown in **Fig. 3-19.**
  d) Distributor housing and engine ground, as shown in **Fig. 3-20.**

One of these four checks should turn up the source of excessive resistance.

IGNITION SYSTEM DIAGNOSIS

CONDITION	CORRECTION
BURNED OR PITTED BREAKER POINTS	
(a) Dirt or oil on point surfaces.	(a) Determine cause and correct condition. Clean distributor cam and apply a light coat of cam lubricant to cam lobes. Replace breaker-point set and adjust as necessary.
(b) Alternator voltage regulator setting too high.	(b) Test voltage regulator and replace if necessary. Replace breaker points and adjust as necessary.
(c) Points misaligned or gap too small.	(c) Align and adjust breaker points.
(d) Faulty coil.	(d) Test and replace coil if necessary. Replace and adjust breaker points.
(e) Ballast resistor not in circuit.	(e) Check wiring and connections in system; correct as required.
(f) Wrong condenser or faulty condenser.	(f) Test condenser and replace if required. Replace and adjust breaker points.
(g) Faulty ignition switch.	(g) Replace.
(h) Bushings worn.	(h) Replace distributor housing if serviced as a unit; replace bushing if not.
IGNITION COIL FAILURE	
(a) Coil damaged by excessive engine heat.	(a) Replace coil and inspect breaker-point condition, replace and adjust if necessary.
(b) Coil tower carbon-tracked.	(b) Replace coil.
(c) Oil leak at tower (oil-filled coils).	(c) Replace coil.

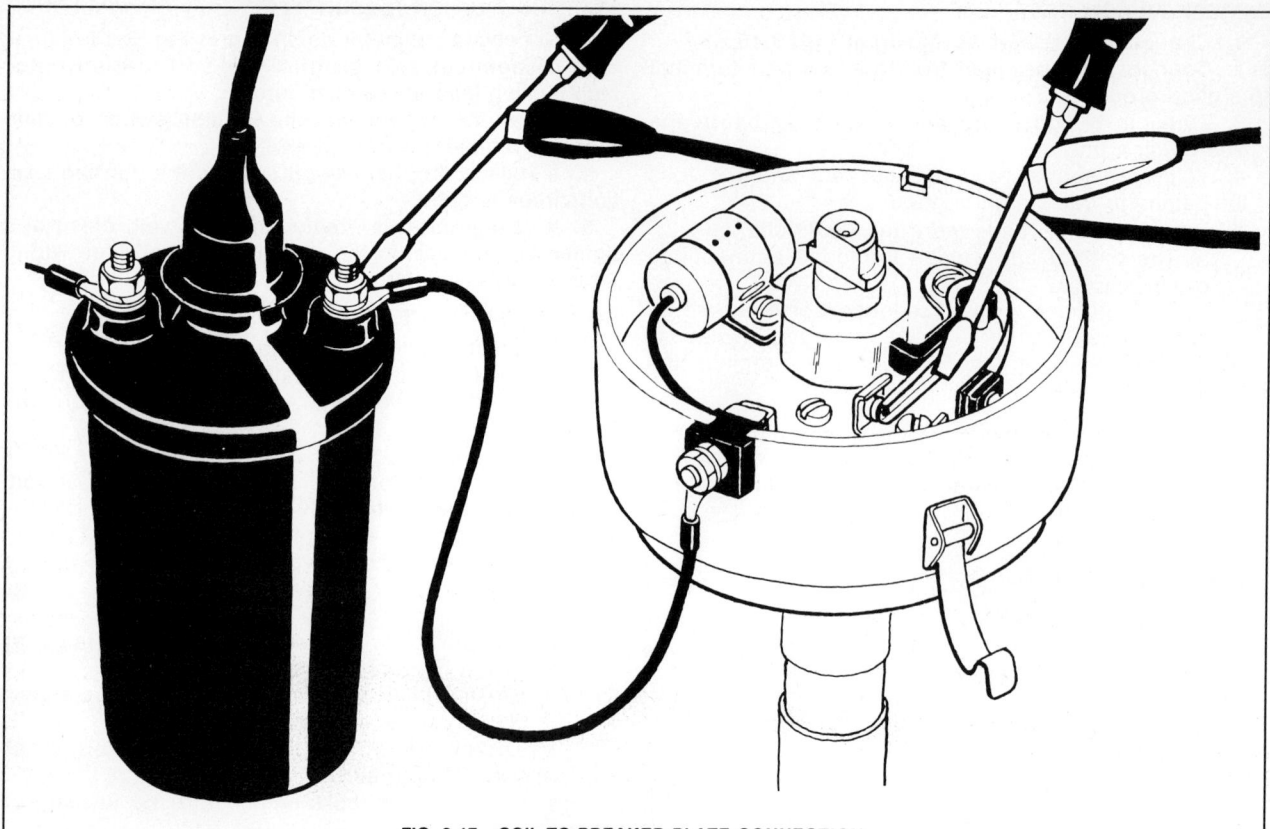

FIG. 3-17 COIL-TO-BREAKER-PLATE CONNECTION

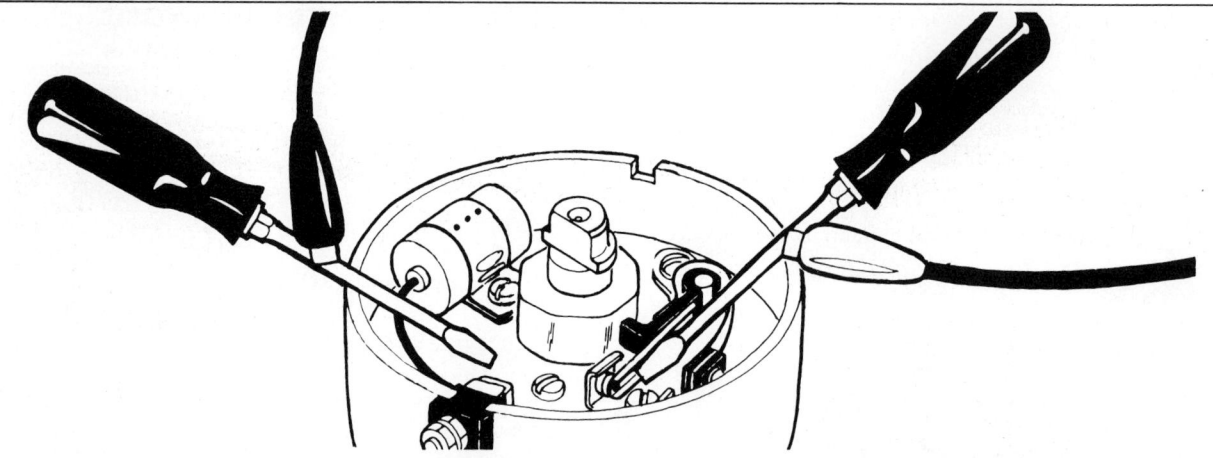

FIG. 3-18 BREAKER-PLATE-TO-BREAKER-POINT CONNECTION

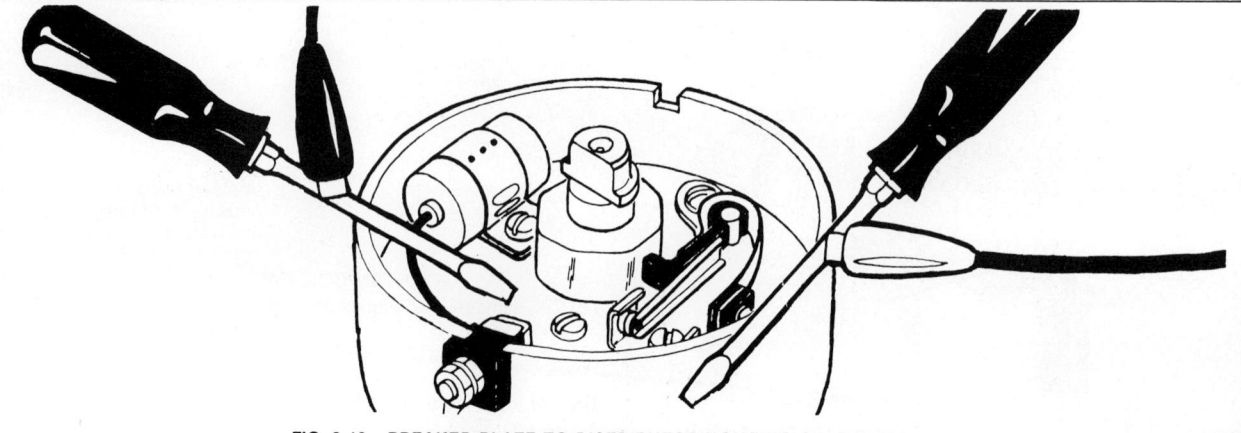

FIG. 3-19 BREAKER-PLATE-TO-DISTRIBUTOR-HOUSING CONNECTION

SECONDARY CIRCUIT TEST

Isolate the secondary circuit problems as follows:

1. Disconnect one spark plug wire—check individual wires for spark intensity one at a time.

2. Install a terminal adapter in the terminal of the disconnected wire.

3. Hold the adapter about 3/16-in. from the manifold, and crank the engine.

4. If the spark jumps the gap with equal and sufficient intensity at all wires, the coil, condenser, rotor, distributor cap and secondary wiring can be considered good.

5. If the spark is not good at some wires, test their resistance values according to the chart following this section.

6. If the spark is equal at all wires, but weak or intermittent, inspect the coil, distributor cap and coil-to-distributor high-tension wire. The wire should be clean, fit snugly and bottom in the tower sockets.

RESISTANCE WIRE TEST

1. Grasp the spark-plug-wire terminal as close as possible to the plug, rotate and remove with a straight, steady pull. *Do not use pliers—do not pull the cable at an angle.*

2. Install the proper adapter between the cable and spark plug.

3. Remove the distributor cap from the distributor with all cables *in place.*

4. Connect an ohmmeter from the plug adapter to the corresponding electrode inside the distributor cap. Compare the ohmmeter reading with the values shown in the following chart.

IGNITION COIL TEST (Fig. 3-21)

A weak ignition coil will affect engine performance when ignition reserve is at a minimum. This can be during starting, low-speed acceleration or at top-speed operation, but the engine will eventually fail to start. Many other ignition system problems will produce the same symptoms as a weak coil; check for the following before replacing the coil:

1. High-resistance connections in either the primary or secondary circuits.

2. Excessive spark plug gaps.

3. High tension leakage through moisture on an unprotected coil terminal.

4. A combination of high engine compression and lean carburetion requiring a substantial voltage increase.

If the coil is still suspect after examining the above areas, it should be tested before being replaced.

COIL OPEN/GROUND CIRCUIT TEST

1. Touch the test leads of a 110-volt test lamp to both primary terminals of the coil. If the lamp does not light, the primary circuit is open.

2. Touch one test lead to the high tension terminal and the other to one of the primary terminals. The lamp should not light, but tiny sparks may appear when the test leads are applied to the terminals. If no sparks are seen, the secondary circuit is open.

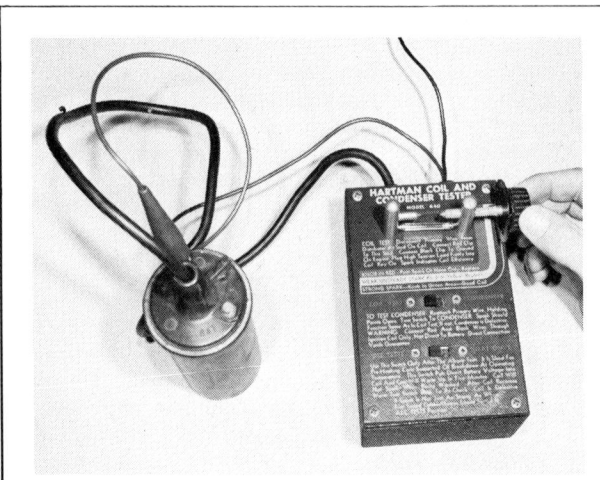

FIG. 3-21   IGNITION COIL SPARK-GAP TEST

MAXIMUM SECONDARY IGNITION WIRE RESISTANCE VALUES (1970-74 Conventional Ignitions)		
	Spark Plug Cables (ohms per foot)	Coil-to-Distributor Cable (ohms)
American Motors	3000-7000	7500-12,500
Chrysler Corp.	15,000*	15,000
General Motors	3000-7000	7500-12,500
Ford, Lincoln, Mercury	12,000	1000 ohms per inch or less

* Must not exceed 30,000 ohms for wires longer than 25 ins.; or 50,000 ohms for wires 25 ins. or shorter.

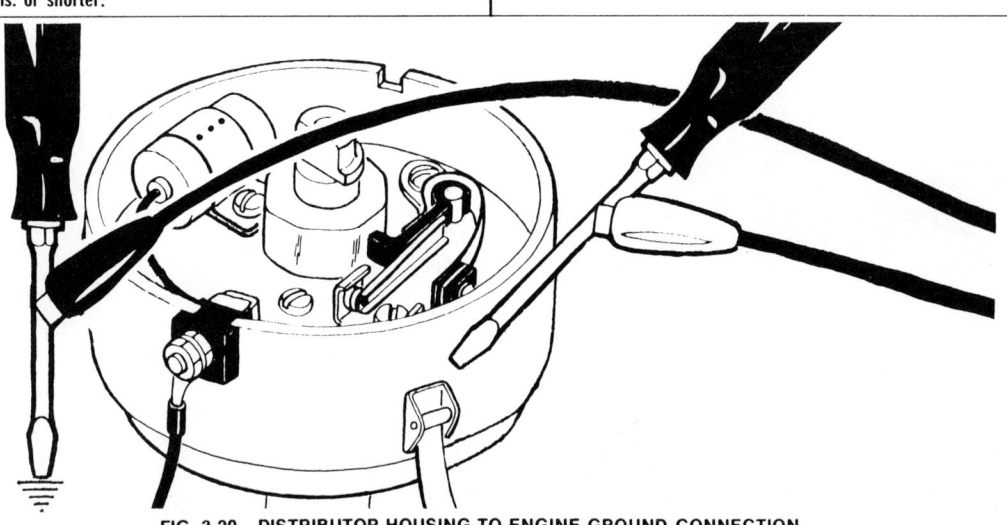

FIG. 3-20   DISTRIBUTOR-HOUSING-TO-ENGINE-GROUND CONNECTION

3. Touch one test lead to a clean area on the metal coil case and the other lead to the primary and high tension terminals. If the lamp lights, or if sparks are seen, the coil windings are grounded.

4. If the coil windings are not open or grounded, use a meter-type coil tester to check for short circuits and other internal defects. Because coil testers vary in design and methods of use, follow the test equipment manufacturer's procedure carefully. Always test the coil at normal operating temperature, because internal defects are not likely to appear on a cold coil test.

DISTRIBUTOR CONDENSER TEST (Fig. 3-22)

A condenser suspected of being defective should be tested with an accurate condenser tester—not to save the replacement cost of a new condenser, but to determine if it is really the cause of the ignition system problem. While condenser testers are usually a specialized piece of test equipment, some of the multi-function engine analyzer units do have a condenser test capability. Regardless of the test unit used, the instructions provided by the test equipment manufacturer should be followed carefully in performing the following three tests. Like the coil, the condenser *must* be tested at normal operating temperature, or defects are not likely to show up.

HIGH SERIES RESISTANCE

Test sequence and connections will depend upon the type of condenser tester used. High series resistance in a distributor condenser slows down the condenser's ability to accept a charge, resulting in excessive voltage being passed across the breaker points when they start to open. This causes rapid point wear, shows up first during starting and low-speed operation, and can eventually cause a complete ignition system failure. New condensers may have a series resistance as low as 0.05-ohms. Although some condenser testers will reject a condenser with a resistance of 0.3-ohm, resistance can usually go to 0.5-ohm without affecting ignition performance.

CAPACITY

Distributor condensers have a capacity rating of 0.18-0.23 microfarads (0.25-0.285 for Chrysler Corporation cars). A condenser with insufficient capacity will cause metal transfer to the positive or breaker arm point; one with excess capacity causes metal transfer to the negative or support point.

LOW INSULATION RESISTANCE

This condition drains enough energy from the ignition system to drop secondary voltage below system requirements, and is usually caused by water absorption, which lowers the winding resistance to a point where the condenser cannot hold a charge. Because distributor condensers are sealed to prevent water absorption, low insulation resistance is not commonly encountered, but is one of those elusive ignition malfunctions that are often overlooked, even when all other possibilities have been ruled out as the cause of an ignition problem.

1970-74 GENERAL MOTORS ENGINES; 1970-74 AMERICAN MOTORS ENGINES
Delco-Remy Breaker-Point Ignition System

Conventional ignitions using a breaker-point distributor were fitted as standard equipment on all 1970-73 and a majority of 1974 General Motors engines, before being replaced by the High Energy Ignition in 1975 (which had been fitted to some 454-cu.-in. engines beginning in mid-1974). American Motors also used the Delco-Remy system on 1970-73 and most 1974 models, before switching to the Prestolite BID electronic ignition on late-model 1974 engines.

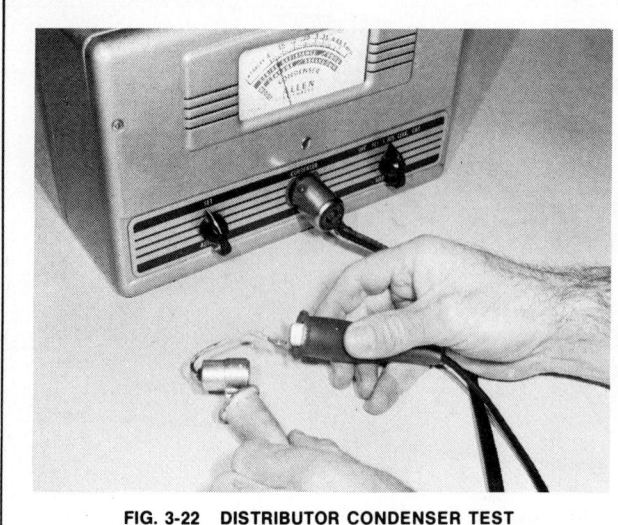

FIG. 3-22   DISTRIBUTOR CONDENSER TEST

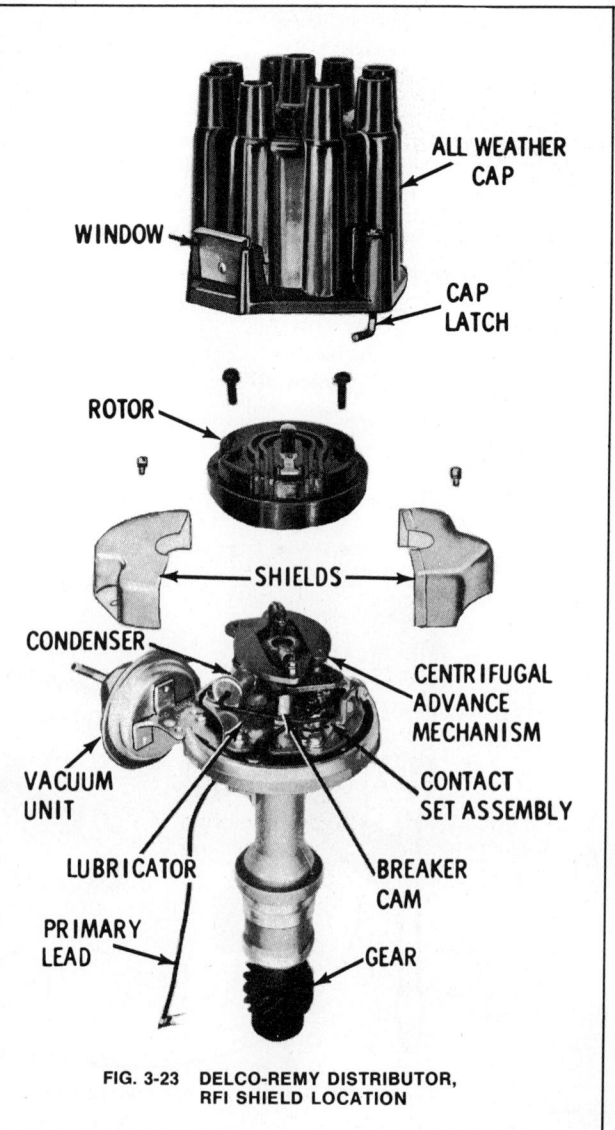

FIG. 3-23   DELCO-REMY DISTRIBUTOR, RFI SHIELD LOCATION

Delco-Remy V-8 distributor design is slightly different from that used by Chrysler Corporation and Ford Motor Company. The molded rotor provides a cover for the centrifugal advance mechanism, which is mounted above the breaker plate assembly. The vacuum advance control is mounted beneath the movable breaker plate, with the breaker points and condenser mounted on top of the breaker plate. A window in the distributor cap permits dwell adjustment while the cap is installed and the engine running.

Breaker-lever spring tension and point alignment on replacement breaker-point/condenser assemblies are preadjusted at the factory and serviced as a complete assembly. To prevent distributor interference with radio operation, all V-8 distributors, except Uni-Set models, use a two-piece RFI shield over the breaker-point/condenser assembly to suppress radio interference. This RFI shield should not be discarded or omitted when servicing the distributor **(Fig. 3-23).** Distributors used with 4- and 6-cyl. engines are similar in design to those used by Chrysler and Ford.

DWELL VARIATION TEST

Excessive wear in the distributor's mechanical parts will cause dwell variations which will affect ignition timing and engine performance. A dwell variation test will determine the mechanical condition of the distributor.

1. Disconnect the distributor vacuum hose and connect a tach-dwell tester. The red lead goes to the DIST terminal of the coil and the black lead to ground.

2. Start the engine and run at idle, then slowly increase engine speed to 1750 rpm and gradually reduce it back to idle.

3. If the dwell varies more than 3° between the idle-speed and 1750-rpm readings, the distributor should be removed and inspected for probable wear in the distributor shaft, bushings or breaker plate. Dwell variations at speeds over 1750 rpm are not an accurate indication of distributor wear.

DISTRIBUTOR REMOVAL—V-8

1. Disconnect the vacuum hose from the vacuum advance unit and the primary lead wire at the coil.

2. Depress the slotted distributor-cap latches on each side with a screwdriver and turn until the latch is free from the distributor housing, then lift the cap up and off. *Do not* remove spark plug cables from the cap towers.

3. Remove the distributor clamp screw and hold-down clamp.

4. Note the rotor position and pull the distributor upward slowly. The distributor shaft will rotate counterclockwise slightly as its gear disengages from that of the camshaft. Note the new rotor position before removing the distributor from the engine. Because the distributor must be replaced in the same position, it will help to scribe a reference mark on the engine block for rotor alignment during installation.

DISTRIBUTOR DISASSEMBLY—V-8 (Fig. 3-24)

1. Remove the attaching screws, lockwashers and flat washers holding the rotor to the advance mechanism and remove the rotor.

2. Unclip the advance springs and remove both advance weights.

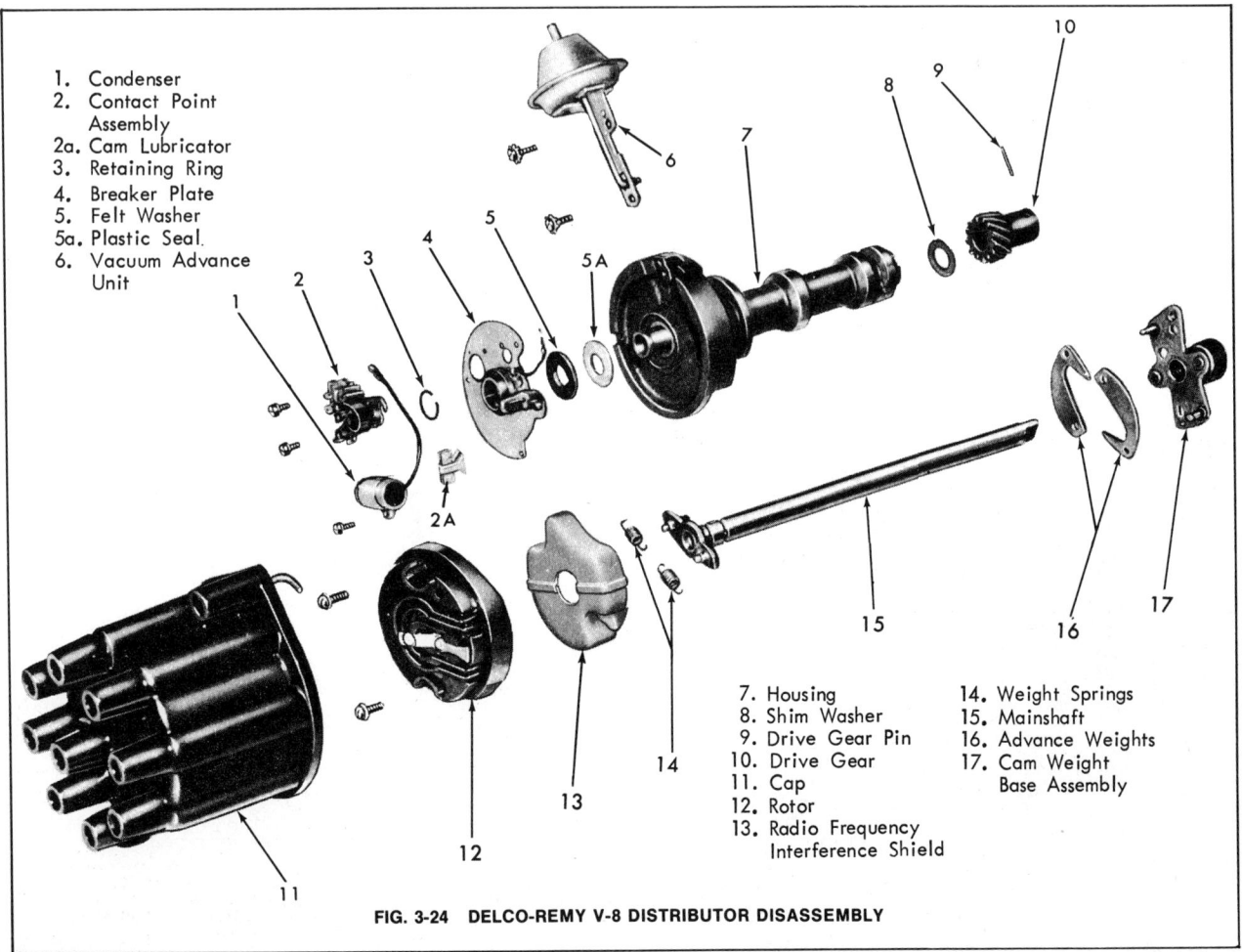

1. Condenser
2. Contact Point Assembly
2a. Cam Lubricator
3. Retaining Ring
4. Breaker Plate
5. Felt Washer
5a. Plastic Seal
6. Vacuum Advance Unit

7. Housing
8. Shim Washer
9. Drive Gear Pin
10. Drive Gear
11. Cap
12. Rotor
13. Radio Frequency Interference Shield
14. Weight Springs
15. Mainshaft
16. Advance Weights
17. Cam Weight Base Assembly

FIG. 3-24   DELCO-REMY V-8 DISTRIBUTOR DISASSEMBLY

3. Unscrew the RFI attaching screws and remove both shields.

4. Support the distributor shaft in a soft-jaw vise and remove the retaining pin from the gear by driving it out with a suitable drift and hammer. Slide the gear and washer off the shaft.

5. Pull distributor shaft and cam-weight base assembly out of the housing.

6. Lift the two wire terminals from the snap lock retainer located between the two breaker-point attaching screws.

7. Remove the breaker-point attaching screws and lift the breaker-point assembly off.

8. Remove the condenser hold-down screw, condenser and bracket from the breaker plate.

9. Remove the spring retainer, and then raise the plate from the distributor housing.

10. Remove the vacuum-advance-unit attaching screws and separate the vacuum advance from the breaker plate.

11. Withdraw the felt washer from around the housing bushing. Housing and bushings are serviced as a complete assembly, and bushing removal should not be attempted; if excessive wear is present, replace the entire unit.

DISTRIBUTOR ASSEMBLY—V-8 (Fig. 3-24)

1. Install the vacuum unit to the distributor housing, with the ground lead terminal under the inner mounting screw.

2. Replace the felt washer (and plastic seal, if used) on the upper bushing, and fit the breaker plate over

the upper bushing and vacuum advance link.

3. Install the retaining ring on the distributor upper housing.

4. Slide the distributor shaft through the housing bushings. Install the tachometer drive on Corvette models.

5. Install the washers and drive gear on the distributor shaft, using a new retaining pin. The pin should fit tightly in the shaft hole to prevent any gear/shaft movement. Since Delco-Remy distributors are fitted with phosphate-coated, hardened drive gears, an identical replacement gear should be used whenever gear wear or damage makes its replacement necessary.

6. Install the breaker-point/condenser assembly and push the lead clips all the way down into the snap lock retainer. The clips must not contact the RFI shield when it is replaced.

7. Lubricate and replace the cam-weight base assembly, then install the RFI shield, advance weights, advance springs and rotor. The rotor is doweled to fit pilot holes in the cam weight assembly and can only be installed in one direction.

DISTRIBUTOR INSTALLATION—V-8

1. Turn the rotor one-eighth turn clockwise, past the

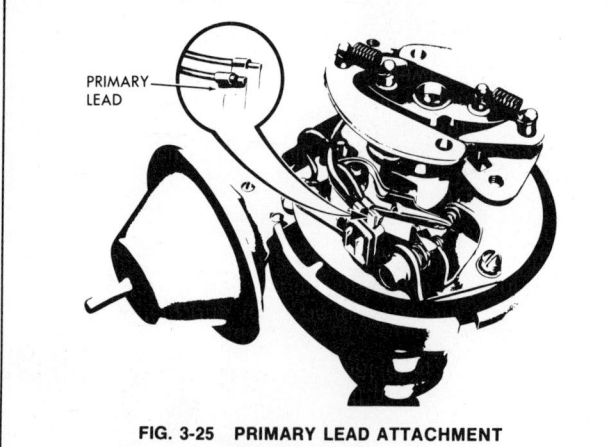

PRIMARY LEAD

FIG. 3-25   PRIMARY LEAD ATTACHMENT

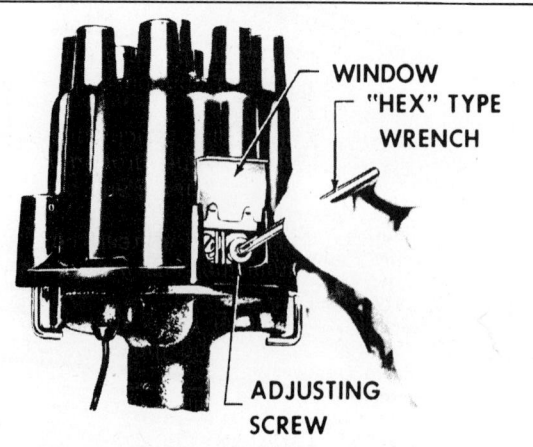

WINDOW
"HEX" TYPE
WRENCH

ADJUSTING
SCREW

FIG. 3-26   DELCO-REMY DWELL ADJUSTMENT

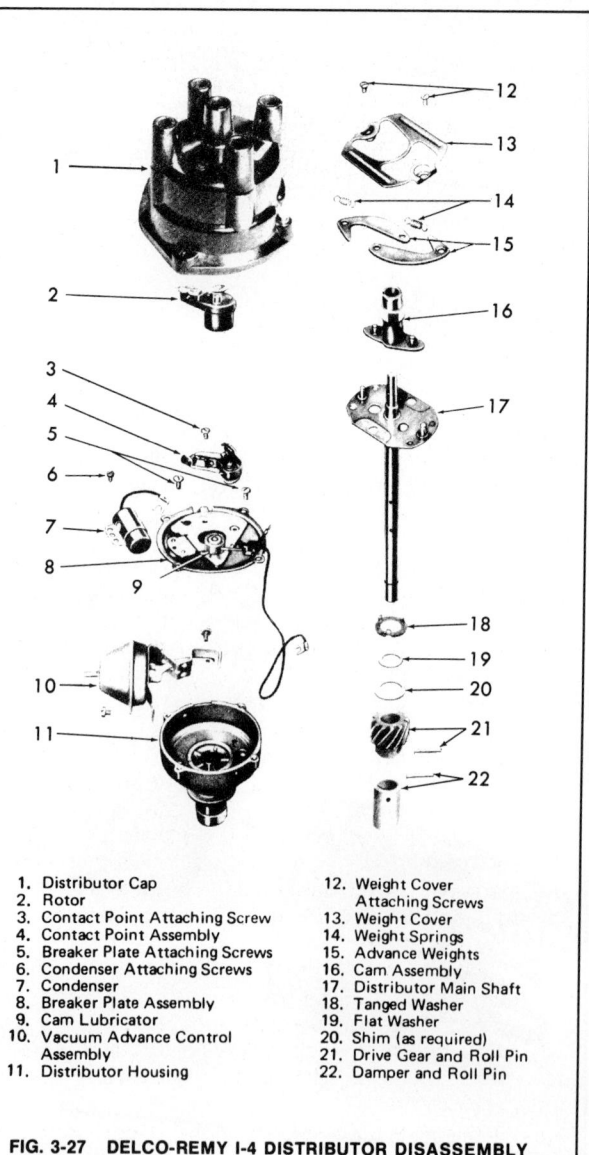

1. Distributor Cap
2. Rotor
3. Contact Point Attaching Screw
4. Contact Point Assembly
5. Breaker Plate Attaching Screws
6. Condenser Attaching Screws
7. Condenser
8. Breaker Plate Assembly
9. Cam Lubricator
10. Vacuum Advance Control Assembly
11. Distributor Housing
12. Weight Cover Attaching Screws
13. Weight Cover
14. Weight Springs
15. Advance Weights
16. Cam Assembly
17. Distributor Main Shaft
18. Tanged Washer
19. Flat Washer
20. Shim (as required)
21. Drive Gear and Roll Pin
22. Damper and Roll Pin

FIG. 3-27   DELCO-REMY I-4 DISTRIBUTOR DISASSEMBLY

reference point noted or scribed during removal, and install the distributor. Shaft may rotate slightly as the drive gear engages the cam gear.

2. Replace the clamp and hold-down bolt and start the engine. If the engine runs unevenly or fails to start, the distributor is 180° out of time. Lift the distributor up sufficiently to disengage the gears and turn the rotor one-half revolution, then reinstall.

3. If the engine has been cranked with the distributor removed, the proper relationship between the distributor shaft and the No. 1 piston must be reestablished:

 a) Install a jumper lead and crank the engine until the timing mark on the harmonic balancer indexes with the 0° timing mark on the engine front cover.

 b) When both No. 1 cylinder valves are closed, the piston will be on top dead center (TDC) in either the firing or exhaust stroke.

 c) Install the distributor. The rotor must point to the No. 1 spark plug terminal in the distributor cap when the distributor is fully seated. If it does not, the relationship between the distributor shaft and No. 1 piston is not correct—repeat Step 3a.

BREAKER-POINT REPLACEMENT—V-8

1. Depress the slotted distributor-cap latch head with a screwdriver and rotate one-quarter turn in either direction to free the latch from the distributor housing, then lift the cap up and off.

2. Remove the attaching screws and rotor.

3. Remove the RFI-shield attaching screws and shield (not used with Uni-Set distributor).

4. Loosen the two screws holding the breaker-point assembly and slide the assembly from the breaker plate.

5. Disconnect the primary and condenser leads from the nylon-insulated snap-lock retainer in the breaker-point assembly.

6. Install a new breaker-point assembly and tighten the attaching screws.

7. Insert the primary and condenser leads in the snap lock retainer and push them all the way down. The primary lead should be located on the retainer side closest to the vacuum advance mechanism, with its wire side facing the vacuum advance unit **(Fig. 3-25).** Improper installation will cause lead interference between the cap, weight base and breaker advance plate. Non-Delco replacement breaker-point sets are usually fitted with a lock screw instead of push-in terminals, and if not installed carefully, can short out if the lock-screw head touches the RFI shield.

8. Replace the RFI shield as follows:

 a) Install the shield half covering the breaker points first. Make sure the shield rests tightly against the breaker plate and that its two register indentations rest on top of the plate.

 b) Check to see that the primary and condenser leads will clear the other RFI shield half; rearrange the leads if needed to provide the necessary clearance.

 c) Install the second RFI half. Make sure the mating flange rests on the outside of the first half, and then replace the attaching screw.

9. Align the rotor so that dowels fit into their proper index holes on the cam weight assembly, and then tighten the screws.

10. Fit the distributor cap in place. Depress and turn the cap latches one-quarter turn in either direction to lock the latches on the distributor housing.

ADJUSTING DWELL SETTING

1. With the vacuum hose disconnected from the distributor, connect the red lead of a dwell-tach to the DIST terminal of the coil and the black lead to ground.

2. Start the engine and run at idle until normal operating temperature is reached.

3. Raise the window in the distributor cap and insert a hex wrench in the adjusting cap-screw head **(Fig. 3-26).**

4. Turn the adjusting screw until the specified dwell angle is obtained (29° to 31°—30° is preferred).

5. Remove the wrench, shut the distributor cap window and reconnect the vacuum hose to the distributor.

DISTRIBUTOR REMOVAL, I-4 AND I-6 ENGINES

1. The distributor cap is bolted directly to the housing. Release the cap hold-down screws and remove cap.

2. Disconnect the vacuum line from the vacuum advance unit and the primary lead wire at the coil.

3. Scribe a realignment mark on the distributor bowl and engine in line with the rotor.

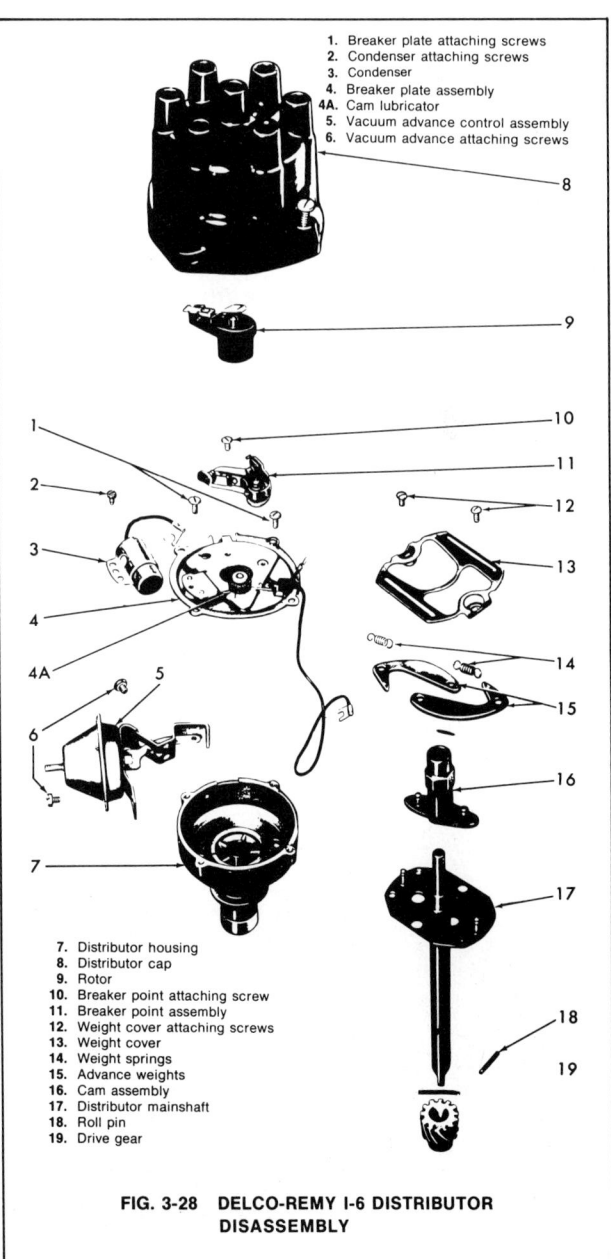

1. Breaker plate attaching screws
2. Condenser attaching screws
3. Condenser
4. Breaker plate assembly
4A. Cam lubricator
5. Vacuum advance control assembly
6. Vacuum advance attaching screws
7. Distributor housing
8. Distributor cap
9. Rotor
10. Breaker point attaching screw
11. Breaker point assembly
12. Weight cover attaching screws
13. Weight cover
14. Weight springs
15. Advance weights
16. Cam assembly
17. Distributor mainshaft
18. Roll pin
19. Drive gear

FIG. 3-28 DELCO-REMY I-6 DISTRIBUTOR DISASSEMBLY

4. Remove the distributor hold-down bolt and clamp, and note the relative position of the vacuum advance unit and the engine, then remove the distributor from the engine by pulling upward slowly.

DISTRIBUTOR DISASSEMBLY,
I-4 (Fig. 3-27) AND I-6 (Fig. 3-28)

1. Remove the rotor by pulling it up and off the distributor shaft.

2. Remove the vacuum-advance-unit attaching screws, and disengage the vacuum advance mechanism from the distributor housing.

3. Disconnect the primary and condenser leads from the breaker-point quick-disconnect terminal and remove the two attaching screws. Remove the breaker points and condenser assembly from the breaker plate.

4. Support the distributor shaft in a soft-jaw vise:

a) I-4—Remove the roll pin from the damper and the roll pin from the drive gear, using a suitable drift and hammer to drive the pins out. Slide the damper cup, drive gear, washers and shims off the drive shaft.

b) I-6—Remove the retaining pin from the drive gear by driving it out with a suitable drift and hammer. Slide the gear and spacer off the distributor shaft.

5. Remove the cam and mainshaft from the distributor housing.

6. Remove the weight cover and stop plate screws.

7. Remove the cover, weight springs and weights, then slide the cam assembly from the mainshaft.

6. Inspect the distributor shaft for excessive wear and check its fit in the bushings in the distributor body. If either shaft or bushings are worn, the shaft or distributor body are replaced as a unit.

DISTRIBUTOR ASSEMBLY,
I-4 (Fig. 3-27) AND I-6 (Fig. 3-28)

1. Lubricate the top end of the distributor shaft with ball bearing grease and replace the cam assembly on the shaft.

2. Replace advance weights on their respective pivot pins and install the weight springs.

3. Replace the weight cover and stop plate.

4. Lubricate the distributor shaft and replace it in the distributor housing.

5. Replace the drive gear on the distributor shaft and make sure the shaft turns freely after installing the retaining pin. Replace the damper and install the roll pin on the I-4 distributor.

6. Replace the breaker plate assembly in the distributor body and install the screws.

7. Replace the condenser and breaker-point set on the breaker plate. Breaker-point pilot must engage the corresponding hole in the breaker plate.

8. Connect the primary and condenser leads to the quick-disconnect terminal.

9. Install the vacuum advance unit to the distributor housing.

10. Check and adjust the breaker-point gap and alignment—see "Breaker Point Replacement" in a following section.

11. Check the breaker-arm spring tension as shown in **Fig. 3-29.**

12. Replace the rotor on the distributor shaft.

DISTRIBUTOR INSTALLATION, I-4 AND I-6

1. Turn the rotor one-eighth turn clockwise, past the reference mark scribed during removal, and install the distributor. The shaft may rotate slightly as the drive gear engages the cam gear.

2. Replace the clamp and hold-down bolt and start the engine. If the engine runs unevenly or fails to start,

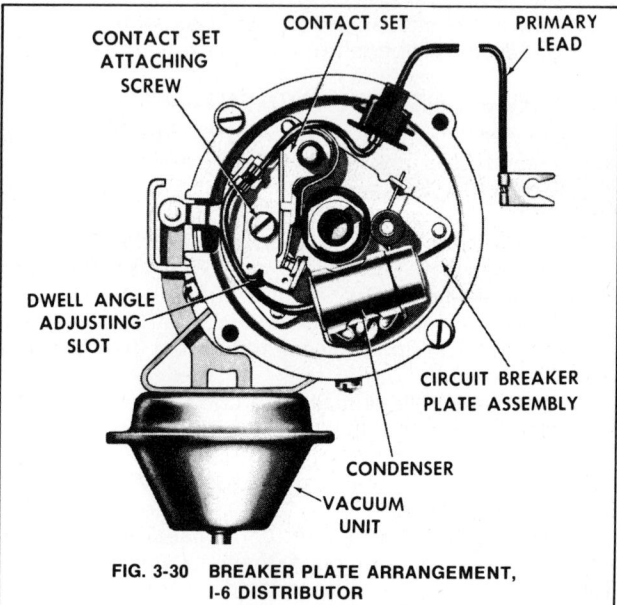

FIG. 3-30   BREAKER PLATE ARRANGEMENT,
I-6 DISTRIBUTOR

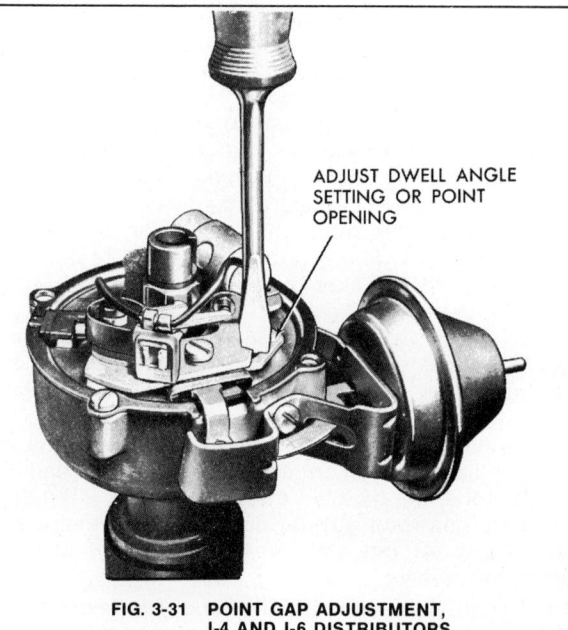

ADJUST DWELL ANGLE
SETTING OR POINT
OPENING

FIG. 3-31   POINT GAP ADJUSTMENT,
I-4 AND I-6 DISTRIBUTORS

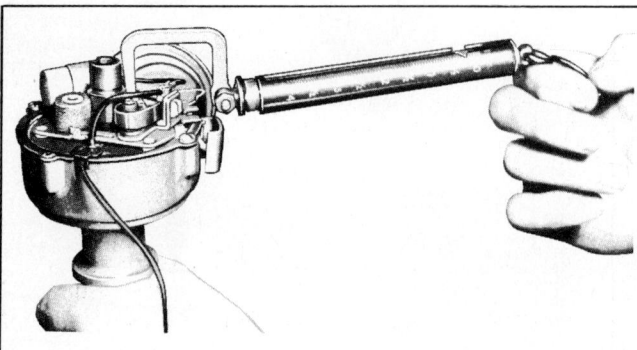

FIG. 3-29   BREAKER-ARM SPRING-TENSION TEST,
I-4 AND I-6 DISTRIBUTORS

the distributor is 180° out of time. Lift the distributor up sufficiently to disengage the gears and turn the rotor one-half revolution, then reinstall.

3. If the engine has been cranked with the distributor removed, the proper relationship between the distributor shaft and the No. 1 piston must be reestablished.

I-4 Engine:

a) Install a jumper lead and crank the engine until the timing mark on the pulley or damper aligns with the fourth mark (8°) from the center toward A on the lower timing belt cover timing pointer.

b) Position the distributor to the cylinder-head opening, with the vacuum advance unit pointing toward the front of the engine and the punch mark on the distributor drive gear in line with the No. 1 distributor cap terminal. Then turn the distributor body counterclockwise approximately one-eighth turn and seat the distributor to engage the drive gear with the camshaft gear.

c) Replace the hold-down clamp and tighten the bolt snugly. Then turn the distributor body slightly, until the breaker points just start to open (0.002-in. maximum), and finish tightening the hold-down bolt.

I-6 Engine:

a) Install a jumper lead and crank the engine until the timing mark on the harmonic balancer indexes with the 0° timing mark on the engine front cover.

b) When both No. 1 cylinder valves are closed, the piston will be on top dead center (TDC) in either the firing or exhaust stroke.

c) Install the distributor. The rotor must point to the No. 1 spark plug terminal in the distributor cap when the distributor is fully seated. If it does not, the relationship between the distributor shaft and No. 1 piston is not correct—repeat Step a.

BREAKER-POINT REPLACEMENT, I-4 AND I-6 (Fig. 3-30)

1. Release the distributor cap hold-down screws and remove the cap.

2. Remove the rotor by pulling it up and off the distributor shaft.

3. Disconnect the primary and condenser lead wires from the quick-disconnect terminal.

4. Remove the breaker-point attaching screw and lift the point set from the breaker plate.

5. Wipe protective film from the new breaker-point set, position on the breaker plate and install the attaching screw. Pilot on the breaker-point set must engage the hole in the breaker plate.

6. Connect the primary and condenser lead wires to the quick-disconnect terminal on the breaker-point set.

7. Check the new breaker points for alignment and breaker-arm spring tension. Hook a spring scale to the breaker arm, and exert sufficient pull at 90° to the breaker arm **(Fig. 3-29)** to barely separate the points.

8. Adjust the spring tension if it's necessary to obtain a reading of 19-23 oz. To decrease pressure, pinch the breaker-arm spring carefully. To increase pressure, remove the arm from the distributor and bend the spring away from the arm, then replace.

9. Position the distributor shaft, with the breaker-arm rubbing block on the high point of a cam lobe, and loosen the attaching screw.

10. Use a screwdriver to move the point support and adjust the breaker-point gap to 0.019-in. for new points and 0.016-in. for used points **(Fig. 3-31)**.

11. Tighten the screw and recheck the setting with a feeler gauge. If the gap is correctly set, replace the rotor and distributor cap and check dwell angle—see "Dwell Variation Test" earlier in this section.

IGNITION COIL AND RESISTOR SPECIFICATIONS

BUICK

Make	Delco-Remy
Coil Number	I-6—1115208
	V-8—1115247
Current Draw, Amps @ 12.6 Volts	
Engine Stopped	3.8
Engine Idling	2.3
Coil Resistance (Ohms) @ 80° F	
Primary	1.28-1.42
Secondary	7200-9500
Resistance Wire	Part of Wiring Harness
Resistance, Ohms @ 80° F	1.80 ± 0.05
Voltage @ Coil (Ignition On and Points Closed)	5.0-5.5

CADILLAC

Amperage Draw (Engine Running)	1.25 Amps
Primary Resistance	1.77-2.01 Ohms
Secondary Resistance	3000-20,000 Ohms
Wiring Harness Primary Resistance @ 80° F	1.3-1.35 Ohms

CHEVROLET

Primary Resistance @ 75° F	I-4—1.41-1.65 Ohms
	I-6—1.41-1.65 Ohms
	V-8—1.77-2.05 Ohms
Secondary Resistance @ 75° F	I-4—3000-20,000 Ohms
	I-6—3000-20,000 Ohms
	V-8—3000-20,000 Ohms
Fixed Ignition Resistor (In Wiring Harness)	I-4—1.8 Ohms
	I-6—1.8 Ohms
	V-8—1.35 Ohms

OLDSMOBILE

Primary Resistance @ 75° F	I-6—1.45-1.63 Ohms
	V-8—1.77-2.05 Ohms
Secondary Resistance @ 75° F	6500-9500 Ohms
Ignition Resistor	
(In Wiring Harness) Resistance @ 80° F	I-6—1.85 Ohms
	V-8—1.35 Ohms

PONTIAC

Coil Number (I-6)	1115208
Primary Resistance @ 75° F	1.40-1.65 Ohms
Secondary Resistance @ 75° F	3000-20,000 Ohms
Coil Number (I-6)	1115414
Primary Resistance	1.4-1.7 Ohms
Secondary Resistance	3000-20,000 Ohms
Coil Number (V-8)	1115410
Primary Resistance @ 75° F	1.7-2.0 Ohms
Secondary Resistance @ 75° F	3000-20,000 Ohms
Coil Number (V-8)	1115424
Primary Resistance @ 75° F	1.77-2.01 Ohms
Secondary Resistance @ 75° F	3000-20,000 Ohms
Coil Number (V-8)	1115432
Primary Resistance @ 75° F	1.8-2.2 Ohms
Secondary Resistance @ 75° F	3000-20,000 Ohms

AMC IGNITION COIL & RESISTOR SPECIFICATIONS

BREAKER-POINT IGNITIONS

Make	Delco-Remy	Delco-Remy	Delco-Remy
Primary Resistance, Ohms@75°F	1.40-1.65	1.77-2.05	1.64-1.80
Secondary Resistance, Ohms@75°F	3000-20,000	3000-20,000	9300-11,800

BID IGNITION SENSOR

Resistance	1.6 to 2.4 Ohms@77°F to 200°F

COIL

Primary Resistance	1 to 2 Ohms
Secondary Resistance	9,000 to 15,000 Ohms
Open Circuit Output	20 Kv minimum

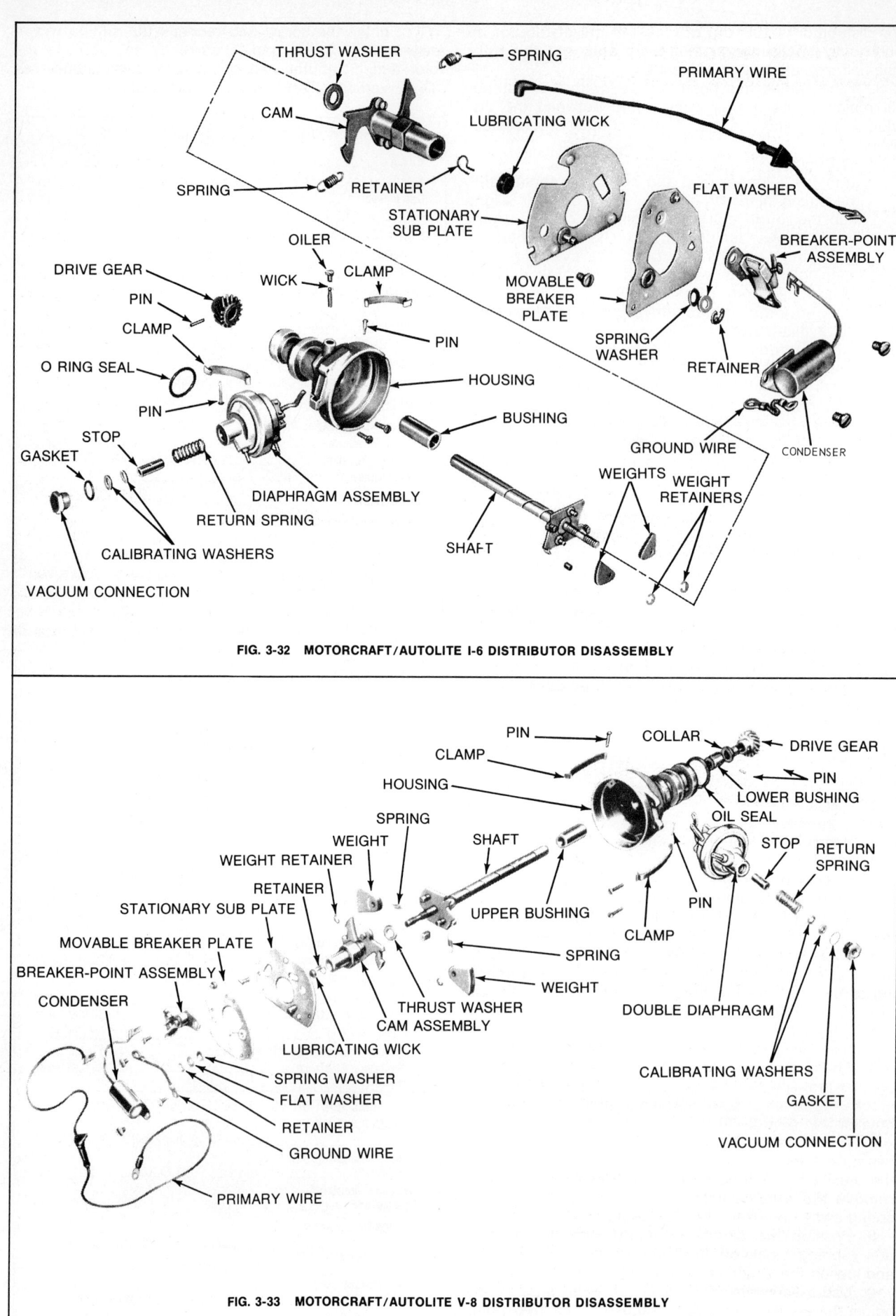

FIG. 3-32 MOTORCRAFT/AUTOLITE I-6 DISTRIBUTOR DISASSEMBLY

FIG. 3-33 MOTORCRAFT/AUTOLITE V-8 DISTRIBUTOR DISASSEMBLY

1970-74 FORD MOTOR COMPANY ENGINES

Motorcraft/Autolite Breaker-Point Ignition System

Conventional ignitions using a variety of breaker-point distributors were fitted to all 1970-73 Ford, Mercury, Lincoln engines and to a majority of 1974 models, except the 400- and 460-cu.-in., which were equipped with the new Ford Solid State Ignition (as were all 200-cu.-in. and larger 1974 engines sold in California). All 1970-74 conventional distributors are dual advance; some of the 1970-72 distributors have a dual-diaphragm vacuum-advance mechanism. Dual-diaphragm vacuum-advance units have two vacuum lines to the advance control unit—one advances timing during high rpm operation, and the other retards timing at idle. Beginning in 1973, a single-diaphragm vacuum-advance control was used. Distributors for high output engines are equipped with two sets of breaker points (dual point distributors).

DISTRIBUTOR REMOVAL, ALL MODELS

1. Disconnect the vacuum line(s) at the distributor and the primary lead wire at the coil.

2. Unclip and remove the distributor cap.

3. Rotate the engine crankshaft until the distributor rotor points toward the cylinder block. Scribe a mark on the block and one on the distributor housing as rotor reference points for installation.

4. Remove the distributor hold-down screw and carefully lift the distributor from the engine. The distributor shaft will rotate slightly as its gear disengages from that in the engine block.

DISTRIBUTOR DISASSEMBLY, I-6 (Fig. 3-32) AND V-8 (Fig. 3-33)

1. Remove the rotor by pulling it up and straight off the distributor shaft.

2. Remove the radio suppression cap, if so equipped.

3. Disconnect the vacuum line(s) and remove the spring clip holding the vacuum-advance diaphragm link to the movable breaker plate (not necessary with dual point distributors).

4. Remove the vacuum-advance attaching screws and remove the unit. With dual point distributors, pull the vacuum advance straight out, then tilt it downward to unhook the linkage.

5. Loosen the terminal nut and disconnect the condenser and primary lead wire from the terminal.

6. Remove breaker-point assembly and condenser.

7. Pull the primary wire grommet and wire through the opening in the distributor bowl and remove.

8. Unscrew and remove the breaker-plate/sub-plate assembly.

9. Mark one weight, spring, bracket and pin.

10. Unhook and remove the weight springs.

11. Remove the lubricating wick from the cam assembly. Reach inside the cam with needlenose pliers and remove the retaining clip.

12. Lift the cam assembly and thrust washer from the distributor shaft.

13. Remove the weight retainers and lift the weights from the distributor housing.

14. Secure the distributor in a soft-jaw vise and tighten it sufficiently to prevent distributor shaft movement.

15. Drive out the distributor drive-gear roll pin carefully, using a suitable drift and hammer. Remove the drive gear, collar and oil seal. If necessary, press out the lower bushing.

16. Withdraw the distributor shaft and press the up-

per bushing from the distributor housing, only if it must be replaced.

17. Inspect the shaft, bushings and housing bore for excessive wear and replace as necessary.

DISTRIBUTOR ASSEMBLY, I-6 (Fig. 3-32) AND V-8 (Fig. 3-33)

1. Replace the distributor shaft and press a new upper bushing in the distributor housing, if the old one was removed.

2. Press a new lower bushing in place, if the old one was removed. Then install the oil seal, collar and drive gear, tapping the roll pin in place snugly.

3. Place the advance weights in the distributor and install the weight retainers. Marked weight is installed on the marked pivot pin.

4. Fit the thrust washer on the distributor shaft and lubricate the grooves in the upper part of the distributor shaft with cam lubricant.

5. Install the marked spring bracket on the cam assembly near the marked spring bracket on the stop plate. When installing a replacement cam assembly, it should be installed with the Hypalon-covered stop in the correct cam-plate control slot. Some advance ranges do not require a Hypalon stop—in this case, make sure the length of the slot on the new cam is identical to the corresponding slot on the old cam. If a cam with the wrong slot size is installed, the maximum advance will be incorrect.

6. Lightly lubricate the distributor cam lobes with special distributor-cam grease, install the retainer clip and felt wick. Oil the wick with SAE 10W engine oil.

7. Install the weight springs, attaching the marked spring to the marked spring bracket.

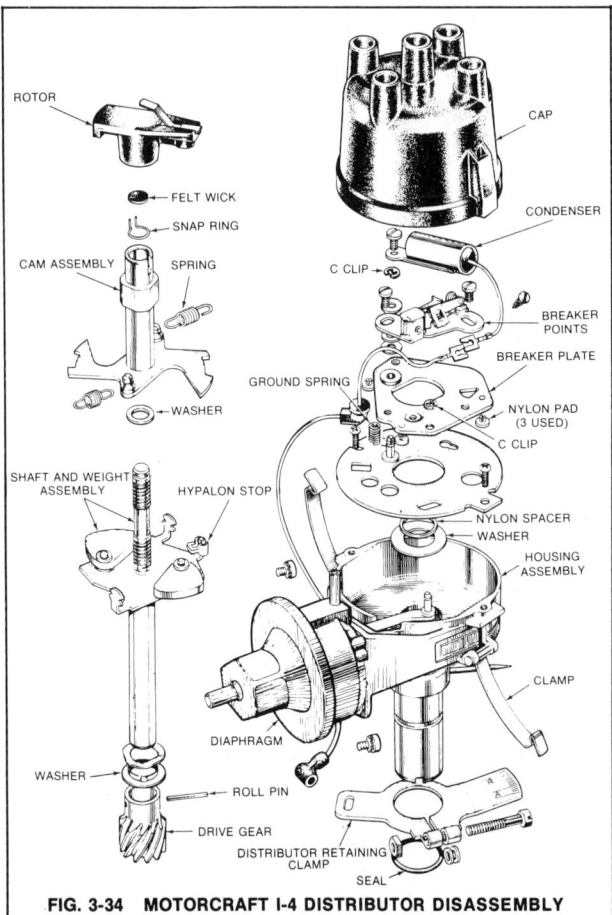

FIG. 3-34 MOTORCRAFT I-4 DISTRIBUTOR DISASSEMBLY

8. Replace the breaker-plate/sub-plate assembly and install the hold-down screws, with the ground wire under the screw from which it was removed.

9. Insert the primary wire through the distributor housing opening and fit the grommet in place securely.

10. Install the breaker-point set and condenser.

11. Connect the primary and condenser lead wires to the breaker-point terminal and tighten the terminal nut.

12. Install the vacuum advance unit and hook the diaphragm linkage to the movable breaker plate.

13. Replace the spring clip holding the diaphragm linkage to the movable breaker plate (not necessary with dual point distributors).

14. Replace the radio suppression cap (if so equipped), rotor and distributor cap.

15. Reconnect the vacuum line(s).

DISTRIBUTOR DISASSEMBLY, MOTORCRAFT I-4 (Fig. 3-34)

1. Remove the rotor by pulling it up and straight off the distributor shaft.

2. Disconnect the vacuum line to the distributor.

3. Loosen the terminal nut and disconnect the condenser and primary lead wire from the terminal.

4. Remove breaker-point assembly and condenser.

5. Pull the primary wire grommet and wire through the opening in the distributor-housing bowl and remove.

6. Unclip and remove the "C" clip which holds the vacuum advance arm to the breaker plate.

7. Remove the two sub-plate screws and lift the plate and wire from the distributor housing.

8. Unhook and remove the weight springs.

9. Remove the lubricating wick from the cam assembly. Reach inside the cam with needlenose pliers and remove the retaining clip.

10. Lift the cam assembly and thrust washer from the distributor shaft.

11. Secure the distributor in a soft-jaw vise and tighten sufficiently to prevent distributor shaft movement.

12. Drive out the distributor drive-gear roll pin carefully, using a suitable drift and hammer. Remove the drive gear and washers.

13. Withdraw the distributor shaft from the housing, with the weights attached.

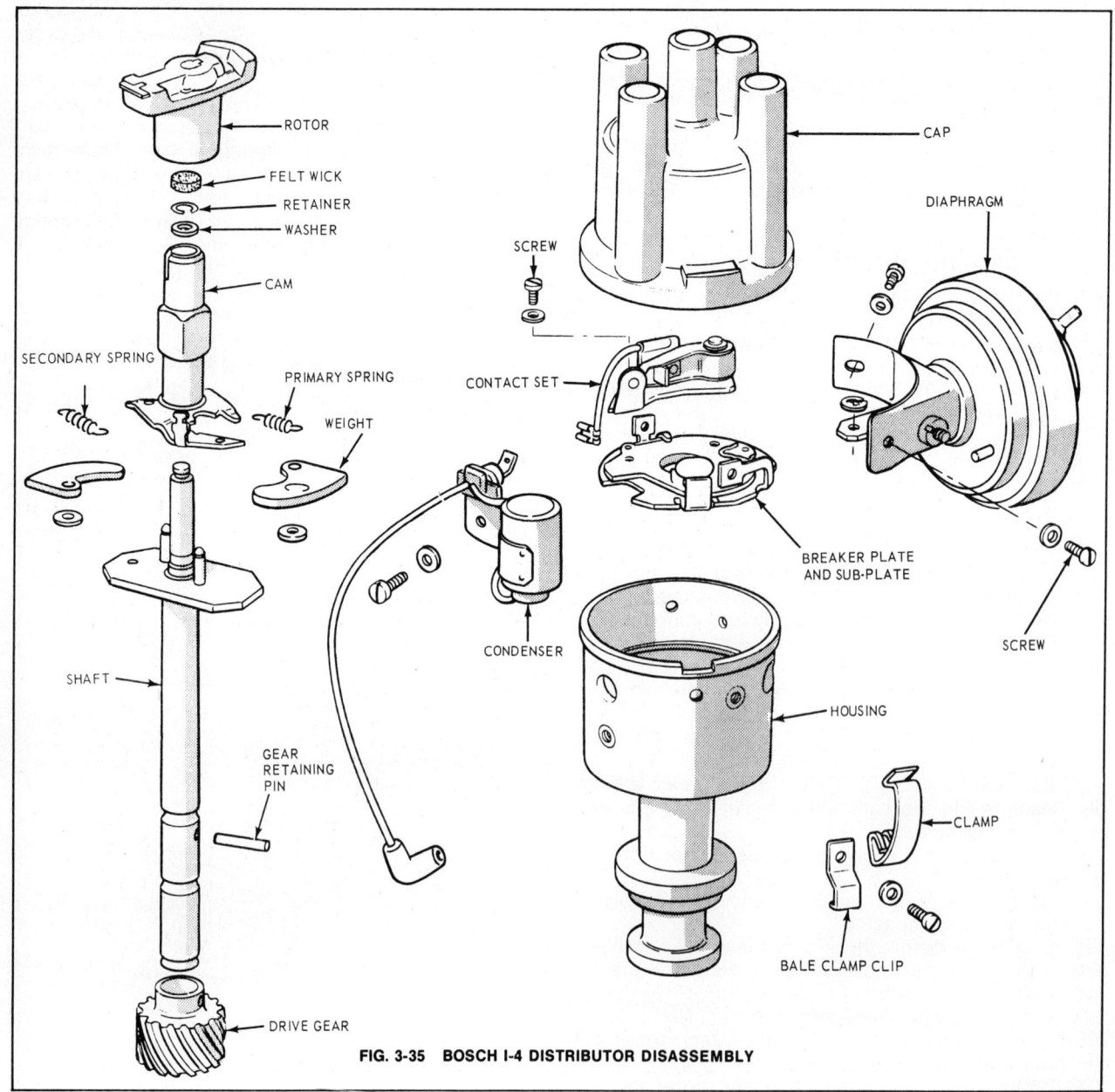

FIG. 3-35 BOSCH I-4 DISTRIBUTOR DISASSEMBLY

DISTRIBUTOR ASSEMBLY, MOTORCRAFT I-4 (Fig. 3-34)

1. Insert distributor shaft in the distributor housing.

2. Replace the drive gear and washers on the distributor shaft and install the roll pin, using a suitable drift and hammer.

3. Slip the upper thrust washer over the distributor shaft and lightly lubricate the upper end of the distributor shaft with cam lubricant.

4. Install the cam assembly and secure the advance weights in place with the weight springs.

5. Lightly lubricate the cam lobes and replace the snap ring and felt wick in the cam assembly.

6. Install the sub-plate assembly and wire in the distributor housing.

7. Insert the primary wire through the distributor-housing bowl opening and fit the grommet in place securely.

8. Install the breaker-point set and condenser.

9. Connect the primary and condenser lead wires to the breaker-point terminal and tighten the terminal nut.

10. Replace the "C" clip to hold the vacuum advance arm to the breaker plate.

11. Replace the distributor rotor, cap and reconnect the vacuum line.

DISTRIBUTOR DISASSEMBLY, BOSCH I-4 (Fig. 3-35)

Service parts are not available for replacement of the distributor shaft, drive gear, bushing or cam on this distributor. Excessive wear and/or damage to any of these components will require replacement of the entire distributor housing/shaft/cam assembly.

1. Remove the rotor by pulling it up and straight off the distributor shaft.

2. Disconnect the vacuum line to the distributor.

3. Disconnect the condenser lead, remove the attaching screw, work the grommet from the housing and remove the condenser assembly.

4. Unclip and remove the "C" clip holding the vacuum diaphragm rod to the breaker plate.

5. Remove the screws holding the vacuum advance to the distributor housing and remove the vacuum advance unit.

6. Remove the breaker points.

7. Remove the screws holding the distributor cap hold-down clips to the distributor body—these also keep the breaker plate assembly in place.

8. Work the breaker plate assembly from the distributor body by prying through the diaphragm-rod housing opening with a screwdriver.

9. Disconnect and remove the primary and secondary advance.

10. Insert a screwdriver in the vacuum-advance rod opening in the distributor housing and pry upward carefully on the lower cam edge to disengage cam retainer.

11. Lift the cam, retainer, washer and felt wick from the distributor shaft, separating wick and retainer from the cam.

12. Lift out the advance weights.

DISTRIBUTOR ASSEMBLY, BOSCH I-4 (Fig. 3-35)

1. Lightly coat the distributor-shaft pivot pins with cam lubricant and install the advance weights.

2. Position the weights, lubricate the upper distributor shaft and install the cam. Replace the cam retainer and felt wick.

3. Carefully install the primary and secondary advance springs in their respective places on the advance mechanism **(Fig. 3-36)**.

4. Position the breaker plate assembly and install the distributor bale clamps and clips with the attaching screws.

5. Fit the condenser wire and grommet through the distributor housing slot and replace the condenser mounting screw.

6. Position the breaker-point assembly and install the screw which holds it to the breaker plate.

7. Connect the diaphragm rod over the breaker plate pin.

8. Replace the vacuum advance unit, install attaching screws and snap "C" clip on the breaker plate pin.

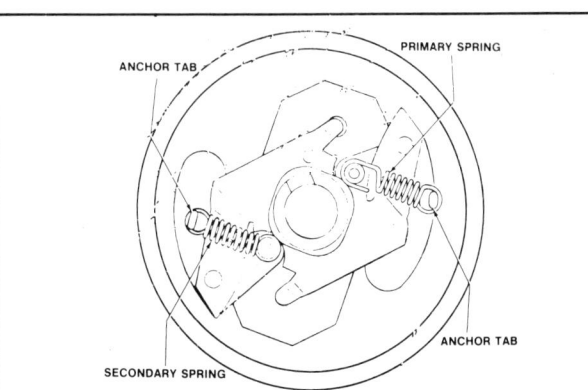

FIG. 3-36 BOSCH ADVANCE SPRING LOCATION

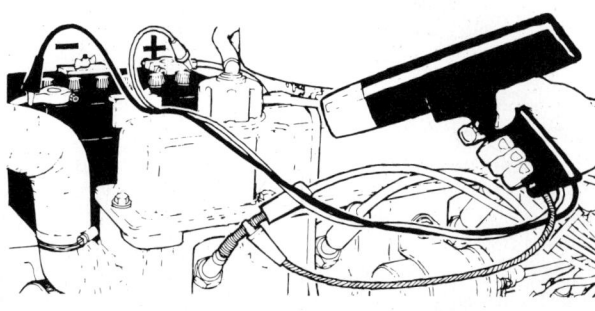

FIG. 3-37 TIMING LIGHT CONNECTIONS

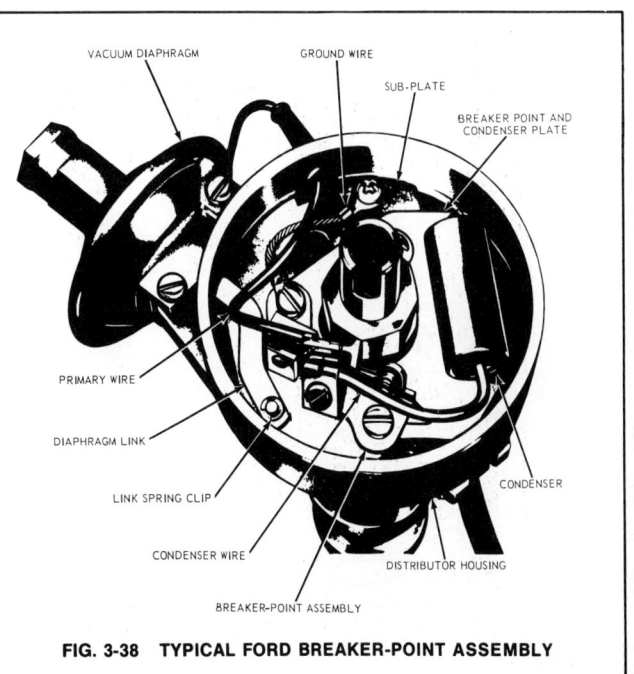

FIG. 3-38 TYPICAL FORD BREAKER-POINT ASSEMBLY

9. Replace the rotor, distributor cap and vacuum line to the distributor.

DISTRIBUTOR INSTALLATION, ALL MODELS

1. Make certain the rubber O-ring seal is fully seated in the distributor shank groove, then turn the distributor until the rotor points to the scribed mark on the distributor housing. Align this scribed mark with the one on the engine.

2. Insert the distributor in the engine, making certain the shaft engages the oil-pump intermediate shaft as it seats. If engine has been cranked with the distributor removed, the proper relationship between the distributor shaft and the No. 1 piston must be reestablished.

a) Rotate the crankshaft until No. 1 piston is at the top of its compression stroke. The TDC mark on the timing pointer should line up with the timing pin on the crankshaft damper.

b) Rotate the distributor rotor to a position just ahead of the No. 1 distributor cap terminal, lower the distributor carefully into the engine opening and engage the oil-pump intermediate shaft.

c) Install, but *do not* tighten, the retaining clamp and bolt. Rotate the distributor to advance the timing to a point where the breaker points are just starting to open; tighten clamp finger-tight.

3. Replace the distributor cap and clamp it in place.

4. Attach the primary lead wire to the coil (the distributor vacuum line(s) is not connected until after the initial timing has been set, but should be pinched shut or plugged with a golf tee or small bolt to prevent a vacuum leak).

5. Connect a timing light **(Fig. 3-37)**, start the engine and run at idle speed.

6. Rotate the distributor housing until the timing mark on the crankshaft damper aligns with the specified timing mark on the pointer.

7. Tighten the distributor hold-down screw and recheck the timing setting with the timing light.

8. If not correct, loosen the hold-down screw and readjust, then recheck. When timing is correct, replace the vacuum line(s) to the distributor.

BREAKER-POINT REPLACEMENT (Fig. 3-38)

When vented, pivoted breaker points are used, they must be accurately aligned to strike squarely; misalignment will cause premature wear, overheating, pitting.

1. Remove the distributor cap and rotor.

2. Loosen the terminal screw nut and remove the primary and condenser leads.

3. Remove the screws holding the breaker-point set and condenser to the breaker plate, then lift the point set and condenser out.

4. Wipe old grease from the cam with a clean, lint-free cloth and sparingly apply a fresh coat of cam lubricant.

5. Attach the new breaker-point set and condenser to the breaker plate—make sure the ground wire is replaced under the breaker-point attaching screw from which it was removed.

6. Connect the primary and condenser lead wires to the breaker-point terminal and tighten the terminal screw.

7. Align the breaker points if necessary. Bend the stationary bracket only when aligning the points.

8. Rotate the distributor shaft until the breaker-point rubbing block rests on the peak of a cam lobe.

9. Insert the tip of a screwdriver in the point-gap adjustment slot **(Fig. 3-39)** and set the breaker-point gap to specifications with a feeler gauge **(Fig. 3-40)**. Tighten the front attaching screw. Repeat for dual points, blocking one set open while adjusting the other set **(Fig. 3-41)**.

10. Replace the radio suppression cap, if used, the rotor and the distributor cap.

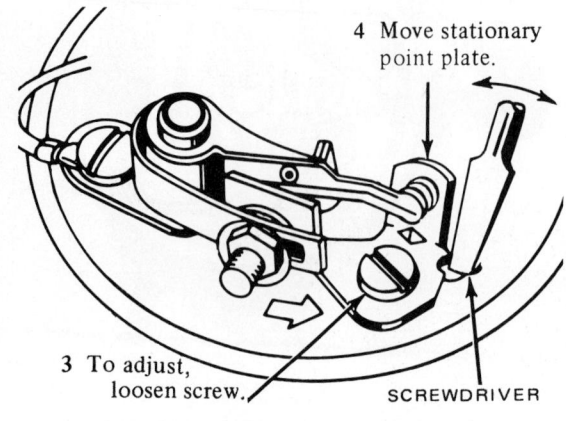

1 Measure gap with feeler gauge.

2 With rubbing block on tip of cam.

FIG. 3-40   SETTING BREAKER-POINT GAP

4 Move stationary point plate.

3 To adjust, loosen screw.

SCREWDRIVER

FIG. 3-39   BREAKER-POINT ADJUSTMENT SLOT

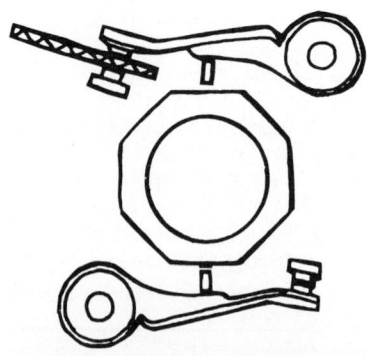

FIG. 3-41   DUAL POINT ADJUSTMENT

IGNITION COIL AND RESISTOR SPECIFICATIONS

FORD, MERCURY, LINCOLN

Primary Resistance @ 75° F	1.40-1.54 Ohms
Secondary Resistance @ 75° F	7600-8800 Ohms
Amperage Draw	
Engine Stopped	4.5 Amps
Engine Idling	2.5 Amps
Primary Circuit Resistor	
Resistance @ 75° F	1.30-1.40 Ohms

11. Connect a dwell-tach meter and check dwell angle. If not within specifications, reset the breaker-point gap and recheck the dwell.

CHECKING DWELL SETTING

1. Disconnect the vacuum line(s) to the distributor.

2. Connect the red lead of a dwell-tach meter to the distributor terminal of the coil and the black lead to ground. Set the dwell-tach selector switch to 4, 6 or 8 cyls., according to the engine under test.

3. Start the engine and run at idle.

4. Compare the dwell reading to specifications. A reading not within specifications indicates an incorrect point gap, a worn rubbing block or cam, or a distortion of the movable contact arm.

5. Reconnect the vacuum line(s) to the distributor.

1970-72 CHRYSLER CORPORATION ENGINES

Chrysler Breaker-Point Ignition System

Conventional ignitions using a breaker-point distributor were fitted to all 1970-71 and a large number of 1972 Chrysler Corporation cars before being replaced by the Chrysler Electronic Ignition in 1973. The Chrysler ignition coil is designed to function with an external ballast resistor **(Fig. 3-42)** as a compensating resistance in the primary circuit. During starter solenoid operation, the ballast resistor is bypassed to permit full battery voltage to the ignition primary circuit. The ballast resistor should be included in all coil tests and replaced if it does not meet factory specifications.

SOLENOID RETARD DISTRIBUTOR

During 1970-71, an ignition retard solenoid was positioned on the side of the distributor to retard ignition timing at closed throttle. This solenoid must be in operation when ignition timing is checked or set. After setting the timing, disconnect the solenoid ground lead and listen to the engine speed. If it increases, the solenoid is operating properly; if engine speed does not increase, the solenoid is defective and must be replaced.

SOLENOID ADVANCE DISTRIBUTOR (Fig. 3-43)

An ignition advance solenoid was used on some 1973 distributors to assist in starting. Since the solenoid receives its power from the starter relay at the same connection which sends current to the starting solenoid, it is only powered during engine cranking, when it advances the spark 7.5°. Once the engine starts, the solenoid is de-energized. A malfunctioning advance solenoid will affect only starting, not drivability. If hard starting is encountered, eliminate the other areas of starting problems (battery, carburetor, ignition, etc.) first. If the starting difficulties persist, test the advance solenoid as follows:

1. Connect a tachometer, disconnect the distributor vacuum line and start the engine.

2. Disconnect the bullet connector and connect a jumper lead between it and the battery—*do not leave this connection on more than 30 seconds at one time.*

3. The jumper lead connection should actuate the solenoid to give an approximate increase of 50 rpm if it is working properly. If no rpm increase is noted, replace the solenoid.

4. Make and break the jumper lead circuit several times to make certain the advance solenoid is working normally, then disconnect the jumper lead and reconnect the bullet connector.

DWELL VARIATION TEST

Excessive wear in the distributor's mechanical parts will cause dwell variations which will affect ignition timing and engine performance. A dwell variation test will determine the mechanical condition of the distributor.

1. Disconnect the distributor vacuum hose and connect a tach-dwell tester. The red lead goes to the DIST terminal of the coil and the black lead to ground.

2. Start the engine and run at idle, then slowly increase engine speed to 1500 rpm and gradually reduce it back to idle.

3. If dwell varies more than 2° between the idle-speed and 1500-rpm readings, the distributor should be removed and inspected for probable wear in the distributor shaft, bushings or breaker plate. Dwell variations at speeds over 1500 rpm are not an accurate indication of distributor wear.

FIG. 3-43 CHRYSLER SOLENOID-ADVANCE DISTRIBUTOR

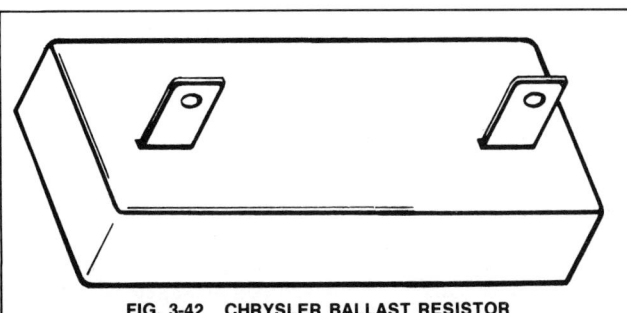

FIG. 3-42 CHRYSLER BALLAST RESISTOR

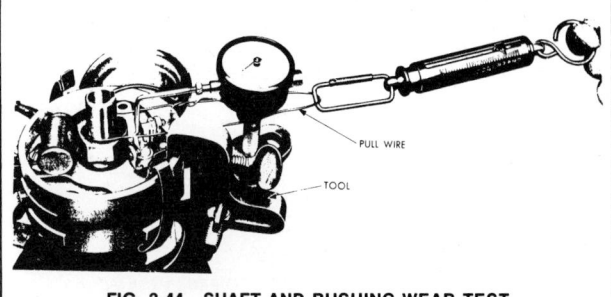

FIG. 3-44 SHAFT AND BUSHING WEAR TEST

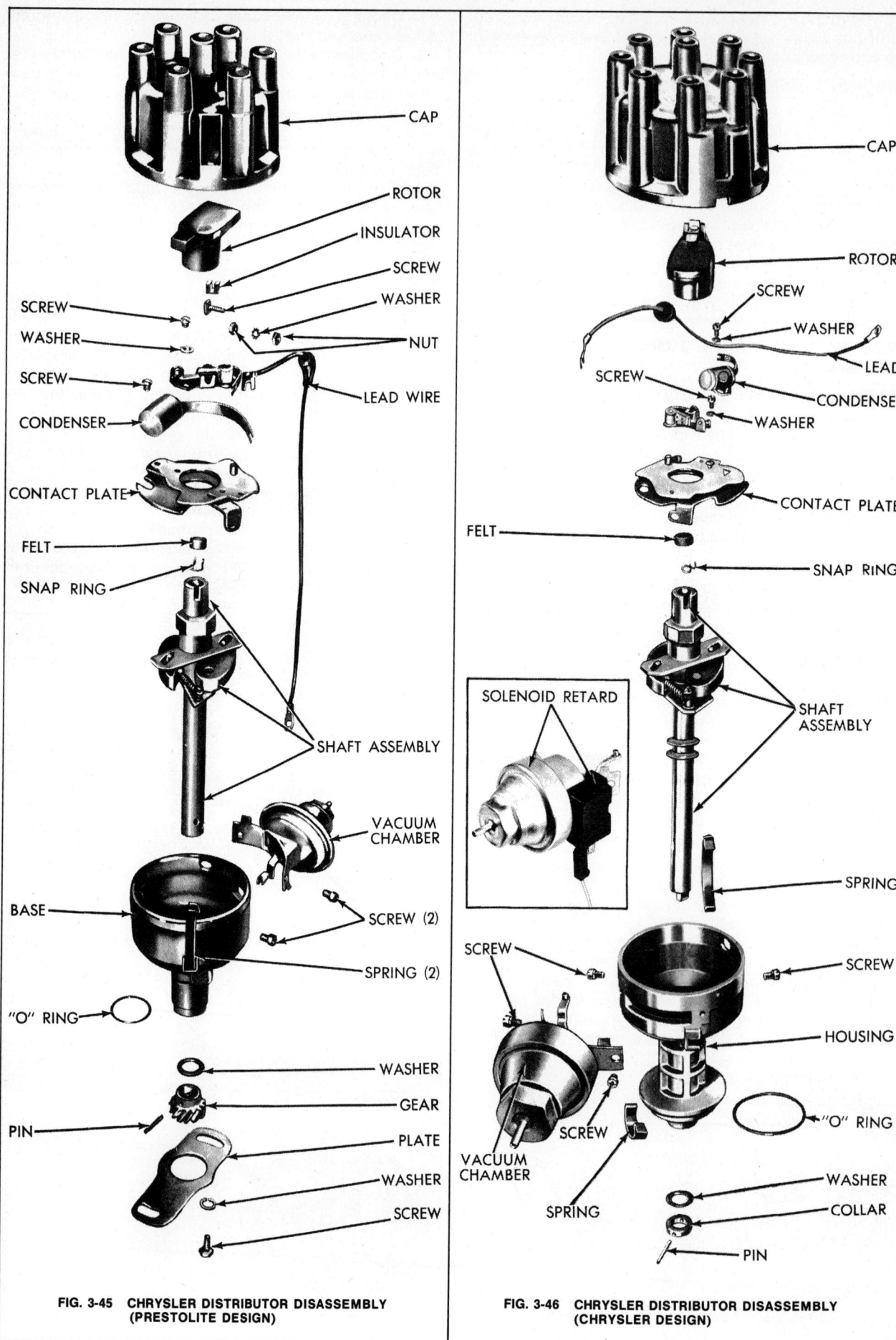

FIG. 3-45 CHRYSLER DISTRIBUTOR DISASSEMBLY (PRESTOLITE DESIGN)

FIG. 3-46 CHRYSLER DISTRIBUTOR DISASSEMBLY (CHRYSLER DESIGN)

DISTRIBUTOR REMOVAL

1. Disconnect the vacuum hose at the distributor and the primary lead wire at the coil.
2. Unclip and remove the distributor cap.
3. Rotate the engine crankshaft until the distributor rotor points toward the cylinder block. Scribe a mark on the block as a rotor reference point for installation.
4. Remove the distributor hold-down screw and carefully lift the distributor from the engine. The distributor shaft will rotate slightly as its gear disengages from that of the camshaft.

DISTRIBUTOR SHAFT
AND BUSHING WEAR TEST (Fig. 3-44)

1. Secure the distributor in a soft-jaw vise by its hold-down arm and tighten sufficiently to prevent distributor movement—no more.
2. Remove the rotor and disconnect the primary lead wire, but do not loosen the removable contact-arm-spring retaining nut.
3. Connect a dial indicator to the distributor housing. With the rubbing block on the highest point of a cam lobe, the plunger arm should rest against the movable breaker-point arm at the rubbing block.
4. Fit a wire loop over the distributor shaft and connect a spring scale. Apply a 5-lb. pull in a straight line, and read the indicator dial.
5. If the indicated side play exceeds 0.006-in., disassemble the distributor and replace the worn parts.

DISTRIBUTOR DISASSEMBLY (Figs. 3-45 & 3-46)

1. Remove the rotor.
2. Remove the screws and lockwashers holding the vacuum advance unit in place. Disengage and remove the vacuum advance unit.
3. Disconnect the primary lead at the terminal screw and remove the lead from the contact plate terminal.
4. Remove the screws and lockwashers holding the contact plate to the housing. Lift out the contact plate, breaker points and condenser as an assembly.
5. Drive out the distributor drive-gear roll pin carefully with a hammer and drift, and slide the gear from the shaft end.
6. Clean any burrs from around the pin hole in the

shaft with a file, and then remove the lower thrust washer.
7. Push the distributor shaft up and remove it through the top of the distributor housing.

DISTRIBUTOR ASSEMBLY (Figs. 3-45 & 3-46)

1. Lubricate and install the upper thrust washer(s) on the shaft and slide the shaft into the distributor housing.
2. Replace the lower thrust washer and old drive gear, securing with the roll pin.
3. Scribe a line on the end of the shaft from edge to center as shown in **Fig. 3-47**. The line must be centered between two gear teeth and should not be scribed completely across the shaft.
4. Now remove the roll pin and old drive gear. Clean any burrs from around the pin hole with a file.
5. Replace the thrust washer and install a new drive gear. Place a 0.007-in. feeler gauge between the gear and thrust washer, and drill a 0.124- to 0.129-in. hole in the gear and shaft, approximately 90° from the old hole, and with the scribe line centered between the two gear teeth. Install the roll pin.
6. Replace the contact plate assembly, aligning the condenser lead, movable contact spring and primary lead. Install the attaching screws.
7. Attach the vacuum-advance-unit arm to the contact plate and replace attaching screws and washers.
8. Test contact-arm spring tension as shown in **Fig. 3-48**. Spring tension should be 17-20 oz. If the pull scale reading is outside these limits, loosen the screw holding the contact arm spring and slide the spring end in or out as required.
9. Lubricate the felt pad located in the top of the distributor cam with one drop of light engine oil, and replace the rotor and distributor cap.

DISTRIBUTOR INSTALLATION

1. Make certain the rubber O-ring seal is fully seated in the distributor shank groove, then turn the distributor until the rotor points to the scribed mark on the cylinder block.
2. Carefully engage the distributor drive gear with the camshaft drive gear. If the engine has been cranked with the distributor removed, the proper relationship between the distributor shaft and the No. 1 piston must be reestablished:

    a) Rotate the crankshaft until No. 1 piston is at the top of its compression stroke. The mark on the inner edge of the crankshaft pulley should line up with the "O" mark on the timing chain cover.

    b) Rotate the distributor rotor to a position just ahead of the No. 1 distributor cap terminal, lower

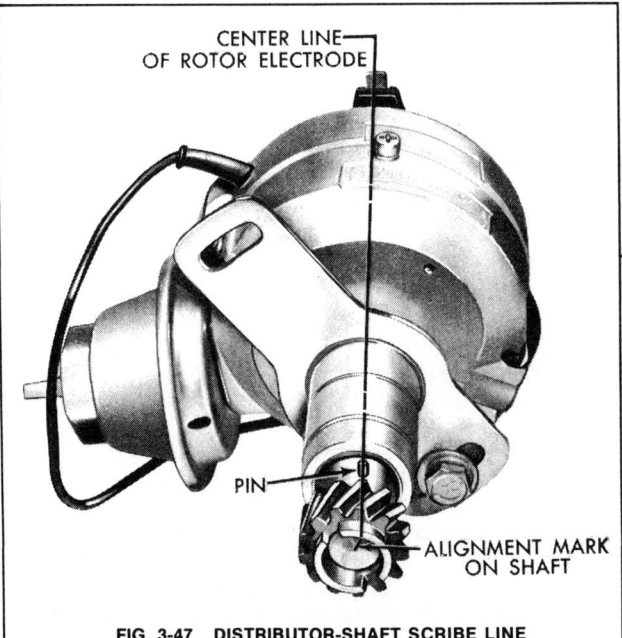

FIG. 3-47   DISTRIBUTOR-SHAFT SCRIBE LINE

CENTER LINE OF ROTOR ELECTRODE

PIN

ALIGNMENT MARK ON SHAFT

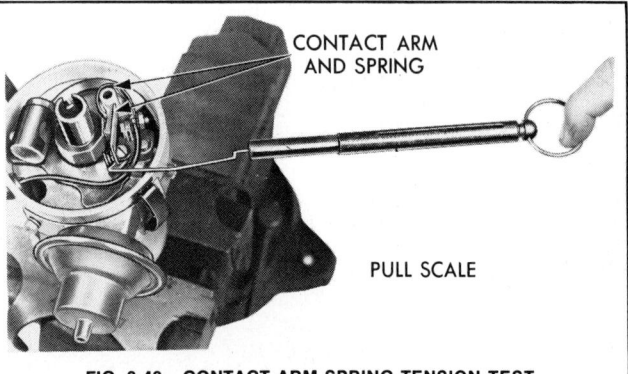

FIG. 3-48   CONTACT ARM SPRING-TENSION TEST

CONTACT ARM AND SPRING

PULL SCALE

the distributor carefully into the engine opening and engage the drive gears.

c) With the distributor fully seated, the rotor should rest under the distributor-cap No. 1 tower, with the breaker points just separating.

3. Replace the distributor cap and clamp it in place.

4. Install and tighten the hold-down-arm screw finger-tight.

5. Attach the primary lead wire to the coil (the distributor vacuum hose is not connected until after initial timing has been set).

6. Connect a timing light **(Fig. 3-49),** start the engine and run at idle speed.

7. Rotate the distributor housing until the timing mark on the crankshaft damper aligns with the specified degree mark on the timing chain cover.

8. Tighten the distributor hold-down screw and re-check the timing setting with the timing light.

9. If not correct, loosen the hold-down screw and readjust, then recheck. When timing is correct, replace the vacuum hose to the distributor.

BREAKER-POINT REPLACEMENT

1. Remove the distributor cap and rotor.

2. Loosen the terminal screw nut and remove the primary and condenser leads.

3. Remove the breaker-plate lockscrew and lift the old breaker-point set and condenser from distributor.

4. Wipe old grease from the cam with a clean, lint-free cloth and sparingly apply a fresh coat of cam lubricant.

5. Install the new breaker-point set. The sleeve at the end of the adjustable bracket should fit over and pivot on the upper contact-plate mounting pin.

6. If point alignment is required, bend the stationary bracket *only.*

7. Set the breaker-point gap with a feeler gauge. Gap is correct when there is a slight drag on the gauge as it is removed. Tighten the lockscrew.

8. Install the condenser, replace the condenser and primary leads, and tighten the terminal screw nut.

9. Replace the rotor and distributor cap.

10. Check dwell with a dwell meter. If dwell is not within specifications, reset the gap and recheck the dwell.

11. If the distributor uses two sets of breaker points, remove and replace in the same way as for a single set. Block one set of points open with a clean insulator while setting the second set **(Fig. 3-50).** Tighten the lock screw and block open the adjusted points while setting the other pair. If the gap is set correctly, the dwell angle should also be within specifications. Check the dwell after setting both point sets to the correct gap.

CHECKING DWELL SETTING

1. Disconnect the vacuum hose to the distributor. Also disconnect the ignition retard solenoid on 1970-71 distributors so equipped.

2. Connect the red lead of a dwell-tach to the distributor terminal of the coil and the black lead to ground. Set the selector switch to 6 or 8 cyls., according to the engine under test.

3. Start the engine and run at idle.

4. Compare the dwell reading to specifications. A reading not within specifications indicates an incorrect point gap, a worn rubbing block or cam, or a distortion of the movable contact arm.

5. Reconnect the vacuum hose to the distributor and reconnect the retard solenoid, if so equipped.

1977-79 AMERICAN MOTORS I-4 ENGINE
Bosch Breaker-Point Ignition System

The only conventional breaker-point ignition presently in use is on the AMC Gremlin and Concord equipped with the I-4 engine **(Fig. 3-51).** All other domestic cars use an electronic ignition.

DISTRIBUTOR REMOVAL

1. Unclip and remove the distributor cap with high-tension cables. Position out of the way.

2. Disconnect the vacuum line from the distributor vacuum advance.

3. Disconnect the primary wiring connector.

4. Rotate the engine crankshaft until the distributor rotor points toward the cylinder block. Scribe a mark on the block and one on the distributor housing as rotor reference points for installation.

5. Remove the distributor hold-down bolt and clamp, and carefully lift the distributor from the engine. The distributor shaft will rotate slightly as its gear disengages from that in the engine block.

DISTRIBUTOR INSTALLATION

1. Clean the distributor mounting area on the drive housing, and install a new mounting gasket.

2. Turn the distributor until the rotor points to the scribed mark on the distributor housing. Align this scribed mark with the one on the engine.

3. Insert the distributor in the engine, making certain the shaft engages with camshaft gear. It may be necessary to move the rotor and distributor shaft slightly to start gear into mesh, but rotor should align with the scribe mark when the distributor is in place. If the engine has been cranked with the distributor removed, the proper relationship between the distributor shaft and the No. 1 piston must be reestablished:

a) Rotate the crankshaft until the No. 1 piston is at the top of its compression stroke. The TDC mark on the timing pointer should line up with the timing pin on the crankshaft damper.

b) Rotate the distributor rotor until the tip points

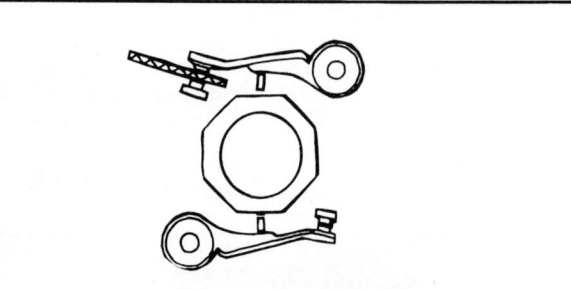

FIG. 3-50   DUAL POINT ADJUSTMENT

IGNITION COIL AND RESISTOR SPECIFICATIONS

CHRYSLER CORPORATION CARS

	Chrysler-Essex	Chrysler-Prestolite
Coil		
Identification Number	2444241	2444242
Primary Resistance @ 70°-80° F	1.41-1.55 Ohms	1.65-1.79 Ohms
Secondary Resistance @ 70°-80° F	9200-10,700 Ohms	9400-11,700 Ohms
Ballast Resistor		2095501
Resistance @ 70°-80° F		0.5-0.6 Ohms
Current Draw (Coil and Ballast Resistor in Circuit)		
Engine Stopped		3.0 Amps
Engine Idling		1.9 Amps

in the direction of the No. 1 terminal, which is indicated by a mark on the edge of the distributor housing. Then turn the rotor ⅛ turn clockwise past the No. 1 terminal and lower the distributor carefully into the engine opening and engage the camshaft gear.

c) Install, but *do not* tighten, the hold-down clamp, bolt and lockwasher. Rotate the distributor to advance the timing to a point where the breaker points are just starting to open; tighten clamp finger-tight.

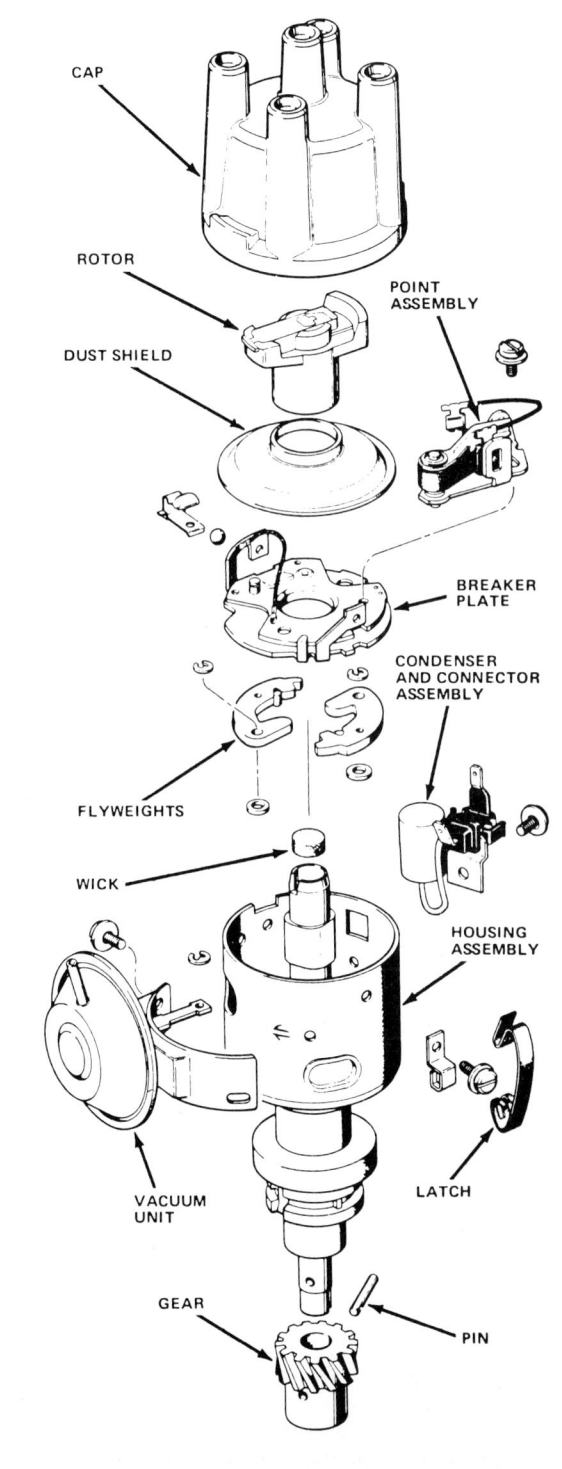

FIG. 3-51 BOSCH I-4 DISTRIBUTOR DISASSEMBLY

CAP
ROTOR
DUST SHIELD
POINT ASSEMBLY
BREAKER PLATE
CONDENSER AND CONNECTOR ASSEMBLY
FLYWEIGHTS
WICK
HOUSING ASSEMBLY
VACUUM UNIT
LATCH
GEAR
PIN

4. Replace the distributor cap, with ignition cables, and clamp it in place.

5. *Do not* connect vacuum line until after the initial timing has been set, but it should be pinched shut or plugged with a golf tee or small bolt to prevent a vacuum leak.

6. Connect a timing light **(Fig. 3-37)**, start the engine and idle at 700 rpm.

7. Rotate the distributor housing until the timing mark on the crankshaft pulley aligns with the specified timing mark on the pointer.

8. Tighten the distributor hold-down bolt and recheck the timing setting with the timing light.

9. If not correct, loosen the hold-down bolt and read-just, then recheck. When timing is correct, replace the vacuum line and tighten the distributor hold-down bolt.

BREAKER POINT REPLACEMENT

1. Remove the distributor cap, with wires attached, and position it aside.

2. Remove the rotor by pulling it straight up, and remove the dust shield.

3. Remove the screws holding the breaker-point set and condenser to the breaker plate, then lift the point set and condenser out.

4. Wipe old grease from the cam with a clean, lint-free cloth, and sparingly apply a fresh coat of cam lubricant.

5. Attach the new breaker-point set and condenser to the breaker plate—make sure the ground wire is re-placed under the breaker-point attaching screw from which it was removed.

6. Connect the primary and condenser lead wires to the breaker-point terminal and tighten the terminal screw.

7. Align the breaker points if necessary. Bend the stationary bracket only when aligning the points.

8. Rotate the distributor shaft until the breaker-point rubbing block rests on the peak of a cam lobe.

9. Adjust gap to 0.45mm (0.018-in.) and tighten the retaining screw.

10. Replace the dust cover, rotor and distributor cap.

11. Connect a dwell-tach meter and check dwell angle. If not within specifications, reset the breaker-point gap and recheck the dwell.

CHECKING DWELL SETTING

1. Disconnect the vacuum line to the distributor.

2. Connect the red lead of a dwell-tach meter to the distributor terminal of the coil and the black lead to ground. Set the dwell-tach selector switch to 4 cyls.

3. Start the engine and run at idle.

4. Compare the dwell reading to specifications. A reading not within specifications indicates an incorrect point gap, a worn rubbing block or cam, or a distortion of the movable contact arm.

5. Reconnect the vacuum line to the distributor.

IGNITION COIL RESISTANCE VALUES

AMERICAN MOTORS I-4 ENGINE

Primary Resistance @ 75° F	1.60 to 1.80 ohms
Secondary resistance @ 75° F	9400 to 11,700 ohms
Open circuit output	20 KV minimum
Required voltage, spark plug	5 to 16 KV

Plug size and type don't tell the whole story. You must "read" the plug.

One of the most valuable skills which you can acquire is the ability to determine engine operating conditions from the appearance of its spark plugs. An inspection of the firing tips of the old plugs at each spark plug change can often be a tip-off that there is something in need of attention that has not yet become a serious problem. Also, when a serious problem does suddenly turn up, a look at the spark plugs will often pinpoint the trouble. By carefully studying the following photos you can familiarize yourself with the most common abnormal plug conditions and their causes. Remember that most of these conditions are caused by engine trouble, not plug trouble. The idea is not to change — for example — to a hotter plug when the type that has served the engine previously begins to oil foul, but to replace the piston rings, valve guides, or whatever, to correct the trouble that's making your plugs look like a petroleum-based fudgesicle.

NORMAL PLUG / Description: Insulator light tan or gray. Few deposits. Indicates proper type and heat range for engine and use. Recommendation: Replace plug at regular intervals with same type and heat range. Plugs showing this reading indicate good longevity and will give acceptable performance.

DETONATION CLUE/ Description: Side electrode snapped off. Plug appears more carbon coated than overheated. Cause: Overheated carbon deposits have begun to cause detonation. Treatment: Remove cylinder head, clean away carbon deposits and check closely for hot spots in the combustion chamber.

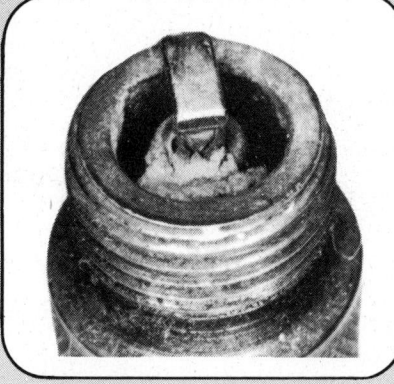

CORE BRIDGING/ Description: Combustion chamber deposits build up between the insulator and plug shell. Cause: Excessive carbon build-up, poor oil, bad oil control, long idling — then rapid acceleration. Treatment: Use good oil, check rings, valve guides, avoid extended idling in traffic if possible.

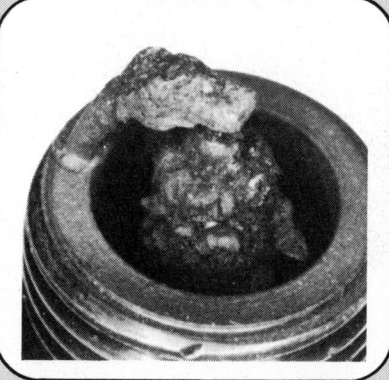

SILICA DEPOSITS/ Description: Hard conductive deposits of fused sand, lead and fuel additives. Cause: Dirt, dust and sand entering with the air/fuel mixture. Treatment: Repair or replace air cleaner on carburetor. Check for any loose bolts, leaks and bad intake gaskets or poorly fitting air cleaners.

SPLASHED DEPOSITS/ Description: Dark spots flecking insulator nose. Cause: Recent tune-up is clearing up old combustion chamber deposits which are splashing onto insulator. Treatment: Condition will soon disappear; however, rapid acceleration could prove harmful by loosening up deposits in the chamber.

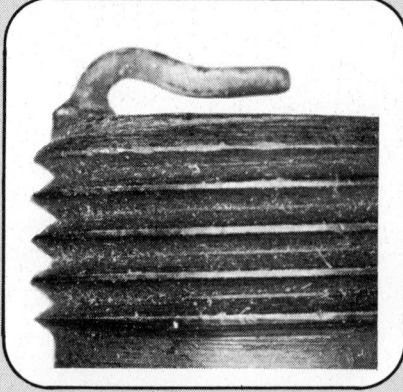

BENT ELECTRODE/ Description: Side electrode has peculiar "question mark" shape. Cause: Using pliers-type gapping tool — especially on filed plugs or worn center electrode. Treatment: Regap plugs or replace those that can't be brought up to specs without deforming the electrode or bending it excessively.

GAP BRIDGING/ Description: Combustion chamber deposits lodged between electrode. Cause: Too much carbon build-up in cylinders, poor oil control or long idling — then all-out acceleration. Treatment: Check your engine for the above trouble then clean and re-install your plugs with proper gapping.

TOO WIDE GAP/ Description: Excessive gap width between insulator nose and electrode. Cause: The action of intense heat, combustion chamber pressures, corrosive gases and spark discharge cause gap to widen. Treatment: Regap plug and then check for adequate secondary resistance in circuit.

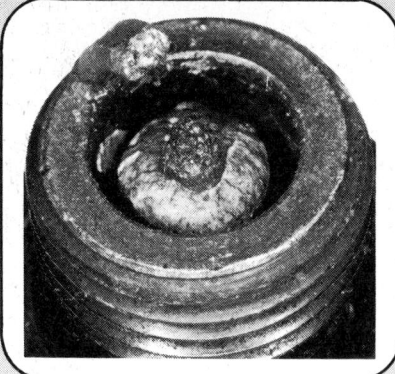

INITIAL PRE-IGNITION/ Description: Electrodes burned away, insulator tip blistered or deformed. Cause: Excessive spark advance, plug too hot, inferior fuel being used. Treatment: Bring timing up to specs, check advance, switch to better gas and try using a colder plug, with a booster gap if available.

SCAVENGE DEPOSITS/ Description: Yellow, white or brownish crust-like deposits over electrodes and insulator. Cause: Typical of chemical make-up of some gasolines, but usually a result of "old fogey" driving. Treatment: Clean and file electrodes, go out and "stand-on-it" to clean out combustion chamber.

ALUMINUM THROW-OFF/ Description: Molten chunks of aluminum imbedded between electrode and insulator. Cause: Pre-ignition causes hot spots on aluminum piston heads. Treatment: Check timing, ignition advance, change to a top grade of gasoline and install colder plugs. Be sure plug is right reach.

OIL FOULED PLUG/ Description: Soft, wet, oily deposits covering insulator and nose of plug. Cause: Excess oil reaching combustion chamber. Treatment: Check or repair worn oil control rings, valve guides, crankcase vent, oil level, oil bath air cleaners. Use hotter plugs. Booster gap plugs will fire longer.

GLAZING/ Description: Hard, glassy, brown coating on insulator tip and electrode. Cause: Fast acceleration after low-speed driving. Treatment: Accelerate slowly after long periods of in-town driving. Glaze is conductive and can ruin plugs, so don't squirrel around the pits. Don't idle engine for long periods.

CARBON FOULED PLUG/ Description: Dry, fluffy black carbon deposits over the entire firing end. Cause: Plug too cold, choke not open, over-rich mixture, low voltage, weak condenser, sticking valves. Treatment: End richness, free the valves, raise voltage, use hotter plug. Check carb float level.

WORN PLUG/ Description: Electrodes are obviously rounded and thinned, insulator pitted and encrusted with old deposits. Cause: Plug has been in service for an extremely long time. Treatment: Be sure to replace your old plugs with a set of new ones after driving approximately 8000 to 12,000 miles.

MECHANICAL DAMAGE/ Description: Insultor nose broken, electrode bent. Cause: Loose object or inadequate piston/valve-to-plug clearance. Treatment: Look for loose parts, check for engine damage, see proper clearance between plugs and engine's moving parts is maintained. Use correct reach plug.

DISTRIBUTOR SPECIFICATIONS

AMERICAN MOTORS

YEAR	ENGINE APPLICATION	DISTRIBUTOR NUMBER	CENTRIFUGAL ADVANCE DIST. DEGREES @ DIST. RPM		VACUUM ADVANCE DIST. DEGREES @ INS. HG.		DWELL ANGLE (Degrees)	INITIAL TIMING @ Engine Idle1
			Start	Finish	Start	Finish		
1970	I-6 199	1110481	0-2@450	11-13@2250	0@5-7	8.5-9.5@14	31-34	3° BTDC
	I-6 232	1110481	0-2@450	11-13@2250	0@5-7	8.5-9.5@14	31-34	3° BTDC
	I-6 232	1110444	2-3@450	12-14@2200	0@5-7	11@16-17	31-34	3° BTDC
	V-8 304	1112018	0-2@500	12-14@2200	NONE	NONE	29-31	5° BTDC
	V-8 304	1111988	0-2@500	12-14@2100	0@5-7	8.5-9.5@14	29-31	5° BTDC
	V-8 360	1111987	0-2@450	11-13@2000	0@5-7	8.5-9.5@14	29-31	5° BTDC
	V-8 360	1111988	0-2@500	12-14@2100	0@5-7	8.5-9.5@14	29-31	5° BTDC
	V-8 390	1111948	0-1@400	14-16@2000	0@4-6	12@18.5	29-31	5° BTDC
	V-8 390	1111987	0-2@450	11-13@2000	0@5-7	8.5-9.5@14	29-31	TDC
1971	I-6 232	1110340	0-2@450	11.5-13.5@2000	0@5-7	10-11.5@15.5-17	31-34	3° BTDC3
	I-6 258	1110340	0-2@450	11.5-13.5@2000	0@5-7	10-11.5@15.5-17	31-34	5° BTDC
	V-8 304	1112028	0-2@450	12.5-14.5@2000	0@5-6	11.5-12.5@18	29-31	2.5° BTDC
	V-8 360	1111948	0-2.5@450	13-15@2000	0@5-6	11.5-12.5@18	29-31	2.5° BTDC
	V-8 360	1112028	0-2@450	12.5-14.5@2000	0@5-6	11.5-12.5@18	29-31	2.5° BTDC
	V-8 401	1111948	0-2.5@450	13-15@2000	0@5-6	11.5-12.5@18	29-31	2.5° BTDC
1972	I-6 232	1110497	0-0.5@500	12-14@2000	0@5-7	6-9@10-11	31-34	5° BTDC
	I-6 258	1110497	0-0.5@500	12-14@2000	0@5-7	6-9@10-11	31-34	3° BTDC
	V-8 304	1112111	0-2@550	13-15@2000	0@5-7	7-9@12.5-16	29-31	5° BTDC
	V-8 360	1112111	0-2@550	13-15@2000	0@5-7	7-9@12.5-16	29-31	5° BTDC
	V-8 401	1112112	0-1@450	12-14@2000	0@5-7	7-9@12.5-16	29-31	5° BTDC
1973	I-6 232	1110522	0-2.5@500	12-14@2200	0@5-7	6.3-9@12.5-13.3	31-34	5° BTDC
	I-6 232	1110523	0-1@500	13-15@2200	0@5-7	6.3-9@12.5-13.3	31-34	5° BTDC
	I-6 258	1110522	0-2.5@500	12-14@2200	0@5-7	6.3-9@12.5-13.3	31-34	3° BTDC
	I-6 258	1110523	0-1@500	13-15@2200	0@5-7	6.3-9@12.5-13.3	31-34	5° BTDC
	V-8 304	1112179	0-1@400	15-17@2200	0@5-7	6.3-8.3@11.5-12.5	29-31	5° BTDC
	V-8 304	1112214	0-2@450	15-17@2200	0@4-6	6.3-8.3@11.5-13	29-31	5° BTDC
	V-8 360	1112112	0-1@500	12-14@2000	0@5-7	6.3-8.3@11.5-12.5	29-31	5° BTDC
	V-8 360	1112115	0-3.3@400	14-16@2300	0@4-6	6.8-8.3@11.8-13	29-31	5° BTDC
	V-8 401	1112112	0-1@500	12-14@2000	0@5-7	6.3-8.3@11.5-12.5	29-31	5° BTDC
	V-8 401	1112115	0-3.3@400	14-16@2300	0@4-6	6.8-8.3@11.8-13	29-31	5° BTDC
1974	I-6 232	1110528	0-2@600	12-15@2200	0@5-7	6.5-9@12.8-13	31-34	5° BTDC
	I-6 232	1110529	0-2@600	12-14@2300	0@5-7	6.5-9@12.8-13	31-34	5° BTDC
	I-6 258	1110528	0-2@600	12-15@2200	0@5-7	6.5-9@12.8-13	31-34	3° BTDC
	I-6 258	1110529	0-2@500	12-14@2300	0@5-7	6.5-9@12.8-13	31-34	3° BTDC
	V-8 304	1112179	0-2@500	15-17@2200	0@5-7	6.8-8.3@11.3-12.8	29-31	5° BTDC
	V-8 304	1112214	0-2.5@500	15-17@2200	0@4-6	6.8-8.3@11.5-13	29-31	5° BTDC
	V-8 360	1112112	0-2@500	12-14@2000	0@5-7	6.8-8.3@11.2-12.8	29-31	5° BTDC
	V-8 360	1112115	0-1.5@400	14-16@2200	0@4-6	6.8-8.3@11.5-13	29-31	5° BTDC
	V-8 401	1112112	0-2@500	12-14@2000	0@5-7	6.8-8.3@11.2-12.8	29-31	5° BTDC
	V-8 401	1112115	0-1.5@400	14-16@2200	0@4-6	6.8-8.3@11.5-13	29-31	5° BTDC
1975	I-6 232	3224968	0-2@600	13-15@2250	0@5-7	7-9@13.1	2	5° BTDC
	I-6 232	3224969	0-2@600	12-14@2250	0@5-7	7-9@13.1	2	3° BTDC
	I-6 258	3224968	0-2@600	13-15@2250	0@5-7	7-9@13.1	2	5° BTDC
	I-6 258	3224969	0-2@500	12-14@2250	0@5-7	7-9@13.1	2	3° BTDC
	V-8 304	3224965	0.4-2.9@500	15-17@2200	0@5-7	6.5-8.5@12.5	2	5° BTDC
	V-8 304	3224966	0-2.5@500	15-17@2200	0@4-6	6.5-8.5@12.7	2	5° BTDC
	V-8 360	3224746	0.4-3@500	14-16@2300	0@4-6	6.5-8.5@12.7	2	5° BTDC
1976	I-6 232	3227331 IDJ-4002-E	0-0.4@500	5.25-7.25@2200	0-2.3@5-7	7-9@12.6	2	8° BTDC
	I-6 258	3227331 IDJ-4002-E	0-0.4@500	5.25-7.25@2200	0-2.3@5-7	7-9@12.6	2	6 BTDC4
	V-8 304	3228263 IDJ-4001-E	0-2.8@500	11-13@2200	0-2.2@4-6	6.5-8.5@12.7	2	10° BTDC
	V-8 304	3228264 IDJ-4001-G	0-2.4@500	13.5-15.5@2200	0-2.7@5-7	6.5-8.5@12.5	2	5 BTDC
	V-8 360	3228265 IDJ-4001-F	0-2.7@500	7.5-9.5@2200	0-2.2@4-6	6.5-8.5@12.7	2	10° BTDC
	V-8 360	3228266 IDJ-4001-H	0-3.75@500	10-12@2200	0-2.2@4-6	6.5-8.5@12.7	2	5 BTDC
	V-8 401	3228265 IDJ-4001-F	0-2.7@500	7.5-9.5@2200	0-2.2@4-6	6.5-8.5@12.7	2	10 BTDC
	V-8 401	3228266 IDJ-4001-H	0-3.75@500	10-12@2200	0-2.2@4-6	6.5-8.5@12.7	2	5 BTDC
1977	I-4 121	0-.231-170-207	0@1050-1350	30@4500	0@2-4	14-18@10.9-9.6	47	12° BTDC5
	I-6 232	IDJ-4002-F	0@700-1100	18-22@4400	0@5-7	14-18@13.1-12.8	2	10° BTDC6
	I-6 258	IDJ-4002-E	0@700-1100	18-22@4400	0@5-7	14-18@13.1-12.8	2	8° BTDC7
	V-8 304	IDJ-4001-E	0@700-1100	22-26@4400	0@4-6	13-17@12.7-11.8	2	10° BTDC
	V-8 304	IDJ-4001-G	0@700-1100	27-31@4400	0@5-7	13-17@12.5-11.4	2	5° BTDC
	V-8 360	IDJ-4001-F	0@700-1100	15-19@4400	0@4-6	13-17@12.7-11.8	2	10° BTDC
	V-8 360	IDJ-4001-H	0@700-1100	20-24@4400	0@4-6	13-17@12.7-11.8	2	5 BTDC
1978	I-4 2L	3250163	0@500	15-17@2200	0@2	4.5-9.5	47° ±3°	12° BTDC8
	I-6 232	3231915	0@425	8-11@2200	0.5-2.5	13@11.2	9	8° BTDC10
	I-6 258	3232434	0@425	8-10.5@2200	0.5@2	9.2@13	9	10° BTDC
	I-6 258	3231915	0@425	8-11@2200	0.5@2.5	13@11.2	9	6° BTDC12
	V-8 304	3233173	0@400	10.9-13.1@2200	0.5@1	13@11.2	9	10° BTDC
	V-8 304	3230443	0@400	10.9-13@2200	0.5@1	9.5-12.5	9	10° BTDC
	V-8 304	3231340	0@400	12.8-16@2200	0.5@1	9.5@12	9	5° BTDC
	V-8 360	3233174	0@400	7-9.2@2200	0.5@1	13.2@11	9	10° BTDC
	V-8 360	3231341	0@375	7-9.2@2200	0.5@1	9.5-12.5	9	10° BTDC
1979	I-4 2L	3250497	0@450	10.8@1800	0@2	11.5@8.5	47° ±3°	12°BTDC
	I-4 2L	3250163	0@450	17@2000	0@2	9@9.5	47° ±3°	8°BTDC
	I-6 232	3231915	0@400	11@2200	0@2	13@11.5	9	10°BTDC13
	I-6 258	3232434	0@400	10.5@2200	0@2	9.5@13	9	8°BTDC
	I-6 258	3231915	0@400	11@2200	0@2	13@11.5	9	4°BTDC12

AMERICAN MOTORS

YEAR	Engine Application	Distributor Number	Centrifugal Advance Dist. Degrees @Dist. RPM Start	Finish	Vacuum Advance Dist. Degrees @Ins. Hg. Start	Finish	Dwell Angle (degrees)	Initial Timing @Engine Idle1
	V-8 304	3234693	0@450	14@2200	0@2	12.8@12	9	5°BTDC
	V-8 304	3233959	0@450	14.5@2200	0@2	17.3@12	9	8°BTDC

1 Refer to vehicle emissions control sticker for engine idle and/or initial timing specification.
2 BID ignition.
3 Automatic. 5° BTDC
4 Automatic. 8° BTDC. 5 California 8°BTDC; Altitude manual 10° BTDC.
6 All Federal 2-bbl. and Matador automatic 6° BTDC; California 2-bbl. 8° BTDC.
7 All Federal 2-bbl. and Matador automatic 6° BTDC; all Altitude and California 1-bbl. 10° BTDC.

8 Calif. Auto.; 8° BTDC.
9 Solid State Ignition.
10 Auto., 10° BTDC.
11 Auto., 8° BTDC; Man., 6° BTDC.
12 Auto., 8° BTDC.
13 MAN., 8°BTDC; Auto. with 2.37 Axle, 12°BTDC.

BUICK

YEAR	ENGINE APPLICATION	DISTRIBUTOR NUMBER	CENTRIFUGAL ADVANCE DIST. DEGREES @ DIST. RPM Start	Finish	VACUUM ADVANCE DIST. DEGREES @ INS. HG. Start	Finish	DWELL ANGLE (Degrees)	INITIAL TIMING @ Engine Idle1
1970	I-6 250	1110463	0@450	17@2100	0@8	10-12@17	32	TDC
	I-6 250	1110464	0@450	15@2100	0@8	10-12@17	32	4° BTDC
	V-8 350	1111986	0@425	17@2300	0@8	7-9@16	30	6° BTDC
	V-8 350	1112006	0@550	15@2300	0@8	7-9@16	30	6° BTDC
	V-8 455	1111984	0@550	17@2300	0@8	7-9@16	30	6° BTDC
	V-8 455	1111962	0@550	12@2300	0@8	7-9@16	30	10° BTDC
1971	I-6 250	1110489	0@500	9-11@2050	0@8	12.5@16	32	4° BTDC
	V-8 350	1112006	0@700-1100	8-10@2300	0@8	7-9@16	30	6 BTDC
	V-8 350	1112037	0@700-800	5-7@2300	0@8	7-9@16	30	10° BTDC
	V-8 350	1112080	0@700-800	7-9@1450	0@8	7-9@16	30	4° BTDC
	V-8 455	1112016	0@350-500	10-12@2300	0@8	7-9@16	30	6° BTDC2
	V-8 455	1112077	0@700-800	8-10@1500	0@8	8-10@16	30	4° BTDC
1972	V-8 350	1112109	0@400-500	6-8@1500	0@8	7-9@16	30	4° BTDC
	V-8 455	1112110	0@500-600	7-9@1450	0@8	7-9@13	30	4° BTDC
	V-8 455	1112016	0@350-500	10-12@2300	0@8	7-9@16	30	4° BTDC3
1973	V-8 350	1112109	0@375-525	7-9@1450	0@8	7-9@16	30	4° BTDC
	V-8 455	1112110	0@375-525	8-10@1500	0@8	7-9.5@13	30	4° BTDC
	V-8 455	1112016	0@350-525	10-12@2300	0@8	7-9@16	30	10° BTDC
1974	I-6 250	1110499	0@550	10.5@2050	0@6	11@14	31-34	8° BTDC
	V-8 350	1112541	0@750	9.5-12@1800	0@6	7-9@16	30	4° BTDC
	V-8 350	1112802	0@750-1050	9.5-12@1800	0@6	7-9@16	4	4° BTDC
	V-8 455	1112542	0@750	11.5-14@2050	0@6.5	7-9.5@13	30	4° BTDC
	V-8 455	1112803	0@750-1050	11.5-14@2050	0@6.5	7-9.5@13	4	4° BTDC
	V-8 455	1112521	0@600	10-12@2300	0@6	7-9@16	30	10° BTDC
	V-8 455	1112520	0@600-1050	10-12@2300	0@6.5	7-9.5@13	4	4° BTDC
1975	V-6 231	____	0@500	8@2050	0@5-7	9@10	4	12° BTDC
	I-6 250	____	0@550	8@2100	0@5-7	9@125	4	10° BTDC
	V-8 260	____	0@650	14@2200	0@4	12@15	4	18° BTDC6
	V-8 350	____	0@750	5-7@2250	0@6.5	5-8@11.5	4	12° BTDC
	V-8 400	____	0@1200	8@2200	0@6	12.5@10.5-13.5	4	16° BTDC
	V-8 455	____	0@750	7-9@2200	0@4	7-10@11	4	12° BTDC
1976	V-6 231	1110661	0-2.2@770	9@2500	0-1@5.3	12.25@12.8	4	12 BTDC
	V-6 231	1110668	0-2.1@700	9@2500	0-1@5.3	11.25@12.8	4	12 BTDC
	V-8 260	1112994	0@325	14@2200	0@4.5	12@10.5	4	14 BTDC
	V-8 260	1112995	0@455	13@2237	0@4	15@11	4	14 BTDC
	V-8 260	1112956	0@325	14@2200			4	18 BTDC
	V-8 260	1103204	0@325	14@2200	0@6	10@14.75	4	18 BTDC
	V-8 260	1103208	0@325	14@2200	0@6	9@10.2	4	18 BTDC
	V-8 260	1103211	0@325	14@2200	0@6	7@9.2	4	18 BTDC
	V-8 350	1112991	0-2.1@875	11@2500	0-1@6.9	10.75@14.3	4	12 BTDC
	V-8 455	1112963	0-2.1@660	9@2200	0-1@4.5	9.75@12	4	12 BTDC
	V-8 455	1112985	0-2.1@660	9@2200	0-.9@4.5	12.75@14.1	4	12 BTDC
1977	V-6 231	1110677	0@1300	20@3600	4-6@--	24@9.5	4	12° BTDC
	V-8 301	____					4	
	V-8 305	____					4	
	V-8 350	1103275	0@1450	20@4400	5.5-7.5@--	24@14	4	12° BTDC
	V-8 403	____					4	
1978	V-6 231	1110695	____	6-9@1800	3@6	12@10-13	4	____
	V-6 231	1110723	____	4-6@2000	4@6	4@5-7	4	____
	V-6 231	1110728	____	7-9@1600	1@5	10@4-8	4	____
	V-6 231	1110730	____	9.5-11.5@2000	4@6	12@7-10	4	____
	V-6 231	1110731	____	6.5-8.5@1800	4@6	8@7-9	4	____
	V-6 231	1110732	____	6.5-8.5@1800	7@9	7@11-13	4	____
	V-6 231	1110735	____	9.5-11.5@2000	2@4	10@11-13	4	____
	V-6 231	1110739	____	6.5-8.5@1800	2@4	10@11-13	4	____
	V-8 301	1103314	____	9.5-11.5@1700	3@5	12.5@11-13	4	____
	V-8 305	1103281	____	9-11@1900	3@5	9@11-13	4	____
	V-8 305	1103282	____	9-11@1900	3@6	10@9-12	4	____
	V-8 350	1103356	0@550	14.3-18@2500	0@2	10@10	5	1
	V-8 350	1103285	____	10-12@2100	3@5	5@7-9	4	____
	V-8 350	1103322	____	13.5-15.5@2000	4@6	12@12-14	4	____
	V-8 350	1103373	____	8.5-10.5@2000	4@5	8@10-12	4	____
	V-8 403	1103324	____	11-12@2250	3@6	12@12-14	4	____
	V-8 305	1103357	0@550	11.8-15.7@2500	0@2	10@10	5	1
	V-8 403	1103325	____	7.5-9.5@2200	5@7	12@11-13	4	____
	V-8 350	1103342	____	6.5-7.5@1800	4@5	10@9-12	4	____
	V-8 350	1103346	____	8.5-10.5@2000	4@6	12@12-14	4	____
	V-8 403	1103347	____	6.5-7.5@1800	4@6	12@12-14	4	____
	V-8 350	1103353	____	10.5-12.5@1800	4@6	8@10-12	4	____
1979	V-6 196	1110765	0@500	7.5@2200	0@6	10@12	4	1
	V-6 196	1110772	0@500	7.5@2200	0@4	12@10	4	1

DISTRIBUTOR SPECIFICATIONS

BUICK

YEAR	ENGINE APPLICATION	DISTRIBUTOR NUMBER	CENTRIFUGAL ADVANCE DIST. DEGREES @DIST. RPM		VACUUM ADVANCE DIST. DEGREES @INS. HG.		DWELL ANGLE (Degrees)	INITIAL TIMING @ Engine Idle1
			Start	Finish	Start	Finish		
1979	V-6 231	1110766	0@840	7.5@1800	0@5	12@11	4	15°BTDC
	V-6 231	1110767	0@840	7.5@1800	0@4	10@12	4	15°BTDC
	V-6 231	1110768	0@500	7.5@1800	0@4	10@12	4	15°BTDC
	V-6 231	1110769	0@500	7.5@1800	0@5	12@11	4	15°BTDC
	V-6 231	1110770	0@840	7.5@1800	0@4	10@9	4	15°BTDC
	V-6 231	1110779	0@840	6-9@1800	0@4	12@9.5	4	15°BTDC
	V-8 301	1110774	0@500	4-6@2200	0@4	10@12	4	1
	V-8 301	1110775	0@500	6-9@1800	0@4	10@9	4	1
	V-8 301	1103314	0@412	9-12@1700	0@5	13@12	4	12°BTDC
	V-8 301	1103400	0@500	7-10@2300	0@5	13@11.5	4	1
	V-8 301	1103399	0@500	9-11@2200	0@5	13@12	4	1
	V-8 305	1103368	0@500	9-11@1900	0@6	5@8	4	4°BTDC
	V-8 305	1103379	0@500	9-11@1900	0@4	10@7.5	4	4°BTDC
	V-8 305	1103281	0@500	9-11@1900	0@6	9@12	4	4°BTDC
	V-8 350	1103322	0@600	13-16@2000	0@6	12@13	4	20°BTDC
	V-8 350	1103323	0@500	8-11@2000	0@5	8@9	4	20°BTD
	V-8 350	1103342	0@500	7-9@2200	0@7	12@12	4	1
	V-8 350	1103346	0@500	8-11@2000	0@6	12@13	4	20°BTDC
	V-8 403	1103324	0@600	10-13@1800	0@6	12@13	4	20°BTDC
	V-8 403	1103325	0@500	6-8@1800	0@5	8@9	4	20°BTDC

1 Refer to vehicle emissions control sticker for idle speed and/or initial timing specification.
2 Stage 1—10° BTDC.
3 Manual transmission—8° BTDC.
4 High Energy Ignition.
5 California, 9@15.
6 California, 9° BTDC.
7 California, 14° BTDC.

CADILLAC

YEAR	ENGINE APPLICATION	DISTRIBUTOR NUMBER	CENTRIFUGAL ADVANCE DIST. DEGREES @ DIST. RPM		VACUUM ADVANCE DIST. DEGREES @ INS. HG.		DWELL ANGLE (Degrees)	INITIAL TIMING @ Engine Idle1
			Start	Finish	Start	Finish		
1970	V-8 472	1111239	0-2.5@400	12-14@2000	0@8	12.25@13	30	7.5° BTDC
1971	V-8 472/500	1112065	0-2@500	11-13@2000	0@8	12.25@13	30	8° BTDC
1972	V-8 472/500	1112018	0-2@500	11-13@2000	0@8	12.6@13	30	8° BTDC
1973	V-8 472/500	1112229	0-2@500	11-13@2000	0@7	12.7@14	30	8° BTDC
1974	V-8 472	1112839	0-2@500	9-11@2500	0@6	8.8@14	30	1
	V-8 472 (Calif.)	1112840	0-2@500	9-11@2500	0@6	8.8@14	30	1
	V-8 500	1112841	0-2@500	8-10@2500	0@6	8.8@14	30	1
	V-8 500 (Calif.)	1112842	0-2@500	8-10@2500	0@6	8.8@14	30	1
1975	V-8 500	1112892	0@330	7.5-10@3000	0@5.5	13.5-14.5@16	2	6° BTDC3
	V-8 500 (Calif.)	1112954	0@330	7.5-10@3000	0@6	9.5-10.5@14	2	6° BTDC3
1976	V-8 350 (Seville)	———	0@200	19.5-22@2500	0@5	13.5-14.5@16	2	10° BTDC3
	V-8 500 (Except Eldorado)	———	0@330	7.5-10@3000	0@5.5	13.5-14.5@16	2	6° BTDC4
	V-8 500 (Eldorado)	———	0@330	8-10@2500	0@6.5	9.5-10.5@13.5	2	6° BTDC4
1977	V-8 350	1103221	0@900	42@5000	0@7.5	24@17.5	2	10°BTDC
	V-8 350	1103222	0@900	42@5000	0@105	18@185	2	8°BTDC
	V-8 425	1103217	0@700	17@4000	0@5	28@15.5	2	18°BTDC
	V-8 425	1103219	0@700	17@4000	0@5	28@15.5	2	18°BTDC
	V-8 425	1103277	0@800	14@5000	0@4	20@12.6	2	18°BTDC
	V-8 425	1103297	0@800	14@5000	0@4	20@12.6	2	18°BTDC
	V-8 425	1103298	0@800	14@5000	0@5	20@9.5	2	18°BTDC
1978	V-8 350	1103307	1.6@450	20-22@2500	0@9.5	8.5-9.5@20.7	2	1
	V-8 350	1103348	1.6@450	20-22@2500	0@5.6	11.5-12.5@20.7	2	1
	V-8 350	1103349	1.6@450	20-22@2500	0@5.6	13.5-14.5@20.7	2	1
	V-8 425	1103331	0.5-3.5@450	6.4-9.5@2500	0@3.5	13.5-14.5@20.7	2	1
	V-8 425	1103332	0.5-3.5@450	6.4-9.5@2500	0@3.5	9.5-10.5@20.7	2	1
	V-8 425	1103334	0.5-3.5@450	7-9.5@2500	0@4.4	13.5-14.5@20.7	2	1
	V-8 425	1103335	1.6@450	6-8@2500	0@3.5	9.5-10.5@20.7	2	1
	V-8 425	1103345	0.5-3.5@450	6.4-9.5@2500	0@3.5	7.5-8.5@20.7	2	1
	V-8 425	1103352	0.5-3.5@450	6.4-9.5@2500	0@5.6	4.5-5.5@20.7	2	1
1979	V-8 350	1103307	0@200	20-22@2500	0@9	7½-9½@17	2	10°BTDC
	V-8 350	1103393	0@200	20-22@2500	0@4	11-12½@13	2	10°BTDC
	V-8 350	1103394	0@200	20-22@2500	0@4	13½-14½@16	2	10°BTDC
	V-8 425	1103334	0@200	7-9½@2500	0@4	13½-14½@16	2	18°BTDC
	V-8 425	1103335	0@200	6-8@2525	0@3	9½-10½@13	2	18°BTDC
	V-8 425	1103389	0@200	7-9½@2000	0@3	13½-14½@16	2	23°BTDC
	V-8 425	1103392	0@200	6½-9½@2400	0@3	9½-10½@14	2	23°BTDC6
	V-8 425	1103332	0@200	6½-9½@2400	0@3	9½-10½@13	2	23°BTDC
	V-8 425	1103395	0@200	5½-9½@2400	0@7	4½-5½@12	2	23°BTDC6

1 Refer to vehicle emissions control sticker for idle speed and/or initial timing specification.
2 High Energy Ignition.
3 California 6° BTDC.
4 EFI 12° BTDC.
5 Figures are for advance. For retard: 0@3 start; 8@9.
6 With ESS connected and fuel economy switch disconnected and plugged.

CHEVROLET

YEAR	ENGINE APPLICATION	DISTRIBUTOR NUMBER	CENTRIFUGAL ADVANCE DIST. DEGREES @ DIST. RPM		VACUUM ADVANCE DIST. DEGREES @ INS. HG.		DWELL ANGLE (Degrees)	INITIAL TIMING @ Engine Idle1
			Start	Finish	Start	Finish		
1970	I-4 153	1110457	0@450	14@1850	0@7	12@15	31-34	TDC
	I-4 153	1110458	0@450	12@1800	0@7	12@15	31-34	4° BTDC
	I-6 230	1110459	0@500	18@2300	0@7	11.5@16	31-34	TDC
	I-6 230	1110460	0@500	16@2300	0@7	11.5@16	31-34	4° BTDC
	I-6 250	1110463	0@450	16@2100	0@7	11.5@16	31-34	TDC
	I-6 250	1110464	0@450	14@2100	0@7	11.5@16	31-34	4° BTDC
	V-8 307	1111995	0@500	14@2150	0@6	7.5@12	29-31	2° BTDC
	V-8 307	1112005	0@400	12@2150	0@8	10@17	29-31	8° BTDC
	V-8 350	1112001	0@400	18@2050	0@7	12@17	29-31	TDC
	V-8 350	1112002	0@450	16@2200	0@7	12@17	29-31	4° BTDC
	V-8 350	1111996	0@475	15@2350	0@10	7.5@17	29-31	TDC
	V-8 350	1111997	0@450	13@2350	0@10	10@17	29-31	4° BTDC
	V-8 350	1111490	0@450	15@2550	0@8	10@17	29-31	4° BTDC
	V-8 350	1111491	0@500	13@2500	0@7	7.5@12		8° BTDC
	V-8 350	1111493	0@500	13@2500	0@7	6@12	29-31	8° BTDC
	V-8 350	1111496	0@600	10@2300	0@7	6@12	29-31	14° BTDC
	V-8 350	1111971	0@475	10@2300	0@7	6@12		14° BTDC
	V-8 400	1111999	0@475	18@2500	0@8	7.5@15.5		TDC
	V-8 400	1112000	0@475	16@2500	0@6	7.5@12	29-31	4° BTDC
	V-8 400	1111492	0@400	16@2200	0@6	7.5@12	29-31	4° BTDC
	V-8 400	1111494	0@350	14@2200	0@6	7.5@12	29-31	8° BTDC
	V-8 400	1111998	0@450	16@2500	0@8	7.5@15.5	29-31	4° BTDC
	V-8 427	1111926	0@400	13@1900	0@7	6@12	28-32	4 BTDC
1971	I-6 250	1110489	0@465	12@2050	0@8	12.5@16	31-34	4° BTDC
	V-8 307	1112039	0@340	10@2100	0@8	10@17	29-31	8° BTDC
	V-8 307	1112005	0@400	12@2150	0@8	10@17	29-31	4° BTDC
	V-8 350	1112042	0@440	14@2150	0@8	10@17	29-31	2° BTDC
	V-8 350	1112005	0@400	12@2150	0@8	10@17	29-31	6° BTDC
	V-8 350	1112044	0@420	11@2100	0@8	7.5@15.5	29-31	4° BTDC
	V-8 350	1112045	0@430	9@2100	0@8	7.5@15.5	29-31	8° BTDC
	V-8 350	1112049	0@535	12@2500	0@8	7.5@15.5	29-31	8° BTDC
	V-8 350	1112038	0@530	12@2400	0@8	7.5@15.5	3	8° BTDC4
	V-8 350	1112074	0@520	10@2500	0@8	7.5@15.5	29-31	12° BTDC
	V-8 350	1112050	0@430	9@2100	0@8	6@15.5	29-31	4° BTDC2
	V-8 400	1112056	0@465	12@2250	0@8	9@17	29-31	8° BTDC
	V-8 402	1112057	0@465	15@2200	0@8	10@17	29-31	8° BTDC
	V-8 454	1112052	0@430	11@1950	0@8	10@17	29-31	8° BTDC
	V-8 454	1112054	0@545	14@2500	0@7	6@12	29-31	12° BTDC
	V-8 454	1112075	0@650	8@2500	0@7	6@12	29-31	8° BTDC
	V-8 454	1112051	0@430	11@1950	0@8	10@17	29-31	8° BTDC
	V-8 454	1112076	0@550	16@2500	0@7	6@12	3	8° BTDC
	V-8 454	1112053	0@545	14@2725	0@7	6@12	3	12° BTDC
1972	I-6 250	1110489	0@465	12@2050	0@8	11.5@16	31-34	4° BTDC
	V-8 307	1112039	0@340	10@2100	0@8	10@17	29-31	8° BTDC
	V-8 307	1112005	0@400	12@2150	0@8	10@17	29-31	4° BTDC
	V-8 350	1112005	0@400	12@2150	0@8	10@17	29-31	6° BTDC
	V-8 350	1112044	0@420	11@2100	0@8	7.5@15.5	29-31	4° BTDC
	V-8 350	1112045	0@430	9@2100	0@8	7.5@15.5	29-31	8° BTDC
	V-8 350	1112049	0@535	12@2500	0@8	7.5@15.5	29-31	8° BTDC
	V-8 350	1112095	0@545	14@2500	0@8	7.5@15.5	29-31	4° BTDC
	V-8 350	1112050	0@435	9@2100	0@8	7.5@15.5	29-31	8° BTDC
	V-8 350	1112101	0@545	14@2500	0@8	7.5@15.5	29-31	4° BTDC
	V-8 400	1112055	0@500	14@2250	0@10	9@17	29-31	2° BTDC
	V-8 400	1112099	0@465	12@2250	0@8	10@17	29-31	6° BTDC
	V-8 402	1112057	0@465	15@2200	0@8	10@17	29-31	8° BTDC
	V-8 454	1112052	0@430	11@1950	0@8	10@17	29-31	8° BTDC
	V-8 454	1112051	0@430	11@1950	0@8	10@17	29-31	8° BTDC
1973	I-6 250	1110499	0@465	12@2050	0@7	6@15	31-34	6° BTDC
	V-8 307	1112102	0@500	10@2100	0@6	7.5@12	29-31	8° BTDC
	V-8 307	1112227	0@500	12@2150	0@6	7.5@12	29-31	4° BTDC
	V-8 350	1112168	0@500	10@2100	0@4	7@7	29-31	8° BTDC
	V-8 350	1112230	0@500	10@2100	0@4	5@5.8	29-31	8° BTDC
	V-8 350	1112093	0@550	9@2100	0@6	7.5@14	29-31	8° BTDC
	V-8 350	1112094	0@550	7@2100	0@6	7.5@14	29-31	12° BTDC
	V-8 350	1112148	0@600	10@2500	0@6	7.5@12	29-31	8° BTDC
	V-8 350	1112098	0@550	7@2100	0@6	7.5@14	29-31	12° BTDC
	V-8 350	1112150	0@600	10@2500	0@6	7.5@12	29-31	8° BTDC
	V-8 400	1112166	0@500	10@2100	0@8	7.5@15.5	29-31	6° BTDC
	V-8 454	1112113	0@550	9@2100	0@6	10@15	29-31	10° BTDC
	V-8 454	1112114	0@550	9@2100	0@6	10@15	29-31	10° BTDC
1974	I-6 250	1110499	0@550	12@2050	0@8	12@14.5-15.5	31-34	I
	V-8 350	1112168	0@500	10@1200	0@4	7@7.5-8.5	29-31	I
	V-8 350	1112093	0@550	9@2100	0@7	7.5@13-14	29-31	I
	V-8 350	1112847	0@550	9@2100	0@4	7@7.5-8.5	29-31	I
	V-8 350	1112852	0@600	10@2500	0@4	7@7.5-8.5	29-31	I
	V-8 350	1112849	0@500	11@2100	0@4	7@7.5-8.5	29-31	I
	V-8 350	1112850	0@500	11@2100	0@4	7@7.5-8.5	29-31	I
	V-8 350	1112851	0@550	9@2100	0@4	7@7.5-8.5	29-31	I
	V-8 350	1112247	0@550	9@2100	0@7	7.5@13-14	29-31	I
	V-8 350	1112853	0@500	10@2500	0@4	7@7.5-8.5	29-31	I
	V-8 400	1112846	0@500	10@2100	0@5	7.5@9.5-10.5	29-31	I
	V-8 400	1112250	0@550	9@2100	0@11	5@14.5-15.5	29-31	I
	V-8 400	1112854	0@500	10@2100	0@5	7.5@9.5-10.5	29-31	I
	V-8 454	1112113	0@550	9@2100	0@7	10@14.2-15.7	29-31	I
	V-8 454	1112114	0@550	9@2100	0@7	10@14.2-15.7	29-31	I
	V-8 454	1112504	0@550	9@2100	0@9	8@15-16	29-31	I
1975	I-6 250	1112863	0@550	8@2100	0@4	9@12	5	10° BTDC
	I-6 250	1110650	0@550	8@2100	0@4	9@12	5	10° BTDC
	I-6 250	1110652	0@550	12@2050	0@5	12@15	5	8° BTDC
	V-8 262	1112933	0@600	11@2000	0@3	8@8	5	8° BTDC
	V-8 350	1112880	0@600	11@2100	0@4	9@12	5	6° BTDC
	V-8 350	1112888	0@550	8@2100	0@4	9@12	5	6° BTDC
	V-8 350	1112883	0@550	11@2300	0@4	7.5@10	5	6° BTDC
	V-8 400	1112882	0@500	7.5@1400	0@8	7.5@15.5	5	8° BTDC
	V-8 454	1112886	0@900	6@2100	0@4	9@7	5	16° BTDC
1976	I-6 250	1110666	0@500	10@2100	0@4	11.5@15	I	6° BTDC
	I-6 250	1112863	0@550	10@2100	0@4	9@12	I	10° BTDC
	V-8 305	1112977	0@500	10@1900	0@3	7.5@7	I	8° BTDC
	V-8 305	1112999	0@500	10@1900	0@4	4.5@7	I	8° BTDC
	V-8 350	1103200	0@600	8@1000	0@4.5	5@8	I	12° BTDC
	V-8 350	1112880	0@600	11@2100	0@400	9@12	I	6° BTDC

DISTRIBUTOR SPECIFICATIONS

CHEVROLET

YEAR	ENGINE APPLICATION	DISTRIBUTOR NUMBER	CENTRIFUGAL ADVANCE DIST. DEGREES @ DIST. RPM		VACUUM ADVANCE DIST. DEGREES @ INS. HG.		DWELL ANGLE (Degrees)	INITIAL TIMING @ Engine Idle1
			Start	Finish	Start	Finish		
1976	V-8 350	1112959	0@600	10@2100	0@6	7@12	1	6° BTDC
	V-8 350	1112979	0@600	8@1000	0@4	6.5@10.5	1	12° BTDC
	V-8 350	1112888	0@550	11@2100	0@5	9@12	1	8° BTDC
	V-8 350	1112905	0@600	11@2100	0@6	7.5@12	1	6° BTDC
	V-8 400	1112882	0@500	7.5@1400	0@8	7.5@15	1	8° BTDC
	V-8 400	1113203	0@500	7.5@1400	0@6	7.5@12	1	8° BTDC
	V-8 454	1112886	0@650	6@2100	0@4	9@7	1	12° BTDC
1977	I-6 250	1110678	0@500	10@2050	0@2	12@15	5	8°BTDC
	I-6 250	1110681	0@500	10@2100	0@2	7.5@12	5	6°BTDC
	I-6 250	1110725	0@500	10@2100	0@2.5	12@12	5	8°BTDC
	V-8 305	1103239	0@600	10@2100	3@2	7.5@10	5	8°BTDC
	V-8 305	1103244	0@500	10@1900	0@2	10@10	5	6°BTDC
	V-8 350	1103246	0@600	11@2100	0@2	9@12	5	8°BTDC
	V-8 350	1103248	0@600	11@2100	0@2	5@8	5	8°BTDC
	V-8 350	1103256	0@600	8@1000	0@2	5@8	5	12°BTDC
1978	I-6 250	1110715	0@500	10@2100	0@4	12@15	5	6° BTDC
	V-6 200	1110696	0@500	10@1900	0@3	8@6.5	5	8° BTDC
	V-6 200	1110737	0@500	11.5-16.7@2500	0@4	8@8	4	1
	V-6 231	1110695	0-3@1000	6-9@1800	0@7-9	12@10	5	15° BTDC
	V-6 231	1110731	0-2@1000	6-9@1800	0@4-6	8@7-9	5	8° BTDC
	V-6 231	1110736	0@500	10-16@2500	0@4	8@8	4	1
	V-8 305	1103281	0@500	10@1900	0@4	9@12	5	4° BTDC
	V-8 305	1103282	0@500	10@1900	0@4	10@10	5	4° BTDC
	V-8 305	1103357	0@550	11.8-15.7@2500	0@2	10@10	5	1
	V-8 350	1103337	0@550	8@1200	0@4	12@10	5	6° BTDC
	V-8 350	1103353	0@550	8@1200	0@4	10@10	5	6° BTDC
	V-8 350	1103356	0@550	14.3-18@2500	0@2	10@10	5	1
	V-8 350	1103285	0@600	11@2100	0@4	5@8	5	8° BTDC
	V-8 350	1103291	–	–	0@4	5@8	5	12° BTDC
	V-8 350	1103286	0@550	11@2300	0@4	9@12	5	6° BTDC
1979	I-6 250	1110716	0@500	10@2100	0@4	10@10	5	8°BTDC
	I-6 250	1110748	0@500	10@2100	0@4	7.5@12	5	10°BTDC
	V-6 200	1110737	0@500	10@1900	0@5	15@16	5	8°BTDC
	V-6 200	1110756	0@700	7@1900	0@5	15@16	5	14°BTDC
	V-6 231	1110695	0@840	7.5@1800	0@6.7	12@18.3	5	15°BTDC
	V-6 231	1110731	0@840	7.5@1800	0@8.4	8@14	5	15°BTDC
	V-8 267	1103370	0@700	7@1900	0@5	15@16	5	10°BTDC
	V-8 267	1103371	0@500	10@1900	0@5	15@16	5	4°BTDC
	V-8 305	1103281	0@500	10@1900	0@4	9@12	5	4°BTDC
	V-8 305	1103282	0@500	10@1900	0@6.7	10@16.9	5	4°BTDC
	V-8 305	1103285	0@600	11@2100	0@4	5@8	5	4°BTDC
	V-8 305	1103368	0@500	10@1900	0@6.7	10@16.9	5	4°BTDC
	V-8 305	1103379	0@500	10@1900	0@5	5@13.5	5	4°BTDC
	V-8 350	1103285	0@600	11@2100	0@4	5@8	5	8°BTDC
	V-8 350	1103291	0@600	8@1000	0@4	5@8	5	12°BTDC
	V-8 350	1103337	0@550	11@2300	0@6.7	12@16.9	5	8°BTDC
	V-8 350	1103353	0@550	11@2300	0@4	10@10	5	6°BTDC

1 Refer to vehicle emissions control sticker for idle speed and/or initial timing specification.
2 8° for automatic transmission.
3 Transistorized ignition.
4 12° for automatic transmission.
5 High Energy Ignition.
6 8° for automatic transmission.

CHEVROLET CHEVETTE/VEGA/MONZA

YEAR	ENGINE APPLICATION	DISTRIBUTOR NUMBER	CENTRIFUGAL ADVANCE DIST. DEGREES @ DIST. RPM		VACUUM ADVANCE DIST. DEGREES @ INS. HG.		DWELL ANGLE (Degrees)	INITIAL TIMING @ Engine Idle1
			Start	Finish	Start	Finish		
1970	I-4 140	1110435	0@472	11@2000	0@7	12@15	31-34	6° BTDC2
	I-4 140	1110492	0@595	12@2000	0@7	12@15	31-34	6° BTDC
1971	I-4 140	1110435	0@472	11@2000	0@7	12@15	31-34	6° BTDC2
	I-4 140	1110492	0@595	12@2000	0@7	12@15	31-34	6° BTDC
1972	I-4 140	1110496	0@800	11@2400	0@7	12@15	31-34	8° BTDC3
1973	I-4 140	1110496	0@800	11@2400	0@7	12@15	31-34	8° BTDC3
1974	I-4 140	1110496	0@800	11@2400	0@7	12@15	31-34	8° BTDC3
1975	I-4 140	1112862	0@810	11@2400	0@5	12@12	4	10° BTDC5
	V-8 262	1112933	0@600	11@2000	0@3	8@8	4	8° BTDC
	V-8 350	1112880	0@600	11@2100	0@4	9@12	4	6° BTDC
1976	I-4 85	1110654	0@600	10@2400	0@4	7@8.5	4	10° BTDC
	I-4 85	1110655	0@600	10@2400	0@5	6@12	4	10° BTDC
	I-4 85	1110658	0@600	10@2400	0@5	13@14.5	4	8° BTDC
	I-4 97.6	1110657	0@600	10@2400	0@5	12@12	4	10° BTDC
	I-4 97.6	1110659	0@750	8@2400	0@4	13@12	4	12° BTDC
	I-4 122	1110649	0@1000	8.5@1800	6	6	4	10° BTDC
	I-4 140	1112862	0@810	11@2400	0@5	12@11	4	10° BTDC
	V-8 305	1112983	0@550	11@2600	0@4	7.5@10	4	6° BTDC
1977	I-4 85	1110703	0@600	12@2650	0@2	15@12	4	12°BTDC
	I-4 97.6	1110687	0@600	12@2400	0@2	13@12	4	8°BTDC
	I-4 97.6	1110693	0@600	12@2400	0@2	7@8	4	8°BTDC
	I-4 97.6	1110702	0@600	12@2400	0@2	15@12	4	8°BTDC
	I-4 140	1110538	0@425	17@2000	0@2.5	12@10	4	TDC

CHEVROLET CHEVETTE/VEGA/MONZA

YEAR	ENGINE APPLICATION	DISTRIBUTOR NUMBER	CENTRIFUGAL ADVANCE DIST. DEGREES @ DIST. RPM		VACUUM ADVANCE DIST. DEGREES @ INS. HG.		DWELL ANGLE (Degrees)	INITIAL TIMING @ Engine Idle1
			Start	Finish	Start	Finish		
	I-4 140	1110539	0@425	17@2000	0@2.5	12@10	4	TDC
	V-8 305	1103239	0@600	10@2100	0@2	7.5@10	4	8°BTDC
	V-8 305	1103244	0@500	10@1800	0@2	10@10	4	6°BTDC
	V-8 305	1103252	0@500	10@1800	0@2	9@12	4	1
1978	I-4 97.6	1110705	0@600	10@2400	0@4	15@12	4	8° BTDC
	I-4 97.6	1110706	0@600	8-12@2500	0@4	7@8	4	1
	I-4 97.6	1110707	0@600	10@2400	0@4	7@8	4	8° BTDC
	I-4 97.6	1110712	0@600	10@2400	0@4	13@12	4	8° BTDC
	I-4 97.6	1110713	0@600	11@2625	0@4	15@12	4	8° BTDC
	I-4 151	1103328	0@600	10@2200	0@3.5	10@9	4	14° BTDC
	I-4 151	1103329	0@600	10@2200	0@3.5	10@12	4	14° BTDC
	I-4 151	1103326	8	8	8	8	4	14° BTDC
	I-4 151	1103365	8	8	8	8	4	14° BTDC
	V-6 196	1110695	0-3@1000	6-9@1800	0@3.6	12@10-13	4	15° BTDC
	V-6 231	1110695	0-3@1000	6-9@1800	0@3.6	12@10-13	4	15° BTDC
	V-8 305	1103281	0@500	10@1900	0@4	10@12	4	4° BTDC
	V-8 305	1103282	0@500	10@1900	0@4	10@12	4	6° BTDC
1979	I-4 98	1110740	0@760	8@1625	0@6.7	15@16.9	4	18°BTDC
	I-4 98	1110741	0@760	8@2625	0@6.7	7@13.5	4	18°BTDC
	I-4 98	1110742	0@600	10@2400	0@8.4	8@19.4	4	12°BTDC
	I-4 98	1110743	0@600	12@2850	0@6.7	15@16.9	4	12°BTDC
	I-4 98	1110744	0@600	10@2400	0@6.7	15@16.9	4	12°BTDC
	I-4 98	1110759	0@600	12@1850	0@6.7	9@12.1	4	12°BTDC
	I-4 98	1110760	0@760	8@2625	0@8.5	8@19.4	4	18°BTDC
	I-4 151	1110726	0@500	9@2000	0@4	10@10	4	12°BTDC
	I-4 151	1110757	0@600	9@2000	0@4	10@10	4	12°BTDC
	I-4 151	1103365	0@850	10@2325	0@5	8@11	4	14°BTDC
	V-6 196/200	1110695	0@840	7.5@1800	0@4	12@10	4	15°BTDC
	V-6 196/200	1110731	0@840	7.5@1800	0@5	8@8	4	15°BTDC
	V-8 305	11103282	0@500	10@1900	0@4	10@10	4	4°BTDC
	V-8 305	11103285	0@600	11@2100	0@4	10@10	4	4°BTDC
	V-8 305	1103379	0@600	10@1900	0@3	10@8	4	4°BTDC

1 Refer to vehicle emissions control sticker for idle speed and/or initial timing specification.
2 RPO L-11, 10° BTDC.
3 RPO 2-11 manual, 10° BTDC; automatic, 12° BTDC.
4 High Energy Ignition.
5 Automatic, 12° BTDC.
6 Vacuum retard.
7 2° for automatic transmission. California, 2° for manual.
8 Electronic Fuel Control System.

CHRYSLER CORPORATION

YEAR	ENGINE APPLICATION	DISTRIBUTOR NUMBER	CENTRIFUGAL ADVANCE DIST. DEGREES @ DIST. RPM		VACUUM ADVANCE DIST. DEGREES @ INS. HG.		DWELL ANGLE (Degrees)	INITIAL TIMING @ Engine Idle1
			Start	Finish	Start	Finish		
1970	I-6 225	2875822	1.5@550	12-14@2000	0.5-3.5@10	5.25-7.75@15	41-46	TDC
	I-6 225	2875826	1.5@550	12-14@2000	0.5-3.5@7	5.25-7.75@10	41-46	TDC
	V-8 318	3438255	1-6@550	14-16@2100	1-4@10.5	8.25-10.75@15	30-34	TDC
	V-8 318	3438255	1-6@550	12-14@2100	1.25-4.25@12	8.25-10.75@15	30-34	TDC
	V-8 383	3438231	0.3-8@550	14-16@2200	0.5-4@7.5	9.3-11.8@12	28.5-32.5	TDC3
	V-8 383	3438233	0.4-6@600	10-12@2300	0.5-4.3@10.5	9.7-12@15.5	28.5-32.5	TDC3
	V-8 440	3438222	0.4-6@600	10-12@2300	0.5-4.3@10.5	9.7-12@15.5	28.5-32.5	TDC3
	V-8 440	3438314	0.4-5@650	9-14@2400	0.5-3.5@11	9.5-12.5@15.5	4	5° BTDC
	V-8 426	2875987 IBS-4014E	0.4-5@650	14-16@1600	0-3.5@9	6.7-9.2@13.5	4	TDC
	V-8 426	2875989 IBS-4014F	0.4-2@600	11.5-13.5@1600	0-3.5@9	6.7-9.2@13.5	4	5° BTDC
1971	I-6 198	3438509	1-6.5@550	12-14@2000	0.5-3@7	6-8.5@11	41-46	2.5° BTDC
	I-6 198	3438524	2-6@700	12-14@2000	0.5-3.5@7	5.25-7.75@10	41-46	2.5° BTDC
	I-6 225	2875822	1.5@550	12-14@2000	0.5-3.5@10	5.25-7.75@15	41-46	TDC
	I-6 225	2875826	1.5@550	12-14@2000	0.5-3.5@7	5.25-7.75@10	41-46	TDC
	I-6 225	3438440	0.5-3.5@800	12-14@2200	0.5-3.5@10	5.25-7.75@15	41-46	2.5° BTDC
	I-6 225	3438442	0.5-3.5@800	12-14@2200	0.5-3@7	5.25-7.75@10	41-46	2.5° BTDC
	V-8 318	3438255	1-6@550	14-16@2100	1-4@10.5	8.25-10.75@15	30-34	TDC
	V-8 318	3438225	1-6@550	14-16@2100	1.25-4.25@12	8.25-10.75@15	30-34	TDC
	V-8 318	3438453	0-4@600	14-16@2100	1-4@9.5	8-10.5@15	30-34	TDC
	V-8 340	3438522 IBS-4018C	0.5-4@650	10-12@2000	0.5-3.5@7	7-10@11	4	5° BTDC
	V-8 340	3438517 IBS-4018C	0.5-4@600	10-12@2100	0.5-3.5@9	7-10@12.5	30-34	5° BTDC
	V-8 340	3438517	0.5-4@600	10-12@2100	0.5-3.5@9	7-10@12.5	30-34	5° BTDC
	V-8 340	3438615 IBS-4018D	0.5-4@700	13-15@2200	0.5-3.5@7	7-10@11	4	2.5° BTDC
	V-8 340	3438617 IBS-4018E	0.5-3.5@700	13-15@2200	0.5-3.5@9	7-10@12.5	30-34	2.5° BTDC
	V-8 360	3438422	1-6@550	14-16@2100	1-4@9.5	8-10.5@15	30-34	2.5° BTDC
	V-8 360	3438453	0-4@600	14-16@2100	1-4@9.5	8-10.5@15	30-34	2.5° BTDC
	V-8 383	3438534	1-4.5@600	12-14@2000	1-3.5@9	8-10@15	28.5-32.5	TDC3
	V-8 383	3438544	0.5-3.5@700	12-14@2000	1-3.5@9	8-10@15	28.5-32.5	TDC3
	V-8 383	3438690	0.5-3.5@700	12-14@2400	1-4@10.5	8-10@15	28.5-32.5	TDC3
	V-8 440	3438559	0.5-3.5@700	10-12@2400	1-4.5@12	8-10@16	28.5-32.5	5° BTDC
	V-8 440	3438572	0-3.5@600	8-10@2200	0.5-4.3@10.5	9.7-12@15.5	28.5-32.5	TDC
	V-8 440	3438694	0.5-4@700	8-10@2200	0.5-4.3@10.5	9.7-12@15.5	28.5-32.5	2.5° BTDC
	V-8 440	3438577	1-3@700	4.5-6.5@2200	1-4@10.5	7.5-10@15	4	5° BTDC
	V-8 426	2875987 IBS-4017B	0.4-5@650	14-16@1600	0-3.5@9	6.7-9.2@13.5	4	TDC
	V-8 426	3438579 IBS-4017E	0-4@600	13-15@1600	0-3.5@9	6.7-9.2@13.5	4	2.5° BTDC
1972	I-6 198	3656237	0-5@550	12-14@2000	0.5-3@7	6-8.5@11	41-46	2.5° BTDC
	I-6 198	3656243	1-4.5@650	12-14@2000	0.5-3@7	6-8.5@11	41-46	2.5° BTDC
	I-6 225	3656252	0.5-4.5@550	12-14@2000	0.5-3.5@10	5-8@15	41-46	TDC
	I-6 225	3656260	0.5-4.5@700	12-14@2000	0.5-3.5@10	5-8@15	41-46	TDC
	I-6 225	3656257	0.5-4.5@550	12-14@2000	0.5-3@7	5-7.5@9.5	41-46	TDC
	I-6 225	3656266	0.5-3.5@700	12-14@2000	0.5-3@7	5-7.5@9.5	41-46	TDC

DISTRIBUTOR SPECIFICATIONS

CHRYSLER CORPORATION

YEAR	ENGINE APPLICATION	DISTRIBUTOR NUMBER	CENTRIFUGAL ADVANCE DIST. DEGREES @ DIST. RPM Start	Finish	VACUUM ADVANCE DIST. DEGREES @ INS. HG. Start	Finish	DWELL ANGLE (Degrees)	INITIAL TIMING @ Engine Idle[1]
1972	V-8 318	3656272	1-6@550	14-16@2100	1-4@9.5	8-10.5@15	30-34	TDC
	V-8 318	3656275	0-4@600	14-16@2100	1-4@9.5	8-10.5@15	30-34	TDC
	V-8 318	3656390	1-6@550	14-16@2100	1-4.5@12	8-10.5@15	30-34	TDC
	V-8 318	3656429	1-6@550	13-15@1900	0-3@9	7-10@14	2	TDC
	V-8 318	3656435	0-4@600	13-15@1900	0-3@9	7-10@14	2	TDC
	V-8 318	3656587	1-6@550	14-16@2100	1-4.5@12	7-10@14.5	2	TDC
	V-8 340	3656278	1-5@650	11.5-13.5@2400	0.5-3.5@9	7-10@12.5	2	TDC
	V-8 360	3656272	1-6@550	14-16@2100	1-4@9.5	8-10.5@15	30-34	TDC
	V-8 360	3656429	1-6@550	13-15@1900	0-3@9	7-10@14	2	TDC
	V-8 360	3656435	0-4@600	13-15@1900	0-3@9	7-10@14	2	TDC
	V-8 400	3656656	1-5@650	12-14@2000	1-4@10.5	8-10.5@15.5	28-32	5° BTDC
	V-8 400	3656332	0.5-4@650	10-12@2000	1-4@10.5	8-10.5@15.5	30-34	10° BTDC
	V-8 400	3656335	1-5@650	13-15@2250	1-4@10.5	8-10.5@15.5	2	5° BTDC[6]
	V-8 400	3656338	0.5-4@650	10.5-12.5@2500	1-4@10.5	8-10.5@15.5	2	10° BTDC
	V-8 440	3656344	0.5-4@650	10-12@2000	1-4@10.5	8-10.5@15.5	30-34	10° BTDC
	V-8 440	3656350	1-5@650	12-14@2000	1-4@10.5	8-10.5@15.5	28.5-32.5	5° BTDC
	V-8 440	3656341	0.5-4@650	10.5-12.5@2500	1-4@10.5	8-10.5@15.5	2	10° BTDC
	V-8 440	3656347	1-5@650	13-15@2250	1-4@10.5	8-10.5@15.5	2	5° BTDC[7]
	V-8 440	3656353	0-3.5@650	8-10.5@2150	1-4@10.5	8-10.5@15.5	2	2.5° BTDC
1973	I-6 198	3656859	0-5@550	12-14@2000	0.5-3@7	7-10@11	2	TDC
	I-6 225	3755037	0.5-4.5@550	12-14@2000	0.5-3@9.5	7-10@15	2	2.5° BTDC
	I-6 225	3755042	0.5-4.5@550	12-14@2000	0.5-3@9.5	7-10@15	2	TDC
	V-8 318	3656763	1-4.5@525	13-15@1900	0.5-3@9	9.5-12.5@15	2	TDC
	V-8 340	3656771	0.5-3.5@600	11-13@2000	0.5-3.5@9	7-10@12.5	2	5° BTDC[3]
	V-8 360	3656780	0.5-3.5@500	13-15@1750	0.5-3@9	9.5-12.5@15	2	TDC
	V-8 400	3656791	0.5-3.5@550	13-15@1950	1-4@10.5	8-10.5@15.5	2	10° BTDC
	V-8 400	3755308	0-2.5@600	13.5-15.5@2150	1-4@10.5	8-10.5@15.5	2	10° BTDC
	V-8 400	3656802	0.5-4@600	10.5-12.5@2500	1-4@10.5	8-10.5@15.5	2	7.5° BTDC
	V-8 440	3755157	0.5-4@650	10.5-12.5@2500	1-4@10.5	8-10.5@15.5	2	10° BTDC
1974	I-6 198	3656859	0.5-4@550	11.5-14@2000	0.5-2.5@7	7-10@11.5	2	2.5° BTDC
	I-6 225	3755037	1-4@550	11.5-14@2000	0.5-2@9	7-10@15.5	2	TDC
	I-6 225	3755042	1-4@550	11.5-14@2000	0.5-2.5@7	7-10@15.5	2	TDC
	I-6 225	3755467	0.5-3.5@550	12-14@2000	0.5-2@9	7-10@15.5	2	TDC
	I-6 225	3755470	0.5-3.5@550	12-14@2000	0.5-2.5@7	7-10@11.5	2	TDC
	V-8 318	3656763	1.5-5.5@550	13.5-16@2100	0.5-2.5@9	9.5-12.5@15.5	2	TDC
	V-8 360	3755475	0.5-4@550	11.5-14@2000	0.5-2.5@7	10-12@12.5	2	5° BTDC
	V-8 360	3755486	1-5@600	12-14@2000	0.5-2.5@8	10-12@13.5	2	5° BTDC
	V-8 400	3755681	1-4.5@650	13.5-16@2150	0.5-2.5@8	9-11@14	2	7.5° BTDC[5]
	V-8 400	3755512	0.5-3.5@650	9.5-12@2000	0.5-2.5@8	9-11@14	2	5° BTDC
	V-8 400	3755508	1-4.5@650	11.5-14@2000	0.5-2.5@8	9.5-12@16	2	5° BTDC[3]
	V-8 440	3755518	0.5-3.5@650	9.5-12@2000	0.5-2.5@8	9-11@14	2	10° BTDC
	V-8 440	3755522	0.5-3@650	8-10@2000	0.5-2.5@8	9-11@14	2	10° BTDC
1975	I-6 225	3874082	1-4.5@600	11.5-14@2200	0.5-2.5@7	7-10@11.5	2	1
	V-8 318	3874090	1.5-5.5@600	11.5-14@2200	0.5-2.5@7	10-12.5@12.5	2	1
	V-8 318	3874298	0.5-3.5@700	13.5-16@2100	0.5-2.5@9	9.5-12.5@15.5	2	1
	V-8 360	3874115	1-3.5@600	10-12@2000	0.5-2.5@7	10-12@12.5	2	1
	V-8 360HP	3874097	1-4.5@650	13.5-16@2150	0.5-2.5@7	10-12@12.5	2	1
	V-8 400	3874101	0.5-3@600	10-12@2000	0.5-2.5@8	9-11@14	2	1
	V-8 400	3874110	1-3.5@600	10-12@2000	0.5-2.5@8	9-11@14	2	1
	V-8 440	3874173	1-3.5@600	8-10@2000	0.5-2.5@8	9-11@14	2	1
1976	I-6 225	3874598	1-4.5@600	9.5-11.5@2300	0.5-2.5@7	7-10@11.5	2	2° BTDC
	I-6 225	3874714	1-4.5@450	7-9@2500	0.5-2.5@7	7-10@11.5	2	6° BTDC
	V-8 318	3874754	0-4@500	11.5-13.5@2400	0.5-2.5@8	10-12@13.5	2	2° BTDC[8]
	V-8 360	3874115	1-3.5@600	10-12@2000	0.5-2.5@7	10-12@12.5	2	6° BTDC
	V-8 360	3874097	1-4.5@650	13.5-16@2150	0.5-2.5@7	10-12@12.5	2	2° BTDC
	V-8 400	3874110	1-3.5@600	10-12@2000	0.5-2.5@8	9-11@14	2	6° BTDC
	V-8 400	3874786	1-2.5@1200	2.5-5@2400	NONE	NONE	2	8° BTDC
	V-8 400	3874101	0.5-3@600	10-12@2000	0.5-2.5@8	9-11@14	2	10° BTDC
	V-8 440	3874596	0.5-4@600	8-10.9@2000	0.5-2.5@8	9-11@14	2	8° BTDC
	V-8 440	3874173	1-3.5@600	8-10@2000	0.5-2.5@8	9-11@14	2	10° BTDC
1977	I-6 225	3874714	6-4.8@1000	13.8-17.8@5000	1.6-5@7	7.3-9.8@11.5	2	12° BTDC[9]
	I-6 225	3874876	4-4.4@1200	7.4-11.4@5000	4-.3@8	10-12@10	2	12° BTDC
	I-6 225	3874929	2.8-6.8@1200	19.4-13.4@4600	1.6-5@7	7.3-9.8@11.5	2	12° BTDC
	I-6 225	4091039	4-4.4@1200	7.4-11.4@5000	1.6-5@7	7.3-9.8@11.5	2	12° BTDC
	I-6 225	4091101	2-2.4@1200	11.6-15.6@4120	2-1@9	7.5-9.5@12.5	2	8° BTDC
	V-8 318	3874909	4-4.4@1200	15.2-19.2@4600	1.6-5.2@8	10-12@13.5	2	8° BTDC
	V-8 318	4091140	–	–	–	–	2	6° BTDC[9]
	V-8 360	3874115	2.6-6.2@1200	20-24@4000	1.6-5.2@7	10-12@12.5	2	6° BTDC
	V-8 360	3874917	1.2-4@1000	16-20@4000	1.6-5.2@7	10-12@12.5	2	10° BTDC
	V-8 360	4091015	–	–	–	–	2	10° BTDC
	V-8 400	4091017	–	–	–	–	2	10° BTDC
	V-8 440	4091019	–	–	–	–	2	8° BTDC
1978	I-6 225	3874876	0.2-2.2@600	3.7-5.7@2500	0.8-2.5@7	7.3-9.8@11.5	2	12° BTDC
	I-6 225	3874929	1.4-3.4@600	9.7-11.7@2300	0.8-2.5@7	7.3-9.8@11.5	2	2° ATDC
	I-6 225	4091101	1.0-1.2@600	7.5-9.5@2060	1.0-3.0@9	7.5-9.5@12.5	2	8° BTDC
	V-8 318	4091140	–	–	–	–	10	16° BTDC
	V-8 360	3874115	1.3-3.1@600	10-12@2000	0.8-2.6@7	10-12@12.5	2	6° BTDC
	V-8 360	3874858	1.4-3.4@600	6.5-8.5@2400	0.8-2.6@7	10-12.5@12.5	2	6° BTDC
	V-8 360	4091140	–	–	–	–	10	6° BTDC
	V-8 400	4091709	–	–	–	–	10	20° BTDC
	V-8 440	3874173	1.3-3.1@600	8-10@2000	0.5-2.5@8	9-11@14	2	8° BTDC
	V-8 440	4091711	–	–	–	–	10	16° BTDC
1979	I-6 225	3874876	0.2-2.2@600	3.7-5.7@2500	0.8-2.5@7	7.3-9.8@11.5	2	12°BTDC
	I-6 225	4091101	1.0-1.2@600	5.8-7.8@2060	1.0-3.0@9	7.5-9.5@12.5	2	8°BTDC
	V-8 318/360	4091140	–	–	–	–	10	16°BTDC

1 Refer to vehicle emissions control sticker for idle speed and/or initial timing specification.
2 Electronic ignition.
3 Automatic, 2.5° BTDC.
4 Dual point distributor. One set 27°-32°; both 37°-42°.
5 Wagons, 5° BTDC.

6 4-bbl. manual, TDC; 4-bbl. manual (Calif.), 2.5° BTDC; 4-bbl. automatic (Calif.), 5° BTDC.
7 Manual, 2.5° BTDC.
8 Automatic, 2° ATDC.
9 8° BTDC California.
10 Electronic Lean Burn.

CHRYSLER
1978 ELECTRONIC LEAN BURN SYSTEM

VACUUM ADVANCE SCHEDULE

SPARK CONTROL COMPUTER	SPARK TIMER ADVANCE SCHEDULE (Deg.)	THROTTLE ADVANCE SCHEDULE (Deg.) 100°F	140°F	OPERATING VACUUM RANGE (Ins.)	ADVANCE OFF Idle (Deg.)2	ACCUMULATION Time (Min.)	ADVANCE AFTER ACCUMULATION Time (Deg.)	SPEED ADVANCE (Deg.)3 2000 PRM	4000 RPM	DELAY TIME (Sec.)
4091730	8	7-9	3-6	0-12	NONE	8	28-32	4-8	8-12	60
4091731	8	4-6	2-4	0-14	7-11	8	23-27	4-8	10-14	60
4091732	8	5-7	2-5	0-14	NONE	8	26-30	0-3	2-6	60
4091786	8	5-7	2-4	0-15.5	5-9	7	18-22	0-1	0-2	60
4091787	8	5-7	2-4	0-10	NONE	8	23-27	2-5	7-11	60
4091788	8	7-9	4-6	0-14	7-11	8	20-24	1-5	4-8	60
4091791	8	4-6	1-4	0-12	NONE	8	20-24	7-11	8-12	60
4091923	8	5-7	2-5	0-14	8-12	8	24-28	1-4	6-10	60
4091924	8	9-11	5-8	0-14	NONE	8	21-25	10-15	16-21	60
4091954	8	5-7	2-5	0-15.5	NONE	8	18-22	0-1	0-2	60
4091955	8	7-9	4-6	0-14	7-11	7	20-24	1-5	4-8	60
4111012	8	0	0	0-15.5	NONE	8	18-22	4-8	6-10	60
4111013	8	9-11	5-8	0-14	NONE	8	21-25	10-14	16-21	60
4111014	8	5-7	2-5	0-12	2-6	8	18-22	8-12	12-16	60
4111015	8	5-7	2-5	0-14	2-6	8	18-22	8-12	12-16	60
4111159	8	5-7	2-5	0-15.5	NONE	8	18-22	0-1	0-2	60
4111169	NONE	5-7	—	0-10	5-9	8	16-20	1-5	4-8	NONE
4111170	NONE	5-7	2-5	0-10	5-9	8	16-20	1-5	4-8	NONE
4111172	NONE	—	2-5	0-10	5-9	8	16-20	1-5	4-8	NONE
4111217	8	0	0	4-14	6-10	7	18-22	8-12	12-16	60
4111218	8	0	0	4-14	2-6	7	18-22	8-12	12-16	60
5206467	8	0	0	0-14	NONE	8	18-22	6-10	18-22	60
5206501	8	0	0	0-14	6-10	7	18-22	6-10	18-22	60
5206516	8	4-6	4-6	0-14	2-6	8	18-22	6-10	18-22	60
5206525	8	4-6	4-6	0-14	2-6	8	18-22	5-9	13-17	60
5206526	8	0	0	0-14	2-6	8	18-22	6-10	18-22	60
5206666	8	4-6	4-6	0-14	6-10	7	18-22	5-9	13-17	60

1Test transducer core out 1 in.
2Carb switch isolated with paper.
3Ground carb switch & disconnect throttle transducer before checking.

1979 ELECTRONIC SPARK CONTROL SYSTEM

SPARK CONTROL COMPUTER	ENGINE APPLICATION	VACUUM ADVANCE Range (IN.)	BASIC TIMING (Deg.) Crank	Electrical	SPEED ADVANCE (Deg.)1 1100 Rpm	2000 Rpm	ZERO TIME 0+FFSET (Deg.)	ACCUMULATOR TIME (Min.)	VACUUM ADVANCE Full Accumulator (Deg.) 1100 Rpm	1500 Rpm	THROTTLE MAXIMUM ADVANCE2 (Deg.)
5206721	I-4 140	0-10	10	5	0-3	8-12	6-10	8	18-22	23-27	0
5206784	I-4 140	0-10	10	5	0-3	8-12	2-6	8	18-22	23-27	0
5206785	I-4 140	0-10	10	5	0-3	8-12	3-7	8	18-22	28-32	0
5206790	I-4 140	0-10	10	5	0-3	8-12	0-3	8	18-22	28-32	0
5206793	I-4 140	0-10	10	0	0-3	8-12	0-3	8	18-22	23-27	0
4111373	I-6 225	5-11	10	5	0-2	1-4	0-3	8	11-15	18-22	6-10
4111392	V-8 318	4-13	10	6	0-1	1-5	8-12	8	16-20	23-27	3-7
4111440	V-8 318	4-12	10	6	0-1	1-5	8-12	8	12-16	18-22	3-7
4111492	V-8 318	4-13	10	6	0-1	1-5	8-12	8	16-20	23-27	3-7
4111540	V-8 318	4-12	10	6	0-1	1-5	8-12	8	12-16	18-22	3-7
4111574	V-8 318	4-13	10	6	0-1	1-5	0-3	8	16-20	23-27	3-7
4111650	V-8 318	4-12	10	6	0-1	1-5	18-22	8	12-16	18-22	3-7
4111674	V-8 318	4-13	10	6	0-1	1-5	0-3	8	16-22	23-27	3-7
4111750	V-8 318	4-12	10	6	0-1	1-5	18-22	0	12-16	18-22	3-7
4111439	V-8 360	4-12	10	6	2-6	6-10	0-3	8	8-12	18-22	6-10
4111441	V-8 360	4-12	12	0	3-7	8-12	6-10	8	11-17	18-22	0
4111442	V-8 360	4-12	10	6	2-6	6-10	6-10	8	8-12	18-22	6-10
4111575	V-8 360	4-10	10	6	2-6	6-10	2-6	8	11-15	18-22	6-10
4111652	V-8 360	4-14	12	0	0-1	11-15	0-3	8	17-21	26-30	3-7
4111656	V-8 360	4-14	12	0	3-7	8-12	18-22	0	13-17	18-22	0
4111657	V-8 360	0-12	10	0	1-5	11-15	0-3	8	17-21	26-30	3-7

1Ground carb. switch and disconnect throttle transducer before checking.
2Throttle open 20°

FORD, MERCURY, LINCOLN

YEAR	ENGINE APPLICATION	DISTRIBUTOR NUMBER	CENTRIFUGAL ADVANCE DIST. DEGREES @ DIST. RPM Start	Finish	VACUUM ADVANCE DIST. DEGREES @ INS. HG. Start	Finish	DWELL ANGLE (Degrees)	INITIAL TIMING @ Engine Idle1
1970	I-6 170	C9DF-B	0-1.5@500	14@2050	0@5	8@25	35-40	6° BTDC
	I-6 170	D0DF-E	0-1.5@500	19@2650	0-1@5	11@25	35-40	6° BTDC
	I-6 200	D0DF-C	0-1.5@350	16@2800	0-1@5	7@25	35-40	6° BTDC
	I-6 240	C8AF-A	0-1.5@500	10@2000	0@5	8@25	35-40	6° BTDC
	I-6 240	C8AF-B	0-1.5@500	11@2500	0-1@5	9@25	35-40	6° BTDC
	I-6 250	D0OF-A	0-1.5@350	16@2175	0-1@5	9@25	35-40	6° BTDC
	V-8 302	C9ZF-E	0-1.75@750	11@2000	0-1@5	7@25	30-33	16° BTDC
	V-8 302	D0AF-T	0-1.5@500	14@3150	0@5	11.5@25	24-29	6° BTDC
	V-8 302	D0AF-Y	0-1.5@500	14@2325	0@5	11@25	24-29	6° BTDC
	V-8 351	D0AF-AC	0-2@500	14@2000	0@5	9.5@25	24-29	1
	V-8 351	D0AF-H	0-0.5@350	14@2375	0@5	8@25	24-29	10° BTDC
	V-8 351	D0OF-T	0-1.5@500	14@2300	0-2@5	12.5@25	24-29	10° BTDC
	V-8 351	D0OF-U	0-0.5@350	14@2275	0-1@5	12.5@25	24-29	10° BTDC
	V-8 351	D0OF-V	0@500	14@2300	0-1@5	10.5@25	24-29	10° BTDC
	V-8 351	D0OF-Z	0@500	8	0@5	10.5@25	24-29	10° BTDC
	V-8 390	C7AF-AA	0@350	14@2425	0@5	11.5@20	24-292	10° BTDC
	V-8 390	C8AF-M	0@350	11@2050	0-1@5	12.5@25	24-292	10° BTDC
	V-8 390	C8AF-R	0-2@500	14@2375	0@5	12.5@25	24-29	10° BTDC
	V-8 428	D0AF-M	0-2@500	14@2175	0@5	12.5@25	24-29	6° BTDC
	V-8 428	D0ZF-C	0@500	14@2150	0@5	11@25	30-33	6° BTDC

DISTRIBUTOR SPECIFICATIONS

FORD, MERCURY, LINCOLN

YEAR	ENGINE APPLICATION	DISTRIBUTOR NUMBER	CENTRIFUGAL ADVANCE DIST. DEGREES @ DIST. RPM Start	Finish	VACUUM ADVANCE DIST. DEGREES @ INS. HG. Start	Finish	DWELL ANGLE (Degrees)	INITIAL TIMING @ Engine Idle1
1970	V-8 428	D0ZF-G	0@500	14@2075	0-1@5	9.5@20	30-33	6° BTDC
	V-8 429	C8VF-C	0@500	14@2975	0@5	12@25	24-29²	6° BTDC
	V-8 429	C9AF-Y	0@350	14@2775	0-1@5	8.5@25	24-29²	6° BTDC
	V-8 429	C9ZF-D	0@500	11@2000	0@5	10@25	24-29²	6° BTDC
	V-8 429	D0AF-Z	0@500	14@2950	0@5	11@25	24-29²	10° BTDC
	V-8 429	D00F-AB	0@500	8	0-1@5	8.5@25	24-29²	10° BTDC
	V-8 429	D00F-AA	0-1.5@500	16@2200	0-1@5	8.5@25	5	1
	V-8 429	D00F-Y	0@350	14@2525	0-1@5	8.5@25	5	1
	V-8 460	D0VF-B	0@500	11@2575	0-1@5	12@25	26-31	6° BTDC
1971	I-6 170	C9DF-B	0@350	14@2050	0@5	8@25	33-38	6° BTDC
	I-6 170	D1AF-CA	0@350-750	18@2500	0-1@5	8@25	33-38	6° BTDC
	I-6 200	D1DF-GA	0@350-500	14@2500	0@5	7@25	33-38	6° BTDC
	I-6 200	D0DF-C	0@350	16@2800	0@5	7@25	33-38	6° BTDC
	I-6 200	D1DF-BB	0@350	14@2500	0-1@5	7.5@25	33-38	6° BTDC
	I-6 240	C8AF-B	0@350-500	11@2600	0-1@5	9@25	33-38	6° BTDC
	I-6 240	D1AF-CA	0-0.5@350-750	18@2500	0-1@5	8@25	33-38	6° BTDC
	I-6 250	D10F-AB	0-0.5@350	14@2500	0-1@5	7.5@25	3	6° BTDC
	I-6 250	D10F-BB	0-1@750	14@2500	0-1@5	7.5@25	3	6° BTDC
	I-6 250	D10F-CA	0-1.5@350	14@2500	0-1@5	10@25	3	6° BTDC
	V-8 302	D0AF-AE	0.2@750	13@2500	0-1.5@5	2.5@25	24-29	6° BTDC
	V-8 302	D0AF-Y	0-1.75@750	14@2325	0-0.75@5	11@25	24-29	6° BTDC
	V-8 302	D1DF-EA	0-0.5@350	13@2500	0-1.5@5	11.5@25	24-29	6° BTDC
	V-8 302	D00F-AC	0-0.5@350	13@2500	0-1@5	5@25	24-29	6° BTDC
	V-8 302	D12F-AA	0-0.5@350	11@2500	0-1.5@5	2.5@25	32-35	16° BTDC
	V-8 351	D00F-G	0-0.5@350	13@2500	0-1@5	10.5@25	24-29	6° BTDC
	V-8 351	D10F-LA	0-0.5@350	18@2500	0-1@5	10.5@25	24-29	6° BTDC
	V-8 351	D10F-GA	0-0.5@350	13@2500	0-1@5	11@25	24-29	6° BTDC
	V-8 351	D00F-U	0-0.5@350	14@2275	0-1@5	12.5@25	24-29	6° BTDC
	V-8 351	D00F-T	0-0.5@350	14@2300	0.2@5	12.5@25	24-29	6° BTDC
	V-8 351	D00F-V	0-0.5@350	14@2300	0-1@5	10.5@25	24-29	6° BTDC
	V-8 351	D1AF-GA	0-0.5@350	11@2500	0-0.5@5	2.5@25	24-29	6° BTDC
	V-8 351	D1AF-HA	0-0.5@350	18@2500	0-0.5@5	9.3@25	24-29	6° BTDC
	V-8 351	D1AF-KB	0-0.5@350	15@2500	0-0.5@5	9.5@25	24-29	6° BTDC
	V-8 390	D1AF-LB	0-0.5@350	18@2500	0.2@5	9@25	24-29	6° BTDC
	V-8 400	D00F-U	0-0.5@350	14@2275	0-1@5	12.5@25	24-29²	10° BTDC4
	V-8 429	C8VF-C	0@350	14@2975	0-0.75@5	12@25	24-29²	4° BTDC
	V-8 429	D1MF-FA	0@350	13@2500	0-0.75@5	11@25	24-29²	4° BTDC
	V-8 429	D0AF-Z	0@350	14@2950	0@5	11@25	24-29²	4° BTDC
	V-8 429	D00F-AA	0@350	16@2200	0-1.25@5	8.5@25	5	10° BTDC
	V-8 429	D1AF-NA	0@350	14@2500	0-1@5	8.5@25	27.5-29.5	10° BTDC
	V-8 460	D1VF-AA	0@350	13@2500	0@5	8.5@25	27-31.5	10° BTDC
1972	I-6 170	D2DF-AA	0-2@500	11-13.5@2000	0@5	4.5-7.5@20	35-39	1
	I-6 170	D2DF-BA	0-2@500	11-13.5@2000	0@5	4.5-7.5@20	35-39	1
	I-6 200	D2DF-CA	0-1@500	10.5-12.5@2000	0@5	4.5-7.5@20	35-39	1
	I-6 200	D2DF-EA	0-1@500	10.5-12.5@2000	0@5	4.5-7.5@20	35-39	1
	I-6 200	D2DF-DA	0.5-2.5@500	11-13.5@2000	0@5	4.5-7.5@20	35-39	1
	I-6 200	D2DF-FA	0-1@500	11-13.5@2000	0@5	4.5-7.5@20	35-39	1
	I-6 240	D2AF-BA	0-1@500	6-8@2000	0@5	6.5-9.5@20	35-39	1
	I-6 250	D20F-PA	0-2@500	12.5-15@2000	0@5	6.5-9.5@20	35-39	1
	I-6 250	D20F-DA	0-1.5@500	8-10@2000	0@5	6.5-9.5@20	35-39	1
	I-6 250	D20F-EA	0-1@500	8-10.5@2000	0@5	6.5-9.5@20	35-39	1
	V-8 302	D20F-AA	0-0.5@500	11-13.5@2000	0@5	10.5-12.5@20	26-30	1
	V-8 302	D2AF-CA	0-1@500	8.5-11@2000	0@5	2.5-5.5@20	26-30	1
	V-8 302	D20F-HA	0-1@500	8.5-11@2000	0@5	2.5-5.5@20	26-30	1
	V-8 302	D20F-JA	0-1@500	8.5-11@2000	0@5	2.5-5.5@20	26-30	1
	V-8 302	D20F-LA	0-0.5@500	11-13.5@2000	0@5	10.5-12.5@20	26-30	1
	V-8 302	D20F-RA	0-1@500	8.5-11@2000	0@5	2.5-5.5@20	26-30	1
	V-8 351	D2AF-KA	1-3@500	10.5-12.5@2000	0@5	10-13@20	26-30	1
	V-8 351	D2ZF-AA	0-1.5@500	10-12.5@2000	0@5	10-12.5@20	26-30	1
	V-8 351	D2ZF-CA	0-1@500	10-12.5@2000	0@5	10-12.5@20	26-30	1
	V-8 351	D2ZF-EA	—	—	—	—	26-30	1
	V-8 351	D2ZF-FA	—	—	—	—	26-30	1
	V-8 351	D2ZF-GC	0-0.5@500	8-11@2000	0@5	6.5-9.5@20	26-30	1
	V-8 351	D2ZF-HA	0-1@500	12-14@2000	0@5	6.5-9.5@20	26-30	1
	V-8 351	D2ZF-JA	0-1@500	11.5-13@2000	0@5	8.5-11.5@20	26-30	1
	V-8 351	D2ZF-PA	0-1@500	11-13.5@2000	0@5	6.5-9.5@20	26-30	1
	V-8 400	D2AF-RA	0.5-2.5@500	7-9@2000	0@5	10-13.5@20	26-30	1
	V-8 400	D2AF-SA	0.5-2.5@500	7-9@2000	0@5	10.5-13.5@20	26-30	1
	V-8 429	DZMF-EA	0-1@500	7-9@2000	0@5	8-11.5@20	26-30	1
	V-8 429	DZMF-FA	0-1@500	7-9.5@2000	0@5	8.5-11.5@20	26-30	1
	V-8 429	DZMF-MA	0-1@500	11-14.5@2000	0@5	6.5-9.5@20	26-30	1
	V-8 429	DZMF-NA	0-1@500	11.5-14.5@2000	0@5	6.5-9.5@20	26-30	1
	V-8 460	D2VF-AA	0-1@500	8-10.5@2000	0@5	9-12@20	26-30	1
	V-8 460	D2VF-BA	0-1@500	9-11.5@2000	0@5	9-12@20	26-30	1
1973	I-6 250	D30F-BA	0.5-2.5@500	12-14@2000	0-1.5@5	6.5-9.25@20	33-39	1
	I-6 250	D30F-LA	0-1.5@500	9.25-12@2000	0-1.5@5	6.5-9.25@20	33-39	1
	I-6 250	D30F-RA	0-1.5@500	7.5-10@2000	0.5-3.5@5	6.5-9.25@20	33-39	1
	V-8 302	D30F-DA	0-1@500	8.5-11@2000	0-1.25@5	2.5-5.25@20	24-30	1
	V-8 302	D30F-EA	0-1@500	8.25-11@2000	0.2@5	2.5-5.25@15	24-30	1
	V-8 302	D30F-JA	0-1.25@500	9.5-12@2000	0-1.25@5	2.5-5.25@20	24-30	1
	V-8 302	D3BF-BA	0-1@500	9.5-12@2000	0-1@5	8.5-11.25@20	24-30	1
	V-8 302	D30F-HA	0-1@500	9.5-12@2000	0-0.5@5	2.5-5.25@20	24-30	1
	V-8 302	D30F-PA	0-1@500	9.5-12.5@2000	0-1.5@5	2.5-5.25@20	24-30	1
	V-8 302	D3UF-GA	0-1@500	9.5-12@2000	0-1@5	2.5-5.25@20	24-30	1
	V-8 351	D3AF-AA	0-1.5@500	14-16.5@2000	0.2@5	10.5-13.25@20	24-30	1
	V-8 351	D3ZF-CA	0-1.25@500	9-11.5@2000	0-1.25@5	10.5-13.25@20	24-30	1
	V-8 351	D3ZF-GA	0-1@500	8.25-11@2000	0-1@5	9.5-12.5@20	24-30	1
	V-8 351	D30F-FA	0-1@500	10.5-13@2000	0-3@5	2.5-5.25@20	24-30	1
	V-8 351	D30F-GA	0-1@500	11-13.5@2000	0-3.5@5	2.5-5.25@20	32-356	1
	V-8 400	D3AF-BA	0-1.5@500	12-14.5@2000	0-1.5@5	10-13.25@20	24-30	1
	V-8 400	D3MF-GA	0-1@500	8-10.5@2000	0.5-4.5@5	10.5-13.5@20	24-30	1
	V-8 429	D3MF-DA	0-1@500	8.25-10.5@2000	0-1@5	8.5-11.25@20	24-30	1
	V-8 429	D3SF-BA	0-1@500	11.25-13.5@2000	0-1@5	8.5-11.25@20	24-30	1
	V-8 429	D3VF-CA	0-1@500	7.25-10@2000	0-1.25@5	8.5-11.25@20	24-30	1
	V-8 429	D3MF-BA	0-1@500	8.5-11@2000	0-1.25@5	4.5-7.25@20	24-30	1
	V-8 460	D3VF-AA	0-1@500	5-7.5@2000	0-2.25@5	8.5-11.25@20	24-30	1
	V-8 460	D3VF-CA	0-1@500	7.25-10@2000	0-1.25@5	8.5-11.25@20	24-30	1
	V-8 460	D3VF-BA	0-1@500	10-12.25@2000	0-1.5@5	4.5-7.25@20	24-30	1

FORD, MERCURY, LINCOLN

YEAR	ENGINE APPLICATION	DISTRIBUTOR NUMBER	CENTRIFUGAL ADVANCE DIST. DEGREES @ DIST. RPM		VACUUM ADVANCE DIST. DEGREES @ INS. HG.		DWELL ANGLE (Degrees)	INITIAL TIMING @ Engine Idle1
			Start	Finish	Start	Finish		
	V-8 460	D3MF-AA	0-1@500	10-12.5@2000	0-1@5	6.5-9.25@20	24-30	1
	V-8 460	D3MF-CA	0-1.5@500	10-12.5@2000	0-1@5	6.5-9.5@20	24-30	1
1974	I-6 200	D3DF-HA	0-1.5@500	10-12.5@2000	0@5	4.5-7.5@20	33-39	1
	I-6 250	D3DF-FA	0-1.5@500	8-10.5@2000	0@5	6.5-9.3@20	33-39	1
	I-6 250	D30F-RA	0-1.5@500	7.5-10@2000	0@5	6.5-9.3@20	33-39	1
	I-6 250	D4DE-LA	0-1.5@500	7-9.5@2000	0@5	6.5-9.3@20	33-39	1
	I-6 250	D4DE-RA	0-1.5@500	7.5-10.5@2000	0@5	6.5-9.3@20	33-39	1
	V-8 302	D3BF-DA	0-1.3@500	11.5-13.5@2000	0@5	8.5-11.3@20	26-30	1
	V-8 302	D3UF-EA	0-1.3@500	12.3-14.5@2000	0@5	6.5-9.3@20	26-30	1
	V-8 302	D30F-DA	0-1@500	8.5-11@2000	0@5	2.5-5.3@20	26-30	1
	V-8 302	D4DE-MA	0-0.5@500	10.5-13.5@2000	0@5	8.5-11.5@20	26-30	1
	V-8 302	D30F-HB	0-1.5@500	10.5-13.5@2000	0@5	8.5-11.5@20	26-30	1
	V-8 351	D3AF-AA	0-1.5@500	14-16.5@2000	0@5	10.5-13.3@20	26-30	1
	V-8 351	D30F-FA	0-1@500	10.5-13@2000	0@5	2.5-5.3@20	26-30	1
	V-8 351	D30F-GA	0-1@500	11-13.5@2000	0@5	2.5-5.3@20	26-30	1
	V-8 351	D3ZF-GA	0-1@500	8.3-11@2000	0@5	9.5-12.5@20	26-30	1
	V-8 351	D4AE-AA	0-0.5@500	8.4-11@2000	0@5	9.5-12.5@20	26-30	1
	V-8 400	D40E-CA	0-0.5@500	8-10.5@2000	0@5	10.5-13.5@20	26-30	1
	V-8 460	D4AE-HA	0-1.5@500	10-12.5@2000	0@5	6.5-9.5@20	26-30	1
	V-8 460	D4VE-CA	0-0.5@500	8.3-10.5@2000	0@5	8.5-11.5@20	26-30	1
1975	I-6 200	D5DE-AA	0-2@725	10.5-13.25@2500	0@3	4.75-7.25@6.5	7	1
	I-6 200	D5DE-UA	0-2@700	9.25-12.25@2500	0@3	4.75-7.25@6.5	7	1
	I-6 200	D5DE-VA	0-2@700	10-12.5@2500	0@3	4.75-7.25@6.5	7	1
	I-6 250	D5DE-AC	0-2@575	11.75-14.25@2150	0@4	6.75-9.25@12.7	7	1
	I-6 250	D5DE-DA	0-2@700	8-11@2500	0@3	4.75-7.25@5.3	7	1
	I-6 250	D5DE-FA	0-4@580	10-12.25@2500	0@4.1	2.75-5.25@8.5	7	1
	I-6 250	D5DE-YA	0-2@635	13.5-16.25@2500	0@5.25	6.75-9.25@12.75	7	1
	V-8 302	D5DE-AD	0-2@650	8.75-11.25@2500	0@4.3	10.75-13.25@12	7	1
	V-8 302	D5DE-LA	0-2@700	9.75-12.75@2500	0@4.3	8.75-11.25@18	7	1
	V-8 302	D5DE-ZA	0-2@660	8.25-10.75@2380	0@6	8.75-11.25@14.25	7	1
	V-8 351	D5AE-BA	0-4@1800	16-22@4250	0@4	13.5-19.5@9	7	1
	V-8 351	D5AE-EA	0-5@1900	16-21@4250	0@3	13-19@7	7	1
	V-8 351	D5DE-HA	0-4@1100	21-26@4000	0@4.5	15-21@13	7	1
	V-8 351	D5DE-MA	0-2@700	8.5-11@2500	0@4.5	10.75-13.25@19.7	7	1
	V-8 351	D5DE-SA	0-2@525	14-16.5@2500	0@3	10.75-13.25@14.5	7	1
	V-8 400	D5AE-BA	0-4@1800	16-23@4300	0@4	13.5-19.5@9	7	1
	V-8 400	D5AE-DA	0-5@1950	16-22@4300	0@4	16-22@9	7	1
	V-8 460	D4VE-CA	0-4@1650	12.6-16.7@2500	0@4	10-16@10	7	1
1976	I-4 140	D6EE-AA	0-2.3@650	11.0-12.5@2500	0@4	9@7.2	7	1
	I-4 140	D6EE-BA	0-5@650	5.5@2500	0@5	10@9	7	1
	I-4 140	D6EE-DA	0-2.5@600	11.5-16.0@2500	0@4	10.5@8	7	1
	V-6 170	76TF-EA	0-5@550	13.2-18.5@2500	0@5	7@9.5	7	1
	V-6 170	76TF-FA	0-2@650	11.5-16.6@2500	0@5.5	7@9.5	7	1
	V-6 170	76TF-GA	0-2@650	11.3-16.2@2500	0@5.6	10@12.5	7	1
	V-6 170	76TF-JA	0-2@680	11.8@2000	0@6	4@6.3	7	1
	I-6 200	D6DE-BA	0-2@550	15.0-19.2@2500	0-3@4.5	11.25@14	7	1
	I-6 250	D6DE-AA	0-2@700	18.0-22.0@2500	0-7@4	8.75@11.2	7	1
	I-6 250	D6DE-GA	0-2@500	6.5-11.0@2500	0-3@4	11.2@9.5	7	1
	I-6 250	D6DE-KA	0-1@500	13.0@2500	0-2@3	7.2@6.7	7	1
	I-6 250	D5DE-ACA	0-2@600	14.2@2500	0-5@6	9.25@12.5	7	1
	V-8 302	D6DE-JA	0-3.5@500	18.3-23.0@2500	0-3.75@5	13.25@12.2	7	1
	V-8 302	D5DE-AFA	0-2.5@550	10.4-15.2@2500	0-3@5.6	13.2@13.1	7	1
	V-8 302	D5DE-AGA	0-2@680	13.5@2500	0-4@5	15@12.7	7	1
	V-8 351W	D6DE-CA	0-3@600	11.0-15.4@2500	0-6@5	13.2@12.7	7	1
	V-8 351W	D6DE-LA	0-3.2@500	18.8-23.5@2500	0-4@4	15.25@10.6	7	1
	V-8 351W	D6OE-AA	0-2@550	13.0@2000	0@4.5	10.5@13	7	1
	V-8 351M	D6AE-BA	0-3@525	14.0-18.6@2500	0-1.25@5	9.5@15	7	1
	V-8 351M	D6AE-CA	0-3@500	11.5-16.2@2500	0-2.5@4	10@7.5	7	1
	V-8 351M	D5OE-FA	0-3@500	11.5@2500	0-1@5	13@16	7	1
	V-8 400	D6AE-AA	0-2@500	12.5-17.0@2500	0-3.5@4.3	10.5@7	7	1
	V-8 460	D6VE-AA	0-2@500	15.5-20.0@2500	0-2@5	10@10	7	1
	V-8 460	D6VE-BA	0-3@520	21.2-25.8@2500	0-3.5@3.8	9.3@7	7	1
1977	I-6 200	D7BE-EA	0-2@1100	10.4-14.5@2500	0-2@3 / 0-6@4.2	17.5-22.5@11	7	6°BTDC
	I-6 250	D7BE-CA	0-2@900	13.0-17.1@2500	0-2@3 / 0-7@4	25.5-30.5@11	7	4°BTDC8
	I-6 250	D7BE-DA	0-2@1000	6.1-10.6@2500	0-2@3 / 0-6@4.2	17.5-22.5@11	7	6°BTDC
	I-6 250	D7BE-FA	0-2@1000	5.5-10.0@2500	0-2@3.1 / 0-7@4	9.5-14.5@6.5	7	8°BTDC
	V-8 302	D7DE-CA	0-2@900	14.2-18.4@2500	0-2@3 / 0-7@4	25.5-30.5@11	7	6°BTDC
	V-8 302	D7DE-DA	0-2@1000	12.0-16.0@2500	0-2@3 / 0-6@4.2	17.5-22.5@11	7	6°BTDC
	V-8 302	D7DE-GA	0-2@1050	5.9-10.2@2500	0-2@3 / 0-7@5.5	21.5-26.5@16	7	12°BTDC
	V-8 302	D7DE-HA	2-+1@1100	4.5-9.0@2500	0-4@5	25@15 / 30@14	7	12°BTDC
	V-8 302	D7ZE-BA	0-2@850	16.7-21.3@2500	0-2@3.5 / 0-7@5.5	21.5-26.5@15.2	7	4°BTDC
	V-8 351	D7AE-BA	0-2@850	22.0-27.0@4500	0-2@3.5 / 0-6@4.8	22.5-30.5@12	7	9°BTDC
	V-8 351	D7AE-CA	0-2@1400	3.0-8.2@2500	0-2@3 / 0-7@4.2	22.5-30.5@11	7	9°BTDC
	V-8 351	D7DE-CA	0-2@900	25.0-31.0@5000	0-2@3 / 0-7@4	22.5-30.5@11	7	8°BTDC
	V-8 351	D7DE-FA	0-2@850	10.6-15.3@2500	0-2@3 / 0-7@4.7	25.5-30.5@13.5	7	4°BTDC
	V-8 351	D7OE-CA	0-2@900	27.0-32.0@5000	0-2@3.5 / 0-6@5.5	25.5-30.5@14.5	7	8°BTDC
	V-8 400	D6AE-AA	0-4@1000	23.2@5000	0-2@3.0 / 0-8@4.5	18.5-25@9.0 / 25-39.5@11.5	7	8°BTDC
	V-8 400	D7AE-DA	0-2@900	12.0-16.5@2500	0-2@3.2 / 0-6@5.5	25.5-30.5@14.5	7	8°BTDC
	V-8 460	D6VE-CA	0-2@900	10.5-15.2@2500	0-2@3.5 / 0-6@5.5	21.5-26.5@15	7	16°BTDC
1978	I-6 250	D8BE-CA	0-1@1000	2.2-4.7@2500	0-1@3	8.7-11.2@11.5	7	1

FORD, MERCURY, LINCOLN

YEAR	ENGINE APPLICATION	DISTRIBUTOR NUMBER	CENTRIFUGAL ADVANCE DIST. DEGREES @DIST. RPM		VACUUM ADVANCE DIST. DEGREES @INS. HG.		DWELL ANGLE (Degrees)	INITIAL TIMING @Engine Idle
			Start	Finish	Start	Finish		
1978	I-6 250	D8BE-JA	0-1@550	7.5-10.5@2500	0-1@3.5	6.7-9.2@13	7	1
	I-6 250	D8DE-CA	0-1@475	6.5-9@2500	0-1@2	10.7-13.2@10.8	7	1
	V-8 302	D7DE-AA	0-1@525	9.5-12.5@2500	0-1@3	12.5-15@11	7	1
	V-8 302	D8AE-GA	0-1@450	5.7-8.3@2500	0-1@5.5	13.2-15.2@16.5	7	1
	V-8 302	D8DE-EA	0-1@450	9.5-12.7@2500	0-1@3	10.7-13.2@14	7	1
	V-8 302	D8ZE-CA	0-1@575	9.5-11.5@2500	0-1@3	12.7-15.2@11.5	7	1
	V-8 351	D7AE-UA	0-1@650	7.5-10.5@2500	0-5@4	10.7-13.5@15	7	1
	V-8 351	D8AE-CA	0-1@1100	7-9.5@2500	0-1@3	14.5-17.5@14	7	1
	V-8 400	D7AE-UA	0-1@650	7.5-10.5@2500	0-5@4	10.7-13.5@15	7	1
	V-8 400	D8AE-BA	0-1@450	11-14@2500	0-2@3.5	15.7-16.8@14.5	7	1
1979	I-6 200	D8BE-EA	0-1@550	7-9.5@2500	0-1@4.5	8.7-11.2@12.5	7	1
	I-6 200	D9TE-BA	0-1@550	7-9.5@2500	0-1@4.5	8.7-11.2@12.5	7	1
	I-6 250	D8BE-JA	0-1@550	7.5-10.5@2500	0-1@3.5	6.8-9.2@13.0	7	1
	I-6 250	D8DE-CA	0-1@475	6.5-9@2500	0-1@2.0	10.7-13.2@10.8	7	1
	I-6 250	D9DE-CA	0-1@1000	3.5-6.5@2500	0-1@3.0	8.7-11.2@11.5	7	1
	V-8 302	D7DE-AA	0-1@525	9.5-12.5@2500	0-1@3.0	12.7-15.2@11.0	7	1
	V-8 302	D8DE-EA	0-1@450	9.5-12.2@2500	0-1@3.0	10.7-13.2@14.0	7	1
	V-8 302	D9AE-AAA	0-2.8@500	10.6-13.2@2500	±.5@2.3	12.7-15.2@25.0	7	1
	V-8 302	D9AE-ABA	0-2@580	9.2-12.2@2500	±.5@2.8	6.7-9.2@25.0	7	1
	V-8 302	D9AE-ZA	0-3@500	12.2-14.7@2500	±.5@1.8	14.7-17.2@25.0	7	1
	V-8 302	D9BE-CA	0-1@700	7.5@2500	0-1@4.0	12@14.0	7	1
	V-8 302	D9ZE-CA	0@450	11.5@2500	0@4.0	16@16.0	7	1
	V-8 302	D97E-CA	0-1@450	10-13@2500	0-1@4.0	7.5-8.5@13.0	7	1
	V-8 351	D7AE-UA	0@730	7.5-10.2@2500	±.5@2.3	10.7-13.2@25.0	7	1
	V-8 351	D80E-AA	0-2.7@500	13.7-16.3@2500	±.5@2.0	12.2-15.2@25.0	7	1
	V-8 351	D9AE-PA	0@550	4.4-7.1@2500	±.5@2.0	14.7-17.2@25.0	7	1
	V-8 351	D9SE-AA	0-2@500	3.6-6.1@2500	±.5@2.8	14.7-17.2@25.0	7	1
	V-8 400	D80E-AA	0-2.7@500	13.7-16.3@2500	±.5@2.0	12.2-15.2@25.0	7	1
	V-8 400	D9AE-ACA	0-2@725	7.5-10.2@2500	±.5@2.4	6.7-9.2@25.0	7	1
	V-8 400	D9AE-YA	0-2@630	9.7-12.6@2500	±.5@2.0	14.7-17.2@25.0	7	1

1 Refer to engine decal for idle speed and/or initial timing specification.
2 Single diaphragm distributor, 26°-31°.
3 Single diaphragm distributor, 34°-39.5°; dual diaphragm, 33°-38°.
4 California, 6° BTDC.

5 Isolate and set individual points to 25°-25.5° to obtain 30°-33° combined.
6 Dwell reading made with both sets of points operating.
7 Electronic ignition
8 6° BTDC for manual transmission.

FORD PINTO, MUSTANG II AND MERCURY BOBCAT

YEAR	ENGINE APPLICATION	DISTRIBUTOR NUMBER	CENTRIFUGAL ADVANCE DIST. DEGREES @ DIST. RPM		VACUUM ADVANCE DIST. DEGREES @ INS. HG.		DWELL ANGLE (Degrees)	INITIAL TIMING @ Engine Idle1
			Start	Finish	Start	Finish		
1971	I-4 1600	D1F2-B	0-0.5@400	12-14@2500	0@5	8@25	38-42	1
	I-4 2000	D1F2-A	0-0.5@350	9.8-11.8@2500	0@5	7.5@25	38-42	1
	I-4 2000	D1F2-B	0-0.5@350	10.5-12.5@2500	0@5	10@25	36-40	1
	I-4 1600	721F-YA	0-0.5@500	10-12@2000	0@5	5-8@20	38-42	1
1972	I-4 1600	721F-TA	0-0.5@500	10-12@2000	0@5	5-8@20	36-40	1
	I-4 2000	72HF-DC	0.5-2.5@500	12-14@2000	0@5	5.5-7.5@20	36-40	1
	I-4 2000	72HF-FA	0.5-2.5@500	11.5-14@2000	0@5	5-7.5@20	36-40	1
	I-4 2000	72HF-SC	0-0.5@500	13.5-15.5@2000	0@5	5-7.5@20	36-40	1
1973	I-4 1600	731F-AHA	0-0.5@500	9.5-11.5@2000	0-2@5	-10.5-13.25@20	37-41	1
	I-4 2000	73HF-AA	0.5-2.5@500	12-14@2000	0-2@5	5.5-7.5@20	37-41	1
	I-4 2000	73HF-BA	0-1@500	12-14@2000	0-2@5	5.5-7.5@20	37-41	1
	I-4 2000	73HF-GA	0-0.5@500	9-11@2000	0-2@5	5.5-7.5@20	37-41	1
1974	I-4 2000	74HF-EA	1-3@500	12-14@2000	0@5	4-6@20	37-41	1
	I-4 2000	74HF-LA	0-1@500	9.5-11.5@2000	0@5	4-6@20	37-41	1
	I-4 2300	D42E-AA	0-1@500	11.5-14@2000	0@5	4.5-7.5@20	37-41	1
	I-4 2300	D42E-BA	0-1@500	11.5-14@2000	0@5	4.5-7.5@20	37-41	1
	I-4 2300	D42F-DA	0-1@500	11.5-14@2000	0@5	4.5-7.5@20	37-41	1
	I-4 2300	D42F-KA	0-1@500	11.5-14@2000	0@5	2.5-5.5@20	37-41	1
	V-6 2800	74TF-LA	0@500	8-10@2000	0@5	2-4@20	38	1
	V-6 2800	74TF-MA	0@500	8-10@2000	0@5	2-4@20	38	1
	V-6 2800	74TF-SA	0@500	8-10@2000	0@5	2-4@20	38	1
1975	I-4 2300	D52E-EA	0@675	11.5-14@2250	0@4	2.75-5.25@7	2	1
	I-4 2300	D52E-EA	0@715	11.5-14@2150	0@4	2.75-5.25@7.5	2	1
	I-4 2300	D52E-AA	0-2@600	10.25-13@2500	0@4.8	2.75-5.25@7.5	2	1
	I-4 2300	D52E-CA	0-2.3@600	10.25-12.75@2400	0@4.75	13-15.75@15	2	1
	V-6 2800	D5TF-EA	0-2@650	8-10@2000	0@4.25	2-3@6.75	2	1
	V-6 2800	D5TF-MA	0-2@660	6.5-9.5@2500	0@4.25	5-7@9.5	2	1
	V-6 2800	D5TF-NA	0-2@650	9-12@2500	0@4.25	5-7@9.5	2	1
	V-8 302	D52E-BA	0-2@540	8.25-11.5@2500	0@5	8.25-11.25@7.5	2	1
	V-8 302	D5DE-KA	0-2@775	8.25-10.75@2350	0@6	8.75-11.25@14.5	2	1
1976	I-4 2300	D6EE-AA	0-2.5@650	11.0-12.5@2500	0-3.5@4	6.5-9@7.2	2	1
		D6EE-BA	0-.5@650	0.5-5.5@2500	0-4@5	6-10@9	2	1
		D6EE-DA	0-2.5@600	11.5-16.0@2500	0-3.5@4	7.5-11@8	2	1
	V-6 2800	76TF-EA	0-.5@550	13.2-18.5@2500	0-3@5	7@7.5	2	1
		76TF-FA	0-2@650	11.5-16.6@2500	0-3@5.5	4.5-7@9.5	2	1
		76TF-GA	0-2@650	11.3-16.2@2500	0-5@5.6	8-10@12.5	2	1
		76TF-JA	0-2@680	9.8-11.8@2000	0-5@4	4@6.3	2	1
	V-8 302	D5DE-AFA	0-2.5@550	10.4-15.2@2500	0-3@5.5	10.8-13.2@15	2	1
		D6DE-JA	0-3.5@500	18.3-23.0@2500	0-3.7@5	13.2@12.2	2	1

FORD PINTO, MUSTANG II AND MERCURY BOBCAT

YEAR	ENGINE APPLICATION	DISTRIBUTOR NUMBER	CENTRIFUGAL ADVANCE DIST. DEGREES @ DIST. RPM Start	Finish	VACUUM ADVANCE DIST. DEGREES @ INS. HG. Start	Finish	DWELL ANGLE (Degrees)	INITIAL TIMING @ Engine Idle[1]
1977	I-4 2300	D7EE-CA	0-2@1600	10.5@5000	0-1@2.3 0-6@4.7	21.5-26.5@15.75	2	6° BTDC[3]
	I-4 2300	D7EE-DA	0-2@1020	12.0-16.5@2500	0-1@1.75 0-6@3.7	21.5-26.5@12.4	2	6° BTDC[3]
	I-4 2300	D7EE-EA	0-2@1050	11.6-16.0@2500	0-1@2 0-6@4.35	21.5-26.5@15.75	2	6° BTDC[3]
	I-4 2300	D7EE-GA	0-2@1050	12.0-16.5@2500	0-1@2.25 0-6@4.75	21.5-26.5@15.75	2	20° BTDC
	I-4 2300	D7EE-HA	0-2@1550	0.2-5.4@2500	0-1@2 0-6@4.75	21.5-26.5@15.75	2	20° BTDC
	V-6 2800	77TF-AA	0-2@1250	11.2-16.0@2500	0-2@4 0-6@5.8	16-20@12	2	8° BTDC[4]
	V-6 2800	77TF-CA	0-2@1200	13.0-18.4@2500	0-2@4.5 0-6@5.6	10-14@10	2	12° BTDC
	V-6 2800	77TF-DA	0-2@1200	11.7-16.6@2500	0-2@4.5 0-6@5.6	10-14@10	2	6° BTDC
	V-8 302	D7DE-GA	0-2@850	5.9-10.3@2500	0-2@3 0-7@5.5	21.5-26.5@16	2	12° BTDC
	V-8 302	D7ZE-BA	0-2@850	16.7-21.3@2500	0-2@3.5 0-7@5.5	21.5-26.5@15.2	2	4° BTDC
	V-8 302	D7ZE-CA	0-2@1150	12.1-16.1@2500	0-2@2.2 0-6@4.5	25.5-30.5@16	2	12° BTDC
1978	I-4 140	D7EE-CA	0-1@800	5-7.5@2500	0-.5@2.3	10.7-13.2@15.75	2	1
	I-4 140	D7EE-DA	0-1@510	11.5-14@2500	0-.5@1.75	10.7-13.2@12.4	2	1
	I-4 140	D7EE-EA	0-1@575	11.5-14@2500	0@2	10.7-13.2@15.75	2	1
	V-6 170.8	77TF-AA	0-1@625	8-10.5@2100	0-1@4	8-10@12	2	1
	V-6 170.8	77TF-CA	0-1@575	9.5-12.5@2500	0-1@3.5	5-7.5@8.5	2	1
	V-6 170.8	77TF-HA	0-1@600	11-12@2100	0-1@4.5	5-7@10	2	1
	I-6 200	D7BE-EA	0-1@500	11.2-13.7@2450	0-1@3	8.7-11.2@13.5	2	1
	I-6 200	D7BE-GA	0-1@500	6.2-8.7@2500	0-1@3	4.7-7.2@7	2	1
	I-6 200	D8BE-EA	0-1@550	7-9.5@2500	0-1@4.5	8.7-11.2@12.5	2	1
	I-6 200	D8BE-FA	0-1@550	7-9.5@2500	0-1@3.5	8.7-11.2@13.5	2	1
	V-8 302	D7DE-AA	0@550	9.5-12.5@2500	0-1@3	13.2-15.2@12	2	1
	V-8 302	D7DE-CA	0@450	12.5-15@2500	0-1@4	12.2-15.2@11	2	1
	V-8 302	D7DE-JA	0-1@550	8.2-10.7@2500	0-1@3	10.7-13.2@16	2	1
	V-8 302	D8DE-EA	0@450	9.5-12.2@2500	0-1@3	10.7-13.2@13	2	1
	V-8 302	D8ZE-BA	0-1@425	13.2-16@2500	0-1@3.5	10.7-13.2@14	2	1
	V-8 302	D8ZE-CA	0-1@575	9.5-11.5@2500	0-1@2.5	9.7-12.2@15.7	2	1
1979	I-4 140	D7EE-CA/HA	0-2.10@1240	5-7.5@2500	±.5@2.3	10.7-13.2@15.75	2	1
	I-4 140	D7EE-DA	0-2.10@530	11.5-14@2500	±.5@1.75	10.7-13.2@12.4	2	1
	I-4 140	D7EE-EA	0-3@500	11.2-14@2500	±.5@2.0	10.7-13.2@15.75	2	1
	I-4 140	D9ZE-EA	0-2.5@490	10.5-13@2500	±.5@1.8	8.7-11.2@14.80	2	1
	I-4 140	D9ZE-FA	0-2.5@490	10.5-13@2500	±.5@1.8	10.7-13.2@16.20	2	1
	V-6 170.8	77TF-CA	0-1@575	9.5-12.5@2500	0-1@3.5	5-7@8.5	2	1
	V-6 170.8	79TF-FA	0-1@600	10-12@2500	0-1@4.5	2-4@10	2	1
	V-8 302	D8DE-EA	0-1@450	9.2-12.2@2500	0-1@2.5	10.7-13.2@14.3	2	1
	V-8 302	D8ZE-CA	0-1@575	6-8.7@2500	0-1@2.0	10.7-13.2@15.3	2	1
	V-8 302	D9ZE-CA	0-1@450	9.5-12.2@2500	0-1@2.8	14.7-17.2@15.5	2	1

1 Refer to engine decal for idle speed and/or initial timing Specification.
2 Electronic ignition
3 20° BTDC for automatic transmission.
4 12° BTDC for automatic transmission.

OLDSMOBILE

YEAR	ENGINE APPLICATION	DISTRIBUTOR NUMBER	CENTRIFUGAL ADVANCE DIST. DEGREES @ DIST. RPM Start	Finish	VACUUM ADVANCE DIST. DEGREES @ INS. HG. Start	Finish	DWELL ANGLE (Degrees)	INITIAL TIMING @ Engine Idle[1]
1970	I-6 250	1110464	0-2@510	13-15@2100	0@6	10.5-13@15.5	31-34	4° BTDC
	I-6 250	1110463	0-3@500	15-17@2100	0@6	10.5-13@15.5	31-34	TDC
	V-8 350	1111975	0-2@400	10-12@2000	0@8-10	8.2-10.8@23	30	10° BTDC2
	V-8 350	1111976	0-2@405	14-16@2000	0@8-10	11.2-13.8@25	30	10° BTDC
	V-8 455	1111977	0.4-2.4@500	10-12@2000	0@10-13	7.2-12.8@25	30	8° BTDC
	V-8 455	1111978	0-2@540	5.5-7.5@1650	0@9-11	8.3-10.8@24	30	10° BTDC
	V-8 455	1111979	0-3.5@375	14-16@1500	0@10-13	7.2-12.8@25	30	8° BTDC
	V-8 455	1111980	0-2@400	13-15@2000	0@8-10	11.2-13.8@25	30	8° BTDC
	V-8 455	1111981	0.4-2.4@700	6-8@1500	0@10-13	7.2-12.8@25	30	8° BTDC
	V-8 455	1111982	0-2@550	9-11@1800	0@10-13	7.2-12.8@25	30	12° BTDC
1971	I-6 250	1110489	0-2@635	11-13@2050	0@7-9	10.5@16.5-18	31-34	4° BTDC
	V-8 350	1112079	0-2@385	16-18@2050	0@6-8	13@16-17.5	30	10° BTDC
	V-8 350	1112085	0.6-2.6@600	12-14@2000	0@6-8	13@16-17.5	30	12° BTDC
	V-8 350	1112079	0-2@385	16-18@2050	0@6-8	13@16-17.5	30	10° BTDC
	V-8 455	1112033	0-2@400	13-15@2000	0@8-10	12.5@18.5-20.5	30	8° BTDC
	V-8 455	1112036	0.4-2.4@500	10-12@2000	0@6-8	13@16-17.5	30	12° BTDC
	V-8 455	1112034	0.8-4@450	12-14@1500	0@6-8	13@16-17.5	30	10° BTDC
	V-8 455	1112033	0-2@400	13-15@2000	0@8-10	12.5@18.5-20.5	30	8° BTDC
	V-8 455	1112078	0-2@500	7-9@1950	0@8-10	13@18.5-20.5	30	10° BTDC
1972	I-6 250	1110489	0-2@635	11-13@2050	0@7	10.5@16.5-18	31-34	4° BTDC
	V-8 350	1112079	0-2@385	16-18@2050	0@6	13@16-17.5	30	10° BTDC
	V-8 350	1112085	0.6-2.6@600	12-14@2000	0@6	13@16-17.5	30	12° BTDC
	V-8 455	1112033	0-2@400	13-15@2000	0@8	12.5@18.5-20.5	30	10° BTDC
	V-8 455	1112034	0.8-4@450	12-14@1500	0@8	13@16-17.5	30	10° BTDC
	V-8 455	1112036	0.4-2.4@500	10-12@2000	0@8	13@16-17.5	30	12° BTDC
	V-8 455	1112078	0-2@500	7-9@1950	0@10	13@18.5-20.5	30	10° BTDC
1973	I-6 250	1110499	0@930	24@4100	0@6	12@14.5-15.5	31-34	6° BTDC
	V-8 350	1112226	0-2@400	14-16@2000	0@3.5	10@12-13	30	14° BTDC3

DISTRIBUTOR SPECIFICATIONS

OLDSMOBILE

YEAR	ENGINE APPLICATION	DISTRIBUTOR NUMBER	CENTRIFUGAL ADVANCE DIST. DEGREES @ DIST. RPM		VACUUM ADVANCE DIST. DEGREES @ INS. HG.		DWELL ANGLE (Degrees)	INITIAL TIMING @ Engine Idle1
			Start	Finish	Start	Finish		
1973	V-8 350	1112225	0-2@380	17-19@2000	0@5	8@10-12	30	10° BTDC
	V-8 350	1112222	0-2@485	14-16@2000	0@5	8@10-12	30	8° BTDC
	V-8 350	1112195	0-2@400	14-16@2000	0@5	8@10-12	30	12° BTDC
	V-8 455	1112197	0-2@540	9-11@1800	0@7	9@15-16.6	30	8° BTDC4
	V-8 455	1112198	0-2@575	7-9@1700	0@7	9@12-14	30	8° BTDC
1974	I-6 250	1110499	0@930	24@4100	0@6	12@14.5-15.5	33	8° BTDC
	V-8 350	1112225	0-4@760	20-22@2100	0@5	16@10-12	30	12° BTDC
	V-8 350	1112226	0-4@800	16-20@2100	0@3.5	20@12-13	30	14° BTDC5
	V-8 350	1112228	0-4@800	16-20@2100	0@4.5	20@12-13	30	12° BTDC
	V-8 350	1112195	0-4@800	16-20@2100	0@5	16@10-12	30	12° BTDC
	V-8 455	1112197	0-4@1080	10-14@2000	0@7	18@15-16.6	30	8° BTDC
	V-8 455	1112531	0-4@1080	10-14@2000	0@6	18@10	30	8° BTDC
	V-8 455	1112506	0-4@1080	10-14@2000	0@7	18@15-16.6	30	8° BTDC
	V-8 455	1112532	0-4@1080	10-14@2000	0@4	20@13	30	8° BTDC
	V-8 455	1112825	0-4@1150	7-11@2000	0@6	18@10	30	10° BTDC
	V-8 455	1112827	0-4@1150	7-11@2000	0@7	24@17	30	10° BTDC
	V-8 455	1112829	0-4@1150	7-11@2000	0@4	20@13	30	10° BTDC
	V-8 455	1112830	0-4@1150	7-11@2000	0@7	24@17	30	10° BTDC
	V-8 455	1112550	0@750	26@3000	0@12	16@18	30	14 BTDC
1975	V-6 231	1110651	0@540	8@2050	0@5-7	9@10	6	12° BTDC
	I-6 250	1112863	0@550	8@2100	0@3.5	3.2-9.5@11-12.5	6	10° BTDC
	I-6 250	1110650	0@550	8@2100	0@3.5	6.7-8.2@11.5-12.5	6	10° BTDC
	V-8 260	1112951	0@325	14@2200	0@4	12@15	6	18° BTDC
	V-8 260	1112956	0@325	14@2200	NONE	NONE	6	16° BTDC8
	V-8 350	1112896	0@550	6@2250	0@6.5	7@11.5	6	12° BTDC
	V-8 350	1112936	0@500	9.5@2000	0@6.5	12@16	6	20° BTDC
	V-8 350	1112953	0@500	9.5@2000	0@8	9@16	6	20° BTDC
	V-8 400	1112500	0@600	10@2200	0@6-8	12.5@11.5	6	16° BTDC
	V-8 400	1112928	0@600	8@2200	0@6-8	12.5@12	6	16° BTDC
	V-8 400	1112958	0@600	8@2200	0@5	12.5@11	6	16° BTDC
	V-8 455	1112937	0@500	6.5@1800	0@8	9@13	6	16° BTDC
	V-8 455	1112952	0@500	7@1800	0@8	9@13	6	12° BTDC
	V-8 455	1112893	0@450	8@1700	0@9	12@19.5	6	8° BTDC
	V-8 455	1112945	0@450	8@1700	0@14.5	5@19	6	8° BTDC
1976	I-4 140	1112862	0@810	11@2400	0@5	12@12	6	12° BTDC
	V-6 231	1110668	0-4.4@718	5.6-9@2500	0.2@5.3	11.2-12.7@12.8	6	12° BTDC
	I-6 250	1110666	0@500	10@2100	0@4	12@15	6	6° BTDC
	I-6 250	1110863	0@550	8@2100	0@3.5	11-13@6.5-7.8	6	10° BTDC
	V-8 260	1112956	0@325	14@2200	NONE	NONE	6	16° BTDC8
	V-8 260	1112994	0@325	14@2200	0@4.5	12@10.5	6	16° BTDC
	V-8 260	1112995	0@455	13@2232	0@4	15@11	6	18° BTDC
	V-8 260	1103204	0@325	14@2200	0@6	10@7.37	6	14° BTDC
	V-8 260	1103211	0@325	14@2200	0@6	7@9.2	6	14° BTDC
	V-8 350	1112991	0-2.3@872	8.7-11@2500	0-2@6.9	12@15.8	6	12° BTDC
	V-8 350	1112936	0@500	9.5@2000	0@6.5	12@15.8	6	20° BTDC
	V-8 350	1112953	0@500	9.5@2000	0@8	9@16	6	20° BTDC
	V-8 350	1103210	0@500	9.5@2000	0@6	12@13.7	6	22° BTDC
	V-8 455	1112937	0@500	6.5@1800	0@8	9@13	6	16° BTDC
	V-8 455	1103212	0@500	6.5@1800	0@8	12@15	6	18° BTDC
	V-8 455	1112988	0@500	6.5@1800	0@8	9@13	6	14° BTDC
	V-8 455	1112952	0@550	7@1800	0@8	9@13	6	12° BTDC
1977	I-4 140	1110538	0@425	8.5@1000	0@5	12@10	6	TDC
	I-4 140	1110539	0@425	16@2200	0@5	12@10	6	2° BTDC
	V-6 231	1110677	0@650	8-11@1800	0@6	11-12.5@10.8	6	12° BTDC
	V-6 231	1110686	0-2@900	8.5-11@1800	0@6	3-4.5@8.8	6	12° BTDC
	V-8 260	1103262	0@450	8.5@1200	0@4	15@11	6	16° BTDC
	V-8 305	1103239	0@600	10@2100	0@4	7.5@10	6	8° BTDC
	V-8 305	1103244	0@500	10@1900	0@4	10@10	6	6° BTDC
	V-8 305	1103252	0@500	10@1900	0@4	9@12	6	8° BTDC
	V-8 350	1103248	0@600	10-12@2100	0@3.5	4-6@7-9	6	6° BTDC
	V-8 350	1103246	0@600	10-12@2100	0@3.5	8.5-9.5@11-13	6	8° BTDC
	V-8 350	1103259	0@600	9.5@2000	0@6	12@13	6	20° BTDC
	V-8 350	1103266	0@500	9.5@2000	0@5	8@11	6	20° BTDC
	V-8 403	1103260	0@500	6.5@1800	0@6	12@13	6	20° BTDC
	V-8 403	1103264	0@500	6.5@1800	0@5	8@11	6	20° BTDC
1978	I-4 151	1103328	0@600	10@2200	0@3.5	10@9	6	14° BTDC
	I-4 151	1103329	0@600	10@2200	0@3.5	10@12	6	14° BTDC
	I-4 151	1103365	0@600	10@2200	0@5	8@11	6	14° BTDC
	V-6 231	1110695	0-3@1000	6-9@1800	0@3-6	12@10-13	6	15° BTDC
	V-6 231	1110731	0-2@1000	6-9@1800	0@2-3	8@7-9	6	15° BTDC
	V-6 231	1110732	0-2@1000	6-9@1800	0@2-3	7@10.6-13	6	15° BTDC
	V-8 260	1103320	0@455	13@2230	0@2	15@11	6	20° BTDC
	V-8 260	1103355	0@455	13@2230	0@2	15@9	6	18° BTDC
	V-8 305	1103282	0@500	10@1900	0@2	10@10	6	4° BTDC
	V-8 305	1103281	0@500	10@1900	0@2	9@12	6	4° BTDC
	V-8 305	1103357	0@550	11.8-15.7@2500	0@	10@10	5	1
	V-8 350	1103346	0@500	9.5@2000	0@6	12@13	6	20° BTDC
	V-8 350	1103353	0-2@625	5.5-6@2250	0@3-6	10@9-12	6	8° BTDC
	V-8 350	1103285	0@600	11@2100	0@4	12@8	6	8° BTDC
	V-8 350	1103222	0@300	14.5@2000	0@6	12@13	6	20° BTDC
	V-8 350	1103223	0@500	9.5@2000	0@5	8@11	6	20° BTDC
	V-8 350	1103356	0@550	14.3-18@2500	0@2	10@10	5	1
	V-8 403	1103224	0@300	11.5@1800	0@6	12@13	6	20° BTDC
	V-8 403	1103325	0@500	6.5@1800	0@6	8@11	6	20° BTDC
	V-8 403	1103347	0@500	6.5@1800	0@6	12@13	6	20° BTDC
1979	I-4 2.5L	1110726	0@500	9@2000	0@3.5	10@8	6	12°BTDC
	I-4 2.5L	1110757	0@600	9@2000	0@3.5	10@8	6	12°BTDC
	I-4 2.5L	1103365	0@600	10@2200	0@5	8@11	6	14°BTDC
	V-6 231	1110766	0@840	7.5@1800	0@4	12@11	6	15°BTDC
	V-6 231	1110767	0@840	7.5@1800	0@3	10@12	6	15°BTDC

OLDSMOBILE

YEAR	ENGINE APPLICATION	DISTRIBUTOR NUMBER	CENTRIFUGAL ADVANCE DIST. DEGREES @ DIST. RPM		VACUUM ADVANCE DIST. DEGREES @ INS. HG.		DWELL ANGLE (Degrees)	INITIAL TIMING @ Engine Idle1
			Start	Finish	Start	Finish		
1979	V-6 231	1110768	0@500	7.5@1800	0@3	10@12	6	15°BTDC
	V-6 231	1110769	0@500	7.5@1800	0@4	12@11	6	15°BTDC
	V-6 231	1110770	0@840	7.5@1800	0@3	10@9	6	15°BTDC
	V-6 231	1110779	0@840	7.5@1800	0@3	12@9.5	6	15°BTDC
	V-8 260	1103320	0@455	13@2230	0@4	15@11	6	20°BTDC
	V-8 260	1103355	0@455	13@2230	0@4	15@9	6	18°BTDC
	V-8 260	1103396	0@455	13@2230	0@5	15@12	6	18°BTDC
	V-8 301	1103314	0@412	10.7@1700	0@4	12.5@12	6	12°BTDC
	V-8 305	1103368	0@500	10@1900	0@4	5@8	6	4°BTDC
	V-8 305	1103379	0@500	10@1900	0@3	10@7.5	6	4°BTDC
	V-8 305	1103281	0@500	10@1900	0@4	9@12	6	4°BTDC
	V-8 305	1103282	0@500	10@1900	0@4	10@10	6	4°BTDC
	V-8 305	1103285	0@600	11@2100	0@4	12@8	6	2°BTDC
	V-8 350	1103322	0@300	14.5@2000	0@6	12@13	6	20°BTDC
	V-8 350	1103285	0@600	11@2100	0@4	12@8	6	8°BTDC
	V-8 350	1103323	0@500	9.5@2000	0@5	8@11	6	20°BTDC
	V-8 350	1103346	0@500	9.5@2000	0@6	12@13	6	20°BTDC
	V-8 350	1103353	0@625	6@2250	0@3	10@9-12	6	8°BTDC
	V-8 403	1103324	0@300	11.5@1800	0@6	12@13	6	20°BTDC
	V-8 403	1103325	0@500	6.5@1800	0@5	8@11	6	20°BTDC
	V-8 403	1103347	0@500	6.5@1800	0@6	12@13	6	20°BTDC

1 Refer to vehicle emissions control sticker for idle speed and/or initial timing specification.
2 W31 engine: 14° BTDC.
3 Engine codes QN, QQ (Olds 88): 12° BTDC.
4 Engine codes UD (Cutlass): 10° BTDC.
5 Engine codes TB, TC, TL, TO (Omega and Cutlass): 12° BTDC.
6 High Energy Ignition.
7 Engine codes QA, QD, QK, QN (Omega and Cutlass): 16° BTDC.
8 Omega: 14° BTDC.
9 All automatic transmissions 12°; all manual transmissions 10°.
10 18° BTDC for automatic transmission.

PONTIAC

YEAR	ENGINE APPLICATION	DISTRIBUTOR NUMBER	CENTRIFUGAL ADVANCE DIST. DEGREES @ DIST. RPM		VACUUM ADVANCE DIST. DEGREES @ INS. HG.		DWELL ANGLE (Degrees)	INITIAL TIMING @ Engine Idle1
			Start	Finish	Start	Finish		
1970	I-6 250	1110463	0-2@450	16@2100	0@6-8	11.5@15-17	31-34	TDC
	I-6 250	1110464	0-2@450	14@2100	0@6-8	11.5@15-17	31-34	4° BTDC
	V-8 350	1112008	0-2@550	13@2350	0@6-8	10@13-14.75	31-34	9° BTDC
	V-8 400	1112007	0-2@400	13@2300	0@8-10	10@15-17	31-34	9° BTDC
	V-8 400	1112009	0-2@400	11@2300	0@8-10	10@15-17	31-34	9° BTDC
	V-8 400	1112010	0-2@550	11@2300	0@8-10	10@15-17	31-34	9° BTDC
	V-8 400	1112011	0-2@600	14@3050	0@8-10	10@15-17	31-34	15° BTDC
	V-8 400	1111148	0-2@400	13@2300	0@8-10	10@15-17	31-34	9° BTDC
	V-8 400	1111176	0-2@550	13@2350	0@8-10	10@15-17	31-34	9° BTDC
	V-8 455	1112012	0-2@400	8@2200	0@8-10	10@15-17	31-34	15° BTDC
	V-8 455	1111105	0-2@400	8@2200	0@8-10	10@15-17	31-34	9° BTDC
1971	I-6 250	1110489	0-2@550	12@2050	0@7-9	11.5@15-17	31-34	4° BTDC
	V-8 350	1112069	0-2@800	11@2300	0@6-8	10@13-14.75	31-34	12° BTDC
	V-8 350	1112083	0-2@600	11@2300	0@6-8	10@13-14.75	31-34	12° BTDC
	V-8 400	1112068	0-2@800	14@2300	0@6-8	10@13-14.75	31-34	9° BTDC
	V-8 400	1112070	0-2@575	11@2300	0@6-8	10@13-14.75	31-34	12° BTDC
	V-8 455	1112071	0-2@800	12@2300	0@8-10	10@15-17	31-34	12° BTDC
	V-8 455	1112072	0-2@825	11@2300	0@8-10	10@15-17	31-34	12° BTDC
	V-8 455	1112073	0-2@500	13@2225	0@6-8	10@13-14.75	31-34	12° BTDC
1972	I-6 250	1110489	0-2@650	12@2050	0@7-9	11.5@15-17	31-34	4° BTDC
	V-8 350	1112005	0-2@600	12@2150	0@7-9	10.3@16.5 17.8	31-34	8° BTDC
	V-8 350	1112039	0-2@650	9-11@2100	0@7-9	10.5@16.5 18	31-34	10° BTDC
	V-8 350	1112140	0-1@800	10-12@2300	0@6-8	10@13-15	31-34	8° BTDC
	V-8 350	1112118	0-1@800	8-10@2300	0@6-8	10@13-15	31-34	10° BTDC
	V-8 400	1112119	0-1@800	11-13@2300	0@8-10	10@15-17	31-34	10° BTDC
	V-8 400	1112121	0-1@700	11-13@2300	0@6-8	10@13-15	2	8° BTDC
	V-8 455	1112122	0-1@800	11-13@2300	0@8-10	10@15-17	31-34	10° BTDC
	V-8 455	1112145	0-1@700	9-11@2300	0@8-10	10@15-17	31-34	10° BTDC
	V-8 455	1112127	0-1@700	9-11@2300	0@8-10	10@15-17	31-34	10° BTDC
	V-8 455	1112133	0-1@575	13-15@2300	0@6-8	10@13-15	31-34	10° BTDC
1973	I-6 250	1110449	0@650	12@2050	0@7	11.5@15	31-34	6° BTDC
	V-8 350	1112201	0@600	12@1800	0@7	12.5@12	31-34	12° BTDC
	V-8 350	1112202	0@700	13@1725	0@7	12.5@12	31-34	10° BTDC
	V-8 350	1112510	0@500	12@1900	0@7	12.5@12	31-34	10° BTDC
	V-8 400	1112511	0@500	12@1900	0@8	12.5@15	31-34	10° BTDC
	V-8 400	1112199	0@610	12@1875	0@8	12.5@15	31-34	10° BTDC
	V-8 400	1112231	0@600	11@2300	0@9	12.5@14	31-34	10° BTDC
	V-8 400	1112233	0@600	11@2300	0@9	12.5@14	2	10° BTDC
	V-8 455	1112191	0@575	9@1950	0@10	12.5@16	31-34	10° BTDC
	V-8 455	1112203	0@600	9@2000	0@10	12.5@16	2	10° BTDC
	V-8 455	1112218	0@600	10@1650	0@6	10@12	31-34	10° BTDC
	V-8 455	1112507	0@600	9@2000	0@5	12.5@11	2	10° BTDC
1974	I-6 250	1110499	0@550	12@2050	0@7	12@15	31-34	6° BTDC
	V-8 350	1112804	0@600	12@1790	0@7	10@14	31-34	12° BTDC
	V-8 350	1112234	0@600	12@1790	0@7	10@14	31-34	12° BTDC
	V-8 350	1112806	0@650	13@1725	0@7	10@14	31-34	10° BTDC
	V-8 350	1112236	0@650	13@1725	0@7	10@14	31-34	10° BTDC
	V-8 350	1112808	0@600	13@1725	0@5	12.5@11	31-34	10° BTDC
	V-8 350	1112235	0@600	13@1725	0@5	12.5@11	31-34	10° BTDC
	V-8 350	1112810	0@600	9@2000	0@9	10@16	2	10° BTDC
	V-8 400	1112231	0@600	11@2300	0@9	12.5@14	31-34	10° BTDC
	V-8 400	1112239	0@600	11@2300	0@9	12.5@14	31-34	10° BTDC

DISTRIBUTOR SPECIFICATIONS

PONTIAC

YEAR	ENGINE APPLICATION	DISTRIBUTOR NUMBER	CENTRIFUGAL ADVANCE DIST. DEGREES @ DIST. RPM Start	Finish	VACUUM ADVANCE DIST. DEGREES @ INS. HG. Start	Finish	DWELL ANGLE (Degrees)	INITIAL TIMING @ Engine Idle1
1974	V-8 400	1112805	0@600	12@1875	0@9	10@16	31-34	10° BTDC
	V-8 400	111223/	0@600	12@1875	0@9	10@16	31-34	10° BTDC
	V-8 400	1112809	0@600	12@1875	0@7	12@12	31-34	10° BTDC
	V-8 400	1112238	0@600	12@1875	0@7	12@12	31-34	10° BTDC
	V-8 400	1112812	0@600	11@2300	0@9	10@16	2	10° BTDC
	V-8 400	1112813	0@600	11@2300	0@9	10@16	31-34	12° BTDC
	V-8 400	1112512	0@600	11@2300	0@9	10@16	31-34	12° BTDC
	V-8 400	1112814	0@600	11@2300	0@7	12.5@11.5	31-34	10° BTDC
	V-8 400	1112240	0@600	11@2300	0@7	12.5@11.5	31-34	10° BTDC
	V-8 455	1112205	0@600	11@2300	0@9	12.5@13.5	31-34	10° BTDC
	V-8 455	1112243	0@600	11@2300	0@9	12.5@13.5	31-34	10° BTDC
	V-8 455	1112807	0@575	9@1950	0@9	10@16	31-34	10° BTDC
	V-8 455	1112513	0@575	9@1950	0@9	10@16	31-34	10° BTDC
	V-8 455	1112821	0@500	12@1900	0@7	10@14	31-34	1
	V-8 455	1112822	0@500	12@1900	0@7	10@14	31-34	1
	V-8 455	1112833	0@600	12@2000	0@9	10@16	31-34	1
	V-8 455	1112834	0@600	12@2000	0@9	10@16	31-34	1
	V-8 455	1112857	0@610	12@1900	———	10@14	31-34	1
	V-8 455	1112856	0@610	12@1900	———	10@14	31-34	1
	V-8 455	1112859	0@575	9@1950	0@7	10@14.5	31-34	1
	V-8 455	1112860	0@575	9@1950	0@7	10@14.5	31-34	1
1975	I-6 250	1112863	0@362	8@2200	0@4	9@12	3	1
	V-8 260	1112951	0@325	14@2200	0@4	12@15	3	1
	V-8 260	1112956	0@325	14@2200	4	4	3	1
	———	1112950	0@600	10@1900	0@7	10@11	3	1
	———	1112498	0@600	8.5@1800	0@6	12@13	3	1
		1112947	0@600	10@1900	0@8	10@15	3	1
	V-8 350	1112896	0@525	6@2250	0@7	8@12	3	1
	V-8 350	1112946	0@500	10.5@1800	0@7	12@15	3	1
	V-8 350	1112500	0@600	10@2200	0@7	12.5@12	3	1
	V-8 350	1112928	0@600	8@2200	0@7	12.5@12	3	1
	V-8 350	1112929	0@500	10@2200	0@7	10@14	3	1
	V-8 400	1112495	0@550	4@2200	0@7	12.5@12	3	1
	V-8 400	1112495	0@550	4@2200	0@7	12.5@12	3	1
	V-8 400	1112930	0@700	10@2200	0@7	12.5@12	3	1
	V-8 400	1112918	0@500	7@2200	0@7	10@11	3	1
	V-8 455	1112949	0@500	7@2200	0@7	10@14	3	1
1976	I-4 140	1112862	0@450	11@2400	0@5	10@14	3	1
	V-6 231	1110661	0@525	8@2050	0@6	9@10	3	1
	V-6 231	1110668	0@637	8@1600	0@6	12@12	3	1
	I-6 250	1110666	0@500	10@2100	0@4	12@15	3	1
	I-6 250	1112863	0@365	8@2200	0@4	9@12	3	1
	V-8 260	1103211	0@600	10@1900	0@6	12@13	3	1
	V-8 260	1112956	0@325	14@2200	———	———	3	1
	V-8 260	1112994	0@325	14@2200	0@5	12@11	3	1
	V-8 260	1112995	0@450	13@2225	0@4	15@11	3	1
	V-8 350	1112495	0@550	4@2200	0@7	12.5@12	3	1
	V-8 350	1112797	0@600	10@1900	0@5	12.5@11	3	1
	V-8 350	1112950	0@600	10@1900	0@7	10@11	3	1
	V-8 350	1112991	0@710	10@2210	0@7	10@13	3	1
	V-8 350	1103206	0@600	8.5@1800	0@7	10@11	3	1
	V-8 400	1103205	0@600	8@2200	0@7	10@11	3	1
	V-8 400	1112500	0@600	10@2200	0@7	12.5@12	3	1
	V-8 400	1112928	0@600	8@2200	0@7	12.5@12	3	1
	V-8 455	1112923	0@500	7@2200	0@7	12.5@12	3	1
	V-8 455	1112930	0@700	5@2200	0@7	12.5@12	3	1
	V-8 455	1112960	0@500	7@2200	0@9	10@16	3	1
	V-8 455	1103207	0@500	7@2200	0@8	10@15	3	1
1977	I-4 140	1110538	0@425	16.5@2300	0@2.5	12@10	3	10°BTDC
	I-4 140	1110539	0@425	16@2200	0@2.5	12@10	3	12°BTDC
	I-4 151	1103239	0@600	10@2200	0@2	10@12	3	14°BTDC
	I-4 151	1103231	0@600	10@2200	0@2	10@12	3	14°BTDC
	I-4 151	1103263	0@600	10@2200	0@2	10@9	3	14°BTDC
	V-6 231	1110677	0@650	10@1800	0@2.5	12@9.5	3	12°BTDC
	V-6 231	1110686	0@700	10@1800	0@2	10@8	3	12°BTDC
	V-8 301	1103272	0@425	10.7@1700	0@2	12.5@12	3	12°BTDC
	V-8 301	1103273	0@500	9.5@1800	0@2	12.5@12	3	16°BTDC
	V-8 350	1103257	0@600	8.5@1800	0@2.5	10@10	3	16°BTDC
	V-8 350	1103259	0@500	10.5@2000	0@3	12@13	3	10°BTDC
	V-8 350	1103266	0@500	10.5@2000	0@2.5	8@11	3	10°BTDC
	V-8 350	1103276	0@400	8.2@1820	0@2.5	10@10	3	10°BTDC
	V-8 400	1103269	0@500	8.5@2300	0@2.5	10@10	3	16°BTDC
	V-8 403	1163264	0@500	8.5@1700	0@2.5	8@11	3	20°BTDC
1978	I-4 2L	1103365	0@600	10@2200	0@5	8@11	3	14° BTDC
	I-4 2L	1103328	0@600	10@2200	0@3.5	10@9	3	12° BTDC
	I-4 2L	1103329	0@600	10@2200	0@3.5	10@9	3	14° BTDC
	V-6 231	1110695	0-3@1000	6-9@1800	0@6	12@13	3	15° BTDC
	V-6 231	1110731	0-2@1000	6-9@1800	0@6	8@9	3	15° BTDC
	V-6 231	1110732	0-2@1000	6-9@1800	0@9	7@13	3	15° BTDC
	V-8 301	1103310	0@500	7@2200	0@4	12.5@12	3	12° BTDC
	V-8 301	1103314	0@412	10.7@1700	0@4	12.5@12	3	12° BTDC
	V-8 305	1103282	0@500	10@1900	0@4	10@10	3	4° BTDC
	V-8 305	1103281	0@500	10@1900	0@4	9@12	3	4° BTDC
	V-8 305	1103357	0@550	11.8-15.7@2500	0@2	10@10	5	1
	V-8 350	1103285	0@600	11@2100	0@4	5@8	3	8° BTDC
	V-8 350	1103337	0@550	8@1200	0@4	12@10	3	8° BTDC
	V-8 350	1103342	2@1000	9.5@2200	0@7	12@13	3	15° BTDC
	V-8 350	1103266		9.5@2000	0@5	8@11	3	20° BTDC
	V-8 350	1103323	———	9.5@2000	0@5	8@11	3	20° BTDC
	V-8 350	1103346	0@500	9.5@2000	0@2	12@13	3	20° BTDC
	V-8 350	1103356	0@550	14.3-18@2500	0@2	10@10	5	1
	V-8 400	1103315	0@500	10@2200	0@5	12.5@11	3	18° BTDC
	V-8 400	1103359	0@500	8.5@2300	0@5	10@10	3	16° BTDC
	V-8 400	1103343	0@400	8.25@1820	0@4	12.5@11	3	16° BTDC
	V-8 400	1103316	0@500	8.5@2300	0@4	12.5@12	3	16° BTDC
	V-8 403	1103264	0@500	6.5@1800	0@5	8@11	3	20° BTDC
	V-8 403	1103325	0@500	6.5@1800	0@5	8@11	3	20° BTDC
	V-8 403	1103347	0@500	6.5@1800	0@6	12@13	3	20° BTDC

PONTIAC

YEAR	ENGINE APPLICATION	DISTRIBUTOR NUMBER	CENTRIFUGAL ADVANCE DIST. DEGREES @ DIST. RPM		VACUUM ADVANCE DIST. DEGREES @ INS. HG.		DWELL ANGLE (Degrees)	INITIAL TIMING @ Engine Idle1
			Start	Finish	Start	Finish		
1979	I-4 2.5L	1103365	0@1000	10@2350	0@2.5	11@11.5	3	14°BTDC
	I-4 2.5L	1110726	0@600	9@2000	0@3.5	10.5@8	3	12°BTDC
	I-4 2.5L	1110757	0@600	9@2000	0@3.5	10.5@8	3	12°BTDC
	V-6 231	1110766	1@975	7.5@1800	0@4	12.5@11.5	3	15°BTDC
	V-6 231	1110767	1@975	7.5@1800	0@3.5	10.5@12.5	3	15°BTDC
	V-6 231	1110768	1@625	7.5@1800	0@3.5	10.5@12.5	3	15°BTDC
	V-6 231	1110769	1@625	7.5@1800	0@4	12.5@12.5	3	15°BTDC
	V-6 231	1110770	1@975	7.5@1800	0@3	10.5@9.5	3	15°BTDC
	V-8 301	1103314	1@525	10.5@1725	0@4	12.5@13	3	12°BTDC
	V-8 301	1103399	1@575	10@2200	0@4	12.5@13	3	12°BTDC
	V-8 301	1103400	1@525	8.5@2350	0@4	12.5@12	3	14°BTDC
	V-8 305	1103281	1@575	10@1900	0@4	10@13	3	4°BTDC
	V-8 305	1103282	1@600	10@1900	0@3.5	11@11	3	4°BTDC
	V-8 305	1103285	1@675	11@2100	0@4	12@7	3	2°BTDC
	V-8 305	1103379	1@575	10@1900	0@2.5	11@8.5	3	4°BTDC
	V-8 350	1103342	1@1100	8.5@2200	0@6	13@15	3	15°BTDC
	V-8 350	1103346	1@650	9.5@2000	0@6	12.5@13.5	3	20°BTDC
	V-8 350	1103353	1.5@600	11@2350	0@3.5	12@11	3	8°BTDC
	V-8 400	1103315	0@500	8.5@2300	0@6	12.5@12	3	18°BTDC
	V-8 403	1103324	2@400	11.5@1800	0@6	12.5@12.5	3	18°BTDC
	V-8 403	1103225	1@700	6.5@1800	0@5	8.5@11.5	3	20°BTDC

1 Refer to vehicle emissions control sticker for idle speed and/or initial timing specification.
2 Unit ignition.
3 High Energy Ignition.
4 No vacuum advance.
5 12° BTDC for California.

HOW TO: Delco-Remy Breaker-Point Replacement

1. To replace breaker points on Delco-Remy V-8 distributor, remove distributor cap. Loosen rotor attaching screws, lift rotor from advance mechanism.

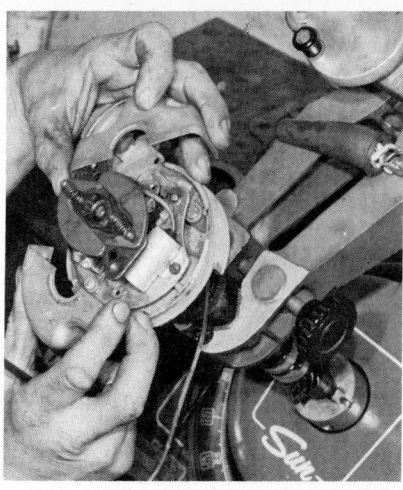

2. Radio frequency interference (RFI) shield is positioned over breaker-point assembly on non-Uni-Set distributors. Remove attaching screws, shield.

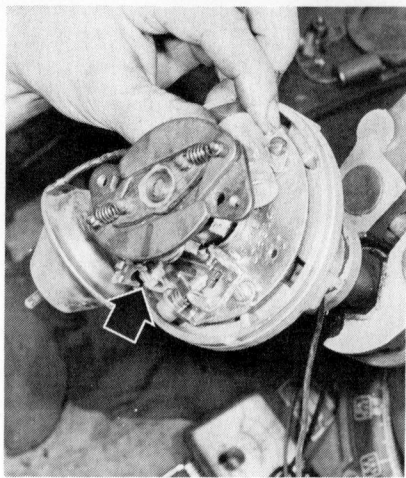

3. Disconnect breaker-point and condenser leads from push-in terminal (arrow). Condenser is held to breaker plate by screw—remove screw and condenser.

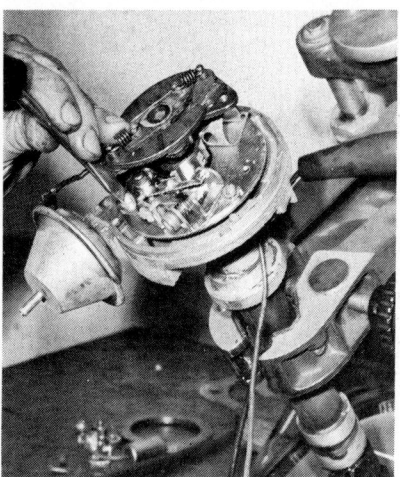

4. Breaker-point assembly is held to breaker plate by a single screw and a pivot pin which fits into breaker plate. Remove screw and point assembly.

5. It is a good idea to clean distributor with solvent to remove dirt and contamination from advance mechanism. Dirt can change the advance curve.

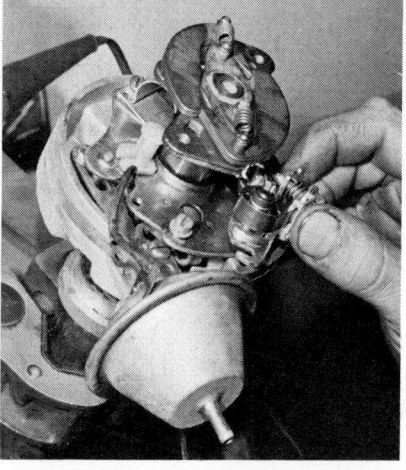

6. Install breaker plate and point attaching screw as shown. Place pivot pin of new point set in plate cutout, and swing into place under attaching screw.

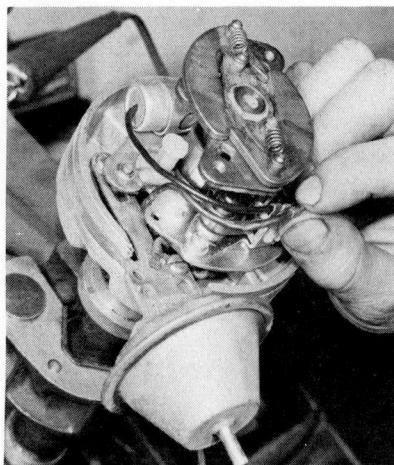

7. Reinstall condenser by slipping into bracket, tightening hold-down screw. Leads must be positioned in push-in terminal, to avoid contacting shield.

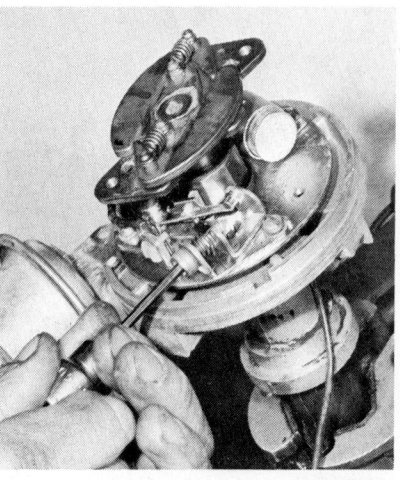

8. If distributor is in car, replace cap, open window and set point dwell with engine running. Here, dwell is set to provide specified gap before replacing.

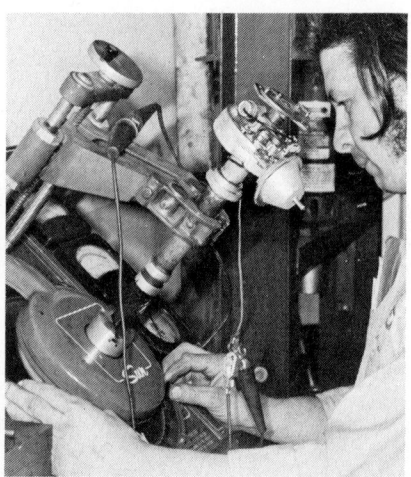

9. A distributor test machine lets you set the dwell off the car. You can also check and adjust the advance curves, if it seems to be necessary.

HOW TO: Motorcraft Breaker-Point Replacement

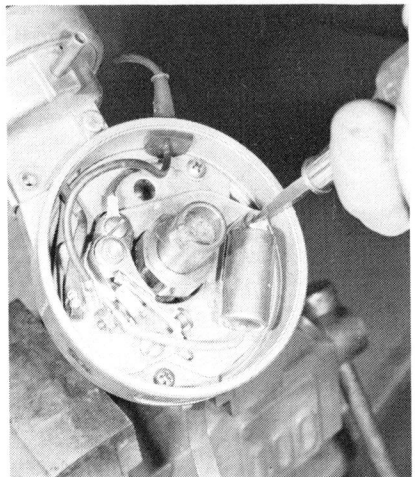

1. To replace breaker-point set on a Motorcraft-Autolite distributor, remove distributor cap and rotor, then remove the condenser attaching screw.

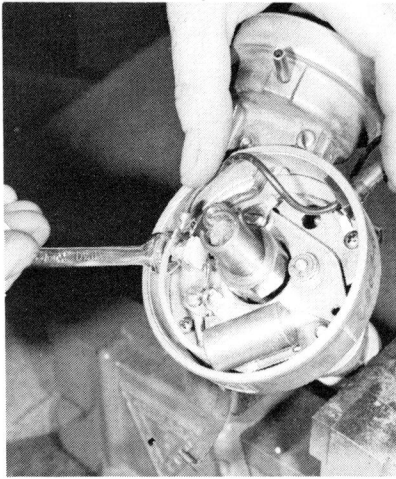

2. Condenser and point assembly leads are attached to this terminal with a nut to hold them in place. Loosen nut and remove leads from terminal.

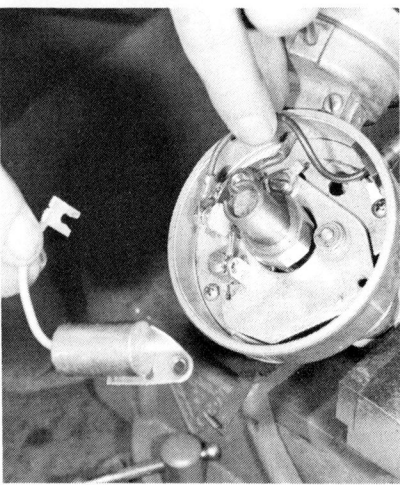

3. You can now remove the condenser and lift the distributor primary-lead wire up and out of the way. *Do not* remove the nut from the terminal.

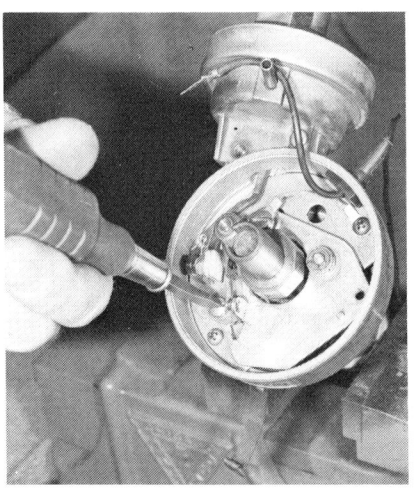

4. Different Motorcraft distributors use slightly different breaker-point assemblies. This one is held in place by two screws. Remove the lower.

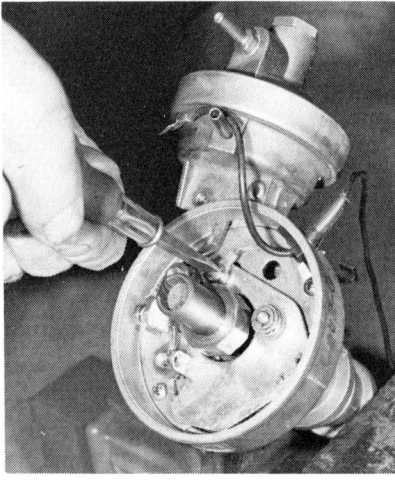

5. The upper attaching screw also provides an attachment point for the ground wire. Remove the screw and lift the ground wire out of the way.

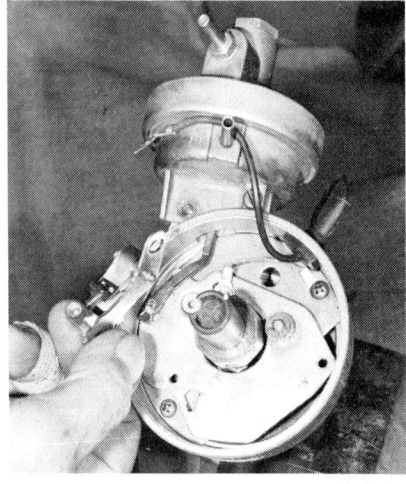

6. Breaker-point assembly can now be lifted from breaker plate. Notice pivot pin on underside of point assembly—this fits into slot on breaker plate.

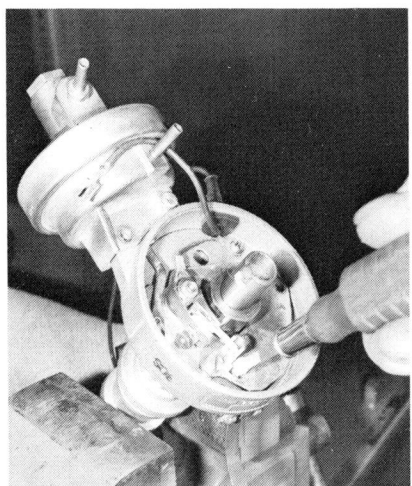

7. Install new breaker-point assembly, replace upper screw with ground lead connected under it. Cam and point rubbing block should be lubricated first.

8. Distributor primary wire is reconnected to the terminal. Install on the outside of the lockwasher, but do not tighten terminal yet.

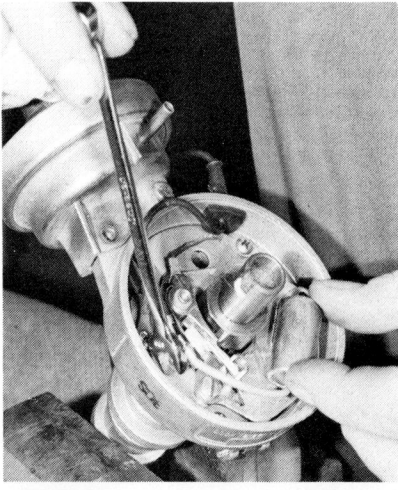

9. Attach new condenser with mounting screw; fit lead between primary lead and lockwasher in terminal assembly. Tighten terminal nut, adjust point gap.

HOW TO: Motorcraft Distributor Stripdown

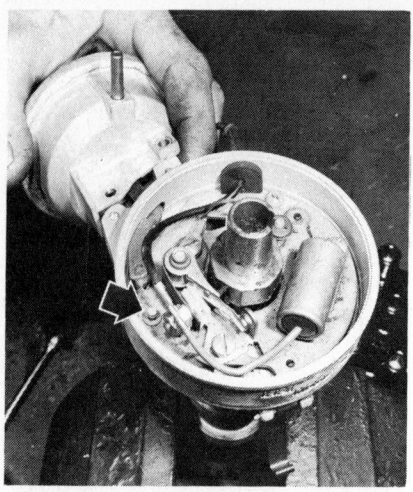

1. To strip down Motorcraft or comparable distributor, remove distributor cap, rotor. Remove vacuum-advance attaching screws, lift advance arm from pivot (arrow).

2. Remove the vacuum advance unit from the distributor housing and loosen the terminal nut which holds condenser and primary wire leads in place.

3. Remove the attaching screws which hold the condenser and the breaker-point assembly in place, then lift each from the breaker plate as shown.

4. Pry the breaker plate up and out of the distributor housing and remove. Do not remove the ground lead attached to the breaker plate.

5. Remove the felt lubricating wick from the cam assembly shaft, then reach inside with needlenose pliers and pull out the tiny wire retaining clip.

6. Primary and secondary advance springs are used to control rate of centrifugal advance. Carefully disengage spring to avoid distorting it, remove.

7. Reverse distributor in vise and carefully tap out both drive gear and collar retaining pins, using suitable drift and hammer. Remove gear, collar, shaft.

8. Slip a small screwdriver blade under the O-ring seal and remove the seal. Install a new O-ring with a little lubricant to help fit it into place.

9. Carefully inspect the breaker plate for signs of wear or a missing plastic support button which lets the upper plate ride on the lower one.

10. Reinstall the distributor shaft, drive gear and collar. Before replacing the cam assembly, make sure that this tanged washer is fitted in place.

11. With cam assembly replaced, install advance weights and advance springs. Replace primary and secondary springs with their respective weights.

12. Check weight operation by revolving shaft and observing movement, then apply a little cam lubricant to the cam assembly before proceeding.

13. Replace wire retaining clip in cam assembly; install felt wick. Fit breaker plate back in distributor housing, remove and clean ground connection.

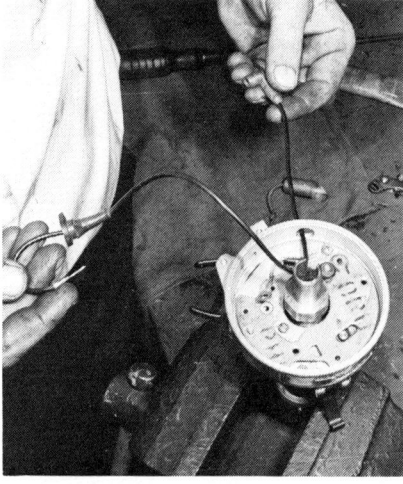

14. Thread the distributor primary lead wire through the hole in the distributor housing and fit the grommet in place—make sure that it is seated snugly.

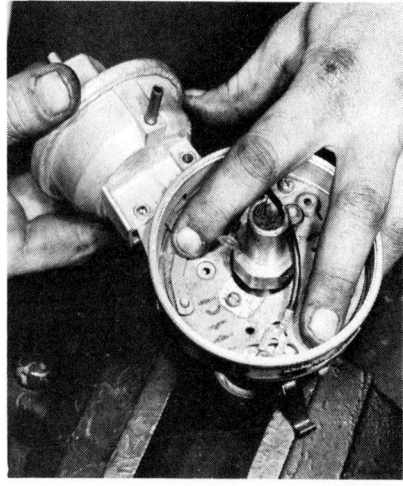

15. Insert the vacuum-advance-unit arm and reconnect on breaker-plate pivot pin. Hold arm in place and replace the advance-unit attaching screws.

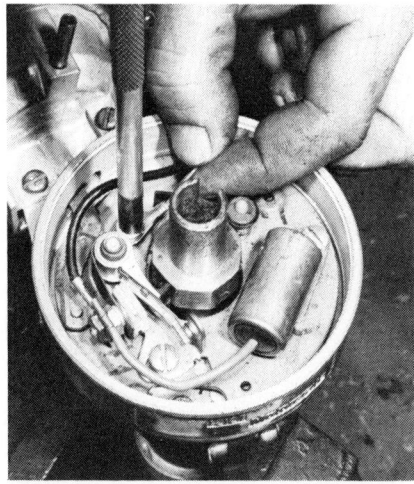

16. Reinstall the condenser and breaker-point assembly, replacing leads in the terminal and tightening the terminal nut. Attach ground lead.

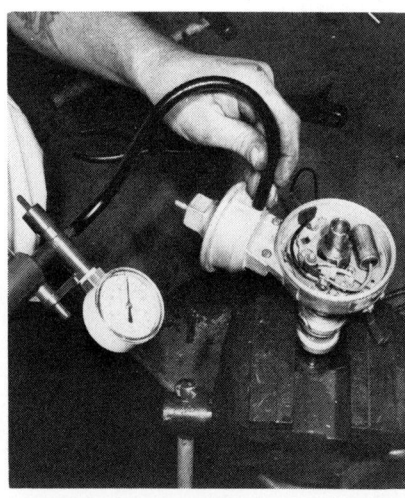

17. The vacuum advance unit can be tested to see if it works by using a hand vacuum pump, but this will not tell you if the advance curve is correct.

18. Replace rotor—note cutout in shaft and plastic insert tang in rotor. Tang must fit into cutout before rotor can be seated. Replace distributor cap.

HOW TO: Motorcraft Distributor Advance Calibration

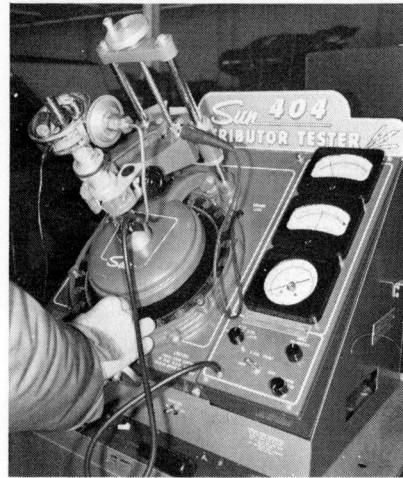

1. To calibrate spark advance, you need distributor test machine. Install distributor, connect per test equipment manufacturer's procedure.

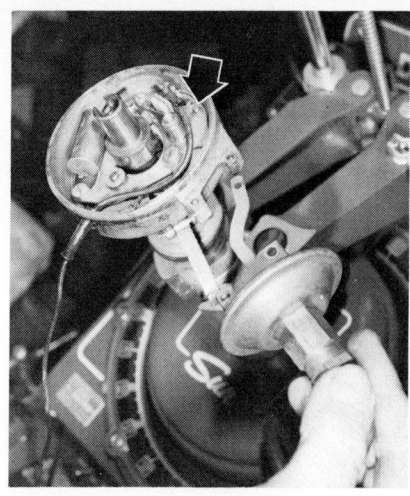

2. Engine timing not constant, too much early advance. Remove vacuum advance screws, pry clip from breaker plate stud (arrow). Press down to disengage lever.

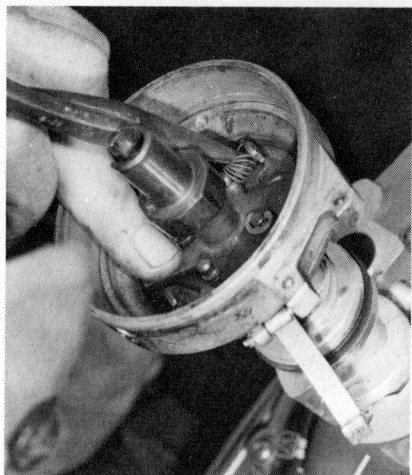

3. Remove points, condenser, breaker plate. Use needlenose pliers to remove tiny retaining clip in cam assembly. Disengage, remove each advance spring.

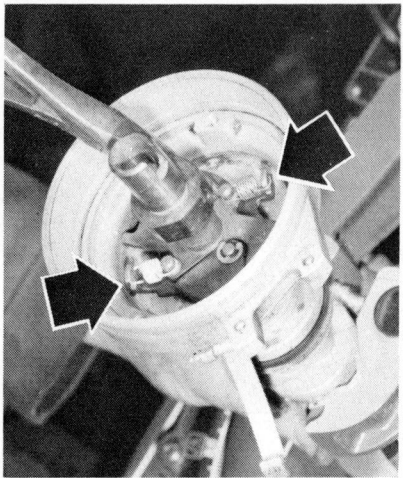

4. Two advance springs control rate of advance. To reduce advance rate, replace with stiffer springs. Bend retaining tabs (arrows) to increase spring tension.

5. Built-in step (shown) limits amount of centrifugal advance. Assembly can be removed and rotated 180° to provide two separate, distinct advance curves.

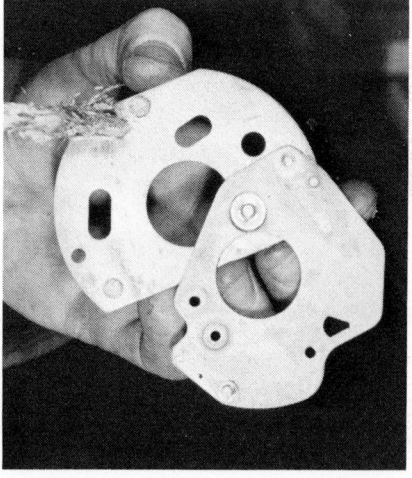

6. Replace retaining clip, felt wick; check breaker plate to make sure three plastic support buttons are intact. If not, replace buttons. Lubricate plate surfaces.

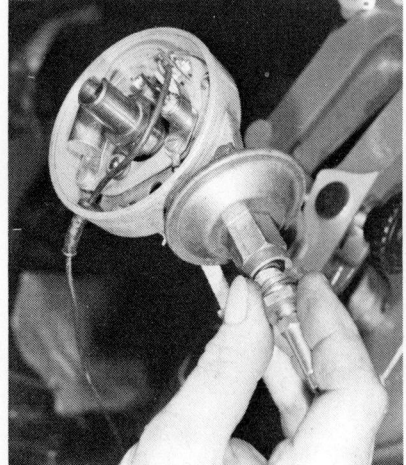

7. Maximum vacuum advance can be altered by changing sleeve; washers control rate of advance, increase spring tension. Vacuum units mostly non-adjustable.

8. Since amount of vacuum advance was beyond specs, washers were changed after reinstalling advance unit to distributor housing, and advance remeasured.

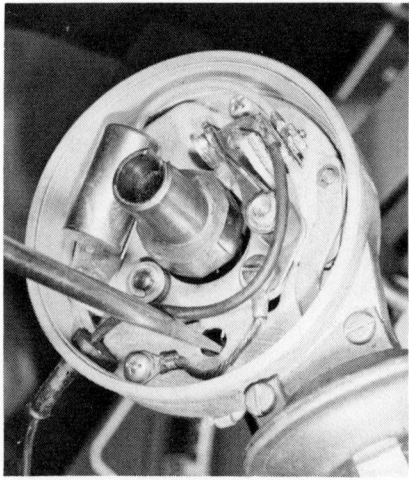

9. Final adjustments in centrifugal advance made by inserting screwdriver into breaker-plate cutout, bending tabs inward to increase, outward to decrease.

HOW TO: Chrysler Distributor Overhaul

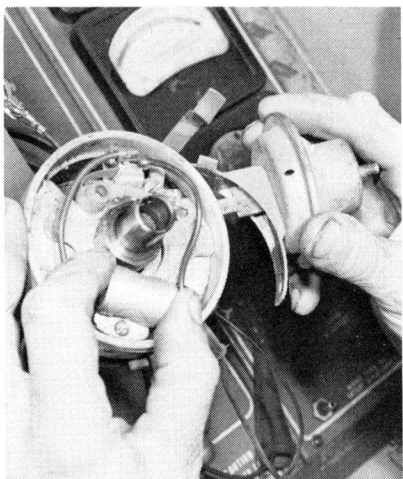

1. Distributor advance is checked in distributor test machine. Screws holding advance unit are removed and advance disengaged from breaker plate.

2. Screw on each side of distributor bowl holds breaker plate in place. These are removed to allow breaker-plate/points/condenser removal as a unit.

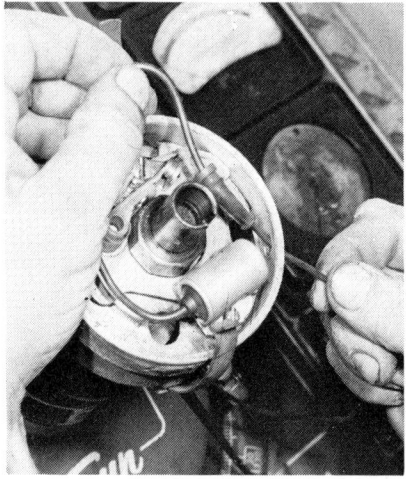

3. Push the rubber grommet out of the hole in the distributor housing and carefully pull the lead wire through after it to prevent any damage.

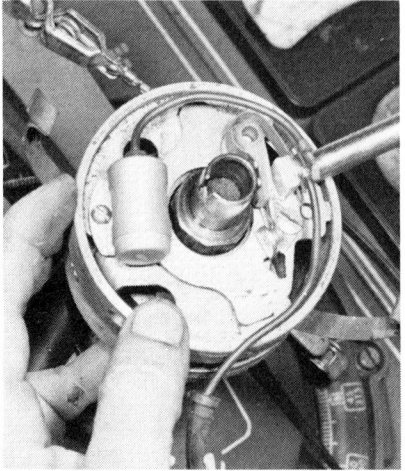

4. The slip-fit breaker plate rests on a lip inside the housing and can now be pried out of distributor housing with the points/condenser as a unit.

5. To remove cam assembly, pull out the felt lubricator and remove the wire clip inside cam assembly, then lift it off the distributor shaft.

6. Centrifugal advance consists of two weights with springs hooked to retainers. Advance is adjusted by changing springs or bending retainers.

7. Cam assembly replacement is the first step in reassembling the distributor. Check any adjustments to advance mechanism after reassembly.

8. With cam assembly seated, fasten tiny wire retaining clip over distributor shaft and install felt pad, adding 2-3 drops of lubricant to it.

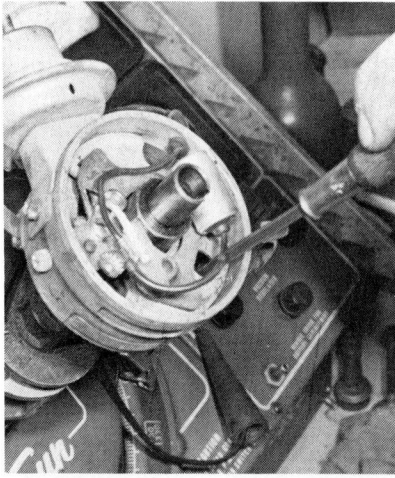

9. Once distributor is assembled, minor advance-curve adjustments are made by inserting screwdriver through breaker-plate opening to bend spring retainers.

INDEX

ELECTRONIC IGNITION SYSTEMS

WHY BREAKERLESS IGNITION?

With the exception of the need for periodic replacement of breaker points, the conventional automotive distributor is dependable and long-lasting. But those reasons which cause the breaker points to wear out are also its greatest weakness. Because the breaker-point rubbing block wears a bit with each revolution of the cam (breaker points open and close 16,000 times per minute at 4000 rpm with an 8-cyl. engine), the gap between the points continually grows smaller. This gradually changes both the dwell and the ignition timing, resulting in gradually deteriorating engine performance. And as the point gap decreases, it becomes far more difficult for the points to actually break the circuit from the coil to ground. As the rubbing block wears, the cam has to travel farther before it starts to open the points, affecting timing in a negative manner. And as the rubbing block continues to wear away, timing becomes more and more retarded. Eventually, the gap becomes so small that the engine misfires, and shortly after, it will simply refuse to run.

Breaker points have another considerable disadvantage—they will only tolerate a certain amount of speed. When the camshaft revolves extremely fast, the points are pushed open so rapidly that their weight causes them to continue opening after the peak of the cam lobe has passed under the rubbing block. This causes the point surfaces to slam back together with such force that the springiness in the point arm causes them to bounce against each other. And when they bounce, they separate, creating another spark from the coil at a time when the engine neither wants nor needs it. Under some circumstances, the points may be still bouncing when the next cam lobe passes under the rubbing block. Because of this, the opening of the points by the cam then produces a very weak spark, or perhaps even no spark at all. This severely limits the top speed of the engine, and can even cause engine damage if the engine is run continually at the speed where the points bounce.

BENEFITS OF ELECTRONIC IGNITIONS

Since 1973, original equipment manufacturers have taken a different approach to ignition systems. The heart of the new electronic ignition systems, offered as standard equipment since 1975, is a special distributor using no breaker points. This breakerless distributor creates magnetic pulses that trigger an electronic control unit to create high voltage in a special coil. The benefits are two-fold—long life and stable timing. This pulse-type distributor is not necessarily a money-saver, because breaker points are inexpensive and easy to replace. Thus, the extra cost of a pulse-type or electronic ignition will never be recovered through elimination of periodic breaker-point replacement. The real value is in increased durability and the ability to exercise far more accurate control over ignition timing between normal tune-up intervals.

Since dwell affects ignition timing, and dwell *is not* adjustable on an electronic ignition system, periodic checks of ignition timing are no longer necessary once the basic timing has been set. This means that after timing is correctly established, there is no need to bother with it, unless the distributor is removed for testing or service.

ELECTRONIC IGNITION SYSTEM OPERATION

Like the conventional automotive ignition system (Fig. 4-1), an electronic ignition (Fig. 4-2) consists of two electrical circuits—the primary (low-voltage) and secondary (high-voltage). Generally speaking, the electronic ignition works like this: When the ignition switch is turned on, current flows from the battery through the ignition switch and to the coil primary windings to energize the coil. As each tooth (leg) of the revolving armature (trigger wheel, reluctor, etc.) approaches the magnetic pickup coil or sensor, it induces a voltage which signals the electronic control module (amplifier) to turn off the coil primary current (Fig. 4-3).

A timing circuit in the control module turns the current on again after the coil field has collapsed. When the current is on, it travels from the battery through the ignition switch to the primary windings of the coil, and then through the electronic module's circuits to ground. When the current is off, the magnetic field which built up in the coil collapses, inducing a high voltage into the coil's secondary windings. High voltage is thus produced each time the coil is built up and collapsed. Secondary current flow is *exactly* like that of a conventional ignition—from the coil high-tension lead to the distributor cap, where the rotor distributes it to the proper spark plug terminal in the distributor cap.

There are minor differences in system operation and major differences in component design among those electronic ignitions offered as factory standard equipment. However, it is important to understand that the spark-advance mechanisms, the entire secondary circuit and that part of the primary circuit from the battery to the BAT terminal of the coil are *exactly the same* as

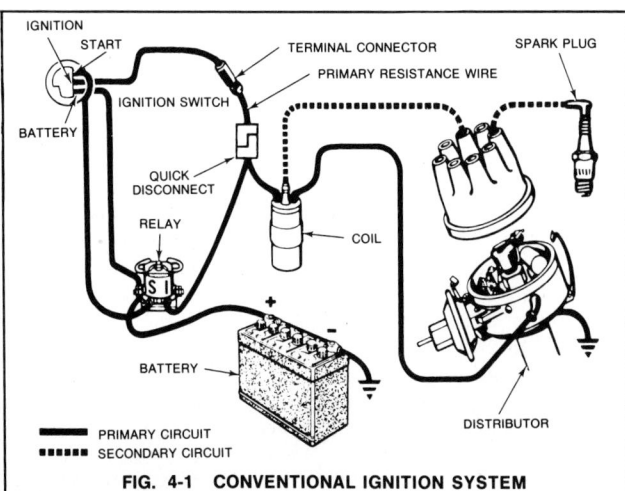

IGNITION
START
TERMINAL CONNECTOR
SPARK PLUG
PRIMARY RESISTANCE WIRE
IGNITION SWITCH
BATTERY
QUICK DISCONNECT
RELAY
COIL
S I
BATTERY
DISTRIBUTOR
⎯⎯ PRIMARY CIRCUIT
▪▪▪▪▪ SECONDARY CIRCUIT

FIG. 4-1 CONVENTIONAL IGNITION SYSTEM

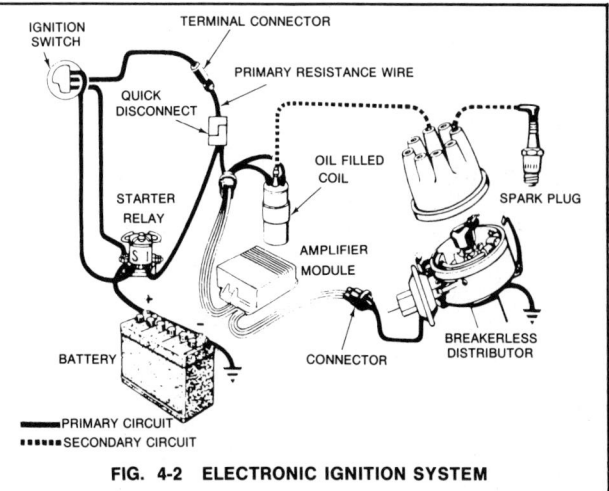

IGNITION SWITCH
TERMINAL CONNECTOR
PRIMARY RESISTANCE WIRE
QUICK DISCONNECT
OIL FILLED COIL
STARTER RELAY
AMPLIFIER MODULE
SPARK PLUG
S I
BATTERY
CONNECTOR
BREAKERLESS DISTRIBUTOR
⎯⎯ PRIMARY CIRCUIT
▪▪▪▪▪ SECONDARY CIRCUIT

FIG. 4-2 ELECTRONIC IGNITION SYSTEM

those in a conventional ignition system. Thus, the same troubleshooting tests and correction procedures used with conventional ignition systems also apply to electronic ignitions *except* for that part of the primary circuit between the BAT terminal of the coil and the final ground at the distributor housing.

The only real difference is that the distributor cam, breaker plate, points and condenser of the convention-

al ignition have been replaced by an armature (trigger wheel, reluctor, etc.), a pickup coil (sensor, stator assembly, etc.) and an electronic control module (amplifier)—test procedures for this part of the secondary system *are different*.

The coil used with an electronic ignition is not interchangeable with that used in a conventional ignition, because its windings have been changed to produce a higher secondary (output) voltage, taking advantage of the improved coil-charging ability of the electronic control module.

The operation, components, troubleshooting and test procedures for each electronic ignition in use are described on the following pages.

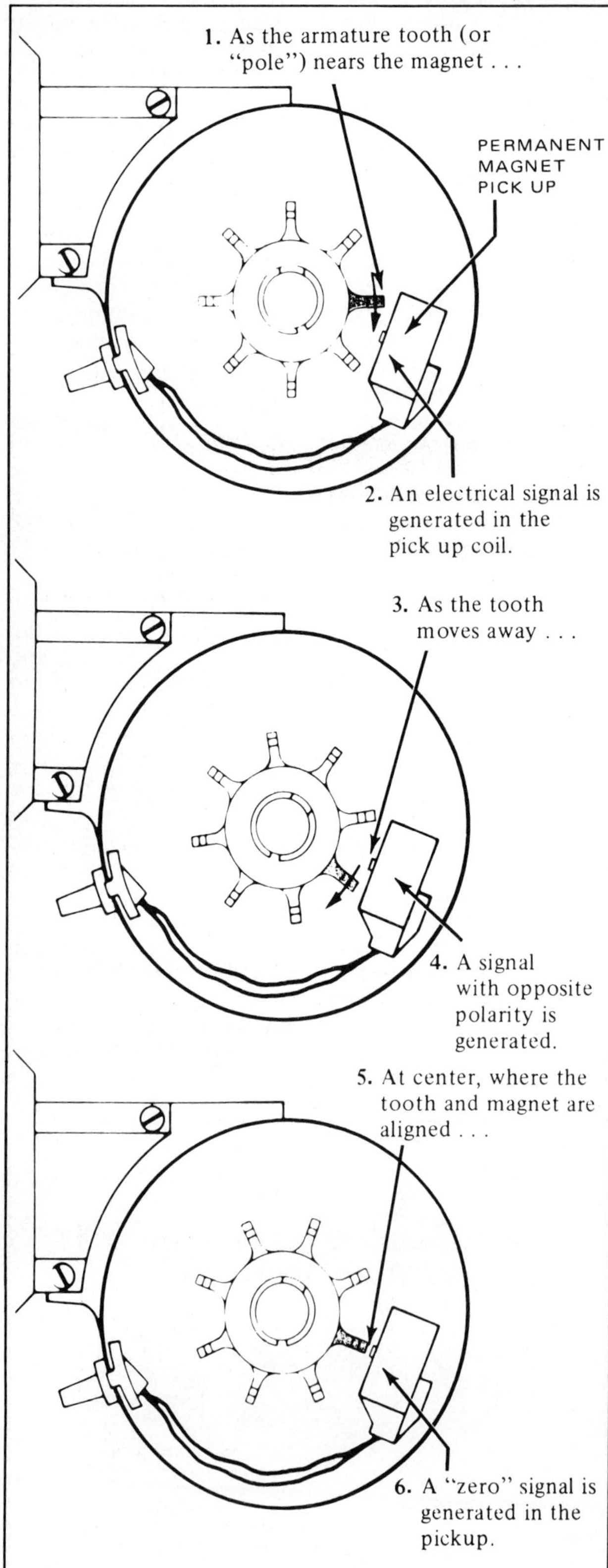

1970-71 CORVETTE OPTION
Delco-Remy Magnetic-Pulse Ignition System
SYSTEM DESCRIPTION (Fig. 4-4)

This transistor-controlled, breakerless ignition system uses a special distributor design, an ignition pulse amplifier and a special coil. The ignition circuit contains two resistance wires—one as a ballast resistor between the negative coil terminal and ground, and the other to provide a voltage drop for the engine run circuit (bypassed during cranking). All other system and circuit components are of standard design **(Fig. 4-5)**.

Resembling a conventional distributor in outward appearance **(Fig. 4-6)**, the internal construction of this magnetic pulse distributor is considerably different. The distributor uses a timer core instead of the usual cam. This core is equipped with eight projections or points, one for each of the engine's cylinders. Surrounding the timer core is a pole piece which also has eight projections. As the distributor shaft rotates, the projections on the timer core line up with the pole piece projections eight times during each revolution. A permanent ring magnet under the pole piece increases the magnetic field whenever the projections line up with each other.

A circular pickup coil is also positioned under the timer core and pole piece. Sensing the increased magnetism each time the projections align, this coil sends a signal to the amplifier **(Fig. 4-7)**, which is mounted separately from the distributor. When the signal is received by the amplifier, primary current flowing through the coil is interrupted and a spark occurs at the spark plug.

The coil was designed specifically for compatibility with the system, even though high voltage in the coil is created in the same manner as in a conventional ignition system. The amplifier consists of transistors, diodes and capacitors connected so they can sense the increased magnetism in the pickup coil and interrupt the coil primary current without using any moving parts.

Centrifugal and vacuum advance in the distributor is similar to that of a conventional distributor. The centrifugal weights advance the timer core, while the vacuum unit moves the pole piece for spark advance. Testing of the advance units either on the engine or on a distributor teststand is the same as with conventional units, although a special amplifier must be used to pick up the distributor signal on a teststand. The ignition coil can also be checked with many coil testers, providing that tester instructions specifically state it will test this special coil.

Tachometer test readings can be made on the primary circuit of this breakerless ignition, but make cer-

1. As the armature tooth (or "pole") nears the magnet . . .

PERMANENT MAGNET PICK UP

2. An electrical signal is generated in the pick up coil.

3. As the tooth moves away . . .

4. A signal with opposite polarity is generated.

5. At center, where the tooth and magnet are aligned . . .

6. A "zero" signal is generated in the pickup.

FIG. 4-3 VOLTAGE INDUCTION

tain that the unit to be used contains circuitry designed for testing transistorized ignitions (not all do) before connecting the tester into the circuit. If the tester is not capable of handling transistorized circuitry, it will not give accurate readings and may cause damage to the ignition system.

TEST PROCEDURES

IGNITION COIL OPEN TEST

For the most reliable readings, the ohmmeter used should have its 20,000-ohm value in the middle third of the scale.

1. Disconnect the battery lead from the negative battery terminal.

2. Connect an ohmmeter across the two primary coil terminals.

3. Primary resistance should range between 0.35 and 0.55 ohms at 75° F. An infinite reading indicates the primary is open.

4. If the primary resistance is good, but the engine continues to miss, the primary open may be of an intermittent type. Replace the coil with a known good coil to see if the engine miss stops.

5. Connect the ohmmeter from the coil high-tension tower to either primary terminal.

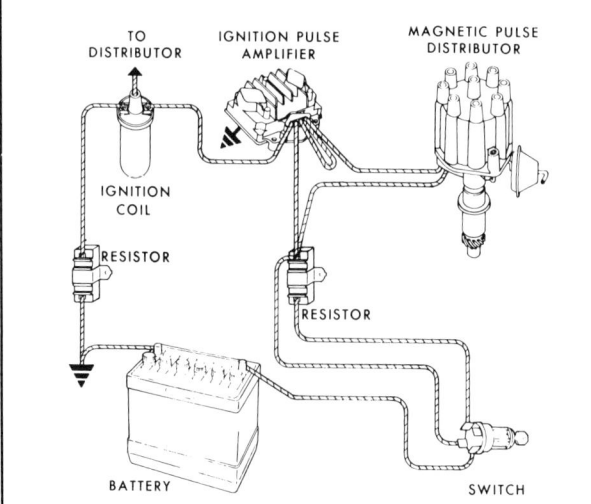

FIG. 4-4 DELCO-REMY MAGNETIC PULSE IGNITION SYSTEM

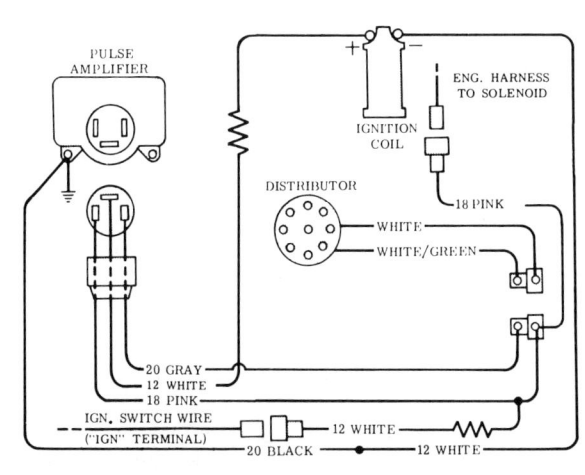

FIG. 4-5 DELCO-REMY MAGNETIC PULSE CIRCUIT DIAGRAM

ELECTRONIC IGNITION SYSTEM DIAGNOSIS

CONDITION	CORRECTION
ENGINE WILL NOT START—FUEL AND CARBURETION GOOD	
(a) Dual ballast resistor malfunctioning.	(a) Test resistance of each section. Compensating resistance: 0.50-0.60 ohms at 70-80°F. Auxiliary resistance: 4.75-5.75 ohms. Replace if faulty. Check wire positions.
(b) Faulty ignition coil.	(b) Inspect for carbonized tower. Test primary and secondary resistances, see specifications for values. Run coil test.
(c) Faulty pickup or improper pickup air gap.	(c) Test pickup coil resistance: 400-600 ohms. Check pickup gap: 0.010-in. feeler gauge should not slip between pickup core and an aligned reluctor blade. (A feeler gauge can, but should not be, forced between a properly adjusted reluctor and pickup.) Pickup core should show no sign of striking reluctor blades. Reset gap if necessary. After resetting gap, run distributor on test stand and apply vacuum advance, making sure that pickup core does not strike reluctor blades.
(d) Faulty wiring.	(d) Visually inspect wiring for brittle insulation. Inspect molded connectors for rubber inside female terminals.
(e) Malfunctioning control unit.	(e) Replace if all above tests are negative. Whenever control unit or ballast resistor is replaced, make sure the dual ballast wires are correctly inserted in the keyed, molded connector.
ENGINE SURGES SEVERELY—NOT LEAN CARBURETION	
(a) Wiring.	(a) Check for loose connection and/or broken conductors in wiring harness.
(b) Pickup leads faulty.	(b) Disconnect vacuum advance. If surging stops, replace pickup.
(c) Ignition coil.	(c) Test for intermittent primary.
ENGINE MISSES—CARBURETION KNOWN GOOD	
(a) Spark plugs.	(a) Check plugs. Clean and regap, if necessary.
(b) Secondary cables.	(b) Test cables with an ohmmeter.
(c) Ignition coil.	(c) Inspect for carbonized tower.
(d) Wiring.	(d) Inspect for loose or dirty connections.
(e) Pickup leads faulty.	(e) Disconnect vacuum advance. If miss stops, replace pickup coil.
(f) Control unit.	(f) Replace if above tests and checks prove negative.

6. Secondary resistance should be 8000-12,500 ohms at 75° F. If the reading is infinite, the coil secondary winding is open.

IGNITION PULSE AMPLIFIER TEST

1. Disconnect and remove the amplifier **(Fig. 4-7)** from the car, then remove its bottom plate.

2. Note the locations of lead connections to the panel board, then remove the attaching screws and lift the panel board from its housing.

3. Note any identifying markings on the two transistors and their respective location on the panel-board/heat-sink assembly.

4. Note the number and position of the insulators placed between the transistors/heat sink and heat sink/panel board.

5. Remove and separate the two transistors and heat sink from the panel board.

6. Examine the panel board for signs of damage.

7. Follow the test procedure specified below in the sequence indicated. Use an ohmmeter containing 1½-volt battery and set it on the low range, unless otherwise directed. Connect the ohmmeter as specified in each procedural step, then reverse the leads to get two readings. The amplifier-circuit diagram is shown in **Fig. 4-8.** A 25-watt soldering iron is necessary and a 60%-tin/40%-lead solder should be used for re-soldering. If necessary, clip away any epoxy and apply new epoxy when finished.

8. Unsolder capacitors C2 and C3 at the locations indicated in **Fig. 4-9.**

    a) Transistors TR1 and TR2—Check each transistor as shown in **Fig. 4-10.** If readings in Steps 1, 2 or 3 are zero, the transistor(s) is shorted. If readings are infinite, the transistor(s) is open.

    b) Trigger Transistor TR3 **(Fig. 4-11)**—If readings in Steps 1, 2 or 3 are zero, the transistor(s) is shorted. If both readings are infinite, the transistor(s) is open.

    c) Diode D1 **(Fig. 4-11)**—If both readings are zero, the diode is shorted. If both readings are infinite, the diode is open.

    d) Capacitor C1 **(Fig. 4-11)**—If both readings are zero, the capacitor is shorted.

    e) Capacitors C2 and C3—Connect the ohmmeter across each capacitor (this check is not shown in **Fig. 4-11,** but should be performed—see **Fig. 4-9** for location). If both readings are zero, the capacitor(s) is shorted.

    f) Resistor R1 **(Fig. 4-11)**—The resistor is open if both readings are infinite.

    g) Resistor R2 **(Fig. 4-11)**—Set the ohmmeter on a scale on which the 1800-ohm value is within, or nearly within, the middle third of the scale. If both readings are infinite, the resistor is open.

    h) Resistor R3 **(Fig. 4-11)**—Set the ohmmeter on a scale on which the 680-ohm value is within, or

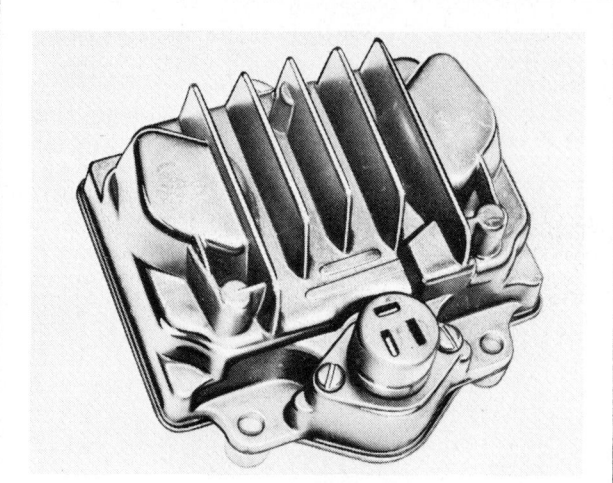

FIG. 4-7 PULSE IGNITION AMPLIFIER

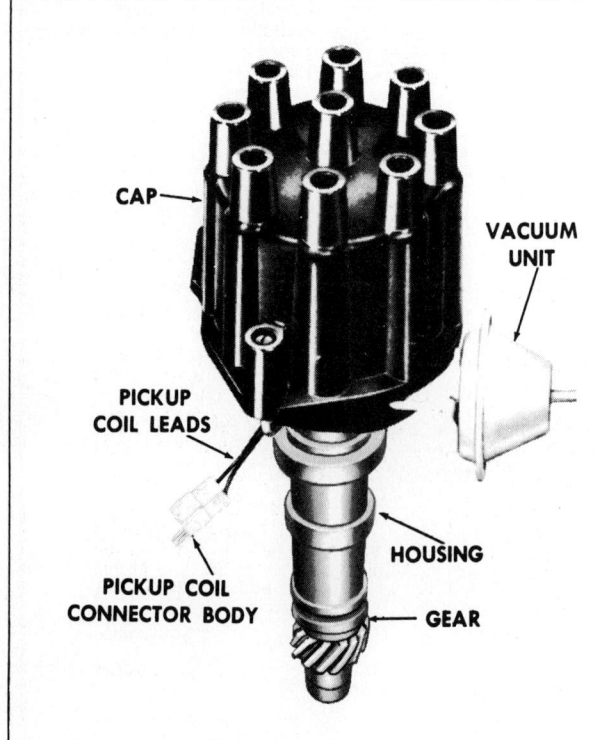

FIG. 4-6 DELCO-REMY MAGNETIC PULSE DISTRIBUTOR

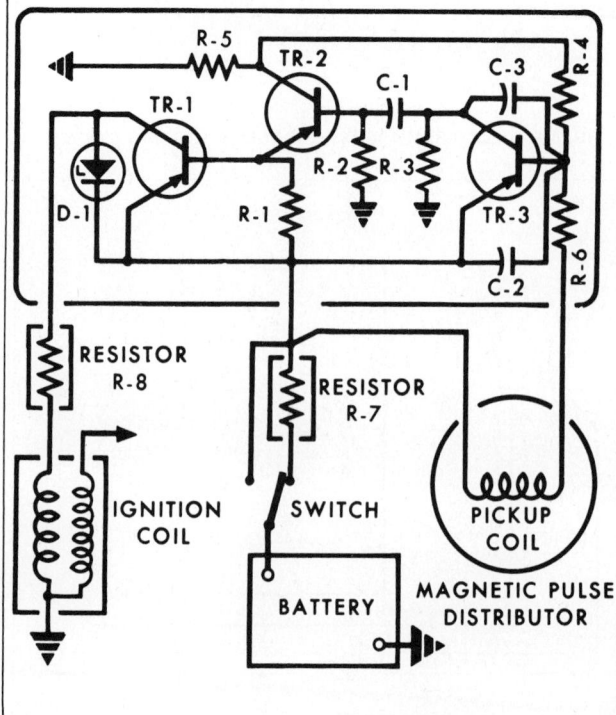

FIG. 4-8 PULSE AMPLIFIER CIRCUITRY

nearly within, the middle third of the scale. If both readings are infinite, the resistor is open.

i) Resistor R4 **(Fig. 4-11)**—Set the ohmmeter on a scale on which the 15,000-ohm value is within, or nearly within, the middle third of the scale. If either reading is infinite, the resistor is open.

j) Resistor R5 **(Fig. 4-11)**—Set the ohmmeter on the lowest range scale. If either reading is infinite, the resistor is open. On some engine applications, this resistor may be located *in the car's*

wiring harness instead of on the panel board.

k) Resistor R6 **(Fig. 4-11)**—Set the ohmmeter on a scale on which the 150-ohm value is within, or nearly within, the middle third of the scale. If both readings are infinite, the resistor is open.

9. If any defective components in the pulse amplifier are found, the entire unit is replaced. If no defective components are found, resolder capacitors C2 and C3 at the locations indicated in **Fig. 4-9.**

10. Before reassembling the pulse amplifier, coat both sides of the flat insulators used between the transistors and heat sink, and the side of the heat sink on which the transistors are mounted, with silicone grease to increase heat dissipation rate and provide better cooling.

11. Replace transistors and heat sink to the panel board, and install attaching screws.

12. Replace all insulators in their proper positions and reinstall the panel board to the amplifier housing.

13. Replace the bottom plate on the amplifier housing and reattach the housing to its proper location.

14. Reconnect the distributor lead to the amplifier housing.

PICKUP COIL TEST

1. Connect an ohmmeter to the pickup coil leads; resistance reading should range between 550 and 650 ohms.

2. Connect one ohmmeter lead to the pickup coil lead and the other lead to the distributor housing. If the reading is not infinite, the pickup coil is grounded and must be replaced.

DISTRIBUTOR REMOVAL

1. Remove the ignition shield over the distributor and coil. If the car is not equipped with a radio, no ignition shield is used.

2. Disconnect the tachometer drive cables and vacuum line from the distributor housing.

3. Disconnect the pickup coil leads at the connector and remove the distributor cap.

4. Rotate the engine crankshaft until the timing mark on the harmonic balancer is indexed with the timing pointer.

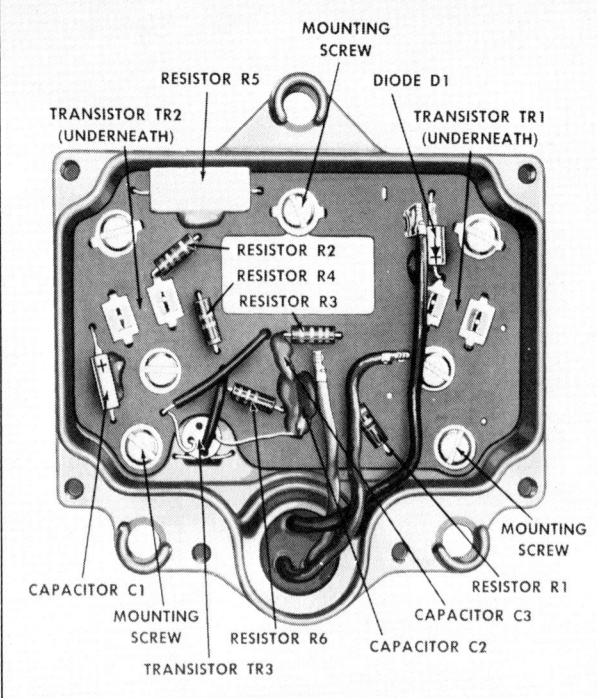

FIG. 4-9 PULSE AMPLIFIER PANEL BOARD

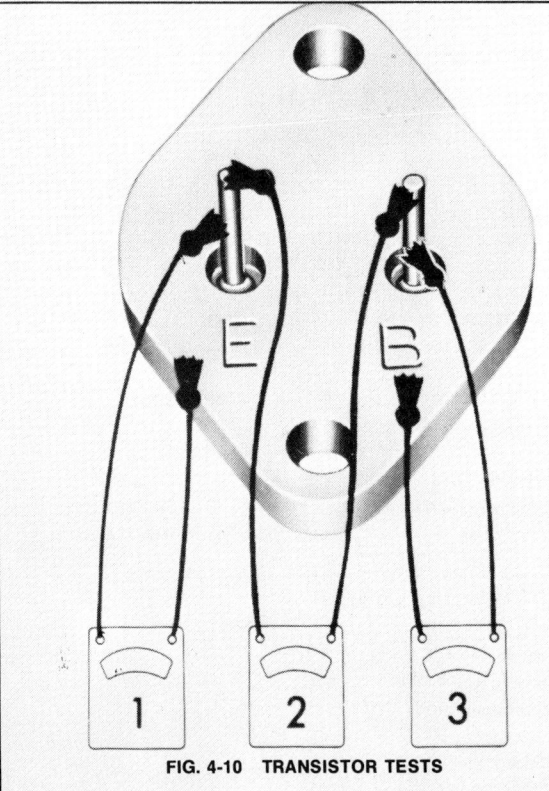

FIG. 4-10 TRANSISTOR TESTS

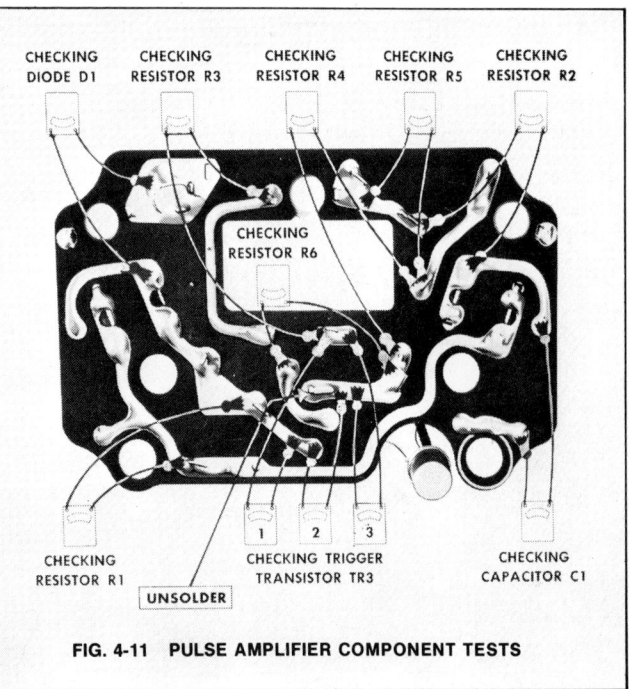

FIG. 4-11 PULSE AMPLIFIER COMPONENT TESTS

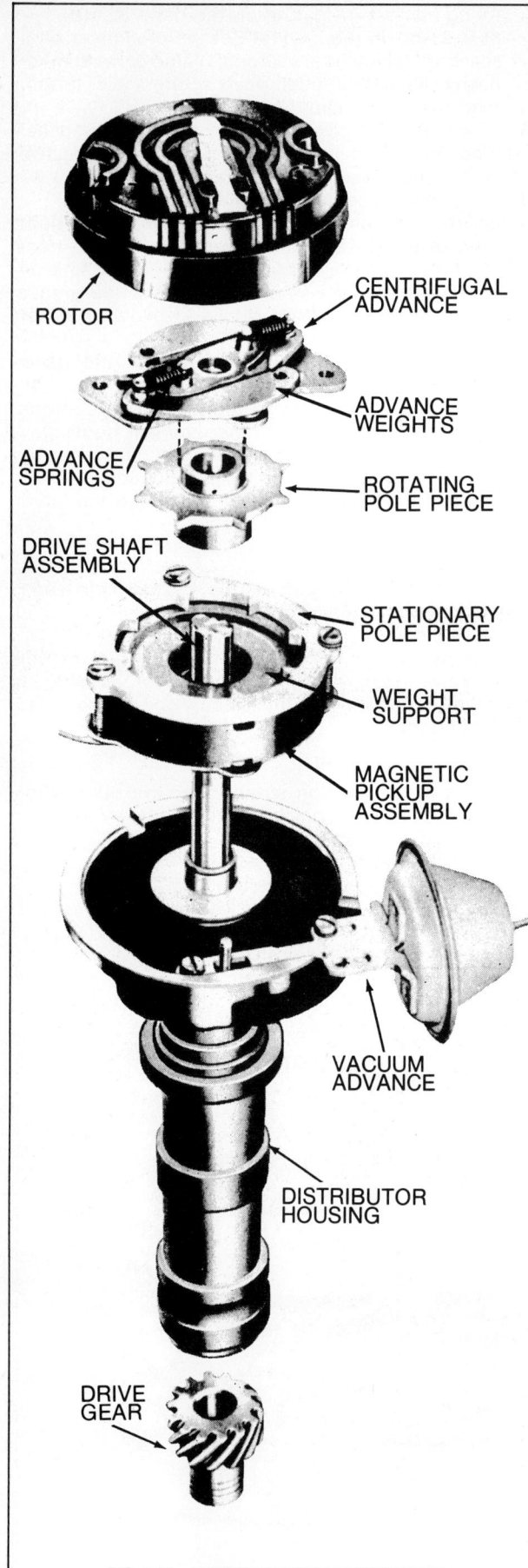

ROTOR

CENTRIFUGAL ADVANCE

ADVANCE WEIGHTS

ADVANCE SPRINGS

ROTATING POLE PIECE

DRIVE SHAFT ASSEMBLY

STATIONARY POLE PIECE

WEIGHT SUPPORT

MAGNETIC PICKUP ASSEMBLY

VACUUM ADVANCE

DISTRIBUTOR HOUSING

DRIVE GEAR

FIG. 4-12   MAGNETIC PULSE DISTRIBUTOR COMPONENTS

5. Remove the distributor hold-down screw and clamp.

6. Lift the distributor from the engine. The distributor shaft will rotate slightly as its gear disengages.

7. Mark the relationship of the rotor and distributor housing so that the rotor can be replaced in the same position when the distributor is reinstalled.

8. If the distributor-to-block gasket did not come off with the distributor, remove it from the engine block.

DISTRIBUTOR DISASSEMBLY (Fig. 4-12)

1. Remove the rotor screws and rotor.

2. Disconnect the advance springs and remove weights.

3. Remove tachometer drive gear from the housing.

4. Use a suitable drift and hammer to tap out the distributor drive-gear roll pin, then remove gear and washer. *Drive gear must be supported to prevent damage to the permanent magnet.*

5. Remove the drive shaft assembly and slide the weight support and timer core from the shaft.

6. Disconnect pickup coil leads at the connector.

7. Remove the retaining ring holding the magnetic pickup assembly to the distributor shaft bushing in the housing and lift the entire assembly from the housing.

8. Remove the brass washer, felt pad and vacuum advance unit.

DISTRIBUTOR ASSEMBLY (Fig. 4-12)

1. Attach the vacuum unit to the distributor housing.

2. Replace the felt pad and brass washer.

3. Position the magnetic pickup coil assembly in the housing and clip the retaining ring in place.

4. Replace the connector at the pickup coil leads.

5. Fit the timer core and centrifugal-weight support on the drive shaft, then install the shaft in the distributor housing.

6. Slide the drive gear into position on the drive shaft; support the shaft and install the roll pin.

7. Replace the tachometer drive gear.

8. Position the advance weights and connect the weight springs.

9. Replace the rotor.

DISTRIBUTOR INSTALLATION

1. Fit a new distributor-to-block gasket on the engine block.

2. Index the distributor rotor with the distributor housing as noted when the distributor was removed.

3. Install the distributor in the engine block with the vacuum diaphragm facing 45° forward on the right side of the engine. Rotor should point toward the No. 1 cylinder contact in the distributor cap.

4. Replace the distributor clamp and screw. Tighten the screw finger-tight.

5. Replace the distributor cap and make certain that all secondary wiring is tightly installed.

6. Connect a timing light and adjust the ignition timing to specifications, then tighten the clamp screw.

7. Reconnect the vacuum line to the distributor and the tachometer drive cables to the housing.

DELCO-REMY MAGNETIC-PULSE IGNITION	
Primary Resistance	0.41-0.51 Ohms
Secondary Resistance	3000-20,000 Ohms
Ignition Resistor (Fixed in Wiring Harness)	0.43-0.68 Ohms
DELCO-REMY UNIT IGNITION	
Coil Model Number	1847953
Primary Resistance @ 75° F	0-0.5 Ohms
Secondary Resistance @ 75° F	6000-9000 Ohms

8. Replace the ignition shield over the distributor and coil.

1973-74 PONTIAC V-8 ENGINE OPTION
Delco-Remy Unit Ignition

SYSTEM DESCRIPTION

The Unit Ignition is quite similar electrically to the Magnetic Pulse Ignition described in the previous section, and almost identical in operation with the present High Energy Ignition provided as standard equipment by GM on all 1975 and later engines. The major differences are the appearance and location of the system's electronic components **(Fig. 4-13).**

A magnetic pickup assembly positioned over the distributor shaft contains a permanent magnet, pole piece with internal teeth and a pickup coil. As a tooth of the timer core, rotating inside the pickup coil, aligns with a tooth of the pole piece, an induced voltage in the pickup coil transmits a signal to the electronic module to open the coil primary circuit. When the primary-circuit current decreases, a high voltage is induced in the coil's secondary windings and sent to the proper spark plug by the rotor.

The entire system is contained in a single unit—the distributor and its cap. Advances in electronic design allowed a reduction in the amplifier size from that of the Magnetic Pulse Ignition to one that's small enough to attach directly to the distributor housing side. Since the coil is a special shape and design, it is a part of the distributor cap. Compactness of the system design reduces system circuitry at the same time **(Fig. 4-14).**

But the most important improvement in the Unit Ignition over the Magnetic Pulse is its resistance to improper secondary circuit connections. Inadvertently cranking the engine, with the high-tension coil wire removed, causes sufficient voltage to destroy the Magnetic Pulse Ignition's transistors. Since the Unit Ignition has no external coil wires, it is foolproof in that respect. Because the coil connections are all internal, a special external terminal is provided on the outside of the cap for connecting a tachometer **(Fig. 4-15).**

Centrifugal and vacuum advance in the Unit Ignition distributor is similar to that of a conventional distributor. The centrifugal weights advance the timer core, while the vacuum unit moves the pole piece for spark

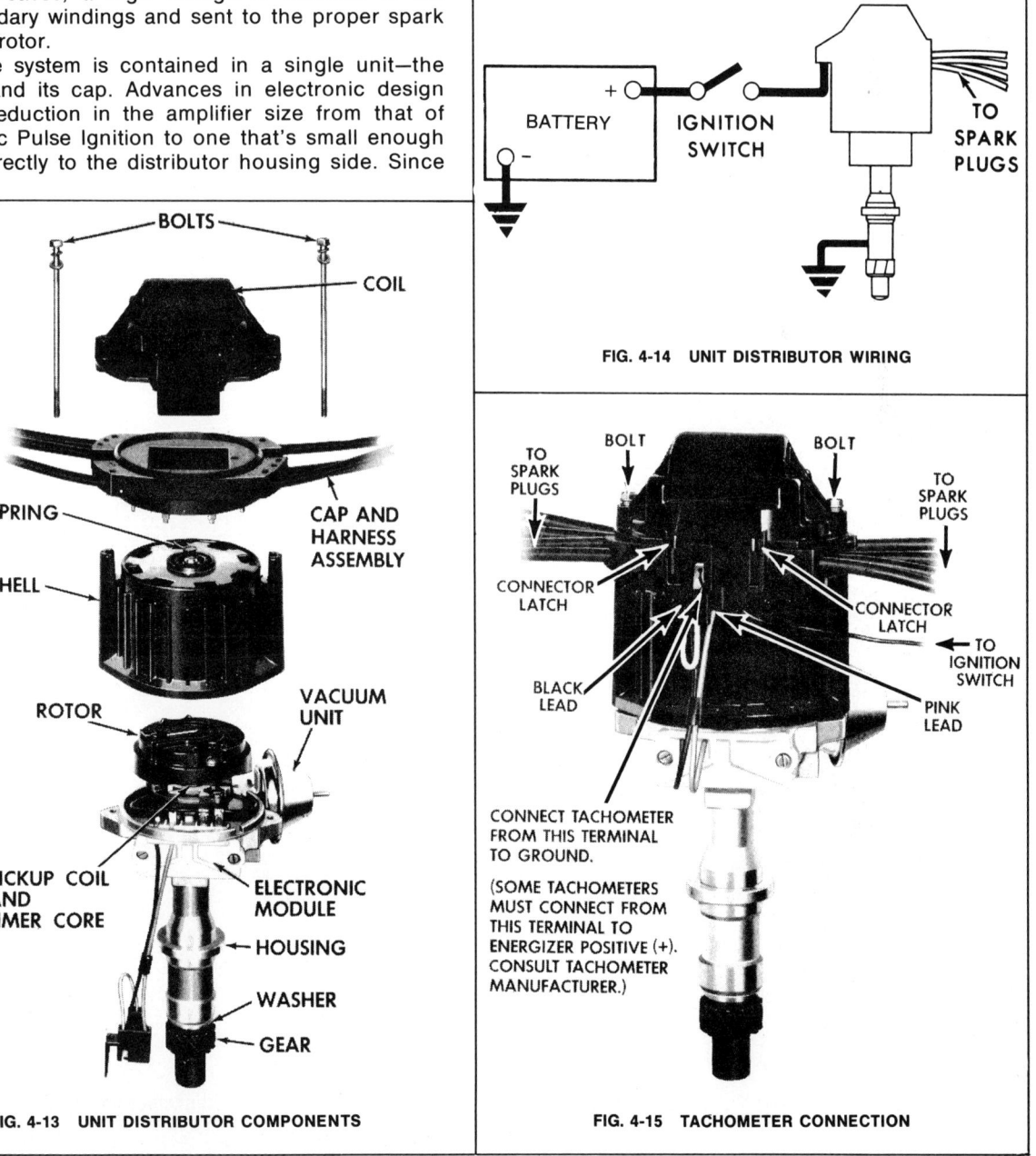

FIG. 4-14   UNIT DISTRIBUTOR WIRING

FIG. 4-13   UNIT DISTRIBUTOR COMPONENTS

FIG. 4-15   TACHOMETER CONNECTION

advance. Testing of the advance units, either on the engine or on a distributor teststand, is the same as with conventional units, although a special amplifier must be used to pick up the distributor signal on a teststand. The ignition coil can also be checked with many coil testers, providing tester instructions specifically state that it will test this special coil.

Tachometer test readings can be made on the primary circuit of this breakerless ignition, but be sure the unit to be used contains circuitry designed for testing transistorized ignitions (not all do) before connecting the tester into the circuit. If the tester is not capable of handling transistorized circuitry, it will not give accurate readings and may cause damage to the ignition system.

Service precaution—You must disconnect the ignition switch connector from the Unit Ignition system when making compression tests.

TEST PROCEDURE

Due to the nature of the Unit Ignition design, test procedures are combined with distributor disassembly. Follow the "Removal" and "Installation" procedures specified for the "Magnetic Pulse Distributor."

COIL/PICKUP-COIL TEST

1. Remove the two through-bolts holding the ignition coil and cap/harness assembly from the distributor cap shell and lift off these components **(Fig. 4-13).**

2. Connect the ohmmeter leads to the coil as shown in **Fig. 4-16.** Conduct tests A through D.

    A & B—Each should read almost zero. If reading is infinite on either A or B, replace the coil.

    C—Should read 6000-9000 ohms. If not within this range, replace the coil.

    D—Should read infinite. If not, replace the coil.

3. Connect the ohmmeter leads to the pickup coil leads as shown in **Fig. 4-17.** Conduct tests A and B.

    A—Should read between 650 and 850 ohms. If not within this range, replace the pickup coil.

    B—Should read infinite. If not, replace the coil.

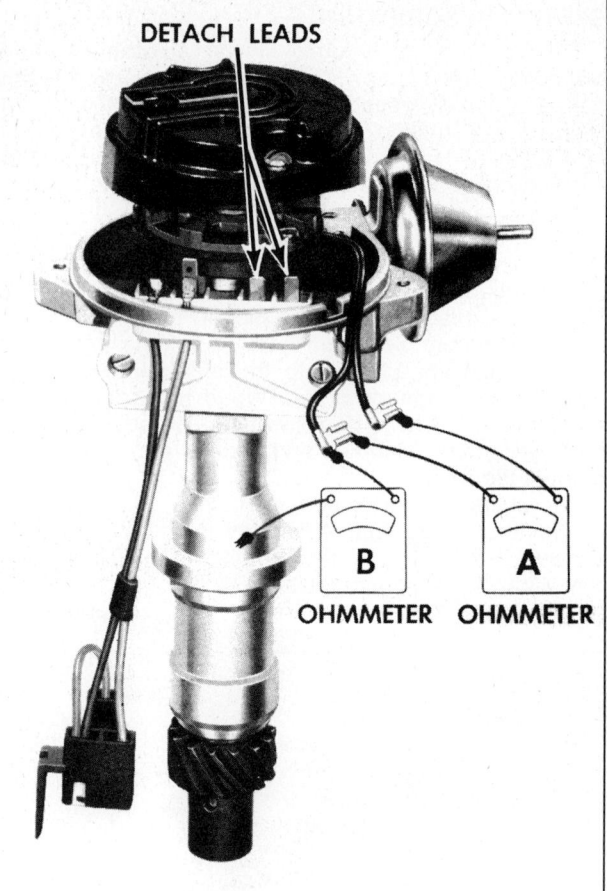

FIG. 4-17 UNIT DISTRIBUTOR PICKUP COIL TEST

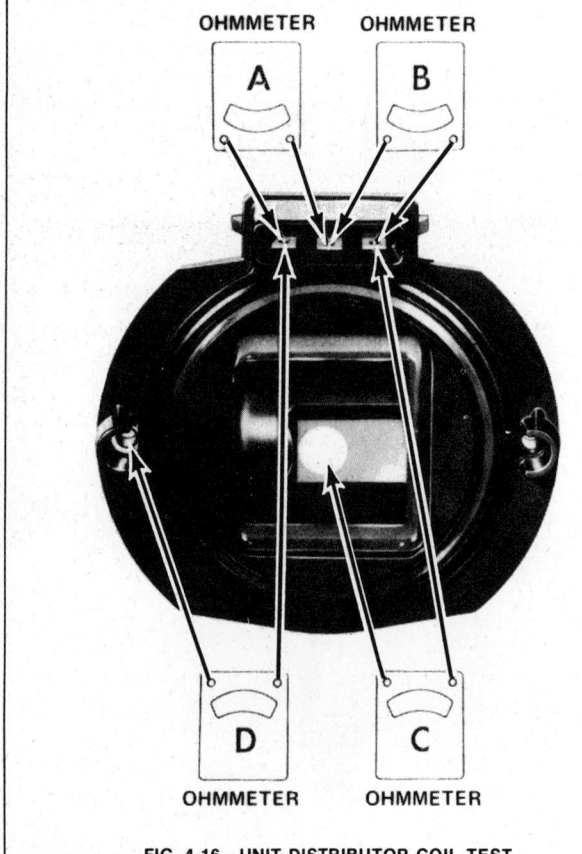

FIG. 4-16 UNIT DISTRIBUTOR COIL TEST

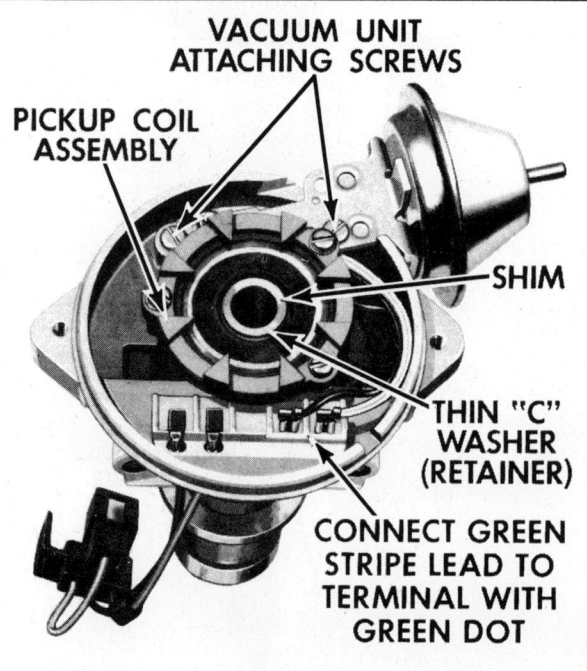

FIG. 4-18 UNIT DISTRIBUTOR PICKUP COIL REPLACEMENT

4. To remove the pickup coil for replacement, support the distributor shaft and use a suitable drift and hammer to tap out the drive-gear retaining pin.

5. Remove the rotor and shaft assembly from the distributor housing.

6. Remove the shim and "C" washer shown in **Fig. 4-18** and disconnect the pickup coil leads. Unscrew and remove the pickup coil assembly.

7. Position a new pickup coil assembly in the distributor housing and replace the attaching screws.

8. Connect the green striped lead to the terminal marked with a green dot, then hook the remaining lead to the other terminal.

9. Replace the "C" washer and shim. Insert the distributor shaft and rotor assembly.

10. Fit the drive gear to the distributor shaft and replace the retaining pin.

11. Replace the distributor cap shell, cap/harness assembly and coil, and secure in place with the through-bolts.

ALL 1975-79 GENERAL MOTORS ENGINES; OPTIONAL: 1974 BUICK, CADILLAC, OLDSMOBILE V-8 ENGINES
Delco-Remy High Energy Ignition System

SYSTEM DESCRIPTION

An outgrowth of the Delco-Remy Magnetic Pulse and Unit Ignitions, the HEI is a pulse-triggered, transistor-controlled, inductive-discharge ignition system. A magnetic pickup assembly, containing a permanent magnet, pole piece with internal teeth and a pickup coil, is located inside the distributor **(Fig. 4-19)**.

As a tooth of the timer core rotating inside the pickup coil aligns with a tooth of the pole piece, an induced voltage in the pickup coil transmits a signal to the electronic module to open the coil primary circuit. When the primary circuit current decreases, a high voltage is induced in the coil's secondary windings and sent to the proper spark plug by the rotor. **Fig. 4-20** shows the wiring diagram for this system.

A capacitor is located in the distributor to provide radio noise suppression. The electronic module controls the dwell period automatically, increasing dwell as engine speed increases. Dwell is thus varied, but cannot be adjusted. Because of the greater amount of energy stored in the coil primary, the HEI system also has a longer spark duration, necessary for firing both lean and EGR (exhaust gas recirculation) diluted air/fuel mixtures.

DISTRIBUTOR

Two types of distributors are used, identical in manner of operation *except* for coil placement and the number of teeth on the rotating timer core and pole piece. V-6/V-8 distributors contain all ignition components in a single unit **(Fig. 4-21)**. Mounted in the distributor cap, the coil is connected directly to the rotor. Those 1975-77 HEI distributors on I-4/I-6 engines have externally mounted coils **(Fig. 4-22)**. Starting with 1978 models, I-4/I-6 HEI distributors use an integral coil/cap design.

IGNITION COIL

The HEI coil is physically smaller than that used with a conventional ignition system **(Fig. 4-23)**, but contains more primary and secondary windings. Interior construction also differs. A conventional coil is constructed in such a manner that the windings surround the iron core, but in the HEI coil the laminated iron core surrounds the windings. Despite the difference in appearance and construction, the HEI coil operates basically the same as a conventional coil, but is more effective in generating higher secondary voltage when the primary circuit is broken.

Correct coil replacement is critical. While all V-8 distributor coils will fit any General Motors HEI distributor, regardless of the car or engine to which it is fitted, the same is not true of HEI coils. For example, the HEI coil fitted to an Oldsmobile Toronado looks and performs identically to that used for the Oldsmobile 88 or 98, but is wound differently. Thus, the coils are not interchangeable in operation, despite the fact they are interchangeable physically. Care should be taken to provide the correct coil number (located on the coil top) when obtaining a replacement.

The ignition coil can also be checked with many coil testers, providing the tester instructions specifically state that it will test this special coil.

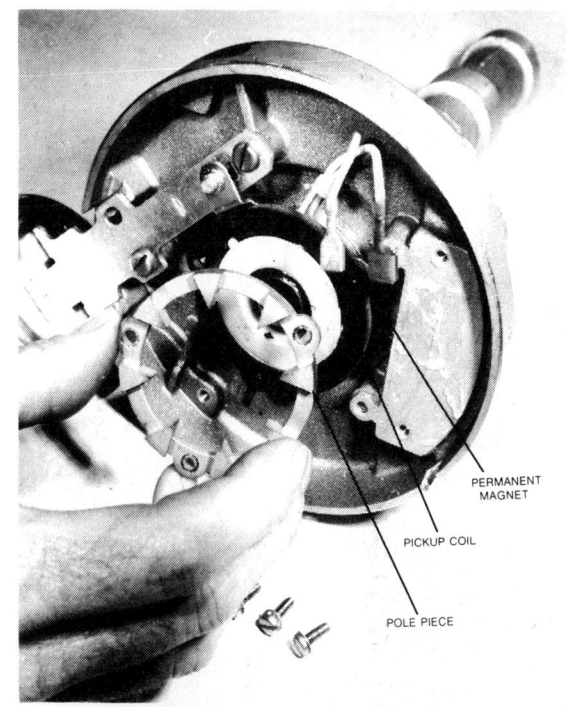

FIG. 4-19 HEI DISTRIBUTOR COMPONENTS

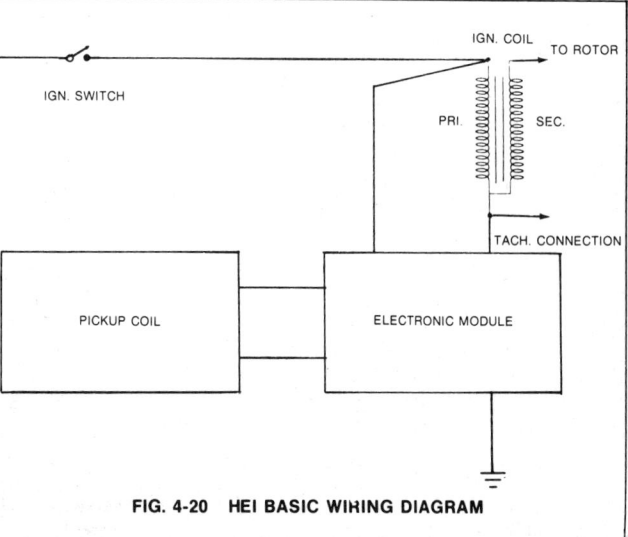

FIG. 4-20 HEI BASIC WIRING DIAGRAM

PICKUP ASSEMBLY

The three-piece pickup assembly consists of: 1) a pickup coil and magnet located between the pole piece and a bottom plate; 2) a stationary pole piece with internal teeth; and 3) a rotating timer core with external teeth.

ELECTRONIC MODULE

Located in the distributor body, the solid-state electronic module contains five complete circuits which control: 1) spark timing; 2) switching; 3) current limiting; 4) dwell control; and 5) distributor pickup. This electronic module delivers full battery voltage to the ignition coil, which is limited to 5-6 amps. The HEI system has no primary resistance wire. The module directs the opening and closing of the coil primary circuit instantly, with no energy lost because of breaker-point arcing or capacitor-charging time lag. This allows the HEI system to deliver up to 35,000 volts to the spark plugs.

As a result of this higher voltage, the HEI system uses 8mm silicone-insulated secondary wiring. Gray in color, the silicone wiring is more heat-resistant and less vulnerable to deterioration than Hypalon-insulated wiring. But because silicone is soft, the wires must be treated with respect.

SERVICE PRECAUTIONS

1. You must disconnect the ignition-switch connector at the distributor when making compression tests.

2. Do not pierce the spark plug lead when connecting an ignition timing light—connect the light at the plug end of the No. 1 spark plug.

3. A "tach" terminal is provided in the distributor cap connector on V-6 and V-8 distributors **(Fig. 4-21)** or on the coil itself on inline 4- and 6-cyl. distributors **(Fig. 4-22)**. Some tachometers connect to this terminal and to ground, while others must connect from the "tach" terminal to the positive battery terminal—follow the test equipment manufacturer's instructions for proper connection. Grounding the "tach" terminal can damage the HEI electronic module.

4. Cadillac uses a diode in the brown wire of the harness near the alternator telltale lamp, similar in appearance to the starter interlock diode, and located near the top of the radio heat sink. This diode prevents feedback through the alternator lead wire to the HEI module. If this diode malfunctions, the approximate 2.7 volts from such feedback will cause engine dieseling.

TEST PROCEDURES

CRANKING TESTS

Before performing any of the following tests, the ignition system must be disabled:

1. 1975-77 I-4/I-6 Engines—Release the two clips and remove the primary connector plug from the coil.

2. All Others—Disconnect the ignition lead from the BAT terminal of the distributor.

Because there is no ballast resistor or bypass circuit, the "Cranking Available Voltage Test" is not necessary

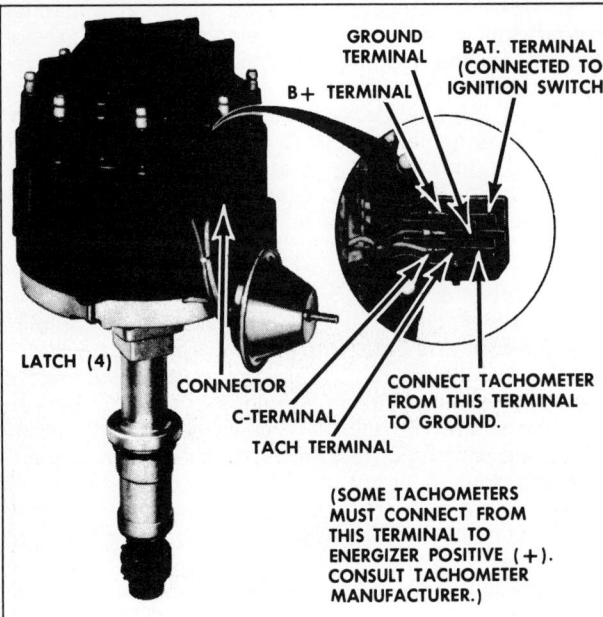

FIG. 4-21   8-CYL. HEI DISTRIBUTOR, WITH TACH CONNECTION

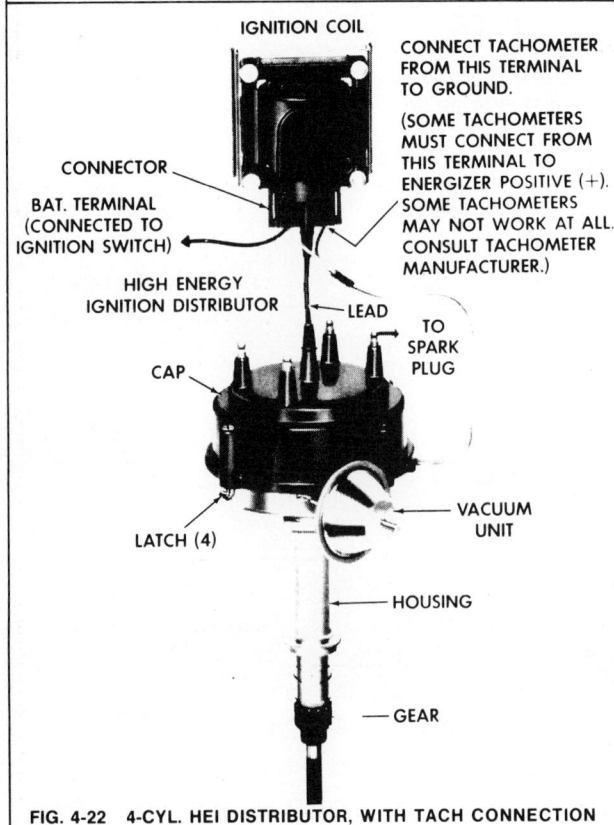

FIG. 4-22   4-CYL. HEI DISTRIBUTOR, WITH TACH CONNECTION

FIG. 4-23   HEI/CONVENTIONAL COIL COMPARISON

unless the engine *will not* start. All tests should be made with the engine at normal operating temperature.

CRANKING AVAILABLE VOLTAGE TEST

1. Remove No. 1 spark plug lead at the plug and hold ¼-in. away from an engine ground with insulated pliers.

2. Crank the engine. If sparking does not occur (no available voltage), test the "Ignition Key Circuit."

IGNITION KEY CIRCUIT TEST

1. Disable the ignition system as described.

2. Connect the positive voltmeter lead to the disconnected ignition switch lead and the negative voltmeter lead to an engine ground.

3. With the ignition switch in the ON position, the voltmeter should read battery voltage. A zero reading indicates an open ignition-switch circuit.

STATIC IGNITION PRIMARY CURRENT DRAW TEST

1. Connect a low-reading ammeter as follows:

(a) 1975-77 I-4/I-6 Engines—No. 1 lead to the distributor coil BAT terminal and the other to the disconnected ignition switch lead.

(b) All Others—No. 1 lead to the disconnected distributor BAT terminal and the other to the disconnected ignition switch lead (use an adapter lead).

2. Turn the ignition switch on. The ammeter should read 0.1- to 0.2-amps. If meter reads greater than 1.0 amps, the module is malfunctioning.

CRANKING IGNITION PRIMARY-CIRCUIT-DRAW TEST

1. With the ammeter connected as in the previous test, crank the engine. The meter should indicate approximately 0.5 to 1.5 amps. If it does not, there are three possible areas of malfunction:

a) Magnetic pickup assembly.
b) Ignition-coil primary circuit.
c) Electronic module.

2. Test individual components as below.

3. Replace the defective components and repeat "Cranking Available Voltage Test."

4. Start the engine and retest for proper ignition system operation.

COMPONENT TESTS

PICKUP-COIL OHMMETER TEST

1. Disconnect the pickup coil leads from the electronic module.

2. Connect the ohmmeter leads as shown in **Fig. 4-24** and calibrate. If the meter reads less than infinity on the X1000 scale, replace the pickup coil.

3. Connect the ohmmeter leads as shown in **Fig. 4-25** and calibrate. If the meter reads less than 500 ohms or more than 1500 ohms, replace the pickup coil.

4. If the meter reads between 500 and 1500 ohms, repeat Steps 2 and 3 while moving the vacuum advance linkage with a screwdriver. If reading is still satisfactory, the pickup coil may be considered good. If reading is not satisfactory, replace the pickup coil.

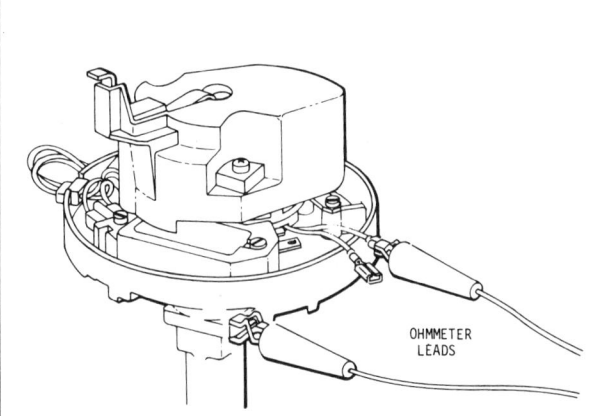

FIG. 4-24 HEI PICKUP COIL—OHMMETER CONNECTION

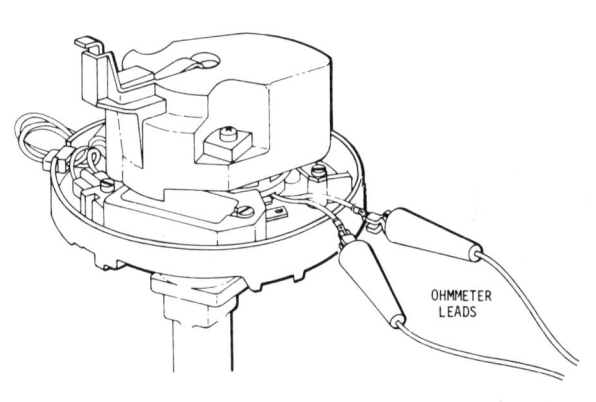

FIG. 4-25 HEI PICKUP COIL—OHMMETER CONNECTION

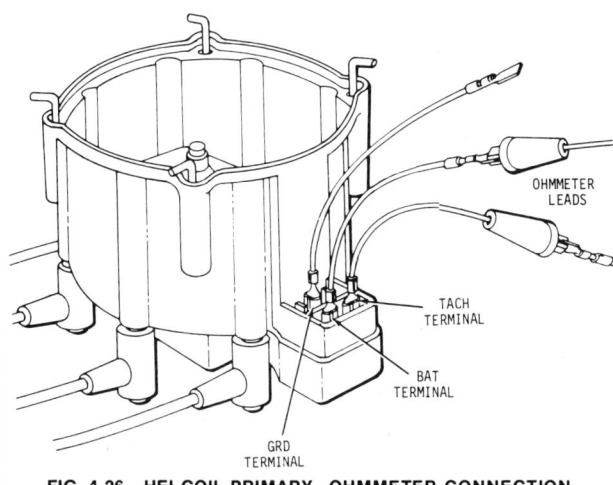

FIG. 4-26 HEI COIL PRIMARY—OHMMETER CONNECTION

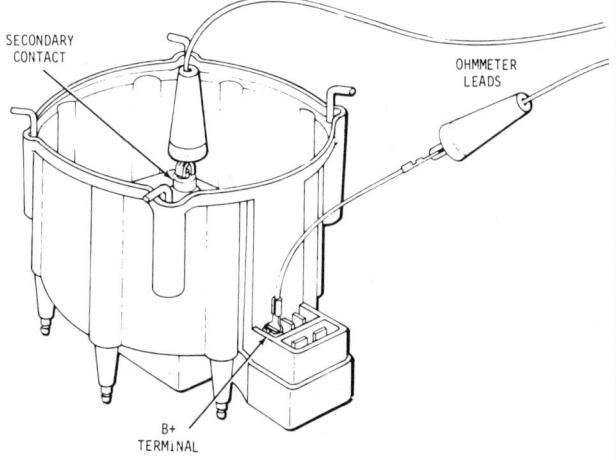

FIG. 4-27 HEI COIL SECONDARY—OHMMETER CONNECTION

IGNITION COIL OHMMETER TEST

1. Remove the distributor cap and wires as an assembly. Test the coil without removing it from the distributor cap to prevent possible damage to the coil primary wires.

2. Connect the adapter leads to the BAT, TACH and GRD coil terminals.

3. Set the ohmmeter to the X1 range, calibrate and connect the leads as shown in **Fig. 4-26.**

    a) BAT and TACH terminals—Reading should be 0.5 ohms.

    b) GRD and TACH terminals—Reading should be infinity.

4. Set the ohmmeter to the X1000 range, calibrate and connect leads as shown in **Fig. 4-27** to the ''B + '' terminal and the secondary contact disc in the distributor cap. Meter should read between 6000 and 20,000 ohms. If the meter reads infinity, remove the coil from the distributor cap and retest.

SERVICE PRECAUTIONS

1. The distributor-cap contact button has a 10,000-ohm resistance. Test specifications of the coil secondary winding alone will be 8000 to 10,000 ohms (V-6 and V-8 only).

2. A small coil spring is located between the coil and the distributor cap. A missing spring will cause an open circuit between the distributor-cap button and the coil secondary contact.

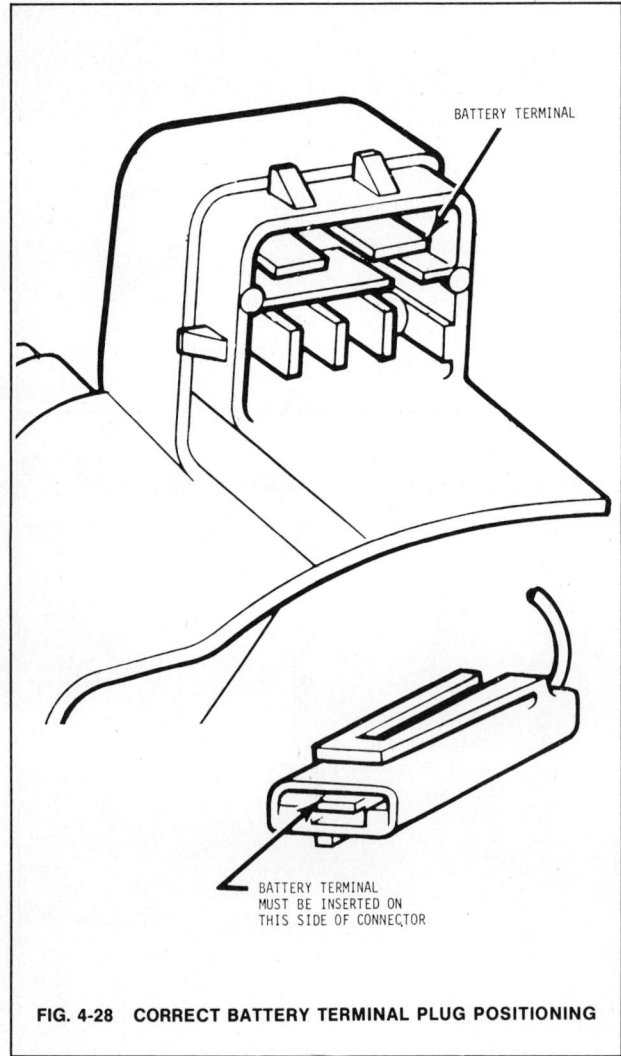

BATTERY TERMINAL

BATTERY TERMINAL
MUST BE INSERTED ON
THIS SIDE OF CONNECTOR

FIG. 4-28 CORRECT BATTERY TERMINAL PLUG POSITIONING

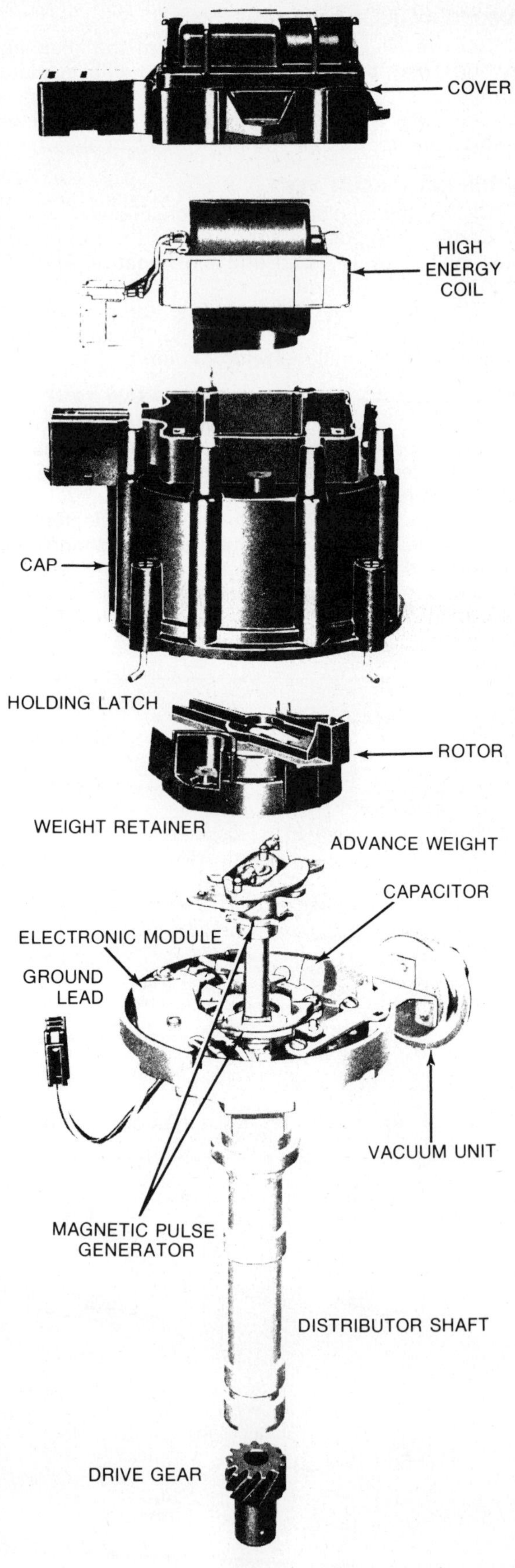

COVER

HIGH ENERGY COIL

CAP

HOLDING LATCH

ROTOR

WEIGHT RETAINER

ADVANCE WEIGHT

CAPACITOR

ELECTRONIC MODULE

GROUND LEAD

MAGNETIC PULSE GENERATOR

VACUUM UNIT

DISTRIBUTOR SHAFT

DRIVE GEAR

FIG. 4-29 8-CYL. HEI DISASSEMBLY

3. A no-start or engine-miss condition can be caused if the distributor battery terminal is incorrectly positioned in the battery-terminal connector plug. The plug is to be positioned as shown in **Fig. 4-28.**

DISTRIBUTOR REMOVAL

1. Disconnect the two wiring-harness connectors at the side of the distributor cap.

2. Remove the distributor cap and position it out of the way.

3. Disconnect the vacuum advance line from the distributor-advance diaphragm unit.

4. Scribe a mark on the engine in line with the rotor and note the position of the distributor housing in relationship to the engine.

5. Remove the distributor hold-down clamp and nut.

6. Withdraw the distributor from the engine. Rotor will turn counterclockwise slightly—note new position.

DISTRIBUTOR DISASSEMBLY (Fig. 4-29)

1. Lift the two retaining tabs and remove the wiring connector from the distributor cap.

2. Remove the coil-cover attaching screws and lift the coil cover off the coil.

3. Remove the four coil attaching screws and lift the coil, with leads intact, from the distributor cap. Coil ground is provided by one of the screws.

4. Remove the ignition coil arc seal. This insulating pad absorbs moisture and must not be left out during reassembly.

5. Depress and turn the four distributor-cap holding latches to remove the cap.

6. Remove the rotor, advance springs, weight retainer and advance weights.

7. Mark the distributor shaft and drive gear to permit proper positioning during reassembly.

8. Support the distributor shaft and use a suitable drift and hammer to tap out the drive-gear roll pin.

9. Remove the drive gear from the distributor shaft and withdraw the shaft assembly from the housing.

10. Disconnect the pickup coil leads from the electronic module.

11. Remove the waved retaining ring, pickup-coil/ pole-piece assembly and the felt washer or wick **(Fig. 4-30).**

12. Disconnect and remove the vacuum advance unit.

13. Disconnect and remove the electronic module, capacitor (radio interference filter) and wiring harness assembly from the distributor housing **(Fig. 4-31).**

SERVICE PRECAUTIONS

1. If the distributor shaft bushing shows evidence of wear, the shaft bushing and distributor housing are replaced as a complete unit—*do not* attempt to remove the bushing from the housing.

2. Do not wipe the grease from the electronic module or its mounting point on the distributor base. The grease is required for proper heat transfer involved in module cooling. If a new module is to be installed, clean off the old grease and replace it with that included with the replacement module. Apply grease both to module metal face and the distributor-housing mounting seat.

DISTRIBUTOR ASSEMBLY (Fig. 4-29)

1. Install the electronic module, capacitor and wiring harness. Ground lead must be *under* the capacitor attaching screw.

2. Position the vacuum advance unit to the distributor housing and replace the screws.

3. Replace the felt washer over the lubricant reservoir at the housing top and lubricate with a few drops of engine oil.

4. Place the shim on top of the felt washer and fit the pickup-coil/pole-piece assembly to the housing, with the vacuum advance arm over the advance actuating pin on the pole piece. Replace the waved ring and connect the pickup coil to the electronic module.

5. Slide the distributor shaft through the housing bushings and rotate to make sure there is even clearance all the way around between the pole piece and shaft projections. If necessary, loosen the pickup coil assembly to provide even clearance, then retighten the screws.

6. Replace the tanged washer and shim, then fit the drive gear on the distributor shaft, with its teeth facing upward.

7. Support the distributor shaft and reinstall the drive-gear roll pin.

8. Install the centrifugal advance weights, weight retainer (with dimple pointing down) and springs.

9. Install the rotor. Make sure the notch on its side engages the tab on the cam weight base.

10. Replace the ignition-coil arc seal in the distributor cap.

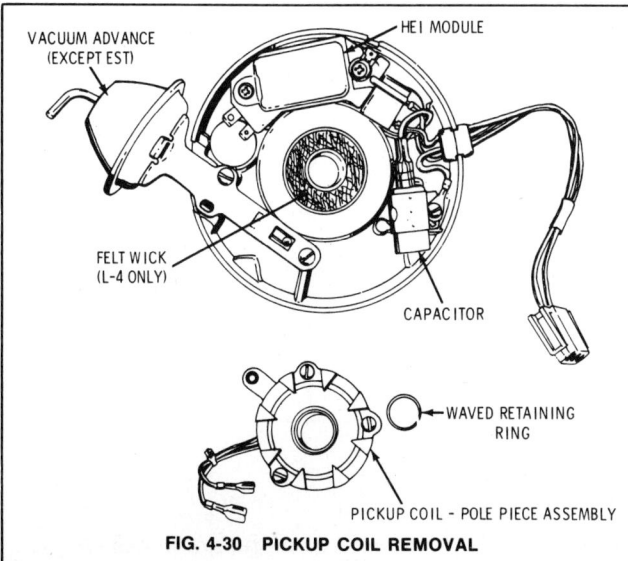

FIG. 4-30 PICKUP COIL REMOVAL

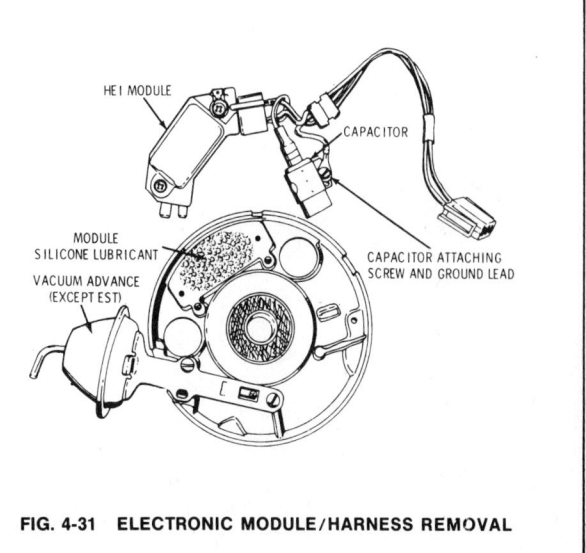

FIG. 4-31 ELECTRONIC MODULE/HARNESS REMOVAL

11. Replace the ignition coil and leads. Install the attaching screws.

12. Replace the coil cover and attaching screws.

13. Replace the wiring connectors. If spark-plug wire replacement is necessary, individual wires *can* be removed from the wiring connector by holding down the grommet of the wire and pressing the retainer tab out of the wire holder. But, since replacement wires are sold only in complete sets, spark plug wires are serviced as a unit.

DELCO-REMY HIGH ENERGY IGNITION

Ignition Coil Output (2000-2500 rpm)	35-38 KV
Ignition Primary Current (Key On):	
Engine Stopped	0.1-0.2 Amps.
Engine Cranking	0.5-1.5 Amps.
Engine @ Idle	0.5-1.5 Amps.
2000-2500 rpm	1.0-2.8 Amps.
Primary Resistance	0.4-0.5 Ohms
Secondary Resistance (Coil and Resistor)	6000-30,000 Ohms
Secondary Wire Resistance	4K-7K per foot
Distributor Cap Resistor	8000-10,000 Ohms
Distributor Pulse Coil Resistance	500-1500 Ohms

1975-76 FORD MOTOR COMPANY ENGINES: 1974 FORD MOTOR COMPANY ENGINES (All Calif. and 400/460-cu.-in. Engines); 1973 LINCOLN ENGINES (Late Models Only); 1978-79 AMERICAN MOTORS ENGINES (6- and 8-Cylinder)

Ford-Motorcraft Solid-State Ignition System

SYSTEM DESCRIPTION

This is a breakerless, pulse-triggered, transistor-controlled system. All 1978-79 AMC 6- and 8-cyl. engines use the 1976 version of this electronic ignition. A magnetic pickup-coil assembly (called a stator) is located inside the distributor, along with an armature which rotates with the distributor shaft **(Fig. 4-32)**.

As a tooth (A) of the rotating armature nears the stator magnetic pickup **(Fig. 4-33)**, an electrical signal is generated in the pickup coil. When the tooth and magnet align (B), a zero signal is generated in the pickup. This zero signal is neither negative nor positive, but more like a break in a circuit. The zero signal

is transmitted to an externally mounted electronic amplifier module **(Fig. 4-34)**, which then breaks the primary circuit, causing the spark plug to fire. As the armature tooth (C) moves away **(Fig. 4-33)**, a signal with opposite polarity is generated. When the primary circuit breaks, it starts an electronic timing circuit in the module. This timing circuit keeps the primary current broken sufficiently to permit the spark to fire. The module then reconnects the primary circuit to allow it to build up enough to fire again. This period is referred to as dwell, but there is no way to adjust it.

DISTRIBUTORS

All V-8 distributors, regardless of engine application or model year, are identical, except for calibration. The I-6 distributor used on 1974 California engines is also of the same design. But I-4, I-6 and V-6 distributors, fitted to 1975 and later engines, use an eccentric-plate, mini-base design. The upper-plate pivot point is located away from the distributor center and produces an eccentric instead of concentric motion to the plate. The rotating armature is also smaller in diameter than that of the V-8 distributor.

The beige phenolic distributor cap was replaced in 1975 with a blue compression-molded alkyd cap, physically interchangeable with the phenolic cap, but possessing a higher dielectric strength and greater resistance to arc tracking.

Rotor design was also changed in 1975. A crown was added on the rotor spring to help center it on the carbon ball in the distributor cap, thus reducing damage due to misassembly. But the spring used on 6-cyl. rotors was not sufficiently strong to keep it in place during rotation. This led to a tendency for the rotor to lift up as the distributor shaft revolved, resulting in eventual rotor and cap damage. Replacement rotors have also turned up with the distributor-shaft index key as much as 5° off, resulting in a cross-firing condition.

IGNITION COIL

Solid State Ignition coils after 1974 use a new polarized connector with a tachometer test lead for connecting an alligator clip to the DIST terminal, which has been renamed "Distributor Electronic Control" or DEC

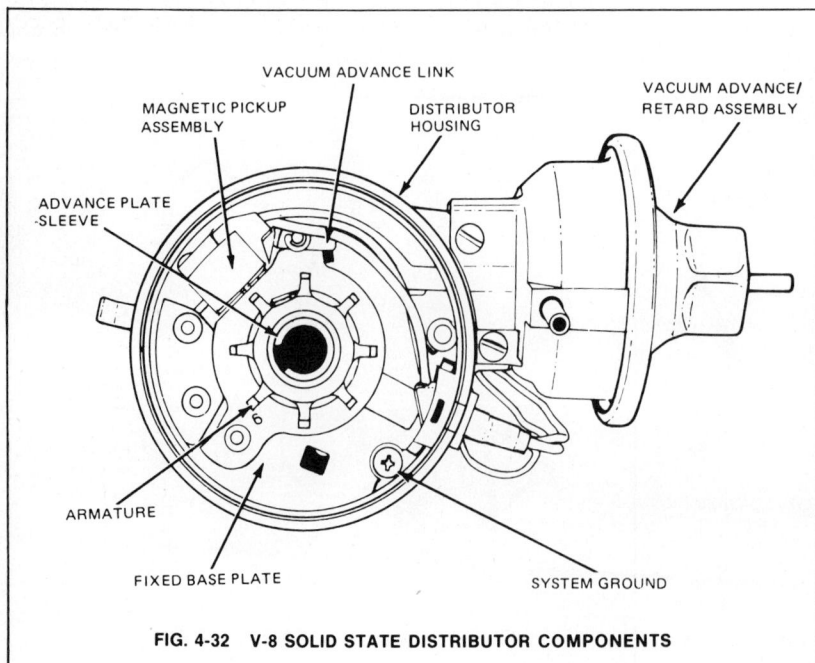

FIG. 4-32 **V-8 SOLID STATE DISTRIBUTOR COMPONENTS**

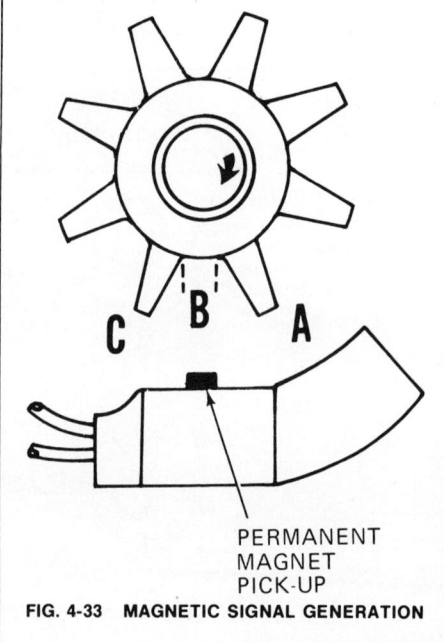

FIG. 4-33 **MAGNETIC SIGNAL GENERATION**

terminal. When checking engine rpm, attach the test clip into the cavity marked TACH TEST, as shown in **Fig. 4-35.** If the coil connector is to be removed, grasp the wires and pull the connector horizontally until it disconnects from the terminals.

CIRCUIT WIRING

Wire color-coding is important to servicing the Solid State Ignition **(Fig. 4-36).** Battery current reaches the electronic module from the ignition switch through the *white* wire during cranking, but through the *red* wire after the engine is running. Distributor signals are transmitted through the *orange* and *purple* wires. Primary current from the coil is carried to the module by the *green* wire. The *black* wire is a ground between the distributor and module. Transient voltage protection for the system is provided by the *blue* wire through 1975; a zenier diode added to the module in 1976 dumps temporary voltage surges before they can damage the module, and the *blue* wire is no longer used. These wires (seven in systems through 1975 and six from 1976 on) feed from the module in two groups, one of which ends in a three-terminal connector, and the other in a four-terminal connector. Both connectors are plugged into the main wiring harness.

SERVICE PRECAUTIONS

1. Internal circuitry changes in the electronic module in both the 1975 and 1976 model years complicate

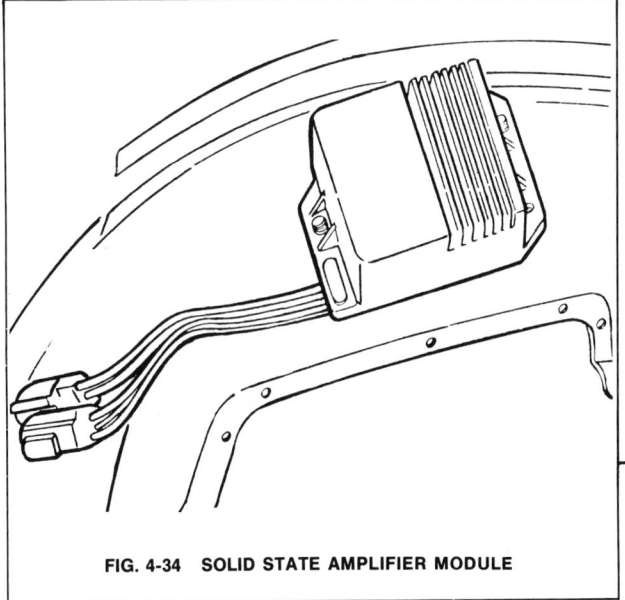

FIG. 4-34   SOLID STATE AMPLIFIER MODULE

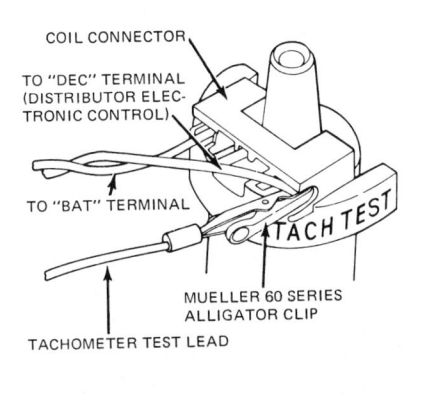

FIG. 4-35   COIL TACHOMETER CONNECTION

system diagnosis, since test equipment connections and procedures differ. Wire continuity and color have not been changed, but the connector shape and terminal arrangement of the 1973-74 connectors was changed in 1975 and again in 1976. Addition of a zenier diode to the electronic module for circuit protection in 1976 resulted in a modification of the three-terminal connector to a two-terminal connector for 1976. The four-terminal connector remained the same for 1976, but the position of the No. 7 and No. 8 distributor wires has been reversed. Because of these changes, modules and wiring harnesses *cannot* be interchanged between model years, and the reader should refer carefully to **Fig. 4-37** when testing a Solid State Ignition.

2. The *orange* and *purple* wires leading from the stator *must* be connected to the *same* color wire at the module. If these connections are crossed in the wiring harness, polarity is reversed and the system will be thrown 22½° out of phase. Unfortunately, many replacement wiring harnesses with crossed connections were distributed before the problem was discovered, and because there is no way to identify an incorrect harness until it is connected, a large number are still on dealers' shelves, and may be sold as good harnesses.

3. The flexible plug carrying the *orange, purple* and *black* wires through the distributor housing is held in place by a small ground-connection screw **(Fig. 4-38).** This screw is the ground for the *black* wire, which grounds the primary circuit, and for the electronic-module control circuits. A loose, dirty or corroded connection at this point will cause a considerable number and variety of difficult-to-diagnose ignition problems.

4. When the ignition switch is on, the module and coil are also on. As a result, the system will generate a spark when the ignition switch is turned off. Other service procedures, such as removing the distributor cap with the ignition switch on, can cause the system to fire. Because of this, the ignition switch should remain off during any underhood operations, unless the test procedure specifies that it be on.

TEST PROCEDURES

First determine that the problem is actually in the ignition system. Then perform the necessary tests (exactly the same as for a conventional system) to elimi-

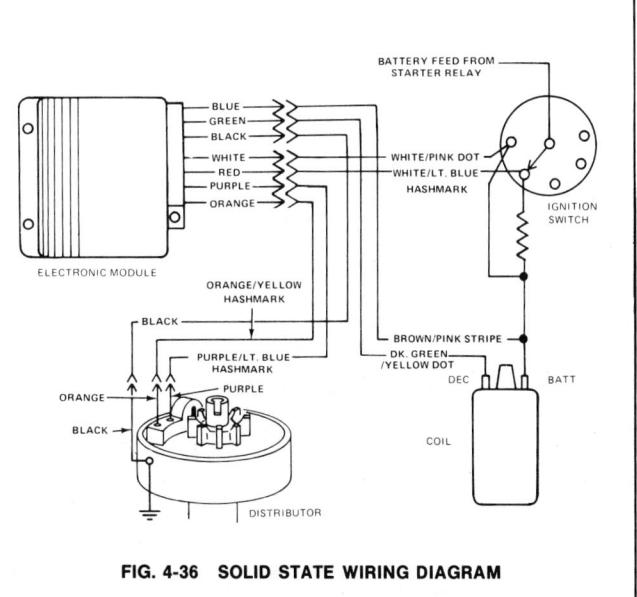

FIG. 4-36   SOLID STATE WIRING DIAGRAM

nate both the secondary circuit and that part of the primary circuit between the battery and BAT terminal of the coil. If the solution is not found, the problem lies in the solid-state portion of the system between the coil and distributor ground. To properly test the connector pins and sockets, three jumper leads are required, as shown in **Fig. 4-39**.

Since there is no way to test the electronic amplifier module, instead, tests are performed on the circuits which feed *into* the module. If *all* input circuits test satisfactory, the module should be presumed to be the cause of the ignition problem and should be replaced with a *known good module* (not necessarily a brand new replacement off the shelf).

1973-74 DIAGNOSIS SEQUENCE (Fig. 4-40)

1. Unplug the four-wire connector at the module and connect a voltmeter as shown in **Fig. 4-41**. With

the voltmeter set at its lowest scale, crank the engine. If the meter needle wiggles slightly, proceed to Step 5.

2. If needle does not wiggle. repeat the test as shown in **Fig. 4-42** at the distributor connector. If the needle wiggles now, repair the harness or connector between the module and distributor.

3. If needle does not wiggle, connect an ohmmeter as shown in **Fig. 4-43** to the same two connector leads. Meter should read between 400 and 800 ohms. If it does not, replace the stator assembly.

4. Switch the ohmmeter to the X1000 scale. Remove the ohmmeter lead from either connector blade and touch it to the distributor housing. Ohmmeter should read over 70,000 ohms. Holding the test lead to the distributor housing, move the other lead to the other parallel connector blade. Ohmmeter should still read over 70,000 ohms. If either reading is less than 70,000 ohms, replace the stator assembly.

5. If both readings are over 70,000 ohms, connect a voltmeter as shown in **Fig. 4-44** and turn the ignition switch to run. Meter should read within 0.4-volt of battery voltage. If more than 0.4-volt below battery voltage, repair the harness or connector between the module connector and the ignition switch.

6. Now connect the voltmeter as shown in **Fig. 4-45** and turn the ignition switch to START. Meter should read within 0.4-volt of battery *cranking* voltage, but not less than 8 volts. If the voltage is below specifications, repair the connectors or harness between the module connector and ignition switch.

7. Connect No. 1 ohmmeter lead to Socket 6 (three-terminal connector) and the other lead to ground. The

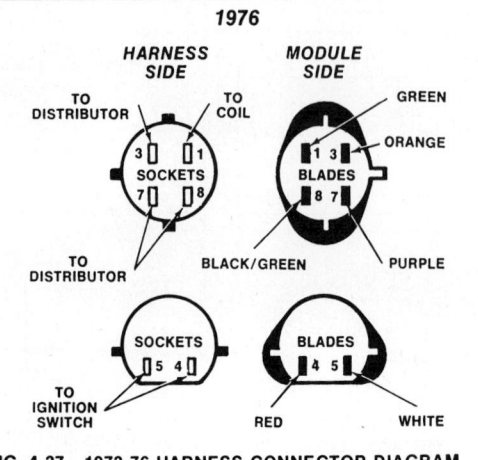

FIG. 4-37   1973-76 HARNESS CONNECTOR DIAGRAM

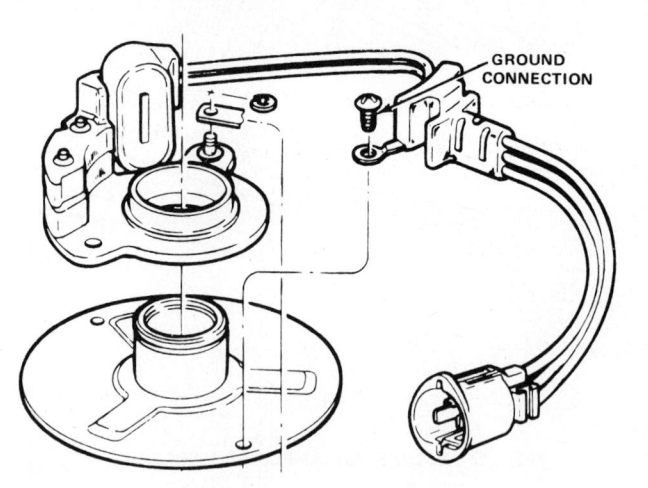

FIG. 4-38   ELECTRONIC MODULE/PRIMARY CIRCUIT GROUND

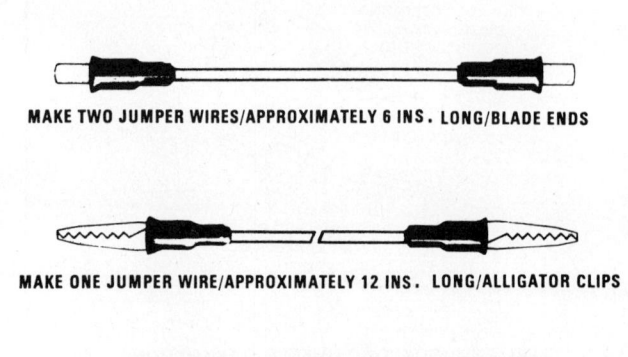

MAKE TWO JUMPER WIRES/APPROXIMATELY 6 INS. LONG/BLADE ENDS

MAKE ONE JUMPER WIRE/APPROXIMATELY 12 INS. LONG/ALLIGATOR CLIPS

FIG. 4-39   REQUIRED JUMPER LEAD CONSTRUCTION

meter should read zero ohms. If not, repeat the check at the distributor blade side of the connector and check the blade connected to the *black* wire. If the meter now reads zero ohms, repair the harness (*black* wire) between the distributor connector and module connector.

8. If the meter shows resistance, remove the distributor cap. Clean and tighten the ground connection **(Fig. 4-38)**. If the meter still shows resistance, replace the stator assembly and wires.

9. Connect the ohmmeter leads to Sockets 4 and 5 of the three-terminal connector. Meter should read 1.0 to 2.0 ohms (coil primary resistance).

10. If resistance is higher or lower than specifications, move the ohmmeter lead from Socket 5 to the coil DEC terminal. If the meter now reads within specifications, repair the harness between the DEC terminal and module (*dark-green/yellow* dot wire).

11. If the resistance still reads outside the 1.0- to 2.0-ohm specification, hold the ohmmeter lead on the coil DEC terminal and move the other lead from Socket 4 to the coil BAT lead. If the meter now reads within specifications, repair the harness between the coil BAT terminal and the module (*brown/pink* spot wire).

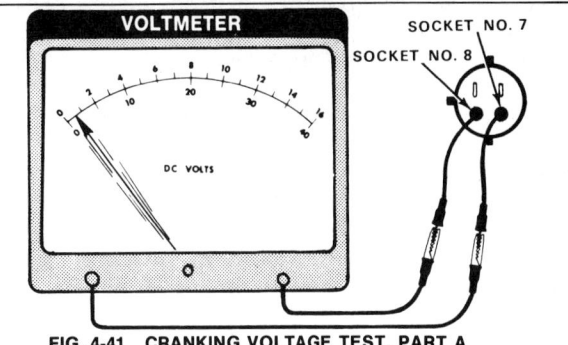

FIG. 4-41   CRANKING VOLTAGE TEST, PART A

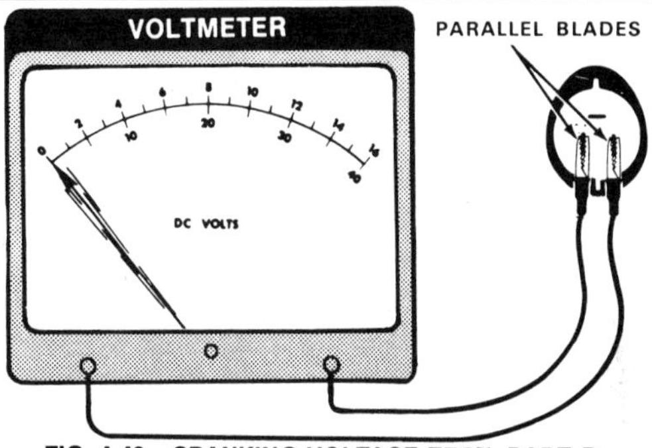

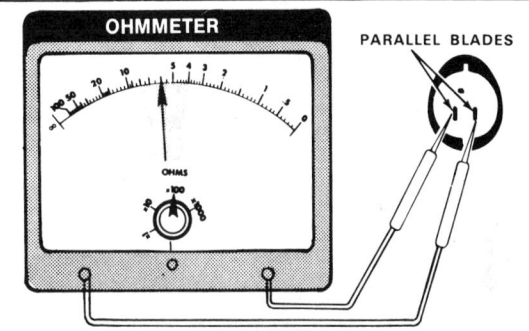

FIG. 4-42   CRANKING VOLTAGE TEST, PART B

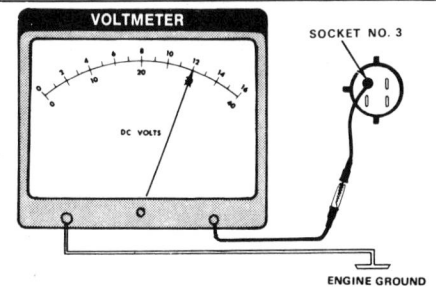

FIG. 4-43   RESISTANCE TEST

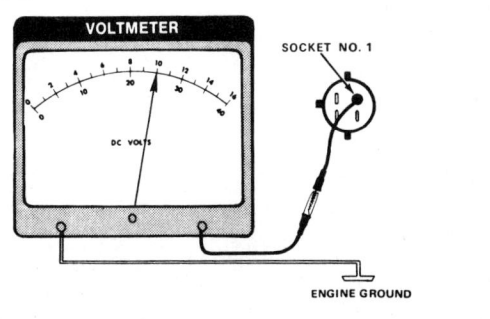

FIG. 4-44   CONTROL VOLTAGE TO MODULE TEST, PART A

CIRCUIT	TEST	BETWEEN	SHOULD BE
Armature and Pickup Coil	Voltage (cranking)	Socket 7 & socket 8; module 4-wire connector	Slight meter wiggle
	Voltage (cranking)	Blades 7D & 8D; distributor 3-wire connector	Slight meter wiggle
	Resistance (key off)	Blades 7D & 8D; distributor 3-wire connector	400-800 ohms
	Resistance (key off)	Blade 7D & ground; distributor 3-wire connector	Over 70,000 ohms
	Resistance (key off)	Blade 8D & ground; distributor 3-wire connector	Over 70,000 ohms
Control Voltages to Module	Voltage (key on)	Socket No. 3 & ground; module 4-wire connector	Battery voltage minus 0.4-volt
	Voltage (cranking)	Socket No. 1 & ground; module 4-wire connector	Battery cranking voltage minus 0.4-volt
Primary Circuit Ground	Resistance (key off)	Socket No. 6 & ground; module 3-wire connector	0 ohms
	Resistance (key off)	Blade 6D & ground; distributor 3-wire connector	0 ohms
Coil and Coil-to-Module Wiring	Resistance (key off)	Socket 4 & socket 5; module 3-wire connector	1.0 to 2.0 ohms
	Resistance (key off)	Socket 4 and DEC terminal of coil; module 3-wire connector	1.0 to 2.0 ohms
	Resistance (key off)	DEC terminal & BATT terminal of coil	1.0 to 2.0 ohms
	Resistance (key off)	DEC terminal and tower of coil	7000-13,000 ohms

FIG. 4-40   1974 SOLID STATE DIAGNOSIS SUMMARY

FIG. 4-45   CONTROL VOLTAGE TO MODULE TEST, PART B

12. If resistance continues to read outside specifications, connect No. 1 ohmmeter lead to the coil DEC terminal and the other to the coil tower. Meter should read 7000 to 13,000 ohms (coil secondary resistance). If the reading is not within specifications, remove the coil for further tests on a coil tester, and replace if test shows it faulty.

13. If coil tests are satisfactory in Step 12, replace the module.

14. Before reconnecting the connectors, dip both sides of each in Lubriplate D.S. or equivalent. The connectors should be completely filled with this grease, then plugged together, and any surplus lubricant wiped from their outside.

1975-76 TEST PROCEDURES (Figs. 4-46 & 4-47)

Refer to **Fig. 4-48** for 1975 test procedure sequence, and **Fig. 4-49** for 1976 test procedure sequence. The first column indicates the connections to be tested, the second column provides the correct meter readings. Further diagnostic tests are specified in column three if meter readings do not agree with column two. Procedures for these additional tests are provided below.

MODULE BIAS TEST

1. Connect one voltmeter lead to Socket #4 and the other to a good engine ground. Turn the ignition switch on. The meter should read battery voltage. If not, repair the voltage feed wiring to the module for running conditions.

BATTERY SOURCE TEST

1. Connect the voltmeter leads from the coil BAT terminal to engine ground without disconnecting the coil.

2. Connect a jumper lead from the coil DEC terminal to ground.

3. Turn off all the lights and accessories and turn on the ignition switch.

4. If the voltmeter reading is between 4.9 and 7.9 volts, the primary circuit from battery to coil is good.

5. If the voltmeter reading is less than 4.9 volts check the primary wiring.

6. If the voltmeter reading is greater than 7.9 volts, replace the resistance wire.

CRANKING TEST

1. Connect one voltmeter lead to Socket #5 and the other to a good engine ground, then crank the engine. If the voltage is not between 8 and 12 volts, repair the voltage feed to the module for starting condition.

STARTING CIRCUIT TEST

1. Connect a jumper lead from Socket #1 to Socket #8, connect voltmeter leads to Socket #1 and Socket #6, then crank the engine. If reading is less than 6 volts, the ignition bypass circuit is open or

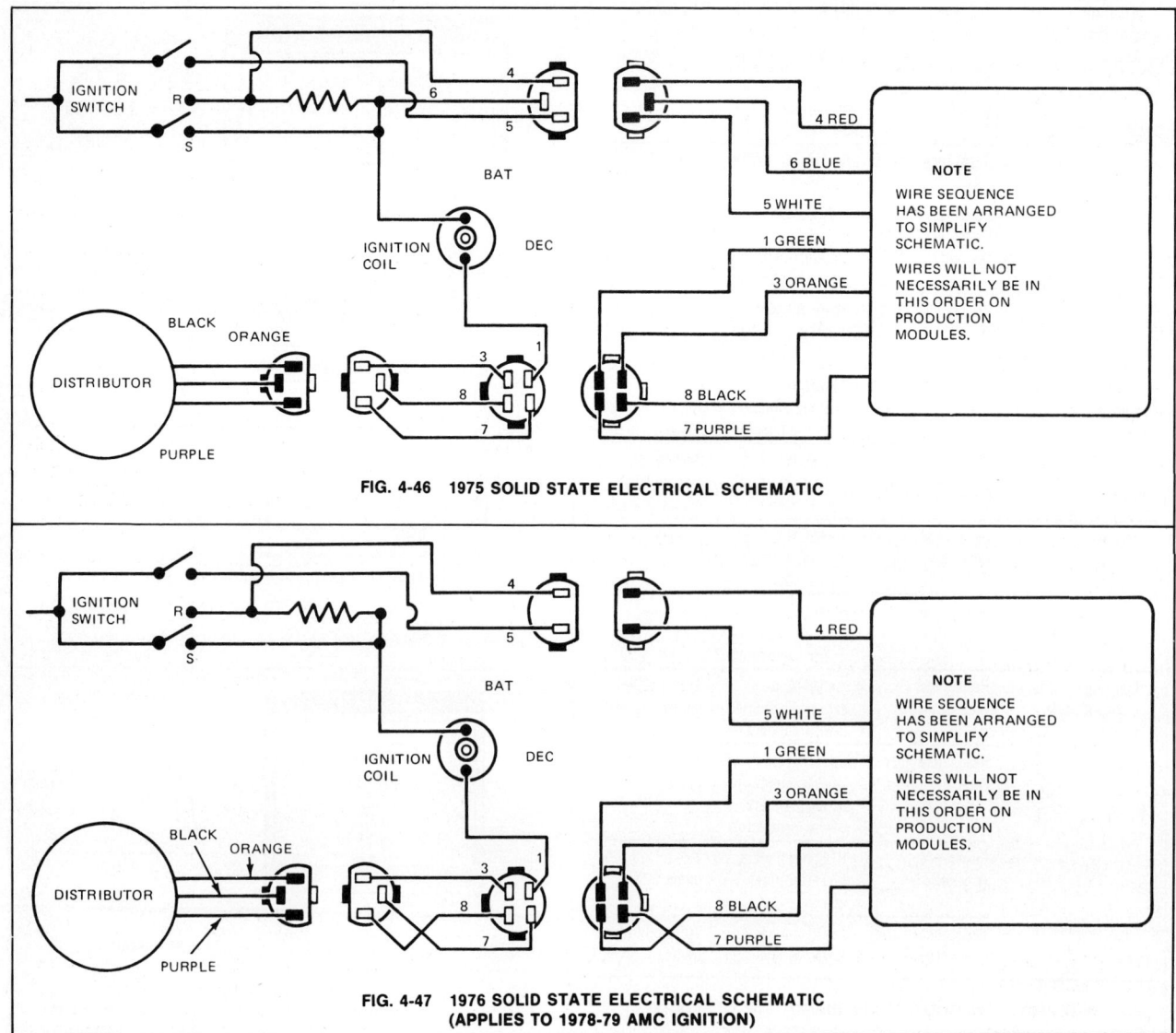

FIG. 4-46 1975 SOLID STATE ELECTRICAL SCHEMATIC

FIG. 4-47 1976 SOLID STATE ELECTRICAL SCHEMATIC
(APPLIES TO 1978-79 AMC IGNITION)

grounded from either the ignition switch or starter sole-noid to Socket #5 or the primary connection at the coil. Determine which and repair.

DISTRIBUTOR HARDWARE TEST

1. Disconnect the three-wire connector at the distributor pigtail.
2. Set the voltmeter on the 2.5-volt scale and connect it to the two parallel blades.
3. When the engine is cranked, the meter needle should wiggle.
4. If the needle does not move, remove the distributor cap and check for a loose armature, missing roll pin or a broken stator.
5. If the hardware is good, replace the magnetic pickup assembly.

MAGNETIC PICKUP TEST

1. Connect an ohmmeter lead to the two parallel blades in the distributor connector. The meter should indicate 400 to 800 ohms resistance.
2. Connect one ohmmeter lead to the third blade (ground) and the other to the distributor bowl. Meter should read zero ohms.
3. Connect one lead to either parallel blade and the other to a good engine ground. Meter should read 70,000 ohms or more.
4. If any of the above steps do not measure to specifications, replace stator assembly and repeat Steps 1-3.
5. If the readings are still not to specifications, replace the harness.

IGNITION COIL TEST

1. Connect one ohmmeter lead to Socket #4 and the other to the coil tower. Meter should read 7000 to 13,000 ohms (coil secondary resistance).
2. Connect the ohmmeter leads to Socket #1 and Pin #6. Meter should read between 1.0 and 2.0 ohms (coil primary resistance).

SHORT TEST

1. Connect the ohmmeter leads to Pin #5 and engine ground. Meter should read 4 ohms or more. If the reading is less than 4 ohms, check for a short to ground at the coil DEC terminal or in the primary wiring to the coil.

TROUBLESHOOTING INTERMITTENT IGNITION PROBLEMS

Electronic ignitions are prone to developing intermittent operational problems—they won't work correctly for you but when a serviceman takes a look, everything runs fine. A few miles down the road out of his sight and your misery returns. This can be frustrating, to say nothing of the inconvenience caused by repeated trips to the service bay with no apparent solution. Most causes of intermittent operation develop in one of three areas: the wiring, module or pickup coil. To help you recreate the problem so that diagnostic procedures will locate the ignition problem, follow the steps listed:

1. Start the engine and systematically wiggle the wires at the coil, distributor and harness connectors. Try disconnecting/reconnecting the wiring connectors.
2. Hold a 250-watt heat lamp an inch or two from the module for several minutes. Apply a few drops of water to the module housing every minute or so; when the water drops begin to boil, remove the heat to prevent module damage.
3. Try tapping the module gently.
4. Shut off the engine, remove the distributor cap

	TEST VOLTAGE BETWEEN	SHOULD BE	IF NOT, CONDUCT
Key On	Socket #4 and Engine Ground	Battery Voltage ± 0.1-Volt	Module Bias Test
	Socket #1 and Engine Ground	Battery Voltage ± 0.1-Volt	Battery Source Test
Cranking	Socket #5 and Engine Ground	8-12 Volts	Cranking Test
	Jumper #1 to #8 Read #6	More Than 6 Volts	Starting Circuit Test
	Pin #7 and Pin #3	0.5-Volt Minimum AC or Any DC Volt Wiggle	Distributor Hardware Test

	TEST VOLTAGE BETWEEN	SHOULD BE	IF NOT, CONDUCT
Key Off	Socket #7 and #3	400-800 Ohms	Magnetic Pickup (Stator) Test
	Socket #8 and Engine Ground	0 Ohms	
	Socket #7 and Engine Ground	More Than 70,000 Ohms	
	Socket #3 and Engine Ground	More Than 70,000 Ohms	
	Socket #4 and Coil Tower	7000-13,000 Ohms	Coil Test
	Socket #1 and Pin #6	1.0-2.0 Ohms	
	Socket #1 and Engine Ground	More Than 4.0 Ohms	Short Test
	Socket #4 and Pin #6	1.0-2.0 Ohms	Resistance Wire Test

FIG. 4-48 1975 PRIMARY TEST SEQUENCE

	TEST VOLTAGE BETWEEN	SHOULD BE	IF NOT, CONDUCT
Key On	Socket #4 and Engine Ground	Battery Voltage ± 0.1-Volt	Battery Source Test
	Socket #1 and Engine Ground	Battery Voltage ± 0.1-Volt	Battery Source Test
Cranking	Socket #5 and Engine Ground	8-12 Volts	Check Supply Circuit (Starting) Through Ignition Switch
	Jumper #1 to #8 Read #6	More Than 6 Volts	Starting Circuit Test
	Pin #3 and Pin #8	0.5-Volt Minimum AC or Any DC Volt Wiggle	Distributor Hardware Test

	TEST VOLTAGE BETWEEN	SHOULD BE	IF NOT, CONDUCT
Key Off	Socket #8 and #3	400-800 Ohms	Magnetic Pickup (Stator) Test
	Socket #7 and Engine Ground	0 Ohms	
	Socket #8 and Engine Ground	More Than 70,000 Ohms	
	Socket #3 and Engine Ground	More Than 70,000 Ohms	
	Socket #4 and Coil Tower	7000-13,000 Ohms	Coil Test
	Socket #1 and Engine Ground	More Than 4.0 Ohms	Short Test

FIG. 4-49 1976 PRIMARY TEST SEQUENCE

and disconnect the distributor connector. Use the heat lamp to warm the stator pickup coil by holding it an inch or two away from the coil. Check the continuity between the parallel blades of the disconnected distributor connector. Resistance should range between 400-1000 ohms. An infinity reading indicates an open circuit; a reading under 400 ohms indicates a short circuit.

5. Try tapping the pickup coil lightly with a screwdriver handle. One of these methods should provide a clue to the nature of your problem.

DISTRIBUTOR REMOVAL—V-8 ENGINE

1. Disconnect the distributor wiring connector from the main wiring harness.

2. Remove the distributor cap with wires intact and place to one side.

3. Disconnect the vacuum advance line at the distributor.

4. Scribe a mark on the distributor housing and one on the engine block to indicate the rotor/distributor and distributor/block positions for use when reinstalling the distributor.

5. Remove the distributor hold-down bolt and clamp.

6. Lift the distributor from the engine block.

DISTRIBUTOR REMOVAL: I-4, I-6 AND V-6 ENGINES

1. Remove the air cleaner on V-6 engines.

2. Remove one Thermactor-pump mounting bolt and the drive belt on I-4 and I-6 engines. Swing the pump to one side and disconnect the Thermactor air filter and lines.

3. Rotate the crankshaft to position the timing mark on the crankshaft damper with the timing pointer.

4. Remove the distributor cap and make sure the rotor and armature are lined up with the index mark located on the top of the magnetic pickup and the marks on the distributor housing **(Fig. 4-50)**.

5. Disconnect the vacuum advance line(s) from the distributor and ignition lead from the wiring harness.

6. Remove the distributor hold-down bolt and distributor from the engine block. If the hex shaft which rotates the oil pump sticks in the distributor shaft, withdraw it from the pump.

DISTRIBUTOR DISASSEMBLY: V-8 ENGINES (Fig. 4-51)

1. Remove the distributor cap and rotor.

2. Use a small gear puller or two screwdrivers to lift or pry the armature from the advance plate sleeve.

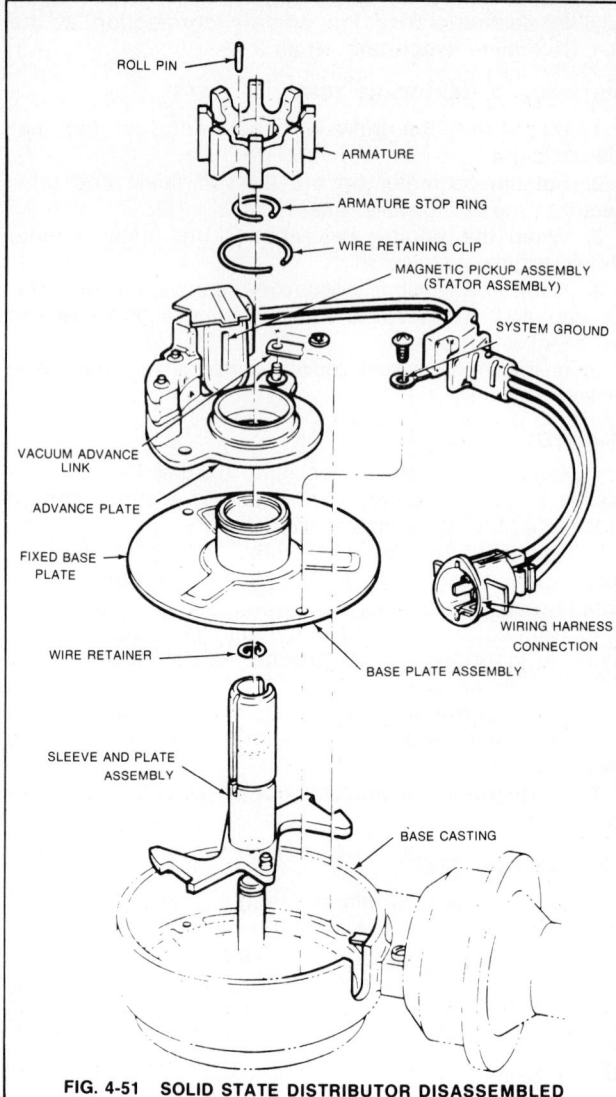

FIG. 4-51   SOLID STATE DISTRIBUTOR DISASSEMBLED

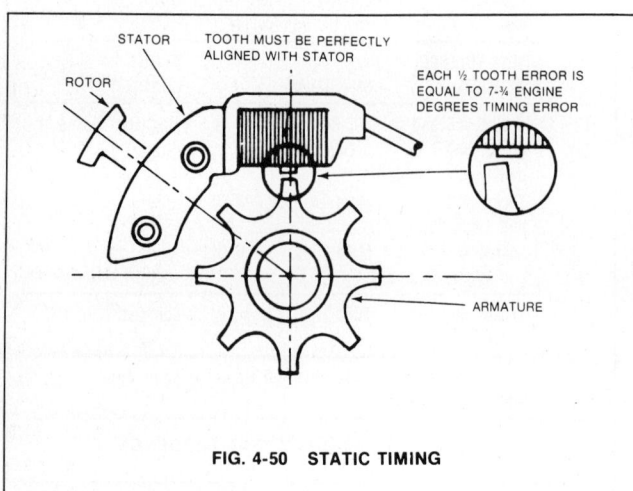

FIG. 4-50   STATIC TIMING

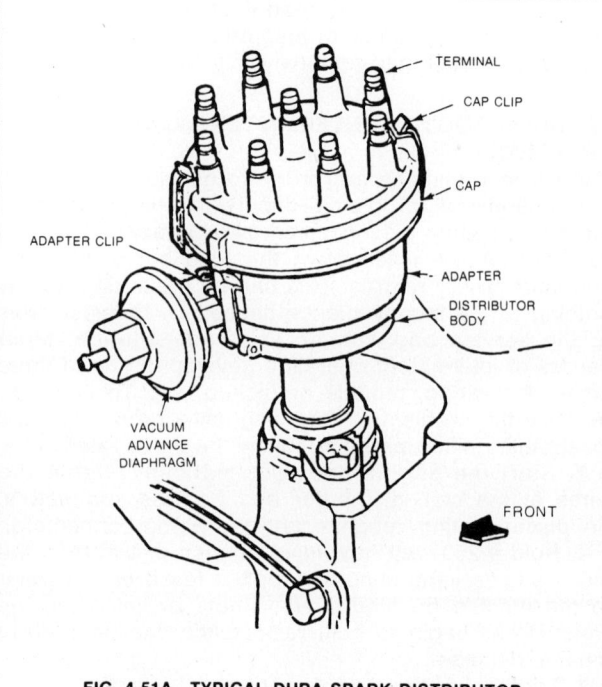

FIG. 4-51A   TYPICAL DURA SPARK DISTRIBUTOR

3. Remove the armature roll pin, armature stop ring and wire retaining clip.

4. Remove the snap ring holding the vacuum advance linkage to the stator assembly.

5. Remove the system ground screw and lift the wiring plug out of housing slot.

6. Lift the vacuum advance arm (or link) from the stator assembly, moving it out against the distributor housing.

7. Remove the fixed-base-plate screw and lift the plate from the distributor.

8. Remove the distributor-shaft wire-retainer clip, disconnect the advance weight springs and remove springs and weights.

9. Lift the sleeve-and-plate assembly from the distributor shaft.

10. If drive gear replacement is required, support the shaft and use a suitable drift and hammer to tap out the roll pin.

DISTRIBUTOR DISASSEMBLY: I-4, I-6 AND V-6 ENGINES

Disassembly procedure is similar to the V-8, mentioned earlier, except that the stator assembly is permanently mounted to the base plate assembly and is removed/serviced as a single unit.

DISTRIBUTOR ASSEMBLY—ALL MODELS

1. Replace the drive gear on the distributor shaft and install the roll pin.

2. Replace the sleeve-and-plate assembly on the distributor shaft.

3. Position the advance weights and replace the springs. Install the wire retainer clip in the distributor shaft.

4. Replace the base-plate/stator assembly and install the vacuum advance arm over the connecting post. Install the snap ring over the advance arm.

5. Slide the wiring grommet into the slot at the edge of the lower plate and install the ground screw.

6. Replace the retaining and snap rings.

7. Replace the armature on the advance plate sleeve, pressing it into position. Install the roll pin.

8. Replace the rotor and distributor cap.

DISTRIBUTOR INSTALLATION—ALL MODELS

1. Make sure the engine was not cranked while the distributor was removed. If it was, time the engine as follows:

   a) Rotate the crankshaft until the No. 1 piston is on top dead center (TDC) after the compression stroke.

   b) Align the initial timing mark on the timing pointer with the timing pointer on the crankshaft damper.

2. If the engine was not cranked, align the rotor/distributor and distributor/block marks and lower the distributor into the engine block. Make sure the oil-pump intermediate shaft engages the distributor shaft properly on V-8 models. If the oil-pump drive shaft was removed on I-4, I-6 and V-6 models, coat one end of the shaft with heavy grease and insert it into the distributor-shaft hex hole, then replace the distributor in the engine block.

3. Install the distributor hold-down clamp and bolt.

4. Reconnect the vacuum line(s) and wiring harness.

5. Replace the Thermactor belt on I-4 and I-6 engines, and adjust to specifications. Connect all Thermactor hoses and filters.

6. Replace the air cleaner on V-6 engines.

7. Check and adjust initial timing to specifications.

MOTORCRAFT-FORD SOLID STATE IGNITION

Primary Resistance @ 75° F	1.0-2.0 Ohms
Secondary Resistance @ 75° F	7000-13,000 Ohms
Primary Circuit Resistor: Resistance @ 75° F	1.30-1.40 Ohms

AMC Solid State Ignition

Primary Resistance	1.13 to 1.23 ohms
Secondary Resistance	7700 to 9300 ohms
Open Circuit Output	20 KV Minimum
Distributor Sensor	400 to 800 ohms

1977-79 FORD MOTOR COMPANY ENGINES

Dura Spark I, II, III

SYSTEM DESCRIPTION

Two variations of the 1976 Solid-State Ignition were introduced on 1977 Ford engines. Dura Spark I is used on all 1977 California engines except the 2.3L, and all 1978 California engines except the Versailles 302-cu.-in. V-8. Dura Spark II is used on all other 1977-78 Ford engines except the Versailles 302 cid. Both Dura Spark systems use the same distributor, **Fig. 4-51A.**

Dura Spark I is essentially a higher energy system to cope with California emissions laws. It features an all-new electronic control module and a new coil. Since there is an energy increase, Dura Spark I also has special primary wiring, a new distributor cap and adapter, high-energy secondary wiring and wide-gap spark plugs. In operation, Dura Spark I senses current flow through the coil and adjusts for maximum spark intensity according to engine rpm. If the module senses that the ignition switch is ON and the distributor is not turning, coil current shuts off automatically after about one second. When this occurs, the key must be turned to the START or OFF position, then ON again.

Dura Spark II uses a ballast resistor value of 1.10 instead of 1.35 ohms to boost energy output and the Dura Spark I rotor, distributor cap and adapter, new secondary wiring and wide-gap spark plugs. The Dura Spark II amplifier works differently from that used with Dura Spark I. The amplifier module and the coil are ON when the ignition switch is ON. Because of this, the ignition system will generate a spark when the switch is turned OFF. It is recommended that the ignition switch remain OFF during any underhood work. Just removing the distributor cap with the ignition switch ON may cause the system to fire.

With some Dura Spark II applications, the module incorporates either altitude compensation or economy modes. This permits the module to modify basic engine timing according to altitude/engine load conditions, **Fig. 4-51B.**

A cranking retard feature is incorporated for 1979 in Dura Spark II ignitions used with all non-California, non-turbocharged 2.3L engines fitted with automatic transmissions. During engine cranking, the slow rpm signal of the distributor magnetic pickup actuates a new circuit in the ignition module to retard crank timing by 18°. The ignition module used with this system can be identified by the use of a *white* 4-pin connector and a *white* wiring grommet located at the base of the module. It is not interchangeable with other FoMoCo ignition modules.

Dura Spark III is fitted to all 1979 non-California 351-W engines equipped with EEC II. It uses the same electronic control distributor as the 1978-79 Lincoln Versailles (**Fig. 4-51E**). The ignition module contains fewer circuits; those removed from the module are now located in the EEC II electronic control assembly (ECA). The Dura Spark III module can be identified by the *brown* wiring grommet at the base of the module, and is not interchangeable with other FoMoCo modules.

SERVICE AND TESTING

Dura Spark I and Dura Spark II systems, **Fig. 4-51C**, are basically the same as the 1976 Solid-State Ignition. Service and testing procedures remain the same as for 1976—**see page 4-15.**

When a distributor rotor must be replaced, the brass electrode tip on non-EEC rotors and the twin brass blades on EEC rotors (**Fig. 4-51E**) should be coated with Dow III silicon grease or G.E. G-627 compound. Apply this coating approximately 1/32-in. thick. EEC

distributor caps have a brass crosshatch surface which must be coated with the same materials.

DUAL MODE IGNITION DIAGNOSIS

The dual mode timing feature used on some 1978 and later Ford, Lincoln and Mercury models is accomplished by a special ignition module with additional circuits and a 3-wire pigtail, which connects to either a vacuum switch or a barometric pressure switch. Calibration of the distributor provides basic timing; the module provides a retard mode when required.

1. Disconnect the vacuum or pressure switch connector and check initial timing in the usual manner. If the timing is to specifications as shown on the emissions decal, the problem is not caused by the dual mode module or switch.

2. Reconnect the switch and check ignition timing again for altitude application, if fitted with the pressure switch. Timing should be as specified on the emissions decal, minus 3-6° at altitudes up to 4300 ft.

3. To check for performance application, disconnect the vacuum switch line and connect a hand vacuum pump to the switch. When more than 10 ins. of vacuum are applied, basic timing should be to specifications; less than 6 ins. should put the timing at 3-6° less than specified.

4. If timing is not correct when Steps 2 or 3 are performed, substitute a new switch and repeat Steps 2 or 3 as required.

5. If this does not correct the problem, replace the original switch and substitute a new dual mode module.

ELECTRONIC ENGINE CONTROL (EEC) SYSTEM

The Lincoln Versailles uses an electronic engine control (EEC) system to control ignition timing, EGR flow

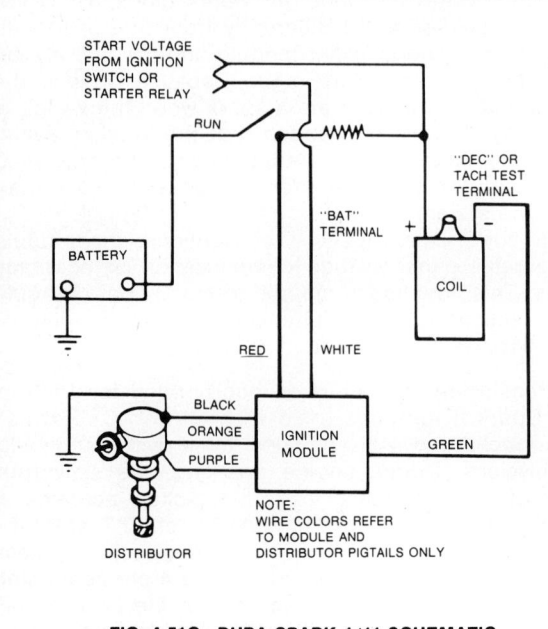

FIG. 4-51B DUAL MODE TIMING SCHEMATIC

FIG. 4-51C DURA SPARK 1/11 SCHEMATIC

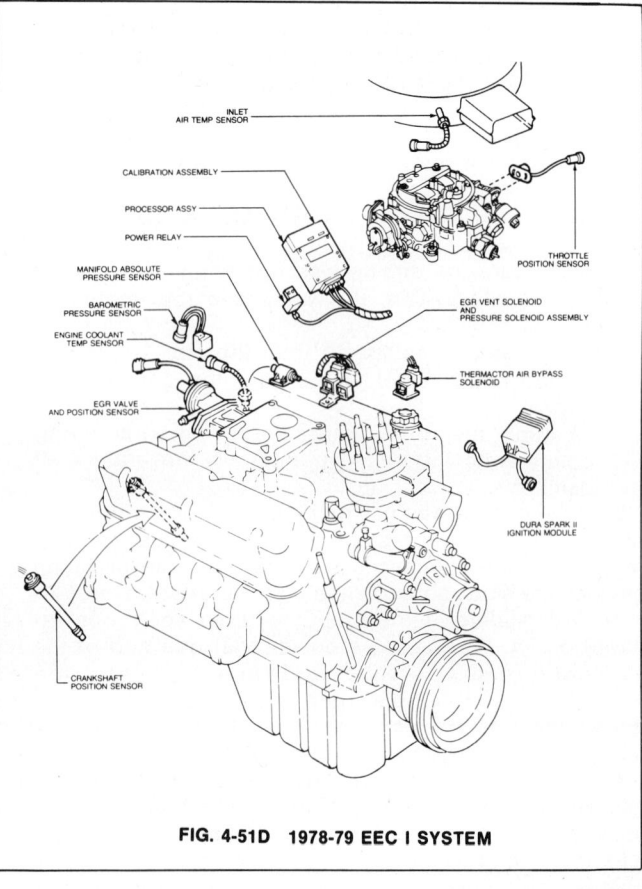

FIG. 4-51D 1978-79 EEC I SYSTEM

rate and Thermactor air-flow. This system consists of an Electronic Control Assembly (ECA), seven sensors, a Dura Spark II ignition module/coil, an air pressure operated EGR system, and a modified distributor assembly, **Fig. 4-51D.** Since all ignition timing is controlled by the ECA, the EEC distributor does not contain conventional mechanical or vacuum advance mechanisms.

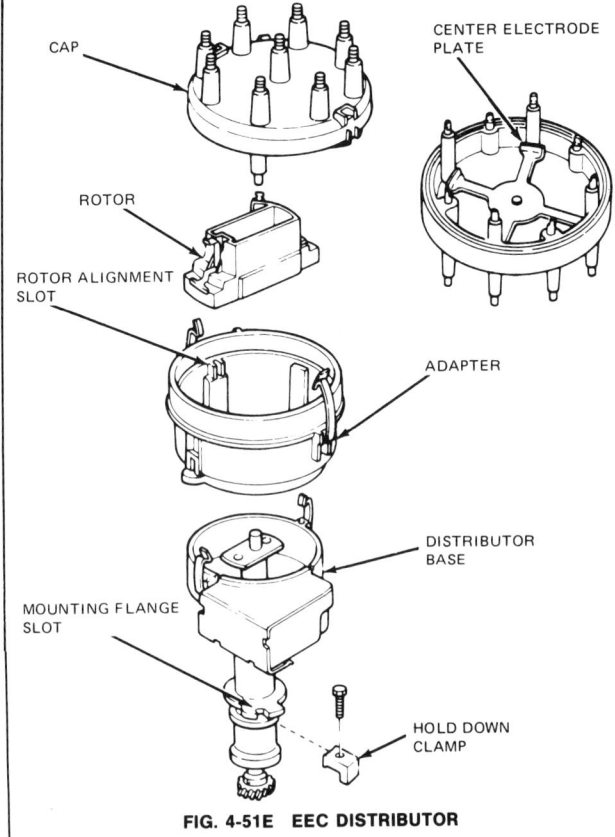

FIG. 4-51E EEC DISTRIBUTOR

The EEC distributor rotor/cap electrodes use a two-level design, **Fig. 4-51E,** to provide advance capability from TDC to 60° BTDC. As the rotor turns, one of its high-voltage pickup arms aligns with a spoke of the center electrode plate in the distributor cap. This allows high voltage to travel from the plate to the appropriate spark plug.

The distributor cap has two sets of numbers molded into its top. The inner ring is used with the Versailles 302 cid: the outer ring will be used with later model 351/400-cu.-in. applications. For this reason, the Versailles 302-cu.-in. spark plug wires are *not* connected to the cap in their actual firing order (1-5-4-2-6-3-7-8).

With the appearance of the EEC II system on 1979 California Ford and non-California Mercury vehicles using the 351-W engine, the original EEC system is redesignated as EEC I. All 1979 non-California Lincoln Versailles using the 302-cu.-in. engine use the EEC I system with the addition of a dual-mode ignition module **(Fig. 4-51B).** EEC II differs from EEC I in that it includes the canister purge function and incorporates a feedback carburetor and three-way catalyst.

The EEC II system consists of an Electronic Control Assembly (ECA), seven sensors, a series of control solenoids, and a vacuum-operated EGR and Thermactor air system **(Fig. 4-51F).** The 1979 EEC II system also uses the 7200 VV feedback carburetor equipped with a controllable air/fuel mixture, an oxygen sensor located in the exhaust manifold to provide a "rich/lean" signal to the ECA, a 4-lobe pulse ring integral with the crankshaft damper, and a crankshaft position (CP) sensor connected to the timing bracket pointer.

EEC SERVICE AND DIAGNOSIS

The EEC distributor is factory-installed in such a way as to prevent movement of the assembly. No adjustment is necessary, as the ECA controls all changes in timing.

Two special diagnostic test units are required to troubleshoot the EEC system: an EEC Diagnostic Tester (T78L-50-EEC-1) and a Digital Volt/Ohmmeter (DVOM) (T78L-50-DVOM). These are both available from Owatonna Tool Co., Owatonna, Minnesota, Attn: Ford Order Desk.

Different test equipment is required for the EEC II system: the Rotunda T79L-50-DVOM Digital Volt-Ohm

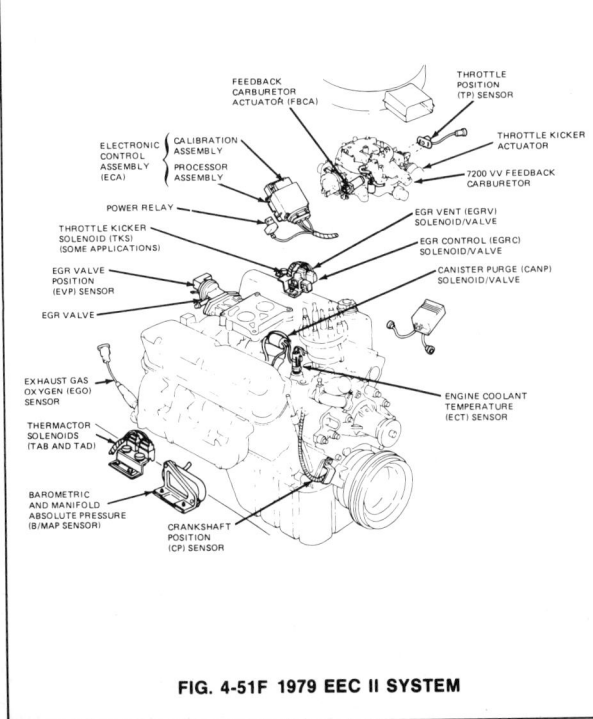

FIG. 4-51F 1979 EEC II SYSTEM

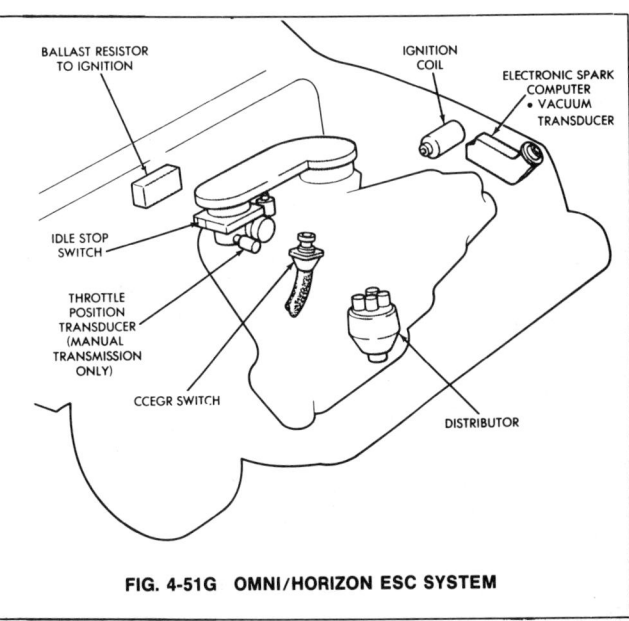

FIG. 4-51G OMNI/HORIZON ESC SYSTEM

Meter and the Rotunda T79L-50-EEC II Diagnostic Tester. These are available from Ford Motor Company.

Once the engine has warmed up to normal operating temperature, it may not restart after being shut down. This hot engine restart problem is usually due to an intermittent short or open—in either the crankshaft sensor or its wiring harness. If the wiring harness tests out satisfactorily, check the sensor resistance when hot. It should range between 100-550 ohms; if not, replace the sensor.

An intermittent or complete loss of ignition may be caused by a poor ground at the power relay attached to the ECA. The two hex-headed screws holding the relay in place provide the ground and should be retorqued to 30-60 in.-lbs. This will usually solve the problem.

DURA SPARK I, II SPECIFICATIONS

	I	II
Primary Resistance (Ohms)	.71-.77	1.13-1.23
Secondary Resistance (Ohms)	7350-8250	7700-9300
Primary Circuit Ballast Resistor (Ohms)	None	1.05-1.15
Rotor Air Gap Voltage Drop (Kv Max.)	8.0	8.0

CHRYSLER CORPORATION I-4 ENGINES ELECTRONIC IGNITION SYSTEM

SYSTEM DESCRIPTION

The electronic ignition fitted to Omni/Horizon I-4 engines is an integral part of the Electronic Spark Control (ESC) system, **(Fig. 4-51G),** and differs considerably from the Chrysler Electronic Ignition used on I-6 and V-8 engines. The distributor contains a Hall Effect Pickup Assembly, which tells the ESC module when to fire the spark plugs. There is no advance mechanism within the distributor, and since the Hall Effect Pickup Assembly is permanently mounted, only a fixed amount of advance is available in the ignition system during the START mode. Once the engine starts, the RUN mode takes over, and the amount of advance is now determined by the ESC—according to data received from the sensors. For further information on the operation and testing of the Omni/Horizon ESC system, see the 1976-79 Chrysler Emission Systems sections of the Emission Controls chapter.

The ignition coil uses an external ballast resistor, **(Fig. 4-51H),** which must be included in any coil tests. The ballast resistor is a compensating resistance in the ignition primary circuit. High resistance during low-speed operation reduces voltage in the primary ignition

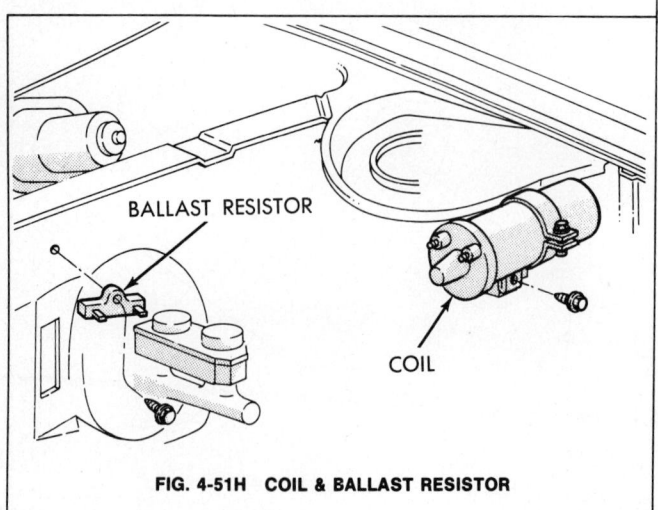

FIG. 4-51H   COIL & BALLAST RESISTOR

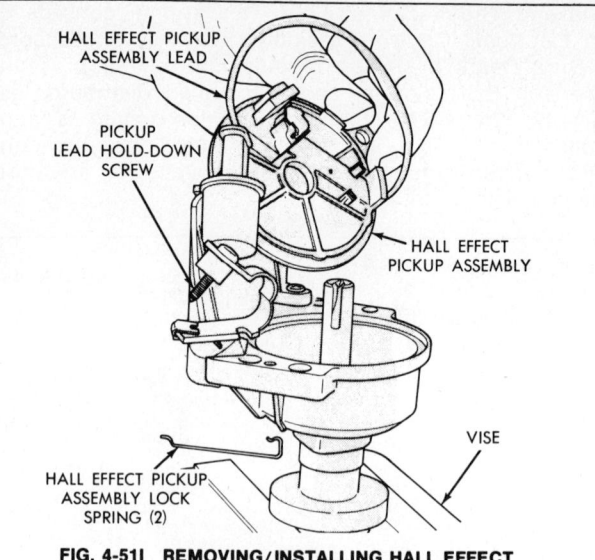

FIG. 4-51I   REMOVING/INSTALLING HALL EFFECT PICKUP ASSEMBLY

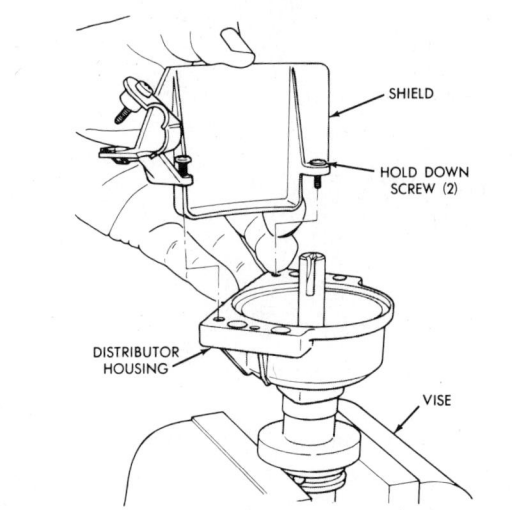

FIG. 4-51J   REMOVING/INSTALLING DISTRIBUTOR SHIELD

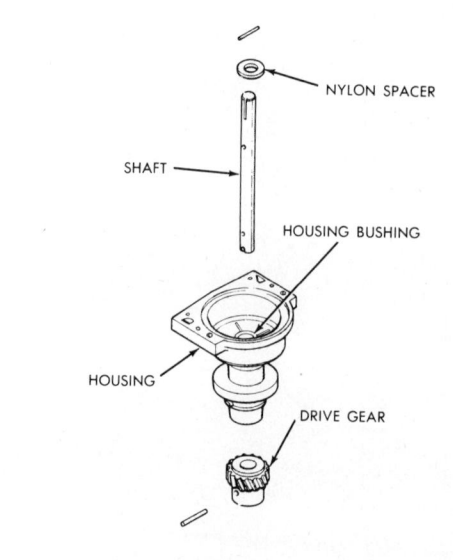

FIG. 4-51K   DISTRIBUTOR HOUSING AND SHAFT

circuit to protect the coil. As engine rpm increases, resistance decreases and voltage in the primary circuit increases. The ballast resistor is bypassed during starting to permit full battery voltage to the primary circuit. The distributor cap is retained to the housing by two hold-down screws, and a special press-on rotor is used. For removal and replacement of the distributor, see Distributor Procedures under the following section: "Chrysler Corporation I-6/V-8 Engines."

DISTRIBUTOR OVERHAUL

1. Remove the distributor cap and pull the rotor from the distributor shaft.

2. Remove the pickup lead screw and two lock springs, then lift out the pickup assembly **(Fig. 4-51I).**

3. Remove the shield from the distributor housing **(Fig. 4-51J).**

4. Mark the position of the drive gear on the distributor shaft. Support the drive gear and drive out the roll pin with a punch.

5. Slip the drive gear of the end of the shaft and separate the shaft from the housing **(Fig. 4-51K).**

6. To reassemble, reverse the above procedure.

CHRYSLER CORPORATION I-6/V-8 ENGINES ELECTRONIC IGNITION SYSTEM

SYSTEM DESCRIPTION

Introduced as an option on some 1972 Chrysler Corporation engines and provided as standard equipment the following year, the Chrysler Electronic Ignition system **(Fig. 4-52)** consists of:

1. Battery.
2. Ignition switch.
3. Dual ballast resistor.
4. Electronic control unit.
5. Coil.
6. Distributor.
7. Wiring, insulator and connectors.

The primary ignition circuit includes:

1. Battery.
2. Ignition switch.
3. Compensating (0.5-ohm) side of ballast resistor.
4. Primary coil windings.
5. Electronic-control unit with power-switching transistor.
6. Car frame.

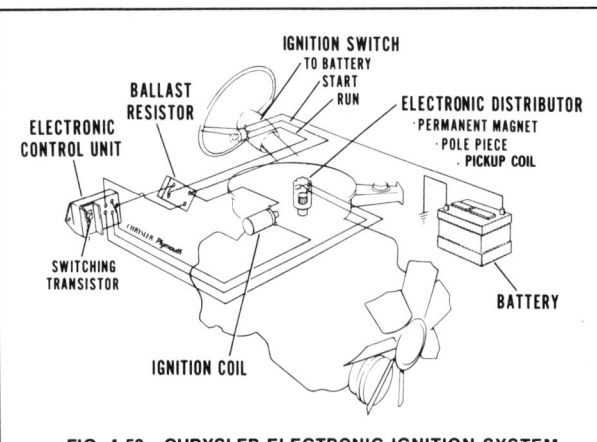

FIG. 4-52 CHRYSLER ELECTRONIC IGNITION SYSTEM

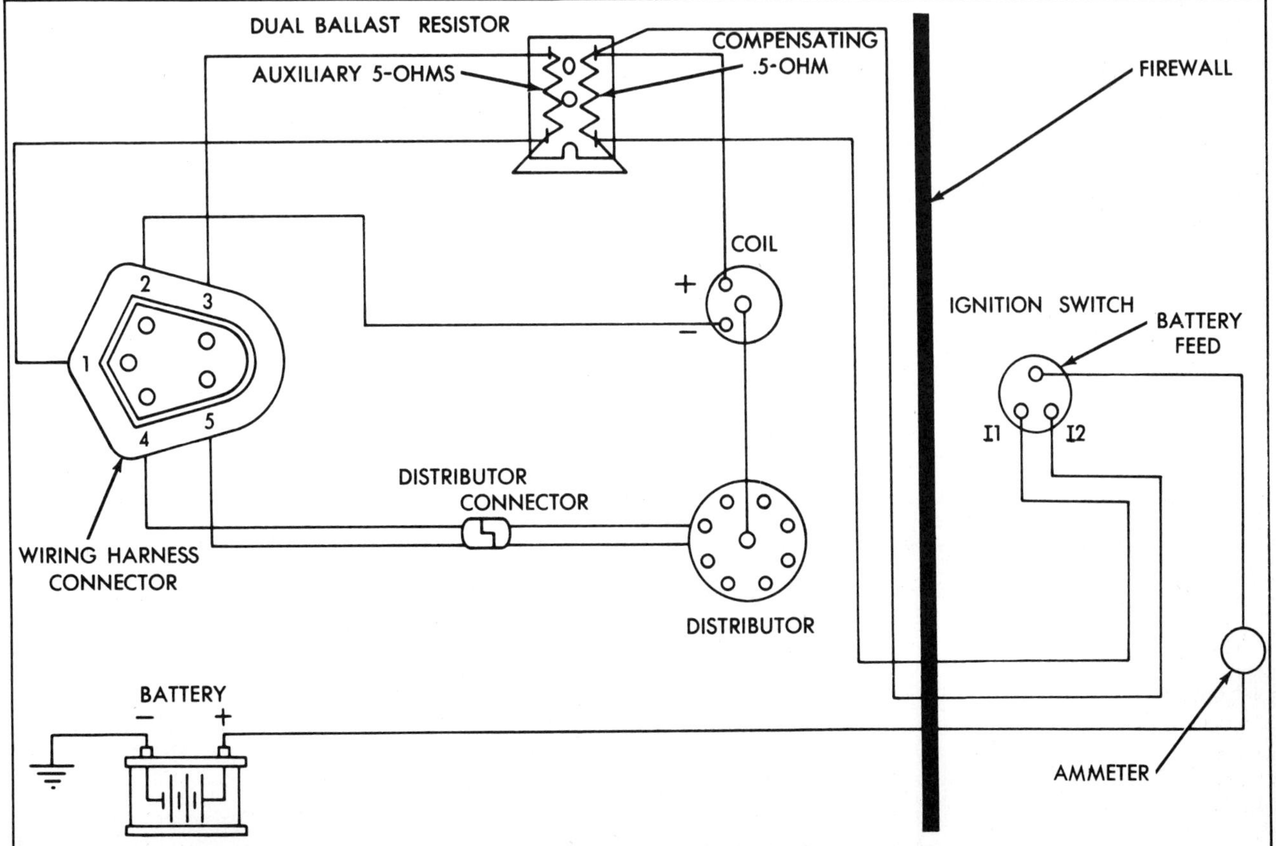

FIG. 4-54 CHRYSLER ELECTRONIC IGNITION CIRCUIT DIAGRAM

The secondary ignition circuit is unchanged from that of the conventional Chrysler ignition system.

NOTE: For Chrysler Corporation I-6 and V-8 engines equipped with the Electronic Lean Burn/Electronic Spark Control System, refer to the Chrysler section of the "Emission Controls" chapter.

DISTRIBUTOR

Chrysler's electronic ignition distributor is very similar in external appearance to that of its conventional breaker-point distributor; in fact, the distributor housing, cap, rotor and advance mechanism are the same. The difference is noted after removing the distributor cap and rotor. The cam and breaker points have been replaced by a toothed reluctor and a magnetic pickup-coil assembly. Gear-like in appearance, the reluctor is attached to the distributor shaft and has one tooth for each cylinder in the engine—six teeth for 6-cyl. engines and eight teeth for 8-cyl. engines. The pickup device is mounted to the breaker plate and contains a pickup coil, pole piece and permanent magnet.

A normally weak magnetic field created by the permanent magnet is strengthened when a reluctor tooth rotates into alignment with the pole piece. This induces a positive voltage in the pickup coil which signals the electronic control unit to cut off primary current flow in the coil. As primary current flow is cut off, the primary field collapses and induces high voltage in the coil secondary, which is sent to the proper spark plug. As the reluctor tooth rotates away from the pole piece, pickup coil voltage becomes negative and the electronic control unit switches primary current back on. This rapid increase and decrease of the magnetic field creates the tiny electrical impulses which trigger the switching transistor in the control unit to interrupt the flow of primary circuit current.

ELECTRONIC CONTROL UNIT

Mounted on the fenderwell or firewall, the electronic control unit contains the power switching transistor which controls primary current flow. The switching transistor is positioned on top of the control unit and should not be touched when the ignition switch is on, because it carries enough voltage to produce a nasty shock. Speed-limiter circuitry was contained in some pre-1973 control units to limit engine rpm. This single electronic control unit was replaced by three different ones, according to engine application, and identifiable by the color of the heat sink on their faces.

DUAL BALLAST RESISTOR

The compensating side of the dual ballast resistor maintains constant primary current with variation in engine speed. But during starting, this resistance is by-passed, allowing full battery voltage to be applied to the ignition coil. The auxiliary side protects the control unit by limiting voltage to the electronic part of the primary circuit.

PICKUP CIRCUIT

The pickup circuit senses the proper timing for the power switching transistor in the control unit. As the reluctor rotates with the distributor shaft, it produces a voltage pulse in the magnetic pickup each time a spark plug should be fired. This pulse passes through the pickup coil to the switching transistor, causing the transistor to interrupt primary-circuit current flow. This primary break induces a high voltage in the secondary coil circuit, which fires the spark plug. The time duration, when the switching transistor stops current flow in the primary circuit, is determined by the electronic circuitry in the control unit. This is what determines dwell, and why dwell is not adjustable.

The Chrysler system does not use a condenser, but a radio suppression capacitor was added in 1973 and mounted on the firewall near the dual ballast resistor.

TEST PROCEDURE

Chrysler recommends the use of its C-4166 tester unit with adaptors C-4166-1 or C-4166-A, but the system can also be tested with a voltmeter having a 20,000-ohm/volt rating and an ohmmeter using a 1½-volt battery for its operation. Both voltmeter and ohmmeter should be calibrated before use.

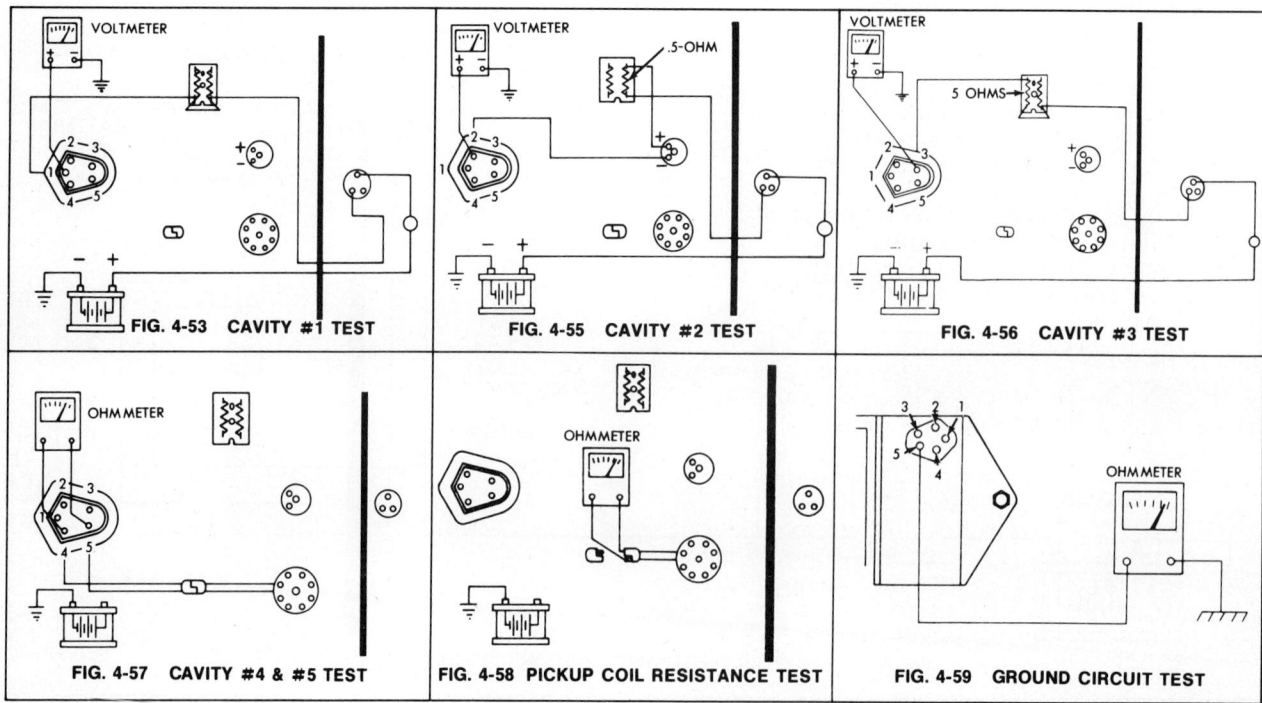

FIG. 4-53 CAVITY #1 TEST

FIG. 4-55 CAVITY #2 TEST

FIG. 4-56 CAVITY #3 TEST

FIG. 4-57 CAVITY #4 & #5 TEST

FIG. 4-58 PICKUP COIL RESISTANCE TEST

FIG. 4-59 GROUND CIRCUIT TEST

When ignition problems are present, visually check all secondary cables at the coil, distributor and spark plugs for cracks and proper connection. The secondary portion of the Chrysler ignition system is tested in the same manner as a conventional ignition. The following test sequences should be performed in the order listed. By the process of elimination, a new electronic control unit should be installed if everything else checks out good but the engine still misfires or refuses to start.

PRIMARY CIRCUIT CONTINUITY TEST

1. Inspect the primary wire at the ignition coil and ballast resistor for a tight connection.

2. Test the battery voltage with a voltmeter—voltage should be at least 12 volts.

3. Make sure that the ignition switch is in the OFF position, then disconnect the multi-wiring connector from the electronic control unit.

4. Turn the ignition switch to ON.

5. Connect the voltmeter negative lead to a good ground.

6. Connect the voltmeter positive lead to the No. 1 wiring-harness connector cavity **(Fig. 4-53)**. Available voltage at cavity No. 1 should come within 1 volt of the previous battery voltage reading (all accessories off). If more than a 1-volt difference exists, check the entire circuit shown in **Fig. 4-54**.

7. Repeat Step 6 with cavity No. 2. If the voltmeter reading differs from the battery voltage reading by more than 1 volt, check entire circuit as in **Fig. 4-55**.

8. Repeat Step 6 with cavity No. 3. If the voltmeter reading differs from the battery voltage reading by more than 1 volt, check entire circuit as in **Fig. 4-56**.

9. Turn the ignition switch off.

DISTRIBUTOR PICKUP COIL TEST

1. Make sure the ignition switch is off.

2. Connect an ohmmeter to the No. 4 and No. 5 wiring-harness connector cavities as shown in **Fig. 4-57**. The resistance reading should range between 150 and 900 ohms.

3. If the ohmmeter reading is outside this range, disconnect the distributor dual-lead connector and check the resistance **(Fig. 4-58)**. If the reading still is not within the specified range, replace the pickup coil.

4. Connect one ohmmeter lead to a good ground and the other to either connector of the distributor lead. Ohmmeter should show an open circuit; if it does give a reading, replace the pickup coil.

ELECTRONIC CONTROL GROUND CIRCUIT TEST

The electronic control unit is grounded to the firewall or fender panel by the two screws holding it. Engine vibration has a tendency to loosen these screws, causing a loss of ground.

1. Make sure the ignition switch is off.

2. Connect one ohmmeter lead to a good ground and the other to the control unit continuity pin No. 5, as shown in **Fig. 4-59**. The ohmmeter should show a zero reading.

3. If the ohmmeter does not show a zero reading, tighten the screws and retest. If the ohmmeter still gives a reading, remove the control unit and lightly file or sand the back of each attachment flange and the firewall/fender-panel area where the unit is attached.

4. Reinstall the control unit and retest. If the ohmmeter still gives a reading, replace the control unit.

AIR GAP CHECK/ADJUSTMENT (Fig. 4-60)

1. Align one reluctor tooth with the pickup coil tooth

and loosen the pickup-coil hold-down screw.

2. Insert an 0.008-in. *non-magnetic* feeler gauge between the pickup tooth and the reluctor tooth (1977 and later, 0.006-in).

3. With a screwdriver blade inserted in the air-gap adjustment slot, adjust the air gap until contact is made between the gauge and both teeth.

4. Tighten the hold-down screw and remove the feeler gauge. If force is required to remove the gauge, the air gap is incorrectly set.

5. Check the air gap setting with a 0.010 *non*-magnetic feeler gauge (1977 and later, 0.008-in.) This should not fit into the air gap, and *should not be forced to fit* into the air gap.

6. Apply vacuum to the vacuum advance unit and rotate the distributor shaft. The pickup pole should not hit the reluctor teeth. If hitting does occur, the air gap is incorrectly set. If hitting occurs on one side of the reluctor only, the distributor shaft is probably bent. Replace the governor and the shaft assembly.

A poor electrical connection between the distributor and the electronic control unit is a rather common cause of engine misfiring or failure to start. The dual lead connector should be checked for a perfectly tight, non-corroded fit, as well as for circuit continuity—a loose connection here will cause an intermittent miss or stumble that may not necessarily show up on a scope test.

If the problem does not show up during this test procedure, it is likely that either the control unit or coil is malfunctioning—both rarely fail at the same time. Before replacing the control unit, check that no foreign matter has lodged in or is blocking the female terminal cavities in the wiring harness connector. If this check proves clear, perform the test below to see whether a replacement control unit or coil will restore secondary voltage.

IGNITION SECONDARY/COIL TEST

1. Disconnect the high-voltage cable from the center coil tower.

2. Crank the engine, holding the high-voltage cable approximately 3/16-in. from it.

3. If arcing does not occur, replace the control unit.

4. After replacing the control unit, crank the engine again, holding the cable as in Step 2.

5. If arcing still does not occur, the control unit was good, but the coil should be replaced.

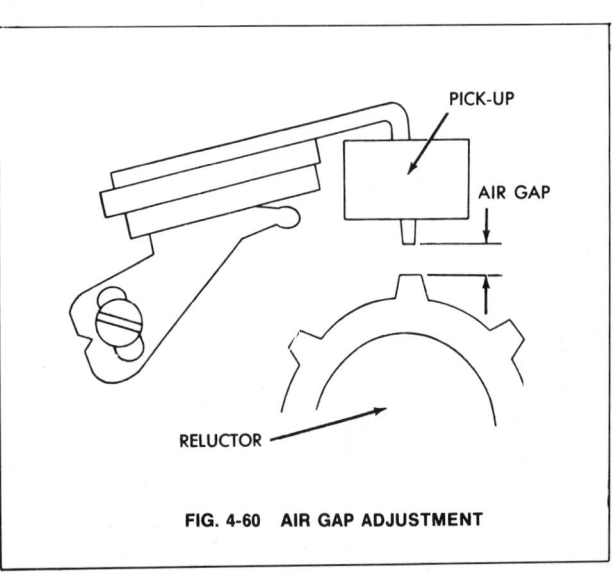

FIG. 4-60 AIR GAP ADJUSTMENT

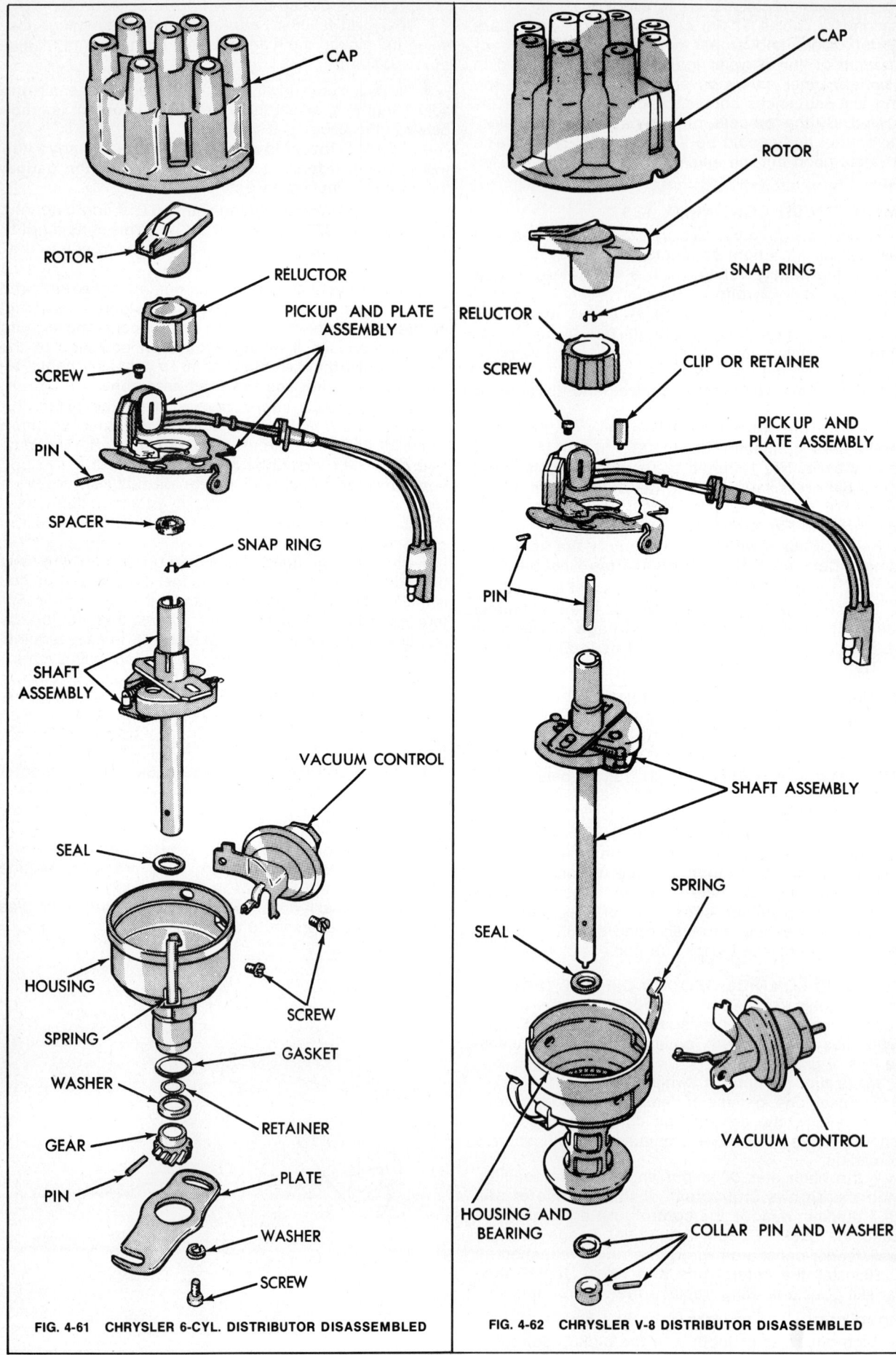

FIG. 4-61 CHRYSLER 6-CYL. DISTRIBUTOR DISASSEMBLED

FIG. 4-62 CHRYSLER V-8 DISTRIBUTOR DISASSEMBLED

DISTRIBUTOR SERVICE PROCEDURES

DISTRIBUTOR REMOVAL

1. Disconnect the vacuum lead at the distributor and the distributor-pickup lead wire at the wiring harness connector.

2. Unfasten retaining clips and remove the distributor cap.

3. Rotate the engine crankshaft until the distributor rotor points toward the engine block.

    a) I-6—Scribe a mark on the block as a rotor reference point for reinstallation.

    b) V-8—Scribe a mark on the distributor housing to indicate the rotor position as a reference point for reinstalling the distributor.

4. Remove the distributor hold-down screw and carefully lift the distributor from the engine. The distributor shaft will rotate slightly as its gear disengages from that of the camshaft.

DISTRIBUTOR SHAFT AND BUSHING WEAR TEST

1. Secure the distributor in a soft-jaw vise by its hold-down arm and tighten the vise sufficiently to prevent distributor movement—no more.

2. Remove the rotor and attach a dial indicator to the distributor housing so that the indicator plunger arm rests against the reluctor.

3. Fit one end of a wire loop around the reluctor sleeve, just above the reluctor, and connect a spring scale. The wire loop must be down against the reluctor top to guarantee a straight pull, and must not interfere with either the indicator or indicator holding bracket.

4. Apply a straight-line 1-lb. pull toward the dial indicator and a 1-lb. pull away from the indicator. Read total movement on the dial.

5. If the indicated side-play exceeds 0.006-in., replace the distributor shaft assembly or housing.

DISTRIBUTOR DISASSEMBLY (Figs. 4-61 & 4-62)

1. Remove the distributor cap and rotor.

2. Remove the screws and lockwashers holding the vacuum advance unit in place. Disengage and remove the vacuum advance unit.

3. Pry the reluctor up and off the distributor shaft, using two screwdrivers (maximum blade width 7/16-

in.). Work slowly and carefully to avoid damaging or distorting the reluctor teeth.

4. Remove the screws and lockwashers holding the lower plate to the housing and lift out the upper plate, lower plate and pickup coil as an assembly. Do not remove the distributor-cap spring clamps.

5. Drive out the distributor drive-gear roll pin carefully with a hammer and suitable drift, then slide the gear from the shaft end.

6. Clean any burrs from around the pin hole in the shaft with a file and remove the lower thrust washer.

7. Push the distributor shaft up and remove it through the top of the distributor housing.

8. Inspect all components for wear or damage. *Do not* interpret the sharp reluctor teeth as wear—there is *no* reluctor tooth wear because of the air gap between the reluctor and the pole piece. Since correct reluctor tooth configuration is important to the alignment with the pole piece tooth, *do not* file or tamper with the reluctor teeth.

9. The electronic distributor uses the same side-pivot plate found in the conventional Chrysler distributor. When plate wear occurs, the single pivot gradually loosens and will eventually permit the plate to tilt or lean as the vacuum advance starts. This leaning movement can pull the pickup coil in and downward, allowing the pole piece tooth to contact the revolving reluctor. This will break the reluctor, the pole piece, or both, causing the engine to stop. Inspect the side-pivot movement carefully and replace if excessive lean or tilt appears to be developing.

DISTRIBUTOR ASSEMBLY (Figs. 4-61 & 4-62)

1. Lubricate and test the advance weights and inspect weight springs for distortion.

2. Check all bearing surfaces and pivot pins for binding, roughness or excessive looseness.

3. Lubricate and install the upper thrust washer(s) on the shaft and slide the shaft into the distributor housing.

4. Replace the lower thrust washer and old drive gear, securing with the roll pin.

5. Scribe a line on the end of the shaft from edge to center as shown in **Fig. 4-63**. The line must be cen-

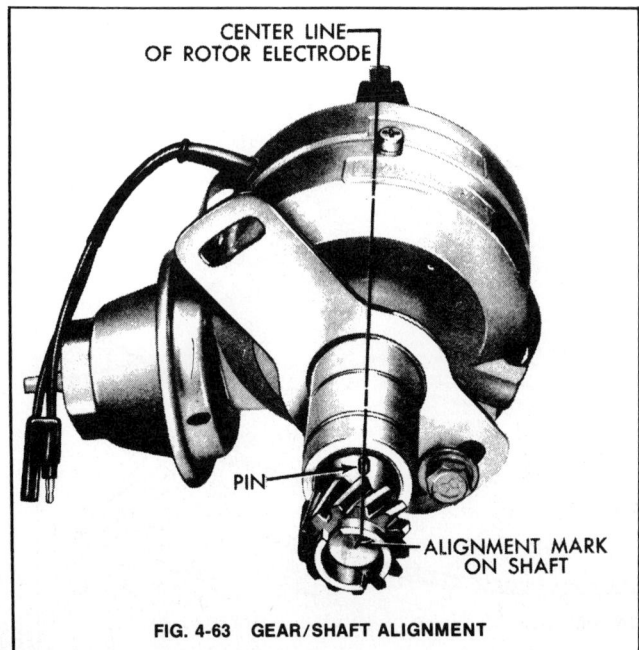

CENTER LINE OF ROTOR ELECTRODE

PIN

ALIGNMENT MARK ON SHAFT

FIG. 4-63 GEAR/SHAFT ALIGNMENT

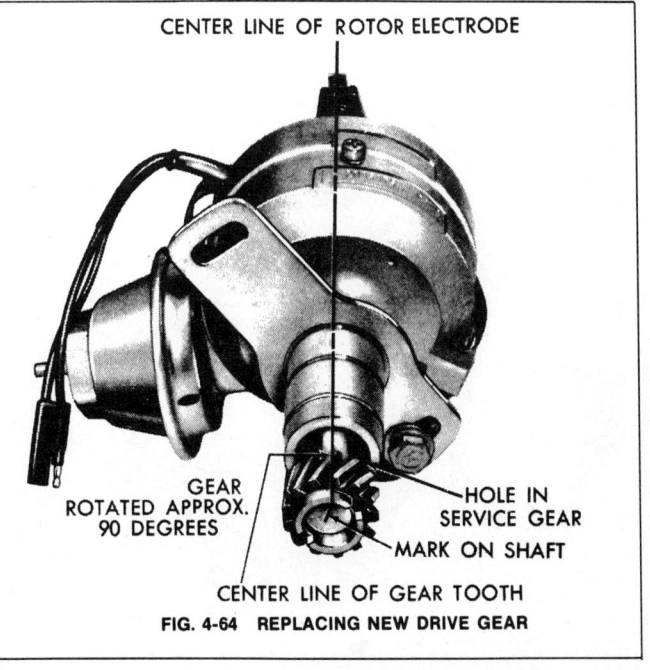

CENTER LINE OF ROTOR ELECTRODE

GEAR ROTATED APPROX. 90 DEGREES

HOLE IN SERVICE GEAR

MARK ON SHAFT

CENTER LINE OF GEAR TOOTH

FIG. 4-64 REPLACING NEW DRIVE GEAR

tered between two gear teeth, but should not be scribed completely across the shaft.

6. Now remove the roll pin and old drive gear. Clean any burrs from around the pin hole with a file.

7. Replace the thrust washer and install a new drive gear. Place a 0.007-in. feeler gauge between the gear and thrust washer, and drill a 0.124- to 0.129-in. hole in the gear and shaft approximately 90° from the old hole, with the scribe line centered between the two gear teeth **(Fig. 4-64).** Install the roll pin.

8. Replace the lower/upper plate and pickup coil assembly and install the attaching screws.

9. Attach the vacuum advance arm to the pickup plate and replace the attaching screws and washers.

10. The same reluctor is used on all V-8 distributors, but distributor shaft rotation is clockwise on the small V-8's and counterclockwise on the large V-8's. To install the reluctor correctly, check its face. There are two engraved arrows and roll pin slots, one on each side of the shaft hub, but offset slightly from each other. Reluctors used on 6-cyl. distributors have only one roll pin slot and are not subject to incorrect installation.

11. Determine the direction of distributor shaft rotation and fit the roll pin into the sleeve beside the corresponding arrow.

12. Slide the reluctor down on the reluctor sleeve and press it into place firmly. Installing the roll pin in the wrong sleeve slot will throw the reluctor rotation off balance and affect the air gap adjustment sufficiently to cause poor engine performance. This is difficult to detect because the air gap will check out to specifications when the distributor shaft is not rotating.

13. Replace the snap ring inside the shaft assembly, lubricate the felt wick and replace.

14. Replace the rotor, fit the distributor cap over the housing and lock the cap clamps in place.

PICKUP COIL REPLACEMENT

1. Follow earlier "Distributor Disassembly" procedure (Steps 1-4).

2. Depress the retainer clip on the underside of the lower plate and move it away from the attaching stud to remove the upper plate and pickup coil assembly.

3. The pickup coil and upper plate are serviced as an assembly—*do not* try to separate them.

4. Lubricate the upper-plate support pins on the lower plate with a small amount of cam lubricant.

5. Fit the new upper-plate/pickup-coil assembly on the lower plate, install the retainer clip and lock it into place.

6. Follow "Distributor Assembly" procedure (Steps 8-14).

DISTRIBUTOR INSTALLATION

1. Make sure that the rubber O-ring seal is fully seated in the distributor shank groove, then turn the distributor until the rotor points to the scribed mark on the cylinder block (I-6) or distributor housing (V-8).

2. Carefully engage the distributor drive gear with the camshaft drive gear. If the engine has been cranked with the distributor removed, the proper relationship between the distributor shaft and the No. 1 piston must be reestablished:

   a) Rotate the crankshaft until No. 1 piston is at the top of its compression stroke. The mark on the inner edge of the crankshaft pulley should line up with the "O" mark on the timing chain cover.

   b) Rotate the distributor rotor to a position just ahead of the No. 1 distributor cap terminal, lower the distributor carefully into the engine opening and engage its drive gear with that of the camshaft.

   c) With the distributor fully seated, the rotor should rest under the distributor cap No. 1 tower.

3. Replace the distributor cap and clamp it in place.

4. Install and tighten the hold-down arm screw finger-tight.

5. Attach the distributor dual-connector lead to the wiring harness connector and make certain the fit is as tight as possible.

6. Connect a timing light **(Fig. 4-65),** start the engine and run at idle speed.

7. Rotate the distributor housing until the timing mark on the crankshaft damper aligns with the specified degree mark on the timing chain cover.

8. Tighten the distributor hold-down screw and recheck the timing setting with the timing light.

9. If not correct, loosen the hold-down screw and readjust, then recheck. When timing is correct, replace the vacuum line to the distributor.

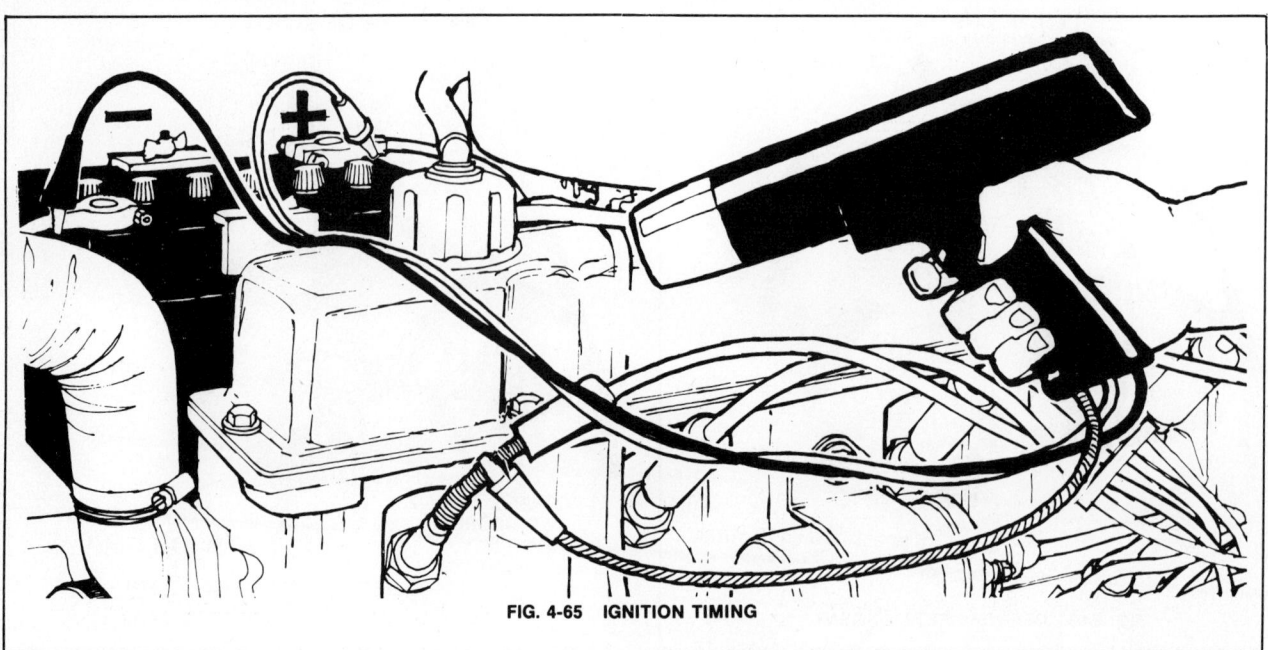

FIG. 4-65 IGNITION TIMING

CENTRIFUGAL AND VACUUM ADVANCE

Attempting to adjust either advance mechanism without the use of an appropriate stroboscope-type distributor tester can result in permanent damage to the engine from an incorrect spark advance curve. Advance curves are specified by the manufacturer for both distributor advance functions, according to their engine application, and are provided in the specifications section at the end of Chapter 3 for use by those with test bench facilities for checking and adjusting the distributor advance to manufacturer's specifications. In order to test electronic distributors for their centrifugal advance curve, the appropriate adapter specified by the distributor tester manufacturer *must* be connected to the distributor stand and the instructions provided for its use followed exactly.

CHRYSLER ELECTRONIC IGNITION

Coil	Chrysler Prestolite	Chrysler Essex
Identification	2444242	2444241
Primary Resistance @ 70°-80° F	1.60-1.79 Ohms	1.41-1.62 Ohms
Secondary Resistance @ 70-80 F	9400-11,700 Ohms	8000-11,200 Ohms [1]
Ballast Resistor		3656199
Resistance @ 70°-80° F:		
Compensating (Coil Side)		0.50-0.60 Ohms
Auxiliary (Control-Unit Side)		4.75-5.75 Ohms

[1] 1978 on, 8000-12,200 Ohms

1974-77 AMERICAN MOTORS ENGINES
AMC-Prestolite Breakerless Inductive Discharge (BID) Ignition System

SYSTEM DESCRIPTION

The Prestolite BID ignition is a variation of the Prestolite electronic ignition introduced on International Harvester engines in 1974. Installation as standard equipment on AMC engines began in late 1974 cars and has been continued to date. A breakerless, inductive discharge system **(Fig. 4-66),** the BID distributor is conventional in design and function, except for the sensor and trigger wheel which replace the breaker points, condenser and distributor cam. Centrifugal and vacuum advance systems are also conventional in design and operation.

When the ignition switch is turned to the START or ON position, the control unit is activated and AC current is sent to the distributor sensor, which develops an electromagnetic field as a result. As the leading edge of a

trigger wheel leg enters the sensor field, it causes a reduction in the sensor's oscillation strength, which continues to diminish as the leg nears alignment with the sensor.

When the oscillation strength is reduced to a predetermined level, a demodulator circuit switches, activating a power transistor in series with the coil primary circuit to switch off the primary circuit, introducing high voltage in the coil secondary winding. The high voltage is then distributed to the spark plugs in a conventional manner—by the rotor, distributor cap and ignition wires.

CONTROL UNIT

A solid-state, moisture-resistant module, all control-unit components are permanently sealed in a potting material to prevent damage from vibration and weather conditions. The unit has built-in reverse polarity protection, transient voltage protection and current regulation. As a result, no resistance wire or ballast resistor is required in the primary circuit. Because full battery

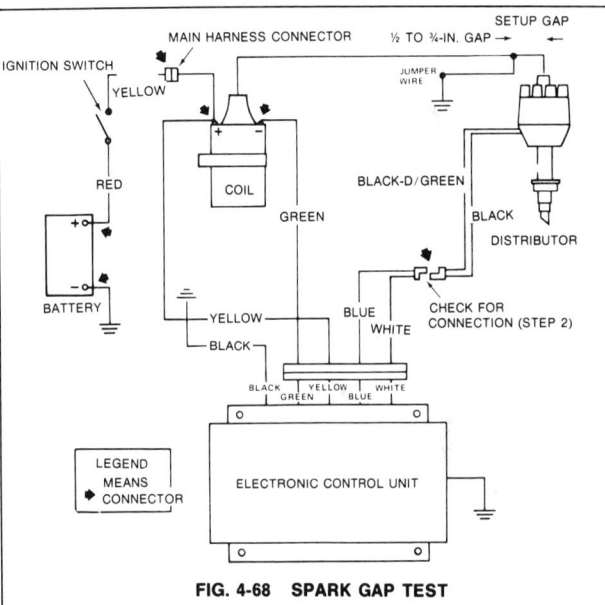

FIG. 4-68   SPARK GAP TEST

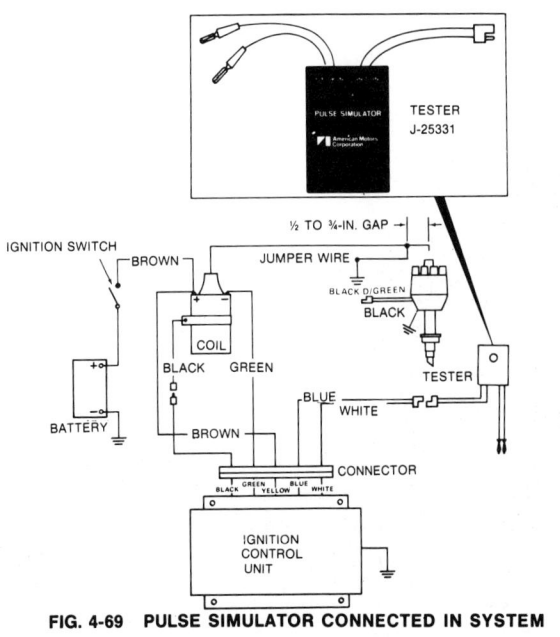

FIG. 4-69   PULSE SIMULATOR CONNECTED IN SYSTEM

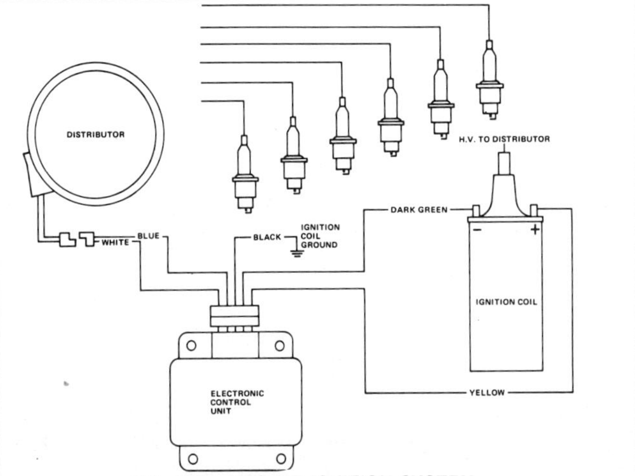

FIG. 4-66   AMC BID IGNITION SYSTEM

voltage is present at the coil positive terminal when the ignition switch is in the ON or START position, an ignition system bypass during cranking is not required. Primary coil current is electronically regulated by the control unit, which is non-repairable and must be serviced as a unit.

IGNITION COIL

The BID ignition coil is an oil-filled, hermetically sealed unit of standard construction, and should be tested at operating temperature, because malfunctions may not be located when the coil is cold.

DISTRIBUTOR SENSOR/TRIGGER WHEEL

The sensor is a small coil wound of fine wire which receives an AC signal from the electronic control unit. There are no wear surfaces between the trigger wheel and sensor, thus dwell remains constant and requires no adjustment. The control unit determines dwell as the angle between the trigger-wheel legs.

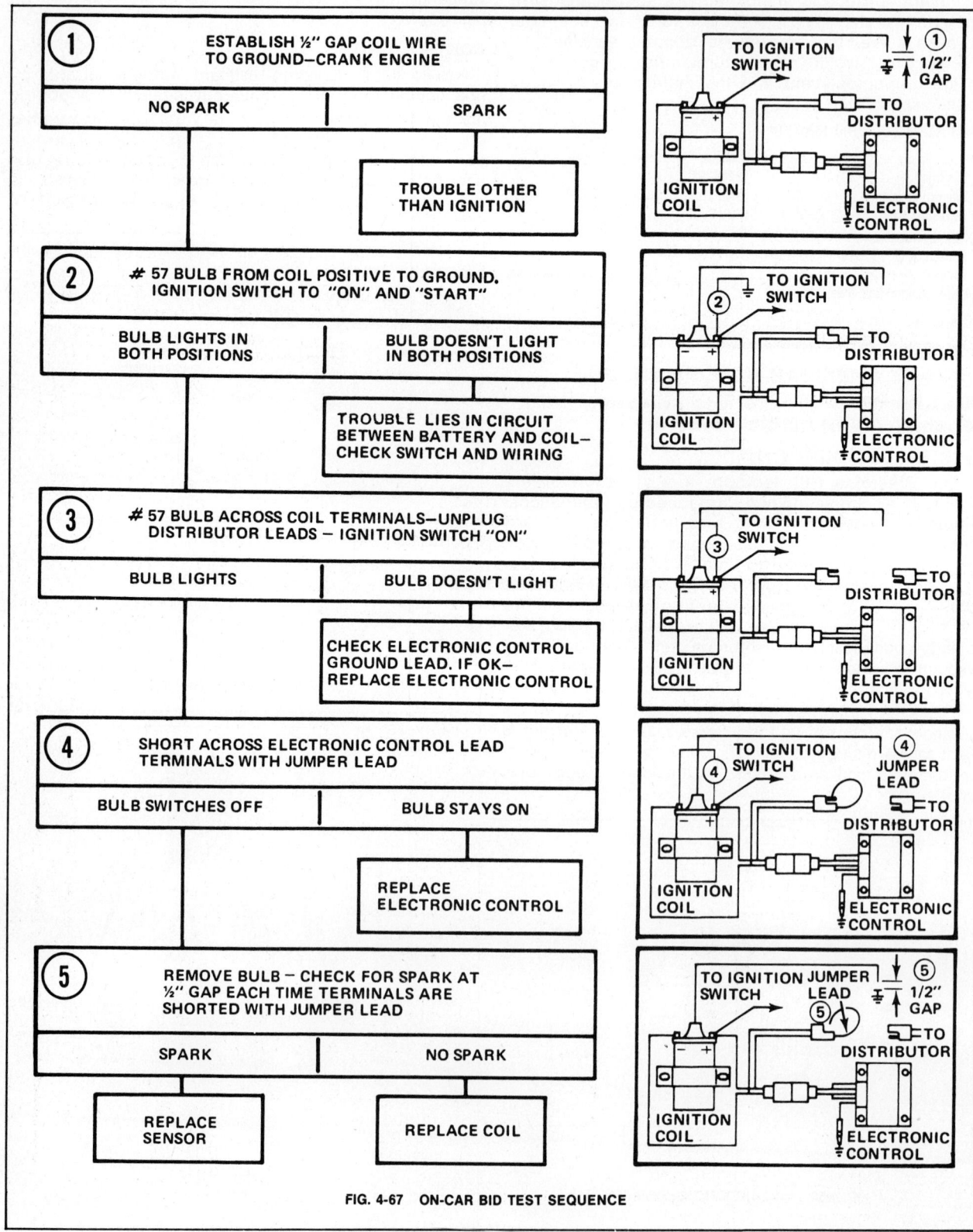

FIG. 4-67   ON-CAR BID TEST SEQUENCE

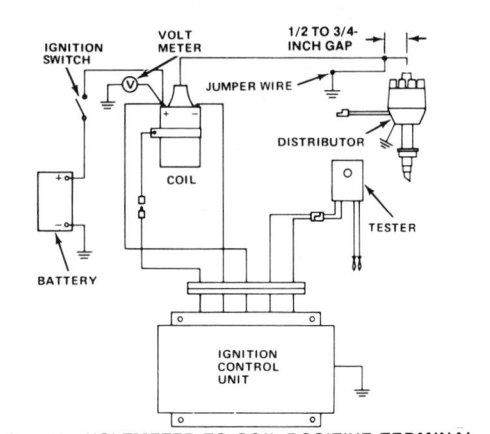

FIG. 4-70 VOLTMETER TO COIL POSITIVE TERMINAL

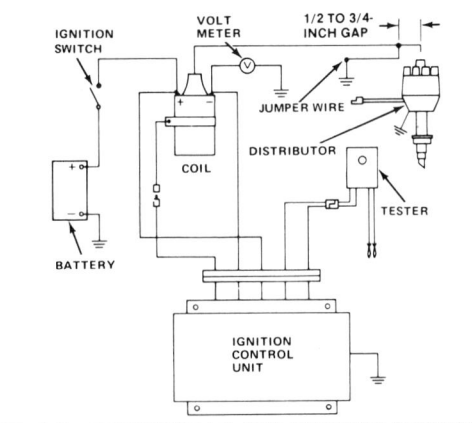

FIG. 4-71 VOLTMETER TO COIL NEGATIVE TERMINAL

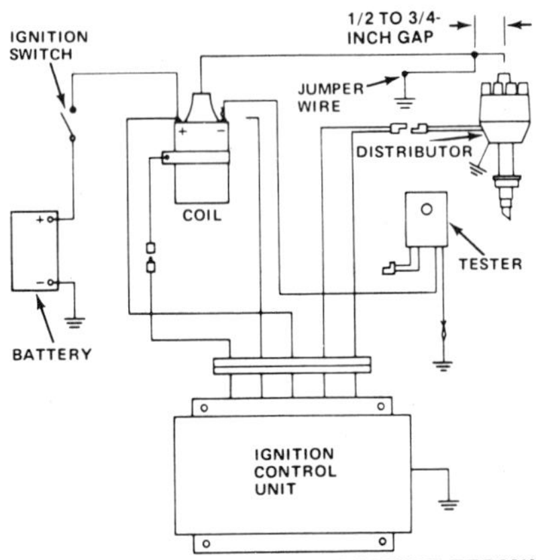

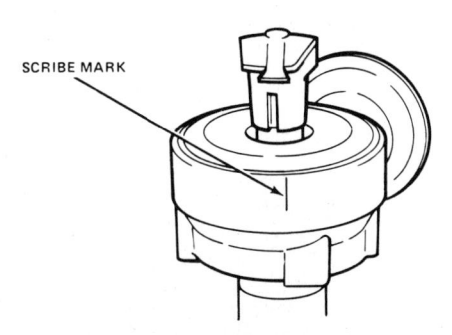

FIG. 4-72 TESTER TO COIL NEGATIVE TERMINAL

FIG. 4-73 ROTOR POSITION REFERENCE MARK

TEST PROCEDURES

To perform a simple on-car test, follow **Fig. 4-67**, using a jumper lead and a No. 57 light bulb. If this does not solve the ignition problem, or if a more comprehensive test is desired, proceed to the "Ignition System Test."

IGNITION SYSTEM TEST

A special Electronic Ignition Pulse Simulator (AMC Tester J-25331) is required for a complete ignition system test.

1. Connect a voltmeter to the battery. Voltage should read 12-13 volts for a fully charged battery. If the battery does not meet voltage specifications, charge or replace it with a fully charged battery for the duration of the test procedure.

2. Visually inspect the primary and secondary wiring for loose connections, damaged insulation, correct routing, etc.

3. Disconnect the high-tension cable from one spark plug using insulated pliers. Hold the plug cable ½- to ¾-in. from the engine, and crank. If a spark jumps the gap, the ignition system is functioning satisfactorily. If not, replace the cable and continue the test procedure.

4. Disconnect the high-tension coil cable from the center tower of the distributor cap. See **Fig. 4-68** for wiring diagram. Clip one end of a jumper lead over the cable, ½- to ¾-in. from the metal tip and ground the other end to the engine. Crank the engine and note the gap between the jumper lead clip and the ignition cable terminal. If spark occurs, the distributor cap or rotor is malfunctioning. Replace and repeat Step 3.

5. If no spark occurs between the jumper lead clip and ignition cable terminal, test the coil secondary wire with an ohmmeter. Meter should read 5000 to 10,000 ohms resistance. If the coil wire tests satisfactory, proceed to Step 6. If not, replace the coil wire and repeat Step 4.

6. Disconnect the distributor primary wires (black and dark green) from the control unit connector. Crimp with pliers to assure a tight fit and reconnect. Crank the engine and note the gap between the jumper lead clip and ignition cable terminal. If a spark occurs, the ignition system is now functioning.

7. From this point on, use of the Pulse Simulator is required. If a spark still does not occur, disconnect the same distributor primary wires and connect to Tester J-25331 as shown in **Fig. 4-69.** Turn the ignition switch on, cycle the test button and note the gap. If spark occurs, the distributor sensor is faulty and must be replaced.

8. If no spark occurs, connect a voltmeter between the coil positive (+) terminal and ground, as shown in **Fig. 4-70.** With the ignition switch on, the voltmeter should read battery voltage. If voltage reading is lower than battery voltage, there is a high resistance between the battery/ignition-switch/coil circuit. Correct before proceeding.

9. Connect the voltmeter between the coil negative (-) terminal and ground, as shown in **Fig. 4-71.** With the ignition switch on, voltage should read 5 to 8 volts. More than 8 volts indicates a defective control unit or coil. If the reading is satisfactory, press the tester button and read the voltmeter, which should increase to 12-13 volts. If voltage does not switch up and down, the control unit is malfunctioning and must be replaced. If the voltage switches correctly, but no spark occurs between the jumper lead clip and ignition cable terminal, continue the test sequence.

10. Disconnect the tester from the control unit and turn off the ignition switch. Remove the wire from the coil negative (-) terminal and connect one tester lead clip in its place, and the other to ground **(Fig. 4-72)**. Turn the ignition switch on and cycle the test button. The spark should jump the gap—if not, replace the ignition coil.

DISTRIBUTOR REMOVAL

1. Unclip and remove the distributor cap with the high-tension wires left connected and set to one side out of the way.

2. Disconnect the vacuum advance line and primary wiring connector from the distributor.

3. Scribe a mark on the distributor housing in line with the rotor tip and note the position of the rotor and distributor in relation to the engine as a reference for installation **(Fig. 4-73)**.

4. Remove the distributor hold-down bolt and clamp.

5. Withdraw the distributor from engine.

DISTRIBUTOR DISASSEMBLY (Fig. 4-74)

1. Secure the distributor housing in a soft-jaw vise and remove the rotor and dust shield.

2. Remove the trigger wheel. A small gear puller should be used. Puller jaws must grip the trigger-wheel inner shoulder to prevent damage. A thick flat washer or nut is used as a spacer to avoid pressing against the center shaft **(Fig. 4-75)**.

3. Loosen the sensor lockscrew. On factory-installed sensors, the screw has a tamper-proof head design which can be removed either with AMC tool J-25097 or a pair of needlenose pliers. Replacement sensor screws have a standard slotted head.

4. Lift the sensor-lead grommet from the distributor housing and pull the leads from the slot around the sensor-spring pivot pin. Lift and release the spring to clear the leads, then slide the sensor from the bracket **(Fig. 4-76)**.

5. The vacuum advance unit is *not* to be removed unless replacement is necessary. In this case, remove the retaining screw and slide the vacuum unit from the distributor housing.

6. To remove the distributor shaft, support the shaft to prevent damage and drive the retaining pin from the drive gear, using a suitable drift and hammer. Slide the drive gear and shims from the shaft and withdraw the shaft and spacers from the housing.

DISTRIBUTOR ASSEMBLY (Fig. 4-74)

1. If the distributor shaft was removed, replace it in the distributor housing, position shims and drive gear on the lower end, and replace the retaining pin.

2. Assemble the sensor, sensor guide, flat washer and retaining screw. Install the screw just enough to hold the assembly together, taking care that it does not project below the bottom of the sensor.

3. Replace the sensor assembly on the vacuum-advance-unit bracket. Locate the sensor tip in the summing bar, position the sensor spring and route the leads around the spring pivot pin **(Fig. 4-76)**.

4. Install the sensor-lead grommet in the distributor housing and check the lead position to make sure the trigger wheel will not make contact.

5. Fit the sensor positioning gauge over the yoke and against the flat of the shaft, then move the sensor assembly to the side to position the gauge. Tighten the

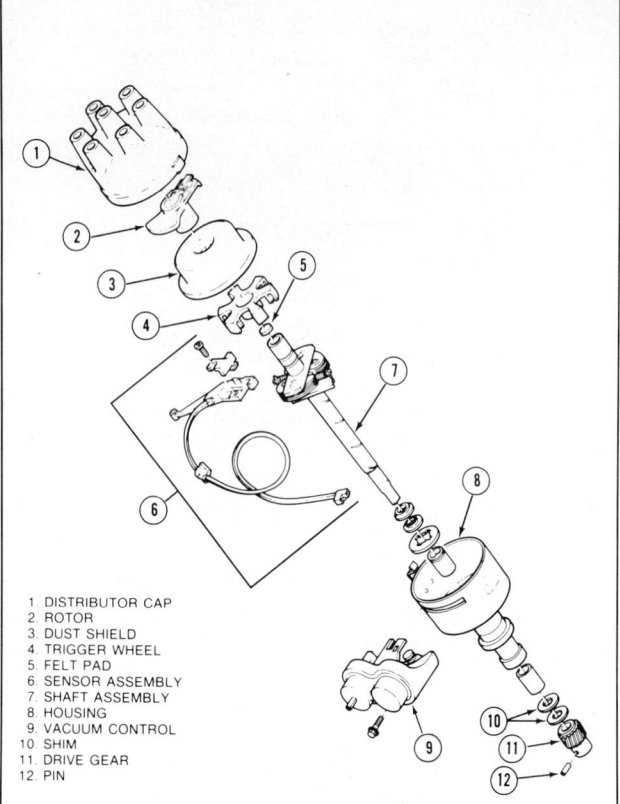

1. DISTRIBUTOR CAP
2. ROTOR
3. DUST SHIELD
4. TRIGGER WHEEL
5. FELT PAD
6. SENSOR ASSEMBLY
7. SHAFT ASSEMBLY
8. HOUSING
9. VACUUM CONTROL
10. SHIM
11. DRIVE GEAR
12. PIN

FIG. 4-74   AMC BID DISTRIBUTOR DISASSEMBLED

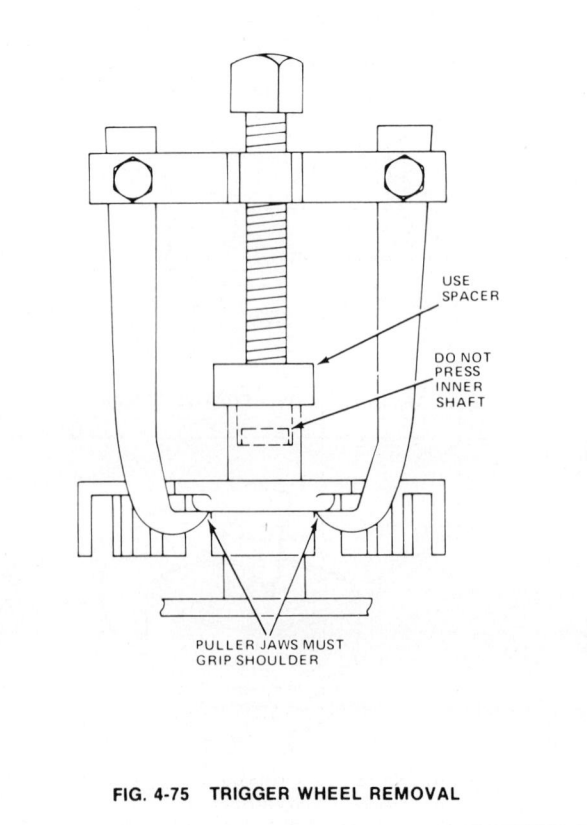

USE SPACER

DO NOT PRESS INNER SHAFT

PULLER JAWS MUST GRIP SHOULDER

FIG. 4-75   TRIGGER WHEEL REMOVAL

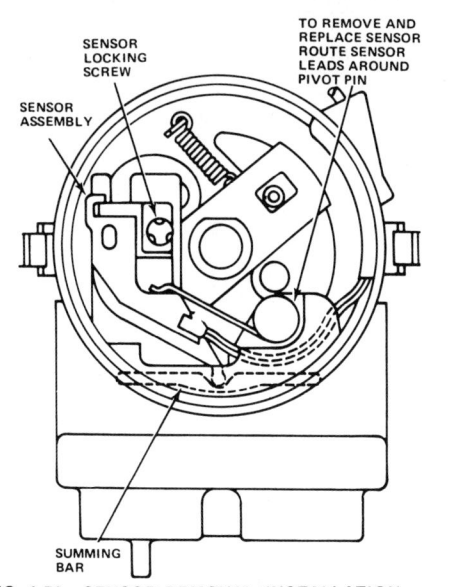

FIG. 4-76 SENSOR REMOVAL/INSTALLATION

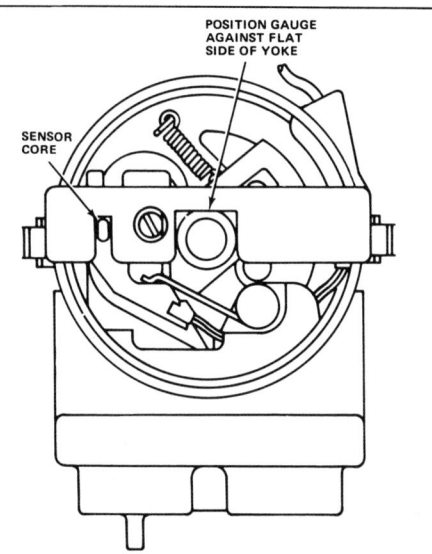

FIG. 4-77 POSITIONING SENSOR

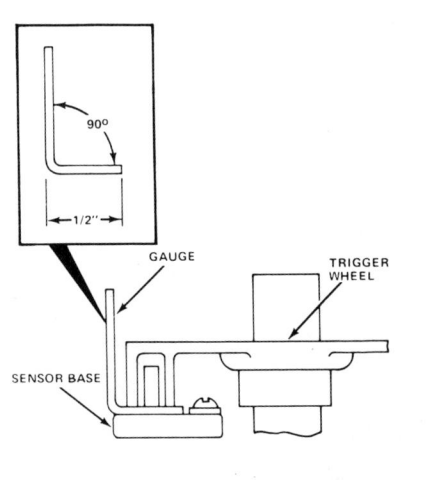

FIG. 4-78 TRIGGER WHEEL/SENSOR CLEARANCE

retaining screw and check the sensor location by removing/replacing the gauge. No sensor side movement should be evident. Torque the retaining screw to 5-10 in.-oz. and recheck the sensor position. Remove the positioning gauge **(Fig. 4-77)**.

6. Place the trigger wheel on the yoke. Make sure the sensor core is positioned in the center of the trigger-wheel legs and that the legs cannot touch the sensor core.

7. Support the distributor shaft and press the trigger wheel on the yoke.

8. Bend the 0.050-in. wire furnished with the replacement sensor assembly as shown in **Fig. 4-78.** Use the bent wire as a gauge to measure the clearance between the sensor base and the trigger wheel legs. Trigger wheel should just touch the wire. If not, readjust the trigger wheel position until it does.

9. Lubricate the felt wick in the top of the yoke with 3-5 drops of SAE 20W oil, and replace the distributor dust shield and rotor.

DISTRIBUTOR INSTALLATION

1. Install a new distributor gasket in the engine block counterbore and set the distributor in the engine.

2. Align the rotor tip with the distributor housing scribe mark, then turn the rotor one-eighth turn counterclockwise beyond the scribed mark **(Fig. 4-73)**.

3. Slide the distributor the rest of the way into the engine and align the vacuum advance unit in the same location relative to the engine as when removed. Rotor and shaft may move slightly when engaging the distributor drive gear with the camshaft gear and oil-pump drive tang, but the rotor should still line up with the scribe mark once the distributor is in place.

4. If the engine was cranked with the distributor removed, reestablish timing by rotating the crankshaft until the timing mark on the crankshaft pulley lines up with top dead center (TDC) mark on timing quadrant.

5. Turn the distributor shaft to align the rotor tip with the No. 1 terminal in the distributor cap, then turn the rotor one-eighth turn counterclockwise past the No. 1 terminal.

6. Replace the distributor hold-down clamp, bolt and lockwasher. *Do not* tighten the bolt.

7. Replace the distributor cap with the high-tension cables. Make sure the housing tang engages the cap slots before fitting the cap on the housing. Incorrect cap positioning can cause damage to the cap or rotor.

8. Connect the distributor primary wiring connector.

9. Connect a timing light to the No. 1 spark plug and time the engine to specifications, then tighten the distributor hold-down bolt. Recheck the timing **(Fig. 4-65)**, and replace the distributor vacuum line. 🦫

IGNITION COIL AND RESISTOR SPECIFICATIONS	
AMC-BID IGNITION	
COIL	
Primary Resistance	1.0-2.0 Ohms
Secondary Resistance	8000-12,000 Ohms
Open Circuit Output	20 KV Minimum
SENSOR	
Resistance @ 77° F	1.8 Ohms (± 10%)
Use accurate ohmmeter and check across sensor lead terminals.	

HOW TO: HEI V-8 Distributor Stripdown

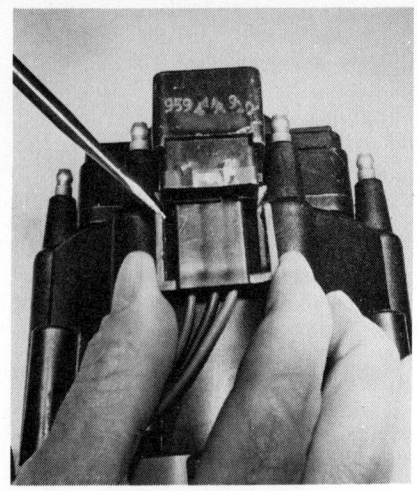

1. Unclip distributor module connector lead from the distributor cap housing. Carefully pry the connector free with a screwdriver.

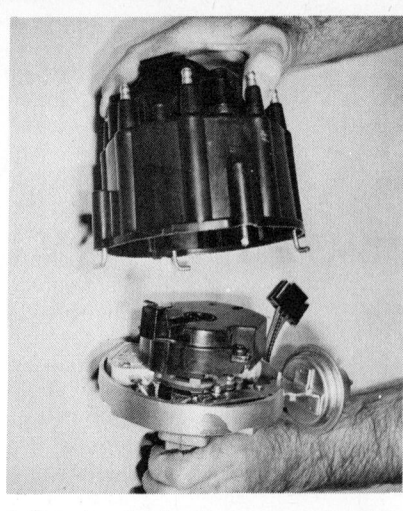

2. Four turn latches hold cap to housing. Latches will turn 90° in one direction only. Remove rotor cap from advance weight assembly.

3. Remove coil cover. Coil is grounded at the screw (arrow), but grommet can vibrate loose. Screwdriver points to additional ground on '76 coils.

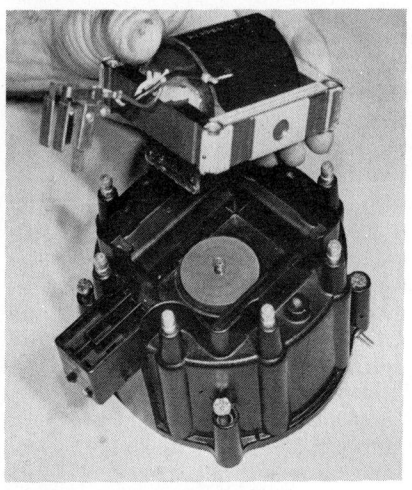

4. Enclosed coil creates heat and moisture, so a large rubber seal under it absorbs moisture and prevents shorting. Replace if seal has lost flexibility.

5. With seal removed, carbon button and spring can be lifted out. HEI system has not been in use long enough to tell if spring will retain proper tension.

6. To remove module, pull lead grommet (1) from housing cutout, unclip connection (2). Remove screws, lift out module. Silicone grease is necessary on both.

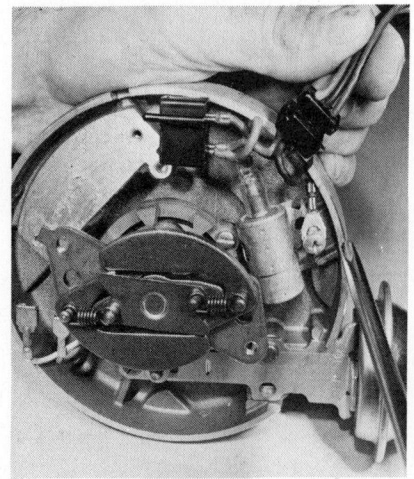

7. Remove screw holding capacitor in place. Capacitor, bracket, module connector harness can be lifted out as a single unit, and replaced the same way.

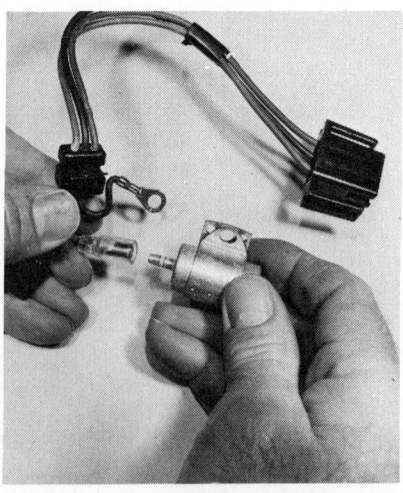

8. Disconnect capacitor from module connector harness by pulling apart. Slip old capacitor from bracket, center new one and plug back into harness.

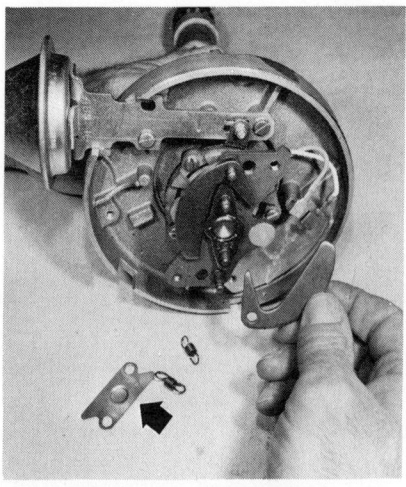

9. Centrifugal advance is similar to conventional Delco-Remy. HEI uses thin weight retainer (arrow); dimple side is down on shaft.

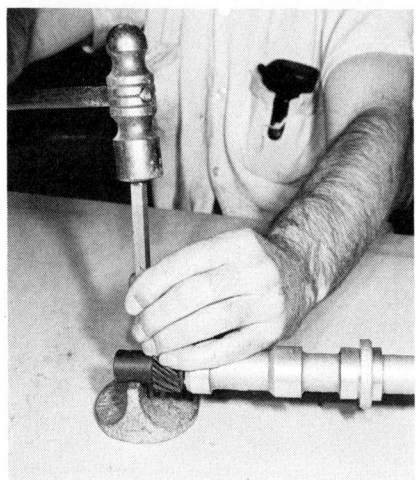

10. Support distributor shaft and tap out drive-gear retaining pin. Housing is fitted with two brass bushings; care must be taken not to damage them.

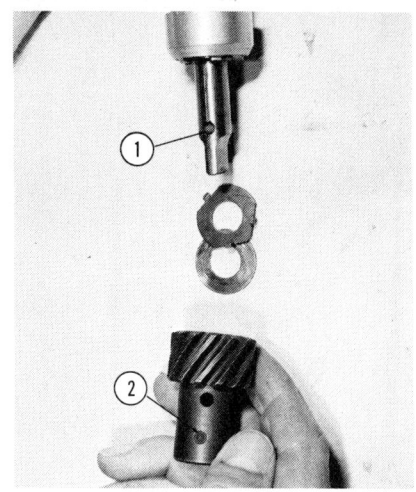

11. Drive gear, shim, tanged washer now slip off shaft end. Clean shaft at (1) to remove any burrs. Note the dimple (2) in the drive gear.

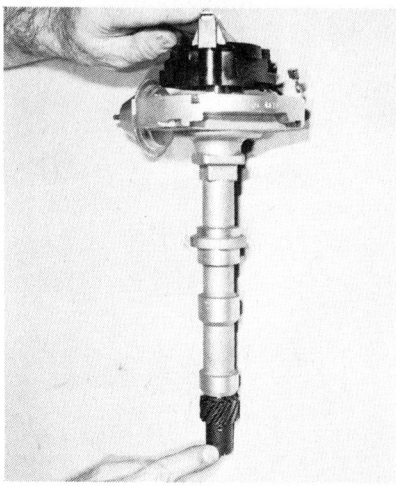

12. Dimple in drive gear must be lined up with rotor, as shown, when reinstalling shaft, or you will have firing problems when distributor is replaced.

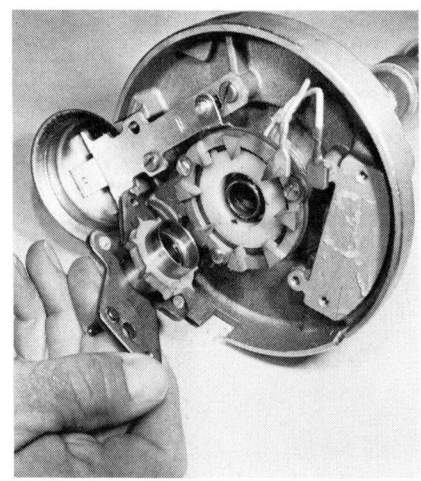

13. Before removing the shaft, start with the rotating pole piece/weight retainer. Its teeth should not touch stationary teeth when the unit is replaced.

14. Remove screws holding stationary teeth, lift off. Remove magnetic rubber ring (arrow). Retaining screws have sufficient adjustment if teeth contact.

15. Take out pickup coil; if it tests out with more than 800 ohms resistance, you can expect problems. Like a coil, this unit should be tested hot.

16. This tiny wavy washer must be pried carefully from its slot at the top of the distributor shaft, an ingenious way of holding things together.

17. Remove vacuum advance screws, lift off pickup coil retainer. Felt washer, lubricant reservoir are located beneath, with a plastic shield. Lubricate washer.

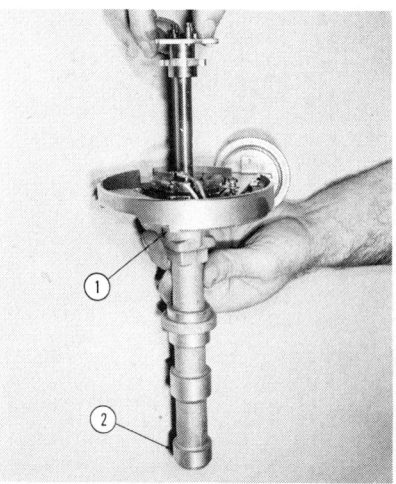

18. Temporarily fit weight assembly in place to provide a handle when inserting distributor shaft. Brass bushings are inside housing at points marked 1 and 2.

HOW TO: Motorcraft Solid State Distributor Stripdown

1. To disassemble the Solid State distributor, remove cap and rotor. Pry armature from shaft with a pair of screwdrivers as shown. Work carefully.

2. As armature is removed from shaft, note the tiny roll pin. This may come off with the armature or it may stay attached to the shaft—don't lose it.

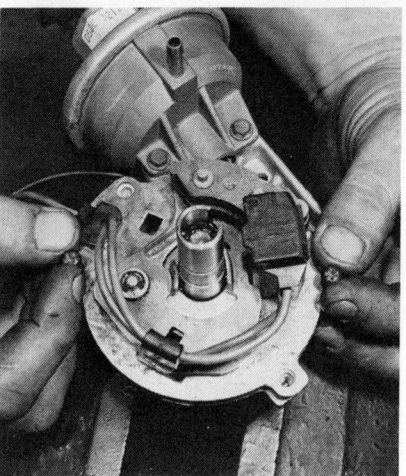

3. Two screws hold the stator assembly and plate to this 6-cyl. distributor. Plate and stator assembly are removed as a unit and serviced that way.

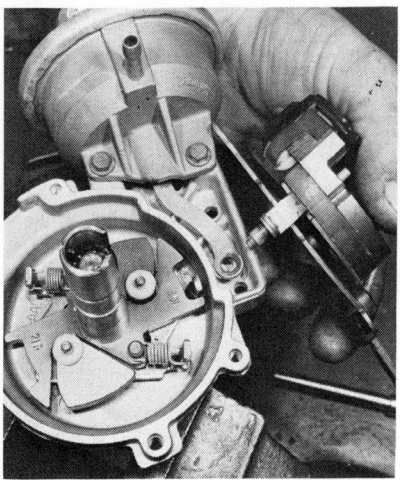

4. To remove the plate/stator assembly, the pivot pin which engages the vacuum advance arm must be lifted out of the attachment hole as shown above.

5. Stator/plate assembly shown at left is used in 4-cyl. models. Stator at right fits the 6- and 8-cyl. distributors. Ground point (circle) causes many problems.

6. Vacuum advance unit is now detached from distributor housing. Remove cap-head screws, lift advance unit. If unit is functioning okay, this isn't necessary.

7. Centrifugal advance mechanism is exactly like that of a conventional Motorcraft-Autolite distributor. Unclip and remove the advance springs.

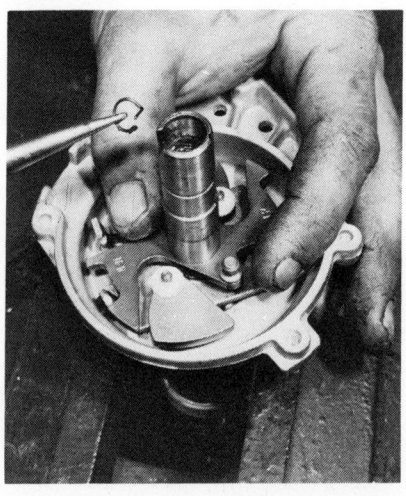

8. Like conventional distributors, a small retaining clip must be removed from inside of sleeve and plate assembly, before assembly can be removed.

9. Lift sleeve and plate assembly off distributor shaft. The centrifugal advance weights are held in place by nylon snap rings and are not to be removed.

10. This tanged washer may come off with sleeve and plate assembly, or it may stay in place to be removed separately. Install it before reassembly.

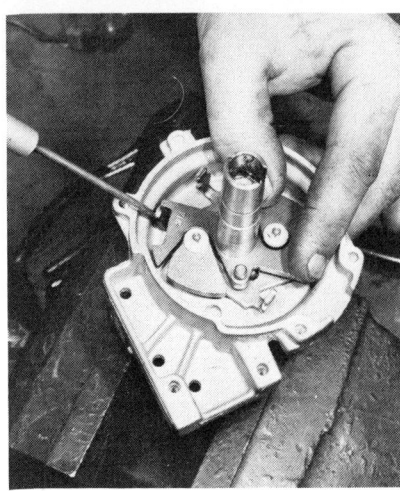

11. Distributor shaft is not to be removed unless bushing wear requires housing replacement or shaft is distorted. Replace sleeve, plate assembly as shown.

12. Reinstall the tiny wire retaining clip inside the sleeve and plate assembly, then install the felt lubricating wick as shown. Lube with engine oil.

13. Check operation of advance weights with sleeve and plate assembly replaced, then install weight retaining springs. Make sure they clip over tanged cutouts.

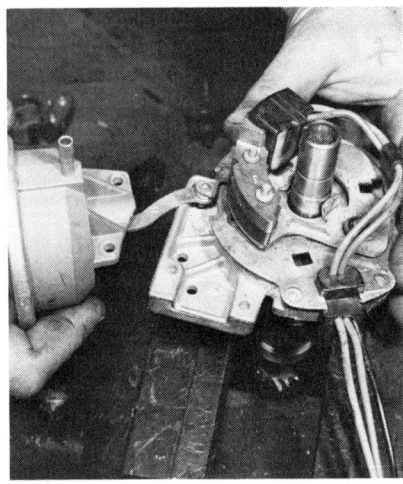

14. Position stator and fixed plate assembly on the distributor housing; reconnect vacuum advance arm. Swing advance unit in place, install screws.

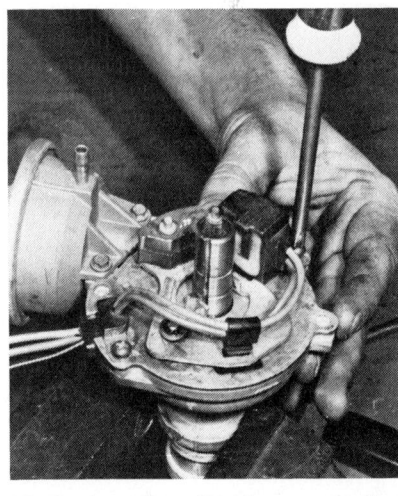

15. Replace the attaching screws that hold the stator and the fixed plate assembly to the distributor housing, and tighten them snugly and evenly.

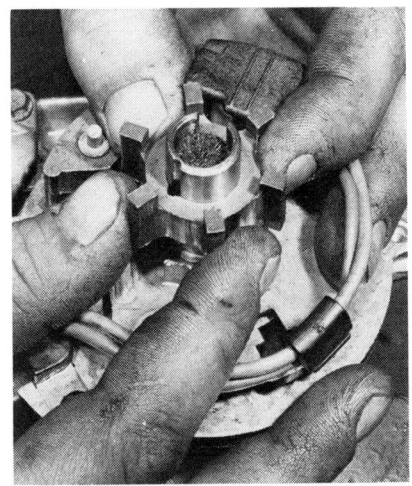

16. To replace armature, position it so that stator pickup tooth is centered between two of the armature legs, and then push it down on the shaft.

17. Using needlenose pliers, insert the armature roll pin in the shaft slot. Use a small punch and light hammer taps to drive flush with armature.

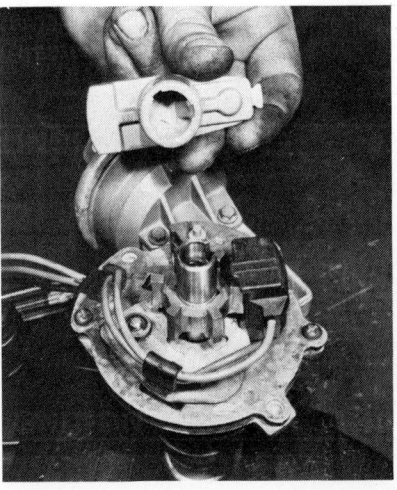

18. Like the conventional distributor rotor, Solid State rotor has a tang which must fit into the shaft cutout for proper replacement. Replace cap.

HOW TO: AMC BID Sensor Replacement

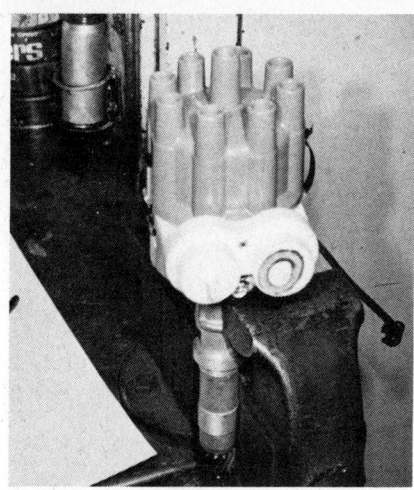

1. All 1975-76 AMC/Jeep vehicles are equipped with the BID ignition system by Prestolite. Only giveaway to eyes is in cap and new vacuum advance unit.

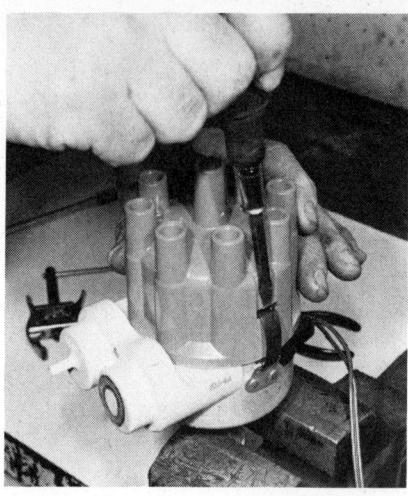

2. While sensor replacement can be made with distributor in the car, you can see what we're doing better this way. Begin by unsnapping the distributor cap.

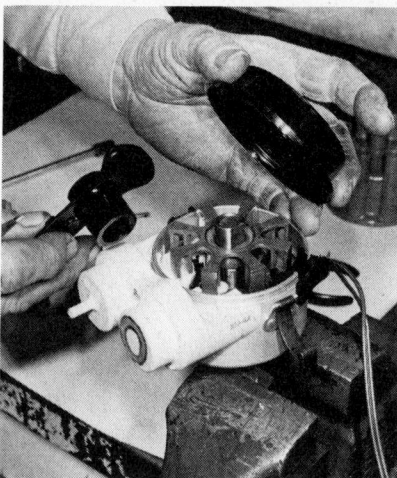

3. After cap has been removed, pull the rotor straight up and off the shaft, then lift off the dust cap. The rotor is a snug fit, so tug at it gently.

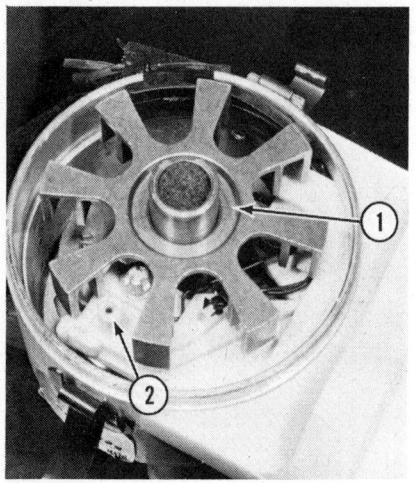

4. A trigger wheel (1) and sensor (2) have replaced the conventional breaker points, condenser and breaker cam in the new BID distributor.

5. Remove the trigger wheel with a battery terminal puller. To avoid pressing against the distributor shaft, use a washer between the shaft and puller.

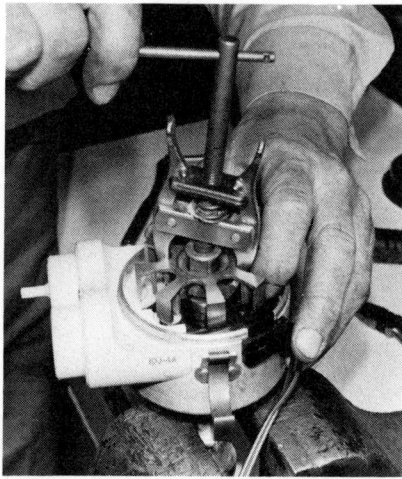

6. Make sure the puller jaws grip the inner shoulder of the trigger wheel before tightening the puller. If they don't, you can break it during removal.

7. To remove tension from the sensor spring, lift it up and out of its guide slot carefully with needlenose pliers; don't let it get away from you.

8. Now lift the sensor lead grommet from its slot in the distributor bowl and carefully free the twin leads from around the spring pivot pin.

9. The factory sensor comes with a special-head screw, which can be removed with needlenose pliers. Replacement sensor has a slotted screw.

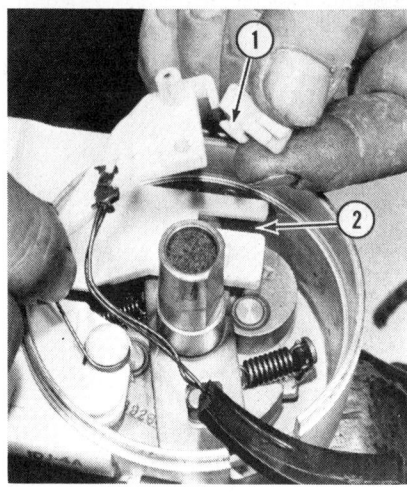

10. The plastic sensor has a guide which separates when the retaining screw and washer are removed. The foot on guide (1) locks into slot (2) on bracket.

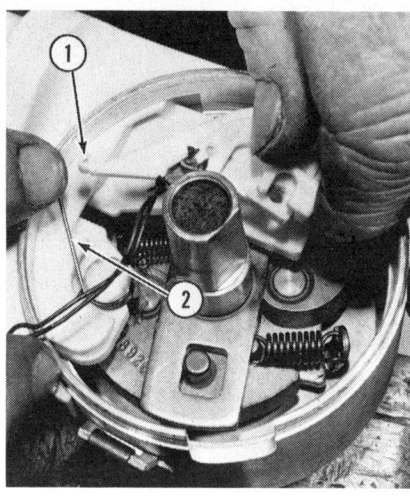

11. The sensor connects mechanically to the vacuum advance, so its pronged end (1) must fit into the slot and under the bracket (2) when replacing the unit.

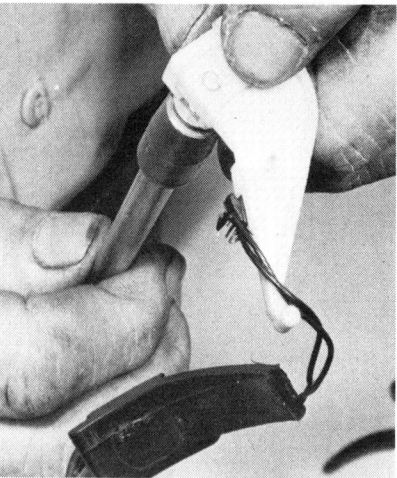

12. Assemble sensor, guide, washer and retaining screw. Install screw just enough to hold two together—it shouldn't protrude through sensor bottom.

13. Sensor prong is inserted to connect with the vacuum advance. Secure the guide foot in the slot, then thread lead wires under the sensor tension spring.

14. Replace grommet, tighten screw and fit placement gauge over shaft/sensor. Adjust until gauge can be removed/replaced without sensor side movement.

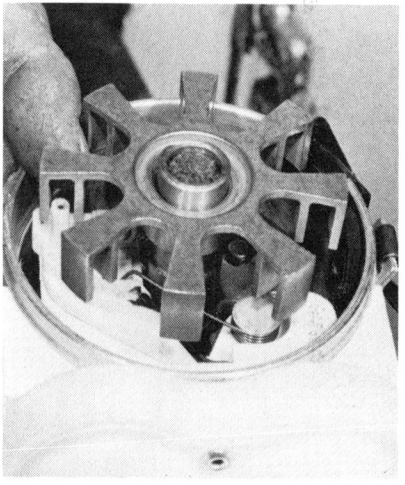

15. Tighten the screw, remove gauge and place trigger wheel in position. If adjusted correctly, trigger-wheel legs should not touch the sensor core.

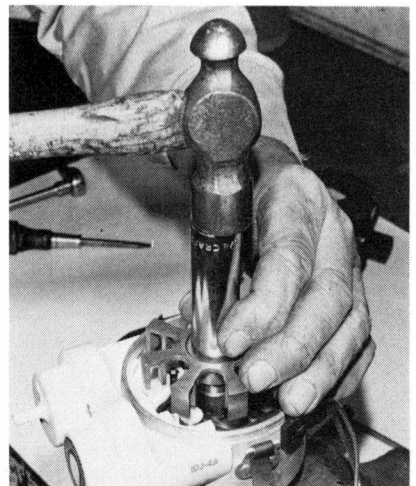

16. Use a socket and hammer to gently work the trigger wheel back onto the distributor shaft. You want a 0.050-in. space between the leg and the sensor.

17. The gauging wire included with the replacement sensor is bent to a 90° angle and is used to check the distance between wheel legs and sensor base.

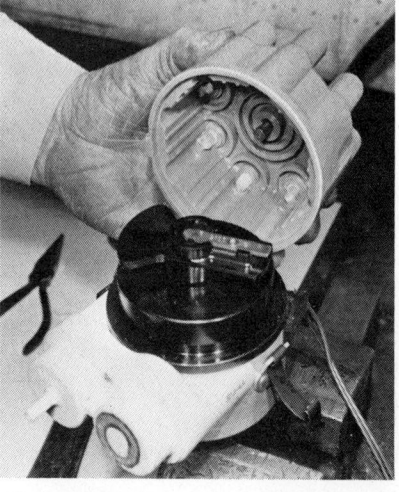

18. Add 3-5 drops of SAE 20W oil to the felt wick in the distributor shaft, then install dust shield and rotor. Replace distributor cap and you're in business.

HOW TO: Chrysler Distributor Overhaul

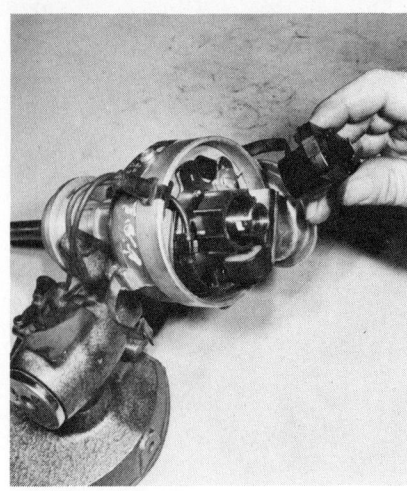

1. Chrysler's electronic ignition distributor has remained unchanged since its introduction in 1973. Unclip and remove distributor cap, then pull rotor off shaft.

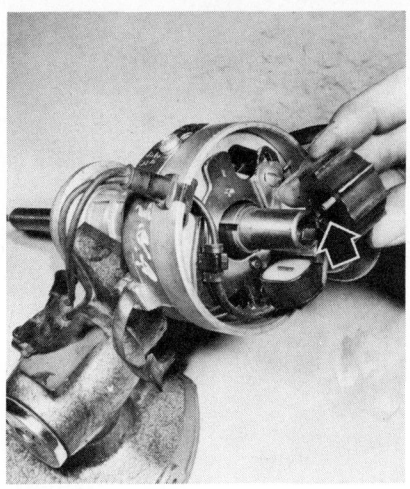

2. If reluctor is a tight fit, use two screwdrivers to pry it loose. Reluctor can generally be worked off sleeve by hand. Note reluctor keeper pin (arrow).

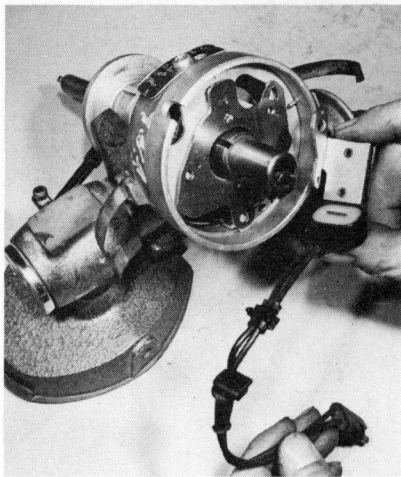

3. Remove screw holding pick-up coil to plate assembly. Pull coil lead and grommet from slot in distributor housing, and remove pick-up coil from distributor.

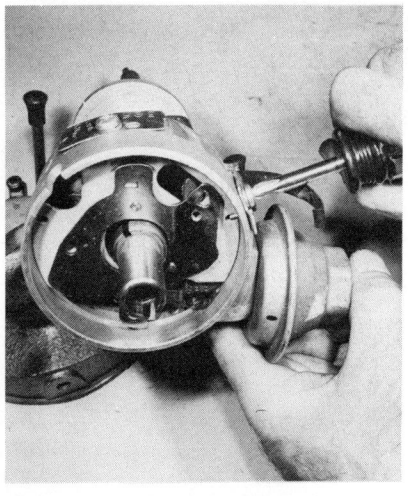

4. Remove two screws and lockwashers which hold vacuum advance diaphragm to distributor housing. Disconnect diaphragm link from plate and remove.

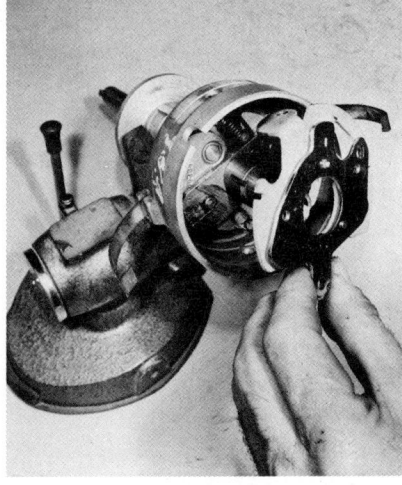

5. Remove two screws and lockwashers holding plate in distributor housing and lift plate out. If a tight fit, it may be necessary to work plate out of housing.

6. For further disassembly, remove felt wick inside reluctor sleeve. There's a small wire snap ring under wick; remove with needle-nose or snap ring pliers.

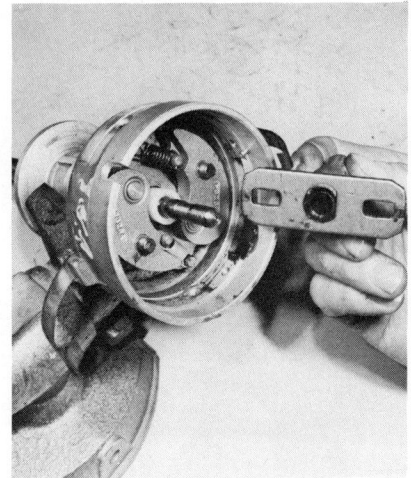

7. After removing wire retainer from distributor shaft, lift reluctor sleeve to disengage from advance weights and remove. Check bushing for wear.

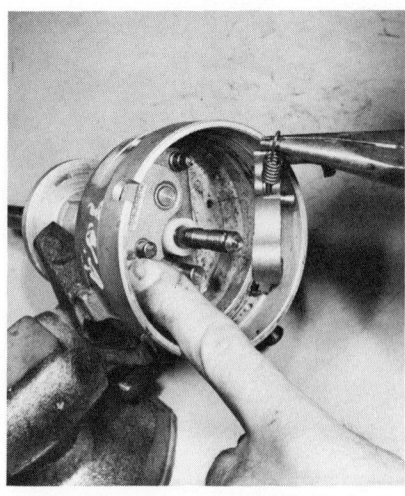

8. To remove advance weights, unclip springs from anchor pins. Lift weight up and off pivot pin. Mark pins, springs and weights for correct reinstallation.

9. Wipe distributor bowl clean with cloth dampened with solvent. Blow distributor bowl dry with compressed air and lubricate anchor and pivot pins.

10. Reinstall weights on pivot pins and clip springs to anchor pins. Remove nylon bushing from distributor shaft and lube shaft lightly; reinstall bushing.

11. Slide reluctor sleeve over shaft and align weights to engage sleeve slots on weight pins. Seat sleeve and install wire retainer over dist. shaft inside sleeve.

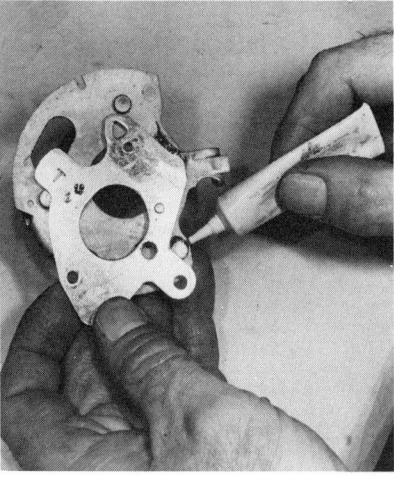

12. Check plate assembly pivot points and replace plate if any are missing or loose, as reluctor could damage pick-up coil when vacuum advance comes in.

13. After lubricating pivot points, reinstall plate assembly and align its retaining holes with those in distributor housing. Install lockwashers and screws.

14. Slide vacuum advance diaphragm into position and tilt diaphragm unit to engage advance link (a) with plate assembly slot (b). Install lockwashers etc.

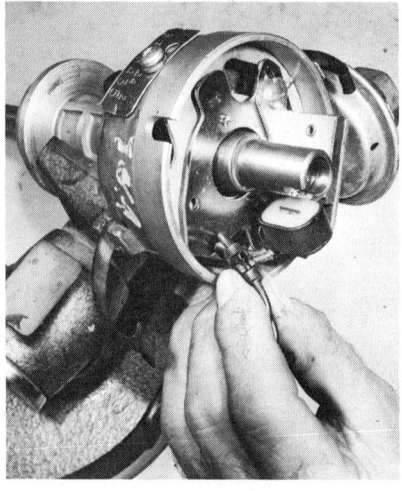

15. Seat pick-up coil assembly on plate and install retaining screw. Press lead wire grommet into housing slot until it is properly seated.

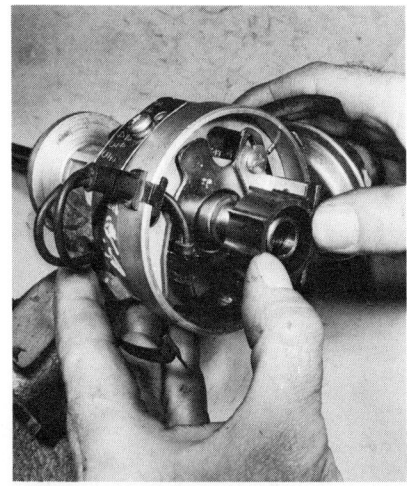

16. There are two keeper pin slots inside reluctor, but only one slot on sleeve. Install reluctor with pin in slot corresponding to direction of shaft rotation.

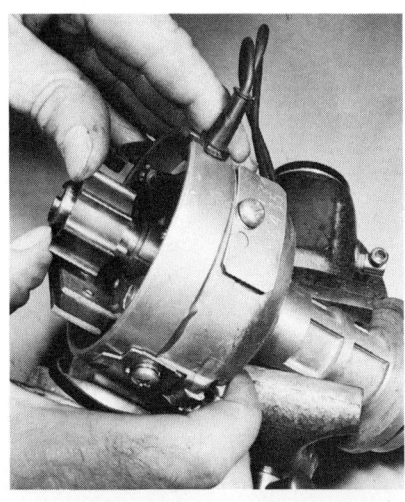

17. Once pin is aligned with sleeve slot, press reluctor firmly into place. Installing keeper pin in wrong reluctor slot will affect timing.

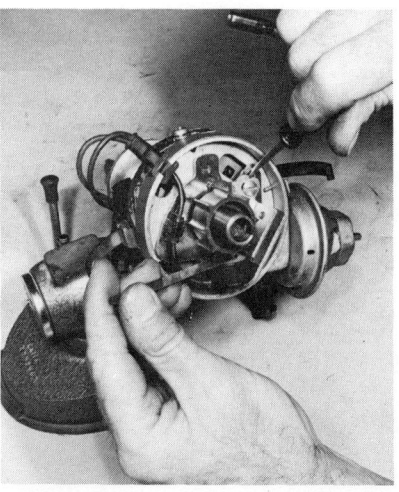

18. Align one reluctor tooth with pick-up coil and adjust air gap with nonmagnetic feeler gauge to .008-in. for 1973-76, and .006-in. for 1977 and later models.

INDEX

FUEL SYSTEMS

The automotive fuel system consists of a fuel tank, a fuel pump, one or more fuel filters, the carburetor, fuel and vacuum lines, and some form of control to prevent the emission of gasoline vapors into the atmosphere. Evaporation control usually is in the form of a charcoal canister, and will be discussed at length in Chapter 6, "Emission Controls."

Except for the carburetor, operation of the fuel system is fairly simple. The fuel tank consists of the tank itself, a filler tube, a fuel-gauge sending-unit assembly and a pressure/vacuum filler cap **(Fig. 5-1)**. Fuel from the tank is drawn through the fuel line by the fuel pump, which forces it to the fuel filter and then to the carburetor.

One fuel filter is located inside the fuel tank, usually on the end of the fuel suction tube **(Fig. 5-1)**. While it normally does not require service, it can be replaced if necessary. A second fuel filter is usually contained somewhere in the fuel line between the fuel pump and carburetor **(Fig. 5-2)**. This has a sealed, disposable paper element which should be replaced at periodic service intervals. A third filter may be located at or inside the carburetor fuel inlet **(Fig. 5-3)**.

ROLLOVER VALVES

Federal Motor Vehicle Safety Standards, effective with the 1976 model year, require that some provision be made to shut off fuel flow to the carburetor float

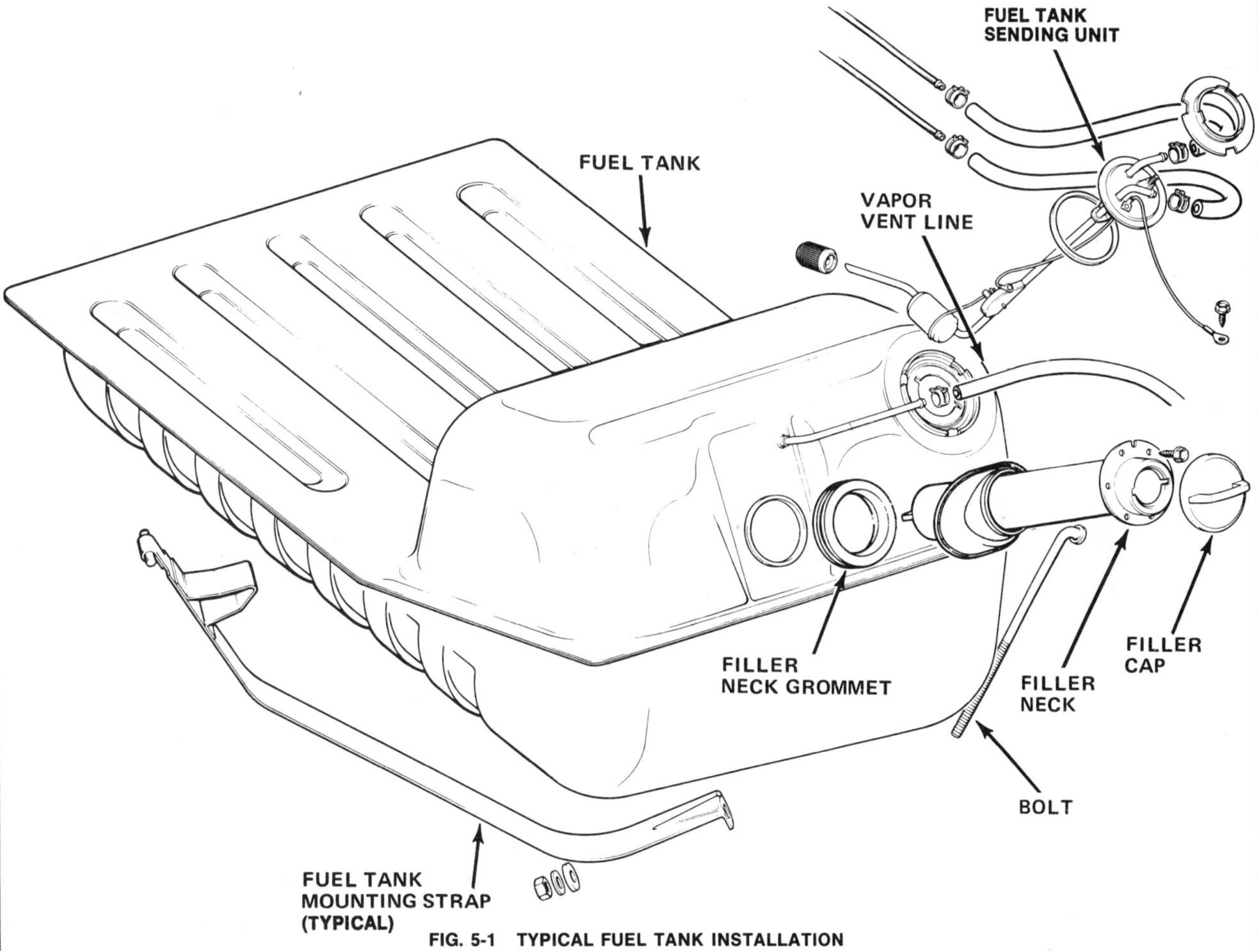

FIG. 5-1 TYPICAL FUEL TANK INSTALLATION

FIG. 5-2 INLINE FUEL FILTER (ARROW)

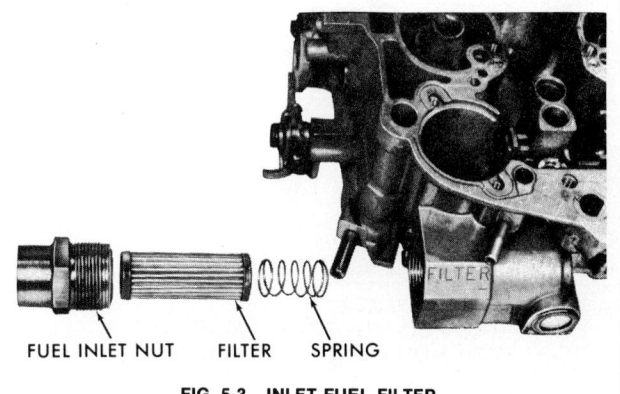

FIG. 5-3 INLET FUEL FILTER

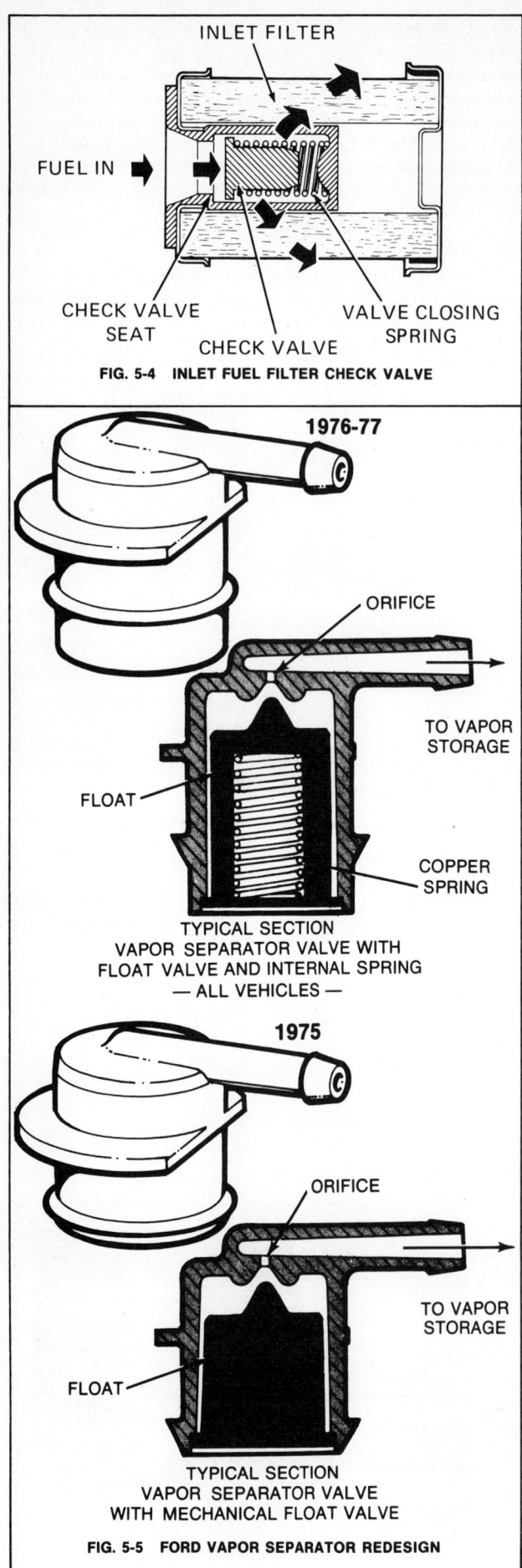

INLET FILTER

FUEL IN

CHECK VALVE
SEAT

CHECK VALVE

VALVE CLOSING
SPRING

FIG. 5-4 INLET FUEL FILTER CHECK VALVE

1976-77

ORIFICE

TO VAPOR
STORAGE

FLOAT

COPPER
SPRING

TYPICAL SECTION
VAPOR SEPARATOR VALVE WITH
FLOAT VALVE AND INTERNAL SPRING
— ALL VEHICLES —

1975

ORIFICE

TO VAPOR
STORAGE

FLOAT

TYPICAL SECTION
VAPOR SEPARATOR VALVE
WITH MECHANICAL FLOAT VALVE

FIG. 5-5 FORD VAPOR SEPARATOR REDESIGN

bowl to prevent the possibility of fuel leaks during a vehicle rollover.

Rochester carburetors (used on all General Motors cars) meet this requirement with a fuel-inlet-filter check valve located behind the fuel-inlet-filter nut and pressed into the inlet neck of the fuel filter **(Fig. 5-4).** The plastic check valve is held in a normally closed position by a small spring, and both are encased in a Viton retainer. When the engine is started and fuel flow pressure from the fuel pump enters the inlet, it pushes the check valve off its seat, allowing fuel to flow past the valve. With the engine off, the check valve closes to shut off fuel flow to the carburetor and prevents excessive fuel flow should the car roll over. Replacement filters for 1976 and later carburetors include the check valve; those for 1975 and earlier carburetors do not have this safety feature. Since the carburetor fuel inlet casting was not changed, filters with or without the check valve will fit old and new carburetors, but a filter with a check valve should not be used in a pre-1976 carburetor. If the car is equipped with a fuel return or vapor bypass line, the check valve can cause a fuel starvation problem.

Ford redesigned its fuel pump, vapor separator and fuel tank cap to meet the 1976 Federal Safety requirements. The 1976 fuel pump incorporates a new valve design at the outlet side to reduce fuel spillage during an accident. The plastic float-valve vapor separator was redesigned so that, whenever gasoline is at the orifice, the orifice is blocked **(Fig. 5-5).** The valve closes when the car is at a 90° angle. The new fuel-tank cap design prevents gasoline pressure from opening a pressure relief valve in the cap during a rollover.

Some Chrysler Corp. cars use a rollover valve in place of the previously used overfill-limiting valve in the vent line between the fuel tank and charcoal canister **(Fig. 5-6).** This valve is not serviceable and must be replaced if not functioning properly. Other models have the rollover valve mounted in the top of the fuel tank **(Fig. 5-6).** When a return line from the fuel filter to the fuel tank is installed, a one-way check valve is incorporated in the line. **(Fig. 5-6).**

American Motors uses a rollover check valve **(Fig. 5-7)** mounted on the right body side-sill behind the rear axle in the Hornet, on the kickup area of the floorpan over the rear axle in the Gremlin, and on the left side-sill forward of the rear axle on all other models. This check valve consists of a stainless steel ball, loose within its guides, which drops to seat a plunger when the assembly is inverted. It may be removed and tested by inverting it while applying 3-psi air to the inlet. Replace the unit if it will not hold the pressure.

Since 1976, American Motors vehicles fitted with 4-bbl. carburetors use an additional check valve in the fuel return system at the fuel filter between the pump and the carburetor. This valve eliminates any possibility of fuel feeding back to the carburetor through the fuel return line. A stainless-steel, spring-assisted check ball closes the orifice. Pressure between 0.1- and 0.6-psi, from the fuel filter side, opens the check valve to permit normal operation of the fuel return system. The check valve unit itself **(Fig. 5-8)** is arrow-marked in the direction of flow and, if reversed in the line, the fuel return system will not operate.

A third rollover check valve is installed in the fuel tank cap **(Fig. 5-9)** used on all AMC Matador models since 1976. This is a stainless steel ball in a plastic housing and mounted on the fuel-tank side of the cap. When the car is tipped sufficiently, the steel ball drops in its orifice to close the vent and prevent fuel leakage. This check valve can also be tested by applying 3-psi air to the plastic housing. When the valve is inverted, the unit should hold the pressure; if not, the cap must be replaced. Carter BBD carburetors used on AMC engines incorporate a rollover check valve in a plastic bowl vent fitting located on the air horn. This valve shuts off the vapor line to the canister in case of a rollover accident.

FUEL PUMPS

Fuel pumps usually operate off an eccentric on the camshaft, with a lever arm, linkage and spring to move the diaphragm up and down. An inlet and outlet valve work with the diaphragm, creating suction on the line from the tank and pressure to push the fuel up to the carburetor **(Fig. 5-10).**

The fuel pump is a quite dependable unit. When one malfunctions, it is usually caused by a cracked or bro-

ken diaphragm, which allows fuel to leak out onto the ground. Worn linkage will also reduce the stroke on the diaphragm so that the pump is unable to deliver fuel in the amounts required. Late-model fuel pumps are no longer serviceable; they all use a crimped edge which cannot be disassembled and must be replaced with a new or rebuilt unit when a malfunction occurs.

FUEL PUMP CAPACITY TEST

To test fuel delivery at the carburetor, take the line loose at the carburetor and slip a tight-fitting rubber hose over this line, letting the hose dangle over the radiator into a quart or larger container. Start the engine and let it idle just on the fuel in the carburetor bowl. As the fuel pump operates, it will squirt fuel into the bucket through the hose. Most fuel pumps should be capable of emitting a pint in 30 seconds, high-capacity pumps will deliver considerably more.

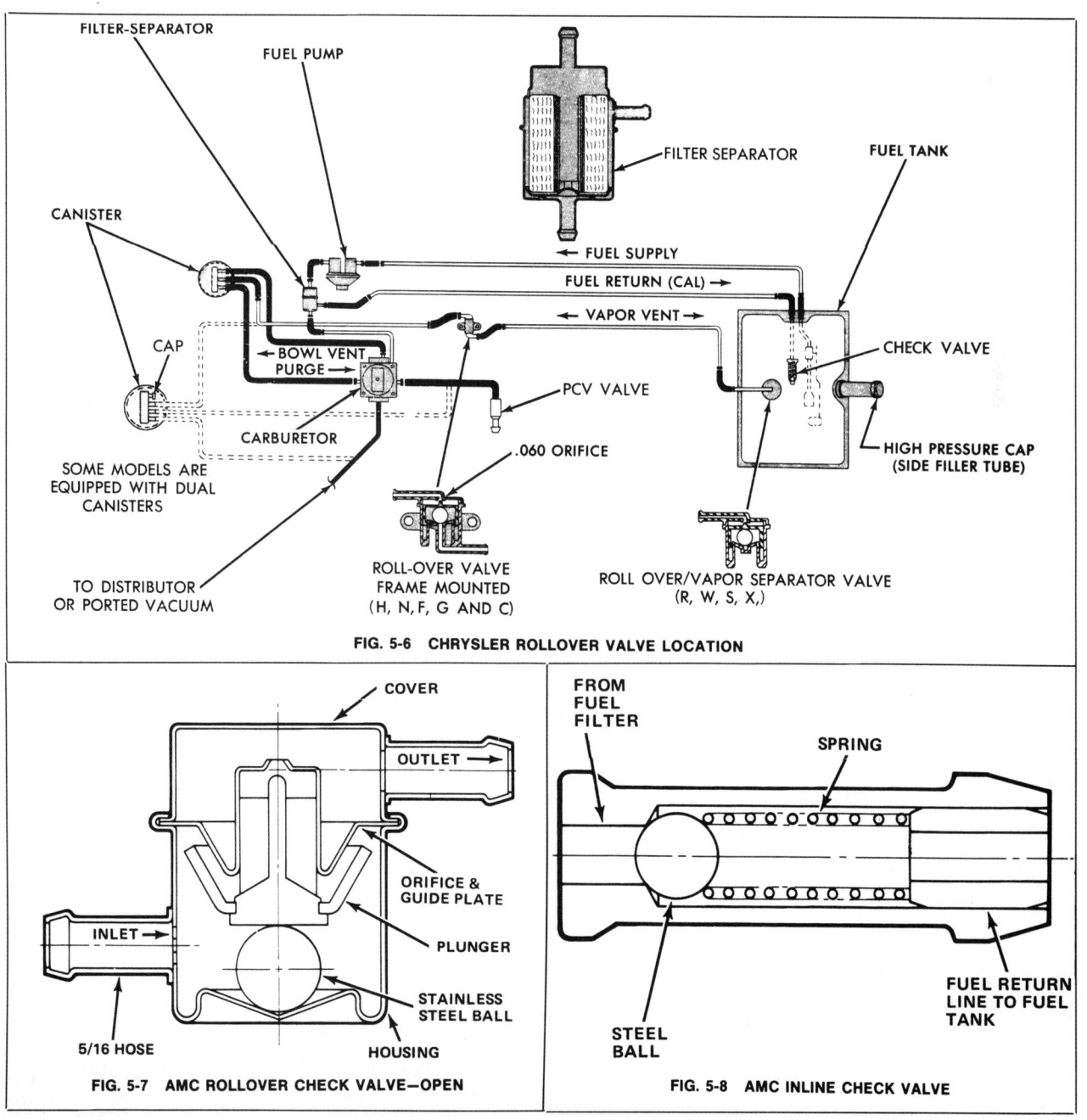

FIG. 5-6 CHRYSLER ROLLOVER VALVE LOCATION

FIG. 5-7 AMC ROLLOVER CHECK VALVE—OPEN

FIG. 5-8 AMC INLINE CHECK VALVE

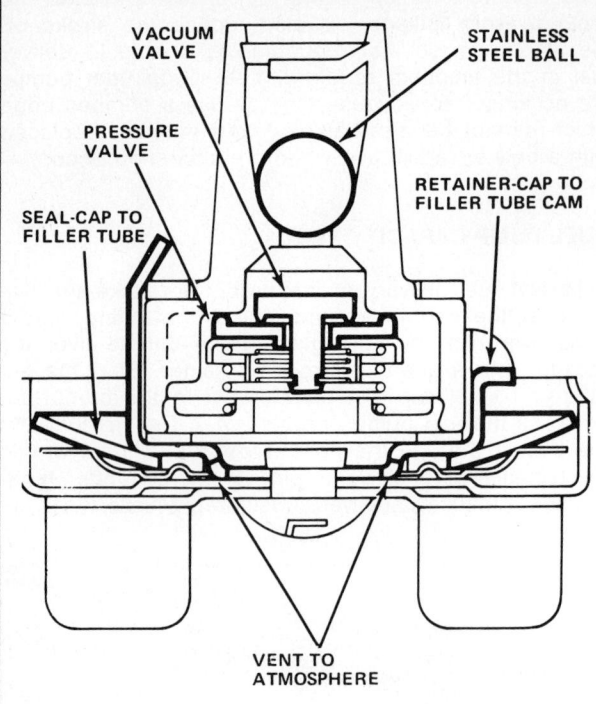

FIG. 5-9 AMC FILLER-CAP CHECK VALVE

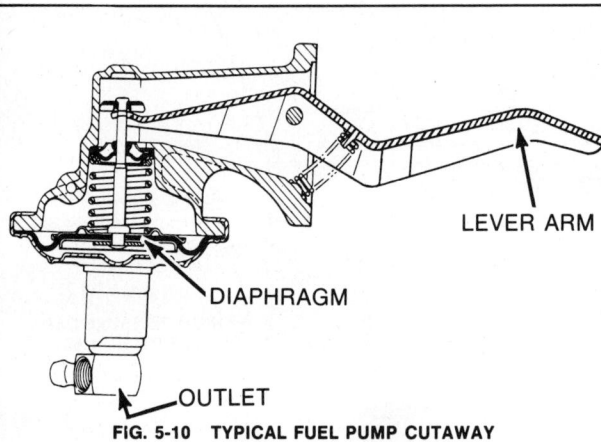

FIG. 5-10 TYPICAL FUEL PUMP CUTAWAY

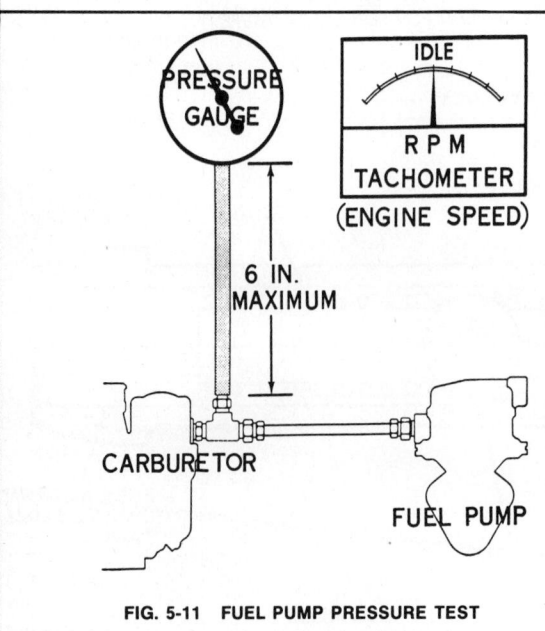

FIG. 5-11 FUEL PUMP PRESSURE TEST

FUEL PUMP PRESSURE TEST (Fig. 5-11)

1. Insert a "T" fitting in fuel line at the carburetor.
2. Connect a fuel pump tester gauge to the "T" fitting, using a piece of hose no longer than 6 ins. to prevent an inaccurate reading caused by the weight of fuel collected in the hose.
3. Vent the pump by operating the engine at idle and momentarily disconnecting the fuel line from the "T" to relieve air trapped in the fuel chamber. If this is not done, the pump cannot operate at full capacity and the resulting pressure reading will be inaccurate.
4. Connect a tachometer, then start the engine and run at idle.
5. Read the pressure gauge and compare the reading to specifications.
6. Shut off the engine. A bleed-back feature in the pump will cause the pressure reading to drop to zero immediately.

FUEL PUMP DIAGNOSIS

CONDITION	CORRECTION
PUMP LEAKS FUEL	
(a) Diaphragm is worn, ruptured or torn.	(a) Replace pump.
(b) Diaphragm mounting plates are loose.	(b) Replace pump.
(c) Loose inlet or outlet line fittings.	(c) Tighten line fittings.
PUMP LEAKS OIL	
(a) Cracked or deteriorated pushrod oil seal.	(a) Replace pump.
(b) Rocker arm pivot pin is loose.	(b) Replace pump.
(c) Pump mounting bolts loose.	(c) Tighten mounting bolts securely.
(d) Pump to block gasket is defective.	(d) Install new gasket
INSUFFICIENT FUEL DELIVERY	
(a) Vent in tank is restricted.	(a) Unplug vent and inspect tank for leaks.
(b) Leaks in fuel line or fittings.	(b) Tighten line fittings.
(c) Dirt or other restriction in fuel tank.	(c) Replace fuel filter and clean out tank.
(d) Diaphragm is worn, ruptured or torn.	(d) Replace pump.
(e) Gas lines frozen.	(e) Thaw lines and drain tank.
(f) Improperly seating valves	(f) Replace pump.
(g) Pump pushrod worn.	(g) Replace pushrod.
(h) Vapor lock.	(h) Install a heat shield wherever lines or pump come near exhaust.
(i) Low pressure.	(i) Replace pump.
(j) Dirty or restricted fuel filter.	(j) Replace filter.
NOISY FUEL PUMP	
(a) Mounting bolts are loose.	(a) Tighten mounting bolts securely.
(b) Rocker arm scored or worn.	(b) Replace pump.
(c) Rocker arm spring weak or broken.	(c) Replace spring.
(d) Stiff inlet hose..	(d) Install new hose about 3 ins. longer than old hose.

FUEL SYSTEM DIAGNOSIS

CONDITION	CORRECTION	CONDITION	CORRECTION

ENGINE CRANKS BUT WILL NOT START

(a) Choke valve does not close sufficiently when cold.

(a) Adjust the choke thermostatic coil.

(b) Choke valve or linkage binds or sticks.

(b) Realign or replace the choke valve or linkage as required. Clean but do not oil.

(c) No fuel in carburetor.

(c) Disconnect fuel line at tank and blow out with compressed air. Reconnect and check for proper operation. If not, replace fuel pump. Fuel filter may be plugged or carburetor float may require adjustment.

(d) Engine is flooded.

(d) Adjust throttle linkage and unloader if choke valve is not opening. If unloader works properly, disassemble and clean carburetor to remove dirt in carburetor float needle and seat. If engine still floods, check float for bent arm.

ENGINE HESITATES ON ACCELERATION

(a) Accelerator pump system defective.

(a) Remove air horn and check pump cup. If cracked, scored or distorted, replace pump plunger. Check discharge ball for proper seating and location.

(b) Dirt in pump passages or pump jet.

(b) Clean and blow out with compressed air.

(c) Float level incorrect.

(c) Check and reset float level to specs. Make sure float needle is not sticking.

(d) Insufficient fuel in carburetor.

(d) Disconnect fuel line at tank and blow out with compressed air. Reconnect and check for proper operation. If not, replace fuel pump. Fuel filter may be plugged or carburetor float may need adjustment.

(e) Carburetor flooding.

(e) Check fuel filters and replace if necessary. If carburetor continues to flood, remove air horn and check float needle and seat for proper seal. If needle set leaks, replace.

ENGINE IDLES ROUGH AND STALLS

(a) Manifold vacuum hoses disconnected, improperly installed or leak.

(a) Check all vacuum hoses, nstall or replace as required.

(b) Carburetor loose on intake manifold.

(b) Tighten carburetor-to-manifold bolts to specs.

(c) Dirt in idle channels.

(c) Clean fuel system and carburetor.

(d) Secondary throttle valve out of alignment.

(d) Loosen screws, align valves and tighten screws.

(e) Defective intake manifold gasket.

(e) Replace manifold gasket.

ENGINE STARTS HARD WHEN HOT

(a) Choke valve does not open completely.

(a) As choke valve and/or linkage binds, clean or replace as required. Also check and adjust choke thermostatic coil.

(b) No fuel in carburetor.

(b) Check fuel pump for proper operation and replace if necessary. Check and adjust float level.

(c) Gasket between air horn and float bowl leaks.

(c) Torque air horn to float bowl to specs.

(d) Carburetor loose on manifold.

(d) Tighten carburetor-to-manifold bolts to specs.

(e) Air valve sticks open.

(e) Free-up air valve shaft and align air valves. Check air valve spring for closing tension and replace if defective.

(f) Secondary throttle valve lockout.

(f) Free-up and check for proper operation if binding, then adjust secondary throttle valve lockout.

NO POWER—HEAVY ACCELERATION OR HIGH SPEED

(a) Carburetor throttle valve not opening completely.

(a) Adjust linkage

(b) Dirty or plugged fuel filters.

(b) Clean or replace filters.

(c) Secondary throttle valves do not unlock once engine has warmed up.

(c) Free-up and adjust lockout.

(d) Air valves bind, or are stuck open or closed.

(d) Free-up air valve shaft and align air valves. Check air valve spring for closing tension and replace if defective.

(e) Power system inoperative.

(e) Remove air horn and clean piston and cavity of dirt. Check power piston sprina for distortion.

(f) Float level too low.

(f) Check and reset float level to specs.

(g) Float does not drop far enough in bowl.

(g) Check for bind in float hanger and arm; check float alignment in bowl.

ENGINE SURGES OR RUNS UNEVEN

(a) Fuel restriction.

(a) Check hoses and fuel lines for bends or leaks. Check fuel filter and replace if dirty or plugged.

(b) Dirt or water in fuel.

(b) Clean fuel tank, lines and filters. Remove and clean carburetor.

(c) Float level incorrect.

(c) Check for free float and float needle valve operation, and adjust.

(d) Main metering jets or metering rods are dirty, plugged or bent.

(d) Completely disassemble carburetor and clean. Replace bent rods.

(e) Power system inoperative.

(e) Remove air horn and clean piston and cavity of dirt. Check power piston spring for distortion.

(f) Vacuum leakage.

(f) Tighten all hose connections. Torque carburetor to manifold to specs. Replace gasket if defective.

BASIC CARBURETOR SYSTEMS

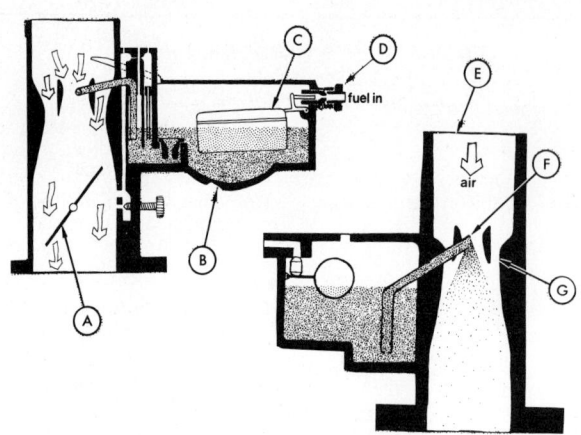

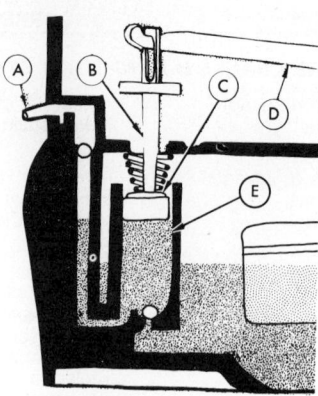

POWER SYSTEM

In some carburetors, a slightly different system is used, one that allows the throttle plate to close completely and routes air through a passageway around the plate to provide idle airflow.

When the throttle is opened suddenly while the engine is idling or running at a steady speed above idle, the rush of additional air into the engine upsets the balance of air to fuel. The fuel, being heavier, cannot respond as quickly as the air. To offset this, another system, called the accelerator pump (B), is used. This consists of an external linkage (D) attached to the throttle and a plunger (C) inside a well (E) filled with gas from the float bowl. When the gas pedal is depressed, the action of the linkage forces the fuel in the accelerator pump well to shoot out of a port (A) into the airstream in the bore. This momentary addition of fuel corrects the imbalance and permits the engine to function normally until the increased suction in the venturi starts drawing more gas from the main nozzle.

FLOAT & CRUISING SYSTEM

The carburetor operates on a simple physical principle. Air, drawn into the engine by the downward suction of a piston in a cylinder, enters the top of the carburetor bore (E). As the air travels downward in the bore, it passes through a slight narrowing of the bore known as the venturi (G). As the air passes through the venturi, it speeds up. This speed-up of air causes a slight drop in pressure in the venturi. The drop in pressure pulls gas from the float bowl (B) through a nozzle (F) into the bore of the carburetor. At this point, the fuel mixes with the air, forming a fine spray of atomized particles. This air/fuel mixture passes through the carburetor into the intake manifold, which distributes the mixture to the cylinders for compression and burning.

As pressure is reduced in the venturi, it causes fuel to be pulled from the float bowl (B). The falling level of the gas causes the float (C) to drop. The float controls a valve called the needle and seat (D), which opens to allow more fuel to enter the float bowl from the fuel pump. This self-metering system keeps a constant supply of fuel available to the carburetor.

Below the point where fuel enters the bore is a movable plate. This throttle plate (A) is controlled by linkage attached to the gas pedal. The opening and closing of the throttle plate controls the amount of air that can pass through the bore and also controls the fuel that is drawn into the airstream. As the throttle plate opens, the air volume entering the intake manifold increases and draws in more fuel, due to the increasingly low pressure created by the venturi. This action causes the engine to speed up and deliver more power. If the throttle plate closes, the amount of air that can enter the engine drops, causing a lessening of the partial vacuum of the venturi, and less gas is pulled into the bore. This is the basic metering system that controls the overall carburetor operation.

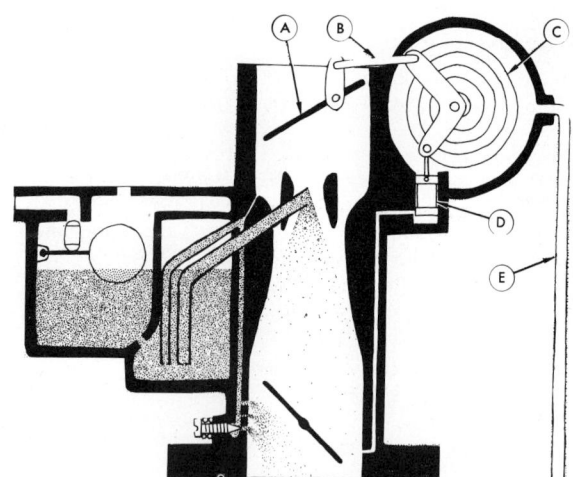

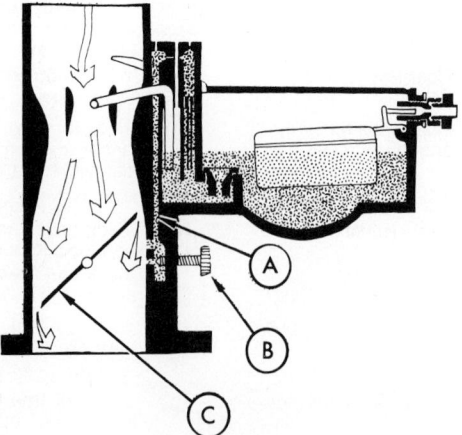

IDLE SYSTEM

When the engine is running at idle speed, or with only slight foot pressure on the gas pedal, the throttle plate is nearly closed. This reduces the intake of air below the point where it will pull fuel from the float bowl through the main metering nozzle. A separate fuel path called the idle circuit (A) is necessary. When the engine is running at idle, the vacuum or low-pressure area is not at the venturi, but is most strongly felt below the throttle plate (C). By providing another route for gasoline to enter the carburetor bore below the throttle plate, sufficient fuel can enter the engine for idle and low-speed operation.

Fuel is drawn through a passageway from the float bowl by the low pressure to a point below the throttle plate. There is an external adjusting screw, called the idle mixture screw (B), located on the outside of the carburetor near the base. This screw regulates the amount of fuel available at the port. Another adjustment screw, the idle speed screw, is also located on the outside of the carburetor. The idle speed screw controls the position of the throttle plate over a small range to adjust the amount of air that is allowed to enter the engine.

CHOKE SYSTEM

At the top of the carburetor bore is another plate which looks much like the throttle plate. This is the choke plate (A). The choke is used to help the engine start when it is cold, and to keep it running until the engine warms up to operating temperature.

When the engine is cold, fuel tends to drop out of the air/fuel mixture and cling to (condense on) the interior surfaces of the intake manifold and the carburetor. This disturbs the balance of air to fuel. To prevent this problem from affecting the engine, the choke plate closes, cutting down on the intake of air. This creates a mixture richer in fuel and aids starting. The choke can be manually or automatically operated. Some older cars and trucks may have manual chokes controlled by a knob on the dashboard, but modern vehicles have automatic chokes. The automatic choke (shown) has a choke plate (A) which is connected to the thermostatic coil spring (C) by a linkage (B). On the other side of the linkage is a choke piston (D). Connected to the body of the choke housing is a tube (E) that runs to the heat stove.

Closing the choke is accomplished by the thermostatic coil (C). The spring is made of a material which relaxes when heated. To set the choke on most cars (when starting a cold engine), depress the gas pedal firmly, all the way to the floor. This positions the linkage to shut the choke plate in the carburetor bore. It also slightly increases the idle speed for cold engine warmup. While the engine is starting, the choke remains closed to block off most of the incoming air. This provides the engine with a rich fuel mixture. As soon as the engine starts, the choke must be partially opened to allow enough air for idle operation. The choke piston does this. By using the vacuum in the lower part of the throttle bore, the choke piston is pulled down, moving the linkage to open the choke slightly. As the engine warms up, the thermostatic spring is warmed by air coming from the heat stove, which is a metal box close to one exhaust manifold. The spring relaxes and opens the choke all the way once the engine has reached operating temperature.

FUEL PUMP REMOVAL/REPLACEMENT

The fuel pump is usually located in the most inaccessible part of the engine compartment, and while locating it may not be difficult, removal/replacement can be a chore. Regardless of the car involved, the procedure is essentially the same. You simply disconnect the lines attached to it and plug them. Then remove the capscrews holding the pump to the engine block, and remove the pump.

Whenever you loosen a line (or reconnect it), always use two wrenches—one to hold the inner fitting and the other to turn the outer fitting. Compare the pump removed from the engine to the replacement pump—there may be some fittings screwed into the old pump which must be removed and installed on the new one. If such fittings are directional, they must be installed on the new pump facing in the same direction as on the old pump.

To install the new pump, remove all gasket material from the pump mounting pad on the engine block. Apply a quantity of oil-resistant sealer to both sides of the new gasket and position it on the pump flange. Install the new pump against the mounting pad and make certain the rocker arm or rod rides on the camshaft or intermediate-shaft eccentric. Pressing the pump tightly against the pad, install the capscrews and alternately torque them to specifications. Reconnect the lines using new clamps, then start the engine and let it idle while you check for leaks.

THE CARBURETOR

The carburetor meters fuel to the incoming air in quantities suitable for all engine speed and load conditions. Its proper operation is essential, as we'll see. The majority of so-called carburetion problems are caused by ignition timing, spark plugs, loss of compression, inadequate fuel delivery to the carburetor or even a clogged air cleaner filter. The carburetor itself seldom gives much trouble during normal operation. Carburetors have so few moving parts that there really isn't much in them to wear out. The throttle shaft, accelerator pump and power valve are probably the biggest offenders. The throttle shaft wears at its bushings from the pressure of the throttle return spring and lets in too much or too little air into the engine when it shouldn't. The accelerator pump plunger wears out and doesn't squirt as much as it should, causing a flat spot when the driver steps on the gas. Power valves using a diaphragm tend to leak, because the diaphragm occasionally develops a pinhole rupture.

The rest of the carburetor has no significant wear points; troubles with it are usually caused by foreign matter reaching the carburetor through the air or through the fuel, or by gummy fuel deposits. The dirt or foreign matter may be rust particles off the sides of the gas tank or dust in the air inside the tank. When dirt is carried up to the carburetor by the fuel, it means trouble. Airborne dirt gets lodged in the air bleeds and passages, upsetting the balance between air and fuel that the carburetor is designed to control. As for the gasoline that passes through it, not all of the substances which compose gasoline will readily pass into the air and turn into smog. The heavier fractions of gasoline turn to a kind of gooey mess which eventually hardens, plugging the tiny jet openings and restricting vital passages.

Carburetor work is primarily disassembly, cleaning and reassembly, without making any adjustments. This is true even when parts such as accelerator pumps and

needle seats are replaced. The old and new parts go back in the same positions; all that is necessary is to make careful checks of specifications. But, if you have not taken the time to learn a little bit about how a carburetor operates, then you're going to cause trouble. You can spend days taking a carburetor apart, putting it back together, running the car and then going through the same procedures again and again, simply because, when you have the carburetor apart, you do not know what to look for.

Descriptions of the "basic systems" (opposite page) which make the carburetor work are essential.

FLOAT SYSTEM (Fig. 5-12)

A float bowl is needed to provide a readily available source of fuel when acceleration demands call for it. A vent in the float bowl allows expanding vapor to escape and maintains a constant atmospheric pressure. To control inlet fuel flow, a needle valve and float arrangement are used. When fuel reaches a predetermined level, the rising float pushes the valve into its seat to shut off further flow.

Either the float arm itself or a tab on the arm moves the needle valve in or out of the seat. The object is to keep fuel in the bowl at just the right level. Too much fuel in the bowl will cause the engine to run rich. Too little fuel causes the engine to run lean, perhaps even creating backfire through the carburetor and igniting an underhood fire.

To adjust float-bowl fuel level to specification, bend the float arm or the tab attached to the arm.

"Float level" specification is a measurement from some part of the carburetor casting to the float, when the float arm is resting on a closed needle.

If the float is attached to the bowl cover, then the measurement is taken between the float and cover,

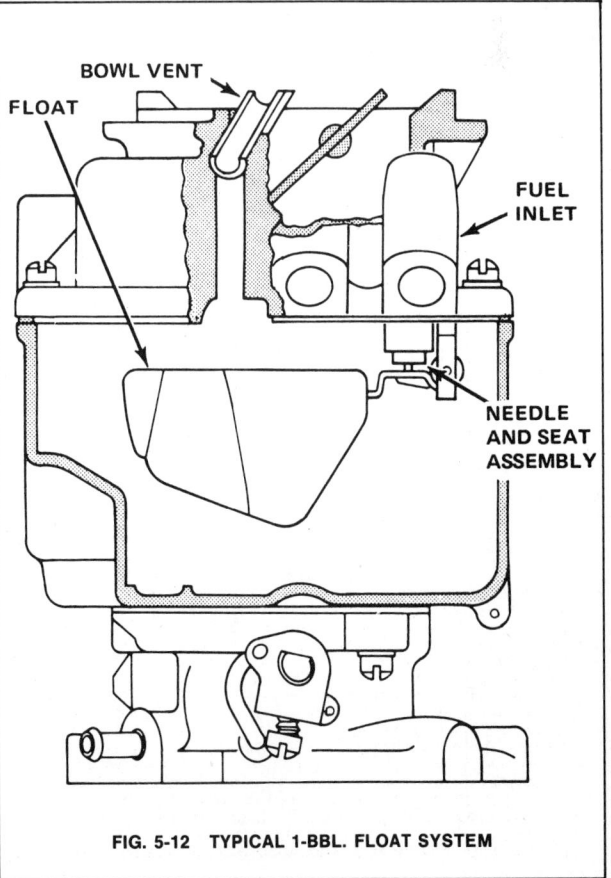

FIG. 5-12 TYPICAL 1-BBL. FLOAT SYSTEM

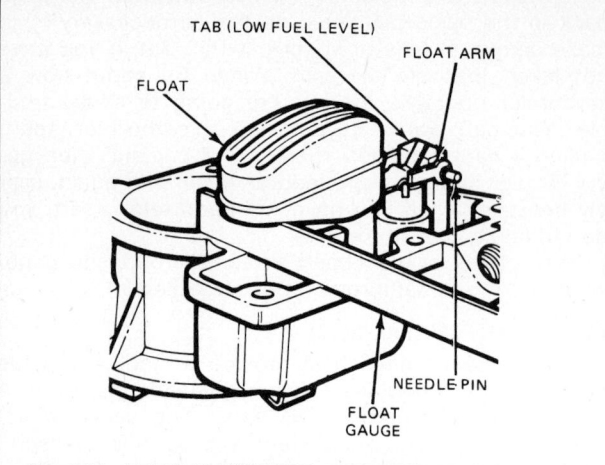

FIG. 5-13 FLOAT ADJUSTMENT—ATTACHED TO BOWL COVER

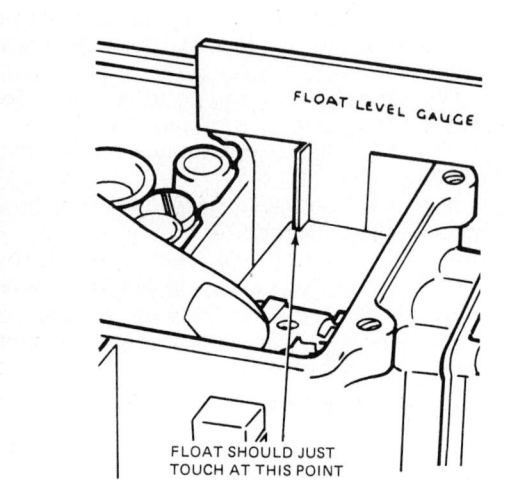

FIG. 5-14 FLOAT ADJUSTMENT—ATTACHED TO BOWL

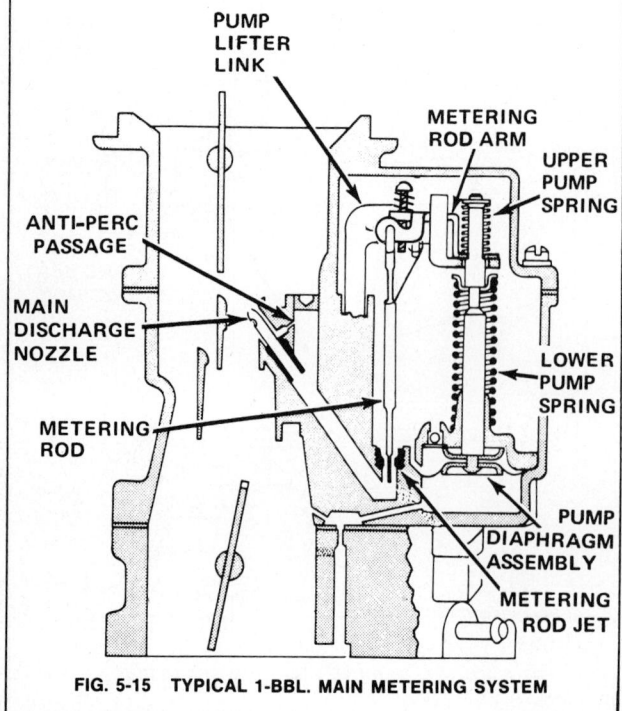

FIG. 5-15 TYPICAL 1-BBL. MAIN METERING SYSTEM

with the cover inverted so that the weight of the float closes the needle **(Fig. 5-13)**.

If the float is attached to the bowl itself, the measurement is taken from the top of the float to the top edge of the bowl, with the float and needle in the closed position **(Fig. 5-14)**. To get the needle and float into the closed position on this type of float system, invert the carburetor, *do not* push the float and needle closed with a finger. Today's Teflon-tipped needles, neoprene-tipped needles and Teflon or neoprene inlet seats will last a long time with only the pressure of the float against them, but the pressure of a finger pushing on the needle may be too much, causing a groove in the neoprene. The neoprene will gradually come back to shape, eliminating the groove, so that a few hours after setting the float level it will change by itself. If the neoprene or Teflon does not come back to shape, the groove may cause flooding, because it provides a place for particles of dirt to lodge, thereby holding the needle off its seat.

To get the float and needle into the closed position on a carburetor with the float attached to the bowl, invert the carburetor and take the measurement. With the carburetor on the car, the easiest way to do it is to pour some gasoline into the bowl until the float rises to its maximum height and then take the measurement. It is important not to confuse fuel level and float level. *Float level* is a measurement from the float to some part of the carburetor bowl or cover. *Fuel level* is an actual wet measurement of how far the fuel is from the top of the bowl. If the float needle and seat are attached to the bowl, then the actual fuel level can be measured with a scale. If they are attached to the bowl cover, then the fuel level cannot be measured in most cases, unless the carburetor manufacturer has provided sight holes in the side of the bowl cover. The fuel level specification, when given, is really nothing more than a double-check to be sure the float level is correctly and accurately set.

When the engine uses fuel and the float drops, it is possible that the needle could fall out of the seat on some carburetors. If this happens, the carburetor will receive just a little more gasoline than it needs, resulting in a flooded condition. To prevent this from happening, there is a small tab on the back side of the float to limit the amount of drop. The float drop measurement is taken with the bowl cover removed from the carburetor. Hold the cover in the normal position and measure from the underside of the bowl cover to the float. If the float is attached to the bowl itself, there is usually no float drop measurement. In this case, the float may be designed so that, at maximum drop, it rests on the bottom of the bowl. Should the little tab that limits float drop become bent, then the float may not drop enough. In this case, the needle will not pull away from the seat sufficiently, resulting in fuel starvation at wide-open throttle.

Dirt is the enemy of any float system. The needle and seat are so sensitive to dirt that the smallest particle can cause flooding. This is the reason Teflon, Viton or neoprene needles and seats are used; these substances have enough "give" to conform to the shape of the speck of dirt and seat around it. Sometimes it does, sometimes it doesn't. If a particle of foreign matter should enter the needle valve and cause it to leak, then enough fuel can be pumped into the engine to kill it, and make restarting almost impossible until the excess fuel evaporates. Keeping the fuel at the right level is very important and an examination of the main metering system tells why.

MAIN METERING SYSTEM (Fig. 5-15)

Now that the float bowl is full of gasoline, the next step is to mix it with air and feed it into the engine. The base of every carburetor is really nothing more than an air valve with a throttle plate(s) hung on a shaft and controlled by the driver's foot on the accelerator pedal. Wide-open throttle means just that—when the driver steps on the gas, he is opening the throttle valve so that the maximum amount of air can enter the engine. But in order for the engine to run, this air has to have gasoline mixed with it in the correct proportion.

This is accomplished by running a tube from the float bowl to the middle of the airstream in the carburetor bore. The end of the tube, called the main nozzle, is positioned so that it is in the center of the venturi, a narrow section in the carburetor bore. Since this section is narrow, it causes reduced pressure at the end of the tube. This reduced pressure draws fuel from the float bowl, through the tube and into the airstream, where it mixes with the air. The fuel/air mixture then passes the throttle valve and is drawn into the combustion chamber.

The main metering system has had many refinements over the years. There may be air bleeds or small baffles in the main nozzle, and there may be vacuum or mechanically operated metering rods in the main jet, a calibrated hole at the bottom of the float bowl. The object of all such refinements is to be certain the engine receives more fuel when it needs it, and less fuel when it doesn't. Metering rods are designed to stay in the main jet when the engine is running at low power. But when the engine is running at maximum power, the rods will lift out of the jet so that the engine gets the fuel it needs. At any point between closed throttle and maximum power, the rods will be partially in or partially out of the jet, thus varying fuel flow according to how much fuel the engine requires at the time **(Fig. 5-16)**

Mechanically operated metering rods are lifted by a lever hooked to the throttle. Vacuum-operated rods are pushed out of the jet by a spring and pulled back down by engine vacuum acting on a piston hooked to the top of the rod. A passage from the intake manifold runs up through the carburetor so that engine vacuum can act on the piston.

Without engine vacuum, the carburetor wouldn't work. This vacuum exists below the throttle valves when the engine is running. A pre-emissions engine in good condition will produce 18- to 21-ins. vacuum; late models may produce as little as 12 ins. As the throttle is opened, engine vacuum drops off until there is zero vacuum at wide-open throttle.

It is rare to have a main metering system plug up completely. If the main nozzle is plugged but the main jet is still open, the carburetor would idle perfectly, but gasp and die completely the moment the throttle was opened. If the driver got his foot off it quick enough, the idle system would take over again and the car would come down to idle perfectly. An idle system is necessary, because at idle the throttle valves are almost completely closed and there is not enough airflow through the venturi to draw fuel out of the main nozzle.

THE IDLE SYSTEM (Fig. 5-17)

At idle, the engine draws air from around the throttle plate, which is just barely open . . . but this air has no fuel in it. Instead, the fuel is coming through the idle port hole in the throttle body just below the throttle plate. An idle mixture needle screws into the outside of the throttle body and is used to regulate the amount of fuel flowing through the port and into the engine.

Fuel enters the idle system through a tube mounted in the carburetor, usually between the float bowl and the carburetor bore. The end of the tube is a calibrated hole called the idle jet. Some idle tubes (jets) can be changed merely by unscrewing them, but others are part of the metering cluster—in that case, the whole cluster must be changed.

As the throttle is opened and the high vacuum beneath the throttle plates starts to fall off, fuel flow through the idle port lessens. To keep the engine from faltering at this critical moment, another hole, called the idle transfer, is uncovered. This feeds more fuel to

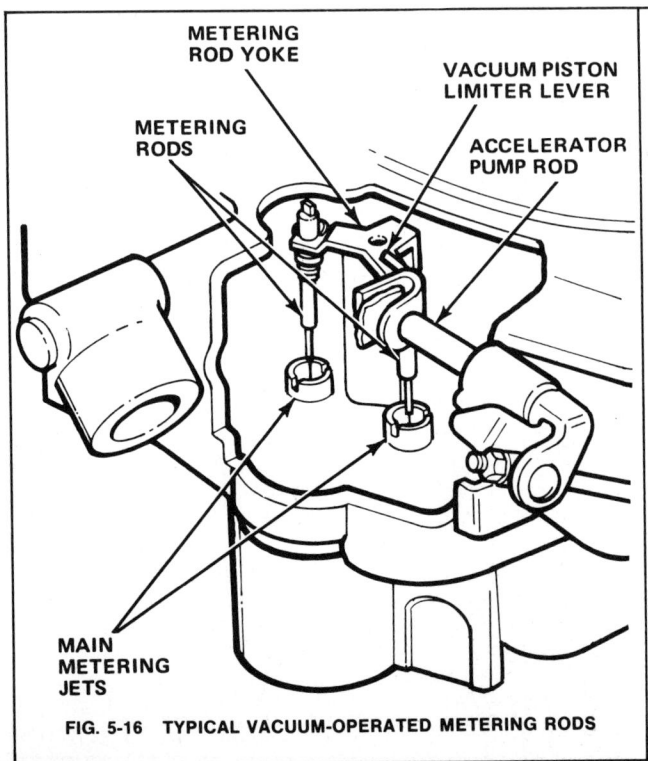

FIG. 5-16 TYPICAL VACUUM-OPERATED METERING RODS

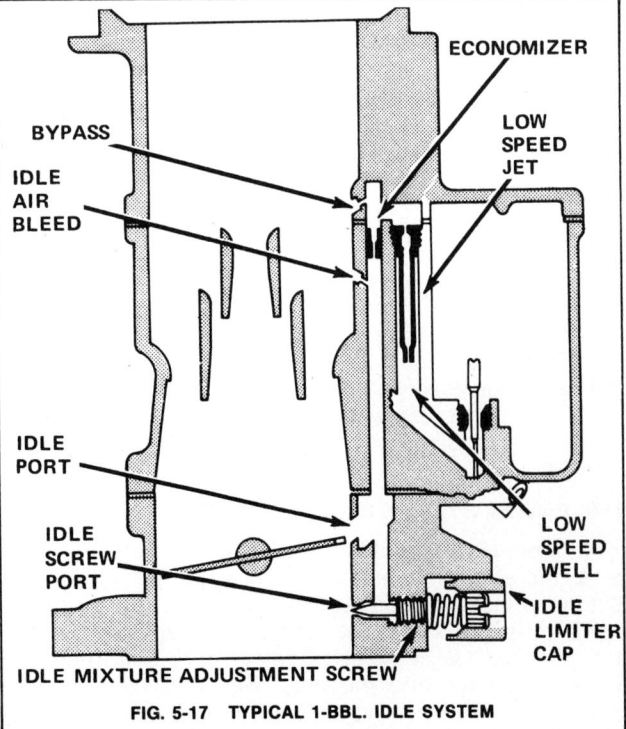

FIG. 5-17 TYPICAL 1-BBL. IDLE SYSTEM

keep the engine going. By that time, sufficient air is coming through the venturi to cause the main metering system to start to take over. But in most carburetor designs, the idle system will continue to feed even at speeds as high as 70 mph.

One very important thing to keep clear is that the engine idles on air from two sources and fuel from one. Air goes into the engine around the partially opened throttle plate and, mixed with fuel, enters through the idle port, controlled by the idle mixture screw. The screw is spring-loaded and the idle mixture is controlled by setting the screw. Engine speed is controlled with a spring-loaded screw on the throttle shaft. When the driver takes his foot off the gas, the throttle will close down to the setting that was made with the idle speed screw. With the wrong setting, the throttle closes too much and the engine will die. If the screw holds the throttle open too far, then the driver will have to use both feet on the brake to keep the car from driving down the street at a 40-mph idle speed.

ACCELERATOR PUMP SYSTEM (Fig. 5-18)

When the throttle opens suddenly, air reacts instantly and rushes past the throttle plates, but the fuel coming out of the main nozzle takes time to catch up. During this period, the engine will run lean and stumble. The problem is solved by using an accelerator pump, which is nothing more than a piston hooked to the throttle linkage. It operates in a cylinder so that, every time the driver steps on the gas, a squirt of fuel goes into each carburetor throat. The pump only squirts when the throttle is moved. At all other times, it does not feed any gas.

The pump system includes an inlet check valve and an outlet check valve so it can draw fuel into its cylinder from the bowl on the upstroke and then squirt this fuel into the carburetor throat on the downstroke. Some pumps are not directly operated by the throttle linkage, but allowed to operate by the linkage. They have a duration spring that actually pushes the pump down. This is done so that the length of time the pump operates is always the same, regardless of how fast the driver opens the throttle.

That well-known "flat spot" on acceleration is usually caused by something wrong in the accelerator pump system. Most often, it is a pump piston that does not fit well in the cylinder, either because the piston is worn or because it is made of leather and the lip of the leather curled up when the piston was installed. Incorrectly adjusted linkage can also be at fault, causing a pump stroke that is either too long or too short. The jet controlling the amount of squirt on an accelerator pump is usually built into the pump nozzle, mounted above the venturi. In an extreme case, which seems to defy the best efforts to correct the problem, it is possible to drill out the pump jet for a little more squirt. With the system as described so far, the carburetor will work fine, until it reaches wide-open throttle. At that point, the engine requires more fuel than is admitted by the main jet.

THE POWER SYSTEM (Fig. 5-19)

With or without metering rods, main metering jets work fine above idle and at almost any cruising speed. But when the engine is really called on to put out with the throttle wide open, the main jet simply does not let sufficient fuel in. In order to admit more fuel, there is another passage into the main well and up into the main nozzle. This passage is closed at all times, except when the throttle is opened enough to allow engine

vacuum to fall below about 10 ins. At that point, a spring opens the power valve and additional fuel is permitted to enter the main well, go through the main nozzle and into the venturi.

Power valves can be either vacuum or mechanically operated. Some carburetors have the power valve located at the bottom of the accelerator pump cylinder so that, when the throttle is wide open, and the accelerator pump bottoms, it tips a little plunger operating the power valve. Other power valves operate off engine vacuum, opposed by a spring. They can be either piston- or diaphragm-operated.

The unfortunate thing about a power valve is that the driver may not determine it is bad until it is too late. If a power valve should fail in the closed position, the engine does not get the fuel it requires at wide-open

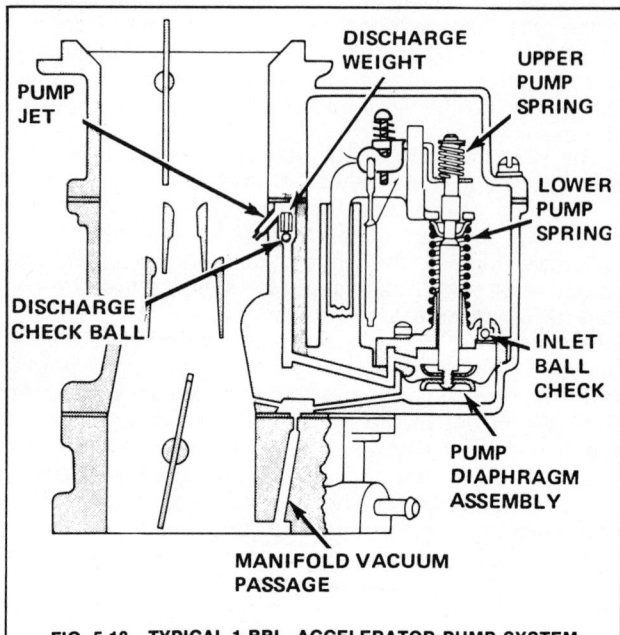

FIG. 5-18 TYPICAL 1-BBL. ACCELERATOR PUMP SYSTEM

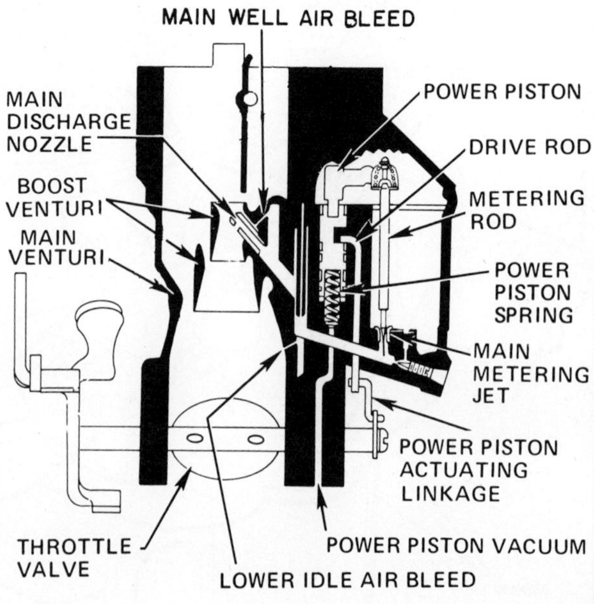

FIG. 5-19 TYPICAL 1-BBL. POWER SYSTEM

throttle—it may even run lean enough to burn a hole in the piston, depending upon how long the engine is operated at wide-open throttle. Vacuum-operated power valves are held closed by engine vacuum and opened by a spring. If they fail, they usually do so in an open position, allowing a lot of fuel to go into the engine at all speeds above idle, and in some designs, even permitting fuel to dribble out onto the top of the engine, which can be a help in troubleshooting the difficulty, but also presents a very real fire hazard.

HIGH-SPEED PULLOVER SYSTEM

To cut down on emissions, main jets must be lean—in many cases so lean that there is not enough fuel supplied under a high-rpm, part-throttle condition. At part throttle, the metering rod hasn't lifted to the high-

speed step because engine vacuum hasn't dropped low enough, even though the engine requires more fuel because of the high rpm.

Rochester carburetors provide this extra fuel with a pullover system, which consists of a passageway from the float bowl up to the air horn, exiting above the choke valve. There is usually one hole for each carburetor throat. Because of their location, these holes are sensitive to air velocity and, anytime there is high air velocity through the carburetor (as at high rpm), the pullover holes feed extra fuel into the airstream. Pullover starts at about 50 mph on part throttle, and is also called High Speed Fuel Feed or Auxiliary Fuel Feed.

CHOKE SYSTEM (Fig. 5-20)

If an engine could be heated up to operating temperature before it was started, a choke would not be necessary. But a cold engine is so cold that fuel condenses on the intake manifold passageways and the walls of the combustion chamber. Fuel by itself will not burn; it has to be mixed with air. And the only way to get an air/fuel mixture into a cold engine is to feed in more fuel than necessary to make up for that which condenses. The choke is an air valve positioned above the main nozzle, so that it can restrict or shut off completely the air entering the engine. This permits the full force of engine suction to operate on the main nozzle so the engine will get the fuel it requires.

The problem with chokes is not in making them work, but in getting them to shut off (open) at the right moment. The choke is closed by a thermostatic spring and opened by this same spring when heat from the exhaust manifold, a hot water tube or electric assist allows it to relax. But this spring control by itself is not sufficient. To get a more positive control, there is often a vacuum piston that opposes the strength of the spring, and the choke valve itself is offset so that the air entering the carburetor tends to push it open. When everything is working correctly, the automatic choke is fine, but when it does not work properly, the engine will lope and blow black smoke from the tailpipe.

Sticking chokes have presented such a problem that

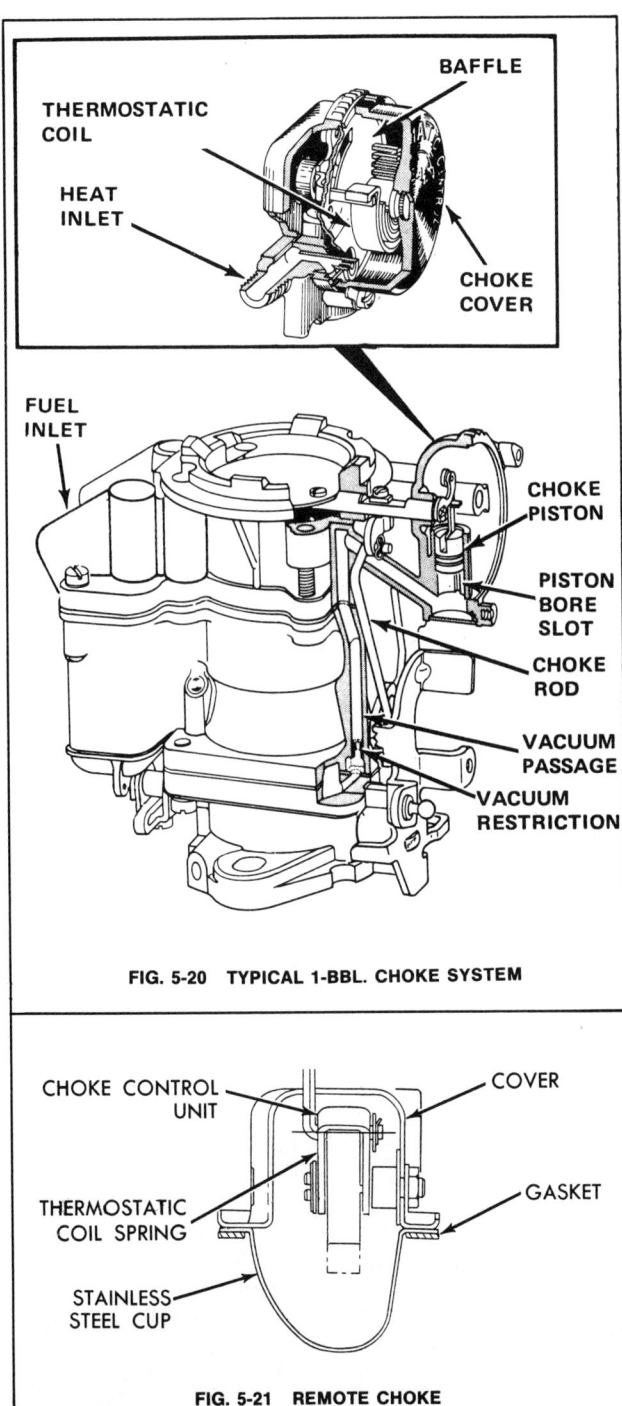

FIG. 5-20   TYPICAL 1-BBL. CHOKE SYSTEM

FIG. 5-21   REMOTE CHOKE

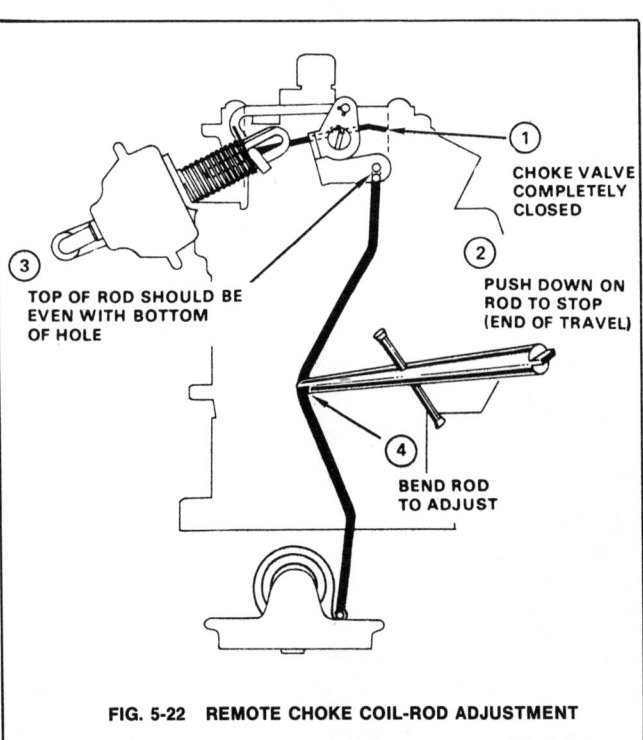

FIG. 5-22   REMOTE CHOKE COIL-ROD ADJUSTMENT

some carburetor manufacturers now coat their choke shafts with Teflon. It seems to work, although the adjustment of a choke continues to be a tricky problem.

The choke itself seldom requires adjustment, unless someone has worked on it, trying to cure a malfunction which appeared to be choke-related, but really wasn't. When a choke does not work correctly, it is usually because evaporating fuel deposits have left gum on the choke shaft, butterfly, etc.

THE REMOTE CHOKE (Fig. 5-21)

Chrysler Corporation through 1978, and most General Motors applications through 1974, use the remote or well-type choke. This is a thermostatic coil mounted in a well on the intake manifold and directly heated by an exhaust passage in the manifold. Adjustment of a remote choke is made by lengthening or shortening the rod connecting it to the carburetor (Fig. 5-22). With few exceptions, all remote chokes push *up* to close the choke, so to obtain more choking action, the rod is bent to make it longer (increasing tension); for less choking action, it is bent to make it shorter (decreasing tension).

INTEGRAL CAP CHOKE

The integral cap choke is mounted on the carburetor. The choke cap contains a thermostatic coil spring which connects to a lever attached to the choke shaft via linkage. This type of choke usually includes a vacuum piston inside the housing (Fig. 5-23). When the engine starts, vacuum pulls on the piston and helps to open the choke by the linkage arrangement. But vacuum pistons have a tendency to gum up and the housing can distort from heat, causing the piston to bind.

To adjust an integral choke, the screws clamping the Bakelite cap to the housing are loosened and the cap rotated either in the direction of rich or lean, as indicated by arrows. Cap rotation increases or decreases tension on the thermostatic coil inside (Fig. 5-24).

Choke caps fitted to the carburetors used on some 1978 and later Corvette engines are riveted to the choke housing, effectively preventing casual choke adjustment by the owner. The riveted cap is to be removed only when the carburetor is overhauled or when the choke cap, coil or housing must be replaced. To remove the cap, drill out the rivets with a No. 21 drill, then remove

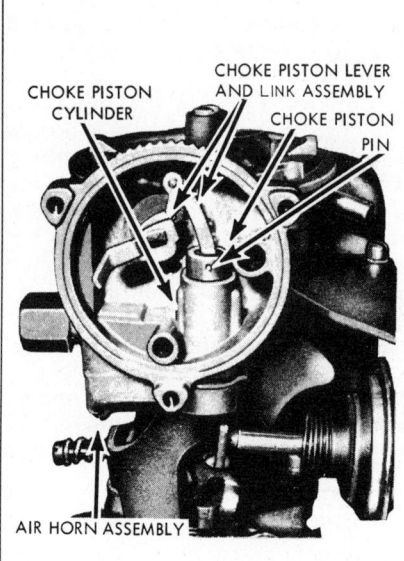

FIG. 5-23 INTEGRAL CHOKE PISTON SYSTEM

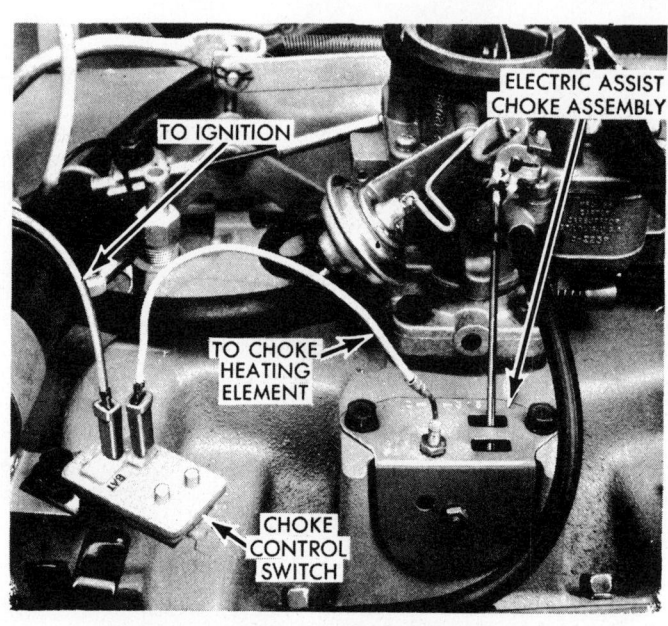

FIG. 5-26 REMOTE CHOKE ELECTRIC ASSIST

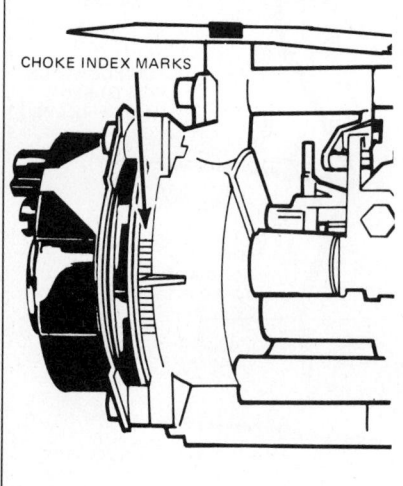

FIG. 5-24 INTEGRAL CHOKE

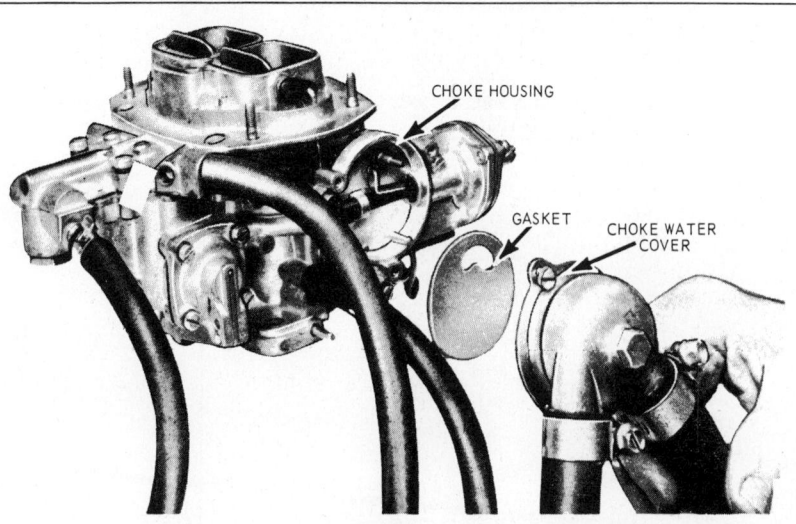

FIG. 5-25 WATER-HEATED INTEGRAL CHOKE

the remainder with a small punch. The new cap is installed with self-tapping screws.

Water-heated cap chokes attempt to shorten choke duration by concentrating engine heat where it is most effective. A heater hose line is run directly against the Bakelite choke cap, or hot coolant is routed directly through the thermostatic coil housing **(Fig. 5-25)**. This has not proven too effective and, for the most part, has been abandoned in favor of an electric assist.

ELECTRIC ASSISTED CHOKE

Remote chokes use a separate heating element connected to the choke thermostatic coil and wired to an external electrical control switch, which is connected in turn to the ignition switch **(Fig. 5-26)**. When the ignition is turned on, the switch senses the outside or ambient temperature and, at about 60° F, the control switch allows current to flow to the heating element, turning on the choke heater. As the temperature reaches approximately 110° F, the control switch shuts off the heating element and lets the choke coil operate on its own.

Integral chokes use a ceramic heating element connected to the choke coil and a bi-metal temperature sensor switch which draws constant power from the alternator **(Fig. 5-27)**. Because this switch remains open at outside temperatures below 60° F, no current reaches the ceramic heater and normal thermostatic spring action takes place. But as the temperature rises above 60° F, the sensor closes and alternator current flows to the ceramic heater **(Fig. 5-28)**. As the heater warms up, it causes the choke coil spring to pull the choke plates open within a period of about 90 seconds. Ground contact is provided by a metal plate or strap located at the rear of the choke assembly. A choke cover gasket *should not* be installed between the electric choke and the choke housing, because it will prevent the electric assist from operating.

Chrysler's electric assist choke has alternated between a single-stage and a dual-stage control, with both types currently in use **(Fig. 5-26)**. The dual-stage control, identified by the resistor attached to the outside of the switch, is designed to shorten choke duration at temperatures above 63° F, and stabilize it in winter weather. The system provides partial power to the choke heater at temperatures below 58° F, by routing some of the electricity through the switch resistor.

An electric assist has no effect on choke adjustment itself, and cannot be adjusted. If faulty, the cap heater or switch must be replaced. On carburetors equipped with an electric assist, look for this type of failure *before* disturbing the actual choke setting.

CHOKE VACUUM BREAK SYSTEMS (Fig. 5-29)

Choke operation has been modified for emission control purposes by the use of a single or dual vacuum break system to help improve air/fuel mixture control while the engine is warming up. When the engine is started, the high vacuum under the choke valve causes additional gas to flow from the carburetor ports, giving a rich mixture for fast starting. Once the engine is running, manifold vacuum is applied to the primary vacuum break unit (and secondary, if so equipped). The primary vacuum break is located on the throttle lever side of the carburetor and opens the choke valve sufficiently to allow the engine to run without loading or stalling. The secondary vacuum break is operated by air cleaner temperature and, at a specified temperature setting, gradually opens the choke valve a little more to prevent stalling. A spring-loaded plunger offsets thermostatic coil tension, balancing further opening of the choke valve against the tension of the choke coil. Since the coil senses engine temperature, it lets the choke valve open gradually against the spring-loaded plunger's tension, making minute adjustments possible automatically. Vacuum break units contain an internal-bleed check valve which delays their operation by a few seconds until the engine will operate on slightly leaner mixtures.

A small bleed hole located beneath a rubber cover on the vacuum tube is incorporated into Rochester carburetors. This acts as a clean-air purge, pulling in a small amount of filtered air to clean the system of fuel vapors or dirt which might otherwise enter the bleed check valve and upset choke operation. Whenever the vacuum break unit is adjusted, this bleed hole should be covered with masking tape to prevent it from working. Applications of the vacuum break principle vary somewhat from one model carburetor to another (front/rear, rich/lean, primary/secondary, primary/auxiliary, etc.), but all current Rochester and the Motorcraft 2150/4350 carburetors use a version operating essentially as described above.

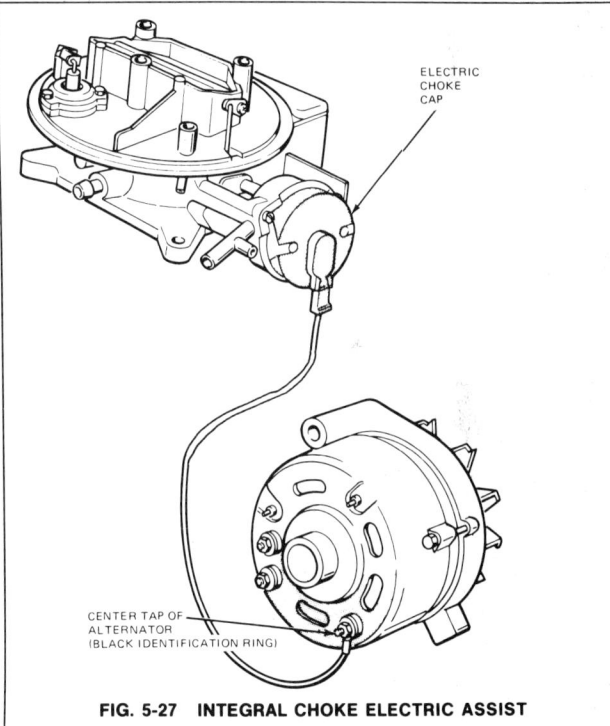

FIG. 5-27   INTEGRAL CHOKE ELECTRIC ASSIST

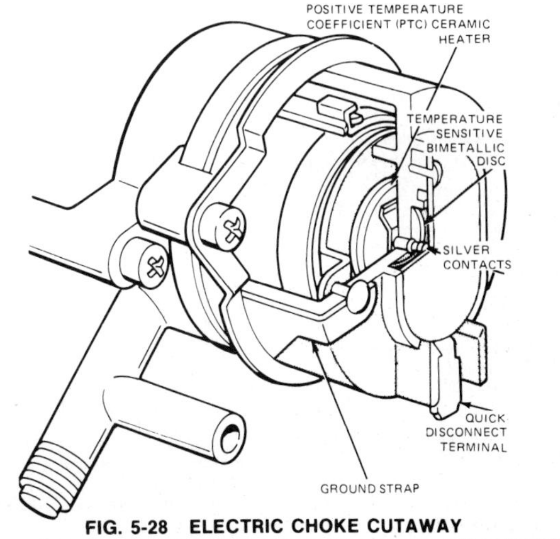

FIG. 5-28   ELECTRIC CHOKE CUTAWAY

CHOKE VACUUM BREAK ADJUSTMENT
HOLLEY 5210-C
Primary (Main) Vacuum Break Adjustment (Fig. 5-29A)

1. Remove the three screws holding the choke coil assembly, and remove the assembly.

2. Close the choke valve by pushing the inside choke coil lever clockwise. Then push the choke shaft against its stop.

3. With the choke in an open position, take out the slack from the linkage.

4. Holding the specified gauge vertically, insert it between the lower edge of the choke valve and the inside wall of the air horn.

5. Turn the adjusting screw to get the specified clearance.

6. Reinstall the choke coil assembly, and set the choke to specificiations.

Secondary Vacuum Break Adjustment (Fig. 5-29B)

1. Remove the three screws holding the choke coil assembly, and remove the assembly.

2. Place the cam follower on the highest step of the fast idle cam.

3. Connect a hand vacuum pump to the diaphragm and apply sufficient vacuum to seat it.

4. To close the choke valve, push the inside choke coil lever counterclockwise.

5. Place a gauge between the lower edge of the choke valve and inside wall of the air horn. Hold the gauge vertically.

6. To adjust, bend the rod at the bottom of the U-shaped bend.

7. Reinstall the choke coil assembly, and set the choke to specifications.

MOTORCRAFT 2150/4350
DELAYED CHOKE PULL-DOWN (Fig. 5-30)

1. Set the throttle on the fast-idle-cam top step and note the position of the choke index mark on the choke cap. Loosen the choke capscrews and rotate the choke 90° rich.

2. Disconnect the diaphragm vacuum line, connect a hand vacuum pump and tape the purge hole after removing the filter cap.

3. Measure gauge pull down dimension at the lower edge of the choke plate in the center of the air horn.

4. Turn the stopscrew on the back of the diaphragm to set adjustment. Loctite 290 is applied to the threads of this screw during manufacture to prevent the screw from vibrating and backing out of adjustment. Attempting to adjust the screw without heating it first with an electric soldering iron to loosen the Loctite 290 can permanently damage the pull down unit.

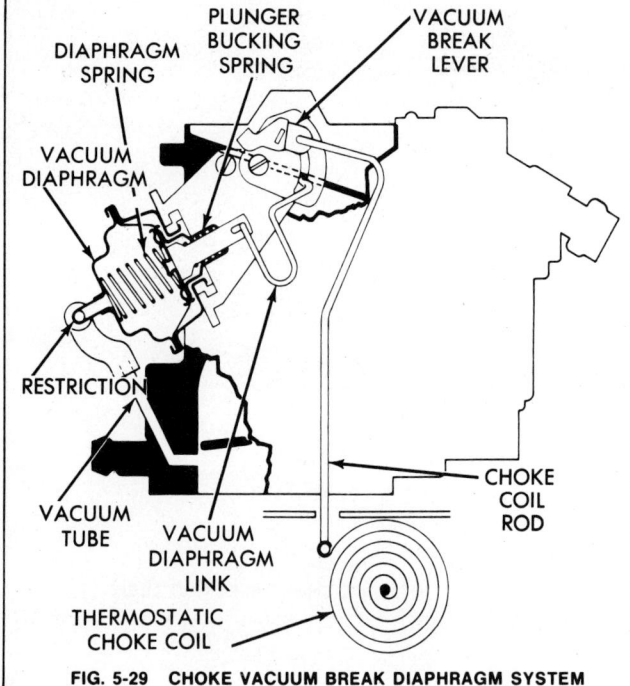

FIG. 5-29   CHOKE VACUUM BREAK DIAPHRAGM SYSTEM

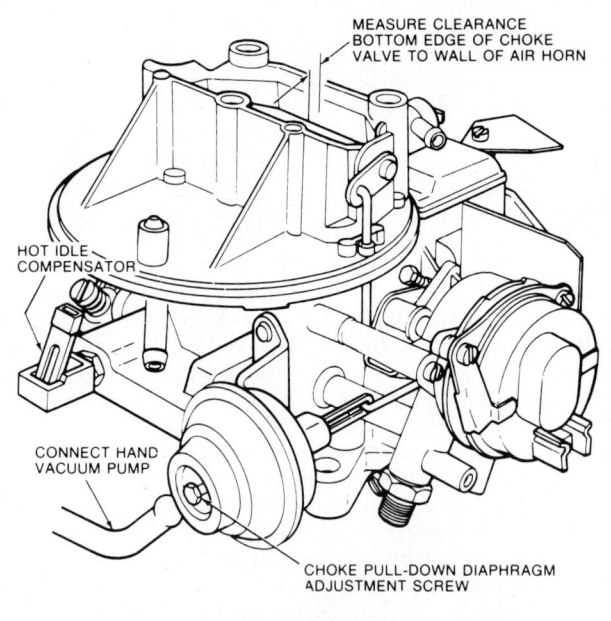

FIG. 5-30 MOTORCRAFT 2150/4350 VACUUM BREAK ADJUSTMENT

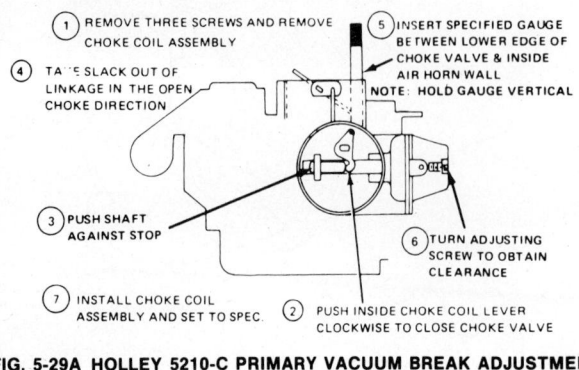

FIG. 5-29A HOLLEY 5210-C PRIMARY VACUUM BREAK ADJUSTMENT

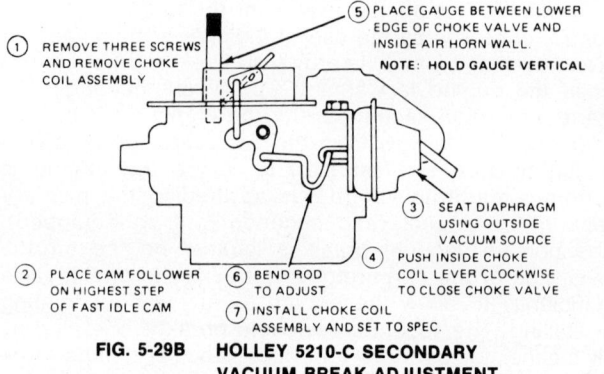

FIG. 5-29B   HOLLEY 5210-C SECONDARY VACUUM BREAK ADJUSTMENT

5. Reset the choke cap to the specified index setting and uncover the purge hole.

MOTORCRAFT 5200/6500
VACUUM CHOKE PULLDOWN

1. Remove the three screws holding the choke coil assembly, and remove the assembly.

2. Set the fast idle adjusting screw on the second step of the fast idle cam (top step, 6500).

3. Push the diaphragm stem against its stop with a screwdriver.

4. Insert the specified gauge rod or drill vertically between the lower edge of the choke valve and the air horn wall.

5. Place one end of a rubber band over the choke operating lever and hook the other end around the vacuum diaphragm cover. This will remove the slack from the choke linkage.

6. Using a hex key, turn the vacuum diaphragm adjusting screw in or out as required to adjust the choke plate-to-air horn clearance to specifications.

7. Remove the rubber band, reinstall the choke assembly, and set the choke to specifications.

MOTORCRAFT 1946
CHOKE PLATE PULLDOWN

1. Place the fast idle cam follower on the highest step of the fast idle cam.

2. Record the choke cap index position. Loosen the retaining screws and rotate the cap 90° in the rich direction. Retighten the screws.

3. Connect a hand vacuum pump to the pulldown diaphragm nipple and apply vacuum to seat it. To check that the pulldown diaphragm is fully retracted, push the small metal plate located in the bottom of the pulldown shaft linkage slot.

4. Insert a drill of the specified diameter between the top of the choke plate and the air horn.

5. To adjust, bend the pulldown linkage rod at the bottom of the U-shaped bend.

6. Return the choke cap to its index position as recorded in Step 2. Remove the vacuum pump and reconnect the vacuum line to the pulldown diaphragm.

ROCHESTER 1ME (Fig. 5-30A)
Vacuum Break Adjustment

1. Place the fast idle cam follower on the highest step of the fast idle cam.

2. Connect a hand vacuum pump to the diaphragm and apply vacuum to seat it. If the diaphragm has a purge bleed hole, cover it with a 1-in. square of masking tape—be sure to remove tape after adjustment.

3. Seat the diaphragm plunger and, if used, be sure the bucking spring is compressed.

4. Push up on the choke coil lever, with the rod in the plunger stem slot.

5. With the choke pushed toward the closed position, place the gauge between the upper edge, at the middle of the choke valve, and the inside wall of the air horn. The gauge must be held vertically.

6. Bend the rod to adjust.

ROCHESTER MV (Fig. 5-31)
Primary (Main) Vacuum Break Adjustment

1. 4-cyl. models—place fast idle screw on the highest step of the fast idle cam.

6-cyl. models—place fast idle cam follower on the highest step of the fast idle cam.

2. Connect a hand vacuum pump to the diaphragm and apply vacuum to seat it. If the diaphragm has a purge bleed hole, cover it with a 1-in. square of masking tape—be sure to remove after adjustment.

3. Seat the diaphragm plunger and push up on the choke coil lever, with the rod in the plunger stem slot.

4. With the choke valve pushed toward the closed position, place the gauge between the lower (upper on 1975 and later) edge of the choke valve and the inside wall of the air horn. The gauge must be held vertically.

5. Bend the rod to adjust.

Auxiliary Vacuum Break Adjustment—1975 and Later

1. 4-cyl. models—place fast idle screw on the highest step of the fast idle cam.

6-cyl. models—place fast idle cam follower on the highest step of the fast idle cam.

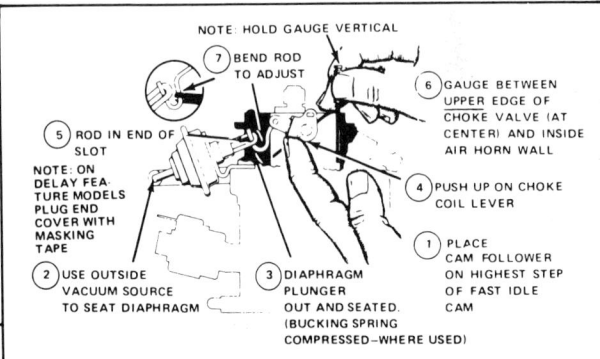

FIG. 5-30A ROCHESTER 1ME VACUUM BREAK ADJUSTMENT

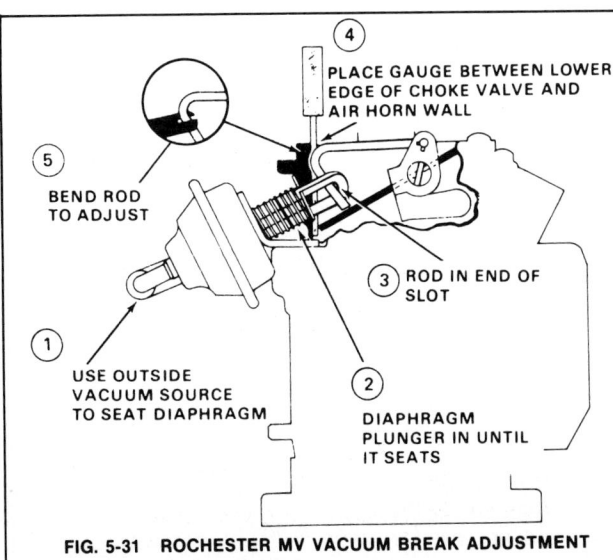

FIG. 5-31 ROCHESTER MV VACUUM BREAK ADJUSTMENT

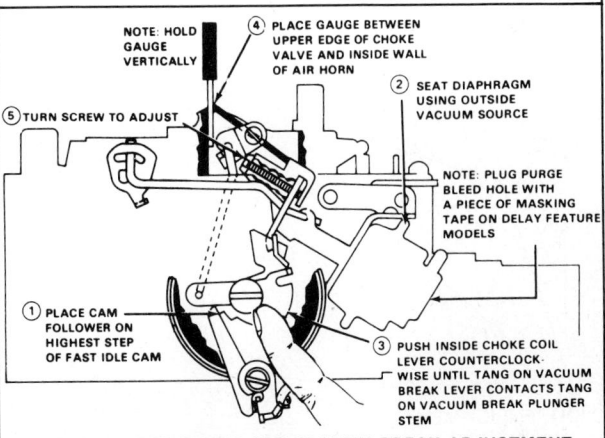

FIG. 5-32 ROCHESTER 2GC VACUUM BREAK ADJUSTMENT

2. Connect a hand vacuum pump to the diaphragm and apply sufficient vacuum to seat it. If the diaphragm has a purge bleed hole, cover it with a 1-in. square of masking tape—be sure to remove after adjustment is complete.

3. Seat diaphragm plunger and place a gauge between the upper edge of the choke valve and the inside wall of the air horn. The gauge must be held vertically.

4. To adjust, bend the rod at the bottom of the U-shaped bend.

ROCHESTER 2GE-2GC (Fig. 5-32)
Primary and Auxiliary Vacuum Break Adjustment

1. Place the fast idle screw on the highest step of the fast idle cam.

2. Connect a hand vacuum pump to the diaphragm and apply vacuum to seat it. If the diaphragm has a purge bleed hole, cover it with a 1-in. square of masking tape—be sure to remove after adjustment.

3. Hold the choke valve toward the closed choke position.

4. Seat the diaphragm plunger and push up on the choke coil lever, with the rod in the plunger stem slot.

5. Place a gauge between the lower (upper on 1975 and later) edge of the choke valve and the inside wall of the air horn.

6. Bend the rod to adjust.

ROCHESTER 2MC (Fig. 5-33)
Vacuum Break Adjustment

1. Place the fast idle cam follower on the highest step of the fast idle cam.

2. Connect a hand vacuum pump to the diaphragm and apply vacuum to seat it. Cover the diaphragm purge bleed hole with a 1-in. square of masking tape—be sure to remove after adjustment is complete.

3. Push the inside choke coil lever counterclockwise until the outside lever tang touches the tang on the vacuum-break plunger stem and compresses the bucking spring. For lean setting, push inside choke lever counterclockwise until tang on outside lever just makes contact with the plunger stem but does not compress the bucking spring.

4. Position the choke rod in the bottom of the choke lever slot. Place a gauge between the upper edge of the choke valve and the inside wall of the air horn.

5. Bend the rod at the end opposite the diaphragm. to adjust for rich setting. Bend the link rod at the plunger stem to adjust for a lean setting.

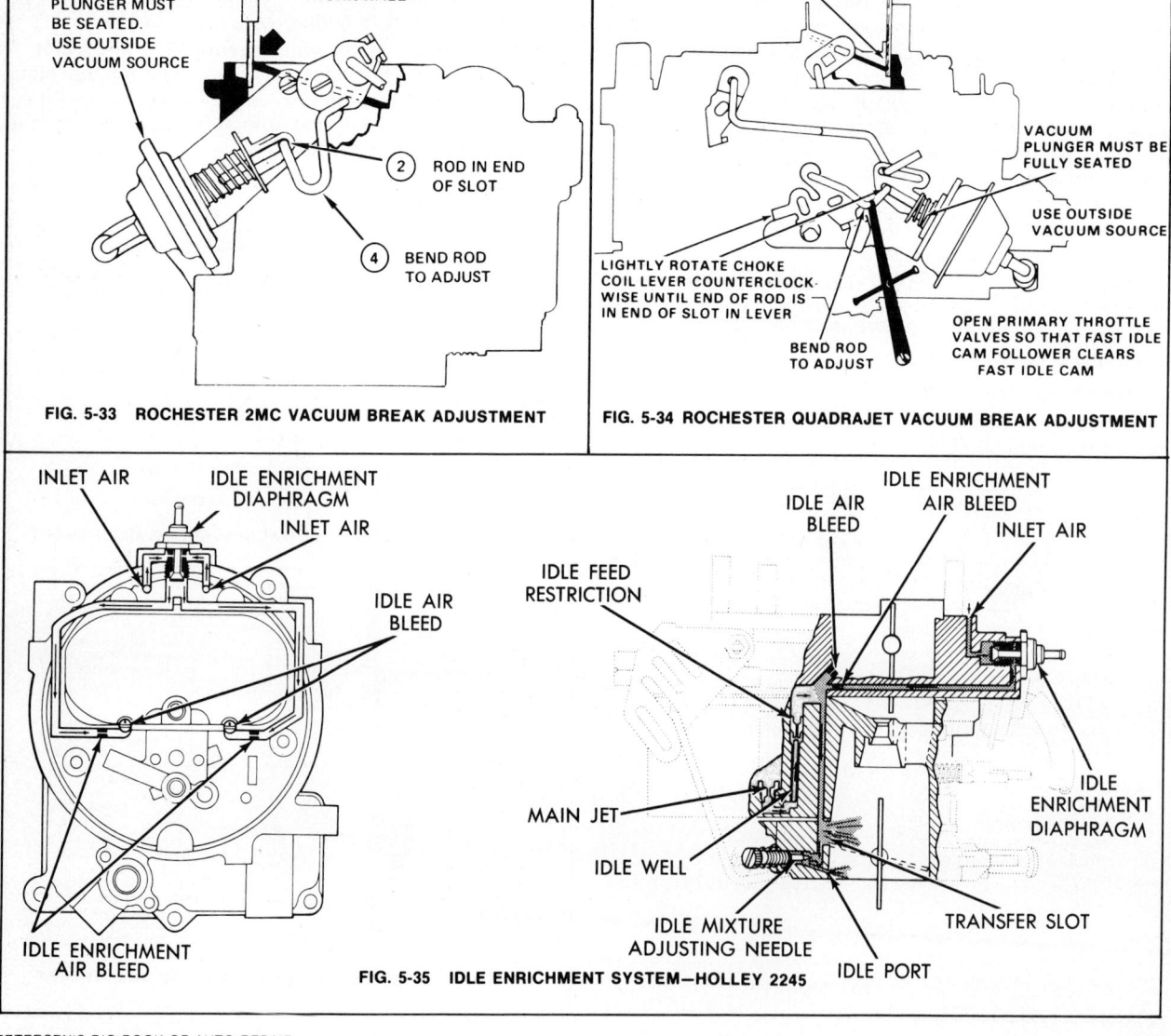

FIG. 5-33 ROCHESTER 2MC VACUUM BREAK ADJUSTMENT

FIG. 5-34 ROCHESTER QUADRAJET VACUUM BREAK ADJUSTMENT

FIG. 5-35 IDLE ENRICHMENT SYSTEM—HOLLEY 2245

ROCHESTER QUADRAJET (Fig. 5-34)
Front Vacuum Break Adjustment (All Models)
1. Remove the thermostatic coil cover and coil assembly from the choke housing.
2. Place the fast idle cam follower on the highest step of the fast idle cam.
3. If the diaphragm has a purge bleed valve hole, cover it with a 1-in. square of masking tape—be sure to remove after adjustment is complete.
4. Connect a hand vacuum pump and apply vacuum to seat the diaphragm. This will require a few seconds on models with a delay feature.
5. Push up on the inside choke coil lever until the vacuum-break-lever tang touches the vacuum break plunger.
6. Place a gauge between the upper edge of the choke valve and the inside wall of the air horn.
7. Turn the adjusting screw on the vacuum break plunger to obtain adjustment to specifications.

Rear Vacuum Break Adjustment (All Cadillac, all Buick and Oldsmobile, except 7045264, Pontiac 7045246 and 7045546 only)
1. Remove the thermostatic coil cover and coil assembly from the choke housing.
2. Place the fast-idle cam follower on the highest step of the fast idle cam.
3. If the diaphragm has a purge bleed valve hole, cover it with a 1-in. square of masking tape—be sure to remove after adjustment is complete.
4. Connect a hand vacuum pump and apply vacuum to seat the diaphragm. This will require a few seconds on models with a delay feature.
5. Push up on the inside choke coil lever, toward a closed choke position, until the plunger is pulled out and seated; the spring will be compressed.
6. Place a gauge between the upper edge of the choke valve and the inside wall of the air horn, with the choke rod in the bottom of the choke lever slot.
7. Bend the vacuum break rod to adjust.

Rear Vacuum Break Adjustment (Buick and Oldsmobile 7045264, all Pontiac except 7045246 and 7045546, all Chevrolet except 454 engine)
1. Remove the thermostatic coil cover and coil assembly from the choke housing.
2. Place the fast idle cam follower on the highest step of the fast idle cam.
3. If the diaphragm has a purge bleed valve hole, cover with a 1-in. square of masking tape—be sure to remove after adjustment is complete.
4. Connect a hand vacuum pump and apply vacuum to seat the diaphragm. This will require a few seconds on models with a delay feature.
5. Push up on the inside choke coil lever toward a closed choke position.
6. Place a gauge between the upper edge of the choke valve and the inside wall of the air horn, with the choke rod in the bottom of the choke lever slot.
7. Bend the vacuum break rod to adjust.

Rear Vacuum Break Adjustment (Chevrolet 454)
1. Remove the thermostatic coil cover and coil assembly from the choke housing.
2. Place the fast idle cam follower on the highest step of the fast idle cam.
3. If the diaphragm has a purge bleed valve hole, cover it with a 1-in. square of masking tape—be sure to remove after adjustment is complete.
4. Connect a hand vacuum pump and apply vacuum to seat the diaphragm. This will require a few seconds on models with a delay feature.

5. Push up on the inside choke coil lever toward a closed choke position.
6. Visually check for a wide-open choke valve (vertical), with the choke rod in the bottom of the choke lever slot.
7. Bend the vacuum break rod to adjust.

COOLANT-CONTROLLED
IDLE ENRICHMENT SYSTEM (CCIE)
Chrysler Corporation has elected to reduce cold engine stalling by using a metering system related to the basic carburetor instead of modifying choke action. Called the Coolant-Controlled Idle Enrichment System (CCIE), shown in **Fig. 5-35,** it is found only on 1975

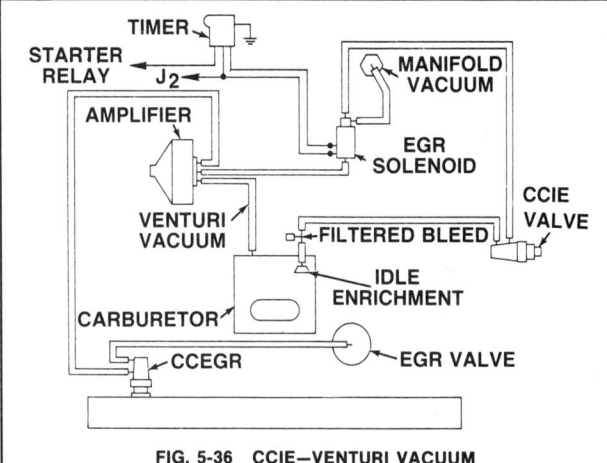

FIG. 5-36   CCIE—VENTURI VACUUM

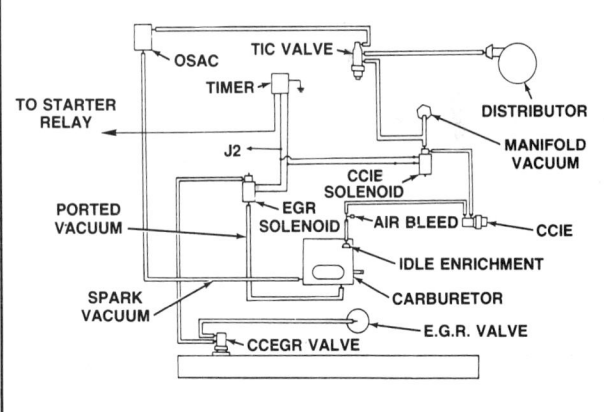

FIG. 5-37   CCIE—PORTED VACUUM

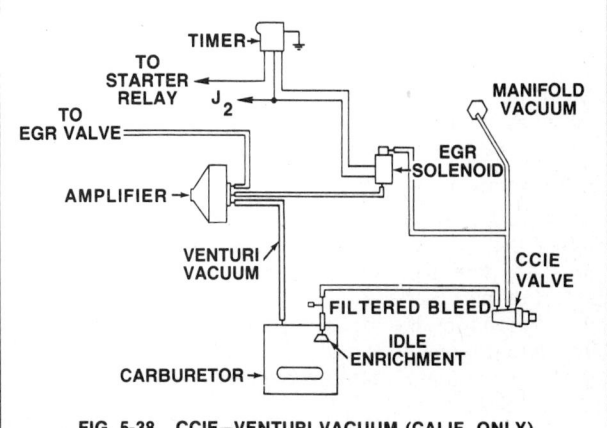

FIG. 5-38   CCIE—VENTURI VACUUM (CALIF. ONLY)

and later carburetors fitted to automatic-transmission-equipped cars (except the 225-cu.-in. engine). A small vacuum-controlled diaphragm, or idle enrichment valve, is mounted near the top of the carburetor to control idle system air. When vacuum is applied, idle system air is reduced. This loss of air in the idle system intensifies a tiny vacuum signal and increases fuel flow, changing the air/fuel ratio and automatically richening the mixture. Three types of system configurations are in use:

1. CCIE—Venturi Vacuum: This system uses manifold vacuum provided by the EGR delay solenoid valve. An electronic timer energizes the solenoid during start-up and for 35 seconds after, when the timer cuts off the solenoid. While the solenoid is energized, it shuts off manifold vacuum from the EGR amplifier, preventing exhaust gas recirculation from taking place. It also applies manifold vacuum to the idle enrichment system through the engine-block coolant valve, which begins idle enrichment if engine block temperature is under 150° F **(Fig. 5-36)**.

2. CCIE—Ported Vacuum: This system uses ported vacuum supplied from a vacuum port on the carburetor, which is to the EGR vacuum solenoid valve. A timer delays ported vacuum to the EGR control valve for 35 seconds after start-up, then permits vacuum flow to the EGR valve via the coolant control valve in the radiator. The coolant-controlled idle enrichment (CCIE) vacuum solenoid valve receives its vacuum signal direct from the intake manifold and, during that 35-second delay, allows vacuum to the CCIE valve, which remains open until engine temperature reaches 150° F **(Fig. 5-37)**.

3. CCIE—Venturi Vacuum: This system is similar to No. 1 described earlier, but is fitted only to cars sold in the state of California. The electronic timer energizes the solenoid during start-up and for 35 seconds thereafter, which prevents manifold vacuum from reaching the EGR amplifier, eliminating exhaust gas recirculation during that time. But during that 35-second interval, a direct tap applies manifold vacuum to the idle enrichment system through the CCIE valve in the engine block, which starts idle enrichment when the engine block temperature is below 98° F **(Fig. 5-38)**.

CCIE TEST PROCEDURES

TIME DELAY TEST

1. Check all system wiring for proper connections.
2. With the ignition off, disconnect wiring from the time delay solenoid valve.
3. Connect a light-type circuit tester with a current draw of 0.5-amp or less across the solenoid valve-connector terminals.
4. Start the engine. The tester should light immediately and remain on for 30 to 40 seconds, then go off.
5. If the test lamp does not light, stays on indefinitely or does not remain on for the 30-40 second interval specified, replace the timer, and repeat the test.

CARBURETOR VALVE TEST

1. With the engine at normal operating temperature, remove the air cleaner. Since vacuum leakage is required for this test, do not plug the vacuum fittings opened by air cleaner removal.
2. Disconnect the hose leading to the idle enrichment diaphragm at the plastic connector. Because the connector contains a filtered bleed, it must be removed from the hose.
3. Start the engine and place the fast-idle-speed screw on the lowest step of the fast idle cam.

4. Connect a hand vacuum pump to the enrichment diaphragm hose and apply vacuum, listening for an engine speed change. If you cannot hear one (Carter carburetors), proceed to Step 5. If the car is equipped with a Holley carb, and no speed change is heard, then replace the valve assembly.
5. Plug the carburetor air inlet passage **(Fig. 5-35)** and listen for an engine speed change. If you hear it, either the diaphragm leaks or the air valve is stuck open. If you cannot hear one, the air valve is stuck closed. In either case, clean the air valve and repeat Step 4. If there is still no change in engine speed, replace the diaphragm.

COOLANT CONTROL VALVE TEST

1. Check the vacuum hoses for proper connection and routing, and inspect the coolant level, adding enough to bring it up to the proper level, if required.
2. Disconnect the molded connector from the coolant control valve and attach a ⅛-in. I.D. hose to the valve's bottom port.
3. With the top radiator-tank temperature under 75° F, try to blow through the hose. If you can, proceed to Step 4. If you cannot blow through the hose, replace the valve.
4. Bring the engine to normal operating temperature and replace the hose used in Step 3 with a hand vacuum pump. Apply 10 ins. of vacuum and watch the pump gauge. If the vacuum level drops more than 1 in. in 15 seconds, replace the valve.

UNLOADER AND FAST IDLE CAM (Fig. 5-39)

One should never go to wide-open throttle on a cold engine, but some drivers do it just the same. Others pump the throttle when trying to start the engine, flooding it as a result. Both conditions are taken care of by the choke unloader, a little tang that opens the choke sufficiently to clean out the engine when the throttle is pushed to a wide-open position.

When the choke is operating, the engine cannot use the extremely rich mixture unless it is run at a faster than normal idle. To accomplish this, a fast idle cam and linkage works in conjunction with the choke to raise the idle speed whenever the choke is operating.

MULTIPLE BARREL CARBURETORS

The systems described to this point are found in the simplest carburetor. Most engines from 1 cyl. up to 6 cyls. have a carburetor with only one throat. Such a carburetor requires only one of each system described. But some 6-cyl. and some V-8 engines are equipped with a two-throat carburetor and, in that case, the main metering system and the idle system must be duplicat-

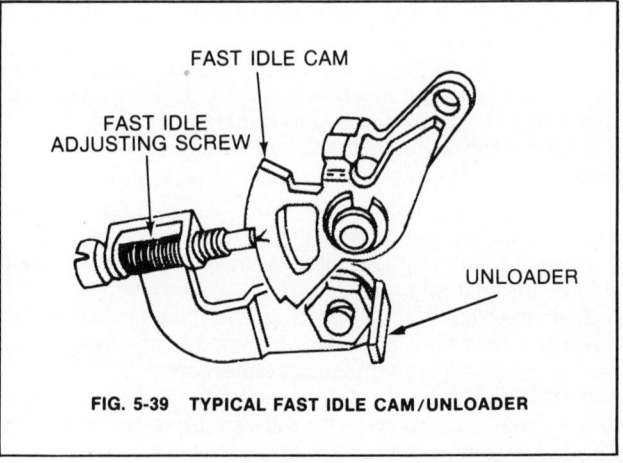

FIG. 5-39 TYPICAL FAST IDLE CAM/UNLOADER

ed for the second throat. The float system does not have to be duplicated, because the bowl has sufficient fuel capacity to serve two main jets easily. The same applies to the accelerator pump system—one pump is used, but it has a nozzle for each throat.

The power system also remains basically the same as in a single-barrel carburetor, except that it feeds two main metering systems instead of one. There is not much change in the choke either; the choke valve is made large enough to cover both carburetor throats. Beyond 2 barrels however, there are some real differences. In a 4-bbl. carburetor, the 2 barrels that the engine normally runs on are called the primaries. The extra 2 barrels only operate at high engine speeds, when needed most.

As pointed out earlier, the carburetor amounts to nothing more than a large air valve. At idle, the air valve or throttle is closed because the engine does not require much air. As it goes faster, it requires increasing quantities of air. At low speeds, only a small throttle opening is needed to make the engine do its job. But at wide-open throttle, the engine will not go as fast as it is capable of running because it does not get enough air. The 4-bbl. carburetor solves this problem. The engine runs at low speeds on the primary barrels, but on the highway the secondary barrels open when the driver steps on the gas, providing all the air the engine needs.

There is no general rule about which systems feed the secondary barrels. There is a main metering system, but there may be a power system or even an idle system, depending upon how the manufacturer designs his carburetor. Secondaries can be controlled either by vacuum or mechanically, with perhaps a velocity valve in addition. Mechanically controlled secondaries start to open when the primaries reach about three-quarter throttle. The secondaries open at a faster rate, so that all 4 barrels reach wide open at the same time. With such a system, it is possible for the driver to open the throttle wide at a low speed when the engine does not require all that air. To prevent this mistake, there is usually an air valve or velocity valve in the secondary barrels above the throttle valve. The air valve does not open until there is a sufficient rush of air past it to raise a weight or compress a spring. The only time

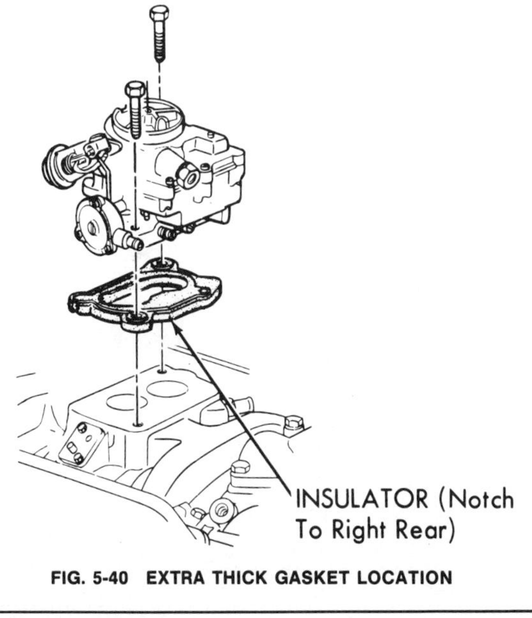

airflow is sufficient is when the engine is going fast, which is the only time secondaries are needed anyway.

Vacuum-controlled secondaries do not have this problem. They are controlled by either manifold or venturi vacuum, so they open only when the engine needs the extra air, regardless of what the driver does or what he wants the car to do. Now the carburetor will work under just about any engine condition, but there are other features that have been added to make it work a little better, and these must be considered whenever adjustment or overhaul is contemplated.

VARIABLE VENTURI CARBURETORS

For 1977, Ford introduced its first variable venturi carburetor, called the Motorcraft 2700VV. Though this is, in a sense, a two-barrel carburetor, it varies venturi size according to engine speed and load. A dual-element venturi valve moves in and out of the airflow, which is squeezed between the carburetor throat wall and the edge of the venturi wall. Free-floating tapered needles—which pass through the calibrated jets in the carburetor body—meter exact air/fuel ratio for any air valve position. The venturi valve is controlled by engine vacuum and throttle positions, and is connected to two main metering rods which control fuel flow.

In operation, air speed through the carburetor is relatively constant, giving more even air/fuel mixtures throughout the engine operating range. In fixed venturi carburetors, airflow speed varies according to throttle opening and engine speed.

Since flow speed remains constant, the variable venturi carburetor does not need supplementary systems, such as an independent idle system, enrich-valve system and choke plate.

A revised 2700 VV carburetor was introduced on some 1979 vehicles. Designated as the 7200 VV, this model uses a feedback control motor, metering valve and revised internal vent system. Incorporated in an Electronic Engine Control System, the 7200 VV varies the air/fuel ratio according to directions from the EEC module.

Overhauling the 2700-7200 VV carburetors requires several special tools, such as a jet wrench (Ford P/N T77L-9533-A), jet plug remover (Ford P/N T77L-9533-B) and jet plug driver (Ford P/N T77L-9533-C). While the carburetor design is not overly complicated, it does use many small parts, involves 108 factory-specified steps, and requires considerable time to disassemble/reassemble. It is not advisable to attempt an overhaul without access to the proper tools; for this reason, no overhaul instructions are provided in this chapter. Exploded drawings of the three main body sections, however, are provided for reference use.

CARBURETOR HEAT

A heated intake manifold improves low-end response. At a low speed, the fuel mixture is moving slowly through the intake passages and droplets of fuel have a tendency to fall out of the airstream. A heated manifold helps keep the fuel vaporized. Heat comes from the exhaust gases which are usually channeled to go up under the carburetor base and heat the intake passages. Because the fuel in the carburetor bowl should not be heated (just the intake passages), carburetors are sometimes installed on the manifold with a large insulating block or extra thick gasket **(Fig. 5-40)**.

ANTI-STALL DASHPOT

A driver who steps on the throttle hard to go across an intersection and then changes his mind may find

INSULATOR (Notch To Right Rear)

FIG. 5-40   EXTRA THICK GASKET LOCATION

that the engine will die when he removes his foot from the throttle. The engine dies because a large load of fuel has started on the way to the cylinders, but letting up on the throttle shuts off the air supply. The excessive fuel then floods the cylinders and kills the engine.

Some carburetors are fitted with an anti-stall dashpot (also called a slow-closing dashpot) which holds the throttle open for a few seconds, allowing it to come down to idle slowly and giving sufficient time for the engine to burn off the rich mixture. Other carburetors use an idle speed high enough to make the use of a dashpot unnecessary.

HOT IDLE COMPENSATORS (Fig. 5-42)

The hot idle compensator is a little air valve in the carburetor main body or air horn which allows fresh air to enter the manifold below the throttle valves and lean the mixture when the engine is hot. This helps to offset rich mixtures caused by fuel vapors, which would otherwise result in a rough idle and/or stalling.

The hot idle compensator consists of a bi-metal strip and valve in a housing. When engine and underhood temperatures reach a predetermined value, the bi-metal strip will lift the valve from its seat, allowing the passage of air. As underhood temperatures return to normal, the bi-metal strip returns to its original position, closing the compensator valve and causing a resumption of normal idle operation.

Hot idle compensators are not adjustable. If one is found open on a cold engine, it must be replaced. When handling the compensator, use care not to bend or otherwise distort the bi-metal strip, or the calibration will be changed, resulting in a good deal of air going into the engine at the wrong time and for the wrong reason.

EXTERNAL BOWL VENTS

Fuel vapors in the float bowl of so-called "emissions carburetors" must be vented externally to the charcoal canister when the engine is not running. If they are not, they will enter the atmosphere as unburned HC pollutants, or enter the intake manifold through the carburetor's internal vent and cause hard starting. External bowl vents are generally mechanically operated poppet valves located in the air horn above the float bowl. These poppet valves are similar in appearance to the anti-percolation vents used some years ago.

The external bowl vent remains open at idle to vent vapors to the canister, and are closed by mechanical linkage or manifold vacuum when the throttle is above idle, venting vapors directly to the air cleaner. If the bowl vent is inoperative or incorrectly adjusted, it will cause hard starting when the engine is warm. Precise adjustment specifications are furnished by carburetor manufacturers, but as a rule of thumb, a clearance of about .015-in. minimum should be maintained between the vent rod and vent valve stem when the throttle is closed.

IDLE STOP SOLENOID (Fig. 5-43)

Also called an anti-dieseling solenoid, this device is fitted to some carburetors to prevent run-on or dieseling when the ignition is turned off. The idle stop solenoid is necessary because of the higher idle speeds required to reduce hydrocarbon emissions during closed throttle deceleration. Such idle speeds (which make the use of the anti-stall dashpot unnecessary) are high enough to cause the engine to continue running under certain conditions, even though the ignition has been shut off. The use of the idle stop solenoid allows

the throttle to close more than it does at normal operating conditions.

Turning on the ignition energizes the solenoid, and its plunger extends to act as a throttle stop. Idle speed adjustments are thus made by adjusting the solenoid plunger instead of the carburetor idle screw. Turning the ignition off de-energizes the solenoid and causes the plunger to retract. The throttle will then close until it is stopped by the carburetor idle screw. The specified idle speed for a de-energized idle stop solenoid is generally 150-400 rpm less than the normal idle speed.

ALTITUDE COMPENSATION

The air/fuel mixture tends to richen when driving in a thinner-than-normal atmosphere, increasing the level of emissions. Beginning with some 4-bbl. carburetors fitted to 1975 engines sold in certain geographic locations in the United States, altitude compensation corrects the air/fuel ratio under such driving conditions. For 1977, the Environmental Protection Agency (EPA) designated 167 counties in 10 western states as high altitude emission control areas. Cars sold in these counties must be tuned differently from those in "low-altitude" areas to meet the EPA specifications. Certain carburetors used on engines sold within these geographic areas have either an auxiliary circuit or device to maintain the proper air/fuel ratio for operation at higher altitudes.

Altitude compensation devices take one of two forms: automatic or manual. Since 1975, the Carter Thermo-Quad has used an altitude-sensitive bellows and valve to control a set of passages which connect both the primary and secondary main air bleeds with a calibrated opening **(Fig. 5-44)**. As the air/fuel mixture begins to richen, the bellows starts to open. This lets additional air enter the main air bleeds, correcting the ratio. Once the outside or atmospheric pressure returns to "normal," the bellows contracts. This closes off the auxiliary air passages and shuts off the system. This circuit works only at cruising speeds.

Carter YF carburetors used on AMC 6-cylinder engines have a manually adjusted auxiliary air bleed. This controls an extra air passage for the idle/main metering circuits, **(Fig. 5-44A)**. Ignition timing should be rechecked whenever the compensator is adjusted, as it may require readjustment.

Some versions of the Rochester Mod-Quad 4-bbl. carburetor use a bellows called an aneroid in conjunction with an adjustable part-throttle (A.P.T.) metering rod assembly. This barometric pressure-sensitive device is an integral part of the A.P.T. assembly on 1975 and

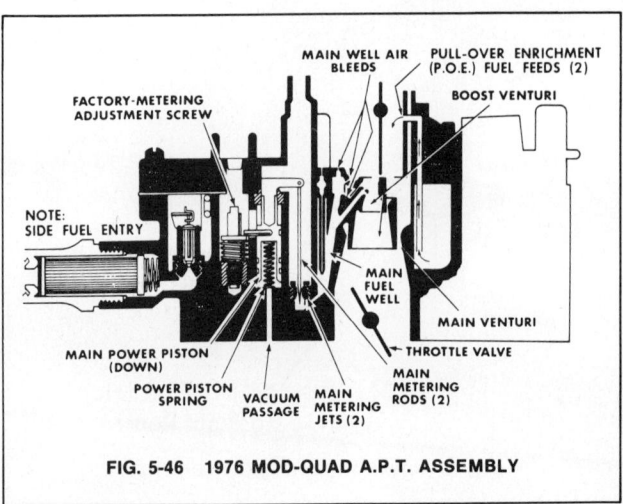

FIG. 5-46 1976 MOD-QUAD A.P.T. ASSEMBLY

some later Mod-Quads fitted in certain geographic areas. The same carburetor body casting is used for nonaneroid-equipped models, with the aneroid cavity containing a filler spool instead. The aneroid compensator senses any change in air pressure and automatically expands or contracts to lower or raise the metering rod in the fixed jet. In this way, its response to a change in air pressure maintains control of the air/fuel ratio during part-throttle conditions. Although the A.P.T. assembly *is* adjustable, it is preset at the factory and *should not* be tampered with, unless it is necessary to replace the metering rod, filler spool or aneroid **(Fig. 5-45)**.

Rochester dropped the A.P.T. metering rod assembly

FIG. 5-42   HOT IDLE COMPENSATOR

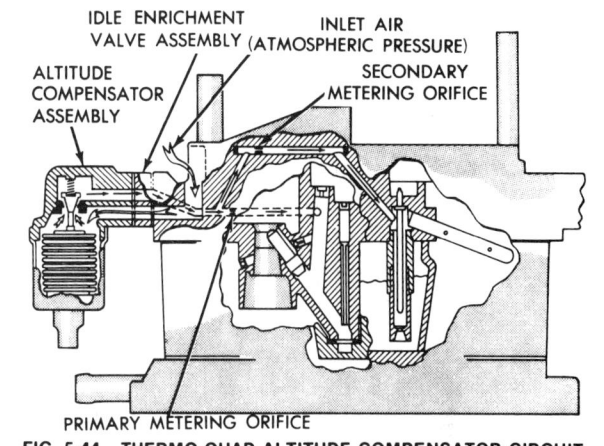

FIG. 5-44   THERMO-QUAD ALTITUDE COMPENSATOR CIRCUIT

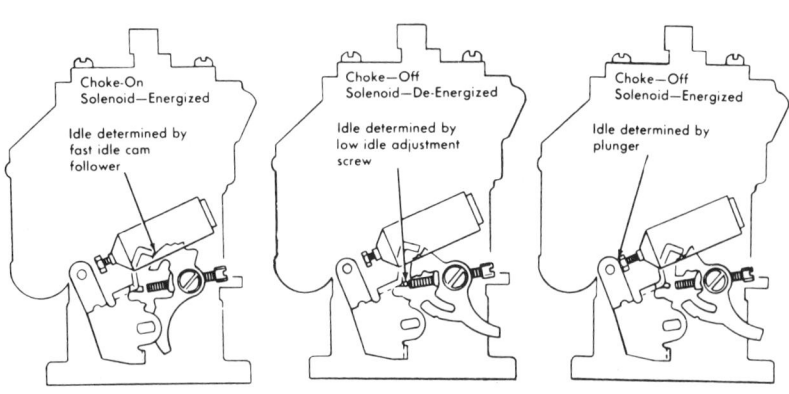

FIG. 5-43   TYPICAL IDLE-STOP-SOLENOID ADJUSTMENT

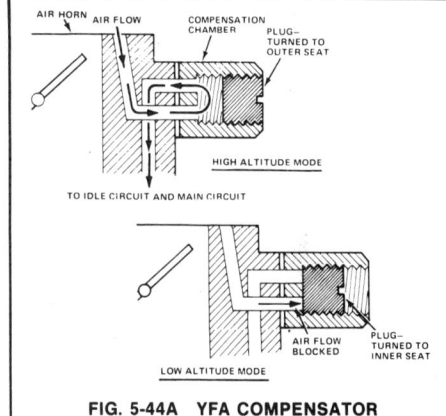

FIG. 5-44A   YFA COMPENSATOR PLUG OPERATION

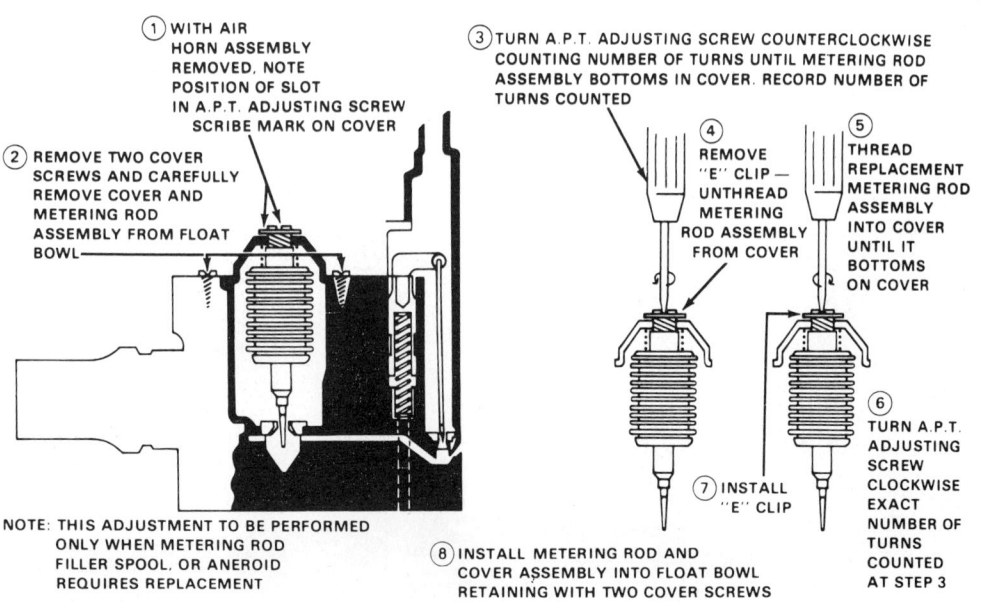

FIG. 5-45   1975 MOD-QUAD ANEROID/A.P.T. ASSEMBLY

on the 1976 Mod-Quad. Although the body casting is identical, a cavity insert is used to replace the aneroid or filler spool, and A.P.T. adjustment is now accomplished by a pin pressed in the side of the main power piston well **(Fig. 5-46).** When the piston is down, the side of the pin stops on top of a flat surface on the adjustment screw, located in the cavity next to the piston. A tension spring beneath the adjustment screw head prevents the screw from turning out of its factory preset adjustment. A.P.T. adjustment on this version of

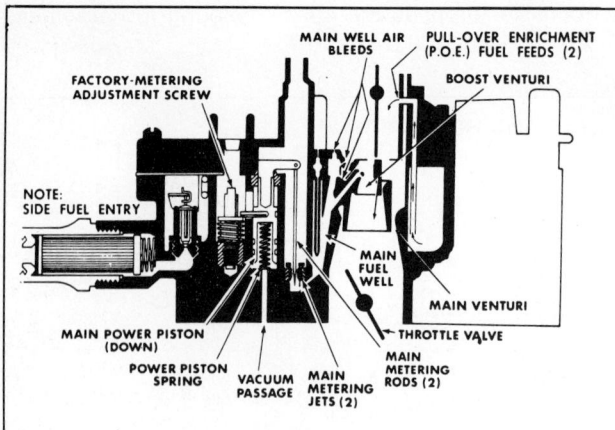

FIG. 5-46 1976 MOD-QUAD A.P.T. ASSEMBLY

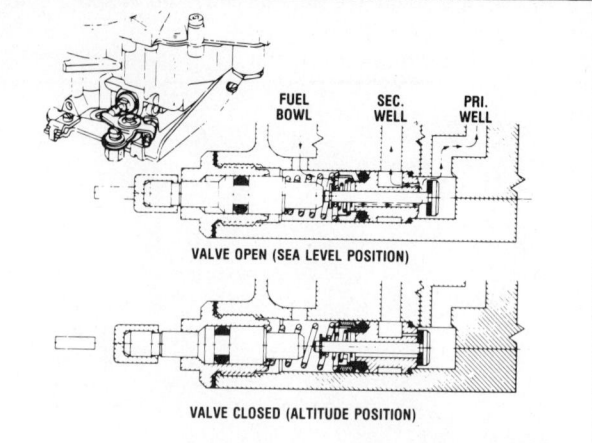

FIG. 5-47A 1977 HOLLEY 5200 ALTITUDE COMPENSATOR

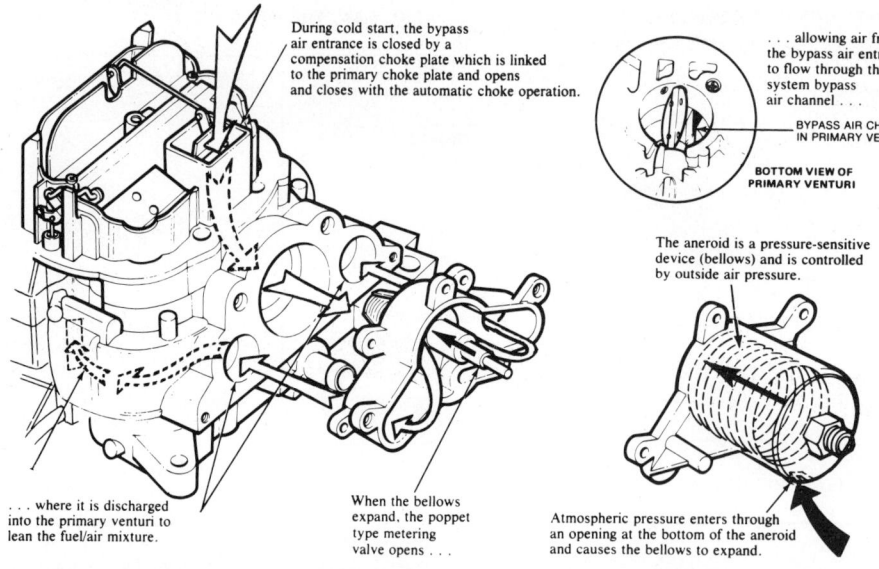

FIG. 5-47 1976 MOTORCRAFT 4350 ALTITUDE COMPENSATION

FIG. 5-48 CADILLAC FUEL INJECTION SYSTEM

FIG. 5-49 FUEL INJECTOR

the 4MC *should not* be attempted; if the float bowl must be replaced, the new bowl assembly will include an adjustment screw already preset by the factory. After 1975, the only altitude compensation model of the Mod-Quad was the M4MEA used by Cadillac through 1977.

The 1976 Motorcraft 4350, fitted to 460-cu.-in. engines sold in the Denver area, uses an aneroid attached to a poppet-type metering valve on the rear of the carburetor. Its operation is described in **Fig. 5-47.** Use of this device was extended to all Motorcraft 4350 and 2150 carburetors sold within the 167-county area on 1977 and later models, as well as 1978 Motorcraft 2700VV carburetors.

The Holley 5200 carburetor used on 1977 Ford 2.3L engines has a fuel metering device which is manually adjusted by the driver for proper altitude compensation **(Fig. 5-47A).** The carburetor valve is operated by a two-position, dash-mounted lever connected to the carburetor by a cable/swivel linkage arrangement. Setting the lever to the ALTITUDE position closes the fuel valve to provide a leaner air/fuel mixture. This mechanical adjustment is not used on 1978 models.

Other carburetors using a manual compensation device are the Carter YF used by AMC and the Carter BBD used by Chrysler. The Carter YF has a manually adjusted auxiliary air bleed with the adjustment plug positioned near the fuel inlet on the air horn. The Cart-

er BBD used on some Dodge/Plymouth vehicles also has manually adjusted air bleeds. The adjustment screw is positioned above the venturi cluster in the air horn.

As 1978 models went into production, the high-altitude emission requirements introduced on the 1977 models were suspended for a minimum of three years. Revised test procedures will accompany their reinstatement, now scheduled for 1981.

FUEL INJECTION

CADILLAC FUEL INJECTION

Starting with mid-1975 models, Cadillac offered an electronically controlled fuel injection system as an option on its large cars and as standard equipment on the Seville. Although complex in appearance **(Fig. 5-48),** it does the same basic job as a carburetor, and provides an air/fuel mixture in the proper ratio for complete combustion under all engine operational conditions. In addition, fuel injection provides more accurate metering of the mixture to the engine under all conditions than a carburetor can, and it permits a considerably quicker response to the driver's demands.

Basically, the system involves electronically actuated fuel-metering valves or injectors which spray a carefully controlled amount of fuel into the engine. These valves **(Fig. 5-49)** are mounted in the intake manifold, with

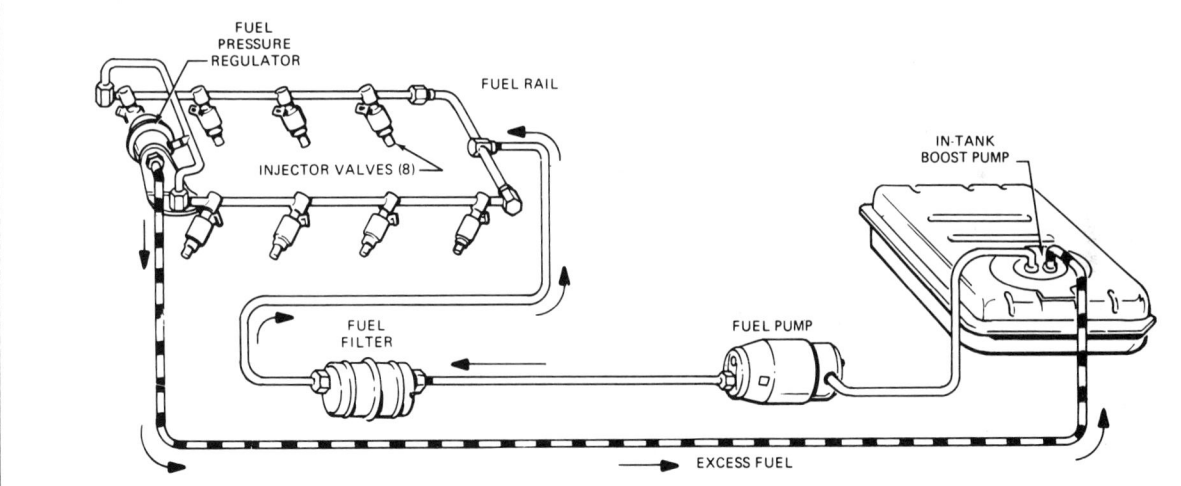

FIG. 5-50 EFI FUEL DELIVERY SUBSYSTEM

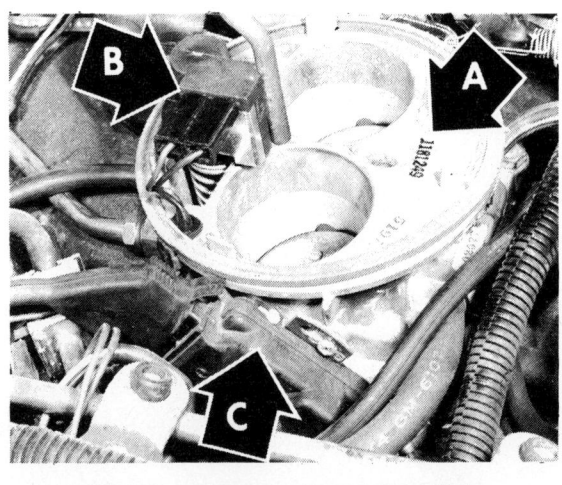

FIG. 5-51 EFI AIR INDUCTION SUBSYSTEM

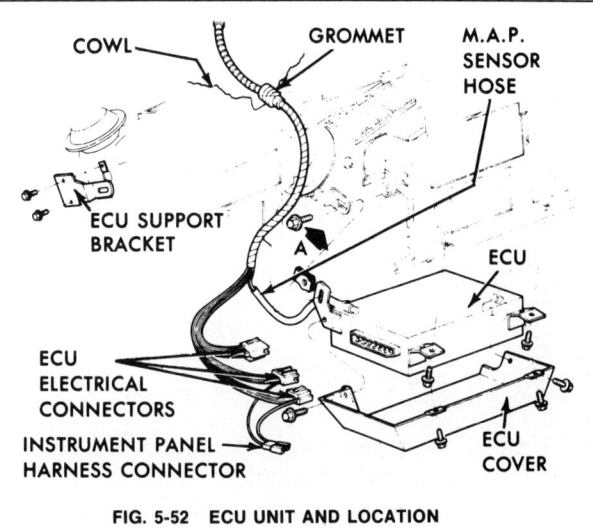

FIG. 5-52 ECU UNIT AND LOCATION

their tips close to the heads of the intake valves. This is called port injection. Injector valves are timed so that the fuel charge is ready for the intake stroke of each cylinder.

Fuel pumped from the tank is supplied to each injector from a pipe called a fuel rail. This is connected to a return line so that any fuel not used by the engine can flow back to the tank. Pressure in the line is maintained by an electric pump mounted just forward of the fuel tank, and an additional booster pump is mounted inside the tank itself to prevent any chance of vapor lock on the suction side of the system.

In some fuel injection systems, the injectors all operate continuously. This type of system is found on several import cars; on other systems, the injectors operate in sequence, as the respective cylinders require their charges. The Cadillac version is a compromise—it divides the 8 cyls. into two groups, which are operated alternately, with all injectors in each group being opened at the same time.

An electronic control unit programs and monitors the operation. Mounted under the dash, this is actually an analog computer. The control unit takes into account such variables as manifold pressure, throttle position, water temperature, underhood air temperature and engine speed. It translates these inputs into opening and closing times for the injector groups, and is thus able to provide accurately metered fuel to the engine. As with a carbureted system, the fuel injection system can be broken down into subsystems, and four major subsystems are used in the Cadillac version.

FUEL DELIVERY SUBSYSTEM (Fig. 5-50)

This system consists of the tank, fuel pumps, filter, pressure regulator and injector valves. The pumps are activated when the ignition switch is turned on and the

---

FIG. 5-53 CADILLAC

ENGINE CRANKS BUT WILL NOT START

(NOTE: The following problems assume that the rest of the car electrical system is functioning properly.)

1. Blown 10 amp in-line fuel pump fuse located below instrument panel near ECU connectors.*
2. Open circuit in 12 purple wire between starter solenoid and ECU.
3. Open circuit in 18 dark green wire between generator "BAT" terminal and ECU (fusible link).*
4. Poor connection at ECU jumper harness (below instrument panel) or at ECU.
5. Poor connection at fuel pump jumper harness (below instrument panel near ECU), 14 dark green wire.*
6. Poor connection at engine coolant sensor or open circuit in sensor or wiring (cold engine only).**
7. Poor connection at distributor trigger (speed sensor).
8. Distributor trigger (speed sensor) stuck closed.
9. Malfunction in chassis-mounted pump.
10. Malfunction in throttle position switch (W.O.T. section shorted). To check, disconnect switch—engine should start.
11. Fuel flow restriction.

HARD STARTING

1. Open engine coolant sensor (cold or partially warm engine only — starts ok hot).**
2. Malfunction in throttle position switch (W.O.T. section shorted). To check, disconnect switch—Engine should start normally.
3. Malfunction in chassis-mounted fuel pump. (Check valves leaking back).
4. Malfunction in pressure regulator.

POOR FUEL ECONOMY

1. Disconnected or leaking MAP sensor hose.
2. Disconnected vacuum hose at fuel pressure regulator or at throttle body.
3. Malfunction of air or coolan sensor.***

ENGINE STALLS AFTER START

1. Open circuit in 12 black/yellow ignition signal wire between fuse block and ECU or poor connection at connector (12 black/yellow wire) located below instrument panel near ECU.
2. Poor connection at engine coolant sensor or open circuit in sensor or wiring (cold or warm engine only)

NO FAST IDLE

1. Bent fast idle valve micro switch causing heater to malfunction and drive valve section down to locked closed position.

engine is cranking or running. If the engine stalls, or the starter does not engage, the pumps shut off 1 to 3 seconds later. Fuel is pumped from the tank, through the filter, the supply line and the pressure regulator to the fuel rail and the injectors.

In the fuel tank, a reservoir directly below the intake of the in-tank pump assures that there will always be a sufficient amount of fuel to the pump, regardless of the car's position. In addition, the return line from the pressure regulator ends in the reservoir, which assures that there will always be an adequate supply of fuel under the pump.

Part of the fuel-gauge sending unit, the in-tank booster pump assures a supply of fuel to the chassis-mounted pump; it also precludes any possibility of vapor lock occuring on the suction side of the system. The chassis-mounted pump is a constant-displacement type and is driven by a 12-volt motor. With a flow rate of 33 gals. per hour under normal operating conditions, it supplies fuel at 39 psi to the injectors. An internal relief valve opens if pressure rises above 55 psi, protecting the rest of the system. The pump is mounted under the car on all models, just forward of the left rear wheel.

The fuel filter has a disposable paper element designed to be replaced every 22,500 miles. On standard Cadillacs, the filter is located in the engine compartment; on the Seville, it is mounted on the frame near the left rear wheel. A valve in the fuel pressure regulator is controlled by spring pressure and vacuum from the intake manifold. As manifold pressure changes with the engine needs, the pressure regulator responds by sending excess fuel back to the tank in order to maintain a constant 39 psi across the injectors.

The injectors are solenoid-operated valves which meter fuel to each cylinder. Pulses from the electronic

EFI SYSTEM DIAGNOSIS

ROUGH IDLE

1. Disconnected, leaking or pinched MAP sensor hose. If plastic harness line requires replacement, replace entire EFI engine harness.
2. Poor connection at air or coolant sensor or open circuit in sensor or wiring (cold engine only).**
3. Poor connection at injection valve(s).
4. Shorted engine coolant sensor.***
5. Speed sensor harness located to close to secondary ignition wires.

PROLONGED FAST IDLE

1. Poor connection at fast idle valve or open circuit in heating element.
2. Throttle position switch misadjusted.
3. Vacuum Leak.

ENGINE HESITATES OR STUMBLES ON ACCELERATION

1. Disconnected, leaking on pinched MAP sensor hose. If plastic harness line requires replacement, replace entire EFI engine harness.
2. Throttle position switch misadjusted.
3. Malfunction in throttle position switch.
4. Intermittent malfunction in distributor trigger (speed sensor).
5. Poor connection at 6 pin connector of ECU.
6. Poor connection at EGR solenoid or open solenoid (cold engine only).

LACK OF HIGH SPEED PERFORMANCE

1. Misadjusted throttle position switch (W.O.T. only).
2. Malfunction in throttle position switch.
3. Malfunction of chassis-mounted fuel pump.
4. Intermittent malfunction in distributor trigger (speed sensor).
5. Fuel filter blocked or restricted.
6. Open circuit in 12 purple wire between starter solenoid and ECU.

*To check, listen for chassis-mounted fuel pump "Whine" (one second only) as key is turned to "ON" position (not to "START" position).

**To check for an "open" circuit in an EFI temperature sensor, connect an ohmmeter to the sensor connector terminals. If the sensor resistance is greater than 1600 ohms, replace the sensor.

***To check for a "closed" (short) circuit in an EFI temperature sensor, connect an ohmmeter to the sensor connector terminals. If the sensor resistance is less than 700 ohms, replace the sensor.

control unit (ECU) open the valve for the time required to inject the proper amount of fuel into each cylinder. The valve sprays the fuel as a mist of fine droplets. These valves require special handling because the metering tips are quite delicate.

AIR INDUCTION SUBSYSTEM (Fig. 5-51)

This system consists of the intake manifold, the throttle body and the fast idle valve. Air enters through the throttle body **(Fig. 5-51, A)** and is distributed through the manifold. Airflow is controlled by the butterfly valves in the throttle body, and additional air for cold starts and warm-up is provided through an electrically controlled fast-idle valve **(Fig. 5-51, B)**.

The dual-plane manifold differs from a carburetor type only in that air is delivered through the runners, there is a port above each cylinder for injector installation, and no exhaust heat passage is used. Provision for exhaust gas recirculation (EGR) is made in the manifold.

The throttle body looks somewhat like a carburetor, because it has two throttle bores and butterfly valves, but it is only an air valve. An adjustable, warm-engine idle screw is incorporated into the body, and the throttle position switch **(Fig. 5-51, C)** is located on an extension of the butterfly valve shaft. A solenoid-operated idle air compensator was added to 1978 throttle bodies. As the air-conditioner clutch engages, the solenoid opens. This provides more air to the engine to control idle speed when the air-conditioner compressor is running.

The fast idle valve incorporates an electric heater, a spring and a plunger, and is connected to a heat-sensitive element. When the engine is first started, the valve opens to allow extra air to enter. As the element warms up, the valve gradually closes, allowing the idle speed to slow. The valve closes completely when the element reaches 140° F. The higher the ambient temperature, the faster the valve will close.

ENGINE SENSOR SUBSYSTEM

Sensors are connected to the electronic control unit to provide it with separate signals, which it analyzes to specify the proper fuel delivery. The Manifold Absolute Pressure (MAP) sensor monitors the changes in intake manifold pressure that result from engine load, speed and barometric pressure (altitude). The sensor is mounted inside the ECU and is connected to the throttle body by a vacuum line. The throttle position switch transmits position and movements of the throttle and the accelerator pedal to the ECU. The switch is mounted on the side of the throttle body. Two temperature sensors monitor air temperature in the intake manifold and coolant temperature in the engine, sending their signals directly to the ECU. The speed sensor is incorporated within the distributor and consists of a magnetic rotor and two reed switches. Two types of information are provided by the speed sensor: synchronization of the ECU with the intake valve timing and engine rpm for scheduling the fuel delivery pulses.

ELECTRONIC CONTROL UNIT (Fig. 5-52)

The ECU receives information from the sensors, encompassing engine coolant temperature, intake-manifold air temperature, intake-manifold absolute pressure, engine speed and firing position, and throttle position and change of position. The ECU processes this information, then sends out command signals that affect electric fuel-pump activation, fast-idle valve activation, injection valve activation and EGR solenoid activation. Air/fuel ratios for all driving conditions are programmed into the ECU, which then sends out the signals to the injectors.

SERVICING THE ELECTRONIC FUEL INJECTION SYSTEM

Before working on the EFI system, it is helpful to first compare its parts with those of a conventionally carbureted system to make the location of possible difficulties and malfunctions easier. The comparison is not a direct interchange, but the following list indicates equivalent parts in the two systems:

CARBURETOR SYSTEM	INJECTION SYSTEM
Accelerator pump	Throttle position switch
Fast idle cam	Electric fast idle valve
Power valve/metering rods	Manifold absolute pressure sensor (MAP)
Metering jets and idle fuel system	Injection valves and ECU

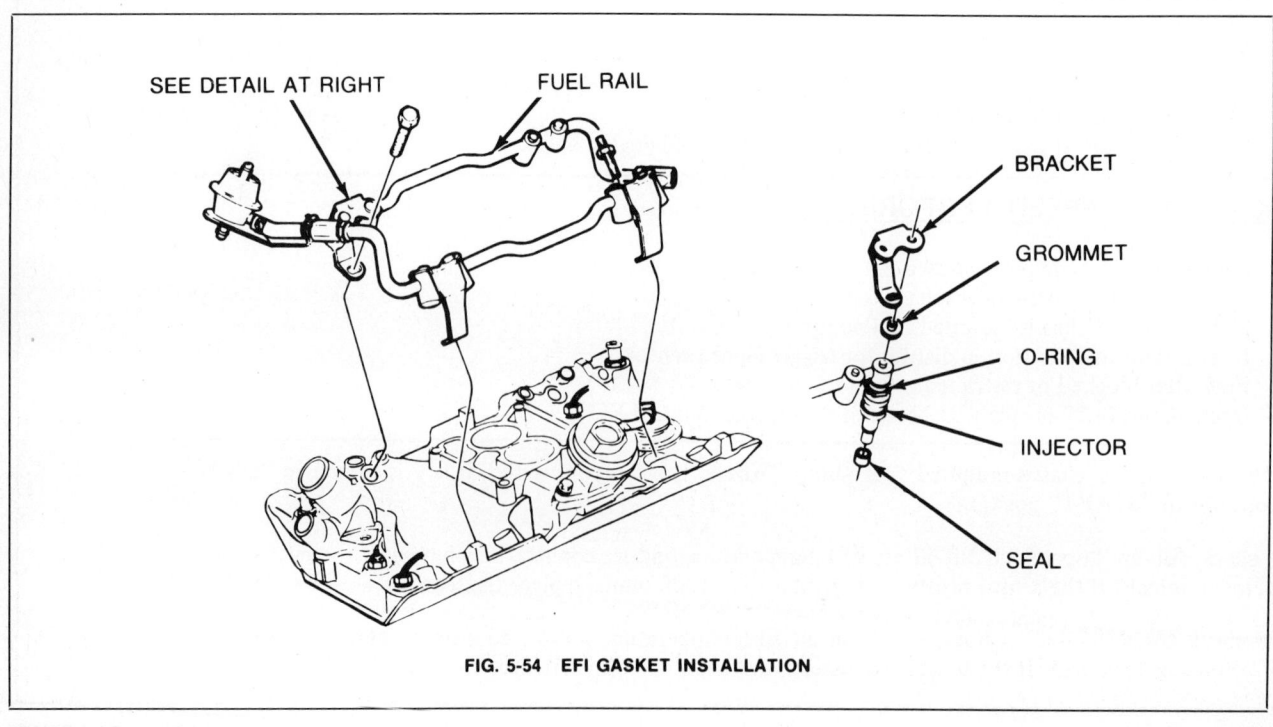

SEE DETAIL AT RIGHT FUEL RAIL

BRACKET

GROMMET

O-RING

INJECTOR

SEAL

FIG. 5-54 EFI GASKET INSTALLATION

Fig. 5-53 presents an EFI Diagnosis Chart prepared by Cadillac to cover specific problems and probable causes that do not require the use of the special test unit designed to troubleshoot the Cadillac EFI system. Without access to one of these special testers, it is not recommended that troubleshooting diagnosis related to the EFI system be attempted. In the vast majority of cases, problems which appear to be injection-related will more likely come from incorrect ignition timing or other non-EFI-related areas.

Should a part of the EFI system malfunction, that part is usually removed and replaced with a new component; adjustment is not recommended and, in many cases, not possible. If it is necessary to dismantle the fuel injection system, remember that the fuel is under pressure. Unless that pressure is relieved before taking a wrench to the system, safety problems could develop. For this reason, a pressure relief valve—the standard Schraeder type of tire valve—has been installed in the system near the fuel pressure regulator. Some fuel will come out with the opening of the valve, but this can be mopped up quickly.

When working on the injection system, be sure to install the special conical gaskets in the fittings between the fuel rails and the injectors and pressure regulator **(Fig. 5-54)**. These gaskets are not installed in production, but must be used anytime the system is taken apart. They cannot be reused, but must be replaced with new ones each time a fitting is disassembled for any reason.

CLOSED-LOOP EFI SYSTEM

Standard on all 1979 and later California Sevilles, the closed-loop EFI system senses the engine's air/fuel ratio and corrects it to the ideal 14.7:1 ratio by means of a feedback signal to the ECU. As shown in **Fig. 5-54A,** an oxygen sensor is positioned in the top of the right exhaust manifold. This produces a varying voltage signal according to the amount of oxygen in the exhaust gas. The sensor is mounted in such a way as to expose one end of its element to the exhaust gas while its center is vented to the atmosphere. This allows the sensor to compare the oxygen content of the exhaust

with that of the atmosphere and signal the specially calibrated ECU as to the richness/leanness of the exhaust gas.

A sensor indicator is provided in the speedometer cluster to remind the driver that sensor replacement is necessary at each 15,000-mile interval. This indicator must be reset each time the sensor is replaced. To reset it, remove the lower steering column cover and locate the reset cable. This is positioned at the left bottom of the speedometer cluster. Pull the cable lightly to reset the warning indicator and replace the cover.

Closed-loop EFI troubleshooting requires additional diagnostic procedures beyond those described in **Fig. 5-53.** Such normal procedures should be performed first to assure that everything else is working properly. If so, perform the following test procedure:

1. Connect a 2-candlepower (or less) test lamp between the fuse block spare cavity and the diagnostic pigtail of the ECU.

2. Start the engine and bring to normal operating temperature. Let the engine run an additional 2½ minutes. If test lamp lights, continue the procedure.

3. Disconnect the exhaust oxygen sensor and connect an ohmmeter between ground and the harness center terminal. If the meter reads less than 1 megaohm, the harness is shorted and must be replaced.

4. With one ohmmeter lead connected to the harness center terminal, connect the other lead to the ECU *red* connector pin J. If the meter reads more than 10 ohms, the harness is open and must be replaced.

5. Connect pin E of the *blue* ECU connector to the oxygen sensor cable shield with a jumper wire and check for continuity.

6. If the problem is not one of continuity, a short or open, replace the oxygen sensor. If the test lamp remains lighted, substitute a known-good ECU. When the test lamp goes out, the problem has been solved.

COSWORTH VEGA FUEL INJECTION SYSTEM

Although the Cosworth Vega, introduced in 1975, is a limited production vehicle, one of the major reasons for its quick response and power is its Electronic Fuel Injection (EFI), a pulse-time manifold injection system

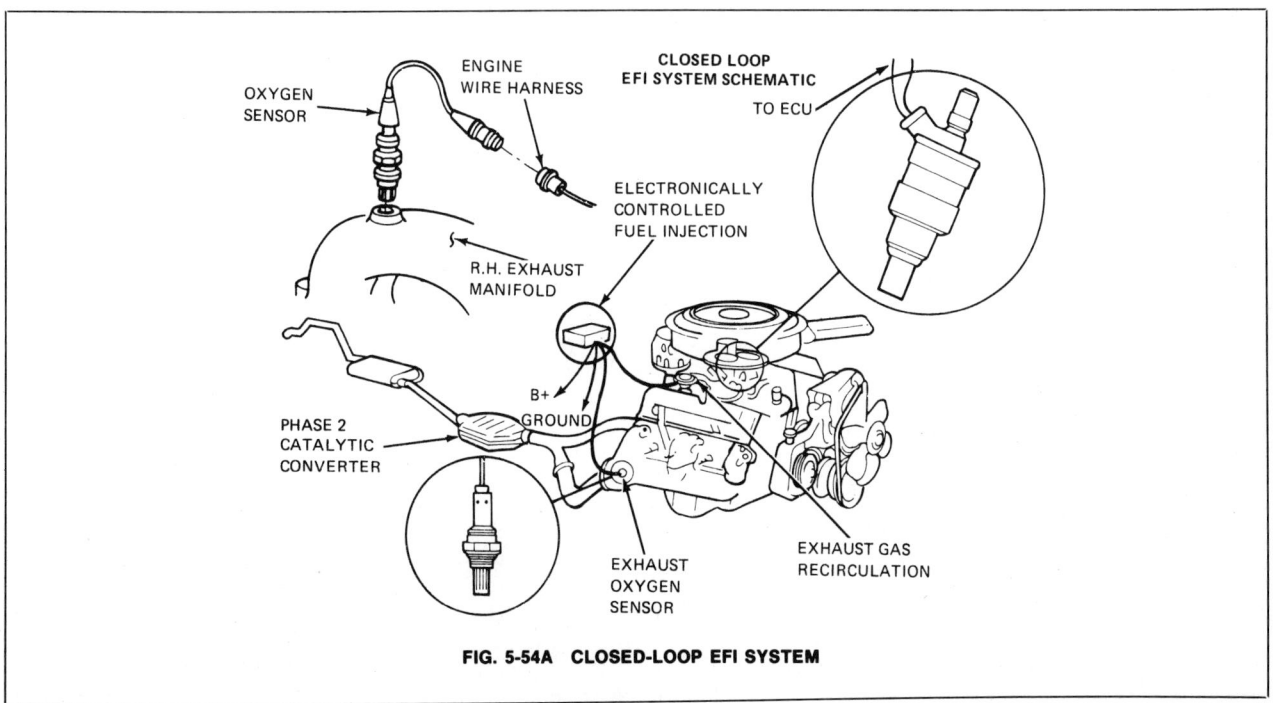

FIG. 5-54A CLOSED-LOOP EFI SYSTEM

(Fig. 5-55) which is composed of four primary subsystems:

1. Electronic Control Unit (ECU).
2. Fuel Delivery Subsystem.
3. Air Induction Subsystem.
4. Engine Sensing Subsystem.

ELECTRONIC CONTROL UNIT (ECU)

A pre-programmed analog computer, the ECU is located under the instrument panel and above the glove compartment. This unit receives and evaluates impulses from the Engine Sensing System, determines the amount and duration of fuel required for engine operation, and thus controls the amount and duration of fuel injected into the engine cylinders. If the ECU is to be disconnected from the power and control harnesses, it is *imperative* that the battery ground cable be disconnected *first* to avoid any accidental shorting of the ECU components, or expensive damage to the ECU may result.

FUEL DELIVERY SUBSYSTEM (Fig. 5-56)

The Cosworth Vega uses two fuel pumps: an electrical in-tank fuel-pump/fuel-gauge metering unit similar to that used on other Vega models and a high-pressure pump mounted on the right side of the underbody in front of the right rear wheel. The in-tank pump can deliver up to 35 gals. per hour, while the external pump is capable of delivering 32 gals. per hour at a nominal pressure of 39 psi. The external pump is not serviceable, but is replaced as a unit if it malfunctions.

The fuel pressure regulator **(Fig. 5-57)** is mounted

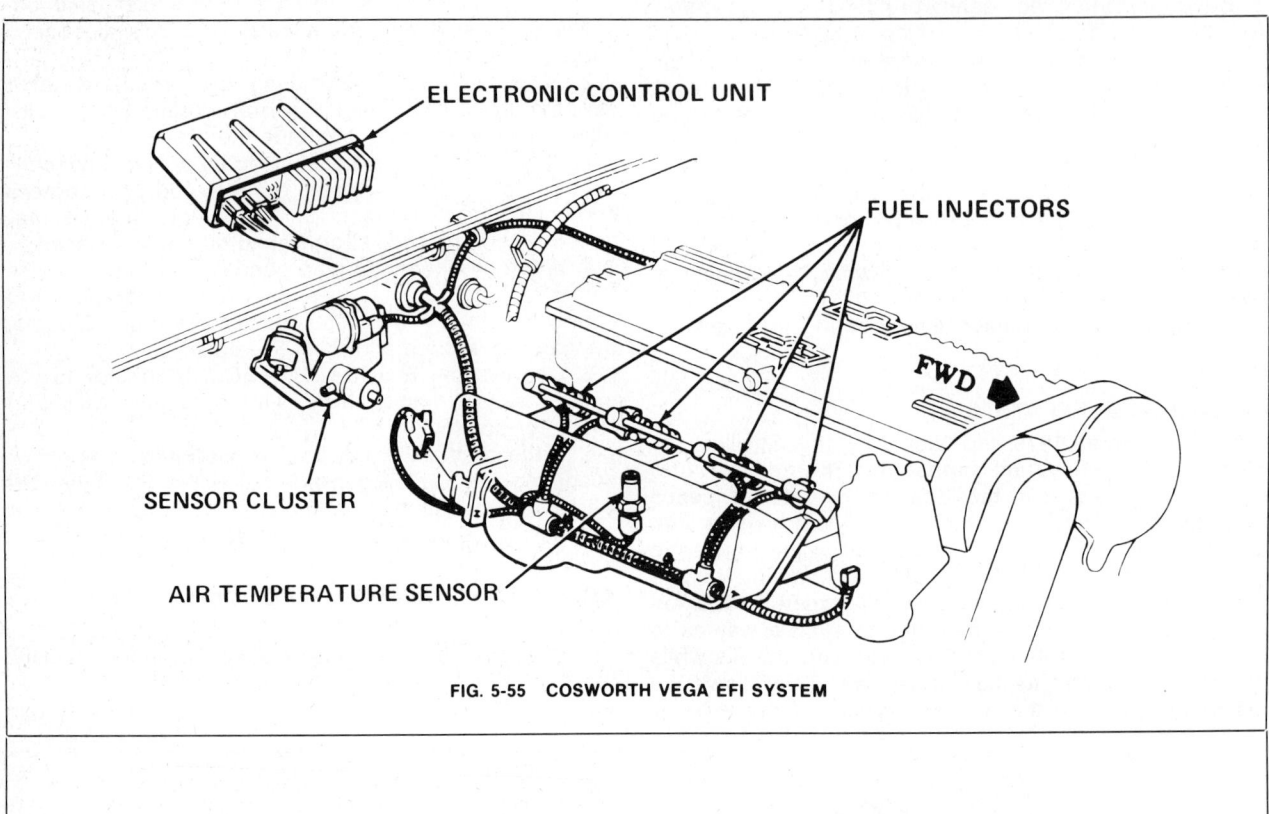

FIG. 5-55 COSWORTH VEGA EFI SYSTEM

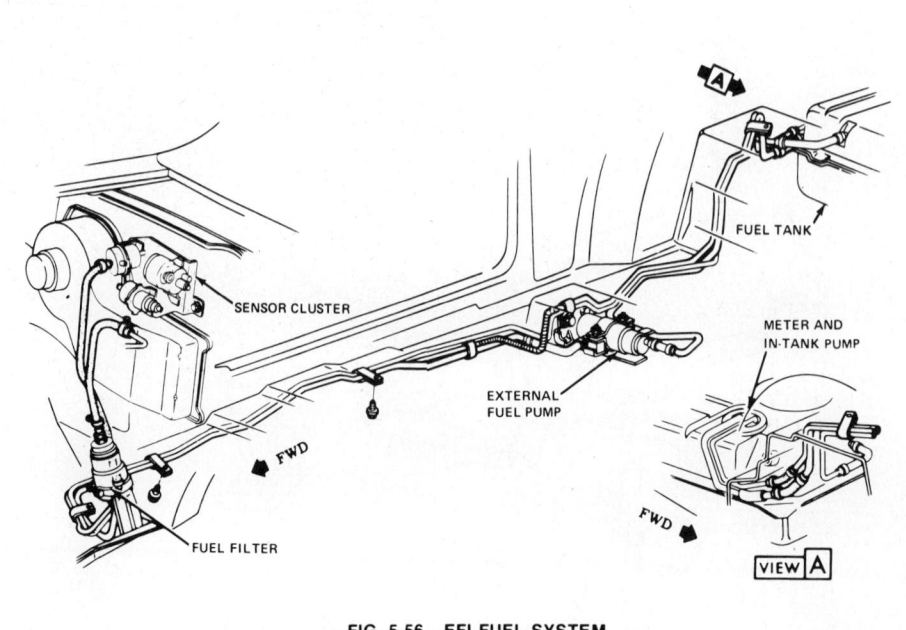

FIG. 5-56 EFI FUEL SYSTEM

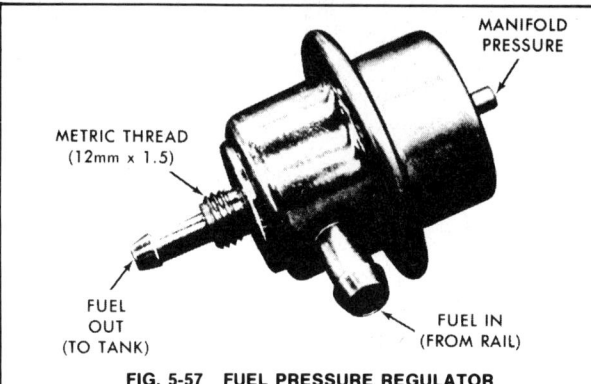

FIG. 5-57 FUEL PRESSURE REGULATOR

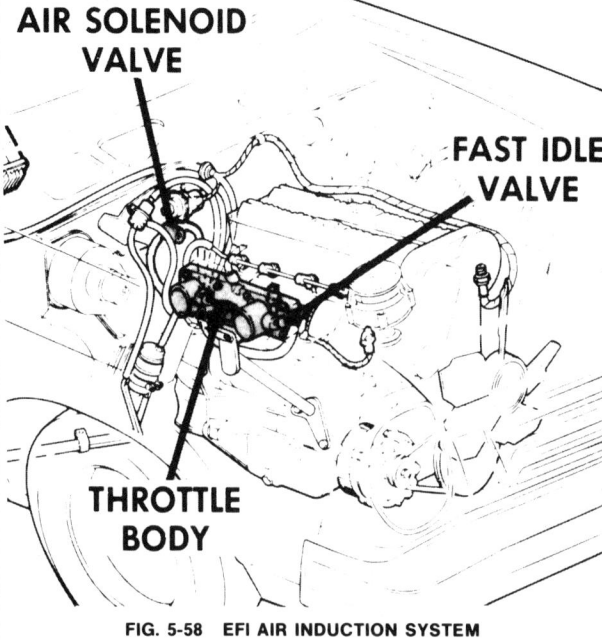

FIG. 5-58 EFI AIR INDUCTION SYSTEM

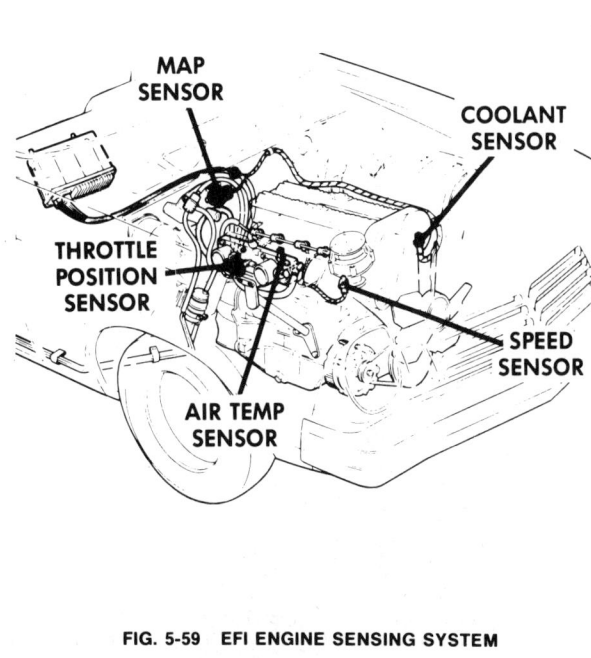

FIG. 5-59 EFI ENGINE SENSING SYSTEM

under the hood on the sensor cluster bracket and maintains fuel at a constant 39-psi pressure to the fuel rail, relative to the intake manifold pressure. Because the fuel pump constantly supplies fuel to the regulator, a return line to the fuel tank is opened by the regulator diaphragm when pressure exceeds 39 psi.

The fuel injector is an electro-mechanical solenoid which meters and atomizes fuel. While capable of opening and closing within 2 milliseconds, the typical injection time for the majority of engine conditions ranges up to 10 milliseconds. The injectors function in pairs—cylinders 1 and 2 as Group One and cylinders 3 and 4 as Group Two. Activating the injectors in pairs produces better cylinder priming. Group injection normally takes place once every 720° of crankshaft rotation, but under a loaded, wide-open throttle condition, all injectors open every 360° of crankshaft rotation to allow maximum power under full load conditions.

The injectors are mounted in a fuel rail and direct the fuel to the top side of the intake valve. While interchangeable between cylinders, the injectors are not compatible with those from other EFI applications (their fuel flow rate is different) and are serviced by replacement only.

The fuel filter uses a throw-away filter element and contains a relief valve which bypasses fuel to maintain flow if the filter element should become clogged or otherwise restricted.

AIR INDUCTION SYSTEM (Fig. 5-58)

The air necessary for combustion is filtered through the air cleaner, passing through the throttle body and intake manifold before entering the combustion chambers. A fast idle valve provides more air to the intake manifold during cold engine conditions. The air solenoid valve controls engine speed during cold-start/engine-warm-up conditions.

ENGINE SENSING SYSTEM (Fig. 5-59)

Five separate sensors are used. The Manifold Air Pressure (MAP) sensor signals the ECU of varying atmospheric and engine pressures. The throttle position sensor informs the ECU of throttle position and throttle motion rate of change. The coolant temperature sensor keeps the ECU informed of engine coolant temperature at the thermostat housing. The air temperature sensor transmits data concerning temperatures at the bottom of the inlet manifold. The engine speed sensor provides data of engine speed and phase. The use of parallel circuits from each sensor to the ECU allow them to operate independently of each other.

SERVICING THE VEGA
ELECTRONIC FUEL INJECTION SYSTEM

Without access to an EFI Diagnostic Analyzer (Bendix J-24706), it is not recommended that troubleshooting diagnosis related to the EFI system be attempted. In the vast majority of such cases, problems which appear to be injection-related will more likely come from incorrect ignition timing, or other non-EFI-related areas.

Should a part of the EFI system malfunction, that part is usually removed and replaced with a new component; adjustment is not recommended, nor is repair, and in many cases it is not possible. If it becomes necessary to dismantle the fuel injection system, remember that the fuel is under pressure from the external fuel pump forward. Unless that pressure is relieved before taking a wrench to the system, safety problems could develop.

SIMPLIFIED CARBURETOR ADJUSTMENT

A carburetor should never be "tinkered" with; if the engine does not run correctly, you should check the rest of the fuel system, the ignition system and certain emission control devices (such as the EGR valve) before blaming the carburetor and attempting to correct the malfunction by adjusting the idle speed/idle mixture/choke action.

The following section presents a simplified approach to carburetor adjustment; a technique that will allow you to adjust *any* carburetor *correctly* on the car. Refer to the emission control information sticker, decal or label found under the hood for up-to-the-minute adjustment specifications where possible; the specifications presented at the end of this chapter are those provided by the manufacturers, but may not agree with the sticker, decal or label because of on-line running changes made during the model year, and should be used only where there is no sticker, decal or label present, or when it has been damaged so that the information is not legible.

ALL 1978 AND LATER GM ENGINES

General Motors has adopted Propane Enrichment (see **Fig. 5-67** for Ford procedure and explanation of technique) as its recommended method of setting idle mixture. Some GM carburetors have been modified to limit the range of idle mixture adjustment on the rich side. This means that backing out the idle mixture needles *will not* richen the mixture by any noticeable extent.

GM does not provide an alternate method in 1978-79 factory manuals. It recommends that idle mixture adjustment should only be necessary because of major carburetor overhaul, throttle body replacement or high idle CO as determined by state or local inspection. It also warns that adjusting the idle mixture by any other method may violate Federal and/or California, or other state laws. Idle mixture screws on some 1979 and later Rochester carburetors are recessed in the throttle body casting. After the mixture is preset at the factory, the mixture screw recess is sealed with a hardened steel plug. This measure has been taken as a means of discouraging owners from changing the factory-adjusted mixture setting in order to improve drivability at the expense of low exhaust emissions.

For the various reasons which are specified herein, no adjustments are provided on the following pages for 1978-79 Buick, Cadillac, Chevrolet, Oldsmobile or Pontiac engines.

BUICK
SIMPLIFIED CARBURETOR ADJUSTMENT PROCEDURE
SERVICE PRECAUTIONS

1. If 1970-72 engines are equipped with a compressor for automatic level control, it should not be operating with the engine running at idle. A regulator valve is included to shut off vacuum at idle. If the compressor is running while idle speed adjustments are being made, the valve is malfunctioning and must be replaced before a satisfactory idle setting can be made.

2. Carburetor adjustments must be performed in DRIVE or, if equipped with manual transmission, NEUTRAL. For safety's sake, be sure to set the parking brake and block the front tires before shifting the transmission.

3. A faulty PCV system can greatly alter air/fuel

ratio, so test the valve and hoses before proceeding with the following adjustments. See "Emission Systems" chapter for test procedure.

4. Refer to "Tune-Up Specifications" chapter for specified idle speeds.

ALL 1970 ENGINES AS SPECIFIED BELOW

I-6 250

1. Connect a tachometer and run the engine until it reaches normal operating temperature and the choke value has fully opened. Leave the air cleaner installed for idle mixture adjustments.

2. Remove and plug the vacuum hose from the distributor to prevent the thermo-vacuum switch from activating full manifold vacuum should the coolant become too hot during the adjustment period.

3. Adjust the solenoid plunger screw until the idle speed agrees with the specified rpm.

4. Shut off the engine and turn in the mixture screw until it lightly seats, then back it out four complete turns.

5. Start the engine and readjust the solenoid screw until the tach reads 830 rpm (manual transmission in NEUTRAL) or 630 rm (automatic in DRIVE).

6. Turn the mixture screw in to obtain the specified idle speed. Connect the distributor vacuum hose.

7. De-energize the idle stop solenoid by disconnecting its wire, and adjust the throttle stopscrew to achieve 400 rpm—manual or automatic. The mixture and idle-stop solenoid screws should not be disturbed at this time.

8. Reconnect the solenoid wire, accelerate the engine to extend the solenoid and double-check the slow idle speed.

V-8 350, 455

1. Connect a tachometer and run the engine until it reaches normal operating temperature and the choke valve has fully opened. Leave the air cleaner installed for idle mixture adjustments.

2. Remove and plug the distributor vacuum hose to prevent the thermo-vacuum switch from activating full manifold vacuum should the coolant become too hot during the adjustment period.

3. Adjust the throttle stopscrew until an idle speed 20 rpm greater than specified is reached.

4. Alternately screw each mixture needle in to get

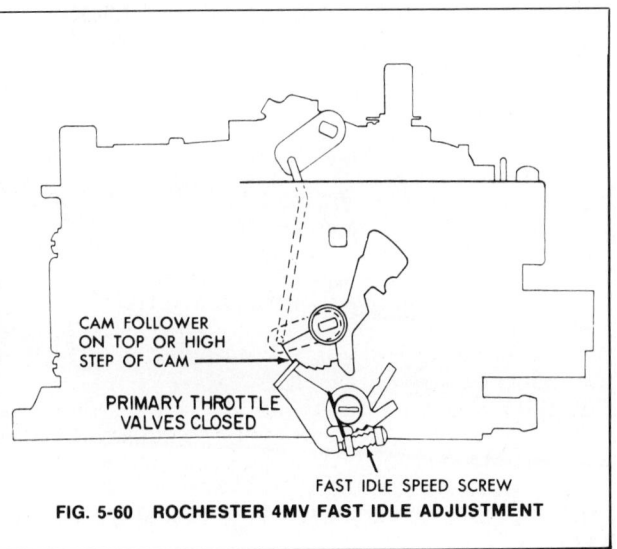

CAM FOLLOWER ON TOP OR HIGH STEP OF CAM

PRIMARY THROTTLE VALVES CLOSED

FAST IDLE SPEED SCREW

FIG. 5-60 ROCHESTER 4MV FAST IDLE ADJUSTMENT

an idle speed of 10 rpm less per needle than the setting obtained in Step 3. This will equal a total of 20 rpm less, or the rpm as specified.

5. With the transmission in DRIVE and the follower on the low step of the fast idle cam, adjust the fast idle to specifications.

6. If the carburetor is fitted with a hot idle compensator, press inward on it and watch the tachometer. If the idle speed drops, the compensator valve is stuck open. Correct and reset the idle.

ALL 1971 ENGINES AS SPECIFIED BELOW
I-6 250

1. Connect a tachometer and run the engine until it reaches normal operating temperature and the choke has fully opened. Leave the air cleaner installed for idle mixture adjustments.

2. Disconnect and plug the distributor vacuum hose, and turn off the engine.

3. Turn in the mixture screw until it lightly seats, then back it out four complete turns.

4. Start the engine and readjust the mixture screw and idle screw to obtain the best idle at 530 rpm (automatic transmission) or 625 (manual).

5. Connect the distributor vacuum hose.

V-8 350, 455

1. Connect a tachometer and run the engine until it reaches normal operating temperature and the choke valve is wide open. Leave the air cleaner installed for idle mixture adjustments.

2. Adjust the throttle stopscrew until the specified idle speed is reached.

3. Alternately adjust the idle mixture needles to get the highest possible tachometer reading.

4. Readjust both throttle stop and mixture as necessary to get an idle speed 50 rpm greater than specified.

5. Turn each idle mixture needle in to reduce the idle speed 25 rpm per needle. This will equal a total of 50 rpm less, or the rpm as specified.

6. Adjust the fast-idle-speed screw on the low step of the fast idle cam to obtain the specified setting **(Fig. 5-60).** Connect the distributor vacuum hose.

ALL 1972-73 ENGINES

1. Connect a tachometer and run the engine until it reaches normal operating temperature. Leave the air cleaner installed for idle mixture adjustments.

2. Disconnect and plug the distributor vacuum hose.

3. Open the throttle until the solenoid plunger extends to touch the throttle lever pad when it is in the idle position.

4. Adjust the solenoid setscrew until the specified rpm is reached.

5. Disconnect the solenoid wire to de-energize the solenoid.

6. Now adjust the idle speed screw to obtain the specified idle speed and reconnect the solenoid wire.

7. Adjust one idle mixture needle until the highest possible tachometer reading is reached, then repeat the procedure with the other mixture needle.

8. At the highest reading, readjust the throttle stopscrew and mixture screws until a reading of 50 rpm over the specified speed is set.

9. Turn one mixture needle in to reduce the idle speed by 25 rpm, then repeat the procedure with the other mixture needle. This will equal a total of 50 rpm, or the rpm setting specified.

10. On 4-bbl. carburetors, adjust the fast idle speed as follows:

a) Automatic Transmission—Low step of fast idle cam, adjust to 700 rpm in DRIVE.

b) Manual Transmission—Low step of fast idle cam, adjust 350 engines to 820 rpm and 455 engines to 920 rpm.

11. Reconnect the distributor vacuum hose.

ALL 1974 ENGINES

1. Disconnect and plug the distributor vacuum hose. Leave the air cleaner installed for idle mixture adjustments.

2. Disconnect and plug the EGR vacuum hose at the EGR valve.

3. Disconnect the vapor canister hose at the air cleaner.

4. Start the engine, disconnect the solenoid wire and adjust the low idle speed to specifications, then reconnect the solenoid and adjust the solenoid screw to the higher specified speed.

5. Adjust the idle speed to 70 rpm above the specified speed for 455 engines and 60 rpm above specifications for 350 engines.

6. Adjust the idle mixture needles inward equally until the engine returns to the specified idle speed, cutting the tabs from the limiter caps if necessary.

7. Reconnect the distributor vacuum, EGR valve and vapor canister hoses.

ALL 1975-76 ENGINES

1. Connect a tachometer and run the engine until it reaches normal operating temperature. Remove the air cleaner on the 2MC carburetor only.

2. Disconnect and plug the distributor vacuum hose (there is no vacuum line to the distributor on California cars).

3. Disconnect the vapor canister hose at the air cleaner.

4. Start the engine, disconnect the solenoid wire and adjust the low idle speed to specifications, then reconnect the solenoid and adjust the solenoid screw to the higher specified speed.

5. 2MC carburetors only: Back each mixture needle out exactly five turns and adjust the idle speed. Turn each needle in one-half turn, and note the idle rpm. Repeat the procedure until rpm reaches specifications. This completes 2MC idle and mixture adjustments—proceed to Step 9.

6. Cut off the mixture-limiter-cap tabs and turn the idle mixture needles out until maximum idle is reached.

7. Reset curb idle speed (if necessary) to obtain 80 rpm more than the specified curb idle speed.

8. Turn the mixture needles inward equally until the specified curb idle is reached.

9. Adjust the fast-idle-speed screw to 900 rpm on low step of cam.

10. If equipped with air conditioning, complete the above adjustments, then turn on the air conditioner. Disconnect the electrical connector at the compressor clutch and adjust the solenoid screw to 650 rpm, then reconnect the electrical connector.

11. Reconnect the distributor vacuum and vapor canister lines.

12. Replace the air cleaner on the 2MC carburetor.

ALL 1977 ENGINES

1. Remove air cleaner, but leave all vacuum hoses attached. On cars with automatic leveling, disconnect and plug vacuum hose to compressor. Disconnect and plug other hoses as indicated on Emission Control Information Label under the hood.

2. Connect a tachometer and run the engine until it reaches normal operating temperature.

3. Disconnect the vacuum advance and plug the hose. Follow instructions on Emission Control Information Label. Then reconnect vacuum advance.

4. Carefully remove caps from the idle mixture screws, being careful not to bend them. Lightly seat each screw, then back both out equally just enough so engine will run.

5. With automatic transmission in DRIVE and manual in NEUTRAL, back out each screw ⅛ turn at a time until maximum idle speed is reached. Repeat the procedure until specifications are reached.

6. Turn mixture screws inward at ⅛ turn increments until specified curb idle speed is reached.

7. Adjust fast idle speed as described on the Emission Control Information Label.

8. Reconnect vacuum hoses, install air cleaner and recheck idle speed. If necessary, reset.

CADILLAC

SIMPLIFIED CARBURETOR ADJUSTMENT PROCEDURE

ALL 1970 ENGINES

1. Disconnect and plug the parking-brake vacuum line at the vacuum release cylinder and the distributor vacuum-advance line at the distributor.

2. Remove the air cleaner, connect a tachometer.

3. Check the dashpot to make sure it does not touch the linkage. Turn the slow-idle-speed screw in 1½ turns after it touches the primary throttle lever.

4. Turn both idle mixture needles inward until they just seat, then back each out six turns.

5. Start the engine and warm it up to normal operating temperature, with the choke fully opened. The air conditioner must be off and the transmission in DRIVE. For safety, set the parking brake and block the wheels.

6. Depress the hot-idle-compensator pin while making the adjustments in Steps 7 and 8.

7. Adjust slow idle screw until rpm reading is 620.

8. Turn one idle mixture needle inward until the idle speed drops off 10 rpm, then repeat the procedure with the other mixture needle. Idle speed should be 600 rpm when needles have been correctly adjusted.

9. Shut off the engine and replace the air cleaner.

10. Reconnect the vacuum lines.

ALL 1971-76 ENGINES

EXCEPT SEVILLE AND OPTIONAL FUEL INJECTION

1. Disconnect and plug the following hoses: the parking-brake vacuum line at the vacuum release cylinder, the distributor vacuum-advance line at the distributor and, if so equipped, the air leveling hose at the air cleaner.

2. Without disturbing the other vacuum hoses, remove the air cleaner and connect a tachometer to the engine.

3. Turn both idle mixture needles inward until they just seat, then back out one six turns (1974 four turns, 1975-76 five turns).

4. Start the engine and warm it up to normal operating temperature, making sure the choke is fully open and the carburetor is on slow idle. The air conditioner must be off and the transmission in DRIVE with the front tires blocked and the parking brake set.

5. An anti-dieseling solenoid replaces the dashpot formerly used. The solenoid, in use from 1971 through

1974, was replaced with a simple idle speed screw for 1975. On solenoid models, open the throttle to allow the solenoid plunger to fully extend, then close the throttle against the extended plunger.

6. Loosen the solenoid jam nut, and set idle speed to 620 rpm for 1971-72 engines, 640 rpm for 1973-74 engines by adjusting the solenoid. Tighten the jam nut. On 1975-76 engines, set idle with idle speed screw to 650 rpm (nationwide) or 620 rpm (California).

7. Alternately turn each mixture needle inward one-quarter turn at a time until the idle speed reaches 600 rpm.

8. Disconnect the solenoid wire and watch its plunger retract from the throttle. The idle should drop from 350 to 400 rpm.

9. Connect the solenoid wire, open the throttle and watch the idle climb back to 600 rpm. If not, readjust solenoid.

10. Shut off the engine, install the air cleaner and connect the vacuum hoses.

ALL 1977 ENGINES

EXCEPT OPTIONAL FUEL INJECTION

1. Disconnect and plug the parking-brake vacuum hose, the distributor vacuum-advance line at the distributor and, if so equipped, the air leveling hose at the air cleaner. Disconnect and plug other hoses as indicated on the Emission Control Information Label under the hood.

2. Without disturbing the other vacuum hoses, remove the air cleaner and connect a tachometer to the engine.

3. Carefully remove the caps from the idle mixture screws, being careful not to bend the screws. Lightly seat the screws, then back each out two turns equally just enough so engine will run.

4. Start the engine and warm it up to normal operating temperature, making sure the choke is fully open and the carburetor is on slow idle. The air conditioner must be off and the transmission in DRIVE with the front tires blocked and the parking brake set.

5. Back out each screw (richer) one-eighth turn at a time until maximum idle speed is reached. Set idle speed screw to 670 rpm (California cars 630 rpm). Repeat procedure.

6. Alternately turn each mixture needle inward one-

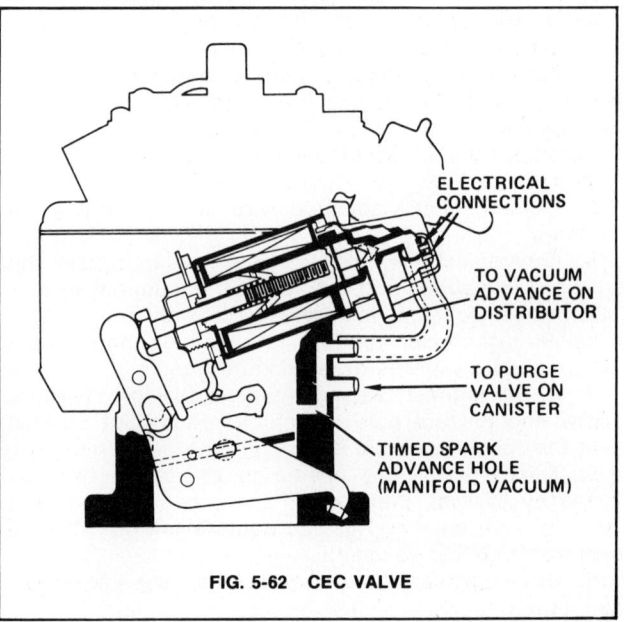

ELECTRICAL CONNECTIONS

TO VACUUM ADVANCE ON DISTRIBUTOR

TO PURGE VALVE ON CANISTER

TIMED SPARK ADVANCE HOLE (MANIFOLD VACUUM)

FIG. 5-62 CEC VALVE

eighth turn at a time until idle speed reaches 600 rpm.

7. Adjust fast idle as described on the Emission Control Information Label.

8. Reconnect vacuum hoses, install air cleaner and recheck idle speed. Reset if necessary.

CHEVROLET

Adjustment procedures and specifications vary, and are provided below on the basis of engine application. Refer to the "Tune-Up Specifications" chapter for specifications. The following four steps must be performed with all carburetors before undertaking the specific adjustment procedure applicable to the engine.

1. Disconnect the vapor canister line marked FUEL TANK (EEC). On Corvette only, remove the fuel tank cap instead.

2. Disconnect and plug the distributor vacuum-advance line at the distributor.

3. Connect a tachometer and start the engine, allowing it to warm up to normal operating temperature. The choke and preheater valves must be fully opened.

4. Turn off the air conditioner and set the transmission in NEUTRAL if manual, DRIVE if automatic, unless specified otherwise. For safety, block the front wheels and set the parking brake.

SIMPLIFIED CARBURETOR ADJUSTMENT PROCEDURE

ALL 1970 ENGINES AS SPECIFIED BELOW

I-4 153 With 1-bbl. Rochester

1. Adjust the idle mixture needle for maximum idle rpm.

2. Set the idle speed screw to obtain 750 rpm manual, 650 rpm automatic.

3. Turn the idle mixture needle inward until the idle speed drops 20 rpm, then back it out one-quarter turn.

4. Readjust the idle speed screw to obtain the specified rpm.

5. Shut off the engine and reconnect the distributor vacuum and vapor canister lines.

I-6 230/250 With 1-bbl. Rochester

1. Turn the idle mixture needle inward until it just seats, then back the needle out four turns.

2. Adjust the solenoid screw to obtain 830 rpm manual, 630 rpm automatic.

3. Turn the idle mixture needle inward until the idle speed reaches 750 rpm manual, 600 rpm automatic.

4. Disconnect the solenoid wire and adjust the idle speed to 400 rpm, then reconnect wire.

5. Shut off the engine and reconnect the distributor vacuum and vapor canister lines.

V-8 307/400 (265 hp) With 2-bbl. Rochester

1. Turn the idle mixture needles inward until they just seat, then back each needle out four turns.

2. Adjust the idle speed screw on manual transmission models to obtain 800 rpm.

3. Adjust the solenoid screw on automatic transmission models to obtain 630 rpm.

4. Turn both idle mixture needles inward equally to obtain 600 rpm automatic, 700 rpm manual.

5. On automatic transmission models, disconnect the solenoid wire and set the idle speed screw to obtain 450 rpm. Reconnect the solenoid.

6. Shut off the engine and reconnect the distributor vacuum and vapor canister lines.

V-8 350 (250 hp) With 2-bbl. Rochester

1. Turn the idle mixture needles inward until they just seat, then back each needle out four turns.

2. Adjust the solenoid screw to obtain an idle speed of 830 rpm manual, 630 rpm automatic.

3. Turn both idle mixture needles inward equally to obtain 600 rpm automatic, 750 rpm manual.

4. Disconnect the solenoid wire and set the idle speed screw to obtain 450 rpm. Reconnect solenoid.

5. Shut off the engine and reconnect the distributor vacuum and vapor canister lines.

V-8 350 (300 hp) and 400 (330 hp) With 4-bbl. Rochester

1. Turn the idle mixture needles inward until they just seat, then back each needle out four turns.

2. Adjust the idle speed screw to obtain 775 rpm manual, 630 rpm automatic.

3. Turn both idle mixture needles inward equally to obtain 600 rpm automatic, 700 rpm manual.

4. Shut off the engine and reconnect the distributor vacuum and vapor canister lines.

V-8 396 (350 hp), 454 (345 hp) & 454 (360 & 390 hp) With 4-bbl. Rochester

1. Turn the idle mixture needles inward until they just seat, then back each needle out four turns.

2. Adjust the idle speed screw to obtain 700 rpm manual, 630 rpm automatic.

3. Adjust the idle mixture needles as follows:

a) Manual transmission—Turn in one mixture needle until the idle speed drops 40 rpm, then adjust the idle speed screw to regain the 700 rpm reading. Repeat procedure with other mixture needle.

b) Automatic Transmission—Adjust the idle mixture needles equally to obtain a 600 rpm reading.

4. Shut off the engine and reconnect the distributor vacuum and vapor canister lines.

ALL 1971 ENGINES AS SPECIFIED BELOW

SERVICE PRECAUTIONS

1. The combination emission control (CEC) solenoid **(Fig. 5-62)** replaces the idle stop solenoid on 1971 carburetors. It *should not* be adjusted unless either the solenoid is replaced because it is defective or if it is removed during a carburetor overhaul. The CEC solenoid is energized through the transmission to provide full vacuum advance in high gear and to increase the idle speed during high gear deceleration. The solenoid is not energized at curb idle and retards the spark in all but high gear to lower hydrocarbon emission. *Do not* adjust idle speed with the CEC solenoid screw.

2. Idle-mixture limiter caps are installed on all 1971 carburetors, except those fitted to Z-28, LT-1 and LS-6 engines. Chevrolet recommends that you do not remove the caps or attempt to adjust the mixture, except when the carburetor is overhauled. Air conditioner is off unless otherwise specified.

3. Follow Steps 1-4 described at the beginning of this section. Refer to the "Tune-Up Specifications" chapter for specifications, if necessary, and proceed with carburetor adjustment according to engine:

I-6 250 With 1-bbl. Rochester

1. Adjust the idle speed screw to obtain 550 rpm manual, 500 rpm automatic.

2. Shut off the engine and reconnect the distributor vacuum and vapor canister lines.

V-8 307 (200 hp), 350 (245 hp) & 400 (255 hp) With 2-bbl. Rochester

1. Adjust the idle speed screw to obtain 600 rpm manual, 550 automatic (air conditioner is on when adjusting the automatic).
2. Shut off the engine, and reconnect the distributor vacuum and vapor canister lines.

V-8 350 (270 hp) With 4-bbl. Rochester

1. Adjust the idle speed screw to obtain 600 rpm manual, 550 automatic (air conditioner is on when adjusting the automatic).
2. With the fast idle cam follower on the second step of the fast idle cam, set the fast idle screw to obtain 1350 rpm manual, 1500 rpm automatic in PARK with the air conditioner off.
3. Shut off the engine and reconnect the distributor vacuum and vapor canister lines.

V-8 350 (Z-28/330 hp & LT-1/330 hp) With 4-bbl. Holley

1. Adjust the idle mixture needles for maximum idle rpm.
2. Adjust the idle speed screw to obtain 700 rpm, manual or automatic.
3. Turn one idle mixture needle inward to obtain a 20 rpm drop in idle speed, then back it out one-quarter turn. Repeat procedure with the other mixture needle.
4. Reset idle speed to 700 rpm.
5. Shut off the engine, and reconnect the distributor vacuum and vapor canister lines.

V-8 402 (LS-3/330 hp) & 454 (LS-5/365 hp) With 4-bbl. Rochester

1. Adjust the idle speed screw to obtain 600 rpm, manual or automatic.
2. With the fast idle cam follower on the second step of the fast idle cam, set the fast idle screw to obtain 1350 rpm manual, 1500 rpm automatic in PARK.
3. Shut off the engine, and reconnect the distributor vacuum and vapor canister lines.

V-8 454 (LS-6/425 hp) With 4-bbl. Holley

1. Adjust the idle mixture needles for maximum idle rpm.
2. Adjust the idle speed screw to obtain 700 rpm, manual or automatic.
3. Turn one idle mixture needle inward to obtain a 20 rpm drop in idle speed, then back it out one-quarter turn. Repeat procedure with the other mixture needle.
4. Reset idle speed to 700 rpm.
5. Shut off the engine and reconnect the distributor vacuum and vapor canister lines.

ALL 1972 ENGINES AS SPECIFIED BELOW

SERVICE PRECAUTIONS

1. All 1972 carburetors are fitted with idle limiter caps; Chevrolet does not recommend attempting to adjust the mixture or removing the caps.
2. The CEC solenoid is retained on the I-6 250-cu.-in. engine, but replaced by an idle stop solenoid on all V-8 engines. *Do not* attempt to set idle rpm with the CEC solenoid.
3. Follow Steps 1-4 described at the beginning of this section. Refer to the ''Tune-Up Specifications'' chapter for specifications, if necessary, and proceed with carburetor adjustment (air conditioner off, unless otherwise specified) according to engine:

I-6 250 With 1-bbl. Rochester

1. Adjust the idle-stop-solenoid screw (this is the

smallest solenoid on the carburetor) to obtain an idle speed of 700 rpm manual, 600 rpm automatic.
2. Shut off the engine and reconnect the distributor vacuum and vapor canister lines.

V-8 307, 350 & 400 With 2-bbl. Rochester

1. Adjust the idle speed screw to obtain an idle speed of 900 rpm manual, 600 rpm automatic.
2. Adjust the fast-idle-cam screw to obtain a fast idle of 1850 rpm (307) or 2200 rpm (350/400) with transmission in NEUTRAL or PARK.
3. Shut off the engine, and reconnect the distributor vacuum and vapor canister lines.

V-8 350 With 4-bbl. Rochester

1. Adjust the idle speed screw to obtain an idle speed of 800 rpm manual, 600 rpm automatic.
2. With the fast idle cam follower on the second step of the fast idle cam, set the fast idle screw to obtain 1350 rpm manual, 1500 rpm automatic in PARK.
3. Shut off the engine, and reconnect the distributor vacuum and vapor canister lines.

V-8 350 With 4-bbl. Holley

1. Adjust the idle-stop-solenoid screw to obtain an idle speed of 900 rpm manual, 700 rpm automatic.
2. Shut off the engine, and reconnect the distributor vacuum and vapor canister lines.

V-8 402/454 With 4-bbl. Rochester

1. Adjust the idle-stop-solenoid screw to obtain an idle speed of 800 rpm manual, 600 rpm automatic.
2. With the fast idle cam follower on the second step of the fast idle cam, adjust the fast idle screw to obtain 1350 rpm manual, 1500 rpm automatic in PARK.
3. Shut off the engine, and reconnect the distributor vacuum and vapor canister lines.

ALL 1973 ENGINES AS SPECIFIED BELOW

Follow Steps 1-4 described at the beginning of this section. Refer to the ''Tune-Up Specifications'' chapter or the vehicle emission control sticker for specification, and proceed with adjustments (air conditioning off, unless otherwise specified) according to engine:

I-6 250 With 1-bbl. Rochester

1. Adjust the idle-stop-solenoid screw to obtain an idle speed of 700 rpm manual, 600 rpm automatic. Do not adjust the idle speed with the CEC solenoid screw.
2. Shut off the engine, and reconnect the distributor vacuum and vapor canister lines.

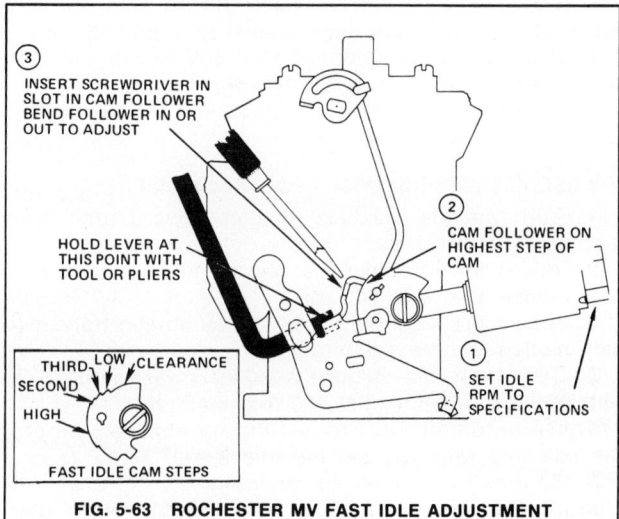

③ INSERT SCREWDRIVER IN SLOT IN CAM FOLLOWER BEND FOLLOWER IN OR OUT TO ADJUST

② CAM FOLLOWER ON HIGHEST STEP OF CAM

HOLD LEVER AT THIS POINT WITH TOOL OR PLIERS

① SET IDLE RPM TO SPECIFICATIONS

THIRD SECOND HIGH — LOW CLEARANCE

FAST IDLE CAM STEPS

FIG. 5-63 ROCHESTER MV FAST IDLE ADJUSTMENT

V-8 307/350/400 With 2-bbl. Rochester

1. Adjust the idle-stop-solenoid screw to obtain an idle speed of 900 rpm manual, 600 rpm automatic.
2. Disconnect the idle-stop-solenoid wire and adjust the idle speed screw (lower step of cam) to specifications. Reconnect the solenoid wire.
3. Shut off the engine, and reconnect the distributor vacuum and vapor canister lines.

V-8 350 (Z-28)

1. Adjust the idle-stop-solenoid screw to obtain an idle speed of 900 rpm manual, 700 rpm automatic.
2. Connect the distributor vacuum-advance line. With the fast idle cam follower on the top step of the fast idle cam, adjust the fast idle screw to obtain a speed of 1300 rpm manual, 1600 rpm automatic in PARK.
3. Shut off the engine, and reconnect the vapor canister line.

V-8 350/454 With 4-bbl. Rochester

1. Adjust the idle-stop-solenoid screw to obtain an idle speed of 900 rpm manual, 600 rpm automatic.
2. Connect the distributor vacuum-advance line. With the fast idle cam follower on the top step of the fast idle cam, adjust the fast idle screw to obtain a speed of 1300 for 350 engines with manual transmissions, 1600 rpm for all others.
3. Shut off the engine, and reconnect the vapor canister line.

ALL 1974 ENGINES AS SPECIFIED BELOW

SERVICE PRECAUTIONS

1. Chevrolet recommends that you follow the specifications on the vehicle emission control sticker if they differ from those given in the "Tune-Up Specifications" chapter, because several changes were made from the initial specifications provided by the factory.
2. Use of the CEC solenoid on 6-cyl. engines has been discontinued, although the idle stop solenoid resembles it closely in appearance.

I-6 250 With 1-bbl. Rochester

1. Adjust the idle-stop-solenoid hex nut to obtain an idle speed of 850 rpm manual, 600 rpm automatic.
2. Break off the limiter cap tabs and turn the idle mixture needle out until the maximum idle speed is reached. Solenoid should be energized and its plunger extended. Reset the speed, if necessary, to the higher specified idle speed.
3. Turn the idle mixture needle in until the lower specified idle speed is reached.
4. With the fast idle lever on the high step of the fast idle cam, bend the fast idle tang on the throttle lever, as required, to set the specified fast idle speed **(Fig. 5-63)**.
5. Shut off the engine, and reconnect the distributor vacuum advance and vapor canister lines.

V-8 262/350/400 With 2-bbl. Rochester

1. Adjust the idle-stop-solenoid screw to obtain an idle speed of 900 rpm manual (800 rpm, 1975), 600 rpm automatic.
2. Disconnect the solenoid wire (de-energize) and, with the idle screw on the low step of the cam, set the idle at 400 rpm (manual) or 600 rpm (automatic). Connect the solenoid wire.
3. Break off the limiter cap tabs and turn the idle mixture needles out equally until the maximum idle speed is reached. Reset speed, if necessary, to the

higher specified idle speed. Solenoid must be energized, with the plunger extended to obtain the higher idle.
4. Turn the mixture needles in equally until the lower specified idle speed is reached.
5. The fast idle speed is set automatically when the low-step idle speed is correctly adjusted.
6. Shut off the engine, and reconnect the distributor vacuum advance and vapor canister lines.

V-8 350 (Z-28) With 4-bbl. Rochester

1. Adjust the idle-stop-solenoid screw to obtain an idle speed of 900 rpm manual, 700 rpm automatic.
2. Break off the limiter cap tabs and turn the idle mixture needles out equally until the maximum idle speed is reached. Reset the speed, if necessary, to the higher specified idle speed.
3. Turn the mixture needles in equally until the lower specified idle speed is reached.
4. Connect the distributor vacuum-advance hose and, with the fast idle lever on the high step of the fast idle cam, adjust the fast idle screw to obtain 1300 rpm manual, 1600 rpm with automatic in PARK.
5. Shut off the engine, and reconnect the distributor vacuum-advance and vapor canister lines.

V-8 350/400 With 4-bbl. Rochester

1. Adjust the idle-stop-solenoid screw to obtain an idle speed of 900 rpm manual (800 rpm, 1975), 600 rpm automatic.
2. Break off the limiter cap tabs and turn the idle mixture needles out equally until the maximum idle speed is reached. Reset the speed, if necessary, to the higher specified idle speed.
3. Turn the mixture needles in equally until the lower specified idle speed is reached.
4. Connect the distributor vacuum-advance hose and, with the fast idle lever on the high step of the fast idle cam, adjust the fast idle screw to 1300 rpm manual, 1600 rpm with automatic in PARK.
5. Shut off the engine, and reconnect the distributor vacuum advance and vapor canister lines.

V-8 454 With 4-bbl. Rochester

1. Adjust the idle-stop-solenoid screw to obtain an idle speed of 800 rpm manual (1974 only), 600 rpm automatic.
2. Break off the limiter cap tabs and turn the idle mixture needles out equally until the maximum idle speed is reached. Reset the speed, if necessary, to the higher specified idle speed.
3. Turn the mixture needles in equally until the lower specified idle speed is reached.
4. Connect the distributor vacuum-advance hose and, with the fast idle lever on the high step of the fast idle cam, adjust the fast idle screw to 1600 rpm manual or 1500 rpm with automatic in PARK.
5. Shut off the engine, and reconnect the distributor vacuum advance and vapor canister lines.

ALL 1975-76 ENGINES AS SPECIFIED BELOW

Follow Steps 1-4 described at the beginning of this Chevrolet section. Refer to the "Tune-Up Specifications" chapter or the vehicle emission control sticker for specifications, and proceed with carburetor adjustments (air conditioning off, unless otherwise specified) according to engine:

I-6 250 With 1-bbl. Rochester

1. Start the engine, check the ignition timing and adjust, if necessary.

2. Connect the vacuum-advance hose to the distributor.

3. With the idle stop solenoid energized (ignition on), set the curb idle to specifications (the higher number) by turning the solenoid in or out.

4. De-energize the solenoid by removing its wire.

5. Set the low idle speed to specifications (the lower number) by turning the hex screw on the end of the solenoid. The transmission must be in DRIVE (automatic) or NEUTRAL (manual).

6. With the vacuum-advance hose connected and the solenoid wire disconnected, cut off the tab on the mixture screw cap. Without removing the cap, turn the screw counterclockwise to obtain maximum idle speed. Turn the screw clockwise to achieve the low idle speed.

7. Shut off the engine, connect the solenoid and the vapor canister line.

V-8 305, 350 & 400 With 2-bbl. Rochester

1. Start the engine, check the ignition timing and correct, if necessary. Return the vacuum-advance hose to the distributor.

2. Shift the transmission into DRIVE (automatic) or NEUTRAL (manual), and turn the idle speed screw to obtain the specified idle speed.

3. With the air cleaner installed, break off the tabs on the mixture screw caps.

4. Adjust the idle to the higher of the two specified in the charts.

5. Turn out the mixture screws an equal amount until a maximum idle speed is achieved. If too high, repeat Step 4 and continue on to Step 6.

6. Turn in (lean) the mixture screws an equal amount to obtain the lower specified idle speed.

7. Shut off the engine, and connect the vapor canister hose.

V-8 350 & 454 With 4-bbl. Rochester

1. Start the engine, check the ignition timing and correct, if necessary. Reconnect the vacuum-advance hose.

2. Remove the wire from the idle stop solenoid and adjust the low idle screw to the specified rpm in either DRIVE (automatic) or NEUTRAL.

3. Reconnect the solenoid wire, and open the throttle to extend the solenoid plunger.

4. Set the curb idle (the higher number) to specifications by turning the plunger screw.

5. Break off the tab from the mixture screw caps.

6. Turn out (enrich) the mixture screws an equal amount, and stop when you've reached maximum idle speed. If the idle is too high, repeat Step 4 and move on to Step 7.

7. Turn in the mixture screws an equal amount to achieve the specified low idle speed.

8. Stop the engine, and connect the vapor canister hose.

ALL 1977 ENGINES

1. Remove the air cleaner with all vacuum hoses attached. Disconnect and plug the distributor vacuum advance line at the distributor, plus other hoses according to Emission Control Label under the hood.

2. Connect a tachometer and start the engine, allowing it to warm up to normal operating temperature. The choke must be fully opened.

3. Turn off the air conditioner and set the transmission in NEUTRAL if manual, DRIVE if automatic, unless specified otherwise. For safety, block the front wheels and set the parking brake.

4. Start the engine, check the ignition timing and adjust, if necessary. Reconnect the vacuum advance line.

5. Remove the cap from the idle mixture screw, being careful not to bend the screw. Lightly seat the screw, then back it out just enough so the engine will run.

6. Back out the screw one-eighth turn at a time until the specified idle speed is reached. Repeat this step to ensure maximum idle speed.

7. Turn in the idle screw at one-eighth turn increments until idle speed reaches specifications on the Emission Control Information Label.

8. Check and adjust the fast idle according to the Emission Control Information Label.

9. Reconnect the vacuum hoses, install the air cleaner and recheck the idle. If necessary, reset idle to specifications.

CHEVROLET VEGA, MONZA

Since the idle mixture adjustment is factory-set for the lowest possible emission level, Chevrolet does not recommend mixture adjustment except after the carburetor has been overhauled. Only idle speed adjustment is provided. Refer to the ''Tune-Up Specifications'' chapter for specifications, but always compare to the vehicle emission control sticker on the particular car, because it contains the latest certified specifications and may vary from those published by Chevrolet and other sources. The following steps must be performed before undertaking idle speed adjustment:

1. Disconnect the fuel tank hose from the top of the vapor canister.

2. Disconnect the distributor vacuum-advance line at the distributor and plug the line.

3. Connect a tachometer and start the engine, allowing it to warm up to normal operating temperature. The choke and preheat valves should be fully open, and the air cleaner left installed.

4. Turn off the air conditioner (leave it on in 1971 models) and set the transmission in NEUTRAL if manual, DRIVE if automatic. For safety, block the front wheels and set the parking brake.

5. Disconnect the electrical connector at the idle stop solenoid.

SIMPLIFIED CARBURETOR ADJUSTMENT PROCEDURE

ALL 1971-76 ENGINES WITH 1-BBL. ROCHESTER MV

1. Adjust the carburetor idle-speed screw (1971-72) or idle-stop-solenoid hex screw (1973 and later) to obtain idle speed specified for ''Solenoid Disconnected.''

2. Adjust the dwell and ignition timing to specifications, if necessary, and recheck the idle speed (1971-74). Reconnect the idle-stop-solenoid wire.

3. 1971-73—Speed up the engine to extend the solenoid plunger. Then adjust the plunger screw to obtain the idle speed specified for ''Solenoid Connected.''

1974-76—Adjust the solenoid plunger by turning the complete solenoid body to obtain the specified curb idle speed.

4. Shut off the engine, and reconnect the distributor vacuum advance and vapor canister lines.

ALL 1973-76 ENGINES WITH 2-BBL. HOLLEY 5210-C

1. Adjust the carburetor low idle screw (**Fig. 5-64**) to obtain the specified low idle speed.

2. Adjust dwell and ignition timing to specifications, if necessary, and recheck the low idle speed (1973-74). Reconnect the idle-stop-solenoid wire.

3. Adjust the curb idle screw located on the throttle

lever **(Fig. 5-64)** to the specified curb idle speed provided for "Solenoid Energized."

ALL 1975 ENGINES WITH 2-BBL. ROCHESTER 2GC

1. Start the engine, check the ignition timing and correct, if necessary. Reconnect the vacuum-advance hose.

2. With the transmission in DRIVE (automatic) or NEUTRAL (manual), adjust the idle speed screw to the specified rpm.

3. Shut off the engine, and reconnect the hose to the vapor canister.

ALL 1977 ENGINES

1. Remove the air cleaner with all vacuum hoses attached. Disconnect and plug the distributor vacuum advance line at the distributor, plus other hoses according to Emission Control Label under the hood.

2. Connect a tachometer and start the engine, allowing it to warm up to normal operating temperature. The choke must be fully opened.

3. Turn off the air conditioner and set the transmission in NEUTRAL if manual, DRIVE if automatic, unless specified otherwise. For safety, block the front wheels and set the parking brake.

4. Start the engine, check the ignition timing and adjust, if necessary. Reconnect the vacuum advance line.

5. Remove the cap from the idle mixture screw, being careful not to bend the screw. Lightly seat the screw, then back it out just enough so the engine will run.

6. Back out the screw one-eighth turn at a time until the specified idle speed is reached. Repeat this step to ensure maximum idle speed.

7. Turn in the idle screw at one-eighth turn increments until idle speed reaches specifications on the Emission Control Information Label.

8. Check and adjust the fast idle according to the Emission Control Information Label.

9. Reconnect the vacuum hoses, install the air cleaner and recheck the idle. If necessary, reset idle to specifications.

CHEVROLET CHEVETTE

Follow the specifications on the vehicle emission control sticker, if they differ from those given in the "Tune-Up Specifications" chapter.

SIMPLIFIED CARBURETOR ADJUSTMENT PROCEDURE

ALL 1976 ENGINES WITH 1-BBL. ROCHESTER 1ME

1 Connect a tachometer and start the engine, allowing it to warm up to normal operating temperature. The choke valve must fully open.

2. Disconnect and plug the distributor vacuum-advance hose at the distributor and the PCV hose at the vapor canister.

3. Turn the air conditioning off, keep the air cleaner on and set the transmission in NEUTRAL if manual, DRIVE if automatic. For safety, be sure to block the front wheels and set the parking brake.

4. On those vehicles not equipped with both automatic transmission and air conditioning:
   a) Set the curb idle speed to specifications by turning the solenoid assembly in or out.
   b) Disconnect the wire from the solenoid.
   c) Shift the transmission in to DRIVE (automatic) or NEUTRAL (manual) and set the low idle speed to specs by turning the hex screw located in the end of the solenoid body.
   d) Reconnect the solenoid wire.

5. On those vehicles having both automatic transmission and air conditioning:
   a) Inspect the solenoid wire. It should be green with a double white strip, not a brown wire. Correct if wrong.
   b) Place the transmission selector in DRIVE and turn the air conditioning off.
   c) Turn the screw into the solenoid body until it bottoms.
   d) Turn the solenoid assembly to achieve a 950 rpm idle.
   e) Turn out the solenoid hex screw to obtain a base speed of 800 rpm (nationwide) or 850 rpm (California).

6. Check the ignition timing and adjust, if necessary.

7. Shut off engine and connect the vacuum hoses.

ALL 1977 ENGINES

1. Remove the air cleaner with all vacuum hoses attached. Disconnect and plug the distributor vacuum advance line at the distributor, plus other hoses according to Emission Control Label under the hood.

2. Connect a tachometer and start the engine, allowing it to warm up to normal operating temperature. The choke must be fully opened.

3. Turn off the air conditioner and set the transmission in NEUTRAL if manual, DRIVE if automatic, unless specified otherwise. For safety, block the front wheels and set the parking brake.

4. Start the engine, check the ignition timing and adjust, if necessary. Reconnect the vacuum advance line.

5. Remove the cap from the idle mixture screw, being careful not to bend the screw. Lightly seat the screw, then back it out just enough so the engine will run.

6. Back out the screw one-eighth turn at a time until the specified idle speed is reached. Repeat this step to ensure maximum idle speed.

7. Turn in the idle screw at one-eighth turn increments until idle speed reaches specifications on the Emission Control Information Label.

8. Check and adjust the fast idle according to the Emission Control Information Label.

9. Reconnect the vacuum hoses, install the air cleaner and recheck the idle. If necessary, reset idle to specifications.

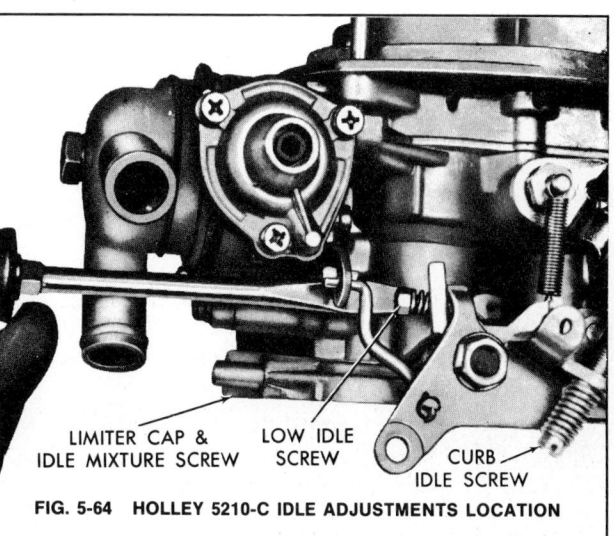

LIMITER CAP & IDLE MIXTURE SCREW LOW IDLE SCREW CURB IDLE SCREW

FIG. 5-64 HOLLEY 5210-C IDLE ADJUSTMENTS LOCATION

OLDSMOBILE

Oldsmobile carburetor adjustments are most easily covered by carburetor type, because minimal changes have been made from 1970 on. Follow the specifications on the vehicle emission control sticker, if they differ from those given in the "Tune-Up Specifications" chapter.

Idle mixture adjustments are factory-set for the lowest possible emission level, and Oldsmobile recommends that no idle mixture adjustment be made unless the needles must be replaced. If a poor idle condition persists, the factory suggests that the car be taken to a shop equipped with a carbon monoxide (CO) meter and that adjustments be made according to the specified CO reading.

A combination emission control (CEC) solenoid **(Fig. 5-62)** is fitted to the 1971 and 1973 1-bbl. carburetor (manual transmission) and *should not* be adjusted unless either the solenoid is replaced because it is defective or is removed during carburetor overhaul. The CEC solenoid *is not* an idle stop solenoid and *should not* be adjusted during a routine tune-up; it is a part of the emission control system and is treated in Chapter 6.

The following steps must be performed before undertaking the specific adjustment procedure according to carburetor:

1. Connect a tachometer and start the engine, allowing it to warm up to normal operating temperature, making sure the choke has opened fully.

2. Disconnect and plug:

a) The distributor vacuum advance line at the distributor.

b) Air vacuum hose from the carburetor base (1970 only).

c) Distributor vacuum line from the CEC solenoid (1971 and 1973 1-bbl. carburetors only).

d) Air cleaner hose at the intake manifold (plug fitting).

e) Exhaust Gas Recirculation (EGR) line at the EGR valve.

f) Fuel tank hose at the vapor canister.

3. Turn off the air conditioner and set the transmission in NEUTRAL if manual, DRIVE if automatic. For safety, block the drive wheels and set the parking brake.

SIMPLIFIED CARBURETOR ADJUSTMENT PROCEDURE

ALL 1970 1-BBL. CARBURETORS

1. With the air cleaner removed, choke fully open, the fast idle cam follower off the fast idle cam, the solenoid connected and the throttle stopscrew not touching the throttle lever, adjust the idle speed screw for the highest possible rpm.

2. Adjust the throttle solenoid plunger to obtain an idle speed 25 rpm greater than the highest idle speed specified.

3. Turn the idle mixture needle inward to bring the idle speed down to the specified rpm.

4. Disconnect the throttle-stop-solenoid wire and adjust the throttle stopscrew to obtain the lower of the specified idle speeds.

5. Reconnect all vacuum lines and hoses.

ALL 1971 & 1973-76 1-BBL. CARBURETORS

1. With 1971 engines, adjust the idle speed screw to obtain the specified rpm.

2. With 1973-later engines, turn the throttle-stop-solenoid hex nut to move the solenoid plunger in or out until the higher specified idle is obtained.

3. Disconnect the solenoid wire and insert a 1/8-in. Allen wrench in the solenoid end; turn until the lower specified idle speed is obtained. If equipped with an automatic transmission, the adjustment should be made with the transmission in PARK.

4. Reconnect all vacuum lines and hoses.

ALL 1970-75 2-BBL. & 4-BBL. CARBURETORS

1. If the carburetor is equipped with a throttle solenoid or vacuum actuator, turn the hex nut to move the solenoid plunger in or out until the higher specified idle speed is reached.

2. Disconnect and plug the solenoid wire or vacuum actuator hose and adjust the throttle stopscrew until the lower specified idle speed is obtained (automatic transmission set in PARK). Replace the wire or hose.

3. On those carburetors not fitted with a solenoid or actuator, adjust the idle speed screw to obtain the specified idle rpm.

4. Reconnect all vacuum lines and hoses.

ALL 1976 ENGINES WITH 2-BBL. ROCHESTER 2GC

1. Set the parking brake, block the drive wheels and start the engine.

2. Allow the engine to warm up to normal operating temperature, making sure the choke has fully opened.

3. Shut off the engine, connect a tachometer and disconnect and plug the vacuum-advance hose from the advance unit.

4. On the V-6 engine, disconnect the emission hose from the air cleaner, and disconnect and plug the EGR vacuum hose at the valve.

5. On 350 V-8's, disconnect the evaporative emission hose from the carburetor.

6. With the air cleaner on, the choke fully open, the air conditioner off and timing properly adjusted, set the idle speed to 600 rpm (automatic in DRIVE, manual in NEUTRAL) On V-6's with manual transmission, disconnect the idle speed solenoid and, with the transmission in NEUTRAL, set the idle at 600 rpm. Connect the solenoid and adjust the solenoid screw to 800 rpm.

7. Shut off the engine, and reconnect the hoses.

ALL 1977 ENGINES

1. Remove the air cleaner with all vacuum hoses attached. Disconnect and plug the distributor vacuum advance line at the distributor, plus other hoses according to Emission Control Label under the hood.

2. Connect a tachometer and start the engine, allowing it to warm up to normal operating temperature. The choke must be fully opened.

3. Turn off the air conditioner and set the transmission in NEUTRAL if manual, DRIVE if automatic, unless specified otherwise. For safety, block the front wheels and set the parking brake.

4. Start the engine, check the ignition timing and adjust, if necessary. Reconnect the vacuum advance line.

5. Remove the cap from the idle mixture screws, being careful not to bend the screws. Lightly seat the screws, then back out just enough so the engine will run.

6. Back out the screws one-eighth turn at a time until the specified idle speed is reached. Repeat this step to ensure maximum idle speed.

7. Turn in the idle screws at one-eighth turn increments until idle speed reaches specifications on the Emission Control Information Label.

8. Check and adjust the fast idle according to the Emission Control Information Label.

9. Reconnect the vacuum hoses, install the air cleaner and recheck the idle. If necessary, reset idle to specifications.

PONTIAC

Pontiac carburetor adjustments are most easily covered by carburetor type, because minimal changes have been made from 1970 on. Follow the specifications on the vehicle emission control sticker if they differ from those given here or in the ''Tune-Up Specifications'' chapter.

A combination emission control (CEC) solenoid **(Fig. 5-62)** is fitted to 1971-73 1-bbl. carburetors (manual transmission) and *should not* be adjusted unless the solenoid is either replaced because it is defective or removed during a carburetor overhaul. The CEC solenoid *is not* an idle stop solenoid and should not be adjusted during a routine tune-up; it is a part of the emission control system and is treated in Chapter 6.

The following steps must be performed before undertaking the specific adjustment procedure according to carburetor:

1976 ENGINE	RPM MAN.	RPM AUTO.	1975 ENGINE	RPM MAN.	RPM AUTO.
140 1-bbl.	825	850	350 2-bbl.	--	690
140 2-bbl.	820	830	350 4-bbl.	925	680
231 2-bbl.	1100	680	350 4-bbl. (Calif.)	--	675
250 1-bbl.	1200	580			
				--	730
250 1-bbl. (Calif.)	--	640	400 2-bbl.	--	730
260 2-bbl.	1075	610	400 4-bbl.	885	690
260 2-bbl. (Calif.)	--	700	400 4-bbl. (Calif.)	885	660
350 2-bbl.	--	680	455 4-bbl.	--	720
350 2-bbl. (Calif.)	--	640	455 4-bbl. (Calif.)	--	745
350 4-bbl.	--	680			
350 4-bbl. (Calif.)	--	675			
400 2-bbl.	--	640			
400 4-bbl.	925	640			
400 4-bbl. (Calif.)	--	640			
455 4-bbl.	--	640			
455 4-bbl. (Calif.)	--	640			
1974 ENGINE	RPM MAN.	RPM AUTO.	1973 ENGINE	RPM MAN.	RPM AUTO.
250 1-bbl.	950	650	250 1-bbl.	800	200
250 1-bbl. (Calif.)	950	630	350 2-bbl.	1100	700
350 2-bbl.	1150	750	400 2-bbl.	--	700
350 2-bbl. (Calif.)	--	720	400 4-bbl.	1200	700
350 4-bbl.	1200	730			
350 4-bbl. (Calif.)		720	455 4-bbl.	1200	700
400 2-bbl.	--	720			
400 2-bbl. (Calif.)	--	690			
400 4-bbl.	1310	720			
400 4-bbl. (Calif.)	--	685			
455 4-bbl.	--	680			
455 4-bbl. (Calif.)	--	675			
455 S.D.	1420	825			

FIG. 5-65 PONTIAC IDLE-SPEED RPM CHART

1. Connect a tachometer and start the engine, allowing it to to warm up to normal operating temperature, with the choke fully open.

2. Disconnect and plug:

   a) Distributor vacuum advance line at distributor.

   b) Hot idle compensator (if so equipped).

   c) Exhaust Gas Recirculation (EGR) line at the EGR valve.

   d) Carburetor EVAP hose from the vapor canister.

   e) Any other open vacuum fittings on the carb.

3. Turn off the air conditioner and set the transmission in NEUTRAL if manual, DRIVE if automatic. Leave the air cleaner in place.

SIMPLIFIED CARBURETOR ADJUSTMENT PROCEDURE
ALL 1970 CARBURETORS—I-6 & RAM AIR IV

1. With solenoid energized, adjust idle-stop-solenoid screw to obtain specified rpm.

2. Adjust the idle mixture needles to obtain the best lean idle at the specified rpm.

3. Disconnect the throttle solenoid wire and adjust the idle speed screw to obtain the specified rpm.

4. Shut off the engine, and reconnect all vacuum lines and hoses.

ALL 1970 CARBURETORS—V-8 350, 400, 455

1. Turn the idle mixture needles inward until they just seat, then back out three to five turns each.

2. Adjust the idle speed screw to obtain the specified idle rpm.

3. Turn the idle mixture needles inward equally to obtain the specified rpm.

4. Shut off the engine, and reconnect all vacuum lines and hoses.

ALL 1971-72 CARBURETORS

1. Turn the idle mixture needles inward until they just seat, then back each out 3½ turns.

2. a) On 4-bbl., manual-transmission applications, disconnect the throttle solenoid wire and adjust the idle speed screw to the specified idle rpm.

   b) On all other applications, set the idle speed screw to obtain the following engine speed increase over specifications: 1) 4-bbl. V-8 manual, 100 rpm; 2) 2-bbl. V-8 manual, 75 rpm; 3) all I-6 manual, 75 rpm; 4) all automatic, 25 rpm.

3. Turn the idle mixture needles inward equally until the specified idle speed is obtained.

4. On 4-bbl., manual-transmission applications, reconnect the throttle solenoid wire, extend the solenoid plunger manually and adjust the screw to the specified idle rpm.

5. Adjust fast idle as follows, with automatic in PARK, manual in NEUTRAL.

   a) 6-cyl.—With the fast idle tang on the top step of the fast idle cam, adjust the fast idle screw to obtain 2400 rpm.

   b) 8-cyl.—With the fast idle screw on the top step of the fast idle cam, adjust the fast idle screw to obtain 1700 rpm.

   c) Fast idle on 2-bbl. carburetors is preset automatically when low idle speed is correctly set.

6. Shut off engine and reconnect all vacuum lines and hoses.

ALL 1973-76 CARBURETORS

1. Disconnect the idle-stop-solenoid wire and insert a 1⅛-in. Allen wrench in the solenoid end; turn until the specified low idle speed is reached.

2. Reconnect the solenoid wire and adjust the solenoid plunger until the specified rpm is reached.

3. To set idle mixture, turn the idle mixture needle(s) inward until just seated, then back out six turns (1973-74), seven turns (1974) or five turns (1975-76), as required.

4. Turn the idle mixture needles inward until the highest possible idle speed is reached.

5. Set idle speed back to rpm listed in **Fig. 5-65.**

6. Turn the idle mixture needle(s) inward (equally) until the engine rpm drops to the specified idle speed.

7. Adjust fast idle as follows:

  a) 1-bbl. Carburetors—Place the fast idle tang on the top step of the fast idle cam and bend the tang to adjust until the specified fast idle rpm is reached.

  b) 2-bbl. Carburetors—The fast idle speed is automatically set when the low idle speed is correctly adjusted.

  c) 4-bbl. Carburetors—Place the cam follower on the top step of the fast idle cam and adjust the fast idle screw until specified rpm is reached.

8. Shut off the engine, and reconnect all vacuum lines and hoses.

ALL 1977 ENGINES

1. Remove the air cleaner with all vacuum hoses attached. Disconnect and plug the distributor vacuum advance line at the distributor, plus other hoses according to the Emission Control Label under the hood.

2. Connect a tachometer and start the engine, allowing it to warm up to normal operating temperature. The choke must be fully opened.

3. Turn off the air conditioner and set the transmission in NEUTRAL if manual, DRIVE if automatic, unless specified otherwise. For safety, block the front wheels and set the parking brake.

4. Start the engine, check the ignition timing and adjust, if necessary. Reconnect the vacuum advance line.

5. Remove the cap from the idle mixture screws, being careful not to bend the screws. Lightly seat the screws, then back out just enough so engine will run.

6. Back out the screws one-eighth turn at a time until the specified idle speed is reached. Repeat this step to ensure maximum idle speed.

7. Turn in the idle screws at one-eighth turn increments until idle speed reaches the specifications on the Emission Control Information Label.

8. Check and adjust the fast idle according to the Emission Control Information Label.

9. Reconnect the vacuum hoses, install the air cleaner and recheck the idle. If necessary, reset idle to specifications.

FORD MOTOR COMPANY

Although Ford has used a variety of carburetors, there is a common procedure for adjusting the idle mixture and idle speed to factory specifications. With Ford-manufactured vehicles from 1972 on, it is very important to use the specifications found on the vehicle emission control decal **(Fig. 5-66)**. Ford makes numerous on-going changes in its specifications during a model year, and the decal may well differ considerably from the factory specifications provided in the "Tune-Up Specifications" chapter in some instances. The decal is located on the engine valve cover, and should be kept free of oil, grease and dirt buildup so that the information is easily legible and the decal remains undamaged.

Idle mixture adjustments are factory-set for the low-est possible emission level, and Ford recommends that no idle mixture adjustment be attempted beyond that provided within the limited range allowed by the idle limiter cap fitted to each idle mixture needle. If a poor idle condition persists, the factory suggests that the car be taken to a shop equipped with an exhaust gas analyzer and that adjustment be made according to the CO reading specified for the engine in question.

For 1975 and later carburetors, Ford recommends the use of its Propane Enrichment technique for idle mixture adjustments. This requires the use of special factory equipment to inject propane gas through the air-cleaner evaporative purge nipple to artificially enrich the idle mixture for adjustment purposes. The technique is described in **Fig. 5-67,** but is not a recommended procedure for use outside a properly equipped service center.

TROUBLESHOOTING LATE-MODEL FORD CARBURETORS

Some late-model Ford, Lincoln and Mercury engines may develop an acceleration hesitation, stumble, or "surge." This problem can be solved by installing a vacuum restrictor (Ford P/N D74212 A225-A) on the proper vacuum line. On 1977 460-cu.-in. engines, cut the EGR vacuum supply line about 3 ins. from the EGR-PVS valve and insert the vacuum restrictor in the line. On 1978 non-California Granadas fitted with the 302-cu.-in. engine and automatic transmission, cut the vacuum line from the PVS valve to the carburetor EGR port at a point approximately 4 ins. from the port and insert the restrictor in the line. It may be necessary to run an idle propane speed gain test and reset the carburetor to specs after installing the restrictor.

Certain 1977 460-cu.-in. engines may prove hard to start during hot weather when they are cold. To solve this problem, remove the vent hose at the carburetor fitting and install a restrictor (Ford P/N D7PZ-9A521-B) in the hose, then reconnect to the carburetor. Engines affected by this problem carry one of the following emissions calibration codes: R7, R8, R17, R19, R20, R21, R22, 7-19A.

SIMPLIFIED CARBURETOR ADJUSTMENT PROCEDURE

ALL 1970-77 CARBURETORS

1. Connect a tachometer and start the engine. Run at 1500 rpm until engine reaches normal operating temperature. Ford recommends a minimum of 20 minutes.

2. Check the choke plate to be certain it is in a fully open position.

3. If the carburetor is equipped with a hot idle compensator, make sure the compensator is seated, or proper idle adjustment will not be possible.

4. The air conditioner must be off and the air cleaner left installed.

5. If a temperature sensing valve is used in the distributor vacuum line, disconnect and plug the vacuum lines from the distributor to the valve and from the valve to the intake manifold.

6. Check the dashpot for freedom of operation—it should not bind.

7. On those 1970-71 engines which list two idle speeds in the specifications, turn the plunger on the electric solenoid to obtain the higher idle speed.

On those 1972-77 engines fitted with an electric solenoid or throttle positioner, turn the adjusting screw in the solenoid mounting bracket **(Fig. 5-68)** until the higher rpm is obtained.

The lower idle speed is set on all 1970-77 engines by disconnecting the solenoid lead wire and adjusting the idle speed screw **(Fig. 5-69)** in the usual manner. Automatic transmission must be in PARK. The idle speed screw must touch the throttle shaft or the throttle plates can jam in their bore when the engine is shut off.

8. Turn the idle mixture needle inward to obtain the smoothest possible idle within the range permitted by the limiter cap. On 2-bbl. and 4-bbl. carburetors, the idle mixture needles should be adjusted inward an equal amount.

9. With the idle speed and mixture adjustments completed, remove the air cleaner and rotate the fast idle cam until the fast-idle adjusting screw rests on the specified step of the fast idle cam. Turn the adjusting screw inward or outward as necessary to set the fast idle rpm to specifications **(Figs. 5-70 & 5-71)**.

10. Check the dashpot adjustment (if so equipped) by measuring the clearance between the throttle lever and the plunger tip with the throttle in a closed position and the plunger depressed. To adjust, turn the dashpot in the direction required to provide the required clearance, and tighten the locknut to retain the adjustment.

11. Replace the air cleaner and reconnect all vacuum lines removed for adjustment purposes.

OPTIMUM IDLE ADJUSTMENT METHOD

1978 California Engines Only—For use when propane enrichment equipment is not available.

Engine speeds must be measured with the air cleaner installed. All vacuum hoses must be connected to the air cleaner assembly when performing carburetor adjustment. Engine idle speed may vary somewhat during the adjustment procedure. Since this is a normal

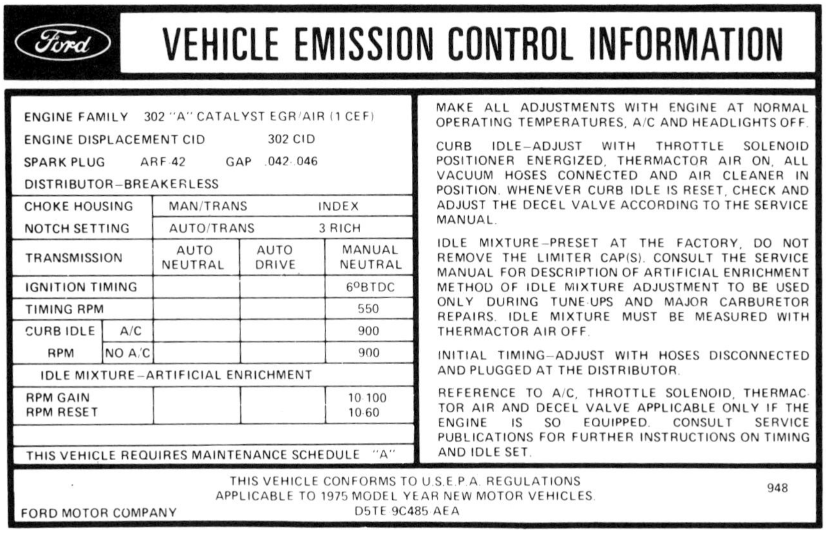

FIG. 5-66 VEHICLE EMISSION CONTROL DECAL

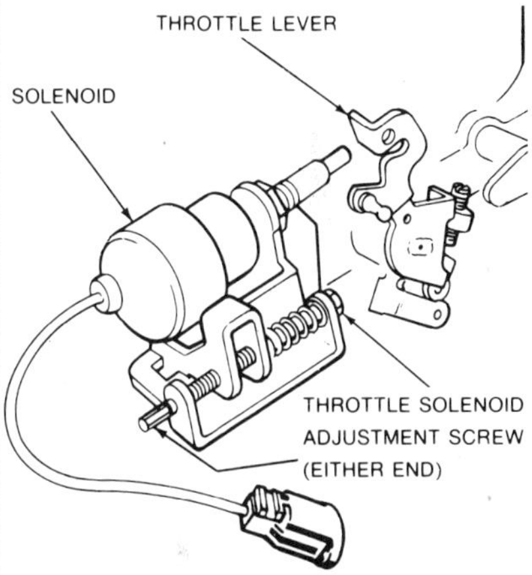

FIG. 5-68 THROTTLE POSITIONER ADJUSTMENT

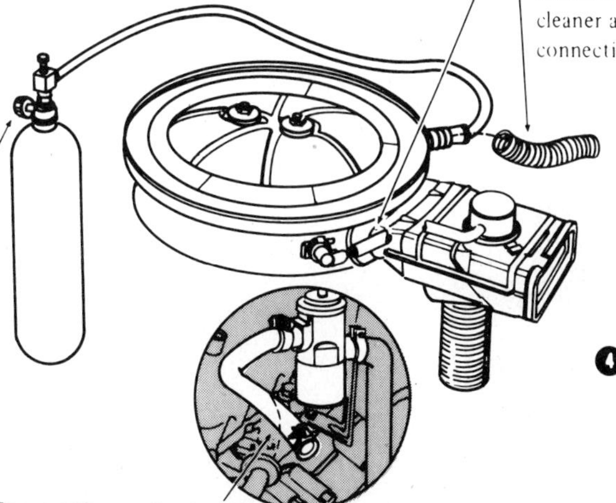

8 If speed increase is to specification, remove Tool from purge connection and re-install all hoses removed from air cleaner. Reconnect thermactor system.

IF SPEED INCREASE IS NOT TO SPECIFICATION, PROCEED TO "ADJUSTMENT"

7 To check proper operation of Tool, continue opening valve until engine speed drops due to over-rich mixture. If speed does not drop, check propane gas supply.

6 Plug Tool T75L-9600-A adapter into purge opening in air cleaner. With engine idling, slowly open propane gas valve until maximum idle speed increase is attained. Note speed increase and compare to specification.

1 Stabilize engine temperature by running at fast idle (kickdown step) until engine thermostat is open (top of radiator tank is warm).

5 Remove thermactor system air supply hose (from bypass valve to check valve) at check valve(s).

2 Disconnect evaporative emission purge hose at air cleaner. When applicable, disconnect PCV hose at air cleaner and cap air cleaner connection.

3 Adjust idle speed to CURB IDLE (or to Idle Mixture Adjust Speed, if given).

4 Make sure transmission is in NEUTRAL, if manual, or in DRIVE if automatic. CAUTION: Depress brake pedal or block wheels when vehicle is in gear with engine running. Disconnect brake vacuum release (if so equipped) and plug fitting.

FIG. 5-67 ARTIFICIAL-ENRICHMENT IDLE MIXTURE PROCEDURE

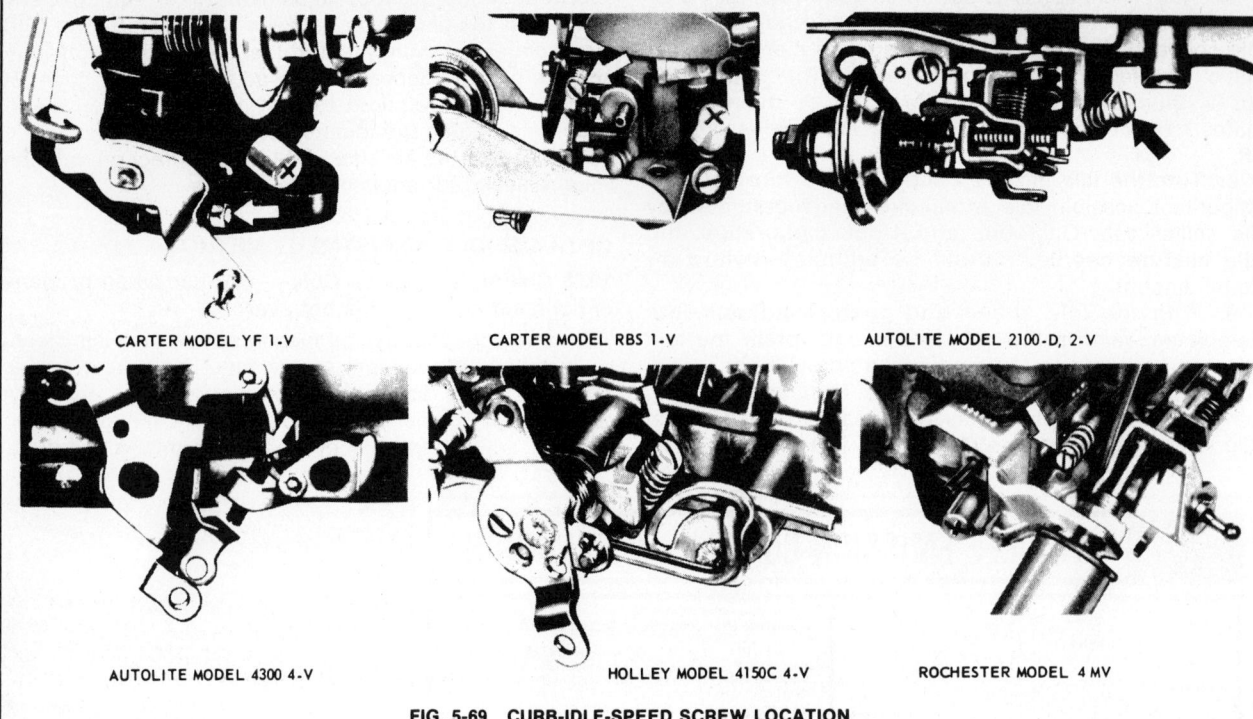

CARTER MODEL YF 1-V   CARTER MODEL RBS 1-V   AUTOLITE MODEL 2100-D, 2-V

AUTOLITE MODEL 4300 4-V   HOLLEY MODEL 4150C 4-V   ROCHESTER MODEL 4 MV

FIG. 5-69 CURB-IDLE-SPEED SCREW LOCATION

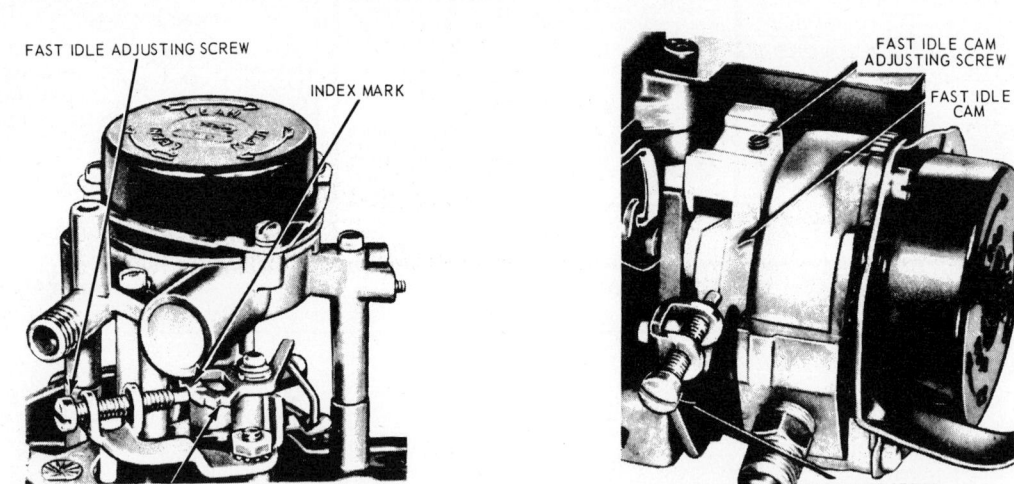

FIG. 5-70 FAST IDLE SPEED ADJUSTMENT—AUTOLITE/MOTORCRAFT 2100/2150 AND 4300/4350

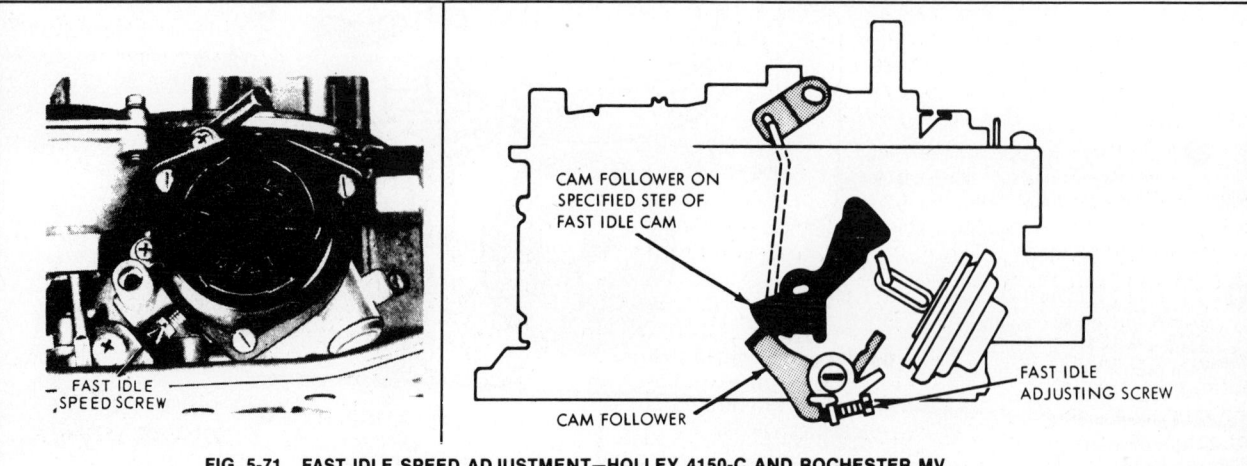

FIG. 5-71 FAST IDLE SPEED ADJUSTMENT—HOLLEY 4150-C AND ROCHESTER MV

condition, the *average* engine speed is used for the purposes of adjustment.

1. Connect a tachometer and start the engine. Run at 1500 rpm until engine reaches normal operating temperature. Shut the engine off.

2. Disconnect the following, if so equipped:

a). Fuel evaporative purge valve signal vacuum hose. *Do not* disconnect at the purge valve, as this may cause damage to the valve. Cap the port and plug the hose.

b). Evaporative emission purge hose. Disconnect at the air cleaner and plug the nipple.

c). Crankcase ventilation closure hose. Disconnect at the air cleaner and plug the nipple.

d). Thermactor dump valve vacuum hose. Disconnect and plug side-mounted hoses. If equipped with a vacuum hose at the top of the valve, check to see if it is connected to intake manifold vacuum. If it is not, remove and plug the hose at the valve. Run a slave hose between the valve fitting and a source of intake manifold vacuum.

3. Remove the idle mixture limiter cap(s).

4. Start the engine and check curb idle rpm. Reset to specification, if necessary.

5. Place the transmission selector lever in the position specified on the engine emission decal for the propane enrichment method. Reset engine rpm to the "alternate idle speed change" rpm, according to the engine decal. Note the new idle speed rpm indicated on the tachometer. If the "alternate idle speed change" is specified as "zero," this step is not required.

6. Readjust the idle mixture screw(s) and idle speed to the best idle at the new idle speed rpm.

7. Adjust the idle mixture screw(s) clockwise until engine speed drops off by the specified "alternate idle speed change" rpm. If this is specified as zero, this step is not required.

8. Shut the engine off. Install new limiter cap(s) on the idle mixture screw(s) at the maximum rich stop. Reconnect all hoses and remove the test equipment.

1979—ALL ENGINES

Idle mixture is preset at the factory and no alternate adjustment instructions are provided by Ford Motor Company.

CHRYSLER CORPORATION

All Chrysler Corporation cars (Dodge, Chrysler, Plymouth, Imperial) from 1970 on are fitted with the Chrysler Cleaner Air System, which incorporates carburetor calibration as an integral part of the emissions control system. Chrysler has long expressed its carburetor adjustment procedure in terms of air/fuel ratio, and recommends the use of an infra-red exhaust-gas analyzer to make accurate idle speed and mixture adjustments. While the highly accurate infra-red analyzer is far too expensive for all but those in the automotive service area to justify its purchase, there are less expensive (and less accurate) exhaust analyzer devices on the market. This is not to say that an analyzer unit is absolutely necessary for carburetor adjustment, but its use *is* necessary if the adjustments made *are to conform* to the emission control requirements.

All necessary information, such as timing, idle rpm, mixture-setting procedure and specified speeds, is clearly spelled out on the vehicle emission control information label located in the engine compartment—the specifications given in the "Tune-Up Specifications" chapter should be used for reference value only. Assuming that an accurate exhaust-gas analyzer of some kind is available, the following adjustment procedure

can be used with any carburetor fitted to a 1970 or later Chrysler Corporation engine, including the Holley 2300 used on the 1970-71 340 and 440 Six-Pack. The twin Carter AFB carburetors fitted to the 1970-71 426 Hemi are adjusted in a conventional manner, except that each carburetor contains a separate idle system, and the two must be adjusted and then synchronized to produce a satisfactory idle.

SIMPLIFIED CARBURETOR ADJUSTMENT PROCEDURE

ALL 1978-79 CHRYSLER CORPORATION ENGINES

Chrysler Corp. has adopted Propane Enrichment (see **Fig. 5-67** for Ford procedure and explanation of technique) as its recommended method of setting idle mixture. In addition, some 1979 Carter BBD carburetors used by Chrysler have tamper-proof idle mixture screws and do not require (or permit) adjustment. For these reasons, Chrysler Corp. does not provide an alternative method of idle mixture adjustment, and no such adjustment procedures are given in this book.

ALL 1970-77 CARBURETORS

1. Connect a tachometer and start the engine (air cleaner installed). Check and adjust ignition timing to specifications, if necessary, while waiting for the engine to reach normal operating temperature. The air conditioner should be off and the transmission placed in NEUTRAL (manual) or DRIVE (automatic).

2. Connect an exhaust-gas analyzer to the engine and insert its probe into the tailpipe as far as possible—Chrysler recommends a minimum of 2 ft. On those cars equipped with a dual exhaust system, place the probe in the left tail pipe—the right pipe contains a heat riser valve. On 1975 and later models, check the vehicle emission control information label to see if the analyzer probe should be installed *ahead* of the catalytic converter. If this is required, a special Chrysler adapter tube/fitting No. C-4349 is necessary to thread the probe into the pipe fitting.

3. If fitted with an air pump system, disconnect the air pump outlet hose and plug the air injection tube to the exhaust manifold.

4. Adjust the idle speed screw inward or outward until the specified idle rpm is obtained. If the carburetor is fitted with a solenoid throttle stop **(Fig. 5-72)**, use the solenoid adjusting screw to obtain the specified rpm, then adjust the idle speed screw until it barely touches the carburetor body stop, and back the screw *out* one full turn to obtain the specified low idle speed setting.

5. Adjust the idle mixture needle by turning it outward one-sixteenth turn at a time—no more—and wait

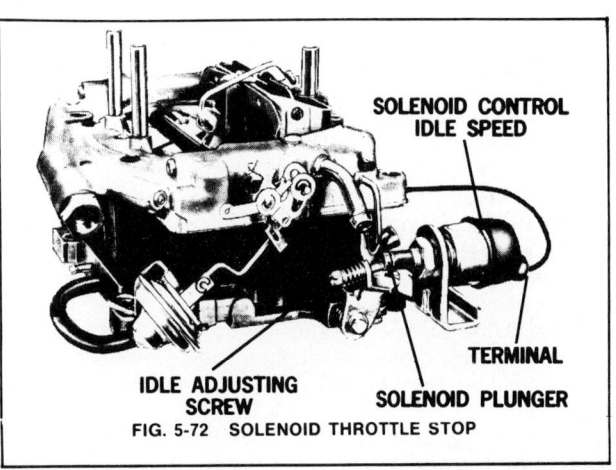

SOLENOID CONTROL IDLE SPEED

IDLE ADJUSTING SCREW

TERMINAL

SOLENOID PLUNGER

FIG. 5-72 SOLENOID THROTTLE STOP

30 seconds to allow the analyzer reading to stabilize. If the carburetor is equipped with two mixture needles, back *each* one out one-sixteenth turn equally. An overly lean mixture will cause the analyzer to indicate rich. To ensure the analyzer is correct, continue to enrich the mixture until so indicated on the meter. *Do not* remove the mixture limiter caps.

6. Slowly lean out the mixture (turn mixture needles inward) until the hydrocarbon (HC) reading levels out and a smooth idle is reached.

7. If the idle speed changes as a result of the mixture adjustment, readjust the idle speed and mixture needle(s) to obtain the desired HC range *and* a smooth idle.

8. Adjust the mixture needle(s) to obtain the desired HC and CO readings, then recheck the idle speed; readjust to specifications, if necessary.

9. Those experienced in working with an exhaust-gas analyzer will find it most efficient to adjust both the idle speed and mixture at the same time to obtain the HC/CO levels specified on the emission label. As the proper CO level is obtained, the lowest HC level *and* the smoothest curb idle should also be obtained. When all three are reached simultaneously, the carburetor is properly balanced.

10. If the idle setting is improperly balanced between the two bores on 2-bbl. and 4-bbl. carburetors, a rough idle and low-speed surge will be present. Correct by turning both mixture needles inward until they just barely seat. Back each needle out 1½ turns as a starting point. Start the engine and set the idle speed to specifications. Watching the CO level on the analyzer scale, adjust the idle speed screw and idle mixture needles to obtain the specified CO percentage, while simultaneously approaching the lowest HC level and smoothest curb idle at the specified rpm setting.

11. If the carburetor is fitted with a dashpot **(Fig. 5-73)**, check its operation by positioning the throttle level so that the actuating tab on the lever contacts the dashpot stem but does not depress it. Wait 30 seconds for the engine to stabilize and read the rpm setting on the tachometer. If the rpm reading is at specifications, the dashpot setting is correct.

If adjustment is required, loosen the locknut and screw the dashpot in or out as required. Tighten the locknut when the specified rpm is reached and check its operation to make sure that the curb idle returns to its specified speed consistently.

12. The Holley carburetor fitted to 1976 Feather Duster and Dart models (6-cyl. only) is fitted with an automatic idle speed (AIS) diaphragm mounted in the position usually occupied by the dashpot **(Fig. 5-74)**. This device maintains a constant hot idle speed, regardless of engine load. When the correct idle speed adjustment is made, open and close the throttle quickly. When engine rpm returns to an idle condition, an idle speed readjustment may be necessary to correct for the proper diaphragm placement within the assembly.

13. To set the fast idle speed, remove the air cleaner and disconnect the carburetor vacuum lines leading to the heated air control and the Orifice Spark Advance (OSAC) valve. If not fitted with an OSAC valve, disconnect the distributor vacuum-advance line and EGR hose. Cap all open carburetor vacuum ports.

14. With the engine off and the car in NEUTRAL, open the throttle and close the choke. Then close the throttle to position the fast idle screw on the highest cam step.

15. Move the fast idle cam until the screw drops to the second highest cam step. Start the engine and

determine the stabilized speed. Adjust the fast idle screw to obtain the specified rpm.

THROTTLE ROD ADJUSTMENT, HOLLEY 2300 TRI-PACK SYSTEM

The Holley 2300 and 2300C carburetor system consists of three 2-bbl. carburetors **(Fig. 5-75)**. The two outboard (front and rear) carburetors are fitted with all the usual carburetion systems except a choke, power enrichment, accelerator pump, idle and spark advance. The center (inboard) carburetor contains these systems, and is connected to the outboard carburetors by adjustable rods controlled by a slotted throttle lever, which permits the outboard carburetor throttle valves to open as vacuum requires and close mechanically according to the center carburetor's control. Idle speed and mixture adjustments are made following the procedure for a single carburetor installation. Throttle synchronization is accomplished as follows:

1. Remove the air cleaner and the outboard throttle rod retaining clips.

2. Disengage the outboard carburetor rods from the throttle levers.

3. With the ignition switch off to de-energize the fast curb idle solenoid, close the throttle valves of all three carburetors and hold them closed.

4. Turn each rod in or out of its threaded sleeve, as required to adjust the rod length, until the rod end can be inserted into the throttle lever smoothly.

5. Fit each connector rod into its corresponding throttle lever and replace the retaining clips.

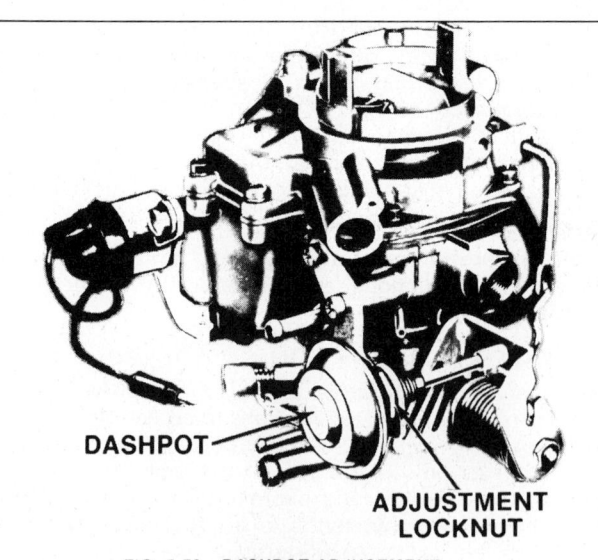

FIG. 5-73 DASHPOT ADJUSTMENT

DASHPOT

ADJUSTMENT LOCKNUT

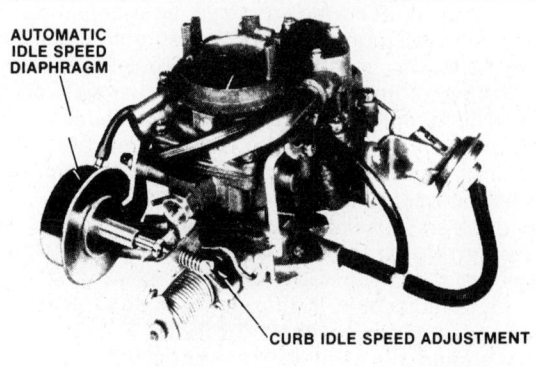

AUTOMATIC IDLE SPEED DIAPHRAGM

CURB IDLE SPEED ADJUSTMENT

FIG. 5-74 AUTOMATIC IDLE SPEED ADJUSTMENT

AMERICAN MOTORS

SIMPLIFIED CARBURETOR ADJUSTMENT PROCEDURE

SERVICE PRECAUTION

American Motors recommends that you observe the following precautions to compensate for fuel and temperature variations that may occur while setting the idle mixture adjustment:

1. Do not idle the engine for more than 3 minutes at a time.

2. If you cannot complete the idle mixture adjustment within 3 minutes, run the engine at 2000 rpm for 1 minute, then return to idle.

3. Check the idle mixture adjustment at the specified rpm, and adjust if required. If you cannot complete the idle mixture check within 3 minutes, repeat Step 2.

ALL 1970-72 ENGINES

1. Connect a tachometer and run the engine until it reaches normal operating temperature. *Do not* remove the air cleaner.

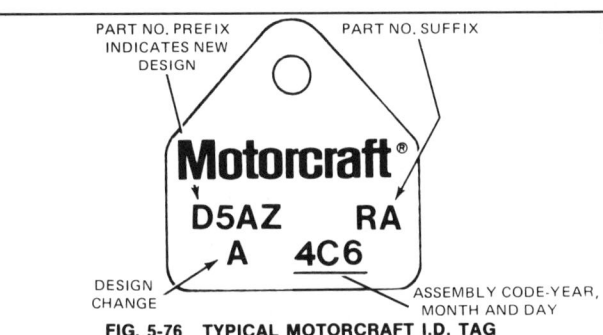

FIG. 5-76 TYPICAL MOTORCRAFT I.D. TAG

(labels: PART NO. PREFIX INDICATES NEW DESIGN; PART NO. SUFFIX; Motorcraft® D5AZ RA; A 4C6; DESIGN CHANGE; ASSEMBLY CODE-YEAR, MONTH AND DAY)

2. If fitted with an "Air-Guard" system, shut the engine off and disconnect the bypass-valve air-inlet hose.

3. Adjust the idle speed to the rpm specified below:

ENGINE/TRANS	1970	1971	1972
6-cyl./Man.	600	600	600 (Calif. 700)
6-cyl./Auto.	550	550	500 (Calif. 750)
V-8/Man.	650	650	750
V-8/Auto.	600	600	700 (except 49-state 304/401—650)

4. Adjust the idle mixture according to the following procedure:

a) Starting from full rich stop(s), turn the mixture screw(s) clockwise until a loss of engine rpm is noted.

b) Turn the mixture screw(s) counterclockwise until the highest rpm reading is obtained within the range of the limiter caps.

c) If the carburetor uses two mixture needles, turn both equally unless the engine demands otherwise.

d) If the idle speed changes more than 30 rpm during the mixture adjustment, reset to specified idle speed rpm and repeat the adjustment.

e) Adjust the final curb idle speed.

5. Reconnect the bypass-valve air-inlet hose on "Air-Guard" systems.

6. The idle speed on 1972 360/401 V-8 engines is set by adjusting the throttle stop solenoid (if so equipped) to the specified figure. Disconnect the solenoid and adjust the idle to 500 rpm, then reconnect the solenoid.

FIG. 5-75 HOLLEY 2300 TRI-PACK CARBURETOR SYSTEM

(labels: THROTTLE CONTROL VACUUM DIAPHRAGM; REAR OUTBOARD CARBURETOR; VACUUM DIAPHRAGM SUPPLY TUBE; CENTER CARBURETOR; FRONT OUTBOARD CARBURETOR; THROTTLE CONTROL VACUUM DIAPHRAGM; DISTRIBUTOR VACUUM ADVANCE TUBE; CRANKCASE VENT TUBE; BOWL VENT TUBE; VACUUM DIAPHRAGM SUPPLY TUBE)

ALL 1973-79 ENGINES

1. Connect a tachometer and run the engine until it reaches normal operating temperature.
2. Remove and discard the idle limiter cap(s).
3. Adjust the idle speed to the rpm specified below:

ENGINE/TRANS	1973	1974	1975	1976	1977	1978	1979
4-cyl./Auto.	–	–	–	–	–	800	800
4-cyl./Man.	–	–	–	–	–	900	900₁
6-cyl./Auto.	550	550	550	550	550	550₂	550
6-cyl./Man.	600	600	600	600	600	600	600₃
6-cyl./Auto. (Calif.)	550	550	700	700	700	700	700
6-cyl./Man. (Calif.)	600	600	600	850	850	850	–
V-8/Auto.	700	700	700	700	600₄	600₅	800
V-8/Man.	750	750	750	750	–	–	600

1 If emissions decal is Code EH, 1000.
2 258 cid, 2V; 600.
3 258 cid, 2V; 700.
4 360 cid, Altitude; 700.
5 Calif. & Altitude; 700.

4. Set idle speed on all V-8's with automatic transmissions and 6-cyl. California engines with automatic transmissions as follows:
   a) 6-cyl. Engines—Loosen the throttle-stop-solenoid locknut and turn the solenoid in or out to obtain the specified idle rpm, then tighten the locknut.
   b) V-8 Engines—Turn the hex screw on the throttle-stop-solenoid carriage to obtain the specified idle rpm.
   c) All—Disconnect the solenoid wire and adjust the curb idle screw to obtain 500 idle rpm, then connect the solenoid wire.
5. Adjust the idle mixture according to the following procedures:
   a) Starting from full rich stop(s), turn the mixture needle(s) clockwise until a loss of engine rpm is noted.
   b) Turn the mixture needles(s) counterclockwise until the highest rpm reading is obtained at the "lean best idle" setting.
   c) If the carburetor uses two mixture needles, turn both equally, unless the engine demands otherwise.
   d) If the idle speed changes more than 30 rpm during the mixture adjustment, reset to 30 rpm above the specified idle speed rpm and repeat the adjustment.
   e) Turn the mixture needle(s) clockwise until the engine speed drops the amount specified below:

ENGINE/TRANS	1973-74	1975	1976	1977	1978	1979
4-cyl./Auto.	–	–	–	–	120	120
4-cyl./Man.	–	–	–	–	120₃	45
6-cyl./Auto.	20	25	25	25₁	25	25
6-cyl./Man.	35	50	50	50₂	50	50
V-8/Auto.	40	20	20	20	20	40
V-8/Man.	40	40	100	–	–	–

1 175 for non-Altitude carburetors, except Matador
2 100 for 232 I-6 California and catalytic-converter-equipped cars.
3 75 for Altitude calibration.

6. Install replacement idle limiter caps.

CARBURETOR OVERHAUL

The only positive approach to cleaning a carburetor is an overhaul—a complete disassembly, replacement of worn and/or defective parts, and reassembly/readjustment. You may be able to operate the carburetor temporarily by running one of the numerous carburetor cleaning agents on the market through the system, but sooner or later, it is going to have to come off the engine for a thorough cleaning.

Carburetor repair kits come in three types—a gasket kit, a light repair kit and an overhaul kit. The light repair kit is usually the best choice for all but the most troublesome carburetor. To order the correct kit, you must know the model number/part number of the carburetor. This is located on a small metal tag attached to the carburetor by one of the air horn screws (**Fig. 5-76**) or stamped on the carburetor body. Particular attention should be paid to replacing the tag when reassembling the carburetor. If it is lost, it is virtually impossible to order the correct kit in many instances.

Carburetor disassembly is a matter of good judgment. If all you plan to do is to remove the air horn and replace a leaking gasket, it is more practical to leave the unit on the engine. Solenoids and dashpots should come off if you are going to clean the main body, because immersing these in carburetor cleaner will ruin them.

A good carburetor cleaning solvent will virtually eat dirt and grease from the carburetor when it is fresh. *Never* put your hands in it, and *do not* let it splash in your eyes. If you do not have a small mesh basket handy for lowering the parts into the solution container, use a small tea strainer available in most department stores. Use this to hold the small parts and hook a metal clothes hanger around the main body and air horn. This will allow you to immerse the parts without the cleaner affecting your skin.

Let the parts stay in the cleaning solution long enough to clean them thoroughly; this can vary from a few minutes to a few hours, depending upon the strength and freshness of the cleaner, and the degree of gum and dirt adhered to the carburetor parts. The cleaning is completed when the parts appear bright and clean-looking. Let them drain, then immerse them once more in a container of fresh, clean solvent. After giving this second solution an opportunity to work its way into all the passages, remove the parts one by one, and blow dry with compressed air.

Before beginning reassembly, make sure you have the specification sheet to make the necessary adjustments as you go. This will accompany the repair or overhaul kit, but the specifications provided at the end of this chapter will enable you to complete the job.

On the following pages, you will find exploded drawings of 15 of the most frequently used carburetor types and photographic overhaul sequences showing exactly how the job is done on 10 of the most popular carburetors—Rochester, Carter and Motorcraft models. Between the exploded drawings and the how-to sequences, you should be able to overhaul any carburetor used during 1970-79 with a minimum of difficulty, as long as you work slowly, do not force components during reassembly and take care not to lose or overlook any parts. ♣

NOTE OF CAUTION

While all versions of a particular carburetor model (Quadrajet, Thermo-Quad, Monojet, etc.) are essentially the same, there are a large number of individual variations according to year and application. Since all auto manufacturers constantly revise the calibraton of the carburetors used from one model year to another, the procedures which follow are to be regarded as representative of the overhaul procedures to follow—not all will contain the same components in the same sequence, or operate exactly the same. To prevent improper functioning when overhauling your carburetor, do not hesitate to check with a dealership or independent carburetor rebuilder should you encounter differences from those shown in our pictorial how-to sequences.

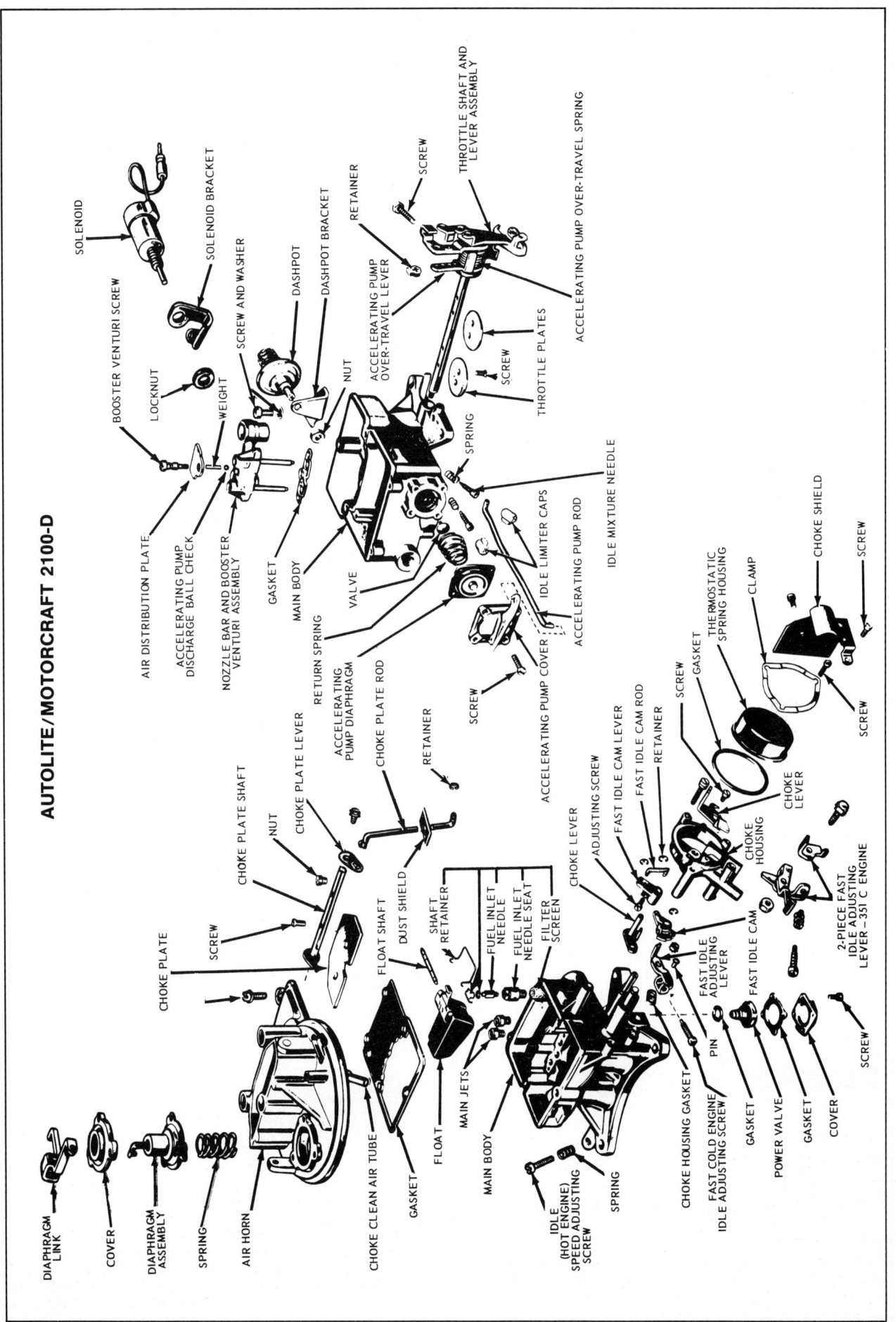

AUTOLITE/MOTORCRAFT 2100-D

MOTORCRAFT 2150

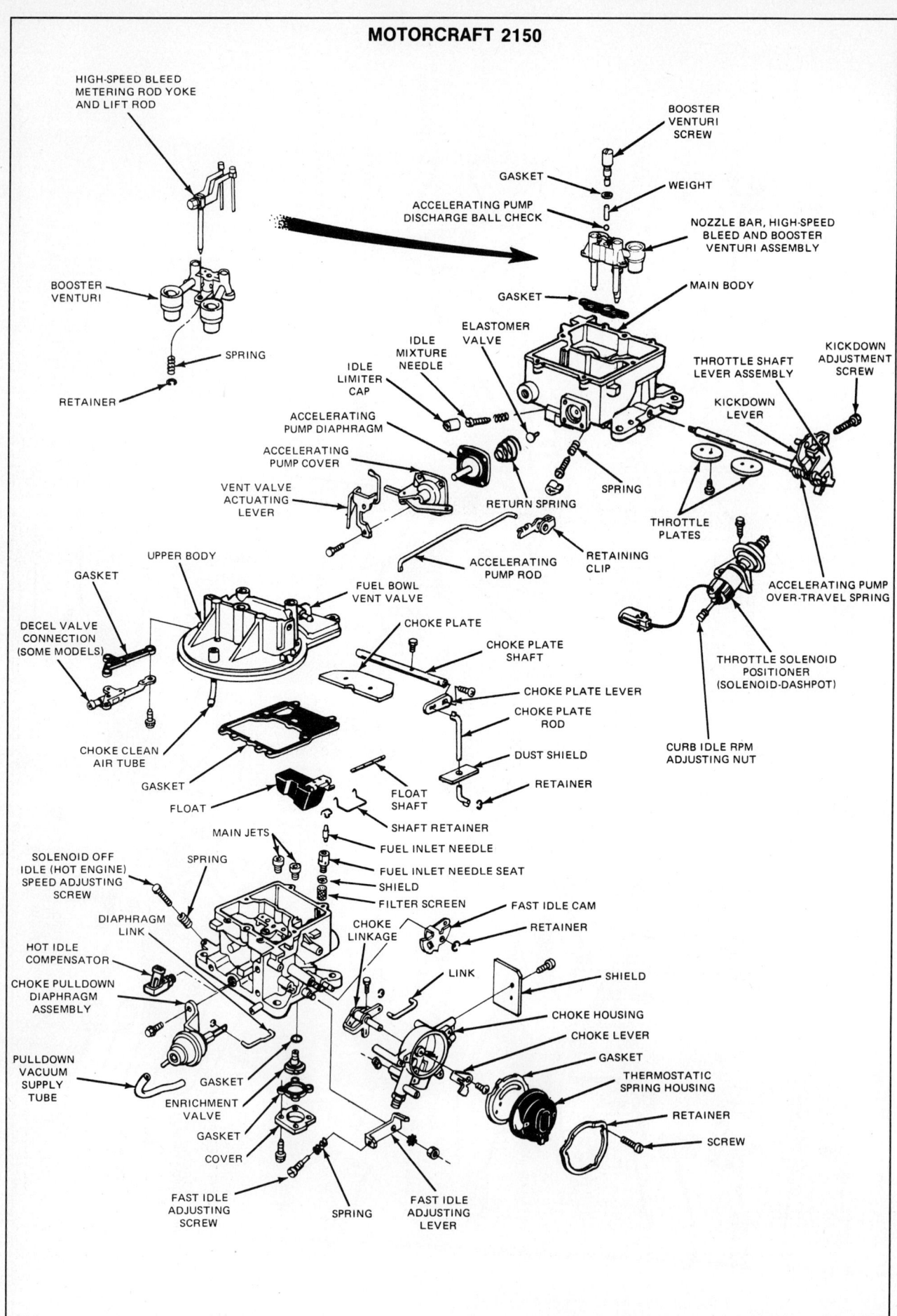

MOTORCRAFT 2700VV

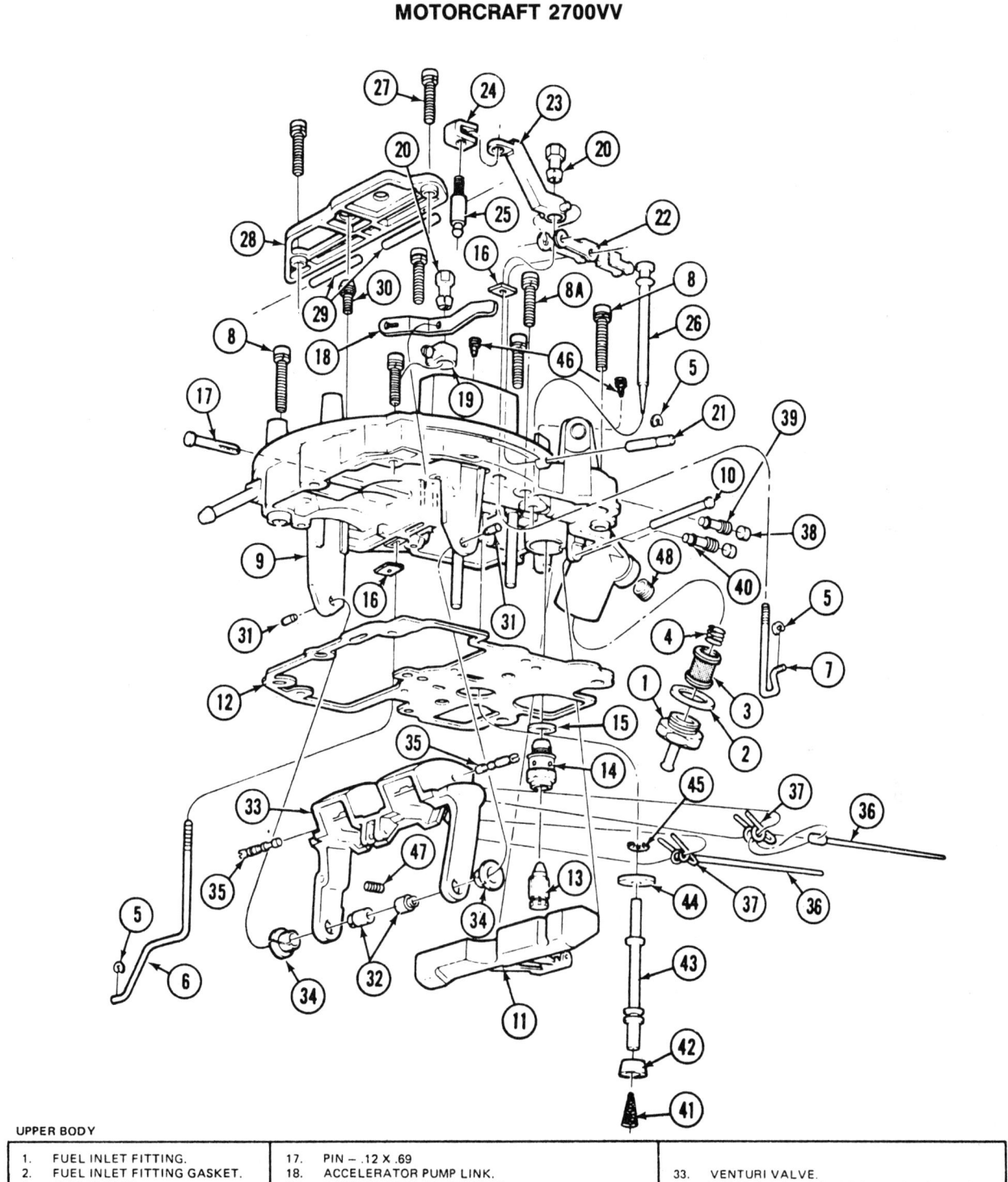

UPPER BODY

1.	FUEL INLET FITTING.	17.	PIN — .12 X .69	33.	VENTURI VALVE.
2.	FUEL INLET FITTING GASKET.	18.	ACCELERATOR PUMP LINK.	34.	VENTURI VALVE PIVOT PIN BUSHING.
3.	FUEL FILTER.	19.	ACCELERATOR PUMP SWIVEL.	35.	METERING ROD PIVOT PIN.
4.	FUEL FILTER SPRING.	20.	NUT — NYLON.	36.	METERING ROD.
5.	1/8 RETAINING E-RING.	21.	CHOKE HINGE PIN.	37.	METERING ROD SPRING.
6.	ACCELERATOR PUMP ROD.	22.	COLD ENRICHMENT ROD LEVER.	38.	CUP PLUG.
7.	CHOKE CONTROL ROD.	23.	COLD ENRICHMENT ROD SWIVEL.	39.	MAIN METERING JET ASSEMBLY.
8.	SCREW (2). 8-32 X .88	24.	CONTROL VACUUM REGULATOR ADJUSTING NUT.	40.	"O" RING.
8A.	SCREW (5) 8-32 X .75	25.	CONTROL VACUUM REGULATOR.	41.	ACCELERATOR PUMP RETURN SPRING.
9.	UPPER BODY	26.	COLD ENRICHMENT ROD.	42.	ACCELERATOR PUMP CUP.
10.	FLOAT HINGE PIN.	27.	SCREW (2) 8-32 X .75	43.	ACCELERATOR PUMP PLUNGER.
11.	FLOAT ASSEMBLY.	28.	VENTURI VALVE COVER PLATE.	44.	INTERNAL VENT VALVE.
12.	FLOAT BOWL GASKET.	29.	ROLLER BEARING.	45.	3/16 RETAINING E-RING.
13.	FUEL INLET VALVE.	30.	VENTURI AIR BYPASS SCREW.	46.	IDLE TRIM SCREW.
14.	FUEL INLET SEAT.	31.	VENTURI VALVE PIVOT PLUG.	47.	VENTURI VALVE LIMITER ADJUSTING SCREW.
15.	FUEL INLET SEAT GASKET.	32.	VENTURI VALVE PIVOT PIN.	48.	PIPE PLUG.
16.	DUST SEAL.	33.	VENTURI VALVE.		

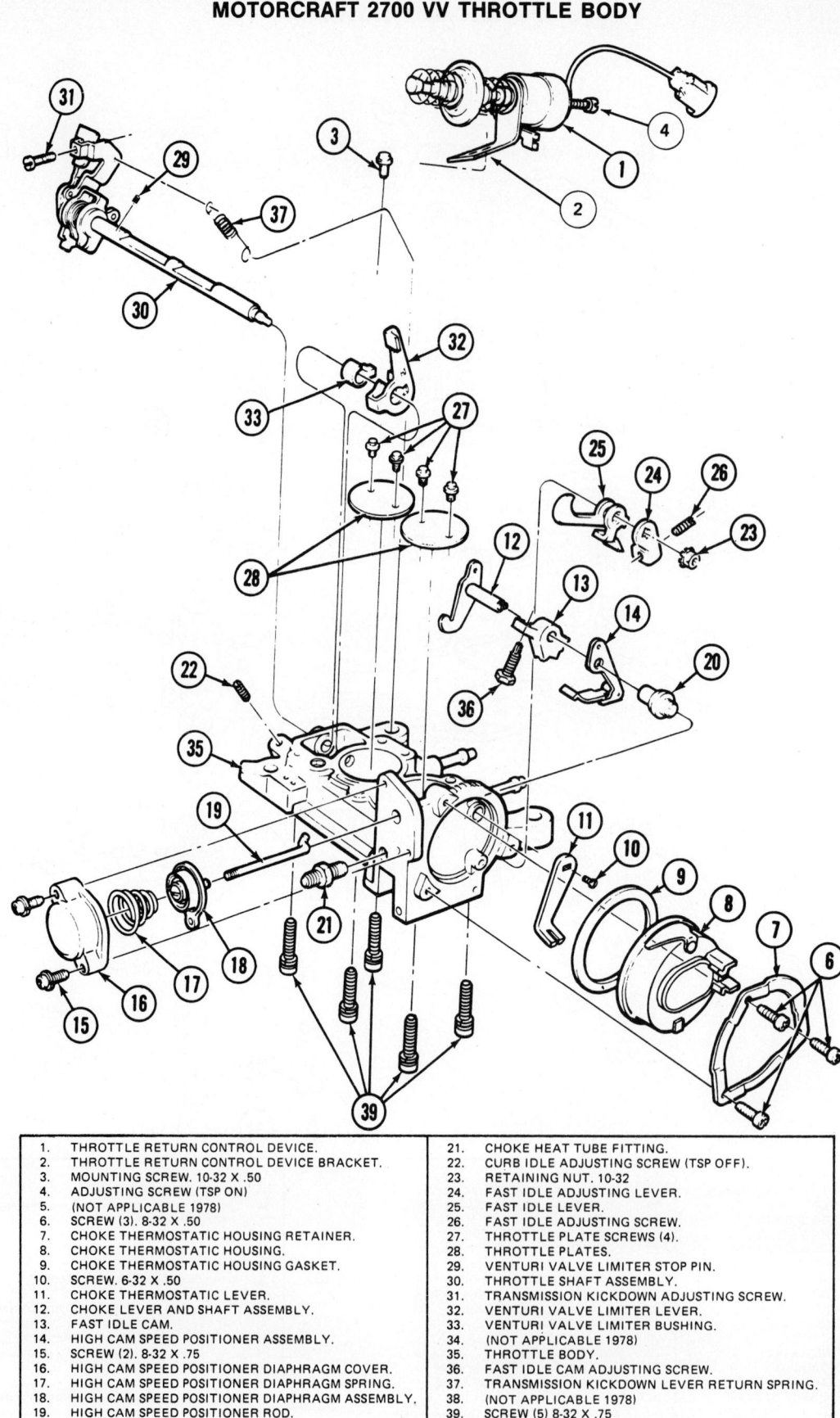

MOTORCRAFT 2700 VV THROTTLE BODY

1.	THROTTLE RETURN CONTROL DEVICE.	21.	CHOKE HEAT TUBE FITTING.
2.	THROTTLE RETURN CONTROL DEVICE BRACKET.	22.	CURB IDLE ADJUSTING SCREW (TSP OFF).
3.	MOUNTING SCREW. 10-32 X .50	23.	RETAINING NUT. 10-32
4.	ADJUSTING SCREW (TSP ON)	24.	FAST IDLE ADJUSTING LEVER.
5.	(NOT APPLICABLE 1978)	25.	FAST IDLE LEVER.
6.	SCREW (3). 8-32 X .50	26.	FAST IDLE ADJUSTING SCREW.
7.	CHOKE THERMOSTATIC HOUSING RETAINER.	27.	THROTTLE PLATE SCREWS (4).
8.	CHOKE THERMOSTATIC HOUSING.	28.	THROTTLE PLATES.
9.	CHOKE THERMOSTATIC HOUSING GASKET.	29.	VENTURI VALVE LIMITER STOP PIN.
10.	SCREW. 6-32 X .50	30.	THROTTLE SHAFT ASSEMBLY.
11.	CHOKE THERMOSTATIC LEVER.	31.	TRANSMISSION KICKDOWN ADJUSTING SCREW.
12.	CHOKE LEVER AND SHAFT ASSEMBLY.	32.	VENTURI VALVE LIMITER LEVER.
13.	FAST IDLE CAM.	33.	VENTURI VALVE LIMITER BUSHING.
14.	HIGH CAM SPEED POSITIONER ASSEMBLY.	34.	(NOT APPLICABLE 1978)
15.	SCREW (2). 8-32 X .75	35.	THROTTLE BODY.
16.	HIGH CAM SPEED POSITIONER DIAPHRAGM COVER.	36.	FAST IDLE CAM ADJUSTING SCREW.
17.	HIGH CAM SPEED POSITIONER DIAPHRAGM SPRING.	37.	TRANSMISSION KICKDOWN LEVER RETURN SPRING.
18.	HIGH CAM SPEED POSITIONER DIAPHRAGM ASSEMBLY.	38.	(NOT APPLICABLE 1978)
19.	HIGH CAM SPEED POSITIONER ROD.	39.	SCREW (5) 8-32 X .75
20.	CHOKE HOUSING BUSHING.		

MOTORCRAFT 2700 VV MAIN BODY

1. Cranking enrichment solenoid.
2. "O" ring seal.
3. Screw. (4) 8-32x.56
4. Venturi valve diaphragm cover.
5. Venturi valve diaphragm spring guide.
6. Venturi valve diaphragm spring.
7. Venturi valve diaphragm assembly.
8. Main body.
9. Venturi valve adjusting screw.
10. Wide open stop screw.
11. Plug expansion.
12. Cranking fuel control assembly.
13. Accelerator pump check ball.
14. Accelerator pump check ball weight.
15. Throttle body gasket.
16. Screw. 6-32x.38
17. Choke heat shield.

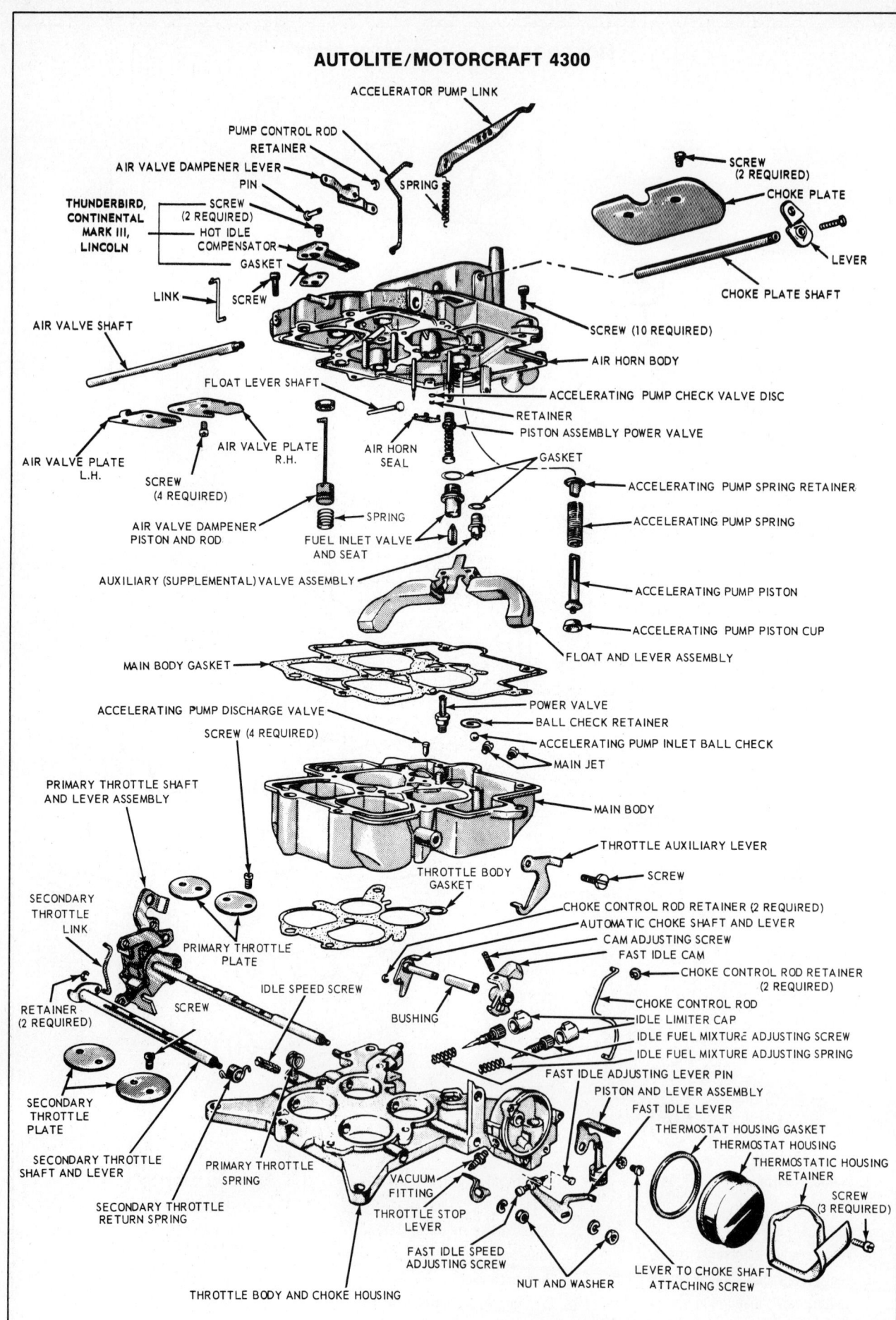

AUTOLITE/MOTORCRAFT 4300

ACCELERATOR PUMP LINK

PUMP CONTROL ROD
RETAINER

AIR VALVE DAMPENER LEVER
PIN

SPRING

SCREW
(2 REQUIRED)

CHOKE PLATE

**THUNDERBIRD,
CONTINENTAL
MARK III,
LINCOLN**

SCREW
(2 REQUIRED)

HOT IDLE
COMPENSATOR

GASKET

LINK

SCREW

LEVER

CHOKE PLATE SHAFT

SCREW (10 REQUIRED)

AIR VALVE SHAFT

AIR HORN BODY

FLOAT LEVER SHAFT

ACCELERATING PUMP CHECK VALVE DISC

RETAINER

PISTON ASSEMBLY POWER VALVE

AIR VALVE PLATE
L.H.

AIR VALVE PLATE
R.H.

AIR HORN
SEAL

GASKET

ACCELERATING PUMP SPRING RETAINER

SCREW
(4 REQUIRED)

ACCELERATING PUMP SPRING

AIR VALVE DAMPENER
PISTON AND ROD

SPRING

FUEL INLET VALVE
AND SEAT

ACCELERATING PUMP PISTON

AUXILIARY (SUPPLEMENTAL) VALVE ASSEMBLY

ACCELERATING PUMP PISTON CUP

FLOAT AND LEVER ASSEMBLY

MAIN BODY GASKET

ACCELERATING PUMP DISCHARGE VALVE

POWER VALVE

BALL CHECK RETAINER

SCREW (4 REQUIRED)

ACCELERATING PUMP INLET BALL CHECK

MAIN JET

PRIMARY THROTTLE SHAFT
AND LEVER ASSEMBLY

MAIN BODY

THROTTLE AUXILIARY LEVER

SCREW

THROTTLE BODY
GASKET

CHOKE CONTROL ROD RETAINER (2 REQUIRED)

AUTOMATIC CHOKE SHAFT AND LEVER

SECONDARY
THROTTLE
LINK

CAM ADJUSTING SCREW

FAST IDLE CAM

PRIMARY THROTTLE
PLATE

CHOKE CONTROL ROD RETAINER
(2 REQUIRED)

RETAINER
(2 REQUIRED)

SCREW

IDLE SPEED SCREW

BUSHING

CHOKE CONTROL ROD

IDLE LIMITER CAP

IDLE FUEL MIXTURE ADJUSTING SCREW

IDLE FUEL MIXTURE ADJUSTING SPRING

FAST IDLE ADJUSTING LEVER PIN

SECONDARY
THROTTLE
PLATE

PISTON AND LEVER ASSEMBLY

FAST IDLE LEVER

THERMOSTAT HOUSING GASKET

THERMOSTAT HOUSING

SECONDARY THROTTLE
SHAFT AND LEVER

PRIMARY THROTTLE
SPRING

THERMOSTATIC HOUSING
RETAINER

SECONDARY THROTTLE
RETURN SPRING

VACUUM
FITTING

THROTTLE STOP
LEVER

SCREW
(3 REQUIRED)

FAST IDLE SPEED
ADJUSTING SCREW

NUT AND WASHER

LEVER TO CHOKE SHAFT
ATTACHING SCREW

THROTTLE BODY AND CHOKE HOUSING

MOTORCRAFT 4350

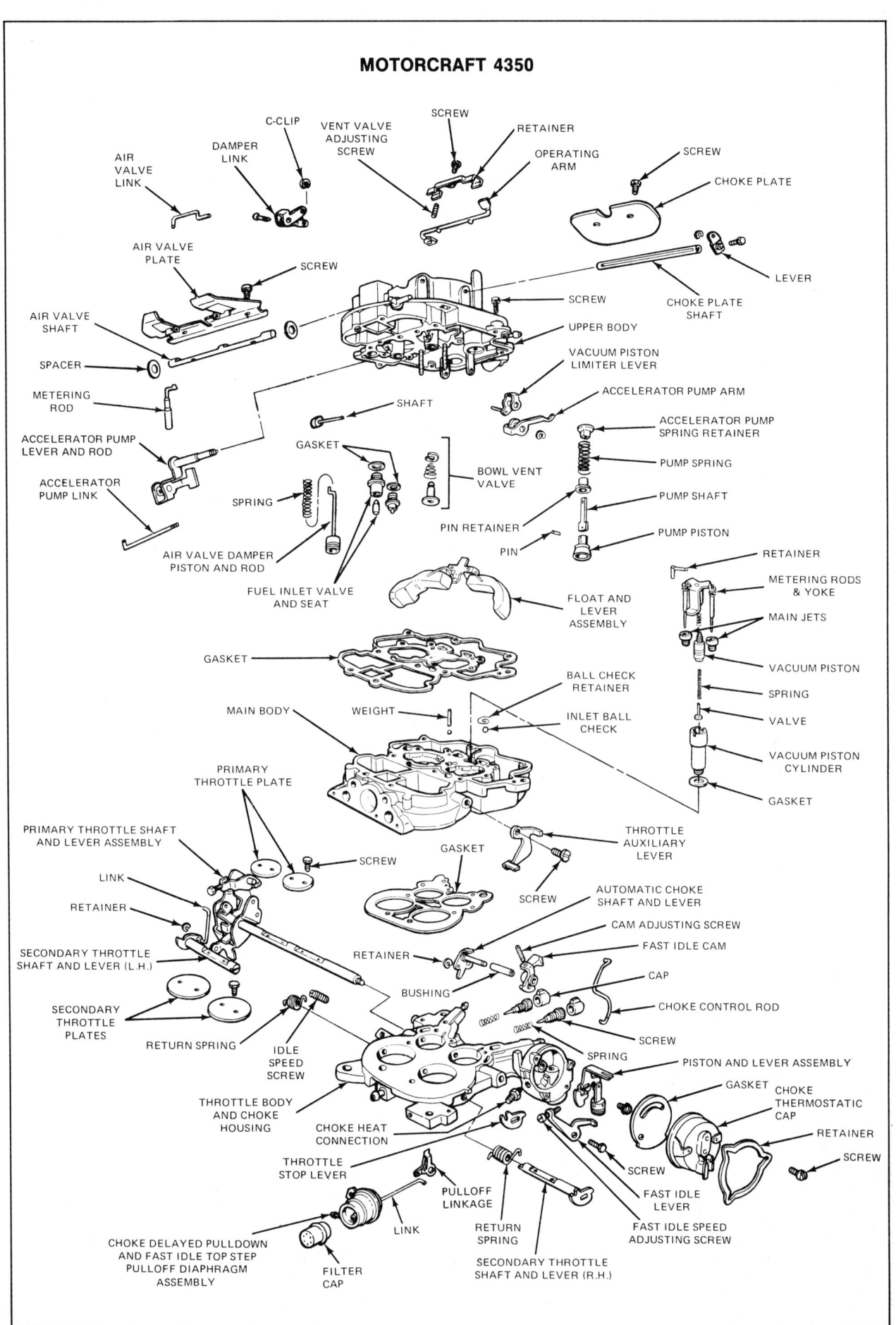

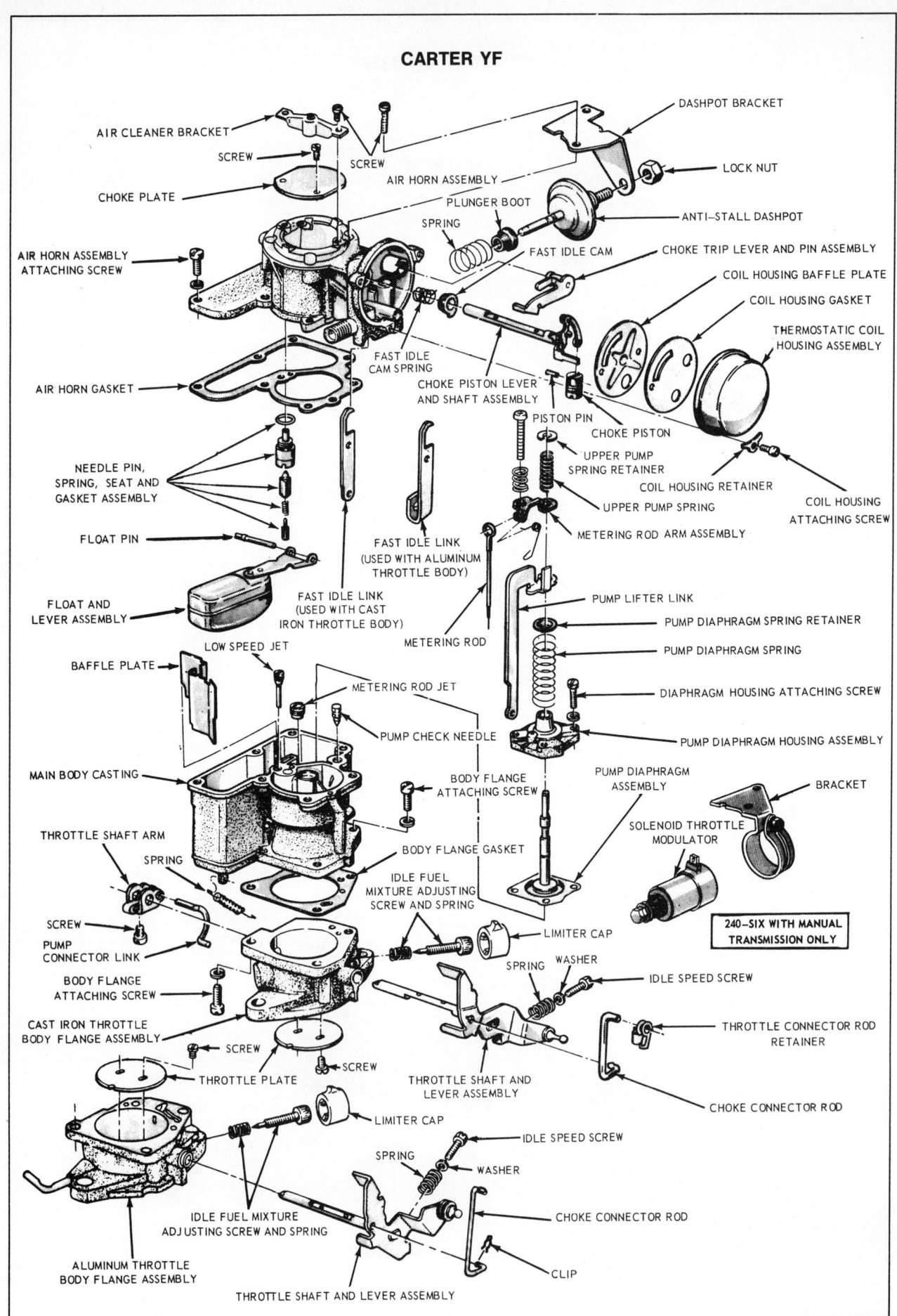

CARTER YF

AIR CLEANER BRACKET
SCREW
SCREW
CHOKE PLATE
AIR HORN ASSEMBLY
PLUNGER BOOT
SPRING
AIR HORN ASSEMBLY
ATTACHING SCREW
AIR HORN GASKET
FAST IDLE CAM SPRING
CHOKE PISTON LEVER
AND SHAFT ASSEMBLY
NEEDLE PIN,
SPRING, SEAT AND
GASKET ASSEMBLY
FLOAT PIN
FLOAT AND
LEVER ASSEMBLY
FAST IDLE LINK
(USED WITH ALUMINUM
THROTTLE BODY)
FAST IDLE LINK
(USED WITH CAST
IRON THROTTLE BODY)
METERING ROD
LOW SPEED JET
BAFFLE PLATE
METERING ROD JET
PUMP CHECK NEEDLE
MAIN BODY CASTING
THROTTLE SHAFT ARM
SPRING
SCREW
PUMP
CONNECTOR LINK
BODY FLANGE
ATTACHING SCREW
CAST IRON THROTTLE
BODY FLANGE ASSEMBLY
SCREW
THROTTLE PLATE
SCREW
BODY FLANGE
ATTACHING SCREW
BODY FLANGE GASKET
IDLE FUEL
MIXTURE ADJUSTING
SCREW AND SPRING
THROTTLE SHAFT AND
LEVER ASSEMBLY
LIMITER CAP
IDLE FUEL MIXTURE
ADJUSTING SCREW AND SPRING
ALUMINUM THROTTLE
BODY FLANGE ASSEMBLY
THROTTLE SHAFT AND LEVER ASSEMBLY
SPRING
WASHER
CLIP
CHOKE CONNECTOR ROD
IDLE SPEED SCREW
DASHPOT BRACKET
LOCK NUT
ANTI-STALL DASHPOT
FAST IDLE CAM
CHOKE TRIP LEVER AND PIN ASSEMBLY
COIL HOUSING BAFFLE PLATE
COIL HOUSING GASKET
THERMOSTATIC COIL
HOUSING ASSEMBLY
PISTON PIN
CHOKE PISTON
UPPER PUMP
SPRING RETAINER
COIL HOUSING RETAINER
UPPER PUMP SPRING
COIL HOUSING
ATTACHING SCREW
METERING ROD ARM ASSEMBLY
PUMP LIFTER LINK
PUMP DIAPHRAGM SPRING RETAINER
PUMP DIAPHRAGM SPRING
DIAPHRAGM HOUSING ATTACHING SCREW
PUMP DIAPHRAGM HOUSING ASSEMBLY
PUMP DIAPHRAGM
ASSEMBLY
BRACKET
SOLENOID THROTTLE
MODULATOR
240-SIX WITH MANUAL
TRANSMISSION ONLY
SPRING
WASHER
IDLE SPEED SCREW
THROTTLE CONNECTOR ROD
RETAINER
CHOKE CONNECTOR ROD

CARTER YFA

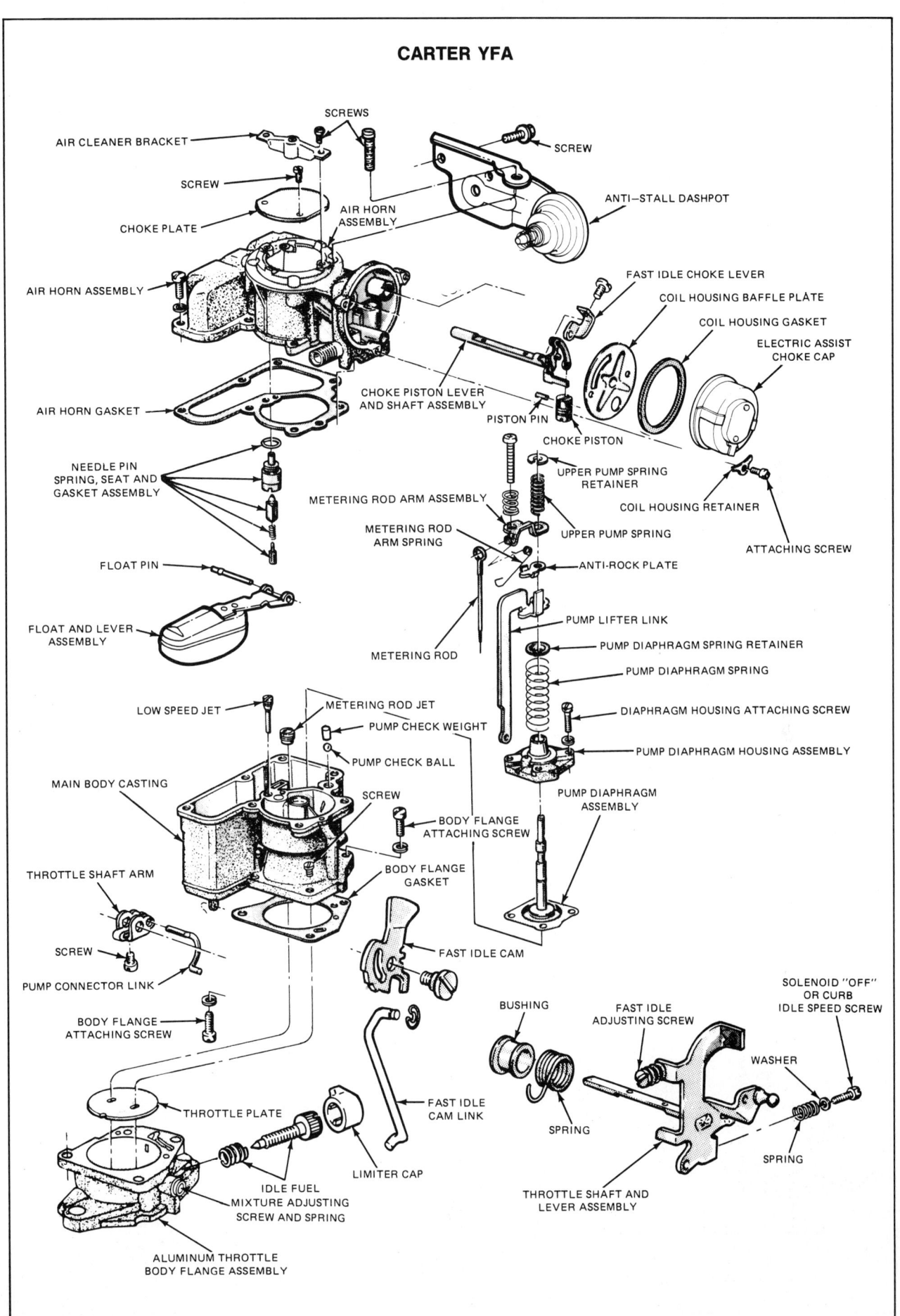

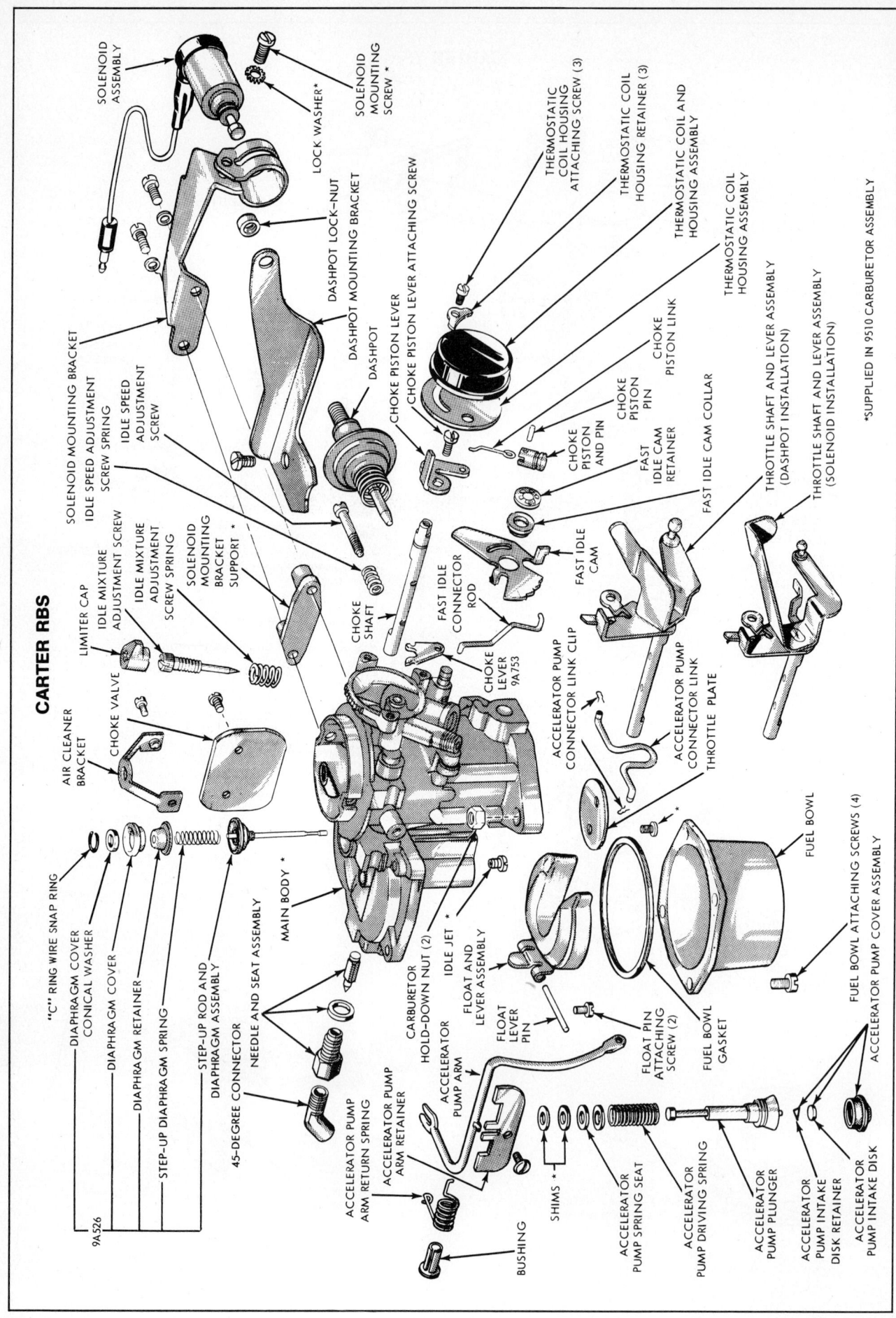

CARTER RBS

SOLENOID ASSEMBLY
LOCK WASHER*
SOLENOID MOUNTING SCREW *
THERMOSTATIC COIL HOUSING ATTACHING SCREW (3)
THERMOSTATIC COIL HOUSING RETAINER (3)
THERMOSTATIC COIL AND HOUSING ASSEMBLY
SOLENOID MOUNTING BRACKET
DASHPOT LOCK-NUT
DASHPOT MOUNTING BRACKET
DASHPOT
CHOKE PISTON LEVER
CHOKE PISTON LEVER ATTACHING SCREW
THERMOSTATIC COIL HOUSING ASSEMBLY
CHOKE PISTON LINK
CHOKE PISTON PIN
IDLE SPEED ADJUSTMENT SCREW SPRING
IDLE SPEED ADJUSTMENT SCREW
CHOKE PISTON AND PIN
CHOKE PISTON RETAINER
FAST IDLE CAM COLLAR
FAST IDLE CAM RETAINER
THROTTLE SHAFT AND LEVER ASSEMBLY (DASHPOT INSTALLATION)
THROTTLE SHAFT AND LEVER ASSEMBLY (SOLENOID INSTALLATION)
*SUPPLIED IN 9510 CARBURETOR ASSEMBLY
SOLENOID MOUNTING BRACKET
IDLE MIXTURE ADJUSTMENT SCREW
IDLE MIXTURE ADJUSTMENT SCREW SPRING
SOLENOID MOUNTING BRACKET SUPPORT *
FAST IDLE CONNECTOR ROD
FAST IDLE CAM
LIMITER CAP
IDLE MIXTURE ADJUSTMENT SCREW
CHOKE SHAFT
CHOKE LEVER 9A753
ACCELERATOR PUMP CONNECTOR LINK CLIP
ACCELERATOR PUMP CONNECTOR LINK
THROTTLE PLATE
AIR CLEANER BRACKET
CHOKE VALVE
"C" RING WIRE SNAP RING
DIAPHRAGM COVER CONICAL WASHER
DIAPHRAGM COVER
DIAPHRAGM RETAINER
STEP-UP DIAPHRAGM SPRING
STEP-UP ROD AND DIAPHRAGM ASSEMBLY
45-DEGREE CONNECTOR
NEEDLE AND SEAT ASSEMBLY
MAIN BODY *
CARBURETOR HOLD-DOWN NUT (2)
IDLE JET *
FUEL BOWL
ACCELERATOR PUMP ARM RETURN SPRING
ACCELERATOR PUMP ARM RETAINER
ACCELERATOR PUMP ARM
FLOAT AND LEVER ASSEMBLY
FLOAT LEVER PIN
FLOAT PIN ATTACHING SCREW (2)
FUEL BOWL GASKET
FUEL BOWL ATTACHING SCREWS (4)
ACCELERATOR PUMP COVER ASSEMBLY
BUSHING
SHIMS *
ACCELERATOR PUMP SPRING SEAT
ACCELERATOR PUMP DRIVING SPRING
ACCELERATOR PUMP PLUNGER
ACCELERATOR PUMP INTAKE DISK RETAINER
ACCELERATOR PUMP INTAKE DISK
9A526

HOLLEY MODEL 1945 1-V CARBURETOR—DISASSEMBLED

Index Number	Part Name
♦	Air Horn
♦♦	Main Body
1	Choke Plate
2	Choke Shaft & Lever Assy.
3	Fast Idle Adj. Screw
4	Throt Body to Main Body
5	Dashpot Bracket Screws
6	Choke Bracket Retainer Screws
7	Pump Clamp Screw
8	Throt Plate Screws
9	Throt Adj. Screw
10	Retaining Plate Screw
11	Choke Plate Screws
12	Air horn to Main body Screws
13	Solenoid Bracket Screws & L.W.
14	Solenoid Adj. Screw
15	Fuel Inlet Fitting Gasket
16	Throt Body Gasket
17	Air horn Gasket
18	Throttle Plate
19	Throt Body & Shaft Assy.
20	Throt Return Spring Bushing
21	Idle Adjusting Needle
22	Float & Hinge Assy.
23	Float hinge Shaft
24	Fuel Inlet Needle & Seat Assy.
25	Main Jet
26	Power Valve Piston
27	Power Valve Assy.
28	Auxil Idle Rich Valve Assy.
29	Pump Rod Seal
30	Pump Discharge Valve
31	Choke Diaph Link Pin
32	Pump Piston Stern
33	Pump Operating Link
34	Choke diaph Link
35	Idle Limiter Cap
36	Pump Piston Cup
37	Choke Diaph
38	Fast Idle Cam Retainer
39	Float Shaft Retainer
40	Power Valve Piston Retainer
41	Idle Needle Spring
42	Fast Idle Adj. Screw Spring
43	Idle Adj. Screw Spring
44	Power Valve Piston Spring
45	Throt Return Spring
46	Pump Drive Spring
47	Mechanical Rod Return Spring
48	Mechanical P.V. Lever Return Spring
49	Solenoid Adj. Screw Spring
50	Pump Lever Nut
51	Dashpot Lock Nut
52	Pump Discharge Valve Weight
53	Fast Idle Cam
55	Return Spring Sleeve
56	Power Valve Rod
57	Fast Idle Rod
58	Pump Rod
59	Pump Lever Nut L.W.
60	Choke Link Washer
61	Pump Rod Clamp
62	Dashpot Bracket
63	Auxil Idle Rich Hose Clamp
64	Choke Vacuum hose
65	Auxil Idle Rich hose
66	Dashpot Assy.
67	Retaining Plate
68	Pump Operating Lever
69	Torsion Spring Lever & hud Assy.
70	Mechanical Power Valve Lever
71	Solenoid Assy.

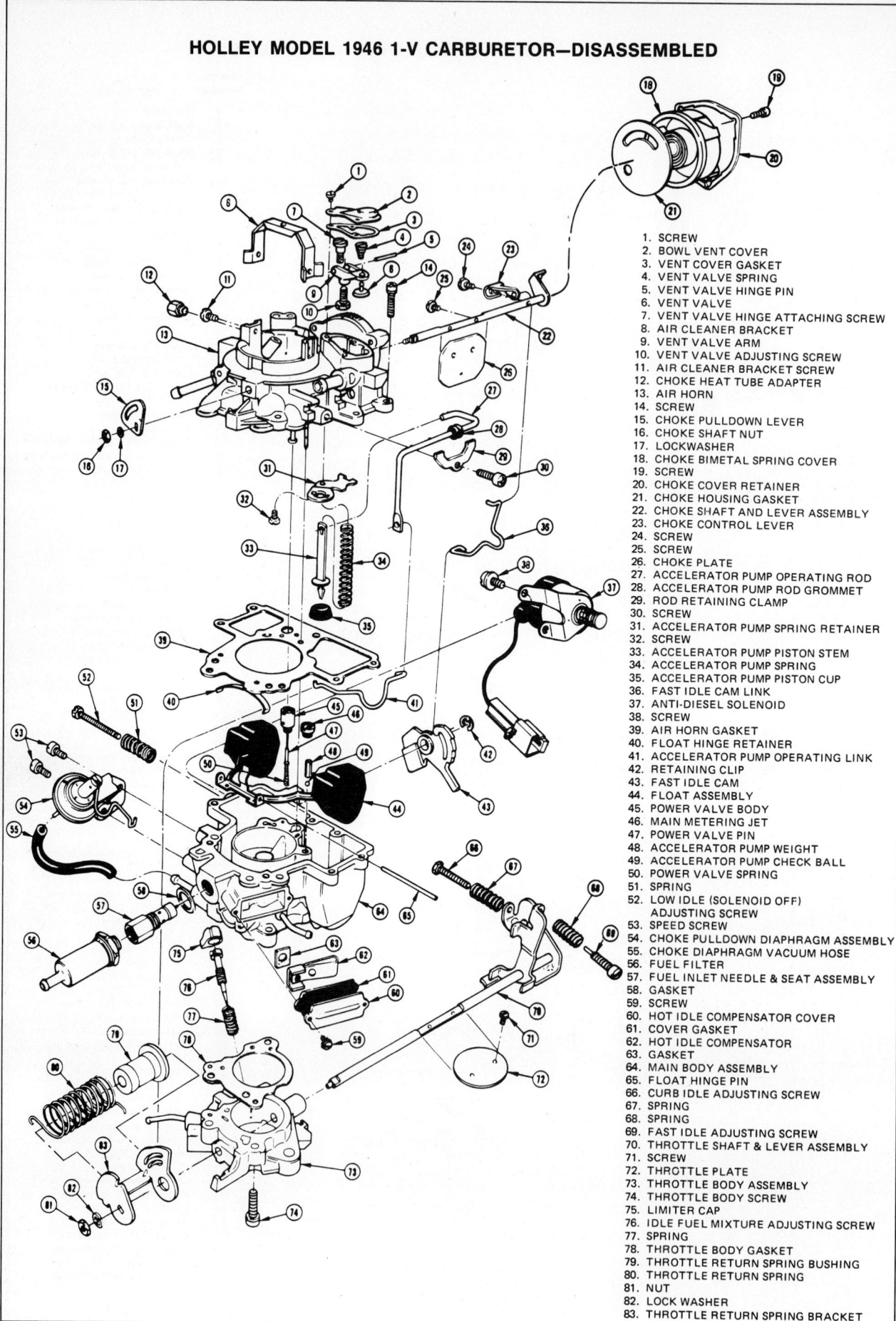

HOLLEY MODEL 1946 1-V CARBURETOR—DISASSEMBLED

1. SCREW
2. BOWL VENT COVER
3. VENT COVER GASKET
4. VENT VALVE SPRING
5. VENT VALVE HINGE PIN
6. VENT VALVE
7. VENT VALVE HINGE ATTACHING SCREW
8. AIR CLEANER BRACKET
9. VENT VALVE ARM
10. VENT VALVE ADJUSTING SCREW
11. AIR CLEANER BRACKET SCREW
12. CHOKE HEAT TUBE ADAPTER
13. AIR HORN
14. SCREW
15. CHOKE PULLDOWN LEVER
16. CHOKE SHAFT NUT
17. LOCKWASHER
18. CHOKE BIMETAL SPRING COVER
19. SCREW
20. CHOKE COVER RETAINER
21. CHOKE HOUSING GASKET
22. CHOKE SHAFT AND LEVER ASSEMBLY
23. CHOKE CONTROL LEVER
24. SCREW
25. SCREW
26. CHOKE PLATE
27. ACCELERATOR PUMP OPERATING ROD
28. ACCELERATOR PUMP ROD GROMMET
29. ROD RETAINING CLAMP
30. SCREW
31. ACCELERATOR PUMP SPRING RETAINER
32. SCREW
33. ACCELERATOR PUMP PISTON STEM
34. ACCELERATOR PUMP SPRING
35. ACCELERATOR PUMP PISTON CUP
36. FAST IDLE CAM LINK
37. ANTI-DIESEL SOLENOID
38. SCREW
39. AIR HORN GASKET
40. FLOAT HINGE RETAINER
41. ACCELERATOR PUMP OPERATING LINK
42. RETAINING CLIP
43. FAST IDLE CAM
44. FLOAT ASSEMBLY
45. POWER VALVE BODY
46. MAIN METERING JET
47. POWER VALVE PIN
48. ACCELERATOR PUMP WEIGHT
49. ACCELERATOR PUMP CHECK BALL
50. POWER VALVE SPRING
51. SPRING
52. LOW IDLE (SOLENOID OFF) ADJUSTING SCREW
53. SPEED SCREW
54. CHOKE PULLDOWN DIAPHRAGM ASSEMBLY
55. CHOKE DIAPHRAGM VACUUM HOSE
56. FUEL FILTER
57. FUEL INLET NEEDLE & SEAT ASSEMBLY
58. GASKET
59. SCREW
60. HOT IDLE COMPENSATOR COVER
61. COVER GASKET
62. HOT IDLE COMPENSATOR
63. GASKET
64. MAIN BODY ASSEMBLY
65. FLOAT HINGE PIN
66. CURB IDLE ADJUSTING SCREW
67. SPRING
68. SPRING
69. FAST IDLE ADJUSTING SCREW
70. THROTTLE SHAFT & LEVER ASSEMBLY
71. SCREW
72. THROTTLE PLATE
73. THROTTLE BODY ASSEMBLY
74. THROTTLE BODY SCREW
75. LIMITER CAP
76. IDLE FUEL MIXTURE ADJUSTING SCREW
77. SPRING
78. THROTTLE BODY GASKET
79. THROTTLE RETURN SPRING BUSHING
80. THROTTLE RETURN SPRING
81. NUT
82. LOCK WASHER
83. THROTTLE RETURN SPRING BRACKET

HOLLEY 4160

1—Lever, Pump Operating	33—Spring Vent Valve Rod	64—Screw, Pump Cam
2—Locknut	34—Valve, Bowl Vent	65—Pump Cam
3—Spring, override	35—Retainer, Clip, Float	66—Screw and Lockwasher,
4—Screw, Pump Adjusting	36—Float	Secondary Stop Lever
5—Screw, Fuel Bowl (Primary)	37—Spring, Float	67—Lever, Secondary Stop
6—Gasket, Bowl Screw	38—Baffle, Float	68—Screws, Secondary Throttle Valves
7—Fuel Bowl (Primary)	39—Needle Valve and Seat	69—Throttle Valves, Secondary
8—Gasket, Fuel Bowl	40—Screws, Fuel Pump Cover	70—Fast Idle Cam Lever
9—Metering Body (Primary Side)	41—Cover Assembly, Fuel Pump	71—Fast Idle Cam
10—Gasket, Metering Body	42—Diaphragm, Fuel Pump	72—Retainer (E-Clip)
11—Fuel Tube (Float Bowl Connecting)	43—Spring, Fuel Pump Diaphragm	73—Choke Diaphragm Link
12—"O" Rings, Fuel Tube	44—Fitting, Fuel Inlet	74—Choke Diaphragm Assembly
13—Screw, Fuel Bowl (Secondary)	45—Gasket, Fuel Inlet, Fitting	75—Choke Vacuum Hose
14—Gasket, Bowl Screw	46—Valve Assembly, Power	76—Choke Diaphragm Bracket Screw
15—Fuel Bowl (Secondary)	47—Gasket, Power Valve	77—Secondary Diaphragm Cover Screw
16—Screw, Metering Body (Secondary)	48—Primary Jets	78—Diaphragm Cover (Machine)
17—Metering Body (Secondary)	49—Needle, Idle Adjusting Mixture	79—Secondary Diaphragm Return Spring
18—Gasket, Metering Body (Secondary)	50—Gasket, Idle Mixture Needle	80—Secondary Diaphragm Assembly
19—Plate, Metering Body (Secondary)	51—Screws, Choke Valve	81—Secondary Diaphragm Housing
20—Gasket, Metering Body Plate	52—Choke Valve	(Machine)
21—Balance Tube	53—Choke Shaft & Lever Assembly	82—Secondary Diaphragm Housing Gasket
22—Washers, Balance Tube	54—Discharge Nozzle Screw, Pump	83—Secondary Diaphragm Assembly
23—"O" Rings, Balance Tube	55—Gasket, Nozzle Screw	Screw
24—Choke Link	56—Nozzle, Pump Discharge	84—Throttle Connecting Rod Retainer
25—Seal, Choke Rod	57—Needle, Pump Discharge Jet	Washer
26—Throttle Body Screws	58—Cotter Pins, Connecting Rods	85—Pump Operating Lever (E-Clip)
27—Main Body	59—Rod, Secondary Connecting	86—Secondary Stop Screw
28—Throttle Body	60—Screw and Lockwasher,	87—Throttle Stop Screw
29—Gasket, Main to Throttle Body	Fast Idle Cam Lever	88—Throttle Stop Screw Spring
30—Screw, Bowl Vent Valve Rod Clamp	61—Lever, Fast Idle Cam	89—Baffle
31—Clamp, Valve Rod	62—Screws, Primary Throttle Valve	90—Limiter Cap
32—Rod, Bowl Vent Valve	63—Throttle Valves, Primary	91—Bowl Vent Valve Assy. (E.C.S.)

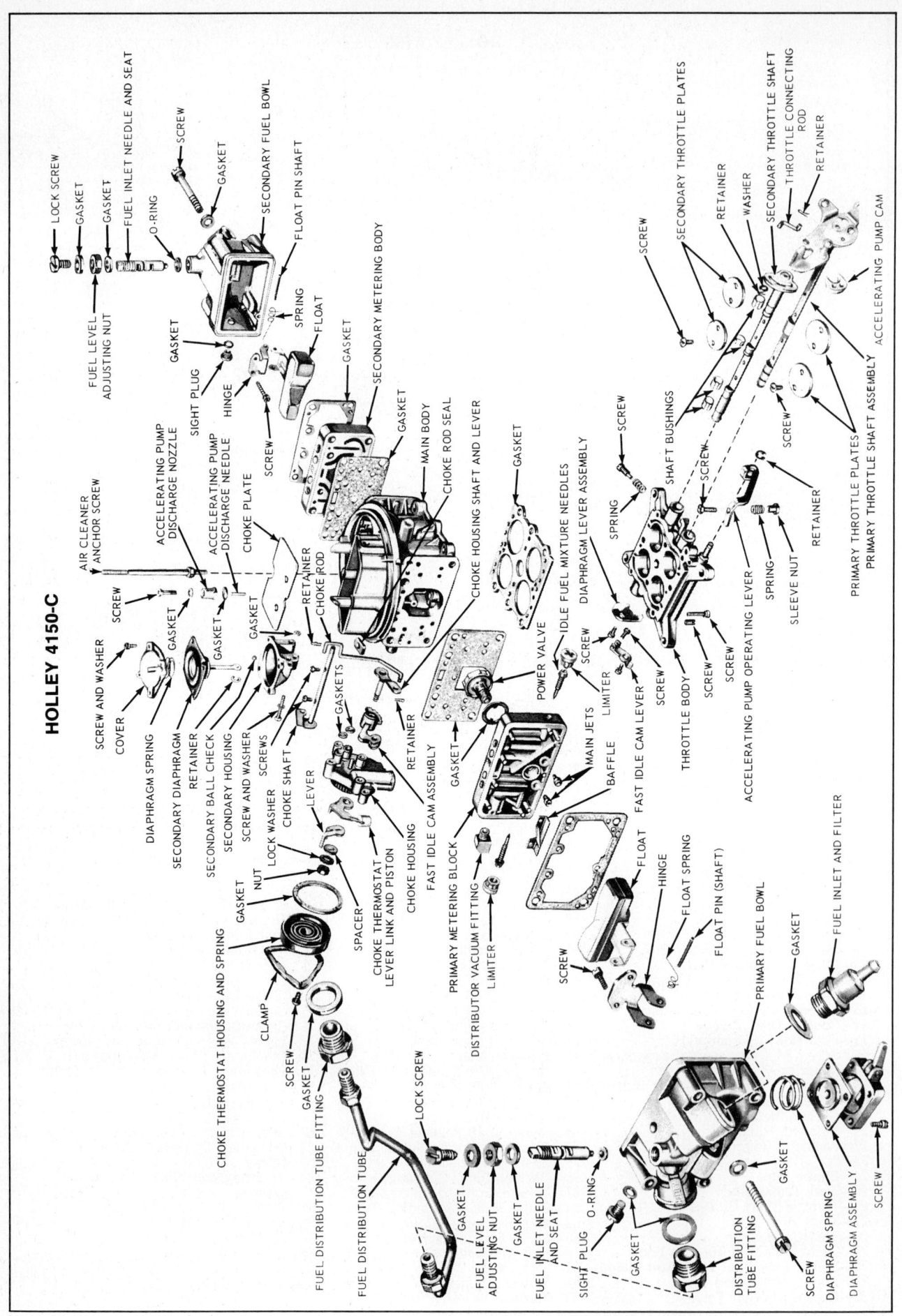

HOLLEY 4150-C

HOLLEY 5200, 5210-C

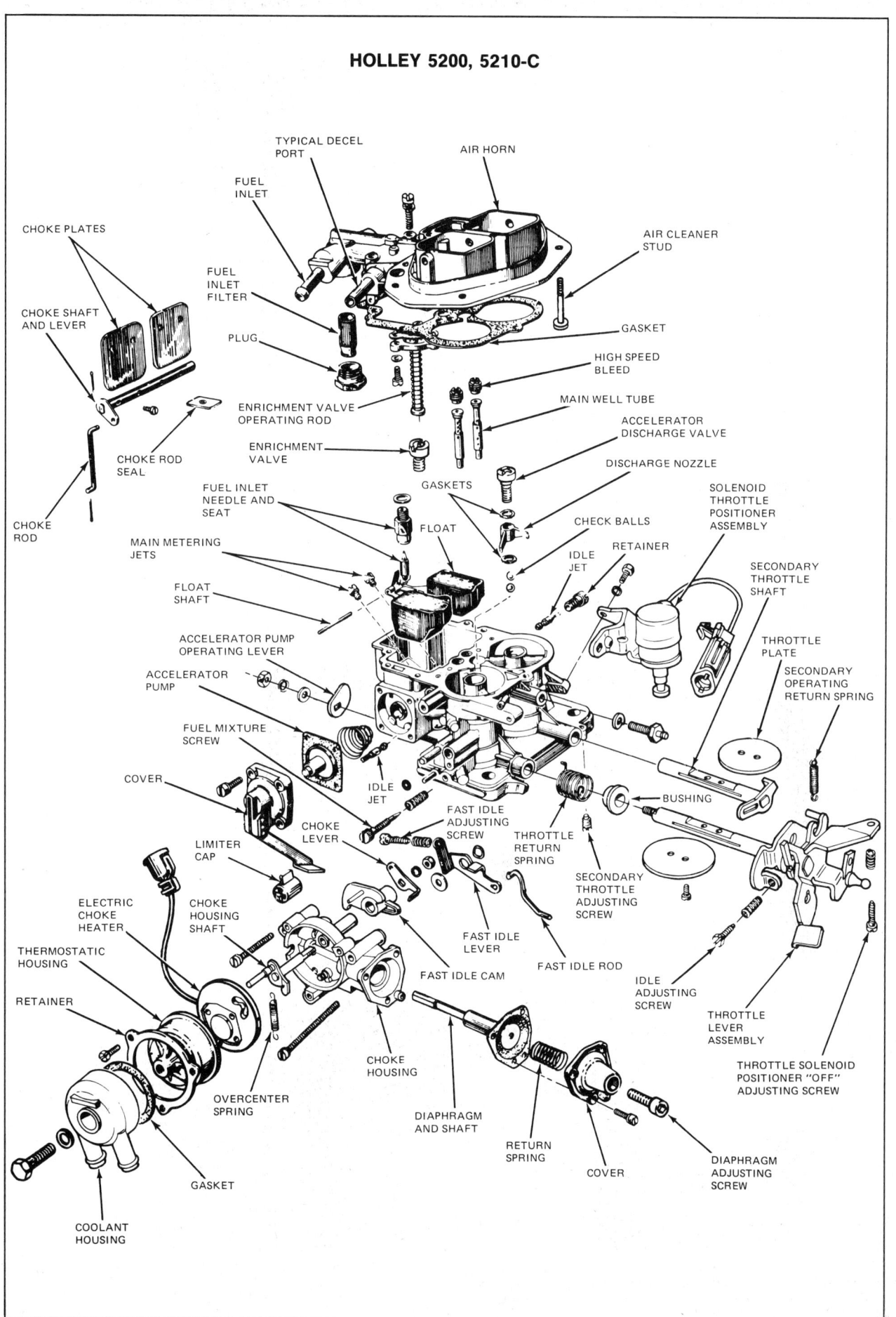

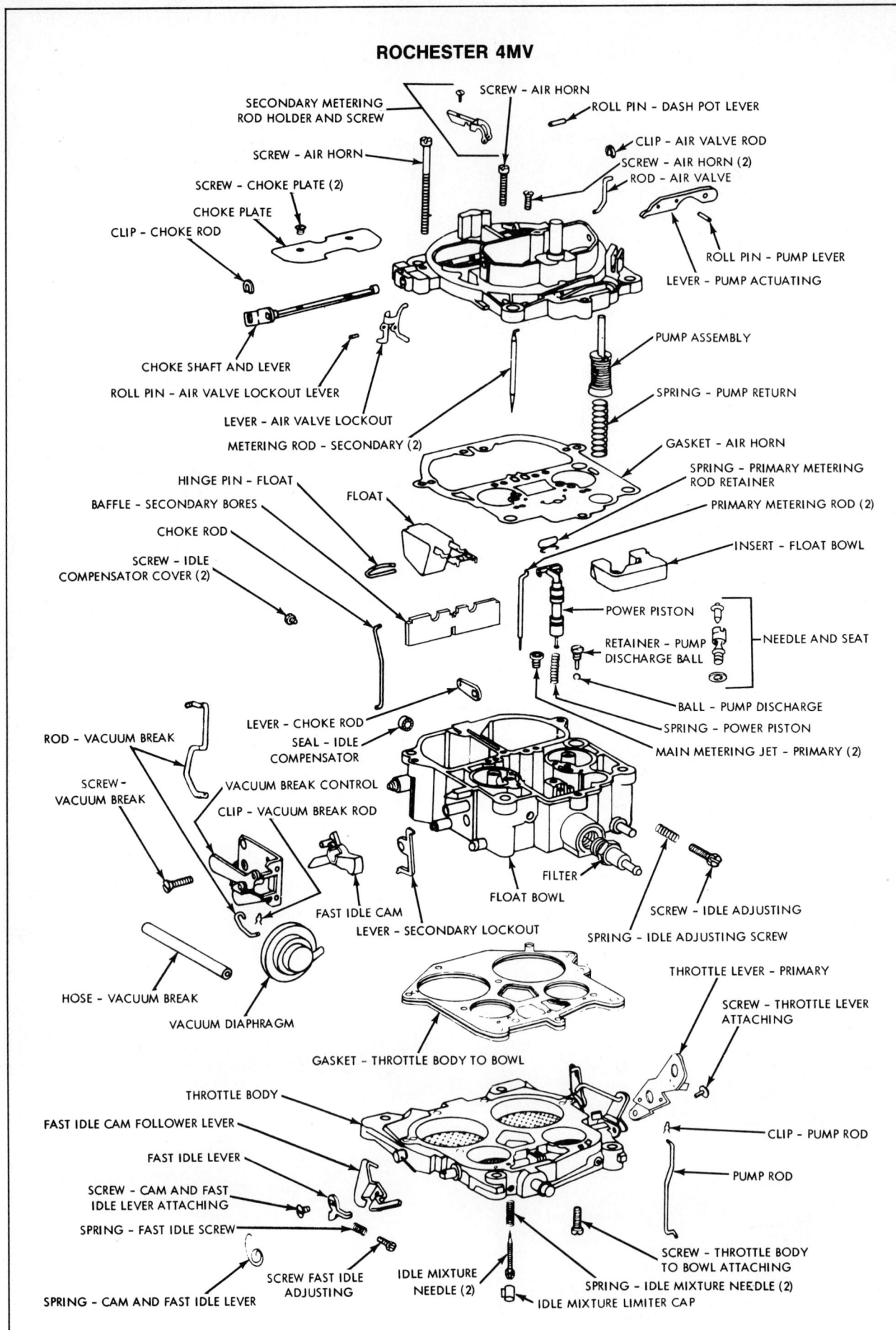

ROCHESTER 4MV

ROCHESTER MV

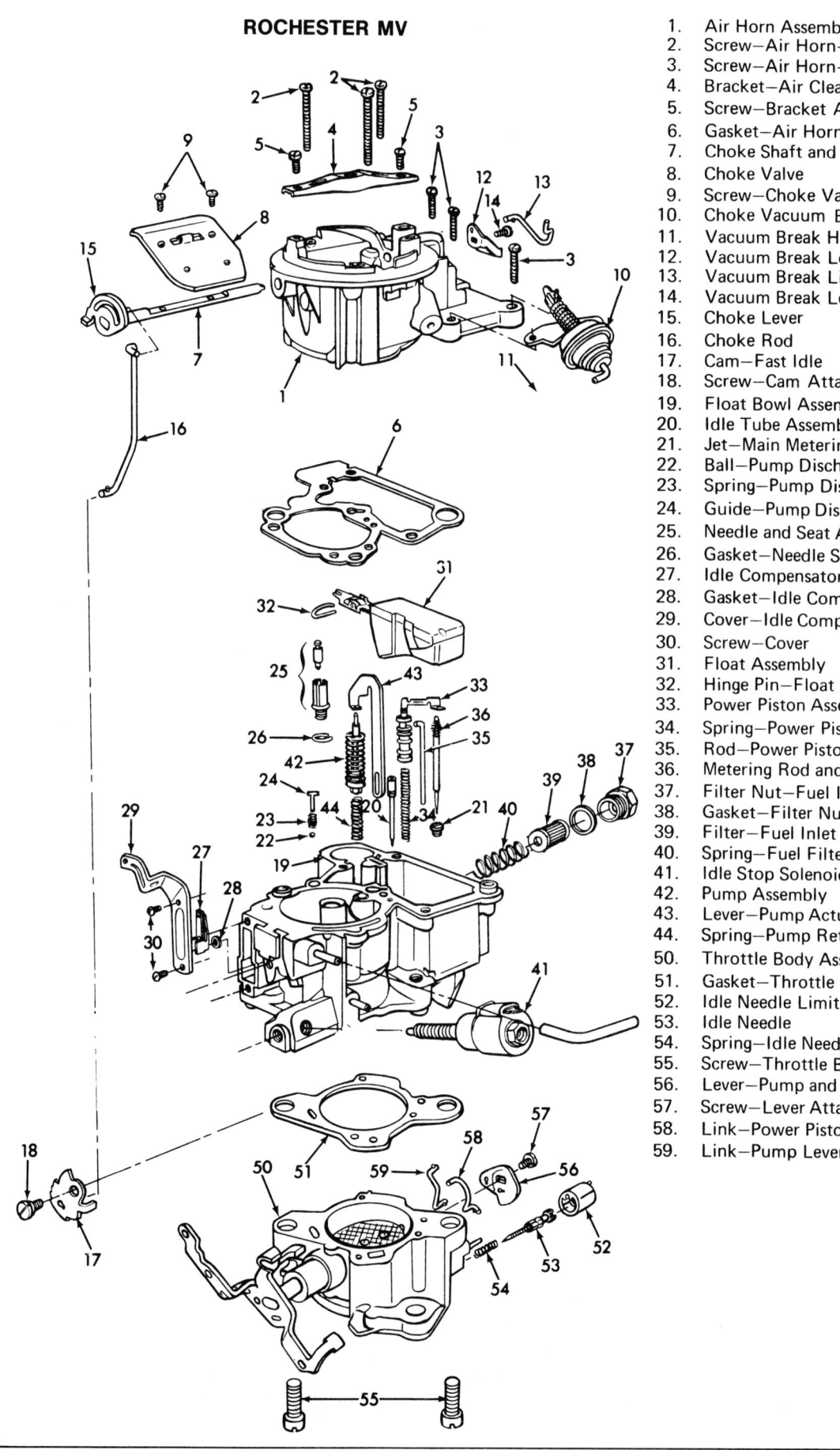

1. Air Horn Assembly
2. Screw—Air Horn—Long
3. Screw—Air Horn-Short
4. Bracket—Air Cleaner Stud
5. Screw—Bracket Attaching
6. Gasket—Air Horn
7. Choke Shaft and Lever Assembly
8. Choke Valve
9. Screw—Choke Valve
10. Choke Vacuum Break, Unit
11. Vacuum Break Hose
12. Vacuum Break Lever
13. Vacuum Break Link
14. Vacuum Break Lever Screw
15. Choke Lever
16. Choke Rod
17. Cam—Fast Idle
18. Screw—Cam Attaching
19. Float Bowl Assembly
20. Idle Tube Assembly
21. Jet—Main Metering
22. Ball—Pump Discharge
23. Spring—Pump Discharge
24. Guide—Pump Discharge
25. Needle and Seat Assembly
26. Gasket—Needle Seat
27. Idle Compensator Assembly
28. Gasket—Idle Compensator
29. Cover—Idle Compensator
30. Screw—Cover
31. Float Assembly
32. Hinge Pin—Float
33. Power Piston Assembly
34. Spring—Power Piston
35. Rod—Power Piston
36. Metering Rod and Spring Assembly
37. Filter Nut—Fuel Inlet
38. Gasket—Filter Nut
39. Filter—Fuel Inlet
40. Spring—Fuel Filter
41. Idle Stop Solenoid
42. Pump Assembly
43. Lever—Pump Actuating
44. Spring—Pump Return
50. Throttle Body Assembly
51. Gasket—Throttle Body
52. Idle Needle Limiter Cap
53. Idle Needle
54. Spring—Idle Needle
55. Screw—Throttle Body
56. Lever—Pump and Power Rods—New
57. Screw—Lever Attaching
58. Link—Power Piston Rod
59. Link—Pump Lever

CARBURETOR SPECIFICATIONS

AMERICAN MOTORS

Year	Carburetor Model	Carburetor Number	Transmission	Dry Float Setting (ins.)	Pump Setting Hole	Main Jet Pri./Sec.	Low Speed Jet	Pump Jet	Unloader (ins.)	Choke Setting	Dash Pot (ins.)	Fast Idle Speed (rpm)
1970	**CARTER**											
	YF	4768S	Manual	29/64	—	120-401/—	#65	#70	21/64	Index	7/64	2300
	YF	4767S	Automatic	29/64	—	120-401/—	#66	#70	19/64	Index	—	2300
	YF	4978S	Automatic	29/64	—	120-398/—	#63	#71	19/64	1NR	—	2300
	YF	4770S	Manual	29/64	—	120-401/—	#63	#70	19/64	Index	3/32	2300
	YF	4769S	Automatic	29/64	—	120-401/—	#63	#70	19/64	Index	—	2300
	WCD	4950S	Manual	7/32	—	120-392/—	#68	#70	3/16	Index	3/32	2000
	WCD	4817S	Automatic	7/32	—	120-392/—	#70	#70	3/16	Index	3/32	2000
	WCD	4816S	Automatic	7/32	—	120-392/—	#70	#70	3/16	Index	3/32	2000
	AUTOLITE											
	2100	ODM2	Manual	3/8	3	49F/—	#64	#66	13/64	Index	1/8	1600
	2100	ODA2	Automatic	3/8	3	48F/—	#66	#66	13/64	2NR	1/8	1600
	2100	ORA2	Automatic	3/8	3	55F/—	#65	#66	13/64	1NR	1/8	1600
	4300	OWM4	Manual	13/16	Center	53/—	#69	#68	19/64	2NR	1/16	1600
	4300	OWA4	Automatic	13/16	Center	53/—	#69	#68	19/64	2NR	1/8	1600
1971	**CARTER**											
	YF	6093S	Manual	29/64	—	120-401/—	#63	#70	19/64	1NR	7/64	2300
	YF	6094S	Automatic	29/64	—	120-401/—	#64	#70	19/64	1NR	—	2300
	YF	6095S	Manual	29/64	—	120-401/—	#63	#70	19/64	1NR	7/64	2300
	YF	6096S	Automatic	29/64	—	120-401/—	#63	#70	19/64	1NR	—	2300
	YF	6038S	Automatic	29/64	—	120-404/—	#63	#70	19/64	1NR	—	2300
	AUTOLITE											
	2100	1DM2	Manual	3/8	3	50F/—	#63	#66	13/64	1NR	1/8	1600
	2100	1DA2	Automatic	3/8	3	49F/—	#66	#66	13/64	2NR	1/8	1600
	2100	1RA2	Automatic	3/8	3	55F/—	#65	#66	13/64	2NR	1/8	1600
	4300	1TM4	Manual	13/16	Center	62F/—	#68	#68	19/64	Index	1/16	1600
	4300	1TA4	Automatic	13/16	Center	62F/—	#70	#68	19/64	Index	1/8	1600
1972	**CARTER**											
	YF	6199S	Manual	29/64	—	120-401/—	#63	#70	19/64	Index	3/32	1600
	YF	6200S	Automatic	29/64	—	120-401/—	#64	#70	19/64	Index	—	1600
	AUTOLITE											
	2100	2DM2	Manual	3/8	3	48F/—	#70	#66	13/64	1NR	7/64	1600
	2100	2DA2	Automatic	3/8	3	47F/—	#70	#73	13/64	2NR	9/64	1600
	2100	2RA2	Automatic	3/8	3	47F/—	#70	#73	13/64	2NR	—	1600
	4300	2TM4	Manual	13/16	Center	61F/—	#71	#70	19/64	1NR	9/64	1600
	4300	2RA4	Automatic	13/16	Center	60F/—	#71	#68	19/64	1NR	—	1600
	4300	2TA4	Automatic	13/16	Center	60F/—	#71	#68	19/64	1NR	9/64	1600

AMERICAN MOTORS

Year	Carb. Model	Carb. Number	Dry Float Setting (Ins.)	Float Drop (Ins.)	Pump Setting Hole	Main Jet Number Or Size Pri./Sec.	Low Speed Jet Number Or Size	Pump Jet Number Or Size	Unloader (Ins.)	Choke Setting (Notches)	External Bowl Vent Opens On	Dashpot (Ins.)
1973	**Carter**											
	YF	6299S	29/64	1.38	—	120-401/—	66	70	9/32	1NR	—	3/32
	YF	6300S	29/64	1.38	—	120-401/—	66	70	9/32	1NR	—	3/32
	YF	6400S	29/64	1.38	—	120-398/—	64	70	9/32	1NR	—	3/32
	YF	6401S	29/64	1.38	—	120-401/—	64	70	9/32	1NR	—	3/32
	YF	6421S	29/64	1.38	—	120-401/—	64	70	9/32	1NR	—	3/32
	YF	6422S	29/64	1.38	—	120-398/—	64	70	9/32	1NR	—	3/32
	Autolite											
	2100	3DA2	3/8	–	A	46F/—	65	73	1/4	2NR	—	9/64
	2100	3DM2	3/8	–	A	47F/—	65	66	1/4	1NR	—	9/64
	2100	3RA2	3/8	–	A	46F/—	65	73	1/4	2NR	—	9/64
	4300	3TA4	3/16	–	Center	61F/—	68	68	9/32	2NR	—	9/64
	4300	3TM4	3/16	–	Center	61F/—	65	70	9/32	2NR	—	9/64
1974	**Carter**											
	YF	6423	.476	1.38	—	120-398/—	64	70	9/32	1NR	—	.095
	YF	6431	.476	1.38	—	120-401/—	64	70	9/32	1NR	—	.095
	YF	6510	.476	1.38	—	120-401/—	66	70	9/32	1NR	—	–
	YF	6511	.476	1.38	—	120-401/—	66	70	9/32	1NR	—	.095
	YF	7000	.476	1.38	—	120-401/—	64	70	9/32	1NR	—	–
	YF	7001	.476	1.38	—	120-401/—	64	70	9/32	1NR	—	–
	Motorcraft											
	2100	4DA2	.400	–	A	48/—	.035	.024	1/4	1NR	—	–
	2100	4DA2-E	.400	–	A	47/—	.035	.024	1/4	1NR	—	–
	2100	4DM2	.400	–	A	48/—	.035	.032	1/4	2NR	—	.140
	2100	4RA2	.400	–	A	47/—	.035	.024	1/4	1NR	—	–
	2100	4RAC-2	.400	–	A	47/—	.035	.024	1/4	1NR	—	–
	4300	4TA4	.820	.50	Center	62/—	.031	.031	9/32	2NR	—	.140
	4300	4TM4	.820	.50	Center	62/—	.031	.028	9/32	2NR	—	.140
1975	**Carter**											
	YF	7039	.476	1.38	—	120-401/—	.033	.028	.275	1NR	—	–
	YF	7041	.476	1.38	—	120-401/—	.033	.028	.275	1NR	—	.075
	YF	7061	.476	1.38	—	120-401/—	.033	.028	.275	1NR	—	–
	YF	7062	.476	1.38	—	120-401/—	.033	.028	.275	1NR	—	.075
	YF	7074	.476	1.38	—	120-401/—	.033	.028	.275	1NR	—	.075
	Motorcraft											
	2100	5DA2	13/32	–	3	47/—	.035	.024	.250	1NR	—	–
	2100	5DMS	13/32	–	3	47/—	.035	.032	.250	2NR	—	.093
	2100	5RAS	13/32	–	3	47/—	.035	.024	.250	1NR	—	–
	4350	5TA4	.900	–	Lower	.072/.144	.038	.026	.325	2NR	—	–

AMERICAN MOTORS

Year	Carb. Model	Carb. Number	Dry Float Setting (Ins.)	Float Drop (Ins.)	Pump Setting Hole	Main Jet Number Or Size Pri./Sec.	Low Speed Jet Number Or Size	Pump Jet Number Or Size	Unloader (Ins.)	Choke Setting (Notches)	External Bowl Vent Opens On	Dashpot (Ins.)
1976	**Carter**											
	YF	7083	.476	1 3/8	—	120-401/—	.036	.028	.275	1NR	1	—
	YF	7084	.476	1 3/8	—	120-401/—	.035	.024	.275	2NR	1	.075
	YF	7085	.476	1 3/8	—	120-401/—	.035	.028	.275	1NR	1	—
	YF	7086	.476	1 3/8	—	120-401/—	.033	.028	.275	2NR	1	—
	YF	7112	.476	1 3/8	—	120-401/—	.033	.028	.275	1NR	1	—
	BBD	8067	.250	—	—	120-389/—	.029	.032	.250	2NR	—	—
	BBD	8073	.250	—	—	120-389/—	.029	.032	.250	1NR	—	.104
	Motorcraft											
	2100	6DA2	13/32	—	3	48/—	.031	.024	.250	1NR	—	—
	2100	6DM2	35/64	—	3	47/—	.031	.032	.250	2NR	—	.075
	2100	6RA2	13/32	—	3	48/—	.031	.024	.250	1NR	—	—
	4350	6TA4	.900	—	Lower	.072/.144	.038	.026	.325	2NR	—	—
1977	**Carter**											
	YF	7151	.476	1 3/8	—	120-401/—	.035	.028	.275	1NR	1	—
	YF	7152	.476	1 3/8	—	120-401/—	.032	.024	.275	1NR	1	—
	YF	7153	.476	1 3/8	—	120-401/—	.035	.028	.275	Index	1	—
	YF	7195	.476	1 3/8	—	120-401/—	.031	.028	.275	1NR	1	—
	YF	7223	.476	1 3/8	—	120-401/—	.033	.0282	.275	Index	1	—
	YF	7111	.476	1 3/8	—	120-398/—	.033	.022	.275	2NR	1	—
	YF	7189	.476	1 3/8	—	120-398/—	.034	.022	.275	1NR	1	—
	BBD	8103	.250	—	—	120-389/—	.0295	.033	.280	1NR	—	—
	BBD	8104	.250	—	—	120-389/--	.0295	.033	.280	1NR	—	—
	BBD	8117	.250	—	—	120-392/—	.031	.033	.280	1NR	—	—
	Motorcraft											
	2100	7RA2	3	—	3	47/—	.031	.024	.250	1NR	—	—
	2100	7RA2C	3	—	3	47/—	.031	.024	.250	1NR	—	—
	2100	7DA2	3	—	3	47/—	.032	.024	.250	Index	—	—
	2150	7RA2A	3	—	3	48/—	.028	.028	.250	1NR	—	—
	Holley											
	5210	7711	.42	—	—	239/183	.022	—	.300	1NR	4	—
	5210	7712	.42	—	—	247/183	.022	—	.300	1NR	4	—
	5210	7799	.42	—	—	235/171	.022	—	.300	Index	4	—
	5210	7846	.42	—	—	NA/NA	.028	—	.300	1NR	4	—
1978	**Carter**											
	YF	7201	.476	1 3/8	—	120-401/—	.034	.028	.275	Index	3rd Step	—
	YF	7228	.476	1 3/8	—	120-401/—	.034	.028	.275	1NR	3rd Step	—
	YF	7229	.476	1 3/8	—	120-401/—	.032	.024	.275	1NR	3rd Step	—
	YF	7235	.476	1 3/8	—	120-401/—	.034	.028	.275	Index	3rd Step	—
	YF	7267	.476	1 3/8	—	120-401/—	.032	.028	.275	1NR	3rd Step	—
	YF	7232	.476	1 3/8	—	120-398/—	.033	.022	.275	2NR	3rd Step	—
	YF	7233	.476	1 3/8	—	120-398/—	.034	.022	.275	1NR	3rd Step	—
	BBD	8128	.250	—	—	120-389/—	.0295	.033	.280	Index	2nd Step	—
	BBD	8129	.250	—	—	120-389/—	.0295	.033	.280	1NR	2nd Step	—
	Motorcraft											
	2100	8DA2	.555	—	3	47/—	.032	.024	.250	Index	—	—
	2100	8RA2	.555	—	3	47/—	.031	.024	.250	1NR	—	—
	2100	8RA2C	.555	—	3	48/—	.029	.024	.250	1NR	—	—
	2150	8DA2A	.555	—	3	48/—	.029	.024	.170	2NR	—	—
	2150	8RA2A	.555	—	3	48/—	.028	.028	.170	2NR	—	—
	Holley											
	5210	8163	.42	—	—	239/183	.022	—	.300	1NR	—	—
	5210	8164	.42	—	—	247/183	.022	—	.300	1NR	—	—
	5210	8165	.42	—	—	235/171	.022	—	.300	Index	—	—
1979	**Carter**											
	YF	7228	.476	1 3/8	—	120-401/—	.034	.028	.275	1NR	3rd Step	—
	YF	7229	.476	1 3/8	—	120-401/—	.032	.024	.275	1NR	3rd Step	—
	BBD	8185	.250	—	—	120-389/—	.0295	.033	.280	1NR	2nd Step	—
	BBD	8186	.250	—	—	120-389/—	.0295	.033	.280	1NR	2nd Step	—
	BBD	8187	.250	—	—	120-389/—	.0295	.033	.280	1NR	2nd Step	—
	BBD	8221	.250	—	—	120-389/—	.0295	.033	.280	1NR	2nd Step	—
	Motorcraft											
	2100	9DA2	.313	—	3	45/—	.032	.024	.300	1NR	.120	—
	Holley											
	5210	8548	.42	—	—	243/179	.022	—	.300	1NR	—	—
	5210	8549	.42	—	—	239/183	.022	—	.300	1NR	—	—
	5210	7846	.42	—	—	235/191	.028	—	.300	1NR	—	—
	5210	8675	.42	—	—	235/171	.022	—	.300	Index	—	—

1 Pressure operated.
2 Thermostatic bleed; .024-in.
3 5/16-in. from machined surface to a point on float 1/8-in. from tip. Needle seated.
4 Vacuum operated.

BUICK

Year	Carb. Model	Trans.	Carb. Number	Float Level (ins.)	Float Drop (ins.)	Accel. Pump Rod (ins.)	Choke Rod (ins.)	Vacuum Break (ins.)	Choke Unloader (ins.)	Main Jet Pri./Sec.	Air Valve Spring (ins.)	Air Valve Dash Pot (ins.)	Fast Idle Speed (rpm)
1970	**ROCHESTER**												
	MV	Manual	7040015	1/4	—	—	.200	.275/—	.350	.106/—	—	—	900
	MV	Automatic	7040014	1/4	—	—	.170	.245/—	.350	.106/—	—	—	650
	2GV	Manual	7040143	15/32	1 7/8	1 15/32	.100	.190/—	.200	.061/—	—	—	7007
	2GV	Automatic	7040142	15/32	1 7/8	1 13/32	.080	.150/.140	.180	.060/—	—	—	6007
	2GV	Automatic (Calif.)	7040446	15/32	1 7/8	1 13/32	.080	.150/.140	.180	.059/—	—	—	6007
	4MV	Manual	7040245	5/16	—	13/32	.130	.215/—	.335	.073/—	1/2 turn	.030	7207
	4MV	Automatic	7040244	5/16	—	13/32	.130	.170/.150	.335	.069/—	1/2 turn	.030	6507
	4MV	Manual	7040243	3/8	—	9/32	.130	.215/.195	.335	.067/—	1/2 turn	.030	7207
	4MV	Automatic	7040240	3/8	—	9/32	.130	.180/.160	.335	.067/—	1/2 turn	.030	6507
	4MV	Stage 1	7040246	5/16	—	9/32	.130	.200/.180	.335	.068/—	1/2 turn	.030	6507
	4MV	Riviera	7040247	3/8	—	9/32	.130	.160/.160	.325	.067/—	1/2 turn	.030	6507
1971	MV	Manual	7041017	1/4	—	—	.180	.225/—	.350	.106/—	—	.050	5507
	MV	Automatic	7041014	1/4	—	—	.160	.225/—	.500	.106/—	—	.050	5007
	2GV	Manual	7040143	15/32	1 7/8	1 15/32	.080	.160/.140	.180	.060/—	—	—	8007

CARBURETOR SPECIFICATIONS

BUICK

Year	Carb. Model	Trans.	Carb. Number	Float Level (ins.)	Float Drop (ins.)	Accel. Pump Rod (ins.)	Choke Rod (ins.)	Vacuum Break (ins.)	Choke Unloader (ins.)	Main Jet Pri./Sec.	Air Valve Spring (ins.)	Air Valve Dash Pot (ins.)	Fast Idle Speed (rpm)
1971	2GV	Automatic	7041142	15/32	1 7/8	1 15/32	.080	.150/.140	.180	.059/—	—	—	6001
	2GV	Automatic	7041442	15/32	1 7/8	1 15/32	.080	.150/.140	.180	.059/—	—	—	6001
	4MV	Manual	7041245	15/32	—	9/32	.130	.170/.150	.335	.069/—	1/2 turn	.030	8201
	4MV	Automatic	7041544	15/32	—	9/32	.130	.170/.150	.335	.068/—	1/2 turn	.030	6501
	4MV	Manual	7041243	13/32	—	1/4	.130	.215/.195	.335	.073/—	1/2 turn	.030	7201
	4MV	Automatic	7041540	3/8	—	1/4	.130	.180/.160	.335	.073/—	1/2 turn	.030	6501
	4MV	Stage 1	7041242	3/8	—	1/4	.130	.200/.160	.335	.075/—	1/2 turn	.030	6501
1972	MV	Manual	7041017	1/4	—	—	.180	.225/—	* .350	.106/—	—	—	5501
	MV	Automatic	7041014	1/4	—	—	.160	.225/—	.500	.106/—	—	—	5501
	2GV	Manual	7079143	15/32	1 7/8	1 15/32	.080	.160/.140	.180	.060/—	—	—	8001
	2GV	Automatic	7042142	15/32	1 7/8	1 15/32	.080	.150/.140	.180	.059/—	—	—	6501
	2GV	Automatic	7042842	15/32	1 7/8	1 15/32	.080	.150/.140	.180	.059/—	—	—	6501
	4MV	Manual	7042245	15/32	—	9/32	.130	.170/.150	.335	.069/—	1/2 turn	.030	8201
	4MV	Automatic (Calif.)	7042944	15/32	—	9/32	130	.170/.150	.335	.068/—	1/2 turn	.030	7001
	4MV	Automatic	7042244	15/32	—	9/32	.130	.170/.150	.335	.068/—	1/2 turn	.030	7001
	4MV	Manual	7042243	13/32	—	1/4	.130	.215/.195	.335	.073/—	1/2 turn	.030	9201
	4MV	Automatic (Calif.)	7042940	3/8	—	1/4	.130	.180/.160	.335	.073/—	1/2 turn	.030	7001
	4MV	Automatic	7042240	3/8	—	1/4	.130	.180/.160	.335	.075/—	1/2 turn	.030	7001
	4MV	Stage 1 (Calif.)	7042942	3/8	—	1/4	.130	.200/.160	.335	.075/—	1/2 turn	.030	9201
	4MV	Stage 1	7042242	3/8	—	1/4	.130	.200/.160	.335	.075/—	1/2 turn	.030	7001

BUICK

YEAR	Carb. Model	Carb. Number	Float Level (Ins.)	Float Drop (Ins.)	Pump Rod (Ins.)	Choke Rod (Ins.)	Choke Lever (Ins.)	Choke Cover/Rod Setting	Choke Unloader (Ins.)	Air Valve Rod (Ins.)	Air Valve Spring (Turns)	Vacuum Break (Ins. or Degs.) Pri.(Front)/Sec.(Rear)	Secondary Opening/Closing (Ins.)	Secondary Lockout (Ins.)
1973 ROCHESTER														
	2GV	7043142	15/32	1 9/32	1 15/32	.080	—	—	.180	—	—	.140/.120	—/—	—
	2GV	7043143	15/32	1 9/32	1 15/32	.080	—	—	.200	—	—	.150/.120	—/—	—
	4MV	7043240	13/32	—	7/16	.130	—	—	—	—	7/16	.215/.160	.070/.020	—
	4MV	7043242	13/32	—	7/16	.130	—	—	—	—	7/16	.200/.180	.070/.020	—
	4MV	7043243	13/32	—	7/16	.130	—	—	—	—	7/16	.215/.195	.070/.020	—
	4MV	7043244	15/32	—	.306	.130	—	—	—	—	11/16	.170/.150	.070/.020	—
	4MV	7043245	15/32	—	.410	.130	—	—	—	—	11/16	.170/.150	.070/.020	—
1974	MV	—	1/4	—	—	.245	—	—	.500	—	—	.300/—	—/—	—
	MV	—	1/4	—	—	.275	—	—	.500	—	—	.350/—	—/—	—
	2GV	7044142	15/32	1 9/32	1 15/32	—	—	—	.180	—	—	.140/.120	—/—	—
	2GV	7044141	15/32	1 9/32	1 15/32	—	—	—	.180	—	—	.160/.120	—/—	—
	2GV	7044144	15/32	1 9/32	1 15/32	—	—	—	.180	—	—	.140/.120	—/—	—
	2GV	7044442	15/32	1 9/32	1 15/32	—	—	—	.180	—	—	.140/.120	—/—	—
	2GV	7044444	15/32	1 9/32	1 15/32	—	—	—	.180	—	—	.140/.120	—/—	—
	4MV	7044240	13/32	—	1/4	.130	—	—	—	—	7/16	.215/.160	.070/.020	—
	4MV	7044241	13/32	—	1/4	.130	—	—	—	—	7/16	.215/.160	.070/.020	—
	4MV	7044242	13/32	—	1/4	.130	—	—	—	—	7/16	.200/.180	.070/.020	—
	4MV	7044244	15/32	—	.306	.130	—	—	—	—	11/16	.170/.150	.070/.020	—
	4MV	7044246	15/32	—	.306	.130	—	—	—	—	11/16	.170/.150	.070/.020	—
	4MV	7044540	13/32	—	1/4	.130	—	—	—	—	7/16	.215/.160	.070/.020	—
	4MV	7044544	15/32	—	.306	.130	—	—	—	—	11/16	.170/.150	.070/.020	—
	4MV	7044546	15/32	—	.306	.130	—	—	—	—	11/16	.170/.150	.070/.020	—
1975	1MV	7045012	11/32	—	—	.160	—	1RL	.275	—	—	.200/.215	—/—	—
	1MV	7045013	11/32	—	—	.275	—	1RL	.275	—	—	.350/.312	—/—	—
	1MV	7045314	11/32	—	—	.230	—	1RL	.275	—	—	.275/.312	—/—	—
	2GC	7045140	15/32	1 9/32	1 3/4	—	—	1NR	.180	—	—	.140/.120	—/—	—
	2GC	7045143	15/32	1 9/32	1 3/4	—	—	1NR	.180	—	—	.140/.120	—/—	—
	2GC	7045145	13/32	1 9/32	1 3/4	—	—	Index	.140	—	—	.120/.120	—/—	—
	2GC	7045147	13/32	1 9/32	1 3/4	—	—	1NL	.140	—	—	.120/.120	—/—	—
	2GC	7045148	13/32	1 9/32	1 3/4	—	—	1NR	.140	—	—	.120/.120	—/—	—
	2GC	7045149	13/32	1 9/32	1 3/4	—	—	1NR	.140	—	—	.120/.120	—/—	—
	2GC	7045448	13/32	1 9/32	1 3/4	—	—	Index	.140	—	—	.120/.120	—/—	—
	2GC	7045449	13/32	1 9/32	1 3/4	—	—	1NL	.140	—	—	.120/.120	—/—	—
	2MC	7045156	5/32	—	9/32	.130	.120	1NR	.285	—	—	.150/.235	—/—	—
	2MC	7045298	5/32	—	9/32	.130	.120	1NR	.285	—	—	.150/.235	—/—	—
	2MC	7045354	3/16	—	5/16	.130	.120	1NR	.300	—	—	.300/.300	—/—	—
	2MC	7045358	3/16	—	5/16	.130	.120	1NR	.300	—	—	.300/.300	—/—	—
	M4MC	7045240	7/16	—	9/32	.095	—	1NR	.240	—	7/16	.135/.120	1/.020	—
	M4MC	7045244	5/16	—	15/32	.095	—	1NR	.240	—	3/4	.130/.115	1/.020	—
	M4MC	7045246	5/16	—	15/32	.095	—	1NR	.240	—	3/4	.130/.115	1/.020	—
	M4MC	7045264	1/2	—	9/32	.260	—	Index	.230	—	1/2	.150/.130	1/.020	—
	M4MC	7045544	5/16	—	15/32	.095	—	1NR	.240	—	3/4	.145/.130	1/.020	—
	M4MCA	7045541	7/16	—	9/32	.095	—	1NR	.240	—	7/16	.135/.120	1/.020	—
	M4MCA	7045548	7/16	—	9/32	.095	—	1NR	.240	—	7/16	.135/.120	1/.020	—
1976	2GC	17056140	15/32	1 5/32	1 11/32	.080	—	1NR	.180	—	—	.140/.100	—/—	—
	2GC	17056143	15/32	1 5/32	1 11/32	.080	—	1NR	.180	—	—	.140/.100	—/—	—
	2GC	17056145	7/16	1 5/32	1 19/32	.080	—	1NR	.140	—	—	.110/.100	—/—	—
	2GC	17056148	7/16	1 5/32	1 19/32	.080	—	1NR	.140	—	—	.120/.100	—/—	—
	2GC	17056149	7/16	1 5/32	1 19/32	.080	—	1NR	.140	—	—	.120/.100	—/—	—
	2GC	17056447	7/16	1 5/32	1 19/32	.080	—	1NR	.140	—	—	.130/.110	—/—	—
	2GC	17056448	7/16	1 5/32	1 19/32	.080	—	1NR	.140	—	—	.120/.100	—/—	—
	2GC	17056449	7/16	1 5/32	1 19/32	.080	—	1NR	.140	—	—	.120/.100	—/—	—
	2MC	17056156	1/8	—	9/32	.105	.120	1NR	.210	—	—	.110/.175	—/—	—
	2MC	17056158	1/8	—	9/32	.105	.120	1NR	.210	—	—	.110/.175	—/—	—
	2MC	17056454	1/8	—	3/16	.105	.120	1NR	.210	—	—	.110/.210	—/—	—
	2MC	17056455	1/8	—	9/32	.120	.120	1NR	.210	—	—	.130/.210	—/—	—
	2MC	17056458	1/8	—	3/16	.105	.120	1NR	.210	—	—	.110/.210	—/—	—
	M4MC	17056240	15/32	—	9/32	.095	.120	1NR	.250	—	7/16	.135/.120	1/.020	.015
	M4MC	17056244	5/16	—	3/8	.095	.120	1NR	.250	—	3/4	.130/.120	1/.020	.015
	M4MC	17056246	5/16	—	3/8	.095	.120	1NR	.250	—	3/4	.130/.120	1/.020	.015
	M4MC	17056540	15/32	—	3/8	.095	.120	1NR	.250	—	7/16	.135/.120	1/.020	.015
	M4MC	17056544	5/16	—	3/8	.095	.120	Index	.250	—	3/4	.130/.130	1/.020	.015
	M4MC	17056546	5/16	—	3/8	.095	.120	Index	.250	—	3/4	.130/.130	1/.020	.015
1977	2GC	17057108	19/32	1 5/32	1 1/16	.260	.120	1NR	.140	—	—	.140/.1302	—/—	—
	2GC	17057110	19/32	1 5/32	1 1/16	.260	.120	1NR	.140	—	—	—/.1302	—/—	—

BUICK

YEAR	Carb. Model	Carb. Number	Float Level (Ins.)	Float Drop (Ins.)	Pump Rod (Ins.)	Choke Rod (Ins.)	Choke Lever (Ins.)	Choke Cover/Rod Setting	Choke Unloader (Ins.)	Air Valve Rod (Ins.)	Air Valve Spring (Turns)	Vacuum Break (Ins. or Degs.) Pri.(Front)/Sec. (Rear)	Secondary Opening/Closing (Ins.)	Secondary Lockout (Ins.)
	2GC	17057140	15/32	1 5/32	1 9/16	.080	.120	1NR	.140	—	—	—/.100	—/—	—
	2GE	17057141	7/16	1 1/2	1 1/2	.080	.120	1NR	.140	—	—	.110/.040	—/—	—
	2GE	17057143	7/16	1 5/32	1 17/32	.080	.120	1NR	.140	—	—	.130/.100	—/—	—
	2GE	17057144	7/16	1 5/32	1 17/32	.080	.120	1NR	.140	—	—	.130/.100	—/—	—
	2GE	17057145	7/16	1 5/32	1 1/2	.080	.120	1NR	.140	—	—	.110/.040	—/—	—
	2GE	17057146	7/16	1 5/32	1 17/32	.080	.120	1NR	.140	—	—	.110/.040	—/—	—
	2GE	17057147	7/16	1 5/32	1 1/2	.080	.120	1NR	.140	—	—	.110/.040	—/—	—
	2GE	17057148	7/16	1 5/32	1 17/32	.080	.120	1NR	.140	—	—	.110/.040	—/—	—
	2GE	17057180	7/16	1 5/32	1 17/32	.080	.120	1NR	.140	—	—	.110/.060	—/—	—
	2GE	17057182	7/16	1 5/32	1 17/32	.080	.120	1NR	.140	—	—	.110/.060	—/—	—
	2GE	17057445	7/16	1 5/32	1 1/2	.080	.120	1NR	.140	—	—	.140/.110	—/—	—
	2GE	17057446	7/16	1 5/32	1 1/2	.080	.120	1NR	.140	—	—	.130/.110	—/—	—
	2GE	17057447	7/16	1 5/32	1 1/2	.080	.120	1NR	.140	—	—	.130/.100	—/—	—
	2GE	17057448	7/16	1 5/32	1 1/2	.080	.120	1NR	.140	—	—	.130/.110	—/—	—
	M2MC	17057172	11/32	— —	3/8	.075	.120	2NR	.240	—	—	.135/.2253	—/—	—
	M4MC	17057241	5/16	— —	3/8	.095	.120	1NR	.240	.015	3/4	—/—	1/.020	.015
	M4MC	17057248	5/16	— —	3/8	.095	.120	Index	.240	.015	3/4	.130/.110	1/.020	.015
	M4MC	17057250	13/32	— —	9/32	.100	.120	2NR	.220	.030	1/2	.135/.180	1/.020	.015
	M4MC	17057253	13/32	— —	9/32	.100	.120	2NR	.220	.030	1/2	.135/.180	1/.020	.015
	M4MC	17057255	13/32	— —	9/32	.100	.120	2NR	.220	.030	1/2	.135/.180	1/.020	.015
	M4MC	17057256	13/32	— —	9/32	.100	.120	2NR	.220	.030	1/2	.135/.180	1/.020	.015
	M4MC	17057550	13/32	— —	9/32	.100	.120	2NR	.220	.030	1/2	.215/.225	1/.020	.015
	M4MC	17057553	13/32	— —	9/32	.100	.120	2NR	.220	.030	1/2	.215/.225	1/.020	.015
	M4MC	17057202	15/32	— —	9/32	.325	.120	2NL	.220	.015	—	.160/—4	1/.020	.015
	M4MC	17057204	15/32	— —	9/32	.325	.120	2NL	.280	.015	7/8	.160/—4	1/.020	.015
	M4MC	17057502	15/32	— —	9/32	.325	.120	2NL	.280	.015	7/8	.165/—5	1/.20	.015
	M4MC	17057504	15/32	— —	9/32	.325	.120	2NL	.280	.015	7/8	.165/—5	1/.020	.015
	M4MC	17057582	15/32	— —	9/32	.325	.120	2NL	.280	.015	7/8	.180/—6	1/.020	.015
	M4MC	17057584	15/32	— —	9/32	.325	.120	2NL	.280	.015	7/8	.180/—6	1/.020	.015
	M4MC	17057258	13/32	— —	9/32	.100	.120	2NR	.220	.030	1/2	.215/.225	1/.020	.015
1978	2GC	17058104	15/32	1 9/32	1 21/32	.260	.120	Index	.325	—	—	—/.160	—/—	—
	2GC	17058105	15/32	1 9/32	1 21/32	.260	.120	Index	.325	—	—	—/.160	—/—	—
	2GC	17058108	19/32	1 9/32	1 21/32	.260	.120	Index	.325	—	—	—/.160	—/—	—
	2GC	17058110	19/32	1 9/32	1 21/32	.260	.120	Index	.325	—	—	—/.160	—/—	—
	2GC	17058112	19/32	1 9/32	1 21/32	.260	.120	Index	.325	—	—	—/.160	—/—	—
	2GC	17058114	19/32	1 9/32	1 21/32	.260	.120	Index	.325	—	—	—/.160	—/—	—
	2GC	17058126	19/32	1 9/32	1 17/32	.260	.120	Index	.325	—	—	—/.150	—/—	—
	2GC	17058128	19/32	1 9/32	1 17/32	.260	.120	Index	.325	—	—	—/.150	—/—	—
	2GC	17058404	1/2	1 9/32	1 21/32	.260	.120	1/2NL	.325	—	—	—/.160	—/—	—
	2GC	17058405	1/2	1 9/32	1 21/32	.260	.120	1/2NL	.325	—	—	—/.160	—/—	—
	2GC	17058408	21/32	1 9/32	1 21/32	.260	.120	1/2NL	.325	—	—	—/.160	—/—	—
	2GC	17058410	21/32	1 9/32	1 21/32	.260	.120	1/2NL	.325	—	—	—/.160	—/—	—
	2GC	17058412	21/32	1 9/32	1 21/32	.260	.120	1/2NL	.325	—	—	—/.160	—/—	—
	2GC	17058414	21/32	1 9/32	1 21/32	.260	.120	1/2NL	.325	—	—	—/.160	—/—	—
	2GE	17058140	7/16	1 5/32	1 19/32	.080	.120	1NR	.140	—	—	.110/.070	—/—	—
	2GE	17058143	7/16	1 5/32	1 9/16	.080	.120	1NR	.140	—	—	.110/.080	—/—	—
	2GE	17058144	7/16	1 5/32	1 5/8	.080	.120	1NR	.140	—	—	.110/.060	—/—	—
	2GE	17058145	7/16	1 5/32	1 19/32	.080	.120	1NR	.160	—	—	.110/.060	—/—	—
	2GE	17058148	7/16	1 5/32	1 19/32	.080	.120	1NR	.150	—	—	.110/.080	—/—	—
	2GE	17058149	7/16	1 5/32	1 19/32	.080	.120	1NR	.150	—	—	.110/.080	—/—	—
	2GE	17058141	7/16	1 5/32	1 19/32	.080	.120	1NR	.140	—	—	.140/.100	—/—	—
	2GE	17058147	7/16	1 5/32	1 19/32	.080	.120	1NR	.140	—	—	.140/.100	—/—	—
	2GE	17058182	7/16	1 5/32	1 19/32	.080	.120	1NR	.140	—	—	.110/.080	—/—	—
	2GE	17058183	7/16	1 5/32	1 19/32	.080	.120	1NR	.140	—	—	.110/.080	—/—	—
	2GE	17058188	7/16	1 5/32	1 5/8	.080	.120	1NR	.140	—	—	.140/.100	—/—	—
	2GE	17058444	7/16	1 5/32	1 19/32	.080	.120	1NR	.140	—	—	.130/.110	—/—	—
	2GE	17058446	7/16	1 5/32	1 19/32	.080	.120	1NR	.140	—	—	.150/.110	—/—	—
	2GE	17058447	7/16	1 5/32	1 19/32	.080	.120	1NR	.140	—	—	.140/.100	—/—	—
	2GE	17058448	7/16	1 5/32	1 9/16	.080	.120	1NR	.140	—	—	.110/.050	—/—	—
	2GE	17058185	7/16	1 5/32	1 19/32	.080	.120	1NR	.140	—	—	.110/.050	—/—	—
	2GE	17058187	7/16	1 5/32	1 19/32	.080	.120	1NR	.140	—	—	.110/.080	—/—	—
	2GE	17058189	7/16	1 5/32	1 19/32	.080	.120	1NR	.140	—	—	.120/.050	—/—	—
	M2MC	17058160	11/32	— —	1/4	.133	.120	2NL	.220	—	—	.149/.227	—/—	—
	M2ME	17058192	1/4	— —	9/32	.074	.120	1NR	.350	—	—	.117/.103	—/—	—
	M2ME	17058496	1/4	— —	3/8	.077	.120	1NR	.243	—	—	.136/.211	—/—	—
	M4ME	17058240	7/32	— —	9/32	.074	.120	Index	.243	.015	3/4	.117/.117	1/.020	.015
	M4ME	17058540	7/32	— —	9/32	.074	.120	Index	.243	.015	3/4	.117/.117	1/.020	.015
	M4ME	17058241	5/16	— —	3/8	.096	.120	1NR	.243	.015	3/4	.121/.103	1/.020	.015
	M4ME	17058250	13/32	— —	9/32	.096	.120	2NR	.220	.030	1/2	.129/.181	1/.020	.015
	M4ME	17058253	13/32	— —	9/32	.096	.120	2NR	.220	.030	1/2	.129/.181	1/.020	.015
	M4ME	17058257	13/32	— —	9/32	.103	.120	2NR	.220	.030	1/2	.136/.231	1/.020	.015
	M4ME	17058258	13/32	— —	9/32	.103	.120	2NR	.220	.030	1/2	.136/.231	1/.020	.015
	M4ME	17058550	13/32	— —	9/32	.103	.120	2NR	.220	.030	1/2	.136/.231	1/.020	.015
	M4ME	17058254	15/32	— —	9/32	.103	.120	3NR	.220	.030	1/2	.136/—	1/.020	.015
	M4ME	17058559	15/32	— —	9/32	.103	.120	3NR	.330	.030	1/2	.142/—	1/.020	.015
	M4ME	17058582	15/32	— —	9/32	.314	.120	2NL	.277	.015	7/8	.179/—	1/.020	.015
	M4ME	17058584	15/32	— —	9/32	.314	.120	2NL	.277	.015	7/8	.179/—	1/.020	.015
	M4ME	17058282	15/32	— —	9/32	.314	.120	Index	.277	.015	7/8	.157/—	1/.020	.015
	M4ME	17058284	15/32	— —	9/32	.314	.120	Index	.277	.015	7/8	.157/—	1/.020	.015
	M4ME	17058228	15/32	— —	9/32	.314	.120	2NL	.277	.015	1	.179/—	1/.020	.015
	M4ME	17058502	15/32	— —	9/32	.314	.120	2NL	.277	.015	7/8	.164/—	1/.020	.015
	M4ME	17058504	15/32	— —	9/32	.314	.120	2NL	.277	.015	7/8	.164/—	1/.020	.015
	M4ME	17058202	15/32	— —	9/32	.314	.120	2NL	.277	.015	7/8	.157/—	1/.020	.015
	M4ME	17058204	15/32	— —	9/32	.314	.120	2NL	.277	.015	7/8	.157/—	1/.020	.015
	M4ME	17058553	15/32	— —	9/32	.103	.120	2NR	.220	.030	1/2	.136/.231	1/.020	.015
1979	**ROCHESTER**													
	E2ME	17059496	5/16	— —	3/8	.139	.120	2NR	.243	—	—	.117/.179	—/—	—
	M2MC	17059134	15/32	— —	1/4	.243	.120	1NL	.243	—	—	.157/—	—/—	—
	M2MC	17059136	15/32	— —	1/4	.243	.120	1NL	.243	—	—	.157/—	—/—	—
	M2ME	17059193	13/32	— —	1/4	.139	.120	2NR	.220	—	—	.103/.090	—/—	—
	M2ME	17059194	11/32	— —	1/4	.139	.120	2NR	.220	—	—	.103/.090	—/—	—
	M2ME	17059190	11/32	— —	1/4	.139	.120	1NR	.243	—	—	.129/.117	—/—	—
	M2ME	17059191	11/32	— —	9/32	.139	.120	2NR	.243	—	—	.103/.103	—/—	—
	M2ME	17059491	11/32	— —	9/32	.139	.120	1NR	.277	—	—	.129/.117	—/—	—
	M2ME	17059492	11/32	— —	9/32	.139	.120	2NR	.277	—	—	.129/.117	—/—	—
	M2ME	17059196	11/32	— —	1/4	.139	.120	2NR	.277	—	—	.103/.090	—/—	—
	M2ME	17059498	11/32	— —	9/32	.139	.120	2NR	.277	—	—	.103/.090	—/—	—
	M2ME	17059180	11/32	— —	1/4	.139	.120	2NR	.243	—	—	.103/.090	—/—	—
	M2ME	17059184	11/32	— —	1/4	.139	.120	2NR	.220	—	—	.103/.090	—/—	—
	M4ME	17059240	7/32	— —	9/32	.074	.120	1NR	.179	.015	3/4	.117/.117	1/.020	.015
	M4ME	17059243	7/32	— —	9/32	.074	.120	1NR	.179	.015	3/4	.117/.117	1/.020	.015
	M4ME	17059241	5/16	— —	3/8	.096	.120	1NR	.243	.015	3/4	.120/.113	1/.020	.015
	M4ME	17059540	7/32	— —	9/32	.074	.120	1NR	.243	.015	3/4	.117/.129	1/.020	.015
	M4ME	17059543	7/32	— —	9/32	.074	.120	1NR	.243	.015	3/4	.117/.129	1/.020	.015
	M4MC	17059553	13/32	— —	9/32	.103	.120	2NR	.220	.030	1/2	.136/.231	1/.020	.015
	M4MC	17059555	13/32	— —	9/32	.103	.120	2NR	.220	.030	1/2	.149/.231	1/.020	.015
	M4MC	17059250	13/32	— —	9/32	.096	.120	2NR	.220	.030	1/2	.129/.183	1/.020	.015
	M4MC	17059253	13/32	— —	9/32	.096	.120	2NR	.220	.030	1/2	.129/.183	1/.020	.015
	M4MC	17059208	15/32	— —	9/32	.314	.120	1NL	.277	.030	7/8	—/.129	1/.020	.015

CARBURETOR SPECIFICATIONS

BUICK

YEAR	Carb. Model	Carb. Number	Float Level (Ins.)	Float Drop (Ins.)	Pump Rod (Ins.)	Choke Rod (Ins.)	Choke Lever (Ins.)	Choke Cover/Rod Setting	Choke Unloader (Ins.)	Air Valve Rod (Ins.)	Air Valve Spring (Turns)	Vacuum Break (Ins. or Degs.) Pri.(Front)/ Sec. (Rear)	Secondary Opening/Closing (Ins.)	Secondary Lockout (Ins.)
1979	M4MC	17059209	15/32	--	9/32	.314	.120	1NL	.277	.030	7/8	—/.129	1/.020	.015
	M4MC	17059210	15/32	--	9/32	.243	.120	1NL	.243	.030	1	.157/—	1/.020	.015
	M4MC	17059211	15/32	--	9/32	.243	.120	2NL	.243	.030	1	.157/—	1/.020	.015
	M4MC	17059228	15/32	--	9/32	.243	.120	1NL	.243	.030	1	.157/—	1/.020	.015

1Center of slot.
2.160 after 22,500 miles.
3.240 after 22,500 miles.
4.245 after 22,500 miles.
5.260 after 22,500 miles.
6.275 after 22,500 miles.
7In Drive, low step of cam.

CADILLAC

Year	Carburetor Model	Carburetor Number	Float Level (in.)	Choke Rod (in.)	Choke Setting	Accel. Pump Rod (in.)	Choke Unloader (in.)	Air Valve Spring (in.)	Air Valve Lockout (in.)	Air Valve Dashpot (in.)	Secondary Throttle Closing Adj. (in.)	Vacuum Break (in.)	Fast Idle Speed (rpm)
1970	ROCHESTER 4MV	7047030	.2404	.090	Index	.344	.300	1/2 Turn	.015	.030	.020	.235	1900-1950
1971	4MV	7041766	.2404	.090	Index	.344	.300	1/2 Turn	.015	.030	.020	.300	1900-1950
1972	4MV	7047231	.2604	.090	Index	.344	.310	9/16 Turn	.015	.030	.020	.140	1900-1950

CADILLAC

Year	Carb. Model	Carb. Number	Float Level (Ins.)	Pump Rod (Ins.)	Choke Rod (Ins.)	Choke Lever (Ins.)	Choke Unloader (Ins.)	Choke Setting (Notches)	Air Valve Spring (Turns)	Air Valve Rod/Dashpot (Ins.)	Secondary Opening/Closing (Ins.)	Secondary Lockout (Ins.)	Vacuum Break Front/Rear Rear (Ins.)
1973	ROCHESTER 4MV	7047331	.2604	.344	.090	—	.310	Index	5/162	.030	1/.020	—	3.200/—
1974	4MV	7044230	1/4	1/4	.110	—	5/16	Index	1/2	.030	1/.020	—	.185/—
	4MV	7044232	23/64	1/4	.110	—	5/16	Index	1/2	.030	1/.020	—	.200/—
	4MV	7044234	1/4	11/32	.110	—	5/16	Index	7/16	.030	1/.020	—	.185/—
	4MV	7044235	23/64	11/32	.110	—	5/16	Index	9/16	.030	1/.020	—	.200/—
	4MV	7044530	1/4	1/4	.110	—	5/16	Index	3/8	.030	1/.020	—	.185/—
	4MV	7044532	23/64	1/4	.110	—	5/16	Index	1/2	.030	1/.020	—	.200/—
1975	M4MEA	7045230	15/32	3/8	.080	.120	.215	2NR	7/16	.030	1/.020	.015	.160/.130
	M4MEA	7045530	15/32	3/8	.080	.120	215	1NR	1/2	.030	1/1.020	.015	.23/.230
1976	M4ME	7056230	13/32	3/8	.080	.120	230	2NR	3/8	.030	1/.020	.015	.160/.160
	M4ME	7056530	7/16	9/32	.080	.120	230	2NR	3/8	.030	1/.020	.015	.160/.160
	M4MEA	7056232	13/32	3/8	.080	.120	230	2NR	3/8	.030	1/.020	.015	.160/.160
1977	M4ME	17057230	13/32	7/16	.080	.120	230	2NR	1/2	.030	1/.020	.015	.14/.120
	M4ME	17057231	17/32	3/8	.080	.120	230	2NR	1/2	.030	1/.020	.015	.140/.140
	M4ME	17057530	13/32	7/16	.080	.120	230	2NR	1/2	.030	1/.020	.015	.150/.150
	M4ME	17057533	13/32	7/16	.080	.120	230	2NR	1/2	.030	1/.020	.015	.150/.150
	M4MEA	17057232	13/32	3/8	.080	.120	230	2NR	1/2	.030	1/.020	.015	.140/.120
	M4MEA	17057233	13/32	3/8	.080	.120	.230	2NR	1/2	.030	1/.020	.015	.140/.140
1978	M4ME	17058232	13/32	3/8	.080	.120	.230	2NR	1/2	.030	1/.020	.015	.150/.165
	M4ME	17058233	13/32	3/8	.080	.120	.230	2NR	1/2	.030	1/.020	.015	.150/.165
	M4ME	17058530	13/32	3/8	.080	.120	.230	2NR	1/2	.030	1/.020	.015	.150/.165
	M4ME	17058531	13/32	3/8	.080	.120	.230	2NR	1/2	.030	1/.020	.015	.150/.165
	M4ME	17058532	13/32	3/8	.080	.120	.230	2NR	1/2	.030	1/.020	.015	.150/.165
	M4ME	17058533	13/32	3/8	.080	.120	.230	2NR	1/2	.030	1/.020	.015	.150/.165
	M4ME	17058535	13/32	3/8	.080	.120	.230	2NR	1/2	.030	1/.020	.015	.150/.165
1979	M4ME	17059230	13/32	9/32	.080	.120	.142	2NL	1/2	.030	1/.020	.015	.142/.234
	M4ME	17059232	13/32	9/32	.080	.120	.142	2NL	1/2	.030	1/.020	.015	.149/.164
	M4ME	17059530	13/32	9/32	.080	.120	.142	2NL	1/2	.030	1/.020	.015	.149/.164
	M4ME	17059532	13/32	9/32	.080	.120	.142	2NL	1/2	.030	1/.020	.015	.149/.164

1 Center of slot.
2 Eldorado 3/8 turn
3 Eldorado .205
4 Eldorado .360

CHEVROLET

Year	Carb. Model	Trans.	Carb. Number	Float Level (ins.)	Float Drop (ins.)	Accel. Pump Rod (ins.)	Choke Rod (ins.)	Vacuum Break (ins.)	Choke Unloader (ins.)	Main Jet Pri./Sec.	Air Valve Dash Pot (ins.)	Idle Vent (ins.)	Fast Idle Speed (rpm)
1970	ROCHESTER M	All	7040011	1/4	—	—	.150	—	—	.106/—	—	.050	2400
	M	All	7040012	1/4	—	—	.150	—	—	.128/—	—	.050	2400
	M	All	7040008	1/4	—	—	.200	—	—	.092/—	—	.50	2400
	MV	All	7040002	1/4	—	—	.190	.230	.350	.104/—	—	.050	2400
	MV	All	7040025	1/4	—	—	.180	.260	.350	.106/—	—	.050	2400
	MV	All	7040022	1/4	—	—	.275	.350	.350	.128/—	—	.050	2400
	MV	All	7040026	1/4	—	—	.275	.350	.350	.128/—	—	.050	2400
	MV	Auto.	7040014	1/4	—	—	.170	.200	.350	.104/—	—	.50	2400
	MV	Man.	7040017	1/4	—	—	.190	.225	.350	.104/—	—	.50	2400
	2GV (1 1/4")	Auto.	7040125	23/32	1 3/4	1 3/8	.100	.140	.325	.049/—	—	.027	2200-2400
	2GV (1 1/4")	Man.	7040105	23/32	1 3/4	1 3/8	.100	.140	.325	.051/—	—	.027	2200-2400
	2GV (1 1/4")	All	7040108	27/32	1 3/4	1 3/8	.095	.130	.215	.052/—	—	.027	2200-2400

CHEVROLET

Year	Carb. Model	Trans.	Carb. Number	Float Level (Ins.)	Float Drop (Ins.)	Accel. Pump Rod (Ins.)	Choke Rod (Ins.)	Vacuum Break (Ins.)	Choke Unloader (Ins.)	Main Jet Pri./Sec.	Air Valve Dash Pot (Ins.)	Idle Vent (Ins.)	Fast Idle Speed (rpm)
	2GV (1 1/4")	Auto.	7040110	27/32	1 3/4	1 1/8	.060	.100	.215	.051/—	—	.020	2200-2400
	2GV (1 1/4")	Auto.	7040112	27/32	1 3/4	1 1/8	.060	.100	.215	.051/—	—	.020	2200-2400
	2GV (1 1/4")	Man.	7040101	27/32	1 3/4	1 1/8	.060	.125	.160	.051/—	—	.020	2200-2400
	2GV (1 1/4")	Man.	7040103	27/32	1 3/4	1 1/8	.060	.125	.160	.051/—	—	.020	2200-2400
	2G	All	7040123	23/32	1 3/4	1 17/32	—	—	—	.066/—	—	.020	2200-2400
	2G	All	7040124	23/32	1 3/4	1 17/32	—	—	—	.067/—	—	.020	2200-2400
	2GV (1 1/2")	Auto.	7040114	23/32	1 3/8	1 17/32	.085	.200	.325	.060/—	—	.020	2200-2400
	2GV (1 1/2")	Auto.	7040116	23/32	1 3/8	1 17/32	.085	.200	.325	.060/—	—	.020	2200-2400
	2GV (1 1/2")	Man.	7040113	23/32	1 3/8	1 17/32	.085	.215	.275	.059/—	—	.020	2200-2400
	2GV (1 1/2")	Man.	7040115	23/32	1 3/8	1 17/32	.085	.215	.275	.059/—	—	.020	2200-2400
	2GV (1 1/2")	Auto.	7040118	23/32	1 3/8	1 17/32	.085	.215	.325	.066/—	—	.020	2200-2400
	2GV (1 1/2")	Auto.	7040120	23/32	1 3/8	1 17/32	.085	.215	.325	.066/—	—	.020	2200-2400
	2GV (1 1/2")	Man.	7040117	23/32	1 3/8	1 17/32	.085	.215	.325	.069/—	—	.020	2200-2400
	2GV (1 1/2")	Man.	7040119	23/32	1 3/8	1 17/32	.085	.215	.325	.069/—	—	.020	2200-2400
	4MV	Auto.	7040202	1/4	—	5/16	.100	.245	.450	.076/—	.020	—	2400
	4MV	Man.	7040203	1/4	—	5/16	.100	.275	.450	.076/—	.020	—	2400
	4MV	Man.	7040207	1/4	—	5/16	.100	.275	.450	.076/—	.015	—	2400
	4MV	Auto.	7040200	1/4	—	5/16	.100	.245	.450	.078/—	.020	—	2400
	4MV	Man.	7040201	1/4	—	5/16	.100	.275	.450	.078/—	.020	—	2400
	4MV	Auto.	7040204	1/4	—	5/16	.100	.245	.450	.078/—	.020	—	2400
	4MV	Man.	7040205	1/4	—	5/16	.100	.275	.450	.078/—	.020	—	2400
HOLLEY													
	2300	Man.	3940929	.350	—	.015	—	.275	.250	#63/—	—	.085	2200
	2300	All	3902353	.350	—	.015	—	—	—	#76/—	—	—	2200
	2300	Auto.	3940930	.350	—	.015	—	.250	.250	#61/—	—	.085	2200
	4150	All	3959164	.350/.50	—	.015	—	.300	.350	#68/76	—	—	2200
	4150	All	3955205	.350/.50	—	.015	—	.350	.350	#82-#78-#80-#82	—	—	2200
	4150	Auto.	3969898	.350	—	.015	—	.350	.350	#70/#76	—	—	2200
	4150	Man.	3967477	.350	—	.015	—	.350	.350	#70/#76	—	—	2200
1971 ROCHESTER													
	MV	Auto.	7041014	1/4	—	—	.160	.200	.350	—/—	—	—	—
	MV	Man.	7041017	1/4	—	—	.180	.230	.350	—/—	—	—	—
	MV	Man.	7041023	1/16	—	—	.120	.200	.350	—/—	—	—	—
	2GV	Auto.	7041024	1/16	—	—	.080	.140	.350	—/—	—	—	—
	2GV	Man.	7041101	13/16	1 3/4	1 3/64	.075	.110	.215	—/—	—	—	—
	2GV	Auto.	7041110	13/16	1 3/4	1 3/64	.040	.080	.215	—/—	—	—	—
	2GV	Auto.	7041102	25/32	1 3/8	1 5/32	.100	.170	.325	—/—	—	—	—
	2GV	Auto.	7041114	25/32	1 3/8	1 5/32	.100	.170	.325	—/—	—	—	—
	2GV	Man.	7041113	23/32	1 3/8	1 5/32	.100	.180	.325	—/—	—	—	—
	2GV	Man.	7041127	23/32	1 3/8	1 5/32	.100	.180	.325	—/—	—	—	—
	2GV	Man.	7041117	23/32	1 3/8	1 5/32	.100	.170	.325	—/—	—	—	—
	2GV	Auto.	7041118	23/32	1 3/8	1 5/32	.100	.170	.325	—/—	—	—	—
	2GV	Man.	7041181	5/8	1 3/4	1 3/8	.080	.120	.180	—/—	—	—	—
	2GV	Auto.	7041182	5/8	1 3/4	1 3/8	.080	.120	.180	—/—	—	—	—
	4MV	Auto.	7041200	1/4	—	—	.100	.260	—	—/—	.020	—	—
	4MV	Auto.	7041202	1/4	—	—	.100	.260	—	—/—	.020	—	—
	4MV	Auto.	7041204	1/4	—	—	.100	.260	—	—/—	.020	—	—
	4MV	Auto.	7041212	1/4	—	—	.100	.260	—	—/—	.020	—	—
	4MV	Man.	7041201	1/4	—	—	.100	.275	—	—/—	.020	—	—
	4MV	Man.	7041203	1/4	—	—	.100	.275	—	—/—	.020	—	—
	4MV	Man.	7041205	1/4	—	—	.100	.275	—	—/—	.020	—	—
	4MV	Man.	7041213	1/4	—	—	.100	.275	—	—/—	.020	—	—
HOLLEY													
	4150	Auto.	3989022 (R-4800A)	6	—	.015₂	—	.350	.350	#70/#76	—	—	2200
	4150	Man.	3989021 (R-4801A)	6	—	.015₂	—	.350	.350	#70/#76	—	—	2200
	4150	Auto.	3986196 (R-4802A)	6	—	.015₂	—	.350	.350	#70/#76	—	—	2200
	4150	Man.	3986195 (R-4803A)	6	—	.015₂	—	.350	.350	#70/#76	—	—	2200
1972 ROCHESTER													
	MV	Auto.	7042014	1/4	—	—	.125	.190	.500	—/—	—	—	2400
	MV	Auto.	7042984	1/4	—	—	.125	.190	.500	—/—	—	—	2400
	MV	Man.	7042017	1/4	—	—	.150	.225	.500	—/—	—	—	2400
	MV	Man.	7042987	1/4	—	—	.150	.225	.500	—/—	—	—	2400
	2GV	Man.	7042111	19/32	19/32	1 1/2	.100	.180	.325	—/—	—	—	1850₃
	2GV	Man.	7042113	19/32	19/32	1 1/2	.100	.180	.325	—/—	—	—	1850₃
	2GV	Man.	7042831	23/32	19/32	1 1/2	.100	.180	.325	—/—	—	—	1850₃
	2GV	Man.	7042833	23/32	19/32	1 1/2	.100	.180	.325	—/—	—	—	1850₃
	2GV	Auto.	7042112	19/32	19/32	1 1/2	.100	.170	.325	—/—	—	—	1850₃
	2GV	Auto.	7042114	19/32	19/32	1 1/2	.100	.170	.325	—/—	—	—	1850₃
	2GV	Auto.	7042118	19/32	19/32	1 1/2	.100	.190	.325	—/—	—	—	1850₃
	2GV	Auto.	7042832	23/32	19/32	1 1/2	.100	.170	.325	—/—	—	—	1850₃
	2GV	Auto.	7042834	23/32	19/32	1 1/2	.100	.170	.325	—/—	—	—	1850₃
	2GV	Auto.	7042838	23/32	19/32	1 1/2	.100	.190	.325	—/—	—	—	1850₃
	2GV	Auto.	7042100	21-32	1 31/32	1 5/16	.040	.080	.215	—/—	—	—	1500₄
	2GV	Auto.	7042820	25/32	1 31/32	1 5/16	.040	.080	.215	—/—	—	—	1500₄
	2GV	Man.	7042101	25/32	1 31/32	1 5/16	.075	.110	.215	—/—	—	—	1350₄
	2GV	Man.	7042821	25/32	1 31/32	1 5/16	.075	.110	.215	—/—	—	—	1350₄
	4MV	Auto.	7042220	1/4	—	3/8	.100	.250	.450	—/—	.020	—	1500₄
	4MV	Auto.	7042216	1/4	—	3/8	.100	.250	.450	—/—	.020	—	1500₄
	4MV	Man.	7042215	1/4	—	3/8	.100	.250	.450	—/—	.020	—	1350₄
	4MV	Man.	7042217	1/4	—	3/8	.100	.250	.450	—/—	.020	—	1350₄
	4MV	Auto.	7042202	1/4	—	3/8	.100	.215	.450	—/—	.020	—	1500₄
	4MV	Auto.	7042203	1/4	—	3/8	.100	.215	.450	—/—	.020	—	1350₄
	4MV	Auto.	7042902	1/4	—	3/8	.100	.215	.450	—/—	.020	—	1500₄
	4MV	Man.	7042903	1/4	—	3/8	.100	.215	.450	—/—	.020	—	1350₄
HOLLEY													
	4150	Auto.	3997788 (R-6233A)	6	—	.015₂	—	.350	.350	#68/#73	—	—	2350₅
	4150	Man.	3999263 (R-6239A)	6	—	.015₂	—	.350	.350	#68/#73	—	—	2350₅

CHEVROLET

Year	Carb. Model	Carb. Number	Float Level (Ins.)	Float Drop (Ins.)	Pump Rod (Ins.)	Choke Rod (Ins.)	Choke Lever (Ins.)	Choke Unloader (Ins.)	Choke Setting (Notches)	Vacuum Break Pri.(front)/Sec.(rear) (Ins.)	Secondary Open/Close (Ins.)	Air Valve Dashpot/Rod (Ins.)	Air Valve Spring (Turns)
1973 ROCHESTER													
	MV	7043014	1/4	--	--	.245	--	.500	--	.300/—	--	--	--
	MV	7043017	1/4	--	--	.275	--	.500	--	.350/—	--	--	--
	MV	7043023	.060	--	--	.110	--	.375	--	.140/—	--	--	--

CARBUROR SPECIFICATIONS

CARBURETOR SPECIFICATIONS

CHEVROLET

Year	Carb. Model	Carb. Number	Float Level (Ins.)	Float Drop (Ins.)	Pump Rod (Ins.)	Choke Rod (Ins.)	Choke Lever (Ins.)	Choke Unloader (Ins.)	Choke Setting (Notches)	Vacuum Break Pri.(front)/Sec.(rear) (Ins.)	Secondary Open/Close (Ins.)	Air Valve Dashpot/Rod (Ins.)	Air Valve Spring (Turns)
1973	MV	7043024	.060	--	--	.085	--	.375	--	.120/—	--	--	--
	MV	7043033	.060	--	--	.110	--	.375	--	.140/—	--	--	--
	MV	7043034	.060	--	--	.085	--	.375	--	.110/—	--	--	--
	MV	7043323	.060	--	--	.110	--	.375	--	.140/—	--	--	--
	MV	7043324	.060	--	--	.085	--	.375	--	.110/—	--	--	--
	MV	7043333	.060	--	--	.110	--	.375	--	.140/—	--	--	--
	MV	7043334	.060	--	--	.085	--	.375	--	.110/—	--	--	--
	2GV	7043100	21/32	1 9/32	1 5/16	.150	--	.215	--	.080/—	--	--	--
	2GV	7043101	21/32	1 9/32	1 5/16	.150	--	.215	--	.080/—	--	--	--
	2GV	7043105	21/32	1 9/32	1 5/16	.150	--	.215	--	.080/—	--	--	--
	2GV	7043111	19/32	1 9/32	1 7/16	.200	--	.250	--	.140/—	--	--	--
	2GV	7043112	19/32	1 9/32	1 7/16	.245	--	.325	--	.130/—	--	--	--
	2GV	7043113	19/32	1 9/32	1 7/16	.200	--	.250	--	.140/—	--	--	--
	2GV	7043114	19/32	1 9/32	1 7/16	.245	--	.325	--	.130/—	--	--	--
	2GV	7043118	19/32	1 9/32	1 7/16	.245	--	.325	--	.130/—	--	--	--
	2GV	7043120	21/32	1 9/32	1 5/16	.150	--	.215	--	.080/—	--	--	--
	4MV	7043200	1/4	--	13/32	.430	--	.450	--	.250/—	1/.020	.015	11/16
	4MV	7043201	1/4	--	13/32	.430	--	.450	--	.250/—	1/.020	.015	11/16
	4MV	7043202	7/32	--	13/32	.430	--	.450	--	.250/—	1/.020	.015	1/2
	4MV	7043203	7/32	--	13/32	.430	--	.450	--	.250/—	1/.020	.015	1/2
	4MV	7043212	7/32	--	13/32	.430	--	.450	--	.250/—	1/.020	.015	3/4
	4MV	7043213	7/32	--	13/32	.430	--	.450	--	.250/—	1/.020	.015	3/4
	HOLLEY												
	5210-C	331156	.420	1 ± 1/8	--	--	--	--	2NR	.300/—	--	--	--
	5210-C	331157	.420	1 ± 1/8	--	--	--	--	1NR	.300/—	--	--	--
	5210-C	331158	.420	1 ± 1/8	--	--	--	--	2NR	.300/—	--	--	--
	5210-C	331159	.420	1 ± 1/8	--	--	--	--	1NR	.300/—	--	--	--
1974	**ROCHESTER**												
	MV	7044014	.295	--	--	.230	--	.500	--	.275/—	--	--	--
	MV	7044017	.295	--	--	.275	--	.500	--	.350/—	--	--	--
	MV	7044023	.060	--	--	.080	--	.375	--	.130/—	--	--	--
	MV	7044024	.060	--	--	.080	--	.375	--	.130/—	--	--	--
	MV	7044033	.060	--	--	.080	--	.375	--	.130/—	--	--	--
	MV	7044034	.060	--	--	.080	--	.375	--	.130/—	--	--	--
	MV	7044314	.295	--	--	.245	--	.500	--	.300/—	--	--	--
	MV	7044323	.060	--	--	.080	--	.375	--	.130/—	--	--	--
	MV	7044324	.060	--	--	.080	--	.375	--	.130/—	--	--	--
	MV	7044333	.060	--	--	.080	--	.375	--	.130/—	--	--	--
	MV	7044334	.060	--	--	.080	--	.375	--	.130/—	--	--	--
	2GV	7044111	19/32	1 9/32	1 9/32	.200	--	.250	--	.140/—	--	--	--
	2GV	7044112	19/32	1 9/32	1 3/16	.245	--	.325	--	.130/—	--	--	--
	2GV	7044113	19/32	1 9/32	1 9/32	.200	--	.250	--	.140/—	--	--	--
	2GV	7044114	19/32	1 9/32	1 3/16	.245	--	.350	--	.130/—	--	--	--
	2GV	7044115	19/32	1 9/32	1 9/32	.200	--	.250	--	.140/—	--	--	--
	2GV	7044116	19/32	1 9/32	1 3/16	.245	--	.325	--	.130/—	--	--	--
	2GV	7044118	19/32	1 9/32	1 3/16	.245	--	.325	--	.130/—	--	--	--
	2GV	7044123	19/32	1 9/32	1 9/32	.200	--	.250	--	.140/—	--	--	--
	2GV	7044124	19/32	1 9/32	1 3/16	.245	--	.325	--	.130/—	--	--	--
	4MV	7044201	3/8	--	13/32	.430	--	.450	--	.250/—	1/.020	.015	7/16
	4MV	7044202	1/4	--	13/32	.430	--	.450	--	.230/—	1/.020	.015	7/8
	4MV	7044203	1/4	--	13/32	.430	--	.450	--	.230/—	1/.020	.015	7/8
	4MV	7044206	1/4	--	13/32	.430	--	.450	--	.230/—	1/.020	.015	7/8
	4MV	7044207	1/4	--	13/32	.430	--	.450	--	.230/—	1/.020	.015	7/8
	4MV	7044208	1/4	--	13/32	.430	--	.450	--	.230/—	1/.020	.015	1
	4MV	7044209	1/4	--	13/32	.430	--	.450	--	.230/—	1/.020	.015	1
	4MV	7044210	1/4	--	13/32	.430	--	.450	--	.230/—	1/.020	.015	1
	4MV	7044211	1/4	--	13/32	.430	--	.450	--	.230/—	1/.020	.015	1
	4MV	7044223	3/8	--	13/32	.430	--	.450	--	.220/—	1/.020	.015	7/16
	4MV	7044500	3/8	--	13/32	.430	--	.450	--	.250/—	1/.020	.015	7/16
	4MV	7044502	1/4	--	13/32	.430	--	.450	--	.230/—	1/.020	.015	7/8
	4MV	7044503	1/4	--	13/32	.430	--	.450	--	.230/—	1/.020	.015	7/8
	4MV	7044506	1/4	--	13/32	.430	--	.450	--	.230/—	1/.020	.015	7/8
	4MV	7044507	1/4	--	13/32	.430	--	.450	--	.230/—	1/.020	.015	7/8
	HOLLEY												
	5210-C	338168	.420	1 ± 1/8	--	--	--	--	3 1/2NR	.400/—	--	--	--
	5210-C	338170	.420	1 ± 1/8	--	--	--	--	3 1/2NR	.400/—	--	--	--
	5210-C	338179	.420	1 ± 1/8	--	--	--	--	2 1/2NR	.300/—	--	--	--
	5210-C	338181	.420	1 ± 1/8	--	--	--	--	2 1/2NR	.300/—	--	--	--
1975	**ROCHESTER**												
	1MV	7045012	11/32	--	--	.160	--	.215	--	.200/.215	--	--	--
	1MV	7045013	11/32	--	--	.275	--	.275	--	.350/.312	--	--	--
	1MV	7045014	11/32	--	--	.230	--	.275	--	.275/.312	--	--	--
	1MV	7045024	1/8	--	--	.080	--	.375	--	.100/.450	--	--	--
	1MV	7045025	1/8	--	--	.080	--	.375	--	.100/.450	--	--	--
	1MV	7045028	1/8	--	--	.080	--	.375	--	.100/.450	--	--	--
	1MV	7045029	1/8	--	--	.080	--	.375	--	.100/.450	--	--	--
	2GC	7045101	19/32	1 7/32	1 19/32	.375	--	.350	--	.130/—	--	--	--
	2GC	7045102	19/32	1 7/32	1 19/32	.380	--	.350	--	.130/—	--	--	--
	2GC	7045105	19/32	1 7/32	1 19/32	.375	--	.350	--	.130/—	--	--	--
	2GC	7045106	19/32	1 7/32	1 19/32	.380	--	.350	--	.130/—	--	--	--
	2GC	7045111	21/32	31/32	1 5/8	.400	--	.350	--	.130/—	--	--	--
	2GC	7045112	21/32	31/32	1 5/8	.400	--	.350	--	.130/—	--	--	--
	2GC	7045114	21/32	31/32	1 5/8	.400	--	.350	--	.130/—	--	--	--
	2GC	7045115	21/32	31/32	1 5/8	.400	--	.350	--	.130/—	--	--	--
	2GC	7045123	21/32	31/32	1 5/8	.400	--	.350	--	.130/—	--	--	--
	2GC	7045124	21/32	31/32	1 5/8	.400	--	.350	--	.130/—	--	--	--
	2GC	7045401	21/32	1 7/32	1 19/32	.380	--	.350	--	.130/—	--	--	--
	2GC	7045405	21/32	1 7/32	1 19/32	.380	--	.350	--	.130/—	--	--	--
	2GC	7045406	21/32	1 7/32	1 19/32	.380	--	.350	--	.130/—	--	--	--
	M4MC	7045200	17/32	--	.275	.300	.120	.325	--	.200/.550	1/.020	.015	9/16
	M4MC	7045202	15/32	--	.275	.300	.120	.325	--	.180/.170	1/.020	.015	7/8
	M4MC	7045203	15/32	--	.275	.300	.120	.325	--	.180/.170	1/.020	.015	7/8
	M4MC	7045206	15/32	--	.275	.300	.120	.325	--	.180/.170	1/.020	.015	7/8
	M4MC	7045207	15/32	--	.275	.300	.120	.325	--	.180/.170	1/.020	.015	7/8
	M4MC	7045208	15/32	--	.275	.300	.120	.325	--	.180/.170	1/.020	.015	7/8
	M4MC	7045209	15/32	--	.275	.300	.120	.325	--	.180/.170	1/.020	.015	7/8
	M4MC	7045210	15/32	--	.275	.300	.120	.325	--	.180/.170	1/.020	.015	7/8
	M4MC	7045211	15/32	--	.275	.300	.120	.325	--	.180/.170	1/.020	.015	7/8
	M4MC	7045222	15/32	--	.275	.300	.120	.325	--	.180/.170	1/.020	.015	7/8
	M4MC	7045223	15/32	--	.275	.300	.120	.325	--	.180/.170	1/.020	.015	7/8

CHEVROLET

Year	Carb. Model	Carb. Number	Float Level (Ins.)	Float Drop (Ins.)	Pump Rod (Ins.)	Choke Rod (Ins.)	Choke Lever (Ins.)	Choke Unloader (Ins.)	Choke Setting (Notches)	Vacuum Break Pri.(front)/Sec.(rear) (Ins.)	Secondary Open/Close (Ins.)	Air Valve Dashpot/Rod (Ins.)	Air Valve Spring (Turns)
	M4MC	7045224	15/32	--	.275	.325	.120	.325	--	.180/.170	1/.020	.015	3/4
	M4MC	7045228	15/32	--	.275	.325	.120	.325	--	.180/.170	1/.020	.015	3/4
	M4MCA	7045502	15/32	--	.275	.300	.120	.325	--	.180/.170	1/.020	.015	7/8
	M4MCA	7045503	15/32	--	.275	.300	.120	.325	--	.180/.170	1/.020	.015	7/8
	M4MCA	7045504	15/32	--	.275	.300	.120	.325	--	.180/.170	1/.020	.015	7/8
	M4MCA	7045506	15/32	--	.275	.300	.120	.325	--	.180/.170	1/.020	.015	7/8
	M4MCA	7045507	15/32	--	.275	.300	.120	.325	--	.180/.170	1/.020	.015	7/8
	HOLLEY												
	5210-C	348659	.420	1±1/8	--	--	--	--	3NR	.325/—	--	--	--
	5210-C	348660	.420	1±1/8	--	--	--	--	4NR	.300/—	--	--	--
	5210-C	348661	.420	1±1/8	--	--	--	--	3NR	.275/—	--	--	--
	5210-C	348662	.420	1±1/8	--	--	--	--	4NR	.275/—	--	--	--
	5210-C	348663	.420	1±1/8	--	--	--	--	3NR	.325/—	--	--	--
	5210-C	348664	.420	1±1/8	--	--	--	--	4NR	.300/—	--	--	--
	5210-C	348665	.420	1±1/8	--	--	--	--	3NR	.275/—	--	--	--
	5210-C	348666	.420	1±1/8	--	--	--	--	4NR	.275/—	--	--	--
1976	**ROCHESTER**												
	1MV	17056012	11/32	--	--	.090	--	.265	--	.110/.215	--	--	--
	1MV	17056013	11/32	--	--	.090	--	.265	--	.110/.215	--	--	--
	1MV	17056014	11/32	--	--	.090	--	.265	--	.110/.215	--	--	--
	1MV	17056015	11/32	--	--	.090	--	.265	--	.110/.215	--	--	--
	1MV	17056016	11/32	--	--	.115	--	.265	--	.140/—	--	--	--
	1MV	17056018	11/32	--	--	.090	--	.265	--	.110/.215	--	--	--
	1MV	17056022	1/8	--	--	.045	--	.215	--	.060/.450	--	--	--
	1MV	17056023	1/8	--	--	.045	--	.215	--	.060/.450	--	--	--
	1MV	17056026	1/8	--	--	.045	--	.215	--	.060/.450	--	--	--
	1MV	17056027	1/8	--	--	.045	--	.215	--	.060/.450	--	--	--
	1MV	17056314	11/32	--	--	.135	--	.265	--	.150/.275	--	--	--
	1ME	17056030	5/32	--	--	.065	--	.200	3NR	.085/—	--	--	--
	1ME	17056031	5/32	--	--	.065	--	.200	3NR	.085/—	--	--	--
	1ME	17056032	5/32	--	--	.065	--	.200	3NR	.085/—	--	--	--
	1ME	17056034	5/32	--	--	.065	--	.200	3NR	.085/▴	--	--	--
	1ME	17056035	5/32	--	--	.065	--	.200	3NR	.085/—	--	--	--
	1ME	17056036	5/32	--	--	.065	--	.200	3NR	.085/—	--	--	--
	1ME	17056330	5/32	--	--	.065	--	.200	3NR	.085/—	--	--	--
	1ME	17056331	5/32	--	--	.065	--	.200	3NR	.085/—	--	--	--
	1ME	17056332	5/32	--	--	.065	--	.200	3NR	.085/—	--	--	--
	1ME	17056334	5/32	--	--	.065	--	.200	3NR	.085/—	--	--	--
	1ME	17056335	5/32	--	--	.065	--	.200	3NR	.085/—	--	--	--
	2GC	17056101	17/32	1 9/32	1 21/32	.260	--	.325	Index	.130/—	--	--	--
	2GC	17056102	17/32	1 9/32	1 21/32	.260	--	.325	Index	.130/—	--	--	--
	2GC	17056103	17/32	1 9/32	1 21/32	.260	--	.325	Index	.130/—	--	--	--
	2GC	17056104	17/32	1 9/32	1 21/32	.260	--	.325	Index	.140/—	--	--	--
	2GC	17056105	17/32	1 9/32	1 21/32	.260	--	.325	Index	.140/—	--	--	--
	2GC	17056108	9/16	1 9/32	1 21/32	.260	--	.325	Index	.140/—	--	--	--
	2GC	17056110	9/16	1 9/32	1 21/32	.260	--	.325	Index	.140/—	--	--	--
	2GC	17056111	9/16	1 9/32	1 11/16	.260	--	.325	Index	.130/—	--	--	--
	2GC	17056112	9/16	1 9/32	1 21/32	.260	--	.325	Index	.140/—	--	--	--
	2GC	17056113	9/16	1 9/32	1 11/16	.260	--	.325	Index	.130/—	--	--	--
	2GC	17056114	21/32	31/32	1 11/16	.260	--	.325	1NR	.130/—	--	--	--
	2GC	17056404	17/32	1 9/32	1 21/32	.260	--	.325	Index	.140/—	--	--	--
	2GC	17056405	17/32	1 9/32	1 21/32	.260	--	.325	Index	.140/—	--	--	--
	2GC	17056430	9/16	1 9/32	1 21/32	.260	--	.325	Index	.140/—	--	--	--
	2GC	17056432	9/16	1 9/32	1 21/32	.260	--	.325	Index	.140/—	--	--	--
	M4ME	17056200	13/32	--	9/32	.190	.120	.270	Index	.240/.160	1/.020	.015	7/8
	M4MC	17056202	13/32	--	9/32	.325	.120	.325	2NL	.185/—	1/.020	.015	7/8
	M4MC	17056203	13/32	--	9/32	.325	.120	.325	3NL	.185/—	1/.020	.015	7/8
	M4MC	17056206	13/32	--	9/32	.325	.120	.325	2NL	.185/—	1/.020	.015	7/8
	M4MC	17056207	13/32	--	9/32	.325	.120	.325	3NL	.185/—	1/.020	.015	7/8
	M4MC	17056210	13/32	--	9/32	.325	.120	.325	2NL	.185/—	1/.020	.015	1
	M4MC	17056211	13/32	--	9/32	.325	.120	.325	2NL	.170/—	1/.020	.015	1
	M4MC	17056226	13/32	--	9/32	.325	.120	.325	2NL	.185/—	1/.020	.015	1
	M4MC	17056228	13/32	--	9/32	.325	.120	.325	2NL	.185/—	1/.020	.015	3/4
	M4MC	17056502	13/32	--	9/32	.325	.120	.325	2NL	.185/—	1/.020	.015	7/8
	M4MC	17056503	13/32	--	9/32	.325	.120	.325	2NL	.185/—	1/.020	.015	7/8
	M4MC	17056506	13/32	--	9/32	.325	.120	.325	2NL	.185/—	1/.020	.015	7/8
	M4MC	17056507	13/32	--	9/32	.325	.120	.325	2NL	.185/—	1/.020	.015	7/8
	M4MC	17056508	13/32	--	9/32	.325	.120	.325	2NL	.185/—	1/.020	.015	3/4
	HOLLEY												
	5210-C	366829	.420	1	--	--	--	.375	2NR	.313/—	--	--	--
	5210-C	366830	.420	1	--	--	--	.375	3NR	.288/—	--	--	--
	5210-C	366831	.420	1	--	--	--	.375	2NR	.313/—	--	--	--
	5210-C	366832	.420	1	--	--	--	.375	3NR	.288/—	--	--	--
	5210-C	366833	.420	1	--	--	--	.375	2NR	.268/—	--	--	--
	5210-C	366834	.420	1	--	--	--	.375	3NR	.268/—	--	--	--
	5210-C	366840	.420	1	--	--	--	.375	3NR	.268/—	--	--	--
	5210-C	366841	.420	1	--	--	--	.375	2NR	.268/—	--	--	--
1977	**ROCHESTER**												
	1ME	17057030	5/32	--	--	.050	.120	.200	3NR	.080/—	--	--	--
	1ME	17057031	5/32	--	--	.050	.120	.200	3NR	.080/—	--	--	--
	1ME	17057032	5/32	--	--	.050	.120	.200	3NR	.080/—	--	--	--
	1ME	17057034	5/32	--	--	.050	.120	.200	3NR	.080/—	--	--	--
	1ME	17057035	5/32	--	--	.050	.120	.200	3NR	.080/—	--	--	--
	1ME	17057042	5/32	--	--	.050	.120	.200	2NR	.080/—	--	--	--
	1ME	17057044	5/32	--	--	.050	.120	.200	2NR	.080/—	--	--	--
	1ME	17057045	5/32	--	--	.050	.120	.200	2NR	.080/—	--	--	--
	1ME	17057332	5/32	--	--	.050	.120	.200	2NR	.080/—	--	--	--
	1ME	17057334	5/32	--	--	.050	.120	.200	2NR	.080/—	--	--	--
	1ME	17057335	5/32	--	--	.050	.120	.200	2NR	.080/—	--	--	--
	1ME	17057013	3/8	--	--	.100	.120	.325	1NR	.125/.230	--	--	--
	1ME	17057014	3/8	--	--	.085	.120	.325	2NR	.120/.200	--	--	--
	1ME	17057015	3/8	--	--	.100	.120	.325	1NR	.125/.230	--	--	--
	1ME	17057016	3/8	--	--	.095	.120	.325	1NL	.125/.230	--	--	--
	1ME	17057018	3/8	--	--	.085	.120	.325	1NR	.120/.215	--	--	--
	1ME	17057020	3/8	--	--	.085	.120	.325	2NR	.120/.200	--	--	--
	1ME	17057310	3/8	--	--	--	.120	--	Index	—/—	--	--	--
	1ME	17057312	3/8	--	--	--	.120	--	Index	—/—	--	--	--
	1ME	17057314	3/8	--	--	.100	.120	.225	Index	.110/.180	--	--	--
	1ME	17057316	3/8	--	--	--	.120	--	--	—/—	--	--	--
	1ME	17057318	3/8	--	--	.100	.120	.225	Index	.110/.180	--	--	--
	2GC	17057104	1/2	1 9/32	1 21/32	.260	.120	.325	Index	.160/—	--	--	--
	2GC	17057105	1/2	1 9/32	1 21/32	.260	.120	.325	Index	.160/—	--	--	--
	2GC	17057107	1/2	1 9/32	1 21/32	.260	.120	.325	Index	.160/—	--	--	--
	2GC	17057108	19/32	1 9/32	1 21/32	.260	.120	.325	Index	.160/—	--	--	--
	2GC	17057109	1/2	1 9/32	1 21/32	.260	.120	.325	Index	.160/—	--	--	--
	2GC	17057110	19/32	1 9/32	1 21/32	.260	.120	.325	Index	.160/—	--	--	--
	2GC	17057111	19/32	1 9/32	1 21/32	.260	.120	.325	Index	.160/—	--	--	--
	2GC	17057112	19/32	1 9/32	1 21/32	.260	.120	.325	Index	.160/—	--	--	--

CARBURETOR SPECIFICATIONS

CHEVROLET

Year	Carb. Model	Carb. Number	Float Level (Ins.)	Float Drop (Ins.)	Pump Rod (Ins.)	Choke Rod (Ins.)	Choke Lever (Ins.)	Choke Unloader (Ins.)	Choke Setting (Notches)	Vacuum Break Pri.(front)/Sec.(rear) (Ins.)	Secondary Open/Close (Ins.)	Air Valve Dashpot/Rod (Ins.)	Air Valve Spring (Turns)
1977	2GC	17057113	19/32	1 9/32	1 21/32	.260	.120	.325	Index	.160/—	--	--	--
	2GC	17057114	19/32	1 9/32	1 21/32	.260	.120	.325	Index	.160/—	--	--	--
	2GC	17057121	19/32	1 9/32	1 21/32	.260	.120	.325	Index	.160/—	--	--	--
	2GC	17057123	19/32	1 9/32	1 21/32	.260	.120	.325	Index	.160/—	--	--	--
	2GC	17057404	1/2	1 9/32	1 21/32	.260	.120	.325	1/2NL	.160/—	--	--	--
	2GC	17057405	1/2	1 9/32	1 21/32	.260	.120	.325	1/2NL	.160/—	--	--	--
	2GC	17057408	21/32	1 9/32	1 21/32	.260	.120	.325	1/2NL	.160/—	--	--	--
	2GC	17057410	21/32	1 9/32	1 21/32	.260	.120	.325	1/2NL	.160/—	--	--	--
	2GC	17057412	21/32	1 9/32	1 21/32	.260	.120	.325	1/2NL	.160/—	--	--	--
	2GC	17057414	21/32	1 9/32	1 21/32	.260	.120	.325	1/2NL	.160/—	--	--	--
	M4MC	17057202	15/32	--	9/32	.325	.120	--	2NL	.160/—	1/.020	.015	--
	M4MC	17057203	15/32	--	9/32	.325	.120	.280	3NL	.160/—	1/.020	.015	7/8
	M4MC	17057204	15/32	--	9/32	.325	.120	.280	2NL	.160/—	1/.020	.015	7/8
	M4MC	17057210	15/32	--	9/32	.325	.120	.280	2²NL	.180/—	1/.020	.015	1
	M4MC	17057211	15/32	--	9/32	.325	.120	.280	3NL	.180/—	1/.020	.015	1
	M4MC	17057228	13/32	--	9/32	.325	.120	.280	2NL	.180/—	1/.020	.015	1
	M4MC	17057502	15/32	--	9/32	.325	.120	.280	2NL	.165/—	1/.020	.015	7/8
	M4MC	17057504	15/32	--	9/32	.325	.120	.280	2NL	.165/—	1/.020	.015	7/8
	M4MC	17057510	15/32	--	9/32	.325	.120	--	2NL	.180/—	1/.020	.015	--
	M4MC	17057528	15/32	--	9/32	.325	.120	--	2NL	.180/—	1/.020	.015	--
	M4MC	17057582	15/32	--	9/32	.325	.120	.280	2NL	.180/—	1/.020	.015	7/8
	M4MC	17057584	15/32	--	9/32	.325	.120	.280	--	.180/—	1/.020	.015	7/8
	HOLLEY												
	5210-C	458102	.420	1	--	--	.085	.350	3NR	.250/.400	--	--	--
	5210-C	458103	.420	1	--	--	.120	.350	3NR	.250/.400	--	--	--
	5210-C	458104	.420	1	--	--	.085	.350	3NR	.250/.400	--	--	--
	5210-C	458105	.420	1	--	--	.120	.350	3NR	.250/.400	--	--	--
	5210-C	458106	.420	1	--	--	.120	.400	3NR	.275/.400	--	--	--
	5210-C	458107	.420	1	--	--	.120	.400	3NR	.275/.400	--	--	--
	5210-C	458108	.420	1	--	--	.120	.400	3NR	.275/.400	--	--	--
	5210-C	458109	.420	1	--	--	.120	.400	3NR	.275/.400	--	--	--
	5210-C	458110	.420	1	--	--	.120	.400	3NR	.300/.400	--	--	--
	5210-C	458112	.420	1	--	--	.120	.400	3NR	.300/.400	--	--	--
1978	**ROCHESTER**												
	1ME	17058031	5/32	--	--	.105	.120	.500	2NR	.150/—	--	--	--
	1ME	17058032	5/32	--	--	.080	.120	.500	3NR	.130/—	--	--	--
	1ME	17058033	5/32	--	--	.080	.120	.500	2NR	.130/—	--	--	--
	1ME	17058034	5/32	--	--	.080	.120	.500	3NR	.130/—	--	--	--
	1ME	17058035	5/32	--	--	.080	.120	.500	3NR	.130/—	--	--	--
	1ME	17058037	5/32	--	--	.080	.120	.500	2NR	.130/—	--	--	--
	1ME	17058042	5/32	--	--	.080	.120	.500	2NR	.160/—	--	--	--
	1ME	17058044	5/32	--	--	.080	.120	.500	2NR	.160/—	--	--	--
	1ME	17058045	5/32	--	--	.080	.120	.500	2NR	.160/—	--	--	--
	1ME	17058332	5/32	--	--	.080	.120	.500	2NR	.160/—	--	--	--
	1ME	17058334	5/32	--	--	.080	.120	.500	2NR	.160/—	--	--	--
	1ME	17058335	5/32	--	--	.080	.120	.500	2NR	.160/—	--	--	--
	1ME	17058336	5/32	--	--	.080	.120	.500	3NR	.130/—	--	--	--
	1ME	17058338	5/32	--	--	.080	.120	.500	3NR	.130/—	--	--	--
	1ME	17058013	3/8	--	--	.180	.120	.500	Index	.200/—	--	--	--
	1ME	17058014	5/16	--	--	.180	.120	.500	Index	.200/—	--	--	--
	1ME	17058020	5/16	--	--	.180	.120	.500	Index	.200/—	--	--	--
	1ME	17058314	3/8	--	--	.190	.120	.400	Index	.245/—	--	--	--
	M2ME	ALL	1/4	--	9/32	.314	.120	.314	Index	.136/—	--	--	--
	2GC	17058102	15/32	1 9/32	1 17/32	.260	.120	.325	Index	.150/—	--	--	--
	2GC	17058103	15/32	1 9/32	1 17/32	.260	.120	.325	Index	.150/—	--	--	--
	2GC	17058104	15/32	1 9/32	1 21/32	.260	.120	.325	Index	.160/—	--	--	--
	2GC	17058105	15/32	1 9/32	1 21/32	.260	.120	.325	Index	.160/—	--	--	--
	2GC	17058107	15/32	1 9/32	1 17/32	.260	.120	.325	Index	.160/—	--	--	--
	2GC	17058109	15/32	1 9/32	1 17/32	.260	.120	.325	Index	.160/—	--	--	--
	2GC	17058404	1/2	1 9/32	1 21/32	.260	.120	.325	1/2NL	.160/—	--	--	--
	2GC	17058405	1/2	1 9/32	1 21/32	.260	.120	.325	1/2NL	.160/—	--	--	--
	2GE	17058143	7/16	1 5/32	1 5/8	.080	.120	.140	1NR	.110/.040	--	--	--
	2GE	17058144	7/16	1 5/32	1 5/8	.080	.120	.140	1NR	.110/.060	--	--	--
	2GE	17058147	7/16	1 5/32	1 5/8	.080	.120	.140	1NR	.140/.100	--	--	--
	2GE	17058447	7/16	1 5/32	1 5/8	.080	.120	.140	1NR	.150/.110	--	--	--
	M4MC	17058202	15/32	--	9/32	.314	.120	.277	2NL	.179/—	1/.020	.015	7/8
	M4MC	17058203	15/32	--	9/32	.314	.120	.277	2NL	.179/—	1/.020	.015	7/8
	M4MC	17058204	15/32	--	9/32	.314	.120	.277	2NL	.179/—	1/.020	.015	7/8
	M4MC	17058210	15/32	--	9/32	.314	.120	.277	2NL	.203/—	1/.020	.015	7/8
	M4MC	17058211	15/32	--	9/32	.314	.120	.277	2NL	.203/—	1/.020	.015	7/8
	M4MC	17058228	15/32	--	9/32	.314	.120	.277	2NL	.203/—	1/.020	.015	7/8
	M4MC	17058502	15/32	--	9/32	.314	.120	.277	2NL	.187/—	1/.020	.015	7/8
	M4MC	17058504	15/32	--	9/32	.314	.120	.277	2NL	.187/—	1/.020	.015	7/8
	M4MC	17058582	15/32	--	9/32	.314	.120	.277	2NL	.203/—	1/.020	.015	7/8
	M4MC	17058584	15/32	--	9/32	.314	.120	.277	2NL	.203/—	1/.020	.015	7/8
	HOLLEY												
	5210-C	10001047	.520	1	--	--	.150	.350	1NR	.325/.400	--	--	--
	5210-C	10001048	.520	1	--	--	.150	.350	2NR	.300/.400	--	--	--
	5210-C	10001049	.520	1	--	--	.150	.350	1NR	.325/.400	--	--	--
	5210-C	10001050	.520	1	--	--	.150	.350	2NR	.300/.400	--	--	--
	5210-C	10001052	.520	1	--	--	.150	.350	2NR	.325/.400	--	--	--
	5210-C	10001054	.520	1	--	--	.150	.350	2NR	.325/.400	--	--	--
	6510-C	10001056	.520	1	--	--	.150	.350	1NR	.325/—	--	--	--
	6510-C	10001058	.520	1	--	--	.150	.350	1NR	.325/—	--	--	--
1979	**ROCHESTER**												
	1ME	17059013	3/8	--	--	.180	.120	.400	Index	.200/—	--	--	--
	1ME	17059014	3/8	--	--	.180	.120	.400	Index	.200/—	--	--	--
	1ME	17059020	3/8	--	--	.180	.120	.400	Index	.200/—	--	--	--
	1ME	17059314	3/8	--	--	.190	.120	.400	Index	.245/—	--	--	--
	M2MC/M2ME	17059130	13/32	--	1/4	--	.120	.243	Index	.157/—	--	--	--
	M2MC/M2ME	17059131	13/32	--	1/4	--	.120	.243	1NL	.157/—	--	--	--
	M2MC/M2ME	17059132	13/32	--	1/4	--	.120	.243	Index	.157/—	--	--	--
	M2MC/M2ME	17059133	13/32	--	1/4	--	.120	.243	1NL	.157/—	--	--	--
	M2MC/M2ME	17059134	13/32	--	1/4	--	.120	.243	1NL	.157/—	--	--	--
	M2MC/M2ME	17059135	13/32	--	1/4	--	.120	.243	1NL	.157/—	--	--	--
	M2MC/M2ME	17059136	13/32	--	1/4	--	.120	.243	1NL	.157/—	--	--	--
	M2MC/M2ME	17059137	13/32	--	1/4	--	.120	.243	1NL	.157/—	--	--	--
	M2MC/M2ME	17059138	9/32	--	1/4	--	.120	.243	1NL	.164/—	--	--	--
	M2MC/M2ME	17059139	9/32	--	1/4	--	.120	.243	1NL	.164/—	--	--	--
	M2MC/M2ME	17059140	9/32	--	1/4	--	.120	.243	1NL	.164/—	--	--	--
	M2MC/M2ME	17059141	9/32	--	1/4	--	.120	.243	1NL	.164/—	--	--	--
	M2MC/M2ME	17059184	11/32	--	1/4	--	.120	.220	1NL	.103/.117	--	--	--

CHEVROLET

Year	Carb. Model	Carb. Number	Float Level (Ins.)	Float Drop (Ins.)	Pump Rod (Ins.)	Choke Rod (Ins.)	Choke Lever (Ins.)	Choke Unloader (Ins.)	Choke Setting (Notches)	Vacuum Break Pri.(front)/Sec.(rear) (Ins.)	Secondary Open/Close (Ins.)	Air Valve Dashpot/Rod (Ins.)	Air Valve Spring (Turns)
	M2MC/M2ME	17059194	11/32	--	1/4	--	.120	.220	1NL	.103/.117	--	--	--
	M2MC/M2ME	17059196	11/32	--	1/4	--	.120	.277	1NR	.129/.117	--	--	--
	M2MC/M2ME	17059430	9/32	--	1/4	--	.120	.243	1NL	.157/—	--	--	--
	M2MC/M2ME	17059432	9/32	--	1/4	--	.120	.243	1NL	.157/—	--	--	--
	M2MC/M2ME	17059491	11/32	--	9/32	--	.120	.243	1NL	—/—	--	--	--
	M2MC/M2ME	17059498	11/32	--	9/32	--	.120	.243	1NL	—/.117	--	--	--
	M2MC/M2ME	17059193	13/32	--	1/4	--	.120	.220	1NL	.103/.090	--	--	--
	M2MC/M2ME	17059180	11/32	--	1/4	--	.120	.243	--	.103/.090	--	--	--
	M2MC/M2ME	17059190	11/32	--	1/4	--	.120	.243	--	.103/—	--	--	--
	M2MC/M2ME	17059434	13/32	--	1/4	--	.120	.243	1NL	.171/—	--	--	--
	M2MC/M2ME	17059436	13/32	--	1/4	--	.120	.243	1NL	.171/—	--	--	--
	2SE	17059674	13/64	--	1/2	.096	.120	.195	2NR	.103/—	--	.025	--
	2SE	17059675	13/64	--	17/32	.096	.120	.195	1NR	.117/—	--	.025	--
	2SE	17059676	13/64	--	1/2	.096	.120	.195	2NR	.103/—	--	.025	--
	2SE	17059677	13/64	--	17/32	.096	.120	.195	1NR	.117/—	--	.025	--
	E2ME	17059496	5/16	--	3/8	.138	.120	.243	2NR	.117/.179	--	--	--
	M4MC	17059203	15/32	--	1/4	.243	.120	.243	1NL	.157/—	1/.020	.015	7/8
	M4MC	17059207	15/32	--	1/4	.243	.120	.243	1NL	.157/—	1/.020	.015	7/8
	M4MC	17059210	15/32	--	9/32	.243	.120	.243	1NL	.157/—	1/.020	.015	1
	M4MC	17059211	15/32	--	9/32	.243	.120	.243	2NL	.157/—	1/.020	.015	1
	M4MC	17059216	15/32	--	1/4	.243	.120	.243	1NL	.157/—	1/.020	.015	7/8
	M4MC	17059217	15/32	--	1/4	.243	.120	.243	2NL	.157/—	1/.020	.015	7/8
	M4MC	17059218	15/32	--	1/4	.243	.120	.243	2NL	.157/—	1/.020	.015	7/8
	M4MC	17059222	15/32	--	1/4	.243	.120	.243	2NL	.164/—	1/.020	.015	1
	M4MC	17059228	15/32	--	9/32	.243	.120	.243	1NL	.164/—	1/.020	.015	7/8
	M4MC	17059502	15/32	--	1/4	.243	.120	.243	2NL	.164/—	1/.020	.015	7/8
	M4MC	17059504	15/32	--	1/4	.243	.120	.243	2NL	.164/—	1/.020	.015	7/8
	M4MC	17059582	15/32	--	11/32	.243	.120	.314	1NL	.203/—	1/.020	.015	7/8
	M4MC	17059584	15/32	--	11/32	.243	.120	.314	1NL	.203/—	1/.020	.015	7/8
	HOLLEY												
	6510-C	10008489	.520	--	--	--	.150	.350	1NL	.250/—	--	--	--
	6510-C	10008490	.520	--	--	--	.150	.350	1NL	.250/—	--	--	--
	6510-C	10008491	.520	--	--	--	.150	.350	2NR	.250/—	--	--	--
	6510-C	10008492	.520	--	--	--	.150	.350	2NR	.250/—	--	--	--
	5210-C	466361	.500	--	--	--	.110	.350	2NR	.245/—	--	--	--
	5210-C	466362	.500	--	--	--	.110	.350	2NR	.250/—	--	--	--
	5210-C	466363	.500	--	--	--	.110	.350	2NR	.245/—	--	--	--
	5210-C	466364	.500	--	--	--	.110	.350	2NR	.250/—	--	--	--
	5210-C	466365	.500	--	--	--	.130	.350	1NR	.300/—	--	--	--
	5210-C	466366	.500	--	--	--	.130	.350	1NR	.300/—	--	--	--
	5210-C	466367	.500	--	--	--	.130	.350	1NR	.300/—	--	--	--
	5210-C	466368	.500	--	--	--	.130	.350	1NR	.300/—	--	--	--
	5210-C	466369	.500	--	--	--	.110	.350	2NR	.245/—	--	--	--
	5210-C	466370	.500	--	--	--	.110	.350	2NR	.250/—	--	--	--
	5210-C	466371	.500	--	--	--	.110	.350	2NR	.245/—	--	--	--
	5210-C	466372	.500	--	--	--	.110	.350	2NR	.250/—	--	--	--
	5210-C	466373	.500	--	--	--	.130	.350	1NR	.300/—	--	--	--
	5210-C	466374	.500	--	--	--	.130	.350	1NR	.300/—	--	--	--
	5210-C	466375	.500	--	--	--	.130	.350	1NR	.300/—	--	--	--
	5210-C	466376	.500	--	--	--	.130	.350	1NR	.300/—	--	--	--

1Center of slot.
2Minimum, wide open throttle.
3Without vacuum advance; low idle at 450 rpm with viscous clutch fan disengaged.
4Without vacuum advance, on second step of cam.
5With vacuum advance.
6Centered on bowl; bowl inverted on engine, fuel level with bottom of sight plug hole

CHEVETTE/MONZA/VEGA

Year	Carburetor Model	Carburetor Number	Float Level (in.)	Float Drop (in.)	Accel. Pump Rod (in.)	Choke Rod (Fast Idle Cam)	Vacuum Break (in.)	Choke Unloader (in.)	Main Jet Pri./Sec.	Idle Jet Pri./Sec.	Pump Position (Hole)	Choke Index Setting	Fast Idle (rpm)
1971	**ROCHESTER**												
	MV	7041023	1/16	—	—	.080	.140	.350	—/—	—/—	—	—	2400[1]
	MV	7041024	1/16	—	—	.120	.200	.350	—/—	—/—	—	—	2400[1]
	2GV	7041181	5/8	1 3/4	1 3/8	.080	.120	.180	—/—	—/—	—	—	2400[1]
	2GV	7041182	5/8	1 3/4	1 3/8	.080	.120	.180	—/—	—/—	—	—	2400[1]
1972													
	MV	7042023	1/8	—	—	.130	.200	.375	—/—	—/—	—	—	2400[1]
	MV	7042993	1/8	—	—	.130	.200	.375	—/—	—/—	—	—	2400[1]
	MV	7042024	1/16	—	—	.700	.120	.375	—/—	—/—	—	—	2800[1]
	MV	7042994	1/16	—	—	.700	.120	.375	—/—	—/—	—	—	2800[1]
	2GV	7042106	19/32	1 7/8	1 1/16	.060	.085	.215	—/—	—/—	—	—	2800[1]
	2GV	7042107	19/32	1 7/8	1 1/16	.080	.100	.215	—/—	—/—	—	—	2400[1]
	2GV	7042826	19/32	1 7/8	1 1/16	.060	.085	.215	—/—	—/—	—	—	2800[1]
	2GV	7042827	19/32	1 7/8	1 1/16	.080	.100	.215	—/—	—/—	—	—	2400[1]
1973													
	MV	7043023	.060	—	—	.110	.140	.375	—/—	—/—	—	—	2000[2]
	MV	7043033	.060	—	—	.110	.140	.375	—/—	—/—	—	—	2000[2]
	MV	7043323	.060	—	—	.110	.140	.375	—/—	—/—	—	—	2000[2]
	MV	7043333	.060	—	—	.110	.140	.375	—/—	—/—	—	—	2000[2]
	MV	7043024	.060	—	—	.085	.120	.375	—/—	—/—	—	—	2200[2]
	MV	7043034	.060	—	—	.085	.120	.375	—/—	—/—	—	—	2200[2]
	MV	7043324	.060	—	—	.085	.120	.375	—/—	—/—	—	—	2200[2]
	MV	7043334	.060	—	—	.085	.120	.375	—/—	—/—	—	—	2200[2]
	HOLLEY												
	5210-C	331157	420	1.0±1/8	—	—	300	—	132/142	55/50	3	1 rich	2000[2]
	5210-C	331159	420	1.0±1/8	—	—	300	—	132/142	55/50	3	1 rich	2000[2]
	5210-C	331156	420	1.0±1/8	—	—	300	—	132/140	55/50	2	2 rich	2200[2]
	5210-C	331158	420	1.0±1/8	—	—	300	—	132/140	55/50	2	2 rich	2200[2]
1974	**ROCHESTER**												
	1MV	7044023	.060	—	—	.080	130	.375	—/—	—/—	—	—	2000[2]
	1MV	7044033	.060	—	—	.080	130	.375	—/—	—/—	—	—	2000[2]
	1MV	7044323	.060	—	—	.080	130	.375	—/—	—/—	—	—	2000[2]
	1MV	7044333	.060	—	—	.080	130	.375	—/—	—/—	—	—	2000[2]
	1MV	7044024	.060	—	—	.080	130	.375	—/—	—/—	—	—	2200[2]
	1MV	7044034	.060	—	—	.080	130	.375	—/—	—/—	—	—	2200[2]
	1MV	7044324	.060	—	—	.080	130	.375	—/—	—/—	—	—	2200[2]
	1MV	7044334	.060	—	—	.080	130	.375	—/—	—/—	—	—	2200[2]
	HOLLEY												
	5210-C	338179	420	1.0±1/8	—	—	300	—	132/142	55/50	3	2 1/2 rich	2000[2]
	5210-C	338181	420	1.0±1/8	—	—	300	—	132/142	55/50	3	2 1/2 rich	2000[2]
	5210-C	338168	420	1.0±1/8	—	—	400	—	130/140	55/50	2	3 1/2 rich	2200[2]
	5210-C	338170	420	1.0±1/8	—	—	400	—	130/140	55/50	2	3 1/2 rich	2200[2]
1975	**ROCHESTER**												
	1MV	7045025	1/8	—	—	.080	.100/.450	.375	—/—	—/—	—	—	2000[2]
	1MV	7045029	1/8	—	—	.080	.100/.450	.375	—/—	—/—	—	—	2000[2]
	1MV	7045024	1/8	—	—	.080	.100/.450	.375	—/—	—/—	—	—	2200[2]

CARBURETOR SPECIFICATIONS

CHEVETTE/MONZA/VEGA

Year	Carburetor Model	Carburetor Number	Float Level (in.)	Float Drop (in.)	Accel. Pump Rod (in.)	Choke Rod (Fast Idle Cam)	Vacuum Break (in.)	Choke Unloader (in.)	Main Jet Sec.	Idle Jet Sec.	Pump Position (Hole)	Choke Index Setting	Fast Idle (rpm)
1975	1MV	7045028	1/8	—	—	.080	.100/.450	.375	— / —	— / —	—	—	2200₂
	2GC	7045101	19/32	1 7/32	1 19/32	.375	.130	.350	— / —	— / —	—	—	3
	2GC	7045105	19/32	1 7/32	1 19/32	.375	.130	.350	— / —	— / —	—	—	3
	2GC	7045401	21/32	1 7/32	1 19/32	.380	.130	.350	— / —	— / —	—	—	3
	2GC	7045405	21/32	1 7/32	1 19/32	.380	.130	.350	— / —	— / —	—	—	3
	2GC	7045102	19/32	1 7/32	1 19/32	.375	.130	.350	— / —	— / —	—	—	3
	2GC	7045106	19/32	1 7/32	1 19/32	.375	.130	.350	— / —	— / —	—	—	3
	2GC	7045402	21/32	1 7/32	1 19/32	.380	.130	.350	— / —	— / —	—	—	3
	2GC	7045406	21/32	1 7/32	1 19/32	.380	.130	.350	— / —	— / —	—	—	3
	HOLLEY												
	5210-C	348659	.420	1.0 ± 1/8	—	—	.325	—	133/140	— / —	—	3 rich	1600₂
	5210-C	348663	.420	1.0 ± 1/8	—	—	.325	—	133/140	— / —	—	3 rich	1600₂
	5210-C	348661	.420	1.0 ± 1/8	—	—	.275	—	135/140	— / —	2	3 rich	1600₂
	5210-C	348665	.420	1.0 ± 1/8	—	—	.275	—	135/140	— / —	2	3 rich	1600₂
	5210-C	348660	.420	1.0 ± 1/8	—	—	.300	—	132/140	— / —	2	4 rich	1600₂
	5210-C	348664	.420	1.0 ± 1/8	—	—	.300	—	132/140	— / —	2	4 rich	1600₂
	5210-C	348662	.420	1.0 ± 1/8	—	—	.275	—	135/140	— / —	2	4 rich	1600₂
	5210-C	348666	.420	1.0 ± 1/8	—	—	.275	—	135/140	— / —	2	4 rich	1600₂
1976	**ROCHESTER**												
	1ME	17056330 17056030	5/32	—	—	.065	.085	.200	— / —	— / —	—	3 rich	2200
	1ME	17056331 17056031	5/32	—	—	.065	.085	.200	— / —	— / —	—	3 rich	2000
	1ME	17056332 17056032	5/32	—	—	.065	.085	.200	— / —	— / —	—	3 rich	2200
	1ME	17056334 17056034	5/32	—	—	.065	.085	.200	— / —	— / —	—	3 rich	2200
	1ME	17056335 17056035	5/32	—	—	.065	.085	.200	— / —	— / —	—	3 rich	2000
	1ME	17056036	5/32	—	—	.065	.085	.200	— / —	— / —	—	3 rich	2200
	1MV	7045024	1/8	—	—	.080	.100/.450	.375	— / —	— / —	—	—	2200
	1MV	7045025	1/8	—	—	.080	.100/.450	.375	— / —	— / —	—	—	2000
	1MV	7045028	1/8	—	—	.080	.100/.450	.375	— / —	— / —	—	—	2200
	1MV	7045029	1/8	—	—	.080	.100/.450	.375	— / —	— / —	—	—	2000
	2GC	7045101	19/32	1 7/32	1 19/32	.375	.130	.350	— / —	— / —	—	—	1600
	2GC	7045102	19/32	1 7/32	1 19/32	.375	.130	.350	— / —	— / —	—	—	1600
	2GC	7045105	19/32	1 7/32	1 19/32	.375	.130	.350	— / —	— / —	—	—	1600
	2GC	7045106	19/32	1 7/32	1 19/32	.375	.130	.350	— / —	— / —	—	—	1600
	2GC	7045401	21/32	1 7/32	1 19/32	.380	.130	.350	— / —	— / —	—	—	1600
	2GC	7045402	21/32	1 7/32	1 19/32	.380	.130	.350	— / —	— / —	—	—	1600
	2GC	7045405	21/32	1 7/32	1 19/32	.380	.130	.350	— / —	— / —	—	—	1600
	2GC	7045406	21/32	1 7/32	1 19/32	.380	.130	.350	— / —	— / —	—	—	1600
	HOLLEY												
	5210-C	348659	.420	1	—	—	.325	—	133/140	— / —	—	3 rich	1600
	5210-C	348660	.420	1	—	—	.300	—	132/140	— / —	2	4 rich	1600
	5210-C	348661	.420	1	—	—	.275	—	135/140	— / —	—	3 rich	1600
	5210-C	348662	.420	1	—	—	.275	—	135/140	— / —	2	4 rich	1600
	5210-C	348663	.420	1	—	—	.325	—	133/140	— / —	—	3 rich	1600
	5210-C	348664	.420	1	—	—	.300	—	132/140	— / —	2	4 rich	1600
	5210-C	348665	.420	1	—	—	.275	—	135/140	— / —	—	3 rich	1600
	5210-C	348666	.420	1	—	—	.275	—	135/140	— / —	2	4 rich	1600
1977	**ROCHESTER**												
	2GC	17057104	1/2	1 9/32	1 21/32	.260	.130₅	.325	—	—	—	—	—
	2GC	17057105	1/2	1 9/32	1 21/32	.260	.130₅	.325	—	—	—	—	—
	2GC	17057107	1/2	1 9/32	1 21/32	.260	.130₅	.325	—	—	—	—	—
	2GC	17057109	1/2	1 9/32	1 21/32	.260	.130₅	.325	—	—	—	—	—
	2GC	17057404	1/2	1 9/32	1 21/32	.260	.140₆	.325	—	—	—	—	—
	2GC	17057405	1/2	1 9/32	1 21/32	.260	.140₆	.325	—	—	—	—	—
	HOLLEY												
	5210-C	458102	.420	1.00 ± 1/8	—	—	.250	.350	239/215	— / —	1	3 rich	2500
	5210-C	458103	.420	1.00 ± 1/8	—	—	.250	.350	243/205	— / —	2	3 rich	2500
	5210-C	458104	.420	1.00 ± 1/8	—	—	.250	.350	239/215	— / —	1	3 rich	2500
	5210-C	458105	.420	1.00 ± 1/8	—	—	.250	.350	243/205	— / —	2	3 rich	2500
	5210-C	458106	.420	1.00 ± 1/8	—	—	.275	.400	243/203	— / —	1	3 rich	2500
	5210-C	458107	.420	1.00 ± 1/8	—	—	.275	.400	4	— / —	2	3 rich	2500
	5210-C	458108	.420	1.00 ± 1/8	—	—	.275	.400	243/203	— / —	1	3 rich	2500
	5210-C	458109	.420	1.00 ± 1/8	—	—	.275	.400	4	— / —	2	3 rich	2500
	5210-C	458110	.420	1.00 ± 1/8	—	—	.300	.400	239/203	— / —	1	3 rich	2500
	5210-C	458112	.420	1.00 ± 1/8	—	—	.300	.400	239/203	— / —	1	3 rich	2500
1978-	**ROCHESTER**												
	1ME	17058031	5/32	—	—	.105	.150	.500	— / —	— / —	—	2 rich	3
	1ME	17058032	5/32	—	—	.80	.130	.500	— / —	— / —	—	3 rich	3
	1ME	17058034	5/32	—	—	.80	.130	.500	— / —	— / —	—	3 rich	3
	1ME	17058035	5/32	—	—	.80	.130	.500	— / —	— / —	—	3 rich	3
	1ME	17058036	5/32	—	—	.80	.130	.500	— / —	— / —	—	3 rich	3
	1ME	17058038	5/32	—	—	.80	.130	.500	— / —	— / —	—	3 rich	3
	1ME	17058042	5/32	—	—	.80	.130	.500	— / —	— / —	—	2 rich	3
	1ME	17058044	5/32	—	—	.80	.130	.500	— / —	— / —	—	2 rich	3
	1ME	17058045	5/32	—	—	.80	.130	.500	— / —	— / —	—	2 rich	3
	1ME	17058332	5/32	—	—	.80	.130	.500	— / —	— / —	—	2 rich	3
	1ME	17058334	5/32	—	—	.80	.130	.500	— / —	— / —	—	2 rich	3
	1ME	17058335	5/32	—	—	.80	.130	.500	— / —	— / —	—	2 rich	3
	2GC	17058102	15/32	1 9/32	1 17/32	.260	.150	.325	— / —	— / —	—	Index	3
	2GC	17058103	15/32	1 9/32	1 17/32	.260	.150	.325	— / —	— / —	—	Index	3
	2GC	17058104	15/32	1 9/32	1 21/32	.260	.160	.325	— / —	— / —	—	Index	3
	2GC	17058105	15/32	1 9/32	1 21/32	.260	.160	.325	— / —	— / —	—	Index	3
	2GC	17058107	15/32	1 9/32	1 17/32	.260	.160	.325	— / —	— / —	—	Index	3
	2GC	17058404	1/2	1 9/32	1 21/32	.260	.160	.325	— / —	— / —	—	1/2 lean	3
	2GC	17058405	1/2	1 9/32	1 21/32	.260	.160	.325	— / —	— / —	—	1/2 lean	3
	2GE	17058141	7/16	1 5/32	1 5/8	.080	—	.140	— / —	— / —	—	1 rich	3
	2GE	17058143	7/16	1 5/32	1 5/8	.080	.110/.040	.140	— / —	— / —	—	1 rich	3
	2GE	17058144	7/16	1 5/32	1 5/8	.080	.110/.060	.140	— / —	— / —	—	1 rich	3
	2GE	17058147	7/16	1 5/32	1 5/8	.080	.140/.100	.140	— / —	— / —	—	1 rich	3
	2GE	17058448	7/16	1 5/32	1 5/8	.080	—	.140	— / —	— / —	—	1 rich	3
	HOLLEY												
	5210-C	10001047	.520	1.00 ± 1/8	—	—	.325/.400	.350	— / —	— / —	—	1 rich	3
	5210-C	10001048	.520	1.00 ± 1/8	—	—	.300/.400	.350	— / —	— / —	—	2 rich	3
	5210-C	10001049	.520	1.00 ± 1/8	—	—	.325/.400	.350	— / —	— / —	—	1 rich	3
	5210-C	10004048	.520	1.00 ± 1/8	—	—	.325/.400	.350	— / —	— / —	—	2 rich	3
	5210-C	10004049	.520	1.00 ± 1/8	—	—	.325/.400	.350	— / —	— / —	—	2 rich	3

CHEVETTE/MONZA/VEGA

| 1978 | 6510-C | 10001056 | .520 | 1.00 ± 1/8 | — | — | .325 | .350 | —/— | —/— | | 1 rich | 3 |
| | 6510-C | 10001058 | .520 | 1.00 ± 1/8 | — | — | .325 | .350 | —/— | —/— | | 1 rich | 3 |

1TCS disconnected and full spark to distributor.
2Vacuum advance disconnected.
3See vehicle emissions control decal under hood.
4Altitude 239/203, California 243/203.
5 .160 above 22,500 miles, except Altitude. Altitude .150 above 22,500 miles.
6 .160 above 22,500 miles.

CHRYSLER CORPORATION

Year	Carburetor Model	Carburetor Number	Transmission	Dry Float Setting Pri./Sec.	Float Drop (ins.)	Choke Unloader (ins.)	Choke Setting	Bowl Vent Valve (ins.)	Accel. Pump Setting (ins.)	Main jet Pri./Sec.	Air Valve Spring Tension	Fast Idle Speed (rpm)
1970	**HOLLEY**											
	1920	R-4351A	Manual	1/—	—	9/32	2 rich	3/32	—	#57/ —	—	1600
	1920	R-4352A	Automatic	1/—	—	9/32	2 rich	3/32	—	#56/ —	—	1800
	1920	R-4353A	Manual	1/—	—	9/32	2 rich	3/32	—	#57/ —	—	1600
	1920	R-4354A	Automatic	1/—	—	9/32	2 rich	3/32	—	#56/ —	—	1800
	2210	R-4371A	Automatic	.200	—	11/64	2 rich	5/64	9/16	#63/#65	—	1700
	4160	R-4367A	Manual	15/64/17/642	—	3	2 rich	5/64	.015	#64/ —	—	2000
	4160	R-4368A	Automatic	15/64/17/642	—	3	2 rich	5/64	.015	#64/ —	—	1800
	4160	R-4369A	Automatic	15/64/17/642	—	3	2 rich	5/64	.015	#64/ —	—	1800
	4160	R-4217A	Manual	15/64/17/642	—	3	2 rich	#72 drill	.015	#64/ —	—	2000
	4160	R-4218A	Automatic	15/64/17/642	—	3	2 rich	#72 drill	.015	#64/ —	—	1800
	2300	R-4375A	Manual	4	—	5/32	2 rich	#38 drill	.015	#64/ —	—	2200
	2300	R-4376A	Automatic	4	—	5/32	2 rich	#38 drill	.015	#63/ —	—	1800
	2300	R-4382AF	Manual	4	—	—	None	—	—	—/ —	—	—
	2300	R-4382AR	Automatic	4	—	—	None	—	—	—/ —	—	—
	2300	R-4374A	Manual	4	—	5/32	2 rich	#38 drill	.015	#64/ —	—	2200
	2300	R-4144A	Automatic	4	—	5/32	2 rich	#38 drill	.015	#63/ —	—	1800
	2300	R-4175AF	Manual	4	—	—	None	—	—	—/ —	—	—
	2300	R-4365AR	Automatic	4	—	—	None	—	—	—/ —	—	—
	4160	R-4366A	Automatic	15/64/17/642	—	3	2 rich	5/64	.015	#64/ —	—	1600
	4160	R-4360A	Automatic	15/64/1m/642	—	3	2 rich	#72 drill	.015	#64/ —	—	1600
	BALL & BALL											
	BBD 1 1/4"	BBD-4721S	Manual	1/4/—	—	1/4	Index	1/32	—	120-309S/ —	—	1600
	BBD 1 1/4"	BBD-4722S	Automatic	1/4/—	—	1/4	Index	1/32	—	120-309S/ —	—	2000
	BBD 1 1/4"	BBD-4895S	Automatic	1/4/—	—	1/4	Index	1/32	—	120-309S/ —	—	2000
	BBD 1 1/4"	BBD-4723S	Manual	1/4/—	—	1/4	Index	1/32	—	120-309S/ —	—	1600
	BBD 1 1/4"	BBD-4724S	Automatic	1/4/—	—	1/4	Index	1/32	—	120-309S/ —	—	2000
	BBD 1 1/2"	BBD-4725S	Manual	5/16/—	—	1/4	2 rich	1/16	1.00	120-329S/ —	—	1700
	BBD 1 1/2"	BBD-4726S	Automatic	5/16/—	—	1/4	2 rich	1/16	1.00	120-306S/ —	—	1700
	BBD 1 1/2"	BBD-4894S	Automatic	5/16/—	—	1/4	2 rich	1/16	1.00	120-306S/ —	—	1700
	BBD 1 1/2"	BBD-4727S	Manual	5/16/—	—	1/4	2 rich	1/16	1.00	120-329S/ —	—	1700
	BBD 1 1/2"	BBD-4728S	Automatic	5/16/—	—	1/4	2 rich	1/16	1.00	120-306S/ —	—	1700
	CARTER											
	AVS	AVS-4736S	Automatic	5/16/—	1/2	1/4	2 rich	3/64	7/16	089/.098	2 turns	1700
	AVS	AVS-4732S	Automatic	5/16/—	1/2	1/4	2 rich	3/64	7/16	089/.098	2 turns	1700
	AVS	AVS-4734S	Automatic	5/16/—	1/2	1/4	2 rich	3/64	7/16	089/.098	2 turns	1700
	AVS	AVS-4737S	Manual	5/16/—	1/2	1/4	2 rich	3/64	7/16	089/.095	2 turns	2000
	AVS	AVS-4738S	Automatic	7/32/—	1/2	1/4	Index	3/64	7/16	101/.095	2 turns	1800
	AVS	AVS-4741S	Automatic	7/32/—	1/2	1/4	Index	3/64	7/16	101/.095	2 turns	1800
	AVS	AVS-4739S	Manual	7/32/—	1/2	1/4	Index	3/4	7/16	101/.095	2 turns	2000
	AVS	AVS-4740S	Automatic	7/32/—	1/2	1/4	Index	3/4	7/16	101/.095	2 turns	1800
	AFB	AFB-4742S	All	7/32/—	3/4	—	2 rich	—	7/16	089/.089	—	—
	AFB	AFB-4745S	Manual	7/32/—	3/4	1/4	2 rich	3/4	7/16	089-.089/.092-.077	—	2000
	AFB	AFB-4746S	Automatic	7/32/—	3/4	1/4	2 rich	3/4	7/16	089-.089/.092-.077	—	2000
1971	**HOLLEY**											
	1920	R-4655A	Manual	1/—	—	9/32	2 rich	1/32	—	#56/ —	—	1600
	1920	R-4656A	Automatic	1/—	—	9/32	2 rich	1/32	—	#55/ —	—	1900
	2210	R-4665A	Manual	.200	—	11/64	2 rich	.015	9/16	#63/ —	—	1800
	2210	R-4666A	Automatic	.200	—	11/64	2 rich	.015	9/16	#62/ —	—	1800
	4160	R-6191A	Manual	15/64/17/642	—	3	2 rich	.015	.015	#64/ —	—	1800
	4160	R-4668A	Automatic	15/64/17/642	—	3	2 rich	.015	015	#64/ —	—	1700
	4160	R-6193A	Manual	15/64/17/642	—	3	2 rich	.015	.015	#64/ —	—	1800
	4160	R-4735A	Automatic	15/64/17/642	—	3	2 rich	.015	.015	#64/ —	—	1700
	2300	R-4789A	All	4	—	—	None	—	—	—/ —	—	—
	2300	R-4791A	Manual	4	—	5/32	Index	#38 drill	.015	#63/ —	—	2600
	2300	R-4792A	Automatic	4	—	5/32	Index	#38 drill	.015	#63/ —	—	2800
	2300	R-4790A	All	4	—	—	None	—	—	—/ —	—	—
	2300	R-4671A	All	4	—	—	None	—	—	—/ —	—	—
	2300	R-4669A	Manual	4	—	5/32	2 rich	#38 drill	.015	#63/ —	—	1800
	2300	R-4670A	Automatic	4	—	5/32	2 rich	#38 drill	.015	#63/ —	—	1800
	2300	R-4672A	All	4	—	—	None	—	—	—/ —	—	—
	BALL & BALL											
	BBS	BBS-4955S	Manual	1/4/—	—	3/16	2 rich	17/64	—	120-429S/ —	—	1900
	BBS	BBS-4956S	Automatic	1/4/—	—	3/16	2 rich	17/64	—	120-429S/ —	—	1800
	BBD 1 1/4"	BBD-4957S	Manual	1/4/—	—	1/4	Index	—	230	120-309S/ —	—	1600
	BBD 1 1/4"	BBD-4958S	Automatic	1/4/—	—	1/4	Index	—	200	120-309S/ —	—	1900
	BBD 1 1/2"	BBD-4961S	Manual	5/16/—	—	1/4	2 rich	3/16	1.00	120-437S/ —	—	1900
	BBD 1 1/2"	BBD-4962S	Automatic	5/16——	—	1/4	2 rich	3/16	1.00	120-437S/ —	—	1700
	CARTER											
	TQ	TQ4972S	Manual	1/—	—	190	2 rich	850	31/64	—/ —	1 1/4 turns	1800
	TQ	TQ4973S	Automatic	1/—	—	190	2 rich	850	31/64	—/ —	1 1/4 turns	1800
	AVS	AVS-6125S	Automatic	7/32/—	1/2	1/4	2 rich	3/4	7/16	089/.089	2 1/2 turns	1700
	AVS	AVS-4966S	Automatic	7/32/—	1/2	1/4	2 rich	3/4	7/16	089/.095	2 1/2 turns	1800
	AVS	AVS-4967S	Manual	7/32/—	1/2	1/4	2 rich	3/4	7/16	101/.095	2 1/2 turns	2100
	AVS	AVS-4968S	Automatic	7/32/—	1/2	1/4	2 rich	3/4	7/16	101/.095	2 1/2 turns	1800
	AFB	AFB-4971S	All	7/32/—	3/4	—	Manual	—	31/64	089/.089	—	—
	AFB	AFB-4969S	Manual	7/32/—	3/4	—	Manual	3/4	31/64	089-.089/.092-.077	—	2300
	AFB	AFB-4970S	Automatic	7/32/—	3/4	—	Manual	3/4	31/64	089-.089/.092-.077	—	2300
	ROCHESTER											
	2GV	—	Automatic	21/32/—	1 3/4	#29 drill	—	—	1 5/64	53c/ —	—	1800
1972	**HOLLEY**											
	1920	R-6364A	Automatic	1	—	5	6	.015	—	#50/ —	—	1900
	1920	R-6365A	Manual	1	—	5	6	.015	—	#50/ —	—	2000
	1920	R-6366A	Automatic	1	—	5	6	.015	—	#50/ —	—	2000
	1920	R-6363A	Manual	1	—	5	6	.015	—	#49/ —	—	2000
	1920	R-6153A	Manual	1	—	5	6	.015	—	#52/ —	—	2000
	1920	R-6154A	Automatic	1	—	5	6	.015	—	#50/ —	—	2000
	1920	R-6155A	Manual	1	—	5	6	.015	—	#56/ —	—	2000
	1920	R-6156A	Automatic	1	—	5	6	.015	—	#55/ —	—	1900
	1920	R-6159A	All	1	—	5	6	.015	—	#49/ —	—	1900
	2210	R-6164A	Automatic	180/—	—	170	6	.015	#3 slot	#65/ —	—	1900

CARBURETOR SPECIFICATIONS

CHRYSLER CORPORATION

Year	Carburetor Model	Carburetor Number	Transmission	Dry Float Setting Pri./Sec.	Float Drop (ins.)	Choke Unloader (ins.)	Choke Setting	Bowl Vent Valve (ins.)	Accel. Pump Setting (ins.)	Main jet Pri./Sec.	Air Valve Spring Tension	Fast Idle Speed (rpm)
1972	2210	R6162A	Automatic	.180/—	—	.170	6	.015	#3 slot	#65/—	—	2000
	2210	R-6368A	Automatic	.180/—	—	.170	6	.015	#3 slot	#65/—	—	1900
	2210	R-6370A	Automatic	.180/—	—	.170	6	.015	#3 slot	#65/—	—	2000
	2300	R-6405A	Manual	4	—	—	6	—	—	—/—	—	—
	2300	R-6404A	Automatic	4	—	.150	6	.015	.015	#62/—	—	1800
	2300	R-6406A	Manual	4	—	—	6	—	.015	—/—	—	—
	4160	R-6160A	Automatic	.110/.204	—	.150	6	.015	.015	#61/—	—	1600
	4160	R-6252A	Manual	.110/.204	—	.150	6	.015	.015	#61/—	—	1800
	4160	R-6253A	Automatic	.110/.204	—	.150	6	.015	.015	#61/—	—	1600
	4160	R-6254A	Manual	.110/.204	—	.150	6	.015	.015	#61/—	—	1800
	4160	R-6255A	Automatic	.110/.204	—	.150	6	.015	.015	#61/—	—	1600
	4160	R-6256A	Manual	.110/.204	—	.150	6	.015	.015	#62/—	—	2000
	4160	R-6257A	Automatic	.110/.204	—	.150	6	.015	.015	#62/—	—	1800
	4160	R-6290A	Automatic	.110/.204	—	.150	6	.015	.015	#61/—	—	1500
	BALL & BALL											
	BBD 1 1/4"	BBD-6149S	Automatic	1/4/—	—	1/4	6	—	.225	120-309S/—	—	1700
	BBD 1 1/4"	BBD-6150S	Manual	1/4/—	—	1/4	6	—	.225	120-309S/—	—	1900
	BBD 1 1/4"	BBD-6151	Automatic	1/4/—	—	1/4	6	—	.225	120-309S/—	—	1800
	BBD 1 1/4"	BBD-6152	Automatic	1/4/—	—	1/4	6	—	.225	120-309S/—	—	2000
	CARTER											
	TQ	TQ-6138S	Manual	1/—	—	.190	6	.815	9/16	—/—	—	1900
	TQ	TQ-6139S	Automatic	1/—	—	.190	6	.815	31/64	—/—	—	1900
	TQ	TQ-6140S	Manual	1/—	—	.190	6	.815	9/16	—/—	—	1900
	TQ	TQ-6090S	Automatic	1/—	—	.190	6	.815	31/64	—/—	—	1900
	TQ	TQ-6165S	Manual	1/—	—	.190	6	.815	9/16	—/—	—	2000
	TQ	TQ-6166S	Automatic	1/—	—	.190	6	.815	31/64	—/—	—	2100

CHRYSLER CORPORATION

Year	Carb. Model	Carb. Number	Dry Float Setting (Ins.)	Choke Unloader (Ins.)	Choke Vacuum Kick (Ins.)	Accel. Pump Stroke (Ins.) Curb Idle/ Sec. Pick-Up	Bowl Vent Valve (Ins.)	Choke Valve Clearance At Fast Idle Cam Position (Ins.)	Sec. Lockout (Ins.)	Main Jet	Air Valve Spring Tension (Turns)
1973	**CARTER**										
	BBD	6316S	1/4	.250	.150	.242/—	—	.095	—	120-866S	—
	BBD	6317S	1/4	.250	.130	.242/—	—	.095	—	120-866S	—
	BBD	6343S	1/4	.250	.150	.242/—	—	.095	—	120-866S	—
	BBD	6344S	1/4	.250	.150	.242/—	—	.095	—	120-866S	—
	TQ	6318S	1 1/16	.190	.160	35/64/23/64	.815	.110	.060-.090	—	1 1/4
	TQ	6319S	1 1/16	.190	.160	31/64/—	.815	.110	.060-.090	—	1 1/4
	TQ	6339S	1 1/16	.190	.160	35/64/23/64	.815	.110	.060-.090	—	1 1/4
	TQ	6340S	1 1/16	.190	.160	31/64/—	.815	.110	.060-.090	—	1 1/4
	TQ	6320S	1 1/16	.190	.160	35/64/23/64	.815	.110	.060-.090	—	1 1/4
	TQ	6321S	1 1/16	.190	.160	31/64/—	.815	.110	.060-.090	—	1 1/4
	TQ	6341S	1 1/16	.190	.160	35/64/23/64	.815	.110	.060-.090	—	1 1/4
	TQ	6342S	1 1/16	.190	.160	31/64/—	.815	.110	.060-.090	—	1 1/4
	TQ	6322S	1 3/16	.190	.160	31/64/—	.815	.110	.060-.090	—	1 1/4
	TQ	6410S	1 3/16	.190	.160	31/64/—	.815	.110	.060-.090	—	1 1/4
	TQ	6324S	1 3/16	.190	.160	31/64/—	.815	.110	.060-.090	—	1 1/4
	TQ	6411S	1 3/16	.190	.160	31/64/—	.815	.110	.060-.090	—	1 1/4
	HOLLEY										
	1920	R-6447A	.260	5	.100	—/—	.015	.065	—	582	—
	1920	R-6448A	.260	5	.080	—/—	.015	.045	—	572	—
	1920	R-6449A	.260	5	.080	—/—	.015	.065	—	572	—
	1920	R-6593A	.260	5	.100	—/—	.015	.065	—	622	—
	1920	R-6450A	.260	5	.100	—/—	.015	.065	—	622	—
	1920	R-6594A	.260	5	.100	—/—	.015	.065	—	612	—
	1920	R-6553A	.260	5	.100	—/—	.015	.065	—	612	—
	1920	R-6595A	.260	5	.100	—/—	.015	.065	—	622	—
	1920	R-6554A	.260	5	.100	—/—	.015	.065	—	622	—
	1920	R-6596A	.260	5	.100	—/—	.015	.065	—	612	—
	2210	R-6452A	.180	.170	.150	.250/—	.015	.110	—	642	—
	2210	R-6575A	.180	.170	.150	.250/—	.015	.110	—	642	—
	2210	R-6454A	.180	.170	.150	.250/—	.015	.110	—	642	—
	2210	R-6472A	.180	.170	.150	.250/—	.015	.110	—	642	—
1974	**CARTER**										
	BBD	6464S	1/4	.325	.150	1/2 /—	—	.095	—	120-389	—
	BBD	6465S	1/4	.325	.110	1/2 /—	—	.095	—	120-389	—
	BBD	6466S	1/4	.325	.150	1/2 /—	—	.095	—	120-389	—
	BBD	6467S	1/4	.325	.110	1/2 /—	—	.095	—	120-389	—
	TQ	6488S	1	.310	.160	35/64/21/64	13/16	.100	.060-.090	—	1 1/4
	TQ	6452S	1	.310	.210	35/64/21/64	—	.100	.060-.090	—	1 1/4
	TQ	6453S	1	.310	.160	31/64/—	—	.100	.060-.090	—	1 1/4
	TQ	6454S	1	.310	.210	35/64/21/64	—	.100	.060-.090	—	1 1/4
	TQ	6455S	1	.310	.160	31/64/—	—	.100	.060-.090	—	1 1/4
	TQ	6489S	1	.310	.160	31/64/—	13/16	.100	.060-.090	—	1 1/4
	TQ	6496S	1	.310	.160	31/64/—	13/16	.100	.060-.090	—	1 1/4
	TQ	6456S	1	.310	.210	35/64/21/64	—	.100	.060-.090	—	1 1/4
	TQ	6457S	1	.310	.160	31/64/—	13/16	.100	.060-.090	—	1 1/4
	TQ	6459	1	.310	.160	31/64/—	13/16	.100	.060-.090	—	1 1/4
	TQ	6460	1	.310	.160	31/64/—	—	.100	.060-.090	—	1 1/4
	TQ	6461S	1	.310	.160	31/64/—	—	.100	.060-.090	—	1 1/4
	TQ	6462S	1	.310	.160	31/64/—	13/16	.100	.060-.090	—	1 1/4
	TQ	6463S	1	.310	.160	31/64/—	13/16	.100	.060-.090	—	1 1/4
	HOLLEY										
	1945	R-6721A	1/32	.250	.140	11/16/—	—	.080	—	621	—
	1945	R-6722A	1/32	.250	.090	13/16/—	—	.080	—	602	—
	1945	R-6723A	1/32	.250	.140	11/16/—	—	.080	—	622	—
	1945	R-6724A	1/32	.250	.080	3/4/—	—	.080	—	622	—
	1945	R-6725A	1/32	.250	.140	11/16/—	—	.080	—	622	—
	1945	R-6726A	1/32	.250	.090	3/4 /—	—	.080	—	622	—
	2245	R-6731A	.180	.170	.150	.255/—	.015	.110	—	651	—
	2245	R-6737A	.180	.170	.150	.255/—	.015	.110	—	642	—

CHRYSLER

Year	Carb. Model	Carb. Number	Dry Float Setting (Ins.)	Choke Unloader (Ins.)	Choke Vacuum Kick (Ins.)	Accel. Pump Stroke (Ins.) Curb Idle/ Sec. Pick-Up	Bowl Vent Valve (Ins.)	Choke Valve Clearance At Fast Idle Cam Position (Ins.)	Sec. Lockout (Ins.)	Main Jet	Air Valve Spring Tension (Turns)
1975	CARTER										
	BBD	8000S	1/4	.280	.130	.500/—	–	.070	–	120-392	–
	BBD	8064S	1/4	.310	.070	.500/—	–	.070	–	120-392	–
	BBD	8001S	1/4	.310	.110	.500/—	–	.070	–	120-392	–
	BBD	8003S	1/4	.310	.110	.500/—	–	.070	–	120-392	–
	BBD	8066S	1/4	.280	.130	.500/—	–	.070	–	120-392	–
	BBD	8062S	1/4	.310	.110	.500/—	–	.070	–	120-392	–
	TQ	9004S	29/32	.310	.100	35/64/21/64	13/16	.100	.060-.090	–	1 1/4
	TQ	9002S	29/32	.310	.100	35/64/21/64	13/16	.100	.060-.090	–	1 1/4
	TQ	9046S	29/32	.310	.100	35/64/21/64	13/16	.100	.060-.090	–	1 1/4
	TQ	9008S	29/32	.310	.100	35/64/21/64	13/16	.100	.060-.090	–	1 1/4
	TQ	9053S	29/32	.310	.100	35/64/21/64	13/16	.100	.060-.090	–	1 1/4
	TQ	9050S	29/32	.310	.100	35/64/21/64	13/16	.100	.060-.090	–	1 1/4
	TQ	9009S	29/32	.310	.100	35/64/21/64	13/16	.100	.060-.090	–	1 1/4
	TQ	9010S	29/32	.310	.100	35/64/21/64	13/16	.100	.060-.090	–	1 1/4
	TQ	9051S	29/32	.310	.100	35/64/21/64	13/16	.100	.060-.090	–	1 1/4
	TQ	9011S	29/32	.310	.100	35/64/21/64	13/16	.100	.060-.090	–	1 1/4
	TQ	9012S	29/32	.310	.100	35/64/21/64	13/16	.100	.060-.090	–	1 1/4
	TQ	9052S	29/32	.310	.100	35/64/21/64	13/16	.100	.060-.090	–	1 1/4
	HOLLEY										
1945		R-7329A	3/64	.250	.130	2 7/32/—	–	.080	–	621	–
1945		R-7017A	3/64	.250	.130	2 7/32/—	–	.080	–	621	–
1945		R-7018A	3/64	.250	.090	2 21/64/—	–	.080	–	611	–
1945		R-7019A	3/64	.250	.130	2 7/32/—	–	.080	–	621	–
1945		R-7020A	3/64	.250	.090	2 21/64/—	–	.080	–	623	–
1945		R-7029A	3/64	.250	.130	2 7/32/—	–	.080	–	621	–
1945		R-7210A	3/64	.250	.090	2 21/64/—	–	.080	–	623	–
2245		R-7226A	3/16	.170	.150	1/4 /—	.015	.110	–	611	–
2245		R-7211A	3/16	.170	.150	1/4 /—	.015	.110	–	651	–
2245		R-7027A	3/16	.170	.150	1/4 /—	.015	.110	–	641	–
1976	CARTER										
	BBD	8071S	1/4	.280	.130	.500/—	–	.070	–	120-389	–
	BBD	8069S	1/4	.310	.070	.500/—	–	.070	–	120-389	–
	BBD	8070S	1/4	.310	.110	.500/—	–	.070	–	120-389	–
	BBD	8077S	1/4	.280	.110	.500/—	–	.070	–	120-392	–
	TQ	9002S	29/32	.310	.100	33/64/ 5/16	–	.100	.060-.090	–	1 1/4
	TQ	9054S	29/32	.310	.100	33/64/ 5/16	–	.100	.060-.090	–	1 1/4
	TQ	9055S	29/32	.310	.100	33/64/ 5/16	–	.110	.060-.090	–	1 1/4
	TQ	9058S	29/32	.310	.100	31/64/—	–	.100	.060-.090	–	1 1/4
	TQ	9059S	29/32	.310	.100	31/64/—	–	.100	.060-.090	–	1 1/4
	TQ	9062S	29/32	.310	.100	33/64/ 5/16	–	.100	.060-.090	–	1 1/4
	TQ	9066S	29/32	.310	.100	33/64/ 5/16	–	.100	.060-.090	–	1 1/4
	TQ	9074S	29/32	.310	.100	33/64/ 5/16	–	.110	.060-.090	–	1 1/4
	TQ	9057S	29/32	.310	.100	33/64/ 5/16	–	.100	.060-.090	–	1 1/4
	TQ	9052S	29/32	.310	.100	33/64/ 5/16	–	.100	.060-.090	–	1 1/4
	HOLLEY										
1945		R-7356A	7	.250	.110	2 7/32/—	–	.080	–	621	–
1945		R-7357A	7	.250	.100	2 21/64/—	–	.080	–	611	–
1945		R-7360A	7	.250	.110	2 7/32/—	–	.080	–	621	–
1945		R-7361A	7	.250	.100	2 21/64/—	–	.080	–	623	–
1945		R-7362A	7	.250	.110	2 7/32/—	–	.080	–	621	–
1945		R-7363A	7	.250	.100	2 21/64/—	–	.080	–	611	–
2245		R-7364A	3/16	.170	.150	17/64/—	.025	.110	–	611	–
2245		R-7366A	3/16	.170	.150	17/64/—	.025	.110	–	641	–
1977	CARTER										
	BBD	8087S	1/4	.280	.100	15/32/—	–	.070	–	–	–
	BBD	8089S	1/4	.280	.130	15/32/—	–	.070	–	–	–
	BBD	8090S	1/4	.280	.130	15/32/—	–	.070	–	–	–
	BBD	8127S	1/4	.280	.110	15/32/—	–	.070	–	–	–
	BBD	8093S	1/4	.310	.130	15/32/—	–	.070	–	–	–
	BBD	8094S	1/4	.310	.070	15/32/—	–	.070	–	–	–
	BBD	8096S	1/4	.310	.110	15/32/—	–	.070	–	–	–
	BBD	8126S	1/4	.310	.110	15/32/—	–	.070	–	–	–
	TQ	9076S	27/32	.310	.150	33/64/ 5/16	13/16	.100	.060-.090	–	1 1/2
	TQ	9077S	27/32	.310	.100	33/64/ 5/16	13/16	.100	.060-.090	–	1 1/2
	TQ	9078S	27/32	.310	.100	33/64/ 5/16	13/16	.100	.060-.090	–	1 1/4
	TQ	9080S	27/32	.310	.100	33/64/ 5/16	13/16	.100	.060-.090	–	1 1/4
	TQ	9081S	27/32	.310	.100	33/64/ 5/16	13/16	.100	.060-.090	–	1 1/4
	TQ	9093S	27/32	.310	.150	33/64/23/64	13/16	.100	.060-.090	–	1 1/4
	TQ	9101S	27/32	.310	.100	33/64/ 5/16	13/16	.100	.060-.090	–	1 1/4
	HOLLEY										
1945		R-7632A	7	.250	.110	2 7/32/—	1/16	.080	–	–	–
1945		R-7633A	7	.250	.110	2 21/64/—	1/16	.080	–	–	–
1945		R-7635A	7	.250	.110	2 21/64/—	–	.080	–	–	–
1945		R-7744A	7	.250	.130	2 21/64/—	1/16	.080	–	–	–
1945		R-7745A	7	.250	.150	2 7/32/—	1/16	.080	–	–	–
1945		R-7746A	7	.250	.110	2 21/64/—	1/16	.080	–	–	–
1945		R-7764A	7	.250	.110	2 21/64/—	1/16	.080	–	–	–
1945		R-7765A	7	.250	.110	2 21/64/—	1/16	.080	–	–	–
2245		R-7671A	3/16	.170	.110	17/64/—	.025	.110	–	–	–
1978	CARTER										
	BBD	8137S	1/4	.280	.100	1/2 /—	.080	.070	–	–	–
	BBD	8177S	1/4	.280	.100	1/2 /—	.080	.070	–	–	–
	BBD	8136S	1/4	.280	.110	1/2 /—	.080	.070	–	–	–
	BBD	8175S	1/4	.280	.160	1/2 /—	.080	.070	–	–	–
	BBD	8143S	1/4	.280	.150	1/2 /—	.080	.070	.075	–	–
	TQ	9147S	29/32	.310	.100	31/64/23/64	–	.100	.075	–	1 1/2
	TQ	9137S	29/32	.310	.100	31/64/23/64	13/16	.100	.075	–	1 1/2
	TQ	9134S	29/32	.310	.100	31/64/23/64	–	.100	.075	–	1 1/2
	TQ	9104S	29/32	.310	.150	31/64/ 5/16	–	.100	.075	–	1 1/2
	TQ	9140S	29/32	.310	.150	33/64/ 5/16	–	.100	.075	–	1 1/2
	TQ	9108S	27/32	.310	.100	33/64/ 5/16	13/16	.100	.075	–	1 1/2
	TQ	9109S	27/32	.310	.100	33/64/ 5/16	–	.100	.075	–	1 1/2
	TQ	9110S	27/32	.310	.100	33/64/ 5/16	–	.100	.075	–	1 1/2
	TQ	9111S	27/32	.310	.100	33/64/ 5/16	13/16	.100	.075	–	1 1/2
	TQ	9112S	29/32	.310	.100	33/64/ 5/16	–	.100	.075	–	1 1/2
	TQ	9148S	29/32	.310	.100	33/64/ 5/16	–	.100	.075	–	1 1/2
	HOLLEY										
1945		R-7988A	7	.250	.110	2 7/32/—	1/16	.080	–	–	–
1945		R-7989A	7	.250	.110	2 21/64/—	1/16	.080	–	–	–
1945		R-8394A	7	.250	.110	2 21/64/—	1/16	.080	–	–	–
1945		R-8010A	7	.250	.130	2 21/64/—	1/16	.080	–	–	–
1945		R-8008A	7	.250	.110	2 21/64/—	1/16	.080	–	–	–
2245		R-7991A	3/16	.170	.110	17/64/—	.025	.110	–	–	–
2245		R-8326A	3/16	.170	.110	17/64/—	.025	.110	–	–	–
2280		R-7990A	5/16	.310	.150	11	.030	.070	–	–	–

CARBURETOR SPECIFICATIONS

CHRYSLER CORPORATION

Year	Carb. Model	Carb. Number	Dry Float Setting (Ins.)	Choke Unloader (Ins.)	Choke Vacuum Kick (Ins.)	Accel. Pump Stroke (Ins.) Curb Idle/ Sec. Pick-Up	Bowl Vent Valve (Ins.)	Choke Valve Clearance At Fast Idle Cam Position (Ins.)	Sec. Lockout (Ins.)	Main Jet	Air Valve Spring Tension (Turns)
1979	**CARTER**										
	BBD	8198S	1/4	.280	.100	1/2 /—	.080	.070	–	–	–
	BBD	8199S	1/4	.280	.100	1/2 /—	.080	.070	–	–	–
	TQ	9195S	29/32	.310	.100	33/64/—	–	.100	.075	–	2
	TQ	9196S	29/32	.310	.100	33/64/—	–	.100	.075	–	2
	TQ	9197S	29/32	.310	.100	33/64/—	–	.100	.075	–	1 1/2
	TQ	9198S	29/32	.310	.100	33/64/—	–	.100	.075	–	2
	TQ	9202S	29/32	.310	.100	33/64/—	–	.100	.075	–	2
	HOLLEY										
	1945	R-8523A	7	.250	.110	1.7/—	1/16	.080	–	–	–
	1945	R-8452A	7	.250	.110	1.605/—	1/16	.080	–	–	–
	1945	R-6555A	7	.250	.110	1.7/—	1/16	.080	–	–	–
	1945	R-8727A	7	.250	.130	1.605/—	1/16	.080	–	–	–
	1945	R-8680A	7	.250	.110	1.605/—	1/16	.080	–	–	–
	2245	R-8450A	3/16	.170	.110	17/64/—	.025	.110	–	–	–
	2245	R-8774A	3/16	.170	.110	17/64/—	.025	.110	–	–	–
	2280	R-8448A	5/16	.310	.150	11	.030	.070	–	–	–

1Use gauge provided in carb rebuild kit.
29/16/13/16 wet setting.
3#25 drill.
4Center float in bowl with fuel bowl inverted.
5Automatically set when fast idle cam is adjusted.
6Thermostatically controlled by electric assist fixed setting.
7Flush with top of bowl gasket.
8Off vehicle at closed throttle, .080-in on vehicle at curb idle.
9Slot #2.
10Slot #3.
11Flush with top of bowl vent casting.

OMNI/HORIZON

Year	Carb. Model	Carb. Number	Trans.	Dry Float Setting (Ins.)	Float Drop (Ins.)	Vacuum Kick (Ins.)	Pump Setting Hole	Choke Setting (Notches)	Throttle Position Transducer	Curb Idle Speed (Rpm)	Fast Idle Speed (Rpm)	Throttle Stop Speed (Rpm)	A/C Idle Speed (Rpm)
1978	**HOLLEY**												
	5200	R-8505A	Man.	.480	1.875	.070	2	2NR	35/64	900	1100	700	—
	5200	R-8376A	Man.	.480	1.875	.070	2	2NR	35/64	900	1100	700	—
	5200	R-8507A	Man.	.480	1.875	.070	2	2NR	35/64	900	1100	—	850
	5200	R-8631A	Man.	.480	1.875	.070	2	2NR	35/64	900	1100	—	850
	5200	R-8439A	Man.	.480	1.875	.070	2	2NR	35/64	900	1100	700	—
	5200	R-8441A	Man.	.480	1.875	.070	2	2NR	35/64	900	1100	—	850
	5200	R-8384A	Man.	.480	1.875	.070	2	2NR	35/64	900	1100	700	—
	5200	R-8386A	Man.	.480	1.875	.070	2	2NR	35/64	900	1100	—	850
	5200	R-8504A	Auto.	.480	1.875	.070	2	2NR	–	900	1100	700	—
	5200	R-8630A	Auto.	.480	1.875	.070	2	2NR	–	900	1100	700	—
	5200	R-8506A	Auto.	.480	1.875	.070	2	2NR	–	900	1100	—	750
	5200	R-8632A	Auto.	.480	1.875	.070	2	2NR	–	900	1100	—	750
	5200	R-8440A	Auto.	.480	1.875	.070	2	2NR	–	900	1100	700	—
	5200	R-8442A	Auto.	.480	1.875	.070	2	2NR	–	900	1100	—	750
	5200	R-8385A	Auto.	.480	1.875	.070	2	2NR	–	900	1100	700	—
	5200	R-8387A	Auto.	.480	1.875	.070	2	2NR	–	900	1100	—	750
1979	**HOLLEY**												
	5200	R-8525A	Man.	.480	1.875	.070	2	2NR	–	900	1400	700	—
	5200	R-8451A	Man.	.480	1.875	.070	2	2NR	–	900	1400	—	850
	5200	R-8531A	Man.	.480	1.875	.070	2	2NR	–	900	1400	700	—
	5200	R-8533A	Man.	.480	1.875	.070	2	2NR	–	900	1400	—	850
	5200	R-8527A	Man.	.480	1.875	.070	2	2NR	–	900	1400	700	—
	5200	R-8529A	Man.	.480	1.875	.070	2	2NR	–	900	1400	—	850
	5200	R-8524A	Auto.	.480	1.875	.040	2	2NR	–	900	1700	700	—
	5200	R-8526A	Auto.	.480	1.875	.040	2	2NR	–	900	1700	—	750
	5200	R-8532A	Auto.	.480	1.875	.040	2	2NR	–	900	1700	700	—
	5200	R-8534A	Auto.	.480	1.875	.040	2	2NR	–	900	1700	—	750
	5200	R-8528A	Auto.	.480	1.875	.040	2	2NR	–	900	1700	700	—
	5200	R-8530A	Auto.	.480	1.875	.040	2	2NR	–	900	1700	—	750

FORD, MERCURY, LINCOLN

Year	Carburetor Model	Carburetor Number	Transmission	Dry Float Setting (ins.)	Pump Setting Hole	Main Jet Pri./Sec.	Power Jet	Pump Jet	Choke Plate Pulldown (ins.)	Choke Setting	Dash Pot (ins.)	Idle Speed (rpm)	Fast Idle Speed (rpm)
1970	**CARTER**												
	YF	D0DF-R	Manual	7/32	—	092/—	—	.028	.225	1 rich	7/64	7501	—
	YF	D0DF-U	Manual	7/32	—	092/—	—	.028	.225	1 rich	7/64	7501	—
	YF	D0DF-N	Automatic	7/32	—	092/—	—	.025	.225	Index	7/64	5502	—
	YF	D0DF-S	Automatic	7/32	—	092/—	—	.025	.225	Index	7/64	5502	—
	YF	D0DF-M	Manual	3/8	—	104/—	—	.028	.265	Index	7/64	7501	—
	YF	D0DF-T	Manual	3/8	—	104/—	—	.028	.265	Index	7/64	7501	—
	YF	D0DF-L	Automatic	3/8	—	101/—	—	.028	.265	Index	7/64	5502	—
	YF	D0DF-V	Automatic	3/8	—	101/—	—	.028	.265	Index	7/64	5502	—
	YF	D0AF-A	Manual	3/8	—	104/—	—	.028	.225	Index	3	800/5004	—
	YF	D0AF-B	Automatic	3/8	—	101/—	—	.031	.225	1 lean	7/64	500	—
	RBS	D0ZF-C	Manual	9/16	—	080/—	—	.026	.190	Index	3	750/5004	—
	RBS	D0ZF-D	Automatic	9/16	—	080/—	—	.028	.190	1 rich	3	600/5004	—
	RBS	D0ZF-F	Automatic	9/16	—	080/—	—	.028	.190	1 rich	7/32	550	—
	AUTOLITE												
	2100	D0AF-C	Manual	7/16	3	48F/—	.033	.024	.150	1 rich	3	800/5004	1400
	2100	D0AF-D	Automatic	7/16	2	48F/—	.033	.024	.150	1 rich	1/8	575	1500
	2100	D0AF-U	Automatic	7/16	2	48F/—	.033	.024	.150	1 rich	3	600/5004	1500
	2100	D0AF-E	Manual	7/16	3	54F/—	.033	.012	.230	2 lean	3	700/5004	1300

FORD, MERCURY, LINCOLN

Year	Carburetor Model	Carburetor Number	Transmission	Dry Float Setting (ins.)	Pump Setting Hole	Main Jet Pri./Sec.	Power Jet	Pump Jet	Choke Plate Pulldown (ins.)	Choke Setting	Dash Pot (ins.)	Idle Speed (rpm)	Fast Idle Speed (rpm)
	2100	D0AF-F	Automatic	7/16	4	55F/—	.035	.012	.200	2 lean	1/8	575	1600
	2100	D0AF-V	Automatic	7/16	4	55F/—	.035	.012	.200	2 lean	3	600/5004	1600
	2100	D0OF-K	Manual	7/16	4	57F/—	.033	.012	.220	Index	3	700/5004	1500
	2100	D0OF-L	Automatic	7/16	3	55F/—	.037	.012	.190	1 rich	1/8	600	1500
	2100	D0OF-M	Automatic	7/16	3	55F/—	.037	.012	.190	1 rich	3	600/5004	1500
	2100	D0AF-Y	Manual	7/16	3	55F/—	.033	.031	.210	1 rich	3	750/5004	1400
	2100	D0AF-Z	Automatic	7/16	3	55F/—	.037	.031	.200	—	1/8	575	1500
	2100	D0AF-AA	Automatic	7/16	3	55F/—	.037	.031	.200	—	3	600/5004	1500
	2100	D0AF-J	Automatic	7/16	3	55F/—	.033	.031	.200	—	1/8	590	1400
	2100	D0AF-T	Automatic	7/16	3	55F/—	.033	.031	.200	—	3	600/5004	1400
	4300	D0OF-Z,AB	Manual	.79-.85	2	61F/.128	.059	.028	.180	Index	3	800/5004	1250
	4300	D0OF-Y,AC	Automatic	.79-.85	2	62F/.128	.059	.028	.200	Index	.080	600	1400
	4300	D0OF-AA,AD	Automatic	.79-.85	2	62F/.128	.059	.028	.200	Index	3	600/5004	1400
	4300	D0AF-M,AD,AJ	Automatic	1.00	3	61F/.116	.059	.035	.160	2 rich	.080	600	1600
	4300	D0AF-R,AE,AK	Automatic	1.00	3	61F/.116	.059	.035	.160	2 rich	3	600/5004	1600
	4300	D0AF-L,AB,AL	Manual	2 5/32	2	64F/.128	.052	.028	.250	Index	.070	700	1400
	4300	D0AF-AG,AM	Automatic	2 5/32	2	63F/.128	.055	.028	.220	Index	.070	600	1300
	4300	D0SF-A,D,E	Automatic	2 5/32	2	63F/.128	.055	.028	.220	Index	.070	600	1300
	4300	D0VF-A,B,C	Automatic	2 5/32	2	62/.116	.049	.028	.230	1 rich	.100	600	1250
	HOLLEY												
	4150-C	D0ZF-Z	Manual	5	—	—/—	—	—	—	Man.	—	—	1900
	4150-C	D0ZF-AA	Manual	5	—	66/79	—	—	—	Man.	.140	725	1900
	4150-C	D0ZF-AB	Automatic	5	—	66/79	—	—	—	Man.	.200	675	2100
	4150-C	D0ZF-AC	Manual	5	—	66/79	—	—	—	Man.	3	725/5004	1900
	4150-C	D0ZF-AD	Automatic	5	—	66/79	—	—	—	Man.	3	675/5004	2100
	4150-C	D0OF-N	Manual	5	—	71/83	—	—	—	Auto.	3	650/5004	2400
	4150-C	D0OF-R	Automatic	5	—	70/83	—	—	—	Auto.	3	700/5004	2200
	4150-C	D0OF-S	Manual	5	—	64/82	—	—	—	Man.	3	700/5004	2200
	ROCHESTER												
	4MV	D0OF-A	Manual	5/8	—	—/—	—	—	—	.0156	—	700	750[7]
	4MV	D0OF-B	Automatic	5/8	—	—/—	—	—	—	.0156	—	650	1850
	4MV	D0OF-E	Automatic	5/8	—	—/—	—	—	—	.0156	3	650/5004	1850
	4MV	D0OF-F	Manual	5/8	—	—/—	—	—	—	.0156	3	700/5004	750[7]
1971	**CARTER**												
	YF	D1DF-MA,KA	Automatic	3/8	—	101/—	—	.031	.200	Index	3	600/5004	2000
	YF	D1DF-GA	Manual	3/8	—	104/—	—	.028	.230	Index	100	750	1750
	YF	D1DF-HA	Manual	3/8	—	104/—	—	.028	.230	Index	3	800/5004	1750
	YF	D1DF-LA,JA	Automatic	3/8	—	101/—	—	.031	.200	Index	100	550	2000
	YF	D1AF-PA	Manual	3/8	—	104/—	—	.028	.200	Index	3	800/5004	1250
	YF	D1AF-RA	Automatic	3/8	—	101/—	—	.031	.230	Index	.100	500	1650
	YF	D1DF-EA	Manual	3/8	—	092/—	—	.028	.200	Index	.100	750	1450
	RBS	D1ZF-LA,HA	Manual	9/16	—	080/—	—	.026	.270	Index	3	750/5004	1600
	RBS	D1ZF-NA,KA	Automatic	9/16	—	080/—	—	.028	.190	1 rich	3	600/5004	1600
	AUTOLITE												
	2100D	D1AF-BA	Manual	7/16	2	47F/—	.031	.024	.150	Index	3	800/5004	1500
	2100D	D1AF-DA	Automatic	7/16	3	47F/—	.031	.024	.170	1 rich	3	600/5004	1400
	2100D	D1ZF-AA	Automatic	7/16	3	47F/—	.031	.024	.150	Index	3	600/5004	1500
	2100D	D1OF-PA	Manual	7/16	3	61F/—	.045	.031	.230	Index	3	700/5004	1500
	2100D	D1ZF-SA	Automatic	7/16	3	54F/—	.037	.031	.200	1 rich	3	600/5004	1500
	2100D	D1OF-RA	Automatic	7/16	3	54F/—	.037	.031	.200	1 rich	3	600/5004	1500
	2100D	D1AF-FA	Manual	7/16	3	54F/—	.036	.031	.220	1 rich	3	600/5004	1300
	2100D	D1AF-JA	Automatic	7/16	3	54F/—	.036	.031	.190	Index	1/8	575	1600
	2100D	D1AF-KA	Automatic	7/16	3	54F/—	.036	.031	.190	Index	3	600/5004	1600
	2100D	D1YF-DA	Automatic	7/16	3	54F/—	.039	.031	.200	Index	3	600/5004	1500
	2100D	D1MF-JA	Automatic	7/16	3	54F/—	.042	.033	.190	1 rich	1/8	600	1500
	2100D	D1MF-FA	Automatic	7/16	3	54F/—	.039	.031	.200	1 rich	1/8	590	1400
	4300	D1OF-EA	Manual	13/16	2	61F/.116	.073	.028	.180	Index	3	825/5004	1250
	4300	D1OF-AAA	Automatic	13/16	2	62F/.116	.073	.028	.200	Index	3	625/5004	1400
	4300	D1OF-MA	Automatic	49/64	2	62F/.128	.059	.028	.220	Index	1/16	600	1350
	4300	D1SF-AA	Automatic	49/64	2	62F/.128	.059	.028	.220	Index	1/16	600	1350
	4300	D1VF-AA	Automatic	49/64	2	62F/.101	.059	.028	.220	1 rich	100	600	1250
	HOLLEY												
	4150-C	D1ZF-VA	Manual	5	2	71/82	—	—	—	Man.	1/8	825	2100
	4150-C	D1ZF-YA	Manual	5	2	71/83	—	—	—	2 rich	7/64	700	2200
	4150-C	D1ZF-XA	Automatic	5	2	70/83	—	—	—	2 rich	3	650/5004	2400
	ROCHESTER												
	4MV	D0OF-A	Manual	11/32	—	—/—	—	—	—	—	—	700	1800[8]
	4MV	D0OF-E	Automatic	11/32	—	—/—	—	—	—	—	3	650/5004	2000[8]
1972	**CARTER**												
	YF	D2DF-AA	Manual	3/8	—	92/—	—	—	.170	Index	100	750	1500
	YF	D2DF-BA	Manual	3/8	—	104/—	—	—	.230	Index	100	750	1750
	YF	D2DF-CA	Manual	3/8	—	104/—	—	—	.230	Index	3	800/5004	1750
	YF	D2DF-DA	Automatic	3/8	—	101/—	—	—	.200	1 rich	100	550	2000
	YF	D2DF-EA	Automatic	3/8	—	101/—	—	—	.200	1 rich	3	600/5004	2000
	YF	D2AF-JA	Automatic	3/8	—	101/—	—	—	.230	1 lean	100	·500	1650
	RBS	D2OF-LA	Manual	56	—	80/—	—	—	.300	Index	3	750/5004	1600
	RBS	D2OF-MA	Automatic	56	—	80/—	—	—	.190	1 rich	3	600/5004	1600
	RBS	D2OF-SA	Automatic	56	—	80/—	—	—	.190	1 rich	3	600/5004	1600
	AUTOLITE												
	2100D	D2OF-KA,KB	Manual	7/16	2A	48F/—	.029	.024	.140	1 rich	3	800/5004	1400
	2100D	D2GF-AA,AB,AC	Automatic	7/16	2A	48F/—	.029	.024	.150	1 rich	1/8	575	1400
	2100D	D2GF-BA,BB,BC	Automatic	7/16	2A	48F/—	.029	.024	.150	1 rich	3	600/5004	1400
	2100D	D2ZF-FA,FB,VA	Automatic	7/16	2A	48F/—	.029	.024	.150	1 rich	3	600/5004	1400
	2100D	D2AF-HA,HB,HC	Automatic	7/16	2A	48F/—	.029	.024	.150	1 rich	1/8	575	1400
	2100	D2ZF-LA	Manual	7/16	3A	61F/—	.045	.031	.240	1 rich	3	750/5004	1400
	2100	D2AF-FB,FC	Automatic	7/16	3A	48F/—	.033	.024	.140	Index	1/8	575	1500
	2100	D2AF-GB,GC	Automatic	7/16	3A	48F/—	.033	.024	.140	Index	3	600/5004	1500
	2100	D2OF-UB	Automatic	7/16	3A	54F/—	.037	.031	.190	1 rich	3	575/5004	1500
	2100	D2WF-CA	Automatic	7/16	3A	54F/—	.037	.031	.190	2 rich	3	575/5004	1500
	2100D	D2MF-FB	Automatic	7/16	4A	54F/—	.037	.031	.180	1 rich	3	625/5004	1500
	2100D	D2MF-FE	Automatic	7/16	4B	53F/—	.039	.031	.170	Index	3	625/5004	1500
	2100D	D2AF-UC	Automatic	7/16	3A	53F/—	.039	.031	.170	Index	3	625/5004	1500
	4300A	D2AF-AA,AB	Automatic	49/64	1	60F/.101	.059	.028	.220	2 rich	3	600/5004	1350
	4300A	D2SF-AA	Automatic	49/64	1	60F/.101	.059	.028	.220	2 rich	3	600/5004	1350
	4300A	D2SF-BA,BB	Automatic	49/64	1	60F/.101	.059	.028	.220	2 rich	3	600/5004	1350
	4300A	D2VF-AA	Automatic	49/64	1	61F/.096	.059	.028	.230	Index	3	625/5004	1250
	4300A	D2VF-BA	Automatic	49/64	1	61F/.096	.059	.028	.230	Index	3	625/5004	1250
	4300A	D2SF-AB,AC	Automatic	49/64	1	60F/.101	.059	.028	.220	1 rich	3	600/5004	1350
	4300A	D2VF-BB	Automatic	49/64	1	61F/.096	.059	.028	.230	Index	3	625/5004	1250
	4300D	D2ZF-GA	Manual	13/16	1	61F/—	.055	.055	.200	Index	3	1000/5004	1200

CARBURETOR SPECIFICATIONS

FORD, MERCURY, LINCOLN

Year	Carburetor Model	Carburetor Number	Transmission	Dry Float Setting (ins.)	Pump Setting Hole	Main Jet Pri./Sec.	Power Jet	Pump Jet	Choke Plate Pulldown (ins.)	Choke Setting	Dash Pot (ins.)	Idle Speed (rpm)	Fast Idle Speed (rpm)
1972	4300D	D2ZF-AA	Manual	13/16	1	61F/—	.063	.063	.200	Index	3	1000/5004	1200
	4300D	D2ZF-BB	Automatic	13/16	1	61F/—	.063	.063	.200	Index	3	700/5004	1200
	4300D	D2AF-LA	Automatic	49/64	1	62F/—	.055	.055	.215	Index	3	700/5004	1200
	4300D	D2ZF-DA	Automatic	13/64	1	61F/—	.063	.063	.200	Index	3	700/5004	1200
1973	**CARTER**												
	YF	D3DF-AB	Manual	3/8	—	.104/—	—	.028	.230	Index	.10	9	1750
	YF	D3DF-BB	Manual	3/8	—	.104/—	—	.028	.230	Index	3	9	1750
	YF	D3DF-GB	Automatic	3/8	—	.101/—	—	.031	.200	1 rich	3	9	2000
	YF	D3DF-FB	Automatic	3/8	—	.101/—	—	.031	.200	1 rich	.10	9	2000
	YF	D3OF-CB	Automatic	9/16	—	.083/—	—	.028	.190	Index	3	9	1700
	YF	D3OF-BC	Manual	9/16	—	.083/—	—	.028	.300	Index	3	9	1600
	YF	D3OF-CC	Automatic	9/16	—	.083/—	—	.028	.190	Index	3	9	1700
	MOTORCRAFT												
	2100D	D3AF-NA	Automatic	7/16	3	54F/—	.037	.031	—	1 rich	3	9	1500
	2100D	D3AF-JA	Automatic	7/16	3	53F/—	.038	.031	—	1 rich	3	9	1500
	2100D	D3AF-XA	Automatic	7/16	3	55F/—	.041	.031	—	3 rich	3	9	1500
	2100D	D3GF-BB	Manual	7/16	2A	47F/—	.034	.024	—	3 rich	3	9	1250
	2100D	D3DF-EA	Manual	7/16	2A	48F/—	.034	.024	—	3 rich	3	9	1400
	2100D	D3OF-EA	Automatic	7/16	2A	49F/—	.033	.024	—	3 rich	3	9	1400
	2100D	D3AF-ABA	Automatic	7/16	2A	49F/—	.033	.024	—	3 rich	3	9	1400
	2100D	D3OF-JA	Automatic	7/16	2A	48F/—	.034	.029	—	3 rich	3	9	1500
	2100D	D3MF-AE	Automatic	7/16	3	54F/—	.039	.031	—	3 rich	3	9	1500
	2100D	D3MF-BA	Automatic	7/16	3	54F/—	.039	.031	—	3 rich	3	9	1500
	2100D	D3MF-DA	Automatic	7/16	3	54F/—	.039	.031	—	3 rich	3	9	1500
	2100D	D3MF-EA	Automatic	7/16	3	54F/—	.039	.031	—	3 rich	3	9	1500
	2100D	D3AF-RA	Automatic	7/16	2	55F/—	.036	.031	—	1 rich	3	9	1500
	2100D	D3AF-RB	Automatic	7/16	2	55F/—	.036	.031	—	3 rich	3	9	1500
	2100D	D3AF-CE	Automatic	7/16	3	52F/—	.039	.031	—	1 rich	3	9	1500
	2100D	D3MF-GA	Automatic	7/16	3	54F/—	.040	.031	—	3 rich	3	9	1500
	2100D	D3AF-PA	Automatic	7/16	3	55F/—	.041	.031	—	3 rich	3	9	1500
	2100D	D3AF-DC	Automatic	7/16	3	54F/—	.043	.031	—	3 rich	3	9	1500
	2100D	D3AF-KA	Automatic	7/16	3	54F/—	.043	.031	—	3 rich	3	9	1500
	2100D	D3ZF-FA	Automatic	7/16	3	54F/—	.042	.031	—	3 rich	3	9	1500
	4300	D3ZF-LA	Manual	13/16	1	60F/60F	.063	.028	.170	Index	—	9	1300
	4300	D3ZF-MA	Automatic	13/16	1	63F/63F	.063	.035	.180	Index	—	9	1300
	4300	D3AF-LA	Automatic	49/64	1	61F/.093	.059	.028	.200	Index	—	9	1350
	4300	D3AF-HA	Automatic	.76	1	62F/.093	.059	.028	.210	Index	—	9	1350
	4300	D3AF-VA	Automatic	49/64	1	62F/.093	.059	.028	.200	Index	—	9	1350
	4300	D3AF-TA	Automatic	7/8	1	61F/.116	.059	.028	.230	Index	—	9	1350
	4300	D3VF-DA	Automatic	49/64	1	61F/.101	.055	.028	.210	Index	—	9	1350
	4300	D3AF-EB	Automatic	.88	1	61F/.116	.059	.028	.200	Index	—	9	1900
	4300	D3ZF-AC	Automatic	.82	1	63F/63F	.063	.035	.180	Index	—	9	1300
	4300	D3ZF-BC	Manual	.82	1	62F/62F	.063	.035	.170	INR	—	9	1300
	4300	D3ZF-DC	Manual	.82	1	62F/62F	.063	.035	.180	Index	—	9	1300
1974	**CARTER**												
	YF	D4DE-EA	Automatic	3/8	—	.104/—	—	—	.200	Index	.100	9	9
	YF	D4DE-JA	Automatic	3/8	—	.101/—	—	—	.200	INR	.100	9	9
	YF	D4DE-JB	Automatic	3/8	—	.101/—	—	—	.200	Index	.100	9	9
	YF	D4DE-ABA	Manual	3/8	—	.101/—	—	—	.230	Index	.100	9	9
	YF	D4DE-KA	Automatic	3/8	—	.101/—	—	—	.200	INR	3	9	9
	YF	D4DE-KB	Automatic	3/8	—	.101/—	—	—	.200	Index	3	9	9
	RBS	D4DE-AB	Automatic	9/16	—	.083/—	—	—	.190	Index	3	9	9
	RBS	D4DE-SB	Manual	9/16	—	.083/—	—	—	.300	Index	3	9	9
	RBS	D4DE-AAA	Automatic	9/16	—	.083/—	—	—	.190	INL	3	9	9
	RBS	D4DE-BB	Manual	9/16	—	.083/—	—	—	.300	Index	3	9	9
	MOTORCRAFT												
	2100D	D4AE-DA	Automatic	7/16	2A	51F/—	—	—	—	INR	—	9	9
	2100D	D4AE-EA	Automatic	7/16	2A	55F/—	—	—	—	3NR	—	9	9
	2100D	D4AE-FA	Automatic	7/16	3A	54F/—	—	—	—	3NR	—	9	9
	2100D	D4OE-FA	Automatic	7/16	2A	55F/—	—	—	—	3NR	—	9	9
	2100D	D4AE-GA	Automatic	7/16	3A	54F/—	—	—	—	3NR	—	9	9
	2100D	D4AE-HB	Automatic	7/16	3A	56F/—	—	—	—	3NR	—	9	9
	2100D	D4DE-NB	Automatic	7/16	2	50/—	—	—	—	3NR	—	9	9
	2100D	D4DE-PA	Manual	7/16	2	49F/—	—	—	—	3NR	—	9	9
	2100D	D4OE-CA	Manual	7/16	2	48F/—	—	—	—	3NR	—	9	9
	2100D	D4DE-LA	Automatic	7/16	2	49F/—	—	—	—	3NR	—	9	9
	2100D	D4DE-RB	Automatic	7/16	2	50F/—	—	—	—	3NR	—	9	9
	2100D	D4ME-BA	Automatic	7/16	3A	56F/—	—	—	—	3NR	—	9	9
	2100D	D4ME-CA	Automatic	7/16	3A	55F/—	—	—	—	3NR	—	9	9
	4300	D4TE-ATA	Automatic	13/16	1	63F/—	—	—	.220	Index	—	9	9
	4300	D4OE-AA	Automatic	13/16	1	63F/—	—	—	.180	Index	—	9	9
	4300	D4AE-AA	Automatic	3/4	1	61F/—	—	—	.230	Index	—	9	9
	4300	D4VE-AB	Automatic	3/4	1	62F/—	—	—	.220	Index	—	9	9
	4300	D4AE-NA	Automatic	3/4	1	61F/—	—	—	.220	Index	—	9	9
	MOTORCRAFT–CARTER												
	TQ	D4AE-BC	Automatic	1 1/1610	Inner	.101/.098	—	—	.150	Index	—	9	9
1975	**CARTER**												
	YFA	D5DE-DA	Manual	3/8	—	.104/—	—	—	.290	2NR	—	9	9
	YFA	D5DE-EA	Manual	3/8	—	.104/—	—	—	.290	2NR	—	9	9
	YFA	D5DE-GA	Automatic	3/8	—	.104/—	—	—	.290	2NR	—	9	9
	YFA	D5DE-MA	Manual	3/8	—	.104/—	—	—	.290	2NR	—	9	9
	YFA	D5DE-ZA	Manual	3/8	—	.104/—	—	—	.290	2NR	—	9	9
	MOTORCRAFT												
	2150	D5DE-AA	Automatic	7/16	2	50F/—	—	—	.140	3NR	—	9	9
	2150	D5DE-BA	—	7/16	2	49F/—	—	—	.140	3NR	—	9	9
	2150	D5DE-JA	Automatic	7/16	2	51F/—	—	—	.140	3NR	—	9	9
	2150	D5ZE-JA	Automatic	7/16	2	49F/—	—	—	.140	3NR	—	9	9
	2150	D5OE-AA	Automatic	7/16	2	56F/—	—	—	.140	3NR	—	9	9
	2150	D5OE-DA	Automatic	7/16	2	56/—	—	—	.140	3NR	—	9	9
	2150	D5DE-HA	Automatic	7/16	3	57F/—	—	—	.140	3NR	—	9	9
	2150	D5DE-UA	Automatic	7/16	2	55F/—	—	—	.140	3NR	—	9	9
	2150	D5OE-BA	Automatic	7/16	3	56F/—	—	—	.125	3NR	—	9	9
	2150	D5OE-CA	Automatic	7/16	3	56F/—	—	—	.125	3NR	—	9	9
	2150	D5OE-GA	Automatic	7/16	2	56F/—	—	—	.125	3NR	—	9	9
	2150	D5AE-AA	Automatic	7/16	3	56F/—	—	—	.125	3NR	—	9	9
	2150	D5AE-EA	Automadic	7/16	3	55F/—	—	—	.125	3NR	—	9	9

FORD, MERCURY, LINCOLN

Year	Carburetor Model	Carburetor Number	Transmission	Dry Float Setting (ins.)	Pump Setting Hole	Main Jet Pri./Sec.	Power Jet	Pump Jet	Choke Plate Pulldown (ins.)	Choke Setting	Dash Pot (ins.)	Idle Speed (rpm)	Fast Idle Speed (rpm)
	2150	D5ME-BA	Automatic	7/16	2	58F/—	—	—	.125	3NR	—	9	9
	2150	D5ME-FA	Automatic	7/16	2	57/—	—	—	.125	3NR	—	9	9
	4350	D5VE-AD	Automatic	15/16	1	421/—	—	—	.160	2NR	—	9	9
	4350	D5VE-BA	Automatic	15/16	1	429/—	—	—	.160	2NR	—	9	9
	4350	D5AE-CA	Automatic	31/32	1	421/—	—	—	.160	2NR	—	9	9
	4350	D5AE-DA	Automatic	31/32	1	429/—	—	—	.160	2NR	—	9	9
1976	**CARTER**												
	YFA	D5DE-DB	Automatic	23/32	—	.104/—	—	—	.290	2NR	—	9	9
	YFA	D6BE-AA	Manual	25/32	—	.104/—	—	—	.260	1NR	—	9	9
	YFA	D5DE-MB	Manual	23/32	—	.104/—	—	—	.290	2NR	—	9	9
	YFA	D6BE-BB	Automatic	25/32	—	.104/—	—	—	.260	2NR	—	9	9
	YFA	D6DE-AB	Manual	23/32	—	.104/—	—	—	.290	Index	—	9	9
	YFA	D6DE-BB	Automatic	23/32	—	.104/—	—	—	.230	Index	—	9	9
	MOTORCRAFT												
	2150	D5DE-AEA	All	7/16	2	51F/—	—	—	—	3NR	—	9	9
	2150	D5DE-AFA	All	7/16	2	49F/—	—	—	—	3NR	—	9	9
	2150	D5WE-FA	Automatic	7/16	2	50F/—	—	—	—	3NR	—	9	9
	2150	D6ZE-JA	Automatic	7/16	2	50F/—	—	—	—	3NR	—	9	9
	2150	D6OE-AA	Automatic	7/16	3	57F/—	—	—	.160	3NR	—	9	9
	2150	D6OE-BA	Automatic	7/16	3	59F/—	—	—	.160	3NR	—	9	9
	2150	D6OE-CA	Automatic	7/16	3	59F/—	—	—	.160	3NR	—	9	9
	2150	D6WE-AA	Automatic	7/16	2	57F/—	—	—	.160	3NR	—	9	9
	2150	D6WE-BA	Automatic	7/16	2	58F/—	—	—	.160	2NR	—	9	9
	2150	D6AE-HA	Automatic	7/16	2	58F/—	—	—	.160	3NR	—	9	9
	2150	D6ME-AA	Automatic	7/16	2	58F/—	—	—	.160	3NR	—	9	9
	4350	D6AE-CA	Automatic	1.0	2	197/—	—	—	.140	2NR	—	9	9
	4350	D6AE-FA	Automatic	1.0	2	192/—	—	—	.140	2NR	—	9	9
	4350	D6AE-DA	Automatic	.96	2	421/—	—	—	.160	2NR	—	9	9
1977	**CARTER**												
	YFA	D5DE-GB	Automatic	1 19/32	—	.104/—	—	—	.290	2NR	—	9	9
	YFA	D7BE-AA	Manual	1 19/32	—	.104/—	—	—	.290	Index	—	9	9
	YFA	D7BE-AB	Manual	1 19/32	—	.104/—	—	—	.290	Index	—	9	9
	YFA	D7BE-BA	Automatic	1 19/32	—	.104/—	—	—	.260	1NR	—	9	9
	YFA	D7DE-DA	Automatic	1 19/32	—	.104/—	—	—	.260	1NR	—	9	9
	YFA	D7BE-FA	Automatic	1 19/32	—	.104/—	—	—	.260	2NR	—	9	9
	YFA	D7BE-GA	Manual	1 19/32	—	.104/—	—	—	.290	Index	—	9	9
	YFA	D7BE-GC	Automatic	1 19/32	—	.104/—	—	—	.290	2NR	—	9	9
	YFA	D7BE-HB	Automatic	1 19/32	—	.104/—	—	—	.290	2NR	—	9	9
	YFA	D7BE-NA	Automatic	1 19/32	—	.104/—	—	—	.260	1NR	—	9	9
	MOTORCRAFT												
	2150	D7BE-PA	Automatic	7/16	—	49F/—	—	—	.142	Index	—	9	9
	2150	D7BE-MA	Manual	7/16	—	49F/—	—	—	.157	Index	—	9	9
	2150	D7AE-CA	Automatic	7/16	—	57F/—	—	—	.180	2NR	—	9	9
	2150	D7AE-KA	Automatic	7/16	—	49F/—	—	—	.142	Index	—	9	9
	2150	D7AE-DA	Automatic	7/16	—	56/—	—	—	.150	2NR	—	9	9
	2150	D7DE-LA	Manual	7/16	—	49F/—	—	—	.157	Index	—	9	9
	2150	D7DE-RB	Automatic	7/16	—	55F/—	—	—	.170	1NR	—	9	9
	2150	D7OE-CA	Automatic	3/8	—	59F/—	—	—	.167	2NR	—	9	9
	2150	D7OE-HA	Automatic	7/16	—	60F/—	—	—	.185	1NR	—	9	9
	2150	D7OE-HB	Automatic	7/16	—	59F/—	—	—	.185	1NR	—	9	9
	2150	D7OE-NA	Automatic	3/8	—	59F/—	—	—	.167	2NR	—	9	9
	2150	D7WE-EA	Automatic	7/16	—	51F/—	—	—	.142	Index	—	9	9
	2700	D7ZE-GO	Automatic	1 3/64	—	—/—	—	—	—	Index	—	9	9
	4350	D7VE-KA	Automatic	1	—	202/—	—	—	.140	2NL	—	9	9
	4350	D7VE-MA	Automatic	1	—	207/—	—	—	.140	2NR	—	9	9
	4350	D7VE-NA	Automatic	1	—	207/—	—	—	.160	2NL	—	9	9
1978	**CARTER**												
	YFA	D8DE-BA	—	25/32	—	.101/—	—	—	.230	2NR	—	9	9
	YFA	D8DE-DA	—	25/32	—	.101/—	—	—	.230	2NR	—	9	9
	YFA	D8DE-EA	—	25/32	—	.101/—	—	—	.200	2NR	—	9	9
	YFA	D8KE-AA	—	25/32	—	.101/—	—	—	.230	2NR	—	9	9
	MOTORCRAFT		—										
	2150	D84E-EA	—	7/16	2 Inb.	49F/—	—	—	.110	3NR	—	9	9
	2150	D8AE-JA	—	3/8	3 Inb.	57F/—	—	—	.167	3NR	—	9	9
	2150	D8BE-ACA	—	7/16	4 Inb.	55F/—	—	—	.155	2NR	—	9	9
	2150	D8BE-ADA	—	7/16	2 Inb.	49F/—	—	—	.110	3NR	—	9	9
	2150	D8BE-AEA	—	7/16	2 Inb.	49F/—	—	—	.110	4NR	—	9	9
	2150	D8BE-AFA	—	7/16	2 Inb.	49F/—	—	—	.110	4NR	—	9	9
	2150	D8DE-HA	—	1 19/32	3 Inb.	48F/—	—	—	.157	Index	—	9	9
	2150	D8KE-EA	—	1 19/32	2 Inb.	50F/—	—	—	.135	3NR	—	9	9
	2150	D8DE-BA	—	3/8	3 Inb.	57F/—	—	—	.167	3NR	—	9	9
	2150	D8OE-EA	—	1 19/32	2 Inb.	51F/—	—	—	.136	Index	—	9	9
	2150	D8OE-HA	—	7/16	3 Inb.	59F/—	—	—	.180	2NR	—	9	9
	2150	D8SE-CA	—	1 19/32	3 Inb.	57F/—	—	—	.150	2NR	—	9	9
	2150	D8ZE-TA	—	3/8	4 Inb.	55F/—	—	—	.135	Index	—	9	9
	2150	D8ZE-UA	—	3/8	4 Inb.	55F/—	—	—	.135	Index	—	9	9
	2150	D8WE-DA	—	7/16	4 Inb.	55F/—	—	—	.143	1NR	—	9	9
	2150	D8YE-AB	—	3/8	3 Inb.	50F/—	—	—	.122	Index	—	9	9
	2150	D8SE-DA	—	7/16	3 Inb.	57F/—	—	—	.147	3NR	—	9	9
	2150	D8SE-EA	—	7/16	3 Inb.	57F/—	—	—	.147	3NR	—	9	9
	2150	D8SE-FA	—	3/8	3 Inb.	57F/—	—	—	.147	3NR	—	9	9
	2150	D8SE-GA	—	3/8	3 Inb.	57F/—	—	—	.147	3NR	—	9	9
	2700VV	D84E-D8	—	1.040	—	—/—	—	—	—	Index	—	9	9
	2700VV	D8BE-EB	—	1.040	—	—/—	—	—	—	Index	—	9	9
	4350	D8VE-FA	—	1.0	2	202/—	—	—	.160	Index	—	9	9
	4350	D8VE-GA	—	1.0	2	202/—	—	—	.160	Index	—	9	9
1979	**CARTER**												
	YFA	D9BE-RA	Manual	.780	—	.104/—	—	—	.180	1NR	—	9	9
	YFA	D9DE-AA	Automatic	.780	—	.101/—	—	—	.230	1NR	—	9	9
	YFA	D9DE-BA	Automatic	.780	—	.101/—	—	—	.230	1NR	—	9	9
	YFA	D9DE-CA	Automatic	.780	—	.101/—	—	—	.260	1NR	—	9	9
	YFA	D9DE-CB	Automatic	.780	—	.101/—	—	—	.260	1NR	—	9	9
	YFA	D9DE-DB	Automatic	.780	—	.101/—	—	—	.260	1NR	—	9	9
	YFA	D9DE-EA	Manual	.780	—	.101/—	—	—	.230	1NR	—	9	9
	MOTORCRAFT												
	2700VV	D84E-KA	Automatic	1 15/32	—	—/—	—	—	—	1NR	—	9	9

CARBURETOR SPECIFICATIONS

████ FORD, MERCURY, LINCOLN ████

Year	Carburetor Model	Carburetor Number	Transmission	Dry Float Setting (ins.)	Pump Setting Hole	Main Jet Pri./Sec.	Power Jet	Pump Jet	Choke Plate Pulldown (ins.)	Choke Setting	Dash Pot (ins.)	Idle Speed (rpm)	Fast Idle Speed (rpm)
1979	7200VV	D9AE-ACA	Automatic	1 15/32	—	—/—	—	—	—	1NR	—	9	9
	7200VV	D9ME-AA	Automatic	1 15/32	—	—/—	—	—	—	1NR	—	9	9

1 800 for air-conditioned cars.
2 600 for air-conditioned cars.
3 Solenoid equipped.
4 Solenoid energized/solenoid de-energized.
5 Parallel with float bowl floor (bowl inverted).
6 Choke rod setting.
7 3rd step of cam.
8 2nd step of cam.
9 Refer to engine decal.
10 Bowl cover inverted, gasket in place—from bottom of float to gasket surface.

████ FORD PINTO, BOBCAT, MUSTANG II ████
(To 2800cc)

Year	Carburetor Model	Carburetor Number	Transmission	Dry Float Setting (ins.)	Main Jet Pri./Sec.	Power Jet	Main-Well Tube Pri./Sec.	Decel Air Bleed	Choke Plate Pulldown (ins.)	Choke Setting (Notches)	Pump Setting (Hole)	Fast Idle Speed (rpm)
1972	AUTOLITE											
	1250	721F-KFA	Manual	1.20	.049/—	.035	— / —	.039	.065-.085	Index	Outer	1700
		721F-KFB										
	HOLLEY											
	5200	D22F-AB,CB	Automatic	.420	.022/.020	.031	F50/F6	.035	.236	1NL	3	1800
	5200	D22F-AC	Automatic	.420	.022/.020	.031	F50/F50	.035	.236	1NL	3	1800
	5200	D22F-BB,DB	Manual	.420	.022/.020	.031	F50/F6	.035	.236	1NL	2	1600
	5200	D22F-BC	Manual	.420	.022/.020	.031	F50/F50	.035	.236	1NL	2	1600
	5200	D22F-EA,GA	Automatic	.420	.024/.020	.015	F50/F6	.035	.236	Index	3	1800
	5200	D22F-EB	Automatic	.420	.024/.020	.015	F50/F50	.035	.236	Index	3	1800
1973	AUTOLITE											
	1250	731F-LCA	Manual	1.20	.050/—	.033	— / —	.039	.065-.085	Index	Outer	1700
	1250	731F-KEA	Manual	1.20	.050/—	.033	— / —	.039	.065-.085	Index	Outer	1700
	HOLLEY											
	5200	D32F-CA	Automatic	.420	.052/.052	.018	F6/F6	—	.158	Index	2	1800
	5200	D32F-BD	Manual	.420	.053/.055	.018	F6/F50	.035	.158	1NL	2	1600
1974	5200	D42F-EA	Manual	.460	.054/.054	—	F6/F6	—	.236	Index	2	1600
	5200	D42E-EB	Manual	.41-.51	.054/.054	—	F50/F6	—	.217-.255	Index	2	1600
	5200	D42E-BA,KA	Manual	.460	.056/.054	—	45R-905/F50	—	.280	1NR	2	1600
	5200	D42F-GA	Automatic	.460	.054/.054	—	F6/F6	—	.236	Index	2	1600
	5200	D42E-AA	Automatic	.460	.056/.054	—	14R-905/F50	—	.280	Index	2	1600
	5200	D42E-CD	Automatic	.460	.052/.055	—	14R-905/F50	—	.255	Index	2	1600
	5200	D42E-AC	Automatic	.460	.056/.054	—	14R-905/F50	—	.255	Index	2	1600
	5200	D4ZE-CA	Manual	.430	.056/.071	—	F50/F50	—	.195	1NR	2	1700
	5200	D4ZE-DC	Manual	.37-.50	.054/.071	—	F50/F50	—	.175-.215	1NR	2	1700
	5200	D4ZE-BC	Automatic	.37-.50	.054/.071	—	F50/F50	—	.175-.215	1NR	2	1700
1975	AUTOLITE											
	2150	D5ZE-BC	Automatic	3/8	49F/—	—	— / —	—	.145	2NR	2	1600
	2150	D5ZE-DC	Automatic	3/8	52F/—	—	— / —	—	.145	2NR	2	1600
	2150	D5ZE-AC	Manual	3/8	50F/—	—	— / —	—	.145	2NR	2	1600
	2150	D5ZE-CC	Manual	3/8	52F/—	—	— / —	—	.145	2NR	3	1600
	HOLLEY											
	5200	D52E-AA	Automatic	.460	1.45/1.32	—	14R-905/F50	—	5.0mm	1NL	2	1800
	5200	D52E-BA	Automatic	.460	1.35/1.32	—	14R-905/F50	—	5.0mm	1NL	2	1800
	5200	D52E-CA	Manual	.460	1.40/1.35	—	14R-905/F50	—	5.0mm	1NL	2	1800
	5200	D52E-DB	Manual	.460	1.35/1.32	—	14R-905/F50	—	5.0mm	1NL	2	1800
	5200	D5ZE-EA	Automatic	.460	1.45/1.32	—	14R-905/F50	—	5.0mm	1NL	2	1800
	5200	D5ZE-FA	Automatic	.460	1.35/1.32	—	14R-905/F50	—	5.0mm	1NL	2	1800
	5200	D5ZE-GA	Manual	.460	1.40/1.35	—	14R-905/F50	—	5.0mm	1NL	2	1800
	5200	D5ZE-HB	Manual	.460	1.35/1.35	—	14R-905/F50	—	5.0mm	1NL	2	1800
1976	MOTORCRAFT											
	2150	D5ZE-BE	Automatic	3/8	52F/—	—	— / —	—	.105	3NR	2	1
	2150	D6ZE-AA	Manual	3/8	51F/—	—	— / —	—	.100	3NR	2	1
	2150	D6ZE-BA	Automatic	3/8	52F/—	—	— / —	—	.100	3NR	2	1
	2150	D6ZE-CA	Manual	13/32	51F/—	—	— / —	—	.110	3NR	2	1
	2150	D6ZE-DA	Automatic	3/8	53F/—	—	— / —	—	.110	3NR	3	1
	HOLLEY											
	5200	D6EE-BA	Automatic	.460	1.37/1.32	—	14R-905/F50	—	6.0mm	1NL	2	1
	5200	D6EE-CA	Manual	.460	1.42/1.32	—	14R-905/F50	—	7.0mm	1NL	2	1
	5200	D6EE-DA	Automatic	.460	1.42/1.32	—	14R-816/F50	—	6.0mm	1NL	2	1
	5200	D6ZE-EA	Manual	.460	1.42/1.32	—	14R-816/F50	—	7.0mm	1NL	2	1
1977	MOTORCRAFT											
	2150	D7YE-AA	Automatic	3/8	48F/—	—	— / —	—	.122	2NR	3 Inb.	1
	2150	D7YE-BA	Manual	3/8	48F/—	—	— / —	—	.114	Index	2 Inb.	1
	2700	D7ZE-BD	Automatic	1 3/64	— / —	—	— / —	—	—	Index	—	1
	2700	D7ZE-GD	Automatic	1 3/64	—	—	— / —	—	—	Index	—	1
	HOLLEY-WEBER											
	5200	D7EE-AA	Manual	29/64	275/227	—	14R905/14R816	—	6.0mm	2NR	2	1
	5200	D7EE-AB	Manual	29/64	275/227	—	14R905/14R816	—	6.0mm	2NR	2	1
	5200	D7EE-DA	Manual	29/64	255/235	—	14R905/14R816	—	6.0mm	2NR	2	1
	5200	D7EE-EA	Automatic	29/64	255/239	—	14R905/14R816	—	6.0mm	Index	2	1
	5200	D7EE-FA	Automatic	29/64	275/255	—	14R905/14R816	—	6.0mm	Index	2	1
	5200	D7EE-GA	Automatic	29/64	263/227	—	14R905/14R816	—	5.0mm	Index	2	1
	5200	D7EE-HA	Manual	29/64	255/239	—	14R905/14R816	—	6.0mm	2NR	2	1
	5200	D7EE-JA	Automatic	29/64	255/239	—	14R905/14R816	—	6.0mm	Index	2	1
	5200	D7EE-KB	Manual	29/64	275/227	—	14R905/14R816	—	6.0mm	2NR	2	1
	5200	D7EE-LA	Automatic	29/64	275/255	—	14R905/14R816	—	6.0mm	Index	2	1
	5200	D7EE-SA	Manual	29/64	255/255	—	14R905/14R816	—	6.0mm	2NR	2	1
	5200	D7EE-TA	Manual	29/64	255/255	—	14R905/14R816	—	6.0mm	2NR	2	1
	5200	D7EE-UA	Automatic	29/64	255/255	—	14R905/14R816	—	6.0mm	Index	2	1
	5200	D7EE-VA	Automatic	29/64	255/255	—	14R905/14R816	—	6.0mm	Index	2	1
	5200	D7EE-AAA	Automatic	29/64	263/227	—	14R905/14R816	—	5.0mm	Index	2	1
	5200	D7EE-BDA	Manual	29/64	247/239	—	14R905/14R816	—	7.0mm	2NR	2	1

FORD PINTO, BOBCAT, MUSTANG II, CAPRI, MUSTANG
(To 2800cc)

Year	Carburetor Model	Carburetor Number	Transmission	Dry Float Setting (Ins.)	Main Jet Pri./Sec.	Power Jet	Main Well Tube Pri./Sec.	Decel Air Bleed	Choke Plate Pulldown (Ins.)	Choke Setting (Notches)	Pump Setting (Hole)	Fast Idle Speed (RPM)
1978 MOTORCRAFT												
	2150	D8BE-MB	—	3/8	50F/—	—	—/—	—	.122	Index	Inb.	1
HOLLEY			—									
	5200	D8BE-FA	—	29/64	171/203	—	14R-905/14R-1004	—	6.0mm	2NR	2	1
	5200	D8BE-HA	—	29/64	147/219	—	14R-905/14R-1004	—	6.0mm	1NR	2	1
	5200	D8EE-CA	—	29/64	147/219	—	14R-905/14R-1004	—	6.0mm	1NR	2	1
	5200	D8EE-DA	—	29/64	163/219	—	14R-905/14R-1004	—	6.0mm	2NR	2	1
	5200	D8EE-JA	—	29/64	163/219	—	14R-905/14R-1004	—	6.0mm	2NR	2	1
	5200	D8EE-KA	—	29/64	147/219	—	14R-905/14R-1004	—	6.0mm	1NR	2	1
	5200	D8ZE-SA	—	29/64	167/199	—	14R-905/14R-1004	—	6.0mm	1NR	2	1
	5200	D8ZE-RA	—	29/64	167/199	—	14R-905/14R-1004	—	6.0mm	1NR	2	1
1979 Motorcraft												
	2700VV	D92E-LB	Automatic	1 15/32	—/—	—	—/—	—	—	1NR	—	1
HOLLEY												
	5200	D9BE-AAA	Manual	.41-.51	171/203	—	14R-905/14R-1004	—	6.0MM	2NR	2	1
	5200	D9BE-ABA	Manual	.41-.51	171/199	—	14R-905/14R-1004	—	6.0MM	2NR	2	1
	5200	D9EE-AMA	Manual	.41-.51	163/219	—	14R-905/14R-1004	—	6.0MM	2NR	2	1
	5200	D9EE-ANA	Automatic	.41-.51	147/219	—	14R-905/14R-1004	—	6.0MM	1NR	2	1
	5200	D9EE-ASA	Manual	.41-.51	147/219	—	14R-905/14R-1004	—	6.0MM	1NR	2	1
	5200	D9EE-AYA	Manual	.41-.51	147/219	—	14R-905/14R-100	—	6.0MM	1NR	2	1
	5200	D9ZE-ND	Manual	.41-.51	259/283	—	14R-974/14R-974	—	6.0MM	2NR	3	1
	6500	D9EE-AFC	Manual	.41-.51	231/207	—	14R-974/14R-974	—	6.0MM	2NR	2	1
	6500	D9EE-AGC	Manual	.41-.51	227/203	—	14R-974/14R-974	—	6.0MM	2NR	2	1
	6500	D9EE-AJC	Automatic	.41-.51	231/207	—	14R-974/14R-974	—	6.0MM	1NR	2	1
	6500	D9EE-AKC	Automatic	.41-.51	231/207	—	14R-974/14R-974	—	6.0MM	1NR	2	1

1See engine decal.

OLDSMOBILE

Year	Carb. Model	Trans.	Carb. Number	Float level (ins.)	Float Drop (ins.)	Accel. Pump Rod (ins.)	Choke Rod Lever (ins.)	Vacuum Break (ins.)	Choke Unloader (ins.)	Secondary Opening/Closing	Air Valve Spring (ins.)	Air Valve Dash Pot (ins.)	Idle Vent (ins.)	Fast Idle Speed (rpm)
1970 ROCHESTER														
	MV	Auto.	7040014	1/4	—	—	.170	.200	.350	—/—	—	—	—	9001
	MV	Man.	7040017	1/4	—	—	.190	.225	.350	—/—	—	—	—	7501
	2GC	Auto.	7040154	9/16	1 3/8	1 3/8	.140	.160	.170	—/—	—	—	—	9002
	2GC	Man.	7040155	9/16	1 3/8	1 3/8	.140	.160	.170	—/—	—	—	—	9002
	2GC	Auto.	7040156	9/16	1 3/8	1 3/8	.140	.160	.170	—/—	—	—	—	9002
	2GC	Auto.	7040159	9/16	1 3/8	1 3/8	.140	.160	.170	—/—	—	—	—	9002
	4MC	All	7040250	1/4	—	—	.120	.200	.200	.070/.020	1/2 turn	.030	—	10003
	4MC	All	7040251	1/4	—	—	.120	.200	.200	.070/.020	3/4 turn	.030	—	9503
	4MC	Auto.	7040252	1/4	—	—	.120	.200	.200	.070/.020	3/4 turn	.030	—	9503
	4MC	Man.	7040253	1/4	—	—	.120	.275	.200	.070/.020	3/4 turn	.030	—	9503
	4MC	All	7040255	1/4	—	—	.120	.325	.200	.070/.020	3/4 turn	.030	—	9503
	4MC	Man.	7040256	1/4	—	—	.120	.325	.200	.070/.020	3/4 turn	.030	—	10503
	4MC	Auto.	7040257	1/4	—	—	.120	.200	.200	.070/.020	3/4 turn	.030	—	9503
	4MC	Auto.	7040258	1/4	—	—	.120	.200	.200	.070/.020	3/4 turn	.030	—	10003
1971	MV	Auto.	7041014	1/4	—	—	160	.200	350	—/—	—	—	—	9003
	MV	Man.	7041017	1/4	—	—	180	.225	350	—/—	—	—	—	7503
	2GC	Man.	7041155	9/16	1 3/8	1 3/8	.140	.200	.170	—/—	—	—	—	10003
	2GC	Auto.	7041156	9/16	1 3/8	1 3/8	.140	.200	.170	—/—	—	—	—	10003
	2GC	Auto.	7041159	9/16	1 3/8	1 3/8	.140	.215	.170	—/—	—	—	—	10003
	4MC	All	7041251	1/4	—	—	.120	.215	.200	.070/—	3/4 turn	.050	—	10503
	4MC	Man.	7041253	1/4	—	—	.120	.275	.200	.070/—	1/2 turn	.050	—	10503
	4MC	Man.	7041256	1/4	—	—	.120	.200	.200	.070/—	3/4 turn	.050	—	10503
	4MC	Auto.	7041257	1/4	—	—	.120	.200	.200	.070/—	3/4 turn	.050	—	10503
	4MC	Auto.	7041252	1/4	—	—	.120	.275	.200	.070/—	3/4 turn	.050	—	10503
1972	2GC	Man.	7042155	17/32	1 3/8	1 3/8	.140	.200	.170	—/—	—	—	—	4
	2GC	Auto.	7042156	17/32	1 3/8	1 3/8	.140	.200	.170	—/—	—	—	—	4
	4MC	All	7042250	1/4	—	—	.120	.200	.200	.070/.020	1/2 turn	.050	—	4
	4MC	All	7042251	1/4	—	—	.120	.200	.200	.070/.020	3/4 turn	.050	—	4
	4MC	Auto.	7042252	1/4	—	—	.120	.200	.200	.070/.020	3/4 turn	.050	—	4
	4MC	Man.	7042953	1/4	—	—	.120	.200	.200	.070/.020	3/4 turn	.050	—	4

OLDSMOBILE

Year	Carb. Model	Carb. Number	Float Level (Ins.)	Float Drop (Ins.)	Pump Rod (Ins.)	Pump Rod Hole	Choke Rod (Ins.)	Choke Lever (Ins.)	Choke Unloader (Ins.)	Vacuum Break (Ins.) Pri. (Front)/ Sec. (Rear)	Secondary Throttle Opening/ Closing	Secondary Lockout (Ins.)	Air Valve Spring (Turns)	Air Valve Dashpot/ Rod (Ins.)	Choke Setting (Notches)
1973 ROCHESTER															
	MV	7043014	1/4	—	—	—	.245	—	.500	.300/—	—/—	—	—	—	—
	MV	7043017	1/4	—	—	—	.275	—	.500	.350/—	—/—	—	—	—	—
	2GC	—	15/32	1 9/32	1 11/32	—	.160	—	.250	.200/—	—/—	—	—	—	—
	4MV	7043250	1/4	—	3/8	—	.120	—	.300	.200/—	.070/.020	.035	1/2	.050	—
	4MV	7043251	1/4	—	3/8	—	.120	—	.300	.200/—	.070/.020	.035	3/4	.050	—
	4MV	7043252	1/4	—	3/8	—	.120	—	.300	.200/—	.070/.020	.035	3/4	.050	—
	4MV	7043254	1/4	—	3/8	—	.120	—	.300	.275/—	.070/.020	.035	3/4	.050	—
	4MV	7043255	1/4	—	3/8	—	.120	—	.300	.200/—	.070/.020	.035	1/2	.050	—
	4MV	7043256	1/4	—	3/8	—	.120	—	.300	.200/—	.070/.020	.035	1/2	.050	—
	4MV	7043259	1/4	—	3/8	—	.120	—	.300	.215/—	.070/.020	.035	3/4	.050	—
	4MV	7043282	1/4	—	3/8	—	.120	—	.300	.215/—	.070/.020	.035	3/4	.050	—
	4MV	7043557	1/4—	—	3/8	—	.120	—	.300	.200/—	.070/.020	.035	3/4	.050	—
	4MV	7043558	1/4	—	3/8	—	.120	—	.300	.200/—	.070/.020	.035	3/4	.050	—
	4MV	7043559	1/4	—	3/8	—	.120	—	.300	.275/—	.070/.020	.035	3/4	.050	—

CARBURETOR SPECIFICATIONS

OLDSMOBILE

Year	Carb. Model	Carb. Number	Float Level (Ins.)	Float Drop (Ins.)	Pump Rod (Ins.)	Pump Rod Hole	Choke Rod (Ins.)	Choke Lever (Ins.)	Choke Unloader (Ins.)	Vacuum Break (Ins.) Pri. (Front)/ Sec. (Rear)	Secondary Throttle Opening/ Closing	Secondary Lockout (Ins.)	Air Valve Spring (Turns)	Air Valve Dashpot/ Rod (Ins.)	Choke Setting (Notches)
1974 **ROCHESTER**															
	MV	7044017	1/4	—	—	—	.275	—	.500	.350/—	—/—	—	—	—	—
	MV	7044314	1/4	—	—	—	.245	—	.500	.300/—	—/—	—	—	—	—
	MV	7044014	1/4	—	—	—	.245	—	.500	.300/—	—/—	—	—	—	—
	4MC	7043255	1/4	—	3/8	Inner	.230	.120	.300	.200/—	.070/.020	.035	1/2	.030	Index
	4MC	7043250	1/4	—	3/8	Inner	.230	.120	.300	.200/—	.070/.020	.035	1/2	.030	Index
	4MC	7043256	1/4	—	3/8	Inner	.230	.120	.300	.200/—	.070/.020	.035	1/2	.030	Index
	4MC	7044559	1/4	—	3/8	Inner	.230	.120	.300	.275/—	.070/.020	.035	3/4	.030	Index
	4MC	7043251	1/4	—	3/8	Inner	.230	.120	.300	.200/—	.070/.020	.035	3/4	.030	Index
	4MC	7044558	1/4	—	3/8	Inner	.230	.120	.300	.200/—	.070/.020	.035	3/4	.030	Index
	4MC	7043252	1/4	—	3/8	Inner	.230	.120	.300	.200/—	.070/.020	.035	3/4	.030	1NR
	4MC	7044557	1/4	—	3/8	Inner	.230	.120	.300	.200/—	.070/.020	.035	3/4	.030	1NR
1975 **ROCHESTER**															
	MV	7045013	11/32	—	—	—	.275	—	.275	.350/.312	—/—	—	—	—	—
	MV	7045012	11/32	—	—	—	.160	—	.275	.200/.215	—/—	—	—	—	—
	MV	7045014	11/32	—	—	—	.160	—	.275	.200/.215	—/—	—	—	—	—
	2GC	7045160	9/16	1 7/32	1 11/32	—	.085	.120	.180	.145/.265	—/—	—	—	—	1NR
	2GC	7045161	9/16	1 7/32	1 11/32	—	.085	.120	.180	.145/.265	—/—	—	—	—	1NR
	2GC	7045143	15/32	1 9/32	1 19/32	—	.080	.120	.180	.140/.120	—/—	—	—	—	1NR
	2GC	7045147	7/16	1 9/32	1 19/32	—	.080	.120	.140	.120/.120	—/—	—	—	—	1NL
	2GC	7045149	7/16	1 9/32	1 19/32	—	.080	.120	.140	.120/.120	—/—	—	—	—	1NR
	2GC	7045449	7/16	1 9/32	1 19/32	—	.080	.120	.140	.120/.120	—/—	—	—	—	1NL
	2MC	7045297	3/16	—	9/32	Inner	.130	.120	.300	.150/.300	—/—	—	—	—	1NR
	2MC	7045354	3/16	—	5/16	Outer	.130	.120	.300	.150/.300	—/—	—	—	—	1NR
	2MC	7045358	3/16	—	5/16	Outer	.130	.120	.300	.150/.300	—/—	—	—	—	1NR
	2MC	7045156	5/32	—	9/32	Inner	.130	.120	.300	.150/.250	—/—	—	—	—	1NR
	2MC	7045598	5/32	—	3/16	Inner	.130	.120	.300	.150/.300	—/—	—	—	—	Index
	2MC	7045298	5/32	—	9/32	Inner	.130	.120	.300	.150/.250	—/—	—	—	—	1NR
	2MC	7045356	5/32	—	3/16	Inner	.130	.120	.300	.150/.300	—/—	—	—	—	Index
	M4MC	7045246	5/16	—	3/8	Outer	.095	.120	.240	.130/.115	1/.020	.015	3/4	.015	1NR
	M4MC	7045546	5/16	—	3/8	Outer	.095	.120	.240	.145/.130	1/.020	.015	3/4	.015	1NR
	M4MC	7045264	17/32	—	9/32	Inner	.130	.120	.235	.150/.260	1/.020	.015	1/2	.030	Index
	M4MC	7045183	3/8	—	9/32	Inner	.130	.120	.235	.190/.140	1/.020	.015	1/2	.030	2NR
	M4MC	7045184	3/8	—	9/32	Inner	.130	.120	.235	.190/.140	1/.020	.015	3/4	.030	2NR
	M4MC	7045185	3/8	—	9/32	Inner	.130	.120	.235	.190/.140	1/.020	.015	3/4	.030	3NR
	M4MC	7045483	3/8	—	9/32	Inner	.130	.120	.235	.275/.180	1/.020	.015	1/2	.030	2NR
	M4MC	7045484	3/8	—	9/32	Inner	.130	.120	.235	.190/.140	1/.020	.015	3/4	.030	2NR
	M4MC	7045550	3/8	—	9/32	Inner	.130	.120	.235	.275/.180	1/.020	.015	1/2	.030	2NR
	M4MC	7045551	3/8	—	9/32	Inner	.130	.120	.235	.190/.140	1/.020	.015	3/4	.030	1NR
	M4MC	7045485	3/8	—	9/32	Inner	.160	.120	.235	.275/.180	1/.020	.015	3/4	.030	3NR
	M4MC	7045250	3/8	—	9/32	Inner	.170	.120	.300	.245/.180	1/.020	.015	1/2	.030	2NR
	M4MC	7045251	3/8	—	9/32	Inner	.170	.120	.235	.190/.140	1/.020	.015	3/4	.030	2NR
1976 **ROCHESTER**															
	MV	17056012	11/32	—	—	—	.100	—	.265	.140/.265	—/—	—	—	—	—
	MV	17056013	11/32	—	—	—	.140	—	.265	.165/.320	—/—	—	—	—	—
	MV	17056014	11/32	—	—	—	.100	—	.265	.140/.265	—/—	—	—	—	—
	MV	17056015	11/32	—	—	—	.140	—	.265	.165/.320	—/—	—	—	—	—
	MV	17056018	11/32	—	—	—	.100	—	.265	.140/.260	—/—	—	—	—	—
	MV	17056314	11/32	—	—	—	.135	—	.265	.165/.320	—/—	—	—	—	—
	2GC	17056143	15/32	1 5/32	1 11/32	—	.080	.120	.180	.140/.100	—/—	—	—	—	1NR
	2GC	17056145	7/16	1 5/32	1 19/32	—	.080	.120	.140	.110/.100	—/—	—	—	—	1NR
	2GC	17056149	7/16	1 5/32	1 19/32	—	.080	.120	.140	.120/.100	—/—	—	—	—	1NR
	2GC	17056447	7/16	1 5/32	1 19/32	—	.080	.120	.140	.130/.110	—/—	—	—	—	1NR
	2GC	17056449	7/16	1 5/32	1 19/32	—	.080	.120	.140	.130/.110	—/—	—	—	—	1NR
	2MC	17056156	1/8	—	9/32	Inner	.105	.120	.210	.110/.175	—/—	—	—	—	1NR
	2MC	17056157	1/8	—	3/16	Outer	.105	.120	.210	.110/.175	—/—	—	—	—	1NR
	2MC	17056158	1/8	—	9/32	Inner	.105	.120	.210	.110/.175	—/—	—	—	—	1NR
	2MC	17056454	1/8	—	3/16	Outer	.105	.120	.210	.110/.210	—/—	—	—	—	1NR
	2MC	17056455	1/8	—	9/32	Inner	.120	.120	.210	.130/.210	—/—	—	—	—	1NR
	2MC	17056456	1/8	—	3/16	Outer	.105	.120	.210	.110/.210	—/—	—	—	—	Index
	2MC	17056457	1/8	—	3/16	Outer	.105	.120	.210	.110/.245	—/—	—	—	—	Index
	2MC	17056458	1/8	—	3/16	Outer	.105	.120	.210	.110/.210	—/—	—	—	—	1NR
	2MC	17056459	1/8	—	3/16	Outer	.105	.120	.210	.110/.210	—/—	—	—	—	Index
	M4MC	17056246	5/16	—	3/8	Outer	.095	.120	.250	.130/.120	1/.020	.015	3/4	.015	1NR
	M4MC	17056250	13/32	—	9/32	Inner	.130	.120	.230	.190/.140	1/.020	.015	1/2	.030	2NR
	M4MC	17056251	13/32	—	9/32	Inner	.130	.120	.230	.190/.140	1/.020	.015	3/4	.030	2NR
	M4MC	17056252	13/32	—	9/32	Inner	.130	.120	.230	.190/.140	1/.020	.015	3/4	.030	2NR
	M4MC	17056253	13/32	—	9/32	Inner	.130	.120	.230	.190/.140	1/.020	.015	1/2	.030	2NR
	M4MC	17056256	13/32	—	9/32	Inner	.130	.120	.230	.190/.140	1/.020	.015	3/4	.030	2NR
	M4MC	17056257	13/32	—	9/32	Inner	.130	.120	.230	.190/.140	1/.020	.015	3/4	.030	2NR
	M4MC	17056258	13/32	—	9/32	Inner	.130	.120	.230	.190/.140	1/.020	.015	1/2	.030	2NR
	M4MC	17056259	13/32	—	9/32	Inner	.130	.120	.230	.190/.140	1/.020	.015	1/2	.030	2NR
	M4MC	17056546	5/16	—	3/8	Outer	.095	.120	.250	.130/.130	1/.020	.015	3/4	.015	Index
	M4MC	17056550	13/32	—	9/32	Inner	.130	.120	.230	.190/.140	1/.020	.015	1/2	.030	2NR
	M4MC	17056551	13/32	—	9/32	Inner	.130	.120	.230	.190/.140	1/.020	.015	3/4	.030	1NR
	M4MC	17056255	13/32	—	9/32	Inner	.130	.120	.230	.190/.140	1/.020	.015	3/4	.030	2NR
	M4MC	17056552	13/32	—	9/32	Inner	.130	.120	.230	.200/.140	1/.020	.015	1/2	.030	2NR
	M4MC	17056553	13/32	—	9/32	Inner	.130	.120	.230	.190/.140	1/.020	.015	3/4	.030	2NR
	M4MC	17056556	13/32	—	9/32	Inner	.130	.120	.230	.190/.140	1/.020	.015	3/4	.030	1NR
HOLLEY															
	5210-C	366829	.41	1	—	—	.32	—	.375	.313/—	—/—	—	—	—	2NR
	5210-C	366830	.41	1	—	—	.32	—	.375	.288/—	—/—	—	—	—	3NR
	5210-C	366831	.41	1	—	—	.32	—	.375	.313/—	—/—	—	—	—	2NR
	5210-C	366832	.41	1	—	—	.32	—	.375	.288/—	—/—	—	—	—	3NR
	5210-C	366833	.41	1	—	—	.32	—	.375	.268/—	—/—	—	—	—	2NR
	5210-C	366834	.41	1	—	—	.32	—	.375	.268/—	—/—	—	—	—	3NR
	5210-C	366840	.41	1	—	—	.32	—	.375	.268/—	—/—	—	—	—	3NR
	5210-C	366841	.41	1	—	—	.32	—	.375	.268/—	—/—	—	—	—	2NR
1977 **ROCHESTER**															
	2GE	17057145	7/16	1 5/32	1 19/32	—	.080	.120	.140	.090/.110	—/—	—	—	—	1NR
	2GE	17057146	7/16	1 5/32	1 19/32	—	.080	.120	.140	.090/.110	—/—	—	—	—	1NR
	2GE	17057148	7/16	1 5/32	1 19/32	—	.080	.120	.140	.090/.110	—/—	—	—	—	1NR
	2GE	17057143	7/16	1 5/32	1 19/32	—	.080	.120	.140	.100/.130	—/—	—	—	—	1NR
	2GE	17057144	7/16	1 5/32	1 19/32	—	.080	.120	.140	.100/.130	—/—	—	—	—	1NR
	2GE	17057446	7/16	1 5/32	1 19/32	—	.080	.120	.140	.110/.130	—/—	—	—	—	1NR
	2GE	17057447	7/16	1 5/32	1 19/32	—	.080	.120	.140	.100/.130	—/—	—	—	—	1NR
	2GE	17057448	7/16	1 5/32	1 19/32	—	.080	.120	.140	.110/.130	—/—	—	—	—	1NR
	2GE	17057445	7/16	1 5/32	1 19/32	—	.080	.120	.140	.110/.140	—/—	—	—	—	1NL
	2GC	17057104	7/16	1 9/32	1 21/32	—	.260	.120	.325	.130/—	—/—	—	—	—	Index
	2GC	17057105	7/16	1 9/32	1 21/32	—	.260	.120	.325	.130/—	—/—	—	—	—	Index
	2GC	17057107	7/16	1 9/32	1 5/8	—	.260	.120	.325	.130/—	—/—	—	—	—	Index
	2GC	17057109	7/16	1 5/8	—	—	.260	.120	.325	.130/—	—/—	—	—	—	Index
	2GC	17057112	19/32	1 9/32	1 21/32	—	.260	.120	.325	.130/—	—/—	—	—	—	Index

OLDSMOBILE

Year	Carb. Model	Carb. Number	Float Level (Ins.)	Float Drop (Ins.)	Pump Rod (Ins.)	Pump Rod Hole	Choke Rod (Ins.)	Choke Lever (Ins.)	Choke Unloader (Ins.)	Vacuum Break (Ins.) Pri. (Front)/ Sec. (Rear)	Secondary Throttle Opening/ Closing	Secondary Lockout (Ins.)	Air Valve Spring (Turns)	Air Valve Dashpot/ Rod (Ins.)	Choke Setting (Notches)
	2GC	17057113	19/32	1 9/32	1 5/8	—	.260	.120	.325	.130/—	—/—	—	—	—	Index
	2GC	17057114	19/32	1 9/32	1 21/32	—	.260	.120	.325	.130/—	—/—	—	—	—	Index
	2GC	17057123	19/32	1 9/32	1 5/8	—	.260	.120	.325	.130/—	—/—	—	—	—	Index
	2GC	17057404	1/2	1 9/32	1 21/32	—	.260	.120	.325	.140/—	—/—	—	—	—	1NL
	2GC	17057405	1/2	1 9/32	1 5/8	—	.260	.120	.325	.140/—	—/—	—	—	—	1NL
	2MC	17057150	1/8	—	11/32	Inner	.085	.120	.190	.090/.160	—/—	—	—	—	2NR
	2MC	17057151	1/8	—	11/32	Inner	.085	.120	.190	.090/.160	—/—	—	—	—	2NR
	2MC	17057156	1/8	—	11/32	Inner	.085	.120	.190	.090/.160	—/—	—	—	—	1NR
	2MC	17057157	1/8	—	3/8	Outer	.090	.120	.190	.100/.190	—/—	—	—	—	1NR
	2MC	17057158	1/8	—	11/32	Inner	.085	.120	.190	.090/.160	—/—	—	—	—	1NR
	M4MC	17057202	15/32	—	9/32	Inner	.325	.120	.280	.160/—	1/.020	.015	7/8	.015	2NL
	M4MC	17057204	15/32	—	9/32	Inner	.325	.120	.280	.160/—	1/.020	.015	7/8	.015	2NL
	M4MC	17057250	13/32	—	9/32	Inner	.100	.120	.220	.135/.180	1/.020	.015	1/2	.030	2NR
	M4MC	17057252	13/32	—	9/32	Inner	.100	.120	.220	.135/.180	1/.020	.015	1/2	.030	2NR
	M4MC	17057253	13/32	—	9/32	Inner	.100	.120	.220	.135/.180	1/.020	.015	1/2	.030	2NR
	M4MC	17057255	13/32	—	9/32	Inner	.100	.120	.220	.135/.180	1/.020	.015	1/2	.030	2NR
	M4MC	17057256	13/32	—	9/32	Inner	.100	.120	.220	.135/.180	1/.020	.015	1/2	.030	2NR
	M4MC	17057257	13/32	—	9/32	Inner	.100	.120	.220	.135/.225	1/.020	.015	1/2	.030	2NR
	M4MC	17057258	13/32	—	9/32	Inner	.100	.120	.220	.135/.225	1/.020	.015	1/2	.030	2NR
	M4MC	17057502	15/32	—	9/32	Inner	.325	.120	.285	.175/—	1/.020	.015	7/8	—	2NL
	M4MC	17057504	15/32	—	9/32	Inner	.325	.120	.285	.175/—	1/.020	.015	7/8	—	2NL
	M4MC	17057550	13/32	—	9/32	Inner	.100	.120	.220	.135/.225	1/.020	.015	1/2	.030	2NR
	M4MC	17057552	13/32	—	9/32	Inner	.100	.120	.220	.135/.225	1/.020	.015	1/2	.030	2NR
	M4MC	17057553	13/32	—	9/32	Inner	.100	.120	.220	.135/.225	1/.020	.015	1/2	.030	2NR
	M4MC	17057582	15/32	—	9/32	Inner	.325	.120	.285	.175/—	1/.020	.015	7/8	—	2NL
	M4MC	17057584	15/32	—	9/32	Inner	.325	.120	.285	.175/—	1/.020	.015	7/8	—	2NL
	HOLLEY														
	5210-C	458102	.42	1	—	—	.085	—	.350	.250/.400	—/—	—	—	—	3NR
	5210-C	458103	.42	1	—	—	.085	—	.350	.250/.400	—/—	—	—	—	3NR
	5210-C	458104	.42	1	—	—	.120	—	.350	.250/.400	—/—	—	—	—	3NR
	5210-C	458105	.42	1	—	—	.120	—	.350	.250/.400	—/—	—	—	—	3NR
	5210-C	458106	.42	1	—	—	.120	—	.400	.275/.400	—/—	—	—	—	3NR
	5210-C	458107	.42	1	—	—	.120	—	.400	.275/.400	—/—	—	—	—	3NR
	5210-C	458108	.42	1	—	—	.120	—	.400	.275/.400	—/—	—	—	—	3NR
	5210-C	458109	.42	1	—	—	.120	—	.400	.275/.400	—/—	—	—	—	3NR
	5210-C	458110	.42	1	—	—	.120	—	.400	.300/.400	—/—	—	—	—	3NR
	5210-C	458112	.42	1	—	—	.120	—	.400	.300/.400	—/—	—	—	—	3NR
1978	**ROCHESTER**														
	2GE	17058140	7/16	1 5/32	1 19/32	—	.080	.120	.140	.110/.070	—/—	—	—	—	1NR
	2GE	17058145	7/16	1 5/32	1 19/32	—	.080	.120	.160	.110/.060	—/—	—	—	—	1NR
	2GE	17058147	7/16	1 5/32	1 19/32	—	.080	.120	.140	.140/.100	—/—	—	—	—	1NR
	2GE	17058182	7/16	1 5/32	1 19/32	—	.080	.120	.140	.110/.080	—/—	—	—	—	1NR
	2GE	17058183	7/16	1 5/32	1 19/32	—	.080	.120	.140	.110/.080	—/—	—	—	—	1NR
	2GE	17058185	7/16	1 5/32	1 19/32	—	.080	.120	.140	.110/.050	—/—	—	—	—	1NR
	2GE	17058187	7/16	1 5/32	1 19/32	—	.080	.120	.140	.110/.080	—/—	—	—	—	1NR
	2GE	17058189	7/16	1 5/32	1 19/32	—	.080	.120	.140	.110/.080	—/—	—	—	—	1NR
	2GE	17058444	7/16	1 5/32	1 19/32	—	.080	.120	.140	.140/.100	—/—	—	—	—	1NR
	2GE	17058446	7/16	1 5/32	1 19/32	—	.080	.120	.140	.130/.110	—/—	—	—	—	1NR
	2GE	17058447	7/16	1 5/32	1 19/32	—	.080	.120	.140	.150/.110	—/—	—	—	—	1NR
	2GE	17058448	7/16	1 5/32	1 9/16	—	.080	.120	.140	.140/.100	—/—	—	—	—	1NR
	2GC	17058102	15/32	1 9/32	1 17/32	—	.260	.120	.325	.130/—	—/—	—	—	—	Index
	2GC	17058103	15/32	1 9/32	1 17/32	—	.260	.120	.325	.130/—	—/—	—	—	—	Index
	2GC	17058104	15/32	1 9/32	1 21/32	—	.260	.120	.325	.130/—	—/—	—	—	—	Index
	2GC	17058105	15/32	1 9/32	1 21/32	—	.260	.120	.325	.130/—	—/—	—	—	—	Index
	2GC	17058107	15/32	1 9/32	1 17/32	—	.260	.120	.325	.130/—	—/—	—	—	—	Index
	2GC	17058108	19/32	1 9/32	1 21/32	—	.260	.120	.325	.130/—	—/—	—	—	—	Index
	2GC	17058109	15/32	1 9/32	1 17/32	—	.260	.120	.325	.130/—	—/—	—	—	—	Index
	2GC	17058110	19/32	1 9/32	1 21/32	—	.260	.120	.325	.130/—	—/—	—	—	—	Index
	2GC	17058111	19/32	1 9/32	1 17/32	—	.260	.120	.325	.130/—	—/—	—	—	—	Index
	2GC	17058113	19/32	1 9/32	1 17/32	—	.260	.120	.325	.130/—	—/—	—	—	—	Index
	2GC	17058121	19/32	1 9/32	1 17/32	—	.260	.120	.325	.130/—	—/—	—	—	—	Index
	2GC	17058123	19/32	1 9/32	1 17/32	—	.260	.120	.325	.130/—	—/—	—	—	—	Index
	2GC	17058126	19/32	1 9/32	1 17/32	—	.260	.120	.325	.130/—	—/—	—	—	—	Index
	2GC	17058128	19/32	1 9/32	1 17/32	—	.260	.120	.325	.130/—	—/—	—	—	—	Index
	2GC	17058404	1/2	1 9/32	1 21/32	—	.260	.120	.325	.140/—	—/—	—	—	—	1/2NL
	2GC	17058405	1/2	1 9/32	1 21/32	—	.260	.120	.325	.140/—	—/—	—	—	—	1/2NL
	2GC	17058408	21/32	1 9/32	1 21/32	—	.260	.120	.325	.140/—	—/—	—	—	—	1/2NL
	2GC	17058410	21/32	1 9/32	1 21/32	—	.260	.120	.325	.140/—	—/—	—	—	—	1/2NL
	M2MC	17058150	3/8	—	1/4	Inner	.065	.120	.203	.203/.133	—/—	—	—	—	2NR
	M2MC	17058151	3/8	—	11/32	Outer	.065	.120	.203	.229/.133	—/—	—	—	—	2NR
	M2MC	17058152	3/8	—	1/4	Inner	.065	.120	.203	.203/.133	—/—	—	—	—	2NR
	M2MC	17058154	3/8	—	11/32	Outer	.065	.120	.203	.146/.245	—/—	—	—	—	2NR
	M2MC	17058155	3/8	—	11/32	Outer	.065	.120	.203	.146/.245	—/—	—	—	—	2NR
	M2MC	17058156	3/8	—	11/32	Outer	.065	.120	.203	.229/.133	—/—	—	—	—	2NR
	M2MC	17058158	3/8	—	11/32	Outer	.065	.120	.203	.229/.133	—/—	—	—	—	2NR
	M2MC	17058450	3/8	—	11/32	Outer	.065	.120	.203	.146/.289	—/—	—	—	—	2NR
	M4MC	17058202	15/32	—	9/32	Inner	.314	.120	.277	.157/—	1/.020	.015	7/8	.015	2NL
	M4MC	17058204	15/32	—	9/32	Inner	.314	.120	.277	.157/—	1/.020	.015	7/8	.015	2NL
	M4MC	17058250	13/32	—	9/32	Inner	.096	.120	.220	.129/.183	1/.020	.015	1/2	.030	2NR
	M4MC	17058253	13/32	—	9/32	Inner	.096	.120	.220	.129/.183	1/.020	.015	1/2	.030	2NR
	M4MC	17058257	13/32	—	9/32	Inner	.103	.120	.220	.136/.230	1/.020	.015	1/2	.030	2NR
	M4MC	17058258	13/32	—	9/32	Inner	.103	.120	.220	.136/.230	1/.020	.015	1/2	.030	2NR
	M4MC	17058259	13/32	—	9/32	Inner	.103	.120	.220	.136/.183	1/.020	.015	1/2	.030	2NR
	M4MC	17058502	15/32	—	9/32	Inner	.314	.120	.277	.164/—	1/.020	.015	7/8	.015	2NL
	M4MC	17058504	15/32	—	9/32	Inner	.314	.120	.277	.164/—	1/.020	.015	7/8	.015	2NL
	M4MC	17058553	13/32	—	9/32	Inner	.103	.120	.220	.136/.230	1/.020	.015	1/2	.030	2NR
	M4MC	17058555	13/32	—	9/32	Inner	.103	.120	.220	.136/.230	1/.020	.015	1/2	.030	2NR
	M4MC	17058582	15/32	—	9/32	Inner	.314	.120	.277	.179/—	1/.020	.015	7/8	.015	2NL
	M4MC	17058584	15/32	—	9/32	Inner	.314	.120	.277	.179/—	1/.020	.015	7/8	.015	2NL
	HOLLEY														
	5210-C	10001047	.52	1	—	—	.150	—	.350	.325/—	—/—	—	—	—	1NR
	5210-C	10001049	.52	1	—	—	.150	—	.350	.325/—	—/—	—	—	—	1NR
	5210-C	10004048	.52	1	—	—	.150	—	.350	.300/—	—/—	—	—	—	2NR
	5210-C	10004049	.52	1	—	—	.150	—	.350	.300/—	—/—	—	—	—	2NR
	6510-C	10001056	.52	1	—	—	.150	—	.350	.325/—	—/—	—	—	—	1NR
	6510-C	10001058	.52	1	—	—	.150	—	.350	.325/—	—/—	—	—	—	1NR
1979	**ROCHESTER**														
	2SE	17059674	13/64	—	1/2	—	.096	.085	.195	.117/—	—/—	.025	—	—	2NR
	2SE	17059675	13/64	—	17/32	—	.096	.085	.195	.117/—	—/—	.025	—	—	1NR
	2SE	17059676	13/64	—	1/2	—	.096	.085	.195	.117/—	—/—	.025	—	—	2NR
	2SE	17059677	13/64	—	17/32	—	.096	.085	.195	.117/—	—/—	.025	—	—	1NR
	M2MC-M2ME	17059134	15/32	—	1/4	Inner	.243	.120	.243	.157/—	—/—	—	—	—	1NL
	M2MC-M2ME	17059135	15/32	—	1/4	Inner	.243	.120	.243	.157/—	—/—	—	—	—	1NL
	M2MC-M2ME	17059136	15/32	—	1/4	Inner	.243	.120	.243	.157/—	—/—	—	—	—	1NL

OLDSMOBILE

Year	Carb. Model	Carb. Number	Float Level (Ins.)	Float Drop (Ins.)	Pump Rod (Ins.)	Pump Rod Hole	Choke Rod (Ins.)	Choke Lever (Ins.)	Choke Unloader (Ins.)	Vacuum Break (Ins.) Pri. (Front)/Sec. (Rear)	Secondary Throttle Opening/Closing	Secondary Lockout (Ins.)	Air Valve Spring (Turns)	Air Valve Dashpot/Rod (Ins.)	Choke Setting (Notches)
1979	M2MC-M2ME	17059137	15/32	—	1/4	Inner	.243	.120	.243	.157/—	—/—	—	—	—	1NL
	M2MC-M2ME	17059150	3/8	—	1/4	Inner	.071	.120	.220	.195/.129	—/—	—	—	—	2NR
	M2MC-M2ME	17059151	3/8	—	11/32	Outer	.071	.120	.220	.243/.142	—/—	—	—	—	2NR
	M2MC-M2ME	17059152	3/8	—	1/4	Inner	.071	.120	.220	.195/.129	—/—	—	—	—	2NR
	M2MC-M2ME	17059154	3/8	—	11/32	Outer	.071	.120	.220	.157/.260	—/—	—	—	—	2NR
	M2MC-M2ME	17059160	11/32	—	1/4	Inner	.110	.120	.195	.129/.203	—/—	—	—	—	2NR
	M2MC-M2ME	17059180	11/32	—	1/4	Inner	.139	.120	.243	.103/.090	—/—	—	—	—	2NR
	M2MC-M2ME	17059190	11/32	—	1/4	Inner	.139	.120	.243	.103/.090	—/—	—	—	—	2NR
	M2MC-M2ME	17059191	11/32	—	9/32	Inner	.139	.120	.243	.103/.090	—/—	—	—	—	2NR
	M2MC-M2ME	17059196	11/32	—	1/4	Inner	.139	.120	.277	.129/.117	—/—	—	—	—	1NR
	M2MC-M2ME	17059450	3/8	—	11/32	Outer	.071	.120	.220	.157/.304	—/—	—	—	—	2NR
	M2MC-M2ME	17059491	11/32	—	9/32	Inner	.139	.120	.277	.129/.117	—/—	—	—	—	1NR
	M2MC-M2ME	17059492	11/32	—	9/32	Inner	.139	.120	.277	.103/.103	—/—	—	—	—	2NR
	M2MC-M2ME	17059498	11/32	—	9/32	Inner	.139	.120	.277	.129/.117	—/—	—	—	—	2NR
	M4M	17059241	5/16	—	3/8	Outer	.096	.120	.243	.120/.113	1/.020	.015	3/4	.015	1NR
	M4MC	17059250	13/32	—	9/32	Inner	.096	.120	.220	.129/.182	1/.020	.015	1/2	.030	2NR
	M4MC	17059253	13/32	—	9/32	Inner	.096	.120	.220	.129/.182	1/.020	.015	1/2	.030	2NR
	M4MC	17059253	13/32	—	9/32	Inner	.096	.120	.220	.129/.182	1/.020	.015	N/A	.030	2NR
	M4MC	17059553	13/32	—	9/32	Inner	.103	.120	.220	.136/.230	1/.020	.015	1/2	.030	2NR

1 ICS solenoid disconnected on low step of cam. Center of slot
2 All transmissions in neutral
3 Vacuum advance disconnected on low step of cam
4 See vehicle emissions control sticker under hood
5 Open primary throttle until actuating link touches tang; bend tang to adjust
6 Altitude manual transmissions
7 Except California

PONTIAC

Year	Carburetor Model	Transmission	Carburetor Number	Float Level (in.)	Float Drop (in.)	Accel. Pump Rod (in.)	Choke Rod (in.)	Vacuum Break (in.)	Choke Unloader (in.)	Main Jet Pri./Sec.	Air Valve Springs (in.)	Air Valve Dash Pot (in.)	Idle Vent (in.)	Fast Idle Speed (rpm)
1970 ROCHESTER														
	MV	Automatic	7040014	1/4	—	—	170	200	350	—/—	—	—	—	—
	MV	Manual	7040017	1/4	—	—	190	230	350	—/—	—	—	—	—
	2GV	Automatic	7040060	11/16	1 3/4	1 11/32	.085	.150	.180	—/—	—	—	—	—
	2GV	Automatic (Calif.)	7040061	11/16	1 3/4	1 11/32	.085	.150	.180	—/—	—	—	—	—
	2GV	Automatic	7040062	9/16	1 3/4	1 11/32	.085	.150	.180	—/—	—	—	—	—
	2GV	Automatic (Calif.)	7040063	9/16	1 3/4	1 11/32	.085	.150	.180	—/—	—	—	—	—
	2GV	Automatic	7040064	11/16	1 3/4	1 11/32	.085	.150	.180	—/—	—	—	—	—
	2GV	Manual	7040066	11/16	1 3/4	1 11/32	.085	.170	.180	—/—	—	—	—	—
	2GV	Manual	7040071	9/16	1 3/4	1 11/32	.085	.160	.180	—/—	—	—	—	—
	2GV	Manual	7040471	9/16	1 3/4	1 11/32	.085	.160	.180	—/—	—	—	—	—
	2GV	Manual	7040072	9/16	1 3/4	1 11/32	.085	.150	.180	—/—	—	—	—	—
	4MV	Automatic	7040262	9/32	—·	—	.100	.400	—	—/—	—	.250	—	—
	4MV	Automatic (Calif.)	7040562	9/32	—	—	.100	.400	—	—/—	—	.250	—	—
	4MV	Manual	7040263	9/32	—	—	.100	.400	—	—/—	—	.250	—	—
	4MV	Manual (Calif.)	7040563	9/32	—	—	.100	.400	—	—/—	—	.250	—	—
	4MV	Automatic	7040264	9/32	—	—	.100	.400	—	—/—	—	.250	—	—
	4MV	Automatic (Calif.)	7040564	9/32	—	—	.100	.400	—	—/—	—	.250	—	—
	4MV	Manual	7040267	9/32	—	—	.100	.400	—	—/—	—	.250	—	—
	4MV	Manual (Calif.)	7040567	9/32	—	—	.100	.400	—	—/—	—	.250	—	—
	4MV	Automatic	7040268	9/32	—	—	.100	.400	—	—/—	—	.250	—	—
	4MV	Automatic (Calif.)	7040568	9/32	—	—	.100	.400	—	—/—	—	.250	—	—
	4MV	Automatic	7040270	9/32	—	—	.100	.245	—	—/—	—	.250	—	—
	4MV	Automatic (Calif.)	7040570	9/32	—	—	.100	.245	—	—/—	—	.250	—	—
	4MV	Manual	7040273	9/32	—	—	.100	.245	—	—/—	—	.250	—	—
	4MV	Manual (Calif.)	7040573	9/32	—	—	.100	.245	—	—/—	—	.250	—	—
	4MV	Automatic	7040274	9/32	—	—	.100	.400	—	—/—	—	.250	—	—
1971	MV	Automatic	7041014	1/4	—	—	.160	.200	.350	—/—	—	—	—	—
	MV	Manual	7041017	1/4	—	—	.180	.225	.350	—/—	—	—	—	—
	2GV	Automatic	7041060	11/16	1 3/4	1 11/32	.085	.125	.180	—/—	—	—	—	—
	2GV	Automatic	7041061	11/16	1 3/4	1 11/32	.085	.125	.180	—/—	—	—	—	—
	2GV	Automatic	7041062	9/16	1 3/4	1 11/32	.085	.105	.180	—/—	—	—	—	—
	2GV	Automatic	7041063	9/16	1 3/4	1 11/32	.085	.105	.180	—/—	—	—	—	—
	2GV	Automatic	7041064	11/16	1 3/4	1 11/32	.085	.130	.180	—/—	—	—	—	—
	2GV	Automatic	7041070	11/16	1 3/4	1 11/32	.085	.125	.180	—/—	—	—	—	—
	2GV	Manual	7041170	9/16	1 3/4	1 11/32	.085	.140	.180	—/—	—	—	—	—
	2GV	Automatic	7041072	9/16	1 3/4	1 11/32	.085	.105	.180	—/—	—	—	—	—
	2GV	Automatic	7041074	11/16	1 3/4	1 11/32	.085	.130	.180	—/—	—	—	—	—
	4MV	Automatic	7041262	9/32	—	—	.100	.240	—	—/—	—	.025	—	—
	4MV	Manual	7041263	9/32	—	—	.100	.240	—	—/—	—	.025	—	—
	4MV	Automatic	7041264	9/32	—	—	.100	.240	—	—/—	—	.025	—	—
	4MV	Manual	7041267	9/32	—	—	.100	.370	—	—/—	—	.025	—	—
	4MV	Automatic	7041268	9/32	—	—	.100	.430	—	—/—	—	.025	—	—
	4MV	Automatic	7041270	9/32	—	—	.100	.430	—	—/—	—	.025	—	—
	4MV	Automatic	7041271	9/32	—	—	.100	.240	—	—/—	—	.025	—	—
	4MV	Manual	7041273	9/32	—	—	.100	.370	—	—/—	—	.025	—	—
1972	MV	Automatic	7042014	1/4	—	—	.160	.200	.500	—/—	—	—	—	2400
	MV	Manual	7042017	1/4	—	—	.180	.230	.500	—/—	—	—	—	2400
	MV	Automatic (Calif.)	7042984	1/4	—	—	.160	.200	.500	—/—	—	—	—	—
	MV	Manual (Calif.)	7042987	1/4	—	—	.180	.230	.500	—/—	—	—	—	—
	2GV	Automatic	7042060	5/8	1 9/32	1 11/32	.085	.122	.180	—/—	—	—	—	—
	2GV	Automatic	7042061	5/8	1 9/32	1 11/32	.085	.122	.180	—/—	—	—	—	—
	2GV	Automatic	7042062	9/16	1 9/32	1 11/32	.085	.105	.180	—/—	—	—	—	—

PONTIAC

Year	Carburetor Model	Transmission	Carburetor Number	Float Level (in.)	Float Drop (in.)	Accel. Pump Rod (in.)	Choke Rod (in.)	Vacuum Break (in.)	Choke Unloader (in.)	Main Jet Pri./Sec.	Air Valve Springs (in.)	Air Valve Dash Pot (in.)	Idle Vent (in.)	Fast Idle Speed (rpm)
	2GV	Automatic	7042064	5/8	1 9/32	1 11/32	.085	.150	.180	— / —	—	—	—	—
	2GV	Automatic	7042100	25/32	1 31/32	1 5/16	.040	.080	215	— / —	—	—	—	—
	2GV	Manual	7042101	25/32	1 31/32	1 5/16	.075	.100	215	— / —	—	—	—	—
	4MV	Automatic	7042262	1/4	—	—	13/32	.100	.290	310	— / —	—	.025	—	—
	4MV	Manual	7042263	1/4	—	—	13/32	.100	.290	310	— / —	—	.025	—	—
	4MV	Automatic	7042264	1/4	—	—	13/32	.100	.290	310	— / —	—	.025	—	—
	4MV	Automatic	7042270	1/4	—	—	7/16	.100	.290	310	— / —	—	.025	—	—
	4MV	Manual	7042273	1/4	—	—	7/16	.100	.290	310	— / —	—	.025	—	—
CARTER														
	WGD	Manual	488062	5/16	—	—	—	—	—	— / —	—	—	—	—

PONTIAC

Year	Carb. Model	Carb. Number	Float Level (Ins.)	Float Drop (Ins.)	Pump Rod (Ins.)	Pump Rod Hole	Choke Rod (Ins.)	Choke Lever (Ins.)	Choke Unloader (Ins.)	Choke Setting (Notches)	Vacuum Break (Ins.) Pri. (Front)/ Aux. (Rear)	Air Valve Rod/Dashpot (Ins.)	Air Valve Spring (Turns)	Air Valve Lockout (Ins.)
1973	ROCHESTER													
	MV	7043014	1/4	–	–	—	.245	—	.500		.300/—	—	–	—
	MV	7043017	3/4	–	–	—	.275	—	.500		.350/—	—	–	—
	2GC	7043062	21/32	1 9/32	1 5/16	—	.085	—	.180	1NL	.167/—	—	–	—
	2GC	7043063	21/32	1 9/32	1 5/16	—	.085	—	.180	1NL	.167/—	—	–	—
	2GC	7043071	23/32	1 9/32	1 5/16	—	.085	—	.180	1NL	.195/—	—	–	—
	2GC	7043072	23/32	1 9/32	1 5/16	—	.085	—	.180	1NL	.167/—	—	–	—
	2GC	7043060	21/32	1 9/32	1 5/16	—	.085	—	.180	1NL	.157/—	—	–	—
	2GC	7043061	21/32	1 9/32	1 5/16	—	.085	—	.180	1NL	.157/—	—	–	—
	2GC	7043066	21/32	1 9/32	1 5/16	—	.085	—	.180	1NL	.180/—	—	–	—
	2GC	7043067	21/32	1 9/32	1 5/16	—	.085	—	.180	1NL	.180/—	—	–	—
	2GC	7043070	23/32	1 9/32	1 5/16	—	.085	—	.180	1NL	.157/—	—	–	—
	4MC	7043263	13/32	–	13/32	Inner	.205	—	.310	Index	.290/—	.025	5/8	.015
	4MC	7043264	13/32	–	13/32	Inner	.205	—	.310	Index	.260/—	.025	1/2	.015
	4MC	7043274	13/32	–	13/32	Inner	.205	—	.310	Index	.290/—	.025	9/16	.015
	4MC	7043262	13/32	–	13/32	Inner	.205	—	.310	Index	.260/—	.025	3/8	.015
	4MC	7043265	13/32	–	13/32	Inner	.205	—	.310	Index	.290/—	.025	9/16	.015
	4MC	7043272	13/32	–	13/32	Inner	.205	—	.310	Index	.290/—	.025	3/8	.015
	4MC	7043270	13/32	–	13/32	Inner	.205	—	.310	Index	—/—	.025	/	.015
	4MC	7043273	13/32	–	13/32	Inner	.205	—	.310	Index	—/—	.025	–	.015
1974	ROCHESTER													
	MV	7044041	.354	–	–	—	.230	—	.500	—	.205/—	—	–	—
	MV	7044017	.354	–	–	—	.275	—	.500	—	.350/—	—	–	—
	MV	7044314	.354	–	–	—	.245	—	.500	—	.300/—	—	–	—
	2GC	7043060	.670	1 3/4	1 5/16	—	.085	—	.180	1NL	.157/—	—	–	—
	2GC	7043062	.670	1 3/4	1 5/16	—	.085	—	.180	1NL	.167/—	—	–	—
	2GC	7043070	.670	1 3/4	1 5/16	—	.085	—	.180	1NL	.157/—	—	–	—
	2GC	7043071	.670	1 3/4	1 5/16	—	.085	—	.180	1NL	.195/—	—	–	—
	2GC	7043072	.670	1 3/4	1 5/16	—	.085	—	.180	1NL	.167/—	—	–	—
	2GC	7044063	.670	1 3/4	1 5/16	—	.085	—	.180	1NL	.157/—	—	–	—
	2GC	7044066	.670	1 3/4	1 5/16	—	.085	—	.180	1NL	.177/—	—	–	—
	2GC	7044067	.670	1 3/4	1 5/16	—	.085	—	.180	1NL	.177/—	—	–	—
	4MC	7043263	.390	–	.410	Inner	.205	—	.310	Index	.290/—	.025	5/8	.015
	4MC	7044262	.390	–	.410	Inner	.205	—	.310	Index	.260/—	.025	3/8	.015
	4MC	7044267	.390	–	.410	Inner	.205	—	.310	Index	.260/—	.025	3/8	.015
	4MC	7044268	.390	–	.410	Inner	.205	—	.310	Index	.260/—	.025	1/2	.015
	4MC	7044269	.390	–	.410	Inner	.205	—	.310	Index	.290/—	.025	1/2	.015
	4MC	7044270	.390	–	.410	Inner	.205	—	.310	Index	.290/—	.025	3/4	.015
	4MC	7044272	.390	–	.410	Outer	.205	—	.310	Index	.290/—	.025	3/4	.015
	4MC	7044273	.390	–	.410	Inner	.205	—	.310	Index	.290/—	.025	3/4	.015
	4MC	7044274	.390	–	.410	Outer	.205	—	.310	Index	.290/—	.025	9/16	.015
	4MC	7044266	.390	–	.410	Inner	.205	—	.310	Index	.260/—	.025	1/2	.015
	4MC	7044560	.390	–	.410	Inner	.205	—	.310	Index	.260/—	.025	3/8	.015
	4MC	7044568	.390	–	.410	Inner	.205	—	.310	Index	.260/—	.025	1/2	.015
1975	ROCHESTER													
	1MV	7045012	11/32	–	–	—	.160	—	.275	—	.200/.215	—	–	—
	1MV	7045013	11/32	–	–	—	.275	—	.275	—	.350/.312	—	–	—
	1MV	7045314	11/32	–	–	—	.230	—	.275	—	.275/.312	—	–	—
	2MC	7045156	5/32	–	9/32	Inner	.130	.120	.275	1NR	.150/.230	—	–	—
	2MC	7045297	3/16	–	9/32	Inner	.130	.120	.275	1NR	.180/.275	—	–	—
	2MC	7045298	5/32	–	9/32	Inner	.130	.120	.275	1NR	.150/.275	—	–	—
	2MC	7045598	5/32	–	9/32	Inner	.160	.120	.275	1NR	.150/.230	—	–	—
	2MC	7045356	5/32	–	9/32	Inner	.160	.120	.275	1NR	.180/.275	—	–	—
	2GC	7045160	9/16	1 7/32	1 3/4	—	.085	—	.180	1NR	.145/.265	—	–	—
	2GC	7045162	9/16	1 7/32	1 13/16	—	.085	—	.180	1NR	.145/.260	—	–	—
	2GC	7045171	9/16	1 7/32	1 13/16	—	.085	—	.180	1NR	.145/.260	—	–	—
	2GC	7045143	5/32	1 7/32	1 13/16	—	.085	—	.180	1NR	.140/.120	—	–	—
	M4MC	7045246	5/16	–	15/32	Outer	.095	—	.240	1NR	.130/.115	.015	1/2	.015
	M4MC	7045546	5/16	–	15/32	Outer	.095	—	.240	1NR	.145/.130	.015	1/2	.015
	M4MC	7045263	1/2	–	9/32	Inner	.130	.120	.230	Index	.150/.260	.025	1/2	.015
	M4MC	7045264	1/2	–	9/32	Inner	.130	.120	.230	Index	.150/.260	.025	1/2	.015
	M4MC	7045268	1/2	–	9/32	Inner	.130	.120	.230	Index	.150/.260	.025	1/2	.015
	M4MC	7045269	1/2	–	9/32	Inner	.130	.120	.230	Index	.150/.260	.025	1/2	.015
	M4MC	7045274	1/2	–	9/32	Inner	.130	.120	.230	Index	.150/.260	.025	1/2	.015
	M4MCA	7045260	1/2	–	9/32	Inner	.130	.120	.230	Index	.150/.260	.025	1/2	.015
	M4MCA	7045262	1/2	–	9/32	Inner	.130	.120	.230	Index	.150/.260	.025	1/2	.015
	M4MCA	7045266	1/2	–	9/32	Inner	.130	.120	.230	Index	.150/.260	.025	1/2	.015
	M4MCA	7045562	1/2	–	9/32	Inner	.130	.120	.230	Index	.150/.260	.025	1/2	.015
	M4MCA	7045564	1/2	–	9/32	Inner	.130	.120	.230	Index	.150/.260	.025	1/2	.015
	M4MCA	7045568	1/2	–	9/32	Inner	.130	—	.230	Index	.150/.260	.025	1/2	.015
	M4MCA	7045566	1/2	–	9/32	Inner	.130	—	.230	Index	.150/.260	.025	1/2	.015
1976	ROCHESTER													
	1MV	—	1/8	–	–	—	.045	—	.215	—	.055/.450	—	–	—
	1MV	—	1/8	–	–	—	.045	—	.215	—	.060/.450	—	–	—
	1MV	—	11/32	–	–	—	.140	—	.265	—	.165/.320	—	–	—
	1MV	—	11/32	–	–	—	.100	—	.265	—	.140/.265	—	–	—
	1MV	—	11/32	–	–	—	.135	—	.265	—	.150/.260	—	–	—
	2MC	—	1/8	–	3/16	Outer	.105	.120	.210	1NR	.110/.175	—	–	—
	2MC	—	1/8	–	9/32	Inner	.105	.120	.210	1NR	.110/.175	—	–	—
	2MC	—	1/8	–	3/16	Outer	.105	.120	.210	1NR/Index	.110/.210	—	–	—
	2GC	—	7/16	1 9/32	1 19/32	—	.080	.120	.140	1NR	.110/.100	—	–	—
	2GC	—	7/16	1 9/32	1 19/32	—	.080	.120	.140	1NR	.120/.100	—	–	—
	2GC	—	7/16	1 9/32	1 19/32	—	.080	.120	.140	1NR	.130/.110	—	–	—
	2GC	—	15/32	1 9/32	1 11/32	—	.080	.120	.180	1NR	.140/.100	—	–	—
	2GC	—	9/16	1 9/32	1 11/32	—	.080	.120	.180	1NR	.165/.285	—	–	—
	M4MC	—	5/16	–	3/8	Outer	.095	.120	.250	1NR	.130/.120	.015	3/4	—
	M4MC	—	5/16	–	3/8	Outer	.095	.120	.250	Index	.130/.130	.015	3/4	—
	M4MC	—	17/32	–	3/8	Outer	.125	.120	.230	1NR	.160/.250	.030	1/2	—

CARBURETOR SPECIFICATIONS

PONTIAC

Year	Carb. Model	Carb. Number	Float Level (Ins.)	Float Drop (Ins.)	Pump Rod (Ins.)	Pump Rod Hole	Choke Rod (Ins.)	Choke Lever (Ins.)	Choke Unloader (Ins.)	Choke Setting (Notches)	Vacuum Break (Ins.) Pri. (Front)/ Aux. (Rear)	Air Valve Rod/Dashpot (Ins.)	Air Valve Spring (Turns)	Air Valve Lockout (Ins.)
1976	M4MC	—	17/32	–	3/8	Outer	.125	.120	.230	1NR	.160/.250	.030	1/2	—
	M4MC	—	17/32	–	3/8	Outer	.125	.120	.230	1NR	.170/.250	.030	5/8	—
	M4MC	—	17/32	–	3/8	Outer	.130	.120	.230	1NR	.150/.260	.030	1/2	—
	M4MC	—	17/32	–	3/8	Outer	.125	.120	.230	1NR	.160/.250	.030	1/2	—
	M4MC	—	17/32	–	3/8	Outer	.120	.120	.230	1NR	.170/.250	.030	1/3	—
1977	**ROCHESTER**													
	2GE	17057108	5/8	1 1/4	1 5/8	—	.260	.120	.325	Index	.160/—	—	–	—
	2GE	17057110	5/8	1 1/4	1 5/8	—	.260	.120	.325	Index	.160/—	—	–	—
	2GC	17057143	7/16	1 5/32	1 19/32	—	.080	.120	.140	1NR	.130/.100	—	–	—
	2GC	17057144	7/16	1 5/32	1 19/32	—	.080	.120	.140	1NR	.130/.100	—	–	—
	2GC	17057145	7/16	1 5/32	1 19/32	—	.080	.120	—	1NR	.110/.040	—	–	—
	2GC	17057146	7/16	1 5/32	1 9/16	—	.080	.120	.140	1NR	.110/.040	—	–	—
	2GC	17057148	7/16	1 5/32	1 9/16	—	.080	.120	.140	1NR	.110/.030	—	–	—
	2GC	17057446	7/16	1 5/32	1 19/32	—	.080	.120	.140	1NR	.130/.110	—	–	—
	2GC	17057447	7/16	1 5/32	1 19/32	—	.080	.120	—		—/—	—	–	—
	2GC	17057448	7/16	1 5/32	1 19/32	—	.080	.120	.140	1NR	.130/.110	—	–	—
	M2MC200	17057172	11/32	–	3/8	Outer	—	.120	.240	2NR	—/.240	—	–	—
	M2MC200	17057173	11/32	–	3/8	Outer	—	.120	.240	2NR	—/.240	—	–	—
	M4MC	17057250	13/32	–	9/32	Inner	.095	.120	.250	2NR	.125/.170	.030	1/2	.015
	M4MC	17057253	13/32	–	9/32	Inner	.095	.120	.205	2NR	.125/.170	.030	1/2	.015
	M4MC	17057255	13/32	–	9/32	Inner	.095	.120	.205	2NR	.125/.170	.030	1/2	.015
	M4MC	17057256	13/32	–	9/32	Inner	.095	.120	.205	2NR	.125/.170	.030	1/2	.015
	M4MC	17057258	13/32	–	9/32	Inner	.095	.120	.205	2NR	.125/.215	.030	1/2	.015
	M4MC	17057262	17/32	–	3/8	Outer	.130	.120	.220	1NR	.150/.240	.030	1/2	.015
	M4MC	17057263	17/32	–	3/8	Outer	.130	.120	.220	1NR	.165/.240	.030	5/8	.015
	M4MC	17057266	17/32	–	3/8	Outer	.130	.120	.220	1NR	.150/.240	.030	1/2	.015
	M4MC	17057274	17/32	–	3/8	Outer	.130	.120	.220	1NR	.150/.240	.030	1/2	.015
	M4MC	17057550	13/32	–	9/32	Inner	.095	.120	.200	2NR	.125/.215	.030	1/2	.015
	M4MC	17057553	13/32	–	9/32	Inner	.095	.120	.200	2NR	.125/.215	.030	1/2	.015
	HOLLEY													
	5210-C	458102	.42	1	–	—	.085	—	.350	3NR	.250/—	—	–	—
	5210-C	458103	.42	1	–	—	.085	—	.350	3NR	.250/—	—	–	—
	5210-C	458104	.42	1	–	—	.085	—	.350	3NR	.250/—	—	–	—
	5210-C	458105	.42	1	–	—	.085	—	.350	3NR	.250/—	—	–	—
	5210-C	458107	.42	1	–	—	.125	—	.350	3NR	.275/.400	—	–	—
	5210-C	458109	.42	1	–	—	.125	—	.350	3NR	.275/.400	—	–	—
	5210-C	458110	.42	1	–	—	.120	—	.350	3NR	.300/.400	—	–	—
	5210-C	458112	.42	1	–	—	.120	—	.350	3NR	.300/.400	—	–	—
	5210-C	458200	.52	1	–	—	.150	—	.400	4NR	.275/—	—	–	—
	5210-C	458201	.52	1	–	—	.150	—	.400	4NR	.300/—	—	–	—
	5210-C	458202	.52	1	–	—	.150	—	.400	4NR	.275/—	—	–	—
	5210-C	458203	.52	1	–	—	.150	—	.400	4NR	.300/—	—	–	—
	5210-C	458204	.52	1	–	—	.150	—	.400	2NR	.275/—	—	–	—
	5210-C	458206	.52	1	–	—	.150	—	.400	2NR	.275/—	—	–	—
1978	**ROCHESTER**													
	2GE	17058145	7/16	1 5/32	1 5/8	—	.080	.120	.160	1NL	.110/.110	—	–	—
	2GE	17058147	7/16	1 5/32	1 5/8	—	.080	.120	.140	1NR	.140/.140	—	–	—
	2GE	17058182	7/16	1 5/32	1 5/8	—	.080	.120	.140	1NR	.110/.110	—	–	—
	2GE	17058183	7/16	1 5/32	1 5/8	—	.080	.120	.140	1NR	.110/.110	—	–	—
	2GE	17058408	21/32	1 9/32	1 21/32	—	.260	.120	.325	1/2NL	.140/.140	—	–	—
	2GE	17058410	21/32	1 9/32	1 21/32	—	.260	.120	.325	1/2NL	.140/.140	—	–	—
	2GE	17058412	21/32	1 9/32	1 21/32	—	.260	.120	.325	1/2NL	.140/.140	—	–	—
	2GE	17058414	21/32	1 9/32	1 21/32	—	.260	.120	.325	1/2NL	.140/.140	—	–	—
	2GE	17058444	7/16	1 5/32	1 5/8	—	.080	.120	.140	1NR	.140/.140	—	–	—
	2GE	17058446	7/16	1 5/32	1 5/8	—	.080	.120	.140	1NR	.140/.140	—	–	—
	2GE	17058447	7/16	1 5/32	1 5/8	—	.080	.120	.140	1NR	.150/.150	—	–	—
	2GE	17058448	7/16	1 5/32	1 5/8	—	.080	.120	.140	1NR	.140/.140	—	–	—
	2GE	17058185	7/16	1 5/32	1 19/32	—	.080	.120	.140	1NR	.110/.110	—	–	—
	2GE	17058187	7/16	1 5/32	1 19/32	—	.080	.120	.140	1NR	.110/.110	—	–	—
	2GE	17058189	7/16	1 5/32	1 19/32	—	.080	.120	.140	1NR	.110/.110	—	–	—
	2GC	17058102	19/32	1 9/32	1 17/32	—	.260	.120	.325	Index	.130/—	—	–	—
	2GC	17058103	19/32	1 9/32	1 17/32	—	.260	.120	.325	Index	.130/—	—	–	—
	2GC	17058108	19/32	1 9/32	1 21/32	—	.260	.120	.325	Index	.130/—	—	–	—
	2GC	17058110	19/32	1 9/32	1 21/32	—	.260	.120	.325	Index	.130/—	—	–	—
	2GC	17058111	19/32	1 9/32	1 5/8	—	.260	.120	.325	Index	.130/—	—	–	—
	2GC	17058112	19/32	1 9/32	1 21/32	—	.260	.120	.325	Index	.130/—	—	–	—
	2GC	17058113	19/32	1 9/32	1 5/8	—	.260	.120	.325	Index	.130/—	—	–	—
	2GC	17058114	19/32	1 9/32	1 21/32	—	.260	.120	.325	Index	.130/—	—	–	—
	2GC	17058121	19/32	1 9/32	1 5/8	—	.260	.120	.325	Index	.130/—	—	–	—
	2GC	17058123	19/32	1 9/32	1 5/8	—	.260	.120	.325	Index	.130/—	—	–	—
	2GC	17058126	19/32	1 9/32	1 17/32	—	.260	.120	.325	Index	.130/—	—	–	—
	2GC	17058128	19/32	1 9/32	1 17/32	—	.260	.120	.325	Index	.130/—	—	–	—
	M2MC-210	17058160	11/32	–	1/4	Inner	.126	.120	.203	2NR	.142/.195	—	–	.015
	M4MC	17058202	15/32	–	9/32	Inner	.314	.120	.277	1NL	.157/—	.015	–	.015
	M4MC	17058204	15/32	–	9/32	Inner	.314	.120	.277	1NL	.157/—	.015	–	.015
	M4MC	17058241	5/16	–	3/8	Outer	.096	.120	.243	1NR	.117/.103	.015	3/4	.015
	M4MC	17058250	13/32	–	9/32	Inner	.088	.120	.203	2NR	.119/.167	.030	1/2	.015
	M4MC	17058253	13/32	–	9/32	Inner	.088	.120	.203	2NR	.119/.167	.030	1/2	.015
	M4MC	17058258	13/32	–	9/32	Inner	.092	.120	.203	2NR	.126/.212	.030	1/2	.015
	M4MC	17058263	17/32	–	3/8	Outer	.129	.120	.220	Index	.164/.260	.030	5/8	.015
	M4MC	17058264	17/32	–	3/8	Outer	.129	.120	.220	1NR	.149/.260	.030	1/2	.015
	M4MC	17058266	17/32	–	3/8	Outer	.129	.120	.220	Index	.149/.260	.030	1/2	.015
	M4MC	17058272	15/32	–	3/8	Outer	.071	.120	.227	2NR	.126/.195	.030	5/8	.015
	M4MC	17058274	17/32	–	3/8	Outer	.129	.120	.220	Index	.149/.260	.030	1/2	.015
	M4MC	17058276	17/32	–	3/8	Outer	.129	.120	.220	Index	.149/.260	.030	1/2	.015
	M4MC	17058278	17/32	–	3/8	Outer	.129	.120	.220	1NR	.149/.260	.030	1/2	.015
	M4MC	17058502	15/32	–	9/32	Inner	.314	.120	.277	2NL	.164/—	.015	–	.015
	M4MC	17058504	15/32	–	9/32	Inner	.314	.120	.277	2NL	.164/—	.015	–	.015
	M4MC	17058553	13/32	–	9/32	Inner	.092	.120	.203	2NR	.126/.212	.030	1/2	.015
	M4MC	17058582	15/32	–	9/32	Inner	.314	.120	.277	2NL	.179/—	.015	7/8	.015
	M4MC	17058584	15/32	–	9/32	Inner	.314	.120	.277	2NL	.179/—	.015	7/8	.015
	HOLLEY													
	5210-C	10001047	.52	1	–	—	.150	—	.350	1NR	.325/—	—	–	—
	5210-C	10001049	.52	1	–	—	.150	—	.350	1NR	.325/—	—	–	—
	5210-C	10004048	.52	1	–	—	.150	—	.350	2NR	.300/—	—	–	—
	5210-C	10004049	.52	1	–	—	.150	—	.350	2NR	.300/—	—	–	—
	6510-C	10001056	.5/2	1	–	—	.150	—	.350	1NR	.325/—	—	–	—
	6510-C	10001058	.5/2	1	–	—	.150	—	.350	1NR	.250/—	—	–	—
1979	**ROCHESTER**													
	2SE	17059674	13/64	–	1/2	—	.096	.085	.195	2NR	.123/—	.025	–	—
	2SE	17059676	13/64	–	1/2	—	.096	.085	.195	2NR	.123/—	.025	–	—
	2SE	17059675	13/64	–	17/32	—	.096	.085	.195	2NR	.123/—	.025	–	—

PONTIAC

Year	Carb. Model	Carb. Number	Float Level (Ins.)	Float Drop (Ins.)	Pump Rod (Ins.)	Pump Rod Hole	Choke Rod (Ins.)	Choke Lever (Ins.)	Choke Unloader (Ins.)	Choke Setting (Notches)	Vacuum Break (Ins.) Pri. (Front)/ Aux. (Rear)	Air Valve Rod/Dashpot (Ins.)	Air Valve Spring (Turns)	Air Valve Lockout (Ins.)
	2SE	17059677	13/64	–	17/32	—	.096	.085	.195	2NR	.123/—	.025	–	—
	M2MC/M2ME	17059134	13/32	–	9/32	Inner	.243	.120	.243	1NL	.157/—	—	–	—
	M2MC/M2ME	17059135	13/32	–	9/32	Inner	.243	.120	.243	1NL	.157/—	—	–	—
	M2MC/M2ME	17059136	13/32	–	9/32	Inner	.243	.120	.243	1NL	.157/—	—	–	—
	M2MC/M2ME	17059137	13/32	–	9/32	Inner	.243	.120	.243	1NL	.157/—	—	–	—
	M2MC/M2ME	17059180	11/32	–	1/4	Inner	.139	.120	.243	2NR	.103/.090	—	–	—
	M2MC/M2ME	17059190	11/32	–	1/4	Inner	.139	.120	.243	2NR	.103/.090	—	–	—
	M2MC/M2ME	17059191	11/32	–	1/4	Inner	.139	.120	.243	2NR	.103/.090	—	–	—
	M2MC/M2ME	17059160	11/32	–	9/32	Inner	.110	.120	.195	2NR	.129/.203	—	–	—
	M2MC/M2ME	17059196	11/32	–	1/4	Inner	.139	.120	.277	1NR	.129/.117	—	–	—
	M2MC/M2ME	17059434	13/32	–	9/32	Inner	.243	.120	.243	2NL	.164/—	—	–	—
	M2MC/M2ME	17059436	13/32	–	9/32	Inner	.243	.120	.243	2NL	.164/—	—	–	—
	M2MC/M2ME	17059492	11/32	–	9/32	Inner	.139	.120	.277	2NR	.129/.117	—	–	—
	M2MC/M2ME	17059498	11/32	–	9/32	Inner	.139	.120	.277	2NR	.129/.117	—	–	—
	M2MC/M2ME	17059430	9/32	–	9/32	Inner	.243	.120	.243	1NL	.171/—	—	–	—
	M2MC/M2ME	17059432	9/32	–	9/32	Inner	.243	.120	.243	1NL	.171/—	—	–	—
	M2MC/M2ME	17059491	11/32	–	9/32	Inner	.139	.120	.277	1NR	.129/.117	—	–	—
	M4MC	17058263	17/32	–	3/8	Outer	.129	.120	.220	Index	.164/.243	.030	5/8	.015
	M4MC	17059250	13/32	–	9/32	Inner	.096	.120	.220	2NR	.129/.183	.030	1/2	.015
	M4MC	17059253	13/32	–	9/32	Inner	.096	.120	.220	2NR	.129/.183	.030	1/2	.015
	M4MC	17059241	5/16	–	3/8	Outer	.096	.120	.243	1NR	.120/.114	.030	3/4	.015
	M4MC	17059271	9/16	–	3/8	Outer	.110	.120	.203	1NR	.142/.227	.030	5/8	.015
	M4MC	17059272	15/32	–	3/8	Outer	.074	.120	.220	2NR	.136/.195	.030	5/8	.015
	M4MC	17059502	15/32	–	1/4	Inner	.243	.120	.243	2NL	.164/—	.015	7/8	.015
	M4MC	17059504	15/32	–	1/4	Inner	.243	.120	.243	2NL	.164/—	.015	7/8	.015
	M4MC	17059553	13/32	–	9/32	Inner	.103	.120	.220	2NR	.136/.231	.030	1/2	.015
	M4MC	17059582	15/32	–	11/32	Outer	.243	.120	.314	1NL	.136/.231	.015	7/8	.015
	M4MC	17059584	15/32	–	11/32	Outer	.243	.120	.314	1NL	.203/—	.015	7/8	.015
	HOLLEY													
	6510-C	10008489	.52	1	–	2	.150	—	.350	2NR	.250/—	—	–	—
	6510-C	10008490	.52	1	–	2	.150	—	.350	2NR	.250/—	—	–	—
	6510-C	10008491	.52	1	–	2	.150	—	.350	2NR	.250/—	—	–	—
	6510-C	10008492	.52	1	–	2	.150	—	.350	2NR	.250/—	—	–	—

1Dry float setting—toe of float with air horn inverted
2Calif. .268.
3Calif. #135.
4Calif. #136
5240 at 22,500-mile tune-up adjustment.
6See emissions label.

TROUBLESHOOTING THE MOTORCRAFT 2700 VV CARBURETOR

TROUBLE	PROBABLE CAUSE	CORRECTION
Rough idle (Hot) — Continued	Venturi valve limiter out of adjustment	Adjust venturi valve limiter
	External vent blocked	Check for kinked hoses.
Rough idle (Cold)	Cold enrichment system sticking	Clean, adjust cold enrichment system.
	Venturi valve sticking open/closed or damaged diaphragm	Clean, repair as required.
	Plugged manifold vacuum restrictor or throttle port	Remove throttle body and check port and restrictor.
Stall, stumble, hesitation (Hot)	Bowl vents blocked	Check internal vent for adjustment and external vent for kinked hoses.
	Venturi valve sticking or damaged diaphragm	Clean, repair as required.
	Throttle solenoid out of adjustment	Adjust
Surge at cruise	Plugged fuel filter	Replace
	Low fuel level	Adjust fuel level to specifications.
	Venturi valve sticking	Clean, repair as required.
	Internal or external valve not functioning	Check internal vent for adjustment and external vent for kinked hoses.
	Leaking jet plugs	Place rubber plugs on end of main well channels. If condition is corrected replace jet plugs.
	Damaged metering rods or springs	Replace
Poor acceleration	Sticking venturi valve /venturi valve diaphragm leaking	Clean, repair as required.
	Limiter lever system out of adjustment	Adjust
	Blocked throttle linkage	Check, repair as required.
	Plugged distributor port	Check, repair as required.
Reduced Hi-speed	Limiter lever out of adjustment	Adjust limiter lever.
	Main metering system plugged	Clean and repair as required.
	Blocked throttle linkage	Check, repair as required.
	Venturi valve diaphragm leaking	Repair as required.
Flooding	Venturi valve sticking	Clean, repair as required.
	Check float drop	Adjust
	Improper float setting	Adjust to specification.
	Damaged inlet system/or	Repair as required.

TROUBLE	PROBABLE CAUSE	CORRECTION
No start (Cold)	Cold enrichment system not functioning	Check linkage for proper operation; clean, repair or replace as required.
	No fuel in bowl	Check by actuating accelerator pump; if no fuel discharge is seen check fuel inlet system.
	Cranking solenoid not operating	Check cranking solenoid. Disconnect connector and use two jumper wires connected from the battery to the connector to hear solenoid click. Repair as required.
	Venturi valve sticking open	Clean, and repair as required.
Hard starting (Cold)	Cold enrichment system not functioning properly	Check and adjust as required.
	Venturi valve stuck open	Clean and repair as required.
	Cranking solenoid not operating	Check cranking solenoid. Disconnect connector and use two jumper wires connected from the battery to the connector to hear solenoid click. Repair as required.
	Venturi valve sticking open/closed or damaged diaphragm	Clean, repair as required.
Stall, stumble, hesitation (Cold)	Cold enrichment system not functioning	Clean, check and adjust.
	Inoperative cold enrichment heat system	Check and repair as required heat tube.
	Accelerator pump not functioning	Check and repair as required.
	Venturi valve sticking (open/or closed)	Clean, check diaphragm repair as required.
Hard starting (Hot)	Venturi valve stuck open	Clean, repair as required.
	Bowl vents plugged	Check internal vent for adjustment and external vent for kinked hoses.
	Sticking cold enrichment system	Check for metering rod seating, bound linkage, or lack of heat to the choke housing.
Rough idle (Hot)	Sticking venturi valve open	Clean, repair as required.
	Improper control vacuum adjustment.	Adjust control vacuum.

HOW TO: Ball & Ball BBD 1¼-in. Overhaul

1. Ball and Ball dual-throat 1¼-in. carburetors were used by Chrysler Corporation, primarily on 318-cu.-in. engines. As with all carbs, the ID tag contains important information.

2. After removing the air horn screws, pull off the hairpin retainer which holds the accelerator pump rod to the pump rocker arm. You can't lose the clip with this tool.

3. Remove clip from the choke operating link, unbolt the choke vacuum diaphragm and disengage link from the choke lever. *Do not* attempt to remove the pressed-on choke lever.

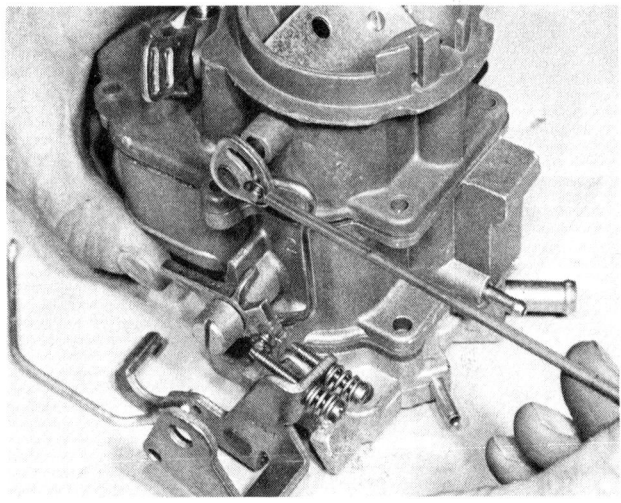

4. Pull retaining hairpin from fast-idle connector rod, and disengage rod from the opposite choke lever. If you use needlenose pliers, take care not to lose tiny clips.

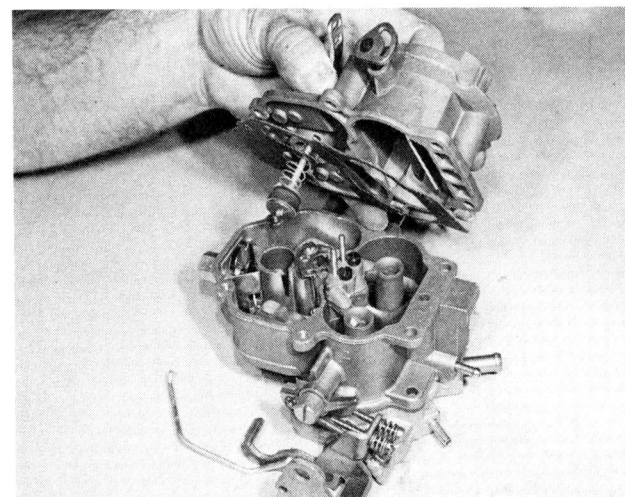

5. With screws removed, lift the air horn straight up and away from main body. Remove and discard the gasket. Remove dashpot, if so equipped, and set main body to one side.

6. Remove the "E" clip and washer which connect the accelerator-pump plunger stem to the pump rocker arm. Plunger stem passes through the closed-bowl vent-valve housing.

HOW TO: Ball & Ball BBD 1¼-in. Overhaul

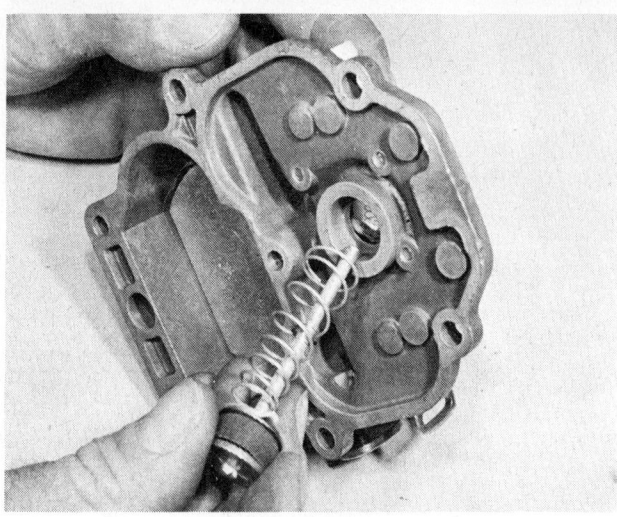

7. Turn air horn over and withdraw pump plunger. Since the plunger is fitted with a leather piston, it should be placed in a cup of gas to prevent leather from drying out.

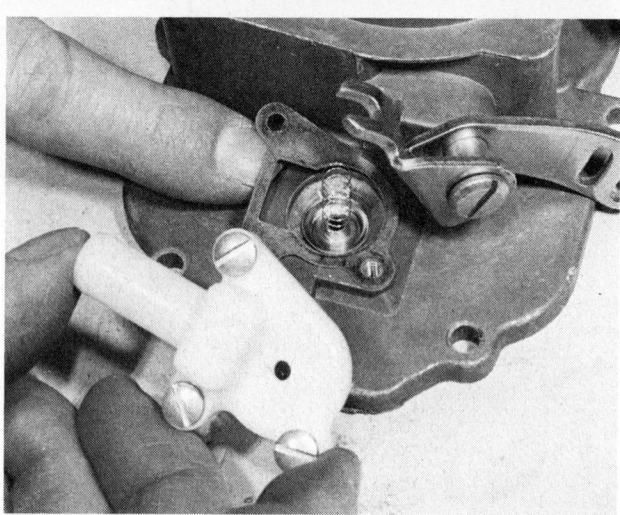

8. Remove the bowl vent-valve housing and screws, and you will find a tiny vent-valve spring. The plastic housing must come off, because cleaning in solvent will damage it.

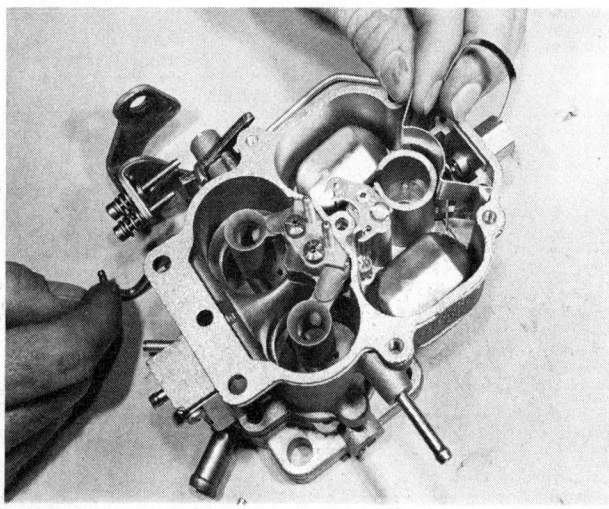

9. Turning to the main body, remove the two float retainer bands. These are quite distinctive in shape and size, so you should have no difficulty in recalling where they fit.

10. Before the dual brass-float assembly can be removed, it is necessary to unscrew and remove the fuel-inlet needle valve, valve seat and the gasket from the main body.

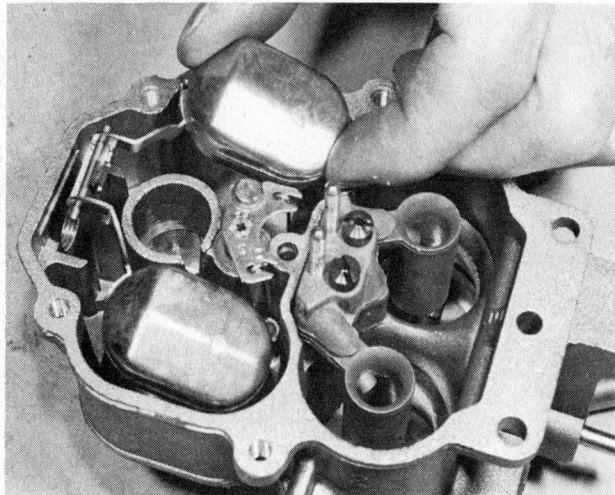

11. Once the fuel-inlet needle valve is out of the way, the float assembly and float fulcrum pin can be removed. Check the brass floats carefully for possible pinhole leaks.

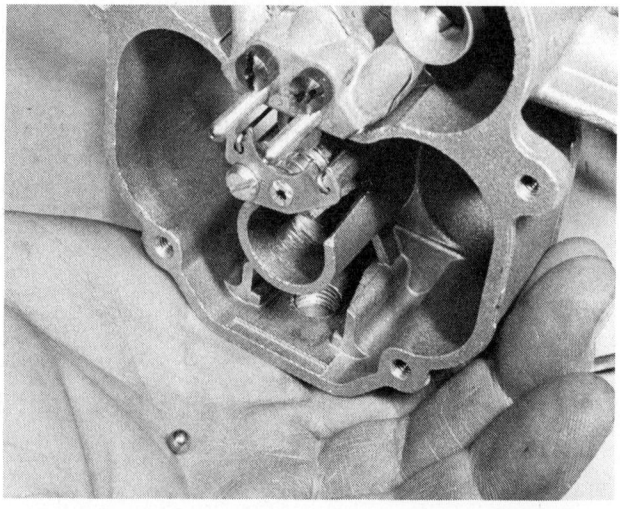

12. Tip main body on its side and catch the accelerator-pump intake check ball as it falls from the bottom of the plunger well. This one is larger than the discharge ball.

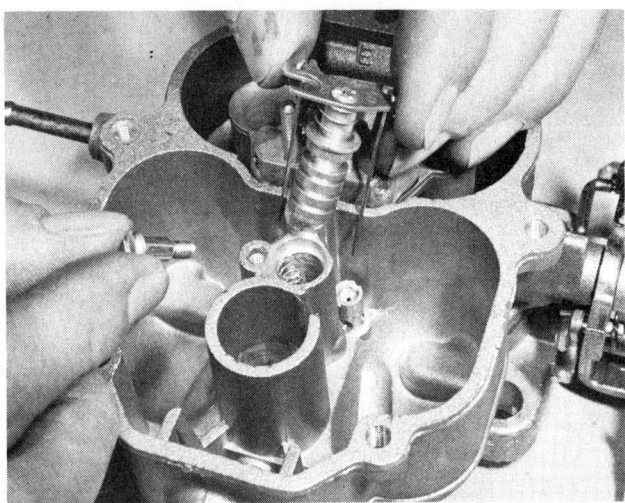

13. Remove the special flanged screw and lift the step-up rods/piston from the cylinder, then remove the piston spring. There's a piston gasket at the bottom of the cylinder.

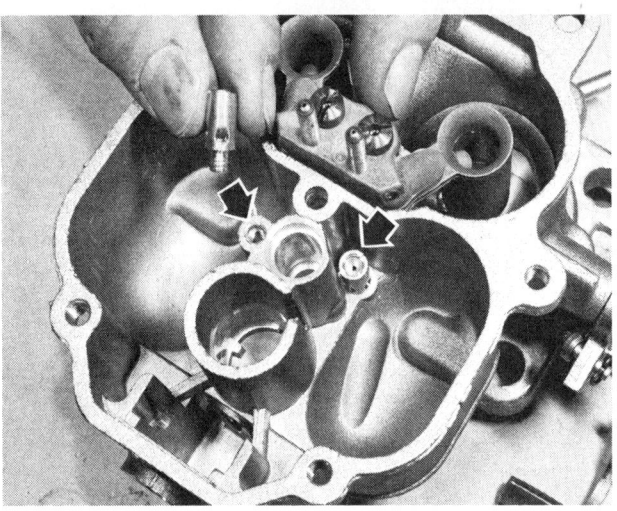

14. The two main metering jets (arrows) are located on either side of step-up-rod piston housing. Use jet remover or wide-blade screwdriver and turn carefully to avoid damage.

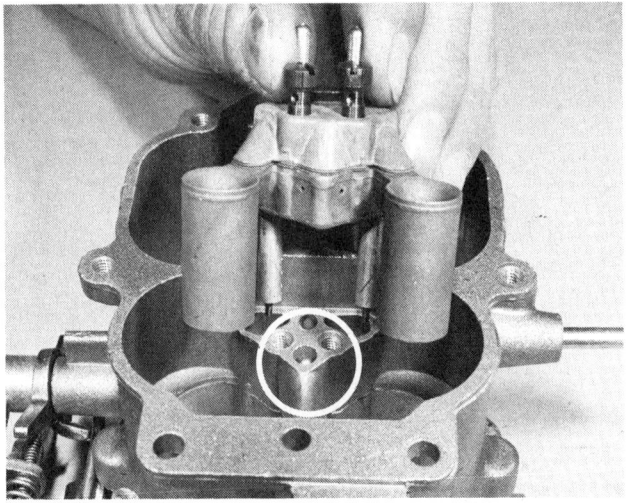

15. Remove the venturi cluster screws, then lift cluster and gaskets up and out of the main body. Remove pump discharge ball (circle). *Do not* remove idle-orifice/main-vent tubes.

16. The hot-idle compensator valve is a thermostatically controlled air bleed which relieves an over-rich condition at idle and is located beneath this odd-shaped cap.

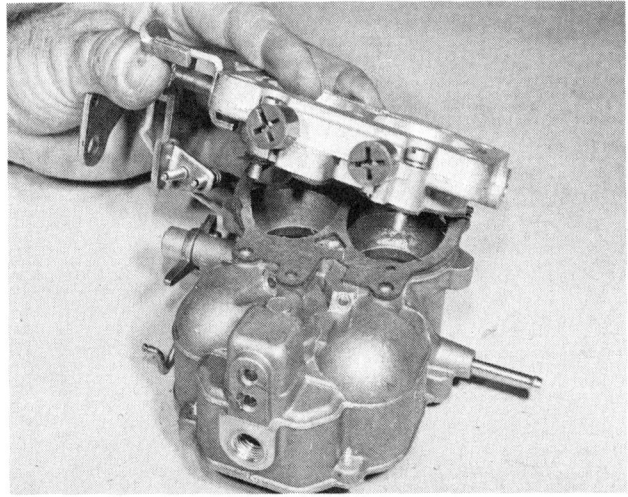

17. Invert the main body and remove the throttle-body-to-main-body screws. Separate the two units and discard the old gasket. Remove idle limiter caps and mixture screws.

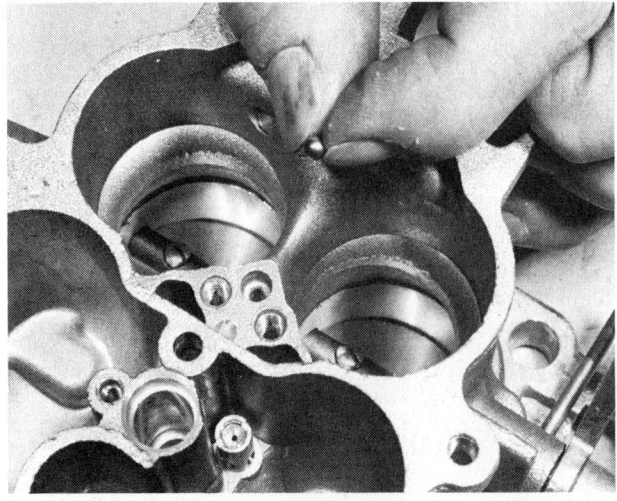

18. To reassemble, replace mixture screws and reattach throttle body with new gasket. Replace main jets, then drop pump-discharge check ball (smaller of the two) back in place.

HOW TO: Ball & Ball BBD 1¼-in. Overhaul

19. Reinstall hot idle compensator. Fit a new gasket between the venturi cluster sections and one under the cluster, then reinstall and tighten the screws securely.

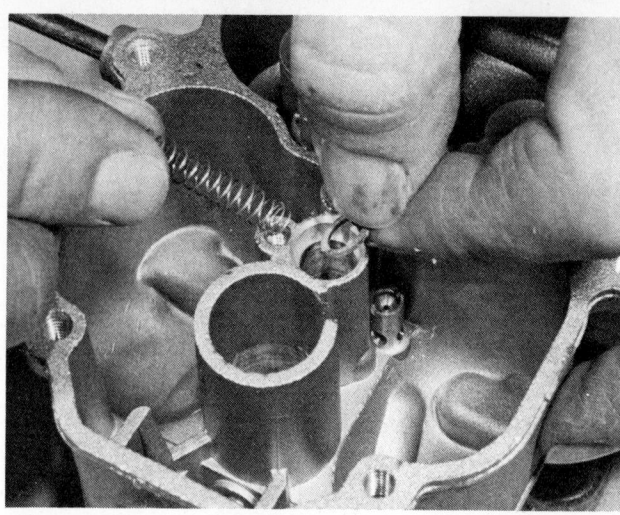

20. Slide the new step-up piston gasket down in position in the piston well, and then install the piston spring. Gasket is an easy item to overlook if you are not careful.

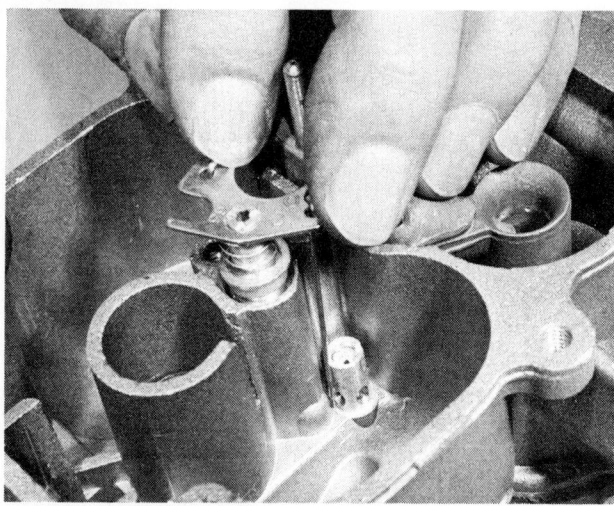

21. Guide step-up rods into the main jets as the piston is reinstalled. If rods stick *up* or are not inserted in jets (shown here), mixture will be too rich at part throttle.

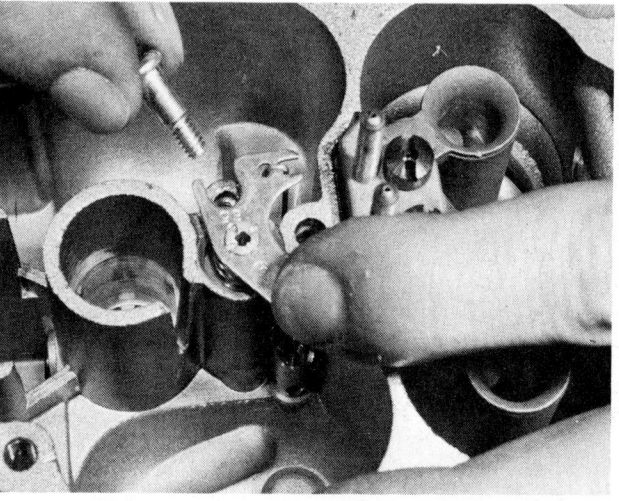

22. With rods positioned in each main metering jet, hold piston/rod assembly down, install retaining screw. Screw has special flanged seat to allow required piston travel.

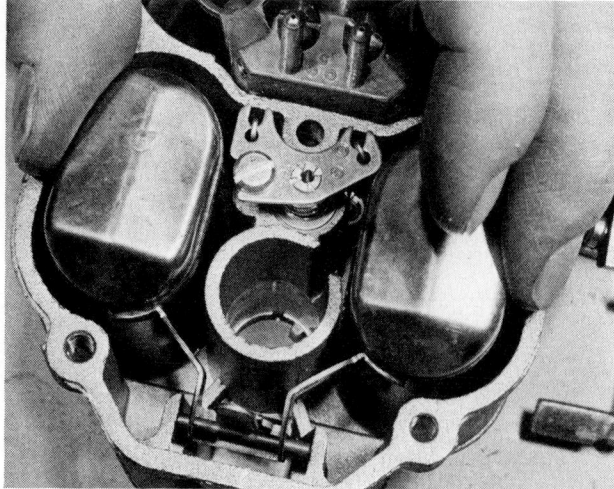

23. Install the dual float assembly, with fulcrum pin and seat in position, then replace the two float retaining bands. Check float action at this point, but do not adjust now.

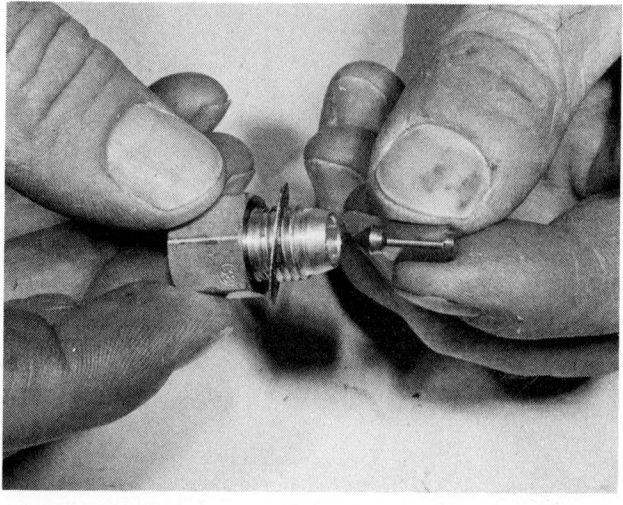

24. BBD carburetors are fitted with a synthetic, rubber-tipped fuel-inlet needle, unaffected by age or temperature, and flexible enough for a good seal to prevent flooding.

25. To replace the accelerator pump, insert the plunger through the air horn and fit the bowl vent/spring over the plunger stem. Hold in place as the vent housing is attached.

26. Lower the pump rocker arm over the plunger stem and replace the washer and "E" clip. Make sure the "E" clip is completely seated around the plunger shaft groove.

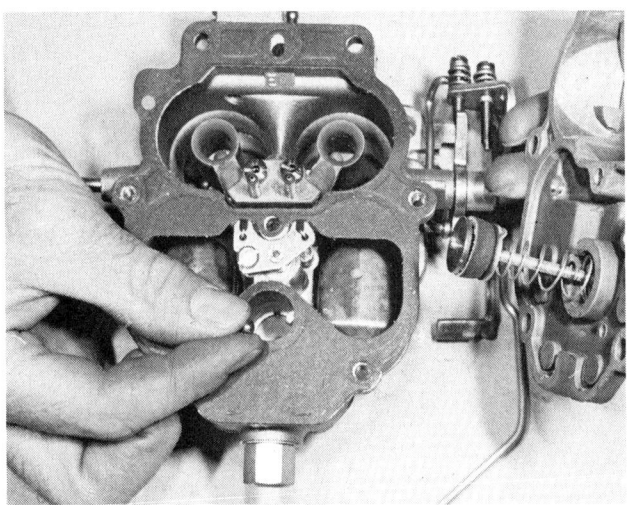

27. Install a new main-body gasket and drop the pump-inlet check ball into the pump well before lowering the air horn in place. Install the air-horn attaching screws.

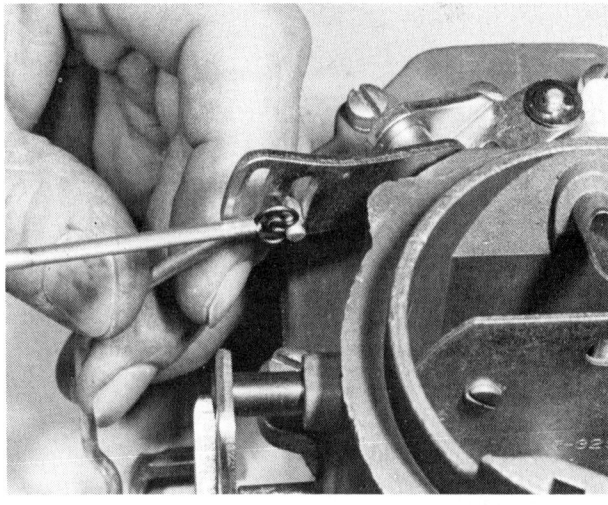

28. Reconnect the accelerator pump rod in the same slot as removed (check specifications if you are not certain where it came from), and replace the hairpin retaining clip.

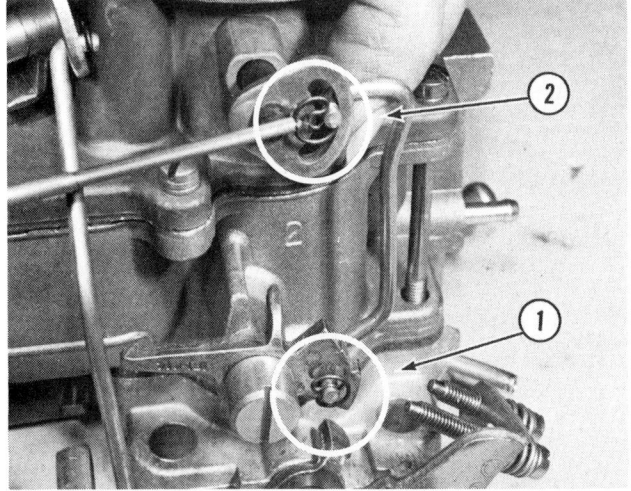

29. Reconnect the fast-idle connector rod to the fast-idle cam (1) and choke lever (2), then install one hairpin retaining clip on each end of the rod; check rod action.

30. Connect choke link to the choke lever and attach the vacuum diaphragm and bracket to the carburetor air horn. Tighten screws, and reconnect the vacuum hose to carburetor.

HOW TO: Carter AVS Overhaul

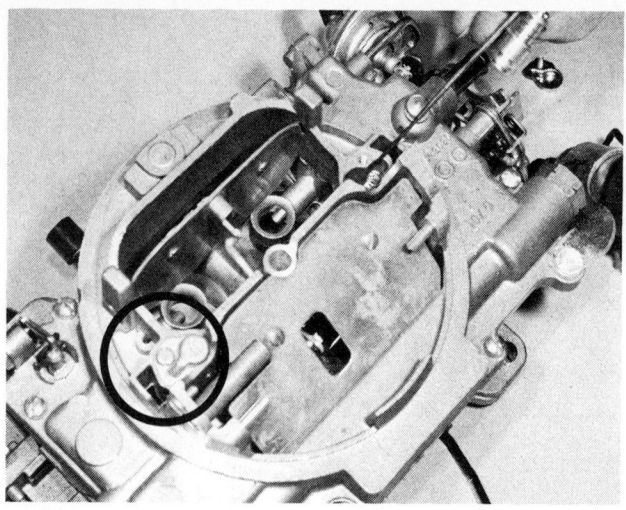

1. Popular in the Sixties, the AVS was offered on 1970-71 Chrysler 383/440 V-8's with automatic transmission. Remove cover plates on each side (circle), step-up piston/rod, spring.

2. Remove hairpin clips which hold fast-idle connector rod to fast-idle cam and choke lever. Disengage rod from cam; swing rod up until you can disengage it from choke operating lever.

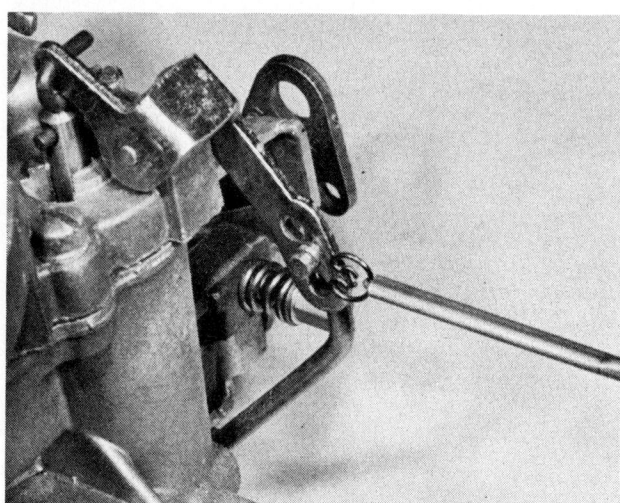

3. On opposite side, remove hairpin clip which holds throttle connector rod in center hole of accelerator-pump rocker arm. Disengage rod from arm and throttle lever; remove.

4. Unhook choke vacuum-diaphragm hose from carburetor body; remove hairpin clip which holds choke operating link to choke lever. Remove screws, diaphragm/bracket assembly.

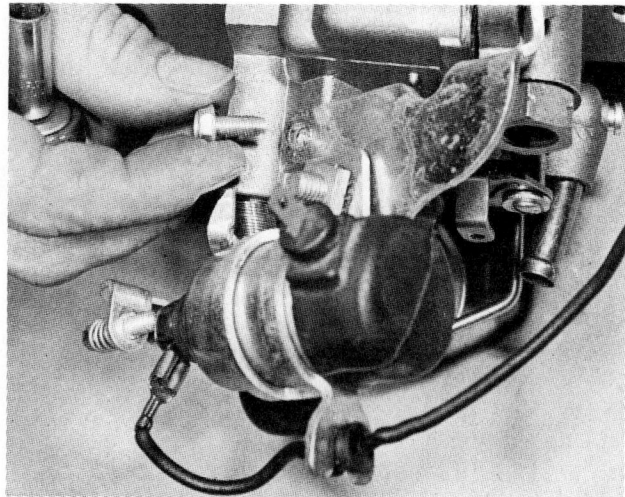

5. Before air horn/main body can be separated, throttle-positioner/idle-stop solenoid (if so equipped) must be removed, because of bracket.

6. Unscrew, remove the eight air-horn attaching screws and carburetor ID tag. Lift air horn straight up and off the main body, taking care not to bend or damage float assemblies.

7. Invert air horn on bench to protect floats; remove one float fulcrum pin, lifting float up and out of air horn bosses. Repeat with other float, marking pump-side float to indicate location.

8. Remove needle valve from each seat; mark the one which goes with marked float. Remove both needle valve seats, marking edge of one which matches marked float and valve.

9. If air horn is to be immersed in cleaning fluid, turn bowl-vent operating lever to provide access to the vent arm, remove rubber vent seal. AVS uses mechanical fuel-bowl vent system.

10. Remove shoulder screw and spring which holds accelerator-pump rocker arm to air horn. This allows arm removal to disengage pump link from plunger stem.

11. Hot-idle compensator valve is fitted to main body to relieve over-rich idle condition at abnormal temperature. Remove the two screws and lift compensator valve off.

12. Remove screws holding each primary venturi cluster (choke and pump side) to main body. Lift venturi straight up and away from main body; discard gaskets.

HOW TO: Carter AVS Overhaul

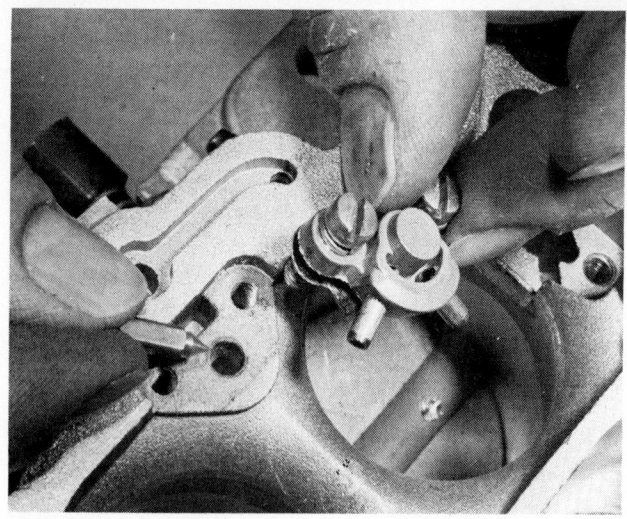

13. Unscrew accelerator-pump jet housing from main body; lift off housing and gasket. Invert main body to remove discharge check needle from the discharge passage. Discard gasket.

14. Carefully remove accelerator-pump intake check valve from fuel bowl (accelerator-pump cylinder side) using wide-blade screwdriver. Also remove accelerator pump spring.

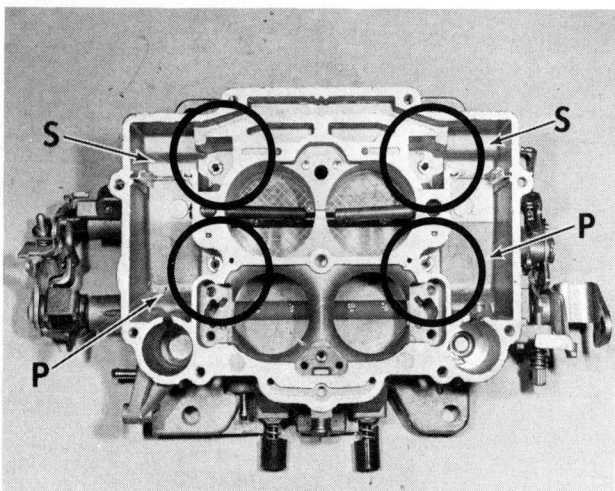

15. Primary (P) and secondary (S) main metering jets are not interchangeable. If removed from main body for cleaning, each must be reinstalled in same location.

16. Remove plastic limiter caps from idle mixture needles. Count the turns required to lightly seat each needle, then back out completely. To reinstall, screw in same number of turns.

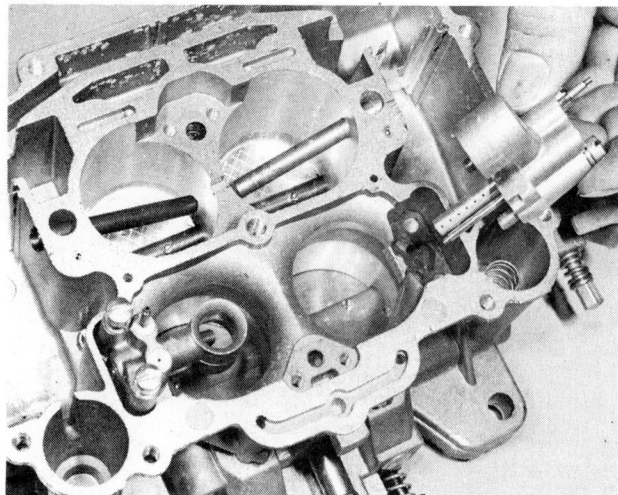

17. After replacing idle mixture needles, place new gasket in position, lower each venturi cluster straight down on gasket. Install and tighten the attaching screws securely.

18. Install accelerator-pump discharge check needle in discharge passage. Position new gasket on mounting surface. Replace accelerator-pump jet housing, tightening screws.

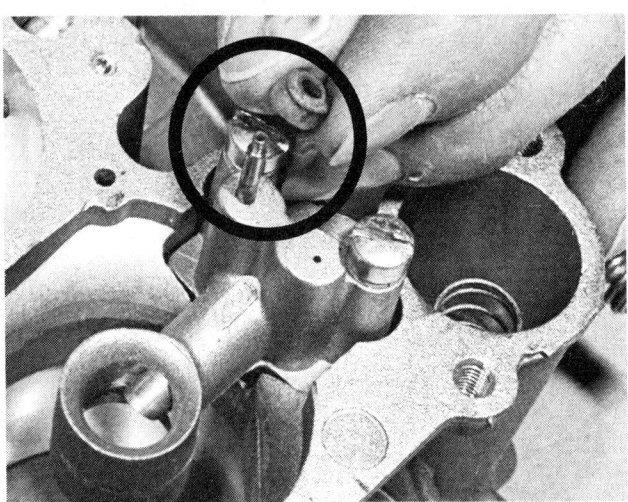

19. If venturi clusters were placed in solvent, these tiny rubber risers (circle) should have been removed. Regardless, risers should each be replaced with new ones.

20. Replace accelerator pump spring (arrow) and reinstall hot idle compensator on a new gasket. Tighten attaching screws securely. Check that valve has not been bent or distorted.

21. Begin air horn reassembly by installing the two needle valve seats. Separate marked seat, valve and float from unmarked set. Reinstall marked seat/needle valve.

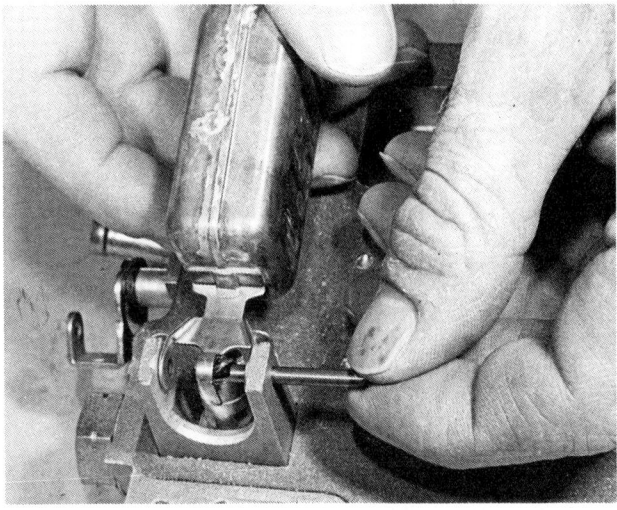

22. Replace brass floats and slide each float fulcrum pin in place from the inside, as shown, to hold floats securely in place. Check that you replaced the needle valves.

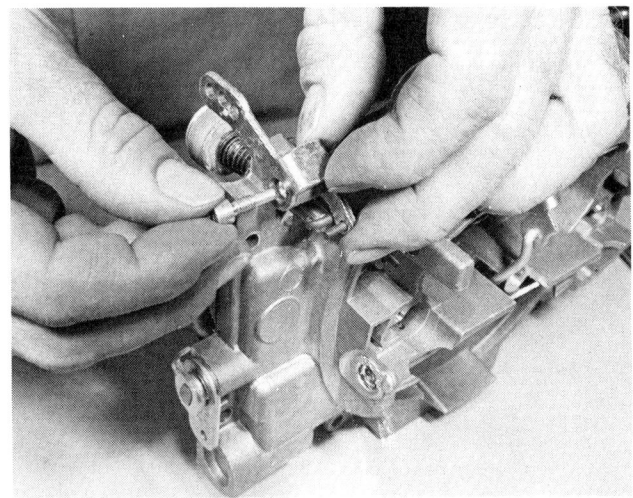

23. Reinstall accelerator pump plunger in air horn housing; depress and hold it in place while engaging pump arm link, swinging arm over housing boss and replacing shoulder screw.

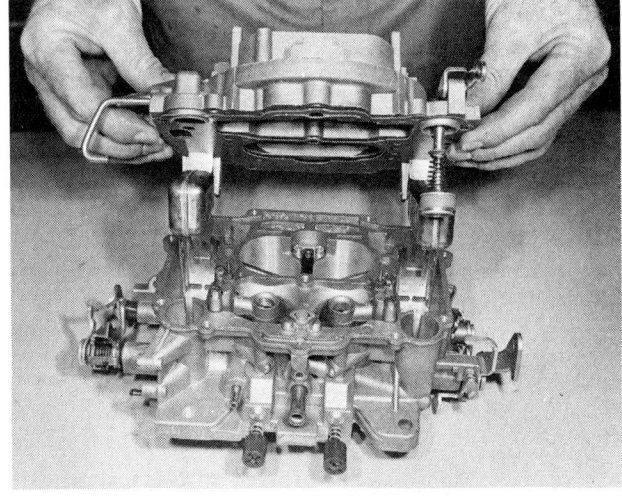

24. Check float and accelerator pump operation. Reinstall rubber bowl-vent valve seal. Position new gasket in place on air horn. Carefully lower assembly down to mate with main body.

HOW TO: Carter AVS Overhaul

25. Replace eight air-horn-to-main-body attaching screws, tighten securely. Reinstall carburetor ID tag on one outboard screw, since it contains necessary information for buying parts.

26. Reattach choke vacuum-diaphragm bracket to main body casting; tighten. Fit choke diaphragm link into choke control lever, replace hairpin clip. Reattach vacuum line.

27. Install accelerator pump rod and engage upper end in pump rocker arm from which it was removed. Replace hairpin clip and check pump link action—should operate smoothly.

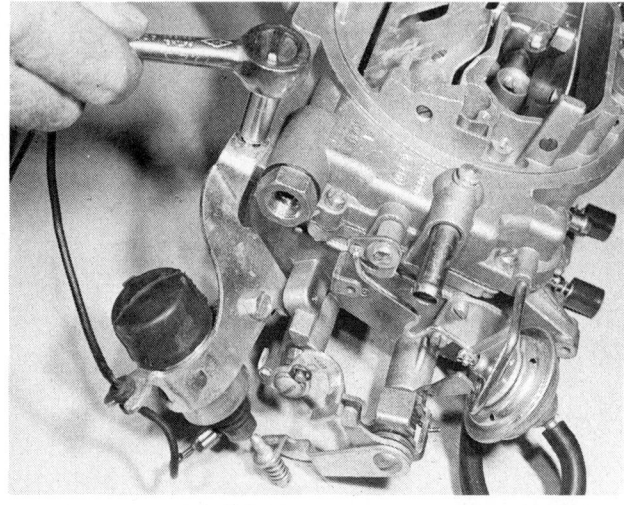

28. Reinstall throttle-positioner/idle-stop solenoid and bracket. Replace cap-head mounting screws, tighten securely. If solenoid, idle screws were not disturbed, adjustment not needed.

29. Replace step-up piston springs in each side of air horn as shown. These are easy to overlook, but piston/rod assembly action will not function if springs have not been replaced.

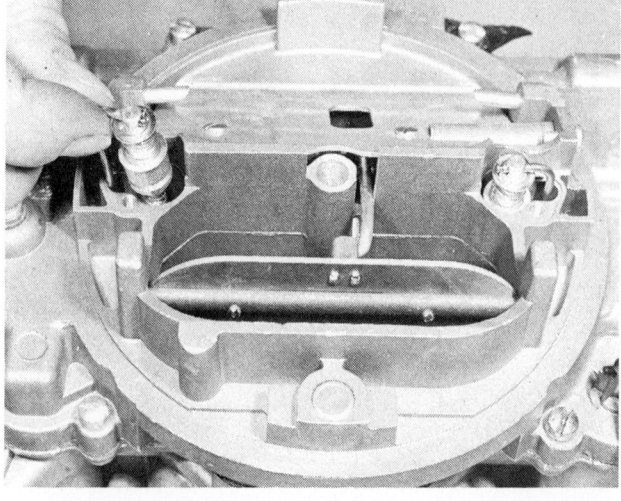

30. Carefully reinstall each piston/rod assembly. These provide a two-stage change from economical low-speed mixtures to richer full-power mixtures. Install cover plates, tighten screws.

HOW TO: Carter YF/YFA Overhaul

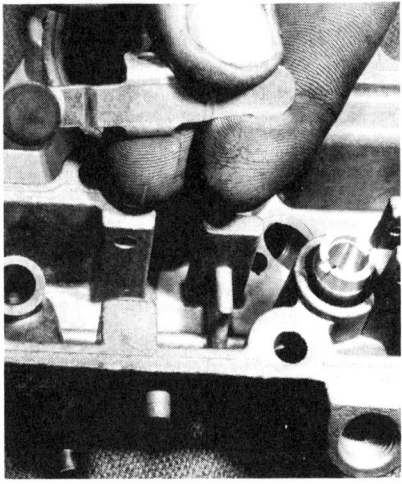

1. Cleaning as you go, disassemble carb to this stage noting location of each part. Vent arm shown has rubber tip; remove it to avoid contact with cleaning solvent.

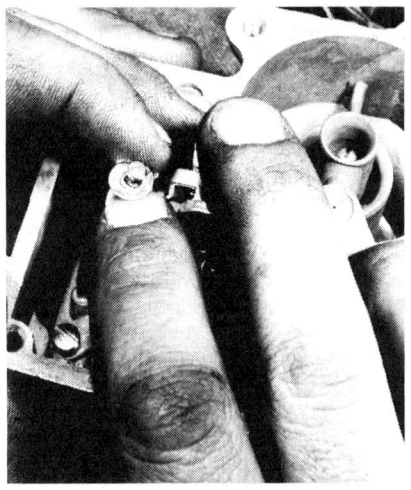

2. Removal of the accelerator-pump/lifter-link assembly is overly complicated. Begin by depressing the pump diaphragm shaft and removing this clip.

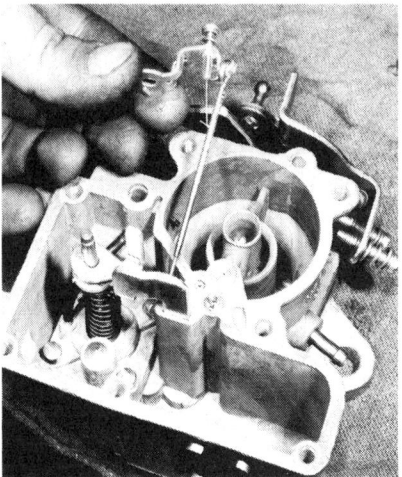

3. This will permit removal of the metering rod and metering arm. The spring-loaded screw *can* be adjusted, but it is advisable *not* to touch the adjustment.

4. This anti-rock plate should be removed before attempting to disengage the accelerator pump. Don't overlook this item during reassembly.

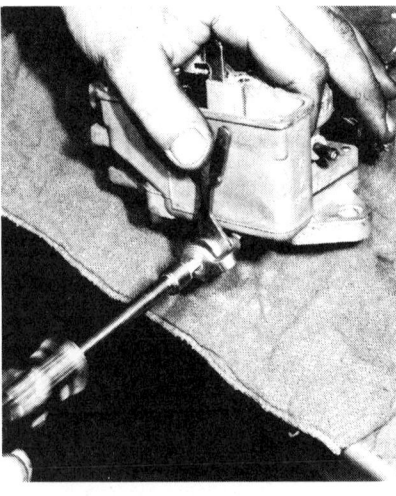

5. The accelerator pump mechanism cannot be removed until the mechanical fuel-bowl vent arm is removed. This device was used only on the 1975 YFA.

6. Rotate throttle shaft until the hex-head screw on the throttle-shaft arm is accessible, then insert the proper size hex-head wrench and loosen the screw.

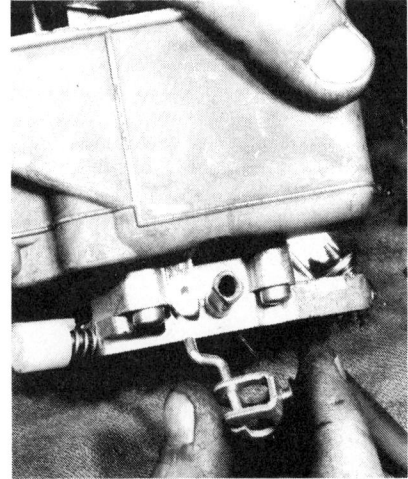

7. Push down on the accelerator pump and link, then hold it with one hand while you disengage the pump connector link and slide off the throttle shaft arm.

8. With the pump link disconnected, you can withdraw the pump lifter link from its slot in the main body housing. Check the link for bends or distortions.

9. The accelerator pump is held in the main body by four screws and a tiny plastic connector hose. Unhook the hose, remove screws and lift out pump.

HOW TO: Carter YF/YFA Overhaul

10. The metering-rod jet is located to the right side of the accelerator pump well. This is unscrewed with a jet remover or wide-blade screwdriver, then removed.

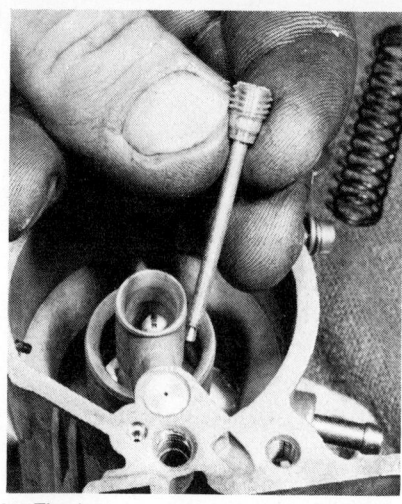

11. The low-speed jet can be unscrewed with a wide-blade screwdriver. When replaced, it should seat flush with the body casting.

12. Remove the body-flange attaching screws to separate the main body from the throttle body. Remove and discard gasket and clean mounting surfaces.

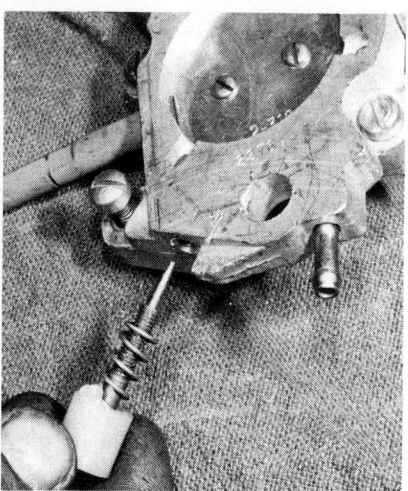

13. To remove the idle mixture screw, break off the limiter cap tab and turn the screw in until it seats, counting the number of turns required, then back.

14. To replace idle mixture screw, turn in until it seats, then back out same number of turns previously counted. Fit gasket, reattach throttle body/main body.

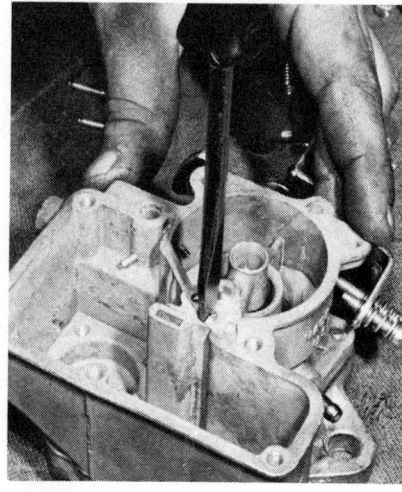

15. Reinstall the metering-rod jet, and then replace the low-speed jet. Make sure both jets seat properly and are not cross-threaded as you screw them in.

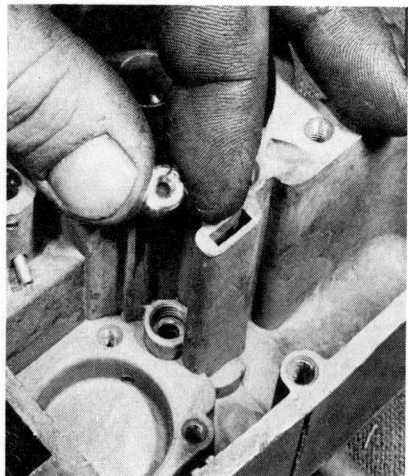

16. Fit plastic washer to new accelerator pump diaphragm. The washer crown must face the diaphragm and seat properly. Diaphragm problems are common.

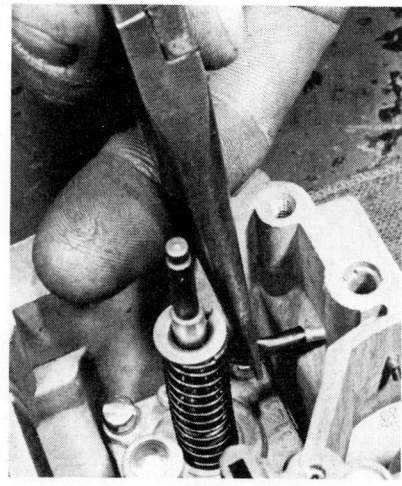

17. Diaphragm housing is notched to fit in body only one way. Install diaphragm, fit spring and retainer in place, reinstall housing, tighten screws, connect hose.

18. After positioning anti-rock plate over the pump diaphragm shaft, reinstall the pump check ball, then drop the pump check weight on top of the ball.

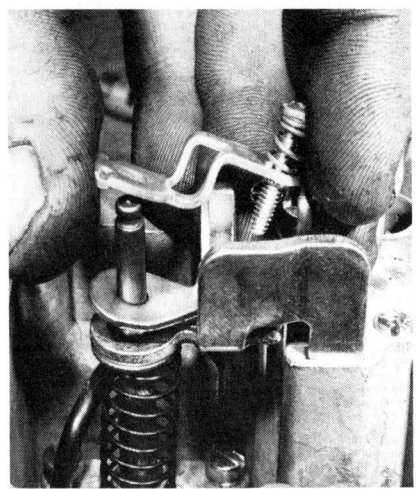

19. Replace metering-rod assembly. Install upper spring and retainer. Depress and hold pump lever while replacing throttle-shaft-arm/connector link.

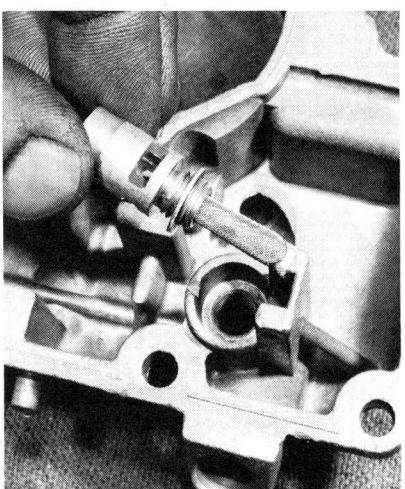

20. Fit a new gasket over the float needle seat and carefully insert a new mesh filter in the seat's threaded end. Replace needle seat in the carburetor and tighten.

21. The spring on the vent shaft must be positioned as shown or vent action will not be correct. Drop the mechanical vent arm in place and insert the vent shaft.

22. Check spring positioning, then slide the shaft all the way in place and secure with the tiny retaining clip. Extra clips come in handy—they often get lost.

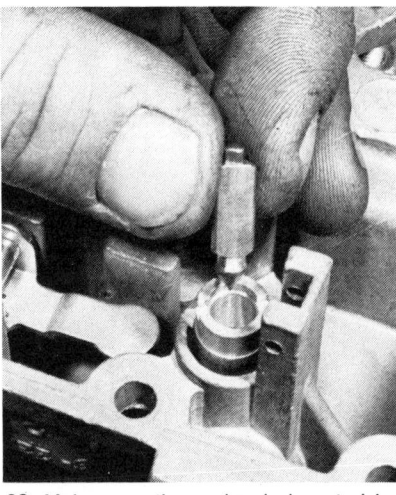

23. Make sure the spring is inserted between the two brass parts of the float needle valve, then drop into needle seat, with its pointed end downward.

24. Replace float and float hanger, and install float pin from the side shown, with the nub end facing you. Install incorrectly and vibration will work it out of place.

25. Position main body gasket and replace air horn. Install two attaching screws, then reconnect and clip the fast idle link to the choke lever.

26. Install the dashpot bracket and the other air horn screws. Position the choke-housing baffle plate so choke piston link protrudes through slotted area.

27. Fit choke housing gasket in place, position cover/thermostatic coil so choke lever engages coil slot, replace retainers and screws, aligning index marks.

HOW TO: Holley 1945 Overhaul

1. Chrysler Corporation cars use Holley 1945 as factory equipment. Begin rebuild of this 1-bbl. carburetor by removing screws holding choke actuator in place.

2. Lift choke actuator up, and angle connecting linkage off choke lever, then remove throttle position solenoid, if so equipped. Neither should be placed in solvent.

3. Remove bowl cover screws. To free the bowl and cover, tap gently with a rubber mallet or a screwdriver handle to break the seal—*do not* pry apart.

4. Remove "E" clip which holds fast idle cam. Leave throttle lever intact, with fast idle and curb idle screws in place—these do not come off for cleaning.

5. Slip fast idle cam from its shaft and off the choke-lever connecting linkage, then remove the link from the choke lever. Choke lever stays in place also.

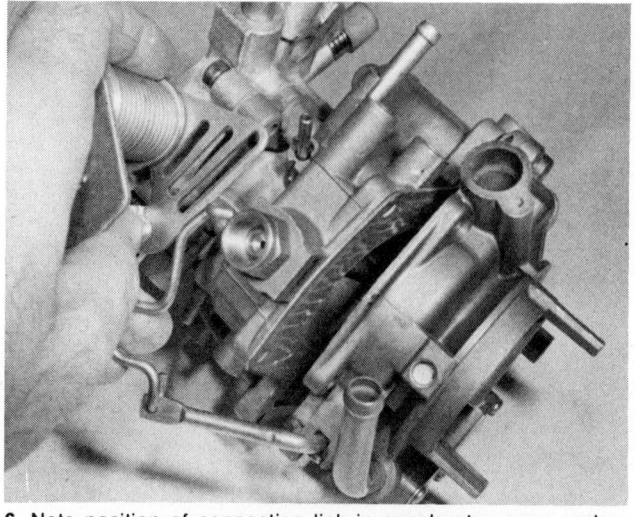

6. Note position of connecting link in accelerator-pump rocker arm; remove nut and lockwasher that hold the arm in place and take it off, angling arm to free it of linkage.

7. Now lift the bowl cover off. Pull straight up and off. The accelerator pump is attached to the cover, along with the vacuum piston assembly.

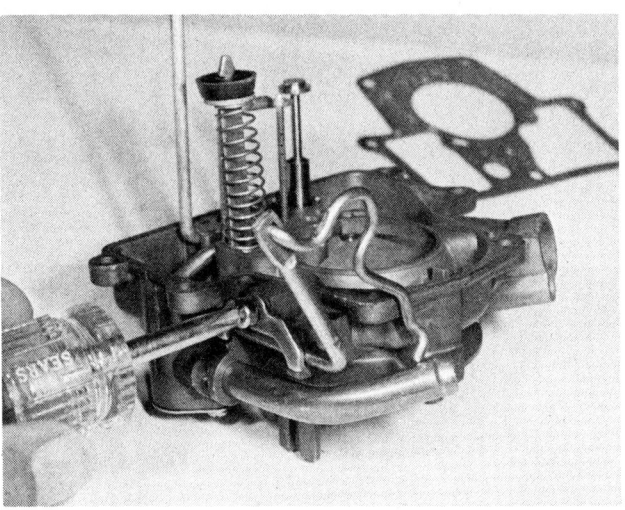

8. Take off the old gasket and discard. Remove screw holding the pump rod retainer in place before attempting to disconnect the accelerator pump from the pump rod.

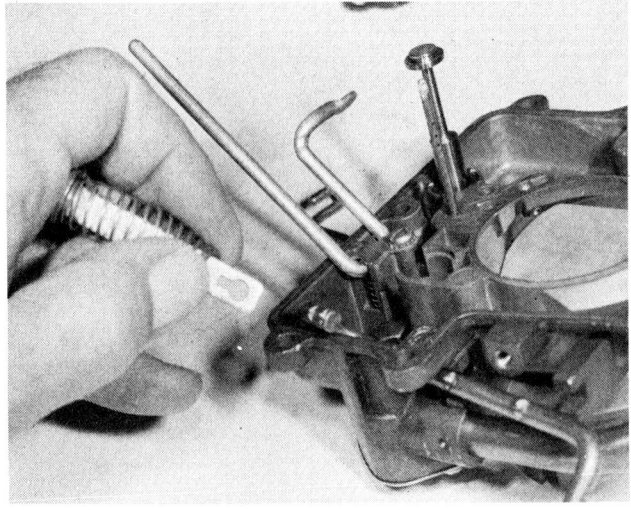

9. Pull up on pump drive spring, rotate pump operating rod slightly and pump assembly will slip off. Note two tangs on end of rod, where pump arm fits for reassembly.

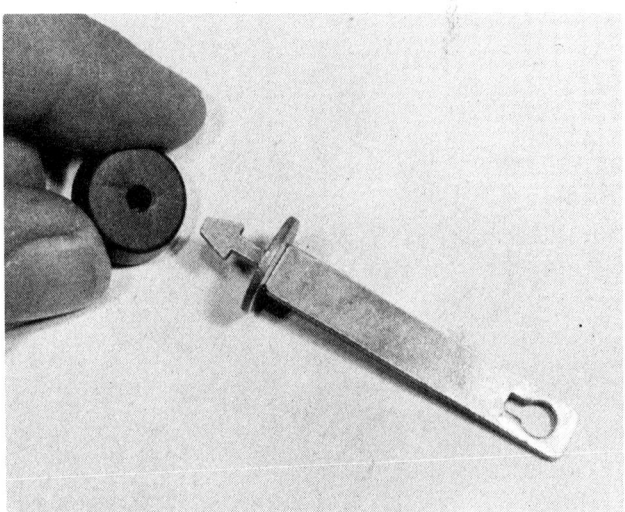

10. Remove pump drive spring, pull off old pump cap. Replace cap with new one furnished in rebuild kit. Install carefully, making sure it fits properly over "arrowhead."

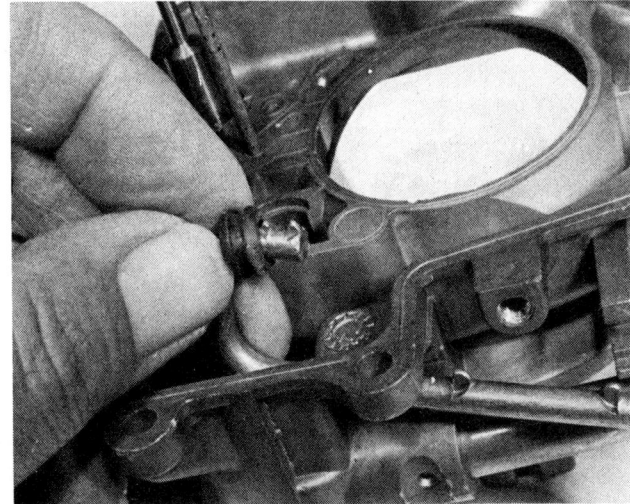

11. Before you can remove the pump operating rod, you must rotate it to free the rubber cover grommet, which must come out before the cover is dunked in cleaner.

12. Turn cover over and remove bowl vent cap. Under the cap, you'll find a spring over the vent adjusting screw. Vent device is held in place by a retaining screw.

HOW TO: Holley 1945 Overhaul

13. Loosen or remove retaining screw, and lift plastic vent device out. Do not touch adjusting screw, because this is factory set and does not require adjustment.

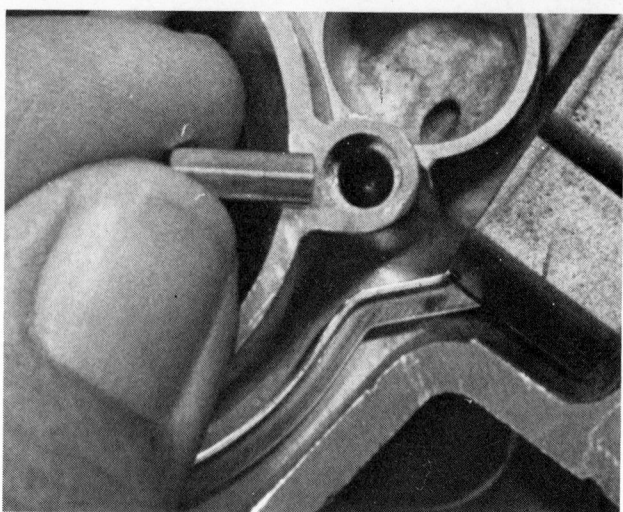

14. A tiny pump discharge check ball is located under this weight. Remove both and set to one side. Normally, a new check ball is included in rebuild kit—weight is reused.

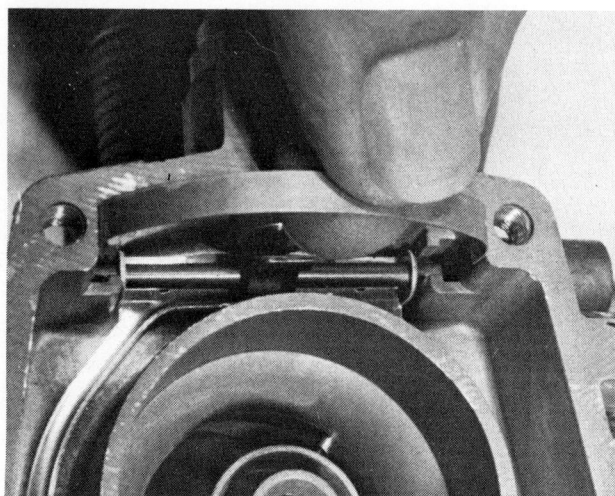

15. A wire float shaft retainer is fitted to hold the dual-lung nitrophyl float in place. This lifts out easily to provide access for float removal.

16. Lift the dual float assembly and the float shaft up and out of the carburetor body. Be careful not to bend the wire arms attached to the two floats.

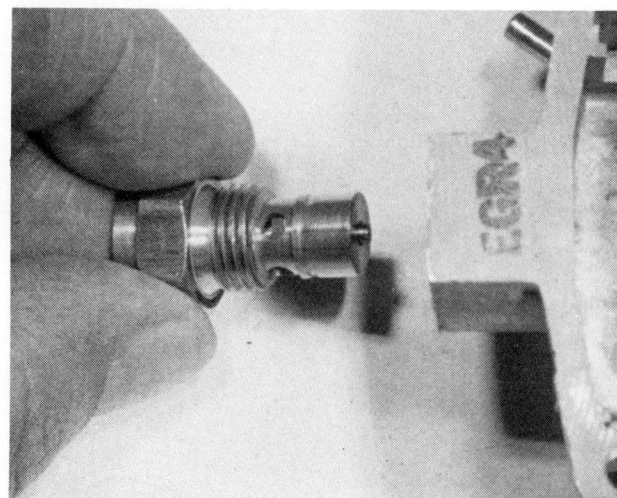

17. Unscrew the fuel inlet fitting and valve. A Viton-tipped fuel-inlet needle in the fitting is held in place by a cap which allows fuel to flow out its sides.

18. Power valve assembly can be removed with a screwdriver blade, but due to close quarters involved, it is better to use a deep socket to prevent valve stem damage.

19. The power valve is a one-piece assembly in some 1945 carburetors; a three-piece assembly in others. Tiny spring must be on valve stem end of three-piece unit.

20. The same removal procedure holds for the main jet. If it must come out, a wide square-point screwdriver can be used, but a jet wrench works best.

21. This completes the carburetor body disassembly. Turn the body over and remove three throttle-body screws, then tap gently to separate throttle and main body units.

22. Lift the throttle body up and off, then remove the old gasket and discard. New gaskets must be installed during reassembly since old ones are prone to leak.

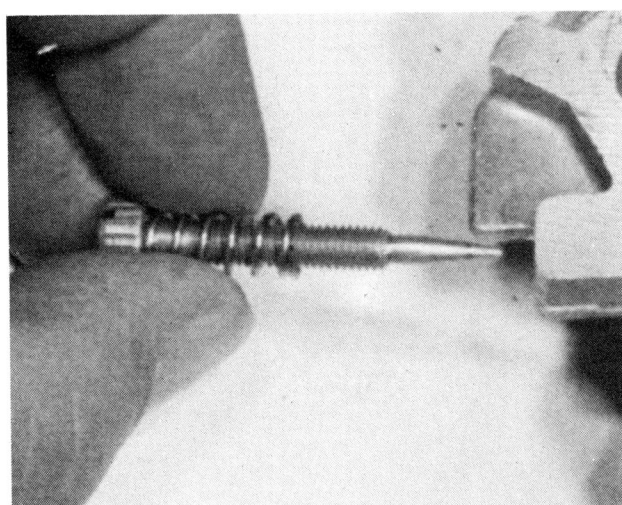

23. Remove the idle limiter cap and turn mixture screw clockwise until it seats, counting number of turns involved. Then turn screw counterclockwise to remove.

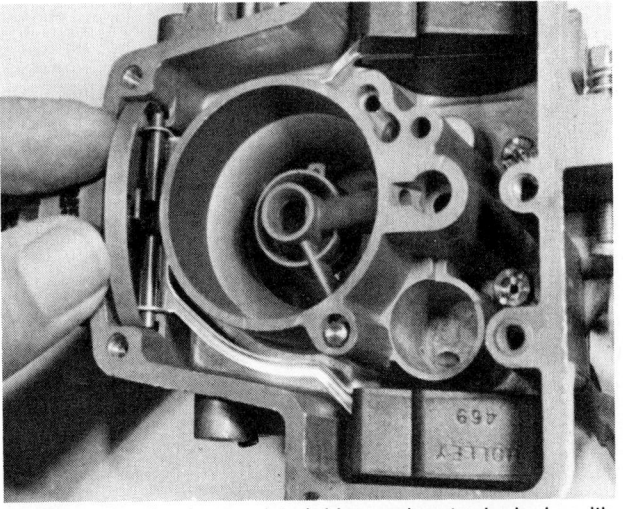

24. Once cleaning is completed, blow carburetor body dry with compressed air. Install main jet, power valve, float assembly. Seat float shaft and fit retainer in place.

HOW TO: Holley 1945 Overhaul

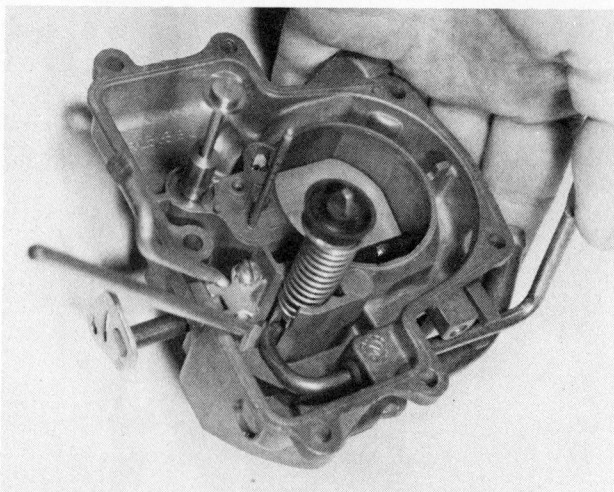

25. Reinstall pump rod and grommet; reconnect pump to pump rod and check action of pump by working the rod. Vacuum piston is staked in place, not normally removed.

26. Drop vent valve and shaft into place; tighten the retaining screw, then set the spring over the adjustment screw before replacing the vent cover.

27. Install new gasket on bowl cover, fit to carburetor body. Make sure accelerator pump goes into pump well and vacuum-piston actuating rod rides under piston flange.

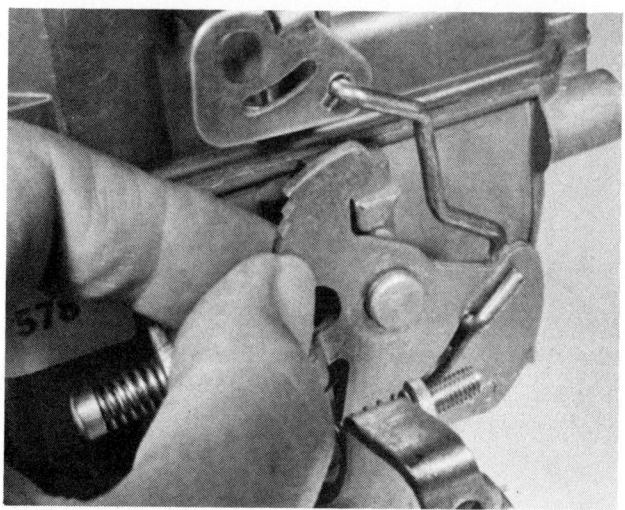

28. Fit fast-idle-cam linkage to choke lever, then slip cam over shaft as shown. After this has been done, replace the large retaining "E" clip.

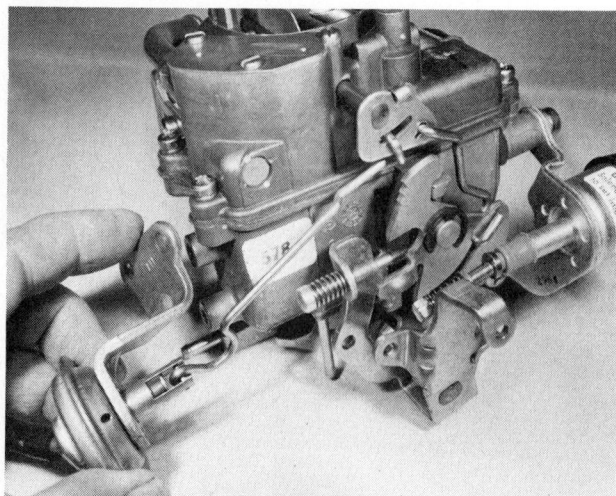

29. Reattach the throttle position solenoid, then connect the choke actuator-linkage arm to the choke lever and fasten the actuator bracket to the carburetor bowl.

30. Connect vacuum hose to the carburetor body fitting. Rebuild is completed. This version of the 1945 is not equipped with the idle enrichment valve used in '75.

HOW TO: Holley 2245 Overhaul

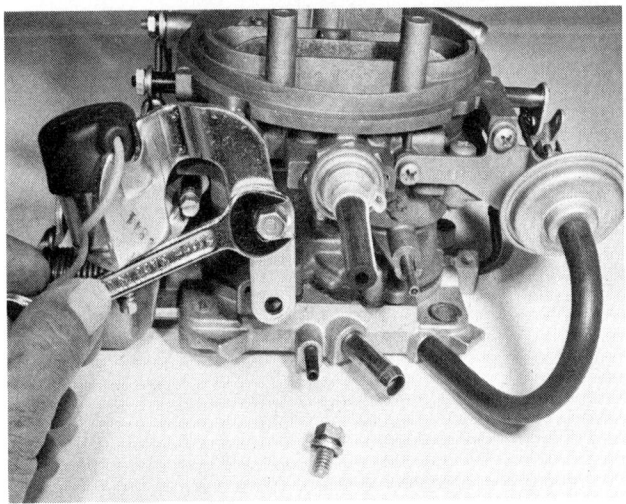

1. Disassembly of Holley 2245 begins with removal of throttle positioner solenoid. You'll need some small wrenches to work on this one, in addition to usual tools.

2. Remove choke pulldown diaphragm and angle unit to free connecting linkage from the choke lever. The solenoid and diaphragm should not be placed in solvent.

3. Remove nut and washer holding rocker arm in place, then pull arm from pump shaft. Disconnect linkage from rocker arm (after noting the slot it is in) and throttle lever.

4. Take off the nut and washer that hold the choke lever to the choke shaft. Disconnect the fast idle rod from the choke lever and the fast idle cam.

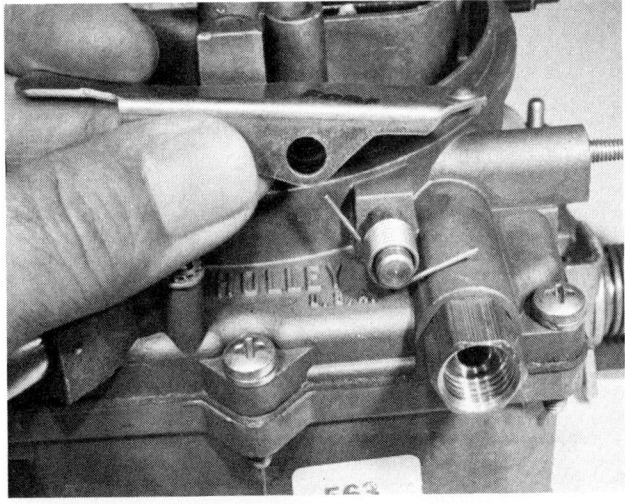

5. Examine bowl vent lever, noting position of spring ends inside, which control lever action. Remove "E" clip and carefully slide the lever/spring off the shaft.

6. Air-horn attaching screws come next; note position of long screw in center. Lift air horn straight up to prevent damage to main well tubes. Do not pry off air horn.

HOW TO: Holley 2245 Overhaul

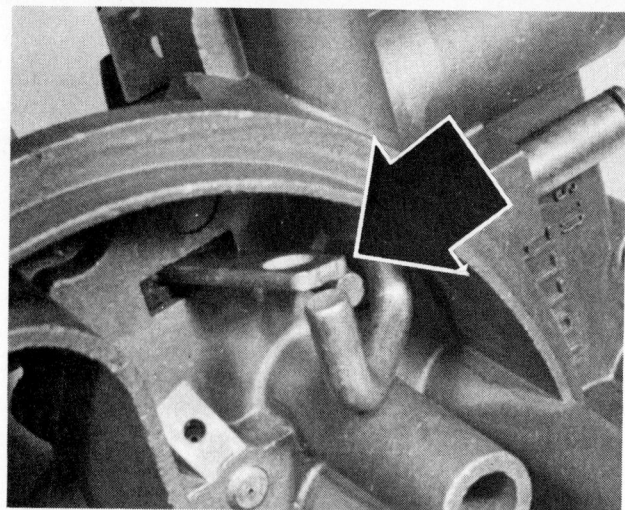

7. To disengage accelerator pump from pump shaft, push up on pump while angling it to one side. This allows pump end to slip off shaft for removal; a washer comes with it.

8. Two screws hold the bowl vent cover in place. Beneath the cover, you'll find the plastic vent device with a small spring and seal underneath it.

9. Remove the screw holding the float retaining plate in place, then slide the float shaft to one side and lift the float up and out of the air horn.

10. Fuel inlet needle comes out next. If you aren't familiar with carburetors, take care not to mix this up with the discharge check needle, which is similar in size/shape.

11. Fuel inlet seat and gasket can be removed with a wide-blade screwdriver. Work carefully in order to avoid damage to the soft, metal seat flanges.

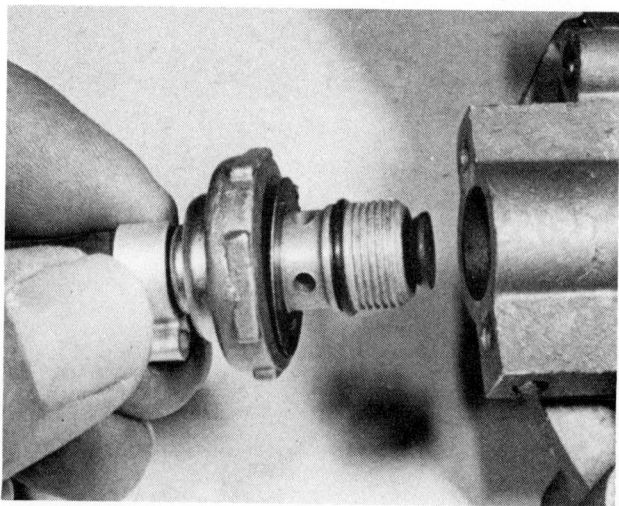

12. Model 2245 carburetors used with automatic transmission cars (1975 only) are equipped with an idle enrichment circuit and vacuum valve—remove valve.

13. Power valve seat is a three-piece unit. Use a wide-blade screwdriver and work carefully to avoid damage to either the seat or power valve needle when removing.

14. If you remove the main jets, be sure to note where each one goes, because the two jets may be of different sizes, depending upon the carburetor application.

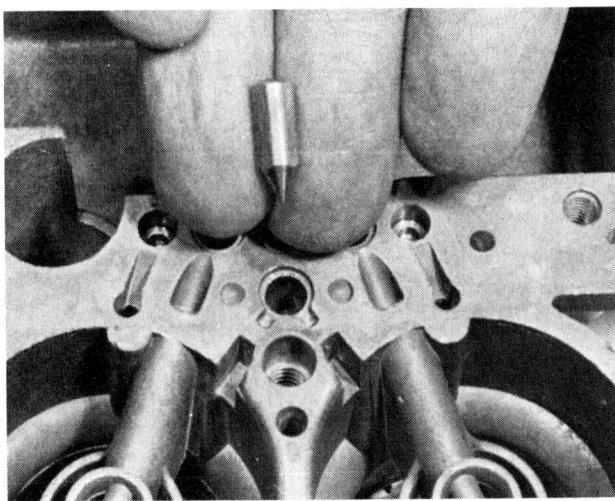

15. The discharge check needle is positioned here. This carburetor does not happen to use a check ball, so do not panic if you cannot find one.

16. Remove attaching screws holding throttle body to main body, and separate. Since gasket is very thick, it will probably pull apart. Clean it off and discard.

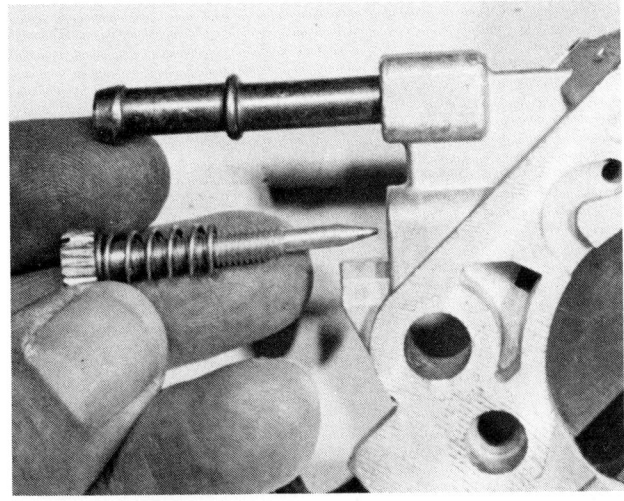

17. To remove idle mixture needles, pry off limiter caps and turn screws in until they seat, counting the number of turns required, then back screws all the way out.

18. Clean in solvent, blow pieces dry with air. Reinstall and seat idle mixture screws. Back out exact number of turns previously counted. Reattach main and throttle bodies.

HOW TO: Holley 2245 Overhaul

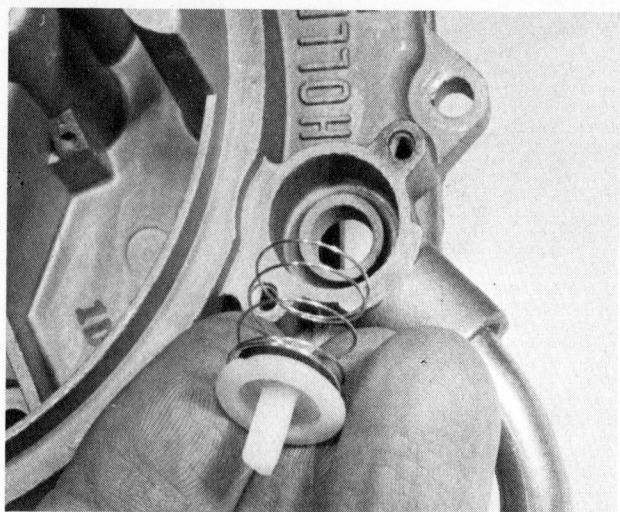

19. Turn the air horn over carefully to prevent bending the main well tubes, and replace the vent valve seat, spring and valve. Fit cover in place, and tighten screws.

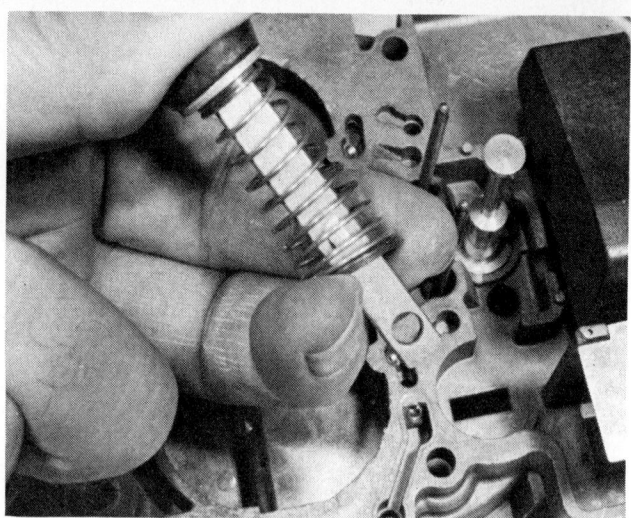

20. Install the float assembly, then replace pump cover, compress spring and fit pump shaft lever through slot in air horn, tilting to one side to reconnect it to the pump.

21. Install a new gasket on the air horn. Gasket should fit over this pin (circle) for proper positioning; pin also keeps it from slipping when the air horn is inverted.

22. Invert air horn and fit to main body, making sure main well tubes and accelerator pump fit into respective places in main body. Replace attaching screws and tighten.

23. Fit spring inside the vent lever and slip the unit onto shaft. Check the lever action and replace the "E" clip. Reinstall the idle enrichment valve.

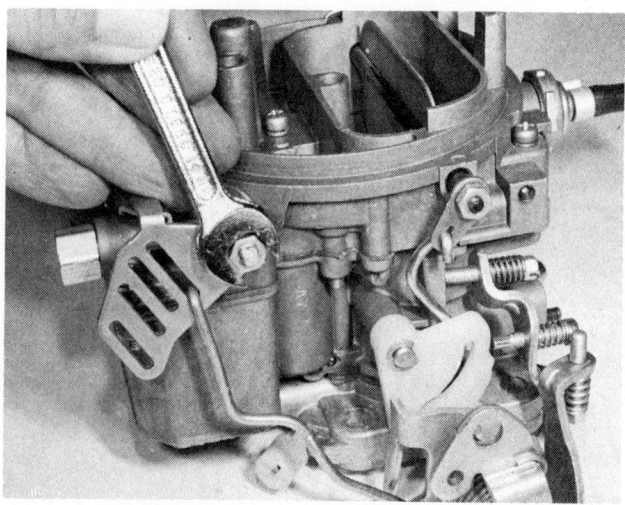

24. Reconnect choke lever and linkage, then install rocker arm and linkage. Replace the throttle positioner solenoid and choke vacuum diaphragm. Rebuild is complete.

HOW TO: Holley 5200/5210-C Overhaul

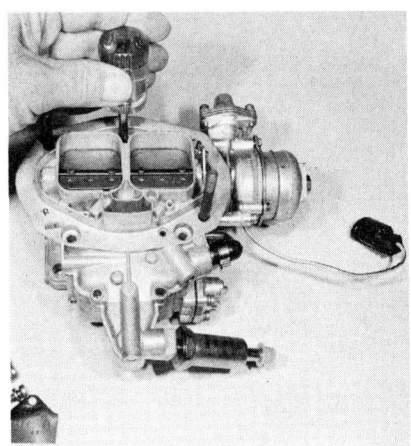

1. The '76 Holley-Weber 5200 is used on Pinto, Bobcat, Mustang II; with minor differences, same carb is designated 5210-C and used by GM. Remove air horn screws.

2. A tiny, hairpin retaining clip (circle) holds lower end of choke rod. Pry choke rod free with screwdriver and remove. Tiny clip is easily lost, so keep an eye on it.

3. Same type of retainer (circle) is used to hold upper end of choke rod in choke lever. These are best removed with the aid of a needlenose pliers instead of a screwdriver.

4. Now separate air horn from main body, lifting it straight up and off. Remove and discard gasket, then remove choke-rod seal and/or plug from the air horn casting.

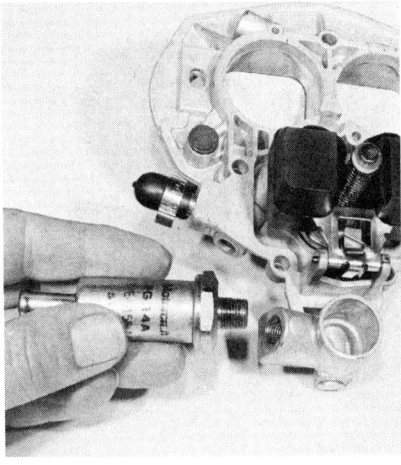

5. Late Ford 5200 carbs use standard throwaway inlet fuel filters; earlier ones were fitted with undersized plastic container with wire mesh screen and plugged easily.

6. Screwdriver points to float-drop adjusting tang; other end of tang is used to adjust float level. Use care when adjusting float to prevent scratching or other damage.

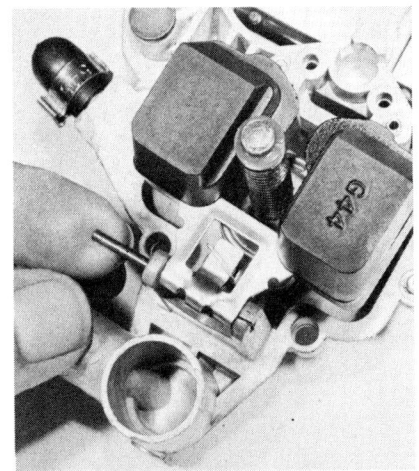

7. Float shaft is a press-fit; tap gently on one end of shaft with a small punch to slide it through the split retainer, then withdraw; next remove the float and the inlet needle.

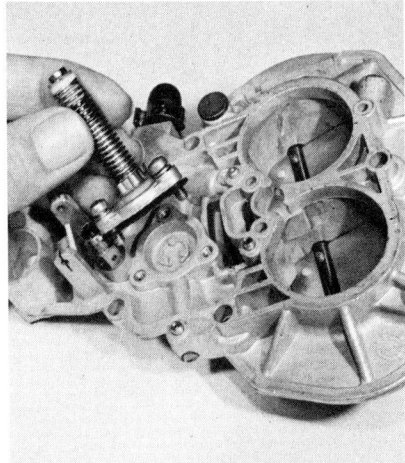

8. Remove the three screws holding power-valve operating rod and attached diaphragm in place. The diaphragm is fragile, and the entire assembly is replaced if it fails.

9. Fuel-inlet valve seat unscrews. Be sure to remove the little gasket underneath it, and to install a new gasket when reassembling the air horn, or you'll have a leak.

HOW TO: Holley 5200/5210-C Overhaul

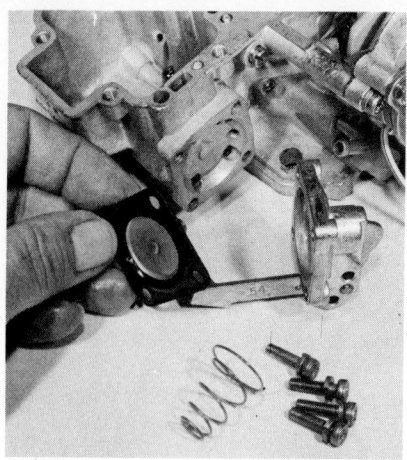

10. Remove four accelerator pump cover screws, cover, diaphragm. Replace diaphragm with new one. Small end of return spring faces carburetor body when replaced.

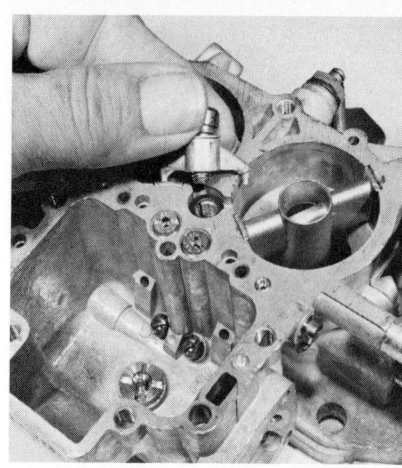

11. Unscrew and remove pump discharge valve, nozzle and gasket. After removing this assembly, turn carburetor over and remove the tiny gasket and the two check balls.

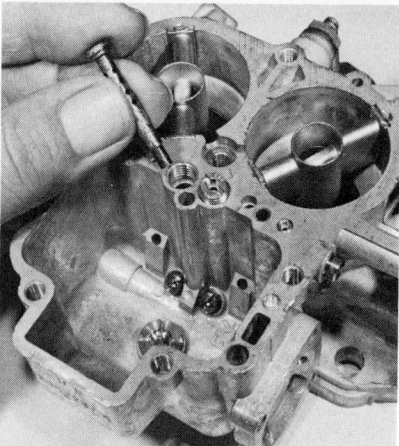

12. Two main well tubes provide air for fuel atomization and are located under the air bleed screws. Primary and secondary are slightly different in size and are color-coded.

13. Remove idle jet at each side of body. Jet fits snugly into retainer plug, but pulls out for cleaning/replacement. Idle jets are color-coded to match main well tubes.

14. Remove the three retaining screws and pull the hot-water choke cover and thermostatic coil assembly from the choke housing. *Do not* attempt to remove housing from coil.

15. Remove choke electric-heater element. This side faces in toward choke housing. Note tiny spring which reacts to electric current provided by the alternator tap.

16. Choke housing must come off if fast idle cam is plastic, since cam can be damaged by solvent. Fast idle cam was redesigned on '76 carburetors to solve sticking problem.

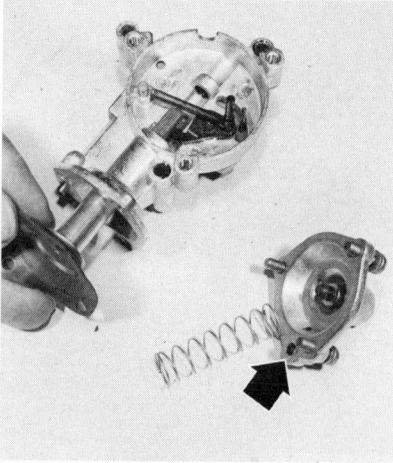

17. When choke vacuum-diaphragm cover and return spring are removed, diaphragm and shaft assembly can be withdrawn. Vacuum inlet (arrow) in cover operates choke pull-down.

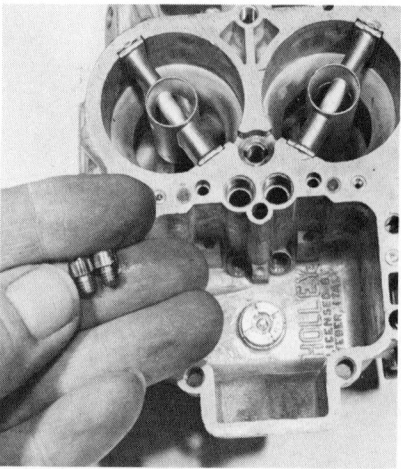

18. Twin main metering jets inside float bowl need not be removed for cleaning purposes, but if they are, use a wideblade screwdriver or jet remover, and work carefully.

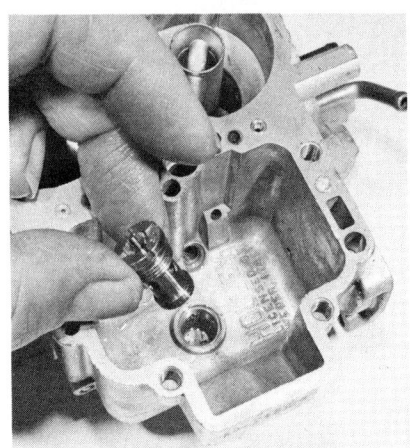

19. Since the power valve stem does not completely seat in the valve, it is tricky to remove undamaged, unless you have a special seat remover. A screwdriver *cannot* be used.

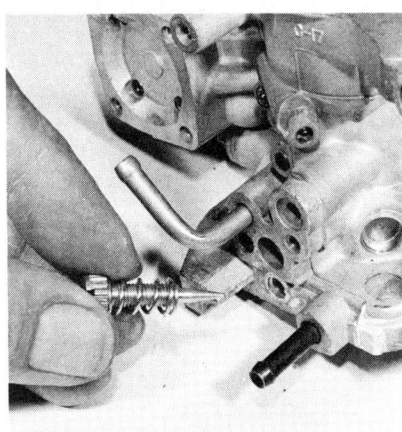

20. Pry off the plastic limiter cap and count the number of turns to the nearest 1/16th required to seat the idle mixture needle, then remove the needle and spring.

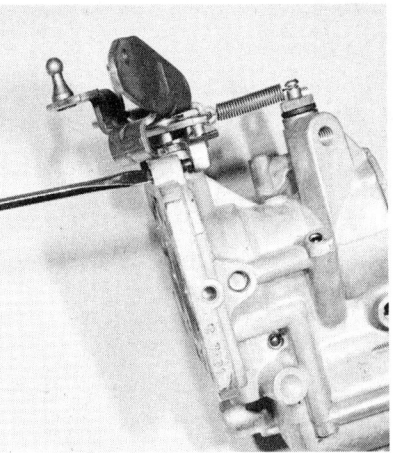

21. If secondary throttle plate does not seat in the bore, turn throttle-stop adjustment screw inward until it touches the lever, then screw it in an extra quarter turn.

22. Reinstall and tighten the power valve snugly—but be careful not to overtighten it—and replace the main metering jets in their respective positions in the fuel bowl.

23. Reinstall the accelerator-pump diaphragm assembly, and reattach the choke housing, after reconnecting the fast idle rod to the throttle lever and fast idle lever.

24. Slide the diaphragm and shaft assembly into the choke housing at a slight angle to clear the shaft and to seat the diaphragm on the housing so it fits over the inlet.

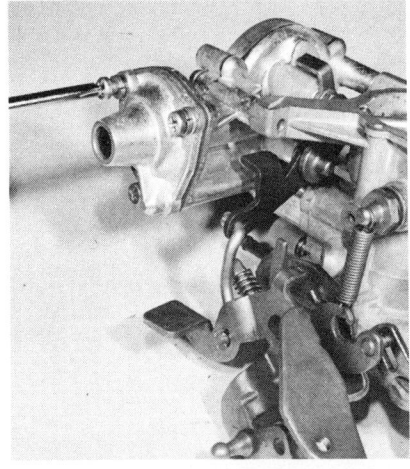

25. While housing will fit in any triangulation, it must be replaced with cover chamber over the inlet in order for vacuum to exert suction to operate choke pulldown.

26. Electric-choke heater plate can only be replaced in one way; connecting wire must fit in housing cutout as shown. Choke plate must also be closed in air horn.

27. Before replacing assembled air horn to main body, make sure that the choke rod seal is correctly installed in its air-horn casting slot and that the choke rod fits through it.

HOW TO: Motorcraft 4300/4350 Overhaul

1. Introduced in 1975, the Motorcraft 4350 is an improved version of the older 4300 series. Spacer plate under carburetor has exhaust gas recirculation (EGR) valve attached.

2. Begin disassembly by removing choke-cover retaining screws. Lift off the cover/thermostatic coil by disconnecting coil loop from choke lever, then remove choke gasket.

3. Pry choke control rod away from carburetor body to disengage lower end from automatic choke lever, then remove upper choke lever, screw and control rod (arrow).

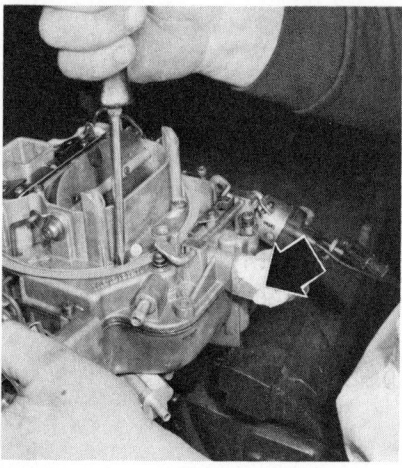

4. Remove air-horn-to-main-body attaching screws. Model 4350 was recalled because of a defect in the fuel inlet—epoxy indicates that the defect has been corrected (arrow).

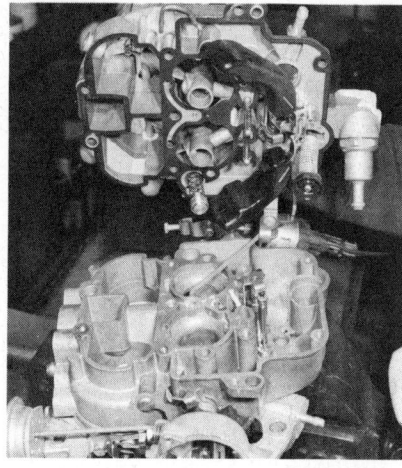

5. Carefully lift the air horn straight up and off the main body, then invert the air horn and set it to one side for further disassembly after the main body has been finished.

6. Carburetor can be inverted to remove accelerator-pump discharge check ball, but the use of a magnetic pencil makes the job much easier and prevents losing small parts.

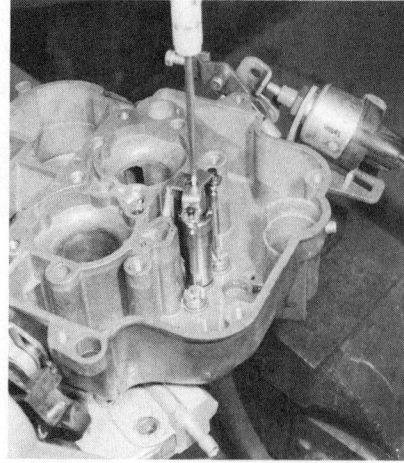

7. This is the main-metering vacuum piston and fuel-metering rod assembly. Although there is an adjustment screw on the piston, you *should not* disturb the setting.

8. To remove main-metering vacuum piston/fuel-metering rod assembly, you must first disengage and remove the white nylon retainer arm pressed into the main body housing.

9. Lift up on the metering rod yoke and assembly comes out of the vacuum piston cylinder. Use caution to prevent disturbing adjustment. Set assembly to one side.

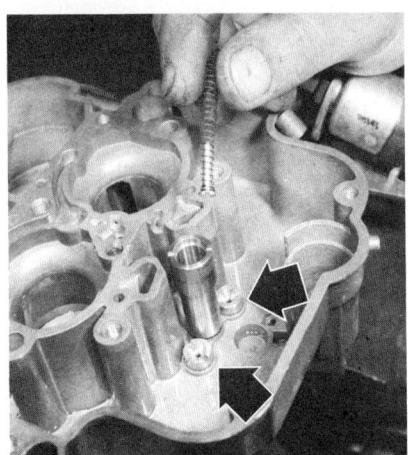

10. Reach into the vacuum piston cylinder and withdraw the spring and valve. Use a jet remover or wide-blade screwdriver to remove the main metering jets (arrows).

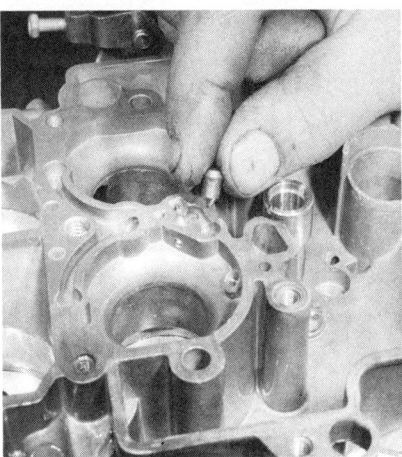

11. Removal of pump discharge needle completes main body disassembly, except on all models fitted with altitude compensation device at rear of body. Remove if fitted.

12. Before the main body can be separated from the throttle body, this screw holding the choke delayed pulldown diaphragm must be removed. Unhook linkage, remove diaphragm.

13. Remove the six throttle-body-to-mainbody screws from bottom of throttle body, separate the two castings. Remove and discard gasket. Do not disassemble linkage.

14. Idle mixture screws can be removed with limiter caps intact, because limiter stops are cast into main body. Turn in until seated, counting the turns, then back out.

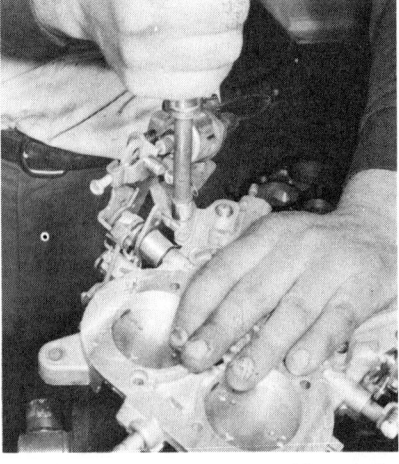

15. Throttle positioner solenoid must be removed before the throttle body is placed in cleaning fluid, or solvent action will damage or even destroy the solenoid.

16. Disassembly of the air horn begins with float removal. Pull the float hinge pin and remove the twin pontoon unit. The float hinge pin must be replaced from this side.

17. Float assembly tends to absorb fuel, which can throw off adjustment. When you remove it, shake and listen for a sloshing sound; replace with new unit if you hear it.

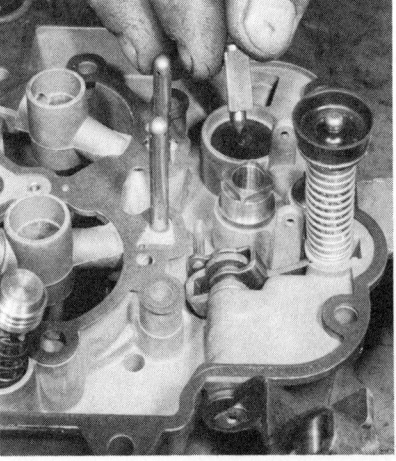

18. With float unit removed, the fuel inlet valve can be withdrawn from the valve seat. If seat is removed to replace the gasket, use an open-end wrench on the seat head.

HOW TO: Motorcraft 4300/4350 Overhaul

19. Accelerator pump piston should be replaced with a new one whenever you overhaul the 4350. To disassemble the pump, depress the spring and slide the arm from its shaft.

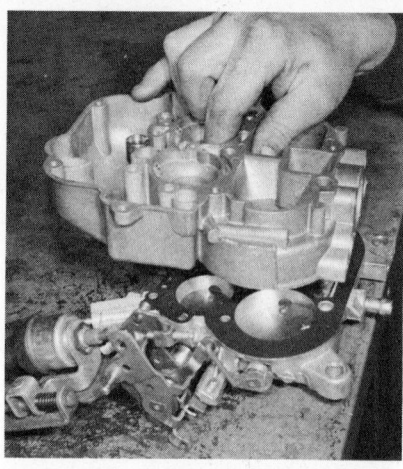

20. Replace throttle positioner solenoid and idle mixture screws, then fit throttle body gasket in place and carefully set main body in position, and replace attaching screws.

21. Reconnect choke vacuum pulldown diaphragm-link rod and secure diaphragm bracket to both main and throttle body with attaching screws. Check linkage for free movement.

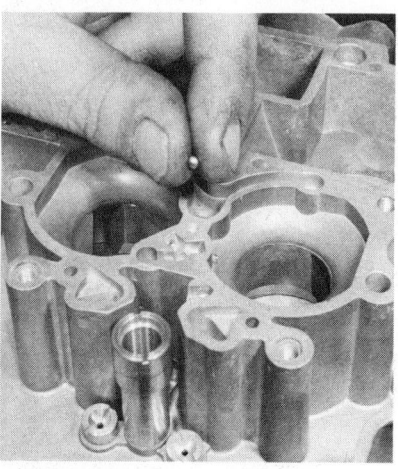

22. Reinstall the two main metering jets and vacuum piston cylinder in the main body, then drop the accelerator-pump discharge check ball back in place— don't forget it.

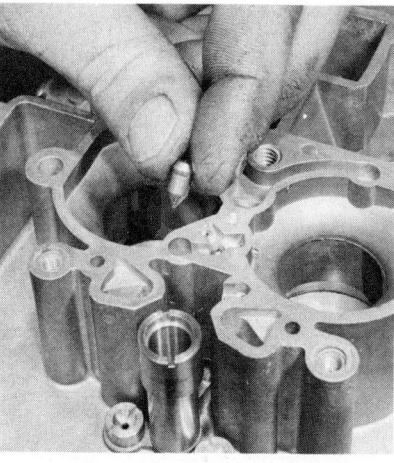

23. Replace inlet weight. Exactly where these particular parts go depends a good deal on model year and carburetor application, but disassembly procedure is basic.

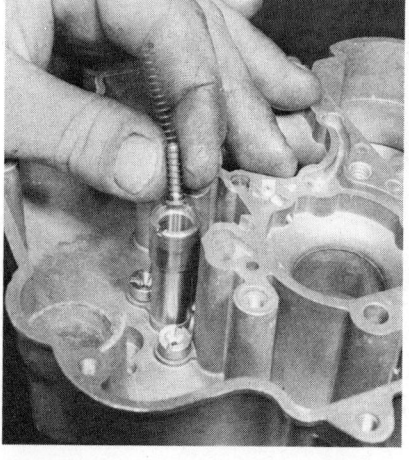

24. Drop the vacuum piston valve and spring in the vacuum piston cylinder before replacing the main-metering-piston/metering-rod assembly in the carburetor fuel bowl.

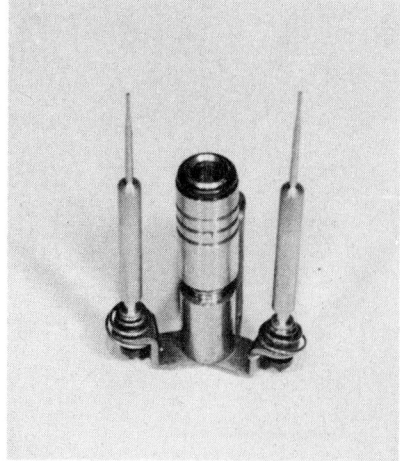

25. The vacuum piston pulls the metering rods down into the main jets to lean the mixture under high engine-vacuum conditions. Any deformity in the rods will cause problems.

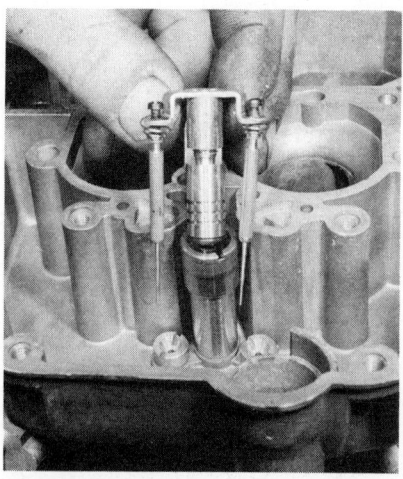

26. Reinstall the vacuum-piston/metering-rod assembly carefully, seating rod ends in the main jets. This particular system is not used on pre-'75 Motorcraft 4-bbl. carburetor models.

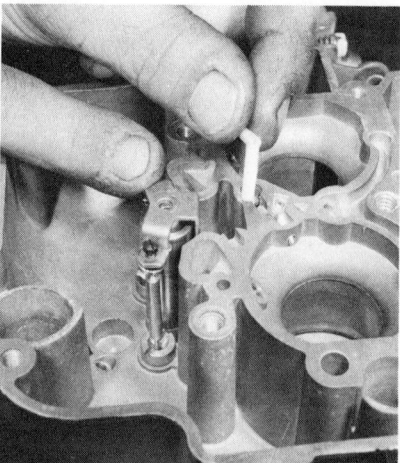

27. Depress vacuum-piston hold-down hanger while replacing nylon retaining pin. Push pin straight down. Unless retainer pin is properly seated, rods won't work correctly.

28. With retainer pin seated, as shown, to hold the hanger in position, make sure the check ball (1) and weight (2) are in place before fitting the air horn to main body.

29. Reassemble the accelerator pump (if disassembled), and fit a new pump piston on the shaft. The air valve damper piston and rod (arrow) should not be disassembled.

30. Install a new air-horn-to-main-body gasket, and then replace the twin-pontoon float assembly in the air horn, making sure to fit the float hinge pin in place as shown.

31. Check float setting with a rebuilding kit "T" gauge or use a steel straightedge as shown. Raise float by bending float lever tab down; bend tab up to lower float.

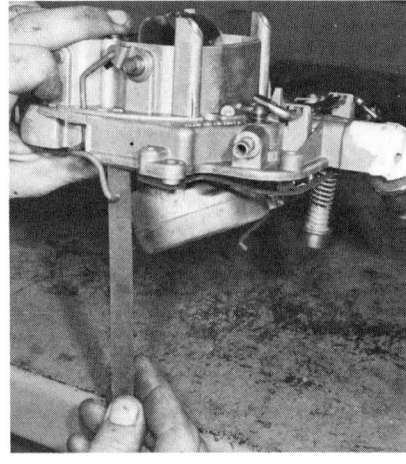

32. Then turn the air horn over and measure the amount of float drop. If the pontoons require alignment, they can be adjusted by slightly twisting in an opposite direction.

33. Carefully position air horn assembly over main body, guiding the accelerator pump plunger and secondary-throttle dashpot piston in place as air horn is lowered.

34. Position throttle lever so that its tang rests against the TSP OFF idle-speed adjustment screw, then insert key end of pump link in throttle lever's corresponding keyed hole.

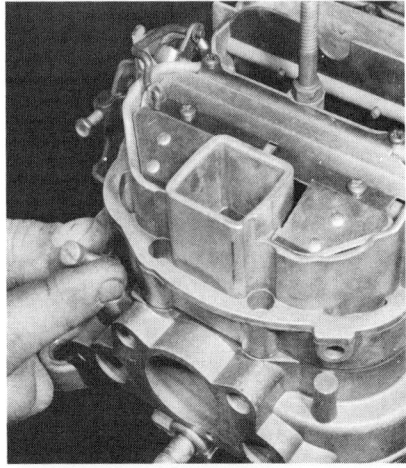

35. Replace choke rod and attach it to the automatic choke lever and upper choke lever, then install the air-horn attaching screws, tightening them snugly and evenly.

36. Fit gasket over choke lever. Reattach lever to the loop end of thermostatic coil in the choke cover. Replace retainers and screws—and adjust cap setting to 90° rich position.

HOW TO: Rochester 2GC Overhaul

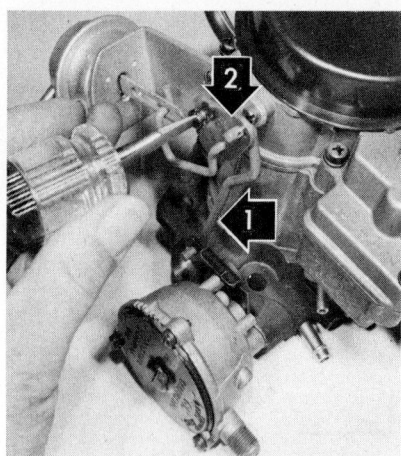

1. Remove screw in choke shaft end to remove choke vacuum-break diaphragm. Disconnect intermediate choke rod (1) from vacuum break lever (2) for access to mounting screws.

2. Remove other vacuum break diaphragm and disconnect linkage from lever on end of choke shaft. Unhook vacuum hose from throttle body tube and set diaphragm aside.

3. Disconnect lower end of pump rod from throttle lever by removing spring clip with pliers. Rotate upper rod end out of hole in pump lever and remove from throttle assembly.

4. Remove the eight air-horn attaching screws and lockwashers. Air horn removal is straightforward on the 2GC, with no hidden attaching bolts or other surprises.

5. Remove fast-idle-cam screw from float bowl, and rotate the choke rod out of the hole in cam. Upper end of choke rod cannot be removed until the air horn has been taken off.

6. Carefully lift air horn straight up and off float body. Note that choke rod is still attached and can now be swiveled out and removed from the choke lever, if desired.

7. Remove two screws holding vent valve cover. Not all 2GC carburetors use external valve which vents to vapor canister. Do not change adjustment provided by screw threaded to nylon plate.

8. Turn air horn over carefully and slide float hinge pin from retainer. This permits float removal, with float needle and pull clip (not used on all 2GC models) attached.

9. If float needle seat is to be removed, use a seat remover tool or a wide-blade screwdriver and work carefully to avoid distorting seat. Remove and replace the gasket.

10. Depress power piston stem (1); it will snap free. *Do not* remove pump plunger unless damaged. To do so, loosen set-screw (2) on plunger inner lever, break swaged end (3).

11. Remove pump-plunger return spring from inside pump well, then invert bowl assembly to remove aluminum check ball located at the bottom of the pump well and set aside.

12. Remove main metering jets and power valve from inside of float bowl, then unscrew and remove venturi cluster and gasket. Plastic main well inserts are also removed.

13. Remove limiter caps from idle mixture needles (if installed) and screw the needle in until it seats, counting the number of turns. Back out all the way and remove.

14. To separate throttle body from fuel bowl, remove the three attaching screws. Choke valve housing can be removed if necessary, but should be left untouched in most cases.

15. It is necessary, however, to remove external choke cover and baffle plate to prevent solvent damage to plastic-choke-cover/thermostatic-coil assembly during cleaning.

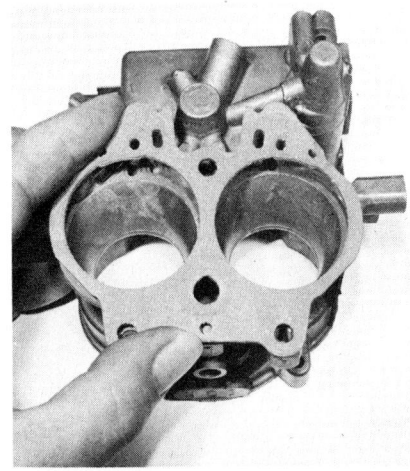

16. Remove old throttle-body-to-fuel-bowl gasket and discard. Position new gasket in place on the bottom of the fuel bowl and align gasket holes with those in the casting.

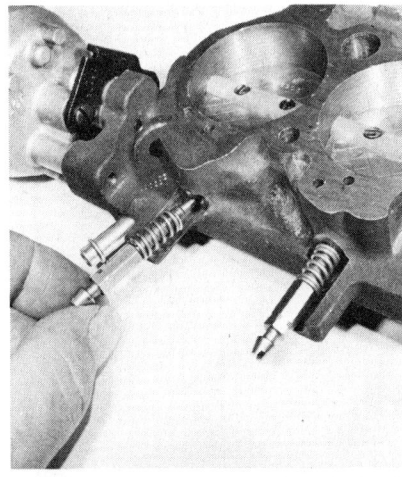

17. Reinstall idle mixture screws to begin reassembly. Screw each all the way in until it seats, then slowly back out the number of turns counted during removal, as described in step 13.

18. Install choke baffle plate in choke housing. Plate has a tanged edge which should face out, toward the choke cover. Make sure choke lever engages baffle plate slot.

HOW TO: Rochester 2GC Overhaul

19. Reinstall thermostatic-coil/cover assembly. Hook coil loop end over choke lever, press cover on housing. Rotate to make sure spring is engaged; replace retaining screws.

20. Replace plastic main-well inserts and retaining springs, then install new gasket on bottom of venturi cluster and seat in place, installing the three attaching screws.

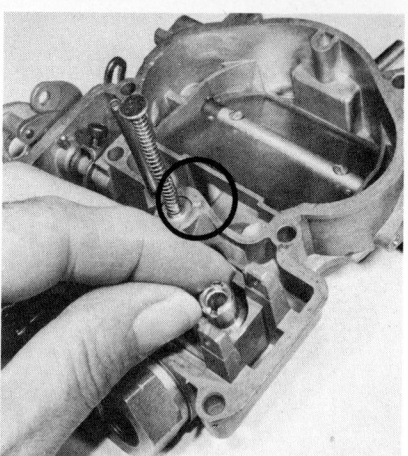

21. Replace power piston and lightly stake in place (circle), then fit a new gasket to the float needle seat and reinstall. Tighten needle seat securely—no more.

22. Insert needle valve in needle seat, then install float assembly on the air horn and insert the hinge pin. Check for float action and free movement of needle in seat.

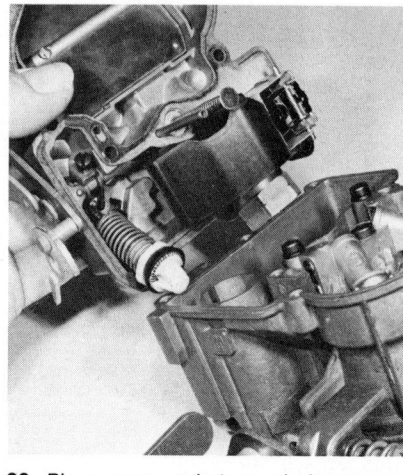

23. Place new gasket on air horn, and invert air horn over fuel bowl, lowering it in place to correctly position accelerator pump plunger in pump well. Tighten screws securely.

24. Replace vent-valve adjustment screw/plate and position vent spring on top of the adjusting screw. Replace cover and gasket, tightening screws securely—no more.

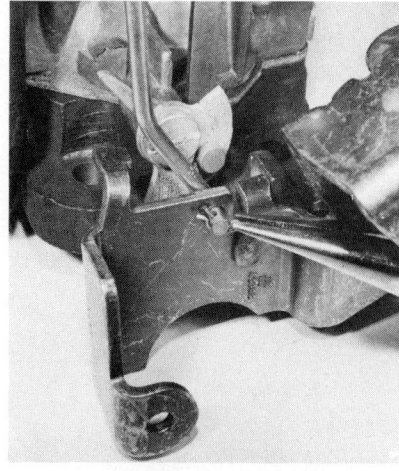

25. Install fast idle cam to lower end of choke rod, and reinstall cam. Rotate pump rod into upper pump lever, fitting lower end to throttle lever; replace spring clip.

26. Replace vacuum break diaphragm, connect linkage to vacuum break lever, as shown, and replace lever on the choke shaft, securing with the screw. Check linkage action.

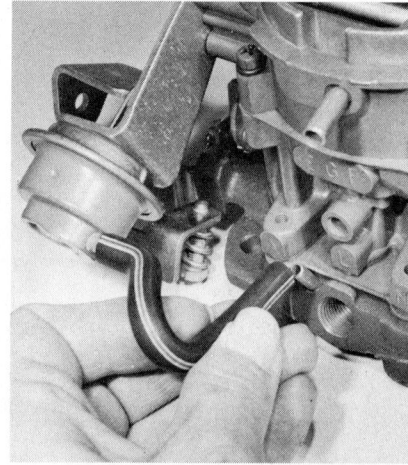

27. Replace other vacuum break diaphragm and link assembly from lever on end of choke shaft, securing diaphragm unit to air horn with attaching screws. Connect vacuum hose.

HOW TO: Rochester M4MC/M4MCA/M4MEA Overhaul

1. Remove retaining screw and disengage upper choke lever from the end of the choke shaft. Rotate the upper choke lever to remove choke rod from the slot in the lever.

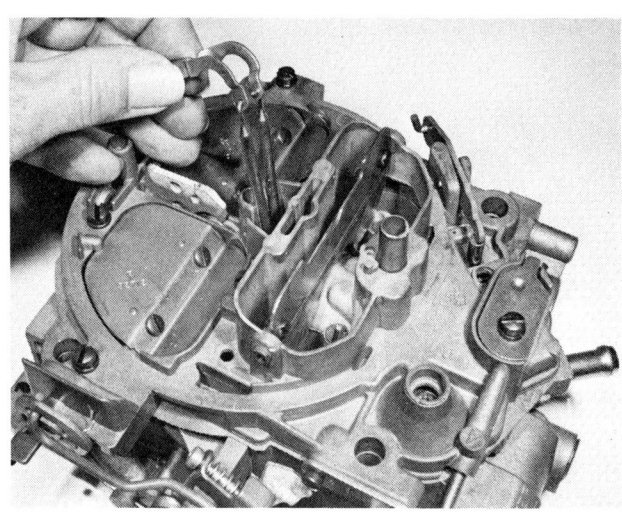

2. Disengage choke rod from lower lever, then remove small screw in the top of the metering rod hanger and lift the secondary metering rods up and out of the air horn.

3. Remove front vacuum-break bracket screws. Diaphragm assembly can now be detached from the air-valve dashpot rod, and the dashpot rod removed from the air valve lever.

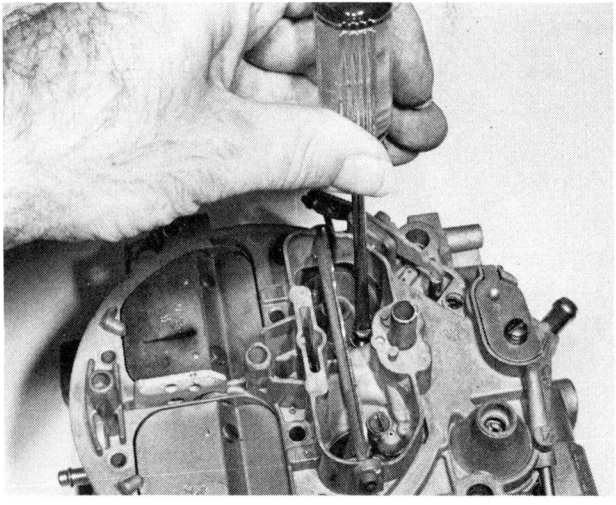

4. Like all Quadrajets, the Mod-Quad has nine air-horn-to-bowl attaching screws, two countersunk screws are located next to the primary venturi and are easy to overlook.

5. Carburetor float chamber is externally vented to the vapor cannister. Remove vent valve cover, gasket and spring which sit atop the hex-head vent adjusting screw.

6. Lift air horn straight up until secondary bleed and accelerating-well tubes clear float bowl, then angle air horn to one side and disengage pump lever from pump rod.

HOW TO: Rochester M4MC/M4MCA/M4MEA Overhaul

7. No further air horn disassembly is required. Loosen air horn gasket carefully, lift one corner to provide access to accelerator pump well and remove the pump plunger.

8. Air horn gasket cannot be stripped from the Mod-Quad as with other carburetors. To remove it, first disengage the auxiliary power-piston/metering-rod assembly.

9. Once the auxiliary metering rod has been removed, swing the auxiliary power piston until it touches the primary power piston. Gasket is slit here and can now be removed.

10. To remove primary and auxiliary power piston assemblies, depress piston stem and let it snap free. This procedure may require several tries before the piston pops up.

11. Remove plastic filler block over the float, then lift the retaining pin to remove the float and needle assembly. Use a seat remover or wide screwdriver to remove seat.

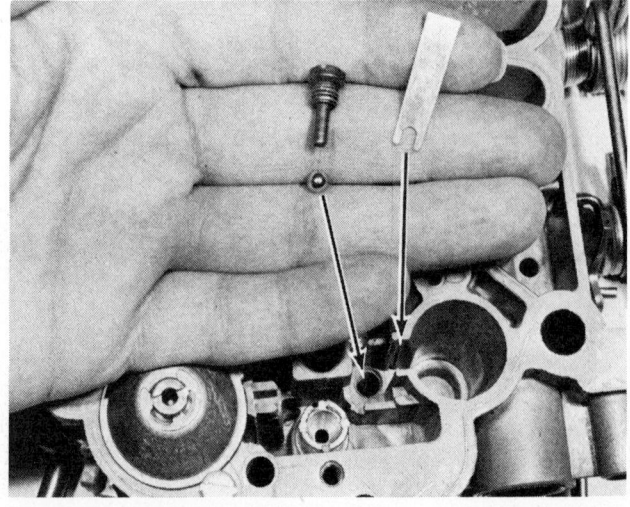

12. Remove the pump discharge check-ball retainer and the check ball, then withdraw baffle from side of pump well. *Do not* remove primary jets unless they are to be replaced.

13. On M4MC/M4MCA/M4MEA versions equipped with adjustable part throttle (APT) and aneroid, remove cover and withdraw unit. Solvent will destroy aneroid.

14. Remove screws and retainer from electric-choke-cover/coil assembly. Pull straight out and remove choke cover/coil from housing. Further disassembly is not required.

15. Remove throttle-body-to-bowl attaching screws and carefully separate the two sections. The heavy throttle-body-to-bowl insulator gasket is removed and discarded.

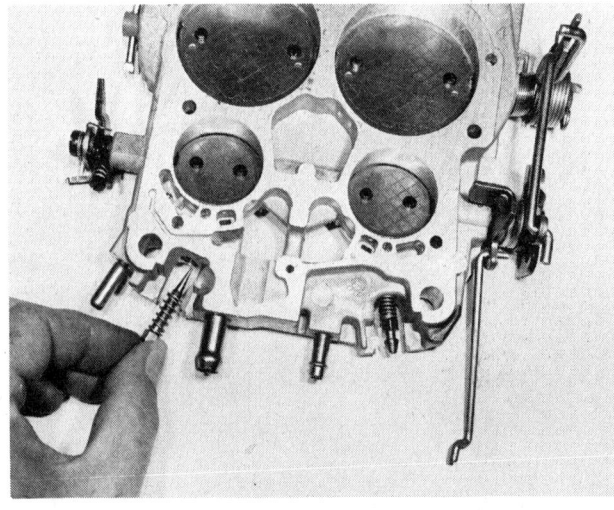

16. Idle mixture needles do not have to be removed, but doing so assures a thorough cleaning of the idle passages. If necessary to remove, destroy the limiter caps.

17. Remove fuel inlet nut, gasket, filter, spring (arrow). Reinstall after cleaning throttle body. Replace idle mixture needles, fit new gasket over locating dowels on bowl.

18. Reattach throttle body to bowl, and install lower end of pump rod in throttle lever. Replace float needle seat (1) and install check ball (2), retainer (3) and baffle.

HOW TO: Rochester M4MC/M4MCA/M4MEA Overhaul

19. APT metering rod with aneroid is very fragile and must be handled carefully. *Do not* change factory-set adjustment. Replace with tang inserted in float bowl cutout.

20. Install float needle by sliding float lever under the needle pull clip. Pull clip should be hooked over the edge of float arm between the two holes and facing pontoon.

21. Install float and adjust level, if necessary. Press filler block in place until it seats; install primary power piston and metering rods with spring in piston well.

22. Make sure primary metering rods drop in place freely, then install the auxiliary power piston and press down firmly on plastic retainer to make sure it seats fully.

23. Position new gasket over the two float bowl dowel pins, then replace auxiliary metering rod. Metering rod must hook on auxiliary piston arm as shown if it is to work.

24. Carefully lifting one edge of gasket, replace accelerator pump spring in pump well, then install the pump plunger. Align stem with hole in gasket and press gasket in place.

25. Carefully replace air horn on float bowl, making sure bleed tubes, accelerating-well tubes, pull-over enrichment tubes and pump plunger fit properly through gasket.

26. Replace the vent valve spring and gasket, then fit cover in place, with dimple on underside seating inside spring. Vent valve *can* be adjusted, but should not require it.

27. Install the nine attaching screws and tighten evenly. These two are best inserted with pliers to avoid dropping into venturi, requiring air horn removal to get them out.

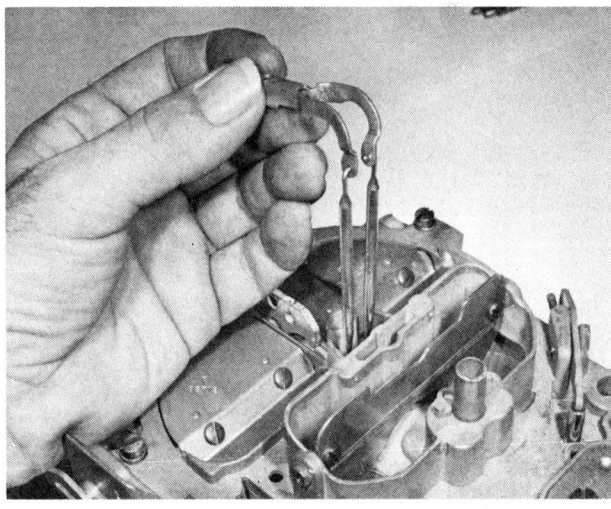

28. Replace the two secondary metering rods in the rod hanger, with upper ends pointing toward each other. Position assembly on air-valve cam follower, replace screw.

29. Fit front vacuum-break diaphragm rod into slot in lever on air-valve shaft end. Install the other end of rod in hole in diaphragm plunger, and replace unit to air horn.

30. Connect lower end of choke rod into lower choke lever inside bowl cavity, then install upper end in upper choke lever and replace to choke shaft, with lever facing to rear.

HOW TO: Rochester Monojet (MV) Overhaul

1. Monojet overhaul performed on '75 Vega model; carburetor is identical to the '74 version except for additional auxiliary vacuum diaphragm. Remove the six air horn screws.

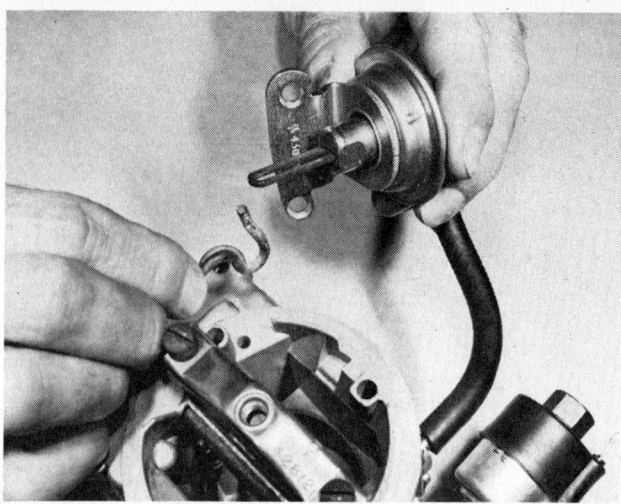

2. To separate air horn from the float bowl, this vacuum diaphragm must be detached. Remove bracket screws, angle the diaphragm arm off the linkage and disconnect the hose.

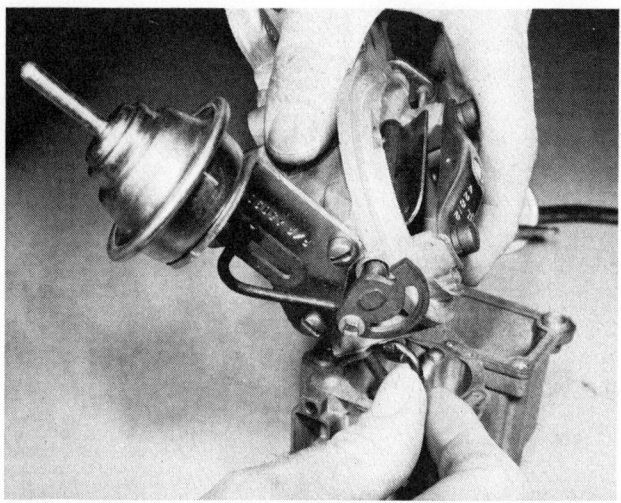

3. Lift air horn up and off the float bowl, then angle, as shown, to permit removal of choke rod from the upper choke lever. No further air horn disassembly is required.

4. Remove and discard the air horn gasket. Lift up on the float hinge pin to remove the float assembly, then remove the hinge pin from the float arm and set to one side.

5. Remove the float needle from the float needle seat, then use a seat removal tool or a screwdriver which completely fills the slot to remove the needle seat and gasket.

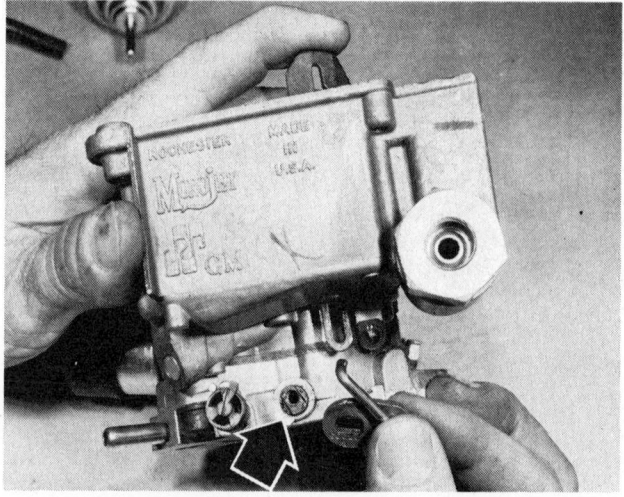

6. To free accelerator pump plunger, remove screw from throttle shaft (arrow), disconnect actuating lever/link. Removal ruins the factory screw—it's set with Loctite.

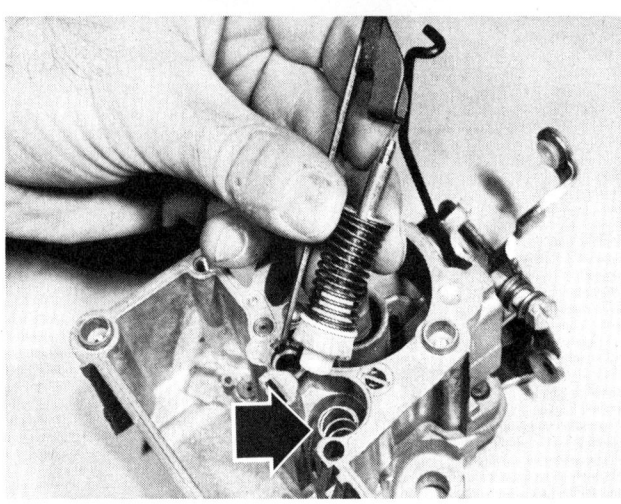

7. With the actuating link detached, the accelerator pump plunger and shaft can be removed. Remember to reach into the pump well and remove the pump return spring (arrow).

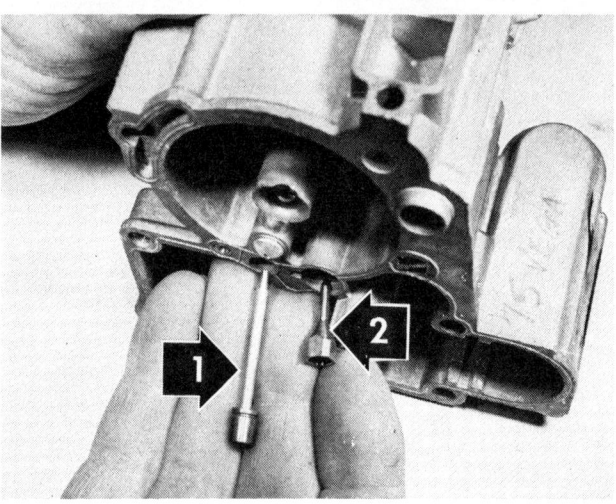

8. Holding your hand over the float bowl, invert it and catch the idle tube assembly (1) and power valve (2) as they fall out. Check idle tube to make certain it is not bent.

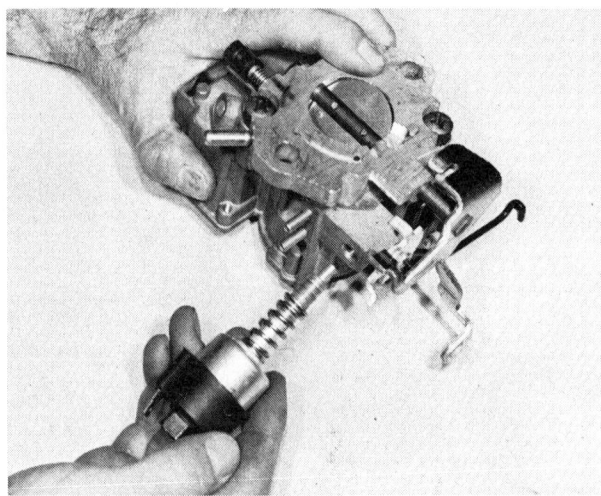

9. With the float bowl still inverted, remove the electrically operated idle-stop solenoid by screwing it in a counterclockwise direction and withdraw from fuel body.

10. Remove fuel inlet nut, filter and spring. A check valve pressed into the filter's inlet neck has been added to '76 models to shut off fuel flow in case of a rollover.

11. Use long-nose pliers to remove the "T" pump discharge guide. The pump discharge ball/spring should also be removed. If necessary, invert fuel bowl for removal.

12. If the main metering jet is to be removed, use a jet remover or a wide-blade screwdriver that will fill the jet slot completely to prevent damage to the jet seat.

HOW TO: Rochester Monojet (MV) Overhaul

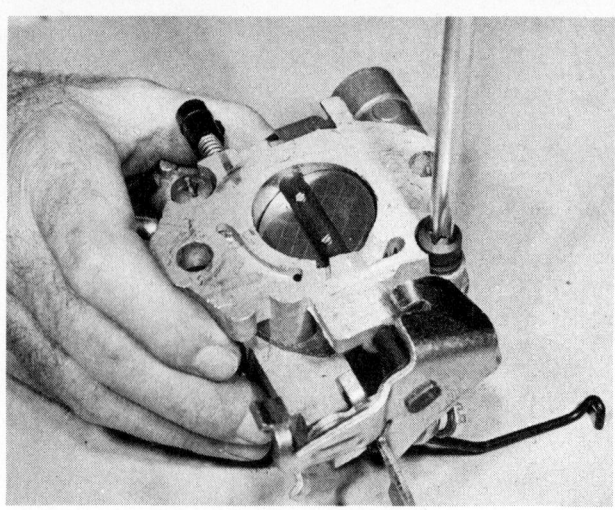

13. To separate throttle body from fuel bowl, invert unit and remove the two hex-head attaching screws. You may have to tap the side of the throttle body to break seal.

14. Monojet uses a thick insulator gasket, and separating the throttle body from the fuel bowl is likely to split the gasket in half. Clean off both halves of body and discard gasket.

15. To remove idle mixture screw, clip limiter stop arm from cap with wire cutters. Turn screw all the way in, counting the number of turns, then back out completely.

16. Install the idle mixture screw, fit a new gasket to the throttle body and install to the fuel bowl. Insert the discharge spring and ball, then replace the "T" guide.

17. Replace accelerator-pump return spring in the pump well, then install pump plunger assembly. You have to hold plunger assembly down while completing the next step.

18. Hold plunger down, reattach actuating link, fit actuating lever back on throttle shaft key. Since old attaching-screw head was ruined during removal, install new one.

19. Screw the idle stop solenoid back in place, and replace the main jet, if removed. Then drop the power valve (1) and idle tube assembly (2) into their respective places.

20. Replace the float needle seat/gasket and tighten snugly. Drop float needle in seat, with pointed end first, and install the float assembly, with hinge pin in the float bowl.

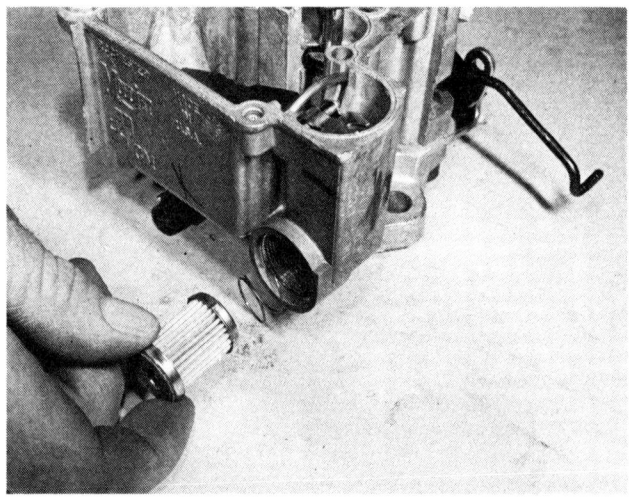

21. Replace fuel inlet filter/spring. On '75 and earlier models, filter gasket faced outward; replacement filters now come with check valve, and its seat faces outward also.

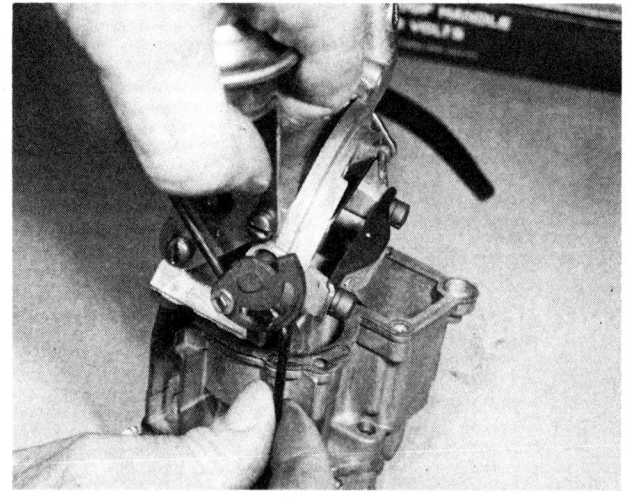

22. Align air horn gasket with locating dowels, press into place. Angle air horn, as shown, to connect choke rod with upper choke lever, then lower air horn onto fuel bowl.

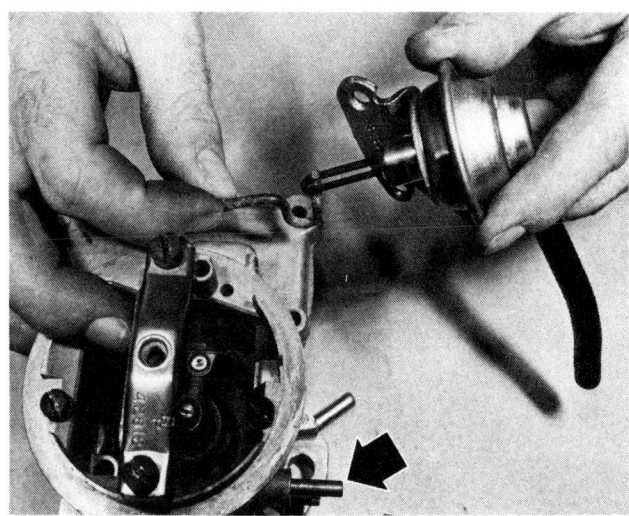

23. Fit auxiliary vacuum-break diaphragm arm over linkage and install bracket to air horn with attaching screws. Connect vacuum hose to its proper fitting (arrow).

24. Check linkage operation and tighten diaphragm bracket snugly. Except for vacuum ports, Monojet design has changed little over the years, and this procedure works with all.

INDEX

EMISSION CONTROLS

BUICK
1970-71 Emission Systems
POSITIVE CRANKCASE VENTILATION (PCV)

A sealed oil-filler cap prevents crankcase gases from escaping under no-vacuum conditions. A tube from the air cleaner goes to the rocker cover, carrying fresh air down into the crankcase. From that point, blowby gases go through the hose into the PCV valve (Fig. 6-1) and then into the manifold. When the PCV system is under zero vacuum, there is no suction on the crankcase, but the gases go from the rocker cover, through the hose and into the air cleaner, where they are drawn into the engine.

CONTROLLED COMBUSTION SYSTEM (CCS)

A series of engine modifications, CCS uses carburetor/choke/distributor calibrations and an increased engine operating temperature to reduce emissions. Ignition timing is retarded and carburetors calibrated to run on a leaner air/fuel mixture. A 190° F/195° F thermostat is fitted to CCS engines, allowing a higher engine temperature to produce better fuel vaporization and a reduced quench (cool) area in the combustion chambers. A thermostatically controlled air cleaner keeps the temperature of the air entering the carburetor at approximately 115° F, reducing engine icing in cold-weather climates and giving better engine warm-up.

TRANSMISSION CONTROLLED SPARK ADVANCE (TCS)

An oil pressure switch in the transmission direct-clutch circuit is pressurized when the transmission is shifted into third or high gear. Oil pressure opens the switch, transmitting an electrical signal to the solenoid valve inserted in the ported carburetor-to-distributor vacuum line. The solenoid valve then closes, shutting off vacuum to the distributor and bleeding off any vacuum in the line (Fig. 6-2).

A three-nipple, thermo-vacuum switch located in the coolant passage at the left front corner of the intake manifold supplies full intake-manifold vacuum to the distributor whenever engine coolant temperature rises above 220° F, causing an increase in engine idle, and in fan and water pump action, to reduce the excess heat. This switch is not used on manual-transmission-equipped cars or on some 350-cu.-in. engines.

EVAPORATIVE EMISSION CONTROL (EEC)

Vapor caused by fuel evaporation in the fuel tank is no longer vented into the atmosphere, but transferred instead to the engine compartment by a vapor line and fed directly into the running engine, or is stored in an activated charcoal accumulator (canister) when the engine is not running (Fig. 6-3). The system includes a fuel-tank overfill protector, a three-point fuel-tank venting system, a liquid vapor separator positioned forward and above the fuel tank, and a pressure-vacuum relief valve in the vapor line.

BUICK
1972 Emission Systems

The following systems are the same as "Buick, 1970-71 Emission Systems": Positive Crankcase Venti-

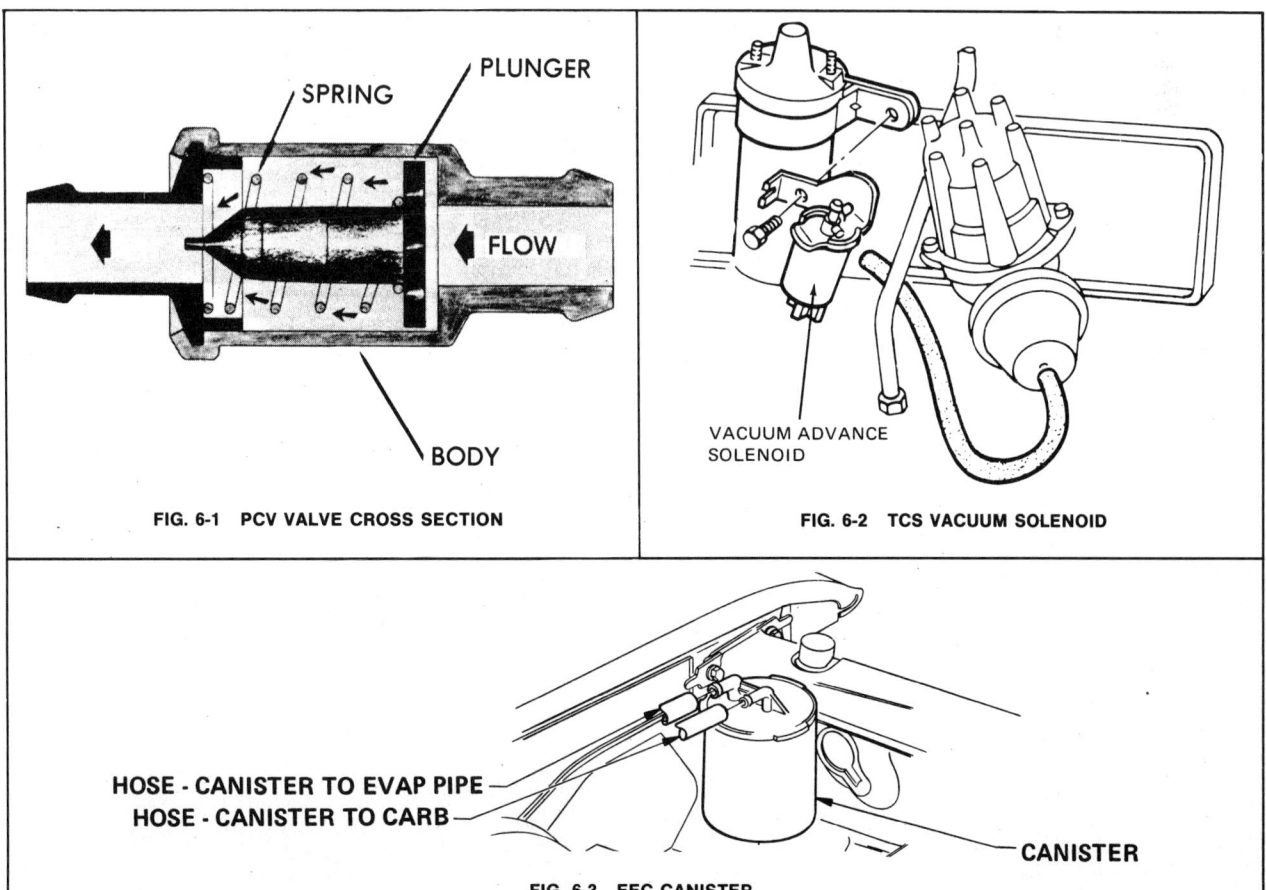

FIG. 6-1 PCV VALVE CROSS SECTION

FIG. 6-2 TCS VACUUM SOLENOID

FIG. 6-3 EEC CANISTER

lation (PCV), Controlled Combustion System (CCS), Transmission Controlled Spark Advance (TCS) and Evaporative Emission Control System (EEC).

EXHAUST GAS RECIRCULATION (EGR)

This system **(Fig. 6-4)** is fitted to all manual-transmission-equipped and all California Buicks. A vacuum-operated recirculation control valve mounted at the right rear of the engine manifold regulates the amount of exhaust gases and the duration of time they enter the intake manifold. When the throttle valves are opened beyond the idle position, vacuum is applied against the EGR-valve actuating diaphragm. As the diaphragm moves up, against spring pressure, it opens the exhaust-gas intake valve, allowing exhaust gases from the manifold crossover exhaust channels to be drawn back into the engine intake. The valve remains closed during idle and deceleration, when excessive exhaust gases added to the air/fuel mixture would cause rough engine idling.

AIR INJECTION REACTOR (AIR)

This system **(Fig. 6-5)** is fitted to all 1972 Buicks, except non-California cars with the 350-cu.-in. engine and automatic transmission. It consists of a belt-driven

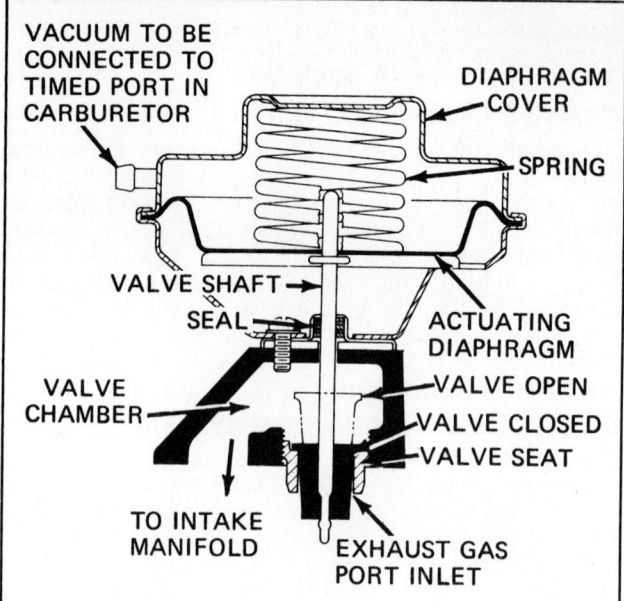

FIG. 6-4 EGR VALVE CROSS SECTION, SINGLE DIAPHRAGM

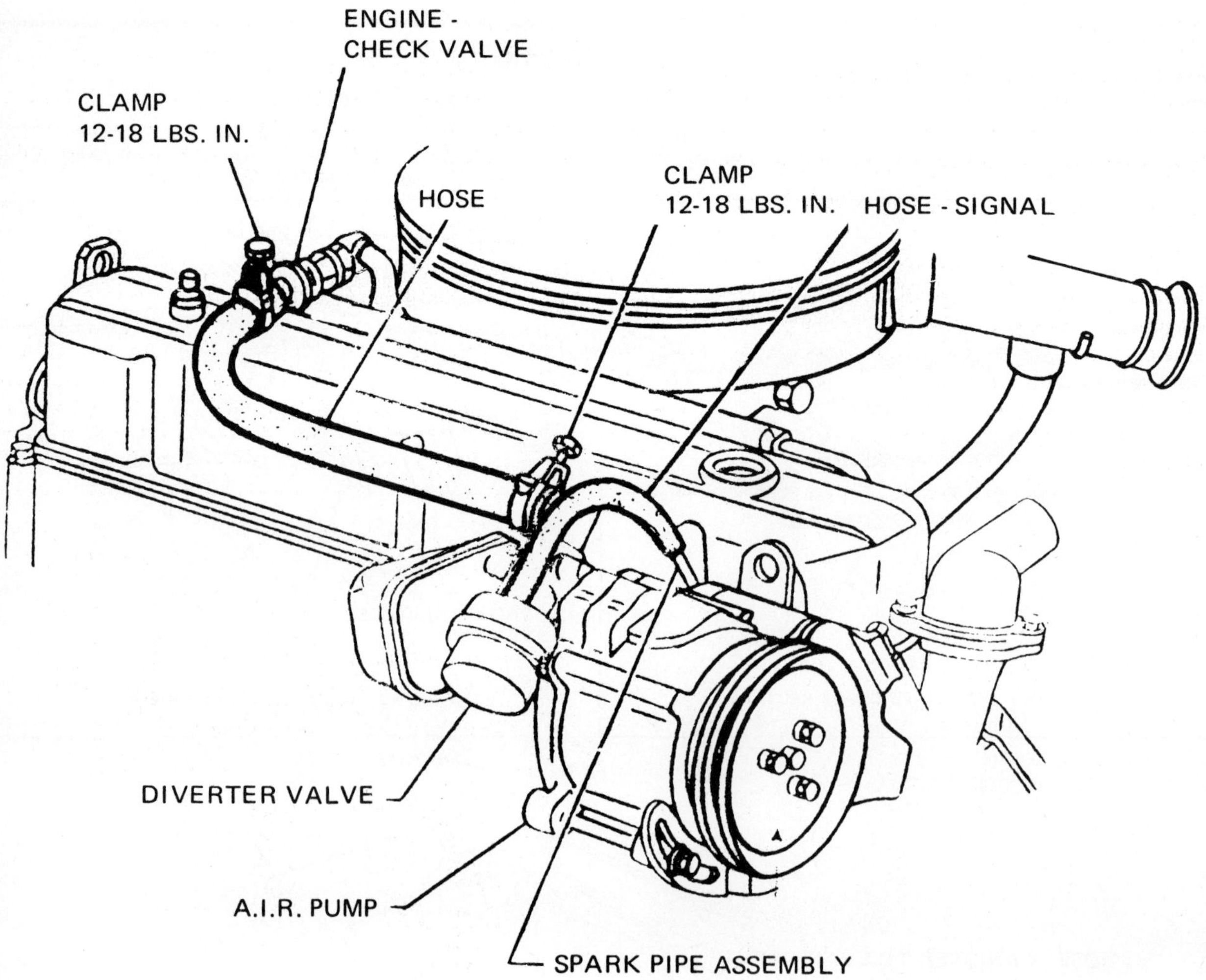

FIG. 6-5 TYPICAL AIR INSTALLATION

air pump (positive-displacement vane type), diverter valve and silencer assembly, check valve, special intake manifold and cylinder head assemblies, and the necessary connecting hoses. The AIR pump is located at the upper left front of the engine. Intake air passes through a centrifugal fan at the front of the pump and is delivered to the intake manifold. During sudden deceleration, vacuum causes a diverter valve at the back of the pump to open, passing pump air into the atmosphere. A screw-on check valve on the left side of the intake manifold contains a one-way diaphragm which prevents hot exhaust gases from backing up in the hose and damaging the pump during periods of pump belt failure, excessive pressure or hose ruptures.

BUICK

1973-74 Emission Systems

The following systems are the same as "Buick, 1970-71 Emission Systems": Positive Crankcase Ventilation (PCV) and Controlled Combustion System (CCS). Air Injection Reactor (AIR) is the same as 1972.

TRANSMISSION CONTROLLED SPARK ADVANCE (TCS)

In 1974, use of the TCS system with I-6 engines is restricted to manual-transmission-equipped models. A thermal switch and a time relay are used with the transmission pressure switch (Fig. 6-6). The thermostatic coolant-temperature switch provides a thermal override below 93° F, while the time relay energizes the solenoid for approximately 20 seconds after the ignition switch is turned on.

EVAPORATIVE EMISSION CONTROL (EEC)

This liquid vapor separator was discontinued in 1973-74. The three-point vent system was changed to a one-point system.

EXHAUST GAS RECIRCULATION (EGR)

Extended to all Buicks for 1973, the EGR system remains the same as that used during 1972, except for the addition of an inline temperature-control valve located in the EGR-valve vacuum line. Designed to sense ambient temperatures above the engine intake manifold, this valve closes at temperatures below 55° F to

block carburetor vacuum from opening the EGR valve until the temperature over the manifold reaches 60° F. The black-and-white plastic valve is marked to indicate its correct placement in the vacuum line.

On engines manufactured after March 15, 1973, the inline temperature-control valve is replaced by a thermal vacuum switch located just behind the thermostat housing. This switch blocks the vacuum signal to the EGR valve whenever coolant temperature is below 67½° F (±7½° F).

For 1974, California 350-cu.-in. engines are fitted with a dual-diaphragm EGR valve (Fig. 6-7).

DISTRIBUTOR VACUUM-ADVANCE SPARK-DELAY SYSTEM

A thermal check/delay valve is located in the hose connecting the carburetor ported-spark port with the thermal vacuum switch "Carburetor" port on all 1974 455 2-bbl. and 350 4-bbl. engines. The valve remains open at underhood temperatures lower than 50° F. Above 50° F, it moves to a restricting position and meters vacuum through a 0.005-in. orifice. Up to 40 seconds are required for full vacuum advance after distributor ported vacuum has been dropped to zero. Above 226° F coolant temperature, the valve is bypassed and vacuum for the advance comes from an intake manifold source.

BUICK

1975 Emission Systems

The Positive Crankcase Ventilation (PCV) system is the same as on 1970-71 Buicks. The Exhaust Gas Recirculation (EGR) system is the same as 1974 Buicks. Although not used on some 1975 Buicks, the Air Injection Reactor (AIR) is the same used in 1972. See 1973-74 for Evaporative Emission Control (EEC).

DISTRIBUTOR VACUUM-ADVANCE SPARK-DELAY SYSTEM

This is restricted to 231-cu.-in. California engines in 1975; the system is identical to that used in 1974 on the 455 2-bbl. and 350 4-bbl. engines or early production models, but later in the year, the thermal vacuum switch is discontinued and the delay valve is relocated between the carburetor ported-spark port and the dis-

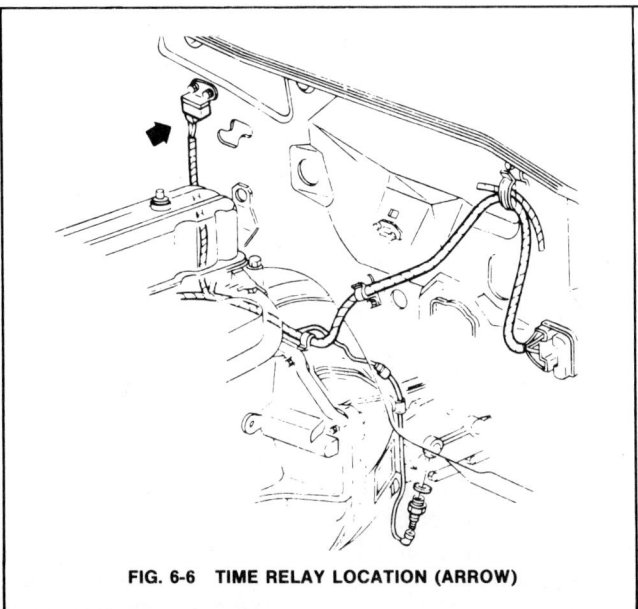

FIG. 6-6   TIME RELAY LOCATION (ARROW)

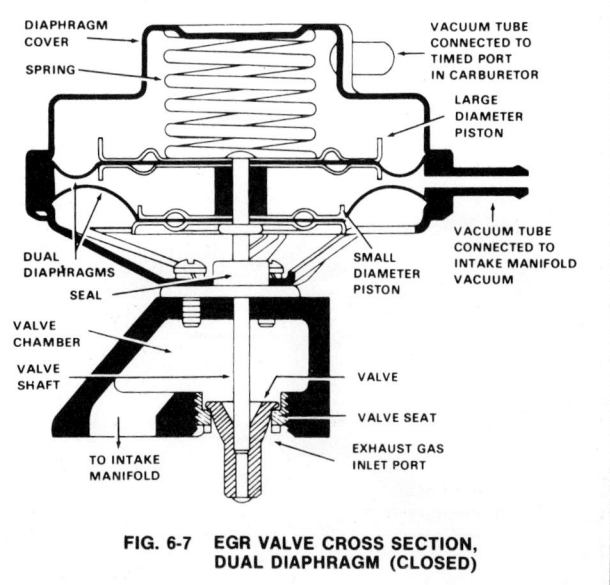

FIG. 6-7   EGR VALVE CROSS SECTION, DUAL DIAPHRAGM (CLOSED)

tributor vacuum-advance unit. The delay to full vacuum advance is 25 seconds.

DISTRIBUTOR VACUUM-ADVANCE RETARD-DELAY VALVE

To improve cold drivability, the 400-cu.-in. engine is fitted with a parallel system of hose plumbing, one branch of which contains a spark-retard delay valve, while the other branch contains a thermal vacuum valve (TVV) which senses engine coolant temperature. When the coolant is warm, the TVV opens, and both vacuum paths are available to the distributor, but at cold coolant temperatures, the TVV closes. This shuts off one of the two vacuum paths. When the throttle is opened, loss of vacuum advance is gradual during a 4-second delay period, instead of immediate.

CHOKE AIR MODULATOR

To provide heated and filtered air to the choke thermostatic-coil housing, all 231, 350 and 455-cu.-in. engines use a modulator valve located in the air cleaner bottom **(Fig. 6-8)**. When the air cleaner temperature is below that specified, the modulator is closed to slow down the rate at which the choke coil is heated. Above the specified temperature, the modulator opens to allow normal air circulation. This heats the coil and opens the choke.

CATALYTIC CONVERTER

All 1975 Buicks are fitted with a catalytic converter to improve fuel economy and drivability.

EARLY FUEL EVAPORATION (EFE)

Added to the exhaust system on most 1975 Buicks, the EFE valve promotes quick heating of incoming fuel by directing exhaust gas flow through the intake-manifold crossover passage directly under the carburetor whenever engine coolant temperatures are below a specified level. The valve operation is the same for all engines, but temperature control and the sensing method used differ.

BUICK

1976 Emission Systems

The Positive Crankcase Ventilation (PCV) system remains the same as for 1970-71 Buicks. Exhaust Gas Recirculation (EGR) and Evaporative Emission Control (EEC) are the same as for 1973-74 systems. The following are carryovers from 1975: Catalytic Converter, Choke Air Modulator and Early Fuel Evaporation (EFE).

SPARK-ADVANCE VACUUM-MODULATOR SYSTEM (SAVM)

A dual-diaphragm regulating valve with three ports, the SAVM **(Fig. 6-9)** controls vacuum to the distributor vacuum advance on all non-California 260-cu.-in. engines. The valve responds only to engine load, and provides two operating conditions:

a) If manifold and ported vacuum are both below 7 ins., the valve output to the distributor is manifold vacuum.

b) If manifold and ported vacuum are both above 7 ins., the valve output to the distributor is ported vacuum.

DISTRIBUTOR THERMAL VACUUM SWITCH (TVS)

Some 350/455-cu.-in. engines have a TVS located in the engine-coolant crossover passage of the intake manifold. When engine temperature exceeds approximately 220° F, the TVS sends manifold vacuum to the vacuum advance. This advance in ignition timing speeds up the engine to increase fan speed and to circulate coolant faster to reduce engine temperature.

BUICK

1977 Emission Systems

The Positive Crankcase Ventilation (PCV) system and Thermostatic Air Cleaner (TAC) are the same as for 1970-71. Air-Injection Reactor (AIR) is essentially the same as 1972, but its use is restricted to California and high-altitude V-6 engines. Evaporative Emission Control (EEC) is the same as the 1973-74 system. The following are carryovers from 1975: Catalytic Converter, Choke Air Modulator and Early Fuel Evaporation (EFE). The Spark Advance Vacuum Modulator (SAVM) system and the Distributor Thermal Vacuum Switch (DTVS) are carryovers from 1976.

EXHAUST GAS RECIRCULATION (EGR)

Two types of EGR systems are used: ported vacuum control and exhaust backpressure modulated. System operation is essentially the same as 1973-74, but a timed carburetor vacuum port regulates EGR in the ported system, while exhaust backpressure regulates flow in the backpressure modulated system. The separate backpressure transducer fitted to some 1976 engines is integrated into EGR valve for 1977 **(Fig. 6-75A)**.

TRANSMISSION CONTROL SPARK (TCS)

Century, Regal and Skylark models equipped with a manual transmission use a solenoid valve and shift linkage-operated transmission switch to control vacuum

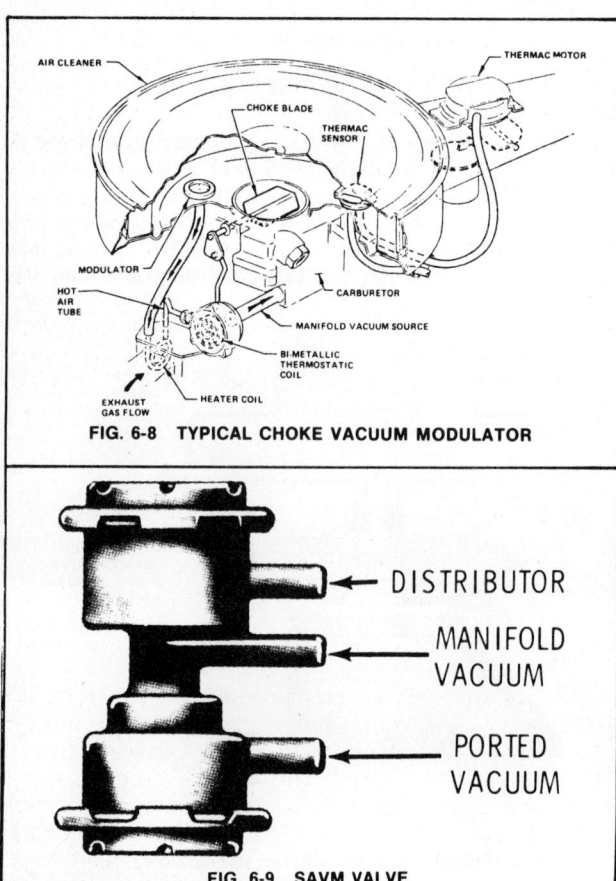

FIG. 6-8   TYPICAL CHOKE VACUUM MODULATOR

DISTRIBUTOR

MANIFOLD VACUUM

PORTED VACUUM

FIG. 6-9   SAVM VALVE

spark advance according to transmission gear. Located in the ported vacuum line to the distributor, the solenoid valve is connected to the transmission switch by an electrical harness. The solenoid valve vents vacuum to prevent distributor vacuum advance in all gears except high.

CHOKE THERMAL VACUUM SWITCH (CTVS)

All 4-bbl. carburetors use a CTVS to provide richer choke operation when carburetor air temperature is under 57° F. The switch controls vacuum to both carburetor vacuum break diaphragms.

DISTRIBUTOR THERMAL VACUUM SWITCH (DTVS)

A vacuum reducer valve (VRV) is incorporated with the DTVS on some V-8 engine applications. Reduced vacuum helps prevent detonation at high operating temperatures.

DISTRIBUTOR VACUUM DELAY VALVE (DVDV)

Some V-8 engines use a DVDV to delay vacuum from the carburetor port to the advance unit by up to 30 full seconds, depending upon calibration for the particular application. The valve is bypassed at coolant temperatures above 220° F when the DTVS valve switches.

BUICK

1978 Emission Systems

The Positive Crankcase Ventilation (PCV) system and Thermostatic Air Cleaner (TAC) are the same as for 1970-71. Evaporative Emission Control (EEC) is the same as the 1973-74 system. The following are carryovers from 1975: Catalytic Converter and Choke Air Modulator. The Transmission Control Spark (TCS) and Distributor Thermal Vacuum Switch carry over from 1977.

SPARK ADVANCE VACUUM MODULATOR (SAVM)

Use is restricted to non-California V-8 403 engines.

EXHAUST GAS RECIRCULATION (EGR)

The ported EGR system is not used in 1978; all EGR valves contain the integral backpressure transducer and are operated according to the exhaust backpressure level.

AIR-INJECTION REACTOR (AIR)

Use is extended to all California V-8 350-cu.-in. engines with Code L, and all California and high-altitude V-8 350-cu.-in. engines with Code R, and V-8 403-cu.-in. engines. California and high-altitude V-6 engines use an internal air distribution system **(Fig. 6-101B)**. AIR passages are case in the intake manifold and are drilled in cylinder heads.

EARLY FUEL EVAPORATION (EFE)

Calibration of the EFE-EGR-TVS is changed for 1978. California V-6 engines and non-California V-8 engines (Code X) use a 120° F ± 3° F opening temperature; non-California V-6 engines use a 90° F ± 3° F calibration.

VACUUM CONTROLS

The operation of various emission control components is modified by one or more of the following vacuum controls:

1. Thermal Vacuum Switch (TVS)
2. Vacuum Delay Valve (VDV)
3. Check Valve
4. Vacuum Modulator Valve (VMV)
5. Vacuum Reducer Valve (VRV)

The exact use and calibration of these devices depends upon the engine and application.

BUICK 1979 Emission Systems

All emission systems are carryover from 1978 except as noted below.

ELECTRONIC FUEL CONTROL (EFC) SYSTEM

A revised version of the 1978 EFC system used on some late model-year California Skyhawks, the 1979 EFC system is fitted to California Century/Regal models equipped with a V-6 231-cu.-in. VIN Code 2 engine. The system consists of an exhaust gas oxygen sensor, an electronic control module (ECM), a controlled air/fuel ratio carburetor, a phase II converter and wide-open throttle switch. An air cleaner TVS and distributor advance/retard system are interrelated in operation, but are not considered to be part of the EFC system. A sensor maintenance reminder (warning flag) is located in the speedometer face to indicate when the oxygen sensor requires replacement.

Before the ECM can control the carburetor air/fuel ratio with the 1979 system, the following three conditions must occur at the same time:

1. EFC operation is subject to a 10-second delay after starting.
2. Coolant temperature must exceed 90° F.
3. The sensor must send a sufficiently strong voltage signal to the ECM. The ECM is programmed to determine when the signal strength is adequate. Prior to EFC operation, the ECU is programmed to provide a pre-calibrated operational condition for the carburetor. If power mixture requirements at wide-open throttle require it, this condition can be overridden by the wide-open throttle switch mounted on the carburetor.

The ECM monitors the sensor voltage and signals the carburetor accordingly. The Rochester Dualjet E2ME Model 210 carburetor contains an electrically operated mixture control solenoid in the fuel bowl. A plunger in the solenoid positions two special stepped metering rods in removable jets to control fuel metering. Cycling of the plunger takes place 10 times per second, providing far more accurate control over the air/fuel mixture than previously possible. The air cleaner TVS controls the secondary choke vacuum break, preventing it from operating at temperatures below 62° F for better drivability.

A first generation electronic control device, the ECM contains a built-in diagnostic system to detect the most common problems which may develop in the EFC system. When a malfunction occurs, a "check engine" light flashes on the instrument panel. When this happens, a diagnostic test lead from the module can be grounded to activate the readout system. Grounding the lead will cause the "check engine" light to flash a trouble code if the system had discovered the malfunction. The self-diagnostic mode does not include all possible malfunctions, but later generation ECMs will most likely be considerably more sophisticated.

The trouble code indicates a problem in a particular circuit and consists of a single flash of the light followed by a pause and then two or more flashes. A longer pause follows and then the light repeats the code twice more. The cycle continues to repeat in this manner until the engine is started or the ignition turned off. When the test lead is grounded with the engine running, the trouble code flashes in sets of three followed by a long pause. If more than one malfunction is affecting EFC operation, the light will flash the first trouble code followed by a pause and then a second trouble code, after which the sequence is repeated.

Once the trouble code has been identified numerically, a diagnostic chart of the same number is consulted to determine which component is at fault. The ECM is connected in such a way as to have a short "memory." Since trouble codes pertaining to intermittent problems may only be recorded in the ECM under certain conditions, a long "memory" is desirable to permit retention of such codes. When the "S" terminal on the ECM is connected directly to a positive battery source, the ECM acquires a long "memory." Since the ECM "S" terminal is connected to a 4-terminal connector located under the dash, a jumper lead connected from the battery source to the 4-terminal connector will provide this feature. When the ECM is connected in this way, there will be a small current drain on the battery at all times regardless of ignition switch position. If the vehicle is to be stored for a long period, the jumper should be disconnected to prevent an excessive drain on the battery.

When a trouble code can be obtained but the light is not on (engine running), it indicates which circuit is malfunctioning intermittently. A physical inspection of the circuit in question should be made to check for poor or corroded connections, etc. The trouble code list for the 1979 EFC system is as follows:

12—No tach signal to ECM
13—Oxygen sensor circuit
14—Shorted coolant sensor circuit
15—Open coolant sensor circuit
21/22—Grounded wide-open throttle switch circuit
22—Grounded idle/wide-open throttle switch circuit
23—Open/shorted carburetor solenoid circuit
51, 52, 53, 55—Faulty ECM
54—Faulty ECM or solenoid

NOTE: A lead from the distributor tach terminal to the ECM has a filter in series. Connect a tach to the 2-terminal (dist.) side only!

DISTRIBUTOR ADVANCE/RETARD SYSTEM

Used with EFC systems, this consists of an electrical relay, water-temperature switch, two solenoids and a dual-diaphragm vacuum advance unit. As long as the coolant is above 150° F, the system works as a conventional distributor. Below that temperature, the system provides spark retard during light throttle operation in order to improve converter operation. It also increases advance during cold acceleration to improve drivability.

EMISSION SYSTEM TEST PROCEDURES
PCV TEST
1. Connect a tachometer and start the engine.
2. Clamp off the crankcase ventilator hose to shut off the airflow completely.
3. If idle speed drops 60 rpm or more, the PCV system is functioning. If idle speed drops less than 60 rpm, install a new valve.

ALTERNATE PCV TEST
1. Remove the PCV valve from the intake manifold or rocker arm cover.
2. Start the engine, and run at idle.
3. Place your thumb over the valve end to check for vacuum. If there is no vacuum at the valve, inspect for plugged hoses.
4. Shut the engine off. Shake the valve and listen for the rattle of the check needle in the valve. If no rattle is heard, replace the valve.

THERMO-AIR-CLEANER VACUUM MOTOR TEST
1. Inspect for plugged, kinked or damaged hoses, and then check for proper connections.
2. With the engine off, the damper door should cut off cold air from the snorkel tube **(Fig. 6-10)**. If not, look for binding linkage.
3. Apply 7-9 ins. of vacuum to the diaphragm motor assembly. Damper door should completely close off the hot air duct **(Fig. 6-11)**. If not, look for a vacuum leak and/or incorrect linkage hookup.
4. With vacuum still applied, clamp off the hose to trap vacuum in the diaphragm assembly. The damper door should continue to close off the hot air duct. If not, replace the diaphragm assembly.

THERMO-AIR-CLEANER SENSOR TEST
1. Check the cold air inlet with the engine off—it should be closed **(Fig. 6-10)**.

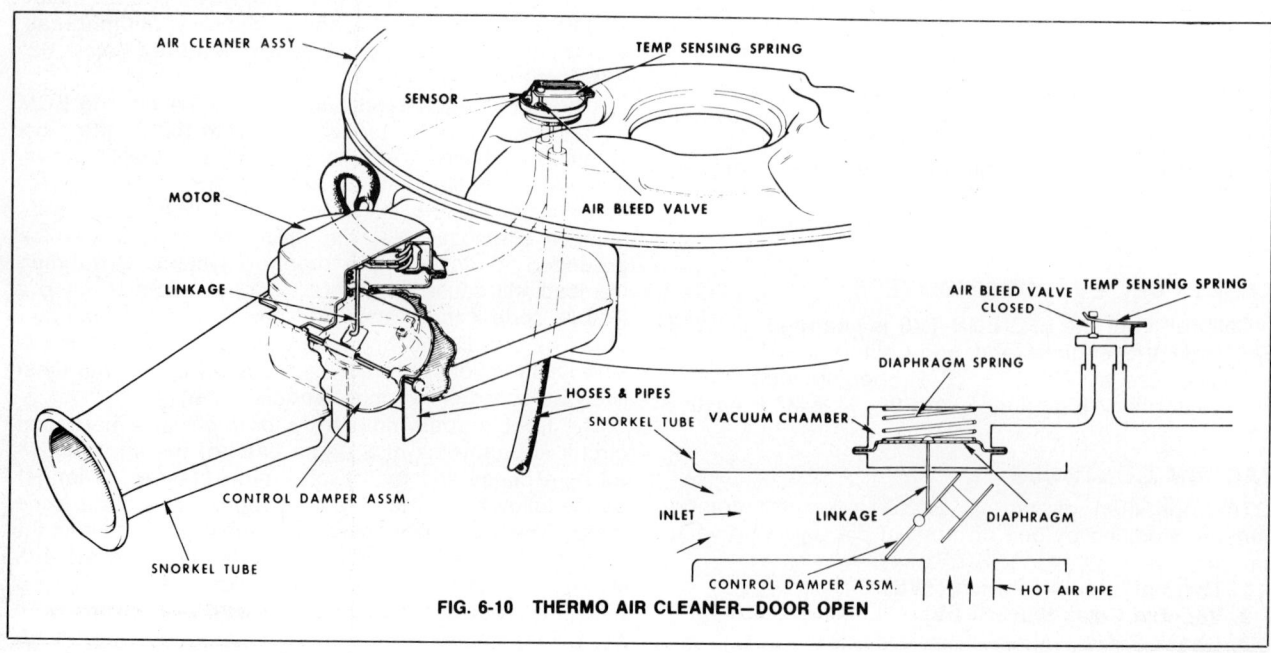

FIG. 6-10   THERMO AIR CLEANER—DOOR OPEN

2. Start cold engine with the air cleaner temperature below 85° F. The cold-air inlet damper should close immediately.

3. As the engine warms up, the cold-air inlet damper should gradually open to allow a mixture of cold and heated air to enter, and the air cleaner should become warm. If not, replace the sensor.

TRANSMISSION CONTROLLED SPARK ADVANCE TEST

1. Connect an ignition timing light and tachometer. Elevate the rear wheels.

2. Start the engine, place the transmission in DRIVE and position the fast idle cam to increase engine speed to 1000 rpm.

3. Check the timing mark—there should be no vacuum advance. A vacuum gauge connected to the distributor vacuum-advance line can also be used—vacuum gauge reading should be zero.

4. Shift the transmission into REVERSE. Make sure the parking brake is applied and that a wheel is blocked in front and back.

5. Check the timing mark or vacuum gauge at 1000 rpm. There should now be full vacuum advance.

6. If not, connect a continuity light between the two TCS solenoid terminals. The test lamp should remain off when the transmission is in REVERSE. The tester must not supply more than 0.8-amps current at 12 volts, or the transmission switch will be damaged. If the test lamp lights, look for a grounded wire between the solenoid and transmission; if the wire is not grounded, replace the transmission switch.

7. Shift the transmission into NEUTRAL—light should go out. If it does not, check for an open circuit. If the circuit is not open, replace the transmission switch.

8. Repeat Steps 6 and 7 with a new switch installed. If vacuum is still not present, replace the TCS solenoid.

CEC VALVE ADJUSTMENT (Fig. 6-12)

Energized through the transmission, the CEC valve acts as a throttle stop by increasing idle speed during high gear operation. The CEC valve also provides full vacuum advance during high gear operation, and is de-energized in all other gears, and at idle for retarded

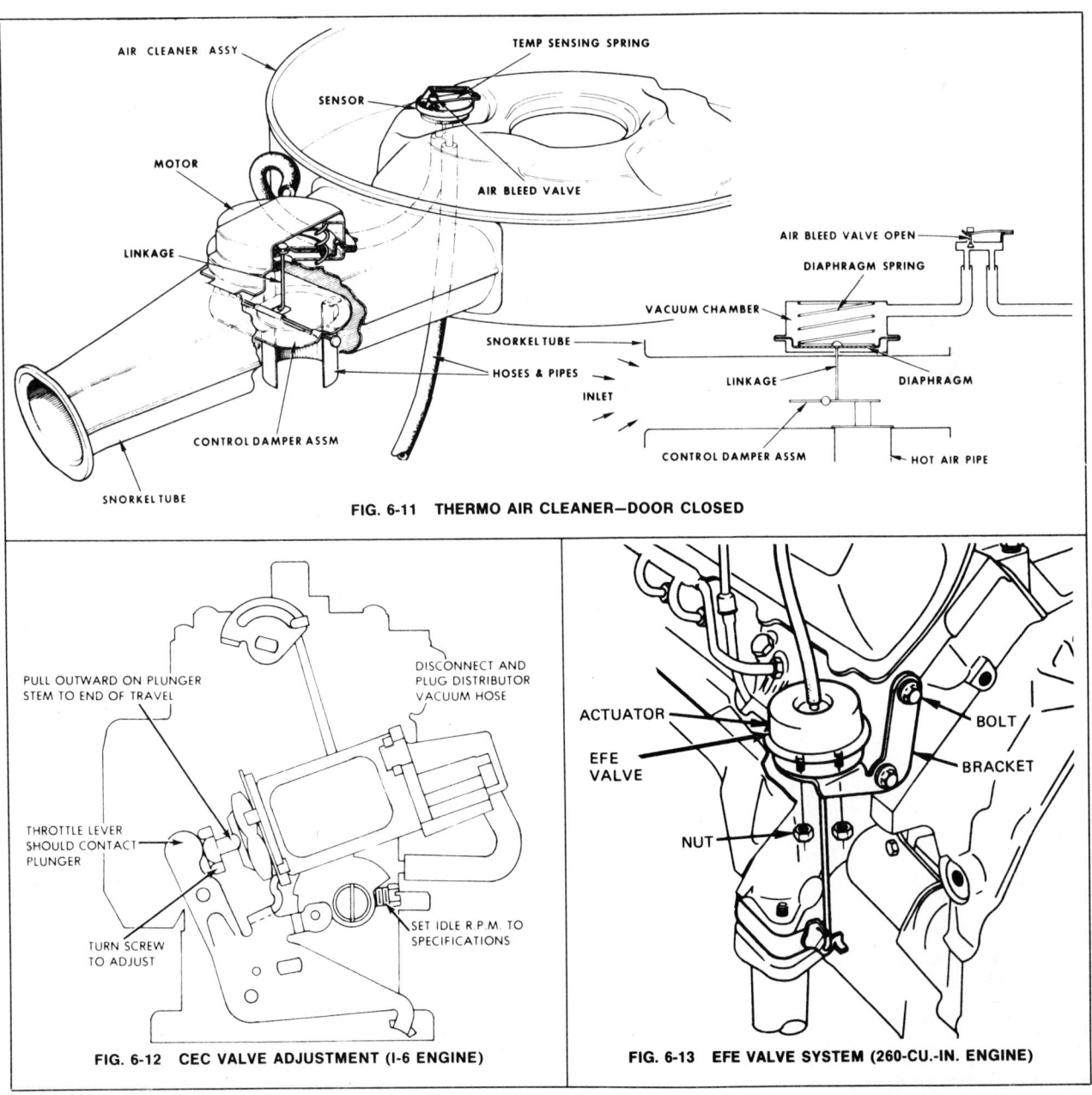

FIG. 6-11 THERMO AIR CLEANER—DOOR CLOSED

FIG. 6-12 CEC VALVE ADJUSTMENT (I-6 ENGINE)

FIG. 6-13 EFE VALVE SYSTEM (260-CU.-IN. ENGINE)

spark timing. The normal idle speed setting is made with the idle stopscrew. The CEC valve should require adjustment only in cases of solenoid replacement, major carburetor overhaul or removal/replacement of the carburetor throttle body.

To adjust the CEC valve:
1. Disconnect and plug the distributor vacuum-advance line; disconnect the fuel tank hose from the vapor canister.
2. Refer to specific instructions for adjustment found on the vehicle emission control sticker; start the engine and connect a tachometer.
3. Manually extend the solenoid valve plunger until it touches the throttle lever.
4. Adjust the plunger length until the specified engine speed is obtained.
5. Reconnect the vacuum advance and vapor canister lines.

EGR VALVE OPERATION TEST
1. Start engine and warm it up to normal operating temperature.
2. Disconnect the EGR thermal-delay system, if used.
3. Apply a vacuum signal to the EGR diaphragm with a hand vacuum pump. The diaphragm shaft should move under a 5-in. vacuum signal and not leak down.
4. If testing a dual diaphragm valve, remove the vacuum line from the lower EGR valve connection.
5. Shut the engine off and apply a 14-in. vacuum signal. Watch for leak-down. If there is no drop in 30 seconds, both diaphragms are functional. If a vacuum drop occurs, one of the diaphragms is leaking. The EGR valve is not serviceable and, if defective, must be replaced.

EGR THERMAL-VACUUM SWITCH TEST
1. With engine coolant below 67° F, start engine.
2. Run at 1500 rpm and immediately feel for EGR-valve stem movement—engine coolant temperature rises quickly.
3. If the stem does not move, the TVS is operating correctly. If stem movement is felt, replace the TVS.

DISTRIBUTOR VACUUM-ADVANCE SPARK-DELAY VALVE TEST
1. Connect a vacuum gauge to the TVS side of the

valve and a hand vacuum pump with gauge to the carburetor side.
2. When vacuum is applied, there should be a 3- to 4-second delay in balancing the two gauge readings. If not, replace the valve.
3. Remove the gauge from the TVS side of the valve, and cover the port with a finger. Apply a 5-in. vacuum signal. The pump gauge should hold steady. If not, the valve should be replaced.
4. Remove the finger, and the gauge reading should drop gradually. If it drops to zero immediately, replace the valve.

EARLY FUEL EVAPORATION SYSTEM TVS SWITCH TEST
At engine temperatures of less than 120° F, manifold vacuum is sent from the TVS port marked "D" or "2" to the EFE actuator to close the heat valve and increase exhaust flow through the intake manifold crossover. Above 120° F, the spring-loaded EFE valve is held open, because there is no vacuum available.
To test the TVS switch:
1. Engine Coolant Below 120° F—Disconnect the "D" or "2" port on the EFE-TVS, and connect a vacuum gauge. Start the engine. If the hoses are properly connected, full manifold vacuum should be present. If not, connect the vacuum gauge to the "C" or "3" port on the TVS. If full manifold vacuum is present here, replace the TVS, using a soft-setting sealant.
2. Engine Coolant Above 120° F—Disconnect the "D" or "2" port on the EFE-TVS, and connect a vacuum gauge. Start the engine. If the hoses are properly connected, less than 5 ins. of vacuum should be present. If more than 5 ins. of vacuum are present, replace the TVS, using a soft-setting sealant.

EARLY FUEL EVAPORATION SYSTEM (250/260-cu.-in. Engines)
When engine temperature is less than the TVS switching temperature, manifold vacuum is directed to the EFE actuator, which closes the EFE heat valve to increase exhaust flow through the intake manifold. The valve starts to close at 5-7 ins. vacuum, and is fully closed at 10-12 ins. vacuum. At engine temperatures above the switching point, the EFE valve remains open, since no vacuum is available.
To test the system:
1. Check the valve for binding and the hoses for cracking, abrasions or deterioration.
2. Connect a hand vacuum pump to the EFE valve actuator **(Fig. 6-13)** and gradually apply vacuum. Watch the valve linkage operation. If it moves only slightly or not at all, replace the valve.

EARLY FUEL EVAPORATION CHECK VALVE (260-cu.-in. Engine)
A check valve is inserted in the vacuum line from the intake manifold to the EFE-TVS switch to hold the highest vacuum reached to keep the EFE heat valve closed until the TVS switches modes. Without this check valve, the EFE heat valve would rattle under conditions of low vacuum, such as heavy acceleration. If this occurs, replace the check valve.

EARLY FUEL EVAPORATION SYSTEM FUNCTIONAL TEST (400-cu.-in. Engine)
1. Connect a remote start switch, and make sure engine coolant temperature is below 120° F.
2. Locate the EFE valve, and note the actuator arm position.

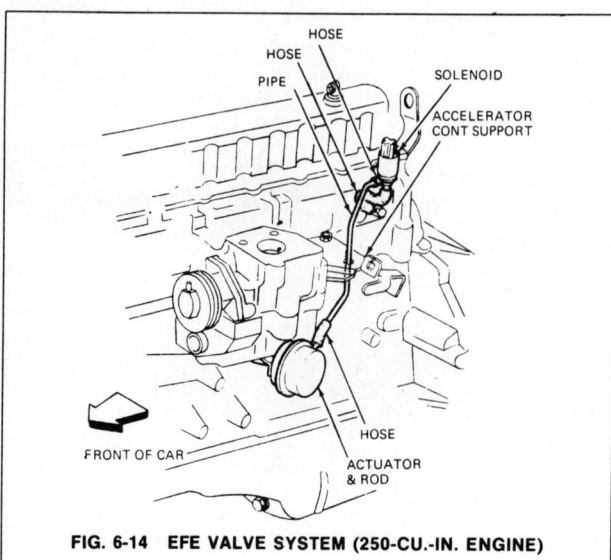

FIG. 6-14 EFE VALVE SYSTEM (250-CU.-IN. ENGINE)

3. Start the engine and watch the valve—it should close as the actuator arm is pulled into the diaphragm housing.

4. If the valve does not close, remove the vacuum hose from the EFE valve and apply 8 ins. or more vacuum, using a hand vacuum pump. If the EFE valve now closes, it's functional. If it doesn't close, replace it.

5. Warm the engine until the coolant exceeds 120° F—the valve should open. If it does not, remove the valve hose. If the valve now opens, there is no air bleed for the diaphragm or the TVV plunger is stuck in the cold mode. In either case, replace the TVV.

EARLY FUEL EVAPORATION SOLENOID
(250-cu.-in. Engine)

1. Visually inspect all hoses, wiring and pipes for proper connections, cracking, abrasions or deterioration. Replace if necessary **(Fig. 6-14)**.

2. Connect a vacuum gauge to the hose at the EFE valve actuator, and start the engine.

3. Disconnect the lead from the engine oil-temperature switch and ground the lead to the engine. The vacuum gauge should read idle vacuum. If it does, go on to Step 5. If not, proceed with Step 4.

4. If idle vacuum is not present, stop the engine and turn the ignition switch to the RUN position. Check for battery voltage at the solenoid with a voltmeter. If battery voltage is present, check the ground circuit with an ohmmeter; if battery voltage is not present, check and repair the power circuit. If the ground circuit is good, replace the solenoid.

5. With the engine running and the oil at normal operating temperature, disconnect the temperature switch lead from ground. The vacuum gauge should read zero. If vacuum is present, replace the solenoid. Reconnect the oil-temperature-switch lead. The vacuum gauge should read zero. If vacuum is present, replace the oil temperature switch.

EXHAUST GAS RECIRCULATION TVS
(250-cu.-in. Engine)

1. Coolant temperature must be above 100° F. Connect a vacuum gauge to the EGR port of the TVS switch and a hand vacuum pump to the carburetor port. If the vacuum gauge does not show a reading when vacuum is applied, replace the valve.

EXHAUST GAS RECIRCULATION TCV
(260-cu.-in. Engine)

All 260-cu.-in. engines are fitted with a temperature sensitive control valve inserted in the vacuum line to the EGR valve. This control valve remains closed at temperatures below 61° F, blocking vacuum to the EGR valve. At temperatures above 76° F, the control valve opens to allow EGR ported vacuum to the EGR valve. To determine the operating condition of the TCV, test vacuum as follows:

1. Tee a vacuum gauge into the EGR valve line. If vacuum is present at temperatures below 61° F, or no vacuum is present at temperatures above 76° F, replace the valve.

DISTRIBUTOR THERMAL
VACUUM SWITCH (TVS) TEST
(350/455-cu.-in. Engines)

1. Connect a vacuum gauge to the "D" port on the TVS **(Fig. 6-15)**.

2. Start the engine and restrict incoming air to the radiator in order to raise coolant temperature.

3. Check the vacuum gauge. If it shows any reading, replace the TVS. If not, continue the procedure.

4. Let the engine run. When the coolant reaches 220° to 230° F, the TVS should switch internally, and the vacuum gauge will indicate a reading. If it does not, replace the TVS and repeat the test procedure.

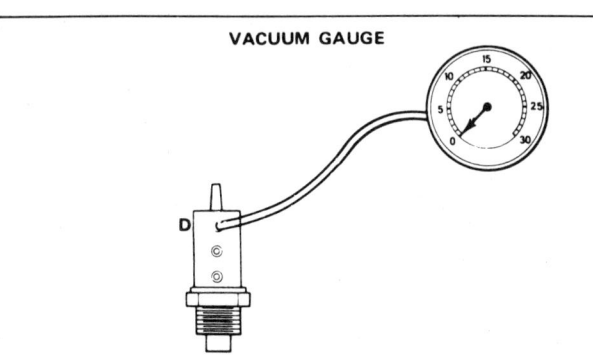

FIG. 6-15 CHECKING DISTRIBUTOR TVS (350/455 ENGINES)

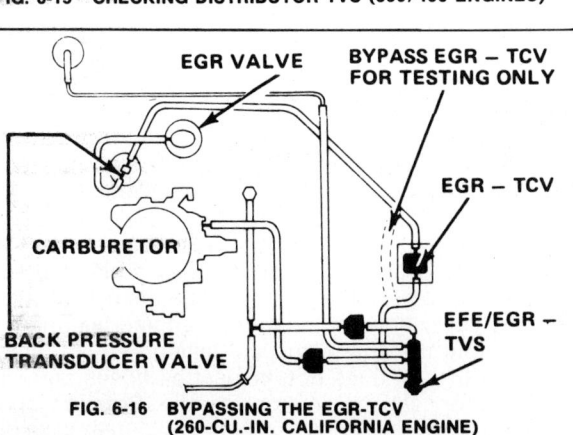

FIG. 6-16 BYPASSING THE EGR-TCV (260-CU.-IN. CALIFORNIA ENGINE)

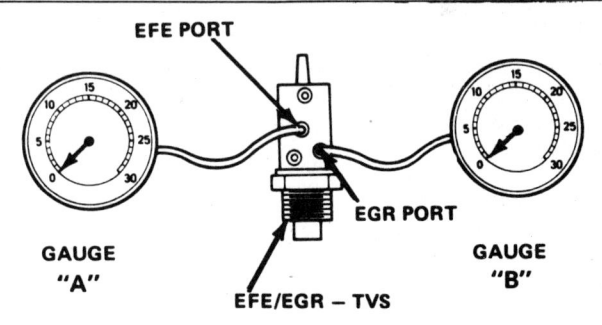

FIG. 6-17 VACUUM GAUGE CONNECTIONS

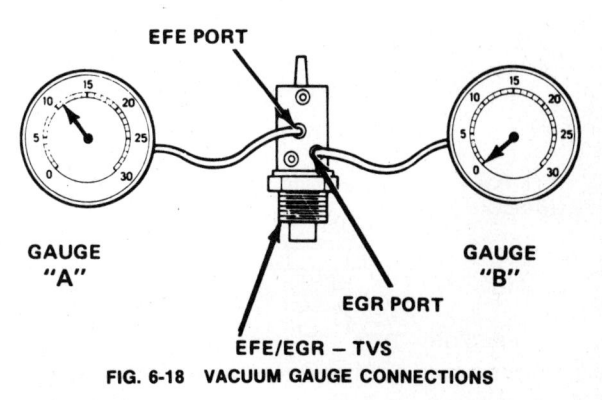

FIG. 6-18 VACUUM GAUGE CONNECTIONS

SPARK ADVANCE VACUUM MODULATOR SYSTEM (Non-California 260-cu.-in. Engine Only)

1. Connect a vacuum gauge to the distributor port, then apply 7 ins. vacuum to the manifold port (Fig. 6-9). The vacuum gauge should read 7 ins. of vacuum and remain constant.

2. Move the vacuum pump to the ported vacuum connection and repeat Step 1. The vacuum gauge should stay at zero until the pump output reaches 7 ins., then follow the pump level upward.

3. Reverse the vacuum gauge and vacuum pump connections in Step 2 and pump up several inches of vacuum. The gauge reading should stay at zero.

4. If the SAVM fails any of these three functional steps, replace it.

EFE/EGR SYSTEM FUNCTIONAL TEST (All 1976 231/350/455-cu.-in. and Early Production California 260-cu.-in. Engines)

In order to determine if the EGR and EFE systems are working properly on 1976 installations, the following functional test procedure must be performed in the indicated order:

1. Engine coolant temperature must be below 120° F (±3° F). For test purposes on the 260-cu.-in. engine (early production), the EGR TCV must be bypassed (Fig. 6-16). Remove the TCV for testing at the end of this procedure.

2. Connect a vacuum gauge (A) to the

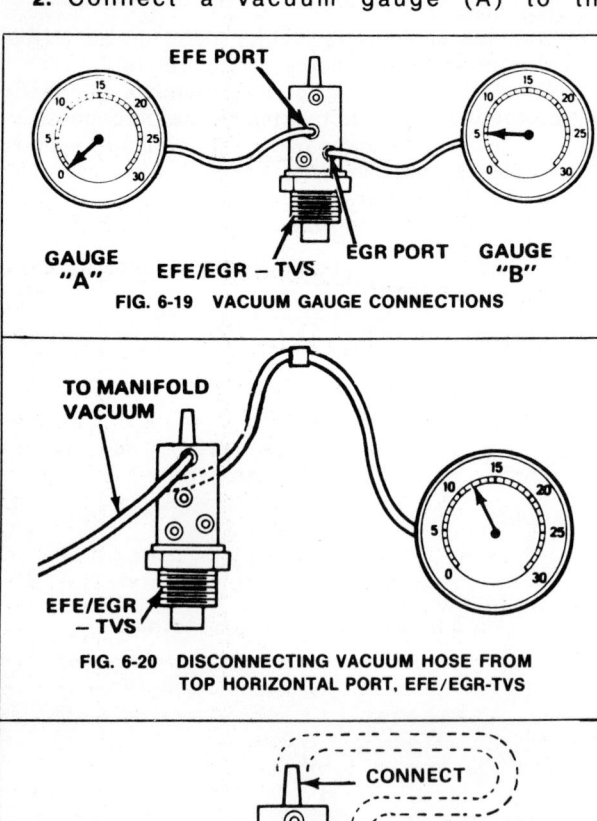

GAUGE "A"   EFE/EGR — TVS   EGR PORT   GAUGE "B"
FIG. 6-19 VACUUM GAUGE CONNECTIONS

TO MANIFOLD VACUUM

EFE/EGR — TVS
FIG. 6-20 DISCONNECTING VACUUM HOSE FROM TOP HORIZONTAL PORT, EFE/EGR-TVS

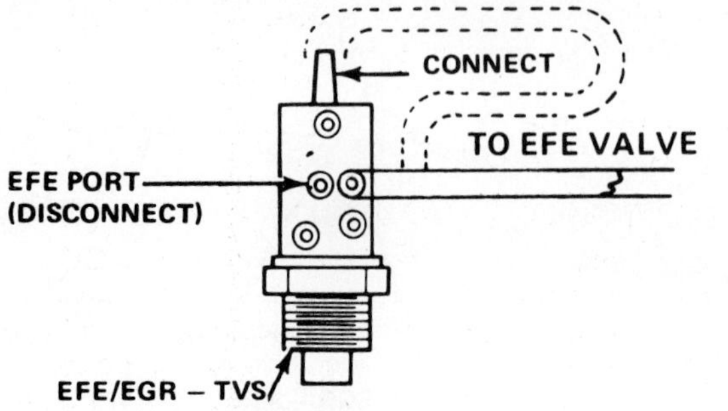

CONNECT
TO EFE VALVE
EFE PORT (DISCONNECT)
EFE/EGR — TVS
FIG. 6-21 CONNECTING EFE HOSE TO TOP PORT OF EFE/EGR-TVS

EFE/EGR-TVS-switch EFE port, and a second vacuum gauge (B) to the EGR port (Fig. 6-17).

3. With the fast-idle cam follower placed on the second step of the fast idle cam, start the engine, set the parking brake and block the drive wheels.

4. Read both gauges. Gauge A should indicate manifold vacuum and gauge B should show no vacuum (Fig. 6-18). If either gauge does not read correctly, replace the EFE/EGR-TVS.

5. Let the engine run long enough to switch the EFE/EGR-TVS internally (5-10 minutes). Gauge readings should change so that "A" shows no vacuum and "B" reads ported vacuum (Fig. 6-19).

6. Disconnect vacuum gauge "A" and connect it to the top port on the TVS. Gauge should now read manifold vacuum (Fig. 6-20).

7. Stop the engine. If the system checks out good so far, skip to Step 9. If Step 6 was unsatisfactory, continue to the next procedure.

8. Disconnect the vacuum gauge from the top TVS port, and connect it to the vacuum hose normally fitted to that port. Start the engine. Gauge should read manifold vacuum. If it does not, check the hose for a plug or leak and replace/repair as required.

9. Replace the fast-idle cam follower on the second step of the fast idle cam, and start the engine.

10. Remove the vacuum line from the EGR valve and watch the valve stem for downward movement with a slight concurrent increase in engine speed. If the stem does not move downward and engine speed does not increase, replace the EGR valve.

11. Reconnect the EGR vacuum line to the valve, and disconnect the EFE port on the EFE/EGR-TVS, connecting the hose to the top port (Fig. 6-21).

12. Start the engine and watch the EFE valve. Remove/replace the hose several times; EFE valve linkage should move back and forth. If it does not (and there is vacuum present), replace the valve.

13. Stop the engine and reconnect all vacuum lines properly.

14. The remainder of the procedure concerns the EGR TCV valve removed from the California 260-cu.-in. (early production) engine. Connect a hand vacuum pump with gauge to the EFE/EGR-TVS side of the EGR TCV.

15. Apply a vacuum. If the valve does not hold it, replace the valve. If it holds, continue the procedure.

16. Warm the valve to 61° F—the vacuum gauge should drop to zero vacuum. If it does, the TCV is operating correctly and can be reinstalled on the engine and the bypass removed. If it does not drop to zero, install a new valve.

DISTRIBUTOR ADVANCE/RETARD SYSTEM FUNCTIONAL TEST

1. Start engine and bring to normal operating temperature. Connect a timing light and check initial timing. It should coincide with that specified on the emission control decal.

2. Disconnect the temperature switch connector located at the coolant outlet housing. This causes an open in the system at normal operating temperature and should result in no change in engine timing.

3. Ground the connector and timing should decrease by about 6°. If it does not, inspect all hoses and wiring for poor connections and/or damage. Proceed to Step 4 if no defects are found.

4. Connect a vacuum gauge to the advance/retard

solenoid outlet port. There should be no vacuum reading unless the solenoid is defective. Before assuming it to be satisfactory, let the engine cool and apply 12 volts to the solenoid connector. The vacuum gauge should read 12 or more ins. Hg.

5. With engine coolant below 120° F, turn the ignition key ON and test solenoid connector with a voltmeter. A reading of 12 volts indicates that the spark control relay is good.

6. Test both sides of the dual-diaphragm vacuum advance unit on the distributor. Draw at least 12 ins. Hg and watch the vacuum unit linkage for movement. If the vacuum reading does not hold, or if the linkage does not move, the diaphragm is defective.

EMISSION SYSTEM COMPONENT REPLACEMENT

AIR CLEANER ASSEMBLY

The air cleaner assembly is not serviceable; if the damper door is malfunctioning, the entire unit must be replaced. The vacuum motor and the air cleaner sensor are replaceable.

VACUUM MOTOR

1. Drill out the center of the two spot welds holding the vacuum motor to the snorkel tube. Use a 1/16-in. drill— *do not* center punch.

2. Enlarge the holes to 5/32-in. Be careful not to damage or distort the air cleaner snorkel.

3. Remove the vacuum-motor retainer strap and lift the vacuum motor, tilting it to one side in order to unhook the linkage at the control door.

4. Drill a 7/64-in. hole in the snorkel tube at the center of the retaining strap end which faces the air cleaner housing.

5. Install a new vacuum motor assembly, using the mounting strap retainer and sheetmetal screw provided with the new motor. Screw must not interfere with the damper assembly operation—shorten if necessary.

AIR CLEANER SENSOR

1. Pry the two sensor retaining clips free and remove the vacuum lines from the sensor.

2. Note the position of the old sensor—the new unit must be installed in the same position to avoid possible interference with the air cleaner element—then remove the old sensor.

3. Install the new sensor and gasket in the air cleaner and replace the retaining clips while supporting the sensor around the center rim to prevent damage to the temperature sensing spring.

4. Replace the vacuum lines.

AIR PUMP REMOVAL/INSTALLATION

TO REMOVE

1. Disconnect the pump and valve hoses.

2. Loosen the pump-to-bracket mounting bolts, and remove the pump drive belt.

3. Remove the pulley-to-hub bolts, and remove the pulley.

4. Remove the air pump from the engine.

TO INSTALL

1. Position the pump on the mounting bracket. Line up the holes and install the bolts loosely.

2. Fit the pulley to the hub and tighten the bolts 72 to 108 in.-lbs.

3. Install the pump belt over the pulley and move the pump until the belt is tensioned to 60-85 lbs. Tighten the bracket bolts.

4. Reconnect the pump and valve hoses.

CENTRIFUGAL FILTER FAN REPLACEMENT

1. Remove the air pump from the engine.

2. Pull the fan from the hub with needlenose pliers. Although it is seldom possible to remove the fan without damage, take care not to let the plastic fragments enter the air intake hole.

3. Draw the new fan evenly into place, using the pulley and bolts as tools. Torque the bolts alternately. Outer edge of the fan must slip into the housing.

4. Replace the pump on the engine. Until the outer diameter sealing lip has worn in, a new fan may be noisy.

DIVERTER VALVE REPLACEMENT

1. Remove the hoses from the diverter valve.

2. Remove the two screws which hold the valve to the pump.

3. Remove the valve and gasket material from the pump. Do not reinstall the valve with a gasket.

4. Fit a new valve to the pump, install the screws and torque 120 to 160 in.-lbs.

5. Connect the hoses to the valve.

CHECK VALVE REPLACEMENT

1. Release the clamp and disconnect the air hose from the check valve, then unscrew and remove the valve.

2. Reinstall and tighten the check valve, then replace the air hose.

EGR VALVE REPLACEMENT

1. Disconnect the EGR-valve vacuum line.

2. Remove the bolt(s) holding the valve to the manifold, and remove the valve.

3. Install a new gasket and valve in the manifold, and tighten the bolt(s).

4. Reconnect the EGR vacuum line to the valve.

CADILLAC

1970-71 Emission Systems

POSITIVE CRANKCASE VENTILATION (PCV)

The PCV system **(Fig. 6-22)** is designed to prevent hydrocarbon contaminants from escaping into the atmosphere. Crankcase vapors are routed through a vacuum-controlled vent on the right rocker-arm cover and into the intake manifold, where they are mixed with the air/fuel mixture and burned in the combustion process. A crankcase-ventilating breather assembly with filter is located between the air cleaner and the left rocker-arm cover and supplies air to the crankcase ventilating system. When the engine is running, air enters the PCV system through the air cleaner and breather, and flows into the left rocker-arm cover and into the valve lifter area, where it combines with the unburned air/fuel mixture and blowby gases. The fumes are then drawn through the right rocker-arm cover and PCV valve into the base of the carburetor and intake manifold.

CONTROLLED COMBUSTION SYSTEM (CCS)

A series of engine modifications, CCS uses carburetor/choke/distributor calibrations and an increased engine-operating temperature to reduce emissions. Ignition timing is retarded, and carburetors are calibrated to run on a leaner air/fuel mixture. A thermostatically controlled air cleaner keeps the temperature of the air entering the carburetor at approximately

130° F, reducing engine icing in cold-weather climates and giving better engine warm-up.

TRANSMISSION CONTROLLED SPARK ADVANCE (TCS)

An oil pressure switch in the transmission direct-clutch circuit is pressurized when the transmission is shifted into third or high gear. Oil pressure opens the switch, transmitting an electrical signal to the solenoid valve inserted in the ported-carburetor-to-distributor-vacuum line. The solenoid valve then closes, shutting off vacuum to the distributor and bleeding off any vacuum in the line.

On 1971 Cadillacs, the TCS system is changed to bypass the solenoid in the PARK and NEUTRAL positions. This permits distributor advance control through a thermal vacuum switch (TVS) to prevent overheating when driving in heavy or slow traffic. The result is a spark advance at fast idle on 1971 Cadillacs, but none on 1970 models.

AIR INJECTION REACTOR (AIR)

This system is fitted to all 1971 Cadillacs. It consists of a belt-driven air pump, diverter valve **(Fig. 6-23)** and

silencer assembly, check valve, special intake-manifold and cylinder-head assemblies, and the necessary connecting hoses. The AIR pump is located at the lower right front of the engine. Intake air passes through a centrifugal fan at the front of the pump, and is delivered to the intake manifold. During sudden deceleration, vacuum causes a diverter valve at the back of the pump to open, passing pump air into the atmosphere. A screw-on check valve fitted to the air injection manifold near the right cylinder head contains a one-way diaphragm which prevents hot exhaust gases from backing up in the hose and damaging the pump during periods of pump belt failure, excessive system pressure or hose ruptures (some later models use a check valve in each air injection manifold).

EVAPORATIVE LOSS CONTROL SYSTEM (ELC)

Vapor caused by fuel evaporation in the fuel tank is not vented into the atmosphere, but transferred instead to the engine compartment by a vapor line and fed directly into the running engine, or stored in an activated charcoal canister when the engine is not running **(Fig. 6-24)**. Liquid fuel is caught by a vapor separator and returned to the tank.

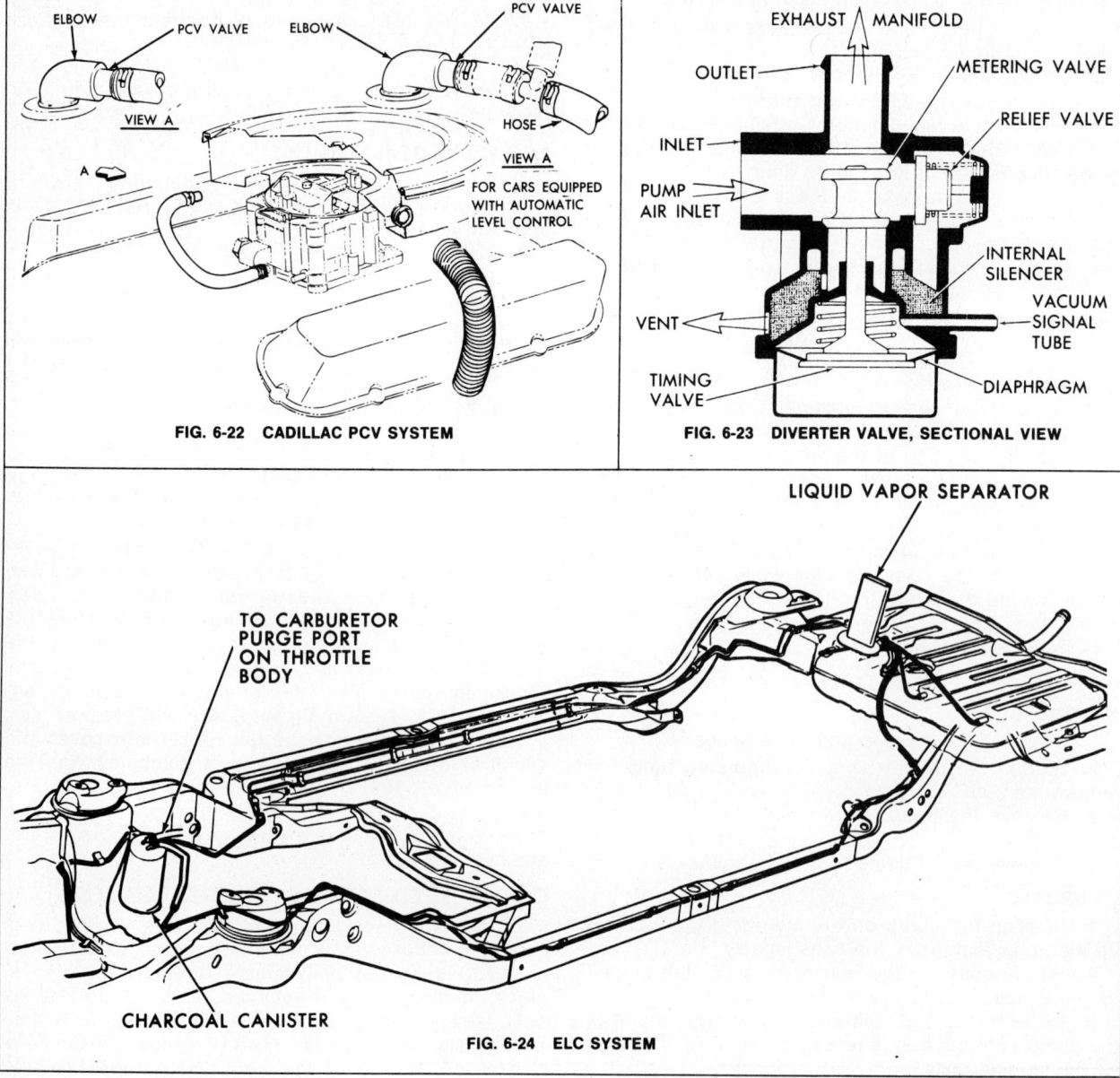

FIG. 6-22 CADILLAC PCV SYSTEM

FIG. 6-23 DIVERTER VALVE, SECTIONAL VIEW

FIG. 6-24 ELC SYSTEM

CADILLAC
1972 Emission Systems

The Positive Crankcase Ventilation (PCV), Air Injection Reactor (AIR) and Evaporative Loss Control (ELC) systems are the same as on 1970-71 Cadillacs.

CONTROLLED COMBUSTION SYSTEM (CCS)

The thermostatically controlled air cleaner is recalibrated to keep the temperature of the air entering the carburetor at approximately 105° F, instead of the 130° F setting of previous years.

SPEED CONTROL SWITCH (SCS)

This distributor vacuum-advance control (Fig. 6-25) replaces the TCS system previously used. The speed control switch controls spark advance at low speeds, shutting off vacuum to the distributor vacuum-advance unit during speeds up to 33±2 mph. A vacuum solenoid positioned by the ignition coil responds to the speed control switch to control the path of vacuum. As the car approaches 33±2 mph, the SCS contacts open, breaking the circuit and de-energizing the vacuum solenoid. The full carburetor vacuum signal is now sent to the distributor vacuum-advance unit, allowing it to function normally for fuel economy. When the car's speed is reduced below 25 mph, the contacts inside the SCS close and the now-energized solenoid again eliminates vacuum to the distributor, shutting off spark advance.

CADILLAC
1973-74 Emission Systems

The same Positive Crankcase Ventilation (PCV) and

Air Injection Reactor (AIR) systems used in 1970-71 remain for these years.

EVAPORATIVE LOSS CONTROL SYSTEM

The previously designated ELC system is now called ECS. The vapor separator is replaced by a dome at the top of the fuel tank, which performs the same function.

CONTROLLED COMBUSTION SYSTEM (CCS)

This system is discontinued, except for the use of the Thermac Air Cleaner.

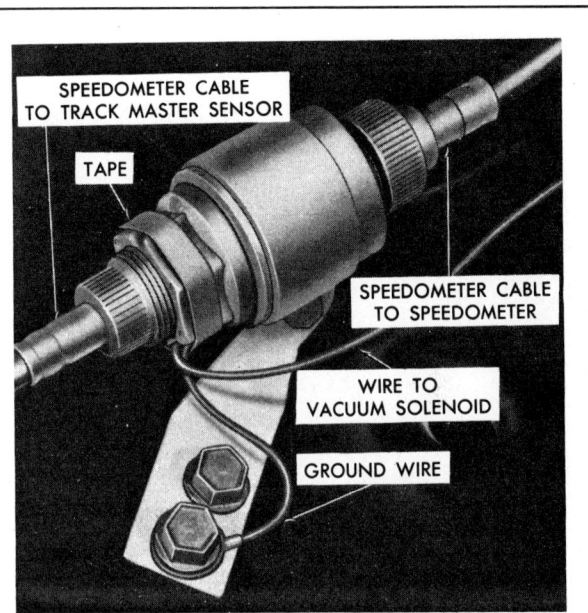

FIG. 6-25   TYPICAL SPEED CONTROL SWITCH

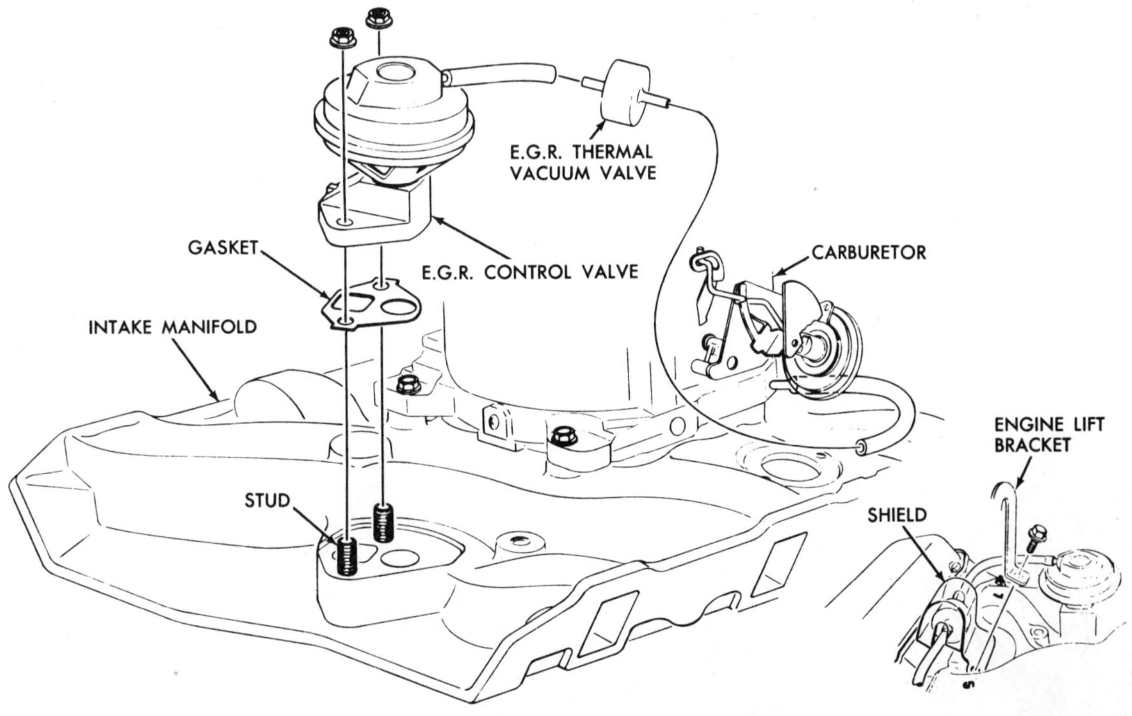

FIG. 6-26   EGR VALVE MOUNTING

EXHAUST GAS RECIRCULATION (EGR)

A vacuum-operated recirculation control valve **(Fig. 6-26)**, mounted at the right rear of the intake manifold, regulates the amount of exhaust gases and the duration of time they enter the intake manifold. When the throttle valves are opened beyond the idle position, vacuum is applied against the EGR-valve actuating diaphragm. At approximately 2 ins. of vacuum, the diaphragm moves upward against the spring tension, and is in a full-up position at approximately 7 ins. of vacuum **(Fig. 6-27)**. As the diaphragm moves upward against spring pressure, it opens the valve in the exhaust gas port, which meters exhaust gas into the intake manifold. The valve remains closed during engine idle, when excessive exhaust gases added to the air/fuel mixture would cause a rough, engine-idle condition, and is delayed at low temperatures by a bi-metal temperature switch positioned inline between the carburetor and the EGR valve. Below 60° F, engine metal temperature, the EGR bi-metal valve is closed, blocking vacuum to the EGR valve; above 60° F, the bi-metal valve is open, allowing EGR ported vacuum to the EGR valve.

EXHAUST BACKPRESSURE TRANSDUCER

All 1974 Cadillacs sold in California are equipped with a backpressure transducer **(Fig. 6-28)** in addition to the EGR valve and TVV valve. The transducer receives its exhaust pressure signal from a small tube leading to the spacer under the EGR valve. It is also connected through the TVV to the EGR vacuum port in the carburetor throttle body, receiving vacuum which it modulates to activate the EGR valve. At idle, exhaust pressure is low and vacuum is zero, resulting in no EGR flow. As airflow increases, so does exhaust pressure; when it is sufficient to overcome the transducer spring preload, the bleed valve is closed, routing the vacuum signal to the EGR valve to force it open. Exhaust pressure decreases as the EGR valve opens, reaching a balanced condition which produces optimum precision in EGR operation.

CADILLAC

1975-76 Emission Systems

The Positive Crankcase Ventilation System (PCV) remains the same as that for 1970-71 models.

AIR INJECTION REACTOR (AIR)

AIR use is restricted to Cadillacs sold in California and to commercial chassis when fitted with the 145-amp alternator.

EVAPORATIVE CONTROL SYSTEM (ECS)

The vapor canister includes a third nipple to accommodate the mechanical fuel bowl vent on 1975-76 carburetors **(Fig. 6-29)**.

EXHAUST GAS RECIRCULATION (EGR)

EGR bi-metal valve changeover temperature is now 64.5° F ± 3.5° F.

EXHAUST BACKPRESSURE TRANSDUCER

This is fitted only on 1975-76 cars using the AIR system or the electronic fuel injection (EFI) option.

CATALYTIC CONVERTER

All 1975-76 Cadillacs are fitted with a catalytic converter to improve fuel economy and drivability.

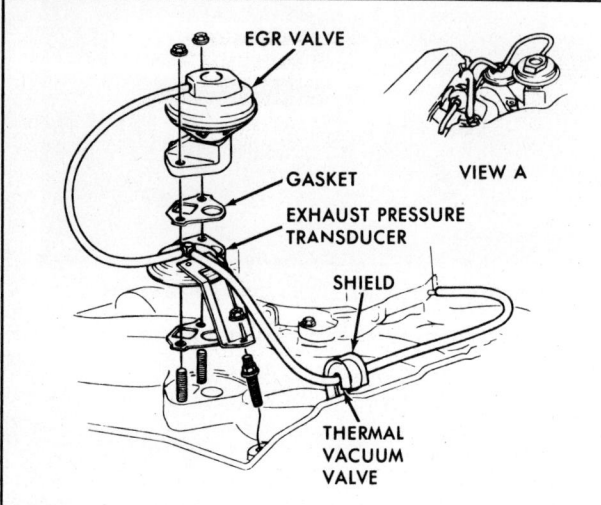

FIG. 6-28 EXHAUST BACKPRESSURE TRANSDUCER MOUNTING

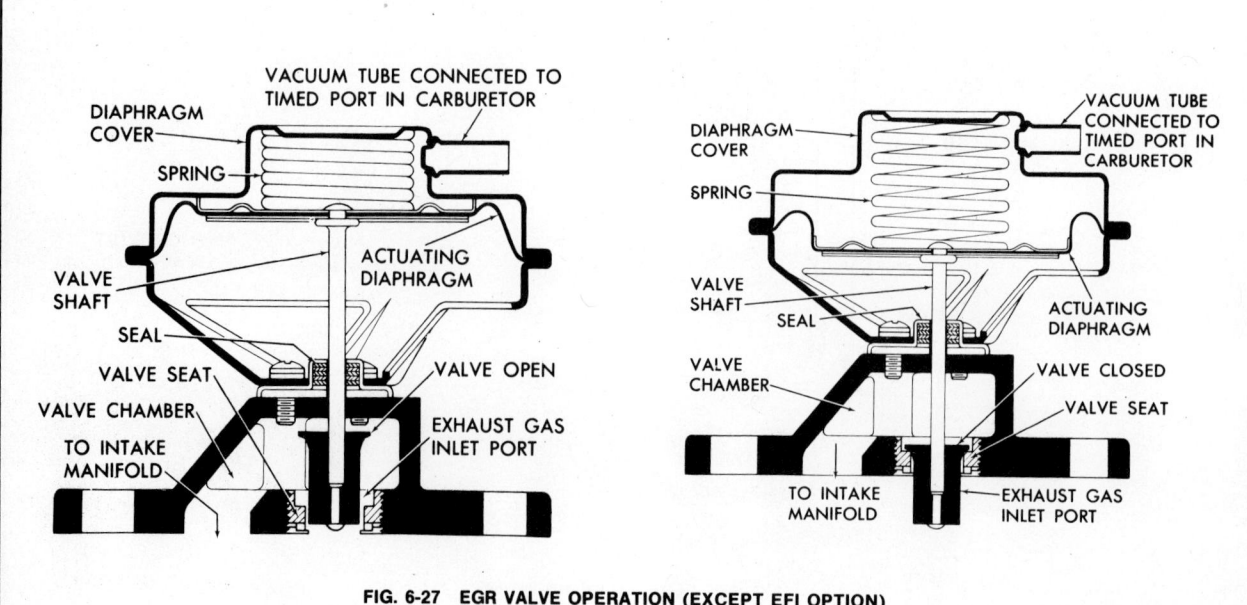

FIG. 6-27 EGR VALVE OPERATION (EXCEPT EFI OPTION)

EARLY FUEL EVAPORATION (EFE)

Installed at the junction of the right-hand exhaust pipe and manifold on all 1975-76 Cadillacs, except those with the EFI option, the EFE valve **(Fig. 6-30)** promotes quick heating of incoming fuel by directing exhaust gas flow through the exhaust crossover passage in the intake manifold during cold engine operation. Heating of the intake manifold provides better fuel vaporization during warm-up. A thermostatic vacuum switch (TVS), located in the upper left front of the cylinder block, allows manifold vacuum to the EFE valve when the coolant temperature is below 150° F. This closes the EFE valve, directing exhaust gases through the crossover passage. As the coolant temperature reaches approximately 150° F, the TVS changes its position to block off manifold vacuum and open the EFE valve to pass exhaust gases through the exhaust system normally.

THERMAL VACUUM SWITCH (TVS)

Three variations are used with 1976 Cadillac models:

1. Non-California Carburetors—A two-port TVS is located in the upper left front of the cylinder block, and controls EFE valve operation, according to engine coolant temperature.

2. California Carburetors—A five-port TVS is used to perform the function of No. 1, and to prevent ported vacuum from reaching the EGR TVV at temperatures below 120° F.

3. All EFI Options—A three-port TVS is used to prevent engine overheating under conditions of very high temperature operation. The three fittings are connected to manifold vacuum, ported vacuum above the throttle valves, and the distributor vacuum-advance diaphragm. When coolant temperature exceeds 220° F, the TVS switches from ported to manifold vacuum, advancing the ignition timing to full vacuum advance at idle.

CADILLAC

1977 Emission Systems

The Positive Crankcase Ventilation (PCV) system remains the same as 1970-71. The Air-Injection Reactor (AIR) system is that used in 1970-71, but use is extended to all EFI-equipped vehicles. The following are carryovers from 1975-76: Evaporative Control system (ECS), Catalytic Converter, Thermal Vacuum Switch (TVS).

EARLY FUEL EVAPORATION (EFE)

The EFE-TVS is recalibrated to 120° F.

EXHAUST GAS RECIRCULATION (EGR)

Three types of valves are used for 1977:

1. Ported vacuum-operated valve on all non-California carbureted cars.

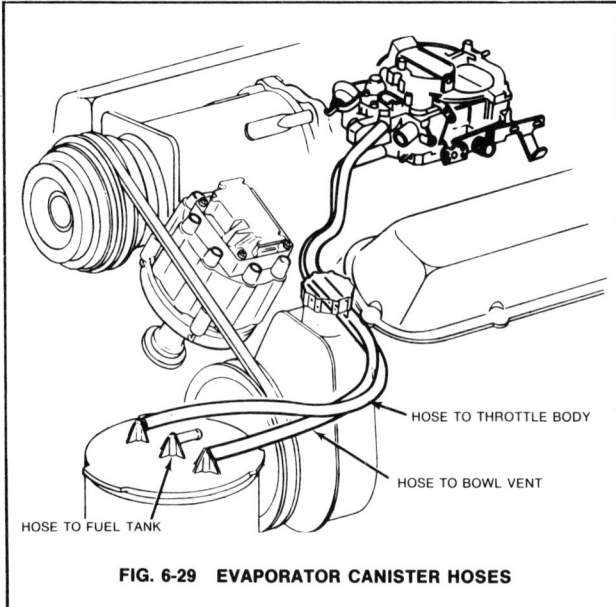

HOSE TO THROTTLE BODY
HOSE TO BOWL VENT
HOSE TO FUEL TANK

FIG. 6-29 EVAPORATOR CANISTER HOSES

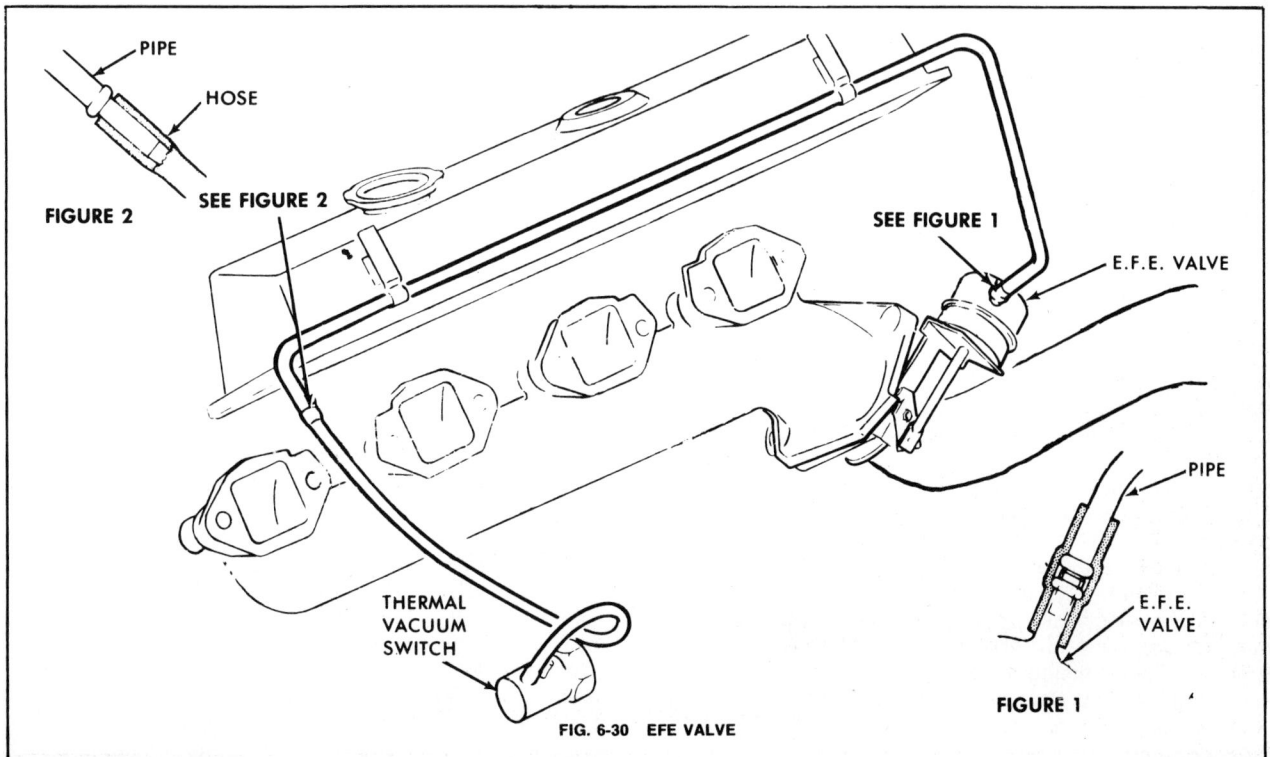

PIPE
HOSE
FIGURE 2
SEE FIGURE 2
SEE FIGURE 1
E.F.E. VALVE
PIPE
E.F.E. VALVE
FIGURE 1
THERMAL VACUUM SWITCH

FIG. 6-30 EFE VALVE

2. Backpressure-operated valve on all California carbureted cars (Fig. 6-75A).

3. Standard valve operated by exhaust pressure transducer on all EFI cars (Fig. 6-28). Four different orifice gaskets may be used, depending upon calibration.

Two temperature-sensitive control valves are installed in the EGR valve vacuum line. A TVS in the coolant crossover blocks vacuum at temperatures under 120° F. A TVV in the right cylinder head blocks vacuum when engine temperature is below 65° F. Both control valves must switch before EGR is activated.

CADILLAC

1978 Emission Systems

The Positive Crankcase Ventilation (PCV) system remains the same as 1970-71. The Air-Injection Reactor (AIR) system is that used in 1970-71, but use is extended to all altitude cars. The following are carryovers from 1975-76: Catalytic Converter, Thermal Vacuum Switch (TVS).

EVAPORATIVE CONTROL SYSTEM (ECS)

A two-stage vapor storage canister is used to absorb and store vapors from the carburetor and fuel tank.

EARLY FUEL EVAPORATION (EFE)

A new EFE-TVS is installed in the thermostat housing of all carbureted engines. The switch is recalibrated to open at 165° F instead of 120° F This allows the EFE valve to remain on longer, resulting in better cold drivability.

EXHAUST GAS RECIRCULATION (EGR)

The integral backpressure transducer EGR valve on carbureted engines is recalibrated to permit EGR at lower speeds. This is accomplished by relocating the control valve spring from above the below the valve diaphragm. Although the new valve appears identical to the previous type, the older valve should not be substituted for the new one.

VACUUM CONTROLS

A secondary vacuum break TVS is used with all 1978 non-California carbureted engines to improve cold drivability. This TVS is installed in the air cleaner and overrides the secondary vacuum break at temperatures below 62° F.

ELECTRONIC SPARK SELECTION (ESS) SYSTEM

Standard on all 1978 Sevilles, the system advances or retards the entire spark curve under predetermined operating conditions. The system consists of an electronic decoder and a modified HEI distributor, now referred to as an ESS distributor. Existing components provide input to the electronic decoder in order to identify basic engine conditions which help determine ignition timing for any operating mode. The fuel economy switch, EGR solenoid and ignition switch furnish data about engine vacuum, coolant temperature and engine cranking, respectively. The modified distributor pickup coil provides the decoder with engine speed and ignition timing data.

A 5-pin module is used, with the additional pin receiving the electronic decoder's signal—which may or may not delay the current shut-off in the coil's primary winding. Spark timing retard is used to improve hot restarting, and on California cars, to shorten converter warm-up time. Spark advance during cruising improves fuel economy.

CADILLAC
1979 EMISSION SYSTEMS

All 1979 emission controls are carryover from 1978 except as noted below:

ELECTRONIC SPARK SELECTION (ESS) SYSTEM

Use is extended to Eldorado, Seville, Limousine, Commercial Chassis and carbureted California Cadillac models. The Eldorado ESS system is identical to that of the Seville in operation, except that maximum advance is set at 1200 rpm (Seville, 1450 rpm). Other Cadillac models require an engine speed of 1350 rpm to obtain maximum advance. As these carbureted cars do not have an EGR solenoid, a three-way coolant temperature switch is used to send a signal to the ESS decoder for spark retard during cold engine operation, and to prevent excessive advance during hot engine operation.

THREE-WAY CONVERTER

Used on all California Sevilles (AIR system is not used on these cars).

EXHAUST GAS RECIRCULATION (EGR)

Revised and recalibrated EGR orifice gaskets are used on EFI-equipped cars.

INTAKE MANIFOLD

Riser tubes have been added to the floor of the intake manifold used with carbureted cars. The risers are designed for more efficient distribution of exhaust gases.

EMISSION SYSTEM TEST PROCEDURES

PCV TEST

1. Remove PCV valve from the rocker arm cover.
2. Start the engine and run at idle.
3. Place a thumb over the valve end to check for vacuum. If there is no vacuum at the valve, inspect for a plugged hose.
4. Shut the engine off. Shake the valve and listen for the rattle of the check needle in the valve. If no rattle is heard, replace the valve.

THERMAC-AIR-CLEANER VACUUM MOTOR TEST

1. Inspect for plugged, kinked or damaged hoses, and then check for proper connections.
2. With the engine off (cold), the damper door in the snorkel tube should block off the cold air inlet (Fig. 6-31). If not, look for binding linkage.
3. Apply 7-9 ins. of vacuum to the diaphragm motor assembly. Damper door should completely close off the hot air duct (Fig. 6-32). If not, look for a vacuum leak and/or incorrect linkage hookup.
4. With vacuum still applied, clamp off the hose to trap vacuum in the diaphragm assembly. The damper door should continue to close off the hot air duct. If not, replace the diaphragm assembly.

THERMAC-AIR-CLEANER SENSOR TEST

1. Check cold air inlet with the engine off—it should be open.
2. Remove the air cleaner cover and tape a suitable thermometer to the air cleaner base next to the sensor. Replace the cover, but do not install the nut.
3. Start the engine; air cleaner temperature must be below 85° F. Damper door should close immediately.

4. When the damper starts to move open, remove the air cleaner cover immediately and record the temperature reading.

5. Replace the air cleaner cover and watch the damper movement.

6. When the damper has moved to a full open position, again remove the air cleaner cover and record the temperature.

7. Compare the readings obtained in Steps 4 and 6 with the following chart:

DAMPER POSITION	TEMPERATURE READING, (°F) 1970-71	TEMPERATURE READING, (°F) 1972-78
Starts to Open	85	85
Full Open	130	105

8. If the sensor does not operate the damper door correctly within the specified range, replace it.

TRANSMISSION CONTROLLED SPARK ADVANCE TEST

1. Connect an ignition timing light and tachometer.

2. Block up rear wheels, start the engine, place the transmission in DRIVE and position the fast idle cam to increase engine speed to 1500 rpm.

3. Check the timing mark—there should be no vacuum advance. A vacuum gauge connected to the distributor vacuum-advance line can also be used—the vacuum gauge should read zero.

4. Now shift the transmission into REVERSE. Make sure the parking brake is applied and that a wheel is blocked in front and back.

5. Check the timing mark or vacuum gauge at 1500 rpm. There should now be full vacuum advance.

6. If not, connect a continuity light between the two TCS solenoid terminals. The test lamp should remain off when the transmission is in REVERSE. The tester must not supply more than 0.8-amps current at 12 volts, or the transmission switch will be damaged. If the test lamp lights, look for a grounded wire between the solenoid and transmission; if the wire is not grounded, replace the transmission switch.

7. Shift the transmission into NEUTRAL—the light should go out. If it does not, check for an open circuit. If a circuit is not open, replace the transmission switch.

8. Repeat Steps 6 and 7 with a new switch installed. If vacuum is still not present, replace the TCS solenoid.

SPEED CONTROL SWITCH SYSTEM TEST

To test SCS operation, the Eldorado must be driven while the test procedure is run—use test lamp leads long enough to allow the lamp to be positioned on the fender, cowl or other visible area outside the engine compartment, with the hood down in position. Other Cadillac models are rear-wheel drive, and the test procedure may be run on a hoist, providing that proper safety precautions are taken.

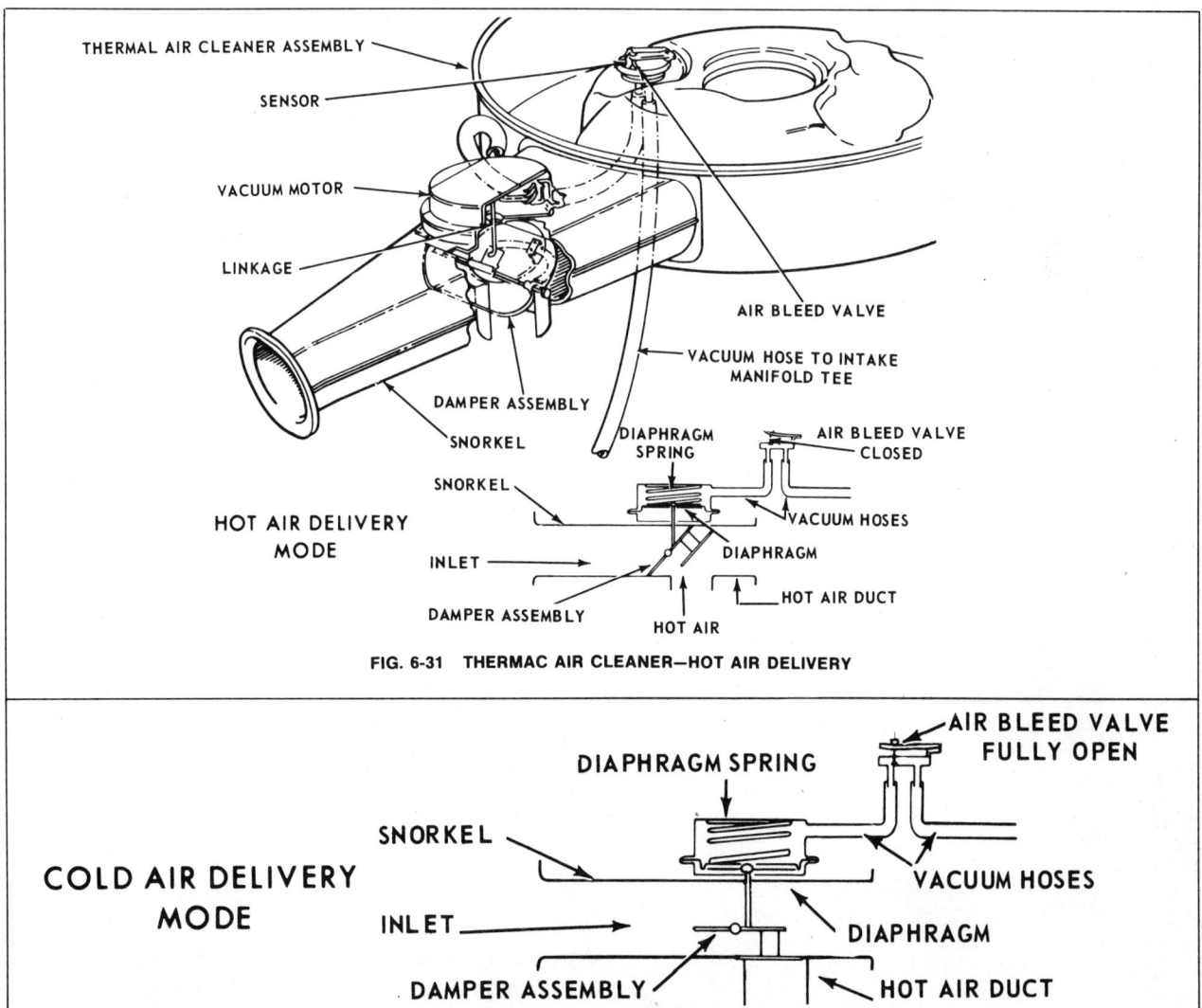

FIG. 6-31 THERMAC AIR CLEANER—HOT AIR DELIVERY

FIG. 6-32 THERMAC AIR CLEANER—COLD AIR DELIVERY

1. Disconnect the double connector at the vacuum solenoid, and connect a test lamp between the two leads.

2. Tape the test lamp to a visible area outside the engine compartment and close the hood.

3. With rear-wheel-drive models on a hoist, or the Eldorado on the road, the test lamp should *go out* at 33±2 mph.

4. Decrease speed and the test lamp should *come on* as speed descends below 25 mph.

5. If the test lamp does not function as indicated in Steps 3 and 4, connect a jumper wire between the 18B wire and ground.

6. If the lamp lights, replace the switch. If it does not light, the circuit is open ahead of the solenoid. Continue the test procedure.

7. Connect a jumper wire between one solenoid terminal and ground.

8. Quickly touch a jumper wire from the positive battery terminal to the other solenoid terminal. A click should be heard each time the jumper wire is connected. If not, replace the solenoid.

EXHAUST GAS RECIRCULATION (EGR) VALVE FUNCTIONAL TEST

1. Remove the air cleaner and plug the manifold vacuum fitting.

2. Disconnect and plug the distributor vacuum-advance line at the distributor and the EGR valve line at the EGR valve.

3. With the air conditioner off, the drive wheels blocked and the transmission in PARK, connect a tachometer and start the engine. Run until the engine reaches normal operating temperature, then position the fast-idle cam follower on the second step of the fast idle cam and note the engine rpm.

4. Connect a hand vacuum pump with gauge to the EGR valve and apply at least 5 ins. vacuum. The EGR valve diaphragm should rise and the engine speed drop at least 250 rpm.

5. If the engine speed does not drop as specified, remove the carburetor and clean the intake manifold EGR ports and EGR valve assembly.

6. Reinstall the EGR valve and repeat Step 4. If engine speed still does not drop as specified, replace the EGR valve.

7. Shut the engine off, remove the tachometer, and reinstall the air cleaner and the vacuum lines to the manifold, distributor and EGR valve.

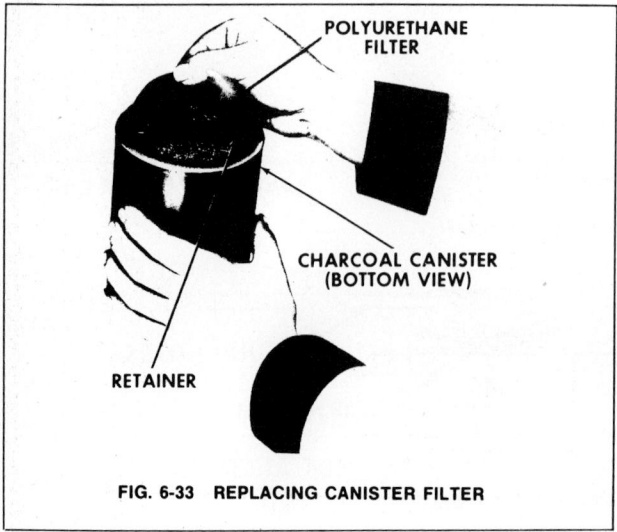

FIG. 6-33 REPLACING CANISTER FILTER

EMISSION SYSTEM COMPONENT REPLACEMENT

AIR CLEANER ASSEMBLY

The air cleaner assembly is not serviceable. If the damper door is malfunctioning, the entire unit must be replaced. The vacuum motor and the air cleaner sensor are replaceable.

VACUUM MOTOR

1. Remove the air cleaner from the engine and drill out the center of each spot weld holding the vacuum motor to the snorkel tube. Use a 1/16-in. drill—*do not* center-punch.

2. Enlarge the holes as required to remove the retainer strap, taking care not to damage or distort the snorkel tube.

3. Remove the retainer strap and lift the vacuum motor assembly slightly from the snorkel tube.

4. Tilt the motor to one side to disengage the valve link and to remove the vacuum motor.

5. Install a new vacuum motor assembly, connecting the link in the valve, and place the motor in position on the snorkel tube.

6. Replace the retainer strap over the new motor and fasten with two sheetmetal screws or pop-rivets. Screws must not interfere with damper assembly operation—shorten if necessary.

AIR CLEANER SENSOR

1. Pry the sensor retainer free, and remove the vacuum lines from the sensor.

2. Note the position of the old sensor—the new unit must be installed in the same position to avoid possible interference with the air cleaner element—then remove the old sensor.

3. Install the new sensor and gasket in the air cleaner, and replace the retainer while supporting the sensor around the center rim to prevent damage to the temperature sensing spring.

4. Replace the vacuum lines.

AIR PUMP REMOVAL/INSTALLATION

TO REMOVE

1. Disconnect the air hose and vacuum line from the pump diverter valve.

2. Remove the pump-to-hub screws, and remove the pulley and drive belt.

3. Remove the mounting bolt at the top of the air pump.

4. Remove the adjusting bolt from the bottom rear of the pump. Lift the pump and diverter valve from the engine as an assembly.

TO INSTALL

1. Lift the pump up through the clearance between the oil filter and the lower radiator hose, rotating it to pass the diverter valve over the oil filter.

2. Position the pump on the mounting bracket and loosely install the upper bolt.

3. Install the adjusting bolt at the lower pump rear—*do not* tighten yet.

4. Replace the pulley and drive belt, then adjust the belt to its proper tension.

5. Torque both mounting and adjusting bolts to 25 ft.-lbs.

6. Replace the air hose and vacuum line to the diverter valve.

CENTRIFUGAL FILTER FAN REPLACEMENT

1. Remove the air pump from the engine.

2. Pull the fan from the hub using needlenose pliers.

Although it is seldom possible to remove the fan without damage, take care not to let the plastic fragments enter the air intake hole.

3. Draw the new fan evenly into place, using the pulley and three mounting screws as tools. Torque the screws alternately to 60 in.-lbs.; this will press the fan onto the hub properly.

4. Replace the pump on the engine. Until the outer diameter sealing lip has worn in, a new fan may be noisy.

DIVERTER VALVE REPLACEMENT

1. Remove the hose and vacuum line from the diverter valve.

2. Remove the two screws which hold the valve body to the pump.

3. Remove the valve and gasket material from the pump.

4. Position a new gasket, and fit the new valve to the pump, tightening the screws securely.

5. Connect the hose and vacuum line to the valve.

CHECK VALVE REPLACEMENT

1. Release the clamp and disconnect the air hose from the check valve, then unscrew and remove the valve from the manifold fitting.

2. Reinstall and tighten the check valve, then replace the air hose.

EGR VALVE REPLACEMENT

1. Disconnect the EGR-valve vacuum line.

2. Remove the bolt(s) holding the valve to the manifold, and remove the valve.

3. Install a new gasket and valve in the manifold, and tighten the bolt(s).

4. Reconnect the EGR vacuum line to the valve.

ECS VAPOR STORAGE CANISTER FILTER REPLACEMENT (Fig. 6-33)

1. Disconnect the top canister hoses, and remove the single screw holding the canister strap bracket to the radiator cradle.

2. Remove the strap and canister from the radiator cradle.

3. Turn the canister over and squeeze the polyurethane filter from under the retainer bar.

4. Squeeze a new filter under the retainer bar and center it on the canister bottom, tucking the edges under the canister lip.

5. Replace the canister on the strap bracket, with its top fittings facing the engine, and secure the strap with the screw.

6. Connect the hoses to the canister nipples. The small diameter hose goes to the carburetor and the large diameter hose to the tank.

CHEVROLET
1970 Emission Systems

POSITIVE CRANKCASE VENTILATION (PCV)

A sealed oil-filler cap prevents crankcase gases from escaping under no-vacuum conditions. A tube from the air cleaner goes to the rocker cover, carrying fresh air down into the crankcase. From that point, blowby gases go through the hose into the PCV valve (**Fig. 6-34**) and then into the manifold. When the PCV system is under zero vacuum, there is no suction on the crankcase, but the gases go from the rocker cover, through the hose and into the air cleaner, where they are drawn into the engine.

CONTROLLED COMBUSTION SYSTEM (CCS)

A series of engine modification, CCS (**Fig. 6-35**) uses carburetor/distributor calibrations to reduce emissions. Temperature-controlled air cleaner keeps the temperature of the air entering the carburetor at approximately 100° F to lean the carburetor.

EVAPORATION EMISSION CONTROL (EEC)

Vapor caused by fuel evaporation in the fuel tank is no longer vented into the atmosphere, but transferred instead to the engine compartment by a vapor line and fed directly into the running engine, or stored in an activated charcoal accumulator (canister) when the engine is not running (**Fig. 6-36**). The system includes a

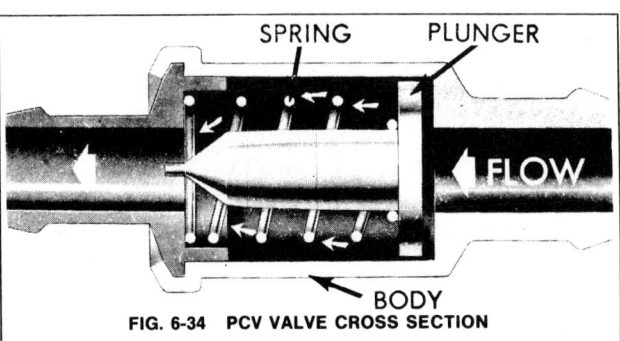

FIG. 6-34 PCV VALVE CROSS SECTION

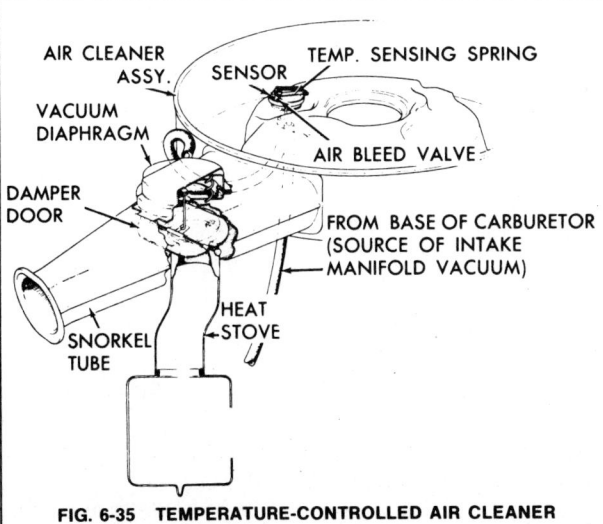

FIG. 6-35 TEMPERATURE-CONTROLLED AIR CLEANER

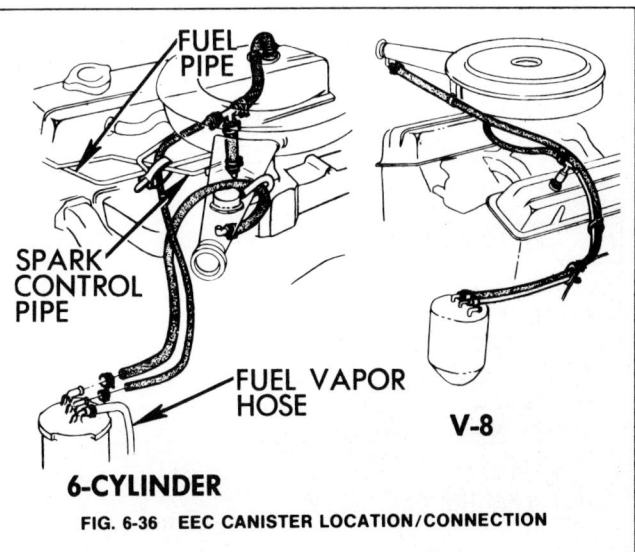

FIG. 6-36 EEC CANISTER LOCATION/CONNECTION

pressure-vacuum, tank-filler-neck cap, a fuel-tank vent/overfill protector, a liquid vapor separator positioned forward and above the fuel tank, and a canister with purge valve and filter.

TRANSMISSION CONTROLLED SPARK ADVANCE (TCS)

Distributor advance is eliminated in low forward gears as shown in the chart in **Fig. 6-37.** When the solenoid vacuum switch is energized, vacuum to the distributor is shut off and the vacuum advance unit vented to the atmosphere by a clean air connection to the carburetor air hose, preventing the advance unit from becoming vacuum-locked at a particular advance position. A temperature override system provides full vacuum in all gears below a specified temperature; control is maintained by a thermostatic water-temperature switch which opens a closed relay in the solenoid-vacuum-switch system. A hot override switch is also used in some applications to provide full vacuum advance for better engine cooling under heavy, slow traffic conditions.

AIR INJECTION REACTOR (AIR)

The AIR system **(Fig. 6-38)** is fitted to some 1970 Chevrolet engines. It consists of a belt-driven air injection pump, an air diverter valve, one air injection tube for each cylinder, one check valve for inline and two check valves for V-8 engines, air manifold assemblies and the necessary connecting hoses. The AIR pump is located as shown in **Fig. 6-39.** Air passes through a centrifugal fan at the front of the pump and is delivered to the intake manifold. During sudden deceleration, vacuum causes a diverter valve **(Fig. 6-40)** at the back of the pump to open, passing pump air into the atmosphere. The check valve contains a one-way diaphragm

which prevents hot exhaust gases from backing up in the hose and damaging the pump during periods of pump belt failure, excessive system pressure or hose ruptures.

CHEVROLET

1971 Emission Systems

The following systems are identical to those used in 1970: Positive Crankcase Ventilation (PCV), Controlled Combustion System (CCS), Evaporation Emission Control System (EEC) and Air Injection Reactor (AIR).

TRANSMISSION CONTROLLED SPARK ADVANCE (TCS)

The vacuum solenoid used in 1970 is changed to a Combination Emissions Control (CEC) solenoid **(Fig. 6-41)** and has two functions: it controls distributor advance and acts as a deceleration throttle stop in high gear to reduce emissions. The CEC solenoid is controlled by a temperature switch, a transmission switch and a time delay relay, just as the 1970 system, but the time delay is extended from 15 to 20 seconds.

System operation is reversed from 1970. Instead of a normally open solenoid position to permit vacuum advance, and a closed position to block it, the CEC version is normally closed to block vacuum advance **(Fig. 6-42)** and opens when energized to permit vacuum advance **(Fig. 6-43).** The temperature switch overrides the system to permit vacuum advance regardless of gear when engine temperature is below 82° F **(Fig. 6-44).** Engines equipped with automatic transmissions and air conditioning use a solid-state timer to engage the air conditioner compressor for 3 seconds, after shutting the ignition off to prevent dieseling or run-on.

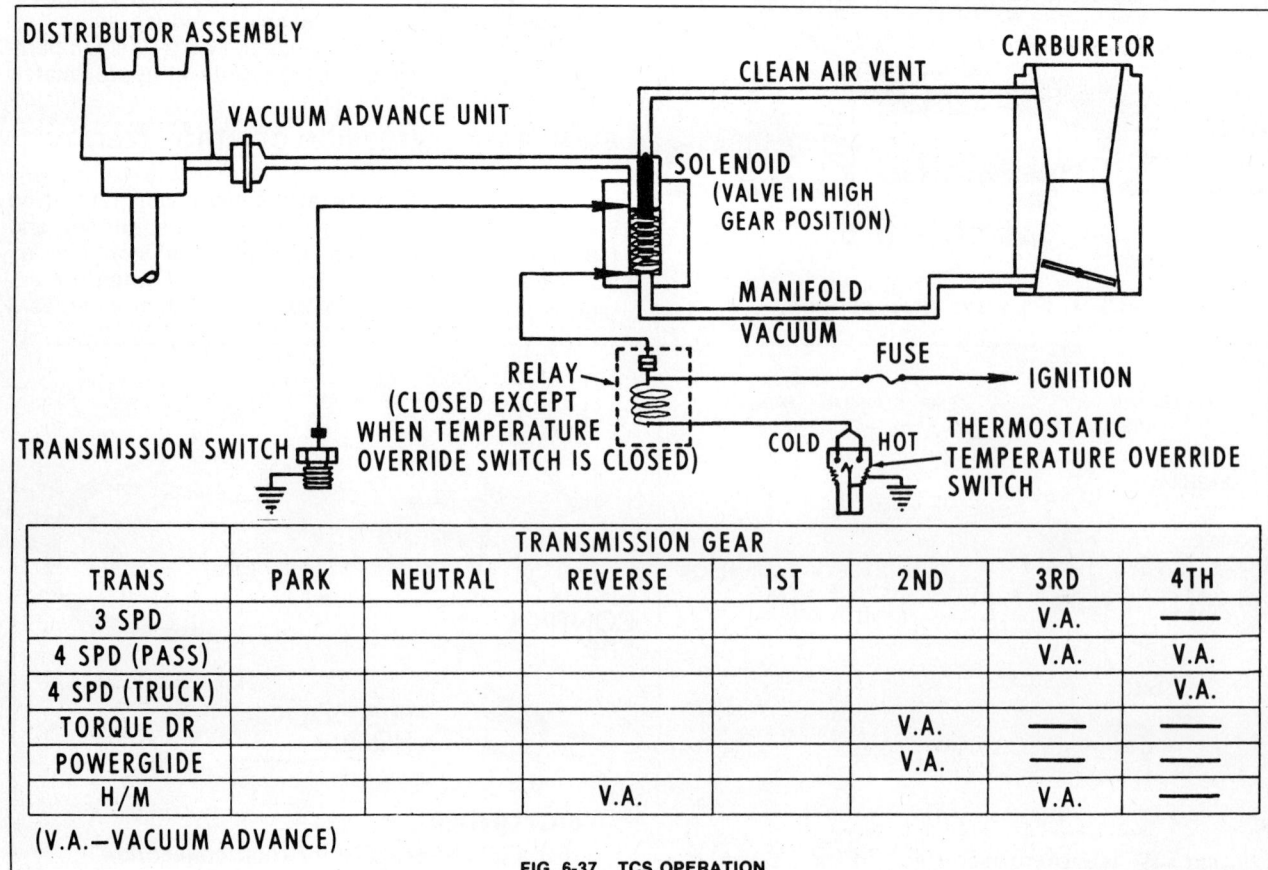

TRANSMISSION GEAR							
TRANS	PARK	NEUTRAL	REVERSE	1ST	2ND	3RD	4TH
3 SPD						V.A.	——
4 SPD (PASS)						V.A.	V.A.
4 SPD (TRUCK)							V.A.
TORQUE DR					V.A.	——	——
POWERGLIDE					V.A.	——	——
H/M			V.A.			V.A.	——

(V.A.—VACUUM ADVANCE)

FIG. 6-37 TCS OPERATION

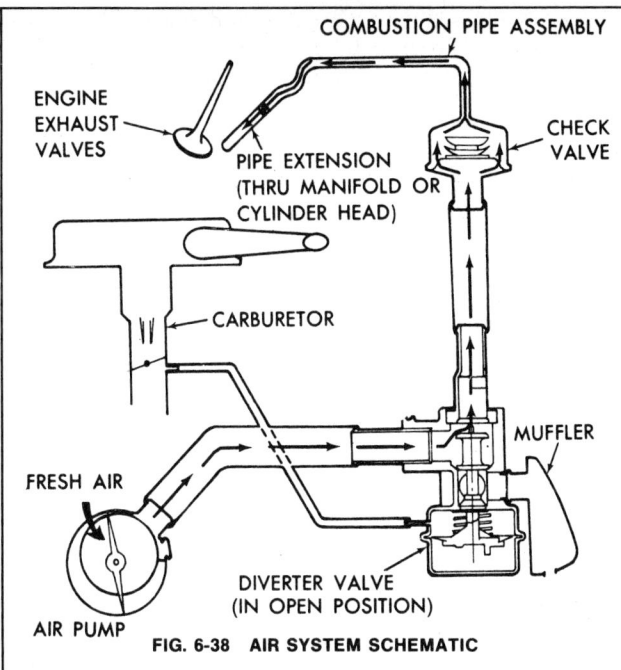

ENGINE EXHAUST VALVES

COMBUSTION PIPE ASSEMBLY

CHECK VALVE

PIPE EXTENSION (THRU MANIFOLD OR CYLINDER HEAD)

CARBURETOR

FRESH AIR

AIR PUMP

MUFFLER

DIVERTER VALVE (IN OPEN POSITION)

FIG. 6-38 AIR SYSTEM SCHEMATIC

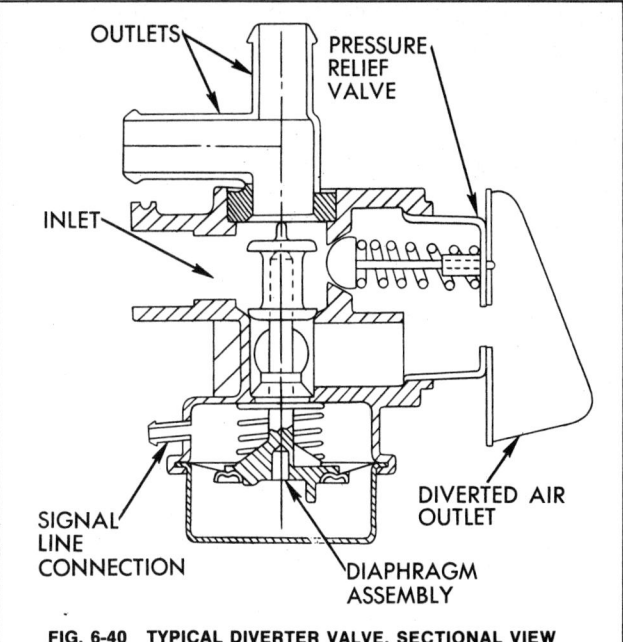

OUTLETS

PRESSURE RELIEF VALVE

INLET

SIGNAL LINE CONNECTION

DIAPHRAGM ASSEMBLY

DIVERTED AIR OUTLET

FIG. 6-40 TYPICAL DIVERTER VALVE, SECTIONAL VIEW

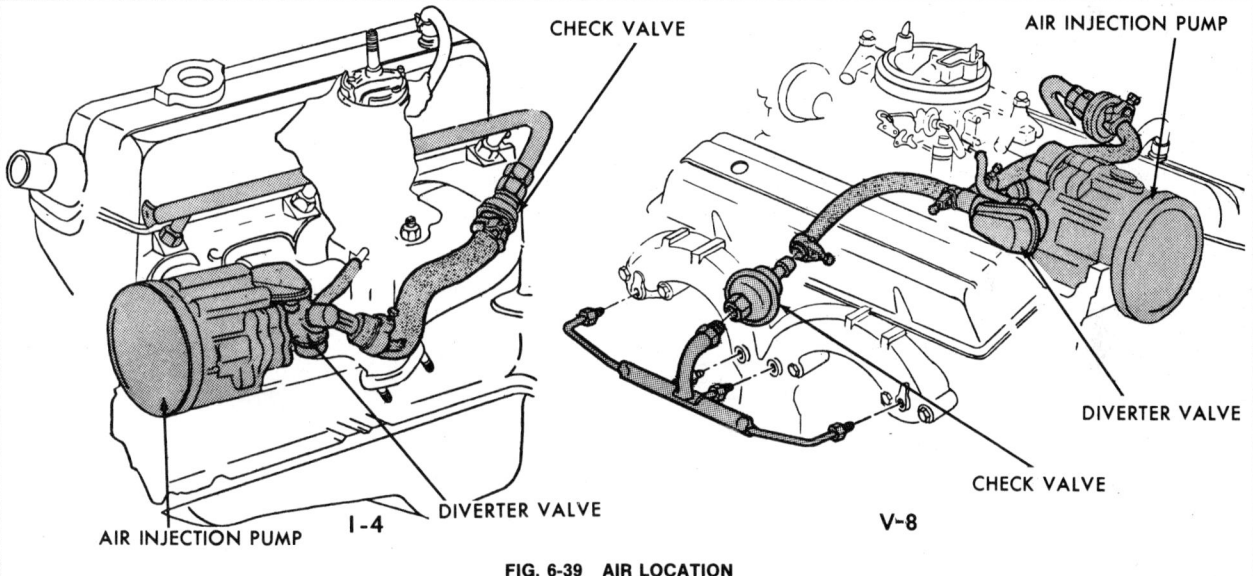

CHECK VALVE

AIR INJECTION PUMP

DIVERTER VALVE

CHECK VALVE

AIR INJECTION PUMP

DIVERTER VALVE

I-4

V-8

FIG. 6-39 AIR LOCATION

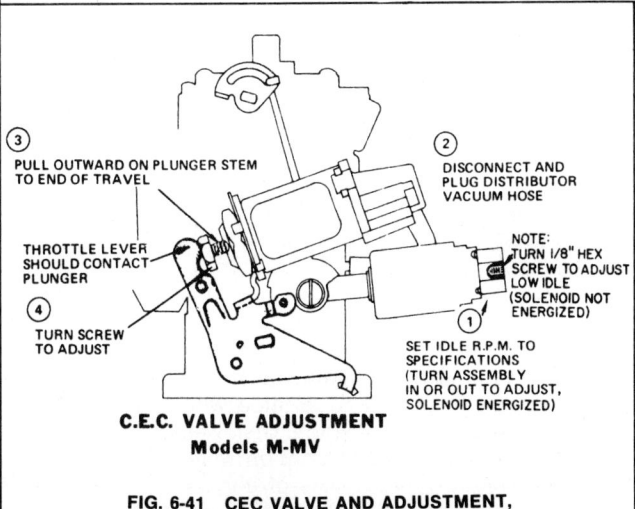

③ PULL OUTWARD ON PLUNGER STEM TO END OF TRAVEL

② DISCONNECT AND PLUG DISTRIBUTOR VACUUM HOSE

THROTTLE LEVER SHOULD CONTACT PLUNGER

④ TURN SCREW TO ADJUST

NOTE: TURN 1/8" HEX SCREW TO ADJUST LOW IDLE (SOLENOID NOT ENERGIZED)

① SET IDLE R.P.M. TO SPECIFICATIONS (TURN ASSEMBLY IN OR OUT TO ADJUST, SOLENOID ENERGIZED)

C.E.C. VALVE ADJUSTMENT Models M-MV

FIG. 6-41 CEC VALVE AND ADJUSTMENT, TYPICAL I-6 MV CARBURETOR

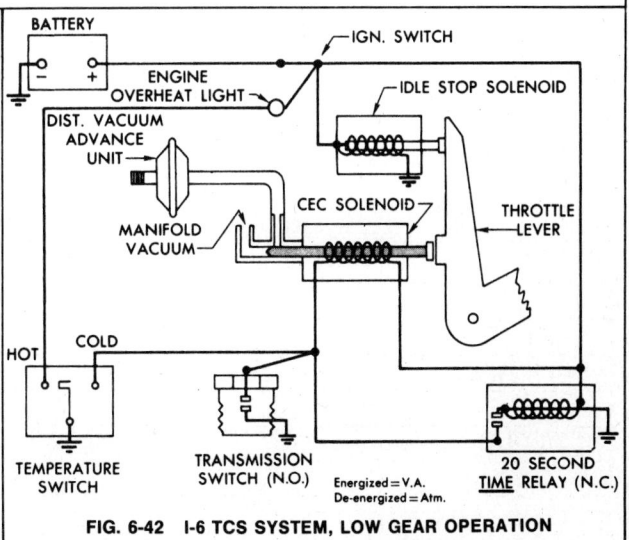

BATTERY

IGN. SWITCH

ENGINE OVERHEAT LIGHT

IDLE STOP SOLENOID

DIST. VACUUM ADVANCE UNIT

CEC SOLENOID

MANIFOLD VACUUM

THROTTLE LEVER

HOT

COLD

TEMPERATURE SWITCH

TRANSMISSION SWITCH (N.O.)

Energized = V.A. De-energized = Atm.

20 SECOND TIME RELAY (N.C.)

FIG. 6-42 I-6 TCS SYSTEM, LOW GEAR OPERATION

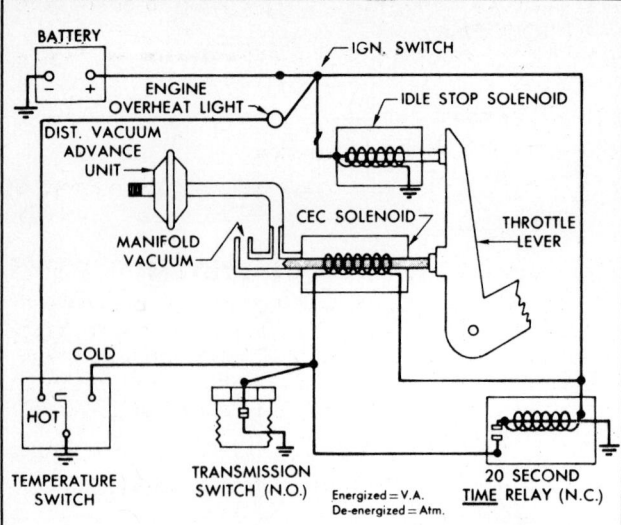

FIG. 6-43　I-6 TCS SYSTEM, HIGH GEAR OPERATION

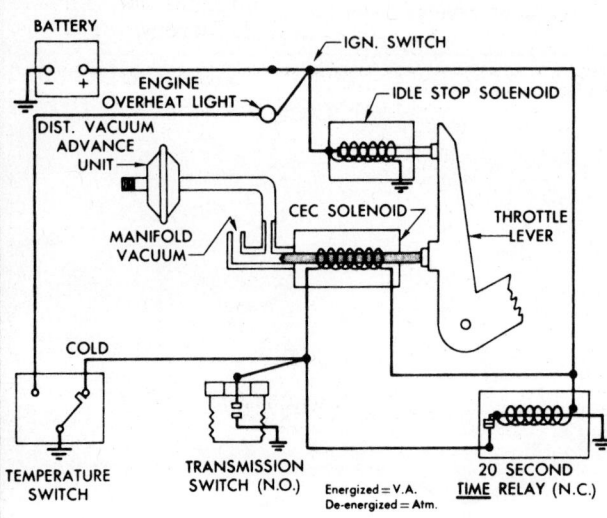

FIG. 6-44　I-6 TCS SYSTEM, COLD OVERRIDE AND TIME RELAY ENERGIZED

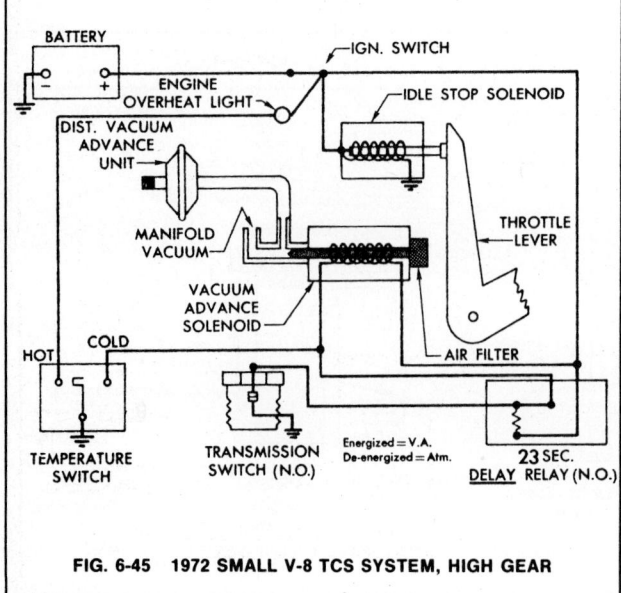

FIG. 6-45　1972 SMALL V-8 TCS SYSTEM, HIGH GEAR

Two throttle settings are required—one for curb idle and one for emission control under deceleration conditions. These settings are described in Chapter 5, and adjustment procedure is shown in **Fig. 6-41.**

CHEVROLET

1972 Emission Systems

The following systems are identical to those used in 1970: Positive Crankcase Ventilation (PCV), Controlled Combustion System (CCS), Evaporation Emission Control System (EEC) and Air Injection Reactor (AIR).

TRANSMISSION CONTROLLED SPARK ADVANCE (TCS)

The CEC valve is restricted to use with the I-6 engine; all V-8 engines return to the use of a vacuum solenoid located on the rear of the inlet manifold to supply or deny vacuum to the distributor vacuum advance unit **(Figs. 6-45 & 6-46)**. On I-6 engines, the delay relay is changed to a time relay, which energizes the CEC solenold for 20 seconds after the ignition key is turned on **(Fig. 6-47)**. The delay relay is used only with the small block V-8 engine, and delay duration is extended from 20 to 23 seconds. In addition to the cold override provision of all systems, Corvette engines are equipped with a hot override feature. When coolant temperatures reach 232° F, the points close to energize the vacuum advance solenoid and send full vacuum to the distributor **(Fig. 6-48)**. Three different temperature switches are used with the V-8 engine—a two-position, single-terminal type with the RPO U14, a three-position, double-terminal type with Corvette engines, and a three-position, double-terminal type with a neutral position is used with all other applications.

CHEVROLET

1973-74 Emission Systems

The following systems are identical to those used in 1970: Positive Crankcase Ventilation (PCV), Controlled Combustion System (CCS), Evaporation Emission Control System (EEC) and Air Injection Reactor (AIR).

TRANSMISSION CONTROLLED SPARK ADVANCE (TCS)

The TCS system on 1973 engines incorporates three changes from that used in 1972 **(Fig. 6-49)**:

1. The small-block V-8 delay relay is changed to a time relay, which energizes the vacuum advance solenoid for 20 seconds after the ignition key is turned on **(Fig. 6-47)**.

2. The thermostatic coolant-temperature switch's operating temperature is raised to 93° F.

3. The switch which engages the air conditioner compressor when the engine is shut off to prevent dieseling or run-on is replaced with an electric throttle contact solenoid, just as that fitted to all other engines. The TCS system for 1973 is used on a) all manual-transmission-equipped cars, b) all station wagon models equipped with a small block V-8 and automatic transmission, and c) all cars fitted with a 307-cu.-in. or larger engine and automatic transmission.

For 1974, TCS is used only on manual-transmission-equipped models, regardless of engine **(Fig. 6-50)**. The CEC solenoid on I-6 applications is replaced by the same vacuum advance solenoid used on the V-8 TCS applications.

EXHAUST GAS RECIRCULATION (EGR)

EGR is added to all 1973 models and continued with minor change in 1974. A vacuum-operated recirculation control valve regulates the amount of exhaust gases and the duration of time they enter the intake manifold. The EGR valve location differs according to engine size/type:

1. Inline engines—Inlet manifold next to carburetor.

2. Small block V-8 engines—Right side of the inlet manifold next to the rocker arm cover.

3. All other engines—Left front corner of the intake manifold in front of the carburetor.

When the throttle valves are opened beyond the idle point, vacuum is applied against the EGR-valve actuating diaphragm. The EGR valve begins to open at approximately 3 ins. of vacuum. As the diaphragm moves up against spring pressure, it opens the exhaust gas intake valve, allowing exhaust gases from the manifold-crossover exhaust channels to be drawn back into the engine intake. The valve remains closed during idle and deceleration, when excessive exhaust gases added to the air/fuel mixture would cause rough engine idling **(Fig. 6-51)**. A thermal vacuum switch (TVS) in the thermostat housing blocks vacuum to the EGR valve until coolant temperature is approximately 100° F. A dual-diaphragm EGR valve **(Fig. 6-52)** is fitted to some 1974 California engines.

CHEVROLET

1975-76 Emission Systems

The Positive Crankcase Ventilation (PCV) system is identical to that used in 1970.

CONTROLLED COMBUSTION SYSTEM

Chevrolet recommends that no attempt be made to adjust carburetor mixture; the idle-mixture-needle limiter caps are not to be removed. The HEI ignition system produces more precise ignition-timing control. An electric choke is used on the Chevette carburetor, as well as the 4-bbl. fitted to the 454-cu.-in. V-8.

EVAPORATIVE EMISSION CONTROL SYSTEM (EEC DESIGNATION NOW ECS)

To prevent against the possibility of fuel draining out through the vapor return line during a rollover accident, the line is re-routed with a fuel control loop just forward of the fuel tank on all but Monza and Corvette models. If the car comes to rest upside down, the loop

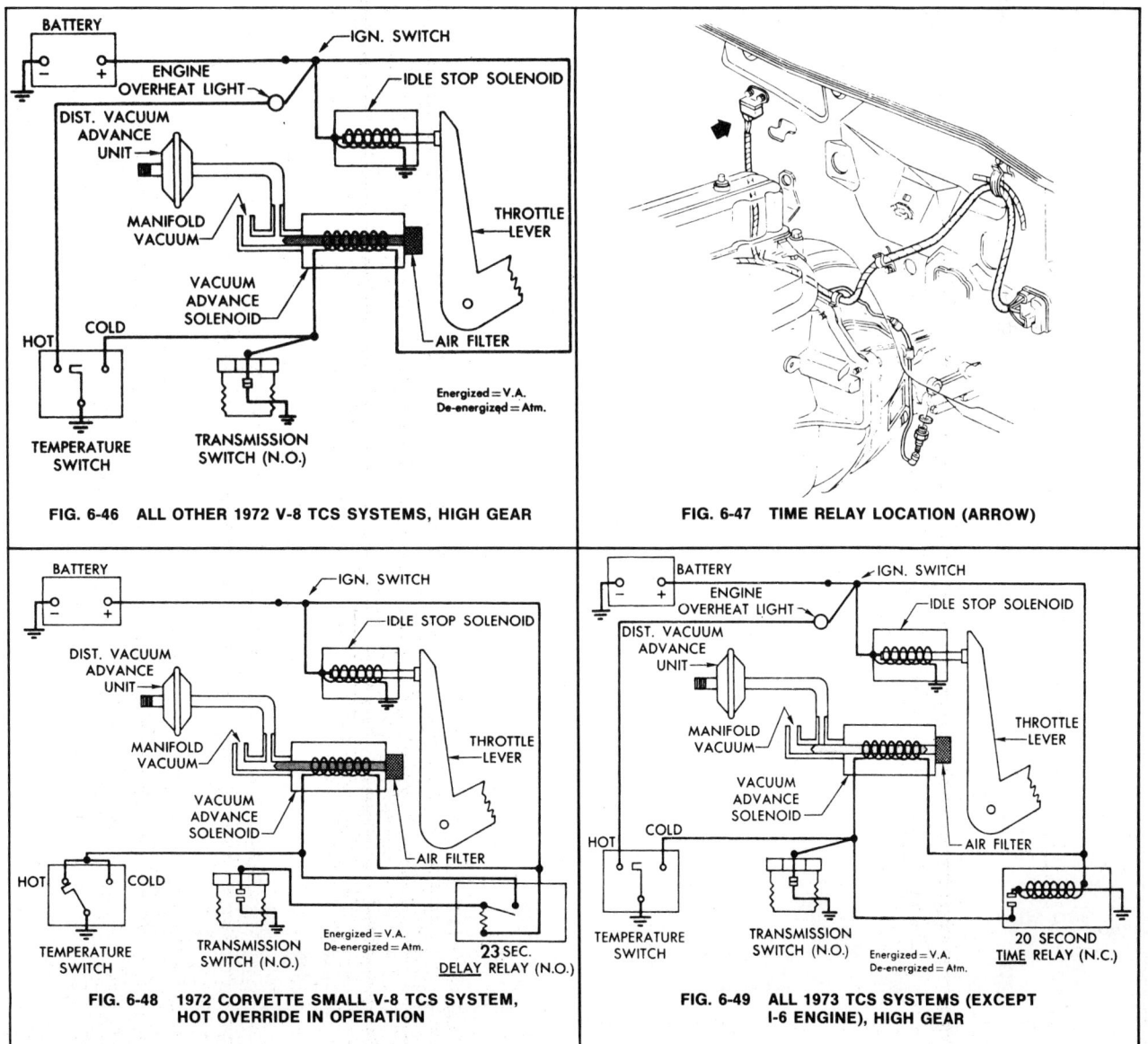

FIG. 6-46   ALL OTHER 1972 V-8 TCS SYSTEMS, HIGH GEAR

FIG. 6-47   TIME RELAY LOCATION (ARROW)

FIG. 6-48   1972 CORVETTE SMALL V-8 TCS SYSTEM, HOT OVERRIDE IN OPERATION

FIG. 6-49   ALL 1973 TCS SYSTEMS (EXCEPT I-6 ENGINE), HIGH GEAR

is higher than the fuel tank and fuel cannot drain out. Corvette and Monza are fitted with a check valve in the vent line at the top connection to the fuel tank.

AIR INJECTION REACTOR (AIR)

The Chevette AIR application uses a different diverter valve design than other Chevrolets. A power-mode diverter valve is included to release pump air into the atmosphere during wide-open throttle conditions, and a vacuum-differential control valve is used to delay the power-mode diverter valve operation for a few seconds after reaching wide-open throttle.

CATALYTIC CONVERTER

All 1975 Chevrolets are fitted with a catalytic converter to improve fuel economy and drivability; some 1976

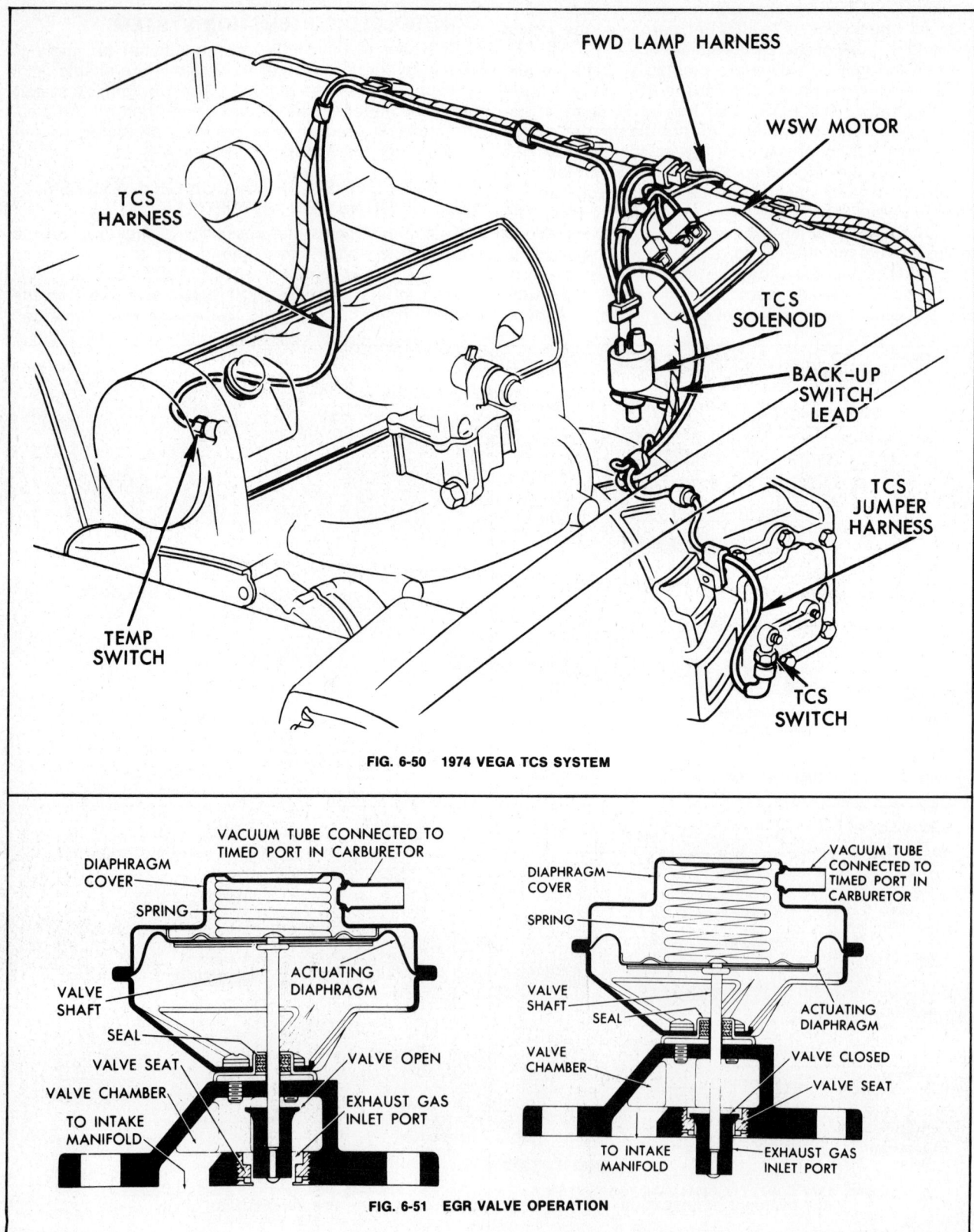

FIG. 6-50 1974 VEGA TCS SYSTEM

FIG. 6-51 EGR VALVE OPERATION

models are not equipped with the catalytic converter.

PULSE AIR INJECTOR REACTOR (PAIR)

An exhaust-emission-control device, utilizing exhaust pressure pulsation to draw air into the exhaust system, the PAIR **(Fig. 6-54)** is fitted to the Cosworth Vega. Fresh air from the clean side of the air cleaner is drawn through the engine fresh-air vent line to provide filtered air. The PAIR system uses a pulse-air shut-off valve **(Fig. 6-53)** through which the filtered air passes on its way to four conventional air check valves **(Fig. 6-55)** located on each of the four exhaust manifold legs next to the cylinder-head exhaust ports.

Engine firing creates a pulsating exhaust-gas flow, which causes pressure or vacuum, depending upon whether the exhaust valve is seated or not. The pressure or vacuum travels through a series of external pipes to the check valves. Pressure forces the disc in the check valve to assume a closed position, and no flow is allowed into the air supply line **(Fig. 6-55, View 1)**. A vacuum causes the disc to open, permitting fresh air to mix with the exhaust gases **(Fig. 6-55, View 2)**.

EARLY FUEL EVAPORATION (EFE)

Added to the exhaust system on 1975 Chevrolets, the EFE valve **(Fig. 6-56)** promotes quick heating of incoming fuel by directing exhaust gas flow through the intake-manifold crossover passage directly under the carburetor whenever engine coolant/oil temperature is below a specified level. Two variations are used as follows:

1. Small block V-8 engines—The EFE system used includes an EFE valve at the flange of the exhaust manifold, a power actuator and actuator rod, and a TVS switch mounted in the thermostat housing. At coolant temperatures below 180° F, manifold vacuum is applied to the actuator, which closes the EFE valve through the actuator rod connection. When coolant

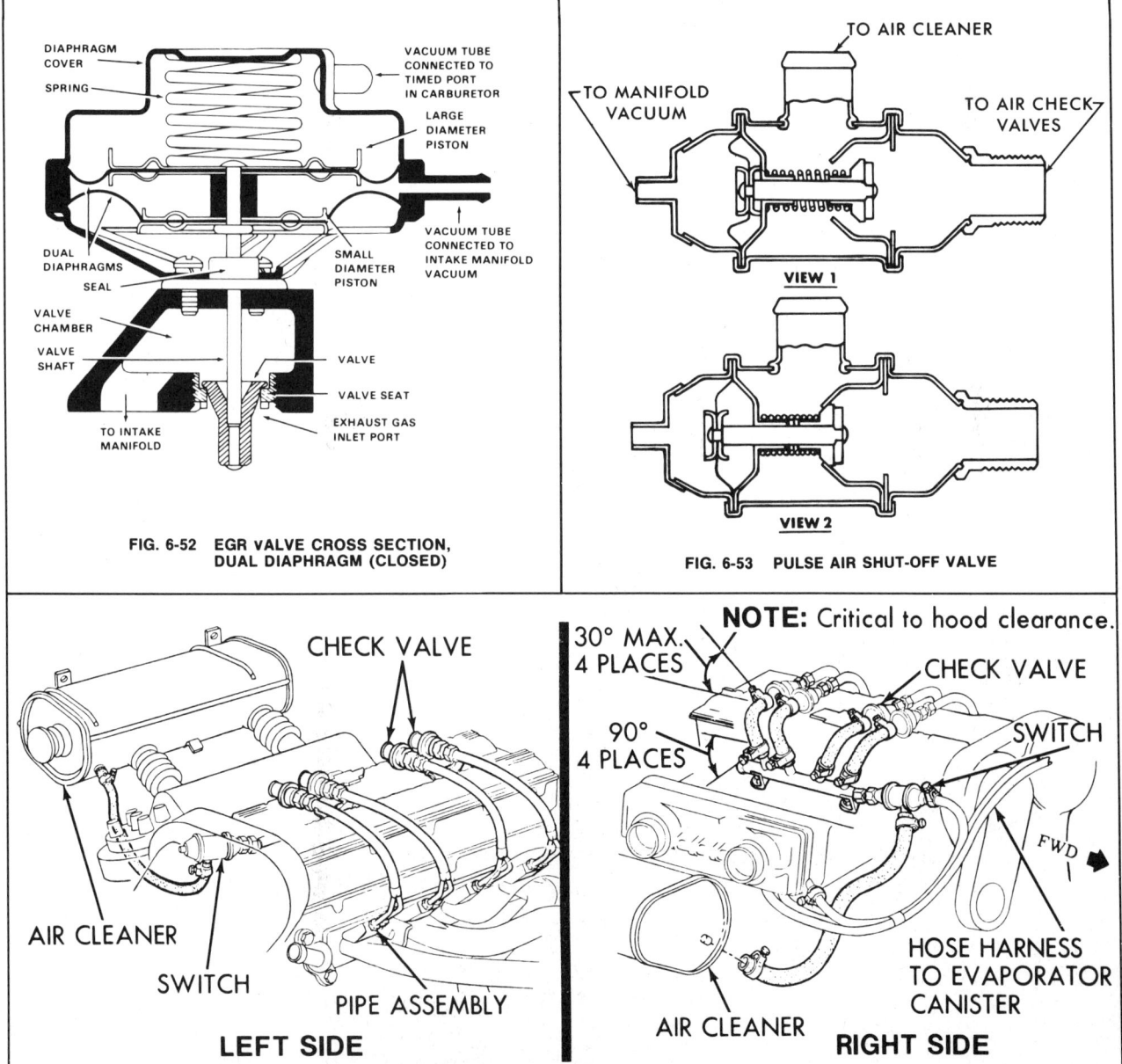

FIG. 6-52   EGR VALVE CROSS SECTION, DUAL DIAPHRAGM (CLOSED)

FIG. 6-53   PULSE AIR SHUT-OFF VALVE

FIG. 6-54   PAIR SYSTEM

temperature exceeds 180° F, vacuum to the power actuator is blocked, allowing the EFE valve to open.

2. All other Chevrolet engines—The EFE system includes an EFE valve at the flange of the exhaust mani-

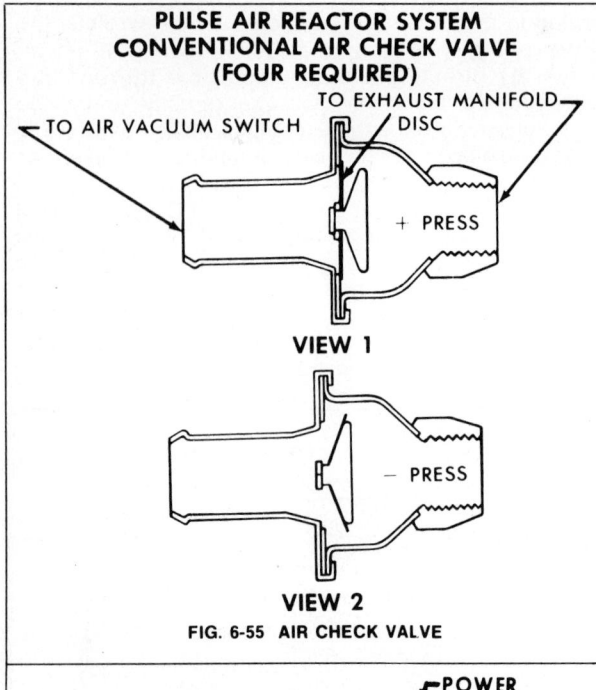

PULSE AIR REACTOR SYSTEM
CONVENTIONAL AIR CHECK VALVE
(FOUR REQUIRED)

TO EXHAUST MANIFOLD

TO AIR VACUUM SWITCH — DISC

+ PRESS

VIEW 1

− PRESS

VIEW 2

FIG. 6-55 AIR CHECK VALVE

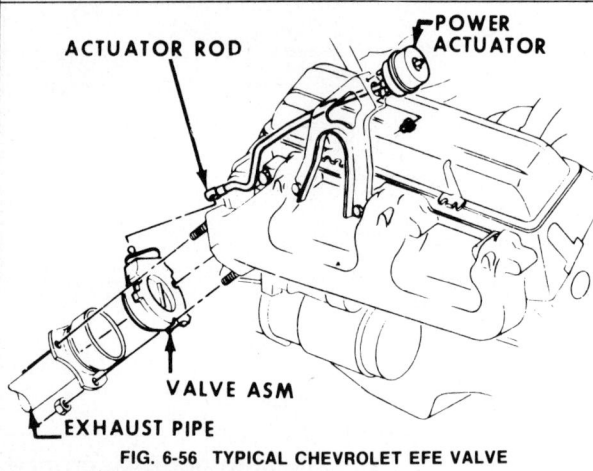

ACTUATOR ROD

POWER ACTUATOR

VALVE ASM

EXHAUST PIPE

FIG. 6-56 TYPICAL CHEVROLET EFE VALVE

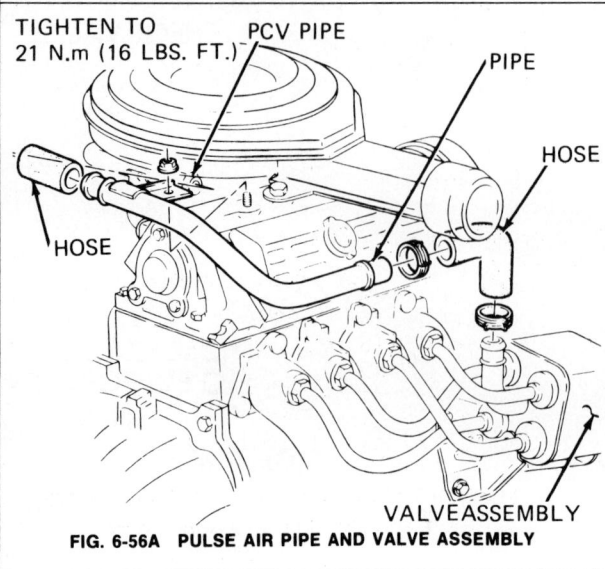

TIGHTEN TO 21 N.m (16 LBS. FT.)

PCV PIPE

PIPE

HOSE

HOSE

HOSE

VALVE ASSEMBLY

FIG. 6-56A PULSE AIR PIPE AND VALVE ASSEMBLY

fold, a power actuator and actuator rod, a TVS switch located on the right-hand side of the cylinder case in front of the oil pressure switch (I-6 engines), or directly above the oil filter (all V-8 engines), and a vacuum solenoid.

A normally closed switch, the TVS is sensitive to oil temperature. With a cold engine (below 150° F, I-6; 100° F, V-8's), the closed TVS energizes the vacuum solenoid and passes manifold vacuum to the power actuator, which closes the EFE valve through the actuator rod connection. When oil reaches the specified temperature, the TVS opens to de-energize the solenoid and block vacuum to the actuator, opening the EFE valve.

The EFE system is dropped from certain 1976 engines and is further refined by replacing the vacuum solenoid and oil-temperature switch control by a TVS inserted in an oil passage in the engine block.

TRANSMISSION CONTROLLED SPARK ADVANCE (TCS)

TCS was reintroduced on 1976 Vegas equipped with a manual transmission, operating in essentially the same manner as that previously used before being dropped from the Chevrolet line with the introduction of the 1975 models.

CHEVROLET
1977 Emission Systems

The Positive Crankcase Ventilation (PCV) system is the same as used in 1970. The Air-Injection Reactor (AIR) system used on some 1977 Chevrolet engines is essentially the same as that used in 1970, although I-4 engines use a new system (see below). Evaporative Emission Control (ECS) system, Catalytic Converter, Early Fuel Evaporation (EFE) and Thermostatic Air Cleaner (TAC) are carryovers from 1975-76.

EXHAUST GAS RECIRCULATION (EGR)

All California and high-altitude V-8 engines are equipped with a backpressure modulated EGR valve.

PULSE AIR-INJECTOR REACTOR (PAIR)

A modification of the 1975-76 Cosworth Vega PAIR system is used on I-4 engines. System operation is the same, but a unit pulse air valve containing a check valve for each port is used **(Fig. 6-56A),** instead of individual valves.

SPARK DELAY VALVE

California 305 V-8 engines use a check valve in the distributor vacuum advance line to delay the ported vacuum spark signal during mild acceleration.

CHEVROLET
1978-79 Emission Systems

The Positive Crankcase Ventilation (PCV) system is the same as used in 1970. Catalytic Converter is a carryover from 1975-76; Thermostatic Air Cleaner (TAC) operates with calibration unchanged from previous years; Pulse Air-Injector Reactor (PAIR) is used on Chevette as in 1977.

EARLY FUEL EVAPORATION (EFE)

Actuator calibration is 150° F for all V-6 engines, except 231-cu.-in. high-altitude and California with manual transmission, 120° F, and 231 cu.-in. low-altitude with automatic transmission, 90° F; Non-California I-4, 110° F; California I-4, 150° F.

EXHAUST GAS RECIRCULATION (EGR)

The system remains essentially that used in 1977, with a positive backpressure EGR valve used on all California and high-altitude V-8 and I-6 engines, and a negative backpressure EGR valve used on some other applications instead of the standard EGR valve. Both backpressure valves have the same function but operate under different backpressure conditions.

AIR INJECTION REACTOR (AIR)

A variation of the standard air pump system is used on V-6 231-cu.-in. California engines similar in design and operation to that fitted in 1977 by Pontiac to its V-6 California and high-altitude engines. See 1977 Oldsmobile Emission systems for details.

ELECTRONIC FUEL CONTROL (EFC) SYSTEM

See 1978-79 Oldsmobile Emission Systems for system operation. For 1979, a variation called the Computer Catalytic Converter or C-4 System is used with all 231-cu.-in. California 2-bbl. engines. It operates essentially the same as the 1978 EFC System, which is carryover for 1979 on 151-cu.-in. California engines.

EMISSION SYSTEM TEST PROCEDURES

PCV TEST

1. Connect the tachometer and start the engine.
2. Clamp off the crankcase ventilator hose to shut off airflow completely.
3. If idle speed drops, the PCV system is functioning. If idle speed does not drop, install a new valve.

ALTERNATE PCV TEST

1. Remove the PCV valve from the intake manifold or rocker arm cover.
2. Start the engine and run at idle.
3. Place a thumb over the valve end to check for vacuum. If there is no vacuum at the valve, inspect for plugged hoses.
4. Shut the engine off. Shake the valve and listen for the rattle of the check needle in the valve. If no rattle is heard, replace the valve.

THERMAC-AIR-CLEANER VACUUM MOTOR TEST

1. With the engine off, check the damper door posi-

tion through the snorkel tube—the passage should be open (**Fig. 6-57, View A**).
2. Remove the air cleaner cover and tape a suitable thermometer to the air cleaner base next to the sensor. Replace the cover, but *do not* install the wing nut.
3. Start the engine; air cleaner temperature must be below 85° F. The damper door should close immediately (**Fig. 6-57, View B**).
4. When the damper starts to move open, remove the air cleaner cover immediately and record the temperature reading. It should be between 85° F and 115° F (**Fig. 6-57, View C**).
5. Replace the air cleaner cover and continue to observe the damper movement.
6. When the damper has moved to a full open position (**Fig. 6-57, View D**), again remove the air

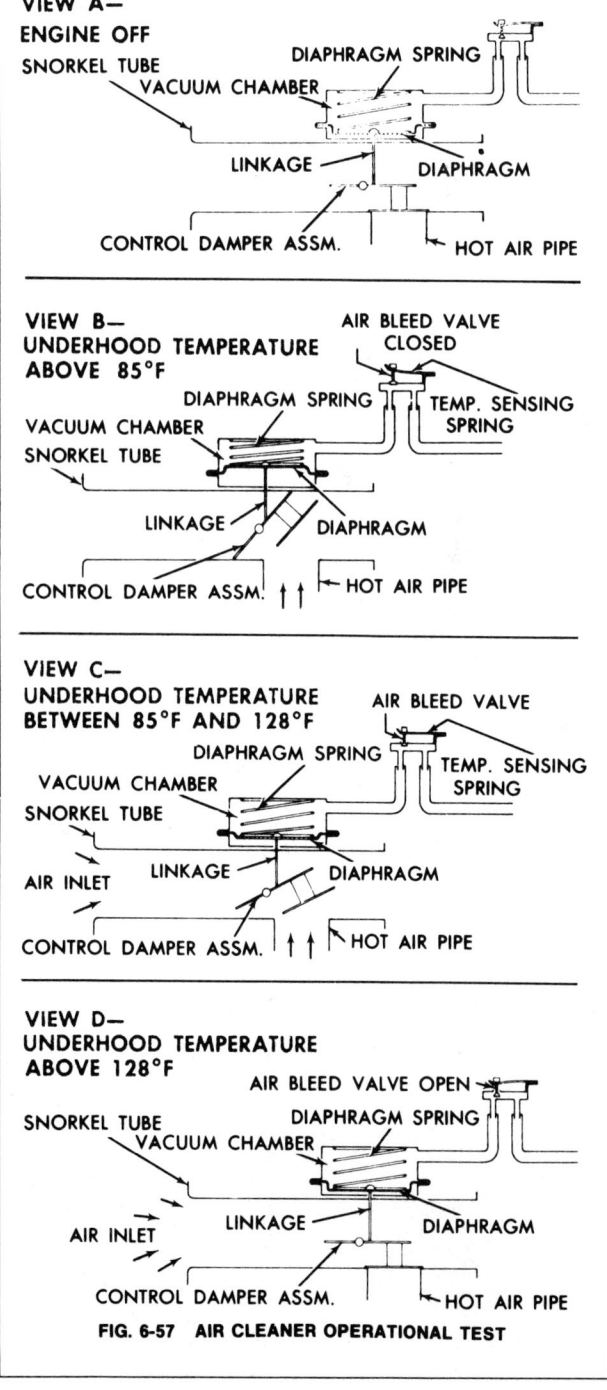

VIEW A—
ENGINE OFF
SNORKEL TUBE — VACUUM CHAMBER — DIAPHRAGM SPRING
LINKAGE — DIAPHRAGM
CONTROL DAMPER ASSM. — HOT AIR PIPE

VIEW B—
UNDERHOOD TEMPERATURE ABOVE 85°F
AIR BLEED VALVE CLOSED
DIAPHRAGM SPRING — TEMP. SENSING SPRING
VACUUM CHAMBER
SNORKEL TUBE
LINKAGE — DIAPHRAGM
CONTROL DAMPER ASSM. — HOT AIR PIPE

VIEW C—
UNDERHOOD TEMPERATURE BETWEEN 85°F AND 128°F
AIR BLEED VALVE
DIAPHRAGM SPRING — TEMP. SENSING SPRING
VACUUM CHAMBER
SNORKEL TUBE
AIR INLET — LINKAGE — DIAPHRAGM
CONTROL DAMPER ASSM. — HOT AIR PIPE

VIEW D—
UNDERHOOD TEMPERATURE ABOVE 128°F
AIR BLEED VALVE OPEN
DIAPHRAGM SPRING
SNORKEL TUBE — VACUUM CHAMBER
AIR INLET — LINKAGE — DIAPHRAGM
CONTROL DAMPER ASSM. — HOT AIR PIPE

FIG. 6-57   AIR CLEANER OPERATIONAL TEST

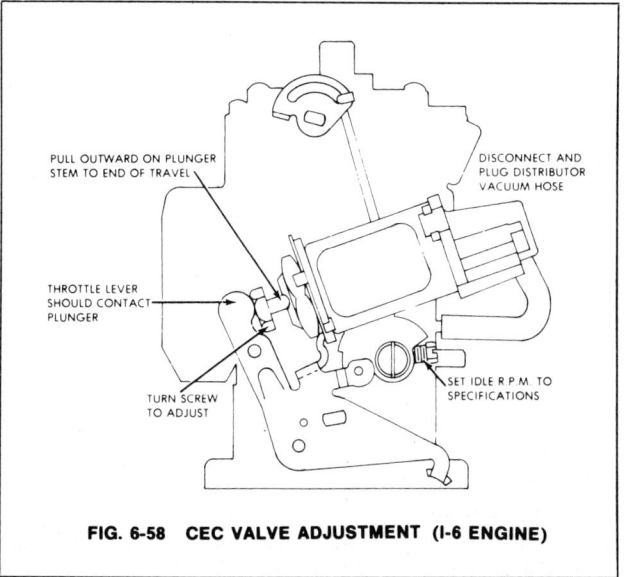

PULL OUTWARD ON PLUNGER STEM TO END OF TRAVEL

DISCONNECT AND PLUG DISTRIBUTOR VACUUM HOSE

THROTTLE LEVER SHOULD CONTACT PLUNGER

TURN SCREW TO ADJUST

SET IDLE R.P.M. TO SPECIFICATIONS

FIG. 6-58   CEC VALVE ADJUSTMENT (I-6 ENGINE)

cleaner cover and record the temperature. It should be in excess of 128° F.

7. If the sensor does not operate the damper door correctly within the specified range, replace it.

TRANSMISSION CONTROLLED SPARK ADVANCE (TCS) COMPONENT TEST

1. Warm the engine to normal operating temperature and place the transmission in low forward gear—advance solenoid should be de-energized. If it energizes, remove the transmission switch connection. If the solenoid now de-energizes, replace the transmission switch.

2. Check the source vacuum and connect a vacuum gauge to the advance solenoid port. Apply 12 volts to the solenoid and it should energize, indicating vacuum to the distributor. With 1970-72 systems, go to Step 4.

3. If the solenoid checks out good on 1973 and later systems, remove the temperature switch connector and check the time relay to be certain that it is cool. Now turn the ignition on and the solenoid should energize for 20 seconds, then de-energize. If it does not de-energize, disconnect the blue lead. If the solenoid now de-energizes, replace the relay.

4. The vacuum advance solenoid should be energized on a cold engine. If it is not, ground the wire from the temperature-switch cold terminal. If the solenoid energizes, replace the temperature sending unit.

5. Warm the engine to normal operating temperature and place the transmission in high on 1970-74 manuals and Powerglides (reverse gear on 1970-73 Hydra-Matics)—solenoid should be energized. If not, remove and ground the connector at the switch. If the solenoid now energizes, replace the switch.

CEC VALVE ADJUSTMENT

Energized through the transmission, the CEC valve (Fig. 6-58) acts as a throttle stop by increasing the idle speed during high gear operation. The CEC valve also provides full vacuum advance during high gear operation, and is de-energized at all other gears and at idle for retarded spark timing. The normal idle speed setting is made with the idle stop screw. The CEC valve should require adjustment only in cases of solenoid replacement, major carburetor overhaul or removal/replacement of the carburetor throttle body.

To adjust the CEC valve:

1. Disconnect and plug the distributor vacuum-

advance line; disconnect the fuel tank hose from the vapor canister.

2. Refer to specific instructions for adjustment found on the vehicle emission control sticker; start the engine and connect a tachometer.

3. Manually extend the solenoid valve plunger until it touches the throttle lever.

4. Adjust the plunger length until the specified engine speed is obtained.

5. Reconnect the vacuum advance and vapor canister lines.

EGR VALVE OPERATIONAL TEST

1. Remove the EGR valve from the engine. Manually depress the valve diaphragm to be sure that valve action is free. If the diaphragm cannot be moved by hand, clean the valve before continuing the test.

2. Apply a 9-in. vacuum signal to the EGR diaphragm tube on top of the EGR valve with a hand vacuum pump. The valve should open fully and remain open with no leak-down while the vacuum is maintained.

3. When testing a dual diaphragm valve, apply a 9-in. vacuum signal to the vacuum tube at the center of the valve. The valve will not open in this test, so check only for leak-down. Replace the valve if required, using one with an identical part number.

EGR THERMAL-VACUUM-SWITCH FUNCTIONAL TEST

The EGR-TVS switch should be closed whenever the coolant temperature is below 100° F. In this position, it will block the ported vacuum signal from reaching the EGR valve.

1. Drain the coolant level below the thermostat housing.

2. Disconnect the vacuum lines and remove the switch from the thermostat housing.

3. If the switch appears to be in good condition, connect a vacuum line to its lower nipple marked "Carb" or "C" and connect a vacuum gauge to the upper nipple marked "EGR" or "E."

4. Submerge the switch in 85° F water, and agitate the water for 2 minutes.

5. Apply a 12-in. vacuum signal to the hose connected to the lower nipple. The switch should be closed: if open, it is defective. Up to 2 ins. leakage in 2 minutes is permitted. If the switch does not operate correctly, replace with a new one.

6. Reinstall the switch in the thermostat housing.

EMISSION SYSTEM COMPONENT REPLACEMENT

AIR CLEANER ASSEMBLY (EXCEPT COSWORTH VEGA)

The air cleaner assembly is not serviceable. If the damper door is malfunctioning, the entire unit must be replaced. The vacuum motor and the air cleaner sensor are replaceable.

VACUUM MOTOR

1. Remove the air cleaner from the engine.

2. Drill out the center of the two spot welds holding the vacuum motor to the snorkel tube. Use a 1/16-in. drill— *do not* center punch.

3. Enlarge the holes to 5/32-in. Be careful not to damage or distort the air cleaner snorkel.

4. Remove the vacuum-motor retainer strap and lift the vacuum motor, tilting it to one side in order to unhook the linkage at the control door.

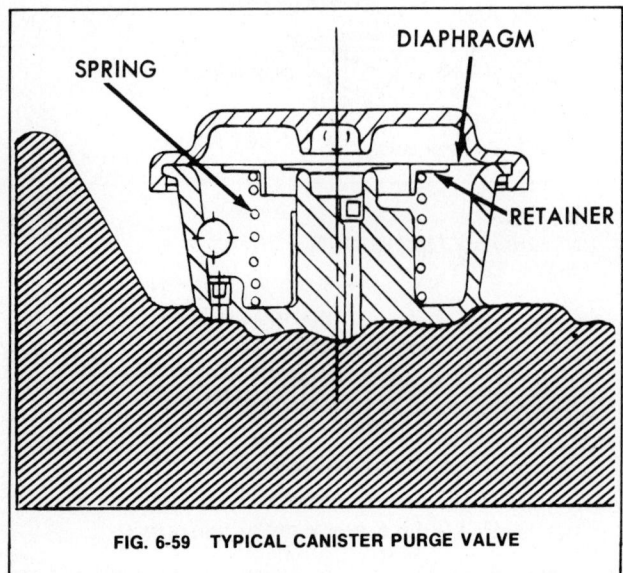

FIG. 6-59   TYPICAL CANISTER PURGE VALVE

5. Drill a 7/64-in. hole in the snorkel tube at the center of the retaining strap end which faces the air cleaner housing.

6. Install a new vacuum motor assembly, using the mounting strap retainer and sheetmetal screw provided with the new motor. Screw must not interfere with the damper assembly operation—shorten if necessary.

AIR CLEANER SENSOR

1. Pry the sensor retaining-clip tabs free, and remove the vacuum lines from the sensor.

2. Note the position of the old sensor—the new unit must be installed in the same position to avoid possible interference with the air cleaner element—then remove the old sensor.

3. Install the new sensor and gasket in the air cleaner, and replace the retaining clip while supporting the sensor around the air cleaner's center rim to prevent damage to the temperature sensing spring.

4. Replace the vacuum lines, and reinstall the air cleaner.

AIR PUMP REMOVAL/INSTALLATION

TO REMOVE

1. Disconnect the pump and valve hoses.

2. Loosen the pump-to-bracket mounting bolts and remove the pump drive belt.

3. Remove the pulley-to-hub bolts, and remove the pulley.

4. Remove the air pump from the engine.

TO INSTALL

1. Position the pump on the mounting bracket. Line up the holes, and install the bolts loosely.

2. Fit the pulley to the hub and tighten the bolts to 25 ft.-lbs.

3. Install the pump belt over the pulley and adjust the tension, then tighten the bracket bolts.

4. Reconnect the pump and valve hoses.

CENTRIFUGAL FILTER FAN REPLACEMENT

1. Remove the air pump from the engine.

2. Pull the fan from the hub with needlenose pliers. Although it is seldom possible to remove the fan without damage, take care not to let the plastic fragments enter the air intake hole.

3. Draw the new fan evenly into place, using the pulley and bolts as tools. Torque the bolts alternately to 25 ft.-lbs. The outer edge of the fan must slip into the housing.

4. Replace the pump on the engine. Until the outer diameter sealing lip has worn in, a new fan may be noisy.

DIVERTER VALVE REPLACEMENT

1. Disconnect the vacuum lines from the valve.

2. Remove the valve from the air pump or elbow.

3. Install new valve and gasket to the pump or elbow, and torque the attaching screws to 85 in.-lbs.

4. Replace vacuum lines to the valve and inspect the system for leakage.

CHECK VALVE REPLACEMENT

1. Disconnect the pump hose from the check valve. Remove and replace with a new check valve, taking care not to bend, twist or distort the air manifold.

EGR VALVE REPLACEMENT

1. Disconnect the vacuum line(s) from the EGR valve.

2. Remove the clamp bolt which holds the valve to the manifold.

3. Remove EGR valve and clamp from manifold.

4. Replace the valve and new gasket to the manifold, torquing the clamp bolt 15 to 20 ft.-lbs. and bending the lock tab over the bolt head.

5. Connect the vacuum line(s) to the EGR valve.

THERMAL VACUUM SWITCH (TVS) REPLACEMENT

1. Disconnect the vacuum lines from the TVS.

2. Remove the switch from the thermostat housing.

3. Apply a non-hardening sealer to the threaded portion of the switch, and install it in the thermostat housing, torquing to 15 ft.-lbs.

4. Turn the TVS head as necessary to align it for proper hose connection, and install the hoses.

EEC/ECS VAPOR CANISTER FILTER REPLACEMENT

1. Disconnect the top canister hoses and loosen the clamps holding the canister in place. Canister removal is from under the car.

2. Remove the canister, and pull the filter from the bottom.

3. Inspect hose connection openings for blockage.

4. Apply vacuum to the purge valve—the valve should hold vacuum without leak-down **(Fig. 6-59).**

5. Install a new filter (on Nova, assemble bottom of canister to canister body).

6. Replace the canister in the mounting clamps, and tighten the clamp bolts.

7. Reconnect the hoses to the canister nipples.

OLDSMOBILE

1970-72 Emission Systems

POSITIVE CRANKCASE VENTILATION (PCV)

A sealed oil-filler cap prevents crankcase gases from escaping under no-vacuum conditions **(Fig. 6-60).** A tube from the air cleaner goes to the rocker cover, carrying fresh air through the air cleaner filter and down into the crankcase. From that point, blowby gases go through the hose into the PCV valve and then into the manifold. When the PCV system is under

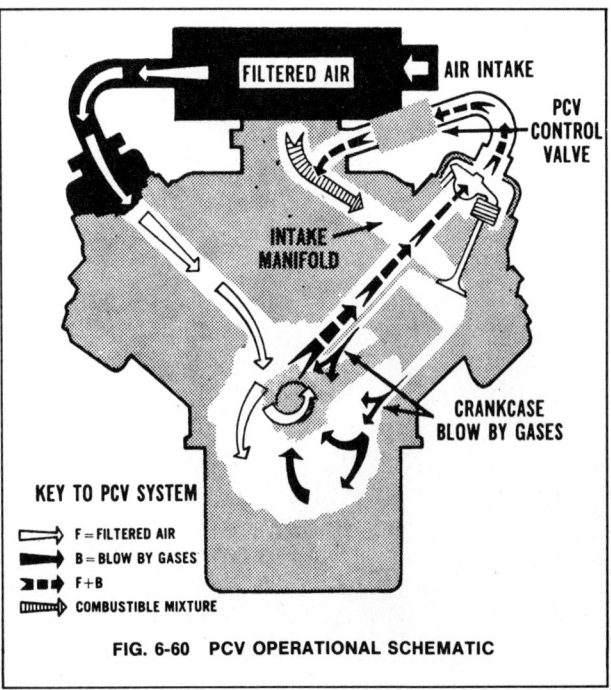

FIG. 6-60 PCV OPERATIONAL SCHEMATIC

zero vacuum, there is no suction on the crankcase, but the gases go from the rocker cover, through the hose and into the air cleaner, where they are drawn into the intake manifold through the carburetor.

CONTROLLED COMBUSTION SYSTEM (CCS)

A series of engine modifications, CCS **(Fig. 6-61)** uses carburetor/choke/distributor calibrations and an increased engine operating temperature to reduce emissions. Ignition timing is retarded and carburetors are calibrated to run on a leaner air/fuel mixture. A 195° F thermostat is fitted to CCS engines, allowing a higher engine temperature to produce better fuel vaporization and a reduced quench (cool) area in the combustion chambers. A thermostatically controlled air cleaner keeps the temperature of the air entering the carburetor at approximately 100° F, reducing engine icing in cold-weather climates and producing better engine warm-up.

Idle-mixture-needle limiter caps are installed on 1971 carburetors, and Oldsmobile recommends that no attempt be made to adjust the carburetor mixture beyond the limits provided: the limiter caps are *not* to be removed for adjustment purposes.

THERMOSTATIC VACUUM SWITCH (TVS)

With the exception of some W30 models, all 1970 F-85 cars fitted with 455-cu.-in. engines use a TVS located in the engine coolant-crossover passage of the intake manifold. When engine temperature exceeds approximately 223° F, the TVS sends manifold vacuum to the distributor vacuum-advance unit. This advance in ignition timing speeds up the engine to increase fan speed and circulate coolant faster to reduce engine temperature.

TRANSMISSION CONTROLLED SPARK ADVANCE (TCS)

The 8-cyl. TCS system controls distributor vacuum advance by means of an oil-pressure-sensitive transmission switch electrically connected to a solenoid valve inserted in the carburetor-to-distributor vacuum line. Whenever the transmission operates in other than high gear, the transmission switch and solenoid valve are both closed, shutting off vacuum to the distributor advance unit. When the transmission shifts to high gear, oil pressure in the direct clutch circuit causes the transmission switch to open, sending an electrical sig-

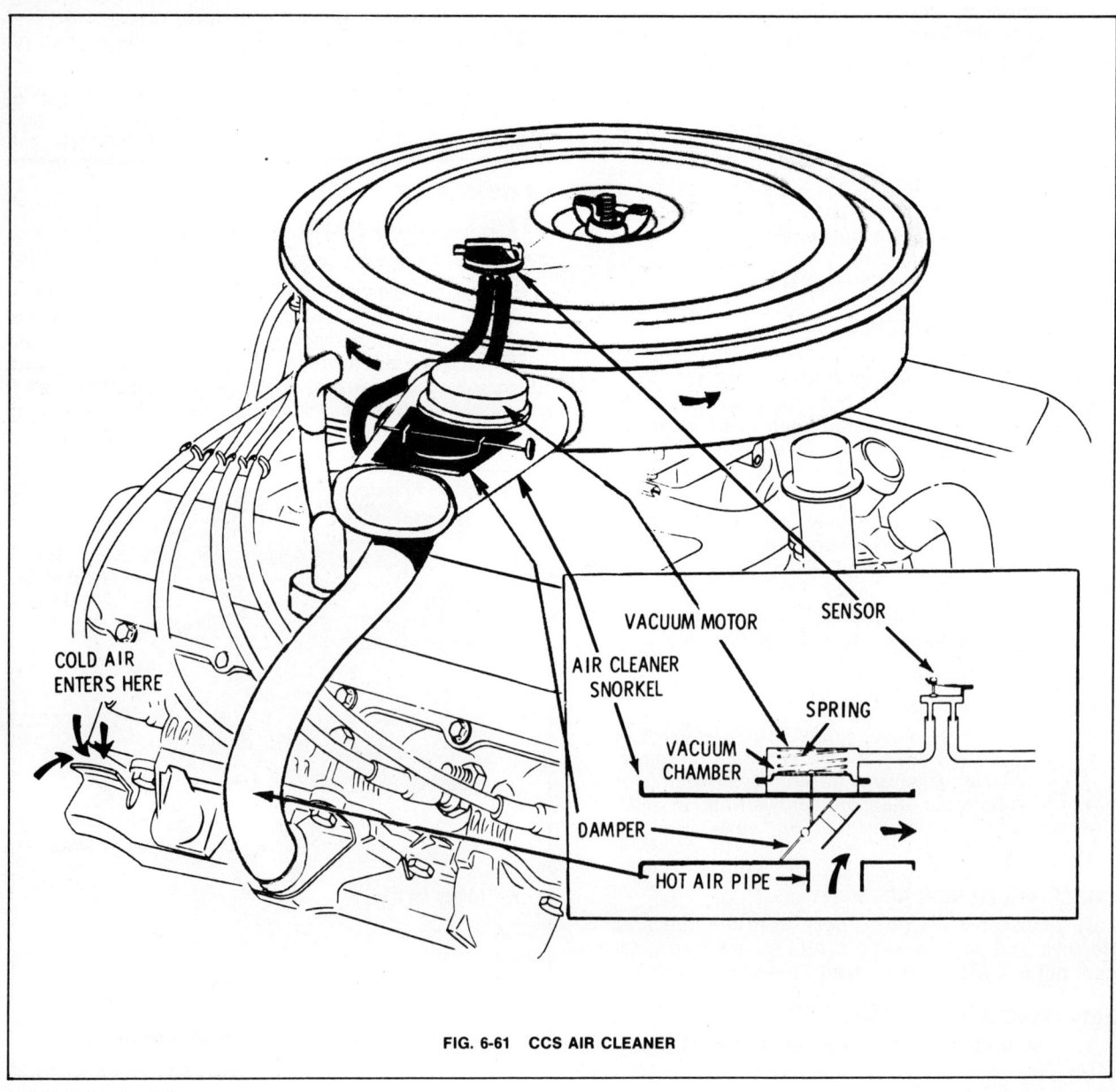

COLD AIR ENTERS HERE

VACUUM MOTOR   SENSOR
AIR CLEANER
SNORKEL   SPRING
              VACUUM
              CHAMBER

DAMPER

HOT AIR PIPE

FIG. 6-61   CCS AIR CLEANER

nal to open the solenoid valve and permiting carburetor vacuum to flow to the distributor, advancing the spark.

The 6-cyl. TCS system is similar, but the transmission switch is externally mounted and operated by the transmission linkage position. A temperature switch is also used on the 6-cyl. TCS system, allowing vacuum to reach the distributor at temperatures under 85° F or above 220° F.

In 1972, the TCS solenoid is used only with the Cutlass when fitted with a 2-bbl. 350-cu.-in. engine without air conditioning. All other TCS systems incorporate the TCS solenoid function in the distributor vacuum-control switch.

DISTRIBUTOR VACUUM CONTROL SWITCH

All 1971-72 cars fitted with air conditioning or heavy-duty cooling options, and all 455-cu.-in. F-85, Cutlass, 4-4-2 and Toronado models, use a distributor vacuum-control switch to advance ignition timing in 3rd or 4th gear, or at high coolant temperatures at idle speed **(Fig. 6-62).** This replaces the thermostatic vacuum switch (TVS) used in 1970.

The solenoid is energized in 1st or 2nd gear, sealing off the carburetor "C" port and opening the vent "V"

port to purge the distributor vacuum-advance unit. In 3rd or 4th gear, the solenoid de-energizes. This lets the solenoid valve plunger seal off the vent port and open the carburetor port, allowing vacuum to pass from the carburetor to the distributor vacuum-advance unit through the vacuum control switch.

When coolant temperature reaches 210° F, the valve plunger moves up to seal off the vent port and open the manifold "M" port. At 218-224° F, full manifold vacuum is sent to the distributor, regardless of transmission gear position. This advances the spark and speeds up water pump operation, circulating the coolant at a faster rate to reduce engine overheating.

EVAPORATIVE CONTROL SYSTEM (ECS)

An evaporative emission control system is fitted to all 1970 cars sold in California. Vapor caused by fuel evaporation in the fuel tank is no longer vented into the atmosphere, but transferred instead to the engine compartment by a vapor line, and fed directly into the running engine, or stored in an activated charcoal accumulator (canister) when the engine is not running. The system includes a fuel-tank overfill protector, fuel-tank venting, a liquid vapor separator positioned forward and above the fuel tank **(Fig. 6-63),** and a pressure-vacuum relief valve in the vapor line. The liquid vapor separator is not fitted to station wagons.

In 1971, the evaporative control system is installed on *all* cars sold, and a fuel standpipe assembly **(Fig. 6-64)** replaces the liquid vapor separator unit (except station wagon models) to perform the same function.

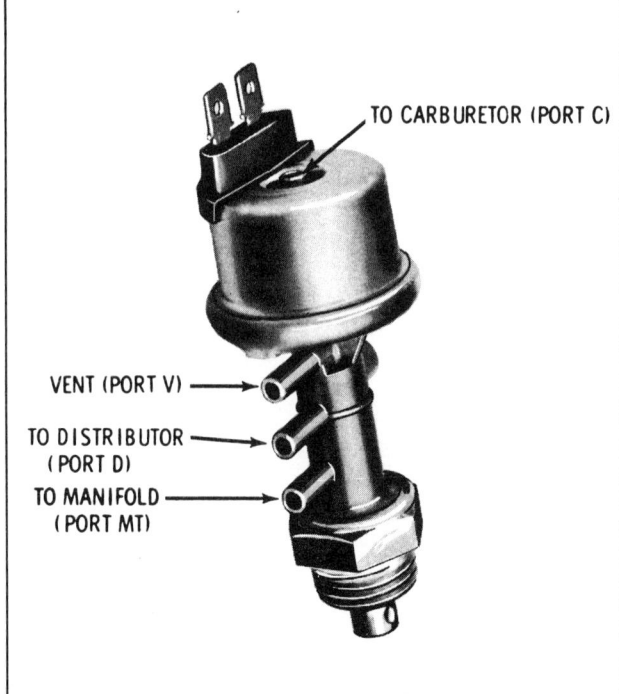

TO CARBURETOR (PORT C)

VENT (PORT V)

TO DISTRIBUTOR (PORT D)

TO MANIFOLD (PORT MT)

FIG. 6-62   DISTRIBUTOR VACUUM-CONTROL SWITCH

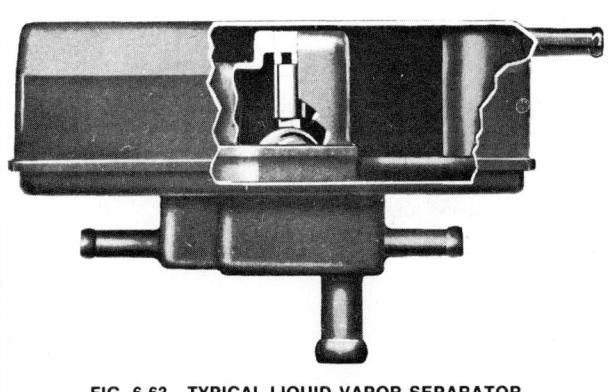

FIG. 6-63   TYPICAL LIQUID VAPOR SEPARATOR

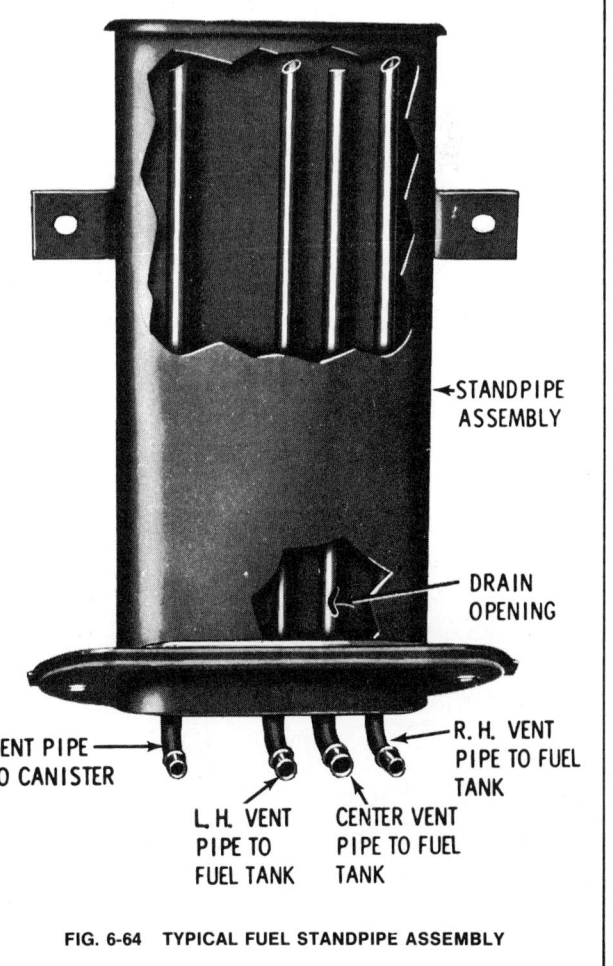

STANDPIPE ASSEMBLY

DRAIN OPENING

VENT PIPE TO CANISTER

L. H. VENT PIPE TO FUEL TANK

CENTER VENT PIPE TO FUEL TANK

R. H. VENT PIPE TO FUEL TANK

FIG. 6-64   TYPICAL FUEL STANDPIPE ASSEMBLY

OLDSMOBILE

1973-74 Emission Systems

The following systems are identical to those used on 1970-72 Oldsmobiles: Positive Crankcase Ventilation (PCV) and Controlled Combustion System (CCS).

THERMAL VACUUM SWITCH (TVS)

All V-8 engines use a coolant-temperature-controlled

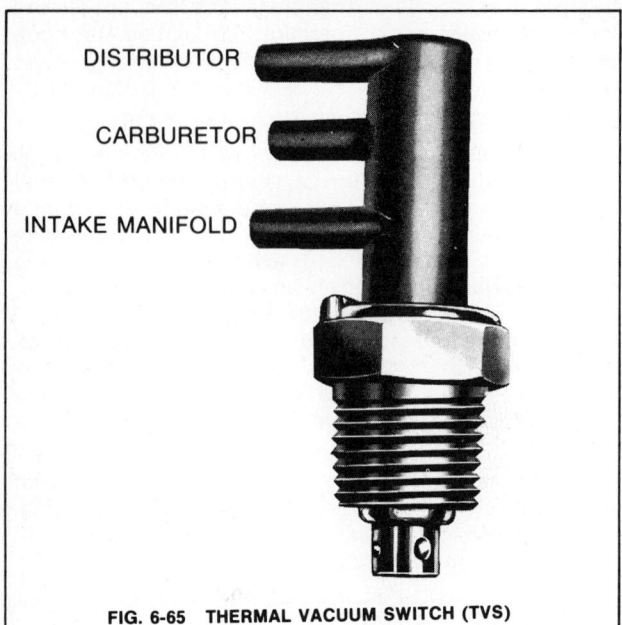

DISTRIBUTOR

CARBURETOR

INTAKE MANIFOLD

FIG. 6-65   THERMAL VACUUM SWITCH (TVS)

TVS **(Fig. 6-65)** connected by vacuum lines to the carburetor, intake manifold and distributor. Carburetor vacuum normally passes through the TVS to the distributor, but when coolant temperature reaches 226° F, the TVS switches to full manifold vacuum, advancing the ignition timing to allow the engine to run cooler. The TVS system used on the 2-bbl. 350-cu.-in. engine incorporates a vacuum reducer installed in the intake manifold line. This keeps the vacuum supplied 3 ins. less than full manifold vacuum. This reduction is necessary because the distributor and EGR valve share the same carburetor vacuum port and the distributor advance is thus calibrated to operate on less than full vacuum.

COMBINED EMISSION CONTROL (CEC)

The I-6 Omega engine with manual transmission uses the CEC system **(Fig. 6-66)** to prevent distributor vacuum advance in 1st and 2nd gears; the TCS system is no longer used. When the CEC solenoid is energized, the solenoid plunger moves outward against the throttle lever. This speeds up the engine and allows ported spark vacuum to the distributor advance unit. The solenoid is energized in one or three ways:

1. The transmission is shifted into 3rd or reverse gear.

2. The temperature override switch opens at coolant temperatures above 93° F.

3. The time delay relay allows vacuum advance for approximately 20 seconds after turning on the ignition.

The CEC solenoid is vented to purge any vacuum that might hold the distributor advanced when the transmission is positioned in 1st or 2nd gear. An idle stop solenoid prevents dieseling (run-on) by permitting

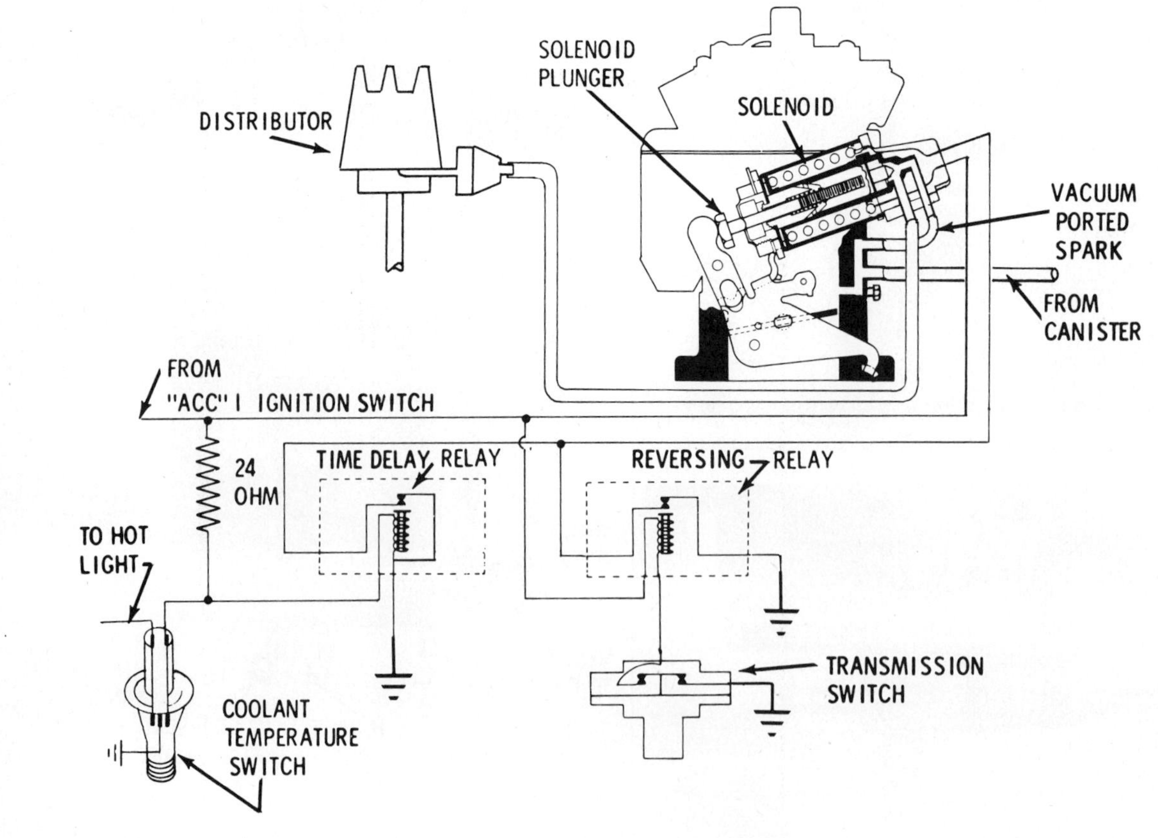

DISTRIBUTOR

SOLENOID PLUNGER

SOLENOID

VACUUM PORTED SPARK

FROM CANISTER

FROM "ACC" IGNITION SWITCH

24 OHM

TIME DELAY RELAY

REVERSING RELAY

TO HOT LIGHT

COOLANT TEMPERATURE SWITCH

TRANSMISSION SWITCH

FIG. 6-66   1974 OMEGA I-6 CEC SYSTEM

the throttle valves to close beyond their normal idle position when the ignition is turned off. Two throttle settings are thus required—one for curb idle and one for emission control. These settings are described in Chapter 5 and the adjustment procedure is shown in **Fig. 6-67.** For 1974, the CEC solenoid is replaced by a vacuum advance solenoid as in 1970-72.

AIR INJECTION REACTOR (AIR)

This system is fitted to all Omega 6-cyl. engines and consists of a belt-driven air pump (positive-displacement vane type), diverter valve and silencer assembly, check valve, special intake-manifold air-injection tubes, and the necessary connecting hoses. The AIR pump is located at the upper left front of the engine. Intake air passes through a centrifugal fan at the front of the pump and is delivered to the intake manifold. During sudden deceleration, vacuum causes a diverter valve at the back of the pump to open, passing pump air into the atmosphere. A check valve located in the line behind the diverter valve contains a one-way diaphragm which prevents hot exhaust gases from backing up in the hose and damaging the pump during periods of pump belt failure, excessive system pressure or hose ruptures.

EXHAUST GAS RECIRCULATION (EGR)

EGR is added to all 1973 models and continued with minor change in 1974. A vacuum-operated recirculation control valve regulates the amount of exhaust gases and the duration of time they enter the intake manifold. The EGR valve location differs according to engine type:

1. Inline engines—Inlet manifold just to the front of the carburetor **(Fig. 6-68).**

2. All V-8 engines—Left side of the intake manifold **(Fig. 6-69).**

When the throttle valves are opened beyond the idle point, vacuum is applied against the EGR-valve actuating diaphragm. The EGR valve begins to open at approximately 2 ins. of vacuum. As the diaphragm moves up against spring pressure, it opens the exhaust-gas intake valve, allowing exhaust gases from the manifold-crossover exhaust channels (V-8) or a drilled hole (I-6) to be drawn back into the engine intake manifold. The valve remains closed during idle and deceleration, when excessive exhaust gases added to the air/fuel mixture would cause rough engine idling.

BACKPRESSURE TRANSDUCER VALVE (BPV)

The BPV is added to all California 1974 V-8 engines to modulate EGR flow to engine load. Exhaust pressure in the BPV probe moves a diaphragm to close off the air bleed **(Fig. 6-70)** to allow maximum exhaust-gas recirculation when the engine load is high. As the engine load decreases, exhaust pressure in the probe decreases, causing the air bleed to open. Vacuum to the EGR valve then bleeds through the air bleed, reducing vacuum flow to the EGR valve and modulating exhaust gas recirculation **(Fig. 6-71).**

DISTRIBUTOR VACUUM VALVE (DVV)

1974 California V-8 and all Toronado engines use a DVV to increase drivability. The DVV directs vacuum to the distributor vacuum-advance unit from the carburetor ported-spark port until the vacuum reaches 8 ins. (7 ins., California). The DVV then switches to direct vacuum from the carburetor EGR port to the distributor vacuum advance.

THERMAL CHECK AND DELAY VALVE

This device is installed in the vacuum advance circuit of all 1974 4-bbl. engines (except California and Toronado models). Located in the vacuum line between the carburetor ported-spark port and the TVS carburetor "C" port, this valve is open whenever the underhood temperature is below 50° F. This sends full distributor ported vacuum to the vacuum advance unit. Above 50° F, the valve is in a restricting position, causing distributor ported vacuum to be metered through a 0.005-in. orifice, thereby delaying full vacuum advance for up to 40 seconds. The valve is bypassed above 226° F coolant temperature when the TVS valve switches. Vacuum comes from the intake manifold el-

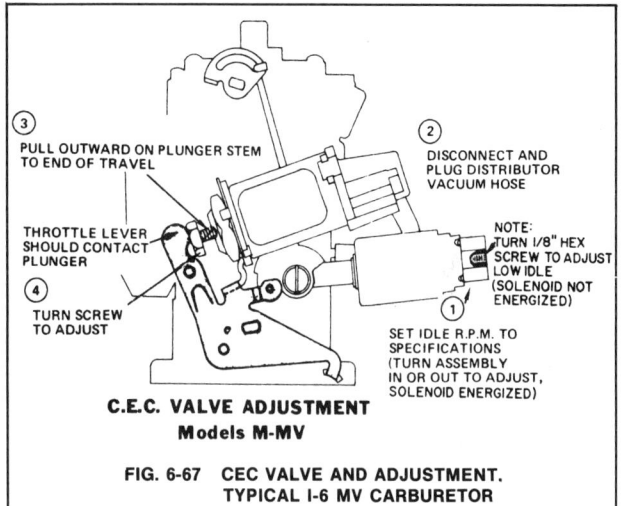

C.E.C. VALVE ADJUSTMENT
Models M-MV

FIG. 6-67   CEC VALVE AND ADJUSTMENT.
TYPICAL I-6 MV CARBURETOR

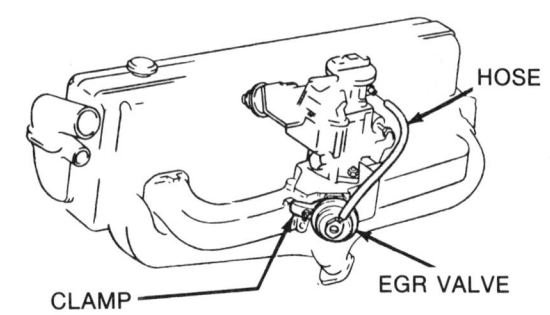

FIG. 6-68   EGR VALVE LOCATION (I-6)

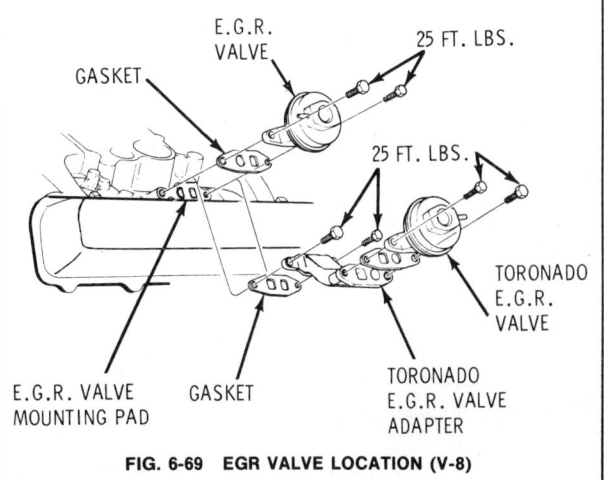

FIG. 6-69   EGR VALVE LOCATION (V-8)

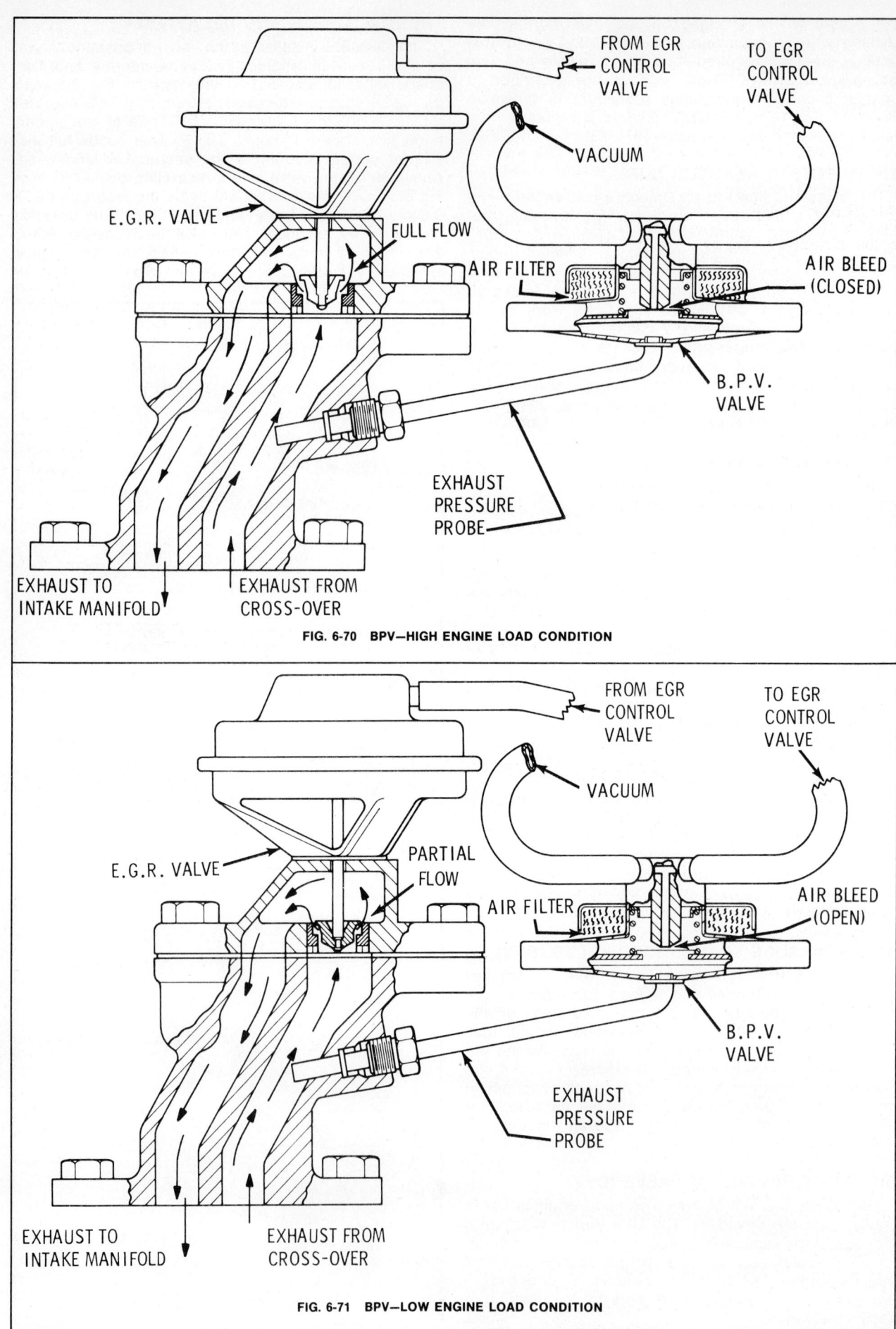

FIG. 6-70   BPV—HIGH ENGINE LOAD CONDITION

FIG. 6-71   BPV—LOW ENGINE LOAD CONDITION

bow during this time. A black plastic cover, fitted over the valve on engines manufactured after March 15, 1973, is used to make the valve more dependent on engine temperature.

VACUUM REDUCER VALVE (VRV)

The VRV is fitted to 1974 2-bbl. 350-cu.-in., 4-bbl. California and Toronado engines. Located between the intake manifold elbow and the TVS-switch manifold ''MT'' port, it reduces intake manifold vacuum 3 ins. This helps to prevent detonation when coolant temperature is above 226° F and the TVS ''MT'' port is open to the distributor vacuum-advance unit. The VRV has one port on its manifold side and two ports on its TVS side; the center port is open to vent at the carburetor air horn, while the outboard port is open to the TVS switch ''MT'' port.

EVAPORATIVE CONTROL SYSTEM (ECS)

The fuel standpipe assembly is eliminated on 1973 and later models.

OLDSMOBILE

1975-76 Emission Systems

The Positive Crankcase Ventilation (PCV) system remains the same as on the 1970-72 models. Air Injection Reactor (AIR) is the same as 1973-74.

THERMAL VACUUM SWITCH (TVS)

Oldsmobile uses the following TVS switches on 1975-76 engines; see **Fig. 6-65** for a typical TVS switch configuration:

1. Exhaust Gas Recirculation Thermal Vacuum Switch (EGR-TVS) is installed on the thermostat housing of all I-6 engines. The TVS opens to pass vacuum to the EGR valve when coolant temperature reaches 100° F.

2. Exhaust Gas Recirculation/Early Fuel Evaporation Thermal Vacuum Switch (EGR/EFE-TVS) is fitted to all V-6 and Omega 350-cu.-in. engines. The same switch is installed to all 350-cu.-in. 2-bbl. and the California Omega 350 4-bbl. engines, but the EFE port is capped, because these engines do not use an EFE valve.

3. Distributor Thermal Vacuum Switch (DTVS) comes in three versions: one for engines without manifold vacuum to the distributor, one for engines with full manifold vacuum spark and one for engines with ported spark. Their operation varies according to the vacuum application, but all are used to increase ignition timing at coolant temperatures of 220° F and above to permit the engine to run cooler.

4. Early Fuel Evaporation Thermal Vacuum Switch (EFE-TVS) is equipped on some engines to activate the heat valve on the exhaust manifold. At coolant temperatures below 120° F, manifold vacuum is sent from the EFE-TVS EFE port to the EFE actuator to close the heat valve and direct exhaust flow through the intake manifold crossover.

5. Early Fuel Evaporation/Exhaust Gas Recirculation Thermal Vacuum Switch (EFE/EGR-TVS) performs the same function as No. 4 above, but is installed only on California 260-cu.-in. and Toronado engines.

6. Early Fuel Evaporation-Distributor Thermal Vacuum Switch (EFE-DTVS) is a combination switch which performs the same function as No. 3, but is installed only on the 1975 400-cu.-in. engine.

7. Choke Thermal Vacuum Switch (CTVS) provides a richer choke operation on I-6 1-bbl., 400-cu.-in. 2-bbl., and all 4-bbl. carburetors when engine coolant temperature measures below 57° F (4-bbl. carburetors), 80° F

(I-6) or 62° F (400-cu.-in.—the CTVS is located in the air cleaner). These are used to override choke vacuum-break operation when coolant is below the specified temperature, improving cold drivability.

THERMOSTATIC AIR CLEANER (TAC)

A part of the Controlled Combustion System (CCS) during 1970-74, this now refers only to the air cleaner assembly, which consists of the air cleaner shell and cover, a temperature sensor, vacuum motor, control damper assembly, and connecting hoses. The temperature sensor controls the vacuum motor, which operates the control damper assembly to regulate the flow of preheated and cool air to the carburetor. Preheating is accomplished by circulating ambient air through the hot air pipe and shroud on the exhaust manifold before passing it through the carburetor. System operation is fully explained under Thermostatic Air Cleaner (TAC) Test on page 6-38.

EARLY FUEL EVAPORATION (EFE)

Added to the exhaust system on most 1975-76 Oldsmobiles, the EFE valve promotes quick heating of incoming fuel by directing exhaust gas flow through the intake-manifold crossover passage directly under the carburetor whenever engine coolant/oil temperature is below a specified level. Two variations are used as follows:

1. Oldsmobile I-6 Engines—The EFE system includes an EFE valve at the flange of the exhaust manifold, a

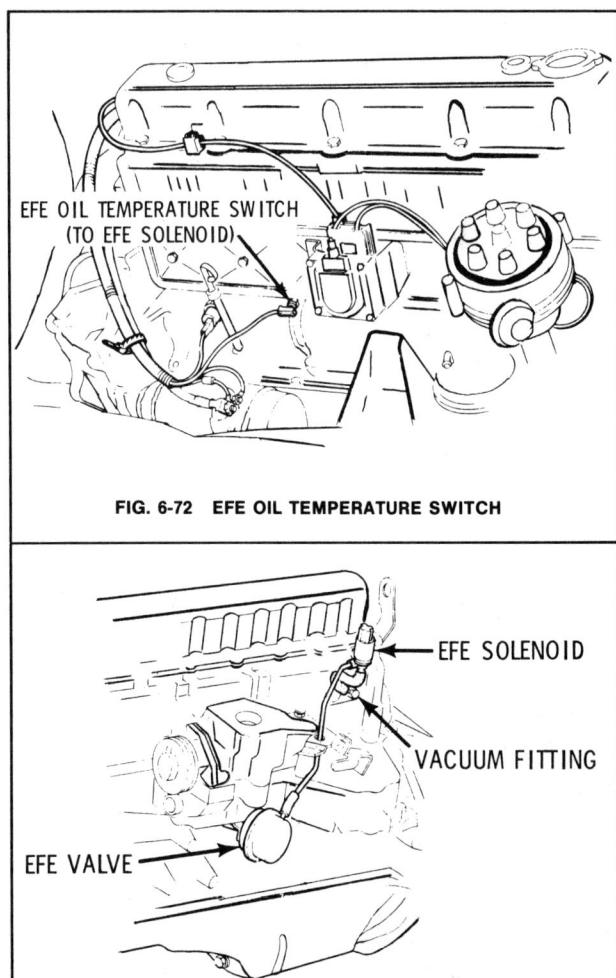

FIG. 6-72 EFE OIL TEMPERATURE SWITCH

EFE OIL TEMPERATURE SWITCH (TO EFE SOLENOID)

EFE SOLENOID

VACUUM FITTING

EFE VALVE

FIG. 6-73 EFE VALVE SOLENOID

power actuator and actuator rod, an EFE oil temperature switch **(Fig. 6-72)**, and an EFE vacuum solenoid **(Fig. 6-73)**. When engine oil temperature reaches 150° F, the solenoid is electrically energized. This closes the vacuum supply to the EFE valve, allowing it to open. An EFE Oil Thermal Vacuum Switch (EFE-OTVS) replaces the temperature switch and vacuum solenoid on 1976 applications; operation and temperature specifications remain unchanged.

2. On all Other Oldsmobile Engines—The EFE system includes an EFE valve at the flange of the exhaust manifold, a power actuator and actuator rod, and a TVS switch mounted in the thermostat housing. At coolant temperatures below 120° F, manifold vacuum is applied to the actuator, which closes the EFE valve through the actuator rod connection. When coolant temperature exceeds 120° F, vacuum to the power actuator is blocked, allowing the EFE valve to open.

VACUUM REDUCER VALVE (VRV)

See 1973-74.

Calibration is changed as follows: intake manifold vacuum is reduced 1½ ins. (from earlier 3-in. reduction) to prevent detonation when coolant temperature exceeds 220° F (from former 226° F).

EXHAUST GAS RECIRCULATION (EGR)

See 1973-74.

An EGR-TVS is used on all 1975-76 I-6 engines to pass vacuum to the EGR valve when coolant temperature reaches 100° F. The Backpressure Transducer Valve, added to all 1974 California V-8 engines to modulate EGR flow to engine load, is retained for 1975-76 (see Backpressure Transducer, 1973-74).

DISTRIBUTOR VACUUM DELAY VALVE (DVDV)

A DVDV valve is located in the vacuum line between the carburetor port and the DTVS "C" port on some V-8 engines. This meters ported vacuum to the distributor through a 0.005-in. orifice to delay full vacuum advance for up to 40 seconds, but is bypassed above 220° F coolant temperature when the DTVS switches.

VACUUM DELAY VALVE (EGR-VDV)

An EGR-VDV is located in the vacuum line to the EGR valve on some V-8 engines. This meters vacuum through a 0.005-in. orifice to delay vacuum from bleeding down too fast at the EGR valve, requiring up to 40 seconds for full vacuum loss at the EGR valve.

CHOKE HOT AIR MODULATOR CHECK VALVE (CHAM-CV)

This check valve **(Fig. 6-74)** is installed in the air cleaner on Omega 350 and Starfire 231 engines. As the valve is closed at air temperatures below 68° F, air heated by the heater coil passes through a 0.005-in. orifice in the modulator. This permits very little hot airflow to reach the choke's bi-metallic thermostatic coil, resulting in a slower choke warm-up. At temperature above 68° F, the modulator opens to pass more airflow and shorten the choke warm-up time.

SPARK ADVANCE VACUUM MODULATOR (SAVM)

A dual-diaphragm regulating valve with three ports, the SAVM **(Fig. 6-75)** controls vacuum to the distributor vacuum advance on some 1976 Oldsmobile engines. The valve responds only to engine load and provides two operation conditions:

a) If manifold and ported vacuum are both below 7 ins., the valve output to the distributor is manifold vacuum.

b) If manifold and ported vacuum are both above 7 ins., the valve output to the distributor is ported vacuum.

CATALYTIC CONVERTER

1975-76 Oldsmobiles are fitted with a catalytic converter to improve fuel economy and drivability.

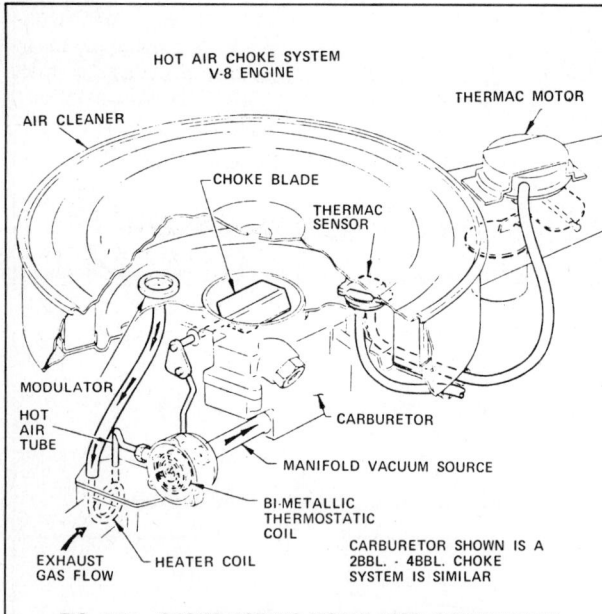

FIG. 6-74 CHOKE HOT-AIR-MODULATOR CHECK VALVE

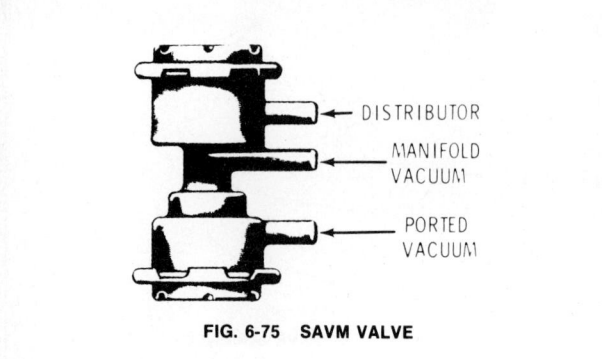

FIG. 6-75 SAVM VALVE

OLDSMOBILE

1977 Emission Systems

The Positive Crankcase Ventilation (PCV) system is identical to that used in 1970-72. The Air Injection Reactor (AIR) and Exhaust Gas Recirculation (EGR) are the same as those used on 1973-74 engines. The following systems are the same as used on 1975-76 engines: Thermal Vacuum Switch (TVS), Distributor Vacuum Delay Valve (DVDV), Vacuum Delay Valve (EGR-VDV) Early Fuel Evaporation (EFE), Spark Advance Vacuum Modulator (SAVM), Thermostatic Air Cleaner (TAC) and Catalytic Converter.

BACKPRESSURE EXHAUST RECIRCULATION (BP-EGR)

Similar to that used on some 1976 models, backpressure transducer has been integrated into the EGR valve on some applications. A small, diaphragm-controlled valve inside the EGR assembly acts as a pressure regulator. It receives backpressure through the hollow shaft and exerts force on the control valve diaphragm **(Fig. 6-75A)**. A metal deflector plate prevents hot exhaust gases from reaching the diaphragm. Any increase in engine load will increase exhaust backpressure, causing the control to close.

PULSE AIR INJECTOR REACTION SYSTEM (PAIR)

Used on the I-4 engine, this system relies on a series of pipes and check valves for air distribution, using the engine exhaust pulses to siphon air into the exhaust port. Unlike the AIR system, it is not an engine-driven pump.

DISTRIBUTOR THERMAL VACUUM SWITCH (DTVS)

Located in the coolant outlet of some engines, this switch opens when coolant temperature reaches 100°F, allowing vacuum to be directed to the EGR valve.

EARLY FUEL EVAPORATION CHECK VALVE (EFE-CV)

A check valve in the vacuum line from the carburetor to the EFE-TVS switch on some 350 V-8 engines. The valve holds the highest vacuum reached to keep the EFE heat valve closed until the TVS mode switches.

CHOKE THERMAL VACUUM SWITCH (CTVS)

Some 350 engines and the 403 V-8 use a choke thermal vacuum switch to give richer choke operation when air temperature is below 62°F. The switch controls vacuum to both carburetor vacuum breaks.

TRAPPED VACUUM SPARK ADVANCE

For I-4 engines, this system improves cold driveaway and engine warm-up. When coolant temperature is below 115°F, full vacuum is supplied through the delay valve to the distributor at a higher vacuum level than would be available during acceleration. A small orifice allows for leakdown to enable restarts in case the engine stalls.

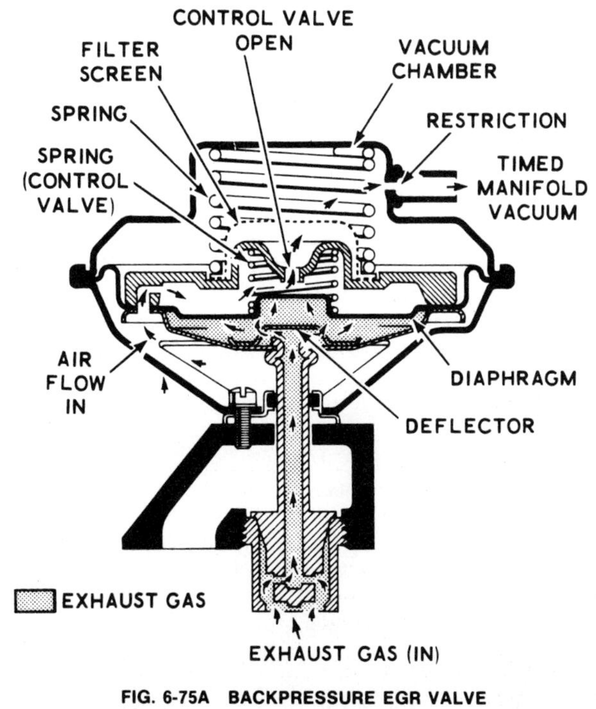

EGR THERMAL CONTROL VALVE (EGR-TCV)

Some V-8 engines have a temperature-sensitive control valve in the vacuum line to the EGR valve. The valve is closed below 61°F, blocking vacuum to the EGR and giving better driveaway and engine warm-up. Above 76°F, the EGR control valve opens, allowing ported vacuum to be directed to the EGR valve.

DIFFERENTIAL VACUUM DELAY/SEPARATOR VALVE (DVDSV)

This valve activates the Air Bypass Valve on California V-6 231 engines when the throttle is opened and closed rapidly.

OLDSMOBILE

1978-79 Emission Systems

The Positive Crankcase Ventilation (PCV) valve is identical to that used in 1970-72. The Air-Injection Reactor (AIR) and Exhaust Gas Recirculation (EGR) systems are the same as those used on 1973-74 engines. The Thermostatic Air Cleaner (TAC), Thermal Vacuum Switch (TVS), Distributor Vacuum Delay Valve (DVDV), Early Fuel Evaporation (EFE) and Spark Advance Vacuum Modulator (SAVM) are the same as used on 1975-76 engines. The Backpressure Exhaust Recirculation (BP-EGR), Differential Vacuum Delay/Separator Valve (DVDSV) and EGR Thermal Control Valve (EGR-TCV) are the same as used on 1977 engines.

ELECTRONIC FUEL CONTROL (EFC) SYSTEM

This system is used to control emissions by precise regulation of the air/fuel ratio and the use of a three-way catalytic converter. It consists of an exhaust gas oxygen sensor, an electronic control unit (ECU), vacuum modulator, controlled air/fuel ratio carburetor (Holley 6510-C) and the three-way converter **(Fig. 6-75B)**. Its use in 1978 is restricted to California I-4 151 engines (Code 1).

Located in the exhaust pipe below the exhaust manifold, an oxygen sensor generates a voltage according to the amount of oxygen in the exhaust gas. Voltage rises with a rich mixture and falls with a lean one. The

FIG. 6-75A BACKPRESSURE EGR VALVE

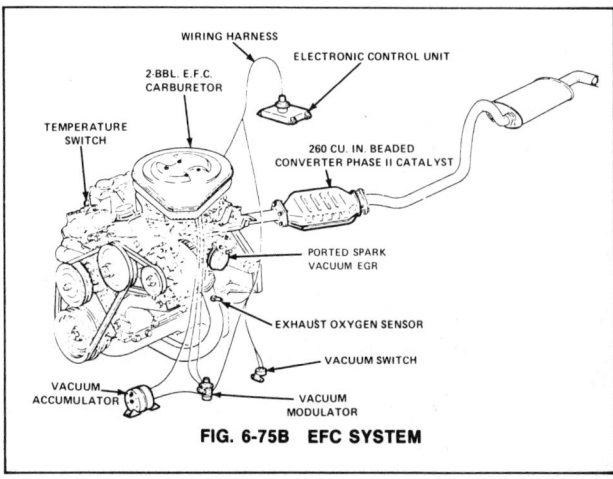
FIG. 6-75B EFC SYSTEM

ECU transforms the voltage output of the sensor into a control signal to the vacuum modulator. The vacuum modulator then signals the carburetor feedback diaphragms. These diaphragms control the air bleed needle and main metering orifice in the carburetor. In this way, the carburetor air/fuel mixture is leaned or is enriched according to the signal from the vacuum modulator.

The three-way converter acts to reduce all three pollutants—NOx, CO and HC. Its efficiency depends upon precise control of the air/fuel ratio, as provided by the EFC system. For proper EFC system operation, it is important that the ECU wiring harness locator clip be aligned with the notch on the ECU. If it is not, proper contact will not be made, although the wiring harness will appear to be properly plugged in. Lack of contact will cause a variety of engine/carburetor malfunctions, and should always be checked first when the vehicle is not running correctly.

DISTRIBUTOR THERMAL VACUUM SWITCH (DTVS)
See 1977

Use is extended to a variety of engines, with calibration dependent upon engine usage.

EARLY FUEL EVAPORATION CHECK VALVE (EFE-CV)
See 1977

Usage is changed to the V-6 231 and V-8 305 engines.

CHOKE THERMAL VACUUM SWITCH (CTVS)
See 1977

Use is extended to the V-6 231 and V-8 260 engines. Calibration is changed to 70° F on 260, 350 and 403 applications; 62° F on 231 engines.

SPARK RETARD DELAY VALVE (SRDV)

This is used in conjunction with the Distributor Thermal Vacuum Switch (DTVS) on I-4 151 engines. It maintains vacuum advance during rapid throttle openings—whenever coolant temperature is below the DTVS switching point of 120° F. A rapid throttle opening causes a sudden decrease in vacuum. The SRDV orifice delays the drop in vacuum to the distributor advance mechanism. The length of delay depends upon the difference in vacuum; the greater the difference, the longer the delay.

COLD ENGINE AIR BLEED-THERMAL VACUUM SWITCH (CEAB-TVS)

This TVS is fitted to I-4 151 engine (Code 1). At temperatures below 170° F, the TVS opens to allow clean air to bleed to the intake manifold. The TVS closes above 170° F to stop the flow.

CANISTER PURGE-THERMAL VACUUM SWITCH (CP-TVS)

This TVS is fitted to V-6 231 engines. At coolant temperatures below 170° F, an internal orifice in the TVS controls canister purge. When coolant temperature exceeds 170° F, the TVS opens. This allows ported manifold vacuum to control canister purging.

DISTRIBUTOR THERMAL CONTROL VALVE (DTCV)

This check valve is fitted to California V-8 260 engines. Located in the manifold vacuum line to the distributor, it allows vacuum to pass at temperatures below 61° F and blocks it at temperatures above 76° F. A Distributor Check Valve (DCV) is also used in the manifold vacuum line between the DTCV and the EGR/DTVS. This holds the highest manifold vacuum to the distributor until either the EGR/DTVS or DTCV switches over. The two devices are used to improve cold engine drivability.

CHOKE VACUUM BREAK-VACUUM DELAY VALVE (CVB-VDV)

Fitted to all I-4 151 engines, this delays a sudden increase in vacuum from reaching the choke vacuum break diaphragm. The length of the delay depends upon the difference in vacuum; the greater the difference, the longer the delay.

EMISSION SYSTEM TEST PROCEDURES
PCV TEST

1. Connect a tachometer and start the engine.
2. Clamp off the crankcase ventilator hose to shut off the airflow completely.
3. If idle speed drops 50-60 rpm, the PCV system is functioning. If the idle speed does not drop, install a new valve.

ALTERNATE PCV TEST

1. Remove the PCV valve from the intake manifold or rocker arm cover.
2. Start the engine and run at idle.
3. Place a thumb over the valve end to check for vacuum. If there is no vacuum at the valve, inspect for plugged hoses.
4. Shut the engine off. Shake the valve and listen for the rattle of the check needle in the valve. If no rattle is heard, replace the valve.

THERMOSTATIC AIR CLEANER (TAC) TEST

1. With the engine off, remove the air cleaner cover and tape a suitable thermometer to the air cleaner base next to the sensor. Until 1973, all sensors were rated at 85° F; sensors used from 1973 through 1975 are color-coded to indicate the temperature rating, with the green sensor activated at 79° F and the blue sensor at 107° F. Only the green sensor was used in 1976. A second green sensor with a different rating is also used for 1977-78. The air cleaner temperature must be below the sensor rating to perform the test correctly.
2. Tee a vacuum gauge in the vacuum line at the motor assembly on the snorkel tube. The control damper door should be open with the engine off.
3. Replace the air cleaner cover without the wing nut and start the engine. The control damper door should close immediately.
4. Watch the control door position; when it reaches full open, remove the air cleaner cover immediately and record the temperature and vacuum gauge reading. Compare readings to the following specifications:

SENSOR	TEMP. (° F)	VACUUM (In. Hg)	DAMPER DOOR POSITION
1970-72	85° or lower	9	CLOSED
	128° or higher	5	OPEN
GREEN	79° or lower	7	CLOSED
	123° or higher	3	OPEN
BLUE	107° or lower	7	CLOSED
	151° or higher	3	OPEN
1977-78 ALTERNATE			
GREEN	75° or lower	7	CLOSED
	151° or higher	3	OPEN

5. If temperature is within specifications, CCS is functioning properly. If not, replace the sensor. If both sensor and vacuum are within specifications, but control door is not working properly, replace the vacuum motor. If both temperature and vacuum are *not* within specifications, the vacuum motor diaphragm is leaking—replace the vacuum motor.

THERMOSTATIC VACUUM SWITCH TEST

1. Disconnect the distributor vacuum hose at the TVS "Dist" port and connect a vacuum gauge.
2. Vacuum gauge should indicate full engine vacuum if the switch is functioning properly.
3. If it does not, remove and replace, using a soft-setting sealant on the threads.

V-8 TCS COMPONENT TEST

1. Disconnect the connector from the switch on the side of the transmission and connect a test lamp from the TCS switch terminal to a 12-volt source. The test lamp should not use a bulb larger than 0.8-amp or it will damage the switch.
2. If a double-terminal switch is used, it is located in the engine compartment. Disconnect the connector and ground one terminal, connecting the test lamp to the other.
3. Automatic Transmission—Test lamp should be off when the transmission is in REVERSE, and on with the transmission in DRIVE (engine running).
Manual Transmission—Test lamp should be off when the transmission is in high gear, and on with the transmission in any lower gear.
4. The manual transmission switch can be adjusted if necessary by loosening the adjustment screws and positioning the switch to obtain the conditions specified in Step 3. Automatic transmission switches must be replaced if they do not function correctly.
5. To test the solenoid, disconnect the hose and the electrical connector.
6. Connect a hose to the distributor vacuum port on the solenoid and blow into it. Air should come from the solenoid carburetor-vacuum port.
7. Plug the solenoid carburetor-vacuum port. Connect a jumper wire from No. 1 terminal to ground. Connect the other terminal to a 12-volt source. Air should now come from the vent port.
8. Plug the vent port. Airflow through the solenoid should be shut off.
9. If the solenoid fails Step 6, 7 or 8, replace it.

6-CYL. TCS COMPONENT TEST

Test the transmission switch and solenoid action as in the "V-8 TCS Component Test." To test the relay and temperature switch:
1. Disconnect the relay and connect a 12-volt source to the No. 1 terminal.
2. Connect a 12-volt test lamp to the No. 2 terminal and to ground. The test lamp should light; if not, replace the relay.
3. Connect the No. 3 terminal to ground. The test lamp should go off. If it remains on, replace the relay.
4. Disconnect the temperature switch connection and connect a 12-volt test lamp to the "G" terminal and to a 12-volt source.
5. With the engine cold, the test lamp should be on. Start the engine and let it idle. The test lamp should go off after a few minutes. If the lamp does not react as specified, replace the temperature switch.

THERMAL VACUUM SWITCH TEST

This is the same unit as the Thermostatic Vacuum Switch used on some 1970 applications, and the test procedure is identical. The primary difference between the Thermal and the Thermostatic Vacuum switches is in the center nipple connection. On the 1970 Thermostatic Vacuum Switch, it is connected to the TCS solenoid, and on the later Thermal Vacuum Switch, it is connected to the carburetor.

COMBINATION EMISSION CONTROL SYSTEM (CEC) COMPONENT TEST

1. To test the solenoid, disconnect the hose and the electrical connector.
2. Connect a hose to the distributor vacuum port on the solenoid and blow through it. Air should come from the solenoid vent port.
3. Plug the solenoid carburetor-vacuum port. Connect a jumper wire from No. 1 terminal to ground. Connect the other terminal to a 12-volt source. Air should now come from the ported spark port.
4. To test the transmission switch, disconnect the switch connector from the transmission side.
5. Connect a test lamp from the switch terminal to a 12-volt source. Do not use a test lamp with a bulb requiring more than 0.8-amp or the switch contacts will be damaged.
6. Test lamp should light when the transmission is placed in 3rd gear, and remain off in 1st or 2nd gear.
7. Check the time delay relay to make sure it is cool, then remove the temperature switch connection on the engine.
8. Turn the ignition on—the solenoid should energize for 20 seconds, then de-energize. If the solenoid does not de-energize, remove the time-relay blue lead. If the solenoid now de-energizes, replace the relay.
9. The temperature switch must be tested with the engine cold. Turn on the ignition and the CEC solenoid should energize and stay energized.
10. If the solenoid does not energize, or if it energizes and then de-energizes after 20 seconds, ground the cold terminal at the temperature switch. If the solenoid now energizes, replace the temperature switch.

CEC SOLENOID ADJUSTMENT (Fig. 6-76)

Energized through the transmission, the CEC solenoid acts as a throttle stop by increasing the idle speed during high gear operation. The CEC solenoid also provides full vacuum advance during high gear operation, and is de-energized at all other gears and at idle for retarded spark timing. The normal idle speed setting is made with the idle stopscrew. The CEC solenoid should require adjustment only in cases of solenoid replacement, major carburetor overhaul or removal/replacement of the carburetor throttle body.
To adjust the CEC solenoid:
1. Disconnect and plug the distributor vacuum-advance line; disconnect the fuel tank hose from the vapor canister.
2. Refer to specific instructions for adjustment found on the vehicle emission control sticker; start the engine and connect a tachometer.
3. Manually extend the solenoid valve plunger until it touches the throttle lever.
4. Adjust the plunger length until the specified engine speed is obtained.
5. Reconnect the vacuum advance and vapor canister lines.

EGR VALVE FUNCTIONAL TEST

1. Remove the air cleaner and plug the manifold vacuum fitting; remove the distributor vacuum line at the distributor and plug; remove the EGR hose from the EGR valve and plug hose.

2. Connect a tachometer. Turn the air conditioner off, block the drive wheels and place the transmission in PARK. Start the engine and warm to normal operating temperature. Place the fast-idle cam follower on the 2nd step of the fast idle cam and record the engine speed.

3. Connect a hand vacuum pump to the EGR valve and apply 9 ins. vacuum. The EGR valve diaphragm should rise and engine speed drop at least 250 rpm with an automatic transmission, 100 rpm with a manual transmission.

4. If engine rpm does not drop as specified, remove and clean the EGR valve assembly and clean the intake manifold ports. Replace EGR valve and repeat Steps 2 and 3. If engine rpm still does not drop the specified amount, replace the EGR valve.

BACKPRESSURE TRANSDUCER FUNCTION TEST

1. Remove the air cleaner and plug the manifold vacuum fitting.

2. Connect a tachometer. Turn the air conditioner off, block the drive wheels and place the transmission in PARK. Start the engine and warm to normal operating temperature. Place the fast-idle cam follower on the high step of the fast idle cam.

3. Check and record the vacuum reading from the carburetor (source) side of the BPV valve.

4. Tee a vacuum gauge to the EGR control side of the BPV. If vacuum is not 1.7 to 2.7 ins., replace the valve. Leave the vacuum gauge installed.

5. Now remove the EGR valve line at the EGR valve, and plug the line. Vacuum gauge should now read the same as the carburetor-side vacuum reading in Step 3. If it's not within 2 ins. of the carburetor vacuum, replace the BPV valve.

DISTRIBUTOR VACUUM VALVE FUNCTIONAL TEST

1. Remove the air cleaner and plug the manifold vacuum fitting.

2. Connect a tachometer. Turn the air conditioner off, block the drive wheels and place the transmission in PARK. Start the engine and warm to normal operating temperature.

3. Remove the "D" port hose from the TVS and attach a vacuum gauge to this port. Tee a second vacuum gauge to the hose at the carburetor EGR port.

4. Gradually open the throttle. The first gauge should read 8 ins. vacuum (7 ins., California) and level off until the second gauge reaches 8 ins. of vacuum (7 ins., California), then both gauges will give the same reading as the throttle is opened, if the valve is functioning correctly. If the readings are not as specified, replace the DVV valve.

THERMAL CHECK & DELAY VALVE FUNCTION TEST

1. Cool valve to at least 40° F to unseat the disc.

2. Connect a hand vacuum pump with gauge to the carburetor side of the valve, and a vacuum gauge to the TVS port.

3. When a vacuum is applied, there should be no delay in the readings between the two gauges. If there is, replace the valve.

VACUUM REDUCER VALVE TEST

1. Connect a vacuum gauge to the "D" port and a hand vacuum pump to the "Man" port.

2. Apply 15 ins. of vacuum; the "D" port reading should be 3 to 4 ins. lower. If not, replace the valve.

6-CYL. VAPOR CANISTER DIAPHRAGM TEST (Fig. 6-77)

1. Tee a vacuum gauge in the line to the canister inlet port marked "Carb."

2. Start the engine and pinch the vacuum source line between vacuum gauge and carburetor. If vacuum gauge bleeds down, replace canister diaphragm.

SPARK ADVANCE MODULATOR (SAVM) TEST

1. Connect a vacuum gauge to the distributor port,

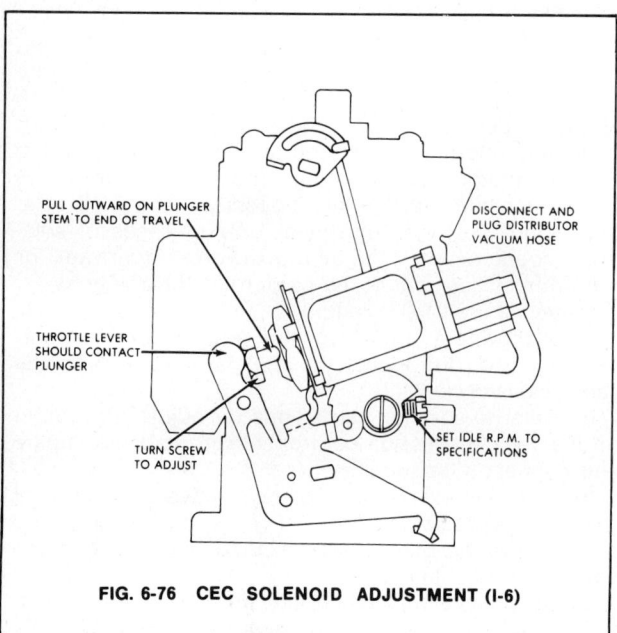

FIG. 6-76 CEC SOLENOID ADJUSTMENT (I-6)

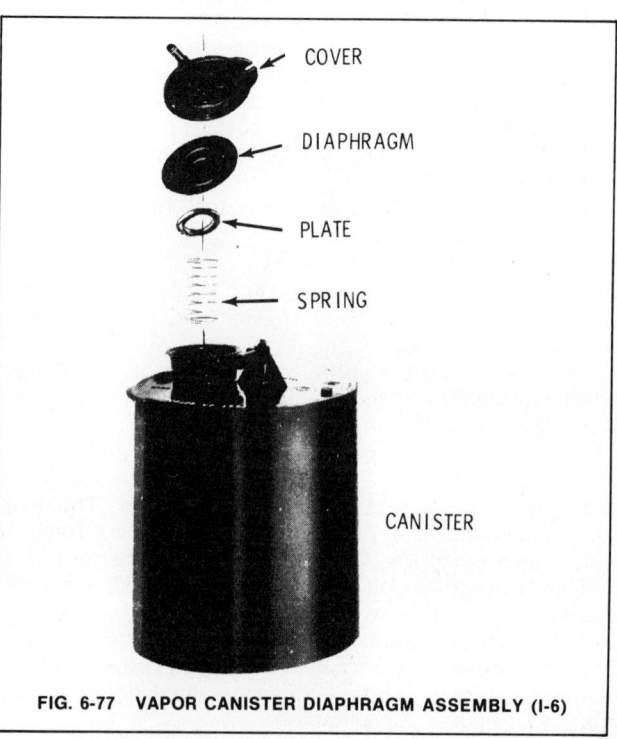

FIG. 6-77 VAPOR CANISTER DIAPHRAGM ASSEMBLY (I-6)

then apply 7 ins. vacuum to the manifold port (**Fig. 6-75**). The vacuum gauge should read 7 ins. of vacuum and remain constant.

2. Move the vacuum pump to the ported vacuum connection and repeat Step 1. Vacuum gauge should stay at zero until the pump output reaches 7 ins., then follow the pump level upward.

3. Reverse the vacuum gauge and vacuum pump connections in Step 2 and pump up several inches of vacuum. The gauge reading should stay at zero.

4. If the SAVM fails any of these three functional steps, replace it.

CHOKE HOT AIR MODULATOR CHECK VALVE (CHAM-CV) TEST

1. Remove the air cleaner cover and tape a suitable thermometer next to the modulator. If the temperature is below 68° F ± 7° F, the valve should be closed. If the temperature is above 68° F ± 7° F, the valve should be open. Replace the valve if it does not perform to these specifications.

DISTRIBUTOR THERMAL VACUUM SWITCH (DTVS) TEST

To test the ported spark or no manifold vacuum versions:

1. Disconnect the distributor vacuum line at the port marked "D" and connect a vacuum gauge.

2. Start the engine and warm to normal operating temperature. Check vacuum reading at idle. If more than 5 ins. are present, replace the DTVS.

To test the full manifold vacuum version:

1. Start the engine and warm to normal operating temperature.

2. Disconnect the distributor vacuum line at port "D" and connect a vacuum gauge. Full manifold vacuum should be present. Reconnect the distributor vacuum line.

3. Disconnect the vacuum-reducer vacuum line from the TVS switch and plug it.

4. Connect a vacuum gauge to the vacuum-reducer valve port of the TVS and check for vacuum with the engine idling.

5. If more than 5 ins. of vacuum are present, replace the DTVS.

EMISSION SYSTEM COMPONENT REPLACEMENT

AIR CLEANER ASSEMBLY

The air cleaner assembly is not serviceable. If the damper control door is malfunctioning, the entire unit must be replaced. The vacuum motor and the air cleaner sensor are replaceable.

VACUUM MOTOR

1. Remove the air cleaner from the engine.

2. Drill out the center of the two spot welds holding the vacuum motor to the snorkel tube. Use a 1/16-in. drill— *do not* center punch.

3. Enlarge the holes to 5/32-in. Be careful not to damage or distort the air cleaner snorkel.

4. Remove the vacuum-motor retainer strap and lift the vacuum motor, tilting it to one side in order to unhook the linkage at the control door.

5. Drill a 7/64-in. hole in the snorkel tube at the center of the retaining strap end which faces the air cleaner housing.

6. Install a new vacuum motor assembly using the mounting strap retainer and sheetmetal screw provided with the new motor assembly. Screw must not interfere with damper door operation—shorten if necessary.

AIR CLEANER SENSOR

1. Pry the sensor retaining-clip tabs free, and remove the vacuum lines from the sensor.

2. Note the position of the old sensor—the new unit must be installed in the same position to avoid possible interference with the air cleaner element—then remove the old sensor.

3. Install the new sensor and gasket in the air cleaner and replace the retaining clip while supporting the sensor around the air cleaner's center rim to prevent damage to the temperature sensing spring.

4. Replace the vacuum lines and reinstall the air cleaner.

AIR PUMP REMOVAL/INSTALLATION

TO REMOVE

1. Disconnect the pump and valve hoses.

2. Loosen the pump-to-bracket mounting bolts and remove the pump drive belt.

3. Remove the pulley-to-hub bolts, and remove the pulley.

4. Remove the air pump from the engine.

TO INSTALL

1. Position the pump on the mounting bracket. Line up the holes, and install the bolts loosely.

2. Fit the pulley to the hub and tighten the bolts to 9 ft.-lbs.

3. Install the pump belt over the pulley, and adjust the tension, then torque mounting bolts to 25 ft.-lbs.

4. Reconnect the pump and valve hoses.

CENTRIFUGAL FILTER FAN REPLACEMENT

1. Remove the air pump from the engine.

2. Pull the fan from the hub with needlenose pliers. Although it is seldom possible to remove the fan without damage, take care not to let the plastic fragments enter the air intake hole.

3. Draw the new fan evenly into place, using the pulley and bolts as tools. Torque the bolts alternately to 9 ft.-lbs. Outer edge of the fan must slip into the housing.

4. Replace the pump on the engine. Until the outer diameter sealing lip has worn in, a new fan may be noisy.

DIVERTER VALVE REPLACEMENT

1. Disconnect the vacuum lines from the valve.

2. Remove the valve from the air pump or elbow.

3. Install the new valve and gasket to the pump or elbow, and torque attaching screws to 7 ft.-lbs.

4. Replace the vacuum lines to the valve, and inspect the system for leakage.

CHECK VALVE REPLACEMENT

1. Disconnect the pump hose from the check valve. Remove and replace with a new check valve, taking care not to bend, twist or otherwise distort the air manifold, and replace the pump hose.

EGR VALVE REPLACEMENT

1. Disconnect the vacuum line from the EGR valve,

and remove the two bolts attaching it to the manifold.

2. Remove the EGR valve and gasket; discard the gasket.

3. Replace the EGR valve on the manifold with a new gasket, and torque the attaching bolts to 25 ft.-lbs.

4. Connect the vacuum line to the EGR valve.

THERMAL VACUUM SWITCH (TVS) REPLACEMENT

1. Disconnect vacuum lines from the TVS.

2. Remove the switch from the manifold or thermostat housing.

3. Apply a soft-setting sealer to the threaded portion of the switch, and install the switch in the manifold or thermostat housing, torquing to 15 ft.-lbs.

4. Turn the TVS head as required to align it for proper hose connection, and reinstall the hoses.

VAPOR CANISTER FILTER REPLACEMENT

1. Disconnect the top canister hoses (two on V-8 canister, three on I-6) and loosen the strap screw (two clamp support bolts on I-6).

2. Remove the canister, and pull the filter from the bottom. On Toronado, the coolant reservoir must be removed for access to the canister.

3. Inspect hose connection openings for blockage.

4. Install a new filter by tucking it under the retainer at the canister bottom and centering it.

5. Replace the canister in the mounting strap, and tighten the strap screw/clamp bolts.

6. Replace the coolant reservoir on Toronado, and reconnect the hoses to the canister nipples.

PONTIAC

1970-71 Emission Systems

POSITIVE CRANKCASE VENTILATION (PCV)

A sealed oil-filler cap prevents crankcase gases from escaping under no-vacuum conditions **(Fig. 6-78)**. A tube from the air cleaner goes to the rocker cover, carrying fresh air through the air cleaner filter and down into the crankcase. From that point, blowby gases go through the hose into the PCV valve and then into the manifold. When the PCV system is under zero vacuum, there is no suction on the crankcase, but the gases go from the rocker cover through the hose into the air cleaner, where they are drawn into the intake manifold through the carburetor. The PCV valve is located at the front of the push rod cover on V-8 engines, and at the rear of the rocker arm cover on 6-cyl. engines.

CONTROLLED COMBUSTION SYSTEM (CCS)

A series of engine modifications, CCS uses carburetor/choke/distributor calibrations and an increased engine operating temperature to reduce emissions. Ignition timing is retarded and carburetors are calibrated to run on a leaner air/fuel mixture. A 190° F thermostat is fitted to CCS engines, allowing a higher engine temperature to produce better fuel vaporization and a reduced quench (cool) area in the combustion chambers. A thermostatically controlled air cleaner keeps the temperature of the air entering the carburetor at approximately 105° F, reducing engine icing in cold-weather climates and producing better engine warm-up. An adjustable off-idle feature in the carburetor is factory-set and should not be adjusted in the field.

Idle-mixture-needle limiter caps are installed on 1971 carburetors, and Pontiac recommends that no attempt be made to adjust carburetor mixture beyond the limits provided; the limiter caps are not to be removed for adjustment purposes.

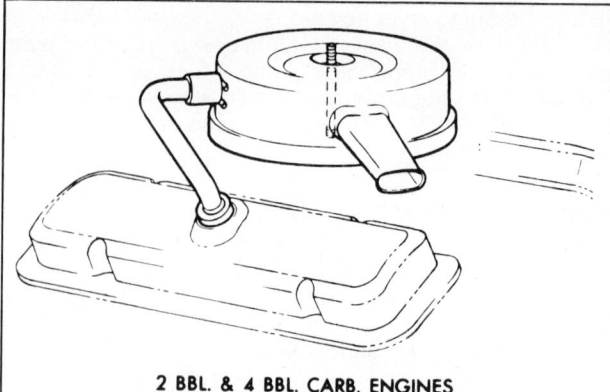

2 BBL. & 4 BBL. CARB. ENGINES

FIG. 6-78 PONTIAC V-8 PCV SYSTEM

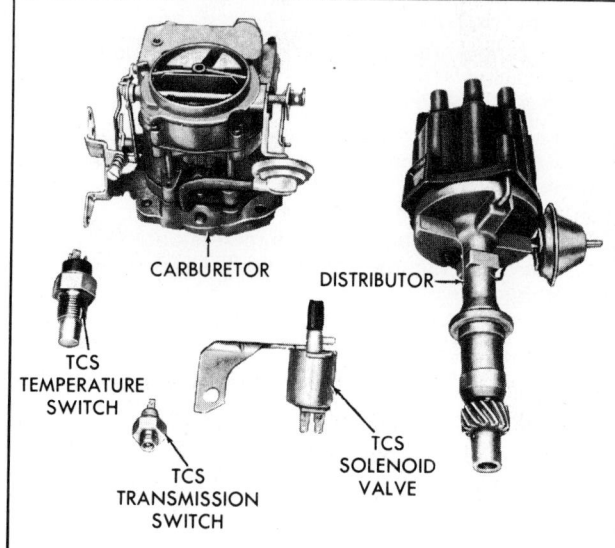

CARBURETOR   DISTRIBUTOR

TCS TEMPERATURE SWITCH

TCS TRANSMISSION SWITCH

TCS SOLENOID VALVE

FIG. 6-79 TYPICAL TCS SYSTEM COMPONENTS

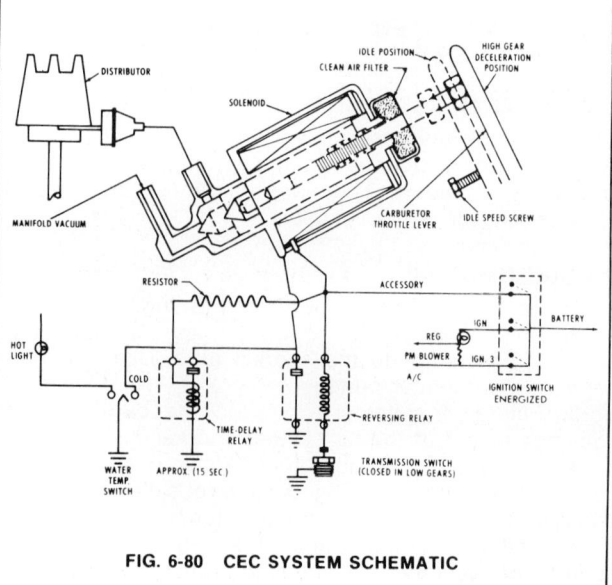

FIG. 6-80 CEC SYSTEM SCHEMATIC

TRANSMISSION CONTROLLED SPARK ADVANCE (TCS)

When used on cars equipped with automatic transmissions, the TCS system controls distributor vacuum advance by means of an oil-pressure-sensitive trans-

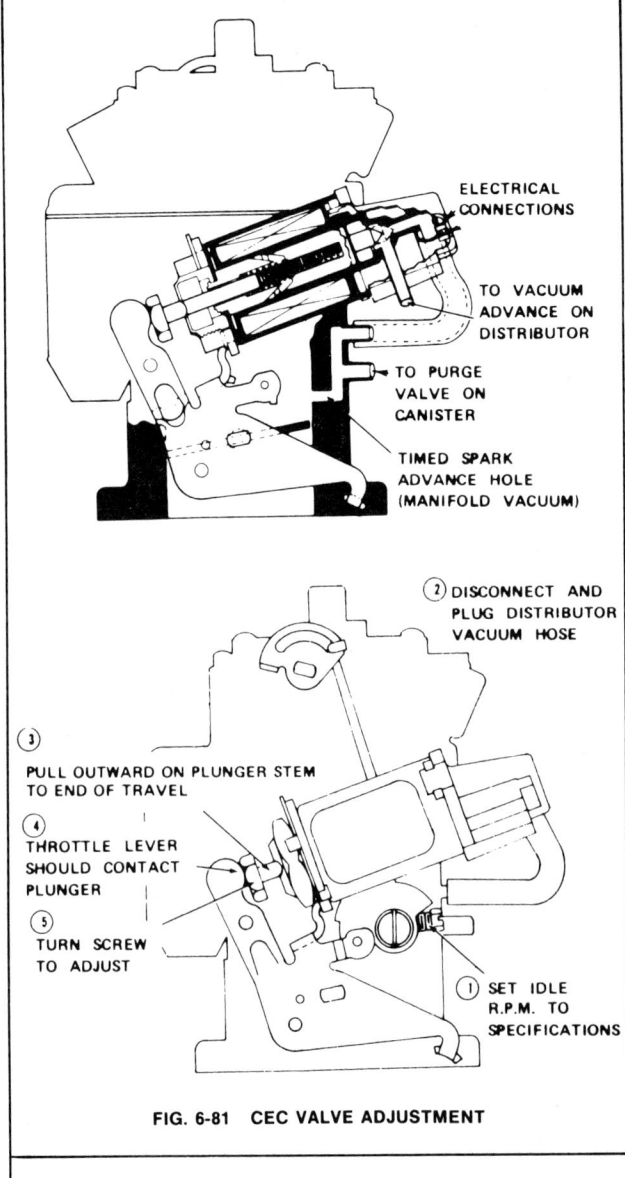

ELECTRICAL CONNECTIONS

TO VACUUM ADVANCE ON DISTRIBUTOR

TO PURGE VALVE ON CANISTER

TIMED SPARK ADVANCE HOLE (MANIFOLD VACUUM)

② **DISCONNECT AND PLUG DISTRIBUTOR VACUUM HOSE**

③ **PULL OUTWARD ON PLUNGER STEM TO END OF TRAVEL**

④ **THROTTLE LEVER SHOULD CONTACT PLUNGER**

⑤ **TURN SCREW TO ADJUST**

① **SET IDLE R.P.M. TO SPECIFICATIONS**

FIG. 6-81 CEC VALVE ADJUSTMENT

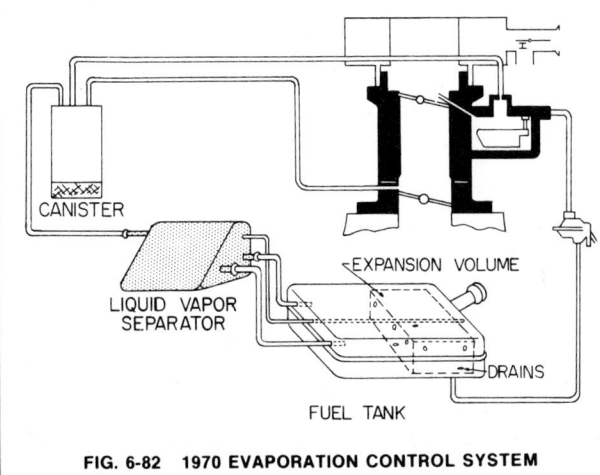

CANISTER

LIQUID VAPOR SEPARATOR

EXPANSION VOLUME

DRAINS

FUEL TANK

FIG. 6-82 1970 EVAPORATION CONTROL SYSTEM

mission switch electrically connected to a solenoid valve inserted in the carburetor-to-distributor vacuum line **(Fig. 6-79)**. Whenever the transmission operates in other than high gear, the transmission switch and solenoid valve are both closed, shutting off vacuum to the distributor vacuum advance. When the transmission shifts to high gear, oil pressure in the direct clutch circuit causes the transmission switch to open, cutting an electrical signal, opening the solenoid valve to permit carburetor vacuum to flow to the distributor, advancing the spark. A temperature switch allows vacuum to reach the distributor at temperatures below 85" F, or above 220" F.

The TCS system used on manual transmission cars is similar, but the transmission switch is externally mounted and operated by the transmission linkage position.

In 1971, all V-8 455-cu.-in. H.O. engines use a throttle-actuated spark advance connected to a Thermostatic Vacuum Switch (TVS). This system provides no vacuum advance at idle unless the coolant temperature rises above 230" F, when full advance is applied to allow the engine to circulate coolant faster to maintain a normal operating temperature.

COMBINATION EMISSION CONTROL SYSTEM (CEC)

The Ventura II introduced in 1971 uses the CEC system of controlling spark advance instead of TCS **(Fig. 6-80)**. When the CEC solenoid is energized, the solenoid plunger moves outward against the throttle lever. This speeds up the engine and allows ported spark vacuum to the distributor advance unit. The solenoid is energized in one of three ways:

1. The transmission is shifted into 3rd or reverse gear.

2. The temperature override switch opens at temperatures below 82° F.

3. The time delay relay allows vacuum advance for approximately 15 seconds after turning on the ignition. This covers temperature conditions above 82" F.

The CEC solenoid is vented to purge any vacuum that might hold the distributor advanced when the transmission is positioned in 1st or 2nd gear. An idle stop solenoid prevents dieseling (run-on) by permitting the throttle valves to close beyond their normal idle position when the ignition is turned off. Two throttle settings are thus required—one for curb idle and one for emission control. These settings are described in Chapter 5 and the adjustment procedure is shown in **Fig. 6-81**.

EVAPORATIVE CONTROL SYSTEM

An evaporative emission control system is fitted to all 1970 cars sold in California and all 1971 cars sold nationwide. Vapor caused by fuel evaporation in the fuel tank is no longer vented into the atmosphere, but transferred instead to the engine compartment by a vapor line and fed directly into the running engine, or stored in an activated charcoal canister when the engine is not running. The system includes a fuel tank overfill protector, three-point fuel tank venting (one-point on station wagon models) and a liquid vapor separator positioned forward and above the fuel tank **(Fig. 6-82)**. The liquid vapor separator is not fitted to station wagon models.

When the Evaporative Control System was extended to all cars in 1971, a fuel standpipe assembly **(Fig. 6-83)** replaced the liquid vapor separator unit to perform the same function. The standpipe assembly is not fitted to station wagon models.

PONTIAC
1972 Emissions Systems

The Positive Crankcase Ventilation (PCV) system remains the same as that used on 1970-71 Pontiacs.

CONTROLLED COMBUSTION SYSTEM (CCS)

This system is redesigned for 1972, incorporating elements from the previous Transmission Controlled Spark Advance and Combination Emission Control systems to form a new Speed Control Spark Advance System (SCS). All 4-speed manual-transmission-equipped V-8 engines retain the TCS system (see 1970-71). All 6-cyl. and V-8 307-cu.-in. engines retain the CEC system (see 1970-71), but the CEC time delay relay is eliminated. Vacuum advance is now permitted approximately 20 seconds after the transmission is shifted into HIGH or DRIVE, and whenever engine temperature is below 82° F.

All other engines use the SCS system. The SCS system contains the same components as the TCS system—a vacuum-advance solenoid valve and temperature sensor switch, but it replaces the TCS transmission switch with an SCS speed-control spark switch. While TCS permits vacuum-controlled spark advance in HIGH or DRIVE only, SCS restricts it to road speeds in excess of 38 mph **(Fig. 6-84)**. The TCS/SCS temperature sensor switch is relocated from the top of the intake manifold to the right of the rear cylinder head between plugs No. 6 and No. 8. This has been recalibrated to permit vacuum controlled advance at engine temperatures below 95° F and above 230° F. Air cleaner operation remains unchanged.

EVAPORATION CONTROL SYSTEM (ECS)

A purge valve, located on the intake manifold next to the water outlet housing, prevents canister purge until coolant temperature reaches 170° F. This improves exhaust emissions during cold starts, but is not fitted to I-6 or to V-8 307-cu.-in. applications.

AIR INJECTION REACTOR (AIR)

This system is fitted to all 250-cu.-in. I-6 engines with automatic transmissions, and consists of a belt-driven air injection pump (positive-displacement vane type), diverter valve and silencer assembly, check valve, and the necessary connecting hoses **(Fig. 6-85)**. The AIR pump is located at the upper right front of the engine. Intake air passes through a centrifugal fan at the front of the pump and is delivered to the intake manifold. During sudden deceleration, vacuum causes a diverter valve at the back of the pump to open, passing pump air into the atmosphere. A check valve located in the line behind the diverter valve contains a one-way diaphragm which prevents hot exhaust gases from backing up in the hose and damaging the pump during periods of pump belt failure, excessive system pressure or hose rupture.

PONTIAC
1973-73½ Emission Systems

The Positive Crankcase Ventilation (PCV) system remains the same as that used on 1970-71 Pontiacs.

CONTROLLED COMBUSTION SYSTEM (CCS)

For 1973, CCS uses three different systems to control ignition timing for emission control:

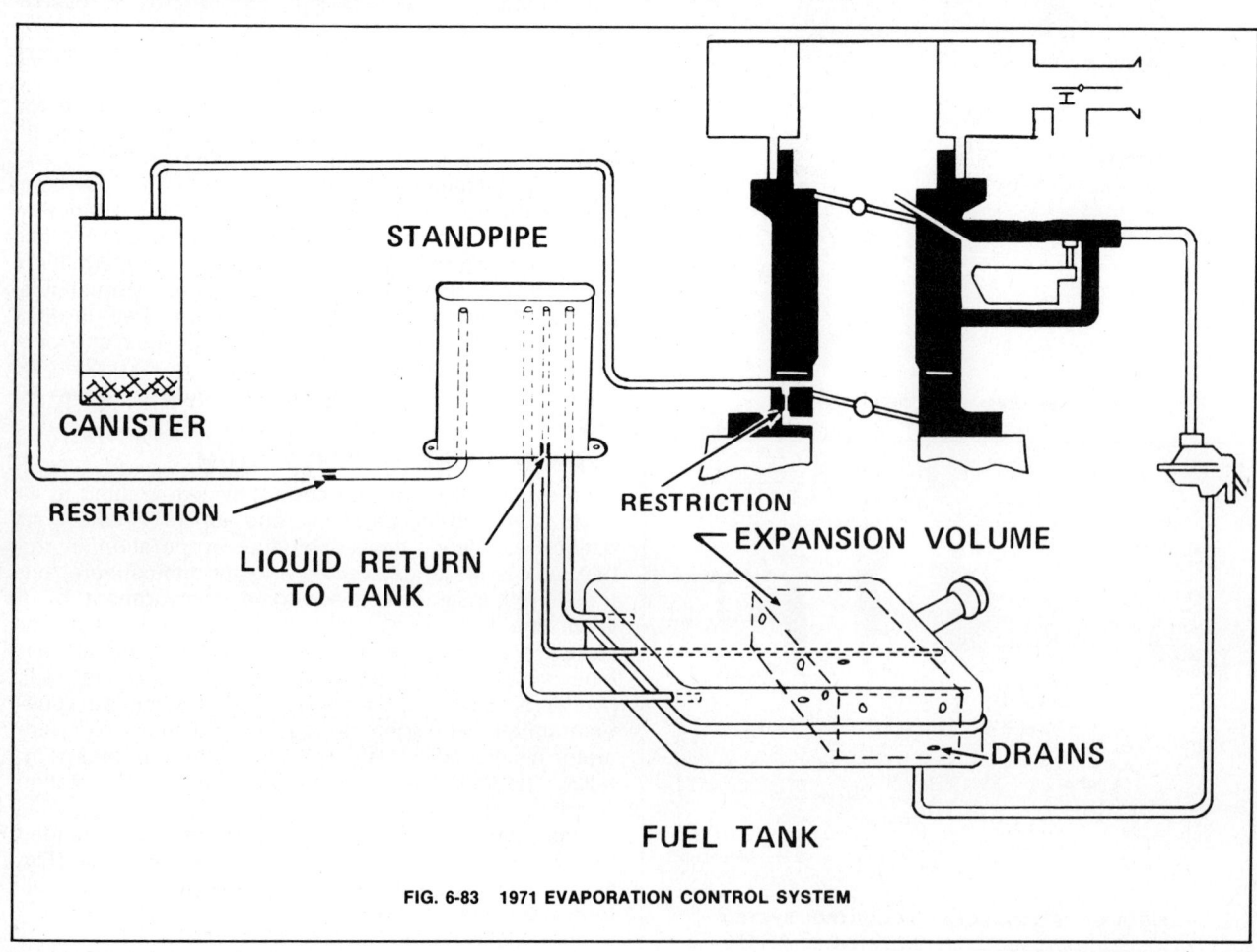

FIG. 6-83 1971 EVAPORATION CONTROL SYSTEM

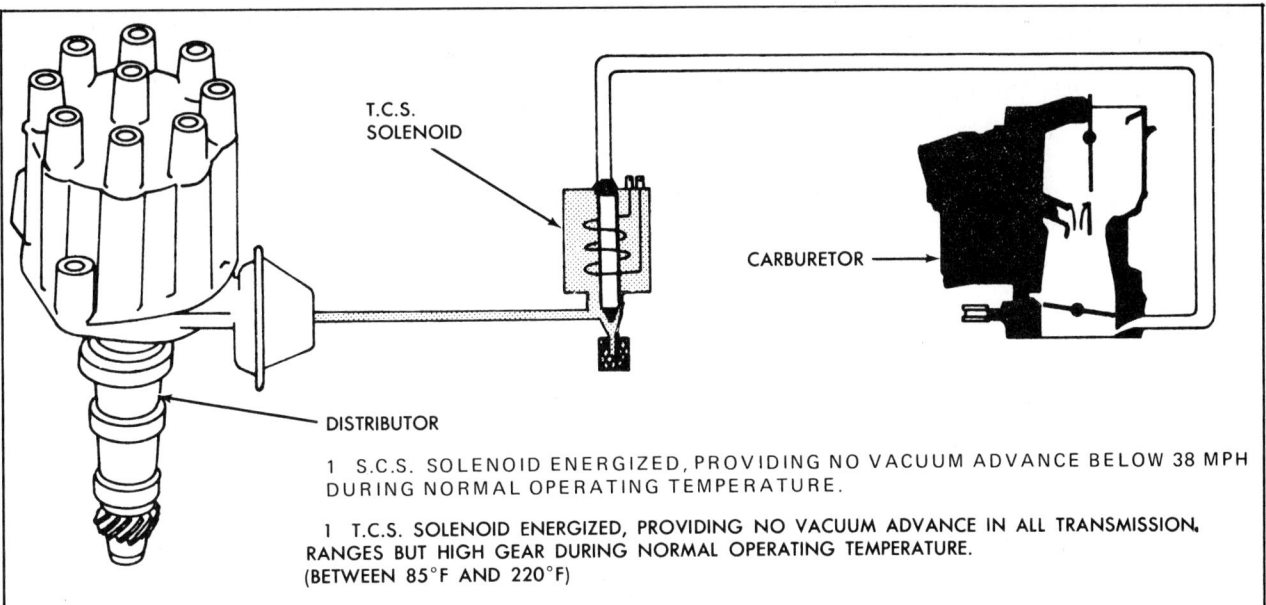

T.C.S.
SOLENOID

CARBURETOR

DISTRIBUTOR

1 S.C.S. SOLENOID ENERGIZED, PROVIDING NO VACUUM ADVANCE BELOW 38 MPH DURING NORMAL OPERATING TEMPERATURE.

1 T.C.S. SOLENOID ENERGIZED, PROVIDING NO VACUUM ADVANCE IN ALL TRANSMISSION RANGES BUT HIGH GEAR DURING NORMAL OPERATING TEMPERATURE.
(BETWEEN 85°F AND 220°F)

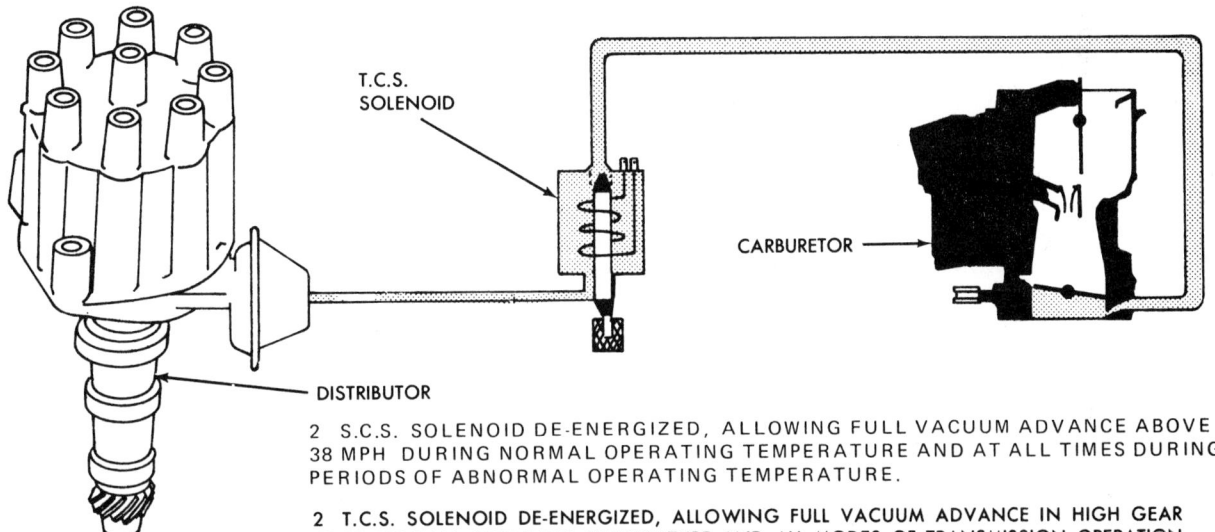

T.C.S.
SOLENOID

CARBURETOR

DISTRIBUTOR

2 S.C.S. SOLENOID DE-ENERGIZED, ALLOWING FULL VACUUM ADVANCE ABOVE 38 MPH DURING NORMAL OPERATING TEMPERATURE AND AT ALL TIMES DURING PERIODS OF ABNORMAL OPERATING TEMPERATURE.

2 T.C.S. SOLENOID DE-ENERGIZED, ALLOWING FULL VACUUM ADVANCE IN HIGH GEAR DURING NORMAL OPERATING TEMPERATURE AND ALL MODES OF TRANSMISSION OPERATION DURING PERIODS OF ABNORMAL ENGINE OPERATING TEMPERATURE.
(BELOW 85°F AND ABOVE 220°F)

FIG. 6-84   TCS/SCS SYSTEM OPERATION

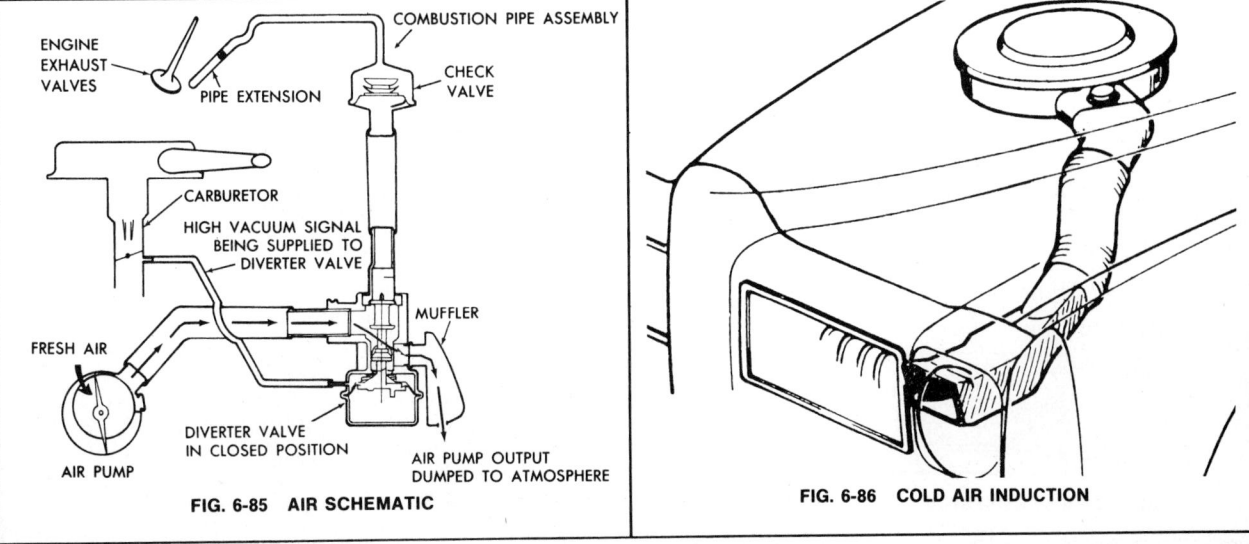

ENGINE
EXHAUST
VALVES

PIPE EXTENSION

COMBUSTION PIPE ASSEMBLY

CHECK
VALVE

CARBURETOR

HIGH VACUUM SIGNAL
BEING SUPPLIED TO
DIVERTER VALVE

MUFFLER

FRESH AIR

DIVERTER VALVE
IN CLOSED POSITION

AIR PUMP

AIR PUMP OUTPUT
DUMPED TO ATMOSPHERE

FIG. 6-85   AIR SCHEMATIC

FIG. 6-86   COLD AIR INDUCTION

1. All V-8 engines use TCS with Exhaust Gas Recirculation (TCS/EGR).
2. All 250-cu.-in. I-6 engines with manual transmissions use CEC with Exhaust Gas Recirculation (CEC/EGR).
3. All 250-cu.-in. I-6 engines with automatic transmissions use Ported Vacuum Advance with Exhaust Gas Recirculation (PVA/EGR).

The operation of each system is described in brief below:

TCS/EGR

Because these two systems are electrically connected, two basic rules apply:
1. When TCS is in operation, there is no EGR.
2. When EGR is in operation, there is no distributor vacuum advance.

The TCS/EGR control system includes the following components:
1. Distributor vacuum solenoid—open when energized—regulates vacuum to the distributor.
2. EGR vacuum solenoid—closed when energized—regulates vacuum to the EGR valve.
3. Time delay relay—connects to the vacuum solenoid—produces a ground circuit for up to 60 seconds after receiving a signal from the TCS transmission switch.
4. Thermal Feed Switch—located at the rear of the engine cylinder head—denies TCS to allow EGR until engine cylinder temperature reaches 125° F. This switch is bypassed during cold starting by the thermal override switch.
5. Thermal Override Switch—located in the right cylinder head—remains closed below 71° F and above 235° F.
6. TCS switch—open in 1st gear—provides ground signal through the thermal feed switch to the time delay relay.

In a typical cold start situation, the system functions as follows:

With coolant temperature below 71° F and the cylinder head temperature below 125° F, the cold/hot thermal override-switch contacts are closed, providing a ground for both solenoids. Thus, *EGR is off and TCS is on.*

When coolant temperature reaches 71° F, the thermal override switch opens to turn off both solenoids. *EGR comes on and TCS goes off.*

When the cylinder head temperature reaches 125° F,

the thermal feed switch closes and both solenoids energize in 33-55 seconds after the transmission shifts into 2nd or an intermediate range. *EGR shuts off and TCS comes on.*

If engine coolant reaches 235° F (hot idle condition), the cold/hot override switch closes both solenoids. Vacuum is supplied to advance ignition timing and provide maximum engine cooling. *EGR is off and TCS is on.*

CEC/EGR

The CEC system functions exactly as that used on the 1971 Ventura II (see "Combination Emission Control System, 1970-71"), with two slight modifications: the thermal override operates at temperatures below 93° F, and the time relay energizes the CEC solenoid valve for 20 seconds after the ignition is turned on. Exhaust Gas Recirculation is not interconnected with the CEC system, but functions independently and is described below.

PVA/EGR

The Ported Vacuum Advance system consists of a direct vacuum line connected from the ported-vacuum carburetor port (located just above the carburetor throttle plates) to the distributor vacuum advance. This causes a retarded vacuum timing advance during idle or closed throttle conditions, and provides full vacuum advance at all other times. EGR is regulated by a ported carburetor vacuum signal, but is not interconnected with the PVA system.

EXHAUST GAS RECIRCULATION (EGR)

EGR is added to all 1973 models. A vacuum-operated recirculation control valve regulates the amount and duration of time that exhaust gases are rerouted to the intake manifold. When the throttle valves are opened beyond the idle point, vacuum is applied against the EGR-valve actuating diaphragm. The EGR valve begins to move up against spring pressure, opening the exhaust-gas intake valve to allow exhaust gases from the manifold-crossover exhaust channels to be drawn back into the engine intake manifold. The valve remains closed during idle and deceleration, when excessive exhaust gases added to the air/fuel mixture would cause rough engine idling. EGR interrelationship with the Controlled Combustion System is discussed under that section.

AUTO-THERM AIR CLEANER

No longer considered a part of the CCS system, the air cleaner is fitted with a cold-air induction system on some V-8 engines (Fig. 6-86). This draws ambient air from just behind the grille area, providing a more uniform air change under normal conditions. Air cleaner air temperature is maintained at approximately 105° F.

EVAPORATION CONTROL SYSTEM (ECS)

A domed fuel tank is fitted to all sedans and coupes (except Firebird), eliminating the need for a standpipe and three-point vent system (Fig. 6-87). The domed tank uses a single vent pipe directly to the vapor canister. A calibrated purge orifice (restriction) in the carburetor is used to transfer vapor from the canister to the engine (as in the previous design) on all applications except the I-6 system; the purge valve on I-6 systems is located on the canister.

1973 MID-YEAR CHANGES

Emission system redesign during the 1973 model

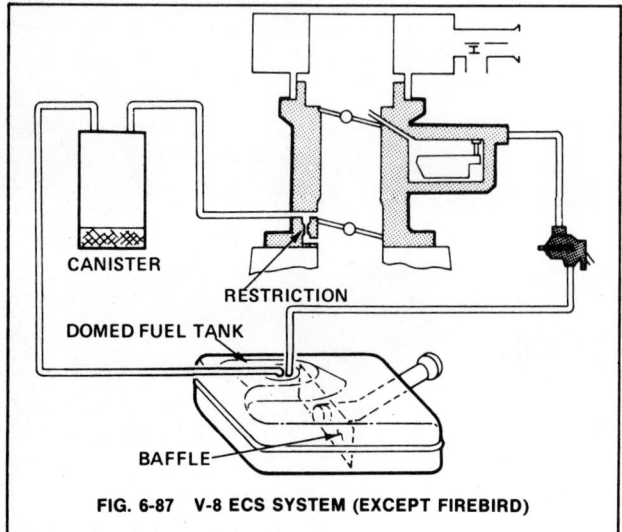

CANISTER
RESTRICTION
DOMED FUEL TANK
BAFFLE

FIG. 6-87   V-8 ECS SYSTEM (EXCEPT FIREBIRD)

year resulted in the following changes:

1. The AIR pump no longer supplies air to the No. 3 and No. 6 cyls. This is accomplished by internal changes to the cylinder heads.

2. The TCS/EGR system is no longer interconnected—each functions independently of the other.

3. A new EGR TVV senses intake manifold temperature. At temperatures below 95° F, EGR is shut off. At temperatures above 95° F, ported vacuum is furnished to the EGR.

4. The TCS thermal-override-switch function range is changed. Vacuum advance is provided at temperatures below 62° F and above 240° F.

AIR INJECTION REACTOR (AIR)

AIR is fitted to all California 250, 350 and 2-bbl. 400-cu.-in. engines for 1973-73½. See 1972.

PONTIAC

1974 Emission Systems

Positive Crankcase Ventilation (PCV) is the same as 1970-71. Air Injection Reactor (AIR)—fitted to all California I-6 and 2-bbl. V-8 engines for 1974—is the same as 1972. For the Evaporation Control System (ECS),

see 1970-71 and 1973-73½. Auto-Therm Air Cleaner and Exhaust Gas Recirculation (EGR), see 1973-73½.

CONTROLLED COMBUSTION SYSTEM (CCS)

TCS/EGR systems are interconnected again on all V-8 engines fitted with automatic transmissions, just as in the pre-1973½ system. Three variations of TCS are used for 1974:

1. V-8 with automatic transmission—Vacuum advance is supplied for 20 seconds following *every* engine start-up, and is available whenever the temperature of the air/fuel mixture is below 62° F. Under normal operating temperatures, the TCS system will allow vacuum advance during high gear and reverse operation. Whenever coolant temperature exceeds 240° F, vacuum advance is available in any gear **(Fig. 6-88)**.

2. V-8 with manual transmission—Manual transmission engines have a ported-spark vacuum source, except during cold operation, when full vacuum advance is provided through the distributor-spark/EGR-thermal valve. Other than these slight modifications, this TCS system operates just as the V-8 automatic transmission system.

3. I-6 with manual transmission—Ported vacuum advance is supplied for 20 seconds following *every* en-

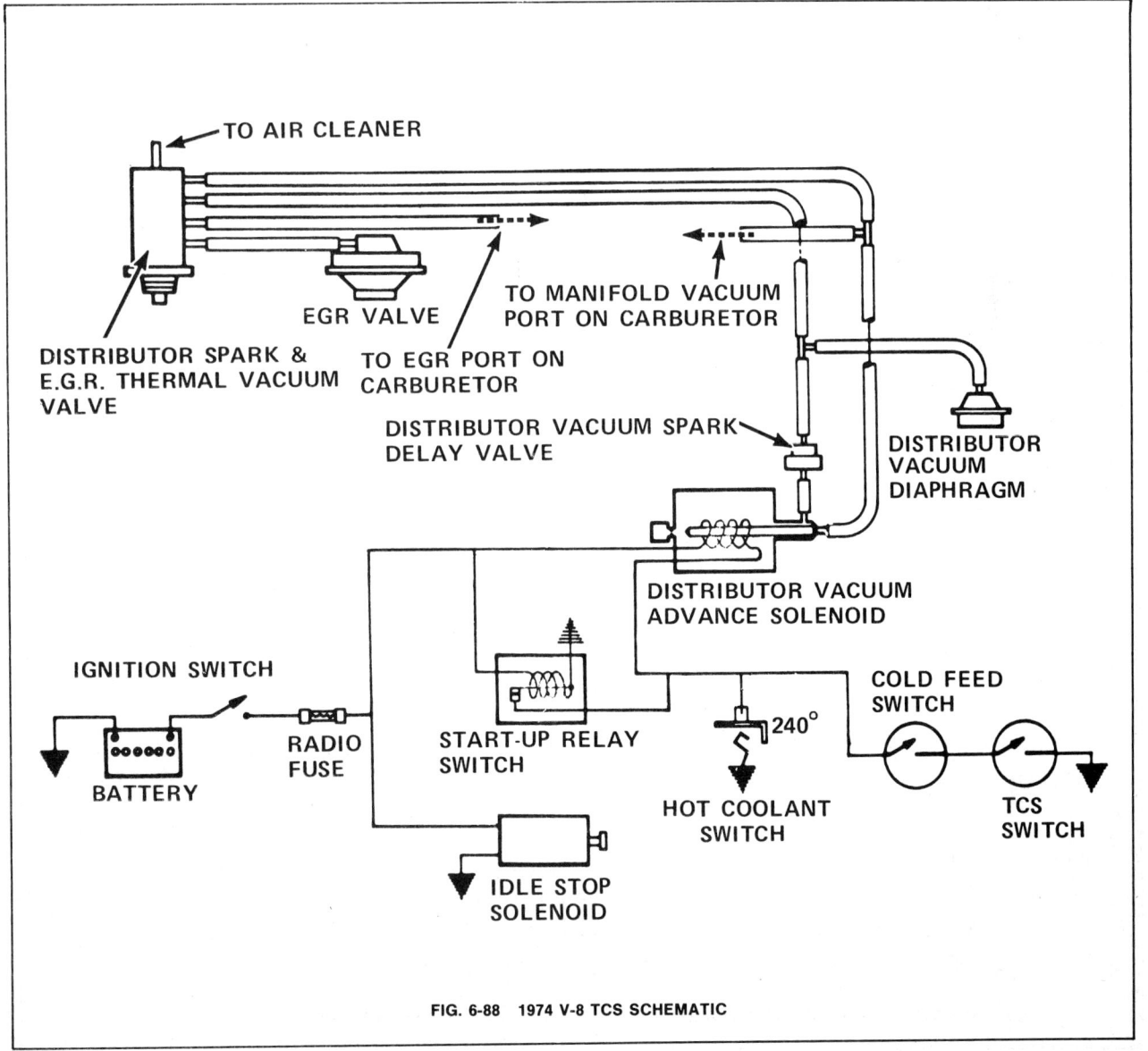

FIG. 6-88   1974 V-8 TCS SCHEMATIC

gine start-up and is available whenever coolant temperature is below 93° F. Under normal operating temperatures, the TCS system allows ported vacuum advance during high gear operation. TCS is not used on the automatic I-6 engine; ported vacuum is supplied whenever the throttle is opened.

EXHAUST GAS RECIRCULATION (EGR)

Four variations are used on 1974 Pontiacs to modulate and/or supplement carburetor vacuum:

1. A vacuum-operated EGR valve is used on most engines.

2. A vacuum bias valve (VBV) and EGR valve are used to reduce EGR under high-manifold-vacuum conditions to reduce surge (only on non-California 2-bbl. 400-cu.-in. engines in Catalina and Grand Ville wagons). See **Fig. 6-89.**

3. A dual-diaphragm EGR valve is used on some 4-bbl. California engines to reduce EGR during high-manifold-vacuum conditions **(Fig. 6-90).**

4. An exhaust backpressure transducer and EGR valve is used on all 2-bbl. California engines to produce maximum EGR during acceleration and reduced EGR under all other conditions **(Fig. 6-91).**

PONTIAC

1975-76 Emission Systems

The Positive Crankcase Ventilation (PCV) system remains unchanged since 1970-71. The Air Injection Reactor (AIR) is the same as 1972. For Evaporative Emission Control System (EECS), see 1970-71 and 1973-73½ systems.

AUTO-THERM AIR CLEANER

Air temperature entering the carburetor is raised to 125° F for 1975-76 models.

CATALYTIC CONVERTER

All 1975 Pontiacs are fitted with a catalytic converter to improve fuel economy and drivability; 1976 Astre/Sunbird 1-bbl. 4-cyl. engines are not equipped with catalytic converters.

EARLY FUEL EVAPORATION (EFE)

A coolant-temperature-sensing thermal vacuum valve (TVV) is used to operate the exhaust manifold heat riser **(Fig. 6-92).** Before engine coolant warms up to 120° F, the TVV sends vacuum to the EFE valve. This

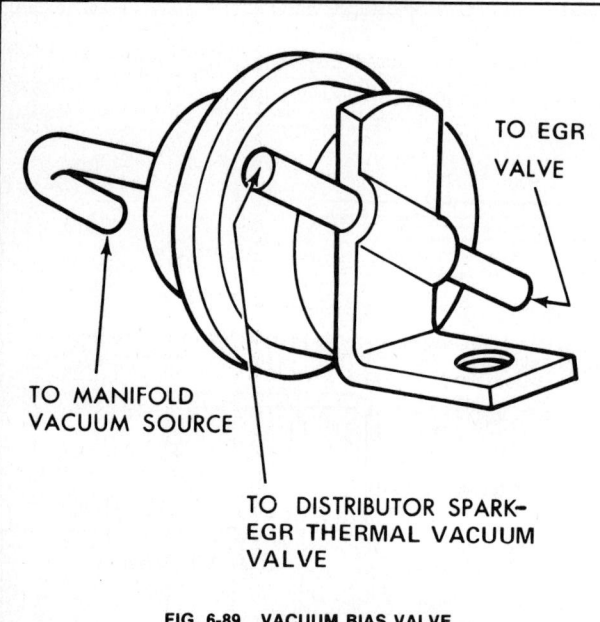

TO EGR VALVE

TO MANIFOLD VACUUM SOURCE

TO DISTRIBUTOR SPARK-EGR THERMAL VACUUM VALVE

FIG. 6-89   VACUUM BIAS VALVE

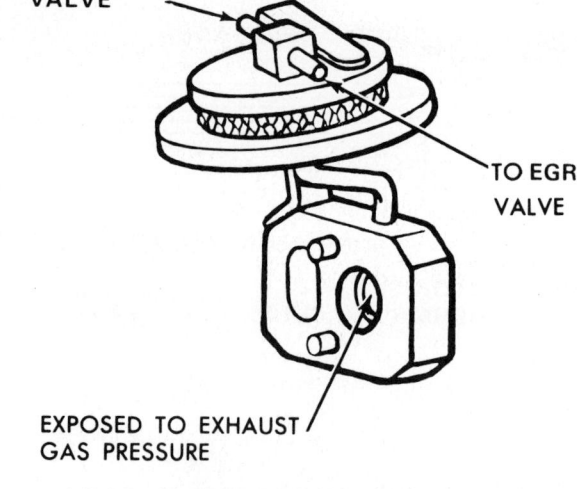

TO DISTRIBUTOR SPARK—EGR THERMAL VACUUM VALVE

TO EGR VALVE

EXPOSED TO EXHAUST GAS PRESSURE

FIG. 6-91   EXHAUST BACKPRESSURE TRANSDUCER

TO INTAKE MANIFOLD VACUUM

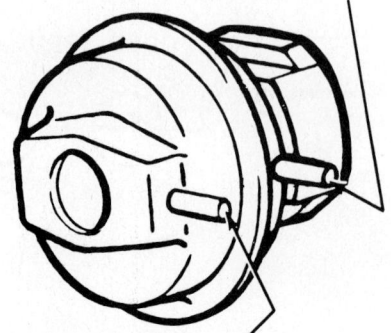

TO CARBURETOR EGR VACUUM PORT

FIG. 6-90   DUAL-DIAPHRAGM EGR VALVE

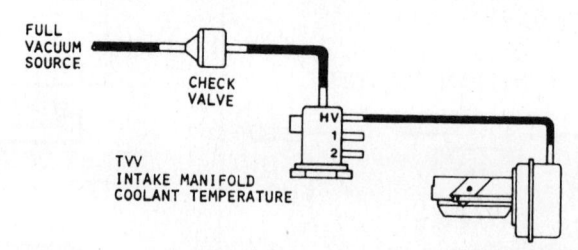

FULL VACUUM SOURCE

CHECK VALVE

HV 1 2

TVV INTAKE MANIFOLD COOLANT TEMPERATURE

E.F.E. VALVE

Engine Coolant Temperature	EFE Thermal Vacuum Valve Position	Exit Path of Exhaust Gas From L.H. Exhaust Manifold
Below 120°F	Closed	Forced to R.H. side through passage in intake manifold
Above 120°F	Open	Via L.H. manifold into crossover pipe

FIG. 6-92   TYPICAL EFE SYSTEM

holds the heat riser closed and forces exhaust gas to pass under the carburetor to warm the air/fuel mixture. After coolant temperature reaches 120° F, vacuum is denied to the EFE valve, which now opens to allow exhaust gas to exit the exhaust system normally.

EXHAUST GAS RECIRCULATION (EGR)

A variety of additional devices are used to further refine the operation of the EGR system for 1975. Numerous and different EGR and Backpressure Transducer (BPT) valves are used, each with its own specific calibration. As such, replacement must be made with the same unit. EGR and BPT valves are therefore not interchangeable.

A central EGR passage is provided on 1975 350-cu.-in. Ventura engines **(Fig. 6-93)**. This feature requires the use of a thicker carburetor gasket, a stainless-steel heat shield and longer carburetor bolts.

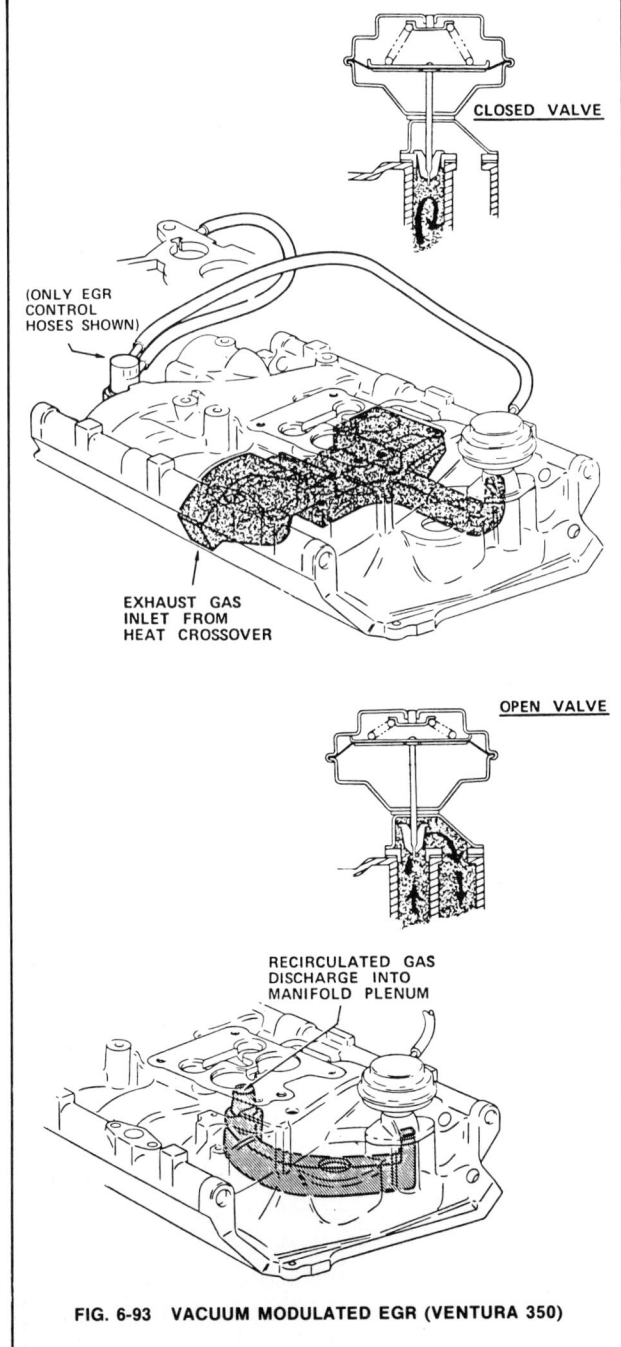

FIG. 6-93   VACUUM MODULATED EGR (VENTURA 350)

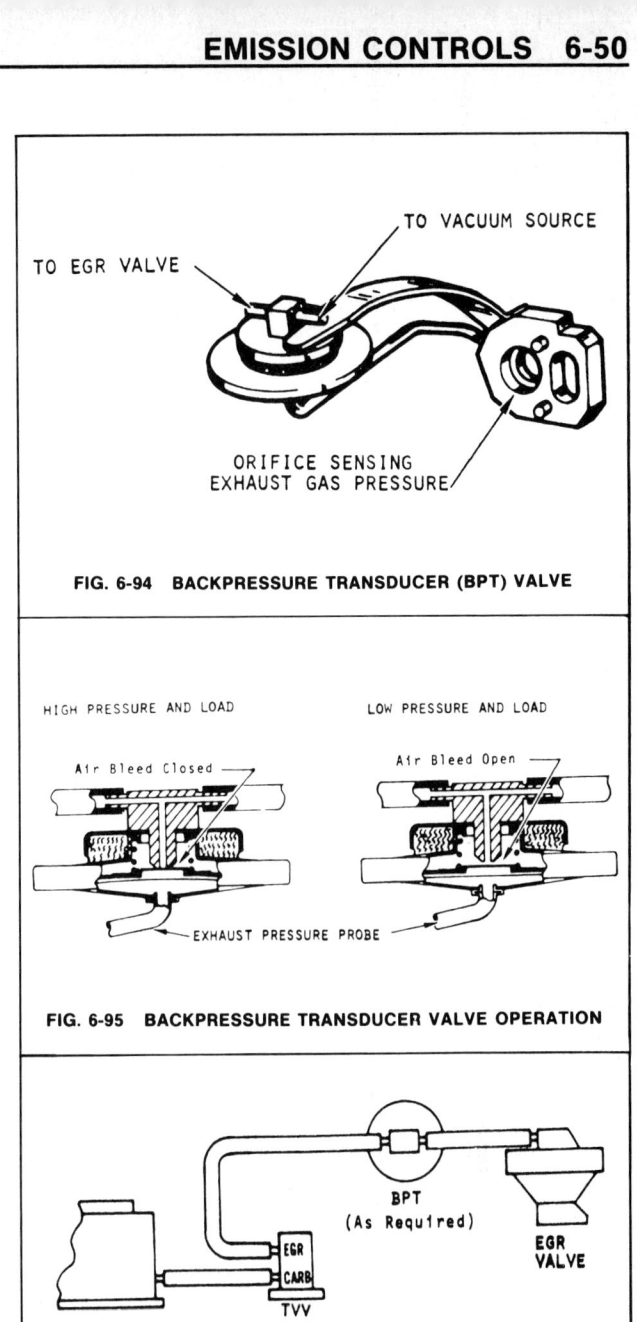

FIG. 6-94   BACKPRESSURE TRANSDUCER (BPT) VALVE

FIG. 6-95   BACKPRESSURE TRANSDUCER VALVE OPERATION

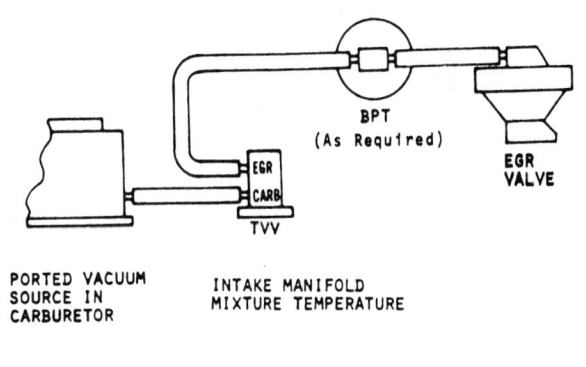

FIG. 6-96   MIXTURE-TEMPERATURE-CONTROLLED EGR SYSTEM

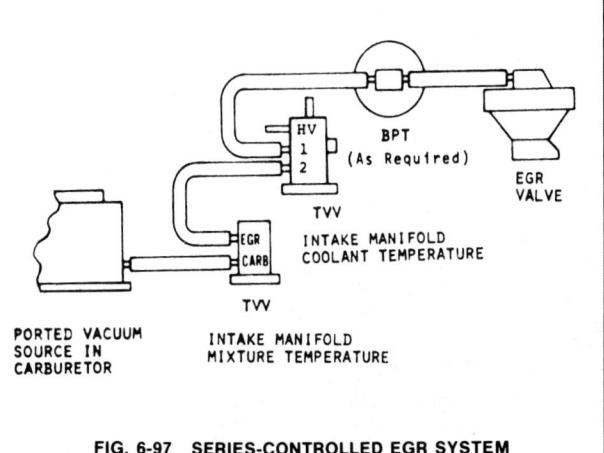

FIG. 6-97   SERIES-CONTROLLED EGR SYSTEM

All V-8 engines use a temperature sensitive control valve (EGR-TCV) installed in the vacuum line to the EGR valve. This EGR-TCV is closed below 61° F to block vacuum to the EGR valve, and open above 76° F to direct ported vacuum to the valve.

All 260-cu.-in. Ventura engines use a Vacuum Delay Valve (VDV) between the carburetor port and the TVS "C" port. When the valve is open, it sends full distributor ported vacuum to the vacuum advance unit. In a restricting position, it causes the ported vacuum to be metered through a 0.005-in. orifice, thereby delaying full vacuum advance for up to 40 seconds. The valve is bypassed above 220° F coolant temperature, when the TVS valve switches.

BACKPRESSURE TRANSDUCER (BPT)

A backpressure transducer is added to modulate EGR valve operation on 260-cu.-in. Ventura engines

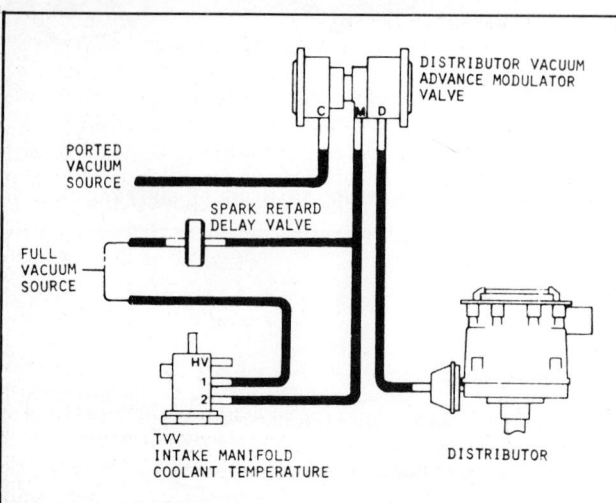

Engine Coolant Temp.	4 Second Spark Retard Delay on Acceleration	Full Vacuum Advance Available
Below 120°F	Yes	Yes
Above 120°F	No	Yes

FIG. 6-98   FULL VACUUM ADVANCE

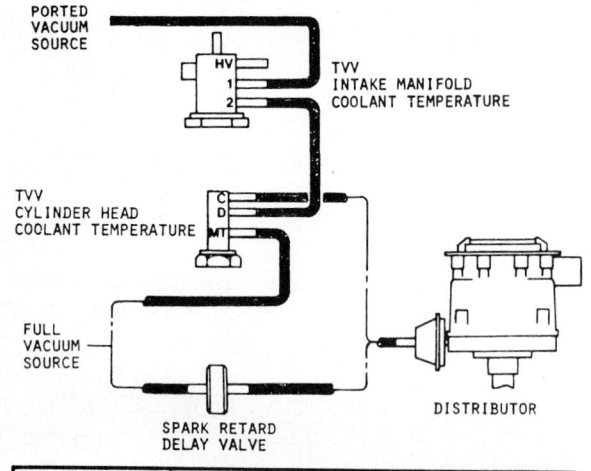

Cyl Head Coolant Temperature	Int Man Coolant Temperature	4-Second Spark Retard Delay on Acceleration	Type of Vac Advance
Below 227°F	Below 120°F	Yes	Full
	Above 120°F	No	Ported
Above 227°F	Above 120°F	No	Full

FIG. 6-101   PORTED VACUUM ADVANCE, WITH HOT COOLANT OVERRIDE PLUS FULL ALLOWANCE WITH 4-SECOND DELAY

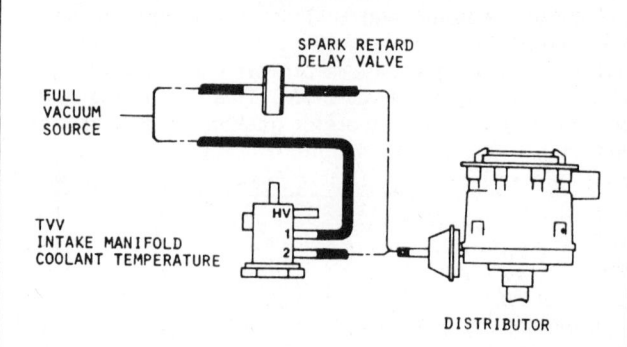

Engine Coolant Temp	4 Second Spark Retard Delay	Modulated Full Vac Adv Available
Below 120°F	Yes	Yes
Above 120°F	No	Yes

Full Vacuum Source at Rear of Carburetor	Ported Vacuum Source at Front of Carb.	Signal that Controls Distributor Vacuum Advance
From 0 to 10 inches	Will be equal to or less than the full vacuum signal	Full vacuum signal
Above 10 inches	Less than 10 inches	Full vacuum signal modulated to a constant 10 inches
	Above 10 inches	Ported vacuum signal

FIG. 6-99   MODULATED FULL VACUUM ADVANCE

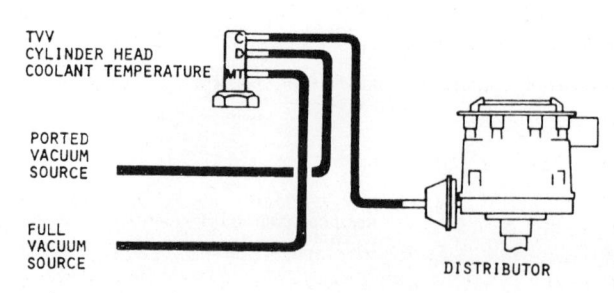

Cyl Head Coolant Temp	Type of Vacuum Advance
Below 227°F	Ported
Above 227°F	Full

FIG. 6-100   PORTED VACUUM ADVANCE

(Fig. 6-94). Exhaust pressure in the BPT probe moves a diaphragm to close off the air bleed (Fig. 6-95) to allow maximum exhaust gas recirculation when the engine load is high. As the engine load decreases, exhaust pressure in the probe decreases, causing the air bleed to open. Vacuum to the EGR valve then bleeds through the air bleed, reducing vacuum flow to the EGR valve and modulating exhaust gas recirculation (Fig. 6-95).

MIXTURE TEMPERATURE CONTROLLED SYSTEM

A thermal vacuum valve (TVV) is installed in the intake manifold to sense air/fuel mixture temperature (Fig. 6-96). At cold engine temperatures, the TVV is closed, shutting off vacuum to the EGR valve. At warm engine temperatures, the TVV is open to pass ported vacuum to the EGR valve.

SERIES CONTROLLED SYSTEM

Series controlled systems use a TVV to sense coolant temperature in series with the TVV, which senses air/fuel mixture temperature (Fig. 6-97). At cold engine temperatures, both TVV valves are closed, shutting off vacuum to the EGR valve. At warm engine temperatures, both TVV valves open to pass ported vacuum to the EGR valve—both valves must open, or no vacuum will reach the EGR valve.

For 1976, EGR theory and application remain unchanged, except for the addition of a heat-sensitive snap-disc valve housed in a stamped steel shield attached to the V-8 intake manifold (except Ventura, Le Mans, Grand Le Mans 260-cu.-in. engines). This snap disc senses engine radiant heat and denies vacuum to the EGR valve on initial start-ups.

DISTRIBUTOR VACUUM ADVANCE SYSTEM

Use of the SCS and TCS systems is discontinued in 1975, with variations of full and ported vacuum used for distributor advance. When full advance is provided, manifold vacuum is present during idle, part throttle and closed throttle operations. Ported advance provides vacuum mainly at part throttle, because the distributor receives vacuum only when the spark port inside the carburetor is uncovered. Most 1975-76 advance systems use one or more auxiliary devices to supplement or modulate the vacuum application. A variety of these and their applications are shown in Figs. 6-98, 6-99, 6-100 & 6-101. For 1976, a spark delay restrictor is used in place of the spark delay valve.

PONTIAC

1977 Emission Systems

The Positive Crankcase Ventilation (PCV) system is the same as 1970-71. See 1970-71 and 1973-73½ for the Evaporative Emission Control system (EECS). The Exhaust Gas Recirculation (EGR) system is the same as 1975-76.

EARLY FUEL EVAPORATION (EFE)

An orifice EFE system is used on some applications. This consists of an orifice restriction in the exhaust crossover pipe. The system functions whenever the engine is running. No maintenance is necessary; a loose orifice which rattles can be rewelded into the pipe. If the orifice cracks or breaks, the entire exhaust crossover pipe is replaced as an assembly.

THERMOSTATIC AIR CLEANER (TAC)

Sensor calibration is changed to 123° F ± 20° F for all models using a vacuum motor. Mechanical air cleaner duct valves equipped with a thermostatic coil on I-4 140/151 engines should open fully at approximately 110° F.

AIR-INJECTION REACTOR (AIR)

The AIR system on 1977 V-6 California and high-altitude engines regulates the injection of air into the exhaust stream with three new devices (Fig. 6-101A):
1. Vacuum Differential Valve (VDV)
2. Air Bypass Valve (ABV)
3. Differential Vacuum Delay/Separator Valve

The Vacuum Differential Valve prevents exhaust system backfiring by dumping pump air when the throttle closes during deceleration. The Bypass Valve operates during deceleration and at high engine loads. This prevents excessive exhaust system temperatures and is operated by the VDV. The DVD/SV delays dumping of pump output under heavy acceleration. This allows injected air to pass, except under conditions of sustained acceleration. The separator function prevents liquid fuel from passing to vacuum components of the AIR system.

PULSE AIR-INJECTION REACTOR (PAIR)

1977 I-4 140/151 engines are equipped with the PAIR system. See 1977 Chevrolet Emission Systems for a full description and testing procedures.

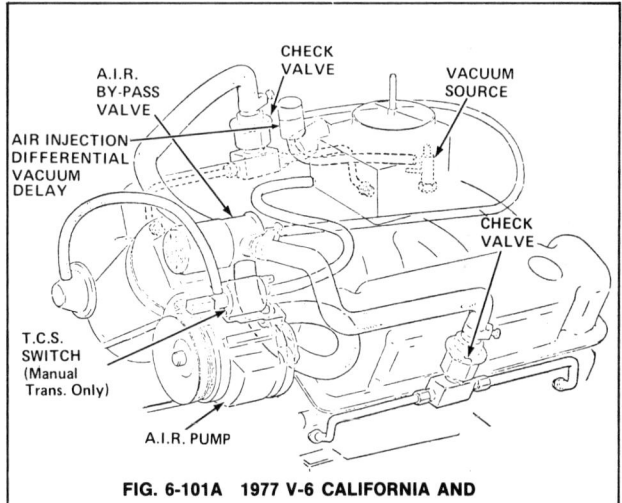

FIG. 6-101A 1977 V-6 CALIFORNIA AND HIGH-ALTITUDE AIR SYSTEM

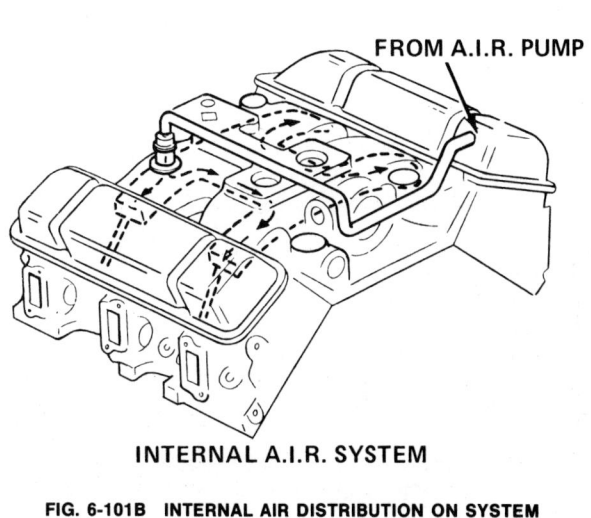

INTERNAL A.I.R. SYSTEM

FIG. 6-101B INTERNAL AIR DISTRIBUTION ON SYSTEM

CATALYTIC CONVERTER

Use is extended to all 1977 Pontiacs.

VACUUM CONTROLS

The operation of various emission control components is modified by one or more of the following vacuum controls:

1. Thermal Vacuum Switch (TVS)
2. Vacuum Delay Valve (VDV)
3. Check Valve
4. Vacuum Modulator Valve (VMV)
5. Vacuum Reducer Valve (VRV)

The exact use and calibration of these devices depends upon the engine and application—nationwide, California, low altitude, high altitude, with air conditioning, without air conditioning, automatic or manual transmission, etc.

PONTIAC

1978-79 Emission Systems

The Positive Crankcase Ventilation (PCV) system is the same as 1970-71. See 1970-71 and 1973-73½ for the Evaporative Emission Control system (EECS). The Exhaust Gas Recirculation (EGR) system is the same as 1975-76. The catalytic converter, Thermostatic Air Cleaner (TAC) and Vacuum Controls are the same as 1977.

AIR-INJECTION REACTOR (AIR)

Use is restricted to certain engines; does not extend across the line as in past years. Where used, it remains as 1977 usage. 1978 V-6 engines with engine Code A use an internal air distribution system to eliminate external plumbing, **Fig. 6-101B.**

PULSE AIR-INECTION REACTOR (PAIR)

Not used on 1978-79 Pontiac engines.

EARLY FUEL EVAPORATION (EFE)

Orifice EFE system is not used on 1978-79 Pontiacs.

ELECTRONIC FUEL CONTROL (EFC) SYSTEM

See 1978-79 Oldsmobile Emission systems for full description and operation of this system. 1978 usage is restricted to California I-4 151-cu.-in. engines (Code 1).

EMISSION SYSTEM TEST PROCEDURES

PCV TEST

1. Connect a tachometer and start the engine.
2. Clamp off the crankcase ventilator hose to shut off the airflow completely.
3. If idle speed drops approximately 60 rpm, the PCV system is functioning. If the idle speed does not drop, install a new valve.

ALTERNATE PCV TEST

1. Remove the PCV valve from the intake manifold or rocker arm cover.
2. Start the engine and run at idle.
3. Place a thumb over the valve end to check for vacuum. If there is no vacuum at the valve, inspect for plugged hoses.
4. Shut the engine off. Shake the valve and listen for the rattle of the check needle in the valve. If no rattle is heard, replace the valve.

AUTO-THERM AIR CLEANER VACUUM-MOTOR TEST

1. Inspect for plugged, kinked or damaged hoses, and then check for proper connections.
2. With the engine off, the damper door in the snorkel tube should cover the hot air pipe **(Fig. 6-102).** If not, look for binding linkage.
3. Apply 9 ins. of vacuum to the diaphragm motor assembly. The damper door should close off the snorkel tube passage completely **(Fig. 6-103).** If not, look for a vacuum leak and/or incorrect linkage hookup.
4. With vacuum still applied, clamp off the hose to trap vacuum in the diaphragm assembly. The damper door should continue to close off the snorkel passage. If not, replace the diaphragm assembly.

AUTO-THERM AIR CLEANER SENSOR TEST

1. Check the cold air inlet with the engine off—it should be open **(Fig. 6-102).**

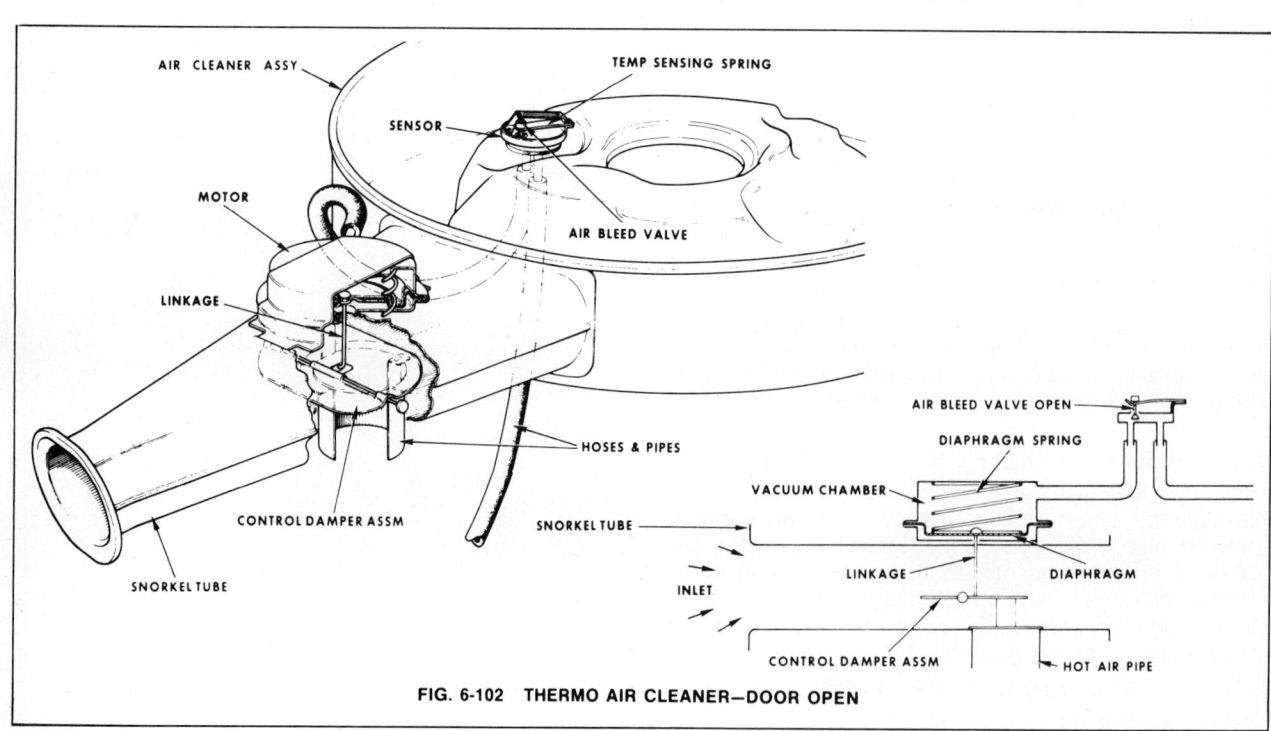

FIG. 6-102   THERMO AIR CLEANER—DOOR OPEN

2. Start the cold engine with air cleaner temperature below 80° F. The cold-air-inlet damper should close immediately.

3. As the engine warms up, the cold-air-inlet damper should gradually open and the air cleaner should become warm. If not, replace the sensor.

1970-71 TRANSMISSION CONTROLLED SPARK ADVANCE TEST

1. Connect an ignition timing light and tachometer.

2. Elevate the rear wheels and start the engine. Place the transmission in DRIVE or HIGH gear, and position the fast idle cam to increase engine speed to 1000 rpm.

3. Use the timing light and check the position of the ignition timing mark—it should indicate advance with the transmission in DRIVE or HIGH gear.

4. Shift the transmission into each lower gear, checking the position of the timing mark each time. The timing mark should remain unchanged from its normal position, indicating no vacuum advance.

COMBINATION EMISSION CONTROL SYSTEM (CEC) COMPONENT TEST

1. To test the solenoid, disconnect the hose and the electrical connector.

2. Connect a hose to the distributor vacuum port on the solenoid and blow through it. Air should come from the solenoid vent port.

3. Plug the solenoid carburetor-vacuum port. Connect a jumper wire from one terminal to ground. Connect the other terminal to a 12-volt source. Air should now come from the ported spark port.

4. To test the transmission switch, disconnect the switch connector from the transmission side.

5. Connect a test lamp from the switch terminal to a 12-volt source. *Do not* use a test lamp with a bulb requiring more than 0.8-amp, or the switch contacts will be damaged.

6. The test lamp should light when the transmission is placed in HIGH gear, and remain off in lower gears.

7. Make sure time delay relay is cool, then remove the temperature switch connection on the engine.

8. Turn the ignition on—the solenoid should energize for 15-20 seconds, then de-energize. If the solenoid does not de-energize, remove the time relay lead. If the solenoid now de-energizes, replace the relay.

9. The temperature switch must be tested with the engine cold. Turn on the ignition and the CEC solenoid should energize and stay energized.

10. If the solenoid does not energize, or if it energizes and then de-energizes after 20 seconds, ground the cold terminal at the temperature switch. If the solenoid now energizes, replace the temperature switch.

CEC SOLENOID ADJUSTMENT

Energized through the transmission, the CEC solenoid acts as a throttle stop by increasing the idle speed during high gear operation. The CEC solenoid also provides full vacuum advance during high gear operation, and is de-energized at all other gears and at idle for retarded spark timing. The normal idle speed setting is made with the idle stopscrew. The CEC solenoid should require adjustment **(Fig. 6-104)** only in cases of solenoid replacement, major carburetor overhaul, or removal/replacement of the carburetor throttle body. To adjust the CEC solenoid:

1. Disconnect and plug the distributor vacuum-advance line; disconnect the fuel tank hose from the vapor canister.

2. Refer to specific instructions for adjustment found on the vehicle emission control sticker; start the engine and connect a tachometer.

3. Manually extend the solenoid valve plunger until it touches the throttle lever.

4. Adjust the plunger length until the specified engine speed is obtained.

5. Reconnect the vacuum advance and vapor canister lines.

1972 CONTROLLED COMBUSTION (CCS) TEST

1. Connect an ignition timing light, elevate the rear wheels and start the engine.

2. With the distributor vacuum-advance line connected and engine temperature between 95° F and

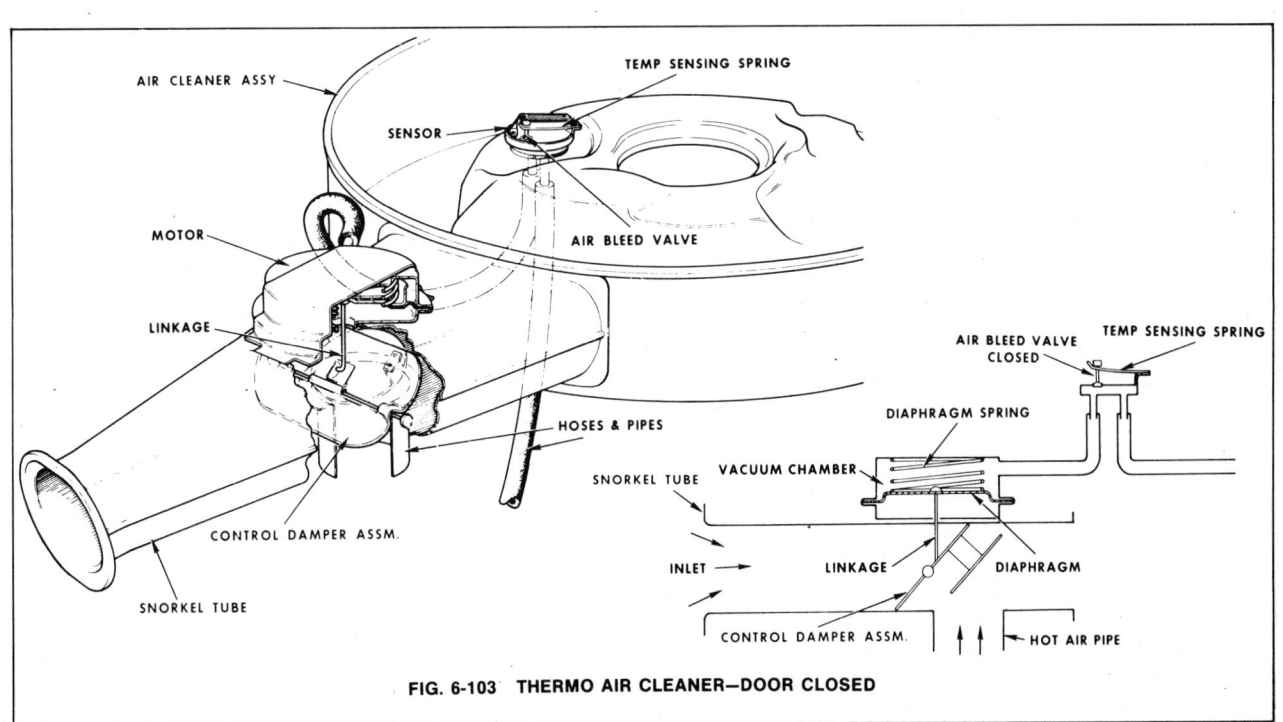

FIG. 6-103 THERMO AIR CLEANER—DOOR CLOSED

230° F, shift the transmission into HIGH gear or DRIVE.

3. Open the throttle while watching the timing mark. The timing mark should advance when the transmission is shifted (TCS), about 20 seconds after shift is made (CEC) or when car speed exceeds 38 mph (SCS).

1973-74 TCS SYSTEM FUNCTIONAL TEST
ALL V-8S WITH MANUAL TRANSMISSION

1. Check hoses for correct routing and kinked or plugged lines; check electrical connections for proper contact.

2. Remove the hot override or the thermal-override-switch terminal and run the engine. Wait 62 seconds and shift the transmission into 1st gear to see if it loses vacuum. If it does, replace the override switch.

3. If vacuum is not lost in 1st gear, remove the transmission switch terminal with the engine running. Wait 62 seconds and check for vacuum. If vacuum is not present, replace the transmission switch.

ALL V-8S WITH AUTOMATIC TRANSMISSION

1. Check hoses for correct routing and kinked or plugged lines; check electrical connections for proper contact.

2. Remove the hot override or the thermal override switch terminal and run the engine in PARK for at least 62 seconds to see if vacuum is lost. If it is, replace the override switch.

3. If vacuum is not lost in PARK, remove the transmission switch terminal with the engine running. Wait 62 seconds and check for vacuum. If vacuum is not present, replace the transmission switch. Check fuse and wiring back to the battery.

ALL 1973-74 V-8S REGARDLESS OF TRANSMISSION

1. Disregard the 62-second interval on all 1974 engines, and Steps 3 and 4 on 1974 I-6 engines.

2. If override and transmission switches check out satisfactory, connect a 12-volt test lamp from the yellow or tan distributor solenoid wire to ground. The lamp should light. If it does not, the distributor solenoid is not receiving voltage.

3. Tee a vacuum gauge to the distributor line connecting to the distributor solenoid and connect a 12-volt test lamp from the blue or black wire to ground. The light should go on. The vacuum gauge should read and the solenoid should energize, producing an audible click. If the light is off (no gauge reading), the solenoid has an open circuit and should be replaced.

3. Connect the 12-volt test lamp from the relay (black wire with white stripe) to ground. The test lamp should light and the solenoid click after 62 seconds. If the light stays off, the relay is defective and should be replaced.

4. Connect the 12-volt test lamp from the thermal delay switch (solid black wire) to ground. The light should go on and the solenoid should click after 33 seconds (white stripe) or 62 seconds (blue stripe). If the light stays off, replace the thermal feed switch.

5. Disconnect the thermal-feed-switch wire from the TCS transmission switch. Run the engine in PARK or NEUTRAL and have someone ground the end of the wire. The solenoid should click and the vacuum gauge should read vacuum after 62 seconds. If no click is heard or no vacuum is present, the wire has an open circuit and must be repaired. If a click and vacuum reading are both present, the TCS transmission switch should be replaced.

1973 EXHAUST GAS RECIRCULATION VALVE FUNCTIONAL TEST

1. Start the engine and run until it is warmed to normal operating temperature. Remove the air cleaner to observe EGR-valve diaphragm action. Place the transmission in NEUTRAL or PARK.

2. Disconnect the EGR electrical connector on manual-transmission-equipped cars.

3. The EGR valve should be closed at idle. Open and close the throttle part way by hand. The EGR valve diaphragm should move out from the engine, indicating proper operation.

4. If the EGR valve diaphragm does not move, check vacuum line connections. Remove the line from the EGR valve and open the throttle. Vacuum should be present. If it is, replace the EGR valve.

5. If no vacuum is present, check the EGR solenoid end of the line connecting the carburetor and distributor solenoid. If vacuum is present there, the EGR solenoid is at fault. If no vacuum is present, either the carburetor-to-solenoid line is plugged, or the carburetor is defective.

6. Check the EGR solenoid for internal plugging. If not plugged, test to see if it is energized by connecting a 12-volt test lamp across its terminals. If the test lamp lights, the solenoid is energized.

7. If the solenoid is energized, remove the override switch terminal. If the test lamp goes out, replace the override switch. If the test lamp stays lit, remove the TCS switch terminal at the transmission. If the test

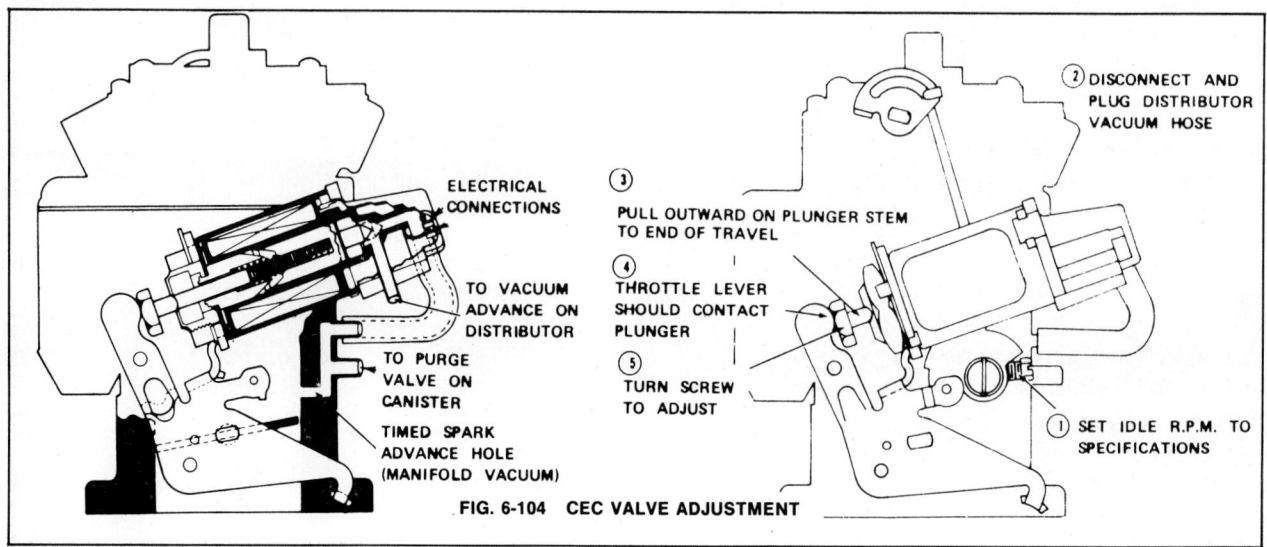

ELECTRICAL CONNECTIONS

TO VACUUM ADVANCE ON DISTRIBUTOR

TO PURGE VALVE ON CANISTER

TIMED SPARK ADVANCE HOLE (MANIFOLD VACUUM)

② DISCONNECT AND PLUG DISTRIBUTOR VACUUM HOSE

③ PULL OUTWARD ON PLUNGER STEM TO END OF TRAVEL

④ THROTTLE LEVER SHOULD CONTACT PLUNGER

⑤ TURN SCREW TO ADJUST

① SET IDLE R.P.M. TO SPECIFICATIONS

FIG. 6-104 CEC VALVE ADJUSTMENT

lamp goes out now, replace the TCS switch. If the test lamp stays lit, check the wiring for a ground.

1974 EXHAUST GAS RECIRCULATION VALVE FUNCTIONAL TEST

1. Perform Steps 1-4 of the 1973 test procedure.
2. If no vacuum is present:
   I-6—Check thermal vacuum switch end of line between the thermal vacuum switch and the carburetor for vacuum.
   V-8—Check distributor-spark/EGR-thermal vacuum valve end of the line, between the valve and the carburetor, for vacuum.
3. If vacuum is present:
   I-6—Check for a stuck thermal vacuum switch or plugged lines.
   V-8—Check for a defective vacuum bias valve, backpressure transducer or distributor-spark/EGR-thermal vacuum valve, or for plugged lines.
   If no vacuum is present, either the carburetor-to-V-8 valve or I-6 switch is plugged, or the carburetor is defective.

1975-78 EXHAUST GAS RECIRCULATION VALVE COMPONENT TEST

EGR VALVE

1. Depress the valve diaphragm, plug the vacuum tube and release the diaphragm.
2. The EGR valve is satisfactory if more than 20 seconds are required for full diaphragm travel—replace if full travel is achieved in less than 20 seconds.

BACKPRESSURE TRANSDUCER VALVE

1. Remove the air cleaner and plug the intake-manifold vacuum fitting.
2. Warm the engine to normal operating temperature and connect a vacuum gauge to the carburetor side of the BPT valve.
3. Place the fast-idle cam follower on the high step of the fast idle cam, with the transmission in PARK. Read and record the vacuum.
4. Tee a vacuum gauge into the line between the BPT and the EGR valves. The vacuum should read between 1.8 and 3.2 ins. (1.7 to 2.7 ins., 260-cu.-in. engine). If not, replace the BPT valve.
5. Remove and plug the EGR line at the EGR valve. If vacuum gauge reading is not the same or higher than Step 4, replace the BPT valve.

EGR-TVV, TWO-PORT TYPE

1. With coolant temperature above 70° F, connect a hand vacuum pump to the lower fitting hose and tee a vacuum gauge to the upper fitting. When vacuum is applied, the upper fitting should read within 1 in. of the applied vacuum. If not, replace the EGR-TVV.

EFE-EGR-TVV, FOUR-PORT TYPE

1. With coolant temperature above 120° F, connect a hand vacuum pump to the bottom port line marked "2" and tee a vacuum gauge to the port marked "1." When vacuum is applied, the "1" port should read within 1 in. of applied vacuum. If not, replace EFE-EGR-TVV.

1975-78 DISTRIBUTOR VACUUM ADVANCE SYSTEM COMPONENT TEST

DISTRIBUTOR VACUUM ADVANCE UNIT

1. Connect an ignition timing light, start the engine and warm it to normal operating temperature.
2. Connect a hand vacuum pump to the distributor advance unit and apply 15 ins. or more vacuum.

3. Advance unit should hold advance for 20 seconds—verify with the timing light. If the engine returns to its initial setting in less than 20 seconds, replace the advance unit.

VACUUM ADVANCE MODULATOR VALVE

1. Remove the air cleaner and plug the manifold vacuum fitting. The TVV should be removed from the air cleaner body rather than attempting to disconnect the secondary vacuum-break lines.
2. Start the engine and warm to normal operating temperature. Remove the line from the modulator-valve DIST fitting and connect a vacuum gauge. Tee a second vacuum gauge into the line between the CARB fitting and the carburetor (Fig. 6-105).
3. The gauge connected to the DIST fitting should read 10 ins. vacuum at idle. Replace the valve if gauge reading is less than 9 ins. or more than 11 ins.
4. Place the transmission in PARK and gradually open the throttle. The reading on both gauges should be the same as the throttle is opened. If not, replace the valve.

EFE-DS-TVV, FOUR-PORT TYPE

1. With coolant temperature above 120° F, connect a hand vacuum pump to the port marked "1" and tee

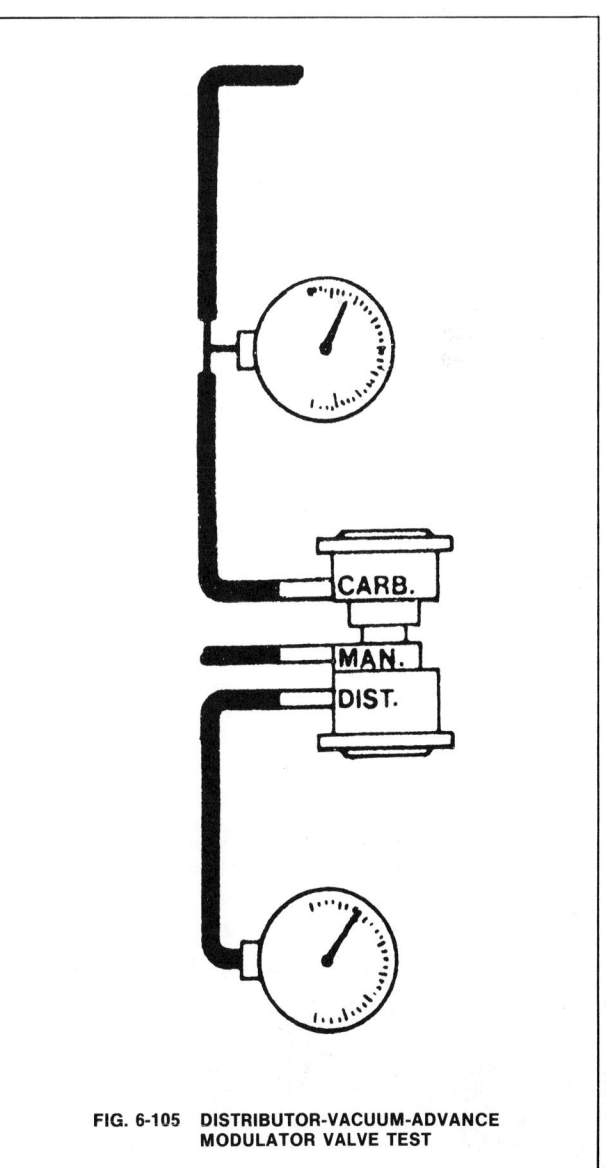

FIG. 6-105   DISTRIBUTOR-VACUUM-ADVANCE MODULATOR VALVE TEST

a vacuum gauge to the port marked ''2.'' When vacuum is applied, the ''2'' port should read within 1 in. of the applied vacuum. If not, replace the EFE-DS-TVV.

DV-TVV, THREE-PORT TYPE

1. With coolant temperature below 227° F, connect a hand vacuum pump to the center or ''C'' fitting and tee a vacuum gauge to each of the remaining two fittings. When vacuum is applied to the ''C'' fitting, the gauge connected to the ''D'' fitting should read within 1 in. of the applied vacuum, and the gauge connected to the ''MT'' fitting should show no reading. If gauges do not read as specified, replace the valve.

EARLY FUEL EVAPORATION (EFE) VALVE FUNCTIONAL TEST

A second person is required to start the engine while you observe the action of the EFE valve.

1. With engine coolant temperature below 120° F, locate and note position of the EFE-valve actuator arm.
2. When the engine is started, the actuator link should be pulled into the diaphragm housing, closing the valve.
3. If the valve does not close, remove the line from the EFE valve and connect a hand vacuum pump.
4. Apply 8 ins. or more vacuum; if the EFE valve still does not close, replace it. If it does close, the problem is not in the EFE valve; proceed with the test.
5. Allow the engine to warm up until coolant temperature exceeds 120° F. If the valve does not open at this point, remove the line from the EFE valve.
6. If the valve now opens, there is no air bleed for the diaphragm, or the thermal vacuum valve plunger is stuck in the cold mode. Replace the TVV.

EMISSION SYSTEM COMPONENT REPLACEMENT

AIR CLEANER ASSEMBLY

The air cleaner assembly is not serviceable; if the damper control door is malfunctioning, the entire unit must be replaced. The vacuum motor assembly and the air cleaner sensor are replaceable.

VACUUM MOTOR

1. Remove the air cleaner from the engine.
2. Drill out the center of the two spot welds holding the vacuum motor to the snorkel tube. Use a 1/16-in. drill— *do not* center punch.
3. Enlarge the holes to 5/32-in. Be careful not to damage or distort the air cleaner snorkel.
4. Remove the vacuum-motor retainer strap and lift the vacuum motor, tilting it to one side in order to unhook the linkage at the control door.
5. Drill a 7/64-in. hole in the snorkel tube at the center of the retaining strap end which faces the air cleaner housing.
6. Install a new vacuum motor assembly, using the mounting strap retainer and sheetmetal screw provided with the new motor assembly. Screw must not interfere with damper door operation—shorten if necessary.

AIR CLEANER SENSOR

1. Pry the sensor retaining-clip tabs free and remove the vacuum lines from the sensor.
2. Note position of the old sensor—the new unit must be installed in the same position to avoid possible interference with the air cleaner element—then remove the old sensor.
3. Install the new sensor and gasket in the air clean-

er and replace the retaining clip while supporting the sensor around the center rim of the air cleaner to prevent damage to the temperature sensing spring.

AIR PUMP REMOVAL/INSTALLATION

TO REMOVE

1. Disconnect the pump and valve hoses.
2. Loosen the pump-to-bracket mounting bolts, and remove the pump drive belt.
3. Remove the pulley-to-hub bolts, and remove the pulley.
4. Remove the air pump from the engine.

TO INSTALL

1. Position the pump on the mounting bracket. Line up the holes and install the bolts loosely.
2. Fit the pulley to the hub and tighten the bolts to 24 ft.-lbs.
3. Install the pump belt over the pulley and adjust the tension, then torque the mounting bolts 20 to 35 ft.-lbs.
4. Reconnect the pump and valve hoses.

CENTRIFUGAL FILTER FAN REPLACEMENT

1. Remove the air pump from the engine.
2. Pull the fan from the hub with needlenose pliers. Although it is seldom possible to remove the fan without damage, take care not to let the plastic fragments enter the air intake hole.
3. Draw the new fan evenly into place, using the pulley and bolts as tools. Torque the bolts alternately to 24 ft.-lbs. Outer edge of the fan must slip into the housing.
4. Replace the pump on the engine. Until the outer diameter sealing lip has worn in, a new fan may be noisy.

DIVERTER VALVE REPLACEMENT

1. Disconnect the vacuum lines from the valve.
2. Remove the valve from the air pump or elbow.
3. Install the new valve and gasket to the pump or elbow, and torque the attaching screws to 85 in.-lbs.
4. Replace the vacuum lines to the valve, and inspect the system for leakage.

CHECK VALVE REPLACEMENT

1. Disconnect the pump hose from the check valve. Remove and replace with a new check valve, taking care not to bend, twist or otherwise distort the air manifold, and then replace the pump hose.

EGR VALVE REPLACEMENT

1. Disconnect the vacuum line from the EGR valve, and remove the bolt attaching it to the manifold.
2. Remove the EGR valve and gasket; discard the gasket.
3. Replace the EGR valve on the manifold with a new gasket, and torque the attaching bolt 12 to 17 ft.-lbs.
4. Connect the vacuum line to the EGR valve.

THERMAL VACUUM SWITCH/VACUUM VALVE (TVS/TVV) REPLACEMENT

1. Disconnect vacuum lines from the TVS or TVV.
2. Remove the switch or valve from the manifold or thermostat housing.
3. Apply a soft-setting sealer to the threaded portion of the switch or valve, and install it in the manifold or thermostat housing. Torque to 15 ft.-lbs.

4. Turn the TVS/TVV head as required to align it for proper vacuum line connection and reinstall the lines.

VAPOR CANISTER FILTER REPLACEMENT (EXCEPT VENTURA)

1. Disconnect the canister hoses carefully to prevent damage to the inlet extensions.

2. Remove the screw from the canister retaining strap(s) and remove the canister.

3. Inspect hose connection openings for blockage, then pull the filter from the retainer at the canister bottom.

4. Install a new filter by tucking it under the retainer and centering it.

5. Replace the canister in the mounting strap, torque the strap screw to 75 in.-lbs. and reconnect the hoses to the canister inlets.

VAPOR CANISTER FILTER REPLACEMENT (VENTURA)

1. Loosen the screw(s) on the strap which holds the canister.

2. Slide the canister (with hoses still attached) from the mounting bracket and remove the mounting bracket screw(s).

3. Inspect hose connection openings for blockage, then pull the filter from the retainer at the canister bottom.

4. Install a new filter by tucking it under the retainer and centering it.

5. Replace the canister mounting-bracket screw(s), and slide the canister back into the mounting bracket.

6. Tighten the mounting bracket screw(s) to 20 ft.-lbs. Install and tighten the screw for the strap holding the canister to 75 in.-lbs.

FORD, MERCURY, LINCOLN

Components and operation of emission controls used on Ford, Lincoln and Mercury engines may differ, depending upon engine application. For this reason, it is quite possible that while you and a neighbor might both own FoMoCo vehicles with the same engine displacement (i.e., 302 cu. ins; 400 cu. ins.; etc.), their emission systems may differ. To identify emission systems, Ford uses a calibration code consisting of a letter/number combination. This calibration is found on a decal or sticker attached to engine rocker cover. Troubleshooting procedures for specific problems affecting Ford-manufactured engines usually carry the emission system calibration code to identify those particular engines with which the procedure may be used. You should note the calibration code in your owner's handbook in case the decal/sticker is defaced, damaged or removed from the engine. Reference to the calibration code is often necessary in order to assure correct component replacement in case of a malfunction.

1970-71 Emission Systems

POSITIVE CRANKCASE VENTILATION (PCV)

All Ford Motor Company vehicles are equipped with

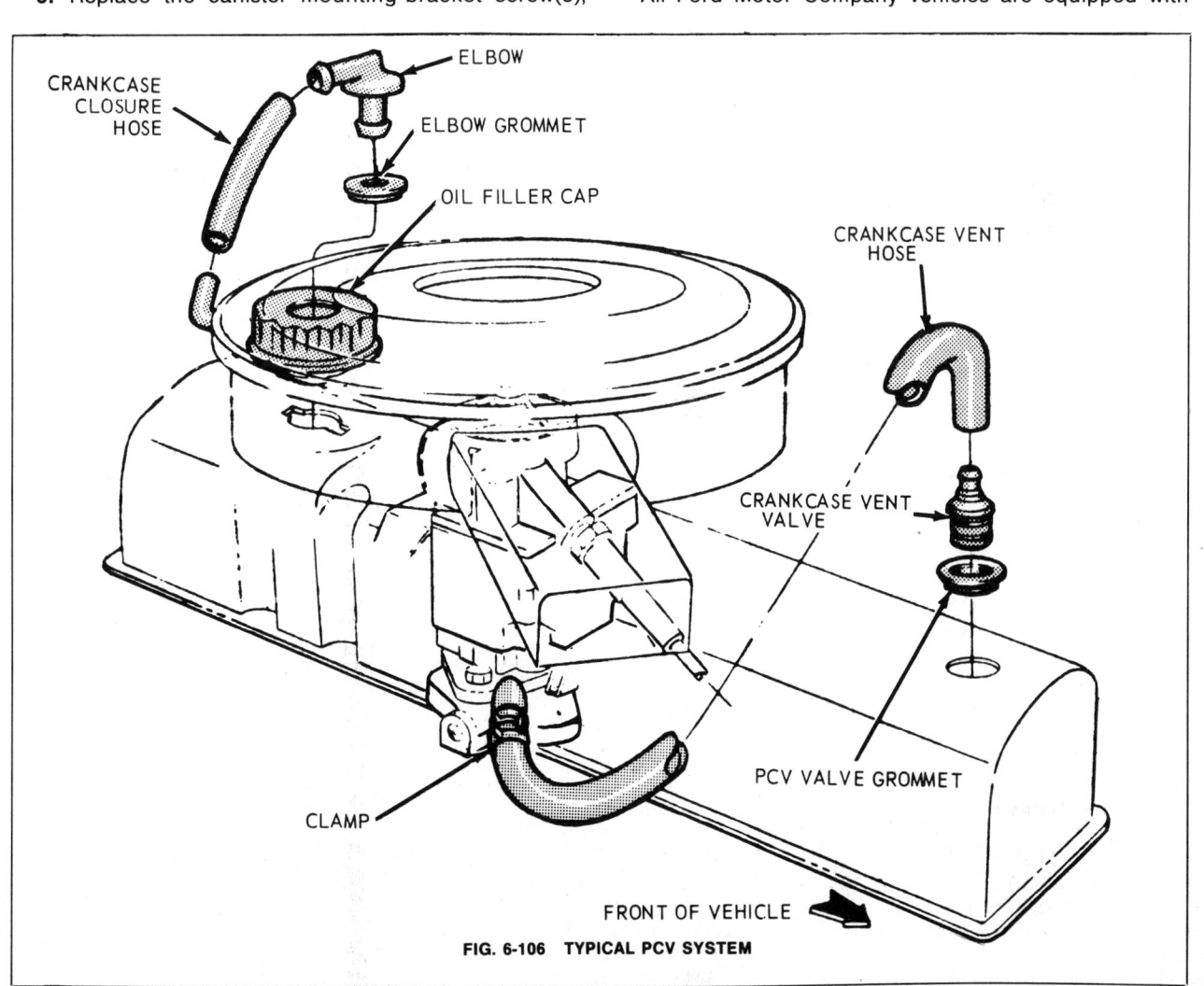

CRANKCASE CLOSURE HOSE

ELBOW

ELBOW GROMMET

OIL FILLER CAP

CRANKCASE VENT HOSE

CRANKCASE VENT VALVE

PCV VALVE GROMMET

CLAMP

FRONT OF VEHICLE

FIG. 6-106 TYPICAL PCV SYSTEM

a closed crankcase ventilation system **(Fig. 6-106)**. A sealed oil-filler cap prevents crankcase gases from escaping under no-vacuum conditions. A tube from the air cleaner goes to the rocker cover, carrying fresh air through the air cleaner filter and down into the crankcase. From that point, blowby gases go through the hose into the PCV valve and then into the manifold. When the PCV system is under zero vacuum, there is no suction on the crankcase, but the gases go from the rocker cover through the hose into the air cleaner, where they are drawn into the intake manifold through the carburetor. A crankcase ventilation filter pack is installed on 1970 351C and all 1971 air cleaner shells, and is clipped to the closure hose **(Fig. 6-107)**.

THERMACTOR AIR INJECTION SYSTEM

A carryover from the late Sixties, use of the Thermactor is restricted to the following high-performance engines as indicated:

1970	1971
302 Boss V-8	302 HO V-8
428 4-bbl. V-8	429 HO V-8
429 Auto. V-8	460 All V-8
460 All V-8	

The Thermactor system uses an air injection pump, a bypass and check valve, external air manifolds, air injector tubes located in the exhaust ports, and necessary connecting hoses to inject fresh air in the exhaust ports to burn raw exhaust fumes. Since the Thermactor system was revived in 1974, a more detailed treatment will be found in that section.

HEATED AIR CLEANER

A temperature-operated duct/valve assembly **(Fig. 6-108)** is used on all engines except the 351C- and 400-cu.-in., which use a vacuum-operated duct/valve system **(Fig. 6-109)** The air-cleaner duct system provides the carburetor with air at 90° F temperature under normal operating conditions. Lincoln and Continental Mark III engines are equipped with a fresh air inlet tube (zip tube) connected to the air cleaner to allow ambient air into the system **(Fig. 6-110)**.

DISTRIBUTOR VACUUM ADVANCE

All distributors are equipped with both centrifugal and vacuum advance. Single-diaphragm advance units are used on the following engine/transmission combinations:

1970	1971
460 Auto.	460 All
429 Auto.	429 4-bbl.
428 CJ Auto.	400 2-bbl. (non-Calif.)
390 2-bbl. (270 hp)	351 2-bbl. (non-Calif.)
351 2-bbl. (Fairlane, Montego)	250 (Calif.)

A dual-diaphragm vacuum advance **(Fig. 6-111)** is used on all other 1970-71 distributors to provide further timing retard during idle conditions. The outer or primary diaphragm uses carburetor vacuum to advance ignition timing, while the inner or secondary diaphragm is operated by intake manifold vacuum for additional retard during closed throttle idle to reduce hydrocarbon emissions. High-performance engines use double breaker-point sets; the resulting dwell increase gives a better spark.

DISTRIBUTOR CONTROL SYSTEMS

The following devices supplement the vacuum diaphragm controls installed on all passenger car distributors. Each device regulates the distributor by changing the vacuum applied to the vacuum advance diaphragm.

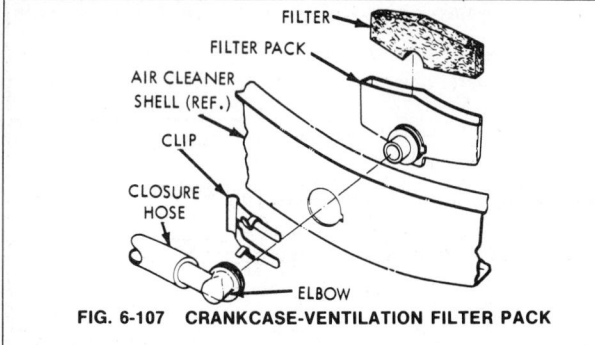

FIG. 6-107 CRANKCASE-VENTILATION FILTER PACK

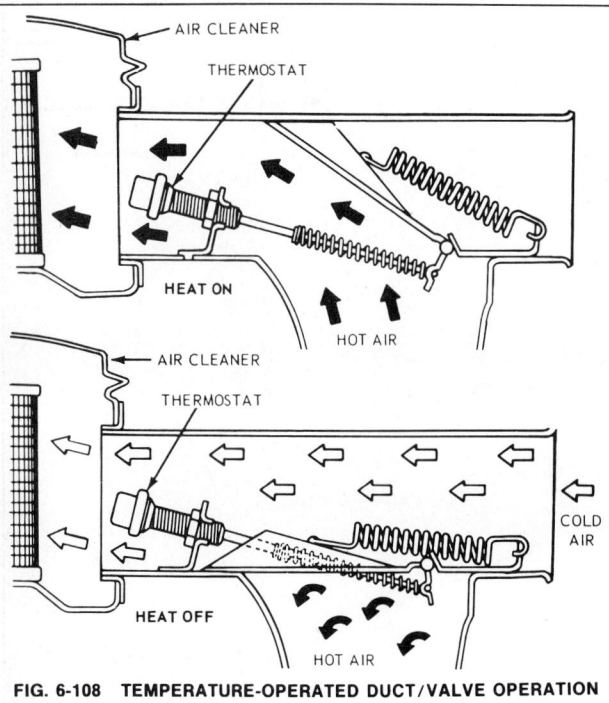

FIG. 6-108 TEMPERATURE-OPERATED DUCT/VALVE OPERATION

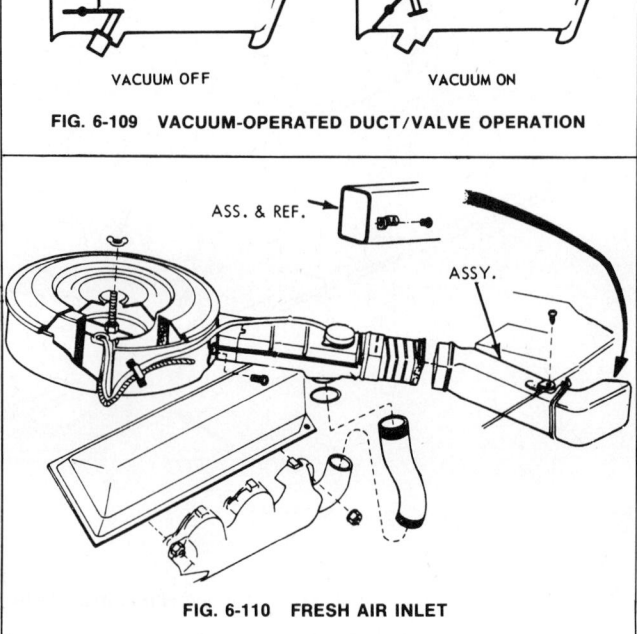

FIG. 6-109 VACUUM-OPERATED DUCT/VALVE OPERATION

FIG. 6-110 FRESH AIR INLET

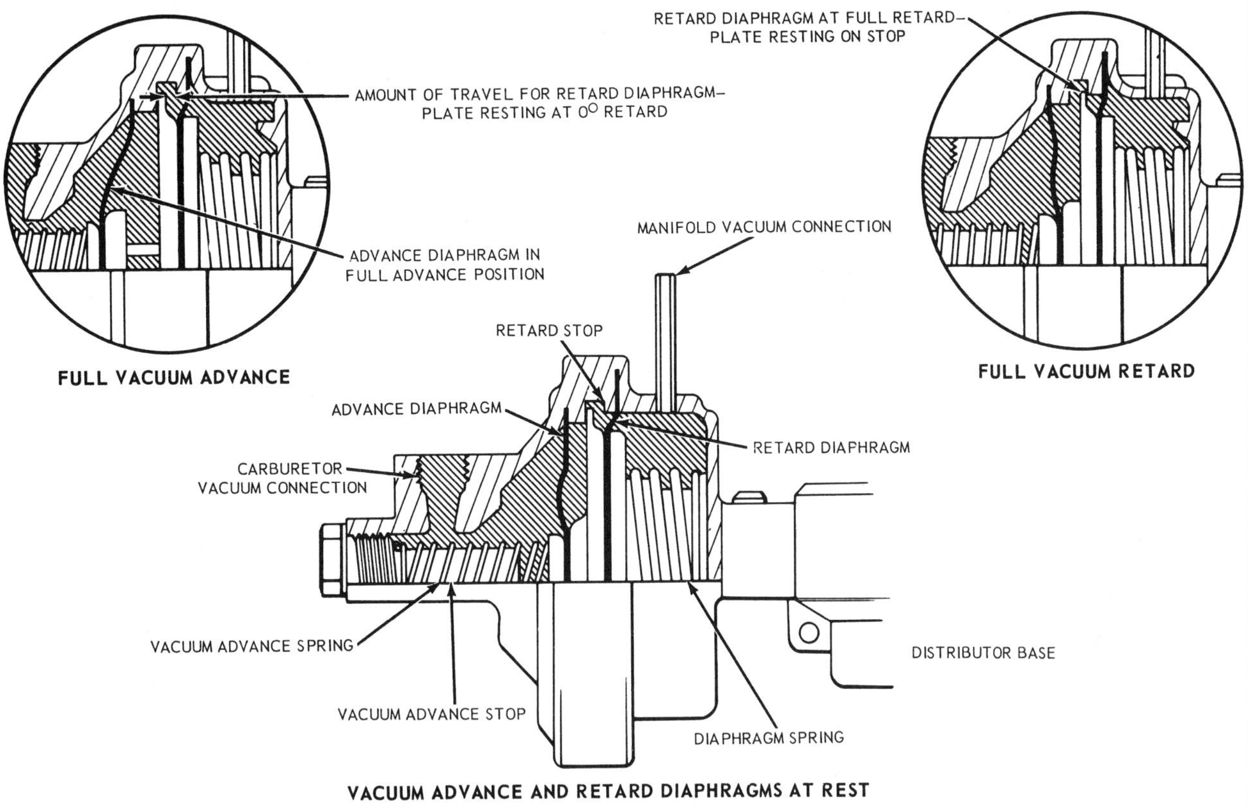

RETARD DIAPHRAGM AT FULL RETARD—
PLATE RESTING ON STOP

AMOUNT OF TRAVEL FOR RETARD DIAPHRAGM—
PLATE RESTING AT 0° RETARD

ADVANCE DIAPHRAGM IN
FULL ADVANCE POSITION

MANIFOLD VACUUM CONNECTION

FULL VACUUM ADVANCE

FULL VACUUM RETARD

RETARD STOP

ADVANCE DIAPHRAGM

RETARD DIAPHRAGM

CARBURETOR
VACUUM CONNECTION

VACUUM ADVANCE SPRING

DISTRIBUTOR BASE

VACUUM ADVANCE STOP

DIAPHRAGM SPRING

VACUUM ADVANCE AND RETARD DIAPHRAGMS AT REST

FIG. 6-111   DUAL-DIAPHRAGM VACUUM ADVANCE MECHANISM

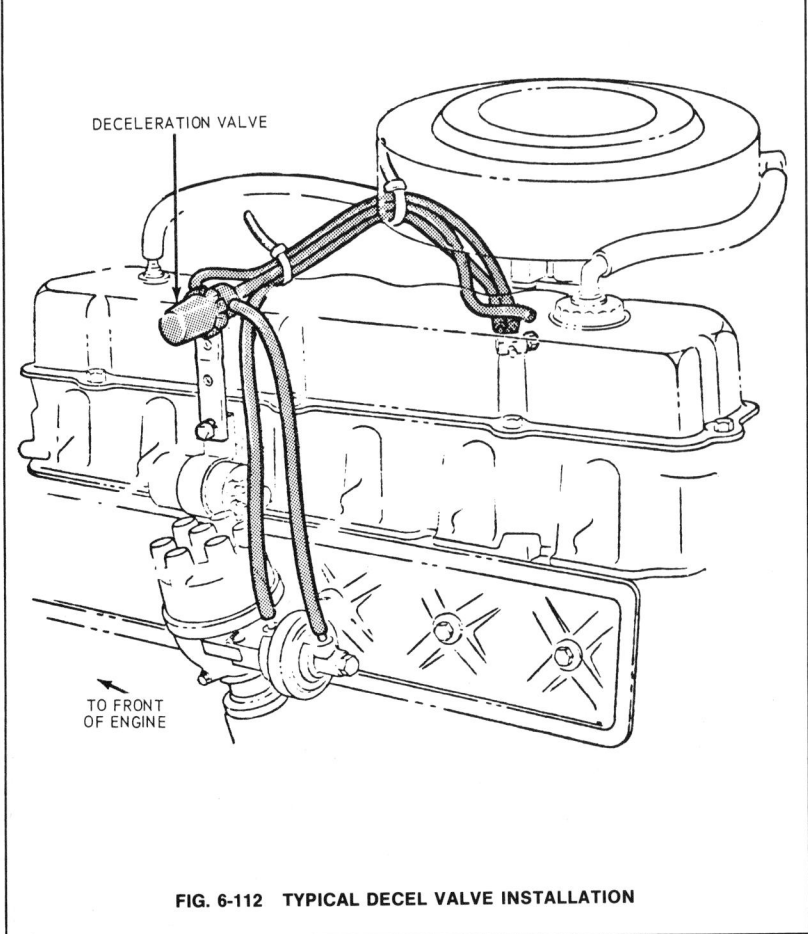

DECELERATION VALVE

TO FRONT
OF ENGINE

FIG. 6-112   TYPICAL DECEL VALVE INSTALLATION

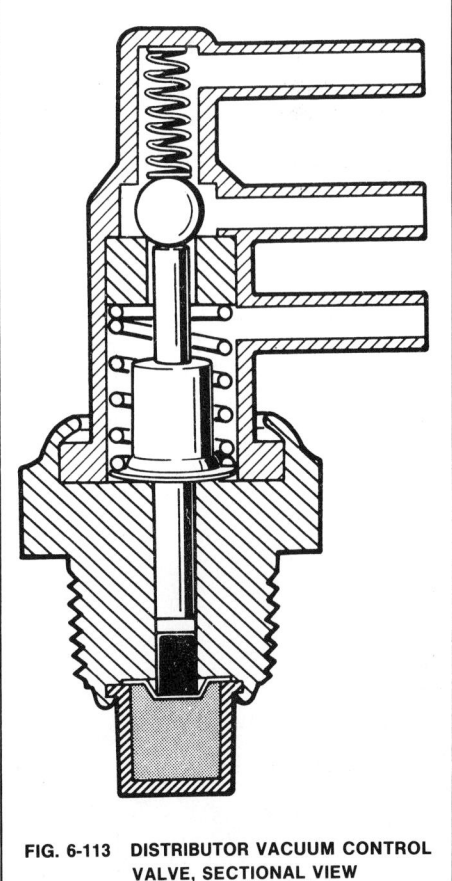

**FIG. 6-113   DISTRIBUTOR VACUUM CONTROL
VALVE, SECTIONAL VIEW**

DISTRIBUTOR VACUUM DECELERATION VALVE

A deceleration valve is fitted to all 1970-71 240-cu.-in. 6-cyl. engines equipped with manual transmissions, and connects to the dual-diaphragm vacuum advance unit **(Fig. 6-112)**. As intake manifold vacuum rises during deceleration, the valve shuts off carburetor vacuum to provide full manifold vacuum to the outer vacuum-advance diaphragm, producing maximum ignition-timing advance to prevent after-burning. When the engine reaches idle, the valve switches vacuum flow from the manifold back to the carburetor.

DISTRIBUTOR VACUUM CONTROL VALVE

This coolant-temperature sensing valve **(Fig. 6-113)** is installed in the coolant outlet elbow of some engines to allow advanced ignition timing under prolonged conditions of idle. The valve usually connects carburetor vacuum with the distributor. When engine coolant temperature rises above a preset level, the valve closes off carburetor vacuum to furnish manifold vacuum. This increases vacuum advance, causing an engine speed increase which continues until coolant temperature returns to normal.

ELECTRONIC DISTRIBUTOR MODULATOR SYSTEM

This system **(Fig. 6-114)** is composed of four major components:

1. A speed sensor connected to the speedometer cable.

2. A thermal switch mounted on the outside of the cowl panel near the front-door hinge pillar.

3. An electronic-control module/solenoid valve combined as a single unit and located inside the passenger compartment on the dash panel.

4. A three-port PVS switch installed in the water jacket.

The system is fitted to the following engine/carburetor combinations:

1970	1971
240 1-bbl.	200 1-bbl.
302 2-bbl.	240 1-bbl.
351 4-bbl.	250 1-bbl.
390 2-bbl.	390 2-bbl.
	429 4-bbl.
	460 4-bbl.

The modulator prevents timing advance below a specified speed, and advance below a specified value

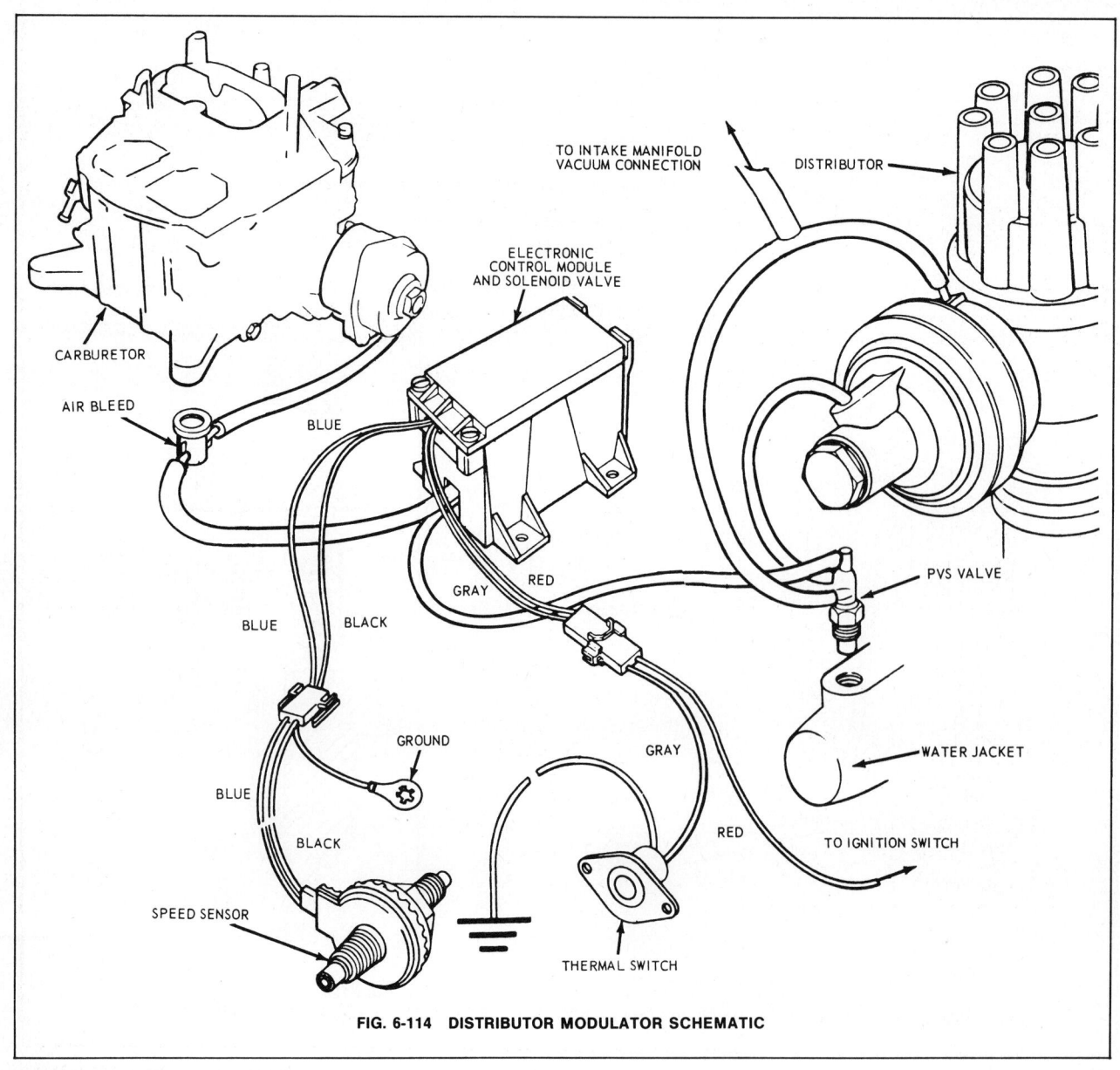

FIG. 6-114   DISTRIBUTOR MODULATOR SCHEMATIC

on deceleration.

EVAPORATIVE EMISSION CONTROL (EEC)

A vapor control system is used on 1970 California cars and all 1971 cars. Fuel vapors are trapped in the sealed fuel tank and vented through an orifice vapor-separator assembly located in the top of the tank **(Fig. 6-115).** The vapors pass through the separator and are directed to a carbon storage canister in the engine compartment by a single vapor line. Canister purge is accomplished by a tube connected to the air cleaner. 1970 system used a separate vapor tank, with connecting lines instead of integrated tank orifice separator.

FORD, MERCURY, LINCOLN

1972 Emission Systems

The Positive Crankcase Ventilation (PCV) system is the same as that used in 1970-71 Ford Motor Company cars.

HEATED AIR CLEANER

Use of the vacuum-operated duct valve is extended to all 460-cu.-in. engines.

DISTRIBUTOR VACUUM ADVANCE

Single-diaphragm vacuum advance units are used on three engines only—2000cc 4-cyl., 351C CJ 4-bbl. and 460 4-bbl.—the remainder are equipped with dual diaphragm units.

DISTRIBUTOR CONTROL SYSTEMS

DISTRIBUTOR VACUUM DECELERATION VALVE

Decel valve design **(Fig. 6-116)** is changed and installed only on the 1600cc and 2000cc 4-cyl. engines. The decel valve is located on the intake manifold next to the carburetor.

For Distributor Vacuum Control Valve, see 1970-71.

ELECTRONIC SPARK CONTROL (ECS)

This is a modified version of the 1970-71 Electronic Distributor Modulator System. The 1972 ECS system **(Fig. 6-117)** controls vacuum advance only at an outside temperature of 65° F or greater. When outside air temperature is below 49° F, normal vacuum advance is provided at all road speeds. At 65° F, the temperature switch closes, cutting off vacuum to the distributor and retarding ignition timing. As the car accelerates, the speed sensor transmits an electrical signal to the electronic amplifier. At a specified speed, the amplifier de-energizes the distributor modulator valve to restore carburetor vacuum to the distributor. When car speed

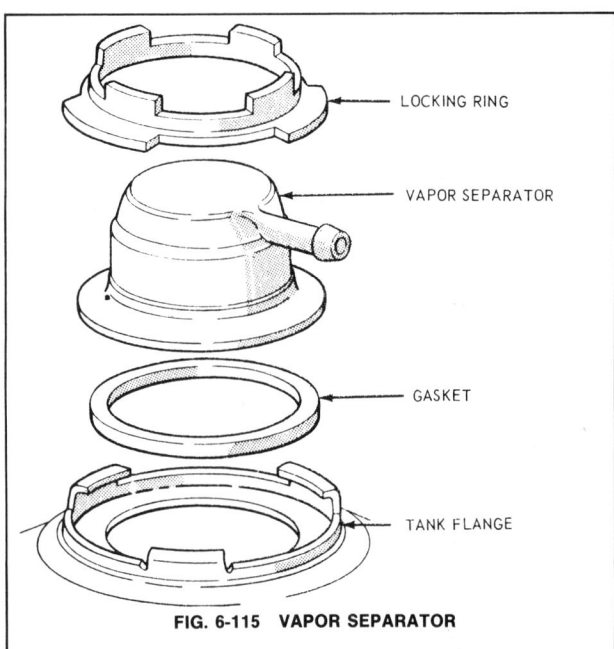

FIG. 6-115 **VAPOR SEPARATOR**

FIG. 6-116 **TYPICAL DECEL VALVE**

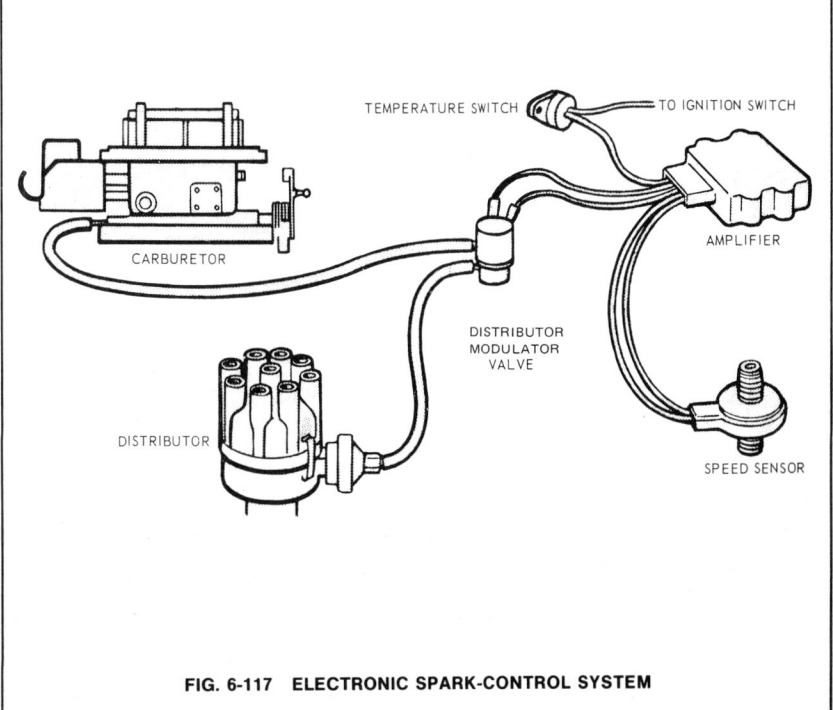

FIG. 6-117 **ELECTRONIC SPARK-CONTROL SYSTEM**

reaches approximately 18 mph during deceleration, the amplifier closes the modulator valve, shutting off vacuum and retarding the timing.

Two different speed-sensor units and four different amplifiers are used, according to system cut-in speeds required for vacuum advance, and must be replaced by an identical unit. The amplifier cases are color-coded as follows, according to speed cut-in:

COLOR	CUT-IN SPEED
Black	23 mph
White	28 mph
Blue	33 mph
Gray	35 mph

On some applications, a ported vacuum switch (PVS)

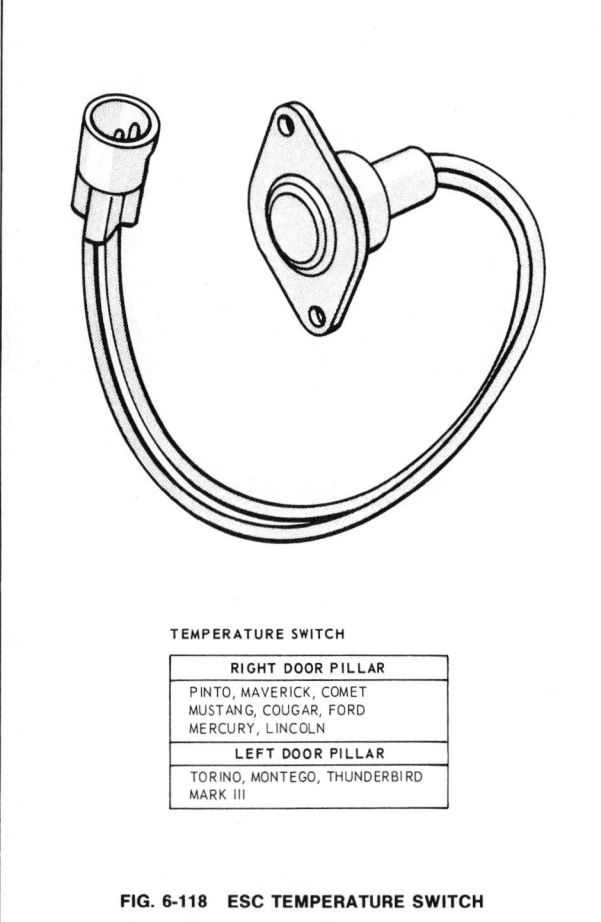

TEMPERATURE SWITCH

RIGHT DOOR PILLAR
PINTO, MAVERICK, COMET MUSTANG, COUGAR, FORD MERCURY, LINCOLN

LEFT DOOR PILLAR
TORINO, MONTEGO, THUNDERBIRD MARK III

FIG. 6-118 ESC TEMPERATURE SWITCH

is used as a bypass or safety override to advance the timing for engine cooling at coolant temperatures of 230° F and above. On other applications, the PVS switch is not used. Component design and locations are shown in **Figs. 6-118, 6-119, 6-120 & 6-121.**

TRANSMISSION REGULATED SPARK CONTROL SYSTEM (TRS)

The TRS system **Fig. 6-122** retards distributor vacuum advance while the car is operating in 1st and 2nd gears. The transmission switch activates the distributor modulator valve (solenoid) to permit vacuum advance only in high gear. The automatic transmission switch is pressure-sensitive, while the manual transmission switch is operated by a linkage detent bar. Like ECS, the TRS system provides full vacuum advance in all gear ranges at temperatures below 49° F (ambient temperature switch), and on some applications, a PVS is installed as a bypass or safety override to provide full vacuum advance at coolant temperatures of 230° F. The TRS system is fitted to the following 1972 engine/transmission combinations:

170-1V	Manual
200-1V	Manual
240 1V	Automatic
250-1V	Manual
302-2V	Manual
351W-2V	Automatic
351C-2V	All
351C-4V CJ	All
351C-4V HO	Manual

EVAPORATIVE EMISSION CONTROL (EEC)

The 1972 system is essentially the same as that used in 1971, but the vapor separator installed on Torino/Montego station wagons is a plastic 90° elbow mounted in a rubber flange atop the fuel tank. Police Interceptor models use a combined electric fuel pump and vapor separator.

FORD, MERCURY, LINCOLN
1973 Emission Systems

The Positive Crankcase Ventilation (PCV) system is the same as that used in 1970-71 Ford Motor Company cars. Electronic Spark Control (ESC) and Transmission Regulated Spark Control (TRS) and Evaporative Emission Control System (EEC) are the same as those of 1972.

IMPROVED COMBUSTION (IMCO) SYSTEM

A series of engine subsystem modifications designed

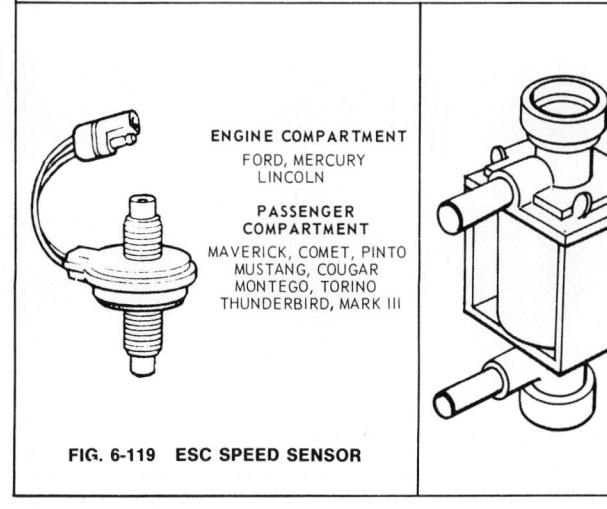

ENGINE COMPARTMENT
FORD, MERCURY
LINCOLN

PASSENGER COMPARTMENT
MAVERICK, COMET, PINTO
MUSTANG, COUGAR
MONTEGO, TORINO
THUNDERBIRD, MARK III

FIG. 6-119 ESC SPEED SENSOR

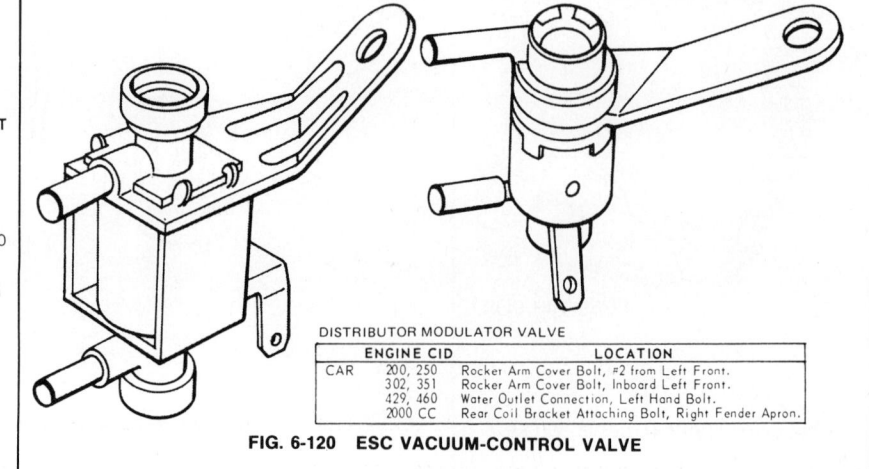

DISTRIBUTOR MODULATOR VALVE

	ENGINE CID	LOCATION
CAR	200, 250	Rocker Arm Cover Bolt, #2 from Left Front.
	302, 351	Rocker Arm Cover Bolt, Inboard Left Front.
	429, 460	Water Outlet Connection, Left Hand Bolt.
	2000 CC	Rear Coil Bracket Attaching Bolt, Right Fender Apron.

FIG. 6-120   ESC VACUUM-CONTROL VALVE

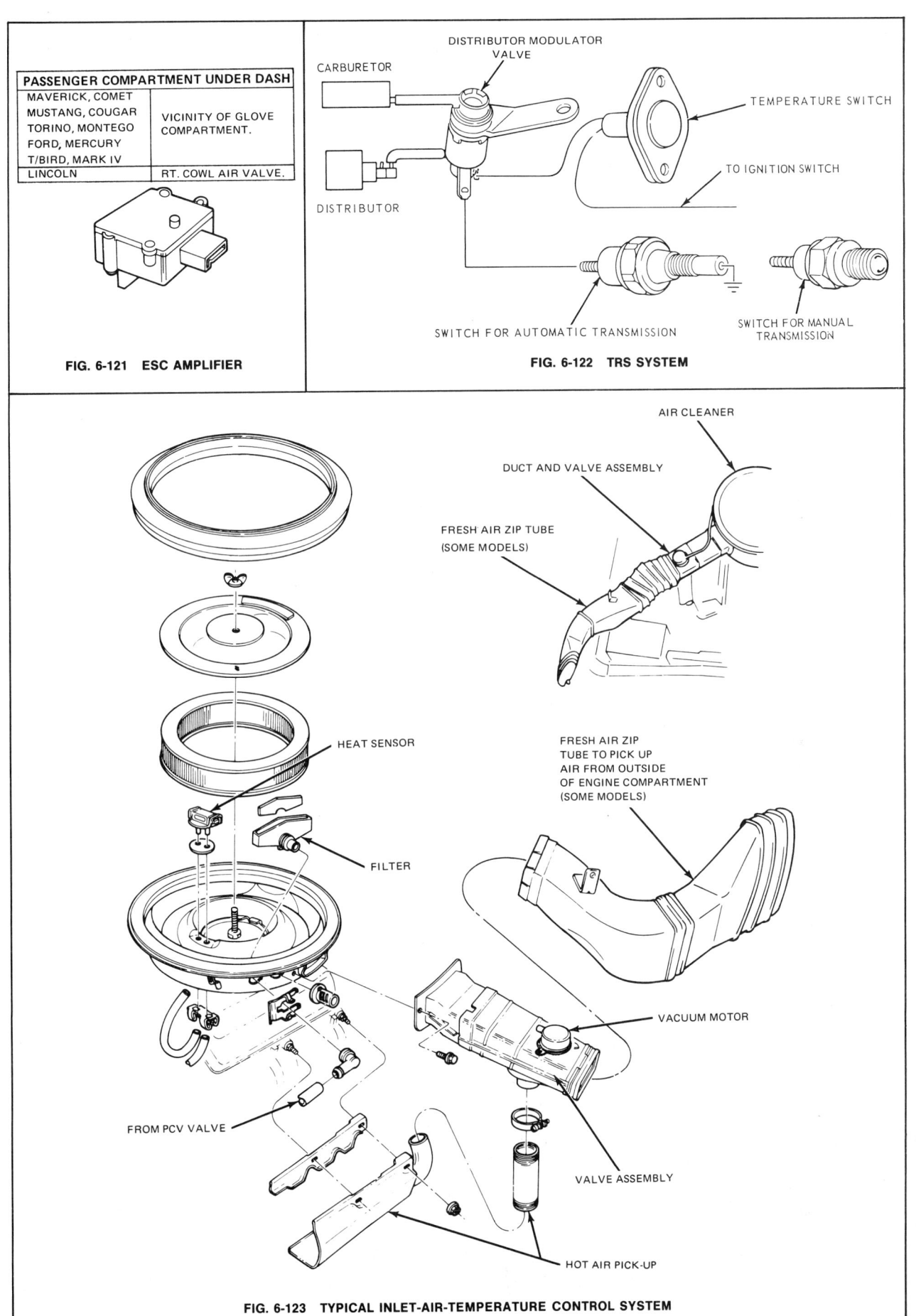

PASSENGER COMPARTMENT UNDER DASH

| MAVERICK, COMET MUSTANG, COUGAR TORINO, MONTEGO FORD, MERCURY T/BIRD, MARK IV | VICINITY OF GLOVE COMPARTMENT. |
| LINCOLN | RT. COWL AIR VALVE. |

FIG. 6-121   ESC AMPLIFIER

CARBURETOR

DISTRIBUTOR MODULATOR VALVE

TEMPERATURE SWITCH

TO IGNITION SWITCH

DISTRIBUTOR

SWITCH FOR AUTOMATIC TRANSMISSION

SWITCH FOR MANUAL TRANSMISSION

FIG. 6-122   TRS SYSTEM

AIR CLEANER

DUCT AND VALVE ASSEMBLY

FRESH AIR ZIP TUBE (SOME MODELS)

HEAT SENSOR

FILTER

FRESH AIR ZIP TUBE TO PICK UP AIR FROM OUTSIDE OF ENGINE COMPARTMENT (SOME MODELS)

VACUUM MOTOR

FROM PCV VALVE

VALVE ASSEMBLY

HOT AIR PICK-UP

FIG. 6-123   TYPICAL INLET-AIR-TEMPERATURE CONTROL SYSTEM

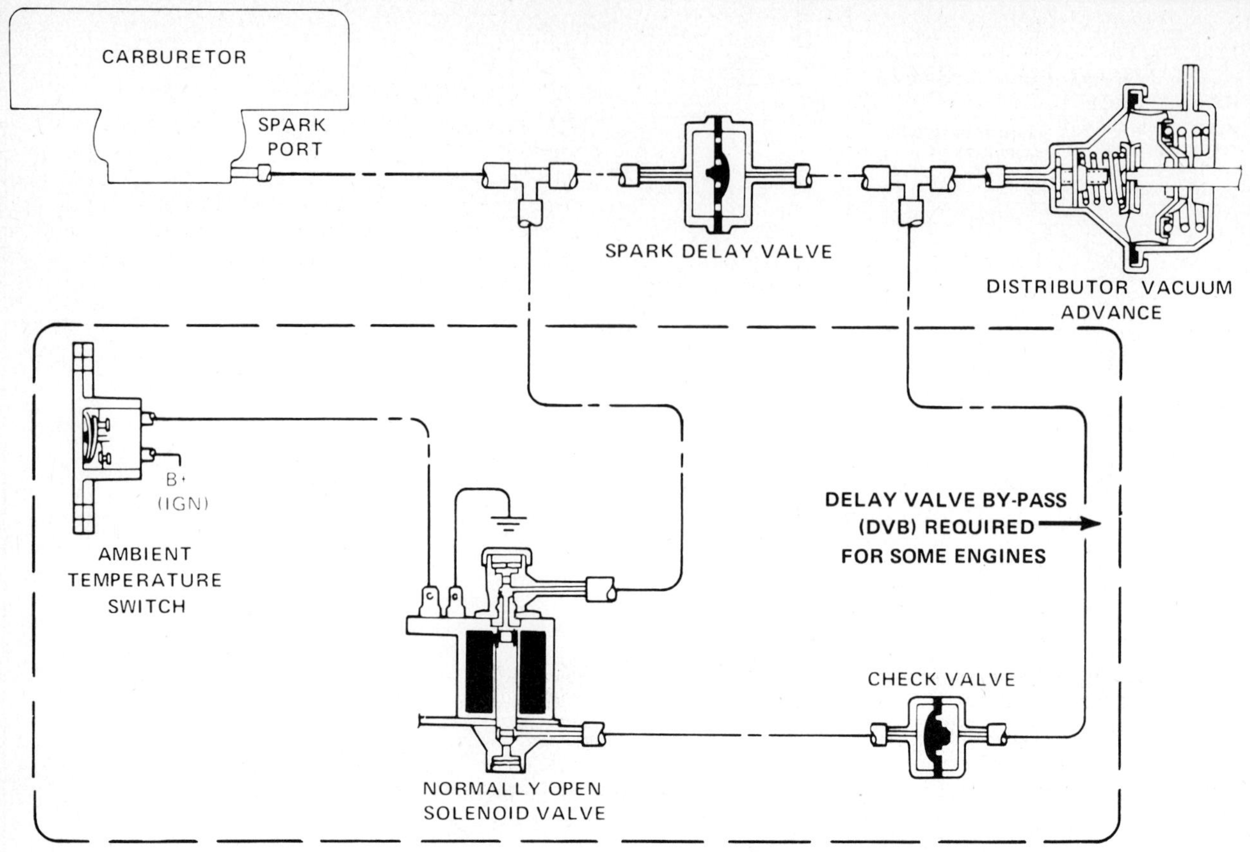

CARBURETOR

SPARK PORT

SPARK DELAY VALVE

DISTRIBUTOR VACUUM ADVANCE

B· (IGN)

AMBIENT TEMPERATURE SWITCH

DELAY VALVE BY-PASS (DVB) REQUIRED FOR SOME ENGINES

CHECK VALVE

NORMALLY OPEN SOLENOID VALVE

FIG. 6-124   TEMPERATURE-ACTUATED VACUUM SYSTEM (TAV)

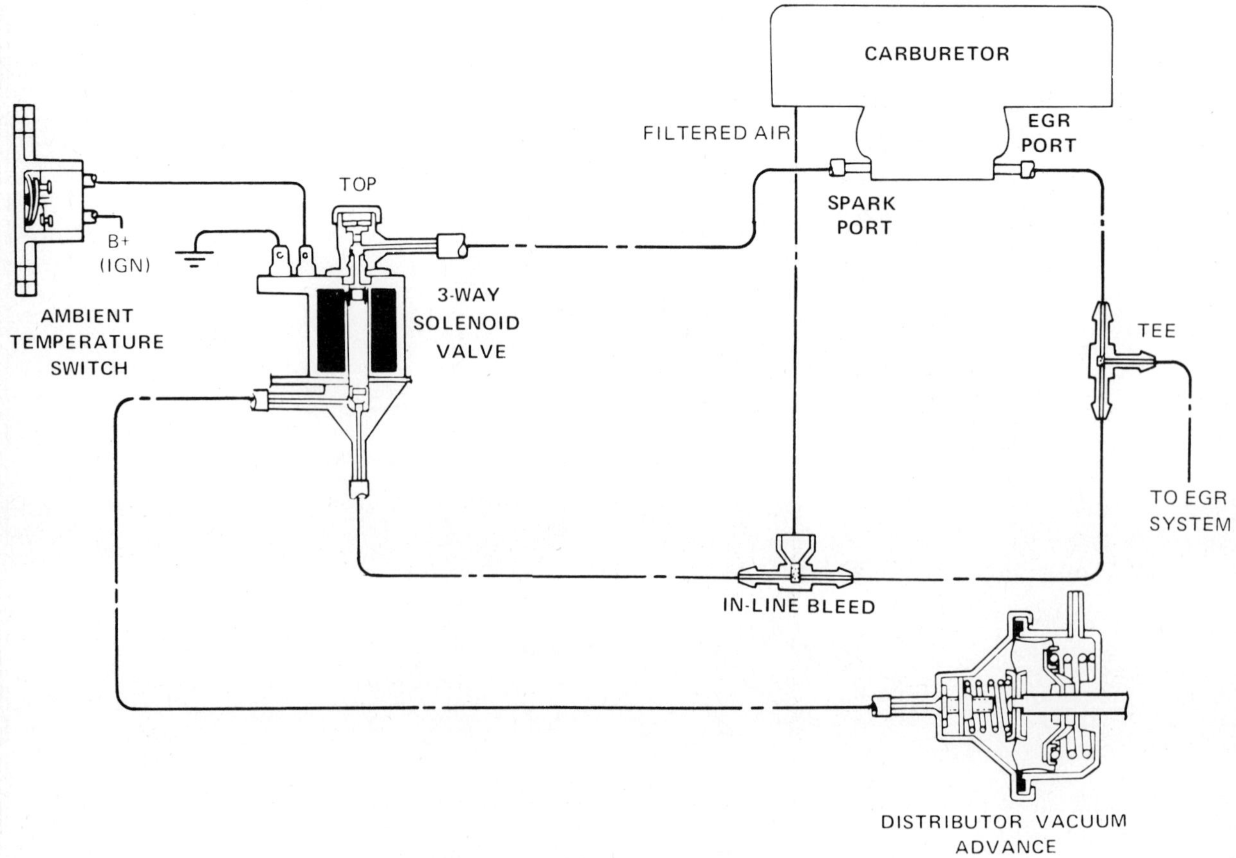

CARBURETOR

FILTERED AIR

EGR PORT

SPARK PORT

TOP

B+ (IGN)

AMBIENT TEMPERATURE SWITCH

3-WAY SOLENOID VALVE

TEE

TO EGR SYSTEM

IN-LINE BLEED

DISTRIBUTOR VACUUM ADVANCE

FIG. 6-125   SPARK DELAY VALVE SYSTEM

for control of hydrocarbons and carbon monoxide emissions, IMCO includes:

1. Inlet air temperature regulation.
2. Carburetor and distributor calibrations.
3. Improvements to the:
   a) Intake and exhaust manifolds and ports
   b) Cylinder heads
   c) Pistons
   d) Camshaft
   e) Engine cooling system

The IMCO modifications are tailored to the individual requirements of each model engine, transmission and car combination.

INLET AIR TEMPERATURE REGULATION

This maintains the temperature of the air entering the carburetor at approximately 100° F (75° F on some engines) whenever the required heated or cool air is available **(Fig. 6-123)**. Air temperature maintained at a constant and moderately high temperature improves engine warm-up, minimizes carburetor icing and permits a leaner carburetor air/fuel mixture. A vacuum

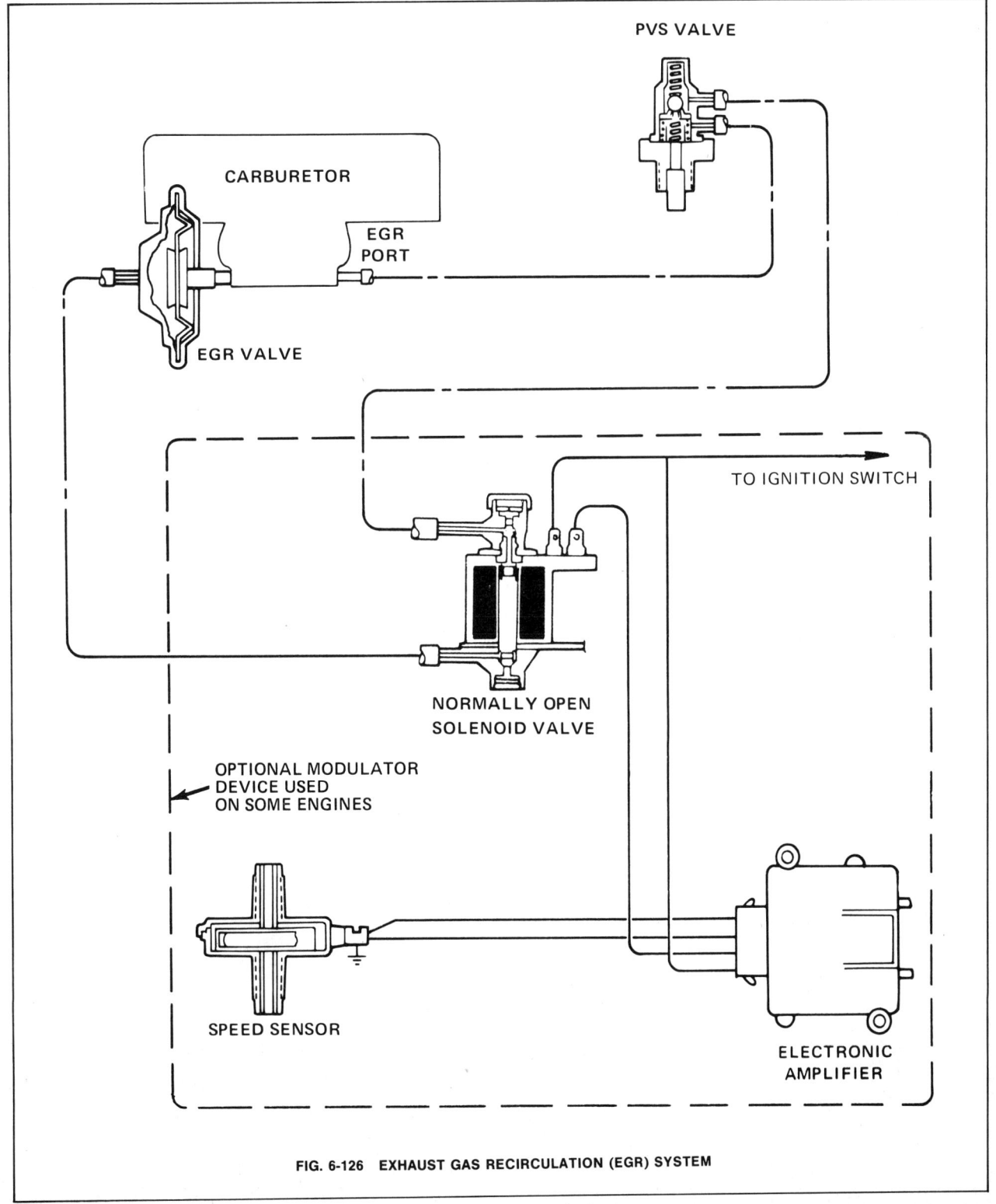

FIG. 6-126 EXHAUST GAS RECIRCULATION (EGR) SYSTEM

motor is used on some applications to overcome the low manifold vacuum encountered during heavy engine loading, and a fresh air inlet (zip) tube is fitted to some engines to pick up outside air.

TEMPERATURE ACTIVATED VACUUM (TAV)

The TAV system **(Fig. 6-124)** matches vacuum advance to engine requirements by switching between two vacuum signals. As it selects between the carburetor spark-port vacuum or carburetor EGR vacuum, the system can only be used in conjunction with Exhaust Gas Recirculation (EGR). When outside temperature is above 60° F, the three-way solenoid valve is energized, allowing EGR vacuum to control distributor advance. If outside air temperature is below 49° F, the solenoid valve is de-energized and spark port vacuum controls distributor advance. An inline bleed purges the TAV vacuum line of gasoline vapors.

SPARK DELAY VALVE SYSTEM (SDV)

This system **(Fig. 6-125)** delays vacuum advance during some vehicle acceleration modes. A bi-directional flow device, the spark delay valve retards spark port vacuum during mild acceleration conditions by means of a sintered metal disc, resulting in a lagging advance during acceleration. During deceleration or very heavy

acceleration, spark port vacuum decreases, causing the pressure difference across the restrictor disc to reverse. This opens a check valve to prevent a delay in the vacuum signal by the restrictor disc. Since spark advance is insufficient during acceleration at low ambient temperatures, a spark delay bypass, controlled by a temperature switch, is required on some engines.

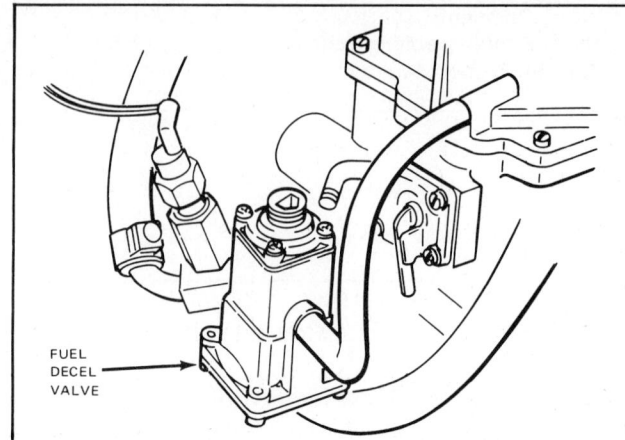

FIG. 6-127   TYPICAL FUEL DECEL VALVE INSTALLATION

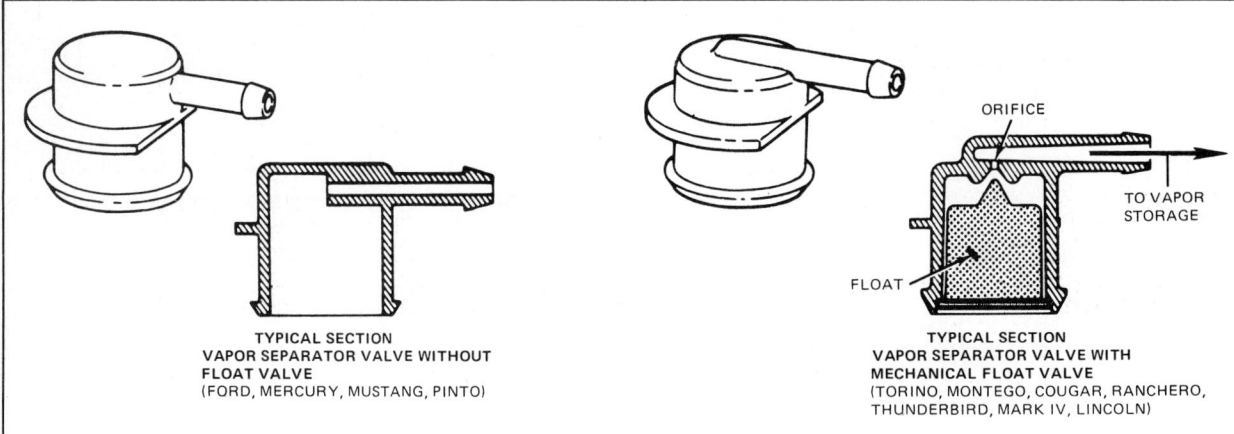

FIG. 6-128   EEC VAPOR SEPARATORS

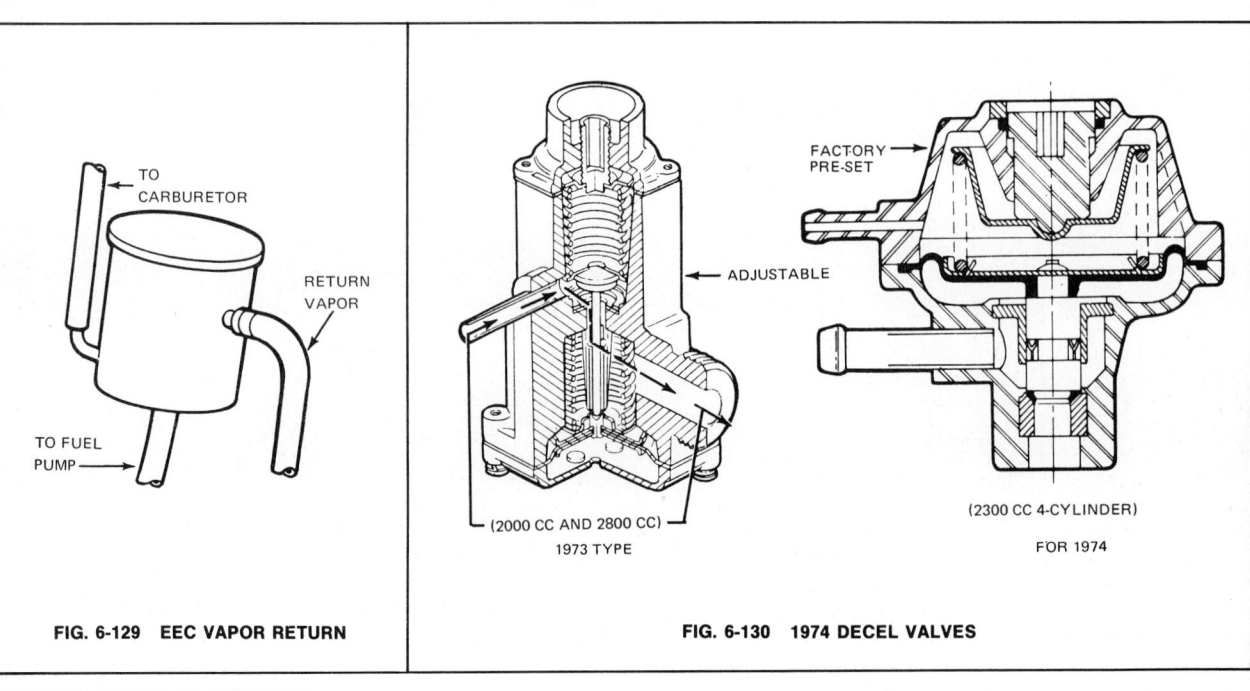

FIG. 6-129   EEC VAPOR RETURN

FIG. 6-130   1974 DECEL VALVES

EXHAUST GAS RECIRCULATION (EGR)

EGR **(Fig. 6-126)** is used on all 1973 engines except the 1600cc, 2000cc and 2600cc models. A vacuum-operated EGR flow-control valve is attached to a carburetor spacer. A variety of applications are used, but typically, the exhaust gases flow from the exhaust crossover through the EGR valve and spacer into the intake manifold below the carburetor. Where exhaust gases cannot be picked up as described, they are picked up from a choke stove located on or near the exhaust manifold.

A coolant valve (EGR PVS) remains closed until coolant temperature reaches either 60° F or 125° F, depending upon the engine. A high-speed EGR modulator subsystem includes a speed sensor, electronic module and solenoid vacuum valve to provide acceptable engine operation at high-speed cruising conditions, and is controlled as a function of vehicle speed.

FUEL DECEL VALVE (FDV)

This device **(Fig. 6-127)** is attached to the intake manifold and connects to the carburetor float bowl to meter a richer air/fuel mixture into the intake whenever intake manifold vacuum exceeds 20 ins., such as that occurring under deceleration.

FORD, MERCURY, LINCOLN
1974 Emission Systems

The Positive Crankcase Ventilation (PCV) system is the same as that used in 1970-71 Ford Motor Company cars.

HEATED AIR CLEANER

The vacuum-operated duct valve is used on all 1974 engines except the 2000cc Pinto.

EVAPORATIVE EMISSION CONTROL (EEC)

Some models of the 90°-plastic-elbow vapor separator contain a mechanical float valve **(Fig. 6-128)**. A vapor return line has been added from the vapor separator to the fuel tank **(Fig. 6-129)**.

DECELERATION VALVE SYSTEM

A second type of valve is added to that used in 1973 **(Fig. 6-130)**.

SPARK DELAY VALVE

SDV's are used in many places on 1974 engines to slow airflow in vacuum lines. All 1974 SDV's use an internal sintered orifice/filter pack and cannot be used as 1973 replacements.

EXHAUST HEAT CONTROL VALVE

Essentially, this is a thermostatically controlled exhaust heat-riser valve **(Fig. 6-131)** which routes hot exhaust gases under the carburetor when the engine is cold. This heats the air/fuel-mixture delivery passages to produce better control over the air/fuel ratio. As the engine warms up, the valve opens and reduces exhaust gas flow to prevent excessive heat.

THERMACTOR SYSTEM

The Thermactor air injection pump system **(Fig. 6-132)** is revived for use on all California cars and some non-California models. It consists of a belt-driven air pump with impeller-type, centrifugal air-filter fan, an air bypass valve, a check valve, an external air manifold or a cylinder-head/exhaust manifold with internal air passages, and the necessary connecting hoses.

The air pump supplies fresh air, under pressure, to the exhaust port near each exhaust valve. This extra oxygen added to the hot exhaust gases causes more complete burning and a reduction in emissions. The air bypass valve **(Fig. 6-133)** prevents a backfire during deceleration by momentarily dumping pump air outside the system. The exhaust-gas check valve prevents a reverse exhaust gas flow in the event of low pressure or pump malfunctions. The check valve is mounted on the air manifold for external systems, the air crossover manifold for internal systems, and the intake manifold on 351C- and 400-cu.-in. engines.

EXHAUST GAS RECIRCULATION

In addition to the spacer-entry EGR system used in 1973 **(Fig. 6-134)**, two variations are introduced on 1974 engines.

FLOOR ENTRY EGR SYSTEM

The EGR valve is mounted on the rear of the intake manifold **(Fig. 6-135)** and controls exhaust gases from cast EGR passages in the exhaust crossover passage.

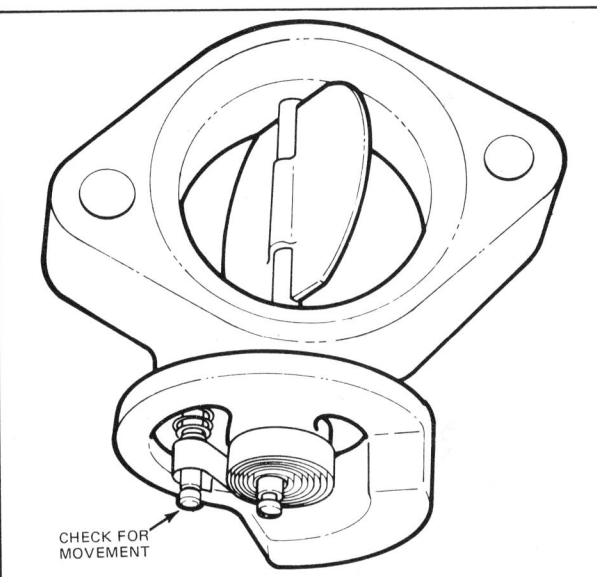

CHECK FOR MOVEMENT

FIG. 6-131 EXHAUST HEAT CONTROL VALVE

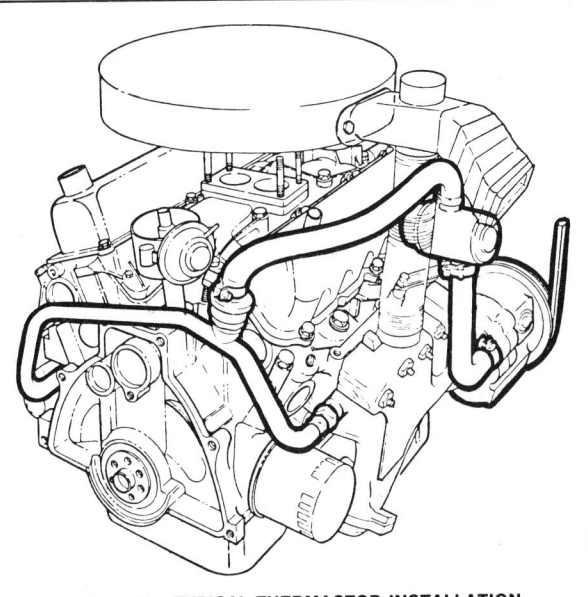

FIG. 6-132 TYPICAL THERMACTOR INSTALLATION

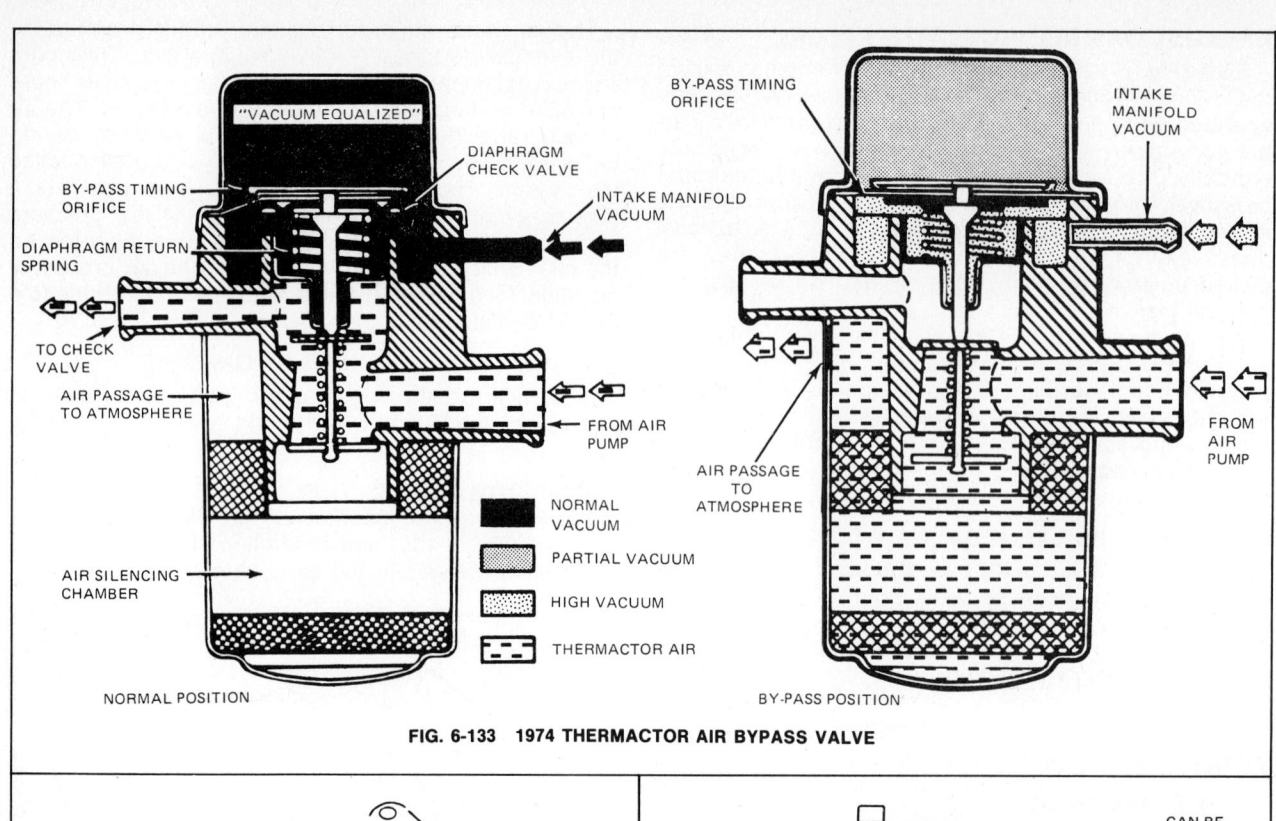

FIG. 6-133   1974 THERMACTOR AIR BYPASS VALVE

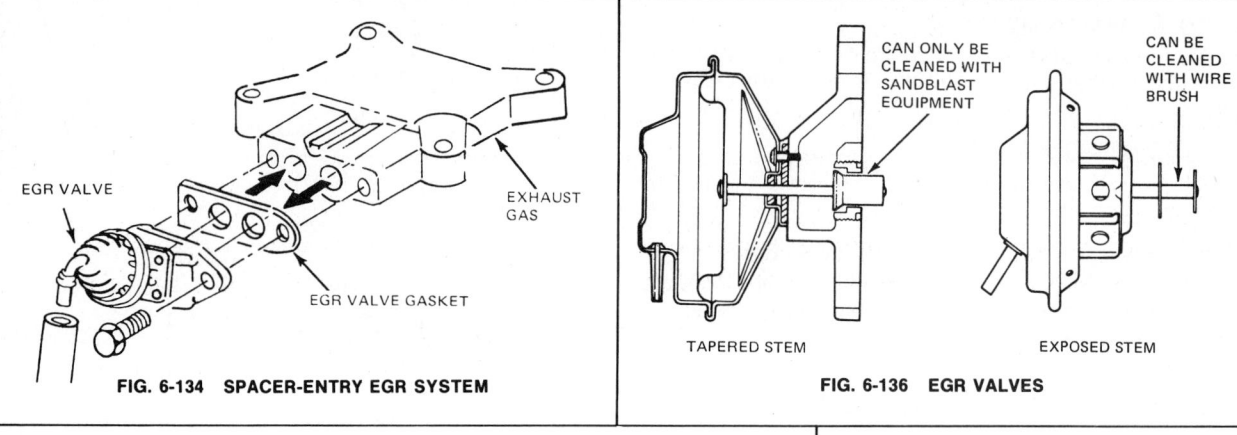

FIG. 6-134   SPACER-ENTRY EGR SYSTEM

FIG. 6-136   EGR VALVES

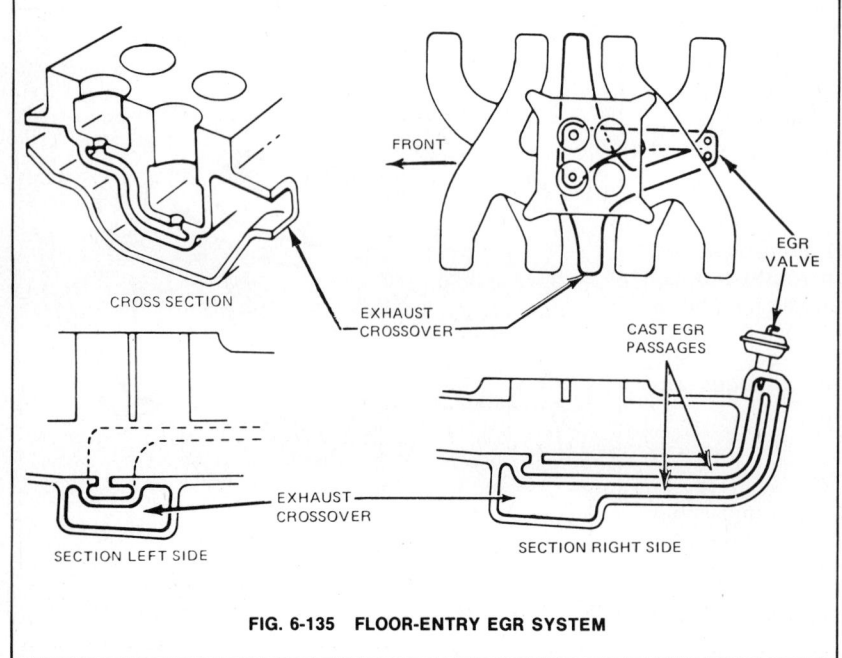

FIG. 6-135   FLOOR-ENTRY EGR SYSTEM

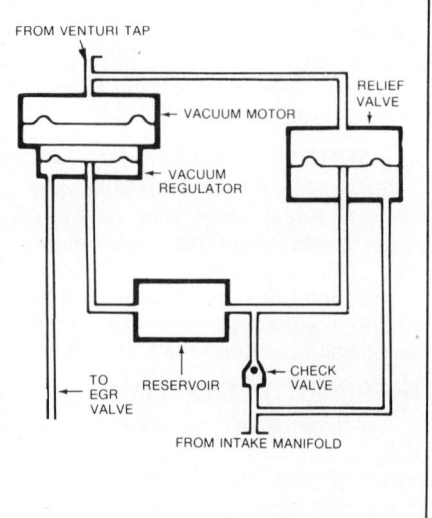

FIG. 6-137   VENTURI-VACUUM-AMPLIFIER EGR SYSTEM

Unlike the internal stem/sealing surfaces of the spacer-mounted EGR valve, the floor entry valve has an exposed stem **(Fig. 6-136)**

VENTURI VACUUM AMPLIFIER SYSTEM

A relatively weak venturi vacuum signal from the carburetor throat shapes a strong intake manifold vacuum signal to operate the EGR valve **(Fig. 6-137)**. The amplifier contains a vacuum reservoir and check valve to maintain an adequate vacuum supply despite any manifold vacuum variations. Whenever the venturi vacuum signal is equal or greater than intake manifold vacuum, a relief valve dumps the output EGR signal, closing the EGR valve at wide-open-throttle acceleration.

EGR/CCS SYSTEM

This system **(Fig. 6-138)** sequentially switches vacuum signals to regulate distributor vacuum advance and EGR valve operation according to engine coolant temperature:

BELOW 82° F COOLANT TEMPERATURE

The EGR/PVS valve sends carburetor port EGR vacuum through a one-way check valve to the distributor advance unit, shutting off carburetor EGR vacuum to the EGR valve **(Fig. 6-139)**.

ABOVE 95° F COOLANT TEMPERATURE

The EGR/PVS valve sends carburetor EGR vacuum to the EGR valve instead of to the distributor. The SDV valve delays carburetor vacuum and the check valve blocks the vacuum signal from the SDV to the EGR/PVS **(Fig. 6-140)**.

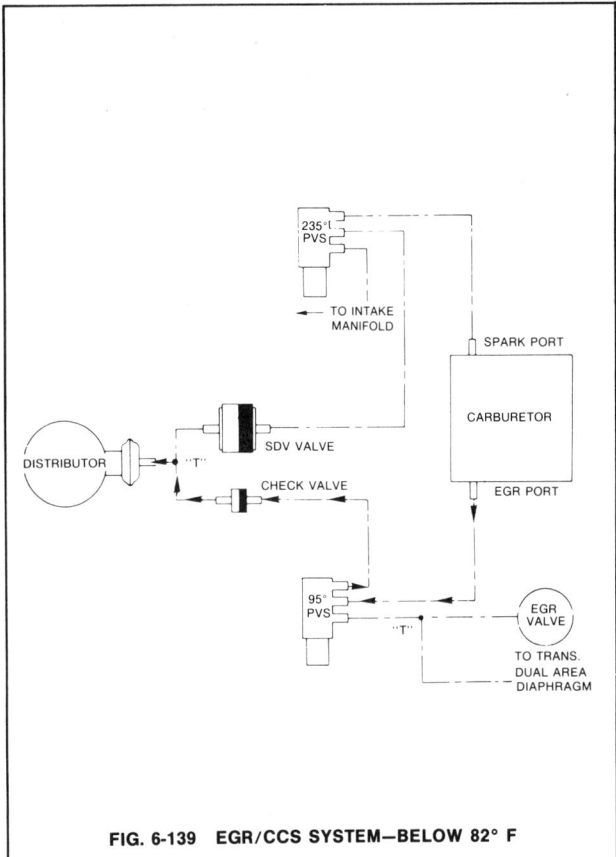

FIG. 6-139 EGR/CCS SYSTEM—BELOW 82° F

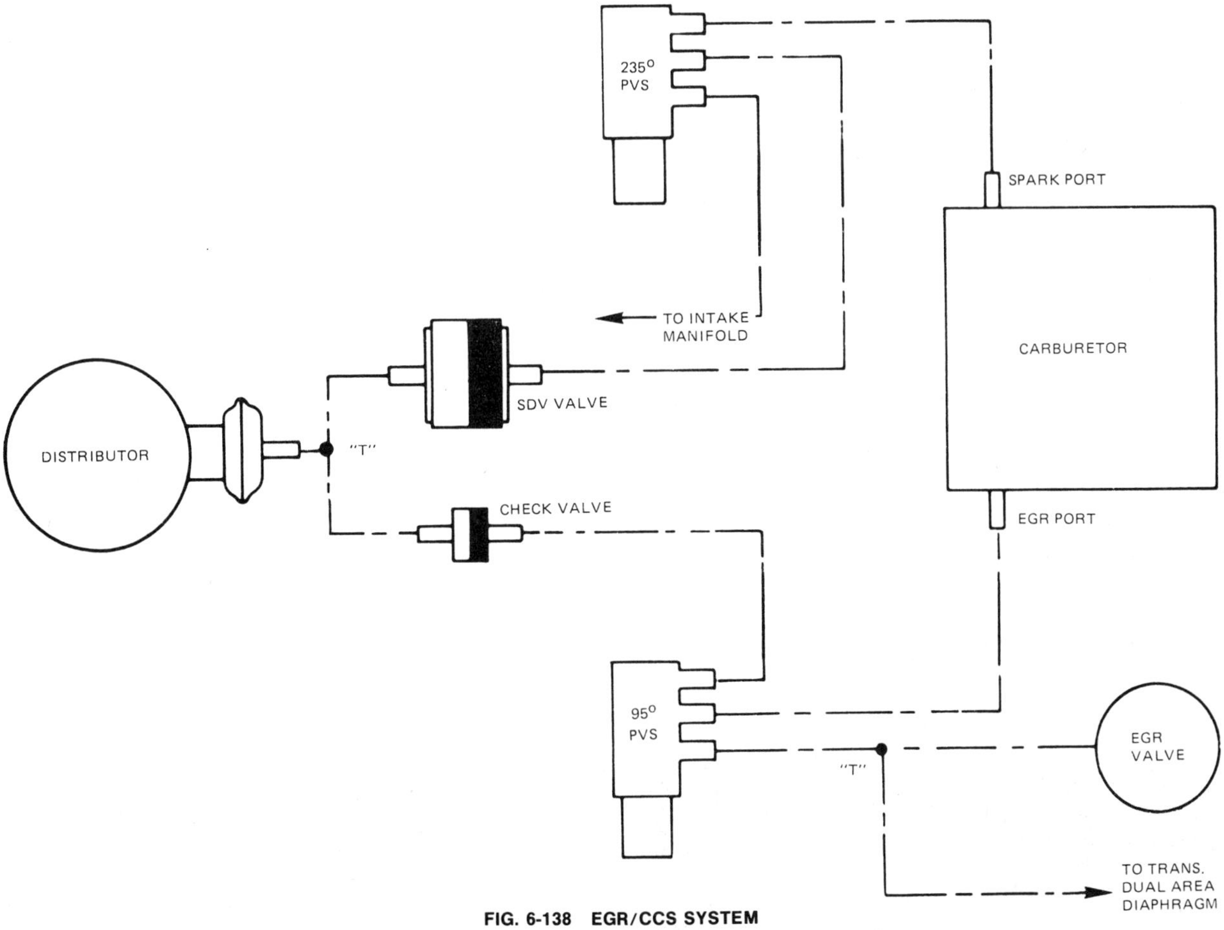

FIG. 6-138 EGR/CCS SYSTEM

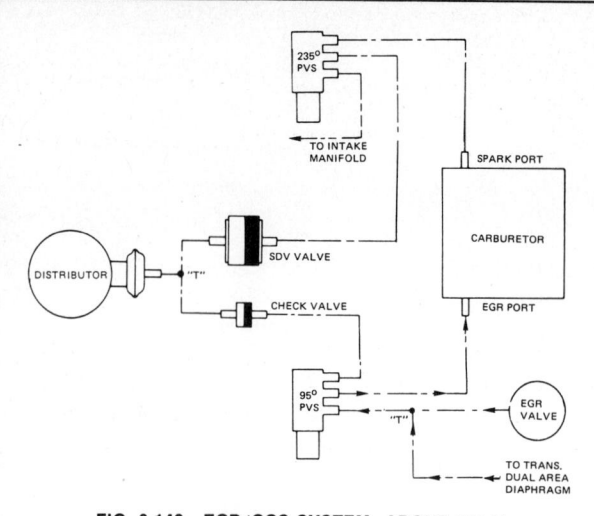

FIG. 6-140   EGR/CCS SYSTEM—ABOVE 95° F

COOLANT TEMPERATURE ACTIVATED SYSTEM

This is a modified version of the 1973 TAV system and functions in essentially the same manner **(Fig. 6-141)**. The ambient temperature level which activates the three-way solenoid valve to send EGR vacuum to the distributor advance is raised from 60° F to 65° F **(Fig. 6-142)**. A latching relay allows only a single cycle each time the ignition is switched on.

FORD, MERCURY, LINCOLN

1975 Emission Systems

The Positive Crankcase Ventilation (PCV) and Evaporative Emission Control (EEC) systems are identical to those used on 1970-71 Ford Motor Company cars. For Spark Delay Valve and Cold Temperature Actuated Vacuum System (CTAV), see 1974.

HEATED AIR CLEANER

A Cold Weather Modulator is used in some air clean-

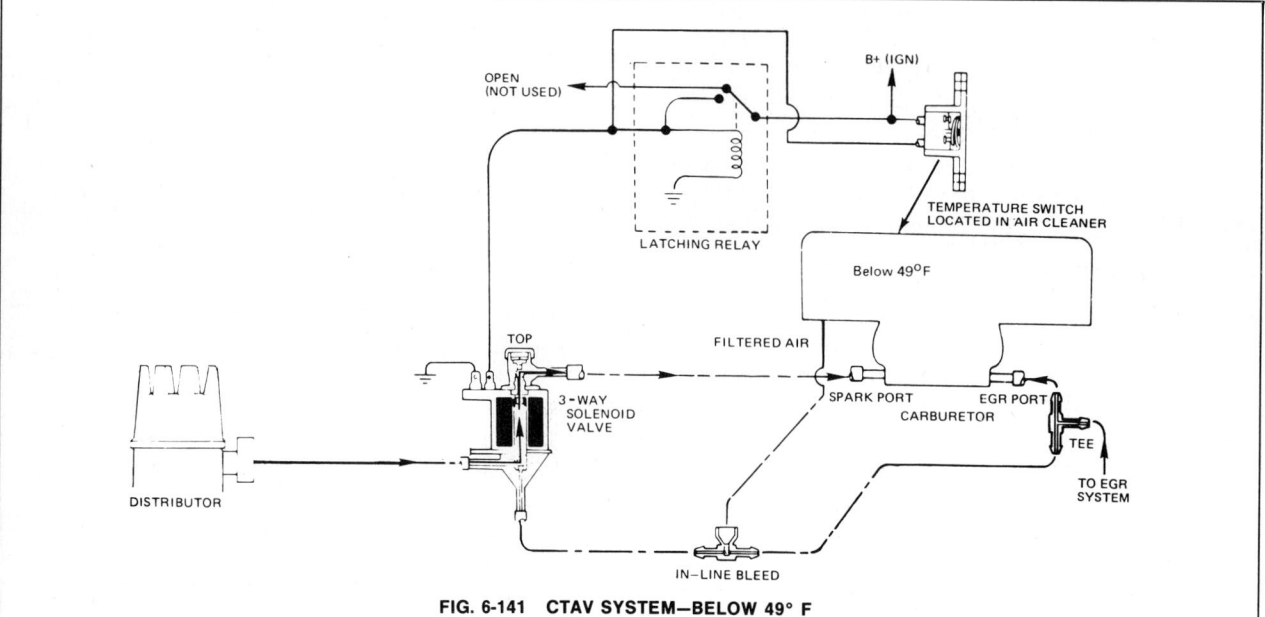

FIG. 6-141   CTAV SYSTEM—BELOW 49° F

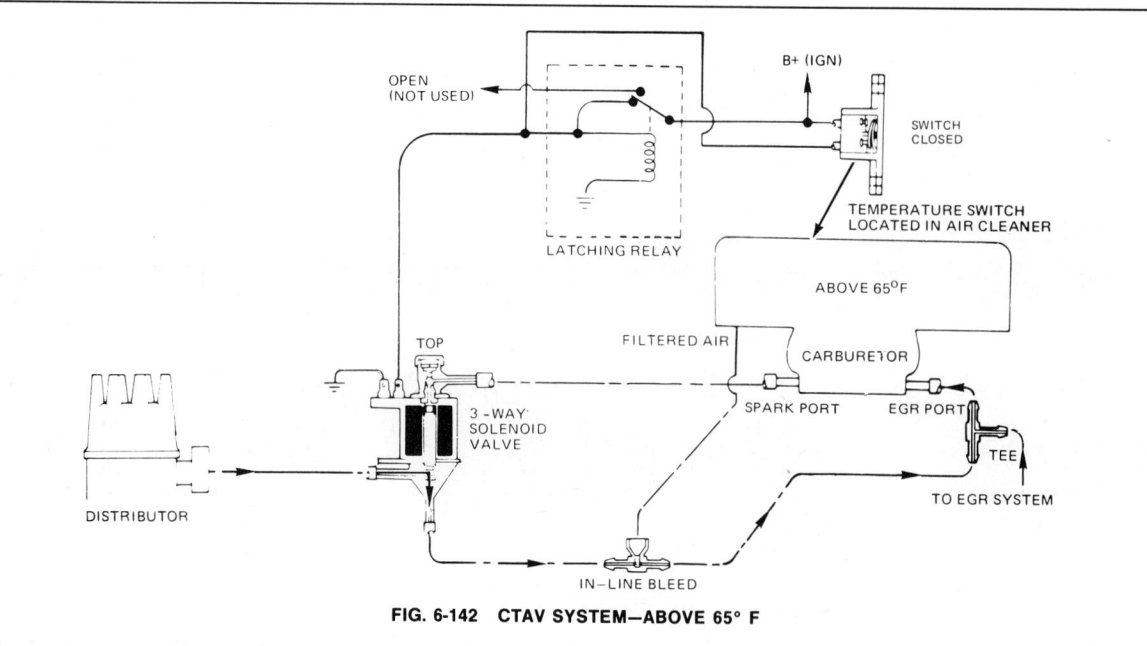

FIG. 6-142   CTAV SYSTEM—ABOVE 65° F

ers. Inserted in the vacuum line between the bi-metal sensor and the vacuum duct motor to prevent the duct door from opening to non-heated intake air, its operation is shown in **Fig. 6-143.**

Engines equipped with CTAV systems and those with Thermactor air pumps using catalytic converters are also fitted with an Air Cleaner Temperature Switch. This contains a bi-metal switch operated by temperature changes. Two types are used **(Fig. 6-144)**; Type 1 with normally closed and Type 2 with normally open contacts. Switch operation is described under each respective system.

DECELERATION VALVE SYSTEM

The 1973-74 decel valve is used on 1975 2300cc 2-bbl. and 2800cc 2-bbl. engines. On Mustang II with

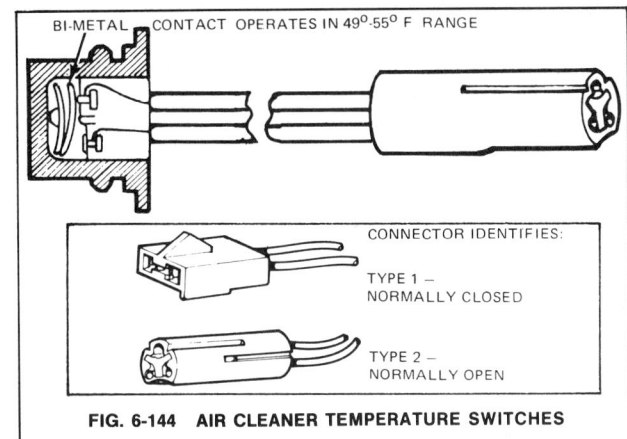

BI-METAL CONTACT OPERATES IN 49°-55° F RANGE

CONNECTOR IDENTIFIES:

TYPE 1 — NORMALLY CLOSED

TYPE 2 — NORMALLY OPEN

FIG. 6-144   AIR CLEANER TEMPERATURE SWITCHES

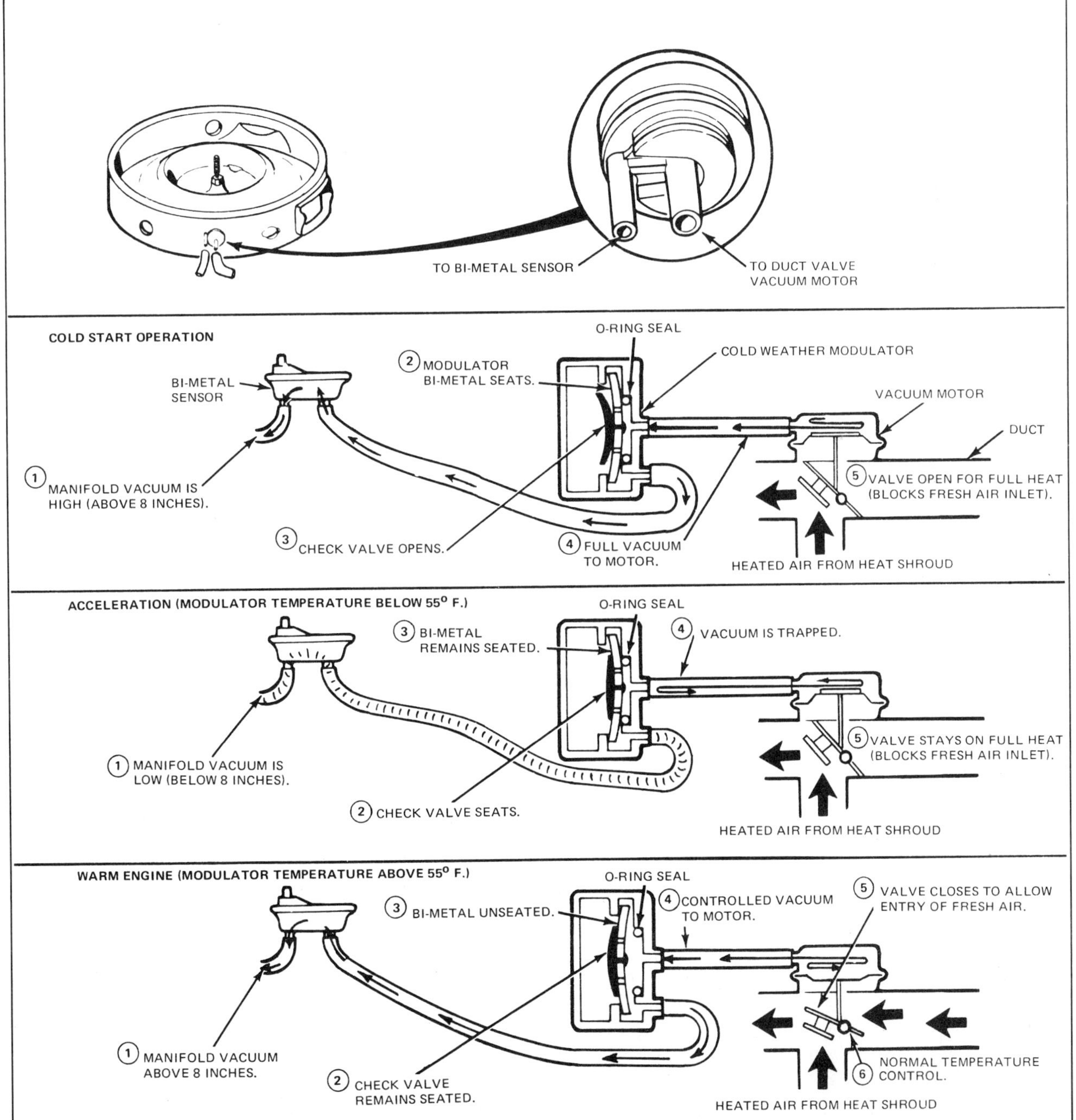

TO BI-METAL SENSOR

TO DUCT VALVE VACUUM MOTOR

COLD START OPERATION

O-RING SEAL

② MODULATOR BI-METAL SEATS.

COLD WEATHER MODULATOR

VACUUM MOTOR

DUCT

BI-METAL SENSOR

① MANIFOLD VACUUM IS HIGH (ABOVE 8 INCHES).

③ CHECK VALVE OPENS.

④ FULL VACUUM TO MOTOR.

⑤ VALVE OPEN FOR FULL HEAT (BLOCKS FRESH AIR INLET).

HEATED AIR FROM HEAT SHROUD

ACCELERATION (MODULATOR TEMPERATURE BELOW 55° F.)

O-RING SEAL

③ BI-METAL REMAINS SEATED.

④ VACUUM IS TRAPPED.

① MANIFOLD VACUUM IS LOW (BELOW 8 INCHES).

② CHECK VALVE SEATS.

⑤ VALVE STAYS ON FULL HEAT (BLOCKS FRESH AIR INLET).

HEATED AIR FROM HEAT SHROUD

WARM ENGINE (MODULATOR TEMPERATURE ABOVE 55° F.)

O-RING SEAL

④ CONTROLLED VACUUM TO MOTOR.

⑤ VALVE CLOSES TO ALLOW ENTRY OF FRESH AIR.

③ BI-METAL UNSEATED.

① MANIFOLD VACUUM ABOVE 8 INCHES.

② CHECK VALVE REMAINS SEATED.

⑥ NORMAL TEMPERATURE CONTROL.

HEATED AIR FROM HEAT SHROUD

FIG. 6-143   COLD WEATHER MODULATOR OPERATION

the 2800cc engine, the fuel deceleration system is interconnected with vehicle speed, preventing the system from operating at deceleration speeds below 11 mph. This prevents decel valve operation at idle speed **(Fig. 6-145)**.

EXHAUST HEAT CONTROL VALVE

Vacuum diaphragm control replaces the thermostatic spring operation of the heat riser (control) valve except 2300cc and 460 engines for 1975 **(Fig. 6-146)**. A PVS valve activates the vacuum diaphragm according to coolant temperature.

ELECTRIC PORTED VACUUM SWITCH

These are used with some Thermactor/converter systems, and combine vacuum switching and electrical signaling in one device. Used in two types—electrical contacts normally closed or normally open.

COLD START SPARK ADVANCE (CSSA)

Installed on some 1975 460-cu.-in. and California 2300cc engines, this system **(Fig. 6-147)** provides intake manifold vacuum to the distributor advance unit whenever engine coolant temperature is below 125° F.

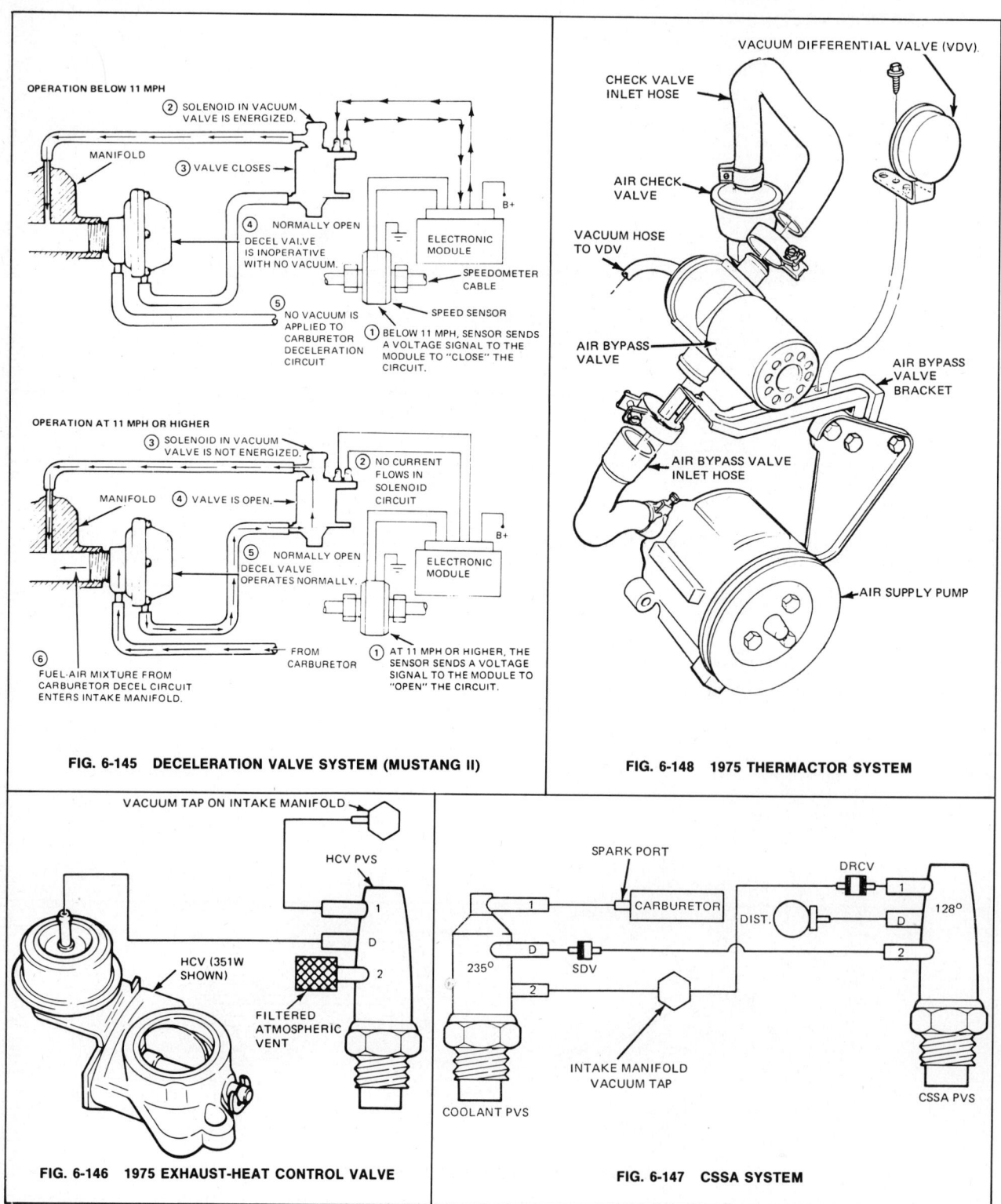

FIG. 6-145 DECELERATION VALVE SYSTEM (MUSTANG II)

FIG. 6-148 1975 THERMACTOR SYSTEM

FIG. 6-146 1975 EXHAUST-HEAT CONTROL VALVE

FIG. 6-147 CSSA SYSTEM

THERMACTOR SYSTEM

The Thermactor system **(Fig. 6-148)** is used on all 1975 cars. Its operation is essentially the same as in 1974, but the changes noted below have been made:

1. The 1975 air pump no longer contains a pressure relief valve. The air bypass valve now controls this function.

2. Larger pump ports are provided for reduced outlet air temperature.

3. A pump muffler is installed on air pumps used with Mustang II engines.

4. Two air bypass valves are used, one for non-catalytic converter-equipped systems and one for catalytic-equipped systems. Operation of the new catalytic-converter bypass valve is described in **Fig. 6-149**.

5. Catalytic-converter-equipped systems also incorporate a Vacuum Differential Valve (VDV). Its operation is described in **Fig. 6-150**.

6. A Cold Engine Lockout is fitted to catalytic-equipped systems. This uses an electrically operated vacuum solenoid located in the vacuum line to the bypass valve and described in **Fig. 6-151**.

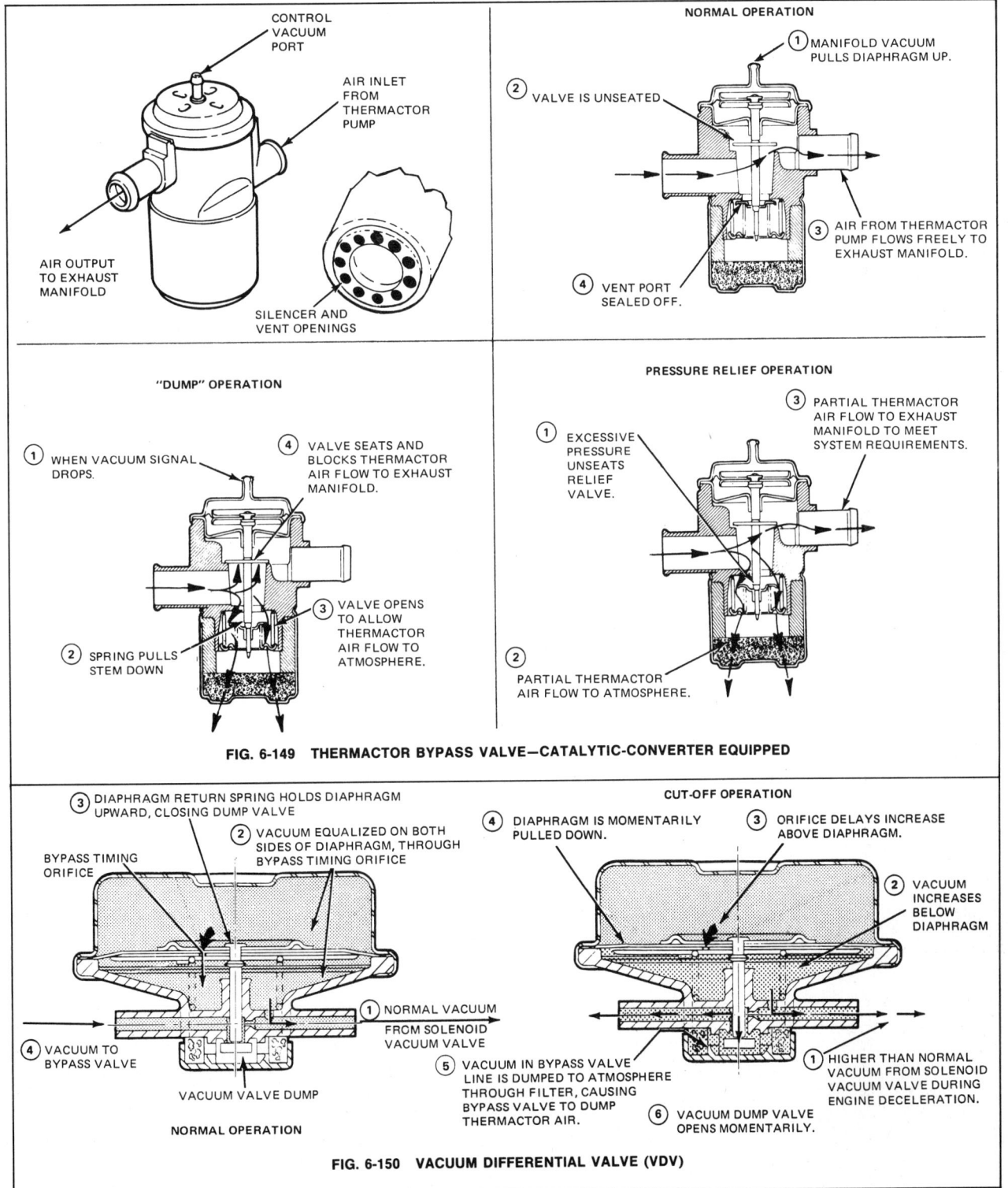

FIG. 6-149   THERMACTOR BYPASS VALVE—CATALYTIC-CONVERTER EQUIPPED

FIG. 6-150   VACUUM DIFFERENTIAL VALVE (VDV)

CATALYTIC CONVERTER

All 1975 Ford Motor Company cars are equipped with a catalytic converter in the exhaust system to reduce emissions and improve drivability.

EXHAUST GAS RECIRCULATION (EGR)

A redesigned spacer-entry EGR system **(Fig. 6-152)** replaces the three systems used in 1974. Operation of this system is essentially the same as the 1973-74 spacer entry EGR, but a dual-connector vacuum amplifier replaces the earlier single connector type on some EGR systems **(Fig. 6-153)**. Three different EGR valves are used for 1975 **(Fig. 6-154),** and a new EGR Backpressure System is installed in late 1975 models as a running change on some applications—see "1976 Emission Systems" for details.

FORD, MERCURY, LINCOLN
1976 Emission Systems

The Positive Crankcase Ventilation (PCV) system remains unchanged from 1970-71. For Cold Temperature Activated Vacuum System (CTAV), see 1974 Emission Controls. Heated Air Cleaner, Cold Start Spark Advance (CSSA) and Deceleration Valve System are identical to those used in 1975.

EVAPORATIVE EMISSION CONTROL (EEC)

A new vapor separator with internal spring is used for rollover fuel safety.

COOLING PVS-VENT RETARD SYSTEM

This system **(Fig. 6-155)** prevents distributor vacuum

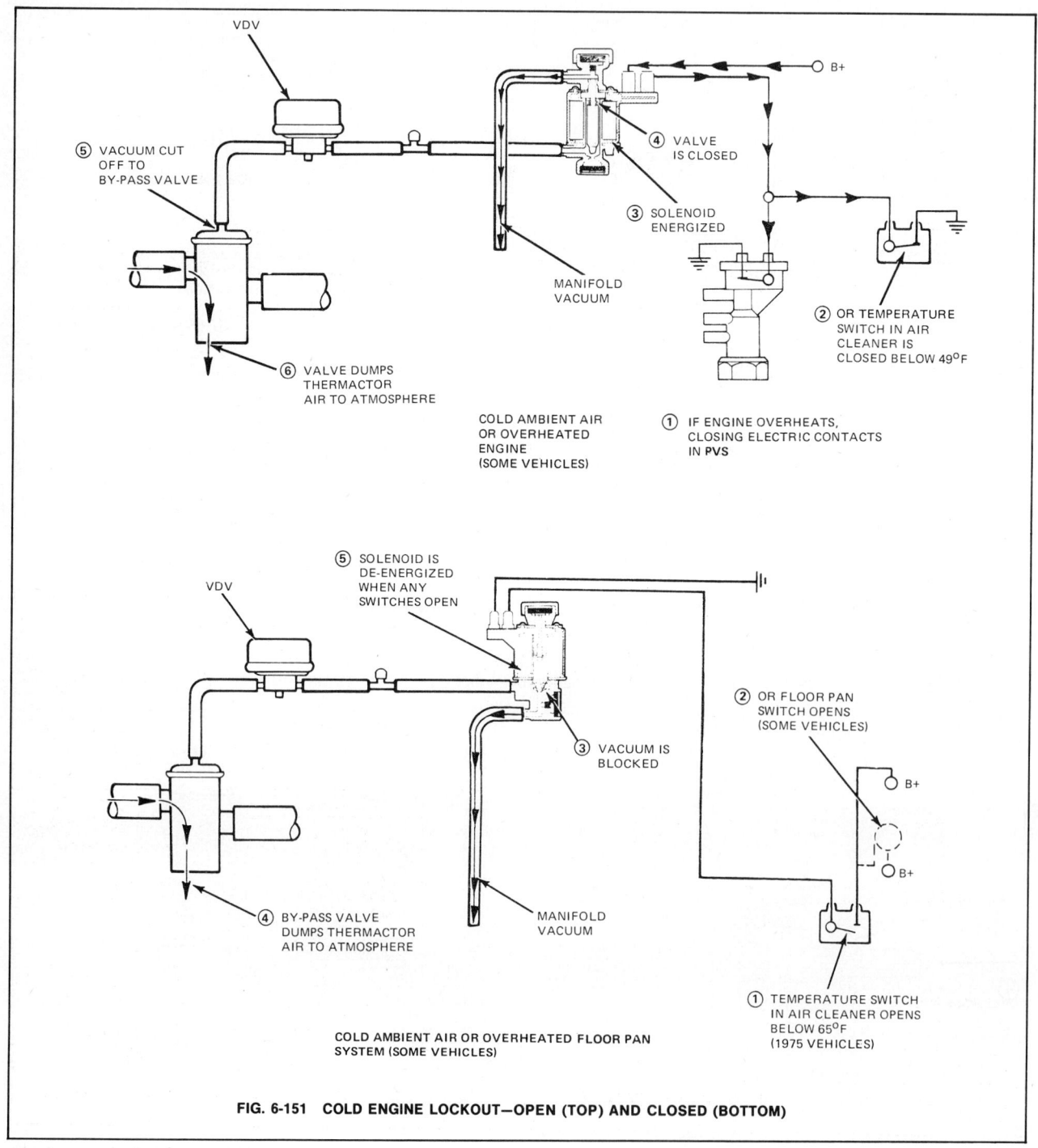

FIG. 6-151   COLD ENGINE LOCKOUT—OPEN (TOP) AND CLOSED (BOTTOM)

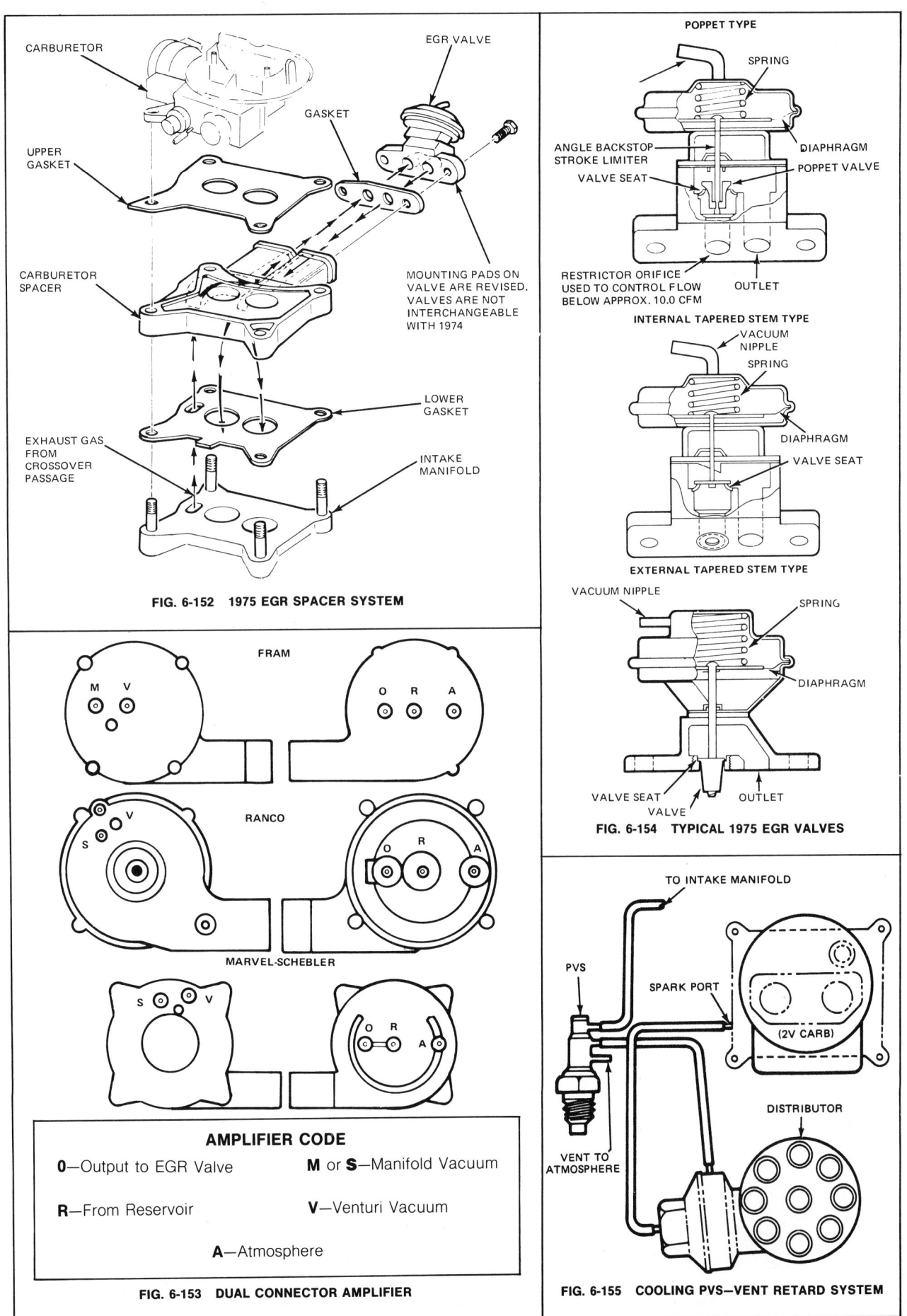

CARBURETOR

EGR VALVE

GASKET

UPPER GASKET

CARBURETOR SPACER

MOUNTING PADS ON VALVE ARE REVISED. VALVES ARE NOT INTERCHANGEABLE WITH 1974

LOWER GASKET

EXHAUST GAS FROM CROSSOVER PASSAGE

INTAKE MANIFOLD

FIG. 6-152 1975 EGR SPACER SYSTEM

POPPET TYPE

SPRING

ANGLE BACKSTOP STROKE LIMITER

DIAPHRAGM

VALVE SEAT

POPPET VALVE

RESTRICTOR ORIFICE USED TO CONTROL FLOW BELOW APPROX. 10.0 CFM

OUTLET

INTERNAL TAPERED STEM TYPE

VACUUM NIPPLE

SPRING

DIAPHRAGM

VALVE SEAT

EXTERNAL TAPERED STEM TYPE

VACUUM NIPPLE

SPRING

DIAPHRAGM

VALVE SEAT

OUTLET

VALVE

FIG. 6-154 TYPICAL 1975 EGR VALVES

FRAM

M V

O R A

RANCO

S V

O R A

MARVEL-SCHEBLER

S V

O R A

AMPLIFIER CODE

0—Output to EGR Valve   **M** or **S**—Manifold Vacuum

R—From Reservoir   **V**—Venturi Vacuum

A—Atmosphere

FIG. 6-153 DUAL CONNECTOR AMPLIFIER

TO INTAKE MANIFOLD

PVS

SPARK PORT

(2V CARB)

DISTRIBUTOR

VENT TO ATMOSPHERE

FIG. 6-155 COOLING PVS—VENT RETARD SYSTEM

retard at a specified coolant temperature, venting vacuum to atmospheric pressure.

COOLANT SPARK CONTROL (CSC) SYSTEM

CSC prevents distributor vacuum advance when engine coolant is below a specified temperature, venting vacuum to atmospheric pressure (Fig. 6-156).

SPARK DELAY VALVE (SDV)

All 1975-76 mono-delay spark delay valves contain an internal sintered orifice to slow the flow of air in one direction, a check valve permitting free airflow in the opposite direction, and a filter. These can be used as replacements on previous model years (Fig. 6-157).

To improve emission control on some engine applications, a dual-delay SDV is used for 1976. This has twin connections on one side and a single connection on the other (Fig. 6-158), and is used to delay vacuum advance during acceleration and provide extra advance during deceleration.

EXHAUST HEAT CONTROL VALVE

Some 1976 applications replace the heat control valve with a spacer. (See 1975 Emission Controls.) Three different temperature ranges are used and can be identified by the following PVS identification chart:

PVS BODY COLOR	OPENING TEMP. (°F)
Black	92-98
Blue	125-131
Purple	157-163

DELAY VALVE BYPASS (DVB) SYSTEM

Full spark port vacuum is provided to the distributor advance unit below the PVS opening temperature. Above that temperature, the two top ports of the four-port PVS close, sending the vacuum signal through the spark delay valve (Fig. 6-159).

DUAL SIGNAL SPARK ADVANCE (DSSA)

A spark delay valve and a check valve are used to provide an improved spark/EGR function under mild acceleration conditions (Fig. 6-160). EGR port vacuum is applied to the EGR valve and spark port vacuum to the distributor advance unit under steady speed or cruising conditions. The check valve functions to prevent spark port vacuum from reaching the EGR valve, causing excessive EGR flow. It also prevents EGR port

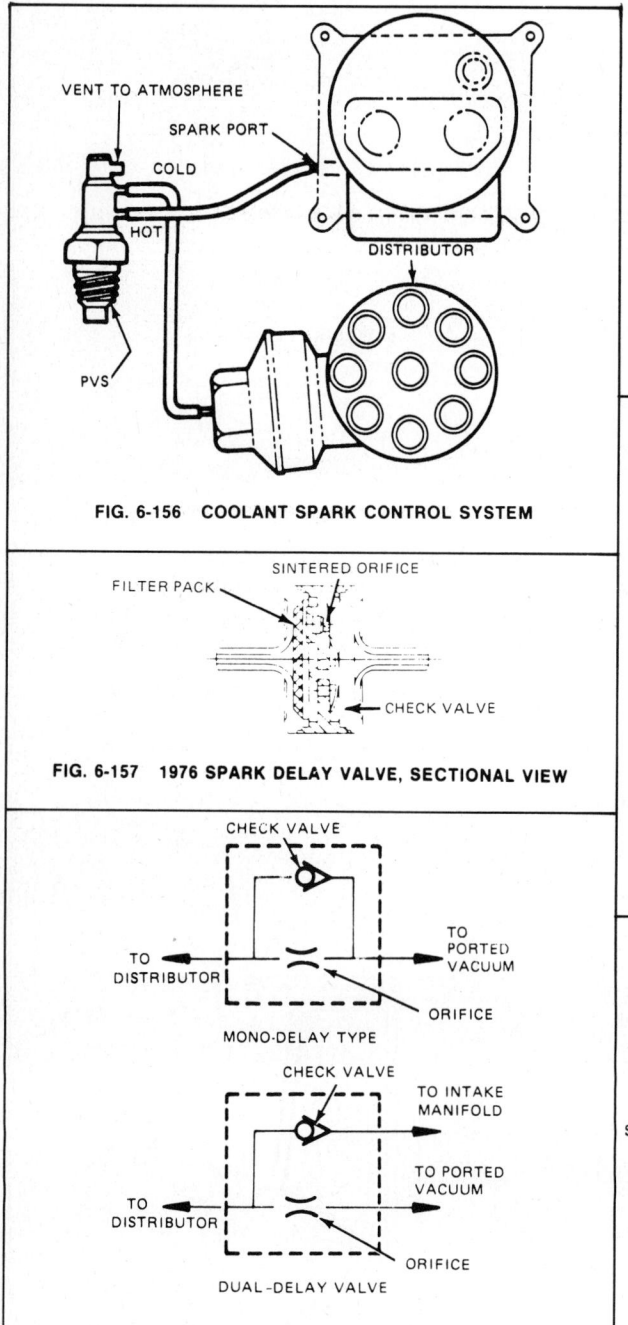

FIG. 6-156 COOLANT SPARK CONTROL SYSTEM

FIG. 6-157 1976 SPARK DELAY VALVE, SECTIONAL VIEW

FIG. 6-158 SPARK DELAY VALVE, MONO AND DUAL RELAY SCHEMATIC

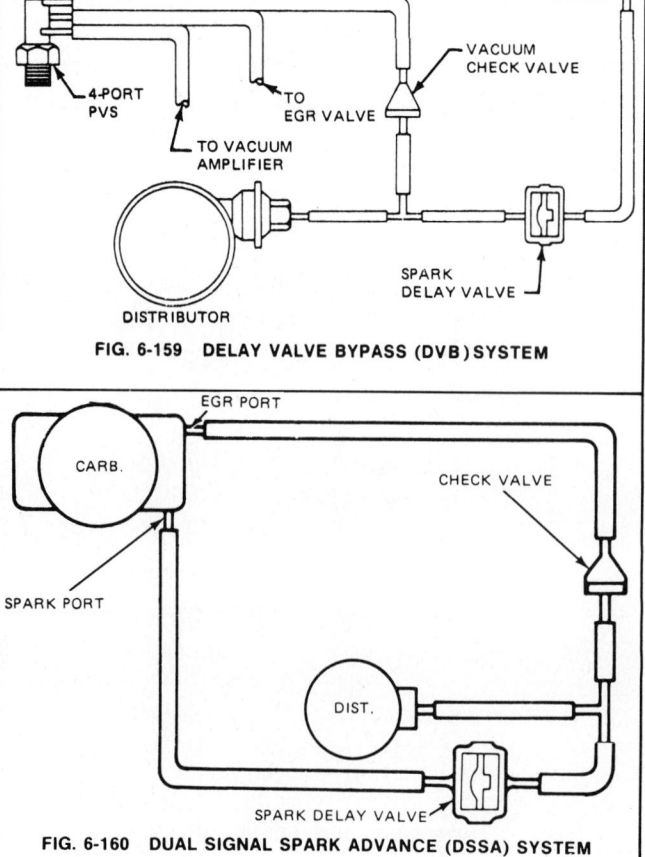

FIG. 6-159 DELAY VALVE BYPASS (DVB) SYSTEM

FIG. 6-160 DUAL SIGNAL SPARK ADVANCE (DSSA) SYSTEM

vacuum from diluting spark port vacuum, which would weaken the desired signal. The spark delay valve allows full EGR vacuum to the distributor advance unit during mild acceleration.

THERMACTOR SYSTEM

The Thermactor system is used on all 1976 cars. Its operation is essentially the same as in 1975, but the changes noted below have been made:

1. Three air bypass valves are used for 1976—one for non-catalytic systems and two for catalytic-equipped systems. The 1974-75 valves are retained, with a new one containing an integral vacuum differential (VDV) function and vent **(Fig. 6-161)**. A separate VDV is not required with the use of this valve. With the vent blocked, the valve functions exactly as a timed bypass with VDV as used in previous years. But when the vent is open to atmospheric pressure and 4 ins. or more of vacuum are applied, the valve immediately dumps pump air.

2. A Differential Valve Delay Valve (DVDV) is installed in series with the Vacuum Differential Valve (VDV) to delay air bypass during low manifold vacuum periods **(Fig. 6-162)**.

3. The exhaust check valve has been redesigned, as shown in **Fig. 6-163**.

4. A vacuum check valve is installed in the line between the intake manifold fitting and the solenoid-switch inlet side in some Thermactor applications **(Fig. 6-164)**. This prevents air bypass under all but cold vehicle conditions.

CATALYTIC CONVERTER

All 1976 Ford Motor Company cars are equipped with

catalytic converters in the exhaust system to reduce emissions and improve drivability. A number of applications use two catalytic converters.

EXHAUST GAS RECIRCULATION (EGR)

Although minor changes are made to the 1976 EGR system, the subsystems operate and function in the same manner as in 1975. Two new subsystem devices are installed for 1976.

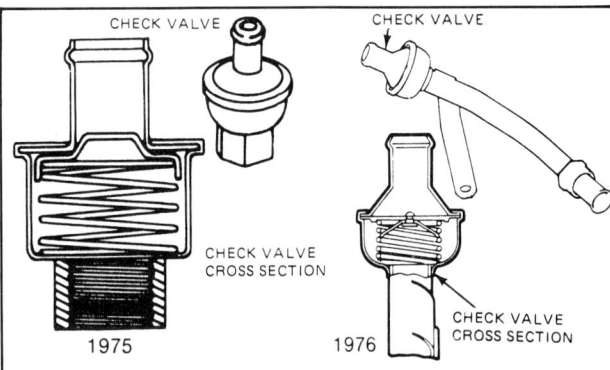

FIG. 6-163   THERMACTOR CHECK VALVE REDESIGN

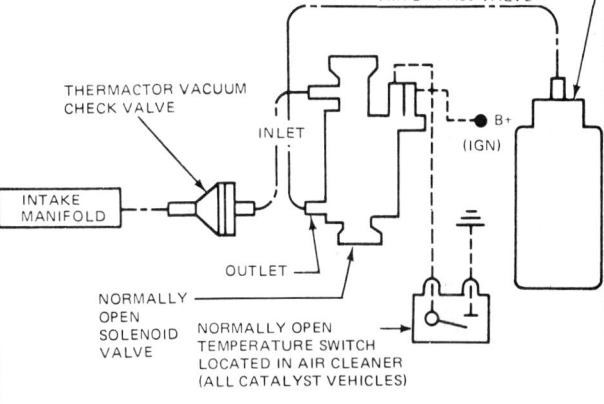

FIG. 6-164   THERMACTOR VACUUM CHECK VALVE

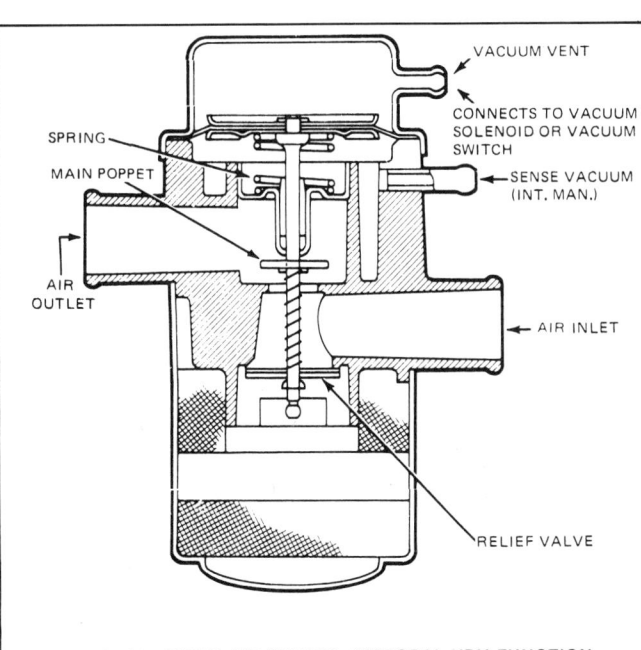

FIG. 6-161   TIMED AIR BYPASS, INTEGRAL VDV FUNCTION

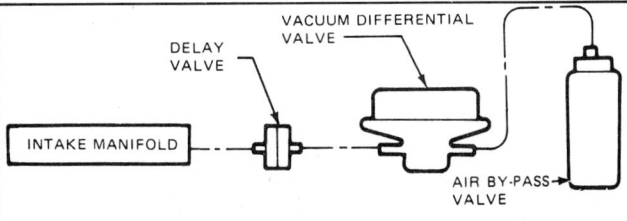

FIG. 6-162   DIFFERENTIAL VALVE DELAY VALVE (DVDV) SYSTEM

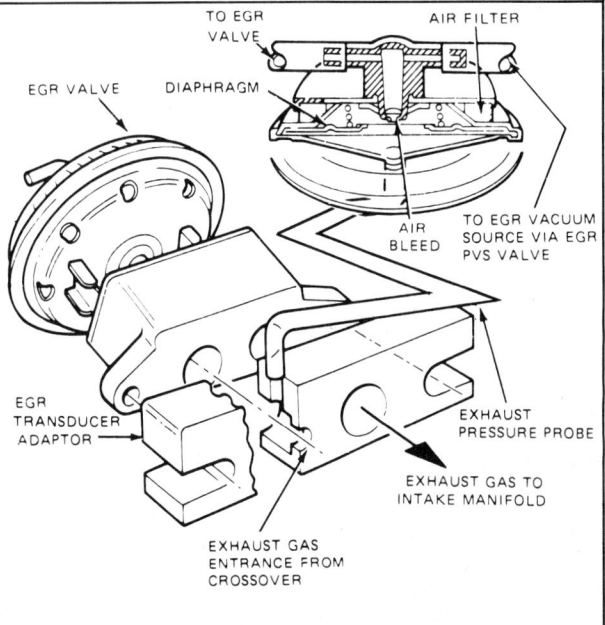

FIG. 6-165   EGR BACKPRESSURE TRANSDUCER

1. The EGR Backpressure System is found on a few late-model 1975 cars and all 1976 351-M, 400 and 460-cu.-in. engines, and the California 2800cc engine when equipped with manual transmission. The transducer unit modulates EGR flow between idle and heavy engine load conditions by making EGR source vacuum respond to exhaust pressure **(Fig. 6-165)**.

2. An EGR Load Control (WOT) Valve is installed between the EGR valve and carburetor EGR port on 400-cu.-in. engines. This closes off the EGR valve when maximum engine power is necessary at near wide-open-throttle (WOT) conditions, opening it again for normal flow when the engine load is reduced.

FORD, MERCURY, LINCOLN
1977 Emission Systems

All systems used for 1977 are essentially the same as those for 1976, with the exceptions noted.

EXHAUST GAS RECIRCULATION (EGR)

A new combined EGR/backpressure transducer valve is used on many engines. It provides greater EGR flow capability and requires no service adjustments. If valve operation is restricted by foreign matter, it is replaced, not cleaned. Functional testing of the valve must be done on the engine.

THERMACTOR SYSTEM

California engines fitted with the 2700 VV carburetor use a vacuum vent valve to prevent fuel from entering the Thermactor system. A distributor vacuum vent valve is also used on California 302 V-8 engines to delay vacuum spark advance during light acceleration. External appearance of these two vacuum vent valves is identical, but they differ internally and should not be confused if removed from the engine during servicing.

POSITIVE CRANKCASE VENTILATION (PCV)

A new high-flow PCV valve is installed in place of the factory-provided standard flow valve at the first specified maintenance interval. This interval and the correct valve number is provided on the emission decal for those engines concerned. This valve is required as the fuel mixture tends to richen with increased mileage. The new valve leans out the richer fuel mixture to remain within the specified emission levels.

FORD, MERCURY, LINCOLN
1978 Emission Systems

All systems used for 1978 are essentially the same as those for 1977, with the exceptions noted.

THERMACTOR SYSTEM

With the addition of a suction-type, or pulse air-injection system on 1978 Fairmont/Zephyr 200 I-6 engines, the Thermactor system is now designated as I or II. **Thermactor I**—this air pump system is a carryover from 1977 but uses a new air bypass valve. The valve works in the same way as prior valves, but is installed directly on the air pump, instead of in the pump hose system. This was done to meet differing vehicle design requirements. A backfire suppressor valve is also used on some California calibrations. This valve allows extra air to enter the system during periods of sudden deceleration to lean out an otherwise enriched mixture and prevent a backfire condition.

Thermactor II—a simplified method of air injection, this system uses an air inlet valve, silencer, and connecting tubes and hoses. The system is installed between the air cleaner and exhaust manifold. System operation is essentially the same as the PAIR system used on the Cosworth Vega and later GM I-4 engines—see 1975-76 Chevrolet Emission Systems for a full operational description.

The air inlet or reed valve is similar in appearance to a Thermactor check valve, but the two are not interchangeable. The silencer unit is used to absorb any pulsation noise created in the exhaust ports and manifold. If damaged or burned by excessive temperatures, the air inlet valve and/or silencer are replaced—no adjustment or service is possible. Air inlet valve failure will result in poor engine performance accompanied by air cleaner noise. Install a new valve and silencer in this case and inspect all hoses/clamps. You should also check the carburetor for exhaust gas and/or silencer material contamination. If found, remove and clean the carburetor.

FEEDBACK CARBURETOR ELECTRONIC CONTROL

Fitted only to 1978 2.3L California Pinto/Bobcat engines, this system is used to vary the air/fuel mixture according to input signals from an exhaust gas sensor, engine coolant temperature sensor, engine rpm and throttle position switches. System operation is essentially the same as the Electronic Fuel Control described under the 1978 Oldsmobile Emission Systems, but uses the 11 components shown in **Fig. 6-165A.**

The Electronic Control Unit receives input from the four sensors and provides a control signal to the vacuum solenoid regulator, which in turn controls the feedback carburetor to vary the mixture by positioning a vacuum-operated metering rod. Four operating modes are possible:

1. No Conversion—Thermactor air is dumped during cold start-up and no control is exercised by the system.

2. Open Loop—when the throttle is either wide open or closed, or when coolant temperature is below 125° F, a fixed control signal is provided to the carburetor.

3. Closed Loop—once the engine reaches normal operating temperature and the vehicle is in cruising mode, the electronic control is functional and responds to the content of the exhaust gas.

4. Wide-Open Throttle—power enrichment is provided by the control system during this operational mode.

This electronic control system requires special equipment for testing and diagnosis: a Rotunda T-78L-50-FBC-1 tester unit and a Rotunda T78L-50-DVOM digital volt-ohmmeter.

EVAPORATIVE EMISSION SHED SYSTEM

To meet new EPA testing standards, Ford has designed a new system to control and retain fuel vapors **(Fig. 6-165B)**. System design and component usage differs according to vehicle application. New components added to certain applications are described below; other components retained from the previous system perform the same functions as before.

1. Purge Control Valve—controls fuel vapor flow according to engine operating mode. Spark port, EGR port, or intake manifold vacuum may be used to operate the valve as required. Vacuum is transmitted to the valve by a PVS; some applications use a 2-port PVS while others use a 4-port PVS.

2. Purge Regulator Valve—looks like a PCV valve and closely controls the rate of purge flow for better drivability.

3. Air Cleaner Vapor Dam—a device installed at the air cleaner zip tube opening to trap fuel vapors passed from the carburetor when the engine is off. The vapors are heavier than air and remain in the bottom of the air cleaner for purging when the engine is started.

4. Fuel Bowl Solenoid Vent Valve—a normally open valve located in the carburetor vent-to-canister line,

this shuts off the vent line when the engine is running.

5. Fuel Bowl Thermal Vent Valve—a normally closed bimetal valve also located in the carburetor vent-to-canister line, this prevents fuel tank vapors from venting through the carburetor except when underhood temperatures are hot and the engine is off.

6. Auxiliary Fuel Bowl Vent Tube—this second vent tube is teed into the primary fuel bowl vent tube and vents the fuel bowl to the air cleaner when other vents are closed.

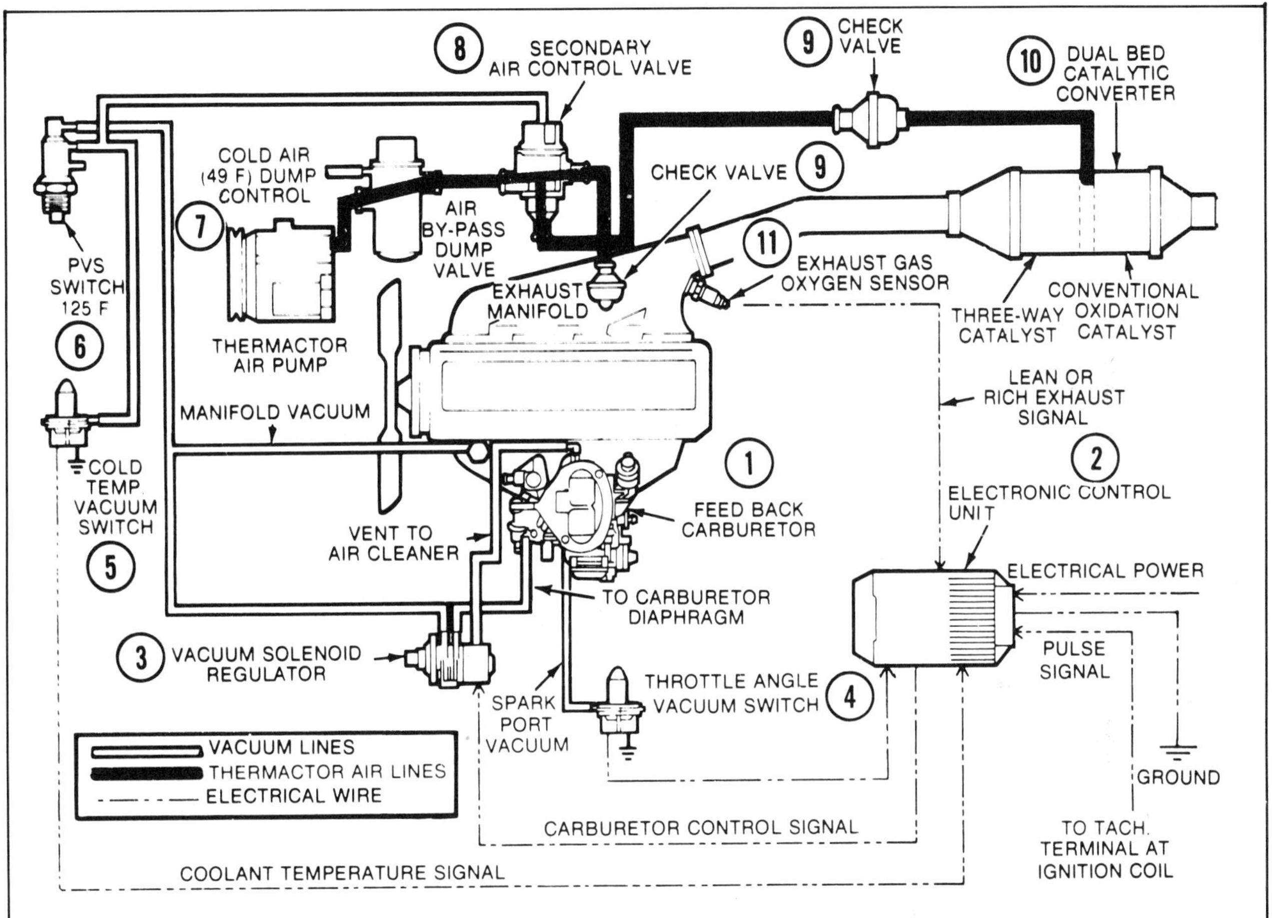

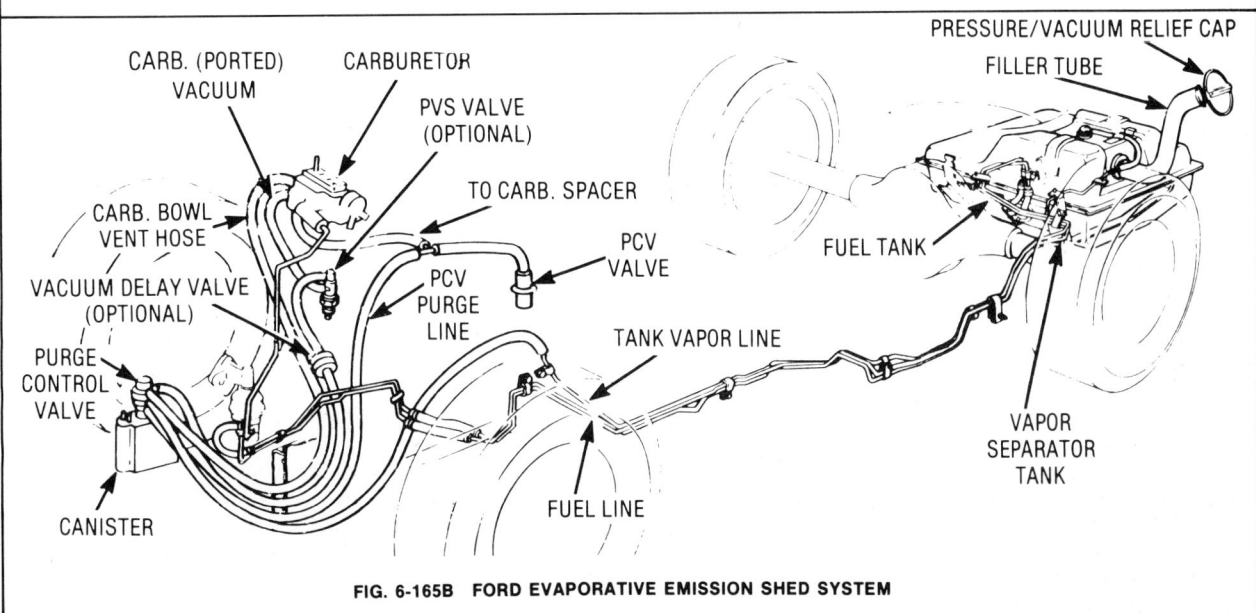

FIG. 6-165A FEEDBACK CARBURETOR ELECTRONIC CONTROL SCHEMATIC

FIG. 6-165B FORD EVAPORATIVE EMISSION SHED SYSTEM

FORD, MERCURY, LINCOLN
1979 Emission Systems

All systems used for 1979 are essentially the same as those for 1978, with the exceptions noted.

Feedback Carburetor Control Electronic

Use is extended to all EEC II equipped 351-W engines, using a variation of the 2700 VV carburetor. The electronically controlled 2700 VV is redesignated the 7200 VV. A Feedback Carburetor Actuator (FBAC) or stepper motor mounted on the right side of the carburetor **(Fig. 6-165C)** is controlled by a signal from the ECA. This motor varies the position of the carburetor metering valve to regulate the control vacuum acting on the fuel bowl. The vacuum lowers the pressure in the fuel bowl to lean the air/fuel mixture.

The electronic control system used with all 1979 California Mustang-Capri 2.3L turbocharged engines is basically the same as that fitted to 1978-79 Pinto-Bobcat 2.3L engines and requires use of the same test equipment. Essential differences are:

1. A vacuum switch signals the ECU to go into open loop operation when the throttle is closed or the coolant temperature is under 125° F.

2. An idle/decel vacuum switch is incorporated into the system.

3. The EGO sensor blinking rich, vacuum regulator blinking: sub-routine engine test speed is changed from 2200-2800 to 2500-2800 rpm.

Cold Start Spark Hold (CSSH) System

To improve cold engine acceleration, this system al-

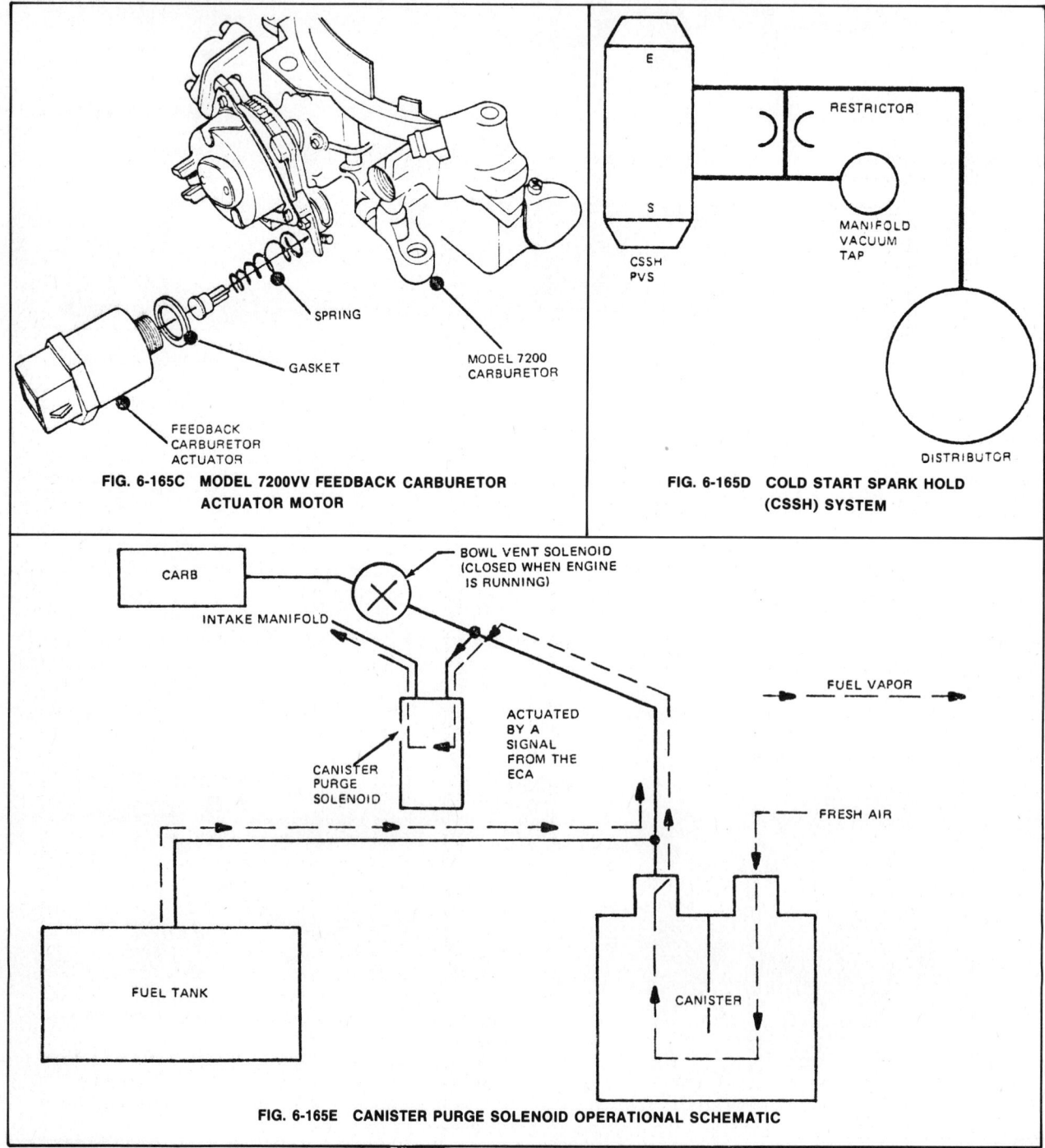

FIG. 6-165C MODEL 7200VV FEEDBACK CARBURETOR ACTUATOR MOTOR

FIG. 6-165D COLD START SPARK HOLD (CSSH) SYSTEM

FIG. 6-165E CANISTER PURGE SOLENOID OPERATIONAL SCHEMATIC

lows a brief hold on spark advance during acceleration with a cold engine. At engine coolant temperatures of less than 128° F, the CSSH-PVS is closed, routing the distributor vacuum signal through the restrictor **(Fig. 6-165D).** High vacuum acting on the distributor diaphragm during a cold start provides the maximum spark advance. During cold acceleration, this high vacuum in the distributor diaphragm is bled down through the restrictor slowly, giving a modified vacuum advance during the beginning of the acceleration period.

EEC II EGR System

The EEC II EGR system consists of three major components: an EGR valve/sensor assembly, two EGR control solenoids, and an EGR cooler assembly. EGR flow rate is controlled by the EEC electronic control assembly (ECA), which recalculates flow requirements about 10 times per second. The EGR valve is mounted on the intake manifold, and is operated by engine manifold vacuum. It contains a position sensor which indicates the position of the valve step to the ECA by means of an electrical signal. The valve and sensor are serviced when necessary as individual components.

Two solenoid valves are mounted on the left valve cover; one is a vacuum valve and the other a vent valve. These are controlled by the ECA and operate in tandem to increase, maintain or decrease EGR flow by applying, trapping or venting vacuum in the system lines. An EGR cooler assembly is mounted on the right valve cover. EGR flow is routed from the exhaust manifold through the cooler to the EGR valve. As exhaust gases pass through the cooler, engine coolant reduces their temperature. This gives better engine operation by improving the EGR flow characteristics.

Canister Purge (CANP) System

A CANP solenoid is used with the EEC II system **(Fig. 165-E).** Located in a line between the intake manifold purge fitting and the charcoal canister, the CANP solenoid controls the vapor flow from the canister to the intake manifold on a signal from the ECA. CANP solenoids are calibrated for their particular application and can be distinguised from a similar-appearing carburetor bowl vent solenoid by their use of a two-lead electrical connector.

Dual Catalytic Converters

All 1979 Ford and Mercury vehicles equipped with a Feedback Carburetor Control (or EEC II) system use a dual catalytic converter system. The larger converter is known as a three-way catalyst (TWC), as it combines with the smaller converter to promote reactions of HC, CO and NOx. All California 2.3L turbocharged engines use a smaller converter attached to the exhaust mani-

fold outlet as the second of the two converters. This smaller catalyst is called a Light-Off Oxidation Catalyst or LOC unit, and reaches operating temperature almost immediately because of its location at the manifold. Other 2.3L engine applications use a conventional oxidation converter or COC as the second catalyst, instead of the LOC. The COC may be located in the same shell as the TWC, with a Thermactor air inlet to a mixing chamber between the catalysts. This type of converter unit is also called a dual-bed converter.

EMISSION SYSTEM TEST PROCEDURE

POSITIVE CRANKCASE VENTILATION (PCV) VALVE TEST

1. Remove the PCV valve from the intake manifold or rocker arm cover.
2. Start the engine and run at idle.
3. Place a thumb over the valve end to check for vacuum. If there is no vacuum at the valve, inspect for plugged hoses.
4. Shut the engine off. Shake the valve and listen for the rattle of the check needle in the valve. If no rattle is heard, replace the valve.

DUAL DIAPHRAGM DISTRIBUTOR TEST (ON ENGINE)

VACUUM ADVANCE

1. Disconnect both distributor-advance-unit diaphragm lines; plug the line removed from the inner diaphragm.
2. Connect a tachometer and ignition timing light, start the engine and set the fast-idle cam follower on the first step of the fast idle cam.
3. Check the timing setting using the timing light, then connect the outer diaphragm line. If the timing does not advance immediately, adjust as required.

VACUUM RETARD

1. Bring engine idle speed back to 550-600 rpm.
2. Check the timing setting using the timing light, then unplug the inner diaphragm line and reconnect to its fitting. If the timing does not retard immediately, replace the advance unit, because the retard portion is out of calibration or the diaphragm is leaking. No adjustment is possible with the retard diaphragm.

DISTRIBUTOR VACUUM DECELERATION VALVE TEST

1. Connect a tachometer, start the engine and check the idle speed.
2. Remove the plastic cover from the VDV to expose the adjustment screw **(Fig. 6-166).**
3. Turn the adjusting screw counterclockwise slowly, without applying excessive inward pressure. Idle speed should increase 1000 rpm suddenly between five and six turns of the screw. If not, push inward on the end of the valve spring retainer and release.
4. Once the valve has been triggered, turn the adjusting screw clockwise until the idle speed drops back to that noted in Step 1, then turn the screw one additional clockwise turn.
5. Now increase engine speed to 2000 rpm, hold for 5 seconds and release the throttle. If the engine does not return to idle in 4 seconds or less, turn the adjusting screw another one-quarter turn clockwise and repeat Step 4.
6. Continue adjusting the screw by quarter-turn clockwise increments until the engine returns to idle within 4 seconds. If this requires more than *one complete turn,* replace the valve.

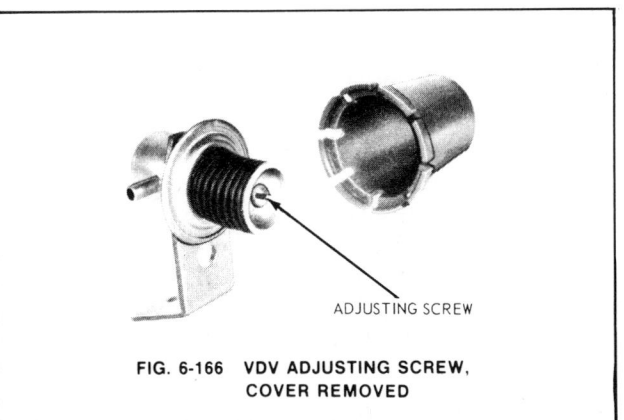

FIG. 6-166   VDV ADJUSTING SCREW, COVER REMOVED

DISTRIBUTOR VACUUM COOLANT VALVE TEST

1. Connect a tachometer, start the engine and warm to normal operating temperature. The choke plate must be in a vertical position.

2. Note engine rpm with the transmission in NEUTRAL and the throttle in a curb idle position.

3. Disconnect the intake-manifold vacuum line at the VCV and plug. Note the idle rpm—if no change occurs, the valve is satisfactory to this point in the test. If an idle change occurs with the line disconnected, replace the VCV.

4. Replace the vacuum line, check the coolant level (add if necessary) and cover the radiator to induce a high temperature condition. Run the engine until an above-normal temperature is indicated by the red light or indicator gauge scale. If idle speed does not increase by 100 rpm or more, replace the VCV.

ELECTRONIC DISTRIBUTOR MODULATOR SYSTEM TEST

1. Connect a tachometer and tee a vacuum gauge to the carburetor spark port, start the engine and run

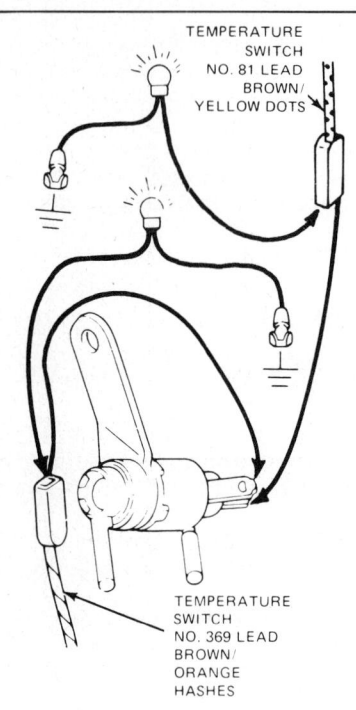

FIG. 6-168   TESTING TRANSMISSION/ TEMPERATURE SWITCH

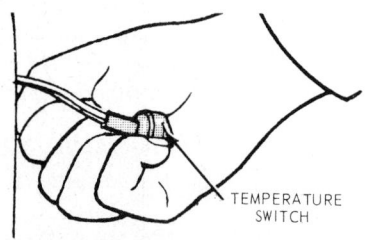

FIG. 6-169   WARMING TEMPERATURE SWITCH BY HAND

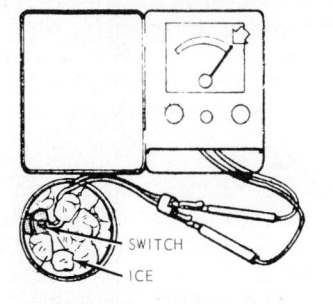

FIG. 6-170   TEMPERATURE SWITCH— LOW TEMPERATURE TEST

Thermal Switch	Open .... 68 Max. (°F.)
	Close .... 58 Min. (°F.)
Speed Sensor	Resistance .... 40-60 ohms @ Room Temperature
	Coil Resistance to Case .... Open Circuit

System Operating Limits

ENGINE	TRANSMISSION	VACUUM ADVANCE CUT-IN SPEED ON ACCELERATION
200-1V	Auto.	23 ± 2.3 mph
240-1V	Auto.	23 ± 2.3 mph
250-1V	Auto.	23 ± 2.3 mph
390-2V	Auto.	23 ± 2.3 mph
429-4V	Auto.	28 ± 2.8 mph
460-4V	Auto.	28 ± 2.8 mph

On deceleration, the vacuum advance cut-out speed for all of the above engines is approximately 18 mph.

FIG. 6-167   DISTRIBUTOR MODULATOR SYSTEM SPECIFICATIONS

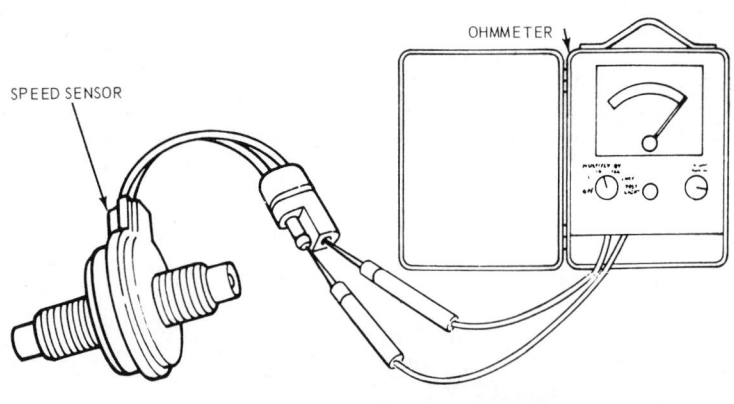

FIG. 6-171   SPEED SENSOR CONTINUITY CHECK

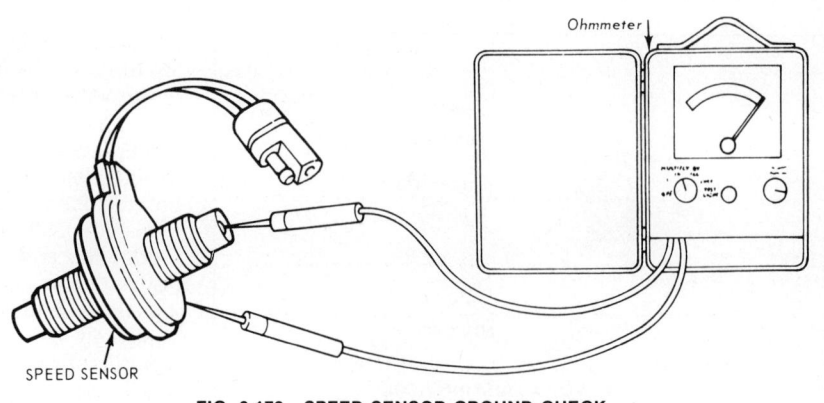

FIG. 6-172   SPEED SENSOR GROUND CHECK

at approximately 1500 rpm. Note the vacuum reading and remove the gauge.

2. Bypass the modulator lines at the rear of the engine, connect the vacuum gauge to the distributor primary diaphragm and note the vacuum reading. If vacuum is lacking or considerably less than the reading in Step 1, check for pinched or leaking vacuum lines.

3. If the two vacuum readings obtained are approximately the same, remove the bypass and connect the vacuum lines from the firewall to rear of engine.

4. Run the engine at normal idle until normal operating temperature is reached. The thermal switch must be above 65° F.

5. Elevate the rear wheels and slowly accelerate to 34 mph. If vacuum occurs between the speed range specified in **Fig. 6-167,** system is functioning properly.

6. If vacuum occurs *before* 20 mph, check the electrical connections inside the car which attach to the modulator box. Then disconnect the thermal switch and recheck the vacuum. If vacuum is now present, replace the modulator assembly. If vacuum is not present, replace the thermal switch.

7. If no vacuum occurs in Step 5 *at any speed,* check the electrical and vacuum line connections inside the car which attach to the modulator box, and repair if necessary.

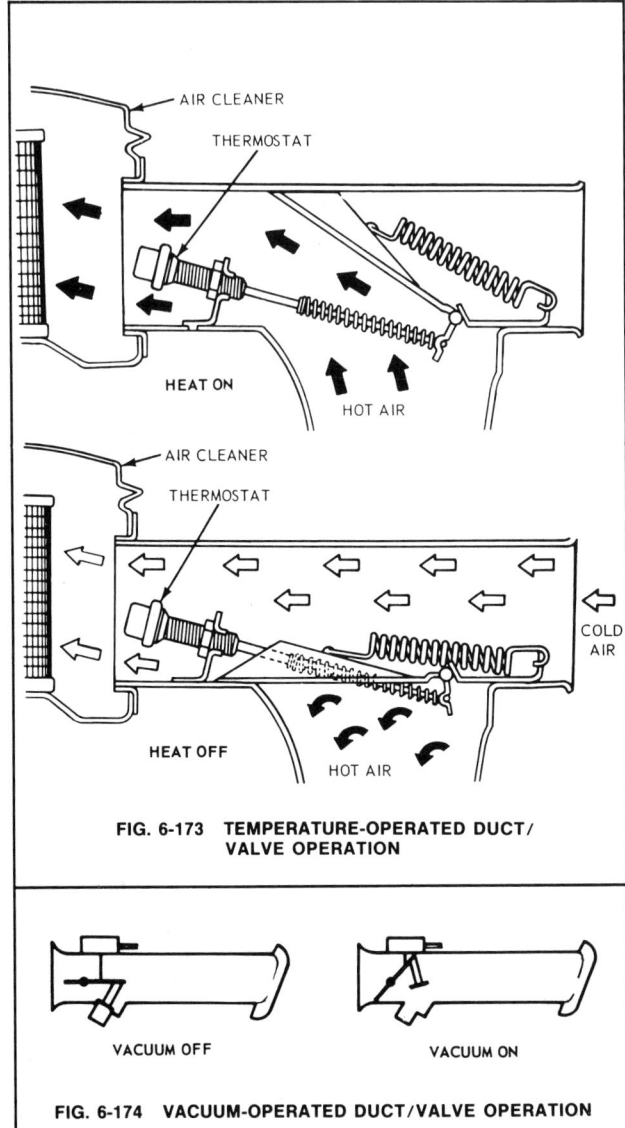

FIG. 6-173 TEMPERATURE-OPERATED DUCT/ VALVE OPERATION

FIG. 6-174 VACUUM-OPERATED DUCT/VALVE OPERATION

8. If the connections are good, replace the modulator and recheck the vacuum as in Step 5. If no vacuum is present, replace the sensor.

TRANSMISSION REGULATED SPARK SYSTEM COMPONENT TEST

TRANSMISSION SWITCH

Disconnect the transmission switch lead from the distributor-modulator-valve blade terminal and connect it in series to the positive battery terminal with a test light **(Fig. 6-168).** Start the engine, apply the foot brake and move the transmission through all positions. The test light should stay *on* in all but high gear (manual transmission) or reverse (automatic transmission). If the light does not go out in this position (according to transmission type), the circuit is grounded or the transmission switch is defective. If the light does not come on at all, the circuit is open, or the transmission switch is defective. Repair/replace as required, and retest.

TEMPERATURE SWITCH

Connect one end of a test light to the temperature switch lead and the other to ground. Warm the switch by hand **(Fig. 6-169)** and, when the switch temperature reaches body temperature, the test lamp should light. Cool the switch with an aerosol spray and the test lamp should go out. If the light does not come on when warmed, the circuit is either open or grounded, or the temperature switch is defective. If it does not go out when cooled, the switch is defective.

ELECTRONIC SPARK CONTROL COMPONENT TEST

TEMPERATURE SWITCH

Disconnect the temperature-switch multiple plug and connect an ohmmeter to both wire terminals. Warm the switch in the palm of your hand **(Fig. 6-169)** and, if the ohmmeter registers a reading, the switch is good. To check the lower temperature range, chill the switch with freon or use cracked ice **(Fig. 6-170).** There should be no ohmmeter reading at temperatures below 49° F.

POWER SUPPLY TEST

Check the temperature switch connector of the instrument panel wiring by grounding one test lamp lead and connecting the other to the wire (red-yellow hash-marked). Turn the ignition switch on and the test lamp should light. If it does not light, the ignition switch or the wiring is defective. If repair/replacement does not solve the problem, replace the electronic amplifier.

SPEED SENSOR TEST

1. Disconnect the speed sensor multiple plug and connect an ohmmeter as shown in **Fig. 6-171** to check continuity. Room temperature resistance of the speed sensor is 40-60 ohms.

2. Connect the ohmmeter as shown in **Fig. 6-172** to check speed sensor resistance to ground. Since no continuity exists between the case and the black wire, the resistance should read an open circuit.

TEMPERATURE-OPERATED AIR CLEANER DUCT/VALVE TEST

1. With the air cleaner installed on a cold engine and the engine compartment temperature below 100° F, the valve plate should be in the *heat on* position **(Fig. 6-173).** If it is not, check for binding or mechanical interference.

2. Remove the air cleaner and immerse the air tube end in sufficient water to cover the thermostat capsule.

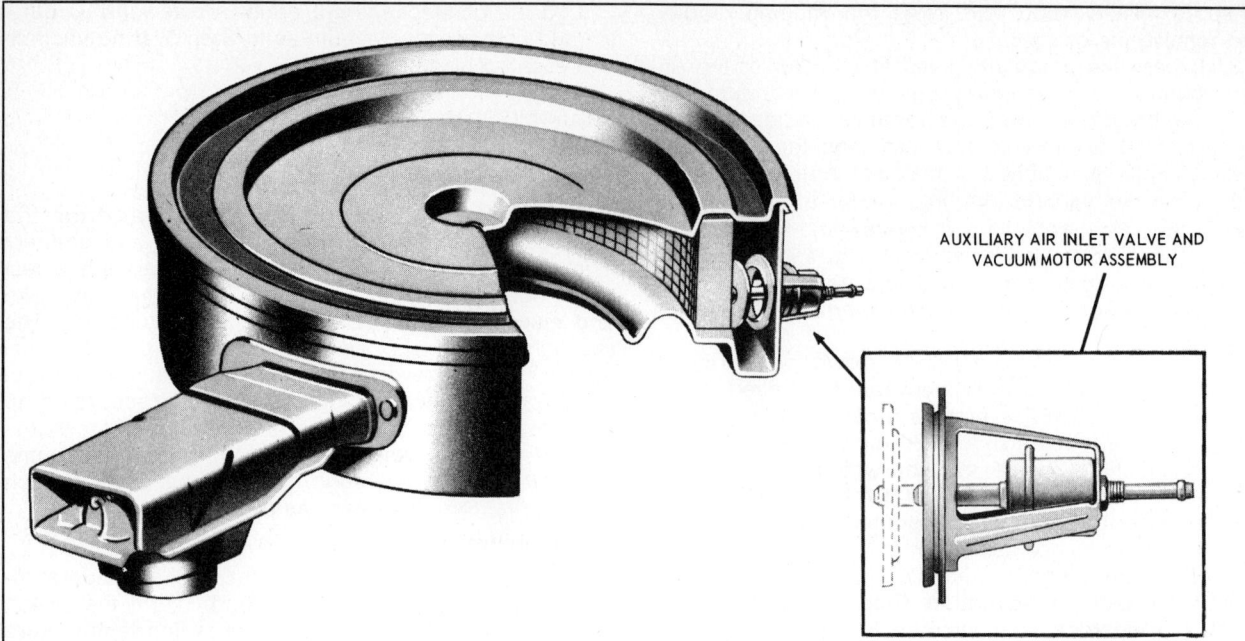

AUXILIARY AIR INLET VALVE AND
VACUUM MOTOR ASSEMBLY

FIG. 6-175   AIR-CLEANER VACUUM-MOTOR TEST

Basic No. 9D475	Type	Start-to-Open Inches HG	Basic No. 9D475	Type	Start-to-Open Inches HG
D3AE-LA	TS	2.5	D42E-BB	P	2.7
D3VE-AA	TS	2.5	D42E-CD	TS	2.8
D4AE-AA	P	2.9	D42E-DB	TS	4.7
D4AE-BA	P	2.9	D42E-DC	P	2.7
D4AE-CA	P	2.0	D42E-EB	TS	2.8
D4AE-DA	M	3.6	D42E-FA	P	2.9
D4AE-EA	P	2.9	D5AE-AA	TS	3.5
D4AE-FA	P	2.9	D5DE-AA	TS	2.5
D4AE-GA	P	2.0	D5EE-CA	P	2.0
D4DE-AB	P	2.9	D5ME-BA	TS	2.5
D4DE-EA	P	2.9	D50E-AA	TS	3.0
D4DE-FA	P	2.7	D5TE-CA	TS	2.5
D4DE-GA	TS	2.5	D5TE-CB	TS	2.9
D4DE-HA	TS	3.0	D5TE-DA	P	2.5
D40E-AA	P	2.9	D5TE-EA	TS	3.0
D40E-BA	P	2.9	D5TE-FA	TS	3.0
D40E-CA	P	2.9	D5UE-BA	TS	3.5
D40E-DA	P	2.7	D5UE-CA	P	2.0
D40E-EA	P	4.8	D5VE-CA	P	2.5
D4TE-AA	P	2.9	D5VE-DA	P	2.5
D4TE-BA	P	2.7	D5VE-EA	TS	2.5
D4TE-DA	P	1.7	D5VE-FA	P	2.5
D4TE-EA	P	2.5	D5VE-GA	P	2.5
D4TE-FA	TS	2.5	D5ZE-AA	TS	2.0
D4TE-HA	P	2.5	D52E-DA	TS	2.8
D4TE-JA	TS	3.0	D52E-EA	TS	2.8
D4TE-KA	TS	3.0	D52E-FA	TS	4.7
D4UE-AA	P	2.9	D52E-GA	TS	2.8
D4UE-BA	P	2.0	D52E-HA	TS	2.6
D4UE-CA	P	2.0	D52E-JA	TS	4.7
D4ZE-AA	M	3.6	D52E-JS	TS	4.7
D4ZE-BA	M	3.6	D52E-KA	TS	3.8
D4ZE-CA	M	3.6	D52E-LA	TS	3.0
D42E-AG	TS	2.8	D58E-AA	TS	2.9

P — Poppet TS — Tapered Stem M — Modulator

FIG. 6-176   1975-76 EGR VALVE SPECIFICATIONS

3. Heat the water to a temperature of 100° F, wait 5 minutes for the temperature to stabilize, and then check the valve position—it should still be in the *heat on* mode.

4. Repeat Step 3, with water temperature increased to 135° F. The valve plate should now be in the *heat off* position **(Fig. 6-173)**.

5. If the valve plate does not meet the requirements, and no mechanical binding or other interference is noted, replace the duct/valve assembly.

VACUUM-OPERATED AIR CLEANER DUCT/VALVE TEST

1. Check the duct valve position with the engine off. It should be open (vacuum off) as shown in **Fig. 6-174**.

2. Start the engine—the valve plate should close (vacuum on) during engine idle as shown in **Fig. 6-174**. If the valve does not close, check the bi-metal switch inside the air cleaner shell to see that the bleed valve is seated and that all vacuum lines are connected.

3. Rapidly open and close the throttle several times. The valve plate should open during throttle opening. If it does not, check for binding or other mechanical interference.

4. If a bi-metal switch malfunction is suspected, remove it and immerse in 80° F water. If the bleed valve does not unseat, replace the switch.

VACUUM-OPERATED AIR CLEANER, AUXILIARY AIR INLET VALVE

1. Start the engine and note the position of the vacuum motor plate **(Fig. 6-175)**. It should be fully closed.

2. Disconnect the vacuum line from the vacuum motor. The plate should open completely.

3. If the plate does not open, check the line for vacuum. There should be a minimum of 15 ins. available. If vacuum is not the problem, replace the vacuum motor.

TEMPERATURE ACTIVATED VACUUM SYSTEM (TAV) OPERATIONAL TEST

1. Connect a tachometer and tee a vacuum gauge into the line at the distributor primary vacuum port. Air temperature must be 65° F or higher so that the temperature switch is closed.

2. Start the engine, shift the transmission to NEUTRAL or PARK and check the vacuum gauge. There should be *no* reading.

3. Increase engine speed to 1500 rpm and note the vacuum gauge, which should now read 5 ins. or more of vacuum.

4. Verify the gauge reading by disconnecting the EGR port line and plugging the line to the carburetor. The vacuum gauge should now read zero. Unplug and reconnect the line.

5. Disconnect one electrical lead at the vacuum valve. The vacuum gauge should now read above 6 ins. with engine speed at 1500 rpm, indicating that vacuum source switching has taken place.

SPARK DELAY VALVE TEST

1. Remove the spark delay valve from the system and connect a vacuum gauge at one port, and a hand vacuum pump at the other.

2. Apply 10 ins. of vacuum and compare the time required for the vacuum gauge to record an 8-in. reading to the table below.

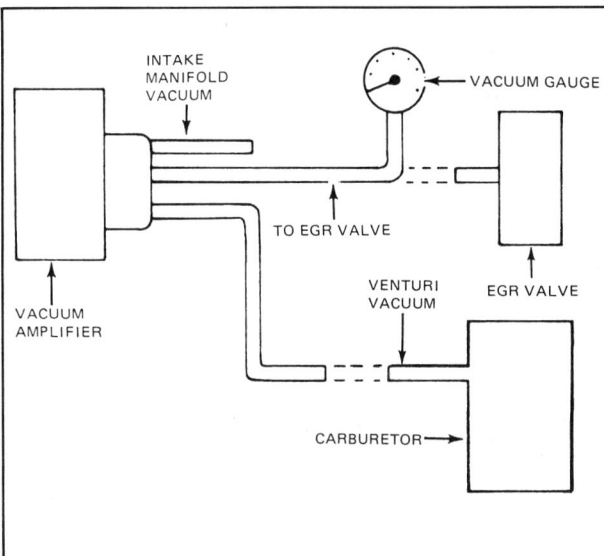

FIG. 6-177 1974 VACUUM AMPLIFIER BIAS TEST

PART NUMBER PREFIX & SUFFIX (Basic No. 9E451)	CODE NUMBER ON UNIT	AMPLIFICATION RATIO OF UNIT	BIAS RATING OF UNIT (In. Hg)	SERVICE BIAS SPECIFICATION
Stamped in Yellow				
D52E-B1A,-B2A,-B3A	10-0	10:1	0	0-0.5
D52E-A1A,-A2A,-A3A	10-5	10:1	0.5	0.2-0.8
D5TE-A1A,-A2A,-A3A	10-1	10:1	1.0	0.7-1.3
D5TE-B1A,-B2A,-B3A	10-15	10:1	1.5	1.2-1.8
D50E-A1A,-A2A,-A3A	10-2	10:1	2.0	1.7-2.3
Stamped in White				
D5DE-A1A,-A2A,-A3A	14-0	14:1	0	0-0.5
D5DE-B1A,-B2A,-B3A	14-1	14:1	1.0	0.7-1.3
D5TE-C1A,-C2A,-C3A	14-2	14:1	2.0	1.7-2.3
D5AE-A1A,-A2A,-A3A	14-3	14:1	3.0	2.7-3.3
Stamped in Red				
D5TE-D3A	18-0	18:1	0	0-0.5

NOTE: The different numerals in the suffix denote alternate vendor sources: "1" for Fram, "2" for Marvel Schebler, "3" for Ranco.

FIG. 6-178 1975-76 EGR VALVE SPECIFICATIONS

VALVE DESCRIPTION		TIME IN SEC.	
COLOR	I.D.#	Min.	Max.
BLACK & GRAY	1	1	4
BLACK & BROWN	2	2	5
BLACK & WHITE	5	4	12
BLACK & YELLOW	10	5,8	14
BLACK & BLUE	15	7	16
BLACK & GREEN	20	9	20
BLACK & ORANGE	30	13	24
BLACK & RED	40	15	28

CHECK VALVE TEST

1. Remove the check valve from the system and connect a hand vacuum pump to the side port and a vacuum gauge to the other port.

2. Apply vacuum. The vacuum gauge should show an immediate reading.

3. Reverse the connections, apply vacuum. There should be no reading. Replace the check valve if it fails either test.

EGR SYSTEM OPERATIONAL TEST

1973 EGR VALVE

1. Tee a vacuum gauge to the EGR valve, start the engine and warm the coolant to 125° F or more.

2. Open and close the throttle rapidly. The vacuum gauge reading should increase as the engine speed increases.

3. If vacuum increases, open the throttle again and watch the EGR valve stem action. If the system is functioning properly, the valve stem will begin to move at 3 to 4 ins. of vacuum, and will reach wide-open position at 8 to 10 ins. If the stem does not move with 3 to 4 ins. of vacuum applied, replace the EGR valve.

4. Switch the carburetor EGR port line to a manifold vacuum source. The EGR stem should move outward again, but engine idle should be rough and accompanied by a drastic rpm loss, even to the point of stalling, if the EGR valve is operating properly. If no change occurs in engine rpm or idle quality, replace the EGR valve.

1974-75 EGR VALVE

1. Disconnect the EGR vacuum line from the EGR valve, and connect a hand vacuum pump.

2. Gradually apply vacuum to the EGR valve while watching the valve stem for movement. 1974 valves should start to move within ½ to 1 in. of the diaphragm signal vacuum. For 1975-76 valves, refer to **Fig. 6-176** for the specified start-to-open vacuum, according to valve part number. If the valve does not meet the start-to-open specification, replace it.

3. Apply at least 8 ins. of vacuum to the EGR valve with the engine on. As the valve moves to the full extent of travel, engine idle should roughen, engine speed should decrease and/or stop completely. If this does not happen, the EGR flow is plugged. Remove and clean the EGR valve; reinstall and retest.

4. If the engine quality still does not change, replace the EGR valve and install a *new* gasket. If this does not change the idle quality either, the problem is *not* with the EGR valve.

VENTURI VACUUM AMPLIFIER SYSTEM

Single vacuum-plug amplifiers have built-in calibration, and no adjustment is possible. To test for an amplifier malfunction:

1. Connect a vacuum gauge as shown in **Fig. 6-177.**

With the engine at curb idle speed, the gauge should read within ±0.3-in. of the specified bias as shown in **Fig. 6-178.**

2. Increase engine speed to 1500-2000 rpm and release the accelerator. As the engine returns to idle, the vacuum reading should return to the bias as in Step 1. If the bias has changed, replace the amplifier. If vacuum increases more than 1 in. during the acceleration period, replace the amplifier.

3. Disconnect the external reservoir line at the amplifier and cap. Rev the engine rapidly to 1500-2000 rpm and the vacuum reading should increase to 4 ins. or more. If not, replace the amplifier.

Dual vacuum plug amplifiers are tested in a similar manner:

1. Disconnect the output hose connecting the amplifier to the EGR valve from the amplifier, and connect a vacuum gauge to the hose.

2. Disconnect the reservoir vacuum hose and tee with the source vacuum line. Connect the source hose to manifold vacuum. If a vacuum solenoid valve or vacuum-operated switch is installed between the amplifier and the EGR valve, bypass it when connecting the vacuum gauge.

3. Increase engine speed to 1500-2000 rpm and release the accelerator. When the engine returns to curb idle speed, disconnect the vacuum line at the carburetor venturi. The vacuum gauge reading should be within ±0.3-in. of the specified bias value shown in **Fig. 6-178.** If not, replace the amplifier.

4. Increase engine speed to 1500-2000 rpm and release the accelerator. If the output vacuum gauge shows an increase of more than 1 in. during acceleration, replace the amplifier.

5. Connect the carburetor venturi hose and read the vacuum gauge. If the reading is greater than ½-in. above the bias value in Step 3, check the idle speed and reset to vehicle emission control sticker specifications, if necessary.

6. Increase engine speed to 1500-2000 rpm and release the accelerator. Note vacuum gauge connected to the EGR hose. If the vacuum does not increase 4 ins. or more during acceleration and then return to specified bias, replace the amplifier.

7. Connect the "R" nipple to manifold vacuum, the "S" nipple to spark port vacuum, the "V" nipple to venturi vacuum and the "C" nipple to a vacuum gauge. Increase engine speed to 1500-2000 rpm and release the accelerator. When the engine returns to curb idle speed, disconnect the vacuum hose at the venturi and check the spark port vacuum—it should not exceed 2 ins. Vacuum gauge reading should be less than ½-in.

EGR-PVS SYSTEM

1. Remove the EGR-PVS valve from the engine, and connect a hand vacuum pump to its top port.

2. Cool the valve to below 60° F with cold water, ice or freon.

3. Apply 20 ins. of vacuum to the valve. It should retain at least 19 ins. for 5 minutes.

4. With the hand vacuum pump still connected and the PVS holding vacuum, immerse the valve in water and heat. The vacuum should drop to zero as the water temperature reaches the valve's opening temperature (60° F or 125° F, depending on PVS calibration).

HIGH-SPEED EGR MODULATOR SUBSYSTEM

1. Tee a vacuum gauge to the EGR valve, elevate the rear wheels and start the engine. Warm to a cool-

ant temperature above 125° F. The vacuum gauge should read zero.

2. Shift the transmission into HIGH gear (manual) or DRIVE (automatic). As speed increases, vacuum should also increase.

3. Apply the throttle until the speedometer reaches approximately 67 mph. If the vacuum drops to zero, the system is functioning properly.

4. If not, test the speed sensor as in the Electronic Spark Control Component Test.

FUEL DECEL VALVE TEST

1. Tee a vacuum gauge to the decel line at the carburetor and connect a tachometer. For 2300cc engines, connect the vacuum gauge as shown in **Fig. 6-179.**

2. Make sure that ignition timing, idle mixture and idle speed are set to specifications.

3. Start engine, run at 3000 rpm for 5 seconds.

4. Release the throttle, and the vacuum gauge reading should drop to zero in 2 to 5 seconds.

5. If the decel valve does not perform within specifications, check the idle vacuum with a vacuum gauge. Idle vacuum should not exceed 18½ ins. for a dual diaphragm distributor or 19½ ins. for a single diaphragm distributor.

6. If the idle vacuum is within specification but the decel valve operation is not, the decel valve must either be replaced or adjusted (the decel valve used with 2300cc engines is *adjustable* for 1975).

FUEL DECEL VALVE ADJUSTMENT

1. To reduce the opening duration, turn the nylon adjuster, located at the top of the decel valve body, inward (clockwise).

2. To increase the opening duration, turn the nylon adjuster outward (counterclockwise).

3. Replace the fast idle cam on the kickdown step and make sure that fast idle speed is to specifications. Vacuum gauge should show no reading.

4. Repeat the Fuel Deceleration Valve Test. If the decel valve cannot be adjusted to operate within specifications, it must be replaced.

EXHAUST HEAT CONTROL VALVE

1974 Bi-Metal Type—Manually rotate the valve shaft to check for binding. Lubricate the shaft ends with a graphite lubricant.

1975-76 Vacuum-Operated Type—Tee a vacuum gauge into the heat-control-valve line. Start the engine and warm to normal operating temperature. With the engine idling, the vacuum gauge should read under 3 ins. Apply 15 to 20 ins. of vacuum to the valve-vacuum-motor actuator motor and the valve should close. Hold vacuum for 60 seconds. The valve should not leak down more than 2 ins. of vacuum in this time, and must return to the open position when the actuator motor is vented (vacuum source removed). If the valve does not open, replace the valve assembly. Refer to the table below for exact specifications.

Cu. Ins.	Start Closing at (In. Hg Vacuum)	Completely Closed* (In. Hg Vacuum)
351 W, 302	1-3	6 or less
All Other Applications	3-6	10 or less

*NOTE: Valve is closed if the shaft lever comes within 0.065 (feeler gauge) of the stop.

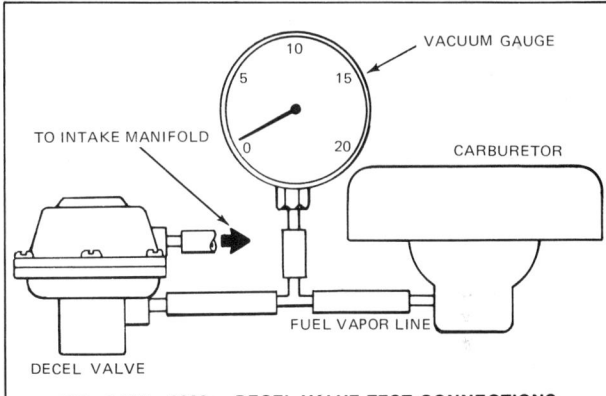

FIG. 6-179 2300cc DECEL VALVE TEST CONNECTIONS

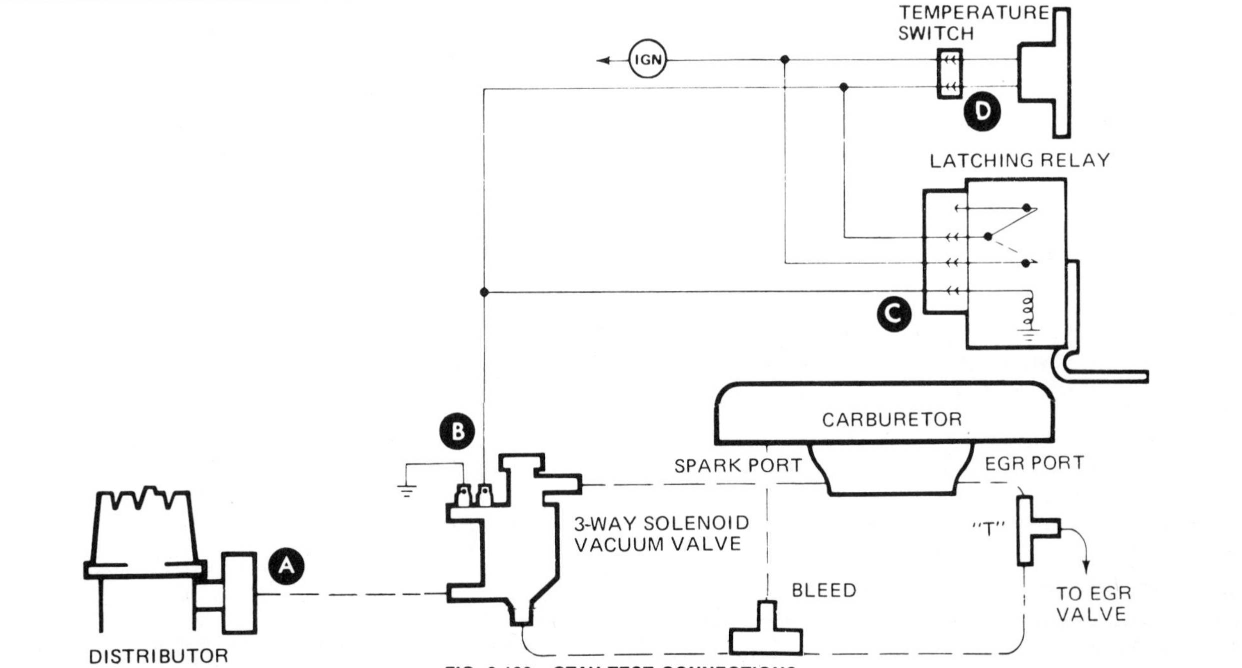

FIG. 6-180 CTAV TEST CONNECTIONS

COLD TEMPERATURE ACTUATED VACUUM SYSTEM (CTAV) TEST

1. Connect a tachometer to the engine and a vacuum gauge to the hose at "A" in **Fig. 6-180.** The temperature sensing switch must be over 65° F. Disconnect the lead at "B."

2. Start the engine and rev to 1500 rpm. The vacuum gauge should read approximately 15 ins. If no vacuum is present, check the vacuum source back to the carburetor spark port.

3. Connect the lead to "B." If vacuum is now present, check the vacuum valve ground and electrical source back to the ignition switch. If no vacuum is present, rev the engine to 3000 rpm. The vacuum gauge should read approximately 9 ins., indicating that the vacuum system is functioning satisfactorily. If no vacuum is present, check the vacuum source back to the carburetor EGR port.

4. Turn the engine off and connect one test lamp lead at "B" and the other to ground. Disconnect the connector at "D" and turn the ignition on. If the test lamp lights, replace the latching relay.

5. If the test lamp does not light, reconnect the connector at "B." The test lamp should light. If it does not, check the temperature switch and electrical source back to the ignition switch.

6. Disconnect the connector at "D." If the test lamp does not light, replace the latching relay.

7. Connect the test lamp to the temperature switch terminal at "D." Cool the switch to below 49° F with an aerosol can or freon. The light should go out when the temperature switch is cooled, indicating that the system is working properly. If the test lamp stays on, replace the temperature switch.

EGR BACKPRESSURE TRANSDUCER SYSTEM TEST

1. Connect a tachometer and start the engine. Slowly open and close the throttle halfway (3000 rpm) and note the EGR valve-stem movement. If the EGR valve stem moves, the system is functioning properly.

2. If the EGR valve stem does not move, disconnect the vacuum supply hose to the transducer and connect a vacuum gauge to the TVS switch.

3. Slowly open and close the throttle again. Note the vacuum gauge reading. If vacuum is less than 4 ins., check the TVS switch operation and/or test for vacuum at the EGR port.

4. If the vacuum exceeds 4 ins., remove the EGR valve and transducer and clean both components and passages.

5. Replace the EGR valve and transducer and repeat Step 1. If the EGR valve stem does not move, replace the transducer.

EVAPORATIVE EMISSION SHED SYSTEM TEST

This diagnostic test procedure does not apply to engine applications equipped with EEC II.

1. Disconnect purge hose from purge control valve "T" or "F" fitting, intake manifold fitting, or carburetor spacer according to system usage. Cap the fitting and start the engine.

2. Disconnect the vacuum signal hose from the purge control valve.

3. Remove the canister fresh air vent cap and connect a vacuum gauge to the fresh air connector. Replace the purge control valve if the vacuum gauge indicates the presence of vacuum after one minute.

4. Connect a vacuum gauge to the vacuum signal hose. Run the engine at 2000 rpm for 10-20 seconds.

The vacuum gauge should read at least 5 ins. of vacuum if the system is okay. If it does not, check individual component operation of the PVS, purge control, spark delay and retard delay valve.

5. Replace the vacuum signal hose vacuum gauge with a hand vacuum pump. Drive 5 ins. of vacuum with the engine idling and check the vacuum gauge at the canister fresh air connector. Replace the purge control valve if vacuum is not indicated.

6. Remove all test equipment and reconnect all hoses and canister fresh air vent cap. Fuel bowl vent line must have a continuous downward slope to its canister connection.

EMISSION SYSTEM COMPONENT REPLACEMENT

AIR CLEANER ASSEMBLY

CRANKCASE VENTILATION FILTER

1. Remove the retainer clip and unsnap the air-cleaner closure elbow from the air cleaner body.

2. Remove the air cleaner cover and unclip the crankcase-ventilation-filter retainer.

3. Lift the filter retainer from the air cleaner and remove the filter pack.

4. Clean the retainer and install a new filter pack.

5. Replace the crankcase-ventilation-filter assembly in the air cleaner and install the retainer clip.

6. Reconnect the closure hose to the air cleaner shell and replace the clip.

7. Install the air cleaner cover and torque the steel wing nuts 15 to 25 in.-lbs.; plastic wing nuts 20 to 30 in.-lbs.

DUCT/ VALVE ASSEMBLY, TEMPERATURE OPERATED

1. Unscrew the hex-head capscrews holding the duct/valve assembly to the air cleaner body, and lift the assembly off.

2. Unscrew thermostat from its mounting bracket.

3. Install a new thermostat, and check its operation before replacing the duct/valve assembly to the air cleaner body.

4. Replace the duct/valve assembly on the air cleaner body and tighten the capscrews securely.

5. Install the vacuum override motor (if used) and check its operation.

AIR PUMP ASSEMBLY

The air-pump rotor vanes and bearing clearances are factory-set and not adjustable; bearings are sealed and permanently lubricated. Adjustment, lubrication and/or overhaul of the air pump are not required. If the pump fails or becomes excessively noisy, replace the unit.

AIR PUMP CENTRIFUGAL FILTER FAN

1. Loosen the air-pump adjusting-arm bracket and mounting bolts to relieve drive belt tension.

2. Remove the pulley attaching bolts and drive pulley from the air pump shaft.

3. After prying the outer disc loose, pull the fan off with pliers—*do not* remove the metal drive hub.

4. Draw the new fan evenly into place, using the pulley and bolts as tools. Tighten the bolts alternately, making sure the outer edge of the fan slips into the housing.

5. Adjust drive belt tension and tighten the bracket and mounting bolts. Until the outer diameter sealing lip has worn in, a new fan may be noisy.

CHRYSLER, DODGE, PLYMOUTH, IMPERIAL
1970-72 Emission Systems

POSITIVE CRANKCASE VENTILATION (PCV)

A completely closed crankcase ventilation system **(Fig. 6-181)** draws unfiltered air from the air cleaner, through a hose and to the crankcase inlet air cleaner, where it is filtered before circulating through the engine. Manifold vacuum draws the air from the cylinder head cover and into the combustion chamber, where it is expelled with exhaust gases. A PCV valve is located in the outlet vent to regulate the flow of crankcase ventilation at various throttle positions.

CLEANER AIR SYSTEM (CAS)

Chrysler's emission control approach for 1970-71 is described as the Cleaner Air System, or CAS, and includes carburetor/choke/distributor calibrations, an idle speed solenoid, a distributor retard solenoid and lower engine compression ratios. In addition to these, the following subsystem comprises the remainder of the Cleaner Air System:

HEATED AIR SYSTEM

A heated air intake is provided on all engines except the 340, 426 Hemi, 440 3-2-bbl. and those engines equipped with a fresh-air scoop option. This system **(Fig. 6-182)** is basically a twin airflow circuit, as described below:

1. At underhood temperatures of 10° F or below, airflow takes place through the heat stove, passing through a flexible hose into the bottom of the snorkel, where it enters the air cleaner.

2. At underhood temperatures of 100° F or higher, airflow takes place through the snorkel directly into the air cleaner.

3. At underhood temperatures between 10° F and 100° F, airflow is a mixture from both circuits. The snorkel air-control valve maintains a temperature range between 95° F and 105° F at the air cleaner thermostat (sensor). Modulation of the induction air temperature is accomplished by intake manifold vacuum in conjunction with the thermostat (sensor) and a vacuum diaphragm assembly which controls operation of the air control valve.

A dual-snorkel air cleaner is used on some engines and operates like the single snorkel unit except under wide-open-throttle conditions, when both snorkels open. The non-heated snorkel connects to manifold vacuum by means of a tee in the vacuum line between the carburetor and the air-cleaner temperature sensor.

EVAPORATION CONTROL SYSTEM (ECS)

Installed on all 1970 Chrysler Corporation cars sold in California and all 1971 cars nationwide, this closed fuel system **(Fig. 6-183)** controls fuel expansion and directs fuel vapors to the carburetor or back to the fuel supply tank. Fuel vapors are transmitted through the crankcase-inlet air cleaner to the crankcase, where they settle to the bottom and are drawn along with normal crankcase vapors to the carburetor base for combustion.

The fuel tank is equipped with a pressure-vacuum filler cap, an overfill tank protector and a vent in each of the four tank corners connected to a standpipe-type liquid vapor separator. Carburetors are fitted with a closed carburetor-bowl vent system, with 6-cyl. models connected to the crankcase by a connecting nipple on

the fuel pump, and 8-cyl. models by a hose from the carburetor bowl to the crankcase-inlet air cleaner.

Two additional components are added to the ECS for 1972. To prevent the fuel tank from being overfilled, a brass needle-type overfill limiting valve located in the vapor vent line is used in all fuel systems except Satel-

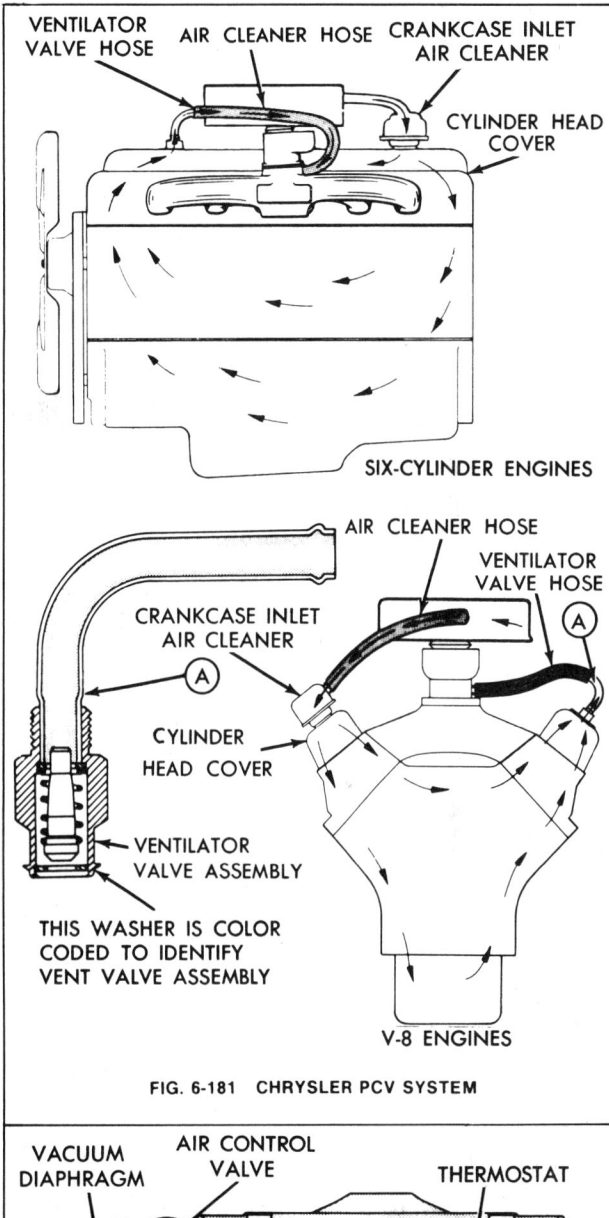

FIG. 6-181 CHRYSLER PCV SYSTEM

FIG. 6-182 HEATED AIR INLET SYSTEM

lite and station wagon models. A charcoal vapor canister is added to all systems to absorb and retain fuel vapors until the canister is purged through the PCV line when the engine is running **(Fig. 6-184)**.

OXIDES OF NITROGEN (NOx) CONTROL SYSTEM

Installed on all California cars in 1971-72, the NOx Control System **(Fig. 6-185)** replaces the solenoid-con-

trolled spark advance previously used by Chrysler Corporation. During 1971-72, the heart of the NOx system is a solenoid vacuum valve **(Fig. 6-186)** which controls vacuum spark advance. On manual transmission cars, this valve is connected to a transmission switch to eliminate vacuum advance in all but high gear. In any other gear position, the valve is energized, shutting off vacuum to the distributor. In high gear, the transmission switch breaks the electrical circuit to the solenoid,

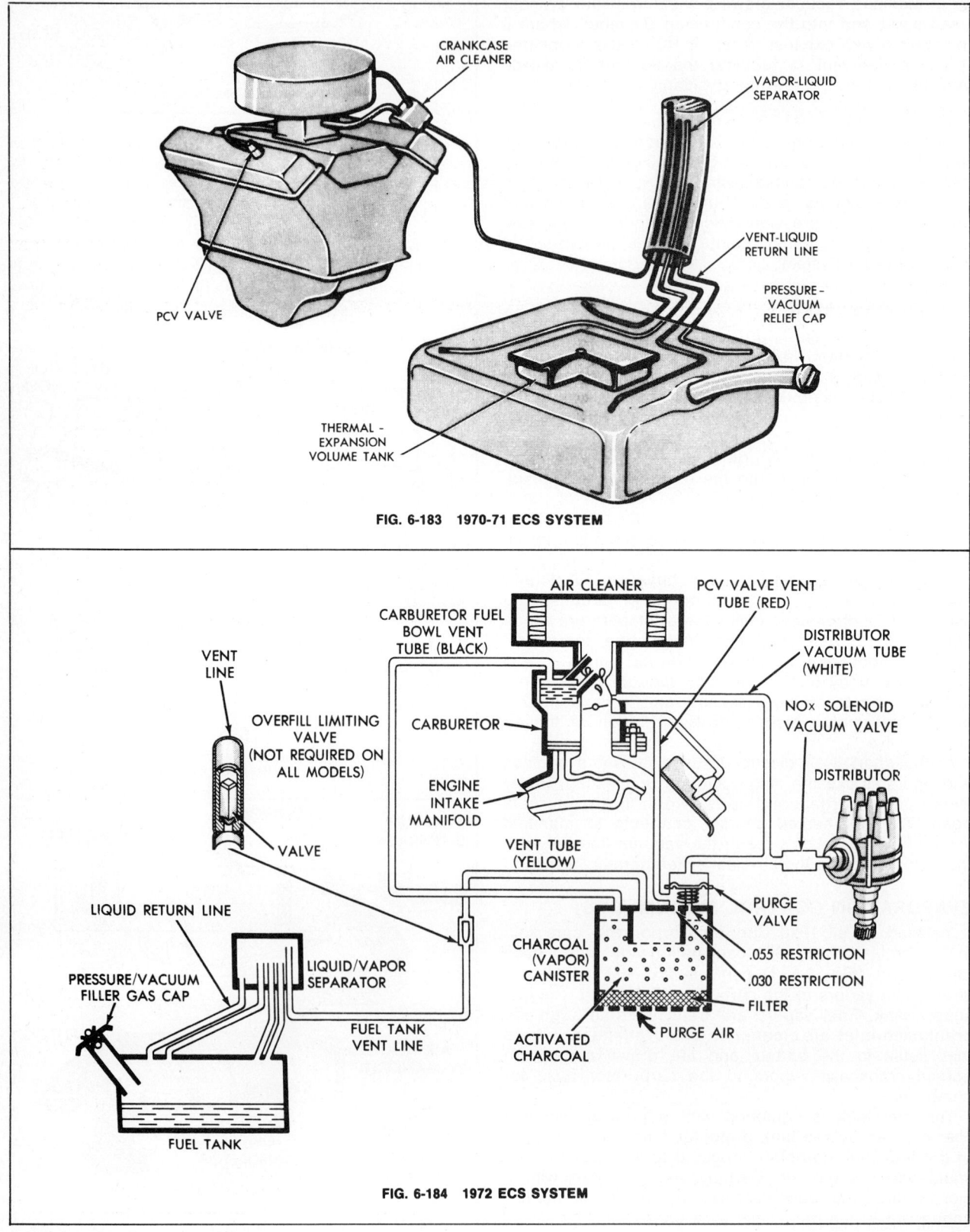

FIG. 6-183   1970-71 ECS SYSTEM

FIG. 6-184   1972 ECS SYSTEM

the spring in the valve opens the passageway and vacuum is allowed to the distributor advance unit. The only additional control on manual transmission cars is a thermal switch mounted on the firewall to sense the temperature in the fresh-air cowl inlet. The thermal switch is not used on 1972 applications. Below 70° F, the thermal switch breaks the circuit to the solenoid valve, which permits normal vacuum advance; above that temperature, the thermal switch makes the connection and lets the NOx system operate as described earlier.

Automatic transmission cars are different—they have an increased-overlap camshaft to produce more exhaust gas contamination in the cylinder, reducing peak combustion chamber temperatures, which are a primary cause of NOx emissions. In addition to the special camshaft, these engines are fitted with a 185° F thermostat, a move directly opposite to that made to reduce hydrocarbons, which had resulted in the use of 195° F thermostats previously. A solenoid vacuum valve is also used, but the control mode is different. A control module, vacuum switch, thermal switch and speed switch all work together to signal the solenoid when to turn distributor vacuum on or off.

All 8-cyl. engines transmit exhaust gases through floor jets below the carburetor to the intake manifold.

Each jet contains an orifice permitting the introduction of a controlled amount of exhaust gas to be drawn in by engine vacuum to dilute the incoming air/fuel mixture (Fig. 6-187). All 6-cyl. engines use a slightly different method, delivering the exhaust gases from the exhaust manifold plenum chamber located at the "hot spot" below the carburetor riser.

When engine coolant reaches a specified overheat temperature, a vacuum bypass valve bypasses the NOx system to provide manifold vacuum to the distributor, advancing ignition timing until the overheat condition is corrected. This valve is used only on 1971 383 2-bbl. engines equipped with automatic transmissions and no air conditioning and on 1972 440 engines equipped with automatic transmissions and air conditioning.

AIR INJECTION SYSTEM

An exhaust-port air injection system (Fig. 6-188) is fitted to all California 198, 225, 400 and 440-cu.-in. engines to provide a controlled amount of air for exhaust gas oxidation. The system consists of a belt-driven air pump, check valve, diverter/pressure-relief valve and injection tubes. The pump is mounted at the front of the engine, where intake air passes through a centrifugal fan at its front and is delivered to the intake manifold. During sudden deceleration, vacuum causes

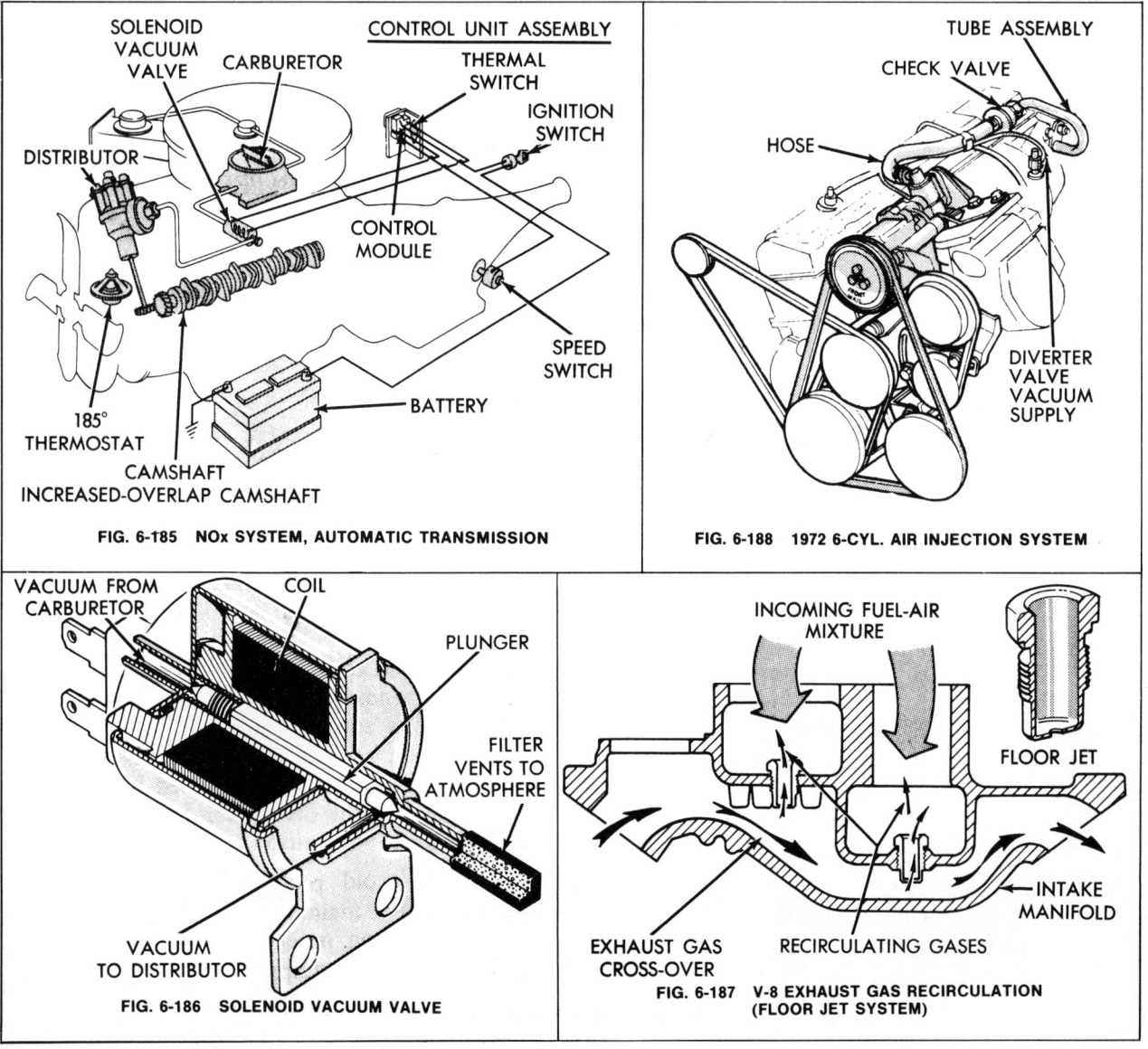

FIG. 6-185 NOx SYSTEM, AUTOMATIC TRANSMISSION

FIG. 6-188 1972 6-CYL. AIR INJECTION SYSTEM

FIG. 6-186 SOLENOID VACUUM VALVE

FIG. 6-187 V-8 EXHAUST GAS RECIRCULATION (FLOOR JET SYSTEM)

a diverter valve at the back of the pump to open, passing pump air into the atmosphere. A check valve located in the 6-cyl. engine head and the 8-cyl. engine injection-tube assembly contains a one-way diaphragm which prevents hot exhaust gases from backing up in the hose and damaging the pump during periods of pump belt failure, excessive system pressure or hose rupture.

CHRYSLER, DODGE, PLYMOUTH, IMPERIAL
1973-74 Emission Systems

The Positive Crankcase Ventilation (PCV) system is the same as that used on 1970-72 models. For Heated Air System, see the Cleaner Air System for 1970-72.

EVAPORATION CONTROL SYSTEM (ECS)

A new vapor canister with three connecting lines and no purge valve is used (Fig. 6-189). Purge valve elimination is made possible by adding another ported vacuum connection on the carburetor to use the carburetor throttle plates as a purge valve, improving hot idle quality. Limited production, high-performance engines continue to use the 1972 two-stage canister with integral purge valve during 1973.

EXHAUST GAS RECIRCULATION (EGR)

The use of the EGR system (Fig. 6-190) is extended to all engines. Two different applications are added to the 1972 NOx Floor Jet System:

1. Ported Vacuum Control—A vacuum-actuated, poppet-type EGR valve modulates exhaust gas flow from the exhaust gas crossover to the incoming air/fuel mixture. A slot-type carburetor port, connected directly to the EGR valve, receives an increasing amount of manifold vacuum as the throttle plates open. In this system, flow rate depends upon manifold vacuum, exhaust gas backpressure and throttle position. The valve opening point is calibrated above available manifold vacuum at wide open throttle to prevent EGR operation and provide maximum performance. A plenum-mounted temperature control valve reduces EGR action at low temperatures for improved drivability.

2. Venturi Vacuum Control—A vacuum-actuated, poppet-type EGR valve modulates exhaust gas flow from the exhaust gas crossover to the incoming air/fuel mixture. The control signal comes from a vacuum tap at the throat of the carburetor vent. An amplifier is required to boost the vacuum signal sufficiently to operate the EGR valve, and its presence is a fast way of identifying the type of EGR control system used on 1973-74 cars. To prevent EGR at wide open throttle, a dump diaphragm compares venturi with manifold vacuum and, at wide open throttle, dumps the internal reservoir to limit output reaching the EGR valve to manifold vacuum. In this system, flow rate depends upon engine intake airflow (venturi signal), intake vacuum and exhaust backpressure. A plenum-mounted temperature control valve reduces EGR action at low temperatures for improved drivability.

Three major changes characterize the 1974 EGR

1. Use of the Floor Jet System is discontinued.

2. A Coolant Control EGR (CCEGR) Valve mounted in the radiator top tank or in the thermostat housing replaces the plenum-mounted valve previously used. The CCEGR valve blocks vacuum flow to the EGR valve whenever coolant temperature is below 65° F (95° F on some models), preventing exhaust gas from recirculating (Fig. 6-191).

3. An EGR Delay System fitted to some engines uses a firewall-mounted electric timer to control an engine-mounted vacuum solenoid and prevent EGR for approximately 35 seconds after turning the ignition on (Fig. 6-192).

ORIFICE SPARK ADVANCE CONTROL (OSAC)

This temperature-actuated vacuum control (Fig. 6-

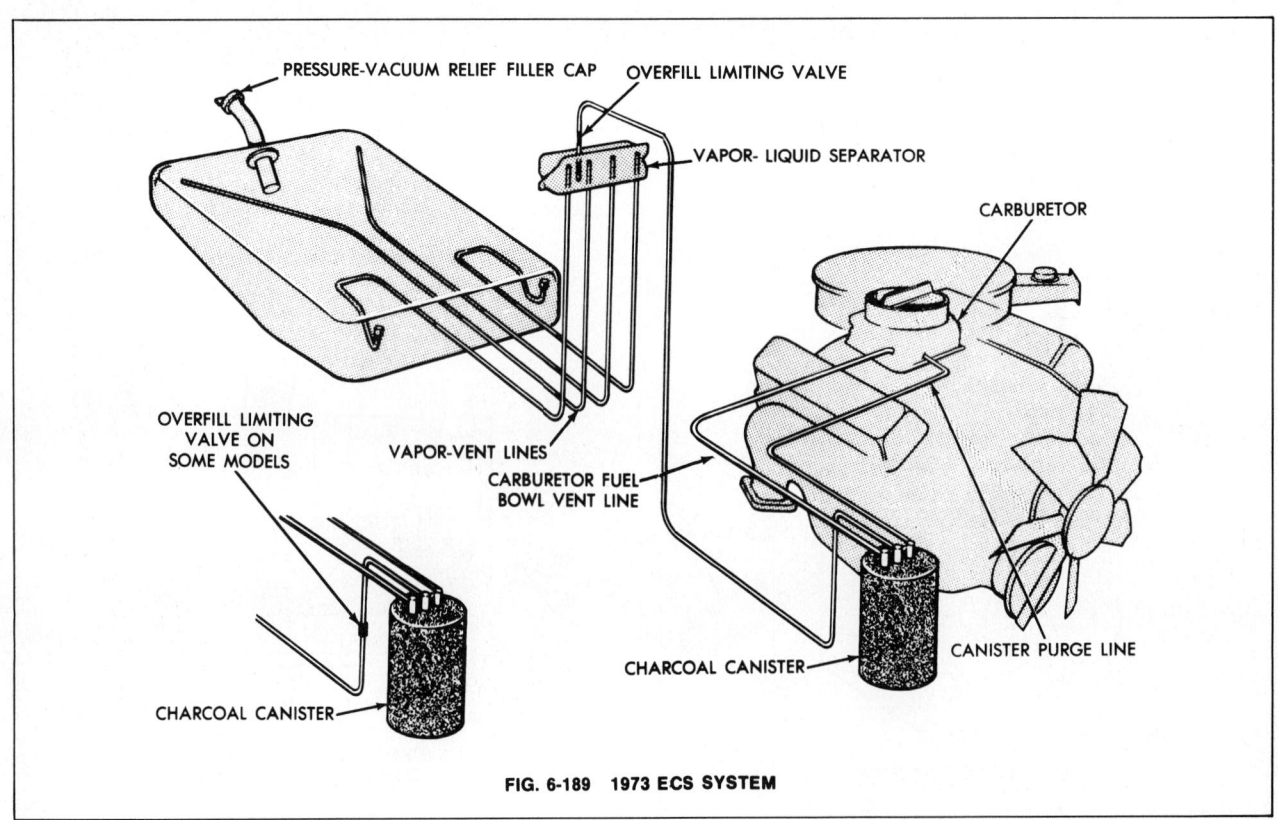

FIG. 6-189 1973 ECS SYSTEM

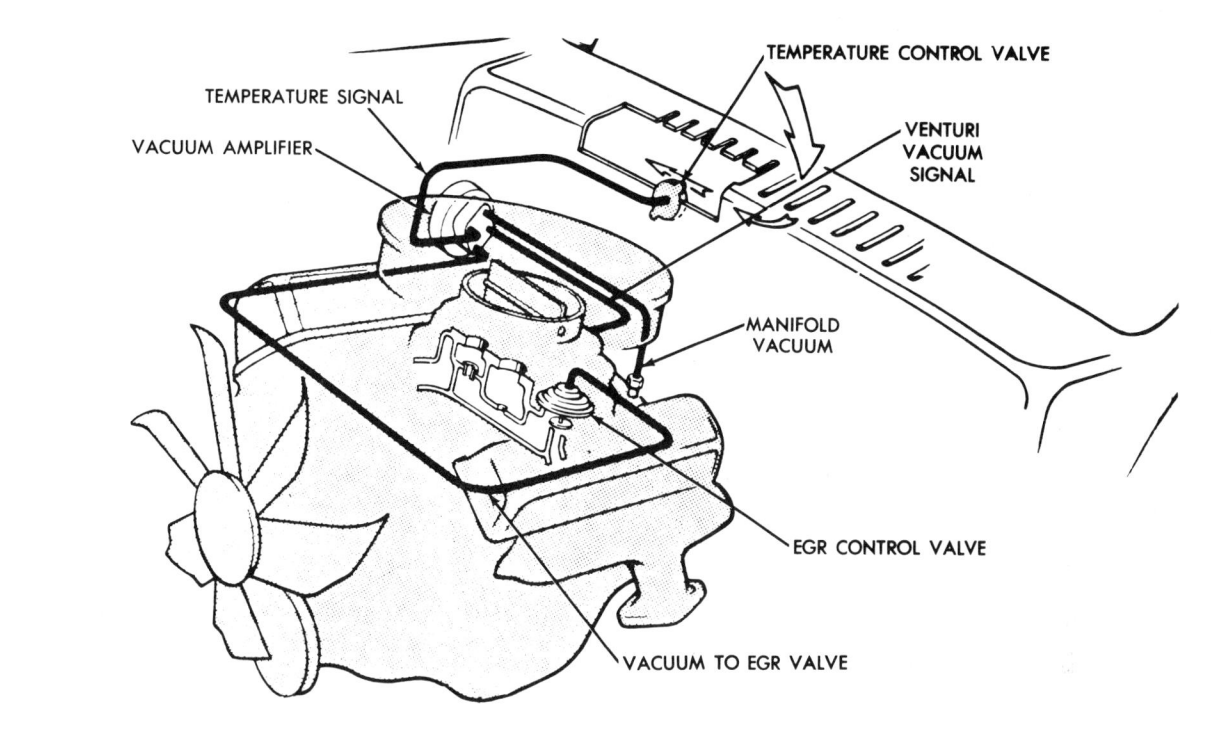

FIG. 6-190   1973 VENTURI VACUUM EGR SYSTEM

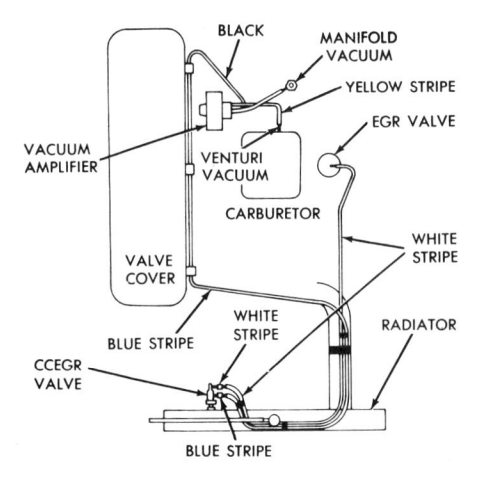

FIG. 6-191   TYPICAL EGR/CCEGR SYSTEM

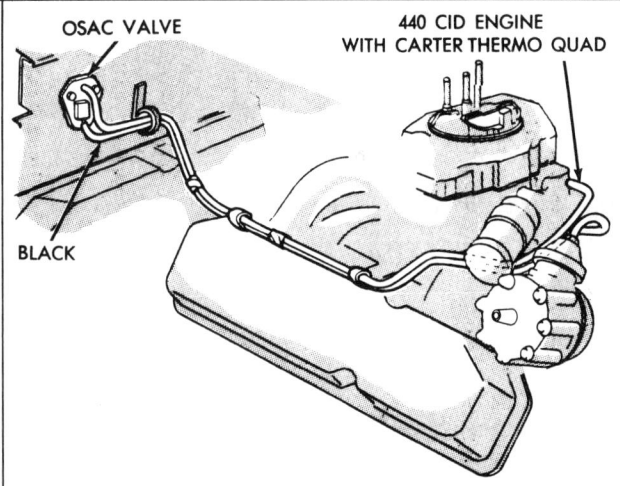

FIG. 6-193   TYPICAL 1973 OSAC VALVE SYSTEM

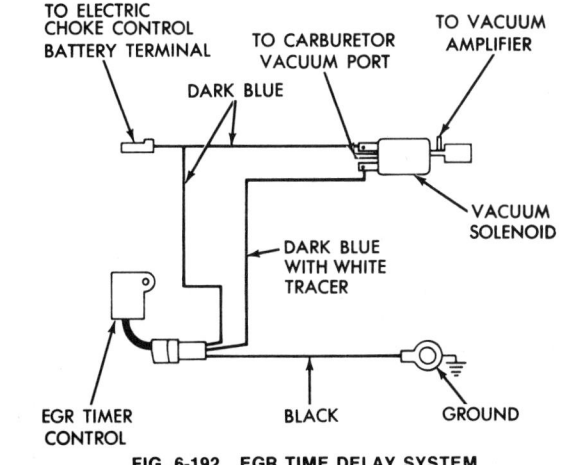

FIG. 6-192   EGR TIME DELAY SYSTEM

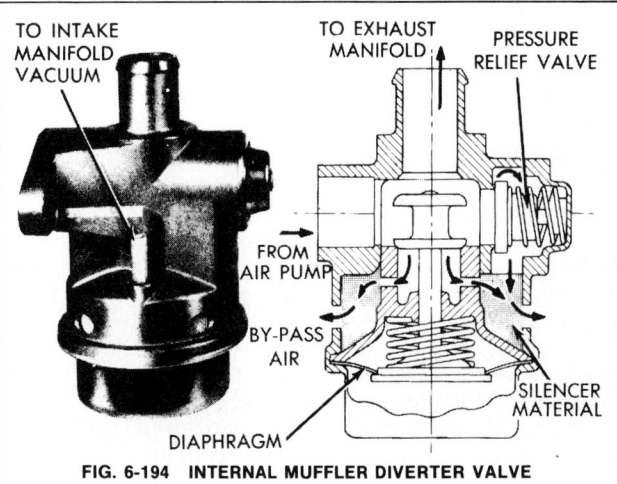

FIG. 6-194   INTERNAL MUFFLER DIVERTER VALVE

193) is mounted on the firewall on 1973 cars and in the air cleaner housing of 1974 vehicles, replacing the previously used solenoid vacuum valve. When going from idle to part throttle, a small opening in the OSAC valve delays the change in ported vacuum to the distributor by about 17 seconds, but when reversing the sequence (part throttle to idle), the change is instantaneous. Since vacuum is provided by a tap just above the carburetor throttle plates, manifold vacuum is not present under idle conditions, but as soon as the throttle plates open slightly, the system starts operating, providing the temperature is 58° F or higher. A temperature-operated vacuum bypass or Thermal Ignition (TIC) valve is used on some applications to increase engine idle at coolant temperatures above 225° F and provide additional engine cooling.

AIR INJECTION SYSTEM

Installed on all California 225, 360 and 440-cu.-in. engines for 1973 and all California 440-cu.-in. engines for 1974, the air injection system is an option on these engines in other states. An internal muffler-type diverter valve **(Fig. 6-194)** replaces the external type previously used, but system operation remains the same.

CHRYSLER, DODGE, PLYMOUTH, IMPERIAL
1975-76 Emission Systems

The Positive Crankcase Ventilation (PCV) system is the same as that used on 1970-72 models. For Orifice Spark Advance Control (OSAC), see 1973-74.

EVAPORATION CONTROL SYSTEM (ECS)

All 1976 vehicles are equipped with a rollover check valve located in the fuel-tank vent line between the fuel tank and the charcoal canister to prevent fuel leakage if the car is overturned in an accident. See Chapter 5, "Fuel Systems" for details, and **Fig. 5-6.**

HEATED AIR CLEANER

System operation remains the same as in previous years, but temperature control has been recalibrated from 10°, 100° and 95°-105° F to 10°, 90° and 85°-95° F for 1975 models, and 50°, 80° and 70° F (85° F on 360 HP and 4-bbl. 440 HP engines) for 1976.

EXHAUST GAS RECIRCULATION (EGR)

See 1973-74. The CCEGR valve used with 2-bbl. 360-cu.-in. engines is relocated in the engine block and opens at 125° F; other CCEGR applications remain mounted in the radiator top tank and open at 65° F. An EGR maintenance reminder light is added to the instrument panel and is designed to come on at 15,000-mile intervals to remind the driver that the EGR system should be serviced.

AIR INJECTION SYSTEM
CATALYTIC CONVERTER

All 1975-76 engines either use an air pump, a catalytic converter or both. Air Injection System operation remains unchanged. To prevent catalytic converter damage by excessive heat resulting from a system failure, a Catalyst Protection System is provided on all converter-equipped cars **(Fig. 6-195).** When engine speed exceeds 2000 rpm, an electronic speed switch energizes a throttle positioner solenoid to hold the throttle plates in a slightly open position. This increases airflow to the engine to reduce the amount of unburned hydrocarbons fed to the catalyst, and during a deceleration condition, the plates remain slightly open

until engine rpm drops below 2000, when the solenoid is de-energized and returns the throttle to the normal curb idle position.

ELECTRONIC LEAN BURN SYSTEM (ELB)

Introduced on the 1976 4-bbl, 440-cu.-in. engine in the middle of the model year, the ELB system **(Fig. 6-196)** makes possible the elimination of EGR, OSAC, Air Injection, the distributor vacuum-advance unit and, on cars not sold in California, the catalytic converter. To accomplish this, the engine's ignition system is controlled by a computer to instantly calculate constantly changing engine variables, ignite the spark plugs at precisely the right moment and thus produce complete combustion of very lean (up to 18:1) air/fuel mixtures. The ELB uses seven sensors to supply the necessary data to the computer:

1. A Start Pick-Up device **(Fig. 6-196)** in the distributor causes the plugs to fire at a fixed advance, but only during cranking.

2. A Run Pick-Up device **(Fig. 6-196)**, also located in the distributor, supplies the basic timing signal.

3. A Coolant Temperature Sensor located on the water pump housing signals the computer when engine coolant temperature is below 150° F and when it exceeds 225° F.

4. An Air Temperature Sensor housed in the computer body determines the temperature of the air admitted to the air cleaner from the fresh air system and the amount of extra ignition advance in conjunction with the Throttle Position Transducer signal.

5. The Throttle Position Transducer is located on the carburetor and provides two signals, one for throttle position and the other for rate of change. Extra advance is allowed when the throttle plates start to open and right up until they reach wide open throttle. This signal is monitored by the Air Temperature Sensor and advance is modified according to air cleaner temperature.

6. The Carburetor Switch Sensor is located on the end of the idle-stop solenoid plunger and tells the computer whether the engine is at idle, off idle or at cruising speed. Its signal also controls the Vacuum Transducer circuit.

7. The Vacuum Transducer tells the computer how much manifold vacuum is present. The higher the vac-

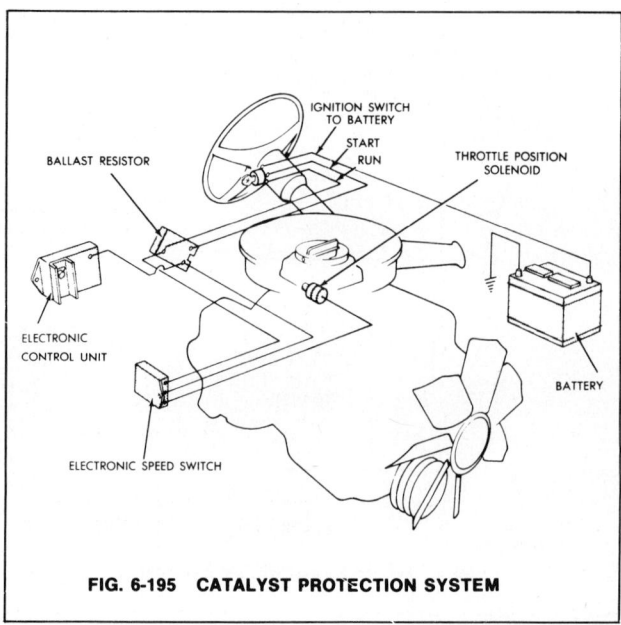

FIG. 6-195 CATALYST PROTECTION SYSTEM

uum, the more advance given, but the duration the Carburetor Switch Sensor is open controls the maximum rate of advance.

The Spark Control Computer **(Fig. 6-197)** consists of two electronic printed-circuit boards, the Program Schedule Module and the Ignition Control Module. The Program Schedule Module receives simultaneous signals from all seven sensors and computes engine operation to direct the Ignition Module to advance or retard spark plug firing accordingly. This is all done in a matter of milliseconds, and the advance curves obtainable are infinite and variable instead of the conventional constant curve.

ELB OPERATION

The instant the ignition key is turned to the ON position, the Start Pick-Up contacts the Ignition Module of the computer and extra ignition advance is provided during cranking to help the engine start. As soon as it

does start, the Run Pick-Up takes over and signals the computer, which maintains the extra advance for about 1 minute. During those 60 seconds, the extra advance is slowly eliminated and the Coolant Temperature sensor signals the computer to prevent any advance until the coolant reaches normal operating temperature. At this point, all sensors are transmitting their information and, although the Run Pick-Up sensor's signals create the basis for the maximum advance available at any engine speed, the other sensors' inputs serve to modify it. Should the coolant temperature rise above 225° F, the computer provides extra advance to cause the engine to run faster for increased cooling. If the computer should fail for any reason, the system will continue to operate in what is called the Limp-In Mode, permitting the driver to continue on until repairs can be made, but fuel economy and engine performance in this mode will be very poor. Should the Start Pick-Up

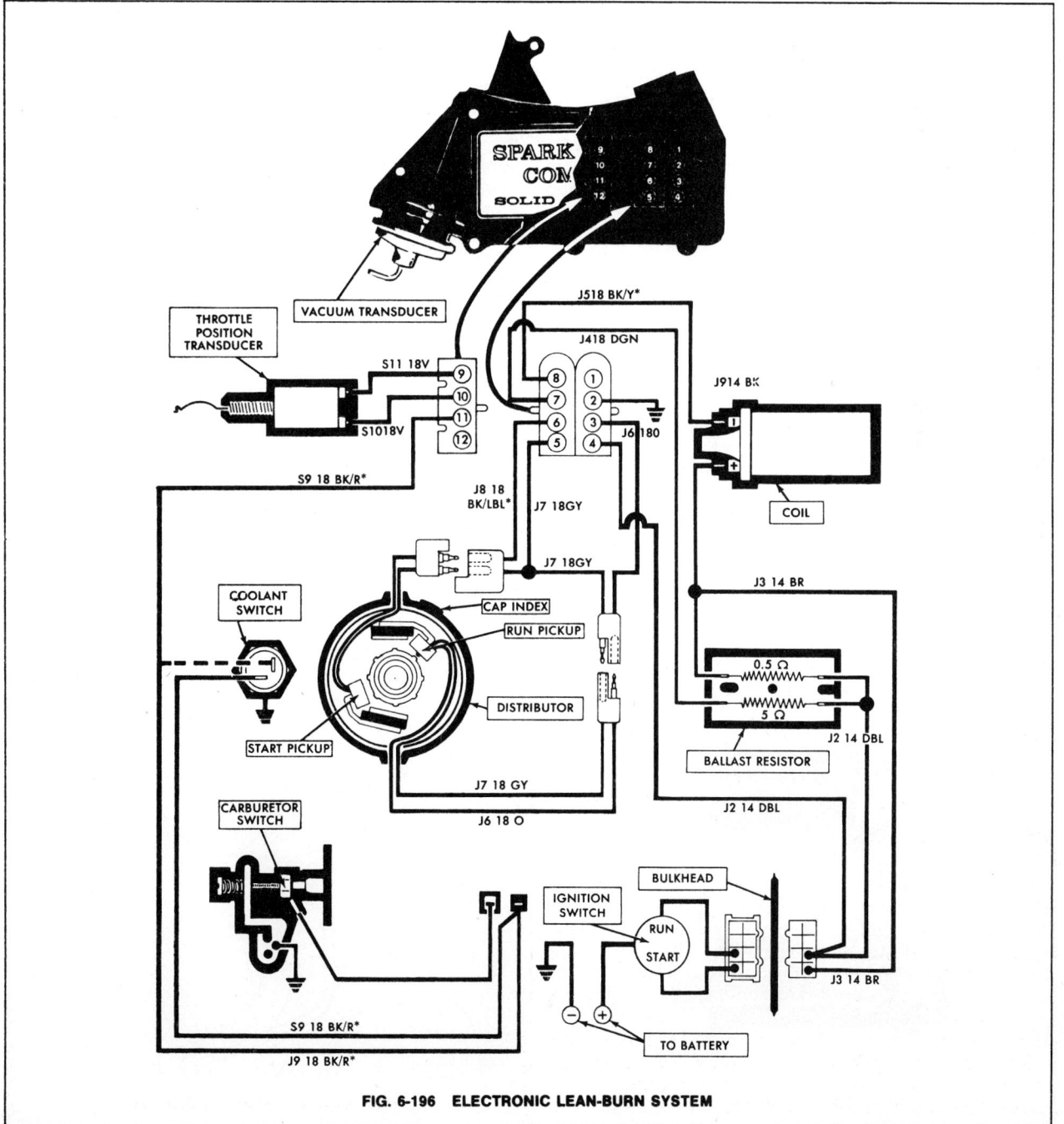

FIG. 6-196 ELECTRONIC LEAN-BURN SYSTEM

or Ignition Control Module function of the computer also fail, the engine will neither start nor run.

Electrical interference with the Spark Control Computer can cause backfiring, pinging and/or rough idling of 1976-77 400/440-cu.-in. engines when equipped with the 100-watt alternator. This can be corrected by repositioning the alternator ground (black) lead to move it away from the computer.

CHRYSLER, DODGE, PLYMOUTH
1977 Emission Systems

The Positive Crankcase Ventilation (PCV) system is the same as used on 1970-72 models. Orifice Spark Advance Control (OSAC) is the same as 1973-74 models. The Heated Air Cleaner is the same as 1975. Evaporation Control System (ECS) and Electronic Lean Burn (ELB) are carryovers from 1976.

CATALYTIC CONVERTER

The catalyst protection system is not used. Some engines have a mini-oxidation converter positioned between the engine exhaust manifold and the main underfloor converter. This small converter is designed to control NOx emissions, and is the first of the "three-way" converter systems to appear. Two designs are used: a mini-ox or single biscuit converter and a hybrid or double biscuit converter.

EXHAUST GAS RECIRCULATION (EGR)

The maintenance reminder light system was dropped in the 1976 model year. Both the ported vacuum and floor jet control systems are discontinued; all 1977 Chrysler Corporation cars use a venturi vacuum control system. The CCEGR valve is color-coded according to calibration, as follows:

Blue—opens at 75° F
Black—opens at 98° F
Yellow—opens at 125° F

Valve location differs according to engine. It may be found in the cylinder head (I-6), intake manifold (318/360 V-8), water pump housing (400/440 V-8), or radiator top tank.

AIR-INJECTION SYSTEM

Air injection is used with all California engines. A vacuum actuated, air switching valve is used on 225,

318 and 360-cu.-in. engines to prevent pump output from interfering with EGR system operation. During engine warmup, air is injected at the exhaust ports. As the engine warms up, airflow is switched by a coolant control engine vacuum switch (CCEVS) to a point downstream in the exhaust system where it can assist oxidation in the main catalyst without interfering with EGR. The CCEVS contains a bleed hole to permit a small amount of pump output to be injected at the exhaust ports at all times to help in CO and HC reduction.

CCEVS valve calibration is changed and valves are not color-coded according to calibration, as follows:

NEUTRAL .... OPEN BELOW 138° F
ORANGE .... OPEN BELOW 108° F
GREEN .... OPEN BELOW 86° F

All Omni/Horizon engines built through January 23, 1978 are equipped with the Air Injection System. California engines built after that date are equipped with Air Injection, while non-California engines are fitted with the Aspirator Air System.

ASPIRATOR AIR SYSTEM (Fig. 6-198)

All catalyst-equipped, non-California engines (except the I-6 225 and V-8 360 4-bbl. high-altitude calibrations) use an aspirator valve instead of an air-injection pump. This valve uses exhaust pressure pulsation to draw air into the exhaust system. The valve draws fresh air from the clean side of the air cleaner. This air passes a spring-loaded, one-way diaphragm in the valve to mix with exhaust gases during negative (vacuum) pulses which take place in the exhaust ports and manifold passages. When the pressure becomes positive, the diaphragm closes to prevent exhaust gases from passing back to the air cleaner. The aspirator system is efficient at idle and slightly off-idle speeds, since negative pulses are maximum during these modes. At higher engine speeds, the valve remains closed.

CHRYSLER, DODGE, PLYMOUTH
1978 Emission Systems

The Positive Crankcase Ventilation (PCV) system is the same as 1970-72 models; Orifice Spark Advance Control (OSAC) is the same as 1973-74; Evaporative

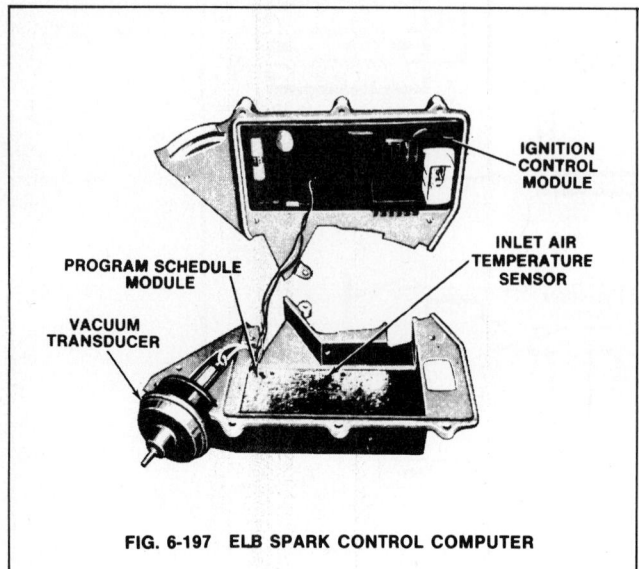

FIG. 6-197 ELB SPARK CONTROL COMPUTER

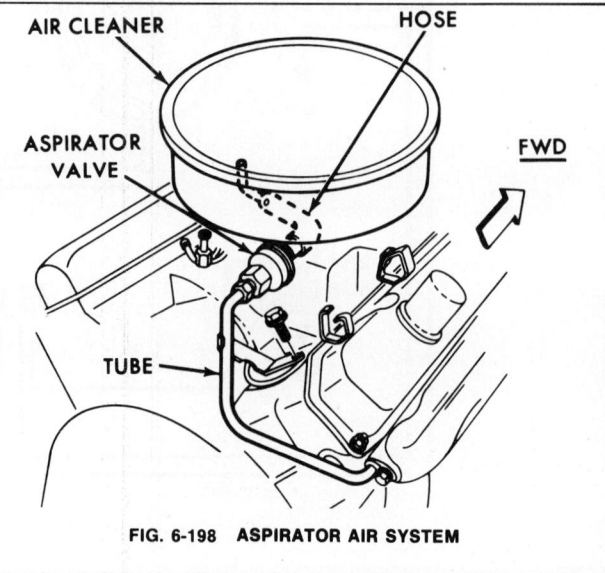

FIG. 6-198 ASPIRATOR AIR SYSTEM

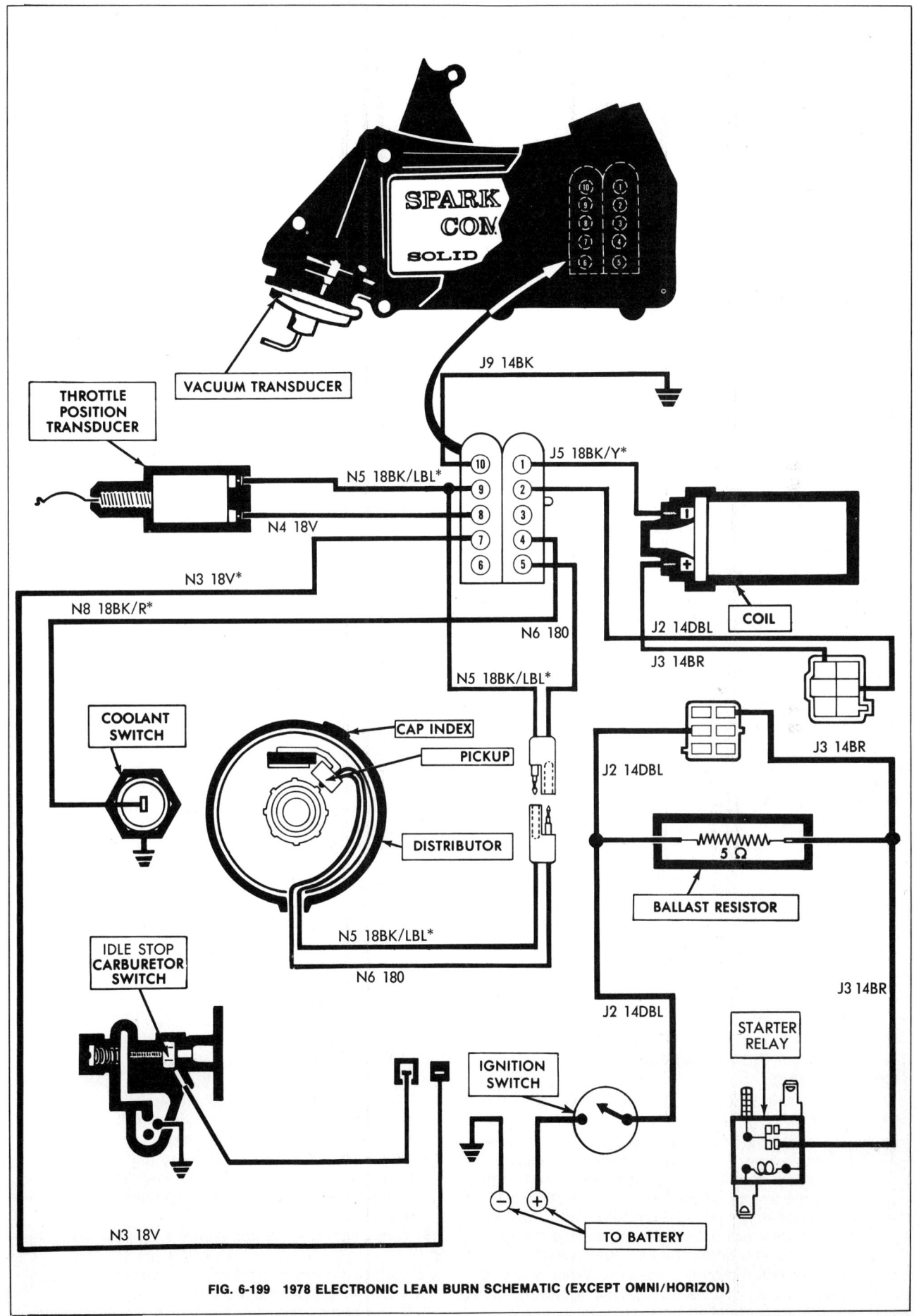

FIG. 6-199 1978 ELECTRONIC LEAN BURN SCHEMATIC (EXCEPT OMNI/HORIZON)

Control System is the same as 1976. The Aspirator Air System and Catalytic Converter are carryovers from 1977.

AIR INJECTION SYSTEM

Use of the 1977 air switching valve is extended to all 225/360-cu.-in. high-altitude engines. Two types of valves are used and are color coded according to application: Green for I-6 engines and Yellow for V-8 engines.

EXHAUST GAS RECIRCULATION

Ported vacuum control is used again on some applications, with venturi vacuum control on others. Both use the same type EGR valve, only the control method differs. A red CCEGR valve is added to those used in 1977. It is calibrated at 150° F and a ±5° F tolerance is applied to all valves used.

ELECTRONIC LEAN BURN (ELB) (Fig. 6-199)

The dual pick-up distributor is replaced by a single pick-up unit. The single pick-up coil controls both "start" and "run" modes. A second generation ELB spark control computer uses a single printed circuit board, with all components connected to the computer case by a single 10-pin wiring connector. The use of the air temperature sensor is discontinued.

When fitted to the Omni/Horizon, the ELB system is combined with a distributor containing a Hall Effect Pickup Assembly. This type of electronic ignition differs from Chrysler electronic ignition, and is discussed in Chapter 4. Test procedures for Omni/Horizon vehicles with the ELB system differ somewhat from those used with all other ELB applications and are provided separately.

CHRYSLER, DODGE, PLYMOUTH
1979 Emission Systems

All 1979 emission systems are carryovers from 1978, except as noted below.

AIR INJECTION SYSTEM

A blue-coded air switching valve is added for use with some California applications.

ELECTRONIC SPARK CONTROL (ESC) SYSTEM

For 1979, the Electronic Lean Burn (ELB) system is redesigned as Electronic Spark Control (ESC). System design and operation is essentially the same as in 1978 (Fig. 6-199). However, when the coolant switch has a TIC function, it is connected to cavity 6 in the 10-pin connector by a wire designated as N10 18BK/W.

EMISSION SYSTEM TEST PROCEDURES
Electronic Lean Burn (ELB) System Troubleshooting

Operation of the 1976-78 ELB system has resulted in considerable difficulty on the part of many drivers. System troubleshooting requires a special test analyzer which has not always been available when necessary. In addition, many problems elude the analyzer to the point where the owner often despairs of ever having the system function properly. From feedback provided by dealers, Chrysler has issued several service bulletins dealing with problems within the ELB fuel system which can result in common owner complaints. While some of these could also be caused by ignition system problems, the following guide is presented as a means of

diagnosing fuel system problems which can cause the ELB system to function in an erratic manner.

1. Engine turns over when cold, but does not start.
  a) Check for proper choke closing.
2. Engine turns over when hot, but does not start.
  a) Check for excessive float level, flooded engine or vapors in the carburetor bowl.
3. Engine starts when cold, runs up, and then dies.
  a) Check choke vacuum kick for a too-wide setting.
  b) Check the fast idle speed and/or fast idle cam for proper adjustment.
  c) Check for an intake vacuum leak.
  d) Check for a low float level or fuel pump pressure.
4. Engine dies on kickdown after a cold start.
  a) Check for an improperly adjusted choke vacuum kick, fast idle speed and/or fast idle cam setting.
5. Engine starts when cold, runs up, but idles slowly and spits out black smoke.
  a) Check for an excessively narrow choke vacuum kick setting.
  b) Check the fast idle speed and/or fast idle cam settings.
6. Engine starts when cold, but will not run up, and dies when the ignition key is released.
  a) Check for binding choke linkage.
7. Engine starts when cold, then stalls as transmission is shifted into gear.
  a) Check adjustment of choke vacuum kick, fast idle speed and/or fast idle cam.
8. Engine hesitates or stalls during initial acceleration.
  a) Check adjustment of choke vacuum kick and/or choke control switch.
  b) Check for low float level, weak accelerator pump output or incorrectly adjusted lockout.
  c) Make sure throttle plates are closing properly.
9. Engine hesitates or stalls after initial acceleration.
  a) Check for low float level, weak accelerator pump output or malfunctioning choke control switch.
10. Cold engine backfires intermittently.
  a) Check for plugged heat crossover system.
11. Engine stumbles or hesitates when under light accelerator pedal.
  a) Check for a vacuum leak.
  b) Check for weak accelerator pump output, low float level, sticking or binding metering rods, or a plugged carburetor idle/low-speed system.
  c) Check heated air cleaner system for a stuck snorkel valve.
12. Engine stumbles or hesitates under heavy accelerator pedal.
  a) See No. 11.
  b) Check for a plugged fuel filter, damaged fuel lines, or a malfunctioning fuel pump.
13. Warm engine surges at a steady low speed.
  a) Check for a vacuum leak, obstructed carburetor idle/low-speed system, low float level, stuck PCV valve, or air cleaner snorkel valve.
14. Warm engine surges at a steady high speed.
  a) Check for a vacuum leak, low float level, or obstructed fuel supply (damaged lines, plugged filter, defective pump).
15. Warm engine does not respond on light acceleration.
  a) Check for stuck metering rod carrier or secondary throttle plates that are not opening.
16. Warm engine stumbles and backfires intermittently.

a) Check for low float level, loose carburetor nee-dle valve seats or a malfunctioning air cleaner.

1976-79 ELB Ignition System Starting Test

This test procedure will determine whether the igni-tion system is the cause of a no-start condition.

1. Disconnect the coil high tension lead at the dis-tributor cap and hold its end about ¼-in. from a good engine ground.

2. Use an assistant or a remote start switch to crank the engine while checking for a spark at the coil lead.

3. If the ignition system is functioning satisfactorily, there will be a constant, bright blue spark. Continue cranking the engine while you slowly move the spark-ing lead away from the engine ground. If arcing occurs at the coil tower, replace the coil. If no arcing occurs, the ignition system is not responsible for the failure to start condition.

4. If there is no spark, or only a weak one, proceed to the Failure To Start Test below.

Failure To Start Test (Except OMNI/HORIZON)

Measure battery voltage before starting this test. The battery specific gravity must be a minimum of 1.220 (temperature corrected) if the necessary voltage to op-erate the starting/ignition systems is to be available.

Wiring connectors differ in 1978-79 systems. Con-nector terminals to be tested are listed for the 1976-77 system in the body of the test procedure, with 1978-79 terminals provided in parentheses.

1. Disconnect the coolant switch wiring harness connector.

2. Insulate the carburetor switch from the curb idle adjustment screw with a piece of paper.

3. Connect a voltmeter negative lead to a good en-gine ground.

4. Turn the ignition key to the RUN position. Mea-sure voltage at the carburetor switch terminal. If volt-age is greater than 5 volts, but less than 10 volts, move to Step 6. When voltage exceeds 10 volts, check for continuity between terminal 2 (10) of the dual connec-tor and ground.

5. If voltage is less than 5 volts, turn the ignition switch OFF and disconnect the connector located under the spark control computer. Turn the ignition back to RUN and measure voltage at terminal 4 (2) of the dual connector. If it is not within 1 volt of the previously measured battery voltage, check the wiring between terminal 4 (2) of the connector and ignition switch for an open, shorted or poor connection.

6. Return the ignition switch to an OFF position and disconnect the connector from under the spark control computer. Check for continuity between terminal 11 (7) of the connector and the carburetor switch terminal with an ohmmeter (with 1978-79 systems, also check for continuity between terminal 10 of the connector and ground). If there is continuity, replace the spark control computer with a known good unit; if not, check for an open or poor connection. Continue to the next step if the engine still will not start.

7. Turn the ignition switch to the RUN position and use the positive voltmeter lead to measure voltage at terminals 7 (1) and 8 (ground) of the disconnected computer lead. If it is not within 1 volt of the previously measured battery voltage:

a) Check terminal 7 (1) wiring and connections to the ignition switch. For 1976-77 systems only, also check the 5 ohm side of the ballast resistor.

b) Check terminal 8 wiring and connections to the ignition switch. Also check the ½-ohm side of the ballast resistor and the primary coil windings.

8. Turn the ignition switch to the OFF position. Use an ohmmeter to measure resistance between terminals 5 (5) and 6 (9) of the dual connector. If resistance is between 150-900 ohms, move to Step 9. If not, discon-nect the "start pick-up" coil leads from the distributor (1978-79 system has one pick-up coil lead assembly). This is the larger of the two connectors. Measure re-sistance at the leads to the distributor. If resistance is now within specifications, there is an open, shorted, or bad connection between the distributor connector and the connector terminals. If resistance is not within specs, replace the "start pick-up" (pick-up) coil.

9. Ground one ohmmeter lead and use the other to check continuity at each lead terminal to the distribu-tor. If continuity exists, replace the "start pick-up" (pick-up) coil. If there is no continuity, reconnect the distributor leads.

10. Remove the distributor cap and check the "start pick-up" (pick-up) coil air gap. Adjust to specifications if necessary.

11. Replace the distributor cap, reconnect all wiring connectors and attempt to start the engine. If the en-gine will not start, replace the spark control computer with a known good unit. Should the engine still refuse to start, reinstall the original computer unit and repeat the test procedure—you probably performed one or more steps incorrectly.

Failure to Start Test—OMNI/HORIZON

Measure battery voltage before starting this test. The battery specific gravity must be a minimum of 1.220 (temperature-corrected) if the necessary voltage to op-erate the starting/ignition systems is to be available.

1. Disconnect the lead at the coil negative terminal and the coil secondary wire at the distributor cap.

2. Turn the ignition key ON and briefly touch the negative coil terminal with a jumper lead while holding the coil secondary wire ¼-in. from a good engine ground. This should produce a spark. If it does not, check for voltage at the positive coil terminal with a voltmeter. If the voltage reads 9 volts, replace the coil. If it reads less than 9 volts, inspect the ballast resistor, wiring and connections. Should a no-start condition still exist, move to Step 3.

3. Turn the ignition key OFF, reconnect the lead to the coil negative terminal and disconnect the 3-wire harness at the distributor.

4. Turn the ignition key ON, ground one voltmeter lead and touch the other to pin B (top center) of the 3-wire harness leading to the spark control computer. If battery voltage is obtained, move to Step 7; if not, continue with Step 5.

5. Turn the ignition key OFF and disconnect the 10-wire harness to the spark control computer. Use an ohmmeter to check for continuity between pin B of the 3-wire harness to the spark control computer and pin 3 of the disconnected 10-wire harness. Repair the wire if the ohmmeter shows no continuity.

6. Now turn the key ON and measure voltage between pins 2 and 10 of the disconnected 10-wire harness. If battery voltage is shown, replace the spark control computer; if not, check the wiring and connections.

7. Turn the key OFF and reconnect the 10-wire har-ness. Turn the key back ON and short pin A to C of the 3-wire harness with a jumper lead, while holding the coil secondary wire ¼-in. from a good engine ground. A spark at this point means that the Hall Effect Pickup

Assembly is defective. If there is no spark, turn the key OFF and disconnect the 10-wire harness to the spark control computer.

8. Check for continuity with an ohmmeter between pin C of the 3-wire harness to the spark control computer, and pin 9 of the disconnected 10-wire harness connector. Then check for continuity between pin A of the 3-wire harness and pin 5 of the disconnected 10-wire harness. Replace the spark control computer if continuity exists. If no continuity exists, look for damaged or defective wires, repair and repeat Step 7.

1976-77 ELB Poor Performance Test—Run Pick-up Function

1. Start the engine and run for two minutes. Disconnect the "start pick-up" lead at the distributor. This is the larger of the two. Move to the next step if the engine stops.

2. Reconnect the leads and turn the ignition OFF. Disconnect the dual connector under the spark control computer. Use an ohmmeter to measure resistance between terminals 3 and 5 of the connector. If resistance is between 150-900 ohms, move to Step 4.

3. If resistance is not within specifications, disconnect the "run pick-up" (smaller) coil leads at the distributor and measure lead resistance to the distributor. If resistance is now within specifications, look for an open, shorted, or bad connection in the wires between the distributor connection and terminals 3 or 5 of the dual connector. If resistance is still out of specification, replace the run pick-up coil and repeat Step 1. Move to Step 4 if the engine still does not run.

4. Disconnect the run pick-up coil at the distributor. Ground one ohmmeter lead and check for continuity at each terminal lead to the distributor with the other ohmmeter lead. If there is continuity, replace the run pick-up coil and repeat Step 1. Move to Step 5 if the engine still does not run.

5. Remove the distributor cap and check the run pick-up coil air gap. Adjust to specifications if necessary and repeat Step 1. Move to Step 6 if the engine still does not run.

6. Replace the distributor cap, connect all wiring connectors and repeat Step 1. If the engine will not run, replace the computer with a known good unit, and repeat Step 1. Should the engine still refuse to run, reinstall the original computer and repeat the test procedure—you probably performed one or more steps incorrectly.

ELB/ESC Poor Performance Test

1976-77 START TIMER/1978-79 START UP ADVANCE TEST

This procedure requires the use of an adjustable timing light to determine the total amount of timing advance at the crankshaft.

1. Connect an adjustable timing light.

2. 1976-77—Have an assistant start the engine, snap the throttle open and close, and place the transmission selector in DRIVE position.

1978-79—Connect a jumper lead between the carburetor switch and engine ground, then start the engine.

3. 1976-77—Check the timing mark as soon as the transmission is placed in DRIVE. Adjust the timing light until basic ignition timing as specified is seen at the timing plate.

1978-79—Check the timing mark as soon as the engine is started. Adjust the timing light until basic ignition timing as specified is seen at the timing plate.

4. The timing light meter will now show the amount of advance indicated by specifications. Watch the timing for 90 seconds and adjust the timing light so that basic timing is maintained.

5. Any additional timing should reduce to basic timing after about 60 seconds. If it does, perform the *Throttle Advance Schedule Test*. If timing does not increase and/or does not return to basic timing, replace the Spark Control Computer.

ELB/ESC Poor Performance Test

1976-79 THROTTLE ADVANCE SCHEDULE TEST

Basic timing and curb idle must be within specifications before this test can be performed. Connect an adjustable timing light to check total advance at the crankshaft. Disconnect the throttle position transducer from the wiring harness, then start and run the engine for two minutes. Increase engine rpm to specified level (see emissions decal) and adjust timing light to show basic timing at the timing indicator. The extra advance shown on the timing light meter should be within specifications. If not, replace the spark control computer. Now proceed with the following test.

Connector terminals to be tested are listed for 1978 and later systems in the body of the test procedure, with 1976-77 terminals provided in parentheses.

1. With ignition switch OFF, disconnect the single connector from the bottom of the spark control computer.

2. Measure the resistance between terminals 8 (9) and 9 (10) of the connector with an ohmmeter. If resistance is between 60 and 90 (50 and 90) ohms, reconnect the connector to the spark control computer and perform Step 4 for 1976-77 systems; Step 5 for 1978 and later systems.

3. If resistance is not within specifications, disconnect the throttle position transducer and measure resistance at the transducer terminals. If resistance now reads as in Step 2, there is an open, short, or poor connection between the connector terminals and those connecting to the transducer. If resistance still is not within specifications, replace the transducer.

4. (1976-77 only) Reconnect all leads. Turn ignition switch to RUN but do not start engine. Ground a negative voltmeter lead and touch one terminal of the throttle position transducer with the positive lead. Watch the voltmeter while opening/closing the throttle. Repeat with the other transducer terminal. Either terminal should show between a 0.5 and 2-volt change which verifies transducer operation. But lack of the specified change may be caused by the spark control computer, so proceed to the next step before replacing the unit.

5. Place the throttle linkage on the fast idle cam and ground the carburetor switch with a jumper lead. Disconnect the transducer wiring harness and connect it to a known-good transducer of the same type. Compress the test transducer core until it is fully bottomed out and then start the engine. Wait about 90 seconds and then extend the core approximately one inch.

6. Adjust the timing light to show basic timing at the timing plate. The timing light meter should show the extra advance specified. Compress the transducer core again and timing should return to its basic setting. If timing advanced and returned properly, move to Step 7. If timing did not advance and/or did not return, replace the spark control computer.

7. Return the timing light meter to zero. Have an assistant compress/extend the test transducer core about one inch several times while you watch the timing marks. Look for an extra advance of 7 to 12° for about a second, then a return to the basic setting. If there is no advance/return, replace the spark control computer. For 1976-77 systems, also replace the transducer if it did not pass Step 4, since the computer is not at fault.

8. Replace the test transducer with the original one and reconnect all wiring.

ELB/ESC Poor Fuel Economy/High Idle Speed Test

COOLANT SWITCH TEST

1. Ground one ohmmeter lead to the engine and connect the other lead to the coolant switch terminal to check for continuity. 1976-77 switches have two terminals to be tested; 1978 and later switches have only one.

2. When the engine is cold (below 150°F), ohmmeter should indicate continuity on the terminal to which the black wire connects. With 1976-77 switches, there should be no continuity on the terminal with the orange wire. Replace the coolant switch if there is no continuity on black wire terminals, or if there is continuity on orange wire terminal.

3. Run the engine to bring it to normal operating temperature and recheck the terminals. There should be no continuity on any terminal. If there is, replace the coolant switch.

EMISSION SYSTEM TEST PROCEDURES

PCV TEST

1. Start the engine and let it idle. On 198- and 225-cu.-in. engines, clamp off the carburetor bowl vent to the fuel pump hose.

2. Remove the PCV valve from the rocker cover. If the valve is not plugged, the air passing through the valve will cause a hissing noise, and a strong vacuum can be felt when a finger is placed over the valve inlet (Fig. 6-200).

3. Replace the PCV valve and remove the crankcase inlet air cleaner. Hold a piece of stiff paper over the rocker cover opening. After crankcase pressure has been reduced, the paper should be sucked tightly against the rocker cover opening. If it is not, the ventilator hose, vent tube and lower carburetor passage must be cleaned.

4. Shut the engine off and remove the PCV valve

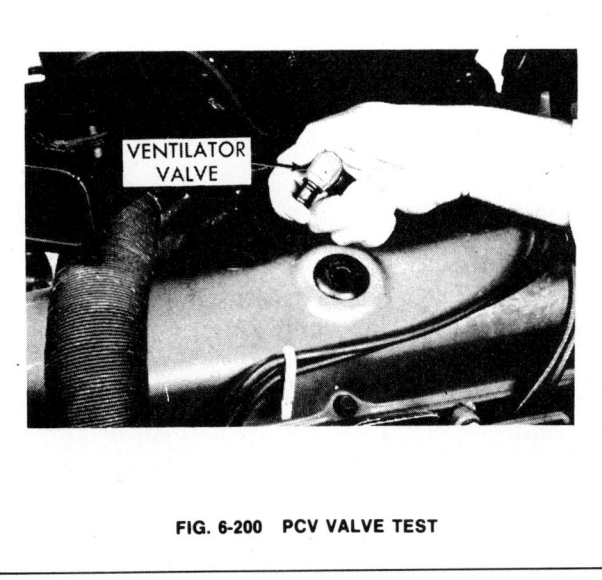

FIG. 6-200 PCV VALVE TEST

from the rocker cover again. Shake it vigorously, and a clicking noise should be heard, indicating that the check valve is free. If no noise is heard, replace the PCV valve.

HEATED AIR SYSTEM TEST

1. Check all hoses and connections to make sure they are correctly attached and in good condition.

2. With a cold engine and the engine compartment temperature below 75° F, the snorkel heat-control door or valve plate should be in the *up* or *heat on* position.

3. Start the engine and warm to normal operating temperature. When the air temperature entering the snorkel is 105° F or greater, the door should be in the *down* or *heat off* position.

4. Remove the air cleaner and let it cool to 80° F. Connect a hand vacuum pump and apply 20 ins. of vacuum to the thermostatic sensor. If the door does not rise to the *up* or *heat on* position, check the vacuum diaphragm operation.

5. Connect a hand vacuum pump directly to the vacuum diaphragm. Hand pump must have a gauge, and a bleed valve should be inserted in the line between the pump and the vacuum diaphragm. Apply 2 ins. of vacuum and shut off the line. The vacuum diaphragm should hold at least 10 ins. of vacuum for at least 5 minutes.

6. Release the vacuum on the vacuum diaphragm. Using the bleed valve and hand vacuum pump, slowly build vacuum back up and watch the door operation. It should lift off the snorkel bottom when 5 ins. of vacuum have been applied, and it should be in the full up position when no more than 9 ins. have been applied. If the vacuum diaphragm does not function within specifications, replace it; if the vacuum diaphragm operates satisfactorily, but proper temperature is not maintained, replace the sensor.

1971-72 NOx CONTROL SYSTEM TEST

MANUAL TRANSMISSION

1. Place the transmission in neutral. The plenum chamber must be at least 78° F. Turn the ignition switch to the RUN position.

2. Hold the solenoid vacuum valve and disconnect the wire from the B + connector at the ballast resistor. The valve should de-energize. Reconnect the wire and the valve should energize.

3. Place the transmission in high gear, then disconnect the B + connector at the ballast resistor and reconnect it immediately. The solenoid should not energize, indicating that the system is working electrically.

4. Now disconnect the solenoid-vacuum-valve blade terminal connections and connect a jumper lead from the ballast resistor piggyback connector to one of the valve blade terminals.

5. Connect a jumper lead from the other blade terminal to ground. If the solenoid does not energize with the ignition switch in the RUN position, replace it.

6. Disconnect the dual plug from the thermal switch and connect the plug sockets with a jumper lead. The solenoid vacuum valve should energize when the transmission is placed in neutral and the ignition switch is turned to the RUN position. If the solenoid vacuum valve will not energize with the thermal switch connected, but does energize when the plug is jumped, replace the thermal switch.

7. With the ignition switch in the RUN position and the transmission in neutral, remove the transmission switch connector and connect it to ground with a jumper lead. If the valve functions when this is done,

check the switch torque in the transmission housing—180 in.-lbs. are required for proper grounding. If torque is not the problem, replace the transmission switch.

AUTOMATIC TRANSMISSION

Because of the variables involved with the components used on automatic-transmission-equipped cars, no specific values are given with regard to temperature, vacuum or speed specifications. All are subject to variation among 1971-72 cars, and exact values are not considered necessary to functionally check the NOx system operation.

1. Start the engine and warm to normal operating temperature. Plenum chamber temperature must be above 78° F. Elevate the rear wheels to clear the floor.

2. Tee a vacuum gauge between the distributor and the solenoid vacuum valve. Disconnect the vacuum line at the vacuum switch on the control module and plug.

3. Run the engine at 850 rpm—the vacuum gauge should read zero.

4. Disconnect the control-module "T" connector electrical lead, and the vacuum gauge should read ported vacuum. Reconnect the wire, and the gauge should drop to zero.

5. Unplug and reconnect the vacuum line to the vacuum switch, then disconnect the single wire lead from the control module to the speed switch. The vacuum gauge should read ported vacuum.

6. Place the transmission in DRIVE—the sharp acceleration should drop the vacuum reading to zero at once. Accelerate the engine speed to 40 mph, and vacuum gauge should read ported vacuum once engine rpm stabilizes.

7. Reconnect the speed switch lead; disconnect and plug the vacuum line at the vacuum switch. The vacuum gauge should read zero.

8. Accelerate engine speed to over 30 mph. The vacuum gauge should indicate normal vacuum when a speed of approximately 30 mph is reached (this may vary considerably, depending upon the engine and the speed switch installed).

9. If no solenoid action takes place during the preceding steps, replace the control module.

EXHAUST GAS RECIRCULATION (EGR) TEST

1. Inspect all hose connections between the EGR valve, amplifier, intake manifold and the carburetor.

2. Connect a tachometer, start the engine and warm to normal operating temperature. Air temperature must be above 68° F.

3. Let the engine idle with the transmission in neutral and the carburetor throttle closed.

4. Abruptly accelerate the engine to 2000-2500 rpm, watching the EGR valve stem for movement. Repeat this several times to confirm the stem movement.

5. Connect a hand vacuum pump to the EGR valve and apply at least 10 ins. of vacuum. Engine should be warm and idling in neutral. Idle speed should drop 150 rpm or more when the vacuum signal is applied. If the speed change does not take place, or is less than the minimum specified, remove the EGR valve for inspection and cleaning.

6. Inspect the floor jets visually through the carburetor, using a flashlight. If the passage in the jet does not show an open path through the orifice, remove, clean and reinstall the jet.

CCEGR VALVE TEST

1. Disconnect the CCEGR-valve vacuum lines, and

remove the valve from the radiator top tank or engine thermostat housing. Place it in water at a temperature below 40° F, making sure that the threaded part is covered.

2. Connect a hand vacuum pump to the CCEGR valve nipple to which the blue or yellow striped hose connects. Apply a minimum vacuum signal of 10 ins. and hold. If the vacuum reading drops more than 1 in. in 1 minute, replace the valve.

EGR TIME DELAY SYSTEM TEST (THROUGH 1974 MODEL YEAR)

This test must be performed within 30 seconds once the ignition is turned on. One lead of a test lamp is connected to ground for each step of the test. The other lead is connected in turn as follows:

1. To the black wire in the timer connector. If the test lamp lights, check the wire from the timer to ground.

2. To the dark blue wire in the timer connector. If the test lamp does not light, check the wiring from the timer to vacuum switch and electric choke control.

3. To the dark blue wire with white tracer in the timer connector. If test lamp lights, replace timer.

4. To the dark blue wire with white tracer in the solenoid connector. If the test lamp lights, inspect the wiring from the timer to the solenoid.

5. To the dark blue wire in the solenoid connector. If the bulb lights, replace the solenoid. If it does not light, inspect the wiring from the vacuum solenoid to the electric choke control.

EGR TIME DELAY SYSTEM TEST (1975-77)

1. Inspect all wiring for proper connections.

2. With the ignition switch off, disconnect the wiring connector from the time-delay solenoid valve.

3. Connect a test lamp across the connector terminals. The test lamp current draw should not exceed 0.5-amp or the timer will be overloaded.

4. Start the engine. The test lamp should light immediately and stay on for 30 to 40 seconds. If the test lamp does not light, if it remains on indefinitely or does not meet delay time specifications above, replace the timer.

5. If the timer is replaced, repeat the test sequence on the new timer.

EGR MAINTENANCE REMINDER SYSTEM

This is a combination switch/counting device **(Fig. 6-201)** mounted inline with the speedometer cable about midway between the transmission and the speedometer head. At 15,000-mile increments, it activates an

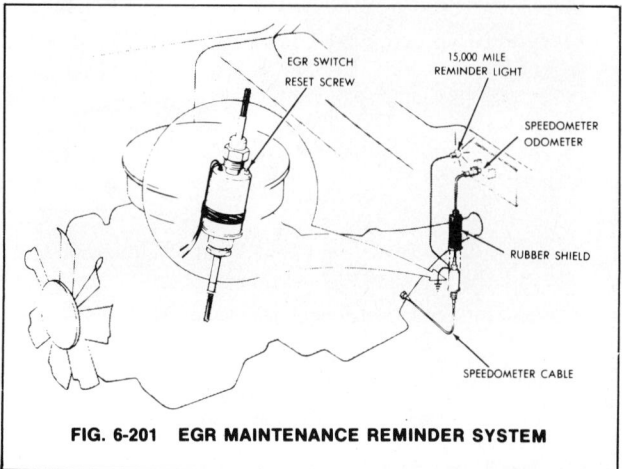

FIG. 6-201 EGR MAINTENANCE REMINDER SYSTEM

indicator lamp on the instrument panel to remind the driver that the EGR system should be serviced.

To reset the device and deactivate the signal warning light, locate the unit and pull back the protective rubber boot shield for access to the EGR switch reset screw. Approximately one-quarter turn with a screwdriver shuts off the indicator lamp, resets the switch and zeros the counter to begin another 15,000-mile counting increment.

OSAC VALVE TEST

1. Inspect all hoses and connections between the OSAC valve, the carburetor and the distributor. Replace any that may leak air.

2. Start the engine and warm to normal operating temperature. Tee a vacuum gauge into the OSAC valve line leading to the distributor.

3. Set the parking brake and increase engine speed to 2000 rpm, with the transmission in neutral. The vacuum gauge should show a very gradual increase, requiring 15-20 seconds to stabilize. If the vacuum reading reaches manifold vacuum immediately, or if no vacuum increase is noted, replace the valve.

THERMAL IGNITION CONTROL (TIC) VALVE

1. Connect a tachometer, start the engine and warm to normal operating temperature. The choke should be open.

2. For the purposes of this test *only*—set idle speed to 600 rpm.

3. Disconnect the line from the TIC No. 2 port **(Fig. 6-202)** and plug the hose. There should be no change in engine speed. If idle speed drops 100 rpm or more, replace the valve. Reconnect the vacuum line to the No. 2 port.

4. Block the radiator front to increase coolant temperature, but *do not* overheat the engine. If the engine idle speed does not increase 100 rpm or more before the temperature gauge has reached the top of the normal bar on its scale, replace the TIC valve.

5. Uncover the radiator and idle the engine to restore the coolant temperature to normal, then readjust the idle rpm to specifications.

EMISSION SYSTEM COMPONENT REPLACEMENT

AIR CLEANER ASSEMBLY

VACUUM DIAPHRAGM REPLACEMENT

1. Remove the air cleaner unit from the engine.

2. Disconnect the vacuum line from the diaphragm. Tip the diaphragm forward slightly to disengage the lock tangs, then rotate counterclockwise.

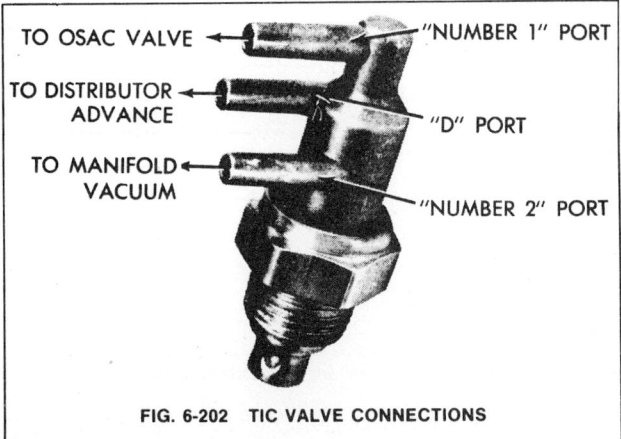

FIG. 6-202 TIC VALVE CONNECTIONS

3. With the diaphragm free from the snorkel tube, slide the assembly to one side to disconnect the operating rod from the heat control valve.

4. Check the heat control valve for freedom of operation and the hinge pin for foreign matter. Clean if necessary.

5. Insert the diaphragm operating rod through the snorkel, and engage the heat control valve.

6. Locate the diaphragm tangs in the snorkel tube opening and turn clockwise until the diaphragm is secured in place.

7. Connect a hand vacuum pump and apply 9 ins. of vacuum to the diaphragm nipple. The heat control valve should move freely under vacuum. If you operate the valve by hand, it will cock the operating rod and prevent proper system operation.

SENSOR REPLACEMENT

1. With the air cleaner removed from the engine, disconnect the sensor vacuum lines.

2. Remove the two retaining clips and discard, then remove the sensor with its gasket and discard.

3. Place a new sensor gasket on the air cleaner housing and replace the new sensor unit. Support the sensor on the outer diameter while installing the new retainer clips furnished. Make sure that the gasket is properly compressed to form an air seal.

AIR INJECTION PUMP REMOVAL/INSTALLATION

TO REMOVE

1. Disconnect the air and vacuum lines from the diverter valve.

2. Loosen the air pump pivot and adjusting bolts, then remove the drive belt from the pulley.

3. Remove the air pump pivot and adjusting bolts from the pump brackets, and lift the air pump assembly from the engine.

4. Remove the pulley brackets and diverter valve from the air pump housing.

TO INSTALL

1. Replace the air pump pulley and brackets on the air pump housing. Torque pulley screws to 35 in.-lbs. and bracket bolts to 30 ft.-lbs.

2. Attach the diverter valve to the air pump housing.

3. Fit the air pump assembly on the engine and loosely replace the pump pivot and adjusting bolts.

4. Replace the drive belt on the air pump pulley and adjust tension. Torque mounting bolts to 30 ft.-lbs.

5. Reconnect the air line and vacuum hose to the diverter valve.

DIVERTER VALVE REPLACEMENT

1. With the air pump removed from the engine, unscrew the screws holding the diverter valve to the air pump housing.

2. Remove the diverter valve and the gasket material from both the pump and valve flanges.

3. Install a new gasket on the pump flange.

4. Replace the diverter valve and torque the screws to 95 in.-lbs. before reinstalling the air pump assembly to the engine.

CENTRIFUGAL FILTER FAN REPLACEMENT

1. With the air pump assembly removed from the engine, insert needlenose pliers between the plastic filter fins, and break the fan from the hub. *Do not* use a screwdriver blade between the pump and the filter. *Do not* try to remove the metal drive hub.

2. Position a new fan over the shaft and draw into place, using the pulley and bolts as tools. Tighten the

bolts alternately, and make sure the outer edge of the fan slips into the housing. A new fan is likely to make noise for 20-30 miles until it seats properly.

CHECK VALVE REPLACEMENT

1. Release the clamp and disconnect the air line from the check valve inlet.
2. Remove the screws holding the injection tube to the exhaust manifold, and lift the injection tube assembly from the engine.
3. Clean gasket material from the exhaust manifold and the injection tube flanges.
4. Fit new gaskets on the exhaust manifold flanges and replace the injection tube assembly. Torque flange-mounting and injection-tube bracket screws to 200 in.-lbs.
5. Reconnect the air line to the check valve inlet and secure with the clamp.

VAPOR CANISTER FILTER REPLACEMENT

1. Remove the lines attached to the top of the vapor canister.
2. Loosen the attaching bracket bolts and remove the canister.
3. Turn the canister over and pull the fiberglass filter out from under the retainer bar.
4. Tuck a new filter under the retainer bar and center it in the canister bottom.
5. Replace the canister in the attaching bracket, and tighten the bolts.
6. Reconnect the lines to the canister nipples.

AMERICAN MOTORS

1970-72 Emission Systems

POSITIVE CRANKCASE VENTILATION (PCV)

All AMC vehicles are equipped with a closed crankcase ventilation system **(Figs. 6-203 & 6-204)**. A non-vented oil-filler cap prevents crankcase gases from escaping under no-vacuum conditions. A tube from the air cleaner goes to the rocker cover, carrying fresh air through the air cleaner filter and down into the crankcase. On AMC 6-cyl. engines, the air passes through a wire gauze filter in the hose connection between the air cleaner and the cylinder head cover; on V-8 engines, it passes through a wire mesh filter in the oil filler cap. When manifold vacuum is low, a calibrated amount of air is reverse-flowed through the PCV valve. Crankcase vapors are drawn through the air cleaner element into the carburetor and burned along with the air/fuel mixture. American Motors PCV valves are color-coded to engine application **(Fig. 6-205)**.

THERMOSTATICALLY CONTROLLED AIR CLEANER (TAC)

Installed on all 1970-71 V-8 engines equipped with either Shift-Command automatic transmission or a manual transmission with 4-bbl. carburetor, and all 1972 engines, the air cleaner thermostatically controls the temperature of the air entering it **(Fig. 6-206)**. When this air is less than 120° ±10° F, the valve plate in the snorkel air tube is maintained in a *heat on* position by the valve plate spring. This closes off air from the engine compartment, and air is drawn instead from the exhaust manifold shroud. As the air temperature reaches 110° F, the thermostat begins to open, pulling the valve plate down to allow cooler air from the engine compartment to enter the air cleaner. Once air temperature reaches 120° to 130° F, the valve plate

should be in the *heat off* position to permit only engine compartment air to enter. On 6-cyl. applications, a PCV wire gauze filter is included in the air cleaner connecting hose. This must be removed from inside the air cleaner cover before attempting to remove the molded air inlet hose, or damage will result to the hose.

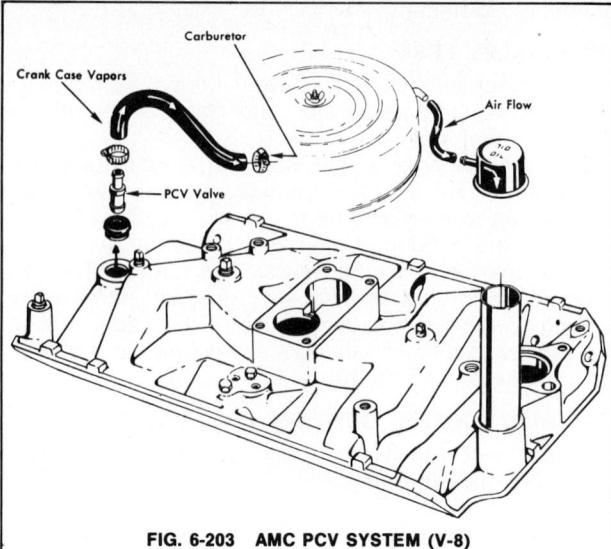

FIG. 6-203 AMC PCV SYSTEM (V-8)

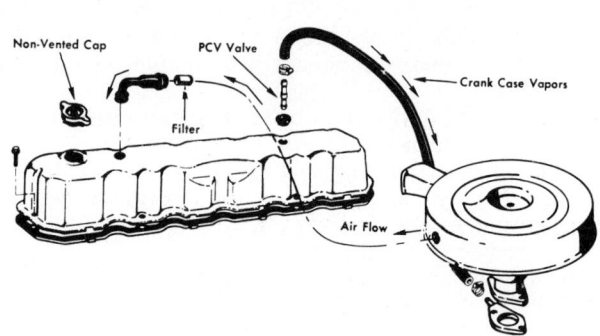

FIG. 6-204 AMC PCV SYSTEM (I-6)

ENGINE MANIFOLD VACUUM			Airflow 232-258 304-360 390-401	CFM 199-232
		In. Hg	Black Color Valve	Silver Color Valve
IDLE		20	1.3-1.7	1.3-1.7
TEST	Min. Flow	18	1.3-1.7	1.3-1.7
POINT		16	1.3-1.7	1.3-1.7
		14	1.5-2.0	1.3-1.7
		12	1.7-2.5	1.3-1.7
		10	2.1-2.8	1.3-1.7
		8	2.4-3.4	1.3-1.7
CRANKING*		6	2.7-3.7	1.3-1.7
SPEED				
TEST	Max. Flow	4	3.2-4.2	1.7
POINT		2	3.3-4.4	1.7

*Coil secondary wire removed and grounded, carburetor throttle at curb idle.

FIG. 6-205 AMC PCV-VALVE FLOW CHART

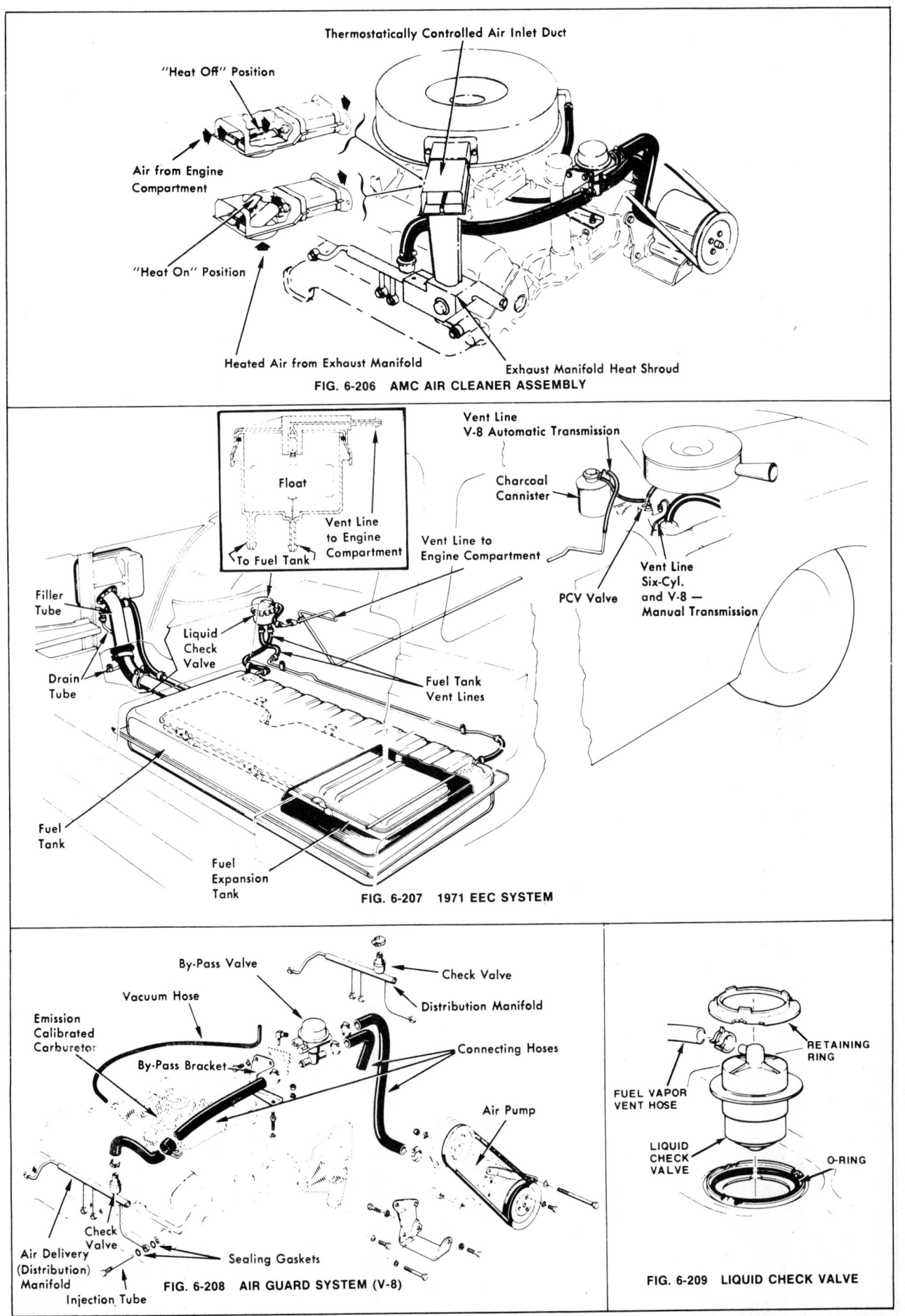

Thermostatically Controlled Air Inlet Duct

"Heat Off" Position

Air from Engine Compartment

"Heat On" Position

Heated Air from Exhaust Manifold

Exhaust Manifold Heat Shroud

FIG. 6-206   AMC AIR CLEANER ASSEMBLY

Float

Vent Line to Engine Compartment

To Fuel Tank

Vent Line V-8 Automatic Transmission

Charcoal Cannister

Vent Line to Engine Compartment

PCV Valve

Vent Line Six-Cyl. and V-8 — Manual Transmission

Filler Tube

Liquid Check Valve

Drain Tube

Fuel Tank Vent Lines

Fuel Tank

Fuel Expansion Tank

FIG. 6-207   1971 EEC SYSTEM

By-Pass Valve

Vacuum Hose

Check Valve

Distribution Manifold

Emission Calibrated Carburetor

By-Pass Bracket

Connecting Hoses

Air Pump

Check Valve

Air Delivery (Distribution) Manifold

Sealing Gaskets

Injection Tube

FIG. 6-208   AIR GUARD SYSTEM (V-8)

RETAINING RING

FUEL VAPOR VENT HOSE

LIQUID CHECK VALVE

O-RING

FIG. 6-209   LIQUID CHECK VALVE

DISTRIBUTOR VACUUM ADVANCE

In 1970, a dual-diaphragm vacuum advance is used on distributors fitted to all 199, 232, 304, 360 and 390-cu.-in. engines to provide further timing retard during idle conditions. The outer or primary diaphragm uses carburetor vacuum to advance ignition timing, while the inner or secondary diaphragm is operated by intake manifold vacuum for additional retard during closed throttle idle to reduce hydrocarbon emissions.

DECEL VALVE

A deceleration valve is fitted to all 199, 232 and 390-cu.-in. engines in 1970 equipped with manual transmissions, and is connected to the dual-diaphragm vacuum advance unit. As intake manifold vacuum rises during deceleration, the valve shuts off carburetor vacuum to provide full manifold vacuum to the outer vacuum-advance diaphragm, producing maximum ignition timing advance to prevent after-burning. When the engine reaches idle, the valve switches vacuum flow from the manifold back to the carburetor.

EVAPORATIVE EMISSION CONTROL (EEC)

Installed on all AMC 1970 California cars and nationwide on all 1971-72 cars, this closed fuel-tank vent system **(Fig. 6-207)** prevents raw fuel vapor from entering the atmosphere by routing it into the PCV system, where it is burned with the air/fuel mixture. The 1970 EEC system includes the fuel tank with integral expansion tank, a fuel tank vent with check valve and a fuel-tank filler cap with a two-way relief valve calibrated to open when a pressure of 0.5 to 1.0 psi or a vacuum of 0.25 to 0.5 ins. occurs within the tank. A charcoal vapor canister is added to 1971 cars fitted with a V-8 engine and the Shift-Command transmission; 1971-72 Gremlin fuel tanks do not include the integral expansion tank.

AIR GUARD SYSTEM

This system **(Fig. 6-208)** is fitted to all 1970-72 AMC V-8 engines equipped with manual transmissions. It consists of a belt-driven air pump with integral relief valve, a bypass valve, check valve, distribution manifolds, injection tubes and the necessary connecting hoses. Intake air passes through a centrifugal fan at the front of the pump and is delivered to the intake manifold. During sudden deceleration, vacuum causes the bypass valve to open, passing pump air into the atmosphere. The check valves on each side of the intake manifold contain one-way diaphragms which prevent hot exhaust gases from backing up in the hose and damaging the pump during periods of pump belt failure, excessive system pressure or hose ruptures.

TRANSMISSION-CONTROLLED SPARK (TCS)

TCS is used on all 1971-72 California cars and all 1971 nationwide cars with the 304-cu.-in. engine and automatic transmission, and 1972 360-cu.-in. engines with automatic transmission. A transmission switch, operated by the speedometer gear speed, opens when car speed exceeds 30 mph, breaking the ground circuit to the solenoid vacuum valve. With the valve de-energized, ported vacuum is applied to the distributor to provide normal vacuum advance. At speeds below 25 mph, the transmission switch closes, completing the ground circuit to the solenoid vacuum valve, which vents ported vacuum to the atmosphere. Manual applications operate in essentially the same manner, except that the transmission switch is manually operated by the shifter shaft and the solenoid vacuum valve is de-energized when the transmission is shifted into high gear.

COOLANT TEMPERATURE OVERRIDE SWITCH

Located in the thermostat housing, this thermal switch is fitted to all 1972 V-8 engines with automatic transmission to route either intake manifold vacuum or carburetor ported vacuum to the distributor advance unit. At temperatures below 160° F, intake manifold vacuum is transmitted; at temperatures above 160° F, carburetor ported vacuum is sent.

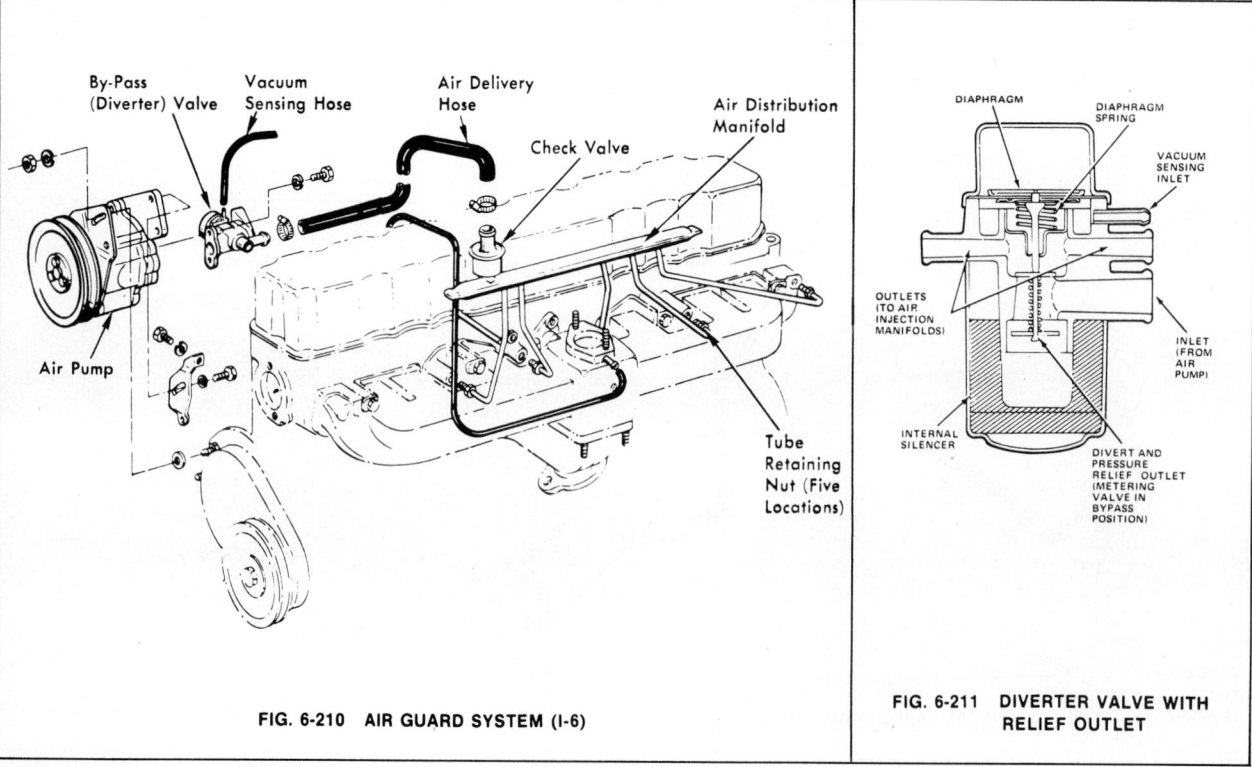

FIG. 6-210 AIR GUARD SYSTEM (I-6)

FIG. 6-211 DIVERTER VALVE WITH RELIEF OUTLET

AMERICAN MOTORS
1973-74 Emission Systems

The Positive Crankcase Ventilation (PCV) and Thermostatically Controlled Air Cleaner (TAC) systems are the same as those used in 1970-72.

EVAPORATIVE EMISSION CONTROL (EEC)

Vapor storage canister use is extended to all cars. The 1973 I-6 canister contains an integral purge valve, but this is dropped for 1974. All canisters use a replaceable filter pad through which outside air is drawn into the canister. A new liquid check valve, mounted in the top of the fuel tank, picks up vapor directly from the tank, passing it to the storage canister through a vent hose **(Fig. 6-209).**

AIR GUARD SYSTEM

System use is extended to 1973 I-6 engines installed in Matador station wagons. The air pump previously used is retained on 1973 V-8 engines; a different pump

without the integral relief valve is fitted to the I-6 engines **(Fig. 6-210).** The I-6 relief valve assembly is part of the diverter valve. In 1974, the I-6 pump replaces the previously used V-8 pump. The pressure relief valve for both is included in a new diverter valve **(Fig. 6-211)** which incorporates an internal silencer.

TRANSMISSION-CONTROLLED SPARK (TCS)

TCS use is extended to all engines except the 401-cu.-in.; the 1973 system is the same as that used in 1971-72. An adjustable TCS control switch, operated by governor oil pressure, is added in 1974 to all applications **(Fig. 6-212).** The TCS control switch is located on the right rear of I-6 blocks and on a bracket at the rear of the right valve cover on V-8s. The ambient temperature override switch is eliminated for 1974.

COOLANT TEMPERATURE OVERRIDE (CTO)

The CTO switch is relocated on 1974 I-6 engines to a boss on the left front side of the engine block. The V-8 switch location is the same, but the 304-cu.-in. engine

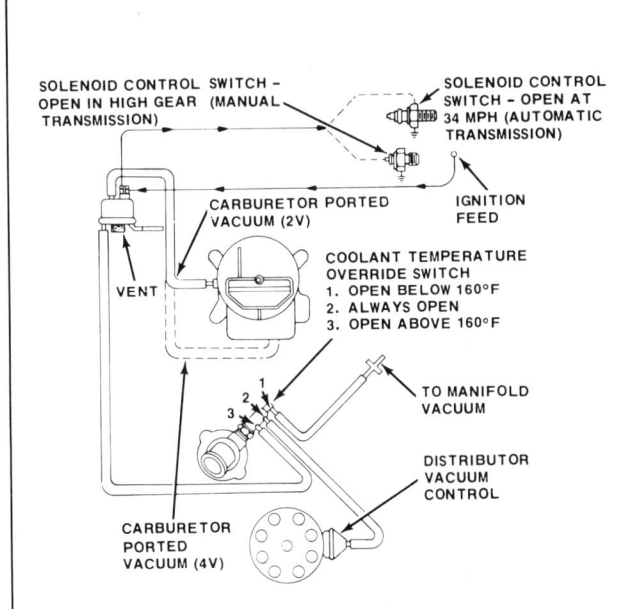

FIG. 6-212 1974 V-8 TCS SYSTEM

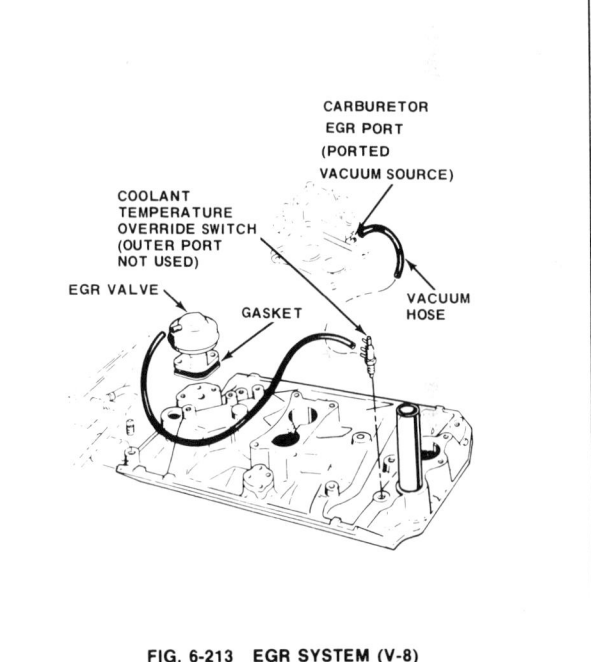

FIG. 6-213 EGR SYSTEM (V-8)

VENDOR PART NUMBER		VACUUM REQUIRED (Ins.) Hg		
(Located on Valve)		AMC Part Number	Open Start	Open (max.)
7046390		3227072	2.8 to 3.2	4.5 to 6.6
7040176	Nationwide	3218739	2.8 to 3.2	5.3 to 5.7
7030881		3219052	2.8 to 3.2	6.9 to 7.3
17050472		3223981	1.8 to 2.2	3.8 to 4.2
	California			
7043589		3225951	1.8 to 2.2	2.8 to 3.4
7051782		3227598	1.8 to 2.2	6.0
17050471		3223980	1.8 to 2.2	5.5

FIG. 6-215 EGR-VALVE VACUUM SIGNAL VALUES

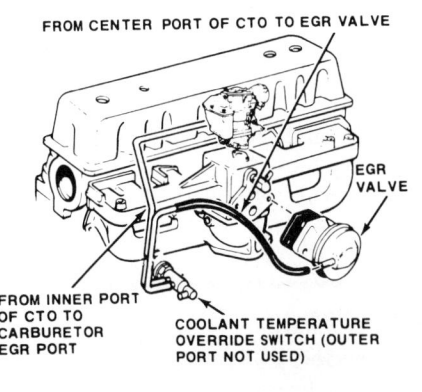

FIG. 6-214 EGR SYSTEM (I-6)

with manual transmission now has a switching temperature of 115° F instead of the previous 160° F.

EXHAUST GAS RECIRCULATION (EGR)

This system (Figs. 6-213 & 6-214) is installed on all 1973 V-8's and those I-6 engines used in the Matador. A vacuum-operated recirculation control valve, mounted at the rear of the intake manifold on V-8 engines and the intake manifold side of I-6 engines, regulates the amount of exhaust gases and the duration of time they enter the intake manifold. When the throttle valves are opened beyond the idle position, vacuum is applied against the EGR-valve actuating diaphragm. As the diaphragm moves up against spring pressure, it opens the exhaust-gas intake valve, allowing exhaust gases from the manifold crossover exhaust channels (V-8) or from below the riser area (I-6) to be drawn back into the engine intake. The valve remains closed during idle and deceleration, when excessive exhaust gases added to the air/fuel mixture would cause rough idling.

The 1973 EGR system operation is modified by the following devices:

1. Coolant Temperature Override Switch—This CTO is located beside the oil filler tube on V-8 engines and at the left side of the engine block on I-6 engines. The outer port is open and not used, the inner port connects to the carburetor EGR fitting, and the center port connects to the EGR valve. When coolant temperature is under 115° F (160° F on the 1973 304-cu.-in. with manual transmission), no vacuum is applied to the EGR valve. Above that temperature, the vacuum signal is allowed to pass, subject to regulation by the Low and High Temperature Signal Modulators.

2. Low Temperature Vacuum Signal Modulator—Located at the left side of the front upper crossmember, the LTVSM is connected to the EGR signal line. When ambient temperature is below 60° F, the modulator opens, causing a weakened vacuum signal to the EGR valve and decreasing the amount of exhaust gas recirculated. This device is not used on 1974 systems.

3. High Temperature Vacuum Signal Modulator—Located at the rear of the engine compartment, the HTVSM is also connected to the EGR signal line. This modulator opens when engine compartment temperature reaches 115° F, reducing the vacuum signal to the EGR valve and decreasing the amount of exhaust gas recirculated. This device is not used after 1973.

1974 California EGR Changes:

1. The EGR valves used on California cars have different-value operating characteristics and are not interchangeable (Fig. 6-215).

2. An exhaust backpressure sensor is used with all I-6 and the 304-360-cu.-in. V-8 engines with automatic transmission. Different sensors are fitted to single and dual exhaust systems, compensating for differences in exhaust backpressure between the two systems (Fig. 6-216).

3. Some 258- and 304-cu.-in. engines have a stainless-steel restrictor plate under the sensor, with gaskets used on both sides of the restrictor plate (Fig. 6-217).

AMERICAN MOTORS

1975-76 Emission Systems

The Positive Crankcase Ventilation (PCV) system is the same as used in 1970-72 AMC cars. Evaporative Emission Control System (EEC), Exhaust Gas Recirculation (EGR) and Air Guard System, see 1973-74.

THERMOSTATICALLY CONTROLLED AIR CLEANER (TAC)

A polyurethane-foam PCV air-inlet filter is located in a retainer in the air cleaner housing (Fig. 6-218) on I-6 engines, and in the sealed oil filler cap on V-8 engines.

TRANSMISSION-CONTROLLED SPARK ADVANCE (TCS) SYSTEM

See 1973-74. This system is used only on 1975-76 California cars.

COOLANT TEMPERATURE OVERRIDE (CTO)

Changed to a two-port switch (Fig. 6-219). Opening temperature is indicated by color: 115° F versions have a black body or paint dab; 160° F versions have a yellow body or paint dab.

CATALYTIC CONVERTER

The following are equipped with a catalytic converter system for 1975-76 to reduce emissions and improve drivability:

One Converter	Two Converters
All California I-6 engines	All California V-8 engines
Nationwide, 2-bbl. V-8 engines	Nationwide 4-bbl. V-8 engines
Matador I-6 engines with manual transmission	

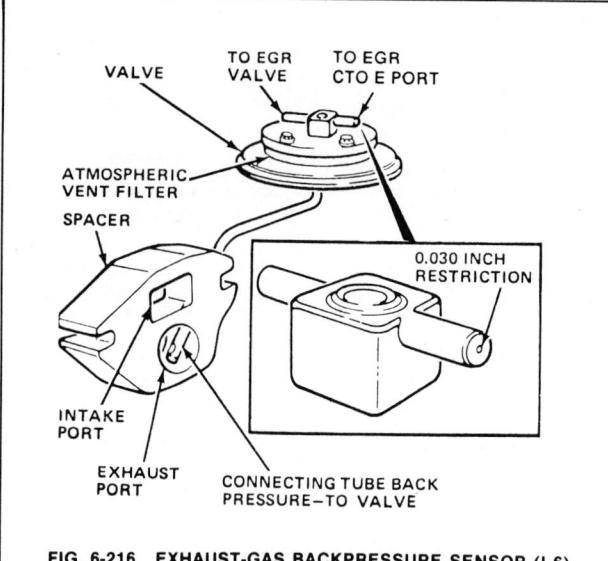

FIG. 6-216   EXHAUST-GAS BACKPRESSURE SENSOR (I-6)

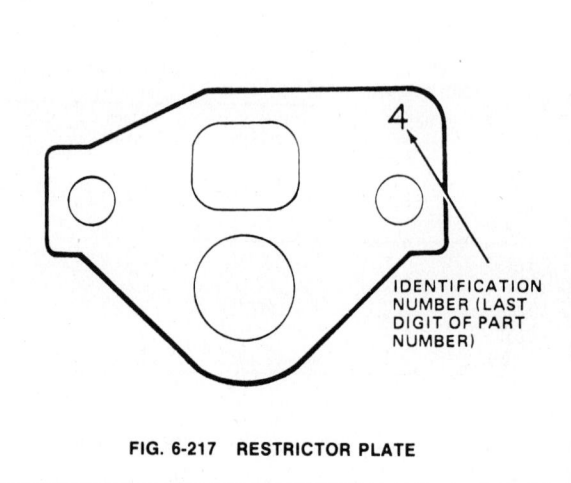

FIG. 6-217   RESTRICTOR PLATE

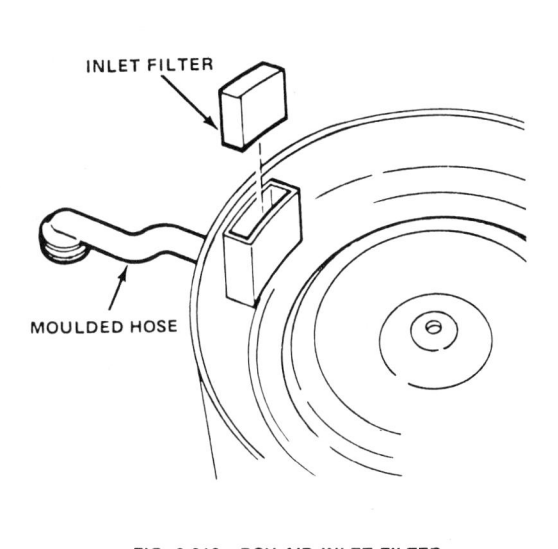

FIG. 6-218   PCV AIR INLET FILTER

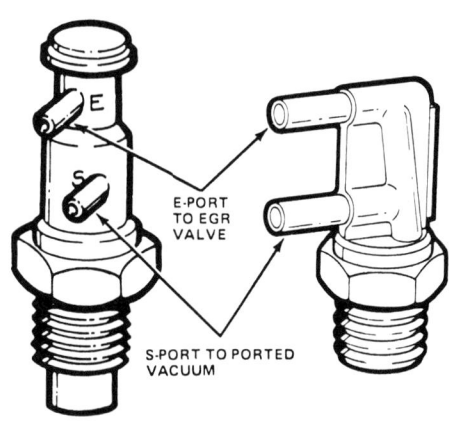

FIG. 6-219   TWO-PORT CTO SWITCH

AMERICAN MOTORS
1977-78 Emission Systems

The Positive Crankcase Ventilation (PCV) system is the same as used in 1970-72 AMC cars. PCV valve flow rates for 1978 differ, as shown in **Fig. 6-219A.** Evaporative Emission Control system (EEC) is the same as 1973-74.

EXHAUST GAS RECIRCULATION (EGR)

The system remains essentially the same as that used in 1973-74, but all 1977 AMC vehicles use a combined back-pressure sensor/EGR valve. No restrictor plate **(Fig. 6-217)** is used, since the new design eliminates the separate sensor and spacer. The I-4 engine introduced in mid-1977 uses a standard EGR valve without backpressure sensor. All such engines use the restrictor plate, except those calibrated for high altitude.

AIR GUARD SYSTEM

Use is extended to all engine applications. System operation is essentially the same as that used in 1973-74, but air pressure in the system is maintained at about 5 psi for nationwide engines, and 7.5 psi for California engines. A vacuum delay valve (VDV) is used on all 1978 California I-6 engines to reduce diverter valve dump mode operating time. The VDV is located between the diverter valve and its manifold source.

THERMOSTATICALLY CONTROLLED AIR CLEANER (TAC) SYSTEM

Use is extended to all engine applications. The mechanical TAC system **(Fig. 6-220 and 6-221)** is used only on 1977 I-6 engines equipped with a 1-bbl. carburetor (except Pacer). All other 1977 and all 1978 engines use the vacuum-operated TAC **(Fig. 6-222 and 6-223.)** Ambient air induction was introduced on 1977 I-4 engines and extended to all 1978 engines.

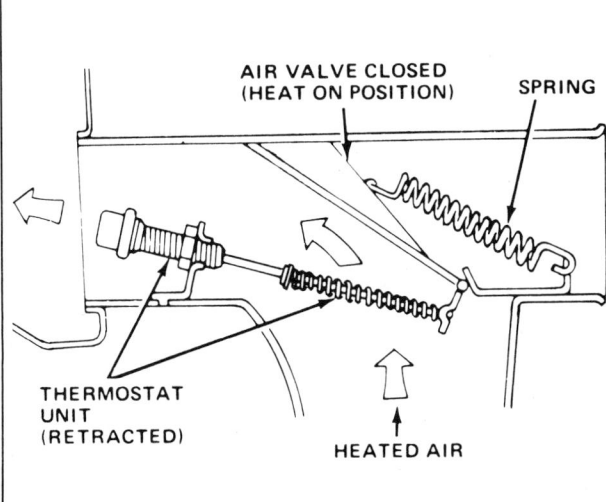

FIG. 6-220   TAC SYSTEM (I-6)—CLOSED POSITION

Engine Manifold Vacuum (in. Hg)	Air Flow (CFM)		
	Yellow Four-Cylinder Six-Cylinder		Black Eight-Cylinder
	1978	1979	
16			1.34-1.63
13	1.30-1.90	1.20-1.70	
7			2.70-3.79
5	1.21-2.26	1.30-1.20	
3			3.30-4.39
2	1.28-2.56	1.40-2.45	

FIG. 6-219A   1978/79 AMC PCV VALVE FLOW RATES

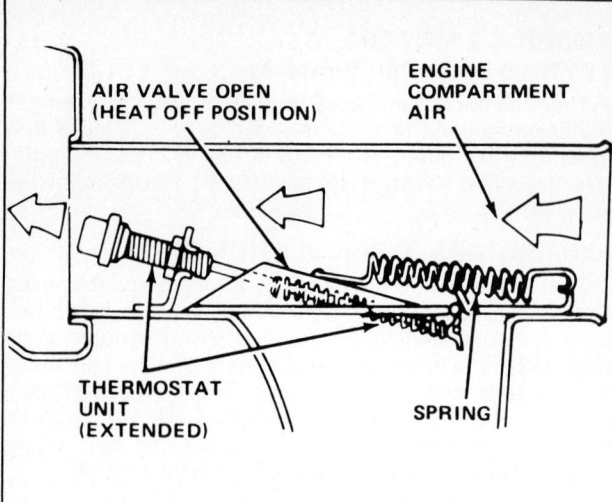

FIG. 6-221 TAC SYSTEM (I-6)—OPEN POSITION

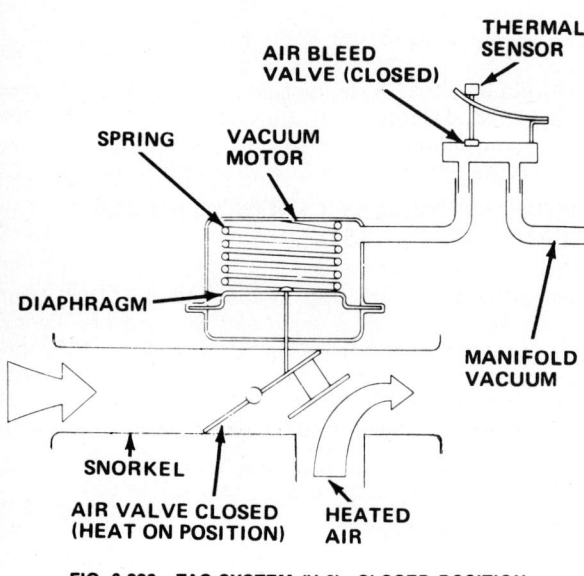

FIG. 6-223 TAC SYSTEM (V-8)—CLOSED POSITION

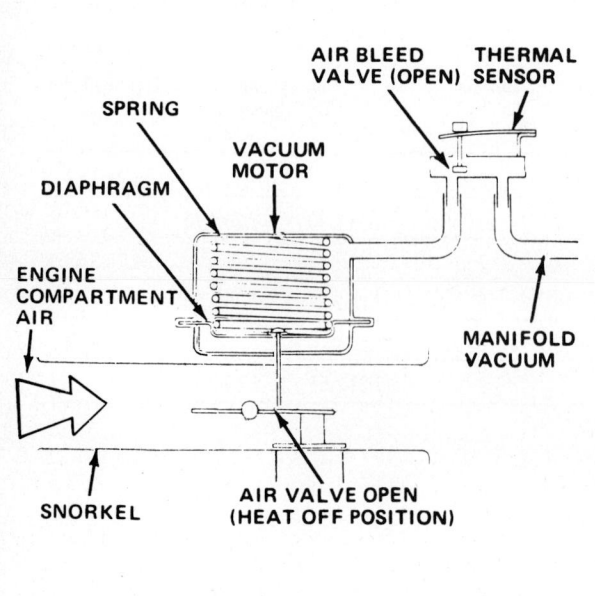

FIG. 6-222 TAC SYSTEM (V-8)—OPEN POSITION

CATALYTIC CONVERTER

All 1977 and later I-6 and V-8 engines use a monolithic-type warm-up converter in addition to the standard pellet-type main converter. Those AMC vehicles equipped with dual pellet-type converters will have dual warm-up converters. Since this smaller converter is an integral part of the manifold-to-converter pipe, replacement of the entire unit is made as a single assembly in cases of converter failure, damage and/or pipe damage. For 1978, a pressed-in plug replaces the threaded plug installed in the bottom of the pellet-type converter housing.

TRANSMISSION CONTROLLED SPARK (TCS)

For 1977, TCS is used on all California cars, all high-altitude cars with automatic transmission, and certain nationwide models. TCS usage for 1978 is restricted to I-6 and V-8 California cars, and certain non-California models. System operation is essentially the same as that used in 1973-74, but the solenoid control switch on automatic transmission applications is recalibrated to open at 33-37 mph.

AMERICAN MOTORS
1979 Emission Systems

All 1978 emission systems are carry-over for 1979 except as noted below.

AIR GUARD SYSTEM

System operation is essentially the same as 1978, but air pressure ratings have been changed. Air pressure for 1979 systems is rated at 5 psi for non-California I-6 engines with automatic transmission, and 7.5 psi for all other I-6 & V-8 non-California and California engines.

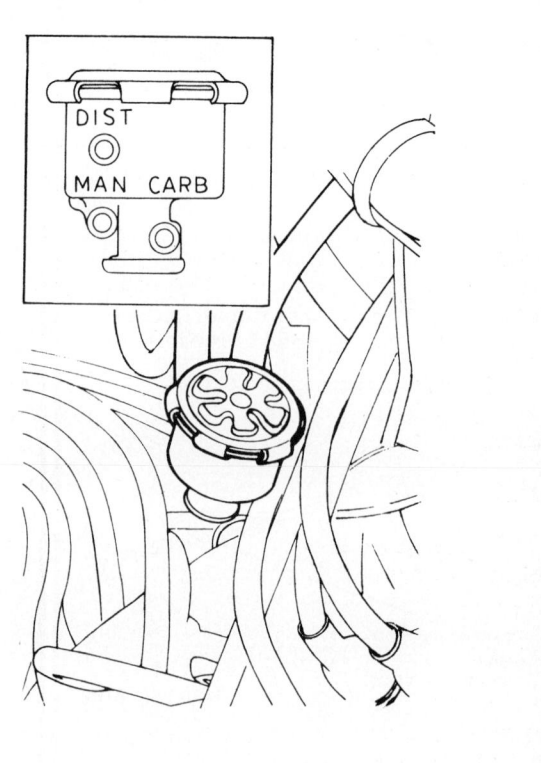

FIG. 6-223A NON-LINEAR VACUUM REGULATOR VALVE

POSITIVE CRANKCASE VENTILATION (PCV) SYSTEM

PCV valve flow rates for some 1979 applications differ, as shown in **Fig. 6-219A**.

NON-LINEAR VACUUM REGULATOR (NLVR) VALVE

This device, **Fig. 6-223A**, is fitted to certain AMC engine and mounted in series between the distributor and vacuum source port. It combines regulated vacuum during idle and carburetor port vacuum under engine load to provide a regulated vacuum signal output to control spark advance. As engine load increases, the vacuum signal also increases. When it exceeds 7.5 in. Hg at 70-80° F, the NLVR switches from manifold to ported vacuum output.

TRANSMISSION CONTROLLED SPARK (TCS)

TCS system operation, specifications and testing procedures are the same as 1978, but apply only to California 258-cu.-in. 6-cyl. engines with automatic transmission.

EMISSION SYSTEM TEST PROCEDURES

PCV TEST

AMC recommends a valve flow test. To perform this test, a PCV Valve Tester J-23111 is required. *Do not* perform Steps 6 through 8 on vehicles equipped with the BID Ignition.

1. Remove the PCV valve from the V-8 intake manifold or I-6 cylinder head cover.
2. Connect the PCV valve to the tester hose and place it in a horizontal position.
3. Connect the tester to an intake manifold fitting which will provide manifold vacuum. The fitting should be centrally located on the intake manifold, if possible.
4. Start the engine and note the flow rate on the tester gauge at idle. Lightly tap the PCV valve while checking the flow rate.
5. Compare the flow rate reading obtained with **Fig. 6-205**.
6. Shut the engine off. Remove and ground the coil secondary wire (conventional ignition only) and set the carburetor throttle at curb idle.
7. Crank the engine and note the flow rate on the tester gauge.
8. Compare the flow rate reading obtained with **Fig. 6-205**.
9. If the PCV valve does not meet the flow rate specifications, replace it.

ALTERNATE PCV TEST

If PCV Valve Tester J-23111 is not available, the PCV valve may be checked according to the following procedure:

1. Remove the PCV valve from the intake manifold or cylinder head cover.
2. Start the engine and run at idle.
3. Place a thumb over the valve end to check for vacuum. If there is no vacuum at the valve, inspect for plugged hoses.
4. Shut the engine off. Shake the valve, and listen for the rattle of the check needle in the valve. If no rattle is heard, replace the valve.

THERMOSTATICALLY OPERATED AIR CLEANER OPERATION TEST

SIX-CYLINDER AIR CLEANER

1. Remove the air cleaner cover and place the snor-

kel tube in cold water. The thermostat unit must be covered.
2. Heat the water slowly to 105° F—the air valve should be in the *heat on* (closed) position **(Fig. 6-220)**.
3. Continue heating the water until the temperature reaches 130° F—the air valve should be in the *heat off* (open) position **(Fig. 6-221)**.
4. If the air valve does not open and close at specified temperatures, inspect for binding or a disconnected spring. If the air valve is mechanically sound, the thermostat is defective and the air cleaner cover assembly must be replaced.

EIGHT-CYLINDER AIR CLEANER

1. Remove the entire air cleaner assembly from the engine and let it cool to room temperature, if needed.
2. Look through the air cleaner snorkel tube to check air valve position—it should be completely open to outside air **(Fig. 6-222)**.
3. Replace the air cleaner assembly on the engine. Connect the hot air tube and manifold vacuum line.
4. Start the engine and note the air valve position—it should now be completely closed to outside air **(Fig. 6-223)**.
5. Note the air valve position again when the engine has warmed to normal operating temperature—it should be completely open to outside air **(Fig. 6-222)**.
6. If the air valve does not close at room temperature with vacuum applied, inspect for vacuum leaks, disconnected vacuum motor linkage or mechanical binding in the snorkel.
7. If the air valve mechanism operates without binding and no vacuum leaks are found, connect a hose from the vacuum motor to an intake manifold vacuum source.
8. If the air valve does not close, replace the vacuum motor. If the air valve does close, replace sensor.

DISTRIBUTOR DUAL VACUUM ADVANCE TEST

DISTRIBUTOR VACUUM

1. Leave the vacuum advance lines connected to the distributor and connect a tachometer and ignition timing light.
2. Start the engine and check the position of the timing marks at idle with the timing light.
3. Increase engine speed to 2000 rpm and recheck the timing mark position. Compare the amount of advance with that specified (see Distributor Specifications, Chapter 3).
4. If the total advance at 2000 rpm is less than that specified, disconnect the vacuum advance line and check for maximum centrifugal advance as specified. If the centrifugal advance is to specifications, replace the vacuum advance unit.

DISTRIBUTOR RETARD

1. Disconnect the distributor vacuum lines and plug the retard line.
2. Increase engine speed by adjusting the curb idle screw until a 10° BTDC reading is noted on the timing mark scale.
3. Remove the retard line plug and reconnect, noting the change in ignition timing with the timing light. If the maximum retard is not to specifications, replace the vacuum advance unit. Reset curb idle speed to specifications.

TCS SYSTEM OPERATIONAL TEST SEQUENCE

The following six-step test sequence is accomplished using a probe-type current tester, a jumper lead and a vacuum gauge. All test connections are shown in **Fig. 6-224.**

1. Turn the ignition switch on and disconnect the TCS harness connector located at the left-front fender panel. Ground the tester wire lead and insert the tester probe in the open-feed-wire female terminal—test point A. If the tester does not light, inspect the ignition feed circuit through the main harness connector and the 20-amp accessory fuse.

2. Connect the harness-connector female terminal to the ambient-temperature-override-switch male terminal with a jumper lead. Ground the tester lead and insert the probe in the open female terminal of the ambient-temperature override switch—test point B. If the tester does not light, replace the switch.

3. Disconnect the solenoid-vacuum-valve wire connector. Ground the tester lead and touch the probe tip to each terminal of the wire connector in turn—test point C. If the tester does not light at one of the two terminals, the ignition feed wire to the TCS harness connector is defective.

4. Connect the tester lead to the positive battery terminal and insert the tester probe in the side of the wire connector which did not light in Step 3 (solenoid-vacuum-valve ground wire)—test point D. If the tester does not light, the solenoid switch at the transmission or its wiring is defective. Reconnect the solenoid-vacuum-valve connector.

5. Disconnect the vacuum line from the CTO switch center port (marked "D") and connect a vacuum gauge—test point E. Start the engine, and the vacuum gauge should read manifold vacuum. As soon as the engine coolant temperature reaches approximately 160° F (yellow color code) or 115° F (black color code), the vacuum reading should drop by 4 to 6 ins. If the vacuum gauge does not read manifold vacuum with a cold engine, or does not drop as specified, replace the CTO switch.

6. Disconnect the vacuum line from the solenoid-vacuum-valve front port and connect a vacuum gauge—test point F. Elevate the rear wheels. Place manual transmission cars in high gear and increase engine speed above idle—the vacuum gauge should read ported vacuum. Place automatic transmission cars in DRIVE and note the vacuum gauge while gradually increasing engine rpm. When the speedometer reaches approximately 34 mph, the vacuum gauge should indicate ported vacuum. If no vacuum is shown, either the solenoid vacuum valve is defective or no carburetor ported vacuum is being applied. Disconnect the carburetor line from the spark port and check the carburetor for vacuum.

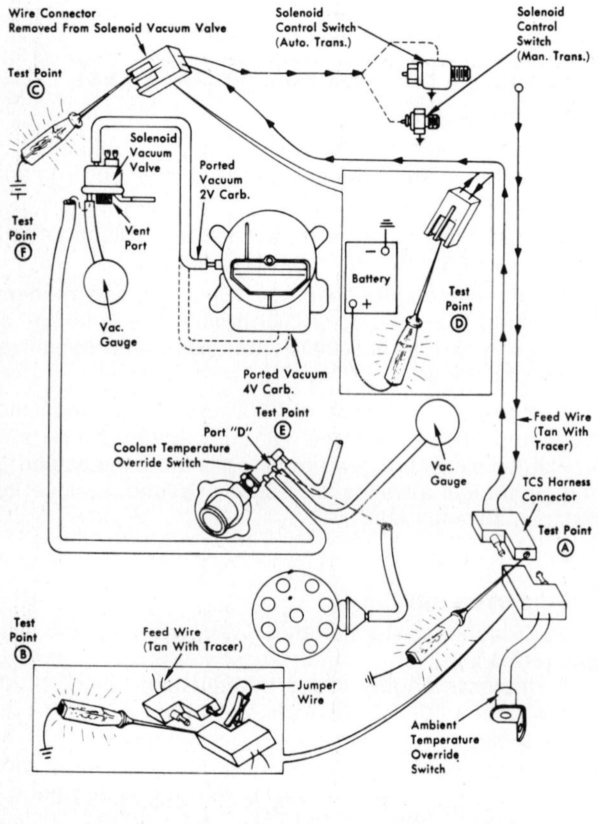

EGR VALVE OPERATIONAL TEST

1. Connect a tachometer, start the engine and warm to normal operating temperature. With the engine at idle, manually depress the EGR valve diaphragm, and the engine rpm should immediately drop about 200 rpm. If there is no rpm drop and the engine is operating properly, exhaust gases are not reaching the combustion chamber. If there is no rpm drop, but engine idle quality is poor, the EGR valve is not shutting off the exhaust gas flow.

2. Tee a vacuum gauge in the EGR valve line close to the valve, and lightly rest your fingers against the EGR valve while gradually increasing engine speed.

3. Check the vacuum gauge as engine speed is increased and note the vacuum reading when the valve begins to move. Compare the reading obtained to the EGR values shown in **Fig. 6-215.**

4. Continue to increase engine speed and note the vacuum necessary to completely depress the EGR valve diaphragm. Compare the vacuum reading as in Step 3. If the EGR valve is not operating within specifications, replace it.

EGR CTO SWITCH TEST

1. Connect a tachometer, disconnect the vacuum line at the backpressure sensor and connect a vacuum gauge to the line.

2. Start the engine and run at 1500 rpm. If vacuum is indicated on the vacuum gauge, replace the CTO switch.

3. Operate the engine at idle while coolant temperature exceeds 115° F (black color code) or 160° F (yellow color code). Increase engine speed to 1500 rpm. If the vacuum gauge does not show carburetor ported vacuum, replace the EGR CTO switch.

EGR BACKPRESSURE SENSOR TEST

1. Connect a vacuum gauge in the vacuum line between the EGR valve and the exhaust backpressure sensor.

2. Connect a tachometer, start the engine and idle. If vacuum is indicated on the vacuum gauge, check the vacuum line connections for manifold vacuum and the carburetor for partially open throttle plates—either condition will interfere with backpressure sensor operation.

3. Increase engine speed to 2000 rpm. If the engine coolant temperature is below 115° F, no vacuum should be indicated. If coolant temperature is above

FIG. 6-224 TCS TEST SEQUENCE CONNECTIONS

115° F (black color code) or 160° F (yellow color code), ported vacuum should be indicated.

4. If no vacuum is indicated at any temperature, check the inlet side of the backpressure sensor for vacuum. Remove the backpressure sensor and check the spacer port/tube for restrictions. If vacuum reaches the backpressure sensor inlet side, but no restrictions are found, replace the backpressure sensor.

NLVR VALVE TEST

1. Tee a vacuum gauge into the NLVR distributor port.
2. Run the engine at idle. The vacuum gauge should indicate 7-ins. Hg.
3. Open the throttle and note the vacuum gauge as the engine speed increases. It should indicate ported vacuum from the carburetor.

EMISSION SYSTEM COMPONENT REPLACEMENT

I-6 AIR GUARD PUMP REMOVAL/INSTALLATION

TO REMOVE

1. Disconnect all hose connections at the air pump.
2. Loosen the adjustment bolt, and move the pump inward to remove the drive belt.
3. Loosen and remove the front mount bracket-to-pump and bracket-to-engine bolts.
4. Loosen the rear mount bracket-to-power-steering bolts.
5. Pull the pump down and forward, and remove it.

TO INSTALL

1. Position the pump in place, and reinstall the rear mount bracket-to-power-steering bolts.
2. Replace the front mount bracket-to-engine and bracket-to-pump bolts finger-tight.
3. Replace the power-steering and air-pump drive belts. Install the adjusting bolt, tension drive belts, and tighten the adjusting bolt.
4. Torque the mounting bolts to 20 ft.-lbs., and connect the hose(s) to the air pump.

V-8 AIR GUARD PUMP REMOVAL/INSTALLATION

TO REMOVE

1. Disconnect the air-pump output hose from the pump.
2. Loosen the bracket-to-pump bolts and adjusting strap screw to remove the drive belt, then remove the screw and bolts.
3. Remove the pump.

TO INSTALL

1. Position the air pump in place, and install the bracket-to-pump bolts, but *do not* tighten.
2. Replace the drive belt and adjust tension.
3. Tighten all mounting bolts and the adjusting strap screw to 20 ft.-lbs. torque.

CENTRIFUGAL FILTER FAN REPLACEMENT

1. Remove the pulley attaching bolts and drive pulley from the air pump shaft.
2. After prying the outer disc loose, pull the fan off with needlenose pliers—*do not* remove the metal drive hub.
3. Draw the new fan evenly into place, using the pulley and bolts as tools. Tighten the bolts alternately, making sure the outer edge of the fan slips into the housing.
4. Reinstall the air pump to the engine. Until the

outer diameter sealing lip has worn in, a new fan may be noisy.

DIVERTER VALVE REPLACEMENT (TO 1973)

1. Remove the hoses from the diverter valve.
2. Remove the two screws which hold the valve to the pump body.
3. Remove the valve and gasket material from the pump.
4. Fit a new valve to the pump, install screws and tighten.
5. Connect the hoses to the valve.

DIVERTER VALVE REPLACEMENT (FROM 1974)

1. The diverter valve is suspended between hoses connected to the air pump and air injection manifold. Disconnect the hoses and vacuum line, install the new valve and replace the hoses and vacuum line.

EGR VALVE REPLACEMENT

1. Remove the air cleaner assembly (V-8 engines only).
2. Disconnect the vacuum lines and remove the manifold retaining nuts.
3. Lift off the EGR valve, gasket, spacer, attached exhaust backpressure sensor, restrictor plate and gaskets.
4. Discard all gasket materials, and clean all mating surfaces.
5. Using new gaskets, assemble the EGR valve, spacer and attached backpressure sensor, and the restrictor plate. The restrictor plate is calibrated for the engine/exhaust system and *must not* be replaced with a different one. If a new restrictor plate is required for any reason, make certain that the plate carries the same identification number as the one being replaced **(Fig. 6-217).**
6. Install the retaining bolts and torque to 13 ft.-lbs.
7. Reconnect all vacuum lines and replace the air cleaner (on V-8 engine).

I-6 EGR CTO REPLACEMENT

1. Drain the radiator of coolant, and disconnect the vacuum lines. Attempting to remove the CTO switch from the block without draining hot coolant can result in serious burns.
2. Remove the CTO switch with a ⅞-in. open-end wrench.
3. Install the new CTO switch in the engine block, and reconnect the vacuum lines.
4. Replace the ccolant, and purge the air from the cooling system.

V-8 EGR CTO REPLACEMENT

1. Drain the radiator of coolant, and remove the air cleaner assembly. Attempting to remove the CTO switch without draining hot coolant can result in serious burns.
2. Remove the coil-bracket attaching screw, then tip the coil away from the CTO switch and disconnect the vacuum lines.
3. Remove the CTO switch with a ⅞-in. open-end wrench.
4. Install the new CTO switch, and replace the coil-bracket attaching screw.
5. Reconnect the vacuum lines, and install the air cleaner.
6. Replace the coolant, and purge the air from the cooling system.

INDEX

COOLING SYSTEMS

During engine operation, internal combustion temperatures often reach as high as 4500°, creating far more heat than the cylinder walls, heads and pistons can safely absorb without causing permanent damage. Since such high temperatures destroy the lubricating qualities of oil, the engine will fail if the excessive heat is not removed. This is the job of the automotive cooling system, designed to maintain the engine at its most efficient operating temperature at all engine speeds and under all engine load/driving conditions. But removal of too much heat will reduce the engine's thermal efficiency, so most cooling systems are designed to transfer and dissipate approximately 35% of the heat generated during combustion. They also provide a means of heating the passenger compartment and cooling the automatic transmission fluid.

COOLING SYSTEM OPERATION (Fig. 7-1)

The basic engine is enclosed in a container or water jacket filled with a mixture of glycol and water, which absorbs the excess heat. Passages cast into the engine block allow the coolant to circulate around cylinder walls, valve seats, valve guides, the combustion chamber top and wherever else heat must be removed. Because some areas in an engine may run hotter than others, deflection guides may be included in the passages, and distribution tubes or water nozzles used to direct coolant to potential dead or hot spots.

There is a limit to how much heat a given amount of coolant can absorb before it begins to boil away, and so the fluid must be constantly circulated by a belt-driven pump, mounted at the front of the cylinder block **(Fig. 7-2).** Extremely simple in design, the pump is a housing with an inlet and outlet for coolant travel, and contains an impeller or flat plate fitted with a number of blades or vanes mounted on the pump shaft. Rota-

tion of the pump impeller pushes cooler coolant into the cylinder block, forcing the hotter coolant out. Because it is belt-driven, the faster the engine runs, the faster the water pump works. A cooling fan located on the end of the water pump shaft (and driven by the same belt) draws cool air in from outside the car **(Fig. 7-2).** To assure that all the air that is drawn in passes through the radiator, a fan shroud is often used to increase cooling system efficiency.

A temperature-sensitive valve or thermostat, placed in the coolant outlet passage, controls the flow of engine coolant, provides fast engine warm-up and regulates coolant temperatures. When the coolant is cold, the valve remains closed. Because this prevents coolant from circulating through the radiator, the coolant in the engine circulates within the block and warms quickly. As coolant temperature rises, the valve opens to allow coolant flow into the radiator, where the heat is dissipated through the radiator walls **(Fig. 7-3).**

As coolant is heated, it expands in volume. The use of a coolant recovery system permits this fluid expansion to overflow into the recovery reservoir **(Fig. 7-4).** When the engine cools, the coolant contracts in volume and vacuum draws any that has overflowed into the bottle or reservoir back into the radiator. This assures that the radiator will not boil over, and so remain filled to capacity at all times, maintaining the specified level of cooling efficiency.

COOLING SYSTEM COMPONENTS
RADIATOR

When hot coolant is pumped into the radiator, it is brought in contact with a large volume of air, causing a transfer of heat from the coolant to the air. Forced into the radiator's inlet tank, it filters through tiny heat

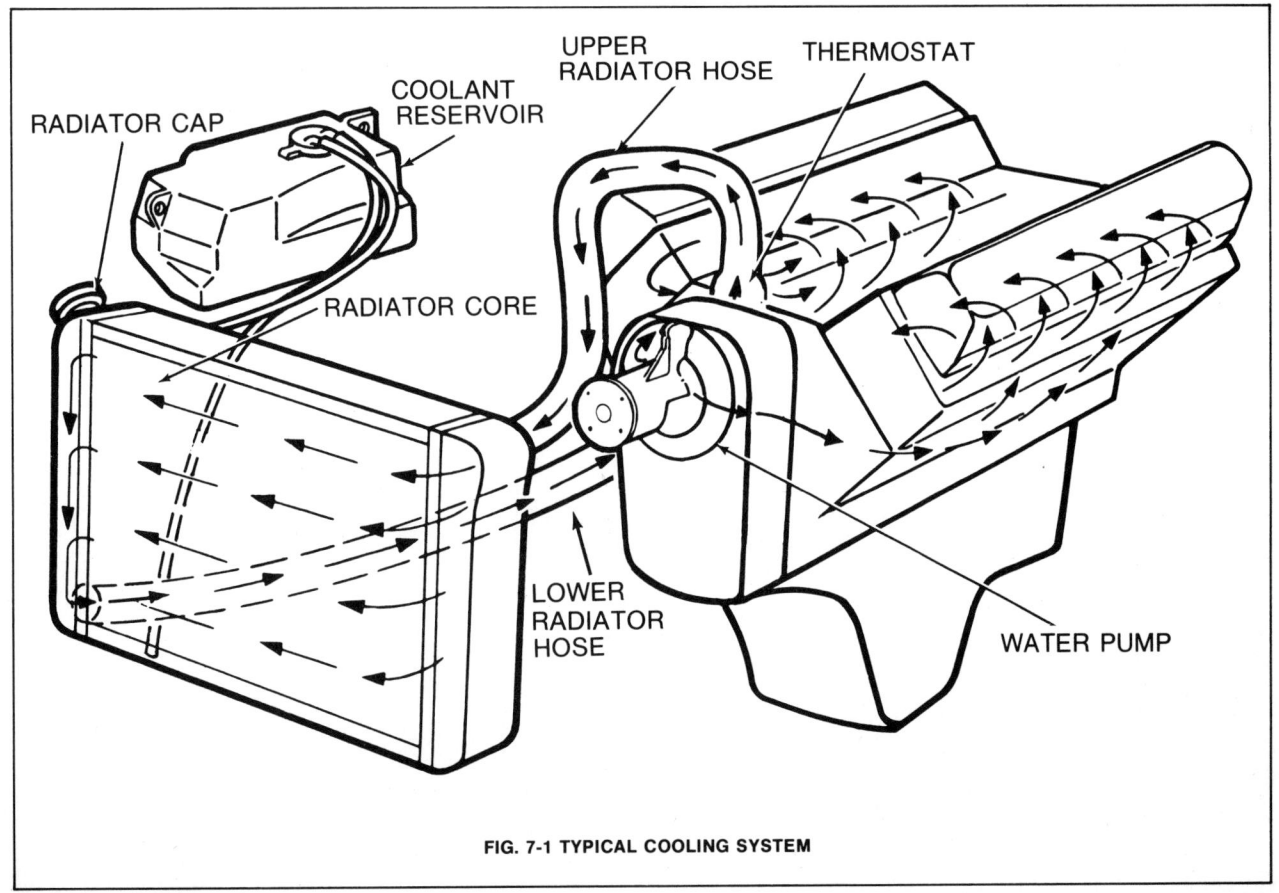

RADIATOR CAP

COOLANT RESERVOIR

UPPER RADIATOR HOSE

THERMOSTAT

RADIATOR CORE

LOWER RADIATOR HOSE

WATER PUMP

FIG. 7-1 TYPICAL COOLING SYSTEM

conductive tubes in the core on its way to the outlet tank for return to the engine block. Two types of radiator designs are used—downflow and crossflow.

Downflow—A conventional vertical-flow design, the expansion (inlet) tank is located at the top of the core and connected by a flexible hose to the coolant outlet housing on the engine. Coolant passes from the inlet tank and down through the core to the bottom (outlet) tank, also connected by a flexible hose to the water pump inlet port. This permits coolant circulation through the radiator when the thermostat is open. The outlet tank on automatic-transmission-equipped cars contains a heat exchanger or transmission oil cooler unit through which automatic transmission fluid is circulated for cooling. All 1970-79 American Motors (except Pacer) and Chrysler Corp. cars, some 1970-72 General Motors cars and some 1970-79 Ford Motor Company cars use the downflow radiator design **(Fig. 7-5)**.

Crossflow—Turn the conventional downflow radiator on its side and you have the crossflow design. With the header tanks on each side (instead of top and bottom), the coolant travels horizontally instead of vertically. The header tank fitted with the radiator cap is the outlet tank, equivalent to the lower tank of the downflow design, and contains a transmission fluid oil cooler on automatic-transmission-equipped models. The crossflow design has two distinct advantages: it permits the use of a lower styling profile and reduces pressure against the radiator cap, which prevents the cap from "blowing" if a blockage occurs and the radiator overheats. This design is used by some 1970-72 GM cars, all 1973 and later GM cars, the AMC Pacer, and some 1970-79 Ford Motor Company models **(Fig. 7-5)**.

RADIATOR CAP

Radiators are pressurized to allow the cooling system to operate at higher than atmospheric pressure. This improves cooling efficiency and prevents evaporation and surge losses. The pressure cap increases air pressure in the system by several pounds per square inch, allowing coolant to be circulated at higher temperatures without boiling. With the greater difference between the coolant and the outside air, heat passes from the coolant faster.

A pressure cap contains a relief valve and a vacuum valve, and seats tightly over both the filler mouth and its edges. A calibrated spring in the relief valve holds the valve closed, producing pressure in the system. If the pressure exceeds the amount for which the system was designed, the valve blows off its seat, relieving the excessive pressure. When the engine has been shut off and cools, a vacuum might form, dropping the inside pressure sufficiently to cause outside air pressure to collapse it. If this happens, the vacuum valve opens to introduce air into the system before any damage can be done **(Fig. 7-6)**.

FAN

The cooling fan, located on the end of the water pump shaft, will be one of three basic types: the fixed drive, flexible blade or automatic clutch fan.

While the fixed drive fan rotates at engine-rpm/water-pump speed, the flexible fan's blades automatically change pitch in relation to engine rpm. As rpm increase, pitch decreases to save power and reduce airflow; as rpm decrease, pitch increases to accelerate airflow and the rate of cooling.

The automatic clutch uses a hydraulic device to vary fan speed relative to engine temperature. This allows the use of a high-delivery fan to provide adequate cooling at lower engine speeds, while at the same time, overcooling, excessive noise and power loss at high speeds are eliminated.

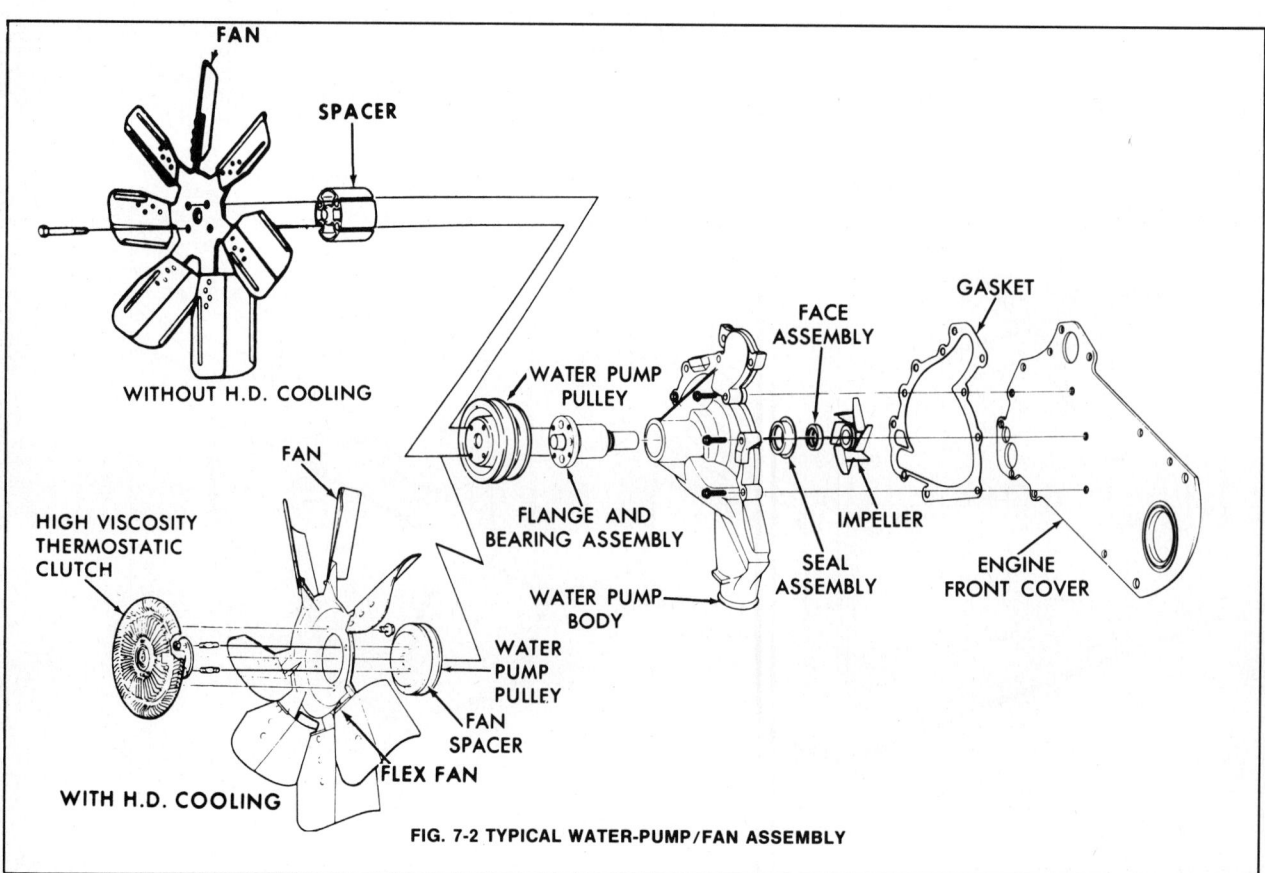

FIG. 7-2 TYPICAL WATER-PUMP/FAN ASSEMBLY

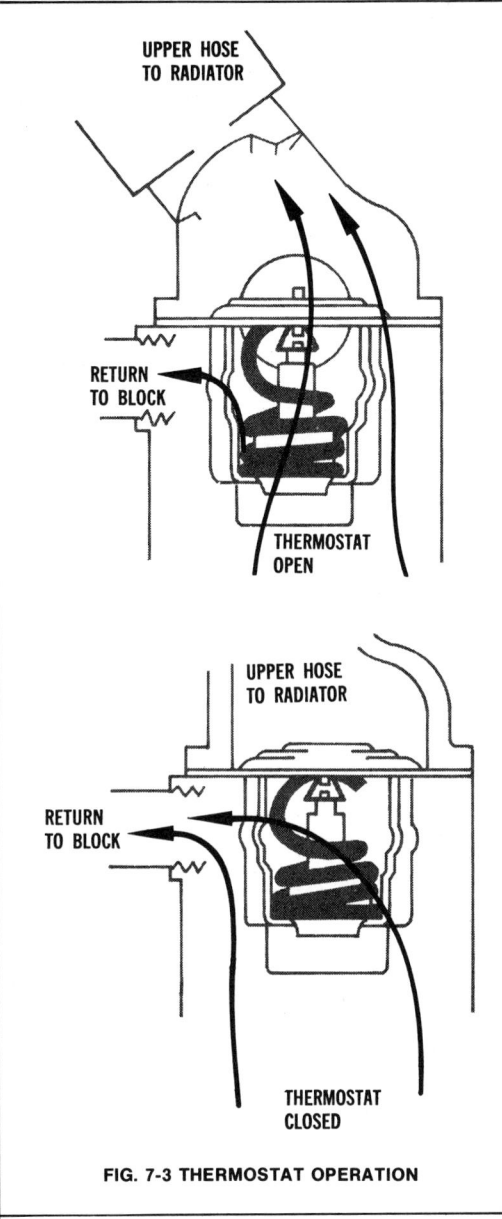

FIG. 7-3 THERMOSTAT OPERATION

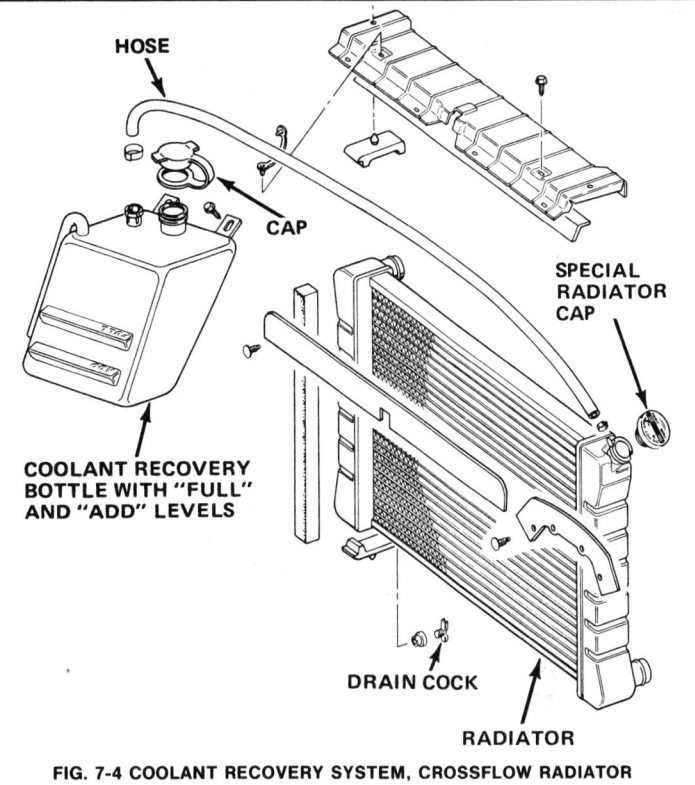

FIG. 7-4 COOLANT RECOVERY SYSTEM, CROSSFLOW RADIATOR

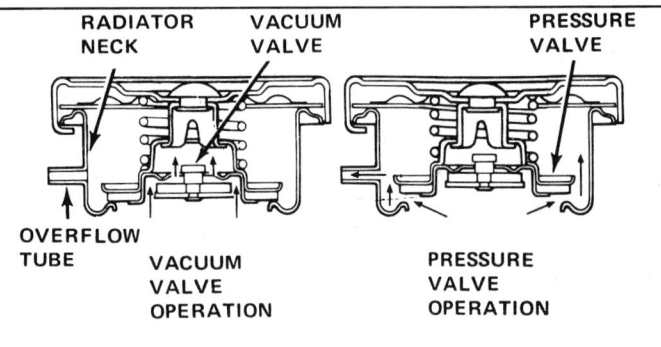

FIG. 7-6 RADIATOR CAP OPERATION

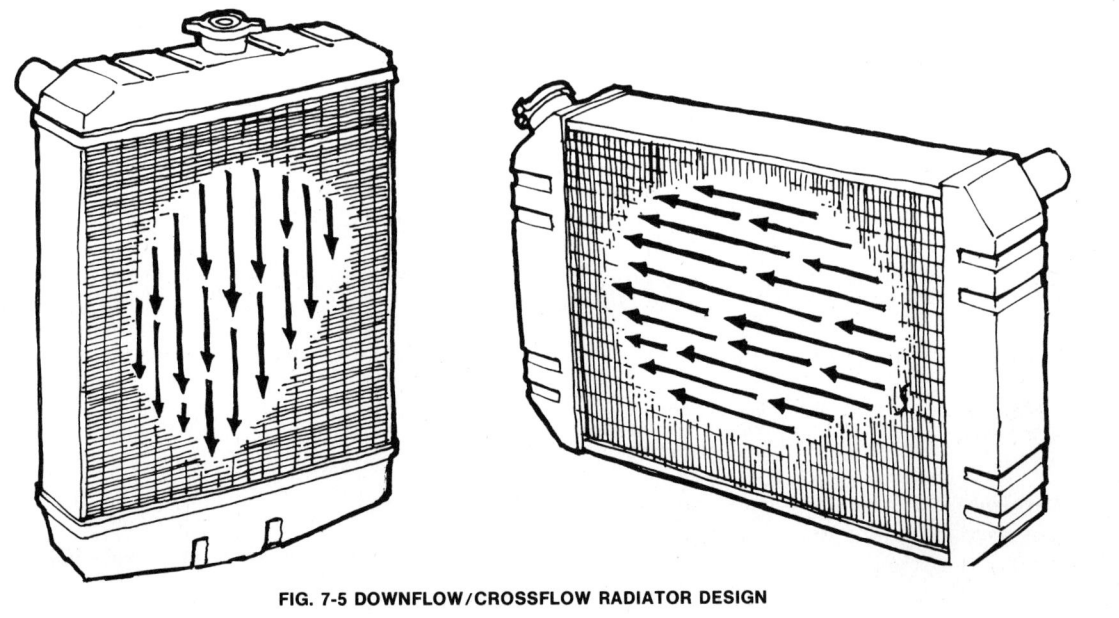

FIG. 7-5 DOWNFLOW/CROSSFLOW RADIATOR DESIGN

A reservoir in the clutch housing contains silicon-base oil during the disengaged mode (cold engine or high speed driving). A temperature-sensitive, bi-metallic coil positioned on the clutch front in the airstream regulates silicon fluid flow from the reservoir to the clutch working chamber. As engine temperature rises, so does the bi-metallic coil temperature, moving a control valve to permit fluid flow. When sufficient silicon fluid passes to the working chamber to cause a resistance between the drive and driven plates, the automatic clutch becomes fully engaged, controlling fan speed relative to the drive pulley and radiator-core airflow temperature **(Fig. 7-7)**.

Fixed drive or flexible blade fans are generally used with standard cooling systems, while the automatic fan clutch is usually fitted to heavy-duty cooling systems or cars equipped with air conditioning.

Used only with 4-cylinder engines, electrically driven fans are actuated by a switch in the radiator. This turns off the fan automatically when its use is not required, but the fan is also electrically interlocked with air conditioning when so equipped. Whenever the air conditioning is on, the fan is also on. The electric fan has several advantages: there is no fan belt to replace or adjust, less fan noise and less power drain on the engine.

THERMOSTAT

This consists of a restriction valve, operated by a wax pellet or powder element, which expands when heated and contracts when cooled. The pellet is con-nected to the valve by a piston, which exerts pressure against a rubber diaphragm, forcing the valve open when the pellet is heated. As the pellet cools, a spring closes the valve **(Fig. 7-8)**. The thermostat is generally located in a housing attached to the engine block where the upper radiator hose connects, but on Ford V-6 engines, it is located on the bottom of the water pump housing **(Fig. 7-9)**.

Each thermostat is designed to open and close at predetermined temperatures (often stamped on the unit) and should be replaced if not operating within specifications. Engines should not be operated without a thermostat, because engine warm-up time increases, causing poor warm-up performance and leading to crankcase dilution, which may result in sludge formation. The thermostat should be installed with the word(s) FRONT, UP or TO RAD in the direction of the radiator; incorrectly installed, it will act as a baffle and force the coolant to change direction in order to pass by the valve. This will lead to overheating and possible engine damage.

HOSES

Rubber or neoprene hoses carry the coolant from the engine to the radiator and back, and to the heater core and back. Some hose installations are spring-reinforced to prevent a collapse caused by suction. Whether rigid or preformed, cooling system hoses are the most fragile part of the system, and should be inspected and replaced periodically.

COOLING SYSTEM DIAGNOSIS

CONDITION	CORRECTION	CONDITION	CORRECTION
ENGINE OVERHEATS		**ENGINE DOES NOT REACH NORMAL OPERATING TEMPERATURE**	
(a) Belt tension is too low.	(a) Adjust belt tension to specs.	(a) Radiator leaks	(a) Check radiator for leaks. Also check system for pressure.
(b) Timing set incorrectly.	(b) Reset timing to specs.	(b) Coolant reservoir/hose leaks.	(b) Replace reservoir or hose.
(c) Timing retarded by faulty distributor vacuum advance unit or thermal vacuum switch.	(c) Check thermal advance for defective switch or distributor vacuum advance unit. Check hose for kinks, partial collapse or poor connections.	(c) Hoses or connections are loose or damaged.	(c) Reseat or replace hoses/clamps.
		(d) Water pump seal leaks.	(d) Repair water pump or replace.
		(e) Water pump gasket leaks.	(e) Replace gasket.
(d) Loss of system pressure.	(d) Test system and cap for pressure. If cap is not defective, inspect for leaks and repair when found.	(f) Radiator cap defective.	(f) Test cap for pressure and replace.
(e) Radiator fins obstructed.	(e) Clean radiator fins of debris, bugs, etc.	(g) Radiator filler neck distorted.	(g) Use wooden block and mallet to reform neck evenly to fit cap.
(f) Cooling system passages blocked by rust or scale.	(f) Flush system and add fresh coolant.	(h) Cylinder head gasket leaks.	(h) Replace gasket.
(g) Reservoir hose is pinched or kinked.	(g) Replace hose and prevent kinking by rerouting if necessary.	(i) Improper cylinder head screw torque.	(i) Retorque screws to specs.
(h) Lower radiator hose has collapsed.	(h) Replace.	(j) Cylinder block core plug leaks.	(j) Replace core plug.
COOLANT LOSS		(k) Cracked cylinder head/block, or warped cylinder head/block gasket surface.	(k) Resurface if possible; replace if not.
(a) Thermostat stuck in closed position.	(a) Replace thermostat.	(l) Heater core leaks.	(l) Replace core.
(b) Leaking hoses or poor connections.	(b) Check hoses and connections. Tighten and/or replace if necessary.	(m) Thermostat stuck open.	(m) Install new thermostat—make sure it's correct type and heat range.
(c) Heater core leaks.	(c) Replace heater core.		
(d) Water temperature sending unit is leaking.	(d) Replace unit.	(n) Heater water control valve leaks.	(n) Replace valve.
(e) Radiator leaks.	(e) Check radiator for leaks, especially bottom half.	(o) Coolant level too low.	(o) Add coolant.

COOLANT

Coolant is a mixture of ethylene-glycol-base anti-freeze and distilled water. Glycol lowers the coolant freezing point to prevent engine damage from below-freezing temperatures, and raises the coolant boiling point to increase the efficiency of heat transfer. This reduces coolant loss during heat-soak conditions, and reduces the possibility of cavitation damage caused by a vacuum formation.

In order to provide adequate protection against corrosion and assure correct operation of the temperature indicator, manufacturers recommend that cooling system protection be maintained at -20° F. If the glycol content of the coolant is less than that required for

-20° F protection (44%), the coolant boiling point will be less than that required by the temperature indicator. Should it be necessary to add coolant for any reason, a sufficient amount of glycol-base antifreeze should be mixed with water to maintain the -20° F protection.

COOLING SYSTEM MAINTENANCE
CHECKING COOLANT LEVEL

Coolant level should be checked with the engine cool. If a coolant recovery system is used, it is advisable to check the level by removing the reservoir cap; removing the radiator cap unnecessarily will allow air to enter, promoting the formation of corrosion. Coolant

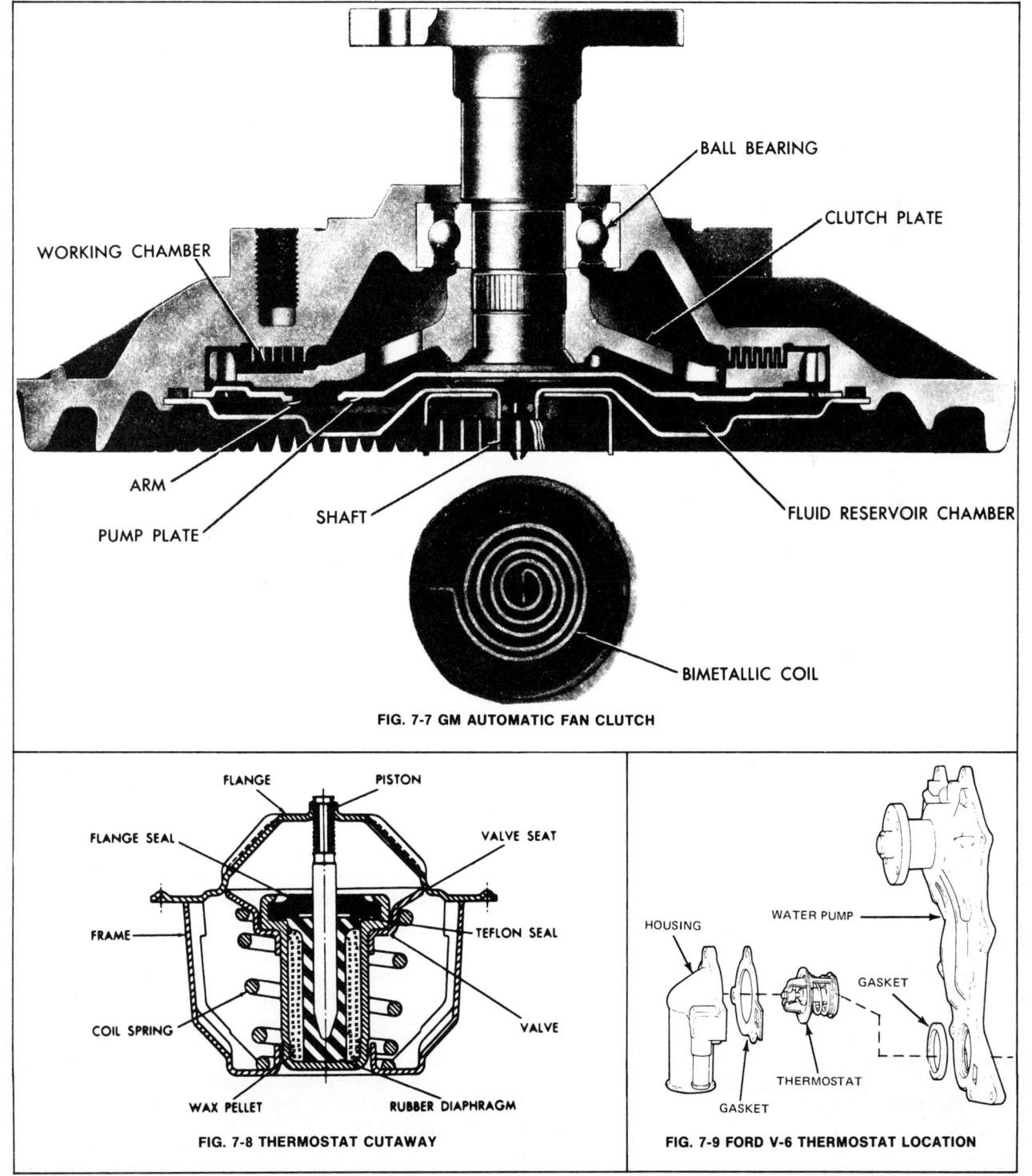

FIG. 7-7 GM AUTOMATIC FAN CLUTCH

FIG. 7-8 THERMOSTAT CUTAWAY

FIG. 7-9 FORD V-6 THERMOSTAT LOCATION

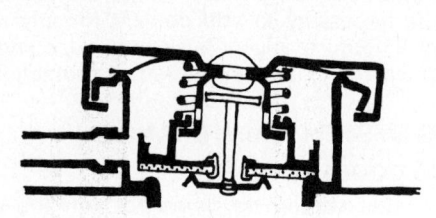

FIG. 7-10 CAP/NECK DEFORMITY

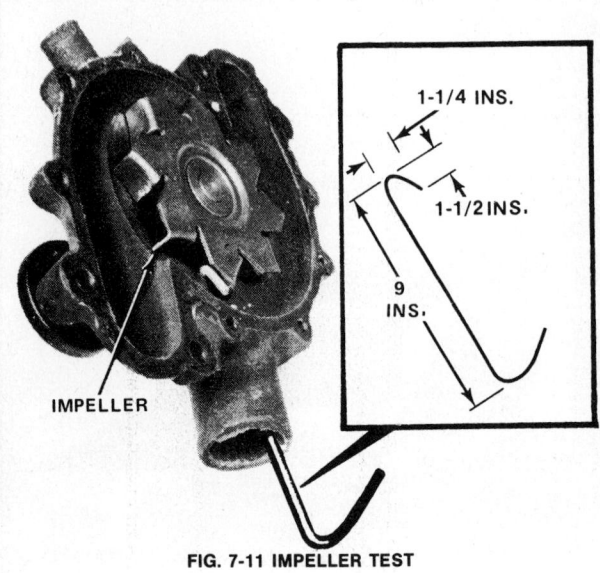

IMPELLER

1-1/4 INS.

1-1/2 INS.

9 INS.

FIG. 7-11 IMPELLER TEST

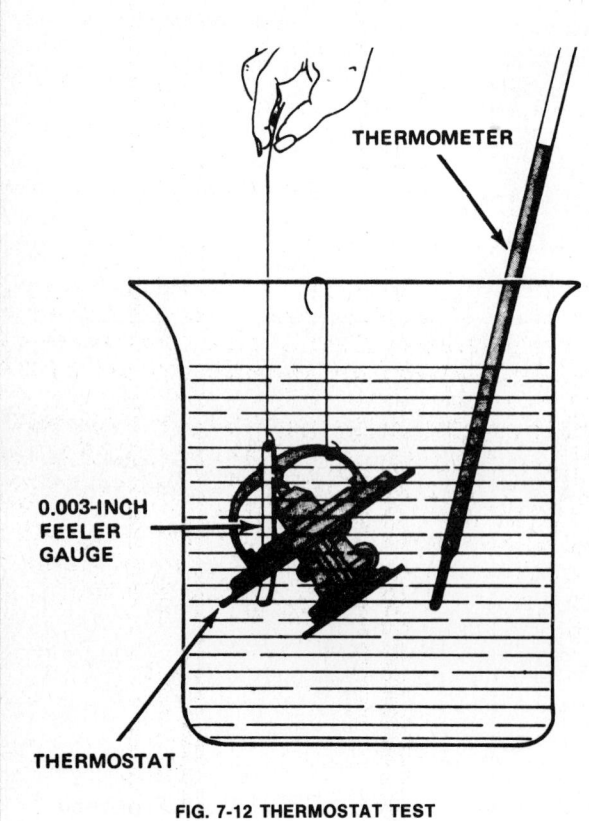

THERMOMETER

0.003-INCH FEELER GAUGE

THERMOSTAT

FIG. 7-12 THERMOSTAT TEST

recovery reservoirs are marked with designations such as COLD FULL, HOT FULL or ADD to indicate whether or not the system requires additional fluid.

If the radiator cap must be removed for any reason when the coolant is hot, a heavy rag or towel should be wrapped over and around the cap, and the cap turned slowly to the first notch to relieve system pressure (pressure can also be reduced by spraying the radiator with cool water before cap removal). Then push down and turn the cap, disengaging the locking tabs and removing it. Move to one side as the cap is removed; hot coolant is likely to blow out of the upper radiator hose and tank, and can cause bad burns if it comes in contact with your skin.

Maintaining the correct coolant level is important to proper system operation, because the sealing ability of the radiator cap is impaired when the coolant level is too high, and system protection is lowered when the level is too low. In a crossflow design, the coolant should be maintained 3 ins. below the filler neck seat when cold, and 1½ ins. below it when hot. The downflow radiator level should be 1½ ins. cold and ¼- to ½-in. hot. If the coolant is maintained at too high a level, fluid expansion when hot will cause an overfull condition, and the excess coolant will be expelled from the system through the overflow pipe.

If repeated coolant loss is noted, look for loose hose connections, defective hoses, gasket leaks or freeze plug deterioration. These can often be detected by the appearance of rusty-looking or grayish-white stains, especially if a leak is so small that immediate evaporation of the hot coolant occurs, preventing a tell-tale drip. If none of these conditions are found, check the radiator cap and filler neck seat for their sealing ability—inspect the rubber cap seal for tears or cracks and check for bent or distorted pressure cap or seat cams **(Fig. 7-10)**.

HOSE INSPECTION

Hoses should be checked at periodic and regular intervals. If any hose has swelled excessively, is cracked or feels brittle when squeezed, it should be replaced to prevent a rupture while driving. A good rule of thumb is to drain, flush and refill the cooling system with new coolant every two years, replacing all hoses at the same time.

SYSTEM OPERATIONAL CHECKS

Warm the engine to normal operating temperature and squeeze the upper radiator hose. If a pressure surge is not felt, look for a plugged vent hole in the water pump housing. Shut off the engine and feel the radiator. The inlet tank should be hot and the outlet tank warm, with an even temperature progression from warm to hot between the two tanks. If a cold spot is felt, it indicates a clogged section of the core.

COOLING SYSTEM COMPONENT TESTS

WATER PUMP IMPELLER (Fig. 7-11)

1. Open the drain cock at the bottom of the radiator and remove the radiator cap to drain the coolant. The coolant must be siphoned from early-model Vega radiators not fitted with a drain cock.

2. Loosen the fan belt and disconnect the lower radiator hose from the water pump housing inlet.

3. Bend a stiff clothes hanger, as shown in **Fig. 7-11,** and position it in the water pump inlet to block impeller movement.

4. Holding the hanger in place, try turning the fan. If the fan can be turned and the impeller held with the

hanger, the water pump is defective. If the impeller cannot be held with the hanger while the fan is turning, the pump is good.

5. If the pump is not defective, reconnect the hose to the pump inlet, close the radiator drain cock, replace and adjust the fan belt and refill the radiator with coolant to the proper level.

THERMOSTAT OPERATION (Fig. 7-12)

1. Open the drain cock at the bottom of the radiator and remove the radiator cap. Drain until the coolant level is below that of the upper hose/thermostat housing, then close the drain cock.

2. Remove the thermostat housing bolts and lift off the outlet housing. Remove the gasket and thermostat.

3. Attach a wire or string to a 0.003-in. feeler gauge, and insert the gauge between the thermostat valve and seat.

4. Submerge and suspend the thermostat in a container of coolant so that it does not touch the sides or bottom, then suspend a thermometer in the same way.

5. Heat the coolant, applying a slight tension on the feeler gauge. When the valve opens 0.003-in., the feel-er gauge will slip free. Note the coolant temperature—it should be between 192-199° F.

6. Continue heating the coolant until the thermostat valve is fully open—this should occur between 215-220° F. Remove the thermostat, place in a container of coolant heated to 180° F, and the valve should close. If the thermostat does not perform according to these specifications, install a new thermostat and gasket.

PRESSURE CAP

1. Remove the radiator pressure cap and check that its seating surfaces are clean.

2. Wet the rubber gasket with water and install the pressure cap on a cap tester, using the appropriate adapter **(Fig. 7-13)**.

3. Operate the tester plunger until the pressure rating stamped on the face of the cap is indicated on the tester gauge.

4. If the gauge needle holds steady for 30 seconds or more, or falls very slowly in that time, the cap is good. If the needle drops rapidly, the cap is defective and must be replaced with a new one of the same type and pressure rating.

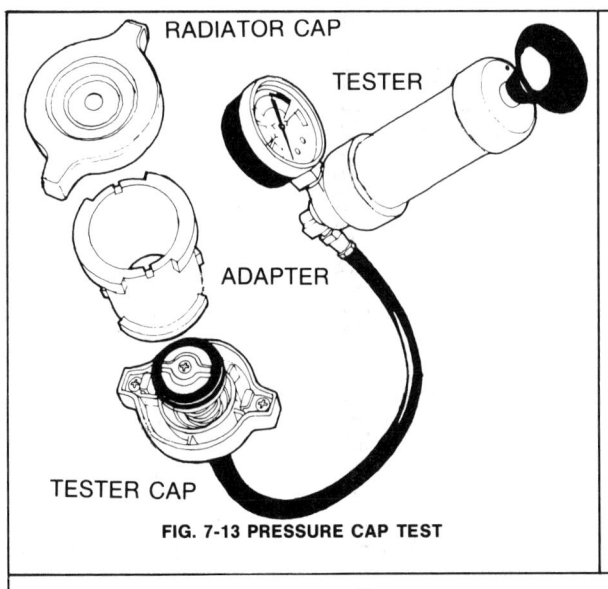

FIG. 7-13 PRESSURE CAP TEST

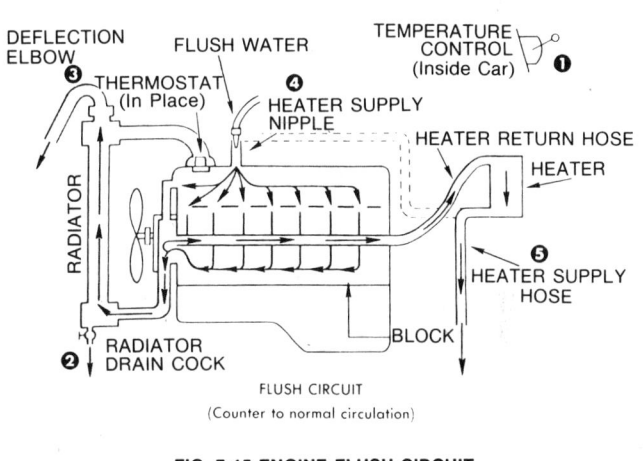

FIG. 7-15 ENGINE FLUSH CIRCUIT

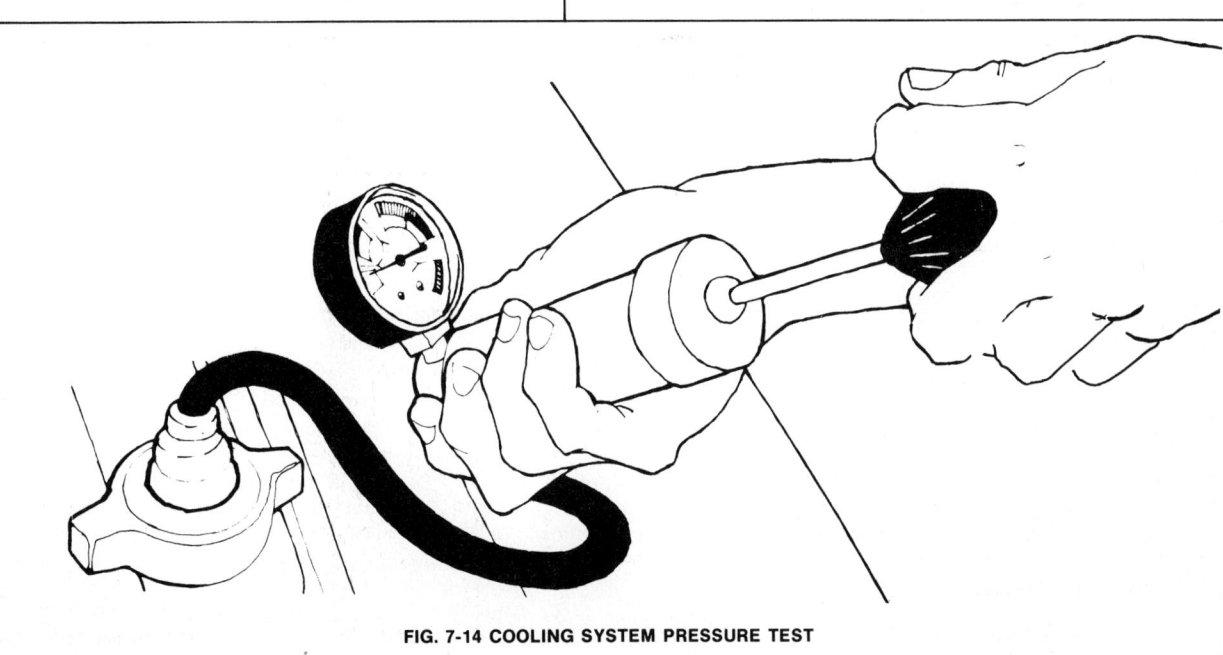

FIG. 7-14 COOLING SYSTEM PRESSURE TEST

COOLING SYSTEM PRESSURE (Fig. 7-14)

1. Start and run the engine until it reaches normal operating temperature, then shut it off.

2. Remove the radiator pressure cap and inspect the coolant level. If necessary, add a sufficient quantity to bring it up to the specified hot level.

3. Wipe the inside of the filler neck clean and examine the sealing seat for any nicks, dents, dirt or other damage/contamination.

4. Check the overflow tube for internal restrictions. If the tube is opaque instead of translucent, run a wire through it to make sure that the passage is clear.

5. Inspect the filler neck cams. Bent cam(s) will affect the seating of the pressure cap valve and thus prevent the tester unit from sealing properly, so the cam(s) should be reformed with a pair of pliers before proceeding

6. Connect the pressure tester to the radiator filler neck and apply system pressure, as indicated on the pressure cap, to the cooling system. If the connecting hoses swell out of shape during the test, they should be replaced.

7. a) If the tester gauge reading holds steady for at least two minutes, the system is intact, with no external leakage present. But this does not rule out the possibility of an internal leak, and if the cooling system continues to lose coolant despite a satisfactory test result, a "Combustion Leakage Test" should be performed.

b) A gauge needle that drops slowly instead of holding steady indicates the presence of a small leak or seepage of some kind. Check the water pump, radiator and heater hoses, connections, clamps and gaskets. If no signs of external leakage are found, there may be one or more tiny leaks in the radiator core.

c) A fluctuating needle indicates a combustion leak, usually a defective head gasket. This can also cause the needle to drop quickly after pressure is applied to the system. In this case, check first for external leaks. If none are found, disconnect the tester and run the engine to assure that the thermostat is open and that the coolant has expanded. Reconnect the tester and apply one-half system pressure with the engine running. Accelerate the engine rapidly while watching the tester needle. If it fluctuates at this point, a defective head gasket is allowing exhaust gas to mix with the coolant. The leaking cylinder can be isolated by shorting out each spark plug. The gauge needle will stop fluctuating when the spark plug wire of the leaking cylinder is removed.

d) If the needle does not fluctuate, but an abnormal amount of fluid comes out of the tailpipe during the test, the source of the leak could be a defective head gasket, a cracked engine block or a cylinder head that is cracked near the exhaust ports.

e) When the tester gauge shows a pressure drop, but no external leakage can be located, run the engine briefly and check for an internal leak by removing the oil and/or automatic transmission dipstick(s) and inspecting for signs of water mixed with the oil/fluid. If water globules appear on the dipstick(s), there is a serious internal leak allowing crankcase oil/transmission fluid to enter the cooling system.

COMBUSTION LEAKAGE TEST

If the cooling system passes the pressure test, but continues to lose coolant and no source of the leakage can be located, perform the following procedure:

1. Drain a sufficient amount of coolant to permit thermostat removal, and remove it.

2. Disconnect the water-pump drive belt.

3. Add sufficient coolant to the engine to bring its level to within ½-in. of the top of the thermostat housing or inlet tank.

4. Start the engine and accelerate rapidly to about 3000 rpm several times while watching the coolant. If bubbles appear in the coolant, exhaust gas is leaking; if bubbles cannot be seen, there are no internal leaks. Shut off the engine to prevent overheating, since the water pump is not working.

OIL COOLER LEAKAGE TEST

Should the presence of transmission fluid be noted in the coolant, or coolant in the transmission fluid, check the transmission fluid level and perform the following test:

1. Disconnect the transmission-to-cooler lines at the radiator, and plug one cooler fitting.

2. Remove the radiator pressure cap, and add sufficient coolant (if required) so that bubbles can be easily seen.

3. Apply 50 to 200 psi of compressed air to the other cooler fitting while watching the filler neck. If bubbles appear in the coolant, the radiator must be removed and repaired.

RADIATOR CLEANING AND FLUSHING

It is possible to clear a clogged radiator by solvent cleaning and flushing. While this procedure *does not always* clean out the obstructions in the core passages, it *is* worth a try before removing the radiator and sending it to a radiator shop for a boil-out. Carrying out the following procedure every 24 months, when the manufacturer-recommended coolant change is made, will help remove rust, scale and other deposits before they have an opportunity to clog the radiator.

CLEANING PROCEDURE

A good cleaning solution will help to loosen rust and scale before the cooling system is flushed. While there are a number of different solutions for this available on the market, pick one with a brand name you recognize and follow the specific procedure recommended by the manufacturer. The procedure which follows *applies only* to the use of GM Cooling System Cleaner, available from any GM dealer.

1. Drain the coolant from the cooling system and engine block.

2. Remove the thermostat, and replace its housing.

3. Add the No. 1 (liquid) part of the cleaner to the radiator and fill with water until it is 3 ins. below the top of the overflow pipe.

4. Run the engine at moderate speed, with the radiator covered, until coolant temperature reaches 180°F, then remove the radiator cover and continue running the engine for 20 minutes—*do not* let it boil.

5. Add the No. 2 (powder) part of the cleaner to the radiator and continue running the engine another 10 minutes. Shut the engine off and wait a few minutes, then open the engine-block drain cock(s) and disconnect the lower radiator hose.

6. After the cleaning solution has drained completely, close the drain cock(s) and reconnect the lower radiator hose in preparation for flushing.

FLUSHING PROCEDURE

While reverse flushing is recommended by manufacturers, the process requires a special flushing gun, and those not familiar with its use and operation can easily damage the cooling system by over-zealous use of the pressure. An equally satisfactory method requiring no special equipment or knowledge is detailed below and in **Fig. 7-15**:

1. Set the heater temperature control to HIGH. If the car is equipped with air conditioning, it has a vacuum-operated heater valve and the engine must run at idle during the flushing procedure described, because a vacuum valve will only stay open with the engine running. Be sure to keep a close watch on the engine temperature gauge in this case.

2. Open the radiator drain cock and let the radiator drain— *do not* open the engine drain cock(s).

3. Remove the radiator pressure cap and place a deflection elbow in the filler neck to prevent excessive splash into the engine compartment.

4. Remove the hose from the heater supply nipple at the engine block and point it downward for draining purposes.

5. Connect the water supply to the heater supply nipple at the engine block. This does not have to be a positive connection; an ordinary garden hose will work as long as most of the water can be directed into the engine.

6. Turn on the water, make sure it is cold, and flush for 3-5 minutes without the engine running (with the

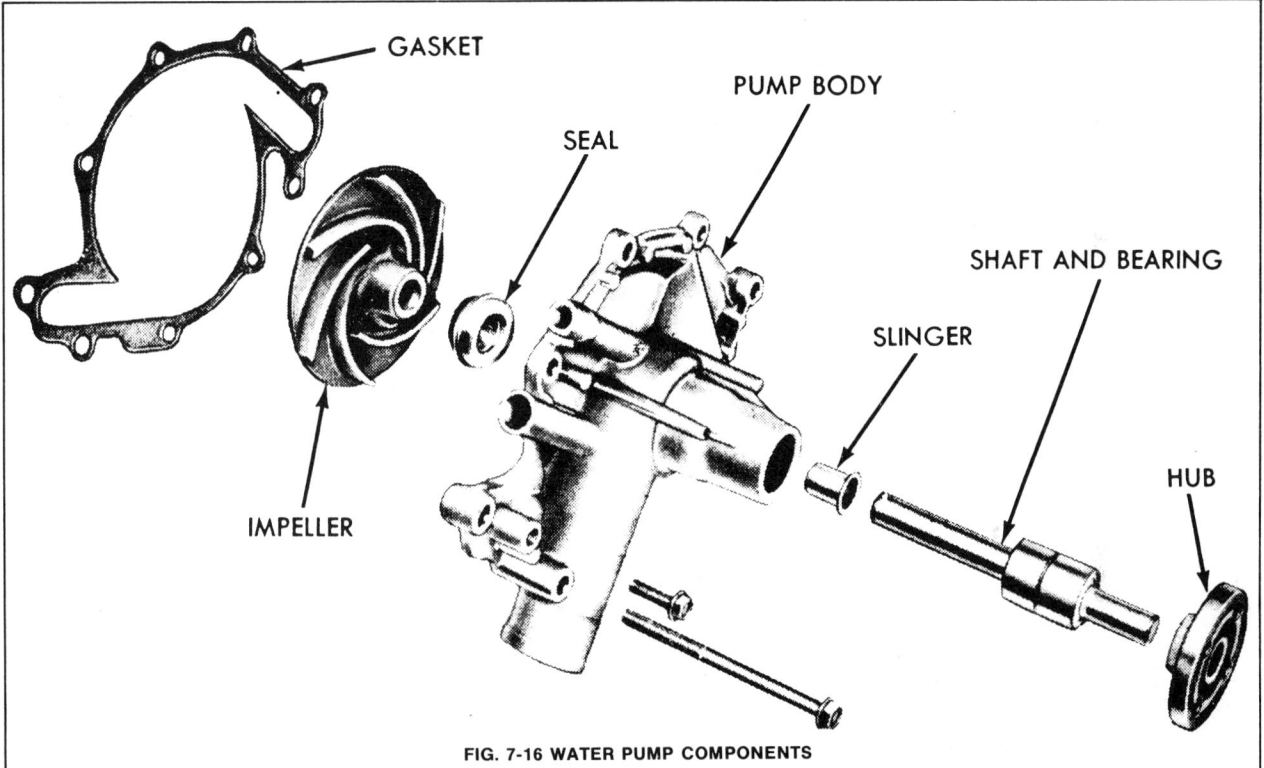

FIG. 7-16 WATER PUMP COMPONENTS

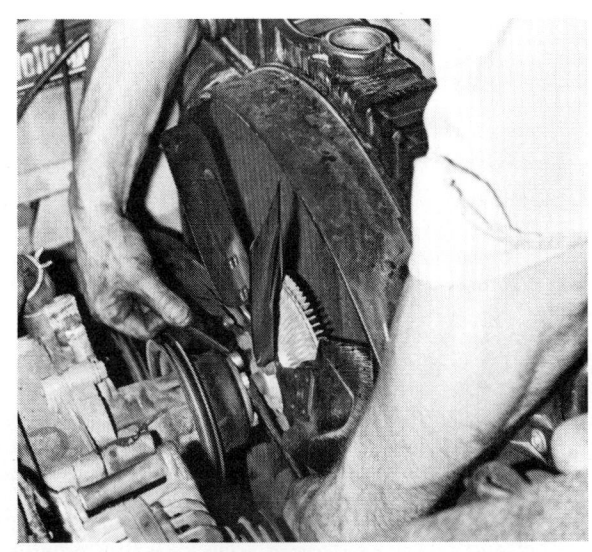

FIG. 7-17 FAN REMOVAL

FIG. 7-18 WATER PUMP REMOVAL

engine running if equipped with a vacuum-operated heater valve). Squeeze the outlet or upper radiator hose during the last minute of flushing to remove any trapped liquid.

7. Turn off the water and close the radiator drain cock. Reconnect the heater supply hose to its nipple on the engine block and remove the deflection elbow from the radiator filler neck. Refill the system with coolant to its normal level.

COOLING SYSTEM COMPONENT REPLACEMENT

WATER PUMP/FAN REMOVAL/INSTALLATION

All water pumps are serviced as a complete assembly. Pump failure is generally caused by bearing/bushing wear, allowing the shaft to rotate off-center. This will eventually damage the pump seal and cause a leak **(Fig. 7-16).** When the pump is replaced due to bearing or shaft failure, manufacturers recommend that the fan unit be replaced at the same time. Fan assemblies must remain in proper balance, or they may fail and fly apart during operation, causing a very dangerous situation. Should the water pump shaft fail, there is no guarantee that proper fan balance exists.

Make certain the correct replacement pump is used, since the pump impeller must be compatible with the drive ratio of the pulley system, or overheating/heater-core failure may result. Water pump removal is simple; getting to the pump for removal is the problem. Due to the large variety of different engine compartment configurations, it is impractical to attempt to describe specific removal procedures for individual installations. Therefore, the following generalized procedure is provided as a guide in assisting with water pump replacement. If only the fan requires servicing, follow Steps 2, 3 and 8 below.

TO REMOVE

1. Drain the cooling system. On some installations, it

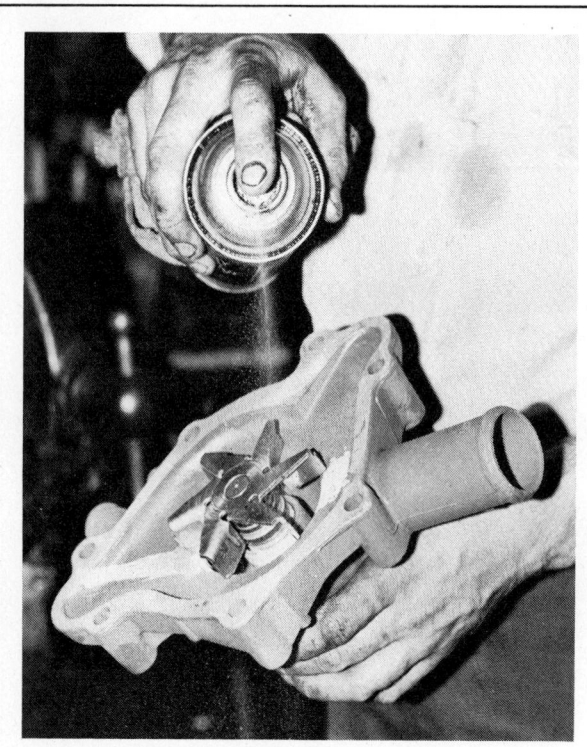

FIG. 7-19 GASKET SPRAY ADHESIVE

may be necessary to remove the battery and fan shroud for access to the pump.

2. Loosen the alternator, air pump, power steering pump and air-conditioning-compressor idler pulley (if so equipped) and remove all drive belts. It may also be necessary to remove one or more of these units from their mounting in order to provide sufficient access to reach the pump.

3. Loosen and remove the fan blade, spacer or fluid unit, pulley and bolts as an assembly **(Fig. 7-17).** If a fan clutch is removed, be sure to keep it in an ''in-car'' or vertical position. Laying it down on a bench will cause the silicone fluid to drain into the fan drive bearing, ruining the lubricant and causing silicone leakage.

4. Disconnect and remove all hoses from the water pump housing.

5. If necessary, remove the air pump and/or compressor-bracket-to-water-pump bolts and tie the compressor/air pump out of the way.

6. Remove the water-pump retaining bolts and withdraw the pump from the cylinder-block/timing-cover case **(Fig. 7-18).** If the pump is old and has not been removed before, it may be necessary to tap the pump housing with a mallet to break the seal.

7. Remove and discard the pump-to-engine gasket and clean the engine mating surface thoroughly.

8. Lay the fan on a flat surface, with its leading edge facing down—place fan clutch units against an upright plane, with their leading edge facing inward. If more than 0.090-in. clearance exists between the blade tip which touches the flat surface and the blade tip opposite it, replace the fan. *Never attempt to bend or straighten a fan.*

TO INSTALL

1. Fit a new gasket to the pump housing and apply a sealer coating **(Fig. 7-19).** Install the pump housing on the cylinder-block/timing-cover case and replace the retaining bolts, torquing to specifications.

2. Rotate the pump shaft by hand to make certain it rotates freely; install all hoses to the pump housing.

3. Install the fan blade, spacer or fluid unit, pulley and bolts as an assembly. Torque the fan attaching bolts to specifications.

4. Replace and adjust all drive belts for proper tension. Replace and connect any other units removed to provide working access.

5. Fill the radiator to specifications with a mixture of glycol antifreeze (44%) and distilled water (56%) to provide cooling system protection to -20° F. Recheck coolant level after engine warm-up and inspect for leaks.

RADIATOR REMOVAL/INSTALLATION

TO REMOVE

1. Open the radiator drain cock, with the pressure cap in place, and drain. When the coolant recovery tank is empty, remove the pressure cap to vent the radiator for more rapid draining.

2. Open the engine block drain cock(s) and move the heater temperature selector to a full ON position.

3. Disconnect the upper and lower radiator hoses, and remove from their respective ports. If the hoses are old and do not pull off easily, try twisting them off. When new hoses are to be installed, cut the old ones with a hacksaw for quick, simple radiator removal.

4. If equipped with an automatic transmission, disconnect and remove oil cooler lines from the radiator.

5. If fitted with a fan shroud, remove the shroud attaching screws and separate the shroud from the ra-

diator, positioning toward the engine for maximum access clearance.

6. Remove the radiator attaching screws and lift the radiator from its support brackets and out of the engine compartment.

TO INSTALL

1. If installing a new radiator, remove the old radiator drain-cock/oil-cooler fittings as required, and install them on the new radiator, using oil resistant sealer.

2. Slide the radiator down in position behind the radiator support, and replace the attaching screws.

3. Replace the fan shroud, connect the hoses and the transmission oil-cooler lines.

4. Open the heater valve, and fill the radiator to specifications with a mixture of glycol antifreeze (44%) and distilled water (56%) to provide cooling system protection to -20° F.

5. Recheck coolant and transmission fluid levels after engine warm-up, and inspect for leaks.

COOLING SYSTEM TORQUE SPECIFICATIONS

GENERAL MOTORS	Ft.-Lbs.	In.-Lbs.
Buick Division		
(V-6 & V-8 Engines)		
Water Pump to Timing Chain Cover	7	—
Fan to Pulley	20	—
Fan Shroud to Radiator Panel	10	—
Alternator Bracket to Water Pump		
Timing Chain Cover	20	—
Thermostat Housing	20	—
Cadillac Division		
(All Engines Except Seville)		
Fan Blade Assembly	18	—
Thermostat Housing	10	—
Water Pump to Cylinder Block Screw	22	—
Water Pump to Cylinder Block	15	—
Water Pump Front Cover Screw	—	70
Heater Hose Clamp	—	13
(Seville)		
Fan Blade to Fan Clutch	18	—
Fan and Clutch to Hub Stud Nuts	18	—
Fan and Driven Pulley to Hub Bolts	20	—
Studs to Water Pump Hub	8	—
Thermostat Housing	20	—
Water Pump to Cylinder Block	15	—
Self-Tapping Bolts to Front Cover		
(Oil Before Installing)	13	—
Water Pump to Front Cover (5/16-in. Bolts)	22	—
Water Pump to Timing Chain Cover	7	—
Chevrolet Division		
I-4, I-6 Water Pump (Except Chevette)	15	—
V-6, V-8 Water Pump	30	—
Chevette Water Pump	18-24	—
Thermostat Housing	30	—
Fan to Pump	20	—
Fan to Clutch	15	—
Oldsmobile Division		
4-cyl. Water Pump	15	—
6-cyl. Water Pump	7-10	—
8-cyl. Water Pump	13	—
I-6, V-8 Thermostat Housing	30	—
V-6 Thermostat Housing	20	—
Fan to Pump	20	—
Fan to Clutch	15	—

GENERAL MOTORS	Ft.-Lbs.	In.-Lbs.
Pontiac Division		
4-cyl. Water Pump	15	—
6-cyl. Water Pump	20	—
8-cyl. Water Pump	15-20	—
Thermostat Housing	30	—
Fan to Pump	20	—
Fan to Clutch	15	—
CHRYSLER CORPORATION		
Water Pump Bolts	30	—
Fan Attaching Bolts	—	200
Thermostat Housing	30	—
Shroud Mounting Bolts	—	12
Radiator Mounting Bolts	—	95
Drain Cock	—	150
Oil Cooler Fittings—to radiator	—	110
Lines to Fittings	—	85
Lines to Auxiliary Cooler	—	85
Lines to Connector	—	50
FORD MOTOR COMPANY		
Thermostat Housing	12-15	—
Fan and Spacer to Pulley	12-18	—
Fan to Clutch	10-15	—
Fan Clutch to Water Pump Hub	12-18	—
Oil Cooler Lines	9-12	—
Radiator Bracket Rod to Support, Hose Clamps	—	20-30
Fan Shroud to Radiator	—	24-48
I-4 Water Pump	14-21	—
V-6 Water Pump	7-9	—
V-8 Water Pump (Except 390-428 cu. in.)	12-15	—
V-8 Water Pump (390-428 cu. in.)	20-25	—
I-6 Water Pump (Except 240 cu. in.)	12-15	—
I-6 Water Pump (240 cu. in.)	15-20	—
AMERICAN MOTORS		
Fan Blades and Pulley to Hub	18	—
Oil Cooler Line Radiator Fitting	15	—
Thermostat Housing	13	—
I-6 Water Pump to Front Block	13	—
V-8 Water Pump to Engine Block	25	—
V-8 Water Pump to Front Cover	—	48

INDEX

THE ENGINE

ENGINE CODE LOCATER

When ordering replacement parts for your car's engine, it is imperative to know which particular engine you have. While it is true that you can pull some accessories and match a replacement to what's in your hand, you must bear in mind that between engine variations there are different bolt patterns and electrical specifications to contend with. It's a fact made more critical when you need internal engine parts.

In the chart below, we will tell you where to find your engine code letter. You can give that information to your favorite parts supply store or automotive dealership and be assured of obtaining the proper engine parts.

Your car will have a Vehicle Identification Number (VIN). The VIN contains a letter or letters designating your engine. You will find it on your certificate of ownership (pink slip), registration slip, and on the car itself.

Here's where to find the VIN, and the engine code:

AMERICAN MOTORS CORP

1971—On a machined surface of engine block between #2 and #3 cylinders of 232- and 258-cu.-in. engines. All others are located on the tag attached to right bank cylinder head cover.

1972-1973—The 5th character of VIN located on upper left side of instrument panel, visible through windshield.

1974 through 1979—The 7th character of VIN, located as above.

CHRYSLER CORP.

1970 through 1979—The 5th character of VIN plate located on upper left side of instrument panel, visible through windshield.

FORD MOTOR CO.

1970—The 5th character on decal located on rear face of driver's door.

1971 through 1974—The 5th character on decal located on rear face of driver's door; and 5th character of VIN plate located on upper left side of instrument panel, visible through windshield. On Capri, code is designated separately and found on VIN plate riveted to top of right fender apron.

1975 through 1979—The 6th character of the VIN plate located on upper left side of the instrument panel, visible through windshield.

GENERAL MOTORS CORP.

1970

Chevrolet—Last 2 or 3 letters of code on Protecta-Plate's upper left corner attached to warranty booklet. Also, for 6-cyl. engines, code is stamped on a machined pad, right side of engine at rear of distributor. For V-8's, code is stamped on pad immediately forward at right-hand cylinder head. On 4-cyl. engines, code is stamped on pad on right side of engine opposite #3 cylinder.

Cadillac—No code is necessary, since each model offered no engine options. Each model had a fixed engine choice. Know your model.

Buick—On right side of distributor at rear of distributor for 6-cyl. engines; between 1st and 2nd spark plugs on left bank for 8-cyl. engines.

Oldsmobile—Engine code is found on tape on engine oil filler tube (8-cyl. only). On 6-cyl. engines, code is on right side of engine at rear of distributor.

Pontiac—Same as Olds 6-cyl. locations (see above); on V-8, code is on machined pad on right bank of engine block.

1971
All models—Same as 1970.

1972 through 1979

The 5th character of the VIN plate fastened to the upper left side of trim molding, visible through windshield (including Cadillac). Vegas, through 1977, including Cosworth option, have engine code on pad at right side of cylinder block above starter.

ENGINE OVERHAUL

The rebuilding or overhauling of an automotive engine requires the use of a considerable amount of specialized tools and equipment not generally found in the average home garage. If the engine is to be removed from the car, an engine hoist is required and an engine stand is desirable. Specialized tools are then required for cylinder reconditioning, piston ring installation, valve grinding, etc. Although such equipment and tools can be bought or rented, a stock engine overhaul or rebuild is often best left to the professional shop due to the high purchase or rental costs involved. Rental fees may seem quite reasonable on the surface, but unless the entire job can be done on a start-to-finish basis, daily rental charges add up quickly and can often exceed the price of a professional overhaul before you are finished. While space limitations do not permit covering specific overhaul techniques for each and every different engine in use, a generalized procedure is provided in this chapter (followed by necessary specifi-

cations) for those who do wish to do their own engine work, and is divided into two sections—cylinder head and engine block reconditioning.

CYLINDER HEAD RECONDITIONING

This can be accomplished without removing the entire engine from the car. The following procedures assume that: A) All necessary accessories and manifolds have already been removed from the engine; B) the cylinder head(s) has been removed and cleaned; C) the camshaft has been removed from ohc heads; and D) the head has been placed on a suitable and clean workbench.

HEAD DISASSEMBLY

1. With the head inverted on the workbench, number the valve faces from front to rear with a felt-tip marking pen.

2. Disconnect and remove the rocker arms **(Fig. 8-1).** Wiring the set of rockers with its corresponding

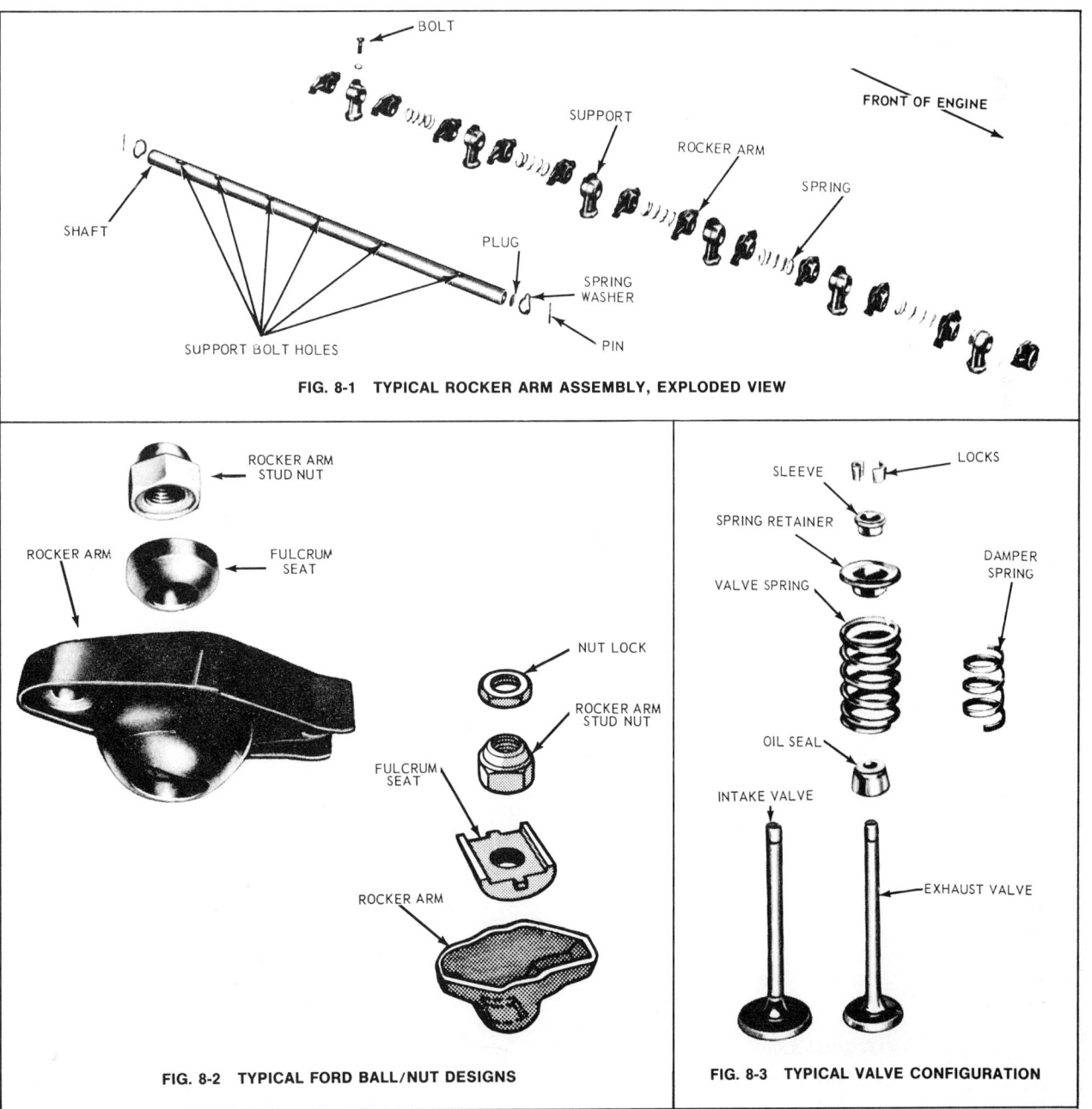

FIG. 8-1 TYPICAL ROCKER ARM ASSEMBLY, EXPLODED VIEW

FIG. 8-2 TYPICAL FORD BALL/NUT DESIGNS

FIG. 8-3 TYPICAL VALVE CONFIGURATION

balls and nuts **(Fig 8-2),** use a tag or tape to identify each with its corresponding valve.

3. Compress the valve springs with a valve-spring compressor tool and remove the valve locks/keepers with a pair of needlenose pliers.

4. Release the compressor tool and remove the valve and its components as shown in **Fig 8-3.** Some valve arrangements will not use all of these parts; thus

FIG. 8-4 VALVE GUIDE-TO-STEM MEASUREMENT

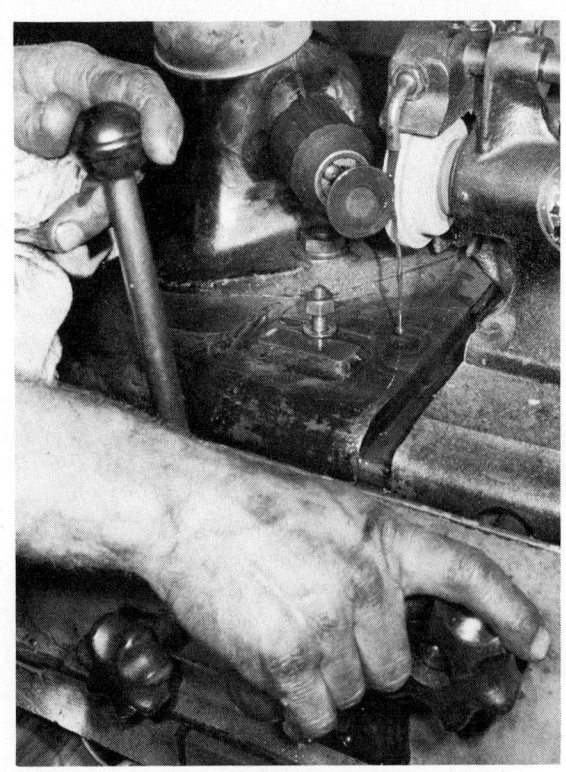

FIG. 8-5 VALVE GRINDING

the exact valve component configuration will vary from one engine design to another. Repeat Steps 3 and 4 for each valve.

5. Remove the valves and place them in sequence in a rack made by drilling holes in a yardstick or other suitable length of wood.

CLEANING AND INSPECTION

1. Clean the valve stems and valve guide bores (for bores, a rifle-cleaning brush and rod work well) with solvent to remove any gum/varnish, and replace each in its correct position in the head.

2. Secure a dial indicator at a 90° angle to the valve stem near the guide, as shown in **Fig. 8-4,** and move the valve off its seat.

3. Rock the stem back and forth to measure the guide-to-stem clearance. Check all valves in this manner. If valve stem-to-guide clearance is excessive, the guides must be replaced, reamed or knurled, depending upon guide design.

a) Where the guides are separate units, pressed or shrunk into the head, they can be removed and replaced by a machine shop.

b) In cases where the guides are an integral part of the head and not removable, they must be reamed to the next larger size and fitted with oversize valves.

c) If the guides are not excessively worn or otherwise distorted, it may be possible to knurl rather than replace them. Knurling is a process which displaces and raises the metal as a means of reducing clearance, and must be done by a machine shop.

4. Clean the accumulated carbon buildup from the combustion chambers, valve ports, valve stems and head. Clean dirt and gasket cement from the machined surface of the head.

5. Inspect the head for cracks in the combustion chambers and valve ports, and for cracks in the gasket surface at each coolant passage.

6. If possible, the head should be hot-tanked to remove any corrosion, grease and scale from the coolant passages; degrease the other components.

7. With the cylinder head inverted, place a straight-edge across the center and both diagonals of its gasket surface to check for warpage. If warpage exceeds 0.006-in. over the total surface, or 0.003-in. over any 6-in. span, the head should be resurfaced. Because milling a V-8 head will change the mounting position of the intake manifold, the manifold flange should also be milled proportionately to retain correct relationships.

8. Check the valve springs by lining them up on a flat surface. If any spring varies more than 1/16-in. out of square, it should be replaced.

9. Use a valve spring tester or have a machine shop test the pressure of each spring at installed and compressed height. Compressed height is installed height minus valve lift. Refer to specifications.

VALVE AND SEAT GRINDING

If the old valves are not excessively worn, burned, distorted or otherwise damaged, they can be reground to specifications. Where valve seat inserts are used and are worn beyond resurfacing, they must be replaced by a machine shop.

1. Reface the intake and exhaust valves to the specified angle with a valve grinder **(Fig. 8-5).** If a 1/32-in. margin does not remain after refacing, as shown in **Fig. 8-6,** the valve must be replaced.

2. Square and resurface the valve stem tip if necessary by grinding, but *do not* remove more than 0.010-in. or the valve will have to be replaced.

3. Fit the correct size pilot in the valve guide and reface the valve seat with a coarse stone of the proper angle **(Fig. 8-7)**. Use a fine stone to dress the seat to the specified angle **(Fig. 8-8)**. Seat runout should be kept to a maximum of 0.0025-in. as measured by a dial indicator **(Fig. 8-9)**.

4. Fit the resurfaced valves in their respective guides and move each one up and down several times rapidly to check their action and seating **(Fig. 8-10)**.

HEAD REASSEMBLY

1. Lightly lubricate each valve stem as the valve is replaced in the valve guide from which it was removed.

2. Install new oil seals or deflectors, if used. On some head designs, this is best accomplished after Step 3 **(Fig. 8-11)**.

3. Replace the valve springs, dampers and spring retainers. Compress the components, using the valve-spring compressor tool, and install the locks/keepers using wheel bearing grease to keep them in place **(Fig. 8-12)**. Release the compressor tool and repeat this step for each valve.

4. Lightly tap each valve spring from side to side with a mallet to make sure it is properly seated.

5. Inspect the rocker arm(s), balls, studs and nuts for signs of excessive wear, galling, burning or scoring. If any defect is noted, replace the component. When exhaust ball replacement is required, use the intake ball from the same cylinder and install a new intake ball—the use of new rocker balls on exhaust valves should be avoided if possible.

6. If push rods are used, check their ends for wear, and replace if necessary—all push rods must be equal in length and straight. Check for straightness by roll-

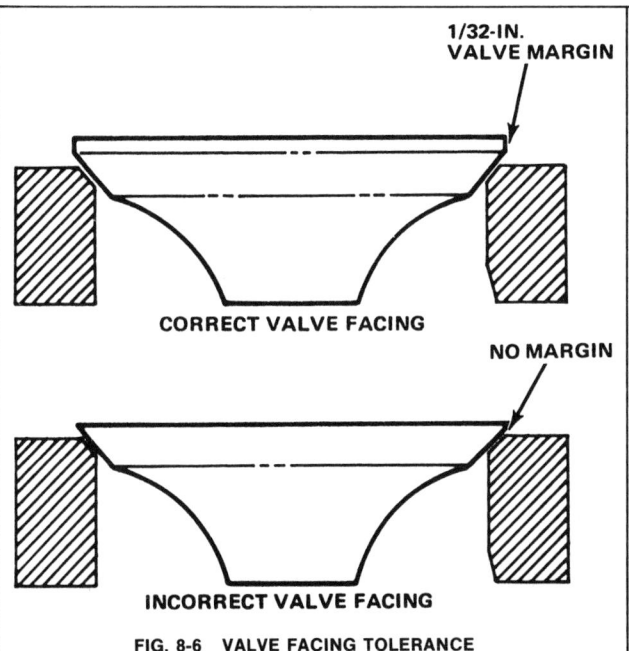

FIG. 8-6 VALVE FACING TOLERANCE

FIG. 8-7 PILOT SHAFT/STONE INSTALLATION

FIG. 8-8 DRESSING THE VALVE SEAT

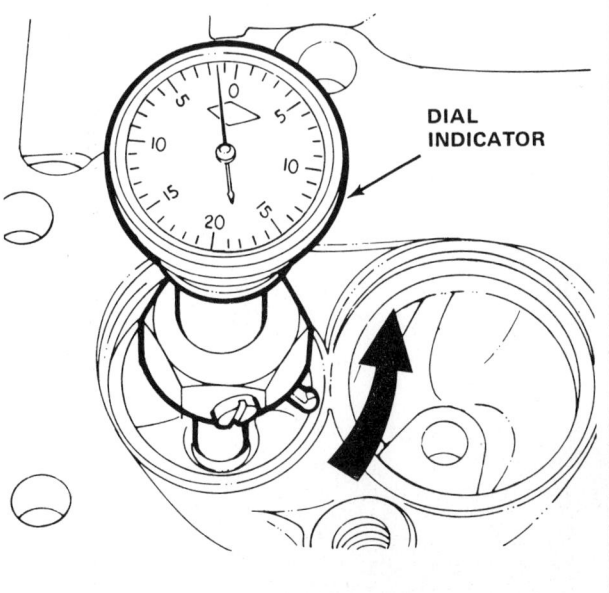

FIG. 8-9 VALVE SEAT RUNOUT

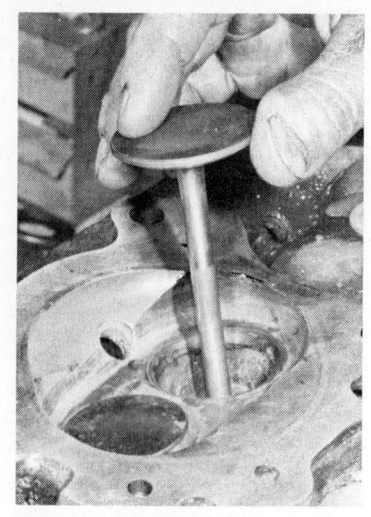

FIG. 8-10   TESTING VALVE ACTION

FIG. 8-11   INSTALLING OIL SEAL

FIG. 8-12 REPLACING LOCKS/KEEPERS

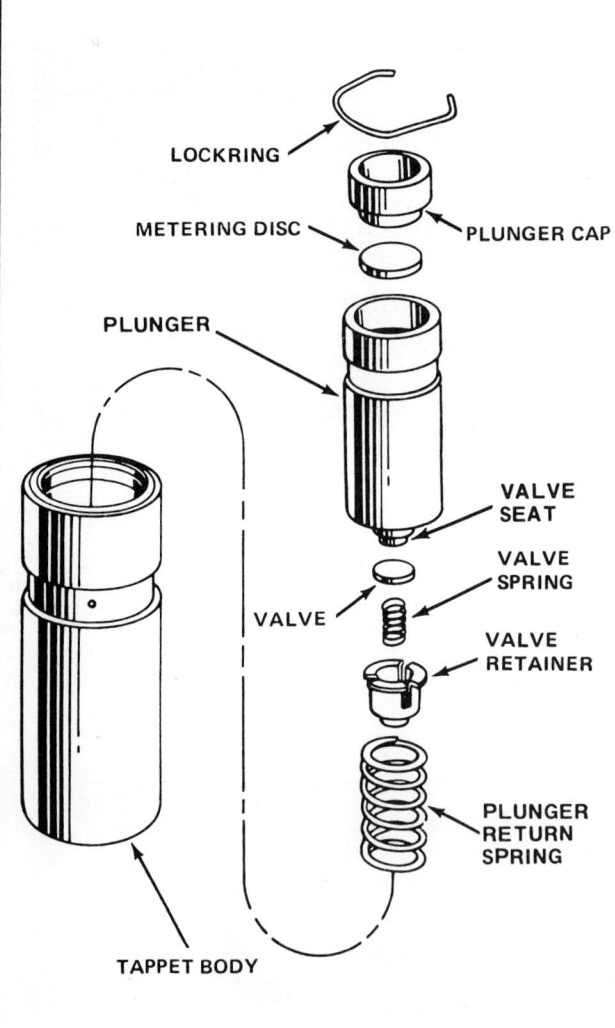

LOCKRING

METERING DISC

PLUNGER

PLUNGER CAP

VALVE SEAT

VALVE

VALVE SPRING

VALVE RETAINER

PLUNGER RETURN SPRING

TAPPET BODY

FIG. 8-13   TYPICAL HYDRAULIC LIFTER, EXPLODED VIEW

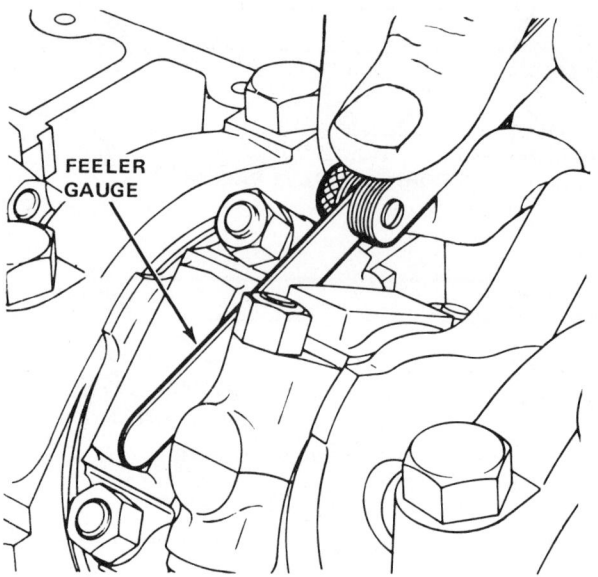

FEELER GAUGE

FIG. 8-14   CONNECTING ROD SIDE CLEARANCE (V-6, V-8)

FIG. 8-14A CONNECTING ROD SIDE CLEARANCE (I-4, I-6)

ing each push rod across a piece of glass. If the rolling rod emits a definite clicking sound, then the push rod is bent and should be replaced. Where push rod wear due to lack of oil is evident, the corresponding lifter should be inspected carefully.

7. Remove, clean and inspect the valve lifters **(Fig. 8-13)** for scuffing on the side and face, and for concave face wear. A straightedge placed across the face of several lifters positioned in an upright position is the most practical test. If concave wear is noted, the corresponding camshaft lobe is worn, and both camshaft and all lifters should be replaced.

8. If lifter wear is insignificant, you may want to check the operation of hydraulic lifters with a leak down test. A machine shop will perform the test for you.

9. If the lifters check out okay, lubricate them and install them in their original bores. Reinstall the push rods in the same bores from which they were removed.

10. Reinstall rocker arm assemblies and torque each retaining screw one turn at a time until the specified torque setting is obtained.

11. Install the reconditioned cylinder head and a new gasket to the engine block. Torque the head bolts in the proper sequence and to specifications.

12. Replace the cylinder head cover and gasket.

ENGINE BLOCK RECONDITIONING

The entire engine should be removed from the car. While it is possible to perform some or all of the reconditioning/overhaul procedures with the engine in the car, the considerable increase in time required, as well as the difficulty of working under and above the block in sequential steps, makes removal advisable. The procedure specified below assumes that: A) All accessories, manifolds and head(s) have already been removed from the engine block; B) the block is mounted on a suitable workstand, preferably an engine stand; and C) the oil pan and oil pump have been removed and the engine block drained of lubricant.

MAIN AND CONNECTING ROD BEARING SERVICE

If misaligned or bent, connecting rods will cause abnormal piston, ring, cylinder wall, bearing or crankshaft journal wear. Rod alignment should be checked if any wear pattern or damage indicates the possibility of a misaligned connecting rod.

1. With the engine block inverted in the engine stand, rotate the crankshaft until two adjacent connecting rods (V-6, V-8) are at the bottom of their strokes. On an inline engine, rotate the crank until one rod

reaches the bottom of its stroke. Check rod side clearance for two rods on the V engines by spreading the two rods at the rod caps with a screwdriver and inserting a snug-fitting feeler gauge between the two as shown in **Fig. 8-14.** On an inline engine, insert the gauge between the rod cap and crankpin **(Fig. 8-14A).** Rods that do not meet clearance specs should be machined or replaced.

2. Remove the bearing cap from the rear main bearing, and inspect the bearing inserts and the crankshaft journal for visible wear **(Fig. 8-14B).** Upper insert can be removed by rotating it out of the rod. If visible wear exists, inserts must be replaced and crank should be checked for trueness.

NOTE: Bearing caps should not be mixed, so scribe or tag each rod cap and its corresponding rod with its appropriate cylinder number *before removal.* The rear main-bearing cap can be marked with a No. 1 and, moving forward, the others should be marked in sequence. This procedure will ensure correct replacement later, if the crank is removed.

When replacing inserts, both halves (upper and lower) must be replaced.

CAUTION: To protect the rod journal while the cap is off, place pieces of rubber hose or plastic tubing over the rod bolts.

3. To check for trueness of crank, clean off each journal as you go, and measure its diameter with a micrometer, as shown in **Fig. 8-15,** and compare readings to specifications.

4. If any rod journal disagrees with specifications, either replace the crankshaft or have it reconditioned, and fit with new oversize bearing inserts.

5. With either used or new inserts, measure the clearance between each insert and journal with Plastigage. Plastigage is a soft, wax-like plastic and, when compressed, it determines this clearance. Clean each journal and insert of all oil, because Plastigage is soluble in oil.

IMPORTANT: When checking bearings and/or clearance, loosen only one bearing cap at a time and, when finished, torque it down before going on to the next.

6. Place a length of Plastigage across the full width (parallel to crank) of the crankshaft journal.

7. Install the bearing cap, with insert, and torque to specifications.

REMEMBER: To ensure accuracy, *do not* rotate the crank with Plastigage in place.

8. Remove the bearing cap, and use the scale furnished on the Plastigage package to measure the width of the compressed Plastigage at its widest point **(Fig. 8-16).**

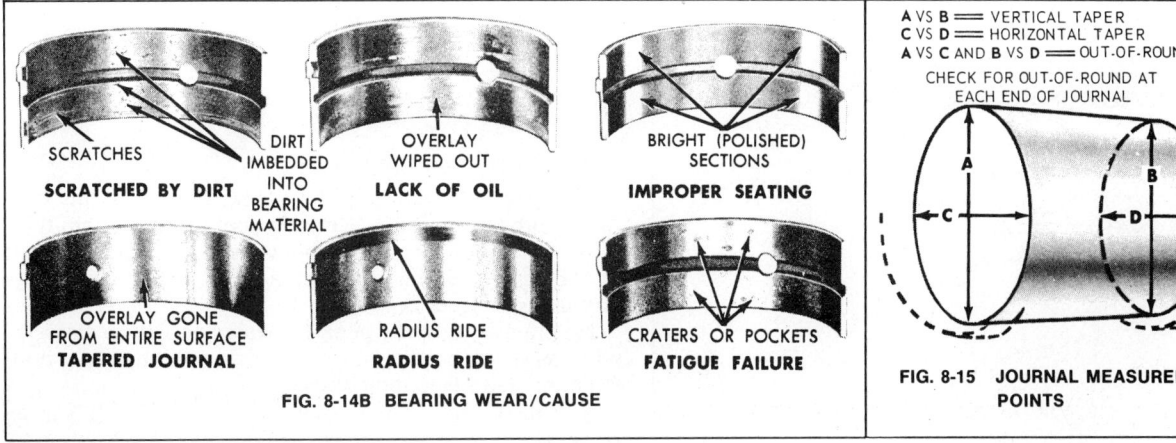

SCRATCHES
SCRATCHED BY DIRT DIRT IMBEDDED INTO BEARING MATERIAL

OVERLAY WIPED OUT
LACK OF OIL

BRIGHT (POLISHED) SECTIONS
IMPROPER SEATING

OVERLAY GONE FROM ENTIRE SURFACE
TAPERED JOURNAL

RADIUS RIDE
RADIUS RIDE

CRATERS OR POCKETS
FATIGUE FAILURE

FIG. 8-14B BEARING WEAR/CAUSE

A VS B ══ VERTICAL TAPER
C VS D ══ HORIZONTAL TAPER
A VS C AND B VS D ══ OUT-OF-ROUND
CHECK FOR OUT-OF-ROUND AT EACH END OF JOURNAL

FIG. 8-15 JOURNAL MEASUREMENT POINTS

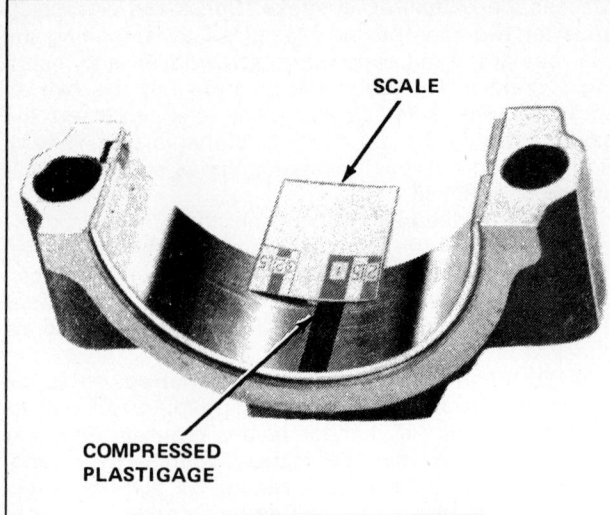

**COMPRESSED
PLASTIGAGE**

FIG. 8-16   PLASTIGAGE MEASUREMENT

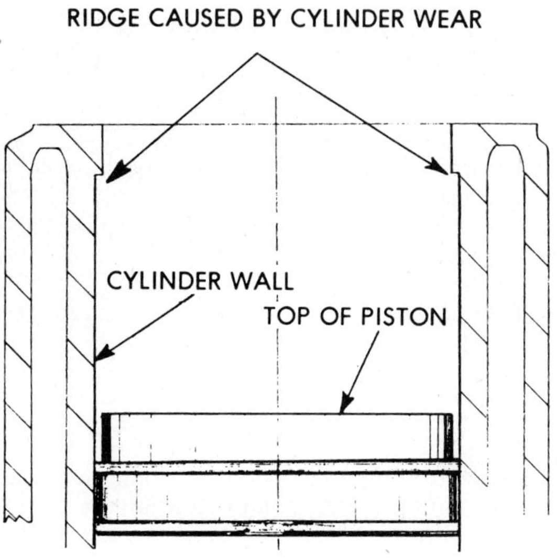

RIDGE CAUSED BY CYLINDER WEAR

CYLINDER WALL
TOP OF PISTON

FIG. 8-17   PISTON WALL RIDGE

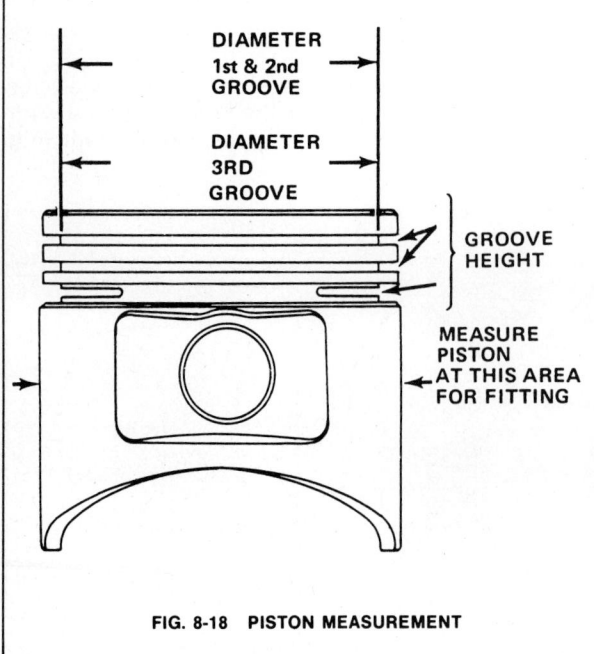

FIG. 8-18   PISTON MEASUREMENT

NOTE: If the Plastigage tapers at its middle or end, it indicates a taper or irregularity of the journal or insert. The difference in measurement between the narrowest and widest points of the Plastigage gives you the amount of journal or insert taper. Measure the journal again with a micrometer if difference is greater than 0.001-in. However, main bearing journals seldom wear unevenly and are rarely out-of-round, so if the difference is greater than 0.001-in., then you can usually blame the bearing.

9. Rotate the crankshaft 90° and repeat Steps 5 through 7 to check journal eccentricity.

10. Torque down the first main-bearing cap, proceed to the next main bearing and repeat Steps 2 through 8 until each has been inspected, measured and serviced. When this is complete, do the same for the rod bearings, one at a time.

IMPORTANT: To ensure proper installation, note the position of each cap before removal.

11. If bearing clearance is within specs, then the bearing insert is okay. If not within specs, replace both upper and lower inserts.

12. After all bearings have been approved or replaced, coat each with engine oil to ensure proper lubrication.

13. With all bearing caps torqued to specs, rotate the crankshaft to make sure there's no excessive drag.

ENGINE BLOCK STRIPDOWN

1. Locate each piston in turn near the bottom of its stroke, and use a ridge reamer to remove the ridge of carbon at the top end of the cylinder wall **(Fig. 8-17).** If this is not done, ring damage will occur when new rings are installed on the pistons.

2. Remove the piston and connecting rod assemblies from the top of the cylinder bores, taking care not to scratch the connecting rod journals or the cylinder walls. If the pistons do not come out easily, tap the connecting rod boss gently with a wooden hammer handle until the piston is forced out.

IMPORTANT: As you remove the pistons, scribe or tag each with its cylinder number, and note which side of the piston faces forward. Each piston/rod assembly must return to its original cylinder.

3. With all bearing caps and inserts removed and marked, lift the crankshaft out of the engine block. Inspect all oil passages and holes to make sure they are free of sludge and open to oil flow.

4. If freeze plugs and/or oil gallery plugs are to be removed and replaced:

    a) Drill a hole in the center of the freeze plug and pry it out with a suitable drift or screwdriver.

    b) Remove the threaded oil gallery plugs with a wrench.

    c) Remove the pressed-in oil gallery plugs by drilling a hole in them and threading a sheetmetal screw in the hole. Apply pliers to the screw and pull the plug out.

ENGINE BLOCK INSPECTION

1. If possible, hot-tank the block to remove any corrosion grease or scale from the coolant passages, then visually inspect for cracks between the cylinders, next to the main bearing saddles, next to the freeze plugs and along the bottom of the cylinders.

2. Check the block deck for warpage with a straight-edge as described in "Step 7, Cleaning and Inspection, Cylinder Head Reconditioning."

3. Check the cylinder wall taper from top to bottom of each cylinder, using an outside micrometer or telescope gauge. Subtract the bottom reading from the top one and compare the amount of taper to specifications.

4. Measure across the cylinder bore, parallel to and perpendicular to the crankshaft, for an out-of-round condition. Subtract the parallel from the perpendicular measurement and compare to specifications.

5. If taper and out-of-round conditions are within specifications, the cylinder bore can be corrected by honing; if not, the cylinder must be bored and honed, and an oversize piston fitted.

ENGINE BLOCK RECONDITIONING

1. To hone the cylinder walls correctly (and this operation is critical for proper ring seating), use a flexible, self-aligning hone, moving it up and down at a speed sufficient to produce a uniform 60° crosshatch pattern on the cylinder wall. This operation should be performed by a qualified machine shop.

2. Scrub the cylinder bores with a hot-water/detergent solution and wipe with a clean, lint-free cloth moistened with engine oil, then recheck piston fit.

3. Lightly coat new freeze plugs with sealer and tap them into place, staking the edges. A piece of pipe that is slightly smaller than the plug makes a good driver.

4. Lightly coat threaded oil gallery plugs with sealer, and install them with a wrench. On blocks using press-in plugs, drill and tap the holes to accept threaded plugs. If press-in plugs are preferred, use a large drift as a driver, and install.

PISTON RING REPLACEMENT

1. Remove the old rings from the piston, using a ring expander tool.

2. Remove the retaining clips and piston pins from floating-type pistons; press out press-fit piston pins with the appropriate tools, taking care not to distort the piston.

3. Measure the connecting rods from the inside of one end to the inside of the other with calipers; if any rod differs in length from the others, replace it.

4. Use a ring-groove cleaning tool to clean carbon and varnish from the piston ring grooves, cleaning the oil drain openings in the oil ring grooves and pin boss. *Do not* cut metal from the grooves or lands, because this will change the ring groove clearances and destroy the ring-to-land seating.

5. Use an inside micrometer to measure the cylinder bore inside diameter at a point 2½ ins. below the top of the bore.

6. Use an outside micrometer to measure the piston diameter at right angles to the piston pin at the pin centerline **(Fig. 8-18)**.

7. The difference between the two measurements is the piston-to-bore clearance; if clearance is excessive, an oversize piston will be required, along with further honing or a cylinder rebore to bring the clearance into specifications.

8. After inspecting the connecting-rod small-end bushings, piston pins and piston bores for excessive wear/damage, measure the inside diameter of the piston bosses and connecting-rod small ends, and the outside diameter of the piston pins. If any parts are not within specifications, replace. When all are within specifications, reassemble the pistons to the connecting

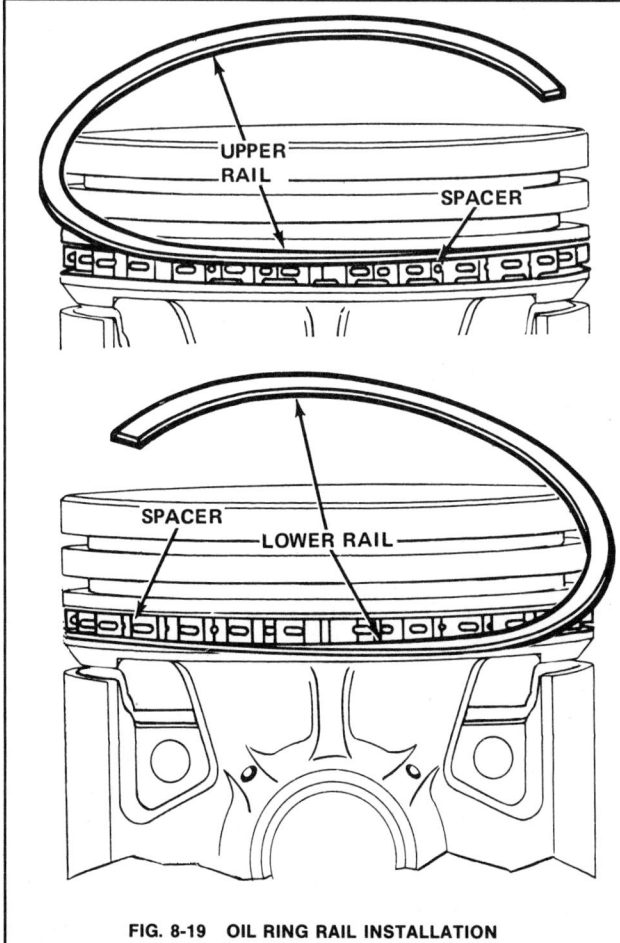

FIG. 8-19 OIL RING RAIL INSTALLATION

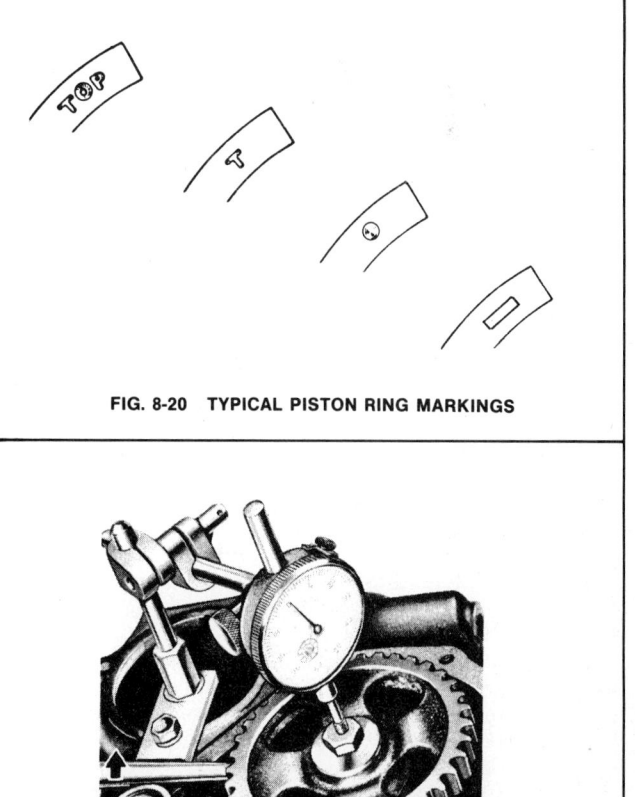

FIG. 8-20 TYPICAL PISTON RING MARKINGS

FIG. 8-21 CHECKING CAMSHAFT END PLAY

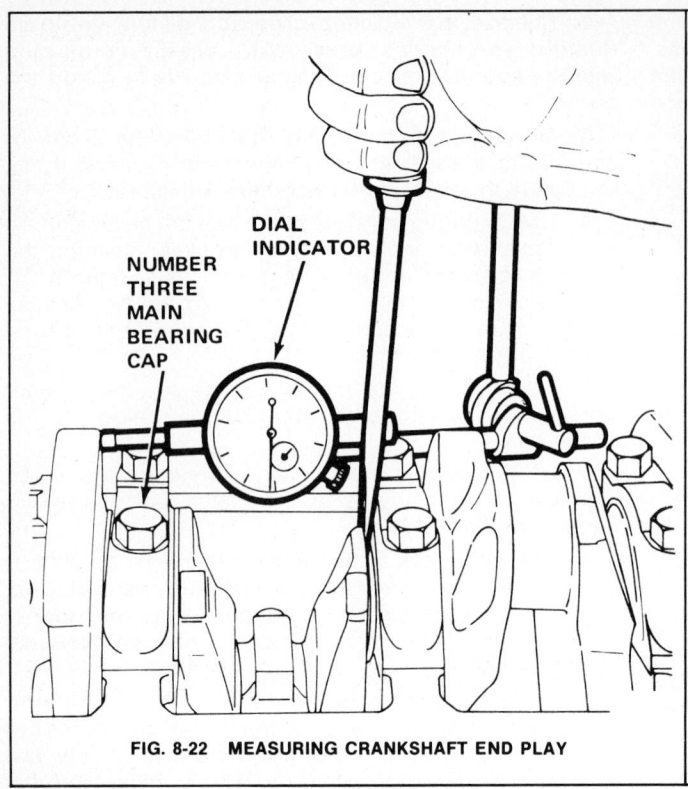

FIG. 8-22 MEASURING CRANKSHAFT END PLAY

FIG. 8-23 INSTALLING PISTONS

rods, using an arbor press and appropriate tools to replace press-fit pins without distorting the piston.

9. Fit each new ring in its groove and place a feeler gauge snugly between the ring and land. Roll the ring around to make sure it moves freely, removing any burrs or deposits with a fine file. Compare the feeler gauge setting to specifications. If the ring groove edges are worn, they can be recut by a machine shop to use an oversize ring or standard ring and spacer. Spacers must be installed *above* the ring in every case. Grooves that are too deep will require the use of a filler or expander behind the ring.

10. Compress the ring and place it (just the ring) in the cylinder bore. Measure ring gap with a feeler gauge fitted snugly in the ring opening and compare to specifications.

11. Install oil control rings as specified by the ring manufacturer. A ring installation tool is not required to install the rails, because they are rolled in place **(Fig. 8-19).**

12. Use a ring installer to expand the lower compression ring and fit it in its piston groove. Compression rings are marked with a variety of symbols **(Fig. 8-20)** to indicate correct installation. Follow the proper instructions provided with the new rings.

13. Repeat Step 12 to install upper compression ring.

ENGINE REASSEMBLY

1. Lubricate the camshaft lobes and journals, and slide the camshaft into the block carefully to avoid cam bearing damage (unless the engine is an ohc design).

2. Install the camshaft thrust plate and tighten the retaining bolts.

3. Check the camshaft end play with a dial indicator attached so that the indicator point is on the cam-sprocket attaching screw **(Fig. 8-21).** Push the camshaft to the rear of the engine and zero the indicator. Pull the camshaft forward and release it. If end play is excessive, install shims behind the thrust plate or replace the plate.

4. Place the rear main seal in its groove and press it into its seat. Use a piece of pipe with a diameter equal to the crankshaft journal to hold the seal seated, then trim the seal ends flush.

5. Lubricate and install the main bearings, then gently lower the crankshaft in position. Replace the main caps and torque to specifications.

6. Attach a dial indicator, as shown in **Fig. 8-22,** and pry the crankshaft back and forth, noting the indicator readings. End play is the difference between the high and low readings. If end play is excessive, the crankshaft must be replaced.

7. Fit the connecting-rod bearing inserts into the rods and rod caps. Install hose/tubing on the rod bolts to prevent cylinder wall damage during installation, and lubricate the pistons. Position the compression ring gaps 180° from each other, with the oil rail gap in line with the piston pin centerline.

8. Lubricate the piston rings with a liberal amount of engine oil, and fit a ring compressor tool around the piston and rings. Press into the cylinder bore using a wooden hammer handle **(Fig. 8-23)** until the connecting rod seats around the crankshaft journal.

9. Remove the hose/tubing from the rod bolts and install the rod caps finger-tight. To ensure lubrication on initial start-up, make sure all bearings are coated with engine oil. Install all pistons in this manner, then torque the rod cap nuts to specifications.

10. Assemble the timing chain, crankshaft and camshaft sprockets, and install with the timing marks aligned. Replace the timing chain cover with a new gasket, and torque to specifications.

11. Fill the oil pump with oil, and replace with its pickup tube. Install the oil pan and gasket. Torque to specifications.

12. Mount the flywheel and crankshaft damper or pulley on the crankshaft. Turn the engine right side up and replace the cylinder head(s) as in ''Steps 8-12, Head Reassembly.''

TURBOCHARGED ENGINES

Carbureted engines use atmospheric pressure to push a mixture of air and fuel into the intake manifold and then into the combustion chamber of each cylinder. This mixture is compressed and then ignited. The greater the compression of the mixture, the more power is created during combustion. High compression engines such as those used during the late Sixties are the most efficient. But the requirements of emission controls in the Seventies resulted in lower compression ratios. High compression engines tend to emit excessive quantities of NOx and cannot run on lead-free gasoline.

Since high compression engines are no longer practical, auto manufacturers have turned to the turbocharger as a means of increasing mixture compression. This exhaust gas-operated turbine device pressurizes air to push the air-fuel mixture into the engine cylinders with a pressure greater than that of the atmosphere. The amount of pressurization above atmospheric pressure is known as the ''boost.'' The result of turbocharging the conventional internal combustion engine used in passenger vehicles is an approximate horsepower increase of 35-50%.

Turbochargers have been most popular with racers and other aftermarket users since World War II. During the 1950's, mechanically-operated pumps called superchargers were used on a handful of domestic cars (Kaiser, Studebaker, Packard and Ford) but they were not very reliable or durable in operation. A turbine pump was installed on some Oldsmobile and Corvair models during the Sixties, but the concept of turbocharging did not meet with popular acceptance.

Several factors, however, have combined to bring about the reemergence of turbocharging as a factory-installed option. The large V-8 engines are being phased out of production and use as car lines are downsized. They are handicapped by emission controls to the point of being inefficient and the government's insistence on regulating the mileage new cars get from a gallon of gasoline make them impractical from the manufacturers' standpoint. Turbocharging is seen as a practical answer to the problem of developing more powerful small engines.

As applied by Buick and Ford, the turbocharger is an ''on-demand'' system used to boost engine output during acceleration or heavy load conditions. In this way, turbocharging improves engine performance while maintaining near-normal fuel economy and emission levels during light-to-moderate load conditions.

The turbocharger is a centrifugal pump driven by hot exhaust gases which are routed from the combustion chamber to the turbine wheel. When these hot gases hit the turbine wheel blades, they expand and cause the wheel to turn. This pulls air in against the center of the wheel where it is propelled outward from the wheel blades by centrifugal force and into a diffuser chamber. The diffuser chamber slows down the speed of the air and causes an increase in pressure as it routes the air into the intake manifold. Typical turbocharger system operation is shown in **Fig. 8-24.**

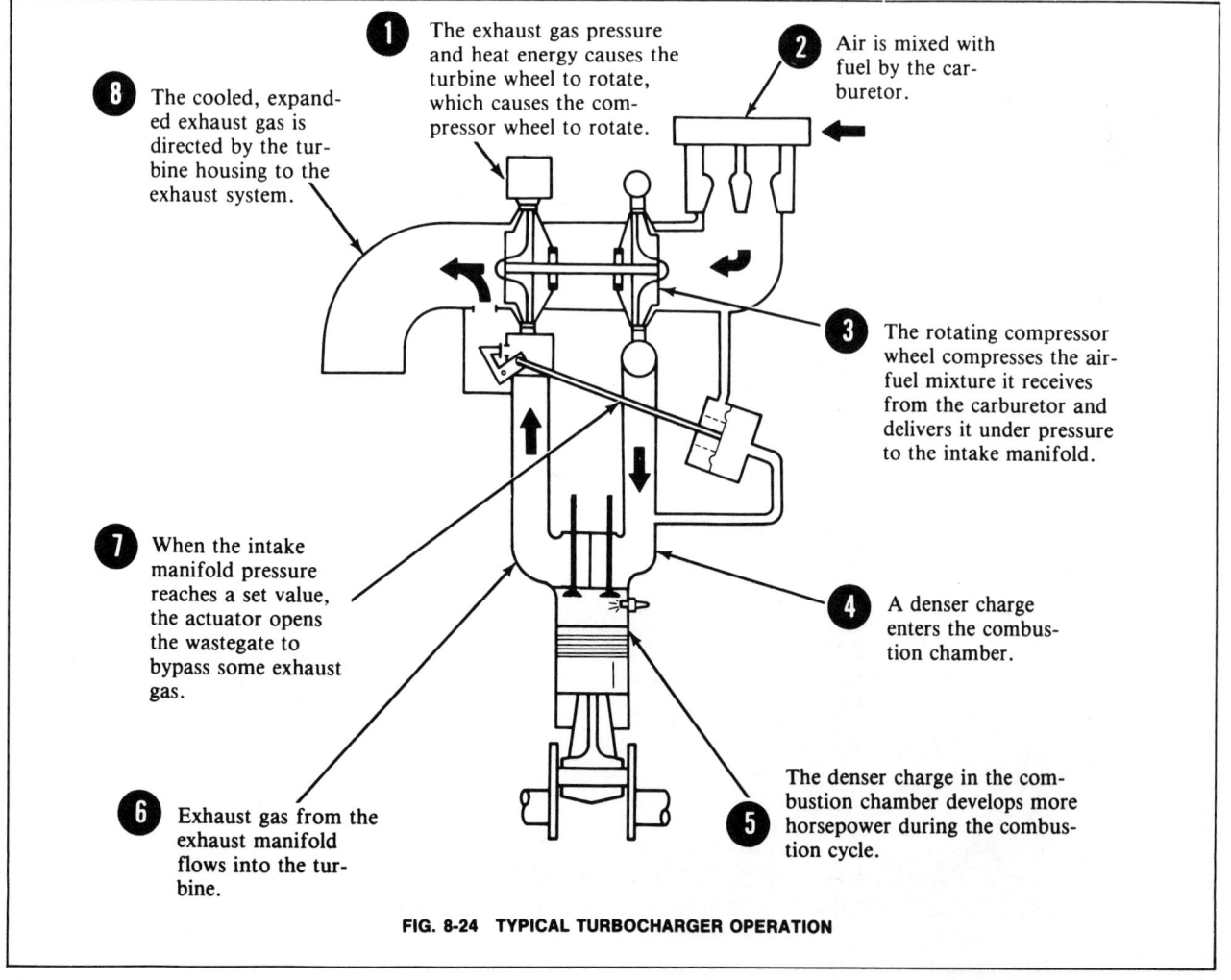

1. The exhaust gas pressure and heat energy causes the turbine wheel to rotate, which causes the compressor wheel to rotate.

2. Air is mixed with fuel by the carburetor.

8. The cooled, expanded exhaust gas is directed by the turbine housing to the exhaust system.

3. The rotating compressor wheel compresses the air-fuel mixture it receives from the carburetor and delivers it under pressure to the intake manifold.

7. When the intake manifold pressure reaches a set value, the actuator opens the wastegate to bypass some exhaust gas.

4. A denser charge enters the combustion chamber.

6. Exhaust gas from the exhaust manifold flows into the turbine.

5. The denser charge in the combustion chamber develops more horsepower during the combustion cycle.

FIG. 8-24 TYPICAL TURBOCHARGER OPERATION

A turbocharger may run at speeds exceeding 100,000 rpm. Lubrication of the turbocharger bearings is therefore vital for cooling as well as reducing friction. Turbo units currently in use are lubricated by engine oil through oil feed and return lines between the turbocharger housing and the engine. For this reason, it is necessary to flush the turbo unit with clean engine oil whenever a basic engine bearing has been damaged. If turbocharger damage occurs, flush the engine oil and change the oil filter as a part of the repair procedure.

Rapid acceleration to top engine rpm immediately upon start-up and/or immediate shut-down of an engine after sustained high-speed operation can cause a lack of proper lubrication. If this happens, it can result in damage to both the turbocharger and the engine.

Engine detonation and boost control are two common problems with a turbocharged engine. Detonation or premature combustion of the air-fuel mixture may result from the excessive heat created by compression. This can cause engine damage. Boost control is necessary to prevent uncontrolled compression from causing

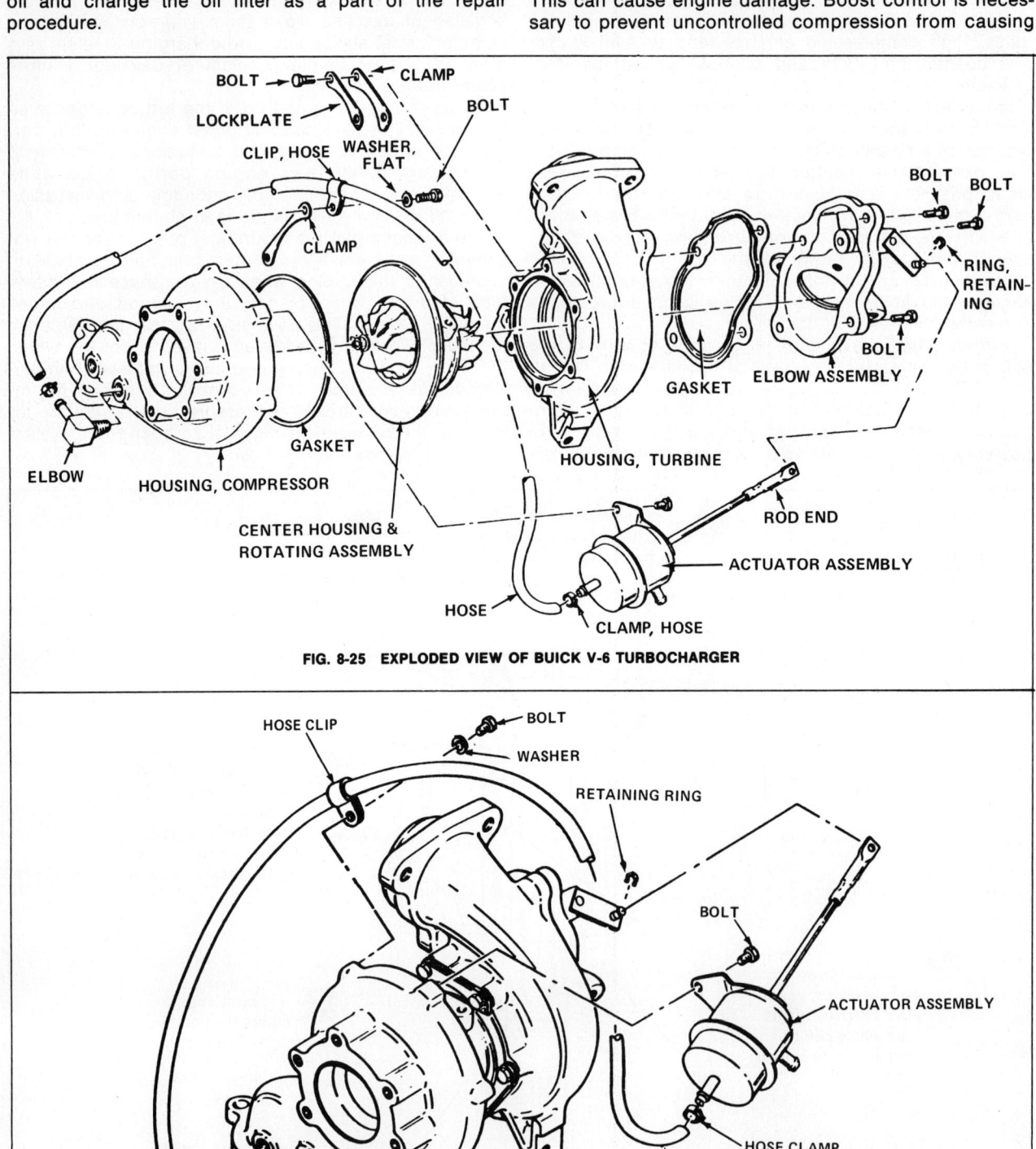

FIG. 8-25 EXPLODED VIEW OF BUICK V-6 TURBOCHARGER

FIG. 8-26 WASTEGATE ACTUATOR ASSEMBLY

engine damage. Various methods have been devised to avoid detonation and to control the maximum boost. The methods currently in use will be discussed under the appropriate engine application.

BUICK TURBOCHARGED V-6 ENGINE (Fig. 8-25)

Buick reintroduced the turbocharger on domestic engines in 1978. The Buick turbocharger was installed on the new even-firing 231-cu.-in. V-6 engine. The turbocharged version of this engine differs very little from the normally aspirated or unblown version. The major changes in the turbocharged application were stronger pistons, a new piston ring design and crankshaft journals with rolled fillets for additional strength. Both versions use the same compression ratio and are equipped with the same emission controls.

Two applications of the turbo V-6 are available; one equipped with a 2-bbl. carburetor and the other with a 4-bbl. carburetor. While the normal V-6 is rated at 105 hp, the turbocharged versions are rated at 150 and 165 hp respectively when the turbo is in use. Maximum boost of the 2-bbl. version is 7-8 psi, while the 4-bbl. version has a boost of 8-9 psi.

A wastegate in the turbine housing controls maximum boost. This device is operated by an actuator unit containing a spring-loaded diaphragm which reacts to manifold pressure **(Fig. 8-26)**. When the wastegate opens, it routes part of the exhaust gas flow to the exhaust system. This reduces the turbocharger speed and thus the amount of boost pressure created.

Buick mounted the turbocharger on a special intake manifold to reduce the lag between throttle opening and the increase in boost pressure. The carburetor is mounted on a plenum chamber attached to the com-

pression inlet **(Fig. 8-27)**. This eliminates the need to pressurize the carburetor and fuel delivery system.

Detonation is controlled by use of an electronic spark timing system **(Fig. 8-28)**. The system operates with a solid-state control module located on the engine fan shroud. When a detonation sensor mounted in the intake manifold signals the ESC controller that detonation is about to occur, the controller signals the ignition module in the distributor. Timing is then retarded until 20 seconds after detonation, when it returns to the setting required by road speed and engine load conditions. Turbocharger operation is indicated to the driver by yellow and orange instrument panel lights.

TURBOCHARGED ENGINE DIAGNOSIS

Although the turbocharger is a precision device, its operation is really quite simple, although noisy to some degree. Most operational malfunctions will be those of a basic engine nature. For this reason, you should first troubleshoot normal engine problems before blaming the turbocharger for poor engine operation. Pay particular attention to the following areas:

1. Inspect all vacuum lines and wiring for proper routing and connections.

2. Inspect the carburetor and wastegate linkage for damage or restricted movement.

3. Inspect the transmission detent cable for correct adjustment. The chart shown in **Fig. 8-29** directs your attention to specific turbocharger problems which may occur, as well as the steps necessary to further diagnose or correct the cause.

WASTEGATE/BOOST PRESSURE TEST (Fig. 8-26)

1. Check the wastegate actuator mechanical linkage for damage.

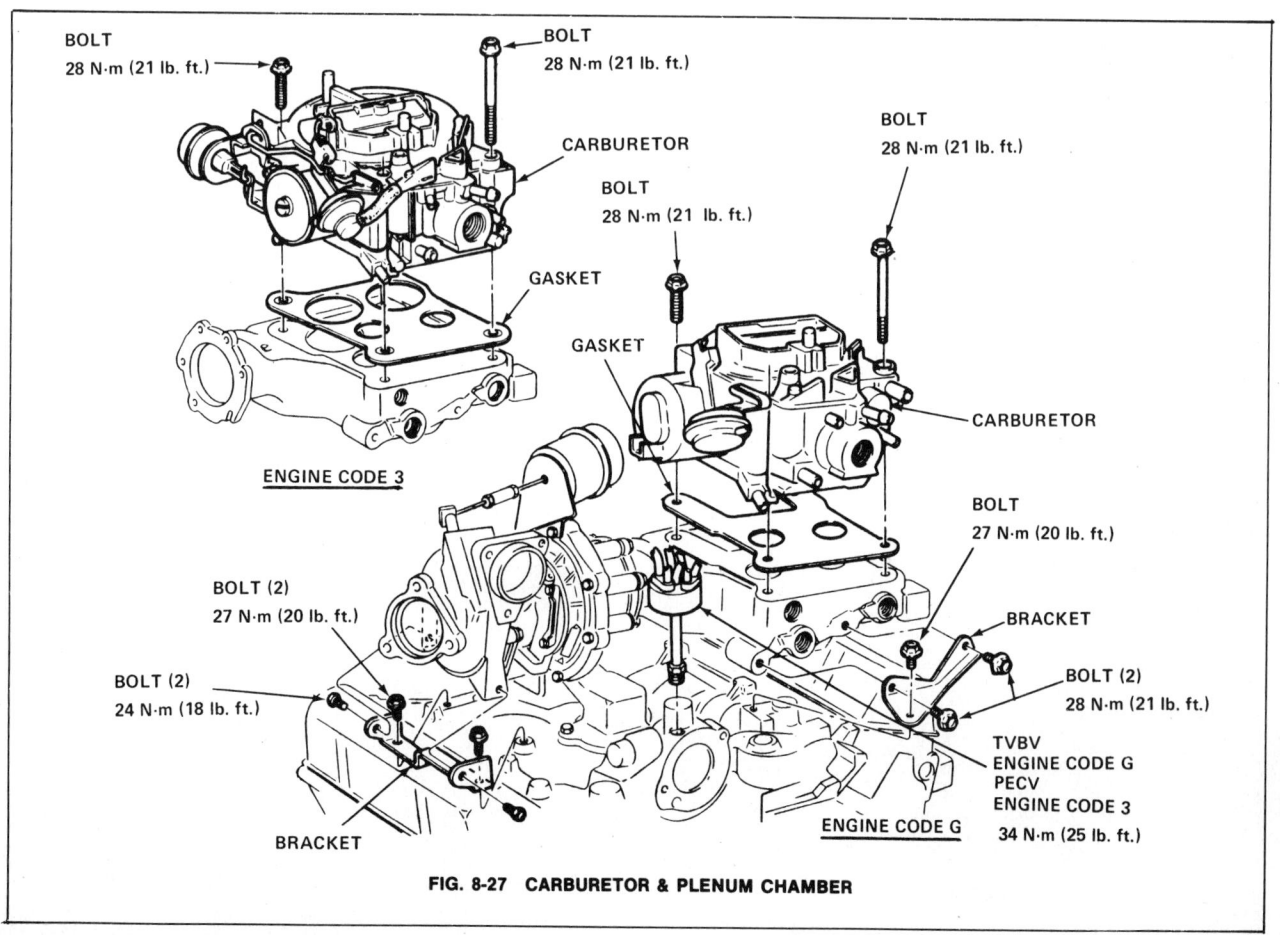

FIG. 8-27 CARBURETOR & PLENUM CHAMBER

2. Inspect the compressor housing-to-actuator-to-PCV tee hoses for damage, restriction or poor connections.

3. Connect a hand vacuum/pressure pump in place of the compressor housing-to-actuator hose and apply 8 psi pressure to the actuator assembly. The actuator rod should move sufficiently to operate the linkage. If it does not, replace the actuator assembly.

4. Remove the test equipment and replace the hose.

TVBV/PECV/PEVR TESTS

A manometer is required for these 3 tests. While the average car owner would not normally include it in his repair tool kit, owners of a turbocharged engine should have one available for troubleshooting. The 2-bbl. turbocharged engine uses a TVBV while the 4-bbl. application is fitted with a PECV or PEVR. Test as appropriate according to engine.

Turbocharger Vacuum Bleed Valve (TVBV)

1. Check the TVBV valve and hoses for deterioration or damage.

2. Disconnect and plug the vacuum line to the carburetor remote power enrichment port. Tee one manometer hose into the distributor vacuum line between the carburetor and TVBV. Tee the other manometer hose into the distributor vacuum line between the TVBV and distributor.

3. Start the engine and run at idle. The manometer scale should read no more than a 14-in. H$_2$O difference.

4. Tee the manometer into the vacuum line from the air cleaner sensor to the TVBV and the vacuum line from the TVBV to the air cleaner vacuum motor. Re-

peat Step 3. If the engine is at normal operating temperature and no vacuum is present at the air cleaner vacuum motor, connect manifold vacuum to the input port and recheck.

5. Plug the EGR vacuum line at the EGR valve. Tee one manometer hose into the vacuum line between the carburetor EGR signal port to the TVBV. Tee the other manometer hose into the vacuum line between the TVBV and the EGR-EFE switch.

6. Start the engine and crack the throttle slightly. The manometer scale should read no more than a 14-in. H$_2$O difference.

7. Disconnect all lines at the TVBV. Connect one manometer hose to the center vent port and vent the other manometer hose to the atmosphere.

8. Start the engine and run at idle. The manometer should show no pressure difference.

9. Replace the TVBV is any manometer reading differs from those specified.

Power Enrichment Control Valve (PECV)

1978 Applications

1. Check the PECV valve and hoses for deterioration or damage.

2. Tee one manometer hose into the center port vacuum line between the tee and the PECV. Connect the other manometer hose directly to the inboard port vacuum line.

3. Start the engine and run at idle. The manometer scale should read no more than a 12-in. H$_2$O difference.

4. Disconnect all lines at the PECV. Connect one manometer hose to the outboard port and vent the

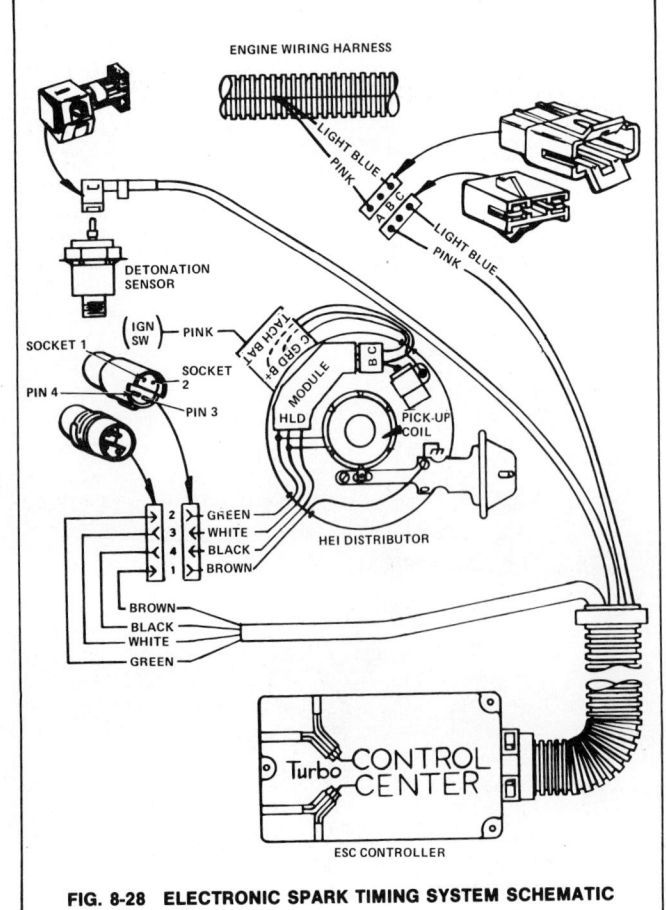

FIG. 8-28 ELECTRONIC SPARK TIMING SYSTEM SCHEMATIC

PROBLEM	CORRECTION
Engine Detonation	1. Free jammed or blocked actuator linkage.
	2. Check hoses between compressor housing, actuator and PCV tee for damage or loose connections.
	3. Perform wastegate/boost pressure test.
	4. Perform TVBV/PECV/PEVR tests.
	5. Inspect turbocharger internal operation.
Engine Lacks Power	1. Inspect exhaust for leaks or restrictions.
	2. Perform TVBV/PECV/PEVR tests.
	3. Check for kinked or collapsed plenum coolant hoses.
	4. Perform wastegate/boost pressure test.
	5. Inspect turbocharger internal operation.
Engine Surges	1. Perform TVBV/PECV/PEVR tests.
	2. Check for loose bolts on compressor side of turbocharger assembly.
Excessive Oil Consumption (Blue Exhaust Smoke.)	1. Check turbocharger oil inlet connections.
	2. Check turbocharger oil drain hose for restrictions or leaks.
	3. Inspect turbocharger internal operation.
Excessive Engine Noise	1. Inspect for exhaust leaks.
	2. Check turbocharger oil supply for restrictions.
	3. Inspect turbocharger internal operation.

FIG. 8-29 TURBOCHARGED ENGINE DIAGNOSIS

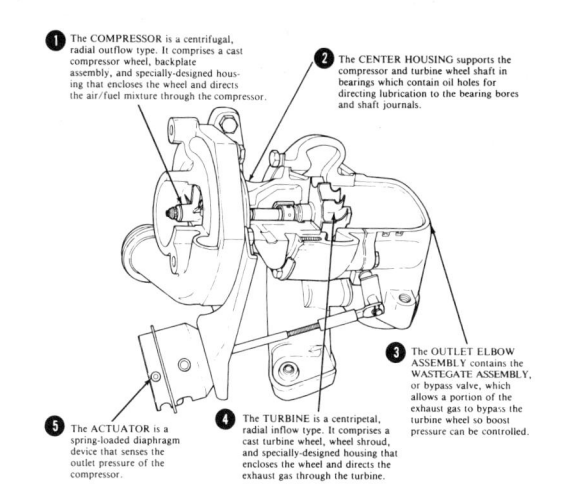

1. The COMPRESSOR is a centrifugal, radial outflow type. It comprises a cast compressor wheel, backplate assembly, and specially-designed housing that encloses the wheel and directs the air/fuel mixture through the compressor.

2. The CENTER HOUSING supports the compressor and turbine wheel shaft in bearings which contain oil holes for directing lubrication to the bearing bores and shaft journals.

3. The OUTLET ELBOW ASSEMBLY contains the WASTEGATE ASSEMBLY, or bypass valve, which allows a portion of the exhaust gas to bypass the turbine wheel so boost pressure can be controlled.

4. The TURBINE is a centripetal, radial inflow type. It comprises a cast turbine wheel, wheel shroud, and specially-designed housing that encloses the wheel and directs the exhaust gas through the turbine.

5. The ACTUATOR is a spring-loaded diaphragm device that senses the outlet pressure of the compressor.

FIG. 8-30 FORD TURBOCHARGER CROSS SECTION

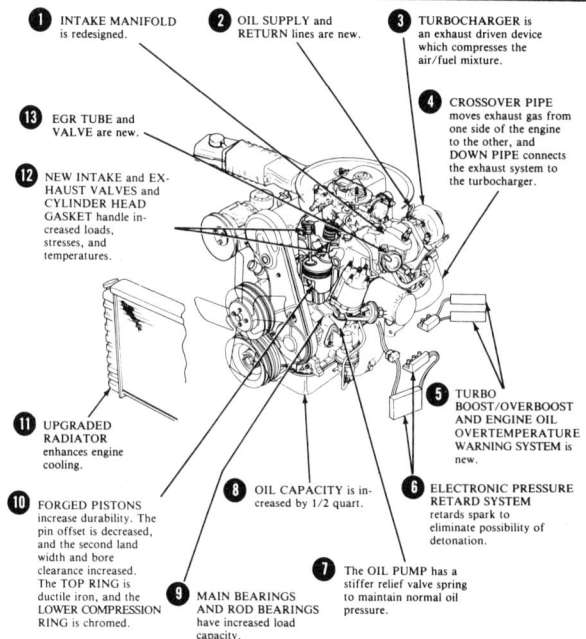

1. INTAKE MANIFOLD is redesigned.

2. OIL SUPPLY and RETURN lines are new.

3. TURBOCHARGER is an exhaust driven device which compresses the air/fuel mixture.

4. CROSSOVER PIPE moves exhaust gas from one side of the engine to the other, and DOWN PIPE connects the exhaust system to the turbocharger.

5. TURBO BOOST/OVERBOOST AND ENGINE OIL OVERTEMPERATURE WARNING SYSTEM is new.

6. ELECTRONIC PRESSURE RETARD SYSTEM retards spark to eliminate possibility of detonation.

7. The OIL PUMP has a stiffer relief valve spring to maintain normal oil pressure.

8. OIL CAPACITY is increased by 1/2 quart.

9. MAIN BEARINGS AND ROD BEARINGS have increased load capacity.

10. FORGED PISTONS increase durability. The pin offset is decreased, and the second land width and bore clearance increased. The TOP RING is ductile iron, and the LOWER COMPRESSION RING is chromed.

11. UPGRADED RADIATOR enhances engine cooling.

12. NEW INTAKE and EXHAUST VALVES and CYLINDER HEAD GASKET handle increased loads, stresses, and temperatures.

13. EGR TUBE and VALVE are new.

FIG. 8-31 FORD INTEGRATED ENGINE TURBOCHARGING SYSTEM

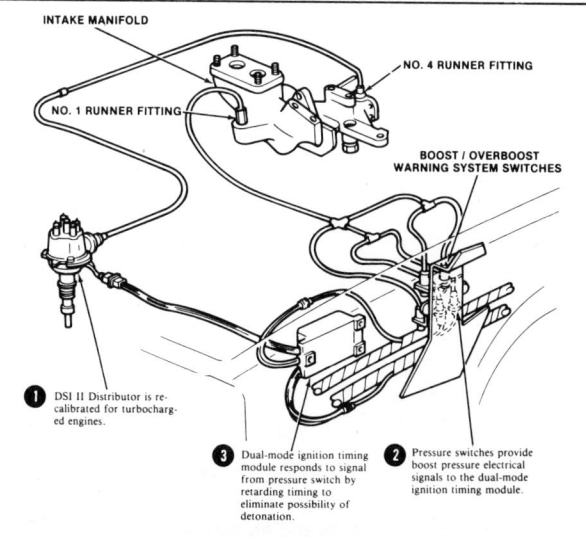

INTAKE MANIFOLD

NO. 1 RUNNER FITTING

NO. 4 RUNNER FITTING

BOOST / OVERBOOST WARNING SYSTEM SWITCHES

1. DSI II Distributor is recalibrated for turbocharged engines.

3. Dual-mode ignition timing module responds to signal from pressure switch by retarding timing to eliminate possibility of detonation.

2. Pressure switches provide boost pressure electrical signals to the dual-mode ignition timing module.

FIG. 8-32 ELECTRONIC PRESSURE RETARD SYSTEM

other manometer hose to the atmosphere.

5. Start the engine and run at idle. The manometer should show no pressure difference.

6. Replace the PECV if any manometer reading differs from those specified.

Power Enrichment Vacuum Regulator (PEVR)

1979 and later Applications

1. Check the PEVR valve and hoses for deterioration or damage.

2. Tee one manometer hose between the input port and the yellow-striped line connected to it. Connect the other manometer hose directly to the PEVR output port.

3. Start the engine and run at idle. The manometer scale should read no more than a 14-in. H_2O difference; if it does, replace the PEVR valve.

TURBOCHARGER INTERNAL INSPECTION

1. Remove the exhaust outlet pipe from the turbocharger elbow assembly.

2. Operate the actuator linkage by hand and use a mirror to watch the wastegate movement.

3. Replace the elbow assembly if the wastegate does not open and close properly in Step 2.

4. If further inspection is necessary, it is recommended that you leave removal/disassembly of the turbocharger unit to a properly qualified and equipped repair shop. If the compressor or turbine wheel blades are bent, nicked or otherwise damaged or distorted, it can result in rotating assembly imbalance and/or failure of the center housing rotating assembly, compressor or turbine housings. Clearance checks performed with a dial indicator are critical and must be measured accurately.

FORD TURBOCHARGED I-4 ENGINE

Ford introduced a turbocharged 2300cc engine as an optional powerplant for 1979 Mustang/Capri models. The five major components of the turbocharger are shown in **Fig. 8-30.** Unlike the Buick V-6 application, internal components of the 2300cc I-4 Ford engine have been revised considerably to accept the turbocharger and many are not interchangeable with those used in normally-aspirated (unblown) 2300cc engines. A number of such components are described in **Fig. 8-31,** which shows the integrated engine turbocharging system used by Ford.

Engine detonation and overboost are controlled by means of an electronic pressure retard system. Its operation is described in **Fig. 8-32.** Turbocharger system operation is indicated to the driver by red and green instrument panel lights; green for satisfactory and red for overboost conditions. A warning buzzer is also used to provide an audible signal of overboost operation.

TURBOCHARGED ENGINE DIAGNOSIS

Although the turbocharger is a precision device, its operation is really quite simple, although noisy to some degree. Most operational malfunctions will be those of a basic engine nature. For this reason, you should first troubleshoot normal engine problems before blaming the turbocharger for poor engine operation. Pay particular attention to the following areas:

1. Inspect all vacuum lines and wiring for proper routing and connections.

2. Inspect the carburetor and wastegate linkage for damage or restricted movement.

To test boost pressure, follow the sequence of steps shown in **Fig. 8-33.** When a malfunction is suspected in the electronic pressure retard system, follow the sequence of steps shown in **Fig. 8-34**. If the conditions shown in Step 6 are not met, perform the following procedure:

1. Substitute a new pressure switch assembly (do not install) and retest. An rpm drop during retest indicates a faulty pressure switch assembly.

2. If there is no rpm drop in Step 1, reconnect the original pressure switch assembly, substitute a new dual-mode ignition module (do not install) and retest. An rpm drop during the retest indicates that the original module is good. If there is no rpm drop, replace the original module with the new one.

TURBOCHARGER INTERNAL INSPECTION

1. Remove the exhaust outlet pipe from the turbocharger elbow assembly.

2. Operate the actuator linkage by hand and use a mirror to watch the wastegate movement.

3. Replace the elbow assembly if the wastegate does not open and close properly in Step 2.

4. If further inspection is necessary, it is recommended that you leave removal/disassembly of the turbocharger unit to a properly qualified and equipped repair shop. If the compressor or turbine wheel blades are bent, nicked or otherwise damaged or distorted, it can result in rotating assembly imbalance and/or failure of the center housing rotating assembly, compressor or turbine housings. Clearance checks performed with a dial indicator are critical and must be measured accurately.

DIESEL ENGINES

DESCRIPTION

The Oldsmobile 5.7-liter 4-cycle diesel engine first appeared in 1978 production models as an optional powerplant. Quite similar in design to the 5.7-liter (350-cu.-in.) gasoline engine, its firing order is 1-8-4-3-6-5-7-2, with odd cylinder numbers on the left bank, and even cylinder numbers on the right. The cylinder heads, combustion chamber, fuel distribution system, air intake manifold and ignition system represent the main differences between the diesel and gasoline versions.

The higher compression ratio necessary to ignite diesel fuel requires the use of a heavy-duty engine block, crankshaft, main bearings, rods, pistons and pins. Since diesel fuel ignites from the heat developed in the combustion chamber during the compression stroke, no spark plugs or high voltage ignition are necessary. A 4.3-liter diesel engine made available for 1979 vehicles is identical to the 5.7-liter diesel, except for piston/valve head diameters, which are the same as those in the 260-cu.-in. engine. In addition, the crankshaft counter-weights on the 4.3-liter are ⅛-in. smaller in diameter than those used on the 5.7-liter crankshaft.

DIESEL ENGINE OPERATION

A diesel engine requires a high compression ratio. This increases internal heat to a temperature of approximately 1000 degrees F. Fuel injected into the cylinder is ignited by the hot air, causing it to burn, expand and produce power. Unlike the gasoline engine, whose air-fuel mixture remains nearly constant despite changes in engine speed or load, the air-fuel mixture used by a diesel engine consists of one constant (air) and one variable (fuel). This means that the amount of air available is unchanged while the amount of fuel provided is changed to control speed and power. Thus,

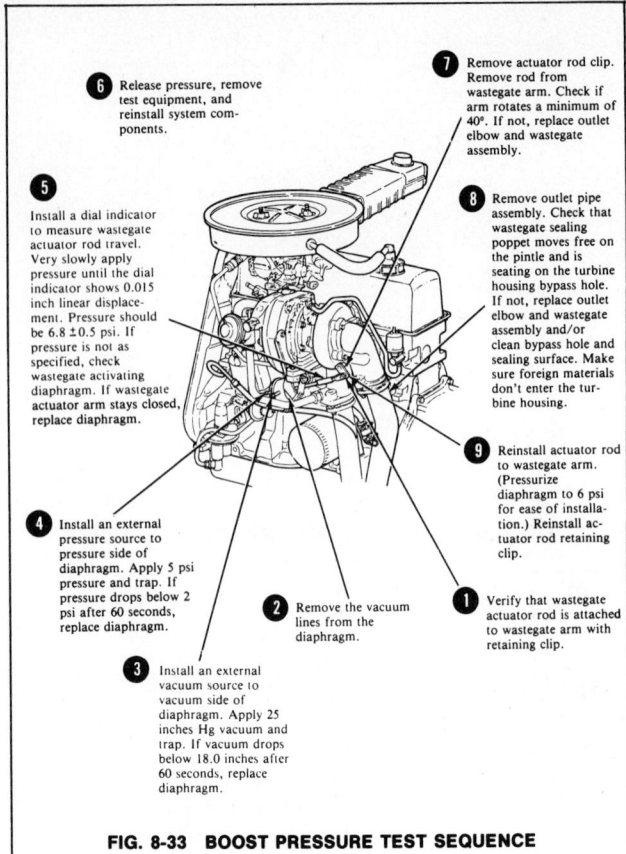

6 Release pressure, remove test equipment, and reinstall system components.

5 Install a dial indicator to measure wastegate actuator rod travel. Very slowly apply pressure until the dial indicator shows 0.015 inch linear displacement. Pressure should be 6.8 ±0.5 psi. If pressure is not as specified, check wastegate activating diaphragm. If wastegate actuator arm stays closed, replace diaphragm.

7 Remove actuator rod clip. Remove rod from wastegate arm. Check if arm rotates a minimum of 40°. If not, replace outlet elbow and wastegate assembly.

8 Remove outlet pipe assembly. Check that wastegate sealing poppet moves free on the pintle and is seating on the turbine housing bypass hole. If not, replace outlet elbow and wastegate assembly and/or clean bypass hole and sealing surface. Make sure foreign materials don't enter the turbine housing.

9 Reinstall actuator rod to wastegate arm. (Pressurize diaphragm to 6 psi for ease of installation.) Reinstall actuator rod retaining clip.

4 Install an external pressure source to pressure side of diaphragm. Apply 5 psi pressure and trap. If pressure drops below 2 psi after 60 seconds, replace diaphragm.

2 Remove the vacuum lines from the diaphragm.

1 Verify that wastegate actuator rod is attached to wastegate arm with retaining clip.

3 Install an external vacuum source to vacuum side of diaphragm. Apply 25 inches Hg vacuum and trap. If vacuum drops below 18.0 inches after 60 seconds, replace diaphragm.

FIG. 8-33 BOOST PRESSURE TEST SEQUENCE

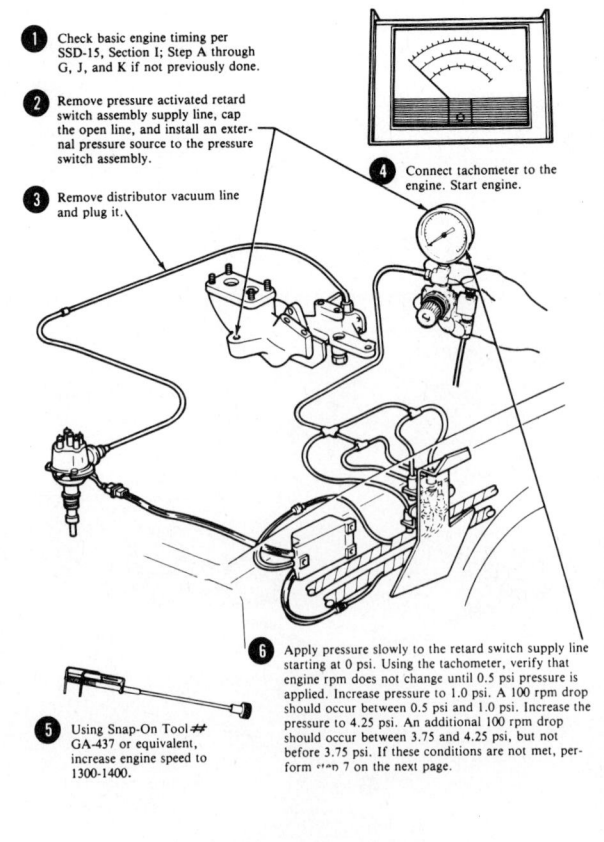

1 Check basic engine timing per SSD-15, Section I; Step A through G, J, and K if not previously done.

2 Remove pressure activated retard switch assembly supply line, cap the open line, and install an external pressure source to the pressure switch assembly.

3 Remove distributor vacuum line and plug it.

4 Connect tachometer to the engine. Start engine.

5 Using Snap-On Tool # GA-437 or equivalent, increase engine speed to 1300-1400.

6 Apply pressure slowly to the retard switch supply line starting at 0 psi. Using the tachometer, verify that engine rpm does not change until 0.5 psi pressure is applied. Increase pressure to 1.0 psi. A 100 rpm drop should occur between 0.5 psi and 1.0 psi. Increase the pressure to 4.25 psi. An additional 100 rpm drop should occur between 3.75 and 4.25 psi, but not before 3.75 psi. If these conditions are not met, perform step 7 on the next page.

FIG. 8-34 ELECTRONIC PRESSURE RETARD SYSTEM TEST SEQUENCE

a diesel engine may operate with a mixture as lean as 80:1 at idle to as rich as 20:1 under conditions of full load.

FUEL SYSTEM

Fuel is provided by a camshaft driven fuel injection pump. This is mounted on top of the engine **(Fig. 8-35)**. It is a high-pressure, rotary pump which injects a metered quantity of diesel fuel to each cylinder at the proper time. All delivery pipes from the pump to the cylinder injection nozzles are the same length. This is necessary to prevent any cylinder-to-cylinder differences in timing. The necessary timing advance is pro-

vided under all operating conditions by the injection pump. A rotary fuel metering valve operated by the throttle cable controls the quantity of fuel delivered. As the accelerator pedal is depressed, the throttle cable opens the metering valve, increasing the amount of fuel provided at the injection nozzles. A fuel filter is located between the injection pump and the fuel pump **(Fig. 8-35)**. Excess fuel is returned to the rear-mounted fuel tank by a fuel return line, just as in gasoline engine applications.

ELECTRICAL SYSTEM

Two types of electrical systems are used with the Oldsmobile diesel engine. The system used with the Cutlass 88-98 is shown in **Fig. 8-36**. The Oldsmobile Toronado and other applications (including the 4.3-litre engine) use the system shown in **Fig. 8-37**. Glow plug usage differs according to the electrical system used, **Fig. 8-38,** and should not be interchanged.

A standard Delco design starting motor is used, but it is larger in size and capacity. The starting motor provided with the diesel engines will crank at least 100 rpm when the engine is cold, or 240 rpm minimum when the engine is hot. Two 12-volt batteries are connected in parallel to provide the greater electrical load required by the glow plugs and starting motor. A standard Delcotron (alternator) supplies charging current to both batteries at the same time. There are no relays or switches in the diesel charging circuit.

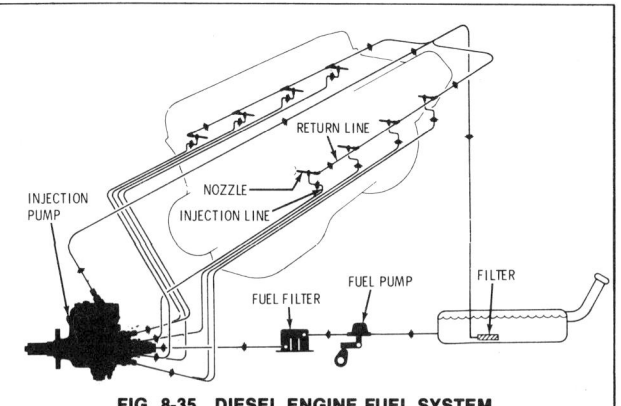

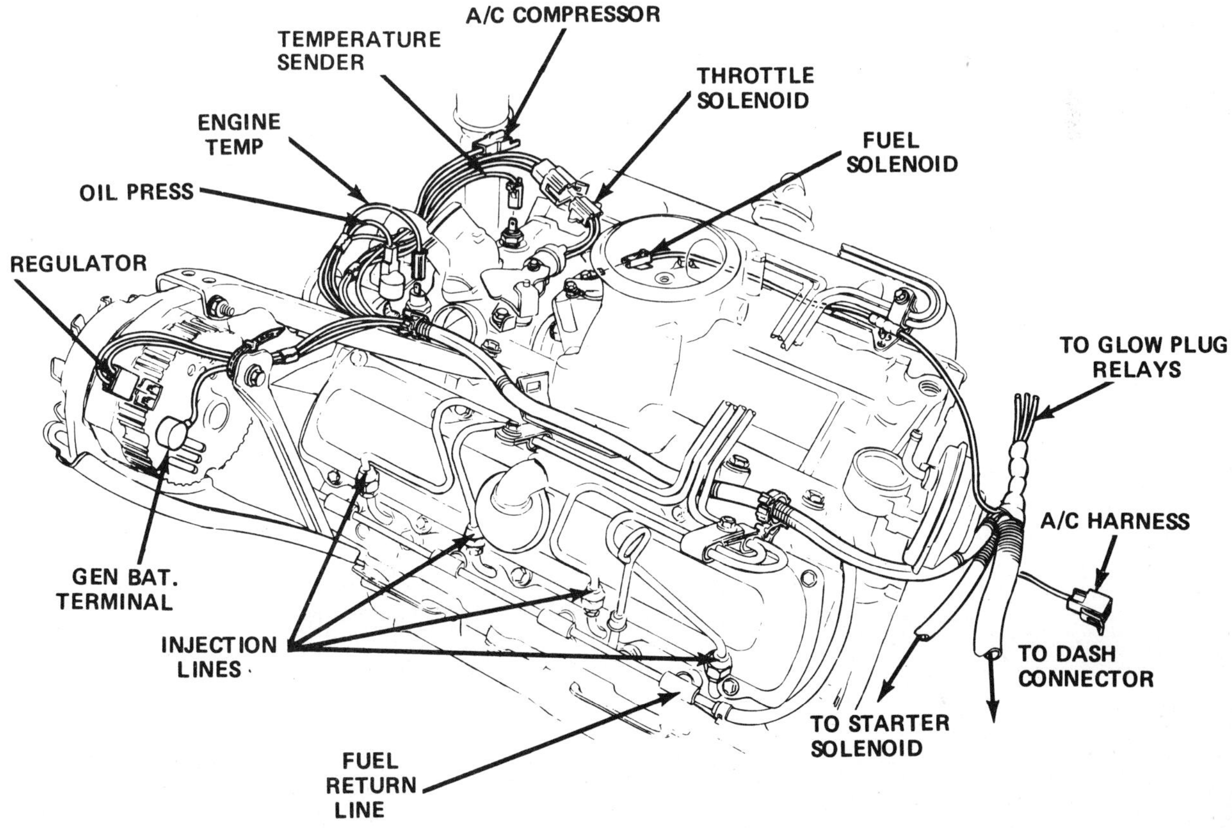

FIG. 8-35 DIESEL ENGINE FUEL SYSTEM

FIG. 8-36 OLDS DIESEL ELECTRICAL SYSTEM, 1ST TYPE

ENGINE LUBRICATION & COOLING

Lubrication is similar to that of the gasoline engine, except that engine oil is routed from the oil filter through an oil cooler in the radiator tank and back to the oil filter base. From this point, it is sent to the engine oil galleries. The filter base contains a by-pass valve which opens at approximately 12 psi to permit continuous oil flow should the cooler or cooler line become restricted/blocked. Engine oil pressure is tested as shown in **Fig. 8-39.**

Cooling is identical to that of the gasoline engine. The radiator tank contains two oil coolers, one for the ATF and the other for engine oil.

EMISSION CONTROLS

The Oldsmobile diesel engines use only a PCV system, as shown in **Fig. 8-40.** This functions in the same manner as a PCV system installed on a gasoline engine.

SERVICE PROCEDURES

Special tools are required to set the engine slow idle speed, check the injection pump housing fuel pressure, and replace the injection pump adapter seal. These procedures should be attempted only by shops which are properly equipped with the necessary special tools. The following five procedures can be accomplished without special tools.

ENGINE TIMING ADJUSTMENT

Diesel engines do not have an ignition system. Engine timing is accomplished by aligning a mark on the flange of the injection pump with one on the top of the injection pump adapter **(Fig. 8-41).** No adjustment is necessary when the marks are in alignment. The engine must be OFF when working on the timing.

1. Loosen, but do not remove, the three pump retaining nuts.
2. Use a ¾-in. end wrench on the boss at the front of

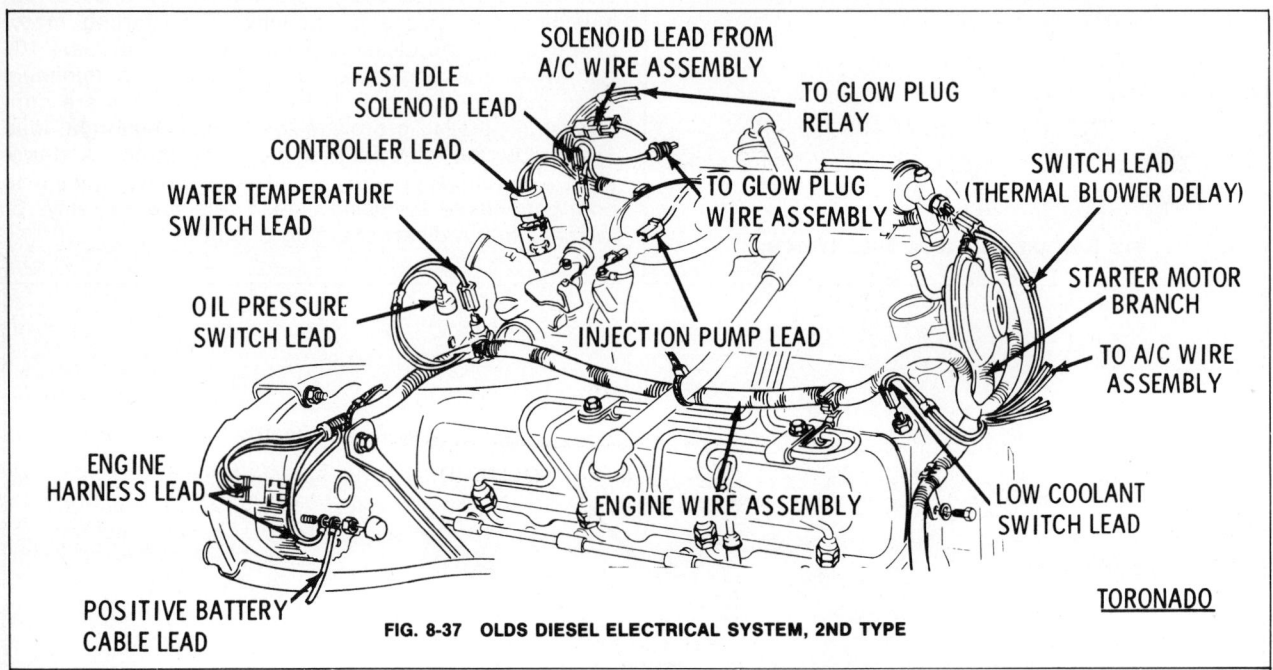

FIG. 8-37   OLDS DIESEL ELECTRICAL SYSTEM, 2ND TYPE

DIESEL ENGINE GLOW PLUG IDENTIFICATION

The second type diesel glow plug control system uses 6 volt glow plugs with controlled pulsing current applied to them for starting. The first type system used steady current applied to 12 volt glow plugs. In either case the correct glow plug should be used for proper starting. The illustration shows the glow plug identification.

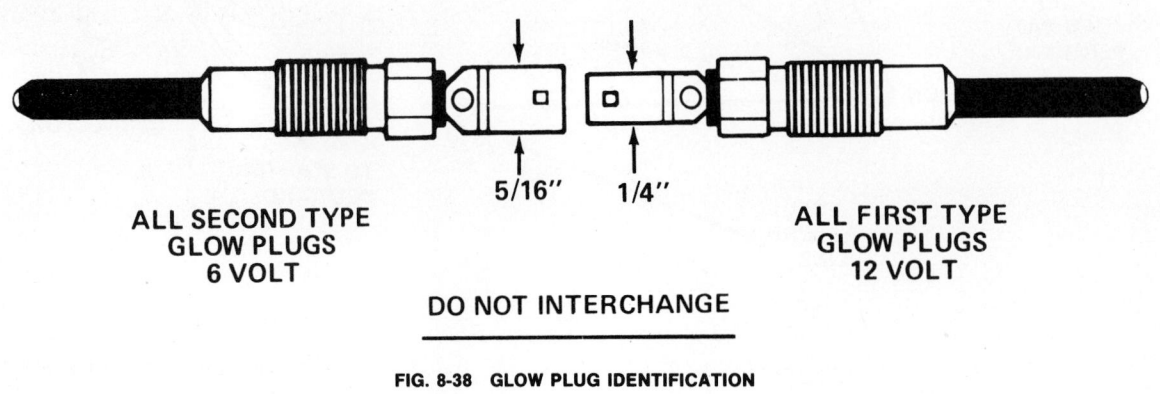

FIG. 8-38   GLOW PLUG IDENTIFICATION

the pump to rotate the injection pump until the line on its flange aligns with the adapter mark.

3. Retighten and torque the retaining nuts to 35 ft.-lbs.

4. Adjust the throttle rod.

THROTTLE ROD ADJUSTMENT

1. Unclip the cruise control rod (when equipped) and remove the throttle rod from the bellcrank.

2. Disconnect the T.V. or detent cable from the bell-crank.

3. Loosen the throttle rod locknut and shorten the rod several turns.

4. Rotate the bellcrank to the full throttle stop. Lengthen the throttle rod until the injection pump lever touches the injection pump full throttle stop.

5. Release the bellcrank and tighten the throttle rod locknut.

6. Reconnect the T.V. or detent cable (and cruise control rod when equipped) to the bellcrank, then adjust.

TRANSMISSION T.V. CABLE/DETENT CABLE ADJUSTMENT

The Turbo Hydra-Matic 200 is equipped with a T.V. cable; the Turbo Hydra-Matic 350 uses a detent cable **(Fig. 8-42).**

1. Remove the throttle rod from the bellcrank and push the snaplock to a disengaged position.

2. Rotate and hold the bellcrank at the full throttle stop position.

3. Push the snaplock in until it's flush with the cable end fitting.

4. Release the bellcrank and reconnect the throttle rod.

TRANSMISSION VACUUM VALVE ADJUSTMENT (THM 350 ONLY)

1. Remove the throttle rod from the bellcrank.

2. Loosen the vacuum valve adjusting bolts sufficiently to disengage the valve from the injection pump shaft.

3. Hold the injection pump lever against the injection pump full throttle stop and rotate the valve to a full throttle position.

4. Insert a .090-in. plug gauge as shown in **Fig. 8-43** to hold the valve in its full throttle position.

5. Turn the assembly clockwise until it touches the injection pump lever shaft and hold it there.

6. Tighten the attaching bolts, remove the plug gauge and release the lever.

7. Reconnect the throttle rod to the bellcrank.

CRUISE CONTROL SERVO RELAY ROD ADJUSTMENT

1. Adjust the relay rod to a minimum slack, then place the clip in the first free hole nearest the bellcrank but within the servo bail.

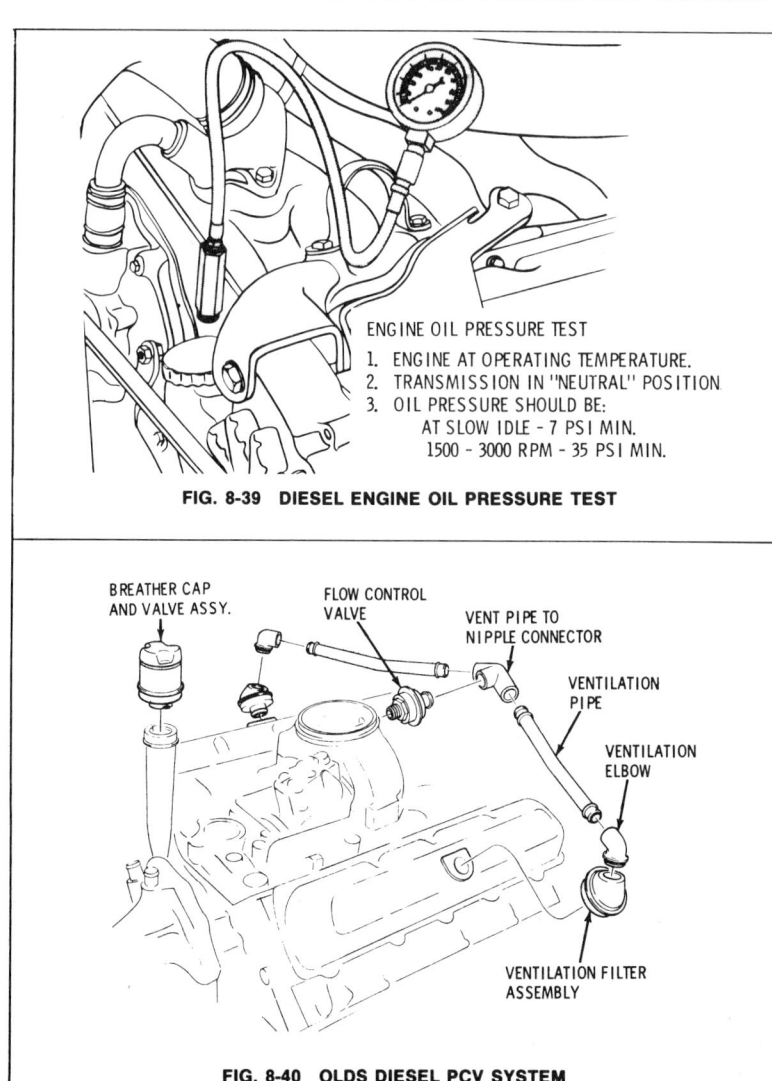

FIG. 8-39 DIESEL ENGINE OIL PRESSURE TEST

FIG. 8-40 OLDS DIESEL PCV SYSTEM

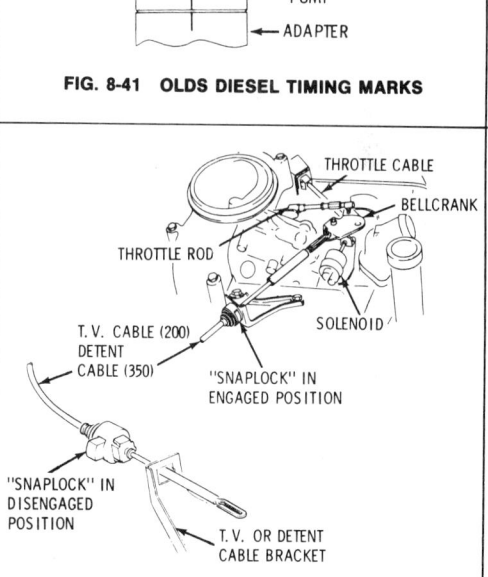

FIG. 8-41 OLDS DIESEL TIMING MARKS

FIG. 8-42 T.V./DETENT CABLE ADJUSTMENT

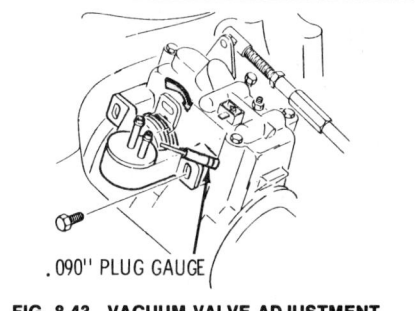

FIG. 8-43 VACUUM VALVE ADJUSTMENT

ENGINE SPECIFICATIONS

AMERICAN MOTORS VALVE ACTION & TIMING

YEAR	ENGINE DISP./H.P.	ROCKER RATIO	LOBE LIFT (Int./Exh.)	VALVE LIFT ZERO LASH (Int./Exh.)	INTAKE VALVE TIMING OPENS (° BTDC)	CLOSES (° ABC)	DURATION (Deg.)	EXHAUST VALVE TIMING OPENS (° BBC)	CLOSES (° ATC)	DURATION (Deg.)	OVERLAP (Deg.)
1970	199-232/ALL	1.50	.254/.254	.381/.381	12.50	51.50	244	52.5	10.5	244	23
	304-360/ALL	1.60	.265/.265₁	.425/.425	18.50	67.50	266	60.5	25.5	266	44
	390/ALL	1.60	.287/.287₁	.457/.457	18.00	68.00	266	66.0	20.0	266	38
1971	232-258/ALL	1.50	.254/.254	.381/.381	12.50	66.50	259.00	53.50	55.50	289.00	68.00
	304-360/ALL	1.60	.266/.266	.425/.425	14.45	68.45	263.30	56.45	56.45	293.30	71.30
	401/ALL	1.60	.286/.286	.457/.457	25.57	90.75	296.32	80.80	42.75	303.55	68.32
1972	232-258/ALL	1.60	.254/.254	.372/.372	12.30	64.30	256.92	53.12₃	23.80₃	256.92₃	35.92₃
	304-360/ALL	1.60	.266/.266	.425/.425	14.75₂	68.75₂	263.50₂	56.75₂	26.75₂	263.50₂	41.50₂
	401/ALL	1.60	.286/.286	.457/.457	25.57	90.75	296.32	80.80	42.75	303.55	68.32
1973	232-258/ALL	1.60	.254/.254	.372/.372	12.12	64.80	256.92	53.12	23.80	256.92	35.92
	304-360/ALL	1.60	.266/.266	.425/.425	14.75	68.75	263.50	56.75	26.75	263.50	41.50
	401/ALL	1.60	.286/.286	.457/.457	25.57	90.75	296.32	80.80	42.75	303.55	68.32
1974	232-258/ALL	1.50	.248/.248	.372/.372	12.12	64.80	256.92	53.12	23.80	256.92	35.92
	304-360/ALL	1.50	.283/.283	.425/.425	14.75	68.75	263.50	56.75	26.75	263.50	41.50
	401/ALL	1.50	.305/.305	.457/.457	25.57	90.75	296.32	80.80	42.75	303.55	68.32
1975	232-258/ALL	1.60	.232/.232	N/A	12.12	64.80	256.92	53.12	23.80	256.92	35.92
	304-360/ALL	1.60	.266/.266	N/A	14.75	68.75	263.50	56.75	26.75	263.50	41.50
	401/ALL	1.60	.286/.286	N/A	25.57	90.75	296.32	80.80	42.75	303.55	68.32
1976	232-258/ALL	1.60	.232/.232	N/A	12.12	64.80	256.92	53.12	23.80	256.92	35.92
	304-360/ALL	1.60	.266/.266	N/A	14.75	68.75	263.50	56.75	26.75	263.50	41.50
	401/ALL	1.60	.286/.286	N/A	25.57	90.75	296.32	80.80	42.75	296.32	68.32
1977	121	N/A	N/A	.402/.382	41.8	77.8	299.5	75.3	63.3	318.6	105.0
	232-258/1-bbl.	1.60	N/A	.375/.375	12.12	64.80	256.92	53.12	23.80	256.92	35.92
	258/2-bbl.	1.60	N/A	.400/.400	14.58	68.79	263.37	55.59	27.78	263.37	42.36
	304-460	1.6153	N/A	.430/.430	14.75	68.75	263.50	56.75	26.75	263.50	41.50
1978	121	N/A	N/A	.402/.382	41.8	77.80	299.50	75.30	63.30	318.60	105.00
	232/258 1-bbl.	1.60	N/A	.375/.375	12.12	64.80	256.92	53.12	23.80	256.92	35.92
	258 2-bbl.	1.60	N/A	.400/.400	14.58	68.79	263.37	55.59	27.78	263.37	42.36
	304/360	1.6153	N/A	.430/.430	14.75	68.75	263.30	56.75	26.75	263.50	41.50
1979	121	N/A	.396/.366	.402/.382	25	61	266	42	30	252	55
	232-258/1-bbl.	1.60	N/A	.375/.375	12.12	64.80	256.92	53.12	23.80	256.92	35.92
	258/2-bbl.	1.60	N/A	.400/.400	14.58	68.79	263.37	55.59	27.78	263.37	42.36
	304	1.60	N/A	.400/.400	12	65	257	53	24	257	36

₁Dealer high performance cam available: lifts .296/.296, timing 46/76/302/70/52/302/98.
₂California valve timing is 14.74/68.75/263.49/56.77/56.75/293.52/71.49.
₃California exhaust valve timing is 53/30,30/55,30/285,12/64.12.

AMERICAN MOTORS INTAKE VALVES & SPRINGS

YEAR	ENGINE DISP./H.P.	SEAT/FACE ANGLE (Degs.)	OVERALL LENGTH	HEAD DIA.	STEM DIA.	STEM-TO-GUIDE CLEARANCE	OUTER SPRING PRESSURE LENGTH CLOSED (Lbs. @ Ins.)	OPEN (Lbs. @ Ins.)	INNER SPRING PRESSURE LENGTH CLOSED (Lbs. @ Ins.)	OPEN (Lbs. @ Ins.)
1970	199/128-232/ALL	30/29	4.899	1.787	.3715-.3725	.0010-.0030	95-105@1.812	188-202@1.437	NONE	NONE
	304/210	30/29	4.899	1.787	.3715-.3725	.0010-.0030	85-93@1.812	193-207@1.387	NONE	NONE
	360/245,290	30/29	4.899	2.025	.3715-.3725	.0010-.0030	85-93@1.812	193-207@1.387	NONE	NONE
	390/325,340	30/29	4.899	2.025	.3715-.3725	.0010-.0030	90-98@1.812	183-195@1.365	NONE	NONE
1971	232/135-258/150	30/29	4.899	1.787	.3715-.3725	.0010-.0030	95-105@1.812	188-202@1.437	NONE	NONE
	304/210	30/29	4.899	1.787	.3715-.3725	.0010-.0030	90-98@1.812	183-194@1.359	NONE	NONE

AMERICAN MOTORS INTAKE VALVES & SPRINGS

YEAR	ENGINE DISP./H.P.	SEAT/FACE ANGLE (Degs.)	OVERALL LENGTH	HEAD DIA.	STEM DIA.	STEM-TO-GUIDE CLEARANCE	OUTER SPRING PRESSURE LENGTH CLOSED (Lbs. @ Ins.)	OPEN (Lbs. @ Ins.)	INNER SPRING PRESSURE LENGTH CLOSED (Lbs. @ Ins.)	OPEN (Lbs. @ Ins.)
	360-401/ALL	30/29	4.899	2.025	.3715-.3725	.0010-.0030	90-98@1.812	183-194@1.359	NONE	NONE
1972	232/100-258/110	30/29	4.899	1.787	.3715-.3725	.0010-.0030	95-105@1.812	188-202@1.437	NONE	NONE
	304/150	30/29	4.899	1.787	.3715-.3725	.0010-.0030	80-88@1.812	210-226@1.365	NONE	NONE
	360-401/ALL	30/29	4.899	2.025	.3715-.3725	.0010-.0030	80-88@1.812	210-226@1.365	NONE	NONE
1973	232/100-258/110	30/29	4.899	1.787	.3715-.3725	.0010-.0030	95-105@1.812	188-202@1.437	NONE	NONE
	304/150	30/29	4.899	1.787	.3715-.3725	.0010-.0030	80-88@1.812	210-226@1.365	NONE	NONE
	360-401/ALL	30/29	4.899	2.025	.3715-.3725	.0010-.0030	80-88@1.812	210-226@1.365	NONE	NONE
1974	232/100-258/110	30/29	4.899	1.787	.3715-.3725	.0010-.0030	95-105@1.812	188-202@1.437	NONE	NONE
	304/150	30/29	4.899	1.787	.3715-.3725	.0010-.0030	80-88@1.812	210-226@1.365	NONE	NONE
	360-401/ALL	30/29	4.899	2.025	.3715-.3725	.0010-.0030	80-88@1.812	210-226@1.365	NONE	NONE
1975	232/100-258/110	30/29	4.7895-4.8045	1.787	.3715-.3725	.0010-.0030	95-105@1.812	188-202@1.437	NONE	NONE
	304/150	30/29	4.7895-4.8045	1.787	.3715-.3725	.0010-.0030	80-88@1.812	210-216@1.437	NONE	NONE
	360-401/ALL	30/29	4.8095-4.8245	2.025	.3715-.3725	.0010-.0030	80-88@1.812	210-216@1.437	NONE	NONE
1976	232/90-258/95	30/29	4.7895-4.8045	1.787	.3715-.3725	.0010-.0030	95-105@1.812	188-202@1.437	NONE	NONE
	304/120	30/29	4.7895-4.8045	1.787	.3715-.3725	.0010-.0030	80-88@1.812	210-216@1.437	NONE	NONE
	360/ALL	30/29	4.7895-4.8045	2.025	.3715-.3725	.0010-.0030	80-88@1.812	210-216@1.437	NONE	NONE
1977	121	44.75/45.33	5.409-5.390	₁	.3531-.3526	.0026-.0012	53@1.701	166@1.299	18@1.488	39@1.086
	232-258/1-bbl.	30/29	4.899	1.787	.3715-.3725	.0010-.0030	95-105@1.786	188-202@1.411	NONE	NONE
	258/2-bbl.	30/29	4.899	1.787	.3715-.3725	.0010-.0030	64-72@1.786	196-210@1.386	NONE	NONE
	304	30/29	4.899	1.787	.3715-.3725	.0010-.0030	80-88@1.812	205-221@1.382	NONE	NONE
	360	30/29	4.899	2.025	.3715-.3725	.0010-.0030	80-88@1.812	205-221@1.382	NONE	NONE
1978	121	44.75/45.33	5.390-5.409	₁	.3526-.3531	.0012-.0026	53@1.701	166@1.299	18@1.488	39@1.086
	232/258 1-bbl.	30/29	4.899	1.787	.3715-.3725	.0010-.0030	64-72@1.786	188-202@1.411	NONE	NONE
	258 2-bbl.	30/29	4.899	1.787	.3715-.3725	.0010-.0030	64-72@1.786	188-202@1.411	NONE	NONE
	304	30/29	4.899	1.787	.3715-.3725	.0010-.0030	64-72@1.786	206-220@1.356	NONE	NONE
	360	30/29	4.899	2.025	.3715-.3725	.0010-.0030	64-72@1.786	206-220@1.356	NONE	NONE
1979	121	45°/45°20′	5.390-5.409	₁	.3526-.3531	.0012-.0026	53.35@1.70	166.46@1.30	17.52@1.49	39.02@1.09
	232-258/1-bbl.	30/29	4.7895-4.8045	1.787	.3715-.3725	.0010-.0030	64-72@1.79	188-202@1.411	NONE	NONE
	258/2-bbl.	30/29	4.7895-4.8045	1.787	.3715-.3725	.0010-.0030	64-72@1.79	188-202@1.411	NONE	NONE
	304	30/29	4.7895-4.8045	1.787	.3715-.3725	.0010-.0030	64-72@1.79	188-202@1.411	NONE	NONE

₁1.496-1.484

AMERICAN MOTORS EXHAUST VALVES & SPRINGS

YEAR	ENGINE DISP./H.P.	SEAT/FACE ANGLE (Degs.)	OVERALL LENGTH	HEAD DIA.	STEM DIA.	STEM-TO-GUIDE CLEARANCE	OUTER SPRING PRESSURE LENGTH CLOSED (Lbs. @ Ins.)	OPEN (Lbs. @ Ins.)	INNER SPRING PRESSURE LENGTH CLOSED (Lbs. @ Ins.)	OPEN (Lbs. @ Ins.)
1970	199/128	44/44	4.892	1.406	.3718-.3725	.0010-.0027	95-105@1.812	188-202@1.437	NONE	NONE
	232/145-155	44/44	4.892	1.406	.3718-.3725	.0010-.0027	95-105@1.812	188-202@1.437	NONE	NONE
	304/210	45/44.5	4.892	1.406	.3715-.3725	.0010-.0030	85-93@1.812	193-207@1.387	NONE	NONE
	360/245-290	45/44.5	4.907	1.625	.3715-.3725	.0010-.0030	85-93@1.812	193-207@1.387	NONE	NONE
	390/325-340	45/44.5	4.907	1.625	.3715-.3725	.0010-.0030	90-98@1.812	183-195@1.365	NONE	NONE
1971	232/135-258/150	45/44.5	4.892	1.406	.3718-.3725	.0010-.0030	95-105@1.812	188-202@1.437	NONE	NONE
	304/210	45/44.5	4.892	1.406	.3718-.3725	.0010-.0030	95-105@1.8i2	188-202@1.437	NONE	NONE
	360/ALL-401/330	45/44.5	4.910	1.680	.3715-.3725	.0010-.0030	90-98@1.812	183-195@1.359	NONE	NONE
1972	232/100-258/110	45/44	4.7895-4.8045	1.406	.3718-.3725	.0010-.0030	95-105@1.812	188-202@1.437	NONE	NONE
	304/150	45/44	4.7895-4.8045	1.406	.3715-.3725	.0010-.0030	80-88@1.812	210-226@1.365	NONE	NONE
	360/ALL-401/255	45/44	4.7895-4.8045	1.680	.3715-.3725	.0010-.0030	80-88@1.812	210-226@1.365	NONE	NONE
1973	232/100-258/110	45/44	4.892	1.406	.3718-.3725	.0010-.0027	95-105@1.812	188-202@1.437	NONE	NONE
	304/150	45/44	4.892	1.406	.3715-.3725	.0010-.0030	80-88@1.812	210-226@1.365	NONE	NONE
	360/ALL-401/255	45/44	4.910	1.680	.3715-.3725	.0010-.0030	80-88@1.812	210-226@1.365	NONE	NONE
1974	232/100-258/110	45/44	4.892	1.406	.3718-.3725	.0010-.0027	95-105@1.812	188-202@1.437	NONE	NONE
	304/150	45/44	4.892	1.406	.3715-.3725	.0010-.0030	80-88@1.812	210-226@1.365	NONE	NONE
	360/ALL-401/235	45/44	4.910	1.680	.3715-.3725	.0010-.0030	80-88@1.630	210-226@1.183	NONE	NONE
1975	232/100-258/110	44.5/44	4.7895-4.8045	1.406	.3715-.3725	.0010-.0030	95-105@1.812	188-202@1.437	NONE	NONE
	304/150	44.5/44	4.7895-4.8045	1.406	.3715-.3725	.0010-.0030	80-88@1.812	210-216@1.437	NONE	NONE
	360/ALL-401/255	44.5/44	4.8095-4.8245	1.680	.3715-.3725	.0010-.0030	80-88@1.812	210-216@1.437	NONE	NONE
1976	232/90-258/95	44.5/44	4.7895-4.8045	1.406	.3715-.3725	.0010-.0030	95-105@1.812	188-202@1.437	NONE	NONE
	304/120	44.5/44	4.7895-4.804	1.406	.3715-.3725	.0010-.0030	80-88@1.812	210-216@1.437	NONE	NONE
	360/ALL	44.5/44	4.8095-4.8245	1.680	.3715-.3725	.0010-.0030	80-88@1.812	210-216@1.437	NONE	NONE
1977	121	44.75/45.33	5.400-5.380	₁	.3528-.3522	.0030-.0015	53@1.701	160@1.319	18@1.488	37@1.106
	232-258/1-bbl.	44.5/44	4.892	1.406	.3718-.3725	.0010-.0027	95-105@1.786	188-202@1.411	NONE	NONE
	258/2-bbl.	44.5/44	4.892	1.406	.3718-.3725	.0010-.0027	64-72@1.786	196-210@1.386	NONE	NONE
	304	44.5/44	4.892	1.406	.3718-.3725	.0010-.0027	80-88@1.812	205-211@1.382	NONE	NONE

ENGINE SPECIFICATIONS

AMERICAN MOTORS EXHAUST VALVES & SPRINGS

YEAR	ENGINE DISP./H.P.	SEAT/FACE ANGLE (Degs.)	OVERALL LENGTH	HEAD DIA.	STEM DIA.	STEM-TO-GUIDE CLEARANCE	OUTER SPRING PRESSURE LENGTH CLOSED (Lbs.@Ins.)	OUTER SPRING PRESSURE LENGTH OPEN (Lbs.@Ins.)	INNER SPRING PRESSURE LENGTH CLOSED (Lbs.@Ins.)	INNER SPRING PRESSURE LENGTH OPEN (Lbs.@Ins.)
1978	360	44.5/44	4.910	1.680	.3718-.3725	.0010-.0027	80-88@1.812	205-211@1.382	NONE	NONE
	121	44.75/45.33	5.380-5.400	1	.3522-.3528	.0015-.0030	53@1.701	160@1.319	18@1.488	37@1.106
	232/258 1-bbl.	44.3/44	4.892	1.406	.3718-.3725	.0010-.0027	64-72@1.786	188-202@1.411	NONE	NONE
	258 2-bbl.	44.3/44	4.892	1.406	.3718-.3725	.0010-.0027	64-72@1.786	196-210@1.386	NONE	NONE
	304	44.3/44	4.892	1.406	.3718-.3725	.0010-.0027	64-72@1.786	206-220@1.356	NONE	NONE
	360	44.3/44	4.910	1.680	.3718-.3725	.0010-.0027	64-72@1.786	206-220@1.356	NONE	NONE
1979	121	45°/45°20′	5.400-5.419	1.287-1.299	.3522-.3528	.0016-.0030	53.35@1.70	160.28@1.32	17.52@1.49	37.15@1.11
	232-258/1-bbl.	44.5/44	4.7970	1.401-1.411	.3715-.3725	.0010-.0030	64-72@1.786	188-202@1.411	NONE	NONE
	258/2-bbl.	44.5/44	4.7970	1.401-1.411	.3715-.3725	.0010-.0030	64-72@1.786	188-202@1.411	NONE	NONE
	304	44.5/44	4.7970	1.401-1.411	.3715-.3725	.0010-.0030	64-72@1.786	188-202@1.411	NONE	NONE

1 1.299-1.287

CHRYSLER CORPORATION VALVE ACTION & TIMING

YEAR	ENGINE DISP./H.P.	ROCKER RATIO	LOBE LIFT (Int./Exh.)	VALVE LIFT ZERO LASH (Int./Exh.)	INTAKE VALVE TIMING OPENS (° BTDC)	INTAKE VALVE TIMING CLOSES (° ABC)	INTAKE VALVE TIMING DURATION (Deg.)	EXHAUST VALVE TIMING OPENS (° BBC)	EXHAUST VALVE TIMING CLOSES (° ATC)	EXHAUST VALVE TIMING DURATION (Deg.)	OVERLAP (Deg.)
1970	198-225/ALL	1.50	.263/.263	.395/.395	10	50	240	50	6	240	16
	318/ALL	1.50	.248/.265	.373/.399	10	50	240	58	10	248	20
	340/ALL	1.50	.295/.302	.429/.444	22	66	268	74	22	276	44
	383/290-330; 440/350	1.50	.283/.290	.425/.435	18	58	256	66	14	260	32
	383/335	1.50	.283/.290	.425/.435	21	67	268	79	25	284	46
	426/425	1.50	.310/.315	.467/.481	36	68	284	80	24	284	60
	440/375-390	1.50	.300/.305	.425/.458	21	67	268	79	25	284	46
1971	198-225/ALL	1.50	—	.406/.414	16	48	244	54	10	244	26
	318/ALL	1.50	1/1	.373/.399	10	50	240	52	16	248	26
	340/ALL	1.50	1/1	.429/.444	22	66	268	74	22	276	44
	360/ALL 383/275; 440/335	1.50	1/1	.410/.412	16	56	252	60	16	256	32
	383/300; 440/370-385	1.50	1/1	.425/.435	18	62	260	68	20	268	38
	426/425	1.50	1/1	.450/.458	21	67	268	79	25	284	46
				.490/.481	36	68	284	80	24	284	60
1972	198-225/ALL	1.50	1/1	.406/.414	16	48	244	54	10	244	26
	318/ALL	1.50	1/1	.373/.400	10	50	240	52	16	248	26
	340/ALL	1.50	1/1	.429/.444	22	66	268	74	22	276	44
	360/ALL 400/190; 440/225-245	1.50	1/1	.410/.412	16	56	252	60	16	256	32
	400/255; 440/280	1.50	1/1	.434/.430	18	62	260	68	20	268	38
		1.50	1/1	.449/.464	21	67	268	79	25	284	46
1973	198-255/ALL	1.50	1/1	.406/.414	16	48	244	54	10	244	26
	318/ALL	1.50	1/1	.373/.400	10	50	240	52	16	248	26
	340/ALL	1.50	1/1	.429/.444	22	66	268	74	22	276	44
	360/ALL	1.50	1/1	.410/.412	16	56	252	60	16	256	32
	400-440/ALL	1.50	1/1	.434/.430	18	62	260	68	20	268	38
	400/260	1.50	1/1	.449/.464	21	67	268	79	25	284	46
1974	198-255/ALL	1.50	1/1	.406/.414	16	48	244	54	10	244	26
	318/ALL	1.50	1/1	.373/.400	10	50	240	52	16	248	26
	360/180-200	1.50	1/1	.410/.412	16	56	252	60	16	256	32
	360/245	1.50	1/1	.429/.444	22	66	268	74	22	276	44
	400-440/ALL	1.50	1/1	.434/.430	18	62	260	68	20	268	38
1975	225/ALL	1.50	1/1	.406/.414	16	48	244	54	10	244	26
	318/ALL	1.50	1/1	.373/.400	10	50	240	52	16	248	26
	360/180-190	1.50	1/1	.410/.412	18	54	252	57	15	252	33
	360/230	1.50	1/1	.429/.444	22	66	268	74	22	276	44
	400-440/ALL	1.50	1/1	.434/.430	18	62	260	68	20	268	38
1976	225/ALL	1.50	1/1	.406/.414	16	48	244	54	10	244	26
	318/ALL	1.50	1/1	.373/.400	10	50	240	52	16	248	26
	360/ALL	1.50	1/1	.410/.410	18	54	252	57	15	252	33
	400-440/ALL	1.50	1/1	.434/.430	18	62	260	68	20	268	38

CHRYSLER CORPORATION VALVE ACTION & TIMING

YEAR	ENGINE DISP./H.P.	ROCKER RATIO	LOBE LIFT (Int./Exh.)	VALVE LIFT ZERO LASH (Int./Exh.)	INTAKE VALVE TIMING OPENS (° BTDC)	CLOSES (° ABC)	DURATION (Deg.)	EXHAUST VALVE TIMING OPENS (° BBC)	CLOSES (° ATC)	DURATION (Deg.)	OVERLAP (Deg.)
1977	225/ALL	1.50	1/1	.406/.414	16	48	244	54	10	244	26
	318/ALL	1.50	1/1	.373/.400	10	50	240	52	16	248	26
	360/ALL	1.50	1/1	.410/.410	18	54	252	57	15	252	33
	400-440/ALL	1.50	1/1	.434/.430	20	60	260	70	18	268	38
1978	104.7/ALL	NONE	—	.406/.406	14	56	250	51	13	244	27
	225/ALL	1.50	1/1	.406/.414	16	48	244	54	10	244	26
	318/ALL	1.50	1/1	.373/.400	10	50	240	52	16	248	26
	360/ALL	1.50	1/1	.410/.410	18	54	252	57	15	252	33
	400/ALL	1.50	1/1	.434/.430	20	60	260	70	18	268	38
	440/ALL	1.50	1/1	.434/.430	20	60	260	70	18	268	38
1979	104.7/ALL	NONE	1/1	.406/.406	14	56	250	51	13	244	27
	225/ALL	1.5	1/1	.406/.414	16	48	244	54	10	244	26
	318/ALL	1.5	1/1	.373/.400	10	50	240	52	16	248	26
	360/ALL	1.5	1/1	.410/.410	18	54	252	57	15	252	33

1 Divide valve lift by rocker arm ratio to determine lobe lift.

CHRYSLER CORPORATION INTAKE VALVES & SPRINGS

YEAR	ENGINE DISP./H.P.	SEAT/FACE ANGLE (Degs.)	OVERALL LENGTH	HEAD DIA.	STEM DIA.	STEM-TO-GUIDE CLEARANCE	OUTER SPRINGS PRESSURE LENGTH CLOSED (Lbs. @ Ins.)	OPEN (Lbs. @ Ins.)	INNER SPRINGS PRESSURE LENGTH CLOSED (Lbs. @ Ins.)	OPEN (Lbs. @ Ins.)
1970	198-225/ALL	45/45	4.688-4.703	1.62	.372-.373	.001-.003	49-57@1.69	137-150@1.31	NONE	NONE
	318/ALL	45/45	4.90	1.78	.372-.373	.001-.003	78-88@1.69	170-184@1.31	NONE	NONE
	340/ALL	45/45	4.90	2.02	.372-.373	.0015-.0035	80-90@1.69	235-249@1.22	DAMPER	DAMPER
	383/ALL	45/45	4.87	2.08	.372-.373	.001-.003	121-129@1.86	192-208@1.43	NONE	NONE
	426/ALL	45/45	5.316-5.331	2.25	.309-.310	.002-.004	110-120@1.86	300-320@1.38	DAMPER	DAMPER
	440/ALL	45/45	4.87	2.08	.372-.373	.001-.003	100-110@1.86	236-256@1.43	DAMPER	DAMPER
1971	198-225/ALL	45/45	4.77	1.62	.372-.373	.001-.003	49-57@1.69	137-150@1.31	NONE	NONE
	318/ALL	45/45	4.97	1.78	.372-.373	.001-.003	78-88@1.69	170-184@1.31	NONE	NONE
	340/ALL	45/45	4.99	2.02	.372-.373	.0015-.0035	80-90@1.69	231-245@1.31	NONE	NONE
	360/ALL	45/45	4.99	1.88	.372-.373	.001-.003	78-88@1.69	170-184@1.31	NONE	NONE
	383/275-440/335	45/45	4.86	2.08	.372-.373	.001-.0027	121-129@1.86	192-208@1.437	NONE	NONE
	383/300-440/370-385	45/45	4.86	2.08	.3718-.3725	.0015-.0032	100-110@1.86	236-256@1.359	DAMPER	DAMPER
	426	45/45	5.41	2.25	.3085-.3095	.002-.004	110-120@1.86	300-320@1.375	DAMPER	DAMPER
1972	198-225/ALL	45/45	4.77	1.62	.372-.373	.001-.003	63@1.65	160@1.24	NONE	NONE
	318/ALL	45/45	4.97	1.78	.372-.373	.001-.003	92@1.65	189@1.28	NONE	NONE
	340/ALL	45/45	4.98	1.88	.3715-.3725	.0015-.0035	96@1.65	238@1.22	DAMPER	DAMPER
	360/ALL	45/45	4.98	1.88	.372-.373	.001-.003	92@1.65	195@1.24	NONE	NONE
	400/190-440/225-240	45/45	4.86	2.08	.372-.373	.001-.0027	125@1.86	200@1.42	NONE	NONE
	400/255-440/280	45/45	4.86	2.08	.3718-.3725	.0015-.0032	105@1.86	234@1.40	DAMPER	DAMPER
1973	198-255/ALL	45/45	4.77	1.62	.372-.373	.001-.003	63@1.65	160@1.24	NONE	NONE
	318/ALL	45/45	4.97	1.78	.372-.373	.001-.003	92@1.65	189@1.28	NONE	NONE
	340/ALL	45/45	4.98	1.88	.3715-.3725	.0015-.0035	96@1.65	238@1.22	DAMPER	DAMPER
	360/ALL	45/45	4.98	1.88	.372-.373	.001-.003	92@1.65	195@1.24	NONE	NONE
	400-440/ALL	45/45	4.86	2.08	.3723-.3730	.001-.0027	125@1.86	200@1.42	NONE	NONE
	400/175-260	45/45	4.86	2.08	.371-.372	.0015-.0032	105@1.86	234@1.40	DAMPER	DAMPER
1974	198-255/ALL	45/45	4.77	1.62	.372-.373	.001-.003	60@1.65	160@1.24	NONE	NONE
	318/ALL	45/45	4.97	1.78	.372-.373	.001-.003	92@1.65	189@1.28	NONE	NONE
	360/180-200	45/45	4.98	1.88	.372-.373	.001-.003	92@1.65	195@1.24	NONE	NONE
	360/245	45/45	4.98	1.88	.372-.333	.001-.003	96@1.65	238@1.24	NONE	NONE
	400-440/ALL	45/45	4.86	2.08	.3723-.3730	.0010-.0027	125@1.86	200@1.42	NONE	NONE
1975	225/ALL	45/45	4.77	1.62	.372-.373	.001-.003	63@1.65	162@1.24	NONE	NONE
	318/ALL	45/45	4.97	1.78	.372-.373	.001-.003	92@1.65	185@1.28	NONE	NONE
	360/180	45/45	4.98	1.88	.372-.373	.001-.003	92@1.65	195@1.24	NONE	NONE
	360/190	45/45	4.98	1.88	.3715-.3725	.0015-.0035	113@1.65	195@1.24	NONE	NONE
	360/230	45/45	4.98	1.88	.372-.373	.001-.0030	96@1.65	238@1.22	NONE	NONE
	400-440/ALL	45/45	4.86	2.08	.3723-.3730	.001-.0027	125@1.86	200@1.43	NONE	NONE
1976	225/ALL	45/45	4.77	1.62	.372-.373	.001-.003	63@1.65	192@1.24	NONE	NONE
	318/ALL	45/45	4.97	1.78	.372-.373	.001-.003	92@1.65	185@1.28	NONE	NONE
	360/ALL	45/45	4.98	1.88	.3715-.3725	.0015-.0035	92@1.65	195@1.24	NONE	NONE
	400-440/ALL	45/45	4.86	2.08	.3723-.3730	.001-.0027	125@1.86	200@1.43	NONE	NONE
1977	225/ALL	44.5-45/45-45.5	4.77	1.62	.372-.373	.001-.003	63@1.65	162@1.24	NONE	NONE
	318/ALL	44.5-45/45-45.5	4.97	1.78	.372-.373	.001-.003	92@1.65	185@1.28	NONE	NONE
	360/ALL	44.5-45/45-45.5	4.98	1.88	.372-.373	.001-.003	92@1.65	195@1.24	NONE	NONE
	400-440/ALL	44.5-45/45-45.5	4.86	2.08	.372-.373	.001-.003	125@1.86	200@1.43	NONE	NONE

ENGINE SPECIFICATIONS

CHRYSLER CORPORATION INTAKE VALVES & SPRINGS

YEAR	ENGINE DISP./H.P.	SEAT/FACE ANGLE (Degs.)	OVERALL LENGTH	HEAD DIA.	STEM DIA.	STEM-TO-GUIDE CLEARANCE	OUTER SPRINGS PRESSURE LENGTH CLOSED (Lbs. @ Ins.)	OPEN (Lbs. @ Ins.)	INNER SPRINGS PRESSURE LENGTH CLOSED (Lbs. @ Ins.)	OPEN (Lbs. @ Ins.)
1978	104.7/ALL	45/45.3	3.89	1.33-1.34	.313-.314	.001-.003	38.80@1.28	100.48@.878	15.89@1.13	48.49@.720
	225/ALL	44.5-45/45-45.5	4.77	1.62	.372-.373	.001-.003	65@1.65	162@1.24	NONE	NONE
	318/ALL	44.5-45/45-45.5	4.97	1.78	.372-.373	.001-.003	92@1.65	185@1.28	NONE	NONE
	360/ALL	44.5-45/45-45.5	4.98	1.88	.372-.373	.001-.003	92@1.65	195@1.24	NONE	NONE
	400-440/ALL	44.5-45/45-45.5	4.86	2.08	.372-.373	.001-.003	125@1.86	200@1.43	NONE	NONE
1979	104.7/ALL	45/45 33′	3.89	1.33-1.34	.313-.314	.001-.003	38.8@1.28	100.48@.878	15.89@1.13	48.49@.720
	225/ALL	45/45	4.77	1.62	.372-.373	.001-.003	63@1.65	162@1.24	NONE	NONE
	318/ALL	45/45	4.97	1.78	.372-.373	.001-.003	92@1.65	185@1.28	NONE	NONE
	360/ALL	45/45	4.98	1.88	.372-.373	.001-.003	92@1.65	195@1.24	NONE	NONE

CHRYSLER CORPORATION EXHAUST VALVES & SPRINGS

YEAR	ENGINE DISP./H.P.	SEAT/FACE ANGLE (Degs.)	OVERALL LENGTH	HEAD DIA.	STEM DIA.	STEM-TO-GUIDE CLEARANCE	OUTER SPRINGS PRESSURE LENGTH CLOSED (Lbs. @ Ins.)	OPEN (Lbs. @ Ins.)	INNER SPRINGS PRESSURE LENGTH CLOSED (Lbs. @ Ins.)	OPEN (Lbs. @ Ins.)
1970	198-225/ALL	43/43	4.688-4.703	1.355-1.365	.371-.372	.002-.004	49-57@1.69	137-150@1.31	NONE	NONE
	318/ALL	43/43	4.90	1.563	.371-.372	.002-.004	78-88@1.69	170-184@1.31	NONE	NONE
	340/ALL	43/43	4.90	1.60	.371-.372	.002-.004	80-90@1.69	235-249@1.22	DAMPER	DAMPER
	383/ALL	45/45	4.87	1.75	.371-.372	.002-.004	121-129@1.86	192-208@1.44	NONE	NONE
	426/ALL	45/45	4.75-4.77	1.94	.308-.309	.003-.005	110-120@1.86	300-320@1.36	DAMPER	DAMPER
	440/ALL	45/45	4.87	1.75	.371-.372	.002-.004	100-110@1.86	236-256@1.36	NONE	NONE
1971	198-225/ALL	45/43	4.80	1.36	.371-.372	.002-.004	49-57@1.69	137-150@1.31	NONE	NONE
	318/ALL	45/45	4.97	1.50	.371-.372	.002-.004	78-88@1.69	170-184@1.31	NONE	NONE
	340/ALL	45/45	4.97	1.60	.3705-.3715	.0025-.0045	80-90@1.69	231-245@1.31	DAMPER	DAMPER
	360/ALL	45/45	4.99	1.60	.371-.372	.002-.004	78-88@1.69	170-184@1.31	NONE	NONE
	383/275;440/335	45/45	4.89	1.75	1	2	121-129@1.86	192-208@1.44	NONE	NONE
	383/300;440/ 370-385	45/45	4.89	1.75	3	4	100-110@1.86	236-256@1.36	DAMPER	DAMPER
	426/ALL	45/45	4.86	1.94	.3075-.3085	.003-.005	110-120@1.86	300-320@1.36	DAMPER	DAMPER
1972	198-225/ALL	45/43	4.80	1.36	.371-.372	.002-.004	63@1.65	160@1.24	NONE	NONE
	318-360/ALL	45/43	4.90	1.60	.371-.372	.002-.004	92@1.65	193@1.25	NONE	NONE
	340/ALL	45/43	4.90	1.60	.3705-.3715	.0025-.0045	96@1.65	241@1.21	DAMPER	DAMPER
	400/190-440/225-245	45/45	4.87	1.75	1	2	125@1.86	200@1.42	NONE	NONE
	400/255-440/280	45/45	4.87	1.75	3	4	105@1.86	234@1.40	DAMPER	DAMPER
1973	198-225/ALL	45/43	4.80	1.36	.371-.372	.002-.004	63@1.65	160@1.24	NONE	NONE
	318/ALL	45/43	5.00	1.50	.371-.372	.002-.004	92@1.65	193@1.25	NONE	NONE
	340/ALL	45/43	5.00	1.60	.371-.372	.0025-.0045	96@1.65	241@1.21	DAMPER	DAMPER
	360/ALL	45/43	5.00	1.60	.371-.372	.002-.004	92@1.65	195@1.24	NONE	NONE
	400-440/ALL	45/45	4.89	1.74	1	2	125@1.86	200@1.42	NONE	NONE
	400/260	45/45	4.89	1.74	3	4	105@1.86	234@1.40	DAMPER	DAMPER
1974	198-225/ALL	45/47	4.80	1.36	.371-.372	.002-.004	60@1.65	160@1.24	NONE	NONE
	318/ALL	45/47	5.00	1.50	.371-.372	.002-.004	92@1.65	193@1.25	NONE	NONE
	360/180-200	45/47	5.00	1.60	.371-.372	.002-.004	92@1.65	195@1.24	NONE	NONE
	360/245	45/47	5.00	1.60	.3705-.3715	.0025-.0045	96@1.65	238@1.24	NONE	NONE
	400-440/ALL	45/45	4.89	1.74	1	2	125@1.86	200@1.42	NONE	NONE
1975	225/ALL	45/47	4.80	1.36	.371-.372	.002-.004	63@1.65	162@1.24	NONE	NONE
	318/ALL	45/47	5.00	1.50	.371-.372	.002-.004	92@1.65	193@1.25	NONE	NONE
	360/180	45/47	5.00	1.60	.371-.372	.002-.004	92@1.65	195@1.24	NONE	NONE
	360/190	45/47	5.00	1.60	.371-.372	.002-.004	113@1.65	195@1.24	NONE	NONE
	360/230	45/47	5.00	1.60	.3705-.3715	.0025-.0045	96@1.65	238@1.22	NONE	NONE
	400-440/ALL	45/45	4.89	1.74	1	2	125@1.86	200@1.43	NONE	NONE
1976	225/ALL	45/47	4.80	1.36	.371-.372	.002-.004	63@1.65	162@1.24	NONE	NONE
	318/ALL	45/47	5.00	1.50	.371-.372	.002-.004	92@1.65	193@1.25	NONE	NONE
	360/ALL	45/47	5.00	1.60	.371-.372	.002-.004	92@1.65	195@1.40	NONE	NONE
	400-440/ALL	45/47	4.86	2.08	1	2	125@1.86	200@1.43	NONE	NONE
1977	225/ALL	44.5-45/47-47.5	4.80	1.36	.371-.372	.002-.004	63@1.65	162@1.24	NONE	NONE
	318/ALL	44.5-45/47-47.5	5.00	1.50	.371-.372	.002-.004	92@1.65	193@1.25	NONE	NONE
	360/ALL	44.5-45/47-47.5	5.00	1.60	.371-.372	.002-.004	92@1.65	195@1.24	NONE	NONE
	400-440/ALL	44.5-45/47-47.5	4.89	1.74	1	2	125@1.86	200@1.43	NONE	NONE
1978	104.7/ALL	45/43.3	3.87	1.22-1.23	.312-.313	.002-.003	38.80@1.28	100.48@.878	15.89@1.13	48.49@.720
	225/ALL	44.5-45/47-47.5	4.80	1.36	.371-.372	.002-.004	63@165	162@1.24	NONE	NONE
	318/ALL	44.5-45/47-47.5	5.00	1.50	.371-.372	.002-.004	92@165	193@1.25	NONE	NONE
	360/ALL	44.5-45/47-47.5	5.00	1.60	.371-.372	.002-.004	92@165	195@1.24	NONE	NONE
	400-440/ALL	44.5-45/45-45.5	4.89	1.74	.3713-.37205	.0020-.00376	125@186	200@1.43	NONE	NONE

CHRYSLER CORPORATION EXHAUST VALVES & SPRINGS

YEAR	ENGINE DISP./H.P.	SEAT/FACE ANGLE(Degs.)	OVERALL LENGTH	HEAD DIA.	STEM DIA.	STEM-TO-GUIDE CLEARANCE	OUTER SPRING PRESSURE LENGTH CLOSED (Lbs. @ Ins.)	OPEN (Lbs. @ Ins.)	INNER SPRING PRESSURE LENGTH CLOSED (Lbs. @ Ins.)	OPEN (Lbs. @ Ins.)
1979	104.7/ALL	45/45 33'	3.87	1.22-1.23	.312-.313	.002-.003	38.8@1.28	100.48@.878	15.89@1.13	48.49@.720
	225/ALL	45/47	4.80	1.36	.371-.372	.002-.004	63@1.65	162@1.24	NONE	NONE
	318/ALL	45/47	5.00	1.50	.371-.372	.002-.004	92@1.65	193@1.25	NONE	NONE
	360/ALL	45/47	5.00	1.60	.371-.372	.002-.004	92@1.65	195@1.25	NONE	NONE

1 Tapered stem. Hot end-.3713-.3720; cold end-.3723-.3730.
2 Hot end-.0020-.0037; cold end-.0010-.0027.
3 Tapered stem. Hot end-.3708-.3715; cold end-.3718-.3725.
4 Hot end-.0025-.0042; cold end-.0015-.0032.
5 Cold end; .3723-.3730.
6 Cold end; .0010-.0027.

FORD MOTOR COMPANY VALVE ACTION AND TIMING

ENGINE DISP./HP	ROCKER RATIO	LOBE LIFT (Int./Exh.)1	VALVE LIFT ZERO LASH (Int./Exh.)	INTAKE OPENS (°BTDC)	INTAKE CLOSES (°ABC)	INTAKE DURATION (Degs.)	EXHAUST OPENS (°BBC)	EXHAUST CLOSES (°ATC)	EXHAUST DURATION (Degs.)	OVERLAP (Degs.)
1970										
170/105	1.50	.2320/.2320	.348/.348	9	51	240	42	18	240	27
200/120	1.50	.2320/.2320	.348/.348	9	51	240	42	18	240	27
240/150	1.61	.2320/.2490	.376/.400	12	62	254	60	28	268	40
250/155	1.50	.245/.245	.368/.368	10	62	252	49	25	254	35
302/220	1.61	.2303/.2375	.368/.381	16	70	266	44	20	244	36
302/290	1.61	.2900/.2900	.477/.477	40	65	285	68	22	270	31
351W/250	1.60	.260/.278	.418/.407	11	65	256	68	22	270	33
351C/250	1.73	.235/.235	.400/.400	12	66	258	66	20	266	32
351/300	1.73	.247/.247	.420/.450	14	72	266	70	22	270	34
390/265	1.73	.2470/.2490	.430/.430	13	63	256	63	23	266	36
428/335	1.73	.2780/.2830	.481/.490	18	72	270	82	28	290	46
428/360	1.73	.2780/.2830	.481/.490	18	72	270	82	28	290	46
429/320	1.75	.253/.278	.443/.486	16	60	256	70	20	270	36
429/360	1.75	.289/.289	.443/.486	16	60	256	70	20	270	36
429/370	1.75	.289/.289	.443/.486	16	60	256	70	20	270	36
429/375	1.75	.289/.289	.443/.486	16	60	256	70	20	270	36
460/365	1.76	.253/.278	.443/.486	16	60	256	70	20	270	36
1971										
98/75	1.54	.2108/.2176	.2967/.3199	17	51	248	51	17	248	34
122/100	1.60	.2519/.2519	.3993/.3993	18	70	268	64	24	268	42
170/100	1.50	.2320/.2320	.348/.348	9	51	240	42	18	240	27
200/115	1.50	.2320/.2320	.348/.348	9	51	240	42	18	240	27
250/145	1.50	.245/.245	.368/.368	10	62	252	49	25	254	35
240/140	1.61	.2330/.2490	.376/.400	12	62	254	60	28	268	40
302/210	1.60	.2303/.2375	.3680/.2810	16	70	266	44	20	244	36
351/240W	1.60	.260/.278	.418/.448	11	65	256	68	22	270	33
351/240C	1.73	.235/.235	.407/.407	12	66	258	66	20	266	32
351/285C	1.73	.247/.262	.427/.453	18	70	268	81	19	280	37
351/330C BOSS	1.73	.245/.260	.491/.491	50	94	324	102	42	324	92
390/255	1.73	.2470/.2490	.4270/.4300	13	63	256	63	23	266	36
400/260	1.73	.247/.250	.427/.433	17	59	256	71	21	272	38
429/320	1.73	.2530/.2780	.4430/.4860	16	60	256	70	20	270	36
429/360	1.73	.2530/.2780	.4430/.4860	16	60	256	70	20	270	36
429/370CJ	1.73	.289/.289	.500/.500	32	70	282	90	26	296	58
429/275SCJ	1.73	.298/.298	.515/.515	40.5	79.5	300	88.5	31.5	300	72
460/365	1.73	.2530/.2780	.430/.4860	16	60	256	70	20	270	36
1972										
98/54	1.54	.2108/.2176	.3247/.3351	17	51	248	51	17	248	34
122/86	1.60	.2512/.2512	.3993/.3993	24	64	268	70	18	268	42
170/82	1.50	.2320/.2320	.348/.348	9	51	240	42	18	240	27
200/91	1.50	.2320/.2320	.348/.348	9	51	240	42	18	240	27
240/103	1.61	.2490/.2490	.400/.400	18	70	268	58	30	268	48
250/98	1.50	.245/.245	.368/.368	10	62	252	49	25	254	35
302/140	1.61	.2303/.2375	.368/.380	16	70	266	44	20	244	36
351/153W	1.61	.260/.278	.418/.448	11	65	256	68	22	270	33
351/163C	1.71	.235/.235	.400/.400	12	66	258	66	20	266	32
351/177C	1.73	.235/.235	.400/.400	12	66	258	66	20	266	32
351/248C	1.73	.247/.262	.480/.488	14	76	270	78	32	290	46
351/262C	1.73	.247/.262	.480/.488	14	76	270	78	32	290	46
351/266C	1.73	.247/.262	.480/.488	14	76	270	78	32	290	46
400/172	1.71	.247/.250	.422/.427	17	59	256	71	21	272	38
429/205	1.71	.2530/.2780	.442/.486	8	68	256	62	28	270	36
429/212	1.71	.2530/.2780	.442/.486	8	68	256	62	28	270	36
460/200	1.71	.2530/.2780	.442/.486	8	68	256	70	20	270	28
460/212	1.71	.2530/.2780	.442/.486	8	68	256	70	20	270	28
460/224	1.71	.2530/.2780	.442/.486	8	68	256	70	20	270	28
1973										
98/54	1.54	.2108/.2176	.3247/.3351	17	51	248	51	17	248	34
122/86	1.60	.2512/.2512	.3993/.3993	24	64	268	70	18	268	42
200/84	1.50	.2533/.2320	.380/.348	28	56	264	39	15	234	43
250/88	1.50	.2533/.2320	.380/.348	26	58	264	37	17	234	43
302/135	1.61	.2303/.2375	.368/.380	16/202	70/702	266/2702	44/442	20/242	244/2482	36/442
302/137	1.61	.2303/.2375	.368/.380	16/202	70/702	266/2702	44/442	20/242	244/2482	36/442
302/138	1.61	.2303/.2375	.368/.380	16/202	70/702	266/2702	44/442	20/242	244/2482	36/442
302/141	1.61	.2303/.2375	.368/.380	16	70	266	44	20	244	36
351/158	1.61	.2595/.2782	.418/.448	15	65	256	68	26	270	41
351/161	1.71	.2333/.2333	.400/.400	12	66	258	66	20	266	32
351/177	1.73	.2312/.2312	.400/.400	11°30'	66°30'	258	50°30'	35°30'	266	47
351/266	1.73	.2470/.2620	.480/.488	14	76	270	78	32	290	46
400/163	1.71	.2470/.2500	.422/.427	17	59	256	71	21	272	38
400/168	1.71	.2470/.2500	.422/.427	17	59	256	71	21	272	38
400/171	1.71	.2470/.2500	.422/.427	17	59	256	71	21	272	38
429/197	1.71	.2530/.2780	.442/.486	8	68	256	62	28	270	36
429/198	1.71	.2530/.2780	.442/.486	8	68	256	62	28	270	36
429/201	1.71	.2530/.2780	.442/.486	8	68	256	62	28	270	36
429/202	1.71	.2530/.2780	.442/.486	8	68	256	62	28	270	36
460/202	1.71	.2530/.2780	.442/.486	8	68	256	62	28	270	36
460/208	1.71	.2530/.2780	.442/.486	8	68	256	62	28	270	36

ENGINE SPECIFICATIONS

FORD MOTOR COMPANY VALVE ACTION AND TIMING

ENGINE DISP./HP	ROCKER RATIO	LOBE LIFT (Int./Exh.)1	VALVE LIFT ZERO LASH (Int./Exh.)	INTAKE VALVE TIMING OPENS (°BTDC)	CLOSES (°ABC)	DURATION (Degs.)	EXHAUST VALVE TIMING OPENS (°BBC)	CLOSES (°ATC)	DURATION (Degs.)	OVERLAP (Degs.)
460/219	1.71	.2530/.2780	.442/.486	8	68	256	62	28	270	36
460/244	1.73	.2786/.2884	.482/.500	18	72	270	86	26	292	44
460/267	1.73	.2786/.2884	.482/.500	18	72	270	86	26	292	44
1974										
122/80	1.60	.2512/.2512	.3993/.3993	24	64	268	70	18	268	42
140/88	1.4-1.6	.2666/.2666	.400/.400	22	66	268	64	24	268	46
170.8/105	1.46	.2555/.2555	.373/.373	20	56	256	62	14	256	34
200/84	152/151	.2434/.2305	.380/.348	28	56	264	39	15	234	43
250/91	152/151	.2434/.2305	.380/.348	26	58	264	37	17	234	43
302/140	1.61	.2303/.2375	.368/.380	16/202	70/702	266/2702	44/442	20/242	244/2482	36/442
351/162	1.61	.2595/.2782	.418/.448	15	65	256	68	26	274	41
351/163	1.71	.2380/.2380	.407/.407	19°30'	58°30'	258	58°30'	27°30'	266	47
351/255	1.73	.2470/.2620	.480/.490	14	76	270	78	32	290	46
400/170	1.73	.24070.2503	.428/.433	17	59	256	71	21	272	38
460/195	1.71	.2530/.2780	.442/.486	8	68	256	62	28	270	36
460/215	1.71	.2530/.2780	.442/.486	8	68	256	62	28	270	36
460/220	1.71	.2530/.2780	.442/.486	8	68	256	62	28	270	36
1975										
140/87	1.4-1.6	.2666/.2666	.400/.400	22	66	268	64	24	268	46
170.8/97	1.48	.2555/.2555	.373/.373	20	56	256	62	14	256	34
200/75	1.52/1.51	.2434/.2305	.380/.348	28	56	264	39	15	234	43
250/85	1.52/1.51	.2434/.2305	.380/.348	26	58	264	37	17	234	43
302/122	1.61	.2303/.2375	.368/.380	20	70	270	44	24	248	44
351W/154	1.61	.2595/.2782	.418/.448	15	62	260	68	26	274	41
351/148	1.73	.2380/.2380	.406/.406	19°30'	58°30'	258	58°30'	27°30'	266	47
400/158	1.7	.2407/.2503	.427/.433	17	59	256	65	27	272	44
460/216	1.71	.2530/.2780	.442/.486	8	68	256	62	28	270	36
1976										
140/92	1.4-1.6	.2666/.2666	.400/.400	22	66	268	64	24	268	46
170.8/103	1.46	.2555/.2555	.373/.373	20	56	256	62	14	256	34
200/81	1.51	.2302/.2302	.367/.367	20	52	254	59	15	254	35
250/90	1.51	.2302/.2302	.367/.367	18	54	252	57	17	254	35
302/138	1.61	.2436/.2656	.382/.398	16	48	244	57	19	256	35
351W/154	1.61	.2595/.2782	.418/.448	23	53	256	58	18	256	41
351M/152	1.73	.2380/.2380	.406/.406	19°30'	58°30'	258	58°30'	27°30'	266	47
400/180	1.73	.2407/.2503	.427/.433	17	59	256	65	27	272	44
460/202	1.71	.25	.437/.481	8	68	256	62	28	270	36
1977										
140/ALL	1.4-1.6	.2437/.2437	.4000/.4000	22	66	268	64	24	268	46
170.8/ALL	1.46	.2555/.2555	.3730/.3730	20	56	256	62	14	256	36
200/ALL	1.51	.245/.245	.367/.367	20	52	254	59	15	254	35
250/ALL	1.51	.245/.245	.367/.367	18	54	252	57	17	254	35
302/ALL	1.61	.2373/.2474	.382/.398	16	48	244	57	19	256	35
351W/ALL	1.61	.2600/.2600	.415/.415	23	53	256	58	18	256	41
351M/ALL	1.73	.235/.285	.406/.406	19.5	58.5	258	58.5	27.5	266	47
400/ALL	1.73	.2474/.2474	.428/.428	17	59	256	65	27	272	44
460/ALL	1.71	.253/.278	.437/.481	8	68	256	62	28	270	36
1978										
140/ALL	1.4-1.6	.2437/.2437	.400/.400	22	66	268	64	24	268	46
170.8/ALL	1.46	.2555/.2555	.373/.373	20	56	256	62	14	256	34
200/ALL	1.52	.245/.245	.367/.367	20	52	254	59	15	254	35
250/ALL	1.52	.245/.245	.367/.367	18	54	252	57	17	254	35
302/ALL	1.61	.2373/.2474	.382/.398	16	48	244	57	19	256	35
351W/ALL	1.61	.260/.260	.419/.419	23	53	256	58	18	256	41
351M/ALL	1.73	.235/.285	.406/.406	19°30'	58°30'	258	58°30'	27°30'	266	47
400/ALL	1.73	.2474/.2474	.428/.432	17	59	256	65	27	272	44
460/ALL	1.71	.253/.278	.437/.481	8	68	256	62	28	270	36
1979										
140/ALL	1.4-1.6	1	.400/.400	22	66	268	64	24	268	46
170.8/ALL	1.46	1	.373/.373	28	66	274	68	26	274	54
200/ALL	1.52	1	.367/.367	20	52	254	59	15	254	35
250/ALL	1.52	1	.367/.367	18	54	252	57	17	254	35
302/ALL	1.58	1	.375/.391	16	48	244	57	19	256	35
351W/ALL	1.73	1	.419/.419	23	53	256	58	18	256	41
351M/49S	1.73	1	.428/.433	17	59	256	65	27	272	44
351M/49CA.	1.73	1	.406/.406	19	58	258	58	27	266	47
400/ALL	1.73	1	.428/.433	17	59	58	256	65	27	272
44										

1Divide valve lift by rocker arm ratio.   2Manual/automatic.

FORD MOTOR COMPANY INTAKE VALVES & SPRINGS

ENGINE DISP./H.P.	SEAT/FACE ANGLE (Degs.)	OVERALL LENGTH	HEAD DIA.	STEM DIA.	STEM-TO-GUIDE CLEARANCE	OUTER SPRING PRESSURE LENGTH CLOSED (Lbs. @ Ins.)	OPEN (Lbs. @ Ins.)	INNER SPRING PRESSURE LENGTH CLOSED (Lbs. @ Ins.)	OPEN (Lbs. @ Ins.)
1970									
170/105	45/44	4.260	1.642-1.657	.3100-.3107	.0008-.0025	51-57@1.59	142-158@1.22	NONE	NONE
200/120	45/44	4.260	1.642-1.657	.3100-.3107	.0008-.0025	51-57@1.59	142-158@1.22	NONE	NONE
240/150	45/44	4.260	1.772-1.787	.3416-.3423	.0010-.0027	78-84@1.70	187-207@1.30	NONE	NONE
250/155	45/44	4.260	1.642-1.657	.3100-.3107	.0008-.0025	51-57@1.59	142-158@1.22	NONE	NONE
302/220	45/44	5.050	1.773-1.783	.3416-.3423	.0010-.0027	71-79@1.66	171-189@1.23	NONE	NONE

FORD MOTOR COMPANY INTAKE VALVES & SPRINGS

ENGINE DISP./H.P.	SEAT/FACE ANGLE (Degs.)	OVERALL LENGTH	HEAD DIA.	STEM DIA.	STEM-TO-GUIDE CLEARANCE	OUTER SPRING PRESSURE LENGTH		INNER SPRING PRESSURE LENGTH	
						CLOSED (Lbs. @ Ins.)	OPEN (Lbs. @ Ins.)	CLOSED (Lbs. @ Ins.)	OPEN (Lbs. @ Ins.)
302/290	45/44	5.050	2.223-2.238	.3416-.3423	.0010-.0027	88-96@1.82	299-331@1.32	NONE	NONE
351W/250	45/44	5.070	1.834-1.852	.3416-.3423	.0010-.0027	76-84@1.82	199-221@1.42	DAMPER	DAMPER
351C/250	45/44	5.231	2.046	.3416-.3423	.0010-.0027	76-84@1.82	199-221@1.42	DAMPER	DAMPER
351/300	45/44	5.070	1.834-1.852	.3416-.3423	.0010-.0027	85-95@1.82	271-299@1.32	DAMPER	DAMPER
390/265	45/44	5.446	2.022-2.037	.3711-.3718	.0010-.0027	85-95@1.82	209-231@1.38	DAMPER	DAMPER
428/335	45/44	5.446	2.022-2.037	.3711-.3718	.0010-.0027	80-90@1.82	255-280@1.32	DAMPER	DAMPER
428/360	30/29	5.446	2.082-2.097	.3711-.3718	.0010-.0027	88-96@1.82	299-331@1.32	DAMPER	DAMPER
429/320	45/44	5.288	2.075-2.090	.3416-.3423	.0010-.0027	76-84@1.81	240-266@1.33	NONE	NONE
429/360	45/44	5.288	2.075-2.090	.3416-.3423	.0010-.0027	76-84@1.81	240-266@1.33	NONE	NONE
429/370	45/44	5.288	2.075-2.090	.3416-.3423	.0010-.0027	76-84@1.81	240-266@1.33	NONE	NONE
429/375	45/44	5.288	2.075-2.090	.3416-.3423	.0010-.0027	76-84@1.81	240-266@1.33	NONE	NONE
460/365	45/44	5.288	2.075-2.090	.3416-.3423	.0010-.0027	76-84@1.81	240-266@1.33	NONE	NONE

1971

ENGINE DISP./H.P.	SEAT/FACE ANGLE	OVERALL LENGTH	HEAD DIA.	STEM DIA.	STEM-TO-GUIDE CLEARANCE	OUTER CLOSED	OUTER OPEN	INNER CLOSED	INNER OPEN
98/75	45/44	4.277	1.497-1.507	.3100	.0008-.0030	44-49@1.263	118@.957	NONE	NONE
122/100	45/44	4.4744	1.6535	.3149	.0015-.0025	67@1.417	144@1.059	NONE	NONE
170/100	45/44	4.26	1.660-1.642	.3107-.3100	.0008-.0025	51-57@.0025	142-158@1.22	NONE	NONE
200/115	45/44	4.26	1.660-1.642	.3107-.3100	.0008-.0025	51-57@1.59	142-158@1.22	NONE	NONE
250/145	45/44	4.26	1.660-1.642	.3107-.3100	.0008-.0025	51-57@1.59	142-158@1.22	NONE	NONE
240/140	45/44	4.72	1.772-1.787	.3423-.3416	.0010-.0027	76-84@1.70	187-207@1.30	NONE	NONE
302/210	45/44	5.050	1.773-1.783	.3416-.3423	.0010-.0027	71-79@1.660	171-189@1.230	NONE	NONE
351/240W	45/44	5.070	1.834-1.852	.3416-.3423	.0010-.0027	79-87@1.790	204-226@1.340	NONE	NONE
351/240C	45/44	5.231	2.032-2.050	.3416-.3423	.0010-.0027	76-84@1.820	199-221@1.420	NONE	NONE
351/285C	45/44	5.231	2.183-2.198	.3416-.3423	.0010-.0027	85-95@1.820	271-299@1.320	NONE	NONE
351/330C BOSS	45/44	5.231	2.183-2.198	.3416-.3423	.0010-.0027	88-96@1.820	299-311@1.320	DAMPER	DAMPER
390/255	45/44	5.446	2.022-2.037	.3711-.3718	.0010-.0027	85-95@1.820	209-231@1.380	DAMPER	DAMPER
400/260	45/44	5.231	2.032-2.050	.3416-.3423	.0010-.0027	76-84@1.820	215-237@1.390	DAMPER	DAMPER
429/320	45/45	5.288	2.075-2.090	.3416-.3423	.0010-.0027	76-84@1.810	240-266@1.330	NONE	NONE
429/360	45/45	5.288	2.075-2.090	.3416-.3423	.0010-.0027	76-84@1.810	240-266@1.330	NONE	NONE
429/370CJ	30/29	5.275	2.242-2.248	.3416-.3423	.0010-.0027	88-96@1.820	300-330@1.330	NONE	NONE
429/375SCJ	30/29	5.275	2.242-2.248	.3416-.3423	.0010-.0027	88-96@1.820	300-330@1.330	NONE	NONE
460/365	45/45	5.288	2.075-2.090	.3416-.3423	.0010-.0027	76-84@1.810	240-266@1.330	NONE	NONE

1972

ENGINE DISP./H.P.	SEAT/FACE ANGLE	OVERALL LENGTH	HEAD DIA.	STEM DIA.	STEM-TO-GUIDE CLEARANCE	OUTER CLOSED	OUTER OPEN	INNER CLOSED	INNER OPEN
98/54	45/44	4.277	1.497-1.507	.3102	.0008-.0027	47.5-52.5@1.263	122@.953	NONE	NONE
122/86	45/44	4.397	1.647-1.663	.3159-.3167	.0008-.0025	64-73@1.418	170-183@1.02	NONE	NONE
170/82	45/44	4.26	1.642-1.660	.3107-.3100	.0008-.0025	51-57@1.59	142-158@1.22	NONE	NONE
200/91	45/44	4.26	1.642-1.660	.3107-.3100	.0008-.0025	51-57@1.59	142-158@1.22	NONE	NONE
240/103	45/44	4.720	1.772-1.787	.3416-.3423	.0010-.0027	80@1.70	197@1.30	NONE	NONE
250/98	45/44	4.26	1.642-1.660	.3416-.3423	.0010-.0027	54.60@1.58	142-158@1.22	NONE	NONE
302/140	45/44	5.050	1.773-1.791	.3423-.3423	.0010-.0027	76-84@1.69	190-210@1.31	NONE	NONE
351/153W	45/44	5.070	1.843	.3416-.3423	.0010-.0027	80@1.69	200@1.31	NONE	NONE
351/163C	45/44	5.231	2.041	.3416-.3423	.0010-.0027	80@1.82	210@1.42	NONE	NONE
351/177C	45/44	5.231	2.041	.3416-.3423	.0010-.0027	80@1.82	210@1.42	NONE	NONE
351/248C	45/44	5.231	2.190	.3416-.3423	.0010-.0027	90@1.82	277@1.34	DAMPER	DAMPER
351/262C	45/44	5.231	2.190	.3416-.3423	.0010-.0027	90@1.82	277@1.34	DAMPER	DAMPER
351/266C	45/44	5.231	2.190	.3416-.3423	.0010-.0027	90@1.82	277@1.34	DAMPER	DAMPER
400/172	45/44	5.231	2.032-2.050	.3416-.3423	.0010-.0027	76-84@1.82	215-237@1.39	NONE	NONE
429/205	45/45	5.288	2.075-2.090	.3416-.3423	.0010-.0027	76-84@1.81	218-240@1.33	NONE	NONE
429/212	45/45	5.288	2.075-2.090	.3416-.3423	.0010-.0027	76-84@1.81	218-240@1.33	NONE	NONE
460/200	45/45	5.288	2.075-2.090	.3416-.3423	.0010-.0027	76-84@1.81	218-240@1.33	NONE	NONE
460/212	45/45	5.288	2.075-2.090	.3416-.3423	.0010-.0027	76-84@1.81	218-240@1.33	NONE	NONE
460/224	45/45	5.288	2.075-2.090	.3416-.3423	.0010-.0027	76-84@1.81	218-240@1.33	NONE	NONE

1973

ENGINE DISP./H.P.	SEAT/FACE ANGLE	OVERALL LENGTH	HEAD DIA.	STEM DIA.	STEM-TO-GUIDE CLEARANCE	OUTER CLOSED	OUTER OPEN	INNER CLOSED	INNER OPEN
98/54	44/45	4.277	1.497-1.507	.3102	.0008-.0027	47.5-52.5@1.263	122@.953	NONE	NONE
122/86	44/45	4.379	1.647-1.663	.3159-.3166	.0008-.0025	64-73@1.418	170-183@1.02	NONE	NONE
200/84	44/45	4.26	1.660-1.642	.3107-.3100	.0008-.0025	58@1.55	146@1.20	NONE	NONE
250/88	44/45	4.26	1.660-1.642	.3107-.3100	.0008-.0025	58@1.55	146@1.20	NONE	NONE
302/135	44/45	5.050	1.782	.3423-.3416	.0010-.0027	80@1.69	200@1.31	NONE	NONE
302/137	44/45	5.050	1.782	.3423-.3416	.0010-.0027	80@1.69	200@1.31	NONE	NONE
302/138	44/45	5.050	1.791-1.773	.3423-.3416	.0010-.0027	76-84@1.69	190-210@1.31	NONE	NONE
302/141	44/45	5.050	1.782	.3423-.3416	.0010-.0027	80@1.69	200@1.31	NONE	NONE
351/158	44/45	5.070	1.843	.3423-.3416	.0010-.0027	80@1.79	200@1.34	NONE	NONE
351/161	44/45	5.231	2.041	.3423-.3416	.0010-.0027	80@1.82	210@1.42	NONE	NONE
351/177	44/45	5.231	2.041	.3423-.3416	.0010-.0027	80@1.82	210@1.42	NONE	NONE
351/266	44/45	5.231	2.041	.3423-.3416	.0010-.0027	90@1.82	277@1.34	DAMPER	DAMPER
400/163	44/45	5.231	2.041	.3423-.3416	.0010-.0027	80@1.82	226@1.39	NONE	NONE
400/168	44/45	5.231	2.041	.3423-.3416	.0010-.0027	80@1.82	226@1.39	NONE	NONE
400/171	44/45	5.231	2.041	.3423-.3416	.0010-.0027	80@1.82	226@1.39	NONE	NONE
429/197	44/45	5.198	2.083	.3423-.3416	.0010-.0027	80@1.81	229@1.33	NONE	NONE
429/198	44/45	5.198	2.083	.3423-.3416	.0010-.0027	80@1.81	229@1.33	NONE	NONE
429/201	44/45	5.198	2.083	.3423-.3416	.0010-.0027	80@1.81	229@1.33	NONE	NONE
429/202	44/45	5.288	2.090-2.075	.3423-.3416	.0010-.0027	80@1.81	229@1.33	NONE	NONE
460/202	44/45	5.198	2.083	.3423-.3416	.0010-.0027	80@1.81	229@1.33	NONE	NONE
460/208	44/45	5.198	2.090-2.075	.3423-.3416	.0010-.0027	76-84@1.81	218-240@1.33	NONE	NONE
460/219	44/45	5.198	2.090-2.075	.3423-.3416	.0010-.0027	76-84@1.81	218-240@1.33	NONE	NONE
460/244	59/60	5.185	2.200-2.194	.3423-.3416	.0010-.0027	92@1.82	315@1.33	NONE	NONE
460/267	59/60	5.185	2.197	.3423-.3416	.0010-.0027	92@1.82	315@1.32	NONE	NONE

1974

ENGINE DISP./H.P.	SEAT/FACE ANGLE	OVERALL LENGTH	HEAD DIA.	STEM DIA.	STEM-TO-GUIDE CLEARANCE	OUTER CLOSED	OUTER OPEN	INNER CLOSED	INNER OPEN
122/80	44/45	4.379	1.647-1.663	.3159-.3166	.0008-.0025	64-73@1.418	170-183@1.02	NONE	NONE
140/88	44/45	4.757	1.730-1.740	.3420-.3427	.0006-.0023	71-79@1.56	179-198@1.16	NONE	NONE
170.8/105	44/45	4.157	1.562-1.577	.3157-.3167	.0008-.0025	60-68@1.58	138-149@1.22	NONE	NONE
200/84	44/45	4.26	1.660-1.642	.3107-.3100	.0008-.0025	57@1.58	156@1.20	NONE	NONE
250/91	44/45	4.26	1.660-1.642	.3107-.3100	.0008-.0025	57@1.58	156@1.20	NONE	NONE
302/140	44/45	5.050	1.791-1.773	.3423-.3416	.0010-.0027	76-84@1.69	190-210@1.31	NONE	NONE
351/162	44/45	5.070	1.843	.3423-.3416	.0010-.0027	75@1.79	200@1.34	NONE	NONE
351/163	44/45	5.231	2.041	.3423-.3416	.0010-.0027	80@1.82	210@1.42	NONE	NONE
351/255	44/45	5.231	2.041	.3423-.3416	.0010-.0027	90@1.82	277@1.34	DAMPER	DAMPER
400/170	44/45	5.231	2.041	.3423-.3416	.0010-.0027	80@1.82	226@1.39	NONE	NONE
460/195	44/45	5.198	2.090-2.075	.3423-.3416	.0010-.0027	76-84@1.81	218-240@1.33	NONE	NONE
460/215	44/45	5.198	2.090-2.075	.3423-.3416	.0010-.0027	76-84@1.81	218-240@1.33	NONE	NONE
460/220	44/45	5.198	2.090-2.075	.3423-.3416	.0010-.0027	76-84@1.81	218-240@1.33	NONE	NONE

1975

ENGINE DISP./H.P.	SEAT/FACE ANGLE	OVERALL LENGTH	HEAD DIA.	STEM DIA.	STEM-TO-GUIDE CLEARANCE	OUTER CLOSED	OUTER OPEN	INNER CLOSED	INNER OPEN
140/87	44/45	4.757	1.735	.3420-.3427	.0006-.0023	71-79@1.56	179-181@1.16	NONE	NONE
170.8/97	44/45	4.157	1.5695	.3157-.3167	.0008-.0025	60-68@1.585	138-149@1.22	NONE	NONE
200/75	44/45	4.260	1.642-1.660	.3100-.3107	.0008-.0025	57@1.58	156@1.20	NONE	NONE
250/85	44/45	5.050	1.642-1.660	.3100-.3107	.0008-.0025	57@1.58	156@1.20	NONE	NONE

ENGINE SPECIFICATIONS

FORD MOTOR COMPANY INTAKE VALVES & SPRINGS

ENGINE DISP./H.P.	SEAT/FACE ANGLE(Degs.)	OVERALL LENGTH	HEAD DIA.	STEM DIA.	STEM-TO-GUIDE CLEARANCE	OUTER SPRING PRESSURE LENGTH CLOSED (Lbs. @ Ins.)	OPEN (Lbs. @ Ins.)	INNER SPRINGS PRESSURE LENGTH CLOSED (Lbs. @ Ins.)	OPEN (Lbs. @ Ins.)
302/122	44/45	5.050	1.782	.3416-.3423	.0017-.0027	76-84@1.69	190-210@1.31	NONE	NONE
351W/154	44/45	5.070	1.843	.3416-.3423	.0010-.0027	75@1.79	200@1.34	NONE	NONE
351M/148	44/45	5.231	2.041	.3416-.3423	.0010-.0027	80@1.82	226@1.39	NONE	NONE
400/158	44/45	5.231	2.041	.3416-.3423	.0010-.0027	80@1.82	226@1.39	NONE	NONE
460/216	44/45	5.198	2.0825	.3416-.3423	.0010-.0027	80@1.81	253@1.33	NONE	NONE

1976

ENGINE DISP./H.P.	SEAT/FACE ANGLE(Degs.)	OVERALL LENGTH	HEAD DIA.	STEM DIA.	STEM-TO-GUIDE CLEARANCE	CLOSED (Lbs. @ Ins.)	OPEN (Lbs. @ Ins.)	INNER CLOSED	INNER OPEN
140/92	44/45	4.787	1.73-1.74	.3420-.3427	.0006-.0023	71-79@1.56	179-198@1.16	NONE	NONE
170.8/103	44/45	4.157	1.562-1.577	.3157-.3167	.0008-.0025	60-68@1.585	138-139@1.222	NONE	NONE
200/181	44/45	4.260	1.642-1.660	.3100-.3107	.0008-.0025	57@1.58	156@1.20	NONE	NONE
250/90	44/45	5.050	1.642-1.660	.3100-.3107	.0008-.0025	57@1.58	156@1.20	NONE	NONE
302/138	44/45	5.050	1.773-1.791	.3416-.3423	.0010-.0027	76-84@1.69	190-210@1.31	NONE	NONE
351W/154	44/45	5.070	1.782	.3416-.3423	.0010-.0027	75@1.79	200@1.34	NONE	NONE
351M/152	44/45	5.231	2.041	.3416-.3423	.0010-.0027	80@1.82	226@1.39	NONE	NONE
400/180	44/45	5.231	2.041	.3416-.3423	.0010-.0027	80@1.82	226@1.39	NONE	NONE
460/202	44/45	5.198	2.0825	.3416-.3423	.0010-.0027	80@1.81	217.5-240.5@1.33	NONE	NONE

1977

ENGINE DISP./H.P.	SEAT/FACE ANGLE(Degs.)	OVERALL LENGTH	HEAD DIA.	STEM DIA.	STEM-TO-GUIDE CLEARANCE	CLOSED (Lbs. @ Ins.)	OPEN (Lbs. @ Ins.)	INNER CLOSED	INNER OPEN
140/ALL	44.5-45/45.5-45.75	4.787	1.735	.3427-.3420	.0006-.0023	71-79@1.56	179-198@1.16	NONE	NONE
170.8/ALL	44.5-45/45.5-45.75	4.157	1.5695	.3167-.3157	.0008-.0025	60-68@1.585	138-149@1.222	NONE	NONE
200/ALL	44.5-45/45.5-45.75	4.26	1.760-1.742	.3107-.3100	.0008-.0025	57@1.58	156@1.20	NONE	NONE
250/ALL	44.5-45/45.5-45.75	4.26	1.760-1.742	.3107-.3100	.0008-.0025	57@1.58	156@1.20	NONE	NONE
302/ALL	44.5-45/45.5-45.75	5.050	1.791-1.733	.3423-.3416	.0010-.0027	76-84@1.69	190-210@1.21	NONE	NONE
351W/ALL	44.5-45/45.5-45.75	5.070	1.782	.3423-.3416	.0010-.0027	75@1.79	192@1.37	NONE	NONE
351M/ALL	44.5-45/45.5-45.75	5.231	2.041	.3423-.3416	.0010-.0027	80@1.82	226@1.39	NONE	NONE
400/ALL	44.5-45/45.5-45.75	5.231	2.041	.3423-.3416	.0010-.0027	80@1.82	226@1.39	NONE	NONE
460/ALL	44.5-45/45.5-45.75	5.198	2.0825	.3423-.3416	.0010-.0027	80@1.81	217.5-240.5@1.33	NONE	NONE

1978

ENGINE DISP./H.P.	SEAT/FACE ANGLE(Degs.)	OVERALL LENGTH	HEAD DIA.	STEM DIA.	STEM-TO-GUIDE CLEARANCE	CLOSED (Lbs. @ Ins.)	OPEN (Lbs. @ Ins.)	INNER CLOSED	INNER OPEN
140/ALL	44.3-45/45.3-45.5	4.787	1.730-1.740	.3420-.3427	.0006-.0023	71-79@1.56	159-175@1.16	NONE	NONE
170.8/ALL	44.3-45/45.3-45.5	4.157	1.562-1.577	.3157-.3167	.0008-.0025	60-68@1.585	138-149@1.222	NONE	NONE
200/ALL	44.3-45/45.3-45.5	4.26	1.742-1.760	.3100-.3107	.0008-.0025	57@1.58	156@1.20	NONE	NONE
250/ALL	44.3-45/45.3-45.5	4.26	1.742-1.760	.3100-.3107	.0008-.0025	57@1.58	156@1.20	NONE	NONE
302/ALL	44.3-45/45.3-45.5	5.050	1.773-1.791	.3416-.3423	.0010-.0027	76-84@1.69	190-210@1.31	NONE	NONE
351W/ALL	44.3-45/45.3-45.5	5.050	1.782	.3416-.3423	.0010-.0027	75@1.79	192@1.37	NONE	NONE
351M/ALL	44.3-45/45.3-45.5	5.231	2.041	.3416-.3423	.0010-.0027	80@1.82	226@1.39	NONE	NONE
400/ALL	44.3-45/45.3-45.5	5.231	2.041	.3416-.3423	.0010-.0027	80@1.82	226@1.39	NONE	NONE
460/ALL	44.3-45/45.3-45.5	5.198	2.0825	.3416-.3423	.0010-.0027	80@1.81	217.5-240.5@1.33	NONE	NONE

1979

ENGINE DISP./H.P.	SEAT/FACE ANGLE(Degs.)	OVERALL LENGTH	HEAD DIA.	STEM DIA.	STEM-TO-GUIDE CLEARANCE	CLOSED (Lbs. @ Ins.)	OPEN (Lbs. @ Ins.)	INNER CLOSED	INNER OPEN
140/ALL	45/45 30'	4.787	1.735	.3423-.3426	.001-.0027	71-79@1.56	159-175@1.16	NONE	NONE
170.8/ALL	45/45 30'	4.157	1.562-1.577	.3157-.3167	.0008-.0025	60-68@1.585	138-149@1.222	NONE	NONE
200-250/ALL	45/45	4.260	1.742-1.760	.3100-.3107	.0008-.0025	57@1.58	156@1.20	NONE	NONE
302/ALL	45/45 30'	5.070	1.780	.3400	.0010-.0027	80@1.70	200@1.30	NONE	NONE
351W/ALL	45/45	5.231	2.041	.3400	.0010-.0027	75@1.79	192@1.37	NONE	NONE
351M/ALL	45/45	5.231	2.041	.3400	.0010-.0027	80@1.82	226@1.39	NONE	NONE
400/ALL	45/45 30'	5.231	2.041	.3416-.3423	.0010-.0027	80@1.82	226@1.39	NONE	NONE

FORD MOTOR COMPANY EXHAUST VALVES & SPRINGS

ENGINE DISP./H.P.	SEAT/FACE ANGLE (Degs.)	OVERALL LENGTH	HEAD DIA.	STEM DIA.	STEM-TO-GUIDE CLEARANCE	OUTER SPRING PRESSURE LENGTH CLOSED (Lbs. @ Ins.)	OPEN (Lbs. @ Ins.)	INNER SPRING PRESSURE LENGTH CLOSED (Lbs. @ Ins.)	OPEN (Lbs. @ Ins.)
					1970				
170/105	45/44	4.260	1.381-1.396	.3098-.3105	.0010-.0027	51-57 @ 1.59	142-158 @ 1.22	NONE	NONE
200/120	45/44	4.260	1.381-1.396	.3098-.3105	.0010-.0027	51-57 @ 1.59	142-158 @ 1.22	NONE	NONE
240/150	45/44	4.720	1.552-1.567	.3416-.3423	.0010-.0027	78-84 @ 1.70	187-204 @ 1.30	NONE	NONE
250/155	45/44	4.260	1.381-1.396	.3098-.3105	.0010-.0027	51-57 @ 1.59	142-158 @ 1.22	NONE	NONE
302/220	45/44	4.990	1.442-1.457	.3411-.3418	.0010-.0027	71-79 @ 1.66	171-189 @ 1.23	NONE	NONE
302/290	45/44	5.070	1.708-1.713	.3411-.3418	.0015-.0032	88-96 @ 1.82	299-331 @ 1.32	NONE	NONE
351W/250	45/44	5.070	1.650-1.660	.3411-.3418	.0015-.0032	76-84 @ 1.82	199-221 @ 1.42	DAMPER	DAMPER
351C/250	45/44	5.050	1.6595	.3411-.3418	.0015-.0032	76-84 @ 1.82	199-221 @ 1.42	DAMPER	DAMPER
351/300	45/44	5.050	1.705-1.715	.3411-.3418	.0015-.0032	85-95 @ 1.82	271-299 @ 1.32	DAMPER	DAMPER
390/265	45/44	5.426	1.551-1.566	.3706-.3713	.0015-.0032	85-95 @ 1.82	209-231 @ 1.38	DAMPER	DAMPER
428/335	45/44	5.426	1.551-1.566	.3706-.3713	.0015-.0032	80-90 @ 1.82	255-280 @ 1.32	DAMPER	DAMPER
428/360	45/44	5.426	1.645-1.660	.3706-.3713	.0015-.0032	80-90 @ 1.82	255-280 @ 1.32	DAMPER	DAMPER
429/320	45/44	5.080	1.646-1.661	.3416-.3423	.0010-.0027	76-84 @ 1.81	240-266 @ 1.33	NONE	NONE
429/360	45/44	5.080	1.646-1.661	.3416-.3423	.0010-.0027	76-84 @ 1.81	240-266 @ 1.33	NONE	NONE
429/370	45/44	5.080	1.646-1.661	.3416-.3423	.0010-.0027	76-84 @ 1.81	240-266 @ 1.33	NONE	NONE
429/375	45/44	5.080	1.646-1.661	.3416-.3423	.0010-.0027	76-84 @ 1.81	240-266 @ 1.33	NONE	NONE
460/365	45/44	5.080	1.646-1.66	.3416-.3423	.0010-.0027	76-84 @ 1.81	240-266 @ 1.33	NONE	NONE
					1971				
98/75	45/44	4.268	1.240-1.250	.3089-.3096	.0017-.0039	44-49 @ 1.263	118 @ .957	NONE	NONE
122/100	45/44	4.372	1.417	.3156-.3163	.0018-.0035	60-64 @ 1.417	144.4 @ 1.059	NONE	NONE
170/100	45/44	4.26	1.381-1.396	.3100-.3107	.0010-.0027	51-57 @ 1.590	142-158 @ 1.222	NONE	NONE
200/115	45/44	4.26	1.381-1.396	.3100-.3107	.0010-.0027	51-57 @ 1.590	142-158 @ 1.222	NONE	NONE
250/145	45/44	4.26	1.381-1.396	.3100-.3107	.0010-.0027	51-57 @ 1.590	142-148 @ 1.222	NONE	NONE
240/140	45/44	4.72	1.552-1.567	.3416-.3423	.0010-.0027	76-84 @ 1.70	187-207 @ 1.30	NONE	NONE
302/210	45/44	4.99	1.442-1.457	.3416-.3423	.0010-.0027	71-79 @ 1.660	171-189 @ 1.230	NONE	NONE
351/240W	45/44	4.99	1.533-1.548	.3416-.3423	.0010-.0027	79-87 @ 1.790	204-226 @ 1.340	NONE	NONE

FORD MOTOR COMPANY EXHAUST VALVES & SPRINGS

ENGINE DISP./H.P.	SEAT/FACE ANGLE (Degs.)	OVERALL LENGTH	HEAD DIA.	STEM DIA.	STEM-TO-GUIDE CLEARANCE	OUTER SPRING PRESSURE LENGTH CLOSED (Lbs. @ Ins.)	OPEN (Lbs. @ Ins.)	INNER SPRING PRESSURE LENGTH CLOSED (Lbs. @ Ins.)	OPEN (Lbs. @ Ins.)
351/240C	45/44	5.050	1.650-1.660	.3416-.3423	.0010-.0027	76-84 @ 1.820	199-221 @ 1.420	NONE	NONE
351/285C	45/44	5.050	1.705-1.715	.3416-.3423	.0010-.0027	85-95 @ 1.820	271-299 @ 1.320	DAMPER	DAMPER
351/330C BOSS	45/44	5.050	1.705-1.715	.3416-.3423	.0010-.0027	88-96 @ 1.820	299-331 @ 1.320	DAMPER	DAMPER
390/255	45/44	5.426	1.551-1.566	.3706-.3713	.0015-.0032	85-95 @ 1.820	209-231 @ 1.380	DAMPER	DAMPER
400/260	45/44	5.050	1.650-1.660	.3416-.3423	.0010-.0027	76-84 @ 1.820	215-237 @ 1.390	NONE	NONE
429/320	45/45	5.080	1.646-1.661	.3416-.3423	.0010-.0027	76-84 @ 1.810	240-266 @ 1.330	NONE	NONE
429/360	45/45	5.080	1.646-1.661	.3416-.3223	.0010-.0027	76-84 @ 1.810	240-266 @ 1.330	NONE	NONE
429/3700J	45/45	5.068	1.722-1.728	.3416-.3223	.0010-.0027	88-96 @ 1.820	300-330 @ 1.320	NONE	NONE
429/375SCJ	45/45	5.068	1.722-1.728	.3416-.3223	.0010-.0027	88-96 @ 1.820	300-330 @ 1.320	NONE	NONE
460/365	45/45	5.080	1.646-1.661	.3416-.3223	.0010-.0027	76-84 @ 1.810	240-266 @ 1.330	NONE	NONE

1972

ENGINE DISP./H.P.	SEAT/FACE ANGLE (Degs.)	OVERALL LENGTH	HEAD DIA.	STEM DIA.	STEM-TO-GUIDE CLEARANCE	CLOSED (Lbs. @ Ins.)	OPEN (Lbs. @ Ins.)	CLOSED (Lbs. @ Ins.)	OPEN (Lbs. @ Ins.)
98/54	45/44	4.265	1.234-1.244	.3093	.0017-.0036	47-52 @ 1.263	122 @ .953	NONE	NONE
122/86	45/44	4.356	1.411-1.419	.3149-.3156	.0018-.0035	64-73 @ 1.418	170-183 @ 1.020	NONE	NONE
170/82	45/44	4.26	1.381-1.399	.3098-.3105	.0010-.0027	51-57 @ 1.59	142-158 @ 1.22	NONE	NONE
200/91	45/44	4.26	1.381-1.399	.3098-.3105	.0010-.0027	51-57 @ 1.59	142-158 @ 1.22	NONE	NONE
240/103	45/44	4.720	1.552-1.567	.3416-.3423	.0010-.0027	80 @ 1.70	197 @ 1.30	NONE	NONE
250/98	45/44	4.26	1.381-1.399	.3098-.3105	.0010-.0027	61-67 @ 1.55	142-158 @ 1.22	NONE	NONE
302/140	45/44	4.990	1.442-1.460	.3411-.3418	.0015-.0032	76-84 @ 1.69	190-210 @ 1.31	NONE	NONE
351/153W	45/44	5.070	1.533-1.548	.3411-.3418	.0015-.0032	75 @ 1.79	200 @ 1.34	NONE	NONE
351/163C	45/44	5.050	1.650-1.660	.3411-.3418	.0015-.0032	80 @ 1.82	210 @ 1.42	NONE	NONE
351/177C	45/44	5.050	1.650-1.660	.3411-.3418	.0015-.0032	80 @ 1.82	210 @ 1.42	NONE	NONE
351/248C	45/44	5.050	1.705-1.715	.3411-.3418	.0015-.0032	90 @ 1.82	281 @ 1.33	DAMPER	DAMPER
351/262C	45/44	5.050	1.705-1.715	.3411-.3418	.0015-.0032	90 @ 1.82	288 @ 1.33	DAMPER	DAMPER
351/266C	45/44	5.050	1.705-1.715	.3411-.3418	.0015-.0032	90 @ 1.82	288 @ 1.33	DAMPER	DAMPER
400/172	45/44	5.050	1.650-1.660	.3411-.3418	.0015-.0032	76-84 @ 1.82	215-237 @ 1.39	NONE	NONE
429/205	45/45	5.080	1.646-1.661	.3416-.3423	.0010-.0027	76-84 @ 1.81	218-240 @ 1.33	NONE	NONE
429/212	45/45	5.080	1.646-1.661	.3416-.3423	.0010-.0027	76-84 @ 1.81	218-240 @ 1.33	NONE	NONE
460/224	45/45	5.080	1.646-1.661	.3416-.3423	.0010-.0027	76-84 @ 1.81	218-240 @ 1.33	NONE	NONE
460/224	45/45	5.080	1.646-1.661	.3416-.3423	.0010-.0027	76-84 @ 1.81	218-240 @ 1.33	NONE	NONE
460/224	45/45	5.080	1.646-1.661	.3416-.3423	.0010-.0027	76-84 @ 1.81	218-240 @ 1.33	NONE	NONE

1973

ENGINE DISP./H.P.	SEAT/FACE ANGLE (Degs.)	OVERALL LENGTH	HEAD DIA.	STEM DIA.	STEM-TO-GUIDE CLEARANCE	CLOSED (Lbs. @ Ins.)	OPEN (Lbs. @ Ins.)	CLOSED (Lbs. @ Ins.)	OPEN (Lbs. @ Ins.)
98/54	44/45	4.265	1.234-1.244	.3093	.0017-.0036	47.5-52.5 @ 1.26	122 @ .953	NONE	NONE
122/86	44/45	4.356	1.411-1.418	.3149-.3156	.0018-.0035	64-73 @ 1.42	170-183 @ 1.020	NONE	NONE
200/84	44/45	4.26	1.399-1.381	.3105-.3098	.0010-.0027	64 @ 1.55	150 @ 1.20	NONE	NONE
250/88	44/45	4.26	1.399-1.381	.3105-.3098	.0010-.0027	58 @ 1.55	144 @ 1.20	NONE	NONE
302/135	44/45	4.99	1.451	.3418-.3411	.0015-.0032	80 @ 1.69	200 @ 1.31	NONE	NONE
302/137	44/45	4.99	1.451	.3418-.3411	.0015-.0032	80 @ 1.69	200 @ 1.31	NONE	NONE
302/138	44/45	4.99	1.460-1.442	.3418-.3411	.0015-.0032	76-84 @ 1.69	190-210 @ 1.31	NONE	NONE
302/141	44/45	4.99	1.451	.3418-.3411	.0015-.0032	80 @ 1.69	200 @ 1.31	NONE	NONE
351/158	44/45	5.070	1.541	.3418-.3411	.0015-.0032	75 @ 1.79	200 @ 1.34	NONE	NONE
351/161	44/45	5.050	1.654	.3418-.3411	.0015-.0032	80 @ 1.82	210 @ 1.42	NONE	NONE
351/177	44/45	5.050	1.654	.3418-.3411	.0015-.0032	80 @ 1.82	210 @ 1.42	NONE	NONE
351/266	44/45	5.050	1.654	.3418-.3411	.0015-.0032	80 @ 1.82	210 @ 1.42	NONE	NONE
400/163	44/45	5.050	1.654	.3418-.3411	.0015-.0032	80 @ 1.82	226 @ 1.39	NONE	NONE
400/168	44/45	5.050	1.654	.3418-.3411	.0015-.0032	80 @ 1.82	226 @ 1.39	NONE	NONE
400/171	44/45	5.050	1.654	.3418-.3411	.0015-.0032	80 @ 1.82	226 @ 1.39	NONE	NONE
429/197	44/45	4.983	1.661-1.646	.3423-.3416	.0010-.0027	80 @ 1.81	229 @ 1.33	NONE	NONE
429/198	44/45	4.983	1.6535	.3423-.3416	.0010-.0027	80 @ 1.81	229 @ 1.33	NONE	NONE
429/201	44/45	4.983	1.661-1.646	.3423-.3416	.0010-.0027	80 @ 1.81	229 @ 1.33	NONE	NONE
429/202	44/45	5.080	1.661-1.646	.3423-.3416	.0010-.0027	80 @ 1.81	229 @ 1.33	NONE	NONE
460/202	44/45	4.983	1.6535	.3423-.3416	.0010-.0027	80 @ 1.81	229 @ 1.33	NONE	NONE
460/208	44/45	4.983	1.661-1.646	.3423-.3416	.0010-.0027	76-84 @ 1.81	218-240 @ 1.33	NONE	NONE
460/219	44/45	4.983	1.661-1.646	.3423-.3416	.0010-.0027	76-84 @ 1.81	218-240 @ 1.33	NONE	NONE
460/244	44/45	4.978	1.728-1.722	.3423-.3416	.0010-.0027	92 @ 1.82	315 @ 1.32	DAMPER	DAMPER
460/267	44/45	4.978	1.725	.3423-.3416	.0010-.0027	92 @ 1.82	315 @ 1.32	DAMPER	DAMPER

1974

ENGINE DISP./H.P.	SEAT/FACE ANGLE (Degs.)	OVERALL LENGTH	HEAD DIA.	STEM DIA.	STEM-TO-GUIDE CLEARANCE	CLOSED (Lbs. @ Ins.)	OPEN (Lbs. @ Ins.)	CLOSED (Lbs. @ Ins.)	OPEN (Lbs. @ Ins.)
122/80	44/45	4.356	1.411-1.418	.3149-.3156	.0018-.0035	64-73 @ 1.42	170-183 @ 1.020	NONE	NONE
140/88	44/45	4.777	1.490-1.510	.3411-.3418	.0015-.0032	71-79 @ 1.56	179-198 @ 1.16	NONE	NONE
170.8/105	44/45	4.161	1.261-1.276	.3149-.3156	.0018-.0035	60-68 @ 1.58	138-149 @ 1.22	NONE	NONE
200/84	44/45	4.26	1.399-1.381	.3105-.3098	.0010-.0027	57 @ 1.58	148 @ 1.23	NONE	NONE
250/91	44/45	4.26	1.399-1.381	.3105-.3098	.0010-.0027	64 @ 1.55	154 @ 1.20	NONE	NONE
302/140	44/45	4.99	1.460-1.442	.3418-.3411	.0015-.0032	76-84 @ 1.69	190-210 @ 1.22	NONE	NONE
351/162	44/45	5.070	1.451	.3418-.3411	.0015-.0032	75 @ 1.79	200 @ 1.34	NONE	NONE
351/163	44/45	5.050	1.654	.3418-.3411	.0015-.0032	80 @ 1.82	210 @ 1.42	NONE	NONE
351/255	44/45	5.050	1.654	.3418-.3411	.0015-.0032	90 @ 1.82	281 @ 1.33	DAMPER	DAMPER
400/170	44/45	5.050	1.654	.3418-.3411	.0015-.0032	80 @ 1.82	226 @ 1.39	NONE	NONE
460/195	44/45	4.983	1.661-1.646	.3423-.3416	.0010-.0027	76-84 @ 1.81	218-240 @ 1.33	NONE	NONE
460/215	44/45	4.983	1.661-1.646	.3423-.3416	.0010-.0027	76-84 @ 1.81	218-240 @ 1.33	NONE	NONE
460/220	44/45	4.983	1.661-1.646	.3423-.3416	.0010-.0027	76-84 @ 1.81	218-240 @ 1.33	NONE	NONE

1975

ENGINE DISP./H.P.	SEAT/FACE ANGLE (Degs.)	OVERALL LENGTH	HEAD DIA.	STEM DIA.	STEM-TO-GUIDE CLEARANCE	CLOSED (Lbs. @ Ins.)	OPEN (Lbs. @ Ins.)	CLOSED (Lbs. @ Ins.)	OPEN (Lbs. @ Ins.)
140/87	44/45	4.777	1.500	.3411-.3418	.0015-.0032	71-79 @ 1.56	179-198 @ 1.16	NONE	NONE
170.8/97	44/45	4.161	1.2685	.3149-.3156	.0018-.0035	60-68 @ 1.585	138-149 @ 1.222	NONE	NONE
200/75	44/45	4.260	1.381-1.399	.3098-.3105	.0010-.0027	57 @ 1.58	148 @ 1.23	NONE	NONE
250/85	44/45	4.260	1.381-1.399	.3098-.3105	.0010-.0027	64 @ 1.55	154 @ 1.20	NONE	NONE
302/122	44/45	4.990	1.451	.3411-.3418	.0015-.0032	76-84 @ 1.60	190-210 @ 1.22	NONE	NONE
351W/154	44/45	5.070	1.541	.3411-.3418	.0015-.0032	75 @ 1.79	200 @ 1.34	NONE	NONE
351M/148	44/45	5.050	1.6545	.3411-.3418	.0015-.0032	80 @ 1.82	226 @ 1.39	NONE	NONE
400/158	44/45	5.050	1.6545	.3411-.3418	.0015-.0032	80 @ 1.82	226 @ 1.39	NONE	NONE
460/216	44/45	4.983	1.6535	.3416-.3423	.0010-.0027	80 @ 1.87	253 @ 1.33	NONE	NONE

1976

ENGINE DISP./H.P.	SEAT/FACE ANGLE (Degs.)	OVERALL LENGTH	HEAD DIA.	STEM DIA.	STEM-TO-GUIDE CLEARANCE	CLOSED (Lbs. @ Ins.)	OPEN (Lbs. @ Ins.)	CLOSED (Lbs. @ Ins.)	OPEN (Lbs. @ Ins.)
140/92	44/45	4.817	1.49-1.51	.3411-.3418	.0015-.0032	71-79 @ 1.56	179-198 @ 1.16	NONE	NONE
170.8/103	44/45	4.161	1.261-1.276	.3149-.3156	.0018-.0035	60-68 @ 1.585	138-149 @ 1.222	NONE	NONE
200/81	44/45	4.26	1.642-1.660	.3100-.3107	.0008-.0025	57 @ 1.58	156 @ 1.20	NONE	NONE
250/90	44/45	5.050	1.642-1.660	.3100-.3107	.0008-.0025	57 @ 1.58	156 @ 1.20	NONE	NONE
302/138	44/45	5.050	1.773-1.791	.3416-.3423	.0010-.0027	76-84 @ 1.69	190-210 @ 1.31	NONE	NONE
351W/154	44/45	5.070	1.451	.3411-.3418	.0015-.0032	75 @ 1.79	200 @ 1.34	NONE	NONE
351M/152	44/45	5.050	1.6545	.3411-.3418	.0015-.0032	80 @ 1.82	226 @ 1.39	NONE	NONE
400/180	44/45	5.050	1.6545	.3411-.3418	.0015-.0032	80 @ 1.82	226 @ 1.39	NONE	NONE
460/202	44/45	4.983	1.6535	.3416-.3423	.0010-.0027	80 @ 1.81	253 @ 1.33	NONE	NONE

ENGINE SPECIFICATIONS

FORD MOTOR COMPANY EXHAUST VALVES & SPRINGS

ENGINE DISP./H.P.	SEAT/FACE ANGLE (Degs.)	OVERALL LENGTH	HEAD DIA.	STEM DIA.	STEM-TO-GUIDE CLEARANCE	OUTER SPRING PRESSURE LENGTH CLOSED (Lbs. @ Ins.)	OPEN (Lbs. @ Ins.)	INNER SPRING PRESSURE LENGTH CLOSED (Lbs. @ Ins.)	OPEN (Lbs. @ Ins.)
1977									
140/ALL	44.5-45/45.5-45.75	4.807	1.500	.3418-.3411	.0015-.0032	71-79 @ 1.56	179-198 @ 1.16	NONE	NONE
170.8/ALL	44.5-45/45.5-45.75	4.161	1.2685	.3156-.3149	.0018-.0035	60-68 @ 1.585	138-149 @ 1.222	NONE	NONE
200/ALL	44.5-45/45.5-45.75	4.26	1.399-1.381	.3105-.3098	.0010-.0027	57 @ 1.58	148 @ 1.23	NONE	NONE
250/ALL	44.5-45/45.5-45.75	4.26	1.399-1.381	.3105-.3098	.0010-.0027	64 @ 1.55	154 @ 1.20	NONE	NONE
302/ALL	44.5-45/45.5-45.75	4.99	1.460-1.442	.3418-.3411	.0015-.0032	76-84 @ 1.60	190-210 @ 1.20	NONE	NONE
351W/ALL	44.5-45/45.5-45.75	5.070	1.451	.3418-.3411	.0015-.0032	80 @ 1.60	206 @ 1.18	NONE	NONE
351M/ALL	44.5-45/45.5-45.75	5.050	1.6545	.3418-.3411	.0015-.0032	80 @ 1.82	226 @ 1.39	NONE	NONE
400/ALL	44.5-45/45.5-45.75	5.050	1.6545	.3418-.3411	.0015-.0032	80 @ 1.82	226 @ 1.39	NONE	NONE
460/ALL	44.5-45/45.5-45.75	4.983	1.6535	.3423-.3416	.0010-.0027	80 @ 1.81	253 @ 1.33	NONE	NONE
1978									
140/ALL	44.3-45/45.3-45.5	4.807	1.490/1.510	.3411/.3418	.0015-.0032	71-79@1.56	159-175@1.16	NONE	NONE
170.8/ALL	44.3-45/45.3-45.5	4.161	1.261/1.276	.3149/.3156	.0018-.0035	60-68@1.585	138-149@1.222	NONE	NONE
200/ALL	44.3-45/45.3-45.5	4.260	1.381/1.399	.3098/.3105	.0010-.0027	57@1.58	148@1.23	NONE	NONE
250/ALL	44.3-45/45.3-45.5	4.260	1.381/1.399	.3098/.3105	.0010-.0027	57@1.58	156@1.20	NONE	NONE
302/ALL	44.3-45/45.3-45.5	4.990	1.442/1.460	.3411/.3418	.0015-.0032	76-84@1.60	190-210@1.20	NONE	NONE
351W/ALL	44.3-45/45.3-45.5	5.070	1.451	.3418/.3441	.0015-.0032	76-84@1.60	190-210@1.20	NONE	NONE
351M/ALL	44.3-45/45.3-45.5	5.050	1.6545	.3411/.3418	.0015-.0032	83@1.68	226@1.25	NONE	NONE
400/ALL	44.3-45/45.3-45.5	5.050	1.6545	.3411/.3418	.0015-.0032	83@1.68	226@1.25	NONE	NONE
460/ALL	44.3-45/45.3-45.5	4.983	1.6535	.3416/.3423	.0010-.0027	80@1.81	253@1.33	NONE	NONE
1979									
140/ALL	45/45 30'	4.807	1.500	.3411-.3418	.0015-.0032	71-79@1.56	159-175@1.16	NONE	NONE
170.8/ALL	45/45 30'	4.161	1.261-1.276	.3149-.3156	.0018-.0035	60-68@1.585	138-149@1.222	NONE	NONE
200-250/ALL	45/45	4.260	1.381-1.399	.3098-.3105	.0010-.0027	57@1.58	156@1.20	NONE	NONE
302/ALL	45/45	4.990	1.450	.3418-.3441	.0015-.0032	80@1.70	200@1.30	NONE	NONE
351W/ALL	45/45	5.010	1.439-1.463	.3411-.3418	.0015-.0032	80@1.60	200@1.20	NONE	NONE
351M/ALL	45/45	5.050	1.6545	.3411-.3418	.0015-.0032	83@1.68	226@1.25	NONE	NONE
400/ALL	45/45 30'	5.050	1.6545	.3411-.3418	.0015-.0032	83@1.68	226@1.25	NONE	NONE

GENERAL MOTORS VALVE ACTION & TIMING

DISPLACEMENT/ HORSEPOWER	ROCKER RATIO	LOBE LIFT (INT./EXH.)	VALVE LIFT ZERO LASH (INT./EXH.)	INTAKE VALVE TIMING OPENS (°BTC)	CLOSES (°ABC)	DURATION (degrees)	EXHAUST VALVE TIMING OPENS (°BBC)	CLOSES (°ATC)	DURATION (degrees)	OVERLAP (degrees)
1970										
BUICK DIVISION										
250/155	1.75	.222/.222	.3880/.3880	62	94	336	92.5	63.5	330	125.5
350/230	1.55	.243/.257	.3818/.3984	24	78	282	84	40	304	64
350/285	1.55	.243/.257	.3818/.3984	24	78	282	84	40	304	64
350/315	1.55	.243/.257	.3818/.3984	24	78	282	84	40	304	64
455/350	1.55	.250/.295	.3873/.4584	18	95	293	93	49	322	67
455/360	1.55	.250/.295	.3873/.4584	18	95	293	93	49	322	67
455/370	1.55	.250/.295	.3873/.4584	18	95	293	93	49	322	67
CADILLAC DIVISION										
472/375	1.65	.266/.275	.440/.454	18	114	312	70	58	308	76
500/400	1.65	.266/.275	.440/.454	18	114	312	70	58	308	76
CHEVROLET DIVISION										
153/90	1.75	.2270/.2270	.3973/.3973	17.5	54.5	252	57	15	252	32.5
230/140	1.75	.1896/.1896	.3317/.3317	16	48	244	46.5	17.5	244	33.5
250/155	1.75	.2217/.2217	.3880/.3880	16	48	244	46.5	17.5	244	33.5
307/200	1.50	.2600/.2733	.3900/.4100	28	72	280	78	30	288	58
350/250	1.50	.2600/.2733	.3900/.4100	28	72	280	78	30	288	58
350/300	1.50	.2600/.2733	.3900/.4100	28	72	280	78	30	288	58
350/350	1.50	.2600/.2733	.4500/.4600	52	114	346	98	62	340	114
350/360	1.50	.3057/.3234	.4586/.4850	42.7	94.3	317	112.9	53.2	346.2	96
350/370	1.50	.2600/.2733	.4586/.4850	42.7	94.3	317	112.9	53.2	346.2	96
400/265	1.70	.2235/.2411	.3900/.4100	28	72	280	78	30	288	58
402/330	1.70	.2343/.2343	.3983/.3983	28	78	286	75	31	286	59
402/350	1.70	.2714/.2824	.4614/.4800	56	114	350	110	62	352	118
402/375	1.70	.3057/.3057	.4614/.4800	56	114	350	110	62	352	118
454/345	1.70	.2343/.2529	.3983/.4300	30	70	280	77	61	318	91
454/360	1.70	.2655/.2824	.4616/.4800	56	114	350	110	62	352	118
454/390	1.70	.2714/.2824	.4616/.4800	56	114	350	110	62	352	118
454/450	1.70	.3057/.3057	.5197/.5197	44	92	316	86	36	302	80
454/460	1.70	.3412/.3647	.5197/.5498	62	105	347	106	73	359	135
OLDSMOBILE DIVISION										
250/155	1.75	.222/.222	.388/.388	16	48	244	46.5	17.5	244	33.5
350/250	1.60	.250/.250	.400/.400	20	58	258	68	24	272	44
350/310	1.60	.250/.250	.400/.400	16	54	250	64	20	264	36
350/325	1.60	.295/.295	.474/.474	40	88	308	86	42	308	82
455/310	1.60	.272/.272	.435/.435	20	58	258	68	24	308	82
455/320	1.60	.777/.272	.435/.435	20	58	258	68	24	308	82
455/365	1.60	.294/.294	.472/.472	30	84	294	78	38	296	68
455/370	1.60	.294/.294	.472/.472	24	81	285	74	33	287	57
455/375	1.60	.272/.272	.435/.435	22	60	262	68	26	274	48
455/390	1.60	.294/.294	.472/.472	24	81	285	74	33	287	57
455/400	1.60	.294/.294	.472/.472	24	81	285	74	33	287	57
PONTIAC DIVISION										
250/155	1.5	.258/.258	.388/.388	16	48	244	46.5	17	244	33.5
350/255	1.5	.251/.275	.376/.412	22	67	269	72	25	277	47
400/265	1.5	.251/.275	.376/.412	22	67	269	72	25	277	47
400/290	1.5	.276/.276	.410/.414	30	63	273	77	25	282	55
400/330	1.5	.273/.276	.410/.414	23	70	273	78	31	289	54
400/345	1.5	.414/.413	.414/.413	31	77	288	90	32	302	63

GENERAL MOTORS VALVE ACTION & TIMING

DISPLACEMENT/ HORSEPOWER	ROCKER RATIO	LOBE LIFT (INT./WXH.)	VALVE LIFT ZERO LASH (INT./EXH.)	INTAKE VALVE TIMING OPENS (°BTC)	CLOSES (°ABC)	DURATION (degrees)	EXHAUST VALVE TIMING OPENS (°BBC)	CLOSES (°ATC)	DURATION (degrees)	OVERLAP (degrees)
400/350	1.5	.273/.275	.410/.413	23	70	273	78	31	289	54
400/366	1.5	.275/.275	.414/.413	31	77	288	90	32	302	63
400/370	1.5	.350/.350	.527/.527	42	86	308	95	45	320	87
455/360	1.5	.275/.275	.414/.413	31	77	288	90	32	302	632
455/370	1.5	.273/.275	.410/.413	23	70	273	78	31	289	54

1971

BUICK DIVISION

250/145	1.75	3	.388/.388	16	48	244	46.5	17.5	244	33.5
350/230	1.55	3	.381/.398	24	78	282	84	40	304	64
350/260	1.55	3	.381/.398	28	74	282	84	40	304	68
455/315	1.60	3	.387/.456	12	102	294	98	62	340	98
455/330²	1.60	3	.387/.456	12	102	294	98	62	340	74
455/345 STG.I	1.55	3	.490/.490	32	114	326	102	66	348	74

CADILLAC DIVISION

472/345	1.65	3	.440/.468	34	100	314	78	56	314	90
500/365	1.65	3	.440/.468	34	100	314	78	56	314	90

CHEVROLET DIVISION

140/90	4	3	.419/.430	22	58	260	92	48	320	70
140/110	4	3	.436/.436	25	71	276	101	55	336	80
250/145	1.75	3	.388/.388	16	48	244	46.5	17.5	244	33.5
307/200	1.50	.2600/.2733	.390/.410	28	72	280	78	30	288	58
350/245	1.50	.2600/.2733	.390/.410	28	72	280	78	30	288	58
350/270	1.50	.2600/.2733	.390/.410	28	72	280	78	30	288	58
350/330¹	1.50	.3057/.3234	.458/.485	42°40'	94°20'	317	112°50'	53°23'	346°13'	96°3'
400/255	1.70	.2235/.2411	.390/.410	28	72	280	78	30	288	58
402/300	1.70	.2343/.2343	.398/.430	28	78	286	75	31	286	59
454/365	1.70	.2714/.2824	.461/.480	28	114	350	110	62	352	118
454/425¹	1.70	.2714/.2824	.519/.519	44	92	316	86	36	302	80

OLDSMOBILE DIVISION

250/145	1.75	3	.388/.388	16	48	244	46.5	17.5	244	33.5
350/240	1.6	3	.400/.400	14	56	250	66	18	264	32
350/260	1.6	3	.472/.472	30 5	75	285	71	36	287	66
455/280	1.6	3	.435/.435	20	58	258	68	24	272	44
455/320	1.6	3	.435/.435	20	58	258	68	24	272	44
455/340	1.6	3	.474/.472 9	44 6	84	308	84	44	308	88
455/350W-30	1.6	3	.475/.475	56 7	92	328	96	52	328	108
455/350 TOR.	1.6	3	.440/.440	22	60	262	68	26	274	48

PONTIAC DIVISION

250/145	1.75	3	.388/.388	16	48	244	46.5	17.5	244	33.5
307/200	1.50	.2600/.2733	.390/.410	28	72	280	78	30	288	58
350/250	1.5	3	.376/.412	265	63	269	72	25	277	51
400/265	1.5	3	.410/.413	236	70	273	78	31	289	54
400/300	1.5	3	.410/.413	236	70	273	78	31	289	54
455/280	1.5	3	.410/.413	236	70	273	78	31	289	54
455/325	1.5	3	.410/.413	236	70	273	78	31	289	54
455/335	1.5	3	.414/.413	317	77	288	90	32	302	63

1972

BUICK DIVISION

350/150	1.55	3	.3818/.3984	24	78	282	84	40	304	64
350/155	1.55	3	.3818/.3984	24	78	282	84	40	304	64
350/175	1.55	3	.3818/.3984	24	78	282	84	40	304	64
350/180	1.55	3	.3818/.3984	24	78	282	84	40	304	64
350/190	1.55	3	.3818/.3984	24	78	282	84	40	304	64
455/225⁴	1.6	3	.3873/.456	12	102	294	98	62	340	74
455/250⁴	1.6	3	.3873/.456	12	102	294	98	62	340	74
455/260⁴	1.6	3	.3873/.456	12	102	294	98	62	340	74
455/270⁴	1.6	3	.3873/.456	12	102	294	98	62	340	74

CADILLAC DIVISION

472/220	1.72	3	.490/.490	34	100	314	78	56	314	90
500/235	1.72	3	.490/.490	34	100	314	78	56	314	90

CHEVROLET DIVISION

140/80⁵	—	.4199/.4301	.4199/.4302	22	58	260	92	48	320	70
140/90	—	.4369/.4369	.4367/.4379	28	70	278	91	55	326	83
250/110⁷	1.75	.2217/.2217 12	.3880/.3880 10	16	48	244	46°30'	17°30'	244	33°30'
307/130⁸	1.50	.2600/.2733	.3900/.4100 11	28	72	280	78	30	288	58
350/165⁸	1.50	.2600/.2733	.3900/.4100 11	28	72	280	78	30	288	58
350/175⁸	1.50	.2600/.2733	.3900/.4100 11	28	72	280	78	30	288	58
350/200⁸	1.50	.3057/.3234	.3900/.4100 11	28	72	280	78	30	288	58
350/255	1.50	.3057/.3234	.4586/.4850	42°40'	94°20'	317	112°50'	53°23'	346°13'	96°03'
400/170⁸	1.50	.2235/.2411	.3900/.4100 11	28	72	280	78	30	288	58
402/210	1.70	.2343/.2343	.3983/.4300	30	70	280	77	61	318	91
402/240	1.70	.2343/.2343	.3983/.4300	28	78	286	75	31	286	59
454/230	1.70	.2714/.2824	.4614/.4800	56	114	350	110	62	352	118
454/270	1.70	.2714/.2824	.4614/.4800	56	114	350	110	62	352	118

OLDSMOBILE DIVISION

350/160	1.60	3	.400/.400	16	54	250	64	20	264	36
350/175	1.60	3	.400/.400	16	54	250	64	20	264	36
350/180	1.60	3	.400/.400	16	54	250	64	20	264	36
350/200	1.60	3	.400/.400	16	54	250	64	20	264	36
455/225	1.60	3	.435/.435	20	58	258	68	24	272	44
455/250	1.60	3	.472/.472	30	75	285	71	36	287	66
455/265	1.60	3	.474/.474	44	84	308	84	44	308	88
455/270	1.60	3	.474/.474	44	84	308	84	44	308	88
455/300	1.60	3	.475/.475	56	92	328	96	52	328	108

PONTIAC DIVISION

250/110	1.75	.2217/.2217	.388/.388	16	48	244	46.5	17.5	244	33.5
307/130	1.50	.2600/.2733	.390/.409	28	72	280	78	30	288	58
350/160	1.50	3	.374/.407	26	63	269	72	25	277	51
350/175	1.50	3	.374/.407	26	63	269	72	25	277	51
400/175	1.50	3	.374/.407	26	63	269	72	25	277	51
400/200	1.50	3	.403/.406	23	70	273	78	31	289	54
400/200	1.50	3	.403/.406	23	70	273	78	31	289	54
400/250	1.50	3	.403/.406	23	70	273	78	31	289	54
455/185	1.50	3	.404/.408	30	63	273	77	23	282	55
455/200	1.50	3	.404/.408	30	63	273	77	23	282	55

ENGINE SPECIFICATIONS

GENERAL MOTORS VALVE ACTION & TIMING

DISPLACEMENT/ HORSEPOWER	ROCKER RATIO	LOBE LIFT (INT./EXH.)	VALVE LIFT ZERO LASH (INT./EXH.)	INTAKE VALVE TIMING OPENS (°BTC)	CLOSES (°ABC)	DURATION (degrees)	EXHAUST VALVE TIMING OPENS (°BBC)	CLOSES (°ATC)	DURATION (degrees)	OVERLAP (degrees)
455/220	1.50	3	.403/.406	23	70	273	78	31	289	54
455/250	1.50	3	.403/.406	23	70	273	78	31	289	54
455/300	1.50	3	.408/.406	31	77	288	90	32	302	63

1973

BUICK DIVISION

DISPLACEMENT/ HORSEPOWER	ROCKER RATIO	LOBE LIFT (INT./EXH.)	VALVE LIFT ZERO LASH (INT./EXH.)	INTAKE OPENS (°BTC)	CLOSES (°ABC)	DURATION (degrees)	EXHAUST OPENS (°BBC)	CLOSES (°ATC)	DURATION (degrees)	OVERLAP (degrees)
350/150	1.55	3	.3818	24	78	282	84	40	304	64
350/175	1.55	3	.3818	24	78	282	84	40	304	64
350/190	1.55	3	.3818	.24	78	282	84	40	304	64
455/225	1.6	3	.3873	14	99	293	97	54	331	68
455/250	1.6	3	.3873	14	99	293	97	54	331	68
455/260	1.6	3	.3873	14	99	293	97	54	331	68
455/270	1.6	3	.3873	14	99	293	97	54	331	68

CADILLAC DIVISION

472/220	1.72	3	.490/.490	34	100	314	78	56	314	90
500/235	1.72	3	.490/.490	34	100	314	78	56	314	90

CHEVROLET DIVISION

140/72	—	.4199/.4301	.4199/.4302	22	58	260	92	48	320	70
140/85	—	.4369/.4369	.4367/.4379	28	70	278	91	55	326	83
250/100	1.75	.2217/.2217 12	.3880/.3880	16	48	244	46°30'	17°30'	244	33°30'
307/115	1.50	.2600/.2733	.3900/.4100	28	72	280	78	30	288	58
350/145	1.50	.2600/.2733	.3900/.4100 11	28	72	280	78	30	288	58
350/175	1.50	.2600/.2733	.3900/.4100 11	28	72	280	78	30	288	58
350/245	1.50	.3000/.307	.4500/.4600	52	114	346	98	62	340	114
350/250	1.50	.3000/.307	.4500/.4600	52	114	346	98	62	340	114
400/150	1.50	.2235/.2411	.3900/.4100 11	28	72	280	78	30	288	58
454/245	1.70	.2588/.2588	.4400/.4400	55	111	346	105	63	348	118
454/275	1.70	.2588/.2588	.4400/.4400	55	111	346	105	63	348	118

OLDSMOBILE DIVISION

250/100	1.75	3	.388/.338	16	48	244	46	17	244	33
350/160	1.60	3	.440/440	22	60	262	68	26	274	48
350/180	1.60	3	.440/.440	22	60	262	68	26	274	48
455/225	1.60	3	.435/.435	20	58	258	68	24	272	44
455/250	1.60	3	.440/.440	22	60	262	68	26	274	48
455/265	1.60	3	.474/.474	44	84	308	84	44	308	88
455/270	1.60	3	.474/.474	44	84	308	84	44	308	88
455/300	1.60	3	.475/.475	56	92	328	96	52	328	108

PONTIAC DIVISION

250/100	1.75	.2217/.2217	.388/.388	16	48	244	46.5	17.5	244	33.5
350/150	1.50	3	.377/.413	26	63	269	72	25	277	51
350/175	1.50	3	.377/.413	26	63	269	72	25	277	51
400/170	1.50	3	.377/.413	26	63	269	68	29	277	55
400/185	1.50	3	.377/.413	26	63	269	68	29	277	55
400/230	1.50	3	.410/.415	30	63	273	77	25	282	55
455/250	1.50	3	.410/.414	23	70	273	78	31	289	54
455/310	1.50	3	.470/.470	42	86	308	95	45	320	87

1974

BUICK DIVISION

250/100	1.5	3.12	.3880/.3880	16	48	244	46.5	17.5	244	33.5
350/150 13	1.5	3	.3818/.3984	19	70	269	79	33	292	54
350/175 13	1.5	3	.3818/.3984	19	70	269	79	33	292	54
455/175 13	1.5	3	.3873/.445	10	90	280	92	45	317	55
455/190 13	1.5	3	.3873/.445	10	90	280	92	45	317	55
455/210 13	1.5	3	.3873/.445	10	90	280	92	45	317	55
455/230 13	1.5	3	.3873/.445	10	90	280	92	45	317	55
455/245 13	1.5	3	.3873/.445	10	90	280	92	45	317	55

CADILLAC DIVISION 13

472/205	1.72	3	.457/.473	21	111	312	73	55	308	76
500/210	1.72	3	.457/.473	21	111	312	73	55	308	76

CHEVROLET DIVISION 13

122/130	—	3	.3550/.3550	39	64	283	70	30	280	68
140/75	—	.4199/.4301	.4199/.4302	22	58	260	92	48	320	70
140/85	—	.4369/.4369	.4367/.4379	28	70	278	91	55	326	83
250/100	1.75	.2217/.2217 12	.3880/.3880	16	48	244	46.5	17.5	244	33.5
350/145	1.50	.2600/.2733	.3900/.4100	28	72	280	78	30	288	58
350/160	1.50	.2600/.2733	.3900/.4100	28	72	280	78	30	288	58
350/185	1.50	.2600/.2733	.3900/.4100	28	72	280	78	30	288	58
350/195	1.50	.2600/.2733'	.3900/.4100	28	72	280	78	30	288	58
350/245	1.50	.3000/.3066	.4500/.4600	52	114	346	98	62	340	114
350/250	1.50	.3000/.3066	.4500/.4600	52	114	346	98	62	340	114
400/150	1.50	.2235/.2411	.3900/.4100	28	72	280	78	30	288	58
400/180	1.50	.2235/.2411	.3900/.4100	28	72	280	78	30	288	58
454/235	1.70	.2588/.2588	.4400/.4400	55	111	346	105	63	348	118
454/270	1.70	.2588/.2588	.4400/.4400	55	111	346	105	63	348	118

OLDSMOBILE DIVISION 13

250/100	1.75	3.12	.388/.338	16	48	244	46.5	17.5	244	33.5
350/180	1.60	3	.440/.440	22	60	262	68	26	274	48
350/200	1.60	3	.440/.440	22	60	262	68	26	274	48
455/210	1.60	3	.435/.435	20	58	258	68	24	272	44
455/230	1.60	3	.435/.435	20	58	258	68	24	272	44
455/275	1.60	3	.474/.474	28	78	286	74	33	287	61

PONTIAC DIVISION 13

250/100	1.75	.2217/.2217 12	.388/.388	16	48	244	46.5	17.5	244	33.5
350/155	1.50	3	.377/.413	26	63	269	72	25	277	51
350/170	1.50	3	.377/.413	26	63	269	72	25	277	51
350/200	1.50	3	.377/.413	26	63	269	72	25	277	51
400/175	1.50	3	.377/.413	26	63	269	68	29	277	55
400/190	1.50	3	.377/.413	26	63	269	68	29	277	55

GENERAL MOTORS VALVE ACTION & TIMING

DISPLACEMENT/ HORSEPOWER	ROCKER RATIO	LOBE LIFT (INT./EXH.)	VALVE LIFT ZERO LASH (INT./EXH.)	INTAKE VALVE TIMING OPENS (°BTC)	CLOSES (°ABC)	DURATION (degrees)	EXHAUST VALVE TIMING OPENS (°BBC)	CLOSES (°ATC)	DURATION (degrees)	OVERLAP (degrees)
400/200	1.50	3	.410/.415	30	63	273	77	25	282	55
400/225	1.50	3	.410/.415	30	63	273	77	25	282	55
455/215	1.50	3	.410/.414	23	70	273	78	31	289	54
455/250	1.50	3	.410/.414	23	70	273	78	31	289	54
455/290 SD	1.50	3	.410/.410	38	83	301	95	38	313	76

1975

BUICK DIVISION

231/110	1.55	3	.4011/.3768	17	73	270	68	29	277	75
250/105	1.75	3	.3880/.4051	16	48	244	64	50	294	66
260/110	1.60	3	.3995/.4000	14	48	242	56	14	250	28
350/145	1.55	3	.3818/.3984	19	70	269	79	33	292	52
350/165	1.55	3	.3818/.3984	19	70	269	79	33	292	52
455/205	1.60	3	.3873/.4450	10	90	280	76	37	293	47

CADILLAC DIVISION

500/190	1.72	3	.457/.473	21	111	312	73	55	308	76

CHEVROLET DIVISION

140/78	—	3	.4367/.4379	28	20	278	91	55	326	83
140/87	—	3	.4199/.4302	22	58	260	92	48	320	70
122/110	—	3	.355/.355	38	62	280	70	30	280	68
250/105	1.75	3	.3880/.4051	16	48	244	64	50	294	66
262/110	1.50	3	.3727/.3900	26	66	272	74	26	280	52
350/155	1.50	3	.3900/.4100	28	72	280	78	30	288	58
400/175	1.50	3	.3900/.4100	28	72	280	78	30	288	58
454/215	1.70	3	.4400/.4400	55	111	346	105	63	348	118

OLDSMOBILE DIVISION

231/110	1.55	3	.4011/.3768	17	73	270	68	29	277	75
250/105	1.75	3	.3880/.4051	16	48	244	64	50	294	66
260/110	1.60	3	.395/.400	14	48	242	56	14	250	28
350/165	1.55	3	.3818/.3984	19	70	269	79	33	292	52
350/170	1.60	3	.400/.400	16	54	250	64	20	264	36
400/175	1.50	3	.410/.415	30	63	273	77	25	282	55
455/190	1.60	3	.435/.435	20	58	258	68	24	272	44

PONTIAC DIVISION

250/105	1.75	3	.388/.4051	16	48	244	64	50	294	66
260/110	1.60	3	.395/.400	14	48	242	56	14	250	28
350/145	1.55	3	.3818/.3984	19	70	269	79	33	292	52
350/155	1.50	3	.377/.413	26	63	269	72	25	277	51
350/165	1.55	3	.3818/.3984	19	70	269	79	33	292	52
350/175	1.50	3	.377/.413	26	63	269	72	25	277	51
400/170	1.50	3	.410/.415	30	63	273	77	25	282	55
400/185	1.50	3	.377/.415	26	63	269	69	33	282	59
455/200	1.50	3	.410/.414	23	70	273	78	31	289	54

1976

BUICK DIVISION

231/105	1.55	3	.3768/.3768	17	73	270	68	29	277	75
260/110	1.60	3	.395/.400	14	48	242	56	14	250	28
350/145	1.55	3	.3818/.3984	13.5	51	244.5	54	33	267	46.5
350/165	1.55	3	.3818/.3984	13.5	51	244.5	54	33	267	46.5
455/205	1.60	3	.3873/.4930	10	90	280	76	37	293	47

CADILLAC DIVISION

350/170	1.55	3	.3818/.3984	19	70	269	79	33	292	52
500/190	1.72	3	.457/.473	21	111	312	72	55	308	76
500/215	1.72	3	.457/.473	21	111	312	72	55	308	76

CHEVROLET DIVISION

85/52	1.6	3	.3712/.3712	32	72	284	74	30	284	62
97.6/60	1.6	3	.3712/.3712	32	72	284	74	30	284	62
122/110	1.1	3	.3550/.3550	38	62	280	70	30	280	68
140/70	1.1	3	.4000/.4150	34	74	288	76	36	292	70
140/84	1.1	3	.4000/.4150	34	74	288	76	36	292	70
250/105	1.75	3	.3880/.4051							
262/110	1.5	3	.3727/.3900	26	66	272	74	26	280	52
305/140	1.5	3	.3900/.4100	28	64	272	78	30	288	58
350/145	1.5	3	.3727/.4100	28	64	272	78	30	288	58
350/165	1.5	3	.3900/.4100	28	72	280	78	30	288	58
400/175	1.5	3	.3900/.4100	28	72	280	78	30	288	58
454/225	1.7	3	.3983/.4300	42	94	316	93	61	334	103

OLDSMOBILE DIVISION

140/78	—	3	.4199/.4302	22	58	260	92	48	320	70
140/87	—	3	.4367/.4379	28	70	278	91	55	326	83
231/105	1.55	3	.4011/.3768	17	73	270	68	29	277	75
250/105	1.75	3	.3880/.4051	16	48	244	64	50	294	66
260/110	1.60	3	.395/.400	14	48	242	56	14	250	28
350/140	1.55	3	.3818/.3984	19	70	269	79	33	292	52
350/155	1.55	3	.3818/.3984	19	70	269	79	33	292	52
350/170	1.60	3	.400/.400	16	54	250	64	20	264	36
455/190	1.60	3	.435/.435	20	58	258	68	24	272	44

PONTIAC DIVISION

140/70	—	3	.4199/.4302	22	58	260	92	48	320	70
140/84	—	3	.4367/.4379	28	70	278	91	55	326	83
231/105	1.55	3	.4010/.3768	17	73	270	68	29	277	75
250/105	1.75	3	.3880/.4051	16	48	244	64	50	294	66
260/110	1.60	3	.395/.400	14	48	242	56	14	250	28
350/140	1.55	3	.3818/.3984	13.5	51	244.5	54	33	267	46.5
350/155	1.55	3	.3818/.3984	13.5	51	244.5	54	33	267	46.5
350/160	1.50	3	.377/.413	22	67	269	72	25	277	47
350/165	1.50	3	.377/.413	26	63	269	72	25	277	51
400/170	1.50	3	.377/.415	26	63	269	68	29	277	55
400/185	1.50	3	.377/.415	30	63	273	77	25	282	55
455/200	1.50	3	.377/.414	23	70	273	78	31	289	54

ENGINE SPECIFICATIONS

GENERAL MOTORS VALVE ACTION & TIMING

DISPLACEMENT/ HORSEPOWER	ROCKER RATIO	LOBE LIFT (INT./EXH.)	VALVE LIFT ZERO LASH (INT./EXH.)	INTAKE VALVE TIMING			EXHAUST VALVE TIMING			OVERLAP (degrees)
				OPENS (°BTC)	CLOSES (°ABC)	DURATION (degrees)	OPENS (°BBC)	CLOSES (°ATC)	DURATION (degrees)	
1977										
BUICK DIVISION										
231/105	1.55	3	.383/.366	17	73	270	68	29	277	46
350/ALL	1.55	3	.323/.339	13.5	51	244.5	54	33	267	46.5
403/185	1.55	3	.400/.400	16	54	250	64	20	264	36
CADILLAC DIVISION										
350/180	1.6	3	.400/.400	22	72	274	70	38	280	30
425/ALL	1.72	3	.457/.473	11	90	281	63	34	277	44
CHEVROLET DIVISION										
85/57	1.6	3	.3712/.3712	29	75	284	71	33	284	62
97.6/63	1.6	3	.3712/.3712	29	75	284	71	33	284	62
140/84	1.00	3	.4000/.4150	34	74	288	76	36	292	70
250/110	1.75	3	.3880/.4051	16	48	244	64	50	294	66
305/145	1.50	3	3727/1.4100	28	64	272	78	30	288	58
350/160-170-180	1.50	3	.3900/.4100	28	72	280	78	30	288	58
350/210	1.50	3	.4500/.4600	52	114	346	98	62	340	114
OLDSMOBILE DIVISION										
140/84	1.00	3	.4000/.4150	34	74	288	76	36	292	70
231/105	1.00	3	.4011/.3768	17	73	270	68	29	277	75
260/110	1.6	3	.395/.400	14	48	242	56	14	250	28
305/145	1.50	3	.3727/.4100	28	64	272	78	30	288	58
350/170 (Calif.)	1.50	3	.3900/.4100	28	72	280	78	30	288	58
350/170 (Federal)	1.6	3	.400/.400	16	54	250	64	20	264	36
403/200	1.6	3	.400/.400	16	54	250	64	20	264	36
PONTIAC DIVISION										
140/84	NONE	3	.4000/.4150	34	74	288	76	36	292	70
151/88	1.75	3	.406/.406	33	81	294	76	38	294	71
231/105	1.55	3	.383/.366	17	73	270	68	69	277	46
301/135 (Manual)	1.5	3	.377/.377	31	81	292	64	30	274	61
301/135 (Auto.)	1.5	3	.364/.364	27	67	274	62	32	274	59
305/145	1.50	3	.3727/.4100	28	64	272	78	30	288	58
350/170 (Calif.)	1.50	3	.3900/.4100	28	72	280	78	30	288	58
350/170 (Federal)	1.6	3	.400/.400	16	54	250	64	20	264	36
400/180	1.5	3	.364/.364	29[14]	55[15]	264[16]	62[17]	22[18]	264[19]	51[20]
403/185	1.6	3	.400/.400	16	54	250	64	70	264	36
1978										
BUICK DIVISION										
196/ALL	1.55	3	.323/.366	18	48	246	68	29	277	47
231/105	1.00	3	.383/.366	17	73	270	68	29	277	46
231 TURBO	1.00	3	.383/.366	17	73	270	68	29	277	46
301/140	1.50	3	.364/.364	27	67	274	62	32	274	59
305/ALL	1.50	3	.3727/.4100	28	64	272	78	30	288	58
350/155	1.60	3	.323/.339	13.5	51	244.5	54	33	267	46.5
350/160	1.50	3	.3900/.4100	28	72	280	78	30	288	58
350/170	1.60	3	.400/.400	16	38	234	64	17	261	33
403/185	1.60	3	.400/.400	16	54	250	64	20	264	36
CADDILAC DIVISION										
350/170	1.60	3	.400/.400	22	72	274	70	38	280	30
425/ALL	1.72	3	.457/.473	11	90	281	63	34	277	44
CHEVROLET DIVISION										
98/63	1.60	3	.3866/.3866	28	76	284	72	32	284	60
98/68	1.60	3	.3866/.3866	31	73	284	69	35	284	66
151/85	1.75	3	.406/.406	33	81	294	76	38	294	71
196/90	1.55	3	.323/.366	18	48	246	68	29	277	47
200/95	–	3	.373/.410	34	86	300	88	52	320	86
231/105	1.00	3	.383/.366	17	73	270	68	29	277	46
250/110	1.75	3	.388/.405	16	48	244	64	50	294	66
305/145	1.50	3	.3727/.4100	28	64	272	78	30	288	58
350/160	1.50	3	.3900/.4100	28	72	280	78	30	288	58
350/185	1.50	3	.3900/.4100	28	72	280	78	30	288	58
350/220	1.50	3	.4500/.4600	52	114	346	98	62	340	114
OLDSMOBILE DIVISION										
151/85	1.75	3	.406/.406	33	81	294	76	38	294	71
231/105	1.55	3	.4011/.3768	17	73	270	68	29	277	75
260/110	1.60	3	.395/.400	14	48	242	56	14	250	28
305/145	1.50	3	.3727/.4100	28	64	272	78	30	288	58
350/160	1.50	3	.390/.410	28	72	280	78	30	288	58
350/170	1.60	3	.400/.400	16	54	250	64	20	264	36
350/DIESEL	1.60	3	.375/.376	16	38	234	64	17	261	33
403/190	1.60	3	.400/.400	16	54	250	64	20	264	36
PONTIAC DIVISION										
151/ALL	1.75	3	.406/.406	33	81	294	76	38	294	71
231/105	1.55	3	.383/.366	17	73	270	68	69	277	46
301/140	1.50	3	.364/.364	27	67	274	62	32	274	59
301/140	1.50	3	.364/.364	14	54	248	41	27	248	41
305/145	1.50	3	.3727/.4100	28	64	272	78	30	288	58
350/155	1.60	3	.323/.339	13.5	51	244.5	54	33	267	46.5
350/170	1.60	3	.400/.400	16	54	250	64	20	264	36
350/160	1.50	3	.390/.410	28	72	280	78	30	288	58
400/180	1.50	3	.364/.364	21	73	274	77	41	298	62
400/180	1.50	3	.364/.364	29	55	264	62	22	264	51
400/220	1.50	3	.364/.364	16	78	274	79	39	298	55
403/185	1.60	3	.400/.400	16	54	250	64	20	264	36
1979										
BUICK DIVISION										
196/ALL	1.55	3	.341/.366	16	53	249	68	29	277	45
231/ALL	1.55	3	.357/.366	16	63	259	68	29	277	45
301/ALL	1.75	3	.364/.364	14	54	248	41	27	248	41
305/ALL	1.50	3	.373/.410	28	64	272	78	30	288	58
350/160	1.55	3	.323/.339	13.5	51	244.5	54	33	267	46.5

GENERAL MOTORS VALVE ACTION & TIMING

DISPLACEMENT/ HORSEPOWER	ROCKER RATIO	LOBE LIFT (Int./Exh.)	VALVE LIFT ZERO LASH (Int./Exh.)	INTAKE VALVE TIMING OPENS (°BTC)	INTAKE VALVE TIMING CLOSES (°ABC)	INTAKE VALVE TIMING DURATION (degrees)	EXHAUST VALVE TIMING OPENS (°BBC)	EXHAUST VALVE TIMING CLOSES (°ATC)	EXHAUST VALVE TIMING DURATION (degrees)	OVERLAP (degrees)
350/195	1.50	3	.390/.410	28	72	280	78	30	288	58
350/225	1.50	3	.400/.400	16	54	250	64	20	264	36
403/ALL	1.50	3	.400/.400	16	54	250	64	20	264	36
CADILLAC DIVISION										
350/R	1.60	3	.400/.400	16	54	250	64	20	264	36
350/Diesel	1.60	3	.375/.376	16	38	234	64	17	261	33
425/ALL	1.72	3	.457/.473	11	90	281	63	34	277	44
CHEVROLET DIVISION										
98/70	1.6	3	.3866/.3866	28	76	284	72	32	284	60
98/74	1.6	3	.3866/.3866	31	73	284	69	35	284	66
151/ALL	1.75	3	.406/.406	33	81	294	76	38	294	71
196/105	1.55	3	.341/.366	16	53	249	68	29	277	45
200/94	1.50	3	.373/.410	34	86	300	88	52	320	86
231/115	1.55	3	.357/.366	16	63	259	68	29	277	45
250/115	1.75	3	.388/.4051	16	48	244	64	50	294	66
267/130	1.50	3	.373/.410	28	64	272	78	30	288	58
305/130	1.50	3	.373/.410	28	64	272	78	30	288	58
350/160-195	1.50	3	.390/.410	28	72	280	78	30	288	58
350/225	1.50	3	.450/.460	52	114	346	98	62	340	114
OLDSMOBILE DIVISION										
151/ALL	1.75	3	.406/.406	33	81	294	76	38	294	71
231/ALL	1.55	3	.357/.366	16	63	259	68	29	277	45
260/ALL	1.60	3	.395/.400	14	48	242	56	14	250	28
260/Diesel	1.60	3	.375/.376	16	38	234	64	17	261	33
305/ALL	1.50	3	.373/.410	28	64	272	78	30	288	58
350/R	1.60	3	.400/.400	16	54	250	64	20	264	36
350/L	1.50	3	.390/.410	28	72	280	78	30	288	58
350/Diesel	1.60	3	.375/.376	16	38	234	64	17	261	33
403/ALL	1.60	3	.400/.400	16	54	250	64	20	264	36
PONTIAC DIVISION										
151/ALL	1.75	3	.406/.406	33	81	294	76	38	294	71
231/ALL	1.55	3	.357/.366	16	63	259	68	29	277	45
301/ALL	1.75	3	.364/.364	14	54	248	41	27	248	41
305/ALL	1.50	3	.373/.410	28	64	272	78	30	288	58
350/R	1.60	3	.400/.400	16	54	250	64	20	264	36
350/X	1.50	3	.390/.410	13.5	51	244.5	54	33	267	46.5
350/L	1.50	3	.390/.410	28	72	280	78	30	288	58
400/ALL	1.50	3	.364/.364	16	78	274	79	39	298	55
403/ALL	1.60	3	.400/.400	16	54	250	64	20	264	36

1 Solid Valve Lifters.
2 Auto Transmission Cam 23/70/273/78/31/289/54.
3 Divide rocker arm ratio into valve lift.
4 No rockers, direct acting tappetss. Intake clearance .014-.016 cold, exhaust .029-.031 cold.
5 Manual transmission only; automatic uses 350/240 cam.
6 Manual transmission only; automatic uses 34/80/294/76/40/296/74.
7 Without Air only; Air conditioning uses 34/80/294/76/40/296/74.
8 Without Air only; Air conditioning uses .472/.472.
9 Manual transmission only; automatic uses .472/.472.
10 .3880/.4051 in California.

11 .4006/.4001 in California.
12 California camshafts .2217/.2315.
13 These figures do not represent a change from 1973, reference point was changed from .004 in valve lift to .004 in cam lift.
14 Firebird—manual transmission 21°; W72 16°.
15 Firebird—manual transmission 73°; W72 78°.
16 Firebird—manual transmission and W72 274°.
17 Firebird—manual transmission 77°; W72 79°.
18 Firebird—manual transmission 41°; W72 39°.
19 Firebird—manual transmission and W72 298°.
20 Firebird—manual transmission 62°; W72 55°.

GENERAL MOTORS INTAKE VALVES & SPRINGS

DISPLACEMENT/ HORSEPOWER	INTAKE OVERALL LENGTH	INTAKE HEAD DIAMETER	INTAKE STEM DIAMETER	INTAKE STEM TO GUIDE CLEARANCE	INTAKE OUTER SPRING PRESSURE & LENGTH CLOSED (LB. @ IN.)	INTAKE OUTER SPRING PRESSURE & LENGTH OPEN (LB. @ IN.)	INTAKE INNER SPRING PRESSURE & LENGTH CLOSED (LB. @ IN.)	INTAKE INNER SPRING PRESSURE & LENGTH OPEN (LB. @ IN.)	ANGLE OF SEAT/FACE (Deg.)
				1970					
BUICK DIVISION									
250/155	4.902-4.922	1.715-1.725	.3410-.3417	.0010-.0027	56-64 @ 1.66	180-192 @ 1.27	NONE	NONE	46/45
350/230	4.994-5.024	1.870-1.880	.3725 ± .0005	.0015-.0025	70-80 @ 1.727	173-187 @ 1.340	NONE	NONE	45/45
350/285	4.994-5.024	1.870-1.880	.3725 ± .0005	.0015-.0025	70-80 @ 1.727	173-187 @ 1.340	NONE	NONE	45/45
350/315	4.994-5.024	1.870-1.880	.3725 ± .0005	.0015-.0025	70-80 @ 1.727	173-187 @ 1.340	NONE	NONE	45/45
455/350	4.994-5.024	2.00	.3725 ± .0005	.0015-.0025	70-80 @ 1.727	178-187 @ 1.340	NONE	NONE	45/45
455/360	4.994-5.024	2.125	.3725 ± .0005	.0015-.0025	70-80 @ 1.727	173-187 @ 1.340	NONE	NONE	45/45
455/370	4.994-5.024	2.00	.3725 ± .0005	.0015-.0025	70-80 @ 1.727	173-187 @ 1.340	NONE	NONE	45/45
CADILLAC DIVISION									
472/375	5.230	2.000	.3415-.3425	.0005-.0025	60-65 @ 1.946	155-165 @ 1.496	NONE	NONE	45/44
500/400	5.230	2.000	.3415-.3425	.005-.0025	60-65 @ 1.946	155-165 @ 1.496	NONE	NONE	45/44
CHEVROLET DIVISION									
153/90	4.902-4.922	1.715-1.725	.3410-.3417	.0010-.0027	78-86 @ 1.66	170-180 @ 1.26	DAMPER	DAMPER	46/45
230/140	4.902-4.922	1.715-1.725	.3410-.3417	.0010-.0027	56-64 @ 1.66	170-184 @ 1.33	NONE	NONE	46/45
250/155	4.902-4.922	1.715-1.725	.3410-.3417	.0010-.0027	56-64 @ 1.66	180-192 @ 1.27	NONE	NONE	46/45
307/200	4.902-4.922	1.715-1.725	.3410-.3417	.0010-.0027	76-84 @ 1.70	194-206 @ 1.25	DAMPER	DAMPER	46/45
350/250	4.870-4.889	1.935-1.945	.3410-.3417	.0010-.0027	76-84 @ 1.70	194-206 @ 1.25	DAMPER	DAMPER	46/45
350/300	4.870-4.889	1.935-1.945	.3410-.3417	.0010-.0027	76-84 @ 1.70	194-206 @ 1.25	DAMPER	DAMPER	46/45
350/350	4.870-4.889	1.935-1.945	.3410-.3417	.0010-.0027	76-84 @ 1.70	194-206 @ 1.25	DAMPER	DAMPER	46/45
350/360	4.870-4.889	2.017-2.023	.3410-.3417	.0010-.0027	76-84 @ 1.70	194-206 @ 1.25	DAMPER	DAMPER	46/45
350/370	4.870-4.889	1.935-1.945	.3410-.3417	.0010-.0027	76-84 @ 1.70	194-206 @ 1.25	DAMPER	DAMPER	46/45
400/265	4.870-4.889	1.935-1.945	.3410-.3417	.0010-.0027	76-84 @ 1.70	194-206 @ 1.25	DAMPER	DAMPER	46/45
402/330	5.215-5.235	2.060-2.070	.3715-.3722	.0010-.0027	69-81 @ 1.88	228-252 @ 1.38	26-34 @ 1.78	81-91 @ 1.28	46/45
402/350	5.215-5.235	2.060-2.070	.3715-.3722	.0010-.0027	69-81 @ 1.88	228-252 @ 1.38	26-34 @ 1.78	81-99 @ 1.28	46/45
402/375	5.215-5.235	2.060-2.070	.3715-.3722	.0010-.0027	69-81 @ 1.88	228-252 @ 1.38	26-34 @ 1.78	81-99 @ 1.28	46/45
454/345	5.215-5.235	2.060-2.070	.3715-.3722	.0010-.0027	94-106 @ 1.88	303-327 @ 1.38	N.A.	N.A.	46/45
454/360	5.215-5.235	2.060-2.070	.3715-.3722	.0010-.0027	69-81 @ 1.88	228-252 @ 1.25	26-34 @ 1.78	81-99 @ 1.28	46/45
454/390	5.215-5.235	2.060-2.070	.3715-.3722	.0010-.0027	69-81 @ 1.88	228-252 @ 1.25	26-34 @ 1.78	81-99 @ 1.28	46/45
454/450	5.204-5.224	2.185-2.195	.3712-.3717	.0010-.0027	69-81 @ 1.88	228-252 @ 1.25	26-34 @ 1.78	81-99 @ 1.28	46/45
454/460	5.226-5.251	2.185-2.195	.3715-.3722	.0010-.0027	69-81 @ 1.88	181-205 @ 1.32	37-45 @ 1.78	92-110 @ 1.22	46/45
OLDSMOBILE DIVISION									
250/155	4.902-4.922	1.715-1.725	.3410-.3417	.0010-.0027	56-64 @ 1.660	180-192 @ 1.270	NONE	NONE	46/45
350/250	4.703	2.067-2.077	.3425-.3432	.0010-.0027	76-84 @ 1.670	180-194 @ 1.270	NONE	NONE	30/30

ENGINE SPECIFICATIONS

GENERAL MOTORS INTAKE VALVES & SPRINGS

DISPLACEMENT/ HORSEPOWER	INTAKE OVERALL LENGTH	INTAKE HEAD DIAMETER	INTAKE STEM DIAMETER	INTAKE STEM TO GUIDE CLEARANCE	INTAKE OUTER SPRING PRESSURE & LENGTH CLOSED (LB. @ IN.)	OPEN (LB. @ IN.)	INTAKE INNER SPRING PRESSURE & LENGTH CLOSED (LB. @ IN.)	OPEN (LB. @ IN.)	ANGLE OF SEAT/FACE (Deg.)
350/310	4.703	2.067-2.077	.3425-.3432	.0010-.0027	76-84 @ 1.670	180-194 @ 1.270	NONE	NONE	30/30
350/325	4.703	2.067-2.077	.3425-.3432	.0010-.0027	76-84 @ 1.670	180-194 @ 1.270	NONE	NONE	30/30
455/310	4.707	1.990-2.000	.3425-.3432	.0010-.0027	76-84 @ 1.670	180-194 @ 1.270	NONE	NONE	46/45
455/320	4.707	1.990-2.000	.3425-.3432	.0010-.0027	76-84 @ 1.670	180-194 @ 1.270	NONE	NONE	46/45
455/365	4.703	1.990-2.000	.3425-.3432	.0010-.0027	76-84 @ 1.670	180-194 @ 1.270	DAMPER	DAMPER	30/30
455/370	4.703	1.990'2.000	.3425-.3432	.0010-.0027	76-84 @ 1.670	180-194 @ 1.270	DAMPER	DAMPER	30/30
455/375	4.703	2.067-2.077	.3425-.3432	.0010-.0027	76-84 @ 1.670	180-194 @ 1.270	DAMPER	DAMPER	30/30
455/390	4.707	1.990-2.000	.3425-.3432	.0010-.0027	76-84 @ 1.670	180-194 @ 1.270	DAMPER	DAMPER	46/45
455/400	4.703	2.067-2.077	.3425-.3432	.0010-.0027	76-84 @ 1.670	180-194 @ 1.270	DAMPER	DAMPER	30/30
PONTIAC DIVISION									
250/155	4.912	1.715-1.725	.3410-.3417	.0010-.0027	56-64 @ 1.66	180-192 @ 1.27	NONE	NONE	46/45
350/255	4.993	1.957-1.963	.3412-.3419	.0016-.0033	60-66 @ 1.58	123-133 @ 1.21	32-38 @ 1.54	89-99 @ 1.17	45/44
400/265	4.993	1.957-1.963	.3412-.3419	.0016-.0033	60-66 @ 1.58	123-133 @ 1.21	32-38 @ 1.54	89-99 @ 1.17	45/44
400/290	5.089	1.957-1.963	.3412-.3419	.0016-.0033	60-66 @ 1.58	128-138 @ 1.17	32-38 @ 1.54	94-104 @ 1.13	45/44
400/330	5.068	1.957-1.963	.3412-.3419	.0016-.0033	63-69 @ 1.56	132-142 @ 1.15	35-41 @ 1.52	97-107 @ 1.11	30/29
400/345	5.093	2.107-2.113	.3412-.3419	.0016-.0033	56-66 @ 1.59	126-140 @ 1.17	54-60 @ 1.52	119-129 @ 1.11	30/29
400/350	5.073	2.107-2.113	.3412-.3419	.0016-.0033	63-69 @ 1.56	132-142 @ 1.15	35-41 @ 1.52	97-107 @ 1.11	30/29
400/366	5.093	2.107-2.113	.3412-.3419	.0016-.0033	56-66 @ 1.59	126-140 @ 1.18	54-60 @ 1.52	119-129 @ 1.11	30/29
400/370	5.207	2.107-2.113	.3412-.3419	.0016-.0033	71-81 @ 1.82	216-230 @ 1.29	37-43 @ 1.75	106-116 @ 1.22	30/29
455/360	4.992	2.107-2.113	.3412-.3419	.0016-.0033	63-69 @ 1.56	133-143 @ 1.15	35-41 @ 1.52	98-108 @ 1.11	30/29
455/370	4.992	2.107-2.133	.3412-.3419	.0016-.0033	63-69 @ 1.56	133-143 @ 1.15	35-41 @ 1.52	98-108 @ 1.11	30/29

1971

DISPLACEMENT/ HORSEPOWER	INTAKE OVERALL LENGTH	INTAKE HEAD DIAMETER	INTAKE STEM DIAMETER	INTAKE STEM TO GUIDE CLEARANCE	INTAKE OUTER SPRING PRESSURE & LENGTH CLOSED (LB. @ IN.)	OPEN (LB. @ IN.)	INTAKE INNER SPRING PRESSURE & LENGTH CLOSED (LB. @ IN.)	OPEN (LB. @ IN.)	ANGLE OF SEAT/FACE (Deg.)
BUICK DIVISION									
250/145	4.902-4.922	1.715-1.725	.3410-.3417	.0010-.0027	56-64 @ 1.66	180-192 @ 1.27	NONE	NONE	46/45
350/230	5.024-4.994	1.880-1.870	.3720-.3730	.0015-.0035	70-80 @ 1.727	173-187 @ 1.340	NONE	NONE	45/45
350/260	5.024-4.994	1.880-1.870	.3720-.3730	.0015-.0035	70-80 @ 1.727	173-187 @ 1.340	NONE	NONE	45/45
455/315	5.155-5.125	2.005-1.995	.3720-.3730	.0015-.0035	67-77 @ 1.890	170-184 @ 1.450	NONE	NONE	45/45
455/330	5.155-5.125	2.005-1.995	.3720-.3730	.0015-.0035	67-77 @ 1.890	170-184 @ 1.450	NONE	NONE	45/45
455/345 STG. 1	5.155-5.125	2.130	.3720-.3730	.0015-.0035	115 @ 1.890	280 @ 1.450	NONE	NONE	45/45
CADILLAC DIVISION									
472/345	5.230	2.000	.3415-.3425	.0005-.0025	60-65 @ 1.946	155-165 @ 1.496	NONE	NONE	45/44
500/365	5.230	2.000	.3415-.3425	.0005-.0025	60-65 @ 1.946	155-165 @ 1.496	NONE	NONE	45/44
CHEVROLET DIVISION									
140/90	4.578-4.598	1.615-1.625	.3410-.3417	.0010-.0027	71-79 @ 1.746	183-197 @ 1.310	DAMPER	DAMPER	46/45
140/110	4.578-4.598	1.615-1.625	.3410-.3417	.0010-.0027	71-79 @ 1.746	183-197 @ 1.310	DAMPER	DAMPER	46/45
250/145	4.902-4.922	1.715-1.725	.3410-.3417	.0010-.0027	55-64 @ 1.66	180-192 @ 1.27	NONE	NONE	46/45
307/200	4.902-4.922	1.715-1.725	.3410-.3417	.0010-.0027	76-84 @ 1.70	194-206 @ 1.25	NONE	NONE	46/45
350/245	.4.870-4.889	1.935-1.945	.3410-.3417	.0010-.0027	76-84 @ 1.70	194-206 @ 1.25	NONE	NONE	46/45
350/270	4.870-4.889	1.935-1.945	.3410-.3417	.0010-.0027	76-84 @ 1.70	194-206 @ 1.25	NONE	NONE	46/45
350/330	4.870-4.889	2.017-2.023	.3410-.3417	.0010-.0027	76-84 @ 1.70	194-206 @ 1.25	NONE	NONE	46/45
400/255	4.870-4.889	1.935-1.945	.3410-.3417	.0010-.0027	76-84 @ 1.70	194-206 @ 1.25	NONE	NONE	46/45
402/300	5.215-5.235	2.060-2.070	.3715-.3722	.0010-.0027	69-81 @ 1.88	228-252 @ 1.38	26-34 @ 1.78	81-99 @ 1.28	46/45
454/365	5.215-5.235	2.060-2.070	.3715-.3722	.0010-.0027	69-81 @ 1.88	228-252 @ 1.38	26-34 @ 1.78	81-99 @ 1.28	46/45
454/425	5.215-5.235	2.185-2.195	.3715-.3722	.0010-.0027	69-81 @ 1.88	228-252 @ 1.38	26-34 @ 1.78	81-99 @ 1.28	46/45
OLDSMOBILE DIVISION									
250/145	4.902-4.922	1.715-1.725	.3410-.3417	.0010-.0027	56-64 @ 1.66	180-192 @ 1.27	NONE	NONE	46/45
350/240	4.740	1.870-1.880	.3425-.3432	.0010-.0027	76-84 @ 1.670	180-194 @ 1.270	NONE	NONE	46/45
350/260	4.740	1.870-1.880	.3425-.3432	.0010-.0027	76-84 @ 1.670	180-194 @ 1.270	NONE	NONE	46/45
455/280	4.707	1.990-2.000	.3425-.3432	.0010-.0027	76-84 @ 1.670	189-204 @ 1.235	NONE	NONE	46/45
455/320	4.707	1.990-2.000	.3425-.3432	.0010-.0027	76-84 @ 1.670	180-194 @ 1.270	NONE	NONE	46/45
455/340	4.707	2.067-2.077	.3425-.3432	.0010-.0027	115-125 @ 1.670 [1]	281-308 @ 1.196 [2]	NONE	NONE	30/29
455/350 W-30	4.707	2.067-2.077	.3425-.3432	.0010-.0027	115-125 @ 1.670 [3]	281-308 @ 1.196 [4]	DAMPER	DAMPER	30/29
455/350 TOR.	4.707	2.067-2.077	.3425-.3432	.0010-.0027	76- 84 @ 1.670	191-206 @ 1.230	DAMPER	DAMPER	30/29
PONTIAC DIVISION									
250/145	4.902-4.922	1.715-1.725	.3410-.3417	.0010-.0027	56- 64 @ 1.66	180-192 @ 1.27	NONE	NONE	46/45
307/200	4.902-4.922	1.715-1.725	.3410-.3417	.0010-.0027	76- 84 @ 1.70	194-206 @ 1.25	NONE	NONE	46/45
350/250	4.982	1.96	.3412-.3419	.0016-.0033	54- 68 @ 1.589 [7]	119-133 @ 1.212	28-38 @ 1.549	87- 97 @ 1.172	45/44
400/265	4.982	1.96	.3412-.3419	.0016-.0033	54- 68 @ 1.589 [7]	119-133 @ 1.212	28-38 @ 1.549	87- 97 @ 1.172	45/44
400/300	4.960	2.11	.3412-.3419	.0016-.0033	57- 71 @ 1.568 [6]	128-142 @ 1.157	31-41 @ 1.528	86-106 @ 1.117	30/29
455/280	4.881	1.96	.3412-.3419	.0016-.0033	54- 68 @ 1.590	125-139 @ 1.179	28-38 @ 1.550	92-102 @ 1.139	45/44
455/325	4.881	2.11	.3412-.3419	.0016-.0033	57- 71 @ 1.568	128-142 @ 1.157	31-41 @ 1.528	86-106 @ 1.117	30/29
455/335	4.960	2.11	.3412-.3419	.0016-.0033	59- 73 @ 1.560	130-144 @ 1.146	33-43 @ 1.520	98-108 @ 1.106	30/29

1972

DISPLACEMENT/ HORSEPOWER	INTAKE OVERALL LENGTH	INTAKE HEAD DIAMETER	INTAKE STEM DIAMETER	INTAKE STEM TO GUIDE CLEARANCE	INTAKE OUTER SPRING PRESSURE & LENGTH CLOSED (LB. @ IN.)	OPEN (LB. @ IN.)	INTAKE INNER SPRING PRESSURE & LENGTH CLOSED (LB. @ IN.)	OPEN (LB. @ IN.)	ANGLE OF SEAT/FACE (Deg.)
BUICK DIVISION									
350/150	4.994-5.024	1.870-1.880	.3720-.3730	.0015-.0035	70-80 @ 1.727	173-187 @ 1.340	NONE	NONE	45/45
350/155	4.994-5.024	1.870-1.880	.3720-.3730	.0015-.0035	70-80 @ 1.727	173-187 @ 1.340	NONE	NONE	45/45
350/175	4.994-5.024	1.870-1.880	.3720-.3730	.0015-.0035	70-80 @ 1.727	173-187 @ 1.340	NONE	NONE	45/45
350/180	4.994-5.024	1.870-1.880	.3720-.3730	.0015-.0035	70-80 @ 1.727	173-187 @ 1.340	NONE	NONE	45/45
350/190	4.994-5.024	1.870-1.800	.3720-.3730	.0015-.0035	70-80 @ 1.727	173-187 @ 1.340	NONE	NONE	45/45
455/225	5.125-5.155	1.995-2.005	.3720-.3730	.0015-.0035	67-77 @ 1.890	170-184 @ 1.450	NONE	NONE	45/45
455/250	5.125-5.155	1.995-2.005	.3720-.3730	.0015-.0035	67-77 @ 1.890	170-184 @ 1.450	NONE	NONE	45/45
455/260	5.125-5.125	1.995-2.005	.3720-.3730	.0015-.0035	67-77 @ 1.727	170-184 @ 1.450	NONE	NONE	45/45
455/270	5.125-5.125	1.995-2.005	.3720-.3730	.0015-.0035	67-77 @ 1.727	170-184 @ 1.450	NONE	NONE	45/45
CADILLAC DIVISION									
472/220	5.231	2.000	.3413-.3420	.0010-.0027	60-65 @ 1.946	163-173 @ 1.456	NONE	NONE	45/44
500/235	5.231	2.000	.3413-.3420	.0010-.0027	60-65 @ 1.946	163-173 @ 1.456	NONE	NONE	45/44
CHEVROLET DIVISION									
140/80	4.590-4.610	1.615-1.625	.3410-.3417	.0010-.0027	71-79 @ 1.746	183-197 @ 1.310	DAMPER	DAMPER	46/45
140/90	4.590-4.610	1.615-1.625	.3410-.3417	.0010-.0027	71-79 @ 1.746	183-197 @ 1.310	DAMPER	DAMPER	46/45
250/110	4.902-4.922	1.715-1.725	.3410-.3417	.0010-.0027	55-64 @ 1.66	180-192 @ 1.27	NONE	NONE	46/45
307/130	4.902-4.922	1.715-1.725	.3410-.3417	.0010-.0027	76-84 @ 1.70	194-206 @ 1.25	DAMPER	DAMPER	46/45
350/165	4.870-4.889	1.935-1.945	.3410-.3417	.0010-.0027	76-84 @ 1.70	194-206 @ 1.25	DAMPER	DAMPER	46/45
350/175	4.870-4.889	1.935-1.945	.3410-.3417	.0010-.0027	76-84 @ 1.70	194-206 @ 1.25	DAMPER	DAMPER	46/45
350/200	4.870-4.889	1.935-1.945	.3410-.3417	.0010-.0027	76-84 @ 1.70	194-206 @ 1.25	DAMPER	DAMPER	46/45
350/255	4.870-4.889	1.935-1.945	.3410-.3417	.0010-.0027	76-84 @ 1.70	194-206 @ 1.25	DAMPER	DAMPER	46/45
400/170	4.870-4.889	1.935-1.945	.3410-.3417	.0010-.0027	76-84 @ 1.70	194-206 @ 1.25	DAMPER	DAMPER	46/45
402/210	5.215-5.235	2.060-2.070	.3715-.3722	.0010-.0027	84-96 @ 1.88	205-225 @ 1.48	DAMPER	DAMPER	46/45
402/240	5.215-5.235	2.060-2.070	.3715-.3722	.0010-.0027	84-96 @ 1.88	205-225 @ 1.48	DAMPER	DAMPER	46/45
454/230	5.215-5.235	2.060-2.070	.3715-.3722	.0010-.0027	69-81 @ 1.88	228-252 @ 1.38	26-34 @ 1.78	81-99 @ 1.28	46/45
454/270	5.215-5.235	2.060-2.070	.3715-.3722	.0010-.0027	69-81 @ 1.88	228-252 @ 1.38	26-34 @ 1.78	81-99 @ 1.28	46/45

GENERAL MOTORS INTAKE VALVES & SPRINGS

DISPLACEMENT/ HORSEPOWER	INTAKE OVERALL LENGTH	INTAKE HEAD DIAMETER	INTAKE STEM DIAMETER	INTAKE STEM TO GUIDE CLEARANCE	INTAKE OUTER SPRING PRESSURE & LENGTH CLOSED (LB. @ IN.)	OPEN (LB. @ IN.)	INTAKE INNER SPRING PRESSURE & LENGTH CLOSED (LB. @ IN.)	OPEN (LB. @ IN.)	ANGLE OF SEAT/FACE (Deg.)
OLDSMOBILE DIVISION									
350/160	4.740	1.870-1.880	.3425-.3432	.0010-.0027	76-84 @ 1.670	180-194 @ 1.270 5	NONE 6	NONE	45/46
350/175	4.740	1.870-1.880	.3425-.3432	.0010-.0027	76-84 @ 1.670	180-194 @ 1.270 5	NONE 6	NONE	45/46
350/180	4.740	1.870-1.880	.3425-.3432	.0010-.0027	76-84 @ 1.670	180-194 @ 1.270 7	NONE 6	NONE	45/46
350/200	4.740	1.870-1.880	.3425-.3432	.0010-.0027	76-84 @ 1.670	180-190 @ 1.270 7	NONE 6	NONE	45/46
455/225	4.707	1.990-2.000	.3425-.3432	.0010-.0027	76-84 @ 1.670	180-194 @ 1.270	NONE	NONE	45/46
455/250	4.703	2.067-2.077	.3425-.3432	.0010-.0027	76-84 @ 1.670	199-214 @ 1.198	DAMPER	DAMPER	30/30
455/265	4.707	1.990-2.000	.3425-.3432	.0010-.0027	76-84 @ 1.670	189-204 @ 1.235	NONE	NONE	45/46
455/270	4.703	2.067-2.077	.3425-.3432	.0010-.0027	115-125 @ 1.670	281-308 @ 1.196	DAMPER	DAMPER	30/30
455/300	4.703	2.067-2.077	.3425-.3432	.0010-.0027	115-125 @ 1.670	281-301 @ 1.195	DAMPER	DAMPER	30/30
PONTIAC DIVISION									
250/110	4.902-4.922	1.715-1.725	.3410-.3417	.0010-.0027	56-64 @ 1.66	180-192 @ 1.27	NONE	NONE	46/45
307/130	4.902-4.922	1.715-1.725	.3410-.3417	.0010-.0027	76-84 @ 1.70	194-206 @ 1.25	DAMPER	DAMPER	46/45
350/160	4.982	1.957-1.963	.3412-.3419	.0016-.0033	54-68 @ 1.590	125-139 @ 1.179	28-38 @ 1.550	93-103 @ 1.139	45/44
350/175	4.982	1.957-1.963	.3412-.3419	.0016-.0033	54-68 @ 1.590	125-139 @ 1.179	28-38 @ 1.550	93-103 @ 1.139	45/44
400/175 (L65)	4.982 12	1.963-1.957 12	.3412-.3419	.0016-.0033	54-68 @ 1.590 9	119-133 @ 1.213 8	28-38 @ 1.550 10	88-98 @ 1.173 11	45/44 12
400/200 (L65)	4.982 12	1.963-1.957 12	.3412-.3419	.0016-.0033	54-68 @ 1.590 9	119-133 @ 1.213 8	28-38 @ 1.550 10	88-98 @ 1.173 11	45/44 12
400/200 (L78)	4.960	2.107-2.113	.3412-.3419	.0016-.0033	58-72 @ 1.568 9	129-143 @ 1.158 8	32-42 @ 1.528 10	96-106 @ 1.118 11	30/29
400/250 (L78)	4.960	1.957-1.963	.3412-.3419	.0016-.0033	58-72 @ 1.568 9	129-143 @ 1.158 8	32-42 @ 1.528 10	96-106 @ 1.118 11	30/29
455/185	4.880	1.957-1.963	.3412-.3419	.0016-.0033	54-68 @ 1.590	125-139 @ 1.180	28-38 @ 1.550	93-103 @ 1.140	45/44
455/200	4.880	2.107-2.113	.3412-.3419	.0016-.0033	54-68 @ 1.590	125-139 @ 1.180	28-38 @ 1.550	93-103 @ 1.140	45/44
455/220	4.880	2.107-2.113	.3412-.3419	.0016-.0033	58-72 @ 1.569	129-143 @ 1.159	32-42 @ 1.529	96-106 @ 1.119	30/29
455/250	4.880	2.107-2.113	.3412-.3419	.0016-.0033	58-72 @ 1.569	129-143 @ 1.159	32-42 @ 1.529	96-106 @ 1.119	30/29
455/300	4.960	2.107-2.113	.3412-.3419	.0016-.0033	59-73 @ 1.561	131-145 @ 1.146	33-43 @ 1.521	98-108 @ 1.06	30/29

1973

DISPLACEMENT/ HORSEPOWER	INTAKE OVERALL LENGTH	INTAKE HEAD DIAMETER	INTAKE STEM DIAMETER	INTAKE STEM TO GUIDE CLEARANCE	INTAKE OUTER SPRING CLOSED (LB. @ IN.)	OPEN (LB. @ IN.)	INTAKE INNER SPRING CLOSED (LB. @ IN.)	OPEN (LB. @ IN.)	ANGLE OF SEAT/FACE (Deg.)
BUICK DIVISION									
350/150	4.994-5.024	1.870-1.880	.3720-.3730	.0015-.0035	70-80 @ 1.727	173-187 @ 1.340	NONE	NONE	45/45
350/175	4.994-5.024	1.870-1.880	.3720-.3730	.0015-.0035	70-80 @ 1.727	173-187 @ 1.340	NONE	NONE	45/45
350/190	4.994-5.024	1.870-1.880	.3720-.3730	.0015-.0035	70-80 @ 1.727	173-187 @ 1.340	NONE	NONE	45/45
455/225	5.125-5.155	1.995-2.005	.3720-.3730	.0015-.0035	65-79 @ 1.890	167-187 @ 1.450	NONE	NONE	45/45
455/250	5.125-5.155	1.995-2.005	.3720-.3730	.0015-.0035	65-79 @ 1.890	167-187 @ 1.450	NONE	NONE	45/45
455/260	5.125-5.125	1.995-2.005	.3720-.3730	.0015-.0035	65-79 @ 1.727	167-187 @ 1.450	NONE	NONE	45/45
455/270	5.125-5.125	1.995-2.005	.3720-.3730	.0015-.0035	65-79 @ 1.727	167-187 @ 1.450	NONE	NONE	45/45
CADILLAC DIVISION									
472/220	5.230	2.000	.3413-.3420	.0010-.0027	60-65 @ 1.946	163-173 @ 1.456	NONE	NONE	45/44
500/235	5.230	2.000	.3413-.3420	.0010-.0027	60-65 @ 1.946	163-173 @ 1.456	NONE	NONE	45/44
CHEVROLET DIVISION									
140/72	4.590-4.610	1.615-1.625	.3410-.3417	.0010-.0027	71-79 @ 1.746	183-197 @ 1.310	DAMPER	DAMPER	46/45
140/85	4.590-4.610	1.615-1.625	.3410-.3417	.0010-.0027	71-79 @ 1.746	183-197 @ 1.310	DAMPER	DAMPER	46/45
250/100	4.902-4.922	1.715-1.725	.3410-.3417	.0010-.0027	55-64 @ 1.66	180-192 @ 1.27	NONE	NONE	46/45
307/115	4.870-4.889	1.935-1.945	.3410-.3417	.0010-.0027	76-84 @ 1.70	194-206 @ 1.25	DAMPER	DAMPER	46/45
350/145	4.870-4.889	1.935-1.945	.3410-.3417	.0010-.0027	76-84 @ 1.70	194-206 @ 1.25	DAMPER	DAMPER	46/45
350/175	4.870-4.889	1.935-1.945	.3410-.3417	.0010-.0027	76-84 @ 1.70	194-206 @ 1.25	DAMPER	DAMPER	46/45
350/245	4.870-4.889	2.017-2.023	.3410-.3417	.0010-.0027	76-84 @ 1.70	194-206 @ 1.25	DAMPER	DAMPER	46/45
350/250	4.870-4.889	2.017-2.023	.3410-.3417	.0010-.0027	76-84 @ 1.70	194-206 @ 1.25	DAMPER	DAMPER	46/45
400/150	4.870-4.889	1.935-1.945	.3410-.3417	.0010-.0027	76-84 @ 1.70	194-206 @ 1.25	DAMPER	DAMPER	46/45
454/245	5.215-5.235	2.060-2.070	.3715-.3722	.0010-.0027	74-86 @ 1.88	288-312 @ 1.38	DAMPER	DAMPER	46/45
454/275	5.215-5.235	2.060-2.070	.3715-.3722	.0010-.0027	74-86 @ 1.88	288-312 @ 1.38	DAMPER	DAMPER	46/45
OLDSMOBILE DIVISION									
250/100	4.902-4.922	1.715-1.725	.3410-.3417	.0010-.0027	56-64 @ 1.66	180-192 @ 1.27	NONE 14	NONE	45/46
350/160	4.667	1.870-1.880	.3425-.3432	.0010-.0027	76-84 @ 1.670	180-194 @ 1.270 13	NONE 14	NONE	45/46
350/180	4.667	1.870-1.880	.3425-.3432	.0010-.0027	76-84 @ 1.670	180-194 @ 1.270 15	NONE	NONE	45/46
455/225	4.667	1.990-2.000	.3425-.3432	.0010-.0027	76-84 @ 1.670	180-194 @ 1.270	NONE	NONE	45/46
455/250	4.667	1.870-1.880	.3425-.3432	.0010-.0027	76-84 @ 1.670	199-214 @ 1.198	NONE	NONE	45/46
455/265	4.667	1.990-2.000	.3425-.3432	.0010-.0027	76-84 @ 1.670	189-204 @ 1.235	DAMPER	DAMPER	45/46
455/270	4.703	2.067-2.077	.3425-.3432	.0010-.0027	115-125 @ 1.670	281-308 @ 1.196	DAMPER	DAMPER	30/30
455/300	4.703	2.067-2.077	.3425-.3432	.0010-.0027	115-125 @ 1.670	281-301 @ 1.195	DAMPER	DAMPER	30/30
PONTIAC DIVISION									
250/100	4.902-4.922	1.715-1.725	.3410-.3417	.0010-.0027	56-64 @ 1.66	180-192 @ 1.27	NONE	NONE	46/45
350/150	4.864	1.957-1.963	.3412-.3419	.0016-.0033	54-68 @ 1.590	125-139 @ 1.179	28-38 @ 1.550	93-103 @ 1.139	45/44
350/175	4.864	1.957-1.963	.3412-.3419	.0016-.0033	54-68 @ 1.590	125-139 @ 1.179	28-38 @ 1.550	93-103 @ 1.139	45/44
400/170	4.864	1.963-1.957	.3412-.3419	.0016-.0033	54-68 @ 1.590	119-133 @ 1.213	28-38 @ 1.550	88-98 @ 1.173	45/44
400/185	4.864	1.963-1.957	.3412-.3419	.0016-.0033	54-68 @ 1.590	119-133 @ 1.213	28-38 @ 1.550	88-98 @ 1.173	45/44
400/230	4.864	2.107-2.113	.3412-.3419	.0016-.0033	58-72 @ 1.568	129-143 @ 1.158	32-42 @ 1.528	96-106 @ 1.118	30/29
455/250	4.780	2.107-2.113	.3412-.3419	.0016-.0033	58-72 @ 1.569	129-143 @ 1.159	32-42 @ 1.529	96-106 @ 1.119	30/29
455/310	4.960	2.107-2.113	.3412-.3419	.0016-.0033	59-73 @ 1.561	131-145 @ 1.146	33-43 @ 1.521	98-108 @ 1.06	30/29

1974

DISPLACEMENT/ HORSEPOWER	INTAKE OVERALL LENGTH	INTAKE HEAD DIAMETER	INTAKE STEM DIAMETER	INTAKE STEM TO GUIDE CLEARANCE	INTAKE OUTER SPRING CLOSED (LB. @ IN.)	OPEN (LB. @ IN.)	INTAKE INNER SPRING CLOSED (LB. @ IN.)	OPEN (LB. @ IN.)	ANGLE OF SEAT/FACE (Deg.)
BUICK									
250/100	4.902-4.922	1.715-1.725	.3410-.3417	.0010-.0027	56-64 @ 1.660	180-192 @ 1.270	NONE	NONE	46/45
350/150	4.994-5.024	1.870-1.880	.3720-.3730	.0015-.0035	70-80 @ 1.727	173-187 @ 1.340	NONE	NONE	45/45
350/175	4.994-5.024	1.870-1.880	.3720-.3730	.0015-.0035	70-80 @ 1.727	173-187 @ 1.340	NONE	NONE	45/45
455/175	5.125-5.155	1.995-2.005	.3720-.3730	.0015-.0035	65-79 @ 1.890	167-187 @ 1.450	NONE	NONE	45/45
455/190	5.125-5.155	1.995-2.005	.3720-.3730	.0015-.0035	65-79 @ 1.890	167-187 @ 1.450	NONE	NONE	45/45
455/210	5.125-5.155	1.995-2.005	.3720-.3730	.0015-.0035	65-79 @ 1.890	167-187 @ 1.450	NONE	NONE	45/45
455/230	5.125-5.155	1.995-2.005	.3720-.3730	.0015-.0035	65-79 @ 1.890	167-187 @ 1.450	NONE	NONE	45/45
455/245	5.125-5.155	1.995-2.005	.3720-.3730	.0015-.0035	65-79 @ 1.890	167-187 @ 1.450	NONE	NONE	45/45
CADILLAC DIVISION									
472/205	4.985	2.000	.3413-.3420	.0010-.0027	60-65 @ 1.946	156-166 @ 1.489	NONE	NONE	45/44
500/210	4.985	2.000	.3413-.3420	.0010-.0027	60-65 @ 1.946	156-166 @ 1.489	NONE	NONE	45/44
CHEVROLET DIVISION									
122/130	4.942-4.953	1.398-1.408	.2788-.2795	.0010-.0027	41-49 @ 1.30	104-116 @ .92	26-34 @ 1.25	78-81 @ .875	46/45
140/75	4.590-4.610	1.615-1.625	.3410-.3417	.0010-.0027	71-79 @ 1.746	183-197 @ 1.310	DAMPER	DAMPER	46/45
140/85	4.590-4.610	1.615-1.625	.3410-.3417	.0010-.0027	71-79 @ 1.746	183-197 @ 1.310	DAMPER	DAMPER	46/45
250/100	4.902-4.922	1.715-1.725	.3410-.3417	.0010-.0027	55-64 @ 1.66	180-192 @ 1.27	NONE	NONE	46/45
350/145	4.870-4.889	1.935-1.945	.3410-.3417	.0010-.0027	76-84 @ 1.70	194-206 @ 1.25	DAMPER	DAMPER	46/45
350/160	4.870-4.889	1.935-1.945	.3410-.3417	.0010-.0027	76-84 @ 1.70	194-206 @ 1.25	DAMPER	DAMPER	46/45
350/185	4.870-4.889	1.935-1.945	.3410-.3417	.0010-.0027	76-84 @ 1.70	194-206 @ 1.25	DAMPER	DAMPER	46/45
350/195	4.870-4.889	1.935-1.945	.3410-.3417	.0010-.0027	76-84 @ 1.70	194-206 @ 1.25	DAMPER	DAMPER	46/45
350/245	4.870-4.889	2.017-2.023	.3410-.3417	.0010-.0027	76-84 @ 1.70	194-206 @ 1.25	DAMPER	DAMPER	46/45
350/250	4.870-4.889	2.017-2.023	.3410-.3417	.0010-.0027	76-84 @ 1.70	194-206 @ 1.25	DAMPER	DAMPER	46/45
400/150	4.870-4.889	1.935-1.945	.3410-.3417	.0010-.0027	76-84 @ 1.70	194-206 @ 1.25	DAMPER	DAMPER	46/45
400/180	4.870-4.889	1.935-1.945	.3410-.3417	.0010-.0027	76-84 @ 1.70	194-206 @ 1.25	DAMPER	DAMPER	46/45
454/235	5.215-5.235	2.060-2.070	.3715-.3722	.0010-.0027	74-86 @ 1.88	288-312 @ 1.38	DAMPER	DAMPER	46/45
454/270	5.215-5.235	2.060-2.070	.3715-.3722	.0010-.0027	74-86 @ 1.88	288-312 @ 1.38	DAMPER	DAMPER	46/45

ENGINE SPECIFICATIONS

GENERAL MOTORS INTAKE VALVES & SPRINGS

DISPLACEMENT/ HORSEPOWER	INTAKE OVERALL LENGTH	INTAKE HEAD DIAMETER	INTAKE STEM DIAMETER	INTAKE STEM TO GUIDE CLEARANCE	INTAKE OUTER SPRING PRESSURE & LENGTH CLOSED (LB. @ IN.)	OPEN (LB. @ IN.)	INTAKE INNER SPRING PRESSURE & LENGTH CLOSED (LB. @ IN.)	OPEN (LB. @ IN.)	ANGLE OF SEAT/FACE (Deg.)
OLDSMOBILE DIVISION									
250/100	4.902-4.922	1.715-1.725	.3410-.3417	.0010-.0027	56-64 @ 1.66	180-192 @ 1.27	NONE	NONE	46/45
350/180	4.667	1.870-1.880	.3425-.3432	.0010-.0027	76-84 @ 1.670	180-194 @ 1.270	NONE	NONE	45/46
350/200	4.667	1.870-1.880	.3425-.3432	.0010-.0027	76-84 @ 1.670	180-194 @ 1.270	NONE	NONE	45/46
455/210	4.667	1.870-1.880	.3425-.3432	.0010-.0027	76-84 @ 1.670	180-194 @ 1.270	NONE	NONE	45/46
455/230	4.667	1.870-1.880	.3425-.3432	.0010-.0027	76-84 @ 1.670	180-194 @ 1.270	NONE	NONE	45/46
455-275	4.703	2.067-2.077	.3425-.3432	.0010-.0027	76-84 @ 1.670	180-190 @ 1.270	DAMPER	DAMPER	60/60
PONTIAC DIVISION									
250/100	4.902-4.922	1.715-1.725	.3410-.3417	.0010-.0027	56-64 @ 1.66	180-192 @ 1.27	NONE	NONE	46/45
350/155	4.864	1.957-1.963	.3412-.3419	.0016-.0033	54-68 @ 1.586	125-139 @ 1.179	28-38 @ 1.550	93-103 @ 1.139	45/44
350/170	4.864	1.957-1.963	.3412-.3419	.0016-.0033	54-68 @ 1.586	125-139 @ 1.179	28-38 @ 1.550	93-103 @ 1.139	45/44
350/200	4.864	1.957-1.963	.3412-.3419	.0016-.0033	54-68 @ 1.586	125-139 @ 1.179	28-38 @ 1.550	93-103 @ 1.139	45/44
400/175	4.864	1.957-1.963	.3412-.3419	.0016-.0033	54-68 @ 1.590	119-133 @ 1.213	28-38 @ 1.550	88-98 @ 1.173	45/44
400/190	4.864	1.957-1.963	.3412-.3419	.0016-.0033	54-68 @ 1.590	119-133 @ 1.213	28-38 @ 1.550	88-98 @ 1.173	45/44
400/200	4.864	2.107-2.113	.3412-.3419	.0016-.0033	58-72 @ 1.568	129-143 @ 1.158	32-42 @ 1.528	96-106 @ 1.118	30/29
400/225	4.864	2.107-2.113	.3412-.3419	.0016-.0033	58-72 @ 1.568	129-143 @ 1.158	32-42 @ 1.528	96-106 @ 1.118	30/29
455/215	4.785	2.107-2.113	.3412-.3419	.0016-.0033	58-72 @ 1.569	129-143 @ 1.159	32-42 @ 1.529	96-106 @ 1.119	30/29
455/250	4.785	2.107-2.113	.3412-.3419	.0016-.0033	58-72 @ 1.569	129-143 @ 1.159	32-42 @ 1.529	96-106 @ 1.119	30/29
455/290 SD	4.985	2.107-2.113	.3412-.3419	.0016-.0033	66-74 @ 1.82	168-181 @ 1.41	37-43 @ 1.75	79-88 @ 1.34	45/44

1975

DISPLACEMENT/ HORSEPOWER	INTAKE OVERALL LENGTH	INTAKE HEAD DIAMETER	INTAKE STEM DIAMETER	INTAKE STEM TO GUIDE CLEARANCE	CLOSED (LB. @ IN.)	OPEN (LB. @ IN.)	CLOSED (LB. @ IN.)	OPEN (LB. @ IN.)	ANGLE OF SEAT/FACE (Deg.)
BUICK DIVISION									
231/110	4.660-4.690	1.625	.3402-.3412	.0015-.0035	64 @ 1.727	164 @ 1.340	NONE	NONE	45/45
250/105	4.902-4.922	1.715-1.725	.3410-.3417	.0010-.0027	54-60 @ 1.660	180-192 @ 1.270	NONE	NONE	46/45
260/110	4.912	1.715-1.725	.3410-.3417	.0010-.0027	50-64 @ 1.660	180-192 @ 1.270	NONE	NONE	46/45
350/145	4.994-5.024	1.870-1.880	.3720-.3730	.0015-.0035	75 @ 1.727	72 @ 1.890	NONE	NONE	45/45
350/165	4.994-5.024	1.870-1.880	.3720-.3730	.0015-.0035	75 @ 1.727	72 @ 1.890	NONE	NONE	45/45
455/205	5.125-5.155	1.995-2.005	.3720-.3730	.0015-.0035	180 @ 1.340	177 @ 1.450	NONE	NONE	45/45
CADILLAC DIVISION									
500/190	4.985	2.000	.3413-.3420	.0010-.0027	60-65 @ 1.946	156-166 @ 1.489	NONE	NONE	45/44
CHEVROLET DIVISION									
140/78	4.590-4.610	1.615-1.625	.3410-.3417	.0010-.0027	71-79 @ 1.746	183-197 @ 1.310	DAMPER	DAMPER	46/45
140/87	4.590-4.610	1.615-1.625	.3410-.3417	.0010-.0027	71-79 @ 1.746	183-197 @ 1.310	DAMPER	DAMPER	46/45
122/110	4.938-4.958	1.3975-1.4075	.2788-.2795	.0010-.0027	41-49 @ 1.300	104-116 @ 0.920	26-34 @ 1.25	78.5-80 @ .875	46/45
250/105	4.902-4.922	1.715-1.725	.3410-.3417	.0010-.0027	50-64 @ 1.660	180-192 @ 1.270	NONE	NONE	46/45
262/110	4.902-4.922	1.715-1.725	.3410-.3417	.0010-.0027	76-84 @ 1.70	194-206 @ 1.25	DAMPER	DAMPER	46/45
350/145	4.870-4.889	1.935-1.945	.3410-.3417	.0010-.0027	76-84 @ 1.70	194-206 @ 1.25	DAMPER	DAMPER	46/45
350/155	4.870-4.889	1.935-1.945	.3410-.3417	.0010-.0027	76-84 @ 1.70	194-206 @ 1.25	DAMPER	DAMPER	46/45
400/175	4.870-4.889	1.935-1.945	.3410-.3417	.0010-.0027	76-84 @ 1.70	194-206 @ 1.25	DAMPER	DAMPER	46/45
454/215					84-96 @ 1.80	210-230 @ 1.40	DAMPER	DAMPER	46/45
OLDSMOBILE DIVISION									
231/110	4.660-4.690	1.625	.3402-.3412	.0015-.0035	64 @ 1.727	64 @ 1.340	NONE	NONE	45/45
250/105	4.902-4.922	1.715-1.725	.3410-.3417	.0010-.0027	56-64 @ 1.660	180-192 @ 1.270	NONE	NONE	46/45
260/110	4.667	1.522	.3425-.3432	.0010-.0027	76-84 @ 1.670	180-194 @ 1.270	NONE	NONE	45/46
350/165	4.994-5.024	1.87-1.88	.3720-.3730	.0015-.0035	75 @ 1.727	180 @ 1.340	NONE	NONE	45/45
350/170	4.667	1.80-1.88	.3425-.3432	.0010-.0027	76-84 @ 1.670	180-194 @ 1.270	NONE	NONE	45/46
400/175	4.8645	2.107-2.113	.3412-.3419	.0016-.0033	N/A	N/A	NONE	NONE	30/29
455/190	4.703	1.90-2.00	.3425-.3432	.0010-.0027	76-84 @ 1.670	180-190 @ 1.270	NONE	NONE	45/46
PONTIAC DIVISION									
250/105	4.902-4.922	1.715-1.725	.3410-.3417	.0010-.0027	50-64 @ 1.66	180-192 @ 1.27	NONE	NONE	46/45
260/110	4.912	1.715-1.725	.3410-.3417	.0010-.0027	50-64 @ 1.66	180-192 @ 1.27	NONE	NONE	46/45
350/145	4.667	1.517-1.527	.3425-.3432	.0010-.0027	76-84 @ 1.67	180-194 @ 1.27	NONE	NONE	45/46
350/155	4.8645	2.107-2.113	.3412-.3419	.0016-.0033	59.6-73.6 @ 1.56	124.7-138.7 @ 1.18	33.3-43.3 @ 1.52	95.5-102.5 @ 1.14	30/29
350/165	5.009	1.870-1.880	.3720-.3730	.0015-.0035	70-80 @ 1.727	173-187 @ 1.34	NONE	NONE	45/45
350/175	4.8645	2.107-2.113	.3412-.3419	.0016-.0033	59.6-73.6 @ 1.56	124.7-138.7 @ 1.18	33.3-43.3 @ 1.52	95.5-102.5 @ 1.14	30/29
400/170	4.8645	2.107-2.113	.3412-.3419	.0016-.0033	63-77 @ 1.54	128-142 @ 1.16	36.4-46.4 @ 1.50	95.7-105.7 @ 1.12	30/29
400/185	4.8645	2.107-2.113	.3412-.3419	.0016-.0033	63-77 @ 1.54	128.1-142.1 @ 1.13	36.4-46.4 @ 1.50	95.7-105.7 @ 1.09	30/29
455/200	4.7155	2.107-2.113	.3412-.3419	.0016-.0033	58-72 @ 1.57	128.8-142.8 @ 1.16	31.4-41.4 @ 1.53	96-106 @ 1.12	30/29

1976

DISPLACEMENT/ HORSEPOWER	INTAKE OVERALL LENGTH	INTAKE HEAD DIAMETER	INTAKE STEM DIAMETER	INTAKE STEM TO GUIDE CLEARANCE	CLOSED (LB. @ IN.)	OPEN (LB. @ IN.)	CLOSED (LB. @ IN.)	OPEN (LB. @ IN.)	ANGLE OF SEAT/FACE (Deg.)
BUICK DIVISION									
231/105	4.66-.469	1.625	.3402-.3412	.0015-.0032	64 @ 1.727	164 @ 1.340	NONE	NONE	45/45
260/110	4.912	1.715-1.725	.3410-.3417	.0010-.0027	50-64 @ 1.66	180-192 @ 1.27	NONE	NONE	46/45
350/145	4.994-5.024	1.87-1.88	.3720-.3730	.0015-.0035	75 @ 1.727	180 @ 1.340	NONE	NONE	45/45
350/165	4.994-5.024	1.87-1.88	.3720-.3730	.0015-.0035	75 @ 1.727	180 @ 1.340	NONE	NONE	45/45
455/206	5.125-5.155	1.995-2.005	.3720-.3730	.0015-.0035	72 @ 1.890	177 @ 1.450	NONE	NONE	45/45
CADILLAC DIVISION									
350/170	4.994-5.024	1.87-1.88	.3720-.3730	.0015-.0035	25 @ 1.727	180 @ 1.340	NONE	NONE	45/45
500/190	4.985	2.000	.3413-.3420	.0010-.0027	60-65 @ 1.946	156-166 @ 1.489	NONE	NONE	45/44
500/215	4.985	2.000	.3413-.3420	.0010-.0027	60-65 @ 1.946	156-166 @ 1.489	NONE	NONE	45/44
CHEVROLET DIVISION									
85/52	3.8679-3.8880	1.5303-1.5405	.3138-.3144	.0018-.0021	64-72 @ 1.26	167-179 @ .886	NONE	NONE	46/45
97.6/60	3.8679-3.8880	1.5303-1.5405	.3138-.3144	.0018-.0021	64-72 @ 1.26	167-179 @ .886	NONE	NONE	46/45
122/110	4.938-4.958	1.3975-1.4075	.2788-.2795	.0010-.0027	41-49 @ 1.30	104-116 @ .92	26-34 @ 1.25	78.5-80 @ .875	46/45
140/70	4.590-4.610	1.615-1.625	.3410-.3417	.0010-.0027	71-79 @ 1.746	183-197 @ 1.310	DAMPER	DAMPER	46/45
140/84	4.590-4.610	1.615-1.625	.3410-.3417	.0010-.0027	71-79 @ 1.746	183-197 @ 1.310	DAMPER	DAMPER	46/45
250/105	4.902-4.922	1.715-1.725	.3410-.3417	.0010-.0027	76-86 @ 1.66	170-180 @ 1.26	NONE	NONE	46/45
262/110	4.928-4.953	1.715-1.725	.3410-.3417	.0010-.0027	76-84 @ 1.70	194-206 @ 1.25	DAMPER	DAMPER	46/45
305/140	4.928-4.953	1.715-1.725	.3410-.3417	.0010-.0027	76-84 @ 1.70	194-206 @ 1.25	DAMPER	DAMPER	46/45
350/145	4.928-4.953	1.715-1.725	.3410-.3417	.0010-.0027	76-84 @ 1.70	194-206 @ 1.25	DAMPER	DAMPER	46/45
350/165	4.870-4.889	1.935-1.945	.3410-.3417	.0010-.0027	76-84 @ 1.70	194-206 @ 1.25	DAMPER	DAMPER	46/45
400/175	4.870-4.889	1.935-1.945	.3410-.3417	.0010-.0027	76-84 @ 1.70	194-206 @ 1.25	DAMPER	DAMPER	46/45
454/225	5.215-5.235	2.060-2.070	.3715-.3722	.0010-.0027	84-96 @ 1.80	210-230 @ 1.40	DAMPER	DAMPER	46/45
OLDSMOBILE DIVISION									
140/78	4.59-4.61	1.615-1.625	.3410-.3417	.0010-.0027	71-79 @ 1.746	183-197 @ 1.310	NONE	NONE	46/45
140/87	4.59-4.61	1.615-1.625	.3410-.3417	.0010-.0027	71-79 @ 1.746	183-197 @ 1.310	NONE	NONE	46/45
231/105	4.66-4.69	1.625	.3402-.3412	.0015-.0035	64 @ 1.727	164 @ 1.340	NONE	NONE	45/45
250/105	4.902-4.922	1.715-1.725	.3410-.3417	.0010-.0027	56-64 @ 1.660	180-192 @ 1.270	NONE	NONE	46/45
260/110	4.667	1.522	.3425-.3432	.0010-.0027	76-84 @ 1.670	180-194 @ 1.270	NONE	NONE	45/46

GENERAL MOTORS INTAKE VALVES & SPRINGS

DISPLACEMENT/ HORSEPOWER	INTAKE OVERALL LENGTH	INTAKE HEAD DIAMETER	INTAKE STEM DIAMETER	INTAKE STEM TO GUIDE CLEARANCE	INTAKE OUTER SPRING PRESSURE & LENGTH CLOSED (LB. @ IN.)	OPEN (LB. @ IN.)	INTAKE INNER SPRING PRESSURE & LENGTH CLOSED (LB. @ IN.)	OPEN (LB. @ IN.)	ANGLE OF SEAT/FACE (Deg.)
350/140	4.994-5.024	1.870-1.880	.3720-.3730	.0015-.0035	75 @ 1.727	180 @ 1.340	NONE	NONE	45/45
350/155	4.994-5.024	1.870-1.880	.3720-.3730	.0015-.0035	75 @ 1.727	180 @ 1.340	NONE	NONE	45/45
350/170	4.667	1.870-1.880	.3425-.3432	.0010-.0027	76-84 @ 1.670	180-194 @ 1.270	NONE	NONE	45/46
455/190	4.703	1.990-2.000	.3425-.3432	.0010-.0027	76-84 @ 1.670	180-194 @ 1.270	NONE	NONE	45/45
PONTIAC DIVISION									
140/70	4.59-4.61	1.615-1.625	.3410-.3417	.0010-.0027	71-79 @ 1.746	183-197 @ 1.310	NONE	NONE	46/45
140/84	4.59-4.61	1.615-1.625	.3410-.3417	.0010-.0027	71-79 @ 1.746	183-197 @ 1.310	NONE	NONE	46/45
231/105	4.66-4.69	1.625	.3402-.3412	.0015-.0035	59-69 @ 1.727	158-170 @ 1.340	NONE	NONE	45/45
250/105	4.912	1.715-1.725	.3410-.3417	.0010-.0027	78-86 @ 1.66	170-180 @ 1.26	NONE	NONE	46/45
260/110	4.667	1.517-1.527	.3425-.3432	.0010-.0027	76-84 @ 1.67	180-194 @ 1.27	NONE	NONE	46/45
350/140	5.009	1.870-1.880	.3720-.3730	.0015-.0035	70-80 @ 1.727	173-187 @ 1.340	NONE	NONE	45/45
350/155	5.009	1.870-1.880	.3720-.3730	.0015-.0035	70-80 @ 1.727	173-187 @ 1.340	NONE	NONE	45/45
350/160	4.8645	2.107-2.113	.3412-.3419	.0016-.0033	59.6-73.6 @ 1.56	124.7-138.7 @ 1.18	33.3-43.3 @ 1.52	95.5-105.5 @ 1.14	30/29
350/165	4.8645	2.107-2.113	.3412-.3419	.0016-.0033	59.6-73.6 @ 1.56	124.7-138.7 @ 1.18	33.3-43.3 @ 1.52	95.5-105.5 @ 1.14	30/29
400/170	4.8645	2.107-2.113	.3412-.3419	.0016-.0033	63-77 @ 1.54	128.1-142.1 @ 1.16	36.4-46.4 @ 1.50	95.7-105.7 @ 1.12	30/29
400/185	4.8645	2.107-2.113	.3412-.3419	.0016-.0033	63-77 @ 1.54	128.1-142.1 @ 1.16	36.4-46.4 @ 1.50	95.7-105.7 @ 1.09	30/29
455/200	4.7155	2.107-2.113	.3412-.3419	.0016-.0033	58-72 @ 1.57	128.8-142.8 @ 1.16	31.4-41.4 @ 1.53	96-106 @ 1.12	30/29
1977									
BUICK DIVISION									
231/105	4.660-4.690	1.625	.3402-.3412	.0015-.0035	64@1.727	164@1.340	NONE	NONE	45/45
301/135	5.0785	1.720	.3425-.3418	.0010-.0027	78-86@1.66	162-170@1.296	NONE	NONE	46/45
350/ALL	5.024-4.994	1.880-1.870	.3720-.3730	.0015-.0035	75@1.727	180@1.340	NONE	NONE	45/45
403/185	4.667	1.880-1.850	.3432-.3425	.0010-.0027	76-84@1.670	180-194@1.270	NONE	NONE	45/46
CADILLAC DIVISION									
350/180	4.667	1.880-1.870	.3432-.3425	.0010-.0027	76-74@1.670	180-194@1.270	NONE	NONE	45/44
425/180-195	4.985	2.000	.3420-.3413	.0010-.0027	60-65@1.946	156-166@1.489	NONE	NONE	45/44
CHEVROLET DIVISION									
85/57	3.8679-3.8880	1.5303-1.5405	.3138-.3144	.0018-.0021	64-72@1.26	167-179@.886	NONE	NONE	46/45
97.6/63	3.8679-3.8880	1.5303-1.5405	.3138-.3144	.0018-.0021	64-72@1.26	167-179@.886	NONE	NONE	46/45
140/84	4.590-4.610	1.615-1.625	.3410-.3417	.0010-.0027	71-79@1.746	183-197@1.310	NONE	NONE	46/45
250/110	4.902-4.922	1.715-1.725	.3410-.3417	.0010-.0027	78-86@1.66	170-180@1.26	NONE	NONE	46/45
305/145	4.902-4.922	1.715-1.725	.3410-.3417	.0010-.0027	76-84@1.70	194-206@1.25	DAMPER	DAMPER	46/45
350/160-170-180	4.870-4.889	1.935-1.945	.3410-.3417	.0010-.0027	76-84@1.70	194-206@1.25	DAMPER	DAMPER	46/45½
350/210	4.870-4.889	2.017-2.023	.3410-.3417	.0010-.0027	76-84@1.70	194-206@1.25	DAMPER	DAMPER	45/45
OLDSMOBILE DIVISION									
140/84	4.590-4.610	1.615-1.625	.3410-.3417	.0010-.0027	71-79@1.746	183-197@1.310	DAMPER	DAMPER	45/45
231/105	4.660-4.690	1.625	.3402-.3412	.0015-.0035	64@1.727	164@1.340	NONE	NONE	45/45
260/110	4.667	1.522	.3432-.3425	–	76-84@1.670	180-194@1.270	NONE	NONE	45/46
305/145	4.902-4.922	1.715-1.725	.3410-.3417	.0010-.0027	76-84@1.70	194-206@1.25	DAMPER	DAMPER	46/45
350/170 (Calif.)	4.870-4.889	1.935-1.945	.3410-.3417	.0010-.0027	76-84@1.70	194-206@1.25	DAMPER	DAMPER	45/45
350/170 (Federal)	4.667	1.880-1.85	.3432-.3425	.0010-.0027	76-84@1.670	180-194@1.270	NONE	NONE	45/46
403/200	4.667	1.880-1.85	.3432-.3425	.0010-.0027	76-84@1.670	180-194@1.270	NONE	NONE	45/46
PONTIAC DIVISION									
140/84	4.590-4.610	1.615-1.625	.3410-.3417	.0010-.0027	71-79@1.746	183-197@1.310	NONE	NONE	46/45
151/88	4.924	1.720	.3425-.3418	.0010-.0027	78-86@1.66	172-180@1.254	NONE	NONE	46/45
231/105	4.660-4.690	1.625	.3402-.3412	.0015-.0035	64@1.727	164@1.340	NONE	NONE	45/45
301/135 (Manual)	5.0785	1.720	.3425-.3418	.0010-.0027	78-86@1.66	165-173@1.283	NONE	NONE	46/45
301/135 (Auto.)	5.0785	1.720	.3425-.3418	.0010-.0027	78-86@1.66	162-170@1.296	NONE	NONE	46/45
305/145	4.902-4.922	1.715-1.725	.3410-.3417	.0010-.0027	76-84@1.70	194-206@1.25	DAMPER	DAMPER	46/45
350/170 (Calif.)	4.870-4.889	1.935-1.945	.3410-.3417	.0010-.0027	76-84@1.70	194-206@1.25	DAMPER	DAMPER	45/45
350/170 (Federal)	4.667	1.880-1.850	.3432-.3425	.0010-.0027	76-84@1.670	180-194@1.270	NONE	NONE	45/46
400/180	4.8645	2.113-2.107	.3419-.3412	.0016-.0033	68@1.549	131@1.185	40@1.509	97@1.145	30/29
403/185	4.667	1.880-1.850	.3432-.3425	.0010-.0027	76-84@1.670	180-194@1.270	NONE	NONE	45/46
1978									
BUICK DIVISION									
196/ALL	4.660-4.690	1.625	.3402-.3412	.0015-.0035	59-69@1.727	159-169@1.340	NONE	NONE	45/45
231/105	4.660-4.690	1.625	.3402-.3412	.0015-.0035	59-69@1.727	159-169@1.340	NONE	NONE	45/45
231/TURBO	4.660-4.690	1.625	.3402-.3412	.0015-.0035	59-69@1.727	159-169@1.340	NONE	NONE	45/45
301/140	5.0785	1.720	.3418-.3425	.0010-.0027	78-86@1.660	162-170@1.296	NONE	NONE	46/45
305/ALL	4.902-4.922	19	.3410-.3417	.0010-.0027	76-84@1.700	174-186@1.250	DAMPER	DAMPER	46/45
350/155	4.994-5.042	21	.3720-.3730	.0015-.0035	70-80@1.727	170-180@1.270	NONE	NONE	45/45
350/160	4.870-4.889	23	.3410-.3417	.0010-.0027	76-84@1.700	194-206@1.250	DAMPER	DAMPER	46/45
350/170	4.667	22	.3425-.3432	.0010-.0027	76-84@1.670	180-194@1.270	NONE	NONE	45/46
403/185	5.0185	21	.3425-.3432	.0010-.0027	77-83@1.670	145-159@1.295	NONE	NONE	45/46
CADILLAC DIVISION									
350/170	4.667	21	.3425-.3432	.0010-.0027	74-76@1.670	180-194@1.270	NONE	NONE	45/44
425/180	4.985	2.000	.3413-.3420	.0010-.0027	60-65@1.946	156-166@1.489	NONE	NONE	45/44
CHEVROLET DIVISION									
98/63	3.8679-3.880	17	.3138-.3144	.0018-.0021	64-72@1.260	167-179@.886	NONE	NONE	46/45
98/68	3.8679-3.880	17	.3138-.3144	.0018-.0021	64-72@1.260	167-179@.886	NONE	NONE	46/45
151/85	4.924	1.720	.3418-.3425	.0010-.0027	78-86@1.660	172-180@1.254	NONE	NONE	46/45
196/90	4.660-4.690	1.625	.3402-.3412	.0015-.0035	59-69@1.727	159-169@1.340	NONE	NONE	45/45
200/95	4.9229-4.9469	18	.3410-.3417	.0010-.0027	76-84@1.700	194-206@1.250	SPRING DAMPER	SPRING DAMPER	46/45
231/105	4.660-4.690	1.625	.3402-.3412	.0015-.0035	59-69@1.727	159-169@1.340	NONE	NONE	45/45
250/110	4.902-4.922	19	.3410-.3417	.0010-.0027	78-86@1.660	170-180@1.260	NONE	NONE	46/45
305/145	4.902-4.922	19	.3410-.3417	.0010-.0027	76-84@1.700	194-206@1.250	SPRING DAMPER	SPRING DAMPER	46/45
350/160	4.870-4.889	23	.3410-.3417	.0010-.0027	76-84@1.700	194-206@1.250	SPRING DAMPER	SPRING DAMPER	46/45
350/185	4.870-4.889	23	.3410-.3417	.0010-.0027	76-84@1.700	180-188@1.250	SPRING DAMPER	SPRING DAMPER	46/45
350/220	4.870-4.889	24	.3410-.3417	.0010-.0027	76-84@1.700	196-204@1.250	SPRING DAMPER	SPRING DAMPER	46/45
OLDSMOBILE DIVISION									
151/85	4.924	1.720	.3418-.3425	.0010-.0027	78-86@1.660	172-180@1.254	NONE	NONE	46/45
231/105	4.660-4.690	1.625	.3402-.3412	.0015-.0035	59-69@1.727	159-169@1.340	NONE	NONE	45/45
260/110	4.667	1.522	.3425-.3432	–	76-84@1.670	180-194@1.270	NONE	NONE	45/46
305/145	4.902-4.922	19	.3410-.3417	.0010-.0027	76-84@1.700	174-186@1.250	DAMPER	DAMPER	46/45
350/160	4.870-4.889	23	.3410-.3417	.0010-.0027	76-84@1.700	194-206@1.250	DAMPER	DAMPER	46/45
350/170	4.667	22	.3425-.3432	.0010-.0027	76-84@1.670	180-194@1.270	NONE	NONE	45/46
350/DIESEL	5.0185	21	.3425-.3432	.0010-.0027	77-83@1.670	145-159@1.295	NONE	NONE	45/46
403/190	5.0185	21	.3425-.3432	.0010-.0027	77-83@1.670	145-159@1.295	NONE	NONE	45/46
PONTIAC DIVISION									
151/ALL	4.924	1.720	.3418-.3425	.0010-.0027	78-86@1.660	172-180@1.254	NONE	NONE	46/45
231/105	4.660-4.690	1.625	.3402-.3412	.0015-.0035	59-69@1.727	159-169@1.340	NONE	NONE	45/45
301/140	5.0785	1.720	.3418-.3425	.0010-.0027	78-86@1.660	162-170@1.296	NONE	NONE	46/45
305/145	4.902-4.922	19	.3410-.3417	.0010-.0027	76-84@1.700	174-186@1.250	DAMPER	DAMPER	46/45
350/155	4.994-5.042	21	.3720-.3730	.0015-.0035	70-80@1.727	170-180@1.270	NONE	NONE	45/45
350/160	4.870-4.889	23	.3410-.3417	.0010-.0027	76-84@1.700	174-186@1.250	DAMPER	DAMPER	46/45
350/170	4.870-4.889	23	.3410-.3417	.0010-.0027	76-84@1.700	174-186@1.250	DAMPER	DAMPER	46/45

ENGINE SPECIFICATIONS

GENERAL MOTORS INTAKE VALVES & SPRINGS

DISPLACEMENT/ HORSEPOWER	INTAKE OVERALL length	INTAKE HEAD DIAMETER	INTAKE STEM DIAMETER	INTAKE STEM TO GUIDE CLEARANCE	INTAKE OUTER SPRING PRESSURE & LENGTH CLOSED (Lb. @ In.)	OPEN (Lb. @ In.)	INTAKE INNER SPRING PRESSURE & LENGTH CLOSED (Lb. @ In.)	OPEN (Lb. @ In.)	ANGLE OF SEAT/FACE (Deg.)
400/ALL	4.8645	24	.3412-.3419	.0016-.0033	63-73@1.549	126-136@1.185	35-45@1.509	92-102@1.145	30/29
403/185	4.667	20	.3425-.3432	.0010-.0027	76-84@1.670	180-194@1.270	NONE	NONE	45/46

1979

DISPLACEMENT/ HORSEPOWER	INTAKE OVERALL length	INTAKE HEAD DIAMETER	INTAKE STEM DIAMETER	INTAKE STEM TO GUIDE CLEARANCE	CLOSED (Lb. @ In.)	OPEN (Lb. @ In.)	CLOSED (Lb. @ In.)	OPEN (Lb. @ In.)	ANGLE OF SEAT/FACE (Deg.)
BUICK DIVISION									
196/ALL	4.660-4.690	1.705-1.715	.3401-.3412	.0015-.0035	59-69@1.727	159-169@1.340	NONE	NONE	45/45
231/ALL	4.660-4.690	1.705-1.715	.3401-.3412	.0015-.0035	59-69@1.727	159-169@1.340	NONE	NONE	45/45
301/ALL	5.070	1.720	.3400	.0017-.0027	78-86@1.660	170@1.260	NONE	NONE	46/45
305/ALL	4.902-4.922	19	.3410-.3417	.0017-.0037	76-84@1.700	194-206@1.250	DAMPER	DAMPER	45/46
350/160	4.994-5.024	21	.3723-.3730	.0015-.0035	70-8@1.727	173-187@1.340	NONE	NONE	45/45
350/195	4.870-4.889	23	.3410-.3417	.0017-.0037	76-84@1.700	194-206@1.250	DAMPER	DAMPER	45/46
350/225	4.667	1.870-1.880	.3425-.3432	.0017-.0027	76-84@1.727	180-194@1.270	NONE	NONE	45/44
403/ALL	4.667	1.990-2.000	.3425-.3432	.0017-.0027	76-84@1.727	145-159@1.295	NONE	NONE	45/44
CADILLAC DIVISION									
350/R	4.667	1.870-1.880	.3425-.3432	.0010-.0027	76-84@1.670	180-194@1.270	NONE	NONE	45/44
350/DIESEL	5.120	1.875	.3425-.3432	.0010-.0027	77-83@1.670	144-158@1.300	NONE	NONE	45/44
425/ALL	4.985	2.000	.3413-.3420	.0010-.0027	60-65@1.946	156-166@1.489	NONE	NONE	45/44
CHEVROLET DIVISION									
98/70	3.8679-3.880	1.5305-1.5405	.3138-.3144	.0018-.0021	64-72@1.260	167-179@.8860	NONE	NONE	46/45
98/74	3.8679-3.880	1.5305-1.5405	.3138-.3144	.0018-.0021	64-72@1.260	167-179@.8860	NONE	NONE	46/45
151/ALL	4.557	1.72	.3418-.3425	.0010-.0027	78-86@1.660	172-180@1.250	NONE	NONE	46/45
196/105	4.698-4.728	1.71	.3402-.3412	.0015-.0035	59-69@1.7270	174-190@1.340	DAMPER	DAMPER	45/45
200/94	4.9229-4.9469	1.595-1.605	.3410-.3417	.0010-.0027	76-84@1.700	174-186@1.250	DAMPER	DAMPER	46/45
231/115	4.698-4.728	1.71	.3402-.3412	.0015-.0035	59-69@1.727	174-190@1.340	DAMPER	DAMPER	45/45
250/115	4.902-4.922	1.715-1.725	.3410-.3417	.0010-.0027	78-86@1.660	170-180@1.260	NONE	NONE	46/45
267/130	4.902-4.922	1.715-1.725	.3410-.3417	.0010-.0027	76-84@1.700	174-184@1.250	DAMPER	DAMPER	46/45
305/130	4.902-4.922	1.715-1.725	.3410-.3417	.0010-.0027	76-84@1.700	174-186@1.250	DAMPER	DAMPER	46/45
350/160-195	4.870-4.889	1.935-1.945	.3410-.3417	.0010-.0027	76-84@1.700	180-188@1.250	DAMPER	DAMPER	46/45
350/225	4.870-4.889	2.017-2.023	.3410-.3417	.0010-.0027	76-84@1.700	196-204@1.250	DAMPER	DAMPER	46/45
OLDSMOBILE DIVISION									
151/ALL	4.920	1.720	.3400	.0010-.0027	78-86@1.660	172-180@1.254	NONE	NONE	46/45
231/ALL	4.660-4.690	1.705-1.715	.3402-.3412	.0015-.0035	59-69@1.727	162-174@1.340	NONE	NONE	45/45
260/ALL	4.667	1.517-1.527	.3425-.3432	.0010-.0027	76-84@1.670	180-194@1.270	NONE	NONE	45/44
260/DIESEL	5.029	1.522	.3425-.3432	.0010-.0027	77-83@1.670	144-158@1.300	NONE	NONE	45/44
305/ALL	4.902-4.922	19	.3410-.3417	.0010-.0037	76-84@1.700	194-206@1.250	DAMPER	DAMPER	46/45
350/R	4.667	1.870-1.880	.3425-.3432	.0010-.0027	76-84@1.670	180-194@1.270	NONE	NONE	45/44
350/L	4.870-4.880	23	.3410-.3417	.0010-.0037	76-84@1.700	194-206@1.250	DAMPER	DAMPER	46/45
350/DIESEL	5.120	1.875	.3425-.3432	.0010-.0027	77-83@1.670	144-158@1.300	NONE	NONE	45/44
403/ALL	4.667	1.990-2.000	.3425-.3432	.0010-.0027	76-84@1.670	180-194@1.270	NONE	NONE	45/44
PONTIAC DIVISION									
15/ALL	4.920	1.720	.3418-.3425	.0010-.0027	78-86@1.660	172-180@1.254	NONE	NONE	46/45
231/ALL	4.660-4.690	1.705-1.715	.3402-.3412	.0015-.0035	59-69@1.727	162-174@1.340	NONE	NONE	45/45
301/ALL	5.070	1.720	.3400	.0017-.0027	78-86@1.660	170@1.260	NONE	NONE	46/45
305/ALL	4.902-4.922	19	.3410-.3417	.0010-.0037	76-84@1.700	194-206@1.250	DAMPER	DAMPER	46/45
350/R	4.994-5.042	21	.3720-.3730	.0015-.0035	70-80@1.727	170-180@1.270	NONE	NONE	45/45
350/X	4.870-4.889	23	.3410-.3417	.0010-.0027	76-84@1.700	174-186@1.250	DAMPER	DAMPER	46/45
350/L	4.870-4.889	23	.3410-.3417	.0010-.0027	76-84@1.700	194-206@1.250	DAMPER	DAMPER	46/45
400/ALL	4.8645	24	.3412-.3419	.0016-.0033	63-73@1.549	126-136@1.185	35-45 @ 1.509	92-102 @ 1.145	30/29
403/ALL	4.667	20	.3425-.3432	.0012-.0027	76-84@1.670	180-194@1.270	NONE	NONE	45/44

1 Used on manual transmission only. Automatic transmission uses 76-84 @ 1.670.
2 Used on manual transmission only. Automatic transmission uses 199-214 @ 1.198.
3 Used without air conditioning only. With AC uses 76-84 @ 1.670.
4 Used without air conditioning only. With AC uses 199-214 @ 1.198.
5 191-206 @ 1.230 in engines with manual transmission.
6 Damper installed in engines with manual transmission.
7 199-214 @ 1.198 in engines with manual transmissions.
8 Auto transmission only; manual transmission, 124-138 @ 1.188.
9 Auto transmission only; manual transmission, 53-67 @ 1.598.
10 Auto transmission only; manual transmission, 50-62 @ 1.528.
11 Auto transmission only; manual transmission, 116-128 @ 1.118.
12 Auto transmission only; manual transmission L65 engines use same valves as L78 engines.
13 191-206 @ 1.230 in engines with manual transmissons.
14 Damper installed in engines with manual transmissions.
15 199-214 @ 1.198 in engines with manual transmissions.
16 45 on 350/180 engine.

17 1.5303-1.5405
18 1.5950-1.6050
19 1.7150-1.7250
20 1.8500-1.8800
21 1.8700-1.8800
22 1.8800-1.8850
23 1.9350-1.9450
24 2.0170-2.0230

GENERAL MOTORS EXHAUST VALVES & SPRINGS

DISPLACEMENT / HORSEPOWER	EXHAUST OVERALL LENGTH	EXHAUST HEAD DIAMETER	EXHAUST STEM DIAMETER	EXHAUST STEM TO GUIDE CLEARANCE	EXHAUST OUTER SPRING PRESSURE LENGTH CLOSED (lb. @ in.)	OPEN (lb. @ in.)	EXHAUST INNER SPRING PRESSURE LENGTH CLOSED (lb. @ in.)	OPEN (lb. @ in.)	ANGLE OF SEAT/FACE (deg.)

1970

DISPLACEMENT / HORSEPOWER	EXHAUST OVERALL LENGTH	EXHAUST HEAD DIAMETER	EXHAUST STEM DIAMETER	EXHAUST STEM TO GUIDE CLEARANCE	CLOSED (lb. @ in.)	OPEN (lb. @ in.)	CLOSED (lb. @ in.)	OPEN (lb. @ in.)	ANGLE OF SEAT/FACE (deg.)
BUICK DIVISION									
250/155	4.913-4.933	1.495-1.505	.3410-.3417	.0010-.0027	56- 64 @ 1.66	180-192 @ 1.27	NONE	NONE	46/45
350/230	5.014-5.044	1.495-1.505	.3723-.37301	.0015-.00322	70- 80 @ 1.727	173-187 @ 1.340	NONE	NONE	45/45
350/285	5.014-5.044	1.495-1.505	.3723-.37301	.0015-.00322	70- 80 @ 1.727	173-187 @ 1.340	NONE	NONE	45/45
350/315	5.014-5.044	1.495-1.505	.3723-.37301	.0015-.00322	70- 80 @ 1.727	173-187 @ 1.340	NONE	NONE	45/45
455/350	5.014-5.044	1.625	.3723-.37301	.0015-.00322	70- 80 @ 1.727	173-187 @ 1.340	NONE	NONE	45/45
455/360	5.014-5.044	1.750	.3723-.37301	.0015-.00322	70- 80 @ 1.727	173-187 @ 1.340	NONE	NONE	45/45
455/370	5.014-5.044	1.625	.3723-.37301	.0015-.00322	70- 80 @ 1.727	173-187 @ 1.340	NONE	NONE	45/45
CADILLAC DIVISION									
472/375	5.245	1.625	.3415-.3420	.0010-.0025	60-65 @ 1.946	155-165 @ 1.496	NONE	NONE	45/44
500/400	5.245	1.625	.3415-.3420	.0010-.0025	60-65 @ 1.946	155-165 @ 1.496	NONE	NONE	45/44
CHEVROLET DIVISION									
153/90	4.913-4.933	1.495-1.505	.3410-.3417	.0015-.0032	78- 86 @ 1.66	170-180 @ 1.26	NONE	NONE	46/45
230/140	4.913-4.933	1.495-1.505	.3410-.3417	.0015-.0032	56- 64 @ 1.66	180-192 @ 1.27	NONE	NONE	46/45
250/155	4.913-4.933	1.495-1.505	.3410-.3417	.0015-.0032	56- 64 @ 1.66	180-192 @ 1.27	NONE	NONE	46/45
307/200	4.913-4.933	1.495-1.505	.3410-.3417	.0012-.0029	76-84 @ 1.70	194-206 @ 1.25	DAMPER	DAMPER	46/45
350/250	4.9913-r.933	1.495-1.505	.3410-.3417	.0012-.0029	76-84 @ 1.70	194-206 @ 1.25	DAMPER	DAMPER	46/45
350/300	4.913-4.933	1.495-1.505	.3410-.3417	.0012-.0029	76-84 @ 1.70	194-206 @ 1.25	DAMPER	DAMPER	46/45
350/350	4.913-4.933	1.595-1.605	.3410-.3417	.0012-.0029	76-84 @ 1.70	194-206 @ 1.25	DAMPER	DAMPER	46/45
350/360	4.913-4.933	1.495-1.505	.3410-.3417	.0012-.0029	76-84 @ 1.70	194-206 @ 1.25	DAMPER	DAMPER	46/45
350/370	4.913-4.933	1.495-1.505	.3410-.3417	.0012-.0029	76-84 @ 1.70	194-206 @ 1.25	DAMPER	DAMPER	46/45
400/265	4.913-4.933	1.495-1.505	.3410-.3417	.0010-.0027	76-84 @ 1.70	194-206 @ 1.25	DAMPER	DAMPER	46/45
402/330	5.345-5.365	1.715-1.725	.3713-.3720	.0010-.0027	69-81 @ 1.88	228-252 @ 1.38	26-34 @ 1.78	81- 99 @ 1.28	46/45
402/350	5.345-5.365	1.715-1.725	.3713-.3720	.0010-.0027	69-81 @ 1.88	228-252 @ 1.38	26-34 @ 1.78	81- 99 @ 1.28	46/45
402/375	5.345-5.365	1.715-1.725	.3713-.3720	.0010-.0027	69-81 @ 1.88	228-252 @ 1.38	26-34 @ 1.78	81- 99 @ 1.28	46/45

GENERAL MOTORS EXHAUST VALVES & SPRINGS

DISPLACEMENT/ HORSEPOWER	EXHAUST OVERALL LENGTH	EXHAUST HEAD DIAMETER	EXHAUST STEM DIAMETER	EXHAUST STEM TO GUIDE CLEARANCE	EXHAUST OUTER SPRING PRESSURE LENGTH CLOSED (lb. @ in.)	OPEN (lb. @ in.)	EXHAUST INNER SPRING PRESSURE LENGTH CLOSED (lb. @ in.)	OPEN (lb. @ in.)	ANGLE OF SEAT/FACE (deg.)
454/345	5.345-5.365	1.715-1.725	.3713-.3720	.0010-.0027	94-106 @ 1.88	303-327 @ 1.38	N.A.	N.A.	46/45
454/360	5.345-5.365	1.715-1.725	.3713-.3720	.0010-.0027	69-81 @ 1.88	228-252 @ 1.25	26-34 @ 1.78	81-99 @ 1.28	46/45
454/390	5.345-5.365	1.715-1.825	.3713-.3720	.0010-.0027	69-81 @ 1.88	228-252 @ 1.25	26-34 @ 1.78	81-99 @ 1.28	46/45
454/450	5.345-5.365	1.875-1.885	.3705-.3710	.0010-.0027	69-81 @ 1.88	228-252 @ 1.25	26-34 @ 1.78	81-99 @ 1.28	46/45
454/460	5.380-5.405	1.875-1.885	.3713-.3720	.0010-.0027	69-81 @ 1.88	181-202 @ 1.32	37-45 @ 1.78	92-110 @ 1.22	46/45
OLDSMOBILE DIVISION									
250/155	4.913-4.933	1.495-1.505	.3410-.3417	.0010-.0027	56-64 @ 1.66	180-192 @ 1.27	NONE	NONE	46/45
350/250	4.695	1.619-1.629	.3420-.3427	.0015-.0032	76-84 @ 1.670	180-194 @ 1.270	NONE	NONE	46/45
350/310	4.695	1.619-1.629	.3420-.3427	.0015-.0032	76-84 @ 1.670	180-194 @ 1.270	NONE	NONE	46/45
350/325	4.695	1.619-1.629	.3420-.3427	.0015-.0032	76-84 @ 1.670	180-194 @ 1.270	NONE	NONE	46/45
455/310	4.695	1.619-1.629	.3420-.3427	.0015-.0032	76-84 @ 1.670	180-194 @ 1.270	NONE	NONE	46/45
455/320	4.695	1.619-1.629	.3420-.3427	.0015-.0032	76-84 @ 1.670	180-194 @ 1.270	NONE	NONE	46/45
455/365	4.695	1.619-1.629	.3420-.3427	.0015-.0032	76-84 @ 1.670	180-194 @ 1.270	DAMPER	DAMPER	46/45
455/370	4.695	1.619-1.629	.3420-.3427	.0015-.0032	76-84 @ 1.670	180-194 @ 1.270	DAMPER	DAMPER	46/45
455/375	4.695	1.619-1.629	.3420-.3427	.0015-.0032	76-84 @ 1.670	180-194 @ 1.270	DAMPER	DAMPER	46/45
455/390	4.695	1.619-1.629	.3420-.3427	.0015-.0032	76-84 @ 1.670	180-194 @ 1.270	DAMPER	DAMPER	46/45
455/400	4.695	1.619-1.629	.3420-.3427	.0015-.0032	76-84 @ 1.670	180-194 @ 1.270	DAMPER	DAMPER	46/45
PONTIAC DIVISION									
250/155	4.923	1.495-1.505	.3410-.3417	.0010-.0027	56-64 @ 1.66	180-192 @ 1.27	NONE	NONE	46/45
350/255	4.982	1.657-1.663	.3412-.3419	.0021-.0038	60-66 @ 1.58	129-139 @ 1.17	32-38 @ 1.54	94-104 @ 1.13	45/44
400/265	4.982	1.657-1.663	.3407-.3414	.0021-.0038	60-66 @ 1.58	129-139 @ 1.17	32-38 @ 1.54	94-104 @ 1.13	45/44
400/290	5.089	1.657-1.663	.3407-.3414	.0021-.0038	60-66 @ 1.58	129-139 @ 1.17	32-38 @ 1.54	94-104 @ 1.13	45/44
400/330	5.078	1.657-1.663	.3407-.3414	.0021-.0038	60-66 @ 1.58	129-139 @ 1.17	32-38 @ 1.54	94-104 @ 1.13	45/44
400/345	5.082	1.767-1.773	.3407-.3414	.0021-.0038	56-66 @ 1.59	125-139 @ 1.18	54-60 @ 1.52	118-128 @ 1.11	45/44
400/350	4.987	1.657-1.663	.3412-.3419	.0021-.0038	56-66 @ 1.59	125-139 @ 1.18	54-60 @ 1.52	118-128 @ 1.11	45/44
400/366	5.082	1.767-1.773	.3407-.3414	.0021-.0038	56-66 @ 1.59	125-139 @ 1.18	54-60 @ 1.52	118-128 @ 1.11	45/44
400/370	5.082	1.767-1.773	.3407-.3414	.0021-.0038	71-81 @ 1.82	216-230 @ 1.29	37-43 @ 1.75	106-116 @ 1.22	45/44
455/360	4.991	1.767-1.773	.3407-.3414	.0021-.0038	60-66 @ 1.58	129-139 @ 1.17	32-38 @ 1.54	94-104 @ 1.13	45/44
455/370	4.991	1.767-1.773	.3407-.3414	.0021-.0038	63-69 @ 1.56	133-143 @ 1.15	35-41 @ 1.52	98-108 @ 1.11	45/44

1971

DISPLACEMENT/ HORSEPOWER	EXHAUST OVERALL LENGTH	EXHAUST HEAD DIAMETER	EXHAUST STEM DIAMETER	EXHAUST STEM TO GUIDE CLEARANCE	EXHAUST OUTER SPRING PRESSURE LENGTH CLOSED (lb. @ in.)	OPEN (lb. @ in.)	EXHAUST INNER SPRING PRESSURE LENGTH CLOSED (lb. @ in.)	OPEN (lb. @ in.)	ANGLE OF SEAT/FACE (deg.)
BUICK DIVISION									
250/145	4.913-4.933	1.495-1.505	.3410-.3417	.0010-.0027	56-64 @ 1.66	180-192 @ 1.27	NONE	NONE	46/45
350/230	5.044-5.014	1.495-1.505	.3730-.3723	.0015-.0032	65-75 @ 1.727	168-182 @ 1.340	NONE	NONE	45/45
350/260	5.044-5.014	1.495-1.505	.3730-.3723	.0015-.0032	65-75 @ 1.727	168-182 @ 1.340	NONE	NONE	45/45
455/315	5.175-5.145	1.630-1.620	.3730-.3723	.0015-.0032	67-77 @ 1.890	170-184 @ 1.450	NONE	NONE	45/45
455/330	5.175-5.145	1.630-1.620	.3730-.3723	.0015-.0032	67-77 @ 1.890	170-184 @ 1.450	NONE	NONE	45/45
455/345 STG 1	5.175-5.145	1.755	.3730-.3723	.0015-.0032	115 @ 1.890	280 @ 1.450	NONE	NONE	45/45
CADILLAC DIVISION									
472-345	5.245	1.625	.3415-.3420	.0010-.0025	60-65 @ 1.946	155-165 @ 1.496	NONE	NONE	45/44
500/365	5.245	1.625	.3415-.3420	.0010-.0025	60-65 @ 1.946	155-165 @ 1.496	NONE	NONE	45/44
CHEVROLET DIVISION									
140-90	4.576-4.596	1.370-1.380	.3410-.3417	.0010-.0027	71-79 @ 1.746	183-197 @ 1.310	DAMPER	DAMPER	46/45
140-110	4.576-4.596	1.370-1.380	.3410-.3417	.0010-.0027	71-79 @ 1.746	183-197 @ 1.310	DAMPER	DAMPER	46/45
250-145	4.913-4.933	1.495-1.505	.3410-.3417	.0010-.0027	56-64 @ 1.66	180-192 @ 1.27	NONE	NONE	46/45
307-200	4.913-4.933	1.495-1.505	.3410-.3417	.0012-.0029	76-84 @ 1.70	194-206 @ 1.25	NONE	NONE	46/45
350-245	4.913-4.933	1.495-1.505	.3410-.3417	.0012-.0029	76-84 @ 1.70	194-206 @ 1.25	NONE	NONE	46/45
350-270	4.913-4.933	1.495-1.505	.3410-.3417	.0012-.0029	76-84 @ 1.70	194-206 @ 1.25	NONE	NONE	46/45
350-330	4.913-4.933	1.495-1.505	.3410-.3417	.0012-.0029	76-84 @ 1.70	194-206 @ 1.25	NONE	NONE	46/45
400-255	4.913-4.933	1.495-1.505	.3410-.3417	.0012-.0027	76-84 @ 1.70	194-206 @ 1.25	NONE	NONE	46/45
402-300	5.345-5.365	1.715-1.725	.3713-.3720	.0012-.0027	69-81 @ 1.88	228-252 @ 1.38	26-34 @ 1.78	81-99 @ 1.28	46/45
454-365	5.345-5.365	1.715-1.725	.3713-.3720	.0012-.0027	69-81 @ 1.88	228-252 @ 1.38	26-34 @ 1.78	81-99 @ 1.28	46/45
454-425	5.345-5.365	1.715-1.725	.3713-.3720	.0012-.0027	69-81 @ 1.88	228-252 @ 1.38	26-34 @ 1.78	81-99 @ 1.28	46/45
OLDSMOBILE DIVISION									
250-145	4.913-4.933	1.495-1.505	.3410-.3417	.0010-.0027	56-64 @ 1.66	180-192 @ 1.27	NONE	NONE	46/45
350-240	4.728	1.557-1.567	.3420-.3427	.0015-.0032	76-84 @ 1.670	180-194 @ 1.270	DAMPER	DAMPER	46/45
350-260	4.728	1.557-1.567	.3420-.3427	.0015-.0032	84-76 @ 1.670	180-194 @ 1.270	DAMPER	DAMPER	46/45
455280	4.695	1.619-1.629	.3420-.3427	.0015-.0032	76-84 @ 1.670	189-204 @ 1.235	DAMPER	DAMPER	46/45
455-320	4.695	1.619-1.629	.3420-.3427	.0015-.0032	76-84 @ 1.670	180-194 @ 1.270	DAMPER	DAMPER	46/45
455-340	4.695	1.619-1.629	.3420-.3427	.0015-.0032	115-125 @ 1.6703	281-308 @ 1.1964	DAMPER	DAMPER	46/45
455-350W-30	4.695	1.619-1.629	.3420-.3427	.0015-.0032	115-125 @ 1.6705	281-308 @ 1.1966	DAMPER	DAMPER	46/45
455-350 TOR	4.695	1.619-1.629	.3420-.3427	.0015-.0032	76-84 @ 1.670	191-206 @ 1.230	DAMOER	DAMPER	46/45
PONTIAC DIVISION									
250/145	4.913-4.933	1.495-1.505	.3410-.3417	.0010-.0027	56-64 @ 1.66	180-192 @ 1.27	NONE	NONE	46/45
307/200	4.913-4.933	1.495-1.505	.3410-.3417	.0012-.0029	76-84 @ 1.70	194-206 @ 1.25	NONE	NONE	46/45
350/250	4.970	1.663-1.657	.3414-.3407	.0021-.0038	54-68 @ 1.589	125-139 @ 1.176	28-38 @ 1.549	93-103 @ 1.136	45/44
400/265	4.970	1.663-1.657	.3414-.3407	.0021-.0038	54-68 @ 1.589	125-139 @ 1.176	28-38 @ 1.549	93-103 @ 1.136	45/44
400/300	4.948	1.773-1.767	.3414-.3407	.0021-.0038	58-72 @ 1.5687	128-142 @ 1.157	31-41 @ 1.528	96-106 @ 1.114	45/44
455/280	4.869	1.663-1.657	.3414-.3407	.0021-.0038	54-68 @ 1.590	125-139 @ 1.175	28-38 @ 1.550	93-103 @ 1.135	45/44
455/325	4.869	1.663-1.657	.3414-.3407	.0021-.0038	58-72 @ 1.568	128-142 @ 1.157	31-41 @ 1.528	96-106 @ 1.115	45/44
455/335	4.948	1.663-1.657	.3414-.3407	.0021-.0038	59-73 @ 1.560	130-144 @ 1.146	33-43 @ 1.520	98-108 @ 1.106	45/44

1972

DISPLACEMENT/ HORSEPOWER	EXHAUST OVERALL LENGTH	EXHAUST HEAD DIAMETER	EXHAUST STEM DIAMETER	EXHAUST STEM TO GUIDE CLEARANCE	EXHAUST OUTER SPRING PRESSURE LENGTH CLOSED (lb. @ in.)	OPEN (lb. @ in.)	EXHAUST INNER SPRING PRESSURE LENGTH CLOSED (lb. @ in.)	OPEN (lb. @ in.)	ANGLE OF SEAT/FACE (deg.)
BUICK DIVISION									
350/150	5.014-5.044	1.495-1.505	.3723-.3730	.0015-.0032	70-80 @ 1.727	173-187 @ 1.340	NONE	NONE	45/45
350/155	5.014-5.044	1.495-1.505	.3723-.3730	.0015-.0032	70-80 @ 1.727	173-187 @ 1.340	NONE	NONE	45/45
350/175	5.014-5.044	1.495-1.505	.3723-.3730	.0015-.0032	70-80 @ 1.727	173-187 @ 1.340	NONE	NONE	45/45
350/180	5.014-5.044	1.495-1.505	.3723-.3730	.0015-.0032	70-80 @ 1.727	173-187 @ 1.340	NONE	NONE	45/45
350/190	5.014-5.044	1.495-1.505	.3723-.3730	.0015-.0032	70-80 @ 1.727	173-187 @ 1.340	NONE	NONE	45/45
455/225	5.145-5.175	1.620-1.630	.3723-.3730	.0015-.0032	73-83 @ 1.890	191-205 @ 1.450	DAMPER	DAMPER	45/45
455/250	5.145-5.175	1.620-1.630	.3723-.3730	.0015-.0032	73-83 @ 1.890	191-205 @ 1.450	DAMPER	DAMPER	45/45
455/260	5.145-5.175	1.620-1.630	.3723-.3730	.0015-.0032	73-83 @ 1.890	191-205 @ 1.450	DAMPER	DAMPER	45/45
455/270	5.145-5.175	1.620-1.630	.3723-.3730	.0015-.0032	73-83 @ 1.890	191-205 @ 1.450	DAMPER	DAMPER	45/45
CADILLAC DIVISION									
472/220	5.246	1.625	.3413-.3418	.0012-.0027	60-65 @ 1.946	163-173 @ 1.456	NONE	NONE	45/44
500/235	5.246	1.625	.3413-.3418	.0012-.0027	60-65 @ 1.946	163-173 @ 1.456	NONE	NONE	45/44
CHEVROLET DIVISION									
140/80	4.576-4.596	1.370-1.380	.3410-.3417	.0010-.0027	71-79 @ 1.746	183-197 @ 1.310	DAMPER	DAMPER	46/45
140/90	4.576-4.596	1.370-1.380	.3410-.3417	.0010-.0027	71-79 @ 1.746	183-197 @ 1.310	DAMPER	DAMPER	46/45
250/110	4.913-4.933	1.495-1.505	.3410-.3417	.0015-.0032	56-64 @ 1.66	180-192 @ 1.27	NONE	NONE	46/45
307/130	4.913-4.933	1.495-1.505	.3410-.3417	.0012-.0029	76-84 @ 1.68	194-206 @ 1.17	DAMPER	DAMPER	46/45
350/165	4.913-4.933	1.495-1.505	.3410-.3417	.0012-.0029	76-84 @ 1.70	194-206 @ 1.25	DAMPER	DAMPER	46/45

ENGINE SPECIFICATIONS

GENERAL MOTORS EXHAUST VALVES & SPRINGS

DISPLACEMENT/ HORSEPOWER	EXHAUST OVERALL LENGTH	EXHAUST HEAD DIAMETER	EXHAUST STEM DIAMETER	EXHAUST STEM TO GUIDE CLEARANCE	EXHAUST OUTER SPRING PRESSURE LENGTH		EXHAUST INNER SPRING PRESSURE LENGTH		ANGLE OF SEAT/FACE (deg.)
					CLOSED (lb. @ in.)	OPEN (lb. @ in.)	CLOSED (lb. @ in.)	OPEN (lb. @ in.)	
350/175	4.913-4.933	1.495-1.505	.3410-.3417	.0012-.0029	76-84 @ 1.70	194-206 @ 1.25	DAMPER	DAMPER	46/45
350/200	4.913-4.933	1.495-1.505	.3410-.3417	.0012-.0029	76-84 @ 1.70	194-206 @ 1.25	DAMPER	DAMPER	46/45
350/255	4.891-4.910	1.595-1.605	.3410-.3417	.0012-.0029	76-84 @ 1.70	194-206 @ 1.25	DAMPER	DAMPER	46/45
400/170	4.913-4.933	1.595-1.605	.3410-.3417	.0012-.0027	76-84 @ 1.70	194-206 @ 1.25	DAMPER	DAMPER	46/45
402/210	5.345-5.365	1.715-1.725	.3713-.3720	.0012-.0027	84-96 @ 1.88	205-225 @ 1.48	DAMPER	DAMPER	46/45
402/240	5.345-5.365	1.715-1.725	.3713-.3720	.0012-.0027	84-96 @ 1.88	205-225 @ 1.48	DAMPER	DAMPER	46/45
454/230	5.345-5.365	1.715-1.725	.3713-.3720	.0012-.0027	69-81 @ 1.88	228-252 @ 1.38	26-34 @ 1.78	81-99 @ 1.28	46/45
454/270	5.345-5.365	1.715-1.725	.3713-.3720	.0012-.0027	69-81 @ 1.88	228-252 @ 1.38	26-34 @ 1.78	81-99 @ 1.25	46/45
OLDSMOBILE DIVISION									
350/160	4.728	1.617-1.627	.3420-.3427	.0015-.0032	76-84 @ 1.670	180-194 @ 1.270 8	DAMPER	DAMPER	30/30
350/175	4.728	1.617-1.627	.3420-.3427	.0015-.0032	76-84 @ 1.670	180-194 @ 1.270 8	DAMPER	DAMPER	30/30
350/180	4.728	1.617-1.627	.3420-.3427	.0015-.0032	76-84 @ 1.670	180-194 @ 1.270 9	DAMPER	DAMPER	30/30
350/200	4.728	1.617-1.627	.3420-.3427	.0015-.0032	76-84 @ 1.670	180-194 @ 1.270 9	DAMPER	DAMPER	30/30
455/225	4.675	1.679-1.689	.3420-.3427	.0015-.0032	76-84 @ 1.620	180-194 @ 1.270	DAMPER	DAMPER	30/30
455/250	4.675	1.679-1.689	.3420-.3427	.0015-.0032	76-84 @ 1.620	199-214 @ 1.270	DAMPER	DAMPER	30/30
455/265 TOR	4.675	1.679-1.689	.3420-.3427	.0015-.0032	76-84 @ 1.620	189-204 @ 1.270	NONE	NONE	30/30
455/270	4.675	1.679-1.689	.3420-.3427	.0015-.0032	115-125 @ 1.620	281-308 @ 1.270	DAMPER	DAMPER	30/30
455/300 W30	4.675	1.679-1.689	.3420-.3427	.0015-.0032	115-125 @ 1.620	280-308 @ 1.270	DAMPER	DAMPER	30/30
PONTIAC DIVISION									
250/110	4.913-4.923	1.495-1.505	.3410-.3417	.0015-.0032	56-64 @ 1.66	180-192 @ 1.27	NONE	NONE	46/45
307/130	4.913-4.923	1.495-1.505	.3410-.3417	.0012-.0029	76-84 @ 1.70	194-206 @ 1.25	DAMPER	DAMPER	46/45
350/160	4.971	1.77	.3407-.3414	.0021-.0038	54-68 @ 1.590	125-139 @ 1.175	28-38 @ 1.550	94-104 @ 1.135 11	45/44
350/175	4.971	1.77	.3407-.3414	.0021-.0038	54-68 @ 1.590	125-139 @ 1.175 10	28-38 @ 1.550	94-104 @ 1.135 11	45/44
400/175 (L65)	4.971	1.77	.3407-.3414	.0021-.0038	54-68 @ 1.590 12	126-140 @ 1.177 10	38-38 @ 1.550 11	93-103 @ 1.137 15	45/44
400/200 (L65)	4.971	1.77	.3407-.3414	.0021-.0038	54-68 @ 1.590 12	126-140 @ 1.177 13	28-38 @ 1.550 14	93-103 @ 1.137 15	45/44
400/200 (L78)	4.949	1.77	.3407-.3414	.0021-.0038	58-72 @ 1.568 12	129-143 @ 1.154 13	32-42 @ 1.528 14	97-107 @ 1.114 15	45/44
400/250 (L78)	4.949	1.77	.3407-.3414	.0021-.0038	58-72 @ 1.568 12	129-143 @ 1.154 13	32-42 @ 1.528 14	97-107 @ 1.114 15	45/44
455/185	4.780	1.77	.3407-.3414	.0021-.0038	54-68 @ 1.590 12	126-140 @ 1.175 13	28-38 @ 1.550	94-104 @ 1.135	45/44
455/200	4.780	1.77	.3407-.3414	.0021-.0038	54-68 @ 1.590	126-140 @ 1.175	28-38 @ 1.550	94-104 @ 1.135	45/44
455/220	4.780	1.77	.3412-.3419	.0021-.0038	58-72 @ 1.569	129-143 @ 1.155	32-42 @ 1.529	97-107 @ 1.115	45/44
455/250	4.780	1.77	.3412-.3419	.0021-.0038	58-72 @ 1.569	129-143 @ 1.155	32-42 @ 1.529	97-107 @ 1.115	45/44
455/300	4.949	1.77	.3412-.3419	.0021-.0038	59-73 @ 1.561	131-145 @ 1.147	33-43 @ 1.521	98-108 @ 1.107	45/44

1973

DISPLACEMENT/ HORSEPOWER	EXHAUST OVERALL LENGTH	EXHAUST HEAD DIAMETER	EXHAUST STEM DIAMETER	EXHAUST STEM TO GUIDE CLEARANCE	EXHAUST OUTER SPRING CLOSED	EXHAUST OUTER SPRING OPEN	EXHAUST INNER SPRING CLOSED	EXHAUST INNER SPRING OPEN	ANGLE OF SEAT/FACE
BUICK DIVISION									
350/150	5.014-5.044	1.495-1.505	.3723-.3730	.0015-.0032	70-80 @ 1.727	173-187 @ 1.340	NONE	NONE	45/45
350/175	5.014-5.044	1.495-1.505	.3723-.3730	.0015-.0032	70-80 @ 1.727	173-187 @ 1.340	NONE	NONE	45/45
350/190	5.014-5.044	1.495-1.505	.3723-.3730	.0015-.0032	70-80 @ 1.727	173-187 @ 1.340	NONE	NONE	45/45
455/225	5.145-5.175	1.620-1.630	.3723-.3730	.0015-.0032	67-77 @ 1.890	170-184 @ 1.450	NONE	NONE	45/45
455/250	5.145-5.175	1.620-1.630	.3723-.3730	.0015-.0032	67-77 @ 1.890	170-184 @ 1.450	NONE	NONE	45/45
455/260	5.145-5.175	1.620-1.630	.3723-.3730	.0015-.0032	67-77 @ 1.890	170-184 @ 1.450	NONE	NONE	45/45
455/270	5.145-5.175	1.620-1.630	.3723-.3730	.0015-.0032	67-77 @ 1.890	170-184 @ 1.450	NONE	NONE	45/45
CADILLAC DIVISION									
472/220	5.246	1.625	.3413-.3418	.0012-.0027	70-75 @ 1.946	163-178 @ 1.456	NONE	NONE	45/44
500/235	5.246	1.625	.3413-.3418	.0012-.0027	60-65 @ 1.946	163-173 @ 1.456	NONE	NONE	45/44
CHEVROLET DIVISION									
140/72	4.576-4.596	1.370-1.380	.3410-.3417	.0010-.0027	71-79 @ 1.746	183-197 @ 1.310	DAMPER	DAMPER	46/45
140/85	4.576-4.596	1.370-1.380	.3410-.3417	.0010-.0027	71-79 @ 1.746	183-197 @ 1.310	DAMPER	DAMPER	46/45
250/100	4.913-4.933	1.495-1.505	.3410-.3417	.0010-.0027	56-64 @ 1.66	180-192 @ 1.27	NONE	NONE	46/45
307/115	4.913-4.933	1.495-1.505	.3410-.3417	.0010-.0027	76-84 @ 1.68	194-206 @ 1.15	DAMPER	DAMPER	46/45
350/145	4.913-4.933	1.495-1.505	.3410-.3417	.0012-.0027	76-84 @ 1.70	194-206 @ 1.26	DAMPER	DAMPER	46/45
350/175	4.913-4.933	1.495-1.505	.3410-.3417	.0012-.0027	76-84 @ 1.70	194-206 @ 1.26	DAMPER	DAMPER	46/45
350/245	4.891-4.910	1.595-1.605	.3410-.3417	.0012-.0029	76-84 @ 1.70	194-206 @ 1.25	DAMPER	DAMPER	46/45
350/250	4.891-4.910	1.595-1.605	.3410-.3417	.0012-.0029	76-84 @ 1.70	194-206 @ 1.25	DAMPER	DAMPER	46/45
400/150	4.913-4.933	1.595-1.605	.3410-.3417	.0012-.0027	74-86 @ 1.88	228-312 @ 1.38	DAMPER	DAMPER	46/45
454/245	5.345-5.365	1.715-1.725	.3713-.3720	.0010-.0027	74-86 @ 1.88	228-312 @ 1.38	DAMPER	DAMPER	46/45
454/275	5.345-5.365	1.715-1.725	.3713-.3720	.0010-.0027	74-86 @ 1.88	228-312 @ 1.38	DAMPER	DAMPER	46/45
OLDSMOBILE DIVISION									
250/100	4.913-4.933	1.495-1.505	.3410-.3417	.0010-.0027	56-64 @ 1.66	180-192 @ 1.27	NONE	NONE	45/46
350/160	4.675	1.617-1.627	.3420-.3427	.0015-.0032	76-84 @ 1.670	180-194 @ 1.270 8	NONE	NONE	59/60
350/180	4.675	1.617-1.627	.3420-.3427	.0015-.0032	76-84 @ 1.670	180-194 @ 1.270 9	NONE	NONE	59/60
455/225	4.675	1.627-1.617	.3420-.3427	.0015-.0032	76-84 @ 1.620	180-194 @ 1.270	NONE	NONE	59/60
455/250	4.675	1.627-1.617	.3420-.3427	.0015-.0032	76-84 @ 1.620	199-214 @ 1.270	NONE	NONE	59/60
455/265	4.675	1.679-1.689	.3420-.3427	.0015-.0032	76-84 @ 1.620	189-204 @ 1.270	NONE	NONE	59/60
455/270	4.675	1.679-1.689	.3420-.3427	.0015-.0032	115-125 @ 1.620	281-308 @ 1.270	DAMPER	DAMPER	59/60
455/300	4.675	1.679-1.689	.3420-.3427	.0015-.0032	115-125 @ 1.620	280-308 @ 1.270	DAMPER	DAMPER	59/60
PONTIAC DIVISION									
250/100	4.913-4.923	1.495-1.505	.3410-.3417	.0010-.0027	56-64 @ 1.66	180-192 @ 1.27	NONE	NONE	46/45
350/150	4.864	1.66	.3407-.3414	.0021-.0038	54-68 @ 1.590	125-139 @ 1.175	28-38 @ 1.550	94-104 @ 1.135	45/44
350/175	4.864	1.66	.3407-.3414	.0021-.0038	54-68 @ 1.590	125-139 @ 1.175	28-38 @ 1.550	94-104 @ 1.135	45/44
400/170	4.864	1.95	.3407-.3414	.0021-.0038	54-68 @ 1.590	126-140 @ 1.177	28-38 @ 1.550	93-103 @ 1.137	45/44
400/185	4.864	1.95	.3407-.3414	.0021-.0038	54-68 @ 1.590	126-140 @ 1.177	28-38 @ 1.550	93-103 @ 1.137	45/44
400/230	4.864	2.10	.3407-.3414	.0021-.0038	58-72 @ 1.568	129-143 @ 1.154	32-42 @ 1.528	97-107 @ 1.114	45/44
455/250	4.785	1.65	.3407-.3414	.0021-.0038	58-72 @ 1.569	129-143 @ 1.155	32-42 @ 1.529	97-107 @ 1.115	45/44
455/310	4.969	1.77	.3412-.3419	.0021-.0038	59-73 @ 1.561	131-145 @ 1.147	33-43 @ 1.521	98-108 @ 1.107	45/44

1974

DISPLACEMENT/ HORSEPOWER	EXHAUST OVERALL LENGTH	EXHAUST HEAD DIAMETER	EXHAUST STEM DIAMETER	EXHAUST STEM TO GUIDE CLEARANCE	EXHAUST OUTER SPRING CLOSED	EXHAUST OUTER SPRING OPEN	EXHAUST INNER SPRING CLOSED	EXHAUST INNER SPRING OPEN	ANGLE OF SEAT/FACE
BUICK DIVISION									
250/100	4.913-4.933	1.495-1.505	.3410-.3417	.0010-.0027	56-64 @ 1.660	180-192 @ 1.270	NONE	NONE	46/45
350/150	5.014-5.044	1.495-1.505	.3723-.3730	.0015-.0032	70-80 @ 1.727	173-187 @ 1.340	NONE	NONE	45/45
350/175	5.014-5.044	1.495-1.505	.3723-.3730	.0015-.0032	70-80 @ 1.727	173-187 @ 1.340	NONE	NONE	45/45
455/175	5.145-5.175	1.620-1.630	.3723-.3730	.0015-.0032	67-77 @ 1.890	170-184 @ 1.450	NONE	NONE	45/45
455/190	5.145-5.175	1.620-1.630	.3723-.3730	.0015-.0032	67-77 @ 1.890	170-184 @ 1.450	NONE	NONE	45/45
455/210	5.145-5.175	1.620-1.630	.3723-.3730	.0015-.0032	67-77 @ 1.890	170-184 @ 1.450	NONE	NONE	45/45
455/230	5.145-5.175	1.620-1.630	.3723-.3730	.0015-.0032	67-77 @ 1.890	170-184 @ 1.450	NONE	NONE	45/45
455/245	5.145-5.175	1.620-1.630	.3723-.3730	.0015-.0032	67-77 @ 1.890	170-184 @ 1.450	NONE	NONE	45/45
CADILLAC DIVISION									
472/205	4.998	1.625	.3411-.3418	.0012-.0029	60-65 @ 1.946	159-169 @ 1.473	NONE	NONE	45/44
500/210	4.998	1.625	.3411-.3418	.0012-.0029	60-65 @ 1.946	159-169 @ 1.473	NONE	NONE	45/44
CHEVROLET DIVISION									
122/130	4.942-4.953	1.195-1.205	.2788-.2795	.0010-.0027	41-49 @ 1.30	104-116 @ .92	26-34 @ 1.25	78-81 @ .875	46/45
140/75	4.576-4.596	1.370-1.380	.3410-.3417	.0010-.0027	71-79 @ 1.746	183-197 @ 1.310	DAMPER	DAMPER	46/45
140/85	4.576-4.596	1.370-1.380	.3410-.3417	.0010-.0027	71-79 @ 1.746	183-197 @ 1.310	DAMPER	DAMPER	46/45

GENERAL MOTORS EXHAUST VALVES & SPRINGS

DISPLACEMENT/ HORSEPOWER	EXHAUST OVERALL LENGTH	EXHAUST HEAD DIAMETER	EXHAUST STEM DIAMETER	EXHAUST STEM TO GUIDE CLEARANCE	EXHAUST OUTER SPRING PRESSURE LENGTH CLOSED (lb. @ in.)	OPEN (lb. @ in.)	EXHAUST INNER SPRING PRESSURE LENGTH CLOSED (lb. @ in.)	OPEN (lb. @ in.)	ANGLE OF SEAT/FACE (deg.)
250/100	3.913-4.933	1.495-1.505	3410-3417	0010-0027	56-64 @ 1.66	180-192 @ 1.27	NONE	NONE	46/45
350/145	4.913-4.933	1.495-1.505	3410-3417	0010-0027	76.84 @ 1.61	194-206 @ 1.16	DAMPER	DAMPER	46/45
350/160	4.913-4.933	1.495-1.505	3410-3417	0010-0027	76.84 @ 1.61	194-206 @ 1.16	DAMPER	DAMPER	46/45
360/185	4.913-4.933	1.495-1.505	3410-3417	0010-0027	76.84 @ 1.61	194-206 @ 1.16	DAMPER	DAMPER	46/45
350/195	4.913-4.933	1.495-1.505	3410-3417	0010-0027	76.84 @ 1.61	194-206 @ 1.16	DAMPER	DAMPER	46/45
350/245	4.891-4.910	1.595-1.605	3410-3417	0010-0027	76.84 @ 1.70	194-206 @ 1.25	DAMPER	DAMPER	46/45
350/250	4.891-4.910	1.595-1.605	3410-3417	0010-0027	76.84 @ 1.70	194-206 @ 1.25	DAMPER	DAMPER	46/45
400/150	4.913-4.933	1.495-1.505	3410-3417	0010-0027	76.84 @ 1.61	194-206 @ 1.16	DAMPER	DAMPER	46/45
400/180	4.913-4.933	1.495-1.505	3410-3417	0010-0027	87.84 @ 1.61	194-206 @ 1.16	DAMPER	DAMPER	46/45
454/235	5.345-5.365	1.715-1.725	3713-3720	0010-0027	74-86 @ 1.88	228-312 @ 1.38	DAMPER	DAMPER	46/45
454/270	5.345-5.365	1.715-1.725	3713-3720	0010-0027	74-86 @ 1.88	228-312 @ 1.38	DAMPER	DAMPER	46/45
OLDSMOBILE DIVISION									
250/100	4.913-4.933	1.495-1.505	3410-3417	0010-0027	56-64 @ 1.66	180-192 @ 1.27	NONE	NONE	46/45
350/180	4.675	1.617-1.627	3420-3427	0015-0032	76.84 @ 1.670	180-194 @ 1.270	NONE	NONE	59/60
350/200	4.675	1.617-1.627	3420-3427	0015-0032	76.84 @ 1.620	180-194 @ 1.270	NONE	NONE	59/60
455/210	4.675	1.617-1.627	3420-3427	0015-0032	76.84 @ 1.620	180-194 @ 1.270	NONE	NONE	59/60
455/230	4.675	1.617-1.627	3420-3427	0015-0032	76.84 @ 1.670	180-194 @ 1.270	NONE	NONE	59/60
455/275	4.695	1.619-1.629	3420-3427	0015-0032	87.84 @ 1.670	180-194 @ 1.270	DAMPER	DAMPER	45/46
PONTIAC DIVISION									
250/100	4.913-4.933	1.495-1.505	3410-3417	0010-0027	56-64 @ 1.66	180-192 @ 1.27	NONE	NONE	46/45
350/155	4.864	1.66	3407-3414	0021-0038	54-68 @ 1.590	125-139 @ 1.175	28-38 @ 1.550	94-104 @ 1.135	45/44
350/170	4.864	1.66	3407-3414	0021-0038	54-68 @ 1.590	125-139 @ 1.175	28-38 @ 1.550	94-104 @ 1.135	45/44
350/200	4.864	1.66	3407-3414	0021-0038	54-68 @ 1.590	125-139 @ 1.175	28-38 @ 1.550	94-104 @ 1.135	45/44
400/175	4.864	1.66	3407-3414	0021-0038	54-68 @ 1.590	126-140 @ 1.177	28-38 @ 1.550	93-103 @ 1.137	45/44
400/190	4.864	1.66	3407-3414	0021-0038	54-68 @ 1.590	126-140 @ 1.177	28-38 @ 1.550	93-103 @ 1.137	45/44
400/200	4.864	1.66	3407-3414	0021-0038	58-72 @ 1.568	129-143 @ 1.154	32-42 @ 1.528	97-107 @ 1.114	45/44
400/225	4.864	1.66	3407-3414	0021-0038	58-72 @ 1.568	129-143 @ 1.154	32-42 @ 1.528	97-107 @ 1.114	45/44
455/215	4.785	1.66	3407-3414	0021-0038	58-72 @ 1.569	129-143 @ 1.154	32-42 @ 1.529	97-107 @ 1.115	45/44
455/250	4.785	1.66	3407-3414	0021-0038	58-72 @ 1.569	129-143 @ 1.154	32-42 @ 1.529	97-107 @ 1.115	45/44
455/290 SD	4.969	1.77	3412-3419	0021-0038	66-74 @ 1.82	168-181 @ 1.41	37-43 @ 1.75	79-88 @ 1.34	45/44

1975

DISPLACEMENT/ HORSEPOWER	EXHAUST OVERALL LENGTH	EXHAUST HEAD DIAMETER	EXHAUST STEM DIAMETER	EXHAUST STEM TO GUIDE CLEARANCE	EXHAUST OUTER SPRING CLOSED	OPEN	EXHAUST INNER SPRING CLOSED	OPEN	ANGLE OF SEAT/FACE
BUICK DIVISION									
231/110	4.683-4.713	1.425	3405-3412	0015-0032	64 @ 1.727	182 @ 1.340	DAMPER	DAMPER	45/45
250/105	4.913-4.933	1.495-1.505	3410-3417	0010-0020	50-64 @ 1.660	180-192 @ 1.270	NONE	NONE	46/45
260/110	4.923	1.495-1.505	3420-3427	0010-0020	50-64 @ 1.660	180-192 @ 1.270	NONE	NONE	46/45
350/145	5.001-5.031	1.545-1.555	3723-3730	0015-0032	70 @ 1.727	175 @ 1.340	DAMPER	DAMPER	45/45
350/165	5.001-5.031	1.545-1.555	3723-3730	0015-0032	70 @ 1.727	175 @ 1.340	DAMPER	DAMPER	45/45
455/205	5.139-5.169	1.682-1.692	3723-3730	0015-0032	72 @ 1.890	177 @ 1.450	DAMPER	DAMPER	45/45
CADILLAC DIVISION									
500/190	4.998	1.625	3411-3418	0012-0029	60-65 @ 1.946	159-169 @ 1.473	NONE	NONE	45/44
CHEVROLET DIVISION									
140/78	4.576-4.596	1.37-1.38	3410-3417	010-020	71-79 @ 1.746	183-197 @ 1.310	DAMPER	DAMPER	46/45
140/87	4.576-4.596	1.37-1.38	3410-3417	010-020	71-79 @ 1.746	183-197 @ 1.310	DAMPER	DAMPER	46/45
122/110	4.9375-4.9575	1.195-1.205	2788-2795	010-020	41-49 @ 1.300	104-116 @ 0.920	26-34 @ 1.25	78.5-80 @ .875	46/45
250/105	4.913-4.933	1.495-1.505	3410-3417	010-027	50-64 @ 1.660	180-192 @ 1.270	NONE	NONE	46/45
262/110	4.913-4.933	1.495-1.505	3410-3417	010-027	76.84 @ 1.610	194-206 @ 1.160	DAMPER	DAMPER	46/45
350/145	4.910-4.930	1.495-1.505	3410-3417	00-027	76.84 @ 1.610	194-206 @ 1.160	DAMPER	DAMPER	46/45
350/155	4.910-4.930	1.495-1.505	3410-3417	010-027	76.84 @ 1.610	194-206 @ 1.160	DAMPER	DAMPER	46/45
400/175	4.910-4.930	1.495-1.505	3410-3417	010-027	76.84 @ 1.610	84-96 @ 1.80	DAMPER	DAMPER	46/45
454/215	5.345-5.365	1.715-1.725	3713-3720	010-027	194-206 @ 1.160	210-230 @ 1.40	DAMPER	DAMPER	46/45
OLDSMOBILE DIVISION									
231/110	4.683-4.713	1.425	3405-3412	0015-0032	64 @ 1.727	182 @ 1.340	DAMPER	DAMPER	45/45
250/105	4.913-4.933	1.495-1.505	3410-3417	0010-0027	56-64 @ 1.660	180-192 @ 1.270	NONE	NONE	46/45
260/110	4.680	1.300	3420-3427	0010-0020	76.84 @ 1.670	180-194 @ 1.270	NONE	NONE	59/60
350/165	5.001-5.031	1.545-1.555	3723-3730	0015-0032	70 @ 1.727	175 @ 1.340	NONE	NONE	45/45
350/170	4.675	1.617-1.627	3420-3427	0015-0032	76.84 @ 1.670	180-194 @ 1.270	NONE	NONE	59/60
400/175	4.8645	1.657-1.663	3407-3414	0021-0038	N/A	N/A	NONE	NONE	45/44
455/190	4.675	1.617-1.627	3420-3427	0015-0032	76.84 @ 1.670	180-194 @ 1.270	NONE	NONE	59/60
PONTIAC DIVISION									
250/105	4.913-4.933	1.495-1.505	3410-3417	.0010-0020	50-64 @ 1.66	180-192 @ 1.270	NONE	NONE	46/45
260/110	4.923	1.495-1.505	3410-3427	.0010-0020	50-64 @ 1.66	180-192 @ 1.270	NONE	NONE	46/45
350/145	4.680	1.295-1.305	3420-3427	.0015-0032	76-84 @ 1.67	180-194 @ 1.270	NONE	NONE	59/60
350/155	4.8645	1.657-1.663	3407-3414	.0021-0038	59.6-73.6 @ 1.56	130.8-144.8 @ 1.15	33.3-43.3 @ 1.52	98.2-108.2 @ 1.11	45/44
350/165	5.016	1.545-1.555	3723-3730	.0015-0032	65-75 @ 1.727	168-182 @ 1.340	NONE	NONE	45/45
350/175	4.8645	1.657-1.663	3407-3414	.0021-0038	59.6-73.6 @ 1.56	130.8-144.8 @ 1.15	33.3-43.3 @ 1.52	98.2-108.2 @ 1.11	45/44
400/170	4.8645	1.657-1.663	3407-3414	.0021-0038	63-77 @ 1.54	134.6-148.6 @ 1.12	36.4-46.4 @ 1.50	101.6-111.6 @ 1.08	45/44
400/185	4.8645	1.657-1.663	3407-3414	.0021-0038	63-77 @ 1.54	133.8-147.8 @ 1.12	36.4-46.4 @ 1.50	101.6-111.6 @ 1.08	45/44
455/200	4.8645	1.657-1.663	3407-3414	.0021-0038	58-72 @ 1.57	134.6-148.6 @ 1.15	31.5-41.5 @ 1.53	96.5-106.5 @ 1.11	45/44

1976

DISPLACEMENT/ HORSEPOWER	EXHAUST OVERALL LENGTH	EXHAUST HEAD DIAMETER	EXHAUST STEM DIAMETER	EXHAUST STEM TO GUIDE CLEARANCE	EXHAUST OUTER SPRING CLOSED	OPEN	EXHAUST INNER SPRING CLOSED	OPEN	ANGLE OF SEAT/FACE
BUICK DIVISION									
231/105	4.683-4.713	1.425	3405-3412	0015-0032	64 @ 1.727	182 @ 1.340	DAMPER	DAMPER	45/45
260/110	4.923	1.495-1.505	3410-3417	0010-0020	50-64 @ 1.66	180-192 @ 1.270	NONE	NONE	46/45
350/145	5.001-5.031	1.545-1.555	3723-3730	0015-0032	70 @ 1.727	175 @ 1.340	NONE	NONE	45/45
350/165	5.001-5.031	1.545-1.555	3723-3730	0015-0032	70 @ 1.727	175 @ 1.340	NONE	NONE	45/45
455/205	5.139-5.169	1.682-1.692	3723-3730	0015-0032	72 @ 1.890	177 @ 1.450	NONE	NONE	45/45
CADILLAC DIVISION									
350/170	5.001-5.031	1.545-1.555	3723-3730	0015-0032	70 @ 1.727	175 @ 1.340	NONE	NONE	45/45
500/190	4.998	1.625	3411-3418	0012-0029	60-65 @ 1.946	159-169 @ 1.473	NONE	NONE	45/44
500/215	4.998	1.625	3411-3418	0012-0029	60-65 @ 1.946	159-169 @ 1.473	NONE	NONE	45/44
CHEVROLET DIVISION									
85/52	3.8856-3.9057	1.2547-1.2650	3130-3130	0026-0029	64-72 @ 1.26	167-179 @ .886	NONE	NONE	46/45
97.6/60	3.8856-3.9057	1.2547-1.2650	3130-3136	0026-0029	64-72 @ 1.26	167-179 @ .886	NONE	NONE	46/45
122/110	4.9575	1.195-1.205	2788-2795	0010-0027	41-49 @ 1.30	104-116 @ .92	26-34 @ 1.25	78.5-80 @ .875	46/45
140/70	4.576-4.596	1.370-1.380	3410-3417	0010-0027	71-79 @ 1.746	183-197 @ 1.310	DAMPER	DAMPER	46/45
140/84	4.576-4.596	1.370-1.380	3410-3417	0010-0027	71-79 @ 1.746	183-197 @ 1.310	DAMPER	DAMPER	46/45
250/105	4.913-4.933	1.495-1.505	3410-3417	0010-0027	76.86 @ 1.660	170-180 @ 1.260	NONE	NONE	46/45
262/110	4.913-4.933	1.495-1.505	3410-3417	0010-0027	76.84 @ 1.160	194-206 @ 1.160	DAMPER	DAMPER	46/45
305/140	4.913-4.933	1.495-1.505	3410-3417	0010-0027	76.84 @ 1.160	194-206 @ 1.160	DAMPER	DAMPER	46/45
350/145	4.913-4.933	1.495-1.505	3410-3417	0010-0027	76.84 @ 1.160	195-206 @ 1.160	DAMPER	DAMPER	46/45
350/165	4.910-4.930	1.495-1.505	3410-3417	0010-0027	76.84 @ 1.160	195-206 @ 1.160	DAMPER	DAMPER	46/45
400/175	4.910-4.930	1.495-1.505	3410-3417	0010-0027	76.84 @ 1.160	84-96 @ 1.800	DAMPER	DAMPER	46/45
454/225	5.345-5.365	1.715-1.725	3713-3720	0010-0027	84-96 @ 1.800	210-230 @ 1.400	DAMPER	DAMPER	46/45

ENGINE SPECIFICATIONS

GENERAL MOTORS EXHAUST VALVES & SPRINGS

DISPLACEMENT/ HORSEPOWER	EXHAUST OVERALL LENGTH	EXHAUST HEAD DIAMETER	EXHAUST STEM DIAMETER	EXHAUST STEM TO GUIDE CLEARANCE	EXHAUST OUTER SPRING PRESSURE LENGTH CLOSED (lb. @ in.)	OPEN (lb. @ in.)	EXHAUST INNER SPRING PRESSURE LENGTH CLOSED (lb. @ in.)	OPEN (lb. @ in.)	ANGLE OF SEAT/FACE (deg.)
OLDSMOBILE DIVISION									
140/78	4.576-4.596	1.370-1.380	.3410-.3417	.0010-.0027	71-79 @ 1.746	183-197 @ 1.310	NONE	NONE	46/45
140/87	4.576-4.596	1.370-1.380	.3410-.3417	.0010-.0027	71-79 @ 1.746	183-197 @ 1.310	NONE	NONE	46/45
231/105	4.683-4.713	1.425	.3405-.3412	.0015-.0032	65 @ 1.727	182 @ 1.340	NONE	NONE	45/45
250/105	4.913-4.933	1.495-1.505	.3410-.3417	.0010-.0027	56-64 @ 1.660	18u-192 @ 1.270	NONE	NONE	46/45
260/110	4.680	1.300	.3420-.3427	.0010-.0020	76-84 @ 1.670	180-194 @ 1.270	NONE	NONE	59/60
350/140	5.001-5.031	1.545-1.555	.3723-.3730	.0015-.0032	70 @ 1.727	175 @ 1.340	NONE	NONE	45/45
350/155	5.001-5.031	1.545-1.555	.3723-.3730	.0015-.0032	70 @ 1.727	175 @ 1.340	NONE	NONE	45/45
350/170	4.675	1.617-1.627	.3420-.3427	.0015-.0032	76-84 @ 1.670	180-194 @ 1.270	NONE	NONE	59/60
455/190	4.675	1.617-1.627	.3420-.3427	.0015-.0032	76-84 @ 1.670	180-194 @ 1.270	NONE	NONE	59/60
PONTIAC DIVISION									
140/70	4.576-4.596	1.370-1.380	.3410-.3417	.0010-.0027	71-79 @ 1.746	183-197 @ 1.310	NONE	NONE	46/45
140/84	4.576-4.596	1.370-1.380	.3410-.3417	.0010-.0027	71-79 @ 1.746	183-197 @ 1.310	NONE	NONE	46/45
231/105	4.683-4.713	1.425	.3405-.3412	.0015-.0032	59-69 @ 1.727	174-190 @ 1.340	DAMPER	DAMPER	45/45
250/105	4.923	1.495-1.505	.3410-.3417	.0010-.0027	78-86 @ 1.66	170-180 @ 1.26	NONE	NONE	46/45
260/110	4.680	1.295-1.305	.3420-.3427	.0015-.0032	76-84 @ 1.67	180-194 @ 1.27	NONE	NONE	31/30
350/140	5.016	1.545-1.555	.3723-.3730	.0015-.0032	65-75 @ 1.727	168-182 @ 1.34	NONE	NONE	45/45
350/155	5.016	1.545-1.555	.3723-.3730	.0015-.0032	65-75 @ 1.727	168-182 @ 1.34	NONE	NONE	45/45
350/160	4.8645	2.107-2.113	.3412-.3419	.0016-.0033	59.6-73.6 @ 1.56	124.7-138.7 @ 1.18	33.3-43.3 @ 1.52	95.5-102.5 @ 1.14	30/29
350/165	4.8645	2.107-2.113	.3413-.3419	.0016-.0033	59.6-73.6 @ 1.56	124.7-138.7 @ 1.18	33.3-43.3 @ 1.52	95.5-102.5 @ 1.14	30/29
400/170	4.8645	2.107-2.113	.3412-.3419	.0016-.0033	63-77 @ 1.54	128.1-142.1 @ 1.16	36.4-46.4 @ 1.50	95.7-105.7 @ 1.12	30/29
400/185	4.8645	2.107-2.113	.3412-.3419	.0016-.0033	63-77 @ 1.54	128.1-142.1 @ 1.13	36.4-46.4 @ 1.50	95.7-105.7 @ 1.09	30/29
455/200	4.7155	2.107-2.113	.3412-.3419	.0016-.0033	58-72 @ 1.57	128.8-142.8 @ 1.16	31.4-41.4 @ 1.53	96 -106 @ 1.12	30/29

1977

DISPLACEMENT/ HORSEPOWER	EXHAUST OVERALL LENGTH	EXHAUST HEAD DIAMETER	EXHAUST STEM DIAMETER	EXHAUST STEM TO GUIDE CLEARANCE	EXHAUST OUTER SPRING PRESSURE LENGTH CLOSED (lb. @ in.)	OPEN (lb. @ in.)	EXHAUST INNER SPRING PRESSURE LENGTH CLOSED (lb. @ in.)	OPEN (lb. @ in.)	ANGLE OF SEAT/FACE (deg.)
BUICK DIVISION									
231/105	4.683-4.713	1.425	.3405-.3412	.0015-.0032	64 @ 1.727	182 @ 1.340	DAMPER	DAMPER	45/45
301/135	5.0785	1.50	.3425-.3418	.0010-.0027	78-86 @ 1.66	162-170 @ 1.296	NONE	NONE	45/45
350/ALL	5.031-5.001	1.555-1.545	.3730-.3723	.0015-.0034	70 @ 1.727	175 @ 1.340	NONE	NONE	45/45
403/185	4.675	1.627-1.617	.3427-.3420	.0015-.0032	76-84 @ 1.670	180-194 @ 1.270	NONE	NONE	59/60
CADILLAC DIVISION									
350/180	4.675	1.507-1.497	.3427-.3420	.0015-.0032	76-84 @ 1.670	180-194 @ 1.270	NONE	NONE	30/30
425/180-195	4.998	1.625	.3418-.3411	.0012-.0029	60-65 @ 1.946	159-169 @ 1.473	NONE	NONE	45/44
CHEVROLET DIVISION									
85/57	3.8856-3.9057	1.2547-1.2650	.3130-.3136	.0026-.0029	64-72 @ 1.26	167-179 @ .886	NONE	NONE	46/45
97.6/63	3.8856-3.9057	1.2547-1.2650	.3130-.3136	.0026-.0029	64-72 @ 1.26	167-179 @ .886	NONE	NONE	46/45
140/84	4.576-4.596	1.370-1.380	.3410-.3417	.0010-.0027	71-79 @ 1.746	183-197 @ 1.310	NONE	NONE	46/45
250/110	4.913-4.933	1.495-1.505	.3410-.3417	.0010-.0027	76-86 @ 1.66	170-180 @ 1.26	NONE	NONE	46/45
305/145	4.913-4.933	1.495-1.505	.3410-.3417	.0010-.0027	76-84 @ 1.61	194-206 @ 1.16	DAMPER	DAMPER	46/45
350/160-170-180	4.910-4.930	1.495-1.505	.3410-.3417	.0010-.0027	76-84 @ 1.61	194-206 @ 1.16	DAMPER	DAMPER	46/45
350/210	4.891-4.910	1.595-1.605	.3410-.3417	.0010-.0027	76-84 @ 1.70	194-206 @ 1.25	DAMPER	DAMPER	46/45
OLDSMOBILE DIVISION									
140/84	4.576-4.596	1.370-1.380	.3410-.3417	.0010-.0027	71-79 @ 1.746	183-197 @ 1.310	DAMPER	DAMPER	46/45
231/105	4.683-4.713	1.425	.3405-.3412	.0015-.0032	64 @ 1.727	182 @ 1.340	DAMPER	DAMPER	45/45
260/110	4.680	1.300	.3427-.3420	—	76-84 @ 1.670	180-194 @ 1.270	NONE	NONE	59/60
305/145	4.913-4.933	1.495-1.505	.3410-.3417	.0010-.0027	76-84 @ 1.61	194-206 @ 1.16	DAMPER	DAMPER	46/45
350/170 (Calif.)	4.910-4.930	1.495-1.505	.3410-.3417	.0010-.0027	76-84 @ 1.61	194-206 @ 1.16	DAMPER	DAMPER	46/45
350/170 (Federal)	4.675	1.627-1.617	.3427-.3420	.0015-.0032	76-84 @ 1.670	180-194 @ 1.270	NONE	NONE	59/60
403/200	4.675	1.627-1.617	.3427-.3420	.0015-.0032	76-84 @ 1.670	180-194 @ 1.270	NONE	NONE	59/60
PONTIAC DIVISION									
140/84	4.576-4.596	1.370-1.380	.3410-.3417	.0010-.0027	71-79 @ 1.746	183-197 @ 1.310	NONE	NONE	46/45
151/88	4.920	1.500	.3425-.3418	.0010-.0027	78-86 @ 1.66	172-180 @ 1.254	NONE	NONE	45/45
231/105	4.683-4.713	1.425	.3405-.3412	.0015-.0032	64 @ 1.727	182 @ 1.340	DAMPER	NONE	45/45
301/135 (Manual)	5.0785	1.50	.3425-.3418	.0010-.0027	78-86 @ 1.66	165-173 @ 1.283	NONE	NONE	45/45
301/135 (Auto.)	5.0785	1.50	.3425-.3418	.0010-.0027	78-86 @ 1.66	162-170 @ 1.296	NONE	NONE	45/45
305/145	4.913-4.933	1.495-1.505	.3410-.3417	.0010-.0027	76-84 @ 1.61	194-206 @ 1.16	DAMPER	DAMPER	46/45
350/170 (Calif.)	4.910-4.930	1.495-1.505	.3410-.3417	.0010-.0027	76-84 @ 1.61	194-206 @ 1.16	DAMPER	DAMPER	46/45
350/170 (Federal)	4.675	1.627-1.617	.3427-.3420	.0015-.0032	76-84 @ 1.670	180-194 @ 1.270	NONE	NONE	59/60
400/180	4.8645	1.663-1.657	.3414-.3407	.0021-.0038	68 @ 1.549	131 @ 1.185	40 @ 1.509	97 @ 1.145	45/44
403/185	4.675	1.627-1.617	.3427-.3420	.0015-.0032	76-84 @ 1.670	180-194 @ 1.270	NONE	NONE	59/60

1978

DISPLACEMENT/ HORSEPOWER	EXHAUST OVERALL LENGTH	EXHAUST HEAD DIAMETER	EXHAUST STEM DIAMETER	EXHAUST STEM TO GUIDE CLEARANCE	EXHAUST OUTER SPRING PRESSURE LENGTH CLOSED (lb. @ in.)	OPEN (lb. @ in.)	EXHAUST INNER SPRING PRESSURE LENGTH CLOSED (lb. @ in.)	OPEN (lb. @ in.)	ANGLE OF SEAT/FACE (deg.)
BUICK DIVISION									
196/ALL	4.683-4.713	1.425	.3405-.3412	.0015-.0032	59-69 @ 1.727	174-190 @ 1.340	DAMPER	DAMPER	45/45
231/105	4.683-4.713	1.425	.3405-.3412	.0015-.0032	59-69 @ 1.727	174-190 @ 1.340	DAMPER	DAMPER	46/45
231/TURBO	4.683-4.713	1.425	.3405-.3412	.0015-.0032	59-69 @ 1.727	174-190 @ 1.340	DAMPER	DAMPER	46/45
301/140	5.0785	1.500	.3418-.3425	.0010-.0027	78-86 @ 1.660	162-170 @ 1.296	NONE	NONE	46/45
305/ALL	4.913-4.933	1.500	.3410-.3417	.0010-.0027	76-84 @ 1.610	184-196 @ 1.160	DAMPER	DAMPER	45/45
350/155	5.001-5.031	1.500	.3723-.3730	.0015-.0032	65-75 @ 1.727	168-182 @ 1.340	NONE	NONE	45/45
350/160	4.910-4.930	1.500	.3410-.3417	.0015-.0032	76-84 @ 1.610	184-196 @ 1.160	DAMPER	DAMPER	46/45
350/170	4.675	1.622	.3420-.3427	.0015-.0032	77-83 @ 1.670	145-159 @ 1.294	NONE	NONE	59/60
403/185	4.675	1.622	.3420-.3427	.0015-.0032	76-84 @ 1.670	180-194 @ 1.270	NONE	NONE	59/60
CADILLAC DIVISION									
350/170	4.675	1.497-1.507	.3420-.3427	.0015-.0032	76-84 @ 1.670	180-194 @ 1.270	NONE	NONE	30/30
425/180	4.998	1.625	.3411-.3418	.0012-.0029	60-65 @ 1.946	159-169 @ 1.473	NONE	NONE	45/44
CHEVROLET DIVISION									
98/63	3.8856-3.9057	1.2547-1.2650	.3130-.3136	.0026-.0029	64-72 @ 1.260	167-179 @ .886	NONE	NONE	46/45
98/68	3.8856-3.9057	1.2547-1.2650	.3130-.3136	.0026-.0029	64-72 @ 1.260	167-179 @ .886	NONE	NONE	46/45
151/85	4.920	1.500	.3418-.3425	.0010-.0027	78-86 @ 1.660	172-180 @ 1.254	NONE	NONE	45/45
196/90	4.683-4.713	1.425	.3405-.3412	.0015-.0032	59-69 @ 1.727	174-190 @ 1.340	DAMPER	DAMPER	45/45
200/95	4.910-4.930	1.375-1.385	.3410-.3417	.0010-.0027	76-84 @ 1.700	194-206 @ 1.250	DAMPER	DAMPER	45/45
231/105	4.683-4.713	1.425	.3405-.3412	.0015-.0032	59-69 @ 1.727	174-190 @ 1.340	DAMPER	DAMPER	46/45
250/110	4.913-4.933	1.495-1.505	.3410-.3417	.0010-.0027	76-86 @ 1.660	170-180 @ 1.260	NONE	NONE	46/45
305/145	4.913-4.933	1.495-1.505	.3410-.3417	.0010-.0027	76-84 @ 1.610	184-196 @ 1.160	DAMPER	DAMPER	46/45
350/160	4.910-4.930	1.495-1.505	.3410-.3417	.0010-.0027	76-84 @ 1.610	184-196 @ 1.610	DAMPER	DAMPER	46/45
350/185	4.870-4.889	1.935-1.945	.3410-.3417	.0010-.0027	76-84 @ 1.700	180-188 @ 1.250	DAMPER	DAMPER	46/45
350/220	4.870-4.889	2.017-2.023	.3410-.3417	.0010-.0027	76-84 @ 1.700	196-204 @ 1.250	DAMPER	DAMPER	46/45
OLDSMOBILE DIVISION									
151/85	4.920	1.500	.3418-.3425	.0010-.0027	78-86 @ 1.660	172-180 @ 1.254	NONE	NONE	45/45
231/105	4.683-4.713	1.425	.3405-.3412	.0015-.0032	59-69 @ 1.727	174-190 @ 1.340	DAMPER	DAMPER	46/45
260/110	4.680	1.295-1.305	.3420-.3427	—	76-84 @ 1.670	180-194 @ 1.270	NONE	NONE	59/60
305/145	4.913-4.933	1.495-1.505	.3410-.3417	.0010-.0027	76-84 @ 1.610	184-196 @ 1.160	DAMPER	DAMPER	46/45
350/160	4.910-4.930	1.495-1.505	.3410-.3417	.0010-.0027	76-84 @ 1.610	194-206 @ 1.160	DAMPER	DAMPER	46/45
350/170	4.675	1.617-1.627	.3420-.3427	.0015-.0032	76-84 @ 1.670	180-194 @ 1.270	NONE	NONE	59/60
350/DIESEL	5.0275	1.617-1.627	.3420-.3427	.0015-.0032	77-83 @ 1.670	145-159 @ 1.294	NONE	NONE	59/60
403/190	4.675	1.617-1.627	.3420-.3427	.0015-.0032	76-84 @ 1.670	180-194 @ 1.270	NONE	NONE	59/60

GENERAL MOTORS EXHAUST VALVES & SPRINGS

DISPLACEMENT/ HORSEPOWER	EXHAUST OVERALL LENGTH	EXHAUST HEAD DIAMETER	EXHAUST STEM DIAMETER	EXHAUST STEM TO GUIDE CLEARANCE	EXHAUST OUTER SPRING PRESSURE & LENGTH		EXHAUST INNER SPRING PRESSURE & LENGTH		ANGLE OF SEAT/FACE (Deg.)
					CLOSED (Lb.@In.)	OPEN (Lb.@In.)	CLOSED (Lb.@In.)	OPEN (Lb.@In.)	
PONTIAC DIVISION									
151/ALL	4.920	1.500	.3418-.3425	.0010-.0027	78-86@1.660	172-180@1.254	NONE	NONE	46/45
231/105	4.683-4.713	1.425	.3405-.3412	.0015-.0032	59-69@1.727	174-190@1.340	IN ASSEMBLY	IN ASSEMBLY	45/45
301/140	5.0785	1.500	.3418-.3425	.0010-.0027	78-86@1.660	162-170@1.296	NONE	NONE	46/45
305/145	4.913-4.933	1.495-1.505	.3410-.3417	.0010-.0027	76-84@1.610	184-196@1.160	DAMPER	DAMPER	46/45
350/155	5.001-5.031	1.545-1.555	.3723-.3730	.0015-.0032	65-75@1.727	168-182@1.340	NONE	NONE	45/45
350/160	4.910-4.930	1.495-1.505	.3410-.3417	.0010-.0027	76-84@1.610	184-196@1.160	DAMPER	DAMPER	46/45
350/170	4.675	1.617-1.627	.3420-.3427	.0015-.0032	76-84@1.670	180-194@1.270	NONE	NONE	59/60
400/ALL	4.8645	1.657-1.663	.3407-.3414	.0021-.0038	63-73@1.549	126-136@1.185	35-45@1.509	92-102@1.145	45/44
403/185	4.675	1.617-1.627	.3420-.3427	.0015-.0032	76-84@1.670	180-194@1.270	NONE	NONE	59/60

1979

DISPLACEMENT/ HORSEPOWER	EXHAUST OVERALL LENGTH	EXHAUST HEAD DIAMETER	EXHAUST STEM DIAMETER	EXHAUST STEM TO GUIDE CLEARANCE	CLOSED (Lb.@In.)	OPEN (Lb.@In.)	CLOSED (Lb.@In.)	OPEN (Lb.@In.)	ANGLE OF SEAT/FACE (Deg.)
BUICK DIVISION									
196/ALL	4.683-4.713	1.495-1.505	.3405-.3412	.0015-.0032	59-69@1.727	174-190@1.340	DAMPER	DAMPER	45/45
231/ALL	4.683-4.713	1.495-1.505	.3405-.3412	.0015-.0032	59-69@1.727	174-190@1.340	DAMPER	DAMPER	45/45
301/ALL	5.070	1.500	.3400	.0017-.0027	78-86@1.660	162-170@1.260	NONE	NONE	46/45
305/ALL	4.913-4.933	1.500	.3410-.3417	.0017-.0037	76-84@1.700	194-206@1.250	DAMPER	DAMPER	46/45
350/160	4.893-4.908	1.545-1.555	.3723-.3730	.0015-.0032	67-77@1.727	170-184@1.450	NONE	NONE	45/45
350/195	4.910-4.930	1.500	.3410-.3417	.0017-.0037	76-84@1.700	194-206@1.250	DAMPER	DAMPER	46/45
350/225	4.675	1.497-1.507	.3420-.3427	.0015-.0032	76-84@1.670	180-194@1.270	NONE	NONE	31/30
403/ALL	4.675	1.497-1.507	.3420-.3427	.0015-.0032	76-84@1.670	180-194@1.270	NONE	NONE	31/30
CADILLAC DIVISION									
350/R	4.675	1.497-1.507	.3420-.3427	.0015-.0032	76-84@1.670	180-194@1.270	NONE	NONE	31/30
350/Diesel	5.029	1.625	.3420-.3427	.0015-.0032	77-83@1.670	144-183@1.300	NONE	NONE	31/30
425/ALL	4.998	1.625	.3411-.3418	.0012-.0029	60-65@1.946	159-169@1.473	NONE	NONE	45/44
CHEVROLET DIVISION									
98/70	3.8856-3.9057	1.2547-1.2650	.3130-.3136	.0026-.0029	64-72@1.26	167-179@.886	NONE	NONE	46/45
98/74	3.8856-3.9057	1.2547-1.2650	.3130-.3136	.0026-.0029	64-72@1.26	167-179@.886	NONE	NONE	46/45
151/ALL	4.489	1.500	.3418-.3425	.0010-.0027	78-86@1.66	172-180@1.25	NONE	NONE	46/45
196/105	4.703-4.733	1.500	.3405-.3412	.0015-.0032	59-69@1.727	174-190@1.34	DAMPER	DAMPER	45/45
200/94	4.910-4.930	1.375-1.385	.3410-.3417	.0010-.0027	76-84@1.70	184-196@1.16	DAMPER	DAMPER	46/45
231/115	4.703-4.733	1.500	.3405-.3412	.0015-.0032	59-69@1.727	174-190@1.34	DAMPER	DAMPER	45/45
250/115	4.913-4.933	1.495-1.505	.3410-.3417	.0010-.0027	78-86@1.66	170-180@1.26	NONE	NONE	46/45
267/130	4.910-4.930	1.495-1.505	.3410-.3417	.0010-.0027	76-84@1.70	184-196@1.16	DAMPER	DAMPER	46/45
305/130	4.913-4.923	1.495-1.505	.3410-.3417	.0010-.0027	76-84@1.70	184-196@1.16	DAMPER	DAMPER	46/45
350/160-195	4.910-4.930	1.495-1.505	.3410-.3417	.0010-.0027	76-84@1.61	186-194@1.16	DAMPER	DAMPER	46/45
350/225	4.890-4.910	1.595-1.605	.3410-.3417	.0010-.0027	76-84@1.70	197-209@1.25	DAMPER	DAMPER	46/45
OLDSMOBILE DIVISION									
151/ALL	4.920	1.500	.3418-.3425	.0010-.0027	78-86@1.660	172-180@1.250	NONE	NONE	46/45
231/ALL	4.700	1.500	.3402-.3412	.0015-.0032	59-69@1.727	162-174@1.340	DAMPER	DAMPER	45/45
260/ALL	4.675	1.295-1.305	.3420-.3427	.0015-.0032	76-84@1.670	180-194@1.270	NONE	NONE	31/30
260/Diesel	5.029	1.300	.3420-.3427	.0015-.0032	77-83@1.670	144-183@1.300	NONE	NONE	31/30
305/ALL	4.913-4.933	1.500	.3410-.3417	.0010-.0037	76-84@1.610	194-206@1.160	DAMPER	DAMPER	46/45
350/R	4.675	1.497-1.507	.3420-.3427	.0015-.0032	76-84@1.670	180-194@1.270	NONE	NONE	31/30
350/L	4.910-4.930	1.500	.3410-.3417	.0010-.0037	76-84@1.610	194-206@1.160	DAMPER	DAMPER	46/45
350/DIESEL	5.029	1.625	.3420-.3427	.0015-.0032	77-83@1.670	144-183@1.300	NONE	NONE	31/30
403/ALL	4.675	1.497-1.507	.3420-.3427	.0015-.0032	76-84@1.670	180-194@1.270	NONE	NONE	31/30
PONTIAC DIVISION									
151/ALL	4.920	1.500	.3418-.3425	.0017-.0027	78-86@1.660	172-180@1.254	NONE	NONE	46/45
231/ALL	4.700	1.500	.3405-.3412	.0015-.0032	59-69@1.727	162-174@1.340	DAMPER	DAMPER	45/45
301/ALL	5.0785	1.500	.3418-.3425	.0010-.0027	76-86@1.660	162-170@1.296	NONE	NONE	46/45
305/ALL	4.913-4.933	1.500	.3410-.3417	.0010-.0037	76-84@1.670	180-194@1.270	DAMPER	DAMPER	46/45
350/R	4.675	1.497-1.507	.3420-.3427	.0015-.0032	76-84@1.670	180-194@1.270	NONE	NONE	31/30
350/X	4.910-4.930	1.500	.3410-.3417	.0010-.0027	76-84@1.610	194-206@1.160	DAMPER	DAMPER	46/45
350/L	4.910-4.930	1.500	.3410-.3417	.0010-.0027	76-84@1.700	194-206@1.250	DAMPER	DAMPER	46/45
400/ALL	4.8645	1.657-1.663	.3407-.3414	.0021-.0038	63-73@1.549	126-136@1.185	34-45@1.509	92-102@1.145	45/44
403/ALL	4.675	1.617-1.627	.3420-.3427	.0015-.0032	76-84@1.670	180-194@1.270	NONE	NONE	59/60

1 Foot-end .372-.373; head-end .371-.375.
2 Foot-end .0015-.0035; head-end .0025-.0045
3 Used on manual transmission only. Automatic transmission uses 76-84 @ 1.670.
4 Used on manual transmission only. Automatic transmission uses 199-214 @ 1.198.
5 Used without air conditioning only. With A/C uses 76-84 @ 1.670.
6 Used without air conditioning only. With A/C uses 199-214 @ 1.198
7 Turbo Hydra-matic only. Manual transmission uses 52-66 @ 1.598; 124-138 @ 1.184; 50-62 @ 1.528; 116-128 @ 1.114.
8 Automatic transmission only. With manual transmission 191-206 @ 1.230.

9 Automatic transmission only. With manual transmission 199-214 @ 1.98.
10 Turbo Hydra-Matic only. With manual or M35 automatic transmission 126-140 @ 1.77.
11 Turbo Hydra-Matic only. With manual or M35 automatic transmission 93-103 @ 1.137.
12 Automatic transmission only. With manual transmission 53-67 @ 1.598.
13 Automatic transmission only. With manual transmission 124-138 @ 1.184.
14 Automatic transmission only. With manual transmission 50-62 @ 1.528.
15 Automatic transmission only. With manual transmission 116-128 @ 1.114.

ENGINE TORQUE SPECIFICATIONS (FT.-LBS.)

	YEAR/ENGINE	CYLINDER HEAD BOLTS	MANIFOLDS INTAKE	MANIFOLDS EXHAUST	MAIN BEARING BOLTS	ROD BEARING BOLTS	CRANKSHAFT BOLTS	FLYWHEEL TO CRANKSHAFT PULLEY BOLT
BUICK	75-76/231	85	40	25	1	42	60	200-310
	77/231	80	45	25	100	40	60	175
	ALL/250	95	30	25	65	35	60	—
	75-76/260	85	25	25	120	42	40	160
	77/301	90	40	35	100	35	95	160
	77/305	65	30	20	70	45	60	60
	70-72/350	75	55	18	95	35	60	120
	73/350	80	55	18	115	35	60	140
	74-76/350	80	45	28	115	40	60	140
	77/350[15]	80	45	25	100	40	60	175
	77/350[16]	130[17]	40[17]	25	80[18]	42	60[19]	200-310
	77/350[20]	65	30	20	70	45	60	60
	77/403	130[17]	40[17]	25	80[18]	42	60[19]	200-310
	70-74/455	100	65	18	115	45	60	200
	75-76/455	100	45	28	115	45	60	200
CADILLAC	76/350	85	25	25	1	42	40	160
	77/350	130[17]	40[17]	25	80[18]	42	60	310
	77/425	95	30	35[21]	90	40	75	—
	ALL/472-500	115	30	35	90	40	75	—

ENGINE SPECIFICATIONS

ENGINE TORQUE SPECIFICATIONS (FT.-LBS.)

YEAR/ENGINE	CYLINDER HEAD BOLTS	MANIFOLDS INTAKE	MANIFOLDS EXHAUST	MAIN BEARING BOLTS	ROD BEARING BOLTS	CRANKSHAFT BOLTS	FLYWHEEL TO CRANKSHAFT PULLEY BOLT
CHEVROLET 76-77/85-97.6		13-18	13-18[2]	40-52	34-40	40-52	65-85
71-77/140	60	30	30	65	35	60	80
70/153	95	30	25	65	35	60	—
ALL/250	95	30	25	65	35	60	—
ALL/262, 307							
305, 350, 400	60-70	30	[4]	75[3]	45	60	60
ALL/402-455	80[5]	30	30	105	50	65	85
OLDSMOBILE 76-77/140	60	30	30	65	35	60	80
75-77/231	85	40	25	[1]	42	60	200-310
77/231	80	45	25	100	40	60	175
ALL/250	95	30	25	65	35	60	—
75-76/260	85	25	25	120	42	40	160
77/260	85[17]	40[17]	25	80[18]	42	60[19]	200-310
77/305	65	30	20	70	45	60	60
70-74/350	80-85	35	25	[1]	42	60[6]	160
75-76/350	85	25	25	[1]	42	40	160
77/350[20]	65	30	20	70	45	60	60
77/350[22]	130	40[17]	25	80[18]	42	60[19]	200-310
77/403	130	40[17]	25	80[18]	42	60[19]	200-310
70-74/455	80-85	35	25	120	42	60[6]	160
75-76/455	85	25	25	110	42	40	160
PONTIAC 76/140	60	30	30	65	35	60	80
77/151	95	40	23	65	30	55	160
75-76/231	85	40	25	[1]	42	60	200-310
77/231	80	45	25	100	40	60	175
ALL/250	95	30	25	65	35	60	—
75-76/260	85	25	25	120	42	40	160
77/301	85	35	40	70[25]	30	95	160
77/305	65	30	20	70	45	60	60
70-76/350	95	40	30	100[7]	43	95	160
77/350[20]	65	30	20	70	45	60	60
77/350[22]	130[17]	40[17]	25	80[18]	42	60[19]	200-310
77/350[24]	100	35	40	100[26]	40	95	160
70-76/400	95	40	30	100[7]	43	95	160
77/400	100	35	40	100[26]	40	95	160
77/403	130[17]	40[17]	25	80[18]	42	60[19]	200-310
ALL/455	95	40	30	100[7]	43	95	160
FORD, LINCOLN, MERCURY 70-76/170-200-240	70-75	—	13-18	60-70	19-24	75-85	85-100
70-76/250	70-75	—	13-18	60-70	21-26	75-85	85-100
77/200-250	27	–	18-24	60-70	21-26	75-85	85-100
ALL/97.6	65-70	12-15	15-18	65-70	30-35	50-55	24-28
ALL/122	65-80	12-15	12-15	65-75	29-34	47-51	39-43
ALL/140	80-90	14-21	16-23	80-90	30-36	54-64	80-114
70-76/170.8	65-80	15-18	14-18	65-75	21-25	47-51	92-103
77/170.8	[28]	15-18[29]	20-30	65-75	21-25	47-51	92-103
70-73/302	65-72	23-25	12-16	60-70	19-24	75-85	70-90
74-76/302	65-72	19-27	12-16	60-70	19-24	75-85	35-50
77/302	–	23-25	18-24	60-70	19-24	75-85	70-90
70-73/351	95-100	23-25[8]	12-22	95-105	40-45	75-85	70-90
74-76/351W	105-112	19-27	18-24	95-105	40-45	75-85	35-50
77/351W	–	23-25	18-24	95-105	40-45	75-85	70-90
74-76/351C-M	95-105	22-32	12-22	95-105	40-45	75-85	70-90
77/351M-400	[30]	22-32[31]	18-24	95-105	40-45	75-85	70-90
70-73/428	80-90	32-35	18-24	95-105	53-58	75-85	70-90
70-73/429-460	130-140	25-30	28-33	95-105	40-45	75-85	70-90
70-73/429 Boss	90-95	25-30	28-33	70-80	85-90	75-85	70-90
ALL/400	95-105	22-32	12-16	95-105	40-45	75-85	70-90
70-76/460	130-140	22-32	28-33	95-105	40-45	75-85	35-50
77/460	[32]	22-32[33]	28-33	95-105	40-45	75-85	70-90
DODGE, CHRYSLER, PLYMOUTH, IMPERIAL 70-76/170-198-225	70	10	10	85	45	55	[9]
77/225	70	120[34]	200[34]	85	45	55	[9]
70-76/318-340-360	95	35	15-20	85	45	55	[12]
77/318-360	95	45	15-25	85	45	55	100
70-76/383-400-440	70	40	30	85	45	55	135
77/400-440	70	45	40	85	45	55	135
ALL/426	75	[11]	35	100[10]	75	70	135
AMERICAN MOTORS 77/121	65[36]	18	18	58[35]	41	65	65
70-76/199-232-258	[13]	18-28	18-28	75-80	25-30	95-120	50-60
77/232-258	95-115	18-28	18-28	75-85	30-35	95-120	50-60
70-76/304-360-390-401	100-120	37-47	20-30	90-105	[14]	95-120	50-60
77/304-360	100-120	37-47	20-30	90-105	30-35	95-120	50-60

[1] 1-4, 80; 5, 120.
[2] End bolts, 19-25.
[3] Where 4 main bolts are used, torque outer bolts to 65.
[4] End bolts: 15-20; center bolts: 25-30.
[5] If aluminum heads, torque long bolts to 75, short bolts to 65.
[6] With manual transmission, 80.
[7] Rear main, 120.
[8] ⅜-in. bolts, 28-32; ¼-in. bolts, 6-9.
[9] Press fit.
[10] Cross bolt mains, 45.
[11] Center bolts: 6; others, 4.
[12] 1970 318, 340 cu.-in. engines, 100.
[13] 1970-72, 80; 1973-76, 95-115
[14] 304, 360 cu. ins., 390; 390, 401 cu. ins., 35-40; all '75-'76, 26-30.
[15] Code engines H and J. Code is 5th character of vehicle ID number.
[16] Code engine K. Code is 5th character of vehicle ID number.
[17] Clean and dip entire bolt in engine oil before tightening.
[18] 120 on No. 5 bearing.
[19] 90 for manual transmission.
[20] Code engine L. Code is 5th character of vehicle ID number
[21] 112 for short bolt.
[22] Code engine R. Code is 5th character of vehicle ID number.
[23] 40 for bolting intake to exhaust manifold; 30 for nut from manifold to cylinder head; 40 for bolt to cylinder head.
[24] Code engine P. Code is 5th character of vehicle ID number
[25] 100 for rear main.
[26] 120 for rear main.
[27] Torque in sequence: Step 1—50-55; Step 2—60-65; Step 3—70-75.
[28] Torque in sequence: Step 1—29-40; Step 2—40-51; Step 3—65-80.
[29] Torque in sequence Step 1—3-6; Step 2—6-11; Step 3—11-15. Retorque to 15-18 when engine is hot.
[30] Torque in sequence Step 1—751 Step 2—95-105.
[31] 19-25 for 5/16.
[32] Torque in sequence: Step 1—70-80; Step 2—100-110; Step 3—130-140.
[33] Retorque to specifications after engine is hot.
[34] Inch pounds.
[35] 47 for rear bearing.
[36] 73 warm.

TORQUE SEQUENCES FOR CYLINDER HEAD BOLTS

The bolts that secure the cylinder head to the block often vary in length and, consequently, are easily misplaced. To ensure proper installation, tag each bolt with a location number (corresponding with the numbers on the applicable diagram) before removal.

AMERICAN MOTORS

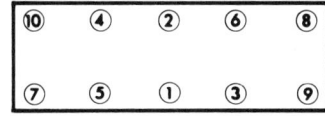

I-4

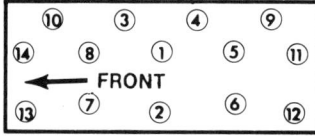

All V-8's

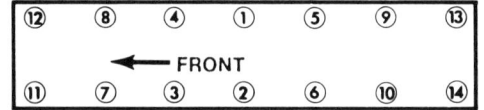

All I-6's

CHRYSLER CORPORATION

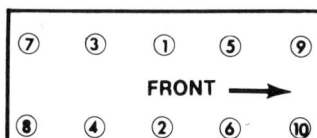

V-8—318, 340, 360 cu.-in.

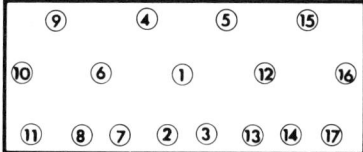

V-8—426 Hemis

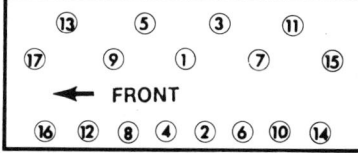

V-8—383, 400, 440 cu.-in.

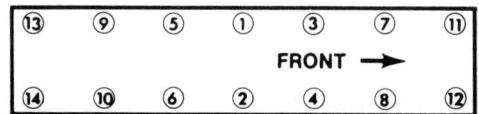

All I-6's

FORD MOTOR COMPANY

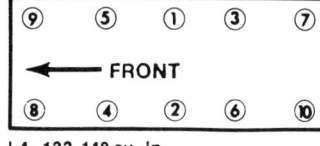

I-4—122, 140 cu.-in.

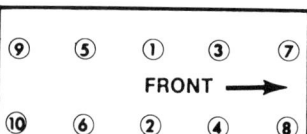

All V-6's

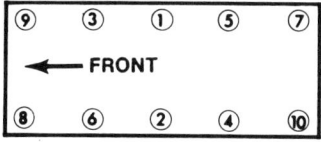

I-4—98 cu.-in.

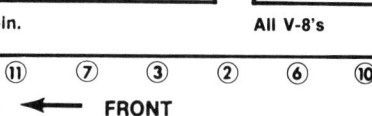

All V-8's

I-6 — 240 cu.-in.

I-6 —170, 200, 250 cu.-in.

GENERAL MOTORS

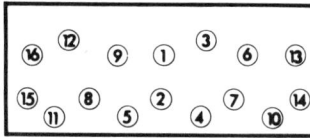

V-8—396, 402, 454 cu.-in. (Chevrolet)

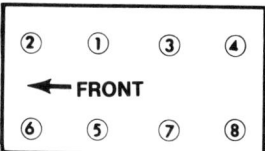

All V-6's

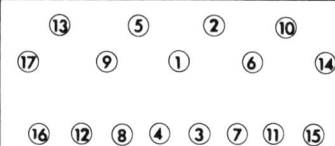

V-8—262, 305, 307, 350, 400 cu.-in. (Chev)

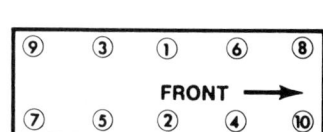

V-8— All Pontiacs, Buicks

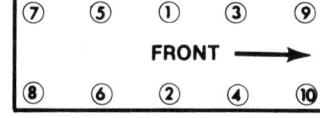

V-8—350, 455 cu.-in. (Oldsmobile)

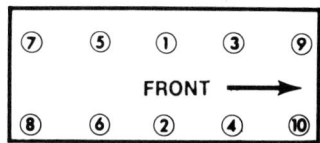

V-8—All Cadillacs

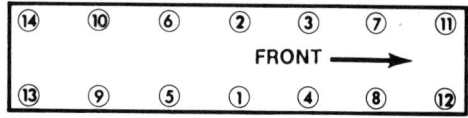

All I-6's

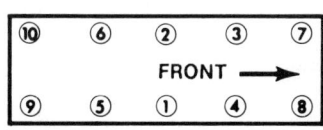

All I-4's

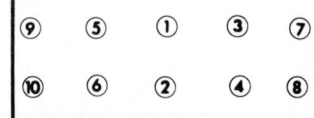

V-8—301

COORDINATING THE DISTRIBUTOR WITH THE PLUGS

If a situation arises where you must disconnect the secondary wiring between the distributor cap and spark plugs, then don't depend upon your memory to return them to the proper places. Locate your car's engine on the chart below and familiarize yourself with the cylinder locations. Follow the plug wire from the No. 1 cylinder up to its connection at the distributor and, with a piece of tape, label the wire with an indelible "1." Once you've established this as your proper starting place, label the other wires and distributor cap towers with their respective cylinder numbers. Using the specified firing order as your map, depart from tower No. 1, and move in a clockwise or counterclockwise direction (as specified by the chart) to the next wire, and label it with the next number in the firing order. When all 4, 6 or 8 towers have been identified, remove the wires.

If you're reading this after the fact and you realize that you can't coordinate the distributor with the spark plug, don't give up. There's still hope. Some distributor caps have a small "1" molded into the No. 1 tower. If you find one, you're in luck. Merely locate the No. 1 spark plug, and join the plug to the tower with a wire and, as described above, go to the next cylinder in the firing order. Choose a wire of the proper length, and connect the tower to the proper plug. If you can't find the number on the cap, then run a wire from the No. 1 plug to any cap tower and, traveling in the right direction, connect the next plug in the firing order to the next tower and so on until complete. Try to start the car (but don't prolong the effort). If the attempt fails, move each wire to the next (in the prescribed direction) and try again. You can move the wires one complete rotation and, within that rotation, you'll hit upon the correct positioning and the car will start.

CYLINDER NUMBERING, FIRING ORDER AND VALVE SEQUENCE

MAKE	CYLINDER NUMBERS (front to rear)[1]	FIRING ORDER	DISTRIBUTOR Rotation[2]	VALVE SEQUENCE[3]
AMERICAN MOTORS I-4's	1-2-3-4	1-3-4-2	C	IE-IE-IE-IE
AMERICAN MOTORS I-6's	1-2-3-4-5-6	1-5-3-6-2-4	C	EI-IE-IE-IE-EI-IE
AMERICAN MOTORS V-8's	L 1-3-5-7 R 2-4-6-8	1-8-4-3-6-5-7-2	C	EI-IE-EI-IE
BUICK I-6	1-2-3-4-5-6	1-5-3-6-2-4	C	EI-IE-EI-IE-EI-IE
BUICK V-6	L 1-3-5 R 2-4-6	1-6-5-4-3-2	C	EI-EI-IE
BUICK V-8's	L 1-3-5-7 R 2-4-6-8	1-8-4-3-6-5-7-2	C	EI-IE-EI-IE
CADILLAC V-8's	L 2-4-6-8 R 1-3-5-7	1-5-6-3-4-2-7-8	C	EI-IE-IE-IE[4]
CHEVROLET I-4's	1-2-3-4	1-3-4-2	C	IE-IE-IE-IE[5]
CHEVROLET I-6	1-2-3-4-5-6	1-5-3-6-2-4	C	EI-IE-EI-IE-EI-IE
CHEVROLET V-8's, except below	L 1-3-5-7 R 2-4-6-8	1-8-4-3-6-5-7-2	C	EI-IE-EI-IE
CHEVROLET V-8's—396, 402, 454 cu.-in.	L 1-3-5-7 R 2-4-6-8	1-8-4-3-6-5-7-2	C	IE-IE-IE-IE
CHRYSLER CORP. I-6's	1-2-3-4-5-6	1-5-3-6-2-4	C	EI-EI-EI-IE-IE-IE
CHRYSLER CORP. V-8—318 cu.-in.	L 1-3-5-7 R 2-4-6-8	1-8-4-3-6-5-7-2	C	L EI-EI-EI-EI, R IE-IE-IE-IE
CHRYSLER CORP. V-8—340, 360 cu.-in.	L 1-3-5-7 R 2-4-6-8	1-8-4-3-6-5-7-2	C	EI-IE-EI-IE
CHRYSLER CORP. V-8's—383, 400, 426, 440	L 1-3-5-7 R 2-4-6-8	1-8-4-3-6-5-7-2	CC	EI-IE-EI-IE
FORD MOTOR CO. I-4—98 cu.-in.	1-2-3-4	1-2-4-3	CC	EI-IE-EI-IE
FORD MOTOR CO. I-6's, except 240 cu.-in.	1-2-3-4-5-6	1-5-3-6-2-4	C	EI-IE-IE-EI-EI-IE
FORD MOTOR CO. I-6—240 cu.-in.	1-2-3-4-5-6	1-5-3-6-2-4	C	EI-EI-EI-EI-EI-EI
FORD MOTOR CO. V-6	L 4-5-6 R 1-2-3	1-4-2-5-3-6	C	L IE-EI-EI, R IE-IE-EI
FORD MOTOR CO. V-8—302 cu.-in.	L 5-6-7-8 R 1-2-3-4	1-5-4-2-6-3-7-8	CC	L EI-EI-EI-EI, R IE-IE-IE-IE
FORD MOTOR CO. V-8's—351, 400 cu.-in.	L 5-6-7-8 R 1-2-3-4	1-3-7-2-6-5-4-8	CC	L EI-EI-EI-EI, R IE-IE-IE-IE
FORD MOTOR CO. V-8's—390, 428 cu.-in.	L 5-6-7-8 R 1-2-3-4	1-5-4-2-6-3-7-8	CC	EI-EI-IE-IE
FORD MOTOR CO. V-8's—429, 460 cu.-in.	L 5-6-7-8 R 1-2-3-4	1-5-4-2-6-3-7-8	CC	L EI-EI-EI-EI, R IE-IE-IE-IE
OLDSMOBILE I-6	1-2-3-4-5-6	1-5-3-6-2-4	C	EI-IE-EI·IE-EI-IE
OLDSMOBILE V-6	L 1-3-5 R 2-4-6	1-6-5-4-3-2	C	EI-EI-IE
OLDSMOBILE V-8	L 1-3-5-7 R 2-4-6-8	1-8-4-3-6-5-7-2	CC[6]	IE-IE-EI-EI
PONTIAC I-6	1-2-3-4-5-6	1-5-3-6-2-4	C	EI-IE-EI-IE-EI-IE
PONTIAC V-6's	L 1-3-5 R 2-4-6	1-6-5-4-3-2	C	EI-EI-IE
PONTIAC V-8's	L 1-3-5-7 R 2-4-6-8	1-8-4-3-6-5-7-2	CC[7]	EI-IE-EI-IE

1 L signifies left (as viewed from driver's seat) bank of cylinders, R signifies right.
2 Direction of distributor rotation is indicated by C (clockwise) or CC (counterclockwise).
3 Valve sequence identifies valves from front to rear, "E" for exhaust, "I" intake.
  Where sequence differs from one head to the other (on some V-6's and V-8's), left head (viewed from driver's seat) is signified by "L", right by "R".
4 Cadillac Seville uses Oldsmobile 350-cu.-in. engine— IE-IE-EI-EI.
5 Cosworth Vega has intake valves on right side, exhaust on left.
6 Omega 350-cu.-in. V-8—clockwise.
7 350-cu.-in. (Ventura II), 307 cu.-in. V-8's clockwise; all other V-8's counterclockwise.

CONVERSION FROM FRACTIONAL INCHES TO MILLIMETERS

inch		mm	inch		mm
1/64	0 015 625	0 396 875	33/64	0 515 625	13 096 875
1/32	0 031 250	0 793 750	17/32	0 531 250	13 493 750
3/64	0 046 875	1 190 625	35/64	0 546 875	13 890 625
1/16	0 062 500	1 587 500	9/16	0 562 500	14 287 500
5/64	0 078 125	1 984 375	37/64	0 578 125	14 684 375
3/32	0 093 750	2 381 250	19/32	0 593 750	15 081 250
7/64	0 109 375	2 778 125	39/64	0 609 375	15 478 125
1/8	0 125 000	3 175 000	5/8	0 625 000	15 875 000
9/64	0 140 625	3 571 875	41/64	0 640 625	16 271 875
5/32	0 156 250	3 968 750	21/32	0 656 250	16 668 750
11/64	0 171 875	4 365 625	43/64	0 671 875	17 065 625
3/16	0 187 500	4 762 500	11/16	0 687 500	17 462 500
13/64	0 203 125	5 159 375	45/64	0 703 125	17 859 375
7/32	0 218 750	5 556 250	23/32	0 718 750	18 256 250
15/64	0 234 375	5 953 125	47/64	0 734 375	18 653 125
1/4	0 250 000	6 350 000	3/4	0 750 000	19 050 000
17/64	0 265 625	6 746 875	49/64	0 765 625	19 446 875
9/32	0 281 250	7 143 750	25/32	0 781 250	19 843 750
19/64	0 296 875	7 540 625	51/64	0 796 875	20 240 625
5/16	0 312 500	7 937 500	13/16	0 812 500	20 637 500
21/64	0 328 125	8 334 375	53/64	0 828 125	21 034 375
11/32	0 343 750	8 731 250	27/32	0 843 750	21 431 250
23/64	0 359 375	9 128 125	55/64	0 859 375	21 828 125
3/8	0 375 000	9 525 000	7/8	0 875 000	22 225 000
25/64	0 390 625	9 921 875	57/64	0 890 625	22 621 875
13/32	0 406 250	10 318 750	29/32	0 906 250	23 018 750
27/64	0 421 875	10 715 625	59/64	0 921 875	23 415 625
7/16	0.437 500	11 112 500	15/16	0 937 500	23 812 500
29/64	0 453 125	11 509 375	61/64	0 953 125	24 209 375
15/32	0 468 750	11 906 250	31/32	0 968 750	24 606 250
31/64	0 484 375	12 303 125	63/64	0 984 375	25 003 125
1/2	0. 500 000	12 700 000	1	1 000 000	25 400 000

METRIC CONVERSIONS

FT.-LBS. X .1383 = METER-KILOGRAMS

Ft. Lbs.	0	1	2	3	4	5	6	7	8	9
	Mkgs	Mkgs	Mkgs	Mkgs	Mkgs	Mkgs	Mkgs	Mkgs	Mkgs	Mkgs
0	0	.14	.28	.42	.55	.69	.83	.97	1.11	1.25
10	1.38	1.52	1.66	1.80	1.94	2.07	2.21	2.35	2.49	2.63
20	2.77	2.90	3.04	3.18	3.32	3.46	3.60	3.73	3.87	4.01
30	4.15	4.29	4.43	4.56	4.70	4.84	4.98	5.12	5.26	5.39
40	5.53	5.67	5.81	5.95	6.09	6.22	6.36	6.50	6.64	6.78
50	6.92	7.05	7.19	7.33	7.47	7.61	7.75	7.88	8.02	8.16
60	8.30	8.44	8.57	8.71	8.85	8.90	9.13	9.27	9.40	9.54
70	9.68	9.82	9.96	10.09	10.23	10.37	10.51	10.65	10.79	10.92
80	11.01	11.20	11.34	11.48	11.62	11.75	11.89	12.03	12.17	12.31
90	12.45	12.59	12.73	12.86	13.00	13.14	13.28	13.42	13.55	13.69
100	13.83	13.97	14.11	14.25	14.38	14.52	14.66	14.80	14.94	15.08
110	15.21	15.35	15.49	15.63	15.76	15.90	16.04	16.18	16.32	16.46

CONVERSION FROM MILLIMETERS TO INCHES

mm	inch	mm	inch	mm	inch
1	0 039 370 08	36	1 417 322 8	71	2 795 275 6
2	0 078 740 16	37	1 456 692 9	72	2 834 645 7
3	0 118 110 24	38	1 496 063 0	73	2 874 015 7
4	0 157 480 31	39	1 535 433 1	74	2 913 385 8
5	0 196 850 39	40	1 574 803 1	75	2 952 755 9
6	0 236 220 47	41	1 614 173 2	76	2 992 126 0
7	0 275 590 55	42	1 653 543 3	77	3 031 496 1
8	0 314 960 63	43	1 692 913 4	78	3 070 866 1
9	0 354 330 71	44	1 732 283 5	79	3 110 236 2
10	0 393 700 8	45	1 771 653 5	80	3 149 606 3
11	0 433 070 9	46	1 811 023 6	81	3 188 976 4
12	0 472 440 9	47	1 850 393 7	82	3 228 346 5
13	0 511 811 0	48	1 889 763 8	83	3 267 716 5
14	0 551 181 1	49	1 929 133 9	84	3 307 086 6
15	0 590 551 2	50	1 968 503 9	85	3 346 456 7
16	0 629 921 3	51	2 007 874 0	86	3 385 826 8
17	0 669 291 3	52	2 047 244 1	87	3 425 196 8
18	0 708 661 4	53	2 086 614 2	88	3 464 566 9
19	0 748 031 5	54	2 125 984 2	89	3 503 937 0
20	0 787 401 6	55	2 165 354 3	90	3 543 307 1
21	0 826 771 7	56	2 204 724 4	91	3 582 677 2
22	0 866 141 7	57	2 244 094 5	92	3 622 047 2
23	0 905 511 8	58	2 283 464 6	93	3 661 417 3
24	0 944 881 9	59	2 322 834 6	94	3 700 787 4
25	0 984 252 0	60	2 362 204 7	95	3 740 157 5
26	1 023 622 0	61	2 401 574 8	96	3 779 527 6
27	1 062 992 1	62	2 440 944 9	97	3 818 897 6
28	1 102 362 2	63	2 480 315 0	98	3 858 267 7
29	1 141 732 3	64	2 519 685 0	99	3 897 637 8
30	1 181 102 4	65	2 559 055 1	100	3 937 008
31	1 220 472 4	66	2 598 425 2		
32	1 259 842 5	67	2 637 795 3		
33	1 299 212 6	68	2 677 165 3		
34	1 338 582 7	69	2 716 535 4		
35	1 377 952 8	70	2 755 905 5		

FORMULA TO CONVERT mm TO INCHES: Divide 25.4 into known mm.

CONVERSION FROM DECIMAL INCHES TO MILLIMETERS

inch	mm	inch	mm	inch	mm
1	25 4	36	914 4	71	1 803 4
2	50 8	37	939 8	72	1 828 8
3	76 2	38	965 2	73	1 854 2
4	101 6	39	990 6	74	1 879 6
5	127 0	40	1 016 0	75	1 905 0
6	152 4	41	1 041 4	76	1 930 4
7	177 8	42	1 066 8	77	1 955 8
8	203 2	43	1 092 2	78	1 981 2
9	228 6	44	1 117 6	79	2 006 6
10	254 0	45	1 143 0	80	2 032 0
11	279 4	46	1 168 4	81	2 057 4
12	304 8	47	1 193 8	82	2 082 8
13	330 2	48	1 219 2	83	2 108 2
14	355 6	49	1 244 6	84	2 133 6
15	381 0	50	1 270 0	85	2 159 0
16	406 4	51	1 295 4	86	2 184 4
17	431 8	52	1 320 8	87	2 209 8
18	457 2	53	1 346 2	88	2 235 2
19	482 6	54	1 371 6	89	2 260 6
20	508 0	55	1 397 0	90	2 286 0
21	533 4	56	1 422 4	91	2 311 4
22	558 8	57	1 447 8	92	2 336 8
23	584 2	58	1 473 2	93	2 362 2
24	609 6	59	1 498 6	94	2 387 6
25	635 0	60	1 524 0	95	2 413 0
26	660 4	61	1 549 4	96	2 438 4
27	685 8	62	1 574 8	97	2 463 8
28	711 2	63	1 600 2	98	2 489 2
29	736 6	64	1 625 6	99	2 514 6
30	762 0	65	1 651 0	100	2 540 0
31	787 4	66	1 676 4		
32	812 8	67	1 701 8		
33	838 2	68	1 727 2		
34	863 6	69	1 752 6		
35	889 0	70	1 778 0		

Tune-Up Specifications

American Motors 4

YEAR	ENGINE CU. INS.	HP	CARBURETOR MAKE	TYPE	FLOAT LEVEL (INS.)	INITIAL TIMING STD. TRANS	AUTO. TRANS.	DISTRIBUTOR POINT GAP (INS.)	DWELL
1979	121		Holley	2-bbl.	.420	12°BTDC	12°BTDC[2]	.018	44-50°
1978	121		Holley	2-bbl.	.420	8° BTDC	10° BTDC	.018	44-50°
1977	121	80	Holley	2-bbl.	.42	12° BTDC[1]	12° BTDC[2]	.018	44-50°

1 Altitude 10° BTDC; California 8° BTDC. 2 California 8° BTDC. 3 In Neutral. 4 In Drive.

American Motors 6

YEAR	CU. INS.	HP	MAKE	TYPE	FLOAT LEVEL	STD. TRANS	AUTO. TRANS.	POINT GAP	DWELL
1979	232		Carter	1-bbl.	.476	8°BTDC	10°BTDC[18]	12	12
	258		Carter	1-bbl.	.476	—	8°BTDC	12	12
	258		Carter	2-bbl.	.250	4°BTDC	8°BTDC	12	12
1978	232		Carter	1-bbl.	.476	8° BTDC	10° BTDC	12	12
	258		Carter	1-bbl.	.476	10° BTDC	10° BTDC	12	12
	258		Carter	2-bbl.	.250	6° BTDC	8° BTDC	12	12
1977	232	90	Carter	1-bbl.	.476	8° BTDC[16]	10° BTDC	12	12
	258	95	Carter	1-bbl.	.476	6° BTDC[17]	8° BTDC[17]	12	12
	258	120	Carter	2-bbl.	.476	6° BTDC	8° BTDC	12	12
1976	232	90	Carter	1-bbl.	.476	8° BTDC	8° BTDC	12	12
	258	95	Carter	1-bbl.	.476	6° BTDC	8° BTDC	12	12
	258	120	Carter	2-bbl.	.250	6° BTDC	8° BTDC	12	12
1975	232	100	Carter	1-bbl.	15/32	5° BTDC[11]	5° BTDC[11]	12	-
	258	110	Carter	1-bbl.	15/32	5° BTDC[11]	5° BTDC[11]	12	-
1974	232	100	Carter	1-bbl.	15/32	5° BTDC[1]	5° BTDC[1]	.016	31°-34°
	258	110	Carter	1-bbl.	15/32	3° BTDC[1]	3° BTDC[1]	.016	31°-34°
1973	232	100	Carter	1-bbl.	29/64	5° BTDC[1]	5° BTDC[1]	.016	31°-34°
	258	110	Carter	1-bbl.	29/64	3° BTDC[1]	3° BTDC[1]	.016	31°-34°
1972	232	100	Carter	1-bbl.	29/64	5° BTDC[1]	5° BTDC[1]	.016	31°-34°
	258	110	Carter	1-bbl.	29/64	3° BTDC[1]	3° BTDC[1]	.016	31°-34°
1971	232	135	Carter	1-bbl.	29/64	3° BTDC[1]	5° BTDC[1]	.016	31°-34°
	258	150	Carter	1-bbl.	29/64	5° BTDC[1]	5° BTDC[1]	.016	31°-34°
1970	199	128	Carter	1-bbl.	29/64	3° ± 1° BTDC[1]	3° ± 1° BTDC[1]	.016	31°-34°
	232	145	Carter	1-bbl.	29/64	3° ± 1° BTDC[1]	3° ± 1° BTDC[1]	.016	31°-34°
	232	155	Autolite	2-bbl.	7/32	3° ± 1° BTDC[1]	3° ± 1° BTDC[1]	.016	31°-34°

1 At 500 rpm (vacuum advance hose disconnected).
2 600 with Exhaust Gas Recirculation (EGR).
3 550 with Exhaust Gas Recirculation (EGR).
4 California cars 700 rpm.
5 California cars 600 rpm.
6 Place in drive, set parking brake firmly, do not accelerate engine.
7 Lowest cylinder must be more than 75% of highest cylinder pressure.
8 Maximum variation 10 psi between cylinders.
9 Matador Wagons 600 rpm.
10 Matador 650 rpm.

American Motors V-8

YEAR	CU. INS.	HP	MAKE	TYPE	FLOAT LEVEL	STD. TRANS	AUTO. TRANS.	POINT GAP	DWELL
1979	304		Motorcraft	2-bbl.	.780	5°BTDC	8°BTDC	7	7
1978	304		Motorcraft	2-bbl.	.780	—	10° BTDC	7	7
	360		Motorcraft	2-bbl.	.780	—	10° BTDC	7	7
1977	304	120	Motorcraft	2-bbl.	.78	—	10° BTDC[8]	7	7
	360	140	Motorcraft	2-bbl.	.78	—	10° BTDC[8]	7	7
1976	304	120	Motorcraft	2-bbl.	13/32	5° BTDC	10° BTDC[8]	7	7
	360	140	Motorcraft	2-bbl.	13/32	—	10° BTDC[8]	7	7
	360	180	Motorcraft	4-bbl.	.90	—	10° BTDC[8]	7	7
	401	N/A	Motorcraft	4-bbl.	.90	—	10° BTDC[8]	7	7
1975	304	150	Motorcraft	2-bbl.	13/32	5° BTDC	5° BTDC	7	—
	360	285	Motorcraft	2-bbl.	13/32	5° BTDC	5° BTDC	7	—
	360	295	Motorcraft	4-bbl.	9/100	—	5° BTDC	7	—
	401	345	Motorcraft	4-bbl.	9/100	—	5° BTDC	7	—
1974	304	150	Motorcraft	2-bbl.	13/32	5° BTDC[1]	5° BTDC[1]	.016	29°-31°
	360	175	Motorcraft	2-bbl.	13/32	5° BTDC[1]	5° BTDC[1]	.016	29°-31°
	360	195	Motorcraft	4-bbl.	13/16	5° BTDC[1]	5° BTDC[1]	.016	29°-31°
	360	220	Motorcraft	4-bbl.	13/16	5° BTDC[1]	5° BTDC[1]	.016	29°-31°
	401	235	Motorcraft	4-bbl.	13/16	5° BTDC[1]	5° BTDC[1]	.016	29°-31°
1973	304	150	Autolite	2-bbl.	3/8	5° BTDC[1]	5° BTDC[1]	.016	29°-31°
	360	175	Autolite	2-bbl.	3/8	5° BTDC[1]	5° BTDC[1]	.016	29°-31°
	360	195	Autolite	4-bbl.	13/16	5° BTDC[1]	5° BTDC[1]	.016	29°-31°
	401	255	Autolite	4-bbl.	13/16	5° BTDC[1]	5° BTDC[1]	.016	29°-31°
1972	304	150	Autolite	2-bbl.	3/8	5° BTDC[1]	5° BTDC[1]	.016	29°-31°
	360	175	Autolite	2-bbl.	3/8	5° BTDC[1]	5° BTDC[1]	.016	29°-31°
	360	175	Autolite	4-bbl.	13/16	5° BTDC[1]	5° BTDC[1]	.016	29°-31°
	401	175	Autolite	4-bbl.	13/16	5° BTDC[1]	5° BTDC[1]	.016	29°-31°
1971	304	210	Autolite	2-bbl.	3/8	2.5° BTDC[1]	2.5° BTDC[1]	.016	29°-31°
	360	245	Autolite	2-bbl.	3/8	2.5° BTDC[1]	2.5° BTDC[1]	.016	29°-31°
	360	285	Autolite	4-bbl.	13/16	2.5° BTDC[1]	2.5° BTDC[1]	.016	29°-31°
	401	330	Autolite	4-bbl.	13/16	2.5° BTDC[1]	2.5° BTDC[1]	.016	29°-31°
1970	304	210	Autolite	2-bbl.	3/8	5° ± 1° BTDC[1]	5° ± 1° BTDC[1]	.016	29°-31°
	360	245	Autolite	2-bbl.	3/8	5° ± 1° BTDC[1]	5° ± 1° BTDC[1]	.016	29°-31°
	360	290	Autolite	4-bbl.	13/16	5° ± 1° BTDC[1]	5° ± 1° BTDC[1]	.016	29°-31°
	390	325	Autolite	4-bbl.	13/16	5° ± 1° BTDC[1]	5° ± 1° BTDC[1]	.016	29°-31°
	390	340	Autolite	4-bbl.	13/16	TDC ± 1°[1,2]	TDC ± 1°[1,2]	.016	29°-31°

1 Set at 500 rpm with distributor vacuum advance hose disconnected and plugged.
2 390-cu.-in., 4-bbl.; effective with engine code 209x26 (type 2 distributor).
3 California cars—700 rpm.
4 Lowest cylinder pressure must be more than 75% of highest cylinder.

NOTE: The spark plug brands listed are those used by the car manufacturers as original factory equipment. For equivalent replacements, consult the spark plug substitution charts at your auto parts store.

When examining your spark plugs at tune-up time, a reference to pages 3-4/3-5 and 3-27/3-28 will help show how your driving conditions are affecting your plug life and wear. You may need a hotter or colder plug than original equipment.

| MAKE | SPARK PLUG | | | IDLE SPEED | | FUEL PUMP PRESSURE | COMPRESSION |
	TYPE	GAP (INS.)	TORQUE (FT.-LBS.)	STD. TRANS.[3]	AUTO. TRANS.[4]	(PSI)	(PSI)
Champion	N8L	.033-.037	22	900	800	4-6	116-160
Champion	N8L	.033-.037	22	600	550	4-6	116-160
Champion	N8L	.033-.037	22	900	800	5.0-6.5	135
Champion	N13L	.033-.038	25-30	600	550	4-5	140
Champion	N13L	.033-.038	25-30	—	700	4-5	150
Champion	N13L	.033-.038	25-30	700	600	4-5	150
Champion	N13L	.033-.037	25-30	600	550	4-5	140
Champion	N13L	.033-.037	25-30	600	550	4-5	150
Champion	N13L	.033-.037	25-30	600	600	4-5	150
Champion	N12Y	.033-.037	25-30	600[15]	550[14]	4.0-5.0	140
Champion	N12Y	.033-.037	25-30	600	550[14]	4.0-5.0	150
Champion	N12Y	.033-.037	25-30	600	600[14]	4.0-5.0	150
Champion	N12Y	.033-.037	25-30	850	550[13,14]	4.0-5.0	140
Champion	N12Y	.033-.037	25-30	850[15]	550[13,14]	4.0-5.0	150
Champion	N12Y	.033-.037	25-30	600	700[13,14]	4.0-5.0	150
Champion	N12Y	.033-.037	25-30	600	550[13,14]	4-5	140
Champion	N12Y	.033-.037	25-30	600	550[13,14]	4-5	150
Champion	N12Y	.033-.037	25-30	700[2]	600[3]	4-5.5 @ 500 rpm	7
Champion	N12Y	.033-.037	25-30	700[2]	600[3]	4-5.5 @ 500 rpm	7
Champion	N12Y	.033-.037	25-30	700[9]	600[10]	4-5 @ 500 rpm	7
Champion	N12Y	.033-.037	25-30	700[9]	600[10]	4-5 @ 500 rpm	7
Champion	N12Y	.033-.037	25-30	600[4]	550[5,6]	4-5 @ 500 rpm	7
Champion	N12Y	.033-.037	25-30	600[4]	550[5,6]	4-5 @ 500 rpm	7
Champion	N12Y	.033-.037	25-30	700	600[2]	4-5 @ 500 rpm	185[8]
Champion	N12Y	.033-.037	25-30	700	600[2]	4-5 @ 500 rpm	185[8]
Champion	N14Y	.033-.037	25-30	600	550	4-5 @ 500 rpm	145[8]
Champion	N14Y	.033-.037	25-30	600	550	4-5 @ 500 rpm	145[8]
Champion	N14Y	.033-.037	25-30	600	550	4-5 @ 500 rpm	145[8]

11 3° BTDC on California cars.
12 Electronic ignition standard.
13 Set idle with transmission in drive and parking brake applied. Do not accelerate engine.
14 700 rpm on California cars.

15 850 rpm on California cars.
16 10° BTDC on California cars.
17 10° BTDC over 4000 ft.
† In neutral.
†† In drive.

18 With 2.37 Axle, 12° BTDC.

Champion	N12Y	.033-.038	25-30	800	600	5-6.5	140
Champion	N12Y	.033-.037	25-30	—	600	5-6.5	140
Champion	N12Y	.033-.037	25-30	—	600	5-6.5	140
Champion	RN12Y	.033-.037	25-30	—	600[3]	5.0-6.5	140
Champion	RN12Y	.033-.037	25-30	—	600[3]	5.0-6.5	140
Champion	N12Y	.033-.037	25-30	750	700	5.0-6.5	140
Champion	N12Y	.033-.037	25-30	—	700	5.0-6.5	140
Champion	N12Y	.033-.037	25-30	—	700	5.0-6.5	140
Champion	N12Y	.033-.037	25-30	—	700	5.0-6.5	140
Champion	N12Y	.033-.037	25-30	750	700[6]	5-6.5 @ 500 rpm	140
Champion	N12Y	.033-.037	25-30	750	700[6]	5-6.5 @ 500 rpm	140
Champion	N12Y	.033-.037	25-30	—	700[6]	5-6.5 @ 500 rpm	140
Champion	N12Y	.033-.037	25-30	—	700[6]	5-6.5 @ 500 rpm	140
Champion	N12Y	.033-.037	25-30	750	700	5-6.5 @ 500 rpm	4
Champion	N12Y	.033-.037	25-30	700	750	5-6.5 @ 500 rpm	4
Champion	N12Y	.033-.037	25-30	700	750	5-6.5 @ 500 rpm	4
Champion	N12Y	.033-.037	25-30	700	750	5-6.5 @ 500 rpm	4
Champion	N12Y	.033-.037	25-30	750	700	5-6.5 @ 500 rpm	4
Champion	N12Y	.033-.037	25-30	750	700	5-6.5 @ 500 rpm	4
Champion	N12Y	.033-.037	25-30	750	700	5-6.5 @ 500 rpm	4
Champion	N12Y	.033-.037	25-30	750	700	5-6.5 @ 500 rpm	4
Champion	N12Y	.033-.037	25-30	750	650[3]	5-6.5 @ 500 rpm	4.5
Champion	N12Y	.033-.037	25-30	750	700	5-6.5 @ 500 rpm	4.5
Champion	N12Y	.033-.037	25-30	750	700	5-6.5 @ 500 rpm	4.5
Champion	N12Y	.033-.037	25-30	750	650[3]	5-6.5 @ 500 rpm	4.5
Champion	N12Y	.033-.037	25-30	750	650	5-6.5 @ 500 rpm	185[4,5]
Champion	N12Y	.033-.037	25-30	750	650	5-6.5 @ 500 rpm	185[4,5]
Champion	N12Y	.033-.037	25-30	750	650	5-6.5 @ 500 rpm	185[4,5]
Champion	N12Y	.033-.037	25-30	750	650	5-6.5 @ 500 rpm	200[4,5]
Champion	N12Y	.033-.037	25-30	650	600	5-6.5 @ 500 rpm	145[4,5]
Champion	N12Y	.033-.037	25-30	650	600	5-6.5 @ 500 rpm	145[4,5]
Champion	N12Y	.033-.037	25-30	650	600	5-6.5 @ 500 rpm	145[4,5]
Champion	N12Y	.033-.037	25-30	650	600	5-6.5 @ 500 rpm	145[4,5]
Champion	N12Y	.033-.037	25-30	650	600	5-6.5 @ 500 rpm	145[4,5]

5 Maximum variation: 10 psi between cylinders.
6 Set idle with transmission in drive and parking brake applied. Do not accelerate engine.

7 Electronic ignition standard.
8 5° BTDC on California cars.   † In neutral.   †† In drive.

Buick, Oldsmobile, Pontiac V-6

YEAR	CU. INS.	HP	MAKE	TYPE	FLOAT LEVEL (INS.)	STD. TRANS.	AUTO. TRANS.	POINT GAP (INS.)	DWELL
1979	231		Rochester	2-bbl.	11/32	15°BTDC	15°BTDC	1	1
	196		Rochester	2-bbl.	11/32	15°BTDC	15°BTDC	1	1
1978	231		Roch.	2-bbl.	.438	15° BTDC	15° BTDC	1	1
	196		Roch.	2-bbl.	.438	—	15° BTDC	1	1
1977	231	105	Roch.	2-bbl.	7/16[4]	12° BTDC	12° BTDC	1	1
1976	231	105	Roch.	2-bbl.	7/16[3]	12° BTDC	12° BTDC	1	1
1975	231	110	Roch.	2-bbl.	5/32	12° BTDC	12° BTDC	1	1

1 High Energy Ignition
2 Skyhawk fuel pump is electric; psi should be 3.0-4.5.
3 Carburetor #17056143 is 15/32-in.
4 Carburetors #17057112 through 17057123 should be 19/32-in.; #17057404 & 05 should be 1/2-in

Buick Turbo V-6

YEAR	CU. INS.	HP	MAKE	TYPE	FLOAT LEVEL (INS.)	STD. TRANS.	AUTO. TRANS.	POINT GAP (INS.)	DWELL
1979	231		Rochester	2-bbl.	11/32	—	15°BTDC	1	1
	231		Rochester	4-bbl.	7/32	—	15°BTDC	1	1
1978	231		Roch.	2-bbl.	.438	—	15° BTDC	1	1
	231		Roch.	4-bbl.	.438	—	15° BTDC	1	1

Buick V-8

YEAR	CU. INS.	HP	MAKE	TYPE	FLOAT LEVEL (INS.)	STD. TRANS.	AUTO. TRANS.	POINT GAP (INS.)	DWELL
1979	301	125	Rochester	2-bbl.	13/32	—	12°BTDC	10	10
	301	128	Rochester	4-bbl.	13/32	—	12°BTDC	10	10
	305	130	Rochester	2-bbl.	15/32	—	4°BTDC	10	10
	305	140	Rochester	4-bbl.	15/32	—	4°BTDC	10	10
	350	165	Rochester	4-bbl.	13/32	—	15°BTDC	10	10
	350	195	Rochester	4-bbl.	15/32	—	20°BTDC	10	10
	350	225	Rochester	4-bbl.	5/16	—	8°BTDC	10	10
	403	180	Rochester	4-bbl.	15/32	—	20°BTDC	10	10
1978	301		Roch.	2-bbl.	.344	—	12° BTDC	10	10
	305		Roch.	2-bbl.	.438	—	4° BTDC	10	10
	305		Roch.	4-bbl.	.469	—	4° BTDC	10	10
	350		Roch.	4-bbl.	.406	—	20° BTDC	10	10
	403		Roch.	4-bbl.	.406	—	20° BTDC	10	10
1977	301	135	Roch.	2-bbl.	11/32	—	12° BTDC	10	10
	305	145	Roch.	2-bbl.	19/32	—	8° BTDC	10	10
	350	135	Roch.	2-bbl.	15/32	—	12° BTDC	10	10
	350	155[11]	Roch.	4-bbl.	5/16[14]	—	12° BTDC	10	10
	403	185	Roch.	4-bbl.	13/32	—	12° BTDC	10	10
1976	260	110	Roch.	2-bbl.	1/8	—	12° BTDC	10	10
	350	140	Roch.	2-bbl.	15/32	—	12° BTDC	10	10
	350	155	Roch.	4-bbl.	5/16	—	12° BTDC	10	10
	455	205	Roch.	4-bbl.	15/32	—	12° BTDC	10	10
1975	260	110	Roch.	2-bbl.	5/32	—	12° BTDC	10	—
	350	145	Roch.	2-bbl.	9/16	—	12° BTDC	10	—
	350	165	Roch.	4-bbl.	1/2	—	12° BTDC	10	—
	455	205	Roch.	4-bbl.	1/2	—	12° BTDC	10	—
1974	350	150	Roch.	2-bbl.	15/32	N/A	4° BTDC	.016	30° ± 1°
	350	175	Roch.	4-bbl.	15/32	N/A	4° BTDC	.016	30° ± 1°
	455	175	Roch.	2-bbl.	3/8	N/A	4° BTDC	.016	30° ± 1°
	455	210	Roch.	4-bbl.	3/8	N A	4° BTDC	.016	30° ± 1°
	455	245[9]	Roch.	4-bbl.	3/8	N A	4° BTDC	.016	30° ± 1°
1973	350	150	Roch.	2-bbl.	15/32	4° BTDC	4° BTDC	.016	30° ± 1°
	350	175	Roch.	4-bbl.	13/32[5]	4° BTDC	4° BTDC	.016	30° ± 1°
	455	225	Roch.	4-bbl.	3/8	4° BTDC	4° BTDC	.016	30° ± 1°
	455	Stage 1 260	Roch.	4-bbl.	15/32	10° BTDC	10° BTDC	.016	30° ± 1°
1972	350	150-155	Roch.	2-bbl.	15/32	4° BTDC[6]	4° BTDC[6]	.016	30° ± 2°
	350	175-195	Roch.	4-bbl.	15/32	—	4° BTDC[6]	.016	30° ± 2°
	455	225-260	Roch.	4-bbl.	13/32[5]	4° BTDC[6]	4° BTDC[6]	.016	30° ± 2°
	455	270 Stage 1	Roch.	4-bbl.	3/8	8° BTDC[6]	10° BTDC[6]	.016	30° ± 2°
1971	350	230	Roch.	2-bbl.	—	6° BTDC[6]	10° BTDC[6]	.016	30° ± 2°
	350	260	Roch.	4-bbl.	15/32	—	4° BTDC[6]	.016	30° ± 2°
	455	315	Roch.	4-bbl.	15/32	6° BTDC[6]	4° BTDC[6]	.016	30° ± 2°
	455	330	Roch.	4-bbl.	13/32[5]	6° BTDC[6]	4° BTDC[6]	.016	30° ± 2°
	455	345 Stage 1	Roch.	4-bbl.	3/8	10° BTDC[6]	10° BTDC[6]	.016	30° ± 2°
1970	350	260	Roch.	2-bbl.	15/32	6° BTDC[6]	6° BTDC[6]	.016	30° + 1°
	350	285	Roch.	4-bbl.	5/16	6° BTDC[6]	6° BTDC[6]	.016	30° + 1°
	350	315	Roch.	4-bbl.	5/16	6° BTDC[6]	6° BTDC[6]	.016	30° + 1°
	455	350	Roch.	4-bbl.	3/8	6° BTDC[6]	6° BTDC[6]	.016	30° + 1°
	455	360 Stage 1	Roch.	4-bbl.	5/16	10° BTDC[6]	10° BTDC[6]	.016	30° + 1°

1 Lowest cylinder must be within 75% of highest cylinder.
2 Lowest cylinder must be within 70% of highest cylinder.
3 Air conditioning off.
4 LeSabre, Centurion 600 rpm.
5 Manual transmission only; automatic transmission float level is ⅜-in.
6 Set at idle with distributor vacuum advance hose disconnected and plugged.
7 600 rpm idle stop solenoid disconnected.
8 500 rpm idle stop solenoid disconnected.

Cadillac V-8

YEAR	CU. INS.	HP	MAKE	TYPE	FLOAT LEVEL (INS.)	STD. TRANS.	AUTO. TRANS.	POINT GAP (INS.)	DWELL
1979	350		7	7	7	—	12	6	6
	425		7	7	7	—	12	6	6
	425		Rochester	4-bbl.	.406	—	12	6	6
1978	350		7	7	7	—	12	6	6
	425		7	7	7	—	12	6	6
	425		Roch.	4-bbl.	.406	—	12	6	6

SPARK PLUG (see note on first page)				IDLE SPEED		FUEL PUMP PRESSURE	COMPRESSION
MAKE	TYPE	GAP (INS.)	TORQUE (FT.-LBS.)	STD. TRANS.†	AUTO. TRANS.††	(PSI)	(PSI)
AC	R46TSX	.060	25	800	600	3-4.5	N/A
AC	R46TSX	.060	15-25	800	600	3	N/A
AC	R46TSX	.060	25	600	600	5.5-6.5	N/A
AC	R46TSX	.060	15-25	—	6	4.25-5.75	N/A
AC	R46TC[5]	.040	15-25	600	600	4.2-5.7[2]	N/A
AC	R44SX	.060	15-25	800	600	4.0-5.0[2]	N/A
AC	R445X	.060	15-25	600	600	3-4.5	N/A

5 Some cars may be equipped with R46TSX; if so, gap to .060-in.   6 See emissions decal.
†In neutral.   ††In drive.

AC	R46TSX	.060	15-25	—	580	5	N/A
AC	R44TSX	.060	15-25	—	650	5	N/A
AC	R44TSX	.060	15-25	—	650	5.5-7	N/A
AC	R44TSX	.060	15-25	—	650	5.5-7	N/A

AC	R46TSX	.060	25	—	650	7-8.5	1
AC	R46TSX	.060	25	—	650	7-8.5	1
AC	R45TS	.045	15	—	600	7.5-9.0	1
AC	R45TS	.045	15	—	500	7.5-9.0	1
AC	R46TSX	.060	25	—	550	3	1
AC	R46SZ	.060	25	—	1100	5.5-6.5	1
AC	R45TS	.045	15	—	500	7.5-9.0	1
AC	R46SZ	.060	25	—	1100	5.5-6.5	1
AC	R46TSX	.060	25	—	650	5.5-6.5	1
AC	R45TS	.045	15	—	600	5.5-6.5	1
AC	R45TS	.045	15	—	600	5.5-6.5	1
AC	R46SZ	.060	25	—	650	5.5-6.5	1
AC	R46SZ	.060	25	—	650	5.5-6.5	1
AC	R46TS	.040	15-25	—	600	4.25-5.75	2
AC	R45TS	.045	15-25	—	500	7.5-9.0	2
AC	R46TS	.040	15-25	—	600	5.0-6.5	2
AC	R46TS	.040	15-25	—	600[12]	5.0-6.5 [13]	2
AC	R46TS	.040	15-25	—	600[12]	4.25-5.75[13]	2
AC	R44SX	.060	15-25	—	600	4.0-5.0	2
AC	R45TSX	.060	15-25	—	600	5.0-6.5	2
AC	R45TSX	.060	15-25	—	600	7.5-9.0	2
AC	R45TSX	.060	15	—	600	3.5-4.5	2
AC	R45TSX	.060	15	—	600	4.25-5.75	2
AC	R45TSX	.060	15	—	600	4.25-5.75	2
AC	R45TSX	.060	15	—	600	4.25-5.75	2
AC	R45TS	.040	15	N/A	650[3]	4.25-5.75	2
AC	R45TS	.040	15	N/A	650[3]	4.25-5.75	2
AC	R45TS	.040	15	N/A	650[3]	4.25-5.75	2
AC	R45TS	.040	15	N/A	650[3]	4.25-5.75	2
AC	R45TS	.040	15	N/A	650[3]	4.25-5.75	2
AC	R45TS	.040	15	800[7]	650[8]	4.25-5.75	2
AC	R45TS	.040	15	800[7]	650[8]	4.25-5.75	2
AC	R45TS	.040	15	900[7]	650[8]	4.25-5.75	2
AC	R45TS	.040	15	900[7]	650[4]	4.25-5.75	2
AC	R45TS	.040	15	800[7]	650[8]	3	2
AC	R45TS	.040	15	—	650[8]	3	2
AC	R45TS	.040	15	900[7]	650[8]	4.5	2
AC	R45TS	.040	15	900[7]	650[8]	4.5	2
AC	R45TS	.030	15	800	—	3	1
AC	R45TS	.030	15	—	600	3	1
AC	R44TS	.030	15	700	600	4.5	1
AC	R44TS	.030	15	700	600	4.5	1
AC	R44TS	.030	15	700	600	4.5	1
AC	R45TS	.030	15	700[3]	600[3]	3	1
AC	R45TS	.030	15	700[3]	600[3]	3	1
AC	R45TS	.030	15	700[3]	600[3]	3	1
AC	R44TS	.030	15	700[3]	600[3]	4.5	1
AC	R44TS	.030	15	700[3]	600[3]	4.5	1

9 Stage 1 engine.
10 High Energy Ignition, no points used.
11 170 hp on California and high-altitude models.
12 550 on Riviera, Electra and Estate Wagon.
13 6-7.5 psi on Riviera, Electra and Estate Wagon.
14 Check fifth digit of engine code: "J" engines are 5/16-in.; "L" engines, 15/32-in.; "R" engines, 13/32-in.
†In neutral.
††In drive.

AC	R47SX	.080	25	—	12	39[7]	160
AC	R45NSX	.060	25	—	12	39[7]	140-165
AC	R45NSX	.060	25	—	12	5.25-6.5	140-165
AC	R47SX	.080	25	—	12	39[7]	N/A
AC	R45NSX	.060	25	—	12	39[7]	140-165
AC	R45NSX	.060	25	—	12	5.25-6.5	140-165

Cadillac V-8

| YEAR | ENGINE | | CARBURETOR | | FLOAT LEVEL (INS.) | INITIAL TIMING | | DISTRIBUTOR | |
	CU. INS.	HP	MAKE	TYPE		STD. TRANS	AUTO. TRANS.	POINT GAP (INS.)	DWELL
1977	350	180	7	7	7	—	10° BTDC[10]	6	—
	425	N/A	7	7	7	—	18° BTDC	6	—
	425	180	Roch.	4-bbl.	13/32[11]	—	18° BTDC	6	—
1976	350	180	7	7	7	—	10° BTDC[9]	6	—
	500	200	7	7	7	—	12° BTDC	6	—
	500	190	Roch.	4-bbl.	13/32[8]	—	6° BTDC	6	—
1975	500	N/A	Roch.	4-bbl.	15/32	—	6° BTDC	6	—
1974	472	205	Roch.	4-bbl.	1/4	—	10° BTDC	.016	28°-32°
	500	210	Roch.	4-bbl.	23/64	—	10° BTDC	.016	28°-32°
1973	472	220	Roch.	4-bbl.	1/4	—	8° BTDC[5]	.016	28°-32°
	500	235	Roch.	4-bbl.	23/64	—	8° BTDC[5]	.016	28°-32°
1972	472	345	Roch.	4-bbl.	1/4	—	8° BTDC[5]	.016	28°-32°
	500	365	Roch.	4-bbl.	23/64	—	8° BTDC[5]	.016	28°-32°
1971	472	345	Roch.	4-bbl.	15/64	—	8° BTDC[5]	.016	28°-32°
	500	365	Roch.	4-bbl.	23/64	—	8° BTDC[5]	.016	28°-32°
1970	472	375	Roch.	4-bbl.	15/64	—	7.5° BTDC[5]	.016	28°-32°
	500	400	Roch.	4-bbl.	15/64	—	7.5° BTDC[5]	.016	28°-32°

2 Air conditioner off.
3 At engine cranking speed.
5 At 600 rpm with distributor vacuum advance hose disconnected and plugged.

6 High Energy Ignition, no points used.
7 Electronic fuel injection.
8 7/16-in. on California cars.

Chevy 4

| YEAR | ENGINE | | CARBURETOR | | FLOAT LEVEL (INS.) | INITIAL TIMING | | DISTRIBUTOR | |
	CU. INS.	HP	MAKE	TYPE		STD. TRANS	AUTO. TRANS.	POINT GAP (INS.)	DWELL
1979	151	90	Rochester	2-bbl.	.520	12°BTDC	12°BTDC	12	12
	98	74	Holley	2-bbl.	1/2	12°BTDC	18°BTDC	12	12
	98	70	Holley	2-bbl.	1/2	12°BTDC	18°BTDC	12	12
1978	151	85	Holley	2-bbl.	.460	14° BTDC	14° BTDC	12	12
	98	68	Roch.	1-bbl.	.156	8° BTDC	8° BTDC	12	12
	98	63	Roch.	1-bbl.	.156	8° BTDC	8° BTDC	12	12
1977	140	84	Holley	2-bbl.	.46	0° BTDC	2° BTDC	12	12
	85	52	Roch.	1-bbl.	5/32	12° BTDC	12° BTDC	12	12
	98	60	Roch.	1-bbl.	5/32	8° BTDC	8° BTDC	12	12
1976	122	110	9	9	9	12° BTDC	—	12	12
	140	70	Roch.	1-bbl.	11/32	8° BTDC	10° BTDC	12	12
	140	84	Holley	2-bbl.	.46	10° BTDC	12° BTDC	12	12
	85	52	Roch.	1-bbl.	5/32	10° BTDC	10° BTDC	12	12
	98	60	Roch.	1-bbl.	5/32	8° BTDC	10° BTDC	12	12
1975	140	78	Roch.	1-bbl.	1/16	8° BTDC	10° BTDC	12	—
	140	87	Holley	2-bbl.	13/32	10° BTDC	12° BTDC	12	—
	122	110	9	—	—	12° BTDC[10]	—	12	—
1974	140	75	Roch.	1-bbl.	1/16	10° BTDC	12° BTDC	.019	31°-34°
	140	85	Holley	2-bbl.	13/32	10° BTDC	12° BTDC	.019	31°-34°
1973	140	72	Roch.	1-bbl.	.06	8° BTDC[2]	8° BTDC[2]	.019	31°-34°
	140	85	Holley	2-bbl.	.42	10° BTDC[2]	12° BTDC[2]	.019	31°-34°
1972	140	80	Roch.	1-bbl.	1/8[7], 1/16[8]	8° BTDC[2]	6° BTDC[2,4]	.019	31°-34°
	140	90	Roch.	2-bbl.	19/32	8° BTDC[2]	8° BTDC[2]	.019	31°-34°
1971	140	90	Roch.	1-bbl.	1/4	6° BTDC[2]	6° BTDC[2]	.019	31°-34°
	140	110	Roch.	1-bbl.	19/32	6° BTDC[2]	10° BTDC[2]	.019	31°-34°

1 At cranking speed, throttle wide open; maximum variation is 20 psi between cylinders.
2 At idle with vacuum advance hose disconnected and plugged.
3 1200 rpm on 4-speed transmission cars.
4 California cars 4° BTDC.

5 California cars with 3-speed transmission, idle speed 850 rpm.
6 800 rpm on cars with air conditioning.
7 Manual transmission cars only.
8 Automatic transmission cars only.
9 Has Bendix fuel injection.

Chevy, Buick, Olds, Pontiac Inline-6

| YEAR | ENGINE | | CARBURETOR | | FLOAT LEVEL (INS.) | INITIAL TIMING | | DISTRIBUTOR | |
	CU. INS.	HP	MAKE	TYPE		STD. TRANS	AUTO. TRANS.	POINT GAP (INS.)	DWELL
1979	250	115	Rochester	1-bbl.	3/8	8°BTDC	10°BTDC	12	12
1978	250	110	Roch.	1-bbl.	.375	6° BTDC	10° BTDC	12	12
1977	250	110	Roch.	1-bbl.	3/8	6° BTDC	8° BTDC	12	12
1976	250	105	Roch.	1-bbl.	11/32	6° BTDC	10° BTDC	12	12
1975	250	105	Roch.	1-bbl.	19/64	10° BTDC	10° BTDC	12	—
1974	250	100	Roch.	1-bbl.	19/64	8° BTDC	6° BTDC	.019	31°-34°
1973	250[5]	100	Roch.	1-bbl.	1/4	6° BTDC[2]	6° BTDC[2]	.019	31°-34°
1972	250[6]	145	Roch.	1-bbl.	1/4	4° BTDC[2,4]	4° BTDC[2,4]	.019	31°-34°
1971	250	145	Roch.	1-bbl.	1/4	4° BTDC[2]	4° BTDC[2]	.019	31°-34°
1970	230[3]	140	Roch.	1-bbl.	1/4	TDC[2]	4° BTDC[2]	.019	31°-34°
	230	155	Roch.	1-bbl.	1/4	TDC[2]	4° BTDC[2]	.019	31°-34°

1 At cranking speed; throttle wide open—maximum variation 20 psi between cylinders.
2 At idle with distributor vacuum advance hose disconnected and plugged.
3 Only available in Chevrolet.

4 0° BTDC—K-20 Suburban models for California.
5 Not available in Buick in '73.
6 Not available in Buick/Olds in '72.
7 Idle solenoid disconnected/idle solenoid connected.

Chevy Small V-6

| YEAR | ENGINE | | CARBURETOR | | FLOAT LEVEL (INS.) | INITIAL TIMING | | DISTRIBUTOR | |
	CU. INS.	HP	MAKE	TYPE		STD. TRANS	AUTO. TRANS.	POINT GAP (INS.)	DWELL
1979	200	94	Rochester	2-bbl.	5/16	8°BTDC	14°BTDC	1	1
	196	105	Rochester	2-bbl.	11/32	15°BTDC	15°BTDC	1	1
1978	200	95	Roch.	2-bbl.	.438	8° BTDC	8° BTDC	1	1
	196	90	Roch.	2-bbl.	.438	15° BTDC	15° BTDC	1	1

1 HEI ignition.
2 See emissions decal.

SPARK PLUG (see note on first page)				IDLE SPEED		FUEL PUMP PRESSURE	COMPRESSION
MAKE	TYPE	GAP (INS.)	TORQUE (FT.-LBS.)	STD. TRANS.†	AUTO. TRANS.††	(PSI)	(PSI)
AC	R47SX	.080	25	—	650	39_7	N/A
AC	R45NSX	.060	25	—	650	39_7	140-165
AC	R45NSX	.060	25	—	650	5.25-6.5	140-165
AC	R46SX	.080	25	—	600	39_7	N/A
AC	R45NSX	.060	25	—	600	39_7	165-185
AC	R45NSX	.060	25	—	600	5.25-6.5	165-185
AC	R45NSX	.060	25	—	600	5 25-6 5 @ 1800	165-185
AC	R45NS	.035	25	—	600_2	5 25-6 5 @ 1800	165-185
AC	R45NS	.035	25	—	600_2	5 25-6 5 @ 1800	165-185
AC	R46N	.035	25	—	600_2	5 25-6 5 @ 500 rpm	165-185
AC	R46N	.035	25	—	600_2	5 25-6 5 @ 500 rpm	165-185
AC	R46N	.035	25	—	600_2	5 25-6 5 @ 600 rpm	165-185
AC	R46N	.035	25	—	600_2	5 25-6 5 @ 600 rpm	165-185
AC	R46N	.035	25	—	600_2	5 25-6 5 @ 600 rpm	165-185
AC	R46N	.035	25	—	600_2	5 3	165-185
AC	R46N	.035	25	—	600_2	5 3	165-185

9 6° BTDC on California cars.
10 8° BTDC on California cars.
11 17/32-in. on Eldorado.
12 See emissions decal.
† In neutral.
†† In drive.

AC	R43TSX	.060	15	1000	750	5-6.5	140
AC	R42TS	.035	25	800	800	5-6.5	145
AC	R42TS	.035	25	800	800	5-6.5	145
AC	R43T5X	.060	15	650	1000	5-6.5	140
AC	R43TS	.035	7-15	800	800	5-6.5	145
AC	R43TS	.035	7-15	800	800	5-6.5	145
AC	R43TS	.035	15	700	750	3.0-4.5 @ 12.5V	140_1
AC	R43TS	.035	15	875	850	5.0-6.5	145
AC	R43TS	.035	15	$900_{16,\,17}$	850	5.0-6.5	145
AC	R43LTS	.035	15	600	—	9, 11	N/A
AC	R43TSX	.035	15	700	750	3.0-4.5	140_1
AC	R43TSX	.035	15	700	750	3.0-4.5	140_1
AC	R43TS	.035	15	800_{13}	$800_{14,\,15}$	5.0-6.5	145
AC	R43TS	.035	15	800_{13}	800_{14}	5.0-6.5	145
AC	R43TSX	.060	15	700	700	3-4 5	140_1
AC	R43TSX	.060	15	750	750_1	3-4 5	140_1
AC	R43LTS	.060	15	1600	—	$3-4\ 5_{11}$	N/A
AC	R42TS	.033-.038	15	700	750	3-4 5 @ 12.5 volts	140
AC	R42TS	.033-.038	15	700	750	3-4 5 @ 12.5 volts	140
AC	R42TS	.035	15	1000	750	3-4 5 @ 12.6 volts	140_1
AC	R42TS	.035	15	1200	750	3-4 5 @ 12.6 volts	140_1
AC	R42TS	.035	15	1200_5	700_6	3.5 @ 12.5 volts	140_1
AC	R42TS	.035	15	1200	1200	3.5 @ 12.5 volts	140_1
AC	R42TS	.035	15	750_3	650	3-4 5	140_1
AC	R42TS	.035	15	750_3	650	3-4 5	140_1

10 Retarded at 1600 rpm.
11 Additional in-line pump rated at 40 psi at 120 volts.
12 Transistor ignition, no points used.
13 1000 rpm on California cars.
14 950 rpm on cars with air conditioning.
15 850 rpm on California cars.
16 875 rpm on California cars.
17 900 rpm on high-altitude cars.
18 HEI ignition
† In neutral.
†† In drive.

AC	R46TS	.035	25	750	550	4.5-6	130
AC	R46TS	.035	25	750	550	4.5-6	130
AC	R46TS	.035	15	750	550	4.0-5.0	130
AC	R46TS	.035	25_{13}	850	550	5.5-6.5	130
AC	R46TX	.060	15	850	550	4.0-5 0	130_1
AC	R46T	.033-.038	15	850	600	4 0-5.0	130
AC	R46T	.035	15	$700/450_7$	$600\ 450_7$	3.5-4 5	130_1
AC	R46T	.035	15	$700/450_7$	$600\ 450_7$	3.5-4 5	130_1
AC	R46TS	.035	15	550_8	500_{10}	3.5-4 5	130_1
AC	R46T	.035	15	750	600	3-4 5	130_1
AC	R46T	.035	15	750_9	600_{11}	3-4 5	130_1

8 600 rpm on cars equipped with air conditioning (air conditioning off).
9 Idle solenoid connected, air conditioning off.
10 575 rpm on cars equipped with air conditioning (air conditioning off).
11 Idle solenoid connected, air conditioning on.
12 High Energy Ignition; no points used.
13 15 ft.-lbs. with tapered-seat plugs.
† In neutral.
†† In drive.

AC	R45TS	.045	20	2	2	4.25-5.75	N/A
AC	R46TSX	.060	15-25	2	2	4.25-5.75	N/A
AC	R45TS	.045	9-20	2	2	4.25-5.75	N/A
AC	R46TSX	.060	15-25	2	2	4.25-5.75	N/A

Chevy Small V-8

	ENGINE		CARBURETOR		FLOAT LEVEL (INS.)	INITIAL TIMING		DISTRIBUTOR	
YEAR	CU. INS.	HP	MAKE	TYPE		STD. TRANS.	AUTO. TRANS.	POINT GAP (INS.)	DWELL
1979	267	125	Rochester	2-bbl.	13/32	4°BTDC	10°BTDC	7	7
	305	130	Rochester	2-bbl.	9/32	4°BTDC	4°BTDC	7	7
	350	160	Rochester	4-bbl.	15/32	6°BTDC	6°BTDC	7	7
	350	195	Rochester	4-bbl.	15/32	6°BTDC	6°BTDC	7	7
	350	225	Rochester	4-bbl.	15/32	12°BTDC	12°BTDC	7	7
1978	305	145	Roch.	2-bbl.	.594	4° BTDC	4° BTDC	7	7
	350	170	Roch.	4-bbl.	.468	6° BTDC	6° BTDC	7	7
	350	185	Roch.	4-bbl.	.468	6° BTDC	6° BTDC	7	7
1977	305	145[8]	Roch.	2-bbl.	19/32	8° BTDC	8° BTDC[9]	7	7
	350	170[8]	Roch.	4-bbl.	15/32	8° BTDC	8° BTDC	7	7
	350	160[10]	Roch.	4-bbl.	15/32	8° BTDC	8° BTDC	7	7
	350 (L82)	210[11]	Roch.	4-bbl.	15/32	12° BTDC	12° BTDC	7	7
1976	305	140	Roch.	2-bbl.	19/32	6° BTDC	8° BTDC	7	7
	350	145	Roch.	2-bbl.	19/32	—	6° BTDC	7	7
	350	165	Roch.	4-bbl.	1/4	8° BTDC	8° BTDC	7	7
	350 (L48)	180	Roch.	4-bbl.	1/4	8° BTDC	8° BTDC	7	7
	350 (L82)	210	Roch.	4-bbl.	1/4	12° BTDC	12° BTDC	7	7
	400	175	Roch.	4-bbl.	1/4	—	8° BTDC	7	7
1975	262	110	Roch	2-bbl	19/64	8° BTDC	8° BTDC	7	—
	350	145	Roch	2-bbl	19/32	6° BTDC	6° BTDC	7	—
	350	155	Roch	4-bbl	1/4	6° BTDC	6° BTDC	7	—
	350	165	Roch	4-bbl	1/4	6° BTDC	12° BTDC	7	—
	350	205	Roch	4-bbl	1/4	6° BTDC	12° BTDC	7	—
	400	175	Roch	4-bbl	1/4	—	8° BTDC	7	—
1974	350	145	Roch	2-bbl	19/32	0° BTDC	8° BTDC	.019	29°-31°
	350	160	Roch	4-bbl	1/4	4° BTDC	8° BTDC	.019	29°-31°
	350	185/195	Roch	4-bbl	1/4	8° BTDC[6]	8° BTDC	.019	29°-31°
	350	245 250	Roch	4-bbl	1/4	8° BTDC	8° BTDC	.019	29°-31°
	400	150	Roch	2-bbl	19/32	N A	8° BTDC	.019	29°-31°
	400	180	Roch	4-bbl	1/4	N A	8° BTDC	.019	29°-31°
1973	307	115	Roch	2-bbl	21/32	4° BTDC	8° BTDC	.019	29°-31°
	350	145	Roch	2-bbl	19/32	8° BTDC	8° BTDC	.019	29°-31°
	350	175	Roch	4-bbl	7/32	8° BTDC	12° BTDC	.019	29°-31°
	350	190	Roch	4-bbl	7/32	12° BTDC	12° BTDC	.019	29°-31°
	350	245-250	Roch	4-bbl	7/32	8° BTDC	8° BTDC	.019	29°-31°
	350	255(Z-28)	Roch	4-bbl	7/32	8° BTDC	8° BTDC	.019	29°-31°
	400	150	Roch	2-bbl	19/32	—	6° BTDC	.019	29°-31°
1972	307	130	Roch	2-bbl	27/32	4° BTDC[2]	8° BTDC[2]	.019	29°-31°
	350	155	Roch	2-bbl	25/32	6° BTDC[2]	6° BTDC[2]	.019	29°-31°
	350	165	Roch	4-bbl	1/4	6° BTDC[2]	6° BTDC[2]	.019	29°-31°
	350	175	Holley	4-bbl	[4]	4° BTDC[2,3]	8° BTDC[2]	.019	29°-31°
	350	255(Z-28)	Holley	4-bbl	[4]	4° BTDC[2]	8° BTDC[2]	.019	29°-31°
	400	170	Roch	4-bbl	1/4	2° BTDC[2]	6° BTDC[2]	.019	29°-31°
1971	307	200	Roch.	2-bbl	13/16	4° BTDC[2]	8° BTDC[2]	.019	29°-31°
	350	245	Roch.	2-bbl	[5]	2° BTDC[2]	6° BTDC[2]	.019	29°-31°
	350	270	Roch.	4-bbl	1/4	4° BTDC[2,3]	8° BTDC[2]	.019	29°-31°
	350	330	Holley	4-bbl	[4]	8° BTDC[2]	12° BTDC[2]	.019	29°-31°
	400	225	Roch.	2-bbl	23/32	4° BTDC[2]	8° BTDC[2]	.019	29°-31°
1970	302	290	Holley	4-bbl	[4]	4° BTDC[2]	4° BTDC[2]	.019	28°-32°
	307	200	Roch.	2-bbl	23/32	2° BTDC[2]	8° BTDC[2]	.019	28°-32°
	350	250	Roch.	2-bbl	[4]	TDC[2,3]	4° BTDC[2]	.019	28°-32°
	350	300	Roch.	4-bbl	27/32	TDC[2,3]	4° BTDC[2]	.019	28°-32°
	350	350	Roch.	4-bbl	23/32	4° BTDC[2]	—	.019	28°-32°
	350	360	Holley	4-bbl	1/4	14° BTDC[2]	—	.019	28°-32°
	350	370	Holley	4-bbl	1/4	14° BTDC[2]	—	.019	28°-32°
	400	265	Roch.	2-bbl	[4]	4° BTDC[2]	8° BTDC[2]	.019	28°-32°

1 At cranking speed; throttle wide open; spark plugs removed—maximum variation 20 psi between cylinders.
2 At idle with distributor vacuum advance hose disconnected and plugged.
3 8° BTDC on Corvette.
4 Wet fuel level; with float bowl sight plugs removed, fuel level should be at bottom edge of sight plug, but not overflowing.
5 23/32-in. on manual transmission cars; 25/32-in. on automatic transmission cars.
6 Initial timing 4° BTDC in California.

Chevy Big V-8

YEAR	CU. INS.	HP	MAKE	TYPE	FLOAT	STD. TRANS.	AUTO. TRANS.	POINT GAP	DWELL
1976	454	225	Roch.	4-bbl.	3/8	—	12° BTDC	8	8
1975	454	215	Roch.	4-bbl.	3/8	—	16° BTDC	8	8
1974	454	235/270	Roch.	4-bbl.	3/8	10° BTDC	10° BTDC	.019	29°-31°
1973	454	245	Roch.	4-bbl.	1/4	10° BTDC[2]	10° BTDC[2]	.019	29°-31°
1972	402	210	Roch.	4-bbl.	1/4	8° BTDC[2]	8° BTDC[2]	.019	29°-31°
	402	240	Roch.	4-bbl.	1/4	8° BTDC[2]	8° BTDC[2]	.019	29°-31°
	454	270	Roch.	4-bbl.	1/4	8° BTDC[2]	8° BTDC[2]	.019	29°-31°
1971	402	300	Roch.	4-bbl.	1/4	8° BTDC[2]	8° BTDC[2]	.019	29°-31°
	454	365	Roch.	4-bbl.	1/4	8° BTDC[2]	8° BTDC[2]	.019	29°-31°
	454	425	Holley	4-bbl.	[4]	8° BTDC[2]	12° BTDC[2]	.019	29°-31°
1970	396	350[7]	Roch.	4-bbl.	1/4	TDC[2]	4° BTDC[2]	.019	28°-32°
	396	375[7]	Holley	4-bbl.	[4]	4° BTDC[2]	4° BTDC[2]	.019	28°-32°
	402	330[7]	Roch.	4-bbl.	1/4	4° BTDC[2]	4° BTDC[2]	.019	28°-32°
	427	390	Roch.	4-bbl.	1/4	4° BTDC[2]	4° BTDC[2]	.019	28°-32°
	427	400	Holley	3x2-bbl.	[4]	4° BTDC[2]	4° BTDC[2]	.019	28°-32°
	427	430	Holley	4-bbl.	[4]	12° BTDC[2,5]	—	.019	28°-32°
	427	435	Holley	3x2-bbl.	[4]	4° BTDC[2]	4° BTDC[2]	.019	28°-32°
	454	345	Roch.	4-bbl.	1/4	—	6° BTDC[2]	.019	28°-32°
	454	360	Roch.	4-bbl.	1/4	6° BTDC[2]	6° BTDC[2]	.019	28°-32°
	454	390	Roch.	4-bbl.	1/4	6° BTDC[2]	6° BTDC[2]	.019	28°-32°
	454	450	Holley	4-bbl.	[4]	4° BTDC[2]	4° BTDC[2]	.019	28°-32°

1 At cranking speed; throttle wide open; spark plugs removed—maximum variation 20 psi between cylinders.
2 Set at idle rpm with distributor vacuum advance hose disconnected and plugged.
4 Wet fuel level; with float bowl sight plug removed, fuel level should be at bottom edge of sight plug, but not overflowing.
5 Adjust timing at 800 rpm.

MAKE	TYPE	GAP (INS.)	TORQUE (FT.-LBS.)	IDLE SPEED STD. TRANS.†	AUTO. TRANS.††	FUEL PUMP PRESSURE (PSI)	COMPRESSION (PSI)
AC	R45TS	.045	25	12	12	7.5-9	160[1]
AC	R45TS	.045	25	12	12	7.5-9	160[1]
AC	R45TS	.045	25	12	12	7.5-9	160[1]
AC	R45TS	.045	25	12	12	7.5-9	160[1]
AC	R45TS	.045	25	12	12	7.5-9	160[1]
AC	R45TS	.045	25	12	12	7.5-9.0	160[1]
AC	R45TS	.045	25	12	12	7.5-9.0	160[1]
AC	R45TS	.045	25	12	12	7.5-9.0	160[1]
AC	R45TS	.045	15	600	500	7.5-9.0	160[1]
AC	R45TS	.045	15	700	500	7.5-9.0	160[1]
AC	R45TS	.045	15	700	500	7.5-9.0	160[1]
AC	R45TS	.045	25	800	700	7.5-9.0	160[1]
AC	R45TS	.045	15	800	600	7.5-9.0	160[1]
AC	R45TS	.045	15	—	600	7.5-9.0	160[1]
AC	R45TS	.045	25	800	800	7.5-9.0	160[1]
AC	R45TS	.045	25	800	600	7.5-9.0	160[1]
AC	R45TS	.045	25	1000	700	7.5-9.0	160[1]
AC	R45TS	.045	15	—	600	7.5-9.0	160[1]
AC	R44TX	060	15	800	600	3 0-4 5	150[1]
AC	R44TX	060	15	800	600	7 5-9 0	150[1]
AC	R44TX	060	15	800	600	7 5-9 0	160[1]
AC	R44TX	060	15	800	900	7 5-9 0	160[1]
AC	R44TX	060	15	600	700	7 5-9 0	150[1]
AC	R44TX	060	15	—	600	7 5-9 0	160[1]
AC	R44T	033- 038	15	900	600	7 5-9 0	150
AC	R44T	033- 038	15	900	600	7 5-9 0	160
AC	R44T	033- 038	15	900	600	7 5-9 0	160
AC	R44T	033- 038	15	900	700	7 5-9 0	150
AC	R44T	033- 038	15	N A	600	7 5-9 0	160
AC	R44T	033- 038	15	N A	600	7 5-9 0	160
AC	R44T	035	15	900	600	5-6 5 @ Idle	150[1]
AC	R44T	035	15	900	600	7-8 5 @ Idle	160[1]
AC	R44T	035	15	900	600	7-8 5 @ Idle	160[1]
AC	R44T	035	15	900	600	7-8 5 @ Idle	160[1]
AC	R44T	035	15	900	700	7-8 5 @ Idle	160[1]
AC	R44T	035	15	900	600	7-8 5 @ Idle	150[1]
AC	R44T	035	15	—	600	7-8 5 @ Idle	160[1]
AC	R44T	033- 035	15	900	600	5-6 5 @ Idle	150[1]
AC	R44T	033- 035	15	900	600	7-8 5 @ 3600 rpm	160[1]
AC	R44T	033- 035	15	900	600	7-8 5 @ 3600 rpm	160[1]
AC	R44T	033- 035	15	800	600	7-8 5 @ 3600 rpm	160[1]
AC	R44T	033- 035	15	900	700	7-8 5 @ 3600 rpm	150[1]
AC	R44T	033- 035	15	900	600	7-8 5 @ 3600 rpm	160[1]
AC	R46TS	035	15	600	550	5-6 5 @ Idle	150[1]
AC	R46TS	035	15	600	550	7-8 5 @ 3600 rpm	160[1]
AC	R44TS	035	15	600	550	7-8 5 @ 3600 rpm	150[1]
AC	R44TS	035	15	700	700	7-8 5 @ 3600 rpm	150[1]
AC	R44TS	035	15	600	550	7-8 5 @ 3600 rpm	160[1]
AC	R43	035	25	900	750	5-6 5 @ Idle	190[1]
AC	R43	035	25	700	600	5-6 5 @ Idle	150[1]
AC	R44	035	25	750	600	5-6 5 @ Idle	160[1]
AC	R44	035	25	700	600	5-6 5 @ Idle	160[1]
AC	R44	035	25	750	—	5-6 5 @ Idle	160[1]
AC	R43	035	25	750	—	5-6 5 @ Idle	190[1]
AC	R43	035	25	750	—	5-6 5 @ Idle	190[1]
AC	R44	035	25	700	600	5-8 @ Idle	160[1]

7 High Energy Ignition; no points used.
8 10 hp less in California cars.
9 6° BTDC in California cars.
10 L48 (Corvette) engine generates 180 hp.

11 Not available in California.
12 See emissions decal.
† In neutral.
†† In drive.

MAKE	TYPE	GAP	TORQUE	STD. TRANS.	AUTO. TRANS.	FUEL PUMP PRESSURE	COMPRESSION
AC	R45TSX	.060	15	—	600	7.5-9.0	160
AC	R44TX	.060	15	—	650	7.5-9.0	160[1]
AC	R44T	033- 038	15	800	600	7 5-9.0	160
AC	R44T	.035	15	900	600	7-8 5 @ Idle	160
AC	R44T	033- 035	15	750	600	7-8 5 @ 3600 rpm	160
AC	R44T	033- 035	15	750	600	7-8 5 @ 3600 rpm	160
AC	R44T	033- 035	15	750	600	7-8 5 @ 3600 rpm	160
AC	R44TS	035	15	600	600	7-8 5 @ 3600 rpm	160
AC	R42TS	035	15	600	600	7-8 5 @ 3600 rpm	160
AC	R42TS	035	15	700	700	7-8 5 @ 3600 rpm	150
AC	R44T	035	15	700	600	5-8 5	160
AC	R43T	035	15	750	700	5-8 5	160
AC	R44T	035	15	700	700	5-8 5	160
AC	R43N	035	25	800	600	5-8 5	160
AC	R43N	035	25	750	600	5-8 5	160
AC	R43XL	035	25	1000	—	5-8 5	150
AC	R43N 6	035	25	750	750	5-8 5	150
AC	44T	035	15	—	600	5-8 5	160
AC	43T	035	15	700	600	5-8 5	160
AC	43T	035	15	700	600	5-8 5	160
AC	43T	035	15	700	700	5-8 5	150

6 Use AC R43XL when equipped with RPO L89 engine.
7 Actually 402-cu.-in. displacement, but engine is called "396" in Chevelle and Nova, and "400" in Chevrolet and Monte Carlo lines (not to be confused with 400/265 small-block V-8).

8 High Energy Ignition; no points used.
† In neutral.
†† In drive.

Chrysler 4

| YEAR | ENGINE | | CARBURETOR | | FLOAT LEVEL | INITIAL TIMING | | DISTRIBUTOR | |
	CU. INS.	HP	MAKE	TYPE	(INS.)	STD. TRANS	AUTO. TRANS.	POINT GAP (INS.)	DWELL
1979	104.7	70	Holley	2-bbl.	.480	15° BTDC[3]	15° BTDC[3]	[4]	[4]
1978	104.7	75	Holley	2-bbl.	.480	15° BTDC	15° BTDC	[1]	[1]

[1] Electronic lean burn system.
[2] See emissions decal.
[3] Canada, Manual Transmission; 10° BTDC.
[4] Electronic Spark Control System.

Chrysler Slant-6

YEAR	CU. INS.	HP	MAKE	TYPE	FLOAT LEVEL (INS.)	STD. TRANS	AUTO. TRANS.	POINT GAP (INS.)	DWELL
1979	225	100	Holley	1-bbl.	[7]	12° BTDC[16]	12° BTDC[16]	[11]	[11]
	225	110	Carter	2-bbl.	.250	12° BTDC[16]	12° BTDC[16]	[11]	[11]
1978	225	90	Holley	1-bbl.	[7]	12° BTDC	12° BTDC	[11]	[11]
	225	110	Carter	2-bbl.	.250	12° BTDC	12° BTDC	[11]	[11]
1977	225	100[15]	Holley	1-bbl.	[12]	12° BTDC[16]	12° BTDC	[11]	[11]
	225	110	Carter	2-bbl.	1/4	12° BTDC	12° BTDC	[11]	[11]
1976	225	100	Holley	1-bbl.	[12]	6° BTDC[14]	2° BTDC	[11]	[11]
1975	225	95	Holley	1-bbl.	1/32	TDC	TDC	[11]	—
1974	198	95	Holley	1-bbl.	1/32	2.5° BTDC	2.5° BTDC	[11]	[11]
	225	105	Holley	1-bbl.	1/32	TDC	TDC	[11]	[11]
1973	198	95	Holley	1-bbl.	[7]	2.5° BTDC ± 2.5°[2]	TDC ± 2.5°[2]	[11]	[11]
	225	105	Holley	1-bbl.	[7]	TDC ± 2.5°[2,9]	TDC ± 2.5°[2]	[11]	[11]
1972	198	125	Holley	1-bbl.	[7]	2.5° BTDC ± 2.5°[2]	2.5° BTDC ± 2.5°[2]	.017-.023	41°-46°
	225	145	Holley	1-bbl.	[7]	TDC ± 2.5°[2]	TDC ± 2.5°[2]	.017-.023	41°-46°
1971	198	125	Carter	1-bbl.	1/4	2.5° BTDC ± 2.5°[2]	2.5° BTDC ± 2.5°[2]	.017-.023	41°-46°
	225	145	Holley	1-bbl.	[7]	2.5° BTDC ± 2.5°[2]	2.5° BTDC ± 2.5°[2]	.017-.023	41°-46°
1970	198	125	Carter	1-bbl.	1/4	TDC ± 2.5°[2]	TDC ± 2.5°[2]	.017-.023	41°-46°
	225	145	Holley	1-bbl.	[7]	TDC ± 2.5°[2]	TDC ± 2°[2]	.017-.023	41°-46°

[2] Set at curb idle with distributor vacuum advance hose disconnected and plugged
[6] Set with headlights on and air conditioning on (if so equipped)
[7] Use float gauge
[8] National .700 rpm, California cars only.
[9] 2.5° BTDC - 2.5° on engines with distributor = 3438440 and = 343842
[10] 100 psi minimum, must not vary more than 25 psi between cylinders
[11] Electronic ignition system standard
[12] Flush with top of bowl cover gasket.

Chrysler Small V-8

YEAR	CU. INS.	HP	MAKE	TYPE	FLOAT LEVEL (INS.)	STD. TRANS	AUTO. TRANS.	POINT GAP (INS.)	DWELL
1979	318	135	Holley	2-bbl.	5/16	16° BTDC	16° BTDC	[21]	[21]
	318	155	Carter	4-bbl.	1/4	16° BTDC	16° BTDC	[21]	[21]
	360	150	Holley	2-bbl.	3/16	—	12° BTDC	[21]	[21]
	360	195	Carter	4-bbl.	29/32	—	16° BTDC	[21]	[21]
1978	318	140	Holley	2-bbl.	.250	16° BTDC	16° BTDC	[17]	[17]
	318	155	Carter	4-bbl.	.906	16° BTDC	16° BTDC	[17][21]	[17][21]
	360	155	Holley	2-bbl.	.250	—	20° BTDC	[17]	[17]
	360	170	Carter	4-bbl.	.906	—	20° BTDC	[17][21]	[17][21]
1977	318	145[19]	Carter	2-bbl.	1/4	—	8° BTDC	[17]	[17]
	360	155	Holley	2-bbl.	3/16[7]	—	10° BTDC	[17]	[17]
	360[20]	170	Carter	4-bbl.	27/32	—	6° BTDC	[17]	[17]
1976	318	150	Carter	2-bbl.	1/4	—	2° BTDC	[17]	[17]
	360	170	Holley	2-bbl.	3/16[7]	—	6° BTDC	[17]	[17]
	360	175	Carter	4-bbl.	29/32	—	6° BTDC	[17]	[17]
1975	318	145	Carter	2-bbl.	1/4	2° BTDC	2° BTDC	[17]	—
	318	150	Carter	2-bbl.	1/4	2° BTDC	2° BTDC	[17]	—
	360	180	Carter	2-bbl.	3/16	—	6° BTDC	[17]	—
	360	190	Carter	4-bbl.	1	—	6° BTDC	[17]	—
	360	230	Carter	4-bbl.	1	—	2° BTDC	[17]	—
1974	318	150	Carter	2-bbl.	1/4	TDC	TDC	[17]	[17]
	360	180	Holley	2-bbl.	3/16	N A	5° BTDC	[17]	[17]
	360	200	Carter	4-bbl.	1	N A	5° BTDC	[17]	[17]
	360	245	Carter	4-bbl.	1	5° BTDC[3]	5° BTDC	[17]	[17]
1973	318	150	Carter	2-bbl.	1/4	TDC ± 2.5°	TDC ± 2.5°	[17]	[17]
	340	240	Carter TQ	4-bbl.	1	5° ± 2.5°[2]	2.5° ± 2.5°[2]	[17]	[17]
	360	170	Holley	2-bbl.	180[7]	—	TDC ± 2.5°[2]	[17]	[17]
1972	318	150	Carter	2-bbl.	1/4	TDC ± 2.5°[2]	TDC ± 2°[2]	.014-.019	30°-34°
	340	240	Carter TQ	4-bbl.	1	TDC ± 2.5°[2,3]	2.5° BTDC ± 2.5°[2]	[4]	[4]
	360	175	Holley	2-bbl.	180[7]	TDC ± 2.5°[2]	2.5° BTDC ± 2.5°[2]	.014-.019	30°-34°
1971	318	230	Carter or Roch.	2-bbl.	1/4[9]	TDC ± 2.5°[2]	TDC ± 2.5°[2]	.014-.019	30°-34°
	340	275	Carter TQ	4-bbl.	1	5° BTDC ± 2.5°[2]	5° BTDC ± 2.5°[2]	.014-.019	[10]
1970	340	290	Holley	3x2-bbl.	12,13	2.5° BTDC ± 2.5°[2]	2.5° BTDC ± 2.5°[2]	.014-.019	[10]
	360	255	Holley	2-bbl.	14	2.5° BTDC ± 2.5°[2]	2.5° BTDC ± 2.5°[2]	.014-.019	30°-34°
	318	230	Carter	2-bbl.	1/4	TDC ± 2.5°[2]	TDC ± 2.5°[2]	.014-.019	30°-34°
	340	275	Carter	4-bbl.	7/32	5° BTDC ± 2.5°[2]	5° BTDC ± 2.5°[2]	.014-.019	30°-34°[10]

[1] 100 psi minimum per cylinder; must not vary more than 40 psi between cylinders.
[2] Set at curb idle, with distributor vacuum advance hose disconnected and plugged.
[3] 2.5° BTDC on California cars equipped with manual transmission.
[4] Point gap and dwell do not apply on cars equipped with electronic ignition systems.
[5] 700 rpm, manual transmission equipped cars, California only.
[6] Idle solenoid adjusted to obtain idle rpm.
[7] Dry float setting between toe of float and float stop.
[8] 110 psi minimum per cylinder; must not vary more than 40 psi between cylinder[s]
[9] 21/32 on engines equipped with Rochester 2-bbl. carburetor.
[10] 27°-32° one set of points; 37°-42° both sets of points on dual point distributor[s]

Chrysler Big V-8

YEAR	CU. INS.	HP	MAKE	TYPE	FLOAT LEVEL (INS.)	STD. TRANS	AUTO. TRANS.	POINT GAP (INS.)	DWELL
1978	400	190	Carter	4-bbl.	.906	—	20° BTDC	38	38
	440	195	Carter	4-bbl.	.906	—	12° BTDC	38	38

SPARK PLUG (see note on first page)				IDLE SPEED		FUEL PUMP PRESSURE	COMPRESSION
MAKE	TYPE	GAP (INS.)	TORQUE (FT.-LBS.)	STD. TRANS.†	AUTO. TRANS.††	(PSI)	(PSI)
Champion	RN12Y	.035	20	900	900	4-6	N/A
Champion	RN12Y	.035	15-25	2	2	4.4-5.8	N/A
Champion	RBL16Y	.035	10	19	19	3.5-5	10
Champion	RBL16Y	.035	10	19	19	3.5-5	10
Champion	RBL16Y	.035	10	700	700	4-5.5	10
Champion	RBL16Y	.035	10	700	700	4-5.5	10
Champion	RBL-15Y[17]	.035	25-35	700[18]	700[18]	4.0-5.5	10
Champion	RBL-15Y[17]	.035	25-35	700[18]	700[18]	4.0-5.5	10
Champion	RBL-13Y	.035	25-35	750[13]	750	4.0-5.5	10
Champion	BL13Y	.035	15	800	750	3.5-5 @ Idle	10
Champion	N14Y	.035	30	800	750	3.5-5 @ Idle	10
Champion	N14Y	.035	30	800	750	3.5-5 @ Idle	10
Champion	N14Y	.035	30	750	750	3.5-5 @ Idle	10
Champion	N14Y	.035	30	800	800	3.5-5 @ Idle	10
Champion	N14Y	.035	30	750[8]	750	3.5-5 @ Idle	10
Champion	N14Y	.035	30	800	800	3.5-5 @ Idle	10
Champion	N14Y	.035	30	750	750	3.5-5 @ Idle	10
Champion	N14Y	.035	30	750[6]	750[6]	3.5-5 @ 500 rpm	10
Champion	N14Y	.035	30	750[6]	650[6]	3.5-5 @ 500 rpm	10

13 800 rpm in California.
14 2° BTDC in California.
15 90 hp in California.
16 8° BTDC in California.
17 RBL-13Y in California.
18 750 rpm in California.
19 See Emissions Decal.
†In neutral.
††In drive.

Champion	RN12Y	.035	30	22	22	5-7	1
Champion	RN12Y	.035	30	22	22	5-7	1
Champion	RN12Y	.035	30	—	22	5-7	1
Champion	RN12Y	.035	30	—	22	5-7	1
Champion	RN12Y	.035	25-35	700	700	5.75-7.25	1
Champion	RN12Y	.035	25-35	700	700	5.75-7.25	1
Champion	RN12Y	.035	25-35	—	750	5.75-7.25	1
Champion	RN12Y	.035	25-35	—	750	5.75-7.25	1
Champion	RN-12Y	.035	25-35	—	700	5.75-7.25	1
Champion	RN-12Y	.035	25-35	—	700	5.75-7.25	1
Champion	RN-12Y	.035	25-35	—	750	5.75-7.25	1
Champion	RN-12Y	.035	25-35	—	750	6.0-7.5	1
Champion	RN-12Y	.035	25-35	—	700[18]	6.0-7.5	1
Champion	RN-12Y	.035	25-35	—	700[18]	6.0-7.5	1
Champion	N13Y	035	30	750	750	5.0-7.0	1
Champion	N13Y	035	30	750	750	5.0-7.0	1
Champion	N12Y	035	30	—	650	5.0-7.0	1
Champion	N12Y	035	30	—	650	5.0-7.0	1
Champion	N12Y	035	30	—	650	5.0-7.0	1
Champion	N13Y	035	30	750	750	5.0-7.0	1
Champion	N12Y	035	30	—	750	5.0-7.0	1
Champion	N12Y	035	30	850	850	5.0-7.0	1
Champion	N13Y	035	30	750	750	5-7 @ Idle	1
Champion	N12Y	035	30	900	750	5-7 @ Idle	1
Champion	N13Y	035	30	—	750	5-7 @ Idle	1
Champion	N13Y	035	30	750[5]	750	5-7 @ Idle	1
Champion	N9Y	035	30	900[6]	750[6]	5-7 @ Idle	1
Champion	N13Y	035	30	700	700	5-7 @ Idle	1
Champion	N14Y	035	30	750	700	5-7 @ Idle	1
Champion	N9Y	035	30	900[11]	900[11]	5-7 @ Idle	8
Champion	N9Y	035	30	1000	950	5-7 @ Idle	8
Champion	N13Y	035	30	750	700	5-7 @ Idle	1
Champion	N14Y	035	30	750	700	5-7 @ 750 rpm	1
Champion	N9Y	035	30	950	900	5-7 @ 750 rpm	8

11 Adjust with idle solenoid.
12 Center float bowl with fuel bowl inverted.
13 Wet fuel level; with bowl sight plugs removed, fuel level should be at bottom edge of sight plug hole.
14 No. 15 drill (.200-in.).
17 Electronic ignition system standard.
18 750 rpm in California.
19 135 hp in California.
20 360 4-bbl. engine available only in California.
21 Electronic lean burn system.
22 See emissions decal.
†In neutral.   ††In drive.

Champion	RJ13Y	.035	25-35	—	750	5.75-7.25	7
Champion	RJ13Y	.035	25-35	—	750	5.75-7.25	7

Chrysler Big V-8

YEAR	ENGINE CU. INS.	HP	CARBURETOR MAKE	TYPE	FLOAT LEVEL (INS.)	INITIAL TIMING STD. TRANS	AUTO. TRANS.	DISTRIBUTOR POINT GAP (INS.)	DWELL
1977	400	190	Carter	4-bbl.	27/32	—	10° BTDC	11	11
	400	195[33]	Carter	4-bbl.	27/32	—	8° BTDC	11	11
	440	—	Carter	4-bbl.	27/32	—	8° BTDC[36]	11	11
1976	400	175	Holley	2-bbl.	3/16	—	10° BTDC	11	11
	400	210[33]	Carter	4-bbl.	29/32	—	8° BTDC	11	11
	440	205[34]	Carter	4-bbl.	29/32	—	8° BTDC	11	11
1975	400	165	Holley	2-bbl.	3/16	—	10° BTDC	29	—
	400	175	Holley	2-bbl.	3/16	—	10° BTDC	29	—
	400	190	Carter	4-bbl.	1	—	8° BTDC	29	—
	400	235	Carter	4-bbl.	1	—	8° BTDC	29	—
	440	215	Carter	4-bbl.	1	—	8° BTDC	29	—
1974	400	185	Holley	2-bbl.	3/16	N A	5° BTDC	29	29
	400	205	Carter	4-bbl.	1	N A	5° BTDC	29	29
	400	250	Carter	4-bbl.	1	5° BTDC	5° BTDC[30]	29	29
	440	230	Carter	4-bbl.	1	N A	10° BTDC	29	29
	440	275	Carter	4-bbl.	1	N A	10° BTDC[10]	29	29
1973	400	185	Holley	2-bbl.	180[13]	10° BTDC ± 2.5°	10° BTDC ± 2.5°	29	29
	400	220	Carter T9	4-bbl.	1	2.5° BTDC ± 2.5°	7.5° BTDC ± 2.5°	29	29
	440	220	Carter T9	4-bbl.	1	10° BTDC ± 2.5°	10° BTDC ± 2.5°	29	29
	440	280	Carter T9	4-bbl.	1	10° BTDC ± 2.5°	10° BTDC ± 2.5°	29	29
1972	400	190	Holley	2-bbl.	180[13]	5° BTDC ± 2.5°[9]	5° BTDC ± 2.5°[9]	.014-.019[11]	30°-34°
	400	265[1]	Carter	4-bbl.	1	TDC ± 2.5°[9,19]	10° BTDC ± 2.5°[9,10]	.014-.019[11]	30°-34°
	440	225[2,3,4]	Holley	4-bbl.	28	5° BTDC ± 2.5°[9]	10° BTDC ± 2.5°[9,10]	.014-.019[11]	30°-34°
	440	280[5,6]	Holley	4-bbl.	28	2.5° BTDC ± 2.5°[9]	5° BTDC ± 2.5°[9]	.014-.019[11]	30°-34°
	440	330	Holley	3x2-bbl.	18	2.5° BTDC ± 2.5°[9]	2.5° BTDC ± 2.5°[9]	11	11
1971	383	275	Carter	4-bbl.	5/16	TDC° ± 2.5°[9]	2.5° BTDC ± 2.5°[9]	.016-.021	28.5°-32.5
	383	300	Holley or Carter	4-bbl.	21,24	TDC° ± 2.5°[9]	2.5° BTDC ± 2.5°[9]	.016-.021	28.5°-32.5
	440	335	Carter	4-bbl.	7/32	—	5° BTDC ± 2.5°[9]	.016-.021	28.5°-32.5
	440	370	Carter	4-bbl.	7/32	2.5° BTDC ± 2.5°[9]	2.5° BTDC ± 2.5°[9]	.016-.021	28.5°-32.5
	440	385	Holley	3x2-bbl.	18	5° BTDC ± 2.5°[9]	5° BTDC ± 2.5°[9]	.014-.019	20
1970	383	290	Holley or Carter	2-bbl.	22	TDC ± 2.5°[9]	2.5° BTDC ± 2.5°[9]	.016-.019	28.5°-32.5
	383	330	Carter	4-bbl.	5/16[23]	TDC ± 2.5°[9]	2.5° BTDC ± 2.5°[9]	.016-.019	28.5°-32.5
	383	335	Holley	4-bbl.	24	TDC ± 2.5°[9]	2.5° BTDC ± 2.5°[9]	.016-.019	28.5°-32.5
	440	350	Holley	4-bbl.	24	TDC ± 2.5°[9]	2.5° BTDC ± 2.5°[9]	.016-.019	28.5°-32.5
	440	375	Carter	4-bbl.	7/32	TDC ± 2.5°[9]	2.5° BTDC ± 2.5°[9]	.016-.019	28.5°-32.5
	440	390	Holley	3x2-bbl.	18	5° BTDC ± 2.5°[9]	5° BTDC ± 2.5°[9]	.014-.019	20

1 255 hp when equipped with dual snorkel air cleaner.
2 225 hp when equipped with single snorkel air cleaner and single exhaust.
3 230 hp when equipped with dual snorkel air cleaner and single exhaust.
4 245 hp when equipped with dual exhaust.
5 280 hp when equipped with dual snorkel air cleaner (high performance).
6 290 hp when equipped with air grabber (cold air package).
7 100 psi minimum per cylinder; must not vary more than 40 psi between cylinders.
8 110 psi minimum per cylinder; must not vary more than 40 psi between cylinders.
9 Set at curb idle, with distributor vacuum disconnected and plugged.
10 5° BTDC California cars only.

11 Point gap and dwell do not apply on cars equipped with electronic ignition system.
12 Idle solenoid adjusted to obtain idle rpm.
13 Dry float setting between toe of float and float stop.
14 800 rpm, manual transmission cars; California only.
15 Standard air cleaner only; with high performance heated air: 900 rpm.
16 U.S. only. California cars with R-6256-A Holley 4-bbl.: 800 rpm, except high performance heated air.
17 U.S. only. California cars with R-690-A Holley 4-bbl.: 700 rpm, except high performance heated air.

Ford 4

YEAR	CU. INS.	HP	MAKE	TYPE	FLOAT LEVEL	STD. TRANS	AUTO. TRANS.	POINT GAP	DWELL
1979	140	88	Holley	2-bbl.	.453	6°BTDC	20° BTDC	9	9
1978	140	88	Holley	2-bbl.	.453	6° BTDC	20° BTDC	9	9
1977	140	89[10]	Hol.-Web.	2-bbl.	15/32 dry	6° BTDC[12]	20° BTDC	9	9
1976	140	92	Hol.-Web.	2-bbl.	.460	6° BTDC	20° BTDC	9	9
1975	140	87	Hol.-Web.	2-bbl.	27/64	6° BTDC[8]	6° BTDC	9	—
1974	122	80	Hol.-Web.	2-bbl.	27/64	6° BTDC[7]	6° BTDC[7]	.025	37°-41°
	140	82/88[6]	Hol.-Web.	2-bbl.	27/64	6° BTDC	6° BTDC	.025	37°-41°
1973	98	50	Motorcraft	1-bbl.	1-13/64	12° BTDC[5]	—	.025	37°-41°
	122	80	Holley	2-bbl.	27/64	6° BTDC[5]	9° BTDC[5]	.025	37°-41°
1972	98	54	Motorcraft	1-bbl.	1-13/64	12° BTDC[2]	—	.025	36°-40°
	122	85	Motorcraft	2-bbl.	27/64	6° BTDC[2]	6° BTDC[2,3]	.025	36°-40°
1971	98	75	Autolite	1-bbl.	31/64	12° BTDC[2]	—	.025	38°-40°
	122	100	Autolite	2-bbl.	31/64	6° BTDC[2]	6° BTDC[2]	.025	48°-52°

1 Lowest cylinder must be within 75% of highest cylinder.
2 Set at 600 rpm with distributor vacuum advance hose(s) disconnected and plugged.
3 9° BTDC on California automatic transmission cars.
4 Idle set with headlights on high beam and air conditioning on, throttle solenoid connected (higher rpm). Solenoid disconnected for lower rpm.
5 Timing must be set to decal specs, if different from setting listed.
6 Pinto—82 hp @ 4600 rpm; Mustang—88 hp @ 5000 rpm.

Ford Inline-6

YEAR	CU. INS.	HP	MAKE	TYPE	FLOAT LEVEL	STD. TRANS	AUTO. TRANS.	POINT GAP	DWELL
1979	200	85	Holley	1-bbl.	.781	8°BTDC	10° BTDC	20	20
	250	97	Carter	1-bbl.	.781	4°BTDC	10° BTDC	20	20
1978	200	85	Carter	1-bbl.	.781	10° BTDC	10° BTDC	20	20
	250	97	Carter	1-bbl.	.781	4° BTDC	14° BTDC	20	20
1977	200	96[24]	Carter	1-bbl.	25/32	6° BTDC	6° BTDC	20	20
	250	98[25]	Carter	1-bbl.	25/32	4° BTDC	6° BTDC[26]	20	20
1976	200	81[21]	Carter	1-bbl.	25/32	10° BTDC	10° BTDC	20	20
	250	90[22]	Carter	1-bbl.	23/32	6° BTDC[23]	14° BTDC[23]	20	20
1975	200	75	Carter	2-bbl.	9/16	6° BTDC[19]	6° BTDC[19]	20	—
	250	72[18]	Carter	2-bbl.	9/16	6° BTDC[19]	6° BTDC[19]	20	—
1974	200	84	Carter	1-bbl.	9/16	6° BTDC	6° BTDC	.027[17]	33°-39°
	250	91	Carter	1-bbl.	9/16	6° BTDC	6° BTDC	.027[17]	35°-39°
1973	200	84	Carter	1-bbl.	3/8	6° BTDC[7,15]	6° BTDC[7,15]	.027	33°-39°
	250	99	Carter	1-bbl.	3/8	6° BTDC[7,15]	6° BTDC[7,15]	.027	33°-39°
1972	170	82	Motorcraft	1-bbl.	3/8	6° BTDC[7]	6° BTDC[7]	.027	35°-39°
	200	90	Motorcraft	1-bbl.	3/8	6° BTDC[7]	6° BTDC[7]	.027	35°-39°
	250	95	Motorcraft	1-bbl.	9/16	6° BTDC[7]	6° BTDC[7]	.027	35°-39°

MAKE	TYPE	GAP (INS.)	TORQUE (FT.-LBS.)	IDLE SPEED STD. TRANS.†	IDLE SPEED AUTO. TRANS.††	FUEL PUMP PRESSURE (PSI)	COMPRESSION (PSI)
Champion	RJ13Y	.035	25-35	—	750	5.75-7.25	7
Champion	RJ13Y	.035	25-35	—	750	5.75-7.25	7
Champion	RJ13Y [37]	.035	35	—	750	5.75-7.25	7
Champion	J13Y	.035	25-35	—	700 [31]	6.0-7.5	7
Champion	J13Y	.035	25-35	—	700 [31]	6.0-7.5	7
Champion	RJ87P [35]	.035	25-35	—	750	6.0-7.5	7
Champion	J13Y	035	30	—	750	4 0-5 5	7
Champion	J13Y	035	30	—	750	4 0-5 5	7
Champion	J13Y	035	30	—	750	4 0-5 5	7
Champion	J13Y	035	30	—	750	4 0-5 5	7
Champion	RY87P	040	30	—	750	4 0-5 5	7
Champion	J13Y	035	30	N/A	750	4 0-5 5	7
Champion	J13Y	035	30	N/A	900 [31]	4 0-5 5	7
Champion	J11Y	035	30	900	900 [32]	4 0-5 5	7
Champion	J11Y	035	30	N/A	750	4 0-5 5	7
Champion	J11Y	035	30	N/A	800	7 0-8 2	7
Champion	J13Y	035	30	—	700	3 5-5 @ Idle	100 [7]
Champion	J11Y	035	30	800	750	3 5-5 @ Idle	100 [7]
Champion	J11Y	035	30	—	700	3 5-5 @ Idle	100 [7]
Champion	J11Y	035	30	—	800	6-7.5 @ Idle	100 [7]
Champion	J13Y	035	30	700	700	3 5-5 @ Idle	100 [7]
Champion	J11Y	035	30	900 [12 14]	750 [12]	3 5-5 @ Idle	100 [7]
Champion	J11Y	035	30	900	750 [15 16 17]	3 5-7 5 @ Idle	100 [7]
Champion	J11Y	035	30	900	900	3 5-7 5 @ Idle	100 [7]
Champion	J14Y	035	30	750	700	3 5-5 @ Idle	100 [7]
Champion	J14Y	035	30	900	800	3 5-5 @ Idle	110 [8]
Champion	J13Y	035	30	—	750	3 5-5 @ Idle	110 [8]
Champion	J11Y	035	30	900	900	3 5-5 @ Idle	110 [8]
Champion	J11Y	035	30	900	900	6-7 5 @ Idle	110 [8]
Champion	N14Y	035	30	750	650	3 5-5 @ 750 rpm	100 [8]
Champion	J11Y	035	30	700	900	3 5-5 @ 750 rpm	110 [8]
Champion	J11Y	035	30	750	750	3 5-5 @ 750 rpm	110 [8]
Champion	J11Y	035	30	650	650	3 5-5 @ 750 rpm	110 [8]
Champion	J11Y	035	30	900	800	3 5-5 @ 750 rpm	110 [8]
Champion	J11Y	035	30	900	900	6-7 5 @ 750 rpm	110 [8]

18 Wet fuel level; with bowl sight plug removed, fuel level should be at the bottom edge of sight plug hole.
19 2.5° BTDC on California cars equipped with manual transmission.
20 Dwell on dual point distributor is 27°-32° when checking one set of points; 37°-42° when checking dwell with both sets of points operating.
21 7/32-in. on Carter 4-bbl carburetors.
22 5/16-in. on Carter carburetors only. = 7 drill (200-in.) on Holley 2-bbl carburetors
23 7/32-in. float level on cars with manual transmissions
24 15/64-in. on primary float level, 17/64-in. on secondary float level on Holley 4-bbl. carburetors

28 110-in. primary, 9204-in. secondary
29 Electronic ignition system standard
30 2.5° BTDC on California cars equipped with automatic transmission
31 Idle speed 750 in California
32 Idle speed 850 in California
33 185 hp in California.
34 200 hp in California.
35 Those with Bosch plugs use WA95 gapped to .033-in.
36 Lean Burn 12° BTDC.   † In neutral.
37 RJ11Y for H.P. engine.   †† In drive.
38 Electronic lean burn system.

Autolite	AWSF-42	.034	10-15	850	800	5.5-6.5	1
Autolite	AWRF-42	.034	10-15	850	800	5.5-6.5	1
Autolite	AWRF-42	.034	10-15	850	800 [11]	5.5-6.5	1
Autolite	AGRF-52	.032-.036	10-15	750	650	5.5-6.5	1
Motorcraft	AGRF-52	034	15-25	550	550	3.5-4.5	1
Motorcraft	BRF-42	034	15-25	750	650	3.5-4.5	1
Motorcraft	AGRF-52	034	10-15	850	750	3.5-4.5	1
Motorcraft	AGR-32	030	10-15	750 [4]	—	3.5-5.0	1
Motorcraft	BRF-42	034	15-20	750 [4]	650	3.8-5.0	1
Motorcraft	AGR-22	030	10-15	750/500 [4]	—	3.5-5.0	1
Motorcraft	BRF-42	034	15-20	750/500 [4]	650/500 [4]	3.0-5.0	1
Autolite	AGR-22	030	10-15	750/500 [4]	—	3.5-5.0	1
Autolite	BRF-32	034	15-20	750/500 [4]	650/500 [4]	3.0-5.0	1

7 3° BTDC @ 650 rpm in California.
8 10° BTDC in California.
9 Breakerless ignition standard.
10 88 hp in California sedans, 85 hp in California wagons.

11 750 rpm in California.
12 20° BTDC in California.
† In neutral.
†† In drive.

Autolite	BRF-82	.050 [27]	15-20	800	650	5.5-6.5	3
Autolite	BSF-82	.050	15-20	800	600	5.5-6.5	3
Autolite	BRF-82	.050 [27]	15-20	800	650	5.5-6.5	3
Autolite	BRF-82	.050	15-20	800	600	5.5-6.5	3
Autolite	BRF-82	.050	15-20	800	650	5.5-6.5	3
Autolite	BRF-82	.050	15-20	850	600	5.5-6.5	3
Autolite	BRF-82	.044	15-20	800 [19]	650 [19]	5.5-6.5	3
Autolite	BRF-82	.044	15-20	850 [19]	600 [19]	5.5-6.5	3
Autolite	BRF-82	.044	15-20	750 [19]	800 [19]	4.5-5.5	3
Autolite	BRF-82	.044	15-20	800 [19]	600 [19]	4.5-5.5	3
Motorcraft	BRF-82	.034	15-20	750	550	4.5-5.5	3
Motorcraft	BRF-82	.044	15-20	500 [16]	500 [16]	4.5-5.5	3
Autolite	BRF-82	.034	15-20	750 [2]	550 [2]	4-6 @ 500 rpm	3
Autolite	BRF-82	.034	15-20	750 [2]	600 [2]	4-6 @ 500 rpm	3
Autolite	BRF-82	.034	15-20	750	—	4-6 @ 500 rpm	3
Autolite	BRF-82	.034	15-20	800/500 [12 13]	600/500 [12 14]	4-6 @ 500 rpm	3
Autolite	BRF-82	.034	15-20	750/500 [12]	600/500 [12]	4-6 @ 500 rpm	3

Ford Inline-6

YEAR	ENGINE CU. INS.	HP	CARBURETOR MAKE	TYPE	FLOAT LEVEL (INS.)	INITIAL TIMING STD. TRANS	AUTO. TRANS.	DISTRIBUTOR POINT GAP (INS.)	DWELL
1971	170	100	Carter	1-bbl.	3/8	6° BTDC [7]	6° BTDC [7]	.027	33°-38°
	200	115	Carter	1-bbl.	3/8	6° BTDC [7]	6° BTDC [7]	.027	33°-38°
	250	145	Carter	1-bbl.	9/16	6° BTDC [7]	6° BTDC [7]	.025 [11]	34°-37.5°
1970	170	105	Carter	1-bbl.	7/32	6° BTDC [7]	6° BTDC [7]	.027	35°-40°
	200	120	Carter	1-bbl.	3/8	6° BTDC [7]	6° BTDC [7]	.027	35°-40°
	250	155	Carter	1-bbl.	9/16	6° BTDC [7]	6° BTDC [7]	.025	37°-42°

[3] Lowest cylinder must be within 75% of highest cylinder.
[5] Higher idle speed with solenoid energized and lower idle speed with solenoid de-energized.
[6] Set all idle speeds with headlights on high beam and air conditioning off.
[7] Set at 600 rpm with distributor vacuum advance hose(s) disconnected and plugged.
[8] No air conditioning. 800 rpm on cars with air conditioning.
[9] No air conditioning. 600 rpm on cars with air conditioning.

[10] No air conditioning. 600/500 idle rpm with headlights on high beam and air conditioning off; throttle solenoid connected (higher rpm), solenoid disconnected for lower rpm.
[11] Single diaphragm distributor only; .027-in. point gap, 33°-38° dwell on dual diaphragm distributor.
[12] Adjust idle speed with headlights on high beam and air conditioning off; throttle solenoid connected (higher rpm), solenoid disconnected for lower rpm.
[13] 750 rpm on engines not equipped with throttle solenoid.

Ford V-6

1979	170.8	102	Motorcraft	2-bbl.	.375	—	9° BTDC	[3]	[3]
1978	170.8	90	Motorcraft	2-bbl.	.375	10° BTDC	12° BTDC	[3]	[3]
1977	170	93 [9]	Ford [8]	2-bbl. [8]	3/8 [8]	8° BTDC [7]	12° BTDC [7]	[3]	[3]
1976	170	103 [4]	Motorcraft	2-bbl.	3/8	10° BTDC [2]	12° BTDC [5]	[3]	[3]
1975	170.8	97	Motorcraft	2-bbl.	7/16	6° BTDC	10° BTDC [2]	[3]	[3]
1974	170.8	105	Hol.-Web.	2-bbl.	27/64	12° BTDC	12° BTDC	.025	37°-41°

[1] Lowest cylinder must be within 75% of highest cylinder.
[2] 8° BTDC in California.
[3] Solid state ignition standard.

[4] 99 hp in California; 100 hp with automatic transmission in all states.
[5] 6° BTDC in California.
[6] 750 rpm in California.

Ford Windsor V-8

1979	302	140	Motorcraft	2-bbl.	.438	12° BTDC	8° BTDC	[18]	[18]
	351	135	Motorcraft	2-bbl.	.438	—	15° BTDC	[18]	[18]
1978	302	139	Motorcraft	2-bbl. [20]	.438	—	6° BTDC [19]	[18]	[18]
	351	144	Motorcraft	2-bbl.	.438	—	4° BTDC	[18]	[18]
1977	302	139 [23]	Ford 2150A [20]	2-bbl. [20]	7/16 [20]	12° BTDC	8° BTDC [19]	[18]	[18]
	351	149 [25]	Ford 2150A	2-bbl.	7/16	—	9° BTDC [19]	[18]	[18]
1976	302	134 [21]	Ford 2150A	2-bbl.	7/16	12° BTDC [16]	8° BTDC [16]	[18]	[18]
	351	154	Ford 2150A	2-bbl.	7/16	—	12° BTDC	[18]	[18]
1975	302	129 [17]	Motorcraft	2-bbl.	7/16	6° BTDC [19]	6° BTDC [19]	[18]	—
	351	154 [17]	Motorcraft	2-bbl.	7/16	[19]	[19]	[18]	—
1974	302	140	Rawson	2-bbl.	7/16	6° BTDC	6° BTDC	.017	24°-30°
	351	162	Rawson	2-bbl.	7/16	N A	6° BTDC	.017	24°-30°
1973	302	156	Motorcraft	2-bbl.	7/16	6° BTDC [2,14]	6° BTDC [2,14]	.017	24°-30°
	351	177	Motorcraft	2-bbl.	7/16	—	6° BTDC [2]	.017	24°-30°
1972	302	140	Motorcraft	2-bbl.	13/16	6° BTDC [2]	6° BTDC [2]	.017	26°-30°
	351W	266	Motorcraft	2-bbl.	7/16	6° BTDC [2]	6° BTDC [2]	.017	26°-30°
1971	302	210	Autolite	2-bbl.	7/16	6° BTDC [2]	6° BTDC [2]	.021 [6]	24°-29°
	351	240	Autolite	4-bbl.	7/16	6° BTDC [2]	6° BTDC [2]	.021	24°-29°
1970	302	210	Autolite	2-bbl.	7/16	6° BTDC [2]	6° BTDC [2]	.021	24°-29°
	Boss 302	290	Holley	4-bbl.	[9]	16° BTDC [2]	16° BTDC [2]	.020 [7]	30°-33° [8]
	351	250	Autolite	2-bbl.	7/16	10° BTDC [2]	10° BTDC [2]	.021	24°-29°

[1] Lowest cylinder must be within 75% of highest cylinder
[2] Set at 600 rpm with distributor vacuum advance hose(s) disconnected and plugged
[3] Adjust idle speed with headlights on high beam and air conditioning off; throttle solenoid connected (higher rpm), solenoid disconnected for lower rpm.
[4] 575 rpm on engines not equipped with idle solenoid
[6] .017-in. point gap and 26°-31° dwell on single diaphragm distributor

[7] Point gap each set of points
[8] Total dwell, dual point distributor
[9] Wet fuel level; with float bowl sight plugs removed, fuel level should be at bottom edge of sight plug, but not overflowing
[14] Timing must be set to decal specs if different from setting listed
[15] Spark plug gap .054 in California, or with solid state ignition

Ford Cleveland V-8

1979	351M	150	Motorcraft	2-bbl.	.375	—	12° BTDC	[17]	[17]
	400	159	Motorcraft	2-bbl.	.438	—	14° BTDC	[17]	[17]
1978	351M	152	Motorcraft	2-bbl.	.375 [22]	—	TDC [23]	[17]	[17]
	400	166	Motorcraft	2-bbl.	.438	—	TDC [23]	[17]	[17]
1977	351M	161	Motorcraft	2-bbl.	3/8 [22]	—	8° BTDC	[17]	[17]
	400	173 [20]	Motorcraft	2-bbl.	7/16	—	8° BTDC	[17]	[17]
1976	351M	152	Motorcraft	2-bbl.	7/16	—	12° BTDC [18]	[17]	[17]
	400	180	Motorcraft	2-bbl.	7/16	—	10° BTDC	[17]	[17]
1975	351M	148 [15]	Motorcraft	2-bbl.	7/16	—	14° BTDC [16]	[17]	—
	400	158 [15]	Motorcraft	2-bbl.	7/16	—	12° BTDC [16]	[17]	—
1974	351	163	Rawson	2-bbl.	7/16	N/A	14° BTDC	.017 [14]	26°-30°
	351CJ	255	Rawson	4-bbl.	13/16	N/A	20° BTDC	.017	26°-30°
	400	170	Rawson	2-bbl.	7/16	N/A	12° BTDC	[13]	[13]
1973	351	159	Motorcraft	2-bbl.	7/16	—	14° BTDC [2,12]	.017	24°-30°
	351CJ	266	Motorcraft	4-bbl.	13/16	16° BTDC [2,12]	16° BTDC [2,12]	.017	24°-30°
	400	163	Motorcraft	2-bbl.	7/16	—	6° BTDC [2,12]	.017	24°-30°
1972	351	161-177	Motorcraft	2-bbl.	7/16	6° BTDC [2]	6° BTDC [2]	.017	26°-30°
	351CJ	248-266	Motorcraft	4-bbl.	13/16	16° BTDC [2,3]	16° BTDC [2,3]	.020 [5]	26°-30°
	351HO	275	Motorcraft	4-bbl.	13/16	10° BTDC [2]		.020	26°-30°
	400	172	Motorcraft	2-bbl.	7/16	—	8° BTDC [2,4]	.017	26°-30°
1971	351	240	Autolite	2-bbl.	7/16	6° BTDC [2]	6° BTDC [2]	.021 [8]	24°-29°
	351	285	Autolite	4-bbl.	13/16	6° BTDC [2]	6° BTDC [2]	.021	24°-29°
	Boss 351	330	Autolite	4-bbl.	13/16	6° BTDC [2]	6° BTDC [2]	.021	24°-29°
	400	260	Autolite	2-bbl.	7/16	—	10° BTDC [2,4]	.021 [9]	24°-29°

SPARK PLUG (see note on first page)				IDLE SPEED		FUEL PUMP PRESSURE	COMPRESSION
MAKE	TYPE	GAP (INS.)	TORQUE (FT.-LBS.)	STD. TRANS.†	AUTO. TRANS.††	(PSI)	(PSI)
Autolite	BRF-82	.034	15-20	750	—	4-6 @ 500 rpm	3
Autolite	BRF-82	.034	15-20	750[8]	550[10]	4-6 @ 500 rpm	3
Autolite	BRF-82	.034	15-20	750	600	4-6 @ 500 rpm	3
Autolite	BF-82	.034	15-20	750[6,8]	550[9]	4-6 @ 500 rpm	3
Autolite	BF-82	.034	15-20	750[6,9]	550[9]	4-6 @ 500 rpm	3
Autolite	BF-82	.034	15-20	750/500[5,6]	600/500[5]	4-6 @ 500 rpm	3

14 550 rpm on engines not equipped with throttle solenoid.
15 Timing must be set to decal specs if different from setting listed.
16 With throttle solenoid off.
17 Solid state ignition (breakerless) in California.
18 Varies according to application, transmission and exhaust.
19 Varies according to emissions calibration; refer to emissions decal.
20 Solid state ignition standard.
21 78 hp with automatic transmission.

22 81 hp with automatic transmission; 78 hp with automatic transmission in California.
23 8° BTDC with air conditioning.
24 97 hp with automatic transmission.
25 86 hp in California.
26 8° BTDC in California.
27 California; .060-in.
† In neutral.
†† In drive.

Autolite	AWSF-42	.034	10-15	—	650	3.5-5.8	
Motorcraft	AWSF-42	.034	25-30	700	650	3.5-5.8	1
Motorcraft	AWSF-42	.034	15-20	850	700[6]	3.5-5.8	1
Autolite	AGR-42	.032-.036	15-20	850	700	3.5-5.8	1
Motorcraft	AGR-42	.034	14-22	850	700	3.5-4.5	1
Motorcraft	AGR-42	.044	14-22	750	650	3.5-4.5	1

7 On California models, refer to emissions decal.
8 California V-6 Pintos & Bobcats use Motorcraft 2700 Variable Venturi carburetor, with dry float setting of 1 3/64 ins.
9 On California models, 90 hp; 88 hp on California wagons.

† In neutral.
†† In drive.

Autolite	ASF-52	.050	10-15	800	600	5.5-6.5	1
Autolite	ASF-52	.050	10-15	—	650	6.5-8.0	1
Motorcraft	ARF-52[24]	.050	10-15	—	600	5.5-6.5	1
Motorcraft	ARF-52[24]	.050	10-15	—	650	4.0-6.0	1
Motorcraft	ARF-52[24]	.050[24]	10-15	850	650	5.5-6.5	1
Motorcraft	ARF-52[24]	.050[24]	10-15	—	625[19]	4.0-6.0	1
Motorcraft	ARF-42	.042-.046	10-15	750	650[22]	5.5-6.5	1
Motorcraft	ARF-42	.044	10-15	—	650	4.0-6.0	1
Autolite	ARF-42[19]	.044[19]	15-25	900[19]	650[19]	5.5-6.5	1
Autolite	ARF-42[19]	.044[19]	15-25	[19]	[19]	5.5-6.5	1
Motorcraft	BRF-42	.044[15]	15-25	800	650	5.5-6.5	1
Motorcraft	BRF-42	.034[16]	15-25	N A	600	5.5-6.5	1
Autolite	BRF-42	.034	15-20	850[3]	650[3]	4-6 @ 500 rpm	1
Autolite	BRF-42	.034	15-20	—	600[3]	5-7 @ 500 rpm	1
Autolite	BRF-42	.034	15-20	800/500[3]	600/500[3,4]	4-6 @ Idle	1
Autolite	ARF-42	.034	10-15	750/500[3]	575/500[3,4]	5.5-6.5 @ Idle	1
Autolite	BRF-42	.034	15-20	800/500[3]	600/500[3]	4-6 @ 500 rpm	1
Autolite	BRF-42	.034	15-20	775/500[3]	600/500[3]	5-7 @ 500 rpm	1
Autolite	BF-42	.035	15-20	800/500[3]	600/500[3,4]	4-6 @ 500 rpm	1
Autolite	AF-32	.035	10-15	800/500[3]	800/500[3]	4.5-6.5 @ 500 rpm	1
Autolite	AF-32	.035	15-20	700/500[3]	600/500[3,4]	5-7 @ 500 rpm	1

16 Spark plug gap .044 with optional solid state ignition
17 Varies according to application, transmission and exhaust
18 Solid state ignition standard
19 Varies according to emissions calibration; refer to emissions decal
20 California models use Motorcraft 2700 Variable Venturi carburetor with dry float setting of 1 3/64 ins.

21 133 hp with automatic transmission; 130 hp with automatic in California.
22 700 rpm in California.
23 132 hp in California; 129 hp with 4-speed.
24 California models use ARF-52-6, gapped to .060-in.
25 135 hp in California.
† In neutral   †† In drive

Autolite	ASF-52	.050	10-15	—	650	6-8	1
Autolite	ASF-52	.050	10-15	—	575	6-8	1
Motorcraft	ARF-52[21]	.050	10-15	—	650	6.5-7.5	1
Motorcraft	ARF-52[21]	.050	10-15	—	650	6.5-7.5	1
Motorcraft	ARF-52[21]	.050[21]	10-15	—	[16]	6.5-7.5	1
Motorcraft	ARF-52[21]	.050[21]	10-15	—	650[19]	6.5-7.5	1
Motorcraft	ARF-52	.044	10-15	—	650[19]	6.5-7.5	1
Motorcraft	ARF-52	.042-.046	10-15	—	650[19]	6.5-7.5	1
Motorcraft	D4PF-CA[16]	.044[16]	15-25	—	650[16]	5.5-6.5	1
Motorcraft	D4PF-CA[16]	.044[16]	15-25	—	625[16]	5.5-6.5	1
Motorcraft	ARF-42	.044[14]	10-15	N A	700	5.5-6.5	1
Motorcraft	ARF-42	.034	10-15	N A	800	5.5-6.5	1
Motorcraft	ARF-42	.044	10-15	N A	625	5.5-6.5	1
Autolite	ARF-42	.034	10-15	—	700[6]	5-7 @ 500 rpm	1
Autolite	ARF-42	.034	10-15	1000[6]	800[6]	5-7 @ 500 rpm	1
Autolite	ARF-42	.034	10-15	—	625[6]	5-7 @ 500 rpm	1
Autolite	ARF-42	.034	10-15	750 500[6]	575/500[6,7]	5.5-6.5 @ Idle	1
Autolite	ARF-42	.034	10-15	1000 500[6]	700/500[6,3]	5.5-6.5 @ Idle	1
Autolite	ARF-42	.034	10-15	1000 500[6]	—	5.5-6.5 @ Idle	1
Autolite	ARF-42	.034	10-15	—	625/500[6]	5.5-6.5 @ Idle	1
Autolite	ARF-42	.034	10-15	700 500[6]	600/500[6]	5-7 @ 500 rpm	1
Autolite	[10]	.034	10-15	800 500[6]	600/500[6]	5-7 @ 500 rpm	1
Autolite	ARF-42	.034	10-15	825 500[6]	625/500[6]	5-7 @ 500 rpm	1
Autolite	ARF-42	.034	10-15	—	600/500[6]	5-7 @ 500 rpm	1

Ford Cleveland V-8

ENGINE			CARBURETOR		FLOAT LEVEL	INITIAL TIMING		DISTRIBUTOR	
YEAR	CU. INS.	HP	MAKE	TYPE	(INS.)	STD. TRANS	AUTO. TRANS.	POINT GAP (INS.)	DWELL
1970	351	250	Autolite	2-bbl.	7/16	6° BTDC2	6° BTDC2	.021	24°-29°
	351	300	Autolite	4-bbl.	51/64-55/64	6° BTDC2	6° BTDC2	.021	24°-29°

1 Lowest cylinder must be within 75% of highest cylinder.
2 Set at 600 rpm with distributor vacuum advance hose(s) disconnected and plugged.
3 10° BTDC, 650 rpm curb idle speed on Cougars with 12-in. converter.
4 National only; 6° BTDC California cars.
5 Manual transmission only; .017-in. on automatic transmission cars.
6 Adjust idle speed with headlights on high beam and air conditioning off; throttle solenoid connected (higher rpm). Solenoid disconnected for lower rpm.

7 National only; 625/500 rpm California cars only.
8 California only; .017-in. point gap, 26°-31° dwell on automatic transmission cars (national).
9 Point gap (.017-in.) and 26°-31° dwell on single diaphragm distributor.
10 ARF-32 with manual transmission. ARF-42 with automatic transmission.
11 600 rpm on engines without throttle solenoid.
12 Timing must be set to decal specs if different from setting listed.
13 Solid state ignition is standard.

Ford Big V-8

YEAR	CU. INS.	HP	MAKE	TYPE	FLOAT LEVEL (INS.)	STD. TRANS	AUTO. TRANS.	POINT GAP (INS.)	DWELL
1971	390	255	Autolite	2-bbl.	7/16	—	6° BTDC2	.0213	24°-29°
1970	390	270	Autolite	2-bbl.	7/16	10° BTDC2	10° BTDC2	.0213	24°-29°
	428CJ	335	Holley	4-bbl.	9	6° BTDC2	6° BTDC2	.0205	30°-33°6
	428SCJ	360	Holley	4-bbl.	9	6° BTDC2	6° BTDC2	.0213	24°-29°
1969	390	270	Autolite	2-bbl.	31/64	6° BTDC11	6° BTDC11	.017	26°-31°
	390	28010	Autolite	2-bbl.	31/64	6° BTDC11	6° BTDC11	.021	24°-29°
	390	320	Autolite	4-bbl.	13/16	6° BTDC11	6° BTDC11	.017	26°-31°
	428CJ	335	Holley	4-bbl.	9	6° BTDC11	6° BTDC11	.021	24°-29°
1968	390	270	Autolite	2-bbl.	31/64	6° BTDC2	6° BTDC2	.014-.016	26°-28.5°
	390	28010	Autolite	2-bbl.	31/64	—	6° BTDC2	.021	24°-29°
	390	315	Autolite	4-bbl.	25/32	6° BTDC2	6° BTDC2	.016	26°-31°
	390	325	Holley	4-bbl.	9	6° BTDC2	6° BTDC2	.019-.021	24°-29°
	390	335	Holley	4-bbl.	9	6° BTDC2	6° BTDC2	.014-.016	26°-28.5°
	427	390	Holley	4-bbl.	9	—	6° BTDC2	.017	26°-31°
	428	340	Autolite	4-bbl.	25/32	6° BTDC2	6° BTDC2	.01712	26°-31°
	428CJ	335	Holley	4-bbl.	9	6° BTDC2	6° BTDC2	.017	26°-31°

1 Lowest cylinder must be within 75% of highest cylinder.
2 Set at 600 rpm with distributor vacuum advance hose(s) disconnected and plugged.
3 .017-in. point gap and 26°-31° dwell on single diaphragm distributor.
4 Adjust idle speed with headlights on high beam and air conditioning off; throttle solenoid connected (higher rpm), solenoid disconnected for lower rpm.

5 Point gap, each set of points.
6 Total dwell, dual point distributor.
7 600/500 rpm with air conditioning.
8 Throttle solenoid energized.
9 Wet fuel level; with float bowl sight plugs removed, fuel level should be at bottom edge of sight plug hole.

Ford, Lincoln, Mercury Big V-8

YEAR	CU. INS.	HP	MAKE	TYPE	FLOAT LEVEL (INS.)	STD. TRANS	AUTO. TRANS.	POINT GAP (INS.)	DWELL
1978	460	202	Motorcraft	4-bbl.	1.0	—	16° BTDC	24	24
1977	460	19726	Motorcraft	4-bbl.	1.0	—	16° BTDC	24	24
1976	460	202	Motorcraft	4-bbl.	1.0	—	8° BTDC25	24	24
1975	460	21623	Motorcraft	4-bbl	3/4	—	14° BTDC	24	—
1974	460	195/220	Rawson19	4-bbl	3/4	N A	14° BTDC	20	20
1973	429	201	Motorcraft	4-bbl	49/64	—	10° BTDC2	.017	24°-30°
	460	208	Motorcraft	4-bbl	49/64	—	14° BTDC2	.017	24°-30°
1972	429	205/212	Motorcraft	4-bbl	49/64	—	10° BTDC2	.017	26°-30°
	460	200-224	Motorcraft	4-bbl	49/64	—	10° BTDC2,3	.017	26°-30°
1971	429	320	Autolite	2-bbl	49/64	—	6° BTDC2	.0215	24°-29°
	429	360	Autolite	4-bbl	49/64	4° BTDC2	4° BTDC2	.0215	24°-29°
	429CJ	370	Roch.	4-bbl	11/32	10° BTDC2	10° BTDC2	.0205	6,7
	429SCJ	375	Holley	4-bbl	11	10° BTDC2	10° BTDC2	.0205	6,7
	460	365	Autolite	4-bbl	49/64	—	5° BTDC2	.017	26°-31°
1970	429	320	Autolite	2-bbl	7/16	6° BTDC2	6° BTDC2	.0215	24°-29°
	429	36015	Autolite	4-bbl	25/32	6° BTDC2	6° BTDC2	.0215	24°-29°
	429CJ	360	Roch.	4-bbl	5/8	10° BTDC2	10° BTDC2	.0215	24°-29°
	429SCJ	370	Holley	4-bbl	11	10° BTDC2	10° BTDC2	.0215	24°-29°
	Boss 429	375	Holley	4-bbl	11	10° BTDC2	10° BTDC2	.020	30°-33°13
	460	365	Autolite	4-bbl	49/64	—	6° BTDC2	.017	26°-31°

1 Lowest cylinder must be within 75% of highest cylinder.
2 Set at 600 rpm with distributor vacuum advance hose(s) disconnected and plugged.
3 National only; 6° BTDC on California cars and all 3.00 rear axle ratios.
4 Adjust idle speed with headlights on high beam and air conditioning off; throttle solenoid connected (higher rpm), solenoid disconnected for lower rpm.
5 .017-in. gap and 26°-31° dwell on single diaphragm distributor.

6 Isolate and adjust individual points to 25°-25.5° dwell to obtain 30°-33° dwell combined; manual transmission cars only.
7 27.5°-29.5° dwell on automatic transmission cars only.
8 600/500 with air conditioning.
9 700/500 with air conditioning.
10 With fuel return plugged.

Oldsmobile V-8

YEAR	CU. INS.	HP	MAKE	TYPE	FLOAT LEVEL (INS.)	STD. TRANS	AUTO. TRANS.	POINT GAP (INS.)	DWELL
1979	260	100	Rochester	2-bbl.	3/8	18°BTDC	20°BTDC	28	28
	301	125	Rochester	2-bbl.	11/32	—	12°BTDC	28	28
	305	130	Rochester	2-bbl.	15/32	4-BTDC	4°BTDC	28	28
	305	140	Rochester	4-bbl.	15/32	4-BTDC	4°BTDC	28	28
	350	160	Rochester	4-bbl.	13/32	—	8°BTDC	28	28
	350	195	Rochester	4-bbl.	13/32	—	20°BTDC	28	28
	350	225	Rochester	4-bbl.	13/32	—	20°BTDC	28	28
	403	180	Rochester	4-bbl.	13/32	—	20°BTDC	28	28
1978	260	100	Roch.	2-bbl.	.375	18° BTDC	20° BTDC	28	28
	305	140	Roch.	2-bbl.	.438	4° BTDC	4° BTDC	28	28
	305	155	Roch.	4-bbl.	.469	—	4° BTDC	28	28
	350	165	Roch.	4-bbl.	.406	—	20° BTDC	28	28
	403	195	Roch.	4-bbl.	.406	—	20° BTDC	28	28

| SPARK PLUG (see note on first page) | | | | IDLE SPEED | | FUEL PUMP PRESSURE | COMPRESSION |
MAKE	TYPE	GAP (INS.)	TORQUE (FT.-LBS.)	STD. TRANS.†	AUTO. TRANS.††	(PSI)	(PSI)
Autolite	AF-32	.034	10-15	700 500[6]	600/500[6][11]	5-7 @ 500 rpm	[1]
Autolite	BF-42	.034	10-15	700 500[6]	600/500[6][11]	5-7 @ 500 rpm	[1]

14 California engines have solid-state ignitions, with .054-in. spark plug gap.
15 Varies according to application, transmission and exhaust.
16 Varies according to emissions calibration; refer to emissions decal.
17 Solid-state ignition standard.
18 8° BTDC @ 650 rpm on California models.
19 625 rpm on California models.
20 168 hp on California models.
21 California models use AR52-6, gapped to .060-in.

22 7/16-in. on California models.
23 California; 160° BTDC.
† In neutral.
†† In drive.

Autolite	BF-32	.034	15-20	—	600 500[4]	5-7 @ 500 rpm	[1]
Autolite	BF-42	.035	15-20	750 500[4]	575[4][7]	5-7 @ 500 rpm	[1]
Autolite	BF-32	.035	15-20	725[8]	675[8]	4.5-6.5 @ 500 rpm	[1]
Autolite	BF-32	.035	15-20	725[8]	675[8]	4.5-6.5 @ 500 rpm	[1]
Autolite	BF-42	.035	15-20	650	550	4.5-6.5 @ Idle	[1]
Autolite	BF-42	.035	15-20	650	550	4.5-6.5 @ Idle	[1]
Autolite	BF-42	.035	15-20	700	550	4.5-6.5 @ Idle	[1]
Autolite	BF-32	.035	15-20	700	650	4.5-6.5 @ Idle	[1]
Autolite	BF-32	.034	15-20	625	550	4.5-6.5 @ 500 rpm	160-200
Autolite	BF-32	.034	15-20	—	550	4.5-6.5 @ 500 rpm	170-210
Autolite	BF-32	.034	15-20	625	550	4.5-6.5 @ 500 rpm	170-210
Autolite	BF-32	.034	15-20	625	550	4.5-6.5 @ 500 rpm	170-210
Autolite	BF-32	.034	15-20	625	550	4.5-6.5 @ 500 rpm	170-210
Autolite	BF-32	.034	15-20	—	600	4.5-6.5 @ 500 rpm	170-210
Autolite	BF-32	.034	15-20	625	550	4.5-6.5 @ 500 rpm	170-210
Autolite	BF-32	.034	15-20	625	550	4.5-6.5 @ 500 rpm	170-210

10 Premium fuel engine.
11 Set at idle rpm with distributor vacuum advance hose(s) disconnected and plugged.
12 IMCO air system only. .021-in. point gap and 24 -29 dwell on engines equipped with Thermactor air system.

† In neutral.
†† In drive.

Motorcraft	ARF-52[27]	.050	10-15	—	580	7.2-8.2	[1]
Motorcraft	ARF-52-6	.060	10-15	—	650	7.2-8.2	[1]
Motorcraft	ARF-52	.042-.046	10-15	—	650	6.2-7.2	[1]
Motorcraft	ARF-52	.044	10-15	—	650	5.5-6.5	[1]
Motorcraft	ARF-52	.054[21]	10-15	N A	650	5.5-6.5[22]	[1]
Autolite	ARF-42	.034	10-15	—	650[4]	5-7 @ 500 rpm	[1]
Autolite	ARF-42	.034	10-15	—	625[4]	5-7 @ 500 rpm	[1]
Autolite	BRF-42	.034	15-20	—	600/500[4]	5.5-6.5 @ Idle	[1]
Autolite	BRF-42	.034	15-20	—	600/500[4]	5.5-6.5 @ Idle	[1]
Autolite	BRF-42	.034	10-15	—	590[4][8]	5-7 @ 500 rpm[10]	[1]
Autolite	BRF-42	.034	10-15	700[4]	600[4]	5-7 @ 500 rpm[10]	[1]
Autolite	AF-32	.034	10-15	700[4][9]	650[4]	6.5-8.5 @ 500 rpm[10]	[1]
Autolite	AF-32	.034	10-15	650 500[4]	700 500[4]	4.5-6.5 @ 500 rpm	[1]
Autolite	BF-42	.034	10-15	—	600[4]	5-7 @ 500 rpm[10]	[1]
Autolite	BF-42	.035	15-20	850 500[4]	600	5-7 @ 500 rpm	[1]
Autolite	BF-42[14]	.035	15-20	850 500[4]	600	5-7 @ 500 rpm	[1]
Autolite	AF-32	.035	10-15	850 500[4]	600	6.5-8.5 @ 500 rpm[10]	[1]
Autolite	AF-32	.035	10-15	850 500[4]	600	4.5-6.5 @ 500 rpm	[1]
Autolite	AF-32	.035	10-15	850 500[4]	600	4.5-6.5 @ 500 rpm	[1]
Autolite	BF-42	.035	15-20	—	600	5-7 @ 500 rpm	[1]

11 Wet fuel level; with float bowl sight plugs removed, fuel level should be at bottom edge of sight plug.
13 Total dwell, dual point distributor.
14 Mustang only. BRF-42 on Thunderbird engine.
15 Thunderbird option.
19 California engines have Carter carburetors.
20 Solid state ignition is standard, with .054-in. spark plug gap.

21 Spark plug gap .044-in. in California.
22 Fuel pump pressure range 6.2-7.2 in California.
23 Varies according to application, transmission and exhaust.
24 Solid state ignition standard.
25 14° BTDC in California.
26 208 hp on Mark V's.
27 California models use AR-52-6, gapped to .060-in.

† In neutral.
†† In drive.

AC	R46SZ	.060	25	650	500	5.5-6.5	[4]
AC	R46TSX	.060	25	—	650	5.5-6.5	[4]
AC	R45TS	.045	15	600	500	5.5-6.5	[4]
AC	R45TS	.045	15	700	500	5.5-6.5	[4]
AC	R45TS	.045	15	—	500	5.5-6.5	[4]
AC	R46SZ	.060	25	—	550	5.5-6.5	[4]
AC	R46SZ	.060	25	—	500	5.5-6.5	[4]
AC	R46SZ	.060	25	—	500	5.5-6.5	[4]
AC	R46SZ	.060	25	650	550	5.5-6.5	[4]
AC	R45TS	.045	15	600	500	5.5-6.5	[4]
AC	R45TS	.045	15	—	500	5.5-6.5	[4]
AC	R46SZ	.060	25	—	600	5.5-6.5	[4]
AC	R46SZ	.060	25	—	600	5.5-6.5	[4]

Oldsmobile V-8

YEAR	ENGINE CU. INS.	HP	CARBURETOR MAKE	TYPE	FLOAT LEVEL (INS.)	INITIAL TIMING STD. TRANS	AUTO. TRANS.	DISTRIBUTOR POINT GAP (INS.)	DWELL
1977	260	105	Roch.	2-bbl.	1/8	16° BTDC	18° BTDC[19]	.28	28
	305	145	Roch.	2-bbl.	7/16	8° BTDC	8° BTDC[20]	.28	28
	350	160	Roch.	4-bbl.	15/32	—	8° BTDC[20]	.28	28
	350	170	Roch.	4-bbl.	13/32	—	20° BTDC[21]	.28	28
	403	200	Roch.	4-bbl.	13/32	—	20° BTDC[22]	.28	28
1976	260	110	Roch.	2-bbl.	1/8	16° BTDC	18° BTDC	.28	28
	260	110	Roch.	2-bbl.	1/8	14° BTDC	16° BTDC	.28	28
	260	110	Roch.	2-bbl.	1/8	—	14° BTDC	.28	28
	350	N/A	Roch.	2-bbl.	7/16	—	12° BTDC	.28	28
	350	160	Roch.	4-bbl.	5/16	—	12° BTDC	.28	28
	350	N/A	Roch.	4-bbl.	13/32	—	20° BTDC	.28	28
	455	190	Roch.	4-bbl.	13/32	—	16° BTDC	.28	28
	455	N/A	Roch.	4-bbl.	13/32	—	18° BTDC	.28	28
	455	N/A	Roch.	4-bbl.	13/32	—	14° BTDC	.28	28
	455	230	Roch.	4-bbl.	13/32	—	12° BTDC	.28	28
1975	260	110	Roch.	2-bbl.	5/32	16° BTDC	18° BTDC	.28	—
	350	170	Roch.	4-bbl.	9/16	—	12° BTDC	.28	—
	350	180	Roch.	4-bbl.	9/16	—	20° BTDC	.28	—
	455	190	Roch.	4-bbl.	1/2	—	16° BTDC	.28	—
	455	215	Roch.	4-bbl.	1/2	—	12° BTDC	.28	—
1974	350	180/200	Roch.	4-bbl.	1/4	N/A	12° BTDC	.016	30°
	455	210/230	Roch.	4-bbl.	1/4	N/A	8° BTDC	.016	30°
1973	350	160	Roch.	2-bbl.	17/32	—	12° BTDC[5,23]	.016	30°
	350	180	Roch.	4-bbl.	1/4	8° BTDC[5]	12° BTDC[5]	.016	30°
	455	225	Roch.	4-bbl.	1/4	10° BTDC[5]	8° BTDC[5]	.016	30°
1972	350	160[1]	Roch.	2-bbl.	17/32	8° BTDC[5]	8° BTDC[5]	.016	30°
	350	180[2]	Roch.	4-bbl.	1/4	—	12° BTDC[5]	.016	30°
	455	225	Roch.	4-bbl.	1/4	10° BTDC[5]	8° BTDC[5]	.016	30°
	455	250	Roch.	4-bbl.	1/4	10° BTDC[5]	8° BTDC[5]	.016	30°
	455	265	Roch.	4-bbl.	1/4	10° BTDC[5]	8° BTDC[5]	.016	30°
	455	270	Roch.	4-bbl.	1/4	10° BTDC[5]	8° BTDC[5]	.016	30°
	455	300 (W30)[3]	Roch.	4-bbl.	1/4	10° BTDC[5]	10° BTDC[6]	.016	30°
1971	350	240	Roch.	2-bbl.	17/32-18/32	10° BTDC[5]	10° BTDC[5]	.016	30°
	350	260	Roch.	4-bbl.	1/4	12° BTDC[5]	12° BTDC[5]	.016	30°
	455	280	Roch.	2-bbl.	17/32-18/32	8° BTDC[5]	8° BTDC[5]	.016	30°
	455	320	Roch.	4-bbl.	1/4	8° BTDC[5]	8° BTDC[5]	.016	30°
	455	340	Roch.	4-bbl.	1/4	10° BTDC[5]	10° BTDC[5]	.016	30°
	455	350 (W30)	Roch.	4-bbl.	1/4	12° BTDC[6,10]	10° BTDC[6]	.016	30°
	455	350	Roch.	4-bbl.	1/4	10° BTDC[5]	10° BTDC[5]	.016	30°
1970	350	250	Roch.	2-bbl.	9/16	10° BTDC[5,12]	10° BTDC[5,12]	.016	30°
	350	310	Roch.	4-bbl.	1/4	10° BTDC[5]	10° BTDC[5]	.016	30°
	350	325	Roch.	4-bbl.	1/4	14° BTDC[5]	14° BTDC[5]	.016	30°
	455	310	Roch.	2-bbl.	9/16	8° BTDC[5]	8° BTDC[5]	.016	30°
	455	320	Roch.	2-bbl.	9/16	—	8° BTDC[5]	.016	30°
	455	365	Roch.	4-bbl.	1/4	8° BTDC[5,13]	8° BTDC[5,13]	.016	30°
	455	370	Roch.	4-bbl.	1/4	8° BTDC[6,15]	8° BTDC[6,14]	.016	30°
	455	375	Roch.	4-bbl.	1/4	—	12° BTDC[5]	.016	30°
	455	390	Roch.	4-bbl.	1/4	—	8° BTDC[5]	.016	30°
	455	400	Roch.	4-bbl.	1/4	—	12° BTDC[5]	.016	30°

[1] 175 hp with dual exhaust.
[2] 200 hp with dual exhaust.
[3] Ram Air.
[4] Lowest cylinder must be 70% of highest, and not less than 100 psi.
[5] Set at 1100 rpm with distributor and air cleaner vacuum hoses disconnected and plugged.
[6] Set at 850 rpm with distributor and air cleaner vacuum hoses disconnected and plugged.

[7] AC-R45S spark plugs used on manual transmission cars.
[8] With throttle solenoid disconnected/throttle solenoid connected.
[9] Lowest cylinder must be 80% of highest, and not less than 100 psi.
[10] Set at 850 rpm on engines with W-30 option.
[11] 650 rpm on air conditioning equipped cars.
[12] 8° BTDC on engines coded TD, TC, TL.
[13] 12° BTDC on engines coded TW, TV, TU.
[14] 10° BTDC on super premium fuel engines.

Pontiac V-8

YEAR	ENGINE CU. INS.	HP	CARBURETOR MAKE	TYPE	FLOAT LEVEL (INS.)	INITIAL TIMING STD. TRANS	AUTO. TRANS.	DISTRIBUTOR POINT GAP (INS.)	DWELL
1979	301	125	Rochester	2-bbl.	11/32	—	12° BTDC	25	25
	301	128	Rochester	4-bbl.	13/32	14° BTDC	12° BTDC	25	25
	305	130	Rochester	2-bbl.	11/32	4° BTDC	4° BTDC	25	25
	305	140	Rochester	4-bbl.	13/32	—	4° BTDC	25	25
	350	160	Rochester	4-bbl.	15/32	—	8° BTDC	25	25
	350	165	Rochester	4-bbl.	13/32	—	15° BTDC	25	25
	350	195	Rochester	4-bbl.	13/32	—	20° BTDC	25	25
	400	170	Rochester	4-bbl.	9/16	—	18° BTDC	25	25
	403	180	Rochester	4-bbl.	15/32	—	18° BTDC	25	25
	403	185	Rochester	4-bbl.	13/32	—	20° BTDC	25	25
1978	301	130	Roch.	2-bbl.	.344	—	12° BTDC	25	25
	301	130	Roch.	4-bbl.	.469	—	12° BTDC	25	25
	305	140	Roch.	2-bbl.	.594	4° BTDC	6° BTDC	25	25
	350	165	Roch.	4-bbl.	.531	6° BTDC	15° BTDC	25	25
	400	175	Roch.	4-bbl.	.531	18° BTDC	18° BTDC	25	25
	403	180	Roch.	4-bbl.	.406	—	20° BTDC	25	25
1977	301	135	Roch.	2-bbl.	11/32	16° BTDC	12° BTDC	25	—
	305[15]	145	Roch.	2-bbl.	5/8	—	8° BTDC	25	—
	350	170	Roch.	4-bbl.	17/32	—	16° BTDC	25	—
	350	170	Roch.	4-bbl.	13/32	—	20° BTDC	25	—
	400	180	Roch.	4-bbl.	17/32	16° BTDC	16° BTDC	25	—
	400 (T/A)	200	Roch.	4-bbl.	17/32	16° BTDC	16° BTDC	25	—
	403	185	Roch.	4-bbl.	13/32	—	20° BTDC	25	—
1976	260	110	Roch.	2-bbl.	1/8	16° BTDC	18° BTDC	25	—
	350	155	Roch.	2-bbl.	9/16[11]	—	16° BTDC	25	—
	350	170	Roch.	4-bbl.	7/32[12]	—	16° BTDC	25	—
	400	175	Roch.	2-bbl.	9/16	—	16° BTDC	25	—
	400	200	Roch.	4-bbl.	17/32	12° BTDC	16° BTDC	25	—
	455	215	Roch.	4-bbl.	17/32	12° BTDC	16° BTDC	25	—

SPARK PLUG (see note on first page)				IDLE SPEED		FUEL PUMP PRESSURE	COMPRESSION
MAKE	TYPE	GAP (INS.)	TORQUE (FT.-LBS.)	STD. TRANS.†	AUTO. TRANS.††	(PSI)	(PSI)
AC	R46SZ	.060	25	900	550	5.5-6.5	4
AC	R45TS	.045	15	600	500	5.5-6.5	4
AC	R45TS	.045	15	—	500	5.5-6.5	4
AC	R46SZ	.060	25	—	550	5.5-6.5	4
AC	R46SZ	.060	25	—	600	5.5-6.5	4
AC	R46SX	.080	25	750	550	5.5-6.5	4
AC	R46SX	.080	25	750	550	5.5-6.5	4
AC	R46SX	.080	25	—	550	5.5-6.5	4
AC	R45TSX	.060	25	—	600	5.5-6.5	4
AC	R45TSX	.060	25	—	600	5.5-6.5	4
AC	R46SX	.060	25	—	550	5.5-6.5	4
AC	R46SX	.060	25	—	550	5.5-6.5	4
AC	R46SX	.060	25	—	550	5.5-6.5	4
AC	R46SX	.060	25	—	600	5.5-6.5	4
AC	R46TX	080	N/A	700	550	3.5-4.5	4
AC	R45TSX	060	N/A	—	600	5.5-6.5	4
AC	R46SX	080	N/A	—	600	5.5-6.5	4
AC	R46SX	080	N/A	—	600	5.5-6.5	4
AC	R46SX	080	N/A	—	550	5.5-6.5	4
AC	R46S[26]	040	30	N/A	650	4.0-5.0	4
AC	R46S[27]	040	30	N/A	650	5.5-6.5	4
AC	R46S	040	35	—	700/550[8]	5.5-6.5 @ Idle	4
AC	R45S	040	35	1100 650[8]	650/550[8]	5.5-6.5 @ Idle	4
AC	R46S[25]	040	35	1000 750[8]	650/550[8]	5.5-6.5 @ Idle	4
AC	R46S	040	35	600 750[8]	600/650[8]	5.5-6.5 @ Idle	4
AC	R46S[7]	040	35	—	600/650[8]	5.5-6.5 @ Idle	4
AC	R46S	040	35	550/750[8]	600	5.5-6.5 @ Idle	4
AC	R46S	040	35	550/750[8]	600	5.5-6.5 @ Idle	4
AC	R46S[7]	040	35	550/750[8]	550/650[8]	5.5-6.5 @ Idle	4
AC	R46S	040	35	550/750[8]	600	5.5-6.5 @ Idle	4
AC	R45S	040	35	550/1000[8]	550/650[8]	5.5-6.5 @ Idle	4
AC	R46S	040	35	750	600	5.5-6.5 @ Idle	9
AC	R46S[7]	040	35	750	600	5.5-6.5 @ Idle	9
AC	R46S	040	35	750`	600	5.5-6.5 @ Idle	9
AC	R46S	040	35	600	600	5.5-6.5 @ Idle	9
AC	R45S	040	35	600	650	5.5-6.5 @ Idle	9
AC	R45S	040	35	600	600[11]	5.5-6.5 @ Idle	9
AC	R46S	040	35	600	600	5.5-6.5 @ Idle	9
AC	R46S	030	35	750	575[18]	5-6 @ Idle	9
AC	R45S	030	35	650	575	5-6 @ Idle	9
AC	R43S	030	35	750	625	5-6 @ Idle	9
AC	R46S	030	35	675	575	5-6 @ Idle	9
AC	R45S	030	35	—	575	5-6 @ Idle	9
AC	R45S[16]	030	35	675	650[17]	5-6 @ Idle	9
AC	R44S	030	35	750	600	5-6 @ Idle	9
AC	R44S	030	35	—	600	5-6 @ Idle	9
AC	R45S	030	35	—	600	5-6 @ Idle	9
AC	R44S	030	35	—	600	5-6 @ Idle	9

15 12° BTDC on super premium fuel engines.
16 AC-R44S on engines coded TW, TV, TU.
17 700 rpm on engines coded TW, TV, TU.
18 675 rpm on engines coded TD, TC, TL.
19 20° BTDC for Omega and 88.
20 6° BTDC for California cars.
21 18° BTDC for Omega and 88 except wagon.
22 22° BTDC for Cutlass wagon.

23 Vista Cruiser; 10° BTDC.
25 Cutlass with manual transmission; R45S.
26 Cutlass models and station wagons use R45S.
27 Cutlass models with 230/275 hp, 455-cu.-in. engines use R45S.
28 High Energy Ignition; no points used.
† In neutral.
†† In drive.

AC	R46TSX	.060	25	—	650	7.0-8.5	5
AC	R45TSX	.060	25	750	650	7.0-8.5	5
AC	R45TS	.045	15	600	500	7.5-9	5
AC	R45TS	.045	15	—	500	7.5-9	5
AC	R45TS	.045	15	—	500	7.0-8.5	5
AC	R46TSX	.060	25	—	550	7.0-8.5	5
AC	R46SZ	.060	25	—	1100#	7.0-8.5	5
AC	R45TSX	.060	25	—	775	7.0-8.5	5
AC	R46SZ	.060	25	—	1100#	7.0-8.5	5
AC	R46SZ	.060	25	—	1100#	7.0-8.5	5
AC	R46TSX	.060	15	—	550	7.0-8.5	5
AC	R46TSX	.060	15	—	750	7.0-8.5	5
AC	R45TS	.045	25	600	500	7.5-9.0	5
AC	R45TS	.045	25	700	600	7.0-8.5	5
AC	R45TSX	.060	15	775	700	7.0-8.5	5
AC	R46SZ	.060	30	—	550	7.0-8.5	5
AC	R46TSX	.060	15	800	550	7.0-8.5	5
AC	R45TS	.045	25	800	600	7.5-9.0	5
AC	R45TSX	.060	15	—	575	7.0-8.5	5
AC	R46SZ[14]	.080	30	—	600[13]	5.5-6.5	5
AC	R45TSX	.060	15	800	575[13]	7.0-8.5	5
AC	R45TSX	.060	15	800	575[13]	7.0-8.5	5
AC	R46SZ[14]	.080	30	—	600[13]	5.5-6.5	5
AC	R44SX	.080	15	750	550	3.5-4.5	5
AC	R46TSX	.060	15	—	600	5.0-6.5	5
AC	R45TSX	.060	15	—	600	5.0-6.5	5
AC	R46TSX	.060	15	—	550	5.0-6.5	5
AC	R45TSX	.060	15	775	575	5.0-6.5	5
AC	R45TSX	.060	15	775	550	5.0-6.5	5

Pontiac V-8

Year	Cu. Ins.	HP	Make	Carburetor Type	Float Level (Ins.)	Initial Timing Std. Trans.	Initial Timing Auto. Trans.	Distributor Point Gap (Ins.)	Dwell
1975	140	78	Roch	1-bbl.	11/32	10° BTDC	12° BTDC	25	—
	140	87	Holley	2-bbl.	13/32	10° BTDC	12° BTDC	25	—
	260	110	Roch	2-bbl.	5/32	16° BTDC	18° BTDC	25	—
	350	170	Roch	2-bbl.	9/16	—	12° BTDC	25	—
	350	185	Roch	4-bbl.	9/16	12° BTDC	16° BTDC	25	—
	400	180	Roch	2-bbl.	1/2	—	16° BTDC	25	—
	400	190	Roch	4-bbl.	1/2	12° BTDC	12° BTDC	25	—
	455	205	Roch	4-bbl.	1/2	—	16° BTDC	25	—
1974	350	155 170	Roch	2-bbl.	21/32	10° BTDC	12° BTDC	.016	30°
	350	170 200	Roch	4-bbl.	3/8	10° BTDC	12° BTDC	.016	30°
	400	175 190	Roch	2-bbl.	21/32	N A	12° BTDC	.016	30°
	400	200 225	Roch	4-bbl.	3/8	10° BTDC	12° BTDC	.016	30°
	455	215 250	Roch	4-bbl.	3/8	N A	12° BTDC	.016	30°
	455	290	Roch	4-bbl.	3/8	10° BTDC	12° BTDC	.016	30°
1973	350	150	Roch	2-bbl.	5/8	10° BTDC[6]	12° BTDC[6]	.019	30°
	400	170	Roch	2-bbl.	5/8	—	12° BTDC[6]	.019	30°
	400	230	Roch	4-bbl.	1/4	10° BTDC[6]	12° BTDC[6]	.019	30°
	455	250	Roch	4-bbl.	1/4	10° BTDC[6]	12° BTDC[6]	.019	30°
1972	307	130	Roch	2-bbl.	25/32	4° BTDC[6]	8° BTDC[6]	.019	30°
	350	160	Roch	2-bbl.[4]	9/16[1]	8° BTDC[6]	10° BTDC[6]	.019	30°
	400	175[1]	Roch	2 or 4-bbl.	22	8° BTDC[6]	10° BTDC[6]	.019	30°
	455	185[2][3]	Roch	2 or 4-bbl.	22	8° BTDC[6]	10° BTDC[6]	.019	30°
1971	307	200	Roch	2-bbl.	27/32	4° BTDC[6]	8° BTDC[6]	.019	30°
	350	250	Roch	2-bbl.	9/16	8° BTDC[6]	8° BTDC[6]	.019	30°
	400	265	Roch	2-bbl.	11/16	—	12° BTDC[6]	.019	30°
	400	300	Roch	4-bbl.	9/32	8° BTDC[6]	8° BTDC[6]	.019	30°
	455	280	Roch	2-bbl.	11/16	—	8° BTDC[6]	.019	30°
	455	325	Roch	4-bbl.	9/32	—	8° BTDC[6]	.019	30°
	455	335	Roch	4-bbl.	9/32	8° BTDC[6]	8° BTDC[6]	.019	30°
1970	350	255	Roch	2-bbl.	9/16	9° BTDC[6]	9° BTDC[6]	.019	30°
	400	265	Roch	2-bbl.	11/16	9° BTDC[6]	9° BTDC[6]	.019	30°
	400	290	Roch	2-bbl.	11/16	9° BTDC[6]	9° BTDC[6]	.019	30°
	400	330	Roch	4-bbl.	9/32	9° BTDC[6]	9° BTDC[6]	.019	30°
	400	345	Roch	4-bbl.	9/32	9° BTDC[6]	9° BTDC[6]	.019	30°
	400	350	Roch	4-bbl.	9/32	9° BTDC[6]	9° BTDC[6]	.019	30°
	400	366[2][3]	Roch	4-bbl.	9/32	9° BTDC[6]	9° BTDC[6]	.019	30°
	400	370[2][4]	Roch	4-bbl.	9/32	15° BTDC[6]	15° BTDC[6]	.019	30°
	455	360	Roch	4-bbl.	9/32	9° BTDC[6]	9° BTDC[6]	.019	30°
	455	370	Roch	4-bbl.	9/32	9° BTDC[6]	9° BTDC[6]	.019	30°

[1] 200 hp with dual exhaust and 4-bbl. carburetor.
[2] 220 hp with dual exhaust and 4-bbl. carbuetor.
[3] 300 hp with Ram Air.
[4] Automatic transmission cars only. Manual transmission cars equipped with Carter 2-bbl. carburetor, float level 5/16-in.
[5] No cylinder should be less than 80% of highest cylinder.
[6] Set at idle rpm with distributor vacuum advance hose disconnected and plugged; idle solenoid disconnected.
[7] Idle solenoid disconnected/idle solenoid connected.
[8] 625 rpm on 2-bbl. carburetors.
[9] 500/700 on 455 High Output engine (Ram Air).
[10] Idle solenoid connected.

SPARK PLUG (see note on first page)				Idle Speed		Fuel Pump Pressure	Compression
Make	Type	Gap (Ins.)	Torque (Ft.-lbs.)	Std. Trans.	Auto. Trans.	(PSI)	(PSI)
AC	R42TS	035	15	700	750	3.0-4.5	5
AC	R42TS	035	15	700	750	3.0-4.5	5
AC	R46TX	060	15	700	550	3.5-4.5	5
AC	R45TSX	060	15	—	600	5.0-6.5	5
AC	R45TSX	060	15	700	600	5.0-6.5	5
AC	R46TSX	060	15	—	750	5.0-6.5	5
AC	R45TSX	060	15	750	750	5.0-6.5	5
AC	R45TSX	060	15	—	750	5.0-6.5	5
AC	R46TS	040	15	900	650	5.0-6.5	120-160 5
AC	R46TS	040	15	1000	650	5.0-6.5	120-160 5
AC	R46TS	040	15	N A	650	5.0-6.5	120-160 5
AC	R45TS	040	15	1000	650	5.0-6.5	120-160 5
AC	R45TS	040	15	N A	650	5.0-6.5	120-160 5
AC	R44TS	040	15	1000	750	5.0-6.5	120-160 5
AC	R46TS	040	15	900 600[7]	650	3-6.5 @ Idle	120-160 5
AC	R46TS	040	15	—	650	3-6.5 @ Idle	120-160 5
AC	R45TS	040	15	1000 600[7]	650	3-6.5 @ Idle	120-160 5
AC	R45TS	040	15	1000 600[7]	650	3-6.5 @ Idle	120-160 5
AC	R44T	035	15	900 450[7]	600 450[7]	3-6.5 @ Idle	150 5
AC	R46TS	035	15	800	625	3-6.5 @ Idle	120-160 5
AC	R46TS	035	15	600 1000[7]	500 700[7 8]	3-6.5 @ Idle	120-160 5
AC	R45TS	035	15	600 1000[7]	500 600[7 9]	3-6.5 @ Idle	120-160 5
AC	R45TS	035	15	600 900[7]	550 650[7]	5-6.5 @ Idle	150 5
AC	R47S	035	25	800	600	5-6.5 @ Idle	120-160 5
AC	R47S	035	25	—	600	5-6.5 @ Idle	120-160 5
AC	R47S	035	25	600 1000[7]	700	5-6.5 @ Idle	120-160 5
AC	R46S	035	25	—	650	5-6.5 @ Idle	120-160 5
AC	R46S	035	25	—	650	5-6.5 @ Idle	120-160 5
AC	R46S	035	25	600 1000[7]	700	5-6.5 @ Idle	120-160 5
AC	R46S	035	25	800	650	5-8 @ 1000 rpm	150-170 5
AC	R46S	035	25	800	650	5-8 @ 1000 rpm	150-170 5
AC	R46S	035	25	800	650	5-8 @ 1000 rpm	185-210 5
AC	R45S	035	25	950	650	5-8 @ 1000 rpm	185-210 5
AC	R45S	035	25	950	650	5-8 @ 1000 rpm	185-210 5
AC	R45S	035	25	950	650	5-8 @ 1000 rpm	185-210 5
AC	R44S	035	25	950	650	5-8 @ 1000 rpm	185-210 5
AC	R44S	035	25	1000[10]	750[10]	5-8 @ 1000 rpm	185-210 5
AC	R45S	035	25	950	650	5-8 @ 1000 rpm	185-210 5
AC	R45S	035	25	950	650	5-8 @ 1000 rpm	185-210 5

[11] 15/32-in. on the Ventura.
[12] 5/16-in. on the Ventura.
[13] On air-conditioned cars, 550 rpm with A/C off, 650 rpm with A/C on.
[14] R45SX for high-altitude engine.
[15] Available in Ventura only.
[22] ⅜-in. on 2-bbl. carburetor, ¼-in. on 4-bbl.

[23] Ram Air III.
[24] Ram Air IV.
[25] High Energy Ignition, no points used.
† In neutral.
†† In drive.
# In Park.

INDEX

EXHAUST SYSTEMS

Hot exhaust gases are routed from the engine to the rear of the car through the exhaust system. Factory-installed exhaust systems consist of the following components **(Fig. 9-1):**

1. An exhaust or front pipe which connects to the exhaust manifold.

2. A muffler.

3. An outlet or tailpipe assembly.

4. Sufficient brackets and hangers to suspend and isolate the components from contact with the car.

5. Clamps, gaskets and seals where required to connect the components.

In addition to these basic components, engine exhaust or design requirements may necessitate the use of a front or rear crossover pipe, a catalytic converter and/or a resonator unit **(Fig. 9-2).**

THE MUFFLER

Stock mufflers are designed to lower exhaust noise, while passing exhaust gases to the tailpipe. To do this,

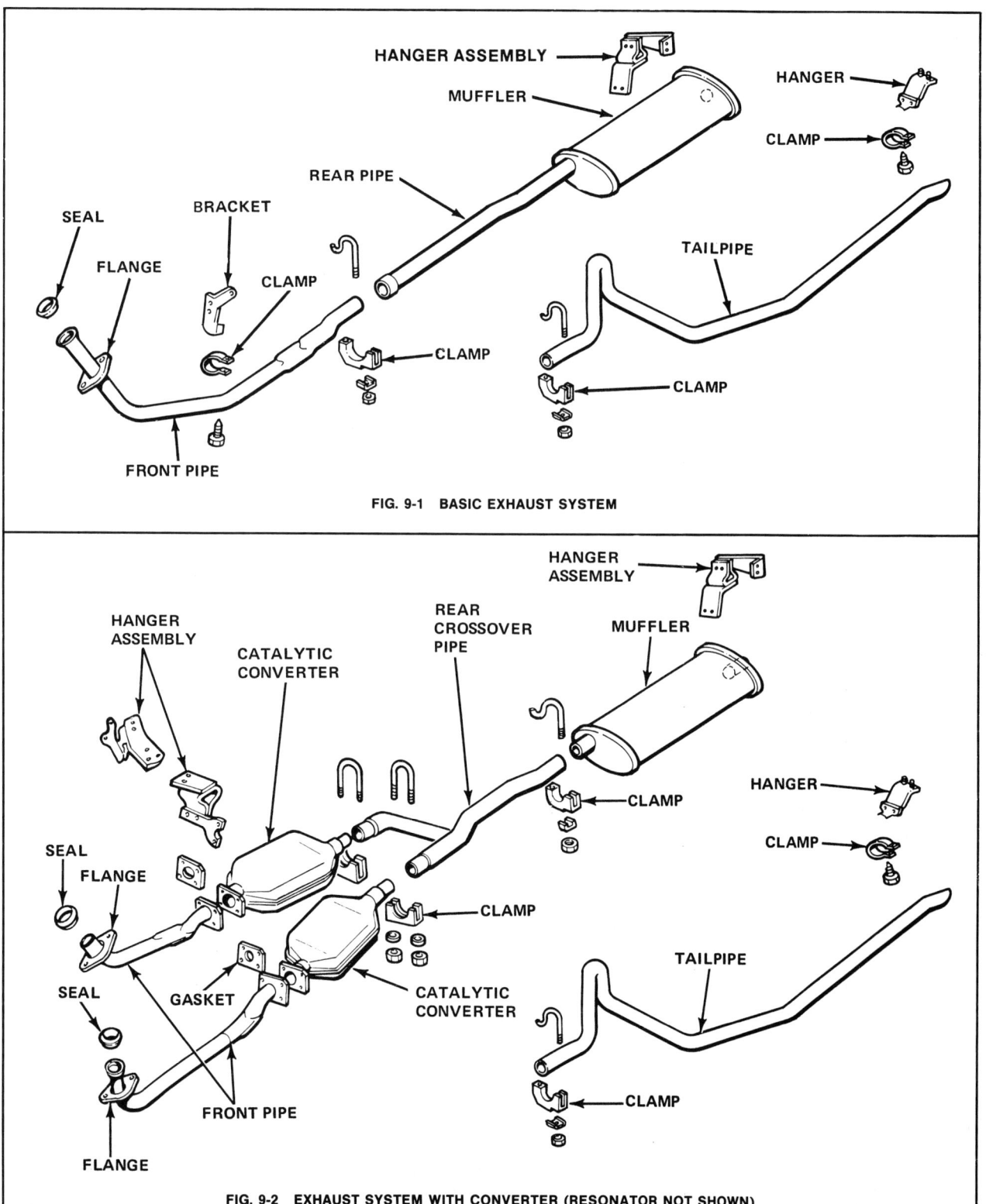

FIG. 9-1   BASIC EXHAUST SYSTEM

FIG. 9-2   EXHAUST SYSTEM WITH CONVERTER (RESONATOR NOT SHOWN)

they contain a series of baffles and noise-absorbing chambers through which the gases must travel before exiting. While mufflers have a restrictive effect on exhaust gases, the restriction is not too great at low engine speeds. But as engine speed increases and more gases are passed through the muffler faster, the backpressure in the system increases, lowering engine efficiency. So, dual exhaust systems are commonly used with higher powered engines **(Fig. 9-3)**.

The dual system cuts the volume of exhaust gases to be muffled in half, but increases noise level—the fewer cylinders serviced by a muffler, the greater the noise. To reduce this additional noise, more baffles and internal restrictions in each muffler are used in a dual exhaust system.

RESONATORS

The resonator is usually just a short-length, straight-through muffler that is either steel- or glass-packed, and is installed in the exhaust system to provide extra sound-muffling for the exhaust. A resonator is usually located to the rear of the muffler and connected by a short pipe. Exhaust gases cool off as they near the rear of the car, causing the volume of gas to be reduced. When a resonator is installed near the end of the exhaust system, the cooler gases are more easily muffled because of this decrease in volume.

EXHAUST SYSTEM PROBLEMS

The exhaust system is subjected to damage from both internal and external forces. The moisture contained in exhaust gases contains corrosives, such as sulfuric acid, that are by-products of combustion. In a car used primarily for stop-and-go driving, the acid-laden moisture collects and attacks the thin metal of the exhaust pipes and muffler shell. Particularly prone to corrosive damage are:

1. Dips in the tailpipe ahead of the rear axle.
2. The section just behind the axle.
3. The rear end of the inlet or front pipe.
4. The bottom of the muffler shell.
5. All joints connecting the components, whether welded or clamped.

Exhaust systems are also attacked from the outside in coastal areas where moisture and humidity levels are high, or where road salt is used to melt snow and ice. If the vehicle is driven off-road, or on roads with potholes and other such defects, physical damage to the exhaust system can be done.

EXHAUST SYSTEM INSPECTION

A corroded or damaged exhaust system is dangerous, because it can allow leakage of poisonous carbon monoxide into the passenger compartment. Periodic exhaust system maintenance is not required, but the system should be inspected whenever the car is on a hoist for other service. If any component is damaged or corroded, or appears unlikely to last until the next inspection, it should be replaced rather than attempting repairs. While small holes in pipes can be brazed, and rusted areas in a muffler covered with sheetmetal and wired, the service life of such repairs is always limited and temporary, as well as dangerous. With the car on a hoist, inspect:

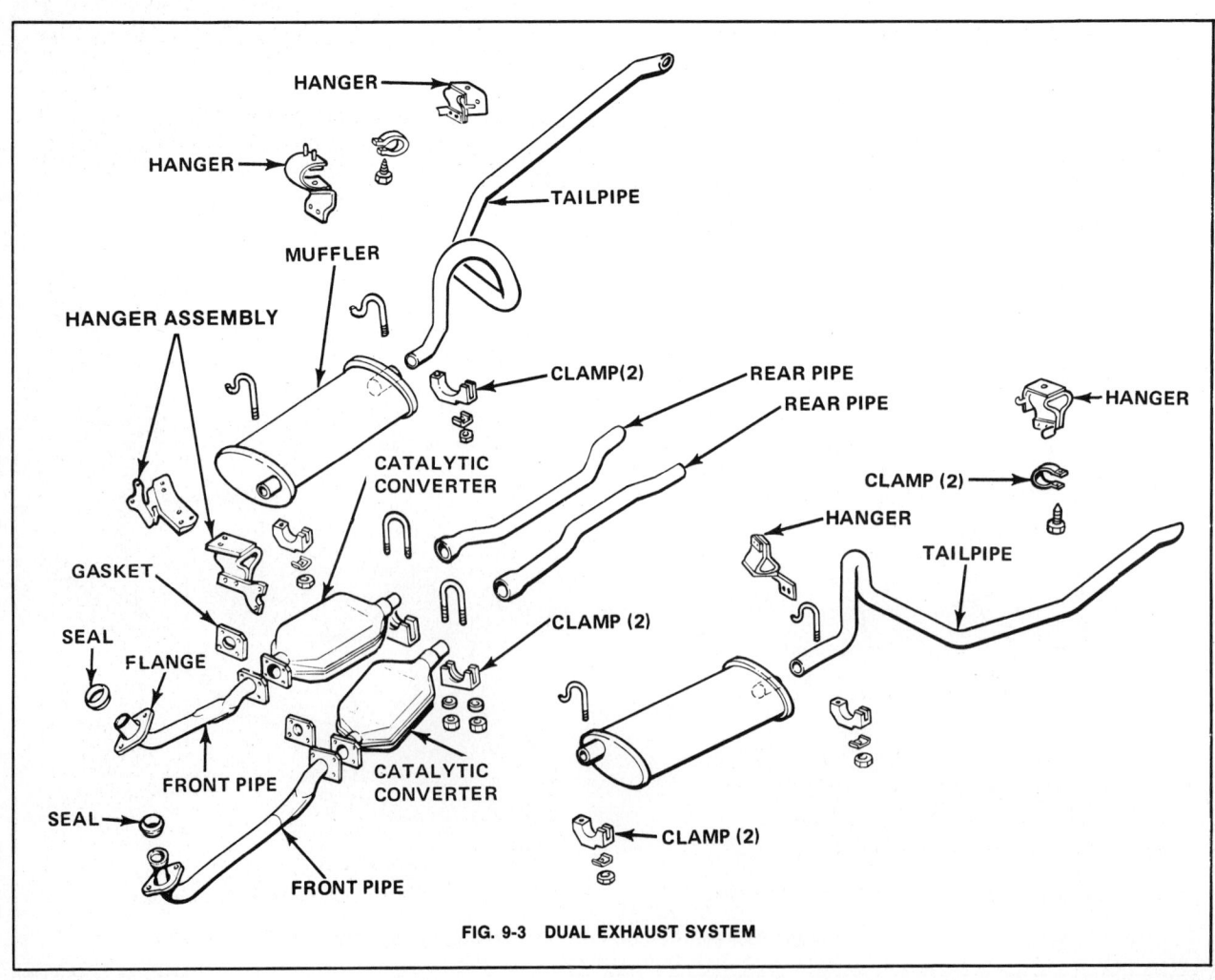

FIG. 9-3 DUAL EXHAUST SYSTEM

1. The inlet pipe(s), catalytic converter(s), muffler(s), resonator(s) and outlet pipe(s) for misalignment, excessive vibration, cracked joints, broken welds or seams, and/or corrosion damage.

2. The clamps, brackets, hangers and insulators for cracks, damage, misalignment, and stripped or corroded bolt threads.

3. Converter exhaust shields for missing/damaged attaching parts (such as clamps or screws). Remove any debris that may have collected in the shield area.

COMPONENT REPLACEMENT

Factory-fitted exhaust system components are often welded together, while service replacement systems are designed to be assembled with clamps. Because of this, the number of basic pieces furnished as an exhaust system replacement may vary from the number used in the factory-fitted system.

Whether installing a complete exhaust system, or just replacing a single component, correct alignment and relationship of the components to each other is important. Annoying noises and rattles can result from an incorrectly assembled exhaust system due to improper clearances or obstructions to the normal flow of exhaust gases. Some manufacturers provide locator tabs and notched flanges on service replacement parts to assist in proper component alignment.

While the number and type of exhaust systems in use varies considerably, depending upon the car, engine and model year, the following general removal/installation procedure can be successfully used.

EXHAUST SYSTEM DIAGNOSIS

CAUSE	CORRECTION
EXCESSIVE EXHAUST NOISE	
(a) Leaks at pipe joints.	(a) Tighten clamps at leaking joints.
(b) Burned or blown-out muffler.	(b) Replace muffler.
(c) Burned or rusted-out exhaust pipe.	(c) Replace exhaust pipe
(d) Exhaust pipe leaks at manifold flange.	(d) Install new gasket and tighten flange bolt nuts
(e) Cracked or broken exhaust manifold.	(e) Replace manifold.
(f) Leak between manifold and cylinder head.	(f) Tighten manifold-to-head stud nuts or bolts.
(g) Restriction in tailpipe or muffler.	(g) Remove restriction or replace component
LEAKING EXHAUST GASES	
(a) Pipe joints leak.	(a) Torque U-bolt to 150 in.-lbs.
(b) Gaskets damaged or improperly installed.	(b) Replace gaskets as required.
(c) Heat tube connections.	(c) Replace gaskets as required. Tighten stud nuts or bolts.
(d) Heat tubes burned or rusted out.	(d) Replace heat tubes.
ENGINE HARD TO WARM UP, OR WILL NOT RETURN TO NORMAL IDLE	
(a) Butterfly valve frozen.	(a) Free valve with a suitable solvent.
(b) Intake manifold crossover passage blocked.	(b) Remove restriction or replace manifold.
NOISY BUTTERFLY VALVE	
(a) Broken thermostatic spring.	(a) Replace spring.
(b) Broken, weak or missing anti-rattle spring.	(b) Replace spring.

EXHAUST SYSTEM REMOVAL

1. With the car raised on a hoist to a comfortable working level, apply penetrating oil to the clamp bolts and nuts of the component to be removed and replaced.

2. If replacing a muffler welded to the exhaust pipe, measure the replacement muffler exhaust-pipe extension. Cut the pipe with a hacksaw, close to the front of the old muffler, allowing sufficient length (usually about 1½ ins.) to install the exhaust pipe in the muffler extension. Where the muffler or resonator is welded to the tailpipe, these units are not usually serviced separately, but are replaced as an integral assembly.

3. Loosen the clamps and supports in the immediate area of the replacement to allow alignment of components during installation. Wire the components to the frame for support.

4. If the tailpipe is to be removed, it may be necessary to raise the rear of the car to relieve body weight from the rear springs and provide sufficient clearance between the pipe and rear axle parts.

5. Remove the component to be replaced. If the

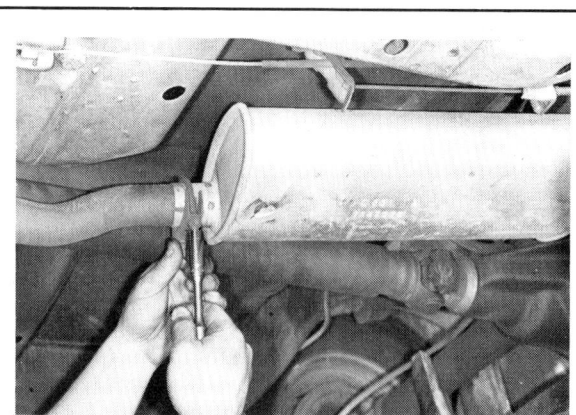

FIG. 9-4   INSTALLING MUFFLER

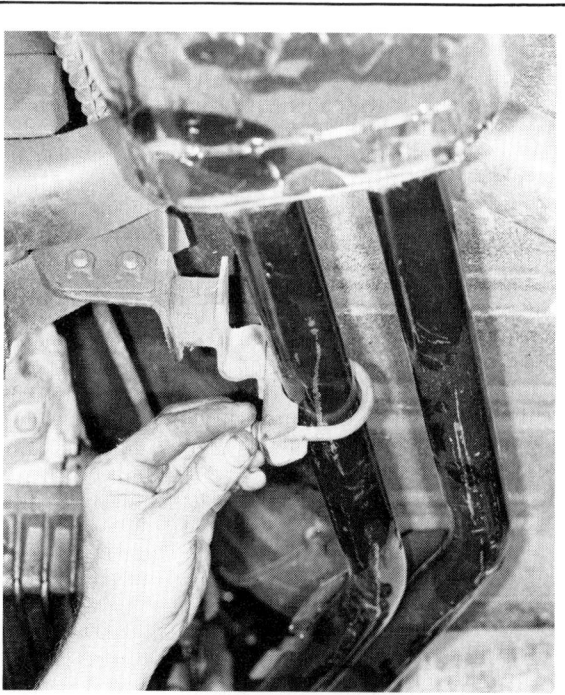

FIG. 9-5   PIPE-TO-BODY CLEARANCE

joint is a slip-on rather than a welded type, and cannot be broken loose with an application of penetrating oil, heat the joint with an oxyacetylene torch and tap apart with a heavy hammer. If a torch is not available, use a tubing cutter if possible. A hammer and chisel will do the job, but it is far slower and more difficult to make a fairly smooth and straight cut.

6. Clean the ends of the pipes and/or muffler to assist in mating of the new and old components.

7. Remove and discard any worn/broken insulators, rusted clamps, hangers, supports or other attaching parts.

8. If replacing the front pipe, use a wire brush or knife to clean the manifold outlet-flange surfaces to remove all gasket debris, or the new installation may leak.

EXHAUST SYSTEM INSTALLATION

1. Install the clamps to be used near their proper places on the existing pipes, leaving them sufficiently loose to move back and forth freely.

2. Connect a new front pipe to the muffler first, then to the manifold flange. Connect a new muffler to the front pipe first, then to the tailpipe. Where alignment tabs are provided, make sure they fit into their corresponding notches **(Fig. 9-4)**.

3. Sliding the clamps in place, align and clamp the component at the front and rear to maintain its correct position and proper clearance (at least ¾-in.) with underbody parts. This will avoid possible overheating of the floorpan, which can cause damage to the passenger compartment carpets, and isolate the exhaust component from possible contact with the underbody or frame, which might cause undesirable vibration noises **(Fig. 9-5)**.

4. Some exhaust manifolds are fitted with a ball flange outlet to provide a tight seal and reduce unnecessary strain on the front pipe connections. On such flanges, tighten the bolts in an alternate manner to assure that the flanges are both parallel and even.

5. When correct alignment and positioning of the components is assured, tighten connections securely.

6. Start the engine and set on a fast idle. Listen for any hissing, intermittent spitting sounds or droning of metal-to-metal contact that might be telegraphed throughout the frame. If any are heard, locate the source and correct.

EXHAUST MANIFOLD HEAT VALVE

A simple butterfly valve, the exhaust manifold heat valve is located in the exhaust manifold and controlled by a thermostatic tension spring and counterweight **(Fig. 9-6)**. This butterfly valve is designed to block the direct exit of exhaust gases from the manifold and force them along passages in the floor of the intake manifold under the carburetor. As the exhaust gases heat up the intake manifold passages, more complete vaporization of the gasoline takes place and warm-up improves. Exhaust heat valves are held in the closed (heat-on) position by the thermostatic tension spring and counterweight **(Fig. 9-7)**. As the engine reaches normal operating temperature, less heat is required under the carburetor. This causes the thermostatic spring to lose tension, opening the valve (heat-off position). The counterweight is offset so that it has a tendency to hold the valve in the closed position, but the valve itself is also offset on a shaft, so that any excess rush of exhaust gases will have a tendency to open it. A combination of these factors results in an exhaust heat-

valve action that forces the correct amount of exhaust gas through the heating passages in the intake manifold to allow the engine to operate without stumbling while sufficiently vaporizing the gasoline to get good mileage. Exhaust heat valves on 1975 and later General Motors, Ford, Lincoln, Mercury, and some 1979 Chrysler Corp. cars, are controlled by a vacuum diaphragm for more precise operation and are considered as part of the car's emission controls—see Chapter 6.

HEAT VALVE PROBLEMS

Under certain conditions, the manifold heat valve can malfunction. When a car is used primarily for stop-and-go driving, the engine seldom warms up completely. Heavy condensation while the engine is cold combines with the extra carbon, caused by running rich on a partial choke setting, to freeze the butterfly valve on its shaft in the closed position. All exhaust gases from the cylinders on the side with the frozen heat valve must therefore pass through the heat riser passages of the intake manifold. Not only does this render half the cylinders practically useless, it also assures an oversupply of heat to the base of the carburetor, which can lead to vapor lock. On factory-equipped dual exhaust systems, the butterfly valve will be located between one of the exhaust manifolds and the front pipe leading to the muffler. If the valve freezes, the exhaust must still pass through the intake manifold risers and into the opposite exhaust manifold.

HEAT VALVE INSPECTION AND MAINTENANCE

1. Start the engine, set the brakes and place the transmission in NEUTRAL or PARK.

2. Accelerate the engine momentarily by operating the throttle linkage while watching the heat valve counterweight.

3. If no movement of the counterweight is noted, the shaft is binding because of accumulated deposits, or the thermostatic tension spring is weak or broken.

4. Shut the engine off. When the manifold is cool, apply a liberal amount of solvent or heat valve lubricant to each end of the valve shaft at the bushings.

5. Allow the solvent/lubricant to soak for several minutes, then operate the valve back and forth by hand until it turns freely. If solvent or lubricant is applied at every oil change, it will prevent the shaft deposits from accumulating and interfering with valve operation.

6. If solvent/lubricant application does not free a binding shaft, or if the tension spring is weak or broken, the heat valve must be removed and repaired or replaced, as necessary.

HEAT VALVE REMOVAL/REPLACEMENT

Depending upon the exhaust system design, the manifold heat valve may be located a) directly in the exhaust manifold neck or b) in a spacer plate positioned between the manifold and front exhaust pipe. The former will require exhaust manifold removal and is repairable; the spacer plate design is serviced as a unit by replacement, not repair.

SPACER PLATE HEAT VALVE REPLACEMENT

1. Disconnect the exhaust pipe and lower it.

2. Remove and replace the defective valve in its spacer plate with a new unit. Use new gaskets.

3. Replace the exhaust pipe gaskets with new ones.

4. Raise the exhaust pipe into position and connect it to the exhaust manifold.

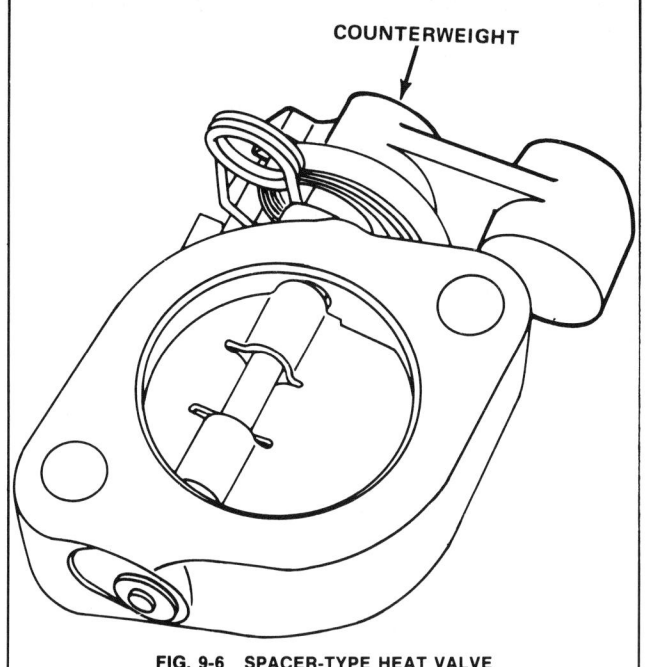

FIG. 9-6 SPACER-TYPE HEAT VALVE

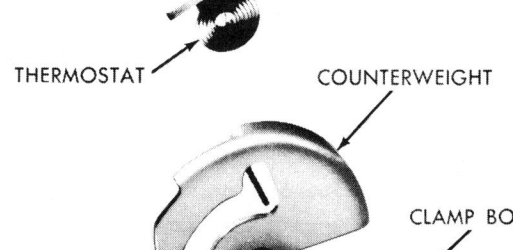

FIG. 9-7 MANIFOLD HEAT VALVE COMPONENTS
(BUTTERFLY INSIDE MANIFOLD NECK)

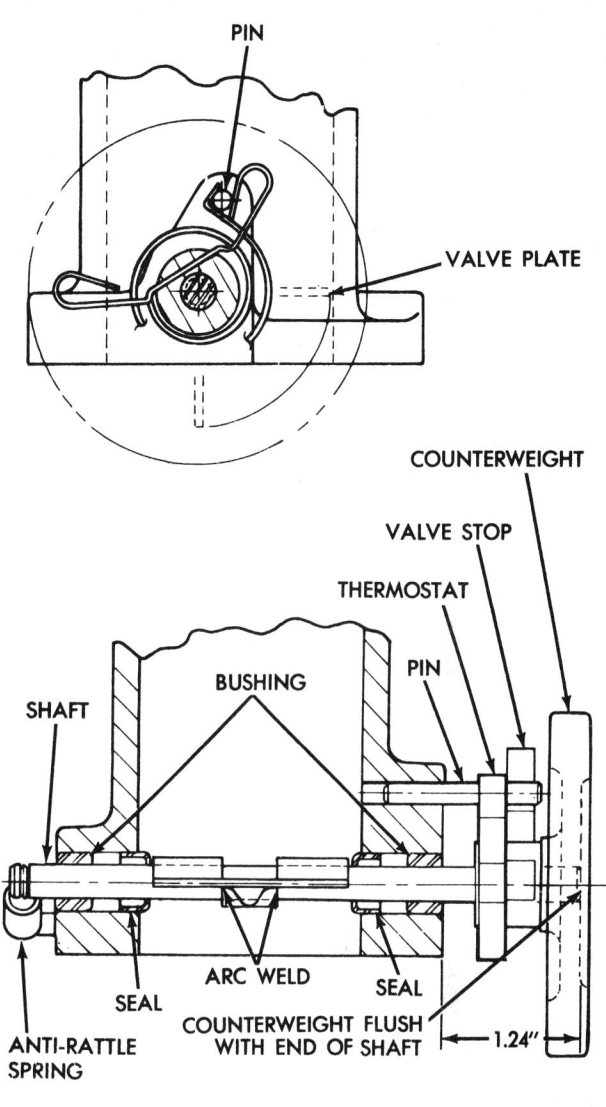

FIG. 9-8 MANIFOLD HEAT VALVE CUTAWAY

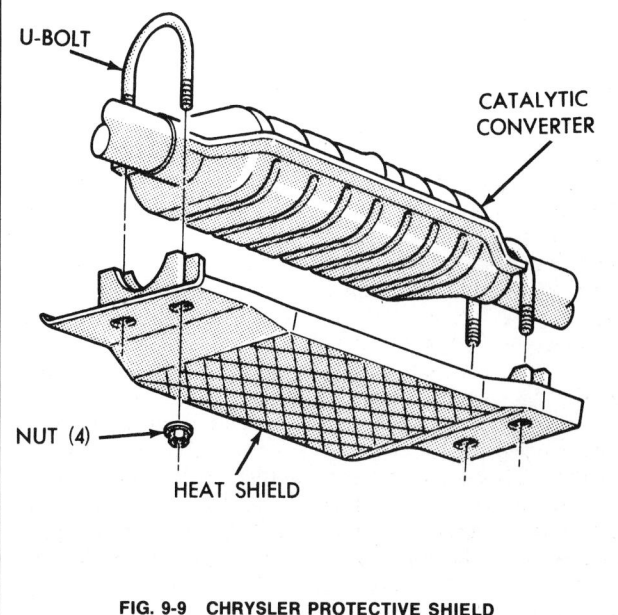

FIG. 9-9 CHRYSLER PROTECTIVE SHIELD

FIG. 9-10 FORD, LINCOLN, MERCURY LOWER SHIELDS

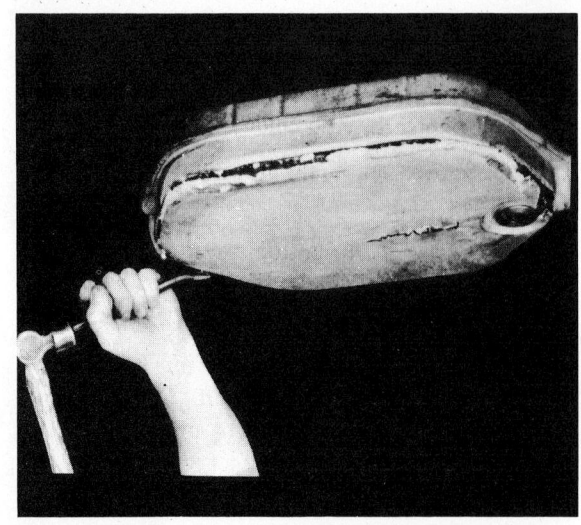

FIG. 9-11 BOTTOM COVER REMOVAL

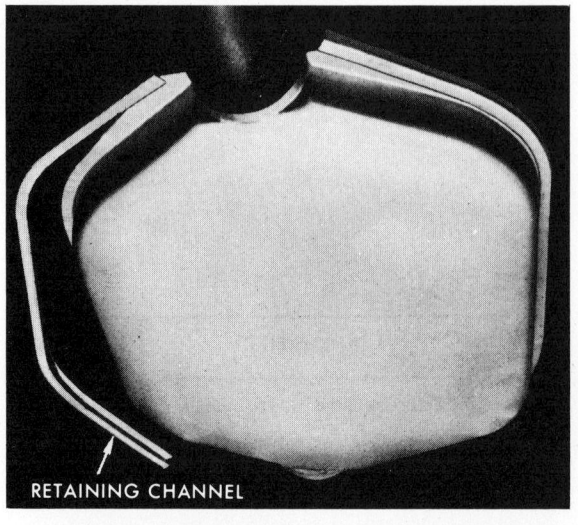

RETAINING CHANNEL

FIG. 9-12 INSTALLING RETAINING CHANNEL

EXHAUST MANIFOLD HEAT VALVE REPLACEMENT

1. Remove the exhaust manifold from the engine after disconnecting the manifold from the front exhaust pipe.

2. With the manifold neck secured in a vise, position the butterfly, as required, and grind off the spot welds from the butterfly and the shaft. If a retaining screw is used instead of a spot weld, cut the shaft on each side of the valve.

3. Remove the counterweight and shaft assembly, and the butterfly **(Fig. 9-8).**

4. Press the bushings and cup seals from the manifold neck.

5. Blow out the vent holes, and clean if necessary.

6. With cupped ends facing outward, press in new cup seals flush with the manifold.

7. Press new bushings in flush with the exhaust manifold's outer edge.

8. Test for a free fit of the shaft in the bushings and seals. Ream bushings to size, if necessary.

9. Fit the valve stop in the counterweight slot. Looped ends must face away from the counterweight shaft hole.

10. Install the thermostatic spring to the counterweight and press the counterweight on the shaft flush with the shaft end.

11. Fit the shaft assembly in the manifold neck, with the butterfly strap facing outward, and hook the spring end to the stop pin.

12. Test its operation, with the butterfly centered between the seals. If satisfactory, arc-weld the plate to the shaft with a stainless steel rod. If a retaining screw is used instead of a spot weld, move the valve as far as possible from the counterweight and tighten the screw. Test its operation again and, if satisfactory, install the anti-rattle spring (where used).

13. Fit a new gasket to the engine studs, and replace the exhaust manifold on the engine.

14. Install the front exhaust pipe to the manifold neck.

CATALYTIC CONVERTER

Where used, the catalytic converter is an integral part of the exhaust system, positioned between the front pipe and the muffler. Removal and replacement procedure is the same as for a muffler or resonator unit, but Ford, Lincoln, Mercury and Chrysler Corporation cars use a protective heat shield which can complicate replacement.

CONVERTER LOWER SHIELD

The Chrysler protective shield, shown in **Fig. 9-9,** attaches beneath the converter inlets with U-bolts, and is fitted to all converter-equipped cars sold in California. Replacement is accomplished by simply removing the U-bolt nuts.

Ford, Lincoln and Mercury converter lower shields **(Fig. 9-10)** are formed and perforated metal sheets. Some installations are factory-clamped in place, and removal is also a simple procedure, but others are factory-welded to the exhaust system. Welded shields are removed with a chisel, taking care not to damage the pipe. The replacement shield is then positioned to the pipe in the same place as the previously removed shield and secured with the correct size and necessary number of Prestole-type clamps. These should be positioned to provide a minimum of ½-in. clearance between the screw tip and frame member where contact is possible.

CONVERTER BOTTOM REPLACEMENT

GM and AMC converter units are not equipped with a lower shield. If the bottom cover of the converter housing is damaged or torn, a repair kit is available to replace it.

1. Remove the bottom cover with a hammer and chisel as shown in **Fig. 9-11.** Cut close to the bottom outside edge; cut depth must be very shallow or the inner converter shell will be damaged. *Do not* remove the fill plug.

2. Remove the insulation and inspect the inner converter shell. If damaged, the entire converter assembly must be replaced.

3. Install new insulation in the replacement cover, and apply sealing compound where the insulation meets the cover edge. Apply additional sealer at the front and rear pipe openings.

4. Fit the replacement cover to the converter and install the retaining channels on both sides of the converter housing **(Fig. 9-12).**

5. Attach the two retaining clamps over the channels at each end of the converter.

INDEX

CLUTCHES AND MANUAL TRANSMISSIONS

THE AUTOMOTIVE CLUTCH

The clutch is used to connect and disconnect the engine from the driveline. Because the internal combustion engine is not capable of developing a high starting torque, it must be permitted to build up enough torque to move the car before it can be successfully connected to the powertrain. The engine's power must be applied gradually for smooth engagement and minimum shock on the driving components. Once engaged, the clutch must transmit 100% of the engine's power to the transmission without slippage. The clutch assembly consists of the following principal components (Fig. 10-1):

1. The clutch pilot bearing.
2. The rear face of the engine flywheel.
3. The clutch driven plate assembly.
4. The clutch pressure plate and cover.
5. The clutch release or throw-out bearing.
6. The clutch fork.
7. The linkage connecting the clutch pedal to the clutch fork.

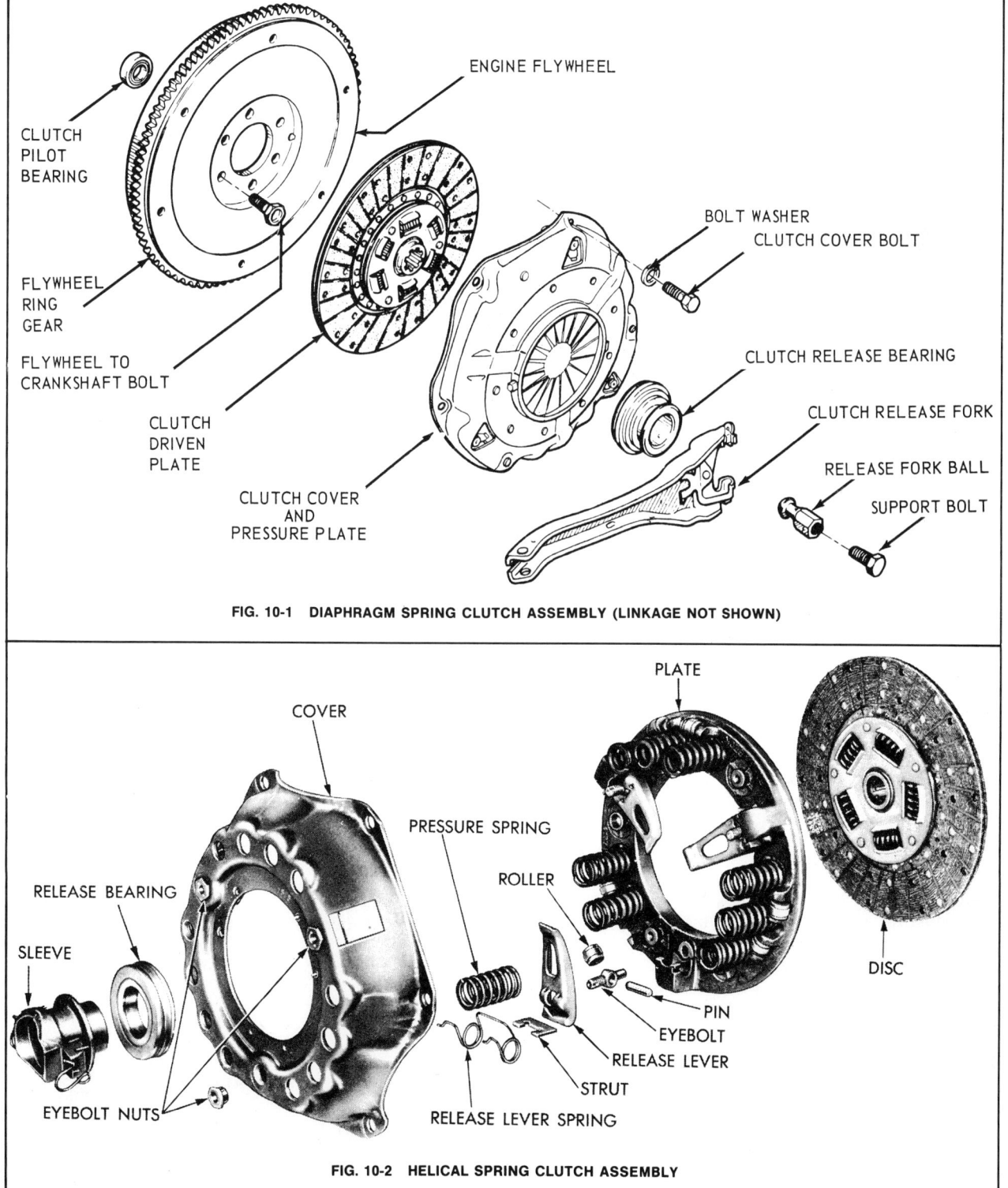

FIG. 10-1 DIAPHRAGM SPRING CLUTCH ASSEMBLY (LINKAGE NOT SHOWN)

FIG. 10-2 HELICAL SPRING CLUTCH ASSEMBLY

CLUTCH PRESSURE PLATES

Two basic types of clutch pressure plates are used: the diaphragm spring and the helical spring design. The diaphragm spring type uses a one-piece conical (Belleville) or diaphragm spring. The inside portion of this spring is slit to produce a series of clutch "fingers" **(Fig. 10-1).** When the clutch release bearing contacts the inner sections of this spring, the applied pressure causes the outer ring of the spring to move away from the flywheel, drawing the pressure plate away from the clutch plate, disengaging the clutch.

The diaphragm spring design may have flat or bent fingers. The bent variation has its integral release fingers bent back toward the transmission to provide a centrifugal assist for quick reengagement at high speeds. It's used mainly in high-performance V-8 powertrains, heavy-duty passenger car applications and all 1979 and later GM clutches. Clutch release bearings should not be interchanged between the two variations. The one used with the bent finger design is shorter in length than that required by the flat finger type. An incorrect release bearing will cause slippage and rapid wear.

The helical spring type uses a system of pressure plate levers which pivot on the cover to force the pressure plate away from the driven plate when contact is made with the release bearing. Lever action thus performs the same function as the dish-shaped diaphragm spring **(Fig. 10-2).** Rollers may be used in this design to increase the normal load on the clutch disc at higher rpm. As rpm increases, the centrifugal force of the rollers causes them to act as wedges between the pressure plate and cover, exerting more force against the disc.

CLUTCH LINKAGE ADJUSTMENT

All normal clutch wear is compensated for by one linkage adjustment, either to the clutch-fork push rod or to the pedal push rod. The clutch pedal must have a certain amount of free travel before the clutch release bearing engages the pressure-plate-spring fingers or levers. This is necessary to prevent clutch slippage, which would take place if the bearing was held in constant contact with the fingers/levers, and to prevent premature bearing failure from constant running. In addition to normal clutch wear adjustment, the pedal free travel must be adjusted whenever the clutch is removed for repair/replacement. The following procedures cover clutch adjustments on all 1970-79 American cars with a clutch and manual transmission.

BUICK

ALL 1970-74 MODELS

1. With the clutch fork on the ball stud, disconnect the return spring from the fork.

2. Hold the equalizer/release rod toward the front of the car while holding the clutch fork toward the rear.

3. Adjust the equalizer/release rod until there is 1/16- to 1/8-in. clearance between the end of the rod and the clutch fork. This will produce ⅝- to ⅞-in. free travel at the pedal.

ALL 1975-79 CENTURYS/REGALS
(Fig. 10-3)

ALL 1975-79 SKYLARKS
(Fig. 10-4)

ALL 1975-79 SKYHAWKS
(Fig. 10-5)

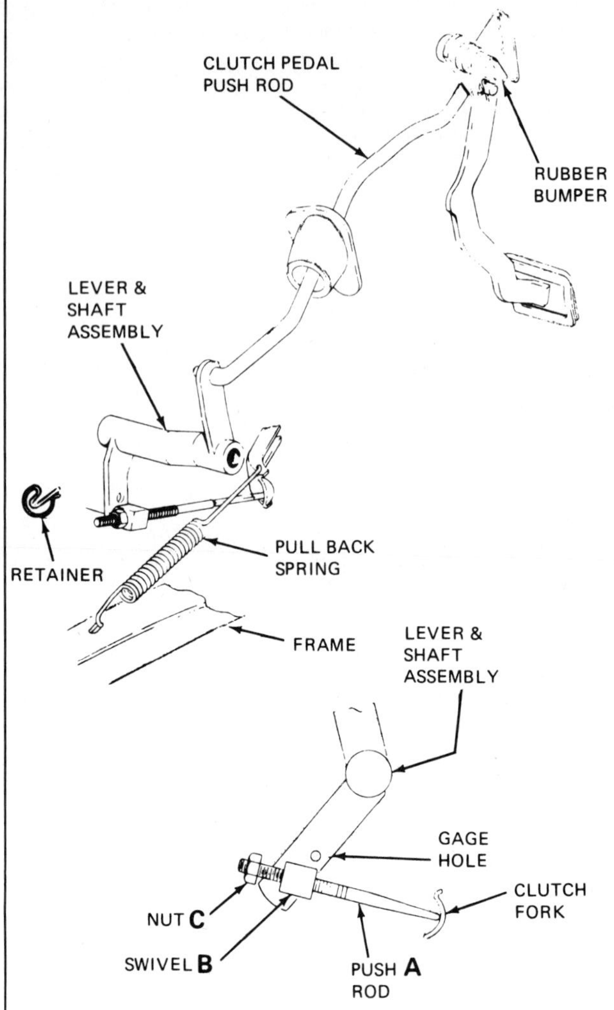

CLUTCH ADJUSTMENT

THE FOLLOWING ADJUSTMENT IS TO BE MADE BEFORE RETURN SPRING IS INSTALLED:

1. ROTATE CLUTCH LEVER & SHAFT ASSEMBLY UNTIL CLUTCH PEDAL IS FIRMLY AGAINST RUBBER BUMPER ON DASH BRACE.

2. PUSH OUTER END OF CLUTCH FORK REARWARD UNTIL THROW-OUT BEARING LIGHTLY CONTACTS BELLEVILLE SPRING FINGERS.

3. INSTALL LOWER PUSH ROD (A) IN FORK AND SWIVEL (B) IN GAGE HOLE. ROTATE ROD (A) CLOCKWISE AS VIEWED FROM FRONT OF VEHICLE TO FINGER TIGHT CONDITION TO REMOVE ALL LASH FROM SYSTEM.

4. REMOVE SWIVEL (B) FROM GAGE HOLE AND INSTALL IN HOLE FURTHEST FROM ₵ OF LEVER & SHAFT ASSEMBLY. INSTALL WASHERS AND RETAINER.

5. TIGHTEN LOCK NUT (C) AGAINST SWIVEL (B) BEING CAREFUL NOT TO CHANGE ROD (A) LENGTH. SEE VIEW A.

6. INSTALL CLUTCH RETAINER SPRING.

7. ABOVE PROCEDURE TO PRODUCE 1.00 ± 30 OF CLUTCH PEDAL "FREE TRAVEL" WHEN MEASURED AT THE CENTER OF THE PEDAL PAD.

FIG. 10-3 CLUTCH LINKAGE ADJUSTMENT (ALL 1975-79 CENTURYS/REGALS)

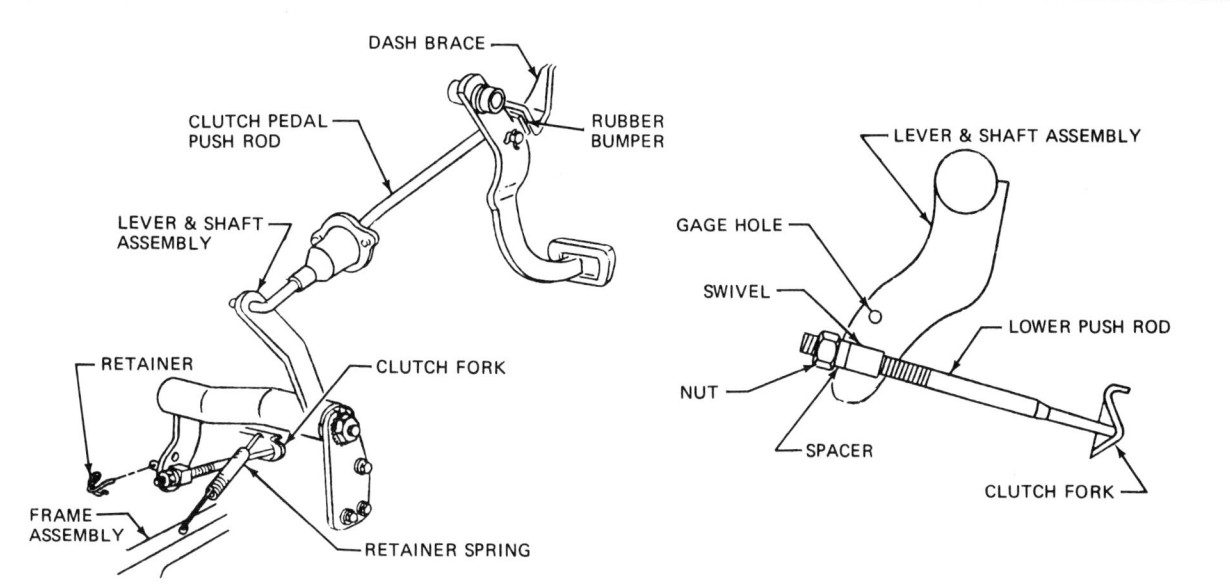

CLUTCH ADJUSTMENT

1 — ROTATE CLUTCH LEVER AND SHAFT ASSEMBLY UNTIL CLUTCH PEDAL IS FIRMLY AGAINST RUBBER BUMPER ON DASH BRACE.
2 — PUSH OUTER END OF CLUTCH FORK REARWARD UNTIL THROW-OUT BEARING LIGHTLY CONTACTS BELLEVILLE SPRING FINGERS.
3 — INSTALL LOWER PUSH ROD IN FORK AND GAGE HOLE, AND INCREASE LENGTH UNTIL ALL LASH IS REMOVED FROM SYSTEM.
4 — INSTALL SWIVEL OR ROD IN HOLE FURTHEST FROM CENTERLINE OF LEVER AND SHAFT ASSEMBLY AND INSTALL RETAINER.
5 — TIGHTEN LOCK NUT & SPACER AGAINST SWIVEL.
6 — INSTALL CLUTCH FORK RETAINER SPRING.
7 — ABOVE PROCEDURE TO PRODUCE 1.15 ± .30 OF CLUTCH PEDAL "FREE TRAVEL" WHEN MEASURED AT THE CENTER OF THE PEDAL PAD.

FIG. 10-4   CLUTCH LINKAGE ADJUSTMENT (ALL 1975-79 SKYLARKS)

ADJUSTMENT PROCEDURE

THE FOLLOWING ADJUSTMENT IS TO BE MADE BEFORE RETURN SPRING IS INSTALLED:

1. PLACE CABLE THROUGH HOLE IN CLUTCH FORK.
2. PULL CABLE UNTIL CLUTCH PEDAL IS FIRMLY AGAINST RUBBER BUMPER.
3. PUSH CLUTCH FORK FORWARD UNTIL THROW-OUT BEARING CONTACTS CLUTCH SPRING FINGERS.
4. SCREW PIN ON CABLE UNTIL IT BOTTOMS OUT ON FORK SURFACE.
5. TURN 1/4 ADDITIONAL REVOLUTION CLOCKWISE & DROP PIN DOWN INTO GROOVE IN FORK.
6. ATTACH RETURN SPRING.
7. ABOVE PROCEDURE TO PRODUCE 7/8 ± 1/4 LASH AT CLUTCH PEDAL.

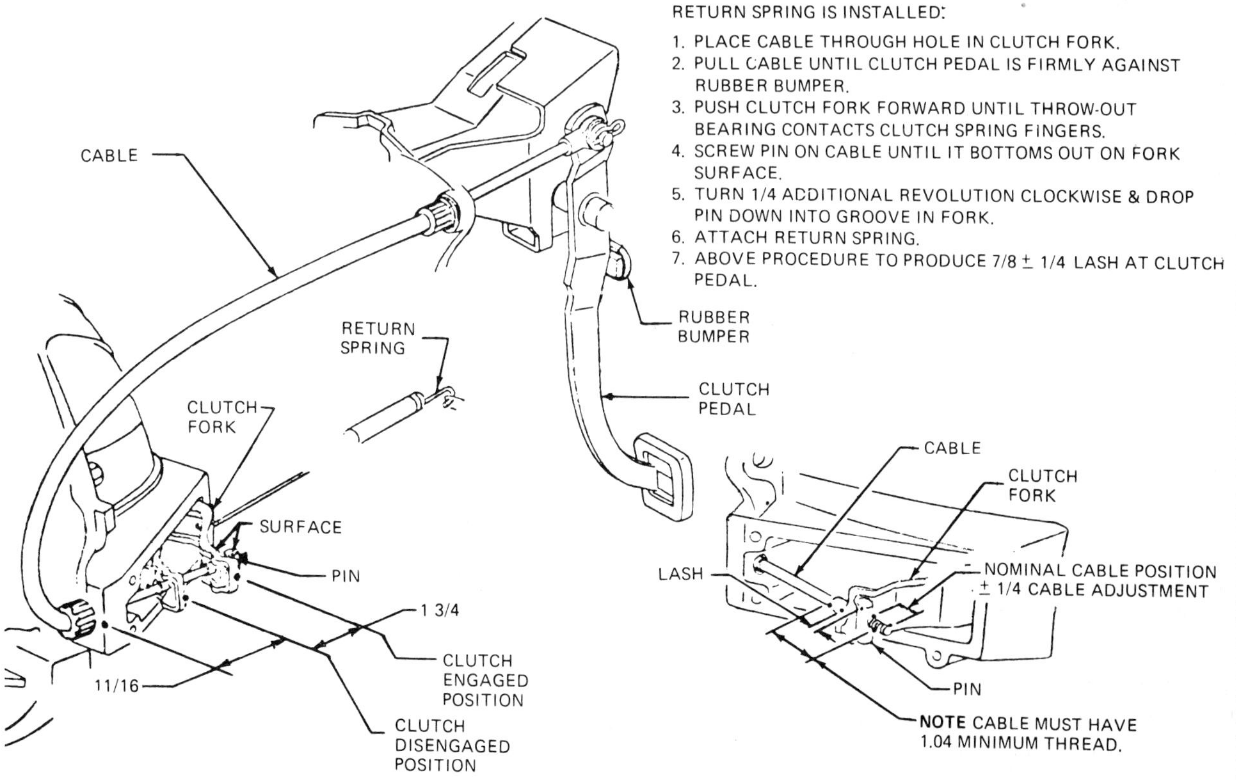

CABLE

RETURN SPRING

CLUTCH FORK

SURFACE

PIN

1 3/4

11/16

CLUTCH ENGAGED POSITION

CLUTCH DISENGAGED POSITION

RUBBER BUMPER

CLUTCH PEDAL

CABLE

CLUTCH FORK

LASH

NOMINAL CABLE POSITION ± 1/4 CABLE ADJUSTMENT

PIN

NOTE CABLE MUST HAVE 1.04 MINIMUM THREAD.

FIG. 10-5   CLUTCH LINKAGE ADJUSTMENT (ALL 1975-79 SKYHAWKS)

CHEVROLET

ALL 1970-74 CORVETTES,
1970 CHEVROLETS
(Fig. 10-6)

1. Disconnect the clutch return (pull-back) spring from the cross shaft lever.

2. Push the clutch pedal against its stop (rubber bumper) and loosen the jam nuts enough to move the adjusting rod.

3. Move the rod (D) until the release bearing lightly contacts the pressure plate fingers.

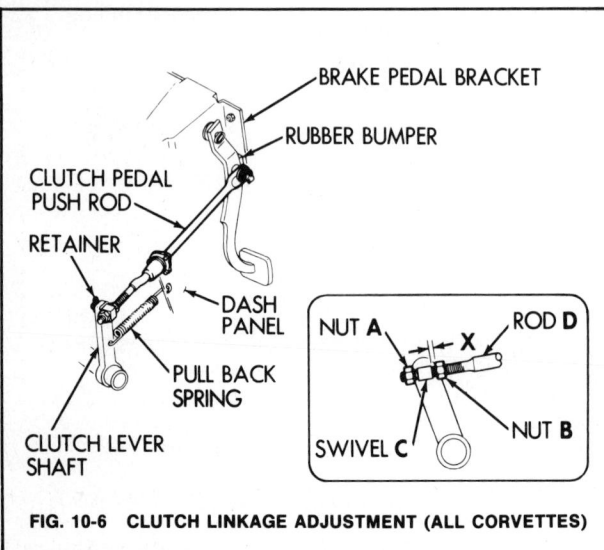

FIG. 10-6 CLUTCH LINKAGE ADJUSTMENT (ALL CORVETTES)

4. Turn the upper nut (B) against the swivel (C), then back off 4½ turns. Secure the swivel by tightening the lower nut.

5. Install the return spring and, using your hand, push down on the clutch pedal. When you feel the first resistance (the point where the release bearing touches the pressure plate spring), don't push any further. Measure the distance the pedal travels (from the pedal pad) before any resistance is felt. This distance is called free travel, and it should agree with the following specifications:

1970 Chevrolet, Corvette	1-1½ ins.
1971 Corvette	1¼-2 ins.
1971 Corvette with heavy-duty clutch	2-2½ ins.
1972 Corvette	1¼-1¾ ins.
1973 Corvette	1¼-1½ ins.
1974 Corvette	1-1½ ins.

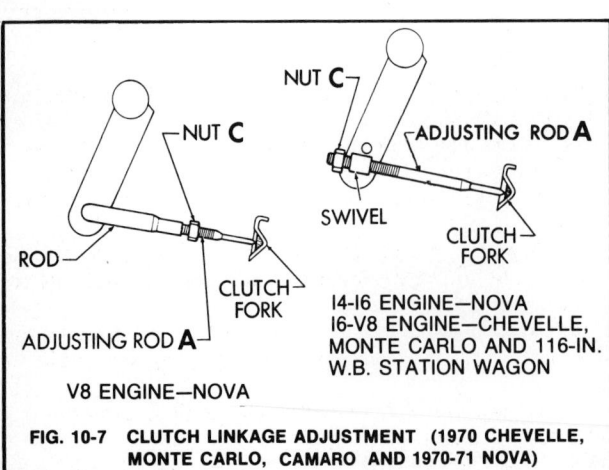

FIG. 10-7 CLUTCH LINKAGE ADJUSTMENT (1970 CHEVELLE, MONTE CARLO, CAMARO AND 1970-71 NOVA)

ALL 1970 CHEVELLES, MONTE CARLOS, CAMAROS;
ALL 1970-71 NOVAS
(Fig. 10-7)

1. Disconnect the return spring from the clutch fork.

2. Push the pedal up against its stop, loosen the locknut (C) and turn the adjusting rod (A) until it pushes against the clutch fork. Continue turning the rod until the release bearing lightly contacts the pressure plate fingers.

3. Turn the rod in the opposite direction by three turns, and tighten the locknut.

4. Install the return spring and measure the pedal free play—the distance the pedal pad travels before any resistance is felt. It should agree with the following specifications; if not, readjust until it does.

1970 Chevelle, Monte Carlo, Camaro	1⅛-1¾ ins.
1970 Nova	1-1⅛ ins.
1971 Nova	1-1½ ins.

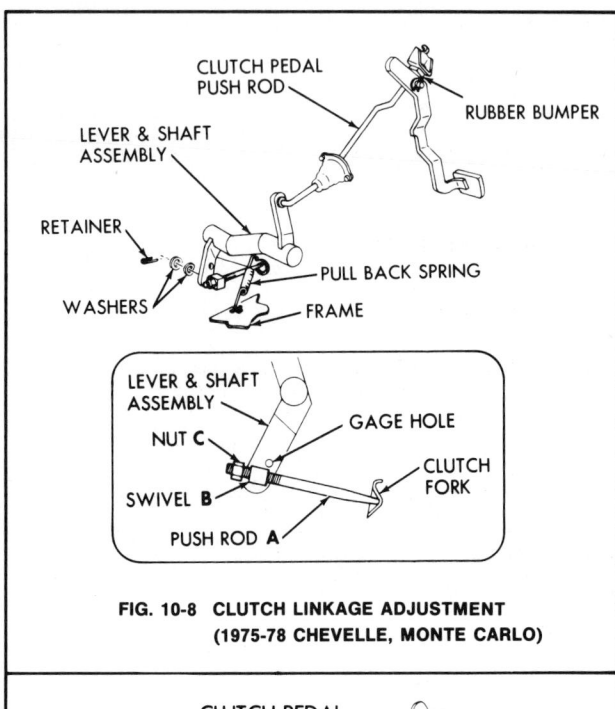

FIG. 10-8 CLUTCH LINKAGE ADJUSTMENT (1975-78 CHEVELLE, MONTE CARLO)

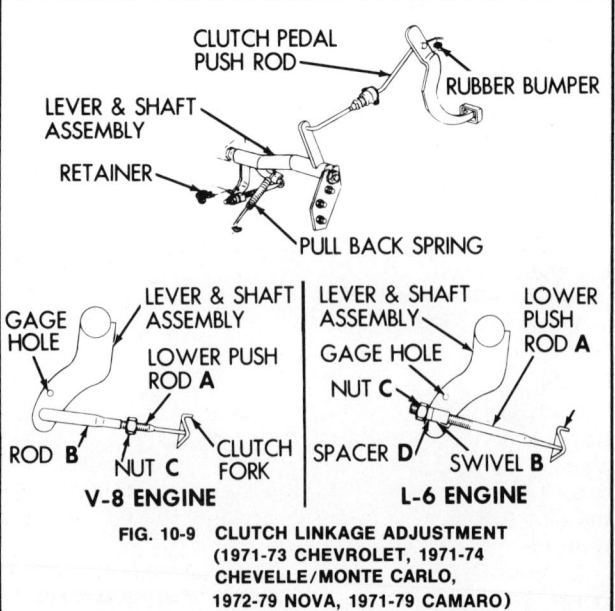

FIG. 10-9 CLUTCH LINKAGE ADJUSTMENT (1971-73 CHEVROLET, 1971-74 CHEVELLE/MONTE CARLO, 1972-79 NOVA, 1971-79 CAMARO)

ALL 1971-73 CHEVROLETS;
ALL 1971-77 CHEVELLES; ALL 1972-77 NOVAS
ALL 1973-79 CAMAROS, MALIBUS, MONTE CARLOS
(Figs. 10-8 & 10-9)

1. Disconnect the return spring from the clutch fork.

2. Push the clutch lever until the pedal firmly contacts its rubber stop.

3. Push the end of the fork to the rear until the release bearing lightly touches pressure plate fingers.

4. Loosen the locknut (C), and lengthen the rod until it aligns with the gage hole in the lever. Without moving the lever, insert the rod in the gage hole, and lengthen the rod until all play has been eliminated from the linkage.

5. Remove the rod from the gage hole, and insert it into the lower hole of the lever. Install the retainer, and tighten the locknut.

6. Install the return spring, and measure the pedal free play—the distance the pedal travels before any resistance is felt. It should agree with the following:

1971-72 Chevrolet, Chevelle, Camaro, Monte
Carlo .... 1⅛-1¾ ins.
1972 Nova .... 1-1½ ins.
1973 Chevrolet .... 1¼-1¾ ins.
1973-77 Nova .... ¾-1⅜ ins.
1973-77 Chevelle .... ¾-1 5/16 ins.
1973-79 Monte Carlo .... ¾-1 5/16 ins.
1973-79 Camaro, Malibu .... ¾-1⅜ ins.

ALL 1975-79 CORVETTES

(Fig. 10-6)

1. Disconnect the return spring from the cross shaft lever.

2. Push the clutch pedal against its rubber stop.

3. Install the swivel (C) and retainer in the clutch lever hole.

4. Loosen the nuts (A & B) on the rod (D) and push on the fork until the release bearing lightly contacts the pressure plate fingers.

5. Tighten the upper locknut (B) until the gap (X) between the nut and the swivel is 0.400-in.

6. When the correct gap is achieved, tighten the lower nut (A) against the swivel.

7. The free travel at the pedal—the distance the pedal travels before any resistance is felt—should be 1-1½ ins. If not, readjust until it is.

ALL MONZAS, VEGAS

(Fig. 10-10)

After replacing the clutch and/or clutch cable, adjust as follows:

1. Loosen the locknut, and turn the ball stud inward until the release bearing contacts the pressure plate springs.

2. Tighten the locknut, being careful not to change the adjustment.

3. Install the ball stud cap.

4. Remove the clutch fork cover and pull on the cable until the clutch pedal rests against the rubber bumper.

5. Push the clutch fork forward until the release bearing touches the clutch spring fingers. Hold in place.

6. Turn the pin on the cable until it bottoms out on the clutch fork, then turn another one-quarter turn, and drop the pin in the fork groove.

7. Hook the return spring and install the clutch fork cover. This will produce 7/8- to 15/16-in. free travel at the pedal.

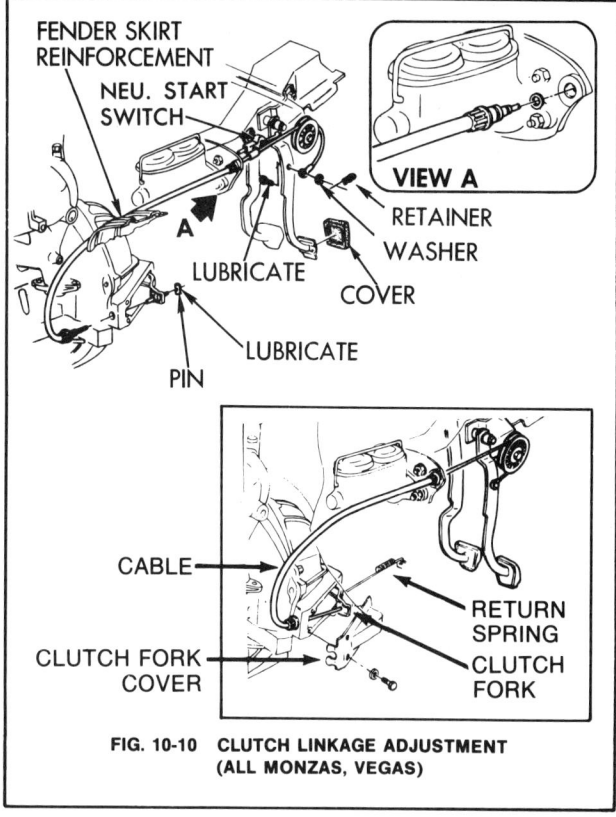

FIG. 10-10 CLUTCH LINKAGE ADJUSTMENT (ALL MONZAS, VEGAS)

To adjust the clutch for normal wear:

1. Remove the ball stud cap, loosen the locknut and turn the stud counterclockwise until there is 7/8- to 15/16-in. free travel at the clutch pedal. This free travel is the distance the pedal travels before any resistance can be felt.

2. Tighten the locknut to 25 ft.-lbs., being careful not to change the adjustment. Install the ball stud cap.

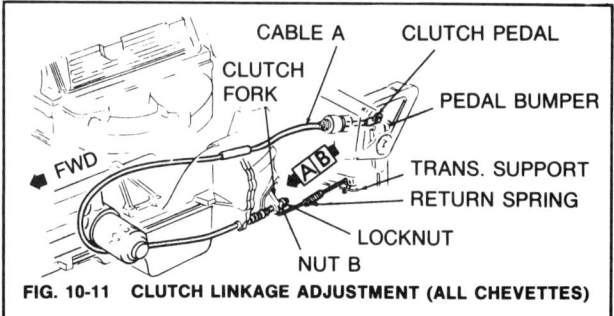

FIG. 10-11 CLUTCH LINKAGE ADJUSTMENT (ALL CHEVETTES)

CHEVETTES

(Fig. 10-11)

After replacing the clutch and/or clutch cable, adjust as follows:

1. Loosen the locknut, and turn the ball stud inward until the release bearing contacts the clutch springs.

2. Tighten the locknut, being careful not to change the adjustment.

3. Remove the clutch fork cover, and pull on the cable until the clutch pedal rests against the rubber pedal bumper.

4. Push the clutch fork forward until the release bearing touches the clutch spring fingers. Hold in place.

5. Thread nut (B) or cable (A) until it bottoms out against the clutch fork.

6. Push the clutch pedal to the floor at least four times to establish cable position at clearance points.

7. Turn nut (B) 4⅓ turns counterclockwise, and thread the locknut on cable (A) until it touches nut (B).

8. Tighten the locknut and attach the return spring. This will produce 0.812±0.25-in. free travel at pedal.

To adjust the clutch for normal wear:

1. Loosen the locknut on the ball stud, and turn the stud counterclockwise until there is ¾- to ⅞-in. free travel at the clutch pedal. This free travel is the distance the pedal travels before resistance can be felt.

2. Tighten the locknut to 25 ft.-lbs., being careful not to change the adjustment.

OLDSMOBILE

ALL 1970 DELTA 88S
1970-72 CUTLASS, 4-4-2
(Fig. 10-12)

1. Located in front of the clutch fork is the adjustable clutch rod. Remove the return spring, loosen the locknut on the rod, and turn the swivel until the correct free travel can be measured at the pedal.

2. Free travel, as measured from the clutch pedal pad, is the distance the pedal travels before any resistance is felt; that is, the distance it travels before the throwout bearing contacts the pressure plate fingers. The free travel should measure ¾- to 1 in.

3. Without upsetting the adjustment, tighten the locknut and install the return spring.

ALL 1973-79 CUTLASSES, OMEGAS
(Fig.10-13)

1. Loosen the lower push-rod swivel locknut, and disconnect the clutch return spring.

2. Rotate the equalizer assembly until the clutch pedal rests against the rubber bumper on the dash brace.

3. Move the clutch-fork outer end to the rear until the release bearing touches the clutch plate.

4. Unclip the lower push-rod swivel, and move the swivel to the gage hole. Replace the retaining clip.

5. Turn the push rod to increase its length until all lash is removed.

6. Replace the swivel in the equalizer lower hole, and install the retaining clip.

7. Tighten the locknut against the swivel. *Do not* change the rod length while tightening.

8. Reinstall the clutch return spring and check the pedal free travel from the center of the pedal. Omega, ⅞-in. to 1½ ins.; Cutlass, ¾-in. to 1¾ ins.

ALL STARFIRES

See Chevrolet section, Monza-Vega adjustment, **Fig. 10-10.** The procedure is identical, but the resulting pedal free travel should be 11/16-in. to 1 1/8 ins.

PONTIAC

ALL 1970-74 FIREBIRDS, TEMPESTS, LE MANS, GTO'S, GRAND AMS, VENTURAS

1. Disconnect the clutch return spring.

2. With the pedal against its stop, loosen the locknut and turn the clutch-fork push rod out of its swivel or the rod end out of the push rod.

3. Turn it rearward against the clutch fork until the throwout bearing touches the pressure plate fingers.

4. Turn the push rod into the swivel or the rod end into the push rod by 3½ turns, then tighten the locknut.

5. Install the return spring, and check the clutch free travel (the distance the pedal moves before resistance is felt) at the pedal. It should measure from 1 to 1½ ins.; if not, readjust until it does.

ALL 1975-79 FIREBIRDS, LE MANS, GRAND PRIX, GRAND AMS, VENTURAS, PHOENIX

1. Disconnect the return spring at the clutch release fork.

2. Loosen the locknut and remove the swivel or push rod end from the countershaft lever, installing it in the upper gage hole in countershaft lever.

3. Rotate the countershaft lever until the clutch pedal is against the rubber bumper on the dash brace.

4. Holding the clutch fork to the rear until the release bearing touches the pressure-plate release levers, turn the push rod until all lash is removed.

5. Reinstall the swivel or push rod end in the countershaft lower lever and tighten the locknut.

6. Reconnect the return spring to the clutch fork; check pedal free travel. It should be ¾-in. to 1¼ ins.

ALL ASTRES, SUNBIRDS

See Chevrolet section, Monza-Vega adjustment. The procedure is identical, but the resulting pedal free travel will be 0.65-1.15 ins.

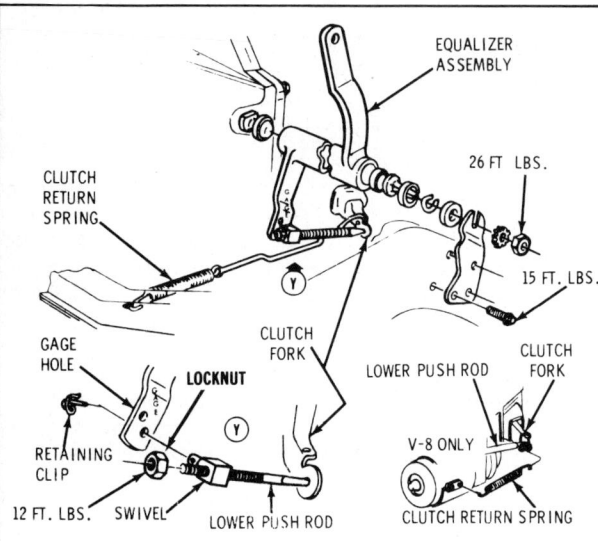

**FIG. 10-13 CLUTCH LINKAGE ADJUSTMENT
(ALL 1973-79 CUTLASS, OMEGAS)**

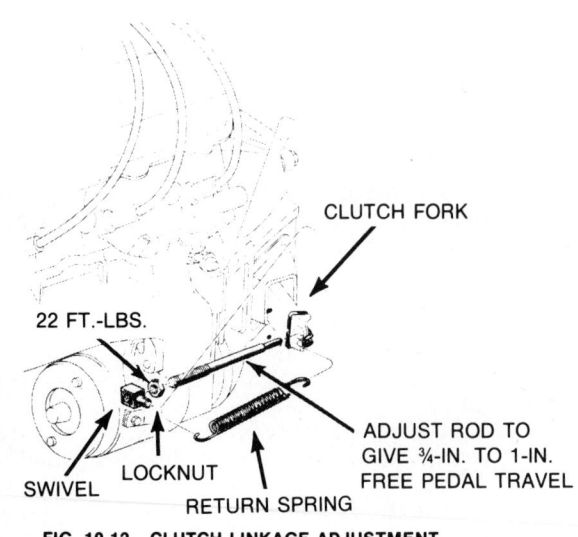

**FIG. 10-12 CLUTCH LINKAGE ADJUSTMENT
(ALL 1970 DELTA 88, 1970-72 CUTLASS, 4-4-2)**

FORD, MERCURY, LINCOLN

ALL FORDS, LINCOLNS, MERCURYS (EXCEPT PINTO/BOBCAT, MUSTANG II, GRANADA/MONARCH, 1975-77 MAVERICK/COMET) (Fig. 10-14)

1. With the clutch return spring disconnected from the clutch release lever, loosen the release lever/rod locknut and adjusting nut.

2. Move the clutch release lever to the rear until it touches the clutch pressure-plate release fingers.

3. Adjust the rod length until it seats in the release lever pocket.

4. Insert a feeler gauge (as specified in "Free Play Adjustment Dimension" below) between the adjusting nut and swivel sleeve, then finger-tighten the nut against the gauge.

5. Tighten the locknut against the adjusting nut without disturbing the adjustment, and remove the feeler gauge.

6. Install the clutch return spring, operate the clutch several times, and recheck the free play dimension. Readjust, if necessary. Free travel at the pedal should be ⅞-in. to 1⅛ ins.

FREE PLAY ADJUSTMENT DIMENSION

1972-74 Torino, Montego, Mustang, Cougar............0.194
1970-71 Ford, Mercury...0.194
1972-77 Maverick, Comet 0.136
1970-71 Fairlane, Montego, Falcon, Mustang, Cougar
    (except 390/428, 429 cu. ins.)......................0.136
    (with 390/428, 429 cu. ins.)..........................0.178

EARLY 1971 PINTO (Fig.10-15)

1. Slide under the car and locate the flexible cable that's attached to the clutch pedal.

2. Pull the cable toward the front of the car and remove the C-clip.

3. Continue pulling on the cable until the free movement has been eliminated from the throwout bearing.

4. Without slackening the cable, place a 0.135-in. spacer against the flywheel boss (engine side) and insert the C-clip into the groove closest to the spacer.

5. Remove the spacer and let go of the cable.

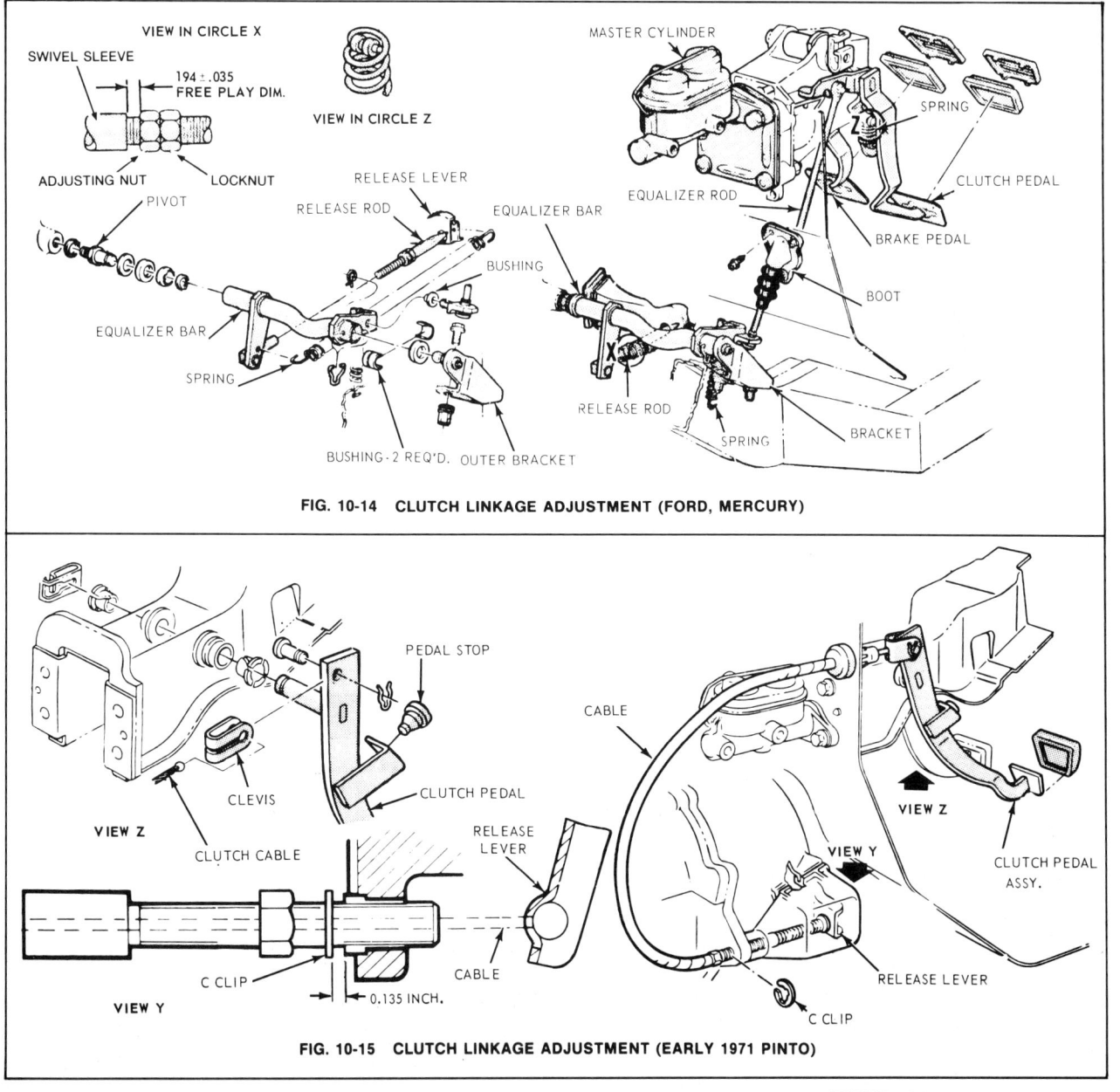

FIG. 10-14 CLUTCH LINKAGE ADJUSTMENT (FORD, MERCURY)

FIG. 10-15 CLUTCH LINKAGE ADJUSTMENT (EARLY 1971 PINTO)

LATE 1971-74 PINTO
(Fig. 10-16)

1. Loosen the cable locknuts and adjusting nut at the flywheel housing, and pull the cable toward the front of the car until all free movement of the release lever is eliminated.

2. Hold the cable in that position and place a ¼-in. spacer against the engine side of the flywheel housing boss.

3. Tighten the adjusting nut against the spacer finger-tight, then tighten the front locknut against the adjusting nut without disturbing adjustment.

4. Torque the locknut 40 to 60 ft.-lbs. and tighten the rear locknut against the flywheel housing boss. Remove the spacer.

5. Check free play travel at the pedal; it should be between 1⅜ and 1⅝ ins.

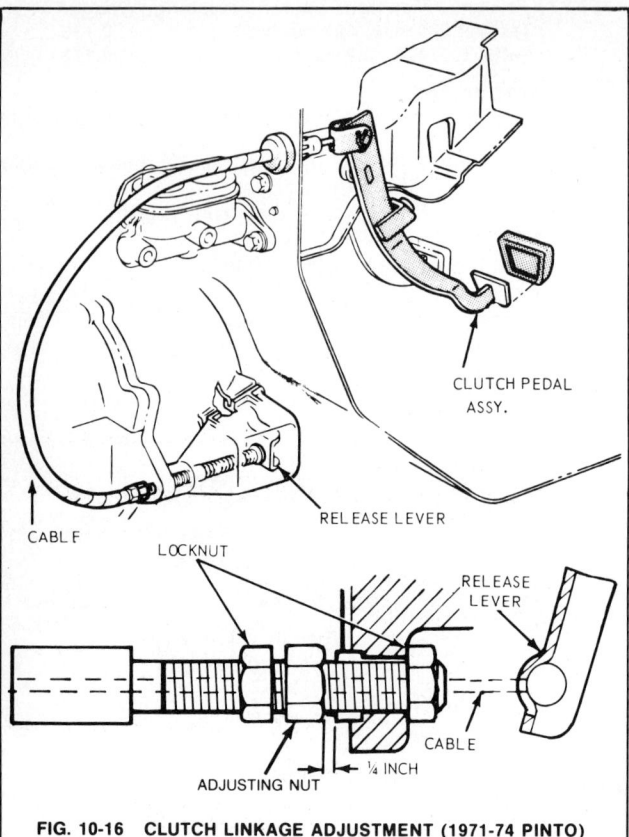

FIG. 10-16 CLUTCH LINKAGE ADJUSTMENT (1971-74 PINTO)

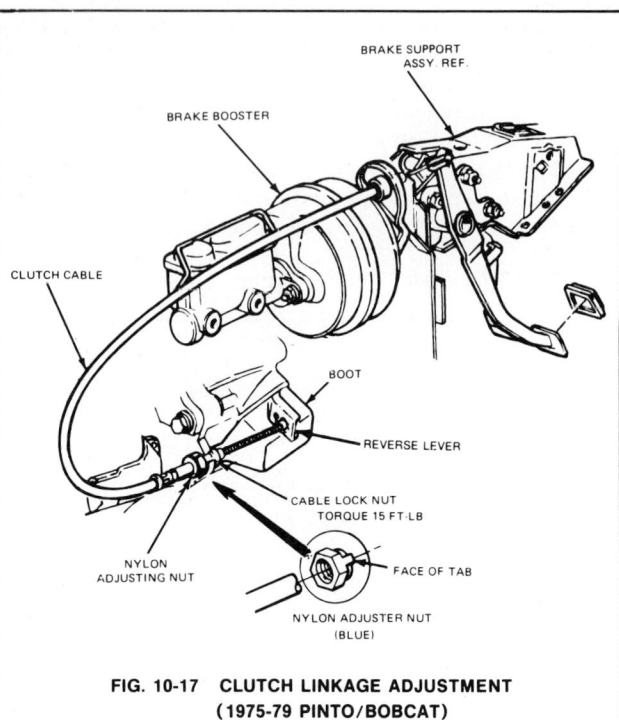

FIG. 10-17 CLUTCH LINKAGE ADJUSTMENT (1975-79 PINTO/BOBCAT)

CLUTCH FREE PLAY ADJUSTMENT

1. WITH CLUTCH CABLE INSTALLED AT BOTH ENDS - PULL CLUTCH CABLE FORWARD BY HAND UNTIL IT STOPS.

2. THEN TURN ADJUSTMENT NUT UNTIL SURFACE A OF NUT CONTACTS SURFACE B OF ADJUSTMENT SLEEVE. - RELEASE HAND FROM CABLE & THEN INDEX ADJUSTMENT NUT INTO NEXT NOTCH OF ADJUSTMENT SLEEVE.

3. PLACE RETENTION SPRING INTO POSITION - MAKE SURE BOTH TABS OF BOTH TABS OF SPRING ARE INSTALLED INTO SLOT OF ADJUSTMENT SLEEVE.

4. BOLT CLUTCH CABLE BRACKET TO FINDER APRON.

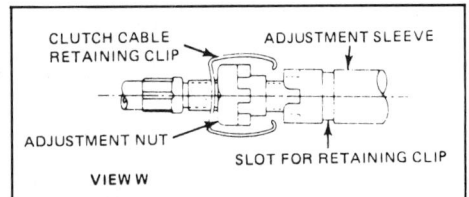

VIEW W

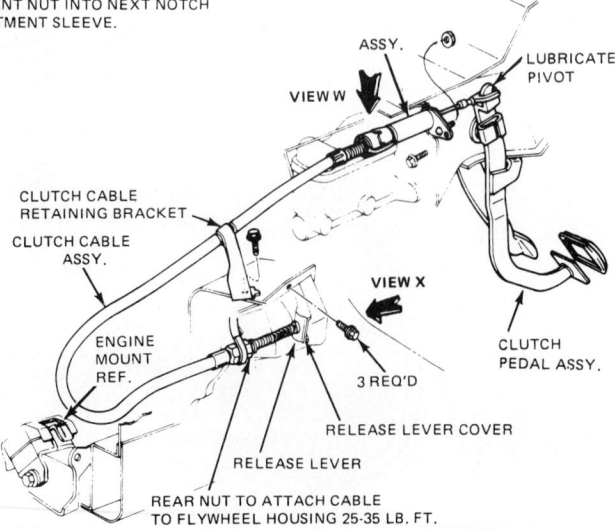

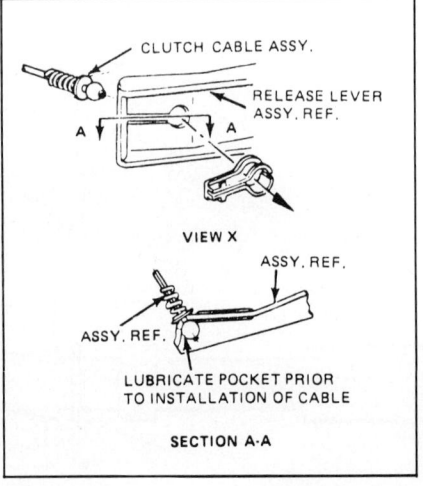

FIG. 10-18 CLUTCH LINKAGE ADJUSTMENT (1974-78 MUSTANG II)

1975-79 PINTO/BOBCAT; 1977-79 AMC I-4 ENGINE

(Fig. 10-17)

1. With the clutch cable locknut on the transmission side of the flywheel housing loosened, pull the cable toward the front of the car until the nylon adjusting nut tabs are clear of the housing boss.

2. Rotate the nut toward the front of the car approximately ¼-in.

3. Release the cable and pull it forward again to eliminate any release lever free movement.

4. Rotate the adjusting nut toward the housing until the index tab faces touch the housing. Index the tabs to drop into the nearest housing groove.

5. Torque the locknut at the rear of the housing boss to 15 ft.-lbs. (25 ft.-lbs. for AMC I-4 engine).

6. Check free play travel at the pedal; it should be between ⅞ and 1⅛ ins. (½ to 1 in. for AMC I-4 engine).

1974-78 MUSTANG II

Adjustment procedure for the 2.3L and 302-cu.-in. engines is shown in **Fig. 10-18**; configuration of the clutch mechanism for the 2800cc engine is slightly different, but adjustment procedure is essentially the same.

1975-77 MAVERICK/COMET; 1975-79 GRANADA/MONARCH

Adjustment procedure for the 200-cu.-in. engine is shown in **Fig. 10-19**; the 250/302-cu.-in. options differ slightly in configuration, but adjustment procedure and free play travel specifications (⅞ to 1⅛ ins.) are the same.

1978 FAIRMONT/ZEPHYR

(Fig. 10-19A)

2.3L Engine

1. Disconnect release lever return spring and remove dust shield.

2. Loosen locknut and adjusting nut at release lever.

3. Position release lever forward to eliminate free movement. Hold release lever forward during adjustment.

4. Place a 0.30-in. spacer against release lever spacer. Finger-tighten adjusting nut against the 0.30-in. spacer.

5. Tighten locknut against adjusting nut and torque locknut to 5-8 ft.-lbs. Remove spacer and operate clutch several times.

6. Check free play travel at the pedal; it should be approximately 1½ ins.

7. Replace dust shield and reconnect return spring.

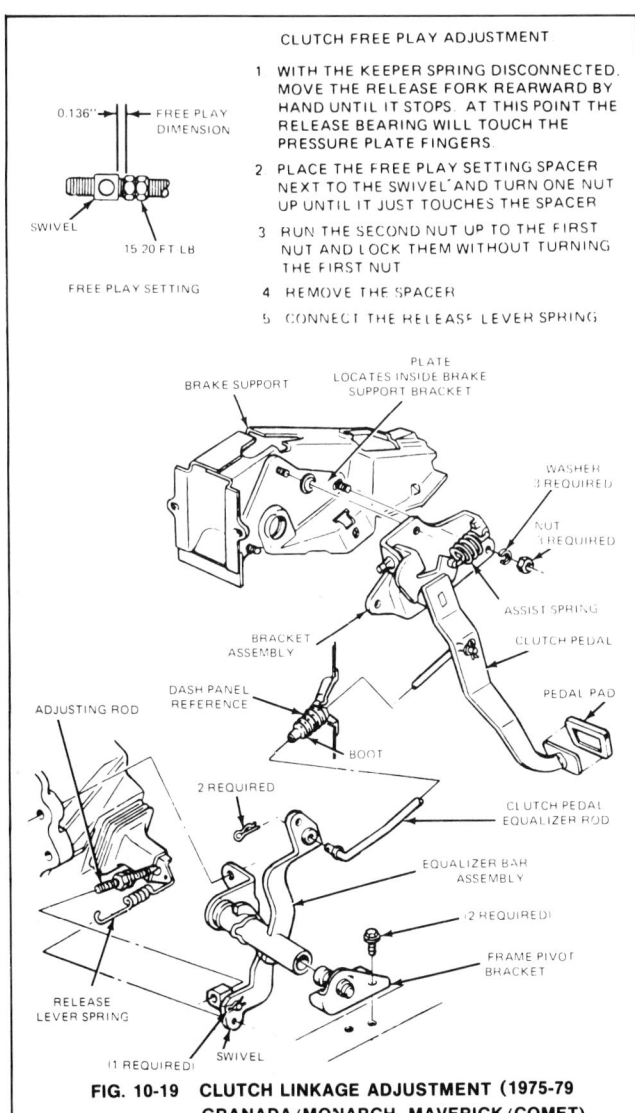

FIG. 10-19 CLUTCH LINKAGE ADJUSTMENT (1975-79 GRANADA/MONARCH, MAVERICK/COMET)

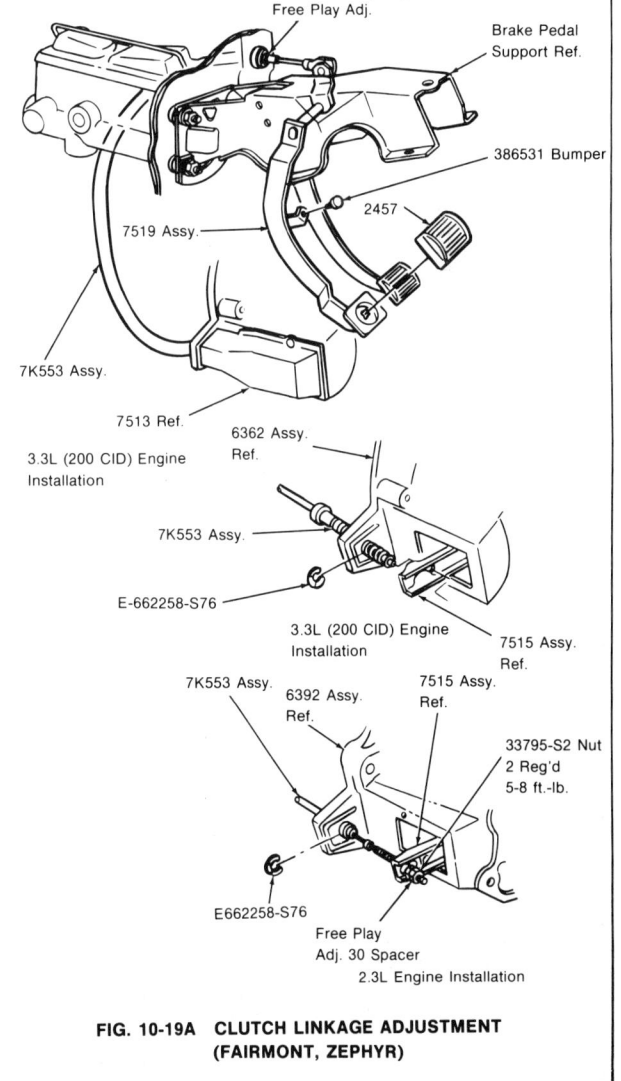

FIG. 10-19A CLUTCH LINKAGE ADJUSTMENT (FAIRMONT, ZEPHYR)

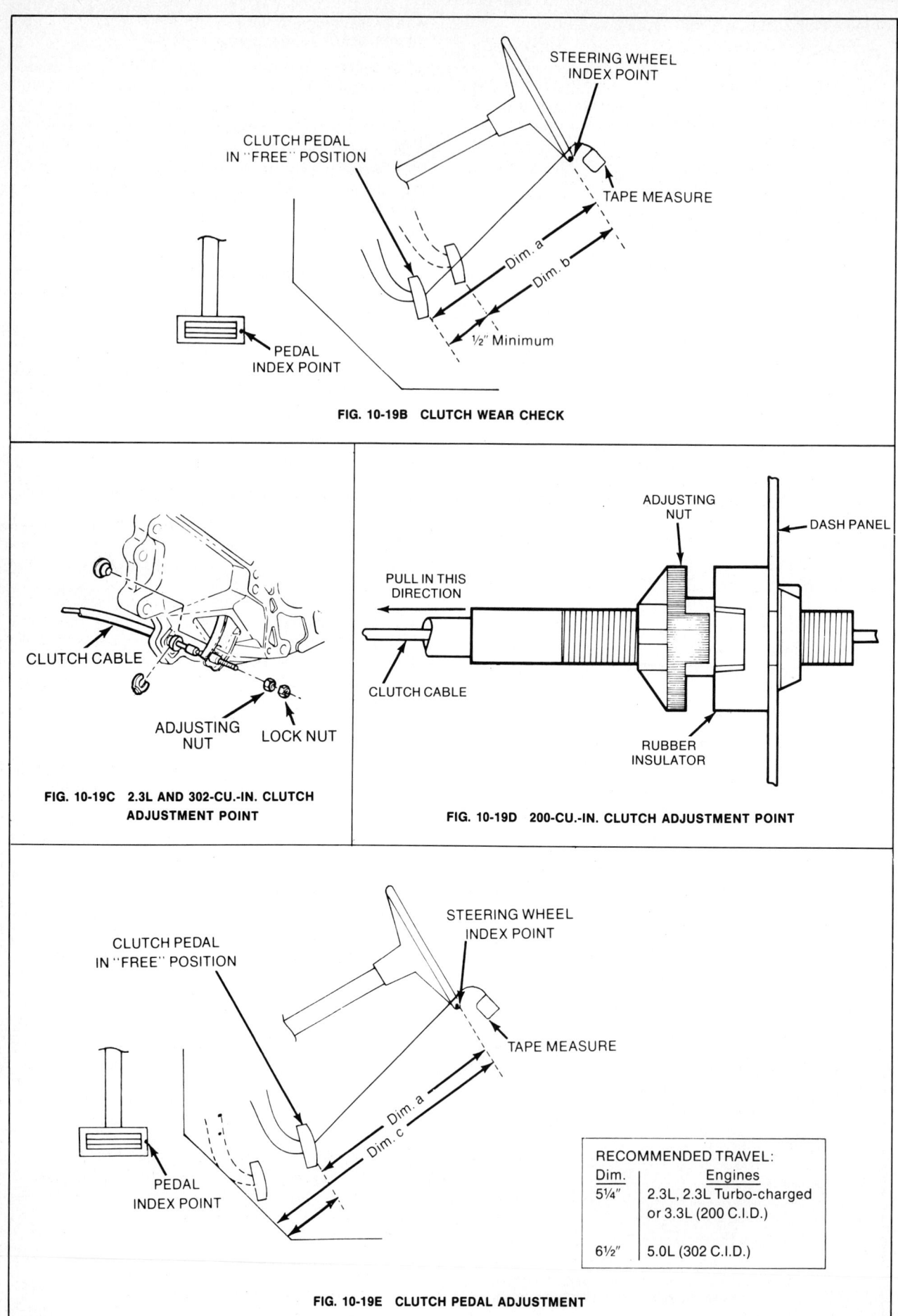

STEERING WHEEL
INDEX POINT

CLUTCH PEDAL
IN "FREE" POSITION

TAPE MEASURE

Dim. a

Dim. b

½" Minimum

PEDAL
INDEX POINT

FIG. 10-19B CLUTCH WEAR CHECK

CLUTCH CABLE

ADJUSTING
NUT

LOCK NUT

**FIG. 10-19C 2.3L AND 302-CU.-IN. CLUTCH
ADJUSTMENT POINT**

ADJUSTING
NUT

DASH PANEL

PULL IN THIS
DIRECTION

CLUTCH CABLE

RUBBER
INSULATOR

FIG. 10-19D 200-CU.-IN. CLUTCH ADJUSTMENT POINT

STEERING WHEEL
INDEX POINT

CLUTCH PEDAL
IN "FREE" POSITION

TAPE MEASURE

Dim. a

Dim. c

PEDAL
INDEX POINT

RECOMMENDED TRAVEL:

Dim.	Engines
5¼"	2.3L, 2.3L Turbo-charged or 3.3L (200 C.I.D.)
6½"	5.0L (302 C.I.D.)

FIG. 10-19E CLUTCH PEDAL ADJUSTMENT

200-cu.-in. Engine

1. Pull clutch cable toward front of car. When nylon adjusting nut no longer touches its rubber insulator, rotate nut about 0.30-in. It may be necessary to remove clutch pedal bumper stop from clutch pedal to free nut from insulator. If so, replace bumper stop before continuing adjustment.

2. Release cable and pull it forward again to eliminate any release lever free movement.

3. Turn adjusting nut toward insulator until the two touch. Index nut tabs into the next notch.

4. Release cable and check free play travel at the pedal; it should be approximately 1½ ins.

1979 Fairmont/Zephyr; Mustang/Capri

The clutch release bearing on these car lines remains in constant contact with the clutch pressure plate. Clutch pedal height therefore replaces clutch free-play adjustment.

Clutch Wear Check

1. Measure and record dimension A shown in **Fig. 10-19B.**

2. Lift and hold the pedal against its upper stop, then measure and record dimension B.

3. Subtract B from A; if the difference is ½-in. or less, adjust the clutch pedal height.

Clutch Pedal Height Adjustment

2.3L and 302-cu.-in. Engines
(Fig. 10-19C)

1. Remove dust shield at transmission clutch cable connection and loosen locknut.

2. Raise pedal by turning adjusting nut clockwise; lower pedal by turning nut counterclockwise.

3. Torque locknut to 5-8 ft.-lbs. and perform Clutch

Pedal Adjustment Check after cycling pedal several times, If within specifications, replace dust shield.

200-cu.-in. Engine
(Fig. 10-19D)

1. Pull clutch cable toward front of car to free nylon adjusting nut free of rubber insulator, blocking clutch pedal in position if necessary.

2. Turn adjusting nut to obtain pedal height of 5¼-in. when cable is released and nut is replaced in rubber insulator.

3. Cycle pedal several times and perform Clutch Pedal Adjustment Check.

Clutch Pedal Adjustment Check

1. To check clutch pedal travel, measure and record dimension A shown in **Fig. 10-19E.**

2. Depress and hold the pedal; measure and record dimension B.

3. Subtract C from A; if clutch is properly adjusted, the difference between C and A will be 5¼ or 6½-ins., as indicated by engine usage in **Fig. 10-19E.**

ALL CHRYSLER CORPORATION CARS
(Fig. 10-20 and 10-20A)

1. On 1970-74 6-cyl. models equipped with the A-903 or A-250 transmission, the gearshift interlock rod must be disconnected by loosening the rod-swivel clamp screw before proceeding with adjustment. See "Gearshift Interlock Adjustment" section which follows. For 1975-79 models, begin with Step 2 below.

2. Adjust the clutch fork rod by turning the self-locking adjusting nut to provide 5/32-in. free movement at the fork end. This will give 1-in. free-play travel at the pedal.

3. Should the adjusting nut refuse to turn easily, the

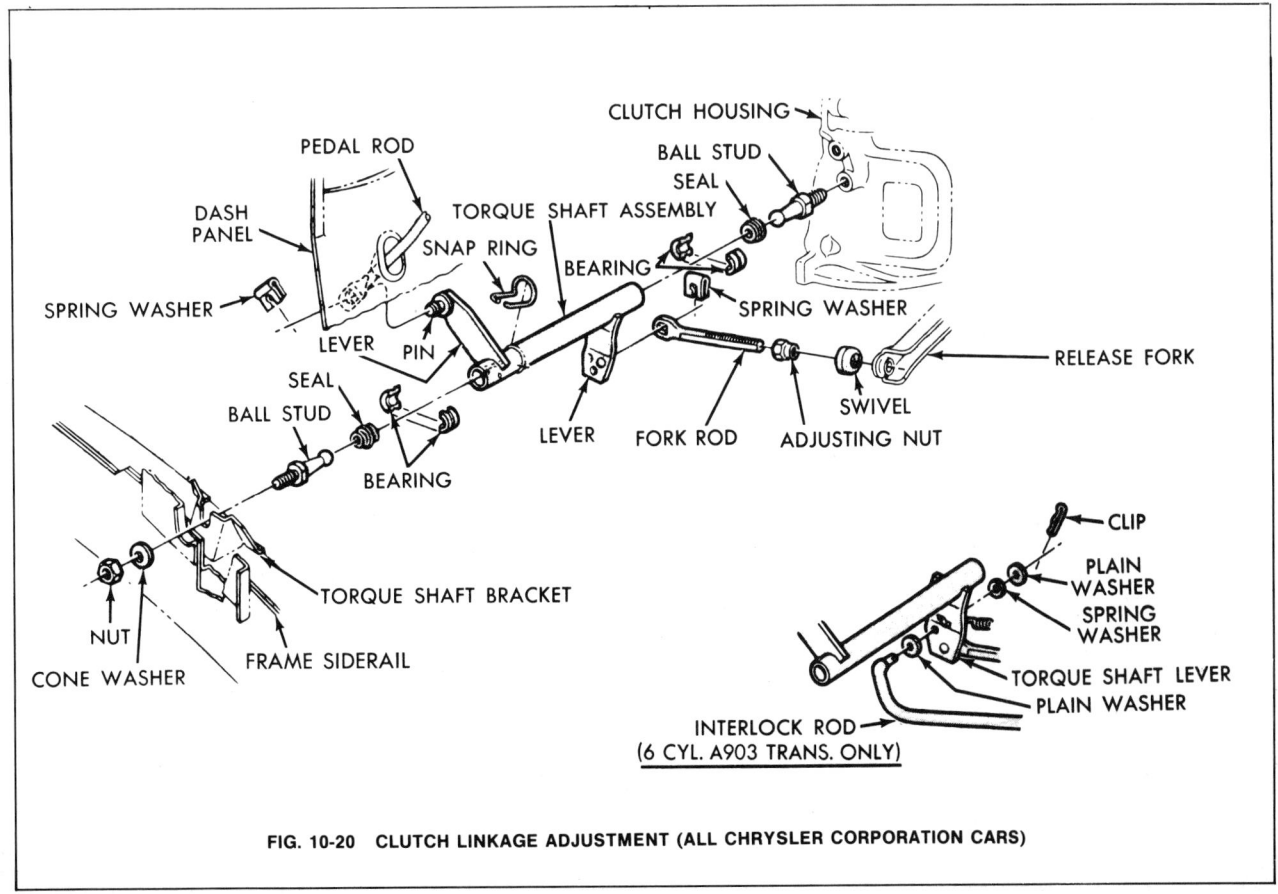

FIG. 10-20 CLUTCH LINKAGE ADJUSTMENT (ALL CHRYSLER CORPORATION CARS)

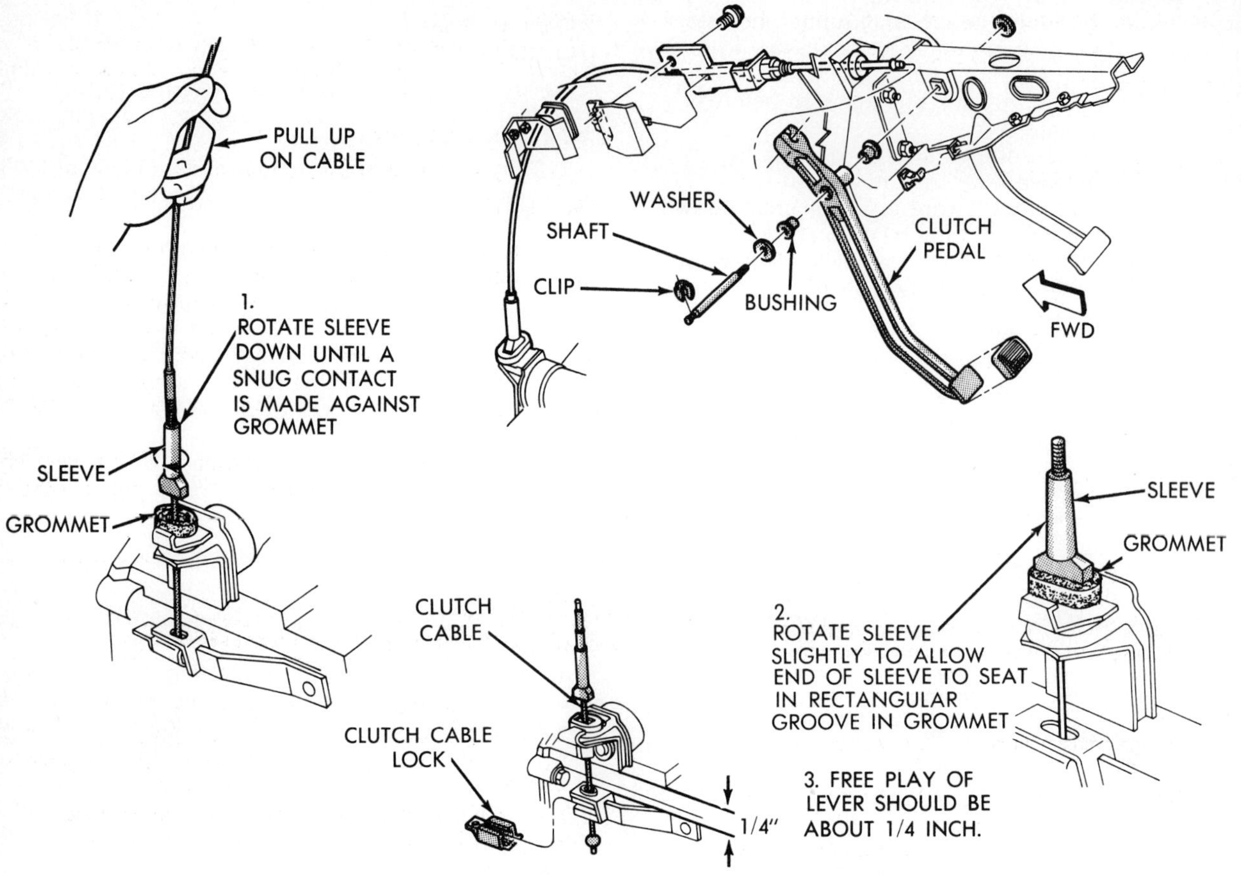

PULL UP
ON CABLE

WASHER

SHAFT

CLIP

BUSHING

CLUTCH
PEDAL

FWD

1.
ROTATE SLEEVE
DOWN UNTIL A
SNUG CONTACT
IS MADE AGAINST
GROMMET

SLEEVE

GROMMET

SLEEVE

GROMMET

CLUTCH
CABLE

CLUTCH CABLE
LOCK

2.
ROTATE SLEEVE
SLIGHTLY TO ALLOW
END OF SLEEVE TO SEAT
IN RECTANGULAR
GROOVE IN GROMMET

1/4"

3. FREE PLAY OF
LEVER SHOULD BE
ABOUT 1/4 INCH.

FIG.10-20A   OMNI/HORIZON CLUTCH FREE PLAY ADJUSTMENT

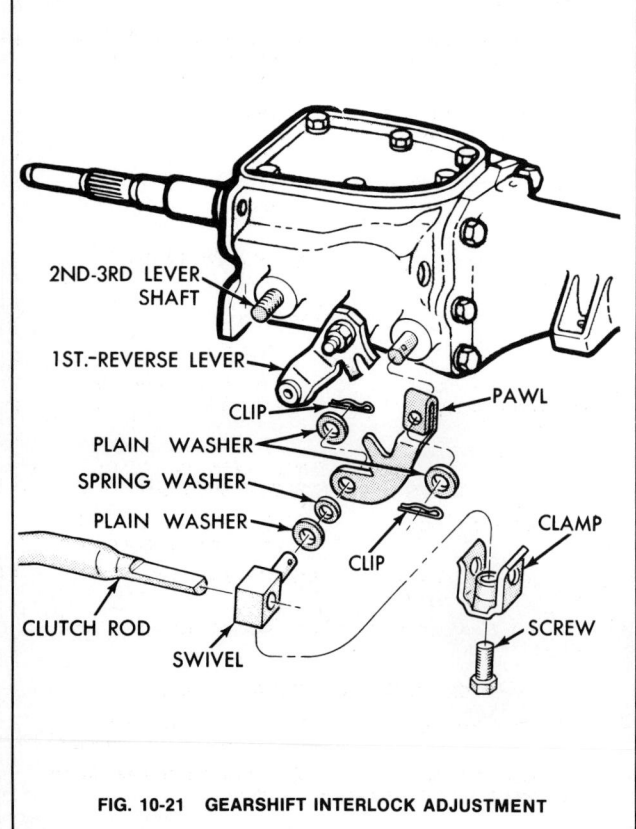

2ND-3RD LEVER
SHAFT

1ST.-REVERSE LEVER

CLIP

PLAIN WASHER

SPRING WASHER

PLAIN WASHER

CLUTCH ROD

SWIVEL

CLIP

PAWL

CLAMP

SCREW

FIG. 10-21   GEARSHIFT INTERLOCK ADJUSTMENT

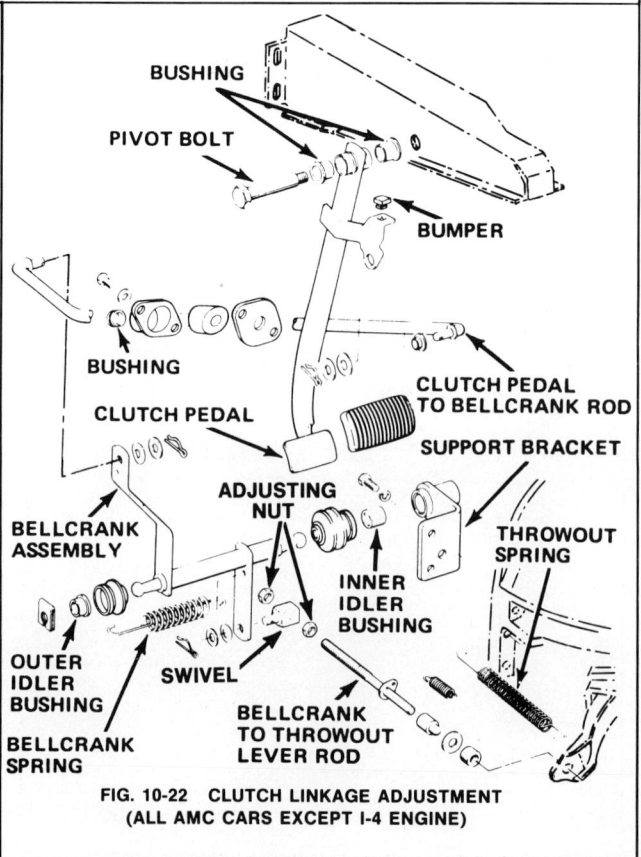

BUSHING

PIVOT BOLT

BUMPER

BUSHING

CLUTCH PEDAL

CLUTCH PEDAL
TO BELLCRANK ROD

SUPPORT BRACKET

ADJUSTING
NUT

THROWOUT
SPRING

BELLCRANK
ASSEMBLY

INNER
IDLER
BUSHING

OUTER
IDLER
BUSHING

SWIVEL

BELLCRANK
SPRING

BELLCRANK
TO THROWOUT
LEVER ROD

**FIG. 10-22   CLUTCH LINKAGE ADJUSTMENT
(ALL AMC CARS EXCEPT I-4 ENGINE)**

swivel is binding on the clutch fork rod. Tapping the swivel should free it and permit adjustment.

4. Omni/Horizon adjustment is described in **Fig. 10-20A**.

GEARSHIFT INTERLOCK ADJUSTMENT
(1970-74 A-903, A-250)
(Fig. 10-21)

1. Disconnect the clutch rod swivel from the interlock pawl.

2. Adjust the clutch-pedal free travel as above.

3. Position the 1st/reverse transmission lever in the middle detent (neutral) and the interlock pawl will enter the 1st/reverse lever slot.

4. Loosen the swivel clamp screw and slide the swivel on the rod to engage the pawl. Install washers and clip.

5. Hold the interlock pawl forward and tighten the swivel clamp screw to 100 in.-lbs. Clutch pedal must be in the full returned position during this adjustment—*do not* pull it to the rear to engage the swivel and pawl.

6. Shift the transmission from neutral to 1st, and from neutral to reverse. The clutch action should be normal.

7. Disengage the clutch, and shift halfway to 1st or reverse. The interlock should hold the clutch to within 1 or 2 ins. of the floor.

AMERICAN MOTORS

ALL AMC MODELS, EXCEPT 1-4 ENGINE
(Fig. 10-22)

1. Disconnect the clutch-rod throwout spring.

2. Loosen the adjusting nuts on each side of the swivel at the end of the bellcrank-to-throwout lever rod.

3. Adjust the bellcrank-to-throwout lever rod to set pedal free play (the distance the pedal moves before any resistance is felt) between ⅞-in. and 1⅛ ins. For 1970-72 cars, 1 in. is preferred; 1⅛ ins. for 1973-79 cars.

4. Tighten the adjusting nuts without disturbing the rod length adjustment, and reconnect the throwout spring.

CLUTCH DIAGNOSIS

CONDITION	CORRECTION	CONDITION	CORRECTION
FAILS TO RELEASE		**RATTLING OR TRANSMISSION CLICK**	
(a) Linkage adjustment is incorrect.	(a) Adjust linkage correctly.	(a) Clutch fork is loose on ball stud or in bearing groove.	(a) Check ball stud and retaining spring—replace if necessary.
(b) Pedal travel is wrong.	(b) Trim bumper stop and adjust linkage.	(b) Oil in driven plate damper.	(b) Replace driven plate.
(c) Linkage is loose.	(c) Replace bushings.	(c) Driven plate damper spring fails.	(c) Replace driven plate.
(d) Pilot bearing is worn or damaged.	(d) Replace bearing.	**THROWOUT BEARING NOISE WHEN CLUTCH IS FULL ENGAGED**	
(e) Faulty driven plate.	(e) Replace driven plate.	(a) Improperly adjusted linkage.	(a) Check and adjust linkage properly.
(f) Fork off ball stud.	(f) Install correctly.	(b) Throwout bearing binds on transmission bearing retainer.	(b) Clean, relubricate and check for nicks, burrs, etc.
(g) Clutch driven plate hub binds on main drive gear spline.	(g) Repair or replace main drive.	(c) Tension between clutch fork spring and ball stud is not sufficient.	(c) Replace fork.
CLUTCH SLIPS		(d) Fork improperly installed.	(d) Remove and reinstall properly.
(a) No lash.	(a) Adjust linkage.	(e) Linkage return spring is weak.	(e) Replace spring.
(b) Driven plate contaminated with oil.	(b) Install new driven plate; locate and correct oil leak.	**CLUTCH IS NOISY**	
(c) Driven plate facing worn or torn.	(c) Replace driven plate.	(a) Throwout bearing is worn.	(a) Replace.
(d) Pressure plate or flywheel warped.	(d) Replace.	(b) Fork is off ball stud causing a heavy clicking noise.	(b) Remove and reinstall properly.
(e) Weak diaphragm spring.	(e) Replace cover assembly.	**PEDAL DOES NOT RETURN WHEN CLUTCH IS DISENGAGED**	
(f) Driven plate not seated correctly.	(f) Make 15-45 starts.	(a) Linkage is binding.	(a) Free linkage; adjust if necessary and lubricate.
(g) Driven plate overheated.	(g) Let cool then check lash.	(b) Pressure plate spring is weak.	(b) Replace spring.
CLUTCH GRABS		(c) Linkage return spring is weak.	(c) Replace spring.
(a) Driven plate facing glazed, burned or oil contaminated.	(a) Replace with new driven plate.	**REQUIRES HIGH PEDAL EFFORT**	
(b) Main drive gear splines worn.	(b) Replace transmission main drive gear.	(a) Linkage is binding.	(a) Free linkage; adjust if necessary and lubricate.
(c) Engine mountings loose.	(c) Check and tighten or replace mountings.	(b) Driven plate is worn excessively.	(b) Replace with new driven plate.
(d) Pressure plate or flywheel warped.	(d) Replace.		
(e) Flywheel or pressure plate burned or resin-smeared.	(e) Sand off if superficial but replace burned or heat checked parts.		

THE MANUAL TRANSMISSION

The manual transmission provides a driver with a necessary selection of gear ratios between the engine and rear wheels to allow the car to operate at its maximum efficiency under a variety of driving conditions and engine loads. Manual transmissions may be provided with 3, 4 or 5 forward speeds and a reverse gear.

Modern units are of constant-mesh design and many are synchronized in all forward speeds. Unfortunately, some 3-speeds are not synchronized in first gear. By synchronizing the speeds of mating parts before engagement is made, gear selection can be made without clashing.

TRANSMISSION GEARS AND SYNCHRONIZERS (Fig. 10-23)

In a constant-mesh design, each gear is in a fixed position on the mainshaft, and those to be synchronized have a cone surface. The synchronizer hub (A) and gear carrier are splined to the mainshaft, while each drive gear (B) can revolve. Three spring-loaded keys (C) slide in slots on the hub. The blocking ring or synchronizer (D), fitted between the hub and the gear, acts in conjunction with the cone surface (F) as a friction clutch. Slots in the synchronizer ring allow the keys to engage and move along with the drive gear. As the synchronizer ring engages the gear cone, it causes the gear to revolve at the same speed as the synchronizer and the outer synchronizer shell (E) rides over the keys to engage the teeth on the gear.

GEAR RATIO

Gear ratio is determined by dividing the number of teeth on the driven gear by the number on the driving gear. If the engine is turning a gear with 15 teeth, and this is meshed with another gear with 29 teeth, the transmission ratio in that gear is 1.93. This means that the engine will turn over 1.93 revolutions for every one revolution of the transmission output shaft (Fig. 10-24).

To determine the transmission gear ratio, simply take each pair of gears in turn and determine the ratio, then multiply the ratios together to get the overall ratio of the transmission. For example, the 3-speed Chevrolet has two pair of gears meshed in low gear. The first pair has 19 and 27 teeth, the second pair 14 and 29. Dividing the driven gear by the driving gear in each pair produces ratios of 1.42 and 2.07. Mutiplying these two ratios together equals 2.939 or 2.94, the overall ratio of the transmission in low gear.

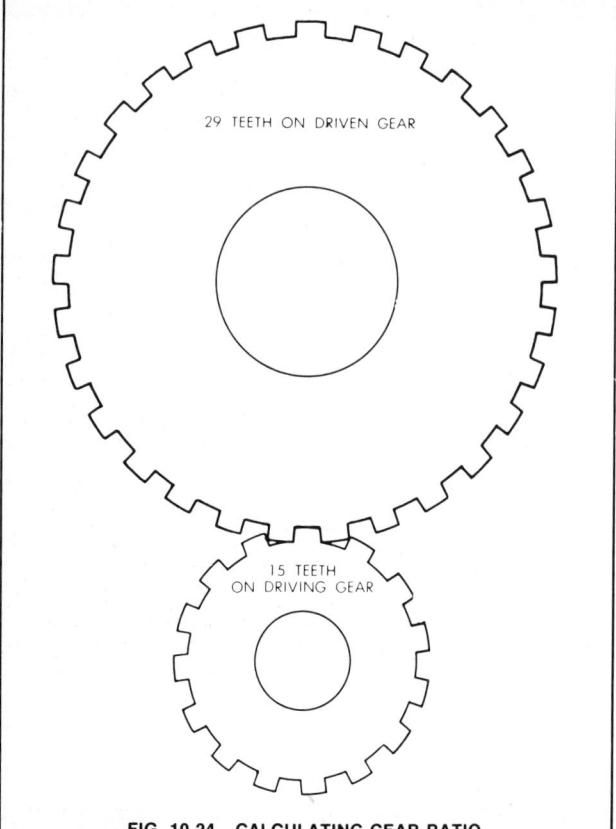

29 TEETH ON DRIVEN GEAR

15 TEETH ON DRIVING GEAR

FIG. 10-24 CALCULATING GEAR RATIO

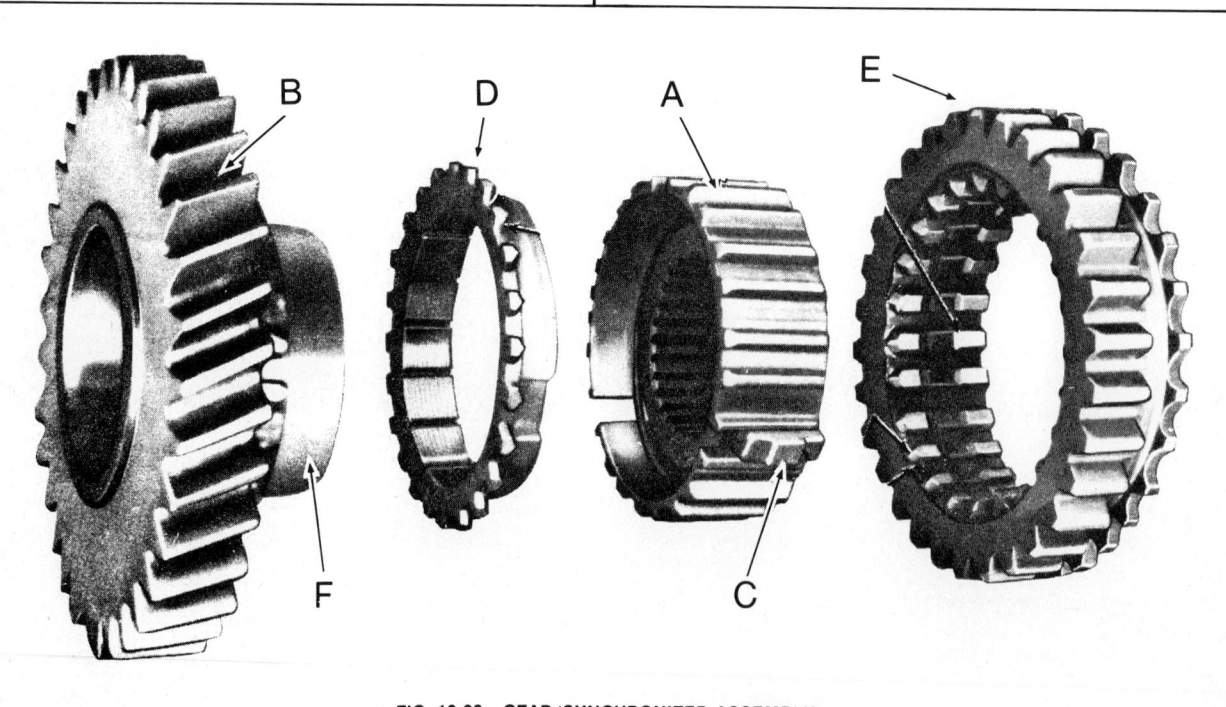

FIG. 10-23 GEAR/SYNCHRONIZER ASSEMBLY

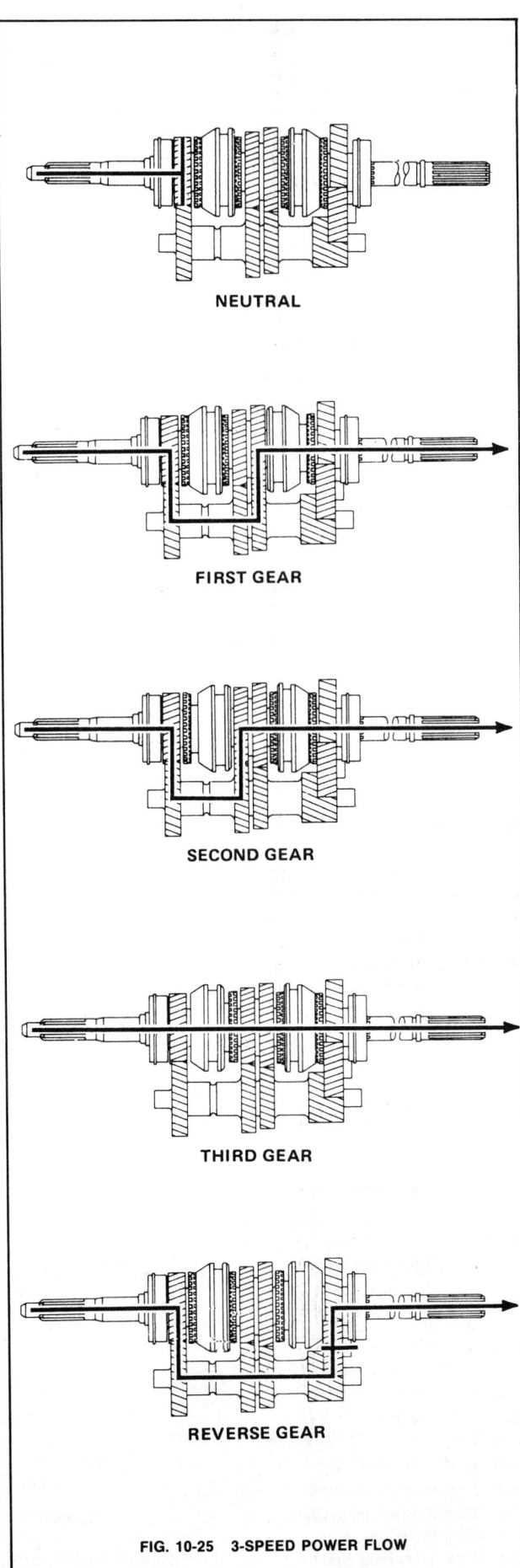

NEUTRAL

FIRST GEAR

SECOND GEAR

THIRD GEAR

REVERSE GEAR

FIG. 10-25   3-SPEED POWER FLOW

With the transmission in second gear, power flow is also going through four gears or two pair, so the same division of teeth and multiplication of ratios give the overall ratio in second gear. In high gear, the power flow is not going through any of the gears, so there is no multiplication—the ratio is 1:1 or direct drive.

POWER FLOW (Fig. 10-25)

NEUTRAL

Engage the clutch, and the drive gear turns the countershaft gear. This gear then turns the second, first and reverse gears, and the reverse idler gear. With both synchronizers neutrally positioned, no power is transmitted to the mainshaft.

FIRST GEAR

Moving the shift selector into first gear moves the rear synchronizer to the front, where it locks its hub to the first gear. Engaging the clutch now transmits power through the shaft and countershaft gears to the first gear. Since first gear is locked with the synchronizer, power is transmitted to the mainshaft. In constant mesh with the countershaft gear, the other gears rotate, but the front synchronizer is still in a neutral position and cannot transmit power when first gear is engaged.

SECOND GEAR

Moving the shift selector into second gear moves the front synchronizer to the rear, where its hub locks to second gear and the rear synchronizer moves back to a neutral position. Engaging the clutch transmits power through the shaft and countershaft gears to second gear. Because second gear is locked with the synchronizer, it transmits power to the mainshaft.

THIRD GEAR

Moving the shift selector into third gear moves the front synchronizer forward, where it locks to the drive-shaft. Engaging the clutch transmits power through the driveshaft directly to the mainshaft, providing a 1:1 ratio. This means that the engine and transmission output shaft are now turning at the same speed.

REVERSE GEAR

Moving the shift selector into reverse moves the front synchronizer to a neutral position, and the rear synchronizer to the rear, where it locks with the reverse gear. Engaging the clutch transmits power to the reverse idler gear. In mesh with the reverse gear, the reverse idler gear transmits the power to the reverse gear and the mainshaft.

4-SPEED TRANSMISSION

Adding another drive gear provides a fourth forward gear and lessens the ratio spread between the gears. High gear is still a 1:1 ratio, or direct drive. Power flow is similar to that of the 3-speed transmission already described, and is shown in **Fig. 10-26.**

OVERDRIVE

Since there is no gear reduction in direct drive or high gear, as used in 3- and 4-speed transmissions, the gear train acts as one solid shaft going through the transmission, with the gears along for a free ride. The overdrive transmission, as currently used on some GM and Chrysler Corporation cars, lets the power flow through the gears in high to produce a ratio greater than 1:1.

The term overdrive is used to describe any gear position resulting in the engine turning slower than the transmission output shaft. Although primarily thought of as an auxiliary unit bolted to the rear of the regular transmission (as used by AMC), the overdrive (fifth gear on the GM transmission, fourth gear on the Chrysler) is obtained by a gear on the transmission output shaft and one on the countergear. When in overdrive, the engine will turn about 20% slower than direct drive. Driving at the legal speed limit of 55 mph with the transmission in overdrive, the engine is working at approximately the same rpm as it would at 44 mph in direct drive.

IDENTIFYING BASIC TRANSMISSION DISORDERS

Many transmission malfunctions show up as one of three basic kinds of internal disorders:

High Shift Effort—If the gears will engage, but excessive effort is necessary to accomplish a shift in any gear, try depressing the clutch and shifting the transmission with the engine not running. If the problem is still present, look for a tight fit between the synchronizer sleeve and hub. Disassemble the transmission and remove the synchronizer keys. If the hub and sleeve do not fit together loosely, replace the entire synchronizer assembly.

Blockout—If the shift lever moves freely until the synchronizer is engaged, but the gear *does not* engage, or *does* engage with a double bump felt through the shift lever, the synchronizer rings or gear cones are probably damaged, causing a blockout. Disassemble the transmission and inspect both the rings and cones with care. If the ring thread is damaged or worn, replace the ring. A discolored gear cone indicates that a synchronizer ring is sticking; polish the cone with 400 grit paper to a bright finish.

Gear Clash—When the sleeve and gear chamfers contact each other in an unsynchronized state, a grating or loud buzzing noise will be heard from the transmission. Clash should not be confused with hard shifting, because they are direct opposites, but if the clash is slight, the shift lever load will build up, only to fall off rapidly just before the grating sound is heard. Examine the sleeve ends for burrs or chipping and, if there is any damage, replace the entire synchronizer/ring assembly as a unit.

3-SPEED MANUAL TRANSMISSION DIAGNOSIS

CONDITION	CORRECTION	CONDITION	CORRECTION
NOISY IN FORWARD SPEEDS		(f) Loose or broken bearing retainer, bearings on main drive gear and output shaft.	See (c)
(a) Low lubricant level.	(a) Top up as required.	(g) Worn or broken blocking ring.	See (c)
(b) Incorrect lubricant in use.	(b) Drain and refill with correct lubricant.	(h) Bent output shaft.	See (c)
(c) Transmission loose or incorrectly aligned.	(c) Tighten attachment bolts and check alignment.	**STICKS IN GEAR**	
(d) Main drive gear or drive gear bearing worn or damaged.	(d) Disassemble transmission and replace drive gear or bearing as required.	(a) Clutch does not release fully.	(a) Adjust clutch properly.
(e) Countergear or needle roller bearings worn or damaged.	(e) Disassemble transmission and replace as necessary.	(b) Low lubricant level.	(b) Top up as required.
NOISY IN REVERSE GEAR		(c) Incorrect lubricant in use.	(c) Drain and refill with correct lubricant.
(a) Reverse gear, reverse idler gear or shaft worn or damaged.	(a) Disassemble transmission and replace gears or shaft as necessary.	(d) Tight main drive gear pilot bearing.	(d) Disassemble transmission and replace parts as necessary for this and remaining causes.
SHIFTS HARD		(e) Frozen synchronizing blocking ring on main drive gear cone.	See (d)
(a) Clutch improperly adjusted.	(a) Adjust clutch correctly.	(f) Damaged teeth on synchronizer sleeve and/or main drive gear.	See (d)
(b) Shift linkage out of adjustment.	(b) Check linkage and adjust for smooth operation.	**FORWARD GEARS CLASH**	
(c) Shift linkage bent; loose or damaged linkage.	(c) Replace damaged linkage; tighten loose linkage.	(a) Clutch does not release fully.	(a) Adjust clutch to release fully.
(d) Shift levers, shafts or forks worn.	(d) Disassemble transmission and replace components as required.	(b) Springs in synchronizer assembly are weak or broken.	(b) Disassemble transmission and replace springs as required.
(e) Blocking rings worn or broken.	(e) Disassemble transmission and replace rings.	(c) Blocking rings and/or cone surfaces are worn.	(c) Disassemble transmission and replace worn components.
JUMPS OUT OF GEAR		**REVERSE GEAR CLASH**	
(a) Shift linkage loose, worn or needs adjustment.	(a) Tighten loose linkage Replace worn linkage, adjust.	(a) Engine idle is set too high.	(a) Reset engine idle.
(b) Transmission loose or incorrectly aligned.	(b) Tighten attachment bolts and check alignment.	(b) Clutch needs adjustment.	(b) Adjust clutch.
(c) Bent or worn shift fork, lever and/or shaft.	(c) Disassemble transmission and replace parts as necessary	(c) Clutch driven plate drags or is distorted.	(c) Adjust if possible; replace if necessary.
(d) Pilot bearing worn.	See (c)	(d) Main drive gear bearing is tight or frozen.	(d) Disassemble transmission and replace bearing.
(e) Detent cam spring weak or notches worn.	See (c)		

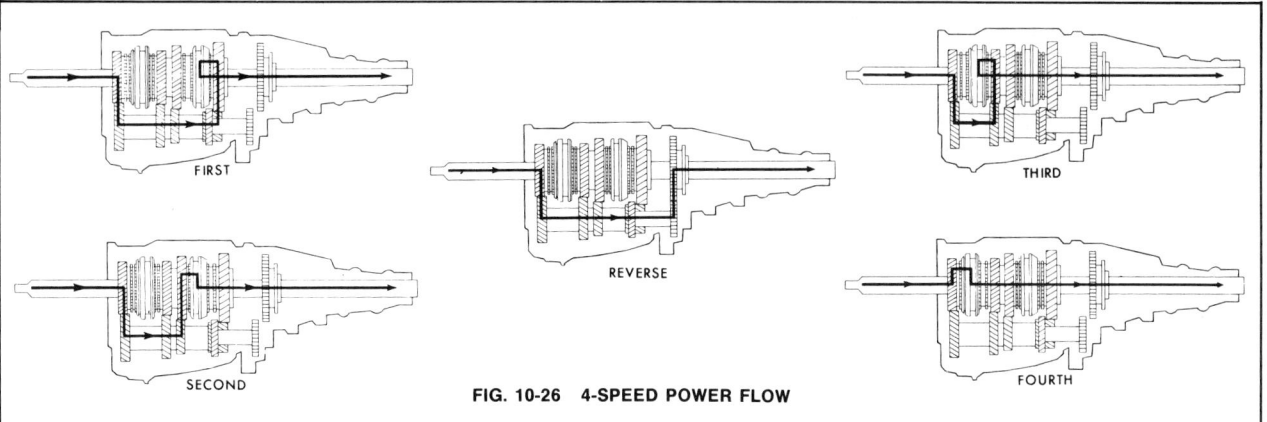

FIRST

THIRD

SECOND

REVERSE

FOURTH

FIG. 10-26 4-SPEED POWER FLOW

4-SPEED MANUAL TRANSMISSION DIAGNOSIS

CONDITION		CORRECTION	

SHIFTS HARD ON DOWNSHIFT

(a) Downshifting at too great rpms.

(a) Shifting into low gear above 45 mph and second above 65 mph makes extra work for synchronizing assemblies. If low or 2nd is used constantly at high speeds, there is the danger of damage from overspeeding the engine.

DISENGAGES FROM GEAR

(a) Dirt between transmission case and clutch housing.

(a) Clean mating surfaces involved.

(b) Does not engage fully.

(b) Check linkage for interference and adjust or replace if damaged.

(c) Clutching teeth worn or defective and/or clutch hub spline worn.

(c) Replace gear, clutch hub and sleeve.

NOISY OPERATION

(a) Worn, scored or broken gears.

(a) Replace gears.

(b) Dirty or worn bearing.

(b) Flush transmission with kerosene. If noise is still there, replace bearings and examine gears—replace if worn or damaged.

(c) Clutch sleeve interferes with countergear.

(c) Replace worn shift forks, countergear and idler gear thrust washers to restore gears and clutch sleeve to proper location. Thrust faces on these gears should be checked for wear and replaced if necessary.

LEAKS LUBRICANT

(a) Too much lubricant in transmission.

(a) Drain to correct level.

(b) Main drive gear bearing retainer loose or broken.

(b) Tighten or replace retainer.

(c) Front main bearing retainer gasket damaged.

(c) Replace gasket.

(d) Cover loose or gasket damaged.

(d) Tighten cover or replace gasket.

(e) Operating shaft seal leaks.

(e) Replace operating shaft seal.

(f) Countershaft loose in case.

(f) Replace case.

(g) Lack of sealant on bolts.

(g) Coat bolts with sealant.

(h) Extension oil seal worn.

(h) Replace seal.

BACKLASH IN ALL REDUCTION GEARS IS EXCESSIVE

(a) Countergear bearings worn.

(a) Replace bearings and shaft.

(b) Too much end-play in countergear.

(b) Replace countergear thrust washers.

NOISY IN ALL REDUCTION GEARS

(a) Insufficient lubricant.

(a) Check and top up to correct level.

(b) Main drive gear or countergear worn or damaged.

(b) Replace gears.

SHIFTS HARD, UP OR DOWN

(a) Clutch binds or releases too slowly.

(a) Adjust or repair clutch.

(b) Shift linkage binds.

(b) Free linkage, lubricate and adjust if necessary.

NOISY IN ALL GEARS

(a) Insufficient lubricant.

(a) Check and top up to correct level.

(b) Countergear bearings worn.

(b) Replace bearings and shaft.

(c) Main drive gear and countershaft drive gear worn or damaged.

(c) Replace gears.

(d) Main drive gear or mainshaft ball bearings damaged.

(d) Replace bearings.

(e) Speedometer gears damaged.

(e) Replace gears.

NOISY IN HIGH GEAR

(a) Front main bearing damaged.

(a) Replace bearing.

(b) Rear bearing damaged.

(b) Replace bearing.

(c) Speedometer gears damaged.

(c) Replace gears.

NOISY IN NEUTRAL WITH ENGINE RUNNING

(a) Front main bearing damaged.

(a) Replace bearing.

(b) Mainshaft pilot bearing damaged.

(b) Replace bearing.

GENERAL MOTORS

General Motors has relied primarily upon the 3-speed Saginaw and Muncie, and the 4-speed Saginaw and Muncie manual transmissions in all but the Chevette, Monza and Vega models. For 1975-77 Camaros and 1975-77 Firebirds see the American Motors section; for 1970-71 Buick, Oldsmobile and Pontiac models equipped with the Ford RAN, see the Ford Motor Company section.

SAGINAW AND MUNCIE 3-SPEED TRANSMISSIONS

The Saginaw and Muncie manual transmissions are representative of the fully synchronized, constant-mesh transmission design. The 3-speed Muncie differs from the 3-speed Saginaw primarily in the Muncie's extra ¼-in. center distance between the mainshaft and the countershaft, and the use of larger bearings, gears, input shaft and mainshaft, but power flow is essentially the same for both. Because their design is almost identical, the overhaul techniques and procedures for these two transmissions are almost identical, and they are treated together, with procedural differences noted where applicable.

SAGINAW 4-SPEED TRANSMISSION

A medium-duty transmission, the Saginaw is the standard 4-speed gearbox for GM cars equipped with 8-cyl. engines. The Saginaw 4-speed differs internally from the Muncie 4-speed, but it can be easily distinguished on the outside by the reverse lever mounted on the side cover rather than in the extension housing, as used by the Muncie.

MUNCIE 4-SPEED TRANSMISSION

The heavy-duty Muncie 4-speed transmission is offered as standard equipment in GM cars equipped with the 400, 454 or 455-cu.-in. engines, and has been offered as an option with most other V-8 GM engines. This design consists of two basic sections—the forward or transmission case contains the forward-speed gear assemblies and their synchronizing mechanisms, while the extension contains the reverse gear assembly.

BORG-WARNER 5-SPEED TRANSMISSION

The 5-speed Borg-Warner was first offered on Chevrolet Vega as an option in 1976. Its use has since been extended to the Buick Skyhawk, Oldsmobile Starfire, Pontiac Astre/Phoenix/Sunbird. This fully synchronized transmission uses 5th gear as an overdrive.

VEGA TRANSMISSIONS

The Vega has used a 3-speed Opel (German) and 4-speed Borg-Warner (1971-72), the 3-speed and 4-speed Saginaw (1973-75), and the new 4-speed 70mm GM transmission (standard equipment on the 1977 Chevette) and the 5-speed Borg-Warner (1977). Overhaul techniques and procedures for each of these transmissions will be found following the Saginaw-Muncie sections.

GM TRANSMISSION OVERHAUL PROCEDURES

SAGINAW & MUNCIE 3-SPEED TRANSMISSIONS

TRANSMISSION DISASSEMBLY (Figs. 10-27 & 10-28)

1. Unbolt and remove the side cover and shift fork assembly.
2. Remove the input-shaft bearing retainer, and discard the old gasket.
3. Remove the bearing-to-case snap ring, pull the input shaft forward, and remove the large snap ring. The slip-fit bearing should now come out easily.
4. Saginaw—Remove the speedometer driven gear from the extension housing, then unbolt the extension from the case.

Muncie—Drive the reverse idler shaft out with a brass drift and remove the reverse idler gear, then unbolt the extension housing from the case.
5. Saginaw—Unclip the E-ring from the reverse idler shaft.
6. Hold the input shaft and drive gear with one hand, and withdraw the mainshaft and extension housing from the case.
7. Separate the drive gear, its pilot bearings and the synchronizer ring (Saginaw only) from the mainshaft assembly.
8. Expand the snap ring retaining the mainshaft rear bearing, and remove the extension housing.
9. Saginaw—Use a dummy shaft to drive the countergear shaft and its Woodruff key from the rear of the case. The dummy shaft will hold the roller bearings in place within the countergear bore.

Muncie—Use a brass drift to drive the countergear shaft and Woodruff key from the case.
10. Saginaw—Remove the countergear, bearings and thrust washers from the case.
11. Saginaw—Drive the reverse idler shaft and Woodruff key through the rear of the case with a long punch.

MAINSHAFT DISASSEMBLY (Figs. 10-29 & 10-30)

If difficulty is encountered in removing any synchronizer hub and gear from the mainshaft, use a hydraulic press—*do not* hammer them off.

1. Remove the hub-to-shaft snap ring and the second/third-speed sliding clutch assembly, synchronizer ring and second speed gear from the front of the mainshaft.
2. Depress the speedometer-drive-gear retaining clip, and slide the gear from the mainshaft.
3. Remove the rear-bearing snap ring from the mainshaft groove, then remove the bearing, spring washer (Saginaw only), reverse-gear thrust washer and reverse gear from the mainshaft.
4. Remove the first/reverse clutch-hub snap ring from the mainshaft, and the clutch assembly, first-speed synchronizer and first gear.

INSPECTION

1. Wash the transmission case inside and out with solvent.
2. Inspect the case for cracks, the front and rear faces for burrs, and the bearing bores.
3. Wash the ball bearing assemblies with solvent. Blow dry with compressed air, taking care not to spin the bearings.
4. Lubricate the bearings with light engine oil, and inspect for roughness by turning each race slowly by hand.
5. Inspect all gear and countergear roller bearings. Replace any that are worn.
6. Inspect the countershaft and reverse idler shaft. Replace if necessary. Replace all worn thrust washers.
7. Check all gears for excessive wear, chips or cracks, and replace any that are worn or damaged.
8. Inspect and replace the reverse gear if the bushing is worn or damaged—bushings *are not* serviced separately.

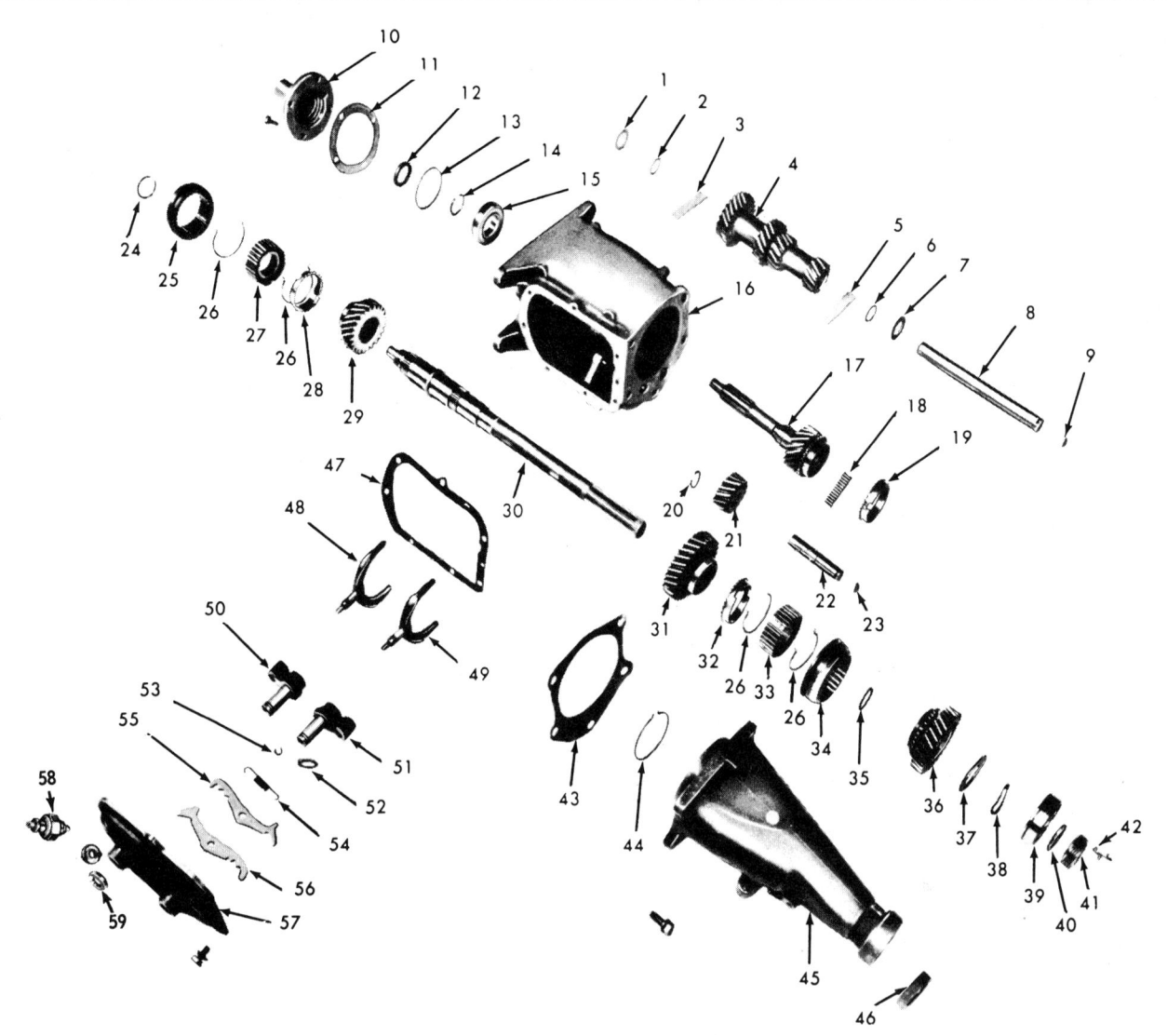

1. Thrust Washer - Front	19. 3rd Speed Blocker Ring	33. 1-2 Synchronizer Hub Assembly	47. Gasket
2. Bearing Washer	20. "E" Ring	34. 1-2 Synchronizer Sleeve	48. 2-3 Shift Fork
3. Needle Bearings	21. Reverse Idler Gear	35. Snap Ring - Hub to Shaft	49. 1st and Reverse Shift Fork
4. Countergear	22. Reverse Idler Shaft	36. Reverse Gear	50. 2-3 Shifter Shaft Assembly
5. Needle Bearings	23. Woodruff Key	37. Thrust Washer	51. 1st and Reverse Shifter Shaft Assembly
6. Bearing Washer	24. Snap Ring - Hub to Shaft	38. Spring Washer	52. "O" Ring Seal
7. Thrust Washer - Rear	25. 2-3 Synchronizer Sleeve	39. Rear Bearing	53. "E" Ring
8. Counter Shaft	26. Synchronizer Key Spring	40. Snap Ring - Bearing to Shaft	54. Spring
9. Woodruff Key	27. 2-3 Synchronizer Hub Assembly	41. Speedometer Drive Gear	55. 2nd and 3rd Detent Cam
10. Bearing Retainer	28. 2nd Speed Blocker Ring	42. Retaining Clip	56. 1st and Reverse Detent Cam
11. Gasket	29. 2nd Speed Gear	43. Gasket	57. Side Cover
12. Oil Seal	30. Mainshaft	44. Snap Ring - Rear Bearing to Extension	58. TCS Switch and Gasket
13. Snap Ring - Bearing to Case	31. 1st Speed Gear	45. Extension	59. Lip Seal
14. Snap Ring - Bearing to Gear	32. 1st Speed Blocker Ring	46. Oil Seal	
15. Clutch Gear Bearing			
16. Case			
17. Clutch Gear			
18. Pilot Bearings			

FIG. 10-27 SAGINAW 3-SPEED TRANSMISSION

9. Check the clutch sleeves for free movement on their hubs.

10. The reverse-idler-gear bushing and countergear anti-lash plate should be inspected; if either are damaged, the entire unit must be replaced, since the bushing and plate are not serviced separately.

CLUTCH KEY/SPRING REPLACEMENT

The two synchronizers are identical in both the Saginaw and Muncie transmissions, but the Muncie synchronizers are assembled on the mainshaft differently.

The fork slot in the second/third sleeve faces the thrust side of the hub, but the fork slot in the first/reverse sleeve faces in a direction opposite to the thrust side of the hub (**Figs. 10-29 & 10-30**).

1. The clutch hubs and sliding sleeves are selected assemblies, and should not be intermixed. But keys or springs may be replaced, if necessary. Mark the hub and sleeve for matching during reassembly.

2. Push the hub from the sleeve, and remove the keys/springs.

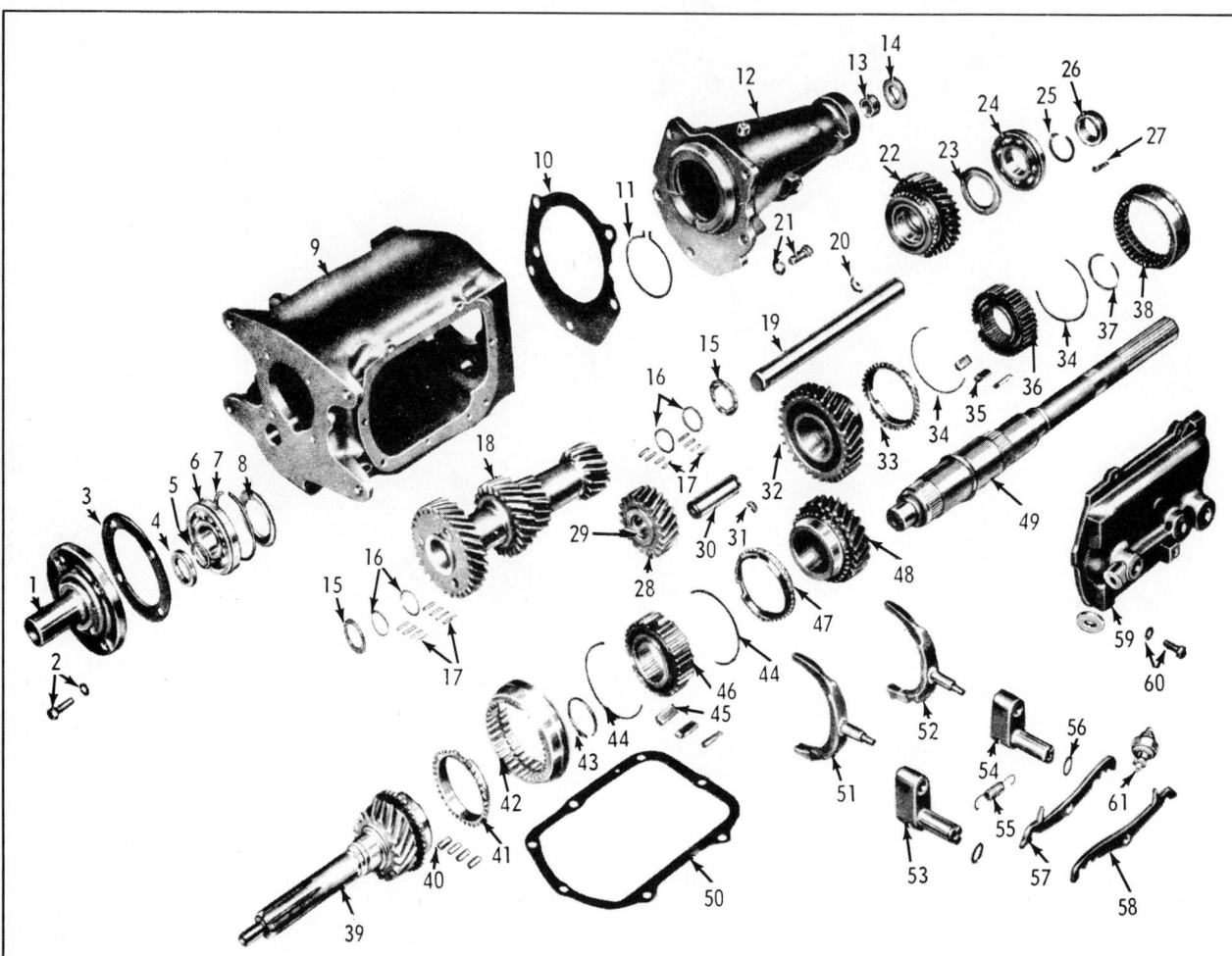

1. Bearing Retainer	21. Bolt (Extension-to-Case)	41. 3rd Speed Blocker Ring
2. Bolt and Lock Washer	22. Reverse Gear	42. 2nd and 3rd Synchronizer Collar
3. Gasket	23. Thrust Washer	43. Snap Ring
4. Oil Seal	24. Rear Bearing	44. Synchronizer Key Spring
5. Snap Ring (Bearing-to-Main Drive Gear)	25. Snap Ring	45. Synchronizer Keys
6. Main Drive Gear Bearing	26. Speedometer Drive Gear	46. 2nd and 3rd Synchronizer Hub
7. Snap Ring Bearing	27. Retainer Clip	47. 2nd Speed Blocker Ring
8. Oil Slinger	28. Reverse Idler Gear	48. 2nd Speed Gear
9. Case	29. Reverse Idler Bushing	49. Mainshaft
10. Gasket	30. Reverse Idler Shaft	50. Gasket
11. Snap Ring (Rear Bearing-to-Extension)	31. Woodruff Key	51. 2nd and 3rd Shifter Fork
12. Extension	32. 1st Speed Gear	52. 1st and Reverse Shifter Fork
13. Extension Bushing	33. 1st Speed Blocker Ring	53. 2-3 Shifter Shaft Assembly
14. Oil Seal	34. Synchronizer Key Spring	54. 1st and Reverse Shifter Shaft Assembly
15. Thrust Washer	35. Synchronizer Keys	55. Spring
16. Bearing Washer	36. 1st and Reverse Synchronizer Hub Assembly	56. O-ring Seal
17. Needle Bearings	37. Snap Ring	57. 1st and Reverse Detent Cam
18. Countergear	38. 1st and Reverse Synchronizer Collar	58. 2nd and 3rd Detent Cam
19. Countershaft	39. Main Drive Gear	59. Side Cover
20. Woodruff Key	40. Pilot Bearings	60. Bolt and Lock Washer

FIG. 10-28 MUNCIE 3-SPEED TRANSMISSION

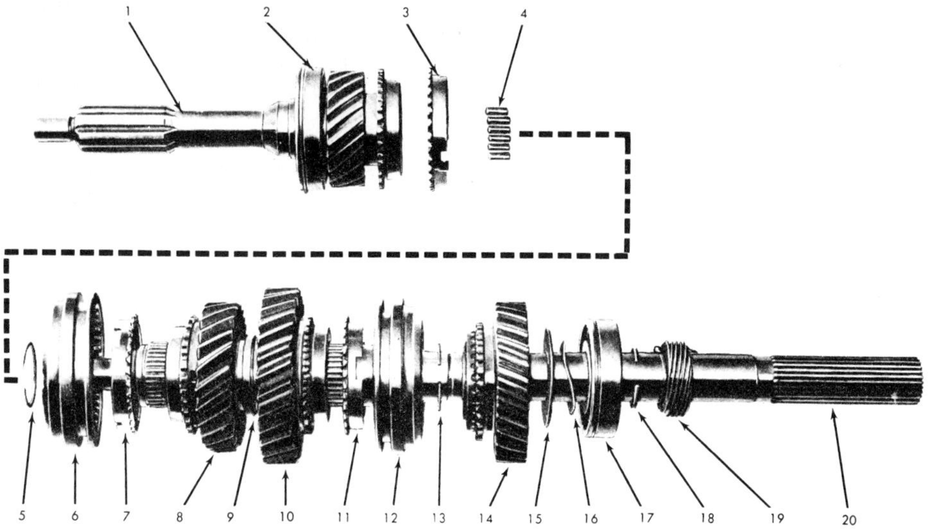

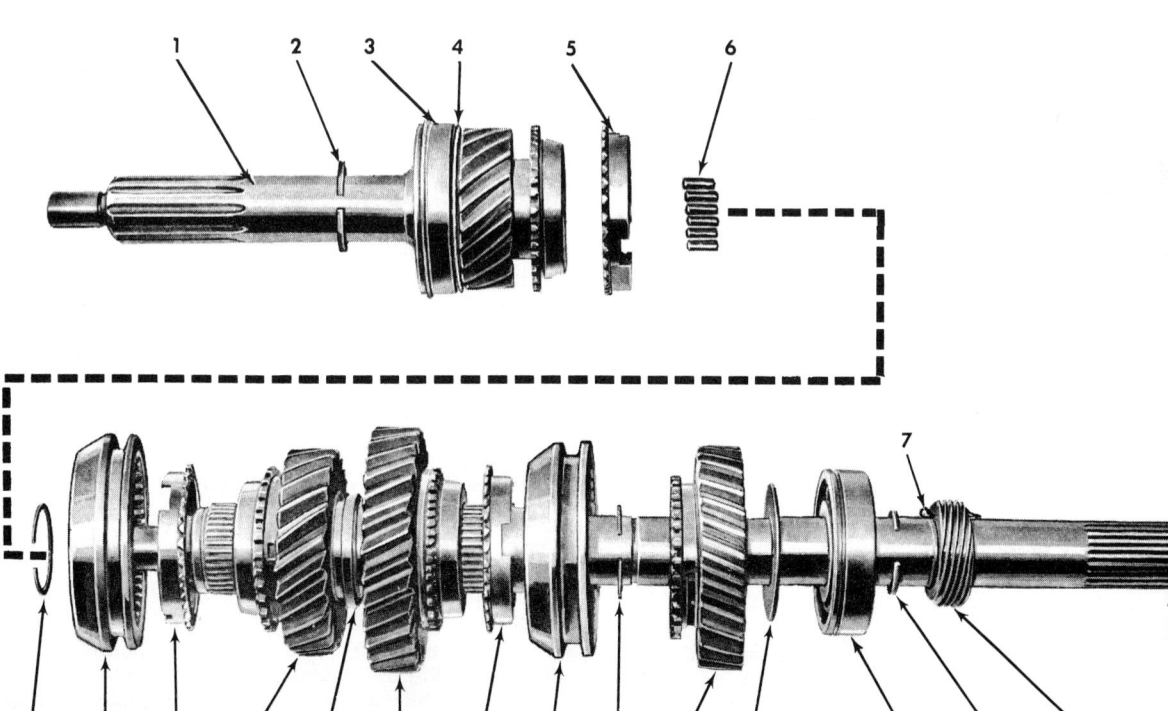

1. Drive Gear
2. Drive Gear Bearing
3. 3rd Speed Blocker Ring
4. Mainshaft Pilot Bearings (14)
5. Snap Ring
6. 2-3 Synchronizer Assembly
7. 2nd Speed blocker Ring
8. 2nd Speed Gear
9. Shoulder (Part of Main Shaft)
10. 1st Speed Gear
11. 1st Speed Blocker Ring
12. 1st Speed Synchronizer Assembly
13. Snap Ring
14. Reverse Gear
15. Reverse Gear Thrust Washer
16. Spring Washer
17. Rear Bearing
18. Snap Ring
19. Speedo Drive Gear and Clip
20. Mainshaft

FIG. 10-29   SAGINAW MAINSHAFT

1. Clutch Gear
2. Snap Ring
3. Clutch Gear Bearing
4. Oil Slinger
5. 3rd Speed Blocker Ring
6. Mainshaft Pilot Bearings (16)
7. Retaining Clip
8. Mainshaft
9. Speedo Drive Gear
10. Snap Ring
11. Rear Bearing
12. Reverse Gear Thrust Washer
13. Reverse Gear
14. Snap Ring
15. 1st Speed Synchronizer Assembly
16. 1st Speed Blocker Ring
17. 1st Speed Gear
18. Shoulder (Part of Mainshaft)
19. 2nd Speed Gear
20. 2nd Speed Blocker Ring
21. 2-3 Synchronizer Assembly
22. Snap Ring

FIG. 10-30   MUNCIE MAINSHAFT

3. Install the keys and position one spring on each side of the hub, making sure the springs engage all three keys. The tanged end of each spring should be inserted in different key cavities.

4. Slide the sleeve onto the hub and align the marks made in Step 1.

OIL SEAL/BUSHING REPLACEMENT

1. If the front bearing retainer requires a new seal, pry out the old one and install a new seal until it seats in its bore.

2. Should the extension housing bushing require replacement, remove the oil seal and drive the old bushing into the housing. Install a new bushing, coat its inside diameter with gear oil and replace the oil seal with a new one.

MAINSHAFT ASSEMBLY

1. With the front of the mainshaft facing you, replace the second gear with its face against the mainshaft shoulder; clutching teeth should face upward.

2. Replace the synchronizer ring with its clutching teeth facing downward over the second gear synchronizing surface. In both transmissions, all three rings are identical, so don't worry about mixing them.

3. Install the second/third synchronizer with the fork slot facing as shown in **Fig. 10-29 or Fig. 10-30.** Press onto the mainshaft splines until it bottoms.

4. With the synchronizer ring notches aligned with the synchronizer assembly keys, replace the synchro hub to mainshaft snap ring.

5. Reverse the position of the mainshaft, and replace the first gear with its face against the mainshaft shoulder; clutching teeth should face upward.

6. Replace the synchronizer ring over the first gear synchronizer surface with its clutching teeth downward.

7. Repeat Steps 3 and 4 with the first/reverse synchronizer. Make sure fork slot is facing down before pushing it onto mainshaft. Remember to align notches on ring with keys on synchronizer assembly.

8. Install the hub-to-mainshaft snap ring, replace reverse gear with its clutching teeth downward, and install the reverse-gear thrust washer and spring washer (Saginaw only).

9. Press the rear ball bearing on the shaft with the snap ring slot downward, and replace the snap ring.

10. Press the speedometer drive gear on the mainshaft, and replace the retaining ring.

TRANSMISSION ASSEMBLY

1. Saginaw—Insert the dummy shaft in the countergear assembly and coat the bearings with grease to hold them in place. Load a row of roller bearings and a thrust washer at each end.

Muncie—Coat the bearings with grease to hold them in place. Load a double row, with a bearing washer between the rows and a thrust washer at each end.

2. Coat the countergear thrust washers with grease, and position them in the transmission case, fitting the washer tangs into the case recesses. Insert the countergear assembly into case.

3. Install the countergear shaft and Woodruff key from the rear of the case. Make sure the shaft picks up both thrust washers and that the tangs do not slip out of the case recesses.

4. Saginaw—Install the reverse idler gear and shaft, inserting the gear through the case rear.

Muncie—Install the reverse idler gear, but *do not* replace the shaft until after reinstalling the mainshaft in the case.

5. Saginaw—Rotate the reverse idler gearshaft until the cutout matches that in the case. Insert the Woodruff key, and tap the shaft flush with the case. *Do not* install the shaft E-clip yet.

6. Expand the extension snap ring, and fit the extension over the rear of the mainshaft and onto the rear bearing. Seat the snap ring in the bearing groove.

7. Wipe the inside of the drive gear cavity with a thin coating of grease, and load the pilot bearings (Saginaw 14; Muncie 16). Install the third-speed synchronizer ring onto the clutch gear, with teeth facing the clutch.

8. Fit the drive gear and third-speed synchronizer ring assembly over the front of the mainshaft, aligning the ring notches with the second/third synchronizer keys. *Do not* assemble the drive gear bearing yet.

9. Install a new gasket to the extension housing, and hold in place with a thin grease coat. Insert the input-shaft drive gear and mainshaft in in the case. The drive gear must engage the countergear anti-lash plate teeth, and on Muncie, make sure oil slinger is on clutch gear.

10. Muncie—Rotate the extension and install the reverse idler shaft and Woodruff key.

11. Install the extension housing to the transmission case, and torque the bolts to 45 ft.-lbs. Use a sealer on all Muncie through-bolts.

12. Install the outer snap ring on the front bearing and seat the bearing in the front case bore.

13. Replace the inner snap ring and bolt the bearing retainer to the case, using a new gasket. The retainer oil-return hole should be at the bottom. Torque Saginaw bolts to 10 ft.-lbs., Muncie bolts to 20 ft.-lbs.

14. Saginaw—Move the reverse idler gear to the rear of the shaft, and install the E-clip in its slot at the front of the gear.

15. Slide the synchronizer sleeves to their neutral position, and replace the cover, gasket and fork assembly to the case. Forks must align with their synchronizer sleeve grooves.

16. Torque Saginaw cover bolts to 10 ft.-lbs., Muncie cover bolts to 20 ft.-lbs. Apply a sealer to all Muncie through-bolts.

17. Turn the input shaft, and shift the transmission through all gears to free rotation in gear.

18. Saginaw—Replace the speedometer driven gear in the extension housing.

SAGINAW 4-SPEED TRANSMISSION

TRANSMISSION DISASSEMBLY
(Fig. 10-31)

1. Unbolt and remove the side cover and shift fork assembly.

2. Unbolt and remove the input-shaft bearing retainer, discarding the old gasket.

3. Remove the bearing-to-case snap ring, pull the input shaft forward and remove the large snap ring. The slip-fit bearing should now come out easily.

4. Unbolt the extension housing from the transmission case.

5. Withdraw the input shaft, drive gear, mainshaft and extension housing from the case.

6. Separate the drive gear, its pilot bearings and the synchronizer ring from the mainshaft assembly.

7. Expand the snap ring retaining the mainshaft rear bearing, and remove the extension housing.

8. Use a dummy shaft to drive the countergear shaft and its Woodruff key from the rear of the case. The

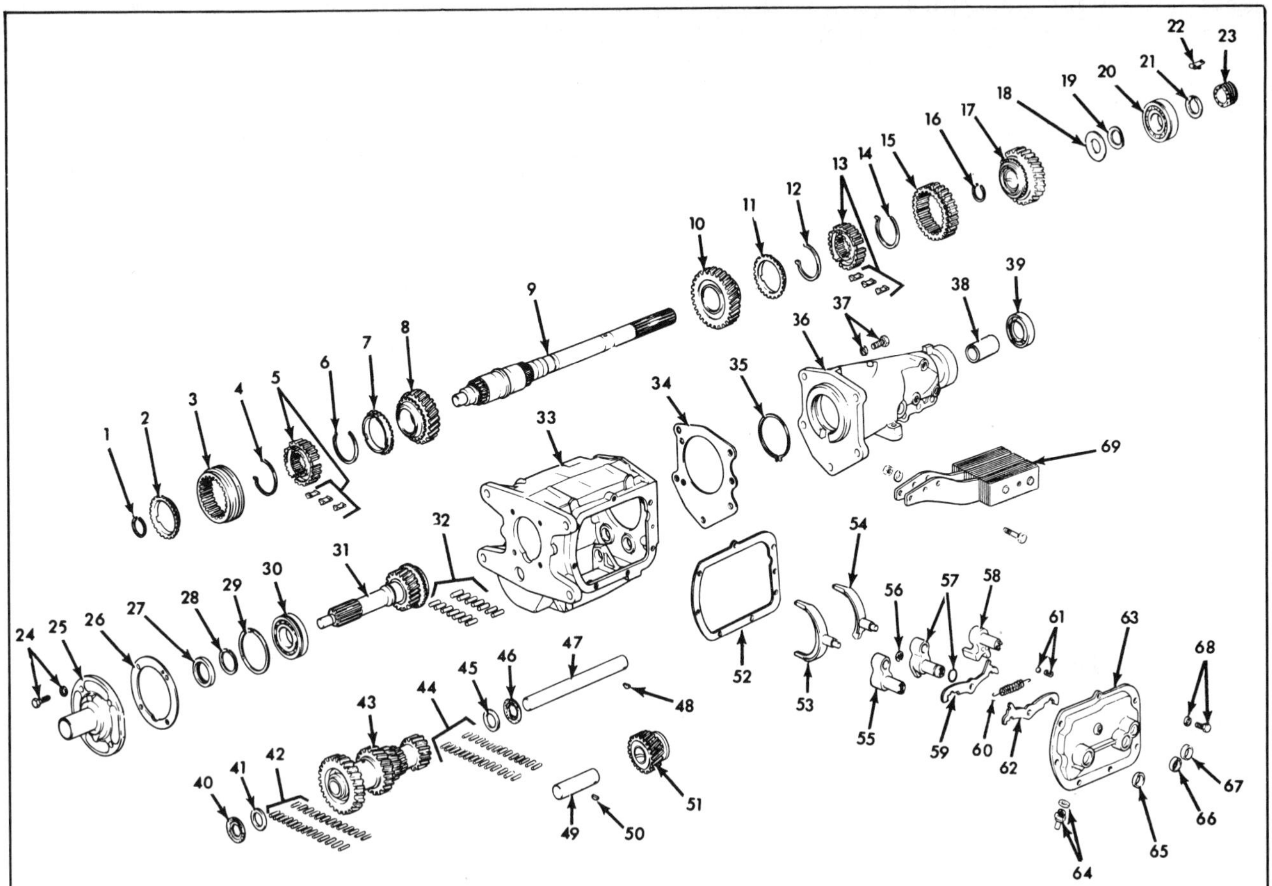

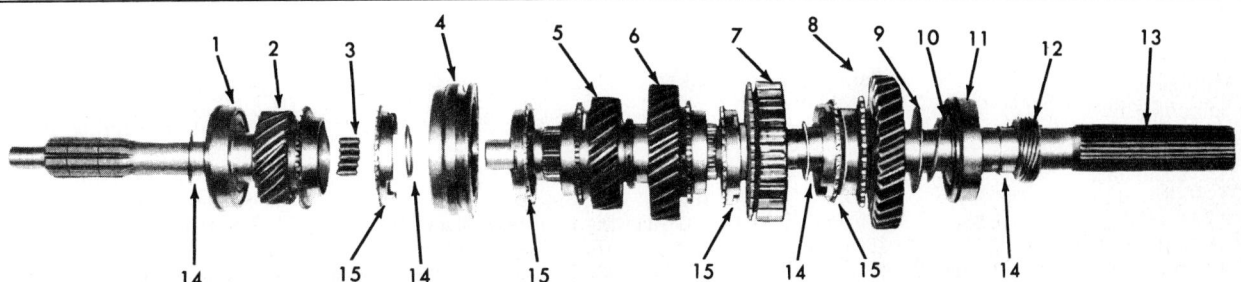

1. Snap ring, Hub to Shaft	24. Bearing Retainer Bolts and Washers (4)	47. Countergear Shaft
2. Synchronizer Ring	25. Front Bearing Retainer	48. Countergear Shaft Key
3. 3–4 Synchronizer Sleeve	26. Bearing Retainer Gasket	49. Reverse Idler Shaft
4. Synchronizer Key Spring	27. Bearing Retainer Oil Seal	50. Idler Shaft Key
5. Synchronizer Hub and Keys	28. Snap Ring	51. Reverse Idler Gear
6. Synchronizer Key Spring	29. Bearing Snap Ring	52. Side Cover Gasket
7. Synchronizer Ring	30. Front Bearing	53. 3–4 Shift Fork
8. Third Gear	31. Drive Gear	54. 1–2 Shift Fork
9. Main Shaft	32. Pilot Bearings	55. 3–4 Shifter Shaft
10. Second Gear	33. Case	56. Retaining "E" Ring
11. Synchronizer Ring	34. Extension to Case Gasket	57. 1–2 Shifter Shaft with "O" Rings
12. Synchronizer Key Spring	35. Rear Bearing to Extension Retaining Ring	58. Reverse Shifter Shaft
13. Synchronizer Hub and Keys	36. Rear Extension	59. 3–4 Detent Cam
14. Synchronizer Key Spring	37. Extension to Case Retaining Bolts and Washers	60. Detent Cam Spring
15. 1–2 Synchronizer Sleeve & Rev. Gear	38. Rear Extension Bushing	61. Reverse Detent Ball & Spring
16. Snap Ring, Hub to Shaft	39. Rear Seal	62. 1–2 Detent Cam
17. First Gear	40. Thrust Washer	63. Shift Cover
18. Thrust Washer	41. Spacer	64. TCS Switch and Gasket
19. Waved Washer	42. Countergear Shaft Roller Bearings	65. Shifter Shaft Seal
20. Ring Bearing	43. Countergear	66. Shifter Shaft Seal
21. Snap Ring, Bearing to Shaft	44. Countergear Shaft Roller Bearings	67. Shift Cover Bolts and Washers
22. Speedometer Gear Clip	45. Spacer	68. Shift Cover Attaching Bolts and Lock Washers
23. Speedometer Drive Gear	46. Thrust Washer	69. Damper Assembly

FIG. 10-31 SAGINAW 4-SPEED TRANSMISSION

1. Drive Gear Bearing	4. 3–4 Synchronizer Assembly	6. Second Speed Gear	8. First Speed Gear
2. Drive Gear	5. Third Speed Gear	7. 1–2 Synchronizer and Reverse Gear Assembly	9. Thrust Washer
3. Mainshaft Pilot Bearings			10. Spring Washer
			11. Rear Bearing
			12. Speedo Drive Gear
			13. Mainshaft
			14. Snap Ring
			15. Synchronizing "Blocker" Ring

FIG. 10-32 SAGINAW MAINSHAFT

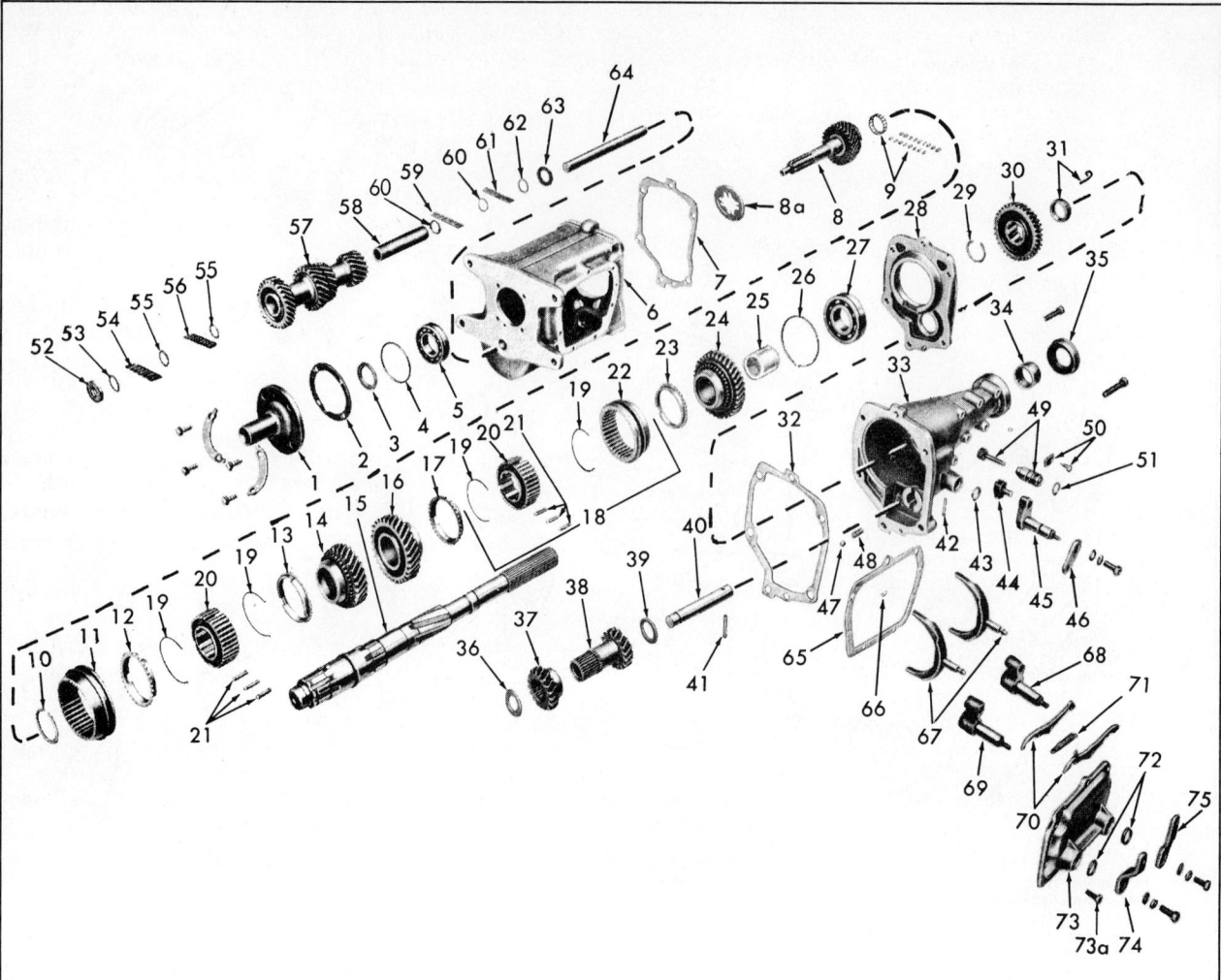

1. Bearing Retainer
2. Gasket
3. Bearing Retaining Nut
4. Bearing Snap Ring
5. Main Drive Gear Bearing
6. Transmission Case
7. Rear Bearing Retainer Gasket
8. Main Drive Gear
8a. Oil Slinger
9. Bearing Rollers (17) and Cage
10. Snap Ring
11. Third and Fourth Speed Clutch Sliding Sleeve
12. Fourth Speed Gear Synchronizing Ring
13. Third Speed Synchronizing Ring
14. Third Speed Gear
15. Mainshaft
16. Second Speed Gear
17. Second Speed Gear Synchronizing Ring
18. First and Second Speed Clutch Assembly
19. Clutch Key Spring

20. Clutch Hub
21. Clutch Keys
22. First and Second Speed Clutch Sliding Sleeve
23. First Speed Gear Synchronizing Ring
24. First Speed Gear
25. First Speed Gear Sleeve
26. Rear Bearing Snap Ring
27. Rear Bearing
28. Rear Bearing Retainer
29. Selective Fit Snap Ring
30. Reverse Gear
31. Speedometer Drive and Clip
32. Rear Bearing Retainer to Case Extension Gasket
33. Case Extension
34. Extension Bushing
35. Rear Oil Seal
36. Reverse Idler Front Thrust Washer (Tanged)
37. Reverse Idler Gear (Front)
38. Reverse Idler Gear (Rear)
39. Flat Thrust Washer
40. Reverse Idler Shaft

41. Reverse Idler Shaft Roll Pin
42. Reverse Shifter Shaft Lock Pin
43. Reverse Shifter Shaft Lip Seal
44. Reverse Shift Fork
45. Reverse Shifter Shaft and Detent Plate
46. Reverse Shifter Lever
47. Reverse Shifter Shaft Detent Ball
48. Reverse Shifter Shaft Ball Detent Spring
49. Speedometer Driven Gear and Fitting
50. Retainer and Bolt
51. "O" Ring Seal
52. Tanged Washer
53. Spacer
54. Bearing Rollers (28)
55. Spacer
56. Bearing Rollers (28)
57. Countergear
58. Countergear Roller Spacer (New Seam Type)

59. Bearing Rollers (28)
60. Spacer
61. Bearing Rollers (28)
62. Spacer
63. Tanged Washer
64. Countershaft
65. Gasket
66. Detent Cams Retainer Ring
67. Forward Speed Shift Forks
68. First and Second Speed Gear Shifter Shaft and Detent Plate
69. Third and Fourth Speed Gear Shifter Shaft and Detent Plate
70. Detent Cams
71. Detent Cam Spring
72. Lip Seals
73. Transmission Side Cover
73a Headed Cam Pin
74. Third and Fourth Speed Shifter Lever
75. First and Second Speed Shifter Lever

FIG. 10-33   MUNCIE 4-SPEED TRANSMISSION

dummy shaft will hold the roller bearings in place within the countergear bore.

9. Remove the reverse-idler-gear stop ring.

10. Drive the reverse idler shaft and Woodruff key through the rear of the case, using a long punch.

11. Remove the countergear, bearings and thrust washers from the case.

MAINSHAFT DISASSEMBLY
(Fig. 10-32)

If difficulty is encountered in removing any synchronizer hub and gear from the mainshaft, use a hydraulic press—*do not* hammer it off.

1. Remove the hub-to-shaft snap ring and the third/fourth-speed sliding-clutch assembly, synchronizer ring and third speed gear from the front of the mainshaft.

2. Depress the speedometer-drive-gear retaining clip, and slide the gear from the mainshaft.

3. Remove the rear-bearing snap ring from the mainshaft groove, then remove bearing, spring washer, thrust washer and first gear from mainshaft.

4. Remove the first/second clutch-hub snap ring from the mainshaft and the clutch assembly, first/second synchronizer ring and second gear.

INSPECTION

1. Wash the transmission case inside and out with solvent.

2. Inspect the case for cracks, the front and rear faces for burrs, and the bearing bores.

3. Wash the ball bearing assemblies with solvent. Blow dry with compressed air, taking care not to spin the bearings.

4. Lubricate the bearings with light engine oil and inspect for roughness by turning the races slowly by hand.

5. Inspect all gear and countergear roller bearings. Replace any that are worn.

6. Inspect the countershaft and reverse idler shaft. Replace if necessary. Replace all worn thrust washers.

7. Check all gears for excessive wear, chips or cracks, and replace any that are worn or damaged.

8. Check the clutch sleeves for free movement on their hubs.

9. The reverse-idler-gear bushing and countergear anti-lash plate should be inspected. If either are damaged, the entire unit must be replaced, since the bushing and plate are not serviced separately.

CLUTCH KEY AND SPRING REPLACEMENT

1. The clutch hubs and sliding sleeves are selected assemblies and should not be intermixed, but keys or springs may be replaced, if necessary. Mark the hub and sleeve for matching during reassembly.

2. Push the hub from the sleeve, and remove the keys/springs.

3. Install the keys and position one spring on each side of the hub, making sure the springs engage the keys. Insert the tanged end of each spring into a key cavity, but not the same cavity for both springs.

4. Fit the key in place to engage both springs, then slide the sleeve onto the hub, and align the marks made in Step 1.

OIL SEAL/BUSHING REPLACEMENT

1. If the front bearing retainer requires a new seal, pry out the old one, and install a new seal until it seats in its bore. Lip of seal must face rear of retainer.

2. Should the extension housing bushing require replacement, remove the oil seal, and drive the old bushing into the housing. Install a new bushing, coat it with gear oil and replace the oil seal with a new one.

MAINSHAFT ASSEMBLY

1. With the front of the mainshaft facing you, replace the third gear with its face against the mainshaft shoulder; clutching teeth should face upward.

2. Replace the synchronizer ring, with its clutching teeth facing downward, over the third-gear synchronizing surface.

3. Install the third/fourth synchronizer with the fork slot facing as shown in **Fig. 10-32.** Press onto the mainshaft splines until it bottoms.

4. With the synchronizer ring notches aligned with the synchronizer assembly keys, replace the snap ring.

5. Reverse the position of the mainshaft, and replace the second gear with its face against the mainshaft shoulder; clutching teeth should face upward.

6. Replace the synchronizer ring over the second-gear synchronizer surface with its clutching teeth downward.

7. Repeat Steps 3 and 4 with the first/second synchronizer.

8. Install the hub-to-mainshaft snap ring, a synchronizer ring (notches down) and first gear with its clutching teeth downward. Install the first-gear thrust washer and spring washer.

9. Press the rear ball bearing on the shaft with the snap ring slot downward, and replace the snap ring.

10. Press the speedometer drive gear on the mainshaft, and replace the retaining ring.

TRANSMISSION ASSEMBLY

1. With the dummy shaft inserted in the countergear assembly, coat the bearings with grease to hold them in place, and load a row of roller bearings and a thrust washer at each end.

2. Coat the countergear thrust washers with grease, and position in the transmission case, fitting the washer tangs into the case recesses.

3. Install the countergear shaft and Woodruff key from the rear of the case. Make sure the shaft picks up both thrust washers and that the tangs do not slip out of the case recesses.

4. Install the reverse idler gear and shaft, inserting the gear through the case side and the shaft and Woodruff key through the case rear.

5. Expand the extension snap ring, and fit the extension over the rear of the mainshaft and onto the rear bearing. Seat the snap ring in the bearing groove.

6. Wipe the inside of the drive gear cavity with a thin coat of grease, and load the 14 pilot bearings.

7. Fit the drive gear and fourth-speed synchronizer ring over the front of the mainshaft, aligning the ring notches with the third/fourth synchronizer keys.

8. Install a new gasket to the extension housing, and hold in place with a thin grease coat. Assemble the drive gear, mainshaft and extension to the case. The drive gear must engage the countergear anti-lash plate teeth.

9. Install the extension housing bolts, and torque to 45 ft.-lbs. Use a sealer on the bottom bolt.

10. Install the outer snap ring on the front bearing, and seat the bearing in the front case bore.

11. Replace the inner snap ring, and bolt the bearing retainer to the case, using a new gasket. The retainer oil-return hole should face downward. Torque bolts to 18 ft.-lbs.

12. Slide the synchronizer sleeves to their neutral position, and replace the cover, gasket and fork assembly to the case. Forks must align with their synchronizer sleeve grooves.

13. Torque cover bolts to 22 ft.-lbs.

14. Turn the input shaft, and shift the transmission through all gears to free rotation in gear.

MUNCIE 4-SPEED TRANSMISSION

TRANSMISSION DISASSEMBLY (FIG. 10-33)

1. Unbolt and remove the side cover and shift fork assembly.

2. Remove the front-bearing retainer bolts and bolt lock strips. Remove the retainer, and discard the old gasket.

3. Shift the transmission into two gears to lock it up, and remove the main-drive-gear retaining nut.

4. Shift the transmission into neutral, and drive the lock pin from the reverse shifter shaft.

5. Pull the shifter shaft out about ⅛-in. to disengage the reverse shifter fork from reverse gear.

6. Unbolt the extension housing from the transmission case, and tap with a plastic or rubber mallet to loosen. When the reverse idler shaft is out as far as it can go, twist the housing to the left. This will disengage the reverse fork from reverse gear. Remove the extension housing, and discard the old gasket.

7. Remove the rear reverse-idler gear, a flat thrust washer, the reverse idler shaft and a roll spring pin.

8. Remove the speedometer drive gear and reverse gear with a puller. Some models use a plastic gear retained by a clip. On these versions, depress the clip, and both the speedometer drive gear and the reverse gear will slide off.

9. Slide the third/fourth-synchronizer clutch sleeve forward to fourth gear position, and remove the rear bearing retainer and mainshaft assembly from the case. It may be necessary to tap the bearing retainer gently with a mallet. The rear reverse-idler gear will pop out of the case when the extension comes loose, and should be removed.

10. Separate the drive gear, its pilot bearings (17) and the synchronizer ring from the mainshaft assembly.

11. Remove the front half of the reverse idler gear and a tanged thrust washer from the case.

12. Remove the main drive bearing. If it does not come out easily, pry snap ring with a screwdriver.

13. Drive the countergear shaft to the rear until it clears the case, then pull the shaft from the case with a revolving motion.

14. Lift the countergear and two tanged thrust washers up and out of the case.

15. Remove 112 rollers, 6 spacers and the roller spacer from the countergear.

MAINSHAFT DISASSEMBLY
(Fig. 10-34)

If difficulty is encountered in removing any synchronizer hub and gear from the mainshaft, use a hydraulic press—*do not* hammer it off.

1. Remove the hub-to-shaft snap ring and the third/fourth-speed sliding-clutch assembly, synchronizer ring and third speed gear from front of mainshaft.

2. Expand the rear-bearing-retainer snap ring, and press the mainshaft from the retainer.

3. Remove the rear, mainshaft snap ring, rear bearing, first gear and sleeve, first-gear synchronizer ring, first/second-synchronizer clutch assembly, second-gear synchronizer ring, second gear from mainshaft.

INSPECTION

1. Wash the transmission case inside and out with solvent.

2. Inspect the case for cracks, the front and rear faces for burrs, and the bearing bores.

3. Wash the ball bearing assemblies with solvent. Blow dry with compressed air, taking care not to spin the bearings.

4. Lubricate the bearings with light engine oil, and inspect for roughness by turning the races slowly by hand.

5. Inspect all gear and countergear roller bearings. Replace any that are worn.

6. Inspect the countershaft and reverse idler shaft. Replace if necessary. Replace all worn thrust washers.

7. Check all gears for excessive wear, chips or cracks, and replace any that are worn or damaged.

8. Check the countergear for a loose damper plate (if used).

9. Check the reverse-idler-gear bushing for excessive wear with a narrow feeler gauge placed between the shaft and the bushing. Clearance should range from 0.003-in. to 0.005-in. The reverse idler gear is serviced as an assembly if the bushing is not within specifications, replace the entire unit.

CLUTCH KEY AND SPRING REPLACEMENT

1. The clutch hubs and sliding sleeves are selected assemblies, and should not be intermixed, but keys or springs may be replaced, if necessary. Mark the hub and sleeve for matching during reassembly.

2. Push the hub from the sleeve, and remove the keys/springs.

3. Position one spring on each side of the hub, and install its tanged ends into the key cavities.

4. Fit the key in place to engage both springs, then slide the sleeve onto the hub, and align the marks made in Step 1.

OIL SEAL AND BUSHING REPLACEMENT

1. If the extension housing bushing requires replacement, remove the oil seal and drive the old bushing into the housing. Install a new bushing, coat with gear oil and replace the oil seal with a new one.

REVERSE-SHIFTER SHAFT SEAL REPLACEMENT

1. Remove the shift fork, and carefully drive the shifter shaft into the case extension, letting the detent ball drop into the case. Remove and replace the seal.

2. Hold the detent ball spring in the detent spring hole, and install the shifter shaft into its opening from inside the extension until the detent plate butts against the inside of the extension housing.

3. With the detent ball on the spring, hold it down and push the shifter shaft back in, away from the case, until it is centered over the ball. Turn until the ball drops into the shaft detent.

4. Install the shift fork.

MAINSHAFT ASSEMBLY

1. With the rear of the mainshaft facing you, install the second gear with its hub facing up (toward shaft rear).

2. Fit a synchronizer ring on either side of the first/second-synchronizer clutch assembly (align clutch keys with keyways), and install on the mainshaft with the sliding-clutch-sleeve taper to the rear.

3. Use a 1¾-in. I.D. pipe or other suitable tool, press the first gear sleeve in place on the mainshaft, then install the first gear with its hub facing to the front of the shaft.

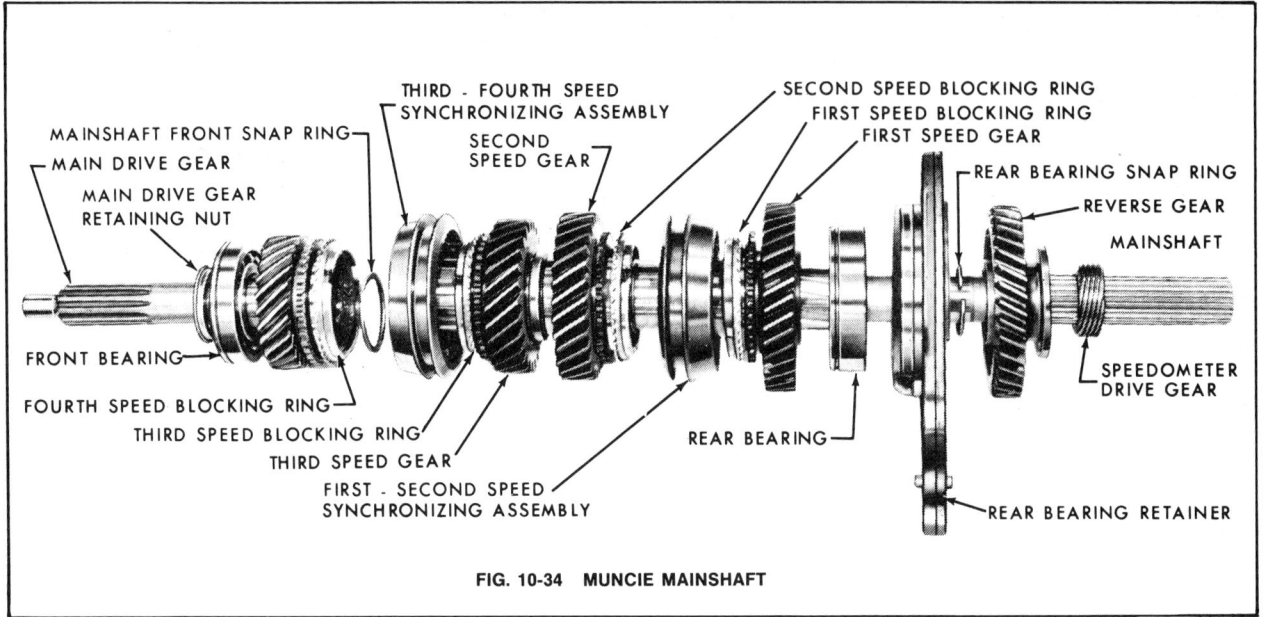

FIG. 10-34 MUNCIE MAINSHAFT

4. Use a 1⅝-in. I.D. pipe or other suitable tool to press the rear bearing in place.

5. Install the selective snap ring in the mainshaft groove behind the rear bearing. The maximum distance between the snap ring and bearing rear face should not exceed 0.005-in. If it does, replace the selective snap ring with a larger size (available in 0.087-in., 0.090-in., 0.093-in. and 0.096-in.).

6. Replace third gear and the third-gear synchronizer ring. The hub and notches should face to the front of the mainshaft.

7. Install the third/fourth-gear clutch assembly with the sleeve taper and hub both facing to the front. The hub keys should correspond with the synchronizer ring notches.

8. Replace the mainshaft snap ring in its groove in front of the third/fourth clutch assembly. Seat the snap ring ends behind the spline teeth.

9. Install the rear bearing retainer, expanding the plate snap ring to engage it in the rear bearing groove.

10. Replace the reverse gear with its shift collar facing to the rear of the mainshaft. On RPO M20 models, replace the two anti-rattle springs.

11. Install the speedometer gear and retaining clip. If a metal gear, press onto the mainshaft until the front side of the gear is 4⅞ ins. from rear bearing retainer.

TRANSMISSION ASSEMBLY

1. With a dummy shaft inserted in the countergear assembly, install a spacer, 28 roller bearings, a second spacer, another 28 bearings and a final spacer at each end.

2. Coat the countergear thrust washers with grease, and position them in the transmission case, fitting the washer tangs into the case recesses.

3. Install the countergear in the case. Make sure the tangs do not slip out of the case recesses.

4. Place the transmission case on its front face, and install the countergear shaft from the rear. The flat on end of the shaft should face the bottom of the case, and should be horizontal with it. When installed, flat should be flush with the end of the case.

5. Check countergear end play with dial indicator. If it exceeds 0.025-in., install new thrust washers.

6. Wipe the inside of the drive gear cavity with a thin coat of grease, and load the 17 pilot bearings.

Replace the oil slinger on the main drive gear with its concave side facing the gear.

7. Install the main drive gear in the transmission case and position it in the front bore.

8. Position a new gasket on the front face of the rear bearing retainer.

9. Replace the synchronizer ring on the main drive gear with its notches facing to the transmission rear.

10. Use grease to hold the tanged thrust washer to the machined face of the ear cast in the case for the reverse idler shaft. Place the front rear-idler gear next to the thrust washers with its hub to the rear of the case.

11. Slide the third/fourth-synchronizer clutch sleeve forward to lower the mainshaft assembly into the case. The notches in the fourth-gear synchronizer ring must correspond with the keys in the clutch assembly, and the main drive gear must engage both the countergear and the anti-lash plate on standard-ratio models.

12. Align the guide pin in the rear bearing retainer with its hole in the rear of the case, and tap the retainer in place with a mallet.

13. Install the rear, reverse idler gear from the rear of the case. The splines must engage with a part of the front gear already in place.

14. Position a gasket on the rear face of the rear bearing retainer, using grease to hold in place.

15. Replace the remaining flat thrust washer on the reverse-idler-gear shaft, and install the shaft, roll pin and thrust washer into the gears, and front boss of the transmission case. Remember to pick up the front tanged thrust washer.

16. Move the reverse shifter shaft to the left side of the extension housing, and rotate the shaft to bring the reverse shift fork forward in the extension.

17. While installing the extension, push in on the shifter shaft to engage the shift fork with the reverse-gear shift collar.

18. Guide the reverse idler shaft into the extension housing. This will allow the extension housing and case to mate. Torque the three upper bolts to 20 ft.-lbs. and the lower ones to 30 ft.-lbs.

19. Line up the reverse-shifter shaft groove with the hole in the case boss, and drive in the lock pin. Replace the shifter lever.

20. With the snap-ring groove in front, press the bearing onto the main drive gear and into the case until several threads can be seen on the drive gear retaining nut.

21. Lock up the transmission in two gears, and replace the main-drive-gear retaining nut. Torque the nut to 40 ft.-lbs., and stake with a center punch, using care not to damage the shaft threads.

22. Replace the main-drive-gear bearing retainer, gasket, bolt lock retainers and bolts (use sealer). Torque bolts to 18 ft.-lbs.

23. Shift the third/fourth clutch sleeve to neutral and the first/second sleeve to second gear.

24. Move the side-cover third/fourth shifter lever to neutral detent and the first/second lever to second gear detent.

25. Install the side cover gasket, and align the side-cover dowel pin with the hole in the transmission case. Install cover bolts, and torque alternately to 25 ft.-lbs.

GENERAL MOTORS 3-SPEED (GERMAN)

TRANSMISSION DISASSEMBLY
(Fig. 10-35)

1. Remove the TCS and back-up lamp switches from the transmission case/extension housing.

2. Remove the shift lever boot and the cotter pins which connect each end of the shift control rod. Detach the control rod and the washers.

3. Pull off the E-clip which holds the selector lever to the rear extension boss.

4. Remove the retaining rings, wave washer and selector ring from the selector shaft, sliding the selector lever/shift idler shaft from the internal shift-lever assembly at the same time.

5. Unbolt the transmission case cover and discard the old gasket. Turn the transmission 180°, and drain the gearbox oil.

6. Unbolt the extension housing, and rotate until the countergear shaft can be seen.

7. Use a punch and hammer to remove the countergear shaft. Work from the front of the transmission, and retrieve the lock ball positioned in the rear of the shaft.

8. Lift the countergear and thrust washers from the transmission case.

9. Remove all lock pins from shifter forks with a ⅛-in. pin punch. Second gear should be engaged to prevent the second/third fork pin from binding.

10. Shift the transmission into third gear and, with the second/third internal lever engaging the shifter shaft, drive the second/third shifter shaft out of the front of the case, and remove the fork.

11. Drive the first/reverse shifter shaft from the case, and remove the fork.

12. Drive the selector-shaft internal-lever lock pins, and remove the shaft and levers.

13. Unclipping the snap ring from the rear-bearing retainer groove, slide the extension housing from the mainshaft assembly.

14. Remove the clutch-drive gear assembly from the case.

15. Move the first/reverse sliding gear to the hub shaft rear, and withdraw the mainshaft assembly from the case. Retrieve the lock pins and detent balls from inside the case.

16. Drive the plugs and springs from the shift-rail detent holes with a pin punch.

17. Angle a punch against the reverse idler shaft

from the front of the case, and gently tap it to the rear and out of the case. Remove the idler gear.

MAINSHAFT DISASSEMBLY

1. The synchronizer hubs and sliding sleeves should not be separated but maintained as a selected assembly. However, the keys and springs may be replaced. Unclip and remove the snap ring from the front of the clutch hub.

2. Depress the retainer clip, and slide the speedometer drive gear from the mainshaft.

3. Unclip and remove the snap ring, Belleville washer and spacer from the mainshaft.

4. Using a press, remove the first/reverse synchronizer assembly, first gear, second/third synchronizer assembly and second gear.

CLUTCH-DRIVE-GEAR BEARING REPLACEMENT

1. Unclip and remove the snap ring holding the bearing on the shaft.

2. Press the drive gear from the bearing.

3. Using a press and a suitable piece of pipe, press a new bearing on the shaft. The slinger must face toward the gear.

4. Reinstall the snap ring.

INSPECTION

1. Wash the transmission case inside and out with solvent.

2. Inspect the case for cracks, the front and rear faces for burrs, and the bearing bores.

3. Wash the ball bearing assemblies with solvent. Blow dry with compressed air, taking care not to spin the bearings.

4. Lubricate the bearings with light engine oil, and inspect for roughness by turning the races slowly by hand.

5. Check all gears for excessive wear, chips or cracks, and replace any that are worn or damaged.

6. Inspect the shift forks for burrs. If any are found, remove with emery cloth.

7. Replace any worn synchronizer rings, key springs or keys.

8. Coat all parts with SAE 90W transmission lubricant before reassembly.

REAR SEAL REPLACEMENT

1. Pry the old seal from the extension housing.

2. Coat the sealing lips of the new seal with SAE 90W gear oil.

3. Install the new seal with a suitable length of pipe and a hammer. Tap the seal slowly and evenly; pipe pressure must be confined to the outer edge of the seal.

MAINSHAFT ASSEMBLY

1. With the front of the mainshaft facing you, replace second gear; it should rotate freely on the shaft.

2. Replace the second/third synchronizer ring over the second gear cone.

3. Fit the front and rear synchronizer key springs into the second/third synchronizer hub. The hooked spring ends must rest in the same slot, with the raised ends resting against the synchronizer rings.

4. Replace the sliding sleeve on the clutch hub with the arrow on each key pointing to the shaft front.

5. Press the second/third synchronizer hub on the mainshaft, and secure with a snap ring.

6. Fit both clutch key springs into the first/reverse synchronizer hub with hooks of both springs in same

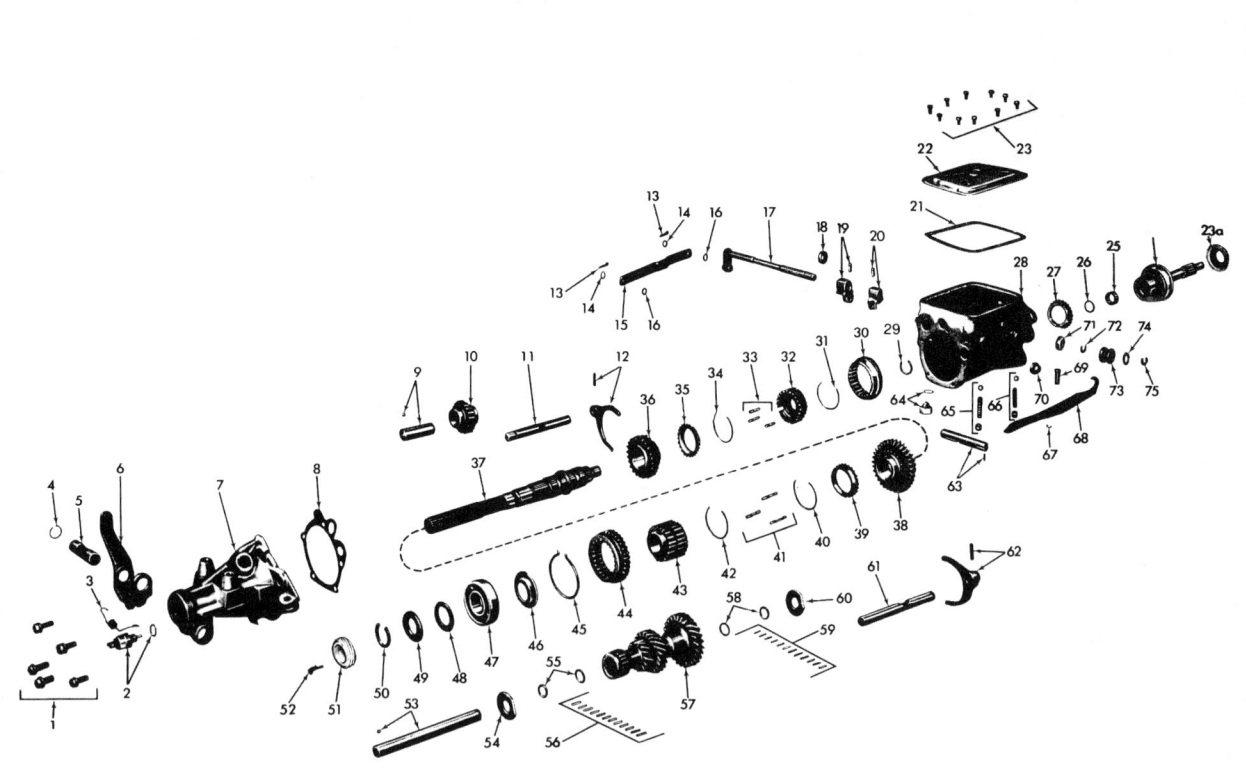

1. Rear Extension to Case Bolts
2. Back-up Lamp Switch and Seal Ring
3. Shift Idler Lever Spring
4. Intermediate Lever Bushing Snap Ring
5. Intermediate Lever Bushing
6. Shift Idler Lever
7. Rear Extension
8. Rear Extension Gasket
9. Reverse Idler Gear Shaft and Lock Ball
10. Reverse Idler Gear and Bushing Assembly
11. 2-3 Speed Shifter Shaft
12. 2-3 Speed Shift Fork and Spiral Pin
13. Cotter Pin
14. Waved Washer
15. Shift Selector Rod
16. Washer
17. Selector Shaft
18. Selector Shaft Seal
19. 2-3 Intermediate Shift Lever and Spiral Pin
20. 1st-Reverse Intermediate Shift Lever and Spiral Pin
21. Cover Gasket
22. Cover Assembly
23. Cover-To-Case Screws
23a. Clutch Drive Gear Seal
24. Clutch Drive Gear Assembly
25. Mainshaft Pilot Bearing Assembly

26. Pilot Bearing Spacer Ring
27. 3rd Gear Synchronizer Ring
28. Transmission Case
29. 2-3 Speed Synchronizer Assembly Retaining Ring
30. 2-3 Speed Synchronizer Sleeve
31. Synchronizer Spring
32. 2-3 Synchronizer Hub
33. 2-3 Synchronizer Keys
34. Synchronizer Spring
35. 2nd Gear Synchronizer Ring
36. 2nd Speed Gear
37. Mainshaft
38. 1st Speed Gear
39. 1st Speed Gear Synchronizer Ring
40. Synchronizer Spring
41. 1st-Reverse Synchronizer Keys
42. Synchronizer Spring
43. 1st-Reverse Synchronizer Hub
44. 1st-Reverse Synchronizer Sleeve
45. Rear Bearing to Extension Locking Ring
46. 1st-Reverse Key Stop Ring
47. Mainshaft Rear Bearing
48. Rear Bearing Spacer
49. Belleville Washer
50. Rear Bearing Retaining Ring
51. Speedo Drive Gear
52. Speedo Drive Clip

53. Countergear Shaft and Lock Ball
54. Countergear Thrust Washer
55. Countergear Bearing Washer
56. Countergear Roller Bearings (24)
57. Countergear
58. Countergear Bearing Washer
59. Countergear Roller Bearings (24)
60. Countergear Thrust Washers
61. 1st-Reverse Shift Shaft
62. 1st-Reverse Shift Fork and Spiral Pin
63. Intermediate Lever Shaft and Pin
64. T.C.S. Switch and Gasket
65. 2-3 Shift Detent Ball, Spring and Hole Plug
66. 1-Reverse Shift Detent Ball, Spring and Hole Plug
67. Pivot Pin Lock Ring
68. Shift Selector Rod
69. Selector Lever Pivot Pin
70. Oil Filler Plug
71. Selector Shaft Oil Seal
72. Selector Shaft Lock Ring
73. Selector Shaft Ring
74. Belleville Washer
75. Selector Shaft Lock Ring

FIG. 10-35 GM 3-SPEED TRANSMISSION (VEGA)

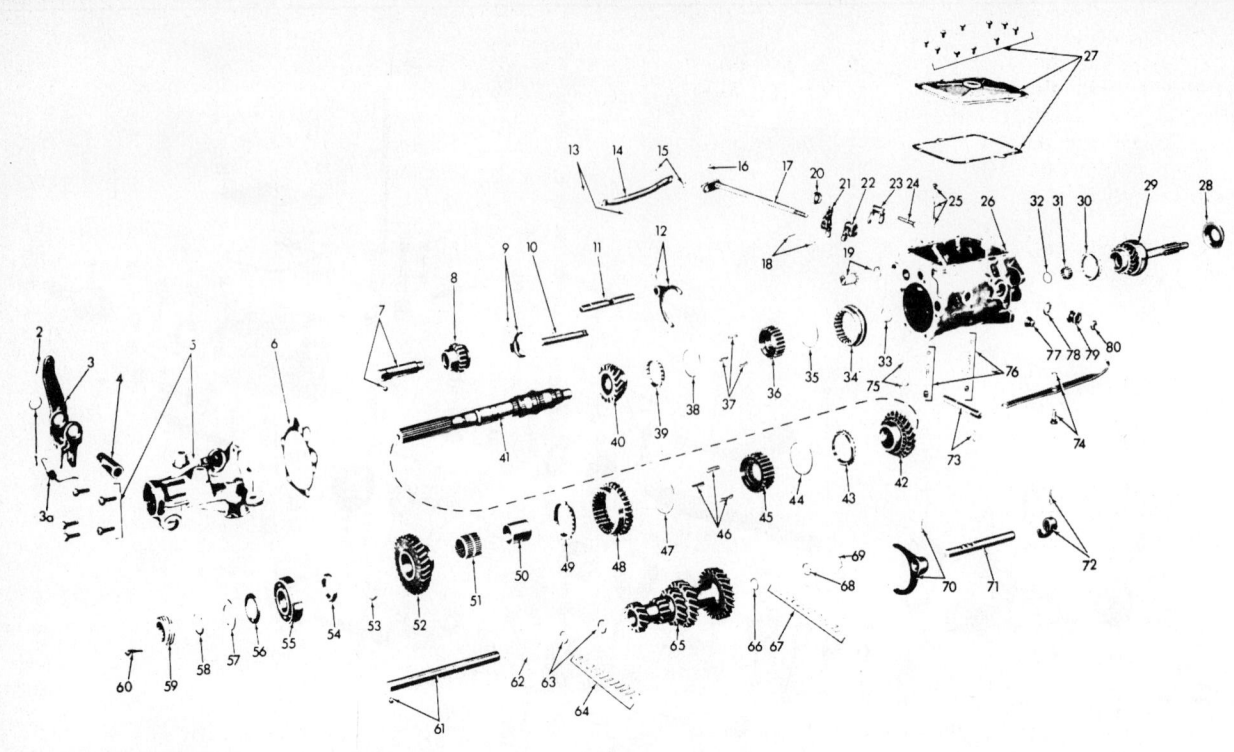

1. Intermediate Lever Bushing Snap Ring
2. Cotter Pin
3. Shift Idler Lever and Spring
4. Intermediate Lever Bushing
5. Rear Extension and Retaining Bolts
6. Rear Extension Gasket
7. Reverse Idler Gear Shaft and Lock Ball
8. Reverse Idler Gear and Bushing Assembly
9. Reverse Idler Gear Shift Fork and Spiral Pin
10. Reverse Idler Gear Shifter Shaft
11. 3-4 Speed Shifter Shaft
12. 3-4 Speed Shift Fork and Spiral Pin
13. Washers
14. Shift Control Rod
15. Washers
16. Cotter Pin
17. Selector Shaft
18. Spiral Pins
19. Back-up Lamp Switch and Seal Ring
20. Selector Shaft Oil Seal
21. 3rd-4th Speed Intermediate Shifter Lever
22. 1st-2nd Intermediate Shift Lever
23. Reverse Intermediate Lever
24. Reverse Intermediate Lever Pin
25. Reverse Shifter Shaft Detent Ball, Spring and Cap
26. Transmission Case

27. Cover Gasket, Cover, and Screws
28. Clutch Drive Gear to Housing Seal
29. Clutch Drive Gear Assembly
30. 4th Gear Synchronizer Ring
31. Mainshaft Pilot Bearing Assembly
32. Pilot Bearing Spacer Ring
33. 3-4 Speed Synchronizer Assembly Retaining Ring
34. 3-4 Speed Synchronizer Sleeve
35. Synchronizer Spring
36. 3-4 Synchronizer Hub
37. 3-4 Synchronizer Keys
38. Synchronizer Spring
39. 3rd Speed Gear Synchronizer Ring
40. 3rd Speed Gear
41. Mainshaft
42. 2nd Speed Gear
43. 2nd Speed Synchronizer Ring
44. Synchronizer Spring
45. 1st-2nd Synchronizer Hub
46. 1st-2nd Synchronizer Keys
47. Synchronizer Spring
48. 1st-2nd Synchronizer Sleeve
49. 1st Speed Synchronizer Ring
50. 1st Speed Gear Bushing
51. 1st Gear Needle Bearing Assembly
52. 1st Speed Gear
53. Rear Bearing to Extension Locking Ring
54. Rear Bearing Spacer Ring (Front)

55. Mainshaft Rear Bearing
56. Rear Bearing Spacer (Rear)
57. Belleville Washer
58. Rear Bearing Retaining Ring (Brg.-to-Mainshaft)
59. Speedo Drive Gear
60. Speedo Drive Clip
61. Countergear Shaft and Lock Ball
62. Countergear Thrust Washer
63. Countergear Bearing Washers
64. Countergear Roller Bearings (24)
65. Countergear
66. Countergear Bearing Washer
67. Countergear Roller Bearings (24)
68. Countergear Bearing Washer
69. Countergear Thrust Washer
70. 1st-2nd Shift Fork and Spiral Pin
71. 1st-2nd Shift Shaft
72. 1st-2nd Selector Lever Cam and Sprial Pin
73. Intermediate Lever Shaft and Pin
74. Shift Selector Rod, Pivot Pin and Lock Ring
75. T.C.S. Switch and Gasket
76. Shifter Shaft Detent Balls, Springs and Hole Plugs
77. Oil Filler Plug
78. Selector Shaft Oil Seal
79. Selector Shaft Adjusting Ring
80. Selector Shaft Lock Nut

FIG. 10-36 GM 4-SPEED BORG-WARNER TRANSMISSION

slot. The raised spring ends should be opposite from each other.

7. Replace the sliding gear and keys on the hub assembly, with the longer key flat and the fork groove on the gear facing to the rear.

8. Slide first gear onto the mainshaft from the rear; it should rotate freely on the shaft.

9. Replace the first/reverse synchronizer ring over the first gear cone.

10. Slide the first/reverse synchronizer assembly on the mainshaft. Install the stop ring, rear-extension retaining ring and rear bearing on the shaft.

11. With the synchronizer ring slots aligned with the keys, support the rear bearing race, and press the components together.

12. Replace the spacer and Belleville washer on the mainshaft, then install the snap ring.

13. Place the speedometer-gear retainer clip on the mainshaft, and install the speedometer gear.

14. Replace the mainshaft assembly in the extension housing, and secure with the retaining ring.

TRANSMISSION ASSEMBLY

1. With a new gasket positioned on the extension housing, slide the mainshaft assembly into the transmission case.

2. Replace two extension housing bolts loosely to prevent the housing from rotating and damaging the new gasket.

3. Slide the lock ring and pilot roller-bearing assembly on the mainshaft through the front of the case. Coat the bearing with bearing grease.

4. Replace the synchronizer ring on the clutch drive gear, and fit the gear into the case to the snap ring stop.

5. Install the first/reverse shifter shaft at the case front with its notches facing down. Push through the shifter fork, and position the fork shoulder toward the case front.

6. Drive the lock pin in place, letting it protrude between 1/16-in. and 5/64-in. above the fork.

7. Repeat Steps 5 and 6 with the second/third shifter shaft.

8. Install the selector shaft, pushing it through the second/third and first/reverse levers. Replace the lock pins as in Step 6.

9. Replace the lock balls and thrust springs in the transmission case bores, and drive the plugs in place.

10. Remove the two bolts from the extension housing, pull the extension back and rotate to expose the reverse-idler-shaft bore.

11. Install the gear in the case and the lock ball in the reverse idler shaft. Drive the shaft into place from the rear of the case.

12. Using a dummy shaft in the countergear, install a spacer, a row of 24 roller bearings and another spacer at each end. Use grease to hold them in place.

13. Coat the two thrust washers with grease, and install them in the transmission case with their lugs fitting into the case slots.

14. Rotate the extension housing to expose the countergear shaft bore.

15. Fit the lock ball in the shaft, and insert it from the rear of the case until it catches the rear thrust washer. Use a small drift placed at the front of the case to catch the other thrust washer and hold it in place.

16. Replace the countergear in the transmission case, and align the lock ball with the case grooves, then tap the shaft through, driving out the dummy shaft.

17. Install the extension housing bolts, and torque to 31 ft.-lbs.

18. Replace the cover with a new gasket, and torque to 48 in.-lbs.

19. Install the gearshift linkages by reversing Steps 2-4 of the ''Transmission Disassembly'' procedure.

20. Reinstall the TCS and back-up lamp switches.

GENERAL MOTORS 4-SPEED BORG-WARNER

TRANSMISSION DISASSEMBLY
(Fig. 10-36)

1. Remove the TCS and back-up lamp switches from the transmission case/extension housing.

2. Remove the cotter pins which connect each end of the shift control rod. Detach the control rod and its washers.

3. Pull off the E-clip which holds the selector lever to the rear extension boss.

4. Remove the locknut and selector ring, sliding the selector-lever/shift-idler shaft from the intermediate shift-lever assembly at the same time.

5. Remove the snap ring from the intermediate shift-lever bushing. Drive the bushing from the lever assembly with a brass drift.

6. Unbolt the transmission case cover, and discard the old gasket.

7. Remove the detent cap, spring and ball, then turn the transmission 180°, and drain the gearbox oil.

8. Unbolt the extension housing, and rotate until the countergear shaft can be seen.

9. Use a punch and hammer to remove the countergear shaft. Work from the front of the transmission, and retrieve the lock ball positioned in the rear of the shaft.

10. Lift the countergear and thrust washers from the transmission case.

11. Remove all lock pins with a 1/8-in. pin punch. Slide the reverse shaft to the back of the case until the selector shaft cutout clears the reverse shaft, then drive the reverse intermediate-shift-lever pivot pin out, and remove the intermediate lever.

12. Shift the transmission gears into neutral, and push the selector shaft inward, turning until the lock pins are positioned vertically. Drive the third/fourth intermediate-lever-cam lock pin out, and repeat with the first/second intermediate-lever-cam pin. This will allow selector shaft removal.

13. Pry the selector-shaft seal rings from the case.

14. Pry the two aluminum gearshift-interlock detents from the outside top of the transmission case, and remove the thrust spring and ball from each.

15. Shift the transmission into first gear, and drive out the lock pins from the shifter forks and selector levers, removing the first/second lever pin first.

16. Drive the first/second shifter shaft from the rear of the transmission, and remove the fork from the sliding sleeve.

17. Drive the third/fourth shifter shaft to the rear until the fork can be removed from the shaft, then drive the shaft out through the front of the case.

18. Remove the clutch drive gear from the transmission case.

19. Withdraw the extension housing and mainshaft assembly from the transmission case.

20. Drive the reverse-idler-gear shaft to the rear until the gear and shaft can be removed from the case. Retrieve the lock ball.

21. Drive the reverse shifter shaft out from the front of the transmission case, and remove the shifter fork.

MAINSHAFT DISASSEMBLY

1. Unclip and remove the snap ring from the rear-bearing retaining groove, and separate the mainshaft assembly from the rear bearing retainer.

2. Depress the retaining clip, and slide the speedometer drive gear from the mainshaft.

3. Remove the needle bearing, spacer ring and synchronizer ring. The sliding sleeve, keys and front clutch-key spring can also be removed.

4. Unclip and remove the snap ring in front of the synchronizer hub.

5. Unclip and remove the snap ring, Belleville washer and spacer from the mainshaft.

6. Remove first gear, the needle bearing, first/second synchronizer assembly and second gear.

7. Remove third-speed synchronizing-hub snap ring, and press the synchronizer assembly and third gear from the mainshaft.

CLUTCH-DRIVE GEAR BEARING REPLACEMENT

1. Unclip and remove the snap ring holding the bearing on the shaft.

2. Press the drive gear from the bearing.

3. Press a new bearing on the shaft. The oil slinger must face toward the gear.

4. Reinstall the snap ring.

INSPECTION

1. Wash the transmission case inside and out with solvent.

2. Inspect the case for cracks, the front and rear faces for burrs, and the bearing bores.

3. Wash the ball bearing assemblies with solvent. Blow dry with compressed air, taking care not to spin the bearings.

4. Lubricate the gearings with light engine oil, and inspect for roughness by turning the races slowly by hand.

5. Check all gears for excessive wear, chips or cracks, and replace any that are worn or damaged.

6. Inspect the shift forks for burrs. If any are found, remove with emery cloth.

7. Replace any worn synchronizer rings, key springs or keys.

8. Coat all parts with SAE 90W transmission lubricant before reassembly.

REAR SEAL REPLACEMENT

1. Pry the old seal from the extension housing.

2. Coat the sealing lips of the new seal with SAE 90W transmission lubricant.

3. Install the new seal with a suitable length of pipe and a hammer. Tap the seal slowly and evenly; pipe pressure must be confined to the outer edge of the seal.

MAINSHAFT ASSEMBLY

1. With the front of the mainshaft facing you, replace third gear; it should rotate freely on the shaft.

2. Replace the third-gear synchronizer ring over the third gear cone.

3. Fit the rear synchronizer key spring into the third/fourth synchronizer hub. The hooked spring end must rest in one slot, with the raised end facing the synchronizer ring.

4. Press the third/fourth synchronizer hub on the mainshaft, and secure with a snap ring.

5. Turn the mainshaft around, and install second gear. It should rotate freely on the shaft.

6. Replace the second-speed synchronizer ring over the second gear cone.

7. Fit both synchronizer key springs into the first/second synchronizer hub. Install the sliding gear and keys on the hub.

8. Slide the first/second-gear synchronizer hub, needle bearing, and inner sleeve on the mainshaft. Replace the spacer, extension-housing retaining ring and rear bearing on the shaft.

9. With the synchronizer ring slots aligned with the keys, support the rear bearing race, and press the components together.

10. Replace the spacer and Belleville washer (concave side facing the bearing) on the mainshaft, then install the snap ring.

11. Place the speedometer-gear retaining clip on the mainshaft, and install the speedometer gear.

12. Fit the mainshaft assembly into the rear bearing retainer until it stops, then install the snap ring.

13. Replace the third/fourth synchronizer assembly on the hub with the raised end of the key springs facing the synchronizer ring and the key arrows toward the front of the shaft.

TRANSMISSION ASSEMBLY

1. Using sealer, install a new gasket on the extension housing, and slide the mainshaft assembly into the transmission case.

2. Slide the spacer ring and needle bearing on the front of the mainshaft. Coat the bearing with bearing grease.

3. Replace the synchronizer ring on the clutch drive gear, and install the gear in the transmission case.

4. Install the first/second shifter shaft with notches down, pushing it through the L-shaped selector dog.

5. Push the first/second selector shaft through the shifter fork with its shoulder to the front of the case. Drive the lock pins in place (selector dog pin first), letting them protrude between 1/16-in. and 5/64-in. above the fork.

6. Install the third/fourth shifter shaft in the same manner, pushing it through the third/fourth shifter fork, and install the lock pin to the same specifications.

7. Push the reverse shifter shaft (with notches up) through the reverse shift fork, and install the lock pin.

8. Replace the selector shaft in the transmission case, pushing it through the third/fourth intermediate lever first, then through the first/second intermediate lever. Install the lock pins.

9. Shift the transmission to neutral, and rotate the selector shaft to engage shifter shafts with the levers.

10. Engage the reverse intermediate lever and the third/fourth intermediate lever, and install the lock pin. Reverse-lever end play on the pin should range between 0.004-in. to 0.012-in.

11. Install the lock balls, thrust springs and detent plugs in the transmission case bores.

12. Rotate the extension housing to expose the reverse-idler-gear shaft bore.

13. Replace the lock ball in the reverse-idler-gear shaft, and install from the rear of the transmission case, positioning the reverse idler gear and reverse shifter fork at the same time. The reverse-idler-gear shift-fork groove and the shifter fork shoulder must face to the front of the mainshaft.

14. Using a dummy shaft in the countergear, install a spacer, a row of 24 roller bearings and another spacer at each end. Use grease to hold them in place.

15. Coat the thrust washers with grease, and install

them in the transmission case with their lugs fitting into the case slots.

16. Rotate the extension housing to expose the countergear shaft bore.

17. Fit the lock ball in the shaft, and insert it from the rear of the case until it catches the rear thrust washer.

18. Replace the countergear in the transmission case, and align the lock ball with the case grooves, then tap the shaft through, driving out the dummy shaft.

19. Install the extension housing bolts, and torque to 31 ft.-lbs.

20. Replace the detent ball, spring and cap in the transmission bore.

21. Replace the cover with a new gasket, and torque to 48 in.-lbs.

22. Install the gearshift linkages by reversing Steps 2-4 of the "Transmission Disassembly" procedure.

23. Reinstall the TCS and back-up lamp switches.

GENERAL MOTORS 4-SPEED (70MM)

TRANSMISSION DISASSEMBLY
(Fig. 10-37)

1. Place the transmission with its bellhousing resting on wooden blocks.

2. Drive out the spring pin retaining the shifter shaft to its arm assembly, and remove the arm assembly.

3. Unbolt and remove the extension housing (all fasteners are metric).

4. Press on the speedometer gear retainer to remove the gear and retainer from the mainshaft.

5. Unclip and remove the shifter-shaft snap ring.

6. Remove the reverse-shifter-shaft cover, detent cap, spring, ball and interlock lock pin.

7. Disengage the reverse lever shaft from the reverse idler, and remove the reverse idler shaft with the gear attached.

8. Unclip and remove the reverse gear and reverse countergear snap rings, then remove both gears.

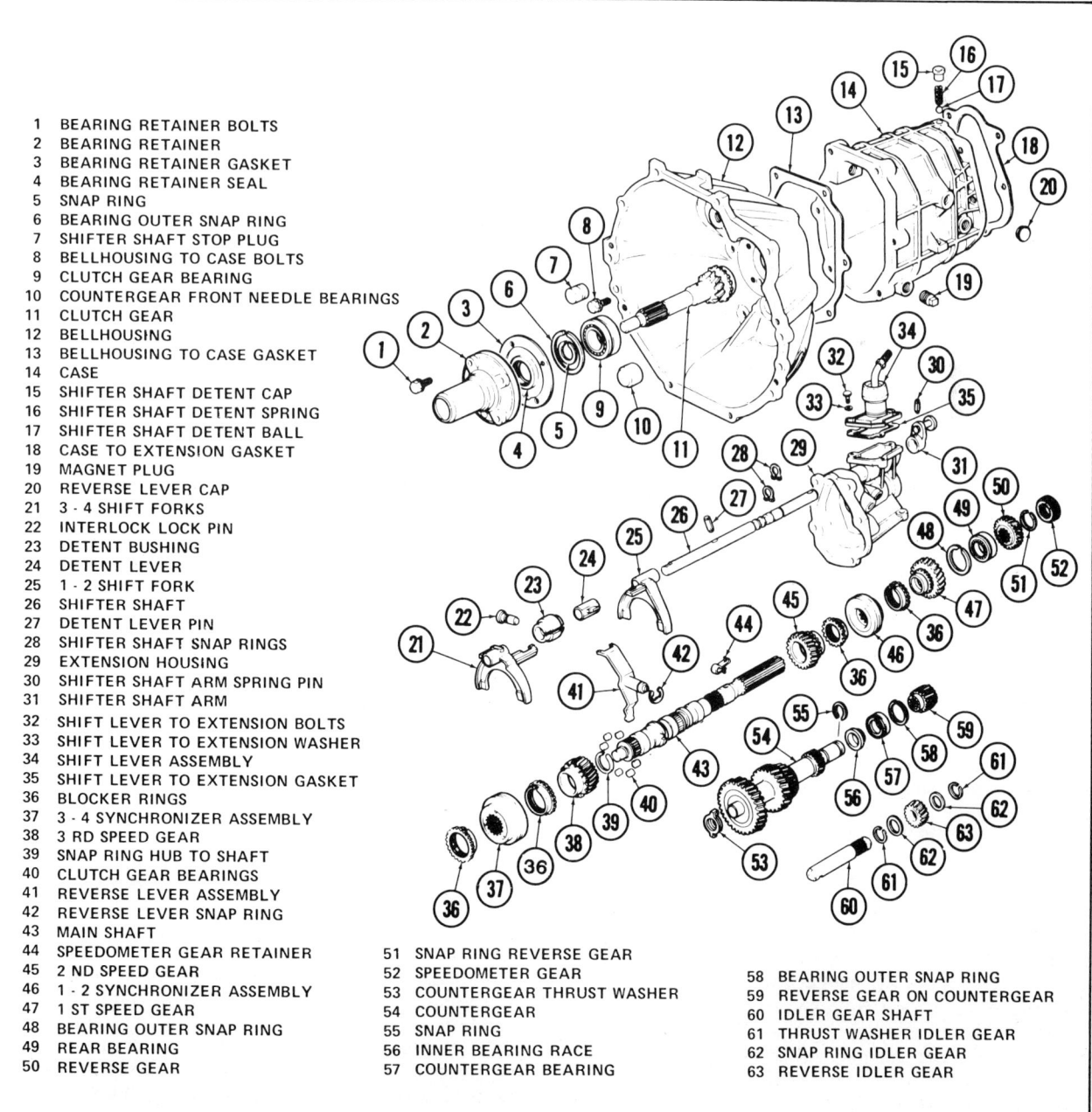

1	BEARING RETAINER BOLTS
2	BEARING RETAINER
3	BEARING RETAINER GASKET
4	BEARING RETAINER SEAL
5	SNAP RING
6	BEARING OUTER SNAP RING
7	SHIFTER SHAFT STOP PLUG
8	BELLHOUSING TO CASE BOLTS
9	CLUTCH GEAR BEARING
10	COUNTERGEAR FRONT NEEDLE BEARINGS
11	CLUTCH GEAR
12	BELLHOUSING
13	BELLHOUSING TO CASE GASKET
14	CASE
15	SHIFTER SHAFT DETENT CAP
16	SHIFTER SHAFT DETENT SPRING
17	SHIFTER SHAFT DETENT BALL
18	CASE TO EXTENSION GASKET
19	MAGNET PLUG
20	REVERSE LEVER CAP
21	3 - 4 SHIFT FORKS
22	INTERLOCK LOCK PIN
23	DETENT BUSHING
24	DETENT LEVER
25	1 - 2 SHIFT FORK
26	SHIFTER SHAFT
27	DETENT LEVER PIN
28	SHIFTER SHAFT SNAP RINGS
29	EXTENSION HOUSING
30	SHIFTER SHAFT ARM SPRING PIN
31	SHIFTER SHAFT ARM
32	SHIFT LEVER TO EXTENSION BOLTS
33	SHIFT LEVER TO EXTENSION WASHER
34	SHIFT LEVER ASSEMBLY
35	SHIFT LEVER TO EXTENSION GASKET
36	BLOCKER RINGS
37	3 - 4 SYNCHRONIZER ASSEMBLY
38	3 RD SPEED GEAR
39	SNAP RING HUB TO SHAFT
40	CLUTCH GEAR BEARINGS
41	REVERSE LEVER ASSEMBLY
42	REVERSE LEVER SNAP RING
43	MAIN SHAFT
44	SPEEDOMETER GEAR RETAINER
45	2 ND SPEED GEAR
46	1 - 2 SYNCHRONIZER ASSEMBLY
47	1 ST SPEED GEAR
48	BEARING OUTER SNAP RING
49	REAR BEARING
50	REVERSE GEAR

51	SNAP RING REVERSE GEAR
52	SPEEDOMETER GEAR
53	COUNTERGEAR THRUST WASHER
54	COUNTERGEAR
55	SNAP RING
56	INNER BEARING RACE
57	COUNTERGEAR BEARING

58	BEARING OUTER SNAP RING
59	REVERSE GEAR ON COUNTERGEAR
60	IDLER GEAR SHAFT
61	THRUST WASHER IDLER GEAR
62	SNAP RING IDLER GEAR
63	REVERSE IDLER GEAR

FIG. 10-37   GM 70MM 4-SPEED TRANSMISSION (CHEVETTE, VEGA)

9. With the transmission positioned on its side, remove the clutch-gear-bearing retainer, and discard the old gasket.

10. Unclip and remove the clutch-gear-ball-bearing-to-bellhousing snap ring.

11. Unbolt the bellhousing, and turn the transmission so that it rests on the bellhousing, as in Step 1.

12. Lift the case off the mainshaft. The mainshaft assembly, countergear and shifter shaft will remain in the bellhousing.

13. Remove the mainshaft with the shifter forks and the countergear meshed with the mainshaft teeth as an assembly.

MAINSHAFT DISASSEMBLY

1. Detach the mainshaft from the shifter shaft assembly and countergear.

2. Remove the clutch gear and synchronizer ring from the mainshaft. Retrieve any pilot bearings that may fall out—there should be 15 in all.

3. Remove the third/fourth-synchronizer-hub snap ring and the third/fourth synchronizer assembly.

4. Remove the synchronizer ring and third gear.

5. Press the ball bearing from the rear of the mainshaft.

6. Remove first gear and the synchronizer ring.

7. Remove the first/second-synchronizer-hub snap ring and the first/second synchronizer assembly.

8. Remove second gear.

INSPECTION

1. Wash the transmission case inside and out with solvent.

2. Inspect the case for cracks, the front and rear faces for burrs, and the bearing bores.

3. Wash the ball bearing assemblies with solvent. Blow dry with compressed air, taking care not to spin the bearings.

4. Lubricate the bearings with light engine oil, and inspect for roughness by turning the races slowly by hand.

5. Inspect the countergear roller bearings, replacing any that are worn.

6. Inspect the countershaft and reverse idler shaft. Replace if necessary. Replace all worn thrust washers.

7. Check all gears for excessive wear, chips or cracks, and replace any that are worn or damaged.

8. Check the clutch sleeves for free movement on their hubs.

9. Inspect the reverse idler bushing. If worn or damaged, replace the entire gear, since the bushing is not serviced separately.

CLUTCH KEY AND SPRING REPLACEMENT

1. The clutch hubs and sliding sleeves are selected assemblies and should not be intermixed, but keys or springs may be replaced if necessary. Mark the hub and sleeve for matching during reassembly.

2. Push the hub from the sleeve, and remove the keys/springs.

3. Fit one spring on each side of the hub so that all three keys are engaged by both springs, then slide the sleeve onto the hub, align the marks made in Step 1.

OIL SEAL AND BUSHING REPLACEMENT

1. Pry the old seal from the rear of the extension housing.

2. Drive the old bushing out and press a new bushing in.

3. Coat the I.D. of the new bushing and seal with SAE 90W transmission lubricant, and install the new seal.

4. If the drive-gear-bearing retainer requires a new seal, pry out the old one and install a new seal until it seats in its bore.

5. Lubricate the I.D. of the seal with SAE 90W transmission lubricant.

MAINSHAFT ASSEMBLY

1. With the rear of the mainshaft facing up, replace the second gear with its face against the mainshaft flange and its clutching teeth facing upward.

2. Fit a synchronizer ring with its clutching teeth facing downward over the second gear synchronizer surface.

3. Install the first/second synchronizer with the fork slot facing down, and press onto the mainshaft splines until it bottoms.

4. With the synchronizer ring notches aligned with the synchronizer assembly keys, replace the synchronizer hub-to-mainshaft snap ring.

5. Install another synchronizer ring with its notches downward and aligned with the first/second-synchronizer-assembly keys.

6. Replace first gear with its clutching teeth facing down.

7. Position the rear (unshielded) ball bearing with its snap ring groove downward, and press onto the mainshaft.

8. Reverse the position of the mainshaft, and replace the third gear with its face against the mainshaft flange and its clutching teeth upward.

9. Install a synchronizer ring over the third-gear synchronizer surface with its clutching teeth downward.

10. Replace the third/fourth synchronizer assembly with its fork slot facing down.

11. Align the synchronizer ring notches with the synchronizer assembly keys, and install a synchronizer-hub-to-mainshaft snap ring.

12. Replace the remaining synchronizer ring, with its notches down, to align with the third/fourth synchronizer assembly keys.

TRANSMISSION ASSEMBLY

1. Install the shielded ball bearing to the clutch gear shaft with an arbor press. The snap ring groove should face upward.

2. Replace the snap ring on the clutch gear shaft.

3. Coat the inside of the clutch gear bore with grease, and install the 15 pilot bearings.

4. Attach the clutch gear to the mainshaft.

5. Secure the detent lever to the shift shaft with a roll pin, and slide the first/second shifter fork onto the shaft until it engages the detent lever.

6. Fit the third/fourth shifter fork to the detent bushing, and slide on the shift shaft to locate below the first/second shifter-fork arm.

7. Install the shifter assembly to the synchronizer sleeve grooves on the mainshaft.

8. Position the bellhousing so that its front rests on the wooden blocks, and install a thrust washer over the countergear shaft hole, locating its tangs in the bellhousing recesses provided.

9. Mesh the mainshaft gears and countershaft gears, and replace in the bellhousing as an assembly.

10. Set the bellhousing on its side, and install the snap ring to the ball bearing on the clutch gear.

11. Bolt the bearing retainer to the bellhousing, using bolt sealer on the retaining bolts. Torque to 105 in.-lbs.

12. Restore the bellhousing to its original position on the wooden blocks. If the reverse lever was removed, reinstall (slot parallel to front of case) with grease to

hold it in place, and replace the reverse-lever snap ring.

13. Fit the roller bearing to the countergear opening, with its snap ring groove inside the case—the snap ring will be on the bearing.

14. Cement a new gasket to the bellhousing.

15. Check the synchronizers to make sure they are in a neutral position, the detent bushing slot is facing outward and the reverse lever is flush with the inside wall of the case.

16. Expand the snap ring in the mainshaft opening of the case, and install it over the mainshaft bearing.

17. Replace the interlock lock pin to retain the shifter shaft in position.

18. Engage the idler shaft with the reverse lever inside the case, and replace the cover to hold the reverse lever in position.

19. Replace the detent ball, spring and cap in the case.

20. Position reverse gear with the gear teeth chamfer facing up, and push onto the mainshaft splines. Install the snap ring.

21. Replace the smaller reverse gear on the countergear shaft with its shoulder against the countergear bearing. Install the snap ring.

22. Install the reverse idler gear to the idler shaft with its gear-teeth chamfer facing downward toward the shaft. Install the thrust washer and snap ring.

23. Replace the snap rings on the shifter shaft.

24. With the retaining loop forward, engage the speedometer gear retainer in the mainshaft hole, and slide the gear over the mainshaft until it locks in place. The gear may have to be heated to 175° F for easy installation.

25. Fit the extension housing and a new gasket to the case, and replace the two partially threaded (pilot) bolts in the upper-right-hand and lower-left-hand corners of the case. Installing the pilot bolts in the incorrect positions can split the case.

26. Replace the shifter shaft arm over the shifter shaft, and align the hole with that in the shaft. Then drive the spring pin in place.

27. Place the transmission case on its side, and install the two pilot bolts in the top-right-hand and bottom-left-hand bellhousing holes.

28. Install the remaining extension and bellhousing bolts, and torque to 25 ft.-lbs.

GENERAL MOTORS 5-SPEED BORG-WARNER T-50

TRANSMISSION DISASSEMBLY
(Fig. 10-38)

1. Remove the selector lever pivot from the transmission case.

2. Unscrew the threaded plug on the case, and remove it with the poppet spring and mesh lock plunger.

3. Unbolt the transmission case/extension housing from the center support, and slide the case forward.

4. Carefully slide the extension housing to the rear. The shifter head, shift rail and selector lever are not secured to the housing, and may drop out, damaging the parts, if care is not used. Remove the housing.

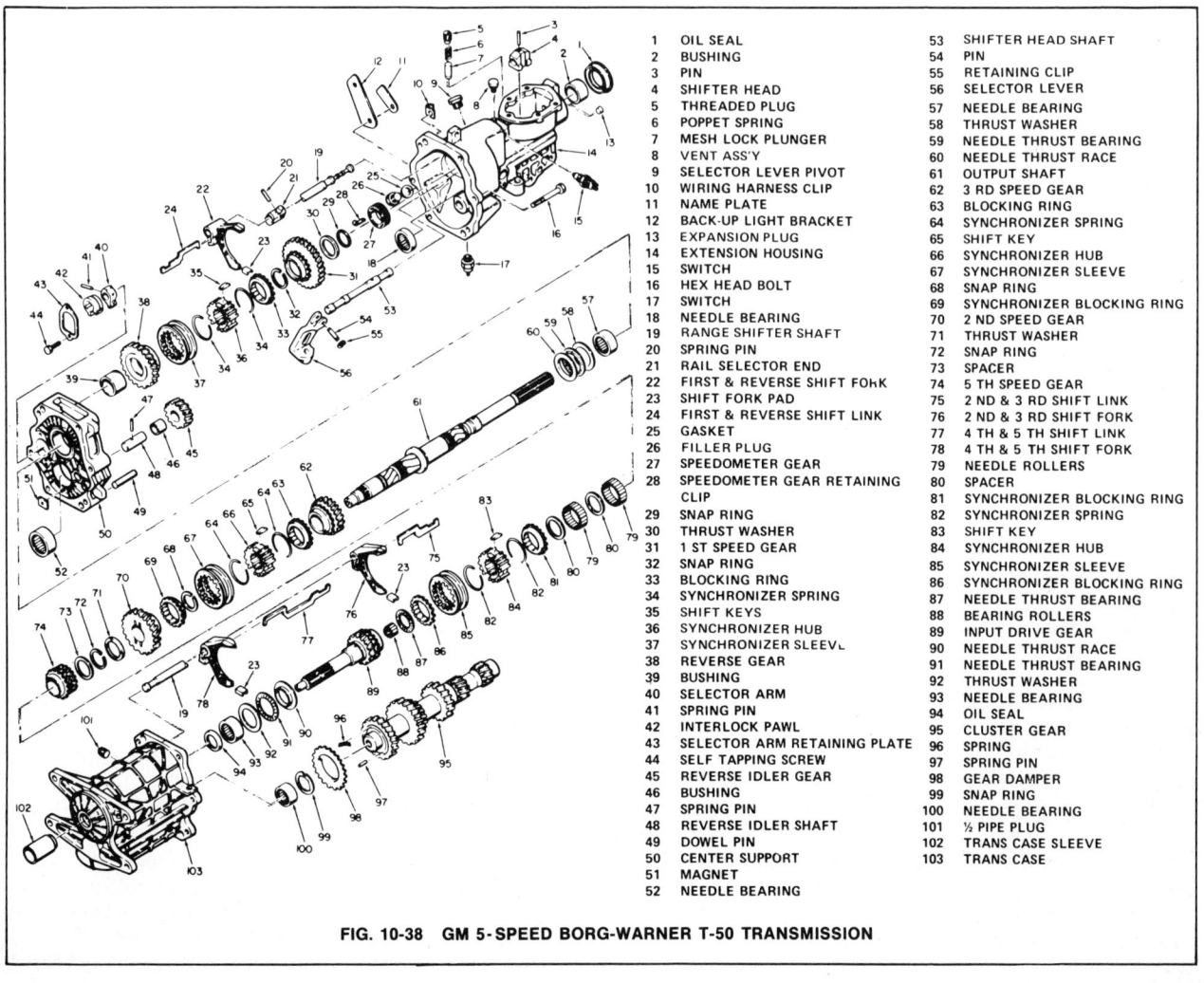

1	OIL SEAL	53	SHIFTER HEAD SHAFT
2	BUSHING	54	PIN
3	PIN	55	RETAINING CLIP
4	SHIFTER HEAD	56	SELECTOR LEVER
5	THREADED PLUG	57	NEEDLE BEARING
6	POPPET SPRING	58	THRUST WASHER
7	MESH LOCK PLUNGER	59	NEEDLE THRUST BEARING
8	VENT ASS'Y	60	NEEDLE THRUST RACE
9	SELECTOR LEVER PIVOT	61	OUTPUT SHAFT
10	WIRING HARNESS CLIP	62	3 RD SPEED GEAR
11	NAME PLATE	63	BLOCKING RING
12	BACK-UP LIGHT BRACKET	64	SYNCHRONIZER SPRING
13	EXPANSION PLUG	65	SHIFT KEY
14	EXTENSION HOUSING	66	SYNCHRONIZER HUB
15	SWITCH	67	SYNCHRONIZER SLEEVE
16	HEX HEAD BOLT	68	SNAP RING
17	SWITCH	69	SYNCHRONIZER BLOCKING RING
18	NEEDLE BEARING	70	2 ND SPEED GEAR
19	RANGE SHIFTER SHAFT	71	THRUST WASHER
20	SPRING PIN	72	SNAP RING
21	RAIL SELECTOR END	73	SPACER
22	FIRST & REVERSE SHIFT FORK	74	5 TH SPEED GEAR
23	SHIFT FORK PAD	75	2 ND & 3 RD SHIFT LINK
24	FIRST & REVERSE SHIFT LINK	76	2 ND & 3 RD SHIFT FORK
25	GASKET	77	4 TH & 5 TH SHIFT LINK
26	FILLER PLUG	78	4 TH & 5 TH SHIFT FORK
27	SPEEDOMETER GEAR	79	NEEDLE ROLLERS
28	SPEEDOMETER GEAR RETAINING CLIP	80	SPACER
		81	SYNCHRONIZER BLOCKING RING
29	SNAP RING	82	SYNCHRONIZER SPRING
30	THRUST WASHER	83	SHIFT KEY
31	1 ST SPEED GEAR	84	SYNCHRONIZER HUB
32	SNAP RING	85	SYNCHRONIZER SLEEVE
33	BLOCKING RING	86	SYNCHRONIZER BLOCKING RING
34	SYNCHRONIZER SPRING	87	NEEDLE THRUST BEARING
35	SHIFT KEYS	88	BEARING ROLLERS
36	SYNCHRONIZER HUB	89	INPUT DRIVE GEAR
37	SYNCHRONIZER SLEEVE	90	NEEDLE THRUST RACE
38	REVERSE GEAR	91	NEEDLE THRUST BEARING
39	BUSHING	92	THRUST WASHER
40	SELECTOR ARM	93	NEEDLE BEARING
41	SPRING PIN	94	OIL SEAL
42	INTERLOCK PAWL	95	CLUSTER GEAR
43	SELECTOR ARM RETAINING PLATE	96	SPRING
44	SELF TAPPING SCREW	97	SPRING PIN
45	REVERSE IDLER GEAR	98	GEAR DAMPER
46	BUSHING	99	SNAP RING
47	SPRING PIN	100	NEEDLE BEARING
48	REVERSE IDLER SHAFT	101	½ PIPE PLUG
49	DOWEL PIN	102	TRANS CASE SLEEVE
50	CENTER SUPPORT	103	TRANS CASE
51	MAGNET		
52	NEEDLE BEARING		

FIG. 10-38 GM 5-SPEED BORG-WARNER T-50 TRANSMISSION

5. Supporting the rail, drive the rail selector pin out and remove the rail.

6. Depress the speedometer-gear retainer clip, and remove the gear and retainer from the output shaft.

7. Expand and remove the snap ring, then remove the thrust washer, first gear and the synchronizer ring from the output shaft.

8. Expand and remove the snap ring behind the synchronizer hub.

9. Remove first/reverse shift link by moving the shift rail to locate the pawl for link removal.

10. Slide the first/reverse synchronizer, shift fork and rail to withdraw the assembly from the transmission.

11. Remove the reverse idler gear from the reverse idler shaft, and slide the reverse gear from the output shaft.

12. Move the interlock pawl until the second/third shift fork and link can be removed.

13. Repeat Step 12 and remove the fourth/fifth shift fork and link.

14. Separate the center support from the output shaft and cluster gear, then remove the needle thrust race and bearing from the output shaft.

15. Remove the cluster gear from the remaining gears.

16. Expand and remove the countershaft snap ring.

17. Remove the spring and gear from the countershaft, and separate the output shaft from the input shaft.

18. Remove the remaining parts from the output shaft.

INSPECTION

1. Wash the transmission case inside and out with solvent.

2. Inspect the case for cracks, the front and rear faces for burrs, and the bearing bores.

3. Inspect all roller bearings in the center support, transmission case and extension housing, and replace if worn.

4. Check all gears for excessive wear, chips or cracks, and replace any that are worn or damaged.

5. Check the clutch sleeves for free movement on their hubs.

6. Replace worn or damaged shift pads on shift forks, if necessary.

CLUTCH KEY AND SPRING REPLACEMENT

Unlike other GM transmissions, the synchronizer assemblies use different hub splines. The hub and sleeve are a selective fit to obtain a maximum backlash of 0.002-in. Mated parts must be kept together to assure a correct sliding fit/backlash.

1. Mark the hub and sleeve for matching during reassembly.

2. Push the hub from the sleeve, and remove the keys/springs.

3. Fit one spring on each side of the hub so that all three keys are engaged by both springs, then slide the sleeve onto the hub, align the marks made in Step 1.

OIL SEAL AND BUSHING REPLACEMENT

1. Pry the old seal from the rear of the extension housing.

2. Drive out the old bushing, and press a new one in place.

3. Coat the I.D. of the new bushing and seal with SAE 90W transmission lubricant, and install the new seal.

4. If the drive-gear-bearing lip seal is to be replaced, pry out the old one, and install a new seal until it seats in its bore.

TRANSMISSION ASSEMBLY

1. Replace third gear on the output shaft with its coned end facing the shaft shoulder.

2. Replace the second/third synchronizer assembly with the sleeve chamfer facing toward the mainshaft front.

3. Install the snap ring in the shaft groove in front of the synchronizer hub.

4. Fit the coned end of the second gear into the synchronizer ring, and position a thrust washer on the face of the gear.

5. Install another snap ring in front of the thrust washer, and seat it in its shaft groove.

6. Replace fifth gear on the output shaft to rest against the thrust washer. Fit one needle spacer over the shaft and into the gear bore. Now install a row of 46 needle bearings, a second spacer, a second row of 46 bearings and a third spacer, using petroleum jelly or light grease to retain them in place.

7. Replace the fourth/fifth synchronizer on the mainshaft with its chamfered sleeve end facing to the transmission front.

8. Place 19 needle bearings into the second step of the input shaft bore, holding them in place with petroleum jelly or light grease. Lower the shaft over the output shaft end carefully to prevent disturbing the bearings.

9. Mesh the cluster gear and input-shaft gear teeth, and assemble on the output shaft.

10. Install a needle thrust washer and thrust plate against the output shaft shoulder.

11. Fit the interlock pawl into the center support bore, and assemble the retaining plate with the hex head screws.

12. Place the needle bearings in the center support races, using petroleum jelly or light grease to hold them in place.

13. Fit the center support over the output shaft and cluster gear.

14. Fit the reverse gear and bushing assembly over the output shaft, resting it on the center support.

15. Install the reverse idler gear and bushing on the reverse idler shaft.

16. Fit the fourth/fifth link into the shift fork, and position the interlock pawl to allow the shift link to be assembled through the center support's outboard slot (as seen from the rear of the transmission). Engage the synchronizer collar and shift fork.

17. Position the interlock pawl to allow the second/third shift link to be assembled in the middle slot, with the shift fork assembled to the link and engaged with the second/third shift collar.

18. Position the interlock pawl to allow the first/reverse shift link to be installed in the inboard slot of the center support.

19. Fit the reverse shift link into the shift fork, and position the selector arm over the shift rail, aligning the spring pin holes. Replace the spring pin.

20. Fit the shift rail through the shift fork from front to rear, with its notches located at the rear.

21. Hook the shift fork over the first/reverse synchronizer sleeve, and slide the synchronizer hub over the output shaft as the shift rail is inserted through the interlock pawl, second/third and fourth/fifth shift forks. Replace the snap ring in the shaft groove.

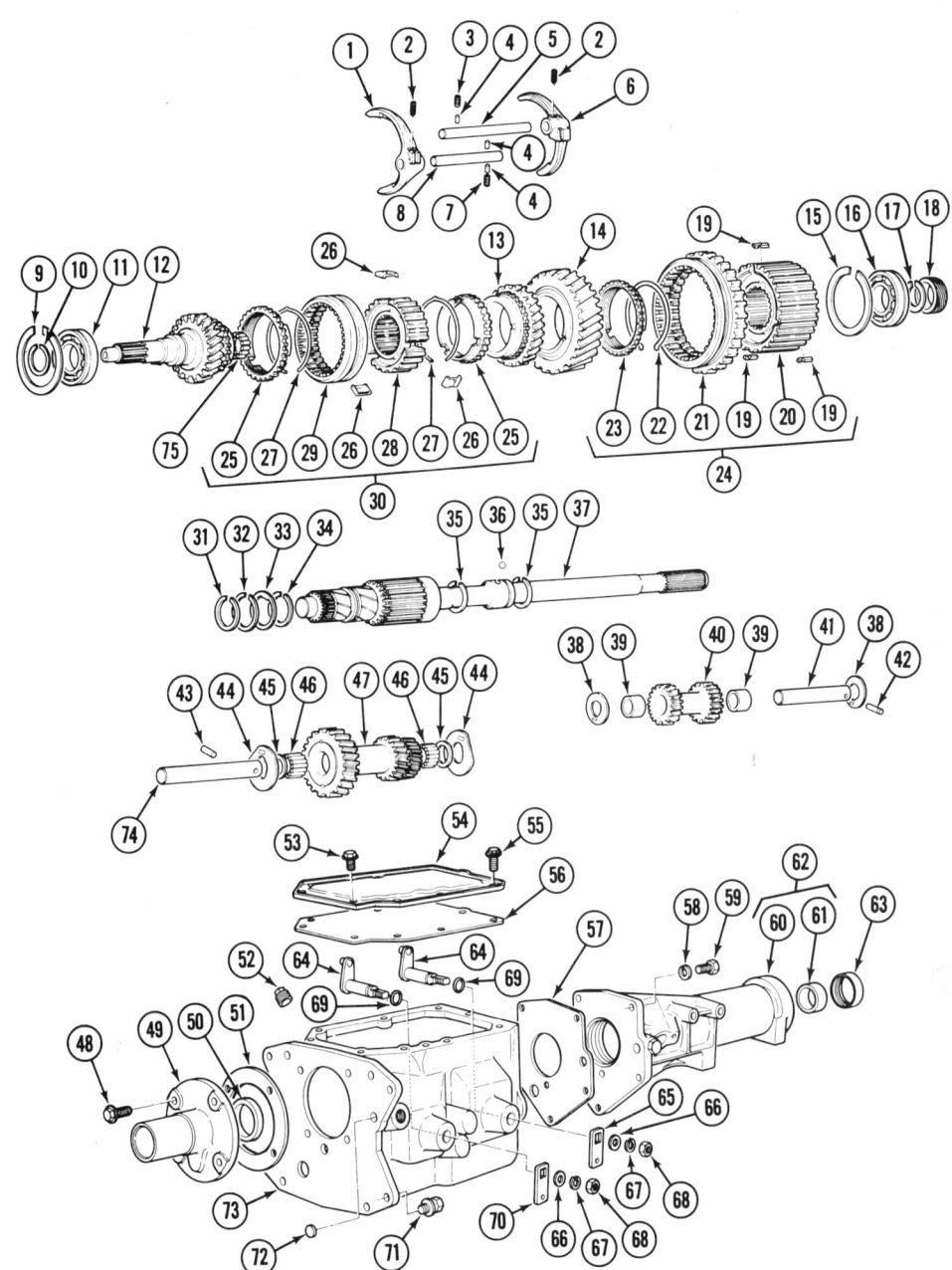

1. **Fork, Second and Third Shifter**
2. **Setscrew, Shifter Fork (2)**
3. **Spring, Upper Detent (Long)**
4. **Plugs, Gear Shift Detent and Interlock (3)**
5. **Shift Rail, First and Reverse**
6. **Fork, First and Reverse Shifter**
7. **Spring, Lower Detent (Short)**
8. **Shift Rail, Second and Third**
9. **Ring, Locating (Snap) Front Bearing**
10. **Ring, Retaining (Snap) Front Bearing to Clutch Shaft**
11. **Bearing, Front**
12. **Shaft, Clutch**
13. **Gear, Second**
14. **Gear, First**
15. **Ring, Locating (Snap) Rear Bearing**
16. **Bearing, Rear**
17. **Ring, Retaining (Snap) Rear Bearing**
18. **Gear, Speedometer Drive**
19. **Insert, First and Reverse Synchronizer (3)**
20. **Hub, First and Reverse**
21. **Sleeve and Gear, First and Reverse**
22. **Spring, Insert, First and Reverse Synchronizer**
23. **Ring, Blocking, First and Reverse Synchronizer**
24. **Synchronizer Assembly, First and Reverse**
25. **Ring, Blocking, Second and Third Synchronizer (2)**

26. **Insert, Second and Third Synchronizer (3)**
27. **Spring, Insert, Second—Third Synchronizer (2)**
28. **Hub, Second and Third**
29. **Sleeve, Second and Third Synchronizer**
30. **Second—Third Synchronizer Assembly**
31. **Ring, Retaining (Snap) Output Shaft**
32. **Ring, Retaining (Snap) First Gear**
33. **Washer, Thrust (Tabbed) First Gear**
34. **Ring, Retaining (Snap) First-Reverse Hub**
35. **Ring, Retaining (Snap) (2) Rear Bearing and Speedometer Gear**
36. **Lock Ball, ¼ Diameter—Speedometer Gear**
37. **Shaft, Output**
38. **Washer, Thrust, Reverse Idler Gear (2)**
39. **Bushing, Reverse Idler Gear (2)**
40. **Gear, Reverse Idler**
41. **Shaft, Reverse Idler Gear**
42. **Pin, Roll, Reverse Idler Gear Shaft**
43. **Pin, Roll, Countershaft**
44. **Washer, Thrust, Countershaft Gear (2)**
45. **Retainer, Countershaft Needle Bearing**
46. **Needle Bearing, Countershaft Gear (50)**
47. **Gear, Countershaft**
48. **Bolt, Front Bearing Cap**
49. **Cap, Front Bearing**

50. **Oil Seal, Front Bearing Cap**
51. **Gasket, Front Bearing Cap**
52. **Plug, Transmission Fill**
53. **Bolt, Top Cover**
54. **Top Cover, Case**
55. **Bolt, Top Cover**
56. **Gasket, Top Cover**
57. **Gasket, Extension Housing**
58. **Lockwasher, Extension Housing Bolt (5)**
59. **Bolt, Extension Housing**
60. **Extension Housing**
61. **Bushing, Extension Housing (Included with Housing)**
62. **Housing Assembly, Extension**
63. **Seal, Oil, Extension Housing**
64. **Shaft, Shifter Fork**
65. **Lever, First and Reverse Shifter**
66. **Flatwasher, Shifter Levers (2)**
67. **Lock, Washer Shifter Levers (2)**
68. **Nut, Hex, Shifter Levers (2)**
69. **O-Ring, Shifter Shaft (2)**
70. **Lever, Second and Third Shifter**
71. **Bolt, Transmission Mounting (4)**
72. **Plug, Expansion**
73. **Case, Transmission**
74. **Countershaft**
75. **Bearings, Clutch Shaft Roller**

FIG. 10-39   FORD RAN/CHRYSLER A-390/AMC 150T DISASSEMBLY

22. Install a synchronizer ring, first gear and a thrust washer on the output shaft behind the first/reverse synchronizer assembly, and secure with a snap ring.

23. Replace speedometer drive gear and retainer clip.

24. Position the rail selector end over the shift rail. Align the holes, and install the spring pin.

25. Fit the selector lever to the shorter shift rail, and install the pin and two retainer clips.

26. Press a new seal into the extension and, using petroleum jelly or light grease to hold in place, install the needle bearings in the extension housing race.

27. Fit the selector lever/shift rail into the extension housing, and insert the shift rail in the shifter head as the rail appears in the housing opening. *Do not* replace the spring pin yet.

28. Apply a 1/32-in. continuous bead of sealer to the transmission case and extension housing faces.

29. Fit the extension housing over the output shaft and slide the end of the rail selector lever into the housing.

30. Place the lipped thrust race, needle thrust washer and flat-thrust-washer race over the input shaft, then fit the case to the front of the center support.

31. Install the bolts to hold the extension housing and transmission case to the center support. Torque bolts to 26 ft.-lbs.

32. Replace the spring pin in the shifter head and shift rail.

33. Install the mesh lock plunger, poppet spring and threaded plug.

34. Coat the selector lever pivot with a sealer (Loctite #92), and install in the transmission case.

FORD MOTOR COMPANY

Ford and Mercury divisions have used the following transmissions since 1970, all representative of the fully synchronized, constant-mesh design:

3-SPEED RAN/RAB—1970-77 Ford/Mercury; 1978 Fairmont/Zephyr; 1975-79 Chrysler Corporation cars; 1978-79 AMC Pacer/Concord/Spirit/AMX; 1974-78 Gremlin/Hornet/Matador; 1970-71 Buick/Oldsmobile/Pontiac. A RAT version was used in 1970-71 Ford/Mercury cars equipped with the 390-cu.-in. and larger engines.

4-SPEED RUG—1970-74 Mustang/Cougar/Torino/Montego. This heavy-duty 4-speed was produced in both close- and wide-ratio versions. Overdrive versions are used for 1977-79 Granada/Monarch and 1979 Fairmont/Zephyr.

4-SPEED 71-72WG (English)—1971-73 1600cc Pinto.

4-SPEED 71-72WG, 74-75WT, 77-79ET (Germany)—All Pinto/Bobcat/Fairmont/Zephyr; 1978 Gremlin with 4-cyl. engine. Uses metric fasteners.

4-SPEED RAD (Borg-Warner SR4)—1975-78 Mustang II, 1979 Mustang/Capri; 1978-79 AMC 6-cyl. engines. Uses metric fasteners.

3-SPEED FORD RAN; CHRYSLER A-390; AMC 150T TRANSMISSIONS

TRANSMISSION DISASSEMBLY (Fig. 10-39)

1. Drain the lubricant by removing the drain plug. On models without a drain plug, remove lower extension-housing bolt.

2. Unbolt and remove the case cover, discarding the old gasket.

150-T—Remove the TCS and back-up lamp switches from the left side of the case/extension housing.

3. Remove the retaining spring and detent plug from

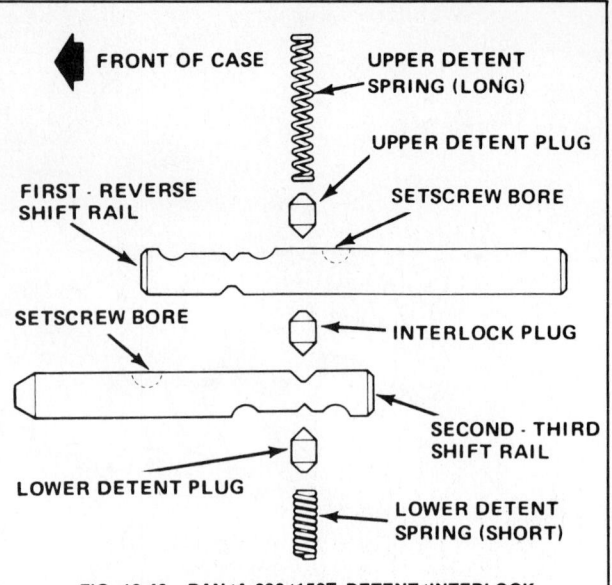

FIG. 10-40 RAN/A-390/150T DETENT/INTERLOCK PLUG ARRANGEMENT

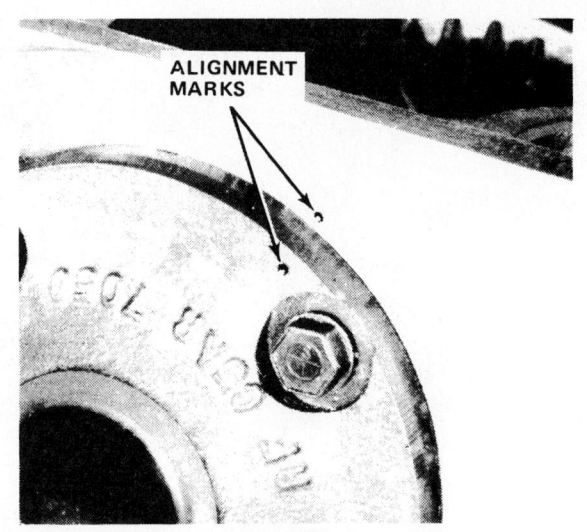

FIG. 10-41 RAN/A-390/150T BEARING-CAP ALIGNMENT MARKS

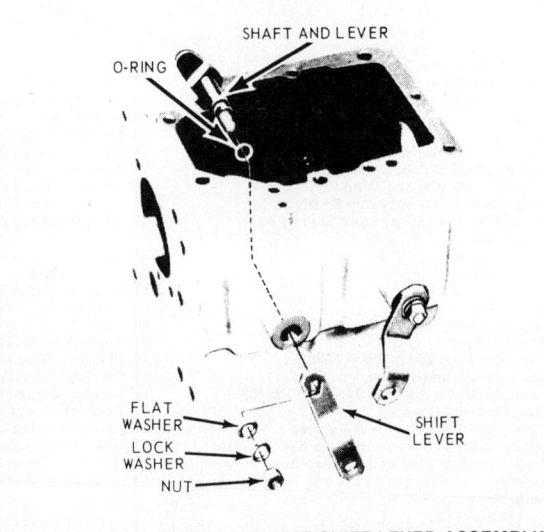

FIG. 10-42 RAN/A-390/150T SHIFT LEVER ASSEMBLY

the transmission case with a pencil-type magnet **(Fig. 10-40)**.

4. Unbolt and remove the extension housing, discarding the old gasket.

150T equipped with overdrive—Remove the pump-drive-key cam and snap ring from the output shaft.

5. Punch an alignment mark on the front bearing retainer and case. Unbolt and remove the retainer, and discard the old gasket **(Fig. 10-41)**.

6. Remove the lubricant filler plug from the right side of the transmission case. Insert a ¼-in. punch in the plug opening, and drive out the roll pin.

7. If the countershaft bore at the front of the case uses an expansion plug, tap the countershaft from the rear of the case with a dummy shaft, and remove the plug.

8. On other models, the countershaft from the rear of the case, and lower the countergear and the thrust washers to the case bottom.

9. Remove the speedometer drive gear. This will be held in place by either a snap ring/lock ball or a retaining clip.

10. Remove the output-shaft-bearing snap ring and bearing.

11. Position both shift levers in the neutral position.

12. Remove the setscrew holding the first/reverse shift fork to the shift rail and slide rail from the rear of the case.

13. Move the first/reverse synchronizer as far forward as possible, then rotate the first/reverse shift fork upward and remove it from the case.

14. Place the second/third shift fork in second gear position to provide access to the setscrew. Remove the setscrew from the fork, and turn the shift rail 90°.

15. 1974-75 models—Remove the seat-belt sensor-switch retaining clamp and bolt.

16. Use the pencil magnet to lift the interlock plug from the case **(Fig. 10-40)**.

17. Remove the second/third shift-rail expansion plug by tapping on the shift-rail inner end or inserting a ¼-in. punch through the rear-case access hole to drive the shift rail out the front. Remove the rail.

18. 1974-75 models—Remove the seat-belt sensor-switch actuator plunger and spring.

19. Lift the second/third shift-rail detent plug and spring from the detent bore **(Fig. 10-40)**.

20. Move the input gear and shaft to the front. Remove the snap ring, then lift the input shaft/gear from the case.

21. Turn the second/third shift fork upward and remove.

22. Lift the output shaft assembly from the top of the case.

23. Lift the reverse idler gear/thrust washers from the case.

24. Remove the countershaft gear, thrust washers and dummy shaft from the case.

25. Expand and remove the output-shaft front snap ring. Slide the synchronizer and second gear from the shaft.

26. Remove the next snap ring and a tanged thrust washer from the output shaft, sliding first gear and a synchronizer ring off the shaft.

27. Remove the last snap ring, and use an arbor press to remove the first/reverse synchronizer hub. This is a press-fit on the output shaft, and *should not* be removed/installed by hammering or prying.

28. On those Fords equipped with a TRS switch, *do not* remove switch from case unless it is damaged.

CLEANING AND INSPECTION

1. Wash the transmission case inside and out with clean solvent.

2. Inspect the case for cracks, worn or damaged bearing bores, damaged threads or other defects.

3. Check the condition of all shift levers, forks, rails and shafts.

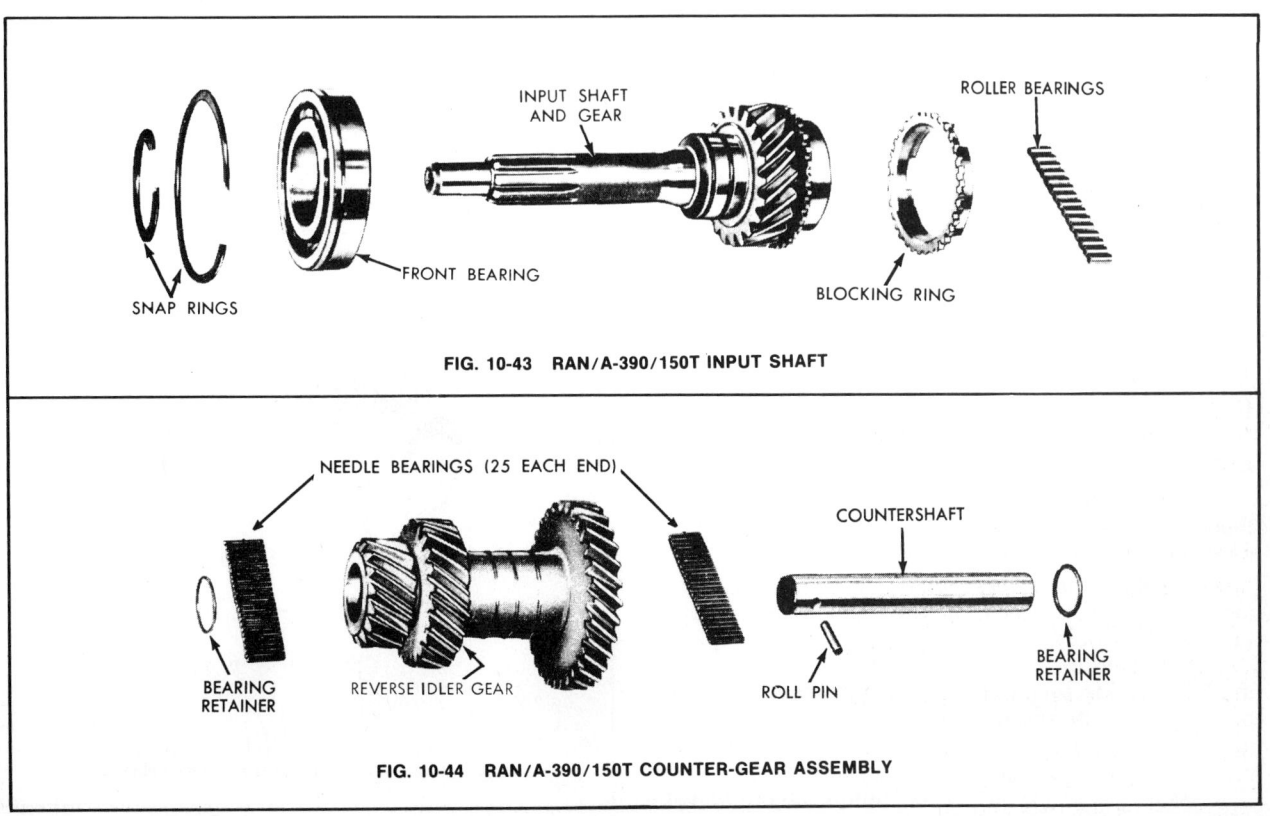

FIG. 10-43   RAN/A-390/150T INPUT SHAFT

FIG. 10-44   RAN/A-390/150T COUNTER-GEAR ASSEMBLY

4. Clean the ball bearings with solvent, and dry with compressed air, holding the bearing assembly to prevent rotation. Lubricate the bearing with a suitable bearing grease.

5. Inspect the ball bearing races for cracks, wear or roughness, and check the balls for looseness, wear, end play or other damage.

6. Check all gears for chipped, worn or broken teeth, and all shafts for wear, scoring or an out-of-round condition.

7. Check the synchronizer sleeves for free movement on their hubs and the synchronizer rings for rounded teeth or enlarged index slots.

SHIFT-LEVER SEAL REPLACEMENT
(Fig. 10-42)

1. Remove the shift lever nut, lockwasher and flat washer, then lift the lever from the shaft, sliding both from the case.

2. Remove and discard the shaft 0-ring seals; lubricate new seals with transmission lubricant, and install them on the shafts.

3. Replace the levers and shafts in the case, position a shift lever on each shaft, and fasten them in place with the flat washer, lockwasher and nut.

INPUT SHAFT BEARING
(Fig. 10-43)

1. Remove the input-shaft-bearing snap ring, and press the shaft from the bearing.

2. Press a new bearing on the shaft, and install the snap ring.

COUNTERSHAFT GEAR BEARINGS
(Fig. 10-44)

1. Lightly coat the bore of the countershaft at each end with grease.

2. Fit the dummy shaft through the bore, and install 25 roller bearings and a retaining washer in each end.

3. Place the countershaft gear, with the dummy shaft and bearings intact, in the transmission case.

4. Set the transmission case in a vertical position, align the gear bore and thrust washers with the case bores, and install the countershaft.

5. Return the case to a horizontal position, and use a feeler gauge to check the countershaft-gear end play. If not within 0.004-in. to 0.018-in., replace the thrust washers.

6. Install the dummy shaft in the countershaft gear after establishing end play with the countershaft in place. Remove the countershaft and let the gear stay at the bottom of the case until the output and input shafts have been replaced.

TRANSMISSION ASSEMBLY
(Figs. 10-39 & 10-40)

1. Position the two reverse-idler-gear thrust washers in the case, with grease to hold them in place.

2. Position the reverse idler gear and dummy shaft, then align the gear bore and thrust washers with the case bore, and install the reverse idler shaft.

3. Measure the reverse-idler-gear end play with a feeler gauge. If not within 0.004-in. to 0.018-in., replace the thrust washers.

4. Lubricate the output shaft with gear oil and press the first/reverse synchronizer and hub assembly on the output shaft with an arbor press. The teeth end of the gear must face the rear of the shaft. Install a synchronizer ring on the first gear cone.

5. Slide the first gear on the output shaft, with the synchronizer ring to the rear, rotating to engage the ring notches with the synchronizer inserts. Install the thrust washer and snap ring.

6. Install a synchronizer ring on the second gear cone.

7. Slide second gear, the synchronizer ring and the second/third synchronizer on the output shaft, with the synchronizer ring to the front. Rotate to engage the ring notches with the synchronizer inserts, and install a snap ring.

8. Lightly wipe the input shaft bore with grease—too much will plug the lubrication holes and block bearing lubrication. Replace the 15 bearings in the bore.

9. RAT model—Install the input gear/bearing through the top of the case, and the bore in the front of the case.

RAN model—Install the input gear/bearing through the front of the transmission case.

10. Replace the snap ring in the input-gear/bearing groove.

11. Place the output shaft assembly in the transmission case with the second/third shift fork on the second/third synchronizer.

12. 1974-75 models—Fit the seat-belt actuating spring inside the plunger, and install in the case bore.

13. Install the detent plug spring and plug in the case. Move the second/third synchronizer to second gear position (towards the transmission rear). Align the fork and install the second/third shift rail while depressing the detent plug. When the rail enters the bore,

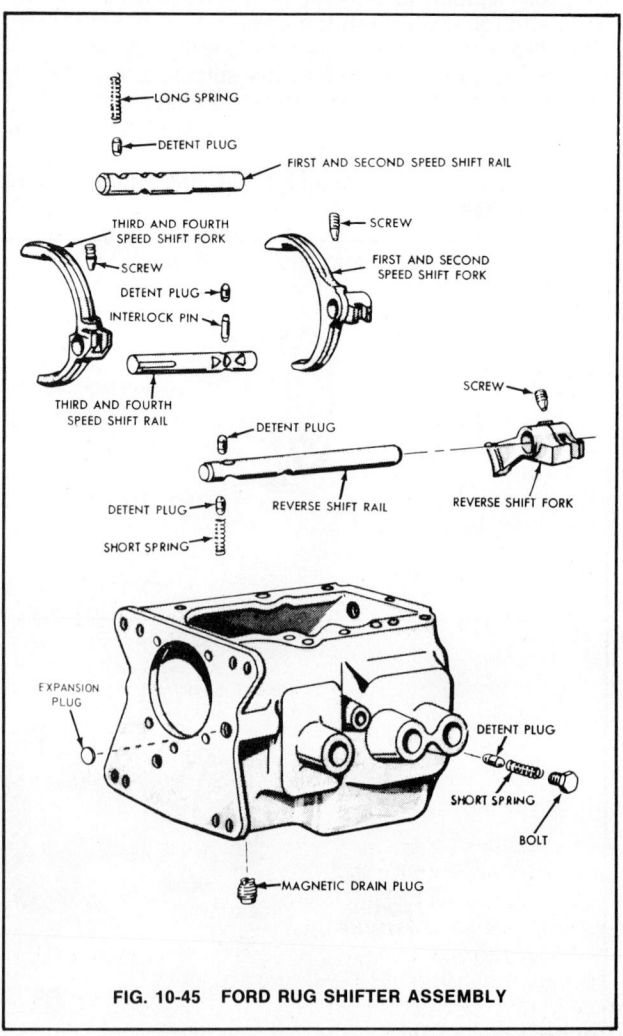

FIG. 10-45 FORD RUG SHIFTER ASSEMBLY

move it inward until the detent plug engages the forward (second gear) notch.

14. Fasten the fork to the shaft with the setscrew, and move the synchronizer to the neutral position.

15. 1974-75 models—Replace the seat-belt sensor switch and oil seal. Install the retaining clamp, and torque bolt to 10-15 ft.-lbs.

16. Replace the interlock plug in the case.

17. Move the first/reverse synchronizer forward to the first gear position, fit the first/reverse shift fork in the first/reverse synchronizer groove. Turn the fork and install the first/reverse shift rail; when center (neutral) notch is lined up with the detent bore, replace the setscrew.

18. Use a *new* shift-rail expansion plug, and install it in the case front.

19. Holding the input shaft and synchronizer ring in place, move the output shaft forward. This will seat the pilot in the input-gear roller bearings.

20. Hold the output shaft, and tap the input gear bearing in place. Use a new gasket, and install the front bearing retainer with the oil return slot facing to the bottom of the case. Torque attaching bolts 30 to 36 ft.-lbs.

21. Replace the snap ring on the rear bearing. Install the bearing on the output shaft, with the snap ring end facing to the rear of the shaft. Press the bearing into place, and install the snap ring.

22. Replace the speedometer drive gear with lock ball/detent or retaining clip, according to design.

23. Position the transmission case vertically, and align the countershaft gear and thrust washers with the case bore.

24. Install the countershaft to push the dummy shaft from the countershaft gear, making sure that the roll pin hole lines up with the case hole. Install the roll pin when the shaft is in place.

25. Some countershafts are a press-fit; others have a countershaft-to-case clearance of 0.020-in. at the front bore and 0.010-in. at the rear bore. On these models, install a new expansion plug in the front-case countershaft bore.

26. Apply sealer to a new extension housing gasket, and fit it to the case. Apply sealer to the extension housing bolts, install the lockwashers, and torque the bolts 42 to 50 ft.-lbs.

27. Replace the filler/drain plugs (where used). The magnetic plug should be installed in the case bottom (where used).

28. With the transmission in gear, pour transmission lubricant over the geartrain while turning the input/output shaft.

29. Replace the remaining detent plug and spring in the case; the cover will hold the spring when replaced.

30. Apply sealer to a new cover gasket. Install the gasket and cover, and torque the bolts 14 to 19 ft.-lbs.

4-SPEED RUG

The following changes were made in all 1979 RUG applications:

1. Aluminum case and extension housing.
2. Shift mechanism is completely enclosed.
3. A single rail serves as the control rod and operates all gear positions.
4. Periodic shift rod adjustment is not required since shift control rod is also the single shift rail.
5. Input/output shaft bearings are slip-fit. Gear arrangement is identical to earlier RUG models. The

procedure for shift lever disassembly of the revised RUG follows Transmission Disassembly/Assembly procedures for the earlier model.

TRANSMISSION DISASSEMBLY
(Figs. 10-45 & 10-46)

1. Drain the lubricant by removing the drain plug. On models without a drain plug, remove the lower extension housing bolt.

2. Unbolt and remove the case cover, discarding the old gasket.

3. Remove the retaining spring and detent plug from the transmission case with a pencil-type magnet.

4. Unbolt and remove the extension housing, discarding the old gasket.

5. Unbolt and remove the input bearing retainer, discarding the old gasket.

6. Drive the countershaft out of the rear with a dummy shaft, and lower the countergear and thrust washers to the case bottom.

7. Position the first/second and reverse shift levers in neutral, and the third/fourth shift lever in third gear.

8. Remove the third/fourth shift-fork setscrew, and tap the inner end of the shift rail to unseat the expansion plug. Remove the plug and the third/fourth shift rail from the case. Be careful not to lose the small pin from the rail.

9. Remove the first/second shift-fork setscrew, and slide the first/second shift rail from the rear of the case.

10. Remove the interlock plug/detent spring with a pencil magnet.

11. Remove the speedometer drive gear. This will either be held in place by a snap ring and lock ball, or a retaining clip.

12. Remove the output-shaft-bearing snap ring and the bearing.

13. Remove the input shaft, bearing and synchronizer ring from the front of the case.

14. With the output shaft positioned to the right side of the case, rotate the shift forks and remove them from the case.

15. Holding the thrust washer and first gear, lift the output shaft assembly from the case.

16. Remove the setscrew from the reverse-gear shift fork, and rotate the shift rail 90°, sliding it from the rear of the case, and removing the reverse shift fork.

17. Use the pencil magnet to remove the reverse detent plug/spring from the case.

18. Rotate and push the reverse-idler-gear shaft from the case with a dummy shaft, removing the reverse idler gear and thrust washers.

19. Remove the countergear and thrust washers with the dummy shaft intact.

20. Expand and remove the output-shaft front snap ring, sliding the third/fourth synchronizer ring and third gear from the shaft.

21. Expand and remove the next snap ring, sliding the thrust washer, second gear and the synchronizer ring from the shaft.

22. Expand and remove the last snap ring. Slide a thrust washer, first gear and the synchronizer from the shaft, and press the first/second synchronizer hub from the shaft with an arbor press. This is a press-fit and *should not* be removed/installed by hammering or prying. If so equipped *do not* remove the TRS switch from case. Removal will damage sealing tape on threads.

CLEANING AND INSPECTION

1. Wash the transmission case inside and out with clean solvent.

2. Inspect the case for cracks, worn or damaged bearing bores, damaged threads or other defects.

3. Check the condition of all shift levers, forks, rails and shafts.

4. Clean the ball bearings with solvent, and dry with compressed air, holding the bearing assembly to prevent rotation. Lubricate the bearing with a suitable bearing grease.

5. Inspect the ball bearing races for cracks, wear or roughness, and check balls for looseness, wear, end play or other damage.

6. Check all gears for chipped, worn or broken teeth, and all shafts for wear, scoring or an out-of-round condition.

7. Check the synchronizer sleeves for free movement on their hubs and the synchronizer rings for rounded teeth or enlarged index slots.

SHIFT-LEVER-CAM AND SHAFT-SEAL REPLACEMENT
(Fig. 10-47)

1. Remove the shift lever nuts, lockwashers and flat washers. Lift the three levers from their shafts, sliding the cam and shaft from the case.

2. Remove and discard the shaft O-ring seals; lubricate new seals with transmission lubricant and install them on the shafts.

3. Replace the levers and shafts in the case, posi-

tion a shift lever on each shaft, and fasten in place.

INPUT SHAFT BEARING
(Fig. 10-48)

1. Remove the input-shaft-bearing snap ring, and press the shaft from the bearing.

2. Press a new bearing on shaft, install snap ring.

COUNTERSHAFT GEAR BEARINGS
(Fig. 10-49)

1. Lightly coat the bore of the countershaft at each end with grease.

2. Fit the dummy shaft through the bore, and install 21 roller bearings and a retaining washer in each end.

3. Place the countershaft gear, with the dummy shaft and bearings installed, in the transmission case.

4. Set the transmission case in a vertical position, align the gear bore and thrust washers with the case bores, and install the countershaft.

5. Return the case to a horizontal position, and use a feeler gauge to check the countershaft-gear end play. If not within 0.004-in. to 0.018-in., replace the thrust washers.

6. Install the dummy shaft in the countershaft gear, after establishing end play with the countershaft in place. Remove the countershaft, and let the gear remain at the bottom of the case until the output and input shafts have been replaced.

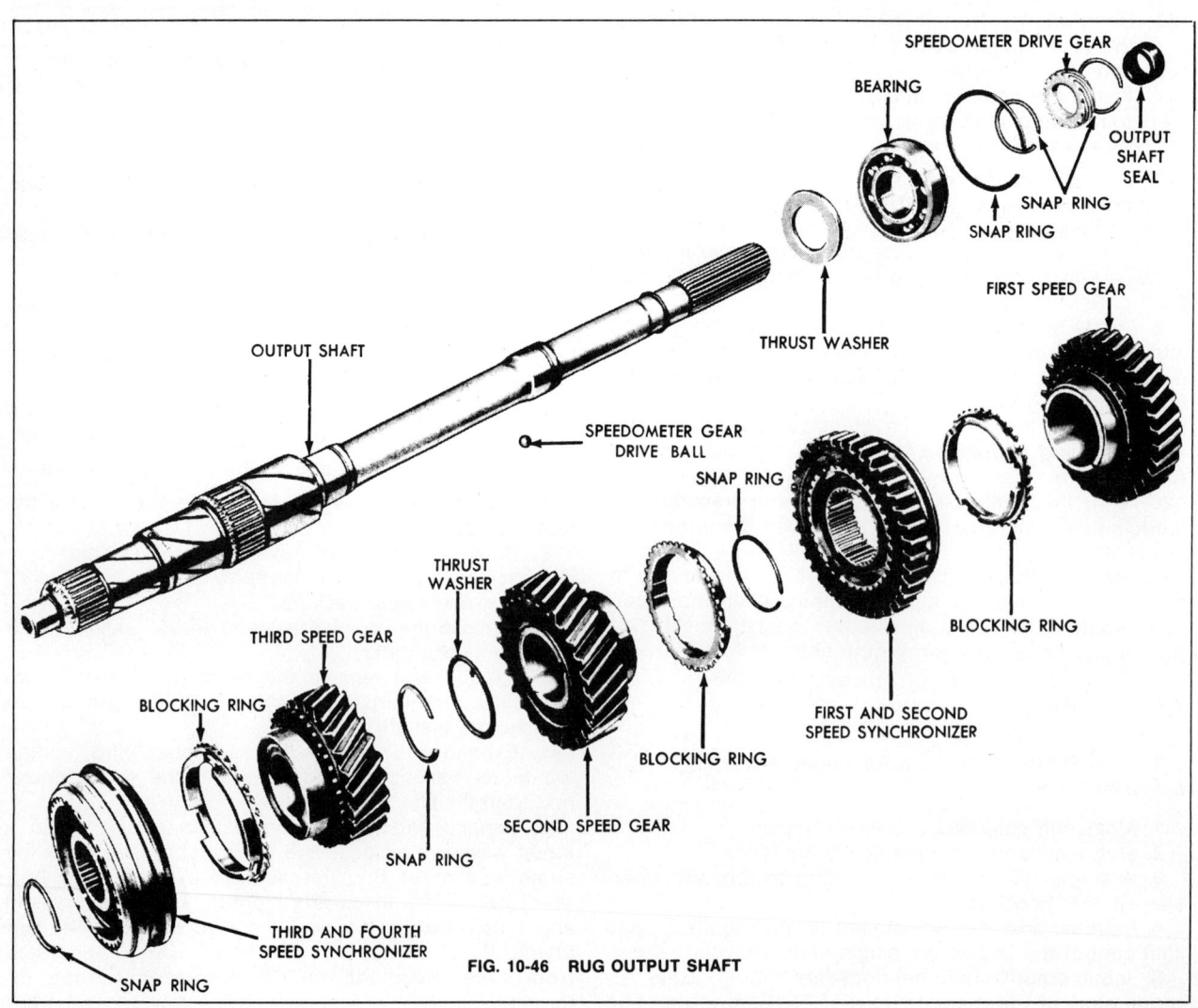

FIG. 10-46 RUG OUTPUT SHAFT

REVERSE-IDLER-GEAR BEARINGS

(Fig. 10-50)

1. Remove the reverse-idler sliding gear from the reverse idler gear.

2. Remove the dummy shaft, two bearing-retaining washers and 44 roller bearings from the reverse-idler-gear bore.

3. Clean and inspect all parts.

4. Lightly coat the bore of the reverse idler gear at each end with grease.

5. Fit the dummy shaft in place, and install 22 roller bearings and a retaining washer at each end.

6. Replace the reverse-idler sliding gear on the reverse idler gear, with shift fork groove facing front.

TRANSMISSION ASSEMBLY

(Figs. 10-45 & 10-46)

1. Position the two reverse-idler-gear thrust washers in the case, with grease to hold them in place.

2. Position the reverse-idler sliding gear, reverse idler gear and dummy shaft, then align the gear bore and thrust washers with the case bore, and install the reverse idler shaft. Shift groove should face to the front.

3. Measure the reverse-idler-gear end play with a feeler gauge. If not within 0.004-in. to 0.018-in., replace the thrust washers.

4. Install the reverse-gear shift-rail detent spring/ plug in the case. With the reverse shift fork on the reverse-idler sliding gear, replace the shift rail from the rear of the case, and install the setscrew.

5. Replace the first/second synchronizer on the front of the output shaft, with its shift groove facing to the rear. The hub should be pressed on, with its teeth end facing to the rear of the shaft.

6. Fit a synchronizer ring over the second gear cone, and install the unit on the output shaft with the ring notches engaging the synchronizer inserts. Install the thrust washer and snap ring.

7. Fit a synchronizer ring over the third gear cone, and install the unit on the output shaft with the coned surface facing to the front.

8. Replace the third/fourth synchronizer on the output shaft, rotating to engage the ring notches with the synchronizer inserts, and install the snap ring.

9. Fit a synchronizer ring over the first gear, and slide the unit on the rear of the output shaft with the synchronizer ring notches engaging the synchronizer inserts.

10. Replace the heavy thrust washer on the rear of the output shaft. Support both thrust washer and first gear, and lower the output shaft assembly into the case.

11. Place the first/second and third/fourth shift forks in the grooves on their respective gears, and rotate in place.

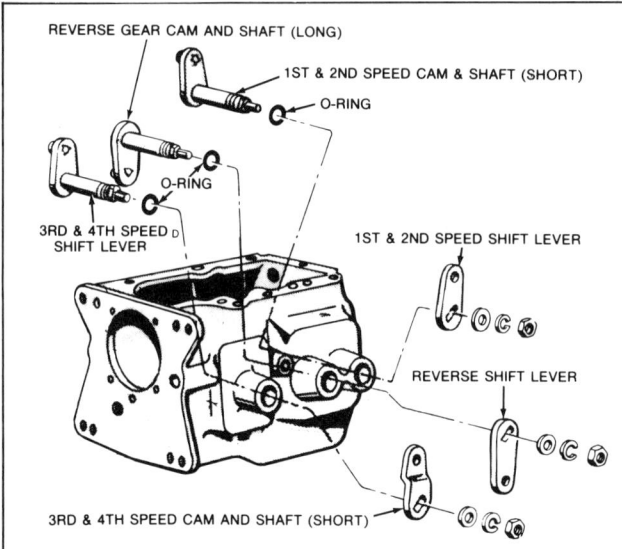

FIG. 10-47 RUG CAM/SEAL REPLACEMENT

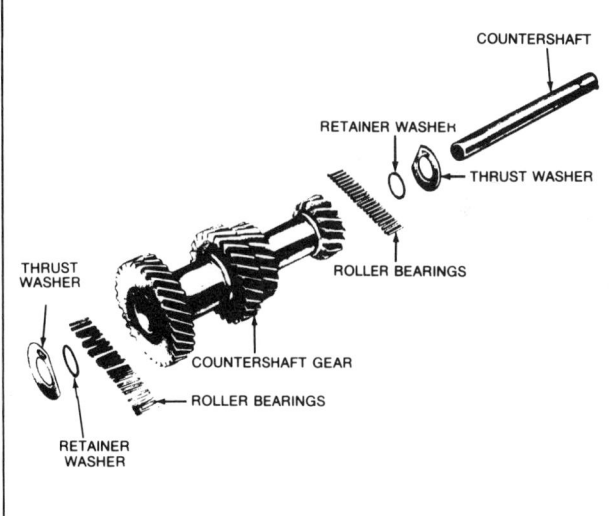

FIG. 10-49 RUG COUNTERSHAFT GEAR

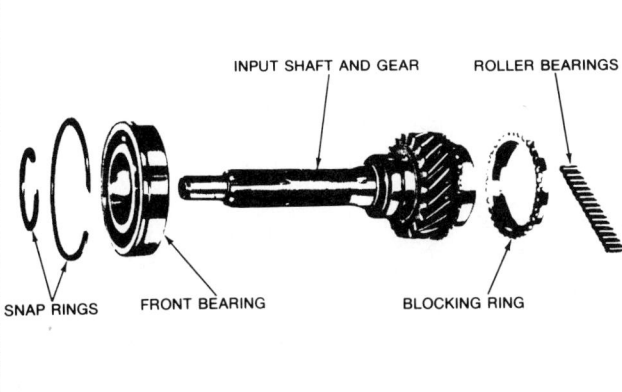

FIG. 10-48 RUG INPUT SHAFT

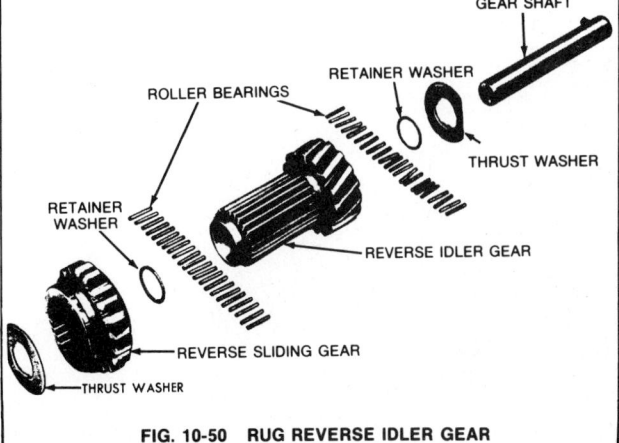

FIG. 10-50 RUG REVERSE IDLER GEAR

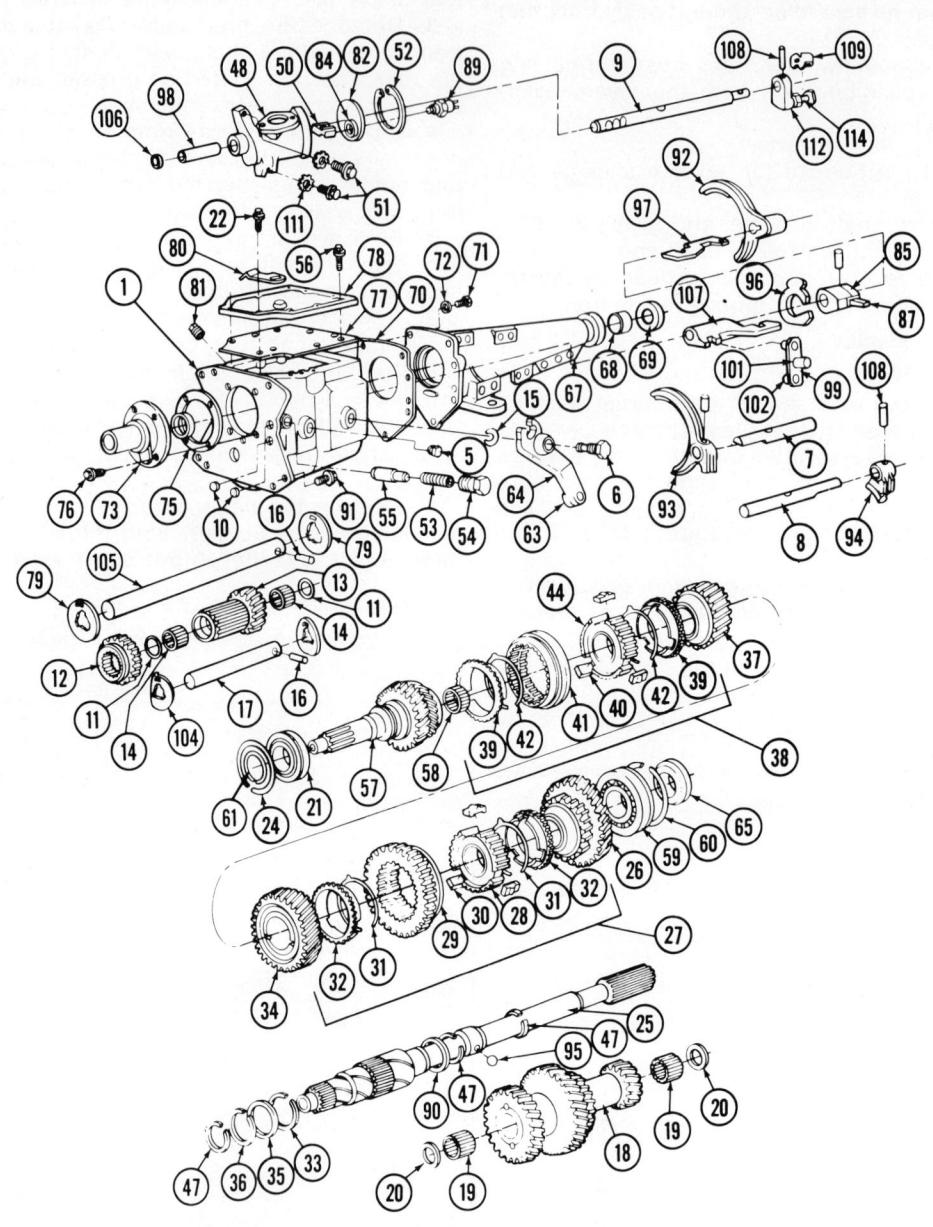

1. TRANSMISSION CASE	30. SYNCHRO. HUB INSERT	59. OUTPUT SHAFT BEARING	90. OUTPUT SHAFT THRUST WASHER
5. PLUG	31. SYNCHRO. RETAINING SPRING	60. SNAP RING	91. SCREW & WASHER ASSY
6. REVERSE RELAY PIVOT PIN	32. SYNCHRO. BLOCKING RING	61. SNAP RING	92. 1ST/2ND SHIFT FORK
7. 3RD/OVERDRIVE SHIFT RAIL	33. SYNCHRO. HUB-SNAP RING	63. SHIFT CONTROL FINGER PIN	93. 3RD/OVERDRIVE SHIFT FORK
8. REVERSE SHIFT RAIL	34. 2ND SPEED GEAR	64. REVERSE SHIFT RELAY LEVER	94. REVERSE SHIFT FORK
9. SHIFT CONTROL ROD	35. THRUST WASHER	65. SPEEDOMETER DRIVE GEAR	95. SPEEDOMETER DRIVE GEAR BALL
10. EXPANSION PLUG	36. RETAINING RING	67. EXTENSION HOUSING	96. SELECTOR INTERLOCK PLATE
11. 3/4 FLAT WASHER	37. OVERDRIVE GEAR	68. EXTENSION BUSHING	97. 1ST/2ND SELECTOR PLATE
12. REVERSE IDLER SLIDING GEAR	38. 3RD/OVERDRIVE GEAR SYNCHRONIZER	69. OIL SEAL	98. SHIFT ROD SLEEVE
13. REVERSE IDLER GEAR	39. SYNCHRO. BLOCKING RING	70. EXTENSION HOUSING GASKET	99. 3RD/OVERDRIVE SHIFT CONTROL LINK
14. IDLER SHAFT BEARING ROLLER	40. SYNCHRO. HUB INSERT	71. BOLT	101. SHIFT CONTROL LINK SHAFT
15. C-CLIP	41. CLUTCH HUB SLEEVE	72. LOCK WASHER	102. SHIFT CONTROL FINGER PIN
16. ROLL PIN	42. SYNCHRO. RETAINING SPRING	73. INPUT SHAFT BEARINGS RETAINER	104. THRUST WASHER
17. REVERSE IDLER GEAR SHAFT	44. 3RD/OVERDRIVE CLUTCH HUB	75. INPUT SHAFT BEARING RETAINER GASKET	105. COUNTER SHAFT
18. COUNTERSHAFT GEAR	47. SNAP RING	76. BOLT	106. SHIFT RAIL LIP SEAL
19. C SHAFT GEAR BEARING ROLLER	48. SHIFT CONTROL HOUSING	77. TRANS. CASE COVER GASKET	107. 3RD/OVERDRIVE SHIFT PAWL
20. WASHER	50. GEARSHIFT LEVER REVERSE STOP	78. TRANS. CASE COVER PLATE	108. ROLL PIN
21. INPUT SHAFT BEARING	51. BOLT	79. THRUST WASHER	109. SHIFT DAMPER BUSHING
22. SCREW	52. SNAP RING	80. RETAINER CLIP	111. LOCK WASHER
24. SNAP RING	53. DETENT SPRING	81. FILLER PLUG	112. SHIFT SHAFT OFFSET LEVER
25. OUTPUT SHAFT	54. SCREW	82. DUST COVER	114. SHIFT SHAFT OFFSET LEVER PIN
26. FIRST SPEED GEAR	55. DETENT PLUNGER	84. TURRET COVER RETAINER	
27. 1ST/2ND GEAR SYNCHRONIZER	56. SCREW	85. CONTROL SELECTOR ARM	
28. 1ST/2ND GEAR CLUTCH HUB	57. INPUT SHAFT	87. SELECTOR PIN	
29. REVERSE SLIDING GEAR	58. M'SHAFT BEARING ROLLERS	89. BACK-UP LAMP SWITCH	

FIG. 10-50A RUG SHIFT RAIL OVERDRIVE TRANSMISSION

12. Fit a detent plug in the detent bore, and move the reverse shift rail into neutral.

13. Apply grease to the third/fourth shift-rail interlock pin, and fit it in the shift rail.

14. With the third/fourth shift fork aligned with the shift rail bore, slide the rail in place with the three detents facing to the outside of the case.

15. Move the front synchronizer to third gear, and replace the third/fourth shift-fork setscrew.

16. Move the front synchronizer to neutral, and replace the third/fourth rail-detent plug, spring and bolt in the left side of the case. Fit the interlock pin in the detent case.

17. Move the first/second shift fork to align with the case bores, and slide the shift rail in place, fastening with the setscrew.

18. Lightly wipe the input shaft bore with grease—too much will plug the lubrication holes and block bearing lubrication. Replace the 15 bearings in the bore.

19. Place the front synchronizer ring in the third/fourth synchronizer, and replace the input shaft gear.

20. Fit a new gasket to the input-shaft bearing retainer. Using sealer, install and torque the attaching bolts 19 to 25 ft.-lbs.

21. Hold the output shaft, and tap the input gear bearing in place. Use a new gasket, and install the front bearing retainer, with the oil return slot facing to the bottom of the case. Torque the attaching bolts 30 to 36 ft.-lbs.

22. Replace the snap ring on the rear bearing. Install the bearing on the output shaft, with the snap ring end facing to the rear of the shaft. Press the bearing into place, and install the snap ring.

23. Replace the speedometer drive gear with lock ball/detent or retaining clip, according to design.

24. Position the transmission case vertically, and align the countershaft gear and thrust washers with the case bore.

25. Install the countershaft to push the dummy shaft from the countershaft gear, making sure the roll pin hole lines up with the case hole.

26. Replace the extension housing, using a new gasket. Apply sealer to the attaching bolts, and torque 42 to 50 ft.-lbs.

27. Replace the filler/drain plugs (where used). The magnetic plug should be installed in the case bottom (where used).

28. With the transmission in gear, pour transmission lubricant over the geartrain while turning the input/output shaft.

29. Replace the remaining detent plug and spring in the case; the cover will hold the spring when replaced.

30. Apply sealer to a new cover gasket. Install the gasket and cover, and torque the bolts 14 to 19 ft.-lbs.

31. Apply sealer to the third/fourth shift rail plug bore, and install a new expansion plug.

4-SPEED RUG WITH SINGLE RAIL SHIFT LEVER
SHIFT LEVER DISASSEMBLY
(Fig. 10-50A)

1. Drain the lubricant by removing the lowest extension housing-to-case bolt and lock washer.

2. Remove the back-up lamp switch and snap ring from the shift control housing.

3. Insert a brass drift through the top of the shift control housing and tap the housing cover free.

4. Use a punch to drive out the roll pin holding the

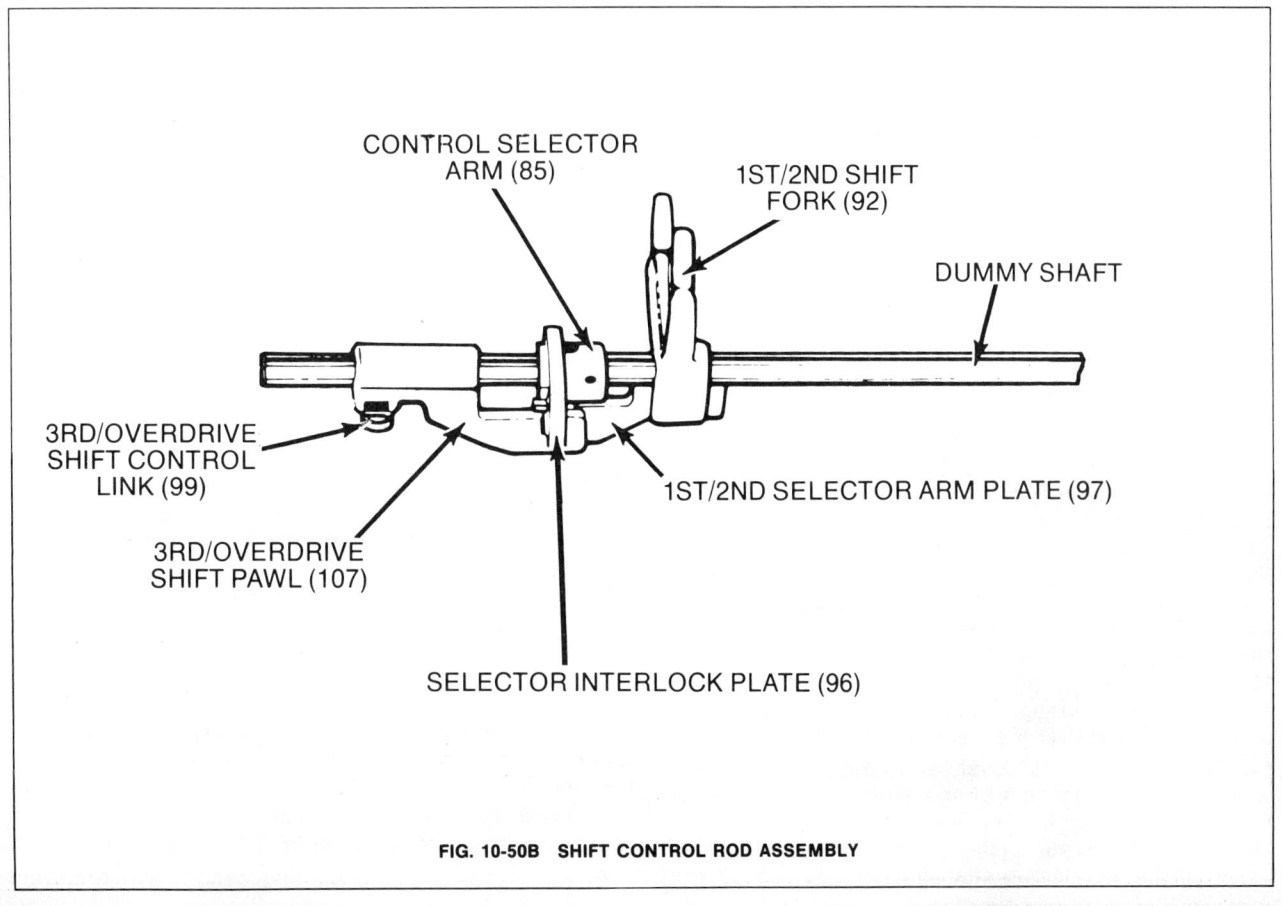

FIG. 10-50B SHIFT CONTROL ROD ASSEMBLY

control selector arm and shift control rod.

5. Remove the case screw holding the detent spring/plunger and withdraw the spring and plunger.

6. Withdraw the shift control rod from the end of the shift control housing.

7. Remove the control selector arm, 1st/2nd selector plate, 3rd/OD shift pawl and 1st/2nd shift fork from the transmission case.

8. Separate and remove the extension housing. Remove the speedometer drive gear/output shaft bearing snap ring and the speedometer drive gear ball.

9. Pry the output shaft slip-fit bearing free and remove.

10. Remove the selector interlock plate.

11. Remove the input shaft bearing retainer, gasket and snap ring, then remove the input shaft bearing.

12. Use a punch to drive out the roll pin holding the 3rd/OD shift fork and shift rail.

13. Tap the 3rd/OD shift rail and remove from front of the transmission case. Remove the 3rd/OD shift fork.

14. Remove the roll pin from the reverse shift fork, slide the reverse shift rail out through the rear of the case and remove the reverse shift fork.

15. Remove the C-clip and pivot pin, then remove the reverse gear shift relay lever.

16. Move the 3rd/OD shift control link to the center of the case and remove.

17. Remainder of transmission disassembly is identical to previous models.

SHIFT LEVER ASSEMBLY

(Fig. 10-50A and 10-50B)

1. Use a dummy shaft to assemble the following: 3rd/OD shift pawl, control selector arm, selector interlock plate, 1st/2nd shift selector plate and 1st/2nd shift fork in the case. Interlock 1st/2nd shift selector plate with the 1st/2nd shift fork before inserting the dummy shaft. The 3rd/OD shift pawl must engage the upper stud on the shift control link, and the roll pin hole in the control selector arm must be positioned to the rear of the case.

2. Install the input shaft bearing and snap ring.

3. Replace the output shaft bearing, snap ring, speedometer drive gear ball, drive gear and snap ring.

4. Attach the input shaft bearing retainer with a new gasket. Oil return notch in both retainer and gasket must face bottom of case. Install and torque attaching bolts.

5. Fit shift rail lip seal to transmission case and attach extension housing with a new gasket. Install and torque attaching bolts.

6. Replace the shift control rod protective sleeve and housing if they were removed.

7. Install shift control rod to replace dummy shaft. Replace roll pin until flush and install the expansion plug in the case front.

8. Replace detent plunger, spring and screw. Torque screw to specifications.

9. Attach the hand shift lever to the shift control housing temporarily. Shift the transmission through the gear range to make sure it works correctly.

10. Remove the shift lever and lubricate the shift stops in the control housing. Rotate the input shaft while pouring lubricant over the transmission gears.

11. Replace the dust cover, snap ring and back-up lamp switch to the end of the shift control housing. Torque lamp switch to specifications.

12. Attach the cover plate to the case with a new gasket. Install and torque attaching bolts to specs.

4-SPEED 71WG, 72WG (ENGLISH)

On the extension housing is an identification tag. If it includes the letters BB or BC, then it is English.

TRANSMISSION DISASSEMBLY
(Fig. 10-51)

1. Unbolt and remove the aluminum cover. Discard the old gasket and set the TRS retaining clip to one side.

2. Pry out the extension housing

3. Unscrew the meshlock plunger setscrew, and remove the spring and detent ball from the side of the case.

4. Remove the roll pin holding the shift boss to the rail with a pin punch. Position the synchronizer hub on the output shaft so that the pin will clear easily when driven out.

5. Remove the shift rail from the back of the case. *Do not* let the shift boss and C-cam drop into the case.

6. Move the first/second and third/fourth synchronizer hubs as far as they will go toward the input shaft bearing.

7. Remove the third/fourth shift-fork-spring pin and fork.

8. Unbolt the extension housing, and tap it to the rear with a soft-faced mallet until the housing can be rotated to align the flange cutout.

9. Tap the countershaft to the rear until it just clears the front of the transmission case. Use a dummy shaft to remove the countershaft, and place the countershaft gear at the bottom of the case.

10. Move the third/fourth synchronizer sleeve forward slightly to provide clearance between the synchronizer and countershaft gear, then remove the extension housing and output shaft assembly. *Do not* move the sleeve too far, because the synchronizer inserts will fall out if you do.

11. Unbolt and remove the bearing retainer from the front of the transmission case. Discard the old gasket, and pry out the retainer oil seal.

12. Remove the input-shaft-gear roller bearings.

13. Expand and remove the input-shaft outer-bearing snap ring, and tap the bearing race inward with a suitable drift. When the bearing clears the bore, remove the input shaft assembly from the case.

14. Lift the countershaft gear and the two thrust washers from the case. Remove the dummy shaft, 40 roller bearings and two retaining washers.

15. Drive out the reverse-idler-gear shaft.

16. Slide the reverse relay lever from its fulcrum pin on the transmission case, but *do not* remove the pin.

OUTPUT SHAFT DISASSEMBLY
(Fig. 10-52)

1. Remove the fourth-gear synchronizer ring. Expand and remove the snap ring from the forward end of the output shaft.

2. Press the third/fourth synchronizer and third gear from the output shaft.

3. Expand and remove the output-shaft rear-bearing snap ring, and withdraw the output shaft assembly from the housing.

4. Remove the speedometer-drive-gear snap ring, and pull the gear (and drive ball beneath it) from the transmission.

5. Press the low/reverse sliding gear, spacer, snap ring and output shaft bearing from the output shaft.

6. Expand and remove the first/second-synchronizer

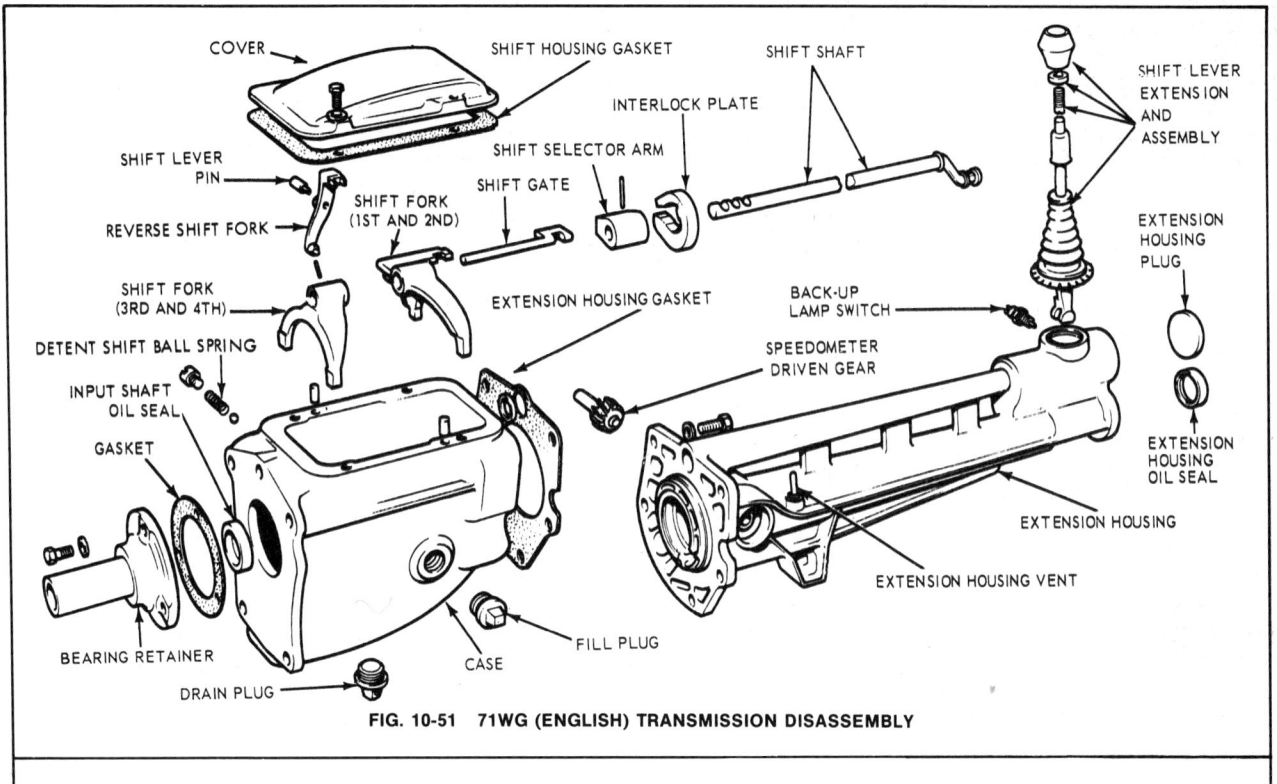

FIG. 10-51   71WG (ENGLISH) TRANSMISSION DISASSEMBLY

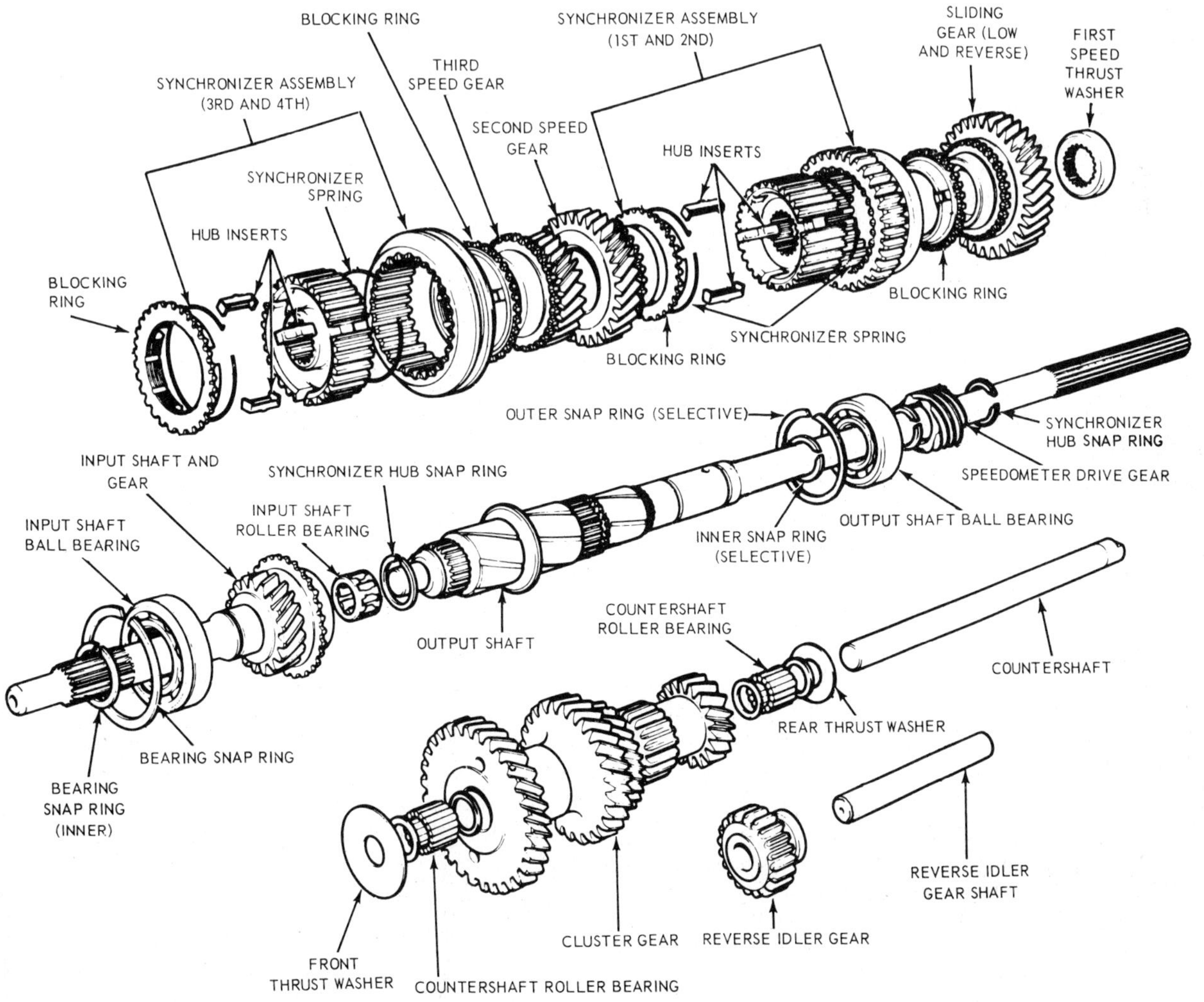

FIG. 10-52   71WG (ENGLISH) OUTPUT SHAFT

snap ring. Press second gear and the first/second synchronizer assembly and synchronizer rings from the output shaft.

7. Separate the synchronizer assemblies by pulling the sleeve from the hub and removing the springs and inserts. If so equipped, don't remove the TRS switch from the case, unless it is to be replaced.

CLEANING AND INSPECTION

1. Wash the transmission case inside and out with clean solvent.

2. Inspect the case for cracks, worn or damaged bearing bores, damaged threads or other defects.

3. Check the condition of all shift levers, forks, rails and shafts.

4. Clean the ball bearings with solvent, and dry with compressed air, holding the bearing assembly to prevent rotation. Lubricate the bearings with a suitable bearing grease.

5. Inspect the ball bearing races for cracks, wear or roughness, and check balls for looseness, wear, end play or other damage.

6. Check all gears for chipped, worn or broken teeth, and all shafts for wear, scoring or an out-of-round condition.

7. Check the synchronizer sleeves for free movement on their hubs, and the synchronizer rings for rounded teeth or enlarged index slots.

INPUT SHAFT AND GEAR

1. Remove and discard the input-shaft inner-bearing snap ring.

2. Inspect the bearing by rotating slowly. If it is noisy, rough, spalled or cracked, press off and replace with a new bearing. Make sure that the load of the press is taken through the inner bearing race and not the balls. If the bearing is good, install a new snap ring.

3. When replacing the bearing, install the new one on the input shaft with the ring groove facing away from the gear. Install the thickest snap ring that the groove will accommodate.

OUTPUT SHAFT ASSEMBLY
(Fig. 10-52)

1. Replace the synchronizer sleeve over the synchronizer hub, and position an insert in each of the three hub slots.

2. Install an insert spring on each side of the synchronizer sleeve and beneath the inserts with both tanged spring ends locating in the same U-section of an insert. Make sure both springs rotate in the same direction when viewed face on.

3. Repeat Steps 1 and 2 with the other synchronizer assembly.

4. Fit a synchronizer ring on the third gear cone, and replace third gear on the output shaft with its dog teeth facing forward. Lubricate the gear cone.

5. Replace the synchronizer assembly on the output shaft with its hub boss facing forward.

6. Press the synchronizer hub in place, and install a new snap ring in front of the hub. Move the synchronizer assembly forward against the snap ring.

7. Replace second gear on the output shaft with the cone and dog teeth to the rear. Lubricate the gear cone. Repeat Steps 1 and 2.

8. Fit a synchronizer ring to the second gear cone, and replace the synchronizer assembly on the output

shaft with reverse gear teeth on the synchronizer sleeve facing to the rear.

9. Position the low/reverse gear on the output shaft, press the synchronizer assembly on the shaft, and secure with a new snap ring.

10. Fit the synchronizer ring to the first gear side of the first/second synchronizer assembly on the output shaft. Install first gear with its cone side facing forward, then lubricate the gear cone.

11. Position the entire assembly in the press, with first gear resting on the press platform. Place the spacer or oil slinger on the output shaft, with its largest diameter next to first gear.

12. Place a new snap ring and the bearing on the output shaft, and press into place. Install a new bearing snap ring in the output shaft groove, using the thickest one that will fit the groove.

13. Replace the output-shaft-detent drive ball, and push the speedometer drive gear on the shaft to clear the snap ring groove, then install a new snap ring.

14. Work the output shaft into the extension housing, and secure with the snap ring.

TRANSMISSION ASSEMBLY
(Fig. 10-51)

1. Position the reverse relay lever on the transmission-case fulcrum pin.

2. Lubricate the idler shaft, install it in the case, replace the idler gear on the shaft, and place the reverse relay lever in the reverse idler groove, tapping the shaft in position with a soft-faced mallet.

3. Fit the dummy shaft into the countershaft gear. Lubricate each end of the gear bore, and install a retaining washer, 20 roller bearings and a second retaining washer at each end.

4. Apply grease to the two countershaft-gear thrust washers, and replace them in the transmission case, installing their tangs into the case recesses provided.

5. Place the countershaft gear in the bottom of the case.

6. Fit the input shaft and gear into the case, and tap the outer bearing race into the bore until the snap ring groove can be seen on the outside of the bore, then install a new outside-bearing snap ring. To prevent bearing damage, tap only on the race, not the input shaft gear.

7. Lubricate and fit the input-shaft roller bearing, and place it in the input-shaft gear recess.

8. Install a new oil seal on the input shaft retainer with the seal lips facing the transmission. Drive it into the retainer until it bottoms.

9. Lubricate the front bearing-retainer seal and the input-shaft-seal journal area, then install a new bearing-retainer gasket.

10. Wrap the input shaft splines with a plastic sleeve to prevent seal damage, and replace the retainer. The oil groove must align with the oil passage in the case.

11. Apply sealer to the bearing-retainer attaching bolts, fit the lockwashers in place, and install the bolts, torquing 12 to 15 ft.-lbs. Remove the plastic protector sleeve from the splines.

12. Lubricate the input-shaft-gear cone, and fit the fourth-gear synchronizer ring over it.

13. Pull the third/fourth synchronizer sleeve forward to clear the countershaft gear, then install the extension housing gasket, and slide the housing and output shaft into place.

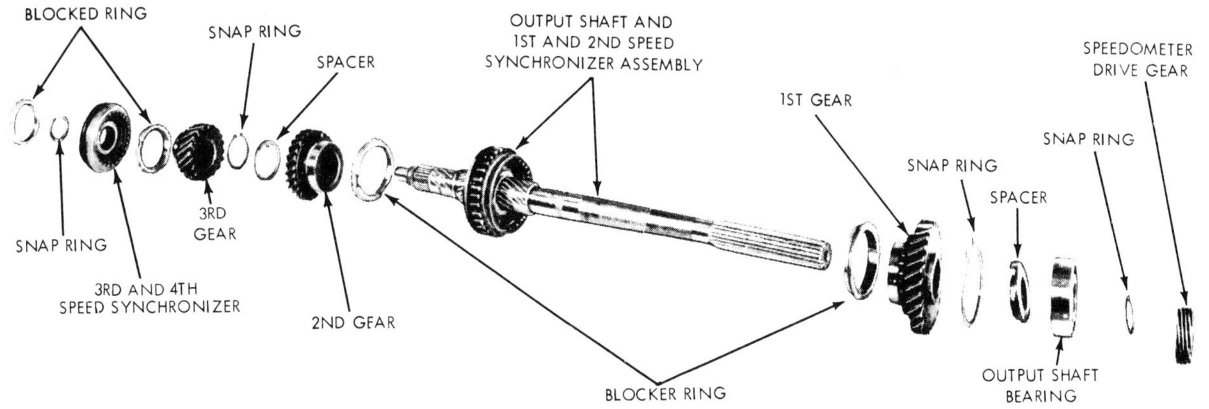

FIG. 10-53   71WG (GERMAN) OUTPUT SHAFT

14. Lift the countershaft gear into mesh with the output/input-shaft gears without disturbing the thrust washers positioned in the case.

15. Align the countershaft gear bore with the countershaft opening, and install the countershaft from the rear, tapping in place with a soft-faced mallet. The countershaft rear lug must fit into the extension-housing flange recess, with the countershaft front flush with the case front when fully installed.

16. Turn the extension housing to align the bolt holes, and push completely in place. Apply sealer to the attaching bolts, and torque 20 to 25 ft.-lbs.

17. Fit the shift forks over the relay lever, and install a new roll pin in the third/fourth shift fork.

18. Place the assembled forks over their respective synchronizer sleeves, and move the synchronizer hubs to neutral. This locates the fork extension arms beneath the reverse-idler-shaft arm.

19. Lubricate the shift-rail oil seal, and slide the rail through the extension housing. Move the shift boss and C-cams to locate the cams in the fork extension-arm cutouts.

20. Install the rail through the forks and boss to align the spring pin holes. Work carefully to avoid damage to the shift-rail oil seal.

21. Replace the detent ball and spring in their bore, and apply sealer to the setscrew before installing it.

22. Drive the roll pin in place to hold the shift boss to the rail.

23. Apply sealer to the extension housing plug, and tap in place.

24. Fit a new cover gasket in place, and install the cover with sealer on the bolts.

25. Connect the TRS-switch wire-retainer clip to the cover with the right front bolt, and torque all bolts 12 to 15 ft.-lbs.

4-SPEED 71WG, 72WG, 74WT, 75WT, 77-79ET (GERMAN)

An identification tag on the transmission will include the suffix AD (71WG, 72WG-AD, etc.) if the box is German. Remember, these fasteners are metric.

TRANSMISSION DISASSEMBLY

1. Unbolt and remove the steel cover. Discard the old gasket, and set the TRS retaining clips to one side.

2. Unscrew the threaded plug, and remove the spring/shift-rail detent plunger from the case front.

3. Drive out the access plug in the rear of the case, using a suitable drift.

4. Drive out the interlock-plate retaining pin from the case by inserting a long drift through the access hole; remove the plate.

5. Tap out the selector-lever-arm roll pin.

6. Gently tap the front of the shift rail to displace the extension housing plug, and withdraw the rail from the housing.

7. Remove the selector arm/shift fork from the case.

8. Unbolt the extension housing, and rotate to align cutaway in the housing flange with countershaft.

9. Tap the countershaft to the rear until it just clears the front of the transmission case. Use a dummy shaft to remove the countershaft, and place the countershaft gear at the bottom of the case.

10. Remove the extension housing and output shaft from the case as a unit.

11. Unbolt the input-shaft-bearing retainer, and remove the input shaft and bearing retainer from the case as a unit.

12. Drive out the reverse-idler-gear shaft and gear from the rear of the case.

13. Pry out the shift rail seal from the rear of the transmission case.

14. If the shift rail bushing in the extension housing is damaged, remove it by driving it out with a 9/16-in. socket and extension. If the bearing is serviceable, *do not* remove it.

15. Lift the remaining shift linkage from the transmission case.

OUTPUT SHAFT DISASSEMBLY
(Fig. 10-53)

1. Remove the fourth-gear synchronizer ring from the front of the output shaft, then expand and discard the snap ring.

2. Press the output shaft from the third/fourth synchronizer assembly and third gear. Support extension housing and output shaft to prevent it from dropping.

3. Remove the snap ring and washer, then slide second gear and the synchronizer ring from the output shaft. Discard the snap ring.

4. Punch alignment marks on the hub and sleeve. Separate the synchronizer assemblies by pulling the sleeve from the hub and removing the springs and inserts. Since the first/second synchronizer assembly is serviced as a unit, disassemble only if replacement is indicated.

5. Expand and remove the output-shaft rear-bearing snap ring, and withdraw the output shaft assembly from the housing.

6. Press first gear from the output shaft, and remove the synchronizer ring. The first/second synchronizer assembly can be left on the shaft; there is no need to remove it unless replacement is necessary.

CLEANING AND INSPECTION

1. Wash the transmission case inside and out with clean solvent.

2. Inspect the case for cracks, worn or damaged bearing bores, damaged threads or other defects.

3. Check the condition of all shift levers, forks, rails and shafts.

4. Clean the ball bearings with solvent, and dry with compressed air, holding the bearing assembly to prevent rotation. Lubricate the bearing with a suitable bearing grease.

5. Inspect the ball bearing races for cracks, wear or roughness, and check balls for looseness, wear, end play or other damage.

6. Check all gears for chipped, worn or broken teeth, and all shafts for wear, scoring or an out-of-round condition.

7. Check the synchronizer sleeves for free movement on their hubs, and the synchronizer rings for rounded teeth or enlarged index slots.

INPUT SHAFT AND GEAR
(Fig. 10-54)

1. Remove the pilot bearing and retainer from the input shaft bore.

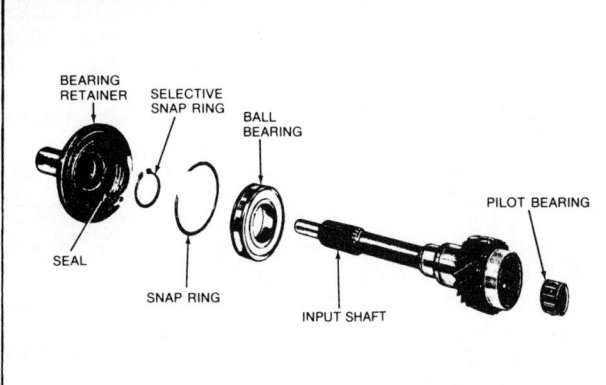

FIG. 10-54   71WG (GERMAN) INPUT SHAFT

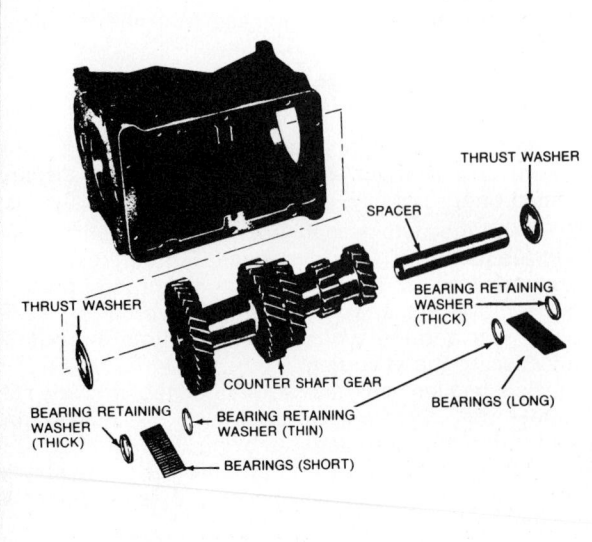

FIG. 10-55   71WG (GERMAN) COUNTERSHAFT GEAR

2. Inspect the ball bearing by rotating slowly. If it is noisy, rough, spalled or cracked, press it off from the input shaft and replace it with a new one. If the bearing is good, install a new snap ring.

3. When replacing the ball bearing, install the new one on the input shaft, with the ring groove facing away from the gear.

4. Pry out the input shaft seal from the bearing retainer, and drive in a new seal until it bottoms.

OUTPUT SHAFT ASSEMBLY
(Fig. 10-53)

1. Replace the synchronizer sleeve over the synchronizer hub, and position an insert in each of the three hub slots.

2. Install an insert spring on each side of the synchronizer sleeve and beneath the inserts, with both tagged spring ends locating in the same U-section of an insert.

3. If the first/second synchronizer assembly was disassembled, repeat Steps 1 and 2 to reassemble it.

4. Fit a synchronizer ring on the first gear side of the first/second synchronizer.

5. Lubricate the first gear cone, and slide the gear on the output shaft so that the coned surface engages the synchronizer ring.

6. Fit the spacer on the output shaft with its larger diameter facing to the rear of the shaft.

7. Place the snap ring and rear bearing on the output shaft, and press into place. Install a new bearing snap ring in the output shaft groove, using the thickest one that will fit the groove.

8. Slide second gear and a synchronizer ring on the output shaft, with the dog teeth to the rear, and replace the washer and snap ring.

9. Slide third gear on the output shaft with its dog teeth facing forward. Lubricate the gear cone, and fit the synchronizer ring on the cone.

10. Place the third/fourth synchronizer assembly on the output shaft with its hub boss to the front, and press in place as far as it will go.

11. Install a snap ring in front of the third/fourth synchronizer assembly, and pull up on the assembly to let the snap ring seat tightly in its groove.

12. Lubricate the input (fourth) gear cone, and install the fourth-gear synchronizer ring.

13. Press the speedometer drive gear on the output shaft.

14. Lubricate the extension-housing bearing bore, and replace the output shaft in the housing, securing it in place with a selective snap ring to eliminate end play.

TRANSMISSION ASSEMBLY

1. Slide the spacer and dummy shaft into the countershaft gear, and install a thin bearing-retainer washer at each end of the dummy shaft. Lubricate and load the 19 long bearings in the small end of the gear and the 19 short bearings in the large end of the gear. Fit a thick retainer washer over each end of the dummy shaft **(Fig. 10-55).**

2. Grease the thrust washers. Place one on each end of the dummy shaft, with the tangs in a position to engage the case slots. Lower the countershaft gear into place, with the washers engaging as required.

3. Lubricate the reverse-idler-gear shaft, and slide it into place, seating the shaft in the case with a soft-faced hammer.

4. Fit the input shaft to the transmission case with a

new bearing retainer O-ring. Gently tap the bearing outer race until the outer snap ring is seated to the case— *do not* tap on the input shaft, or bearing damage will result.

5. Slide the third/fourth synchronizer sleeve forward to the fourth gear position for clearance, then install a new gasket on the extension housing.

6. Lubricate the input-shaft pilot bearing, and install

it in the shaft bore. Slide the extension housing and output shaft in place without disturbing the third/fourth synchronizer.

7. Align the extension-housing flange cutaway with the countershaft bore in the case rear. Lift the countershaft gear into place, and install the countershaft, making sure that both thrust washers are in place. With the countershaft flat pointing to the top of the case, tap

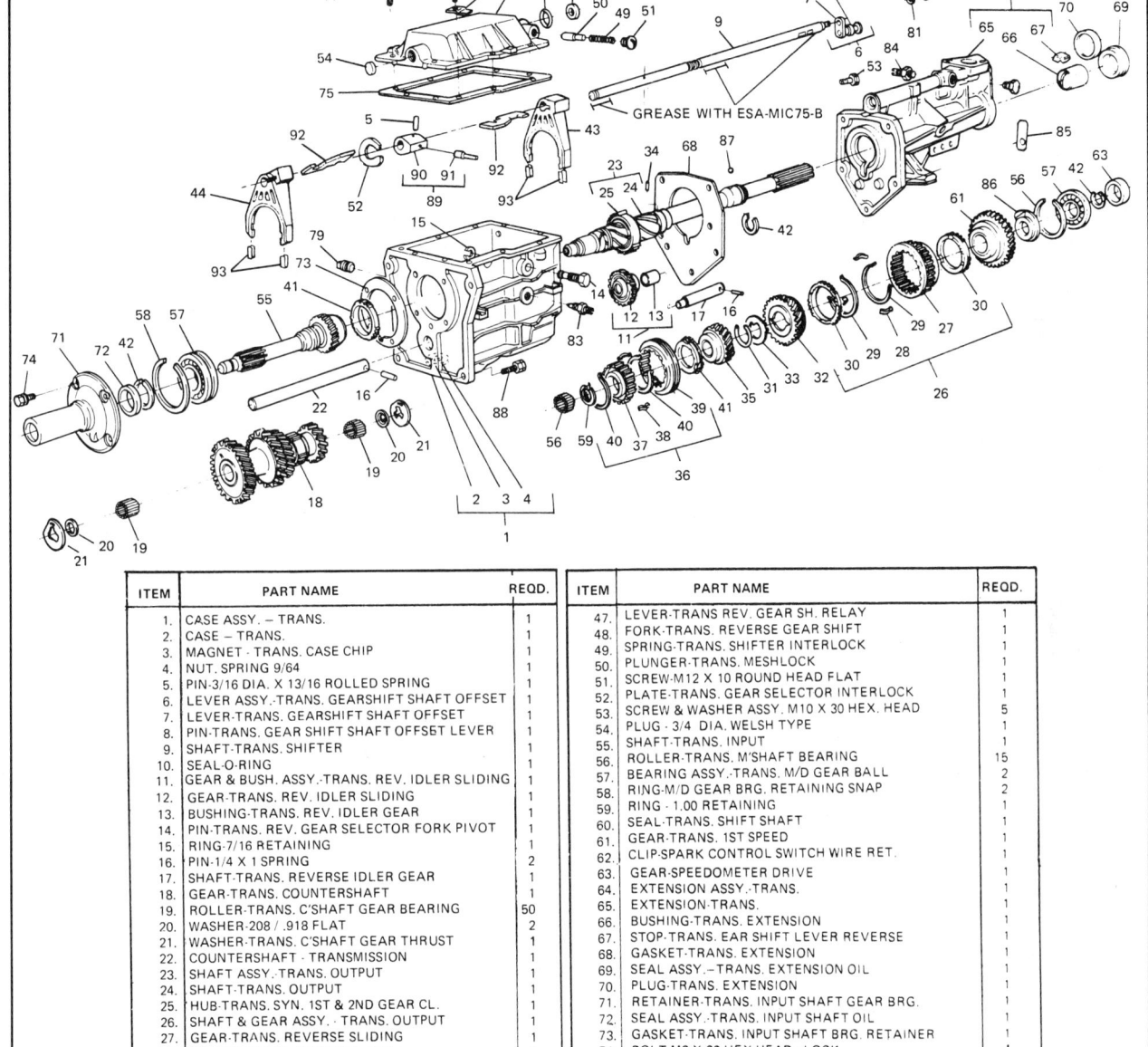

ITEM	PART NAME	REQD.
1.	CASE ASSY. – TRANS.	1
2.	CASE – TRANS.	1
3.	MAGNET · TRANS. CASE CHIP	1
4.	NUT. SPRING 9/64	1
5.	PIN·3/16 DIA. X 13/16 ROLLED SPRING	1
6.	LEVER ASSY.·TRANS. GEARSHIFT SHAFT OFFSET	1
7.	LEVER·TRANS. GEARSHIFT SHAFT OFFSET	1
8.	PIN·TRANS. GEAR SHIFT SHAFT OFFSET LEVER	1
9.	SHAFT·TRANS. SHIFTER	1
10.	SEAL·O·RING	1
11.	GEAR & BUSH. ASSY.·TRANS. REV. IDLER SLIDING	1
12.	GEAR·TRANS. REV. IDLER SLIDING	1
13.	BUSHING·TRANS. REV. IDLER GEAR	1
14.	PIN·TRANS. REV. GEAR SELECTOR FORK PIVOT	1
15.	RING·7/16 RETAINING	1
16.	PIN·1/4 X 1 SPRING	2
17.	SHAFT·TRANS. REVERSE IDLER GEAR	1
18.	GEAR·TRANS. COUNTERSHAFT	1
19.	ROLLER·TRANS. C'SHAFT GEAR BEARING	50
20.	WASHER·208 / .918 FLAT	2
21.	WASHER·TRANS. C'SHAFT GEAR THRUST	1
22.	COUNTERSHAFT · TRANSMISSION	1
23.	SHAFT ASSY.·TRANS. OUTPUT	1
24.	SHAFT·TRANS. OUTPUT	1
25.	HUB·TRANS. SYN. 1ST & 2ND GEAR CL.	1
26.	SHAFT & GEAR ASSY. · TRANS. OUTPUT	1
27.	GEAR·TRANS. REVERSE SLIDING	1
28.	INSERT·TRANS. SYNCHRO. HUB	3
29.	SPRING·TRANS. SYNCHRO. RETAINING	2
30.	RING·TRANS. SYNCHRO BLOCKING	2
31.	RING·TRANS·2ND SPEED GEAR RET. SNAP	1
32.	GEAR·TRANS. 2ND SPEED	1
33.	WASHER · TRANS. 2ND SPEED GEAR THRUST	1
34.	PIN · 1/8 x 3/8 ROLLED SPRING	1
35.	GEAR·TRANS. 3RD SPEED	1
36.	SYNCHRONIZER ASSY. · 3RD & 4th SPEED	1
37.	HUB·TRANS. SYNC. 3RD &4TH GEAR CLUTCH	1
38.	INSERT·TRANS. SYNC. HUB	3
39.	SLEEVE·TRANS. 3RD & 4TH GEAR CLUTCH HUB	1
40.	SPRING·TRANS. SYNCHRO. RETAINING	2
41.	RING·TRANS. SYNCHRO BLOCKING	2
42.	RING·TRANS. M/D GEAR BRG. SHAFT·SNAP	3
43.	FORD·TRANS. 1ST & 2ND GEAR SHIFT	1
44.	FORK·TRANS. 3RD & 4TH GEAR SHIFT	1
45.	LEVER ASSY.·TRANS. REV. GEAR SH. RELAY	1
46.	REING.·TRANS. REV. GEAR SH. RELAY LEVER	2

ITEM	PART NAME	REQD.
47.	LEVER·TRANS REV. GEAR SH. RELAY	1
48.	FORK·TRANS. REVERSE GEAR SHIFT	1
49.	SPRING·TRANS. SHIFTER INTERLOCK	1
50.	PLUNGER·TRANS. MESHLOCK	1
51.	SCREW·M12 X 10 ROUND HEAD FLAT	1
52.	PLATE·TRANS. GEAR SELECTOR INTERLOCK	1
53.	SCREW & WASHER ASSY. M10 X 30 HEX. HEAD	5
54.	PLUG · 3/4 DIA. WELSH TYPE	1
55.	SHAFT·TRANS. INPUT	1
56.	ROLLER·TRANS. M'SHAFT BEARING	15
57.	BEARING ASSY.·TRANS. M/D GEAR BALL	2
58.	RING·M/D GEAR BRG. RETAINING SNAP	2
59.	RING · 1.00 RETAINING	1
60.	SEAL·TRANS. SHIFT SHAFT	1
61.	GEAR·TRANS. 1ST SPEED	1
62.	CLIP·SPARK CONTROL SWITCH WIRE RET.	1
63.	GEAR·SPEEDOMETER DRIVE	1
64.	EXTENSION ASSY.·TRANS.	1
65.	EXTENSION·TRANS.	1
66.	BUSHING·TRANS. EXTENSION	1
67.	STOP·TRANS. EAR SHIFT LEVER REVERSE	1
68.	GASKET·TRANS. EXTENSION	1
69.	SEAL ASSY.–TRANS. EXTENSION OIL	1
70.	PLUG·TRANS. EXTENSION	1
71.	RETAINER·TRANS. INPUT SHAFT GEAR BRG.	1
72.	SEAL ASSY.·TRANS. INPUT SHAFT OIL	1
73.	GASKET·TRANS. INPUT SHAFT BRG. RETAINER	1
74.	BOLT M8 X 20 HEX HEAD · LOCK	4
75.	GASKET·TRANS. CASE COVER	1
76.	COVER · TRANS. CASE	1
77.	SCREW·M6 X 20 HEX. HEAD	8
78.	BOLT·M6 X 32 HEX. WASHER HD. SHOULDER	2
79.	PLUG·1 2·14 PIPE (FILLER)	1
80.	BUSHING·TRANS. GEAR SHIFT DAMPER	1
81.	WASHER·SPRING LOCK ·5/16 FLAT	1
82.	NUT·HEXAGON	1
83.	SWITCH ASS'Y·BACK-UP LAMP	1
84.	SWITCH ASSY.·TRANS. SEAT BELT WARNING SENSOR	1
85.	TAG TRANS. SERVICE IDENTIFICATION	1
86.	WASHER·TRANS. 1ST GEAR THRUST	1
87.	BALL · .25 DIA.	1
88.	SCREW & LOCKWASHER ASSY. M12 X 40	4
89.	ARM ASSY·TRANS. CONTROL SELECTOR	1
90.	ARM·TRANS. CONTROL SELECTOR	1
91.	PIN·TRANS. GEARSHIFT	1
92.	PLATE·TRANS. GEARSHIFT SELECTOR ARM	2
93.	INSERT·TRANS. GEARSHIFT FORK	4

FIG. 10-56   RAD TRANSMISSION DISASSEMBLY

the countershaft into the case until the shaft is flush with the front.

8. Fit the shift forks in their respective synchronizer sleeves, position the interlock lever, and tap a new retainer in place.

9. Lubricate the shift-rail oil seal, and slide the rail through the extension housing, transmission case and the first/second shift fork. Place the selector arm on the rail and slide the rail through the third/fourth shift fork and front of the case until the center detent aligns with the detent plunger bore. Install a new selector-arm retainer pin.

10. Replace the detent plunger, spring and plug with sealer.

11. Fit a new access plug in the case rear.

12. Turn the extension housing to align the bolt holes with the case holes, and loosely install the attaching bolts. Check the shift rail for free movement in the bore. If it binds, turn the extension housing sufficiently to free the rail, then seat the housing in the case.

13. Remove the extension-housing-to-case bolts, apply sealer, and replace. Torque each 33 to 36 ft.-lbs.

14. Replace the O-ring in the transmission-case-face groove, and lubricate the input-shaft journal area. Install the input-shaft bearing retainer, with the oil groove aligned with the case oil passage.

15. Replace the washers on the attaching bolts, and apply sealer to the bolts. Install bolts in the retainer, but do not tighten.

16. Replace the bellhousing, then torque the retainer bolts 8 to 10 ft.-lbs.

17. Apply sealer to a new extension-housing end plug, and tap in place.

18. Fit a new cover gasket in place, and install the cover with the vent to the case rear. Apply sealer to the left-front cover bolt. Attach the three TRS clips to the cover, with a lockwasher between each clip and the cover. Replace all bolts and torque 8 to 10 ft.-lbs.

4-SPEED RAD (BORG-WARNER SR4)

TRANSMISSION DISASSEMBLY
(Fig. 10-56)

1. Drain the lubricant by removing the lower extension housing bolt.

2. Drive the access plug from the rear of the extension housing. Remove the nut, bolt and offset lever, as shown in **Fig. 10-57.**

3. Unbolt and remove the extension housing from the case, discarding the gasket.

4. Unbolt and remove the case cover, shifter forks and shift rod assembly from the case, discarding the gasket.

5. Unbolt and remove the front bearing retainer from the case, discarding the gasket.

6. Unclip the reverse lever assembly from the pivot bolt; remove both.

7. Expand and remove the snap ring holding the input bearing to the input shaft.

8. Expand and remove the outer snap ring from the input bearing.

9. Expand and remove the speedometer-gear-to-output-shaft snap ring, and slide the gear from the shaft, removing the lock ball.

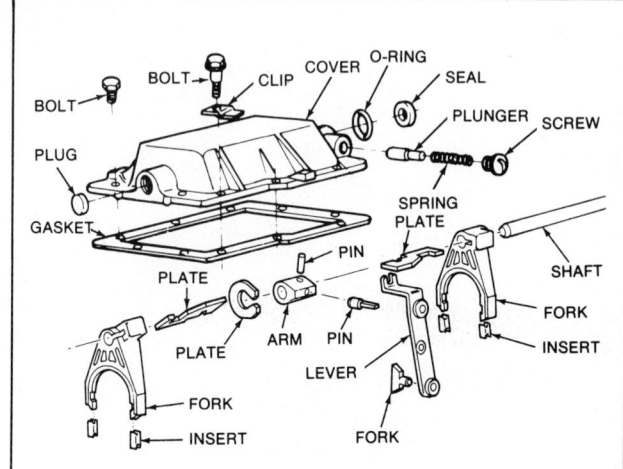

FIG. 10-58 TRANSMISSION COVER DISASSEMBLY

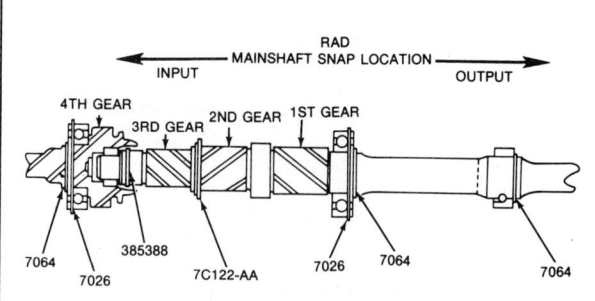

FIG. 10-59 OUTPUT-SHAFT SNAP RING LOCATIONS AND PART NUMBERS

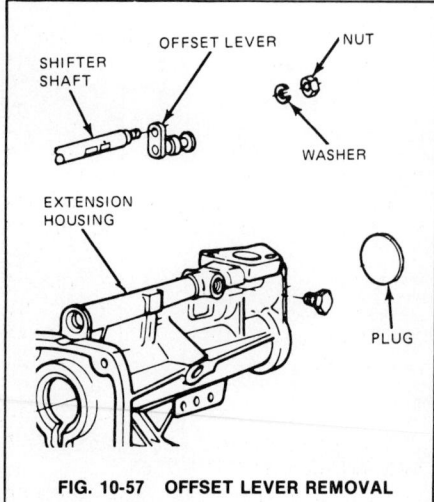

FIG. 10-57 OFFSET LEVER REMOVAL

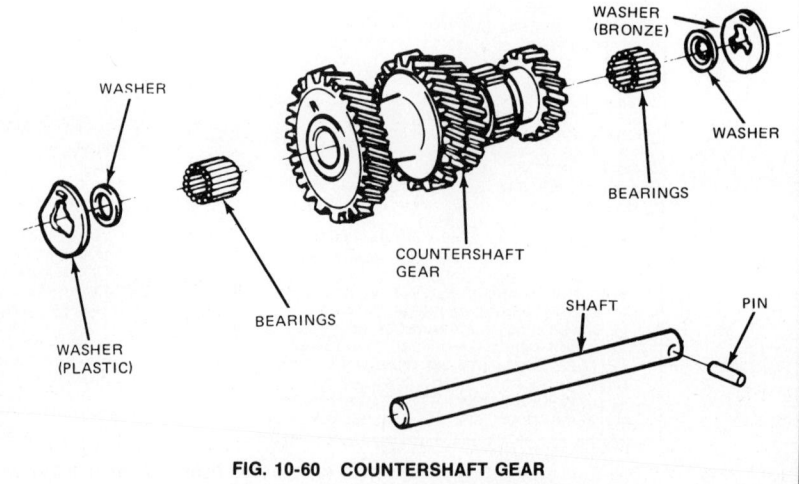

FIG. 10-60 COUNTERSHAFT GEAR

10. Expand and remove the output-shaft-bearing snap ring.

11. Remove the output shaft bearing from the case.

12. Draw the input shaft through the bearing hole in the front of the case, and lift the output shaft and gear assembly from the top of the case.

13. Slide the reverse-idler-gear shaft from the rear of the case, and remove the reverse idler gear.

14. Use a dummy shaft to drive the countershaft out of the rear of the case.

15. Remove the countershaft gear, two thrust washers and the dummy countershaft from the top of the case. *Do not* remove back-up lamp or seat-belt interlock switch (1974-75 models only) unless damaged.

TRANSMISSION COVER DISASSEMBLY

(Fig. 10-58)

1. Remove the detent screw, spring and plunger, then pull the shifter shaft rod to the rear, rotating counterclockwise.

2. Remove the selector and interlock-to-shifter-shaft spring pin.

3. Remove the shifter shaft, manual selector and interlock plate from the cover. Be careful not to damage the seal.

4. Remove both shifter forks.

5. Check the shifter shaft seal and the welch plug—if either is damaged or leaking, replace.

OUTPUT SHAFT DISASSEMBLY

(Fig. 10-59)

1. Mark the synchronizer assembly and ring for alignment.

2. Expand and remove the output-shaft front snap ring, then slide the third/fourth synchronizer assembly, synchronizer rings and third gear from the shaft.

3. Expand and remove the next snap ring and the second-gear thrust washer, sliding second gear and the synchronizer ring from the shaft.

4. *Do not* lose the sliding gear from the first/second synchronizer assembly, because the hub cannot be removed from the output shaft. If damaged, the hub and shaft are replaced as a single unit.

5. Turn the output shaft around, and remove the first-gear thrust washer (an oil slinger type), then the spring pin holding first gear to the shaft. This pin locates and drives the thrust-washer-type oil slinger.

6. Slide first gear and the synchronizer ring from the output shaft, observing the caution in Step 4.

CLEANING AND INSPECTION

1. Wash the transmission case inside and out with clean solvent.

2. Inspect the case for cracks, worn or damaged bearing bores, damaged threads or other defects.

3. Check the condition of all shift levers, forks, rails and shafts.

4. Clean the ball bearings with solvent, and dry with compressed air, holding the bearing assembly to prevent rotation. Lubricate the bearings with a suitable bearing grease.

5. Inspect the ball bearing races for cracks, wear or roughness, and check balls for looseness, wear, end play or other damage.

6. Check all gears for chipped, worn or broken teeth, and all shafts for wear, scoring or an out-of-round condition.

7. Check the synchronizer sleeves for free movement on their hubs, and the synchronizer rings for rounded teeth or enlarged index slots.

COUNTERSHAFT-GEAR-BEARING REPLACEMENT

(Fig. 10-60)

1. Disassemble, clean and inspect all components.

2. Wipe the inside of the countershaft gear bore at each end with a light coat of grease.

3. Install the dummy shaft, and replace the needle bearings and retainer washers at each end.

INPUT-SHAFT POCKET-BEARING REPLACEMENT

1. Remove the input-shaft roller bearings. Clean and inspect all components.

2. Wipe the inside of the input shaft bore with a light coat of grease. If grease is applied too thick, it will plug lubrication holes and prevent bearing lubrication.

3. Install the needle bearings in the input shaft bore.

OUTPUT SHAFT ASSEMBLY

(Fig. 10-59)

1. Fit a synchronizer ring on the first gear cone, and slide both onto the output shaft. The synchronizer inserts must engage the synchronizer ring notches.

2. Replace the spring pin in the shaft to hold the first gear.

3. Repeat Step 1 with the second gear, and install the second-gear thrust washer and a new snap ring.

4. Repeat Step 1 with the third gear. Install the third/fourth synchronizer assembly with the inserts engaging the ring notches, and install a new third/fourth-gear retaining snap ring.

5. Place first-gear thrust washer (oil slinger) on the output shaft, with the oil grooves positioned against the gear, and install the spring pin.

TRANSMISSION ASSEMBLY

(Fig. 10-56)

1. Place the reverse idler gear and reverse-idler-gear shaft in the case.

2. Lubricate the countershaft thrust washers, and position them in the countershaft gear and dummy shaft. The plastic washer should go at the front and the bronze washer at the rear.

3. Set the transmission case upright. Align the countershaft gear bore and thrust washers with the case bore, taking care not to let the dummy shaft fall through the front hole. Install the countershaft through the rear of the case, engaging the thrust washers.

4. Replace the transmission case in a horizontal position, and place the output shaft assembly in the case. Slide a dummy bearing through the front of the case, and engage the output shaft—this will help to align and support the output shaft assembly.

5. Replace the input shaft and fourth-gear synchronizer ring with the notches engaging the synchronizer inserts.

6. Fit a new snap ring to the input shaft bearing O.D., and press the bearing in place. Then install the input-shaft bearing-retainer snap ring.

7. Replace the front bearing retainer with a new gasket. Apply sealer to the bolt threads and torque 11 to 15 ft.-lbs.

8. Set the transmission case upright, and remove the dummy output-shaft bearing. Fit a new snap ring on the output-shaft bearing O.D. and, with the snap ring positioned to the rear, install the bearing on the shaft.

9. Check to make sure that the first-gear thrust washer did not slip out of position, then install a new output-shaft rear-bearing-retainer snap ring.

10. Replace the reverse-idler-gear lever assembly with the fork in the reverse-idler-gear groove.

11. Apply sealer to the reverse-lever pivot bolt and install, aligning the pivot bolt lever and torquing the bolt 15 to 25 ft.-lbs. Replace the retaining spring clip to the pivot bolt.

12. With the transmission tilted forward, pour a light coat of transmission lubricant over the geartrain.

13. Replace the inserts on the shift forks, if removed. Position the inserts so that the two inside projections on each fit into blind holes at fork ends **(Fig. 10-61).**

14. Replace the selector arm plates in the forks. Install both forks in the cover, and lubricate the shifter bore with grease.

15. Fit the manual selector through the interlock plate, and place the two pieces in the cover. The wide leg of the interlock plate should face to the inside of the transmission.

16. Coat the shifter shaft with a light application of grease, align in the cover, and insert the shaft through the forks and the manual selector.

17. Align the manual selector arm and shifter-shaft pin holes, and install the spring pin flush with the selector arm surface.

18. Replace the detent plunger, spring and plug. Torque the plug 8 to 12 ft.-lbs., and check shift-fork operation in each gear position.

19. Fit a new cover gasket in place, and install the cover assembly. Replace the two shouldered locating bolts first, and place the shift rail in first or third gear position. Replace the rest of the bolts, and torque all 7 to 12 ft.-lbs.

20. Fit the speedometer-drive-gear lock ball in the shaft hole, and slide the gear in place. Install the snap ring.

21. Install the extension case with a new gasket, applying sealer to the attaching bolts, and torquing 18 to 27 ft.-lbs.

22. Replace the offset lever assembly on the shift shaft, and install the nut and flat washer. Torque 8 to 12 ft.-lbs.

23. Insert the gearshift lever to check the gear position, then replace the access plug in the rear of the extension housing.

CHRYSLER CORPORATION

Chrysler Corporation cars have used the following transmissions since 1970, all representative of the fully synchronized, constant-mesh design:

3-Speed A-903/A-250—Provided as standard equipment in the 6-cyl. compact Chrysler Corporation cars, the A-903 was furnished from 1970 through 1972, and the A-250 during 1973-74. After 1974, it was replaced by the A-390, a Chrysler version of the Ford 3-speed RAN (see Ford Motor Company section). This was the last factory-offered transmission equipped with the pin-type gear synchronizers **(Fig. 10-62),** once considered the best for competition. The transmission case is a closed type, with the access cover on the top rather than the side.

3-Speed A-230—A heavy-duty 3-speed, the A-230 is standard equipment in 1970-79 Chrysler Corporation cars, both 6-cyl. and V-8 models. Like the GM Saginaw and Muncie, this transmission uses the side cover design in which the shift forks and detent cams can be replaced without removing the transmission from the car.

4-Speed A-833/Overdrive-4—Designed in 1964 to replace the Warner T-10 for use with the powerful V-8 engines of that era, the A-833 was furnished in two ratios through 1975. By changing the gear ratios to provide direct drive in third instead of fourth gear, and giving fourth gear a 0.73 ratio, the A-833 was redesigned into a 3-speed transmission with an overdrive fourth gear for 1976-79. Except for the size of second, third and fourth gears, and the use of an expansion plug on the front of the countershaft bore, the two transmissions are identical, and thus treated together in the following overhaul procedures.

3-SPEED A-903/A-250
TRANSMISSION DISASSEMBLY
(Fig. 10-63)

1. Unbolt and remove the case cover, discarding the gasket.

2. Insert a feeler gauge between the outer and inner synchronizer stop rings to measure synchronizer "float." Make the measurement on two pins 180° apart. The gap or "float" should be between 0.060-in. and 0.117-in., and the same at both points of measurement **(Fig. 10-64).**

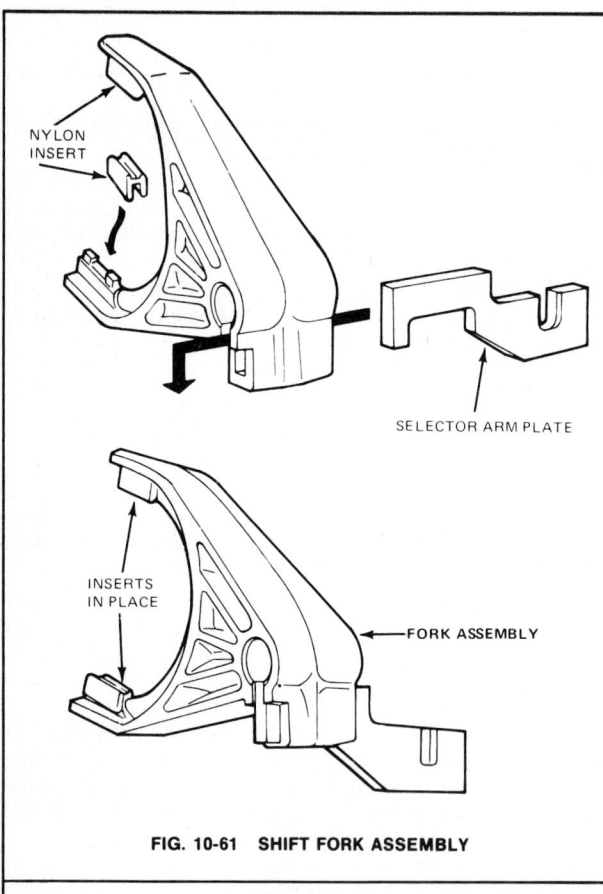

FIG. 10-61   SHIFT FORK ASSEMBLY

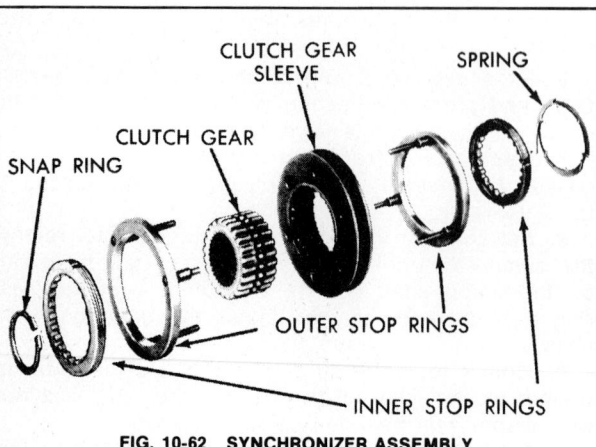

FIG. 10-62   SYNCHRONIZER ASSEMBLY

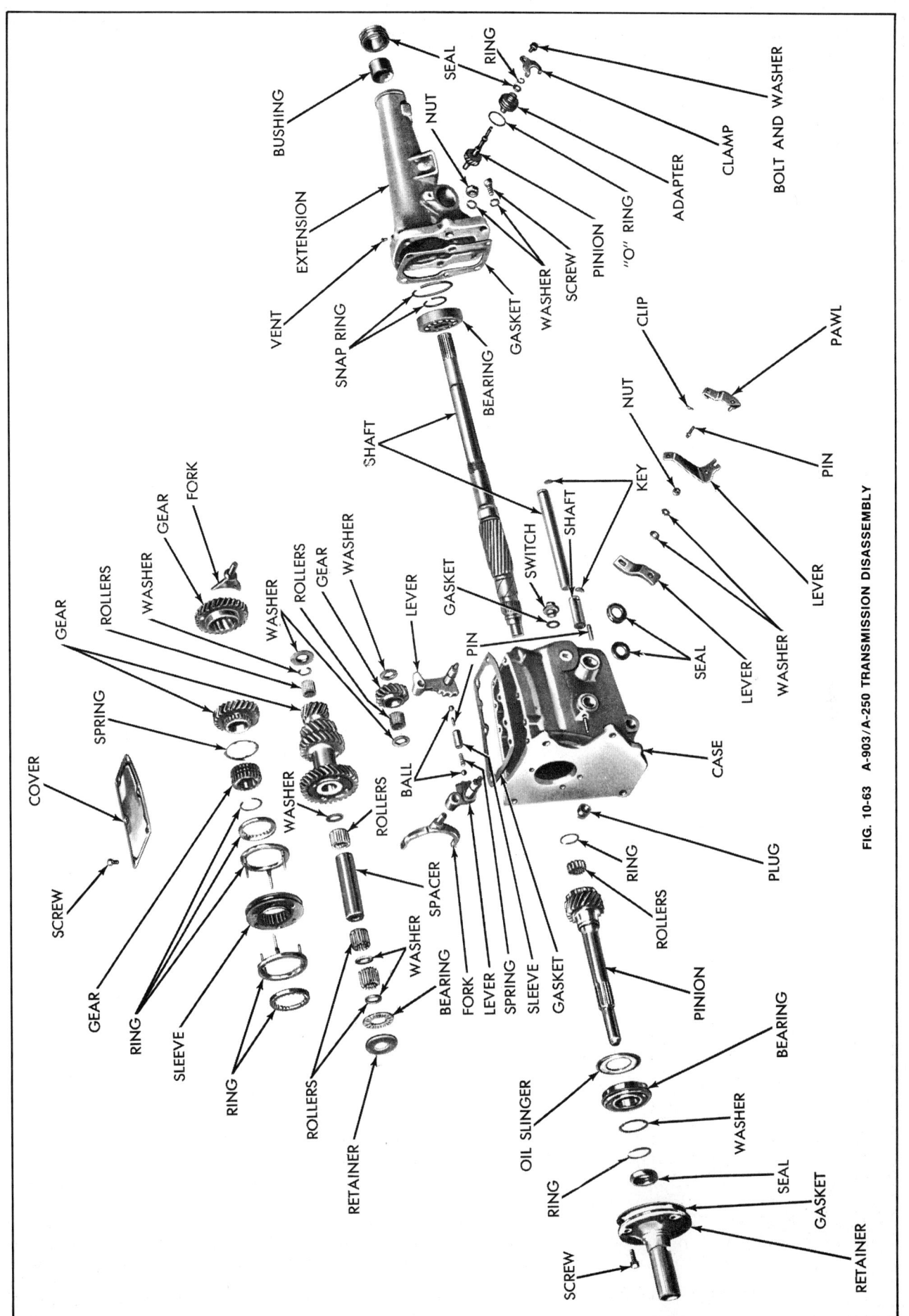

FIG. 10-63 A-903/A-250 TRANSMISSION DISASSEMBLY

3. Unbolt the speedometer pinion retainer from the extension housing, and work the adapter and pinion out carefully.

4. Unbolt and remove the extension housing, discarding the gasket.

5. Unbolt the drive-pinion bearing retainer, and slide it from the pinion. Pry out the retainer seal.

6. Turn the drive pinion until the blank tooth area is next to the countershaft gear to provide clearance for removal.

7. Pull the pinion shaft forward slightly, sliding the synchronizer front-inner stop ring from the pinion splines as the unit is removed from the transmission case.

8. Remove the inner snap ring and washer from the drive pinion shaft.

9. Press the pinion shaft from the bearing with an arbor press, and remove the oil slinger.

10. Remove the snap ring holding the mainshaft pilot bearings in the end of the drive pinion, and remove the bearing rollers.

11. Remove the clutch-gear-retainer snap ring from the mainshaft, turn the case around, and remove the mainshaft-bearing-retainer snap ring from case.

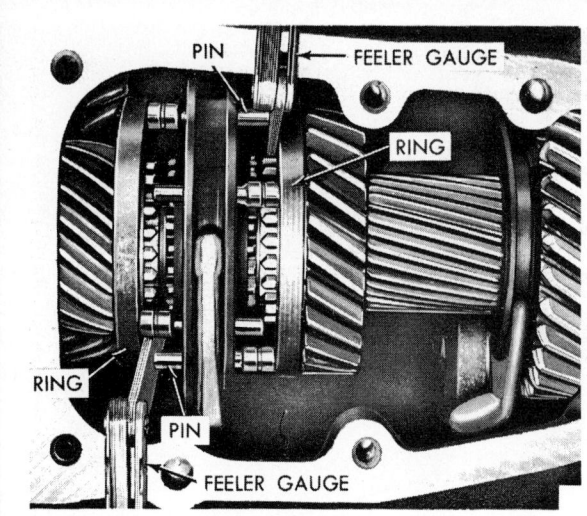

FIG. 10-64 MEASURING SYNCHRONIZER FLOAT

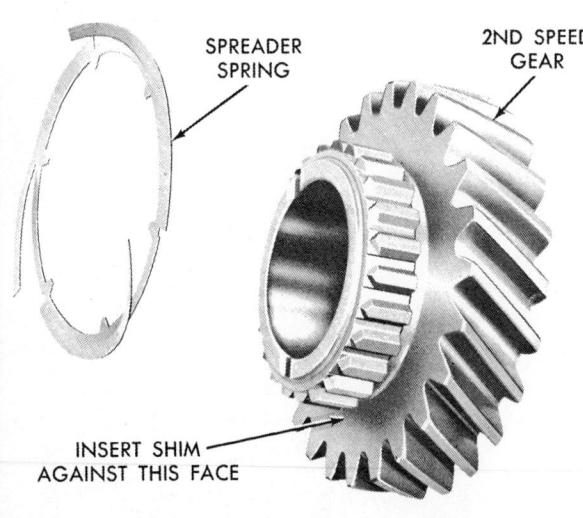

FIG. 10-65 SYNCHRONIZER SHIM LOCATION

12. Slide the mainshaft and rear bearing out of the case, steadying the gears with one hand as they drop free into the case.

13. Remove the mainshaft selective snap ring, and press the bearing off the shaft.

14. Lift out all synchronizer parts, gears and shift forks from inside the transmission case.

15. Measure the countershaft-gear end play with a feeler gauge. If the end play does not range between 0.005-in. and 0.022-in., the thrust washers should be replaced during reassembly.

16. Using a plastic hammer, drive the countershaft slightly to the rear of the case, remove the key, and continue driving the shaft until it can be removed from the case. Don't lose the roller bearings.

17. Lift the countershaft gear and thrust washers from the case.

18. Disassemble the bearing rollers, washers and center spacer from the countershaft gear.

19. Repeat Step 16 to remove the reverse-idler-gear shaft.

20. Lift the reverse idler gear and thrust washers from the case, and remove the roller bearings from the gear.

CLEANING AND INSPECTION

1. Wash the transmission case thoroughly inside and out with clean solvent, and blow dry with compressed air.

2. Inspect the case for cracks, stripped threads in the bolt holes, burrs and nicks on machined mating surfaces.

3. Wash the ball bearings in clean solvent, and blow dry with compressed air, holding the bearings from spinning.

4. Check the bearings and races for roughness, cracks, wear or other defects, and relubricate.

5. Inspect the needle bearings for brinnelling and flat spots, check the bearing spacers for galling or other wear. Replace any bearings or spacers that are not satisfactory.

6. Check all gear teeth on the synchronizer clutch gears and synchronizer stop rings for excessive wear, chipping, nicks or burrs. Inspect the synchronizer stop-ring pins for secure attachment and straightness.

7. Check the main-drive pinion teeth and oil contact area on the pinion shaft.

8. Inspect the shift forks for shank and pad wear; test interlock sleeve and pin for free movement in the shift housing bore.

9. Check the mainshaft gear and bearing mating surfaces for excessive wear or galling; check snap ring grooves for burred edges.

TRANSMISSION ASSEMBLY
(Fig. 10-63)

1. Install a dummy shaft through the countershaft gear spacer, and wipe the bore with a light coat of grease, then insert both in the gear bore.

2. Install 22 bearings, followed by a spacer ring in each end of the gear, using heavy grease to hold them in place. On the A-250 transmission, repeat this step to install a second row of bearings for a total of 88 bearings and four spacers.

3. Coat the thrust washers with heavy grease, and install them in the transmission case with the tanged ends engaging the case grooves provided. If the end play exceeded 0.022-in. when disassembled, use new thrust washers for reassembly.

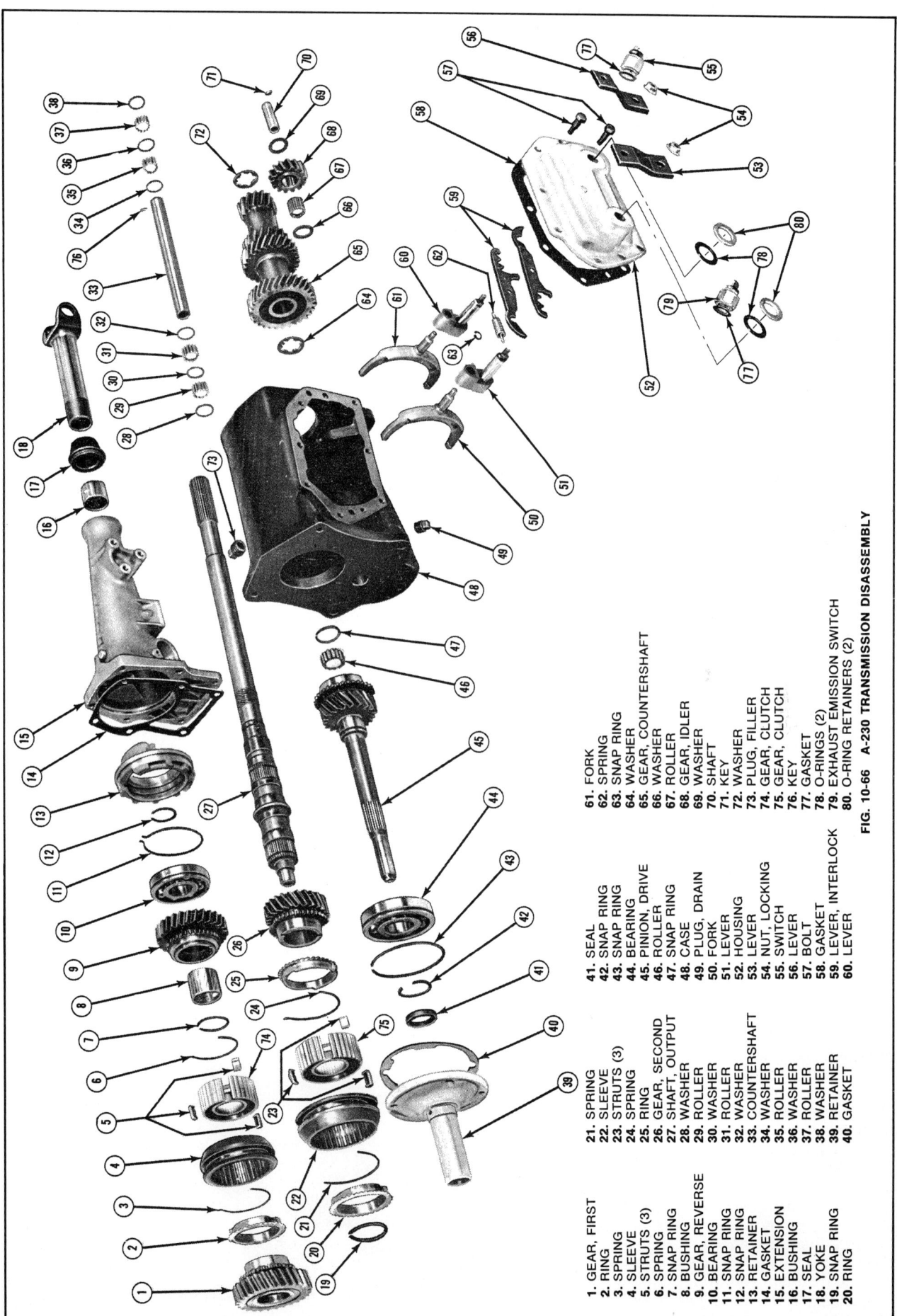

1. GEAR, FIRST
2. RING
3. SPRING
4. SLEEVE
5. STRUTS (3)
6. SPRING
7. SNAP RING
8. BUSHING
9. GEAR, REVERSE
10. BEARING
11. SNAP RING
12. SNAP RING
13. RETAINER
14. GASKET
15. EXTENSION
16. BUSHING
17. SEAL
18. YOKE
19. SNAP RING
20. RING

21. SPRING
22. SLEEVE
23. STRUTS (3)
24. SPRING
25. RING
26. GEAR, SECOND
27. SHAFT, OUTPUT
28. WASHER
29. ROLLER
30. WASHER
31. ROLLER
32. WASHER
33. COUNTERSHAFT
34. WASHER
35. ROLLER
36. WASHER
37. ROLLER
38. WASHER
39. RETAINER
40. GASKET

41. SEAL
42. SNAP RING
43. SNAP RING
44. BEARING
45. PINION, DRIVE
46. ROLLER
47. SNAP RING
48. CASE
49. PLUG, DRAIN
50. FORK
51. LEVER
52. HOUSING
53. LEVER
54. NUT, LOCKING
55. SWITCH
56. LEVER
57. BOLT
58. GASKET
59. LEVER, INTERLOCK
60. LEVER

61. FORK
62. SPRING
63. SNAP RING
64. WASHER
65. GEAR, COUNTERSHAFT
66. WASHER
67. ROLLER
68. GEAR, IDLER
69. WASHER
70. SHAFT
71. KEY
72. WASHER
73. PLUG, FILLER
74. GEAR, CLUTCH
75. GEAR, CLUTCH
76. KEY
77. GASKET
78. O-RINGS (2)
79. EXHAUST EMISSION SWITCH
80. O-RING RETAINERS (2)

FIG. 10-66 A-230 TRANSMISSION DISASSEMBLY

4. Install the countershaft gear in the case, and drive the countershaft through the case from the front to engage the thrust washers and gear bore—thrust washers must remain in place during countershaft installation.

5. Position the countershaft keyway to align with the rear-case-key recess, install the key, and finish driving the countershaft in place until the key is bottomed in the case recess.

6. Install a dummy shaft in the reverse-idler-gear bore, and replace 22 roller bearings with heavy grease to hold them in place.

7. Install the front and rear thrust washers in the case with heavy grease, and lower the reverse idler gear into place with the chamfered end of the gear teeth facing to the front.

8. Slide the reverse-idler-gear shaft into the rear of the case (keyway pointing to the rear), and push through to the case front, displacing the dummy shaft and engaging the thrust washers properly. Install the key in the keyway, and drive the shaft in until the key seats in the case recess.

9. Press the mainshaft bearing in place, and install a snap ring that will allow minimum end play.

10. Move the shift lever to the reverse position, and install the first/reverse gear and shift fork in the case.

11. Assemble the synchronizer parts **(Fig. 10-62)**, second gear and the other shift fork, and hold in one hand. The shift forks must be offset toward the rear of the transmission.

12. Install this gear set in the case, with the machined step on the clutch gear hub to the front, and fit the shift fork into its lever.

13. Work the mainshaft through the gear set carefully until the bearing bottoms in the rear of the case, then replace the synchronizer-clutch-gear snap ring at the front and the mainshaft-bearing snap ring at the rear.

14. If the synchronizer ''float'' exceeds 0.017-in. when disassembled, install synchronizer shims and a spreader spring on the shoulder of the second gear **(Fig. 10-65)** to bring the end play within specifications.

15. Replace the oil slinger on the pinion shaft.

16. Slide the bearing on the pinion shaft with its snap ring groove away from the gear and press in place until fully seated.

17. Replace the keyed washer between the bearing and the retainer snap-ring groove, then install the snap ring. The snap ring must be properly seated and eliminate end play. Four different thicknesses are available for this purpose. Replace the large snap ring on the bearing.

18. Install the 14 roller bearings in the pinion shaft bore, using heavy grease to hold in place, then replace the bearing snap ring.

19. Position the drive pinion to align the blank tooth area with the countershaft gear, and replace the pinion in the case, engaging the inner synchronizer stop ring with the clutch teeth and seating the pinion bearing.

20. Install and seat a new seal in the pinion bearing retainer.

21. Fit a new gasket to the retainer, and replace on the case. Apply sealer to the bolts and torque to 30 ft.-lbs.

22. Fit a new gasket to the extension housing, and slide the housing over the mainshaft, guiding the shaft through the bushing/oil seal. Install and tighten the bolts to 50 ft.-lbs., using sealer on the bolt installed in the one hole tapped through the transmission case.

23. Replace the case cover with a new gasket, and torque the cover attaching bolts to 12 ft.-lbs.

24. Position the speedometer pinion gear and adapter, with the adapter number on its face in the 6 o'clock position, and install in the housing carefully.

25. Replace and torque the drain plug to 25 ft.-lbs. and the back-up light switch to 15 ft.-lbs.

3-SPEED A-230

TRANSMISSION DISASSEMBLY
(Fig. 10-66)

1. Position the transmission in second gear to provide shift fork clearance, then unbolt and remove the cover and shift fork assembly.

2. Unbolt the drive-pinion bearing retainer, and slide it from the drive pinion, discarding the old gasket. Carefully pry the pinion oil seal from bearing retainer.

3. Move the drive pinion forward as far as possible by tapping gently with a hammer and brass drift. This provides maximum clearance for mainshaft removal.

4. Position the cutaway area on second gear next to the countershaft gear, and shift the second/third synchronizer sleeve forward for removal clearance.

5. Unbolt the speedometer pinion-adapter retainer, and remove the retainer, adapter and pinion from the extension housing.

6. Unbolt the extension housing from the transmission case, tap gently with a soft-faced mallet to break the gasket seal, and remove the housing. Discard the gasket.

7. Drive the reverse idler shaft and key from the transmission case, remove the reverse idler gear and the two thrust washers.

8. Withdraw the mainshaft assembly from the rear of the case.

9. Using a plastic hammer, drive the countershaft sufficiently to the rear to remove the key, then drive the shaft out completely, and gently lower the countershaft gear to the bottom of the case to remove the main drive pinion.

10. Remove the pinion-bearing snap ring, and drive the pinion into the case with a soft-faced mallet, removing it from the rear of the case.

11. Remove the countershaft gear through the rear of the case.

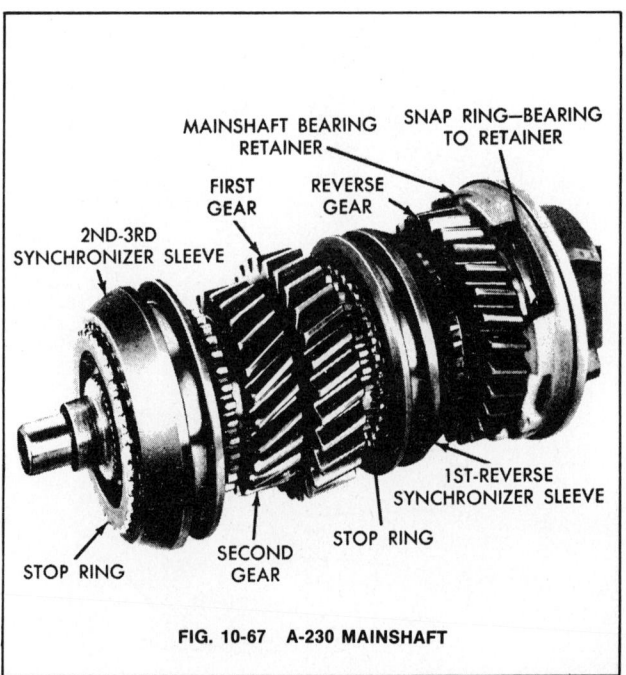

FIG. 10-67 A-230 MAINSHAFT

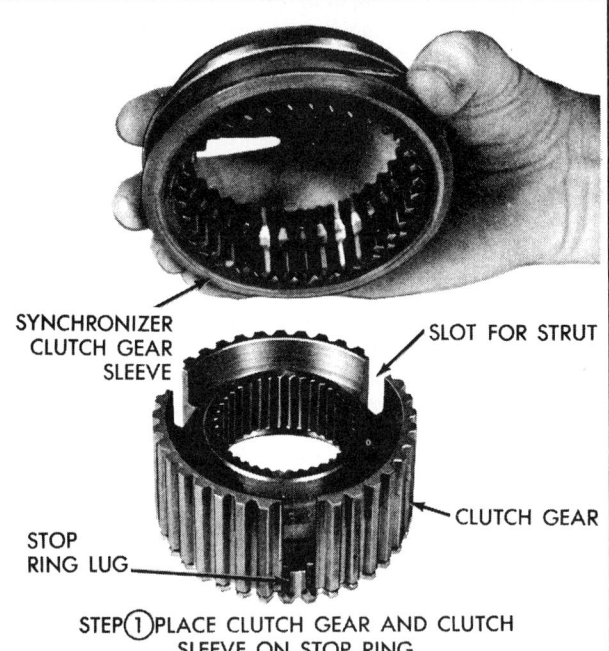

SYNCHRONIZER CLUTCH GEAR SLEEVE

SLOT FOR STRUT

CLUTCH GEAR

STOP RING LUG

STEP ① PLACE CLUTCH GEAR AND CLUTCH SLEEVE ON STOP RING

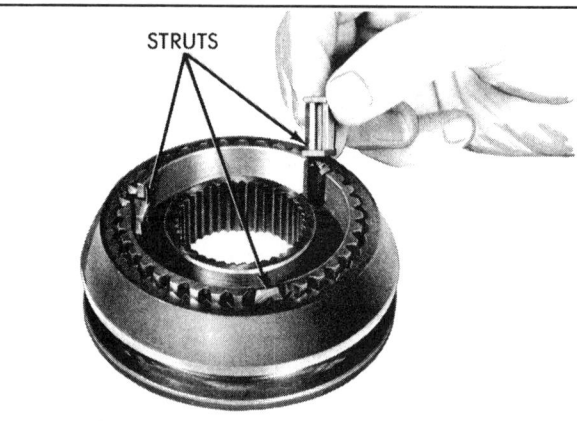

STRUTS

STEP ② INSTALL STRUTS IN CLUTCH GEAR SLOTS

TANG ON SPRING INSIDE STRUT

STEP ③ INSTALL STRUT SPRING

FIG. 10-68 SYNCHRONIZER ASSEMBLY

MAINSHAFT DISASSEMBLY
(Fig. 10-67)

1. Remove the second/third-synchronizer snap ring from the front of the mainshaft, and slide the second/third synchronizer assembly and second synchronizer ring from the mainshaft. Remove the second gear. If the synchronizers are to be disassembled, mark them now for proper assembly later.

2. Expand the mainshaft-bearing-retainer snap ring, and slide the retainer from the bearing race. Then remove the snap ring which holds the bearing to the mainshaft.

3. Place the mainshaft in an arbor press, and support the front side of the reverse gear to press off the bearing.

4. Remove the mainshaft from the press, and slide the mainshaft bearing and reverse gear from the shaft.

5. Remove the first/reverse snap ring, and slide the first/reverse synchronizer assembly and first gear from the mainshaft. Remove the first gear stop ring.

CLEANING AND INSPECTION

1. Wash the transmission case thoroughly inside and out with clean solvent, and blow dry with compressed air.

2. Inspect the case for cracks, stripped threads in the bolt holes, burrs and nicks on machined mating surfaces.

3. Wash the ball bearings in clean solvent, and blow dry with compressed air, holding the bearings from spinning.

4. Check the bearings and races for roughness, cracks, excessive wear or other defects; relubricate.

5. Inspect the needle bearings for brinnelling and flat spots; check the bearing spacers for galling or other wear. Replace any bearings or spacers that are not satisfactory.

6. Check all gear teeth on the synchronizer clutch gears and synchronizer stop rings for excessive wear, chipping, nicks or burrs.

7. Check the main-drive pinion teeth and oil contact area on the pinion shaft.

8. Inspect the shift forks for shank and pad wear; test interlock sleeve and pin for free movement in the shift housing bore.

9. Check the mainshaft gear and bearing mating surfaces for excessive wear or galling; check snap ring grooves for burred edges.

TRANSMISSION ASSEMBLY
(Fig. 10-66)

1. Install a dummy shaft in the countershaft gear bore. Fit a roller thrust washer over the dummy shaft, and insert 22 greased roller bearings in place. Insert a thrust washer and a second row of 22 bearings, then install a thrust washer at the end.

2. Repeat Step 1 with the other end of the countershaft gear, installing a total of 88 roller bearings and 6 thrust washers in the two ends.

3. Coat the rear-countershaft thrust washer with heavy grease, and install it in the transmission case with the washer tangs engaging the case recesses. Place the other thrust washer on the front of the countershaft gear with its tangs facing forward.

4. Place the countershaft gear assembly in the bottom of the case, but do not install the countershaft until the drive pinion is in place.

5. Press the pinion bearing in place with its snap ring groove to the front, and install the snap ring on the shaft.

6. Use grease, and install 15 pilot bearings and the retainer ring in the main-drive-gear bore.

7. Install the drive-pinion/bearing assembly in the case.

8. Position the countershaft gear assembly and thrust washer, and install the countershaft in the rear of the case to engage the thrust washers and counter-shaft gear. Replace the key in the countershaft, and drive the shaft in place until it is flush with the case.

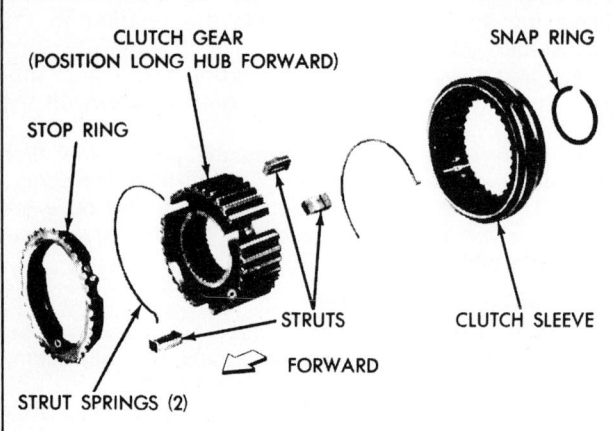

FIG. 10-69   FIRST/REVERSE SYNCHRONIZER

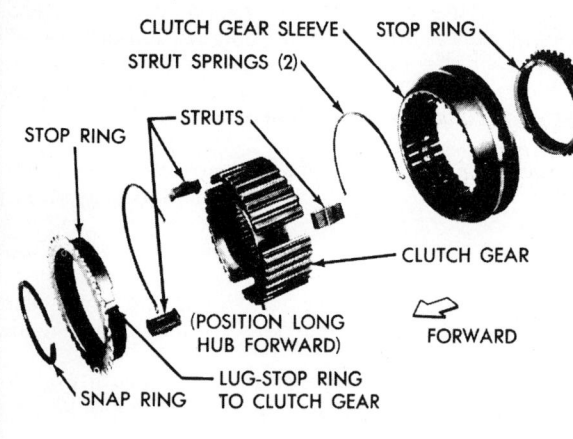

FIG. 10-70   SECOND/THIRD SYNCHRONIZER

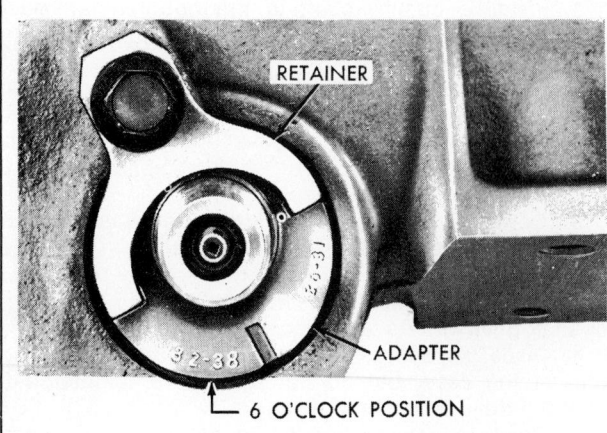

FIG. 10-71   SPEEDOMETER PINION INSTALLATION

9. Tap the drive pinion forward to provide maximum clearance for mainshaft replacement.

10. Reassemble the synchronizer parts, if disassembled **(Figs. 10-68, 10-69 & 10-70).**

11. Slide the first gear and stop ring over the rear of the mainshaft. Seat against the mainshaft flange, which separates first and second gears.

12. Replace the first/reverse synchronizer assembly on the mainshaft, indexing the hub slots with the first-gear stop ring.

13. Replace the clutch-gear snap ring on the main-shaft.

14. Install reverse gear and the rear mainshaft bearing (with its snap ring groove facing forward), and press the bearing on the shaft, supporting the inner race as the bearing is seated to the shoulder.

15. Replace the bearing-retainer snap ring on the mainshaft, and expand it to slide it over the bearing and into the bearing groove.

16. Install second gear on the mainshaft with the thrust surface against the flange, and replace the synchronizer ring and the second/third synchronizer assembly, then install the second/third clutch-gear snap ring.

17. Position the second/third synchronizer sleeve as far forward as possible, and install the front synchronizer ring, using grease to hold it in place. Seat inside the sleeve with the lugs indexed to the struts.

18. Turn second gear until the cutaway section faces the countershaft gear, and carefully insert the mainshaft assembly in the case, tilting as necessary to clear the countershaft gears, and seat in the drive pinion gear.

19. The bearing retainer will bottom to the case without forcing, if everything is correctly assembled. If not, check for a strut, pinion roller bearing or synchronizer ring out of place.

20. Install the dummy shaft in the reverse idler gear, and position 22 greased roller bearings in the bore.

21. Coat the reverse-idler-gear thrust washer with heavy grease, and install in the transmission case.

22. Place the reverse idler gear in the case, and install the reverse idler shaft and key.

23. Replace the extension housing bushing and seal, if necessary. Fit a new gasket to the housing, and install the housing to hold the mainshaft in place.

24. Fit the outer snap ring on the drive pinion bearing, and tap the bearing outer race to seat it—the snap ring *should* touch the case.

25. Install a new oil seal in the front retainer bore.

26. Install the main drive-pinion retainer with a new gasket to the front of the case, coating the bolt threads with sealer and torquing to 30 ft.-lbs.

27. Move the second/third synchronizer sleeve to the second gear position and the first/reverse synchronizer to neutral. Install the shift forks in the cover assembly to the same positions.

28. Replace the gasket and cover assembly, using the special shoulder bolts. The one with the extra-long shoulder is used as a locating dowel pin. Torque the bolts to 15 ft.-lbs.

29. Align the speedometer drive-pinion gear and adapter with the range number stamped on the adapter pointing in the 6 o'clock position, and install in the housing.

30. Fit the retainer in place with the tangs in the adapter-positioning slots, and install the drive-gear-pinion retaining bolt, torquing to 100 in.-lbs. **(Fig. 10-71).**

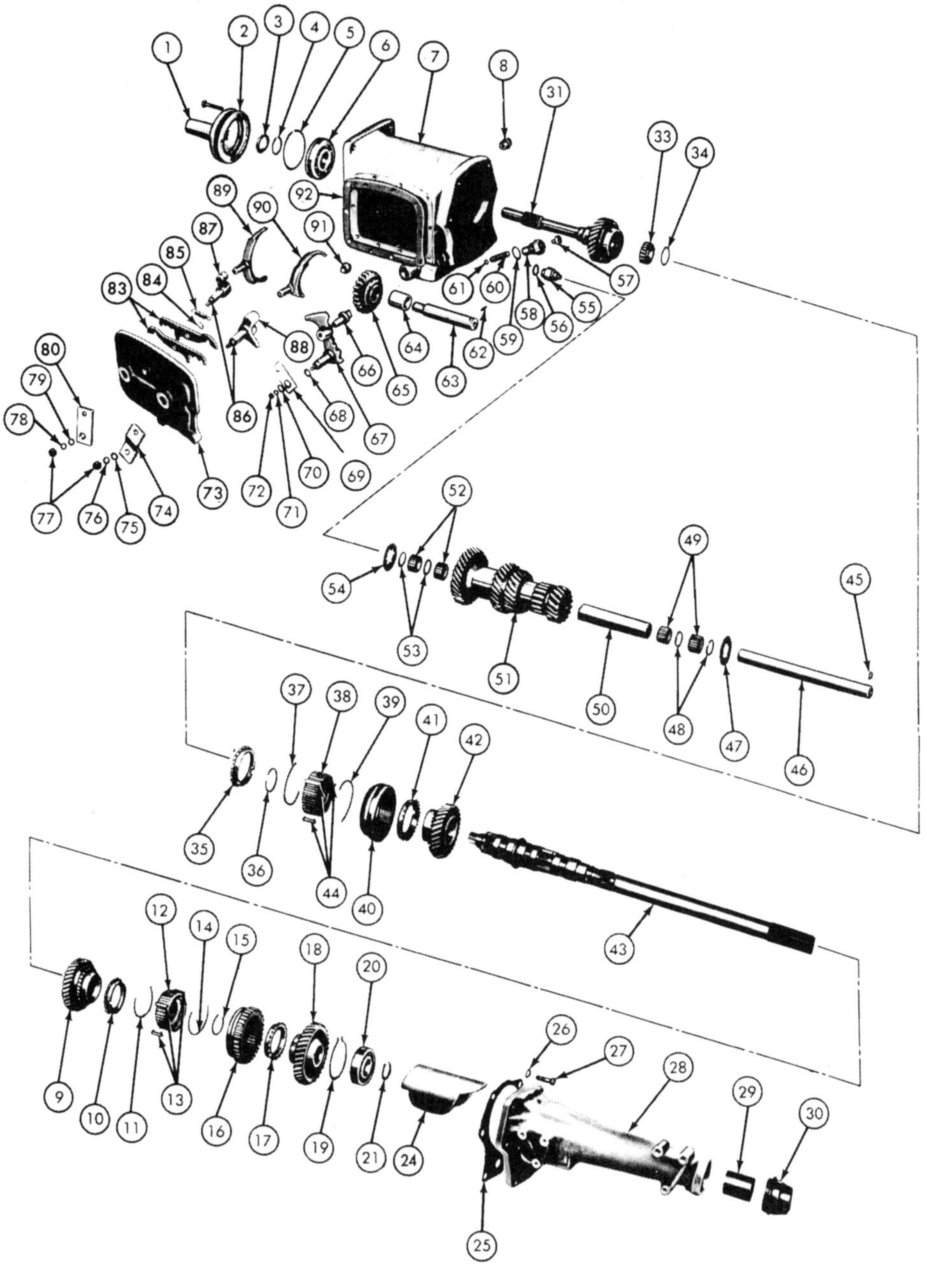

1. Bearing Retainer
2. Bearing Retainer Gasket
3. Bearing Retainer Oil Seal
4. Snap Ring, Bearing (Inner)
5. Snap Ring, Bearing (Outer)
6. Pinion Bearing
7. Transmission Case
8. Filler Plug
9. Gear, 2nd Speed
10. Snap Ring
11. Shift Strut Springs
12. Clutch Gear
13. Shift Struts (3)
14. Shift Strut Spring
15. Snap Ring
16. 1st and 2nd Clutch Sleeve
    Gear
17. Stop Ring
18. 1st Speed Gear
19. Bearing Retainer Ring
20. Rear Bearing
21. Snap Ring
24. Baffle
25. Gasket, Case to Extension
    Housing

26. Lockwasher
27. Bolt
28. Extension Housing
29. Mainshaft Yoke Bushing
30. Oil Seal
31. Main Drive Pinion
33. Needle Bearing Rollers
34. Snap Ring
35. Stop Ring
36. Snap Ring
37. Shift Strut Spring
38. Clutch Gear
39. Shift Strut Spring
40. Clutch Sleeve
41. Stop Ring
42. 3rd Speed Gear
43. Mainshaft (Output)
44. Shift Struts (3)
45. Woodruff Key
46. Countershaft
47. Thrustwasher, Gear (1)
48. Spacer Ring Needle Roller
    Bearing

49. Needle Bearing Rollers
50. Bearing Spacer
51. Countershaft Gear (Cluster)
52. Needle Bearing Rollers
53. Spacer Ring Needle Roller
    Bearing
54. Thrustwasher, Gear (1)
55. Backup Light Switch
56. Backup Light Switch Gasket
57. Plug
58. Retainer, Reverse Detent
    Ball Spring
59. Gasket
60. Spring, Reverse Detent Ball
61. Ball, Reverse Detent
62. Woodruff Key
63. Reverse Idler Gear Shaft
64. Bushing, Reverse Idler Gear
65. Gear, Reverse Idler
66. Fork, Reverse Shifter
67. Reverse Lever
68. Oil Seal, Reverse Lever
    Shaft

69. Reverse Operating Lever
70. Flatwasher
71. Lockwasher
72. Nut
73. Gearshift Control Housing
74. 1st and 2nd Operating Lever
75. Flatwasher
76. Lockwasher Lever
77. Nut, Lever
78. Lockwasher, Lever
79. Flatwasher, Lever
80. 3rd and 4th Operating Lever
83. Interlock Lever (2)
84. "E" Ring
85. Spring
86. Oil Seal (2)
87. 3rd and 4th Lever
88. 1st and 2nd Lever
89. 3rd and 4th Speed Fork
90. 1st and 2nd Speed Fork
91. Drain Plug
92. Gasket, Shift Control
    Housing

FIG. 10-72   A-833/OVERDRIVE-4 TRANSMISSION DISASSEMBLY

4-SPEED A-833/OVERDRIVE-4

TRANSMISSION DISASSEMBLY
(Fig. 10-72)

1. Place the transmission gears in neutral, and remove the reverse shift lever, the cover and the shift fork assembly. Because the forks may remain engaged to the syncrhonizer sleeves when the cover is lifted off, work the forks out carefully.

2. Unbolt and remove the speedometer pinion retainer from the extension housing, and work the adapter and pinion out carefully.

3. Unbolt the extension housing from the transmission case.

4. Move the third/fourth synchronizer sleeve forward, and center the reverse idler gear on its shaft. Tap the extension housing to break the seal, and slide the housing and mainshaft from the rear of the case.

5. Remove the third/fourth-synchronizer clutch-gear snap ring, and slide the synchronizer assembly from the mainshaft **(Fig. 10-73)**. *Do not* separate the synchronizer assemblies unless inspection indicates that a replacement part is necessary.

6. Remove third gear and the synchronizer ring from the mainshaft.

7. Compress the mainshaft-bearing snap ring, and pull the mainshaft and bearing from the extension housing. If the snap ring is in the bearing outer race, you have a heavy-duty model, and the snap ring must be expanded instead of compressed.

8. Remove the snap ring holding the mainshaft bearing on the shaft, and press the bearing off.

9. Remove the bearing, bearing retainer ring, first gear and the first-gear synchronizer ring from the mainshaft.

10. Remove the first/second-synchronizer snap ring, and slide the first/second synchronizer assembly and second gear from the mainshaft.

11. Insert a feeler gauge between the countershaft gear and thrust washer to measure the end play, which should be between 0.015-in. and 0.029-in on the A-833, and 0.005-in. on the Overdrive-4. If end play exceeds this specification, install new thrust washers on reassembly **(Fig. 10-74)**.

12. Remove the reverse-gear shift-lever detent, spring retainer, gasket, plug and detent ball spring from the rear of the case.

13. Drive the reverse-idler-gear shaft from the front to the rear of the case sufficiently to remove the reverse idler gear, then drive the shaft and Woodruff key completely out of the case.

14. Drive the countershaft from the case, and lower the countershaft gear to the bottom of the case to permit main-drive gear removal. The Overdrive-4 uses an expansion plug at the front of the countershaft bore. Punch a hole in the plug, and drive the countershaft to the rear until the Woodruff key can be removed, then drive the countershaft to the front to remove the expansion plug and remove the shaft from the case.

15. Unbolt the main-drive pinion-bearing retainer from the case, and slide the retainer and gasket from the pinion shaft. Gently pry out the bearing-retainer oil seal.

16. Remove the ball-bearing outer snap ring. Drive the pinion into the case with a soft-faced mallet, and lift it out. The heavy-duty model uses a larger bearing which can be removed through the front of the case.

17. Remove the inner snap ring holding the ball bearing, and press the bearing from the pinion.

18. Remove the drive-pinion-bore snap ring and the 16 roller bearings.

19. Lift the countershaft gear from the case and remove.

20. Disassemble the countershaft gear by removing the dummy shaft, 76 needle bearings, thrust washers and spacers.

CLEANING AND INSPECTION

1. Wash the transmission case thoroughly inside and out with clean solvent, and blow dry with compressed air.

2. Inspect the case for cracks, stripped threads in the bolt holes, burrs and nicks on machined mating surfaces.

3. Wash the ball bearings in clean solvent, and blow dry with compressed air, holding the bearings from spinning.

4. Check the bearings and races for roughness, cracks, wear or other defects, and relubricate.

5. Inspect the needle bearings for brinnelling and flat spots; check the bearing spacers for galling or other wear. Replace any bearings or spacers that are not satisfactory.

6. Check all gear teeth on the synchronizer clutch gears and synchronizer stop rings for excessive wear, chipping, nicks or burrs.

7. Check the main-drive-pinion teeth and oil contact area on the pinion shaft.

8. Inspect the shift forks for shaft and pad wear; test the interlock sleeve and pin for free movement in the shift housing bore.

9. Check the mainshaft gear and bearing mating surfaces for excessive wear or galling; check snap ring grooves for burred edges.

TRANSMISSION ASSEMBLY
(Fig. 10-72)

1. Wipe the inside of the countershaft bore with a light coat of grease, and install the spacer and a dummy shaft.

2. Coat the needle bearings with heavy grease, and install a row of 19 roller bearings, a spacer, a second row of 19 roller bearings and a second spacer ring in one end.

3. Turn the countershaft gear around, and repeat Step 2 in the other end, installing a total of 76 bearings and 4 spacers in the two ends.

4. If the countershaft end play exceeded specifications when disassembled (A-833, 0.029-in; Overdrive-4, 0.005-in.), replace the thrust washers with new ones. Coat the washers with heavy grease and position on the ends of the driveshaft with the tangs facing outward, then place the countershaft gear in the case.

5. Press the main drive bearing on the pinion shaft, with the outer groove toward the front, seating the bearing against the gear shoulder.

6. Install and seat a new snap ring on the shaft. Since this snap ring is a selective fit, it should allow minimum end play.

7. Wipe the inside of the pinion shaft bore with a light coat of grease, and install the 16 pilot bearings and the retainer snap ring.

8. Replace the drive pinion and bearing through the case rear, and install in the front bore, tapping lightly in place with a soft-faced mallet, and installing the outer snap ring in the bearing groove. Install the heavy-duty-model drive-pinion/bearing assembly through the front of the case.

9. Insert the countershaft in the case rear bore, and lift the countershaft gear up until its teeth mesh with those on the main-drive pinion gear. The thrust washers must remain in place, with their tangs aligned in the case recesses.

10. Drive the countershaft into the gear, and install the Woodruff key, then continue driving the shaft in until the end is flush with the case rear face. Install a new expansion plug on the Overdrive-4.

11. Replace the reverse-detent spring retainer and gasket, torquing to 50 ft.-lbs. Install the ball, spring, plug and gasket, and torque to 24 ft.-lbs.

12. Position the reverse-idler-gear shaft in the case bore and drive it in until the reverse idler gear can be installed with the shift slot to the rear. The reverse shift fork should engage the slot at the same time.

13. Install the back-up-light switch and gasket, torquing to 15 ft.-lbs.

14. Slide second gear over the mainshaft, with the synchronizer cone to the rear, and seat against the shaft shoulder.

15. Replace the first/second synchronizer assembly, with the synchronizer ring lugs indexed in the hub slots over the mainshaft and up against second gear, then install a new snap ring.

16. Slide the next synchronizer ring over the mainshaft, and index the lugs and slots.

17. Install first gear with the synchronizer cone facing the clutch sleeve gear previously installed.

18. Replace the mainshaft-bearing retainer ring and

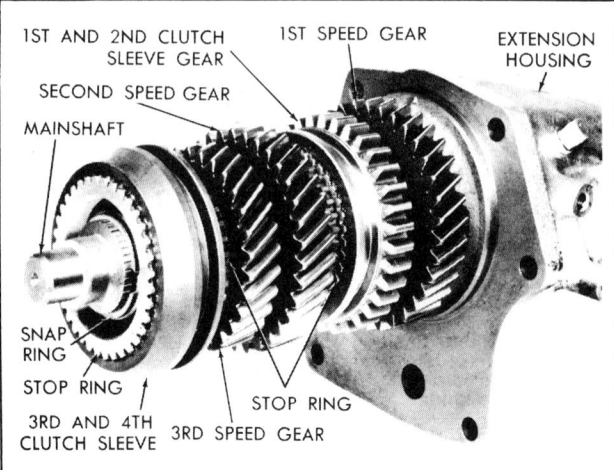

1ST AND 2ND CLUTCH SLEEVE GEAR
1ST SPEED GEAR
EXTENSION HOUSING
SECOND SPEED GEAR
MAINSHAFT
SNAP RING
STOP RING
3RD AND 4TH CLUTCH SLEEVE
STOP RING
3RD SPEED GEAR

FIG. 10-73 A-833 MAINSHAFT

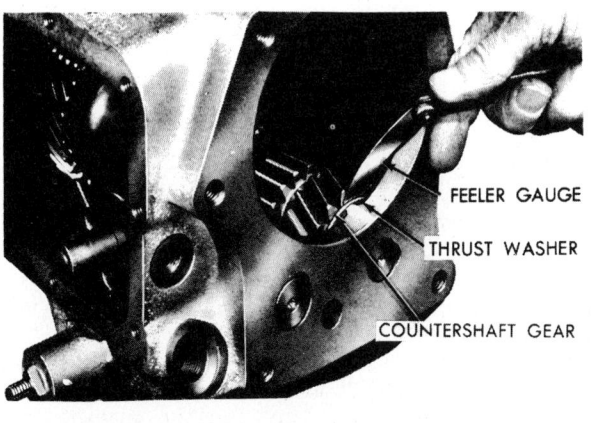

FEELER GAUGE
THRUST WASHER
COUNTERSHAFT GEAR

FIG. 10-74 COUNTERSHAFT GEAR CLEARANCE

mainshaft rear bearing. Press the bearing in place, and install a new inner snap ring to hold the bearing in place. Since this snap ring is a selective fit, it should allow a minimum of end play.

19. Replace the partially assembled mainshaft in the extension housing to engage the bearing retainer ring in the housing groove. Compress the snap ring, and push the mainshaft in until the bearing bottoms against its thrust shoulder in the housing, then seat the ring in its groove. With the heavy-duty model, the ring is expanded instead of compressed.

20. Install third gear on the mainshaft with the synchronizer cone facing forward, followed by the third-gear synchronizer ring.

21. Slide the third/fourth synchronizer assembly on the mainshaft, with the fork slot to the rear, indexing the ring slots with the struts.

22. Replace the retaining snap ring, and use heavy grease to hold the front synchronizer ring over the clutch gear, with the slots and struts indexed correctly.

23. Grease a new extension housing gasket on both sides, and install it on the case.

24. Center the reverse idler gear on its shaft, and move the third/fourth synchronizer sleeve as far forward as possible without losing the struts.

25. Move the drive pinion to the front as far as possible to provide maximum clearance for the mainshaft pilot end.

26. Carefully insert the mainshaft assembly in the case, tilting as necessary to clear the reverse idler and countershaft gears while engaging the drive pinion gear pilot bearings.

27. Move the third/fourth synchronizer sleeve to neutral. If everything is properly assembled, the extension housing will bottom to the case without force. If not, check for a strut, pinion roller or synchronizer ring that is out of place.

28. Replace the extension housing bolts, and torque to 50 ft.-lbs.

29. Replace the drive-retainer oil seal, and install the main-drive pinion-bearing retainer and gasket, coating the bolt threads with sealer, and torquing to 30 ft.-lbs.

30. Move the first/second and third/fourth clutch sleeves to neutral, install a new cover-to-case gasket.

31. Replace the shift-housing/cover assembly, aligning the shift fork shafts with the clutch sleeve grooves. Raise the interlock lever with a screwdriver to let the first/second fork slip under the levers.

32. Install the cover bolts. The one with the longest shoulder acts as a dowel, and passes through the cover and the transmission case at the rear flange center. The two non-shoulder bolts are installed at the lower right. The remaining bolts are shoulder bolts. Torque all to 15 ft.-lbs.

33. Test for correct reverse shifting by placing the transmission in reverse. Turn the input shaft, and move the first/second shift lever in each direction. If the shaft locks or gets harder to turn, the synchro is partly engaged, caused by excessive cam clearance. Install new 1-2 shift lever. Too little clearance would make shift into reverse nearly impossible. Grease the reverse shaft, and replace the operating lever and nut. Torque to 18 ft.-lbs.

34. Align the speedometer-drive pinion gear and adapter with the range number stamped on the adapter pointing in the 6 o'clock position, and install in the housing.

35. Fit the retainer in place, with the tangs in the adapter-positioning slots, and install the drive-gear-pinion retaining bolt, torquing to 100 in.-lbs.

AMERICAN MOTORS

AMC has used the following transmissions; all but the T-96 are fully synchronized, constant mesh designs:

3-Speed T-14 Borg-Warner—1970-74 232, 258, 304-cu.-in. engines, 1976 Gremlins with 232, 258-cu.-in. engines.

3-Speed T-15 Borg-Warner—1970-71 304, 360-cu.-in. engines.

3-Speed T-96 Borg-Warner—1970-71 199, 232-cu.-in. engines. Synchronized only in second and third gears.

3-Speed 150T (FORD RAN/RAB)—1974-76 232, 258, 304-cu.-in. engines; 1977 232, 258-cu.-in. engines; 1979 232-cu.-in. engines. See Ford Motor Company section for overhaul procedures.

4-Speed T-10 Borg-Warner—1970-74 360, 390, 401-cu.-in. engines; 1975-77 Camaros and Firebirds.

4-Speed SR4 Borg-Warner (FORD RAD)—1976½-78 Pacer; 1977-78 232, 258-cu.-in. engines; 1979 6-cyl. and V-8 engines.

4-Speed HR-1—1977-78 Gremlin, 1979 Spirit with I-4.

In addition, AMC introduced an optional auxiliary overdrive unit with the 1975 Pacer. This was also available on 1976 Gremlin/Hornet models and discontinued at the end of the 1976 model year. A hydraulically operated unit, the AMC overdrive is a planetary gearbox manufactured in England by Laycock. Because it is a complicated design, a full discussion of its operation, test procedures and a listing of the special tools necessary to work on it are included in the overhaul section.

3-SPEED T-14/T-15 BORG-WARNER
TRANSMISSION DISASSEMBLY (Fig. 10-75)

1. Unbolt and remove the case cover. Discard the gasket.
2. Unbolt and remove the clutch-gear bearing cap. Discard the gasket. Remove the two front-bearing snap rings.
3. Turn the countergear to align the blank tooth area in the third gear with the countershaft gear, and pull the clutch shaft and front bearing out of the case as an assembly. If the bearing does not slip out easily, use a puller—*do not* hammer or pry out.
4. Press the front bearing from the mainshaft.
5. Unbolt and remove the extension housing. Discard the gasket.
6. Remove the snap ring holding the speedometer drive gear in place, and slide the drive gear off. *Do not* lose the drive ball.
7. Remove the two rear-bearing snap rings, and press the bearing from the shaft.
8. Move the mainshaft assembly to one side to provide access to the shift forks, and remove both.
9. Shift the front synchronizer to second gear position (rear of case), and remove the mainshaft by tilting it up and through the case top.
10. Inspect the shift fork shafts. If their seals do not leak, it is not necessary to remove them.
11. Drive the reverse-idler-gear shaft to the rear slightly, and remove the shaft lock plate, then finish driving the shaft from the case.
12. Drive the countershaft from the case with a dummy shaft.
13. Remove the mainshaft snap ring, and slide the second/third synchronizer assembly and second gear from the shaft front.
14. Slide reverse gear from the mainshaft, and re-

move the rear snap ring, synchronizer assembly and first gear.

CLEANING AND INSPECTION

1. Wash the transmission case thoroughly inside and out with clean solvent.
2. Check the case bearing recesses for wear or scoring, inspecting for cracks and stripped bolt hole threads.
3. Inspect all gears for chipped, cracked or excessively worn teeth. Slide each gear on a new shaft, and if the fit is loose, replace the gear.
4. Wash ball bearings in clean solvent, and blow dry with compressed air, holding bearing from spinning.
5. Examine the bearing for roughness, cracked races and worn balls. Replace if condition is doubtful.
6. Inspect the synchronizer assemblies and synchronizer rings. Look for a pitted condition on the tapered ring area, and for excessive wear or rounded teeth.
7. Use a dial indicator to check the rear face and bore alignment of the clutch-shaft bearing retainer. The total indicator reading should not exceed 0.010-in. on the face, or 0.010-in. on the bore.

TRANSMISSION ASSEMBLY
(Fig. 10-75)

1. Replace first gear and its synchronizer ring on the mainshaft, with the synchronizer ring hub facing to the rear of the shaft.
2. Install the synchronizer assembly on the mainshaft with the collar groove toward first gear, and replace the snap ring. This is a selective-fit snap ring, and must completely fill the groove.
3. Insert a feeler gauge between first gear and the mainshaft collar; if the clearance exceeds 0.012-in. for the T-14, or 0.014-in. for the T-15, replace snap ring.
4. Slide second gear and the synchronizer ring on the mainshaft with their hub facing forward.
5. Install the second-gear synchronizer assembly on the mainshaft, with the end accepting the synchronizer ring facing the rear of the shaft, and replace the snap ring. This is also a selective-fit snap ring, and must fill the groove.
6. Insert a feeler gauge between second gear and the mainshaft collar. If the clearance exceeds 0.018-in. (T-14 and T-15), replace the snap ring.
7. Complete the mainshaft assembly by installing the reverse gear.
8. Install the spacer and a dummy shaft in the countergear bore, and wipe the bore with a light coat of grease. Seat a spacer washer, a row of roller bearings and a second spacer washer in each end of the bore.
9. Place the countershaft gear in the transmission case, and locate a thrust washer on each end so that the tangs are aligned with the case recesses provided. Install the countershaft, positioning it so the slot in the rear of the shaft will face the corresponding slot in the reverse idler shaft and accept the lock plate.
10. Wipe the bore of the reverse idler gear with grease, and install the roller bearings, then place gear in the case, and locate a thrust washer on each end.
11. Install the reverse-idler-gear shaft with the shaft slot facing the countershaft slot, and replace the lock plate.
12. Fit the front synchronizer assembly in the second gear position, and install the mainshaft in the transmission case.
13. Move the mainshaft to one side, and pull the detent levers up to install the shift forks in the shifting assembly.

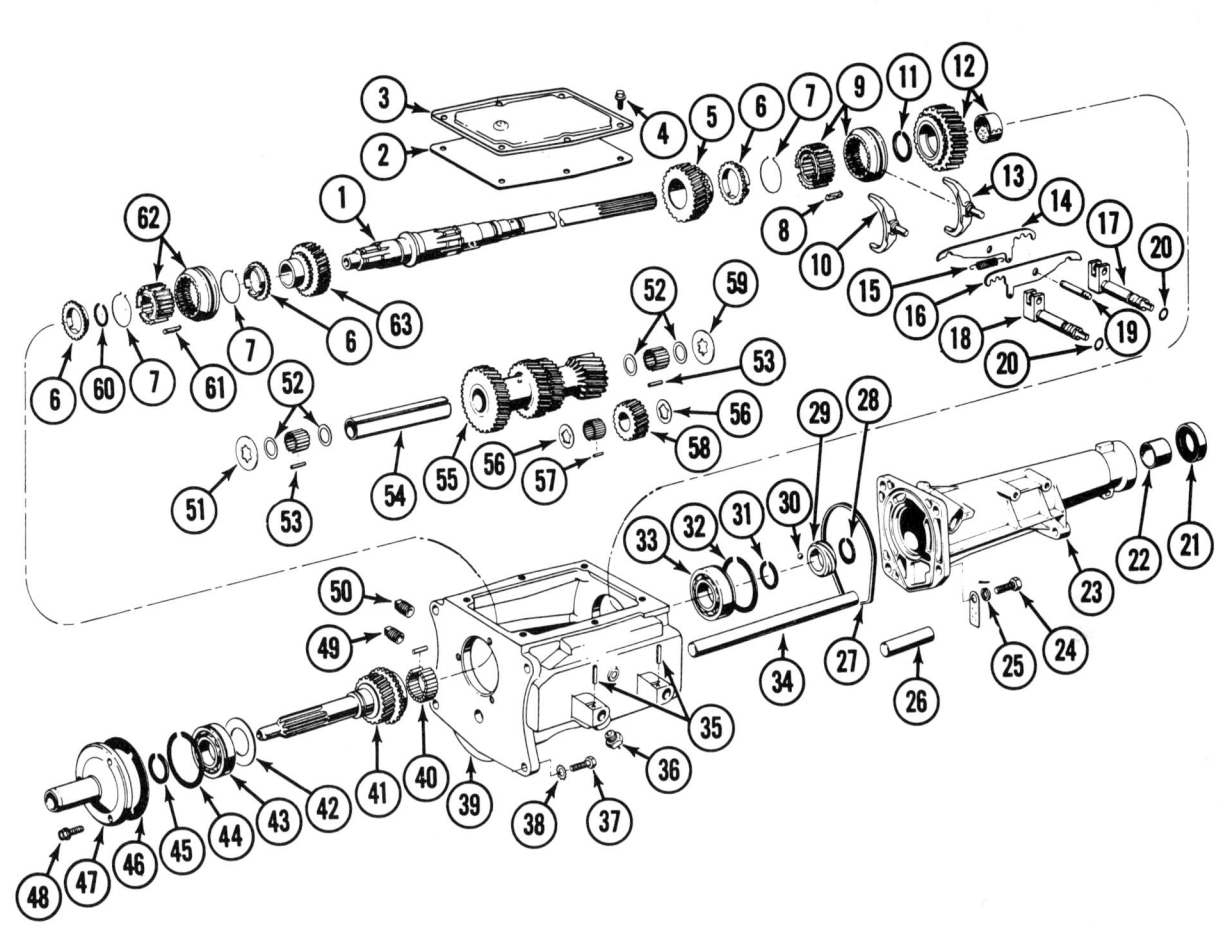

1. Spline Shaft
2. Gasket
3. Case Cover
4. Bolt
5. First Gear
6. Clutch Friction Ring Set
7. Shaft Plate Retaining Spring
8. Clutch Shaft First and
   Reverse Plate
9. First and Reverse Clutch
   Assembly
10. Shifter Second and High Fork
11. Clutch First and Reverse
    Gear Snap Ring
12. Reverse Gear
13. Shifter First and Reverse R Fork
14. Shifter Interlock First and
    Reverse Lever
15. Speed Finder Interlock
    Poppet Spring
16. Shifter Interlock Second and
    Third Lever
17. Shifter Fork First and
    Reverse Shaft
18. Shifter Fork Second and
    Third Shaft
19. Shifter Fork Interlock Lever
    Pivot Pin

20. Shifter Fork Shaft Seal
21. Rear Bearing Cap Oil Seal
22. Rear Bearing Cap Bushing
23. Rear Bearing Cap
24. Bolt
25. Lock Washer
26. Idler Gear Shaft
27. Rear Bearing Cap Gasket
28. Speedometer Drive Gear Ring
29. Speedometer Drive Gear
30. Speedometer Drive Gear Ball
31. Rear Ball Bearing Lockring
32. Rear Ball Bearing Lockring
33. Rear Ball Bearing
34. Countershaft
35. Shifter Fork Retaining Pin
36. Solenoid Control Switch
37. Bolt
38. Lock Washer
39. Case
40. Spline Shaft Pilot Bearing
    Roller
41. Clutch Shaft
42. Front Ball Bearing Washer
43. Front Ball Bearing
44. Front Ball Bearing Lockring
45. Front Ball Bearing Snap Ring
46. Gasket

47. Front Bearing Cap
48. Bolt
49. Drain Plug
50. Filler Pipe Plug
51. Front Countershaft Gear
    Thrust Washer
52. Countershaft Gear Bearing
    Roller Washer
53. Countershaft Gear Bearing
    Roller
54. Countershaft Gear Roller
    Bearing Spacer
55. Countershaft Gear
56. Reverse Idler Gear Bearing
    Roller Washer
57. Reverse Idler Gear Bearing
    Roller
58. Reverse Idler Gear
59. Rear Countershaft Thrust
    Washer (Less Lip)
60. Clutch Second and Third
    Snap Ring
61. Clutch Shaft Second and
    Third Plate
62. Second and Third Clutch
    Assembly
63. Second Gear

FIG. 10-75 T-14/T-15 DISASSEMBLY

14. Press the front bearing on the clutch shaft. Install the speedometer drive ball, drive gear and snap ring.

15. Wipe the inside of the clutch-gear bore with a light coat of grease, and replace its roller bearings.

16. Fit the mainshaft friction ring in place, and install the clutch shaft in the case front.

17. Slide the mainshaft into the clutch-gear pilot bearing, replace the mainshaft rear bearing, using a piece of 1¼-in. pipe to drive the bearing in place until seated. Support the clutch shaft with one hand while seating the bearing.

18. Install the front- and rear-bearing snap rings, and check the assembly to make certain it is secure. Use the thickest snap ring that will fit.

19. Put a new gasket on the clutch-gear bearing cap, and replace it on the transmission case, aligning the cap lubrication hole with the transmission-case lubrication hole. Install the retaining bolts.

20. Fit the extension housing and a new gasket to the rear of the case, and install the retaining bolts.

21. Shift the transmission to check operation in all gears.

22. Replace the case cover and gasket, taking care that the vent is not restricted.

3-SPEED BORG-WARNER T-96
TRANSMISSION DISASSEMBLY
(Fig. 10-76)

1. Unbolt and remove the transmission cover. Discard the gasket.

2. Unbolt and remove the clutch-gear bearing cap. Discard the gasket.

3. Expand and remove the clutch-shaft snap ring and the bearing snap ring.

4. Use a bearing puller and a thrust yoke (to protect the gear), remove the bearing from the clutch shaft, and remove the oil slinger.

5. Unbolt and remove the extension housing from the transmission case.

6. Remove the two snap rings holding the speedometer drive gear on the mainshaft, and press the drive gear from the mainshaft. Retrieve the lock ball positioned on the shaft.

7. Move the mainshaft slightly to the rear of the case to provide clearance for clutch shaft removal. Tilt the clutch shaft to disengage it from the countershaft gear, and withdraw from the case.

8. Remove the second/third shift fork, tilt the mainshaft, and remove the second/third synchronizer snap ring.

9. Slide the second/third synchronizer, second gear and the low/reverse gear from the mainshaft.

10. Lift out the low/reverse shift fork, and remove the mainshaft and rear bearing from the rear of the case.

11. Press the rear bearing from the mainshaft.

12. Remove the reverse idler and countershaft lock plate with a hammer and suitable punch.

13. Use a dummy shaft to drive the countershaft out the rear of the case, and lower the countershaft gears to the bottom of the case.

14. Drive the reverse-idler-gear shaft out the rear of the case, and remove the reverse idler gear, the countershaft gear assembly and the thrust washers.

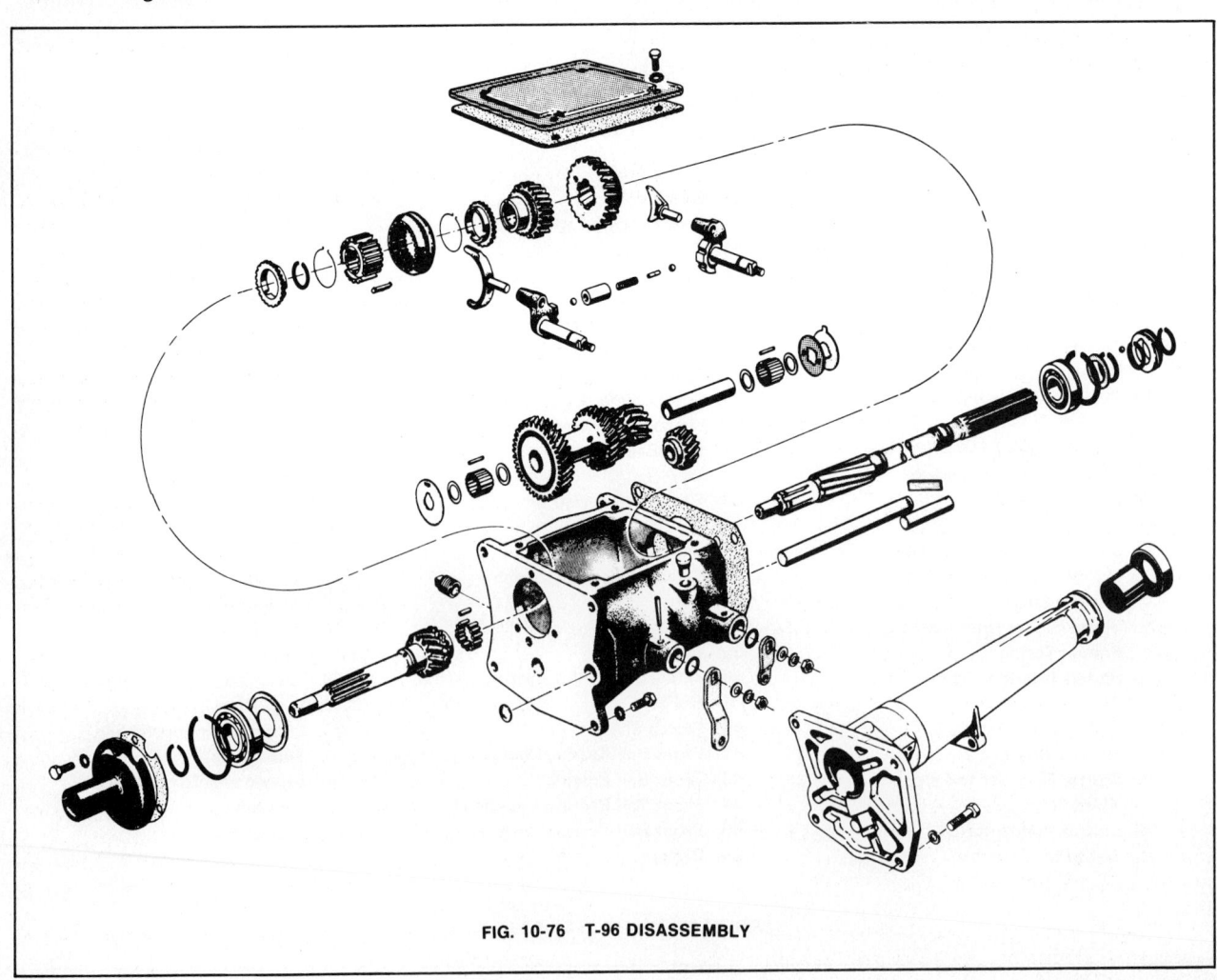

FIG. 10-76 T-96 DISASSEMBLY

15. *Do not* remove the shifter shafts unless the shaft O-ring seals leak.

CLEANING AND INSPECTION

1. Wash the transmission case thoroughly inside and out with clean solvent.

2. Check the case bearing recesses for wear or scoring, inspecting for cracks and stripped bolt-hole threads.

3. Inspect all gears for chipped, cracked or excessively worn teeth. Slide each gear on a new shaft, and if the fit is loose, replace the gear.

4. Wash ball bearings in clean solvent, and blow dry with compressed air, holding bearing from spinning.

5. Examine the bearing for roughness, cracked races and worn balls. Replace if condition is doubtful.

6. Inspect the synchronizer assemblies and synchronizer rings. Look for a pitted condition on the tapered ring area, and for excessive wear or rounded teeth.

7. Use a dial indicator to check the rear face and bore alignment of the clutch-shaft bearing retainer. The total indicator reading should not exceed 0.010-in. on the face, or 0.010-in. on the bore.

TRANSMISSION ASSEMBLY
(Fig. 10-76)

1. Insert the spacer and a dummy shaft in the countershaft gear bore, and install a spacer washer, a row of needle bearings and a second spacer washer in each end, and fit a bronze thrust washer at the front and rear, with grease to hold it in place. The front thrust-washer tang must index with a recess in the transmission case.

2. Place the assembled countershaft gear in the bottom of the transmission case, and install the reverse idler gear with the chamfered side of its teeth facing the case front.

3. Drive the reverse-idler-gear shaft in from the rear of the case. The notched end of the shaft should face the countershaft bore to allow replacement of the lock plate.

4. Install the countershaft, and align the shaft slot with the slot in the reverse idler shaft. Seat the lock plate in place with a hammer and punch.

5. Press the rear bearing on the mainshaft, and install the snap ring.

6. Insert the mainshaft through the rear of the case, and replace the shift forks.

7. Slide the first/reverse gear on the mainshaft, then replace second gear and the synchronizer, with its hub facing to the front.

8. Replace the front mainshaft snap ring. This is a selective fit, and must completely fill the groove.

9. Press the synchronizer hub tightly against the snap ring, and measure the clearance with a feeler gauge. If the distance between second gear and the mainshaft shoulder is not between 0.003 and 0.010-in., replace the snap ring with one that will provide this clearance.

10. Wipe the inside of the clutch-gear bore with grease, and replace the 21 roller bearings to form the pilot bearing.

11. Replace the front synchronizer ring and the clutch shaft on the mainshaft.

12. Align the shift forks and gears while moving the mainshaft rear bearing into the transmission case. Guide the mainshaft end into the clutch-shaft pilot bearing.

13. Replace the rear mainshaft snap ring. This is also a selective fit, and must fill the groove completely.

14. Set the speedometer-drive-gear ball bearing in its mainshaft recess, and slide the drive gear over it, then replace a snap ring at the rear of the drive gear to hold it in place.

15. Fit a new gasket to the extension housing, and replace the housing on the mainshaft.

16. Replace the oil slinger on the countershaft with its concave side facing the rear of the transmission.

17. Install the front bearing and outer snap ring, then replace the inner or clutch-shaft snap ring. This is another selective fit and must completely fill the groove.

18. Fit a new gasket to the clutch-gear bearing cap, and install on the transmission.

19. Measure the synchronizer ring clearance with a feeler gauge. Both clearances should be between 0.036-in. and 0.100-in.

20. Check the transmission assembly by shifting through the gears, then replace the case cover, using a new gasket.

4-SPEED T-10 BORG-WARNER

TRANSMISSION DISASSEMBLY
(Fig. 10-77)

1. Remove the shift rods from the shift levers, and unbolt the shift mechanism from the extension housing.

2. Drain the transmission lubricant, and shift transmission into second gear.

3. Remove the side cover bolts, and withdraw the cover/shift-fork assembly from the case. Discard the gasket.

4. Drive out the tapered, reverse-shift shaft lock pin, using a 1/8-in. punch. Pull the shaft from the case about 1/8-in. to disengage the reverse sliding gear and shift fork.

5. Unbolt the extension housing, and tap with a soft-faced mallet to free it from the adapter plate, pulling the housing to the rear at the same time until the reverse idler gear is free of the reverse idler shaft.

6. Turn the extension housing counterclockwise to disengage the reverse shift fork from the reverse sliding-gear collar, and remove the extension housing.

7. Rotate and pull the rear reverse-idler gear forward to remove from the case. Remove the self-locking bolt beside the gear bore which holds the adapter plate to the transmission case.

8. The reverse-idler-gear shaft is locked in the extension housing by a pin and welch plug. If the shaft does not appear to be worn or damaged, *do not* remove it.

9. Inspect the reverse shift fork, also positioned in the extension housing. If the fork is not worn or damaged, and the reverse-shift-shaft seal does not leak, *do not* remove.

10. Remove the speedometer drive gear, ball bearing and snap rings from the mainshaft, then slide the reverse sliding gear off.

11. Slide the mainshaft and adapter plate sufficiently to the rear to allow center-bearing snap ring removal.

12. Move the third/fourth synchronizer collar forward for mainshaft removal clearance, and slide the mainshaft assembly from the case. The 16 pilot bearings will fall in the case, and should be removed.

13. Lift the reverse front-idler gear and its corresponding thrust washer from the case.

14. Use a dummy shaft to drive the press-fit countershaft from the rear of the transmission case, removing the Woodruff key.

15. Lower the countershaft gear and dummy shaft to the case bottom.

16. Unbolt and remove input-shaft bearing retainer.

17. Remove the input-bearing snap ring, and tap the clutch-shaft/bearing assembly to the rear of the case. Remove through the case side.

18. Remove the clutch-shaft snap ring, and press the bearing from the shaft.

MAINSHAFT DISASSEMBLY

1. Remove the snap ring and flat steel washer from the front of the mainshaft.

2. Slide the third/fourth synchronizer assembly and third gear off the shaft.

3. Remove the snap ring and flat washer holding the center bearing on the mainshaft.

4. Support first gear, and drive the bearing from the mainshaft with a plastic hammer.

5. Remove first gear, the first/second-synchronizer snap ring, the first/second synchronizer assembly and second gear from the mainshaft.

CLEANING AND INSPECTION

1. Wash the transmission case thoroughly inside and out with clean solvent.

2. Check the case bearing recesses for wear or scoring, inspecting for cracks and stripped bolt-hole threads.

3. Inspect all gears for chipped, cracked or excessively worn teeth. Slide each gear on a new shaft, and if the fit is loose, replace the gear.

4. Wash ball bearings in clean solvent, and blow dry with compressed air, holding bearing from spinning.

5. Examine the bearing for roughness, cracked races and worn balls. Replace if condition is doubtful.

6. Inspect the synchronizer assemblies and synchronizer rings. Look for a pitted condition on the tapered ring area, and for excessive wear or rounded teeth.

7. Use a dial indicator to check the rear face and bore alignment of the clutch-shaft bearing retainer. The total indicator reading should not exceed 0.010-in. on the face, or 0.010-in. on the bore.

MAINSHAFT ASSEMBLY

1. Install third gear on the front end of the mainshaft with its tapered cone to the front, then replace the third-gear synchronizer ring.

2. Replace the third/fourth synchronizer assembly on the front of the mainshaft. Hold in place with a selective snap ring which completely fills the groove.

3. Install second gear and the synchronizer ring on the rear of the mainshaft, with its tapered cone to the rear.

4. Replace the first/second synchronizer assembly on the mainshaft, with the tapered hub end to the rear of the shaft. Secure in place with a selective snap ring that will completely fill the groove.

5. Install first gear and its synchronizer ring on the mainshaft.

6. Press the mainshaft center bearing in place, with the snap-ring retainer groove facing first gear.

7. Replace the flat washer and lock ring to hold the bearing in place.

8. With a new gasket on the adapter front face, install the adapter-to-bearing snap ring.

TRANSMISSION ASSEMBLY
(Fig. 10-77)

1. Install the spacer and a dummy shaft in the countershaft gear, and insert a bearing washer, a row of 20 needle bearings, a second washer, a second row of 20 needle bearings and a third washer at each end of the gear.

2. Replace the bronze countershaft-gear thrust washers at each end of the transmission case with heavy grease, indexing the thrust washer tangs with the case recesses provided, then place the countershaft gear in the bottom of the transmission case.

3. Press the clutch shaft bearing in place.

4. Wipe the bore of the clutch-shaft gear with a light coat of grease, and install the 16 roller bearings to form the mainshaft pilot bearing.

5. Place the clutch-shaft assembly in the transmission, and install the flat steel washer in the shaft bore to retain the pilot bearing in place.

6. Position the clutch shaft bearing in the bore, and seat by gently tapping the bearing outer race.

7. Replace the front-bearing snap ring and the clutch-shaft snap ring.

8. Install a new gasket and the clutch-shaft bearing retainer, and torque 15 to 20 ft.-lbs.

9. Replace the front rear-idler gear with its hub facing to the rear, and install the steel thrust washer in front of the gear.

10. Install the Woodruff key in the countershaft slot, lift the counter-gear up to mesh with the clutch shaft gear, and insert the countershaft in the rear of the case, aligning the shaft key with the case recess. Seat the countershaft flush with the rear of the case.

11. Move the first/second synchronizer collar forward to the second gear position and the third/fourth synchronizer collar to the fourth gear position to provide sufficient clearance for mainshaft installation.

12. Install the fourth-gear synchronizer ring on the mainshaft, and insert the shaft assembly into the rear of the case. The synchronizer ring notches must align with the third/fourth synchronizer plates.

13. Align the adapter dowel pin with the transmission case hole, and tap the mainshaft assembly forward. Replace the self-locking adapter-plate bolt, and torque 20 to 30 ft.-lbs.

14. Move the synchronizer assembly sleeves to neutral, and replace the rear reverse-idler gear in the adapter-plate opening to engage the splined portion of the front reverse-idler gear.

15. Install the reverse sliding gear on the mainshaft with its shift sleeve to the rear.

16. Fit a new gasket to the adapter-plate rear face with sealer.

17. Place the speedometer ball bearing in the mainshaft indent, slide the drive gear in place to index with the bearing, and replace the snap ring.

18. Position the reverse-shift-shaft lever in reverse, and pull the shaft out about 3/16-in. for clearance.

19. Place the extension housing over the mainshaft, and slide it toward the case, guiding the reverse-idler-gear shaft into the rear reverse-idler gear and aligning the reverse-sliding-gear sleeve with the reverse shift fork. When the fork and sleeve engage, push the reverse shift shaft back in place.

20. Move the reverse shift lever forward, and continue to install the extension housing, aligning adapter counterbore and dowel pin to extension housing.

21. Install the extension-housing-to-case bolts, and torque 35 to 40 ft.-lbs. Replace the tapered reverse-shift shaft pin.

22. Secure a new cover gasket with sealer. Move the first/second synchronizer sleeve to second gear position and the first/second shift lever forward to the second gear position. Align the synchronizer sleeves and shift forks, and replace the cover assembly.

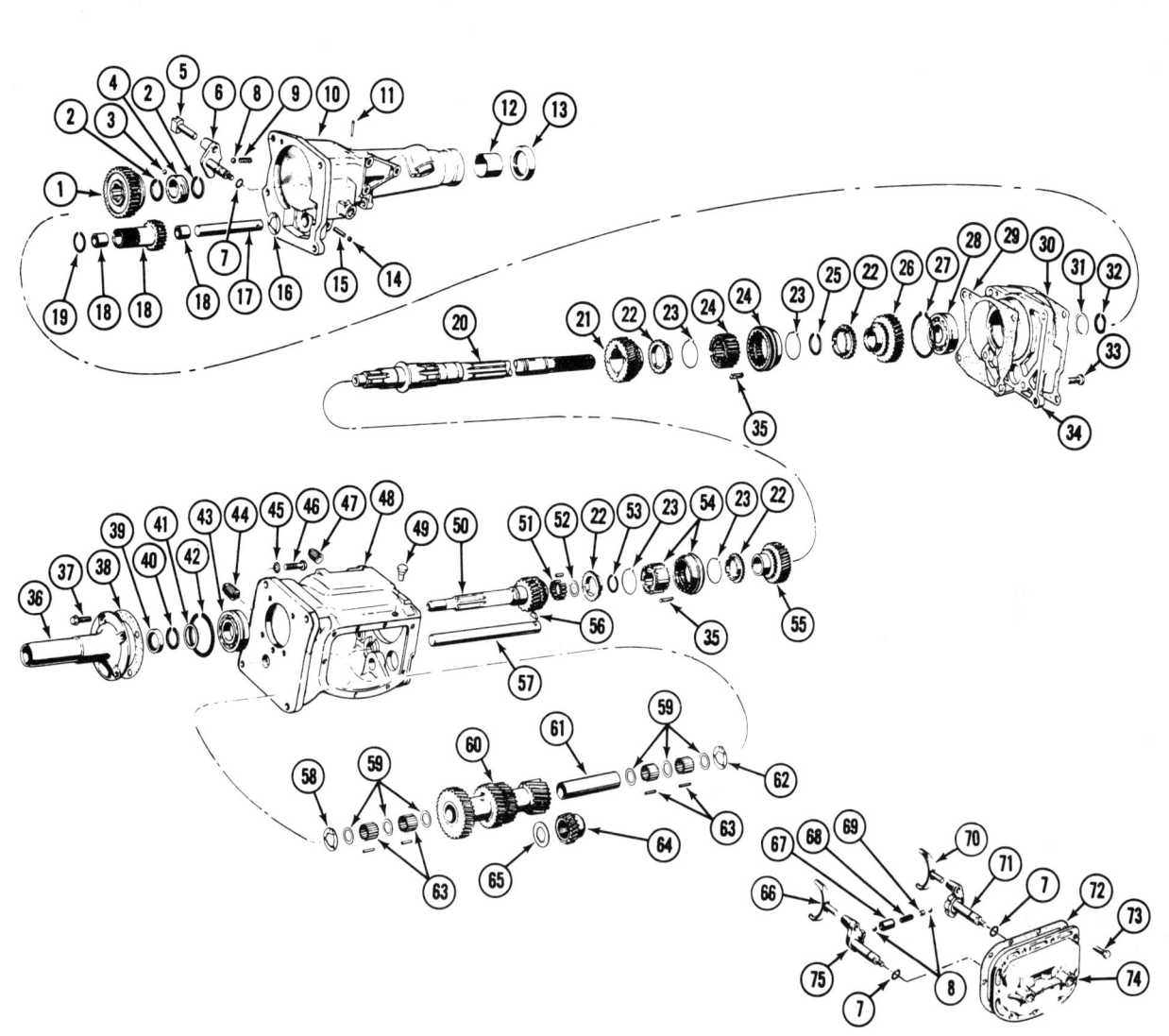

1. Reverse Gear
2. Speedometer Drive Gear Ring
3. Speedometer Drive Gear Ball
4. Speedometer Drive Gear
5. Shifter Reverse Fork
6. Shifter Fork Reverse Shaft
7. Shifter Fork Shaft Seal
8. Speed Finder Interlock Poppet
9. Speed Finder Interlock Poppet Reverse Spring
10. Reverse Gear Housing
11. Shifter Fork Shaft Retaining Pin
12. Reverse Gear Housing Bushing
13. Reverse Gear Housing Seal
14. Idler Gear Shaft Pin Access Plug
15. Idler Gear Shaft Retaining Pin
16. Idler Gear Shaft Thrust Washer
17. Idler Gear Shaft
18. Reverse Idler Gear and Bushings
19. Reverse Idler Rear Snap Ring
20. Spline Shaft
21. Second Gear

22. Clutch Friction Ring Set
23. Shaft Plate Retaining Spring
24. First and Second Gear Clutch Assembly
25. First and Second Snap Ring
26. First Gear
27. Rear Ball Bearing Lockring
28. Rear Ball Bearing
29. Gasket
30. Gasket
31. Rear Ball Bearing Washer
32. Rear Ball Bearing Lockring
33. Bolt
34. Reverse Gear Housing Adapter
35. Clutch Shaft Plate
36. Front Bearing Cap
37. Bolt
38. Front Bearing Cap Shim
39. Front Bearing Oil Seal
40. Front Ball Bearing Snap Ring
41. Front Ball Bearing Washer
42. Front Ball Bearing Lockring
43. Front Ball Bearing

44. Drain Plug
45. Lock Washer
46. Bolt
47. Filler Plug
48. Case
49. Case Breather
50. Clutch Shaft
51. Spline Shaft Pilot Bearing Roller
52. Spline Shaft Pilot Bearing Roller Roller Spacer
53. Third and Fourth Gear Snap Ring
54. Third and Fourth Gear Clutch Assembly
55. Third Gear
56. Key
57. Countershaft
58. Front Countershaft Gear Thrust Washer
59. Countershaft Gear Bearing Roller Washer
60. Countershaft Gear
61. Countershaft Gear Roller Bearing Spacer

62. Rear Countershaft Gear Thrust Washer (Less Lip)
63. Countershaft Gear Bearing Roller
64. Reverse Idler Gear
65. Reverse Idler Gear Thrust Washer
66. Shifter Third and Fourth Gear Fork
67. Speed Finder Interlock Sleeve
68. Speed Finder Interlock Poppet Spring
69. Speed Finder Interlock Pin
70. Shifter First and Second Gear Fork
71. Shifter Fork First and Second Gear Shaft
72. Gasket
73. Bolt
74. Cover
75. Shifter Fork Third and Fourth Gear Shaft

FIG. 10-77   T-10 DISASSEMBLY

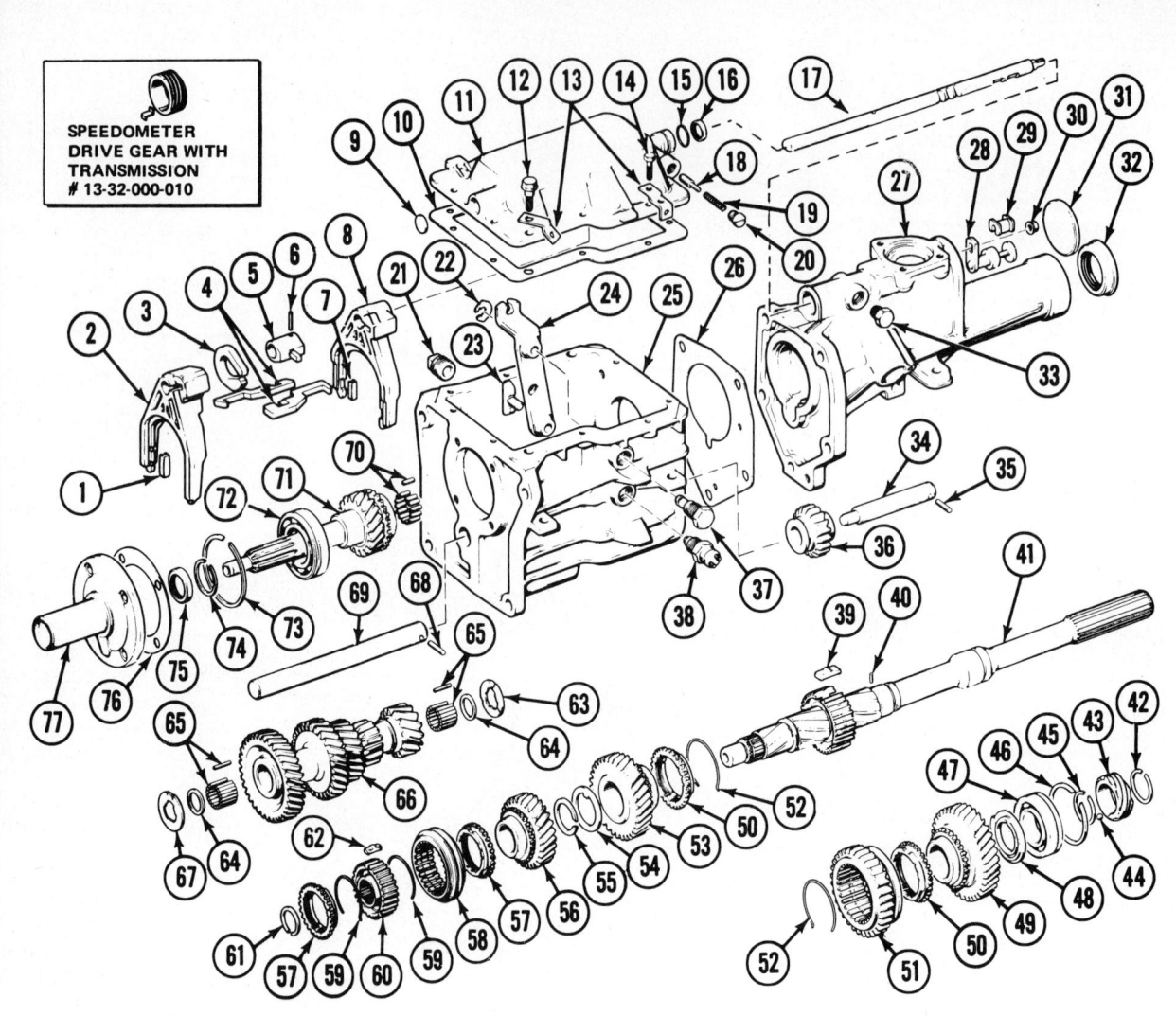

SPEEDOMETER
DRIVE GEAR WITH
TRANSMISSION
13-32-000-010

1. THIRD-FOURTH SHIFT FORK INSERT (2)
2. THIRD-FOURTH SHIFT FORK
3. INTERLOCK PLATE
4. SELECTOR ARM PLATE (2)
5. SELECTOR ARM
6. SELECTOR ARM ROLL PIN
7. FIRST-SECOND SHIFT FORK INSERT (2)
8. FIRST-SECOND SHIFT FORK
9. SHIFT RAIL PLUG
10. TRANSMISSION COVER GASKET
11. TRANSMISSION COVER
12. TRANSMISSION COVER DOWEL BOLT (2)
13. CLIP
14. TRANSMISSION COVER BOLT (8)
15. SHIFT RAIL O-RING SEAL
16. SHIFT RAIL OIL SEAL
17. SHIFT RAIL
18. DETENT PLUNGER
19. DETENT SPRING
20. DETENT PLUG
21. FILL PLUG
22. REVERSE LEVER PIVOT BOLT
    SPRING CLIP
23. REVERSE LEVER FORK
24. REVERSE LEVER
25. TRANSMISSION CASE
26. EXTENSION HOUSING GASKET
27. EXTENSION HOUSING
28. OFFSET LEVER
29. OFFSET LEVER INSERT
30. OFFSET LEVER RETAINING NUT
31. ACCESS PLUG

32. EXTENSION HOUSING OIL SEAL
33. THREADED PLUG
34. REVERSE IDLER SHAFT
35. REVERSE IDLER SHAFT ROLL PIN
36. REVERSE IDLER GEAR
37. REVERSE LEVER PIVOT BOLT
38. BACKUP LAMP SWITCH
39. FIRST – SECOND SYNCHRONIZER
    INSERT (3)
40. FIRST GEAR ROLL PIN
41. OUTPUT SHAFT AND HUB ASSEMBLY
42. SPEEDOMETER GEAR SNAP RING
43. SPEEDOMETER GEAR
44. SPEEDOMETER GEAR DRIVE BALL
45. REAR BEARING RETAINING SNAP RING
46. REAR BEARING LOCATING SNAP RING
47. REAR BEARING
48. FIRST GEAR THRUST WASHER
49. FIRST GEAR
50. FIRST – SECOND SYNCHRONIZER
    BLOCKING RING (2)
51. FIRST-SECOND SYNCHRONIZER
    SLEEVE
52. FIRST-SECOND SYNCHRONIZER
    INSERT SPRING (2)
53. SECOND GEAR
54. SECOND GEAR THRUST WASHER
    (TABBED)
55. SECOND GEAR SNAP RING
56. THIRD GEAR
57. THIRD-FOURTH SYNCHRONIZER
    BLOCKING RING (2)

58. THIRD-FOURTH SYNCHRONIZER
    SLEEVE
59. THIRD-FOURTH SYNCHRONIZER
    INSERT SPRING (2)
60. THIRD-FOURTH SYNCHRONIZER HUB
61. OUTPUT SHAFT SNAP RING
62. THIRD-FOURTH SYNCHRONIZER
    INSERT (3)
63. COUNTERSHAFT GEAR REAR
    THRUST WASHER (METAL)
64. COUNTERSHAFT NEEDLE BEARING
    RETAINER (2)
65. COUNTERSHAFT NEEDLE BEARING (50)
66. COUNTERSHAFT GEAR
67. COUNTERSHAFT GEAR FRONT
    THRUST WASHER (PLASTIC)
68. COUNTERSHAFT ROLL PIN
69. COUNTERSHAFT
70. CLUTCHSHAFT ROLLER BEARINGS (15)
71. CLUTCHSHAFT
72. FRONT BEARING
73. FRONT BEARING LOCATING SNAP
    RING
74. FRONT BEARING RETAINING SNAP
    RING
75. FRONT BEARING CAP OIL SEAL
76. FRONT BEARING CAP GASKET
77. FRONT BEARING CAP

FIG. 10-78 AMC SR4 4-SPEED DISASSEMBLY

23. Apply sealer to the lower right bolt, and install all cover bolts, torquing to 20 ft.-lbs.

24. Check the transmission operation by shifting through the gear range.

4-SPEED SR4 BORG-WARNER TRANSMISSION

TRANSMISSION DISASSEMBLY
(Fig. 10-78)

All threaded holes and bolts are metric, except for the gearshift-lever attaching bolts and fill plug. *Do not* substitute differently threaded bolts if the originals are lost or damaged.

1. Drive out the large extension-housing access plug with a hammer and punch.

2. Reaching through the access hole, unscrew the flanged nut attaching the offset lever to the shift rail, and remove the offset lever.

3. Remove the housing drain bolt, and drain the transmission lubricant.

4. Remove the extension housing, and discard the gasket.

5. Gently pry out the seal from the extension housing with a screwdriver.

6. Unbolt and remove the transmission cover, and discard the gasket. The shift rail and forks are attached as an assembly to the cover. Two of the attaching bolts are alignment dowel bolts.

7. Remove the reverse-lever-to-pivot-bolt spring clip, pivot bolt, reverse lever and fork.

8. Remove the front bearing cap, and discard the gasket.

9. Remove the snap ring holding the speedometer gear in place. Slide the gear and drive ball from the output shaft.

10. Remove the large locating and small retaining snap rings from the front and rear bearings.

11. Using a bearing remover and puller assembly, remove the front and rear bearings from the clutch and output shafts.

12. Withdraw the output shaft and geartrain from the case as an assembly. *Do not* let either synchronizer sleeve assembly separate from the hub.

13. Slide the reverse-idler-gear shaft from the rear of the case, and remove the shaft and reverse idler gear.

14. Drive the countershaft from the rear of the case with a dummy shaft. Remove the countershaft gear and dummy shaft from the case as an assembly.

15. Remove the countershaft thrust washers and any clutch-shaft pilot bearings that may have fallen into the case during disassembly. The front thrust washer is plastic; the rear is metal.

16. Remove the dummy shaft, needle bearing retainers and 50 needle bearings from the countershaft gear.

MAINSHAFT DISASSEMBLY

1. Scribe alignment marks on the third/fourth synchronizer hub and sleeve assembly for alignment reference during reassembly.

2. Remove the output-shaft snap ring and slide the third/fourth synchronizer off the output shaft. If the synchronizer is undamaged, *do not* disassemble.

3. Remove third gear, second-gear retaining snap ring, tabbed thrust washer, second gear and second-gear synchronizer ring.

4. Remove the first-gear thrust washer, and use diagonal cutters to remove the first-gear roll pin from the rear of the output shaft.

5. Remove first gear and the synchronizer ring, then scribe alignment marks on the first/second synchronizer sleeve and output shaft hub.

6. The first/second/reverse hub assembly is machined as a matched unit during manufacture, and *should not* be removed from the output shaft. If damaged, the entire unit is replaced as an assembly.

TRANSMISSION COVER DISASSEMBLY
(Fig. 10-79)

1. Remove the detent plug, spring and plunger.

2. Center the selector arm plates and shift rail.

3. Rotate the shift rail counterclockwise to disengage the selector arm from the selector arm plates. This exposes the selector-arm roll pin.

4. Pull the shift rail to the rear until the selector arm touches the first/second shift fork.

5. Use a 3/16-in. punch to remove the selector-arm roll pin, then pull the shift rail from the cover.

6. Remove the shift forks, selector arm plates, selector arm and roll pin, and the interlock plate from the cover.

7. Pry out the shift-rail oil seal and O-ring with a screwdriver.

8. Drive the shift rail plug out with a hammer and punch.

CLEANING AND INSPECTION

1. Wash the transmission case thoroughly inside and out with clean solvent.

2. Check the case bearing recesses for wear or scoring, inspecting for cracks and stripped bolt-hole threads.

3. Inspect all gears for chipped, cracked or excessively worn teeth. Slide each gear on a new shaft and, if the fit is loose, replace the gear.

4. Wash the ball bearings in clean solvent, and blow dry with low-pressure compressed air, holding the bearing from spinning.

5. Examine the bearings for roughness, cracked races and worn balls. Replace if their condition is doubtful.

6. Inspect the synchronizer assemblies and synchronizer rings. Look for a pitted condition on the tapered ring area, and for excessive wear or rounded teeth.

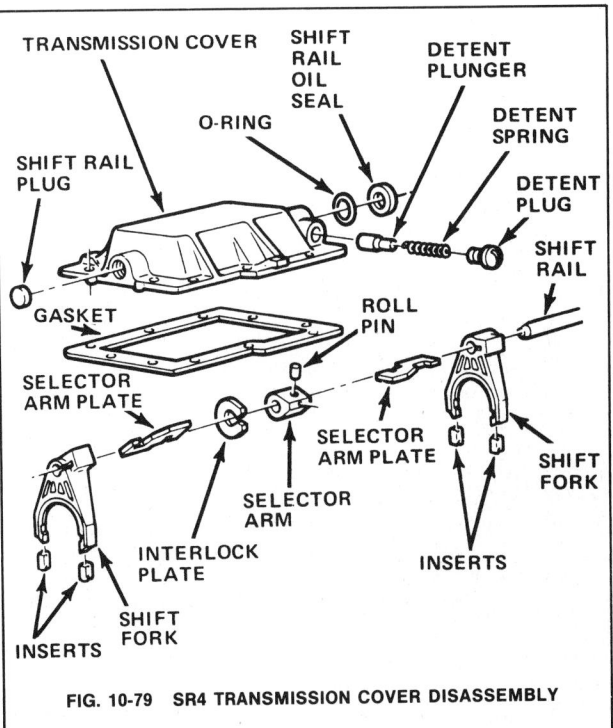

FIG. 10-79 SR4 TRANSMISSION COVER DISASSEMBLY

7. Use a dial indicator to check the rear face and bore alignment of the clutch-shaft bearing retainer. The total indicator reading should not exceed 0.010-in. on the face, or 0.010-in. on the bore.

TRANSMISSION COVER ASSEMBLY
(Fig. 10-79)

1. Replace the nylon inserts and selector arm plates in the shift forks **(Fig. 10-80).**

2. Coat a new shift rail plug with non-hardening sealer, and install it.

3. Coat the shift rail and shift rail bores lightly with petroleum jelly, and install the shift rail until its end is flush with the inside edge of the cover.

4. Place the first/second (larger) shift fork in the cover, with its offset facing to the cover rear, and slide the shift rail through it.

5. Install the selector arm and C-shaped interlock plate in the cover, and slide the shift rail through the arm. The roll pin hole must face down, and the widest part of the arm must face away from the cover.

6. Install the third/fourth shift fork with its offset to the cover rear. The third/fourth shift-fork selector arm plate is positioned under the first/second shift-fork selector arm plate.

7. Slide the shift rail through the third/fourth shift fork and into the bore at the front of the cover.

8. Turn the shift rail until the forward end flat is parallel to, but faces away from, the cover.

9. Align the holes, and install the roll pin flush with the selector arm surface.

10. Install the C-shaped interlock plate, detent plunger, spring and plug.

11. Fit a new O-ring in the shift-rail oil-seal groove.

12. Lubricate a new oil seal with petroleum jelly, and install it.

MAINSHAFT ASSEMBLY

If it is necessary to replace any output shaft gear, the countergear must also be replaced to maintain the proper gear mesh and to prevent noisy operation.

1. Lightly lubricate the output shaft and gear bores with transmission lubricant.

2. Align and install the first/second synchronizer sleeve on the output shaft hub, using the reference marks made at disassembly.

3. Install the synchronizer ring on first gear, and slide the gear and ring on the output shaft. The synchronizer inserts must engage the first-gear synchronizer-ring notches.

4. Install a new first-gear roll pin in the output shaft.

5. Install the synchronizer ring on second gear, and slide the gear and ring on the output shaft. The synchronizer inserts must engage the second-gear synchronizer-ring notches.

6. Replace the second-gear thrust washer and snap ring on the output shaft. The sharp edges of the washer face down, and the tab engages the output shaft notch.

7. Insert a feeler gauge between second gear and the thrust washer to measure end play. If it exceeds 0.014-in., replace the thrust washer and snap ring, and inspect the synchronizer hub for excessive thrust face wear.

8. Install the synchronizer ring on third gear, and slide the gear and ring on the output shaft.

9. Align and install the third/fourth synchronizer on the output shaft, with its machined groove facing forward. The synchronizer inserts must engage the synchronizer ring notches.

10. Replace the output-shaft snap ring, and measure end play between the third/fourth synchronizer hub and the snap ring as in Step 7; the same specification is used.

TRANSMISSION ASSEMBLY
(Fig. 10-78)

Petroleum jelly is recommended rather than grease as an aid in helping to position thrust washers and roller bearings.

1. Install the dummy shaft in the countershaft gear, and wipe the bore with a light coat of petroleum jelly, installing a row of 25 needle bearings and a retainer at each end of the gear.

2. Replace the plastic thrust washer at the front of the transmission case and the metal thrust washer at the rear with petroleum jelly, indexing the thrust washer tangs with the case recesses provided.

3. Insert the countershaft gear assembly in the case, and install the countershaft from the rear of the case to engage thrust washers and countershaft gear properly.

4. Insert the reverse idler gear in the case (shift lever groove toward the front), and install the reverse idler shaft from the rear of the case.

5. Replace the assembled output shaft and geartrain in the case, taking care not to disturb the synchronizer assembly positions.

6. Install the fourth-gear synchronizer ring in the third/fourth synchronizer sleeve, with the inserts and notches engaging.

7. Wipe the bore of the clutch shaft gear with a light coat of petroleum jelly, and install the mainshaft pilot bearing.

8. Replace the clutch shaft assembly in the transmission, and engage it with the third/fourth synchronizer assembly.

9. Position the output-shaft first gear against the case, and install the front bearing, driving it completely into the case to seat.

10. Replace the front-bearing retaining and locating snap rings.

11. Install a new oil seal in the front bearing cap.

12. Align the front bearing-cap groove and gasket cutout with the oil hole in the case, and replace the

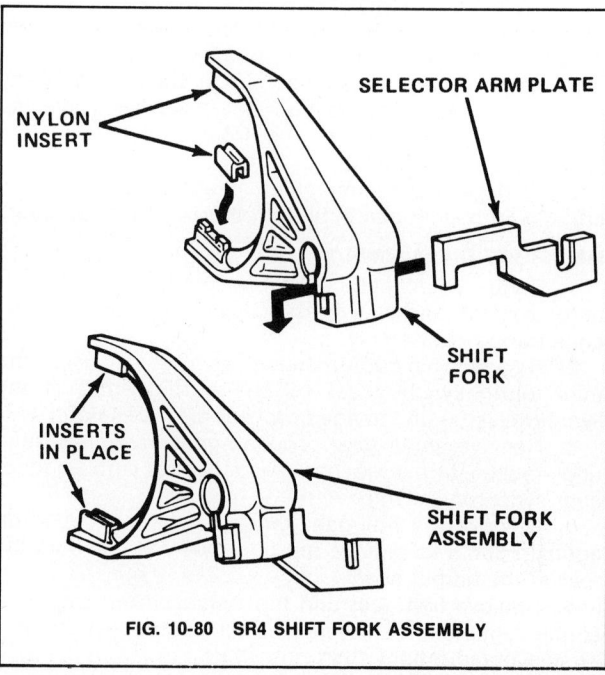

FIG. 10-80 SR4 SHIFT FORK ASSEMBLY

NYLON INSERT

SELECTOR ARM PLATE

SHIFT FORK

INSERTS IN PLACE

SHIFT FORK ASSEMBLY

bearing cap. Coat the bolts with non-hardening sealer, and torque to 13 ft.-lbs.

13. Check that the first-gear thrust washer is properly installed and engages the roll pin, then install the rear bearing, rear-bearing retaining and locating snap rings.

14. Replace the speedometer-gear drive ball in the output shaft, and slide the speedometer gear over it. Install the snap ring.

15. Place the reverse lever in the case. With non-hardening sealer on the pivot bolt, partially install it in the case.

16. Fit the reverse lever on the pivot bolt, install the spring clip, and torque the pivot bolt to 20 ft.-lbs.

17. Check to make sure the reverse lever fork engages the reverse idler gear, then rotate the clutch shaft and output shaft to check for binding.

18. With the reverse lever positioned in neutral, install a new cover gasket, and replace the cover assembly on the case. Install the two cover dowel bolts in the same location from which they were removed. These maintain cover alignment, and misplacement can cause hard shifting.

19. With non-hardening sealer on the cover bolts, tighten all finger-tight, then torque in an alternate pattern to 10 ft.-lbs.

20. Replace the extension housing on the case, using a new gasket. Apply non-hardening sealer on the bolts, install and torque to 23 ft.-lbs.

21. Replace the nylon insert on the offset lever (if removed) and mount the lever on the shift rail. With sealant on the shift rail threads, replace the offset-lever retaining nut, and torque to 10 ft.-lbs.

22. Install the access plug with non-hardening sealer and add three pints of transmission lubricant to the transmission case.

23. Install the filler plug, and torque to 23 ft.-lbs.

24. Install a new extension-housing oil seal.

4-SPEED HR-1 TRANSMISSION

TRANSMISSION DISASSEMBLY

(Fig. 10-80A)

All threaded holes and bolts are metric, except for the fill plug. *Do not* substitute differently threaded bolts if the originals are lost or damaged.

1. Remove bolts attaching the top cover to the trans-

mission case, and remove top cover and gasket.

2. Remove the detent plug with a hex wrench, along with detent spring and plunger.

3. Drive out the access plug at the rear of the case with a punch and hammer.

4. Insert a 5/16-in.-diameter rod in the access hole to push out the interlock plate retaining pin. Remove interlock plate.

5. Remove the selector arm roll with a 5/32-in. pin punch.

6. Tap the forward end of the shift rail until it displaces the large plug at the rear of the extension housing. Remove the shift rail.

7. Remove the selector arm, interlock plate and shift forks. Be sure to note the position of each of these parts for reassembly.

8. Remove the front-bearing-cap attaching bolts and remove the cap and O-ring. Discard the O-ring.

9. Using a screwdriver, pry out the front-bearing-cap oil seal. If the seal does not come out easily, use a small, sharp chisel to partially collapse the seal wall, using extreme care to avoid damage to the seal bore.

10. Remove the front bearing retaining and locating snap rings from the clutch shaft and front bearing.

11. To remove the front bearing, use the tools shown in **Fig. 10-80B.**

12. Unbolt and loosen—don't remove—the extension housing by tapping it with a plastic-tipped hammer.

13. Remove the clutch shaft from the front of the case.

14. Without allowing the third/fourth synchronizer sleeve to separate from the hub, pull out the extension housing and output-shaft geartrain assembly from the rear of the case.

15. Using a screwdriver, pry out the shift-rail oil seal from the seal counterbore at the rear of the case.

16. Remove the mainshaft pilot roller bearing from the clutch shaft bore or from the output-shaft pilot bearing hub.

17. Thread the shaft remover tool into the reverse idler shaft and thread the slide hammer bolt into the shaft remover. Remove as shown in **Fig. 10-80C,** along with gear spacer. Note their positions for reassembly.

18. Remove the shift fork from the reverse lever. Note the position of the fork for reassembly.

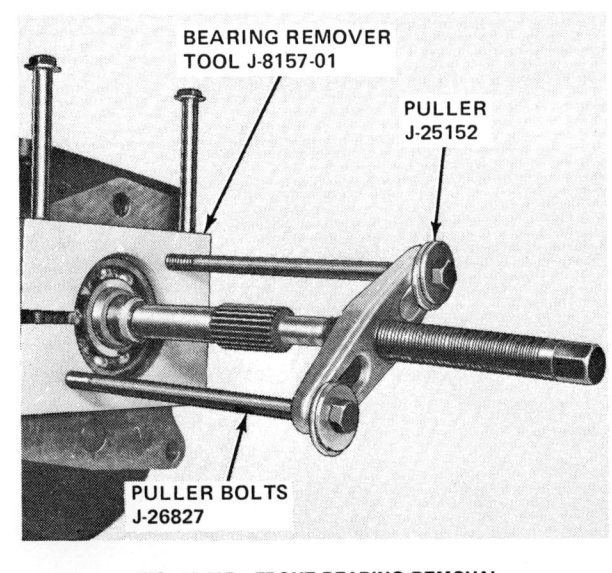

FIG. 10-80B FRONT BEARING REMOVAL

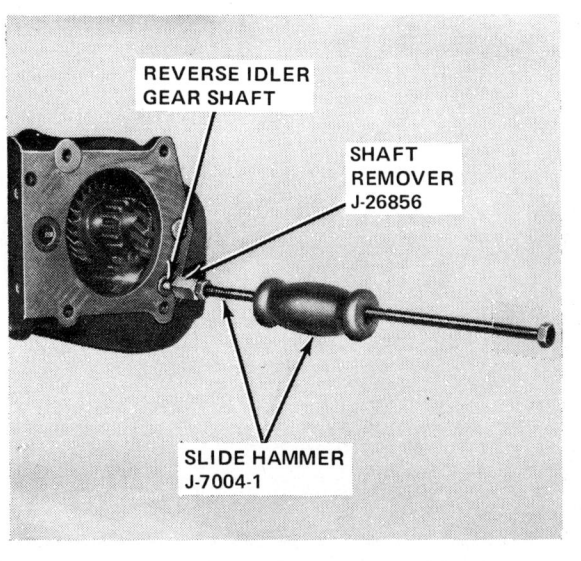

FIG. 10-80C REVERSE IDLER GEARSHAFT REMOVAL

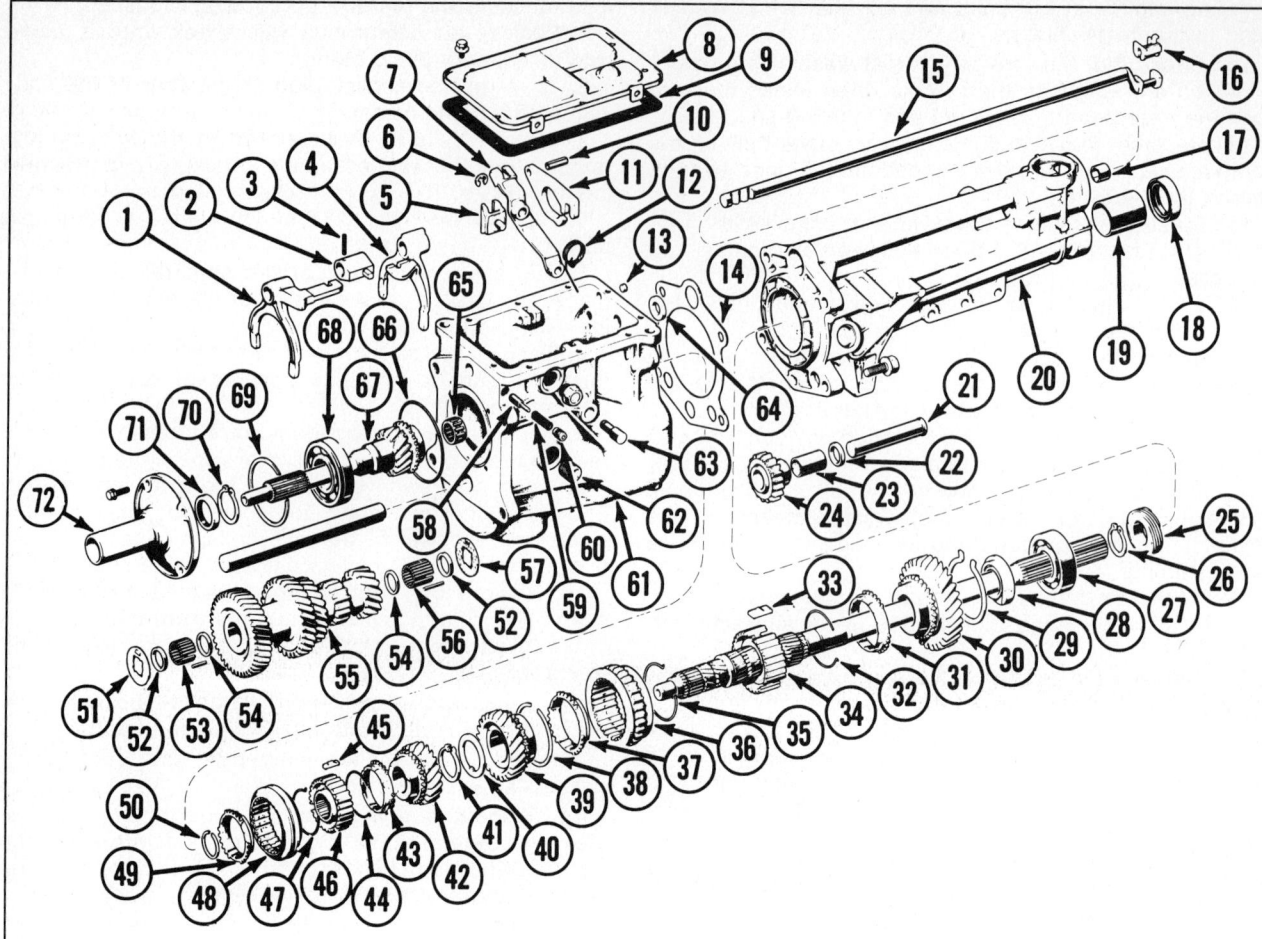

1. THIRD-FOURTH SHIFT FORK
2. SELECTOR ARM
3. SELECTOR ARM ROLL PIN
4. FIRST-SECOND SHIFT FORK
5. REVERSE LEVER SHIFT FORK
6. REVERSE LEVER SPRING CLIP
7. REVERSE LEVER
8. TOP COVER
9. TOP COVER GASKET
10. INTERLOCK PLATE RETAINING PIN
11. INTERLOCK PLATE
12. REVERSE LEVER SPRING
13. INTERLOCK RETAINING PIN ACCESS PLUG
14. EXTENSION HOUSING GASKET
15. SHIFT RAIL
16. SHIFT RAIL INSERT
17. SHIFT RAIL BUSHING (NYLON)
18. EXTENSION HOUSING SEAL
19. EXTENSION HOUSING BUSHING (SERVICED AS PART OF HOUSING)
20. EXTENSION HOUSING
21. REVERSE IDLER GEAR SHAFT
22. REVERSE IDLER GEAR SPACER
23. REVERSE IDLER GEAR BUSHING (SERVICED AS PART OF GEAR)
24. REVERSE IDLER GEAR
25. SPEEDOMETER GEAR
26. REAR BEARING SNAP RING
27. REAR BEARING
28. OIL SLINGER/SPACER
29. OUTPUT SHAFT REAR SNAP RING

30. FIRST GEAR
31. FIRST GEAR BLOCKING RING
32. FIRST-SECOND SYNCHRONIZER INSERT SPRING
33. FIRST-SECOND SYNCHRONIZER INSERT (3)
34. OUTPUT SHAFT AND FIRST-SECOND SYNCHRONIZER HUB ASSEMBLY (SERVICED AS ASSEMBLY ONLY)
35. FIRST-SECOND SYNCHRONIZER INSERT SPRING
36. FIRST-SECOND SYNCHRONIZER SLEEVE
37. SECOND GEAR BLOCKING RING
38. SECOND GEAR STOP RING (INSTALLED ON GEAR)
39. SECOND GEAR
40. SECOND GEAR SPACER
41. SECOND GEAR SNAP RING
42. THIRD GEAR
43. THIRD GEAR BLOCKING RING
44. THIRD-FOURTH SYNCHRONIZER INSERT SPRING
45. THIRD-FOURTH SYNCHRONIZER INSERT (3)
46. THIRD-FOURTH SYNCHRONIZER HUB
47. THIRD-FOURTH SYNCHRONIZER INSERT SPRING
48. THIRD-FOURTH SYNCHRONIZER SLEEVE
49. FOURTH GEAR BLOCKING RING
50. OUTPUT SHAFT FRONT SNAP RING
51. COUNTERSHAFT THRUST WASHER (METAL FACE)
52. COUNTERSHAFT BEARING RETAINER (THICK)

53. COUNTERSHAFT FRONT BEARINGS (SHORT-19 REQD.)
54. COUNTERSHAFT BEARING RETAINER (THIN)
55. COUNTERSHAFT GEAR
56. COUNTERSHAFT REAR BEARINGS (LONG-19 REQD.)
57. COUNTERSHAFT THRUST WASHER (METAL FACE)
58. DETENT PLUNGER
59. DETENT SPRING
60. DETENT PLUG
61. TRANSMISSION CASE
62. FILL PLUG
63. REVERSE LEVER PIVOT (SERVICED AS PART OF CASE)
64. SHIFT RAIL OIL SEAL
65. CLUTCH SHAFT ROLLER BEARING
66. FRONT BEARING CAP O-RING
67. CLUTCH SHAFT
68. FRONT BEARING
69. FRONT BEARING LOCATING SNAP RING
70. FRONT BEARING RETAINING SNAP RING
71. FRONT BEARING CAP OIL SEAL
72. FRONT BEARING CAP

FIG. 10-80A   AMC HR-1 4-SPEED DISASSEMBLY

19. Remove the spring clip that holds the reverse lever on the lever pivot shaft. Remove the lever and the lever spring. Note the spring position for reassembly.

20. Remove the countershaft gear and the loading tool as an assembly. Then remove the loading tool and the 38 needle bearings and 4 bearing retainers. There are two thick and two thin bearing retainers, along with short and long countershaft needle bearings. Again, note their positions for reassembly.

21. Remove the countershaft-gear thrust washers.

OUTPUT SHAFT GEARTRAIN DISASSEMBLY

1. Remove the fourth-gear blocking ring from the third/fourth synchronizer.

2. Using needlenose pliers, remove the output-shaft snap ring. To unseat the snap ring, compress it, then slide it toward first gear until it clears the extension housing.

3. Tap the end of the output shaft with a plastic-tipped hammer to remove the extension housing from the bearing.

4. Remove and discard the output-shaft front snap ring.

5. Remove the third/fourth synchronizer and mark the hub and sleeve for reassembly reference. Separate the sleeve from the hub and remove the synchronizer inserts and insert springs.

6. Remove third gear and the blocking ring.

7. Remove the second-gear snap ring, then second gear and the blocking ring.

8. To unseat the rear-bearing snap ring, use snap ring pliers with 45° angle tips. Then slide the snap ring toward the speedometer drive gear.

9. Using bearing remover J-8157-01 **(Fig. 10-80D)** and an arbor press, remove first gear, the first gear

spacer, the rear bearing and the speedometer gear as an assembly. *Do not* allow the first-gear blocking ring to get caught between the remover and the gear.

10. Remove the first-gear blocking ring.

11. Before removing the first/second synchronizer sleeve from the hub, the inserts and insert springs, mark them for reassembly. *Do not* try to remove the first/second synchronizer from the output shaft—hub and shaft are serviced only as an assembly.

12. Remove the extension-housing oil seal as shown in **Fig. 10-80E**.

CLEANING AND INSPECTION

1. Wash the transmission case thoroughly inside and out with clean solvent.

2. Check the case bearing recesses for wear or scoring, inspecting for cracks and stripped bolt-hole threads.

3. Inspect all gears for chipped, cracked or excessively worn teeth. Slide each gear on a new shaft and, if the fit is loose, replace the gear.

4. Wash the bearings in clean solvent, and blow dry with low-pressure compressed air, holding the bearing from spinning.

5. Examine the bearings for roughness, cracked races and worn balls. Replace if their condition is doubtful.

6. Inspect the synchronizer assemblies and synchronizer rings. Look for a pitted condition on the tapered ring area, and for excessive wear or rounded teeth.

7. Use a dial indicator to check the rear face bore alignment of the clutch-shaft bearing retainer.

OUTPUT SHAFT GEARTRAIN ASSEMBLY

1. Seat the rear bearing in the extension housing bore with a plastic-tipped hammer.

2. Choose the thickest possible output-shaft rear snap ring that will fit in the ring groove. Do not install. The output shaft rear snap ring is a selective-type, and available in varying thicknesses. Trial-fit the snap rings until the proper thickness is obtained.

3. Remove the rear bearing from the extension housing with a long punch or a ratchet handle extension.

4. Lubricate the output shaft, synchronizer components and all gear bores with transmission lubricant. Spread petroleum jelly on the tapered blocking-ring surfaces of all gears.

5. Install the synchronizer spring and inserts in the first/second hub and the first/second synchronizer sleeve over the hub and inserts. Using the alignment

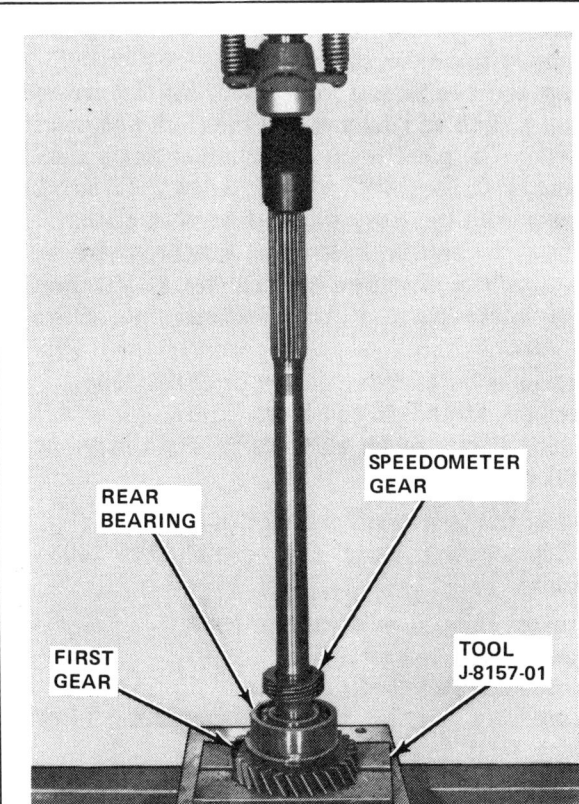

**FIG. 10-80D FIRST GEAR/REAR BEARING/
SPEEDOMETER GEAR REMOVAL**

REAR
BEARING

SPEEDOMETER
GEAR

FIRST
GEAR

TOOL
J-8157-01

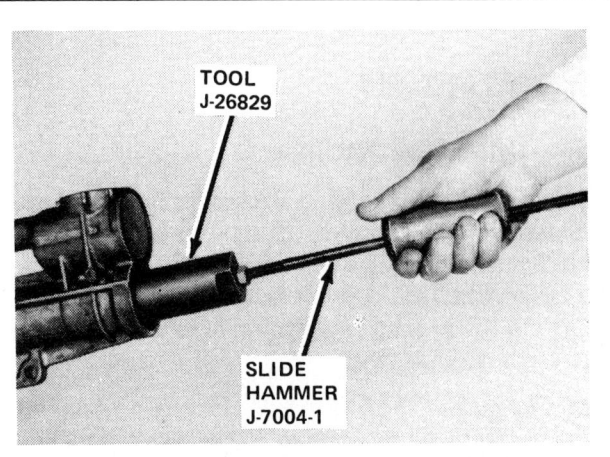

TOOL
J-26829

SLIDE
HAMMER
J-7004-1

FIG. 10-80E EXTENSION HOUSING SEAL REMOVAL

marks made during disassembly, index the hub to the sleeve. Engage the tang end of each insert spring in the same synchronizer insert, but position the open ends of each spring-face away from one another.

6. Replace the blocking ring on the tapered surface of second gear. Install the ring and gear on the output shaft, being sure the synchronizer inserts engage in the blocking ring notches.

7. When installing the second-gear thrust washer and snap ring on the output shaft, make sure the tabbed end of the snap ring is seated in the machined groove of the output shaft.

8. Measure second-gear end play with a feeler gauge. End play should be .004-.014. If it exceeds this figure, replace the thrust washer, snap ring and gear, if necessary.

9. Place the first-gear blocking ring on the tapered surface of the gear. Install the ring and gear on the output shaft, being sure the tapered-gear surface faces the first/second synchronizer hub and that the synchronizer inserts mate with the blocking ring notches.

10. Replace the oil slinger-spacer on the output shaft. Make sure the oil slinger grooves face first gear and that the flat surface of the slinger-spacer are against first gear.

11. The output-shaft rear snap ring selected in Step 2 should now be installed. Position the snap ring over the oil slinger-spacer and against first gear.

12. Seat the rear bearing on the output shaft as shown in **Fig. 10-80F.** Bearing must seat against slinger-spacer, and first gear must seat in the first/second synchronizer hub on output shaft.

13. Completely seat the thickest possible replacement rear-bearing snap ring in the output shaft groove.

14. Install the speedometer gear on the output shaft and mount the output shaft assembly in an arbor press. Place Rear Bearing Installer Tool J-25678-01 over the output shaft and onto the positioning gauge tool **(Fig. 10-80G).**

15. Press the speedometer gear onto the output shaft until the positioning gauge contacts the rear bearing. Release the press and remove the output shaft assembly and tools. Then remove the tools. *Do not* install the speedometer gear without using the positioning gauge tool.

16. Install third gear on the output shaft and the blocking ring on the tapered gear surface.

17. Assemble third/fourth synchronizer hub, sleeve, inserts and insert springs. Index the hub to the sleeve, according to the alignment marks made earlier. Be sure to engage the tang end of each insert spring in the same synchronizer insert, but position the open ends of the springs so they face away from one another.

18. Replace the third/fourth synchronizer assembly on the output shaft. Then install the output-shaft front snap ring.

19. Measure third/fourth synchronizer end play with a feeler gauge. End play should be .004-.014-in. If end play exceeds this figure, replace the snap ring, synchronizer hub and sleeve, if necessary.

20. Insert the assembled output shaft and geartrain into the extension housing. Seat the rear bearing in the extension housing by tapping the front end of the output shaft with a plastic hammer.

21. Compress the output-shaft rear snap ring with needle-nose pliers and install the snap ring in the extension-housing snap ring groove. Be sure it's completely seated.

TRANSMISSION ASSEMBLY

1. Lubricate all components with transmission lubri-

cant, unless noted otherwise.

2. Insert Countershaft Loading Tool J-26826 into the countershaft gear bore, and coat the countershaft needle bearings and bearing retainers with petroleum jelly.

3. Install a thin bearing retainer in the needle bearing bores at each of the countershaft gear. Then install 21 long needle bearings in the bore at the rear and 21 short needle bearings in the bore at the front.

4. Place a thick bearing retainer in each countershaft bore and over the ends of the needle bearings.

5. Coat the replacement countershaft-gear thrust washers with petroleum jelly and position them over the bearing bore at the front of the countershaft gear.

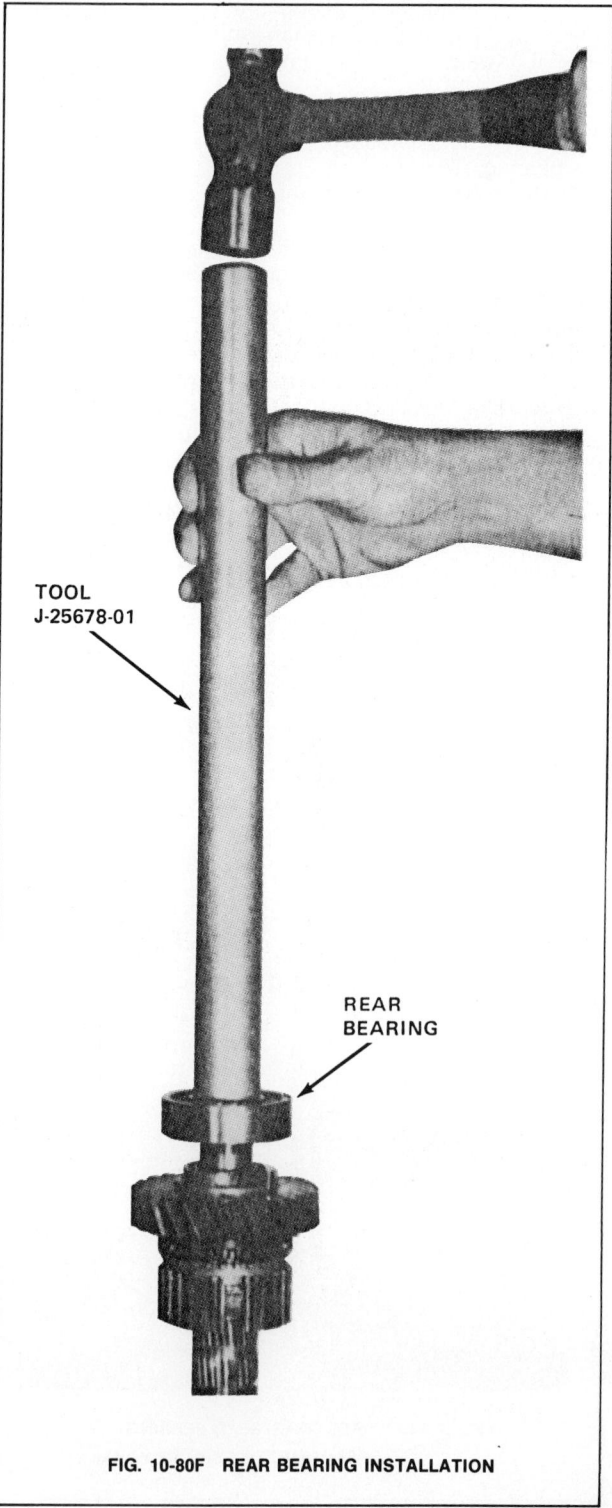

TOOL
J-25678-01

REAR
BEARING

FIG. 10-80F   REAR BEARING INSTALLATION

6. Push the loading tool toward the front of the gear and through the thrust washer. The loading tool should extend only far enough to hold the washer in place.

7. Align the locating notch on the countershaft-gear front thrust washer with the locating notch in the case. Install the gear. Be sure the washer tab and case notch are aligned.

8. Turn the case on end so the rear bearing bore is facing upward. Align the locating tab on the countershaft-gear rear thrust washer with the locating notch. Install the thrust washer between the gear and the case.

9. Align the countershaft-gear rear bore, case rear bore and the rear thrust washer. Insert the countershaft through the case bore and thrust washer, and into the rear bore of the countershaft gear. Be sure the step machined in the rear of the countershaft is in a horizontal position and make certain that the lower step is facing downward.

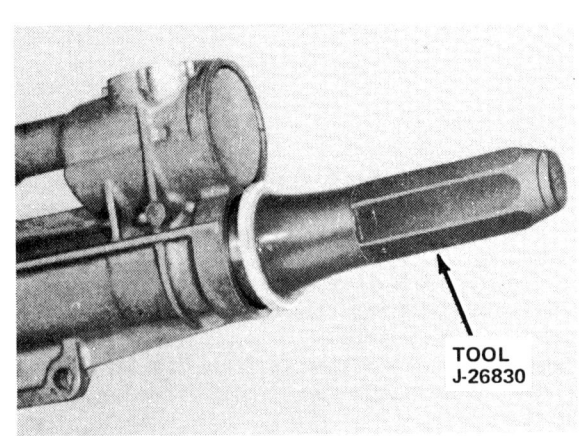

FIG. 10-80H EXTENSION HOUSING SEAL INSTALLATION

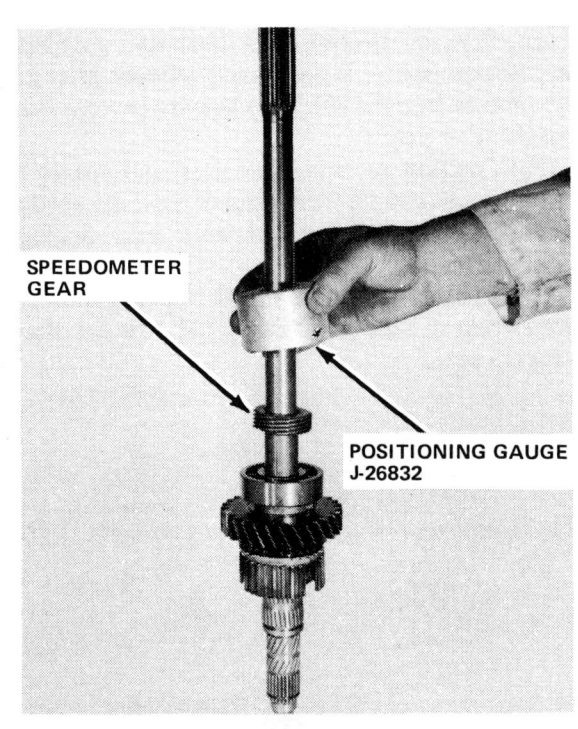

FIG. 10-80G SPEEDOMETER GEAR INSTALLATION

10. Countershaft end play should be .006-.018-in. If figure exceeds this, replace thrust washers.

11. Replace the reverse lever fork in the reverse lever, then install the reverse lever and spring on the pivot shaft and replace the lever retaining spring clip.

12. Place the reverse idler gear and gear spacer in the case. Spacer must be positioned between the idler gear and the rear of the case. Be sure the reverse lever fork engages the idler gear.

13. Install the idler-gear shaft from the rear of the case. Be sure the reverse lever fork remains engaged with the gear during installation.

14. Install a new shift-rail oil seal in the rear counterbore with a suitable-size socket.

15. Coat the output-shaft pilot bearing with petroleum jelly and install in the clutch shaft bore.

16. Install a new gasket on the extension housing.

17. Place the output shaft into the case and install the clutch shaft on the output shaft. Output-shaft pilot hub must be fully engaged in clutch-shaft pilot bearing.

18. Coat the extension housing bolts with a non-hardening sealer.

19. Align the clutch and output shafts in the case, then install the extension housing bolts finger-tight. Be sure the notch in the end of the countershaft is aligned with the recess in the extension housing before installing the attaching bolts. If not aligned, the housing will not seat properly and will cause leaks or a cracked housing.

20. Install the front bearing on the clutch shaft and into the case using Front Bearing Installer J-5590.

21. Install the front bearing retaining and locating snap rings.

22. A new front bearing cap must be installed with Tool J-26540.

23. Place a new front-bearing-cap O-ring on the case and install the front bearing cap.

24. Install the shift forks in the synchronizer sleeves.

25. Position the interlock plate in the case and secure with a new retaining pin.

26. Lubricate the shift rail with transmission lubricant and install. Slide the shift rail into the case and through the first/second shift fork and interlock plate.

27. Replace the selector arm on the shift rail, then slide the shift rail through the third/fourth shift fork and into the case front bore.

28. After installing the selector-arm roll pin in the arm and shift rail, make sure the pin is flush with the selector arm surface.

29. Put the detent plunger, spring and plug in the case. Tighten plug to 13 ft.-lbs.

30. Tighten front bearing-cap bolts to 9 ft.-lbs. and extension housing bolts to 34 ft.-lbs.

31. Place new access plugs in the shift rail bore in the extension housing and in the interlock-plate retaining-pin access hole.

32. Use Tool J-26830 **(Fig. 10-80H)** to install a new extension-housing oil seal.

33. Put in 2.4 pints of transmission fluid and install new gasket and top cover. Tighten cover bolts to 9 ft.-lbs.

AMC MANUAL TRANSMISSION OVERDRIVE
DESCRIPTION

The AMC overdrive (factory option) is an additional gearbox connected between the transmission and driveshaft to provide a higher overall gear ratio than normally produced by the drive gear/pinion. When in use, the overdrive **(Fig. 10-81)** gives a transmission ratio of 0.75:1.00 in overdrive third gear. Engagement and disengagement of the hydraulically operated overdrive are controlled by a solenoid valve located in the overdrive unit. This valve is activated by a control switch mounted in the turn signal lever of 1975-76 Hornet, Gremlin and Pacer 6-cyl. manual-transmission models to which it has been fitted. Overdrive cut-in/cut-out speeds are controlled by a governor speed switch operated by the speedometer cable.

OPERATION
(Fig. 10-82)

Overdrive engagement in first, second and reverse gears is prevented by a third gear switch located in the transmission of 49-state cars. California cars use a TCS switch in the transmission and a third gear relay mounted in the dash panel. At speeds below 38 mph, overdrive engagement is prevented by the governor speed switch. Once engaged, the overdrive will remain engaged unless the control switch is shut off or the car speed drops below the 32-mph cutout point.

A plunger-type kickdown switch mounted on the carburetor base and operated by the throttle linkage is provided in the overdrive electrical-control circuit to provide additional acceleration for highway passing. When the accelerator pedal is fully depressed, the kickdown switch opens, de-energizing the solenoid valve which disengages the overdrive. Once the throttle is released, the kickdown switch closes. This engages the solenoid valve, which re-engages the overdrive. An indicator lamp in the instrument panel lights and remains lit whenever the overdrive is engaged.

OVERDRIVE MAINTENANCE
Lubrication

The overdrive and transmission units share the same lubricating oil supply; a level check for both assemblies should be made at the transmission fill plug every 5000 miles. The fill level of the assembly is the edge of the transmission fill plug, and a correct check can only be made if the lubricant is at normal operating temperature and the overdrive has been cut-in and cut-out at least once before the fill plug is removed. The transmission drain bolt and the overdrive lubrication pan must both be removed in order to drain the assembly. Once refilled, the overdrive should be engaged/disengaged, and the fill level rechecked, adding sufficient lubrication to bring the level to the fill plug edge, if necessary.

Oil Pan and Pressure Filter (Fig. 10-83)

1. Raise the car on a hoist or support on jackstands.

2. Position a support stand under the clutch hous-

ing, and remove the rear crossmember.

3. Remove the oil pan, gasket and filter from the main case.

4. Use a spanner wrench to remove the pressure filter plug and aluminum washer. Discard the washer.

5. Clean the pressure filter and the oil pan filter thoroughly with clean solvent. Drain the filters, and place on a clean, lint-free cloth to air-dry. If the filters are torn, split or plugged, replace.

6. Fit a new aluminum washer on the pressure filter plug.

7. Place the pressure filter in the plug, and install the assembly with the spanner wrench. The plug should be torqued to 16 ft.-lbs.

8. Replace the oil pan, gasket and filter. Torque the oil pan bolts to 6 ft.-lbs.

9. Replace the rear crossmember, and torque the nuts to 30 ft.-lbs.

10. Operate the overdrive, check the fluid level and add fluid, if required.

OVERDRIVE TEST PROCEDURE
Hydraulic Pressure (Fig. 10-84)

1. Raise the car on a hoist or support on jack stands so that the rear wheels are free to rotate.

2. Check the lubricant level, and add fluid, if necessary. Support the clutch housing and remove the rear crossmember.

3. Remove the main-case pressure plug and copper gasket.

4. Connect an adapter fitting and a pressure gauge, using the copper gasket with the adapter fitting.

5. With the overdrive control switch off, start the engine and shift the transmission into third gear. With the engine speed at 25-30 mph, hydraulic pressure should be 20-40 psi.

6. Turn the overdrive on and increase engine speed to 40-45 mph. Hydraulic pressure should increase to 520-540 psi when the overdrive engages.

7. Shut the overdrive off, and the hydraulic pressure should return to 20-40 psi.

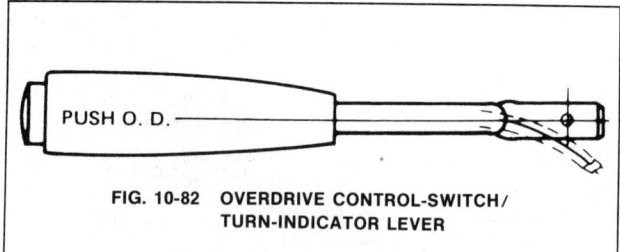

FIG. 10-82 OVERDRIVE CONTROL-SWITCH/ TURN-INDICATOR LEVER

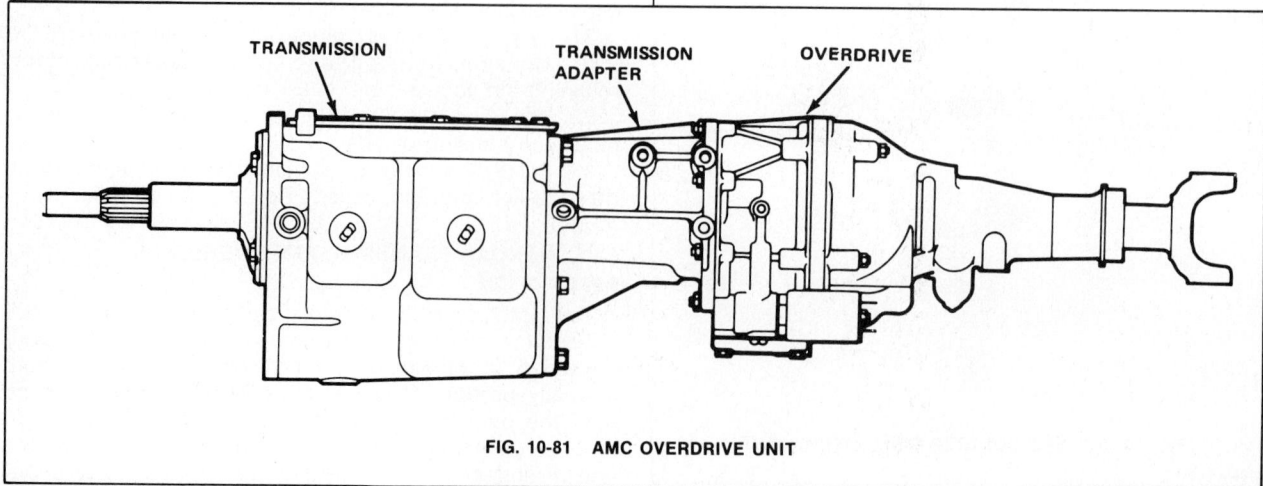

FIG. 10-81 AMC OVERDRIVE UNIT

8. Turn the engine off, remove the adapter/pressure gauge, and replace the main-case pressure port and gasket. Torque the plug to 12 ft.-lbs. Install the crossmember, remove support and lower car.

Solenoid Valve

1. With the car on a hoist or supported on jack stands, disconnect Support the clutch housing and remove rear crossmember.

2. Using a 1-in. open-end wrench (ground down to a ¼-in. thickness) remove the valve and check for cracks, plugged oil-feed holes, broken electrical terminals and/or a seized valve plunger.

3. Soak the valve in clean solvent, and allow to air-dry. Then replace the O-ring seal.

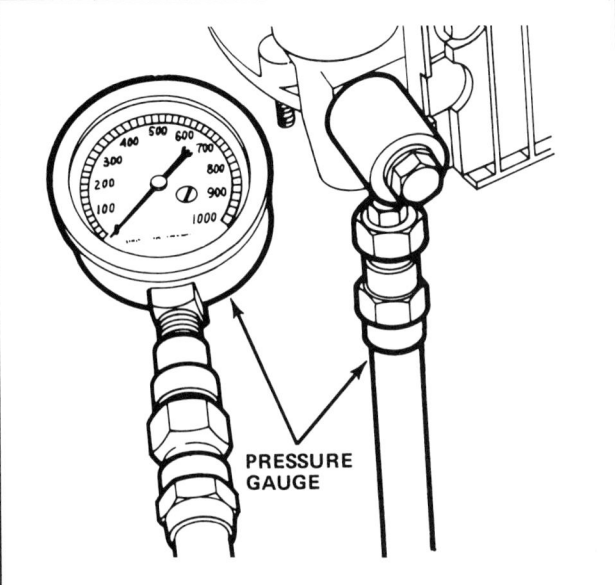

FIG. 10-84   HYDRAULIC-PRESSURE-TEST CONNECTION

4. Connect the solenoid to a 12-volt battery and an ammeter. The solenoid should draw about 2 amps when energized. The valve plunger must move fully forward when energized, and return under spring pressure when de-energized.

5. If defective, replace with a new valve; if not, reinstall in the overdrive unit.

OVERDRIVE OVERHAUL

The following special tools are required for overdrive overhaul. Use of substitutes can result in permanent damage to the components involved and are not recommended: Solenoid wrench, AMC part number J-25304; spanner tool, AMC part number J-25305; relief-valve body/sleeve remover, AMC part number J-25307; overrunning-clutch remover/installer tool, AMC part number J-25308; clutch-hub remover/installer tool, AMC part number J-25315.

OVERDRIVE DISASSEMBLY
(Fig. 10-85)

1. Remove the solenoid valve. If a solenoid valve wrench (AMC J-25304) is not available, use a 1-in. open-end wrench ground down to a thickness not exceeding ¼-in. Attempting removal with pliers or similar tools may damage the solenoid valve body.

2. Remove and discard the self-locking nuts holding the clutch-piston apply bars to the thrust-bearing cover pins.

3. Remove the main-case-to-rear-case nuts, lockwashers and copper gaskets from the studs. Separate the main case from the rear case assembly.

4. Remove the loose clutch return spring from the main case and the clutch brake ring/gaskets. If the brake ring does not come out freely, tap lightly with a soft-faced mallet—*do not* attempt to pry out.

5. Remove the oil pan, gasket, filter and main case pressure plug. Discard the gasket.

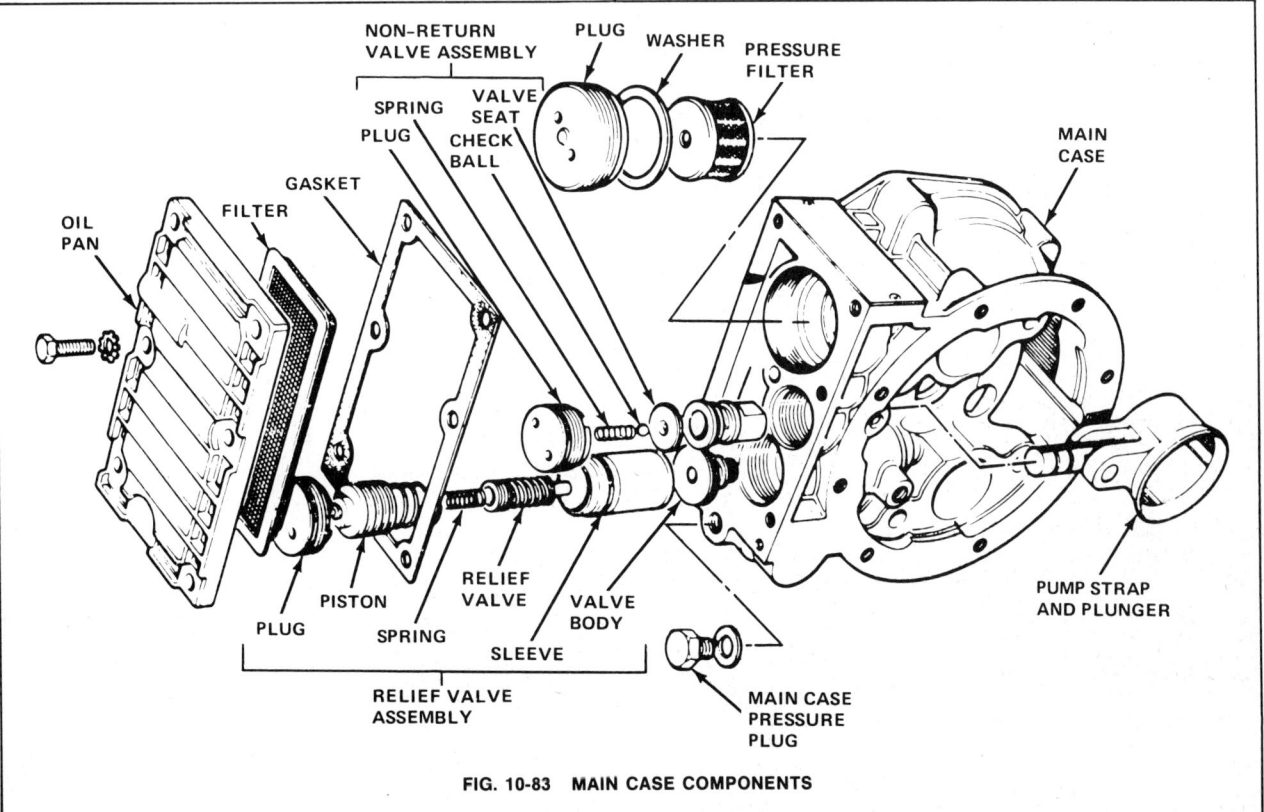

FIG. 10-83   MAIN CASE COMPONENTS

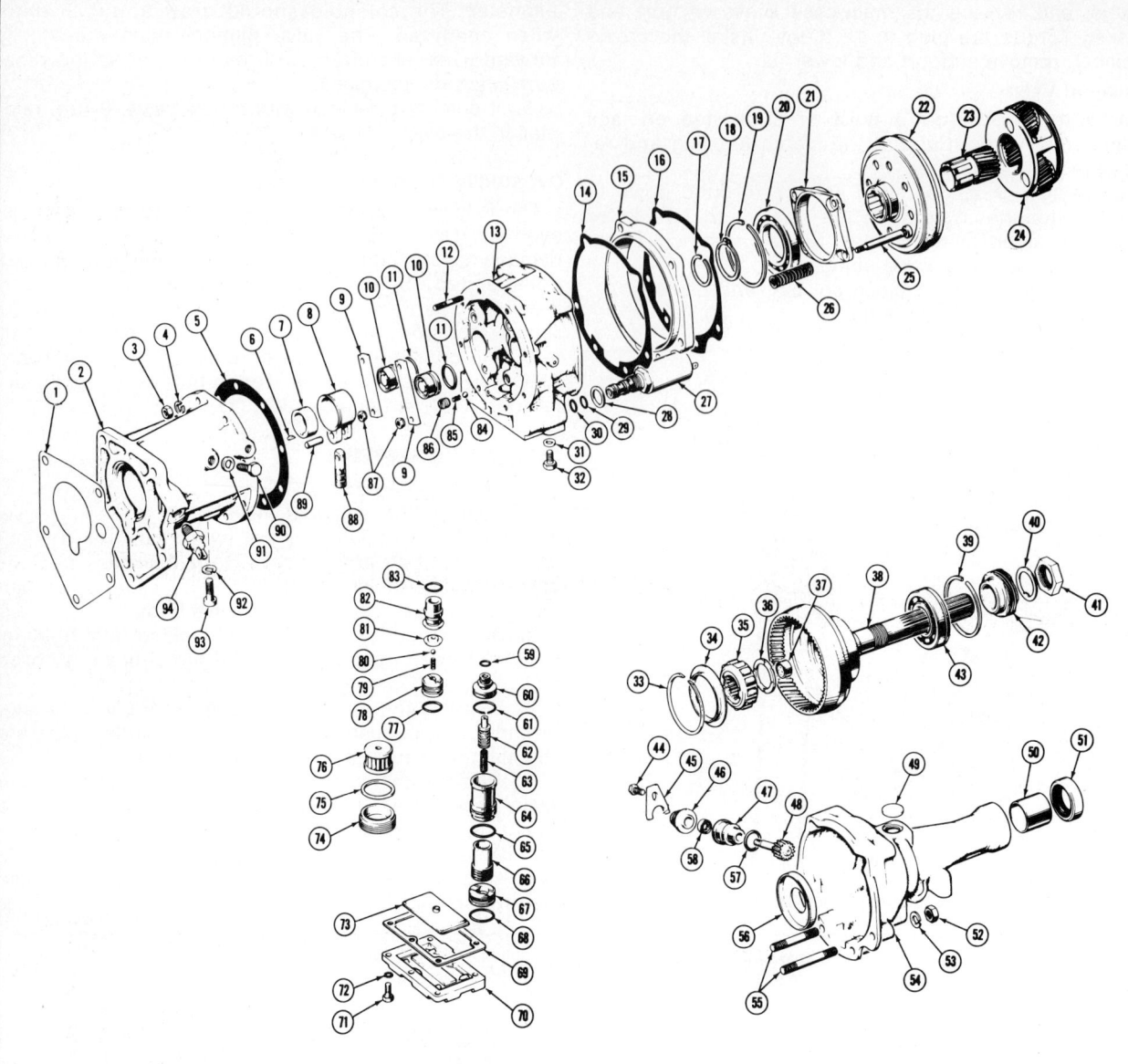

1. Gasket Transmission to Adapter
2. Adapter, Transmission
3. Nut, Self Locking, Main Case Stud
4. Washer, Lock
5. Gasket, Main Case to Transmission Adaptor
6. Key, Pump Strap Cam Drive
7. Cam, Pump Strap
8. Strap, Pump
9. Bar, Clutch Piston Apply
10. Piston, Clutch Apply
11. Seal, Clutch Apply Piston O-Ring
12. Stud, Main Case to Transmission Adapter
13. Main Case
14. Gasket, Clutch Brake Ring (front)
15. Brake Ring, Clutch
16. Gasket, Clutch Brake Ring (rear)
17. Ring, Sun Gear Snap
18. Ring Lock, Sliding Clutch
19. Ring, Thrust Bearing Snap
20. Bearing, Thrust
21. Cover, Thrust Bearing
22. Clutch, Sliding
23. Sun Gear
24. Assembly, Pinion Carrier
25. Bolt, Thrust Bearing Cover (4 reqd.)
26. Spring, Clutch Return (4 reqd.)
27. Solenoid Valve
28. Washer, Solenoid Valve
29. Seal, Solenoid Valve O-Ring
30. Seal, Solenoid Valve O-Ring
31. Gasket, Main Case Pressure Plug
32. Plug, Main Case Pressure

33. Ring, Overrunning Clutch Snap
34. Slinger, Overrunning Clutch Oil
35. Assembly, Overrunning Clutch
36. Washer, Mainshaft Thrust
37. Bushing, Mainshaft Support (Included in Mainshaft)
38. Main Shaft and Annulus Gear
39. Ring, Mainshaft Bearing Snap
40. Washer, Speedometer Drive Gear Tab
41. Nut, Speedometer Drive Gear Lock
42. Gear, Speedometer Drive
43. Bearing, Mainshaft
44. Bolt, Speedometer Adapter Clamp
45. Clamp, Speedometer Adapter
46. Adapter, Speedometer to Governor Speed Switch
47. Adapter, Speedometer Driven Gear
48. Gear, Speedometer Driven
49. Plug, Expansion
50. Bushing, Rear Case (Included in Case)
51. Seal, Rear Case Oil
52. Nut, Self Locking, Main Case to Rear Case Stud
53. Washer, Lock
54. Rear Case
55. Stud, Main Case to Rear Case
56. Washer, Disc (not removed: included in rear case)
57. Seal, Speedometer Adapter O-Ring
58. Seal, Speedometer Adaptor Oil
59. Seal, Relief Valve Body O-Ring (Inner)
60. Body, Relief Valve
61. Seal, Relief Valve Body O-Ring (Outer)
62. Assembly, Relief Valve and Spring
63. Spring, Relief Valve Residual Pressure
64. Sleeve, Relief Valve

65. Seal, Relief Valve Sleeve O-Ring
66. Piston, Relief Valve
67. Plug, Relief Valve Piston
68. Seal, Relief Valve Piston Plug O-Ring
69. Gasket, Oil Pan
70. Oil Pan
71. Bolt, Oil Pan
72. Washer, Lock
73. Filter, Oil Pan
74. Plug, Pressure Filter
75. Washer, Pressure Filter (Aluminum)
76. Filter, Pressure
77. Seal, Pump Body O-Ring
78. Plug, Pump Body
79. Spring, Non-return Valve Ball-seat
80. Ball, Non-return Valve Check
81. Seat, Non-return Valve
82. Body, Pump Plunger
83. Seal, Pump Plunger Body O-Ring
84. Ball, Lubrication Relief Valve Check
85. Spring, Lubrication Relief Valve
86. Plug, Lubrication Relief Valve
87. Nut, Self Locking, Clutch Piston Apply Bar
88. Plunger, Pump
89. Pin, Pump Plunger
90. Bolt, Gearshift Lever Retainer to Adapter
91. Washer, Lock
92. Washer, Lock
93. Bolt, Rear Support Cushion to Adapter
94. Switch, Back-up Light

FIG. 10-85 OVERDRIVE DISASSEMBLY

6. Use a spanner wrench (AMC J-25305) to remove the pressure filter plug and aluminum washer from the main case. Discard the aluminum washer.

7. Remove the pump body plug with the spanner wrench, and take out the non-return-valve ball-seat spring, check ball and valve seat.

8. Clutch apply pistons are removed from the main case bore with pliers **(Fig. 10-86)**. Remove and discard the O-rings from the pistons. Leave the lubrication relief-valve plug, spring and ball intact in the main case.

9. Push the pump body up to unseat it from the main case bore, and slide the pump plunger out carefully. The piston should not be cocked in the body during this step **(Fig. 10-87)**.

10. Remove the body from the main case bore. Note the machined flat on one side—this must align with the oil feed hole and slot in the main case bore during reassembly.

11. Remove the drive cam/key from the pump strap. The pump strap and plunger are serviced as a unit and should not be disassembled.

12. Remove the relief-valve piston plug with the spanner wrench, and take out the piston and the residual pressure spring. These should not be separated, or spring calibration will be affected. Discard the plug O-ring seal. Remove the valve and spring assembly with magnetic or needlenose pliers.

13. Fit the hooked end of the relief-body-valve/sleeve remover tool (AMC J-25307) into the relief-valve body bore located at the bottom of the case bore and under the relief valve sleeve.

14. Hook the tool over the inner edge of the valve body, and slide the tool barrel down to lock the hook end in place, then withdraw with a steady upward pull. The valve body and sleeve will be extracted together. Remove and replace all O-ring seals.

15. Remove the sliding clutch assembly, sun gear

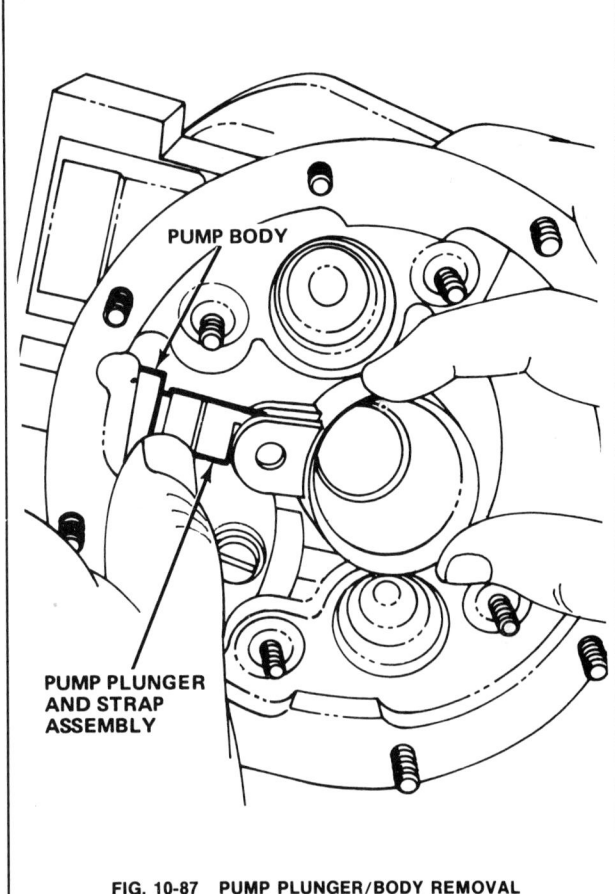

FIG. 10-87   PUMP PLUNGER/BODY REMOVAL

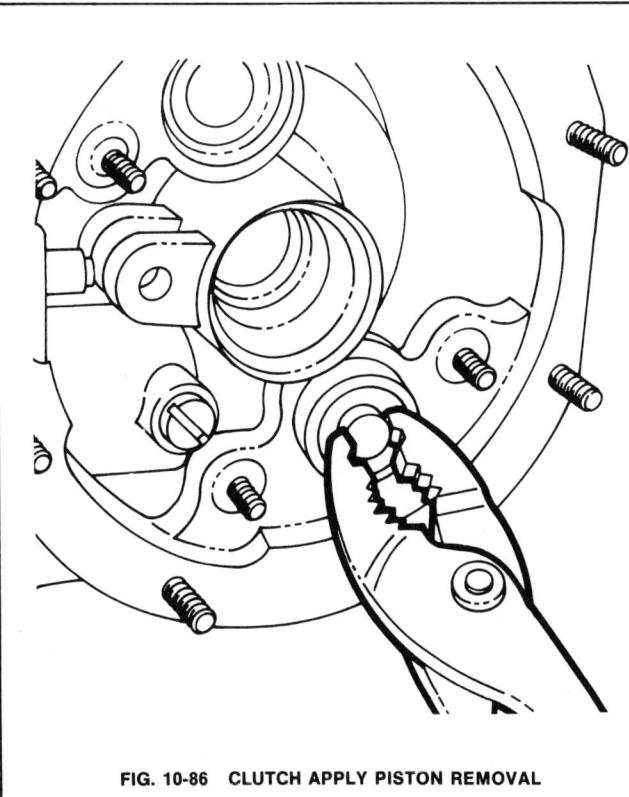

FIG. 10-86   CLUTCH APPLY PISTON REMOVAL

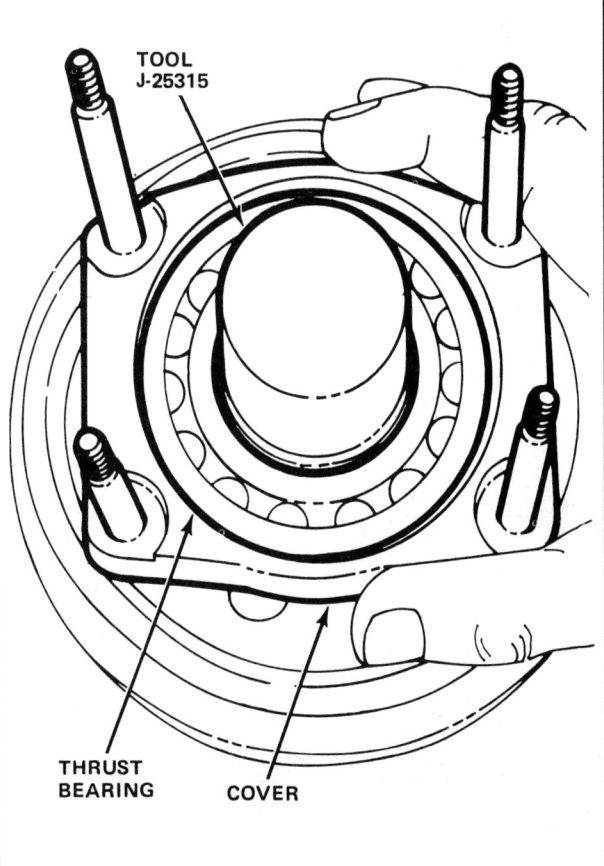

FIG. 10-89   SLIDING CLUTCH/PINION CARRIER REMOVAL

and the thrust-bearing cover assembly from the mainshaft annulus gear, then remove the pinion carrier assembly from the mainshaft annulus gear **(Fig. 10-88)**.

16. Unclip the sun-gear snap ring and the sliding-clutch ring lock to separate the sun gear from the clutch hub.

17. Use the clutch-hub remover/installer (AMC J-25315) to separate the thrust bearing and cover from the sliding clutch hub **(Fig. 10-89)**.

18. Unclip the thrust-bearing snap ring, and press the bearing from the cover. Thrust-bearing cover bolts are not removed.

19. Unclip the overrunning-clutch snap ring, and remove the brass oil slinger **(Fig. 10-88)**.

20. Fit the overrunning-clutch tool (AMC J-25308) into the mainshaft annulus-gear shaft. Use the relief-valve-body tool (AMC J-25307) to pull the overrunning clutch into the clutch tool, then remove as a unit.

21. Remove the mainshaft thrust washer from the mainshaft annulus-gear recess, separate the overrunning clutch from the tool, and disassemble. However, don't remove the tension spring from the cage.

22. Drive or pry out the rear case expansion plug.

23. Support the rear case as shown in **Fig. 10-90** expand the mainshaft-bearing snap ring, and tap the mainshaft to free it from the case.

24. Remove the drive gear locknut, the speedometer tab washer and the drive gear.

25. Press the mainshaft bearing out, pry the rear-case oil seal from the case, and remove the mainshaft-bearing snap ring from the rear-case machined groove. Don't remove the disc washer or rear bushing from the case—they are not serviceable.

CLEANING AND INSPECTION

1. Wash all parts except the sliding clutch thoroughly in clean solvent. Wipe the sliding clutch with a clean, lint-free cloth.

2. Dry all parts, except the solenoid valve and slid-

ing clutch, with compressed air, directing it into all oil passages.

3. Drain and air-dry the solenoid valve on a clean, lint-free cloth.

4. Inspect the main case for:
   a) Cracks in the valve/piston bores.

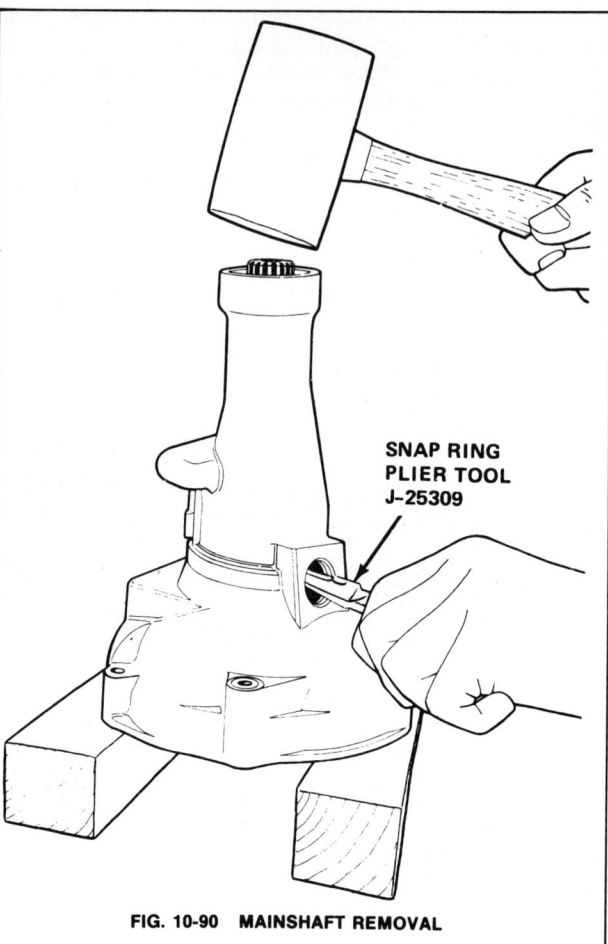

SNAP RING
PLIER TOOL
J-25309

FIG. 10-90   MAINSHAFT REMOVAL

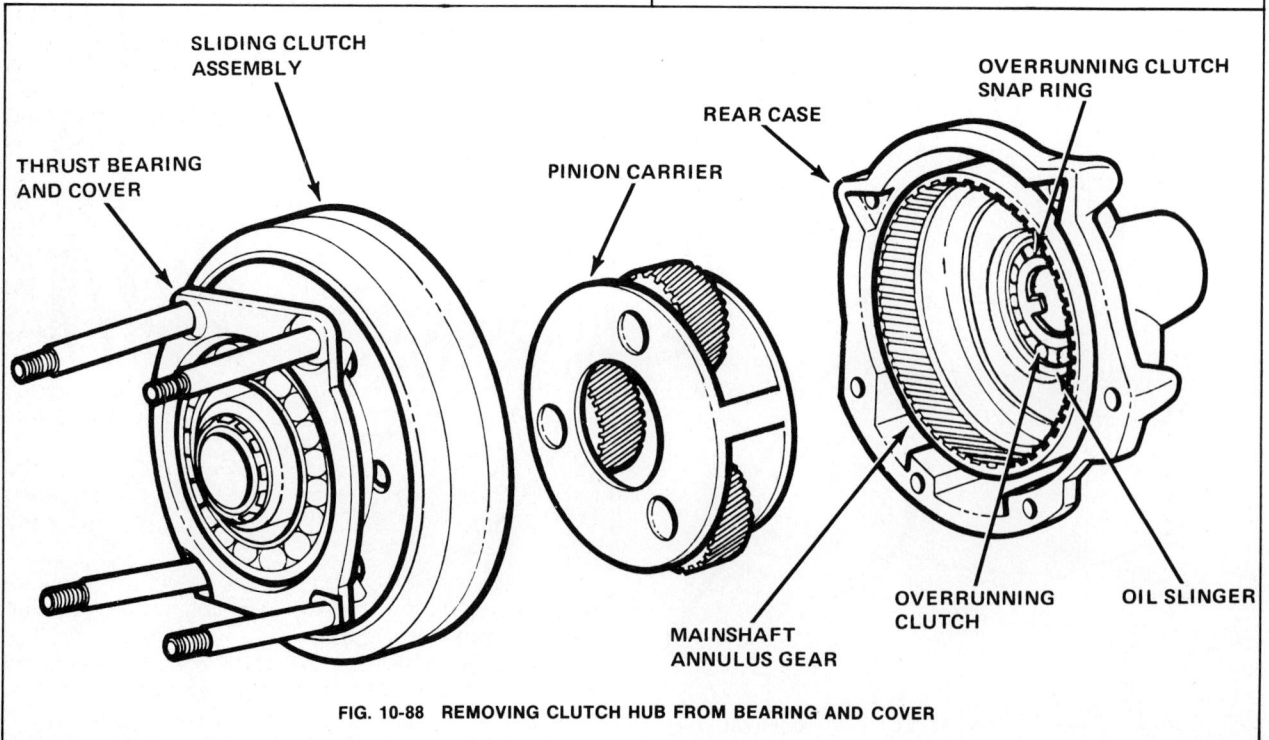

SLIDING CLUTCH
ASSEMBLY

OVERRUNNING CLUTCH
SNAP RING

REAR CASE

THRUST BEARING
AND COVER

PINION CARRIER

OVERRUNNING
CLUTCH

OIL SLINGER

MAINSHAFT
ANNULUS GEAR

FIG. 10-88   REMOVING CLUTCH HUB FROM BEARING AND COVER

b) Nicks, scratches, warpage or grooving in the valve/piston bores and mating surfaces.

c) Worn, stripped or galled plug threads/valve bores/studs.

d) Loose lubrication-valve plug, blocked oil passages or control orifice.

5. Inspect the rear case for:

a) Cracks in the mainshaft-bearing snap-ring groove.

b) Nicks, scratches, warpage in mating surfaces.

c) Worn, stripped or galled stud hole threads.

d) Worn or loose rear bushing/disc washer.

6. Inspect the pump, valves, pistons and bores for:

a) Nicks, burrs, scratches, excessive wear, pitting or corrosion.

b) Weak, distorted or broken springs.

c) Torn, distorted or plugged filters.

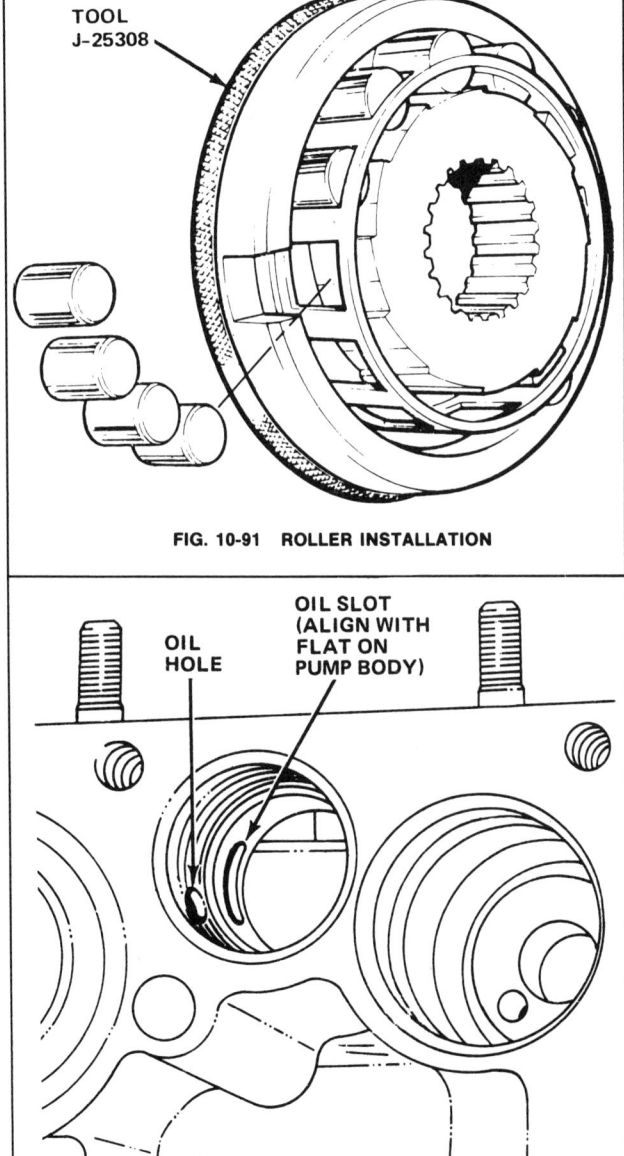

FIG. 10-91 ROLLER INSTALLATION

FIG. 10-92 PUMP-BODY SLOT ALIGNMENT

7. Inspect the clutch brake ring for worn, grooved, distorted or burned surfaces, and cracks in the ring or at the stud holes.

8. Inspect the sliding clutch, thrust bearing and cover for excessive wear, cracks, damaged threads or splines.

9. Inspect the mainshaft pinion carrier or sun gear for chipped, worn or broken teeth/splines, plugged oil holes and worn bearings.

OVERDRIVE ASSEMBLY

(Fig. 10-85)

As with any hydraulic unit, the overdrive should be assembled on a clean working surface. Contamination allowed to enter the overdrive during assembly can cause premature failure of the unit and impair proper operation.

1. Lubricate the mainshaft bearing with transmission fluid, and replace on the mainshaft with its snap ring groove to the rear.

2. Replace the speedometer drive gear on the mainshaft with its shoulder side facing the mainshaft bearing. Install a new washer with its tab in the mainshaft slot, and replace the locknut. Torque to 55 ft.-lbs., then bend the washer against the locknut in two places.

3. Fit a new mainshaft-bearing snap ring to the rear case groove with its butt ends in the expansion plug hole.

4. Lower the rear case onto the upright mainshaft, and tap the case to start the bearing into the case counterbore. Expand the snap ring, and continue tapping until the bearing is fully seated and the snap ring is installed in its groove correctly.

5. Replace the rear-case oil seal, lubricate it with gear oil and install a new expansion plug in the rear case. Secure the plug by striking its center with a flat-faced punch.

6. Lubricate the mainshaft thrust washer, and replace it in the mainshaft annulus-gear recess.

7. Fit the hooked end of the hub spring in the cage locating hole. Hold the cage and turn the hub against spring pressure until the cage tabs align with the slots in hub. When that occurs, seat the cage on the hub. Place the cage in the overrunning-clutch tool (AMC J-25308), and turn the cage clockwise while installing the clutch rollers (**Fig. 10-91**).

8. Lubricate the overrunning clutch assembly with transmission fluid, and place in the mainshaft annulus-gear bore. Remove the clutch tool, and replace the oil slinger with its shoulder facing out. Install the snap ring and seat in its groove.

9. Lubricate the pinion carrier assembly, and place in the mainshaft annulus gear.

10. Press the thrust bearing into the thrust bearing cover, and replace the snap ring. Lubricate with transmission fluid.

11. Install the thrust-bearing cover assembly to the sliding clutch hub with the clutch hub tool (AMC J-25315). Insert the tool into the clutch hub and drive the hub into the bearing.

12. Fit the sun gear in the sliding clutch hub. Replace the sliding-clutch lock ring with its sharp edge facing up, and install the sun-gear snap ring.

13. Install the sliding clutch assembly by rotating the mainshaft annulus gear to engage the sun gear in the pinion gears.

14. Lubricate the clutch apply pistons, install new O-

ring seals, and place the pistons (counterbored-end out) in the main case bores.

15. Lubricate the relief valve assembly, install new O-ring seals on the valve body, sleeve and piston plug, and insert the relief valve body in the main case bore. Align the relief-valve-sleeve oil hole with the bore oil hole, and insert the sleeve with the O-ring facing up **(Fig. 10-92).**

16. Push the sleeve inward to seat the sleeve/valve body, and replace the relief-valve/spring assembly, then insert the residual pressure spring.

17. Replace the relief valve piston and piston plug. Torque to 16 ft.-lbs.

18. Fit the pressure filter in the main case bore, install a new aluminum washer on the filter plug, and torque the plug to 16 ft.-lbs.

19. Lubricate the pump plunger assembly, body and non-return valve seat, and install new O-ring seals on the pump body and plug. Align the pump body flat with the main-case-bore oil hole and insert halfway.

20. Install the pump plunger in the pump body, and push the body in the main case bore until fully seated. Plunger must not cock in the body.

21. Replace the non-return valve seat on the pump body with the check ball seat facing up. Place the check ball in the valve seat.

22. Fit the ball seat spring to the pump body plug, and install the plug and spring. Torque the plug to 16 ft.-lbs.

23. Replace the main-case pressure plug and gasket, the oil pan filter and gasket, and the oil pump cover to the main case. Torque the pressure plug to 13 ft.-lbs., and the pan bolts to 6 ft.-lbs.

24. Secure the rear case assembly upright in a soft-jaw vise, but *do not* overtighten because the case is aluminum. Place new clutch return springs on the thrust-bearing cover bolts.

25. Fit the first clutch brake-ring gasket on the rear case, and install the clutch brake ring into the case with its tapered surface facing to the rear.

26. Fit the second clutch brake-ring gasket on the brake ring. Gaskets and brake ring must align with the rear-case stud holes.

27. Apply a light coat of sealer to the main-case-to-rear-case studs, and lower the main case assembly on the rear case, aligning the thrust-bearing cover bolts with the main-case bolt holes **(Fig. 10-93).**

28. Replace the copper gaskets on the top case studs **(Fig. 10-94),** and install the lockwashers and nuts on all four to 11 ft.-lbs. because the case is under spring pressure.

29. Fit the clutch apply bars on the thrust-bearing cover bolts, and install new locknuts. Torque 8 ft.-lbs.

30. Replace the solenoid valve and tighten securely, but don't overtighten.

31. Lubricate a new drive cam, and install with a new drive key on the transmission output shaft. Install a new snap ring.

32. Pour one pint of transmission fluid in the main-case front-access hole, and replace the assembled overdrive unit on the car.

CLUTCH REMOVAL AND REPAIR—ALL MODELS

Clutch slippage is often caused by insufficient free travel at the clutch pedal. If allowed to go uncorrected, the increased frictional heat caused by the slippage will continue to burn the clutch disc surface and/or score the flywheel and pressure plate facing. It can even affect spring pressure, resulting in a complete overhaul

or replacement. Linkage adjustment will often compensate for normal clutch wear, but if the clutch continues to slip, then it's time to replace the clutch and/or pressure plate. Proceed as follows:

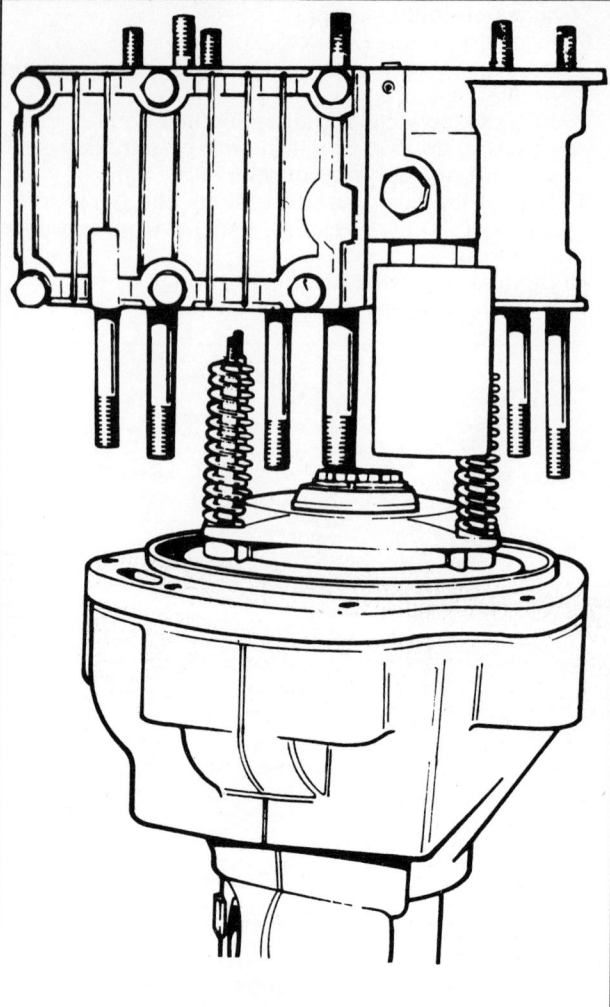

FIG. 10-93   MAIN CASE INSTALLATION

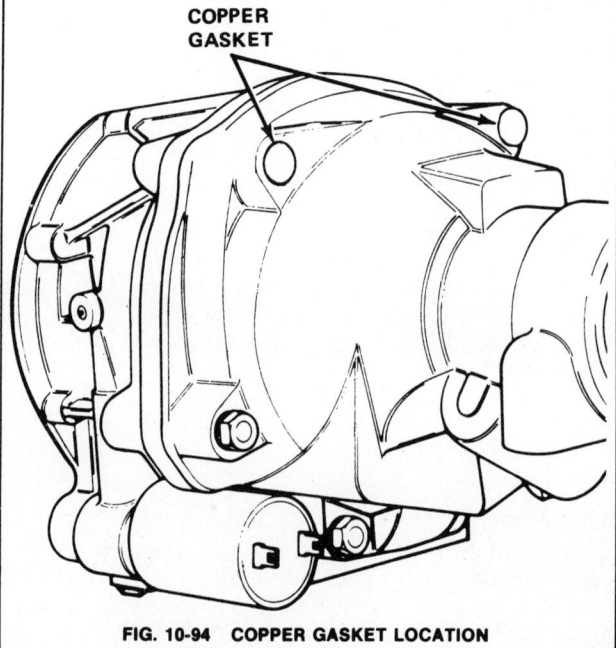

COPPER
GASKET

FIG. 10-94   COPPER GASKET LOCATION

REMOVAL

1. To remove the clutch assembly, raise the car, support it on jackstands, support the engine and remove the transmission according to the following procedure:

a) For proper assembly, mark the driveshaft in relation to the rear universal joint, and disconnect the shaft at the joint. Tape the bearing cups to the trunnion to prevent them from falling off.

b) To avoid scratching the splines, carefully withdraw the shaft yoke from the transmission housing. Quickly cover the end of the housing with a plastic bag and rubberband to prevent oil from leaking out or dirt from getting in.

c) Disconnect the speedometer cable, shift levers, parking brake cable, electrical connections and anything else linking the transmission to the rest of the car.

IMPORTANT: Proper installation of the transmission is ensured if you tag the parts as to location before removing them.

d) With the help of an assistant or a transmission jack, support the transmission, and unbolt the mounts from the crossmember.

e) If necessary, unbolt the crossmember.

f) Remove the transmission from the bellhousing, and pull it straight back until its input shaft clears the clutch splines. Lower it to the ground.

2. If necessary, disconnect any brake or clutch linkages, and disconnect the clutch release fork and spring.

3. To expose the flywheel and clutch assembly, remove the bellhousing or, if applicable, remove only the lower half of the housing or the inspection cover.

4. When the bellhousing has been removed, scribe a mark at the edge of the pressure plate cover, and right next to it make another mark on the edge of the flywheel. The pressure plate and flywheel are balanced as a unit, and these marks assure that they will be returned to the same position; otherwise, the engine will be imbalanced.

5. If the surface of the pressure plate is scored, burned (blue spots) or ridged, then the plate should be replaced along with the clutch disc. The new or rebuilt pressure plate has been balanced by the manufacturer prior to sale and, for non-racing applications, it is quite sufficient. However, for top performance, the flywheel should be removed and balanced with the new plate by a qualified machine shop.

6. If it's necessary to work through an opening at the bottom of the bellhousing, rotate the flywheel gradually to expose the pressure plate bolts. Regardless of bellhousing design, loosen the plate bolts.

CAUTION: The pressure plate bolts should be loosened evenly and gradually. Back out each bolt about one full turn before going on to the next. When spring tension has been relaxed from the plate, the release levers will contact the cover. When that occurs, remove the bolts. To remove the bolts in any other manner would probably bend the clutch plate. As the last bolt is being removed, hold the plate with one hand, and lower the plate and disc from the car.

CLEANING AND INSPECTION

1. With the assembly removed, inspect the components. An oil soaked disc indicates leakage from the rear main oil seal or transmission drive-pinion seal. If this condition exists, correct it before installing a new disc.

2. If the flywheel is scored, ridged, has burn marks or is highly polished, it should be removed and resurfaced by a machine shop. After resurfacing, it should be balanced with the pressure plate. The face of the flywheel should have a uniform wear pattern around its circumference. If there are signs of heavy wear on one side and light wear 180 degrees from that area, you can suspect that the flywheel is sprung or improperly mounted. A closer inspection with a dial indicator (mounted on the clutch housing) should reveal no more than 0.003-in. runout for the circumference. If it does, it should be replaced.

3. As mentioned, the pressure plate should be replaced if its surface shows signs of scoring, burning (blue spots) or ridges. The inner ends of the release levers should be worn uniformly.

4. While the transmission is out, it's a good idea to replace both the clutch plate, disc, the drive-pinion pilot bushing and throwout bearing. The pilot bushing can be removed from the crankshaft with a slide hammer. The new bushing should be soaked in oil and driven into place with a hammer and a piece of wood. When installed, apply some grease in the cavity behind the bushing.

5. The throwout bearing is prelubricated and sealed, so don't immerse it in solvent. Wipe the bearing clean and, while holding the inner race, apply pressure to the outer one and rotate it. If bearing rotation is rough or noisy, replace it. Tap off the old bearing and carefully tap on a new bearing, using a block of wood as a driver. Lightly coat the bearing hub and fork contacts with Lubriplate before installing it on the transmission.

6. The clutch disc should be replaced if it is oil soaked, warped, cracked, broken or worn down to the rivets or, if bonded, less than 1/32-in. thick on either side.

7. The hub splines and those on the transmission drive pinion should fit snugly without signs of excessive wear. The disc must slide smoothly on the splines. If not, lightly file the splines and polish with crocus cloth.

INSTALLATION

1. Before touching the new clutch, make sure your hands are clean and grease free. A bit of grease on the friction surfaces will cause the clutch to chatter. Clean the pressure plate and flywheel surfaces with a non-oil-based solvent just before assembly.

2. If removed, install the flywheel and torque to factory specifications.

3. To align the disc with the pilot bearing, you will need to purchase a wooden pilot shaft from your local auto supply.

4. Position the disc and pressure plate on the flywheel, and insert the shaft through the disc into the pilot bearing. The springs on the disc damper should face to the rear. Most discs are labeled as to flywheel side.

5. Align the two punch marks (on flywheel and plate) made during disassembly, and bolt the plate to the flywheel. Tighten the bolts evenly only a few turns at a time to prevent any clutch cover distortion. When torqued to specifications, withdraw the wooden pilot shaft. Lightly coat the fork pivots with Lubriplate, but *do not* lube the transmission drive pinion.

6. Install the transmission, and adjust the pedal free travel according to earlier directions.

REMEMBER: For clutch and throwout bearing longevity, *do not* ride the clutch, and periodically check and adjust pedal free travel, and lubricate the clutch linkage.

INDEX

AUTOMATIC TRANSMISSIONS

Automatic transmissions select the appropriate gear ratio/torque output according to engine speed and load conditions. To do this, three basic systems are necessary:

1. Torque Converter—This couples the transmission geartrain to the engine, and multiplies engine torque output. The torque converter consists of an engine impeller, geartrain turbine and a stator.

2. Planetary Gear Set—This transmits and multiplies torque by means of differing gear ratios. While the hydraulic system usually selects the ratio, the driver can override the automatic function and manually select the desired gear. Planetaries operate in different ways, but all perform the same functions as manual transmission gears—torque multiplication, torque coupling and speed/direction changes. Gear ratios are obtained by holding one or more planetary gears in position while the others are turned. Multiple disc clutches, sprag (one-way) clutches and friction bands accomplish gear shifting under the direction of the hydraulic system, operating through various servo mechanisms.

3. Hydraulic Control—This provides the fluid linkage which engages the necessary clutches or bands to operate the planetary gear set. Four subsystems are involved in the hydraulic system:

a) Pressure Supply—the front (oil) pump keeps the torque converter full of automatic transmission fluid (ATF), maintaining mainline pressure and circulating fluid to lubricate the transmission components.

b) Pressure Regulator—the pressure regulator valve, throttle valve and governor compose the pressure regulator system. These devices respectively regulate the front pump pressure, control shift points according to engine load and transmit pressure according to road speed.

c) Flow Control—the manual valve and shift valves control mainline pressure routing and accomplish the application/release of reaction members to produce automatic shifting, either up or down range.

d) Valve (Control) Body—The valve body is the master control center or brain of the automatic transmission, housing the valves and directing hydraulic pressure via passages with a variety of orifices, check valves, release valves and spool valves to delay, close off, release or change fluid direction.

POWER FLOW

The manner in which the automatic transmission performs its gear shifting function is a rather complicated sequence which differs somewhat from one design to another. But the basic power flow can and should be understood before attempting to diagnose and service the unit. The following simplified explanation applies to all automatic transmissions currently in use.

DRIVE/LOW

Placing the transmission selector lever in the DRIVE position with the engine running will allow the car to move forward with automatic gear changes. When placed in DRIVE, the manual valve opens mainline pressure flow from the regulator valve to the 1-2 and 2-3 shift valves, the governor valve and the rear clutch. As the car accelerates, throttle pressure increases. Governor pressure works against the 1-2 shift valve to block mainline pressure from the 2-3 shift valve and thus cause an upshift.

DRIVE/SECOND

As soon as governor pressure exceeds throttle pressure, the front band is applied. Once this happens, mainline pressure waits for the governor pressure to move the 2-3 shift valve and obtain direct drive or high gear.

DRIVE/HIGH

When the governor pressure moves the 2-3 shift valve, mainline pressure applies the front clutch. The front-band servo-release circuit branches off the front-clutch-apply circuit, and mainline oil is applied against both sides of the servo piston. Spring force and release oil pressure cause the servo piston to release the band.

DOWNSHIFTS

When throttle pressure overcomes governor pressure, the shift valve cuts off the apply circuit to cause a downshift.

AUTOMATIC TRANSMISSION FLUID (ATF)

Before you attempt to diagnose any transmission problem, you must understand how to evaluate the condition and appearance of automatic transmission fluid. A careful analysis at this point can often eliminate needless repairs. Many malfunctions can be traced back to an improper reading of the dipstick, resulting in an incorrect fluid level.

A commonly used rule-of-thumb in the past has been that a dark coloration of the fluid indicates problems, but some transmission fluids now in use have a darker color and stronger odor than in the past. Regardless of the color, a burned smell indicates that the clutches and/or bands are burned and will require replacement. To determine if the fluid has a burned odor, rub a small quantity of it between two fingers and smell—the odor will tell you if the fluid is good or bad.

CHECKING FLUID LEVEL

Checking the fluid level is easy, but frequently done incorrectly. Unlike the crankcase oil, which must be checked when the engine is cold if you want an accurate level reading, ATF should be checked when the engine is at normal operating temperature. The fluid level increases as its temperature rises, and a level change of more than ¾-in. is normal as fluid temperature increases from 60° F to 182° F. But many owners and some mechanics mistakenly or carelessly check the fluid level with the engine cold, and because the dipstick indicates that the level is low, they add more to bring it up to the FULL mark.

Overfilling results in foaming and a loss of fluid through the vent; slippage and transmission failure inevitably follow. To prevent the possibility of checking the fluid level incorrectly, some dipsticks are marked with a COLD level scale on one side and a HOT level scale on the other, allowing the fluid level to be checked under either condition.

Those who neglect to check the ATF level, and add more than required, will find that the transmission will begin to slip, especially when it is cold or when the car is on a hill. Proper fluid level must be maintained if correct transmission operation without problems is expected. When removing the dipstick to check ATF level, look for the presence of air bubbles—they indicate an air leak in the suction lines which can lead to slippage and erratic operation. If the fluid has a milky pink cast, there is a leak in the radiator/fluid cooler system, which is allowing water to mix with the fluid.

FLUID CHECKING PROCEDURE

1. With the car on a level surface and the parking brake applied, start the engine and run until it reaches normal operating temperature. If it has just completed an extended high-speed trip, been used to pull a trailer or driven through city traffic on a hot day, the car should be parked for about 30 minutes before checking the fluid level, or an accurate indication will not be possible.

2. Move the transmission selector lever through all ranges several times and place in PARK.

3. Remove the transmission dipstick and wipe a small quantity on two fingers, rub together and inspect the odor for a burned smell.

4. Wipe the dipstick clean, replace in the transmission filler tube and remove a second time. Hold it in a horizontal position and read the fluid level—it should be on the FULL mark. If not, add sufficient fluid to bring the level to the FULL mark. Clean the dipstick, reinsert it in the filler tube and recheck the level.

TRANSMISSION FLUID TYPES

Before you add any fluid to your transmission, make sure you know which kind to use—check the manufacturer's recommendations. Chrysler/American Motors specify Dexron, GM recommends Dexron II and Ford uses Types F and CJ. One difference between the four fluids—Dexron/Dexron II permit a smooth clutch engagement; Types F/CJ use a friction modifier to provide a quicker lockup. Incorrect fluid usage will lead to quick deterioration of internal components and an expensive overhaul.

Ford, however, has advised mechanics that Dexron II can be mixed with or substituted for Type CJ fluid, but only in 1977 and later Jatco transmissions used in Granada/Monarch models.

TRANSMISSION FLUID LEAKS

A fluid leak should be suspected if the ATF level is consistently low—inspect the area under the car after it has been parked overnight. This is not always an accurate indicator of leakage, since some leaks occur primarily when the transmission is in operation, and air-flow around the transmission while the car is moving will carry the leaking fluid toward the rear of the car and away from its actual source—the leak may even appear to come from the differential.

1. Wipe the suspected area clean. If the underside of the transmission is especially dirty, degrease.

2. Road-test the car to bring the ATF to normal operating temperature.

3. Stop the car and inspect for leakage with the engine running. This is best done by driving the vehicle onto a hoist, placing the transmission in PARK and setting the brake. With the car elevated, a leakage inspection is easier and more accurate.

4. Shut off the engine and inspect for ATF leakage caused by converter drainback. This situation is common with torque-converter automatic transmissions—the ATF in the converter drains back to the transmission through a faulty check valve in the front pump, artificially raising the transmission fluid level.

5. Refer to the chart to determine possible points of ATF leakage, and remember that where the fluid is located is probably not where the actual source of the leakage is.

VACUUM DIAPHRAGM/MODULATOR LEAKAGE

Vacuum diaphragm/modulator units should be checked for vacuum leaks if throttle pressure problems

AUTOMATIC TRANSMISSION FLUID LEAK POINTS

SOURCE	CAUSE
A. Oil Pan	1. Incorrectly torqued attaching bolts. 2. Oil pan gasket damaged or incorrectly installed. 3. Oil pan gasket mounting face is defective.
B. Extension Housing	1. Incorrectly torqued attaching bolts. 2. Rear seal is damaged or incorrectly installed. 3. Extension housing-to-case gasket is damaged or incorrectly installed. 4. Output shaft O-ring is damaged or missing. 5. Porous casting.
C. Transmission Case	1. Filler pipe O-ring is damaged or missing. 2. Filler pipe bracket is incorrectly installed, "loading" one side of the O-ring seal. 3. Modulator O-ring is damaged or missing. 4. Electrical connector O-ring is damaged or missing. 5. Speedometer gear O-ring is damaged or missing. 6. Incorrectly torqued governor cover bolts. 7. Governor cover gasket is damaged or missing. 8. Manual shaft lip seal is damaged or incorrectly installed. 9. Line pressure tap plug is loose. 10. Parking pawl shaft cup plus is damaged or incorrectly installed. 11. Vent pipe (see E). 12. Porous casting.

D. Leak at Transmission Front	1. Front pump seal leaks. This may be caused by:
	  a. A cut seal lip. Inspect converter hub for nicks, etc.
	  b. The bushing has moved forward and is damaged.
	  c. The garter spring is missing from the seal.
	2. Loose front pump attaching bolts.
	3. Front pump attaching bolt seals damaged or missing.
	4. Front pump housing O-ring damaged or cut.
	5. Converter leak in the weld area.
	6. Porous case.

E. Fluid from Vent Pipe	1. Too much ATF. 2. Water in ATF. 3. Contamination between pump and case, or pump cover and body. 4. Pump-to-case gasket is mispositioned or missing. 5. O-ring/grommet on the filter is cut. 6. Breather hole in the pump cover is plugged. 7. Porous case.

are suspected. On Ford transmissions, remove the vacuum diaphragm unit and connect to a hand vacuum pump. Apply at least 18 ins. of vacuum, with the vacuum hose blocked off. Connect the vacuum hose to the manifold vacuum port on the diaphragm unit—the vacuum gauge should still read the vacuum applied. If it does not, the diaphragm is leaking and must be replaced. On a dual-area diaphragm, connect the vacuum hose to the EGR port and leave the manifold vacuum port open. Holding a finger over the control rod, remove the hose from the vacuum diaphragm and the internal spring should push the rod outward. If it does not, replace the vacuum diaphragm unit.

General Motors vacuum modulators are checked for leakage by turning the units so that the vacuum stem points downward. Check the substance that comes out; if it has the feel of oil, the vacuum diaphragm is faulty, because the only way ATF can be on the vacuum side of the modulator is by a diaphragm leak. If it does not have an oily feel, it is a mixture of gasoline and/or water vapor, and the vacuum modulator must not be changed. Should oil be found on the vacuum side and no external leaks are visible, yet fluid level continually remains low, replace the modulator on the assumption that the diaphragm contains a pin-hole leak.

TRANSMISSION SERVICE

DRAINING THE FLUID

Manufacturers' specifications for replacing the ATF differ, but generally speaking, it is a good idea to change the fluid every 60,000 miles (24,000 on most GM cars) under normal conditions, or every 15,000 miles if the car is: 1) routinely subjected to hauling heavy loads, such as trailers or boat towing or 2) operated constantly in a hot or dusty climate, in mountainous areas or in heavy city traffic involving constant stop-and-go driving.

Transmission drainage is accomplished in one of three ways: by a drain plug, dipstick tube or oil pan removal. The ATF must be hot and the transmission in a level position. On those transmissions fitted with a drain plug in the oil pan or in the bottom of the transmission case, the plug is removed and the transmission allowed to drain, just as when draining crankcase oil. Wipe the plug clean and replace it.

If draining is accomplished by the dipstick tube, remove it from the oil pan side and replace the gasket or O-ring seal when reinstalling the tube. Most transmissions are drained by removing the oil pan. Clean the pan and discard the old gasket. Make sure that both the pan and case gasket surfaces are clean before replacing the pan with a new gasket. Torque the pan attaching bolts to specifications.

CONVERTER DRAINAGE

Torque converters are one-piece welded units with their own separate drain plug(s). To remove the drain plug(s), it is necessary to remove the access cover below the converter, or to lower the bottom part of the converter housing. Turn the engine over until the plug is accessible, and remove it. If the converter uses two drain plugs, remove one and rotate the unit 180° for access to the other. The second drain plug acts as a vent to speed the draining process. Single plug converters can be vented for faster draining by removing the transmission pressure-takeoff plug, but be sure to replace it when draining is completed.

Late-model converters may have no drain plug(s). Such converters cannot be flushed and are designed to be replaced when the ATF is contaminated. A molded

turbine thrust spacer is used inside the THM 200 torque converter. If this spacer breaks, it will cause an erratic or no-shift condition. To determine if a broken spacer is at fault when troubleshooting these conditions, remove the oil pan and check for a deposit of hard black gritty material either in the pan or on the fluid screen. If found, disassemble and clean the entire transmission, flush the oil cooler and lines, and replace the converter and fluid screen, as well as any other parts that may show excessive wear or damage as a result.

SCREENS AND FILTERS

All automatic transmissions are fitted with either a screen or fluid filter located between the valve body and the oil pan. Screens can be cleaned and reused if undamaged, but filters should always be replaced. Screens and filters are retained in various ways—by attaching screws, steel retaining clips or neoprene O-rings. To clean the screen, wash it in clean solvent and blow dry with low-pressure compressed air—*do not wipe dry with a cloth*, because a single piece of lint can cause a transmission malfunction. Screens with holes or those not easily cleaned should be replaced. On Ford C4 transmissions, a tab on the screen serves to hold a small valve/spring in the valve body. Remove the screen carefully and replace the valve and spring when reinstalling the screen.

REFILLING THE TRANSMISSION WITH FLUID

With the drain plugs and oil pan reinstalled, and the transmission in a level position, fill with the type and amount of fluid specified by the manufacturer. Apply the brakes and start the engine, letting it idle for a few minutes. Then move the selector lever slowly through the complete gear range several times, returning it to PARK or NEUTRAL. Check the fluid level on the dipstick and add a sufficient quantity of fluid if necessary to bring the level up to the ADD mark on the dipstick. Allow the transmission to reach normal operating temperature and recheck the fluid level. If necessary, add more fluid to bring the level up to the FULL mark. Inspect the drain plug(s), dipstick tube, oil pan gasket and oil cooler lines at the transmission and radiator for leakage.

TRANSMISSION REMOVAL/REPLACEMENT

Transmission removal is a matter of using good judgment, having the correct tools and equipment at hand, and following a logical procedure. Because the placement of exhaust pipes, crossmembers, catalytic converters, etc., differs considerably with body style, model year and engine application, describing the exact removal/replacement procedure for each particular transmission application is not possible here, nor is it necessary.

Whether you plan to work on a hoist or on a set of jackstands, a transmission jack will be a necessity. You just cannot remove or install a transmission weighing more than you do safely without the use of one. Since the investment in such a specialized piece of equipment is high, it is suggested that you either borrow or rent one. Also determine if the overhaul procedure for the transmission in question will require any specialized tools beyond the use of a torque wrench and spring compressor; if so, arrange to have them available before setting to work. A generalized removal/replacement sequence follows.

TO REMOVE

1. Disconnect the negative battery terminal from the battery.

2. Drain the ATF and replace the oil pan to protect the valve control body.

3. Drain the converter and reinstall the drain plug.

4. Disconnect the transmission-to-driveshaft yokes, remove the output shaft yoke from the transmission extension housing and plug the housing end with a seal installer or a rag.

5. Disconnect all cables, electrical connections, vacuum hose and oil cooler lines from the transmission case.

6. Disconnect the transmission shift linkage as required. When this step is completed, all external connections to the case should have been unhooked.

7. Survey the situation and determine if exhaust pipes, exhaust manifolds, catalytic converters, etc., must be lowered out of the way to provide sufficient access for attaching bolt removal. If so, loosen and move or remove as necessary.

8. Check the starting motor location; if the starter will interfere with the converter housing removal, unbolt and remove the unit.

9. Place the transmission jack beneath the transmission body to support it, and secure it with a safety chain.

10. Remove the transmission mounting-pad bolts or the crossmember, as required.

11. Remove the bolts holding the converter housing to the engine, lower the jack and remove the converter/transmission assembly from under the car.

12. Transfer the transmission case from the jack to a transmission stand or place on a clean workbench.

TO INSTALL

1. Fit the torque converter to the transmission. Make sure the converter engages the pump gear.

2. Place the transmission on the transmission jack, and secure it with a safety chain.

3. Rotate the converter until its attaching studs/holes are aligned with their respective holes/studs on the flywheel.

4. Raise the transmission jack and maneuver the converter and transmission case into position, then install the converter-housing-to-engine attaching bolts, and torque to specifications. Remove the safety chain and jack.

5. Position the transmission mounting pad/crossmember, and install the attaching bolts. Torque to specifications.

6. If exhaust components were removed or lowered, replace and secure.

7. Replace and torque the flywheel-to-converter nuts. Install and connect the starting motor, and torque to specifications, if removed.

8. Connect all linkage, oil cooler lines, speedometer cable, electrical connections, etc.

9. Install the converter housing cover, and torque the attaching bolts to specifications.

10. Install the transmission output-shaft yoke/companion flange, and connect to the driveshaft. Torque all bolts to specifications.

11. Double-check to make certain everything removed has been replaced and securely attached.

12. Fill the transmission with ATF, and make any necessary linkage adjustments.

TRANSMISSION OVERHAUL

On the following pages, you will find pertinent data, diagnosis charts, specifications and a pictorial how-to sequence providing instructions on overhauling each of the automatic transmissions currently in use on American cars from 1970 through 1978. Read the section pertaining to your transmission carefully, and try to determine the malfunctioning area before beginning work. With care and patience in progressing through a series of logical steps, you should have no difficulty in completing an overhaul yourself—removing and replacing the transmission often takes longer than the overhaul.

Make certain you have all the necessary tools on hand, including any special tools indicated, before setting to work. Cleanliness is most important; consequently, an air hose and compressor are highly recommended. If replacement parts are required, be certain to note the transmission model number (usually stamped on a pad on the case housing) and provide this information to the parts department, along with the make, model and year of car.

CAUTION/WARNING:

WHILE ALL TURBO 400'S ARE ESSENTIALLY THE SAME, FOR EXAMPLE, THERE ARE A LARGE NUMBER OF INDIVIDUAL VARIATIONS ACCORDING TO YEAR AND APPLICATION, AND THE TRANSMISSION MODEL NUMBER IS ESSENTIAL IN OBTAINING THE CORRECT REPLACEMENT PARTS. SINCE FORD, GM AND CHRYSLER CONSTANTLY REVISE THE INTERNAL COMPONENTS AND OPERATION IN THEIR AUTOMATIC TRANSMISSIONS (ALTHOUGH THE BASIC DESIGNATION REMAINS THE SAME), THE PROCEDURES WHICH FOLLOW ARE TO BE REGARDED AS REPRESENTATIVE OF THE OVERHAUL PROCEDURE TO FOLLOW—NOT ALL WILL CONTAIN THE SAME COMPONENTS IN THE SAME SEQUENCE, OR OPERATE EXACTLY THE SAME. TO PREVENT ACCIDENTAL DAMAGE WHEN OVERHAULING YOUR AUTOMATIC TRANSMISSION, DO NOT HESITATE TO CHECK WITH A DEALERSHIP OR INDEPENDENT TRANSMISSION SPECIALIST SHOULD YOU ENCOUNTER DIFFERENCES FROM THOSE SHOWN IN OUR PICTORIAL HOW-TO-SEQUENCES.

GENERAL MOTORS
Powerglide

APPLICATIONS

1970-72 Camaro	1970-72 Monte Carlo
1970-72 Catalina	1970-73 Nova
1970-72 Chevelle	1970-72 Tempest
1970-72 Chevrolet	1971-73 Vega
1970-72 Firebird	1971-73 Ventura II

DESCRIPTION

The two-speed Powerglide is contained within a single case/converter housing of aluminum. The transmission automatically shifts into low gear when the selector lever is placed in the DRIVE position. As the car gains speed, the load and throttle position control the upshift to high gear. A passing gear is provided by returning the transmission to low range by means of a forced downshift feature. A manual shifting version of the Powerglide, known as the Torque Drive, is used with I-4 and I-6 Nova models, and is basically similar, but with the automatic shifting provisions removed.

BAND ADJUSTMENT

LOW BAND

(Lower Left Side of Case Under Protective Cap)

1. Remove protective cap from the band adjusting screw. It may be necessary to remove the rear mount bolts from the crossmember and move the transmission slightly to one side to gain sufficient working clearance on Chevelle models.

2. Loosen the adjusting screw locknut one-quarter turn and *hold* in place with a wrench—this is important.

3. Torque the adjusting screw to 70 in.-lbs., then back it off four complete turns if band has been in use for 6000 or more miles, three complete turns if band has been in use less than 6000 miles. The amount of back-off must be exact.

4. Hold the adjusting screw in place and torque the locknut to 15 ft.-lbs.

5. Replace the protective cap and the rear mount bolts, if they were removed.

POWERGLIDE OVERHAUL DIAGNOSIS CHART

CONDITION	CORRECTION
Car does not move in any selector position	1, 2, 3, 18, 19, 20
Engine speed flares, as if clutch is slipping	1, 2, 4, 5, 6, 21, 22, 23
Engine speed flares during upshift	1, 2, 4, 7, 24, 25, 26
Transmission will not upshift	8, 9, 10, 28, 29, 30
Transmission upshifts harshly	4, 7, 11, 12
Downshifts harshly on deceleration	4, 7, 12, 13, 14
Transmission will not downshift	8, 9, 13
Clutch failure—burnt plates	1, 4, 8, 15, 25, 26
Creeps excessively in Drive	10, 12
Creeps in Neutral	10, 21, 25
Vehicle will not move in Reverse	10, 24, 27, 31
Improper shift points	8, 9, 10, 29
Car cannot be push-started	30
Transmission leaks oil	7, 16, 17, 18, 32
Oil is forced out at filler tube	1, 17, 33

KEY

1. Oil level	12. Idle speed too high	23. Converter Stator
2. Oil screen	13. Valves malfunctioning	24. Clutch feed blocked
3. Pressure regulator valve	14. Make pressure tests	25. High clutch
4. Band adjustment	15. Driving too fast in low	26. Front clutch relief valve
5. Servo seal	16. External oil leaks	27. Reverse clutch relief valve
6. Servo blocked	17. Oil cooler or lines	28. Low clutch valve stuck
7. Vacuum modulator or line	18. Front pump	29. Rear pump priming valve
8. Governor	19. Input shaft	30. Rear pump or drive
9. Throttle valve	20. Front pump priming valve	31. Low clutch
10. Throttle linkage	21. Low band	32. Front pump attaching bolts
11. Hydraulic modulator valve	22. Low band linkage	33. Pump circuit leakage

TORQUE SPECIFICATIONS

Transmission Case to Engine	35 ft.-lbs.
Transmission Oil Pan to Case	8 ft.-lbs.
Transmission Extension to Case	25 ft.-lbs.
Speedometer Driven Gear Fitting Retainer	4 ft.-lbs.
Servo Cover to Transmission Case Bolts	20 ft.-lbs.
Front Pump to Transmission Case Bolts	15 ft.-lbs.
Front Pump Cover to Body Attaching Bolts	20 ft.-lbs.
Pinion Shaft Lock Plate Attaching Screws	2½ ft.-lbs.
Governor Body to Hub Attaching Bolts	7 ft.-lbs.
Governor Hub Drive Screw	8 ft.-lbs.
Governor Support to Transmission Case Bolts	10 ft.-lbs.
Valve Body to Transmission Case Bolts	15 ft.-lbs.
Valve Body Suction Screen Attaching Screws	2½ ft.-lbs.
Upper Valve Body Plate Bolts	5 ft.-lbs.
Lower to Upper Valve Body Attaching Bolts	15 ft.-lbs.
Inner Control Lever Allen Head Screw	2½ ft.-lbs.
Parking Lock Pawl Reaction Bracket Attaching Bolts	10 ft.-lbs.
Oil Cooler Plugs at Transmission Case	5 ft.-lbs.
Pressure Test Point Plugs	5 ft.-lbs.
Low Band Adjustment Locknut	15 ft.-lbs.
Converter to Engine Bolts	35 ft.-lbs.
Under Pan to Transmission Case	7½ ft.-lbs.
Oil Cooler Pipe Connectors to Transmission Case or Radiator	10 ft.-lbs.
Oil Cooler Pipe to Connectors	10 ft.-lbs.
Vacuum Modulator to Transmission Case	15 ft.-lbs.
Oil Pan Drain Plug	20 ft.-lbs.
Converter Drain Plug (Taxis)	20 ft.-lbs.
Parking Brake Lock & Range Selector Inner Lever Allen Head Screw	2½ ft.-lbs.

POWERGLIDE TRANSMISSION CASE DISASSEMBLY

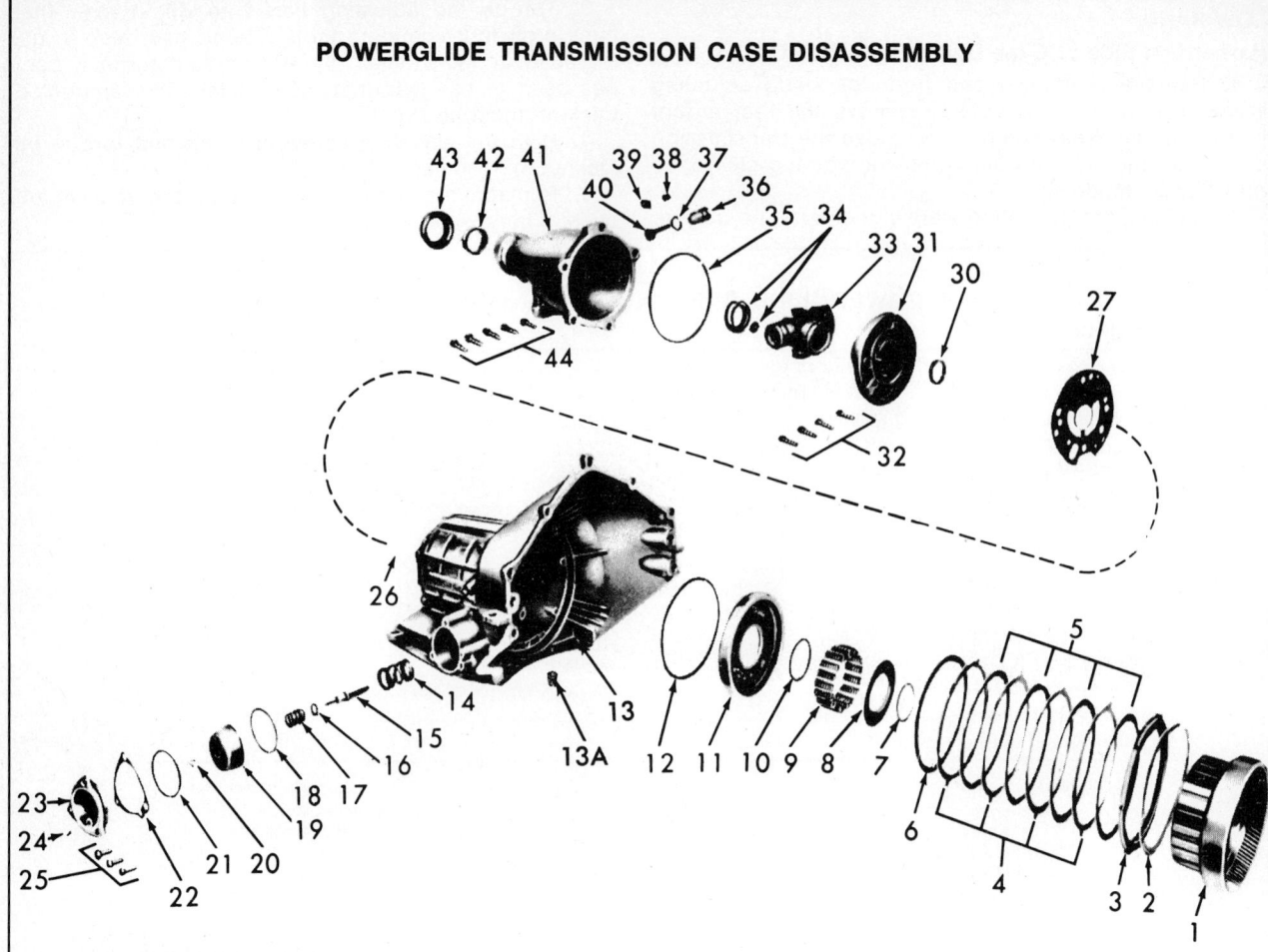

1. Reverse Ring Gear	13. Transmission Case	31. Governor Support
2. Reverse Clutch Pack Snap Ring	13A. Transmission Case Screen	32. Governor Support to Case Attaching Bolts
3. Reverse Clutch Pressure Plate	14. Servo Piston Return Spring	33. Governor Assembly
4. Reverse Clutch Reaction Plates	15. Servo Piston Rod	34. Speedometer Drive Gear and Clip
5. Reverse Clutch Drive Plates	16. Servo Piston Apply Spring Seat	35. Seal
6. Reverse Clutch Cushion Spring	17. Servo Piston Apply Spring	36. Speedometer Shaft Fitting
7. Reverse Clutch Piston Return Spring Retainer Snap Ring	18. Servo Piston Seal Ring	37. Speedometer Shaft Fitting Oil Seal
	19. Servo Piston	38. Lock Plate Attaching Screw
8. Reverse Clutch Piston Return Spring Retainer	20. Servo Piston Rod Spring Retainer	39. Lock Plate
	21. Servo Cover Seal	40. Speedometer Driven Gear
9. Reverse Clutch Piston Return Springs	22. Servo Cover Gasket	41. Transmission Extension
10. Reverse Clutch Piston Inner Seal	23. Servo Cover	42. Extension Bushing
	24. Servo Cover Plug	43. Extension Oil Seal
11. Reverse Clutch Piston Outer Seal	25. Servo Cover Bolts	44. Extension to Case Attaching Screws
	26. Transmission Case Bushing	
12. Reverse Clutch Piston Outer Seal	27. Gasket	
	30. Governor Support Bushing	

POWERGLIDE COMPONENT DISASSEMBLY

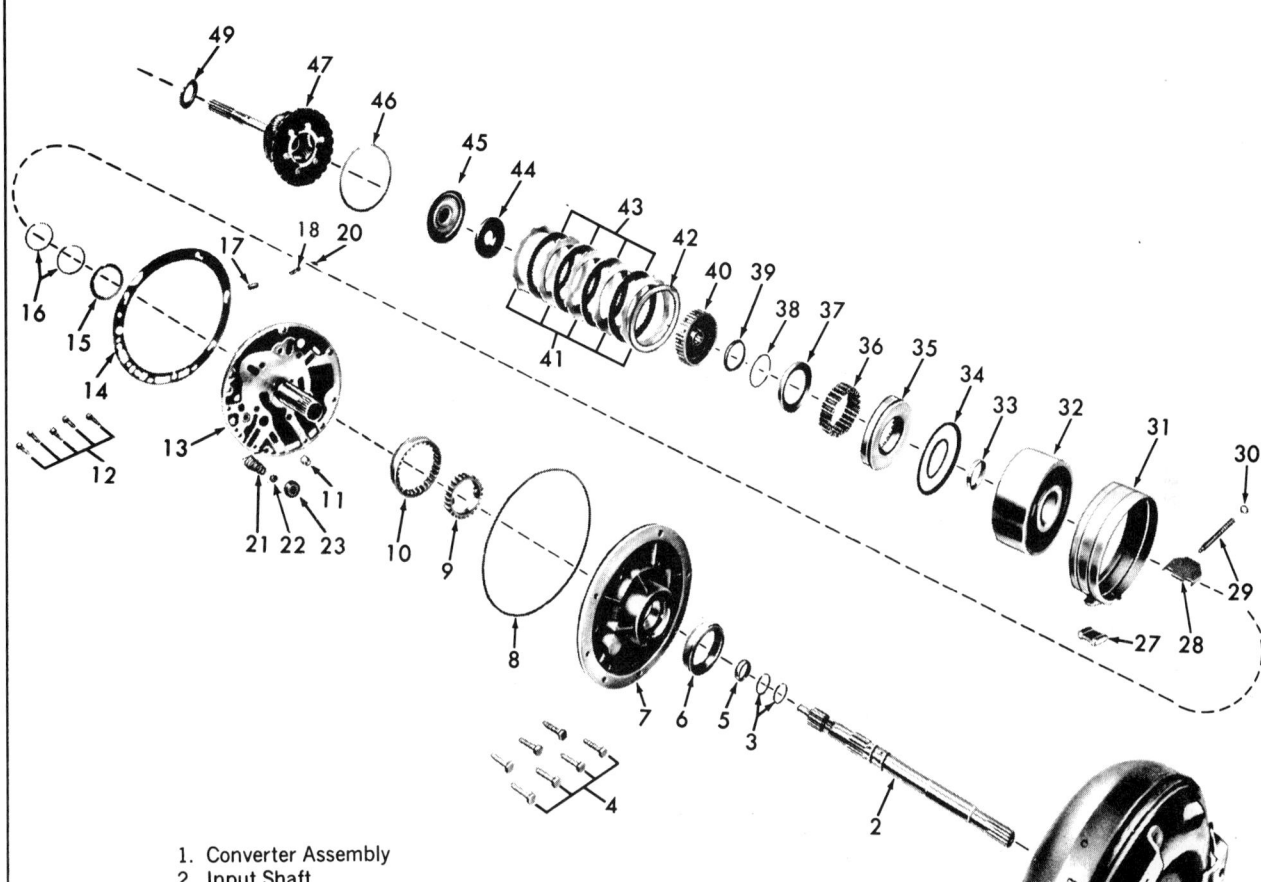

1. Converter Assembly
2. Input Shaft
3. Input Shaft Oil Seals
4. Oil Pump to Case Attaching Bolts and Sealing Washers
5. Low Sun Gear Bushing
6. Pump Oil Seal
7. Oil Pump Body
8. Pump to Case Oil Seal
9. Oil Pump Drive Gear
10. Oil Pump Driven Gear
11. Downshift Timing Valve
12. Oil Pump Cover to Pump Body Attaching Screws
13. Oil Pump Cover and Converter Stator Shaft
14. Oil Pump Gasket
15. Clutch Drum Thrust Washer (Selective Fit)
16. High Clutch Seal Rings
17. Pump Priming Valve
18. Pump Priming Valve Spring
20. Pump Priming Valve Spring Retaining Pin
21. Oil Cooler By-Pass Valve Spring*

22. Oil Cooler By-Pass Valve*
23. Oil Cooler By-Pass Valve Seat*
27. Band Apply Strut
28. Band Anchor Strut
29. Band Anchor Adjusting Screw
30. Band Anchor Adjusting Screw Nut
31. Low Brake Band
32. Clutch Drum
33. Clutch Drum Bushing
34. Clutch Piston Outer and Inner Seals
35. Clutch Piston
36. Clutch Return Springs
37. Clutch Spring Retainer
38. Clutch Spring Retainer Snap Ring
39. Clutch Hub Front Thrust Washer

40. Clutch Hub
41. Clutch Driven Plates (Flat)
42. Clutch Cushion Spring (Waved)
43. Clutch Drive Plates (Waved)
44. Clutch Hub Rear Thrust Washer
45. Low Sun Gear and Clutch Flange Assembly
46. Clutch Flange Retainer Ring
47. Planet Carrier and Output Shaft Assembly
49. Output Shaft Thrust Bearing

*Except air cooled and 11" converter models.

POWERGLIDE VALVE BODY DISASSEMBLY

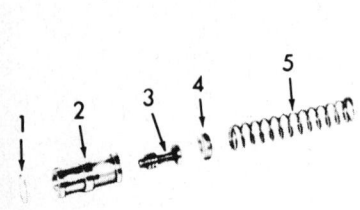
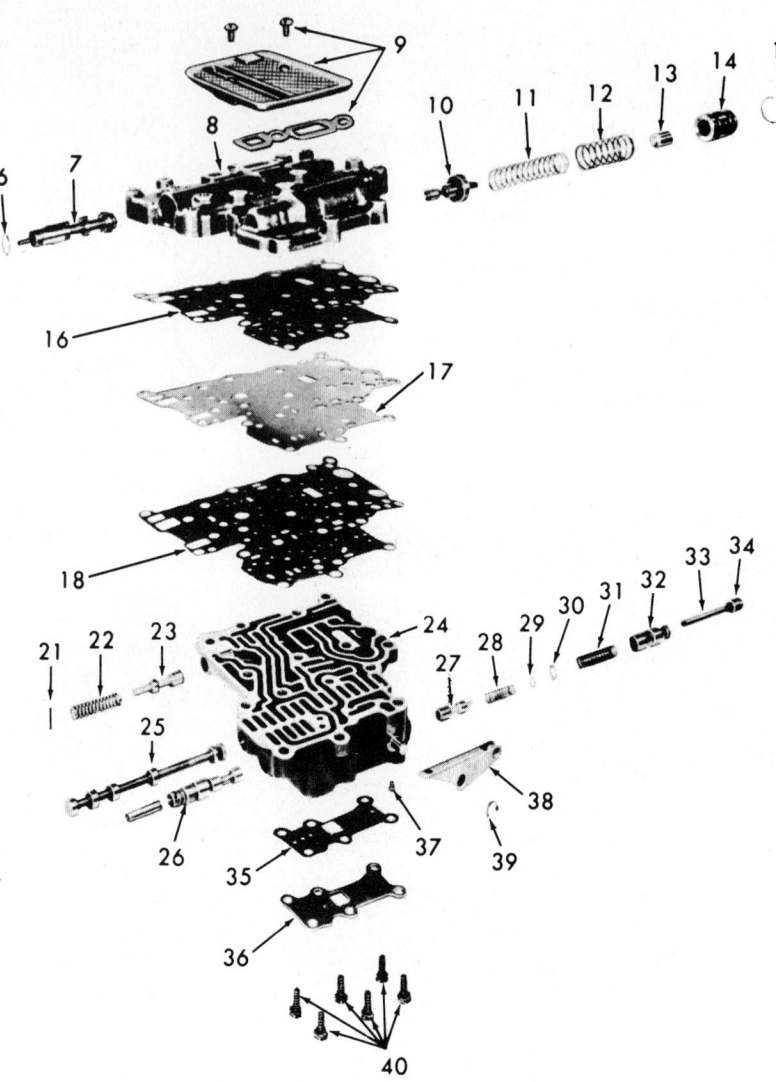

1. Snap Ring
2. Hydraulic Modulator Valve Sleeve
3. Hydraulic Modulator Valve
4. Pressure Regulator Spring Retainer
5. Pressure Regulator Spring
6. Pressure Regulator Spring Seat
7. Pressure Regulator Valve
8. Lower Valve Body
9. Suction Screen, Gasket and Attaching Screws
10. Low and Drive Valve
11. Low and Drive Valve Inner Spring
12. Low and Drive Valve Outer Spring
13. Low and Drive Regulator Valve
14. Low and Drive Regulator Valve Sleeve and Cap
15. Snap Ring
16. Transfer Plate to Lower Valve Body Gasket
17. Transfer Plate
18. Transfer Plate to Upper Valve Body Gasket
21. High Speed Down Shift Timing Valve Stop Pin

22. High Speed Down Shift Timing Valve Spring
23. High Speed Down Shift Timing Valve
24. Upper Valve Body
25. Manual Control Valve
26. Vacuum Modulator Valve, Plunger and Spring (exc. L-4)
27. Throttle Valve
28. Throttle Valve Spring
29. Throttle Valve Spring Seat
30. Throttle Valve Spring Regulator Guide Washer
31. Detent Valve Spring

32. Detent Valve
33. Throttle Valve Spring Regulator
34. Throttle Valve Spring Regulator Nut
35. Upper Valve Body Plate Gasket
36. Upper Valve Body Plate
37. Detent Valve and Spring Retaining Stud
38. Range Selector Detent Lever
39. Snap Ring
40. Upper Valve Body Plate to Upper Valve Body Attaching Bolts and Washers

HOW TO: Powerglide Overhaul

1. Aluminum Powerglide overhaul begins with removal of the oil-pan attaching bolts. Lift oil pan off, discard the old gasket, and clean pan and case flanges of any remaining gasket material.

2. Remove the transmission-oil suction screen and gasket. This throwaway item is replaced with a new one. Late-model screens do not cover this inlet, since it is no longer used.

3. Remove the valve-body-to-case attaching bolts, and carefully lift the valve body from the case, disengaging the servo apply tube from the case bore as the valve body is removed.

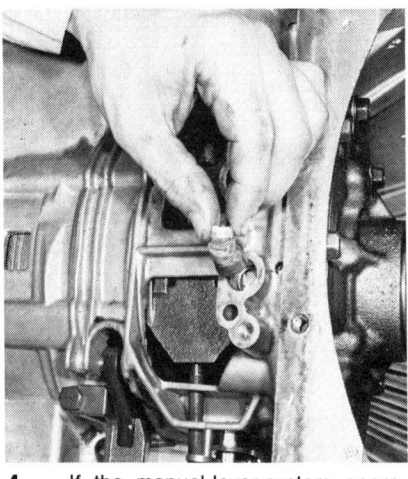

4. If the manual-lever-system operation is satisfactory, leave the assembly intact in the transmission case, but remove this small filter screen and place it in a container of clean solvent.

5. Remove the vacuum modulator and gasket, the vacuum modulator plunger, the dampening spring (4-cyl. model does not use this) and the modulator valve from the transmission case.

6. Remove the seven oil pump bolts, and screw a slide hammer into one of the two threaded puller holes to remove the pump assembly. Use two slide hammers (one on each side).

7. After releasing the low-band-adjuster tension, grasp the input shaft and carefully work it and the clutch assembly from the case. *Do not* lose the low sun gear bushing (1).

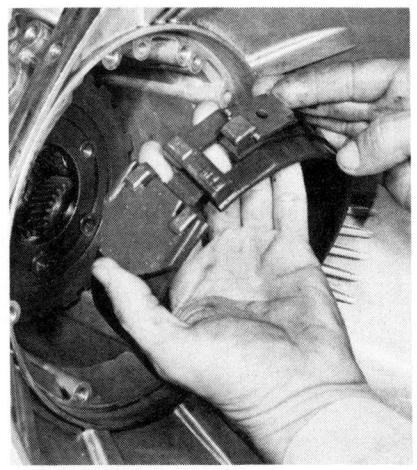

8. Remove the low-brake-band struts and withdraw the band from the transmission case. Carefully inspect the band for signs of excessive wear, burning, scoring or other defects.

9. Unbolting the extension housing from the transmission case, withdraw the housing and gasket from the output shaft. Use a gear puller to remove the speedometer drive gear.

HOW TO: Powerglide Overhaul

10. Unclip the "C" clip from the governor shaft on the weight side of the governor with a small screwdriver, then remove the shaft and governor valve from the opposite side.

11. Loosen the governor drive screw and remove the assembly from the output shaft. Unbolt and remove the governor support body, gasket and extension seal ring from the transmission case.

12. Carefully withdraw the planetary carrier, the output-shaft thrust caged bearing and the reverse ring-gear assembly as a unit from the front of the transmission case.

13. Unclip the reverse-clutch-pack retainer ring with a large screwdriver, then lift out the reverse clutch plates and the waved cushion spring. Inspect all plates for defects.

14. A spring compressor must be installed in the case at this point to remove the large snap ring. Remove tool, and lift out the reverse-piston-spring retainer after unclipping snap ring.

15. This will expose 17 piston return springs. Remove and inspect springs, replacing any that are broken or do not otherwise appear to be functioning properly—a rare problem with Powerglide.

16. The rear piston is easily removed by applying compressed air to the reverse port in the rear of the transmission case as shown. Piston removal without air pressure is a time-consuming task.

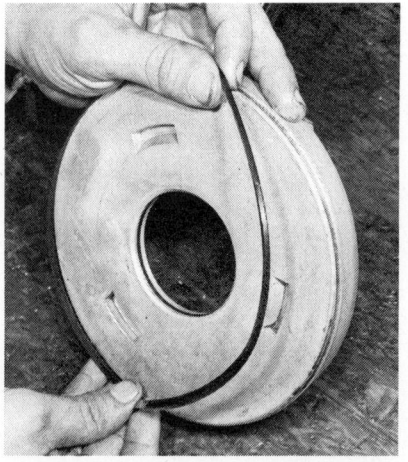

17. Once rear piston is removed from case, inner and outer seal rings should be removed and replaced with new set. Coat piston edge with wax-type lubricant for ease in replacement.

18. Remove the three servo-cover bolts and the servo cover. Push the piston and spring out from inside the case. Clean the servo assembly thoroughly, and replace all O-rings and seals.

19. Reinstall rear piston in transmission case, pushing inward and revolving until you are certain it is fully seated. This is where that wax-type lubricant comes in handy.

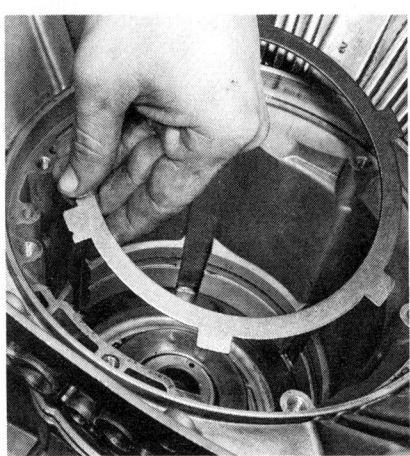

20. Replace springs, retainer and snap ring. Reinstall the cushion spring and begin clutch installation with a steel plate—notched lug fits into a groove located at 7 o'clock position.

21. Align the internal lands and groove of the reverse clutch pack, and engage the reverse ring gear with the plates by turning and jiggling the ring gear until you can feel it seat.

22. Place the output-shaft thrust bearing over the output shaft, secure with a touch of grease and install the output shaft and planetary carrier in the transmission case.

23. The governor is a factory-balanced assembly, and must be replaced as a unit. If it is necessary to replace the internal gasket, unbolt and separate the assembly as shown here.

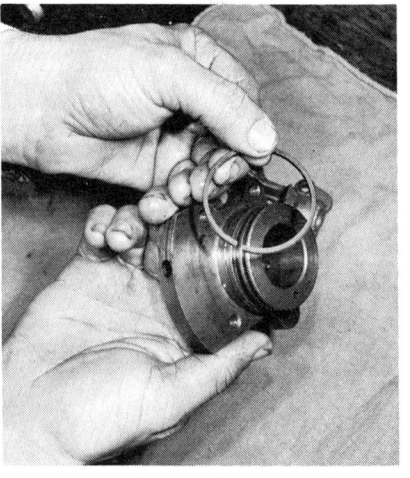

24. Remove and replace the seal rings on the governor hub. These are usually brittle and may break when removed. Install new rings carefully, seating them properly in their grooves.

25. Slide the governor support and gasket on the output shaft, and bolt it to the transmission case. Torque the bolts in an alternate sequence to 10 ft.-lbs. *Do not* overtighten.

26. When installing the governor hub, line up the drive screw with this hole in the output shaft, and slide the hub over it. Tighten the screw carefully to be sure it actually engages the hole.

27. Position the governor body and gasket over the output shaft, and install the four attaching screws. Tighten finger-tight at this point—they will be torqued to the proper value later.

HOW TO: Powerglide Overhaul

28. Reinstall the governor shaft, valve and urethane washer in the governor body assembly, then replace the "C" clip on the opposite side of the assembly, seating it completely.

29. Install the speedometer drive gear on the output shaft. Gear fits over a raised portion of the shaft and will have to be tapped in place gently with a brass or plastic mallet.

30. Check the governor weight for free fit in the body after torquing the governor assembly bolts to 7 ft.-lbs. If the weight sticks or binds, you should loosen the bolts and retorque.

31. *Do not forget* to replace the extension seal ring on the governor support. This is an easy step to overlook, but it can cause all kinds of grief if it is not reinstalled.

32. Wash the extension housing with solvent and air-dry. Inspect for cracks, replace rear bushing and/or oil seal if worn or damaged, and reinstall to the transmission case. Torque to 25 ft.-lbs.

33. Pry the retaining clip (1) from the servo piston assembly, and remove the piston shaft and spring. Clean all parts thoroughly with solvent, then air-dry and reassemble.

34. Remove and replace the metal oil seal on the servo piston before reinstalling the unit in the transmission case. Push the servo assembly into the case as far as it will go.

35. Replace the O-ring seal on the servo cover. Fit cover over the servo piston, align bolt holes and reinstall three attaching bolts. Torque in an alternate sequence to 20 ft.-lbs.

36. Inspect the output shaft and splines for signs of excessive wear or damage, then remove and replace the metallic oil seal rings, seating the new ones properly in their grooves.

37. Start the clutch drum disassembly by removing the retainer ring. With this out of the way, you can remove the low sun gear and the clutch flange from the clutch drum assembly.

38. Remove the hub rear thrust washer and lift out the clutch hub, then remove and inspect the clutch pack plates and the hub front washer for signs of excessive wear or damage.

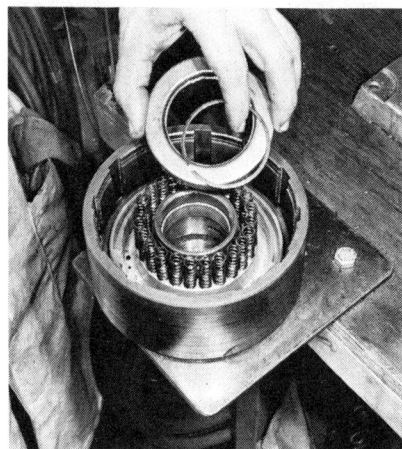

39. Use a spring compressor tool to compress the spring retainer sufficiently to remove the snap ring. Then remove the spring compressor tool and lift the retainer off the springs.

40. Remove and inspect the piston springs, then unseat the piston with a twisting motion as you remove it from the drum. Remove and replace the inner and outer seals with new ones.

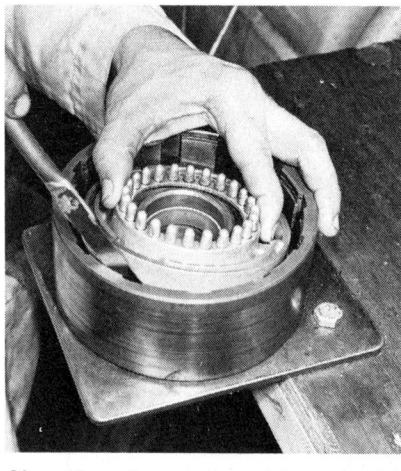

41. Use of a wax-type lubricant stick is also recommended for help in replacing this piston. If such is not available, a feeler gauge will help to seat the piston properly.

42. With the piston seated all the way in the drum, reinstall the piston springs, replace the spring retainer and compress it sufficiently to reinstall the retaining snap ring in its groove.

43. Apply a little grease, and replace the clutch hub front washer, with its lip facing in toward the clutch drum. Then reinstall the clutch hub in the clutch drum, revolving to seat properly.

44. Begin clutch pack reassembly by installing the wave or cushion spring first, if one is used. When installing new composition clutch plates, soak them in transmission fluid first.

45. Reinstall the low sun-gear/clutch-flange assembly and the clutch-hub rear thrust washer. Replace the retainer snap ring, seating it fully in the clutch drum groove.

HOW TO: Powerglide Overhaul

46. Reassemble the input shaft to the clutch drum, and replace the low sun-gear bushing. Set the assembly to one side while you prepare the case for reinstallation of the components.

47. Install the planetary carrier to engage the reverse clutch, then work the band in place and reinstall the band strut supports, tightening the adjuster screw to hold them in place.

48. Replace the output-shaft thrust bearing, and install the clutch drum and input shaft assembly, indexing the low sun gear with the short pinions on the planetary carrier.

49. If the front pump seal requires replacement, pry out the seal and replace it with a new one. Remove the pump-cover attaching bolts, and lift the cover from the body carefully.

50. Mark the pump gears for correct alignment, and remove them from the pump body. Inspect the drive and driven gears and pump body crescent for nicks or damage, then reinstall.

51. Check clearances between O.D. of driven gear and body (0.0035-0.0065-in.), I.D. of driven gear and crescent (0.003-0.009-in.) and the gear end clearance (0.005-0.0015-in.).

52. Inspect the pump body face for nicks, scoring or other damage. Make sure that the oil-cooler bypass-valve spring and seat are intact—these *are not* used on all Powerglides.

53. Carefully replace the pump cover, and loosely install two attaching bolts. Install an alignment band around the pump, and replace the remaining bolts, torquing each to 2½ ft.-lbs.

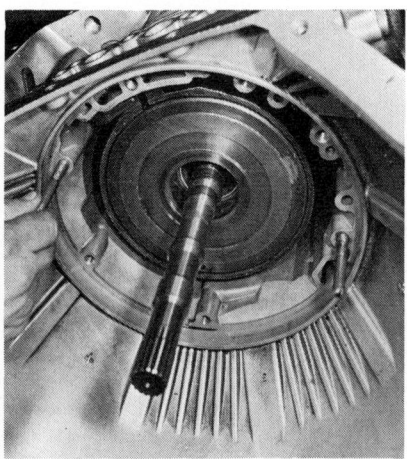

54. Replace the pump-body seal ring. Before installing the pump assembly in the transmission case, screw two guide pins into place, and fit a new pump-to-case gasket over them.

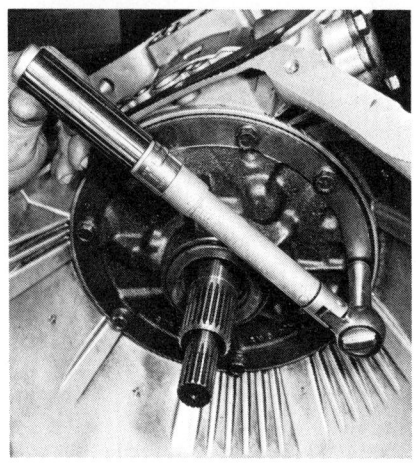

55. Install pump on guide pins, replace attaching bolts and tighten. Then remove guide pins, and install remaining two bolts, torquing them all in alternate sequence to 20 ft.-lbs.

56. Position case screen in its bore, with the filter end facing toward the oil pan. If the filter screen is damaged or cannot be thoroughly cleaned, it should be replaced with a new one.

57. Remove the valve body bolts, and carefully lift the lower body and transfer plate from the upper body, discarding all gaskets. If further valve body disassembly is required, see exploded view.

58. Replace the selector lever detent roller (1), and install the reassembled valve body with a new gasket, carefully guiding the servo apply line (2) into its boss in the case.

59. With the valve body secured in the case, make sure that the manual valve engages the manual-valve actuating lever. Check operation by turning the actuating connector (1).

60. Use a pair of needlenose pliers, as shown, to reconnect the range-selector-detent roller spring to the detent roller lever and to the valve-body attaching arm. Spring ends must engage properly.

61. Replace vacuum modulator valve and spring in transmission case, and screw modulator in place. Make sure modulator gasket is properly installed on modulator unit.

62. Fit new oil screen gasket to valve body, and install new oil suction screen over it. Replace two attaching bolts, and torque each to 2½ ft.-lbs. Replace screen whenever fluid is changed.

63. Replace oil pan, using a new gasket, and install oil-pan attaching screws. Tighten each one in an alternating pattern, and torque to 8 ft.-lbs. Powerglide overhaul is complete.

GENERAL MOTORS
Turbo Hydra-Matic 200
Turbo Hydra-Matic 325

TURBO 325 APPLICATION

Buick:
Riviera 1979
Cadillac:
Eldorado 1979

Oldsmobile:
Toronado 1979

Used with 1979 and later GM front wheel drive vehicles, the 325 was developed from the THM 200. It uses three multiple disc clutches, one roller clutch and a band.

TURBO 200 APPLICATION

1976-77 Chevette,
Omega, Vega, Monza
1979 Chevette, Monza
1976 Skyhawk, Skylark
1976-79 Starfire
1977-79 Phoenix

1978 LeSabre
1978-79 LeMans, Grand Am,
Grand Prix, Sunbird,
Century, Cutlass
1979 Olds 88, 98, Regal
1979 Seville (Diesel)

DESCRIPTION

A fully automatic transmission, the Turbo Hydra-Matic 200 consists of a three-element hydraulic torque converter and compound planetary gear set, with three multiple-disc clutches, a roller clutch and one band. The converter and extension housings are an integral part of the transmission case, and there is no external band adjustment. All fasteners are metric.

Considerable modifications were made in the 200 transmission beginning with the 1979 model year. A new case introduced in 1979 incorporates a 3rd accumulator check valve assembly in the intermediate servo bore. This permits quicker oil exhaust and speeds up the 1-2 upshift. Valve body bolt holes, speedo retainer clip hole and T.V. cable bolt holes are

BOLT TORQUE SPECIFICATIONS

LOCATION	THREAD SIZE	TORQUE Ft.-Lbs.
Pump Body to Pump Cover	8P1.25	18
Pump Assembly to Case	8P1.25	18
Parking Brake Bracket to Case	8P1.25	18
Transmission Oil Pan to Case	8P1.25	12
Manual Shaft to Inside Detent Lever	10P1.5	18
Cooler Connector, Steel	¼ 18NPSF	28
Cooler Connector, Brass	¼ 18NPSF	28
Line Pressure Plug	⅛ 27NPTF	8
Throttle Lever, Link and Bracket to Case	6P1	8
Valve Body Assembly to Case	6P1	8
Oil Screen to Case	6P1	8
Speedometer Driven Gear Retainer to Case	6P1	8

The letter (P) in bolt sizes refers to universal thread size on all GM metric bolts.

TURBO HYDRA-MATIC 200 OVERHAUL DIAGNOSIS CHART

CONDITION	CORRECTION
NO DRIVE IN DRIVE RANGE	
(a) Oil level low.	(a) Top up to correct level. Check for external leaks or defective vacuum modulator. Leaking diaphragm will evacuate oil from unit.
(b) Oil pressure is low.	(b) Check filter assembly as O-ring may be missing or damaged; neck weld may leak or filter might be blocked. Check pump assembly for damage by converter. In rare cases, there might be porosity in intake bore of unit.
(c) Manual linkage is out of adjustment.	(c) Check and adjust linkage.
(d) Faulty control valve assembly.	(d) Reconnect manual valve to manual lever.
(e) Forward clutch not working properly.	(e) Check for cracked piston, missing or damaged seals, or burned clutch plates. Check for stuck or missing clutch housing ball; missing or leaking cup plug; wrong forward clutch piston assembly or wrong number of clutch plates; plugged feed orifice in turbine shaft.
(f) Broken spring or damaged cage in roller clutch assembly.	(f) Replace.
OIL PRESSURE TOO HIGH OR TOO LOW	
(a) Incorrect oil pressure.	(a) Check for misadjusted, binding, unhooked or broken throttle valve cable/lever/bracket assembly. Shift T.V. valve may bind, or # 1 check ball missing or leaking. Check pressure regulator for leaking bore plug, plugged control orifice in the pump cover or a binder valve. If pressure is incorrect only

CONDITION	CORRECTION
	in the intermediate and low ranges, check for binding or plugged intermediate boost valve. If problem is in reverse only, check a binding or plugged reverse boost valve. Defective gears will cause low oil pressure.
1-2 SHIFT: FULL THROTTLE ONLY	
(a) Throttle valve control malfunctioning.	(a) Look for binding, broken, disconnected or misadjusted T.V. cable, plunger, lever, bracket assembly of exhaust ball lifter. If #5 ball seats, full T.V. pressure will be present regardless of throttle valve position.
(b) Control valve assembly faulty.	(b) Valve body spacer plate to cover gasket may leak. It can also be damaged or incorrectly installed.
(c) Porosity in case assembly.	(c) Replace.
NO 1-2 SHIFT: FIRST SPEED ONLY	
(a) Governor assembly faulty.	(a) Governor valve sticks. Feed orifice in spacer plate may be plugged. Governor ball(s) may be missing, O-ring seals missing or leaking, governor driven gear stripped, weights binding on pin.
(b) Control valve assembly faulty.	(b) Check 1-2 shift valve trin to see if it's closed. Governor feed channels may be blocked, leaking or pipes out of position. Check valve body spacer plate-to-cover gasket as it may be leaking, damaged or incorrectly installed. Broken or missing band, intermediate-band anchor pin missing or unhooked from the band.

CONDITION	CORRECTION
(c) Intermediate servo faulty.	(c) Check for missing servo-to-cover oil seal ring, wrong intermediate-band apply pin, incorrect piston/cover.

FIRST & SECOND SPEEDS ONLY, NO 2-3 SHIFT

CONDITION	CORRECTION
(a) Control valve assembly faulty.	(a) Check 2-3 shift train to see if it's stuck. Also Check valve body spacer plate-to-cover gasket as it may be leaking, damaged or incorrectly installed.
(b) Direct clutch defective.	(b) Check for cracked piston/housing, damaged or missing clutch plates, missing or damaged oil seals, backing-plate snap ring out of groove.
(c) Faulty oil pump.	(c) Check pump-to-case gasket, look for plugged or leaking pump channels, missing or leaking rear oil seal ring on pump.
(d) Intermediate servo.	(d) Check for missing or broken servo-to-case oil seal ring on intermediate servo. Exhaust hole in the case between the servo piston-seal rings may be plugged.

DRIVE IN NEUTRAL

CONDITION	CORRECTION
(a) Manual linkage out of adjustment.	(a) Adjust linkage.
(b) Forward clutch does not release.	(b) Replace.
(c) Pump or case faulty.	(c) Check for cross leakage in the pump or forward clutch passages.

NO DRIVE OR SLIPS IN REVERSE

CONDITION	CORRECTION
(a) Oil level low.	(a) Top up oil to proper level.
(b) Manual linkage out of adjustment.	(b) Adjust linkage.
(c) T.V. malfunction.	(c) Binding, misadjusted or faulty throttle valve or cable.
(d) Reverse clutch.	(d) Look for cracked piston, broken or missing seals, burned clutch plates or wrong selective spacer ring.
(e) Direct clutch passages.	(e) Check for plugged, leaking or cross feeding of pump channels, pump oil-seal cover rings damaged or missing, incorrect piston, burned plates, stuck/leaking/missing housing ball check, plugged spacer plate orifices.

ROUGH 1-2 SHIFT

CONDITION	CORRECTION
(a) Incorrect oil pressure.	(a) Replace vacuum modulator assembly. Check for loose fittings or restrictions in line.
(b) Control valve assembly bolts loose.	(b) Torque valve body to case bolts to specs.
(c) Valve body spacer plate-to-cover gasket damaged or mispositioned.	(c) Replace gasket.
(d) Faulty throttle valve assembly.	(d) Adjust cable; check for binding cable, plunger throttle valve.
(e) 1-2 accumulator assembly faulty.	(e) Remove unit and check for damaged oil rings, binding valve, stuck piston, broken or missing spring or damaged bore. Repair accordingly.

CONDITION	CORRECTION
(f) Intermediate servo faulty.	(f) Check for missing or damaged piston-to-case oil seal ring or use of wrong pin.

2-3 SHIFT SLIPS

CONDITION	CORRECTION
(a) Oil level low.	(a) Top up oil to proper level.
(b) Throttle valve malfunctions.	(b) Check for binding or misadjusted cable.
(c) Spacer plate and gaskets.	(c) Check for mispositioned or damaged gaskets, or partial blockage in the direct clutch orifice.
(d) Intermediate servo assembly.	(d) Replace servo-to-case oil seal ring.
(e) Direct clutch feed.	(e) Check for cracked piston or housing, mispositioned gaskets, cut or missing piston seals, damaged or missing pump-cover oil seal rings, burned clutch plates or pump channels cross feeding, leaking or restricted.

ROUGH 2-3 SHIFT

CONDITION	CORRECTION
(a) Throttle valve faulty.	(a) Misadjusted, binding—check and repair/replace as required.
(b) Intermediate servo malfunctioning.	(b) Look for a plugged exhaust hole between the servo piston seals, not allowing piston to complete its stroke.
(c) Direct clutch exhaust valve ball check #4 missing.	(c) Replace.

NO ENGINE BRAKING—2ND GEAR

CONDITION	CORRECTION
(a) Intermediate band broken or burned.	(a) Replace and determine cause.
(b) Intermediate boost valve	

NO ENGINE BRAKING—1ST GEAR

CONDITION	CORRECTION
(a) Reverse gear also missing.	(a) Check for broken or missing piston seals; loose, broken or missing clutch housing snap ring; missing or damaged cup plug/seal between case and low/reverse clutch housing.

NO PART—THROTTLE DOWNSHIFTS

CONDITION	CORRECTION
(a) Throttle valve malfunctioning.	(a) Check for binding shift T.V. valve, misadjusted throttle valve cable, plugged passages for throttle plunger or 2-3 throttle valve bushings.
(b) Valve body.	(b) Plugged spacer plate or damaged/mispositioned gaskets.

INCORRECT SHIFT POINTS

CONDITION	CORRECTION
(a) Throttle valve malfunctioning.	(a) Look for binding in throttle valve, valve cable, valve plunger; missing or mispositioned T.V. exhaust ball #5 and lifter; unhooked or loose lever/bracket assembly.
(b) Governor malfunctioning.	(b) Broken or missing shaft-to-cover seal rings or cover O-rings.

WILL NOT HOLD IN PARK

CONDITION	CORRECTION
(a) Manual linkage needs adjustment.	(a) Adjust linkage.
(b) Internal linkage broken or binding.	(b) Check park pawl, parking bracket, and actuator rod/plunger. Replace as required.
(c) Manual detent roller/spring assembly malfunctioning.	(c) Check for loose bolt holding roller assembly to valve body; damaged, mispositioned or missing pin or roller; loose, worn or damaged inside detent lever and pin assembly.

CONTROL VALVE DISASSEMBLY

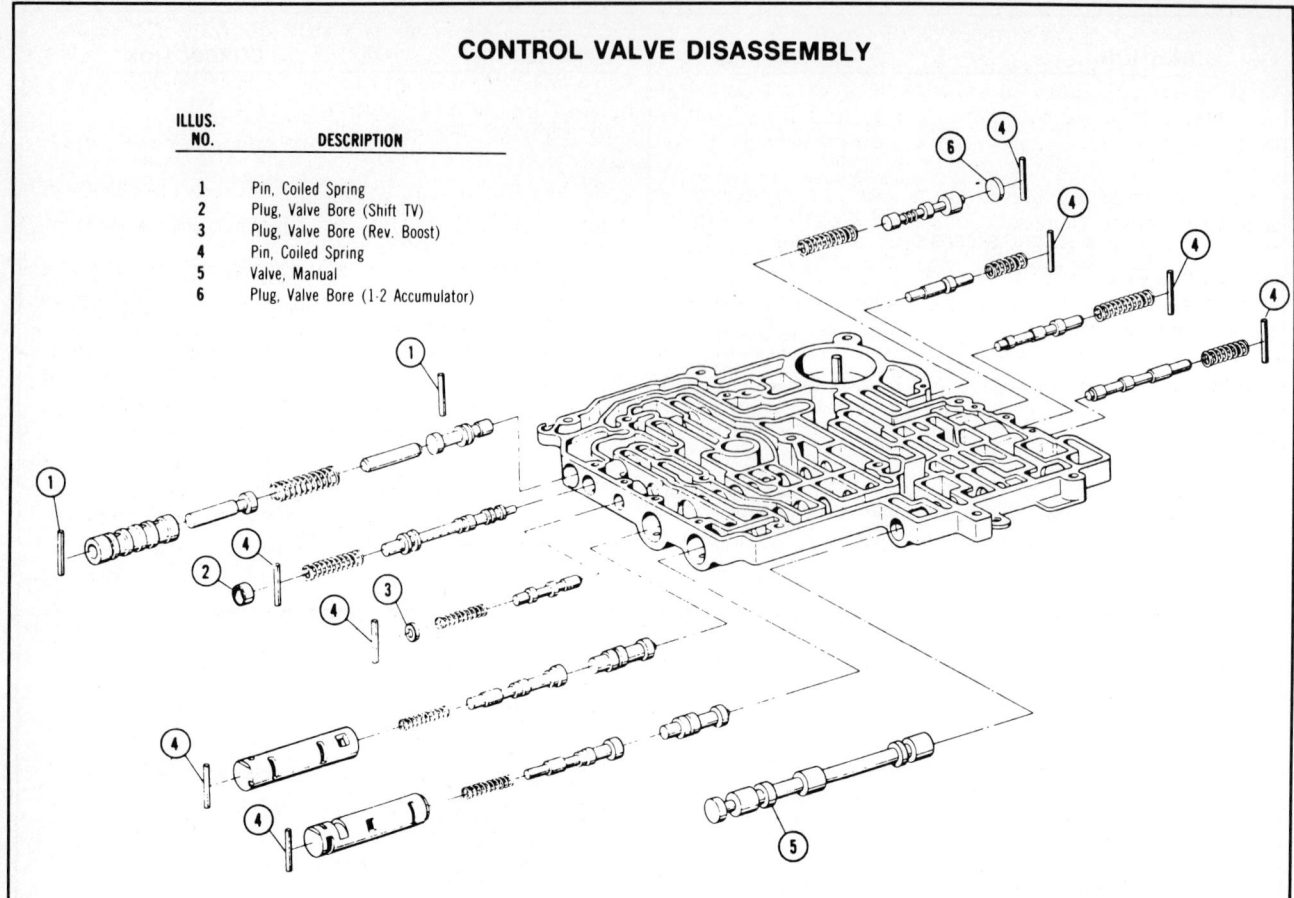

ILLUS. NO.	DESCRIPTION
1	Pin, Coiled Spring
2	Plug, Valve Bore (Shift TV)
3	Plug, Valve Bore (Rev. Boost)
4	Pin, Coiled Spring
5	Valve, Manual
6	Plug, Valve Bore (1-2 Accumulator)

CLUTCH PLATE SPECIFICATIONS

MODELS	DIRECT CLUTCH					FORWARD CLUTCH						LOW & REV. CLUTCH			
	FLAT STEEL PLATE		COMP. FACED PLATE	APPLY RING		WAVED PLATE		FLAT STEEL PLATE		COMP. FACED PLATE	APPLY RING		FLAT STEEL PLATE	COMP. FACED PLATE	APPLY RING	
	NO.	THICKNESS	NO.	I.D.	*WIDTH	NO.	THICKNESS	NO.	THICKNESS	NO.	I.D.	*WIDTH	NO.	NO./TYPE	I.D.	*WIDTH
BR, CX, CN PA, PY PT, PB, PC	4	2.324mm (.091")	4	1	16.99mm (.669")	1	1.585mm (.062")	2	1.969mm (.077")	3	0	17.50mm (.689")	5	4-/ GROOVED	5	24.34mm (.958")
BR, CX (early Models)	3	2.324mm (.091")	3	2	21.44mm (.844")	1	1.585mm (.062")	2	1.969mm (.077")	3	0	17.50mm (.689")	5	4-/ GROOVED	5	24.34mm (.958")
CS (early Models)	4	2.324mm (.091")	4	1	16.99mm (.669")	1	1.585mm (.062")	3	1.969mm (.077")	4	8	13.51mm (.532")	6	5-/NON-GROOVED	4	20.14mm (.793")
BZ, OW, CS	5	2.324mm (.091")	5	9	12.50mm (.492")	1	1.585mm (.062")	3	1.969mm (.077")	4	8	13.51mm (.532")	6	5-/NON-GROOVED	4	20.14mm (.793")
PG, PH, CO, CR CY, BA, OS, OT OR, OZ, CA, OF CU, OX, AS, AX	5	2.324mm (.091")	5	9	12.50mm (.492")	1	1.585mm (.062")	3	1.969mm (.077")	4	8	13.51mm (.532")	7	6-/NON-GROOVED	3	15.94mm (.628")

NOTE: THE DIRECT AND FORWARD CLUTCH FLAT STEEL CLUTCH PLATES AND THE FORWARD CLUTCH WAVED STEEL PLATE SHOULD BE IDENTIFIED BY THEIR THICKNESS.

THE DIRECT AND FORWARD PRODUCTION INSTALLED COMPOSITION-FACED CLUTCH PLATES MUST NOT BE INTERCHANGED. FOR SERVICE, DIRECT AND FORWARD CLUTCH USE THE SAME COMPOSITION-FACED PLATES.

ALL LOW AND REVERSE CLUTCH COMPOSITION-FACED PLATES ARE SERVICED WITH THE GROOVED COMPOSITION-FACED PLATES.

* MEASURE THE WIDTH OF THE CLUTCH APPLY RING FOR POSITIVE IDENTIFICATION.

now 6mm threads instead of 6.3mm. Oil pump gears are 0.100-in. wider and have a different pitch. The direct clutch center seal retainer is changed from an "L" to a "U" shape. Early production models will use the "L" seal with a backing ring, but should be replaced with the new "U" shape retainer when service is required.

Four intermediate servo band apply pins are now available instead of two—this allows a better tuning of the shift feel. The intermediate servo uses a new double piston. The valve body, spacer plate and gaskets have been modified and recalibrated to improve downshift feel during deceleration. The output shaft no longer uses a snap ring for the rear internal gear to locate against—a hub to the rear of the splines serves this purpose. New filler tubes and T.V. cables use a multi-lip seal rather than an O-ring seal. A new front vent is located on top of the case and has replaced the old vent near the rear of the case. The pump-to-case gasket contains the new vent holes; installing the old gasket will cause transmission damage.

BAND ADJUSTMENT
INTERMEDIATE BAND (Lower Right Side of Case)

Special GM tools are required to properly check band adjustment—a dial indicator (GM J-8001) and pin gauge (GM J-25014-1 and J-25014-2).

1. Remove the intermediate servo, and clean the servo bore.

2. Install the dial indicator and pin gauge in the servo bore, and use the servo retaining ring to hold it in place.

3. Set the indicator dial to zero, and align the stepped side of the band apply pin with the torquing arm of the pin gauge.

4. Torque the hex nut on the side of the gauge to 100 in.-lbs. Slide the dial indicator over the band apply pin, and compare the reading to specifications.

5. If the dial indicator reading does not conform to the pin in use, replace the band apply pin with the proper one, as specified.

6. Disassemble the dial indicator and pin gauge, and replace the intermediate servo.

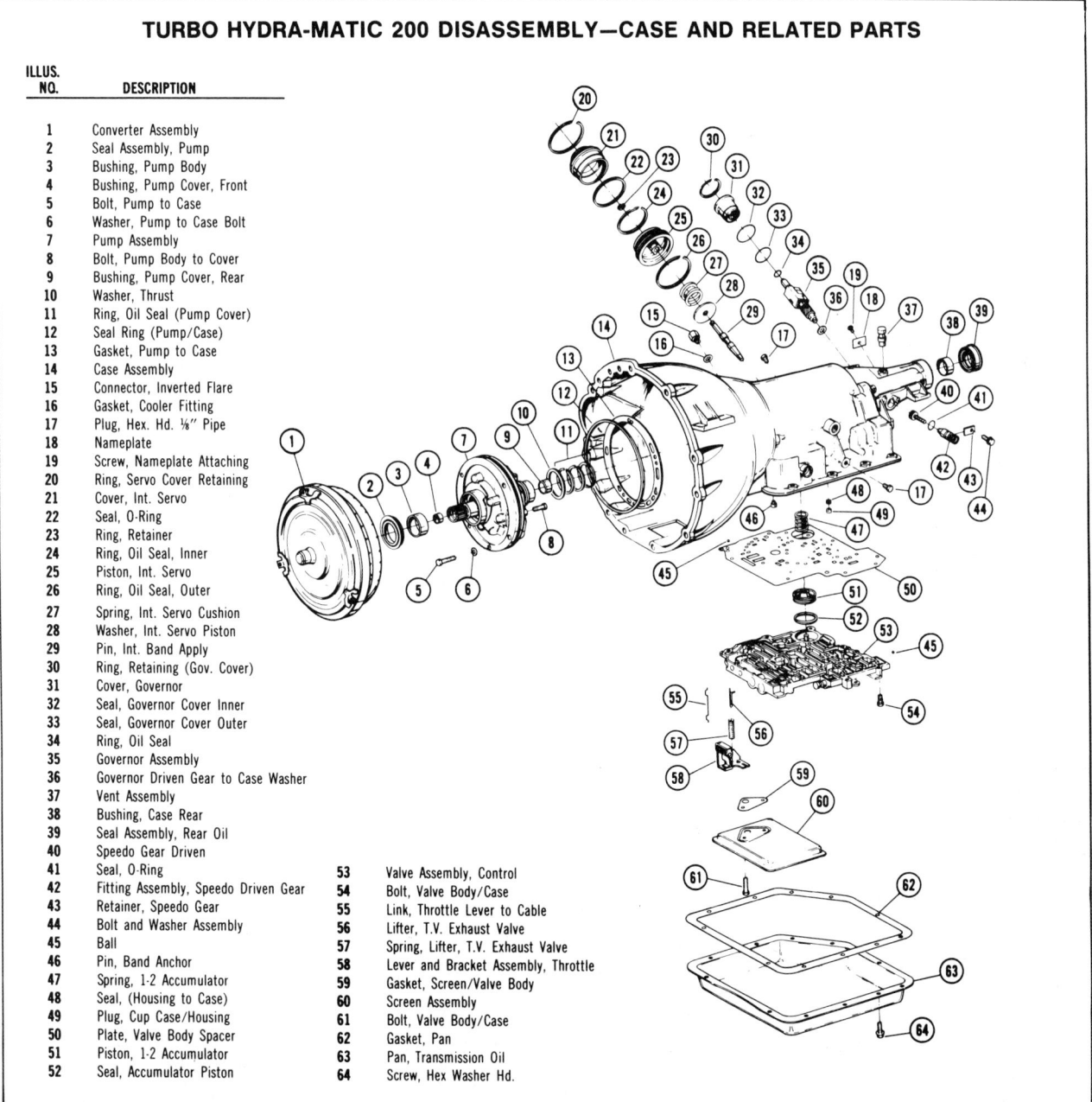

TURBO HYDRA-MATIC 200 DISASSEMBLY—CASE AND RELATED PARTS

ILLUS. NO.	DESCRIPTION
1	Converter Assembly
2	Seal Assembly, Pump
3	Bushing, Pump Body
4	Bushing, Pump Cover, Front
5	Bolt, Pump to Case
6	Washer, Pump to Case Bolt
7	Pump Assembly
8	Bolt, Pump Body to Cover
9	Bushing, Pump Cover, Rear
10	Washer, Thrust
11	Ring, Oil Seal (Pump Cover)
12	Seal Ring (Pump/Case)
13	Gasket, Pump to Case
14	Case Assembly
15	Connector, Inverted Flare
16	Gasket, Cooler Fitting
17	Plug, Hex. Hd. ⅛" Pipe
18	Nameplate
19	Screw, Nameplate Attaching
20	Ring, Servo Cover Retaining
21	Cover, Int. Servo
22	Seal, O-Ring
23	Ring, Retainer
24	Ring, Oil Seal, Inner
25	Piston, Int. Servo
26	Ring, Oil Seal, Outer
27	Spring, Int. Servo Cushion
28	Washer, Int. Servo Piston
29	Pin, Int. Band Apply
30	Ring, Retaining (Gov. Cover)
31	Cover, Governor
32	Seal, Governor Cover Inner
33	Seal, Governor Cover Outer
34	Ring, Oil Seal
35	Governor Assembly
36	Governor Driven Gear to Case Washer
37	Vent Assembly
38	Bushing, Case Rear
39	Seal Assembly, Rear Oil
40	Speedo Gear Driven
41	Seal, O-Ring
42	Fitting Assembly, Speedo Driven Gear
43	Retainer, Speedo Gear
44	Bolt and Washer Assembly
45	Ball
46	Pin, Band Anchor
47	Spring, 1-2 Accumulator
48	Seal, (Housing to Case)
49	Plug, Cup Case/Housing
50	Plate, Valve Body Spacer
51	Piston, 1-2 Accumulator
52	Seal, Accumulator Piston
53	Valve Assembly, Control
54	Bolt, Valve Body/Case
55	Link, Throttle Lever to Cable
56	Lifter, T.V. Exhaust Valve
57	Spring, Lifter, T.V. Exhaust Valve
58	Lever and Bracket Assembly, Throttle
59	Gasket, Screen/Valve Body
60	Screen Assembly
61	Bolt, Valve Body/Case
62	Gasket, Pan
63	Pan, Transmission Oil
64	Screw, Hex Washer Hd.

TURBO HYDRA-MATIC 200 POWERTRAIN COMPONENTS

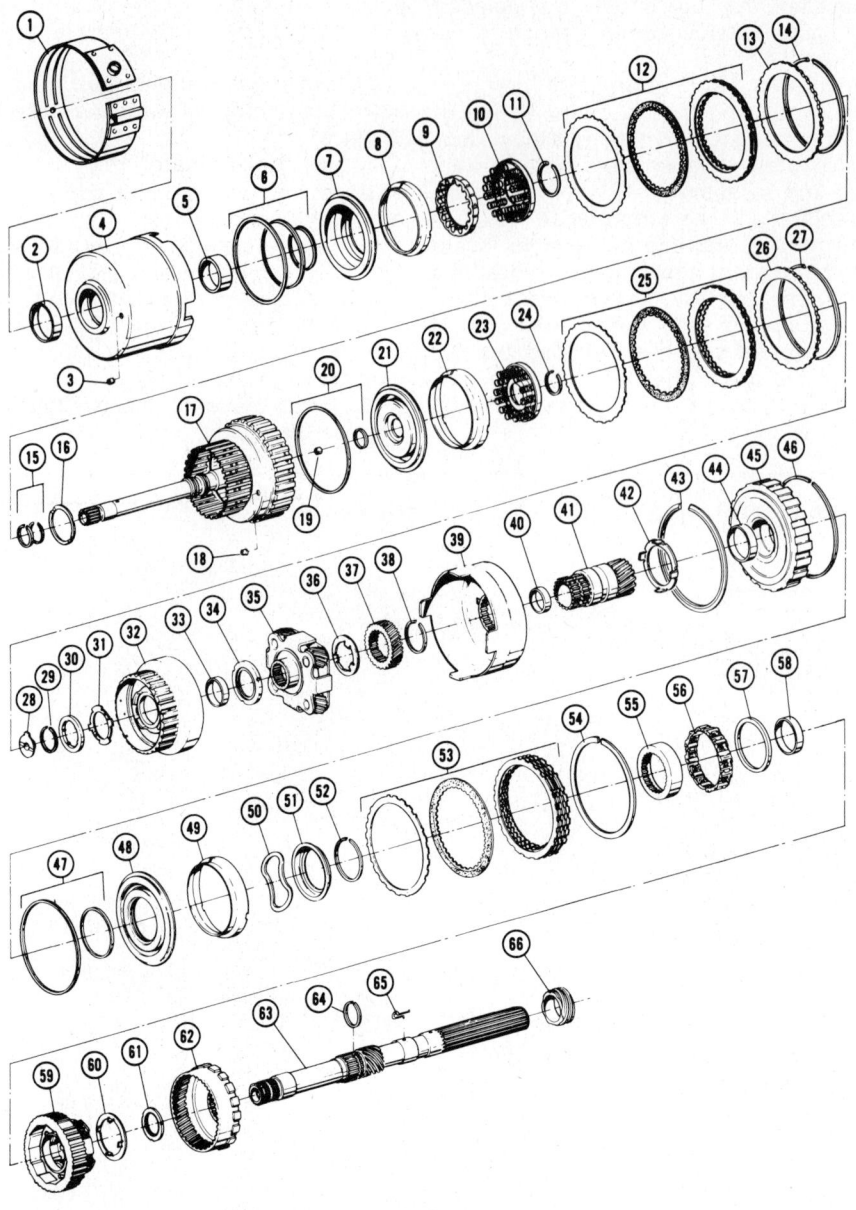

ILLUS. NO.	DESCRIPTION
1	Band Assembly, Intermediate
2	Bushing, Direct Clutch, Front
3	Retainer & Ball Assembly, Check Valve
4	Housing & Drum Assembly, Direct Clutch
5	Bushing, Direct Clutch, Rear
6	Seals, Direct Clutch Piston (Package)
7	Piston Assembly, Direct Clutch
8	Ring, Clutch Apply
9	Guide, Release Spring
10	Retainer & Spring Asm., Direct Clutch
11	Ring, Snap (Spring Retainer)
12	Plate, Direct Clutch
13	Plate, Clutch Backing
14	Ring, Snap
15	Seal, Ring (Turbine Shaft)
16	Washer, Thrust (Dir. to Fwd. Clutch)
17	Housing Assembly, Forward Clutch
18	Retainer & Ball Asm., Check Valve
19	Plug, Cup
20	Seals, Fwd. Cl. Piston (Package)
21	Piston Assembly, Fwd. Clutch
22	Ring, Clutch Apply
23	Retainer & Spring Asm., Fwd.
24	Ring, Snap
25	Plate, Fwd. Clutch
26	Plate, Clutch Backing
27	Ring, Snap
28	Washer, Thrust, Selective Front
29	Ring, Snap (Output Shaft)
30	Washer, Thrust, Selective Rear
31	Washer, Thrust
32	Gear & Bushing Asm., Front Int.
33	Bushing, Front Int. Gear
34	Bearing Asm., Roller (Int. Gear/Carrier)
35	Carrier Asm., Frt. Complete
36	Bearing Asm., Thrust (Frt. Carr./Sun Gr.)
37	Gear, Frt. Sun
38	Ring, Snap (Input Drum to Rear Sun Gear)
39	Drum, Input
40	Bushing, Rear Sun Gear
41	Gear & Bushing Assembly, Rear Sun
42	Washer, Thrust (Drum to Housing)
43	Ring, Snap (Housing to Case)
44	Bushing, Hsg. Asm., Lo & Rev. Cl.
45	Hsg. Asm., Lo & Rev. Cl.
46	Spacer, Housing to Case
47	Seals, Lo & Rev. Piston (Package)
48	Piston Asm., Lo & Rev. Cl.
49	Ring, Clutch Apply
50	Spring, Wave Rev. Cl. Rel.
51	Retainer, Lo & Rev. Cl. Spring
52	Ring, Snap Ret. to Housing
53	Plate, Lo & Rev. Clutch
54	Washer, Lo & Reverse Clutch Selective
55	Race, Lo Roller Cl.
56	Roller Asm., Lo Cl.
57	Washer, Thrust (Rear Carr. to Lo Race)
58	Bushing, Rear Carrier
59	Carrier Assembly, Rear Complete
60	Washer, Thrust (Rear Carr. to Lo Race)
61	Bearing Asm., Roller Thrust (Rear Sun Gear/Rear Internal Gear)
62	Gear, Rear Internal
63	Shaft Output
64	Ring, Snap (Rear Int. Gear to O.P. Shaft)
65	Clip, Speedo Drive Gear
66	Gear Speedo Drive

HOW TO: Turbo Hydra-Matic 200 Overhaul

1. Remove the transmission oil pan and discard the gasket. The pan is stamped with a large warning that metric tools will be required to overhaul this unit, so have them handy.

2. If you discover a considerable amount of metal particles in the oil pan, and the transmission has never been overhauled, it is probably only flashing from the stamped parts.

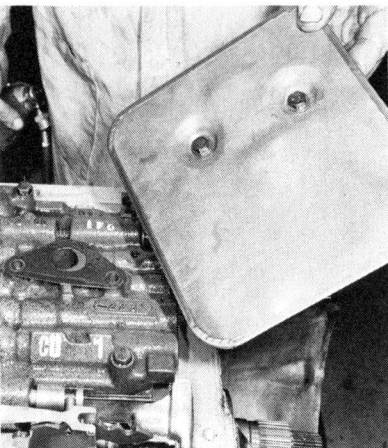

3. Remove the two bolts which hold the oil service screen in place, and discard the gasket. GM recommends fluid/screen changes every 60,000 miles under normal driving conditions.

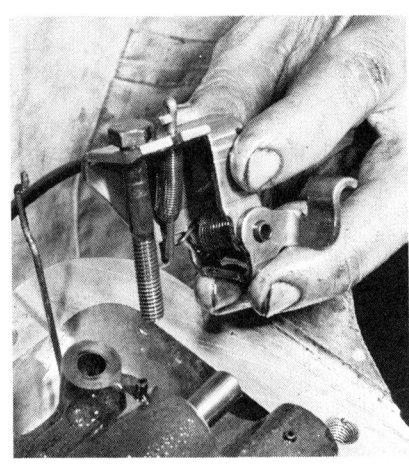

4. Unbolt and remove the throttle lever and bracket assembly, taking care not to bend the throttle lever link. The manual detent roller and spring assembly will be removed next.

5. After removing the remaining valve body bolts, hold the manual valve with a finger and lift the control valve and spacer plate together to prevent losing any of the four check balls inside.

6. The throttle exhaust check ball is located in the transmission case. This should be removed (a magnetic pencil works fine) and placed in a clean parts container.

7. The 1-2 accumulator spring comes out next. Since the transmission contains many stamped and polished parts, keep them separate to avoid nicking or burring of the surfaces.

8. Remove the bolt, washer and retainer which hold the speedometer driven gear in place, and withdraw the driven gear assembly. The nylon gear slips off the assembly. Replace O-ring seal.

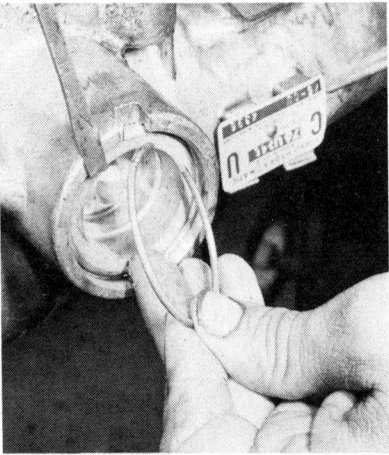

9. Use a screwdriver to pry the governor-control retaining ring free. This is a round snap ring and more annoying to remove than the standard flat variety which is usually used.

HOW TO: Turbo Hydra-Matic 200 Overhaul

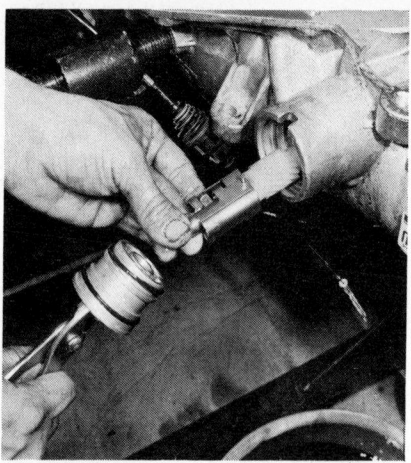

10. Remove the governor cover with pliers and withdraw the governor assembly from the transmission case. You may have to rotate the output shaft counterclockwise for governor removal.

11. Remove intermediate servo in the same way as governor. If necessary, apply compressed air to accumulator port (circle) to remove the cover, then withdraw piston and band apply pin.

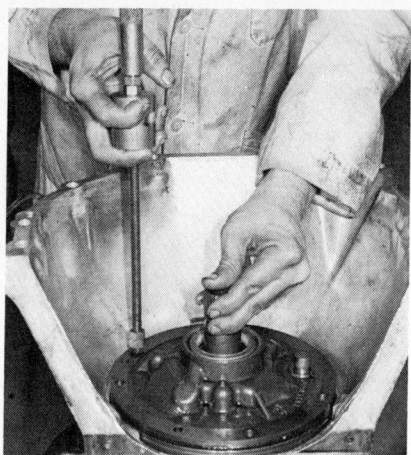

12. Remove the front-pump attaching bolts, and use an oil pump puller to free the pump assembly. Since the thread is metric, a standard puller will not work. The special GM tool is #J-24773.

13. Grasp the turbine shaft and lift the direct/forward clutch assemblies from the transmission case, then work the intermediate band out carefully by pulling from side to side.

14. Push in on the intermediate-band anchor pin and release. It should pop out of the case far enough to grasp and withdraw by hand. If not, use a magnetic pencil as before.

15. Remove the output-shaft-to-turbine-shaft-front-selective-washer snap ring and the selective washer. The washer has a tanged end, and it must be aligned when replaced on the shaft.

16. Withdraw the front internal gear (front selective washer shown). If a rear selective washer and a tanged thrust washer do not come out with the internal gear, remove from the case.

17. The front planetary carrier and roller-thrust-bearing assembly are removed next. Carrier is stamped metal and cannot be disassembled for planetary gear replacement—replace as unit.

18. Withdraw the roller thrust bearing and race, and the front sun gear. Check the thrust bearing and race carefully for any signs of wear, scoring or damage that might impair its operation.

19.   Remove the input drum and the rear sun gear. The input drum is also stamped metal and fits very tightly. Remove the tanged input-drum-to-reverse-clutch-housing thrust washer.

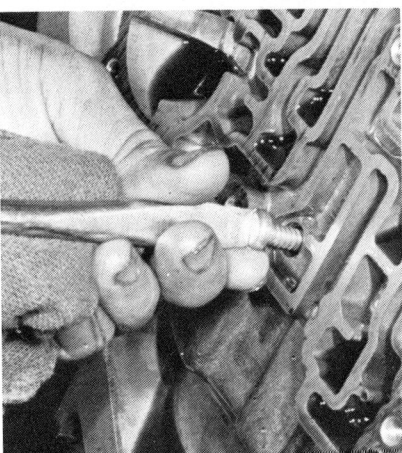

20.   Before attempting to remove low/reverse clutch housing, the housing-to-case-cup plug/seal must be removed. Turn a #14 sheetmetal screw in two to three turns, then pull straight out.

21.   Remove the low/reverse clutch-housing-to-case snap ring. This is a beveled ring, and must be replaced in the case with the beveled side of the ring facing toward the front.

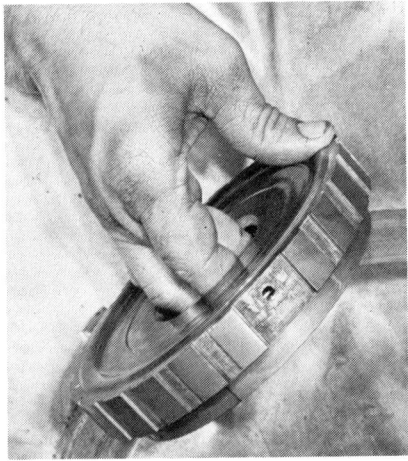

22.   The low/reverse clutch housing can now be removed by moving it back and forth while pulling outward. There is another housing-to-case spacer ring under it to be removed.

23.   Withdraw the low/reverse clutch pack. Check all composition-faced plates for signs of wear, scoring, burning, etc. If new plates are to be installed, soak first in transmission fluid.

24.   The rear planetary carrier, thrust washers and rear internal gear complete the case disassembly. Inspect bearings and carrier clutch/race assembly for signs of wear, scoring or damage.

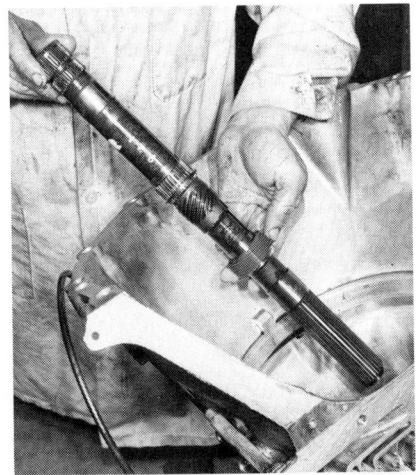

25.   The output shaft can now be withdrawn from the case. Check the splines and gears for wear or damage, then remove the speedometer drive gear from the output shaft.

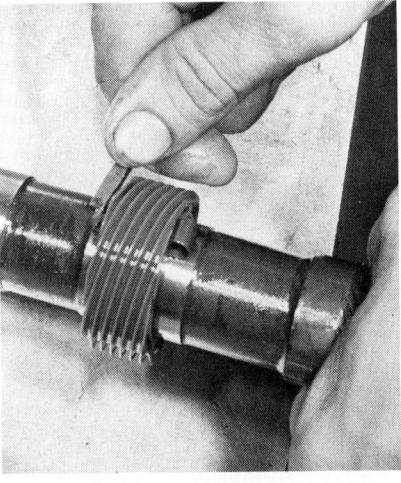

26.   Two types of speedometer drive gears are used. The type of clip retainer and the clip slot size in the gear differ. As a result, they cannot be interchanged. This is Type 1.

27.   Remove the roller clutch/race from the rear carrier. Inspect carefully for wear or damage. If the rollers or energizing springs in the roller clutch are worn, they can be replaced.

HOW TO: Turbo Hydra-Matic 200 Overhaul

28. Use a feeler gauge, as shown, to measure the rear carrier planetary pinion end play. Carrier contains only two gears in this model; end play should be between 0.009- and 0.027-in.

29. Replace all O-ring seals on the intermediate servo assembly, and reinstall the intermediate servo band-apply pin, piston and cover assembly. Apply pin controls the band adjustment.

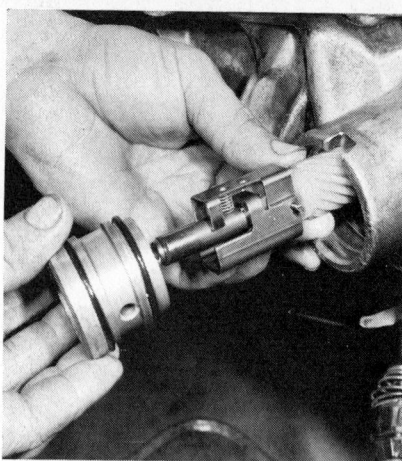

30. Replace the O-ring seals, and insert the governor assembly and washer in the case. Depress and hold the governor cover while reinstalling and seating the retaining snap ring.

31. Replace the speedometer drive gear and retaining clip, then reinstall the rear internal gear (hub end first) on the output shaft. Install the shaft in the transmission case.

32. Replace the roller-thrust-bearing assembly, with its inside diameter race facing against the gear. Reinstall the rear internal-gear snap ring, and make sure it is fully seated.

33. Fit the rear carrier and low/reverse housing together. Install as a unit on the output shaft, aligning the housing feed hole (1) to the reverse-clutch-case feed passage.

34. Reinstall the low/reverse clutch selective washer, then replace the clutch pack, alternating metal and composition plates. Install the housing-case spacer ring and beveled snap ring.

35. Remove the low/reverse housing-to-case seal and cup plug from the screw used to unseat them. Install and seat the case seal, then replace the cup plug flush with the case.

36. Apply a light coating of grease to the four-tanged thrust washer. Seat it on the back of the input drum, engaging the tangs in the cutouts. Replace the sun gear/input drum in the case.

37. Inspect the rear band, and reinstall it in the case, working it in position by compressing and revolving the band back and forth while simultaneously pushing the band inward.

38. Check the front-carrier-pinion end play with a feeler gauge. It should be between 0.009- and 0.027-in. Then install the front sun gear and thrust washer, with the bearings facing the gear.

39. Position the front carrier in the case, and install the thrust bearing by placing its small diameter race against the carrier. Use grease, if necessary, to hold the bearing in place.

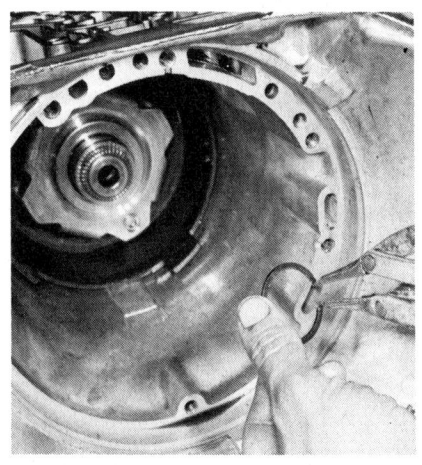

40. Replace the snap ring on the output shaft. Make certain that it is fully seated in the groove, or you will have difficulty installing the remaining components in the case.

41. Replace the tanged thrust washer on the front internal gear, and hold in place with grease. Replace the front internal gear in the case with the rear selective thrust washer.

42. Another snap ring is installed, then grease the turbine-shaft front selective washer, and replace it, with the large tang fitting into the cutout which is provided for it.

43. Install the intermediate band, with the apply lug and anchor pin lug located in the case slot. Install the band anchor, pin-stem end first, seating the stem in the band lug hole.

44. Remove the forward clutch snap ring, the backing plate and the clutch pack from the forward clutch housing. *Do not* intermix the direct and forward clutch composition plates.

45. Compress the retainer/spring assembly to remove the snap ring, then lift the retainer/spring assembly out. Springs are permanently attached to the retainer in this all-stamped design.

HOW TO: Turbo Hydra-Matic 200 Overhaul

46. The forward clutch piston is fitted with an inner and outer seal; remove and replace with new seals. Coat the piston edge with a wax-type lubricant stick for easy replacement.

47. Install retainer/spring assembly, and compress. Install snap ring and waved steel plate. Alternately install composition/steel plates, then replace backing plate and snap ring.

48. Repeat Steps 45, 46 and 47 with direct clutch assembly. Components are the same, but direct clutch piston uses three lip-type seals. Replace these with lips facing upward.

49. Remove and replace the turbine-shaft seal rings if necessary. Factory-assembled transmissions come with Teflon seal ring, while those used as replacements are made of cast iron.

50. Install the forward clutch to the direct clutch, rotating until they seat together. Hold the combined assembly by the turbine shaft, and install it in the case, rotating to seat.

51. Position the front pump over a hole in the workbench, with the pump cover side facing up. Then remove the pump-to-direct-clutch thrust washer from the pump shaft.

52. Remove athe pump cover bolts, and lift the cover from the pump body. Mark drive and driven gears for reassembly, and inspect. Face clearance should be 0.0007- to 0.0021-in.

53. Reassemble the pump body and cover, using an aligning strap. Install attaching bolts, and torque to 18 ft.-lbs. The pressure regulator need not be disassembled unless malfunctioning.

54. In addition to the large pump-to-case outer seal ring (1), remove and replace the two pump-shaft oil seal rings. These are also Teflon, and replacements will be metallic.

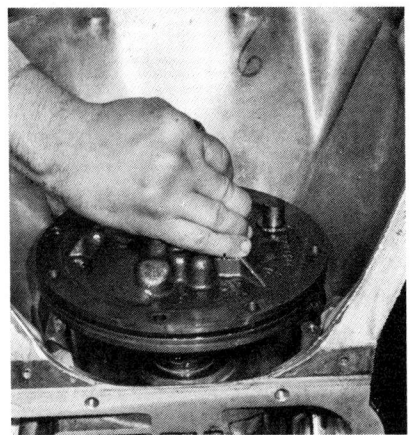

55. Replace the pump-to-direct-clutch thrust washer, and install the pump-to-case gasket on the pump. Use guide pins to lower the pump assembly into the transmission case.

56. After removing the guide pins, install the pump bolts with new washers. Tighten bolts alternately, torquing each to 18 ft.-lbs. Check the turbine shaft for freedom of rotation.

57. Install the throttle-valve exhaust check ball and the accumulator spring in the case. Check to make sure that the low/reverse cup plug and seal have been properly installed.

58. If the control valve is disassembled (see exploded view), reassemble and make sure that the four check balls are properly located in their channels, then replace the spacer plate.

59. Install the control valve assembly to the case. Align the manual detent roller/spring with the pin on the inside of the detent lever. Torque the bolt to 8 ft.-lbs.

60. Install the remaining control valve bolts, and tighten loosely. *Never* install a valve body with an air wrench and snug the bolts completely, because you can overtorque them and cause damage.

61. Install the throttle-lever/bracket assembly, locating the bracket slot with the coiled pin, aligning the plunger through the valve body hole, and the link through the linkage case bore.

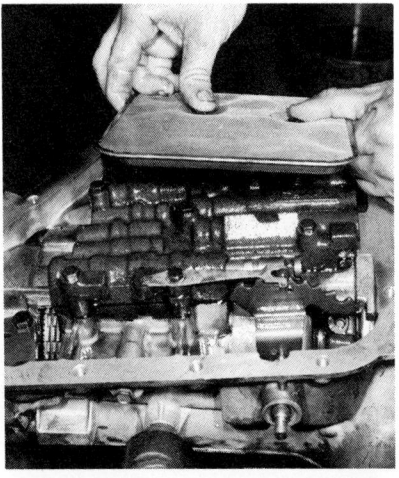

62. Use a thin coat of grease to install a new oil screen gasket on the screen, and replace the screen on the control body. Install and torque the attaching bolts to 8 ft.-lbs.

63. Fit new oil pan gasket to transmission case, and replace oil pan. Torque bolts to 12 ft.-lbs., and Turbo Hydra-Matic 200 overhaul is complete. Replace converter and install in car.

GENERAL MOTORS

Turbo Hydra-Matic 250
Turbo Hydra-Matic 350, 375B, M-38

TURBO 250 APPLICATION
Chevrolet:
Camaro 1974-77
Chevelle 1974-77
Nova 1974-77
Vega 1973-77

TURBO 350, 375B, M-38 APPLICATION
Buick:
Apollo 1973-75
Century 1973-79
Electra 1976-77
LeSabre 1971-79
Regal 1973-79
Skyhawk 1975-79
Skylark 1971-79
Special 1970-72

Chevrolet:
Camaro 1970-79
Chevelle 1970-77
Chevrolet 1970-79
Corvette 1970-79
Monte Carlo 1970-79
Nova 1970-77

Vega 1972-73
Monza 1979

Oldsmobile:
Cutlass 1971-79
Delta 1973
Olds F-85, 1970-72
Omega 1973-79

Starfire 1979
Olds 88 1979

Pontiac:
Astre 1976-77
Firebird 1970-79
Grand Am 1973-75
            1978-79
LeMans 1971-79
Phoenix 1977-79

Sunbird 1976-79
Tempest 1970-72
Ventura 1971-77
Catalina 1978-79
Bonneville 1978-79
Grand Prix 1978-79

DESCRIPTION

The Turbo Hydra-Matic 250 is a fully automatic transmission consisting of a three-element hydraulic torque converter and two planetary gear sets, with three multiple disc clutches, one roller clutch and an adjustable intermediate band. The THM 350 is a heavier duty version, using four multiple disc clutches, two roller clutches and an intermediate overrun band. The THM 375B is identical to the THM 350, but has a longer output shaft and extension housing. The Pontiac version is called the M-38.

BAND ADJUSTMENT

250 INTERMEDIATE BAND (Lower Right Side of Case)

1. Place the selector lever in NEUTRAL.
2. Loosen the locknut one-quarter turn, and torque the adjusting screw to 30 in.-lbs.
3. Back off the adjusting screw exactly three turns.
4. Hold the adjusting screw from moving, and torque the locknut to 15 ft.-lbs.

TURBO HYDRA-MATIC—250/350

TORQUE SPECIFICATIONS

Pump Cover to Pump Body	17 ft. lbs.
Pump Assembly to Case	18-1/2 ft. lbs.
Valve Body and Support Plate	130 in. lbs.
Parking Lock Bracket	29 ft. lbs.
Oil Suction Screen	40 in. lbs.
Oil Pan to Case	130 in. lbs.
Extension to Case	25 ft. lbs.
Modulator Retainer to Case	130 in. lbs.
Inner Selector Lever to Shaft	25 ft. lbs.
Detent Valve Actuating Bracket	52 in. lbs.
Converter to Flywheel Bolts	35 ft. lbs.
Under Pan to Transmission Case	110 in. lbs.
Transmission Case to Engine	35 ft. lbs.
Oil Cooler Pipe Connectors to Transmission Case or Radiator	120 in. lbs.
Oil Cooler Pipe to Connectors	10 ft. lbs.
Gearshift Bracket to Frame	15 ft. lbs.
Gearshift Shaft to Swivel	20 ft. lbs.
Manual Shaft to Bracket	20 ft. lbs.
Detent Cable to Transmission	75 in. lbs.
Intermediate Band Adjust Nut	15 ft. lbs.

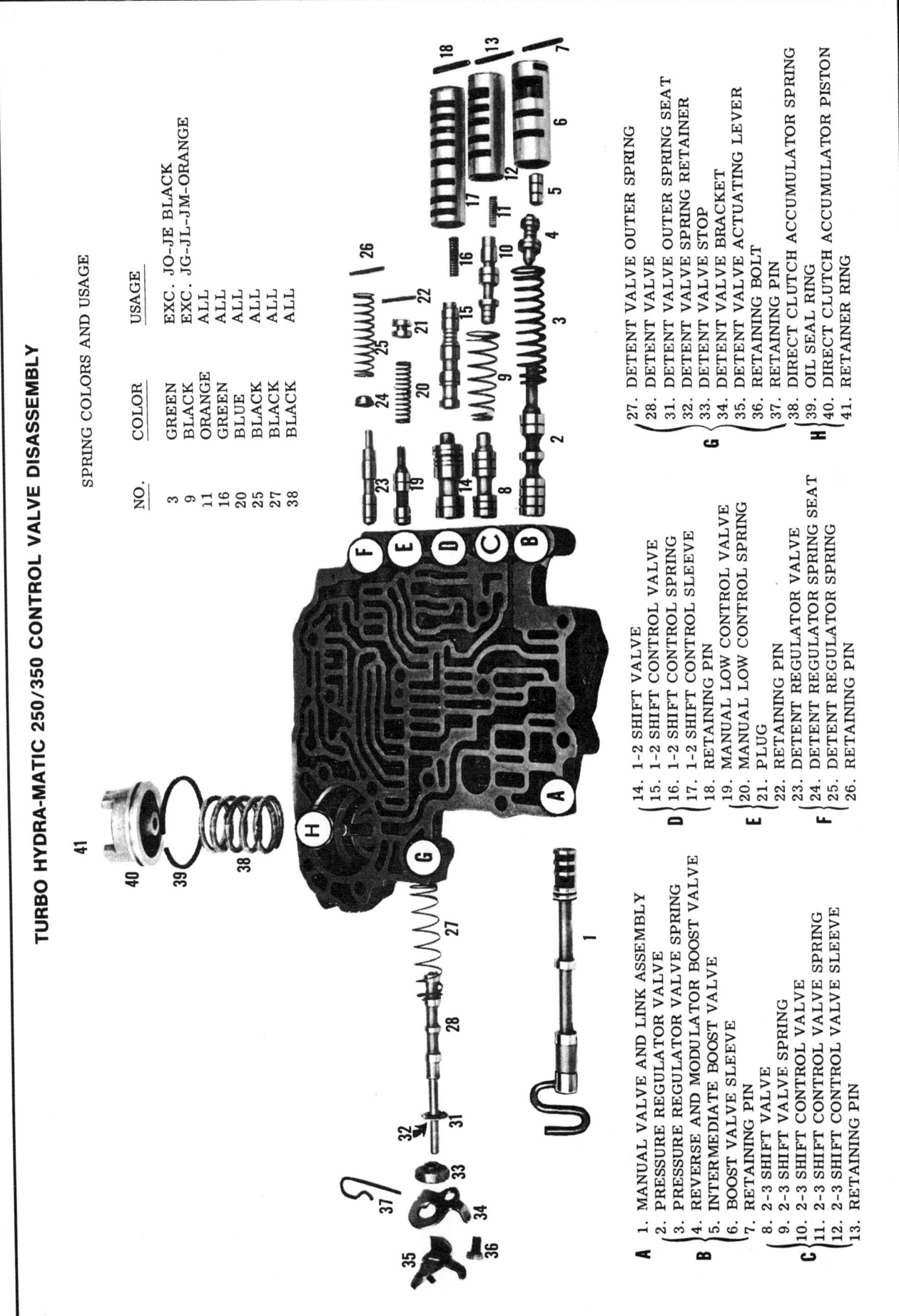

TURBO HYDRA-MATIC 250/350 CONTROL VALVE DISASSEMBLY

SPRING COLORS AND USAGE

NO.	COLOR	USAGE
3	GREEN	EXC. JO-JE BLACK
9	BLACK	EXC. JG-JL-JM-ORANGE
11	ORANGE	ALL
16	GREEN	ALL
20	BLUE	ALL
25	BLACK	ALL
27	BLACK	ALL
38	BLACK	ALL

A
1. MANUAL VALVE AND LINK ASSEMBLY
2. PRESSURE REGULATOR VALVE
3. PRESSURE REGULATOR VALVE SPRING
B
4. REVERSE AND MODULATOR BOOST VALVE
5. INTERMEDIATE BOOST VALVE
6. BOOST VALVE SLEEVE
7. RETAINING PIN
C
8. 2-3 SHIFT VALVE
9. 2-3 SHIFT VALVE SPRING
10. 2-3 SHIFT CONTROL VALVE
11. 2-3 SHIFT CONTROL VALVE SPRING
12. 2-3 SHIFT CONTROL VALVE SLEEVE
13. RETAINING PIN
D
14. 1-2 SHIFT VALVE
15. 1-2 SHIFT CONTROL VALVE
16. 1-2 SHIFT CONTROL SPRING
17. 1-2 SHIFT CONTROL SLEEVE
18. RETAINING PIN
E
19. MANUAL LOW CONTROL VALVE
20. MANUAL LOW CONTROL SPRING
21. PLUG
22. RETAINING PIN
F
23. DETENT REGULATOR VALVE
24. DETENT REGULATOR SPRING SEAT
25. DETENT REGULATOR SPRING
26. RETAINING PIN
27. DETENT VALVE OUTER SPRING
28. DETENT VALVE
31. DETENT VALVE OUTER SPRING SEAT
32. DETENT VALVE SPRING RETAINER
33. DETENT VALVE STOP
34. DETENT VALVE BRACKET
35. DETENT VALVE ACTUATING LEVER
G
36. RETAINING BOLT
37. RETAINING PIN
38. DIRECT CLUTCH ACCUMULATOR SPRING
39. OIL SEAL RING
H
40. DIRECT CLUTCH ACCUMULATOR PISTON
41. RETAINER RING

TURBO HYDRA-MATIC 250/350 DISASSEMBLY—CASE, EXTENSION & PLANET CARRIER

1. WASHER, Input Gear Supt.–Rear to Outer Carrier
2. CARRIER, Output
3. BEARING & RACE, Output Carrier
4. BEARING & RACE, Output Carrier
5. GEAR, Sun
6. BUSHING, Sun Gear
7. BUSHING, Sun Gear
9. SHELL, Sun Gear Drive
10. WASHER, Sun Gear Thrust
11. RING, Sun Gear Drive Shell Retaining (2)
12. WASHER, Low and Reverse Clutch Race and Shell Thrust
13. RACE, Low and Reverse O/Run Clutch Inner
14. CLUTCH, Low and Reverse O/Run
15. RING, Low and Reverse Clutch to Cam Retaining
16. RACE-L/Rev Clutch O/Run
17. SPRING, Low and Reverse Anti-Klunk
18. RING, Low and Reverse Clutch Retaining
19. SUPPORT & CAM, LOW and Reverse Roller Clutch
20. PLATES, L/Rev. Clutch Drive
21. BUSHING, Reaction Carrier
22. CARRIER, Reaction
23. WASHER, Output Ring Gear Front Thrust
24. GEAR, Output Ring
25. BEARING, Output Ring Gear Support to Case
27. PLATES, Low and Reverse Reaction
28. SEAT, Low and Reverse Clutch Piston
29. SPRING, Low and Reverse Clutch Piston Return
30. PISTON, Low and Reverse Clutch
31. SEAL-Clutch Piston Rev. Outer
32. SEAL-Clutch Piston Rev. Center
33. SEAL-Clutch Piston Rev. Inner
34. BUSHING, Output Shaft
35. SHAFT ASSY., Output
38. SLEEVE, Output Shaft Yoke
39. RETAINER, Intermediate Accummulator Piston Cover
40. COVER, Intermediate Clutch Accumulator Piston
41. SEAL, Accumulator Piston Cover
42. SPRING, Intermediate Clutch Accumulator Piston
43. SEAL, Intermediate Clutch Accumulator Piston-Outer
44. PISTON, Intermediate Clutch Accumulator
45. SEAL, Intermediate Clutch Accumulator Piston-Inner
46. VALVE ASSY., Vacuum Modulator
47. SEAL, Vacuum Modulator
48. RETAINER, Vacuum Modulator
49. BOLT (5/16–18 x 11/16)
50. MODULATOR, Vacuum
51. BUSHING-Case
52. SEAL, Extension to Case
53. EXTENSION
54. BUSHING-Extension
55. SEAL–Rear Oil
64. PIN, Gov. Gear Retaining
65. RETAINER, Governor Cover
66. COVER, Governor
67. SEAL, Governor Cover
68. GOVERNOR
69. GEAR, Governor
70. RETAINER–Parking Pawl Shaft
71. SPRING, Lock Pawl
72. BRACKET, Park Link Reaction
73. SEAL, Oil
75. LEVER, Range Selector Inside Detent
76. NUT
77. CLIP–Range Selector Shaft
78. PAWL, Park
79. SHAFT–Parking Pawl
80. SHAFT–Range Selector
81. SPRING, Detent
82. ROD, Actuator
83. LEVER, Shift, Outer
84. HOSE–Vacuum Modulator

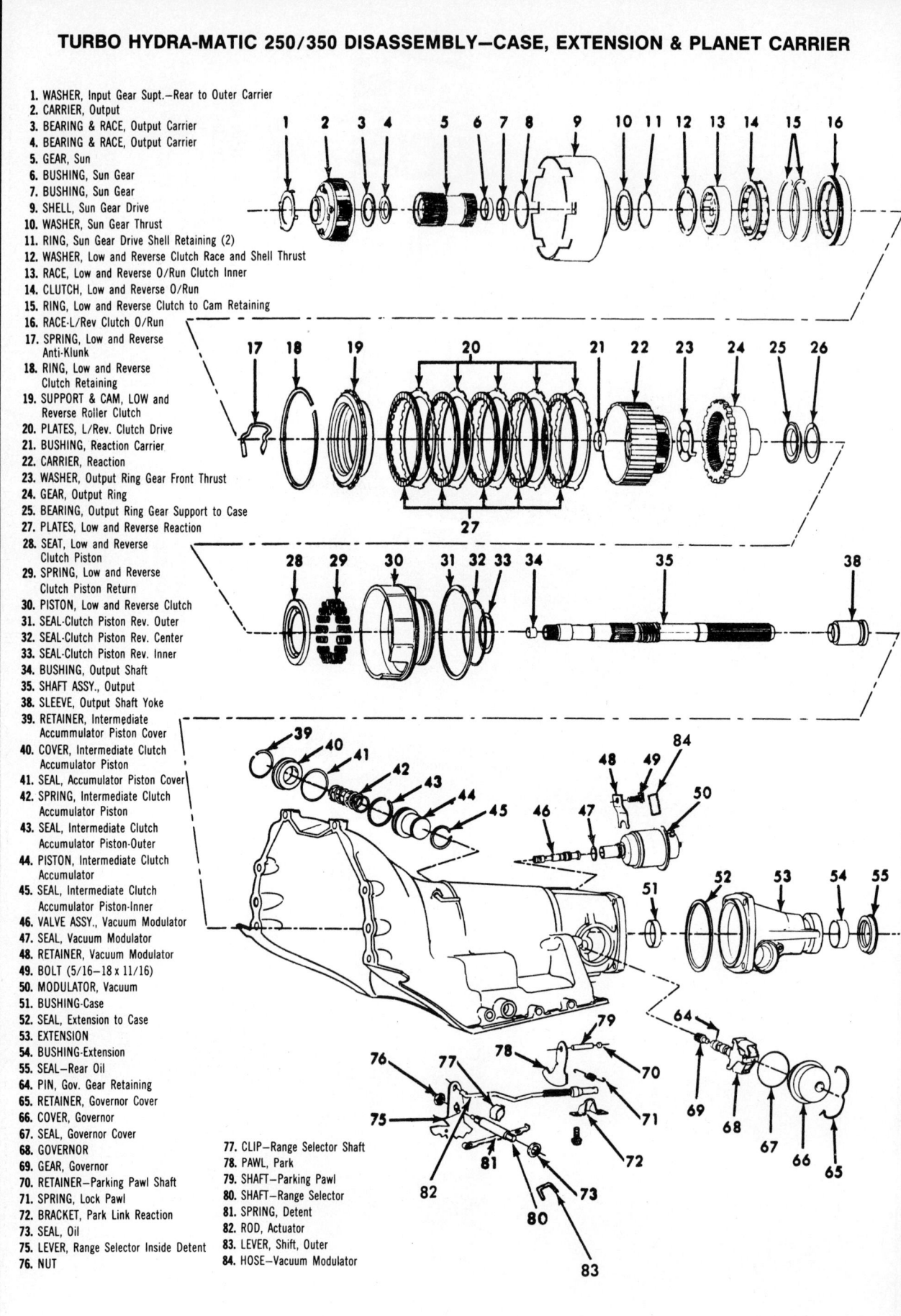

TURBO HYDRA-MATIC 250 DIAGNOSIS CHART

PROBLEM — CAR ROAD TEST

LEGEND
X — PROBLEM AREA VS. CAUSE
* — @ "O" VACUUM ONLY
O — BALLS / #2/3/4 ONLY
L — LOCKED
S — STUCK

Problem columns (left → right):

1. ALL RANGES-SLIPS
2. DRIVE-SLIPS-NO 1ST GEAR
3. LINE PRESSURE-NO 1ST GEAR
4. LINE PRESSURE-ALL LOW
5. LINE PRESSURE-ALL HIGH
6. 1-2 INTERM. PRES. LOW
7. 1-2 INTERM. PRES. HIGH
8. 2-3 INTERM. PRES. LOW
9. 2-3 DIRECT CL. PRES. HIGH
10. 2-3 DIRECT CL. PRES. LOW
11. NO 1-2 UPSHIFT
12. 1-2 U.-EARLY/LATE
13. SLIPS-1-2 UPSHIFT @ W.O.T. ONLY
14. ROUGH-1-2 UPSHIFT
15. NO 2-3 UPSHIFT
16. 2-3 U.-EARLY/LATE
17. SLIPS-2-3 UPSHIFT
18. ROUGH-2-3 UPSHIFT
19. NO-PART TH. DOWN SHIFT
20. NO-FULL TH. DOWN SHIFT
21. 2-3 UPSHIFT-W.O.T. DOWN SHIFT
22. HARSH-DOWN SHIFT
23. L1 RANGE-NO ENG. BRAKING
24. L2 RANGE-NO ENG. BRAKING
25. NEUTRAL-DRIVES IN NEUTRAL
26. REVERSE-DRIVES IN NEUTRAL
27. SLIPS IN REVERSE
28. PARK-NO PARK-RATCHETS
29. NOISY-ALL RANGES
30. 1-2, 2-3 SHIFT NOISY
31. REV. & D, L1 & L2 NOISY
32. HUNTS BETWEEN 2 & 3 AND 3 & 2
33. SPEWS FLUID OUT BREATHER

POSSIBLE CAUSE rows (top → bottom of matrix):

- LOW FLUID LEVEL/WATER IN FLUID
- VACUUM LEAK
- MODULATOR &/OR VALVE
- STRAINER &/OR GASKET
- GOVERNOR-VALVE/SCREEN
- VALVE BODY-GASKET/PLATE
- PRES. REG. &/OR BOOST VALVE
- BALL (#1) SHY
- 1-2 SHIFT VALVE
- 2-3 SHIFT VALVE
- MANUAL LOW CONT'L. VALVE
- DETENT VALVE & LINKAGE
- DETENT REG. VALVE
- 2-3 ACCUMULATOR
- MANUAL VALVE/LINKAGE
- POROSITY/CROSS LEAK
- PUMP-GEARS
- CLUTCH SEAL RINGS
- POROUS/CROSS LEAK
- GASKET SCREEN-PRESSURE
- CASE-POROUS/X LEAK
- 1-2 ACCUMULATOR
- INTERMED. SERVO
- FORWARD CLUTCH ASS'Y
- DIRECT CLUTCH ASS'Y
- INTERMED. BAND ASS'Y
- L & REV. CL. ASS'Y
- L. & R. ROLLER CL. ASS'Y
- PARK PAWL/LINKAGE
- CONVERTER ASS'Y
- GEAR SET & BEARINGS

TURBO HYDRA-MATIC 250/350 DISASSEMBLY

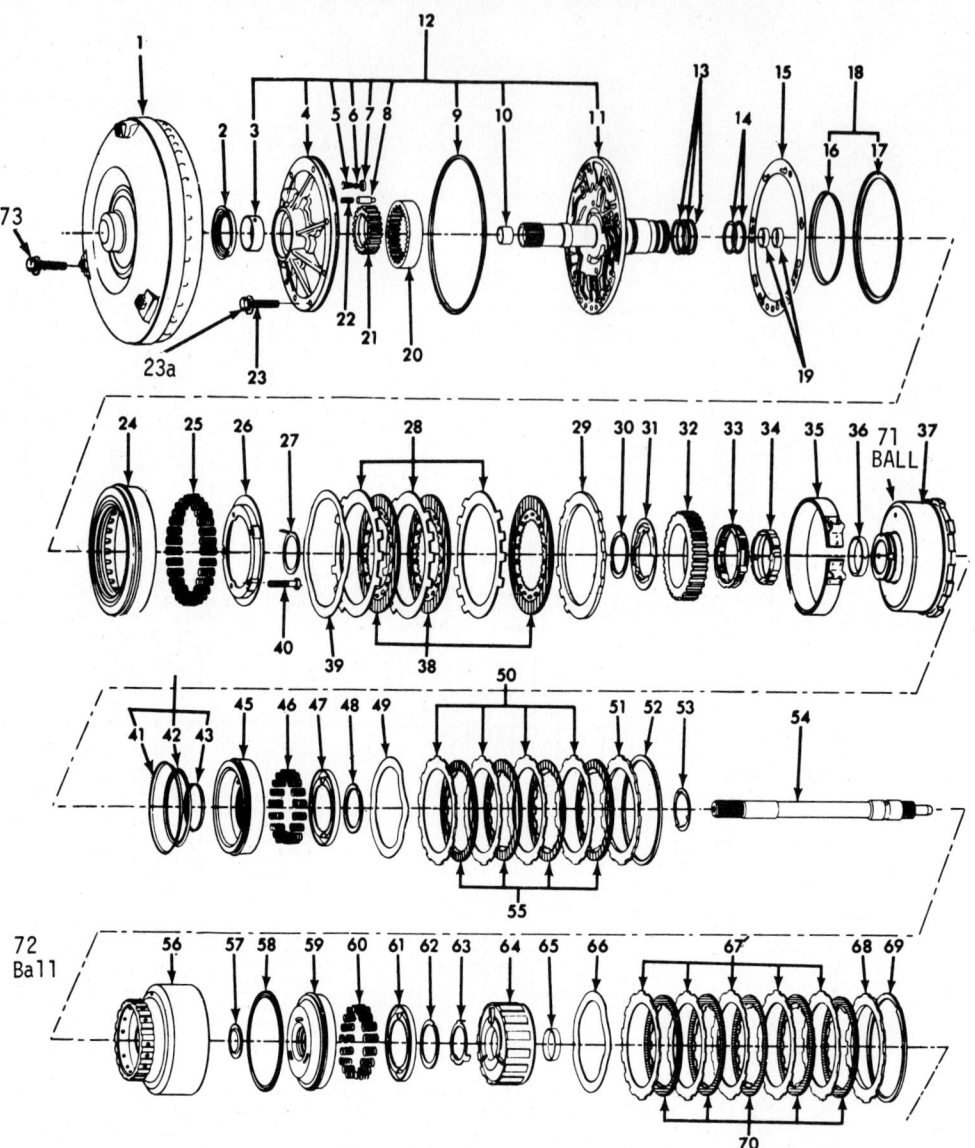

PUMP, FORWARD & DIRECT CLUTCH & CONVERTER

1. CONVERTER ASSY.
2. SEAL, Oil Pump to Conv. Hub
3. BUSHING, Oil Pump Body
4. BODY, Oil Pump
5. SPRING, Oil Pump Cooler
6. BALL, Oil Pump Cooler By-Pass Valve
7. SEAL, Oil Pump Cooler By-Pass Valve
8. VALVE, Oil Pump Priming
9. SEAL, Oil, Pump to Case O-Ring
10. BUSHING, Trans. Stator
11. COVER ASSY., Oil Pump
13. RINGS, Direct Clutch Drum Oil Seal
14. RINGS, Forward Clutch Housing Oil Seal
15. GASKET, Pump Cover to Case
16. SEAL, Intermediate-Clutch Inner
17. SEAL, Intermediate-Clutch Outer
19. BUSHING, Oil Pump Stator Shaft-Rear
20. GEAR, Oil Pump Driven (Part of No. 12)
21. GEAR, Oil Pump Drive (Part of No. 4)
22. VALVE, Oil Pump Priming Valve Part of No. 4
23. BOLT, Oil Pump to Case
23a SEAL, Pump to Case Bolt
24. PISTON, Intermediate Clutch
25. SPRING, Intermediate Clutch Return

26. SEAT, Intermediate Clutch Return Spring
27. WASHER, Pump Cover Thrust
28. PLATES, Intermediate Clutch Reaction
29. PLATE, Intermediate Clutch Backing
30. RING, Intermediate O/Run Clutch Retainer
31. RETAINER, Intermediate O/Run Clutch
32. RACE, Intermediate Clutch O/Run—Outer
33. SPRAG, Intermediate O/Run Clutch
34. RACE, Intermediate O/Run Clutch Inner
35. BAND, Intermediate O/Run Brake
36. BUSHING, Direct Clutch Drum
37. DRUM ASSY., Direct Clutch
38. PLATES, Intermediate Clutch Drive
39. SPRING, Intermediate Clutch Cushion
40. BOLT (5/16-18 x 1-1/2)
41. SEAL, Direct Clutch Piston
42. SEAL, Dir. Clutch Piston—Center
43. SEAL, Direct Clutch Piston—Inner
45. PISTON, Direct Clutch
46. SPRING, Clutch Piston Return
47. SEAT, Direct Clutch Piston Return
48. RETAINER, Direct Clutch Piston Return
49. WASHER, Direct Clutch Piston
50. PLATES, Direct Clutch Driven

51. PLATE, Direct Clutch Pressure
52. RING, Direct Clutch Pressure Plate Retainer
53. WASHER, Direct Clutch Drum to Forward Clutch Housing-Thrust
54. SHAFT
55. PLATES, Direct Clutch Drive
56. DRUM, Forward Clutch
57. SEAL, Inner
58. SEAL, Outer
59. PISTON, Forward Clutch
60. SPRINGS, Forward Clutch Piston Return
61. SEAT, Forward Clutch Piston Return
62. RING, Forward Clutch Seat Retainer
63. WASHER, Input Ring Gear Thrust—Front
64. GEAR, Input Ring
65. BUSHING, Input Ring Gear
66. WASHER, Forward Clutch Piston Cushion
67. PLATES, Forward Clutch Driven
68. PLATE, Forward Clutch Pressure
69. RING, Forward Clutch Pressure Plate Retaining
70. PLATES, Forward Clutch Drive
71. BALL, Direct Clutch Ex.
72. BALL, Forward Clutch Ex.
73. BOLT, Converter Attach.

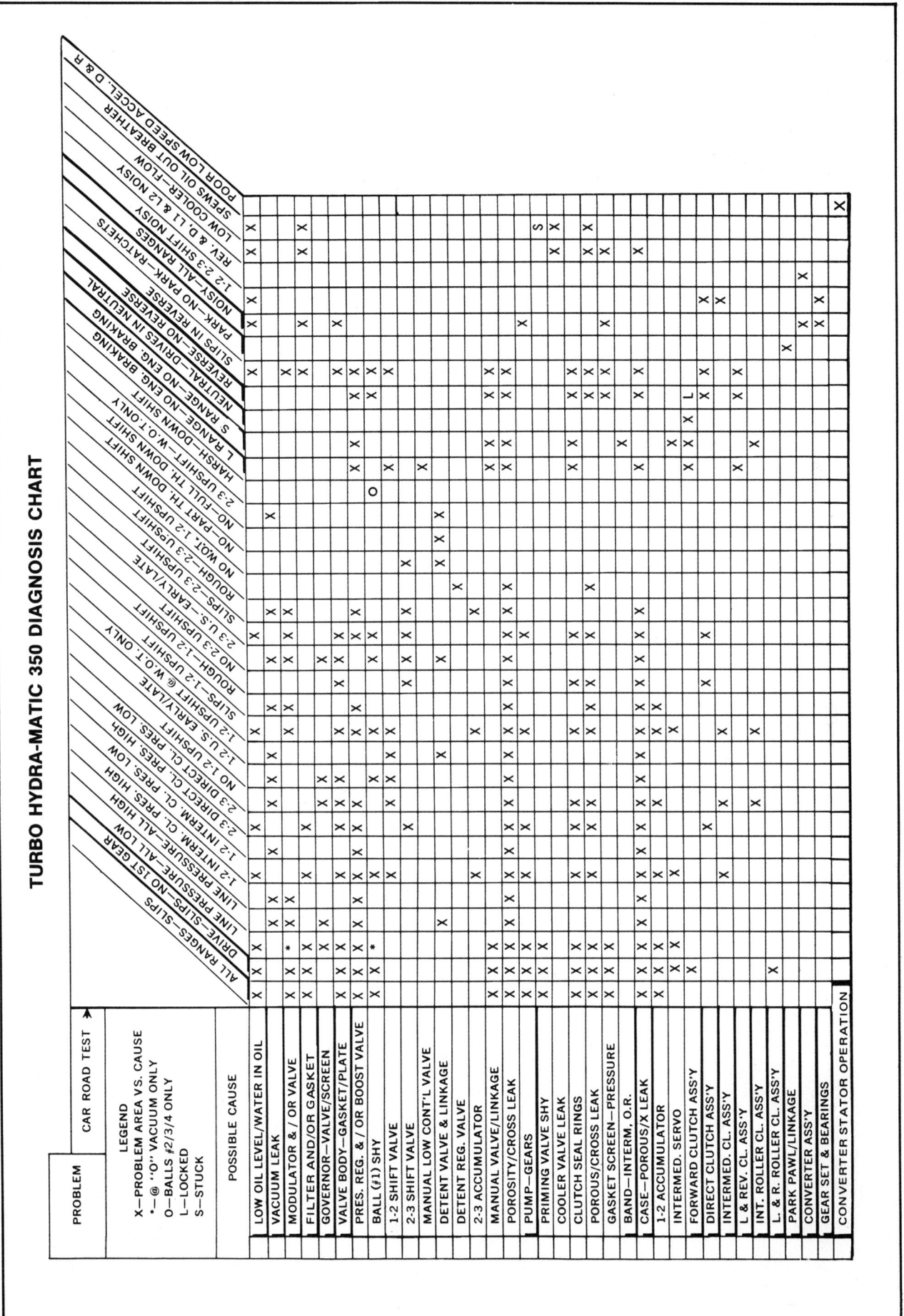

TURBO HYDRA-MATIC 350 DIAGNOSIS CHART

PROBLEM

CAR ROAD TEST

LEGEND
X—PROBLEM AREA VS. CAUSE
•—@ "O" VACUUM ONLY
O—BALLS #2/3/4 ONLY
L—LOCKED
S—STUCK

POSSIBLE CAUSE

Problems (column headings):
- DRIVE—SLIPS—NO 1ST GEAR
- LINE PRESSURE—ALL LOW
- LINE PRESSURE—ALL HIGH
- 1-2 INTERM. CL. PRES. LOW
- 1-2 INTERM. CL. PRES. HIGH
- 2-3 DIRECT CL. PRES. LOW
- 2-3 DIRECT CL. PRES. HIGH
- NO 1-2 UPSHIFT
- 1-2 UPSHIFT @ W.O.T. ONLY
- SLIPS—1-2 UPSHIFT
- ROUGH—1-2 UPSHIFT
- NO 2-3 UPSHIFT
- 2-3 U.S. EARLY/LATE
- SLIPS—2-3 UPSHIFT
- ROUGH—2-3 UPSHIFT
- NO W.O.T. 1-2 UPSHIFT
- NO PART. TH. 1-2 UPSHIFT
- NO—PART TH. DOWN SHIFT
- NO—FULL TH. DOWN SHIFT
- HARSH—DOWN SHIFT
- L RANGE—W.O.T. ONLY
- S RANGE—NO ENG. SHIFT
- NEUTRAL—DRIVES IN NEUTRAL
- REVERSE—NO ENG. BRAKING
- REVERSE—NO REVERSE
- SLIPS IN REVERSE
- PARK—NO PARK
- NOISY—ALL RANGES
- 1-2-3 SHIFT NOISY
- REV. & D, L1 & L2 NOISY
- LOW COOLER—FLOW
- SPEWS OIL OUT BREATHER
- POOR LOW SPEED ACCEL., D & R

Possible Cause (row headings):
- LOW OIL LEVEL/WATER IN OIL
- VACUUM LEAK
- MODULATOR & / OR VALVE
- FILTER AND/OR GASKET
- GOVERNOR—VALVE/SCREEN
- VALVE BODY—GASKET/PLATE
- PRES. REG. & / OR BOOST VALVE
- BALL (#1) SHY
- 1-2 SHIFT VALVE
- 2-3 SHIFT VALVE
- MANUAL LOW CONT'L VALVE
- DETENT VALVE & LINKAGE
- DETENT REG. VALVE
- 2-3 ACCUMULATOR
- MANUAL VALVE/LINKAGE
- POROSITY/CROSS LEAK
- PUMP—GEARS
- PRIMING VALVE SHY
- COOLER VALVE LEAK
- CLUTCH SEAL RINGS
- POROUS/CROSS LEAK
- GASKET SCREEN—PRESSURE
- BAND—INTERM. O.R.
- CASE—POROUS/X LEAK
- 1-2 ACCUMULATOR
- INTERMED. SERVO
- FORWARD CLUTCH ASS'Y
- DIRECT CLUTCH ASS'Y
- INTERMED. CL. ASS'Y
- L & REV. CL. ASS'Y
- INT. ROLLER CL. ASS'Y
- L. & R. ROLLER CL. ASS'Y
- PARK PAWL/LINKAGE
- CONVERTER ASS'Y
- GEAR SET & BEARINGS
- CONVERTER STATOR OPERATION

HOW TO: Turbo Hydra-Matic 350, 375B, M-38 Overhaul

1. Unbolt and remove the bottom pan. Gasket is discarded. Place pan in a container of solvent and soak clean while disassembling transmission.

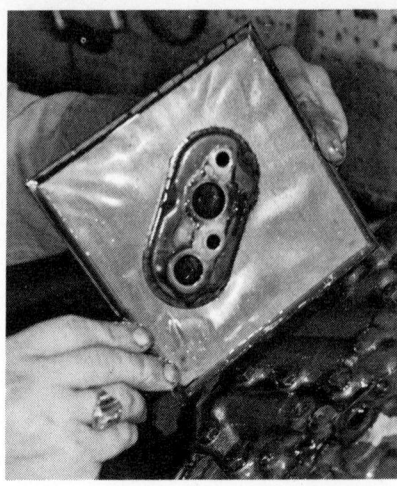

2. Two retainer bolts hold oil pump strainer assembly in place. Size and shape of strainer differs, depending on model and year of transmission.

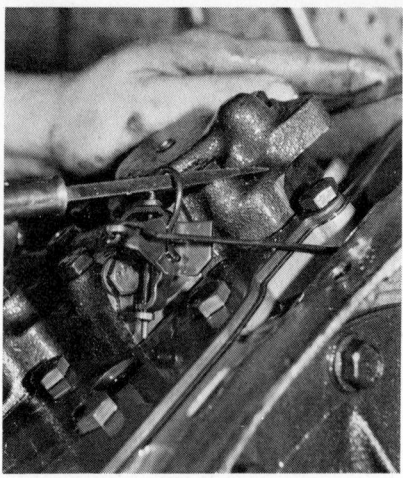

3. Unclip, remove detent control-valve wire. Wire extends through side of transmission body, and seal fitting must be unscrewed to pull wire out.

4. Unbolt and remove the control valve assembly. The exact configuration of this unit also differs according to year and model of transmission.

5. The transfer plate is a two-piece unit. The support plate is removed first, and then the larger spacer plate can be taken off.

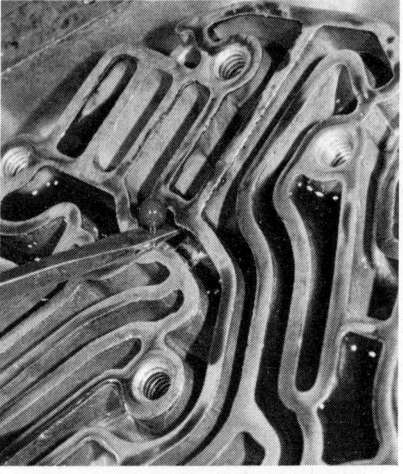

6. You'll find rubber check balls instead of steel ones. Locate and pick all four from cored passages. Place check balls in a cup to prevent losing them.

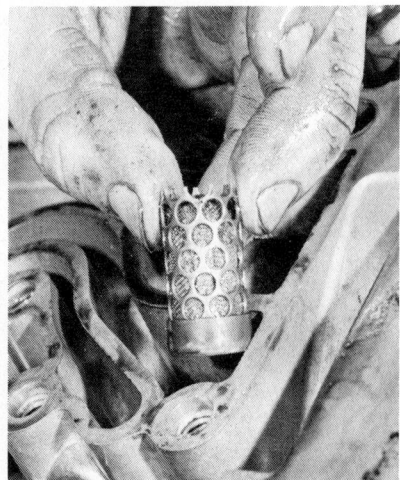

7. Oil-pump pressure screen lifts from oil-pump pressure hole in transmission case. Clean all parts with solvent, and air-dry—*do not* wipe with cloth.

8. Remove front servo piston, pin and spring. Check piston for cracks, porosity and damaged oil-ring groove; make sure servo pin is not bent or damaged.

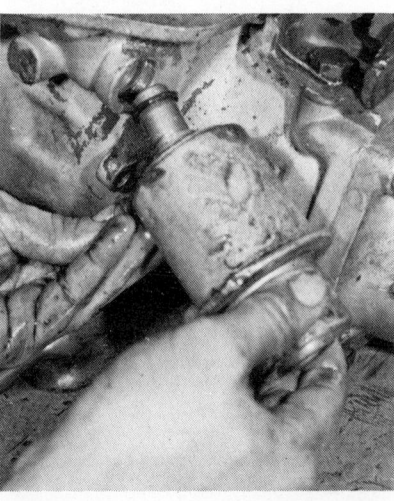

9. The vacuum modulator assembly pulls out when the retainer is removed. The O-ring seal should be replaced with a new one.

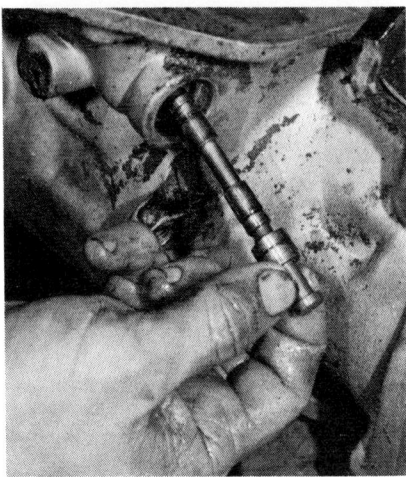

10. The slip-fit vacuum modulator valve can now be withdrawn from the transmission case. Clean and inspect it carefully for burrs and other defects.

11. Unbolt and remove extension housing next. Peel off old gasket, and discard. Use new gaskets for reassembly to prevent possibility of leaks.

12. Speedometer drive gear is held in place by this spring clip. Depress rear of clip with a screwdriver, and gear can be pulled off easily.

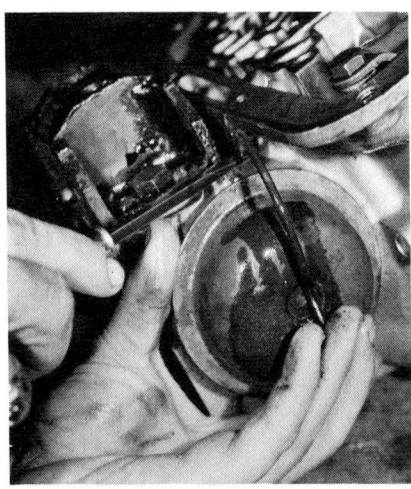

13. Pry off large spring clip holding governor cover in place. Pull governor out of case after removing cover. Some Hydra-Matics use bolted-on cover.

14. To remove the pump assembly, a slide hammer is necessary. This type threads directly into the pump, while some other types use a separate bolt.

15. Draw the pump off the mainshaft; then remove and discard the pump-to-case seal ring and gasket. Place to one side for further disassembly later.

16. Remove the intermediate-clutch cushion spring, clutch-faced and steel reaction plates, and clutch pressure plate. Check condition of all plates.

17. The intermediate overrun brake band is removed next. Pull out and check band surface carefully for signs of burning, scoring and/or cracked areas.

18. Direct and forward clutch assemblies are removed by withdrawing the input shaft. These are also put to one side for further disassembly.

HOW TO: Turbo Hydra-Matic 350, 375B, M-38 Overhaul

19. Planetary geartrain disassembly begins with the input ring gear. There is a three-tanged thrust washer at the front of the ring gears.

20. The next step in disassembly requires the removal of this snap ring, which holds the output carrier in position on the output shaft.

21. With the snap ring removed, the output carrier lifts out fairly easily. Be sure to inspect all of the gear teeth for worn or damaged areas.

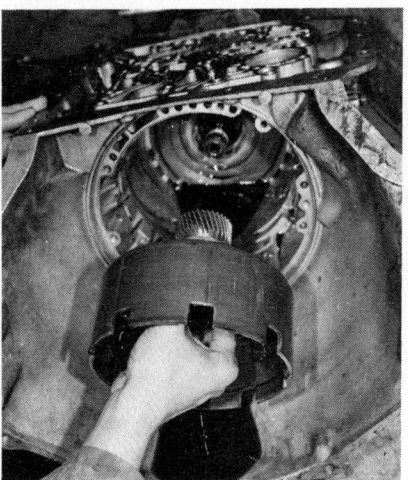

22. The sun-gear drive shell, with sun gear assembly, comes off the output shaft. If the gear is damaged, remove from shell by unclipping snap ring.

23. A large, selective snap ring holds the low/reverse clutch assembly in place, and must be removed before the clutch can be taken out.

24. Low/reverse clutch assembly and support are final units to be removed from transmission case. Place to one side, begin work on the direct clutch.

25. Retaining ring must be removed from the direct clutch in order to get to the clutch plates. Pry the ring up and out with a screwdriver.

26. Remove the pressure plate, faced and steel separator plates, and cushion spring. Inspect all plates carefully, because this is a common problem area.

27. While both sides of the plates shown are worn, one is really gone, pointing up the necessity for a thorough examination of all component parts.

28. To remove the direct-clutch piston assembly, a spring compressor is necessary to allow you to remove the snap ring without difficulty.

29. Once the snap ring is off and the spring compressor removed, the piston return-spring seat lifts off, exposing the 17 clutch-return coil springs.

30. Remove and replace outer and inner seals on the piston, as well as center seal on the direct clutch drum. A little transmission fluid helps here.

31. To reassemble, reseat the clutch piston in the drum by revolving a feeler gauge between the piston inner seal and the drum center seal.

32. Replace return springs and seat, then use compressor to reinstall snap ring. Install cushion spring and one separator plate; alternate others.

33. The same procedure applies to the forward clutch assembly. Inspect surfaces carefully for burning, scoring or wear. If one is bad, replace all.

34. A hydraulic press can take the place of a compressor to help in snap ring removal, as well as in pressing out the output shaft.

35. The piston return seat is lifted out after snap ring removal, exposing 21 springs. Check them to see if any are collapsed or distorted.

36. The forward clutch piston can be removed once springs are taken off its top. As with direct-clutch piston, seal rings are important and are replaced.

HOW TO: Turbo Hydra-Matic 350, 375B, M-38 Overhaul

37. Remove and replace forward-clutch inner and outer piston seal rings. Inspect piston for cracks, and check housing for wear or scoring.

38. When reassembling the direct and forward clutch units, this cushion spring is fitted in place before inserting the faced and steel plates.

39. Loosen oil-pump cover bolts, and lower the pump body to the bench. Remove spring retainer and the 30 intermediate-clutch return springs.

40. Intermediate clutch piston uses an inner and outer seal ring. Remove and replace both with new seal rings dipped in transmission fluid.

41. Lift the pump-cover/stator-shaft assembly off. Check the drive and driven gear teeth for nicks or other damage, and the body for nicks or scoring.

42. Oil-pump priming valve and spring are important, as are cooler bypass valve seat, spring and check ball (arrow). Remember where they fit.

43. Replace gears, pump cover, piston and springs. Lift up body and insert attaching bolts through spring retainer. Torque to 17 ft.-lbs.

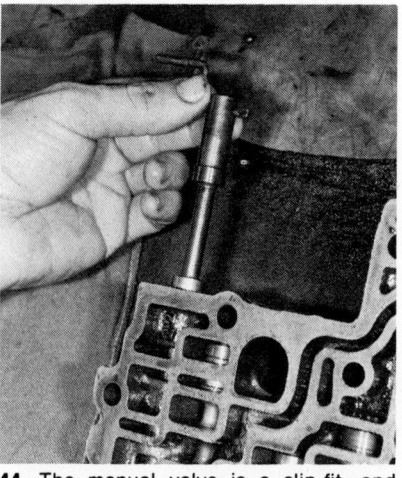

44. The manual valve is a slip-fit, and can be lifted out of valve body as shown. Inspect this and other valves for cracks and free movement.

45. Valve body uses retaining pins to hold valve parts in bore. Press in slightly on valve, and lift out each pin with a magnetic pencil.

46. Detent regulator valve, spring seat and spring are located here. Line up each set as removed to avoid confusion during reassembly.

47. The manual-low control valve, spring and plug come out next. Check carefully for scoring after cleaning valves thoroughly in solvent.

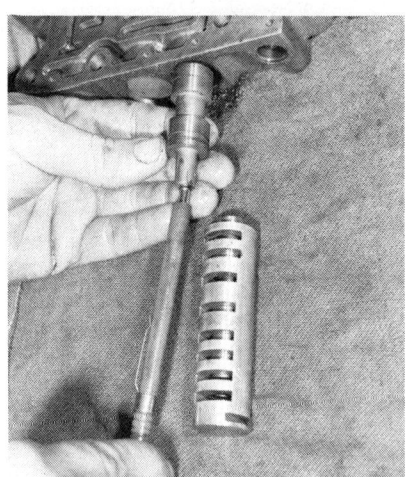

48. The 1-2 shift valve, shift control valve, spring and sleeve are the third set to be removed. Magnet shown is handy to draw valves out of body.

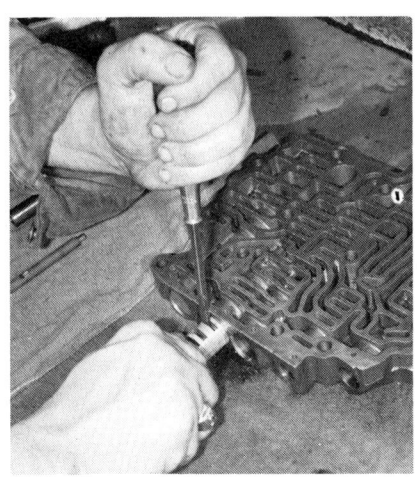

49. If you have difficulty in removing the sleeves, carefully insert a screwdriver, as shown, and pry from one notch to the next until the sleeve is free.

50. The 2-3 shift valve, spring, control valve, spring and sleeve come out here. Sequence begins to get a little confusing with this and the next valve.

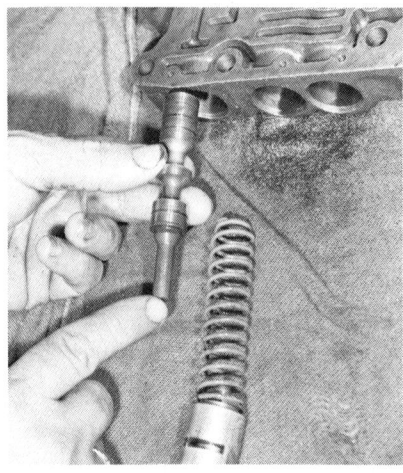

51. Remove the pressure regulator valve, spring, reverse and modulator boost valve, intermediate boost valve and sleeve. Clean and reinstall all valves.

52. Output ring gear and output shaft are inserted in transmission case to begin reassembly sequence. Be sure tanged thrust washer (arrow) is in place.

53. Notched washer will only fit into case one way. Rotate until notches line up with grooves inside case and fit against ring gear.

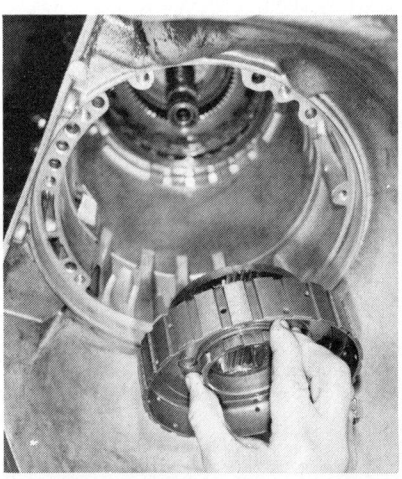

54. Now install the reaction carrier and set it against the large notched washer until the rear planetary assembly fits into the ring gear.

HOW TO: Turbo Hydra-Matic 350, 375B, M-38 Overhaul

55. Low/reverse roller clutch assembly is seated into position next. Rotate until notches fit into case grooves, and it goes in place easily.

56. Install the sun gear and drive shell on output shaft. Rotate, if necessary, to mesh the sun gear properly, and push back into place.

57. Replace the output carrier-to-output-shaft snap ring. Make sure that snap ring is seated completely before proceeding with the next step.

58. Now fit the output carrier into the input ring gear, and position in the transmission case until it meshes with the sun gear assembly.

59. Position the tanged thrust washer on the input ring gear; then couple the forward and direct clutch assemblies together, and insert.

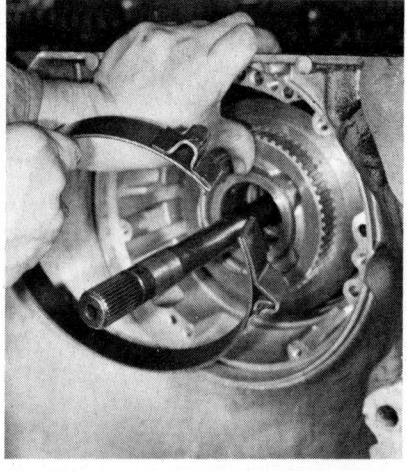

60. Slip the intermediate overrun brake band over the clutch assemblies and slide it into position. No band struts are necessary with this design.

61. To reassemble intermediate clutch plate, install pressure plate, alternate the faced and steel plates and replace the cushion spring.

62. Replace oil seal rings on stator shaft, if necessary, and install oil-pump/stator-shaft assembly over input shaft. Torque to 18½ ft.-lbs.

63. Fit pegged end of spring clip into hole in output shaft, and slide speedometer drive gear on and over clip for accurate positioning.

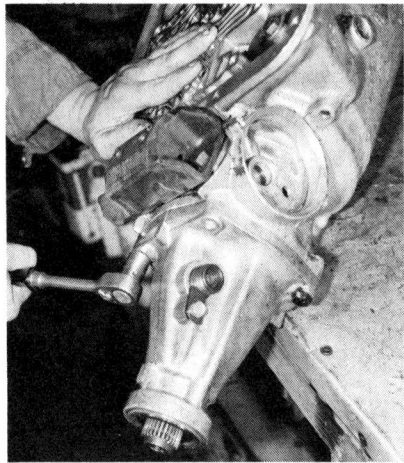

64. The next step is to replace the extension housing on the output shaft, and bolt it to transmission case. Torque bolts to 25 ft.-lbs.

65. Check the governor bore and sleeve for scoring, and reinstall the governor. Fit cover in place (use new O-ring seal) and attach spring clip.

66. Intermediate servo piston, apply pin and spring seat are reinstalled over the spring. It's a good idea to replace the piston seal first.

67. Replace the valve-body spacer plate, using a new gasket, then you can add the spacer support plate and torque everything to 130 in.-lbs.

68. Reinstall valve body so that manual control valve link engages the range selector inner lever. This should be torqued to 130 in.-lbs.

69. Replace oil-pump suction screen or strainer to the valve body, and torque to 40 in.-lbs. Screen is marked "Front" to prevent improper installation.

70. Detent control-valve wire is inserted in transmission case, and reconnected to actuating lever. Retaining pin holds lever to bracket on valve body.

71. Vacuum modulator valve is inserted at rear of case, with the modulator assembly and O-ring seal following. Tighten the holding bracket.

72. Install new pan gasket, and rebolt the oil pan to transmission case. Torque to 130 in.-lbs., and Turbo Hydra-Matic 350, 375B, M-38 overhaul is complete.

GENERAL MOTORS
Super Turbine 375
Turbo Hydra-Matic 400, 425

375 APPLICATION
Buick:

    1970-76 Centurion   1978 Riviera
    1970-77 LeSabre

Oldsmobile:

    1973-77 Delta 88

400 APPLICATION
Buick:

    1970-72 Special

    1978-79 Electra

Cadillac:

    All 1970-79, except Eldorado, Seville (Diesel)

Chevrolet:

    1970-72 Camaro   1970-77 Corvette
    1970-77 Chevelle   1970-77 Monte Carlo
    1970-77 Chevrolet   1970-72 Nova

Oldsmobile:

    1973-77 Cutlass   1970 Olds F-85
    1970-77 Cutlass Supreme   1978-79 Olds 98
    1970-76 Olds 455-cu.-in.

Pontiac:

    1970-77 Bonneville, Firebird, Grand Prix
    1970-73 GTO
    1970-72 Tempest

425 APPLICATION
Cadillac:

    1970-78 Eldorado

Oldsmobile:

    1970-78 Toronado

DESCRIPTION

The Turbo Hydra-Matic 375/400 is a fully automatic transmission with a three-element hydraulic torque converter and compound planetary gear set, with three multiple-disc clutches, one gear unit, one roller clutch and two bands. The 425 is used with Toronado and Eldorado front-wheel-drive vehicles, and is essentially similar internally, but with one sprag and one roller clutch instead of the 400's two roller clutches. The 425 torque converter couples the engine to the planetary gear set by means of a drive and driven sprocket and a link belt. The 425 also uses eight check balls, two more than the 400.

All Turbo Hydra-Matic 400 transmissions from 1977 on use a new forward clutch center seal design without the lip found on older seals. When overhauling a 1977 or later Turbo 400, make sure the seal bears the GM Part Number 8626985 and is installed with its chamfered side facing *upward.*

BAND ADJUSTMENT
REAR BAND
(Internal, Rear Servo)

Special GM tools are required to properly check band adjustment—a band apply pin gauge J-21370-5 and J-21370-6 for the THM 400, and a band apply pin gauge J-21370-6, J-21370-7 and J-21370-8 for the THM 425.

1. Remove rear servo, and clean the servo bore.

2. Install the pin gauge to the transmission case with the attaching screws provided.

3. Apply 25 ft.-lbs. torque, and determine the proper servo pin required from the pin gauge scale in the specifications.

4. Refer to the specifications for the proper selective pin to be used. The identification ring is located on the band lug end of the pin. Proper pin selection is the equivalent of band adjustment.

TURBO HYDRA-MATIC 375/400 SPECIFICATIONS AND BAND APPLY PIN SELECTION CHARTS
TORQUE SPECIFICATIONS

Pump Cover Bolts	18 ft. lbs.
Parking Pawl Bracket Bolts	18 ft. lbs.
Center Support Bolt	23 ft. lbs.
Pump to Case Attaching Bolts	18 ft. lbs.
Extension Housing to Case Attaching Bolts	23 ft. lbs.
Rear Servo Cover Bolts	18 ft. lbs.
Detent Solenoid Bolts	7 ft. lbs.
Control Valve Body Bolts	8 ft. lbs.
Bottom Pan Attaching Screws	12 ft. lbs.
Modulator Retainer Bolt	18 ft. lbs.
Governor Cover Bolts	18 ft. lbs.
Manual Lever to Manual Shaft Nut	8 ft. lbs.
Manual Shaft to Inside Detent Lever	18 ft. lbs.
Linkage Swivel Clamp Nut	43 ft. lbs.
Converter Dust Shield Screws	93 ft. lbs.
Transmission to Engine Mounting Bolts	35 ft. lbs.
Converter to Flywheel Bolts	32 ft. lbs.
Rear Mount to Transmission Bolts	40 ft. lbs.
Rear Mount to Crossmember Bolt	40 ft. lbs.
Crossmember Mounting Bolts	25 ft. lbs.
Line Pressure Take-Off Plug	13 ft. lbs.
Strainer Retainer Bolt	10 ft. lbs.
Oil Cooler Pipe Connectors to Transmission Case or Radiator	12-16 ft. lbs.
Oil Cooler Pipe to Connector	10 ft. lbs.
Gearshift Bracket to Frame	15 ft. lbs.
Gearshift Shaft to Swivel	20 ft. lbs.
Manual Shaft to Bracket	20 ft. lbs.
Downshift Switch to Bracket	30 in. lbs.

BAND APPLY PIN SELECTION CHART

	STEP LOCATION	PIN IDENT.	SIZE
	TOP STEP OR ABOVE	THREE RINGS	LONG
	THIS AREA	TWO RINGS	MED.
J-21370-5	LOWER STEP OR BELOW	ONE RING	SHORT

TURBO HYDRA-MATIC 425 SPECIFICATIONS AND BAND APPLY PIN SELECTION CHARTS
TORQUE SPECIFICATIONS

APPLICATION	FT.-LBS.	APPLICATION	FT.-LBS.
Solenoid Assembly to Pump Or Valve Body	3	Vacuum Modulator Retainer To Case	20
Line Pressure Take-Off	15	Oil Pan To Case	13
Oil Cooler Lines	20	Case Extension To Case	25
Race To Center Support	10	Case To Center Support	25
Solenoid Assembly To Case	10	Manual Shaft To Inside Detent	20
Valve Body To Case	10	Filter To Valve Body	10
Sprocket Cover To Case	10	Transmission Case To Cylinder Block Bolts	30
Pump Assembly To Case	20	Flywheel To Converter Attaching Bolts	35
Pump Body To Cover	20	Support Assembly To Transmission	35
Driven Support To Cover	20	Prop Shaft To Rear Companion Flange	16
Cover Plate To Case	20	Speedometer Driven Gear To Case Attaching Bolt	6
Rear Servo Cover To Case	20	Crossmember To Frame	15
Governor Cover To Case	20	Transmission To Crossmember	60

BAND APPLY PIN SELECTION CHART

STEP LOCATION	PIN IDENT.	SIZE
TOP STEP OR ABOVE	THREE RINGS	LONG
THIS AREA	TWO RINGS	MED.
LOWER STEP OR BELOW	ONE RING	SHORT

J-21370-7

TYPICAL TURBO HYDRA-MATIC 375/400 CONTROL VALVE DISASSEMBLY

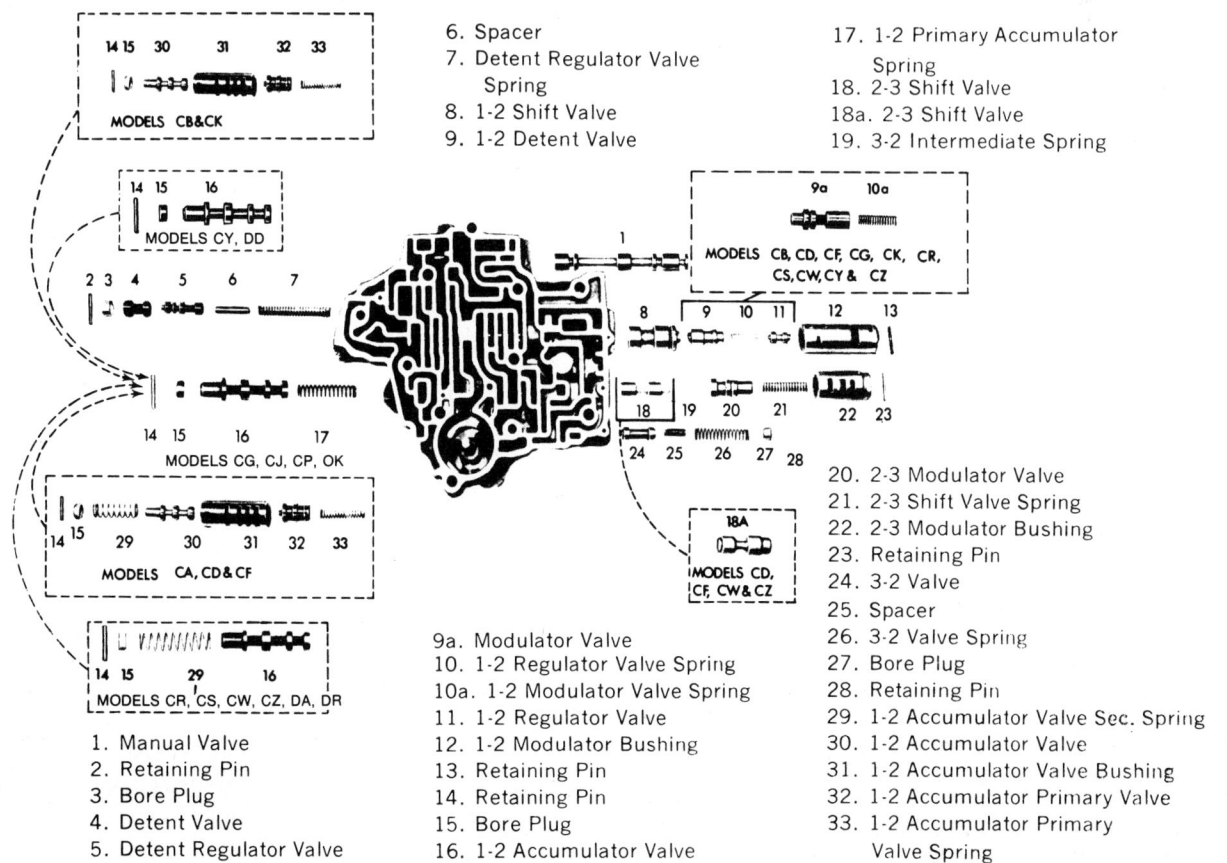

MODELS CB&CK

MODELS CY, DD

MODELS CG, CJ, CP, OK

MODELS CA, CD & CF

MODELS CR, CS, CW, CZ, DA, DR

MODELS CB, CD, CF, CG, CK, CR, CS, CW, CY & CZ

18A MODELS CD, CF, CW & CZ

6. Spacer
7. Detent Regulator Valve Spring
8. 1-2 Shift Valve
9. 1-2 Detent Valve

17. 1-2 Primary Accumulator Spring
18. 2-3 Shift Valve
18a. 2-3 Shift Valve
19. 3-2 Intermediate Spring

9a. Modulator Valve
10. 1-2 Regulator Valve Spring
10a. 1-2 Modulator Valve Spring
11. 1-2 Regulator Valve
12. 1-2 Modulator Bushing
13. Retaining Pin
14. Retaining Pin
15. Bore Plug
16. 1-2 Accumulator Valve

1. Manual Valve
2. Retaining Pin
3. Bore Plug
4. Detent Valve
5. Detent Regulator Valve

20. 2-3 Modulator Valve
21. 2-3 Shift Valve Spring
22. 2-3 Modulator Bushing
23. Retaining Pin
24. 3-2 Valve
25. Spacer
26. 3-2 Valve Spring
27. Bore Plug
28. Retaining Pin
29. 1-2 Accumulator Valve Sec. Spring
30. 1-2 Accumulator Valve
31. 1-2 Accumulator Valve Bushing
32. 1-2 Accumulator Primary Valve
33. 1-2 Accumulator Primary Valve Spring

TURBO HYDRA-MATIC
375/400/425 DIAGNOSIS CHART

CONDITION	CORRECTION	CONDITION	CORRECTION
NO DRIVE IN DRIVE RANGE		(d) Porosity in case assembly.	(d) Replace.
(a) Oil level low.	(a) Top up to correct level. Check for external leaks or defective vacuum modulator. Leaking diaphragm will evacuate oil from unit.	**NO 1-2 SHIFT: FIRST SPEED ONLY**	
		(a) Governor assembly faulty.	(a) Governor valve sticks. Driven gear may also be loose, damaged or worn. If driven gear shows signs of damage, check output shaft drive gear for nicks or rough finish.
(b) Oil pressure is low.	(b) Check filter assembly as O-ring may be missing or damaged; neck weld may leak or filter might be blocked. Check pump assembly for damage by converter. In rare cases, there might be porosity in intake bore of unit.	(b) Control valve assembly faulty.	(b) Check 1-2 shift valve train to see if it's closed. Governor feed channels may be blocked, leaking or pipes out of position. Check valve body spacer plate-to-cover gasket as it may be leaking, damaged or incorrectly installed.
(c) Manual linkage is out of adjustment.	(c) Check and adjust linkage.	(c) Defective case.	(c) Replace leaking or blown-out intermediate clutch plug. Governor feed channel may also be blocked or governor bore could be scored or worn causing cross pressure leak.
(d) Faulty control valve assembly.	(d) Reconnect manual valve to manual lever.		
(e) Forward clutch not working properly.	(e) Check for cracked piston, missing or damaged seals, or burned clutch plates.		
(f) Pump feed circuit to forward clutch faulty.	(f) Check for missing or broken oil seal rings, leak in feed circuits, pump-to-case gasket out of position or damaged. Clutch drum ball check may be stuck or missing.	(d) Intermediate clutch not working correctly.	(d) Replace clutch piston seals. Check center support oil rings as they may be missing or broken. Orifice plug could also be missing.
(g) Broken spring or damaged cage in roller clutch assembly.	(g) Replace.		
OIL PRESSURE TOO HIGH OR TOO LOW		**FIRST & SECOND SPEEDS ONLY, NO 2-3 SHIFT**	
(a) High oil pressure.	(a) Vacuum line or fittings may leak; also check vacuum modulator, modulator valve, pressure regulator and oil pump for correct operation.	(a) Detent solenoid stuck open.	(a) Replace.
		(b) Detent switch faulty.	(b) Replace.
		(c) Control valve assembly faulty.	(c) Check 2-3 shift train to see if it's stuck. Also check valve body spacer plate-to-cover gasket as it may be leaking, damaged or incorrectly installed.
(b) Low oil pressure.	(b) Vacuum line or fittings may be obstructed; also check vacuum modulator, modulator valve, pressure regulator, governor and oil pump for correct operation.	(d) Direct clutch defective.	(d) Replace center support oil rings. Also check clutch piston seals for damage and make sure that piston ball check is not stuck or missing.
1-2 SHIFT: FULL THROTTLE ONLY		**DRIVE IN NEUTRAL**	
(a) Sticking or defective detent switch.	(a) Replace.	(a) Manual linkage out of adjustment.	(a) Adjust linkage.
(b) Detent solenoid is loose, has leaking gasket or sticks open.	(b) Repair and/or replace as necessary.	(b) Forward clutch does not release.	(b) Replace.
(c) Control valve assembly faulty.	(c) Valve body spacer plate to cover gasket may leak. It can also be damaged or incorrectly installed. Check detent valve train for sticking and 3-2 valve for same.	**NO DRIVE OR SLIPS IN REVERSE**	
		(a) Oil level low.	(a) Top up oil to proper level.
		(b) Manual linkage out of adjustment.	(b) Adjust linkage.

CONDITION	CORRECTION	CONDITION	CORRECTION
(c) Incorrect oil pressure.	(c) Replace vacuum modulator assembly.	(e) Rear servo accumulator assembly faulty.	(e) Remove unit and check for damaged oil rings, stuck piston, broken or missing spring or damaged bore. Repair accordingly.
(d) Control valve assembly faulty.	(d) Replace valve body spacer plate-to-gasket. Check 2-3 valve train to see if it's stuck open. Make sure low reverse ball is not missing from case and that reverse feed passage is correctly installed.		
		2-3 SHIFT SLIPS	
		(a) Oil level low.	(a) Top up oil to proper level.
		(b) Incorrect oil pressure.	(b) Replace vacuum modulator assembly. Check for mislocated pump-to-case gasket and replace correctly if necessary.
(e) Rear servo piston seal ring damaged or missing.	(e) Replace ring.		
(f) Reverse or low band defective or burned.	(f) Replace band.		
(g) Direct clutch—clutch plates burned or damaged.	(g) Replace clutch plates. Check to see if caused by stuck ball check in piston. Also check outer seal as it may be damaged too.	(c) Accumulator piston pin leaks at swedge end.	(c) Replace.
		(d) Direct clutch—piston seals leak.	(d) Replace seals and check for leak from center support oil seal rings.
SLIPS IN ALL RANGES		**ROUGH 2-3 SHIFT**	
(a) Oil level low.	(a) Top up oil to proper level.	(a) Oil pressure is too high.	(a) Modulator valve sticks or assembly is defective. Determine which and repair accordingly.
(b) Incorrect oil pressure.	(b) Replace vacuum modulator assembly. Also check for plugged or leaking filter assembly, especially a damaged O-ring.	(b) Front servo accumulator spring missing or broken.	(b) Replace. Check for stuck piston.
(c) Forward and direct clutches burned.	(c) Replace burned clutches and locate cause.	**NO ENGINE BRAKING—2ND GEAR**	
1-2 SHIFT SLIPS		(a) Front band broken or burned.	(a) Replace and determine cause.
(a) Oil level low.	(a) Top up oil to proper level.	**NO ENGINE BRAKING—1ST GEAR**	
(b) Incorrect oil pressure.	(b) Replace vacuum modulator assembly. Check pump pressure regulator valve at same time for correct operation.	(a) Low-reverse check ball missing from case.	(a) Replace.
		(b) Rear servo oil seal ring, bore or piston damaged.	(b) Replace.
(c) Front accumulator oil ring damaged or missing.	(c) Replace.	(c) Rear band apply pin is short or improperly assembled.	(c) Replace correctly.
(d) Control valve assembly bolts are loose.	(d) Torque valve body attaching bolts to correct specs if 1-2 accumulator valve train is not sticking. If valve sticks, replace.	(d) Rear band is broken or burned.	(d) Replace and determine cause.
(e) Rear accumulator oil ring damaged or missing.	(e) Replace.	**NO PART-THROTTLE DOWNSHIFT**	
(f) Mispositioned pump-to-case gasket.	(f) Replace gasket correctly.	(a) 3-2 valve stuck, spring missing or broken.	(a) Free valve and/or replace spring.
(g) Intermediate clutch plug in case leaking excessively.	(g) Replace. If leak continues, there may be porosity between channels.	(b) Oil pressure incorrect.	(b) Check operation of vacuum modulator assembly and replace if necessary.
(h) Intermediate clutch piston seals damaged.	(h) Replace. Clutch plates may also be burned and should be replaced if necessary.	**NO DETENT DOWNSHIFTS**	
		(a) 3-2 valve stuck, spring missing or broken.	(a) Free valve and/or replace spring.
ROUGH 1-2 SHIFT		(b) Detent switch out of adjustment.	(b) Adjust.
(a) Incorrect oil pressure.	(a) Replace vacuum modulator assembly. Check for loose fittings or restrictions in line.	(c) Solenoid inoperative.	(c) Replace.
		(d) Detent valve train sticking.	(d) Replace.
(b) Control valve assembly bolts loose.	(b) Torque valve body to case bolts to specs.	**WILL NOT HOLD IN PARK**	
(c) Valve body spacer plate-to-cover gasket damaged or mispositioned.	(c) Replace gasket.	(a) Linkage needs adjustment.	(a) Adjust linkage.
		(b) Defective parking brake lever and actuator assembly.	(b) Replace.
(d) Intermediate clutch ball missing or not sealing.	(d) Replace or ascertain why sealing is not taking place.	(c) Parking pawl broken.	(c) Replace.

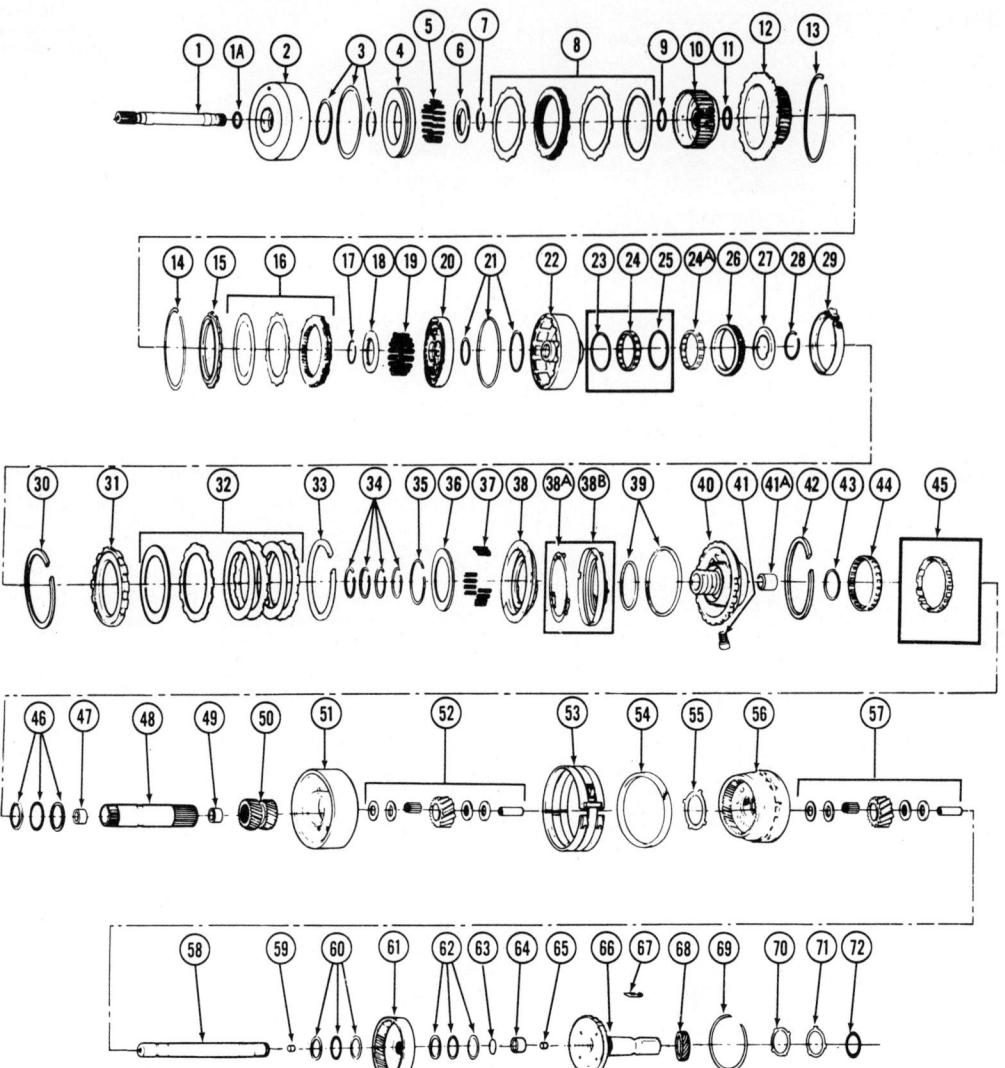

**TURBO HYDRA-MATIC 375/400/425 FORWARD,
DIRECT AND INTERMEDIATE CLUTCH DISASSEMBLY**

ILLUS. NO.	DESCRIPTION
1	Shaft, Turbine
1A	Ring, Oil Seal
2	Housing, Forward Clutch
3	Seal-Forward Clutch (Package)
4	Piston, Forward Clutch
5	Spring, Forward Clutch
6	Retainer, Spring Forward Clutch
7	Ring, Snap-Spring Retainer
8	Plates, Forward Clutch
9	Washer, Thrust, Housing to Hub
10	Hub, Forward Clutch
11	Washer, Thrust, Fwd. Hub to Direct Clutch Hsg.
12	Hub, Direct Clutch
13	Ring, Snap-Forward Clutch
14	Ring, Snap-Direct Clutch
15	Plate, Direct Clutch Backing
16	Plates, Direct Clutch
17	Ring, Snap-Direct Clutch
18	Retainer, Spring-Direct Clutch
19	Spring—Direct Clutch
20	Piston-Direct Clutch
21	Seal-Direct Clutch (Package)
22	Housing-Direct Clutch
23	Bushing, Sprag
24	Sprag Asm., Intermediate Clutch

ILLUS. NO.	DESCRIPTION
25	Bushing, Sprag
26	Race, Intermediate Sprag
27	Retainer, Intermediate Sprag
28	Ring, Snap-Intermediate Sprag
29	Band, Front
30	Ring, Snap-Int. Clutch
31	Plate, Int. Clutch Backing
32	Plates, Int. Clutch
33	Ring, Snap-Center Support
34	Ring, Oil Seal Center Support
35	Ring, Snap-Int. Clutch
36	Retainer, Spring-Int. Clutch
37	Spring-Int. Clutch
38	Piston-Int. Clutch
38A	Guide, Intermediate Clutch Spring
38B	Piston, Intermediate Clutch
39	Seal-Int. Clutch (Package)
40	Support, Center
41	Screw, Center Support Locating
41A	Bushing, Center Support
42	Spacer, Center Support to Case
43	Thrust Washer, Center Support
44	Sprag Assembly-Low Clutch
45	Roller Assembly-Low Clutch
46	Bearing, Thrust (Package), Sun Gear to Center Support
47	Bushing, Sun Gear Shaft

ILLUS. NO.	DESCRIPTION
48	Shaft, Sun Gear
49	Bushing, Sun Gear Shaft
50	Sun Gear
51	Carrier Assembly, Reaction
52	Pinion (Package)
53	Band, Rear
54	Ring, Int. Gear
55	Washer, Thrust, Output Carr. to Reaction Carr.
56	Carrier Assembly, Output
57	Pinion (Package)
58	Shaft, Main
59	Plug, Main Shaft (No longer required.)
60	Bearing, Thrust (Package), Rear Internal Gear to Sun Gear
61	Gear, Rear Internal
62	Bearing, Thrust (Package), Output Shaft to Rear Int. Gear
63	Ring, Snap
64	Bushing, Output Shaft
65	Plug, Output Shaft
66	Shaft, Output
67	Clip, Speedometer Drive Gear
68	Gear, Speedometer Drive
69	Ring, Snap
70	Washer, Thrust, Output Shaft to Case
71	Washer, Selective, Output Shaft to Case
72	Seal, O-Ring Output Shaft

TURBO HYDRA-MATIC 375/400 DISASSEMBLY—CASE AND RELATED PARTS

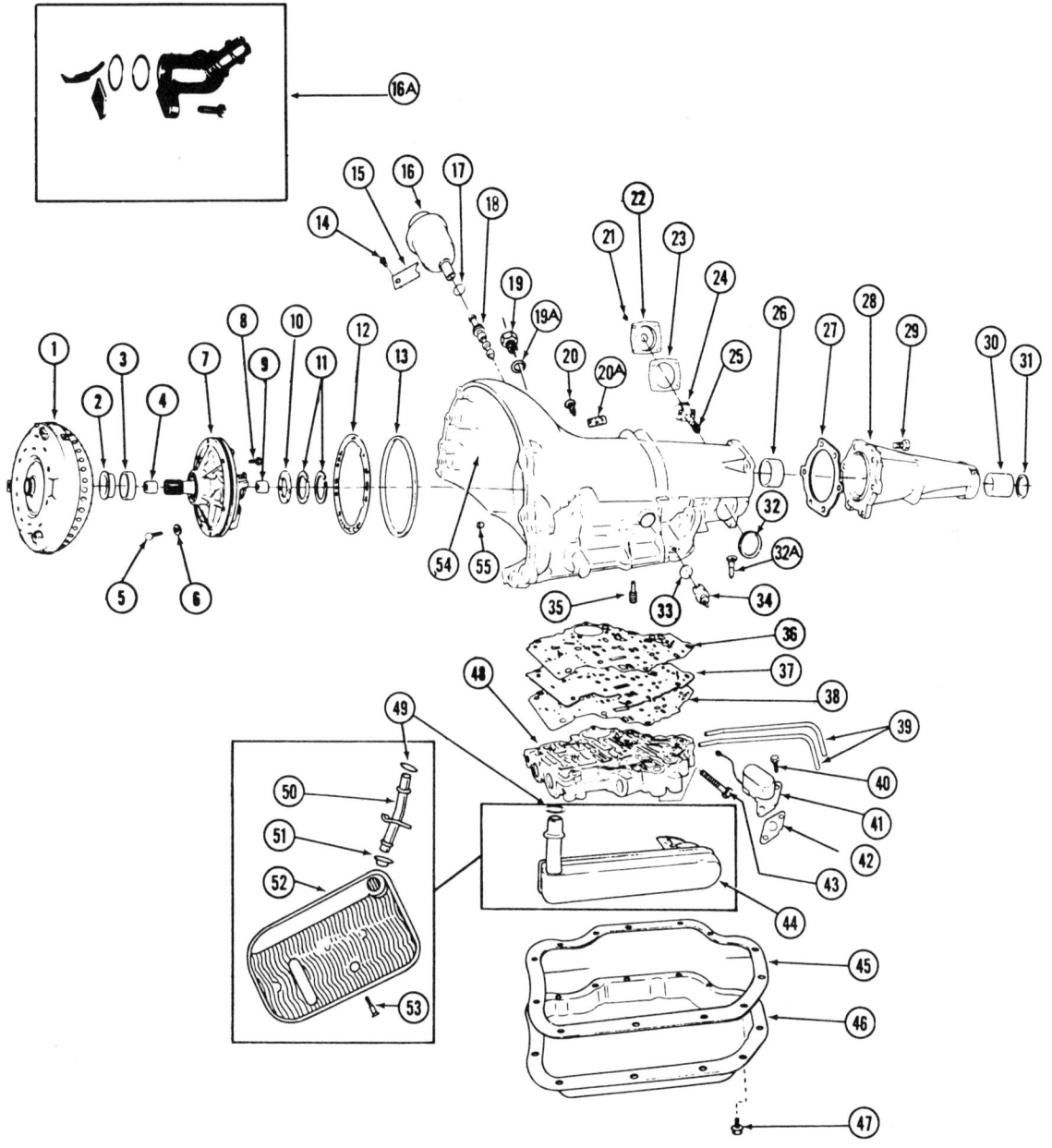

ILLUS. NO.	DESCRIPTION
1	Converter Assembly
2	Seal Assembly, Pump
3	Bushing, Pump Body
4	Bushing, Stator Shaft—Front
5	Bolt, Pump to Case
6	Gasket, Bolt
7	Pump Assembly
8	Bolt, Pump Body to Cover
9	Bushing, Stator Shaft Rear
10	Washer, Thrust
11	Ring, Oil Pump Cover
12	Gasket, Pump to Case
13	"O" Ring, Pump to Case
14	Bolt, Modulator Retainer
15	Retainer, Modulator
16	Modulator Assembly
16A	Modulator Adapter Kit—American Motors
17	Seal "O" Ring
18	Valve, Modulator
19	Connector, Oil Cooler
19A	Gasket, Oil Cooler Connector
20	Screw, Nameplate Attaching
20A	Nameplate
21	Bolt, Governor Cover
22	Cover, Governor
23	Gasket, Governor Cover
24	Governor Assembly
25	Gear, Governor Package
26	Bushing, Case
27	Gasket, Case to Extension
28	Extension Assembly, Case
29	Bolt, Extension
30	Bushing, Case Extension
31	Seal Assembly, Case Extension
32	Plug, Speedo Hole/Steel
32A	Screen Assembly, Governor
33	Seal, "O" Ring
34	Connector, Electrical
35	Screw, Case to Center Support
36	Gasket, Spacer to Case
37	Plate, Valve Body Spacer
38	Gasket, Valve Body to Spacer
39	Pipe, Governor
40	Bolt, Solenoid to Case
41	Solenoid Assembly
42	Gasket, Solenoid
43	Bolt, Valve Body to Case
44	Filter Assembly (First Type)
45	Gasket, Oil Pan
46	Pan, Transmission Oil
47	Screw & Washer Asm., Oil Pan to Case
48	Valve Body Assembly
49	Seal "O" Ring, Pipe to Case
50	Pipe Asm. Trans. Intake to Strainer (2nd Type)
51	Grommet Transmission Strainer to Pipe
52	Filter Assembly (2nd Type)
53	Bolt, Shoulder/Special/Filter to Case
54	Case Assembly
55	Plug .25 Dia. Intermediate Clutch Line

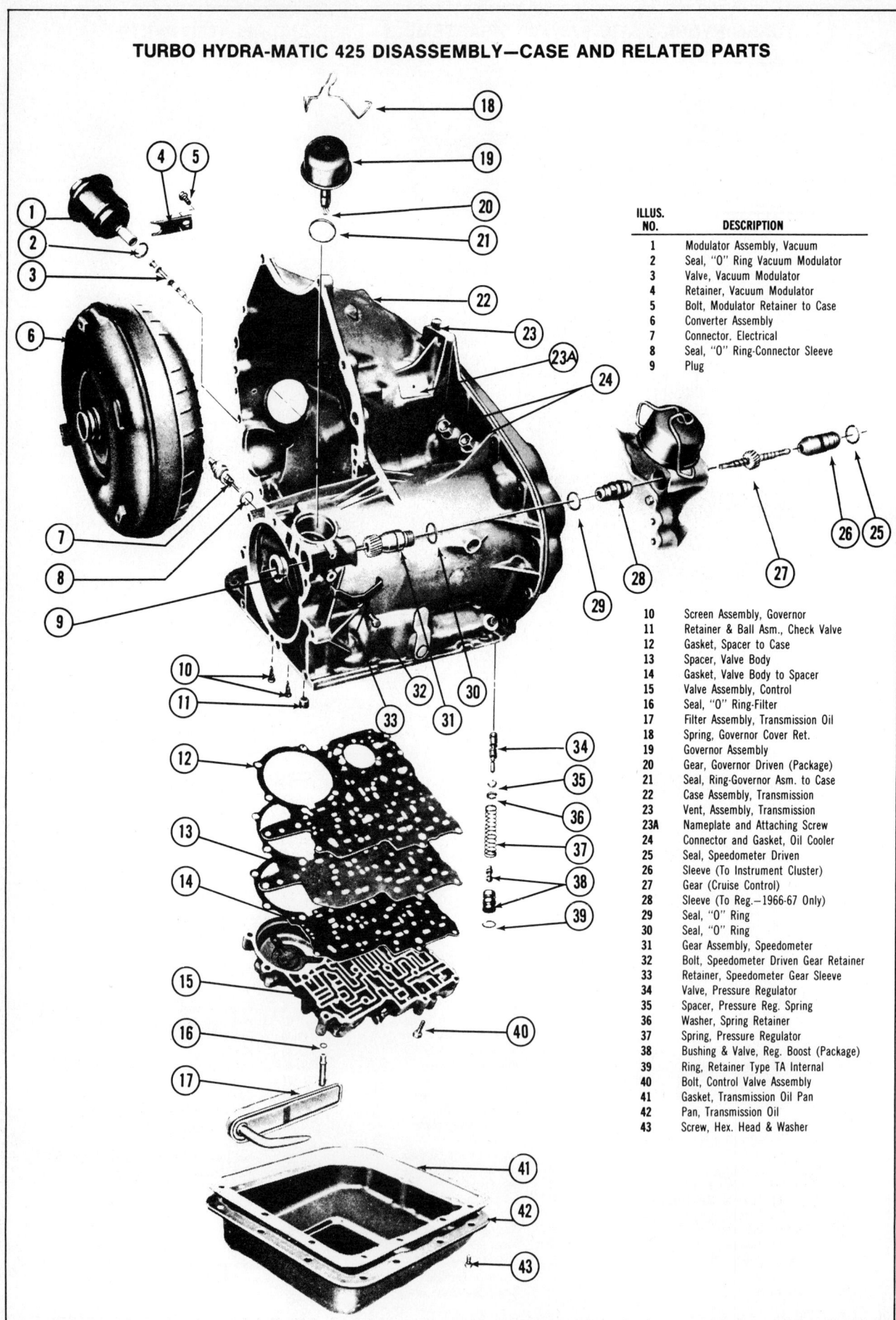

TURBO HYDRA-MATIC 425 DISASSEMBLY—CASE AND RELATED PARTS

ILLUS. NO.	DESCRIPTION
1	Modulator Assembly, Vacuum
2	Seal, "O" Ring Vacuum Modulator
3	Valve, Vacuum Modulator
4	Retainer, Vacuum Modulator
5	Bolt, Modulator Retainer to Case
6	Converter Assembly
7	Connector, Electrical
8	Seal, "O" Ring-Connector Sleeve
9	Plug
10	Screen Assembly, Governor
11	Retainer & Ball Asm., Check Valve
12	Gasket, Spacer to Case
13	Spacer, Valve Body
14	Gasket, Valve Body to Spacer
15	Valve Assembly, Control
16	Seal, "O" Ring-Filter
17	Filter Assembly, Transmission Oil
18	Spring, Governor Cover Ret.
19	Governor Assembly
20	Gear, Governor Driven (Package)
21	Seal, Ring-Governor Asm. to Case
22	Case Assembly, Transmission
23	Vent, Assembly, Transmission
23A	Nameplate and Attaching Screw
24	Connector and Gasket, Oil Cooler
25	Seal, Speedometer Driven
26	Sleeve (To Instrument Cluster)
27	Gear (Cruise Control)
28	Sleeve (To Reg.—1966-67 Only)
29	Seal, "O" Ring
30	Seal, "O" Ring
31	Gear Assembly, Speedometer
32	Bolt, Speedometer Driven Gear Retainer
33	Retainer, Speedometer Gear Sleeve
34	Valve, Pressure Regulator
35	Spacer, Pressure Reg. Spring
36	Washer, Spring Retainer
37	Spring, Pressure Regulator
38	Bushing & Valve, Reg. Boost (Package)
39	Ring, Retainer Type TA Internal
40	Bolt, Control Valve Assembly
41	Gasket, Transmission Oil Pan
42	Pan, Transmission Oil
43	Screw, Hex. Head & Washer

TURBO HYDRA-MATIC 425 CONTROL VALVE DISASSEMBLY

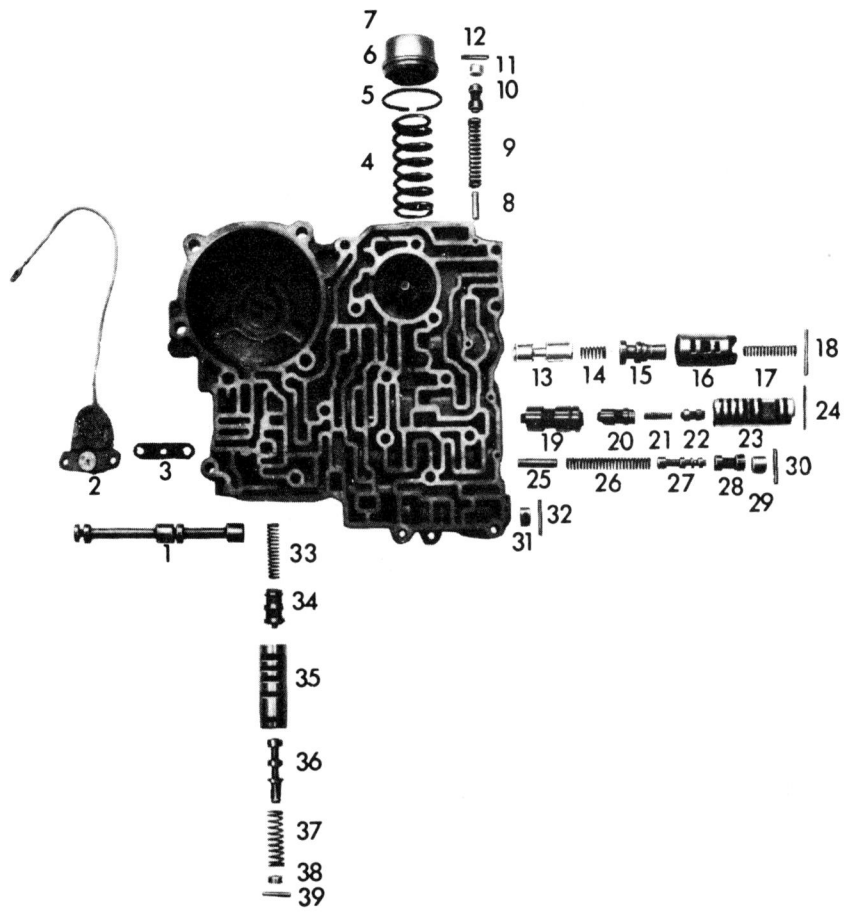

1. MANUAL VALVE
2. DETENT SOLENOID
3. GASKET
4. FRONT ACCUMULATOR SPRING
5. OIL RING
6. ACCUMULATOR PISTON
7. E-RING
8. 3-2 VALVE PIN
9. 3-2 VALVE SPRING
10. 3-2 VALVE
11. 3-2 BORE PLUG
12. RETAINER PIN
13. 2-3 VALVE
14. 3-2 INTERMEDIATE SPRING
15. 2-3 MODULATOR VALVE
16. 2-3 MODULATOR BUSHING
17. 2-3 VALVE SPRING
18. RETAINER PIN
19. 1-2 VALVE
20. 1-2 MODULATOR VALVE

21. 1-2 MODULATOR SPRING
22. 1-2 REGULATOR VALVE
23. 1-2 MODULATOR BUSHING
24. RETAINER PIN
25. DETENT REGULATOR PIN
26. DETENT REGULATOR SPRING
27. DETENT REGULATOR VALVE
28. DETENT VALVE
29. VALVE BORE PLUG
30. RETAINER PIN
31. VALVE BORE PLUG
32. RETAINER PIN
33. 1-2 PRIMARY ACCUMULATOR SPRING
34. 1-2 PRIMARY ACCUMULATOR VALVE
35. 1-2 ACCUMULATOR VALVE BUSHING
36. 1-2 ACCUMULATOR VALVE
37. 1-2 SECONDARY ACCUMULATOR SPRING
38. 1-2 ACCUMULATOR VALVE PLUG
39. RETAINING PIN

HOW TO: Turbo Hydra-Matic 375/400/425 Overhaul

1. The Turbo Hydra-Matic 375/400 is the heavy-duty GM transmission. To overhaul, remove converter, unbolt and remove oil pan and discard gasket.

2. Filter/intake pipe assembly design differs according to model year and application. Rock filter to free intake pipe; then lift assembly off and out.

3. Lift up on control-valve-assembly governor pipes to free them from the transmission case, then remove the control valve assembly from the case.

4. Pressure switch/detent solenoid design also varies. Unclip lead wires from connectors and unbolt solenoid. Be sure to remove and discard the gasket.

5. Remove control-valve-assembly spacer plate and gasket, then locate and remove the six check balls from cored passages in the transmission case.

6. Remove the front servo piston, washer, pin, retainer and spring from the case. Unless servo appears to be giving trouble, do not disassemble the unit.

7. Remove the rear servo cover and gasket. Discard the gasket, and remove the rear servo assembly and accumulator spring from the transmission case.

8. Pry rear oil seal from the extension housing. Unbolt housing and tap gently to break seal, then withdraw housing. Discard gasket and housing seal.

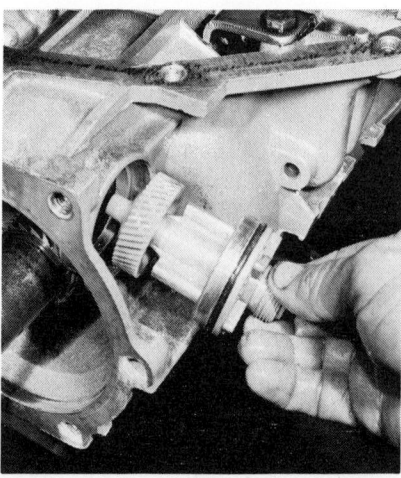

9. Remove the speedometer-driven-gear attaching screw and retainer, and withdraw the gear. Inspect teeth; remove and replace the O-ring seal.

10. Remove the governor-cover attaching screws, cover and gasket. Discard gasket and withdraw the governor assembly from the transmission case.

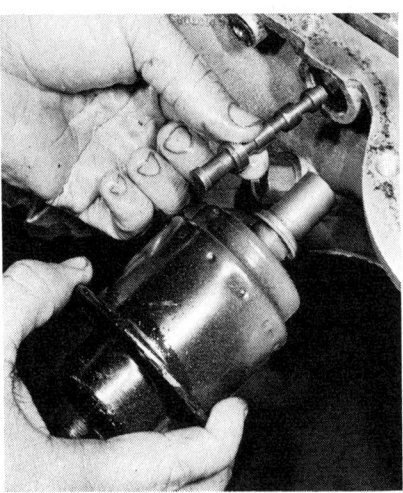

11. Remove the screw and retainer holding the modulator assembly to the case, and withdraw the modulator. Remove and replace the O-ring seal.

12. Remove the pump attaching bolts, and install a threaded slide hammer. Operate slide hammer to pull the pump free from the transmission case.

13. With front pump removed, withdraw forward clutch assembly/turbine shaft from the case. There should be a thrust washer on the rear of the assembly.

14. If not, locate and remove the forward clutch-hub-to-direct-clutch-housing thrust washer, then withdraw the direct clutch assembly from the case.

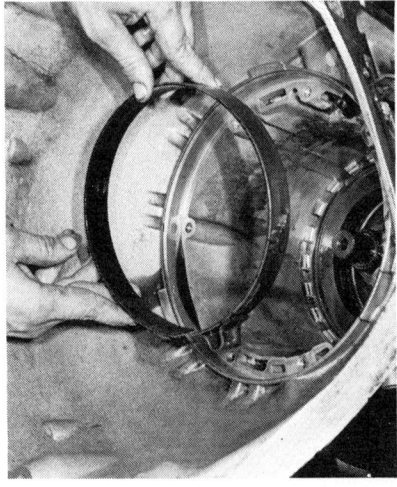

15. Removal of the remaining parts is made easier if you can position the transmission case vertically. Remove the front band assembly.

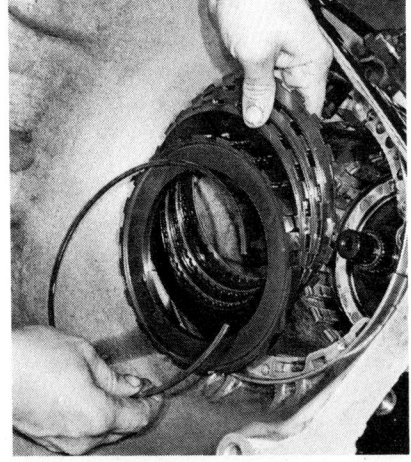

16. Unclip snap ring holding the intermediate clutch pack in place, and withdraw backing plate and six clutch plates from the transmission case.

17. Remove the center support-to-case bolt. This requires the use of a ⅜-in., 12-point thinwall deep socket—nothing else will do the job properly.

18. Pry the center support-to-case retaining snap ring free, and remove it from the transmission case, again positioned vertically.

HOW TO: Turbo Hydra-Matic 375/400/425 Overhaul

19. Tilting transmission case back to a horizontal position, remove entire gear assembly and output shaft—this unit is very heavy, so take care.

20. Remove the rear-unit selective washer, the center support-to-case spacer and the rear band assembly from the transmission case.

21. Check the manual-shaft retaining pin. An ordinary finishing nail, it can slip out and get lost. *Do not* remove pin and manual shaft unless damaged.

22. Begin component disassembly with the gear unit; remove the center support assembly by simply lifting the two apart to separate.

23. Remove the reaction carrier and roller clutch assembly, then lift the front internal gear ring from the output carrier assembly—ring is plastic.

24. The sun gear and the sun gear shaft are both removed from the mainshaft. Inspect the sun-gear tooth pattern for excessive wear and/or damage.

25. A large tanged thrust washer is fitted between the reaction carrier assembly and the output carrier assembly; locate and remove this washer.

26. After cleaning and inspecting all parts, replace the tanged thrust washer, and install the reaction carrier assembly and plastic gear ring.

27. Install the sun gear shaft with its long splines facing downward; then replace the sun gear assembly with its chamfered edge facing downward.

28. This needle bearing thrust washer goes next. Place one race over the shaft, drop the thrust bearing in place and install the other race.

29. Using snap ring pliers, spread and remove the center-support snap ring, then remove the retainer plate positioned underneath the snap ring.

30. Remove the piston from the center support assembly. The thick O-ring seal should also be removed and replaced with a new seal ring.

31. Apply a thin coating of wax-type lubricant to the O-ring seal to make piston installation easier. Fit on the center support and seat properly.

32. The seals on the center support shaft should be removed and replaced before installing the center support to the reaction carrier.

33. Install output-shaft-to-case thrust washer. A small amount of grease holds it in place. Be sure tangs engage the pockets in the reaction carrier.

34. Replace rear band assembly so that two lugs index with two anchor pins. Make sure band seats properly on lugs.

35. Install the support-to-case spacer against the shoulder at the bottom of the case, then replace the entire gear unit assembly in the case.

36. Replace the retaining snap ring, and hold the center support firmly while torquing the case-to-center support bolt 20 to 25 ft.-lbs.

HOW TO: Turbo Hydra-Matic 375/400/425 Overhaul

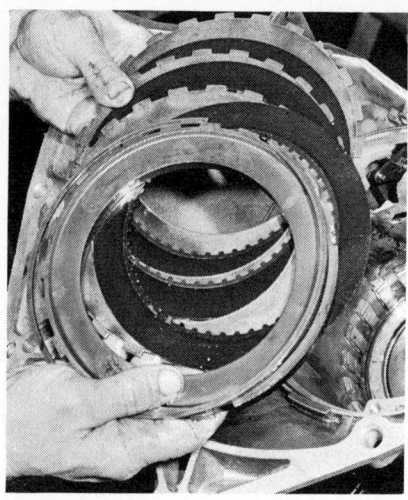

37. Install three steel and three composition intermediate clutch plates. Begin with the waved steel plate (if used) and alternate composition with steel plates.

38. Install backing plate, with ridge facing outward. Replace the front band, with anchor hole placed over band anchor pin and apply lug facing servo hole.

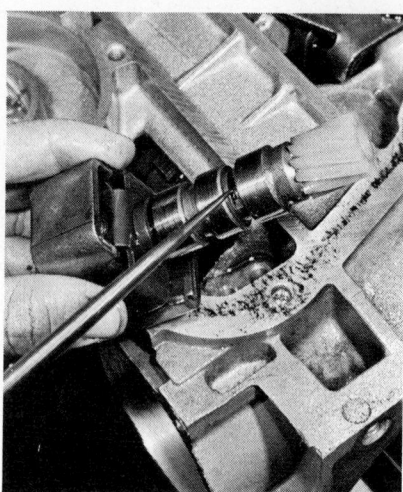

39. Inspect governor valve spring, and install assembly in case. Attach governor cover and gasket, and torque the attaching bolts to 18 ft.-lbs.

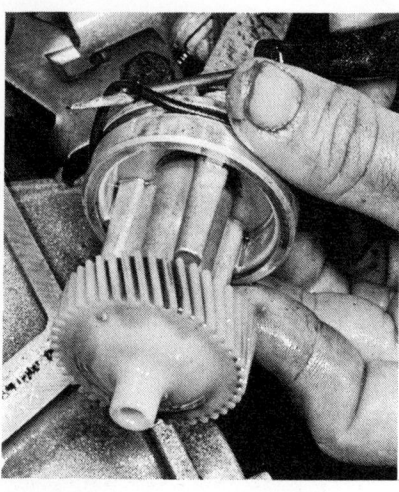

40. Replace the O-ring seal on the speedometer-driven-gear assembly, and install it in the case. Replace gear retainer and the attaching bolt.

41. Install a new extension-housing-to-case gasket on the housing, and replace the housing-to-case seal. Install housing, and torque bolts 20 to 25 ft.-lbs.

42. Drop the rear accumulator spring in the rear servo housing. Change the two O-ring seals on the accumulator, and replace the piston in the housing.

43. Install the servo piston with servo pin, spring and spring retainer in the accumulator piston. Replace gasket and cover; torque bolts 15 to 20 ft.-lbs.

44. Drop front servo spring retainer and spring in housing, then replace the O-ring seal on the servo piston. Replace piston and washer in the case.

45. Remove direct-clutch snap ring and backing plate, then remove and inspect the direct clutch pack, replacing any worn, burned or scored plates.

46. Use a spring compressor to provide access to the snap ring; remove it, and detach the spring compressor. Remove the spring retainer.

47. There are 16 piston release springs in the direct clutch assembly. Remove and inspect them, replacing any that are broken or distorted.

48. Removing the direct clutch piston, replace the piston outer and inner O-ring seals, and the center piston seal in the direct clutch housing.

49. Coat piston edge with wax-type lubricant for easier replacement. Use of a feeler gauge around the O-ring seal also eases installation.

50. Replace the clutch pack, beginning with the waved steel plate. Alternate composition with flat steel plates; install backing plate, flanged side up.

51. Forward clutch assembly is treated in exactly the same way as direct clutch. Do one unit at a time, since pistons can be mistakenly interchanged.

52. Place oil pump in a holding fixture, and remove the pump-cover-to-body attaching bolts, then separate and remove the pump cover from the housing.

53. Since the drive and driven gears must be replaced exactly as removed, scribe an alignment mark across their faces and that of the housing, as shown.

54. Using a straightedge and a feeler gauge, check the pump body-to-gear-face clearance. Clearance should range between 0.0018- and 0.0035-in.

HOW TO: Turbo Hydra-Matic 375/400/425 Overhaul

55. Remove the drive and driven gears, and inspect for scoring, galling or other damage. Also check the pump body face for scoring or nicks.

56. Replace gears according to the alignment marks, and fit pump cover to body housing. Align attaching bolt holes, and torque bolts to 18 ft.-lbs.

57. Pump pressure regulator (located by thumb) need not be disassembled for ordinary overhaul, but oil seal rings (located by finger) must be replaced.

58. Begin disassembly of control valve by removing manual valve. Place components to one side in the order removed to prevent a mix-up when replacing.

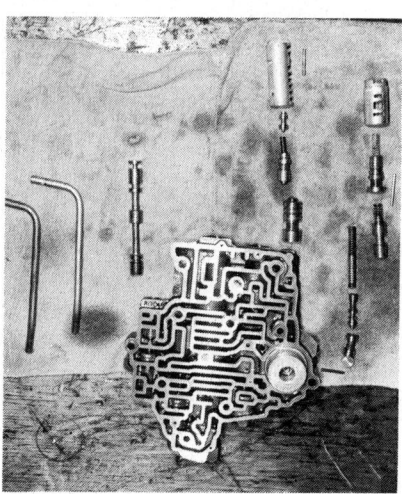

59. This shows one valve body configuration. Because many models of this transmission design are used, check charts for a given valve body design.

60. With converter end of transmission facing upward, install direct clutch and intermediate sprag assembly. Housing hub must bottom on the sun gear.

61. Install thrust washer. Replace forward clutch assembly/turbine shaft to index with direct clutch hub. When seated, clutch is 1¼-in. from pump face.

62. Install front pump assembly and gasket. If turbine shaft cannot be rotated when pulling pump into place, forward and/or direct clutch is not indexed.

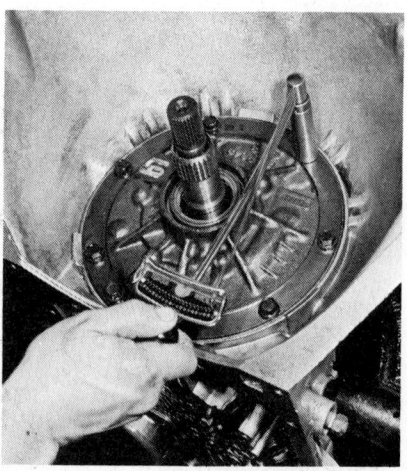

63. When pump is correctly seated, install pump attaching bolts with their seals. Torque each bolt to 18 ft.-lbs., and retest turbine for rotation.

64. If necessary to replace front seal, use a seal remover. Apply a non-hardening sealer on outside of new seal body, then drive it into place.

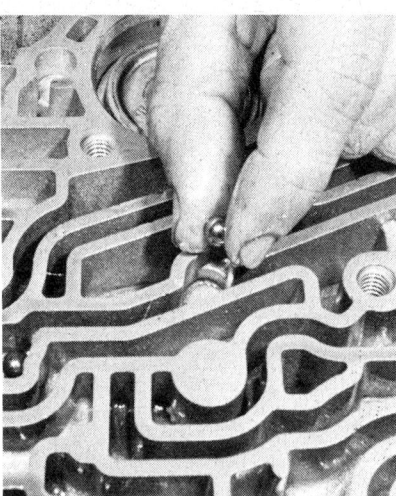

65. Carefully and correctly replace the six check balls, dropping each one in its proper location in the transmission-case cored passages.

66. Install the valve body spacer-to-case gasket and plate, using a pair of threaded studs to locate and hold gasket until valve body is replaced.

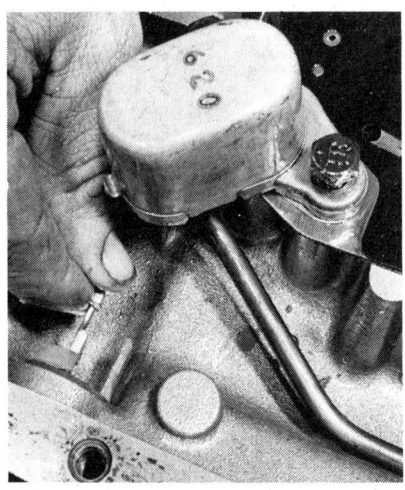

67. Replace the detent solenoid and gasket, with the connector facing the outer edge of the case. Connect lead wires to the electrical connectors.

68. Position valve body on the studs, and replace governor pipes in their respective locations in the transmission case. Press in until pipes seat.

69. Lower the valve body in place, and make sure manual valve properly indexes with manual detent lever pin. Replace governor pipe installation.

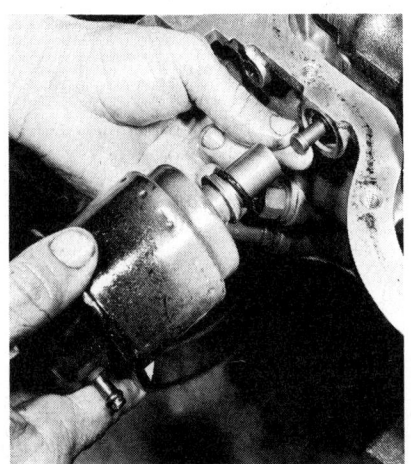

70. Replace vacuum modulator stem in case, with stem end facing outward; then install modulator with new O-ring seal. Torque retainer to 18 ft.-lbs.

71. Install a new O-ring seal on the intake pipe before replacing the filter and intake pipe assembly. Filter should be replaced rather than cleaned.

72. Fit a new bottom pan gasket to the transmission case, and install the bottom pan. Replace and torque the attaching screws to 12 ft.-lbs.

FORD MOTOR COMPANY
Ford C3, C4, C4S
C3 APPLICATION

1975-79 Bobcat	1974-79 Pinto
1974-78 Mustang II	1979 Mustang, Capri
1978-79 Fairmont, Zephyr	

C4, C4S APPLICATION

1975-79 Bobcat	1970-73 Mustang
1971-77 Comet	1974-78 Mustang II
1970-79 Cougar	1971-79 Pinto
1970 Fairlane, Falcon	1971-76 Torino, Elite
1975-79 Granada, Monarch	1978-79 Versailles,
1970-77 Maverick	Fairmont, Zephyr
1970-76 Montego, Galaxie, LTD	1977-79 LTD II
	1979 Mustang, Capri

DESCRIPTION

A light-duty automatic transmission developed specifically for use in Ford subcompact cars, the C3 is fitted to the 2300cc and 2800cc engines. The C3 is very similar in internal design to the C4. Both contain a torque converter, planetary gear train, two multiple disc clutches, a one-way clutch and a hydraulic control system. The C4 has two adjustable bands (the intermediate and the low/reverse), while only the intermediate C3 band is adjustable.

BAND ADJUSTMENT
C4, C4S INTERMEDIATE BAND
(Lower Left Side of Case Toward the Front)

1. Remove and discard the locknut on the band adjusting screw, cleaning the area around the screw.

2. Install a new locknut on the band adjusting screw, and torque to 10 ft.-lbs.

3. Back off the adjusting screw exactly 1¾ turns.

4. Hold the adjusting screw from turning, and torque the new locknut 35 to 45 ft.-lbs.

C4, C4S LOW/REVERSE BAND
(Lower Right Side of Case Toward the Rear)

1. Remove and discard the locknut on the band adjusting screw, cleaning the area around the screw.

2. Install a new locknut on the band adjusting screw, and torque to 10 ft.-lbs.

3. Back off adjusting screw exactly three full turns.

4. Hold the adjusting screw from turning, and torque the new locknut 35 to 45 ft.-lbs.

C3 INTERMEDIATE BAND
(Lower Left Side of Case Toward the Front)

1. Remove the downshift rod from downshift lever.

2. Remove and discard the locknut on the band adjusting screw, cleaning the area around the screw.

3. Install a new locknut on the band adjusting screw, and torque to 10 ft.-lbs.

4. Back off the adjusting screw exactly 1½ turns.

5. Hold the adjusting screw from turning, and torque the new locknut 35 to 45 ft.-lbs.

6. Replace the downshift rod on the downshift lever.

FORD C3, C4, C4S OVERHAUL DIAGNOSIS CHART

CONDITION	CORRECTION	KEY
Excessively slow 1-2 shift.	1, 2, 5, 6, 7, 10, 18, 21, 27	1. Fluid level
Rough 1-2 shifts.	2, 5, 6, 7, 10, 21	2. Vacuum diaphragm unit/tube
Rough 2-3 shifts.	2, 5, 6, 7, 10, 21, 26, 36	3. Manual link
Incorrect/erratic shift points.	1, 2, 3, 4, 5, 12, 18, 21	4. Governor
Rough initial engagement in D1 or D2.	2, 5, 6, 7, 11, 21, 25	5. Valve body
Engine overspeeds on 2-3 shift.	1, 2, 3, 5, 6, 7, 10, 21, 26, 36	6. Pressure regulator
No 1-2, 2-3 upshift.	2, 3, 4, 5, 7, 10, 12, 21, 26, 27	7. Intermediate band
No 3-1 shift in D1, or 3-2 shift in D2.	4, 5	8. Reverse band
No forced downshift.	2, 5, 12	9. Reverse servo
Runaway engine on downshift.	2, 5, 6, 7, 10, 21, 27	10. Intermediate servo
No engine braking in 1st gear or manual low.	3, 4, 5, 8, 9, 18	11. Engine idle speed
Shifts 1-3 in D1 and D2.	2, 4, 5, 7, 10, 18	12. Downshift linkage
Rough 3-2 or 3-1 shift at closed throttle.	2, 5, 6, 10, 11	13. Converter drain plug
Slips or chatters in 1st gear.	1, 2, 5, 6, 21, 25, 27, 31	14. Oil pan and/or filler tube gasket seal
Excessive creep.	11, 23	15. Oil cooler and/or connections
Slips or chatters in 2nd gear.	1, 2, 5, 6, 7, 10, 18, 21, 25, 27	16. Manual or D1 shift-lever shaft seal
Slips or chatters in reverse gear.	1, 2, 5, 6, 8, 9, 10, 18, 26, 27, 36	17. Pipe plug, case side
No drive in D1.	1, 3, 5, 18, 21, 31	18. Check air pressure
No drive in D2.	1, 3, 5, 10, 18, 27, 31	19. Extension-housing-to-case gasket/washers
No drive in L.	1, 3, 5, 9, 10, 18, 27, 31	20. Extension-housing rear oil seal
No drive in R.	1, 3, 5, 8, 9, 10, 18, 26, 27, 36	21. Run a control pressure test
No drive regardless of shifter position.	1, 3, 5, 6, 18, 21, 27, 28	22. Poor engine performance
Lockup in D1.	26, 27, 29	23. Vehicle brakes
Lockup in D2.	8, 9, 26, 27, 29, 31	24. Speedometer driven-gear adapter seal
Lockup in L.	7, 10, 26, 27, 29	25. Forward clutch
Lockup in R.	7, 10, 25, 27, 29	26. Reverse/High clutch
Parking lock does not hold or binds.	3, 29	27. Hydraulic system leakage
Transmission overheats.	2, 6, 15, 21, 33	28. Front pump
Maximum speed too low, poor acceleration.	22, 23, 33	29. Parking brake linkage
Transmission noisy in N and P.	1, 6, 28, 30	30. Planetary assembly
Transmission noisy in any drive position.	1, 6, 25, 28, 30, 31	31. Planetary one-way clutch (sprag)
Fluid leaks.	1, 2, 9, 10, 13, 14, 15, 16, 17, 19, 20, 24, 32, 33, 35, 41	32. Engine rear oil seal
Car moves forward in N.	3, 25	33. Front oil pump seal
		34. Converter one-way clutch
		35. Front-pump-to-case seal/gasket
		36. Reverse/High clutch-piston air bleed valve

C3 SPECIFICATIONS *

SELECTIVE THRUST WASHERS (END PLAY CONTROL)
C3 TRANSMISSION

End Play 1970-78: .007-.032-in. 1979: .001-.025-in. (less gasket)	No. 1 Thrust Washer Front Pump Support (Selective)	Part Numbers	Thickness	ID Number
		74DT-7D014-EA	0.1091-0.1110	5
		74DT-7D014-DA	0.0929-0.0949	4
		74DT-7D014-CA	0.0768-0.0787	3
		74DT-7D014-BA	0.0610-0.0630	2
		74DT-7D014-AA	0.0488-0.0507	1

SELECTIVE SNAP RINGS

	HIGH CLUTCH					FORWARD CLUTCH			
Part Numbers	Thickness		Diameter		Part Numbers	Thickness		Diameter	
	Inches	MM	Inches	MM		Inches	MM	Inches	MM
E 860126-S	.0539	1.37	5.161	131.1	E 860115-S	.0539	1.37	4.925	125.1
E 860127-S	.0681	1.73	5.161	131.1	E 860116-S	.0681	1.73	4.925	125.1
E 860128-S	.0819	2.08	5.161	131.1	E 860117-S	.0819	2.08	4.925	125.1
E 860129-S	.0961	2.44	5.161	131.1	E 860118-S	.0961	2.44	4.925	125.1

CLUTCH PLATES – C3 TRANSMISSION

	Forward Clutch			High Clutch		
Model	Steel	Friction	Clearance	Steel	Friction	Clearance
2.3L	4	4	0.055-0.083	4	4	0.051-0.079
2.8, 3.3L	5	5	0.055-0.083	5	5	0.051-0.079

CHECKS AND ADJUSTMENTS
C3 TRANSMISSION

Operation	Specification
Transmission End Play	1970-78: .007-.032-in.; 1979: .001-.025 (less gasket)
Turbine and Stator End Play	Model 74DT-BKB New or Rebuilt — 0.044 Max., Used—0.060 Max. 1
Front (Intermediate Band) Adjustment	Remove and discard locknut. Install new locknut. Tighten adjusting screw to 10 ft-lbs.torque. Back off 1-1/2 turns. Hold screw and tighten locknut.

1 1977: .023 Max.; Used-.050 Max.

APPROXIMATE REFILL CAPACITY
C3 TRANSMISSION

All Cars With C-3 Transmission	U.S. Measure (Qts)	Imperial Measure (Qts)
All Engines	8	6-1/2

C3 TRANSMISSION TORQUE LIMITS

Item	Ft-Lbs.
Converter Housing to Case	27-39
Extension Housing to Case	27-39
Oil Pump to Converter Housing	7-10
Flywheel to Converter Housing	27-37 2
Main Control to Case	7-9
Plate to Valve Body	7-9
Servo Cover to Case	7-10
Inner Race — OWC — to Case	7-10
Oil Pan to Case	12-17
Governor to Collector Body	7-10
Converter Housing to Engine	28-38
Nut — Downshift Lever — Outer	7-11
Nut — Manual Lever — Inner	30-40
Neutral Switch to Case	12-15
Front Band Adjusting Locknut	35-45
Vacuum Diaphragm Retaining Clip to Case	15-23 ①
Oil Cooler Line or By-pass Tube to Connector	7-10
Connector to Case	10-15
Drain Plug — Converter	28-38 3
Flywheel to Crankshaft	48-53
Filler Tube to Engine Clip	28-38

① In-Lbs. 2 1979, 27-49 3 1979, 20-30

* A reverse servo piston return spring is not used in 1977 model DT-FA C-3 transmissions, nor in any 1978 or later models. The transmission was recalibrated to cover removal of the spring. All other 1977 C-3's do use the spring.

C4, C4S SPECIFICATIONS

TORQUE LIMITS C4 TRANSMISSION

Item	Ft-Lbs.	Item	Ft-Lbs.	Item	In-Lbs.
Converter to Flywheel	23-28	Pressure Gauge Tap	9-15	End Plates to Body	20-35
Converter Hsg. to Trans. Case	28-40	Band Adj. Screw Locknut to Case	35-45	Lower to Upper Valve Body	40-55
Front Pump to Trans. Case	38-40	Yoke to Output Shaft	60-120	Reinforcement Plate to Body	40-55
Overrunning Clutch Race to Case	13-20	Reverse Servo Piston to Rod	12-20 1	Screen and Lower to Upper Valve Body	40-55
Oil Pan to Case	12-16	Converter Drain Plug	20-30	Neutral Switch to Case	55-75
Rear Servo Cover to Case	12-20	Manual Valve Inner Lever to Shaft	30-40	Separator Plate to Lower Valve Body	40-55
Stator Support to Pump	12-20	Downshift Lever to Shaft	12-16	Control Assy. to Case	80-120
Converter Cover to Converter Hsg.	12-16	Filler Tube to Engine	20-25	Gov. Body to Collector Body	80-120
Intermediate Servo Cover to Case	16-22	Filler Tube to Pan	32-42	Cooler Line Fittings	80-120
Diaphragm Assy. to Case Bolt	28-40	Transmission to Engine	40-50	Detent Spring to Lower Valve Body	80-120
Extension Assy. to Trans. Case	28-40	Distributor to Engine	12-20	Upper Valve Body to Lower Valve Body	80-120
Engine to Transmission	23-33 2			Oil Tube Connector	80-120

1 On a Pinto, tighten to 10 ft-lbs. and back off 5/8 turn.

2. 1979 Pinto/Bobcat/Mustang/Capri, 28-38; All Others, 40-50.

SELECTIVE THRUST WASHERS C4 TRANSMISSION

THRUST WASHER NO. 1

Nylon Thrust Washer W/Tangs	Color of Washer
0.053-0.0575	Red
0.070-0.0745	Green
0.087-0.0915	Natural (White)
0.104-0.1085	Black
0.121-0.1255	Yellow

THRUST WASHER NO. 2

No. Stamped On Washer	Metal Thrust Washer
1	0.041-0.043
2	0.056-0.058
3	0.073-0.075
Spacer	0.032-0.036 ①

① This is a selective spacer. The spacer must be installed next to the stator support to obtain correct end play.

CLUTCH PLATES—C4 TRANSMISSION

Model	Forward Clutch			Reverse Clutch		
	External Spline (Steel)	Internal Spline (Comp.)	Free Pack Clear (Inches)	External Spline (Steel)	Internal Spline (Comp.)	Free Pack Clear. (Inches)
PEB	3	4	0.025-0.050	3	3	0.050-0.071
PEA, PEE, PEF	4	5		4	4	
PEJ-B	2	3		2	2	
PEJ-C, D, E, G, H	2	3		3	3	

CHECKS AND ADJUSTMENTS C4 TRANSMISSION

Operation	Specification
Transmission End Play	0.008-0.042 inch (Selective Thrust Washers Available)
Turbine and Stator End Play	New or rebuilt 0.023 max. Used 0.050 max.
Intermediate Band Adjustment	Remove and discard lock nut. Adjust screw to 10 ft-lbs. torque, then back off 1-3/4 turns. Install new lock nut and torque to specification.
Low-Reverse Band Adjustment	Remove and discard lock nut. Adjust screw to 10 ft-lbs. torque, then back off 3 turns. Install new lock nut and torque to specification.
Selective Snap Ring Thickness	0.050-0.054, 0.064-0.068, 0.078-0.082, 0.092-0.096

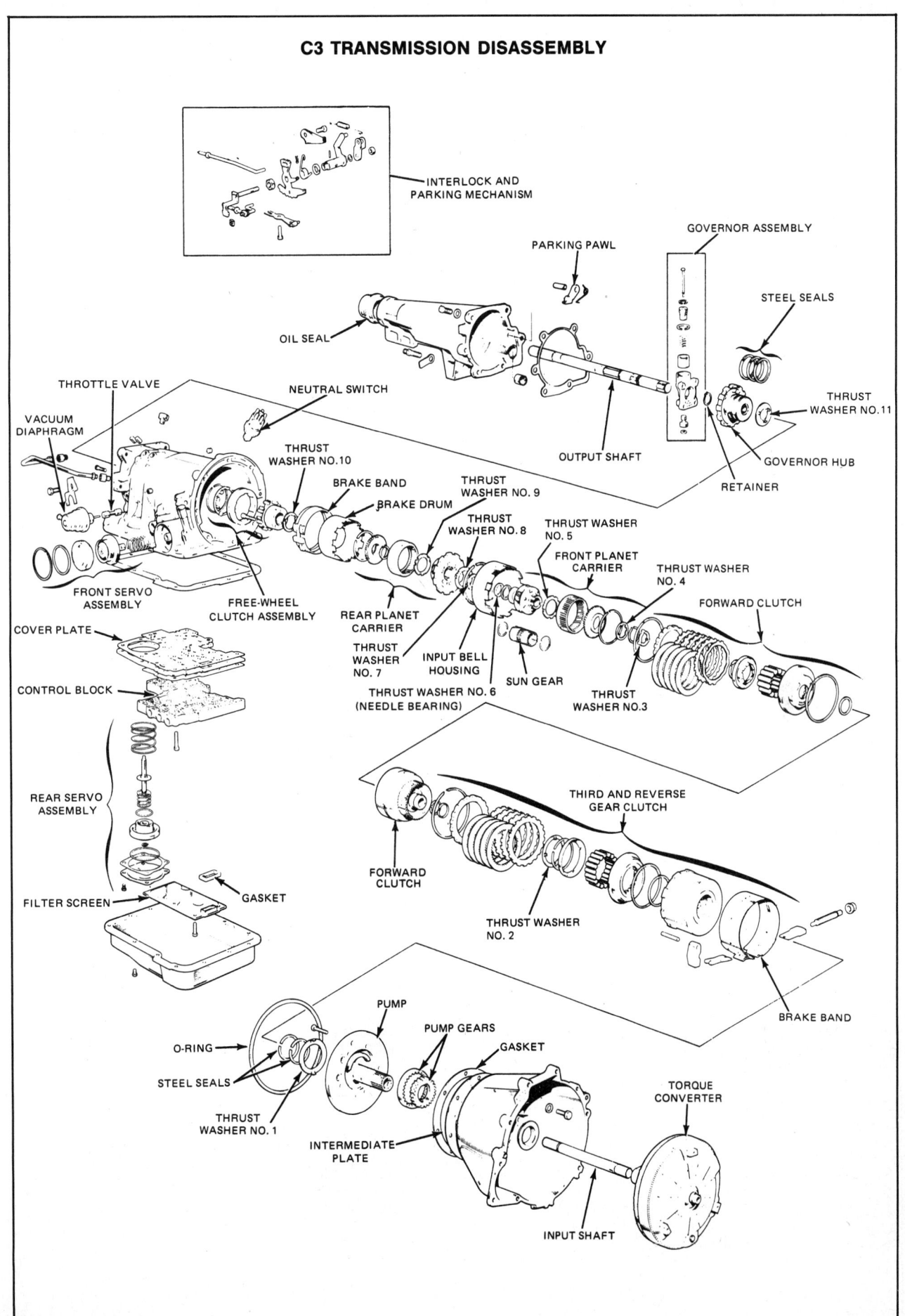

C3 TRANSMISSION DISASSEMBLY

C4, C4S TRANSMISSION DISASSEMBLY

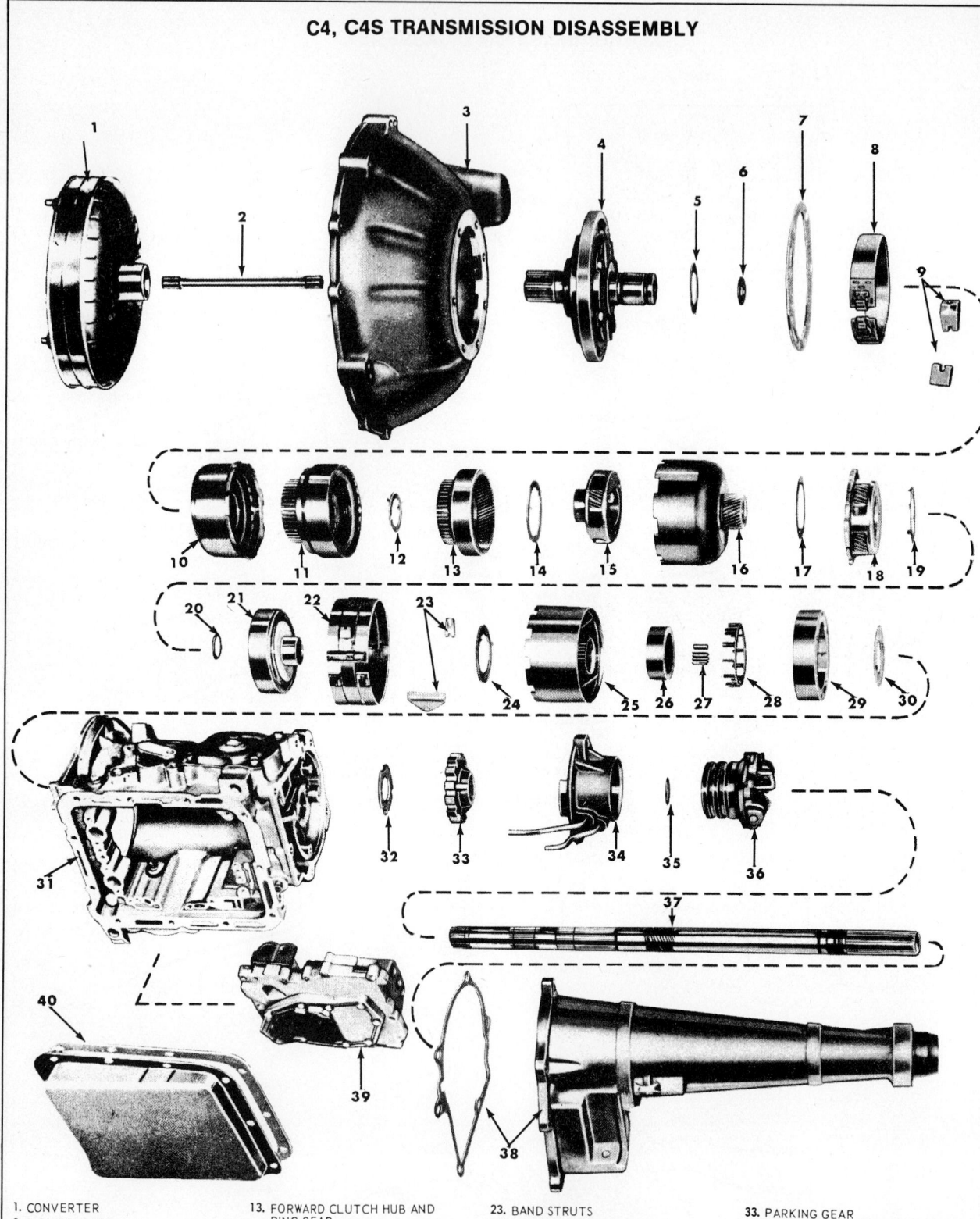

1. CONVERTER
2. INPUT SHAFT
3. CONVERTER HOUSING
4. FRONT PUMP
5. THRUST WASHER NO. 1
6. THRUST WASHER NO. 2
7. FRONT PUMP GASKET
8. INTERMEDIATE BAND
9. BAND STRUTS
10. REVERSE AND HIGH CLUTCH DRUM
11. FORWARD CLUTCH AND CYLINDER
12. THRUST WASHER NO. 3

13. FORWARD CLUTCH HUB AND RING GEAR
14. THRUST WASHER NO. 4
15. FRONT PLANET CARRIER
16. INPUT SHELL, SUN GEAR — AND THRUST WASHER NO. 5
17. THRUST WASHER NO. 6
18. REVERSE PLANET CARRIER
19. THRUST WASHER NO. 7
20. SNAP RING
21. REVERSE RING GEAR AND HUB
22. LOW AND REVERSE BAND

23. BAND STRUTS
24. THRUST WASHER NO. 8
25. LOW AND REVERSE DRUM
26. ONE-WAY CLUTCH INNER RACE
27. ROLLER (12) AND SPRING (12)
28. SPRING AND ROLLER CAGE
29. ONE-WAY CLUTCH OUTER RACE
30. THRUST WASHER NO. 9
31. CASE
32. THRUST WASHER NO. 10

33. PARKING GEAR
34. GOVERNOR DISTRIBUTOR SLEEVE
35. SNAP RING
36. GOVERNOR AND DISTRIBUTOR ASSY (AUTOMATIC ONLY)
37. OUTPUT SHAFT
38. EXTENSION HOUSING AND GASKET
39. CONTROL VALVE BODY
40. OIL PAN AND GASKET

C4, C4S CONTROL (VALVE) BODY DISASSEMBLY

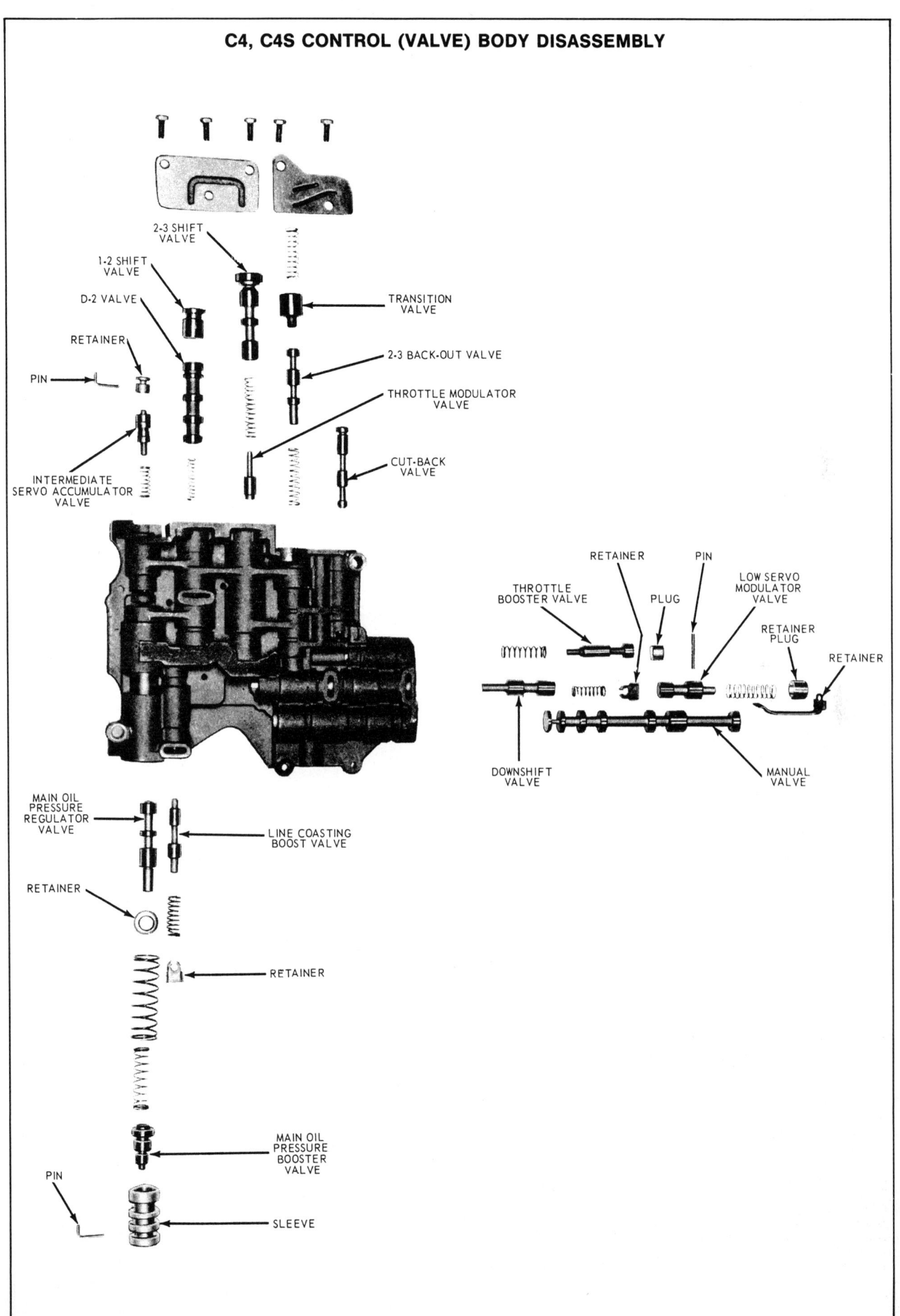

2-3 SHIFT VALVE

1-2 SHIFT VALVE

D-2 VALVE

RETAINER

PIN

TRANSITION VALVE

2-3 BACK-OUT VALVE

THROTTLE MODULATOR VALVE

CUT-BACK VALVE

INTERMEDIATE SERVO ACCUMULATOR VALVE

THROTTLE BOOSTER VALVE

RETAINER

PLUG

PIN

LOW SERVO MODULATOR VALVE

RETAINER PLUG

RETAINER

DOWNSHIFT VALVE

MANUAL VALVE

MAIN OIL PRESSURE REGULATOR VALVE

LINE COASTING BOOST VALVE

RETAINER

RETAINER

MAIN OIL PRESSURE BOOSTER VALVE

PIN

SLEEVE

C3 CONTROL VALVE—BODY DISASSEMBLY

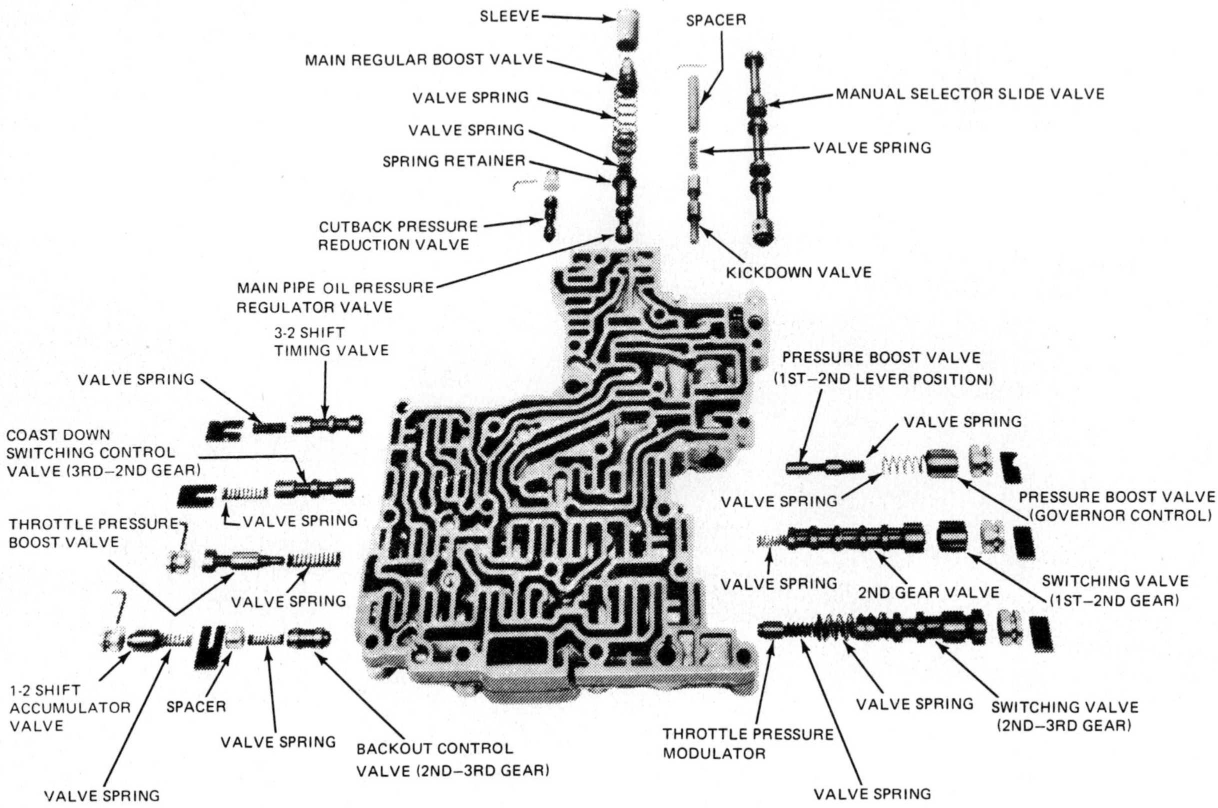

SLEEVE

SPACER

MAIN REGULAR BOOST VALVE

MANUAL SELECTOR SLIDE VALVE

VALVE SPRING

VALVE SPRING

VALVE SPRING

SPRING RETAINER

CUTBACK PRESSURE
REDUCTION VALVE

KICKDOWN VALVE

MAIN PIPE OIL PRESSURE
REGULATOR VALVE

3-2 SHIFT
TIMING VALVE

PRESSURE BOOST VALVE
(1ST–2ND LEVER POSITION)

VALVE SPRING

VALVE SPRING

COAST DOWN
SWITCHING CONTROL
VALVE (3RD–2ND GEAR)

VALVE SPRING

PRESSURE BOOST VALVE
(GOVERNOR CONTROL)

VALVE SPRING

THROTTLE PRESSURE
BOOST VALVE

SWITCHING VALVE
(1ST–2ND GEAR)

VALVE SPRING

VALVE SPRING

2ND GEAR VALVE

1-2 SHIFT
ACCUMULATOR
VALVE

SPACER

SWITCHING VALVE
(2ND–3RD GEAR)

VALVE SPRING

VALVE SPRING

BACKOUT CONTROL
VALVE (2ND–3RD GEAR)

THROTTLE PRESSURE
MODULATOR

VALVE SPRING

VALVE SPRING

VALVE SPRING

HOW TO: Ford C4 Overhaul

1. Unbolt and remove the oil pan and gasket to begin C4 transmission disassembly. Discard gasket. As each part is removed, clean with solvent.

2. Remove the screws holding the valve body in place, and lift it out. A three-piece unit, the valve body is set to one side for servicing later.

3. Remove the seven bolts that hold the converter housing to the transmission case, then lift the housing off and set it to one side.

4. Back off intermediate band adjuster until band struts are loose, and then remove them to eliminate band tension when removing other parts.

5. Pry gently between input shell and forward clutch cylinder to push the front pump assembly forward enough so that it can be easily removed.

6. When the input shaft is withdrawn, the reverse and high clutch drum and the forward clutch cylinder will come out as a unit. Set in solvent for cleaning.

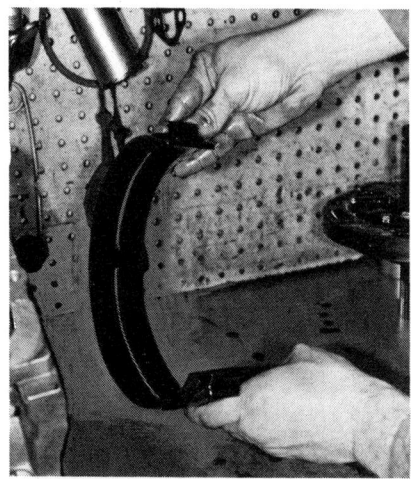

7. Remove the intermediate band, and inspect it carefully for signs of cracking, burning, etc. Problems with this band are fairly common.

8. Lift out thrust washer and forward clutch hub, removing each part carefully to prevent accidental nicking or burring of bearing/mating surfaces.

9. Another thrust washer and the front planet carrier come out next. Planetary gears rarely malfunction, but the carrier should be inspected anyway.

HOW TO: Ford C4 Overhaul`

10. Lift out the input shell with sun gear and two thrust washers. The C4 uses 10 thrust washers between subassemblies; note their positions carefully.

11. Withdraw the reverse planet carrier and the No. 7 thrust washer from their positions inside the low/reverse drum. Clean and inspect carefully.

12. Before the reverse ring gear and hub can be taken out of the housing, a snap ring must be removed from the output shaft. Check gear/hub for defects.

13. Once the low/reverse band adjuster has been backed off, the low/reverse drum can be removed from the input shaft and placed in solvent for cleaning.

14. To withdraw low/reverse band from transmission case, pull band struts out of position. Inspect band surface for defects as you did the intermediate.

15. Removing the transmission vacuum unit is an easy job with the special tool shown here. Without it, you'll have to work at it a little harder.

16. After removing the vacuum unit gasket and control rod, the primary throttle valve is removed. A pencil-type magnet will speed up the process.

17. Unbolt and remove the extension housing from the transmission case, then pull off and throw away the old gasket. Reassemble with new gaskets.

18. To withdraw the output shaft with governor and distributor assembly attached, pull straight back on the shaft. It should come out easily.

19. Unbolt the governor distributor sleeve and carefully pry it away from the transmission case, and remove to expose the parking gear.

20. The parking gear and another thrust washer simply lift out of place. Note that the washer fits between the gear and the transmission case.

21. Lift, do not pry, the parking pawl and its return spring off the retaining pin. If you try to pry the spring off, it will pop into the air and can get lost.

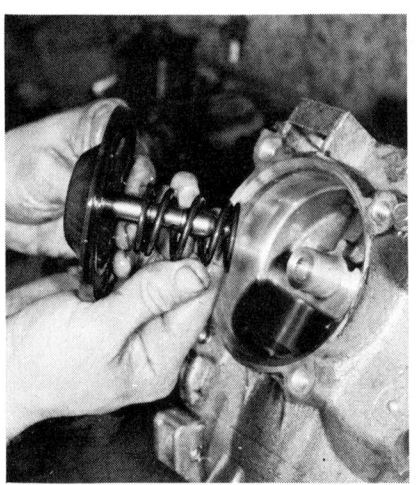

22. Remove the low/reverse servo cover, and lift out the piston and return spring. The piston seal is bonded; if defective, entire piston unit must be replaced.

23. Also remove the intermediate servo on the opposite side of the transmission case. Piston separates from cover, and all seals should be replaced.

24. One-way clutch assembly is only unit remaining in transmission case. When removed, inner/outer races separate, with bearings/springs falling out.

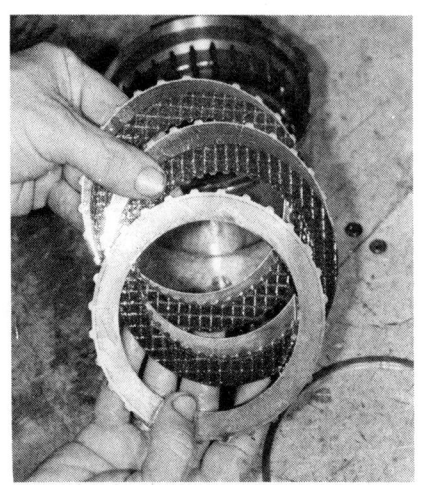

25. After removing retaining snap ring from reverse/high clutch, lift out the drive and driven clutch plates, inspecting all surfaces carefully.

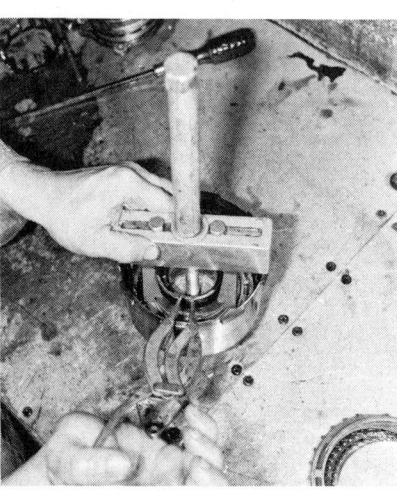

26. Spring compressor is required to remove piston-spring snap ring from clutch hub, because pressure exerted by return springs is considerable.

27. Lift out piston, remove and replace the outer seal from the piston, and the inner seal from the clutch drum before beginning reassembly.

HOW TO: Ford C4 Overhaul

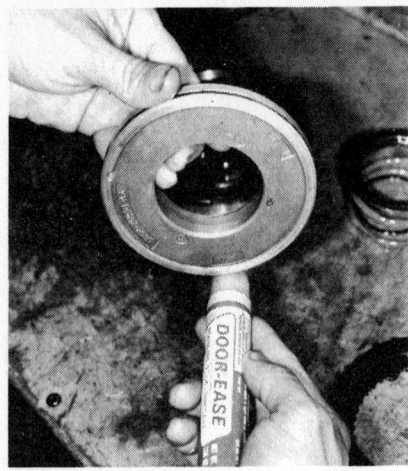

28. Apply a dry stick lubricant, such as Door-Ease, to the new seal surfaces to make the replacement of the piston in the clutch drum easier.

29. Compress return springs, replace snap ring and insert clutch plates alternately, starting with a steel plate. Install pressure plate last.

30. Remove forward-clutch snap ring and plates. Depress disc spring to remove the second snap ring, and lift the disc spring out. Inspect all parts.

31. Lift the clutch piston out next. Remove and replace the outer seal from the piston and the inner seal from the clutch hub. Use a dry-stick lubricant.

32. Install lubricated piston, replace disc spring and snap ring. Insert the thin pressure plate, clutches, thick pressure plate and snap ring.

33. Unbolt the oil screen from the valve body, and lift off both screen and gasket. Take care not to lose the throttle pressure limit valve and spring.

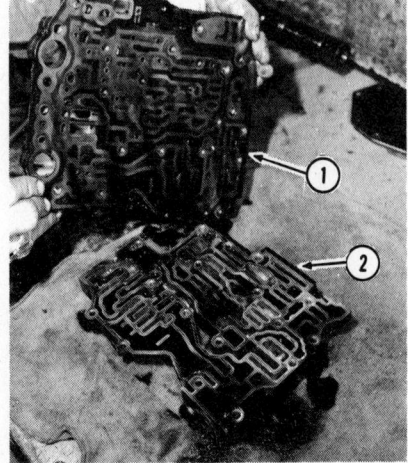

34. To separate the valve body, two attaching screws must be removed from the upper valve body (1) and nine screws from the lower section (2).

35. There are three shuttle valves and a servo check contained within the valve body. Because they are rubber, they cannot be removed with a magnet.

36. Manual-valve retaining ring is unclipped to slide manual valve from the body. Ring holds valve in bore during shipment, and should be discarded.

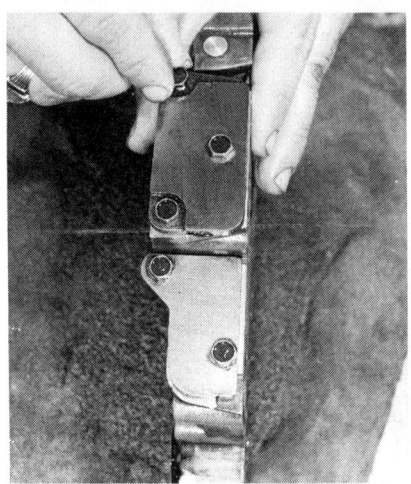

37. Removing these two cover plates provides access to the shift, transition and cut-back valves. Once removed, all five will come out easily.

38. Begin removal with the cut-back valve. As each of the valves is removed, line it up beside the valve body in its correct order of removal.

39. The correct order here is a spring, transition valve, the 2-3 back-out valve and spring. Maintaining the sequence is an absolute necessity.

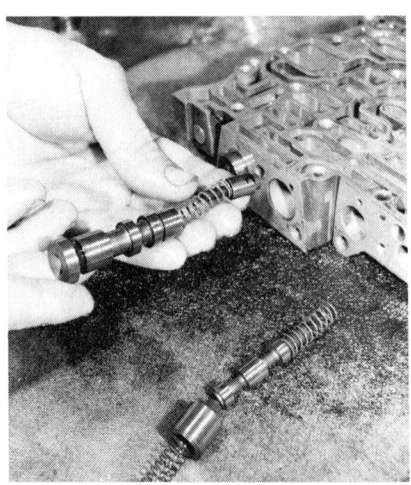

40. A spring separates the 2-3 shift valve and the throttle modulator valve. When replacing these, make certain the long neck fits into the spring.

41. The 1-2 shift valve and D-2 shift valve mate end-to-end, and are followed by a spring. Since spring tension values are different, don't confuse them.

42. Be sure to replace the throttle pressure-limit valve and spring when reassembling the valve body. It fits into place right here.

43. Unbolt and remove the stator support from the front pump housing. Check the support bushings in each end of the stator for excessive wear.

44. Remove the drive and driven gears from the pump housing, and check their teeth and surfaces. These seldom give trouble and should be in good shape.

45. Use a scraper or putty knife to clean off the old gasket completely. Try to get it all without scratching the mounting surface.

HOW TO: Ford C4 Overhaul

46. Remove and discard four seal rings from stator support, installing new ones. You'll need snap ring tool to do the job—these are sharp and brittle.

47. Apply grease around the pump housing, because it helps you to position the new gasket correctly, and will hold it in place during reassembly.

48. Transmission reassembly begins with the installation of the one-way clutch. Insert both races, then alternate bearings with springs until all 12 are in.

49. Locate parking pawl over its retaining pin, and engage the short end of the return spring in the cutout. Hold and secure the other end of spring.

50. Grease the inside surface of the parking gear, and fit the correct thrust washer in place. Then flip it over and insert the gear in the case.

51. Position the governor distributor sleeve, and tap it into place with a hammer. Make sure the two tubes have sufficient clearance in the case.

52. Once the governor distributor sleeve has been bolted down, remove and replace the seal rings on the governor distributor assembly before replacing it.

53. Insert the output shaft into the transmission case. Since new seal rings can make this a tight fit, work it in place as carefully as possible.

54. Replace and bolt the extension housing in place. Torque limits specified by Ford are 28 ft.-lbs., and bolts should be torqued to that specification.

55. Now lubricate the low/reverse servo with clean transmission fluid, and position it in the transmission case bore right over the return spring.

56. A cover seal is installed, but adding a bit of Permatex around the flange is also good insurance against an unwanted leak developing at a later date.

57. Install new seal on intermediate servo cover, and lubricate with clean transmission fluid. Insert return spring and servo; torque bolts to 20 ft.-lbs.

58. Slide low/reverse drum over the case, and fit low/reverse drum over the output shaft. Fit band struts in place, and tighten the adjustment to hold.

59. After positioning a thrust washer in the low/reverse drum, insert the reverse ring gear and hub, then clip the snap ring into place.

60. The reverse planet carrier uses a thrust washer at each end. The one with the tangs goes at the rear of the carrier, and fits into reverse gear.

61. Once the reverse planet carrier is installed in the low/reverse drum, insert the input shaft with the sun gear and work it into place.

62. A thrust washer is fitted to each end of the front planet carrier before installing it in the input shell. The carrier must be seated properly.

63. Another thrust washer is positioned in the forward clutch hub and ring gear, then the assembly is positioned in the reverse/high drum.

HOW TO: Ford C4 Overhaul

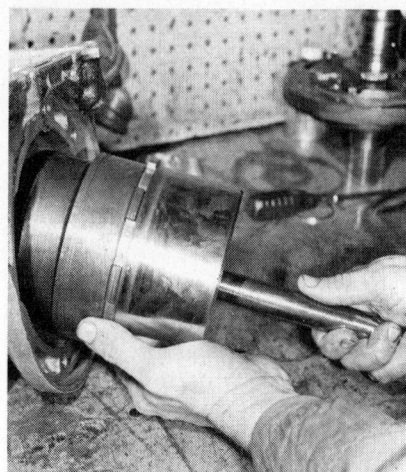

64. Hold gear train package together, with input shaft installed, and insert entire assembly into transmission case to engage the output shaft.

65. After working the intermediate band in place, set the band struts in position, and tighten the adjuster to hold the band correctly.

66. The remaining two thrust washers are fitted at the rear of the front pump assembly, which is then fitted in place over the input shaft.

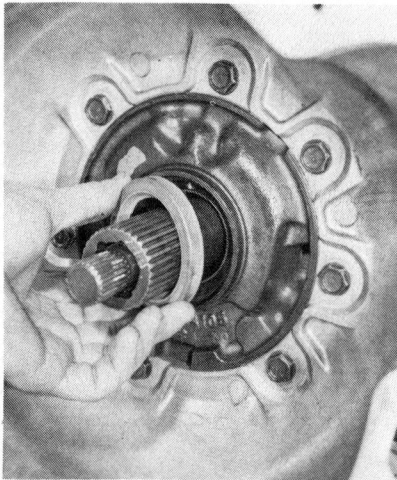

67. Bolt converter housing to transmission case, and torque each bolt 28 to 40 ft.-lbs. in a cross pattern, then remove and replace front pump seal.

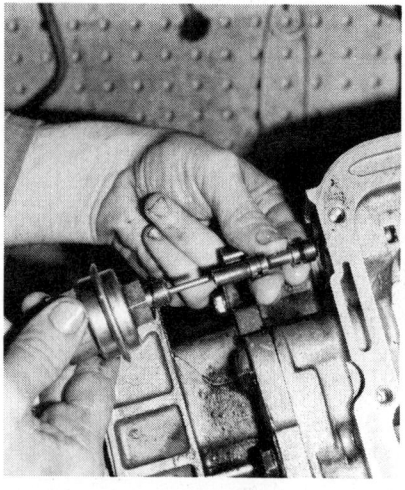

68. Reinstall primary throttle valve, control rod, gasket and transmission vacuum unit at back of case. Some are push-in units, others are bolted on.

69. Locate inner downshift lever between downshift lever stop and valve when reinstalling control valve body. Torque bolts 80 to 120 in.-lbs.

70. The intermediate band adjustment should be made carefully by tightening the adjuster all the way in, and then backing it off exactly 1¾ turns.

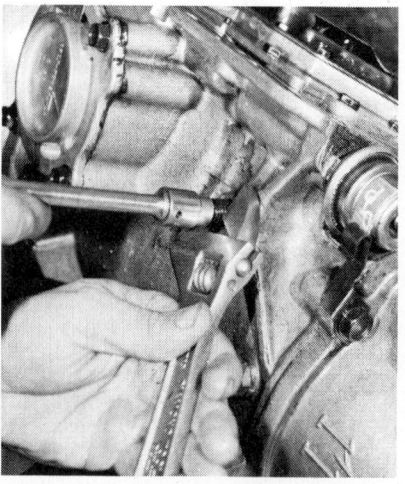

71. The low/reverse band adjustment is made in the same way, but backed off two full turns. Torque adjustment-screw locknuts 35 to 45 ft.-lbs.

72. The final step is to install new oil pan gasket, and fit pan in place, torquing the pan bolts 12 to 16 ft.-lbs. C4 overhaul is complete.

FORD MOTOR COMPANY
Ford C6
APPLICATION
1970-79 Continental
1970-78 Cougar
1975-76 Cougar XR7
1970 Fairlane
1970-79 Ford
1970-79 Lincoln
1970-79 Mercury
1970-76 Montego
1970-78 Mustang, Mustang II
1970-78 Thunderbird
1970-76 Torino, Elite
1977-78 LTD II
1978-79 Mark V

DESCRIPTION
Ford's heavy-duty automatic transmission, the C6 is very similar in design and operation to the smaller C4, but uses a low/reverse clutch instead of the C4's low/reverse band. The hydraulic control system, gear train and clutch combinations are otherwise very similar.

(Type F fluid is used through 1976; all 1977 and later C-6 models use Type CJ fluid.)

BAND ADJUSTMENT

INTERMEDIATE BAND
(Lower Left Side of Case Toward the Front)

1. Remove and discard the adjusting screw locknut. This has a fluid-sealing feature which breaks when the locknut is loosened.

2. Install a new locknut, and torque the adjusting screw to 10 ft.-lbs.

3. Back off the adjusting screw exactly one turn on 1970 models, 1½ turns on 1971 and later models.

4. Hold the adjusting screw from turning, and torque the new locknut 35 to 45 ft.-lbs.

FORD C6 OVERHAUL DIAGNOSIS CHART

CONDITION	CORRECTION
No drive in D, 2 or 1.	3, 5, 17, 20, 24, 26
Rough initial engagement in D or 2.	2, 5, 6, 10, 20, 24
Incorrect/erratic shift points.	1, 2, 3, 4, 5, 11, 17, 20
Rough 1-2 shift.	2, 5, 6, 7, 9, 20
Rough 2-3 shift.	2, 5, 6, 7, 9, 17, 20, 25, 35
1-2 shift too long.	1, 2, 5, 6, 7, 9, 17, 20, 26
Engine overspeeds on 2-3 shift.	1, 2, 3, 5, 6, 7, 9, 20, 25, 35
No 1-2, 2-3 upshift.	2, 3, 4, 5, 7, 9, 11, 20, 25, 26
No 3-1 shift in D.	4, 5
No forced downshift.	2, 5, 11
Runaway engine on downshift.	2, 5, 6, 7, 9, 20, 26
Rough 3-1 or 3-2 shift, closed throttle.	2, 5, 6, 9, 10
Shifts 1-3 in D.	2, 4, 5, 7, 9, 17
No engine braking in 1st gear.	3, 4, 5, 8, 17
Excessive creep.	10
Slips or chatters in 1st gear, D.	1, 2, 5, 6, 20, 24, 26, 30
Slips or chatters in 2nd gear.	1, 2, 5, 6, 7, 9, 17, 20, 24, 26
Slips or chatters in reverse gear.	3, 5, 20, 30
No drive in D.	1, 3, 5, 9, 17, 20, 26
No drive in 2.	1, 3, 5, 17, 20, 26
No drive in 1.	1, 3, 5, 8, 17, 20, 25, 26, 35
No drive in R.	1, 3, 5, 6, 17, 20, 26, 27
No drive regardless of shifter position.	26, 28
Lockup in D.	8, 25, 26, 28, 30
Lockup in 2.	26, 28
Lockup in 1.	24, 26, 28
Lockup in R.	3, 28
Parking lock does not hold or binds.	2, 6, 14, 20, 33, 36
Transmission overheats.	22, 23, 33
Maximum speed too low, poor acceleration.	1, 6, 17
Transmission noisy in any gear position.	1, 6, 24, 27, 29, 30
Transmission noisy in N or P.	1, 12, 13, 14, 15, 16, 18, 31, 32, 34
Fluid leaks.	2, 9, 19, 21
Car moves forward in N.	3, 24

KEY
1. Fluid level
2. Vacuum Diaphragm unit
3. Manual linkage
4. Governor
5. Valve body
6. Pressure regulator
7. Intermediate band
8. Low/reverse clutch
9. Intermediate servo
10. Engine idle speed
11. Downshift linkage
12. Converter drain plugs
13. Oil pan gasket, seal or filler tube
14. Oil cooler and connections
15. Manual/downshift lever shaft seal
16. Case ⅛-in. pipe plugs
17. Perform air-pressure check
18. Extension-housing-to-case gasket
19. Extension-housing rear oil seal
20. Perform control pressure check
21. Speedometer driven-gear-adapter seal
22. Engine performance
23. Vehicle brakes
24. Forward clutch
25. Reverse/High clutch
26. Hydraulic system leakage
27. Front pump
28. Parking linkage
29. Planetary assembly
30. Planetary one-way clutch
31. Engine rear oil seal
32. Front pump oil seal
33. Converter one-way clutch
34. Front-pump-to-case gasket/seal
35. Reverse/High clutch-piston air bleed valve
36. Converter pressure check valves

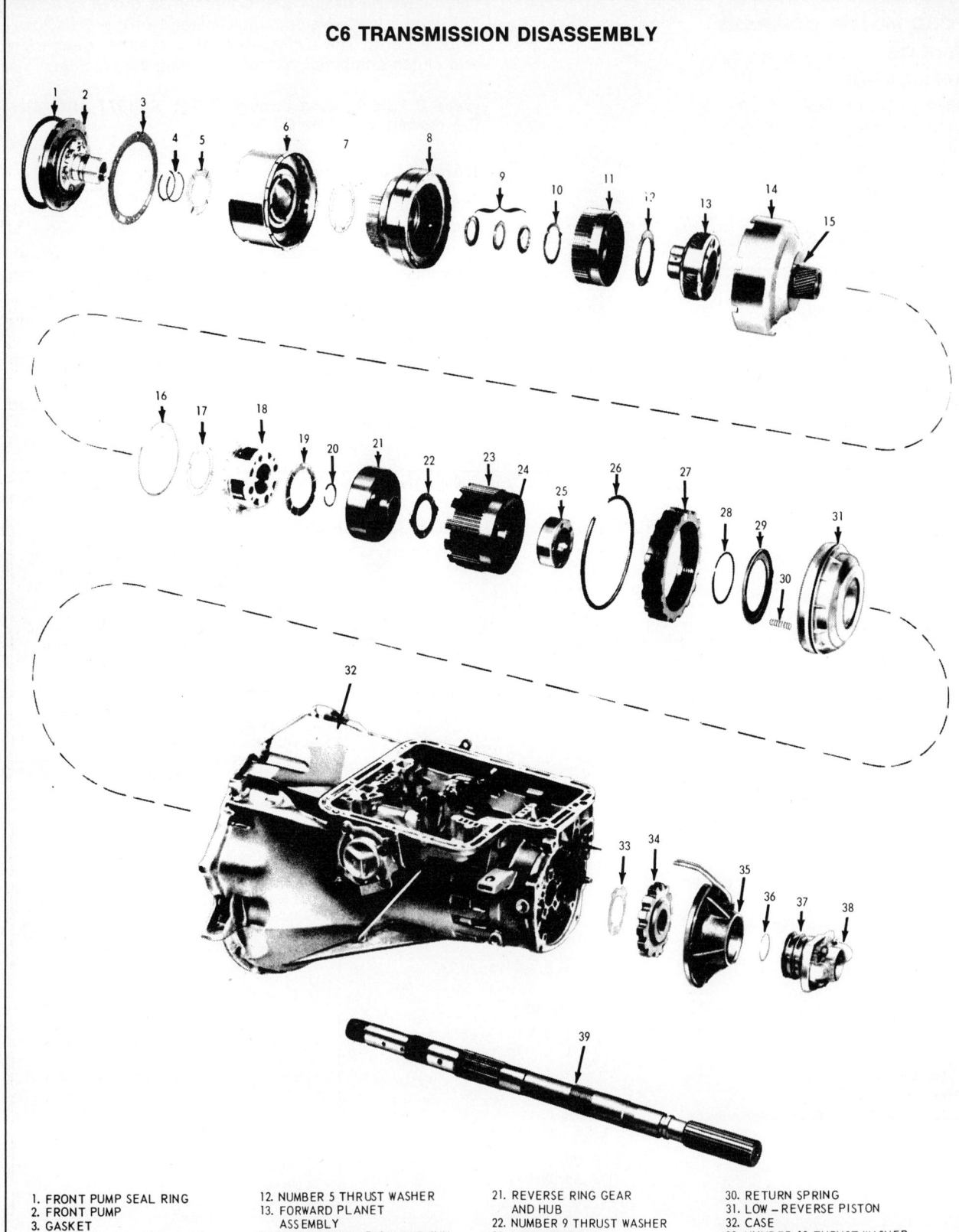

C6 TRANSMISSION DISASSEMBLY

1. FRONT PUMP SEAL RING
2. FRONT PUMP
3. GASKET
4. SEAL
5. NUMBER 1 THRUST WASHER (SELECTIVE)
6. REVERSE – HIGH CLUTCH ASSEMBLY
7. NUMBER 2 THRUST WASHER
8. FORWARD CLUTCH ASSEMBLY
9. NUMBER 3 THRUST WASHER
10. NUMBER 4 THRUST WASHER
11. FORWARD CLUTCH HUB ASSEMBLY

12. NUMBER 5 THRUST WASHER
13. FORWARD PLANET ASSEMBLY
14. INPUT SHELL - 7D064 AND SUN GEAR ASSEMBLY
15. NUMBER 6 THRUST WASHER
16. SNAP RING
17. NUMBER 7 THRUST WASHER
18. REVERSE PLANET ASSEMBLY
19. NUMBER 8 THRUST WASHER
20. REVERSE RING GEAR AND HUB RETAINING RING

21. REVERSE RING GEAR AND HUB
22. NUMBER 9 THRUST WASHER
23. LOW – REVERSE CLUTCH HUB
24. ONE-WAY CLUTCH
25. ONE-WAY CLUTCH INNER RACE
26. SNAP RING
27. LOW–REVERSE CLUTCH
28. SNAP RING
29. LOW – REVERSE PISTON RETURN SPRING RETAINER

30. RETURN SPRING
31. LOW – REVERSE PISTON
32. CASE
33. NUMBER 10 THRUST WASHER
34. PARKING GEAR
35. GOVERNOR DISTRIBUTOR SLEEVE
36. SNAP RING
37. GOVERNOR DISTRIBUTOR
38. GOVERNOR
39. OUTPUT SHAFT

C6 VALVE BODY DISASSEMBLY

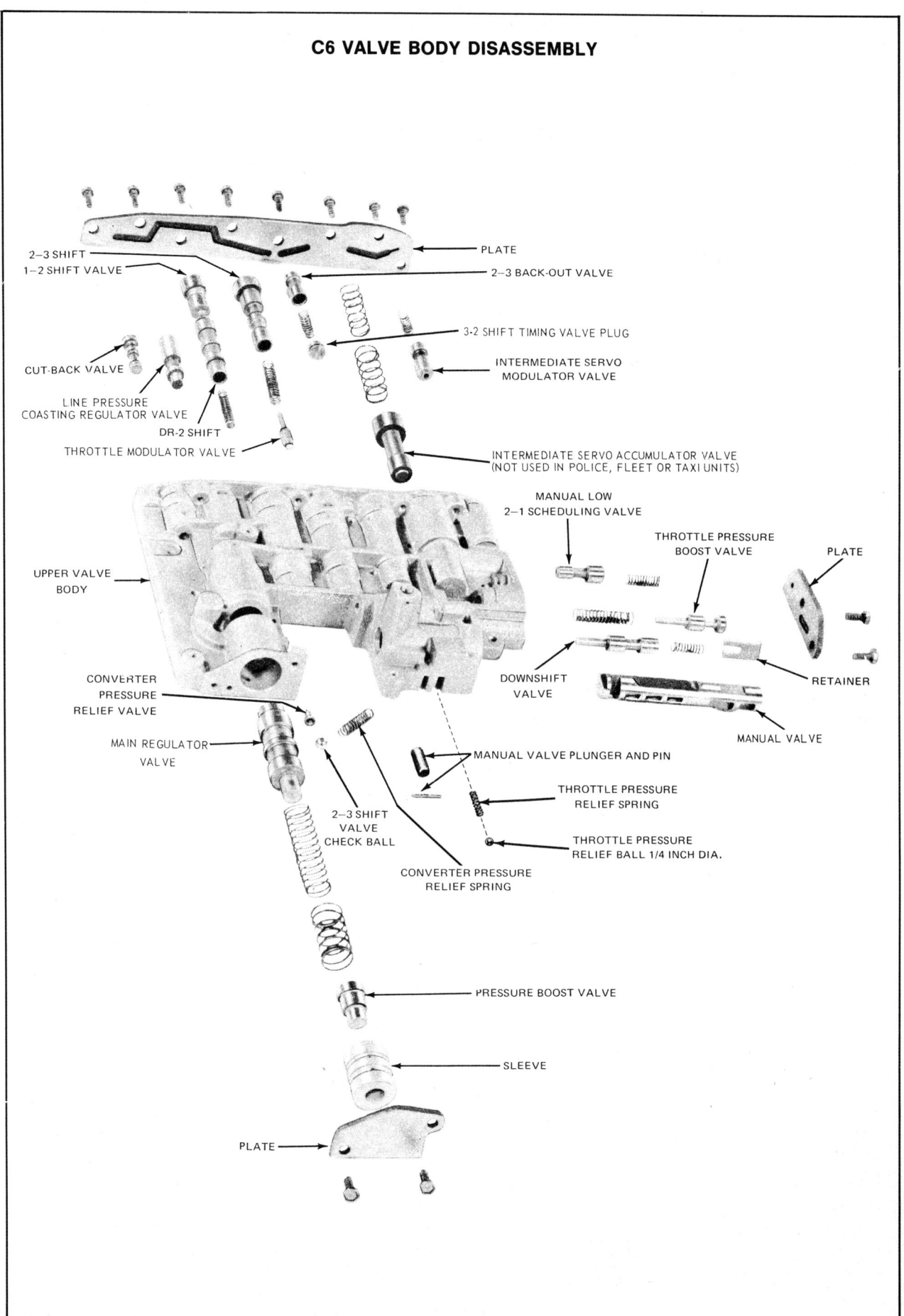

C6 SPECIFICATIONS

SELECTIVE THRUST WASHERS
C6 TRANSMISSION

Identification Color	Thrust Washer Thickness—Inch
Blue	0.056-0.060
Natural (White)	0.073-0.077
Red	0.088-0.092

CHECKS AND ADJUSTMENTS
C6 TRANSMISSION

Operation	Specification	
Transmission End Play	0.008-0.044 (Selective Thrust Washers Available)	
Turbine and Stator End Play	New or rebuilt 0.021 max. Used 0.040 max. ①	
Intermediate Band Adjustment	Remove and discard lock nut. Adjust screw to 10 ft-lbs torque, then back off 1-1/2 turns, install new lock nut and tighten lock nut to specification.	
Forward Clutch Pressure Plate to Snap Ring Clearance	0.031-0.044 ②	
Selective Snap Ring Thicknesses	0.058-0.060, 0.065-0.069, 0.074-0.078, 0.083-0.087, 0.092-0.096	
	Transmission Models	
	PGA, PJA	All Others
Reverse High Clutch Pressure Plate to Snap Ring Clearance	0.022-0.036	0.027-0.043
Selective Snap Ring Thicknesses	0.056-0.060, 0.065-0.069, 0.074-0.078, 0.083-0.087, 0.092-0.096	

① To check end play, exert force on checking tool to compress turbine to cover thrust washer wear plate. Set indicator at zero.

② 1978 on; .021-.046-in.

TORQUE LIMITS
C6 TRANSMISSION

Item	Ft-Lbs.	Item	Ft-Lbs.
Converter to Flywheel	20-30	Converter Cover to Converter Hsg.	30-60
Front Pump to Trans Case	16-30	Pressure Gauge Tap	6-12
Overrunning Clutch Face to Case	18-25	Band Adj. Screw Locknut to Case	35-45
Oil Pan to Case	12-16	Cooler Tube Connector Lock	20-35
Stator Support to Pump	12-16	Converter Drain Plug	14-28
Diaphragm Ret. Clip to Case	12-16	Manual Valve Inner Lever to Shaft	30-40
Guide Plate to Case	12-16	Downshift Lever to Shaft	12-16
Intermediate Servo Cover to Case	14-20	Filler Tube to Engine	20-25
Distributor Sleeve to Case	12-16	Transmission to Engine	40-50
Extension Assy. to Trans. Case	25-35	Engine Rear Cover to Conv. Hsg.	20-30
Oil Connector to Case	10-14	Oil Line Connector to Case Fitting	12-18
Item	**In-Lbs.**	**Item**	**In-Lbs.**
End Plates to Body	20-45	Control Assy to Case	95-125
Inner Downshift Lever Stop	20-45	Gov. Body to Collector Body	80-120
Reinforcement Plate to Body	20-45	Detent Spring to Case	80-120
Screen and Lower Body to Upper Valve Body	40-55		

HOW TO: Ford C6 Overhaul

1. With transmission mounted horizontally, remove 17 pan bolts, lift pan off and discard gasket. Remove eight valve body bolts and lift unit from case.

2. Remove primary throttle valve from the transmission case, then loosen band adjustment screw, and remove two struts holding band in place.

3. Unbolt extension housing and disengage the vent tube; then remove housing and gasket. Discard gasket and clean the gasket mounting surface.

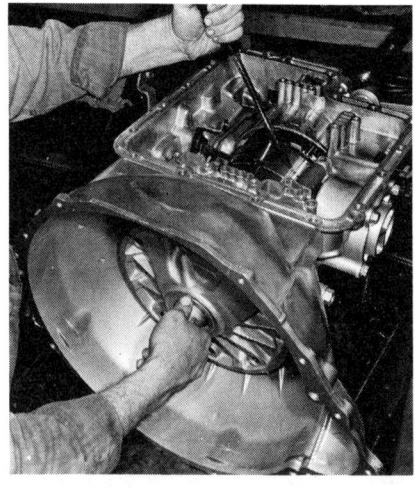

4. Remove front pump attaching bolts, and use a screwdriver, as shown, to pry against the input shell and move the gear train ahead for pump removal.

5. The reverse/high and forward clutch assemblies will come out with the front pump. Remove the forward clutch hub assembly and thrust washers.

6. The #5 thrust washer and forward planetary assembly can be withdrawn from the case. The C6 uses 10 thrust washers; keep track of their location.

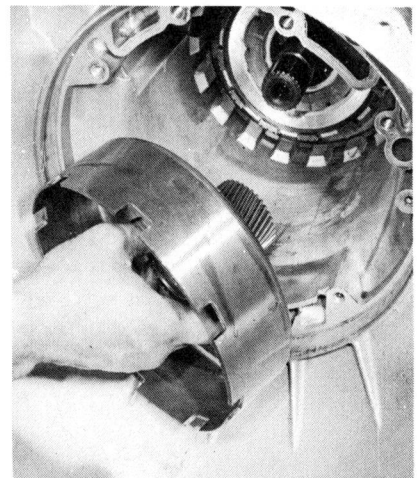

7. Disengage the sun gear from the output shaft, and withdraw input shell and sun gear assembly. There's another thrust washer on the face of rear planet.

8. Pry the large selective snap ring free from the low/reverse clutch hub. Be careful not to damage the surface of the #7 thrust washer (arrow).

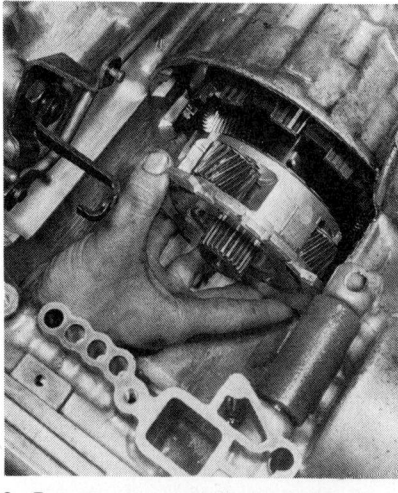

9. Remove the #7 thrust washer and reverse planetary assembly from the low/reverse clutch hub. Use snap ring pliers to remove the hub retaining ring.

HOW TO: Ford C6 Overhaul

10. Withdraw the reverse ring gear and hub assembly and the #9 thrust washer. This empties the low/reverse clutch hub; rotate clockwise to remove it.

11. The output shaft with governor and governor distributor installed can now be removed. Withdraw the shaft by pulling from the rear of the case.

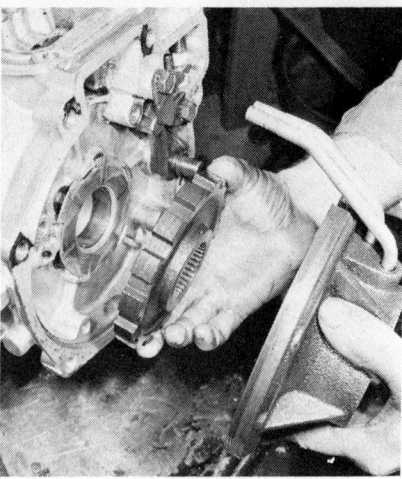

12. Unbolt the governor distributor sleeve, and disengage the tubes. Then remove the sleeve, parking gear and #10 thrust washer (shown on case).

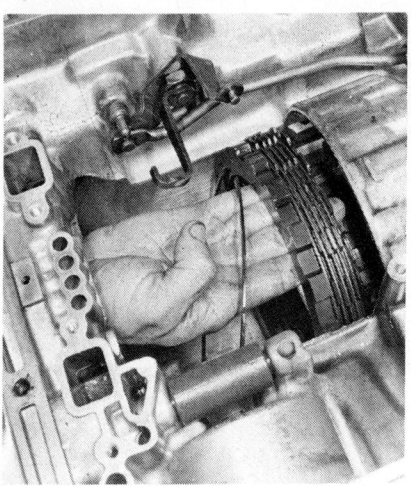

13. Pry the large snap ring free, and remove the ring and the low/reverse clutch pack. This leaves only the low/reverse piston in the case.

14. The low/reverse piston is a real bear to remove. Leave it in case unless bad seals are suspected. Remove snap ring/retainer to free piston springs.

15. Check spring condition, and replace if broken. Tilt transmission case upright to make spring replacement on the piston shafts easier.

16. Reinstall spring retainer and snap ring, then return case to a horizontal position. Vacuum modulator comes off next; tool shown makes removal easy.

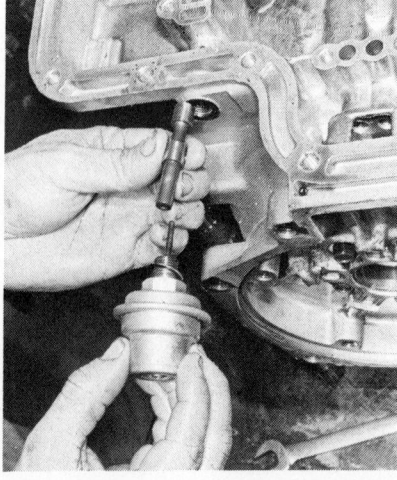

17. Remove vacuum modulator and push rod. Design of this unit varies with model year. Modulator frequently goes bad, and should be replaced with a new one.

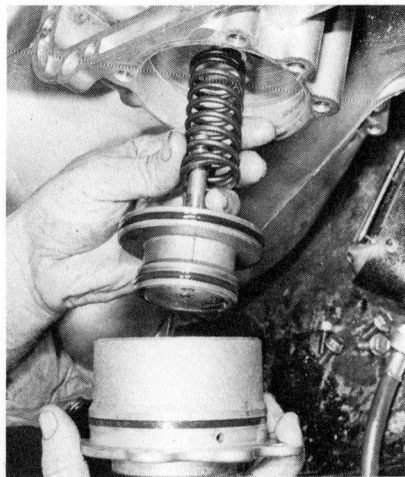

18. Remove the intermediate servo cover. Servo piston and spring should come out easily. If not, apply air pressure to the port in the servo piston rod.

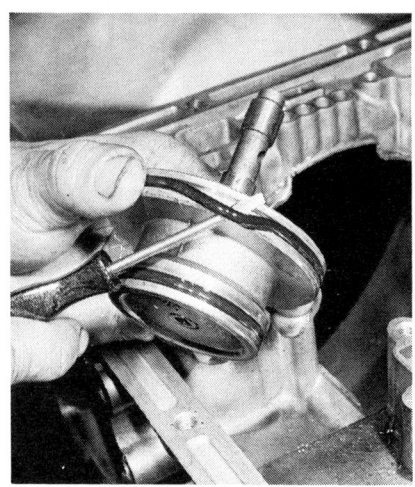

19. Servo cover is fitted with one O-ring seal, servo piston with two O-rings. Remove seals, as shown, and install new ones lubricated with trans fluid.

20. Wipe servo housing clean. Fit piston inside the cover, and place spring on piston rod; then insert assembly, with piston rod in port, and secure with bolts.

21. With #10 thrust washer and parking gear in place, guide distributor sleeve tubes in place in the case and slide sleeve over gear, replacing bolts.

22. Remove the four bolts holding governor assembly in place, and slide housing from output shaft. Governor assembly should be disassembled and inspected.

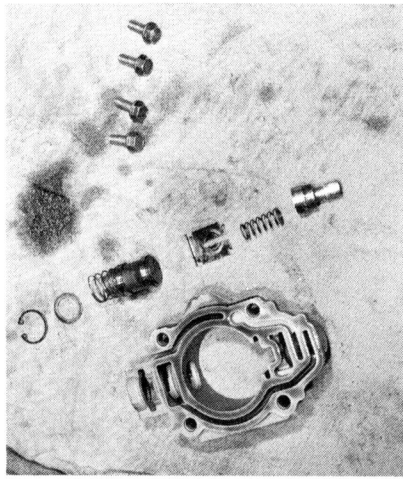

23. Disengage one snap ring and one retaining sleeve, and the components shown can be removed. Check valve surfaces carefully for nicks and burrs.

24. Remove and replace the governor distributor seal rings. Reinstall governor housing assembly to distributor, and torque the bolts to specifications.

25. Forward clutch hub assembly contains a sprag gear (one-way clutch) at the rear. Inspect but do not remove sprag unless it is worn or broken.

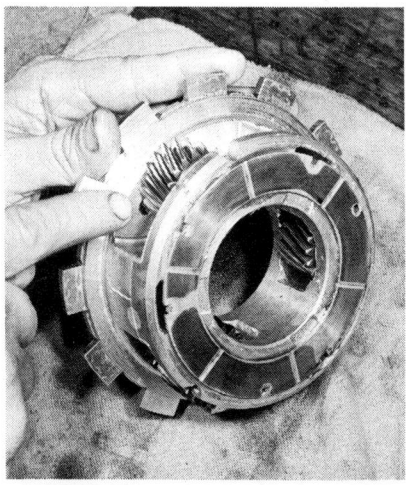

26. Inspect thrust surfaces and planetary gear teeth on both forward and reverse planetary assemblies for excessive wear and/or damaged teeth.

27. Use grease to hold the #8 and #9 thrust washers in place when installing reverse ring gear and planetary assembly in low/reverse clutch hub.

HOW TO: Ford C6 Overhaul

28. Inspect the sun gear teeth and bushing condition, then check the notched edges of the input shell for signs of improper engagement or wear.

29. Install the tanged #5 thrust washer on the front planetary gear, sliding the planetary on the sun gear, with the thrust washer facing outward.

30. Repeat the same procedure used in Step 29 with the #4 thrust washer and the forward clutch hub assembly. Make sure gear teeth engage properly.

31. Inspect the intermediate brake band for burning, scoring or excessive wear. Band replacement is always a good idea when overhauling a transmission.

32. Separate the forward clutch from the reverse/high clutch assembly. Remove snap ring and clutches, then compress the reverse/high spring retainer.

33. With snap ring removed from reverse/high clutch assembly, remove spring compressor. Lift off spring retainer to remove and inspect springs.

34. Use compressed air, if necessary, to free piston from the clutch hub—direct it through piston apply hole in hub. Replace two seals and lubricate edge.

35. Reinstall piston in the clutch hub, and replace all springs in their respective positions, replacing any that are distorted or broken.

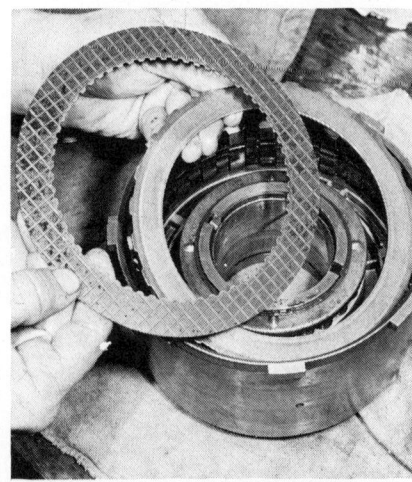

36. Replace spring retainer, compress to install snap ring, then insert clutch pack. Alternate driven with drive plates, and install pressure plate/snap ring.

37. Look for this needle-bearing thrust washer and retaining races in the front of the forward clutch before beginning disassembly. Clean and lubricate.

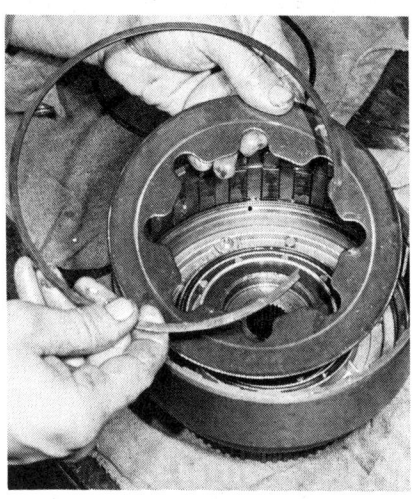

38. Pry snap ring from forward clutch assembly, remove rear pressure plate, clutch pack and forward pressure plate, then second snap ring and disc spring.

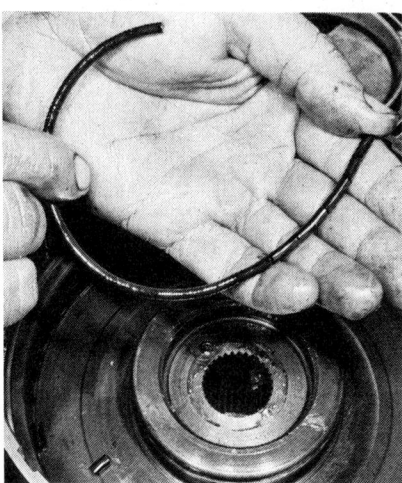

39. Remove the piston, using air pressure if necessary. Replace outer piston seal and inner seal located in clutch cylinder—this one is shot.

40. Coat piston edge with wax-type lubricant, and reinstall in cylinder. Fit disc spring and snap ring in place. Forward pressure-plate lips face down.

41. Remove selective thrust washer from the front pump stator support, and replace the seal rings; then unbolt the stator from the pump housing.

42. Gears must be reinstalled in housing exactly as they are; scribe an alignment mark across the drive and driven gears and the housing.

43. After inspecting both gears for wear or damage, replace in housing according to the scribed marks. Check clearance according to specifications.

44. Before replacing the stator support to the front pump housing, carefully inspect all machined surfaces on both for wear and/or damage.

45. Unbolt and remove the oil screen/gasket from the lower valve body. Wash screen thoroughly in clean solvent, and blow dry with compressed air.

HOW TO: Ford C6 Overhaul

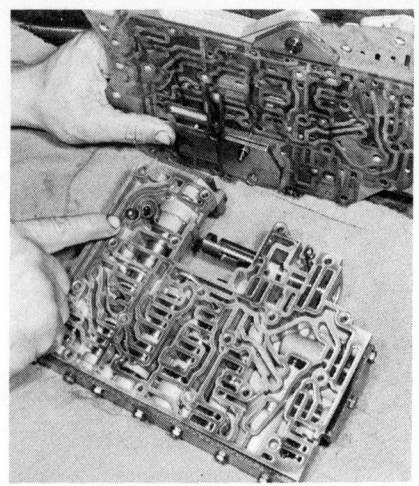

46. Wipe gasket with clean cloth. Remove five upper-to-lower valve-body bolts, then turn unit over to remove seven lower valve-body bolts and separate.

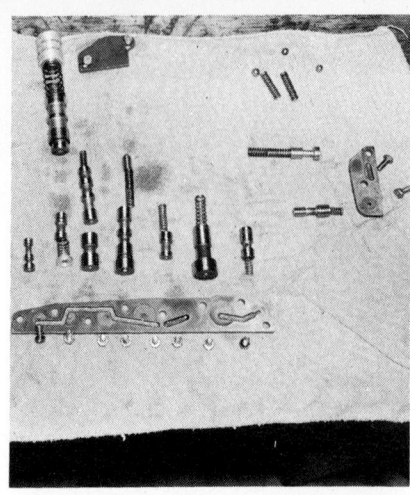

47. Remove the check ball, and carefully disassemble the unit to remove the parts as shown above. Wash valve body, dry with air, and reinstall the parts.

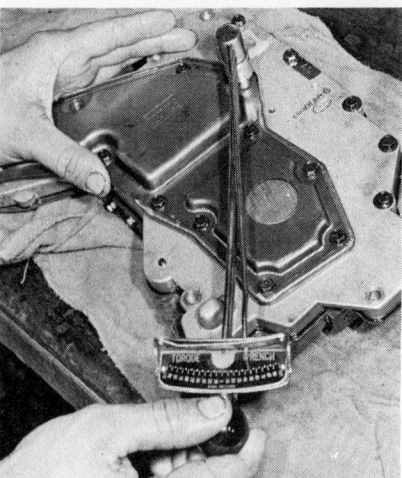

48. Replace upper and lower valve bodies, installing attaching bolts. Torque 40 to 55 in.-lbs.; replace oil screen, and torque to the same specifications.

49. Reinstall the low/reverse clutch pack in the transmission case, and install the snap ring. Alternate clutch and driven plates when installing.

50. Now fit the low/reverse clutch hub, with one-way clutch installed, in the case. Be sure to replace the #9 thrust washer at front of hub.

51. Install the reverse ring gear and hub, the #8 thrust washer, the reverse planetary assembly and the #7 thrust washer in that order.

52. With governor bolted to distributor sleeve, install output shaft through low/reverse clutch hub and through components installed in case.

53. Replace the retaining snap ring which holds all the components in place. Make sure ring seats properly, then check output shaft operation.

54. The sun gear and input shell are replaced next. Rotate sun gear/input shell assembly onto the output shaft to help seat it properly.

55. Remember that needle bearing thrust washer and its two races? Install bearing between races, and insert it in rear of front planetary before replacing.

56. Install forward clutch assembly and #2 thrust washer in the reverse/high clutch assembly, then add intermediate band, and replace in the case.

57. Make sure the assembly engages the output shaft, and replace the strut at each end of the band. Tighten adjustment screw to hold band in place.

58. Fit a new gasket to the rear of the front pump, and install on input shaft with #1 thrust washer (arrow) in place. Work pump until properly seated.

59. Position pump on the case, taking care not to damage the large seal on the housing outside diameter; install and torque bolts to specifications.

60. With a new gasket on the rear of the case, position the extension housing, then install and torque the attaching bolts to specifications.

61. Install the valve body in the case, making sure that the levers properly engage the valves. Torque the eight attaching bolts to specifications.

62. Fit a new oil pan gasket, and replace oil pan on case. Install the 17 oil-pan attaching bolts, and torque on opposite sides to specifications.

63. To adjust band, install locknut and torque adjusting screw 10 ft.-lbs., then back it off exactly 1½ turns; torque locknut to specs while holding screw.

FORD MOTOR COMPANY
Ford FMX, CW

FMX APPLICATION

1970-79 Cougar	1977-79 LTD II, Thunderbird
1970 Fairlane	1971-76 Torino, Elite
1970-79 Ford	
1970 Maverick	
1970-79 Mercury	
1970-76 Montego	
1970-73 Mustang	
1970 Thunderbird	

CW APPLICATION

1974-76 Ford

DESCRIPTION

The Ford FMX automatic transmission bears a marked resemblance to the Borg-Warner design used by American Motors as the Shift-Command, and has been called by a variety of names during its lengthy use by Ford—Select Shift, Cruise-O-Matic, Merc-O-Matic. The CW automatic transmission is similar in appearance to the FMX, but few internal parts are interchangeable. The transmission has limited application in the full-size Ford line from 1974 on. Both the FMX and CW transmissions contain a torque converter, planetary gear train, two multiple disc clutches, a one-way clutch and a hydraulic control system. The FMX has two adjustable bands, the intermediate and the low/reverse, while only the low/reverse CW band is adjustable.

BAND ADJUSTMENT

FMX INTERMEDIATE BAND
(Internal)

1. Drain the transmission fluid, remove the oil pan, the fluid screen and clip.
2. Loosen the front servo adjusting-screw locknut.
3. Pull the servo actuating rod back and insert a ¼-in. spacer between the servo piston stem and adjusting screw. Torque the adjusting screw to 10-in.-lbs.
4. Remove the spacer, and tighten the adjusting screw an extra three-quarter turn.
5. Hold the adjusting screw from turning, and torque the locknut 20 to 25 ft.-lbs.
6. Replace the fluid screen and clip, and install the oil pan with a new gasket.
7. Refill the transmission to the specified level with Type F transmission fluid.

FMX LOW/REVERSE BAND
(Upper Right Side of Case)

1. Clean the dirt from the adjusting screw, and oil the screw threads.
2. Loosen adjusting screw locknut, torque screw to 10 ft.-lbs.
3. Back off the adjusting screw exactly 1½ turns.
4. Hold the adjusting screw from turning, and torque the locknut 35 to 45 ft.-lbs.

CW LOW/REVERSE BAND
(Upper Right Side of Case)

1. Clean the dirt from the adjusting screw, and oil the screw threads.
2. Loosen adjusting screw locknut, torque screw to 10 ft.-lbs.
3. Back off the adjusting screw exactly 1¼ turns.
4. Hold the adjusting screw from turning, and torque the locknut 35 to 50 ft.-lbs.

FORD FMX
Overhaul Diagnosis Chart

CONDITION	CORRECTION
Engagements	
Harsh.	3, 6
Delayed forward.	1, 27
Delayed reverse.	1
None.	1, 11, 12, 13, 15
No forward D.	1, 2, 9, 27
No forward 2.	1, 2, 27
No reverse.	1, 5, 8
No neutral.	3
Upshifts	
No 1-2.	1, 14, 26
No 2-3.	1, 5, 14, 20, 26
Shift points too high.	1, 14
Shift points too low.	1
Upshift Quality	
1-2 delayed followed by 2-3 shift.	1
2-3 slips.	1, 5, 7, 14, 20
1-2 harsh.	2
2-3 harsh.	6
1-2 ties up.	6, 10
Downshifts	
No 2-1 in D.	9, 26
No 2-1 in 1.	8, 26
No 3-2.	7, 26
Shift points too high.	1
Shift points too low.	1

CONDITION	CORRECTION
Forced Downshifts	
2-1 slips.	2, 12, 27
3-2 slips.	1, 5, 7, 20
3-1 shifts above—mph.	1, 7
2-1 harsh.	1, 2, 9
3-2 harsh.	5, 6
Reverse	
Slips or chatters.	1, 3, 5, 8, 20
Tie up.	1, 3
Line Pressure	
Low idle pressure.	1, 13
Low stall pressure.	1, 13, 26
Stall Speed	
Too low (200 rpm or more).	15
Too high D.	1, 2, 9, 11, 15, 21, 22, 27
Reverse too high.	5, 8, 11, 15, 21, 22
Others	
Poor acceleration.	15, 26
Noisy in N.	4, 6, 15, 16
Noisy in P.	4, 15, 16
Noisy in 1st or 2nd only.	16, 18, 23
Noisy in all gears.	15, 16, 18
Parking brake does not hold.	17
Oil out breather/fill tube.	1, 24, 25
Ties up in D, 1.	1, 6
Ties up in 2nd/3rd gear.	1, 6, 10
Chatters—D, 2 or 1.	1, 2, 27

KEY
1. Seal rings missing, leaking or broken
2. Front clutch slipping, worn plates or faulty parts
3. Front clutch seized or distorted plates
4. Front clutch hub thrust washer missing (detectable in N, P, R only)
5. Rear clutch slipping, worn or faulty parts
6. Rear clutch seized or distorted parts
7. Front band worn or broken
8. Rear band worn or broken
9. One-way (sprag) clutch slipping or incorrectly installed
10. One-way (sprag) clutch seized
11. Broken input shaft
12. Pump drive tangs or converter hub broken
13. Pump worn
14. Downshift solenoid
15. Converter
16. Pump
17. Parking linkage
18. Planetary assembly
19. Fluid distributor sleeve in output shaft (V-8)
20. Rear clutch piston ball check leaks
21. Broken output shaft
22. Broken gears
23. Forward sun gear thrust washer missing
24. Breather baffle missing
25. Fluid aerated or overfull
26. Output shaft plug missing (6-cyl.)
27. Front clutch piston check valve leaks

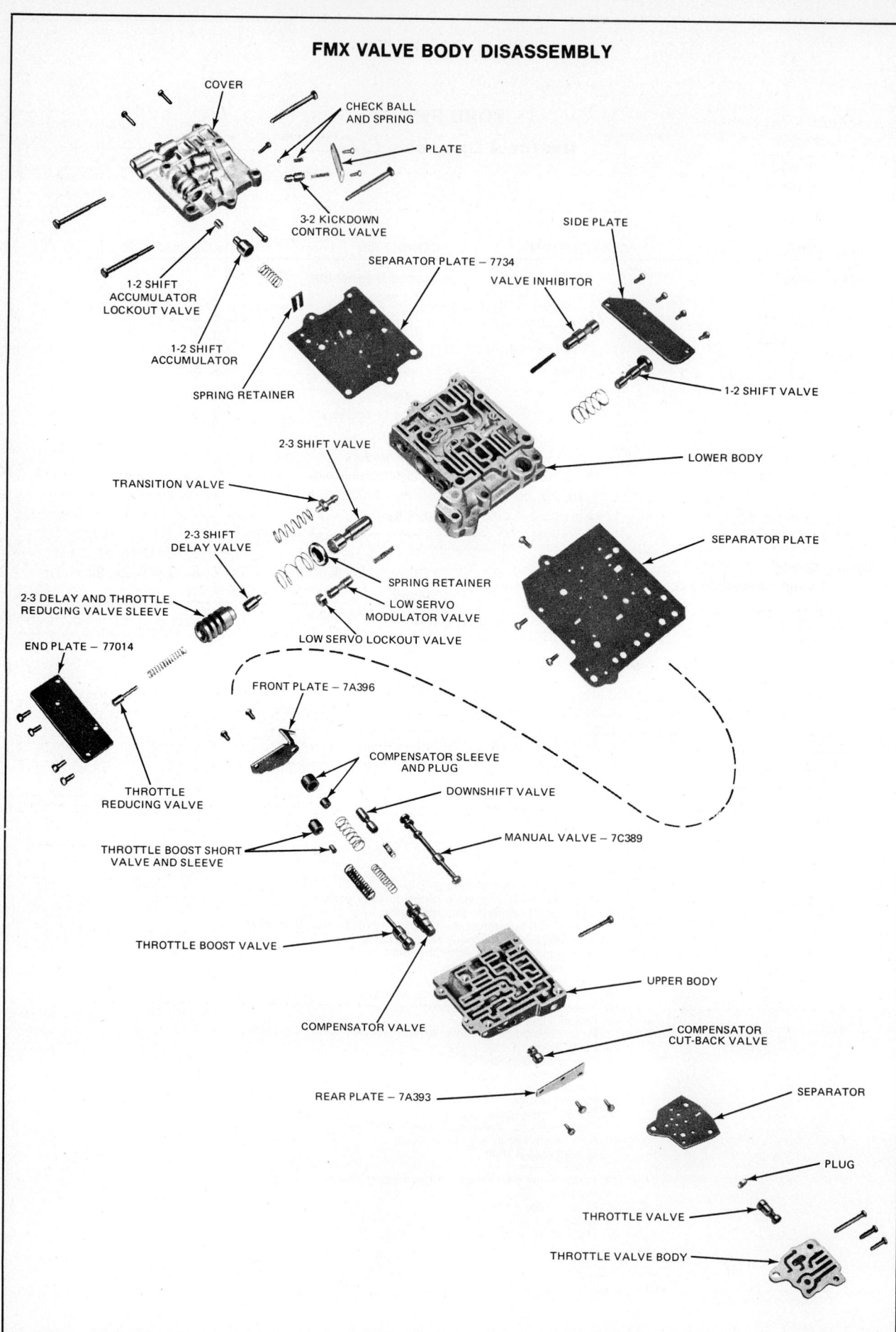

FMX VALVE BODY DISASSEMBLY

COVER

CHECK BALL
AND SPRING

PLATE

3-2 KICKDOWN
CONTROL VALVE

SIDE PLATE

1-2 SHIFT
ACCUMULATOR
LOCKOUT VALVE

SEPARATOR PLATE — 7734

VALVE INHIBITOR

1-2 SHIFT
ACCUMULATOR

SPRING RETAINER

1-2 SHIFT VALVE

2-3 SHIFT VALVE

TRANSITION VALVE

LOWER BODY

2-3 SHIFT
DELAY VALVE

SEPARATOR PLATE

SPRING RETAINER

2-3 DELAY AND THROTTLE
REDUCING VALVE SLEEVE

LOW SERVO
MODULATOR VALVE

LOW SERVO LOCKOUT VALVE

END PLATE — 77014

FRONT PLATE — 7A396

COMPENSATOR SLEEVE
AND PLUG

THROTTLE
REDUCING VALVE

DOWNSHIFT VALVE

THROTTLE BOOST SHORT
VALVE AND SLEEVE

MANUAL VALVE — 7C389

THROTTLE BOOST VALVE

UPPER BODY

COMPENSATOR VALVE

COMPENSATOR
CUT-BACK VALVE

REAR PLATE — 7A393

SEPARATOR

PLUG

THROTTLE VALVE

THROTTLE VALVE BODY

FMX SPECIFICATIONS

APPROXIMATE REFILL CAPACITIES
FMX TRANSMISSION

Qts.	U.S. Measure	Imp. Measure
All Car Lines	11	9 1/4

SELECTIVE THRUST WASHERS
FMX TRANSMISSION

Identification No.	Thrust Washer Thickness – Inch
By Thickness	0.061-0.063
	0.067-0.069
	0.074-0.076
	0.081-0.083

CLUTCH PLATES
FMX TRANSMISSION

Trans. Model	Forward Clutch				Rear Clutch		
	Steel Plates	Friction Plates	Selective Plate Thickness	Selective Plate Identification	Steel Plate	Friction Plates	Free Pack Clearance
PHA	3	4₁	0.0565-0.0605	No Stripe	3₂	3	
			0.0705-0.0745	One Stripe			
PHB	4	5₁	0.0845-0.0885	Two Stripes	4₂	4	0.030-0.055
PHC			0.0985-0.1025	Three Stripes			

① Last plate (Friction) in forward clutch is selective. Install thickest plate in pack that will be a minimum of 0.010 inch below input shaft shoulder in cylinder. All other friction plates in pack are thinnest available.

② Plus one external tabbed waved plate installed next to piston.

CHECKS AND ADJUSTMENTS
FMX TRANSMISSION

Operation	Specification
Transmission End Play Check	0.010-0.029 (Selective Thrust Washers Available)
Turbine and Stator End Play Check	New or rebuilt 0.023 max., Used 0.050 max.
Front Band Adjustment (Use 1/4 inch spacer between adjustment screw and servo piston stem)	Adjust screw to 10 in.-lbs. torque. Remove spacer, hold screw then tighten screw an extra ¾ turn. Torque locknut to 20-25 ft.-lbs.
Rear Band Adjustment	Loosen locknut, adjust screw to 10 ft.-lbs. Back off exactly 1½ turns, hold screw and torque locknut to 35-40 ft.-lbs.
Primary Sun Gear Shaft Ring End Gap Check	0.002-0.009
Rear Clutch Selective Snap Ring Thickness	0.060-0.064, 0.074-0.078, 0.088-0.092, 0.102-0.106

TORQUE LIMITS FMX TRANSMISSION

Item	Ft-Lb.	Item	Ft-Lb.	Item	Ft-Lb.
Converter to Flywheel	23-28	Regulator to Case	17-22	Converter Drain Plug	15-28
Converter Hsg. to Trans. Case	40-50	Planetary Support to Trans. Case	20-30	Rear Band Adjusting Screw Locknut	35-40
Front Pump to Trans. Case	17-22	Control Valve Body to Trans. Case	8-10	Front Band Adjusting Screw Locknut	20-25
Front Servo to Trans. Case	30-35	Diaphragm Assy. to Case	15-23	Manual Valve Inner Lever to Shaft	20-30
Rear Servo to Trans. Case	40-45	Cooler Return Fitting	15-20	Downshift Lever to Shaft	17-20
Oil Pan to Case	10-13	Extension Assy. to Trans. Case	30-40	Filler Tube to Engine	20-25
Converter Cover to Converter Hsg.	12-16	Pressure Gauge Tap	7-15	Transmission to Engine	40-50

Item	In-Lb.	Item	In-Lb.	Item	In-Lb.
Governor to Counterweight	50-60	Front Servo Release Piston	20-30	T.V. Body to Valve Body	20-30
Governor Valve Body Cover Screws	20-30	End Plates to Body	20-30	Lower Valve Body Cover and Plate to Valve Body	20-30
Pressure Regulator Cover Screws	20-30	Stator Support to Pump	25-35		
Control Valve Body Screws (10-24)	20-30	Lower Body and Cover Plate to Valve Body	20-30		

HOW TO: Ford FMX Overhaul

1. Although the FMX three-speed transmission has been in use for several years, the basic design has remained the same with minor modifications. Remove oil pan/gasket to begin the overhaul.

2. To remove transmission oil screen, it's necessary to unclip retainer which holds the screen in place. The screen can be cleaned in solvent, blown dry with compressed air and reused.

3. Gently pry compensator pressure tube from pressure regulator and control valve body, then remove main pressure oil tube from main control-valve assembly, being careful not to bend it.

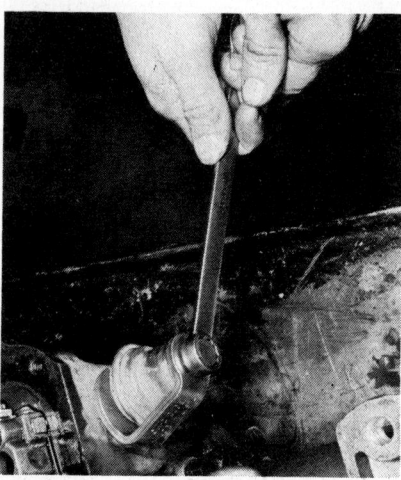

4. Remove the vacuum diaphragm unit and push rod. The special puller tool shown here is available from any automotive parts store, and its use will save both time and trouble.

5. Press inward on the pressure-regulator spring retainer, as shown, and unclip it. Remove the two pressure valves, the valve stop, two springs and the retainer clip from the regulator body.

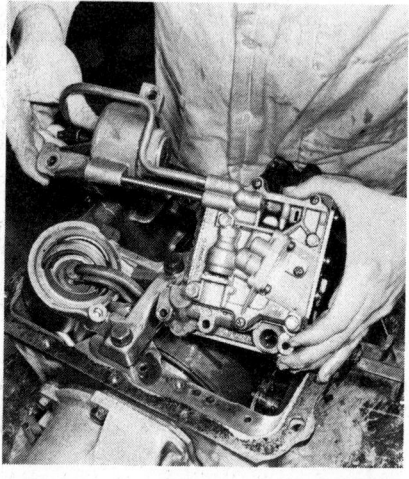

6. Unbolt and remove the pressure regulator body and the main control-valve body with the front servo attached, aligning the levers to allow valve body removal. Detach servo tubes carefully.

7. Remove rear-servo attaching bolts. Hold the actuating and anchor struts with your fingers as you lift the servo unit from the transmission case. Note lockwashers on attaching bolts.

8. Front and rear servo removal exposes case center-support pins; one fits in the side and the other one drops directly into its bore in the center of the case. Different shapes prevent mixups.

9. There is one more small oil-return tube hidden in the bottom of the front servo compartment. This must be removed before you can begin actual case component disassembly procedure.

10. Remove the five bolts holding extension housing to the transmission case, and pull housing off the output shaft. These same bolts are used to hold the rear support to the transmission case.

11. Remove output shaft assembly from case. If necessary, a screwdriver can be placed between ring gear and pinion carrier to pry shaft loose. *Do not* bend the pressure tubes (arrow).

12. Withdraw rear planetary carrier from case, and remove primary sun-gear rear thrust bearing and races (arrow), then squeeze rear band ends together to remove the band from the case.

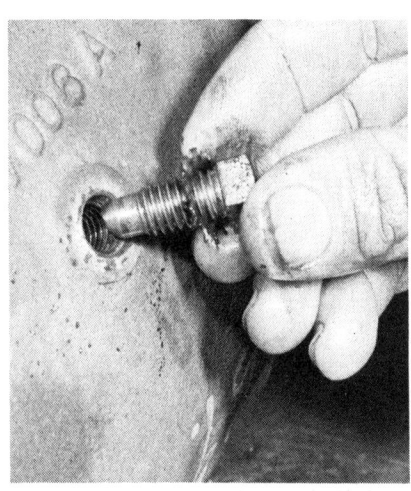

13. You will find a center-support outer bolt located on each side of the transmission case. These must be removed before further disassembly can be accomplished.

14. Once the two outer support bolts have been removed, the center support, front and rear clutches and input shaft can all be removed from the transmission case as a complete assembly.

15. Remove the remaining front-pump-assembly attaching bolts, and pull the front pump/gasket from the case. If the pump refuses to come out easily, tap screw bosses with a soft-faced hammer.

16. Prying the rear-clutch snap ring from its groove, remove the pressure plate, waved cushion spring and clutch pack. Inspect both composition and steel plates for signs of wear/damage.

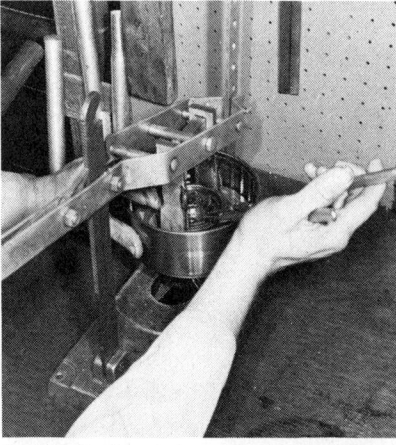

17. You will need a spring compressor tool to depress and hold spring retainer for snap ring removal. A homemade unit is shown here, but tools to do the job can be bought at auto supply stores.

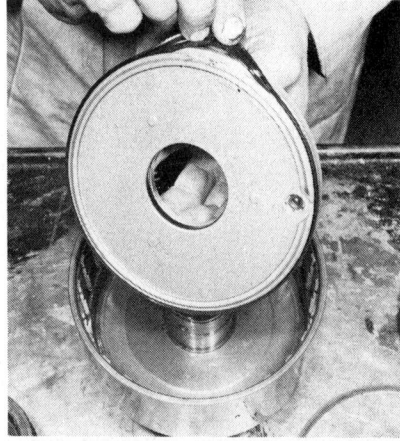

18. Holding one hand over the piston, apply compressed air to one of the holes in center shaft. This will force the piston out of the clutch drum for removal/replacement of inner/outer seals.

HOW TO: Ford FMX Overhaul

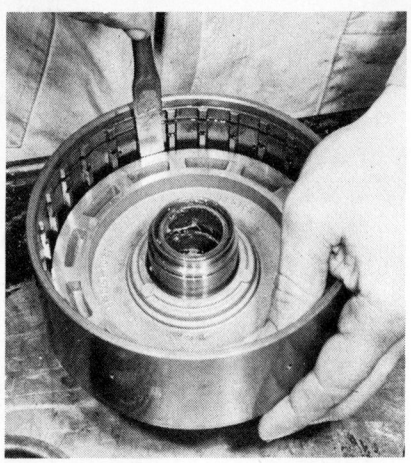

19. Installing the piston works best if its edge is coated with a wax-type lubricant stick. If one is not available, use a feeler gauge, as shown, to properly seat the piston in the drum.

20. Compressing spring retainer, replace snap ring, then reinstall clutch pack, beginning with the external-tabbed waved cushion spring (arrow). Alternate steel/composition plates in that order.

21. Remove the front clutch-cover snap ring, and lift the input shaft from the clutch drum. There should be a thrust washer on the clutch-hub thrust surface. Remove the clutch pack.

22. Remove clutch-release-spring snap ring with a screwdriver. A compressor tool is not required for this step, since you should be able to depress the retainer sufficiently by hand.

23. Remove front clutch piston by directing compressed air through the piston apply hole located inside hub of clutch drum. Remove and replace piston and drum O-ring seals (arrows).

24. Use of a wax-type lubricant stick is shown here. This makes piston reinstallation and seating easy. If not used, be careful when trying to seat piston, or you can damage the new seals.

25. With the piston replaced and seated properly in the front clutch drum, replace the spring retainer. Depress and hold retainer in place while reinstalling snap ring in its groove.

26. Front clutch hub should be replaced in the clutch drum with its deep counterbore facing downward. This is easy enough if you just remember that the side with the lettering faces up.

27. Install the pressure plate in the clutch drum, with its bearing surface facing upward, then alternate the composition/steel plates in that order. Replace the inner thrust washer.

28. Install the turbine shaft in the clutch drum, and replace the large snap ring, making sure it seats correctly. Replace the outer thrust washer, using grease to hold it in place.

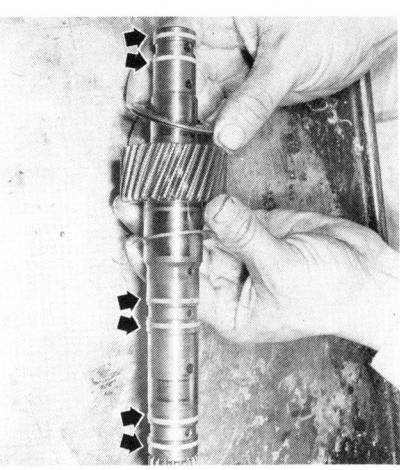

29. Inspect the primary sun-gear shaft. If its Teflon seals (arrows) are worn or damaged, cut them carefully from the shaft with a knife, and replace them with cast iron seal rings.

30. Reinstall the primary sun-gear shaft to the rear clutch drum assembly by rotating it to mesh the clutch plates with the clutch hub serrations; then install front clutch drum assembly.

31. The FMX front pump is a comparatively small unit. Separate the stator from the pump body by removing the stator-support attaching screws. Remove and inspect both drive and driven gears.

32. Inspect all machined surfaces of the stator support, pump body housing, gear pockets and crescent for scoring. Minor burrs and scores can be removed with crocus cloth. Reassemble pump.

33. If you did not separate the front servo from the main control-valve body while removing the assembly from the transmission case, do so now by carefully pulling the two units apart.

34. The three-section, two-separator-plate valve body is shown with cover and first plate removed. If further disassembly is required, refer to earlier drawing, then separate upper and lower body.

35. Apply pressure to the spring-loaded front servo piston, and remove the snap ring. The servo piston retainer, servo piston and return piston can be removed. Replace all oil seals.

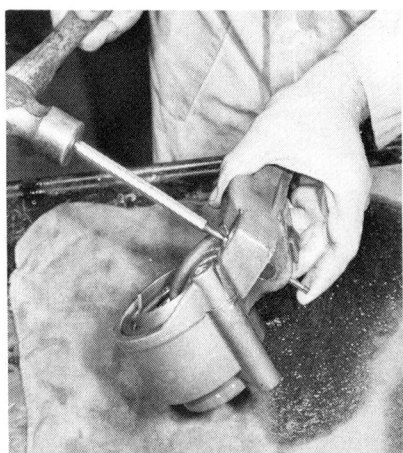

36. To disassemble the rear servo, the actuating lever must be removed. Drive the shaft retaining pin out with a ⅛-in. punch. When the shaft is removed, the needle bearings will fall out.

HOW TO: Ford FMX Overhaul

37. Compress the piston to remove snap ring. Replace the seal, clean the servo body and reassemble with servo spring small end against piston. Compress the retainer and install snap ring.

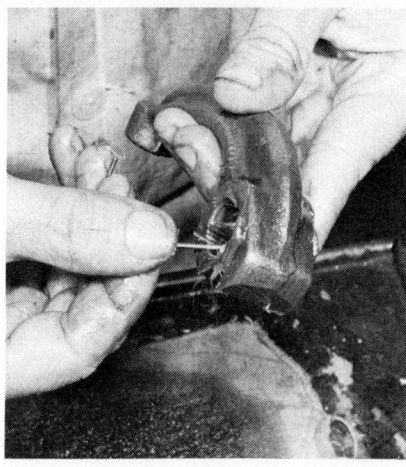

38. To replace needle bearings in the servo lever, use a thin coating of grease in the hub, and install the bearings as shown. Position the lever in the servo body, and install the shaft and pin.

39. Pressure regulator is a three-piece unit. Separate and wash parts thoroughly in clean solvent, then blow dry with compressed air. Inspect for scoring and obstructions, then reassemble.

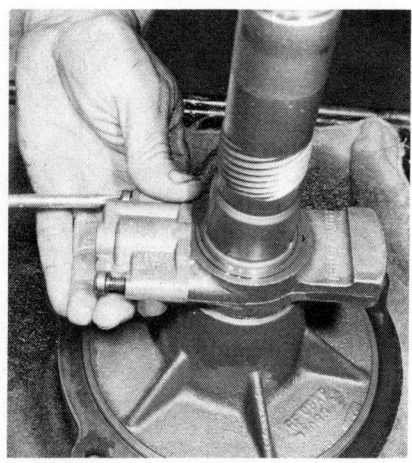

40. Two screws hold governor valve body to the counterweight. Governor should be removed, and small screen located inside the valve body should be cleaned thoroughly before replacing.

41. After inspecting both bands for excessive wear or other damage, begin reassembly by installing the front band in the case, with its anchor end aligned with the anchor in the case.

42. With the thrust washer in place on the input shaft, hold the front and rear clutches from separating, and install the entire assembly in the case while positioning the band on the drum.

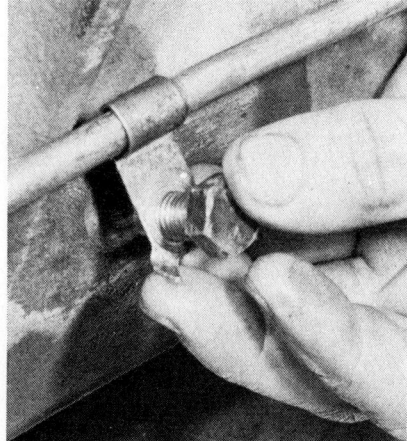

43. Install the center support in the case, and line up the attaching holes with those in the case. Replace the two outside case center-support bolts, and torque each 20 to 30 ft.-lbs.

44. Replace the inside center-support pins (arrows). Compress the ends of the rear band, and install it in the case, sliding the band over the support face as far as it will go.

45. Install the one-piece inner bearing/race assembly in the planetary carrier. Black race must face to the front of the case. Position planetary carrier on the center support, rotate and seat.

46. Position a new rear support-to-case gasket on the rear support, and install, carefully inserting the tubes into their respective case bores as the support is seated to the case.

47. Insert the extension-housing oil-seal replacer and pilot in the housing. Fit a new gasket to the housing, and install the housing to the case. Torque the attaching bolts 30 to 40 ft.-lbs.

48. Wet a new front pump gasket in transmission fluid, and fit it to the case counterbore. Position the front pump, and install the four attaching bolts. Torque each 17 to 22 ft.-lbs.

49. Install the rear band struts in their respective positions, as shown. Use of a little grease on the end of each will help hold them in place while the rear servo unit is reinstalled.

50. Install the rear servo unit, rotating the band until the anchor struts engage properly with servo and band. Install the attaching bolts, and torque each 40 to 45 ft.-lbs.

51. Fit the front servo and main control-valve body back together. Grease will hold the anchor struts in place while the front servo is reinstalled. Rotate band to engage with anchor pin.

52. Once the band struts have engaged the servo properly, replace the two attaching bolts. Move the servo toward the case centerline, and torque the bolts 30 to 35 ft.-lbs.

53. Install valve body bolts, and move the body toward the case center, until clearance between manual valve and manual detent lever pin is less than 0.050-in. Torque the bolts 8 to 10 ft.-lbs.

54. Make sure that the cover screws are torqued 20 to 30 in.-lbs., and install the pressure regulator body. The valves will be reinstalled after the body has been replaced in the case.

HOW TO: Ford FMX Overhaul

55. Torque the pressure regulator attaching bolts 17 to 22 ft.-lbs. Torque values and band adjustment specifications are critical to proper operation of the FMX transmission.

56. Replace the converter pressure (1) and control pressure (2) valves in the pressure regulator and seat; then install a valve stop on the end of (2) and a retainer on the end of (1).

57. Replace pressure valve springs (largest goes at bottom) and fit the retainer clip over them. Engage retainer clip on body lip (circle), then snap bottom of retainer in place.

58. Replace the main pressure oil tube to the pressure regulator first, then install the other end of the tube to the main control-valve body, using gentle taps of a soft-faced hammer to seat it.

59. Replace pressure compensator tube. Fit the fluid screen on the rear clip so tang enters the flange hole. Rotate clockwise, press grommet into pump inlet port, and replace retaining clip.

60. Loosen locknut, pull actuating rod back, and insert ¼-in. spacer. Torque screw to 10 in.-lbs. Remove spacer, tighten screw an extra three-quarter turn, torque locknut 20 to 25 ft.-lbs.

61. Loosen rear-band adjusting-screw locknut. Tighten adjusting screw to 10 ft.-lbs., then back off screw exactly 1½ turns. Hold screw stationary, and tighten locknut. Torque 35 to 40 ft.-lbs.

62. Install oil pan with a new gasket, then insert push rod in the vacuum diaphragm unit, and replace it in the transmission case. Screw diaphragm unit in, and torque 15 to 23 ft.-lbs.

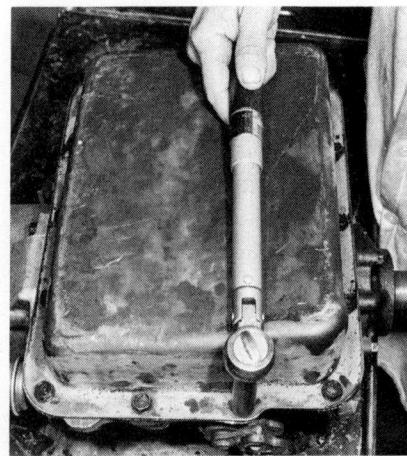

63. Torque the oil-pan-cover attaching bolts 10 to 13 ft.-lbs., and the overhaul is completed. The FMX transmission is now ready to reinstall in the car with the converter unit.

CHRYSLER CORPORATION
Chrysler TorqueFlite

AMERICAN MOTORS
Torque-Command

TORQUEFLITE APPLICATION

All 1970-79 Chrysler Corporation cars equipped with automatic transmission.

TORQUE-COMMAND APPLICATION

All 1972-79 American Motors cars equipped with automatic transmission.

DESCRIPTION

The TorqueFlite/Torque-Command automatic transmission consists of a hydraulic torque converter and compound planetary gear set, with two multiple disc clutches, one overrunning clutch and two servo/bands. The converter housing and transmission case are a single aluminum casting.

There are three basic models of the TorqueFlite/Torque-Command in use: the 727, 904 and 998. The 727 differs considerably internally and is physically larger than the 904/998. Although the 904 and 998 are similar in size, appearance and operation, their internal components are somewhat different, especially the valve bodies and rear band. The 904 uses a single wrap rear band while the 998 has a double wrap band. The 998 also has reinforcing ribs cast into the top of its rear servo boss case. When used with I-4 engines, the 904 is fitted with a dynamic absorber to dampen sympathetic driveline vibrations caused by engine operation.

LOCKUP TORQUE CONVERTER

Introduced by Chrysler on 1978 models, and by AMC on 1979 transmissions, the lockup converter contains an internal mechanism to lock the turbine and impeller in direct drive, thus eliminating the slippage found in conventional converters. This increases fuel economy and reduces the operating temperature of the automatic transmission fluid. In addition to the lockup mechanism within the converter, a lockup module is attached to the valve body. The converter control valve in the valve body has been modified to function within the lockup system. Since the lockup mechanism is internal and cannot be seen, an identifying decal is attached to the front cover of converters so equipped.

CONVERTER REPLACEMENT

Torque converters used since February 1977 no longer have drain plugs. Chrysler recommends three

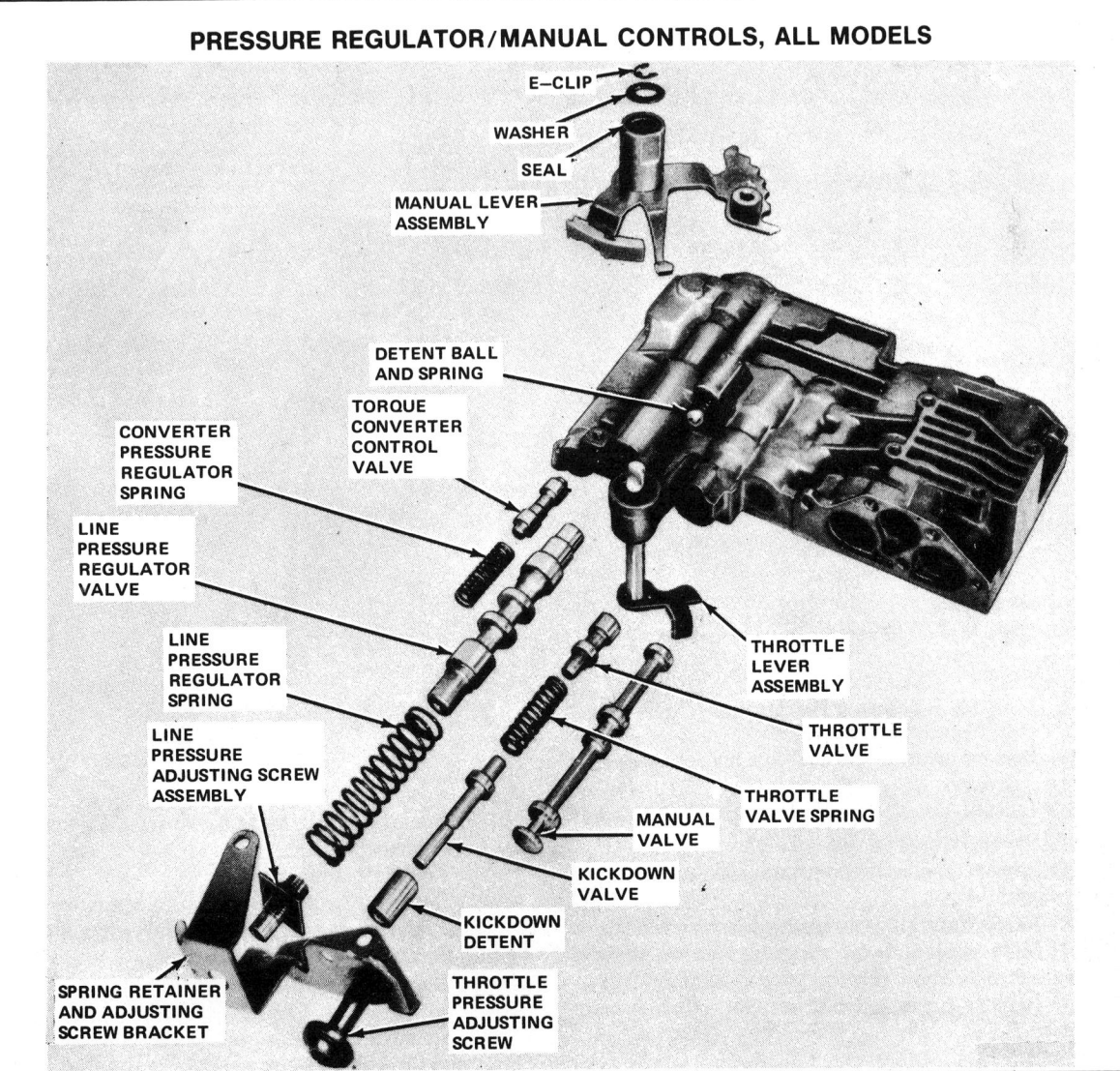

PRESSURE REGULATOR/MANUAL CONTROLS, ALL MODELS

E-CLIP
WASHER
SEAL
MANUAL LEVER ASSEMBLY
DETENT BALL AND SPRING
TORQUE CONVERTER CONTROL VALVE
CONVERTER PRESSURE REGULATOR SPRING
LINE PRESSURE REGULATOR VALVE
LINE PRESSURE REGULATOR SPRING
LINE PRESSURE ADJUSTING SCREW ASSEMBLY
THROTTLE LEVER ASSEMBLY
THROTTLE VALVE
THROTTLE VALVE SPRING
MANUAL VALVE
KICKDOWN VALVE
KICKDOWN DETENT
SPRING RETAINER AND ADJUSTING SCREW BRACKET
THROTTLE PRESSURE ADJUSTING SCREW

situations in which these converters should be replaced when a transmission is overhauled:

1. If the oil pan contains an extensive accumulation of dirt and/or contamination when removed from the transmission.

2. If the ATF is black, burnt, or contains small particles in suspension.

3. If the converter hub is damaged or excessively worn. These recommendations also apply to all 1978 and later AMC vehicles equipped with Torque-Command transmissions.

BAND ADJUSTMENT

FRONT (KICKDOWN) BAND
(Left Side of Case)

1. Loosen the adjusting screw locknut and back it off five turns. The adjusting screw must turn freely in the transmission case.

2. Torque the adjusting screw to 72 in.-lbs.

3. Back off the adjusting screw the number of turns specified for the transmission application.

4. Hold the adjusting screw from turning, and torque the locknut to specifications.

REAR (LOW/REVERSE) BAND
(Internal, Remove Oil Pan)

1. Loosen the adjusting screw locknut and back it off five turns. The adjusting screw must turn freely in the transmission case.

2. Torque the adjusting screw to 72 in.-lbs. or 41 in.-lbs. on 1974-75 198 cu.-in. and 225 cu.-in. engines with A-904 transmission.

3. Back off the adjusting screw the number of turns specified for the transmission application.

4. Hold the adjusting screw from turning, and torque the locknut to specifications.

5. Replace the oil pan with a new gasket, and torque the attaching bolts to 150 in.-lbs.

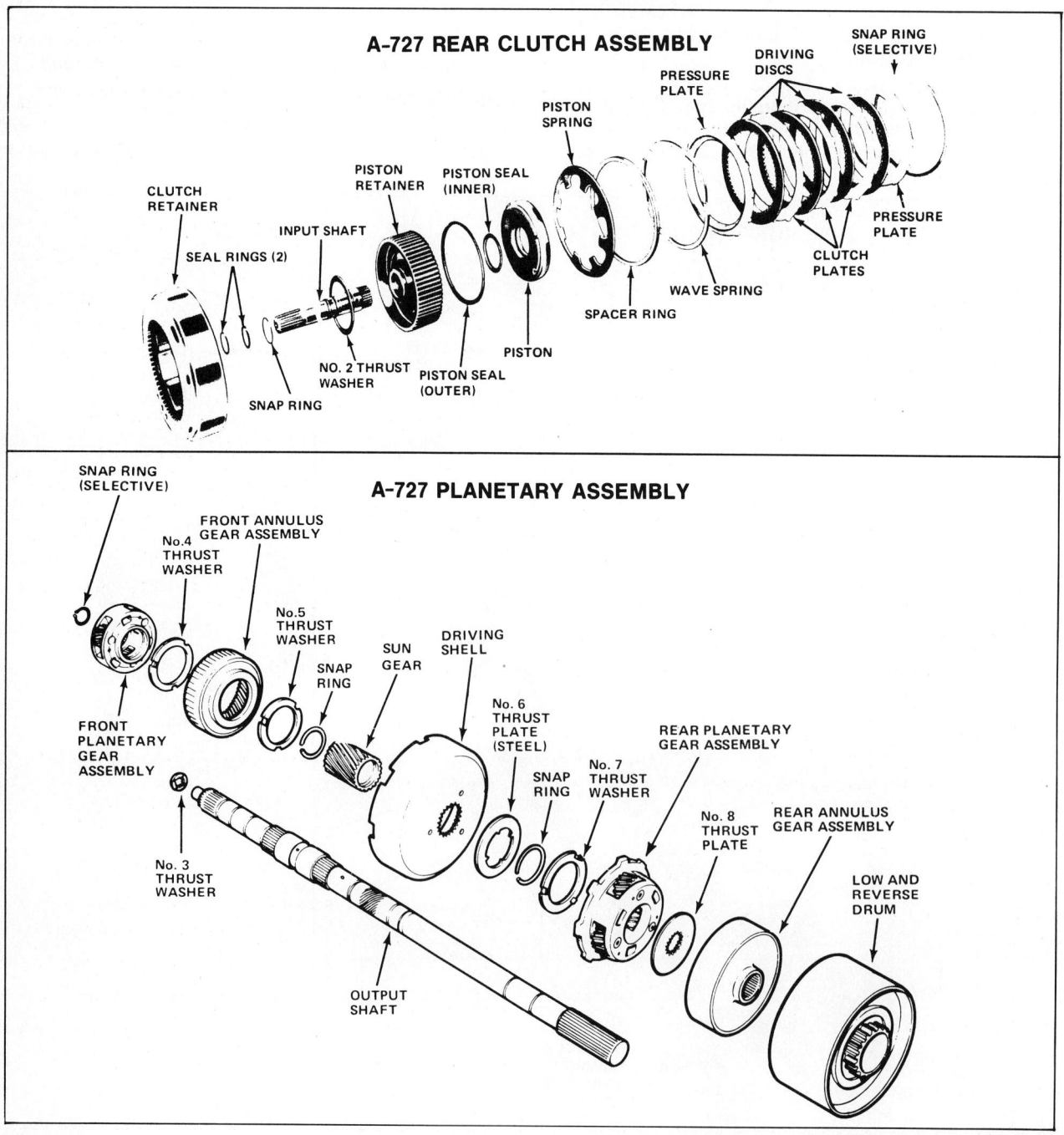

A-727 REAR CLUTCH ASSEMBLY

A-727 PLANETARY ASSEMBLY

TORQUEFLITE/TORQUE-COMMAND OVERHAUL DIAGNOSIS CHART

POSSIBLE CAUSE	DELAYED UPSHIFT	HARSH UPSHIFT	TRANSMISSION OVERHEATS	HARD TO FILL, OIL BLOWS OUT FILLER TUBE	BUZZING NOISE	GRATING, SCRAPING, GROWLING NOISE	DRAGS OR LOCKS	DRIVES IN NEUTRAL	NO DRIVE IN REVERSE	NO DRIVE IN FORWARD DRIVE POSITIONS	NO DRIVE IN ANY POSITION	SLIPS IN ALL POSITIONS	SLIPS IN REVERSE ONLY	SLIPS IN FORWARD DRIVE POSITIONS	SHIFTS ERRATIC	NO KICKDOWN OR NORMAL DOWNSHIFT	3-2 KICKDOWN RUNAWAY	NO UPSHIFT	RUNAWAY UPSHIFT	DELAYED ENGAGEMENT FROM NEUTRAL TO D OR R	HARSH ENGAGEMENT FROM NEUTRAL TO D OR R
1 Engine idle speed too high.			X																		X
2 Hydraulic pressures too low.		X	X						X	X	X	X	X	X	X		X	X	X	X	X
3 Low-reverse band out of adjustment						X	X		X												
4 Valve body malfunction or leakage.					X			X	X	X	X	X	X	X	X	X	X	X	X	X	X
5 Low-reverse servo, band or linkage malfunction.									X								X			X	X
6 Low fluid level.			X		X			X		X	X	X	X	X	X		X	X	X	X	
7 Incorrect gearshift control linkage adjustment.			X					X	X				X	X	X			X		X	
8 Oil filter clogged.				X								X	X	X						X	
9 Faulty oil pump.			X		X							X	X	X	X					X	
10 Worn or broken input shaft seal rings.										X			X	X						X	
11 Aerated fluid.				X	X							X	X	X	X		X	X		X	X
12 Engine idle speed too low.																					X
13 Incorrect throttle linkage adjustment.	X	X														X	X	X	X	X	
14 Kickdown band out of adjustment.	X	X				X											X	X			
15 Overrunning clutch not holding.										X						X		X			
16 Output shaft bearing and/or bushing damaged.						X															
17 Governor support seal rings broken or worn.	X														X		X	X		X	
18 Worn or broken reaction shaft support seal rings.	X								X				X		X		X	X	X	X	
19 Governor malfunction.	X														X	X		X	X	X	
20 Kickdown servo band or linkage malfunction.	X														X	X	X	X	X		
21 Worn or faulty front clutch.	X								X				X		X		X	X	X	X	
22 High fluid level.				X																	
23 Breather clogged.				X X																	
24 Hydraulic pressure too high.			X																		X
25 Kickdown band adjustment too tight.							X														
26 Faulty cooling system.			X																		
27 Insufficient clutch plate clearance.			X							X											
28 Worn or faulty rear clutch.									X	X							X			X	X
29 Rear clutch dragging.							X	X													
30 Planetary gear sets broken or seized.						X	X		X	X	X										
31 Overrunning clutch worn, broken or seized.						X	X			X						X					
32 Overrunning clutch inner race damaged.				X																	

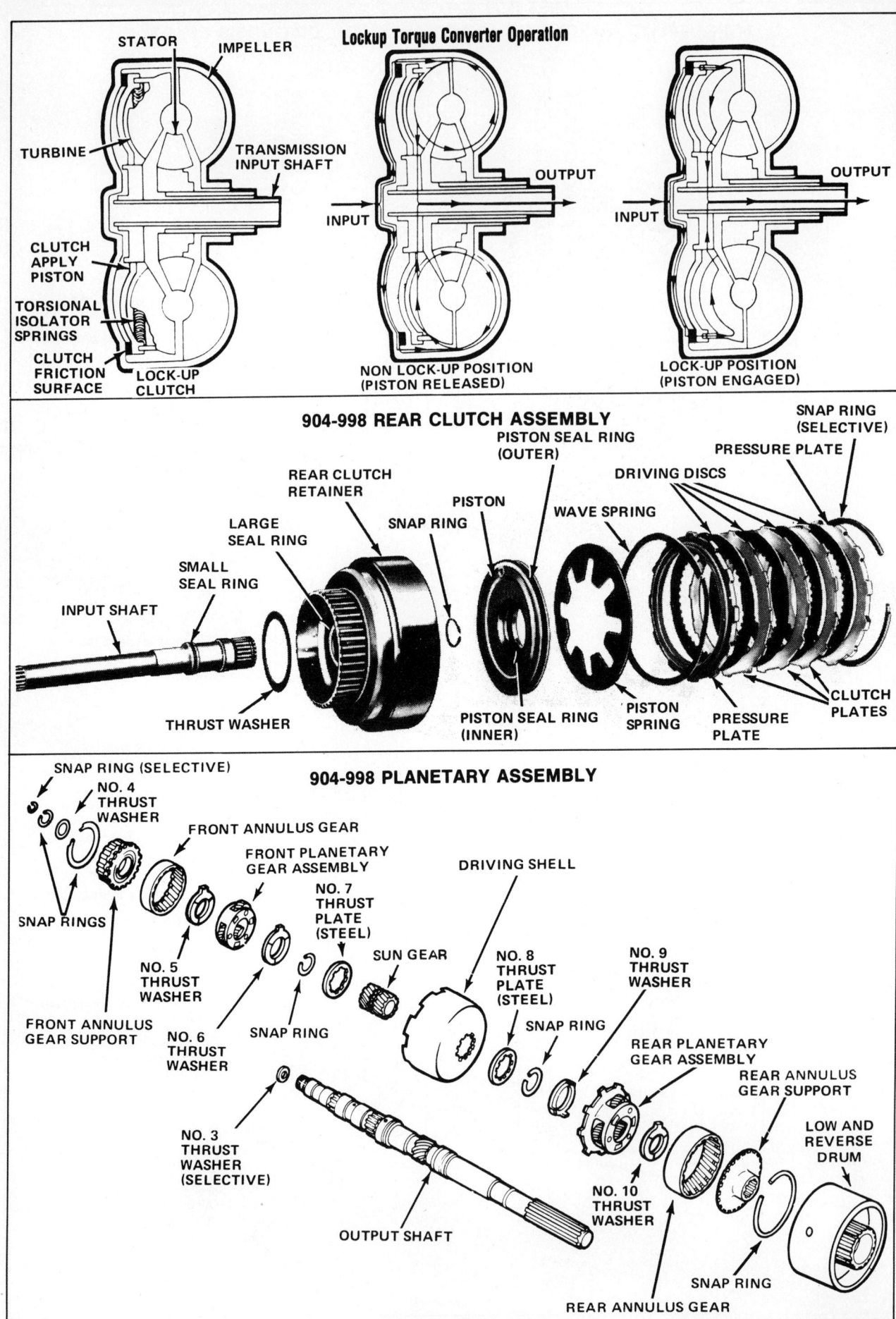

Lockup Torque Converter Operation

STATOR IMPELLER

TURBINE

TRANSMISSION INPUT SHAFT

CLUTCH APPLY PISTON

TORSIONAL ISOLATOR SPRINGS

CLUTCH FRICTION SURFACE

LOCK-UP CLUTCH

OUTPUT

INPUT

NON LOCK-UP POSITION (PISTON RELEASED)

OUTPUT

INPUT

LOCK-UP POSITION (PISTON ENGAGED)

904-998 REAR CLUTCH ASSEMBLY

SNAP RING (SELECTIVE)

PRESSURE PLATE

PISTON SEAL RING (OUTER)

DRIVING DISCS

REAR CLUTCH RETAINER

PISTON

WAVE SPRING

LARGE SEAL RING

SNAP RING

SMALL SEAL RING

INPUT SHAFT

THRUST WASHER

PISTON SEAL RING (INNER)

PISTON SPRING

PRESSURE PLATE

CLUTCH PLATES

904-998 PLANETARY ASSEMBLY

SNAP RING (SELECTIVE)

NO. 4 THRUST WASHER

FRONT ANNULUS GEAR

FRONT PLANETARY GEAR ASSEMBLY

NO. 7 THRUST PLATE (STEEL)

DRIVING SHELL

SUN GEAR

NO. 8 THRUST PLATE (STEEL)

NO. 9 THRUST WASHER

SNAP RINGS

SNAP RING

FRONT ANNULUS GEAR SUPPORT

NO. 5 THRUST WASHER

NO. 6 THRUST WASHER

REAR PLANETARY GEAR ASSEMBLY

REAR ANNULUS GEAR SUPPORT

LOW AND REVERSE DRUM

NO. 3 THRUST WASHER (SELECTIVE)

OUTPUT SHAFT

NO. 10 THRUST WASHER

SNAP RING

REAR ANNULUS GEAR

904 SHIFT & PRESSURE REGULATOR VALVES

2-3 SHIFT VALVE

2-3 SPRING

1-2 SHIFT VALVE

1-2 SPRING

REGULATOR VALVE THROTTLE PRESSURE PLUG

REGULATOR VALVE LINE PRESSURE PLUG

SLEEVE

LINE PRESSURE REGULATOR VALVE END PLATE

SHIFT VALVE END PLATE

998-727 SHIFT & PRESSURE REGULATOR VALVES

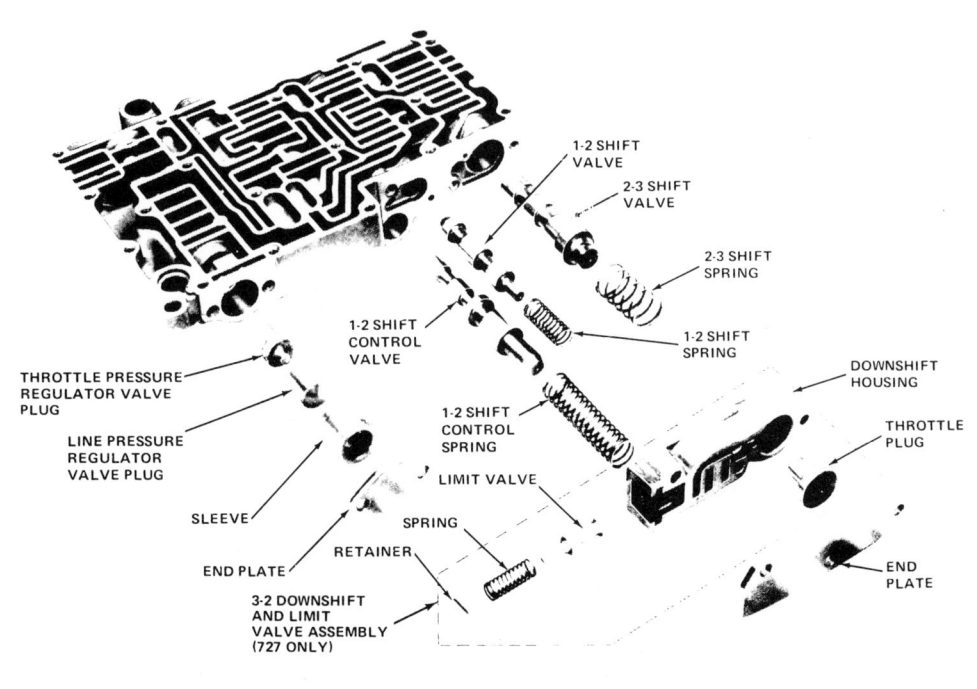

1-2 SHIFT VALVE

2-3 SHIFT VALVE

2-3 SHIFT SPRING

1-2 SHIFT CONTROL VALVE

1-2 SHIFT SPRING

THROTTLE PRESSURE REGULATOR VALVE PLUG

LINE PRESSURE REGULATOR VALVE PLUG

1-2 SHIFT CONTROL SPRING

DOWNSHIFT HOUSING

THROTTLE PLUG

SLEEVE

LIMIT VALVE

END PLATE

SPRING

RETAINER

END PLATE

3-2 DOWNSHIFT AND LIMIT VALVE ASSEMBLY (727 ONLY)

CHRYSLER TORQUEFLITE SPECIFICATIONS
1970

TRANSMISSION MODELS	A-904		A-727	
TYPE	Automatic Three Speed with Torque Converter			
TORQUE CONVERTER DIAMETER............(Std.)	10¾ ins.		11¾ ins.	
(High Perf.)			10¾ ins.	
OIL CAPACITY—TRANSMISSION AND	**U.S.** **Measure**	**Imperial** **Measure**	**U.S.** **Measure**	**Imperial** **Measure**
TORQUE CONVERTER				
Use Automatic Transmission Fluid Labeled				
Type AQ-ATF, Suffix "A" or "Dexron" ..(Std.)	17 Pts.	14 Pts.	19 Pts.	16 Pts.
(High Perf.)			16½ Pts.	13½ Pts.
COOLING METHOD	Water-Heat Exchanger			
LUBRICATION	Pump (Rotor Type)			
CLUTCHES—Engine Cu. Ins..................	198 225 318	225 318 340 383 440 426		
Number of Front Clutch Plates.............	3 3 4	3 3 4 4 4 5		
Number of Front Clutch Discs..............	3 3 4	3 3 4 4 4 5		
Number of Rear Clutch Plates.............	2 2 3	3 3 3 3 3 3		
Number of Rear Clutch Discs..............	3 3 4	4 4 4 4 4 4		
GEAR RATIOS	First	Second	Third	Reverse
	2.45:1	1.45:1	1:1	2.20:1
PUMP CLEARANCES				
Outer Rotor to Case Bore...................	.004 to .008″			
Outer to Inner Tip	.005 to .010″			
End Clearance—Rotors	.0015 to .003″			
PLANETARY ASSY. END PLAY	.006 to .033″		.010 to .037″	
DRIVE TRAIN END PLAY	.030 to .089″		.037 to .084″	
CLUTCH PLATE CLEARANCE				
Front Clutch	.042 to .087″ (3 Disc)		.036 to .086″ (3 Disc)	
	.056 to .104″ (4 Disc)		.024 to .125″ (4 Disc)	
			.066 to .123″ (4 Disc)	
			.022 to .079″ (5 Disc, High Perf.)	
Rear Clutch	.032 to .055″		.025 to .045″	
SNAP RINGS				
Front and Rear Clutches				
Rear Snap Ring (Selective).................	.060 to .062″		.060 to .062″	
	.068 to .070″		.074 to .076″	
	.076 to .078″		.088 to .090″	
Output Shaft (Forward End)..................	.040 to .044″		.048 to .052″	
	.048 to .052″		.055 to .059″	
	.059 to .065″		.062 to .066″	
THRUST WASHERS				
Output Shaft to Input Shaft (Selective)	.052 to .054″ (Natural)		—— ——	
	.068 to .070″ (Red)		—— ——	
	.083 to .085″ (Black)		—— ——	
Reaction Shaft Support to Front Clutch				
Retainer (Selective).........................	——		.061 to .063″ (Green)	
	——		.084 to .086″ (Red)	
	——		.102 to .104″ (Yellow)	
Driving Shell Thrust Plate—Steel (2)	.034 to .036″		——	
Front Planetary Gear to Driving Shell	.060 to .062″		——	
Rear Planetary Gear to Driving Shell.........	.060 to .062″		——	
Front Annulus Gear Support...................	.121 to .125″		——	
Front Clutch to Rear Clutch	.043 to .045″		——	
Front Clutch to Reaction Shaft Support........	.043 to .045″		——	
Output Shaft to Input Shaft...................	——		.062 to .064″	
Driving Shell Thrust Plate—Steel (1)	——		.034 to .036″	
Rear Planetary Gear to Driving Shell...........	——		.062 to .064″	
Front Planetary Gear to Annulus Gear.........	——		.062 to .064″	
Front Annulus Gear to Driving Shell...........	——		.062 to .064″	
Front Clutch to Rear Clutch	——		.061 to .063″	
Rear Planetary Gear to Annulus Gear.........	——		.034 to .036″	

BAND ADJUSTMENTS	Engines	Turns*	Engines	Turns*
Kickdown (Front)..	All	2	All Except 426	2
			426 cu. in.	1½
Low-Reverse (Internal)..	All Except 318	3¼	All	2
	318 cu.-in.	4		

*Backed off from 72 in.-lbs.

1971-79

Transmission Models	A-904		A-727	
TYPE...	Automatic Three Speed with Torque Converter			
TORQUE CONVERTER DIAMETER (Standard)	10¾ ins.		11¾ ins.	
(High Stall Speed)	—		10¾ ins.	
	U.S. Measure	Imperial Measure	U.S. Measure	Imperial Measure
OIL CAPACITY—TRANSMISSION AND TORQUE CONVERTER ....(Standard)	17 Pts.	14 Pts.	19 Pts.	16 Pts.
(High Stall Speed)	—	—	16½ Pts.	13½ Pts.

COOLING METHOD...	Water-Heat Exchanger			
LUBRICATION...	Pump (Rotor Type)			
GEAR RATIOS...	First 2.45:1	Second 1.45:1	Third 1:1	Reverse 2.21:1

SNAP RINGS		
Rear Clutch Snap Ring (Selective)...	.060 to .062″ .068 to .070″ .076 to .078″ ———	.060 to .062″ .074 to .076″ .088 to .090″ .106 to .108″
Output Shaft (Forward End)	.040 to .044″ .048 to .052″ .059 to .065″	.048 to .052″ .055 to .059″ .062 to .066″

	A-904				A-727							
							340 360-2 360-4	383-2 400-2 360-4 H.P.	383-4 400-4 400-4 H.P.		440-6	
CLUTCHES—Engine Cu. Ins.............	198	225	318	360	225	318				440-4	426	
Number of Front Clutch Plates........	3	3	4	5	3	3	3	3	3	4	4	5
Number of Front Clutch Discs.........	3	3	4	5	3	3	3	3	3	4	4	5
Number of Rear Clutch Plates.........	2	2	3	3	3	3	3	3	3	3	3	3
Number of Rear Clutch Discs..........	3	3‡	4	4	4	4	4	4	4	4	4	4
Number of Front Clutch Springs......	1	1	1	1	13	9†	9†	9†	9	9†	9	12
BAND ADJUSTMENTS												
Kickdown (Front) Turns*	2	2	2	2	2½	2½	2½	2½	2½	2½	2½(1)	1½
Low-Reverse (Internal) Turns*........	7(2)(3)	7(2)(3)	4	.4	2	2	2	2	2	2	2	2

*Backed off from 72 in.-lbs.   (2) Backed off from 41 in.-lbs. on 1974-75 models.
(1) 440-4 dual exhaust, 2 turns.   (3) 1971-73 models, torque screw to 72 in.-lbs., and back off 3¼ turns.
‡ 4 with Lock-Up Converter
†11 with Lock-Up Converter

CLUTCH PLATE CLEARANCES

1971

FRONT CLUTCH ... 3 Disc .036 to .087″ 3 Disc .035 to .088″
4 Disc .048 to .109″ 4 Disc .047 to .110″
5 Disc .033 to .075″
REAR CLUTCH...... 3 Disc .026 to .055″ 4 Disc .025 to .045″
4 Disc .032 to .056″

1978-79

FRONT CLUTCH ..3 Disc .074 to .125″ 3 Disc .070 to .129″
4 Disc .067 to .134″ 4 Disc .082 to .151″
5 Disc .075 to .152″
REAR CLUTCH .....3 Disc .032 to .055″
4 Disc .032 to .055″ 4 Disc .025 to .045″

1972-74

FRONT CLUTCH .... 3 Disc .077 to .122″ 3 Disc .076 to .123″
4 Disc .089 to .144″ 4 Disc .088 to 145″
5 Disc .090 to .122″
REAR CLUTCH......3 and 4 Disc .032 to .055″ 4 Disc .025 to .045″

1975-77

FRONT CLUTCH .... 3 Disc .074 to .125″ 3 Disc .070 to .129″
4 Disc .067 to .134″ 4 Disc .082 to .151″
REAR CLUTCH............... 3 Disc .032 to .055″* 5 Disc .090 to .122″**
4 Disc .032 to .055″ 4 Disc .025 to .045″

* .075-.152 for 1976.   ** 1975 only.

THRUST WASHER CHART

THRUST WASHERS	THRUST WASHER NO. AND TRANSMISSION MODEL			
	904-998		727	
Reaction Shaft Support to Front Clutch Retainer	No. 1	.061 to .063	No. 1	Selective .061 to .063—Natural .084 to .086—Red .102 to .104—Yellow
Rear Clutch to Front Clutch Retainer	No. 2	.061 to .063	No. 2	.061 to .063—Natural
Output Shaft to Input Shaft	No. 3	Selective .052 to .054—Tin .068 to .070—Red .083 to .085—Green	No. 3	.062 to .064
Front Annulus Support to Rear Clutch Retainer	No. 4	.121 to .125		——
Front Annulus Support to Front Planetary Gear	No. 5	.048 to .050	No. 4	.059 to .062
Driving Shell to Front Annulus Gear		——	No. 5	.060 to .062
Front Planetary Gear to Driving Shell	No. 6	.048 to .050		——
Sun Gear and Driving Shell Front Thrust Plate	No. 7	.050 to .052	No. 6	.034 to .036
Sun Gear and Driving Shell Rear Thrust Plate	No. 8	.050 to .052		——
Rear Planetary Gear to Driving Shell	No. 9	.048 to .050	No. 7	.059 to .062
Rear Planetary Gear to Rear Annulus Gear		——	No. 8	.034 to .036
Rear Planetary Gear to Rear Annulus Support	No. 10	.048 to .050		——

AMERICAN MOTORS TORQUE SPECIFICATIONS

Service set to torques should be used when assembling components.
Service in use recheck torques should be used for checking a pre-torqued item.

	Service Set To Torque	Service In Use Recheck Torque
Cooler Line Fitting	15	10-30
Cooler Line Nut	25	15-30
Converter Drain Plug	90 in.-lbs.	——
Converter Drive Plate to Crankshaft Bolt	105	95-120
Converter Drive Plate to Torque Converter Bolt	22	20-25
Extension Housing to Transmission Case Bolt	24	——
Extension Housing to Insulator Mounting Bolt	50	——
Governor Body to Support Bolt	100 in.-lbs.	——
Kickdown Band Adjusting Screw Locknut	35*	——
Kickdown Lever Shaft Plug	150 in.-lbs.	——
Neutral Starter Switch	24	——
Oil Filler Tube Bracket Bolt	150 in.-lbs.	——
Oil Pan Bolt	150 in.-lbs.	9-13
Oil Pump Housing to Transmission Case Bolt	175 in.-lbs.	——
Output Shaft Support Bolt	150 in.-lbs.	——
Overrunning Clutch Cam Setscrew	40 in.-lbs.	——
Pressure Test Take-Off Plug	110 in.-lbs.	——
Reaction Shaft Support to Oil Pump Bolt	160 in.-lbs.	——
Reverse Band Adjusting Screw Locknut	35 ft.-lbs.	——
Speedometer Drive Clamp Screw	100 in.-lbs.	——
Transmission to Engine Bolt	28	22-30
Valve Body Screw	35 in.-lbs.	——
Valve Body to Transmission Case Bolt	100 in.-lbs.	——

All torque values given in ft.-lbs. with dry fits, unless otherwise specified.

*1970-73—29 ft.-lbs.

CHRYSLER TORQUE SPECIFICATIONS

TorqueFlite A-904 and A-727	In.-Lbs.		In.-Lbs.
Cooler Line Fitting	110	Neutral Starter Switch	24
Cooler Line Nut	85	Oil Pan Bolt	150
Converter Drain Plug	90	Oil Pump Housing to Transmission	
Converter Drive Plate to Crankshaft Bolt	55	Case Bolt	175
Converter Drive Plate to Torque		Output Shaft Support Bolt	150
Converter Bolt	270	Overrunning Clutch Cam Setscrew	40
Extension Housing to Transmission		Pressure Test Take-Off Plug	110
Case Bolt	24	Reaction Shaft Support to Oil Pump Bolt	160
Extension Housing to Insulator		Reverse Band Adjusting Screw Locknut	30**
Mounting Bolt	50	Speedometer Drive Clamp Screw	100
Governor Body to Support Bolt	100	Transmission to Engine Bolt	28**
Kickdown Band Adjusting Screw		Valve Body Screw	35
Locknut	35*	Valve Body to Transmission Case Bolt	100
Kickdown Lever Shaft Plug	150		

*1970-71—29 ft.-lbs.; 1972-76—35 ft.-lbs.   **1970-71—35 ft.-lbs.; 1972-76—30 ft.-lbs.

AMERICAN MOTORS TORQUE COMMAND SPECIFICATIONS

Transmission Models	904-998		727	
TYPE	Automatic Three-Speed with Torque Converter			
TORQUE CONVERTER DIAMETER (Std.)	10 3/4 ins. 3		11¾ ins.	
	U.S. Measure	Imperial Measure	U.S. Measure	Imperial Measure
OIL CAPACITY—TRANSMISSION AND TORQUE CONVERTER	17 Pts.	14 Pts.	19 Pts.	16 Pts.
Use AMC or Dexron Automatic Transmission Fluid				
COOLING METHOD	Water-Heat Exchanger			
LUBRICATION	Pump (Rotor Type)			
GEAR RATIOS	First	Second	Third	Reverse
	2.45:1	1.45:1	1.00:1	2.20:1
PUMP CLEARANCES				
Outer Rotor to Case Bore	.004 to .008-in.			
Outer to Inner Tip	.005 to .010-in.			
End Clearance-Rotors	.001 to .003-in.		.001 to .002-in.	
GEAR TRAIN END PLAY 1976-78 : 1	.001 to .047-in.		.009 to .044-in.	
INPUT SHAFT END PLAY 1975-78 :	.022 to .091-in.		.036 to .082-in.	
SNAP RINGS				
Front and Rear Clutches				
Rear Snap Ring (Selective)	.060 to .062-in.		.060 to .062-in.	
	.068 to .070-in.		.074 to .076-in.	
	.076 to .078-in.		.088 to .090-in.	
Output Shaft (Forward End)	.040 to .044-in.		.048 to .052-in.	
	.048 to .052-in.		.055 to .059-in.	
	.059 to .065-in.		.062 to .066-in.	
CLUTCH PLATE CLEARANCE				
Front Clutch 1975-78 :	3 Disc 0.074 to 0.125-in.		3 Disc 0.070 to 0.129-in.	
	4 Disc 0.067 to 0.134-in.		4 Disc 0.082 to 0.151-in.	
Rear Clutch 1975-78 :	3 and 4 Disc .032 to .055-in.		4 Disc .025 to .045-in.	
CLUTCH COMPONENT THICKNESS TOLERANCE 1976-78				
Front Clutch				
Lined Plate	.083 to .088-in.		.090 to .095-in.	
Steel Plate	.066 to .071-in.		.066 to .171-in.	
Pressure Plate	.214 to .218-in.		.278 to .282-in.	
Rear Clutch				
Lined Plate	.060 to .065-in.		.060 to .065-in.	
Steel Plate	.066 to .071-in.		.066 to .071-in.	
Flat Pressure Plate	.214 to .218-in.		.278 to .282-in.	
Formed Pressure Plate	.409 to .413-in.		.441 to .445-in.	

	232	258 2		304		360		401
CLUTCHES—Engine Cu. Ins.	STD	STD (904)	HD (727)	STD (998)	HD (727)	STD (727)	HD (727)	STD HD
Number of Front Clutch Plates	3	4	3	4	3	3	4	4
Number of Front Clutch Discs	3	4	3	4	3	3	4	4
Number of Rear Clutch Plates	2	2	3	3	3	3	3	3
Number of Rear Clutch Discs	3	3	4	4	4	4	4	4

· 1972-74 same as '71 Chrysler   ₁1975 same as '72 Chrysler   ₂1972 cars used 998 in place of 727.   ₃ 9½ with I-4 Engine

HOW TO: A727 TorqueFlite Overhaul

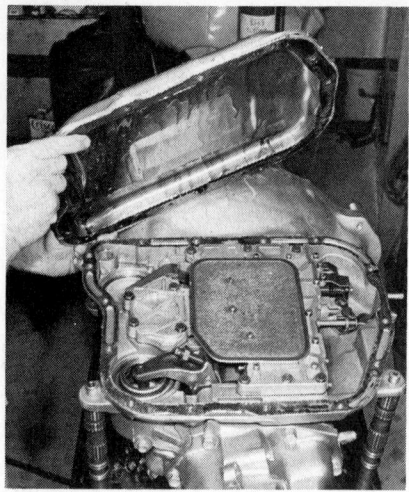

1. Place the transmission on a repair stand. Remove the 10 hex-head oil-pan-to-case bolts. Lift off the oil pan and gasket—discard the gasket.

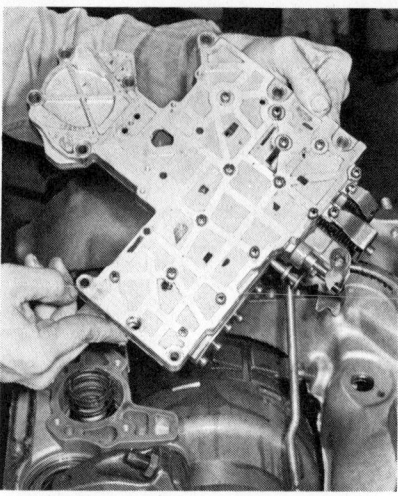

2. Remove/discard oil filter, then unbolt valve body. Disconnect parking lock rod from manual lever, and lift valve body from transmission case.

3. Lift spring from accumulator piston, and withdraw piston from case. Spring is located at small end of piston on the 440 dual-exhaust engine.

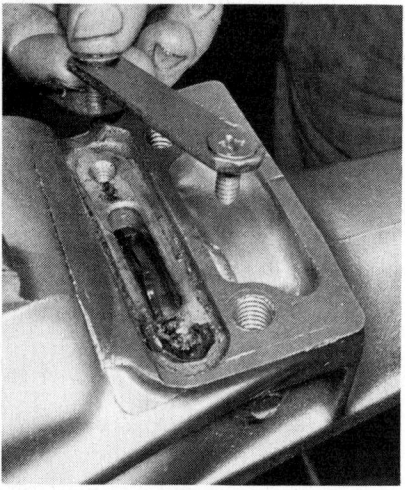

4. Pull parking lock rod forward and out of case before removing extension housing. Unscrew and remove this plate from the transmission mounting pad.

5. Using snap ring pliers, spread the snap ring from the output shaft bearing. Tap or wiggle housing, and pull it off the output shaft and bearing.

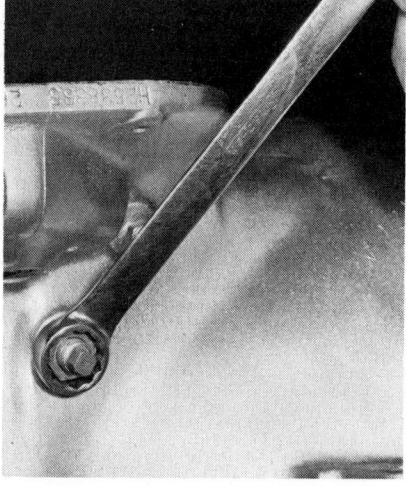

6. Tighten front-band adjusting screw to tighten band on clutch retainer and prevent it from coming out with the pump and damaging the clutches.

7. After removing the oil-pump-housing retaining bolts, install a knocker weight in the threaded holes located in the housing flange, and tighten.

8. Bump the weight outward to free the front pump from the housing, then withdraw the pump and reaction-shaft support assembly from the case.

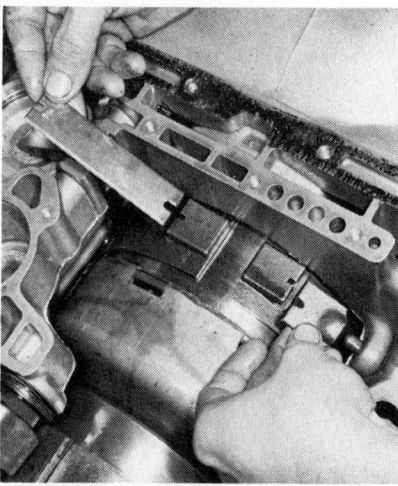

9. Now loosen the front-band adjusting screw, and remove the band strut. On the A727 version, this band strut anchor, shown here, should also be removed.

10. Once the band strut and anchor have been removed, front clutch/band assembly and rear band can be withdrawn with input shaft.

11. This thrust washer may come out with the input shaft, or it may remain on the forward end of the output shaft. Don't lose it. Remove the snap ring.

12. While it is possible to remove the planetaries and driving shell at one time, it's much easier to remove the front planetary/annulus gears first.

13. Now remove the driving shell with the sun gear installed. This thrust washer should be the seventh removed from the transmission case to this point.

14. Unclip another snap ring, and the rear planetary, the rear annulus gear and the low/reverse drum can be removed from the transmission case.

15. With the low/reverse drum out of the case, loosen the rear band adjuster, remove the band strut and link, then withdraw the band from the case.

16. Withdraw output shaft, with governor assembly, from rear of case. *Do not* remove output shaft support unless clutch cam is to be replaced.

17. Overrunning clutch cam is not usually removed unless damaged. To do so, remove setscrew (circle) and output shaft support, then drive cam from case.

18. In order to remove the kickdown (front) servo, an engine-valve-spring compressor is required to override spring pressure for snap ring removal.

HOW TO: A727 TorqueFlite Overhaul

19. Remove rod guide, springs and piston rod from the case, taking care not to damage rod or guide. Withdraw the piston and replace all seals.

20. You can compress the low/reverse (rear) servo without a special tool. Remove the snap ring, spring retainer, servo piston and the plug assembly.

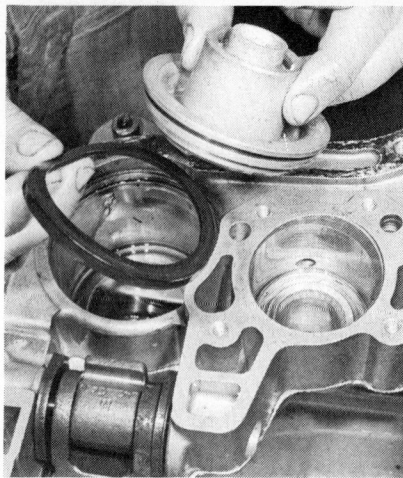

21. The rear servo-piston seal ring should be replaced. If necessary to disassemble piston, remove snap ring at bottom to free plug from piston body.

22. Reinstall the rear servo-piston/plug assembly, then fit the piston spring/retainer cap in place. Depress and hold while installing snap ring.

23. Controlled-load, front servo-piston seal ring is attached to piston proper by piston rod. Replace all three seals before reinstalling.

24. Replace the controlled-load servo, and use the engine-valve-spring compressor to hold the unit in place while the snap ring is installed.

25. Carefully inspect the rear annulus gear, the #8 thrust plate and the rear planetary gear for signs of excessive wear, damaged teeth, etc.

26. Inspect the driving shell for wear or damage, paying particular attention to the sun gear and bushings. Check, as shown, for signs of poor engagement.

27. Inspect bands for signs of wear, cracks, burning, scoring or other defects. Bands are the weak link in almost every automatic transmission.

28. Inspect the thrust faces of both planetary carriers for wear, cracks, scoring or other damage. Check pinions for broken or worn teeth.

29. The oil seal rings on the governor housing should be replaced with new ones. Rings tend to harden with age and crack with transmission heat.

30. Governor disassembly begins by prying this C-clip from one side. With the C-clip removed, the piston can be withdrawn from the other side.

31. With the piston removed, pressure on the snap ring which holds the governor valve is released, and it can be withdrawn from the housing easily.

32. Inspect the valve for nicks, burrs, scoring, etc. Light scratches or small nicks/burrs can be removed by a careful crocus cloth treatment.

33. Reinstall the valve and snap ring, then turn the governor unit over to insert and seat the piston. Replace the C-clip on the piston stem.

34. The output-shaft rear bearing is retained by front and rear snap rings. To remove and/or replace the bearing, unsnap and remove the rear snap ring.

35. Bearing can then be withdrawn from rear of shaft, with no need to remove front snap ring. Clean and regrease or replace with a new bearing.

36. To check the front clutch pack, pry out snap ring and remove pressure plate. These clutch plates have been scored and burned, and must be replaced.

HOW TO: A727 TorqueFlite Overhaul

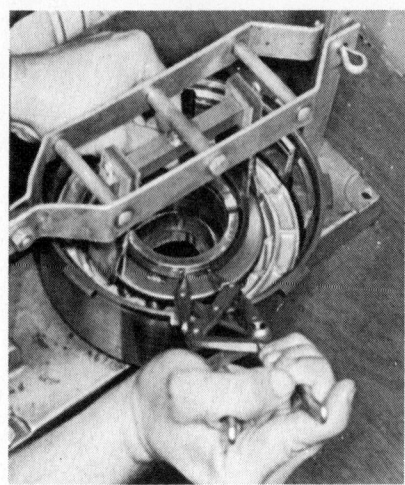

37. To remove the front clutch piston for seal replacement, the spring retainer must be compressed in order to remove the large snap ring easily.

38. Under the spring retainer, you'll find 8, 9 or 13 springs; 9 and 13 spring versions have 12 and 15 shafts respectively. Replace any broken springs.

39. Remove the piston, and replace both outer seal on piston and piston-retainer inner seal with new ones; make sure the seals are properly seated.

40. An application of a dry-stick wax-type lubricant, such as Door-Ease, to the new seal surfaces will make piston replacement in the retainer easy.

41. After reinstalling the piston and seating it in place, turn it to make sure it moves freely; then replace the springs on the piston shafts.

42. Fit retainer and snap ring in place, then reinstall clutch pack. Start with new clutch plate, and alternate with metal driving discs. Replace snap ring.

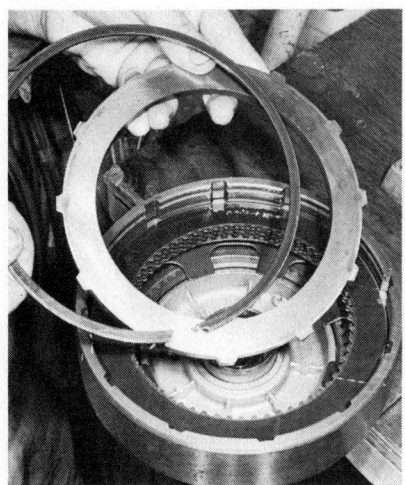

43. Remove selective snap ring holding the pressure plate in the rear clutch retainer, then remove clutch plates, driving discs and inner plate.

44. Inspect the clutch pack for wear or damage, then pry wave spring out. Nylon spacer ring and the piston spring can now be removed.

45. Rear clutch piston is removed from the piston retainer. Inner and outer piston seals are both fitted to the piston, and should be replaced.

46. Apply a coating of the wax-type lubricant, and use a feeler gauge, as shown, while pressing down on the piston to seat it in the retainer.

47. Replace the piston spring, nylon spacer ring and retainer wave ring; then install the clutch pack. Inner pressure-plate lip must face inward.

48. Turn the clutch retainer over, and replace the two oil seal rings; then fit the thrust washer in place, and set the assembly aside for reinstallation.

49. After removing the bolts from the rear side of the reaction shaft support, carefully lift the support up and off the oil pump assembly.

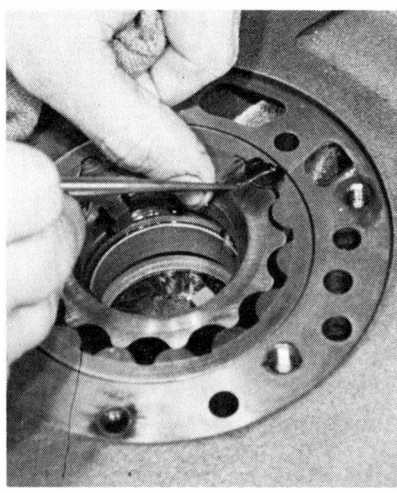

50. Apply a small amount of bluing, and scribe a mark across the inner and outer rotors for correct tooth alignment; then remove both for inspection.

51. Inspect the inner and outer surfaces for scoring or pitting. Check machined surfaces for nicks and burrs, and inspect the rotor teeth for wear.

52. Use the scribed marks to replace and align teeth correctly. Lay a straight-edge across rotors and pump. Clearance limits are 0.001- to 0.002-in.

53. Rotor tip clearance between inner/outer teeth is 0.005- to 0.010-in.; 0.004- to 0.008-in. between outer rotor and pump bore. Replace shaft support seals.

54. Replace reaction shaft support to oil pump body, and reinstall the six attaching bolts. Torque the bolts in alternate sequence to 160 in.-lbs.

HOW TO: A727 TorqueFlite Overhaul

55. Separate the transfer plate from the valve body, and remove the seven check balls and one spring from the valve body locations as circled above.

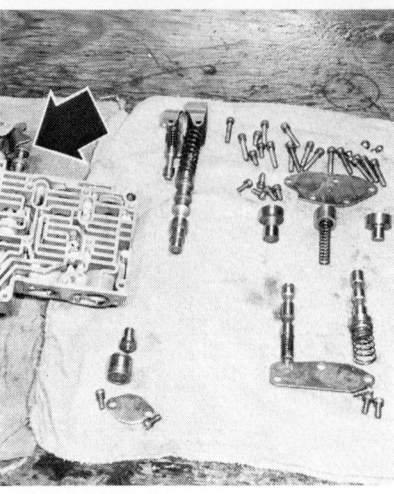

56. For routine cleaning, this is as far as the valve body really needs to be disassembled; pressure regulator system (arrow) does not need to be removed.

57. Clean the separator and transfer plates, then reattach the two to the valve body, torquing all valve-body attaching screws to a value of 35 in.-lbs.

58. Begin transmission case assembly by installing the output shaft and governor assembly. Work new oil seal rings into shaft support carefully.

59. Replace low/reverse clutch band, and install the short strut. Connect the long link and anchor to the band, and tighten adjuster to hold in place.

60. Install the low/reverse drum with rear annulus gear on the output shaft. Be sure #8 thrust washer (arrow) is in place, and install rear planetary.

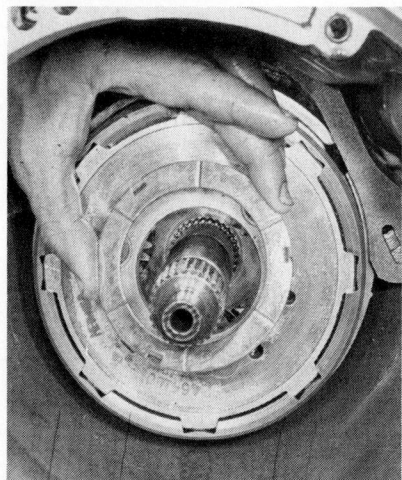

61. The #7 thrust washer is tanged. Put a little grease on it to help hold the washer in place while other components are replaced; then install the washer.

62. Install #6 thrust plate/snap ring on one end of sun gear. Insert gear through driving shell on input shaft; replace #5 washer, snap ring and annulus gear.

63. Fit the #4 thrust washer to rear of front planetary carrier; install on the output shaft, and secure with a snap ring and the #3 thrust washer.

64. The front clutch assembly is installed and engaged with the rear clutch, whose splines must be engaged with those of the front annulus gear.

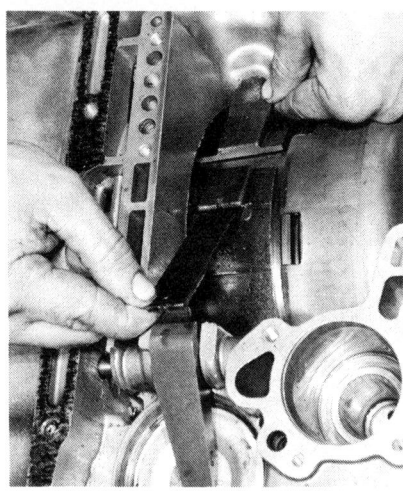

65. Make sure that front clutch-drive lugs engage the driving shell slots. Install the kickdown band in the same manner as the low/reverse band.

66. Replace the O-rings on the accumulator piston, and install the piston and spring in the case—spring goes under piston in 440 dual-exhaust model.

67. To adjust low/reverse band—back off adjusting-screw nut five turns, torque screw to 72 in.-lbs., back off screw as specified, and torque nut to 30 ft.-lbs.

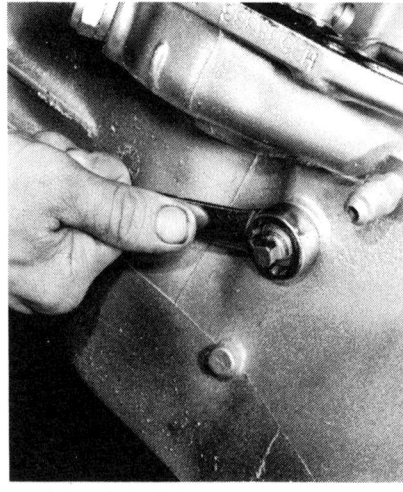

68. To adjust front band—back nut off five turns, torque screw to 72 in.-lbs., then back off screw as specified (page 11-102), and torque nut to 35 ft.-lbs.

69. Replace front pump assembly, and install two studs to position the unit; then replace the attaching bolts, and torque each to 150 in.-lbs.

70. If the front pump seal requires replacement, use a seal puller to remove, as shown, and then install a new seal with its lip facing inward.

71. Position the valve-body manual lever in low to move the parking rod to the rear, and install valve body, working parking rod in place. Install new filter.

72. Replace valve-body attaching bolts, and torque to 100 in.-lbs. Install gearshift lever, and check for binding; fit new gasket and install oil pan.

FORD MOTOR COMPANY

Ford Jatco

APPLICATION

1977-79 Granada, Monarch

DESCRIPTION

Originally developed by Ford Motor Company, Nissan Motor Company and Toyo Kogyo (Mazda) as a joint Japanese/American venture, the Jatco has been used for several years in both Datsun and Mazda vehicles. The Ford version is a 3-speed automatic transmission which uses a torque converter and two planetary gear sets, with two multiple disc clutches, a multiple disc brake, a one-way sprag clutch, and an adjustable intermediate brake band.

Jatco transmissions which require excessive effort to get the shift lever out of the PARK position may suffer from bindup in the shift cable/cable adjustment. If this is not the case, look for a buildup of corrosion between the manual lever shaft and its bore in the transmission case. This will require dropping the oil pan and cleaning the manual lever shaft with fine crocus cloth.

Lubricate each end with type ESA-MIC75-B grease or equivalent before replacing the shaft in the valve body.

The intermediate brake band servo is positioned on the right side of the transmission case next to the fluid filler tube. This allows band adjustment externally by removing the small servo housing cover. A slight amount of fluid will be lost when the cover is removed for band adjustment. Be certain to check the fluid level after replacing the servo cover. Ford specifies use of Type CJ fluid, but has advised mechanics that Dexron II can be mixed with or substituted for Type CJ when necessary.

INTERMEDIATE SERVO BAND ADJUSTMENT

1. Remove the servo cover.
2. Loosen the intermediate servo band adjusting screw locknut and torque the adjusting screw to 10 ft.-lbs.
3. Back off the adjusting screw exactly two turns.
4. Hold the adjusting screw from turning and torque the locknut to 22-29 ft.-lbs.
5. Replace the servo cover with a new gasket. Torque the attaching screws to specifications and check the transmission fluid level. Add fluid if necessary.

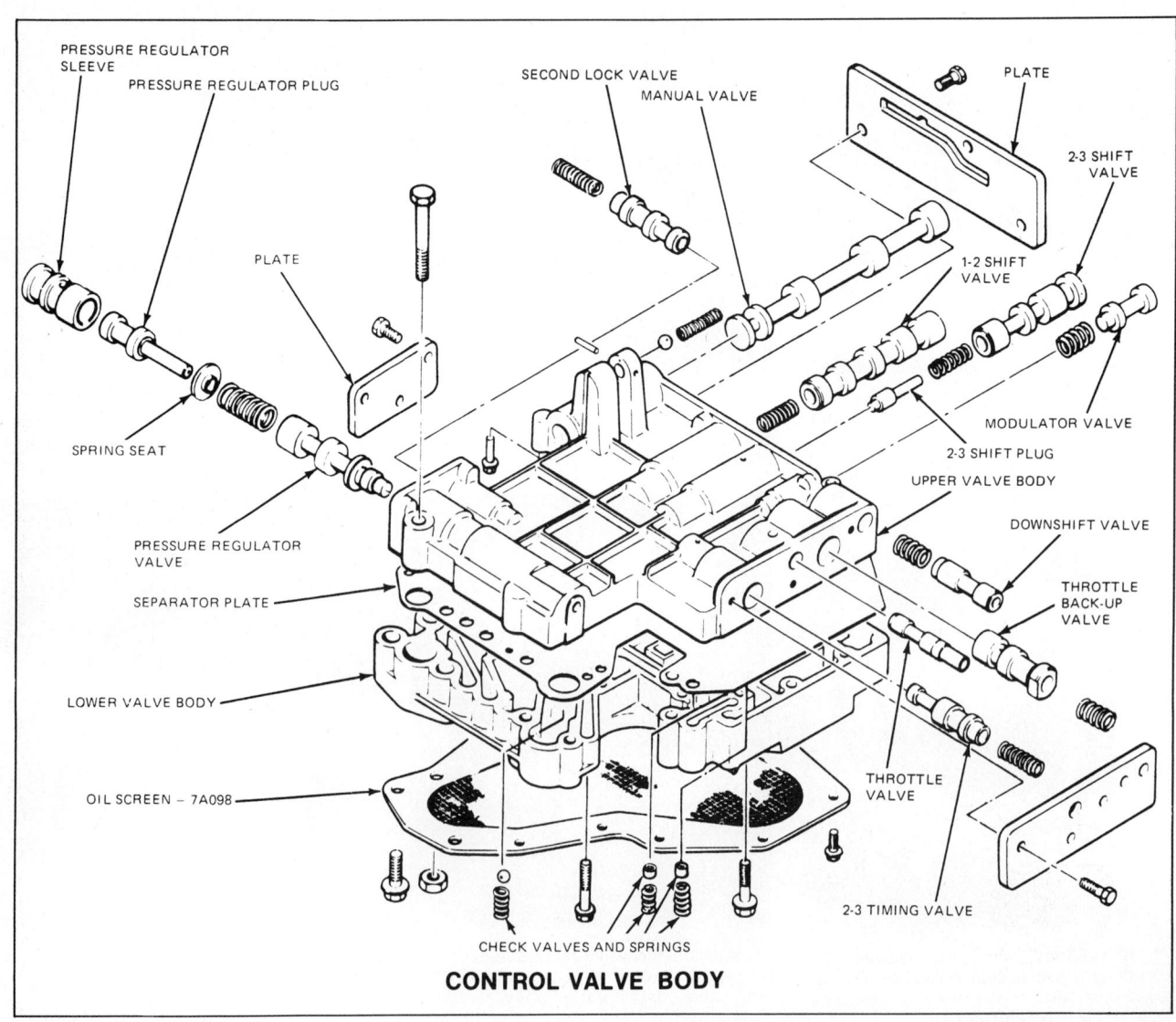

CONTROL VALVE BODY

FORD JATCO

Low and Reverse Brake Disassembled

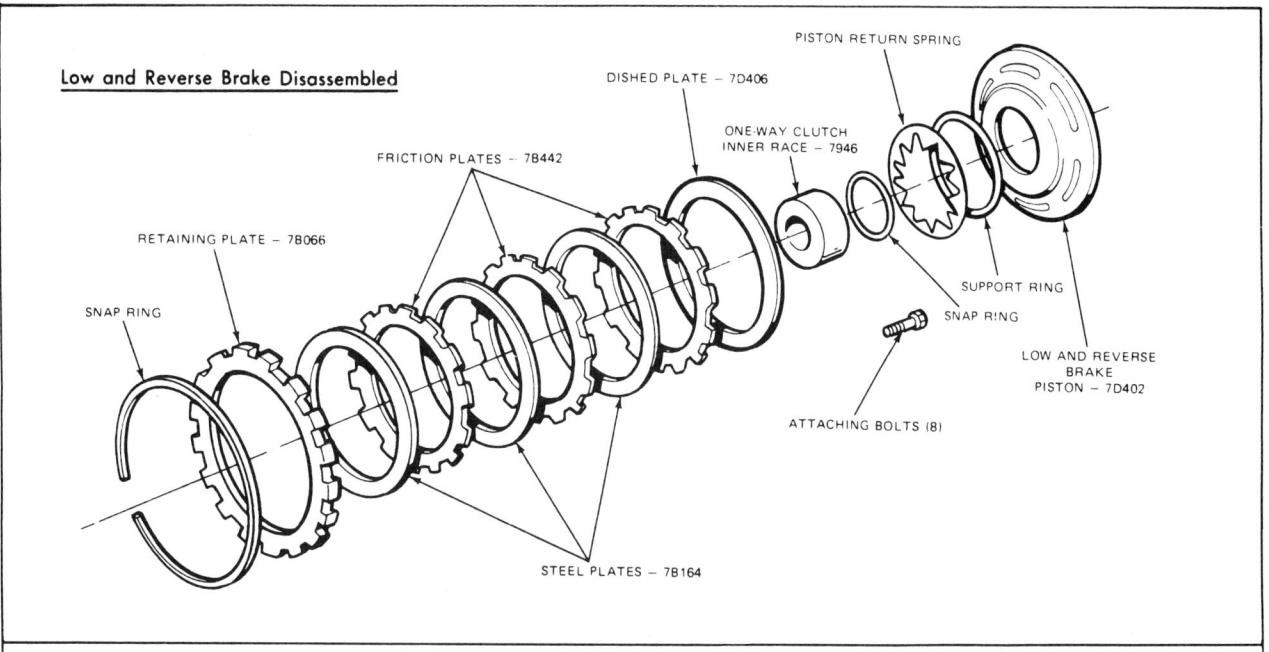

PISTON RETURN SPRING

DISHED PLATE – 7D406

ONE-WAY CLUTCH INNER RACE – 7946

FRICTION PLATES – 7B442

RETAINING PLATE – 7B066

SNAP RING

SNAP RING

SUPPORT RING

ATTACHING BOLTS (8)

LOW AND REVERSE BRAKE PISTON – 7D402

STEEL PLATES – 7B164

Front Clutch Disassembled

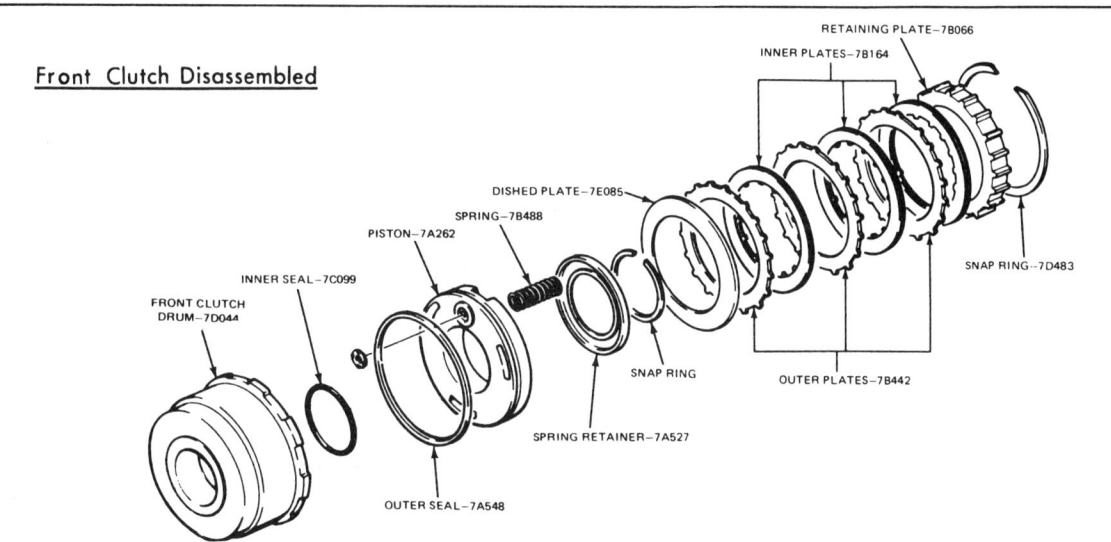

RETAINING PLATE–7B066

INNER PLATES–7B164

DISHED PLATE–7E085

SPRING–7B488

PISTON–7A262

INNER SEAL–7C099

SNAP RING–7D483

FRONT CLUTCH DRUM–7D044

SNAP RING

OUTER PLATES–7B442

SPRING RETAINER–7A527

OUTER SEAL–7A548

Rear Clutch Disassembled

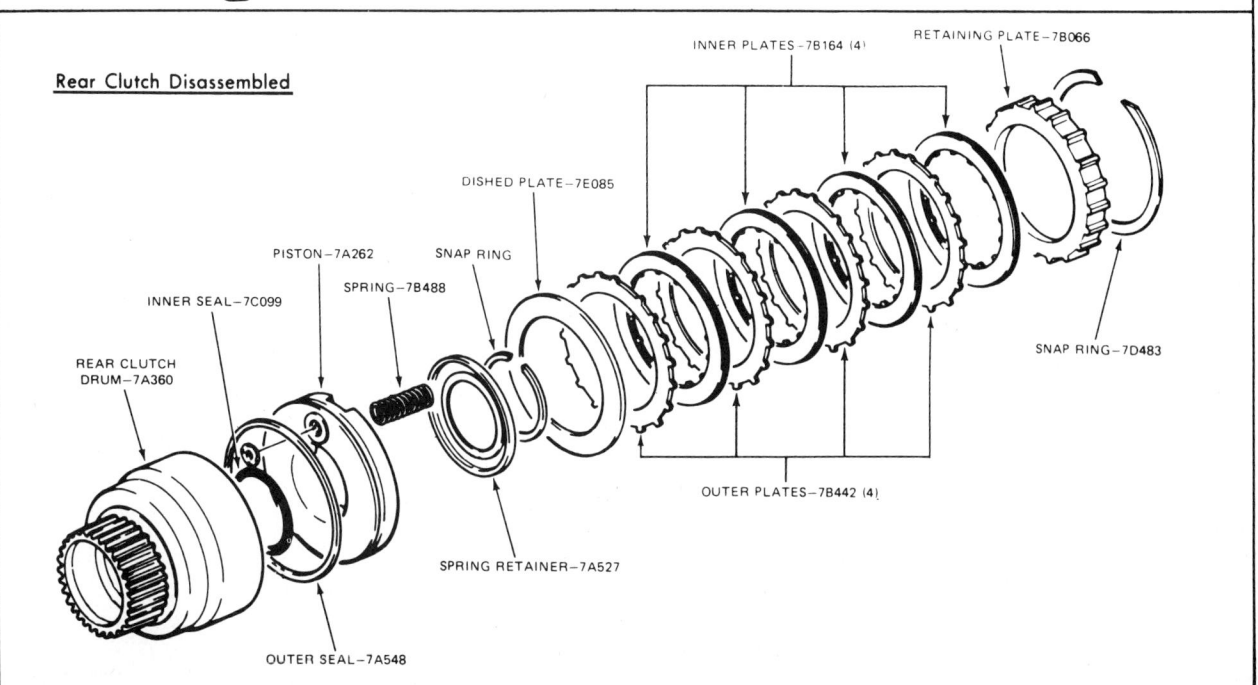

INNER PLATES–7B164 (4)

RETAINING PLATE–7B066

DISHED PLATE–7E085

PISTON–7A262

SNAP RING

INNER SEAL–7C099

SPRING–7B488

SNAP RING–7D483

REAR CLUTCH DRUM–7A360

OUTER PLATES–7B442 (4)

SPRING RETAINER–7A527

OUTER SEAL–7A548

TORQUE SPECIFICATIONS   **JATCO**   ① Apply Motorcraft Sealer or equivalent under bolt heads.

Item	Ft-Lbs	Item	Ft-Lbs
Flywheel to crankshaft	100-115	Lower valve body to upper valve body	2-3
Flywheel to torque converter	29-36	Side plate to control valve body	2-3
Converter housing to engine	29-36	Stud and nut upper to lower control valve body attaching	4-5
Converter housing to transmission case	23-24 ①	Oil screen to lower valve body	2-3
Extension housing to transmission case	15-18	Governor valve body to oil distributor	4-6
Oil pan to transmission case	4-5	Oil pump cover to oil pump housing	4-6
Servo piston rod (when adjusting intermediate band)	9-10	Manual shaft lock nut	22-29
Servo piston rod lock nut	22-29	Oil pressure test plug	7-11
Servo piston retainer to transmission case	4-5	Actuator for parking rod to extension housing	6-8
Servo cover to retainer	4-5	Down shift solenoid	Hand Tight
One-way clutch inner race to transmission case	11-13	Vacuum diaphragm	Hand Tight
Control valve body to transmission case	4-5	Outer manual lever to shaft nut	14-25

GOVERNOR PRESSURE (GOV. P.S.I.)

MPH	2.47:1 Axle Ratio	2.50:1 Axle Ratio
20	19-25	19-25
35	32-39	33-40
50	52-60	53-61

END PLAY SPECIFICATION

Oil Pump Cover to Front Clutch Drum	Total End Play
0.020-0.032	0.010-0.020

REVERSE CLUTCH

Reverse Clutch

Steel	Friction	Clearance
7	7	0.032-0.041

CLUTCH PLATE USAGE

	Forward Clutch			High Clutch		
Model	Steel	Friction	Clearance	Steel	Friction	Clearance
PLA-A	6	6	No Specification	4	4	0.062-0.071

MAIN CONTROL AND GOVERNOR IDENTIFICATION

Vehicle	Engine	Transmission Model	Main Control I.D.	Governor I.D.
Granada/Monarch	250-1V (4.1L)	PLA-A PLA-A2	MA FDI	FD FD

INTERMEDIATE SERVO COMPONENT IDENTIFICATION

Vehicle	Engine	Trans. Model	Servo Piston I.D.	Retainer I.D.	Spring I.D.
Granada/Monarch	250-1V (4.1L)	PLA-A/PLA-A2	F	64-36	None

DIAPHRAGM ASSEMBLY   The Jatco automatic transmission uses a SINGLE AREA vacuum diaphragm.

Operation	Specifications
Total Gear Train End Play	0.010-0.020
Selective Bearing Race Thickness	0.047, 0.055, 0.063, 0.071, 0.079, 0.087
Reverse and High Clutch Pressure	0.062-0.071
Plate-To-Snap Ring Clearance	
Low and Reverse Clutch Pressure Plate	0.032-0.041
To Snap Ring Clearance	

HOW TO: Ford JATCO Overhaul

1. Unbolt the converter housing and remove. Turn the transmission case over and remove the oil pan attaching bolts, pan and gasket.

2. Remove the control valve body attaching bolts and lift body from the case. Unbolt the oil strainer from the control body.

3. Remove the 3 bolts holding the band servo assembly in the case. Lift out servo assembly and remove servo apply spring.

4. Attach a slide hammer to the oil pump and loosen pump from case. Remove slide hammer and lift pump from the case.

5. Loosen the brake band adjusting screw and remove the band strut, then remove the band and forward clutch as an assembly.

6. Remove the rear clutch, clutch hub and front planetary ring gear. This may come out as an assembly or as individual components.

7. Remove the connecting shell and sun gear by rotating it as you pull forward on the assembly. You'll want to have a secure grip on the connecting shell.

8. Use a screwdriver to pry the rear planetary carrier away from the low/reverse brake assembly and withdraw from the case.

9. You'll find this large needle bearing thrust washer located in front of the rear planetary carrier assembly. Again—exercise care in this operation.

HOW TO: Ford JATCO Overhaul

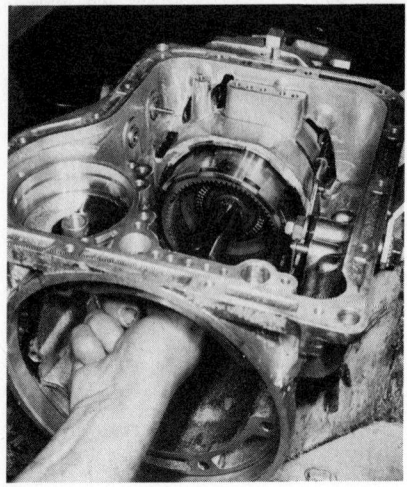

10. Expand and remove the large output shaft snap ring holding the rear planetary carrier to the connecting drum. When expanding snap ring, do it carefully.

11. Turn the connecting drum counterclockwise and the connecting drum clockwise. Remove the drum and one-way clutch race.

12. Unbolt and remove the extension housing-to-case attaching bolts. Remove the extension housing from the transmission case.

13. The parking brake assembly is held in place with E-clip retainers. Unclip and remove the parking brake lever/rod. Do not use unnecessary force.

14. Remove the manual shaft attaching nut to free the manual plate and spacer. Remove the plate and shaft from the case.

15. Remove the case bolts holding the one-way clutch assembly to the rear of the main case and separate from the case.

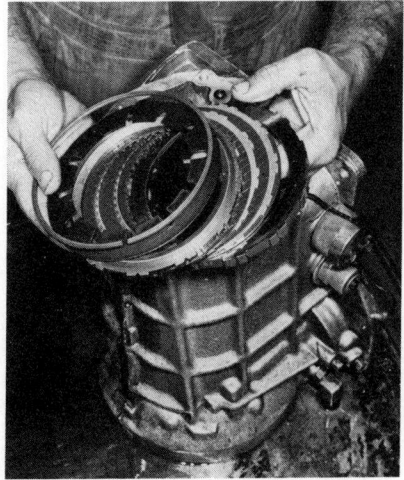

16. Remove the snap ring holding the low/reverse brake assembly to the case. Remove the retaining and clutch plates from the case.

17. After removing the piston, remove the rubber O-ring seals (indicated by arrows 1, 2 and 3) and install new seals before reassembly.

18. Reinstall the piston and check the steel/composition plates for wear, scoring or burning. Replace all if one is bad. Reinstall plates in proper order.

19. Unclip the reverse/high clutch retaining ring and remove the pressure plate, steel/friction/dished plates from the drum.

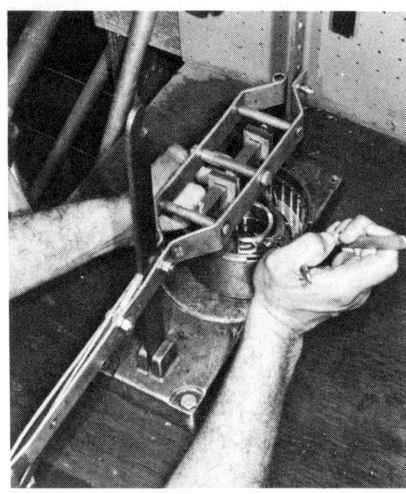

20. Use a spring compressor to hold the spring assembly down while removing the spring retainer snap ring from the clutch drum.

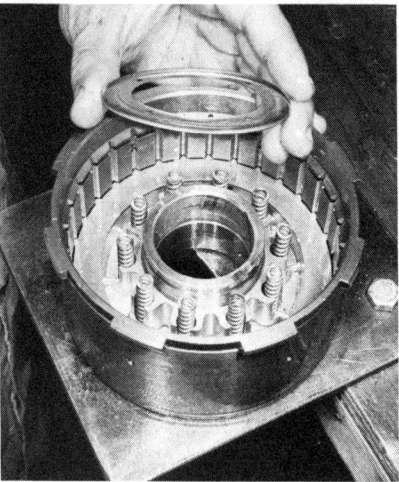

21. Remove the coil spring retainer and the 10 coil springs inside. If any of these coil springs is distorted or broken, replace them all.

22. Remove the piston and replace all O-rings. Replace the coil springs/retainer, then compress them in order to install snap ring.

23. The front clutch is disassembled in the same manner. Remove the large retaining ring and inspect the clutches. Check for any irregularities.

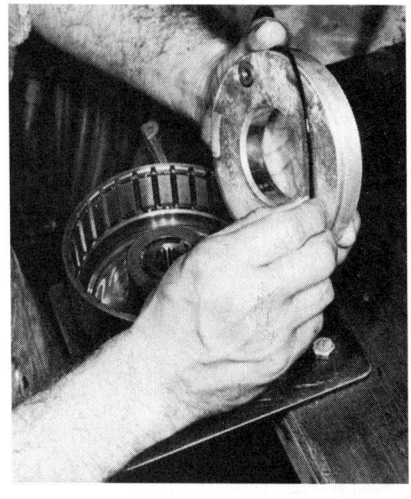

24. Compress the spring assembly to remove the snap ring. Remove retainer and 10 coil springs; replace O-rings and reassemble.

25. Remove the 5 bolts holding the pump cover to its housing. Separate the two and replace stator support seal rings.

26. Inspect drive/driven gears for wear, then replace in pump housing and check clearances with feeler gauge/straight-edge.

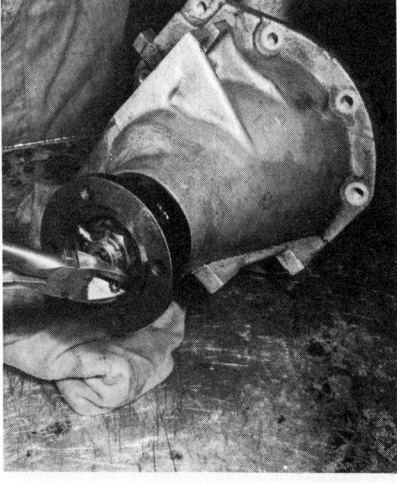

27. To remove output shaft from the extension housing, pull out the cotter pin and remove the attaching nut. Replace rear seal.

HOW TO: Ford JATCO Overhaul

28. Withdraw the output shaft from the rear extension housing. Press on the ball bearing at the rear of the shaft. Notice governor valve (arrow).

29. The governor assembly need not be removed unless it is not functioning. Check governor valve operation as shown.

30. Inspect the three oil distributor slip rings. To remove or replace the slip rings, you must disengage the connecting ends and slip off the shaft.

31. Begin reassembly by installing low/reverse clutch pack. You must replace the pressure plate first, then the clutch plates and retainer.

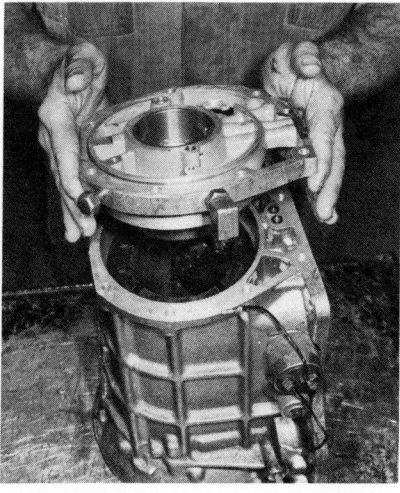

32. Replace the low/reverse snap ring and install the one-way clutch assembly housing to the rear of the transmission case.

33. Install the manual plate and replace the attaching nut. Insert the parking rod, replace retaining arm and install E-clips. This is another job where feel counts.

34. Reinstall rear bearing and insert output shaft into transmission case, rotating shaft to seat oil distributor in case bushing.

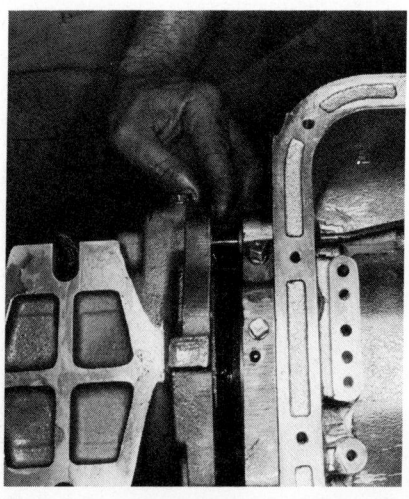

35. Install a new extension housing gasket and slide housing over output shaft. Be sure to align the parking rod with its slot in housing.

36. Seat the extension housing to the transmission case and install the attaching bolts, torquing to factory specifications.

37. Install the low/reverse brake assembly on the output shaft. Rotate assembly until it seats in place correctly. Obviously, you won't want to force it.

38. Slip the drive flange assembly very carefully over the output shaft and rotate to seat inside the low/reverse brake assembly.

39. With your thumb and fingers, fit the rear planetary carrier assembly over the output shaft and engage its tangs in the low/reverse assembly.

40. Install the large snap ring which holds the rear planetary to the connecting drum and replace the needle bearing thrust washer.

41. It's a little different feel, as you replace the shell and ring gear assembly, rotating it to seat against the low/reverse brake assembly.

42. Install the front clutch to the rear clutch, meshing the units, then replace the assembly with input shaft in the case.

43. Insert the brake band in the case around the front clutch drum. Install the strut and tighten adjusting screw to hold band.

44. Drop the servo return spring in the case and install the servo piston/retainer. Torque the attaching bolts to specifications.

45. Replace the front pump and control valve body. Install the oil pan with gasket and attach converter housing. Torque all bolts.

GENERAL MOTORS

180 Transmission

APPLICATION
1978-79 Chevette

DESCRIPTION

Known as the "Strasbourg Transmission," this French-built automatic uses a torque converter and compound planetary gear set, with three multiple disc clutches, a roller (sprag) clutch, and one band to produce three forward and a reverse gear. Upshifts and downshifts are automatic and controlled by vehicle speed, engine vacuum and a cable connected to the accelerator pedal.

Design of the 180 transmission is slightly different from that of other GM automatic transmissions, although its operation is conventional. Stamped components are used, and the second clutch drum contains the ring gear, held in place by internal snap rings. The sprag assembly is also retained inside the third clutch

drum by an internal snap ring. GM provides a special ring compression tool (Part No. J-28456-1 and J-28456-2) to permit separation of these units. They can also be separated by the use of several screwdrivers to compress the ring at various points, but this method is far less efficient.

The rear of the converter housing forms the front of the oil pump, with a wear plate and square-cut oil seal between the two. The band is servo-operated and requires no adjustment in normal use. If the servo assembly is removed from the case, the servo apply bolt must be readjusted to specifications.

SERVO ADJUSTMENT (Internal)

1. Once the servo assembly is reinstalled and the retaining ring replaced, remove the servo compressor tool.

2. Torque the servo adjusting bolt to 40 ft.-lbs. The locknut must remain loose.

3. Back off the servo adjusting bolt exactly 5 turns.

4. Hold the adjusting bolt and sleeve from moving and tighten the locknut snugly.

180 TRANSMISSION TORQUE VALUES

	Torque	
	N·m	Ft.-Lb.
Oil Pan-to-Case	9.8-12.8	7-10
Modulator Assembly	52	38
Extension Housing-to-Case	27.5-34.3	20-25
Oil Pressure Check Plug	6.4-9.8	5-7
Converter Housing-to-Cylinder Block	27-41	20-30
Transmission Support-to-Extension	39-48	29-36
Shift Lever-to-Selector Lever Shaft	20-34	15-25
Detent Cable, Retainer-to-Case	7-10	5-7
Oil Cooler Fittings-to-Case	11-16	8-12
Oil Cooler Fittings-to-Radiator	20-34	15-25
Oil Cooler Hose Clamps-to-Cooler Lines	0.8-1.2	.6-.9
Shifter Ass'y-to-Console	8.5-11	6-8
Neutral Safety Switch-to-Bracket	1.6-2.2	1.2-1.6
Lower Cover-to-Converter Housing	18-22	13-16
Flexplate-to-Converter	41-54	30-40
Transfer Plate-to-Valve Body	7.8-10.8	6-8
Reinforcement Plate-to-Case	7.7-20.6	13-15
Valve Body-to-Case	7.7-20.6	13-15
Servo Cover-to-Case	22.6-25.5	17-19
Converter Housing-to-Oil Pump	17.7-20.6	13-15
Converter Housing-to-Case	32.4-35.3	24-26
Selector Lever Locknut	10.8-14.7	8-11
Governor Body-to-Governor Hub	7.8-9.8	6-7
Servo Adjusting Bolt Locknut	16.7-20.6	12-15
Planetary Carrier Lock Plate	27-48	20-35

HOW TO: General Motors 180 Overhaul

1. Remove fluid filler tube and invert transmission case. Unbolt and remove oil pan. Remove and discard oil pan gasket from case sealing surface.

2. Remove fluid strainer attaching screws. Lift strainer up and off valve body. If strainer gasket does not come off with strainer, remove from valve body.

3. Unbolt valve body (a), transfer plate reinforcement (b), and servo cover (c). Reinforcement plate and servo cover must be removed before valve body.

4. Remove valve body attaching bolts. Lift valve body and transfer plate from trans case. Tilt valve body and disconnect S-link from manual valve.

5. 180 transmission uses two steel check balls located in case passages as shown. Check balls are same size and interchangeable. (Use magnetic pencil.)

6. Remove vacuum modulator by turning counterclockwise with appropriate size modulator removal tool or thin wrench. (Also plunger, valve, sleeve and O-ring.)

7. Transmission mount and balance weight are removed from car with transmission. Unbolt and remove extension housing. Remove and discard gasket.

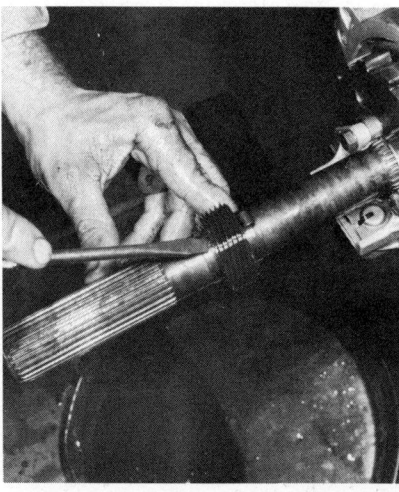

8. To remove speedometer drive gear, depress retaining clip and push clip toward transmission case with screwdriver. Slide gear from output shaft.

9. Unbolt and remove governor unit from output shaft. Shake governor and listen for valve movement. If movement is sluggish or isn't heard, overhaul governor.

HOW TO: General Motors 180 Overhaul

10. Expand and remove governor hub snap ring. Withdraw governor support hub from output shaft. Check oil seal rings on hub for defects or damage.

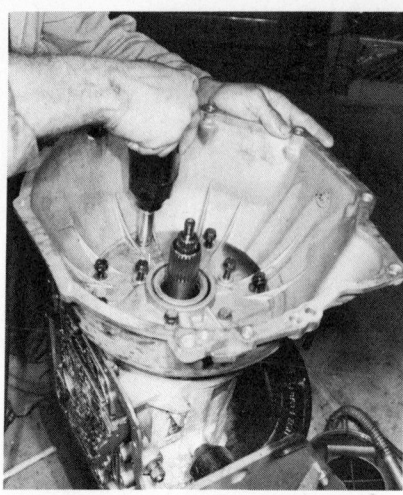

11. Invert transmission case. Remove inner and outer rows of bolts. Lift converter housing up/off case. Rear side of converter housing forms front pump cover.

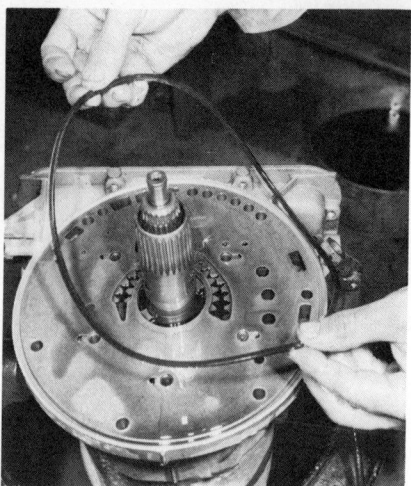

12. Remove large square-cut O-ring seal. Note position of pump wear plate and lift off input shaft. All internal pump components are now exposed.

13. Install metric thread slide hammer in pump bolt hole. Operate slide hammer to free pump and remove with reverse clutch assembly from case as single unit.

14. Withdraw input shaft, second clutch assembly and third clutch drum as single unit. Reverse discs and pressure plate will come out on second clutch drum.

15. Withdraw planetary carrier with attached output shaft, torrington bearings and thrust washer. Stamped carrier contains dual pinion set; possibly replace.

16. Remove reaction sun gear and drum from front of case, and torrington bearing from rear. Servo must be removed before low band can be withdrawn.

17. Servo piston apply pin controls band adjustment. Use compressor tool to depress and hold servo for retaining snap ring removal. Note large servo spring.

18. With servo removed, compress low band slightly and lift from transmission case. Inspect band surface and servo piston apply lugs for wear or damage.

19. Withdraw reverse clutch pack from second clutch. Separate second clutch from input shaft and third clutch drum. Remove thrust washer from shaft.

20. Second clutch drum holds ring gear and large stamped spacer above clutch discs. Remove upper snap ring: pushing screwdriver blade through drum holes.

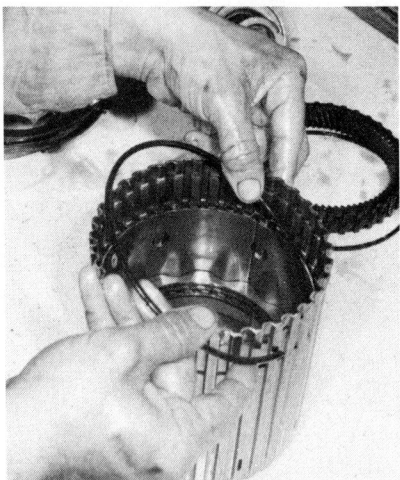

21. Remove ring gear from clutch drum, pry second snap ring free and remove. Snap ring removal is time-consuming if GM compressor tool is not available.

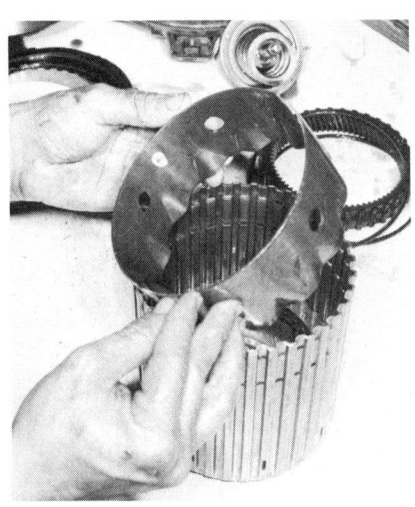

22. Compress and withdraw second clutch spacer positioned under lower snap ring. Remove clutch drive/driven plates and thrust washer. Inspect plates.

23. Compress piston spring retainer and remove snap ring. Replace piston seals, inspect piston check ball and springs. Reinstall piston and retaining snap ring.

24. Install second clutch discs with wave washer first. Driven plate lugs must engage in clutch drum serrations. Install spacer and replace lower snap ring.

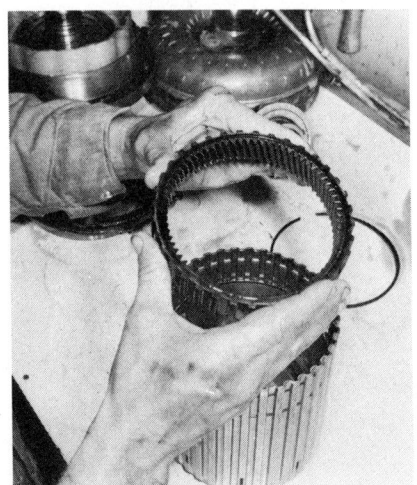

25. Inspect inner and outer ring gear teeth. Install gear in second clutch drum with grooved edge facing upward. Replace upper snap ring.

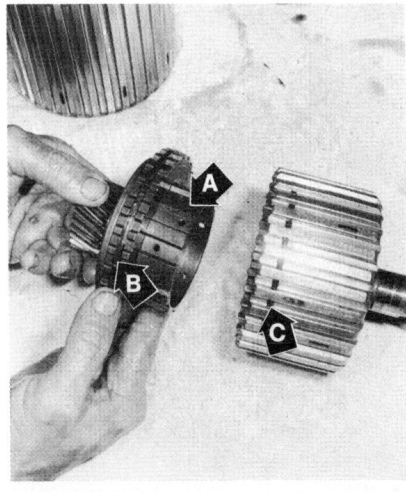

26. If GM compressor tool is not available to separate hub (a) from 3rd clutch drum, depress snap ring (b) through drum slots (c) with screwdriver.

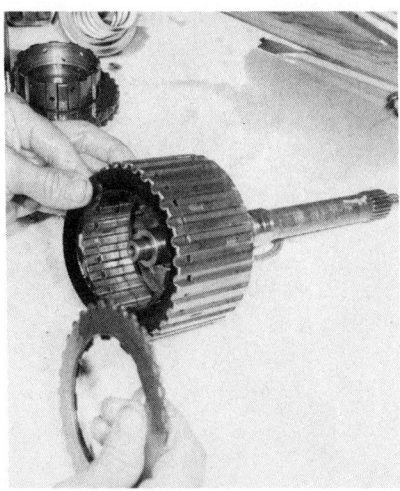

27. Remove thrust washer, torrington bearing and clutch pack from third clutch drum. Discs are quite small. Inspect carefully for wear or damage.

HOW TO: General Motors 180 Overhaul

28. Withdraw roller thrust bearing and spacer from input shaft inside clutch drum. Spacer is located beneath bearing. Check both for wear or damage.

29. Remove snap ring by compressing third clutch retaining plate. Remove retaining plate and check for worn, broken or distorted piston springs.

30. Remove piston from clutch drum. Replace all O-ring seals with new set. Lubricate edge of piston, reinstall in clutch drum and rotate to seat piston.

31. Replace return springs on piston. Reinstall retaining plate and compress for snap ring replacement. Snap ring must engage shaft groove properly.

32. Reinstall conical plate in clutch drum and replace clutch pack. Install thrust washer on clutch hub shaft and replace torrington bearing.

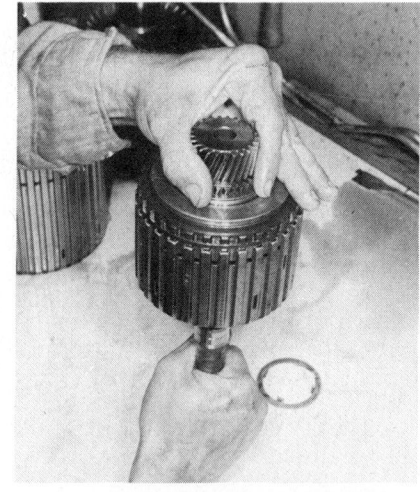

33. Assemble clutch hub, sprag race and retainer assembly to third clutch drum, rotating to mesh and seat. Snap ring must expand to engage slots properly.

34. Invert third clutch housing and turn sprag clockwise to make sure it locks up. Lubricate and install selective thrust washer shown on face of clutch housing.

35. Reassemble input shaft and third clutch drum to second clutch drum. Rotate to engage units and invert. Reverse clutch pack is not now installed.

36. Reverse clutch is positioned at rear of front pump. Compress retaining plate, remove snap ring and check for broken, distorted or worn return springs.

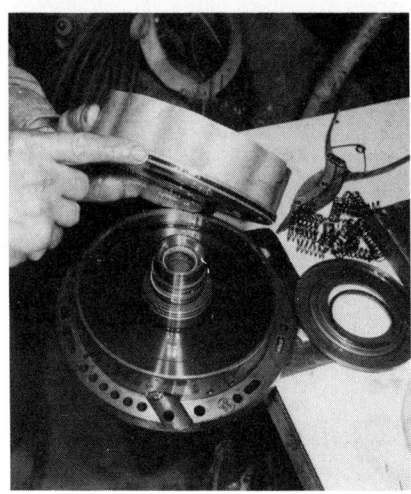

37. Rotate reverse clutch piston and pull upward to remove. Replace O-ring seals on piston. Check pump support seal rings and replace if worn or damaged.

38. Reinstall reverse clutch piston and rotate until completely seated. Replace piston return springs and retaining plate. Install snap ring in shaft groove.

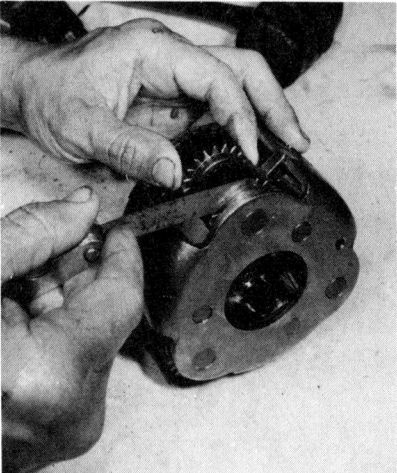

39. Check planetary carrier pinion clearances with feeler gauge. Clearance must be within .005-.035-in. Replace if teeth are worn/damaged, or if excessive play.

40. Don't forget roller thrust bearing positioned on forward end of output shaft inside planetary carrier. Remove, inspect and replace bearing in carrier.

41. Remove, inspect and reinstall pump drive/driven gears. End clearance measured with feeler gauge and straightedge should be between .0005-.0035-in.

42. Begin transmission reassembly by installing low band in case. Rotate band until apply lugs are positioned for engagement with servo apply pin.

43. Install reaction sun gear and drum inside low band. Rotate sun gear assembly to make certain that it engages properly within the low band.

44. Replace output shaft/planetary carrier in transmission case. Rotate planetary carrier to engage reaction sun gear in pinions, and seat completely.

45. Grasp input shaft and lower the second/third clutch assembly into case. Rotate assembly to engage input sun gear in planetary and seat completely.

HOW TO: General Motors 180 Overhaul

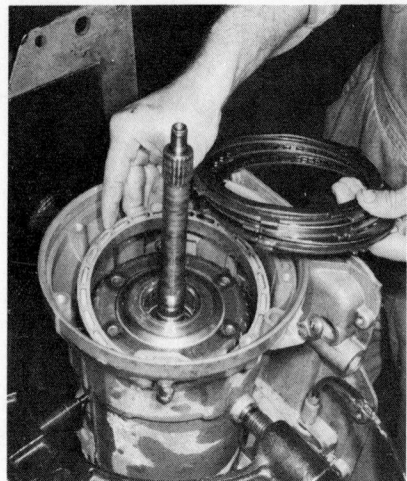

46. Rotate input shaft. Output shaft will turn if components are properly installed. Reinstall reverse clutch drive/driven discs as shown.

47. Install new front pump gasket. Align gasket holes with those in transmission case. Install two guide studs in case to assist in proper pump installation.

48. Replace reverse clutch/front pump assembly in transmission case. Align pump cutout with cooler fitting on case and seat in place.

49. Replace pump wear plate and install new O-ring seal. Seal does not fit completely into case groove, as converter housing is also grooved to accept seal.

50. Fit converter housing to case and install inner and outer row of attaching bolts. Alternately torque inner bolts to 13-17 ft.-lbs.; outer bolts to 22-26 ft.-lbs.

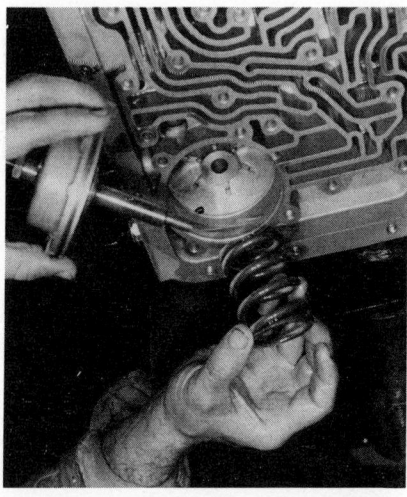

51. Replace servo return spring and install servo piston and apply pin to engage band apply lugs. Compress servo piston to install retaining snap ring.

52. Slide governor support hub on output shaft and rotate to seat hub in case without damaging oil ring seals. Install snap ring in output shaft groove.

53. Align governor body with support hub holes. Install attaching bolts and torque to 6-8 ft.-lbs. Governor valves must move freely when shaft is rotated.

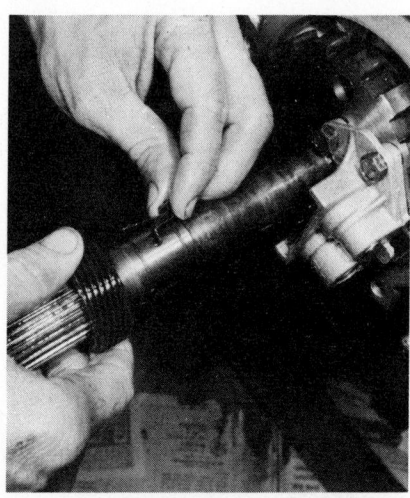

54. Insert speedometer drive gear retaining clip in shaft slot. Slide speedometer drive gear over retaining clip until it snaps in place.

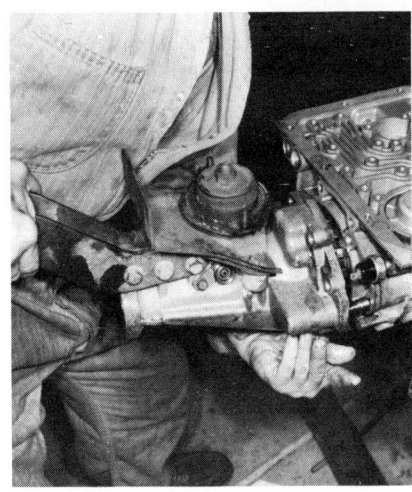

55. Install new extension housing gasket. Slide extension housing over output shaft and align parking pawl shaft. Install and torque bolts to 20-30 ft.-lbs.

56. Replace both check balls in respective cored passages in case as shown. When valve body service is necessary, disassemble according to drawing.

57. Install two guide studs at opposite sides of case. Fit new valve body gasket over studs. These will position and hold gasket for valve body installation.

58. Replace valve body and transfer plate, engaging manual valve with S-link. Install servo cover and reinforcement plate. Replace attaching bolts loosely.

59. Check engagement of manual valve with S-link. Check for proper manual valve operation by operating roller detent (a) through entire gear range.

60. Position new fluid strainer gasket on valve body. Install fluid strainer, replace attaching bolts and torque to factory specifications.

61. Torque all valve body, servo cover and reinforcement plate bolts to factory specs. An alternating pattern to draw components in place prevents warping.

62. Replace modulator valve, sleeve and plunger in case. Install and tighten modulator. Replace oil pan with new pan gasket and install attaching bolts.

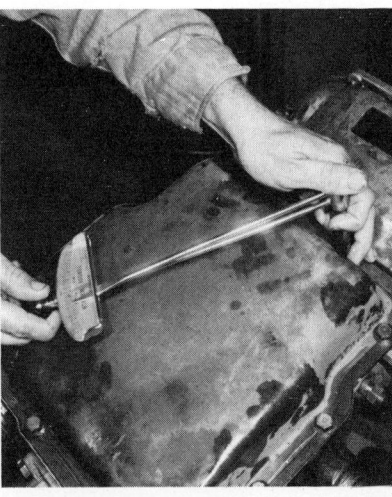

63. Torque all oil pan attaching bolts to factory specifications in an alternating pattern. Invert case and reinstall fluid filler tube.

INDEX

DRIVESHAFTS, REAR AXLES AND TRANSAXLES

THE DRIVESHAFT—REAR WHEEL DRIVE

A steel tube fitted with universal joints at each end and used to transmit power from the transmission output shaft to the rear axle or differential, the drive or propeller shaft differs in length, diameter and type of connection according to the car model, wheelbase and transmission combination used **(Fig. 12-1)**.

A splined slip yoke is used with the universal or U-joint to connect the driveshaft to the transmission, and is held in alignment by a bushing in the transmission extension housing. The slip yoke allows horizontal (in-out) shaft movement as the rear axle moves vertically (up-down) with varying road conditions. The spline is lubricated by the transmission fluid, and an oil seal in the extension housing protects the yoke from road dust and dirt while preventing lubricant leakage **(Fig. 12-2)**. Some automatic transmissions use a slip yoke spline with a center vent hole to prevent O-ring seal damage during installation. Such vent holes **(Fig. 12-3)** should be kept clear of contamination.

At the opposite end of the driveshaft, another U-joint is used to connect the shaft to the rear axle companion flange. This may be attached by bolts, U-bolts or by clamp straps. Some driveshafts incorporate a damper; these are not serviceable, and if replacement is required, the damper and sleeve are replaced as an assembly. Since the driveshaft is a balanced unit, it must be kept completely free of undercoating or other contamination which can alter the balance.

UNIVERSAL JOINTS

Since the angle and length of the driveshaft change with suspension motion, a universal joint is necessary at each end of the driveshaft. There are two types of U-joints in common use on all 1970 and later American cars—the Cardan, or cross and yoke, and the Double Cardan, or constant velocity joint.

CARDAN JOINT

Two Y-shaped yokes connected by an X-shaped crossmember, called a spider or cross, form this simple automotive U-joint **(Fig. 12-4)**. The spider permits the

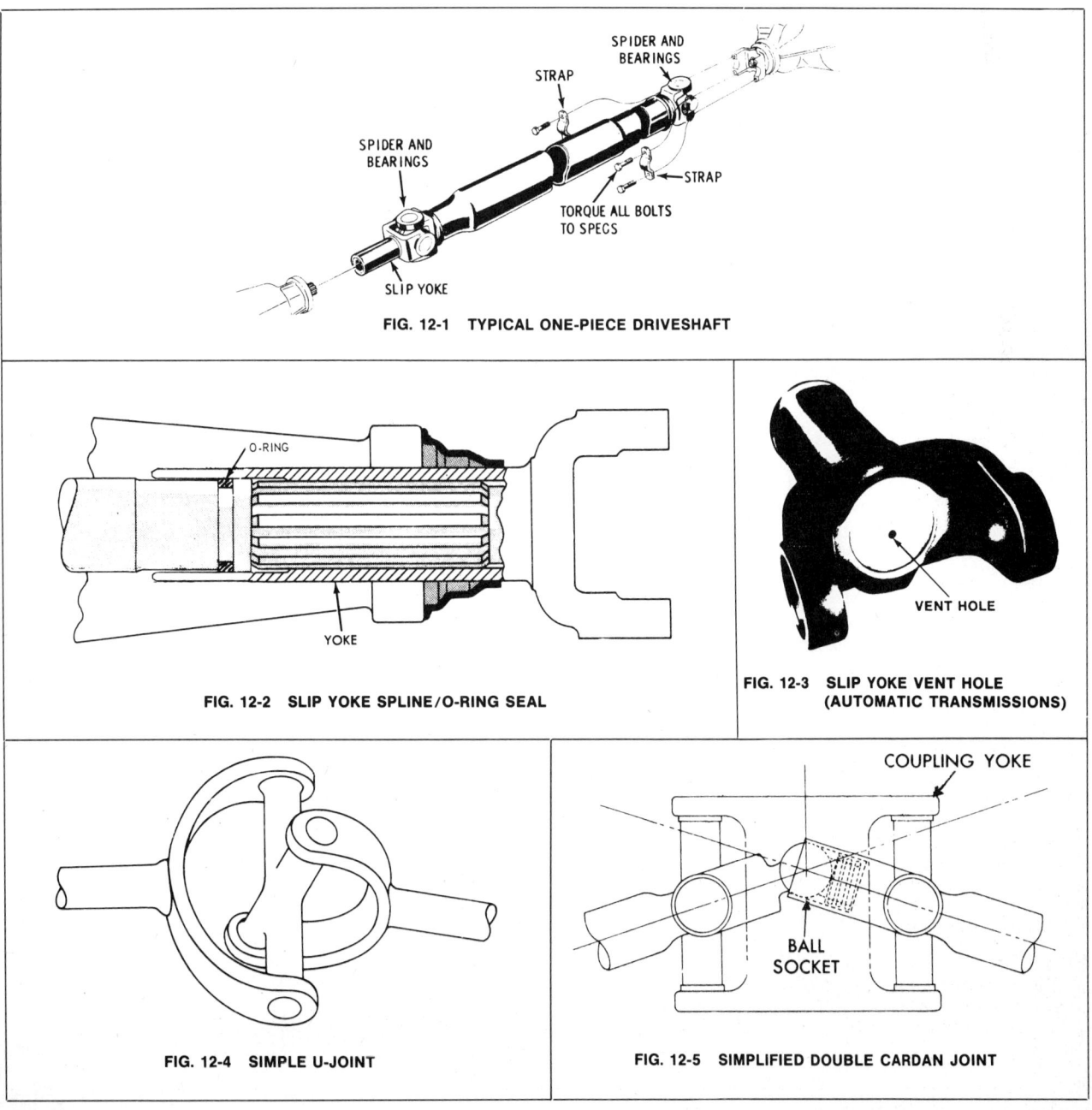

FIG. 12-1   TYPICAL ONE-PIECE DRIVESHAFT

FIG. 12-2   SLIP YOKE SPLINE/O-RING SEAL

FIG. 12-3   SLIP YOKE VENT HOLE
(AUTOMATIC TRANSMISSIONS)

FIG. 12-4   SIMPLE U-JOINT

FIG. 12-5   SIMPLIFIED DOUBLE CARDAN JOINT

two yoke shafts to function at angles to each other. But when torque passes through this joint, it is not transferred at a uniform speed, because the driving shaft rotates at a constant speed, while the driven yoke slows down and speeds up twice during each revolution. This variation in velocity increases as the angle between the two yoke shafts increase, and can lead to driveline vibration if the angle is too great.

The problem is minimized on one-piece driveshafts by arranging U-joints at each end of the shaft placed at 90° angles to each other. The alternating acceleration/deceleration of one U-joint is offset by the alternating deceleration/acceleration of the second joint. As long as the angle between the drive and driven yokes is approximately equal, objectionable vibration can be avoided.

DOUBLE CARDAN JOINT

Where a large angle is required in a driveline, the Cardan joint introduces two vibrations in each revolution of sufficient intensity to cause driveline vibration. To eliminate this problem, two Cardan joints are connected by a coupling yoke that is properly phased for constant velocity and a centering ball socket is located between the two joints to maintain their relative position (**Fig. 12-5**). In this manner, the turning motion at one end forces the other end to turn an equal amount in the opposite direction. Thus, the input speed is the same as the output speed, despite the link yoke's variation in speed.

U-JOINT CONSTRUCTION

All universal joints contain needle roller bearings held in place by round bearing cups. Two methods are used to secure the cross to the yoke—retaining clips and injection molding.

Retaining Clips—Grooves are provided in the bearing cups, and snap rings are installed to hold the cross in the yoke (**Fig. 12-6**). The snap ring may be located either on the inside or the outside of the yoke. In either case, care must be taken to seat the snap ring securely in the groove whenever the U-joint is disassembled. This method of securing the cross to the yoke is used on American Motors, Ford Motor Company and Chrysler Corporation cars; when used on General Motors cars, it is referred to as the "Cleveland" U-joint.

Injection Molding—A groove in the outside diameter of the round bearing cup matches a groove in the inside diameter of the driveshaft yoke-bearing bore. When these grooves are aligned during manufacture, with the bearing cups seated against the ends of the cross, a plastic ring is injection-molded between them, through a hole in the yoke, to hold the bearing cup in place (**Fig. 12-7**). Production universal joints of this type cannot be reassembled once taken apart. A replacement kit is available containing a new cross, bearing cup assemblies and bearing retainer clips (**Fig. 12-8**). This method of securing the cross to the yoke is used on General Motors cars, and referred to as the "Saginaw" U-joint.

U-JOINT LUBRICATION

Cardan U-joints are lubricated for life during manufacture, and grease fittings are not provided for lubrication on the car, although you will generally find lube fittings on replacement U-joints. Where a Double Cardan U-joint is used, a lubrication fitting is provided on the centering ball in the coupling yoke, and should be lubricated according to the manufacturer's recommendations—usually at 6000- to 7500-mile intervals. Should a U-joint become worn or noisy, it must be removed and a replacement U-joint installed.

DRIVESHAFT REMOVAL/REPLACEMENT
TO REMOVE

1. With the car on a hoist, mark the shaft-to-companion-flange relationship for correct reassembly, and disconnect the rear U-joint by removing the flange bolts (**Fig. 12-9**) or the clamp straps (**Fig. 12-10**).
2. Wrap a piece of tape around the U-joint to retain the bearing cups to prevent possible damage and/or loss of the bearing rollers.
3. Place a container under the transmission-output-shaft housing to catch any oil leakage.
4. Remove the driveshaft front yoke from the transmission by pulling the shaft to the rear and passing it under the axle housing.
5. Check for burrs on the transmission-output-shaft spline.

TO REPLACE

1. Check the transmission-extension-housing yoke seal, and replace if necessary.
2. Lightly coat the slip yoke splines with transmission oil.
3. Fit the driveshaft front yoke into the extension housing so that the output shaft splines mate with the driveshaft yoke splines.
4. Align the driveshaft and companion-flange reference marks, and remove the tape from the bearing cups.
5. Connect the exposed bearing cups to the companion flange by replacing the U-bolts, flange bolts or clamp straps, and torque to specifications.

CARDAN U-JOINT REPLACEMENT (Fig. 12-11)
DISASSEMBLY—RETAINING CLIP TYPE

1. Secure the driveshaft yoke in a vise—*do not*

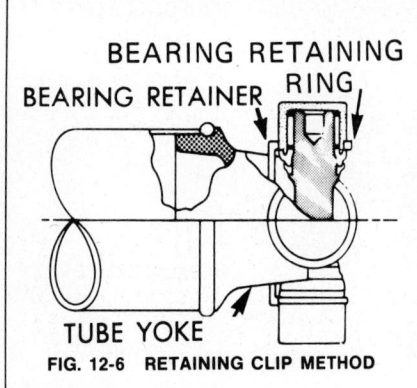

BEARING RETAINING RING

BEARING RETAINER

TUBE YOKE

FIG. 12-6 RETAINING CLIP METHOD

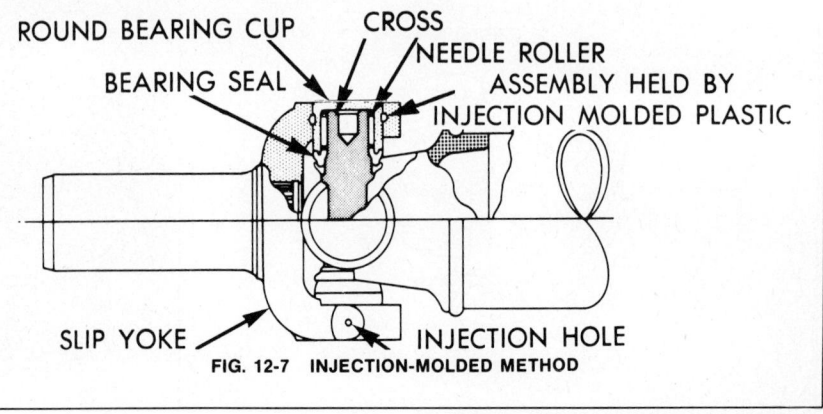

ROUND BEARING CUP   CROSS

NEEDLE ROLLER ASSEMBLY HELD BY INJECTION MOLDED PLASTIC

BEARING SEAL

SLIP YOKE   INJECTION HOLE

FIG. 12-7 INJECTION-MOLDED METHOD

clamp the driveshaft housing in the vise, because excessive pressure can damage it.

2. Apply penetrating oil to the bearing cups, and remove the retaining clips with a screwdriver and needlenose pliers.

3. Remove the driveshaft yoke from the vise, and place a 1 1/8-in. socket against the yoke on one side and a 9/16-in. socket against the bearing cup on the other. Then replace it in the vise **(Fig. 12-11A)**.

4. Tighten the vise until the bearing cup being pushed out by the small socket clears the inside of the yoke.

5. Release the vise and sockets.

6. Position the protruding bearing cup in the vise jaws, and remove it.

7. Repeat Steps 4 to 6 to remove the opposite bearing cup.

8. If the front U-joint is being serviced, remove the yoke from the cross, and repeat Steps 4 to 6 to remove the other two bearing cups and the cross from the driveshaft.

9. Clean the yoke and yoke area of all dirt and grease before reassembling.

REASSEMBLY—RETAINING CLIP TYPE

1. Pack the bearings in the bearing cups with grease, and fill the lubricant reservoir at each end of the cross (unless the new cross is pre-lubricated). Using a squeeze bottle of lubricant will prevent any air pockets from forming in the cross lubricant cavities.

2. Position the replacement cross in the driveshaft yoke, and partially install the bearing cups and new seals in the yoke.

3. Secure the driveshaft yoke in a vise with the 9/16-in. socket, and tighten the vise to press the bearing cup flush with the outside of the yoke.

4. Install a new retainer clip, and seat it securely in the bearing cup groove.

5. Repeat Steps 3 and 4 to install the other driveshaft yoke-bearing cup. If servicing the front U-joint, fit the front yoke over the remaining two cross arms, and repeat the same procedure to install the other two bearing cups.

6. Once the retaining clips are all in place, support the driveshaft yoke in the vise, and tap it lightly with a soft-faced hammer to make sure the clips have seated properly.

7. Remove the driveshaft yoke, and fit the front yoke in the vise, repeating Step 6 with the remaining retaining clips.

DISASSEMBLY—INJECTION MOLDED TYPE

This is accomplished in essentially the same manner as the retaining clip type, but a small pin or punch

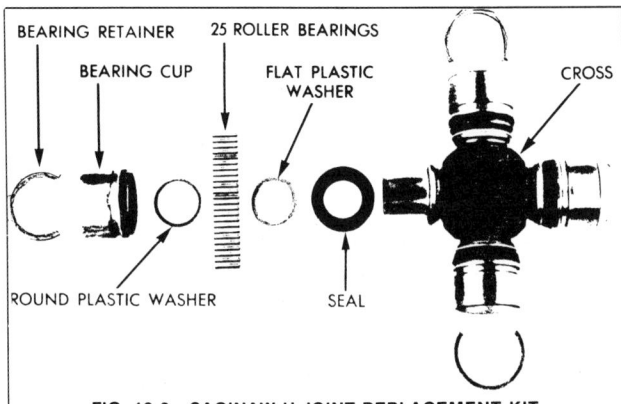

FIG. 12-8 SAGINAW U-JOINT REPLACEMENT KIT

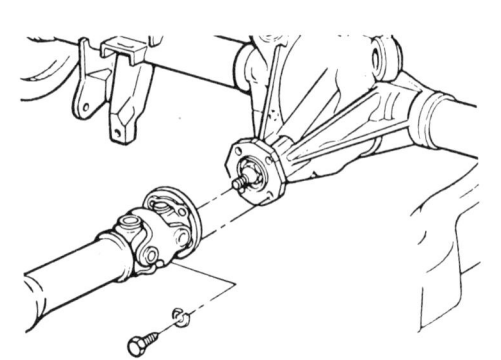

FIG. 12-9 FLANGE ATTACHMENT

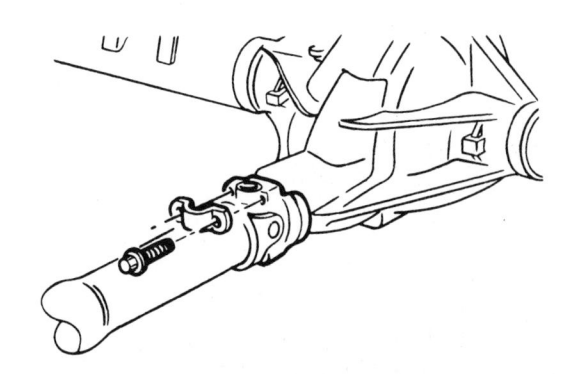

FIG. 12-10 STRAP ATTACHMENT

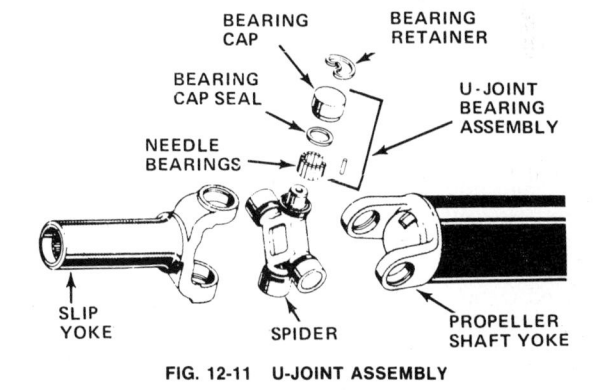

FIG. 12-11 U-JOINT ASSEMBLY

FIG. 12-11A U-JOINT REPLACEMENT

must be driven through the injection holes, and all remains of the sheared, plastic bearing-retainer material must be removed from the yoke ears, or the new bearing cups cannot be properly pressed into place.

REASSEMBLY—INJECTION MOLDED TYPE

1. Fit one bearing cup partially into one side of the yoke, and insert the cross into the yoke so that its arm seats freely in the bearing cup.

2. Partially replace the opposite bearing cup, and use a vise to press the cross ends into the bearing cup, working the yoke to check for free movement of the cross ends in the bearings.

3. When one bearing-cup retainer groove clears the inside of the yoke, stop pressing and install the retaining ring, then continue pressing until the other groove clears the yoke and install that ring.

4. If servicing the front U-joint, repeat the procedure to assemble the front yoke to the driveshaft yoke.

5. Gently tap the yoke ears to loosen the bearings, and seat the retainer clips.

DOUBLE CARDAN U-JOINT REPLACEMENT

The Double Cardan U-joint is serviced in the same manner as the Cardan, but the coupling yoke and flange yokes should all be marked with a punch to provide an alignment guide for correct reassembly. Centering ball replacement on General Motors Double Cardan U-joints requires the use of a special installation tool (Chevrolet J-23996 or Buick J-23677) to properly seat the new ball. Proper seating is vital to joint operation, because the center of a Double Cardan joint is determined by the ball seating tightly in the proper location. To remove and replace the centering ball mechanism:

1. Remove one of the U-joints, as described under "Cardan U-Joint Replacement."

2. Pry the seal from the ball socket, and remove the washers, spring and the three ball seats **(Fig. 12-12)**.

3. Clean the ball seat insert, and inspect the seat insert bushing. If excessively worn, replace the entire coupling yoke/cross assembly.

4. Clean and check the seal, ball seats, spring and washer. Replace the entire set if any parts are excessively worn. The seal should be replaced with a new one whenever the ball seat parts are removed, whether replaced or not.

5. Clean all plastic from the coupling yoke groove, and inspect the surface of the centering ball. If the ball is worn beyond a smooth polish, replace it.

6. Position the inner fingers of tool J-23996 or J-23677 over the centering ball, replace the outer cylinder of the tool and thread the nut in place, drawing the ball from the seat.

7. Position the replacement ball on the stud, and drive in place, using tool J-23996 or J-23677 and a hammer, until the ball seats firmly against the shoulder located on the stud base.

8. Lubricate all parts with the grease provided, and insert the spring, small washer, ball seats (largest opening facing outward), large washer and seal.

9. Lubricate the seal lip, and seat the seal flush, using an appropriate socket and hammer. The sealing lip must tip inward when properly installed.

10. Lubricate the cavity with the grease provided, and reassemble the flange to the centering ball, aligning the reference punch marks.

11. Replace the cross and bearing cups as outlined under "Cardan U-Joint Replacement."

UNIVERSAL JOINT ATTACHMENT TORQUE SPECIFICATIONS

	FT.-LBS.
BUICK	
Strap or U-bolt	15
Flange yoke	75
CADILLAC	
Pinion flange to U-joint flange	70
CHEVROLET	
U-Joint to Companion Flange, except Chevette	70
U-Joint to Companion Flange, Chevette	16
OLDSMOBILE	
Strap attachment	14
Flange yoke	75
PONTIAC	
Strap attachment	14
Flange yoke	85
FORD, LINCOLN, MERCURY	
All except circular flange	8-15
Circular flange	70-90
CHRYSLER	
U-bolt (except 7¼-in axle)	45
U-bolt (7¼-in axle)	40
Clamp screws	170*
AMERICAN MOTORS	
U-bolt clamp	13

* in. lbs.

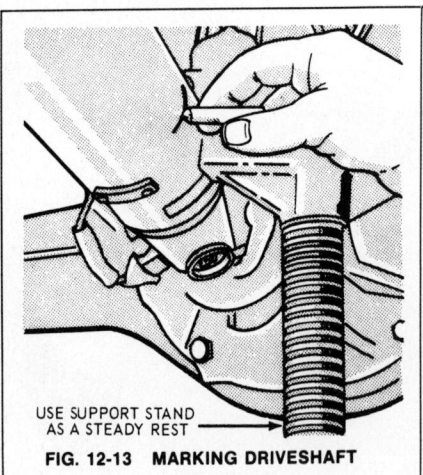

FIG. 12-13 MARKING DRIVESHAFT

USE SUPPORT STAND AS A STEADY REST

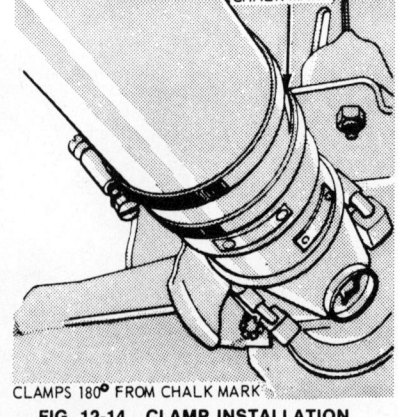

CLAMPS 180° FROM CHALK MARK

FIG. 12-14 CLAMP INSTALLATION

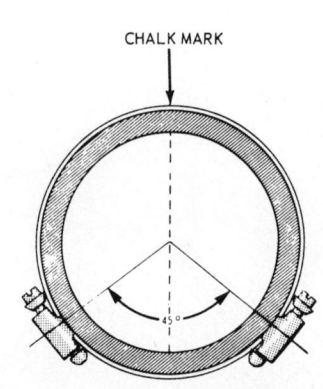

CHALK MARK

FIG. 12-15 CLAMP ROTATION

DRIVESHAFT BALANCING

All driveshafts are balanced units. If the driveshaft is removed for service and a yoke replaced incorrectly, driveline vibration will result. Whenever the driveshaft is to be removed, mark the shaft and yoke and the shaft and companion flange so the components can be reassembled in the same rotational position as they were.

When vibration is encountered after a yoke replace-ment, disconnect the shaft at the slip yoke, rotate the yoke 180° and reconnect to the shaft. Should vibration continue, disconnect the shaft from the rear-axle companion flange, and rotate the flange 180°, then reconnect the shaft and flange.

If this procedure does not eliminate driveshaft vibration, the driveshaft must be balanced. The most accurate method involves the use of an electronic wheel balancer, but this is a very specialized piece of shop

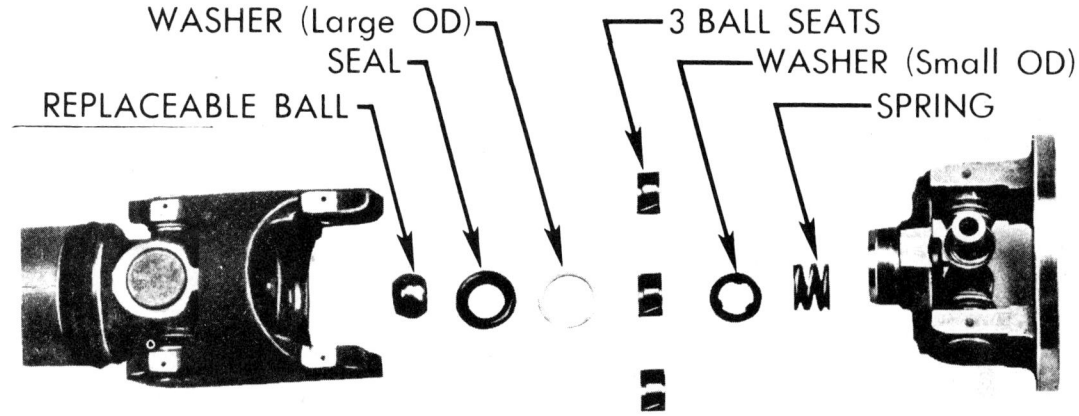

FIG. 12-12   CENTERING BALL COMPONENTS

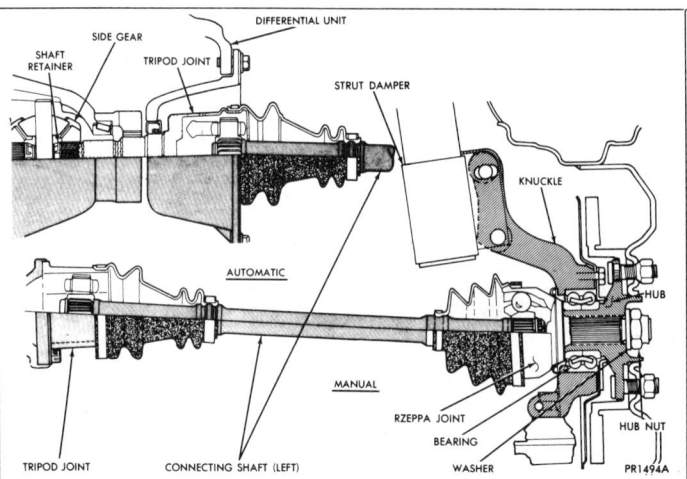

FIG. 12-15A   OMNI/HORIZON DRIVESHAFT COMPONENTS

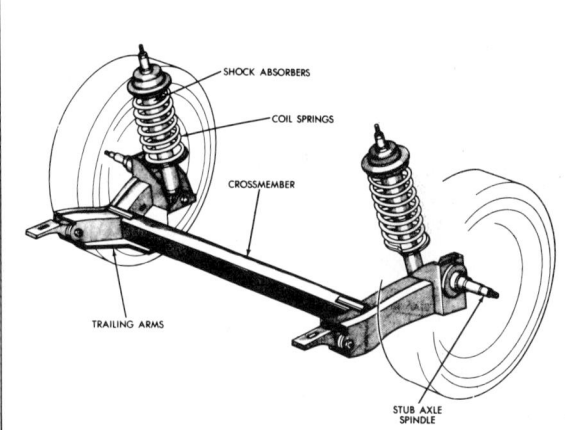

FIG. 12-15C   OMNI/HORIZON REAR AXLE AND SUSPENSION

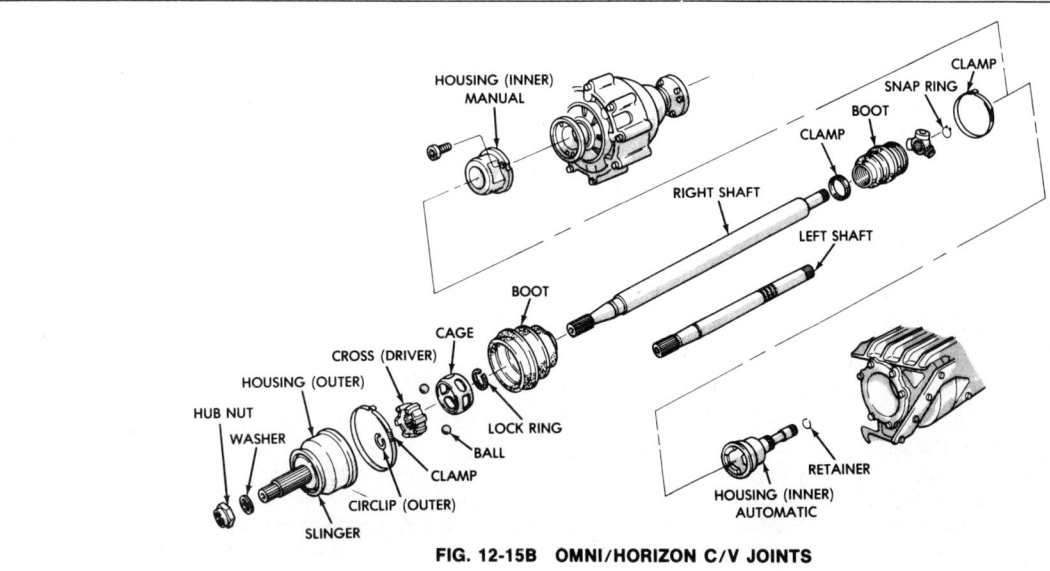

FIG. 12-15B   OMNI/HORIZON C/V JOINTS

equipment which the non-professional is unlikely to find available. The hose clamp methods described below will produce the same results, if the procedure is followed carefully. *Do not* run the engine for prolonged periods while carrying out this procedure, or overheating will result. Exercise extreme caution while working near the rotating driveshaft, or severe injury can result.

1. Raise the car on a twin-post hoist, with its rear supported on the rear axle housing.

2. Remove the rear wheels, and replace the wheel lug nuts with their flat side facing the drum.

3. Start the engine, place the transmission in gear and run at approximately 40 mph.

4. Using a jackstand as a steady rest, slowly move a piece of chalk or crayon toward the rotating driveshaft. The moment the chalk or crayon contacts the driveshaft surface, withdraw it. The resulting mark indicates the driveshaft's heavy spot **(Fig. 12-13)**.

5. Shut off the engine and, when the driveshaft stops rotating, install two worm-type (Whittek) hose clamps as far to the rear of the driveshaft as possible, with their heads located 180° from the heavy spot **(Fig. 12-14)**.

6. Operate the car in gear again, this time at the speed at which vibration is noticeable. If the vibration is not reduced, shut off the engine and move both clamp heads at 45° increments around the shaft until the vibration is at a minimum.

7. Once the point of minimum vibration is found, move the clamp heads an equal distance in opposite directions toward the heavy spot, until the best correction is found **(Fig. 12-15)**; then road-test the car.

8. If this does not result in a satisfactory reduction or elimination of the vibration, repeat Steps 3 to 7 at the front of the driveshaft. Should this fail to eliminate the vibration, the driveshaft should be replaced with a new unit.

THE DRIVESHAFT

FRONT WHEEL DRIVE

Three-piece driveshaft assemblies are used with front wheel drive vehicles **(Fig. 12-15A)**. Each drive shaft is connected to the combination transmission/differential or transaxle by an inner sliding constant velocity or C/V joint, and to the wheel hub by an outer C/V joint **(Fig. 12-15B.)** The C/V joint connecting shafts differ in length and construction, with a short solid shaft on the left side and a longer tubular shaft on the right. The C/V joints are sealed from dirt and other contamination by neoprene boots held in place by clamps at each end. The boots also seal in the special lubricant used in the C/V joints, and should be periodically inspected for damage. When working on the driveshaft, support both ends and be careful not to pinch or otherwise damage the boots.

The rear axle assembly used with Omni/Horizon vehicles is a trailing arm type with stub axle wheel spindles attached. A crossmember welded between the trailing arms **(Fig. 12-15C)** provides anti-rollbar stabilizing action. The rear axle used on front wheel drive Cadillac Eldorado, Oldsmobile Toronado and 1979 Buick Riviera is a straight hollow tube, with the rear wheel spindles pressed into and bolted to the rear hubs instead of ball bearings. The output shaft/drive axle used with the final drive at the front differs considerably in design from rear wheel drive systems, and service instructions are provided in the "Differential Overhaul" section pertaining to the specific car.

OMNI/HORIZON DRIVESHAFT REMOVAL/REPLACEMENT

TO REMOVE MANUAL ASSEMBLY

1. With the vehicle on the floor and the brakes applied, loosen the hub nut.

2. Raise the vehicle on a hoist and remove the hub nut and wheel/tire assembly.

3. Remove the clamp bolt which holds the ball joint stud to the steering knuckle.

4. Place a pry bar between the control arm and knuckle leg to separate the ball joint stud from the steering knuckle.

5. Hold the outer C/V joint housing and move the knuckle hub away to separate the splined shaft from the hub. Support the outer joint/shaft assembly by tying to the control arm.

6. Remove the six 8mm Allen-head screws holding the inner C/V joint to the transaxle drive flange. Chrysler tool L-4550 will expedite screw removal/replacement.

7. Wipe all dirt and grease from the inner C/V joint and drive flange, then untie the outer assembly from the control arm.

8. Hold both C/V joint housings parallel and rotate the outer assembly downward while pivoting the inner assembly upward. This technique helps reduce the loss of the special lubricant used in the inner C/V joint.

TO REPLACE MANUAL ASSEMBLY

1. Wipe all grease from the joint housing, face and screw holes and drive flange.

2. If any lubricant was lost during removal, fill the inner C/V joint housing with required lubricant (Chrysler P/N 4131389 or equivalent).

3. Hold the assembly with the inner housing upward to prevent loss of lubricant and fit it to the drive flange. Rotate the assembly upward and slide the inner housing into the drive flange while supporting the outer drive shaft end.

4. Install *new* Allen-head screws to the drive flange and torque to 25 in.-lbs. **NOTE:** This is important, as improper torquing can allow screws to loosen during vehicle operation, creating a potentially dangerous situation.

5. Position the steering knuckle to accept the splined outer C/V joint shaft and install in the hub.

6. Fit the knuckle assembly and ball joint stud together, then install and torque the clamp bolt to 50 ft.-lbs. Vent the inner boot by inserting a small diameter rod between the boot and shaft. This will return the boot to its original shape.

7. Clean the thread lock groove on the outer axle driveshaft and install the washer and a *new* hub nut (hub nuts should not be reused).

8. Apply the brakes and torque the hub nut to 200 ft.-lbs. then stake the nut in place as shown in **Fig. 12-15D**. Achieving the correct stake is important to maintain proper wheel bearing preload and to prevent the wheel nut from backing off.

TO REMOVE AUTOMATIC ASSEMBLY

1. With the vehicle on the floor and the brakes applied, loosen the hub nut.

2. Raise the vehicle on a hoist and remove the hub nut and wheel/tire assembly.

3. Drain the transaxle differential and remove the cover.

4. When the right driveshaft is to be removed, re-

move the speedometer pinion first.

5. Turn the driveshaft until its circlip tangs can be seen. Compress the tangs with needle nose pliers while prying the shaft into the side gear splined cavity.

6. Remove the clamp bolt which holds the ball joint stud to the steering knuckle.

7. Place a pry bar between the control arm and knuckle leg to separate the ball joint stud from the steering knuckle.

8. Hold the outer C/V joint housing and move the knuckle hub away to separate the splined shaft from the hub.

9. Support the driveshaft at each C/V joint housing and pull outward on the inner joint housing to remove—do not pull on the shaft itself.

TO REPLACE AUTOMATIC ASSEMBLY

1. Install new retaining circlips on the inner joint shaft (circlips should not be reused). Circlip tangs must align with flat on shaft end, or jamming and component damage may occur.

2. Support the inner joint assembly housing and guide the spline into the transaxle.

3. Complete lockup of circlip on the axle side gear with a quick push or thrust. Rotate the driveshaft to check circlip tang position.

4. Position the steering knuckle to accept the splined outer C/V joint shaft and install in the hub.

5. Fit the knuckle assembly and ball joint stud together, then install and torque the clamp bolt to 50 ft.-lbs. Vent the inner boot by inserting a small diameter rod between the boot and shaft. This will return the

boot to its original shape.

6. Replace the speedometer pinion when working on the right driveshaft.

7. Apply a ⅛-in. wide and thick line of room temperature vulcanizing (RTV) gasket material to the gasket area on the differential cover, then replace the cover and torque the attaching screws to 250 in.-lbs.

8. Fill the differential to the bottom of the filler plug with Dexron ATF.

9. Clean the thread lock groove on the outer axle driveshaft and install the washer and a *new* hub nut (hub nuts should not be reused).

10. Apply the brakes and torque the hub nut to 200 ft.-lbs. then stake the nut in place as shown in **Fig. 12-15D**. Achieving the correct stake is important to maintain proper wheel bearing preload and prevent the wheel nut from backing off.

INNER C/V JOINT OVERHAUL (FIG. 12-15A)

TO DISASSEMBLE

1. Remove driveshaft from vehicle.

2. Cut the two clamps holding the boot in place. Discard the boot and clamps.

3. Clean the grease from inside the joint housing and ball/trunion assembly.

4. Check the housing ball raceway and tripod components for excessive wear.

5. Unsnap the retaining ring from the groove at the end of the shaft.

6. Separate the tripod from the shaft splines by tapping lightly with a hammer and brass punch.

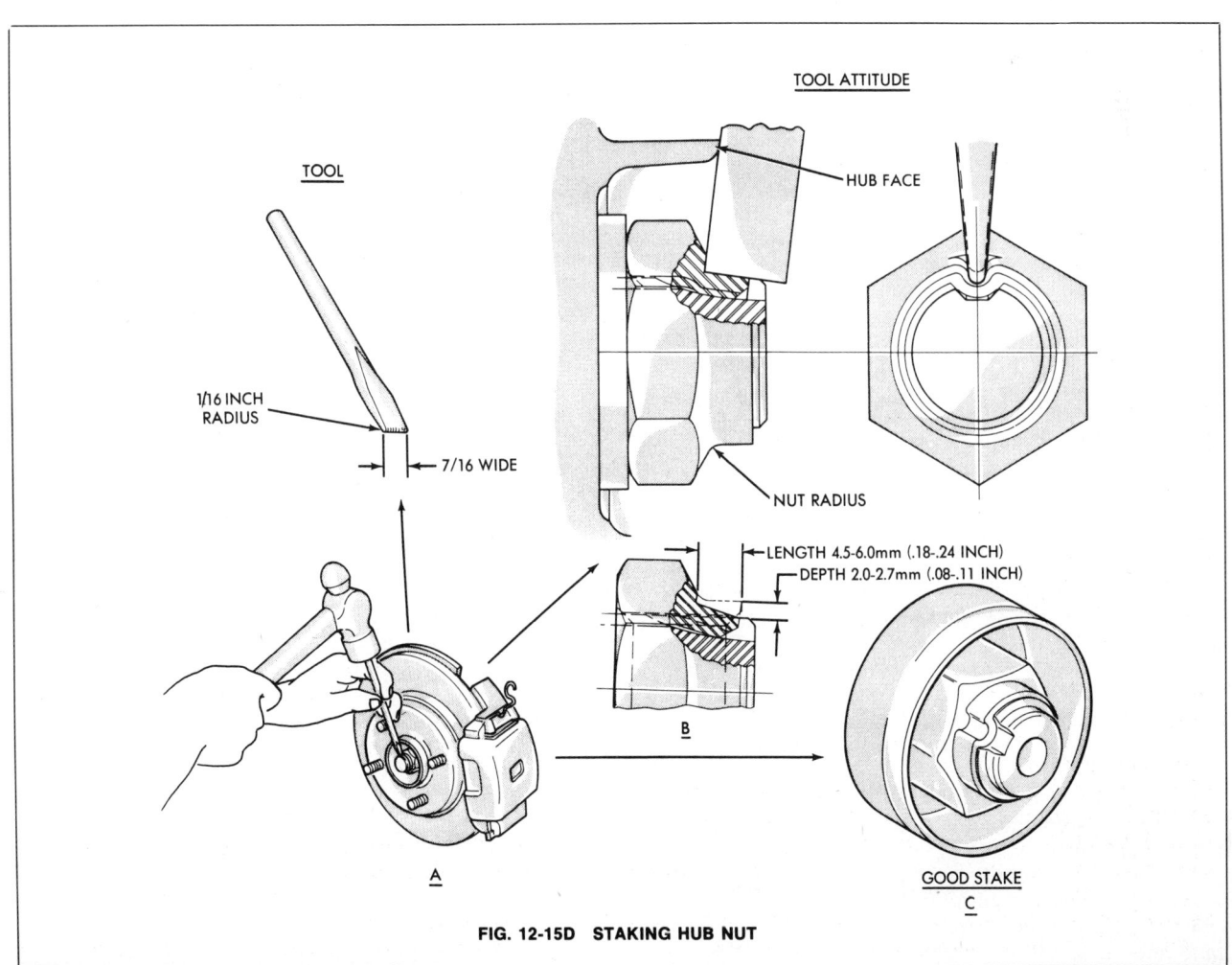

FIG. 12-15D STAKING HUB NUT

TO ASSEMBLE

1. Slide the small boot clamp onto the shaft and install the small end of the new boot over the shaft. Use the new clamps provided in the kit.

2. With tubular shafts, align the boot lip face with the shaft mark. With solid shafts, fit the small end of the boot into the machined groove.

3. Fit the clamp over the boot and secure in place.

4. Replace the tripod on the shaft. Non-chamfered face of the tripod body should face the shaft retainer groove.

5. Lock the tripod assembly on the shaft by installing the retaining ring in the groove.

6. Boot joint kits contain several packets of lubricant. Squeeze two packets into the boot at this time.

7. To install a manual joint housing, fit it over the tripod and slide the large end of the boot over the housing groove.

8. To install an automatic joint housing, squeeze one more packet of grease into the housing, then fit it over the tripod and slide the large end of the boot over the housing groove.

9. Install the large metal clamp on the boot, locate the clamp tags in the slot and squeeze the clamp together as tightly as possible by hand. A pair of pliers can be used to complete the tightening of the clamp, but Chrysler tool C-4124 is recommended.

10. With manual joints, squeeze two more packets of grease into the housing by pushing forward to provide space for the lubricant. Install driveshaft in vehicle.

OUTER C/V JOINT OVERHAUL (FIG. 12-15A)

TO DISASSEMBLE

1. Remove the driveshaft from the vehicle.

2. Cut the two clamps holding the boot in place. Discard boot and clamps.

3. Wipe grease away to expose the joint.

4. Support the shaft in a soft-jaw vise. Hold the outer joing and disconnect it from the internal circlip with a sharp tap of a rubber mallet. Do not remove slinger from housing.

5. Remove and discard circlip in the shaft groove. Do not remove the shaft lock ring unless the shaft is to be replaced.

6. Once the joint has been separated from the shaft, wipe off any excess grease and mark the relative positions of the inner cross, cage and housing with paint.

7. Support the joint in a soft-jaw vise (clamp on the splined shaft) and press down on one side of the inner race. This will tilt the race and allow removal of one ball. Repeat this operation until all six balls have been removed. If the joint is tight, tap the inner race with a hammer and brass drift and pry the balls loose with a screwdriver.

8. Tilt the cage/inner race vertically, locate between the cage windows and pull up and out of the housing, as shown in **Fig. 12-15E.**

9. Turn the inner cross 90° to the cage. Align a race land with the cage window. Lift the land into the cage window and swing inner race out.

TO ASSEMBLE

1. Lubricate all components with light oil.

2. Align the components according to the previously made paint mark.

3. Install one cross land through the cage window. Position it inside and turn 90°.

4. Align opposite cage windows with the housing land and install the cage assembly in the housing, turn-

ing 90°. When correctly assembled, the curved side of the cage windows and the inner cross counterbore should face out and away from the joint.

5. Squeeze one packet of lubricant into the ball races and spread it equally between all sides of the ball grooves.

6. Tilt the cage and inner race assembly to install the balls in the raceway.

7. Support the driveshaft in a soft-jaw vise and slip the small boot clamp over the shaft and lock ring.

8. Slip the small end of the new boot over the lock ring and slide the clamp over the boot groove. Tighten the clamp securely.

9. Fit a new circlip on the shaft. Do not twist or expand the circlip during this step.

10. Compress and hold the circlip while installing the outer joint over the shaft end. Chrysler tool L-4538 will expedite circlip installation by holding it in the proper position.

11. Pull on the joint to make sure that the circlip has seated correctly. If the joint and shaft separate at this point, repeat Step 10.

12. Fit the large boot end over the joint housing and install the metal clamp over the boot groove. Fasten the clamp securely. A pair of pliers can be used to complete the tightening of the clamp, but Chrysler tool C-4124 is recommended.

THE REAR AXLE

DESCRIPTION (Fig. 12-16)

Basically simple in design and operation, the purpose of the rear axle is to convert the driveshaft torque into thrust at the two rear wheels. To turn the driveshaft rotation through the necessary 90° angle, a form of bevel gear, called a ring gear, and drive pinion are used. Located in the large center section (rear end), the pinion is the small gear driven directly from the driveshaft, just behind the rear U-joint. This turns the large ring gear, which turns the rear wheels.

Because one rear wheel must turn faster than the other when the car goes around a corner, a small

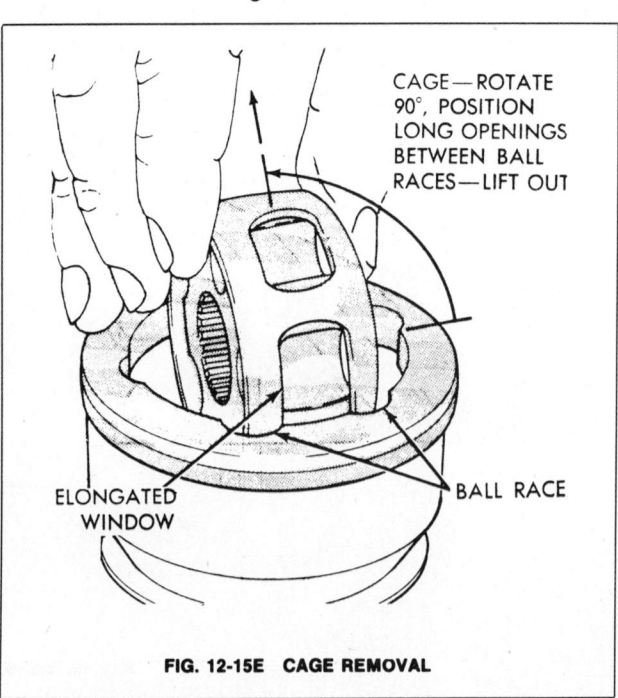

CAGE—ROTATE 90°, POSITION LONG OPENINGS BETWEEN BALL RACES—LIFT OUT

ELONGATED WINDOW

BALL RACE

FIG. 12-15E   CAGE REMOVAL

bevel planetary-gear set (differential) inside the ring gear is used. The ring gear is bolted to the differential outer housing, and the axle shafts to the two rear wheels are splined into side gears, which are connected in turn to the ring through bevel pinions, allowing one wheel to overspeed the other while continuing to supply torque to both wheels **(Fig. 12-17).**

REAR AXLE RATIO

The ratio of the gears (ring and pinion) in a differential has a greater effect on the acceleration and operating economy of the car than any other single factor. Since each car's engine, transmission and wheel size requires a specific speed and torque rate at the axle shaft, the gear ratio of the axle permits tailoring the powertrain to the job.

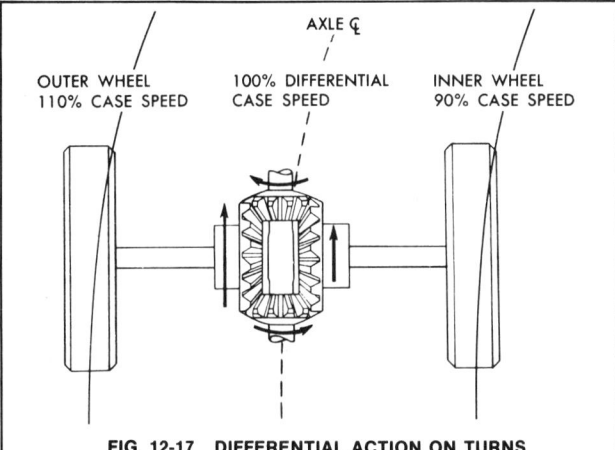

FIG. 12-17 DIFFERENTIAL ACTION ON TURNS

Some rear axle assemblies are either color-coded with a blotch of paint or have either the ratio itself or a code number stamped somewhere on the assembly. Unfortunately, the car owner cannot always rely on these methods of determining axle ratio—even if he has access to the color blotch or number coding. Mistakes may be made during assembly or a previous owner may have switched to a higher or lower gear ratio without bothering to note the change with the proper paint blotch or code number for that particular car. Why is axle ratio so important?

The ratio determines how fast the engine turns in relation to rear wheel rotation or the car speed. For example, with a 3.55:1 ratio, the driveshaft would turn 3.55 times for each 1 full turn of the rear wheels in high gear. Generally speaking, the faster the engine turns in relation to car speed, the snappier the acceleration. Just changing the axle ratio from 3.55 to 4.11 can improve acceleration more than the world's best tune-up. On the other hand, changing the axle ratio from the same 3.55 to 3.10 can improve gasoline economy as much as 1 to 2 mpg.

DETERMINING AXLE RATIO

If you are uncertain of the exact ratio, it can be measured quite simply with the help of a jack and one or two jackstands. Park the car on a level surface, turn off the engine, place the transmission in NEUTRAL, with the parking brake off, and block both front wheels and one rear wheel so the car cannot roll. Jack up the car sufficiently to raise the unblocked wheel off the ground, then place the jackstand near the jack for safety, in case the jack gives way.

Mark the driveshaft or the U-joint just ahead of the

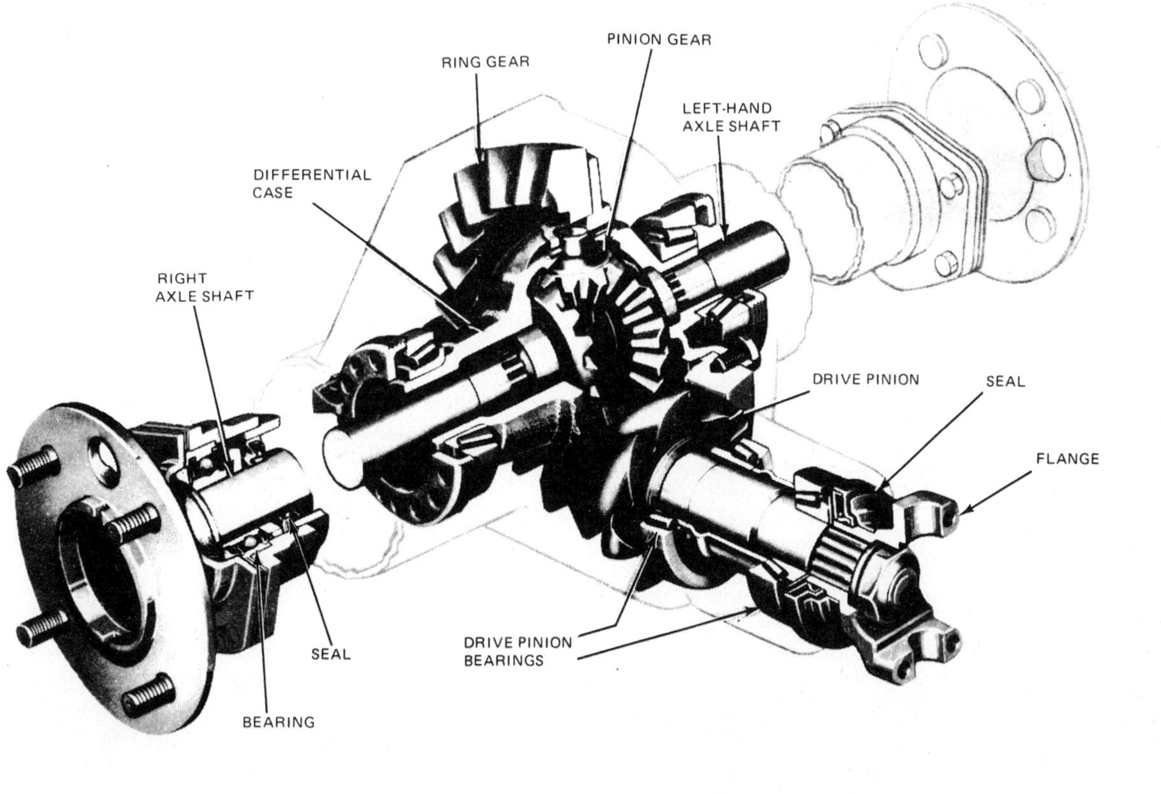

FIG. 12-16 TYPICAL INTEGRAL AXLE ASSEMBLY

differential with a grease pencil or chalk. Make another mark at the base of the tire, then rotate the tire slowly, either forward or backward, while counting the number of revolutions the driveshaft makes. Do this for 10 full turns of the tire until the mark is positioned at the bottom center. The driveshaft will not stop in the same position as when you started, but will be somewhere in the middle of a revolution, and you must determine how far it has gone on this final turn.

Judge the percentage as carefully as you can then divide the driveshaft rotation by the wheel rotation. For example, assume that the driveshaft rotated 15½ times while the tire went 10. Divide the 15.5 by 10 and you get 1.55, but this is only one-half of the axle ratio. When one wheel is stopped and the other turned, the differential operates at twice the rate it would if both wheels were turning. Thus, you must multiply 1.55 x 2 to arrive at the ratio, or 3.10. You'll find that your answer will not come out exactly on one of the ratios available for your car during the particular model year (check your owner's manual), but it will be close enough so that you can determine which it is if your car has optional ratios.

If your car is equipped with a limited-slip differential, you will not be able to turn one rear wheel while the other is parked on the ground. In this case, you must jack up both rear wheels, and they will turn together when you rotate one by hand. In this situation, you should not multiply the ratio by two—dividing the driveshaft turns by the wheel turns will provide the final ratio.

DIAGNOSING REAR AXLE NOISE

Since all rear axles are noisy to some degree, locating the source of the problem to make the necessary correction is the most difficult part of rear axle service. For example, tire noise is often mistaken as coming from the rear axle, even though the faulty tire may be located on the front wheel. Other noises, such as those coming from the wheel bearings, engine, transmission, exhaust, driveshaft vibration, U-joint or body, often appear to be coming from the rear axle.

Before any disassembly of the rear axle is undertaken, a thorough and careful inspection should be made to isolate the source of the noise. Axles can be noisy when they are improperly adjusted or require lubrication. When new gears are set incorrectly, it is possible to adjust the annoying noise out, but remember that noisy gears will not quiet down with additional mileage—the noise will remain the same, or get even worse.

Axle noises usually fall into one of two categories—gear noise or bearing noise. In order to properly diagnose the source of the noise (a task often requiring more than will be spent correcting the problem), a thorough road test is required. A smooth, level blacktop or asphalt road surface should be used, and the car should be driven far enough to warm the axle to normal operating temperature. Drive the car and note the speed at which the objectionable noise appears, then stop the car, and with the transmission in neutral, accelerate the engine slowly until the engine speed corresponds with the car speed at which the noise was noticed. Repeat this several times to determine if the noise is caused by exhaust or other engine conditions.

To distinguish between tire and axle noise, remember that:

1. Tire noise changes with different road surfaces; rear axle noise does not.

2. Tire noise continues while coasting at speeds under 30 mph; rear axle noise does not.

3. Tire noise remains the same when comparing drive and coast conditions; rear axle noise does not.

To distinguish between wheel bearing and axle noise, remember that:

1. Front wheel bearing noise does not change when comparing drive and coast. Holding the car speed constant while lightly applying the brake takes some of the weight off the wheel bearings, and thus causes the noise to diminish.

2. Defective rear-wheel-bearing noise is seldom heard at road speeds above 30 mph, unless the bearing damage is severe. A spalled rear wheel bearing will cause a growling noise with the car coasting and in neutral; a brinelled rear wheel bearing will cause a whirring sound under the same conditions.

To detect drive pinion and differential bearing noise, remember that:

1. These bearings usually cause a rough growl or grating sound, constant in pitch but varying with car speed.

2. Front pinion bearing noise is usually greater under coast conditions, while rear pinion bearing noise is loudest under drive conditions.

3. Differential bearing noise is usually a constant rough tone, much slower than pinion bearing noise.

To detect gear noise, remember that:

1. Side gears and pinions mesh too slowly during normal driving conditions to be heard.

2. Gear noise causes a very pronounced cycling tone throughout a given speed range, and is more noticeable at speeds between 30-40 mph and 50-60 mph.

3. Abnormal gear noise under drive conditions is most often caused by insufficient lubrication, resulting in a scoring of the ring and drive pinion gear. If the noise is heard under coasting conditions at all speeds, it is most likely a loose pinion nut.

A knocking sound at low speeds, or an excessive clunk on acceleration/deceleration, usually results from improper clearance between one or more of the following:

1. Differential side-gear-hub-to-differential-case counterbore.
2. Differential pinion-shaft-to-differential-case.
3. Axle-shaft-to-differential-side-gear splines.
4. Differential side-gear-to-pinion.
5. Worn thrust washers.
6. Drive gear backlash.

The most common causes of objectionable axle noise are improper backlash or differential-bearing-preload adjustment, or a combination of both. When such noise is noticed, remove the center housing cover and inspect the:

1. Differential gear and pinion backlash.
2. Pinion bearing preload.
3. Gear tooth contact pattern.

This information and the road test will provide a basis for more accurately determining what is required to eliminate the noise, and a few simple adjustments may correct the complaint without the necessity of an extensive teardown and overhaul.

AXLE SHAFT REMOVAL/INSTALLATION

Two methods of retaining the axle shaft and rear wheel bearing in place are used on rear-wheel-drive cars. One design has the wheel bearings pressed onto the axle shaft, and the shaft bolted to a retaining plate and the wheel backing plate. The other design uses wheel bearings pressed into the axle tube, and the axle shaft retained with a C-lock installed in the center housing.

AXLE SHAFT REPLACEMENT—RETAINER TYPE PLATE

1. Raise car on a hoist, and remove rear wheels.

2. Remove the brake drum.

3. If the flange contains an access hole with nuts on the backing plate, turn the axle from nut to nut, and remove as shown in **Fig. 12-18**. If the access hole is not provided, the nuts are removed from the back side of the plate.

4. Withdraw the axle shaft by pulling outward on the flange slowly. If the shaft does not come easily, use a rear hub puller as shown in **Fig. 12-19**. Use of a knock-out or slide hammer puller can damage the rear wheel bearing or the thrust block.

5. As the axle shaft is removed from the housing, the wheel bearing may come out in sections **(Fig. 12-20)**. This *does not* mean that the bearing has failed. If the balls and races are good, the same bearing can be reinstalled when the axle shaft is replaced. If you need to replace the bearings, the old one will have to be pressed off of the axle at a machine shop, where the new bearings can also be pressed on.

6. To replace the axle shaft, lightly coat the wheel bearing, housing seal recess and axle-shaft seal surface with wheel bearing grease.

7. Lubricate inner end (splines) of axle shaft, reinstall.

8. Replace the retainer plate nuts, and torque to specifications.

9. Replace the brake drum and wheel, and tighten the lug nuts.

AXLE SHAFT REPLACEMENT—C-LOCK TYPE

1. Raise the car on a hoist. Rear wheel removal is not required.

2. Place a container under the rear axle housing, and remove the differential cover and gasket. Allow the

FIG. 12-18   AXLE SHAFT REMOVAL

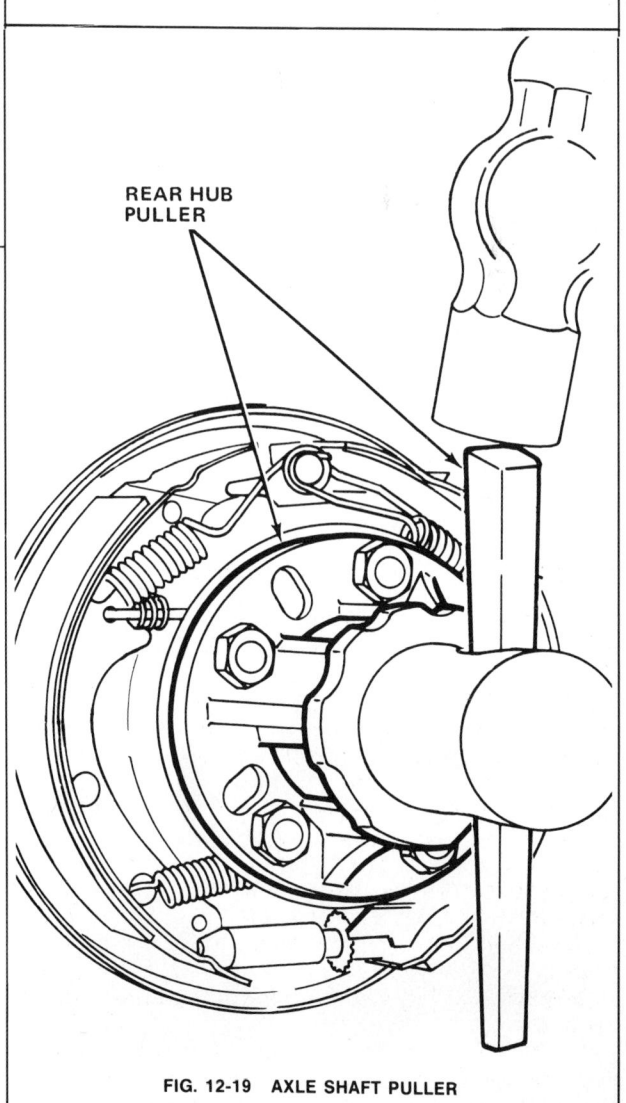

REAR HUB PULLER

FIG. 12-19   AXLE SHAFT PULLER

TORQUE SPECIFICATIONS (Ft.-Lbs.)

	AXLE RETAINER PLATE NUTS	CARRIER COVER BOLTS
BUICK	—	30
CADILLAC	50	30
CHEVROLET	40	23
OLDSMOBILE		
Cutlass	35	25
88 & 98	50	25
PONTIAC	35	25
FORD MOTOR CO.		
Mustang II, Pinto, Maverick, Comet, Granada, Monarch	20-40	25-35
Torino, Montego, Cougar, Mustang	35-55	25-35
All other Ford, Lincoln, Mercury	50-75	25-35
CHRYSLER CORP.		
All Chrysler, Dodge, Plymouth	35	250*
AMERICAN MOTORS	15	32

*in.-lbs.

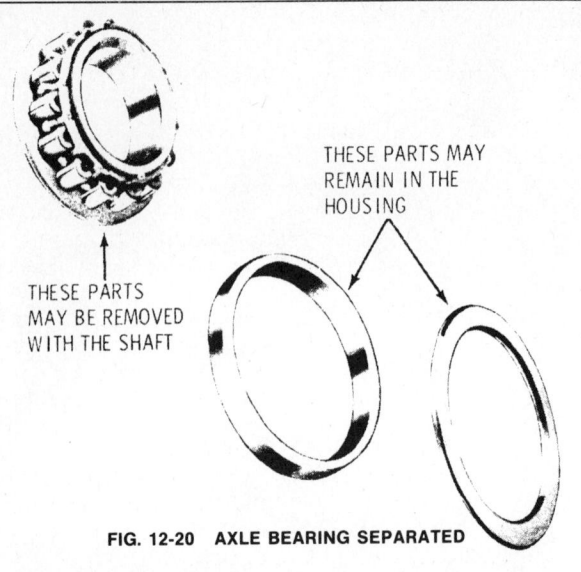

FIG. 12-20 AXLE BEARING SEPARATED

THESE PARTS MAY REMAIN IN THE HOUSING

THESE PARTS MAY BE REMOVED WITH THE SHAFT

lubricant to drain into the container.

3. Wipe the exposed parts dry with a clean, lint-free cloth, and remove the differential pinion lockscrew **(Fig. 12-21)** holding the pinion shaft in place.

4. Rotate the gear housing for access, push each axle shaft inward and remove their C-locks from the button ends of the axle shafts **(Fig. 12-22)**.

5. Reinstall the pinion shaft and lockscrew to hold the differential gears in place.

6. Remove the axle shaft by slowly pulling outward. *Do not* damage the differential oil seal when removing the axle.

7. As the axle shaft is removed, the wheel bearing may come out in sections **(Fig. 12-20)**. This *does not* mean the bearing has failed. If the balls and races are good, the same bearing can be reinstalled when the axle shaft is replaced.

8. Install the axle shaft carefully to avoid damaging the oil seal, and engage the shaft splines with those of the differential side gear.

9. Remove the pinion shaft and lockscrew, and replace the C-lock on the axle-shaft button end. Grasp the wheel and pull the shaft outward to seat the shaft lock in the differential side-gear counterbore.

10. Replace the pinion shaft, and align the shaft hole with the lockscrew hole; then install the lockscrew.

11. Fit a new gasket to the carrier cover, and install. Torque the bolts to specifications in a crosswise pattern to assure uniform draw on the gasket.

12. Refill the axle with the specified lubricant until the level is even with the bottom of the filler hole.

DIFFERENTIAL OVERHAUL
All 1970-79 General Motors Cars (Except Cadillac, Oldsmobile Toronado, Corvette);
All 1970-79 American Motors Cars

The differentials referred to in this section are all fitted with an integral-housing-type rear axle design. As such, all adjustments are made by shims. The following service procedures include all passenger car models. Before proceeding with differential case removal and disassembly, the existing ring-gear-to-pinion backlash should be checked and recorded. This check will indi-

PINION SHAFT

FIG. 12-21 DIFFERENTIAL PINION LOCKSCREW REMOVAL

FIG. 12-22 C-LOCK REMOVAL/REPLACEMENT

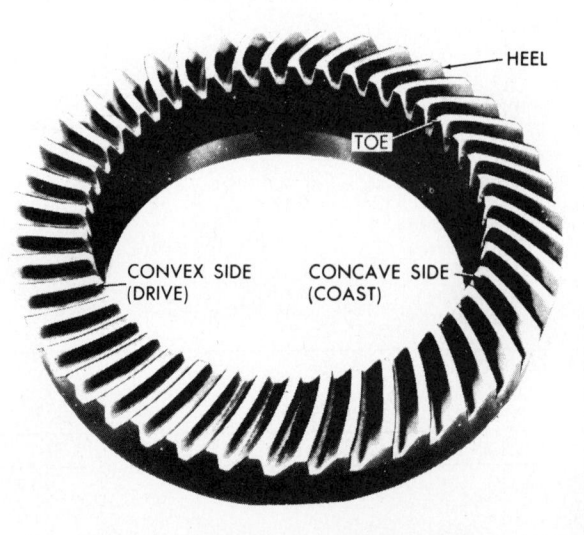

HEEL

TOE

CONVEX SIDE (DRIVE)

CONCAVE SIDE (COAST)

FIG. 12-23 GEAR TOOTH NOMENCLATURE

cate any gear or bearing wear, or incorrect backlash/pinion-depth setting, which can help in determining the cause of axle noise. If the same gears are to be reused, recording the results of this check will allow reinstallation at the same lash setting to avoid changing gear tooth contact.

NOMENCLATURE

The outward curving (convex) side of the ring gear tooth is called the drive side; the concave side is referred to as the coast side. The tooth end closest to the ring gear center is the toe end, while the tooth end farthest from the center is the heel. The toe is smaller than the heel **(Fig. 12-23)**.

GEAR TOOTH CONTACT PATTERN TEST

1. Wipe the carrier free of oil, and clean each tooth of the ring gear with a clean, lint-free cloth.

2. Apply gear marking compound sparingly to all ring gear teeth with a medium stiff brush. The pinion tooth contact area should be visible when a hand load is applied.

3. Torque the bearing cap bolts to 55 ft.-lbs., and expand the brake shoes until a torque of 20 to 30 ft.-lbs. is needed to turn the pinion. If the gears are not properly loaded, the pattern will not be satisfactory.

4. Use a wrench to turn the companion flange one complete revolution, then reverse the direction to rotate the ring gear one complete revolution in the opposite direction.

5. Compare the pattern on the ring gear teeth with

Fig. 12-24, and record the results for later reference.

DIFFERENTIAL REMOVAL/DISASSEMBLY (Fig. 12-25)

1. Perform and record the ''Gear Tooth Contact Pattern Test.''

2. Remove the rear axle shafts.

3. Roll the differential pinions and thrust washers out, then remove the side gears and thrust washers.

4. Mark the side bearing caps, pinions and side gears for correct reassembly.

5. Loosen the differential side-bearing-cap-to-housing bolts until only a few threads are engaged, then pull the caps away from the bearings.

6. Insert a pry bar behind the differential case, and carefully pry forward. At a certain point, the differential case will fall free against the bearing caps.

7. Remove the bearing caps and differential case.

8. Put the right and left bearing outer races and shims in sets with the correct bearing caps for proper reinstallation in their original position.

9. Clean all parts with solvent, and inspect carefully for any signs of excessive wear or damaged teeth.

DRIVE PINION REMOVAL

1. Remove the drive pinion nut and washer.

2. Use a puller to remove the pinion flange from the pinion.

3. Thread the pinion nut part way on the pinion to protect the threads, and replace the differential cover with two screws. Tap the end of the pinion nut with a

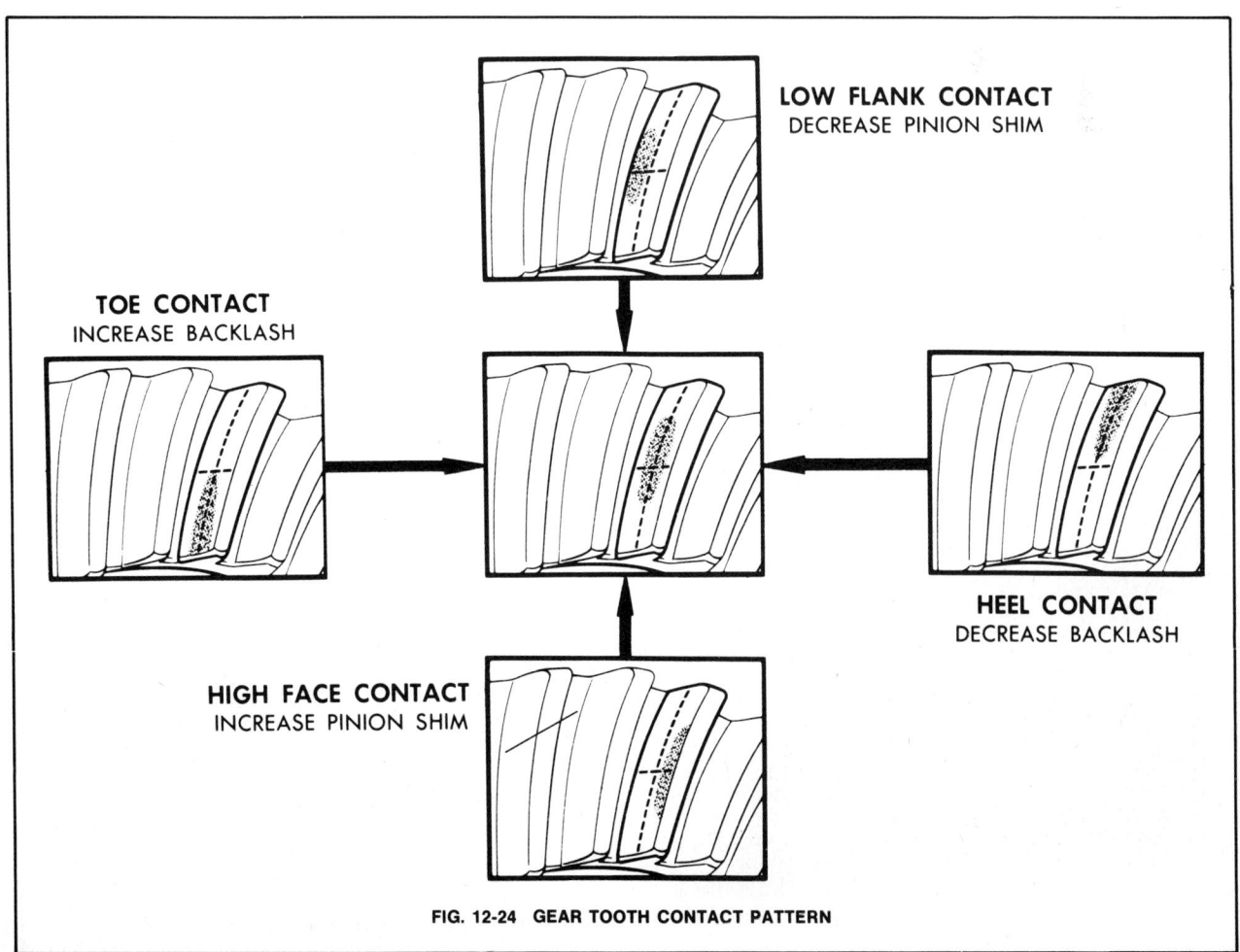

LOW FLANK CONTACT
DECREASE PINION SHIM

TOE CONTACT
INCREASE BACKLASH

HEEL CONTACT
DECREASE BACKLASH

HIGH FACE CONTACT
INCREASE PINION SHIM

FIG. 12-24 GEAR TOOTH CONTACT PATTERN

large hammer and a brass drift **(Fig. 12-26)**.

4. Pry out the pinion oil seal and remove the front pinion bearing.

5. Remove the cover, and lift the drive pinion from the case. Discard oil seal, nut and collapsible spacer.

6. If either the front or rear pinion bearing is to be replaced, drive the appropriate outer race from the carrier housing by placing a drift in the slots provided, and alternately tapping on opposite sides of the bearing cup to prevent cocking.

7. Inspect drive pinion carefully for wear or damage.

RING GEAR REMOVAL

1. Secure the differential case in a vise, and remove

the ring-gear retainer screws (left-hand thread).

2. Reinstall two of the screws at opposing holes, and tap the ring gear off the case, using a hammer and brass drift. *Do not* pry the ring gear from the case, or the machined surfaces will be damaged.

3. Remove the two retainer screws, and extract the ring gear.

4. Inspect the ring gear carefully for signs of wear or damage.

DIFFERENTIAL AND PINION ASSEMBLY

1. Coat the differential case pilot with hypoid lubricant, and align the ring-gear and differential-case bolt holes. It may ease assembly to heat (expand) the ring

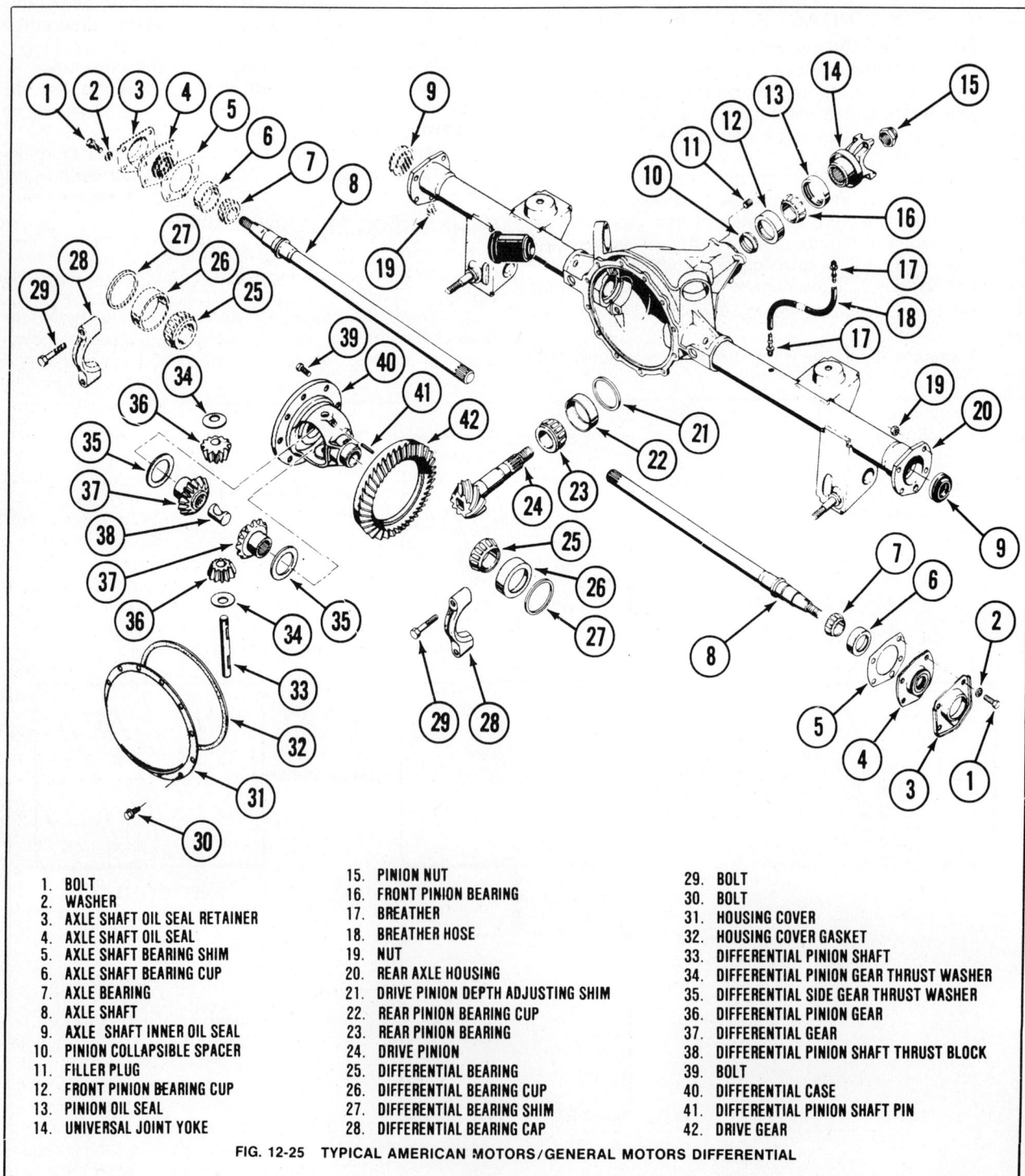

1. BOLT	15. PINION NUT	29. BOLT
2. WASHER	16. FRONT PINION BEARING	30. BOLT
3. AXLE SHAFT OIL SEAL RETAINER	17. BREATHER	31. HOUSING COVER
4. AXLE SHAFT OIL SEAL	18. BREATHER HOSE	32. HOUSING COVER GASKET
5. AXLE SHAFT BEARING SHIM	19. NUT	33. DIFFERENTIAL PINION SHAFT
6. AXLE SHAFT BEARING CUP	20. REAR AXLE HOUSING	34. DIFFERENTIAL PINION GEAR THRUST WASHER
7. AXLE BEARING	21. DRIVE PINION DEPTH ADJUSTING SHIM	35. DIFFERENTIAL SIDE GEAR THRUST WASHER
8. AXLE SHAFT	22. REAR PINION BEARING CUP	36. DIFFERENTIAL PINION GEAR
9. AXLE SHAFT INNER OIL SEAL	23. REAR PINION BEARING	37. DIFFERENTIAL GEAR
10. PINION COLLAPSIBLE SPACER	24. DRIVE PINION	38. DIFFERENTIAL PINION SHAFT THRUST BLOCK
11. FILLER PLUG	25. DIFFERENTIAL BEARING	39. BOLT
12. FRONT PINION BEARING CUP	26. DIFFERENTIAL BEARING CUP	40. DIFFERENTIAL CASE
13. PINION OIL SEAL	27. DIFFERENTIAL BEARING SHIM	41. DIFFERENTIAL PINION SHAFT PIN
14. UNIVERSAL JOINT YOKE	28. DIFFERENTIAL BEARING CAP	42. DRIVE GEAR

FIG. 12-25 TYPICAL AMERICAN MOTORS/GENERAL MOTORS DIFFERENTIAL

gear beforehand in hot water or oil (not over 300°), and smooth the chamfer on the inner ring gear circumference with an Arkansas stone to prevent burrs.

2. Install all bolts, and pull the ring gear in place evenly by tightening the bolts in a criss-cross pattern around the case.

3. When the ring gear is firmly seated to the case, torque the bolts to 90 ft.-lbs.

4. Replace the thrust washers on the side gear hubs, and install in the case.

5. Replace the pinions and thrust washers on opposite sides through the case loading hole, and engage the side gears, rotating until the pinion bores and case shaft are aligned.

6. Install the pinion shaft and lockscrew.

DIFFERENTIAL INSTALLATION/ADJUSTMENT

1. Replace the front pinion oil seal.

2. If the original ring gear, pinion and rear pinion bearing are to be reinstalled, use the original pinion shims. Should any new parts be installed (always replace ring gear and pinion together), use a shim 0.002-in. thinner than the original one. This is just a guide, and it is quite possible that once the unit is assembled, adjusted and checked, the pinion may have to be removed, a new collapsible spacer installed and another size shim installed. The "Gear Tooth Pattern Test" will determine this.

3. Place the shim on the pinion stem, and install the rear bearing.

4. Fit a new collapsible spacer (if used) on the pinion stem, and replace the pinion. Position the front bearing, and press until it touches the spacer.

5. Replace the companion flange, washer and nut, tightening slightly. Check the preload and compare to specifications **(Fig. 12-27)**. Do this in several stages of very small increments, since a one-eighth turn can add drag at the rate of 5 in.-lbs. Tighten a little at a time,

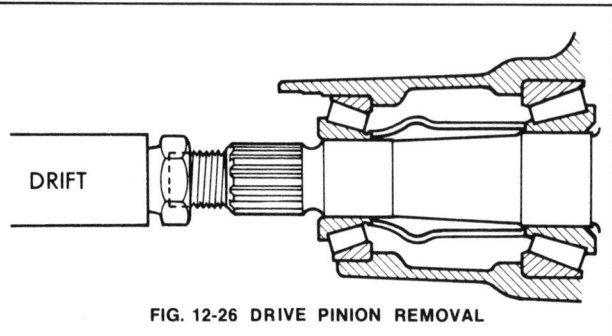

FIG. 12-26 DRIVE PINION REMOVAL

BEARING PRELOAD

Year	Model	Pinion Bearing Preload (in.-lbs.) New	Old	Differential Bearing Preload (in.-lbs.) New	Old
1970-78	Buick (C-type)	20-25	10-15	34-40	20-25
1970-78	AMC (7 9/16-in.)	15-25	—	—	—
1970-78	AMC (8⅞-in.)	17-28¡	—	—	—
1970-72	Oldsmobile (C-type)	24-32	8-12	—	—
1970-72	Oldsmobile (std.)	20-30	5-15	—	—
1973-78	Oldsmobile (all)	24-32	8-12	—	—
1970-72	Chevrolet	20-25	5-10	—	—
1973-78	Chevrolet	15-30	5-10	—	—
1970-72	Pontiac	24-32	10-15	—	—
1973-78	Pontiac	20-25	8-12	—	—

¡ 199-cu.-in.—15-25 in.-lbs.

FIG. 12-27 BEARING PRELOAD SPECIFICATIONS

and repeatedly test for preload. If the torque specifications are exceeded, the collapsible spacer will have to be replaced with another new one.

6. Rotate the pinion several times to make sure the bearings are properly seated, then recheck the preload. If pinion rotation reduces drag, reset the preload to specifications.

7. Lubricate the bearings with axle grease, replace the respective bearing cups and install the differential assembly in the carrier housing. Support the unit to prevent it from falling out.

8. Fit a 0.170-in. service spacer between each bearing race and the housing. When new bearings are installed, add sufficient shims to each spacer to equal a thickness corresponding to that of the original shim pack. If the old bearings are reinstalled, increase the original shim pack thickness by 0.002-in. (one shim) on each side.

9. Insert the shim pack on one side, and tap the other shim pack in place, installing the head bolts into the bearing caps.

10. Rotate the differential case several times to check for proper bearing seating, then apply a torque wrench to the ring-gear attaching bolt, and check bearing preload, comparing to the specifications given in **Fig. 12-27**. If no specifications are provided, the correct preload is established by the gear backlash.

11. Position a dial indicator to read the gear lash at the ring-gear outer edge, checking lash at 90° intervals. The backlash should be between 0.005-in. and 0.008-in., with variations in readings not exceeding 0.002-in.

12. Should backlash variations exceed 0.002-in., check the ring gear and case runout; if this exceeds 0.003-in., look for ring-gear/case deformation or contamination between the gear and the case.

13. If gear lash is not within specifications, decrease the shim thickness on one side, while increasing it on the other by the same amount. The total shim pack thickness should be maintained to prevent changing the preload. Should backlash exceed the upper limit, increase the thickness on the ring gear side; if less than the lower limit, decrease thickness on the ring gear side. Backlash changes about 0.002-in. for each 0.003-in. change in shim pack thickness.

14. Once backlash is correctly adjusted, torque the bearing cap bolts to 60 ft.-lbs.

15. Perform a second "Gear Tooth Contact Pattern Test" and compare to the results of the first one. If the same pattern is not obtained, the pinion shaft shim may have to be changed in order to change the pinion depth.

16. If the test is satisfactory, reinstall the axle shafts, drums, wheels and tires, and fill the housing with lubricant to the proper level.

DIFFERENTIAL OVERHAUL
All 1970-79 Cadillacs
(Except Eldorado)

The standard differential used on all Cadillac cars, except the Eldorado, is a unitized carrier and housing design using two tapered roller bearings and a straight roller straddle bearing to support the pinion and to provide rigidity. As such, adjustments are made by shims. Before proceeding with differential case removal and disassembly, the existing ring-gear-to-pinion backlash should be checked and recorded. This check will indicate any gear or bearing wear, or incorrect backlash/pinion-depth setting, which can help in determining the cause of axle noise. If the same gears are to be reused, recording the results of this check will allow reinstallation at the same lash setting to avoid changing gear tooth contact.

NOMENCLATURE

The outward curving or convex side of the ring gear tooth is called the drive side; the concave side is referred to as the coast side. The tooth end closest to the ring gear center is the toe end, while the tooth end farthest from the center is the heel. The toe is smaller than the heel **(Fig. 12-28)**.

GEAR TOOTH CONTACT PATTERN TEST

1. Loosen and remove all but one of the six pinion-retainer-to-differential-carrier screws.

2. Use a slide hammer to unseat the pinion assembly from the differential carrier, leaving the shim(s) in position.

3. Remove the remaining retainer screw, and slide the pinion out of the carrier.

4. Remove the slide hammer, and clean the ring gear teeth with solvent.

5. Apply a light coat of gear-marking compound to the ring gear teeth.

6. Clean the pinion gear teeth with solvent, and replace the assembly in the housing, installing three of the six bolts, and torque to 30 ft.-lbs.

7. Rotate the ring gear one complete revolution in each direction by hand with a box wrench on the ring-gear-to-case bolts, holding a cloth around the pinion flange to produce drag while turning the ring gear.

8. Compare the pattern on the ring gear teeth with **Fig. 12-28,** and record the results for later reference.

DIFFERENTIAL REMOVAL (Fig. 12-29)

1. Remove the rear axle shafts and disconnect the driveshaft.

2. Drain the lubricant into a container by removing the cover and gasket.

3. Measure the ring gear backlash with a dial indicator at 90° intervals on the ring gear. The backlash should not exceed 0.005-in. to 0.010-in., with variations in the readings not to exceed 0.003-in.

4. Perform and record the ''Gear Tooth Pattern Test.''

5. Remove the differential adjuster locktab, and loosen the differential adjuster nut. Use a dial indicator to measure the total deflection between both bearing caps, loosening the caps, if necessary. Record the reading.

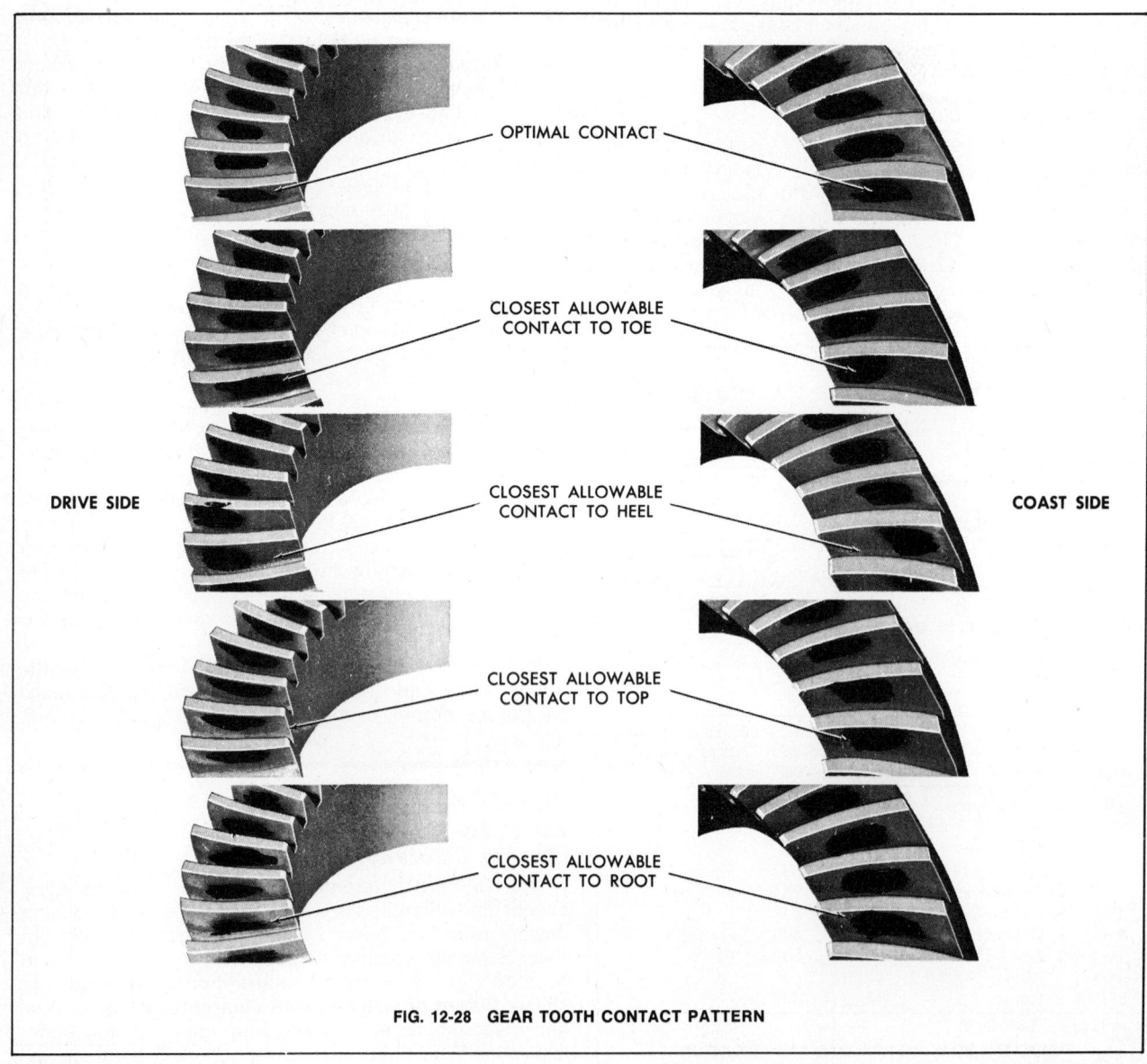

DRIVE SIDE

OPTIMAL CONTACT

CLOSEST ALLOWABLE CONTACT TO TOE

CLOSEST ALLOWABLE CONTACT TO HEEL

CLOSEST ALLOWABLE CONTACT TO TOP

CLOSEST ALLOWABLE CONTACT TO ROOT

COAST SIDE

FIG. 12-28 GEAR TOOTH CONTACT PATTERN

6. Remove both bearing caps, the differential adjuster nut and differential shim(s).

7. Pull the differential gear case from the carrier, and remove the pinion assembly.

8. Unclip and remove the straddle-bearing outer snap ring and the straddle bearing assembly, applying force only to the inner end of the bearing cage.

PINION DISASSEMBLY (Fig. 12-29)

1. Remove the pinion O-ring and discard it.

2. Remove the pinion nut, using a torque multiplier—more than 200 ft.-lbs. are required.

3. Remove the pinion flange, and pry the oil seal from the pinion retainer.

4. Remove the pinion outer bearing.

5. Press the outer cup of the outer bearing from the retainer and the inner bearing outer cup.

6. Remove the pinion bearing collapsible spacer and discard, then remove the pinion inner bearing.

DIFFERENTIAL DISASSEMBLY (Fig. 12-29)

1. Use a gear puller to remove both differential side bearings.

2. Scribe an alignment mark on the differential case

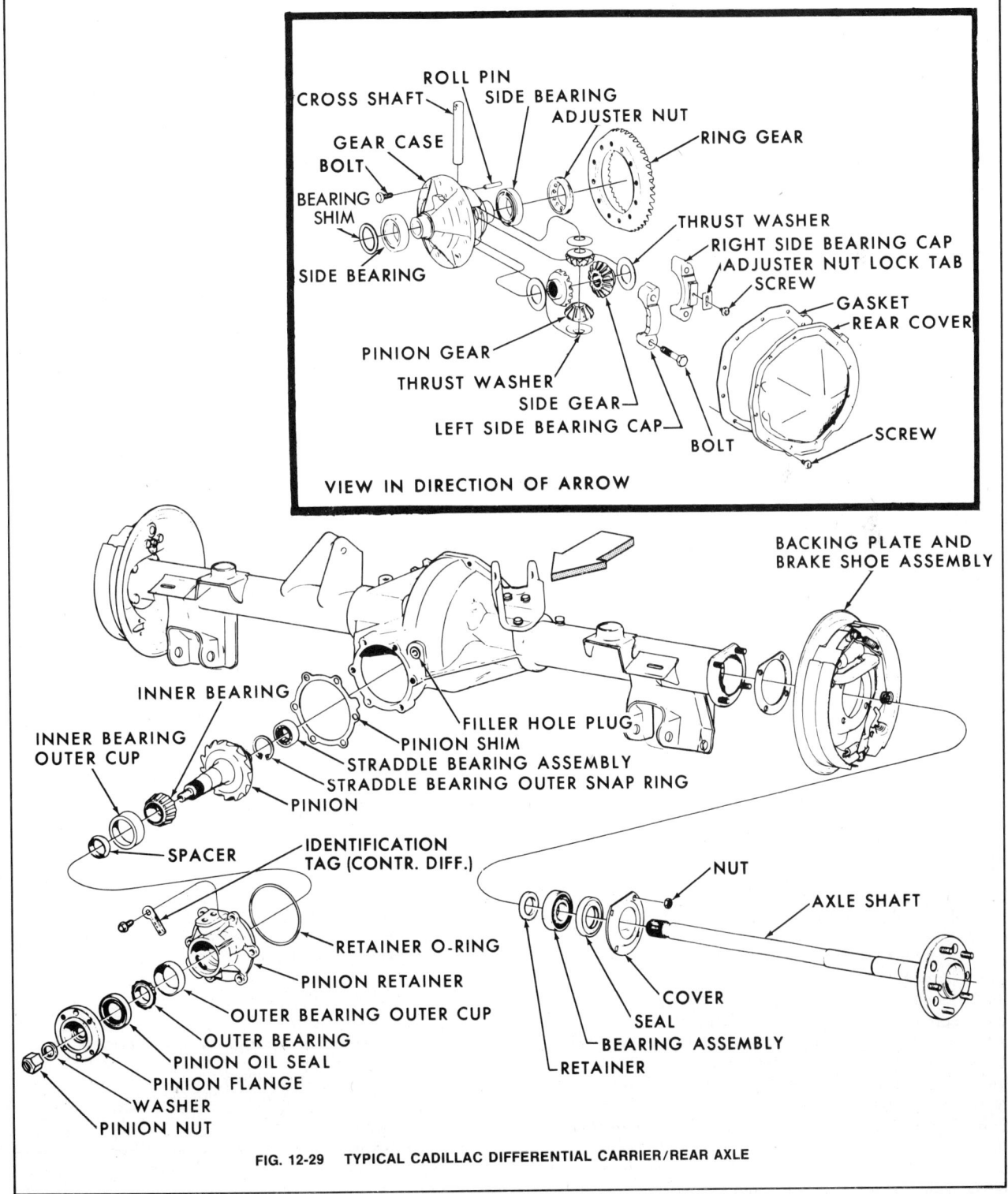

FIG. 12-29 TYPICAL CADILLAC DIFFERENTIAL CARRIER/REAR AXLE

and ring gear, then loosen the ring gear screws (left-hand thread), removing three of them.

3. Install three pilot screws (slotted studs with no heads) in their place, and remove the other nine ring gear screws.

4. Tap on the pilot screws to unseat the ring gear, then remove it from the differential case.

5. Drive out the differential-case roll pin with a ¼-in. drift.

6. Drive out the differential cross shaft with a brass drift.

7. Turn the pinion gears clockwise until they align with the differential case opening, and remove.

8. Remove the differential-pinion-gear thrust washers, the side gears and their thrust washers.

PINION ASSEMBLY (Fig. 12-29)

1. File any staking burrs from the pinion shaft; and lubricate pinion inner bearing with differential lubricant.

2. Use an arbor press to install the inner pinion bearing on the pinion shaft.

3. Install the outer-bearing outer cup and inner-bearing outer cup in the retainer.

4. Fit a new collapsible spacer on the pinion.

5. Lubricate the outer pinion bearing, and install it in the retainer.

6. After packing the pinion-oil-seal inner lip with wheel bearing grease, press the oil seal into the retainer and seat with not more than 1/16-in. protruding above the machined retainer face.

7. Align the pinion flange on the pinion shaft, tap the flange into place and install the pinion nut.

8. Check the preload, which should range between 22 and 30 in.-lbs. for a new bearing and 10 to 15 in.-lbs. for used bearings. Do this in several stages of very small increments, since one-eighth can add drag at the rate of 5 in.-lbs. Tighten a little at a time, and repeatedly test for preload. Never back the pinion nut off to obtain the proper preload; if torque specifications are exceeded, the collapsible spacer will have to be removed and replaced with another new one.

DIFFERENTIAL ASSEMBLY (Fig. 12-29)

1. Coat all differential gears with differential lubricant, and install one side gear with its thrust washer in the differential case.

2. Replace the other side gear and thrust washer, holding them in place.

3. Install a pinion gear and thrust washer in each differential case opening, rotating the gears to align the cross shaft holes with those in the case.

4. Replace the differential cross shaft, and align its hole with the roll pin hole in the case.

5. Replace the roll pin, and install the pilot screws in the ring gear.

6. Align the ring gear and the differential case marks, and replace the nine ring-gear screws finger-tight. Remember they are left-hand threaded.

7. Tap the ring gear in place with a soft-faced mallet, remove the pilot screws and install the regular ring gear screws in their place. It may ease assembly to heat (expand) the ring gear beforehand in hot water or oil (not over 300°), and smooth the chamfer on the inner ring gear circumference with an Arkansas stone, to prevent burrs.

8. Torque the ring gear screws in a criss-cross pattern to 85 ft.-lbs.

9. Lubricate and install the side bearings, with their large diameter on the gear case shoulder.

DIFFERENTIAL INSTALLATION (Fig. 12-29)

1. Replace the straddle bearing and outer race, installing the snap ring.

2. Replace the original pinion shim(s) in the differential carrier, and install a new pinion retainer O-ring.

3. Slide the pinion assembly in the differential carrier, install the retainer screws and torque to 30 ft.-lbs.

4. Replace the differential side-bearing cups, holding in place while the case is installed in the carrier.

5. Thread the adjusting nut in place.

6. Replace the right-side bearing cap and the mounting bolts, but *do not* tighten the bolts.

7. Align the bearing cap threads with those on the adjusting nut, and slide the differential case to the far right until the ring gear and pinion teeth are completely meshed. There should be no backlash at this point.

8. Tighten the adjusting nut until it touches the right differential side bearing, then slide the left side bearing and cup to the far right.

9. Fit a 0.100-in. shim between the left side-bearing cup and the differential case. Insert a feeler gauge between the shim and bearing cup, and measure the clearance; then insert that size shim with the one already installed.

10. Replace the left side-bearing cap and the two mounting bolts; torque to 50 ft.-lbs.

11. Place a dial indicator on the carrier, and measure the deflection of the bearing cap, tightening the adjusting nut until a 0.003-in. to 0.004-in. reading is obtained.

12. Reposition the dial indicator to measure the ring-gear-to-pinion backlash. The reading should range between 0.005-in and 0.010-in., varying by less than 0.003-in. measured at four places around the ring gear. Increase the shim size if the reading is too high, and decrease it if too low. Changing the shim by 0.002-in. will change the backlash by about 0.001-in.

13. Perform a second "Gear Tooth Contact Pattern Test," and compare the results with the first test. If the same pattern is not obtained, the pinion shaft shim will have to be replaced in order to change the pinion depth.

14. If the test is satisfactory, replace the locktab on the adjusting nut, and torque the nut to 18 ft.-lbs.

15. Replace the cover with a new gasket, and torque the cover screws to 30 ft.-lbs. Complete the rear axle assembly.

FINAL DRIVE OVERHAUL
1970-78 Cadillac Eldorado, Oldsmobile Toronado

The Eldorado/Toronado front-wheel-drive system includes the final drive unit, right and left output shafts, and drive axles. The final drive unit uses a spiral-bevel ring-and-pinion gear set and a spur-bevel differential gear set. It functions in a manner similar to that of a standard differential (**Figs. 12-30 & 12-31**). The pinion gear is directly splined to the transmission, with the housing attached to the transmission and secured by a support bracket at its front.

The Cadillac final drive unit is not serviced, but is replaced as an assembly, except for the pinion oil seal, output shaft seal, pinion-bearing-housing O-ring, vent pin, seal-cover/filler-plug gaskets, all of which can be serviced separately.

Oldsmobile provides detailed instructions for final drive disassembly, component replacement and reassembly, but a very extensive list of highly specialized

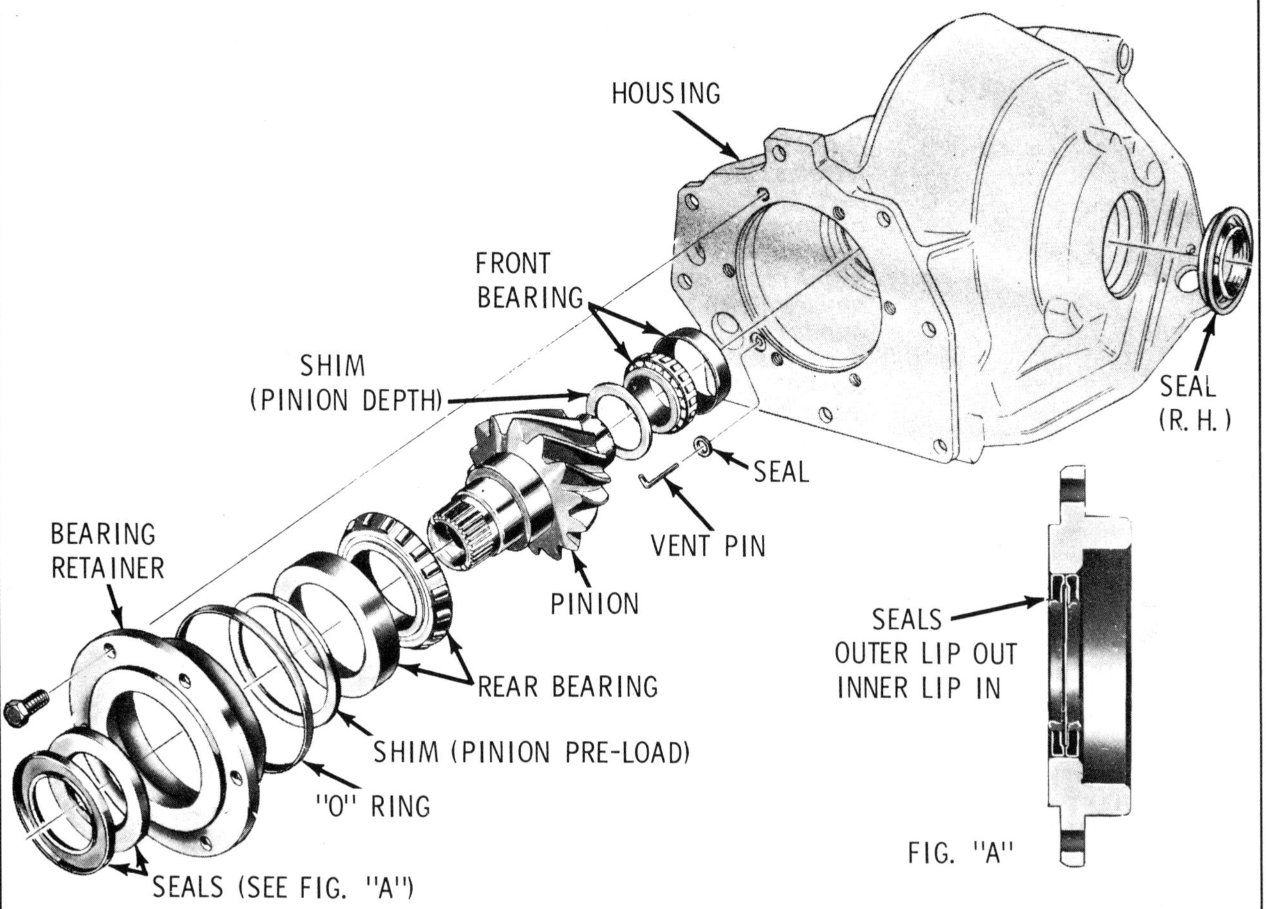

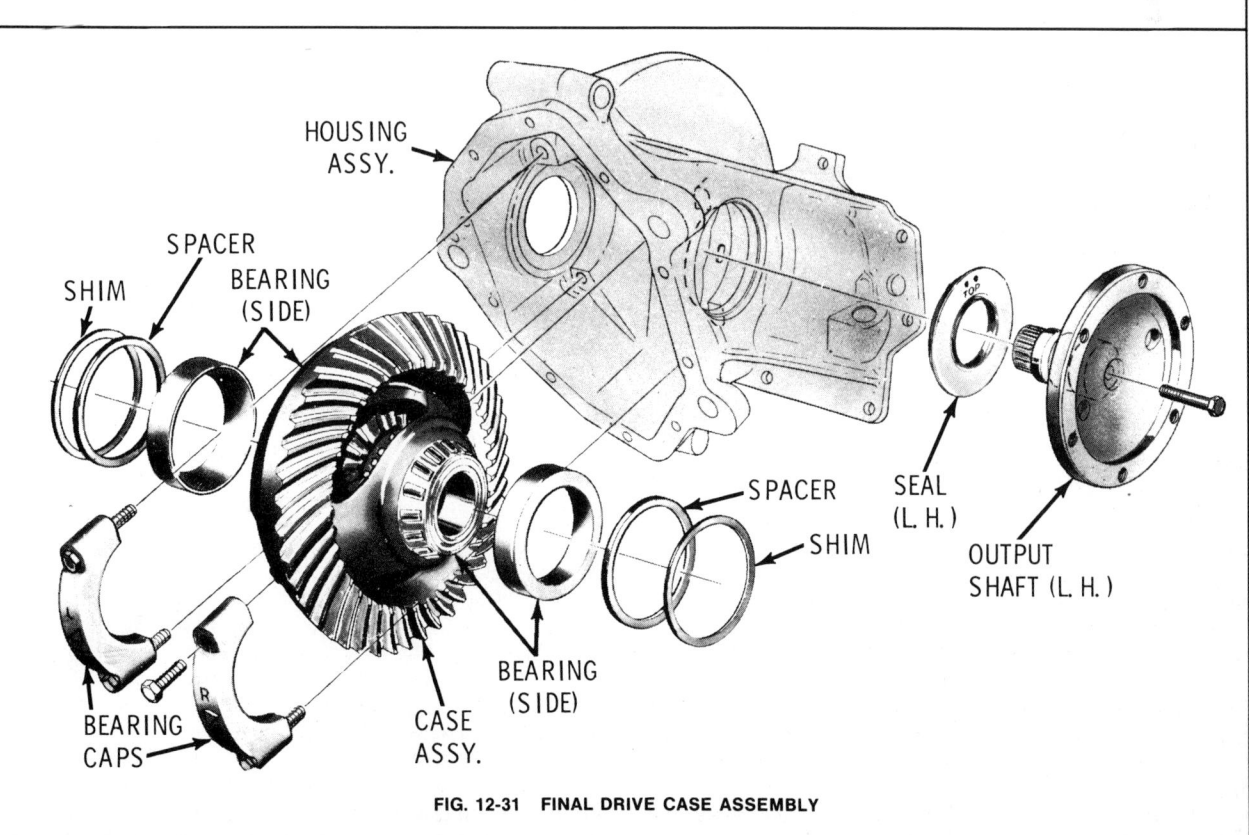

HOUSING

FRONT
BEARING

SHIM
(PINION DEPTH)

SEAL
(R. H.)

SEAL

VENT PIN

BEARING
RETAINER

PINION

SEALS
OUTER LIP OUT
INNER LIP IN

REAR BEARING

SHIM (PINION PRE-LOAD)

"O" RING

FIG. "A"

SEALS (SEE FIG. "A")

FIG. 12-30   FINAL DRIVE PINION ASSEMBLY

HOUSING
ASSY.

SPACER
SHIM   BEARING
(SIDE)

SEAL
(L. H.)

SPACER

OUTPUT
SHAFT (L. H.)

SHIM

BEARING
(SIDE)

BEARING
CAPS

CASE
ASSY.

FIG. 12-31   FINAL DRIVE CASE ASSEMBLY

tools and equipment, obtainable only from Oldsmobile, is required to perform these tasks. Because the overhaul procedure is very complicated and time-consuming, Oldsmobile dealers in many cases recommend replacement as a unit rather than overhaul, due to the labor/parts cost, which is often more expensive than unit replacement. For these reasons, final drive service procedures here are restricted to those which can be accomplished by those not having access to the specialized equipment and tools required to perform a complete final-drive-unit overhaul.

Both Cadillac and Oldsmobile outer constant-velocity drive axle joints can be repacked and their seals replaced, but if any other defect is noted, the joint is replaced as an assembly. The inboard tri-pot joints can also be repacked, and the spider components, seals and housing end-cover O-ring replaced.

Because of the component location in the front-wheel-drive system, the negative battery cable should always be disconnected when working on the right drive axle, because contact between a wrench and the starting motor terminal can short out the starting motor. When working on the drive axles, fit a short piece of rubber hose on the lower-control-arm torsion bar connector to prevent damage to the tri-pot joint seals.

RIGHT OUTPUT-SHAFT/DRIVE-AXLE REMOVAL (Fig. 12-32)

1. Disconnect the negative battery cable.
2. Remove the wheel. If the drive axle is to come off too, remove the cotter pin and loosen, but *do not remove,* the spindle nut.
3. Elevate the car so that its front weight is supported at the lower control arms.
4. Loosen the right-front shock-absorber lower

mounting nut, and pry the shock absorber along the lower mounting stud with a screwdriver until it reaches the nut.

5. Fit a short length of hose on each lower-control-arm torsion-bar connector, and remove the screws holding the right drive axle to the output shaft.
6. Move the inboard drive-axle end to the rear to provide access to the output shaft.
7. Remove the screws holding the output shaft support and support strut **(Fig. 12-33)**.
8. Pull the output shaft outward to disengage the splines, and remove the assembly.
9. Place a block of wood on the end of the drive axle, and tap with a hammer to unseat the axle at the hub.
10. Rotate the axle in and toward the front of the car, guiding it over the front crossmember and out from under the car.

LEFT OUTPUT-SHAFT/DRIVE-AXLE REMOVAL (Fig. 12-32)

1. Disconnect the negative battery cable.
2. Remove the wheel. If the drive axle is to come off too, remove the cotter pin and loosen, but *do not remove,* the spindle nut.
3. Elevate the car so that its front weight is supported at the lower control arms.
4. With the brake applied, remove and discard the drive-axle-to-output-shaft screws and lockwashers.
5. Loosen the shock-absorber upper mounting bolt.
6. Remove the upper-spherical-joint cotter pin and nut and the brake hose clip from the joint stud.
7. Strike the knuckle with a hammer, then lift the upper arm and remove the joint stud from the steering knuckle.

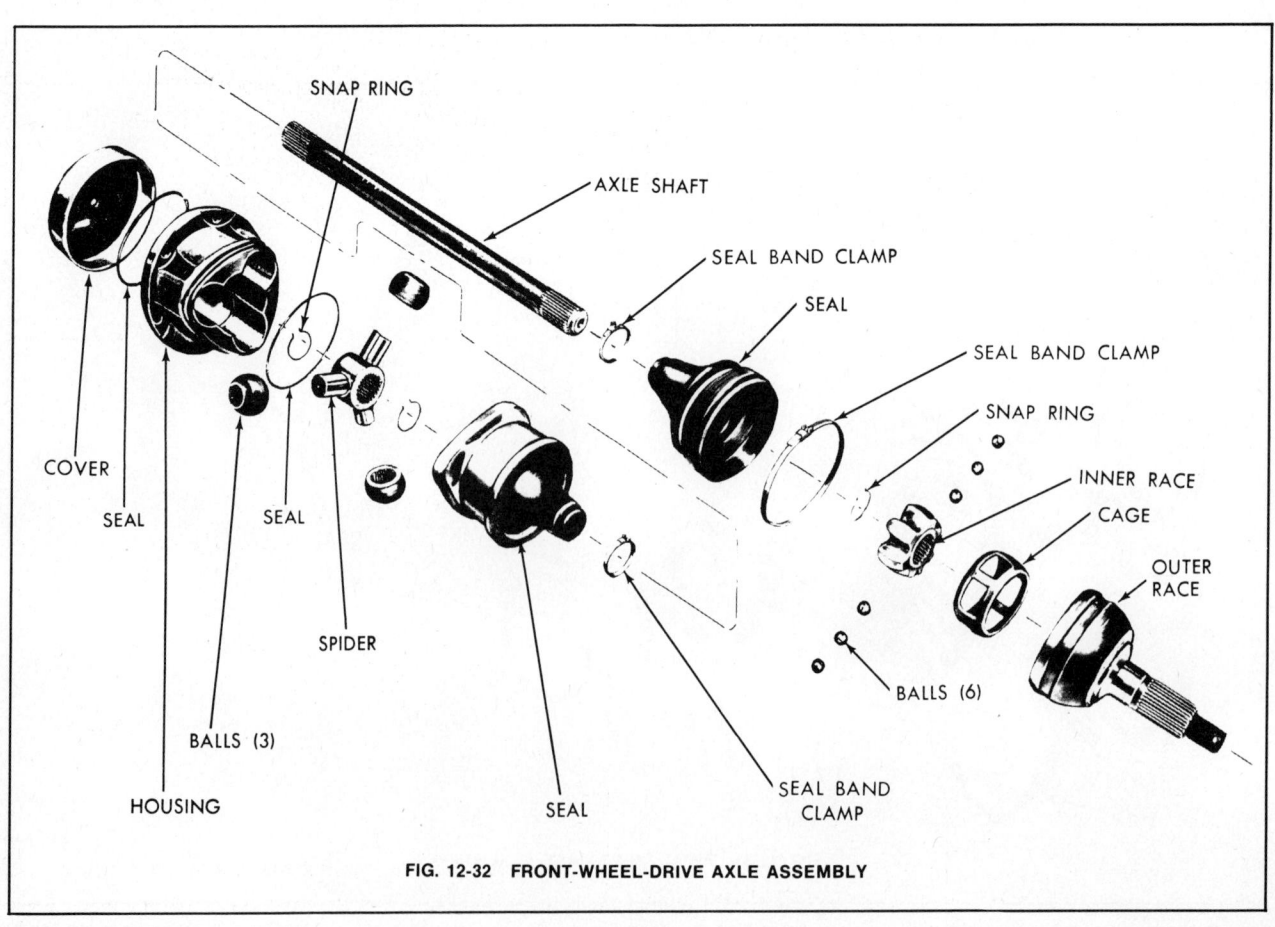

FIG. 12-32 FRONT-WHEEL-DRIVE AXLE ASSEMBLY

8. Remove the brake-hose-to-frame bracket, and carefully tip the disc/knuckle assembly out at the upper end. Wire the assembly to the upper control arm to prevent damage to the brake hose.

9. Rotate the inner drive-axle end to the front of the car.

10. Remove the drive axle from the knuckle, and remove from the car.

11. Install two screws in the output shaft flange to prevent the shaft from rotating, and remove the left output-shaft retainer bolt.

12. Pull the output shaft straight out to remove. *Do not* damage the oil seal surface on the shaft when removing.

OUTER CONSTANT VELOCITY JOINT DISASSEMBLY

1. Secure the axle assembly in a vise, clamping the shaft in the middle. Protect the shaft from the vise jaws, and clamp on the right drive-axle torsional damper with extreme caution to prevent damage.

2. Cut the inner and outer seal bands with a pair of pliers.

3. Slide the seal down the axle to expose the constant velocity joint. Wipe the grease away from the snap ring.

4. Spread the snap ring and slide the joint from the axle spline.

5. Remove the inner-race snap ring, and slide the seal from the axle shaft.

6. Clamp the joint in a vise by its shank, using jaw blocks to prevent damaging the joint shank.

7. Tap on the inner race with a hammer and brass drift until a ball can be removed. Remove the other balls one at a time in the same manner. It may be necessary to pry the last ball out from the cage with a screwdriver.

8. Turn the cage 90°, with the slot aligned with the short land on the outer race, and lift the cage out with the inner race **(Fig. 12-34)**.

9. Turn the short land of the inner race 90° in line with the hole in the cage. Lift the inner race land up through the cage hole, then turn it up and out, separating the parts **(Fig. 12-35)**.

10. Wash all parts thoroughly in solvent, and dry with compressed air. Check the rubber seals for damage or wear, and replace with new ones if necessary.

11. If the following defects are found, replace the entire joint as a unit:

a) Excessive wear or scoring in the outer race ball grooves.

b) Excessive wear, scoring or cracks in the inner race.

c) Damaged housing splines and threads.

d) Nicked, cracked, scored or worn balls.

e) Cracked, broken or excessive brinelling of the cage window flats.

OUTER CONSTANT VELOCITY JOINT ASSEMBLY

1. Fit the inner-race short land in the cage slot, and pivot to install.

2. Pack the joint with drive-axle joint lubricant. Cadillac recommends GM Part #1050802; Oldsmobile suggests #1050169.

3. Replace the cage and inner race in the outer race by aligning the windows on the cage with the outer race lands **(Fig. 12-34)**.

4. Lubricate the inner and outer race, inserting the balls into the outer race one at a time, until all six balls

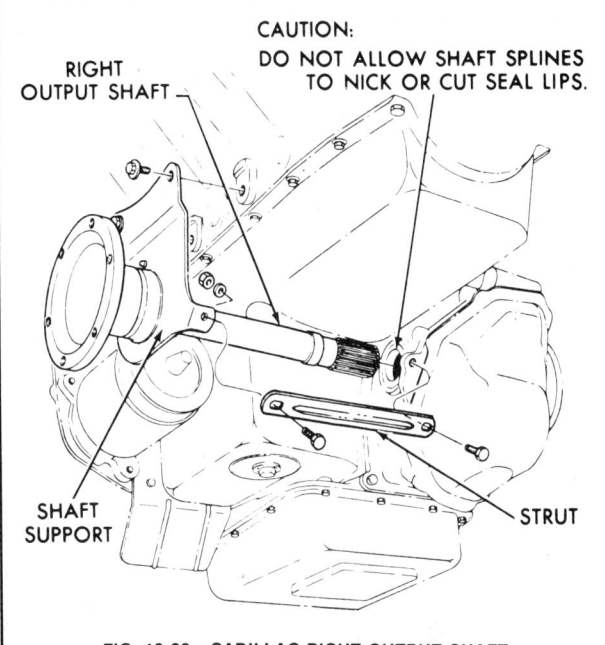

FIG. 12-33 CADILLAC RIGHT OUTPUT SHAFT

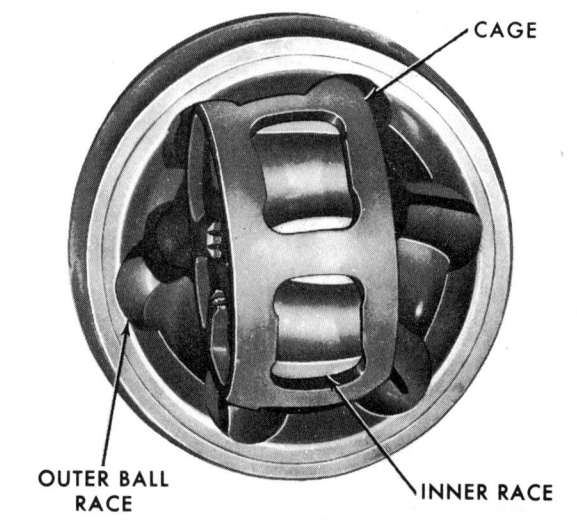

FIG. 12-34 REMOVING CAGE AND INNER RACE

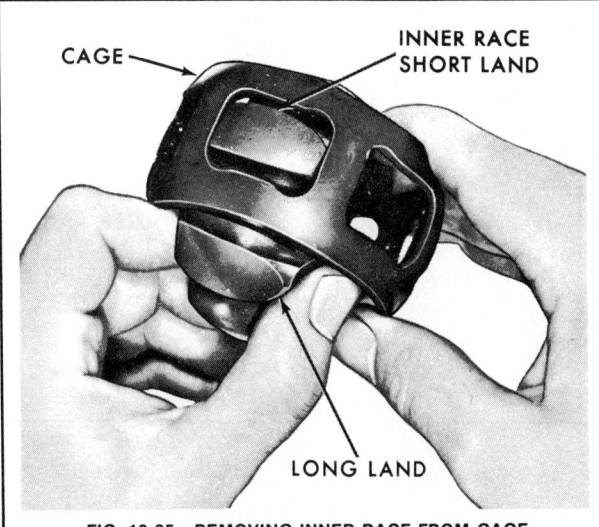

FIG. 12-35 REMOVING INNER RACE FROM CAGE

are replaced. Tilt the inner race and cage to make installation easier.

5. Fit the small end of the seal in the axle shaft groove, and use a seal-clamp-band installation tool to install new seal bands.

6. Pack the inside of the seal with about ¼-lb. of drive-axle joint lubricant, and install the snap ring in the inner race.

7. Fit the axle shaft in the outer constant-velocity-joint splines, and spread the snap ring until it holds the shaft in the second snap-ring groove.

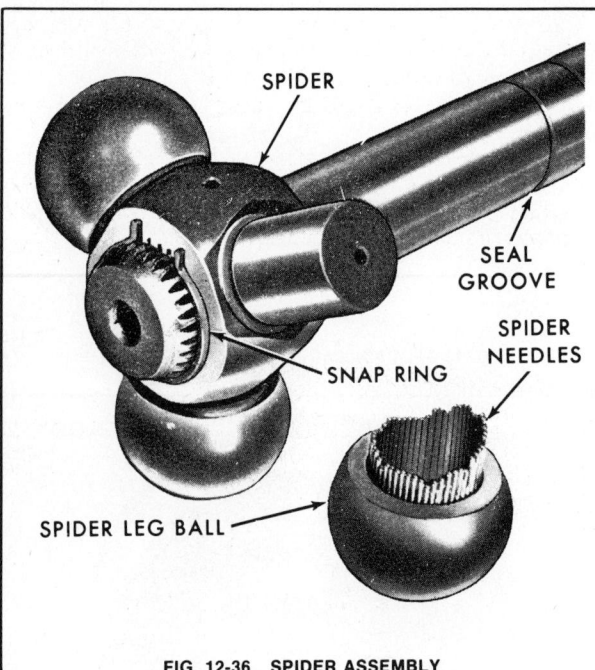

FIG. 12-36 SPIDER ASSEMBLY

FIG. 12-37 SEAL ADAPTER INSTALLATION

8. Place the seal in the outer race groove. Make sure the seal and the outer-race mating surfaces are free of lubricant, or proper sealing will not be possible.

9. Install the large seal-clamp band.

INNER JOINT DISASSEMBLY

1. Place the axle assembly on a clean workbench, and pry up the seal-retainer staked areas, driving the housing off with a hammer and chisel.

2. Holding the axle assembly with one hand and the joint housing with the other, stand both upright on the bench and withdraw the axle from the housing, taking care not to lose the needles and balls from the axle spider. A rubberband can be used to retain the spider balls and needle bearings **(Fig. 12-36)**.

3. Wipe off all excess grease, and set the housing to one side.

4. Clamp the mid-section of the axle shaft in the vise, and remove the snap ring from its end.

5. Slide the spider assembly from the axle shaft, and remove the inner snap ring.

6. Remove the small seal clamp, and slide the boot seal from the axle shaft.

7. Remove all three spider balls. Each contains 53 needle bearings.

8. If the tri-pot housing end cover or O-ring must be removed, secure the housing in a vise and place a 2 x 2 x 8-in. piece of soft wood in the housing.

9. Drive on the wooden block to push the end cover from the housing.

10. Remove and discard the housing O-ring.

11. Wash all parts in clean solvent, and dry with compressed air. Inspect the rubber seals and O-rings for damage or excessive wear, and replace if necessary.

12. Inspect all other components for wear, distortion or other damage. The housing will show a polished area where the balls travel, but unless the wear pattern is suspected as the cause of noise or vibration, it need not be replaced.

INNER JOINT ASSEMBLY

1. Slide a new clamp and seal on the axle shaft, then install the snap ring.

2. Load 53 needle bearings into each spider ball, holding in place with drive axle lubricant, and carefully install each ball on the spider legs. Retain in place with a rubberband until the assembly is installed in the housing.

3. Fit the spider assembly on the axle shaft, and install the outer snap ring.

4. Install and lubricate a new O-ring in the housing, and replace the end cover by tapping around its outer edge.

5. Replace the O-ring in the housing outer groove, and pack the housing one-half full with drive axle lubricant.

6. Remove the rubberband (if used) from the spider assembly, align it with the housing assembly and push into place until it bottoms.

7. Fill the remainder of the housing with lubricant, and swab the inside of the boot seal retainer and housing outer-groove O-ring with lubricant.

8. With the housing positioned as shown in **Fig. 12-37**, alternately tap the seal retainer lobes until they are firmly bottomed, then stake in three places.

9. Draw the inboard joint to its maximum length, and position the seal in the farthest axle groove from the joint.

10. Use a seal-band installer tool to install new seal clamp bands on the end of the seal.

RIGHT OUTPUT-SHAFT/DRIVE-AXLE INSTALLATION

1. Guide the drive axle up and over the front crossmember to engage the splined end in the knuckle and hub.

2. Rotate the drive-axle inner end toward the rear.

3. Apply clean front-wheel-bearing grease between the output-shaft seal lips, and install the output shaft into the final drive unit, indexing the splines.

4. Replace the output shaft support, and torque the bolts to 50 ft.-lbs. (Toronado, 55 ft.-lbs.), then install the self-tapping screw which holds the output-shaft support strut to the final drive housing.

5. Rotate the drive axle toward the front and into place.

6. With the brakes applied to prevent the drive axle from turning, install new screws and lockwashers to retain the drive axle to the output shaft. Torque to 65 ft.-lbs. (Toronado, 75 ft.-lbs.).

7. Replace the drive-axle spindle nut, and lower the car.

8. Torque the drive-axle spindle nut to a minimum 110 ft.-lbs. (Toronado, 200 ft.-lbs.), then tighten (*do not back off*) to align the cotter pin hole with the spindle hole, and install the cotter pin.

9. Connect the negative battery cable, and check the final-drive oil level. Inspect for oil leaks at the output shaft.

LEFT OUTPUT-SHAFT/DRIVE-AXLE INSTALLATION

1. Lubricate the final-drive output-shaft seal between its lips with wheel bearing grease.

2. Replace the output shaft from beneath the car, indexing the output shaft splines carefully with those of the final drive unit to prevent damage.

3. Replace the output-shaft retainer bolt, and torque to 40 ft.-lbs.

4. Guide the drive axle into the car, and connect the spindle to the steering knuckle.

5. Align the output shaft flange with the drive-axle inner-joint flange and, with the brakes applied to pre-

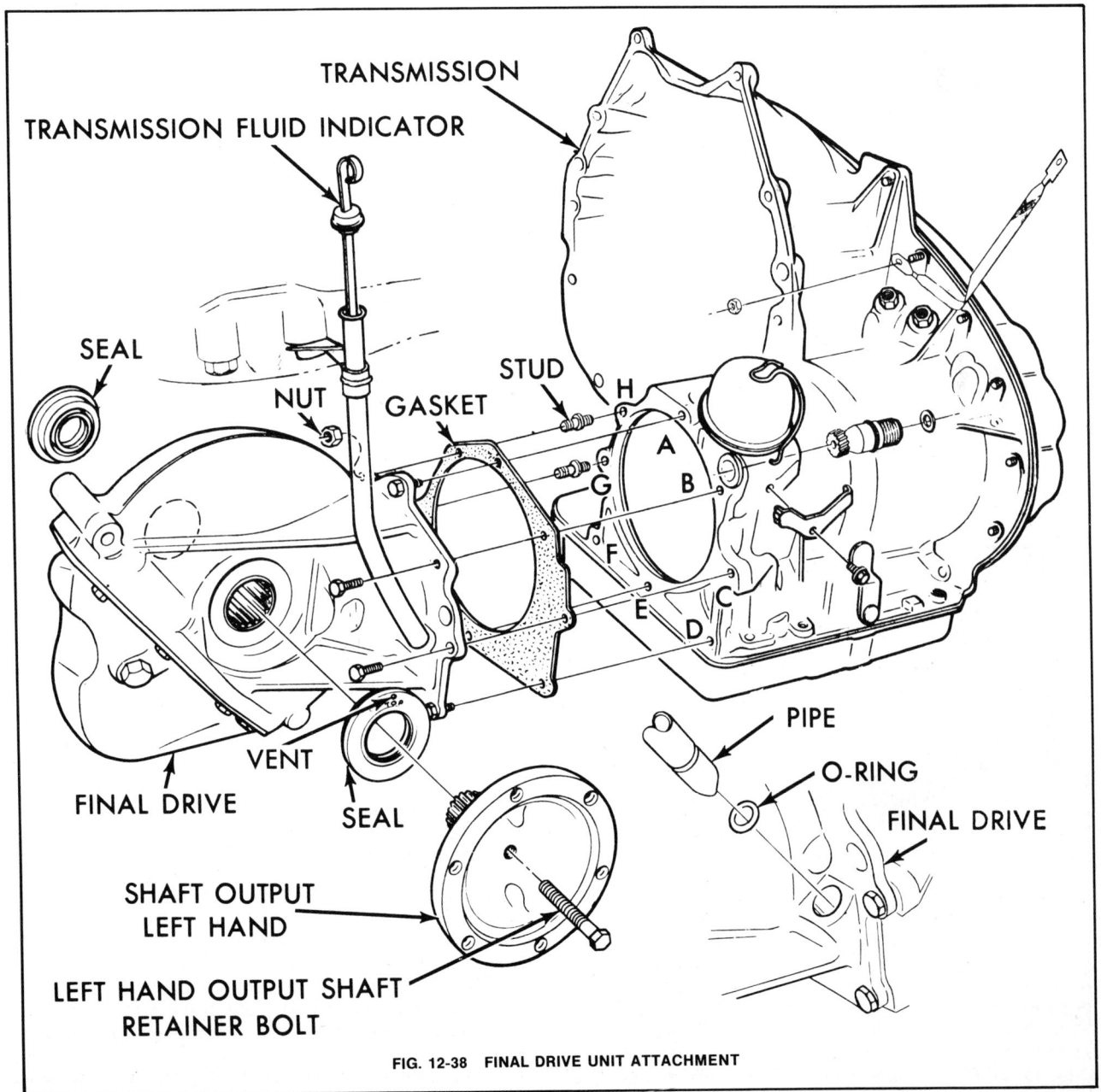

FIG. 12-38 FINAL DRIVE UNIT ATTACHMENT

vent the drive axle from turning, install new screws and lockwashers. Torque to 65 ft.-lbs. (Toronado, 75 ft.-lbs.).

6. Unwire the knuckle assembly, lift the upper control arm and fit the upper spherical joint into the steering knuckle.

7. Replace the brake hose clip on the upper-spherical-joint stud and install the retaining nut. Torque to 60 ft.-lbs., and replace the cotter pin (Toronado—torque lower-ball-joint stud nuts to 95 ft.-lbs.).

8. Install the brake hose bracket, and torque the shock-absorber upper-mounting nut to 75 ft.-lbs.

9. Install the drive-axle spindle washer and nut, and torque to a minimum 110 ft.-lbs. (Toronado, 200 ft.-lbs.), then tighten (*do not* back off) to align the cotter pin hole with the spindle hole, and install the cotter pin.

10. Replace the wheel, connect the negative battery cable and check the final-drive oil level. Inspect for oil leaks at the output shaft.

FINAL DRIVE REMOVAL (Fig. 12-38)

A special adapter fitted to a transmission lift is required to remove and replace the final drive unit. A variety of these are available from lift equipment manufacturers and rental agencies. Attempting to remove and replace the final drive unit without the use of such an adapter can cause serious personal injury, as well as damage to the final drive unit.

1. Disconnect the negative battery cable.

2. Remove the transmission-filler-tube bracket from the final drive bracket, and remove the filler tube.

3. Remove screws ''A'' and ''B'' and nut ''H'' **(Fig. 12-38)** holding the upper part of the final drive housing to the transmission. Use a box-end wrench with a crescent-shaped handle (a starter or manifold wrench) to remove ''H'' easily.

4. Remove the transmission-cooler-line clip from the final-drive support bracket.

5. Remove the locknut, washer and large through-bolt holding the final-drive support bracket to the engine mount bracket.

6. Remove the right output shaft (see ''Right Output-Shaft/Drive-Axle Removal'').

7. Make sure the right-shock-absorber lower sleeve cannot be dislodged from the mounting stud, then place jackstands under the front frame siderails, and lower the hoist. If the shock absorber is not positioned as specified, the lower control arm will drop down.

8. Remove the final drive cover and let the lubricant drain into a container.

9. Remove the screws holding the left drive axle to the output shaft. Compress the drive-axle inner-constant-velocity joint, and wire in this position to provide sufficient clearance for final-drive-unit removal without removing the left output shaft.

10. Remove the left tie-strut-to-crossmember bolt, loosen the strut-to-siderail bolt and swing the strut out to clear the final drive area.

11. Remove the final-drive support bracket, cover and gasket.

12. Position a transmission lift and the special adapter to remove the final drive unit. Follow the lift and adapter manufacturers' instructions and recommendations for use.

13. Slide a drain pan under the transmission, and remove screws ''C,'' ''D,'' ''E'' and ''F'' and nut ''G'' **(Fig. 12-38),** then disengage the final drive splines from the transmission, and let the unit drain.

14. Slide the final drive unit from under the car by rotating the ring gear over the steering linkage and lowering the housing.

PINION-BEARING OIL SEAL REPLACEMENT

1. With the final drive unit removed from the car and positioned on a clean workbench area, remove the pinion-bearing-housing-to-final-drive-case bolts.

2. Apply a steady pull on the pinion-gear splined end with one hand, and rotate the pinion bearing housing with the other.

3. Remove and discard the pinion-bearing-housing O-ring.

4. Check the vent-pin O-ring seal, and replace if necessary.

5. Use a screwdriver to remove the pinion-gear oil seals from the pinion bearing housing.

6. Place the pinion-gear oil seals back-to-back, with the spring on the seals exposed; then install in the housing.

7. Install the pinion bearing housing carefully over the pinion gear, and rotate until it seats correctly in the final drive case.

8. Replace and torque the pinion-bearing-housing-to-final-drive-case bolts to 35 ft.-lbs (Toronado, 45 ft.-lbs.).

10. Install the final drive unit in the case.

FINAL DRIVE INSTALLATION (Fig. 12-38)

1. Lubricate the transmission-side of a new final-drive-to-transmission gasket with transmission fluid, and position on the studs.

2. With the final drive unit secured to the transmission jack adapter, lift it into position and align the unit with the two studs while aligning the final drive and transmission splines. Rotating the left output shaft will help in this alignment procedure.

3. Position the final-drive support bracket as close as possible to its correctly installed position.

4. Replace the large through-bolt, nut and washer finger-tight, then install the long bolt, washer and locknut holding the final-drive support bracket to the engine mount support finger-tight.

5. Replace screws ''C,'' ''D,'' ''E'' and ''F,'' and nut ''G,'' torquing to 25 ft.-lbs. (Toronado, 30 ft.-lbs.).

6. Hold the large through-bolt nut with a wrench, torque bolt to 70 ft.-lbs. (Toronado, 110 ft.-lbs.).

7. Disconnect and remove the transmission jack and adapter assembly from the final drive housing.

8. Replace the final drive cover with a new gasket, and torque the attaching screws to 156 in.-lbs. (Toronado, 30 ft.-lbs.). The Cadillac installation uses two cover gaskets to vent the unit. The thin dark-gray gasket is installed next to the housing, and the slotted light-gray gasket placed on top next to the cover.

9. Place the left drive axle on the output shaft and, with the brakes applied to prevent axle rotation, torque screws to 65 ft.-lbs. (Toronado, 75 ft.-lbs.). Install left tie strut to crossmember, then right output shaft assembly.

10. Torque the remaining support bolts to 20 ft.-lbs. (Toronado, 55 ft.-lbs.).

11. Replace screws ''A'' and ''B,'' and nut ''H,'' torquing to 25 ft.-lbs. (Toronado, 30 ft.-lbs.).

12. Replace the transmission-cooler-line clip to the support bracket. Install a new O-ring seal on the transmission filler tube, and install.

13. Connect the negative battery cable, fill the final drive unit with specified lubricant and start the engine.

14. Check the transmission fluid level, and add as necessary.

15. Inspect output shaft seals, final-drive-to-transmission connection and final drive cover for oil leakage.

FINAL DRIVE OVERHAUL

1979 Riviera, Cadillac Eldorado, Oldsmobile Toronado

Downsizing of these GM models in 1979 led to the use of a final drive assembly somewhat different from the 1970-78 model. The front wheel drive system used on these vehicles includes a final drive unit of metric design, right and left output shafts and drive axles, **(Fig. 12-38A)**. The 8-in. hypoid ring and pinion gear set is rotated by a splined transmission output shaft. Two preloaded tapered roller bearings support the drive pinion in the housing. Right and left output shafts are splined to the side gears and held in place with a snap-lock retainer ring. The right output shaft is longer and requires a support bracket and brace. Both output shafts are connected to and drive the drive axles. Drive axles consist of inner/outer constant velocity joints connected by the axle shaft.

RIGHT OUTPUT SHAFT/SEAL REMOVAL
(Step 12 applies only to the right-hand shaft)

1. Disconnect the negative battery cable.

2. Raise the car on a hoist. Position jack stands under the front frame horns and lower front post when using a twin post hoist.

3. Remove the wheel cover and wheel.

4. Discard the cotter pin, remove the nut and shield from the tie rod pivot and use a puller to separate the tie rod end from the knuckle.

5. The drive axle boots must be treated with extreme care if boot seal protectors are not used. Discard the cotter pin and remove the retainer, nut and washer from the drive axle.

6. Insert a drift through the top of the brake caliper to engage a rotor vane and hold the drive axle from rotating while removing the six drive axle-to-output shaft screws.

7. Discard the cotter pin and push the drive axle inward to remove the nut holding the upper spherical joint.

8. Remove the brake hose clip at the spherical joint stud and reinstall the nut loosely.

9. Rap the knuckle sharply with a hammer and drift to free the spherical joint. It may help to apply pressure during this step by prying on the upper control arm.

10. Remove the nut again and separate the knuckle and joint.

11. Withdraw the drive axle from the knuckle and remove from the car. If boot protectors are used, leave in place.

12. Disconnect the battery cable retainer from the support and remove the shaft support.

13. Unbolt the frame brace and swing it outward, then tap on the flanged end of the output shaft with a brass hammer. When it pops out of the retaining ring, withdraw the output shaft and support assembly. Be careful not to damage the support bearing or the output shaft seal and splines.

14. Pry the seal from the housing. Apply pressure at several points to prevent cocking the seal. Take care not to damage the housing.

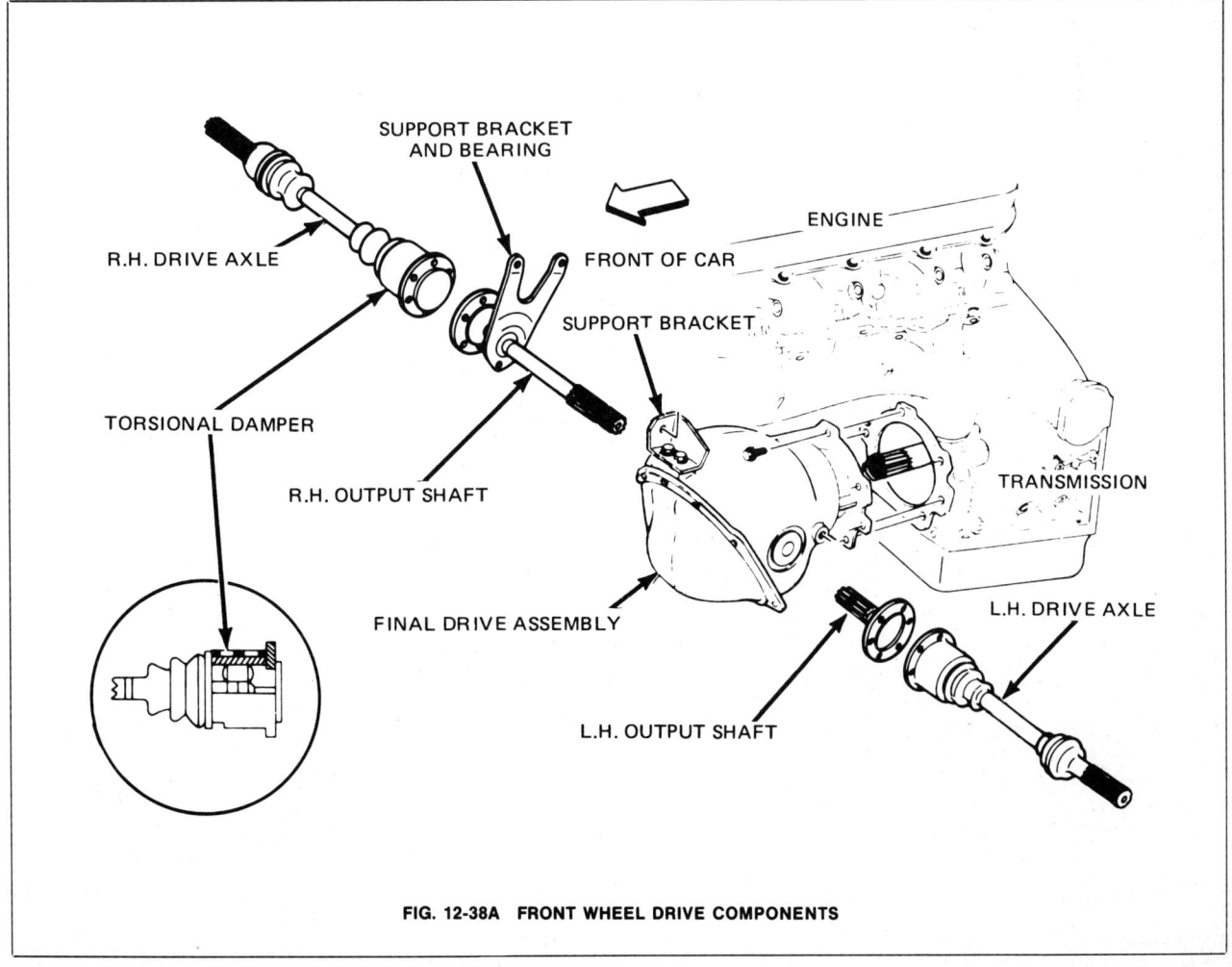

FIG. 12-38A   FRONT WHEEL DRIVE COMPONENTS

OUTPUT SHAFT/SEAL INSTALLATION

(Steps 3, 4 and 5 apply only to right-hand shaft)

1. Install a new seal in the housing and apply wheel bearing grease between the seal lips.

2. Index the output shaft splines with the side gear splines in the final drive assembly. Lightly tap the center of the flanged end with a brass hammer until you feel the shaft snap in place. Make sure it's secured in position and that the splines align properly. Failure to do so will result in a driveline "clunk."

3. Line up the attaching holes in the shaft support with those in the engine block and install the support screws and washers.

4. Move the shaft flange end around until the center location is found. Hold the shaft in this position and torque the screws to 50 ft.-lbs.

5. Replace the battery cable retainer to the support.

6. Guide the drive axle in place and fit the splined axle end into the knuckle.

7. Align the upper spherical joint stud with the knuckle, replace the brake hose clip on the stud and push the drive axle inward, torquing the nut to 60 ft.-lbs. If the cotter pin slot does not align with the nut, tighten (do not back off) the nut up to 1/6th turn or until the slots line up.

8. Replace the output shaft-to-drive axle screws and torque to 60 ft.-lbs.

9. Replace the washer, nut, retainer and new cotter pin. Torque the nut to 130 ft.-lbs. and align the pin slot with the rotating retainer. Bend the pin to prevent the retainer from rattling.

10. Install the tie rod pivot in the knuckle and replace the shield and nut. Torque the nut to 60 ft.-lbs. and align the pin slot as in Step 7.

11. Position the frame brace and replace the bolt and nut. Torque the brace end nuts to 50 ft.-lbs.

12. Remove the boot seal protectors, install the wheel and cover assembly and torque the mounting nuts to 100 ft.-lbs.

13. Lower the car to the ground and reconnect the negative battery cable.

14. Start the engine and run until the differential lubricant is warm. Check the output shaft seals for oil leaks.

FINAL DRIVE ASSEMBLY REMOVAL

1. Disconnect the negative battery cable.

2. Raise the car on a hoist. Position jack stands under the front frame horns and lower front post when using a twin post hoist.

3. Unbolt both frame braces at the front and move outward.

4. Position a suitable drain pan or container beneath the final drive cover. Loosen all 13 cover screws and let the lubricant drain.

5. Remove cover and discard the gasket.

6. Install boot seal protectors or take care not to damage the boot seals. Remove the output shaft-to-drive assembly screws on each side.

7. Separate the output shaft-drive axle flanges. Final drive assembly will be removed with output shaft attached.

8. Unbolt the battery cable retainer at the right output shaft support and remove the support screws at the engine block.

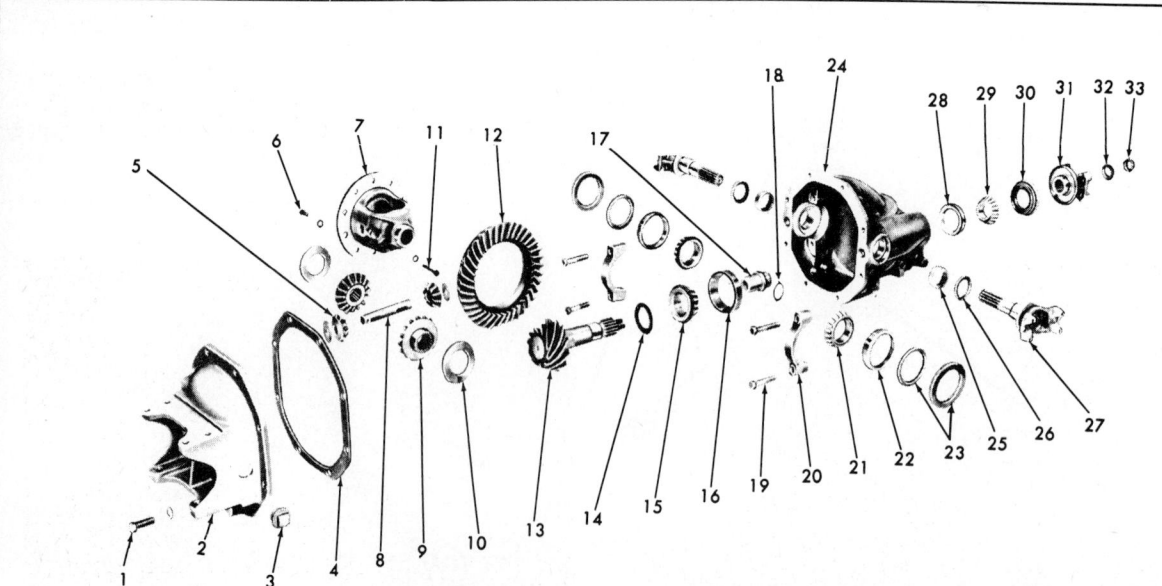

1. Cover Bolt	11. Differential Pinion Pin Retainer	19. Side Bearing Cap Bolt	26. Side Gear Yoke Bearing Seal
2. Carrier Cover	12. Hypoid Ring Gear	20. Side Bearing Cap	27. Side Gear Yoke
3. Filler Plug	13. Hypoid Drive Pinion	21. Differential Side Bearing	28. Pinion Front Bearing Cup
4. Cover Gasket	14. Pinion Bearing Shim	22. Side Bearing Cup	29. Pinion Front Bearing
5. Differential Pinion	15. Pinion Rear Bearing	23. Side Bearing Shim and Spacer	30. Pinion Oil Seal
6. Ring Gear Bolt	16. Pinion Rear Bearing Cup	24. Differential Carrier	31. Companion Flange
7. Differential Case	17. Pinion Bearing Spacer	25. Side Gear Yoke Bearing	32. Pinion Washer
8. Pinion Shaft	18. Side Gear Yoke Snap Ring		33. Pinion Nut
9. Differential Side Gear			
10. Side Gear Thrust Washer			

FIG. 12-39 CORVETTE DIFFERENTIAL CARRIER ASSEMBLY

9. Remove the screw holding the rear of the final drive shield and loosen the support bracket screw holding the front of the shield. Slide the shield out and forward to remove.

10. Remove the remaining final drive-to-transmission screws and the support bracket-to-engine block screw.

11. Separate the steering linkage from the pitman arm with a puller, then push the linkage toward the front of the car.

12. Slide the final drive forward until it comes off the transmission splined shaft, then remove the assembly with output shafts attached. It is not advisable to use the output shafts as handles when removing the final drive. Any weight or pressure applied in this way can cause damage to the seals and/or splines.

FINAL DRIVE ASSEMBLY INSTALLATION

1. Clean all transmission-to-final drive gasket mating surfaces.

2. Fit a new gasket to the final drive assembly. *Do not use* any grease, oil or sealer to hold the gasket in place—it must be perfectly dry.

3. Tie the right output shaft support arm to the shaft flange hole nearest to the twelve o'clock position.

4. Position the final drive assembly (with output shafts attached) and align the final drive/transmission shaft splines. Make sure that the gasket does not slip out of place as you push the final drive assembly to the rear until it seats in place with the transmission.

5. Replace the final drive-to-transmission screws, except for the one in the two o'clock position. Torque to 30 ft.-lbs.

6. Loosen the front support bracket, hold flush on the housing pad and replace the bracket-to-engine block screw, torquing to 50 ft.-lbs.

7. Position the final drive shield and replace the final drive-to-transmission screw in the two o'clock position. Torque the bracket-to-housing screws to 34 ft.-lbs. Bend the shield if necessary to obtain the proper housing clearance.

8. Line up the attaching bolt holes in the shaft support with those in the engine block and install the support screws and washers.

9. Move the shaft flange end around until the center location is found. Hold the shaft in this position and torque the screws to 50 ft.-lbs.

10. Replace the battery cable retainer to the support.

11. Align each drive axle with the output shaft, replace the attaching screws and torque to 60 ft.-lbs.

12. Install the final drive cover with a new gasket and replace the cover screws. Torque to 7 ft.-lbs.

13. Fill the final drive assembly with 3.2 pints of appropriate axle lubricant and torque the filler nut to 30 ft.-lbs.

14. Connect the steering linkage to the pitman arm and torque the nut to 60 ft.-lbs. Align the cotter pin slot with the nut; tighten up to 1/6th turn if necessary, but do not back off.

15. Swing the frame braces into position and replace the attaching bolts and nuts. Torque the nuts at both ends of the brace to 50 ft.-lbs.

16. Remove the boot seal protectors, if used.

17. Lower the car to the ground and reconnect the negative battery cable. Start the engine and check the transmission fluid level. Top up level is necessary.

18. Run the engine until the differential lubricant is warm. Check the output shaft seals for oil leaks.

DIFFERENTIAL OVERHAUL
1970-79 Corvette

DIFFERENTIAL DISASSEMBLY (Fig. 12-39)

1. Remove the two snap rings retaining the side gear yokes to the carrier housing, and pull the yokes from the case **(Fig. 12-40)**.

2. Remove the differential bearing caps and lightly punch an identification mark on the side of each cap and on the face of the case to assure correct reassembly **(Fig. 12-41)**.

FIG. 12-40 SIDE GEAR YOKE REMOVAL

FIG. 12-41 BEARING CAP/CASE MARKING

FIG. 12-42   DIFFERENTIAL REMOVAL

FIG. 12-43   COMPANION FLANGE SEAL REMOVAL

FIG. 12-44   PINION SHAFT REMOVAL/REPLACEMENT

3. Pull the differential assembly from the carrier housing, and remove the bearing shims, marking them for correct reassembly **(Fig. 12-42)**.

4. Remove the pinion lockscrew, shaft, differential pinions and thrust washers, and the side gears/thrust washers from the differential case.

5. Inspect the differential side bearings, the side-gear yoke bearings, and the pinion front and rear bearings for excessive wear, roughness, scoring or other damage. If necessary, remove and replace with new bearing(s).

6. Inspect the ring gear. If necessary to replace, remove the ring gear bolts, and tap the ring gear from the differential case.

DRIVE PINION REPLACEMENT

1. With the differential removed from the carrier housing, remove the companion flange.

2. Remove the pinion and rear bearing, then pry the companion flange seal from the carrier **(Fig. 12-43)**, and remove the front pinion bearing.

3. Pry out and discard the differential side-gear yoke seals, then remove the yoke bearing from the bore by driving out with a hammer and length of 1¾-in. O.D. pipe.

4. Press off the rear-pinion-bearing inner race and roller assembly.

5. Select a pinion shim. If the differential gave no trouble, and the old gears are being reinstalled, the original pinion shim can be used. If the ring and pinion gear set is changed, a new shim should be used.

6. Place the shim on the pinion head, and press the rear bearing in place.

7. Lubricate the pinion bearings, and replace the pinion gear in the carrier housing.

8. Fit a new collapsible pinion-bearing spacer over the pinion shaft and seat it on the rear-bearing inner race.

9. Seat the pinion front-bearing cone and roller on the pinion shaft against the spacer.

10. Lubricate the pinion seal lips, and install the pinion oil seal to seat against the pinion flange, then replace the companion flange.

11. Replace the companion flange washer and nut, tightening slightly. Check the preload and compare to specifications (20 to 30 in.-lbs. for new bearings, 5 to 15 in.-lbs. for old bearings). Do this in several stages of very small increments, since a one-eighth turn can add drag at the rate of 5 in.-lbs. Tighten a little at a time, and repeatedly test for preload. If the torque specifications are exceeded, the collapsible spacer will have to be removed and replaced with another new one—never back off the pinion nut if torque is exceeded.

DIFFERENTIAL ASSEMBLY (Fig. 12-39)

1. If the ring gear was removed, replace it to the differential case and install every other bolt, drawing them up evenly until the ring gear is seated against the flange. It may ease assembly to heat (expand) the ring gear beforehand in hot water or oil (not over 300°), and smooth the chamfer on the inner ring gear circumference with an Arkansas stone, to prevent burrs.

2. Install the remaining ring gear bolts, and tighten.

3. Replace the side gears and thrust washers in the case.

4. Place the pinions and thrust washers in the housing through the loading hole.

5. Mesh the pinion gears with the side gears, and rotate to align the case and pinion shaft bores.

6. Replace pinion shaft and lockscrew **(Fig. 12-44).**

7. Fit a 0.160-in. service spacer between each bearing race and the housing. When new bearings are installed, add sufficient shims to each spacer to equal a thickness corresponding to that of the original shim pack. If the old bearings are reinstalled, increase the original shim-pack thickness by 0.002-in. (one shim) on each side.

8. Insert the shim pack on one side and tap the other shim pack in place, installing the head bolts into the bearing caps.

9. Rotate the differential case several times to check for proper bearing seating, then position a dial indicator to read the gear lash at the ring-gear outer edge, checking lash at 90° intervals. The backlash should be between 0.003-in. and 0.010-in., with variations in readings not exceeding 0.002-in.

10. Should backlash variations exceed 0.002-in., check the ring gear and case runout; if this exceeds 0.003-in., look for ring-gear/case deformation or contamination between the gear and the case.

11. If gear lash is not within specifications, decrease the shim thickness on one side, while increasing it on the other by the same amount. The total shim pack thickness should be maintained to prevent changing the preload. Should backlash exceed the upper limit, increase the thickness on the ring gear side; if less than the lower limit, decrease thickness on the ring gear side.

12. Once backlash is correctly adjusted, tighten the bearing caps securely.

13. Perform a "Gear Tooth Contact Pattern Test." If a correct pattern is not obtained, the pinion shaft shim will have to be changed in order to change the pinion depth.

14. If the test is satisfactory, reinstall the carrier housing.

FORD MOTOR COMPANY DIFFERENTIAL OVERHAUL

Ford, Mercury and Lincoln cars use two different types of differentials: an integral carrier axle and a removable carrier axle. Various ring gear sizes, axle housings and differential cases are used, with the particular application depending primarily upon car model and engine size. All carry an identification tag attached to one of the rear-cover-to-housing or carrier-to-housing bolts, and information provided on the tag should be used to identify the exact model/gear ratio when obtaining replacement parts **(Fig. 12-45).** Before you attempt to work on a Ford Motor Company differential, determine which type you have.

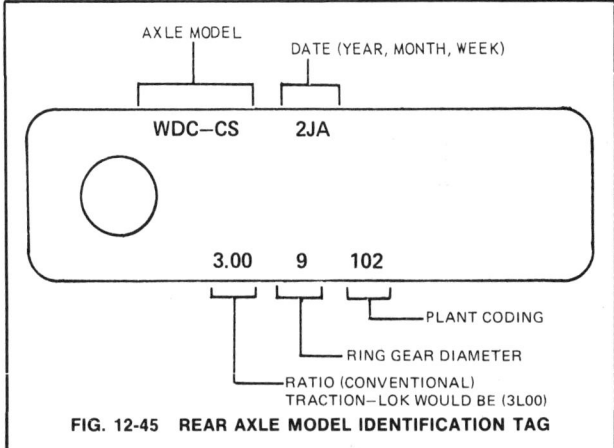

FIG. 12-45 REAR AXLE MODEL IDENTIFICATION TAG

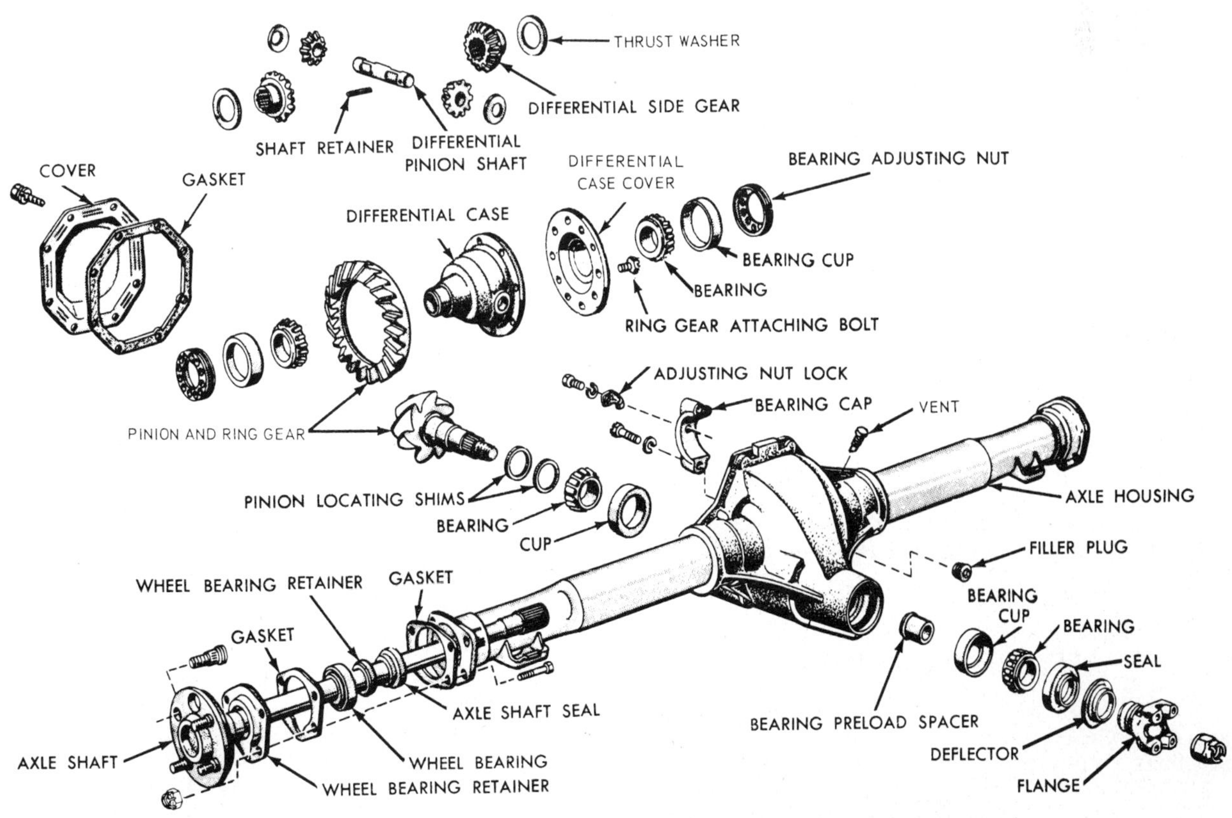

FIG. 12-46 TYPICAL INTEGRAL AXLE (EXCEPT WER)

INTEGRAL CARRIER OVERHAUL

Two basic integral carrier designs are used: the WCY, WDC, WDV, WDW, WFS, WFZ, WGF and WGG in which the axle shafts use an inner and outer bearing retainer, and the light-duty WER, WGX, WGZ, which use C-locks to retain the axle. If the identification tag is missing or damaged, the WER/WGX/WGZ can be identified by the lack of a retainer-bolt access hole in the axle shaft flange.

INTEGRAL CARRIER DISASSEMBLY
ALL EXCEPT WER/WGX/WGZ (Fig. 12-46)

1. Support the car on a hoist to allow the rear axle to drop as far as the suspension will allow.
2. Place a container under the axle housing, remove the carrier cover and let the lubricant drain.
3. Wipe the gear teeth with a clean, lint-free cloth, and paint the gear teeth with red lead or gear marking compound.
4. Use a box wrench on the ring-gear attaching bolts to rotate the ring gear five full revolutions in both directions, or until a clear contact pattern is seen.
5. Compare the pattern obtained to Fig. 12-47. Any combination of the drive/coast patterns that are shown is acceptable.
6. Remove the rear wheels, brake drums and axles, wiring the brake backing plates to the frame rail.
7. Scribe a mark on the driveshaft end yoke and the axle U-joint flange, disconnect them and remove the driveshaft.
8. Remove the bearing-cap nut locks, and mark one bearing cap and the case for correct reassembly.
9. Remove the bearing cap bolts and bearing caps, holding the differential from falling out of the case.
10. Lift the differential case and bearing cups out of the housing.
11. Block the drive pinion flange to prevent it from rotating, and remove the pinion nut and flange.
12. Use a soft-faced mallet to drive the pinion through the front bearing cone, and remove it through the rear of the housing.
13. Drive the pinion front-bearing cone, flange seal and bearing cup out through the front of the housing.
14. Press the pinion rear-bearing cone from the pinion shaft, and measure the thickness of the shim under the cone.

INTEGRAL CARRIER DISASSEMBLY,
WER/WGX/WGZ ONLY (Fig. 12-48)

1. With the car on a hoist, place a container under the axle housing. Loosen the housing cover, and drain the lubricant.
2. Remove the driveshaft after scribing a mark on the end yoke and axle U-joint flange.
3. Position a set of jackstands under the rear frame crossmember, and lower the car until the axle hangs as low as possible.
4. Remove the housing cover and gasket.
5. Wipe the gear teeth with a clean, lint-free cloth, and paint the gear teeth with red lead or gear marking compound.
6. Use a box wrench on the ring-gear attaching bolts to rotate the ring gear five full revolutions in both directions, or until a clear contact pattern is seen.
7. Compare the pattern obtained to Fig. 12-47. Any combination of the drive/coast patterns that are shown is acceptable.
8. Remove the pinion shaft lock and pinion shaft, then push the axle shafts inward, remove the C-locks

and pull the axle shafts from the housing.
9. Remove the two side-bearing adjustment nut locks.
10. Position a dial indicator to check backlash and ring gear runout (see Step 21, "Differential Case Assembly").
11. Mark one differential bearing cap and the case for correct reassembly, then remove the bearing caps, cups, adjusting nuts and the case assembly.
12. Block the drive pinion flange to prevent it from rotating, and remove the pinion nut and flange.
13. Use a hammer and drift to remove the pinion-shaft oil seal through the front of the housing.
14. Press the pinion rear-bearing cone from the pinion shaft, and measure the thickness of the shim under the cone.

DIFFERENTIAL CASE DISASSEMBLY
ALL UNITS

1. Inspect each differential bearing for wear or damage. If satisfactory, it need not be removed. If unsatisfactory, a puller is required to remove it.
2. Scribe the differential case, cover and ring gear for correct reassembly.
3. Remove and discard the ring-gear-to-differential-case bolts.
4. Press the ring gear from the case, or tap off with a soft-faced mallet.
5. Remove the left side of the case, and use a drift to drive out the pinion-shaft lock pin.
6. Drive out the pinion shaft with a brass drift, and remove the gears and thrust washers.
7. Leave the pinion bearing cups intact, unless they are worn or damaged. If necessary to remove them, drive out from the carrier with a drift, and reinstall new ones, seating properly. The cone and roller assembly must also be replaced if the cups are changed.

CLEANING/INSPECTION OF ALL UNITS

All parts should be cleaned in solvent, except synthetic seals. Oil the bearings immediately after cleaning, then inspect all parts for damage, wear or other defects as follows:

1. Gears—Check for scoring or excessive wear. Do not damage the pilot bearing surface of the pinion. Inspect the teeth and thrust surfaces of all gears for wear, since this is a contributing factor to excessive driveline backlash.
2. Bearing Assemblies—Inspect the cups for rings, scoring, galling or excessive wear patterns. Look for roughness in roller operation and step-wear on their ends. Replace any worn components.
3. Differential Bearing Adjusting Nuts—Test the fit of the adjusting nuts in the bearing cap threads.
4. Differential Case—Examine the hubs where the bearings mount—they should be smooth. Also inspect the differential-case bearing shoulders. Check the free rotation of the side gears in their bores.

DIFFERENTIAL CASE ASSEMBLY
ALL UNITS

For WER reassembly, start with Step 4.

1. Lubricate all parts with axle lubricant, and place the side gears in the case with their thrust washers.
2. Install the two pinion gears and thrust washers at opposite sides in the case, meshing with the side gears and aligning the gear holes with the case pinion-shaft holes.

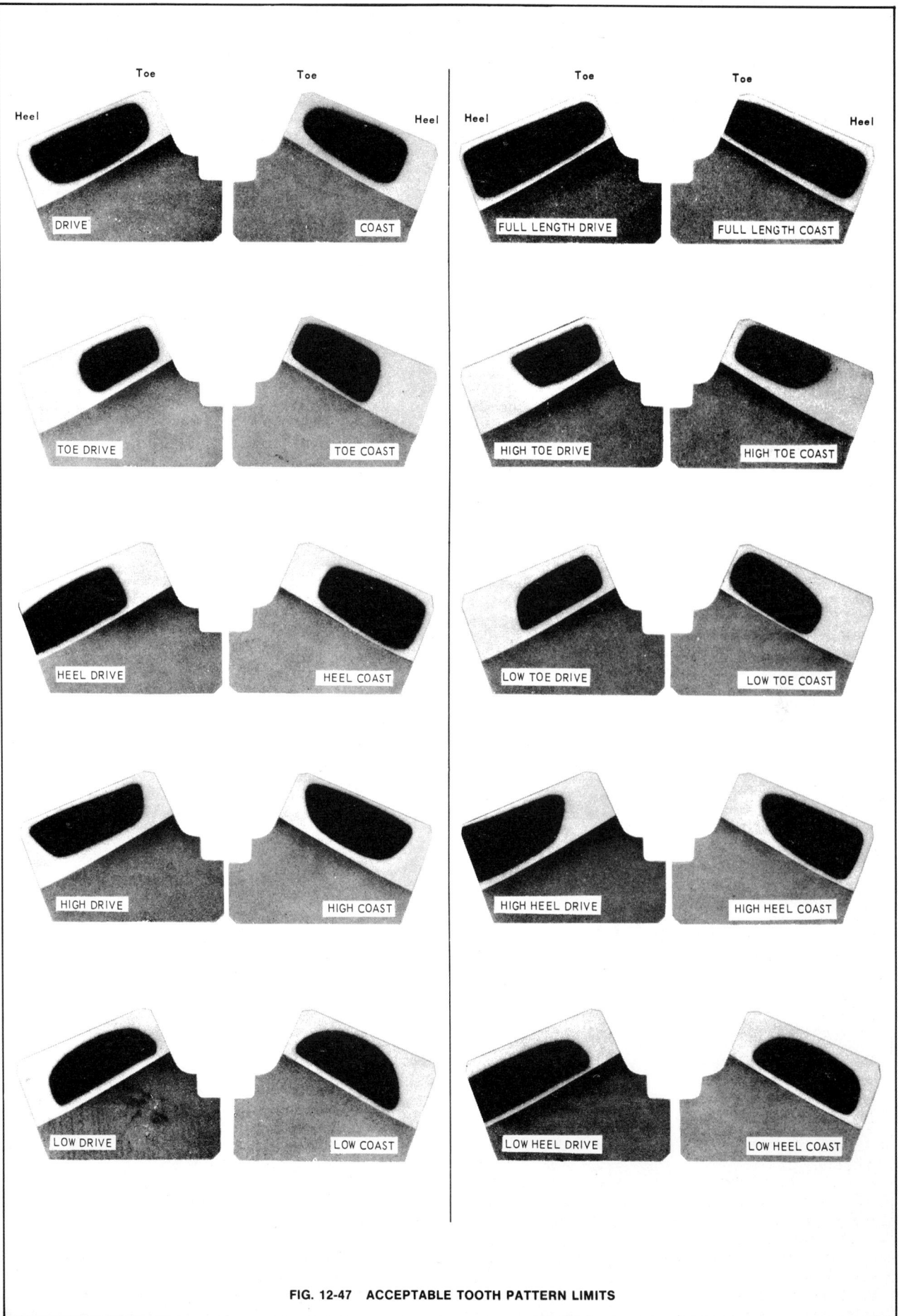

FIG. 12-47 ACCEPTABLE TOOTH PATTERN LIMITS

3. Fit the pinion shaft into the differential case, and align the shaft lock-pin hole with the case pin hole, then drive the shaft in place and install the lock pin.

4. Align the scribed marks on the two halves of the case, and fit together.

5. Position the ring gear on the differential case, and install new bolts. If the bolts used have threads that are coated green, install as is. If the threads are not coated, apply sealer (Loctite) and install. Torque 45 to 60 ft.-lbs. (WER/WGX/WGZ, 70 to 85 ft.-lbs.)

6. Press the differential bearings in place, if they were removed.

7. Select a new shim of the same thickness as that removed from the pinion.

8. Install the shim and pinion rear bearing on the pinion shaft, pressing firmly against the shaft shoulder.

9. Install a new pinion-bearing preload spacer (largest diameter end first) on the pinion shaft.

10. Lubricate the pinion front and rear bearings, and place the front bearing cone in the housing, installing a new pinion oil seal in the carrier.

11. Fit the drive-pinion-shaft flange in the seal, and hold firmly against the pinion front-bearing cone, then insert the pinion shaft into the flange from the rear of the carrier.

12. Install a new pinion shaft nut, and tighten carefully. This pulls the pinion shaft into the front bearing cone and the flange, reducing end play and bringing the flange and bearing cone into contact with the collapsible pinion spacer.

13. Check the pinion-shaft end play, and continue to tighten. As soon as there is drag on the bearings, turn the pinion shaft in both directions several times to set the bearing rollers, and adjust the preload to specifications with a torque wrench. If the preload limit is exceeded (see Step 20), it will be necessary to remove the pinion shaft and install another new collapsible spacer, since backing off the pinion nut removes the compression and can let the front bearing cone turn on the pinion shaft.

14. Lubricate the bearing bores, place the cups on bearings, install differential case assembly in carrier.

15. If the gear teeth have timing marks, position the differential case and ring gear in the carrier to index

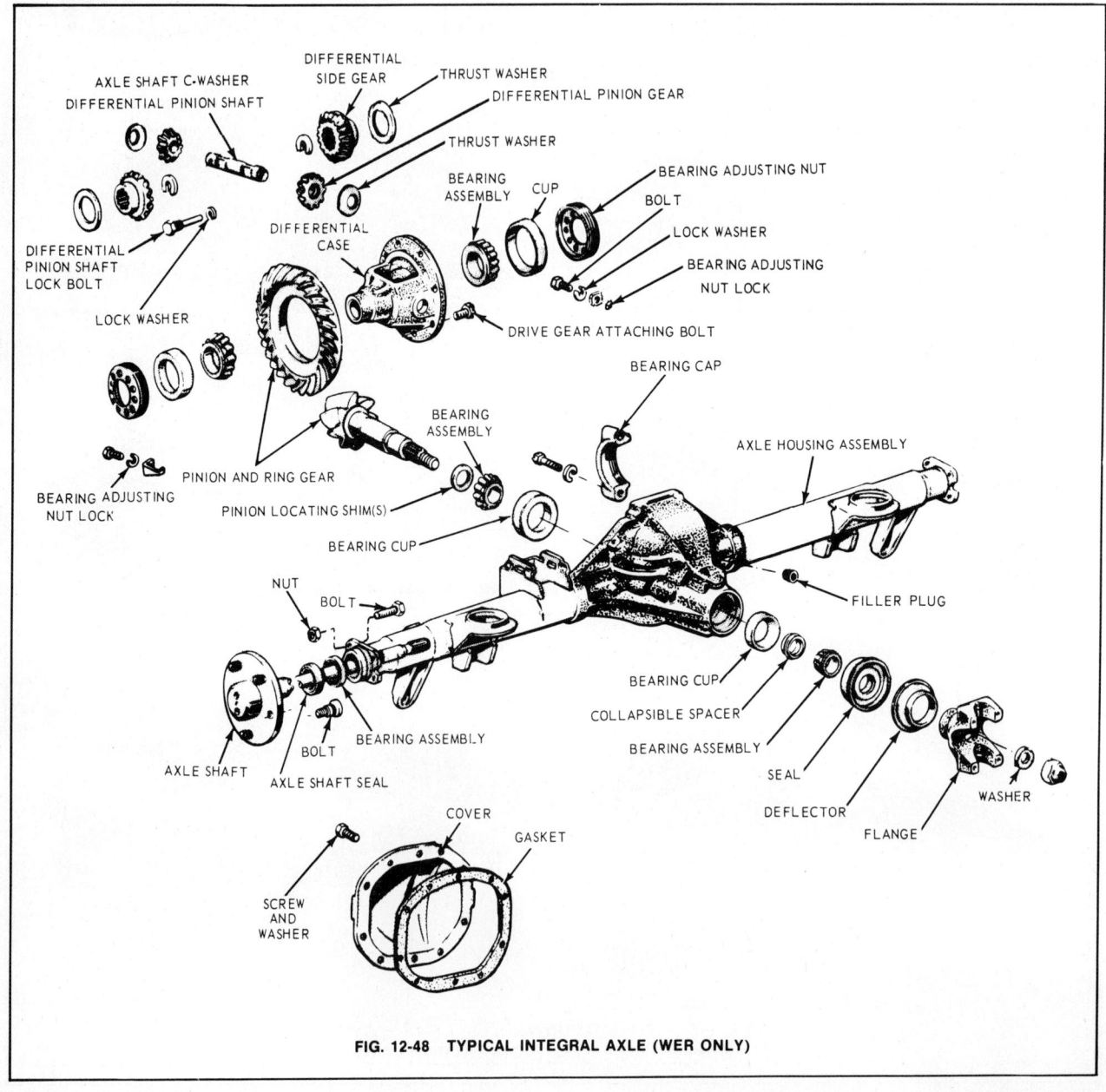

FIG. 12-48   TYPICAL INTEGRAL AXLE (WER ONLY)

the marked teeth with the correspondingly marked pinion gear tooth.

16. Push the differential case in the bores until a slight amount of backlash is felt, then hold the case in place and set the adjusting nuts in the bores to just touch the bearing cups.

17. Replace the bearing caps to match the case marks, and install the cap bolts and lockwashers. Tighten the bolts while turning the adjusting nuts.

18. Torque cap bolts 40 to 55 ft.-lbs (WER, 55 to 70 ft.-lbs., WGX, WGZ, 70-85 ft.-lbs.), then loosen and retorque to 5 ft.-lbs. for adjustment purposes.

19. Loosen the right adjusting nut (pinion side) until it is away from the cup, and tighten the left adjusting nut (ring-gear side) until the ring gear is forced into the pinion with no backlash **(Fig. 12-49)**. Rotate the pinion several times to make sure it does not bind.

20. Tighten right adjusting nut until it touches bearing cup. Bearings must be preloaded with 17 to 27 in.-lbs. (WER, 22 to 32 in.-lbs.) if new bearings, or 6 to 12 in.-lbs. (WER/WGX/WGZ, 8-14 in.-lbs.) if old bearings. Rotate the pinion several times to make sure it does not bind and that the bearings are properly seated in their cups.

21. Torque cap bolts as in Step 18 and measure ring gear backlash with a dial indicator. It should range from 0.008-in. to 0.012-in., with a maximum variation of 0.003-in. between teeth (WGX/WGZ, 0.004-in.).

22. If the backlash is not within specifications, loosen one adjusting nut, and tighten the opposite one an equal amount to move the ring gear nearer or farther from the pinion **(Fig. 12-49)**.

23. Check the tooth contact pattern again, as described in "Integral Carrier Disassembly" procedure. If the pattern is not satisfactory, the differential will have

to be disassembled and a thicker or thinner pinion shim installed.

24. WER/WGX/WGZ—Clean marking compound from gear teeth, and install both side-bearing adjusting nut locks, torquing 12 to 25 ft.-lbs.

25. WER/WGX/WGZ—Replace differential pinion gears and thrust washers.

26. All—If the pattern is satisfactory, replace cover

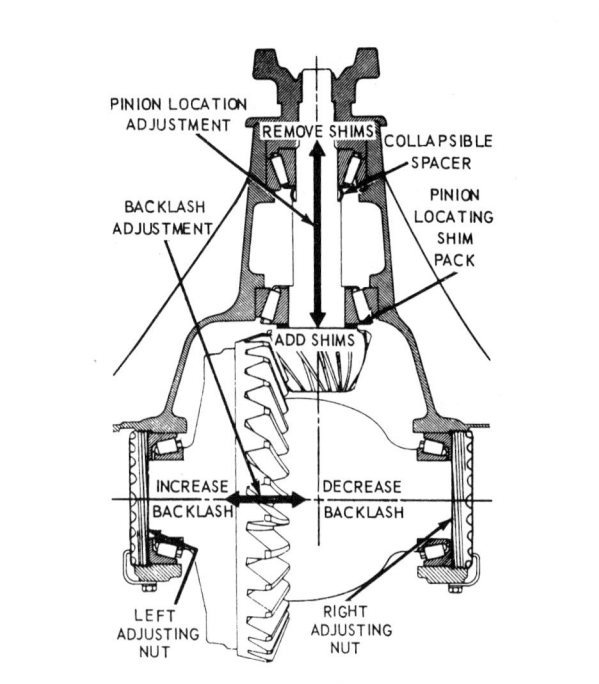

FIG. 12-49 PINION/RING-GEAR TOOTH CONTACT ALIGNMENT

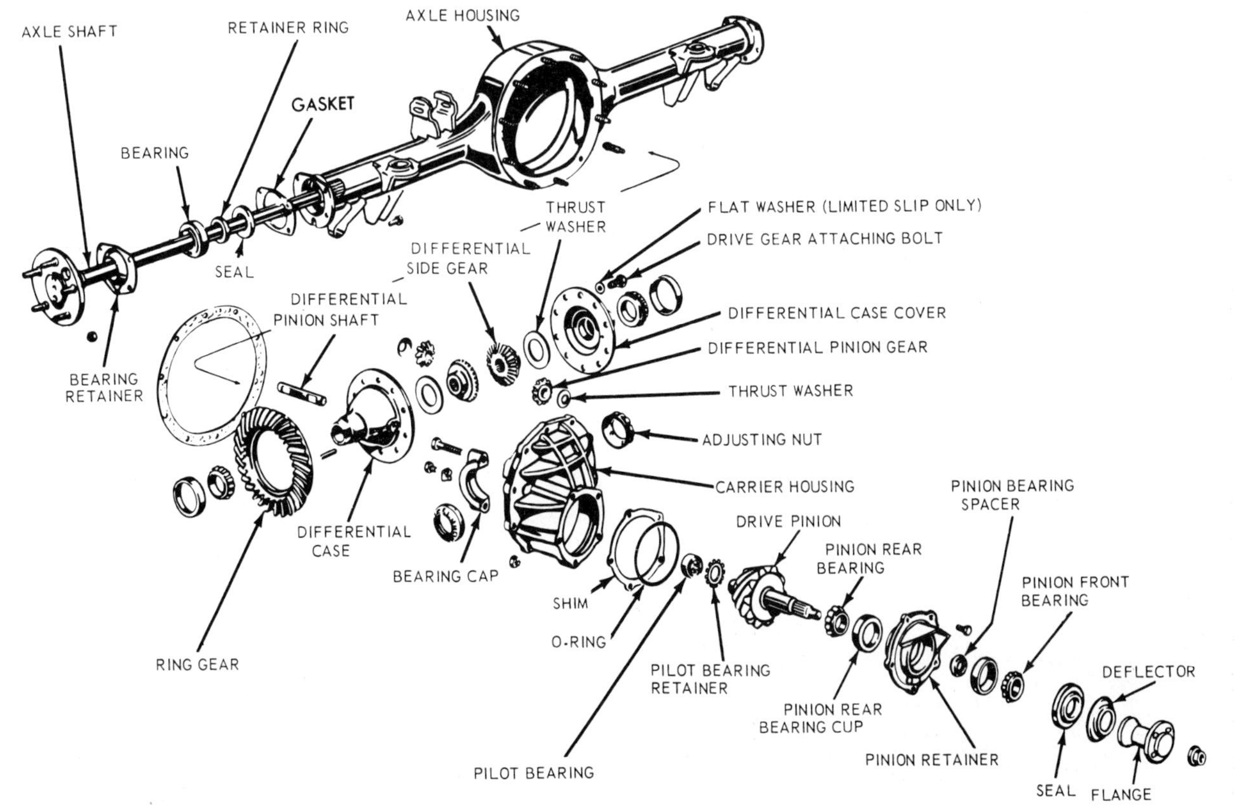

FIG. 12-50 TYPICAL REMOVABLE CARRIER ASSEMBLY

with a new gasket, and reinstall the axle shafts and driveshaft. (WER/WGX/WGZ, reverse this procedure.)

REMOVABLE CARRIER OVERHAUL

The removable carrier axle type is fitted with both a removable differential carrier and pinion housing, and uses four different ring-gear sizes. The semi-floating axle shafts use outer-bearing retainer plates (disc adapters on disc brake applications) to hold the axle in place. The left axle shaft is shorter than the right one, and the axles are therefore not interchangeable.

REMOVABLE CARRIER DISASSEMBLY (Fig. 12-50)

1. With the car on a hoist, remove the wheels, brake drums and axle shafts, wiring the brake backing plates to the frame rails to prevent brake line damage.

2. Scribe a mark on the driveshaft end yoke and the axle U-joint flange, disconnect them and remove the driveshaft.

3. Clean the carrier-to-housing surfaces with a wire brush, and wipe with a cloth moistened in solvent, then place a container under the axle housing, remove the carrier attaching nuts and washers; drain the lubricant.

4. The 9-in. (1973 on) or 9⅜-in. (1971-72) ring gear axle may be fitted with a single sensor (Sure-Track) system on the companion flange, with the sensor mounted in the pinion retainer. Unplug the anti-skid sensor connection (Fig. 12-51).

5. Remove the carrier assembly from the axle housing, and mount it securely in a vise.

6. Perform a "Gear Tooth Pattern Check" as in Steps 3, 4 and 5, "Integral Carrier Disassembly."

7. Mark one differential bearing cap and its support with punch marks for correct reassembly.

8. Mark one bearing-cap adjusting nut and the carrier with punch marks for correct reassembly.

9. Remove the adjusting nut locks, bearing caps and adjusting nuts. Lift the differential case from the carrier.

10. Use a puller to remove the differential bearings. The bearing cups on the 8-in. ring gear have a black oxide coating. While this *does not* indicate a failed or burned condition, these bearings do require a closer than normal inspection to determine if excessive wear or damage is present.

11. Scribe an alignment mark on the differential case, cover and ring gear for correct reassembly.

12. Remove and discard the ring-gear-to-differential-case bolts.

13. Press the ring gear from the differential case, or tap it off with a soft-faced mallet.

14. Drive the pinion-shaft lock pin out with a drift, and separate the differential case halves.

15. Drive the pinion shaft out with a brass drift, and remove the gears and thrust washers.

16. Hold the pinion shaft flange to prevent it from rotating, and remove the pinion nut and flange.

17. Remove the oil deflector and the pinion seal.

18. Remove the pinion bearing, and unbolt the retainer assembly from the carrier housing. Measure and re-

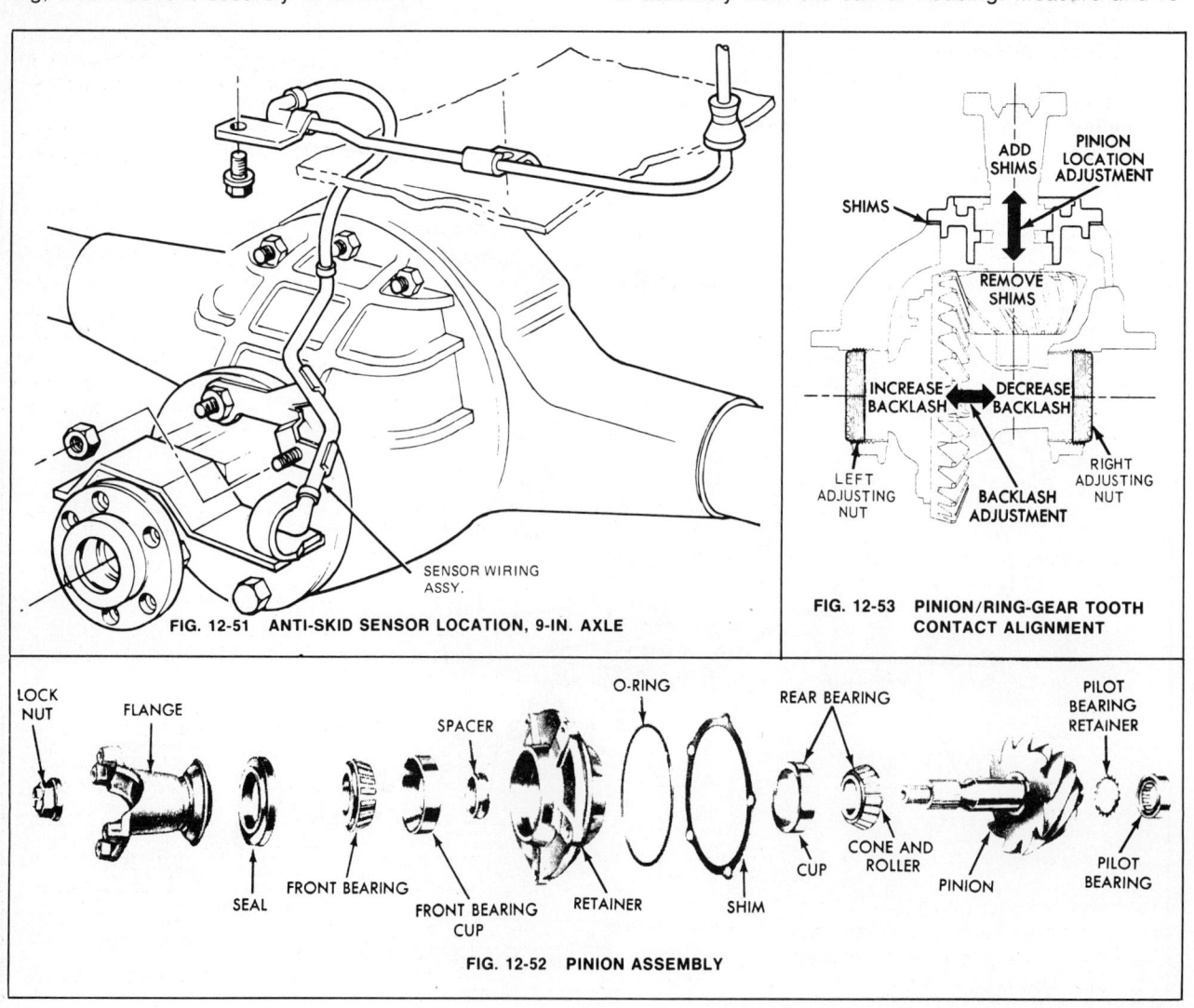

FIG. 12-51 ANTI-SKID SENSOR LOCATION, 9-IN. AXLE

FIG. 12-53 PINION/RING-GEAR TOOTH CONTACT ALIGNMENT

FIG. 12-52 PINION ASSEMBLY

cord the original pinion shim thickness.

19. Install a length of hose on the pinion pilot-bearing surface, and press the pinion shaft from the front pinion-bearing cone.

20. Press the pinion shaft from the rear pinion-bearing cone and roller.

21. Drive out the pilot bearing and bearing retainer as an assembly.

22. Leave the pinion bearing cups intact in the retainer unless they are worn or damaged. The retainer flange and pilot are machined during manufacture. If worn or damaged, press the cups or drive them out carefully, and press new ones in place, seating properly. The cone and roller assembly must also be replaced if the cups are changed.

CLEANING AND INSPECTION

All parts should be cleaned in solvent, except synthetic seals. Oil all bearings immediately after cleaning, then inspect all parts for damage, wear or other defects as follows:

1. Gears—Check for scoring or excessive wear. *Do not* damage the pilot bearing surface of the pinion. Inspect the teeth and thrust surfaces of all gears for wear, since this is a contributing factor in excessive driveline backlash.

2. Bearing Assemblies—Inspect the cups for rings, scoring, galling or excessive wear patterns. Look for roughness in roller operation and step-wear on their ends. Replace any worn components.

3. Differential Bearing Adjusting Nuts—Test the fit of the adjusting nuts in the bearing cap threads.

4. Differential Case—Examine the hubs where the bearings mount—they should be smooth. Also inspect the differential-case bearing shoulders. Check the free rotation of the side gears in their bores.

REMOVABLE CARRIER ASSEMBLY
(Figs. 12-50 & 12-52)

1. Lubricate all differential components with axle lubricant, and install one side gear and its thrust washers in the differential case.

2. Install a pinion thrust washer and pinion gear, installing the pinion shaft into the case far enough to hold them in place.

3. Position the other pinion gear and thrust washer in the case, and completely install the pinion shaft, aligning the lock pin hole with that of the case.

4. Install the other side gear and thrust washer, and replace the differential cover.

5. Replace the pinion-shaft lock pin, and insert the drive pinion to check for free gear rotation.

6. Press the ring gear on the case, and install the retaining bolts. New bolts should be used, and if they have green-coated threads, install as is. If the threads are not coated green, apply sealer (Loctite) and install. Torque 70 to 85 ft.-lbs.

7. Press the differential bearings in place.

8. Install a new pilot bearing in the pinion until it bottoms, then install the retainer with its concave side facing up.

9. Seat the drive pinion's rear-bearing cone and roller on the shaft, and fit a new collapsible spacer in place.

10. With the bearing retainer on the pinion shaft, press the front bearing roller and cone in place, taking care not to crush the bearing spacer.

11. Lubricate a new O-ring, and install it in the pinion retainer groove without twisting it.

12. Install the selected shim on the carrier housing. Use a shim of the same thickness as that removed. The "Gear Tooth Pattern Check" will determine if further shim changes are required.

13. Install the pinion and retainer assembly to the carrier, taking care not to pinch the O-ring.

14. Replace the pinion-retainer attaching bolts, and torque 30 to 45 ft.-lbs.

15. Replace the oil deflector on the pinion shaft against the bearing, and install a new oil seal in the bearing retainer.

16. Replace the U-joint flange, and install a new pinion shaft washer and nut, holding the flange while torquing the nut to a maximum 175 ft.-lbs.

17. Check the pinion bearing preload by rotating the bearing retainer while torquing the nut until drag exists. Using the torque wrench to turn the shaft, read the amount of torque necessary. Preload should be according to the specifications provided in the preceding table ("Pinion Bearing Preload").

18. Do not back off the pinion nut; if excessive preload is present from overtightening, the collapsible bearing spacer will have to be removed and replaced.

19. Lubricate the bearing bores, place the cups on the bearings and install the differential case assembly in the carrier.

20. If the gear teeth have timing marks, position the differential case and ring gear in the carrier to index the marked teeth with the correspondingly marked pinion gear tooth.

21. Push the differential case in the carrier bores until a slight amount of backlash is felt, then hold the case in place and set the adjusting nuts in the bores to just touch the bearing cups.

22. Replace the bearing caps to match the case marks, and install the cap bolts and lockwashers. Tighten the bolts while turning the adjusting nuts.

23. Torque the cap bolts to 70 ft.-lbs., then loosen and retorque to 25 ft.-lbs. for adjustment purposes.

24. Loosen the right adjusting nut (pinion side) until it is away from the cup, and tighten the left adjusting nut (ring-gear side) an equal amount until the ring gear is forced into the pinion with no backlash **(Fig. 12-53)**.

25. Tighten the right adjusting nut until it touches the bearing cup. Torque the cap bolts to specifications in Step 23, and install a dial indicator to measure ring

PINION BEARING PRELOAD (in.-lbs.)				
YEAR	**INTEGRAL CARRIER**		**REMOVABLE CARRIER**	
	NEW	**OLD**	**NEW**	**OLD**
1970-72	1	8-14₂	20-30	8-14₃
1973-79	17-27	8-14₂	17-27	8-14₂

₁ WER axles, 22-32; non-WER, 1970: 22-32, 1971: 20-30, 1972: 15-30.
₂ 1970 7¼-in. axle and 1972-76 6¾-in. axle, 6-12 in.-lbs.
₃ Solid spacer, 13-33 in.-lbs.

DIFFERENTIAL BEARING PRELOAD (Case Spread)				
YEAR	**INTEGRAL CARRIER**		**REMOVABLE CARRIER**	
	NEW	**OLD**	**NEW**	**OLD**
1970-72	.008-.012₂	.006-.010₃, ₁	.008-.012	.005-.008
1973-79	.008-.012₂	.006-.010₃	.008-.012	4

₁ 1970 7¼-in. ring gear, .003-.005; 8.7-in., .006-.010.
₂ 6¾-in. axle, .004-.008.
₃ 6¾-in. axle, .003-.005, 8.7-in., .006-.010.
₄ 6¾-in. axle, .003-.005; 8 or 9-in. axle, .005-.008; Mustang and Pinto, .004-.008.

gear backlash, which should range from 0.008-in. to 0.012-in., with a maximum variation of 0.003-in between teeth.

26. If the backlash is not within specifications, loosen one adjusting nut, and tighten the opposite one an equal amount to move the ring gear nearer or farther from the pinion **(Fig. 12-53).**

27. Check the "Gear Tooth Contact Pattern" again, as described in Steps 3, 4 and 5 of "Integral Carrier Disassembly." If the pattern is not satisfactory, the differential will have to be disassembled, and a thicker or thinner pinion shim installed.

28. Install the side-bearing adjusting nut locks, and torque 12 to 25 ft.-lbs.

29. Install the carrier assembly in the axle housing and torque the stud nuts 25 to 40 ft.-lbs. Replace the axles.

DIFFERENTIAL OVERHAUL
All Chrysler Corporation Cars
(EXCEPT OMNI/HORIZON)

All Dodge, Chrysler and Plymouth cars use a semi-floating, hypoid gear differential. Fitted with a variety of ring gear sizes, all but one utilize an integral housing design, with access to the differential, drive gears and bearings provided by a stamped steel cover bolted to the rear of the axle housing. Ring gear diameter can be identified by the number of cover bolts on 1973 and later models. The 7¼-in. has a 9-bolt cover, the 8¼-in. a 10-bolt cover and the 9¼-in. a 12-bolt cover. The 9¾-in., discontinued at the close of the 1972 model year, also had a 10-bolt cover. The 7¼-in. and 9¾-in. axle shafts are held in place by retainer plates, while the 8¼-in. and 9¼-in. axle shafts use C-locks in the carrier housing.

The 8¾-in. ring gear is also a hypoid gear differential, but is fitted in a removable carrier, with axle shafts held in place by retainer plates.

All Chrysler Corporation differentials have the gear ratio stamped on a small metal tag attached beneath a cover screw or housing-to-carrier bolt. The tag, attached to the 9¾-in. axle housing, is stamped with the number of drive pinion and ring gear teeth. To determine the gear ratio, divide the larger number by the smaller one.

While Chrysler recommends the use of a considerable number of specialized tools to service its

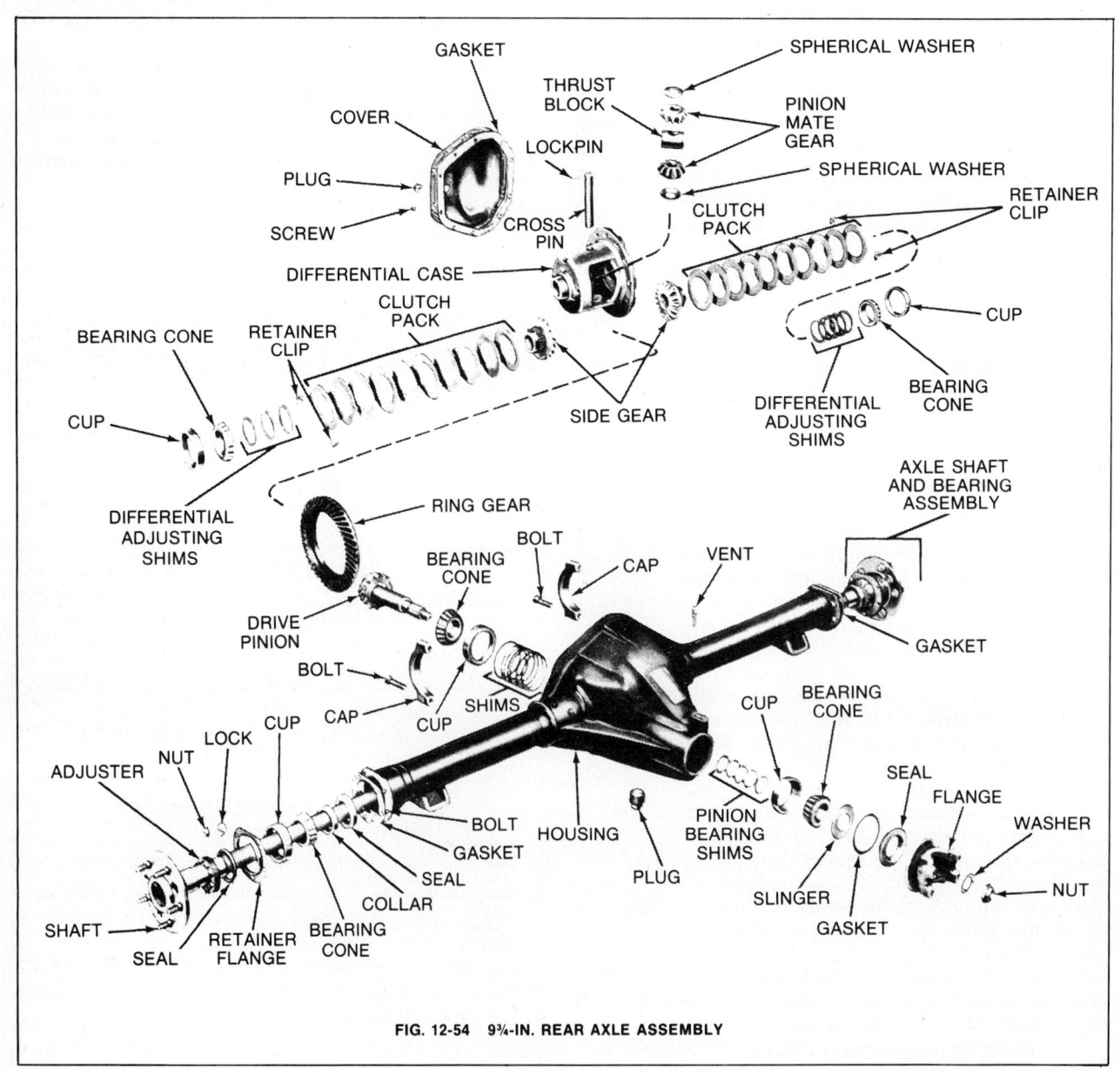

FIG. 12-54 9¾-IN. REAR AXLE ASSEMBLY

rear-axle/differential components, the disassembly/ assembly procedures which follow have been designed and field-tested to perform the work with a minimum of specialized tools. As with all other rear axle work, a torque wrench, case spreader and dial indicator will be necessary. Pay particular attention to the model year of the differential on which you are working, because Chrysler has changed specifications during production runs without materially altering the design. Wherever necessary, these changes are included in the procedures.

9¾-in. REAR AXLE

1970-72 Chrysler Corporation cars equipped with the 426-cu.-in. Hemi or 440-cu.-in. with Power Pak, and 4-speed manual transmission.

DIFFERENTIAL REMOVAL

1. Remove the cover and drain the lubricant.
2. Wipe the housing inside with a cloth moistened in solvent, and blow dry with compressed air.
3. Check the differential side play by fitting a screwdriver between the left side of the housing and the differential case flange. When a prying motion is exerted, there should be no side play.
4. Position a dial indicator on the case side, with the stem loaded slightly when the plunger is at right angles to the back side of the ring gear. Rotate the drive gear several full turns, and mark the case at the point of maximum runout, the total of which should not exceed 0.006-in.
5. Check the differential bearing-cap-to-bearing-cup clearance. A 0.003-in. feeler gauge should not fit between them. If the clearance is 0.003-in or larger, the bearing cup may have turned in the carrier, causing excessive wear.
6. Check to see that the bearing caps and housing seal surface are stamped with identifying letters for proper reassembly; if not, mark them with a punch.
7. After removing the bearing caps, fit a spreader tool in the housing locating holes, install the pilot stud on the housing left side and attach a dial indicator with the stem barely resting against the opposite side of the housing.
8. Tighten the spreader tool until the dial indicator reads 0.015-in., then remove the dial indicator and differential case assembly, using a light prying action on each side of the case, if necessary. A case spread in excess of 0.020-in. will permanently damage the carrier casting.
9. Retain the bearing cups and preload adjustment spacers with their respective bearing cones, unless worn or damaged.

DIFFERENTIAL DISASSEMBLY (Fig. 12-54)

1. Secure the differential case in a holding fixture or a soft-jawed vise. Remove and discard the drive gear screws.
2. Tap the drive gear from the case pilot with a soft-faced mallet, and remove.
3. Remeasure the differential-case flange runout, if the drive gear runout in Step 4, "Differential Removal," exceeded 0.006-in. Replace the differential case and bearings in the housing, remove the spreader tool and replace the bearing caps. Repeat the procedure specified in Step 4; total runout should not exceed 0.003-in.
4. Place the carrier in the vise, with its nose pointing up, and remove the drive-pinion nut and washer.
5. Remove the drive pinion flange with a puller, then remove the slinger, gasket, front pinion bearing and

preload shim pack. Measure and record the shim pack thickness.
6. Press out the drive pinion stem and rear bearing cone assembly.
7. Drive out the front and rear pinion bearing cups with a brass drift and hammer, removing the rear bearing-cup shim pack. Measure and record the shim pack thickness.
8. Remove the rear bearing cone from the pinion stem and the differential bearings from the case hubs with a puller.
9. Remove the shims from behind each bearing; measure and record their thickness.
10. The differential case and its internal parts are serviced only as an assembly. There is no need to further disassemble the case.

CLEANING AND INSPECTION

1. Wash and clean all parts in solvent. Dry all but the bearings with compressed air.
2. Check all machined housing contact surfaces and differential bearing caps for flat, smooth surfaces, free of raised edges.
3. Inspect the axle-shaft oil seal bores and the housing-flange face surface for smoothness, rust and corrosion.
4. Check all gear teeth for wear, chipping or damaged attaching-bolt threads. The drive gear and drive pinion must be replaced in matched sets.
5. Inspect all other differential parts for wear, nicks or burrs. Shims should be checked—if broken, distorted or otherwise damaged, replace them.

DIFFERENTIAL ASSEMBLY

1. Fit the drive gear on the differential case pilot, with the drive-gear and case-flange threaded holes aligned.
2. Install the drive gear screws through the differential case flange, and tap the drive gear flush against the case flange with a soft-faced mallet. It may ease assembly to heat (expand) the ring gear beforehand in hot water or oil (not over 300°), and smooth the chamfer on the inner ring gear circumference with an Arkansas stone, to prevent burrs.
3. Secure the assembly in a soft-jawed vise, and torque each screw in an alternating pattern 100 to 120 ft.-lbs.
4. Fit the differential bearings (without shims) on the differential hub, with the small end facing away from the drive gear, and press into place. *Do not* exert pressure on the bearing cage.
5. Install the bearing cups on their respective cones, and replace the differential case in the carrier.
6. Install the bearing caps in their correct positions, and tighten the bolts finger-tight.
7. Mount a dial indicator, with its stem touching the back of the drive gear. Pry the case assembly as far to one side of the housing as it will go, using a screwdriver inserted between the housing and bearing cup.
8. Reset the dial indicator to zero, and pry in the opposite direction.
9. This indicates the necessary shim thickness between the bearing cups and case. The shim thickness for the bearing cone/differential case is calculated after setting the pinion depth of mesh.
10. Remove the dial indicator, bearing caps and differential case from the housing.

PINION DEPTH OF MESH

The correct pinion depth of mesh is maintained by a shim pack available in thicknesses of 0.003-in., 0.005-

in. and 0.010-in. To determine the correct shim thickness to be used when installing a new gear set, examine the head of the pinion and locate the depth adjustment figure **(Fig. 12-55).** The (+) or (-) mark before the number indicates the variation from the nominal distance between the front of the pinion and the carrier centerline. As an example, if the original pinion was marked with +2, and installed with a 0.035-in. shim pack, and the new pinion is marked -1, increase the shim pack thickness by 0.003-in. to position the new pinion correctly. Thus, a shim pack 0.038-in. thick will give the approximate pinion setting; a pinion depth gauge should be used for the final pinion setting.

Remember that a (+) on the pinion indicates the use of a thinner shim pack, and a (-) on the pinion indicates the use of a thicker shim pack. Should the old pinion and bearing be reinstalled, or the new pinion have the same markings as the old pinion, the original shim thickness can be used.

PINION BEARING PRELOAD

1. Install the original front-pinion-bearing shim pack and the bearing cone, then replace the U-joint flange washer and nut. Torque the nut 250 to 270 ft.-lbs., rotate the pinion several full turns to align, and seat the bearing rollers.

2. Use an in.-lb. torque wrench to rotate the pinion through several full turns, and measure the preload torque, which should be between 10 to 20 in.-lbs. To decrease preload, add shims; to increase it, subtract shims.

3. It will be necessary to recheck the pinion depth of mesh, then remove the U-joint flange nut and washer to install the oil slinger, gasket and oil seal.

4. Replace the U-joint flange, washer and nut, holding the flange while torquing the nut 250 to 270 ft.-lbs.

DIFFERENTIAL-BEARING PRELOAD/DRIVE GEAR & PINION BACKLASH

1. Once the drive pinion and bearing are installed, and the pinion bearing preload established, replace the differential-case/ring-gear assembly with the respective bearing cups.

2. Repeat the procedure specified in Steps 4-10 of "Differential Assembly." The measurement taken prior to installing the drive pinion equals the total clearance; the reading obtained this time equals the thickness of the shim pack required to take up the clearance. Sub-

PRODUCTION
NUMBERS NO
SIGNIFICANCE
PINION DEPTH
ADJUSTMENT
FIGURE
+2
F
0
754
GEAR MATING MARK
(SAME AS ON DRIVE GEAR)

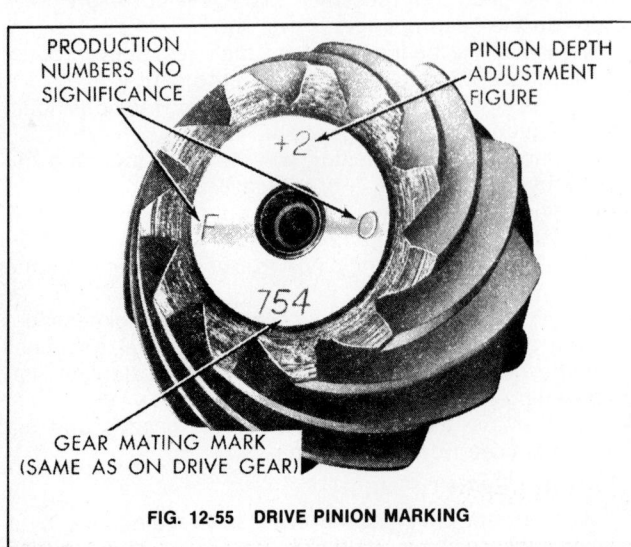

FIG. 12-55 DRIVE PINION MARKING

A
PATTERN CLOSE TO CENTER
TOE
END
HEEL END—DRIVE
SIDE (CONVEX)
HEEL END—COAST
SIDE (CONCAVE)
B
THICKER SPACER NEEDED
TOE
END
HEEL END—DRIVE
SIDE (CONVEX)
HEEL END—COAST
SIDE (CONCAVE)
C
THINNER SPACER NEEDED
TOE
END
HEEL END—DRIVE
SIDE (CONVEX)
HEEL END—COAST
SIDE (CONCAVE)

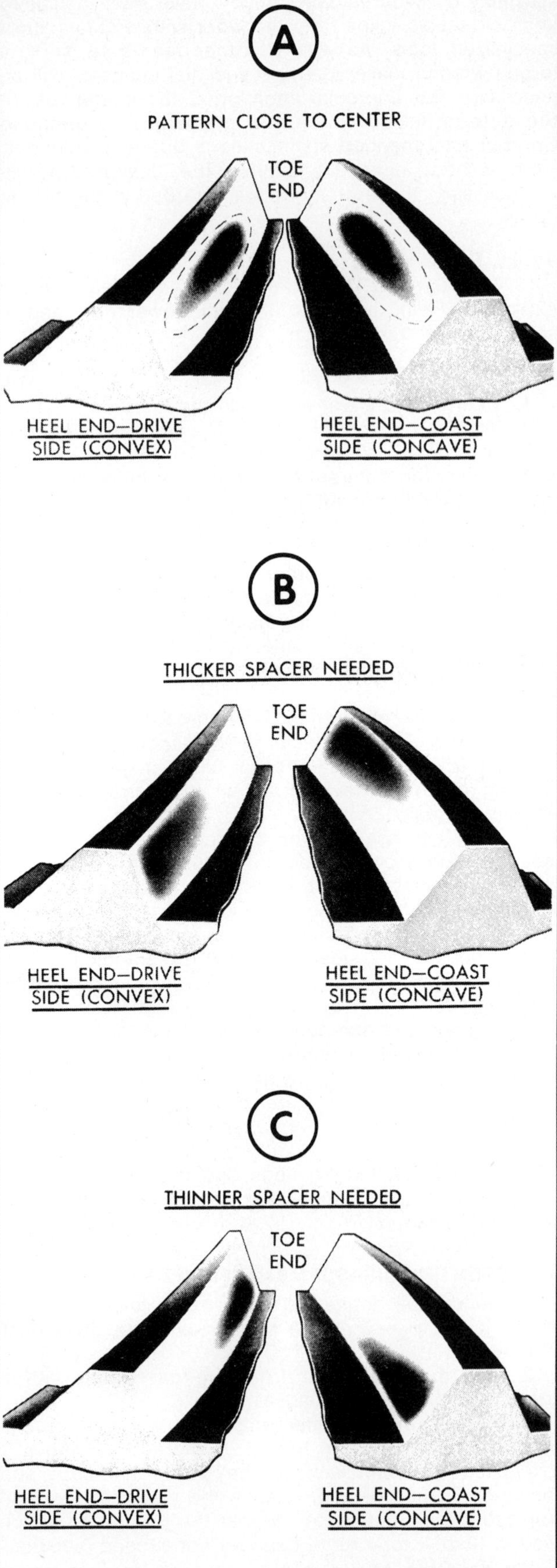

FIG. 12-56 GEAR TOOTH CONTACT PATTERNS

tract this second reading from the first one to determine the amount of shimming necessary.

3. Remove the differential/ring-gear assembly and bearing cones. Install the correct size shim pack between the bearing cone and differential-case hub shoulder, then add an extra 0.015-in. shim to the drive gear side, and replace the differential bearing cones. This 0.015-in. shim pack will produce the correct bearing preload/backlash.

4. Install the spreader tool and mount the dial indicator. Spread the case 0.015-in., and replace the bearing caps according to their alignment marks.

5. Remove the spreader tool and dial indicator, then coat the bearing cap bolts with sealer, and install snugly.

6. Gently tap the drive gear with a soft-faced mallet to seat the differential bearings and cups properly—*do not* nick the ring gear or drive pinion teeth as they mesh.

7. Torque the bearing cap bolts 70 to 90 ft.-lbs.

8. Install the dial indicator to the carrier, with its contact point touching the ring gear teeth, and measure the ring-gear/drive-pinion backlash at 90° intervals. Backlash must be between 0.004-in. and 0.009-in., and should not vary more than 0.002-in. between the four checkpoints.

9. If the backlash is not within specifications, the shim pack thickness on both differential bearing hubs must be changed.

10. Once these adjustments are made, use gear marking compound to coat the drive and coast sides of the drive gear, and turn through one full turn while prying with a screwdriver blade placed between the case and case flange.

11. Compare the tooth pattern to **Fig. 12-56 (A).** If the pattern seems closer to **Fig. 12-56 (B) or (C),** than

it does to (A), then disassemble and increase the shim pack thickness on (B) or decrease the thickness on (C). The shims are located behind rear pinion bearing.

12. Install a new gasket, replace the housing cover and torque the bolts to 20 ft.-lbs. Replace the axle, and fill it with the required amount of lubricant.

8¾-in. REAR AXLE

1970-73 CHRYSLER CORPORATION CARS

The 8¾-in. axle may be fitted with one of three pinion types: a small-stem step pinion, a large-stem step pinion and a large-stem pinion with collapsible spacer. Pinion depth of mesh and bearing preload are determined in the same way, but the adjustment sequence varies. Small-stem pinions have their bearing preload adjusted first, while large-stem pinions have their depth of mesh adjusted first. The large-stem pinion with collapsible spacer must have its spacer replaced if preload is exceeded during adjustment.

CARRIER DISASSEMBLY (Fig. 12-57)

1. Remove the carrier assembly from the housing, and check the differential side play by fitting a screwdriver between the left side of the housing and the differential case flange. When a prying motion is exerted, there should be no side play.

2. Position a dial indicator on the case side, with the stem loaded slightly when the plunger is at right angles to the rear of the ring gear. Rotate the drive gear several full turns, and mark the case at the point of maximum runout, the total of which should not exceed 0.005-in.

3. Hold the companion flange from moving, and remove the drive pinion nut and Belleville washer, then remove the companion flange and the drive-pinion oil seal.

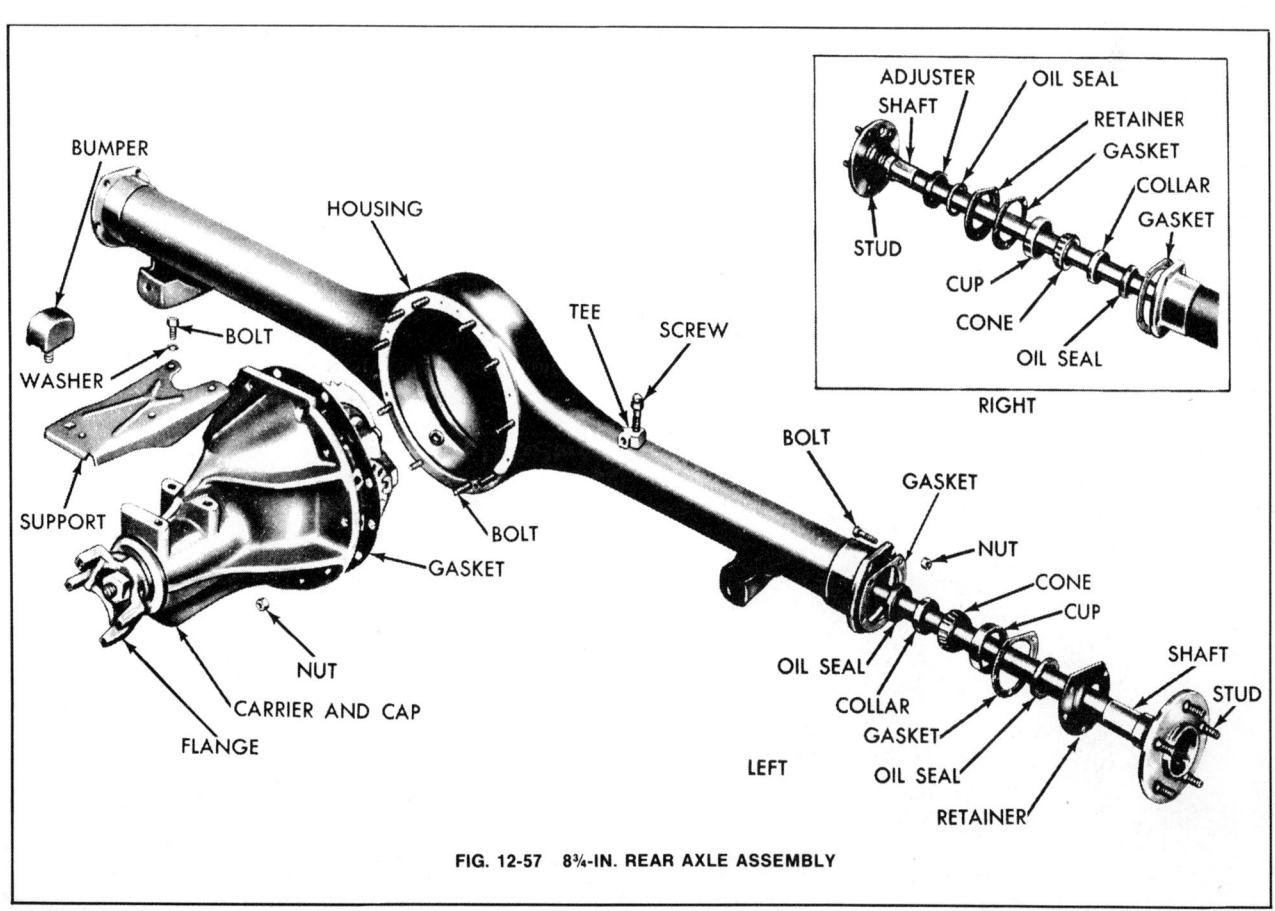

FIG. 12-57 8¾-IN. REAR AXLE ASSEMBLY

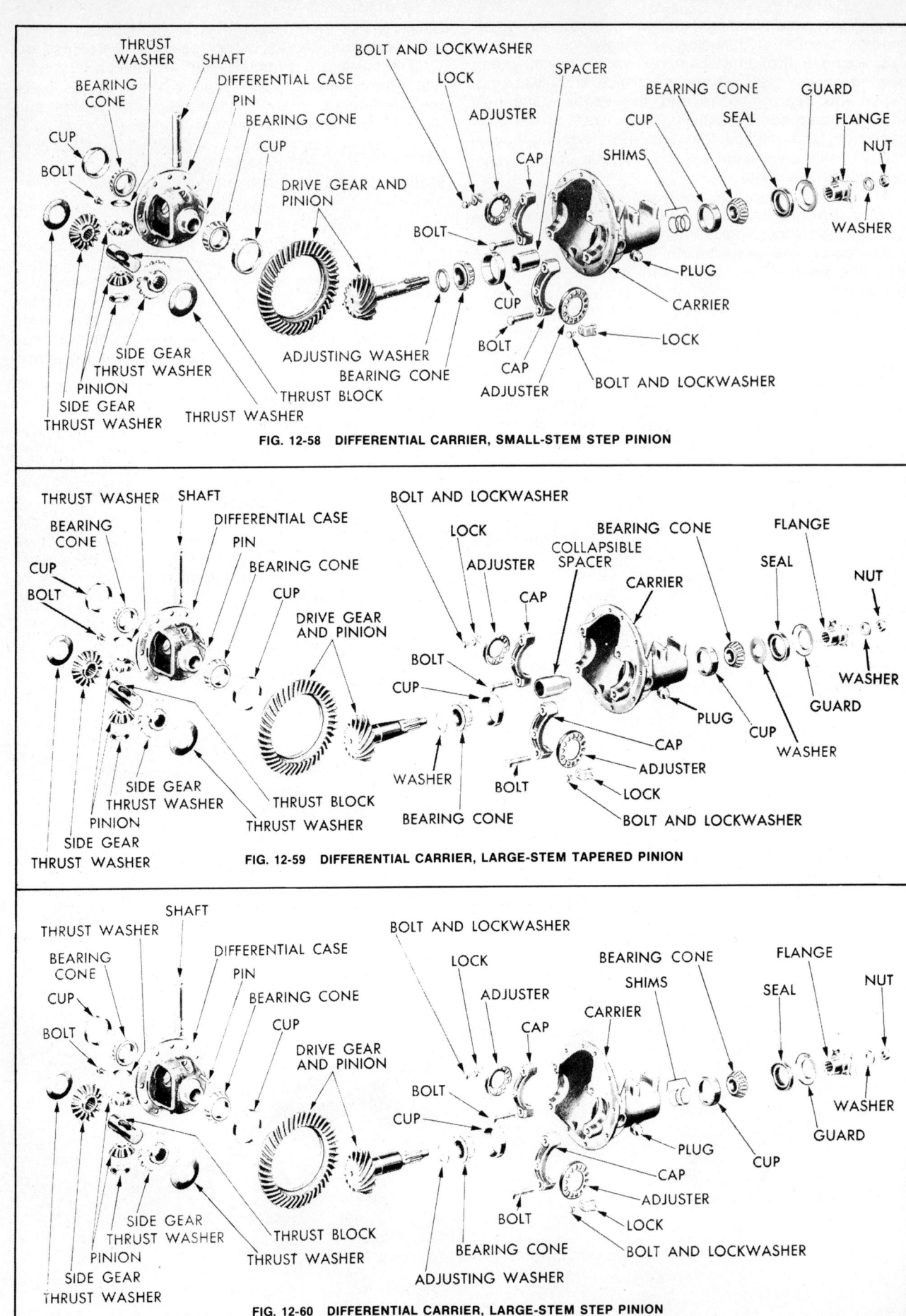

FIG. 12-58 DIFFERENTIAL CARRIER, SMALL-STEM STEP PINION

FIG. 12-59 DIFFERENTIAL CARRIER, LARGE-STEM TAPERED PINION

FIG. 12-60 DIFFERENTIAL CARRIER, LARGE-STEM STEP PINION

4. Place one hand over the carrier nose end, and invert. The front pinion-bearing cone, shim pack and bearing spacer (if used) will drop out.

5. Scribe marks on the drive bearing caps, drive bearing pedestals and bearing adjusters for reassembly, and remove both adjusting lockscrews and locks.

6. Loosen each cap bolt, and back the adjusters off slightly with a spanner wrench to remove the bearing preload. Remove the caps and adjusters.

7. Lift the differential/ring-gear assembly with bearing cups from the carrier, then remove the drive pinion and rear bearing assembly from the carrier.

8. Remove the drive-pinion rear bearing with a puller, and the front and rear pinion-bearing cups with a flat-end brass drift.

DIFFERENTIAL DISASSEMBLY
(Figs. 12-58, 12-59 & 12-60)

1. Secure the differential-case/ring-gear assembly in a soft-jaw vise, and remove the drive gear bolts (left-hand thread), tapping the drive gear loose from the differential case pilot with a non-metallic mallet.

2. Recheck the drive gear runout if it exceeded 0.005-in. in Step 2 of "Carrier Disassembly." Total indicator reading must not exceed 0.003-in. this time, or the differential case must be replaced.

3. Remove the drive-pinion-shaft lock pin from the back of the drive gear flange with a flat-nose drift, then remove the drive pinion shaft and axle-drive-shaft thrust block with a brass drift.

4. Turn the differential side gears, and remove each drive pinion and its thrust washer as it appears in the case opening.

5. Remove the differential side gears and thrust washers.

CLEANING AND INSPECTION

1. Wash and clean all parts in solvent. Dry all but the bearings with compressed air.

2. Check all machined housing contact surfaces and differential bearing caps for flat, smooth surfaces, free of raised edges.

3. Inspect the axle-shaft thrust block for excessive wear or damage. The wear surface on opposite ends of the block must be smooth.

4. Check all gear teeth for wear, chipping or damaged attaching bolt threads. The drive gear and drive pinion must be replaced in matched sets.

5. Inspect all other differential parts for wear, nicks or burrs. Shims should be checked and, if broken, distorted or otherwise damaged, replaced.

DIFFERENTIAL CASE ASSEMBLY

1. Lubricate all parts, and install the differential side gears with thrust washers in the differential case.

2. Replace the thrust washers on both drive pinions, and install the pinion gears to mesh with the side gears.

3. Turn the side gears 90° to align the pinions and thrust washers with the differential pinion-shaft case holes.

4. Install the slotted pinion-shaft end through the pinion-shaft lock-pin-hole side of the case, and insert it into the conical thrust washer and one of the pinion gears.

5. Replace the thrust block through the side gear hub, with its slot centered between the side gears.

6. Hold all components in alignment and push the pinion shaft into the case until the lock pin holes are aligned. Replace the pinion-shaft lock pin from the

pinion-shaft side of the drive gear flange.

7. Relieve the sharp edge of the inside diameter chamfer on the ring gear with an Arkansas stone.

8. Place the drive gear on the differential case pilot, and align the drive gear's threaded holes with those in the differential case flange.

9. Replace the drive gear screws, and tap the drive gear with a non-metallic mallet to seat it against the differential case flange.

10. Secure in a soft-jaw vise, and tighten each ring gear screw to 55 ft.-lbs. in an alternating sequence.

11. Place each differential bearing cone on the differential case hub, with the taper away from the drive gear, and press the bearing cones in place.

12. Place the differential bearing cups squarely in their carrier bores.

PINION BEARING PRELOAD AND DEPTH OF MESH

The correct pinion depth of mesh is maintained by a shim pack available in one thickness—0.002-in. To determine the correct shim thickness to be used when installing a new gear set, examine the head of the pinion, and locate the depth adjustment figure **(Fig. 12-55)**. The (+) or (-) mark before the number indicates the variation from the nominal distance between the front of the pinion and the carrier centerline. As an example, if the original pinion was marked and installed with an 0.086-in. shim pack, and the new pinion is marked +2, decrease the shim pack thickness by 0.002-in. to position the new pinion correctly. Thus, a shim pack 0.084-in. thick will give the approximate pinion setting; a pinion depth gauge should be used for the final pinion setting.

Remember that a (+) on the pinion indicates the use of a thinner shim pack, and a (-) on the pinion indicates the use of a thicker shim pack. Should the old pinion and bearing be reinstalled, or the new pinion have the same markings as the old one, the original shim thickness can be used. Shims will differ in diameter, depending upon which pinion they are designed to be used with.

PINION BEARING PRELOAD (LARGE STEM)

1. Position the rear pinion-bearing cone on the pinion stem, with its small end facing away from the pinion head.

2. Lubricate and press the rear pinion-bearing cone on the pinion shaft.

3. Fit the pinion bearing (and collapsible spacer, if used) through the carrier, and install the front bearing cone and companion flange.

4. Install a new oil seal, replace the Belleville washer with its convex side facing up and, holding the companion flange from turning, torque the pinion nut to remove end play.

5. Turn the pinion to assure that the bearings are seated properly, and torque the pinion nut to 170 ft.-lbs. for 1970-72 models, 210 ft.-lbs. for 1973 models.

6. Use an in.-lb. torque wrench to measure the pinion bearing preload, which should be 30 to 40 in.-lbs. for the original bearing and 20 to 30 in.-lbs. for a new one.

7. When the collapsible spacer is fitted, care must be taken not to exceed the pinion bearing preload, or the unit must be disassembled and a new spacer installed, since correct preload cannot be achieved by backing off the nut.

PINION BEARING PRELOAD (SMALL STEM)

1. Install the bearing in the case with a drift, and assemble the pinion shim on the pinion stem, with its chamfered side facing the gear. If fitted with a tubular spacer, install the spacer and the pinion preload shims on the pinion stem.

2. Replace the pinion assembly in the carrier, and install the front pinion-bearing cone, U-joint flange, Belleville washer (convex side facing up) and the pinion shaft nut.

3. Turn the pinion to assure the bearings are seated properly, and torque the pinion nut to 240 ft.-lbs. for 1970-72 models and 210 ft.-lbs. for 1973 models.

4. Use an in.-lb. torque wrench to measure the pinion bearing preload, which should be 0 to 15 in.-lbs. for the original bearing and 20 to 30 in.-lbs. for a new one.

5. Once the correct pinion depth has been determined, and the proper preload set, remove the drive pinion flange, and install a new oil seal.

6. Replace the pinion flange, washer and nut, torquing to the specifications in Step 3.

DIFFERENTIAL-BEARING PRELOAD/DRIVE GEAR & PINION BACKLASH

1. Replace the differential case in the carrier, with the bearing cups on their respective cones.

2. Replace the bearing caps according to the alignment marks scribed during disassembly, and install the cap bolts, tightening by hand.

3. Replace the bearing adjusters according to the alignment marks scribed during disassembly, and screw in by hand.

4. Square the bearing cups with the bearing cones, using a spanner wrench, and turn the adjusters inward until end play is eliminated but some degree of backlash exists between the drive gear and pinion.

5. Torque one differential-bearing cap bolt on each side 85 to 90 ft.-lbs.

6. Turn the drive gear/ring gear several full revolutions to seat the bearing rollers, and install a dial indicator to the carrier flange, with the indicator pointer touching one drive gear tooth squarely on the drive side.

7. Measure the backlash at 90° positions, determining the point of least backlash, and leave the drive gear at that point until the remainder of adjustments have been made.

8. Turn both bearing adjusters inward equally with a spanner wrench until the backlash between the drive gear and pinion is 0.0005-in. to 0.0015-in.

9. Replace the adjuster lock on the bearing cap on the back face of the drive gear, and torque the lock-screw 15 to 20 ft.-lbs.

10. Turn the bearing adjuster on the tooth side of the drive gear inward one lock hole at a time until the backlash between the drive gear and pinion is 0.006-in. to 0.008-in. to preload the differential bearings and establish the correct backlash.

11. Torque the remaining bearing cap bolts 85 to 90 ft.-lbs.

12. Replace the remaining adjuster locks, lockwashers and attaching screws, torquing 15 to 20 ft.-lbs.

13. Once these adjustments are made, use gear marking compound to coat the drive and coast sides of the drive gear, and turn through one full turn while prying with a screwdriver blade placed between the case and case flange.

14. Compare the tooth pattern to **Fig. 12-56 (A).** If the pattern seems closer to **Fig. 12-56 (B) or (C)** than it does to **(A)**, disassemble and increase the spacer thickness on **(B)** or decrease the thickness on **(C)**. The shims are located behind the rear pinion bearing.

15. Clean the carrier and rear-axle-housing gasket surface, and install the carrier assembly to the axle housing with a new gasket, torquing the nuts to 45 ft.-lbs.

16. Replace the axle shafts and driveshaft, and fill the carrier with the required amount of lubricant.

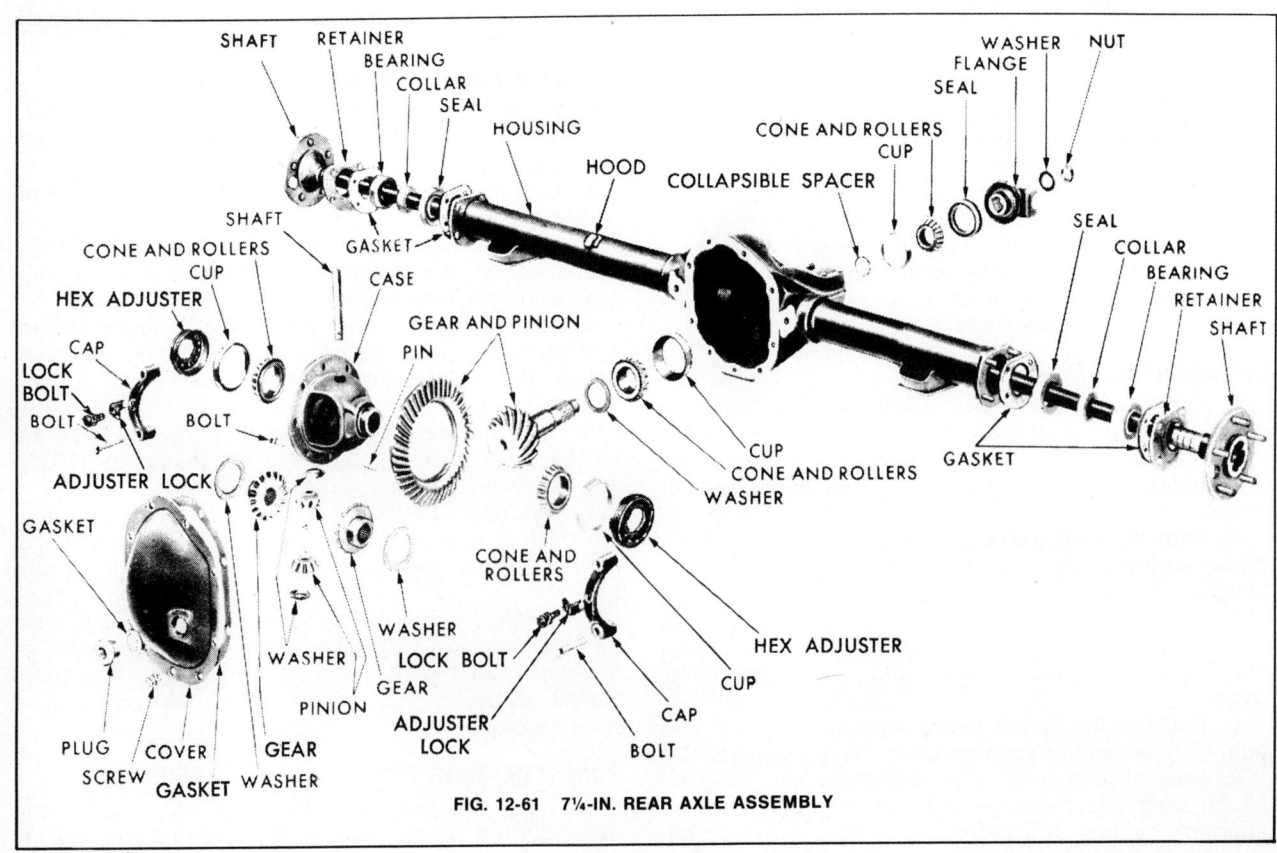

FIG. 12-61 7¼-IN. REAR AXLE ASSEMBLY

7¼-in., 8¼-in. & 9¼-in. REAR AXLE
1970-78 CHRYSLER CORPORATION CARS

Beginning in 1975, the 7¼-in. and 8¼-in. axle differentials use new "balance-life" side gears and pinion gears installed during manufacture. Mixing these with earlier side or pinion gears will result in lock-up or excessive differential backlash. If the "balance-life" side or pinion gears must be replaced, they must be replaced as a *complete* set of two side and two pinion gears.

The drive pinion depth of mesh adjustment of the 7¼-in. and 9¼-in. axles is determined by the use of metal shims between the rear pinion-bearing cone and drive pinion head; on the 8¼-in. axle, the metal shims are located either between the rear pinion-bearing cone and drive pinion head, or between the rear pinion-bearing cup and the carrier casting. Drive pinion preload on all three axles is controlled by a collapsible metal spacer behind the front bearing cone. The 7¼-in. axles manufactured before December 1, 1970, did not use the collapsible spacer.

7¼-in. AXLE
DIFFERENTIAL REMOVAL (Fig. 12-61)

1. Remove the cover and drain the lubricant.
2. Wipe the inside of the carrier housing with a cloth moistened in solvent.
3. Remove the axle shafts, scribe alignment marks on the driveshaft U-joint and axle-housing pinion flange. Disconnect the driveshaft and remove.
4. Check the differential side play by fitting a screwdriver between the left side of the housing and the differential case flange. When a prying motion is exerted, there should be no side play.
5. Position a dial indicator on the case side, with the stem loaded slightly when the plunger is at right angles to the rear of the ring gear. Rotate the drive gear several full turns, and mark the case at the point of maximum runout, total should not exceed 0.005-in.
6. Hold the companion flange from moving, and remove the drive pinion nut and washer, then remove the companion flange, drive-pinion oil seal, bearing cone and collapsible spacer.
7. Scribe the differential bearing caps and housing for reassembly, and remove the adjusting locks from each cap—*do not* remove the cap.
8. Axles manufactured after January 31, 1972, require that a hex shaft be inserted through the axle tube on each side, and the hex adjusters loosened.
9. Install a spreader tool and a dial indicator on the differential assembly, with its stem opposite the axle housing. Spread the housing 0.015-in.
10. Remove the dial indicator, and pry the differential case from the housing, with the differential bearing cups intact and the preload adjusting spacers with their bearing cones. *Do not* remove the spreader tool yet.

DIFFERENTIAL DISASSEMBLY

1. To remove the drive pinion and rear bearing components from the housing, the pinion stem must be driven rearward. This will result in damage to both the bearing rollers and cups, and these will have to be replaced with new components. Discard the collapsible spacer.
2. Remove the front and rear bearing cups using a flat-end brass drift. If used, record size of cup shim, and discard.
3. Secure the differential-case/ring-gear assembly in a soft-jaw vise. Remove the drive gear bolts (left-hand thread), and gently tap the drive gear from the differential case pilot with a non-metallic mallet.
4. Recheck the runout of the differential drive-gear flange if it exceeded 0.005-in. in Step 5 of "Differential Removal." Total indicator reading must not exceed 0.003-in. this time, or the differential case must be replaced.
5. Remove the drive-pinion-shaft lock pin from the drive gear side of the case with a flat-nose drift, then remove the drive pinion shaft with a brass drift.
6. Turn the differential side gears, and remove each drive pinion and its thrust washer as it appears in the case opening.
7. Remove the differential side gears and thrust washers.
8. Remove the differential bearings and rear bearing cone with a puller.

CLEANING AND INSPECTION

1. Wash and clean all parts in solvent, drying all but the bearings with compressed air.
2. Check all machined housing contact surfaces and the differential bearing caps. They must be flat, smooth and free of raised edges.
3. Inspect the axle-shaft oil-seal bores and the housing-flange face surface. They must be smooth, and free of rust or corrosion.
4. Check all gear teeth for wear or chipping. Inspect all bolt holes for damaged threads. The drive gear and drive pinion must be replaced only in matched sets.
5. Inspect all other differential parts for wear, nicks or burrs. If the shims are broken, distorted or otherwise damaged, replace them.

DIFFERENTIAL ASSEMBLY

1. Install the thrust washers on the differential side gears, and replace the gears in the case.
2. Install the thrust washers on the pinion gears, and insert the gears in the case to engage with the side gears.
3. Rotate the side gears to align the pinion gears and washers with the pinion shaft holes in the case, then install the lock pin in the differential case from the drive-gear tooth side.
4. Relieve the sharp edge of the ring-gear inside diameter chamfer with an Arkansas stone.
5. Heat the ring gear with a heat lamp, and replace on the differential case.
6. Install new drive-gear screws, and secure the assembly in a soft-jaw vise. Alternately torque each screw to 55 ft.-lbs.
7. Replace the differential bearing cones.

PINION DEPTH OF MESH

The correct pinion depth of mesh is maintained by a shim pack. To determine the correct shim thickness to be used when installing a new gear set, examine the head of the pinion and locate the depth adjustment figure (**Fig. 12-55**). The (+) or (-) mark before the number indicates the variation from the nominal distance between the front of the pinion and the carrier centerline. As an example, if the original pinion was marked with a 0 and installed with a 0.033-in. shim pack, and the new pinion is marked +2, use a shim that is 0.002-in. thinner. Thus, a shim pack 0.031-in. thick will give the approximate pinion setting.

Remember that a (+) on the pinion indicates the use of a thinner shim pack, and a (-) on the pinion indicates the use of a thicker shim pack. Should the old pinion and bearing be reinstalled, or the new pinion have the same markings as the old pinion, the original shim thickness can be used.

PINION BEARING PRELOAD

If Manufactured Before November 30, 1970

1. Replace the bearings in the carrier, and drive into place.

2. Fit the pinion shim on the pinion stem, with its chamfered side toward the gear, then replace the tubular spacer (if used) and the preload shims on the pinion stem.

3. Install the assembled pinion in the carrier, and replace the front pinion-bearing cone, U-joint flange, Belleville washer (convex side facing up) and the pinion nut.

4. Torque the nut to 240 ft.-lbs., rotating the pinion to seat the bearing rollers. Use an in.-lb. torque wrench, and measure the effort required to turn the pinion. The preload torque should be 0 to 15 in.-lbs. for the original bearing, and 15 to 25 in.-lbs. for the new bearing. A thicker shim pack will decrease preload, and a thinner shim pack will increase it.

5. After establishing the correct pinion preload, remove the companion flange and install a new oil seal.

6. Replace the companion flange, washer and nut, torquing it to 240 ft.-lbs.

If Manufactured After November 30, 1970

1. Install the rear pinion-bearing cone on the pinion stem, with its small side facing away from the pinion head.

2. Install the pinion bearing and collapsible spacer in the carrier, and replace the front bearing cone, taking care not to collapse the spacer while replacing the bearing.

3. Replace the companion flange, install a new oil seal and replace the Belleville washer (convex side facing up) and the pinion nut.

4. Hold the companion flange while tightening the pinion nut and rotating the pinion to assure proper seating of the bearing.

5. Torque the pinion nut to 210 ft.-lbs. and use an in.-lb. torque wrench to measure the pinion bearing preload. This should be 10 to 20 in.-lbs. if the original bearing is used, and 15 to 30 in.-lbs. if a new bearing is installed. If the final pinion-nut torque is less than 210 ft.-lbs. or the pinion bearing preload is not within specifications, the assembly is unacceptable. *Do not back off the pinion nut to reduce pinion bearing preload,* or the assembly will have to be taken apart and a new collapsible spacer installed and adjusted.

RING-GEAR/PINION BACKLASH

If Manufactured Before January 31, 1972

1. With the drive pinion installed and the preload correctly adjusted, replace the differential-case/ring-gear assembly. Use a 0.254-in. spacer on the ring gear side of the axle housing to adjust preload. Use a spacer on the other side sufficiently thick to seat snugly, but allow some end play.

2. Move the differential to the ring gear side, and insert a feeler gauge between the spacer and right side of the housing, taking the measurement above the case centerline.

3. Fit another feeler gauge of the same thickness between the housing and spacer below the centerline. Rotate the differential case several full turns to seat all parts, and remeasure end play.

4. Replace the spacer with one whose thickness

equals that of the feeler gauge/spacer combined to produce zero end play.

5. Position a dial indicator, with its stem parallel to and touching the drive gear side of the ring gear teeth, and measure the backlash at 90° intervals—backlash should range between 0.004-in. and 0.007-in.

6. Remove the differential-case/ring-gear assembly, and install spacers of the proper thickness to the right and left sides.

7. Spread the axle housing 0.015-in. with a spreader tool, replace the differential/ring-gear assembly, and remove the dial indicator and spreader tool.

8. Replace the bearing caps, and torque the cap bolts to 40 ft.-lbs.

9. Recheck the drive gear backlash. If not within specifications, the shim pack thickness on both differential bearing hubs must be changed.

10. Once all adjustments are correctly made, use gear marking compound to coat the drive and coast sides of the drive gear, and turn through one full turn while prying with a screwdriver blade placed between the case and case flange.

11. Compare the tooth pattern to **Fig. 12-56 (A)**. If the pattern seems closer to **Fig. 12-56 (B) or (C)** than it does to (A), disassemble and increase the shim pack thickness on (B) or decrease the thickness on (C). The shims are located behind the rear pinion bearing.

12. Install axle shafts, connect the driveshaft and replace the housing cover using a new gasket and sealant. Torque the cover bolts to 20 ft.-lbs.

If Manufactured After January 31, 1972

The 7¼-in. axles manufactured after January 31, 1972, are somewhat different in design and require a different assembly/adjustment procedure. Threaded adjusters are used instead of shims to control side bearing preload, and Chrysler tool #C-4164 is necessary to adjust the side bearing preload. A different shim is used for the pinion rear bearing, and either side of the shim can be placed against the pinion head. The gear teeth should be indexed to maintain same-tooth contact before beginning adjustments. Seat the differential bearing cups and bearings by turning them in each direction a dozen times each time the adjusters are moved.

1. With the pinion bearing installed and the preload established, replace the differential case, complete with adjusters, caps and bearings. Adjusters should be turned as far out as possible.

2. Torque the top cap screws to 10 ft.-lbs., and tighten the bottom cap screws finger-tight.

3. Using tool #C-4164, check for free adjuster rotation, and turn both adjusters inward until bearing play is eliminated but a slight amount of backlash exists.

4. Position a dial indicator with the stem resting against the drive side of a gear tooth, and check backlash at 90° intervals. After finding the position of least backlash, mark the tooth, and take all readings from that point.

5. Loosen and turn the right adjuster until the backlash is 0.003- to 0.004-in., then tighten the bearing-cap screws to 45 ft.-lbs.

6. Torque the right adjuster, and seat the bearing rollers until the torque remains constant at 70 ft.-lbs.

7. Remeasure backlash; if not within 0.004- to 0.006-in., increase the right adjuster torque and seat the rollers until backlash is correct, then repeat the procedure with the left end.

8. Once these adjustments are made, use gear marking compound to coat the drive and coast sides of

the drive gear, and turn through one full turn while prying with a screwdriver blade placed between the case and case flange.

9. Compare the tooth pattern to **Fig. 12-56 (A).** If the pattern seems closer to **Fig. 12-56 (B) or (C)** than it does to **(A),** disassemble and increase the spacer thickness on **(B)** or decrease the thickness on **(C).** The shims are located behind the rear pinion bearing.

10. Replace the adjuster locks, and torque the lock-screws to 90 in.-lbs.

11. Replace the axle shafts, install a new gasket and the cover on the housing, and torque the cover bolts to 250 in.-lbs.

8¼-in. & 9¼-in. AXLE

DIFFERENTIAL REMOVAL (Figs. 12-62 & 12-63)

1. Remove the cover and drain the lubricant.
2. Wipe the inside of the carrier housing with a cloth moistened in solvent.
3. Remove the axle shafts, scribe alignment marks on the driveshaft U-joint and axle housing pinion

flange, then disconnect and remove the driveshaft.

4. Check the differential side play by fitting a screwdriver between the left side of the housing and the differential case flange. When a prying motion is exerted, there should be no side play.

5. Position a dial indicator on the case side, with its stem loaded slightly when the plunger is at right angles to the rear of the ring gear. Rotate the drive gear several full turns, and mark the case at the maximum runout point. Total runout should not exceed 0.005-in.

6. Hold the companion flange from moving, and remove the drive pinion nut and washer, then remove the companion flange, drive-pinion oil seal, bearing cone and collapsible spacer.

7. Scribe the differential bearing caps and the housing for correct reassembly then remove the adjusting locks from each cap—*do not* remove the cap.

8. Remove the threaded adjusters and then the bearing caps, holding the differential case in place.

9. Remove the differential assembly with the bearing

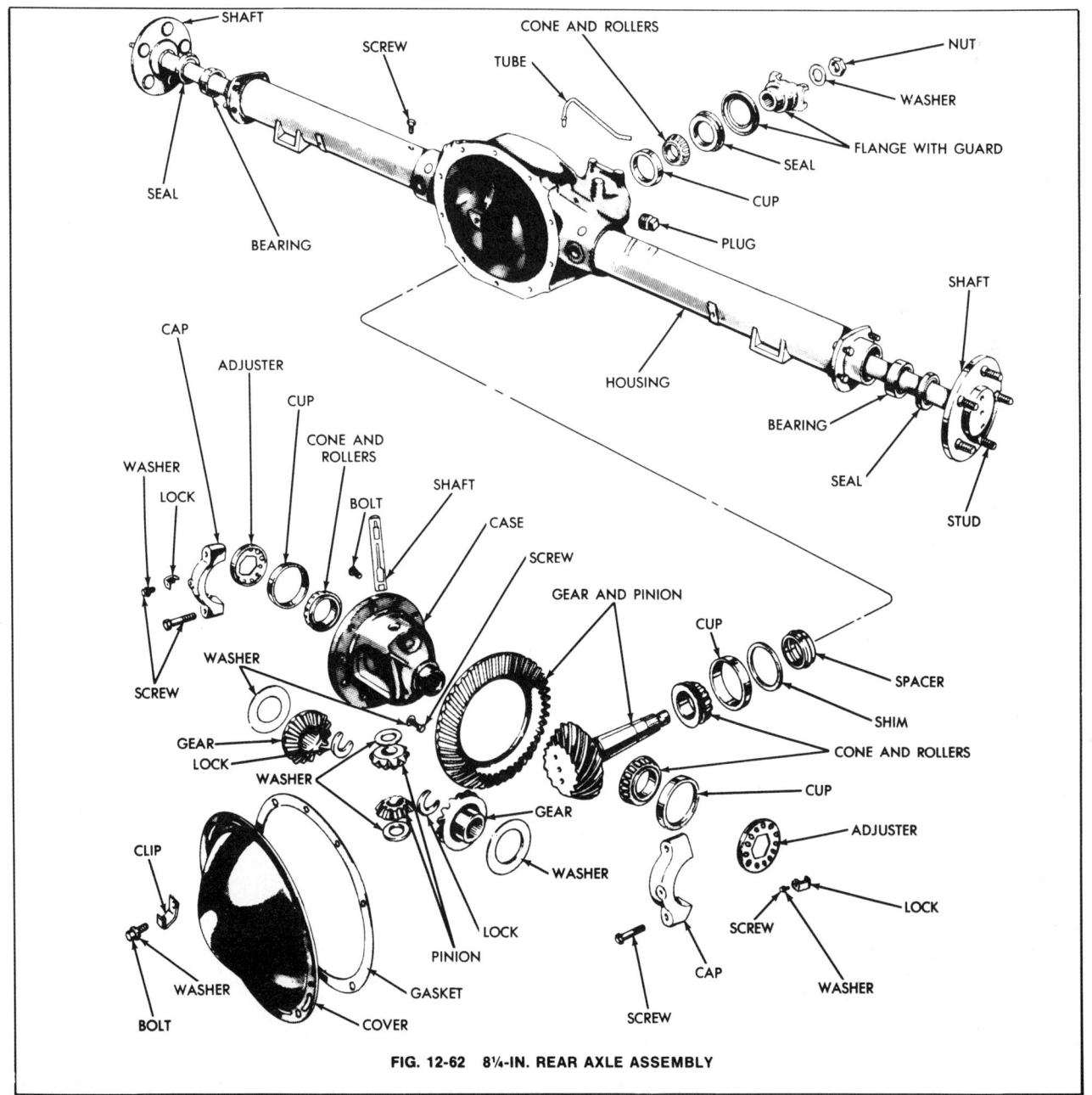

FIG. 12-62   8¼-IN. REAR AXLE ASSEMBLY

cups on their respective cones. Keep the threaded adjusters with their respective bearings on 8¼-in. axles; on 9¼-in. axles, adjusters will remain in the housing.

DIFFERENTIAL DISASSEMBLY

1. To remove the drive pinion and rear bearing components from the housing, drive the pinion stem to the rear. This will destroy the bearing rollers and cups, and new ones will have to be installed upon reassembly. Discard the collapsible spacer.

2. Remove the front and rear bearing cups using a flat-end brass drift.

3. Remove, measure and discard the shim located behind the rear bearing cone.

4. Remove the rear bearing from the pinion stem.

5. Secure the differential-case/ring-gear assembly in a soft-jaw vise. Remove the drive gear bolts (left-hand thread), and gently tap the drive gear from the differential case pilot with a non-metallic mallet.

6. Replace the differential case, cups, caps and adjusters in the housing. Tighten the adjusters to eliminate side play, and snug the differential bearing-cap bolts. Recheck the drive gear runout if it exceeded 0.005-in. in Step 5 of "Differential Removal." Total indicator reading must not exceed 0.003-in. this time, or the differential case must be replaced.

7. Remove the drive-pinion-shaft lockscrew and the drive pinion shaft.

8. Turn the differential side gears, and remove each drive pinion and its thrust washer as it appears in the case opening.

9. Remove the differential side gears and thrust washers.

10. Remove the differential bearings with a puller.

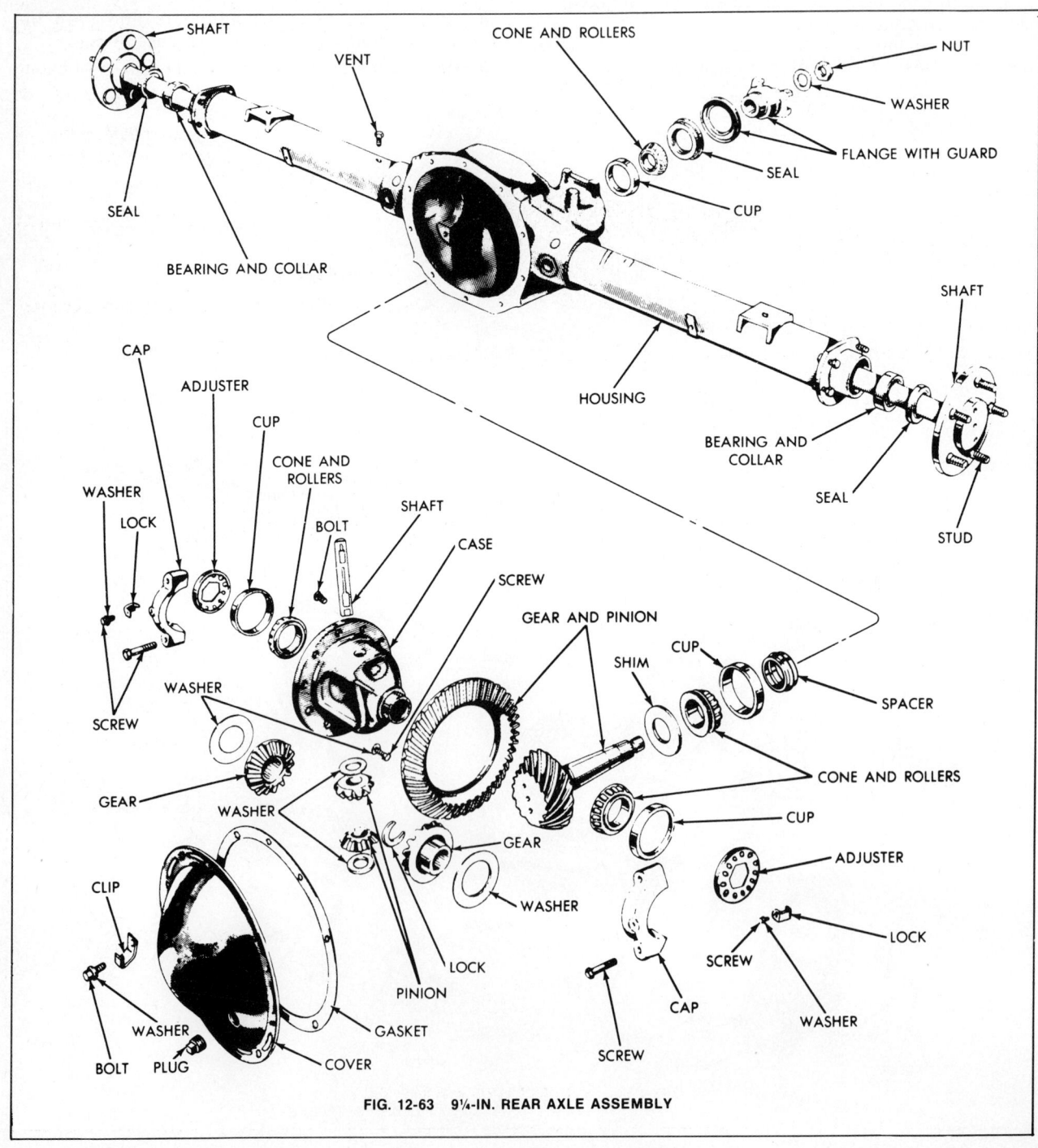

FIG. 12-63   9¼-IN. REAR AXLE ASSEMBLY

CLEANING AND INSPECTION

1. Wash and clean all parts in solvent, drying all but the bearings with compressed air.

2. Check all machined housing contact surfaces and the differential bearing caps. They must be flat, smooth and free of raised edges.

3. Inspect the axle-shaft oil-seal bores and the housing-flange face surface. They must be smooth, and free of rust or corrosion.

4. Check all gear teeth for wear or chipping. The drive gear and drive pinion must be replaced only in matched sets. Inspect all bolt holes for damaged threads.

5. Beginning with the 1975 model year, the 8¼-in. axle uses "balance-life" side and differential pinion gears, which must be replaced in a complete set of four.

6. Inspect all other differential parts for wear, nicks or burrs. If the shims are broken, distorted or otherwise damaged, replace them.

DIFFERENTIAL ASSEMBLY

1. Install the thrust washers on the differential side gears, and replace the assembled gears/washers in the case.

2. Install the thrust washers on the pinion gears, and insert the gears in the case to engage with the installed side gears.

3. Rotate the side gears to align the pinion gears and washers with the pinion shaft holes in the case, then install the pinion shaft through the case, the conical thrust washer and one pinion gear, slotted end first.

4. Fit a thrust block through the side gear hub, with the slot centered between the side gears. Hold all parts aligned, and install the lock pin from the pinion shaft side of the ring gear flange.

5. Relieve the sharp edge of the ring-gear inside diameter chamfer with an Arkansas stone.

6. Heat the ring gear with a heat lamp, and replace on the differential case.

7. Install new drive-gear screws, and secure the assembly in a soft-jaw vise. Alternately torque each screw to 55 ft.-lbs.

8. Press the differential bearing cones in place.

PINION DEPTH OF MESH

The correct pinion depth of mesh is maintained by a shim pack. To determine the correct shim thickness to be used when installing a new gear set, examine the head of the pinion and locate the depth adjustment figure (Fig. 12-55). The (+) or (-) mark before the number indicates the variation from the nominal distance between the front of the pinion and the carrier centerline. As an example, if the original pinion was marked with a 0 and installed with a 0.041 shim pack, and the new pinion is marked -2, use a shim that is 0.002-in. thicker. Thus, a shim pack 0.043-in. thick will give the approximate pinion setting.

Remember that a (+) on the pinion indicates the use of a thinner shim pack, and a (-) on the pinion indicates the use of a thicker shim pack. Should the old pinion and bearing be reinstalled, or the new pinion have the same markings as the old pinion, the original shim thickness can be used.

PINION BEARING PRELOAD

1. Place the selected shim in the axle cup bore, and install the rear bearing cup.

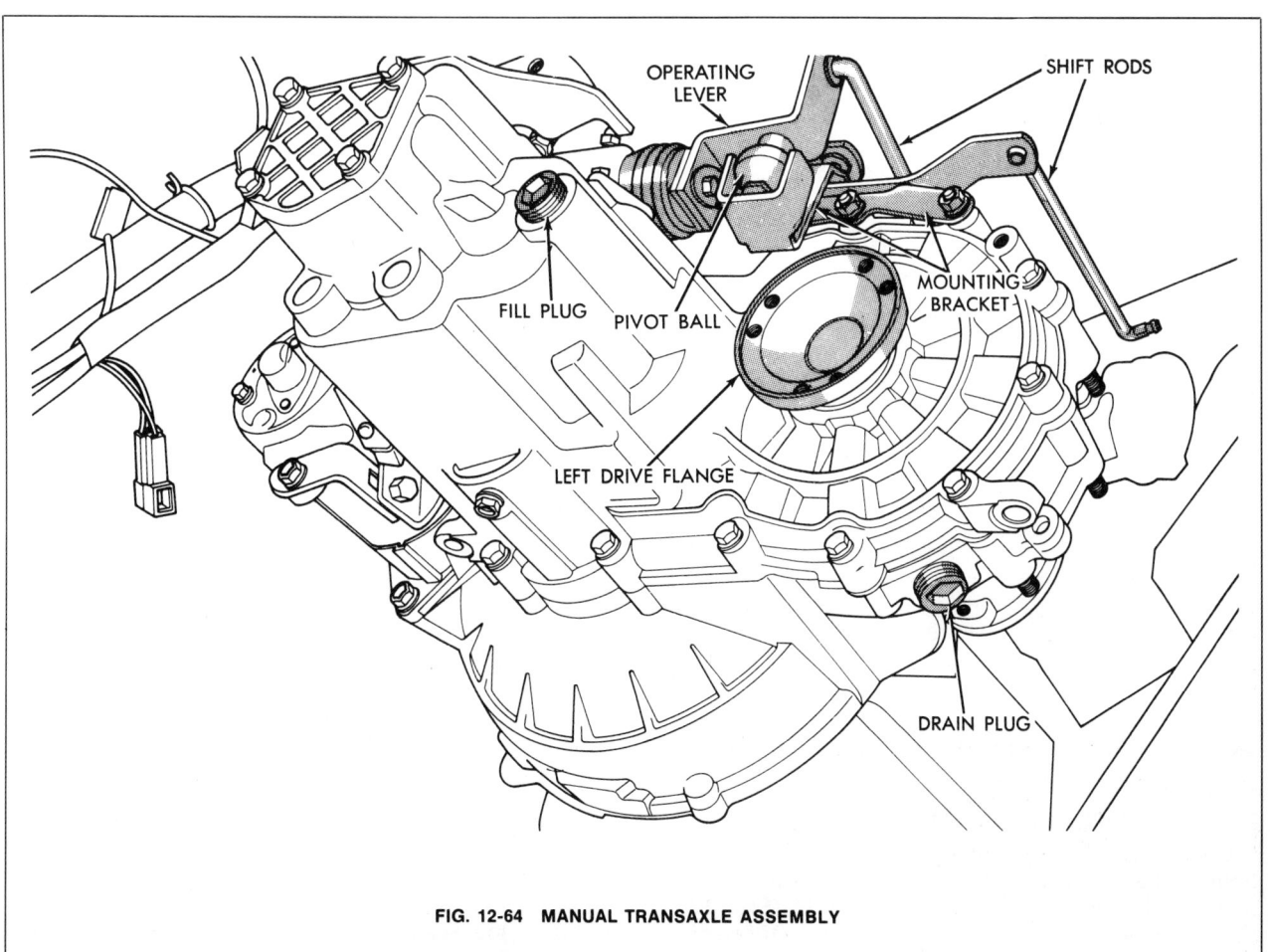

FIG. 12-64 MANUAL TRANSAXLE ASSEMBLY

2. Install the rear pinion-bearing cone on the pinion stem, with its small side facing away from the pinion head.

3. Install the pinion bearing and collapsible spacer in the carrier, and replace the front bearing cone, taking care not to collapse the spacer while replacing the bearing.

4. Replace the companion flange, install a new oil seal and replace the Belleville washer (convex side facing up) and the pinion nut.

5. Hold the companion flange while tightening the pinion nut and rotating the pinion to assure proper seating of the bearing.

6. Torque the pinion nut to 170 ft.-lbs., and use an in.-lb. torque wrench to measure the pinion bearing preload. This should be 10 in.-lbs. over the original figure if the old bearing is used, or 20-30 in.-lbs. for a new bearing. If the final pinion nut torque is less than 170 ft.-lbs. or the pinion bearing preload is not within specifications, the assembly is unacceptable. *Do not* back off the pinion nut to reduce pinion bearing preload, or the assembly will have to be taken apart and a new collapsible spacer installed and adjusted.

RING-GEAR/PINION BACKLASH

If Manufactured Before April 15, 1972

1. With the drive pinion installed and the preload correctly adjusted, replace the differential-case/ring-gear assembly with the respective bearing caps and adjusters. Torque each cap bolt to 10 in.-lbs.

2. Fit a spreader tool and dial indicator on the case, and spread the case 0.005-in.

3. Torque all cap bolts to 60 ft.-lbs., and turn the right adjuster until the spread is removed.

4. Turn the adjuster inward to eliminate free play, and turn the ring gear and pinion several times to seat the bearings.

5. Position a dial indicator, with its stem parallel to and touching the drive gear side of the ring gear teeth, and measure the backlash at 90° intervals, positioning at the point of least backlash.

6. Turn both adjusters inward until the backlash is 0.001-in. to 0.002-in., then turn the right bearing adjuster until minimum backlash is reached—0.006-in. to 0.008-in. When the backlash is correct, the preload will be properly adjusted.

7. Once all adjustments are correctly made, use gear marking compound to coat the drive and coast sides of the drive gear, and turn through one full turn while prying with a screwdriver blade placed between the case and case flange.

8. Compare the tooth pattern to **Fig. 12-56 (A).** If the pattern seems closer to **Fig. 12-56 (B) or (C)** than it does to (A), disassemble and increase the shim pack thickness on (B) or decrease the thickness on (C). The shims are located behind the rear pinion bearing.

9. Install the axle shafts, connect the driveshaft and replace the housing cover using a new gasket and sealant. Torque the cover bolts to 20 ft.-lbs.

If Manufactured After April 15, 1972

Refer to 7¼-in. axles manufactured after Jan. 31, 1972.

OMNI/HORIZON
MANUAL TRANSAXLE OVERHAUL

Gear ratio selection, reduction and differential functions in the front wheel drive Omni/Horizon are combined in a single unit called a transaxle **(Fig. 12-64)** The manual 4-speed transaxle is contained within a two-piece magnesium case, with one piece housing the

transmission function. The clutch and differential are contained in the other piece. To identify the unit for parts replacement, the transaxle part number is stamped into a machined pad on the clutch housing above the engine timing access hole. The last 8 digits of the VIN number are also stamped on the rear edge of the clutch housing.

MANUAL TRANSAXLE
REMOVAL/INSTALLATION

1. On early production models, it is necessary to remove the plug from the timing access hole and rotate the engine until the drilled flywheel mark aligns with the clutch housing pointer.

2. Disconnect the negative battery cable, shift linkage rods, starter wire, ground wire, backup light switch wire and clutch cable **(Fig. 12-65).**

3. Remove the starting motor and the bolt holding the speedometer adapter to the transaxle. Work the speedometer adapter and pinion out of the transaxle (do not disconnect the cable housing).

4. Support the engine with a fixture similar to that shown in **Fig. 12-66.**

5. Loosen the left hub nut and raise the vehicle on the hoist.

6. Disconnect the right driveshaft and tie it out of the way, then remove the left driveshaft.

7. Remove the left splash shield, the small dust cover on the bell housing and the large dust cover bolts at the bell housing.

8. Drain the transaxle fluid.

9. Position a transmission jack underneath the transaxle assembly and chain it in place securely **(Fig. 12-67).**

10. Remove the left engine mount and the transaxle-to-engine attaching bolts.

11. Slide the transaxle to the left and rear until the mainshaft is clear of the clutch.

12. Lower the transaxle on the jack and remove it from under the vehicle. Clean the transaxle exterior with a brush and solvent.

13. To install the transaxle assembly, reverse the above procedure.

14. Adjust the clutch cable **(see 10-13)** and gearshift linkage **(Figs. 10-20A & 12-68).**

TRANSAXLE DISASSEMBLY

This procedure requires the use of several special tools offered by Chrysler according to the part numbers provided here. While it may be possible to complete transaxle disassembly using makeshift tools, it is strongly recommended that the following tools be used: drive flange remover (P/N L-4443), oil seal remover (P/N L-4445), seal installers (P/N L-4446 & C-4171), case remover (P/N L-4443), puller (P/N L-4534) and selector shaft cover remover (P/N L-4441).

1. Remove clutch push rod.

2. Pry out drive flange dust plug with a screwdriver blade.

3. Remove the drive flange snap ring and cone washer.

4. Remove the drive flange with tool No. L-4443, Fig. 12-69.

5. Use oil seal remover No. L-4445 to remove the oil seal.

6. Remove the selector shaft cover with tool No. L-4441.

7. Withdraw the detent spring assembly and remove the selector shaft boot seal.

8. Push the selector shaft through the housing and remove it.

9. Use tool No. L-4445 to remove the selector shaft oil seal.

10. Pry out the mainshaft bearing nut plugs, then remove the clutch release bearing end cover, holding clutch release lever in the upper position to prevent loading the cover and causing damage to the case thread **(Fig. 12-70)**.

11. Withdraw the release bearing and plastic sleeve.

12. Pry the circlip from the torque shaft using two screwdrivers. Withdraw the clutch torque shaft and lift out the return spring and release lever **(Fig. 12-71)**.

13. Use tool No. L-4445 to remove the two clutch torque shaft oil seals.

14. Remove the three mainshaft bearing retainer nuts and washers, letting the studs and clips drop into the case.

15. Remove the case attaching bolts, reverse idler shaft setscrew and backup light switch.

16. Use tool No. 4443 to remove the transaxle case and label all shims according to their location for correct replacement.

17. Once the case is off, remove the two bolts holding

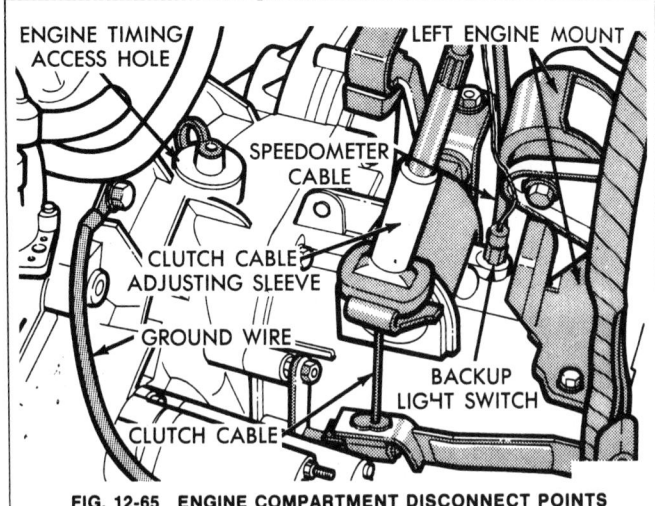

FIG. 12-65 ENGINE COMPARTMENT DISCONNECT POINTS

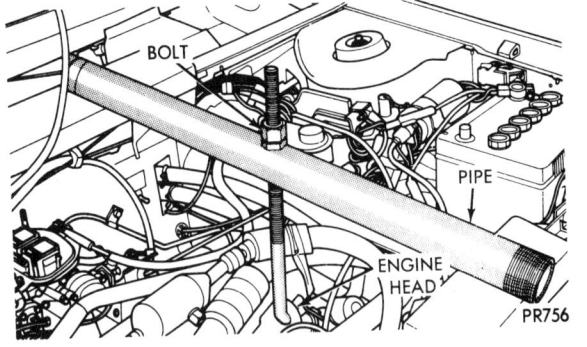

FIG. 12-66 SUGGESTED TYPE OF ENGINE SUPPORT FIXTURE

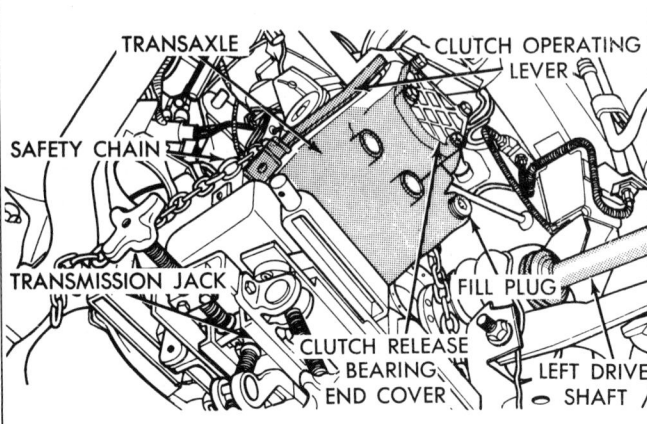

FIG. 12-67 TRANSMISSION JACK POSITIONING

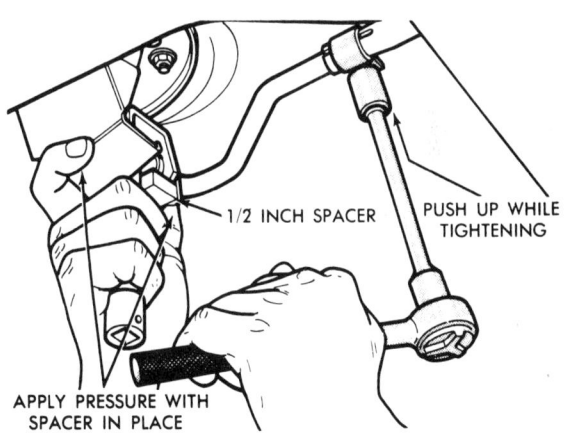

FIG. 12-68 GEARSHIFT LINKAGE ADJUSTMENT

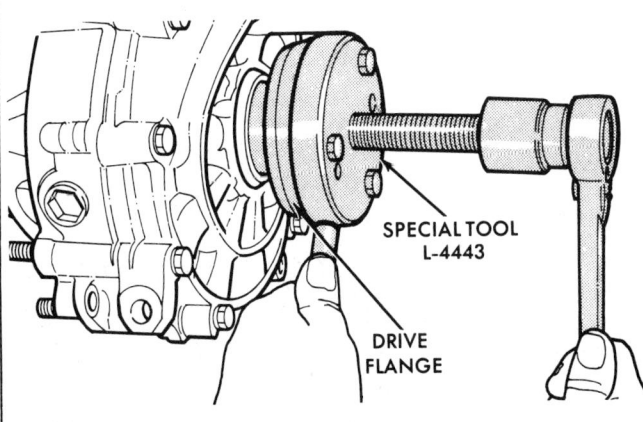

FIG. 12-69 DRIVE FLANGE REMOVAL/INSTALLATION

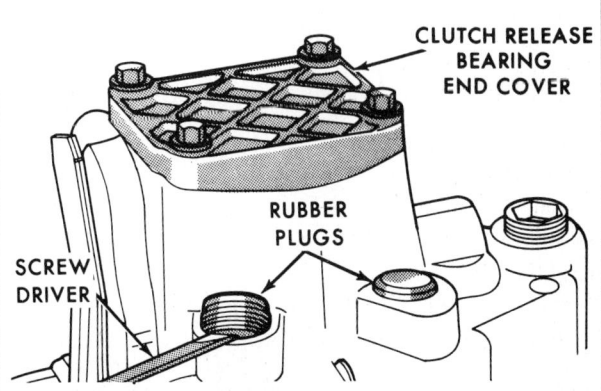

FIG. 12-70 MAINSHAFT BEARING PLUG/CLUTCH RELEASE END COVER

the reverse shift fork supports and lift out the shift fork **(Fig. 12-72)**.

18. Pry the upper and lower E-clips holding the shift forks in place on the shaft and remove the forks.

19. Lift the mainshaft assembly and pinion shaft 4th speed gear straight up until the gear clears the pinion shaft, then remove from the case.

MAINSHAFT DISASSEMBLY/ASSEMBLY (Fig. 12-73)

1. Secure the mainshaft in an upright position in a soft-jaw vise. Remove the mainshaft bearing snap ring and thrust button.

2. Use puller L-4534 to remove the mainshaft bearing and 4th-speed gear. Locate puller jaws under the gear and pull both bearing and gear off at the same time.

3. Remove the 4th gear needle bearing, taking care not to expand cage excessively or it will break.

4. Expand the synchronizer snapring and use puller L-4534 to remove the 3rd/4th synchronizer, 3rd speed gear and 3rd gear needle bearing. Use same care in removing this bearing as in Step 3.

5. If clutch push rod seal and bushing assembly are to be replaced, pry out old units and install new ones flush with shaft edge.

6. Clean and inspect all gears and synchronizer assemblies for excessive wear or spline chipping. Syn-

chronizer springs must be positioned with the tang inside the strut cavity. Note the staggered tang location in **Fig. 12-74**. Check stop rings for high thread wear and/or cracks.

7. To assemble the mainshaft, reverse Steps 1-4. Press gears on the mainshaft in the sequence shown in **Fig. 12-73**, installing snap rings where required.

PINION SHAFT DISASSEMBLY/ASSEMBLY (Fig. 12-75)

1. Expand and remove the pinion shaft snap ring.

2. Remove the 3rd speed gear, 2nd speed gear and needle bearing from the pinion shaft.

3. Place a length of 2x4 across the case and use a pry bar to remove the reverse gear idler shaft.

4. Pry out the plastic thrust button from the end of the

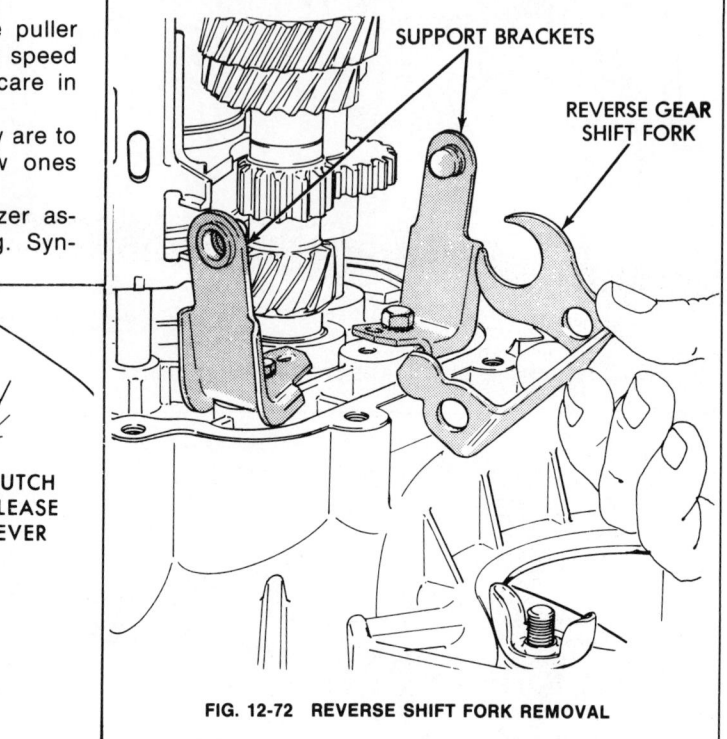

FIG. 12-72 REVERSE SHIFT FORK REMOVAL

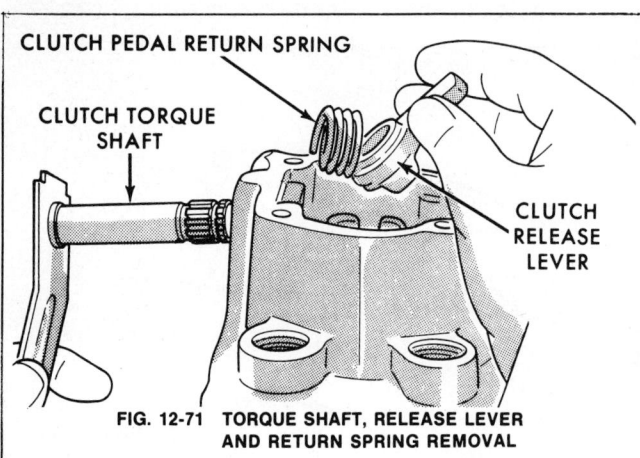

FIG. 12-71 TORQUE SHAFT, RELEASE LEVER AND RETURN SPRING REMOVAL

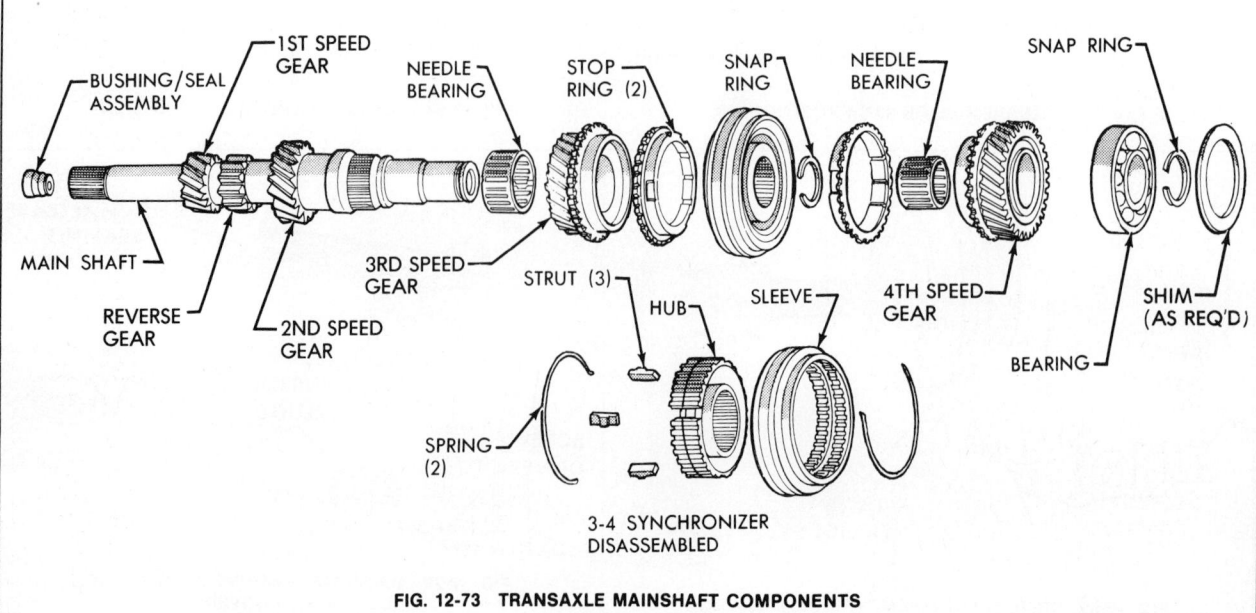

FIG. 12-73 TRANSAXLE MAINSHAFT COMPONENTS

TORQUEFLITE AUTOMATIC TRANSAXLE SPECIFICATIONS

	Metric Measure	U.S. Measure
Type	Automatic Three Speed With Torque Converter and Integral Differential	
Torque Converter Diameter	241 millimetres	9.48 inches
Oil Capacity—Note Two Separate Sumps:		
Differential Sump	1.12 Litres	2.37 pints
Transmission—Torque Converter Sump	6.86 Litres	14.5 pints
Use "DEXRON" Type Automatic Transmission Fluid in **Both** Sumps		
Cooling Method	Water-Heat Exchanger	
Lubrication	Pump (Internal-External Gear Type)	

Gear Ratios	1978	1979
Transmission Portion: First	2.48	2.48
Second	1.48	1.48
Third	1.00	1.00
Reverse	2.10	2.10
Final Drive Portion: Federal	3.48	3.48
California	3.74	3.67

Pump Clearances	(Millimetre)	(Inch)
Outer Gear to Pocket	0.045-.141	.0018-.0056
Outer Gear I.D. to Crescent	0.150-.306	.0059-.012
Outer Gear Side Clearance	0.025-.050	.001-.002
Inner Gear O.D. to Crescent	.160-.316	.0063-.0124
Inner Gear Side Clearance	.150-.306	.0059-.012

End Play	(Millimetre)	(Inch)
Input Shaft	0.76-2.69	.030-.106
Front Clutch Retainer	0.76-2.69	.030-.106
Front Carrier	0.89-1.45	.007-.057
Front Annulus Gear	0.09-0.50	.0035-.020
Planet Pinion	0.15-0.59	.006-.023
Reverse Drum	0.76-3.36	.030-.132

Clutch Clearance and Selective Snap Rings

Front Clutch (Non-Adjustable) Measured from Reaction Plate to "Farthest" Wave	1.7-2.7	.067-.106
Rear Clutch		
Adjustable	0.40-0.94	.016-.037
Selective R.C. Snap Rings (2)	1.53-1.58	.060-.062
	2.01-2.06	.079-.081

Band Adjustment

	1978	1979
Kickdown (Front) Turns (Backed off from 72 inch-pounds)	2.5 Turns	3.5 Turns
Low-Reverse (Rear) non adjustable		

Thrust Washers		(Millimetre)	(Inch)
Reaction Shaft Support (Phenolic) ..	No. 1	1.55-1.60	.061-.063
Rear Clutch Retainer (Phenolic)	No. 2	1.55-1.60	.061-.063
Output Shaft, Steel Backed Bronze ..	No. 3	1.55-1.65	.061-.065
Front Annulus, Steel Backed Bronze	No. 4	2.95-3.05	.116-.120
Carrier, Steel Backed Bronze	Nos. 5, 6, 9, 10	1.22-1.28	.048-.050
Sun Gear Drive Shell, Steel	Nos. 7, 8	0.85-0.91	.033-.036
Rev. Drum, Phenolic	No. 11	1.55-1.60	.061-.063

Tapered Roller Bearing Settings		
Output Shaft	0.0-0.07 Preload	0.0-0028
Transfer Shaft	0.05-0.14 End Play	.002-.0055
Differential	0.15-0.29 Preload	.006-.011

TORQUEFLITE AUTOMATIC TRANSAXLE SPECIFICATIONS

Spacers (Shims) for Tapered Roller Bearing Settings	(Millimetre)	(Inch)
Output Shaft		
36 Thicknesses Available in		
increments of:	0.04	0.0016
over a range of:	7.59-8.99	0.299-0.354
Placed between bearing cones		
Differential		
40 Thicknesses Available in		
increments of:	0.04	0.0016
over a range of:	0.50-2.06	.020-.080
Placed between left cup and retainer		
Transfer Shaft		
31 Thicknesses Available in		
increments of:	0.06	0.0024
over a range of:	1.88-3.68	0.074-0.145
Placed between governor support and transfer gear bearing cone		

BEARING ADJUSTMENT CHART

(1) Select a shim to get less than .010 inch end play. (.025 to .250 mm). **Record shim thickness and end play.** (2) Use the following table to select the required shim for NOMINAL bearing setting:

Bearing Centerline	Specification Inch (mm)	Shim Thickness	End Play	Required Shim For Nominal Bearing Setting		
				Shim Thickness	End Play	Specification
Differential†	.008″ to .009″ tight (.220 ± .070)	"A"	.xxx	"A" +	.xxx +	.0085 inch (.220 mm)
Output Shaft	.001″ to .0015″ tight (.035 tight)	"B"	.yyy	"B" −	.yyy −	.001 inch (.035 mm)
Transfer Shaft	.003″ to .004″ loose (.095 loose)	"C"	.zzz	"C" −	.zzz +	.0035 inch (.095 mm)

†Differential turning torque with proper preload, is 7 to 19 inch-pounds.

(3) Install required shim, oil the bearing, and check turning torque or end play as applicable per chart.

Speedo Pinion
Same for all automatics—21 teeth

TIGHTENING REFERENCE

Item	Qty.	Thread Size	Driver	Torque
A-404 Automatic Transaxle				
Bolt—Bell Housing Cover	3	9.8-M6-1-10	10mm Hex	105 in. lb.
Bolt—Flex Plate to Crank	6	10.9-M10-1-16	16mm Hex	50 ft. lb.
Bolt—Flex Plate to Torque Converter	3	10.9-M10-1.5-11	18mm Hex	40 ft. lb.
Screw Assy. Transmission to Cyl. Block	3	9.8A-M12-1.75-65	18mm Hex	70 ft. lb.
Screw Assy. Lower Bell Housing Cover	3	9.8-M6-1-10	10mm Hex	105 in. lb.
Screw Assy. Manual Control Lever	1	9.8A-M6-1-35	10mm Hex	105 in. lb.
Screw Assy. Speedometer to Extension	1	9.8A-M6-1-14	10mm Hex	105 in. lb.
Nut—Cooler Tube to Transmission	2	1/2-20	5/8 Hex	150 in. lb.
Connector, Cooler Hose to Radiator	2	1/8-27 NPTF	12mm Hex	110 in. lb.
Bolt—Starter to Transmission Bell Housing	3	M10-1.5-30(+)	15mm Hex	40 ft. lb.
Bolt—Throttle Cable to Transmission Case	1	M6-1.0-14	10mm Hex	105 in. lb.
Bolt—Throttle Lever to Transmission Shaft	1	M6-1-25	10mm Hex	105 in. lb.
Bolt—Manual Cable to Transmission Case	1	M8-1.75-30(+)	13mm Hex	250 in. lb.
Bolt—Front Motor Mount	2	M10	15mm Hex	40 ft. lb.
Bolt—Left Motor Mount	3	M10-1.5-25	15mm Hex	40 ft. lb.

pinion shaft. Install puller L-4534 with its jaws under 1st gear. Pinion shaft bearing retainer is notched in two places to accommodate puller jaws. Loosen the remaining components and remove the puller.

5. Lift 2nd gear inner sleeve and 1st/2nd 1st/2nd synchronizer assembly from pinion shaft.

6. Remove the 1st speed gear and needle bearing.

7. Mark the synchronizer hub and sleeve for correct assembly.

8. Check the synchronizer sleeve for excessive spline wear or chipping.

9. Check reverse gear teeth for damage caused by partial engagement.

10. Reassemble synchronizer units as in step 6 of mainshaft assembly.

11. If pinion shaft must be replaced, unbolt shaft retainer.

12. Lift retainer off pinion shaft, remove 1st gear thrust washer and pull pinion shaft from case.

13. Inspect pinion shaft bearing. If replacement is required, press off old bearings and press new ones on **(Fig. 12-76).**

14. To reassemble and replace pinion shaft, reverse the above sequence and install components according to the sequence shown in **Fig. 12-75.** The flat side of the 1st gear thrust washer must face toward 1st gear. Torque pinion shaft retainer bolts to 29 ft.-lbs.

DIFFERENTIAL SERVICE (Fig. 12-77)

The outside diameter of the ring gear on the 3.70 ratio has an identification groove; there is none on the 3.48 ratio ring gear.

1. Remove the differential from the clutch/differential housing.

2. Expand and remove the select fit circlips on each axle shaft to remove and replace the shafts. Install new circlips of the same size when new shafts are installed.

3. Bearing cones and cups should not be removed unless defective. Cones and cups are matched sets and are replaced as assemblies. Chrysler provides a special bearing puller (P/N L-4463), installer (P/N L-4510) and two cup removers (P/N L-4449 & 4450) for this purpose.

4. When replacing the ring gear, drill a ⅛-in. pilot hole in the rivets, then drill them out with a 15/32-in. bit and knock the rivets out. Clean differential housing of all metal particles.

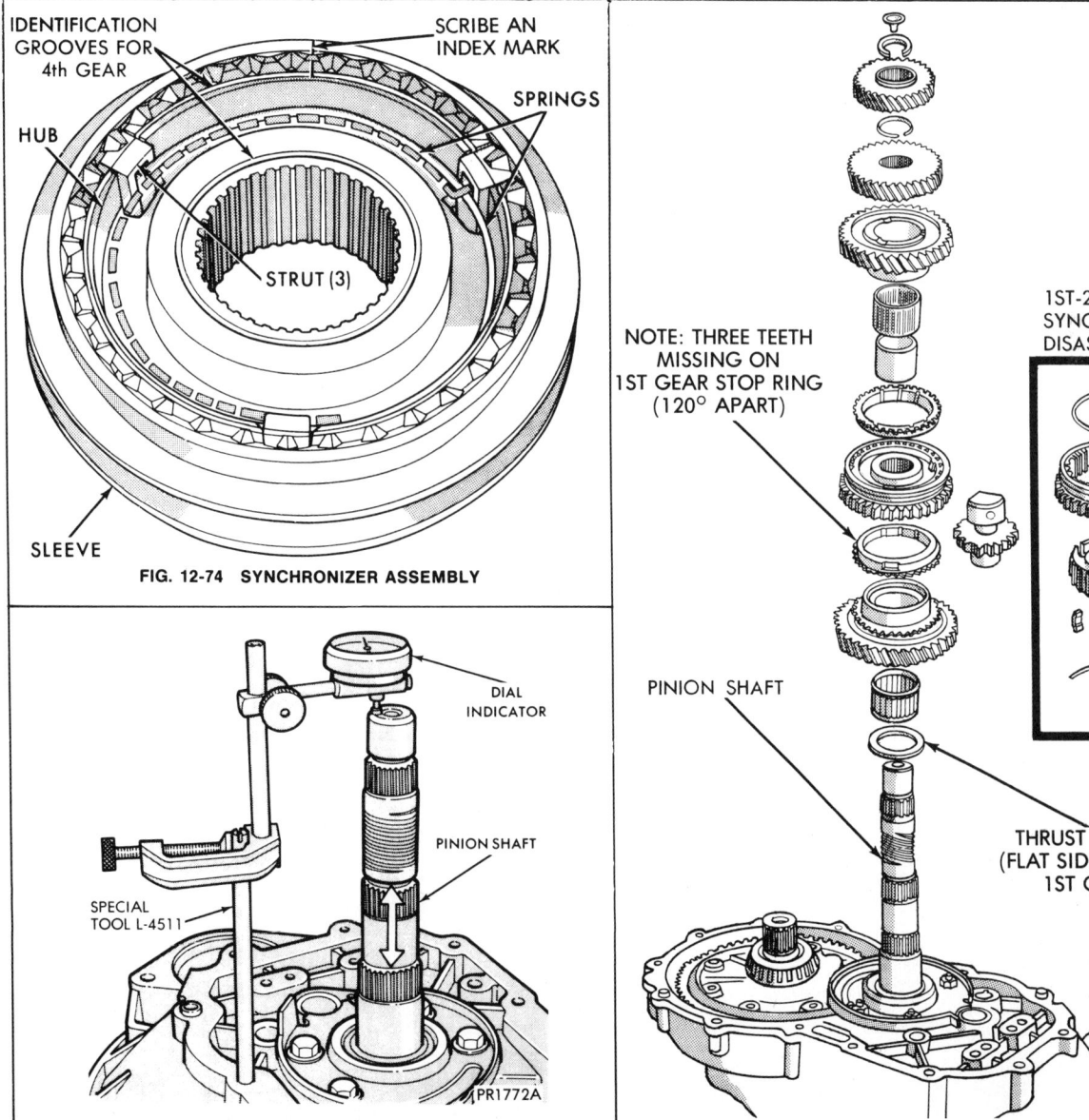

FIG. 12-74 SYNCHRONIZER ASSEMBLY

IDENTIFICATION GROOVES FOR 4th GEAR
SCRIBE AN INDEX MARK
SPRINGS
HUB
STRUT (3)
SLEEVE

FIG. 12-78 DETERMINING PINION BEARING PRELOAD SHIM

DIAL INDICATOR
PINION SHAFT
SPECIAL TOOL L-4511

FIG. 12-75 PINION SHAFT COMPONENTS

NOTE: THREE TEETH MISSING ON 1ST GEAR STOP RING (120° APART)
1ST-2ND SYNCHRONIZER DISASSEMBLED
PINION SHAFT
THRUST WASHER (FLAT SIDE TOWARD 1ST GEAR)

5. Install the new ring gear with the special bolts, washers and nuts provided. Retorque the bolts to 41 ft.-lbs.

6. Whenever the ring gear or drive pinion are replaced, the pinion shaft preload must be adjusted.

PINION SHAFT BEARING PRELOAD ADJUSTMENT

1. Set a 0.024-in. shim in the bearing housing and press in the small bearing cup in the clutch housing.

2. Install the pinion shaft in the case and torque the bearing retainer bolts to 14 ft.-lbs.

3. Attach a dial indicator as shown in **Fig. 12-78** and move the pinion shaft up and down. Note measurement.

4. Add 0.008-in. to measured reading and shim thickness to obtain required bearing preload. For example, if reading is 0.012-in. and installed shim is 0.025-in., the correct bearing preload is 0.008 + 0.012 + 0.025 or 0.045-in.

5. Remove the pinion shaft retainer and shaft. Remove the small bearing cup and the 0.025-in. shim.

6. Install the correct size shim and replace the bearing cup. Install the pinion shaft and retainer, torquing bolts to 29 ft.-lbs.

TRANSAXLE ASSEMBLY

1. After installing pinion shaft, check end play between 3rd gear and snap ring with a flat feeler gauge **(Fig. 12-79)**. If end play exceeds 0.039-in., remove and install the next thicker snap ring available. Six snap rings are available, ranging from 0.098-in. to 0.118-in. in 0.004-in. increments.

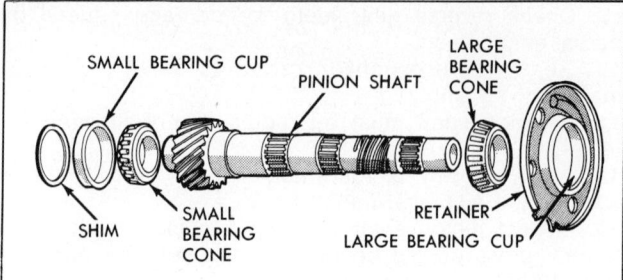

FIG. 12-76 PINION SHAFT BEARING CONFIGURATION

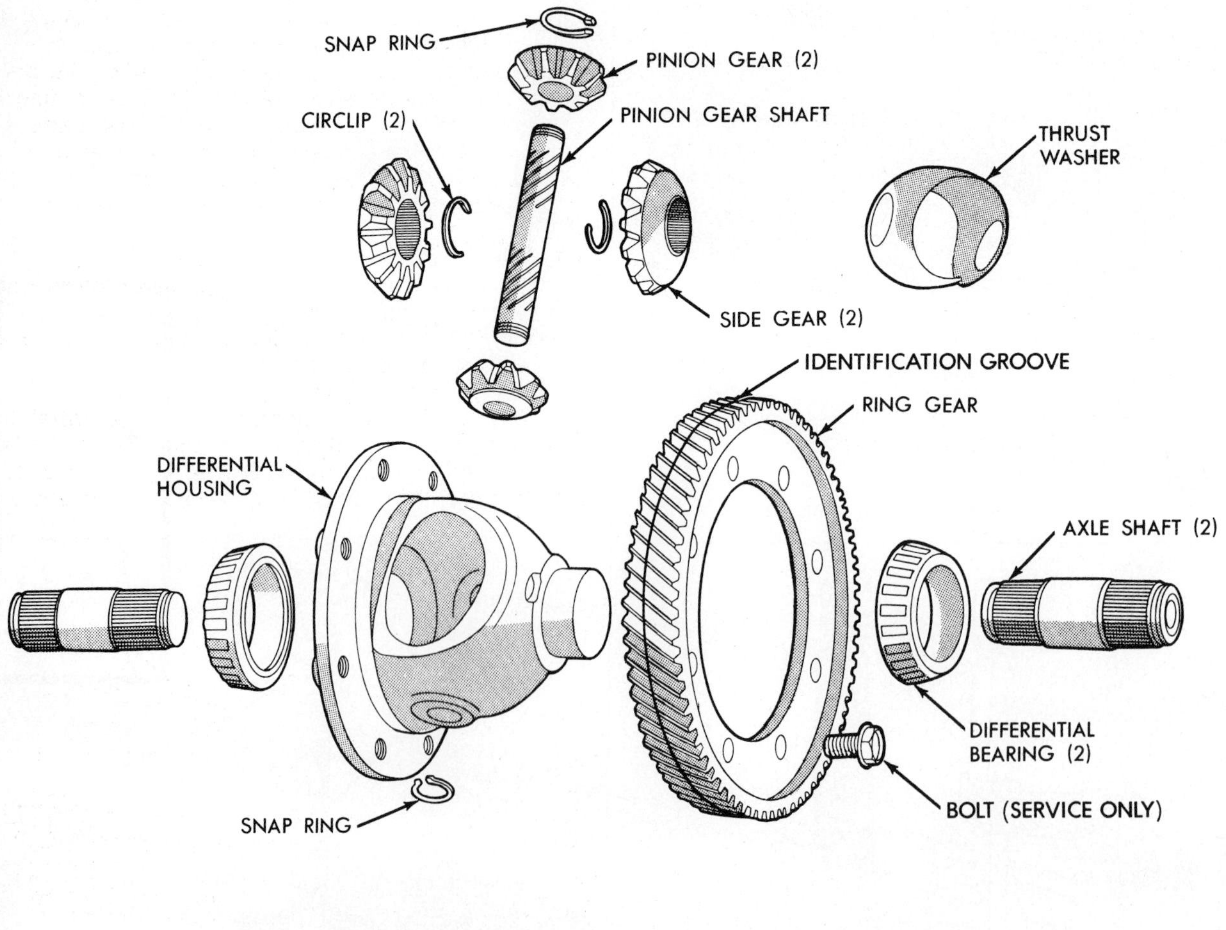

FIG. 12-77 DIFFERENTIAL COMPONENTS

2. Install the mainshaft assembly, taking care not to scratch the needle bearing journal.

3. Replace the 4th speed mainshaft needle bearing, 4th gear and snap ring.

4. If trans case, clutch housing or mainshaft has been replaced with a new unit, mainshaft end play must be checked. This procedure requires the use of two special Chrysler tools (P/N L-4442 and L-4459). Fasten tool No. L-4442 as shown in **Fig. 12-80**. Install tool No. L-4459 on mainshaft and replace transmission housing with a new gasket, torquing the bolts to 14 ft.-lbs. **(Fig. 12-81)**. Install a dial indicator with measuring sleeve and zero the indicator dial **(Fig. 12-82)**. Move the measuring sleeve up and down to determine the amount of play. Select proper shim from table below and remove transmission housing and special tools to continue assembly.

IF DIAL INDICATOR READS:	SELECT THIS SHIM THICKNESS:
.000 to .018	---
.019 to .029	.012
.030 to .041	.024
.042 to .057	.035

5. Assemble shift forks to shift rail **(Fig. 12-83)**. Do not install E-clips at this time.

6. Install shift fork assembly by inserting the forks in their respective synchronizer grooves and slide the shift rail into its housing bore. Install E-clips now.

7. Position the reverse shift fork between the support brackets, **Fig. 12-72,** and torque the bracket bolts to 105 in.-lbs.

8. Fit the shim selected in Step 4 (or original shim if Step 4 was not required) over the mainshaft and install the mainshaft ball bearing.

9. Install the guide pins and replace the transmission housing. Check that the pinion shaft is aligned with the pinion shaft needle bearing in the transmission case and install the mainshaft bearing snap ring. Replace case attaching bolts.

10. Lubricate the axle shaft flange lip seals and install, then replace drive flanges, spring washer and snap ring.

11. Replace selector shaft assembly. Install mainshaft bearing retainer nuts with washers and torque to 155 in.-lbs.

12. Install the clutch torque shaft, return spring and release lever **(Fig. 12-71)**. Replace the two circlips on the torque shaft.

13. Replace the release bearing/sleeve and install the mainshaft bearing retainer end cover and plugs **(Fig. 12-70)**.

14. Replace the selector shift cover and install the backup light switch.

15. Install the detent plunger/spring assembly and hand tighten locknut. Place transmission in neutral and back off the locknut. Tighten the adjusting sleeve until the detent plunger barely makes contact with the gearshift selector. Hold the sleeve in this position and torque the locknut to 175 in.-lbs.

16. Install clutch push rod and shift selector boot seal.

OMNI/HORIZON
AUTOMATIC TRANSAXLE OVERHAUL

A modified version of the Chrysler TorqueFlite automatic transmission, this transaxle is designated as the A-404 and combines a torque converter, fully automatic 3-speed transmission, final drive assembly and differential in a compact unit of metric design. Since the operational requirements of the A-404 differ according to vehicle/engine requirements, some internal parts will differ according to application. For this reason, it is important to refer to the 7-digit part number stamped on the rear of the oil pan flange when replacing components.

The A-404 contains 3 primary areas:

(1) The main centerline plus the valve body, quite similar to that of the conventional TorqueFlite.

(2) A transfer shaft centerline including the governor and parking sprag.

(3) A differential centerline.

The converter, transmission and differential are housed in an integral aluminum casting, but the differential and transmission have separate oil sumps. It is important that the differential oil level be maintained to

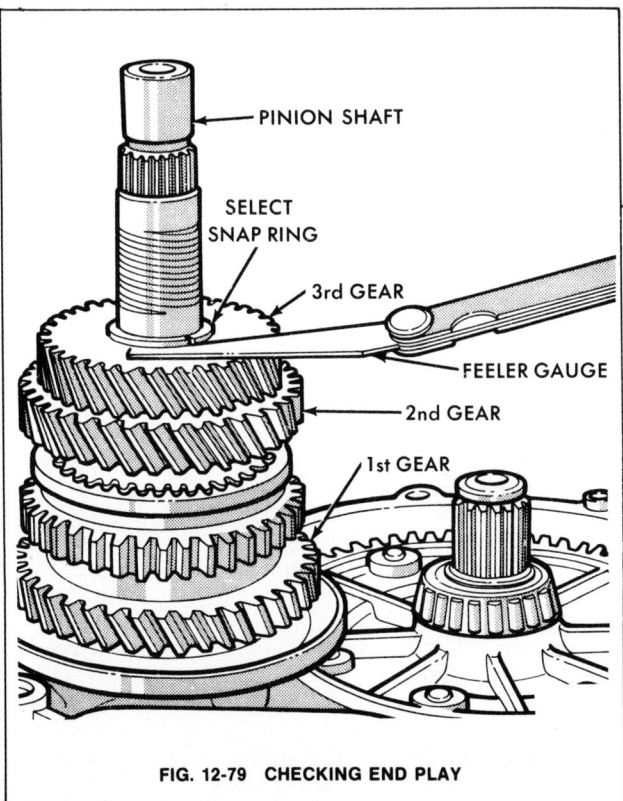

FIG. 12-79 CHECKING END PLAY

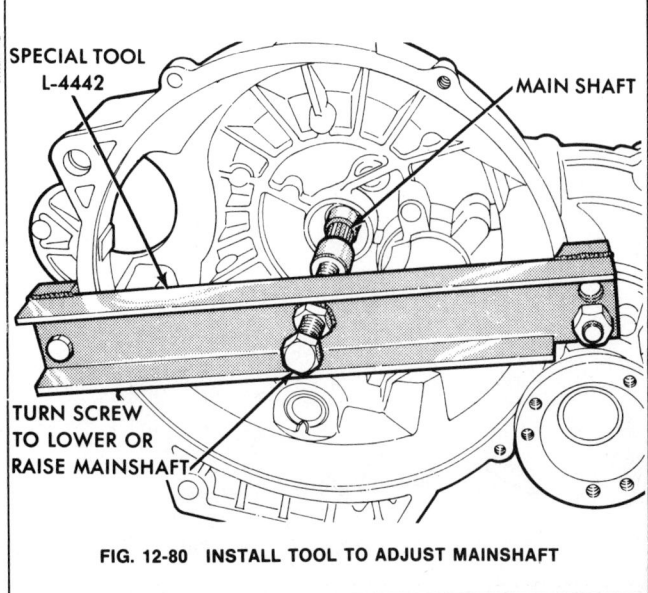

FIG. 12-80 INSTALL TOOL TO ADJUST MAINSHAFT

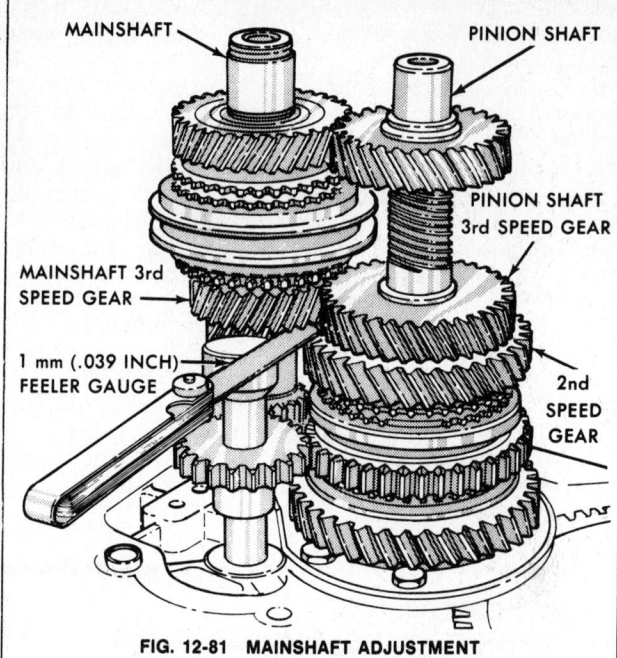

FIG. 12-81 MAINSHAFT ADJUSTMENT

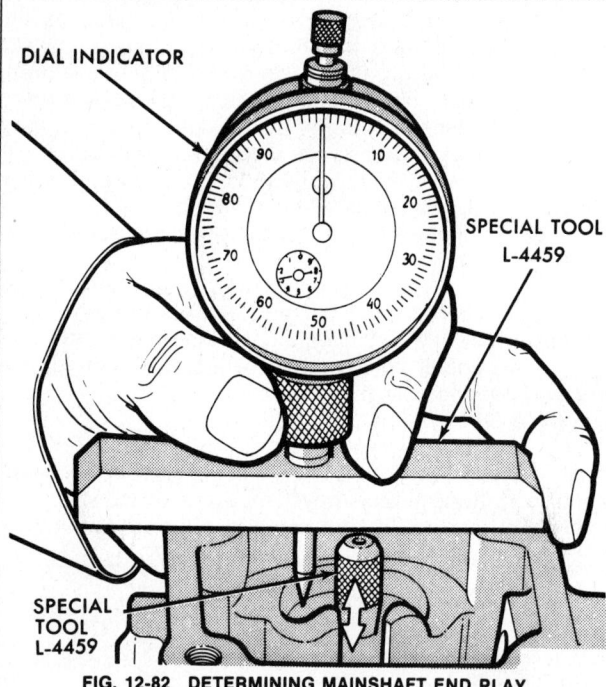

FIG. 12-82 DETERMINING MAINSHAFT END PLAY

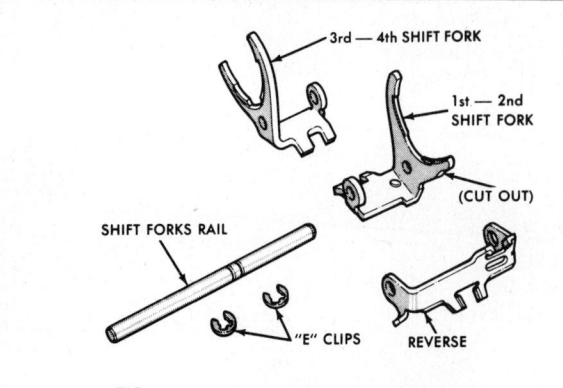

FIG. 12-83 SHIFT FORK/RAIL ASSEMBLY

the fill hole in the differential cover.

The transmission is cooled by circulating the ATF through an oil-to-water type cooler located in the radiator side tank. The transmission sump is vented through a hollow dipstick, while the differential is vented by a spring-loaded cap on the extension housing. The A-404 contains two multiple disc clutches, an overrunning clutch, two servos, a hydraulic accumulator, two bands, and two planetary gear sets. An integral helical gear on the transfer shaft drives the differential ring gear. Final drive gearing may differ according to the gearset used. All 1978-79 non-California models have an overall ratio of 3.48, while the ratio is 3.74 and 3.67 for 1978 and 1979 California models respectively.

BAND ADJUSTMENT
KICKDOWN (FRONT) BAND

1. Loosen the adjusting screw locknut at the left side (top front) of the case and back it off about five turns. Check to see that the adjusting screw turns freely in the transmission case.

2. Torque the adjusting screw to 72 in.-lbs., then back the screw off 2½ turns for 1978 and 3½ turns for 1979 models.

3. Hold the adjusting screw from moving and torque the locknut to 35 ft.-lbs.

LOW-REVERSE (REAR) BAND

This band is not adjustable; it must be visually insepcted to determine its condition. The band is satisfactory if the lining grooves are visible, at least .080-in. deep, and the band end gap is not less than .020-in.

AUTOMATIC TRANSAXLE REMOVAL/INSTALLATION

To avoid damage to the converter drive plate, pump bushing and/or oil seal, the transaxle and converter must be removed from the vehicle as a unit. Since the drive plate will not support any weight, the transaxle must not rest on the plate during removal.

1. Disconnect the positive (+) battery cable and remove the upper transmission cooler tube.

2. Disconnect the throttle and the shift linkage at the transaxle.

3. Support the engine with a fixture similar to that shown in **Fig. 12-66.**

4. Remove the upper bell housing bolts.

5. Remove the hub nuts, raise the vehicle on the hoist and remove the wheel/tire assemblies.

6. Remove the left splash shield, drain the differential and remove the differential cover.

7. Remove the speedometer adapter, cable and pinion as a unit.

8. Remove the sway bar and separate the lower ball joints from the steering knuckle bolts.

9. Remove the driveshafts from the hub, rotate both driveshafts to expose their circlip ends in the transaxle and squeeze the ends of each circlip together while prying each driveshaft from the side gear.

10. Remove each driveshaft.

11. Mark the torque converter and drive plate **(Fig. 12-84)** then remove the converter mounting bolts.

12. Remove the access plug in the right splash shield and rotate the engine.

13. Disconnect the lower cooler tube and the neutral safety switch wire.

14. Remove the front crossmember engine mount bracket.

15. Remove the through bolt in the front engine mount insulator and the bezel housing bolts.

16. Position a transmission jack underneath the transaxle assembly and chain it securely in place **(Fig. 12-67)**.

17. Remove the left engine mount and its through bolt.

18. Lower the transaxle on the jack. You may have to pry the engine for clearance, as shown in **Fig. 12-85**. Remove the transaxle from under the vehicle and clean its exterior with a brush and solvent.

19. To install the transaxle assembly, reverse the above procedure.

20. Fill the differential with Dextron ATF before lowering the vehicle to the floor.

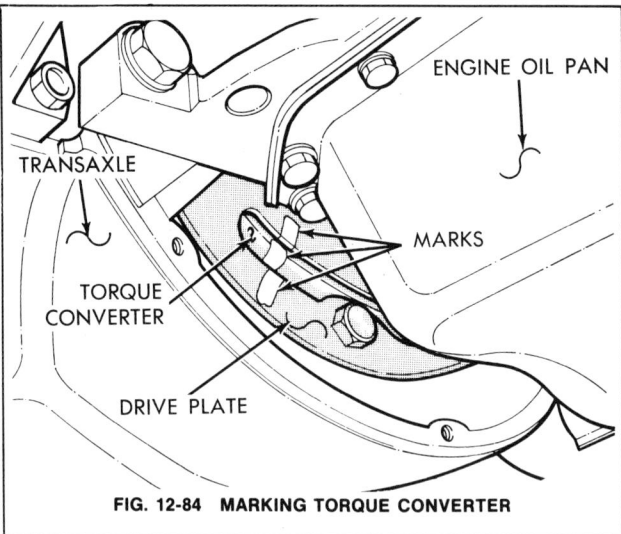

FIG. 12-84 MARKING TORQUE CONVERTER

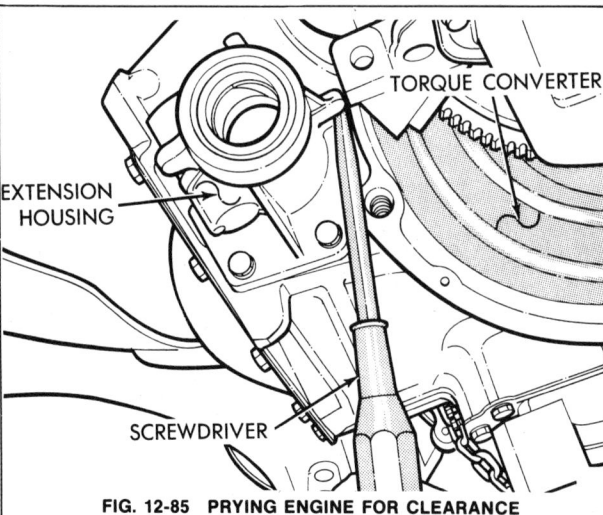

FIG. 12-85 PRYING ENGINE FOR CLEARANCE

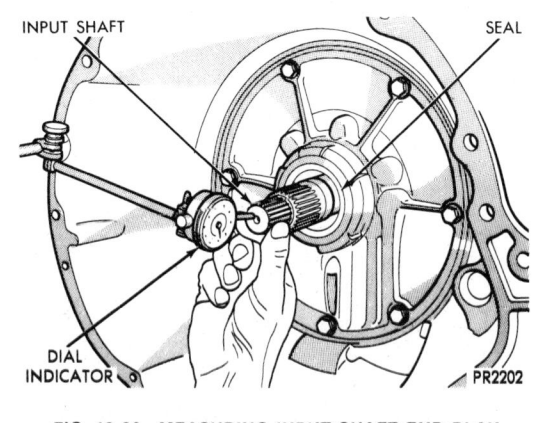

FIG. 12-86 MEASURING INPUT SHAFT END PLAY

AUTOMATIC TRANSAXLE DISASSEMBLY

1. Attach a dial indicator as shown in **Fig. 12-86** and measure input shaft end play. End play in excess of 0.106-in. will require installation of a new thrust washer between the input and output shafts.

2. Unbolt and remove transaxle oil pan. Clean gasket surfaces on the pan and case thoroughly to remove all traces of old gasket.

3. Unbolt, remove and discard the oil filter.

4. Pry off the E-clip holding the parking rod and remove the rod from the transaxle case.

5. Unbolt and remove the valve body from the case with governor tubes attached.

6. If valve body service is required, remove the detent spring attaching screw and the detent spring. Remove the valve body screws and separate the unit in half. Remove the seven steel balls located as shown in **Fig. 12-87,** and refer to **Fig. 12-88** through **12-91** for removal of the remaining components.

7. Pry out and discard the pump oil seal, then tighten the kickdown band adjusting screw.

8. Remove the seven pump bolts and attach a slide hammer to remove the oil pump.

9. Remove the oil pump gasket and loosen the kickdown band adjusting screw.

10. Remove the kickdown band and strut assembly.

11. Withdraw the front clutch, the No. 2 thrust washer and the rear clutch assemblies from the case.

12. Remove the No. 3 thrust washer and expand and remove the front planetary snap ring from the output shaft.

13. Remove the front planetary assembly, the No. 6 thrust washer and the sun gear driving shell with No. 7 thrust washer attached.

14. Withdraw the No. 9 thrust washer, the rear planetary assembly and the No. 10 thrust washer.

15. Remove the overrunning clutch assembly, clutch rollers and springs. Reassemble the clutch as shown in **Fig. 12-92.**

16. Remove the low-reverse band, strut and No. 11 thrust washer. This completes case disassembly.

TRANSAXLE COMPONENT OVERHAUL

1. Support the front pump and remove the reaction shaft support bolts.

2. Separate the pump unit and inspect the inner/outer pump gears for wear or damage.

3. Reinstall the gears and check pump gear clearances with a feeler gauge as shown in **Fig. 12-93**. If

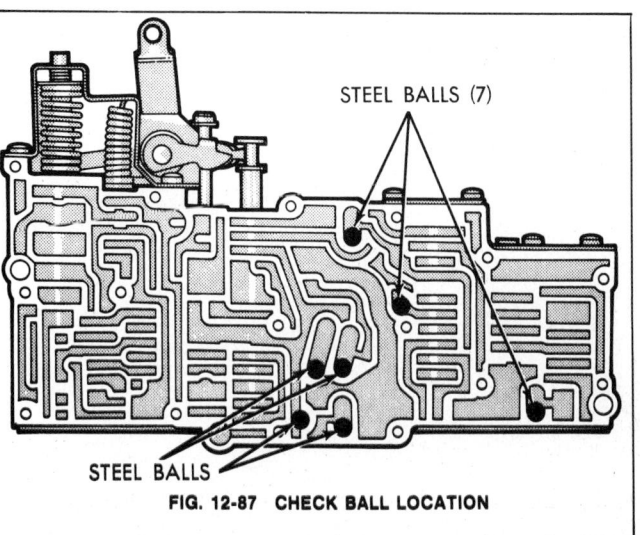

FIG. 12-87 CHECK BALL LOCATION

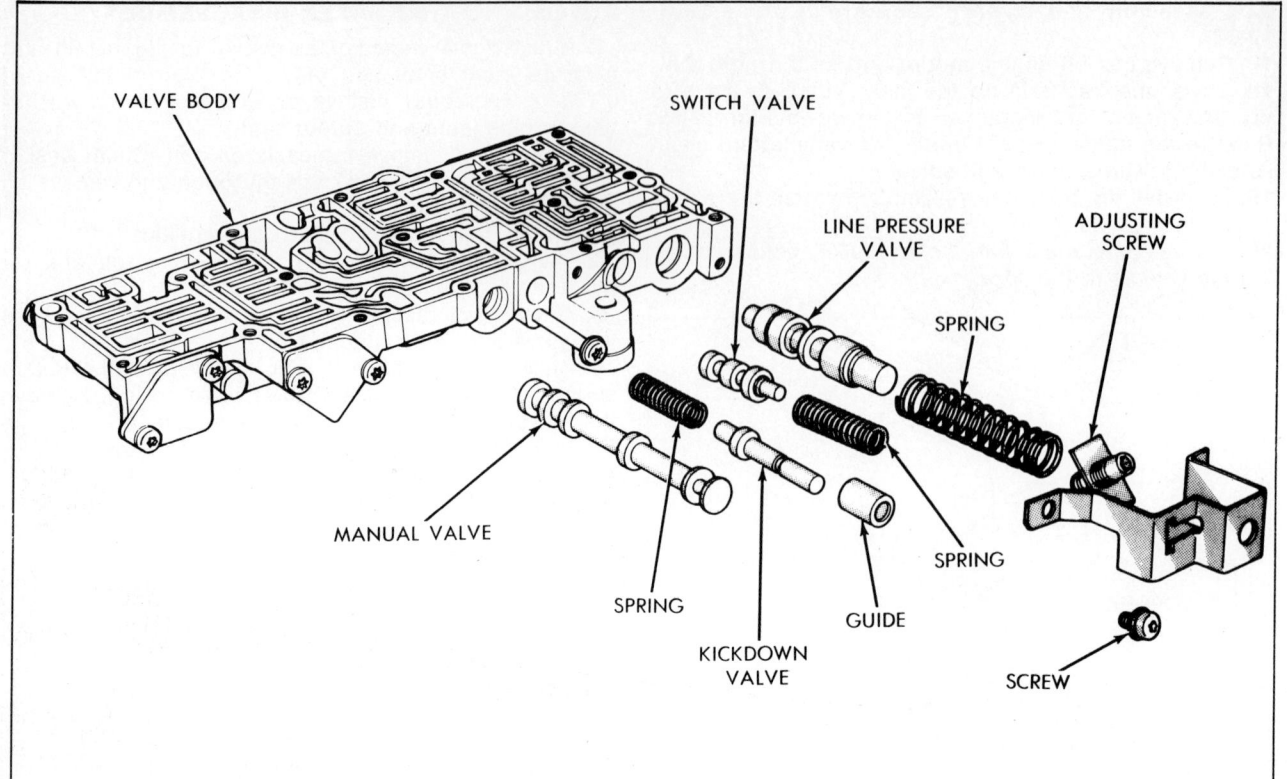

VALVE BODY

SWITCH VALVE

LINE PRESSURE VALVE

ADJUSTING SCREW

SPRING

MANUAL VALVE

SPRING

KICKDOWN VALVE

GUIDE

SPRING

SCREW

FIG. 12-88   PRESSURE REGULATORS & MANUAL CONTROLS

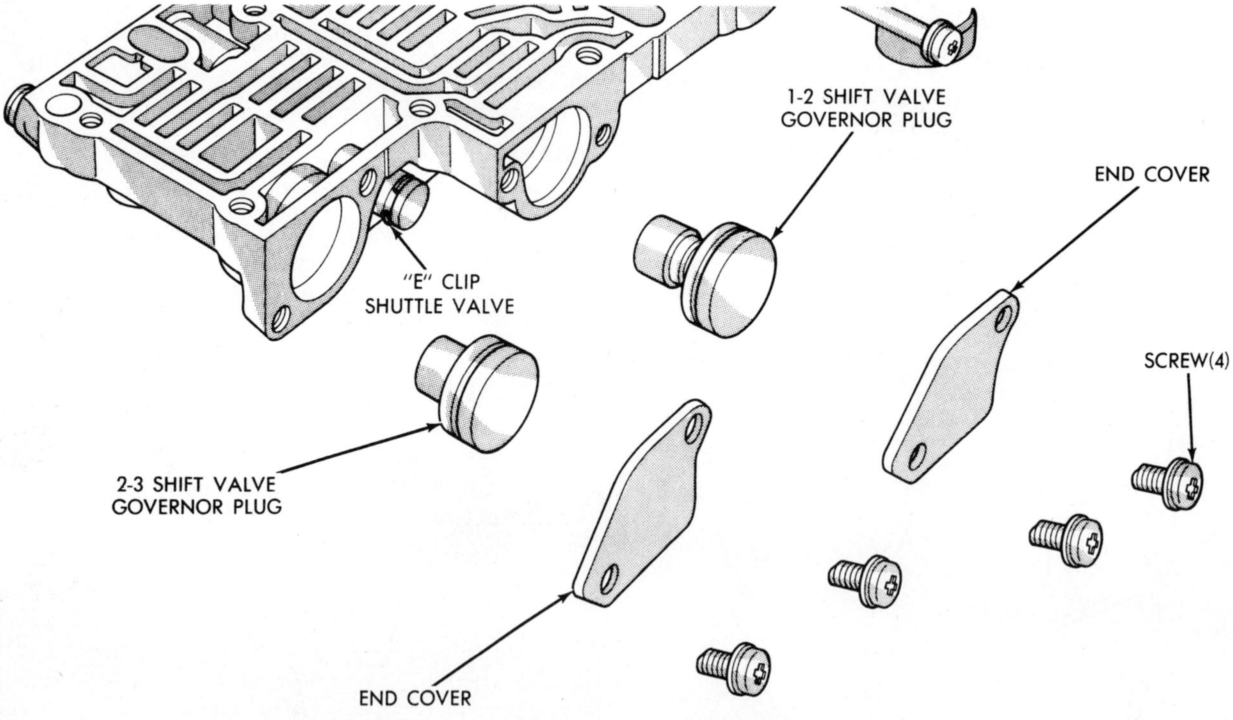

1-2 SHIFT VALVE GOVERNOR PLUG

END COVER

SCREW(4)

"E" CLIP SHUTTLE VALVE

2-3 SHIFT VALVE GOVERNOR PLUG

END COVER

FIG. 12-89   GOVERNOR PLUGS

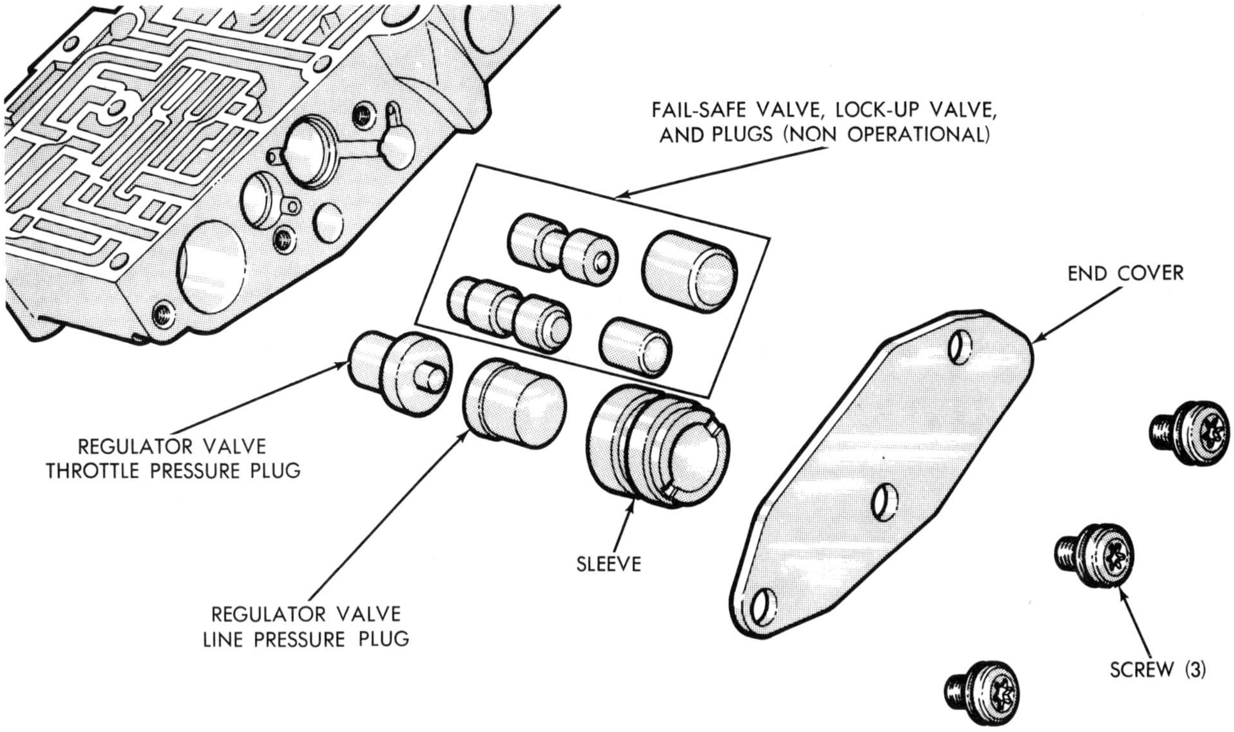

FAIL-SAFE VALVE, LOCK-UP VALVE,
AND PLUGS (NON OPERATIONAL)

END COVER

REGULATOR VALVE
THROTTLE PRESSURE PLUG

SLEEVE

SCREW (3)

REGULATOR VALVE
LINE PRESSURE PLUG

FIG. 12-90   PRESSURE REGULATOR VALVE PLUGS

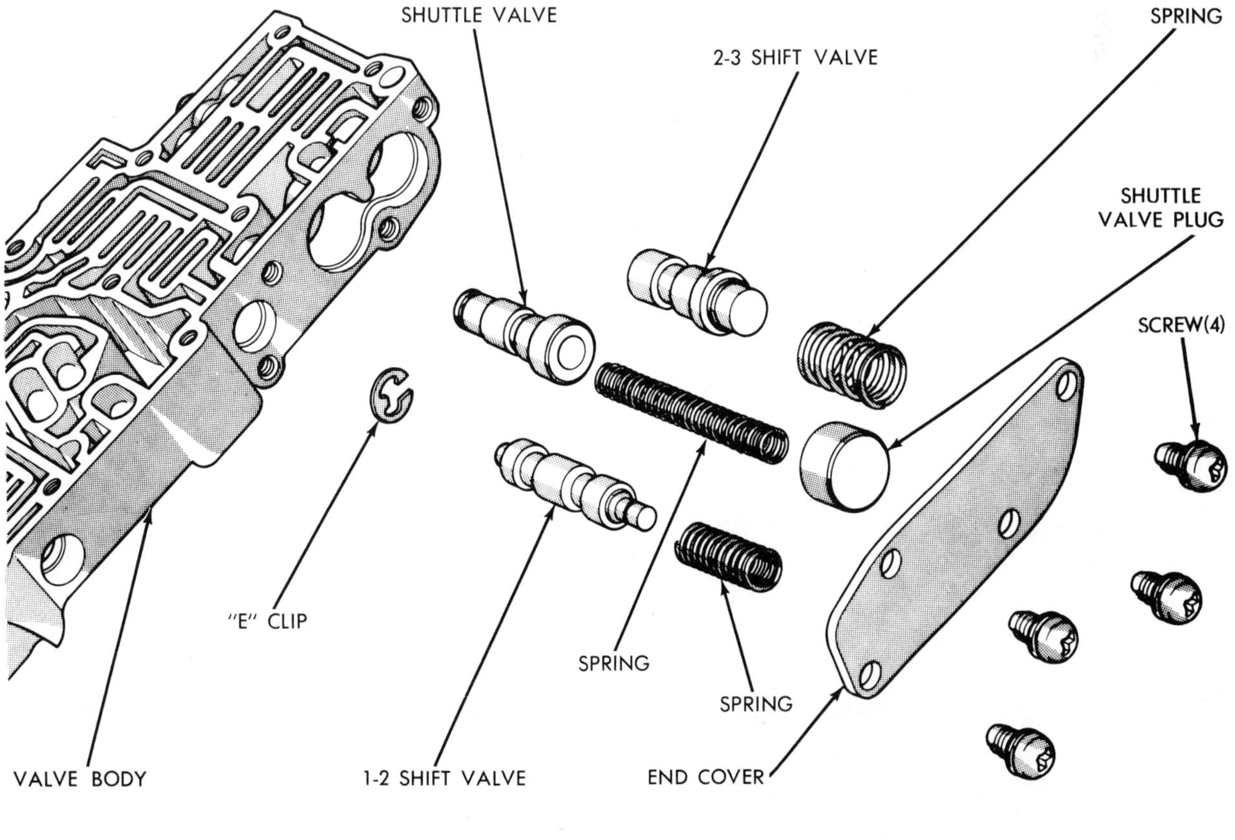

SHUTTLE VALVE

2-3 SHIFT VALVE

SPRING

SHUTTLE
VALVE PLUG

SCREW(4)

"E" CLIP

SPRING

SPRING

VALVE BODY

1-2 SHIFT VALVE

END COVER

FIG. 12-91   SHIFT VALVES & SHUTTLE VALVE

the clearances are within specifications **(see 12-52)**, reattach the reaction shaft to the pump housing and torque the bolts to 250 in.-lbs.

4. Pry the waved snap ring from the front clutch and remove the thick steel plate, two driving discs and three clutch plates.

5. Attach a spring compressor and tighten to compress the clutch return spring while removing the snap ring. Release the compressor and remove the spring retainer, return spring and clutch piston.

6. Replace the oil seals on the piston and clutch retainer shaft, then reinstall piston, spring and retainer.

7. Attach the spring compressor and tighten to compress the return spring while installing the snap ring. Remove the compressor and install the clutch plates and discs as shown in **Fig. 12-94.**

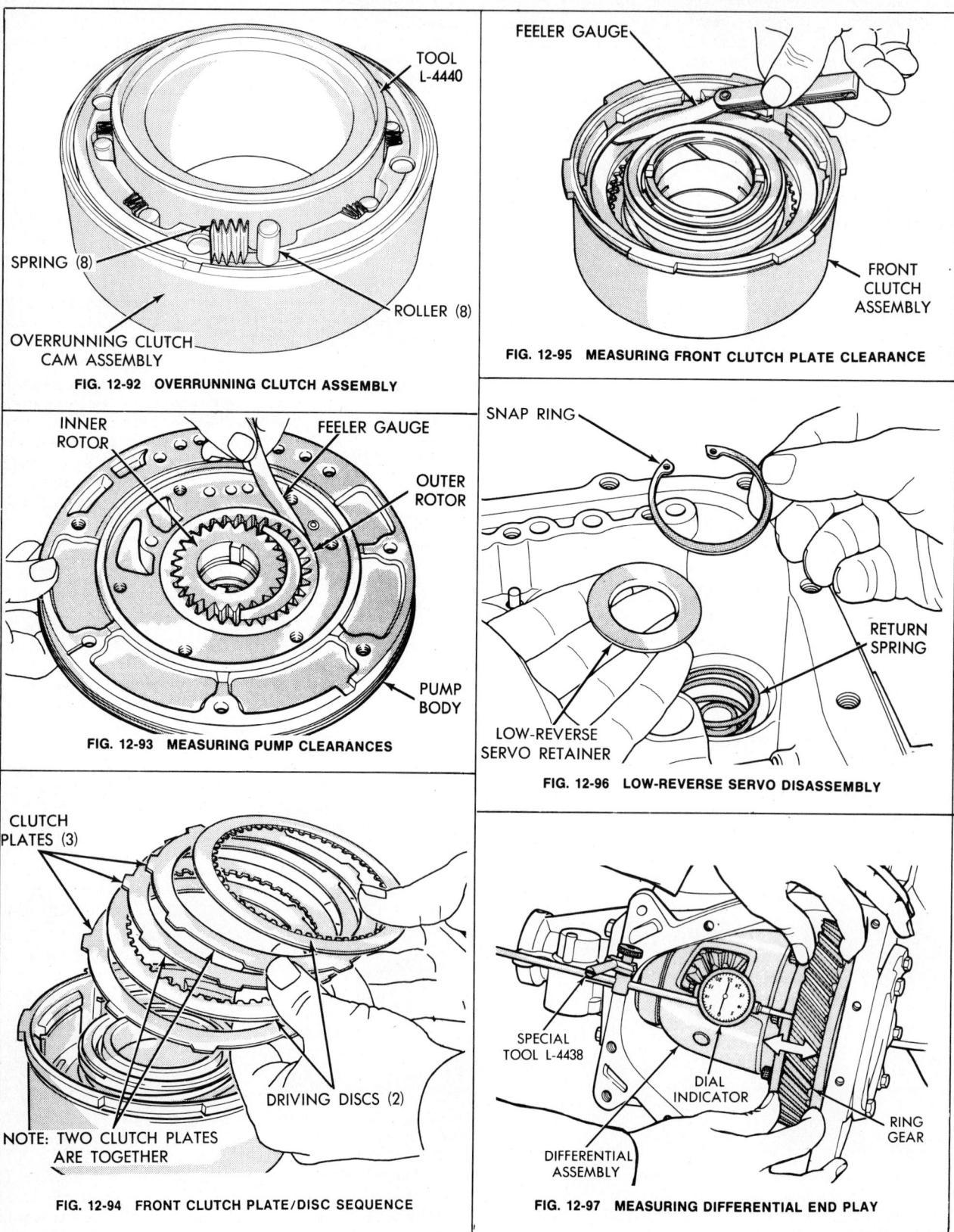

FIG. 12-92 OVERRUNNING CLUTCH ASSEMBLY

FIG. 12-95 MEASURING FRONT CLUTCH PLATE CLEARANCE

FIG. 12-93 MEASURING PUMP CLEARANCES

FIG. 12-96 LOW-REVERSE SERVO DISASSEMBLY

FIG. 12-94 FRONT CLUTCH PLATE/DISC SEQUENCE

FIG. 12-97 MEASURING DIFFERENTIAL END PLAY

8. Measure the front clutch plate clearance as shown in **Fig. 12-95.**

9. Repeat Steps 4-8 with the rear clutch. Components are essentially the same, but differ slightly in size and appearance. The clutch piston is retained by a large waved snap ring which is pried out of the housing with a screwdriver instead of using a spring compressor and snap ring pliers.

10. Remove the snap ring and No. 4 thrust washer from the front planetary gear, then separate the annulus gear from the planetary assembly. The No. 5 thrust washer is located between the two units.

11. Pry the snap ring from the annulus gear and remove the gear support. Inspect all gears and reassemble the planetary and annulus gears with the No. 5 thrust washer between them.

12. Compress the low-reverse servo snap ring and remove it with the servo retainer, return spring and servo assembly **(Fig. 12-96).** Replace the piston lip seal and reassemble the servo.

13. Repeat Step 12 with the accumulator. Replace the accumulator plate and piston seal rings and reassemble the accumulator.

LIMITED SLIP DIFFERENTIAL

TYPE	SERVICE Replace	Repair
GENERAL MOTORS		
Buick Positive Traction (cone)	X	
Buick Positive Traction (disc)		X
Cadillac Controlled Differential	X	
Chevrolet Positraction (Borg-Warner)	X 1	
Chevrolet Positraction (Chevrolet)		X
Chevrolet Positraction (Dana)		X
Chevrolet Positraction (Eaton)		X
Oldsmobile Anti-Spin (cone)	X 2	
Oldsmobile Anti-Spin (disc)		X
Pontiac Safe-T-Track (C-type)	X	
Pontiac Safe-T-Track (non-C-type)		X
FORD MOTOR COMPANY		
Equa-Lok		X
Borg-Warner Traction-Lok		X
CHRYSLER SURE-GRIP	X	
AMERICAN MOTORS		
Twin-Grip (7 9/16-in. axle)	X	
Twin-Grip (8 7/8-in. axle)		X

1 Replace with a Chevrolet or Eaton model.
2 Replace with a disc type.

FIG. 12-99 LIMITED SLIP DIFFERENTIALS

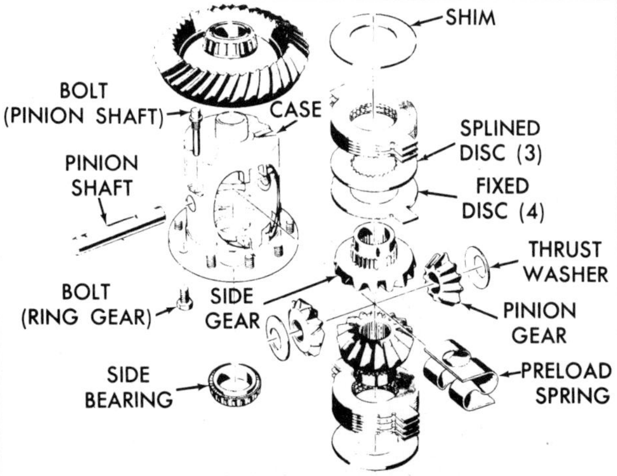

FIG. 12-98 CHEVROLET POSITRACTION (DISC TYPE)

14. Repeat Step 12 with the kickdown servo. The snap ring is pried out with a screwdriver instead of using snap ring pliers. Replace the piston rod guide and piston seals and reassemble the servo.

15. Removal and replacement of the transfer and output shafts and gears requires the use of several special tools and disassembly should not be attempted without them. Remove the rear cover and visually inspect the gear/bearing condition. If further disassembly is indicated, take the unit to a properly equipped repair shop. Reinstall the rear cover after applying a thin coat of room temperature vulcanizing gasket sealer to the cover and then torque the cover screws to 165 in.-lbs.

DIFFERENTIAL OVERHAUL

1. Pry out and discard the extension housing oil seal.
2. Unbolt and remove the differential cover.
3. Remove the six differential bearing retainer bolts and rotate the retainer to remove it.
4. Remove the four extension housing bolts and rotate the housing to remove it from the case. Hold the differential assembly while removing the extension housing to prevent it from falling out.
5. Inspect the differential bearings, pinion and side gears. Bearing and cup replacement requires the use of special tools and should be done by a properly equipped repair shop.
6. To replace the ring gear, remove the eight attaching bolts, tap off the old gear and tap on the new one. Replace attaching bolts and torque each to 70 ft. lbs.
7. Replace the differential in the case, install the extension housing and bearing retainer. Torque all bolts to 250 in.-lbs. Install new extension housing oil seal.
8. Install a dial indicator as shown in **Fig. 12-97** and check end play by moving ring gear back and forth.
9. Coat the cover gasket on both sides with room temperature vulcanizing gasket sealer and install the cover, torquing the bolts to 165 in.-lbs.

AUTOMATIC TRANSAXLE ASSEMBLY

Reverse Steps 1-16 under "Automatic Transaxle Disassembly" and measure the input shaft end play as shown in **Fig. 12-86.** End play should range between 0.030 and 0.106-in.

LIMITED SLIP DIFFERENTIALS

The limited slip differential is used to provide more driving force to the wheel with traction when one wheel starts to spin. Two basic types are used on American cars, a clutch plate and a clutch cone design, with both performing the same function. Limited-slip differential cases are similar to those used with standard differential design, except for a large internal recess beside the side gears, where the clutch pack or cone is located **(Fig. 12-98).**

As shown in **Fig. 12-99,** many limited slip differentials are non-repairable, and are replaced as complete assemblies when they malfunction. Overhaul procedures on repairable limited slip differentials are similar to those of standard differential units, except that the disc/cone assembly is retained by a form of preload spring. When servicing a rear axle containing a limited slip differential, both wheels should be raised off the ground if the engine is to be started. The limited-slip differential is just the opposite of the conventional unit in that engine torque is transferred to the wheel with the most traction. If one wheel is contacting the ground and the other is elevated, engine torque is sent to the contacting wheel, thereby pulling the car off the jack and causing possible injury and damage.

INDEX

BRAKING SYSTEMS

The automotive hydraulic braking system is simply a way in which friction can be applied to stop, slow or hold the car by changing motion to heat, either through drum or disc surfaces. All cars discussed in this volume are equipped with a split or dual brake system as a safety factor; if one should fail, the other will provide an adequate means of stopping the car. The typical drum brake system consists of:

1. Hydraulic master cylinder.
2. Slave or wheel cylinder at each wheel.
3. Brake drum and a pair of lined brake shoes at each wheel.
4. Brake distribution valve, pressure differential valve and warning lamp switch.
5. System of brake line tubing and hoses to carry the hydraulic fluid.

The typical disc brake system consists of:

1. Hydraulic master cylinder.
2. Brake disc at each wheel hub.
3. Brake caliper and a pair of lined pads at each wheel.
4. Metering valve, proportioner and system-failure warning switch, sometimes called a combination switch or valve.
5. System of brake line tubing and hoses to carry the hydraulic fluid.

HYDRAULIC BRAKE OPERATION

Filled with hydraulic fluid, the master cylinder has a piston at what might be called bottom dead center, with the connecting rod linked to the brake pedal (**Fig. 13-1**). Hydraulic lines connect this cylinder with the slave cylinders located at each wheel. As the brake pedal is depressed, the master cylinder piston pushes the fluid through the lines to each slave or wheel cylinder, causing the cylinder pistons to push outward and force the brake shoes against the drum. Since this pressure is equal to all wheel cylinders, effective braking pressure cannot be applied to any one wheel until all the shoes on the wheels are in contact with their respective drums, providing a self-equalizing effect.

Drum brake systems are designed to carry a little pressure in the line when the brakes are not being used. This pressure is maintained by the check valve, sometimes called a residual pressure valve. The large spring in the master cylinder activates it and keeps light pressure in the lines to hold the wheel cylinder pistons out against the shoe tabs. Without this residual pressure, the pistons could vibrate away from the shoes, causing low pedal and a lack of brakes.

Disc brakes *do not* use the check valve because their seals fit much tighter, keeping the pistons from vibrating away from the disc. With a disc/drum combination system, a check valve is necessary in the line to the drum brakes, but not to the disc brakes. In current disc/drum systems, the check valves are located in the master cylinder outlet where the drum brake line attaches.

In addition to properly conditioned hydraulics (no air in the system), the efficiency of any braking system depends upon: 1) proper lining material of adequate thickness, 2) internally smooth and round brake drum (or disc) surfaces, 3) maximum contact between the lining area and drum (or disc) surface, and 4) proper cooling. Besides the force exerted on the shoes by the mechanical and hydraulic leverage, additional pressure between shoes and drum is achieved by self-energizing, where the actual contact of the shoe with the drum is used to apply additional force to the drum.

As the brakes are applied, the friction between lining and drum wants to force the shoes around in the direction of drum rotation. The location of the shoe pivot point determines whether the shoe is forced against the drum (self-energizing) or away from the drum by the rotation of the drum itself. Current brake designs get additional power by linking the two shoes together so that not only are both shoes self-energizing, but the primary shoe exerts pressure on the secondary shoe, pushing the secondary shoe into the drums that much harder. This is known as "servo" action.

A self-adjusting feature eliminates the need for a periodic "setting up the shoes" service procedure. Self-adjusting designs simply use the rotating shoe action in reverse to operate a lever which picks up an extra notch on the star-wheel adjuster nut, if wear allows the shoes to move far enough for the lever to engage. Self-adjusters work only when the car is moving backward with the brakes applied, and *do not* compensate for drum expansion caused by heat. This means that backing up with hot brakes applied can cause the automatic adjuster mechanism to move the rear shoes into a position where they will drag when the drums cool off.

HYDRAULIC SYSTEM SERVICE

MASTER CYLINDERS (FIG. 13-2)

The dual or tandem master cylinders currently in use contain split reservoirs and pressure chambers to sepa-

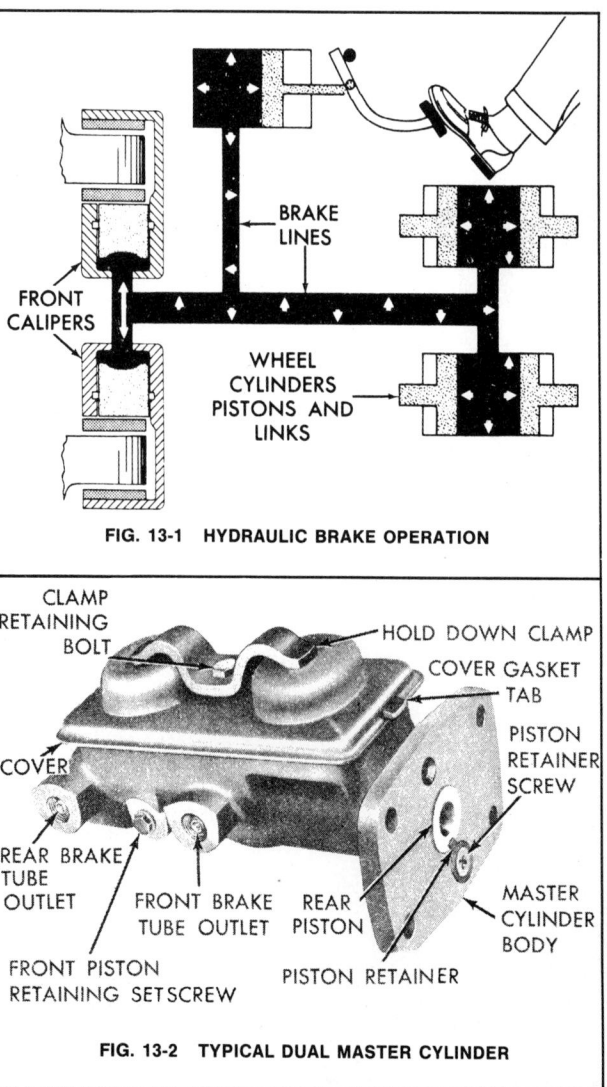

FIG. 13-1 HYDRAULIC BRAKE OPERATION

FIG. 13-2 TYPICAL DUAL MASTER CYLINDER

DRUM BRAKE DIAGNOSIS

CONDITION	CORRECTION	CONDITION	CORRECTION
PEDAL GOES TO FLOOR		(c) Brake shoe return spring weak or broken.	(c) Replace with new shoe return spring.
(a) Fluid level low in reservoir.	(a) Fill and bleed master cylinder.	(d) Brake pedal binds.	(d) Free pedal and lubricate linkage.
(b) Air in hydraulic system.	(b) Fill and bleed system.	(e) Master cylinder cup sticks.	(e) Recondition master cylinder.
(c) Brakes improperly adjusted.	(c) Repair or replace self-adjuster.	(f) Master cylinder relief port is obstructed.	(f) Use compressed air to blow out relief port.
(d) Wheel cylinders leaking.	(d) Recondition or replace wheel cylinder. It may be necessary to replace brake shoes.	(g) Brake drum is bent or out-of-round.	(g) Reface or replace drum.
(e) Loose or broken brake lines.	(e) Tighten all brake fittings or replace brake line.	(h) Stop light switch needs adjustment.	(h) Adjust switch to allow for full return of pedal.
(f) Worn or leaking master cylinder.	(f) Recondition or replace master cylinder and bleed system.	**HARD PEDAL**	
(g) Brake lining excessively worn.	(g) Reline and adjust brakes.	(a) Brake booster is not working.	(a) Replace unit.
BRAKE PEDAL IS SPONGY		(b) Restriction in brake line or hose.	(b) Clean out or replace brake line or hose.
(a) Air in hydraulic system.	(a) Fill master cylinder and bleed hydraulic system.	(c) Frozen brake pedal linkage.	(c) Free and lubricate linkage.
(b) Contaminated or incorrect brake fluid.	(b) Drain, flush and refill with proper brake fluid.	**WHEEL LOCKS**	
(c) Brake drums excessively worn or cracked.	(c) Replace drums.	(a) Brake lining is contaminated with oil or grease.	(a) Reline all brakes.
BRAKES PULL WHEN APPLIED		(b) Brake lining is loose or torn.	(b) Replace damaged linings.
(a) Contaminated lining.	(a) Replace with new lining of original quality.	(c) Wheel cylinder cups stick.	(c) Recondition or replace wheel cylinders.
(b) Front end needs alignment.	(b) Check and align front end.	(d) Wheel bearings out of adjustment.	(d) Clean, pack and adjust wheel bearings to specs.
(c) Brake adjustment incorrect.	(c) Adjust brakes and check fluid.	**BRAKES FADE**	
(d) Unmatched brake linings.	(d) Match primary and secondary linings with same type on all wheels.	(a) Use of inferior linings.	(a) Replace with original quality linings.
(e) Brake shoes are distorted.	(e) Replace shoes.	(b) Brake drums overheat.	(b) Check for dragging brakes.
(f) Restriction in brake hose or line.	(f) Locate and replace plugged hose or brake line.	(c) Contaminated or incorrect brake fluid.	(c) Drain, flush, refill and bleed hydraulic brake system.
(g) Rear spring broken.	(g) Replace.	(d) Saturated brake lining.	(d) Reline all brakes.
BRAKES SQUEAL OR CHIRP		**SURGE BELOW 15 MPH**	
(a) Brake lining glazed or saturated.	(a) Cam grind (glazed only) or replace lining.	(a) Rear brake drum bent or out-of-round.	(a) Reface or replace drum.
(b) Brake shoe retaining spring weak or broken.	(b) Replace with new retaining spring.	**CHATTER FROM 40 TO 80 MPH**	
(c) Brake shoe return spring weak or broken.	(c) Replace with new return spring.	(a) Front brake drum bent or out-of-round.	(a) Reface or replace drum.
(d) Brake shoes are distorted.	(d) Replace shoes.	**SHOE KNOCK**	
(e) Support plate is bent.	(e) Replace with new support plate.	(a) Machine grooves in contact face of brake drum.	(a) Sand, reface or replace brake drum.
(f) Dust in brakes or scored brake drums.	(f) Blow out brake assembly with compressed air and reface drums—machine, do not grind.	(b) Hold-down springs are weak.	(b) Replace with new springs.
(g) Drum or eccentric axle flange pilot out-of-round.	(g) Remove and replace—lubricate support plate contact areas.	**BRAKES DO NOT SELF-ADJUST**	
BRAKES DRAG		(a) Adjuster screw is frozen in thread.	(a) Clean and free all thread areas.
(a) Wheel or parking brake adjustment incorrect.	(a) Adjust brakes and check fluid level.	(b) Adjuster screw is corroded at thrust washer.	(b) Clean threads and replace thrust washer.
(b) Parking brake engaged.	(b) Release parking brake.	(c) Adjuster lever does not engage star wheel properly.	(c) Repair, free up or replace adjuster.
		(d) Adjuster incorrectly installed.	(d) Check and reinstall correctly.

rate front and rear brake systems. Breather and compensating ports allow hydraulic fluid to pass between each pressure chamber and its fluid reservoir under certain operation conditions. A vented cover and flexible diaphragm at the top of the reservoirs prevent contamination from reaching the fluid, yet allow the fluid to expand or contract without direct venting. The master cylinder may or may not have a bleed screw on its outlet flange; if present, this permits bleeding of the brakes (to remove any air from the hydraulic fluid) without disturbing the wheel cylinders.

Starting with the 1978 model year, some GM and Chrysler Corporation cars use a two-piece aluminum master cylinder/molded plastic fluid reservoir assembly. Operation of the master cylinder remains unchanged, but the see-thru reservoir is secured to the master cylinder housing with two rubber grommets which function as seal/retainers. The reservoir should not be removed unless it is damaged or the grommets are leaking. A piston retainer stop pin is used instead of the piston stopscrew **(Fig. 13-3).** Since aluminum is a soft metal and corrosion-prone, the master cylinder body is anodized during manufacture to make its bore resistant to wear and corrosion. *Do not* attempt to hone the bore of an aluminum master cylinder housing. If scratched or corroded, the housing should be replaced as an assembly.

MASTER CYLINDER SERVICE (Fig. 13-3)

While master cylinders used by different automotive manufacturers differ somewhat in external design, all are serviced by essentially the same procedure:

1. Disconnect and remove the master cylinder from the car, discarding the fluid.

2. Secure the unit in a soft-jaw vise, with its outlets facing upward. Remove the secondary piston stop-

screw from beneath the front fluid reservoir.

3. Unclip the lock ring at the front of the bore, and remove the primary piston assembly.

4. Hold a cloth over the bore opening and remove the secondary piston assembly with compressed air inserted through the stopscrew hole. If compressed air is not available, bend about ¼-in. of the end of a piece of wire into a right angle, hook under the piston edge and withdraw it from the bore.

5. Discard all rubber parts, and clean the metal parts in fresh brake fluid.

6. Check the bore and pistons for wear, damage and proper clearance.

7. If the bore is scored or pitted slightly, it can be honed. Clean the unit thoroughly when honing is completed, and blow out all passages with compressed air.

8. Using all new rubber parts, fit the secondary seals in the front piston flat-end grooves, with their lips facing away from each other.

9. Fit a seal protector and seal on the other end of the piston; seal lip should face outward.

10. Lubricate the seals with clean brake fluid, and fit the front spring and retainer to the piston, with the retainer seating in the seal.

11. Replace the piston assembly, spring-end first, in the cylinder bore, and seat with a small wooden rod.

12. Assemble the piston seals on the rear piston, install the bore spring in the bore and push the piston assembly in after it.

13. Install the lock ring and make certain it seats properly in the bore groove.

14. Replace the stopscrew, and fit a new seal on the hub.

15. Bench-bleed the cylinder, replace it on the car, and then bleed the wheel cylinders.

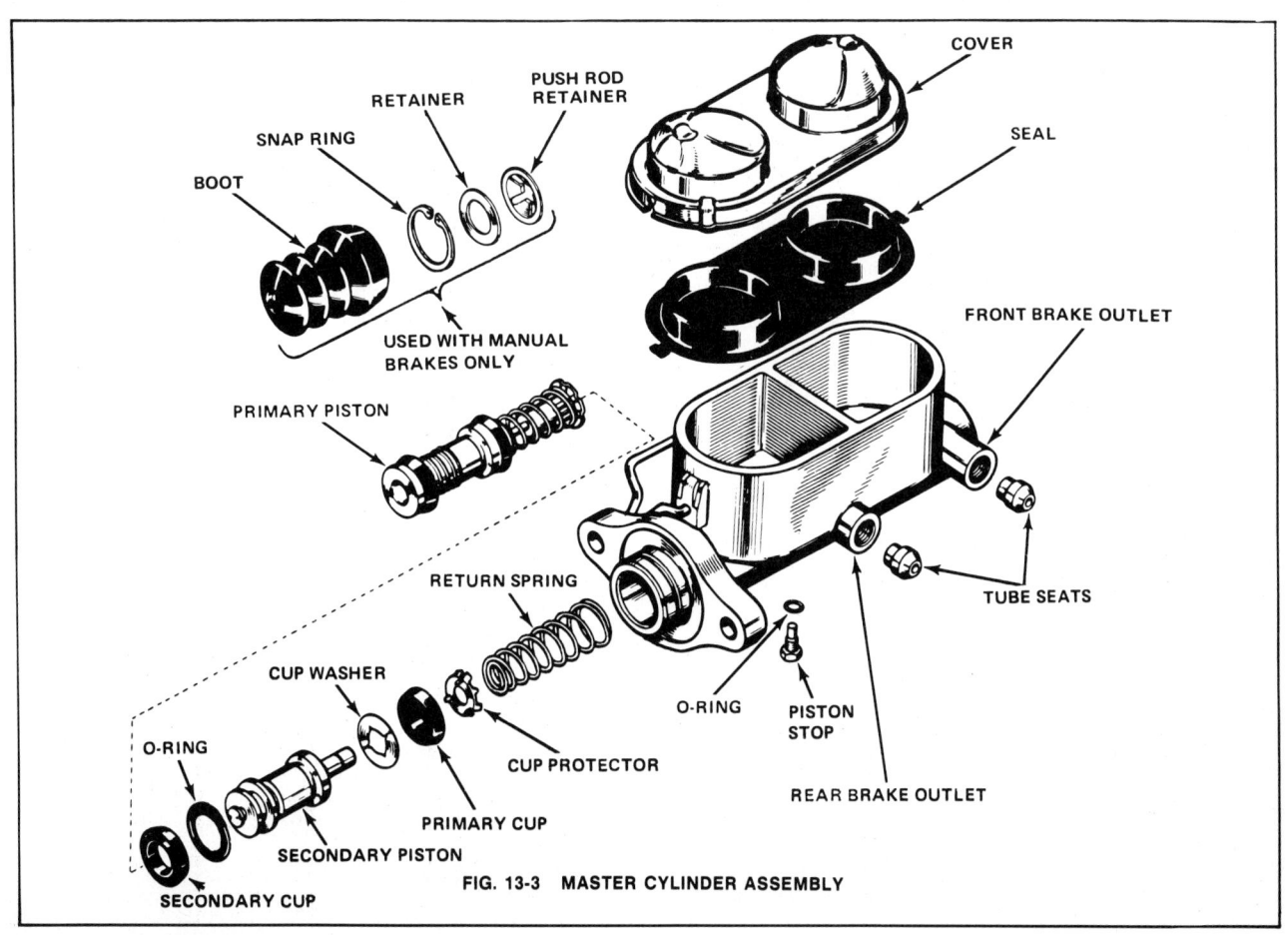

FIG. 13-3   MASTER CYLINDER ASSEMBLY

WHEEL CYLINDER SERVICE (Fig. 13-4)

Like master cylinders, wheel cylinders vary slightly in external shape and design, but all are serviced by essentially the same procedure:

1. Remove the brake drum and brake shoes from the wheel to be serviced.

2. Clean the backing plate and wheel cylinder with a brush or compressed air.

3. Disconnect the brake line from the cylinder, and wrap a clean, lint-free cloth around the end of the line to prevent contamination.

4. Unscrew the cylinder attaching bolts, and remove the cylinder from the backing plate.

5. Pull the cylinder end boots off with pliers, and discard.

6. Remove the pistons, expanders and spring, and discard the seal cups.

7. Check the wheel cylinder bore and pistons for wear or damage. Pistons cannot be reconditioned and should be replaced if their condition is questionable or if new pistons are contained in the rebuild kit used.

8. If the cylinder bore is scored or pitted slightly, it can be honed, but the cylinder should be replaced if corroded. Stained areas should be cleaned with crocus cloth. Support the cloth on a finger, and rotate the cylinder—*do not* slide it back and forth.

9. Wash all metal parts and the cylinder in clean brake fluid.

DISC BRAKE DIAGNOSIS

CONDITION	CORRECTION
PEDAL TRAVEL IS EXCESSIVE	
(a) Air leak or insufficient fluid in hydraulic system or caliper.	(a) Check system for leaks and bleed.
(b) Shoe and lining assembly warped or excessively tapered.	(b) Install new shoe and linings.
(c) Disc runout excessive.	(c) Check disc for runout with dial indicator. Install a new or refinished disc.
(d) Rear brake needs adjustment.	(d) Adjust and check rear brakes.
(e) Wheel bearing adjustment is too loose.	(e) Readjust wheel bearing to specified torque.
(f) Caliper piston seal damaged.	(f) Install new piston seal.
(g) Contaminated or incorrect brake fluid.	(g) Drain and replace with correct fluid.
(h) Power brake unit malfunction.	(h) Replace unit.
BRAKE CHATTER	
(a) Braking disc has excessive thickness variation.	(a) Check disc for thickness variation with a micrometer.
(b) Lateral runout of braking disc is excessive.	(b) Check disc for lateral runout with a dial indicator; replace with new or refaced disc.
(c) Front bearing clearance is too great.	(c) Readjust wheel bearings to specified torque.
REQUIRES EXCESSIVE PEDAL EFFORT	
(a) Brake fluid, oil or grease on linings.	(a) Replace with new linings.
(b) Incorrect or faulty lining.	(b) Remove and replace lining with original quality lining.
(c) Seized or frozen piston(s).	(c) Disassemble caliper and free up piston(s).
(d) Power brake malfunction.	(d) Replace unit.
PULL, GRABBING OR UNEVEN BRAKING ACTION	
(a) Brake fluid, oil or grease on linings.	(a) Replace with new linings.
(b) Linings unmatched.	(b) Replace with correct lining.
(c) Seized or frozen piston(s).	(c) Disassemble caliper and free up piston(s).
(d) Tire pressure insufficient.	(d) Check and inflate tires to recommended pressures.

CONDITION	CORRECTION
(e) Front end needs alignment.	(e) Check and align front end to specs.
(f) Rear spring broken.	(f) Replace.
(g) Restriction in hose or line.	(g) Check hoses and lines and replace.
(h) Caliper incorrectly aligned with braking disc.	(h) Check alignment and remove caliper if necessary to correct alignment when replacing.
BRAKE RATTLE AT LOW SPEEDS ON ROUGH ROADS	
(a) Inboard shoe anti-rattle spring either missing or not properly positioned.	(a) Install new anti-rattle spring or position properly.
(b) Clearance between shoe and caliper is too great.	(b) Replace shoe and lining assemblies.
SCRAPING	
(a) Mounting bolts are too long.	(a) Replace with mounting bolts of correct length.
(b) Wheel bearings are loose.	(b) Readjust wheel bearings to correct specs.
(c) Splash shield is deformed and rubs on rotor.	(c) Bend shield to provide proper clearance.
FRONT BRAKES HEAT UP AND FAIL TO RELEASE	
(a) Pedal linkage sticks.	(a) Free sticking linkage and lubricate.
(b) Seized or frozen piston(s).	(b) Disassemble caliper and free piston(s).
(c) Power brake unit malfunction.	(c) Replace unit.
LEAKING WHEEL CYLINDER	
(a) Worn or damaged caliper piston seal.	(a) Remove and disassemble caliper; install new seal.
(b) Scoring or corrosion on surface of cylinder bore.	(b) Remove and disassemble caliper; hone cylinder bore and install new seal.
PEDAL GOES TO FLOOR—NO BRAKING ACTION	
(a) Air in hydraulic system.	(a) Bleed hydraulic system correctly.
(b) Fluid leak past primary cup in master cylinder.	(b) Recondition master cylinder.
(c) Hose or line leak in system.	(c) Check hoses and lines for leak and repair or replace as required.
(d) Rear brakes need adjustment.	(d) Adjust rear brakes.
(e) Bleeder screw open.	(e) Close bleeder screw and bleed entire system.

10. Shake or blow dry; *do not* wipe, because lint may adhere to the cylinder bore surface.

11. Replace the spring expander assembly, and install new cups with the seal lips facing inward.

12. Replace the pistons with their flat surfaces inward, and press new boots in the counterbore by hand.

13. Reattach the wheel cylinder to the brake backing plate, reconnect the brake line, and replace the shoes and drums, engaging the cylinder push rods.

14. Bleed the cylinder.

PROPORTIONING VALVE (Fig. 13-5)

The proportioning valve maintains proper line-pressure ratios between the front and rear brakes. Factory-adjusted, the valve must be replaced with a new unit if defective. Valve fittings are usually identified with an ''R'' to indicate the rear brake connection and/or an ''M'' or ''F'' for the master cylinder line. Where a combination valve is used, it can be identified by an electrical terminal connecting to the instrument-panel warning light. Combination valves are also serviced by replacement instead of repair.

METERING VALVE (Fig. 13-6)

Some cars fitted with front disc brakes use a metering valve in the front hydraulic brake line to prevent pressure build-up during braking and to provide a balanced braking effort during normal stops. If defective, a metering valve is serviced by replacement.

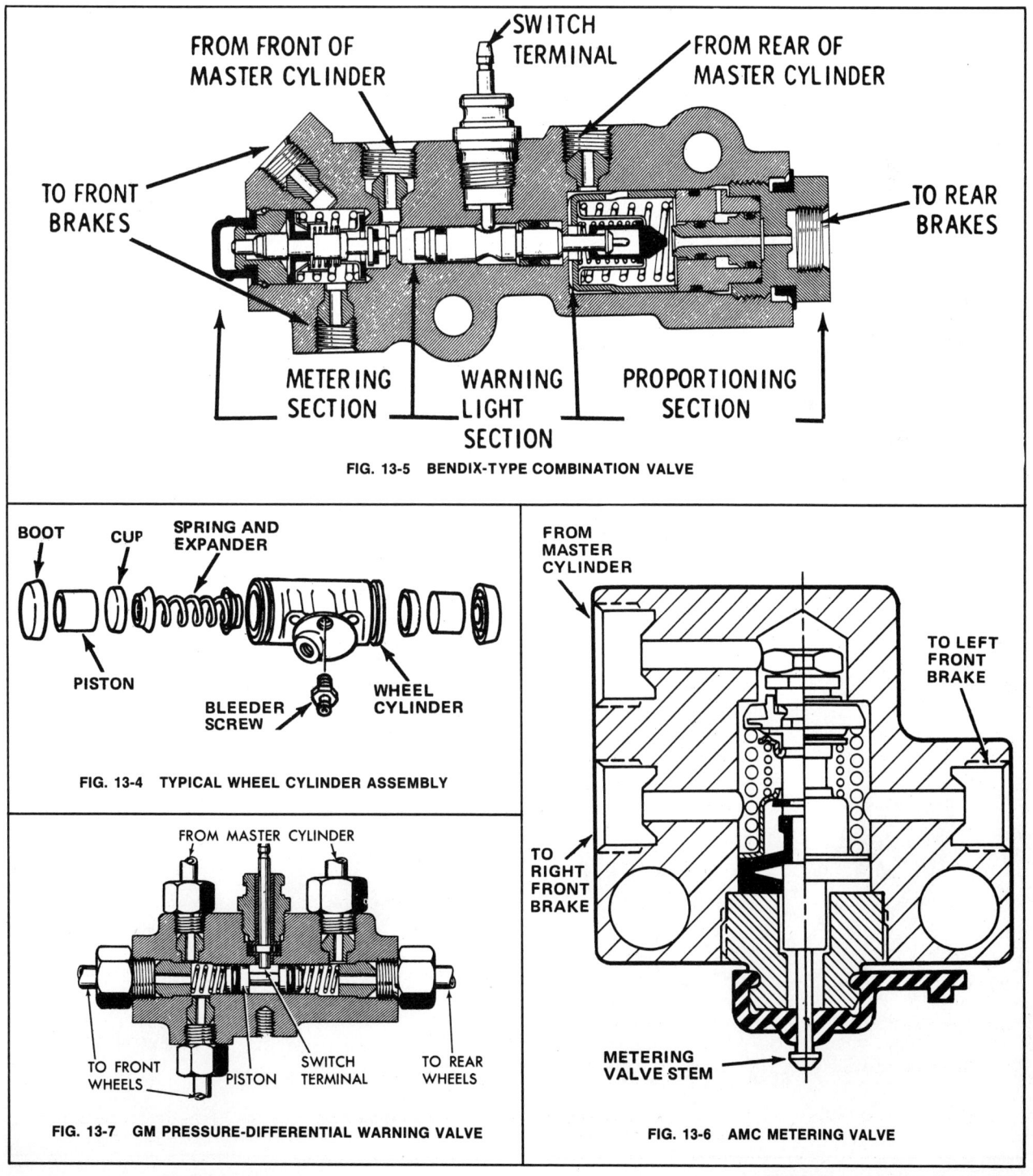

FIG. 13-5   BENDIX-TYPE COMBINATION VALVE

FIG. 13-4   TYPICAL WHEEL CYLINDER ASSEMBLY

FIG. 13-7   GM PRESSURE-DIFFERENTIAL WARNING VALVE

FIG. 13-6   AMC METERING VALVE

PRESSURE-DIFFERENTIAL WARNING VALVE

This unit **(Fig. 13-7)** contains the brake warning-lamp switch mounted in the top center of its housing. A piston assembly directly below it is kept in the center of the bore by equal fluid pressure from the front and rear brake systems. Should a leak develop in either, the fluid pressure decreases and the piston is moved in that direction by the now-unequal pressure. This activates the instrument panel warning lamp. Except for American Motors 1970 (disc/drum) and 1971-76 (drum only) models, all pressure-differential warning valves are self-centering, and the piston will return to its proper position automatically after bleeding the hydraulic system.

Pistons in the valves used on the above-mentioned AMC cars must be centered by the following procedure before bleeding the brakes:

1. Disconnect the wire from the switch terminal, and remove the terminal, plunger spring and plunger. It may be necessary to apply a slight amount of pressure on the brake pedal in order to remove the plunger if warning light was activated by system malfunction.

2. Correct the malfunction and bleed the brakes.

3. Replace the plunger and spring in the valve, with the contact end facing downward.

4. Replace the terminal and reconnect the wire.

If the warning switch is the malfunction, it is serviced by replacement only.

BLEEDING THE HYDRAULIC SYSTEM

The hydraulic system must be bled whenever any work is undertaken on the brake linings, wheel cylinders or master cylinder. Bleeding is necessary to expel any air that may have entered the lines or components. The pressure bleeding method requires specialized equipment, but the gravity method described below is equally satisfactory, although somewhat slower to accomplish. An assistant is required to operate the brake pedal while you bleed each wheel.

Because the front and rear brake systems are separate systems, they are bled separately. *Do not* bleed one front wheel, one rear wheel, etc. Work in a wheel-to-wheel sequence within each system, bleeding the longest line first. *Do not* use the secondary piston stopscrew found on the bottom of some master cylinders to bleed the brakes—loosening or removing this screw can cause damage to the secondary piston or stopscrew.

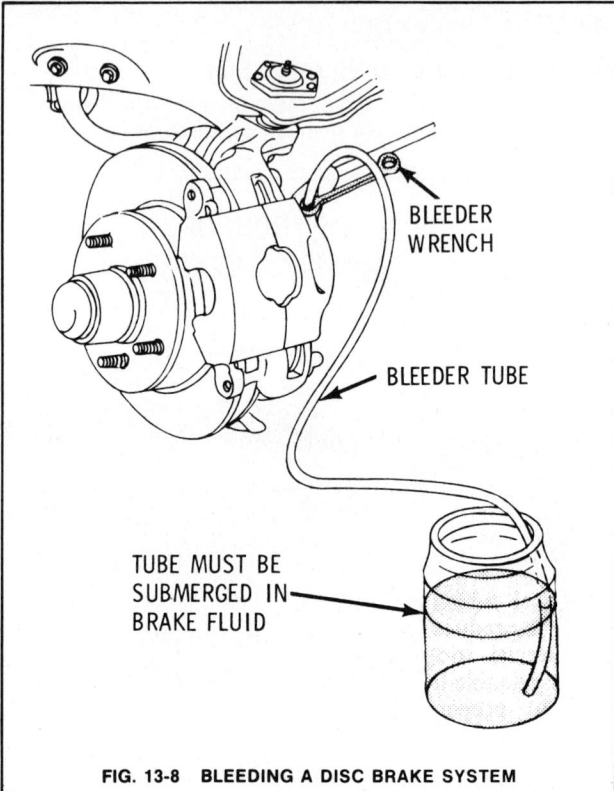

FIG. 13-8 BLEEDING A DISC BRAKE SYSTEM

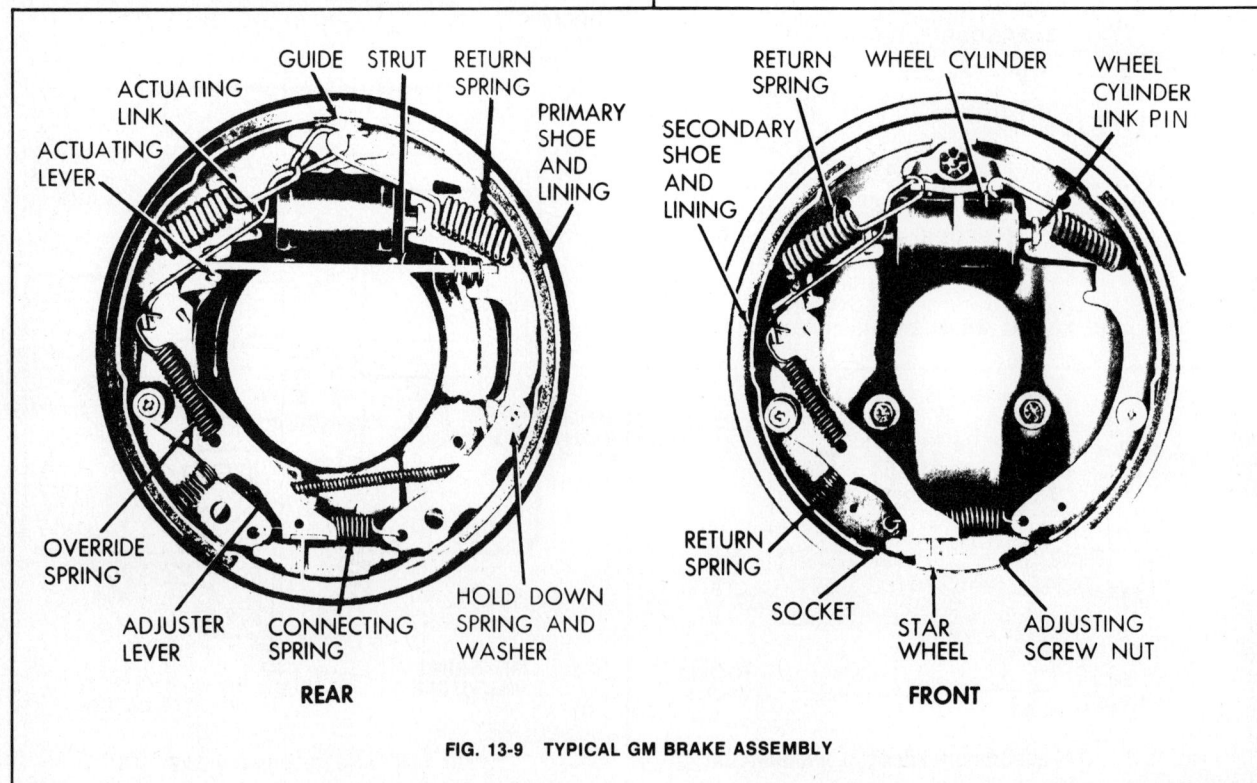

FIG. 13-9 TYPICAL GM BRAKE ASSEMBLY

1. Clean the bleed valve located at each wheel.

2. Fill the master cylinder with fresh brake fluid. *Do not* let the reservoir run dry—watch the level closely while bleeding, and add more fluid if necessary to keep it full.

3. Using a suitable length of tubing, connect one end to the bleed valve at the wheel and place the other end in a container with sufficient fluid to cover the hose end **(Fig. 13-8).**

4. Open the bleed valve as your assistant slowly depresses the brake pedal through its full travel.

5. Close the bleed valve just before the pedal hits bottom, and have the assistant return the pedal slowly to a fully released position.

6. Repeat until the expelled fluid flows in a solid stream without air bubbles.

7. Close the bleed valve tightly, and remove the hose. Repeat the procedure at the wheel cylinder on the opposite side, then bleed the remaining system.

8. After bleeding each wheel cylinder, refill the master cylinder before proceeding to the next wheel, then replace the master cylinder gasket and cover. When all four wheels are bled, bring the master cylinder fluid level to the full position (if marked), or to within ¼-in. of the reservoir tops.

9. On disc brake systems, rotate the disc and depress the brake pedal several times until a normal pedal travel is established. This is necessary to make certain the caliper pistons have returned to their normal unapplied position.

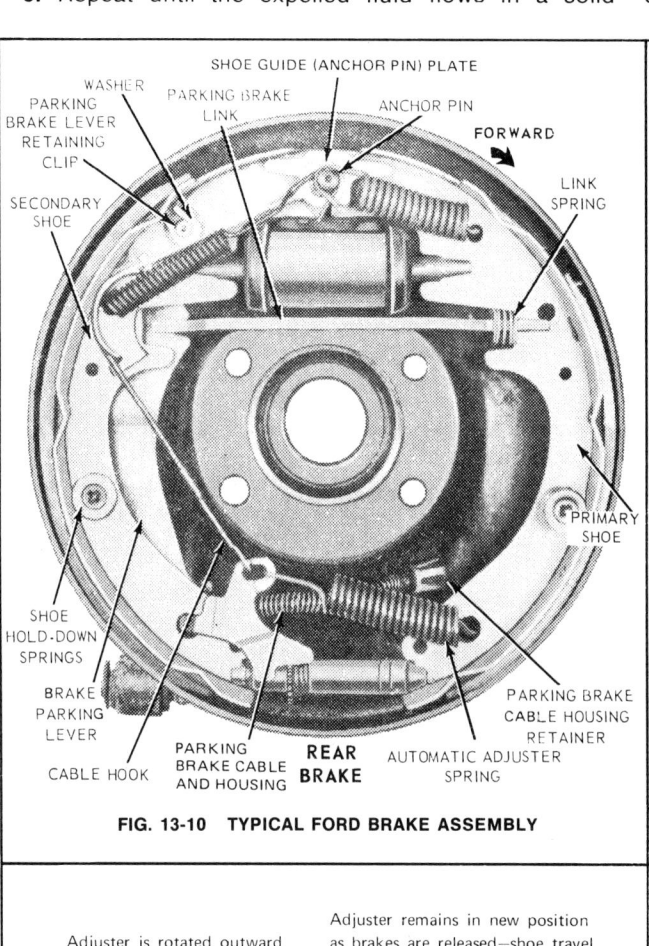

FIG. 13-10 TYPICAL FORD BRAKE ASSEMBLY

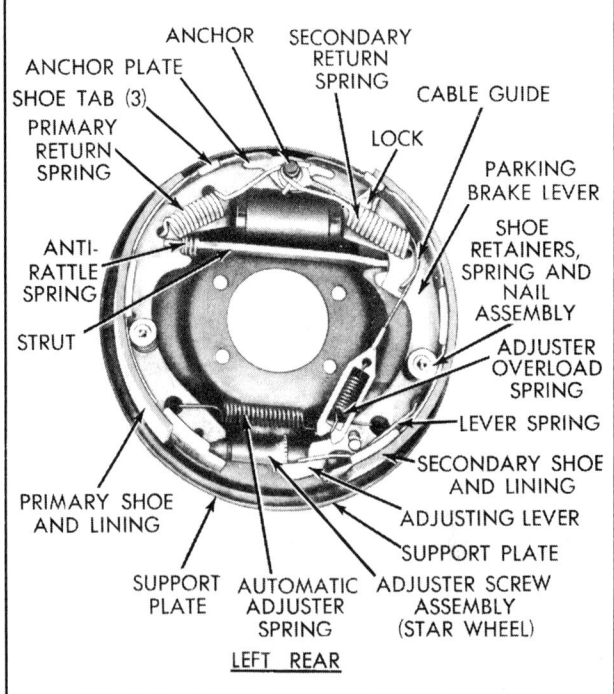

FIG. 13-11 TYPICAL CHRYSLER BRAKE ASSEMBLY

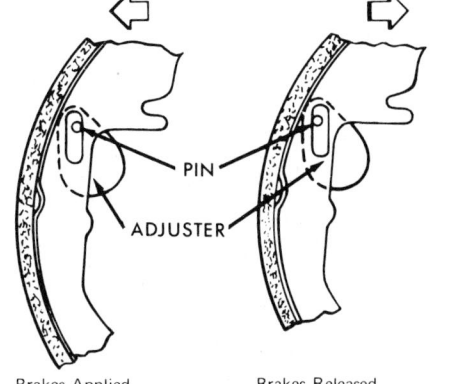

FIG. 13-12 CHEVETTE ADJUSTER OPERATION

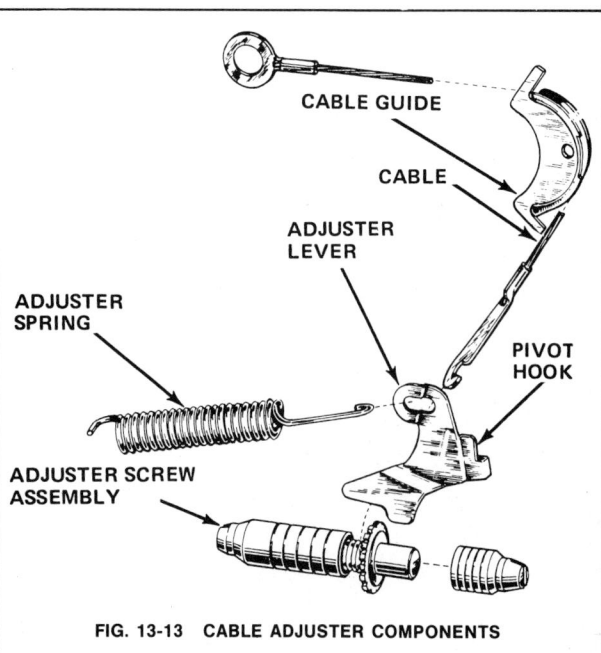

FIG. 13-13 CABLE ADJUSTER COMPONENTS

DRUM BRAKE SERVICE

All American cars equipped with drum brakes use the Bendix duo-servo design **(Figs. 13-9, 13-10 & 13-11)** with a star and screw self-adjusting mechanism, except for the Astre, Monza, Starfire and Vega, which are fitted with an expanding strut adjuster, and the Chevette, which uses a variation of this design providing automatic adjustment **(Fig. 13-12).** A rod-operated lever turns the star wheel on GM car brakes, while AMC, Ford and Chrysler use a cable-operated lever assembly **(Fig. 13-13).** Since this is the only difference in drum brake design, except for size, a generalized adjustment and lining replacement procedure is provided for use with all cars.

STAR AND SCREW SELF-ADJUSTER

Hydraulic drum brakes with star and screw adjusters require adjustment only when the brake linings are changed or removed for wheel cylinder overhaul or replacement. If the self-adjustment mechanism does not operate correctly, the brake drum must be removed and the cause of the malfunction corrected.

BRAKE ADJUSTMENT

1. Remove the rubber plug from the access slot located on the backing plate. On some GM cars, the access slot is located on the front of the drum; on others, there is no access plate, but a lanced area is provided in the backing plate for removal with a hammer and punch. The drum must then be removed, all metal chips blown out with compressed air and a rubber plug installed after adjustment is completed to prevent dirt and water from entering the brakes.

2. Hold the adjuster lever away from the star wheel with a small screwdriver or wire hook. Insert a brake adjustment tool or screwdriver through the access hole and engage the star wheel teeth. Press down on the tool to tighten the brakes (this pushes the star wheel teeth upward) or up on the tool to loosen the brakes—this pushes the star wheel teeth downward **(Figs. 13-14, 13-15 & 13-16).**

3. Once the brake linings are snug against the drum, back the star wheel off just enough to allow the wheel to rotate freely. Count the number of turns as the star wheel is tightened or loosened, because the

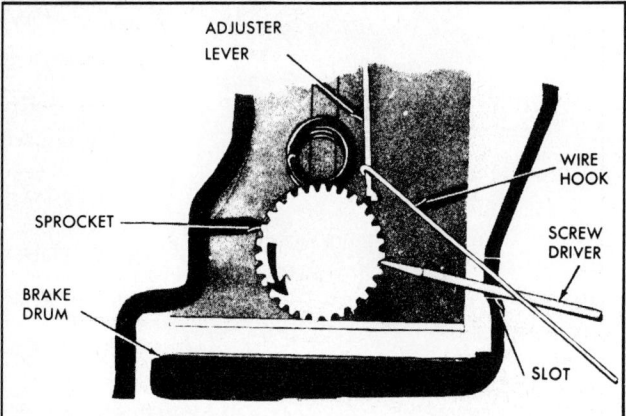

FIG. 13-14 GM BRAKE-DRUM ACCESS HOLE

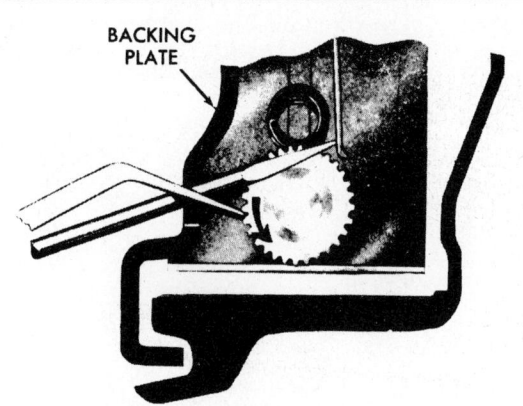

FIG. 13-15 GM FLANGE-PLATE ACCESS HOLE

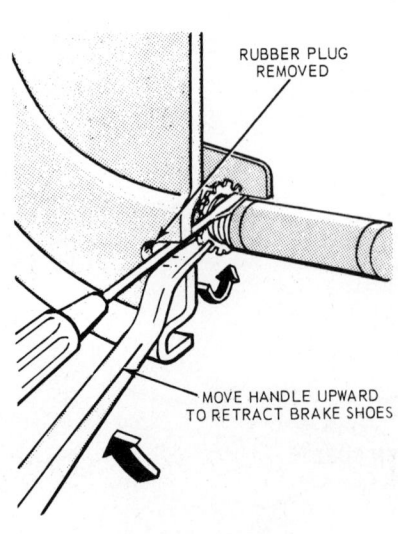

FIG. 13-16 FORD BRAKE ADJUSTMENT

FIG. 13-17 BACKING-PLATE CONTACT SURFACES

other wheel must be adjusted the same number of turns, or the brakes will pull from side to side when applied.

4. When adjustment of all wheels with drum brakes is completed, check the brake pedal travel, and then test-drive the car, making several stops to equalize the wheels.

BRAKE LINING REPLACEMENT

Those unfamiliar with the procedure of removing and replacing drum brake linings will find it useful to work on only one wheel at a time, leaving the other(s) intact to serve as a reference guide.

To Remove

1. Remove the wheel, tire and brake drum from each wheel to be relined.

2. Loosen the parking-brake cable equalizer, if working on the rear brakes. This removes any tension from the cable.

3. Disengage one brake retaining spring by twisting it from the brake-shoe anchor pin with the hollow end of a brake spring tool. If this tool is not available, the spring can be removed with a pair of pliers clamped over the end of the spring and pulled to expand it. Remove the other retaining spring in the same manner. Since the springs are under considerable tension, remove them carefully to prevent possible injury.

4. From behind the backing plate, press the end of one brake hold-down pin while grasping the cup or washer on the front of the plate with a pair of pliers. Pushing inward with the pliers, turn the cup/washer 90° to align its slot with the head of the mounting pin, and remove. Repeat this procedure with the other hold-down pin and cup.

5. This next step differs as follows:
  a) GM—Remove the adjuster link lever, pivot and override spring, then disengage the brake shoes from the wheel cylinder and lift from the backing plate.
  b) Ford/AMC—Lift the brake adjuster lever upward with a screwdriver placed on top of the adjuster screw to provide slack in the adjusting cable. Disconnect the cable from the anchor pin. Separate the brake shoes to disengage them from the wheel cylinder and remove from the backing plate. The adjuster mechanism will come off intact with the shoes. To separate, twist the shoes and the assembly will fall apart.
  c) Chrysler—Remove the cable from the anchor pin, disengage it from the adjuster lever, and remove with the overload spring and cable guide. Disconnect and remove the adjuster lever and return spring. Separate the brake shoes to disengage them from the wheel cylinder and remove from the backing plate.

6. Rear brakes only—Disengage the brake cable from the lever with a pair of pliers.

7. Remove the star wheel adjuster.

To Replace

1. Rear brakes only—Remove the parking brake lever from the old shoe and install on the matching new shoe. Attach the cable to the lever.

2. Lightly coat brake shoe contact points on backing plate with high temperature grease **(Fig. 13-17)**.

3. Install the primary brake shoe on the front of the backing plate and replace the hold-down spring and washer/cup on the mounting pin. Repeat this step with the secondary brake shoe on the other side. Be sure to twist the cup/washer 90° to secure the pin properly.

4. Rear brakes only—Replace the parking brake link between the two shoes.

5. Clean and lightly lubricate the star wheel screw thread. Install it as you put the secondary shoe in place, with the star wheel nearest the secondary shoe and accessible through the backing plate slot.

6. This step differs as follows:
  a) GM—Install the adjuster lever, pivot and override spring as an assembly.
  b) Ford/AMC—Slip the adjuster cable loop over the anchor pin with its crimped side facing toward the backing plate.
  c) Chrysler—Replace the adjuster lever and return spring, then replace the overload spring and cable, with one end engaging the adjuster lever and the other slipping over the anchor pin (under the return springs).

7. Replace the primary brake-shoe return spring in the shoe and, using the tapered end of the brake spring tool or a pair of pliers, slide the other end of the spring over the anchor pin.

8. Replace the adjuster cable guide in the secondary brake shoe, fit the cable in the groove at top.

9. Repeat Step 6 with the secondary brake-shoe return spring.

10. Replace the hooked end of the adjuster spring in

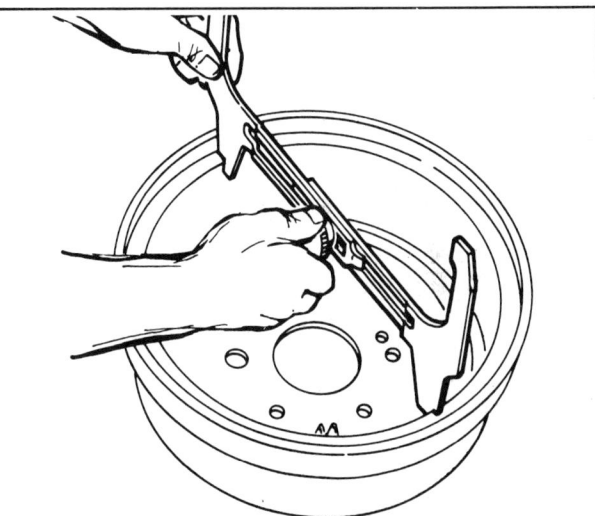

FIG. 13-18 MEASURING BRAKE DRUM INSIDE DIAMETER

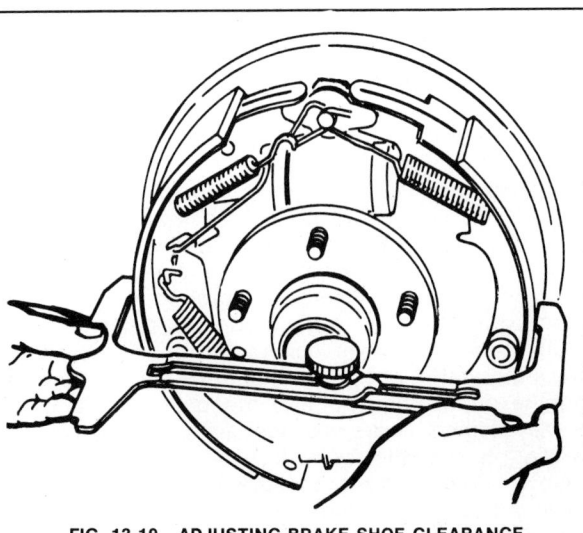

FIG. 13-19 ADJUSTING BRAKE SHOE CLEARANCE

the primary brake-shoe hole and connect the other end, along with the hooked end of the adjuster cable, in the slot at the top of the adjuster lever.

11. Pulling the adjuster lever down and to one side, engage pivot hook in the secondary brake-shoe hole.

12. Inspect the assembly to make certain that everything installed is properly engaged. On cable-actuated adjuster mechanisms, pull up on the cable to free the adjuster lever from the star wheel and release. If correctly installed, the adjuster lever should return to the star wheel and advance it one tooth.

13. Measure the ID of the brake drum with an inside caliper **(Fig. 13-18)** and the outside of the brake shoes with the outside caliper **(Fig. 13-19)**. Adjust the brake shoes to fit snugly inside the drum.

14. Replace the drum and wheel, and adjust the brakes as described under "Star and Screw Self-Adjuster, Brake Adjustment."

EXPANDING STRUT ADJUSTER

Two variations of this design are used on GM subcompacts. The Vega-type adjustment **(Fig. 13-20)** is not automatic, but adjustment occurs, if necessary, whenever the parking brake is applied. This pushes the parking brake strut against the front shoe, and the rod is pulled against the rear shoe. When this happens, a spring lock in the strut/rod assembly allows it to lengthen **(Fig. 13-21)**. Releasing the parking brake relaxes the rod, and brake shoe pressure to the drum is also released. If the shoe-to-drum clearance was sufficient to let the strut and rod slip, the lock will have engaged the rod assembly to hold the new length.

The Chevette-type **(Fig. 13-22)** is automatically adjusted whenever the brakes are applied, whether making a stop in forward, reverse or just standing still. When the brake pedal is depressed, the shoes move outward to touch the drum. As this happens, the automatic adjustment levers **(Fig. 13-12)** follow the shoe. The adjustment pin is smaller than the brake shoe slot so that, when the brakes are released, the shoes return slightly to provide shoe-to-drum clearance.

BRAKE LINING REPLACEMENT

To Remove

1. Remove the wheel, tire and brake drum from each rear wheel. If the drum does not pull off easily on the Vega-type, the brake adjuster assembly must be released. Use a hammer and punch to knock out the lanced area in the web of the drum, and push in on the rod assembly until it clears the secondary shoe. This allows the pull-back spring to pull the shoes inward and free the drum. Clean all metal particles from the brake assembly, and install a rubber hole cover when replacing the drum.

2. Loosen the parking-brake equalizer nut to release tension on the brake cable.

3. Remove the parking brake cable from the parking brake lever, and remove the pull-back spring.

4. Vega-type—Pull the primary and secondary shoes from under the hold-down clips, and remove with the strut and adjuster assembly attached. Separate the shoes to remove the strut and adjuster assembly.

Chevette-type—Reach behind the backing plate and press the end of one brake hold-down pin while grasping the cup on the front of the plate with a pair of pliers. Pushing inward with the pliers, turn the cup 90° to align its slot with the head of the mounting pin and remove. Repeat this procedure with the other hold-down pin and cup. Remove the shoes with the strut and retaining spring as an assembly, and separate.

5. Remove the parking brake lever.

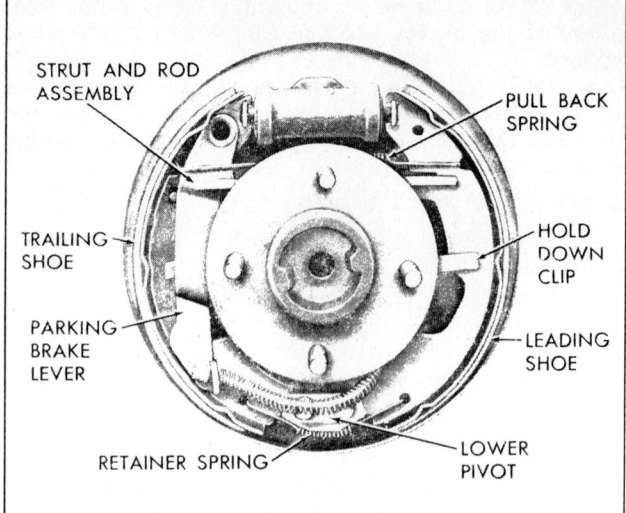

FIG. 13-20 VEGA-TYPE REAR DRUM BRAKE ASSEMBLY

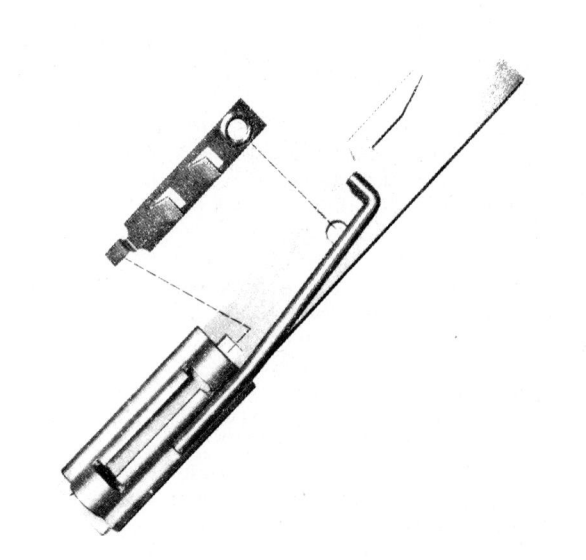

FIG. 13-21 ADJUSTER ASSEMBLY

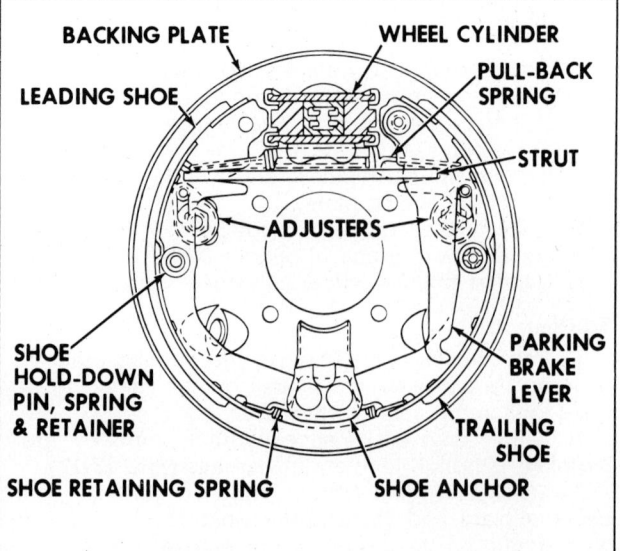

FIG. 13-22 CHEVETTE REAR DRUM BRAKE ASSEMBLY

To Replace

1. Lightly coat the brake-shoe contact points on the backing plate with a high temperature grease. These are located in a position roughly equivalent to those shown in **Fig. 13-17.**

2. Lubricate the fulcrum end of the parking brake lever, and connect it to the secondary shoe.

3. Vega-type only—Install the parking brake strut and adjuster assembly to the shoe.

4. Connect the shoes together with the lower or retaining spring.

5. Replace the shoes to the backing plate in the following manner:

  a) Vega-type—Fit the lower spring under the shoe anchor, guiding the lever/adjuster assembly into place with the hold-down clips in position.

  b) Chevette-type—Install the primary brake shoe on the front of the backing plate, and replace the hold-down spring and cup on the mounting pin. Position the strut, and repeat this step with the secondary shoe. Be sure to twist the cup 90° to secure the pin properly.

6. Engage the shoes with the wheel cylinder, and install the parking brake lever.

7. Replace the pull-back spring and connect the parking brake cable to the parking brake lever.

8. Install the brake drums, wheels and tires.

9. Adjust Vega-type brakes by setting and releasing the parking brake several times; adjust Chevette-type brakes by depressing the brake pedal several times, or until a firm pedal is established. Check the master cylinder reservoir and add fluid, if necessary, to bring it to the correct level.

10. Apply the parking brake one notch from a fully released position, and tighten the equalizer nut until a slight drag is felt when rotating the rear wheels. Release the parking brake completely. If the rear wheels can be rotated without drag, the parking brake adjustment is correct. If not, repeat the adjustment.

DISC BRAKE SERVICE

Caliper disc brakes used on 1970 and later American cars fall into one of the following three categories:

1. A fixed caliper, four-piston type (Bendix, Delco-Moraine, Kelsey-Hayes).

2. A sliding caliper, single-piston type (Bendix, Delco-Moraine, Kelsey-Hayes).

3. A floating caliper, single-piston type (Delco-Moraine, Kelsey-Hayes).

The fixed caliper design uses two pistons mounted in each side of the caliper. Braking friction is created by moving both disc pads hydraulically against the side of the rotating disc. In both the sliding and floating designs, the inside disc pad is moved into contact with the rotor disc by hydraulic force. As the caliper moves slightly along the centerline of the axle, the outside pad is drawn into contact with the disc by a reaction force.

It is best to remove disc brake pads for wear inspection, and on some applications, it may be necessary to remove the caliper in order to remove the pads. When the lining on any pad has worn to a minimum ⅛-in. thickness, both pads on that wheel and on the opposite wheel (both front or both rear) should be replaced. If the lining thickness wears to 1/16-in. or less, permanent damage can be done to the rotor disc, requiring its replacement.

Check pad wear in the floating caliper design carefully. There is a tendency for the lining to wear in a tapered manner, and the lining thickness should be measured at the narrow end. Pads with a taper greater than ⅛-in. from one end to the other should be replaced.

When the caliper is removed for brake pad inspection, *do not* allow it to hang unsupported from the brake hose. Place the caliper on the frame rail or suspension to remove the weight from the hose. If this is not possible because of the car's suspension design, be prepared to wire the caliper to the frame or suspension when it is removed.

FIXED CALIPER DISC BRAKE SERVICE

PAD REPLACEMENT

Before removing the calipers or disc pads, check the master cylinder. If it is full of brake fluid, siphon enough out to prevent the reservoir from overflowing when the fluid in the wheel cylinders is returned as the new pads are installed. *Do not* drain the reservoir completely, or air will enter the system. Be sure to recheck the master-cylinder fluid level after completing work on each wheel, and after the entire job is finished.

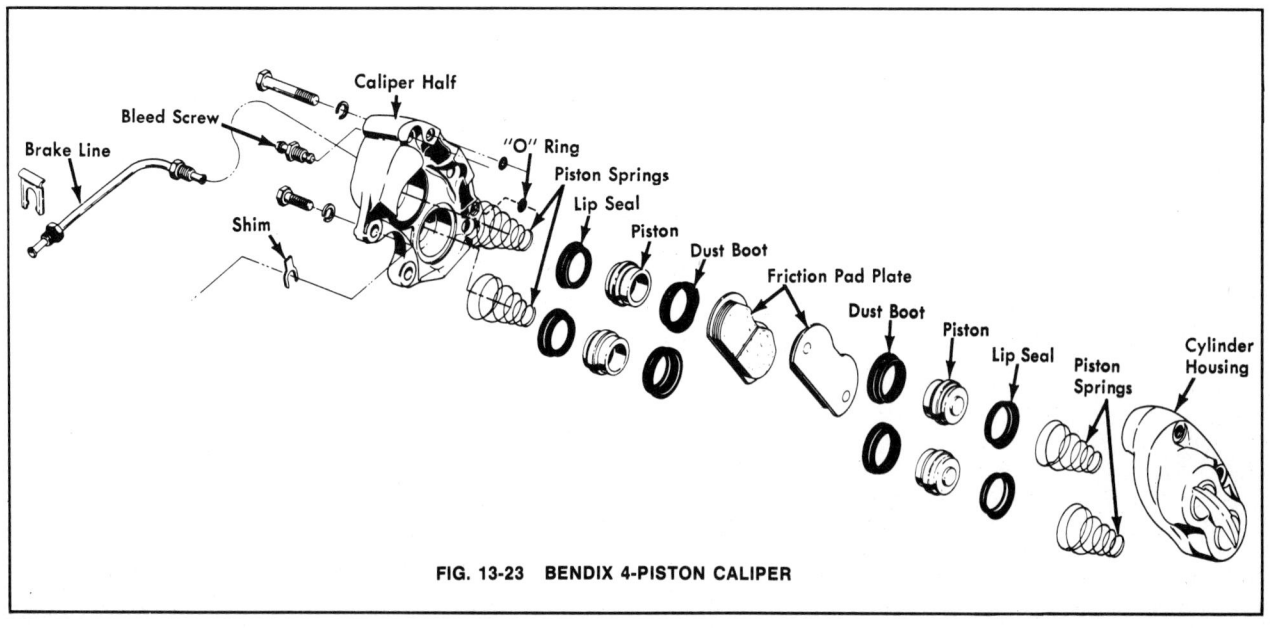

FIG. 13-23 BENDIX 4-PISTON CALIPER

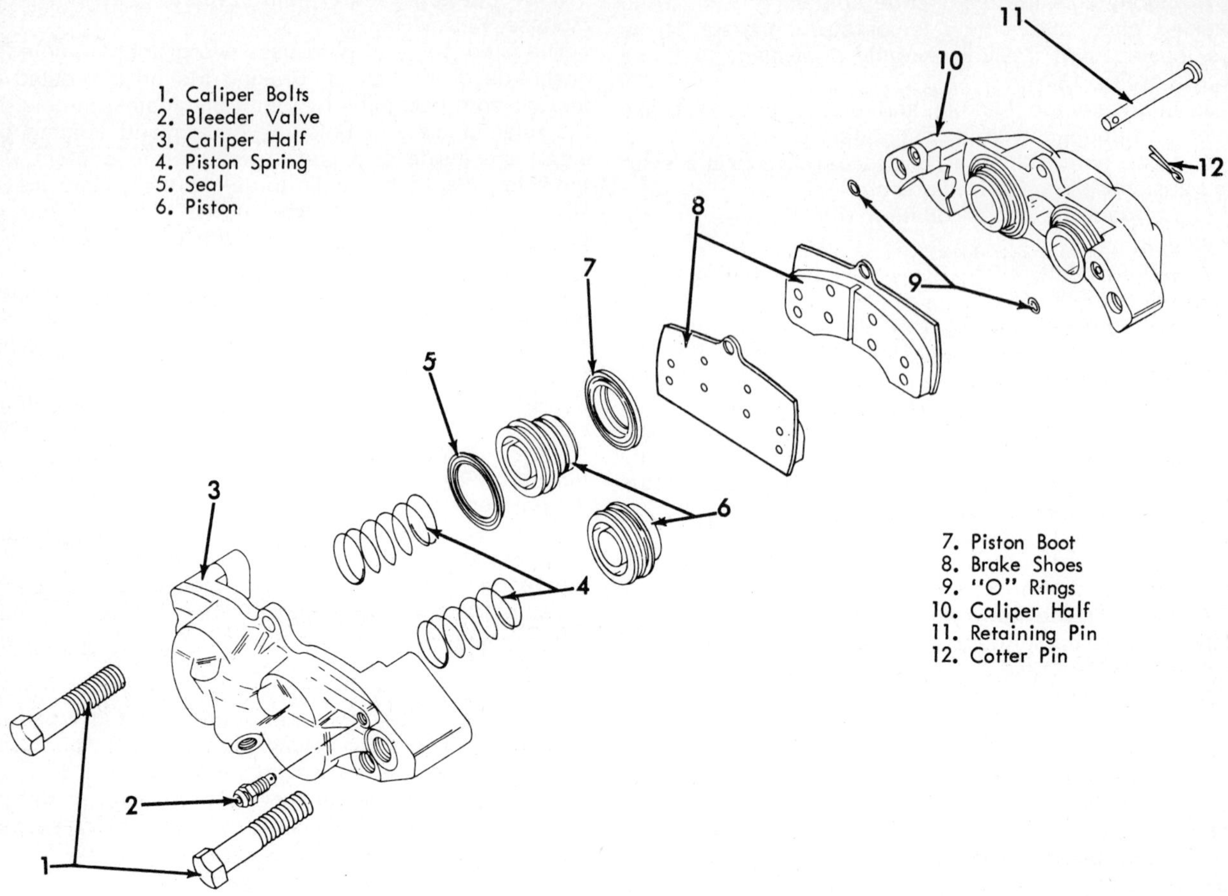

1. Caliper Bolts
2. Bleeder Valve
3. Caliper Half
4. Piston Spring
5. Seal
6. Piston

7. Piston Boot
8. Brake Shoes
9. "O" Rings
10. Caliper Half
11. Retaining Pin
12. Cotter Pin

FIG. 13-24   DELCO-MORAINE 4-PISTON CALIPER

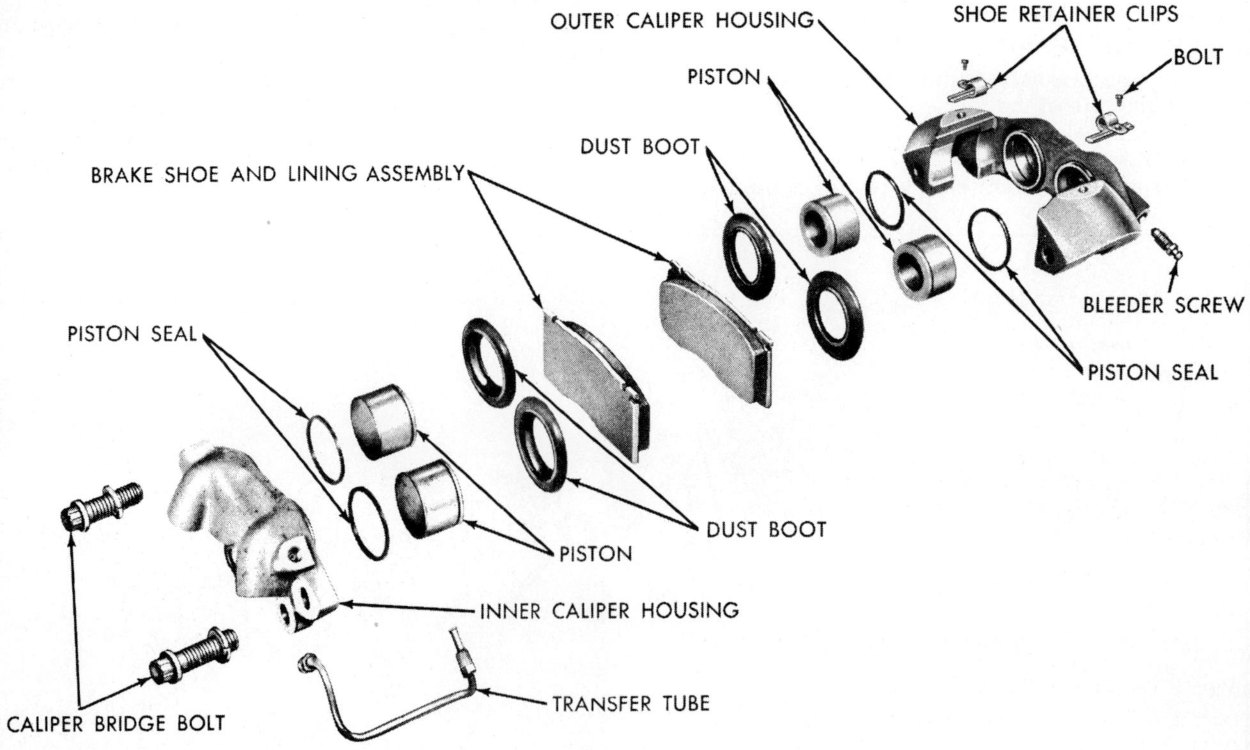

OUTER CALIPER HOUSING

SHOE RETAINER CLIPS

PISTON

BOLT

DUST BOOT

BRAKE SHOE AND LINING ASSEMBLY

BLEEDER SCREW

PISTON SEAL

PISTON SEAL

PISTON

DUST BOOT

INNER CALIPER HOUSING

CALIPER BRIDGE BOLT

TRANSFER TUBE

FIG. 13-25   KELSEY-HAYES 4-PISTON CALIPER

BENDIX
1970 American Motors Cars (Fig. 13-23)

1. Raise the car on a hoist, or block the rear wheels and jack up the front end. Remove the wheels and tires. Work on only one wheel at a time.

2. Remove the caliper bolts and slide the caliper from the disc. If shims are used under the mounting bolts, retrieve and label them ''upper'' or ''lower,'' because they must be replaced in the same location from which they are removed.

3. Wire the caliper assembly to the upper suspension and, using two screwdrivers between the pads, gradually press all pistons toward the bottom of their cylinders. Lift the worn pads from the caliper, and inspect the caliper casting for cracks.

4. Insert the curved edge of the new pad first, with the steel backing plate resting against the pistons.

5. Spread the pads apart as in Step 3 to seat the pistons, and replace the caliper on the disc.

6. Align the caliper bolt holes with those in the mounting bracket, and replace the shims and mounting bolts. Torque to specifications.

DELCO-MORAINE
1970-79 Corvette (Fig. 13-24)

1. Raise the car on a hoist, or block the rear wheels and jack up the front end (reverse this sequence if the rear brakes need service). Remove the wheels and tires. Work on only one wheel at a time.

2. Remove the cotter pin from the end of the pad retaining pin, and slide the retaining pin out. Discard both.

3. Pull the inside pad up and out. Push the spring-loaded pistons back with a putty knife, and install the new pad.

4. Pull the outside pad up and out. Push the pistons back with the putty knife, and install the new pad.

5. Insert a new retaining pin through the caliper and pads, and install a new cotter pin through the retaining pin, bending the cotter pin ends back to secure it.

6. Repeat this procedure at each wheel where new pads are to be installed.

KELSEY-HAYES
1970-72 Valiant, Dart (Fig. 13-25)

1. Raise the car on a hoist, or block the rear wheels and jack up the front end. Remove the wheels and tires. Work on only one wheel at a time.

2. Remove the shoe retainer clips.

3. Force the pistons back in their bore with a pair of water pump pliers placed on the corner of the shoe and the caliper housing.

4. Grasp the tabs on the outer end of the inside shoe with pliers (one pair on each tab), pull outward.

5. Slide the new shoe into the caliper, with the shoe ears resting on the caliper side (lining faces disc). If necessary to push the pistons farther into their bore to install the new pad, use a flat-sided metal bar inserted between the pistons and the disc, and pry the pistons back.

6. Repeat Steps 3, 4 and 5 to replace the outside shoe.

7. Replace the shoe retainer clips on the caliper.

CALIPER OVERHAUL

Since the Bendix **(Fig. 13-23)**, Delco-Moraine **(Fig. 13-24)** and Kelsey-Hayes **(Fig. 13-25)** fixed calipers are essentially similar in design, the following procedure can be used to overhaul any of the three. Where differences in procedure do occur, they are noted.

To Disassemble

1. Raise the car on a hoist, or block the rear wheels and jack up the front end. Remove the wheels and tires. Work on only one wheel at a time.

2. Remove the caliper mounting bolts (and shims, if used). Slide the caliper unit from the disc.

3. Loosen the hydraulic inlet line with a wrench, then unscrew the caliper from the line. Plug the line with a golf tee.

4. Remove the disc pads, and mark each with chalk to identify it for replacement in the same position, unless new pads are to be installed.

5. Open the bleed valve and drain the brake fluid from the caliper.

6. Wipe the outside of the caliper with a cloth moistened in brake fluid (*do not* use solvent) to remove grease and road dirt, then secure the unit in a soft-jaw vise.

7. Bendix—Remove the bridge bolts holding the two halves of the caliper together, and remove the two O-ring seals from the transfer holes.

Delco-Moraine—The rear brake uses only one O-ring seal and transfer hole.

Kelsey-Hayes—An external transfer tube is used instead of the internal passage with O-ring seals. Remove the transfer tube before separating the caliper halves.

8. Remove the lip of each piston dust boot from its

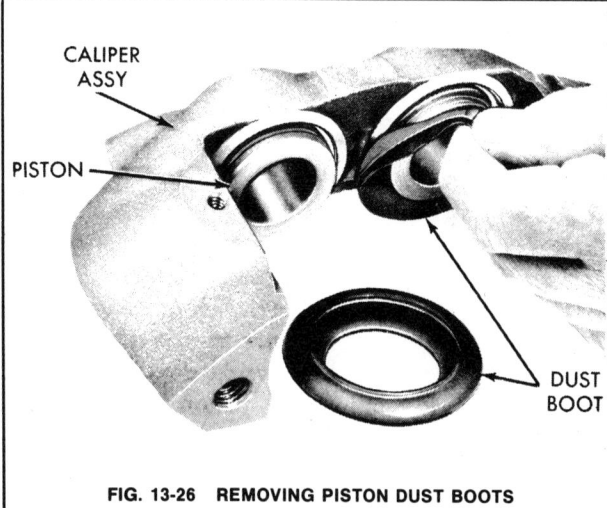

FIG. 13-26 REMOVING PISTON DUST BOOTS

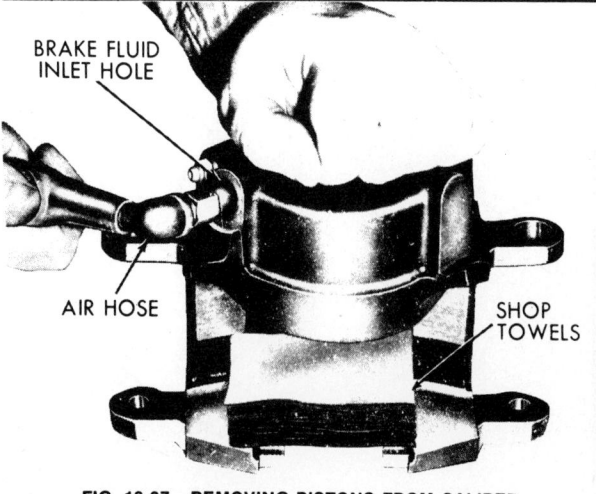

FIG. 13-27 REMOVING PISTONS FROM CALIPER

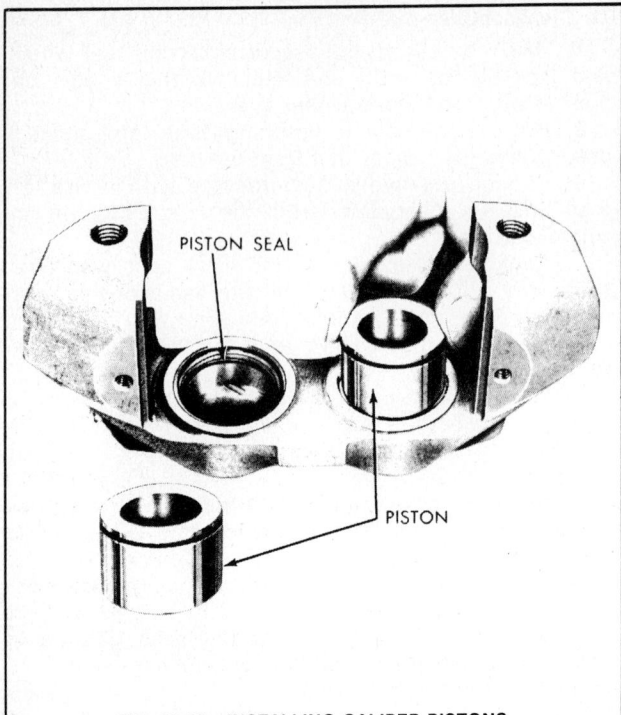

FIG. 13-28   INSTALLING CALIPER PISTONS

groove and pull off **(Fig. 13-26),** then remove the piston assemblies and springs (Bendix/Delco-Moraine only) from each bore. Use compressed air through the brake line, if necessary *(do not pry),* but cover the pistons with a clean cloth wrapped around a block of wood to prevent them from being blown out and damaged **(Fig. 13-27).**

Delco-Moraine—A retaining ring must be removed from the piston boot before it can be removed.

CLEANING AND INSPECTION

1. Clean all metal parts in denatured alcohol, and blow dry with compressed air. If shop air supply is lubricated, *do not* use, because the mineral oil will leave a film on the metal parts. Blow out all caliper and bleeder valve passages.

2. Inspect the caliper cylinder bores for scoring, pitting or corrosion. The same techniques used on wheel cylinders are applicable to the caliper cylinders. If the bore is very rough or pitted, it is corroded, and the caliper must be replaced. A staining condition or very light roughness can be removed with crocus cloth. Place the cloth on your finger and insert it in the bore. Use a rotating motion only—*do not* slide the crocus cloth back and forth in the bore or polish with an abrasive in an attempt to "save" a caliper that needs replacing.

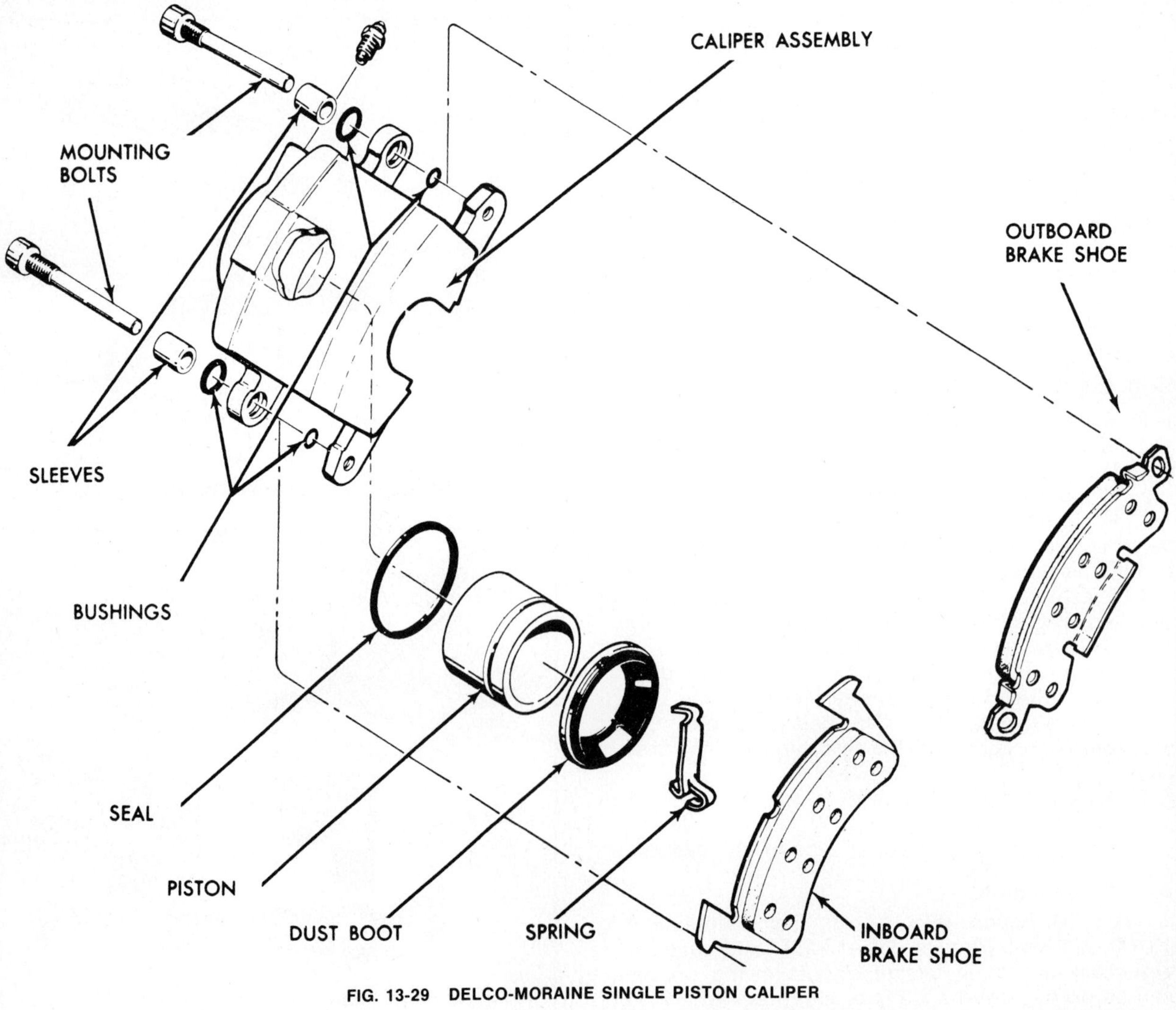

FIG. 13-29   DELCO-MORAINE SINGLE PISTON CALIPER

3. Inspect the condition of the pistons. The outside diameter of the piston is the primary sealing surface in the caliper bore and is plated to a close tolerance. If any surface defects are noted, replace the piston.

4. Use a feeler gauge to check piston clearance in the bore. Specified clearance is between 0.002-in. and 0.006-in. (Corvette, 0.0035-in. to 0.009-in.). If the clearance exceeds this specification, replace the caliper.

To Assemble

1. Lubricate new rubber parts with clean brake fluid.

2. Bendix—Replace the seals in the piston groove nearest to the piston closed end, with the seal lips facing in that direction. Install the boots with their lips facing the seal.

Kelsey-Hayes—Install the seals in the cylinder bore grooves.

3. Lubricate the cylinder bores and pistons with brake fluid. Replace the piston return spring in the bore with its large coil facing inward (Kelsey-Hayes does not use return springs).

4. Replace the piston in the cylinder bore **(Fig. 13-28)**. Work carefully to prevent damage to the seal lip by the edge of the bore.

Delco-Moraine—The seal lip must face the piston spring end, with the fold in the boot facing the seal.

Seat the seal lip in the cylinder bore with a small screwdriver and install the retaining ring, seating it below the caliper's machined face. Compress the dust boot into the cylinder bore and seat completely.

5. Replace the transfer hole O-rings (except Kelsey-Hayes). Align the two caliper halves and fit together. Replace the bridge bolts, and torque to specifications.

Kelsey-Hayes—Install the transfer tube.

6. Replace the disc pads in the caliper and reconnect the caliper to the brake line and then to the hub (see "Pad Replacement"). With Kelsey-Hayes calipers, install the pads after remounting the caliper to the hub.

7. Bleed the brakes (see "Bleeding the Hydraulic System").

SLIDING/FLOATING DISC BRAKE SERVICE

PAD REPLACEMENT

Before removing the calipers or disc pads, check the master cylinder. If it is full of brake fluid, siphon enough out to prevent the reservoir from overflowing when the fluid in the wheel cylinders is returned as the new pads are installed. *Do not* drain the reservoir completely, or air will enter the system. Be sure to recheck the master-cylinder fluid level after completing work on each wheel, and after the entire job is finished.

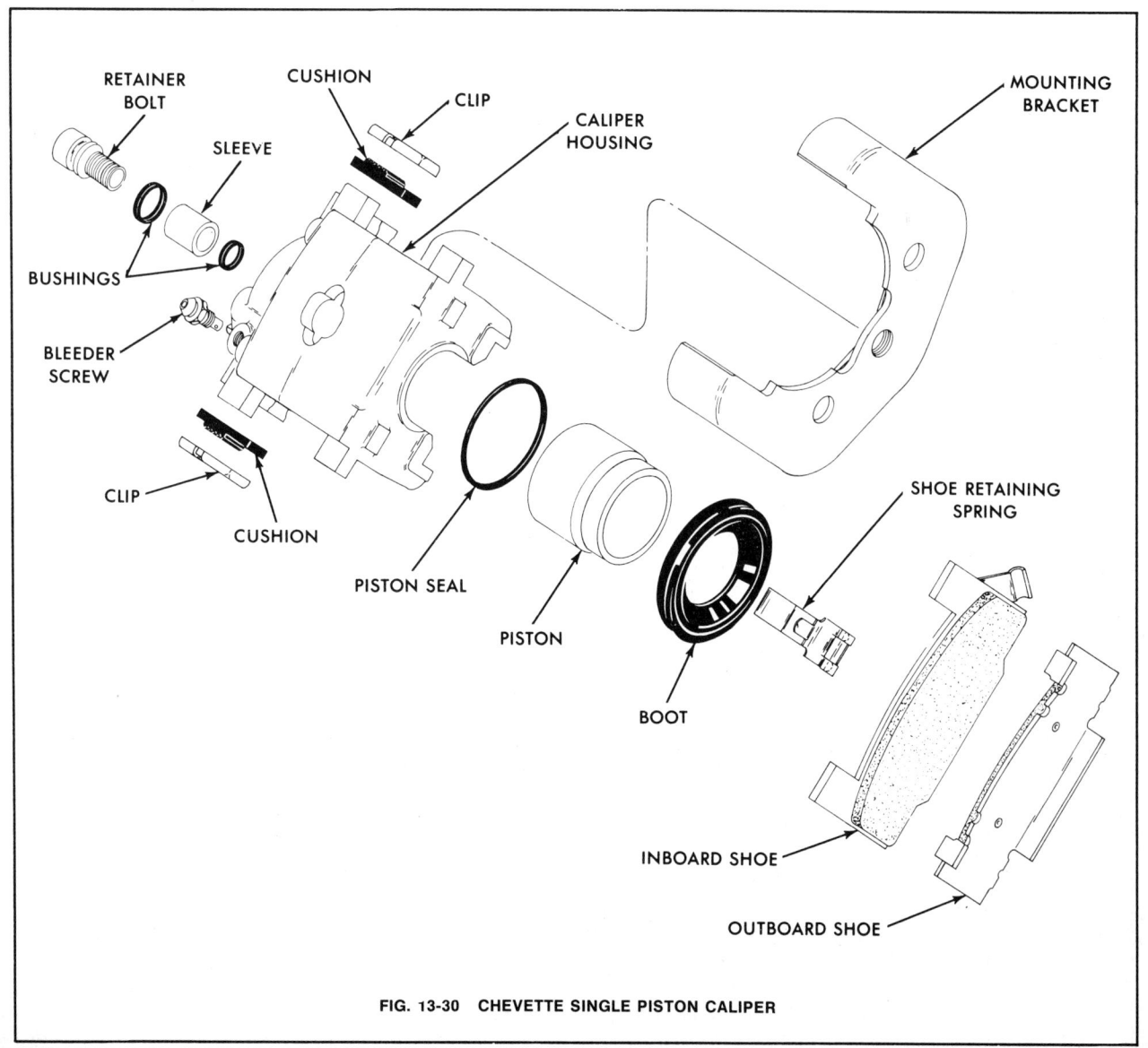

FIG. 13-30 CHEVETTE SINGLE PISTON CALIPER

DELCO-MORAINE 1970-79 (FRONT WHEEL)
General Motors Cars, Except Corvette
(Figs. 13-29 & 13-30)

1. Raise the car on a hoist, or block the rear wheels and jack up the front end. Remove the wheels and tires. Work on only one wheel at a time.
2. Push the piston back in its bore using a "C" clamp as shown in **Fig. 13-31.**
3. Remove the mounting bolts holding the caliper to the support, and lift the caliper from the disc.
4. Remove the two brake shoes, and check the caliper for cracks and seal leakage.
5. Remove the shoe support spring, the two sleeves and four bushings from the caliper. The Chevette version uses one sleeve and two bushings.
6. Clean the caliper mounting-bolt holes and the bushing grooves. Wipe the inside of the caliper clean.
7. Lubricate the new sleeves, rubber bushings, bushing grooves and bolt ends with silicone lubricant.
8. Install the bushings and sleeves.
9. Fit the shoe support spring to the shoe, and place the assembly in the piston cavity **(Fig. 13-32)**, pressing it down against the piston.
10. Install the other pad with its ears over the caliper ears, and bend the shoe ears over those on the caliper with pliers.
11. Screw the caliper onto the brake hose, and replace the caliper assembly on the disc, and align the mounting holes. *Do not* twist or kink the brake hose.
12. Install the caliper-to-mounting-bracket bolts so that they pass under the retaining ears **(Fig. 13-33)** and torque to specifications. Since the Chevette uses a single mounting bolt passing through the caliper, it is simply installed and torqued.

DELCO-MORAINE (REAR WHEEL)
1977-79 Buick, Cadillac; 1979 Oldsmobile, Pontiac
(Fig. 13-30A)

1. Raise the car on a hoist, or block the front wheels and jack up the rear end.
2. Mark relation of wheel to axle flange and remove wheel assembly.
3. Relieve tension on parking brake cable at equalizer by loosening the rear equalizer nut.
4. Remove the spring at the rear of the caliper and compress the prongs on the bracket to permit conduit removal.
5. Remove return spring, locknut, lever/seal, and anti-friction washer. If caliper is to be overhauled, disregard this step.
6. Clean the lever seal area on the caliper surface to remove all contamination.
7. Push the piston back in its bore using a "C" clamp as shown in **Fig. 13-31.** "C" clamp should not touch actuator screw.
8. With clamp in place lubricate the caliper surface under the lever seal with silicone.
9. Install a new anti-friction washer, lever seal and lever. Hex on lever arm must point downward.
10. Rotate the lever toward front of car and hold. Install and torque nut to 25 ft.-lbs. Rotate lever backwards until it stops.
11. Replace lever return spring and remove "C" clamp.

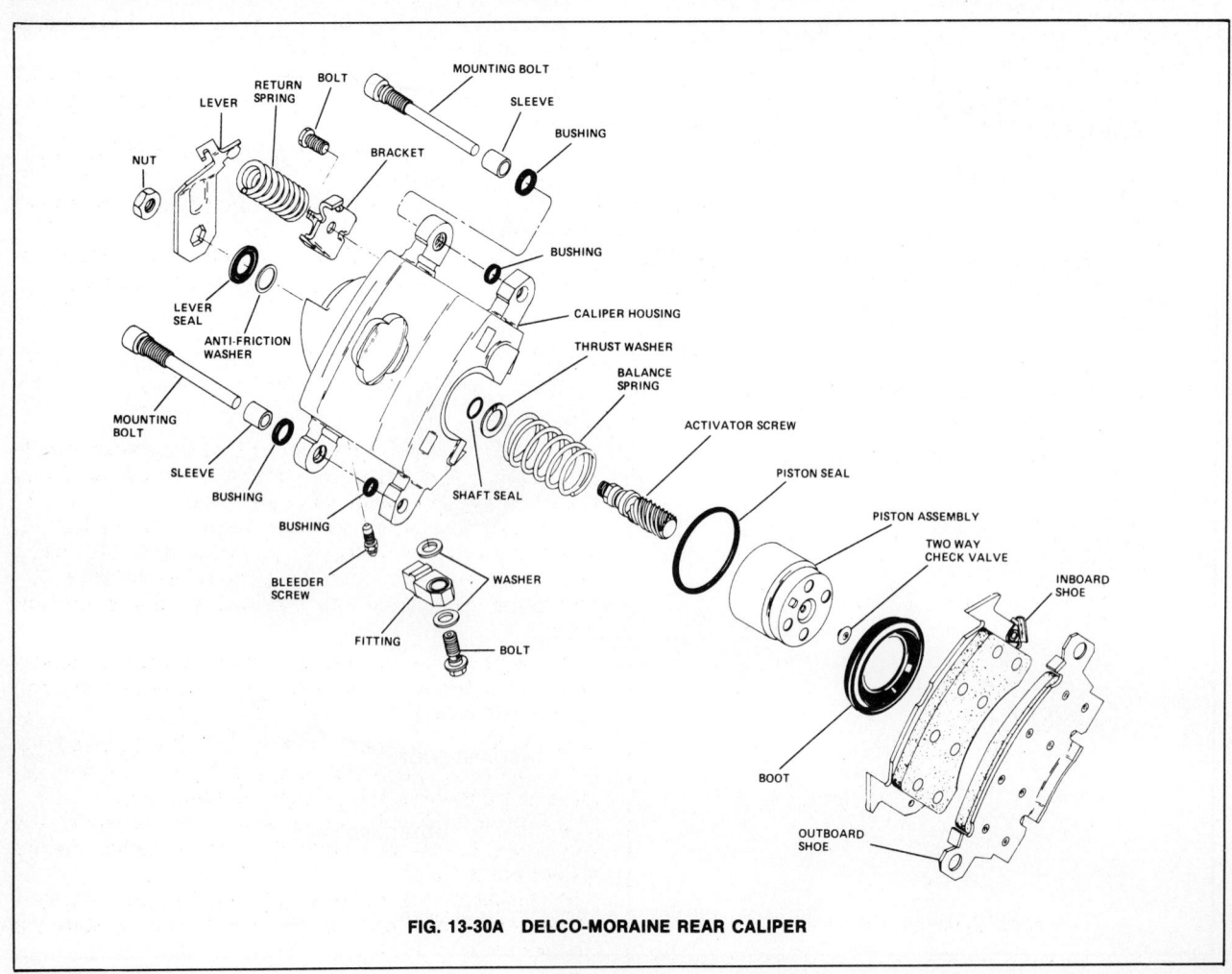

FIG. 13-30A   DELCO-MORAINE REAR CALIPER

12. Disconnect and plug the brake line at the caliper.
13. Remove the mounting bolts holding the caliper to the support, and lift the caliper from the disc.
14. Remove the two brake shoes and check the caliper for cracks and seal leakage.
15. Remove and discard the caliper mounting sleeves and rubber bushings.
16. Remove and discard the piston check valve; install new check valve.
17. Clean the caliper mounting bolt holes and the bushing grooves. Wipe the inside of the caliper clean. Install new prelubed bushings and sleeve.
18. Fit new inner shoe on the piston with its D-tab in

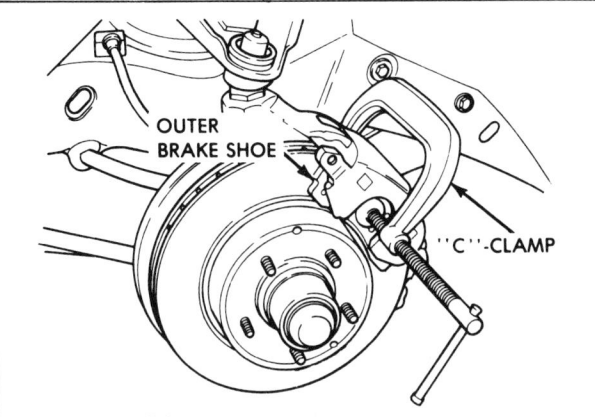

FIG. 13-31 "C" CLAMP LOCATION

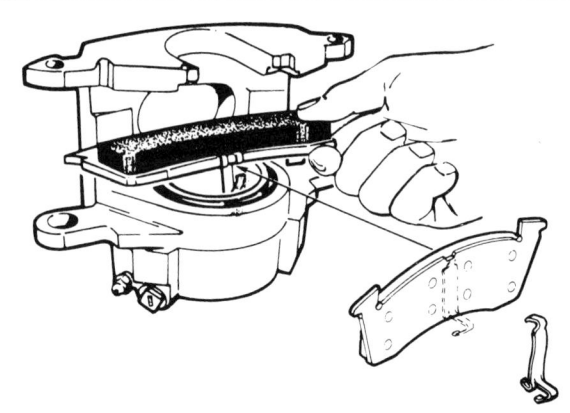

FIG. 13-32 INSTALLING SUPPORT SPRING AND SHOE

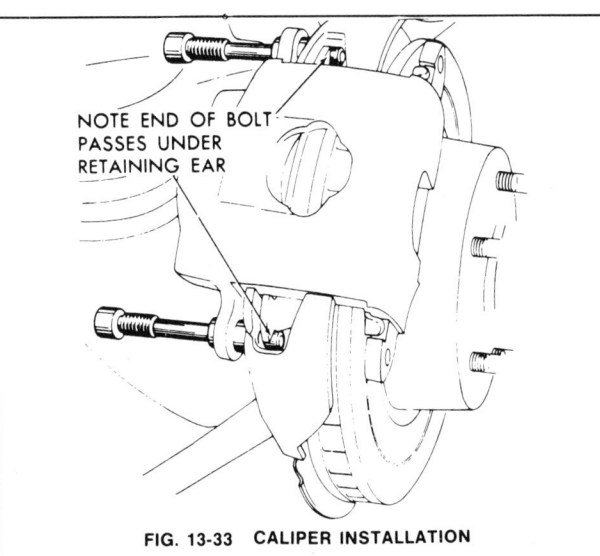

FIG. 13-33 CALIPER INSTALLATION

the piston D-indention. Rotate piston if necessary to align hole with tab.
19. Install new outer shoe assembly.
20. Slide caliper over rotor disc and install mounting bolts under the inner shoe ears. Torque to 30 ft.-lbs.
21. Unplug and reconnect brake line to caliper.
22. Pump brake pedal to seat outer shoe against caliper. Cinch upper ear of outer shoe with pliers until there is no radial clearance between the shoe ears and caliper.
23. Install lever return spring, replace parking brake conduits and cable, and adjust parking brake.
24. Bleed rear brakes and check before replacing wheel/tire assembly.

KELSEY-HAYES

1970-74 American Motors Cars; All Chrysler Corporation Cars, Except Newport, New Yorker, Monaco, Imperial and Fury from 1974, All Valiant and Dart; All Aspen, Volare, LeBaron, Diplomat

(Fig. 13-34)

1. Raise the car on a hoist, or block the rear wheels and jack up the front end. Remove the wheels and tires. Work on only one wheel at a time.
2. Remove the guide pins and positioners from the caliper and adapter. Discard the positioners and inner bushings.
3. Lift the caliper from the disc, and discard the outer bushings.
4. Remove the two shoes from the caliper, and seat the piston in its bore.
5. Lubricate new outer bushings with brake fluid, and install them in the caliper.
6. Install the new shoes, with the outer shoe slipping into the retaining spring, then replace the caliper on the disc.
7. Lubricate new inner bushings with brake fluid, and install in the caliper.
8. Fit new positioners on the guide pins, as shown in **Fig. 13-34.**
9. Install guide-pin/positioner assemblies, and carefully thread into adapter. Torque to specifications.

BENDIX
1974-79 American Motors Cars

(Fig. 13-35)

1. Raise the car on a hoist, or block the rear wheels and jack up the front end. Remove the wheels and tires. Work on only one wheel at a time.
2. Insert a large screwdriver through the caliper inspection port and between the piston and the inside shoe. Pry the piston back into its bore. A large "C" clamp can be used if the piston does not bottom by prying.
3. Remove the support-key retaining screw, using a ¼-in. Allen wrench, and drive out the key and support spring with a drift.
4. Remove the caliper, and support it with wire from the suspension, then pull the two shoes out and remove the anti-rattle spring from the inner shoe.
5. Fit the anti-rattle spring on the rear flange of the new inner brake shoe, with its looped section facing away from the disc.
6. Install the new shoes and seat flanges fully. Replace the caliper on the disc, and align it with the anchor plate.

7. Insert the support key and spring, and seat in place with a drift. Then install the retaining screw, and torque to 15 ft.-lbs.

KELSEY-HAYES FLOATING CALIPER (FORD)

1970-72 Ford, Lincoln, Mercury;
1970-71 Mark III, Thunderbird
(Fig. 13-36)

1. Raise the car on a hoist, or block the rear wheels and jack up the front end. Remove the wheels and tires. Work on only one wheel at a time.

2. Remove the inside shoe hold-down clip and the outer shoe retaining clips.

3. Remove the two locating pins and stabilizer from the rear of the caliper.

4. Lift the caliper from the anchor plate, and remove the outer shoe.

5. Support the caliper from the upper control arm with wire, and remove insulator from the anchor plate.

6. Remove the inner shoe.

7. Fit the new inner shoe to the anchor plate, and install new locating pin insulators. Replace the hold-down clips.

8. Retract the piston into its bore fully, and install the new outer shoe, retaining pins and clips.

9. Position the caliper to the anchor plate, and replace the stabilizer and locating pins.

1970 Fairlane; 1970-71 Montego/Torino; 1970-73 Cougar/Mustang

1. Raise the car on a hoist, or block the rear wheels and jack up the front end. Remove the wheels and tires. Work on only one wheel at a time.

2. Remove the caliper locating pins and stabilizer. Lift the caliper from the disc.

3. Remove the inner shoe hold-down clips, insulator and shoe.

4. Pry off the outer shoe retaining clips, and remove the shoe.

5. Retract the piston into its bore fully, and replace the inner shoe and retaining clips.

6. Fit caliper over the disc, and install outer shoe.

7. Install a new stabilizer, and connect the assembly to the anchor plate.

KELSEY-HAYES SLIDING CALIPER

1972-78 Thunderbird, Montego, Torino;
1973-78 Ford, Mercury, LTD II;
1973-79 Lincoln, Continental, Mark V
1974-79 Pinto, Bobcat;
1974-78 Mustang II;
1976-77 Comet, Maverick;
1976-79 Granada, Monarch;
1977-79 Versailles;
1979 LTD II, Cougar, Thunderbird;
1974 and later Chrysler Newport, New Yorker, Monaco, Imperial, Fury;
1973-76 Valiant, Dart;
1976-79 Aspen, Volare, LeBaron, Diplomat

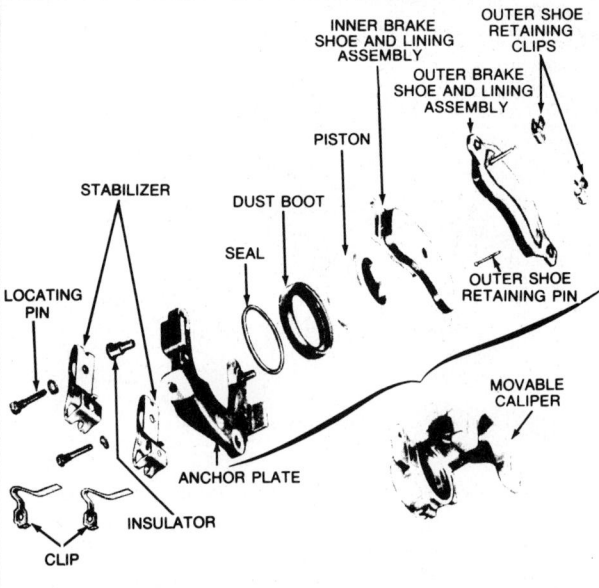

FIG. 13-36   FORD (KELSEY-HAYES) SINGLE PISTON CALIPER

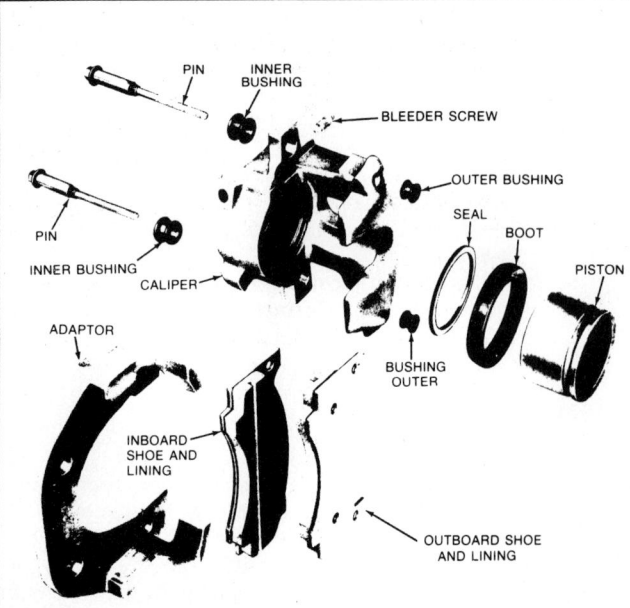

FIG. 13-34   KELSEY-HAYES SINGLE PISTON CALIPER

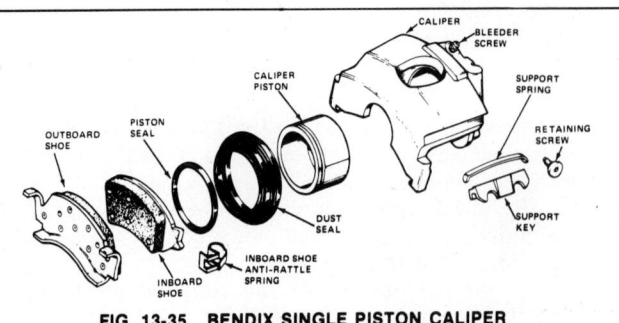

FIG. 13-35   BENDIX SINGLE PISTON CALIPER

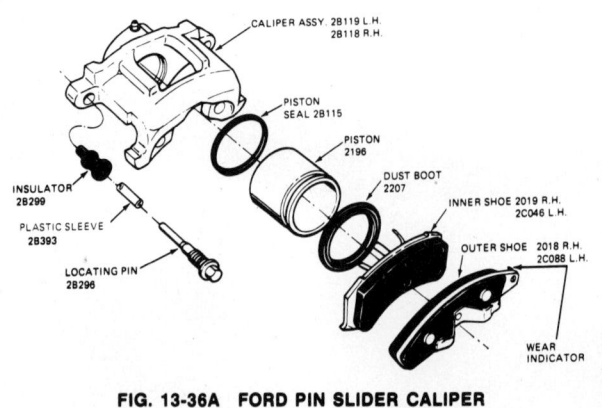

FIG. 13-36A   FORD PIN SLIDER CALIPER

Essentially the same design as that of the Bendix single-piston caliper used on 1974-76 AMC cars, pad replacement is accomplished in a similar manner.

FORD SLIDING PIN CALIPER

**1978-79 Fairmont/Zephyr;
1979 Ford/Mercury/Mustang/Capri (Fig. 13-36A)**

1. Remove and discard 50% of the brake fluid in the primary (large) master cylinder reservoir.

2. Raise the car on a hoist, or block the rear wheels and jack up the front end. Remove the wheels and tires. Work on only one wheel at a time.

3. Remove the caliper locating pins and lift the cali-

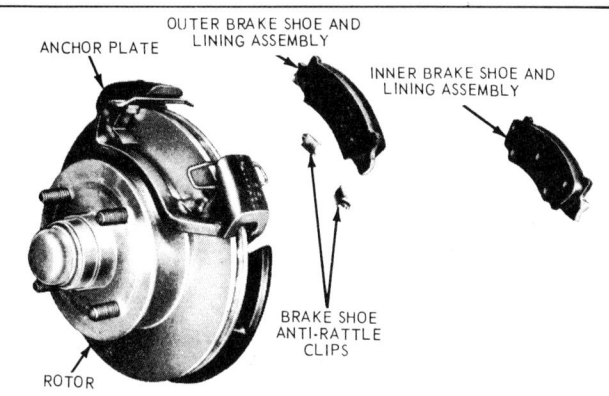

FIG. 13-37   FORD PINTO SINGLE PISTON CALIPER, 1971-73

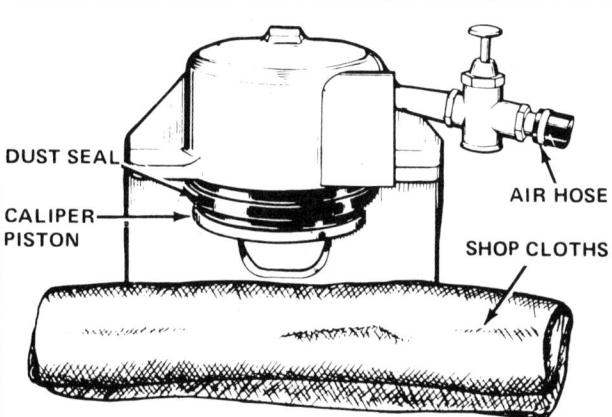

FIG. 13-38   REMOVING THE CALIPER PISTON

per from integral spindle anchor plate/rotor assembly.

4. Remove the outer shoe from the caliper.

5. Remove the inner shoe from the caliper.

6. Suspend the caliper from the inside of the fender housing with a wire.

7. Remove and discard the caliper locating pin insulators and their plastic sleeves.

8. Seat the caliper piston in its bore. This is most efficiently done using a 4-in. C-clamp and a small block of wood 3x1x¾-in.

9. Install *new* locating pin insulators and sleeves in the caliper. Both insulator flanges must straddle the housing holes; sleeves must be completely bottomed in the insulators.

10. Install the inner shoe/lining assembly. These are marked LH or RH, and must be used in the correct caliper. Do not bend shoe clips excessively.

11. Install the correct outer shoe/lining assembly. The wear indicator must face toward front of caliper.

12. Replace the caliper on the anchor plate/rotor. Install locating pins and torque to 30-40 ft.-lbs. for 1978 and 40-60 ft.-lbs. for 1979 applications.

13. Replace wheels and tires. Lower car and top up master cylinder reservoir to "full" mark.

FORD SLIDING CALIPER

**1971-73 Pinto
(Fig. 13-37)**

Brake shoes can be replaced without removing the entire caliper/anchor plate assembly.

1. Raise the car on a hoist, or block the rear wheels and jack up the front end. Remove the wheels and tires. Work on only one wheel at a time.

2. Remove the two cotter pins from the caliper retaining key, and slide the key from the anchor plate, using a drift if necessary.

3. Press the caliper in and up against the support springs, and lift away from the anchor plate. Suspend the caliper from the upper suspension arm.

4. Remove the two shoes and seat the piston fully in its bore.

5. If the brake-shoe anti-rattle clips came out during disassembly, reinstall them and position the new shoes in the anchor plate.

6. Slide the caliper over the brake shoes, hold in place and install the retaining key.

7. Install two new stainless-steel cotter pins in the retaining key.

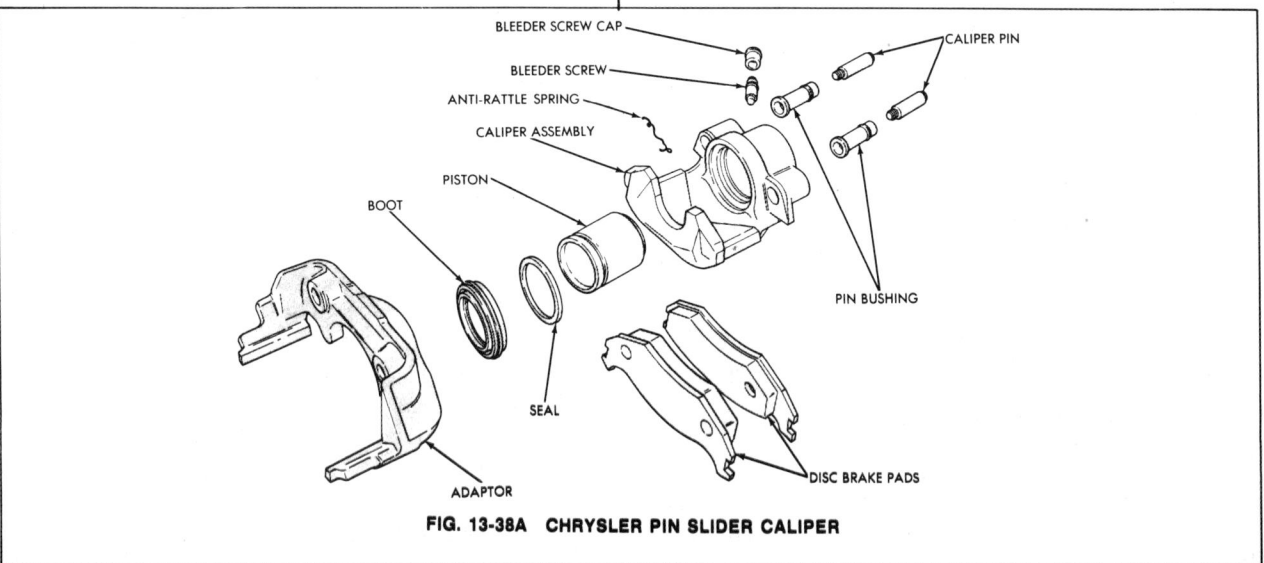

FIG. 13-38A   CHRYSLER PIN SLIDER CALIPER

CHRYSLER PIN SLIDER CALIPER

All Omni/Horizon
(Fig. 13-38A)

1. Raise the car on a hoist, or block the rear wheels and jack up the front end. Remove the wheel covers and wheel/tire assembly. Work on one wheel at a time.

2. Remove the caliper guide pins from the back side of the caliper, then remove the anti-rattle spring.

3. Slide the caliper assembly out and away from the disc. Suspend it in such a way as to prevent hose stress or damage.

4. Remove the outboard shoe from the adaptor.

5. Slide the braking disc from the drive axle flange/studs.

6. Remove the inboard shoe from the adaptor.

7. Push the piston into the caliper bore until it bottoms.

8. Insert the new inboard shoe in the adaptor. The metal part of the shoe must rest completely in the adaptor recess.

9. Replace the braking disc on the drive flange studs and seat.

10. Insert the new outboard shoe in the adaptor.

11. Lower the caliper over the braking disc and adaptor.

12. Install the guide pins through the bushing, caliper and adaptor. Press the guide pins in and thread them into the adaptor.

13. Torque the guide pins to specifications.

14. Bleed the brakes, then replace the wheel/tire assembly and wheel cover.

CALIPER OVERHAUL

Since the Delco-Moraine, Chrysler/AMC version of the Kelsey-Hayes, Ford Sliding Caliper (except 1971-73

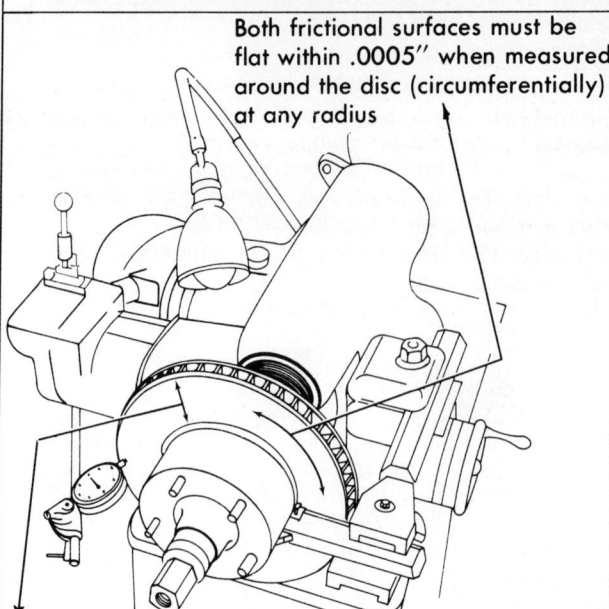

Both frictional surfaces must be flat within .0005" when measured around the disc (circumferentially) at any radius

Both frictional surfaces must be flat within .001" total indicator reading when measured across the surface (radially)

FIG. 13-39 ROTOR MEASUREMENT

OMNI/HORIZON TORQUE VALVES

	1978		1979	
	FT.-LBS.	IN.-LBS.	FT.-LBS.	IN.-LBS.
HYDRAULIC BRAKE LINES				
Tubes to Flexible Hoses....................	– –	80-150	– –	80-150
Tubes to Rear Tees.......................	– –	80-150	– –	80-150
Tubes to w/cyl..........................	– –	80-150	– –	80-150
Fittings to Calipers....................	19-29	– –	19-29	– –
Hoses to Calipers........................	15-35	– –	19-29	– –
Front Brake Hose Intermediate Bracket.......	– –	– –		– –
MASTER CYLINDER				
Master Cylinder to Dash Panel.............	– –	170-230	– –	200-250
Master Cylinder to Booster Front Cover......	– –	170-230	– –	200-250
POWER BRAKE				
Power Brake Assembly to Dash.............	– –	150-220		200-250
Lower Pivot.............................	30	– –	30	– –
Pedal Push Rod Bolt.....................	30	– –	30	– –
WHEEL CYLINDERS				
To Support Plate........................	– –	75 min.	– –	75 min.
Bleed Screw...........................	– –	60-100	– –	60-100
BRAKE SUPPORT PLATE				
To Flange.............................	25-60	– –	35-55	– –
WHEEL STUD NUTS				
All...................................	85	– –	85	– –
CALIPERS				
Adapter Mounting Bolts..................	95-125	– –	70-100	– –
Caliper Retaining Plate Screws.............	– –	170-260	– –	170-260
Splash Shield Mounting Bolts..............	– –	160 min.	– –	160 min.
Bleed Screw...........................		80-170		80-170
CALIPERS—PIN TYPE				
Adapter Mounting Bolts..................	95-125	– –	70-100	– –
Guide Pins............................	25-40	– –	25-40	– –
Splash Shield Mounting Bolts..............	– –	160 min.	– –	200-300
STOPLIGHT SWITCH				
Bracket Screw.........................	– –	75	– –	75

Pinto) and the Bendix single-piston calipers are essentially similar in design **(Figs. 13-34 & 13-35)**, the following procedure can be used to overhaul any of the four. Where differences in procedures do occur, they are noted.

To Disassemble

1. Disconnect and plug the hydraulic brake hose, and remove the caliper according to the procedure specified under ''Pad Replacement'' for the particular caliper.

2. Clean the outside of the caliper with a cloth moistened in clean brake fluid (*do not* use solvent), paying particular attention to the mounting holes, bushing grooves, etc.

3. If shoe support springs are used on the piston, remove them. Also remove any rubber bushings, and drive out any sleeves in the caliper ears with a punch.

4. Place cloths and wood inside the caliper to form a pad, and blow compressed air at low pressure through the fluid inlet hole to remove the piston—*do not* try to pry the piston out, since its outside diameter is the primary sealing surface and prying on the piston will damage it **(Fig. 13-38)**.

5. Remove the piston boot and seal from the caliper bore. *Do not* use a metal tool to pry, because you can damage the bore. A wooden cuticle tool used by manicurists is ideal for this.

6. Blow out all caliper and bleed valve passages with compressed air, and clean the cylinder bore and piston with clean brake fluid.

Cleaning and Inspection

1. Clean all metal parts in denatured alcohol, and blow dry with compressed air. If shop air supply is lubricated, *do not use,* because the mineral oil will leave a film on the metal parts.

2. Inspect the caliper cylinder bore for scoring, pitting or corrosion. The same techniques used on wheel cylinders are applicable to the caliper cylinders. If the bore is very rough or pitted, it is corroded and the caliper must be replaced. A staining condition or very light roughness can be removed with crocus cloth. Use a rotating motion only—*do not* slide the crocus cloth back and forth in the bore, or polish with an abrasive in an attempt to ''save'' a caliper that needs replacing.

3. Inspect the condition of the pistons. The outside diameter of the piston is plated to a close tolerance. If any defects are noted, replace the piston.

4. Use a feeler gauge to check the piston clearance in the bore. Specified clearance is between 0.002-in. and 0.006-in. If the clearance exceeds this specification, replace the caliper.

To Assemble

1. Lubricate new rubber parts with clean brake fluid.
2. Install the seal in the cylinder bore groove.
3. Lubricate the cylinder bore and piston with brake fluid, and install the boot in the piston groove with the fold facing the open piston end.
4. Install the piston in the cylinder bore until it is fully seated.
5. Seat the boot lip around the cylinder counterbore, and replace the brake hose fitting.
6. Lubricate and install new sleeves and bushings.
7. Where shoe support springs are used, replace in the piston, and install the brake shoes.
8. Reconnect the hydraulic line, replace the caliper on the disc, and install the mounting bolts.
9. Bleed the brakes.

FORD FLOATING CALIPER (KELSEY-HAYES)
To Disassemble
(Fig. 13-36)

1. Disconnect and plug the hydraulic brake hose, and remove the caliper according to the procedure specified under ''Pad Replacement.''

2. Clean the outside of the caliper with a cloth moistened in clean brake fluid (*do not* use solvent).

3. Remove the bleed valve, and drain brake fluid.

4. Place shop cloths inside the caliper to form a pad, and blow compressed air at low pressure through the fluid inlet hole to remove the piston—*do not* try to pry the piston out, because its outside diameter is the primary sealing surface, and prying will damage it.

5. Remove the piston boot and seal from the caliper bore. *Do not* use a metal tool to pry, because you can damage the bore. A wooden cuticle tool used by manicurists is ideal for this.

Cleaning and Inspection

1. Clean all metal parts in denatured alcohol, and blow dry with compressed air. If shop air supply is lubricated, *do not* use, because the mineral oil will leave a film on the metal parts.

2. Inspect the caliper cylinder bore for scoring, pitting or corrosion. The same techniques used on wheel cylinders are applicable to the caliper cylinders. If the bore is very rough or pitted, it is corroded and the caliper must be replaced. A staining condition or very light roughness can be removed with crocus cloth. Place the cloth on your finger and insert it in the bore. Use a rotating motion only—*do not* slide the crocus cloth back and forth in the bore or polish with abrasive trying to ''save'' a caliper that needs replacing.

3. Inspect the condition of the pistons. The outside diameter of the piston is plated to a close tolerance. If any defects are noted, replace the piston.

To Assemble

1. Lubricate new rubber parts in clean brake fluid.
2. Install the seal in the cylinder bore groove.
3. Lubricate the cylinder bore and piston with brake fluid, and install the boot in the piston groove.
4. Install the piston in the cylinder bore, open end out, and fit the boot over the piston and into its groove.
5. Reconnect the hydraulic line, replace the anchor plate assembly on the caliper, and replace the locating pins. Torque to specifications.
6. Install the brake shoes and retaining clips, connect the stabilizer, and install the bleed valve. Bleed the brakes.

DISC BRAKE HUB AND ROTOR SERVICE

The hub and rotor assembly is cast as a single unit on all American cars, except the Cadillac Eldorado, Oldsmobile Toronado and Corvette (rear discs only). The hub contains the wheel bearing and wheel mounting studs, while the hollow-cast rotor section with its integral cooling fins provides the contact surface for brake shoe application. In all cases, except the three cars mentioned above, the hub and rotor assembly is serviced as an assembly; if either the hub or the rotor is defective, the entire unit is replaced.

MINIMUM REQUIREMENTS

Proper brake disc tolerances are extremely critical to safe brake operation, and servicing the disc when necessary is very important. In addition to the radial and circumferential specifications described in **Fig. 13-39**, the lateral runout of the brake disc should not exceed a total indicator reading as specified. This is checked by installing a dial indicator to some part of the suspension so that the indicator stylus touches the face of the rotor at about 1 in. from its edge. Tighten the wheel-bearing adjustment nut to remove all bearing play and, with the dial indicator set at zero, turn the rotor one complete revolution, checking the indicator dial as the rotor is turned. Be sure to readjust the wheel bearing after removing the dial indicator **(Fig. 13-40)**.

Measure the rotor thickness with a micrometer at 90° intervals around its circumference at the same distance inward from rotor edge; compare to specifications.

ROTOR REFINISHING

1. If the rotor meets the measured specifications, and its surfaces have heavy rust, scale and/or scoring less than 0.009-in. deep, resurface on a brake lathe with flat sanding discs.

2. If scoring exceeds 0.009-in., or if lateral runout, flatness, parallelism or thickness variation exceed specifications, refinish the rotor on a disc brake lathe to a nondirection cross-hatch micro-finish.

3. If refinishing causes the rotor to fall below the minimum specified thickness, replace it.

BRAKE DRUM SERVICE

Whenever brake drums are removed, they should be cleaned and inspected for defects. Scoring, deep grooving and out-of-round conditions should be corrected, because they reduce braking efficiency and can lead to brake failure. A cracked drum is not suitable for further use and must be replaced—*do not* try to weld it.

RECONDITIONING

Slight scoring conditions can be corrected by polishing with a fine emery cloth; heavy scoring will require a refinishing of the drum surface. When the brake linings are only slightly worn, but drum grooving is present, the drum should be turned on a lathe to remove the grooves, and the lining ridges should be removed with a lining grinder. If brake linings are worn, but not to the point of replacement, and the drum is grooved, it should be polished but not turned until the linings are replaced. Whenever the brake drum is turned, only

enough metal should be removed to restore a smooth and true braking surface. If turning causes the drum to exceed the original diameter by more than 0.060-in. (Chevette, 0.025-in.), discard and install a replacement. Whenever the drum on one side of the axle is refinished, the other drum on that axle should be turned to the same specification.

TAPERED OR OUT-OF-ROUND DRUMS

If a brake drum is more than 0.006-in. out-of-round on the diameter, rough brake application, irregular tire wear and a pulsating brake pedal will result. The drum should be turned on a lathe to restore a true braking surface. An inside micrometer is used to measure for an out-of-round or tapered-wear condition, and measurements should be taken at the open and closed edges of the machined surface, as well as at right angles to each other.

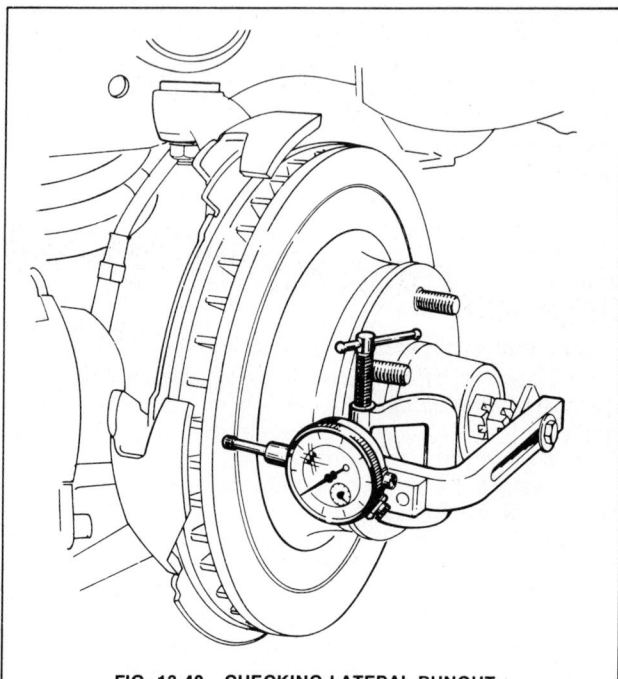

FIG. 13-40 CHECKING LATERAL RUNOUT

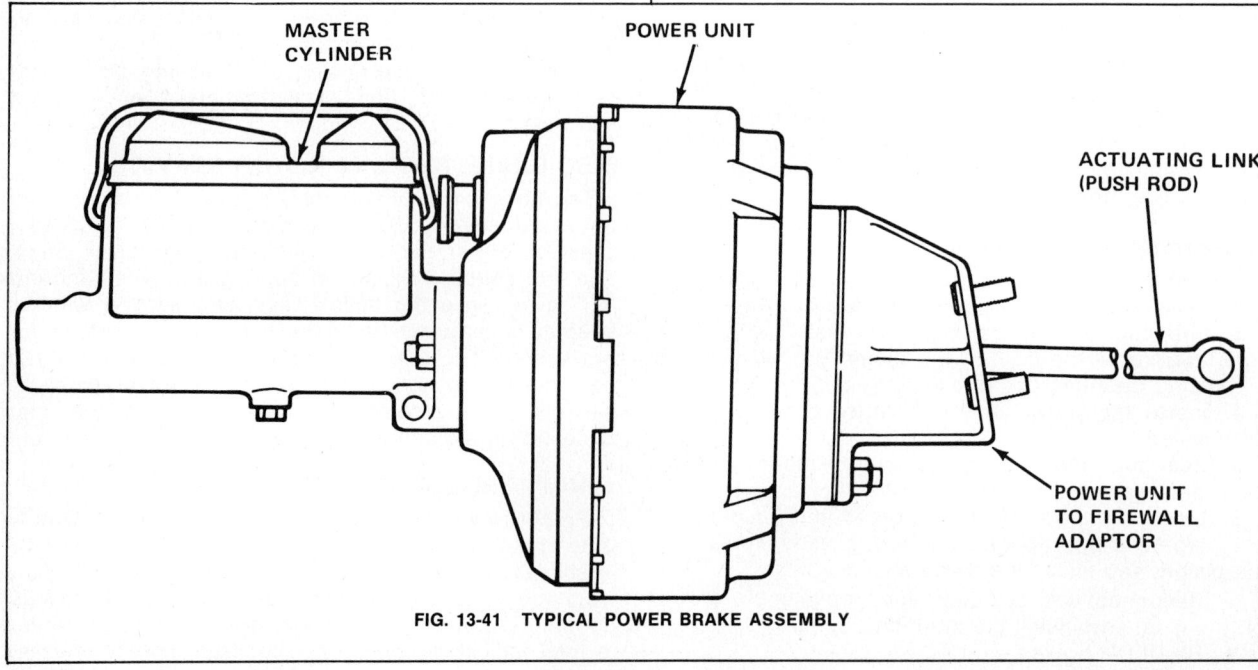

FIG. 13-41 TYPICAL POWER BRAKE ASSEMBLY

1. Place the drum on a level surface.

2. Position the tips of the inside micrometer at the center of the drum face, and move both horizontally and vertically while adjusting the micrometer until maximum contact is made.

3. Turning the drum 45° each time, repeat Step 2 to obtain four readings. The maximum difference between these four readings cannot exceed 0.006-in. or the drum should be refinished.

POWER BRAKES

DESCRIPTION (Fig. 13-41)

Power brake systems differ from conventional brake systems only in the way in which the master cylinder is actuated; the hydraulic and mechanical problems remain the same. Modern power brake units are installed between the master cylinder and brake pedal, and they use a combination of manifold vacuum and atmospheric pressure to assist the driver by reducing the amount of effort and degree of pedal travel necessary to apply the brakes. A vacuum hose connects the diaphragm housing to the intake manifold, and a check valve prevents assist vacuum from being lost during periods of low manifold vacuum.

OPERATION

When the brake pedal is depressed, the vacuum source is cut off and atmospheric pressure enters on one side of the diaphragm, causing the master cylinder pistons to move. Releasing the pedal applies vacuum to both sides of the diaphragm, and the diaphragm and pistons return to a released position. Should the vacuum unit fail, the booster-to-master-cylinder push rod will ensure brake application when the pedal is de-pressed, but requires pressure equal to that of a conventional system.

POWER BRAKE SYSTEM OPERATIONAL TEST

1. With the engine off, pump the brake pedal until the supply vacuum is completely used up, then apply a light but steady pressure on the pedal.

2. With the transmission in NEUTRAL or PARK, start the engine and let it idle. If the system is operating properly, the constant pressure on the pedal should cause it to travel toward the floor.

POWER BRAKE SYSTEM VACUUM LEAK TEST

1. With the transmission in NEUTRAL or PARK, start the engine and let it idle without touching the brakes.

2. Shut the engine off and wait one minute, then depress and release the brake pedal several times. If the same amount or more pedal travel is required with each application, there is a vacuum leak in the system.

POWER BRAKE UNIT OVERHAUL (Fig. 13-42)

Booster units used by American Motors, Chrysler and Ford cars are serviced as an assembly only, and if defective, should be removed and replaced with a new unit. A booster-to-master-cylinder push-rod adjustment is possible, but this is factory-set to the correct height at the time of assembly of the booster unit and, under normal service conditions, does not require further adjustment.

The Delco-Moraine and Bendix booster units used by GM cars are repairable, but because of the specialized equipment required and the difficulty in disassembly and correct assembly, it is recommended that a faulty unit be replaced with a new or rebuilt one.

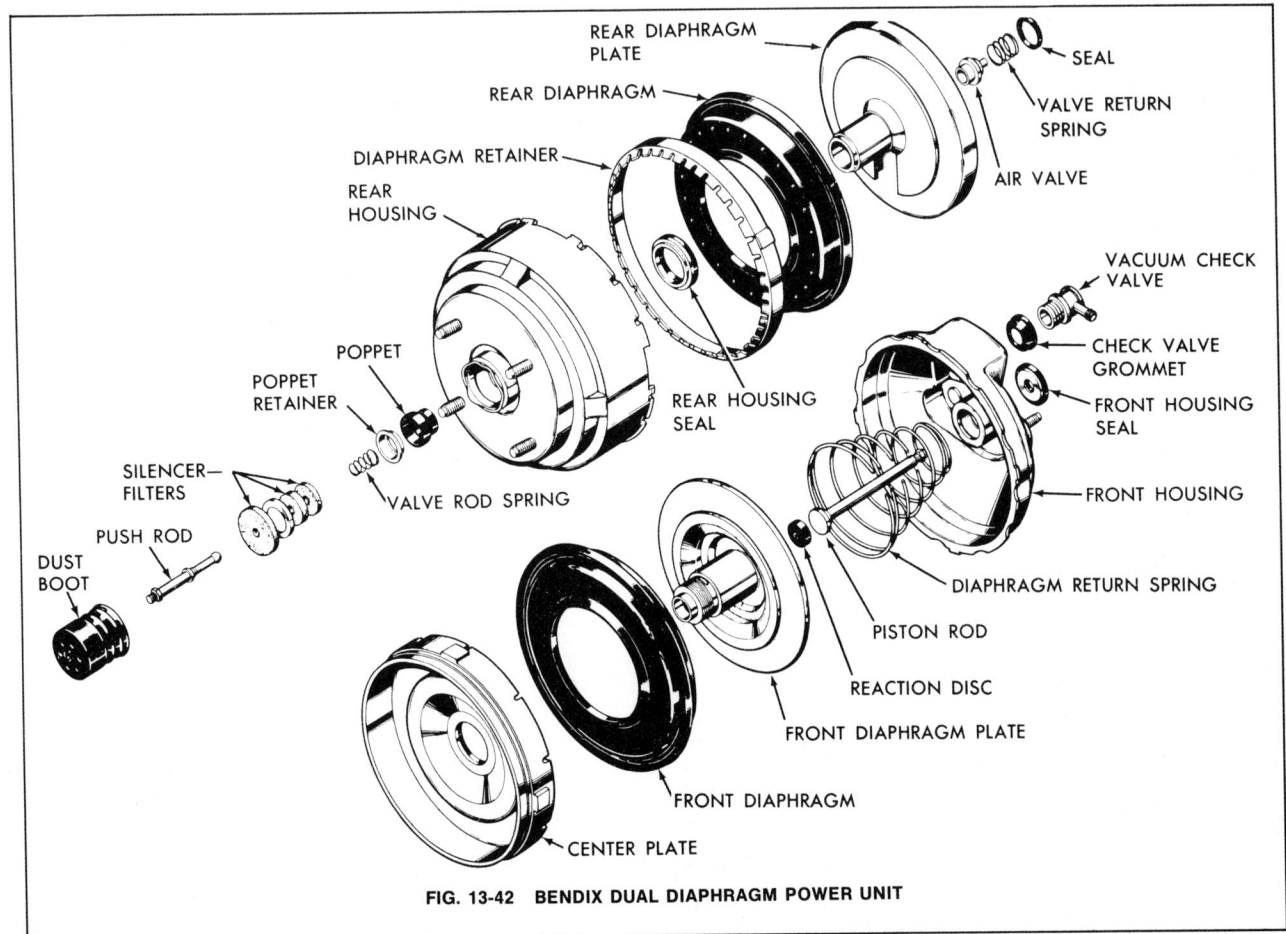

FIG. 13-42 BENDIX DUAL DIAPHRAGM POWER UNIT

INDEX

MANUAL STEERING

To provide the driver with control over front wheel direction, American cars use either a recirculating ball and worm or rack and pinion steering design.

RECIRCULATING BALL AND WORM

As shown in **Fig. 14-1,** the end of the steering input shaft, called the worm or wormshaft, is machined with a continuous spiral groove in which ball bearings ride to move a ball nut assembly up or down the wormshaft. Tubes connecting the lock-nut/sleeve unit allow the balls to constantly recirculate, distributing wear evenly among them, while support for the wormshaft is provided by ball bearing (worm bearing) assemblies at each end of the steering box housing.

Because the wormshaft is coupled directly to the steering column shaft, turning the steering wheel causes the wormshaft to turn in the same direction, moving the ball nut assembly along its length. The balls circulate in one direction for a right-hand turn and in the opposite direction for a left-hand turn. Teeth on the ball nut assembly engage sector teeth on the Pitman or sector shaft and cause it to move the Pitman arm, which transmits the desired directional movement to the steering linkage and thus to the front wheels **(Fig. 14-2).**

Two adjustments are possible on a recirculating ball and worm steering gearbox. A worm-bearing adjuster screw **(Fig. 14-3)** allows worm-bearing preload adjustment, and a sector shaft or lash adjusting screw **(Fig. 14-4)** takes up any excessive play between the sector-shaft gear teeth and those on the ball nut.

RACK AND PINION

This steering design uses an input-shaft pinion gear connected to the steering column shaft by a flexible coupling. Similar to the pinion gear used in a differential, it is cut on an angle and meshed on one side with a steel bar or rack contained in the steering gearbox, as shown in **Fig. 14-5.** The gearbox is positioned between the tie rods in the steering linkage and, with the rack mounted parallel to the front axle, the input shaft pinion causes it to move from side to side as the steering wheel is turned. In this way, it operates directly on the steering linkage, without the use of a Pitman arm, and transmits steering motion to the wheels **(Fig. 14-6).**

Two adjustments are possible on the rack and pinion gear, depending upon design. On the Ford rack and pinion, the support-yoke-to-rack preload and pinion bearing preload can be adjusted. With the Chevette design, the rack-bearing-to-rack preload is adjustable. In each case, the steering gear must be removed from the car for adjustment.

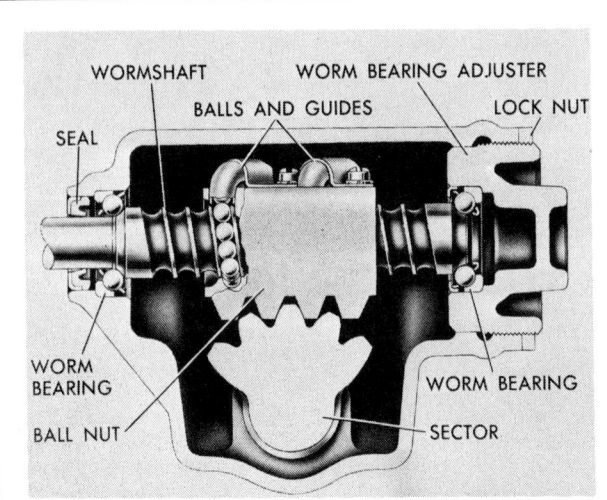

FIG. 14-1   RECIRCULATING BALL AND WORM DESIGN

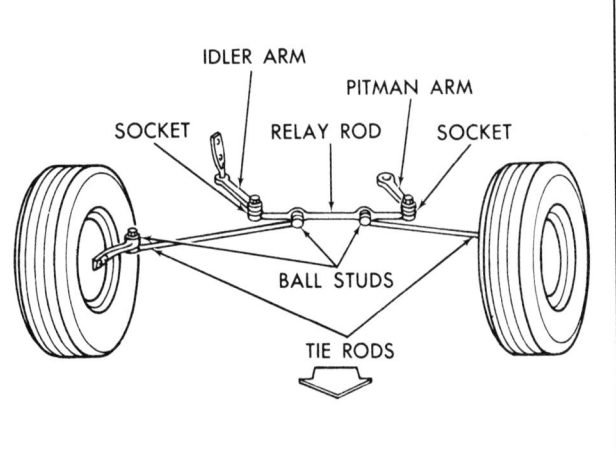

FIG. 14-2   STEERING LINKAGE RELATIONSHIP

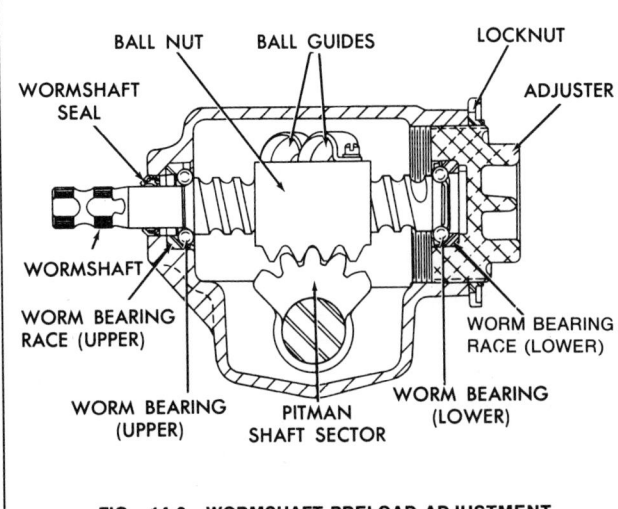

FIG. 14-3   WORMSHAFT PRELOAD ADJUSTMENT

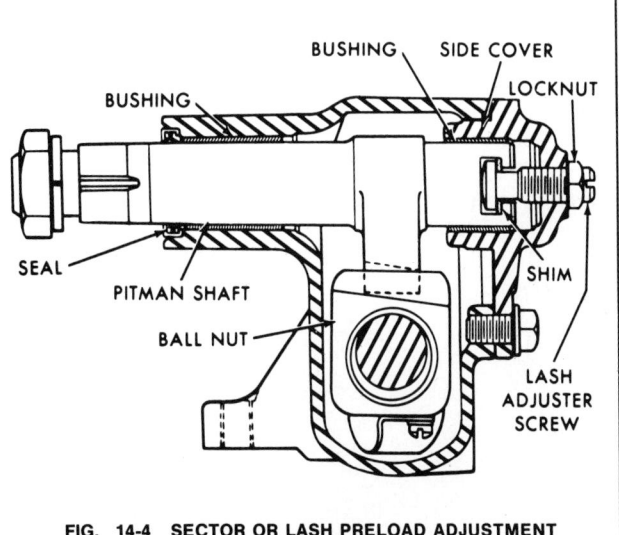

FIG. 14-4   SECTOR OR LASH PRELOAD ADJUSTMENT

STEERING GEAR AND WHEEL ALIGNMENT

Raise the front of the car and check the steering gear, its linkage and the front suspension components before attempting any steering gear adjustments. Should any excessively worn or damaged parts be found, they must be replaced or you will be unable to make the correct adjustments.

Incorrect steering gearbox alignment will also stress the wormshaft and prevent correct steering-gear adjustments. Check both the steering box and its mounting seat, tightening the attachment bolts to specifications if necessary. Should the steering gearbox require realignment, loosen the bolts and it will align itself correctly. If a gap then exists between the steering gearbox and its seat, use shims for alignment instead of trying to draw the box to the seat by excessively tightening the attachment bolts.

With the steering gear set on its high point (straight-ahead position), the front wheels should be in a straight-ahead position, with the Pitman arm pointing directly forward and the steering wheel spokes in their normal position. If the spokes do not come to rest properly, adjust the steering wheel as follows:

WITH RECIRCULATING BALL STEERING

1. Loosen the clamp bolts on each tie-rod adjusting sleeve.

2. If toe-in adjustment is correct, turn both sleeves up or downward the same number of turns until the steering wheel spokes return to their normal position **(Fig. 14-7)**.

3. When toe-in adjustment is not correct, turn both sleeves to lengthen or shorten each tie rod equally until toe-in is set to specifications. If this does not return the steering wheel spokes to their normal position **(Fig. 14-8)**, adjust both sleeves as in Step 2.

4. Once the steering-wheel-spoke position and toe-in adjustments are correct, lubricate the clamps, bolts and nuts, then torque the clamp bolts on both sleeves to specifications, taking care not to change the sleeve position in the process.

WITH RACK AND PINION

1. Loosen the tie-rod-bellows clamp screw (if used) and free the tie rod seal.

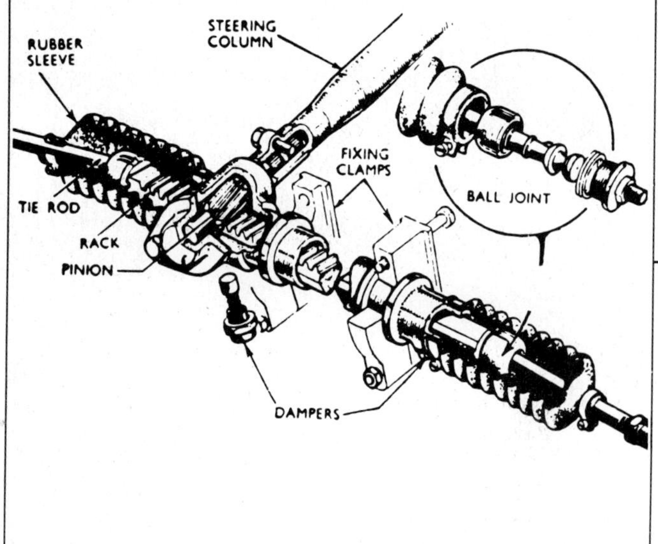

FIG. 14-5 RACK AND PINION GEARBOX

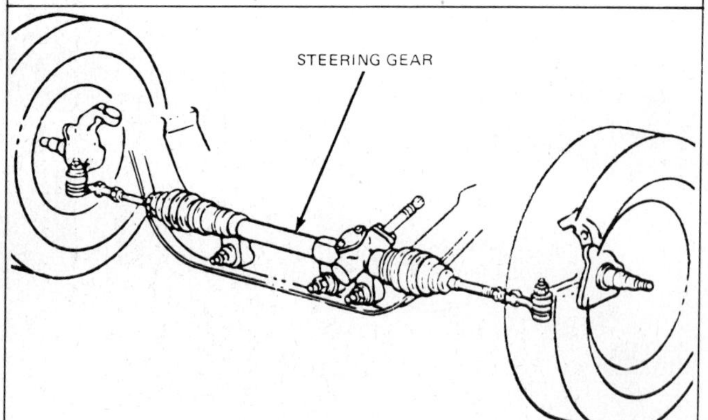

FIG. 14-6 RACK AND PINION STEERING RELATIONSHIP

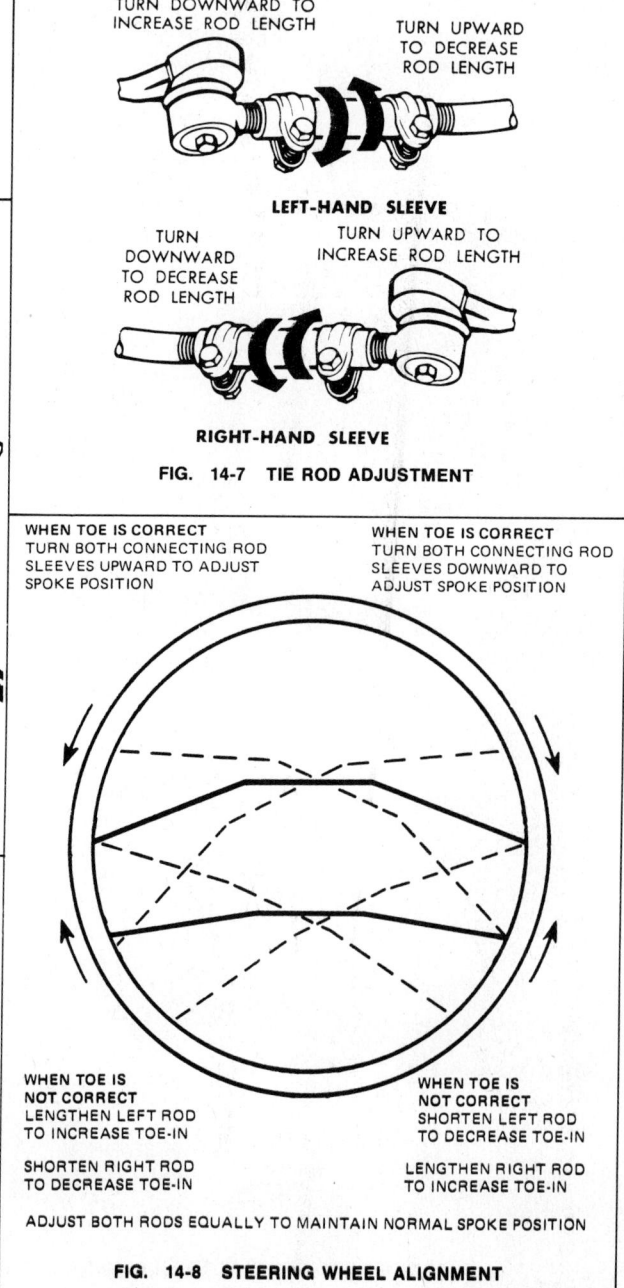

TURN DOWNWARD TO INCREASE ROD LENGTH

TURN UPWARD TO DECREASE ROD LENGTH

LEFT-HAND SLEEVE

TURN DOWNWARD TO DECREASE ROD LENGTH

TURN UPWARD TO INCREASE ROD LENGTH

RIGHT-HAND SLEEVE

FIG. 14-7 TIE ROD ADJUSTMENT

WHEN TOE IS CORRECT TURN BOTH CONNECTING ROD SLEEVES UPWARD TO ADJUST SPOKE POSITION

WHEN TOE IS CORRECT TURN BOTH CONNECTING ROD SLEEVES DOWNWARD TO ADJUST SPOKE POSITION

WHEN TOE IS NOT CORRECT LENGTHEN LEFT ROD TO INCREASE TOE-IN

SHORTEN RIGHT ROD TO DECREASE TOE-IN

WHEN TOE IS NOT CORRECT SHORTEN LEFT ROD TO DECREASE TOE-IN

LENGTHEN RIGHT ROD TO INCREASE TOE-IN

ADJUST BOTH RODS EQUALLY TO MAINTAIN NORMAL SPOKE POSITION

FIG. 14-8 STEERING WHEEL ALIGNMENT

2. Place an open-end wrench on the flat of the tie rod socket to prevent it from turning while the tie-rod jam nut is being loosened, as in **Fig. 14-9.**

3. If toe-in adjustment is correct, turn both tie-rod inner ends up or down the same number of turns until the steering wheel spokes return to their normal position. Use pliers, but *do not* position them on the tie rod threads for adjustment.

4. When toe-in is not correctly set, turning the tie rods to increase the number of threads showing will decrease toe; turning to decrease the number of visible threads will increase toe.

5. Hold flats of the tie rod socket with an open-end wrench and tighten the tie-rod jam nut to 35-50 ft.-lbs. Tighten the bellows clamp screw securely.

MANUAL STEERING DIAGNOSIS

CONDITION	CAUSE	TO CORRECT
Hard Steering or Poor Returnability.	1. Low or uneven front tire pressure.	1. Inflate to recommended pressure.
	2. Incorrect front wheel alignment.	2. Adjust wheel alignment angles; see Chapter 16.
	3. Steering gearbox lubricant level low.	3. Add lubricant as required.
	4. Steering gear shaft adjustment too tight.	4. Adjust to specifications.
	5. Steering linkage needs lubrication.	5. Lubricate suspension components.
Excessive Play in Steering	1. Loose or worn front wheel bearings.	1. Adjust or replace.
	2. Worn ball joints.	2. Replace as required.
	3. Loose or worn steering linkage.	3. Replace defective parts.
	4. Steering gearbox attachment bolts loose.	4. Tighten to specifications.
	5. Loose steering arm at steering knuckle.	5. Tighten to specifications.
	6. Loose steering arm on steering gear shaft.	6. Inspect for damage and replace.
	7. Loose or worn steering gear shaft.	7. Adjust to specifications; if still too loose, replace worn parts.
	8. Loose wormshaft bearing preload.	8. Adjust to specifications.

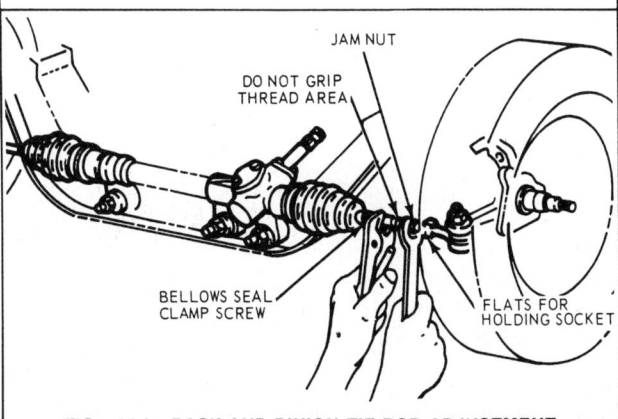

FIG. 14-9   RACK AND PINION TIE-ROD ADJUSTMENT

ALL GENERAL MOTORS MODELS (Except Chevette); ALL AMERICAN MOTORS MODELS (Except Pacer)

Saginaw Recirculating Ball Steering

WORM BEARING AND PITMAN SHAFT PRELOAD ADJUSTMENTS

The manual steering gear is an inline recirculating-ball, worm-and-nut design connected to the steering column shaft by a flexible coupling to permit independent removal of either. The teeth on the Pitman shaft sector and ball nut assembly are designed to fit together tighter when the front wheels are in a straight-ahead position.

A worm bearing adjuster preloads both upper and lower worm thrust bearings, controlling worm bearing adjustment. An adjusting screw moves the Pitman shaft up or down to control ball-nut/Pitman-shaft gear teeth engagement and provides overcenter or Pitman-shaft lash adjustment **(Fig. 14-10)**. Always check and adjust worm bearing preload before making Pitman-shaft preload adjustment. To prevent possible gear damage or failure, adjust in the following sequence:

1. Disconnect the Pitman arm from the steering gear shaft, using an appropriate puller as in **Fig. 14-11.**

2. Loosen the Pitman-shaft adjusting-screw locknut and turn the screw counterclockwise a few turns.

3. Carefully turn the steering wheel in one direction until it stops, then turn back one full turn.

4. Remove the steering-wheel horn-button cap or shroud and fit an in.-lb. torque wrench with a ¾-in. socket on the steering shaft nut to measure worm bearing preload.

5. Rotate the steering wheel through a 90° arc (¼-turn). Torque reading should read between 5 and 8 in.-lbs. for all I-6, V-6 and V-8 applications; 3 to 7 in.-lbs. for I-4 engines.

6. If preload is not within above specifications, loosen the adjuster locknut and turn the adjuster plug. Seen from the bottom of the gear, this plug is turned clockwise to increase preload and counterclockwise to decrease preload.

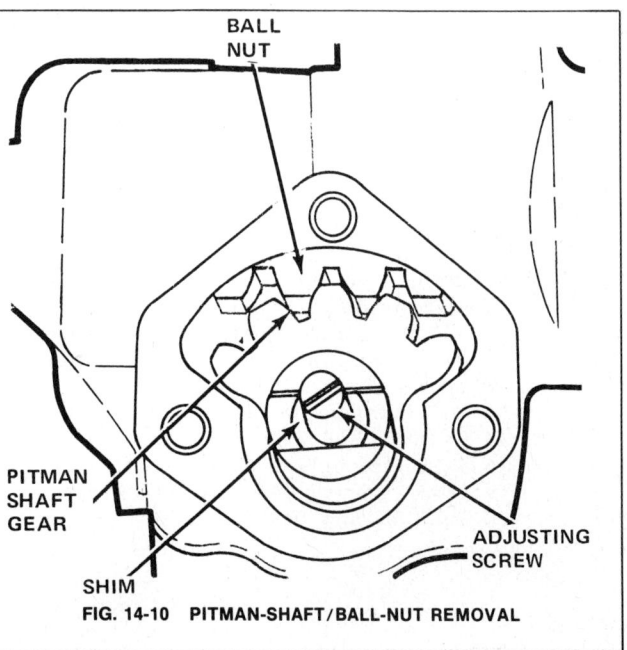

FIG. 14-10   PITMAN-SHAFT/BALL-NUT REMOVAL

FIG. 14-11   REMOVING PITMAN ARM

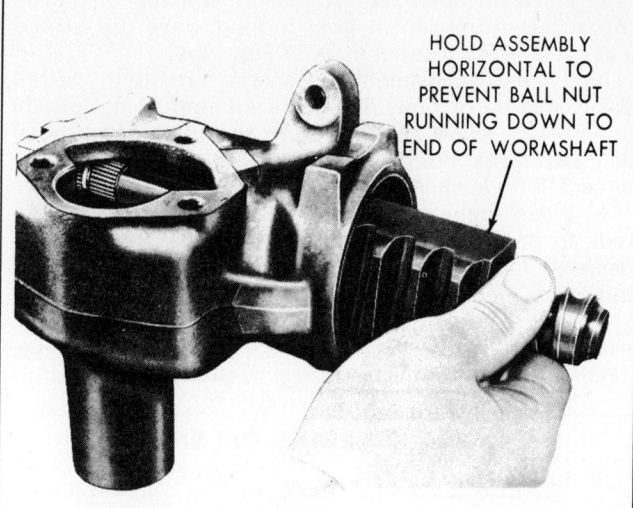

HOLD ASSEMBLY HORIZONTAL TO PREVENT BALL NUT RUNNING DOWN TO END OF WORMSHAFT

FIG. 14-13   WORMSHAFT/BALL-NUT REMOVAL

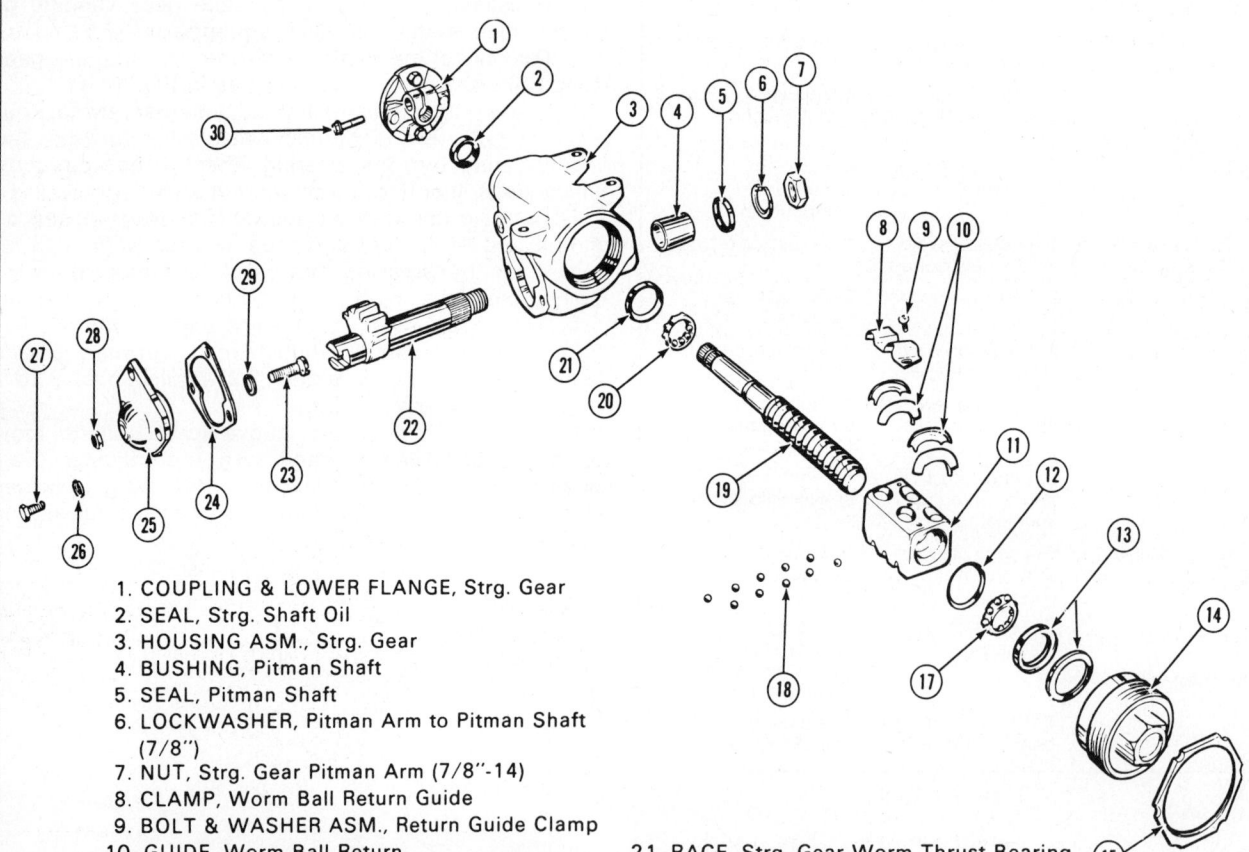

1. COUPLING & LOWER FLANGE, Strg. Gear
2. SEAL, Strg. Shaft Oil
3. HOUSING ASM., Strg. Gear
4. BUSHING, Pitman Shaft
5. SEAL, Pitman Shaft
6. LOCKWASHER, Pitman Arm to Pitman Shaft (7/8")
7. NUT, Strg. Gear Pitman Arm (7/8"-14)
8. CLAMP, Worm Ball Return Guide
9. BOLT & WASHER ASM., Return Guide Clamp
10. GUIDE, Worm Ball Return
11. NUT, Steering Gear Worm Ball
12. RETAINER, Worm Thrust Adj. Lower Bearing
13. RACE, Strg. Gear Worm Thrust Bearing
14. ADJUSTER, Worm Thrust Bearing
15. NUT, Worm Bearing Adjusting
17. BEARING, Strg. Gear Thrust
18. BALL, Steering Gear Worm
19. SHAFT, Steering Gear (w/Balls & Nut)
20. BEARING, Strg. Gear Thrust

21. RACE, Strg. Gear Worm Thrust Bearing
22. SHAFT ASM., Pitman
23. SCREW, Lash Adjuster
24. GASKET, Housing Side Cover
25. COVER, Housing Side
26. LOCKWASHER, Cover to Housing (3/8")
27. BOLT, Cover to Housing (3/8"-16 × 3/4")
28. NUT, Sector Adjusting Screw (7/16"-20 Check)
29. SHIM, PKG., Lash Adjuster
30. BOLT, Shaft Flange to Shaft Clamping

FIG. 14-12   SAGINAW MANUAL GEARBOX

7. Tighten the locknut to 85 ft.-lbs. and recheck preload.

8. Turn the steering wheel slowly from full left to full right, counting the exact number of steering wheel turns.

9. Turn the steering wheel back exactly one-half the number of lock-to-lock turns to locate the steering gear over center, then turn it one-half turn off-center.

10. Loosen the Pitman-shaft adjusting-screw locknut and turn the screw until you have added 4 to 10 in.-lbs. drag in addition to the worm bearing preload already set. Check adjustment as in Steps 4 and 5.

11. Torque the Pitman-shaft adjusting-screw locknut 25 to 35 ft.-lbs. and recheck adjustment as in Steps 4 and 5; total should be between 12 and 16 in.-lbs. for all but I-4 engines (I-4 not to exceed 11 in.-lbs.).

12. Reconnect the Pitman arm to the steering gear shaft and torque the nut to 180 ft.-lbs. (115 ft.-lbs. for AMC; 140 ft.-lbs. for I-4 powered GM vehicles). Stake the nut to the shaft with a punch by dimpling the nut surface near the shaft to lock it in place.

STEERING GEAR REMOVAL/INSTALLATION

TO REMOVE

1. Unbolt the flexible coupling between the steering gearbox and the steering-column shaft.

2. Use a puller to remove the Pitman arm from the Pitman shaft.

3. Unbolt and remove the steering gearbox from the frame siderail.

TO INSTALL

1. Line up the flexible coupling and steering shaft, then bolt the steering gearbox to the frame siderail and torque to 70 ft.-lbs.

2. Fit the Pitman arm to Pitman shaft and torque to 180 ft.-lbs. (115 ft.-lbs. for AMC; 140 ft.-lbs. for I-4 powered GM vehicles).

3. Replace the flexible coupling bolts and torque to 30 ft.-lbs.

STEERING GEAR DISASSEMBLY/ASSEMBLY

Work on a clean bench with clean tools. Drain off excess fluid and clean exterior of gearbox thoroughly with solvent before beginning disassembly. Handle all interior parts **(Fig. 14-12)** carefully to prevent nicks, burrs and scratches.

TO DISASSEMBLE

1. With the steering gearbox secured in a vise, rotate the wormshaft from stop to stop, turning it back exactly halfway to center the gear.

2. Remove the Pitman-shaft adjusting-screw locknut and side-cover attaching bolts. Lift the cover and Pitman shaft assembly from the housing. You may have to turn the wormshaft slightly to permit passage of Pitman shaft through the opening and out of the housing.

3. Remove the adjusting screw locknut and turn the screw clockwise to remove the Pitman shaft from the cover. *Do not* lose shim.

4. Loosen and remove the adjuster plug locknut and adjuster plug assembly.

5. Withdraw the wormshaft and ball nut assembly. Keep the ball nut from running down to either end of the worm, or you may damage the return guides **(Fig. 14-13)**.

6. Carefully pry out the lower bearing retainer with a suitable screwdriver, and remove the bearing from the adjuster plug.

7. Pry out and discard the Pitman-shaft and wormshaft seals.

8. If the ball nut is to be disassembled, hold it clamp-side up and remove both clamp and return guides.

9. Turn the ball nut over a clean container and rotate the wormshaft slowly from side to side to eject the balls, then slide the ball nut assembly from the wormshaft.

TO ASSEMBLE AND ADJUST

1. Install and lubricate the new Pitman-shaft and wormshaft seals.

2. Slide the ball nut on the wormshaft, with the guide holes lining up and the shallow end of the teeth to the left of the steering wheel position.

3. Install the return guides and fill each with an equal number of balls, rocking the shaft from side to side. *Do not* rotate the shaft, or the balls will enter the crossover passages and bind **(Fig. 14-14)**.

4. Replace the guide clamp and tighten its holddown screw.

5. Place the upper bearing over the wormshaft, center the ball nut assembly on the wormshaft and slide into the housing.

6. Fit the lower bearing in the adjuster plug, install the retainer and screw the plug into the housing until almost all end play has been eliminated.

7. Replace the Pitman-shaft adjusting screw and the shim in the slotted end of the Pitman shaft. End play must not exceed 0.002-in. **(Fig. 14-15)**. If clearance is too tight or too loose, use a new shim. An available shim kit contains four different thicknesses—0.063-in., 0.065-in., 0.067-in. and 0.069-in.

8. Lubricate the steering gear with multi-purpose chassis grease and rotate the wormshaft to spread the grease.

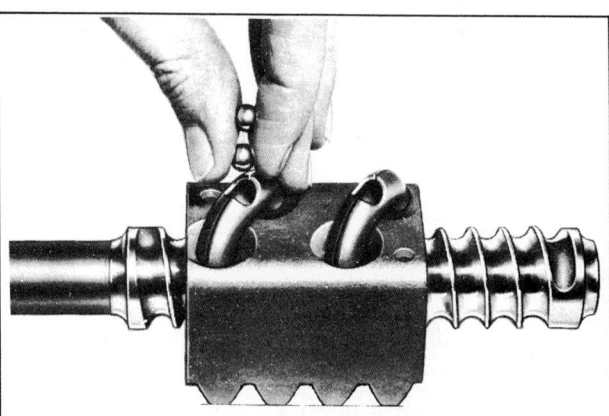

FIG. 14-14   FILLING BALL CIRCUITS

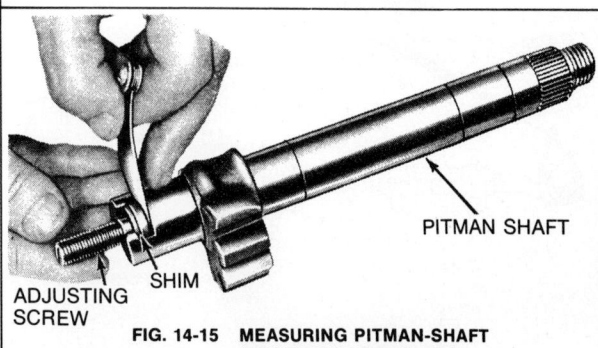

PITMAN SHAFT

SHIM

ADJUSTING SCREW

FIG. 14-15   MEASURING PITMAN-SHAFT ADJUSTING-SCREW END

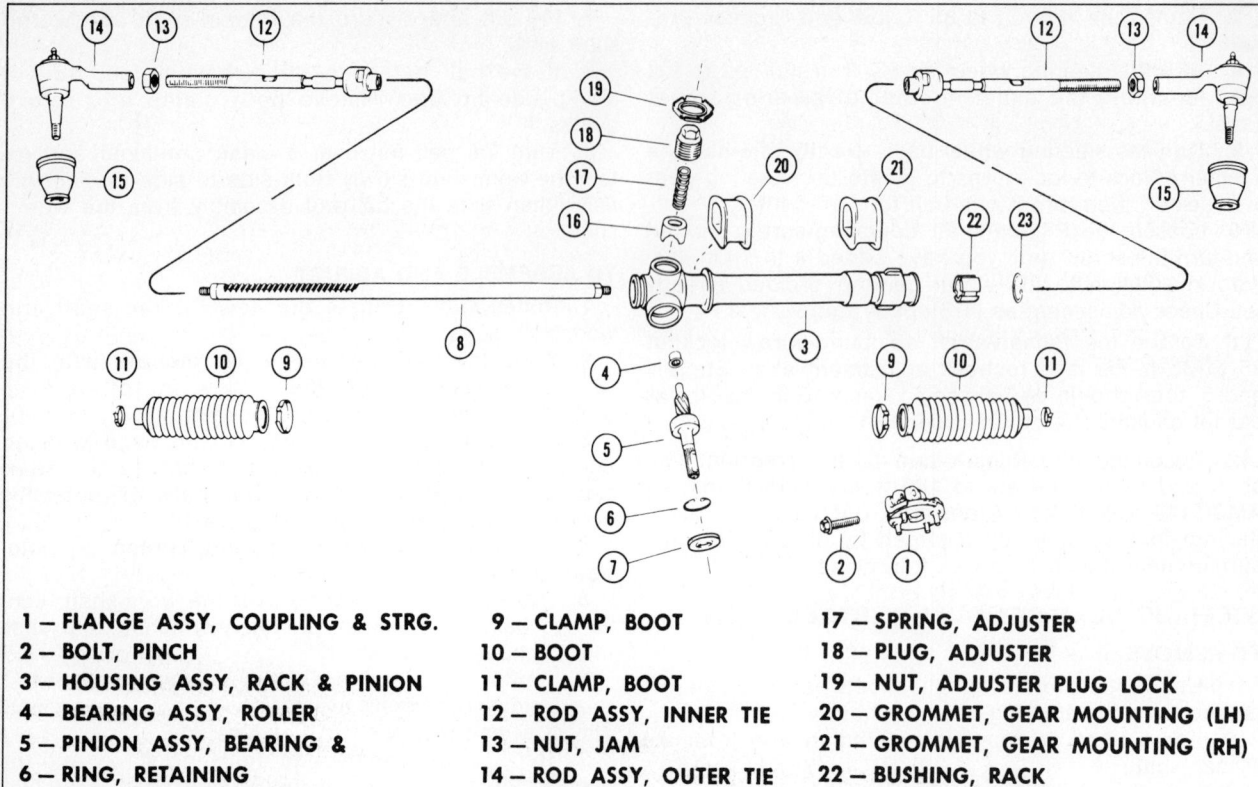

1 — FLANGE ASSY, COUPLING & STRG.
2 — BOLT, PINCH
3 — HOUSING ASSY, RACK & PINION
4 — BEARING ASSY, ROLLER
5 — PINION ASSY, BEARING &
6 — RING, RETAINING
7 — SEAL, STEERING PINION
8 — RACK, STEERING

9 — CLAMP, BOOT
10 — BOOT
11 — CLAMP, BOOT
12 — ROD ASSY, INNER TIE
13 — NUT, JAM
14 — ROD ASSY, OUTER TIE
15 — SEAL, TIE ROD
16 — BEARING, RACK

17 — SPRING, ADJUSTER
18 — PLUG, ADJUSTER
19 — NUT, ADJUSTER PLUG LOCK
20 — GROMMET, GEAR MOUNTING (LH)
21 — GROMMET, GEAR MOUNTING (RH)
22 — BUSHING, RACK
23 — RING, RETAINING

FIG. 14-16   CHEVETTE RACK AND PINION DISASSEMBLY

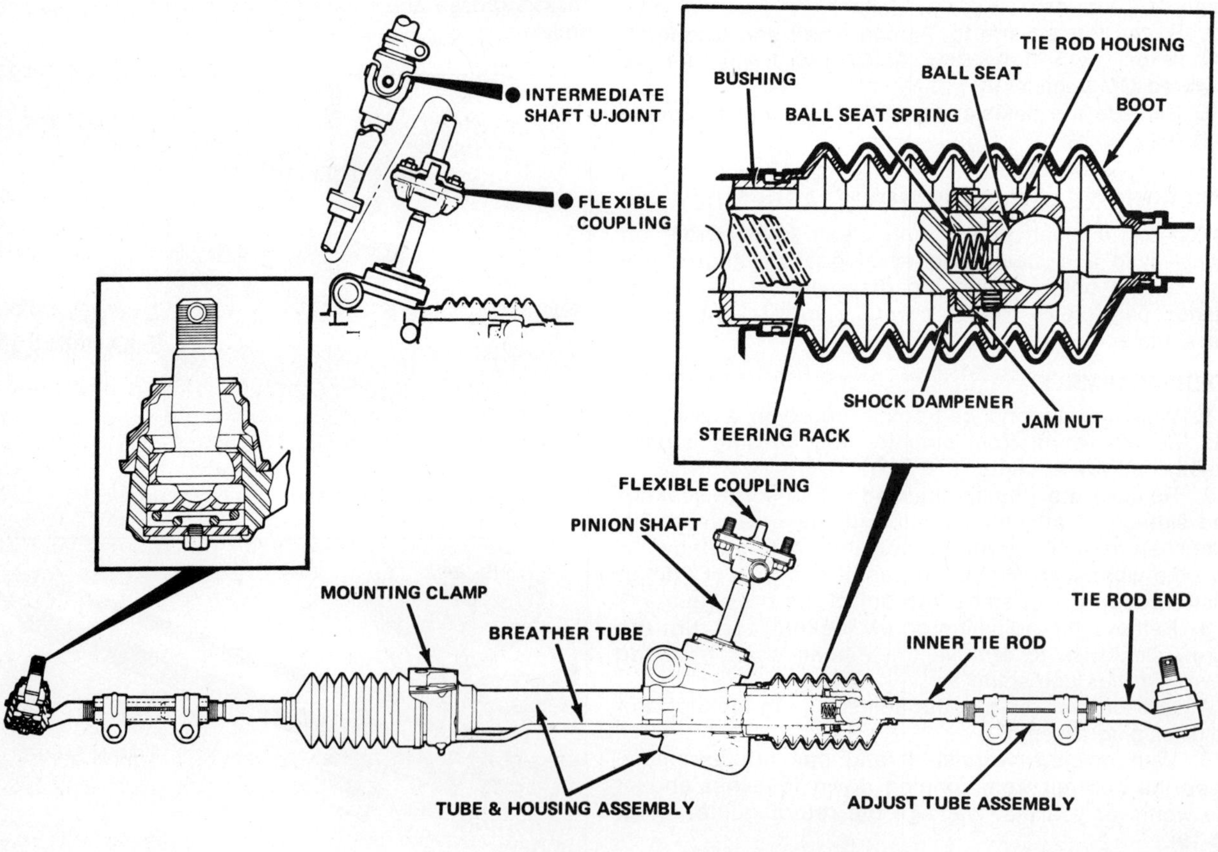

● INTERMEDIATE SHAFT U-JOINT

● FLEXIBLE COUPLING

BUSHING
BALL SEAT SPRING
BALL SEAT
TIE ROD HOUSING
BOOT

SHOCK DAMPENER
JAM NUT

STEERING RACK

FLEXIBLE COUPLING
PINION SHAFT
MOUNTING CLAMP
BREATHER TUBE
TIE ROD END
INNER TIE ROD
TUBE & HOUSING ASSEMBLY
ADJUST TUBE ASSEMBLY

FIG. 14-17   AMC PACER RACK AND PINION STEERING

9. Position the ball nut in its center of travel and install the Pitman shaft, making sure the center sector tooth engages the ball-nut center-tooth space.

10. Pack the housing and side cover bushing with grease, then install the side cover and gasket by turning the adjusting screw counterclockwise through its threaded cover hole.

11. Turn the adjusting screw until it bottoms, then back off one-quarter turn and install a new locknut loosely on the screw.

12. Replace and torque the side cover bolts to 30 ft.-lbs.

13. Turn the gear shaft carefully from stop to stop to check for binding.

14. Adjust as described earlier in the "Worm Bearing and Pitman Shaft Preload Adjustments" section.

1976-79 CHEVETTE ONLY
General Motors Rack and Pinion Steering
RACK BEARING TO RACK ADJUSTMENT

The pinion and much of the rack are encased in a die-cast aluminum housing. The pinion rotates within a sealed, upper ball bearing and a pressed-in, lower roller bearing, both of which provide pinion support. Compression of an adjuster spring maintains rack-to-pinion teeth engagement and provides wear take-up **(Fig. 14-16)**. To adjust:

1. Remove the steering housing from the car and secure the assembly in a soft-jaw vise fitted with pads to prevent housing damage. The adjuster plug should face upward and the pinion assembly toward the front.

2. Remove the adjuster plug locknut, plug and spring. Lift the rack bearing from the housing and inspect it carefully for wear. Replace if wear is excessive.

3. Install the rack bearing, and assemble the adjuster plug and spring in the housing.

4. Turn the adjuster plug inward until it bottoms, then back off 45° to 60°.

5. Fit an in.-lb. torque wrench to the end of the pinion assembly which faces forward. Torque required to turn the pinion should register between 8 and 10 in.-lbs.

6. Turn the adjuster plug in or out as required to adjust pinion torque to the specifications above, then install and torque the locknut to 50 ft.-lbs.

1975-79 PACER ONLY
Saginaw Rack and Pinion Steering
STEERING GEAR DESCRIPTION

The Pacer rack and pinion steering **(Fig. 14-17)** is an integral-tube/housing assembly permanently connected by a plastic, injection bonding process during manufacture. Two thrust bearings and two nylon bushings support the pinion shaft, with a nylon bushing at each end of the rack for support. A preload spring maintains pinion bushing location and compensates for bushing wear. The steering gear must be removed from the car and overhauled when preload adjustment is required.

STEERING GEAR REMOVAL/INSTALLATION
TO REMOVE

1. Disconnect the flexible coupling from the intermediate shaft flange. (The intermediate shaft connects from the flexible coupling to the car.)

2. Turning the steering wheel to full left stop, jack up the left lower control arm 2 ins. or more.

3. Remove the cotter pin and retaining nut from the tie rod end, then unhook the tie rod end.

4. Turning the steering wheel to full right stop, jack up the right lower control arm and repeat Step 3.

5. Loosen the clamp mounting bolts to reduce torsional stress on the clamp.

6. Remove the steering-gear-to-front-crossmember attaching bolts and lower the steering gear assembly.

TO INSTALL

1. Attach the steering gear to the front crossmember. Torque the mounting bracket bolts to 50 ft.-lbs. and the housing bolts to 75 ft.-lbs.

2. Connect the steering arm to the tie rod ends. The steering wheel should be turned in the direction of the tie rod end being connected and the corresponding lower control arm should be supported as it was during removal. Torque the nuts to 50 ft.-lbs.

3. Reconnect the flexible coupling to the intermediate shaft and torque the nuts to 25 ft.-lbs.

STEERING GEAR DISASSEMBLY/ASSEMBLY

Work on a clean bench with clean tools. Drain off excess fluid and clean the exterior of the steering gear thoroughly before beginning disassembly. Handle all interior parts **(Fig. 14-18)** carefully to prevent nicks, burrs and scratches.

TO DISASSEMBLE

1. Mount the steering gear housing in a soft-jaw vise—*do not* clamp any part of the tube.

2. Cut off the large-diameter boot clamps on the housing end of the steering gear; remove the clamps and slide the boots back to expose the rack teeth.

3. Move the rack toward the housing end of the steering gear as far as it will go by rotating the flexible coupling.

4. Remove the flexible-coupling pinch bolt and the coupling from the pinion shaft.

5. Unscrew and remove the adjuster plug locknut.

6. Pull up and rotate the pinion shaft counterclockwise to remove it from the housing. If pinion teeth are damaged, stop disassembly and discard the entire unit; if not, proceed.

7. Remove the contraction plug from the housing by inserting a ¼-in. rod through the upper and lower pinion bushings and tapping.

8. Remove the lower pinion bushing and preload spring from the housing.

9. Center the rack in the tube and housing, and install the pinion shaft and adjuster plug in the housing. Hand-tighten the plug.

10. Loosening both adjuster tube clamps, remove the tubes and tie rod assembly from the inner tie rods.

11. Mark the adjuster-tube position on the inner tie rod and the breather-tube position on the tube and housing for reference during reassembly.

12. Cut and remove the remaining boot clamps and boots.

13. Pull the breather tube from the mounting grommet and remove.

14. Clamping the inner tie rod in a vise, remove the shock dampener rings from the jam nut, and loosen the jam nut.

15. Loosen the tie-rod-housing setscrew and repeat Steps 14 and 15 on the opposite end of the rack.

16. Replace the housing in a vise and remove the inner tie-rod housing.

17. Remove the ball seats and springs, jam nuts and shock-dampener ring from the rack.

18. Remove the adjuster plug and pinion shaft from the housing **(Fig. 14-19).**

19. Remove the lower thrust bearing, bearing race and upper pinion bushing from the housing **(Fig. 14-19).**

20. Pull the steering rack from either end of the housing and remove.

21. Slip a knife blade under the rack bushings and remove with needlenose pliers.

22. Thread the adjuster plug back into the housing and pry out the pinion shaft seal with a screwdriver. Inspect all components for wear or damage, and replace as required.

TO ASSEMBLE

1. Press the new pinion shaft seal into the adjuster plug until it is flush with the plug face.

2. Compress the rack bushings with your fingers and force into the housing. Once in place, bushings will regain their original shape.

3. Install the rack in the housing, after lubricating the rack teeth.

4. Install the upper pinion bushing, pinion-shaft lower race and thrust bearing in the housing. Flanged edge of the race *must* face upward.

5. Center the steering rack in the housing. Distance

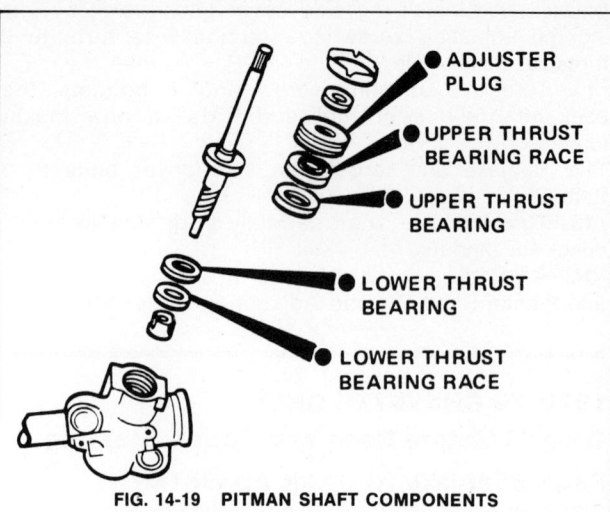

FIG. 14-19 PITMAN SHAFT COMPONENTS

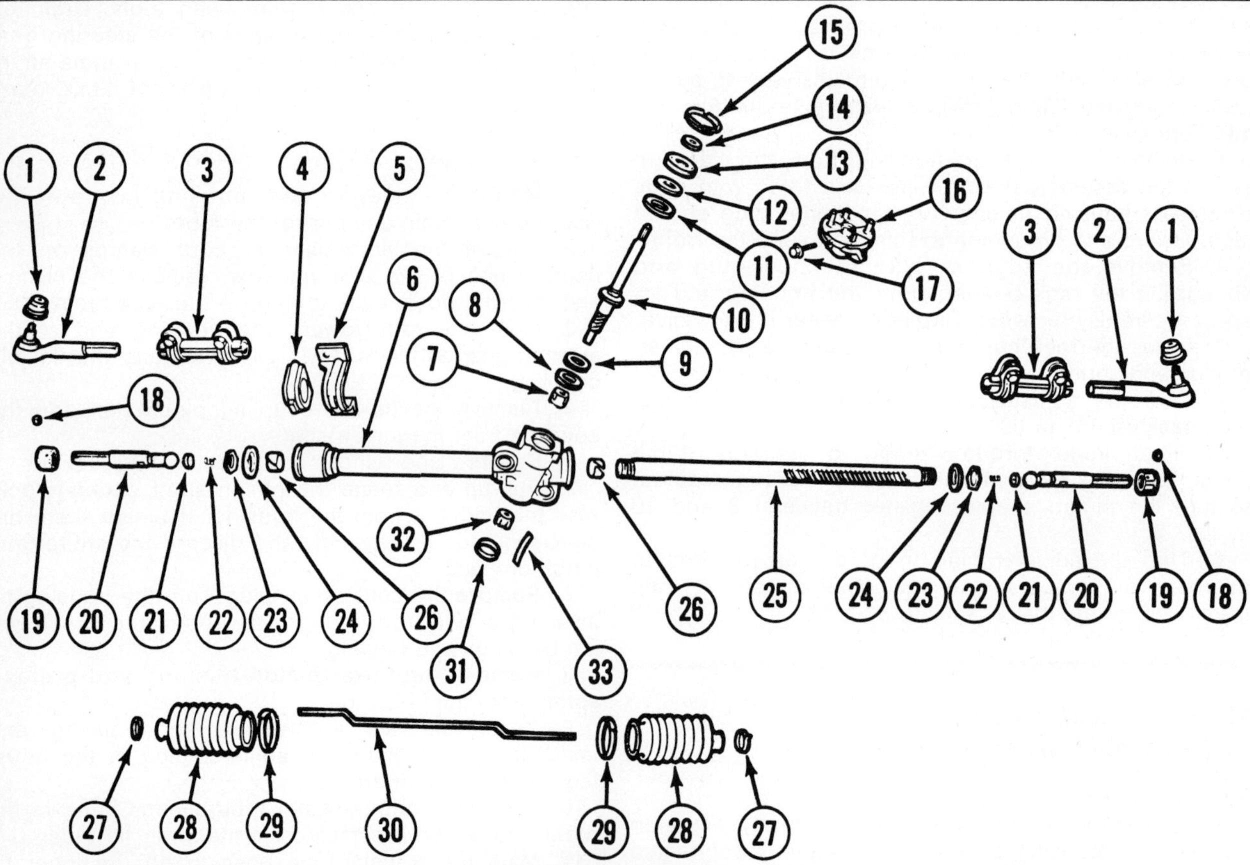

1. TIE ROD SEAL
2. TIE ROD END
3. ADJUSTER TUBE
4. MOUNTING GROMMET
5. MOUNTING CLAMP
6. TUBE AND HOUSING ASSEMBLY
7. UPPER PINION BUSHING
8. LOWER THRUST BEARING RACE
9. LOWER THRUST BEARING
10. PINION SHAFT
11. UPPER THRUST BEARING

12. UPPER THRUST BEARING RACE
13. ADJUSTER PLUG
14. PINION SHAFT SEAL
15. ADJUSTER PLUG LOCKNUT
16. FLEXIBLE COUPLING
17. PINCH BOLT
18. SET SCREW
19. TIE ROD HOUSING
20. INNER TIE ROD
21. BALL SEAT
22. BALL SEAT SPRING

23. JAM NUT
24. SHOCK DAMPENER RING
25. STEERING RACK
26. RACK BUSHING
27. BOOT RETAINER
28. BOOT
29. BOOT CLAMP
30. BREATHER TUBE
31. CONTRACTION PLUG
32. LOWER PINION BUSHING
33. PRELOAD SPRING

FIG. 14-18 AMC RACK AND PINION DISASSEMBLY

between the end of the rack and the housing inner lip should be 4 ins.

6. Install the pinion shaft with the flat on the splined end at about a 10 o'clock position. Turn counterclockwise and push down until the pinion shaft race bottoms on the thrust bearing.

7. Reset the rack distance as in Step 5, with the flat on the pinion shaft at a 3 o'clock position.

8. Install and tighten the adjuster plug until it bottoms. Using the center of the spanning hole as a reference point, mark both housing and adjuster plug.

9. Back the adjuster plug off 3/16- to 1/4-in. in a counterclockwise direction and install the locknut.

10. Hold the adjuster plug from moving and tighten the locknut to 50 ft.-lbs.

11. Partially fill the housing with lubricant, leaving room for the pinion bushing and spring.

12. Install the preload spring, with the center-bearing hump against the housing. Spring should extend ¼-in. from the housing end.

13. Use needlenose pliers to hold the top of the preload spring against the housing and install the bushing, with the chamfered end facing downward.

14. Seat the contraction plug using a drift.

15. Fit the shock dampener rings on the steering rack ends, with the open ends facing outward. Install the jam nuts.

16. Lubricate the inner-tie-rod wear surfaces and pack the tie rod housing with lubricant.

17. Install the inner tie-rod assemblies and torque the tie rod housing to 25 ft.-lbs., rocking the inner tie rod to prevent grease lock. Back off the housing 45°.

18. Torque the housing setscrews to 60 in.-lbs.

19. With the tie rod housing in a vise, tighten the jam nut to 100 ft.-lbs.

20. Replace the shock dampener rings over the jam nuts and install the mounting clamp and grommet, using the alignment mark.

21. Install the boots and line up the tube holes, then replace the boot clamps.

22. Replace the adjuster tubes so that no more than three threads are visible at each end.

23. Install the flexible coupling and torque the pinch bolt to 30 ft.-lbs.

ALL FORD AND MERCURY MODELS (Except PINTO, BOBCAT, MUSTANG II, FAIRMONT, ZEPHYR)

Ford Recirculating Ball Steering

WORM AND SECTOR ADJUSTMENTS

The sector gear and ball nut assembly must be properly adjusted to provide a minimum of steering-shaft end play and backlash between the ball nut and sector gear. The sector (or Pitman) shaft is mounted between a roller bearing in the gearbox housing below the gear and a bushing positioned in the cover above the gear.

A large adjuster plug shown in **Fig. 14-20** is threaded in the cover and controls the worm bearing preload, which should be adjusted first. The sector shaft's mesh load can then be adjusted by means of a screw and locknut arrangement in the housing cover. To prevent possible gear damage or failure, adjust in the following manner:

1. Locate the service identification tag fastened to the steering gear unit and determine the model (**Fig. 14-21**). This information is necessary to determine torque settings.

2. Disconnect the Pitman arm from the steering Pitman-to-idler-arm rod.

3. Loosen the sector-shaft adjusting-screw locknut and turn the screw counterclockwise.

4. Remove the steering-wheel horn-button cap and use an in.-lb. torque wrench on the steering wheel nut to measure bearing preload. For steering gear models SMA-B and SMA-Y, this is 3 to 4 in.-lbs.; for model SMA-F, 5 to 6 in.-lbs.

5. Moving the steering wheel off-center, measure the amount of pull necessary to rotate the steering input shaft one-and-a-half turns to either side of center.

6. If preload is not within the above specifications, loosen the wormshaft-bearing adjuster locknut and turn the adjuster in or out as required to reset preload to specifications.

7. Tighten the locknut and recheck preload against the above specifications.

8. Slowly turn the steering wheel in one direction until it stops. To prevent damage to the ball return guides, turn gently against the stop. Now turn the wheel back until the ball nut is centered. Models SMA-B and SMA-Y will require 2 turns; model SMA-F requires 2¾ turns.

9. Turn the sector-shaft adjusting screw clockwise until the wormshaft rotates past its center or high point.

10. Hold the sector-shaft adjusting screw and torque its locknut 32 to 40 ft.-lbs., then recheck the backlash adjustment.

11. Reconnect the Pitman arm to the steering-arm-to-idler-arm rod, and torque 150 to 225 ft.-lbs.

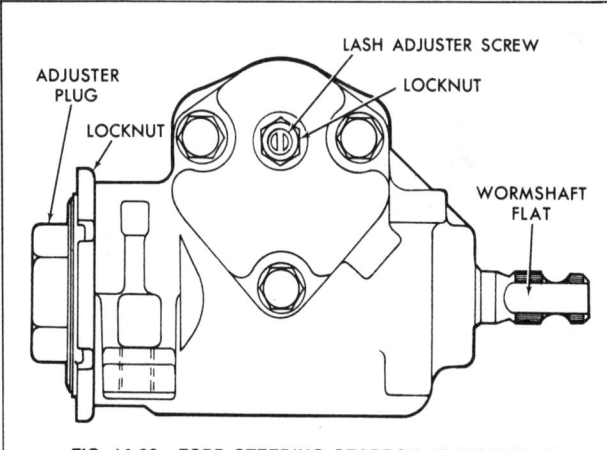

FIG. 14-20 FORD STEERING GEARBOX ADJUSTMENTS

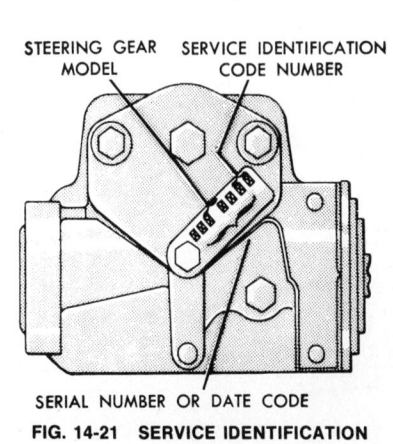

FIG. 14-21 SERVICE IDENTIFICATION

STEERING GEAR REMOVAL/INSTALLATION
TO REMOVE

1. Unbolt the flexible coupling between the steering gearbox and steering column shaft.

2. After removing the nut and lockwasher which holds the Pitman arm to the sector shaft, use a puller to separate the arm from the shaft. Using a hammer on the puller should be avoided—this can cause damage to the steering gear.

3. If necessary, disconnect the clutch linkage or lower the exhaust system to provide adequate clearance for removal.

4. Unbolt and remove the steering gearbox from the siderail.

TO INSTALL

1. Line up the flexible coupling and steering shaft, then bolt the steering gearbox to the siderail and torque 50 to 60 ft.-lbs.

2. Reinstall the clutch linkage or reposition the exhaust system if this step was necessary for removal.

3. Fit the Pitman arm on the sector shaft and replace the attaching nut and lock washer. Align the blind tooth on each, and torque the nut 150 to 225 ft.-lbs.

4. Replace flexible coupling bolts torque nuts 25 to 35 ft.-lbs. on all but Granada/Monarch/Versailles. Torque specifications for these are 10 to 22 ft.-lbs.

STEERING GEAR DISASSEMBLY/ASSEMBLY

Work on a clean bench with clean tools. Drain off excess fluid and clean the exterior of the gearbox thoroughly with solvent before beginning disassembly. Handle all interior parts **(Figs. 14-22 & 14-23)** carefully to prevent nicks, burrs and scratches.

TO DISASSEMBLE

1. After securing the gearbox in a vise, rotate the wormshaft to its center position.

2. Remove the sector-shaft adjusting-screw locknut and housing cover bolts **(Fig. 14-22)**. The sector shaft is removed with the cover and separated from it by turning the screw clockwise. Be sure to keep the shim with the screw.

3. Now loosen the worm-bearing adjuster locknut **(Fig. 14-23)** and remove both the adjuster and wormshaft (steering shaft) upper bearing.

4. Pull the wormshaft and ball nut assembly from the gearbox housing and remove the wormshaft lower bearing. Keep the ball nut from running down to either end of the wormshaft or you may damage the return guides. There is no need to disassemble the ball nut unless binding or tightness is present.

5. If the ball nut must be disassembled, hold it clamp-side up and remove both the clamp and return guides.

6. Turn the ball nut over a clean container and rotate the wormshaft from side to side to eject the balls; then slide the ball nut from the worm.

7. Remove both bearing cups. One should be located in the adjuster and the other in the housing. If they do not come out easily, tap gently with a wooden block to jar the cups loose.

8. If damage to the sector shaft bearing and oil seal is suspected, press them from the housing.

TO REASSEMBLE AND ADJUST

1. Press a new sector shaft bearing into the gearbox housing and install a new oil seal if the old ones were

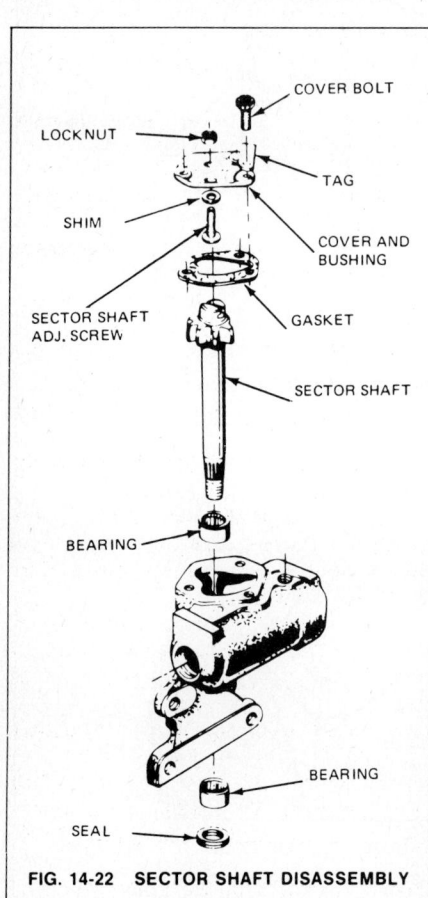

FIG. 14-22 SECTOR SHAFT DISASSEMBLY

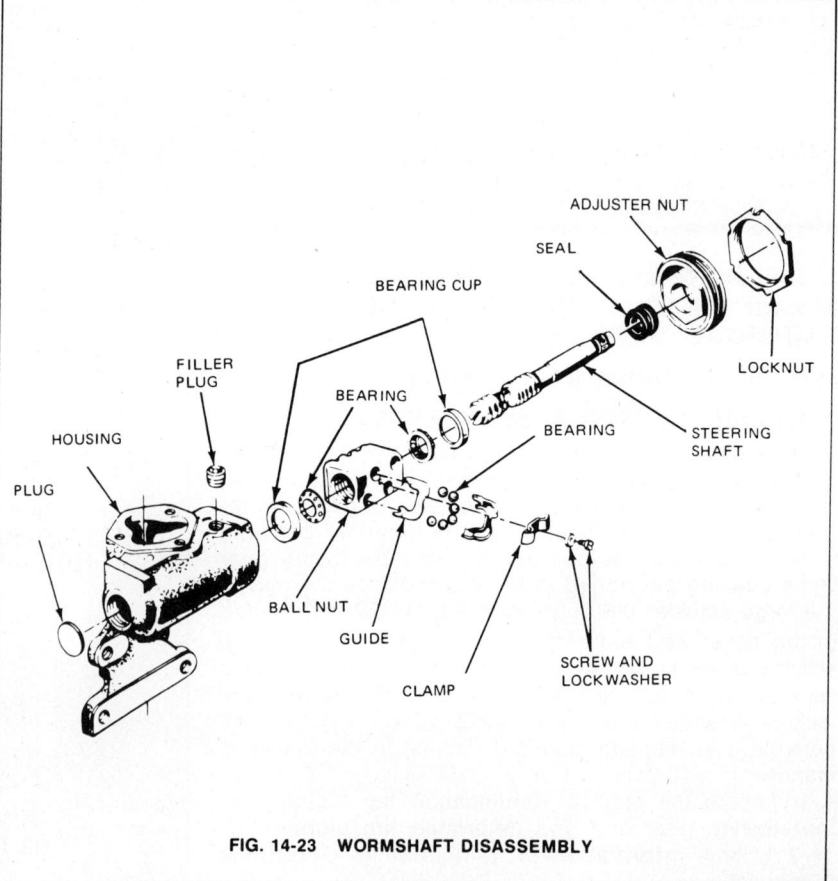

FIG. 14-23 WORMSHAFT DISASSEMBLY

removed; if not, start with the following step.

2. After lubricating the bearing and seal with recommended lubricant, install one bearing cup in the lower end of the gearbox housing and one in the adjuster. Fit a new seal in the bearing adjuster.

3. If the ball guides were removed, reposition them in the ball nut holes and tap lightly with a wooden screwdriver to seat them, if necessary.

4. Half of the balls should be inserted in the hole at the top of one ball guide, and the remaining balls in the other ball guide, rotating the shaft in one direction, then the other, to help distribute them properly.

5. Replacing the ball guide clamp, torque its hold-down screw 42 to 70 in.-lbs. Test the wormshaft for freedom of rotation.

6. Use steering gear lubricant to coat the worm bearings, sector shaft bearings and gear teeth.

7. With the gearbox housing clamped in a soft-jaw vise, put the wormshaft lower bearing in its cup—the sector shaft should be in a horizontal position for this step.

8. Set the wormshaft and ball nut assembly in the housing, then place the upper bearing on the wormshaft, installing the bearing adjuster, adjuster nut and bearing cup.

9. Use an in.-lb. torque wrench to adjust the worm bearing preload 3 to 4 in.-lbs. for models SMA-B, SMA-Y; 5 to 6 in.-lbs. for model SMA-F. Torque the adjuster locknut 60 to 80 ft.-lbs.

10. Position the sector-shaft adjusting screw and shim, checking the clearance between screw head and sector shaft end. If it exceeds 0.004-in., add sufficient shimming to bring the end play into correct tolerance.

11. Fitting a new gasket to the cover, start the sector-shaft adjusting screw in the housing cover.

12. Rotate the sector shaft until the ball nut teeth mesh with the sector gear. Housing should be tilted to allow the ball to tip toward the cover opening.

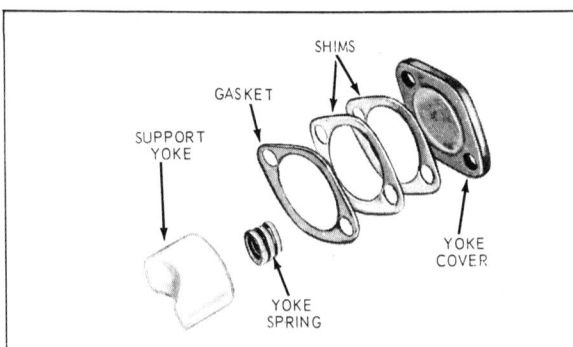

FIG. 14-24   SUPPORT YOKE PRELOAD

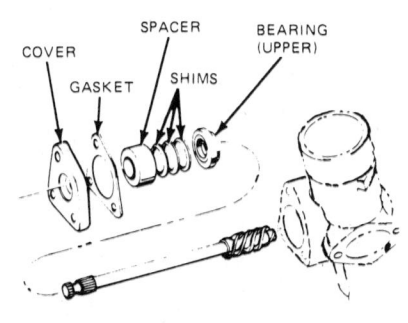

FIG. 14-25   PINION ADJUSTMENT, 1974 AND LATER

13. Lubricate the sector shaft journal, then install both shaft and cover.

14. Turning the cover out of the way, fill the gearbox with the specified amount of recommended gear lubricant. Push the cover and sector shaft into place, and replace the cover bolts, but *do not* tighten unless there is lash between the ball nut and sector gear teeth.

15. Now install sector shaft adjusting screw locknut. Adjust mesh load 7 to 8 in.-lbs. for SMA-B, SMA-Y (1978-79, SMA-Y, 5 to 7 in.-lbs.); 12 to 13 in.-lbs. for SMA-F (1978-79, 10 to 16 in.-lbs.). Torque locknut 32 to 40 ft.-lbs.

PINTO, BOBCAT, MUSTANG II, FAIRMONT, ZEPHYR
Ford Rack and Pinion Steering

SUPPORT-YOKE-TO-RACK PRELOAD

Preload is applied to the rack by a support yoke and yoke spring held in place by a yoke cover on the steering gearbox housing **(Fig. 14-24)**. The amount of preload is determined by the thickness of the shim pack installed under the cover. To adjust:

1. Remove the steering gear unit and clean the exterior thoroughly. With the yoke cover facing upward, secure it in a soft-jaw vise fitted with pads to prevent housing damage.

2. Removing the cover attaching screws, lift off the yoke cover, shims, gasket and yoke spring.

3. Clean the housing flange area and cover.

4. Replace the yoke and cover, but without installing the gasket, shims or spring. Lightly tighten the cover bolts until the cover barely touches the yoke.

5. Using a flat feeler gauge, measure the clearance between the cover and housing flange. Select appropriate shims and add to the gasket to give a combined pack thickness of 0.005- to 0.006-in. greater than the measured clearance or gap.

6. Remove the cover and fit the gasket to the housing flange. Place the selected shims on top of the gasket, insert the yoke spring and replace the cover, torquing the bolts 7 to 10 ft.-lbs. through 1972 models, and 15 to 20 ft.-lbs. from 1973 on.

7. Check gear operation to see that it operates smoothly without slack or binding.

PINION BEARING PRELOAD

1. Clean and mount in a vise, as for the support-yoke-to-rack adjustment.

2. Loosen the yoke cover to relieve yoke-spring pressure on the rack.

3. Removing the pinion cover and gasket, clean the cover flange area thoroughly.

4. From 1974 on, the input shaft goes through the cover **(Fig. 14-25)**. Adjustment is made here; on earlier models, adjustment is made from a bottom cover **(Fig. 14-26)**. Remove the gasket or spacer and shims.

5. Fit a new gasket and install the shims in order of thickness (thinnest at the bottom) until the shim pack is flush with the gasket. If used, the spacer top should be flush with the gasket.

6. Use light pressure on a straightedge to assure correct shim pack height.

7. Add one 0.005-in. shim to the pack to preload the bearing. If a spacer is used, the shim must go under it, because the spacer is to be assembled next to the pinion cover.

8. Install the cover and attaching bolts, torquing 15 to 20 ft.-lbs.

ALL CHRYSLER CORPORATION CARS
Chrysler Recirculating Ball Steering
WORM AND SECTOR ADJUSTMENTS

Essentially the same design as that used on General Motors and American Motors cars, the Chrysler manual steering gear **(Fig. 14-27)** differs primarily in adjustment and torque specifications. In order to properly overhaul this unit, the following special Chrysler tools are recommended: C-3323 (holding fixture), C-3868 (bearing remover), C-3865 (bearing installer), C-3875 (1⅛-in. shaft), C-3880 (adapter set), C-3884 (wrench) and C-4150 (puller).

Before a correct adjustment of the ball nut and sector gear mesh can be made, the worm bearing preload must be properly adjusted. This is controlled by the worm-bearing thrust adjuster threaded into the housing at the upper end of the wormshaft. Adjust in the following sequence:

1. Disconnect the steering arm from the sector (or Pitman) shaft using Chrysler tool C-4150 or an appropriate puller.

2. Loosen the sector-shaft adjusting-screw locknut **(Fig. 14-28)** and back the screw out two full turns to relieve friction load at the mesh point.

3. Remove the horn pad and turn the steering wheel two complete turns from a straight-ahead position, fitting an in.-lb. torque wrench to the steering shaft nut.

4. Read torque while rotating the steering wheel one complete turn toward the straight-ahead position. Torque reading should be between 1½ and 4½ in.-lbs.

5. If not within specifications, loosen the wormshaft adjuster locknut **(Fig. 14-28)** and turn the adjuster clockwise to increase, or counterclockwise to decrease preload.

6. Tighten the locknut and recheck preload against specifications.

7. Slowly turn the steering wheel from lock-to-lock, counting the number of turns required. Turn the steering wheel back exactly halfway, to center the ball nut.

8. Remove all lash between the ball nut and steering sector by turning the sector-shaft adjusting screw clockwise, then torque the adjusting screw locknut to 35 ft.-lbs.

9. Check the sector mesh adjustment by turning the steering wheel one-quarter turn off-center and rotating it through the high spot at the center with the in.-lb. torque wrench fitted to the steering shaft nut. Reading should be between 8¼ and 11¼ in.-lbs. Readjust the sector shaft screw, if necessary to obtain the specified reading.

10. Returning the wheels to a straight-ahead position, reconnect the steering arm to the sector shaft. Torque the retaining nut to 175 ft.-lbs.

STEERING GEAR REMOVAL/INSTALLATION
TO REMOVE

1. Unbolt the flexible coupling between the steering gearbox and the steering-column shaft.

2. Remove the steering-arm retaining nut and lockwasher. Use an appropriate puller or Chrysler tool C-4150 to remove the steering arm from sector shaft.

3. Unbolt and remove the steering gearbox from the frame rail.

TO INSTALL

1. Bolt the steering gearbox to the frame rail and torque to 100 ft.-lbs.

2. Turn the wormshaft by hand to center the sector shaft at its midpoint of travel. Line up the master serrations on the sector shaft with the steering arm splines and install with retaining washer and nut. Torque nut to 175 ft.-lbs.

3. Align the flexible coupling and install the attaching bolts. Torque to 200 in.-lbs.

STEERING GEAR DISASSEMBLY/ASSEMBLY

Work on a clean bench with clean tools. Drain off excess fluid and clean exterior of gearbox thoroughly with solvent before beginning disassembly. Handle all interior parts carefully to prevent nicks, burrs and scratches.

TO DISASSEMBLE

1. Remove the steering gearbox, and secure it in a soft-jaw vise.

2. Loosen the sector-shaft adjusting-screw locknut and back the screw out two full turns to relieve friction load at the mesh point.

3. With the wormshaft in a straight-ahead position, remove the sector-shaft cover bolts.

4. Insert the sector-shaft bearing tool (Chrysler C-3875) into the housing as the sector shaft is removed, to maintain needle bearing integrity.

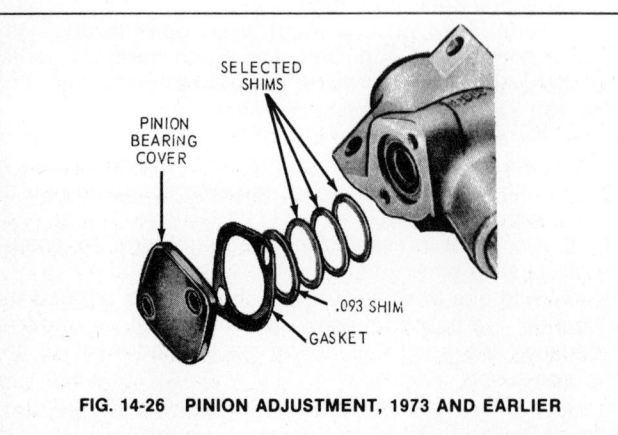

FIG. 14-26 PINION ADJUSTMENT, 1973 AND EARLIER

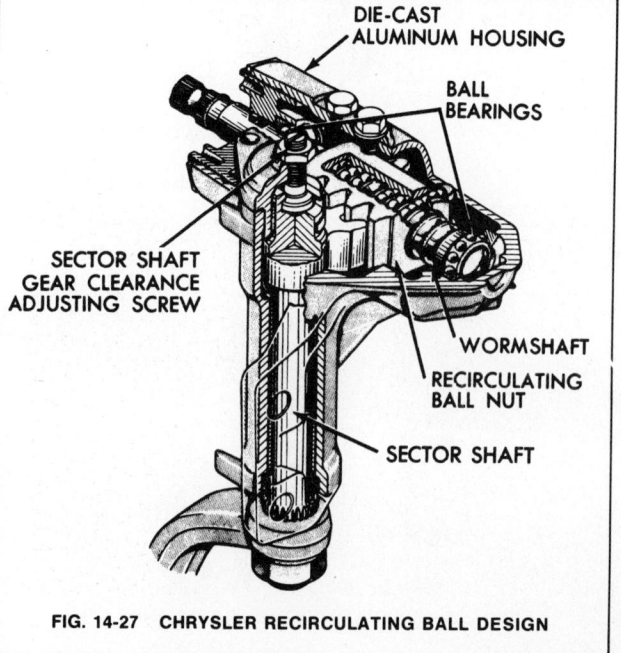

FIG. 14-27 CHRYSLER RECIRCULATING BALL DESIGN

5. Unscrew the sector shaft locknut and turn the adjusting screw clockwise to remove them from the cover.

6. Slide the adjusting screw and shim from the slot in the sector shaft end. *Do not* lose the shim.

7. Remove the adjuster locknut and adjuster plug, holding the wormshaft from turning with Chrysler tool C-3884.

8. Pull the worm and ball nut assembly from the housing. Keep the ball nut from running down to either side of the wormshaft, or you may damage the return guides. The ball nut is not disassembled, but serviced as an assembly with the wormshaft. Test ball nut operation on the wormshaft, and if there is roughness or binding, replace the entire assembly.

9. Set the gear housing in an arbor press to remove the sector-shaft needle bearing. Press both bearings through the housing by inserting Chrysler tool C-3875, with the adapter ring in the lower end of the housing. If the adapter ring is not used, bearings will be crushed.

10. If the housing is equipped with a sector shaft bushing, it is serviced as an assembly; sector shaft covers, which include a needle bearing or bushing, are also serviced as an assembly.

11. To remove the wormshaft oil seal from the adjuster, place a blunt punch behind the seal and tap it out gently, alternating taps from side to side.

12. Wormshaft upper-bearing cup is removed in the same manner, but care must be taken not to cock the cup and distort adjuster counterbore in the process.

13. The lower bearing cup is removed only if necessary. Use Chrysler tool C-3868 if this step is required.

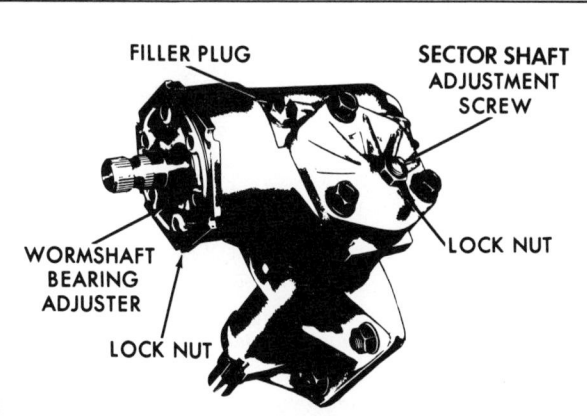

FILLER PLUG

SECTOR SHAFT ADJUSTMENT SCREW

WORMSHAFT BEARING ADJUSTER

LOCK NUT

LOCK NUT

FIG. 14-28   CHRYSLER ADJUSTMENTS

FIG. 14-29   ADJUSTING MESH LOAD

TO REASSEMBLE AND ADJUST

1. Press the sector-shaft lower needle bearing into the housing 7/16-in. below the end of the bore, using Chrysler tool C-3875 and the adapter ring. This provides space for the oil seal.

2. Press the upper needle bearing in the housing flush with the inside end of the bore surface. Chrysler tool C-3875 and adapter ring are also used for this step.

3. Press the wormshaft bearing cups into the housing and adjuster nut using Chrysler tool C-3865.

4. Install the oil seal in the adjuster, with its metal retainer facing up. Drive slightly below the end of the bore, using a suitable sleeve.

5. Clamp the housing in a vise, with the bearing adjuster opening facing upward, and position a thrust bearing in the lower cup in the housing.

6. Hold the ball nut from turning and insert the worm and ball nut assembly into the housing. The end of the worm should rest in the bearing.

7. Set the upper thrust bearing on the wormshaft. Lubricate the adjuster and the housing threads.

8. Slide the adjuster assembly over the wormshaft after taping the shaft splines with plastic tape to prevent them from damaging the seal.

9. Using Chrysler tool C-3884, thread the adapter into the housing and torque to 50 ft.-lbs. while rotating the wormshaft to seat the bearings.

10. Remove the preload by loosening the adjuster, then torque the bearing preload from 1⅛ to 4½ in.-lbs. Tighten the locknut and recheck preload.

11. Fill the housing with 11 oz. of steering gear lubricant, working into all the cavities.

12. Slide the sector-shaft adjusting screw and shim into the slotted end of the shaft, setting the end clearance so that it does not exceed 0.004-in.

13. Turn the adjusting screw counterclockwise in the housing cover to pull the shaft into place and install, but *do not* tighten the locknut.

14. Center the ball nut by rotating the wormshaft.

15. Fit a new gasket to the cover, then install the sector shaft and the cover carefully into the housing, after lubricating both shaft and sector teeth.

16. Install and torque the cover bolts to 25 ft.-lbs.

17. Press the sector shaft seal into the housing with Chrysler tool C-3828.

18. Adjust the mesh load **(Fig. 14-29)** to obtain a torque reading of 8 to 11¼ in.-lbs., as described earlier in the "Worm and Sector Adjustments" section. Torque the locknut to 35 ft.-lbs.

ALL OMNI/HORIZON
Chrysler Rack & Pinion Steering

STEERING GEAR DESCRIPTION

The manual steering gear used on Omni/Horizon models consists of a tubular housing which contains the toothed rack, a pinion, the rack slipper and slipper spring. A helical-cut pinion runs in straddle-mounted ball bearings. The upper bearing is permanently swaged to the pinion shaft, while the lower bearing is incorporated in the pinion housing. This unit is permanently lubricated at the factory and requires no periodic lubrication. It cannot be adjusted or serviced and should a malfunction develop, the complete rack and pinion assembly must be replaced with a new one.

HOW TO: Ford Recirculating Ball Manual Steering Overhaul

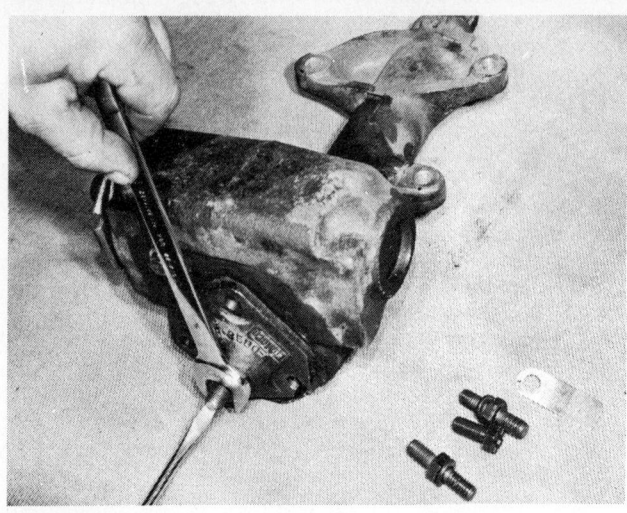

1. Ford recirculating ball steering gearbox is similar in design and operation to that of the Saginaw used on GM cars. Center wormshaft and remove sector cover bolts.

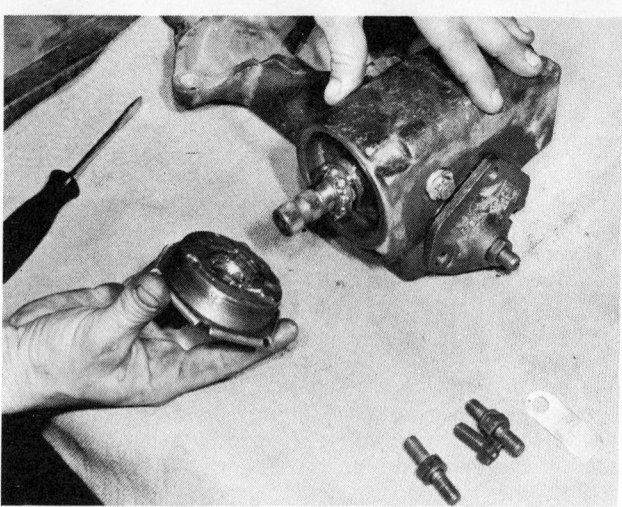

2. Loosen the worm-bearing adjuster locknut and remove the adjuster plug and locknut as an assembly. The wormshaft upper bearing may come out with the adjuster plug.

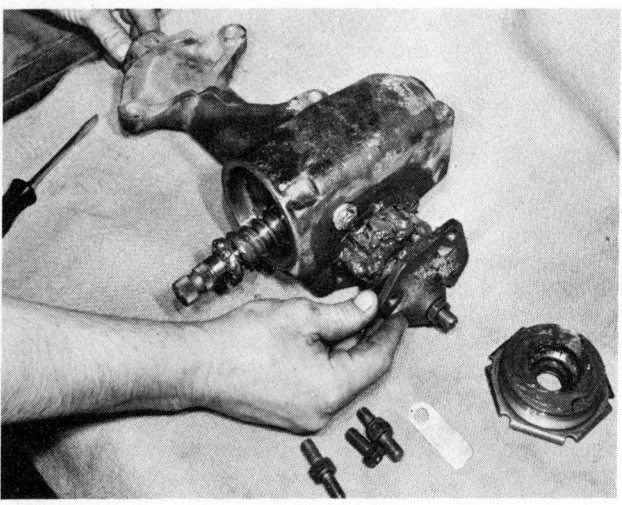

3. Sector shaft and cover can now be removed from gearbox. Clean unit thoroughly with fresh solvent. Remove cover from shaft by turning adjusting screw clockwise.

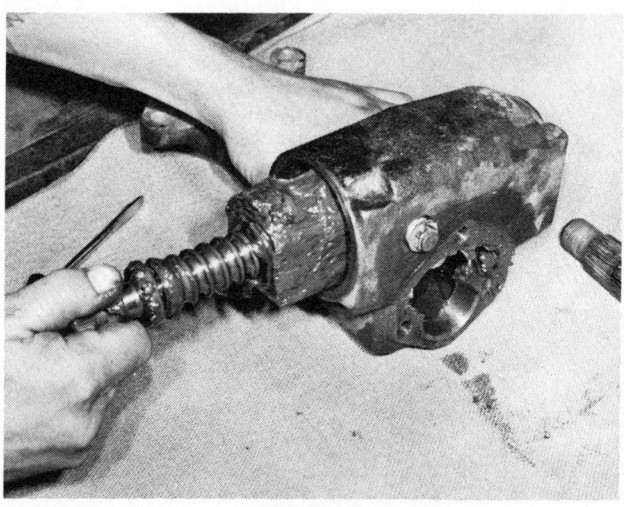

4. With sector shaft removed, wormshaft and ball nut can be withdrawn from housing. Don't let ball nut run to the end of wormshaft. Take out lower bearing.

5. Disassemble only if there is binding or tightness. After cleaning unit, remove ball-nut return-guide screws holding the clamp. Lift clamp and guides off.

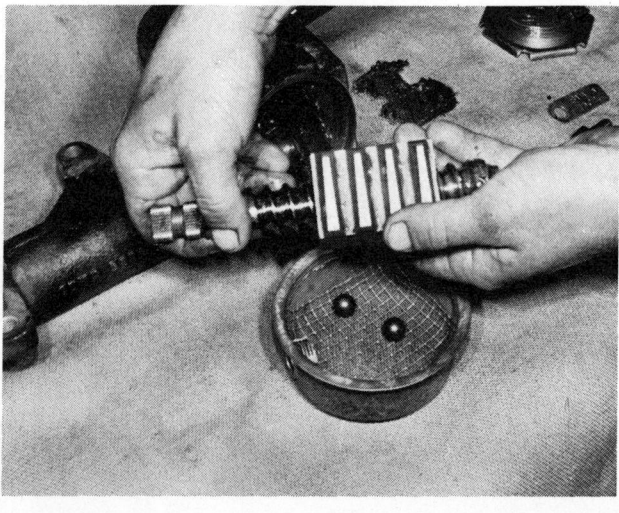

6. Hold ball nut over a clean container, turn it over and rotate wormshaft until all balls drop out, then slide ball nut from wormshaft.

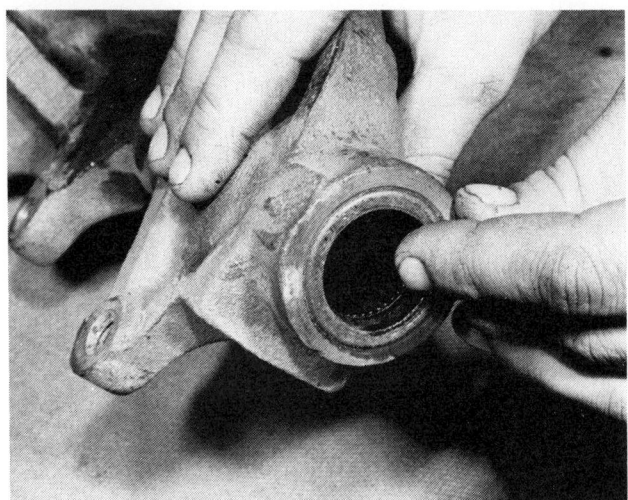

7. This model Ford gearbox uses needle bearings in housing to support wormshaft and sector shaft. Clean housing, check needle bearings; remove and replace only if required.

8. Wormshaft upper bearing race is located at end of adjuster plug. Fit bearing into race, revolve to check operation, then clean bearing and adjuster plug with solvent.

9. Begin reassembly by replacing the sector shaft. Grease the sector teeth lightly with gear lubricant, and insert the shaft in the gearbox housing.

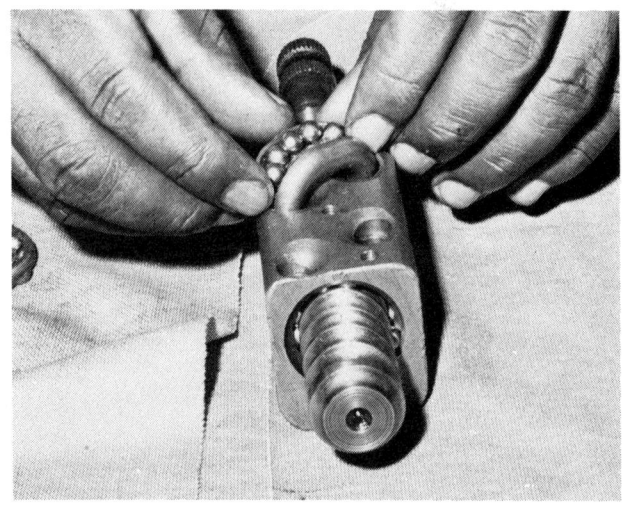

10. If ball nut disassembled, replace balls and guides, secure guide clamp. Lightly lubricate ball nut with gear lubricant; install wormshaft lower bearing, wormshaft.

11. Fit upper bearing on wormshaft and lubricate end of adjuster plug before replacing it. Adjust wormshaft preload with in.-lbs. torque wrench, tighten locknut.

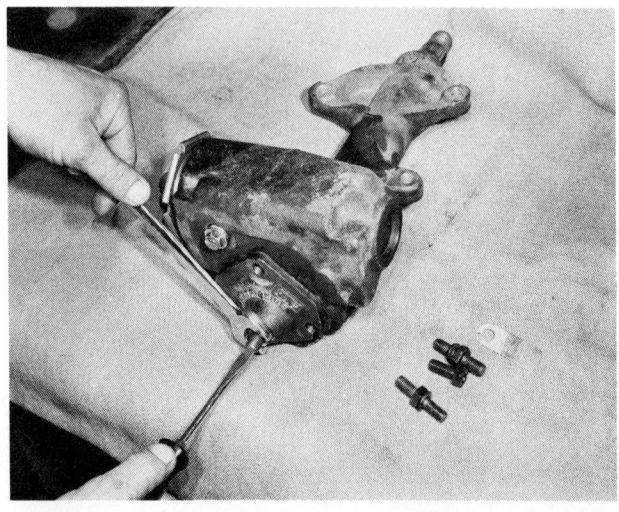

12. Replace sector shaft cover; draw in place by turning sector shaft counterclockwise. Replace bolts, gearbox ID tag. Torque cover bolts to specifications.

HOW TO: Ford Rack And Pinion Overhaul

1. Overhauling a rack and pinion steering gear requires removal of the entire assembly from the car. Remove support yoke cover first, and use caution—it's spring-loaded.

2. Under the support yoke cover, you'll find two or more very thin shims between the cover and housing. Remove cover, shims, gasket and yoke spring. Clean cover flange area.

3. Unbolt and remove pinion bearing cover, shims and gasket. Pinion bearing and spacer are then removed. Don't mix up shims with the ones removed from support yoke cover.

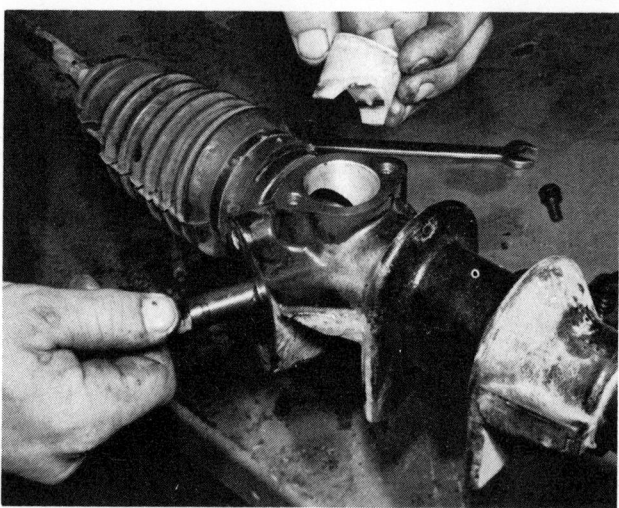

4. Now lift support yoke out and work pinion shaft back and forth carefully to disengage it from rack teeth. Once disengaged, draw pinion shaft straight out.

5. Inspect pinion shaft carefully for nicks, burrs, worn or damaged threads. If pinion shaft checks out satisfactorily, chances are good the rack will too.

6. Inspect rack teeth also. Ball socket at each end of rack is staked with a retaining pin. If rack removal is required, pin must be drilled out.

7. Rack and pinion both checked out good in this case. After aligning the flat on the input shaft with the rack, the bearing, shims and spacer are reinstalled.

8. Replace shim pack with thinnest shim first, add 0.005 shim to preload bearing. Thickest shim goes next to cover. Gasket and cover are replaced, torqued.

9. Install support yoke in the bore and replace the cover without the spring, shims or gasket. Replace the cover and tighten the bolts until the cover just touches the yoke.

10. Measure gap between cover and housing flange, using a feeler gauge. Combined shim-pack/gasket thickness should be 0.005- to 0.006-in. *thicker* than measured gap.

11. Remove cover, reinstall spring, fit gasket to housing flange. Install required shims and hold cover in place while you finger-tighten cover bolts.

12. Torque cover bolts to specifications, then replace rubber boot and tighten clamp. Steering gear assembly can now be replaced on Pinto, Bobcat or Mustang II.

INDEX

POWER STEERING

Automotive power steering systems include two basic components: the steering unit (steering gear) and the hydraulic oil pump **(Fig. 15-1)**. The steering unit may be an integral part of the gearbox (Saginaw), coaxial (Chrysler) or an external linkage-assist unit (Saginaw, Ford). The latter can be replaced without removing the entire steering assembly. Mounted at the front and belt-driven by the engine, the hydraulic pump supplies oil pressure as required to the steering unit.

POWER STEERING UNITS

Integral power steering units vary in design from one manufacturer to another, but all function in essentially the same way, using hydraulic pressure to help in sector (or Pitman) shaft or ball-nut piston movement. Linkage-assist power steering **(Fig. 15-2)** uses a hydraulic cylinder mounted to the steering linkage. A control valve assembly connected to the steering-gear Pitman arm controls the hydraulic assist. As the Pitman arm connector moves the internal spool valve in the control valve assembly against spring tensions, hydraulic pressure is allowed to flow.

POWER STEERING HYDRAULIC PUMPS

All power steering pumps are constant-displacement, delivering from 650- to 1300-lbs. pressure, depending upon type and make of the system and car. Special power-steering fluid or Type "A" Automatic Transmission Fluid is used. This fluid is stored in a reservoir attached to the pump, with a filter in the reservoir to prevent foreign matter from entering the system. A pressure relief valve located in the pump prevents the fluid pressure from exceeding the predetermined maximum pressure of the system. Flexible hoses carry the fluid to the control valve of the steering unit. The small-est (high-pressure) hose carries the fluid to the control valve while the larger hose is the return (low-pressure) hose.

A flow-control valve is combined with the pressure relief valve located inside the pump. When fluid circulation reaches about 2 gals. per minute, this flow-control valve is forced to open a passage between the inlet and outlet sides of the pump. This sends all excess oil back to the intake side of the pump for recirculation. When oil pressure exceeds the fixed pressure limit, the relief valve opens, permitting fluid to flow back to the

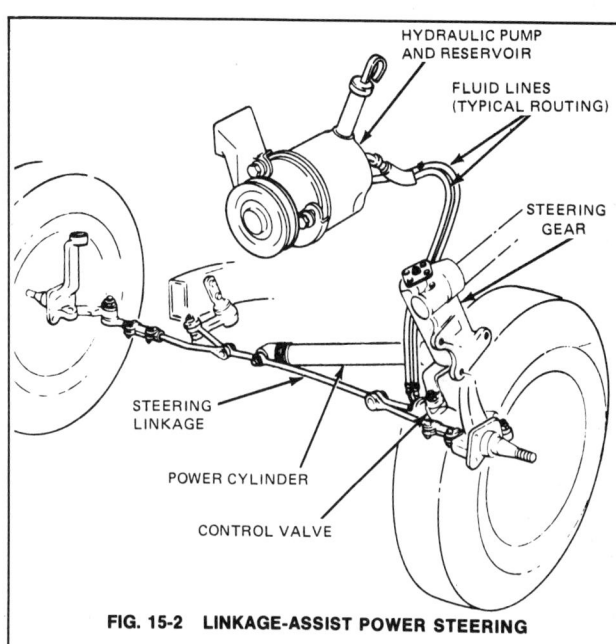

FIG. 15-2   LINKAGE-ASSIST POWER STEERING

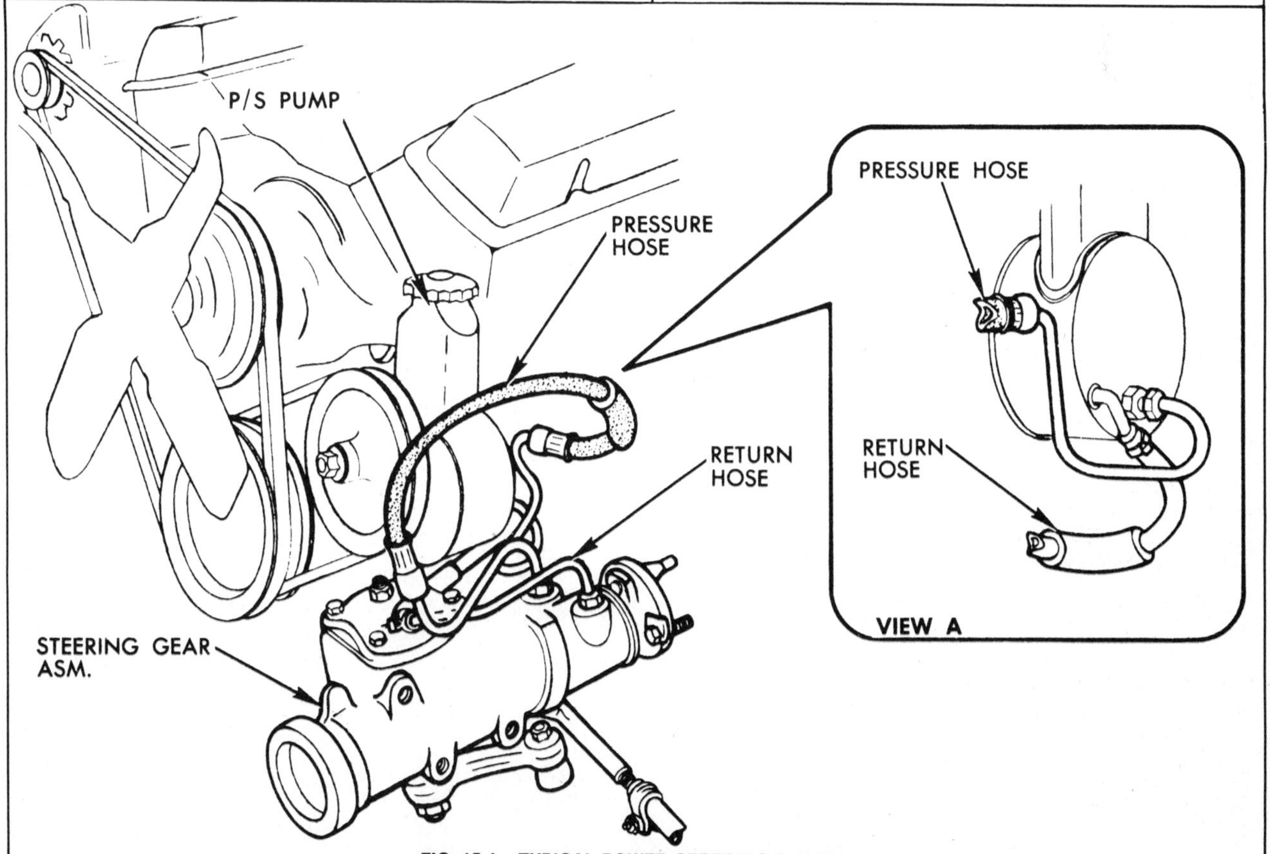

FIG. 15-1   TYPICAL POWER STEERING SYSTEM

POWER STEERING DIAGNOSIS

CONDITION	CORRECTION
HISSING NOISE IN STEERING GEAR	
(a) There's some noise in all power steering systems, one of the most common of which is a slight hiss evident at standstill or park.	(a) A slight hiss is normal and in no way affects steering.
RATTLE OR CHUCKLE NOISE IN STEERING GEAR	
(a) Gearbox is loose on frame.	(a) Check gear-to-frame mounting and tighten bolts to 70 ft.-lbs.
(b) Steering linkage is loose.	(b) Check linkage pivot points for wear and replace if necessary.
(c) Pressure hose is touching another part of car.	(c) Adjust hose position but do not bend steel tubing by hand.
(d) Loose pitman shaft over center adjustment.	(d) Adjust to specs.
SQUAWK NOISE IN STEERING GEAR DURING TURN MANEUVER	
(a) Dampener "O" ring on valve spool cut.	(a) Replace O-ring.
CHIRP NOISE IN PUMP OR BELT SQUEAL	
(a) Loose belt.	(a) Adjust belt tension to specs.
GROWL NOISE IN STEERING PUMP	
(a) Restriction in hoses or steering gear causing excessive back pressure.	(a) Locate restriction and correct, replacing part or hose if necessary.
(b) Scored pressure plates, thrust plate or rotor.	(b) Replace damaged parts and flush system.
(c) Cam ring extremely worn.	(c) Replace cam ring.
GROAN NOISE IN STEERING PUMP	
(a) Low lubricant level.	(a) Fill reservoir to proper level.
(b) Air in the lubricant or a poor pressure hose connection.	(b) Tighten connector to specified torque. Bleed system by operating steering from right to left full turn.
RATTLE OR KNOCK IN STEERING PUMP	
(a) Loose pump pulley nut.	(a) Tighten nut to specified torque.
(b) Vanes not properly installed.	(b) Remove and replace correctly.
(c) Vanes sticking in rotor slots.	(c) Free by removing dirt, varnish or burrs that act as a restriction.
SWISH NOISE IN STEERING PUMP	
(a) Defective flow control valve.	(a) Replace valve.
WHINE NOISE IN STEERING PUMP	
(a) Pump shaft bearing is scored.	(a) Replace housing and shaft and flush system.
POOR STEERING WHEEL RETURN TO CENTER	
(a) Lack of lubrication in linkage and ball joints.	(a) Lubricate linkage and ball joints.
(b) Lower coupling flange rubs against steering gear adjuster plug.	(b) Loosen the pinch bolt and assemble correctly.
(c) Misalignment of steering gear to column.	(c) Align steering column.
(d) Steering linkage binds.	(d) Replace pivots.
(e) Ball joints bind.	(e) Replace ball joints.

CONDITION	CORRECTION
(h) Steering wheel rubs against directional signal housing.	(h) Adjust steering jacket.
CAR WANDERS FROM ONE SIDE OF ROAD TO THE OTHER	
(a) Unbalanced steering gear valve, requires light effort in direction of lead and heavy in opposite direction.	(a) Replace valve.
MOMENTARY INCREASE IN EFFORT WHEN TURNING WHEEL FAST	
(a) Low lubricant level in pump.	(a) Top up with power steering fluid as necessary.
(b) Pump belt slips.	(b) Check belt for wear; tighten or replace, and adjust to tension specs.
(c) High internal leakage.	(c) Check pump pressure; repair or replace.
STEERING WHEEL SURGES WHEN TURNING	
(a) Low lubricant level.	(a) Top up as required.
(b) Loose pump belt.	(b) Adjust belt tension to specs.
(c) Steering linkage hits oil pan at full turn position.	(c) Correct clearance.
(d) Pump pressure is insufficient.	(d) Check pump pressure and replace relief valve if defective.
(e) Flow control valve sticks.	(e) Check for varnish or damage and replace if necessary.
EXCESSIVE WHEEL KICK-BACK OR LOOSE STEERING	
(a) Air in system.	(a) Add power steering fluid to pump reservoir and bleed by operating steering, then check hose connectors for proper torque and adjust as required.
(b) Steering gear loose on frame.	(b) Tighten attaching bolts to specified torque.
(c) Steering gear flexible coupling loose on shaft; rubber disc mounting screws loose.	(c) Tighten flange pinch bolts to 30 ft.-lbs., if serrations are undamaged. Tighten upper flange to coupling nuts to specified torque.
(d) Excess wear in steering linkage.	(d) Replace loose pivots.
(e) Front wheel bearings worn or incorrectly adjusted.	(e) Adjust bearings or replace.
(f) Poppet valve (gear) worn.	(f) Replace.
(g) Thrust bearing preload adjustment (gear) loose.	(g) Adjust to specs with gear out of car.
(h) Excessive over-center lash	(h) Adjust to specs with gear out of car.
HARD STEERING OR LACK OF ASSIST	
(a) Loose pump belt.	(a) Adjust belt tension to specs.
(b) Low oil in reservoir.	(b) Top up to proper level. If excessively low, check lines and joints for evidence of external leakage. Tighten any loose connectors to 30 ft.-lbs.
(c) Steering gear to column misalignment.	(c) Align steering column.
(d) Lower coupling flange rubs against steering gear adjuster plug.	(d) Loosen pinch bolt and assemble correctly.

inlet side and recirculate in the pump without raising the pressure in the rest of the system.

PRELIMINARY POWER STEERING CHECKS

Before beginning any major service operation on a power steering system, the steering gear, linkage and front end should be serviced and lubricated, and the wheel alignment should be checked. Tires must be inflated to correct pressures, belt tension set to factory specifications, and hydraulic fluid level inspected and brought to a proper level if necessary. Before inspecting the pump fluid, it should be brought to operating temperature by turning the wheels back and forth with the engine idling after a brief warm-up period. During inspection, the wheels must be positioned straight ahead.

With the wheels in the straight-ahead position and the engine idling, check the amount of steering effort required. If this is done with a spring scale attached to the rim of the steering wheel, the amount of pull required to turn the wheels from one extreme to the other should not exceed 10 lbs. at any given point. Steering effort can also be checked using a torque wrench on the steering wheel nut—follow directions for this technique in "Manual Steering," Chapter 14.

Check oil-flow and relief-valve operation by turning the steering wheel from one extreme to the other with the engine idling. If these valves are working properly, a slight buzzing noise should be heard. If no buzzing noise is present, a sticking or malfunctioning valve is likely. The steering wheel should not be held in either extreme position for more than 2 or 3 seconds, because the high pressure involved can cause damage to the system if the relief valve is not operating properly.

To assist in pinpointing possible causes of power steering problems, refer to the "Power Steering Diagnosis" chart and **Fig. 15-3**.

**All General Motors Cars (Except Corvette);
All Ford Torino & Elite, Mercury Montego,
1970 Ford Mustang & Mercury Cougar,
1979 Ford LTD II and Thunderbird,
1979 Mercury Cougar and XR-7;
All American Motors Cars (Except Pacer)**

Saginaw Power Steering Gear

STEERING GEAR DESCRIPTION

The rotary-valve, safety power-steering gear provides hydraulic-fluid pressure assists, when turning, by displacing fluid. Because internal gear components are constantly immersed in fluid, periodic lubrication is not required. The hydraulic fluid also acts as a "cushion" which absorbs road shock before it is transmitted to the driver. Except for the pressure and return hoses between gearbox and pump, all fluid passages are internal. The one-piece, rack-piston nut is geared to the sector (or Pitman) shaft and preload is maintained by an adjusting screw located on the end of the shaft gear.

Beginning with the 1977 model year, a similar but slightly smaller power steering gearbox is used on some GM cars. The two can be distinguished by the type of side cover used. The larger unit is designated as the 800-808 model and has a rectangular side cover retained by four bolts. The smaller gearbox is designated as the 605 model and has a circular side cover held in

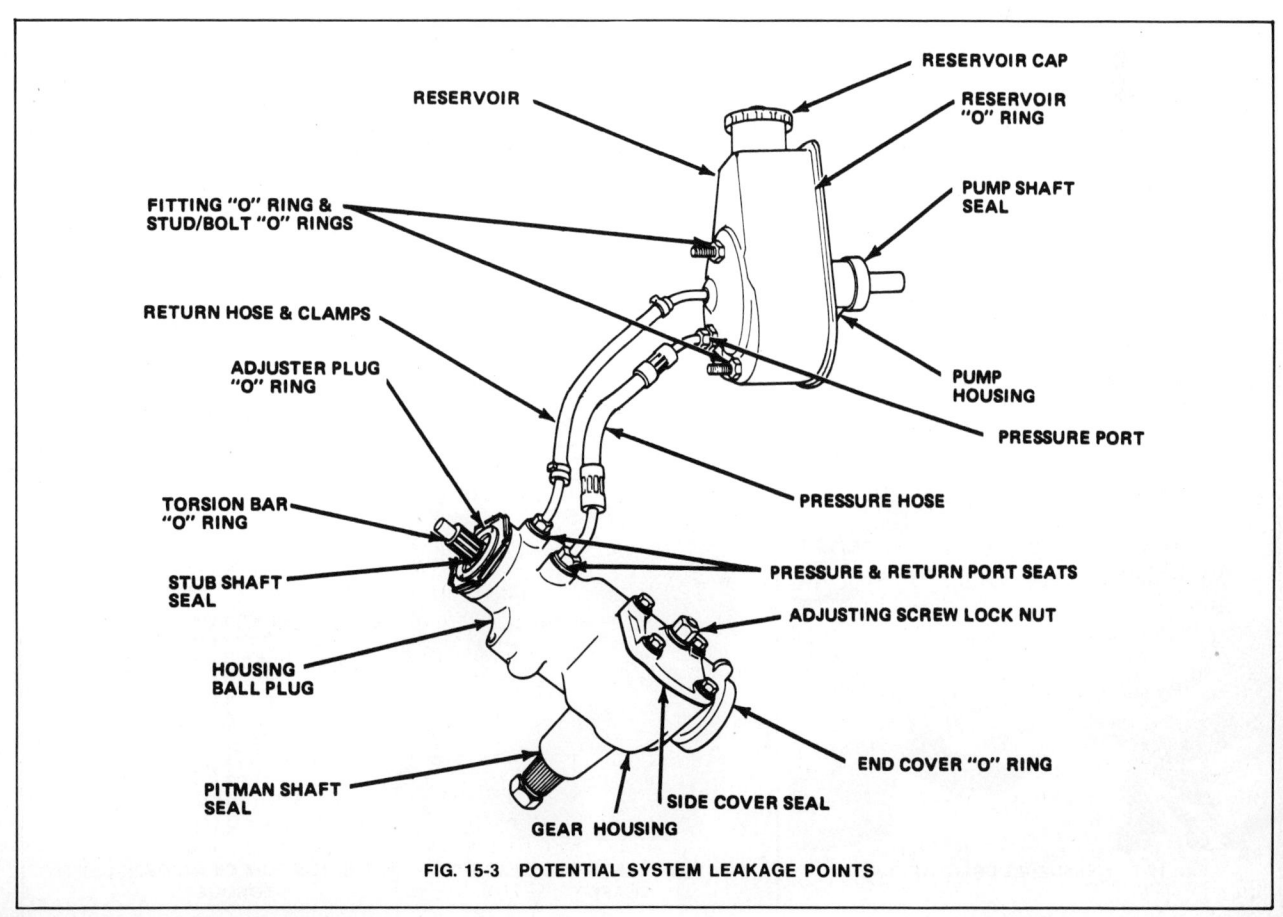

FIG. 15-3   POTENTIAL SYSTEM LEAKAGE POINTS

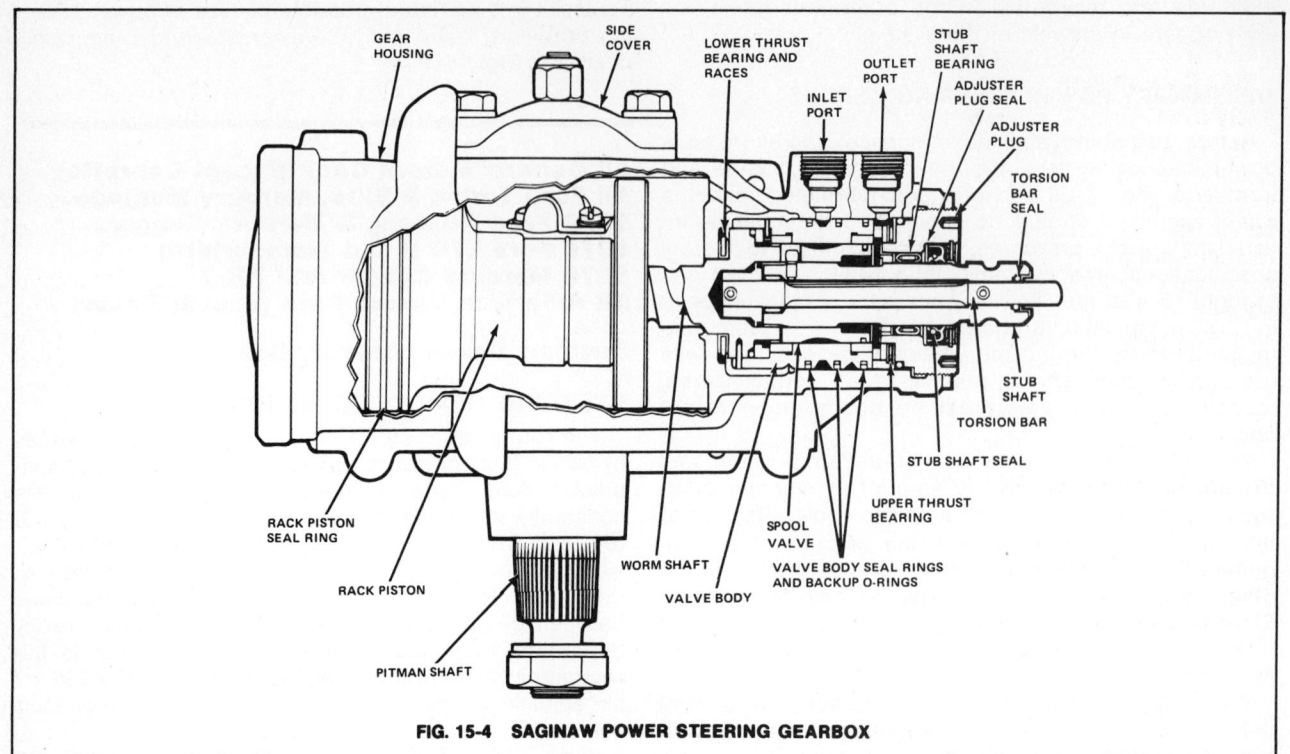

FIG. 15-4   SAGINAW POWER STEERING GEARBOX

FIG. 15-4A   SAGINAW POWER STEERING
GEARBOX INDENTIFICATION

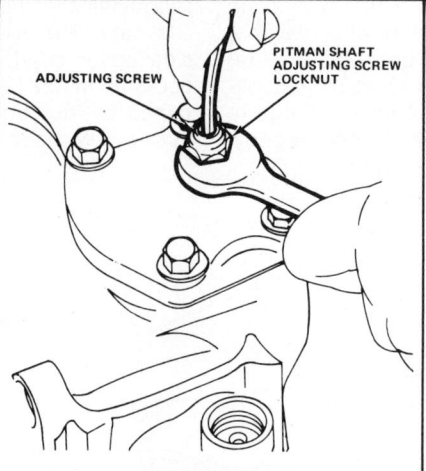

FIG. 15-5   SECTOR SHAFT ADJUSTMENT

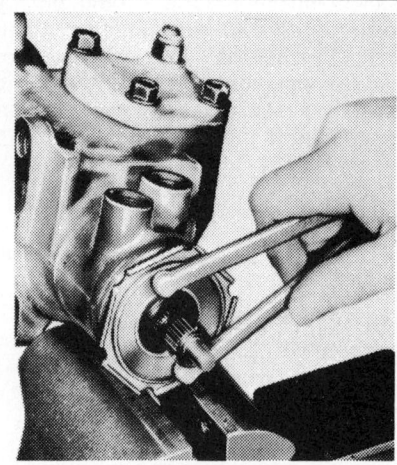

FIG. 15-6   LOOSENING ADJUSTER
PLUG LOCKNUT

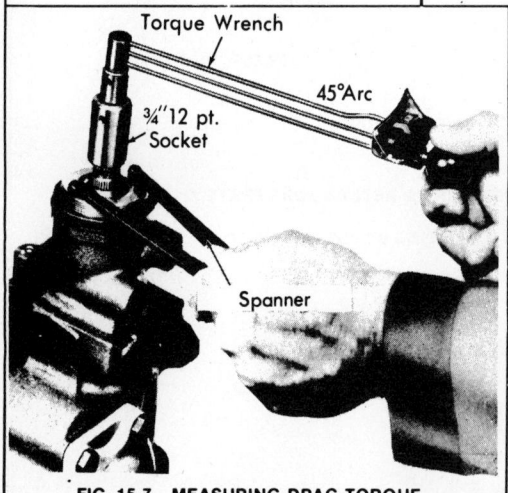

FIG. 15-7   MEASURING DRAG TORQUE

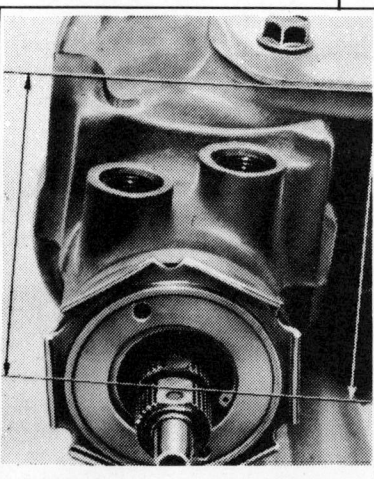

FIG. 15-8   CENTERING GEAR STUB
SHAFT

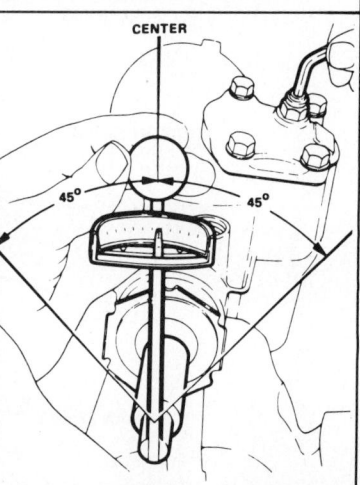

FIG. 15-9   CHECKING OVER-CENTER
TORQUE

place by a retaining snap ring, **(Fig. 15-4A)**. Adjustment of the 605 gearbox is the same as for the 800-808; overhaul procedures are essentially the same.

STEERING GEAR ADJUSTMENTS

All adjustments, other than the sector shaft preload, require removal of the gearbox **(Fig. 15-4)** from the car. Because gear adjustments are made as a corrective rather than a periodic measure, gearbox removal is recommended even for sector shaft adjustments. Since poor handling stability can be caused by an improper adjustment of the worm thrust bearing, as well as an incorrect sector-shaft preload (lash) adjustment, the steering gearbox should be removed and bench-adjusted as required. Checking the gearbox in the car will not pinpoint an incorrect worm-thrust-bearing preload due to the confusing effects of hydraulic fluid.

WORM-THRUST-BEARING PRELOAD

TO ADJUST

1. Loosen the sector-shaft adjusting-screw locknut **(Fig. 15-5)**. Loosen the adjusting screw one-and-a-half turns and retighten the locknut.

2. Loosen the adjuster plug locknut **(Fig. 15-6)**. Loosen the plug one turn.

3. Turn the stub shaft to right stop, then back off one-half turn.

4. Measure drag torque with an in.-lb. torque wrench on the gear stub shaft **(Fig. 15-7)**.

5. Bottom out the adjuster plug, then back off sufficiently to add 3 to 4 in.-lbs. stub-shaft torque in excess of drag torque. Total torque should not exceed 10 in.-lbs.

6. Tighten the adjuster plug locknut securely while holding the adjuster plug in position with the spanner. Since preload torque tends to drop off when the locknut is tightened, recheck the setting.

SECTOR SHAFT PRELOAD

TO ADJUST

1. Center the steering gear by turning the stub shaft one-half the number of turns required from lock-to-lock. Flat side of the stub shaft should face up and parallel with the side cover **(Fig. 15-8)**.

2. Check rotational torque by turning the torque wrench from 45° to 90° each side of center. Note the highest reading.

3. Loosen the sector-shaft (Pitman shaft) adjusting-screw locknut and turn the adjusting screw clockwise while checking the torque setting as in Step 2 above **(Fig. 15-9)**. Total over-center torque should not exceed 18 in.-lbs. for new gears, or 14 in.-lbs. for used gears (400 miles or over).

4. Holding the adjusting screw, tighten the locknut to 35 ft.-lbs., then recheck preload (over-center) adjustment.

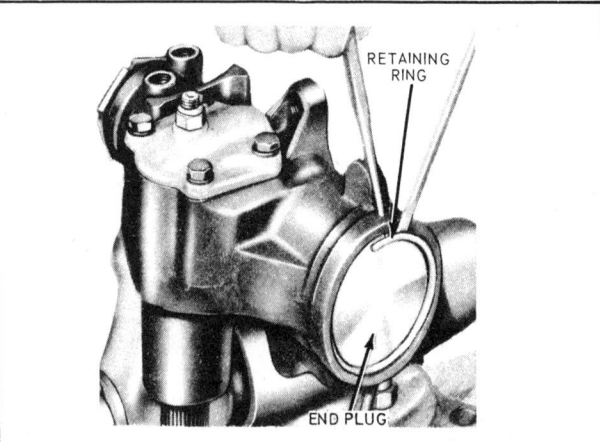

FIG. 15-11 END PLUG AND RETAINING RING

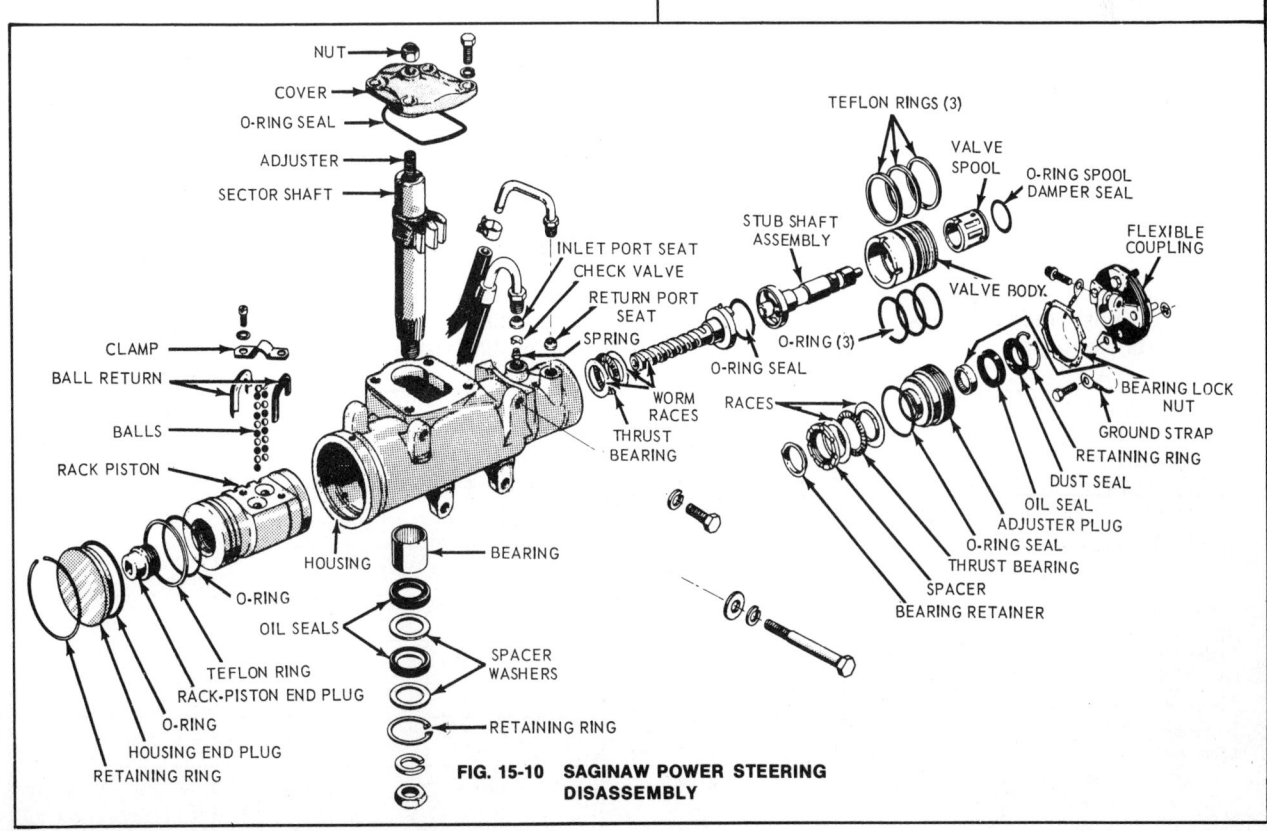

FIG. 15-10 SAGINAW POWER STEERING DISASSEMBLY

STEERING GEAR REMOVAL/INSTALLATION

TO REMOVE

1. Disconnect both pump lines from the steering gearbox. Plug the gear ports and lines to protect against accidental contamination from dirt, grease, etc.

2. Remove the flexible coupling bolts holding the gearbox shaft and column shaft together.

3. Remove the Pitman-arm retaining nut and lock-washer, then disconnect the Pitman arm from the sector shaft using an appropriate puller.

4. On some cars, it may be necessary to remove the clutch-release-lever retracting spring or catalytic converter in order to provide sufficient clearance for gearbox removal.

5. Remove the attaching bolts while supporting the gearbox, and work it free of the flexible coupling and frame rail.

TO INSTALL

1. Turn the steering wheel to position the spokes normally.

2. Fit the flexible coupling in place on the steering shaft, and center the steering-gear input shaft.

3. Slide the input shaft onto the flexible coupling as you work the gearbox into place on the frame siderail. Install the attaching bolts and torque to specifications.

4. With wheels in a straight-ahead position, fit the Pitman arm on the sector shaft. Replace the lockwasher and retaining nut, and torque to specifications.

5. Replace the bolts in the flexible coupling. Torque to specifications.

6. Reconnect and tighten the pressure and return lines. Replace the clutch spring or catalytic converter if removal was required.

7. Unhook the coil wire. Fill the pump reservoir with specified power steering fluid. Crank the engine and continue adding fluid until the level remains constant, then turn the steering wheel from side to side, but without hitting the stops. Shut off the engine and re-check fluid level.

8. Reconnect the coil wire and start the engine. When it reaches operating temperature, turn the steering wheel from stop to stop. Shut off the engine and recheck fluid level, adding more fluid if necessary.

STEERING GEAR DISASSEMBLY/ASSEMBLY

Work on a clean bench with clean tools. Drain off excess fluid and clean the exterior of the gearbox with solvent before beginning disassembly—*do not* use solvent on the seals. Handle all interior parts **(Fig. 15-10)** carefully to prevent nicks, burrs and scratches.

TO DISASSEMBLE

1. Position the gearbox in a soft-jaw vise and tighten securely.

2. Turn the end-plug retaining ring until one end of the ring is opposite the housing hole, then unseat the ring from the hole and work it out of the groove with a screwdriver blade **(Fig. 15-11)**.

3. Use a ¾-in. 12-point socket wrench to rotate the input shaft counterclockwise and force the end plug from the housing. Rotate only as far as necessary, because excessive rotation will allow the balls to fall from their guides and cause the rack-piston to disengage from the sector shaft. Remove and discard the housing O-ring.

4. Turn the input shaft clockwise one-half turn to draw the piston inward.

5. Use a ½-in. drive extension to turn the end plug counterclockwise out of the piston.

6. Remove and discard the sector shaft locknut.

7. Remove the cover attaching screws and turn the sector-shaft adjusting screw until the cover is free of the housing. Remove the cover and discard the O-ring.

8. Rotate the input shaft to center the sector-shaft gear teeth in the housing.

9. Tap the sector shaft end with a soft-face hammer to free it from the housing.

10. Remove the adjuster plug locknut and the adjuster plug.

11. Rotate the stub shaft counterclockwise until the worm is free of the rack-piston. Remove but *do not* disassemble the rack-piston.

12. Pull the stub shaft and valve assembly out of the housing.

13. Lift the worm, lower thrust bearing and races from the housing.

TO ASSEMBLE

1. With the gearbox housing secured in a soft-jaw vise, lubricate the wormshaft, lower thrust bearing and races with steering gear fluid.

2. Position the thrust bearing and races on the worm. Line up the valve-body drive pin on the worm with the pin slot in the valve body. Install a new O-ring seal between the valve body and the worm head.

3. Lubricate the Teflon ring and lower cap O-ring with steering gear fluid. Position the valve assembly/wormshaft as a unit in the housing. To install the assembly, push on the outer valve-body diameter with your fingertips. The fluid return hole in the gear housing will be fully visible when valve is correctly seated.

	AMC	BUICK	CADILLAC	CHEVROLET	FORD	OLDS	PONTIAC
TORQUE SPECIFICATIONS (Ft.-lbs.)							
Gearbox to frame attaching bolts	60	70	55	70*	50-65	70	70
Pitman arm to Pitman shaft	115	180	185	185**	150-225	180-210	185
Flexible coupling bolts	20	20	20	30	20-30	30	35
Sector shaft cover bolts	30***	35	45	30	30-35	35	30
Adjuster locknut	85	75	80	85	50-110	80	85
Sector-shaft adjusting screw locknut	35	23	32	30	30-35	35	32

* Corvette, 30 ft.-lbs.
** Nova and Vega class cars, 140 ft.-lbs.
*** 1977-79 , 45 ft.-lbs.

4. Install and lubricate a new O-ring in the adjuster plug groove and, fitting the plug over the stub shaft end, tighten it just enough to seat all parts.

5. Install the adjuster plug locknut loosely on the adjuster plug and set the preload according to the procedure under "Steering Gear Adjustments."

6. Using a dummy shaft, install the rack-piston until it touches the wormshaft. Turn the stub shaft clockwise until the middle rack groove lines up with the center of the sector-shaft roller bearing. Remove the dummy shaft.

7. Fit and lubricate a new O-ring in the sector shaft cover.

8. Thread the sector shaft cover on the adjusting screw until it bottoms, then back off one-and-a-half turns.

9. Install the sector shaft to mesh the center gear tooth with the rack-piston center groove. Make sure the cover O-ring is in place and then push the cover down onto the housing. If a gasket is used, be sure it is correctly installed. Some models use a metal gasket with a molded rubber section which fits into the cover O-ring groove. Two metal tabs are provided for bending around the side cover edges to prevent incorrect installation and gasket rotation.

10. Replace the lockwashers and cover screws. Torque to specifications.

11. Install a new adjusting-screw locknut and tighten to the halfway point on the adjusting screw.

12. Lubricate and fit a new housing end-plug O-ring.

13. Fit the end plug in the housing and seat against the O-ring seal. Tap with a soft-face mallet to seat properly, if necessary.

14. Replace the retaining ring and adjust the sector shaft preload according to the procedure under "Steering Gear Adjustments." Torque the sector-shaft adjusting-screw locknut to specifications.

ALL CORVETTES

Saginaw Linkage-Type Power Steering Gear

STEERING GEAR DESCRIPTION

The Saginaw power steering used on Corvette **(Fig. 15-12)** is a hydraulically controlled, linkage-type system and consists of an integral pump with fluid reservoir, control valve, power cylinder, connecting fluid lines and steering linkage. The steering gearbox used is a Saginaw manual recirculating ball type, and is adjusted/overhauled according to procedures in Chapter 14. Should the control valve or power cylinder require other than a ball seat or seal replacement, Chevrolet recommends the entire unit be discarded and a new one installed.

CONTROL VALVE BALANCING

This procedure is used to correct a complaint that more steering effort is required in one direction than the other. To balance the control valve:

1. Unhook the piston rod from the frame, and start the engine.

2. If the piston rod does not extend:
   a) Rotate the adjusting nut clockwise until the rod starts to move outward.
   b) Rotate the nut counterclockwise until the rod starts to move inward.
   c) Rotate nut clockwise to exactly one-half the rotation needed to change piston rod direction.

3. If the piston rod does start to extend:
   a) Rotate the adjusting nut counterclockwise until the rod starts to retract, then turn it clockwise until the rod begins to extend again.
   b) Rotate the nut counterclockwise to exactly one-half the rotation needed to change piston rod direction.

4. Once the rod is balanced, it should move in and out manually.

5. Shut off the engine and reconnect the piston rod to the frame. Torque the nut to 23 ft.-lbs.

6. Restart the engine. The front wheels should not turn in either direction from center. If they do, the valve adjustment is still incorrect and the procedure must be repeated.

7. Once the control valve is correctly balanced, grease the valve end and install the dust cap.

CONTROL VALVE REMOVAL/INSTALLATION

TO REMOVE

1. Elevate the wheels and remove the relay-rod-to-control-valve clamp bolt.

2. Disconnect the pump-to-control-valve hose connections and drain, then disconnect the valve-to-power-cylinder hoses and drain.

3. Unhook the control valve from the Pitman arm by removing the retaining nut from the ball-stud-to-Pitman-arm connection.

4. Turn the Pitman arm to the right to provide control valve clearance and unscrew the valve from the relay rod. Remove the control valve.

TO INSTALL

1. Connect the control-valve-to-relay rod and center the Pitman arm.

2. Replace the retaining nut; torque to 140 ft.-lbs.

3. Reconnect all hoses and replace the relay-rod-to-control-valve clamp.

4. Fill the pump reservoir with power steering fluid and bleed air from the system.

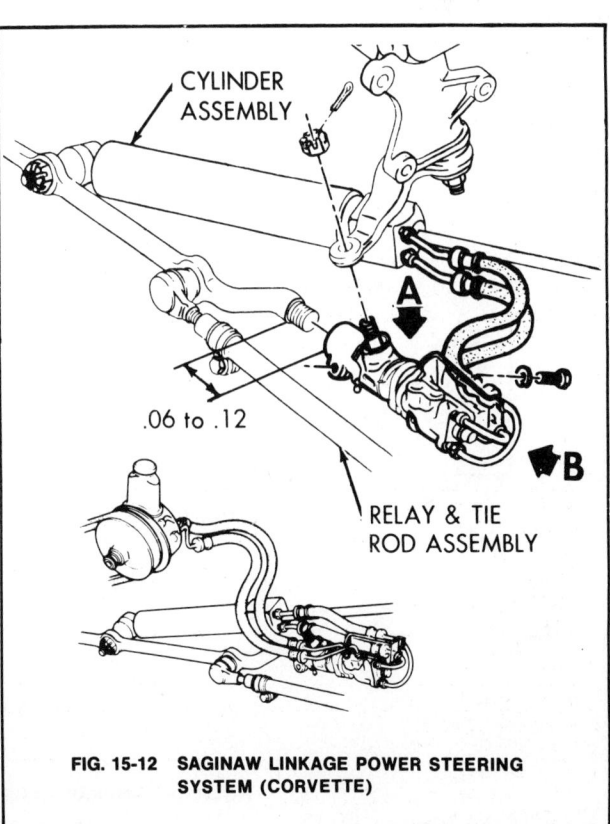

FIG. 15-12   SAGINAW LINKAGE POWER STEERING SYSTEM (CORVETTE)

POWER CYLINDER REMOVAL/INSTALLATION

TO REMOVE

1. Elevate the front wheels and disconnect the hydraulic lines from the power cylinder. Drain the lines and discard the fluid.

2. Remove cotter pin, nut, retainer and grommet from the power cylinder rod at the frame bracket.

3. Remove cotter pin, nut and ball stud at the relay rod end, and remove the power cylinder from the car.

TO INSTALL

1. Position the power cylinder on the frame bracket and replace grommet, retainer, nut and cotter pin.

2. Reconnect the ball stud at the relay rod, and install the nut and cotter pin.

3. Reconnect the hydraulic lines, fill the pump reservoir with fluid and bleed air from the system.

ALL AMERICAN MOTORS PACERS

Saginaw Rack and Pinion
Power Steering Gear

STEERING GEAR DESCRIPTION

The Saginaw rack-and-pinion power steering gear consists of an integral tube and housing assembly containing the steering rack and piston, the pinion shaft, the valve body assembly and the adjuster plug assembly. The tube and housing assembly is similar in design to that used with the manual steering gear on the AMC Pacer, but the permanently attached steering rack-piston operates inside the power cylinder section of the tube **(Fig. 15-13)**. The valve body is an open-center, three-position rotary type, which directs fluid to either side of the power cylinder to provide hydraulic assist. Wheel resistance and car weight during a turning maneuver cause a torsion bar to deflect, rotating the stub shaft and spool valve within the valve body. This rotational motion aligns directional passages which carry fluid into the power cylinder, where it acts on the rack-piston to move left or right as required.

STEERING GEAR ADJUSTMENT

As with the manual version of this rack and pinion design, two thrust bearings and two nylon bushings support the pinion shaft, with a nylon bushing at each end of the rack for support. A preload spring maintains pinion bushing location and compensates for bushing wear. The steering gear must be removed from the car and overhauled when preload adjustment is required.

STEERING GEAR REMOVAL/INSTALLATION

TO REMOVE

1. Disconnect the flexible coupling from the intermediate shaft flange.

2. Turning the steering wheel to full left stop, jack up the left control arm 2 ins. or more.

3. Remove the cotter pin and retaining nut from the tie rod end, then unhook the tie rod end.

4. Turning the steering wheel to full right stop, jack up the right lower control arm and repeat Step 3.

5. Disconnect and cap the power steering hoses at the housing.

6. Remove the steering-gear-to-front-crossmember attaching bolts and lower the steering gear assembly.

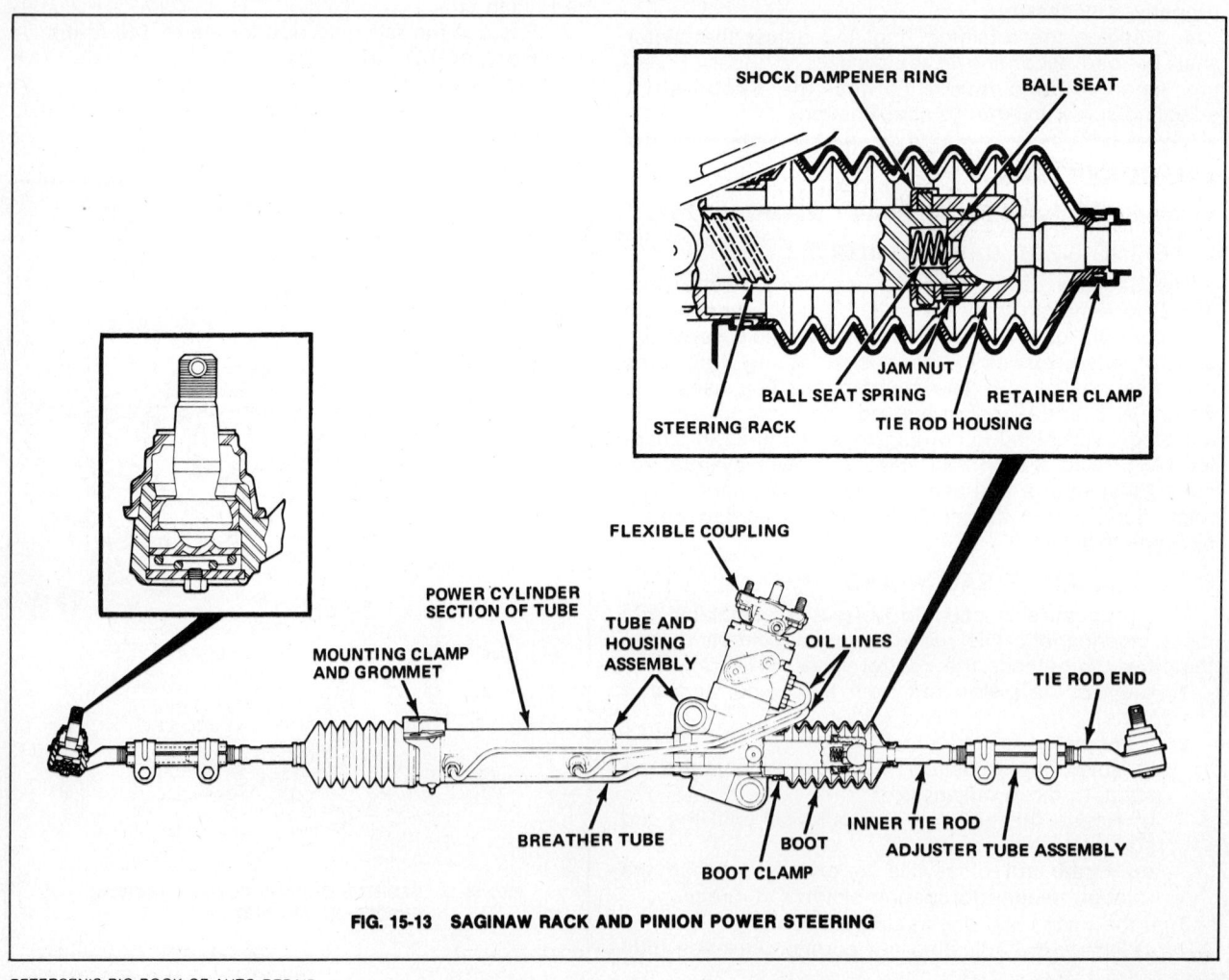

FIG. 15-13 SAGINAW RACK AND PINION POWER STEERING

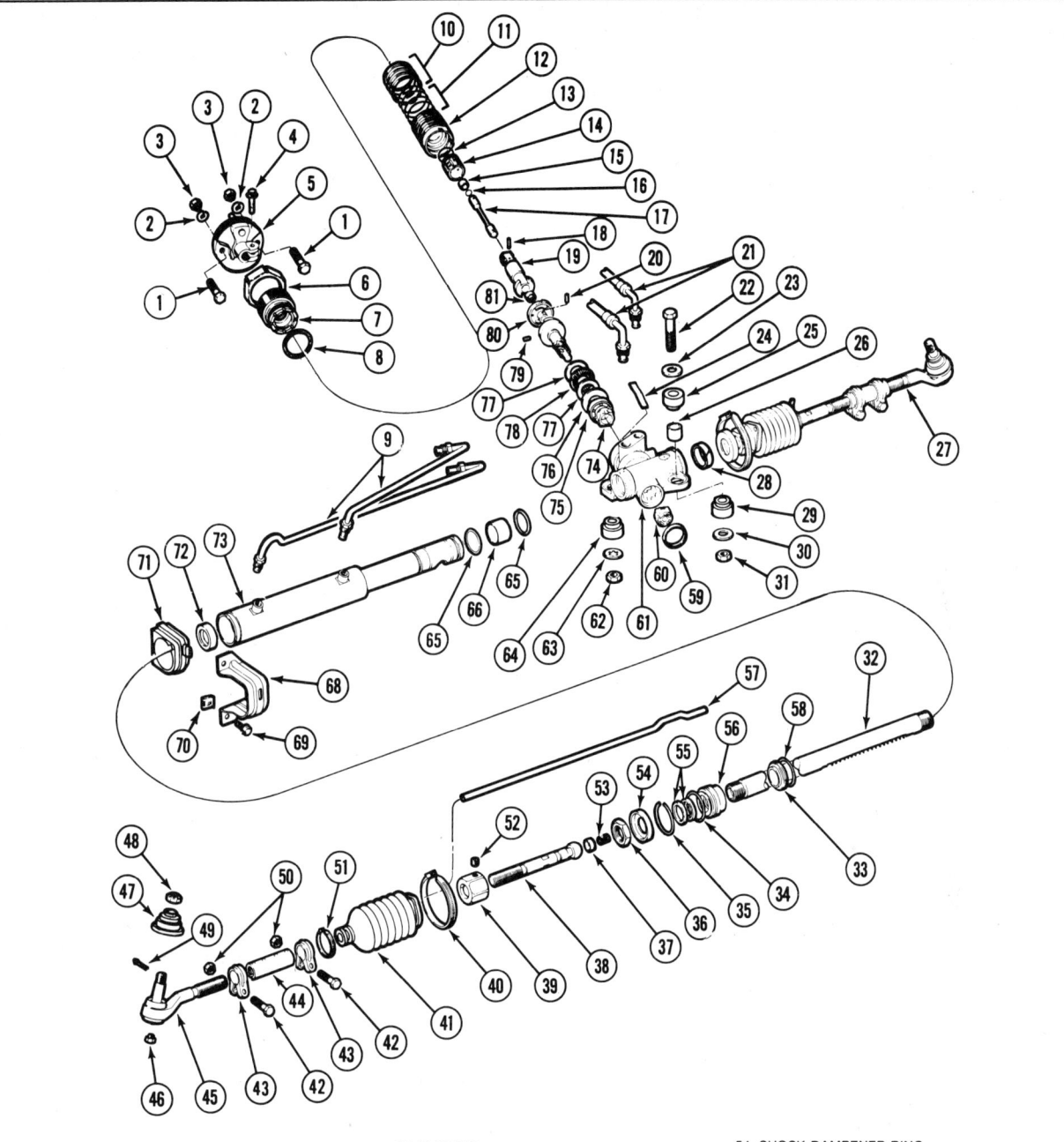

1. FLEXIBLE COUPLING-TO-INTERMEDIATE
   SHAFT ATTACHING BOLT
2. LOCKWASHER
3. NUT
4. PINCH BOLT
5. FLEXIBLE COUPLING
6. ADJUSTER PLUG LOCKNUT
7. ADJUSTER PLUG ASSEMBLY
8. ADJUSTER PLUG O-RING
9. OIL LINES
10. VALVE BODY SEAL RINGS
11. VALVE BODY O-RINGS
12. VALVE BODY
13. SPOOL VALVE DAMPER O-RING
14. SPOOL VALVE
15. TORSION BAR BUSHING (INCLUDED IN
    STUB SHAFT)
16. TORSION BAR SEAL RING (INCLUDED IN
    STUB SHAFT)
17. TORSION BAR (INCLUDED IN STUB SHAFT)
18. DRIVE PIN (INCLUDED IN STUB SHAFT)
19. STUB SHAFT
20. DRIVE PIN (INCLUDED IN STUB SHAFT)
21. POWER STEERING HOSES
22. MOUNTING BOLT
23. WASHER
24. PRELOAD SPRING
25. GROMMET

26. BUSHING
27. STEERING LINKAGE (ASSEMBLED)
28. RACK BUSHING
29. GROMMET
30. WASHER
31. NUT
32. STEERING RACK
33. RACK PISTON
34. BULKHEAD O-RING
35. BULKHEAD RETAINING RING
36. JAM NUT
37. BALL SEAT
38. INNER TIE ROD
39. INNER TIE ROD HOUSING
40. BOOT CLAMP
41. BOOT
42. ADJUSTER TUBE CLAMP BOLT
43. ADJUSTER TUBE CLAMP
44. ADJUSTER TUBE
45. TIE ROD END
46. LUBE PLUG
47. TIE ROD END SEAL
48. TIE ROD END NUT
49. COTTER PIN
50. ADJUSTER TUBE CLAMP NUT
51. BOOT CLAMP
52. TIE ROD HOUSING SETSCREW
53. BALL SEAT SPRING

54. SHOCK DAMPENER RING
55. BULKHEAD SEALS (LIP TYPE)
56. BULKHEAD
57. BREATHER TUBE
58. RACK PISTON SEAL RING
59. CONTRACTION PLUG
60. LOWER PINION BUSHING
61. HOUSING (INCLUDED IN TUBE AND
    HOUSING ASSEMBLY)
62. NUT
63. WASHER
64. GROMMET
65. MOUNTING CLAMP
66. BOLT
67. MOUNTING CLIP
68. MOUNTING GROMMET
69. INNER RACK SEAL
70. TUBE AND POWER CYLINDER (INCLUDED IN
    TUBE AND HOUSING ASSEMBLY)
71. UPPER PINION BUSHING
72. PINION SHAFT SEAL (LIP TYPE)
73. SUPPORT WASHER
74. CONICAL THRUST BEARING RACE
75. THRUST BEARING
76. DRIVE PIN (INCLUDED IN STUB SHAFT)
77. SHAFT CAP (INCLUDED IN STUB SHAFT)
78. TORSION BAR BUSHING (INCLUDED IN
    STUB SHAFT)

FIG. 15-14   SAGINAW POWER RACK AND PINION DISASSEMBLY

TO INSTALL

1. Attach the steering gear to the front crossmember. Torque the mounting bracket bolts to 50 ft.-lbs. and the housing bolts to 55 ft.-lbs.

2. Replace power steering hoses, tighten securely.

3. Connect the steering arm to the tie rod ends. The steering wheel should be turned in the direction of the tie rod end being connected, and the corresponding lower control arm should be supported as during removal. Torque nuts to 50 ft.-lbs.

4. Reconnect the flexible coupling to the intermediate shaft and torque the nuts to 25 ft.-lbs.

STEERING GEAR DISASSEMBLY/ASSEMBLY

Work on a clean bench with clean tools. Drain off the excess fluid and clean the exterior of the steering gear thoroughly before beginning disassembly. Handle all interior parts **(Fig. 15-14)** carefully to prevent nicks, burrs and scratches.

TO DISASSEMBLE

1. Mount the steering gear housing in a soft-jaw vise—*do not* clamp it on any part of the tube.

2. Cut the large-diameter boot clamps on the housing end of the steering gear. Remove the clamps and slide the boots back to expose the rack teeth.

3. Move the rack toward the housing end of the steering gear as far as it will go by rotating the flexible coupling.

4. Remove the flexible-coupling pinch bolt and the coupling from the pinion shaft.

5. Unscrew and remove the adjuster plug locknut.

6. Pull straight up on the stub shaft to remove the valve body assembly. *Do not disassemble the valve body.*

7. Grip the pinion shaft with pliers and rotate counterclockwise while pulling upward. Remove the pinion shaft and inspect the teeth. If the pinion teeth are damaged, stop disassembly and discard the entire unit; if not, proceed with the next step.

8. Remove the contraction plug from the housing by inserting a ¼-in. rod through the upper and lower pinion bushings and tapping.

9. Remove the lower pinion bushing and preload spring from the housing.

10. Center the rack in the tube and housing, and install the pinion shaft.

11. Replace the valve body and adjuster plug in the housing. Hand-tighten the plug.

12. Loosening both adjuster tube clamps, remove the tubes and tie rod assembly from the inner tie rods.

13. Mark the adjuster tube position on the inner tie rod and mark the breather tube position on the tube and housing for reference during reassembly.

14. Cut and remove the remaining boot clamps and boots.

15. Clamping the inner tie rod in a vise, remove the shock dampener rings from the jam nut; loosen the jam nut.

16. Loosen the tie-rod-housing setscrew and repeat Steps 15 and 16 on the opposite end of the rack.

17. Replace the housing in a vise and remove the inner tie-rod housing.

18. Remove the ball seats and springs, jam nuts and shock dampener rings from the rack.

19. Remove the adjuster plug and valve body from the housing.

20. Remove the pinion shaft by rotating it counterclockwise while pulling upward.

21. Remove the pinion thrust bearing, bearing races and support washer from the housing.

22. Pull the breather tube from the mounting grommet and remove.

23. Force the bulkhead retaining ring from the groove, then pry the ring out of the tube with a screwdriver.

24. Remove the steering rack from the tube/housing assembly. This will force the bulkhead out of the tube at the same time.

25. Slip a knife blade under the rack bushings and remove with needlenose pliers.

26. The inner rack seal will be damaged when the steering rack is removed. Drive the seal from the tube.

27. Remove the upper pinion bushing and pinion shaft seal. Inspect all components for wear or damage, and replace as required.

TO ASSEMBLE

1. Install the split-type nylon rack bushing by compressing it with your fingers and forcing it into the housing. Once in place, the bushing will regain its original shape.

2. Install the inner rack seal on the steering rack. Wrap the rack teeth with paper to prevent the teeth from cutting the seal, and slide the seal in place, with its metal surface facing *away* from the rack piston. Remove the paper protector when the seal has cleared the teeth.

3. Lubricate the outside diameter of the inner rack seal, bulkhead retaining ring and rack teeth, then install the piston seal ring on the rack piston.

4. Install the steering rack into the tube and bottom the seal, using the rack piston as a seal driver.

5. Install the upper pinion bushing, with its chamfered side facing down, and fit the pinion shaft seal in the housing, with its spring facing upward.

6. Position the support washer on top of the pinion shaft seal and tap lightly with a 1¼-in. socket, extension and hammer until both the seal and washer are fully seated.

7. Lubricate the pinion-shaft thrust bearing and races with petroleum jelly; install in race-bearing-race sequence.

8. Center the steering rack in the housing/tube assembly, with rack teeth parallel to the housing bore. Set the rack end 4 ins. from the machined inner-housing face.

9. Fit the pinion shaft into the housing bore with a drive pin set between the 3 and 4 o'clock positions, pushing the pinion down until it bottoms.

10. Center the steering rack to a 4-in. setting—the pinion-shaft drive pin should now be at 12 o'clock. If not, remove and repeat Steps 8 through 10.

11. Line up the valve-body notch with the drive pin in the pinion shaft, and install the valve body in the housing. Correct installation will expose the fluid return hole in the housing. If not visible, the pinion shaft is not fully seated.

12. Install and tighten the adjuster plug in the housing until it bottoms.

13. Adjust the thrust bearing preload, using the spanner hole for reference. Mark the plug and housing, then back off the plug 3/16- to 1/4-in. Replace the locknut and torque to 80 ft.-lbs.

14. Install the O-ring and seal in the bulkhead, with the seal lips facing inward. Slide the bulkhead into the tube until it bottoms against the counterbore.

15. Replace the bulkhead retaining ring with the opening ¼-in. from the access hole in the tube.

16. Turn the housing over in a vise and fill it with lubricant up to the housing bore.

17. Install the preload spring, with the center bearing hump against the housing. Spring must enter the upper pinion bushing and extend ¼-in. from the housing end.

18. Use needlenose pliers to hold the top of the preload spring against the housing, and install the lower pinion bushing, with the flat end facing out. Tap both to seat fully in the housing.

19. Install and seat the contraction plug.

20. Fit the shock dampener rings on the steering rack ends, with the open ends facing outward. Install the jam nuts.

21. Lubricate the inner tie-rod wear surfaces and pack the tie rod housing with lubricant.

22. Install the inner tie-rod assemblies, and torque the tie rod housing to 25 ft.-lbs., rocking the inner tie rod to prevent grease lock. Back off the housing 45°.

23. Torque the housing setscrews to 60 in.-lbs.

24. With the tie rod housing in a vise, tighten the jam nut to 100 ft.-lbs.

25. Replace the shock dampener rings over the jam nuts, and install the mounting clamp and grommet, using the alignment mark.

26. Install the boots and line up the tube holes, then replace the boot clamps.

27. Replace the adjuster tubes so that no more than three threads are visible at each end.

28. Install the flexible coupling, and torque the pinch bolt to 30 ft.-lbs.

ALL FULL-SIZE FORDS, MERCURYS; ALL FORD THUNDERBIRDS; 1974-79 MERCURY COUGAR/LTD II; ALL LINCOLNS
Ford Integral Power Steering

STEERING GEAR DESCRIPTION

A torsion-bar type of hydraulic assist system, the Ford integral power steering gearbox contains a one-piece rack-piston and worm meshed to teeth on the sector shaft (Pitman shaft) gear **(Fig. 15-15)**. A rotary-valve sleeve assembly (control valve) is contained in a separate housing, but is attached to the gearbox. Using relative rotational motion of the input shaft and valve sleeve, the control valve directs fluid flow.

In a wheels-straight-ahead position, the torsion bar holds the valve spool in a center position, since no power assist is necessary. But when the steering wheel is turned in either direction, wheel resistance and car weight cause the torsion bar to deflect. Because this changes the position of the valve spool, fluid is directed, under pressure, to the appropriate piston end in the housing. This pressure difference on the piston helps to move the sector shaft, thus assisting in the turning effort. But when the turning effort is released, the torsion bar forces the spool valve back to its centered position. This equalizes pressure on both sides of the piston, and the wheels are returned to a straight-ahead position. Steering gear ratio is 17:1, except for 1979 Ford/Mercury sedans, which use a 14:1 ratio. If the steering gear unit must be replaced on 1979 vehicles, make certain that one with the proper ratio is installed.

STEERING GEAR ADJUSTMENT

TO ADJUST SECTOR SHAFT PRELOAD IN CAR

1. Remove the Pitman-arm retaining nut and lockwasher. Using a puller, disconnect the Pitman arm from the sector (Pitman) shaft.

2. Disconnect the fluid return line at the reservoir. Place the end of the line in a clean container and turn the steering wheel from left to right to discharge fluid from the gearbox. Cap the reservoir-return fitting.

3. Turn the steering wheel to 45° from left stop and, with an in.-lb. torque wrench on the steering wheel nut, slowly rotate the steering wheel approximately one-eighth turn, checking torque required for the turn.

4. Now turn the steering wheel back to center and check the torque reading as you rotate the sector shaft back and forth across its center position.

5. Loosen the sector-shaft adjusting-screw locknut and turn the adjusting screw until the over-center reading is 11 to 12 in.-lbs. more than at the 45° reading. Holding the screw in place, tighten the locknut 35 to 45 ft.-lbs.

6. Recheck the torque readings, reconnect the Pitman arm and torque the retaining nut to specifications. Install the steering-wheel hub cover.

7. Reconnect the fluid return line to the pump reservoir; fill to appropriate level. Check and adjust belt tension, if necessary. Bolts and nut should be torqued 30 to 40 ft.-lbs., if belt tension is adjusted.

TO CHECK ROTARY VALVE CENTERING IN CAR

1. Install a pressure gauge (0 to 2000 psi) in the pressure line between the pump outlet port and the gearbox inlet port. Gauge valve must be fully open.

2. Check pump-reservoir fluid level. Add more fluid if necessary.

3. Starting the engine, turn the steering wheel from lock-to-lock several times to bring the fluid to operating temperature. Shut off the engine and recheck the fluid level.

4. Center the steering wheel and restart the engine, running at 1000 rpm. Fit an in.-lb. torque wrench to the steering wheel nut and apply torque in each direction to get a gauge reading of 250 psi.

5. Torque readings should be the same in each direction at 250 psi. If they differ by more than 4 in.-lbs., remove the steering gearbox and replace the input shaft and control assembly.

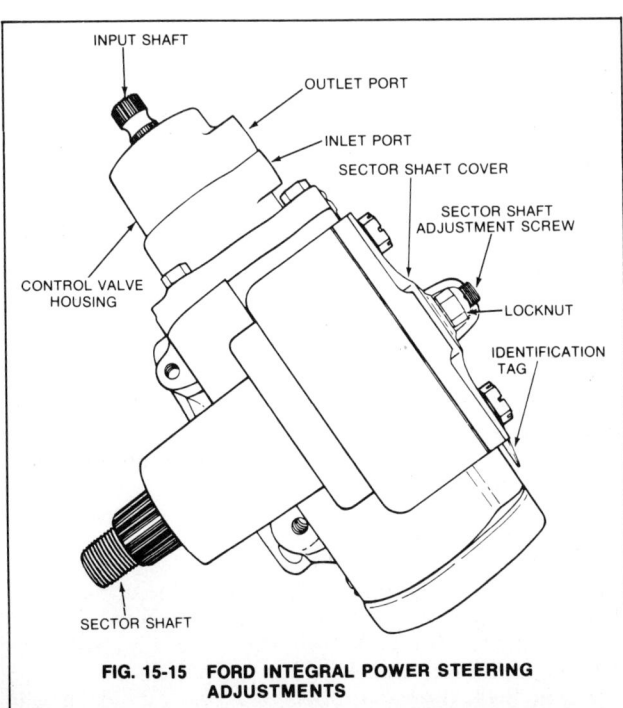

FIG. 15-15 FORD INTEGRAL POWER STEERING ADJUSTMENTS

STEERING GEAR REMOVAL/INSTALLATION

TO REMOVE

1. Disconnect the pressure and return lines from the steering gearbox. Plug the ends of the lines and gearbox ports.

2. Unhook the flexible coupling to separate the steering gear shaft from the column shaft.

3. After removing the Pitman-arm retaining nut and washer, use a puller to disconnect the Pitman arm from the sector shaft.

4. If the car is fitted with manual transmission, remove the clutch-release-lever retracting spring for access to the steering gearbox.

5. Unbolt the steering gearbox from the frame rail.

6. Work the gearbox shaft free from the flexible coupling and remove.

TO INSTALL

1. Make sure the steering wheel spokes are in a normal position.

2. Center the steering-gearbox input shaft and slide it into the flexible coupling, positioning the gearbox on the frame siderail.

3. Install the attaching bolts and torque 60 to 65 ft.-lbs.

4. With the wheels in a straight-ahead position, install the Pitman arm to the sector shaft. Replace the retaining washer and nut, and torque to specifications.

5. Position the flexible coupling to couple the input and steering column shafts. Install the attaching bolts and torque 20 to 30 ft.-lbs.

6. Reconnect the pressure and return lines to the steering gearbox, and torque to specs.

7. Fill the fluid reservoir and disconnect the coil wire. Turn on the ignition and turn the steering wheel from lock-to-lock to distribute the fluid.

8. Recheck fluid level and replace the coil wire. Start the engine and turn the steering wheel from left to right, checking for fluid leaks.

STEERING GEAR DISASSEMBLY/ASSEMBLY

Ford suggests that complete steering-gearbox disassembly will not be necessary in most cases, and that only faulty subassemblies be completely disassembled. Work on a clean bench with clean tools. Drain off excess fluid and clean the gearbox exterior thoroughly with solvent before beginning disassembly. Handle all interior parts carefully to prevent nicks, burrs and scratches. In order to properly overhaul this unit, the following special Ford tools are recommended: T75L-3517-A2 (ring pusher), T75L-3517-A1 (mandrel), T75L-3517-A3 (spacer set), T75L-3517-A4 (sizing tube), T59L-100-B (slide hammer), T58L-101-A (puller attachment), T65P-3524-A1, A2, A3 (bearing removers), T65P-3576-B (sector shaft installer), T64P-3504-L and M (tube seat remover/replacer set).

TO DISASSEMBLE

1. Drain the gearbox by holding the unit upside down over a container. Turn the input shaft back and forth to help discharge the fluid.

2. Secure the gearbox in a soft-jaw vise, clamping onto the mounting pads of housing to prevent damage.

3. Remove the sector-shaft adjusting-screw locknut and turn the input shaft to either stop, then back until the gear is centered (approximately 1¾ turns).

4. Remove the sector-shaft cover bolts, brake-line bracket and identification tag.

5. Using a soft mallet, loosen the sector shaft by tapping its lower end. Lift off the cover and shaft as an assembly, and discard the O-ring.

6. Remove the cover from the sector shaft by turning it counterclockwise.

7. Unbolt the valve housing. Separate the valve housing from the gearbox while holding the piston to keep it from spinning off the shaft.

8. Remove and discard the control valve seals. Stand the valve body upright, with the piston end down. Rotate the input shaft counterclockwise out of the piston to let the ball bearings drop into the piston.

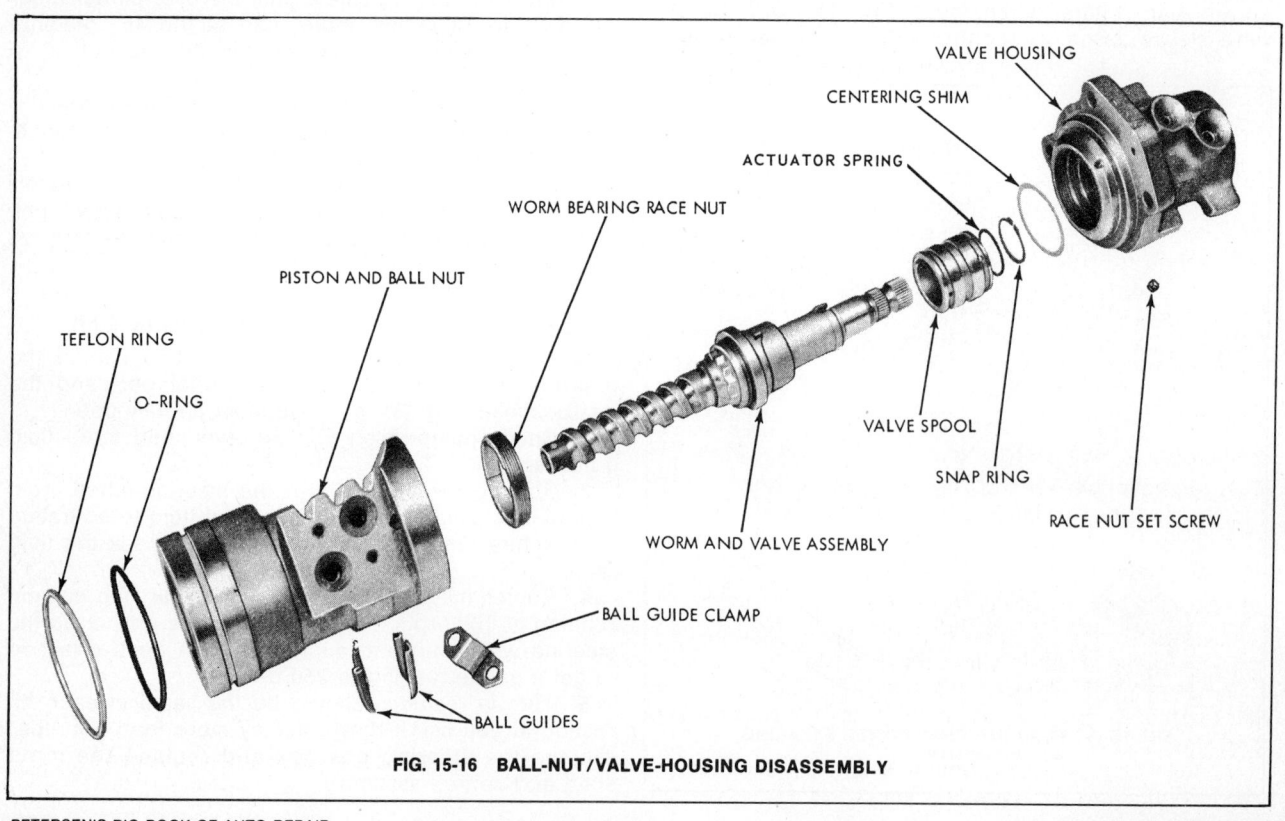

FIG. 15-16 BALL-NUT/VALVE-HOUSING DISASSEMBLY

9. Placing a clean cloth over the open piston end, turn the piston upside down to remove the balls.

10. Unscrew and remove the ball guide clamp and guides. Use **Fig. 15-16** as guide for further disassembly.

11. Loosen the Allen-head race-nut screw in the valve housing and remove the worm-bearing race nut.

12. Slide the input shaft and worm/valve assembly from the valve housing. Use extreme care in this step, because the valve sleeve and housing are a close fit, and tilting the spool valve while withdrawing it can cause sleeve damage.

VALVE HOUSING OVERHAUL

1. Use tools T59L-100-B and T58L-101-A to remove and discard the dust seal at the rear of the housing **(Fig. 15-17)**.

2. Remove the snap ring and turn the housing upside down. Tap the bearing and seal from the housing using tools T65P-3524-A2 and A3. Discard the seal.

3. If the fluid inlet and outlet tube seats are damaged, remove with tool T64P-3504-L. Coat the new seats with petroleum jelly and install them in the housing with tool T64P-3504-M.

4. Coat the bearing and seal surface of the housing with petroleum jelly. Install and seat the bearing, making sure it rotates freely.

5. Lubricate a new oil seal and fit it in the housing with the metal side facing out. Drive it into the housing until the outer edge of the seal almost clears the snap ring groove.

6. Install the snap ring by tapping until it seats in the groove.

7. Set the dust seal in the housing, rubber side facing out. Drive the seal in and seat it behind the undercut in the input shaft.

WORM AND VALVE SLEEVE OVERHAUL

1. Slip a small knife blade under the valve sleeve rings and cut them off.

2. Secure the worm end of worm/valve-sleeve assembly in a soft-jaw vise.

3. Installing tool T75L-3517-A1 over the sleeve, slide one valve sleeve ring over it.

4. Sliding tool T75L-3517-A2 over the mandrel, push down on the tool rapidly to force the ring down the ramp to the fourth valve-sleeve groove. Repeat this three times, adding one of the spacers (tool T75L-3517-A3) under the mandrel each time. The spacer is used to line up the tool with the appropriate valve-sleeve groove.

5. Using one spacer as a pilot for installing the sizing tube (tool T75L-3517-A4), slowly fit it over the sleeve-valve end of the wormshaft and onto the valve sleeve rings. Be careful not to bend the rings as the tube is slid over them.

6. Remove the sizing tube and check ring condition—they must turn freely in the grooves.

PISTON/BALL NUT OVERHAUL

1. Remove the Teflon piston ring and O-ring.

2. Lubricate and install a new O-ring.

3. Install the new Teflon piston ring, but do not stretch it excessively.

STEERING GEAR HOUSING OVERHAUL

1. Remove the snap ring and spacer washer from the lower end of the housing **(Fig. 15-18)**.

2. Using tools T59L-100-B and T58L-101-A, remove the lower seal and washer, then remove the upper seal and washer.

3. Lubricate both the sector-shaft seal bore of the housing and the new seals with power steering fluid.

Install the inner seal in the housing, with the lip facing inward, and press it into place. Fit a 0.090-in. washer on top and relubricate the housing bore.

4. Position the outer seal in the housing, with the lip facing inward, and press it into place. Fit a 0.090-in. washer on top of the seal.

5. Replace the snap ring, pressing it in to locate the seals properly while seating the snap ring in the groove.

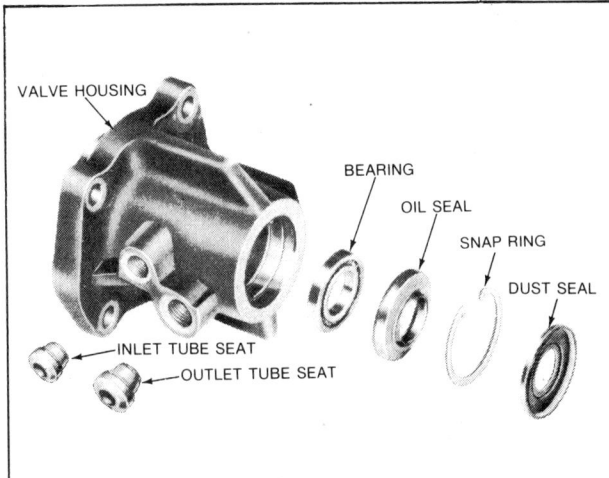

FIG. 15-17   VALVE HOUSING DISASSEMBLY

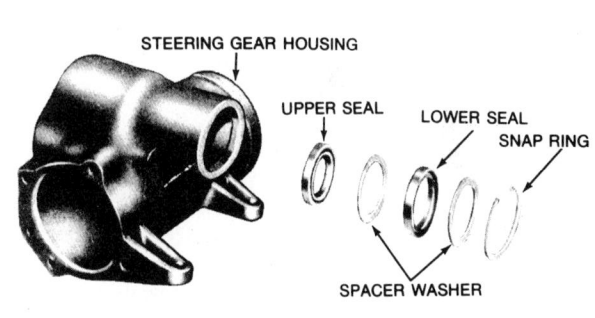

FIG. 15-18   STEERING GEAR HOUSING DISASSEMBLY

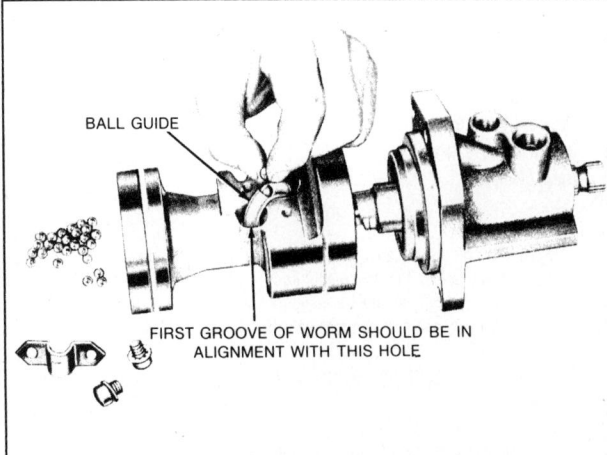

FIG. 15-19   RECIRCULATING BALL REPLACEMENT

TO ASSEMBLE

1. Secure the valve housing, with flanged end facing up **(Fig. 15-16)**. Lubricate the valve sleeve rings and carefully install the worm-and-valve assembly in the housing.

2. Install the race retaining nut in the housing, and torque to specifications.

3. Install the race nut setscrew through the valve housing, and torque to specifications.

4. With the piston on the bench, and ball guide holes facing up, install the wormshaft into the piston. The first groove must line up with the hole nearest the piston center **(Fig. 15-19)**.

5. With the ball guide in the piston, turn the worm clockwise and place 27-29 balls in the guide (the exact number depends upon design). Do not rotate the input shaft more than 3½ turns off right stop, or the balls will fall out.

6. Replace the clamp to hold the guides in place, and tighten the holding screw to specifications.

7. Coat the Teflon seal on the piston with petroleum jelly, and fit the new control valve seals on the valve housing.

8. Sliding the piston and valve into the housing, line up the lubricating passage in the valve housing with the passage in the gearbox housing. Install the attaching bolts, but *do not* tighten.

9. Turn the ball nut until the teeth are in the same plane as the sector teeth. Torque the valve housing bolts to specifications.

10. Place the sector-shaft-cover O-ring in the steering gearbox housing and turn the input shaft to its center position.

11. Coating the sector shaft journal with petroleum jelly, place the sector shaft and cover assembly in the housing.

12. Replace the brake line bracket, identification tag and sector-shaft cover bolts, torquing to specifications.

13. Adjust the gear input-shaft meshload 2 to 8 in.-lbs., using a torque wrench.

FORD INTEGRAL POWER STEERING GEAR TORQUE LIMITS (FT-LBS.)

DESCRIPTION	TORQUE
Sector Shaft Cover Bolts	55-70
Meshload Adjusting-Screw Lock Nut	35-45
Ball-Return-Guide Clamp Screw	42-70*
Valve Housing to Gear Housing Screw	35-50
Race Retaining Nut	**
Setscrew Race Nut	15-25*
Piston End Cap	70-110
Pressure Hose to Gear	16-25
Return Hose to Gear	25-34
Hose Clamps	1-2

* In.-lbs.
** Specified Torque—Because the length of the tool required to torque the nut will affect the observed torque reading on the torque wrench, the torque reading should be computed using the length of the torque wrench and the nominal specified torque as follows:

$$\text{Torque (using tool T66P-3553-B)} = \frac{\text{Length of Torque Wrench} \times 72 \text{ ft-lbs.}}{\text{Length of Torque Wrench} + 5.5 \text{ ins.}}$$

Example: With 13-in. torque wrench

$$\frac{13 \text{ ins.} \times 72 \text{ ft-lbs.}}{13 \text{ ins.} + 5.5 \text{ ins.}} = \frac{13 \times 72 \text{ ft-lbs.}}{18.5} = 0.703 \times 72 = 50 \text{ ft-lbs.}$$

ALL FORD MAVERICKS, GRANADAS, 1970 MUSTANGS; ALL MERCURY COMETS, MONARCHS, 1970 COUGARS; ALL LINCOLN VERSAILLES

Ford Non-Integral Power Steering System (Bendix Linkage Type)

STEERING GEAR DESCRIPTION

Ford non-integral steering **(Fig. 15-20)** is a hydraulically controlled, linkage-type system and consists of an integral pump with fluid reservoir, control valve, power cylinder, connecting fluid lines and steering linkage. The steering gearbox used is a Ford manual recirculating-ball type, and is adjusted/overhauled according to procedures in Chapter 14.

CONTROL VALVE CENTERING SPRING ADJUSTMENT

TO ADJUST

1. With the car elevated, remove the two control-valve, spring-cap attaching screws, lockwashers and the spring cap.

2. Torque the centering-spring adjusting nut 90 to 100 in.-lbs., then loosen the nut one-quarter turn, making certain it rotates 90° on the bolt threads.

3. Place the spring cap and a new gasket on the valve housing. Lubricate and install the attaching screws and washers. Torque screws 72 to 100 in.-lbs.

4. Lower the car and start the engine. Attach a spring scale to the steering wheel rim; effort required to turn the steering wheel in either direction should not exceed 6.5 lbs.

CONTROL VALVE REMOVAL/INSTALLATION

TO REMOVE

1. Disconnect all fluid line fittings from the control valve, and drain the lines into a container, turning the steering wheel back and forth gently to force all fluid from the system.

2. Locate the clamping nut and bolt at the right end of the sleeve, and loosen.

3. Remove the roll pin from the steering-arm-to-idler-arm rod through the slot in the sleeve.

4. Remove the cotter pin and control-valve ball-stud nut. Using a puller, disconnect the ball stud carefully from the Pitman arm **(Fig. 15-21)**.

5. Turning the front wheels fully to the left, unthread the control valve from the center-link, steering-arm-to-idler-arm rod.

TO INSTALL

1. Thread the control valve onto the center link until only four threads remain visible on the link.

2. Placing the ball stud in the Pitman arm, measure the distance between the center of the grease plug in the sleeve and the center of the stud at inner end of the left spindle connecting rod. This should be exactly 5⅞ ins.; if not, disconnect the ball stud and turn the valve on the center link to increase or decrease distance.

3. With the ball stud in the Pitman arm, align the hole in the steering-arm-to-idler-arm with the slot in the valve sleeve; install the roll pin in the rod hole, locking the valve in position on the rod.

4. Torque valve-sleeve clamp bolt 13 to 17 ft.-lbs.

5. Replace the ball stud nut and torque 35 to 47 ft.-lbs.; install a new cotter pin.

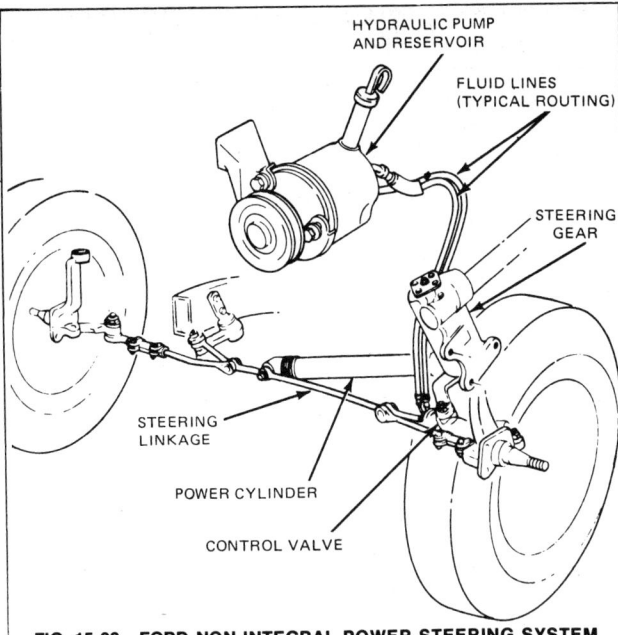

FIG. 15-20 FORD NON-INTEGRAL POWER STEERING SYSTEM

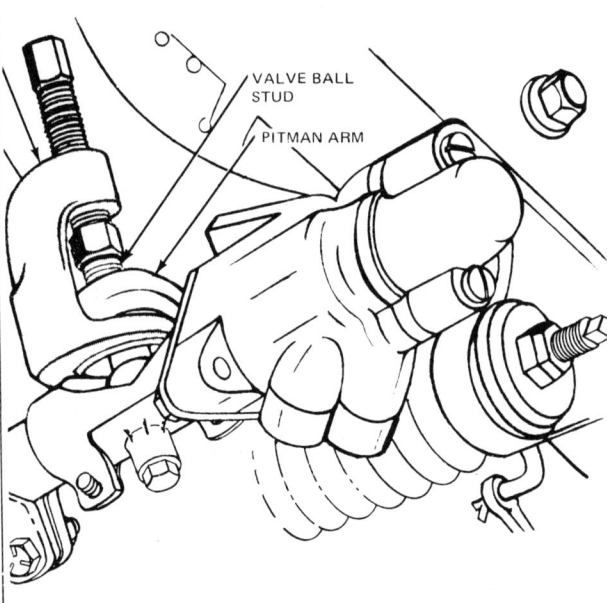

FIG. 15-21 DISCONNECTING BALL STUD

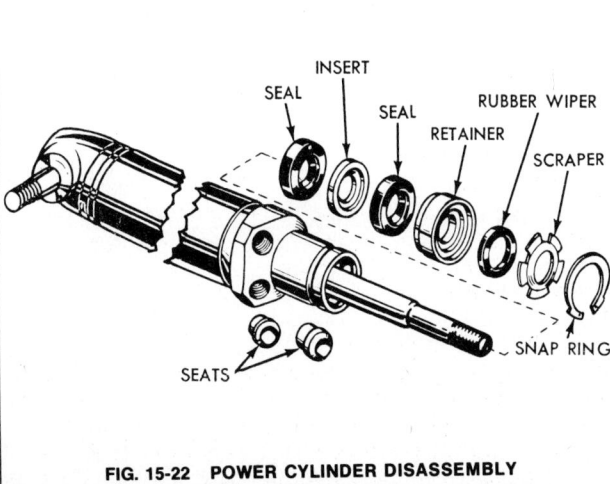

FIG. 15-22 POWER CYLINDER DISASSEMBLY

6. Reconnect the fluid lines to the control valve; tighten all fittings to specifications.

7. Fill the fluid reservoir to the cross-hatched area on the dipstick. Start and idle the engine to warm the power steering fluid.

8. Turning the steering wheel slowly from lock-to-lock, inspect the system for leakage. Stop the engine and check the control valve and hose connections for leaks, then check the fluid level, and refill if necessary.

POWER CYLINDER REMOVAL/OVERHAUL/INSTALLATION

TO REMOVE AND OVERHAUL

1. Unhook fluid lines from the power cylinder; drain fluid into a container.

2. Remove the pal nut, attaching nut, washer and insulator from the power-cylinder rod end.

3. Remove the cotter pin and castellated nut which holds the power cylinder stud to the center link.

4. Use a puller to disconnect the power cylinder stud from the center link.

5. Remove the insulator sleeve and washer from the power-cylinder rod end.

6. Check the fittings and power cylinder seat for nicks, burrs, etc. Replace as required.

7. Remove the snap ring from the rod end. Pull the piston rod out and remove the scraper, rubber wiper, retainer and seals **(Fig. 15-22)**. If a pick is used for seal removal, use care not to damage the shaft or seal seat.

TO INSTALL

1. Use a repair kit when replacing the seals. Coat with the power steering fluid and push the piston rod all the way in. Use a 6-in. piece of 15/16-in. OD electrical conduit to install the parts in the power cylinder; replace the snap ring. Make sure the seal is installed so that the garter spring points to the bottom of the seal cavity and the flat side of the plastic retainer faces the inner seal.

2. Replace the washer, sleeve and insulator on the power-cylinder rod end.

3. Pulling the rod out as far as it will go, insert it in the frame bracket. Compress the rod sufficiently to install the stud in the center link. Replace the castellated nut and install a new cotter pin.

4. Fasten the power cylinder rod with insulator, washer, nut and pal nut; torque nuts to specifications.

5. Reconnect the fluid lines to their respective cylinder ports, and fill the reservoir to the correct level with the engine idling.

6. Bleed air from the system by turning the steering wheel lock-to-lock several times.

7. Stop the engine and check fluid level. Fill as required, replacing the dipstick and cap.

8. Start the engine and inspect for leakage.

CONTROL VALVE DISASSEMBLY/ASSEMBLY

Work on a clean bench with clean tools. Drain off excess solvent and clean the exterior of the control valve thoroughly before beginning disassembly. Handle all parts **(Fig. 15-23)** carefully to prevent nicks, burrs and scratches.

TO DISASSEMBLE

1. Clamp the unit by its sleeve flanges in a soft-jaw vise.

2. Remove the centering spring cap from the valve housing.

3. Unscrew the adjusting nut from the end of the valve spool bolt and remove washers, spacer, centering spring, adapter and bushing from the valve housing.

4. Unbolt and remove the valve housing and gasket from the sleeve.

5. Removing the plug from the valve sleeve, push the valve spool out of the housing and remove the spool seal.

6. Lift the spacer, bushing and seal from the sleeve end of the valve housing—the stop pin will fall out of

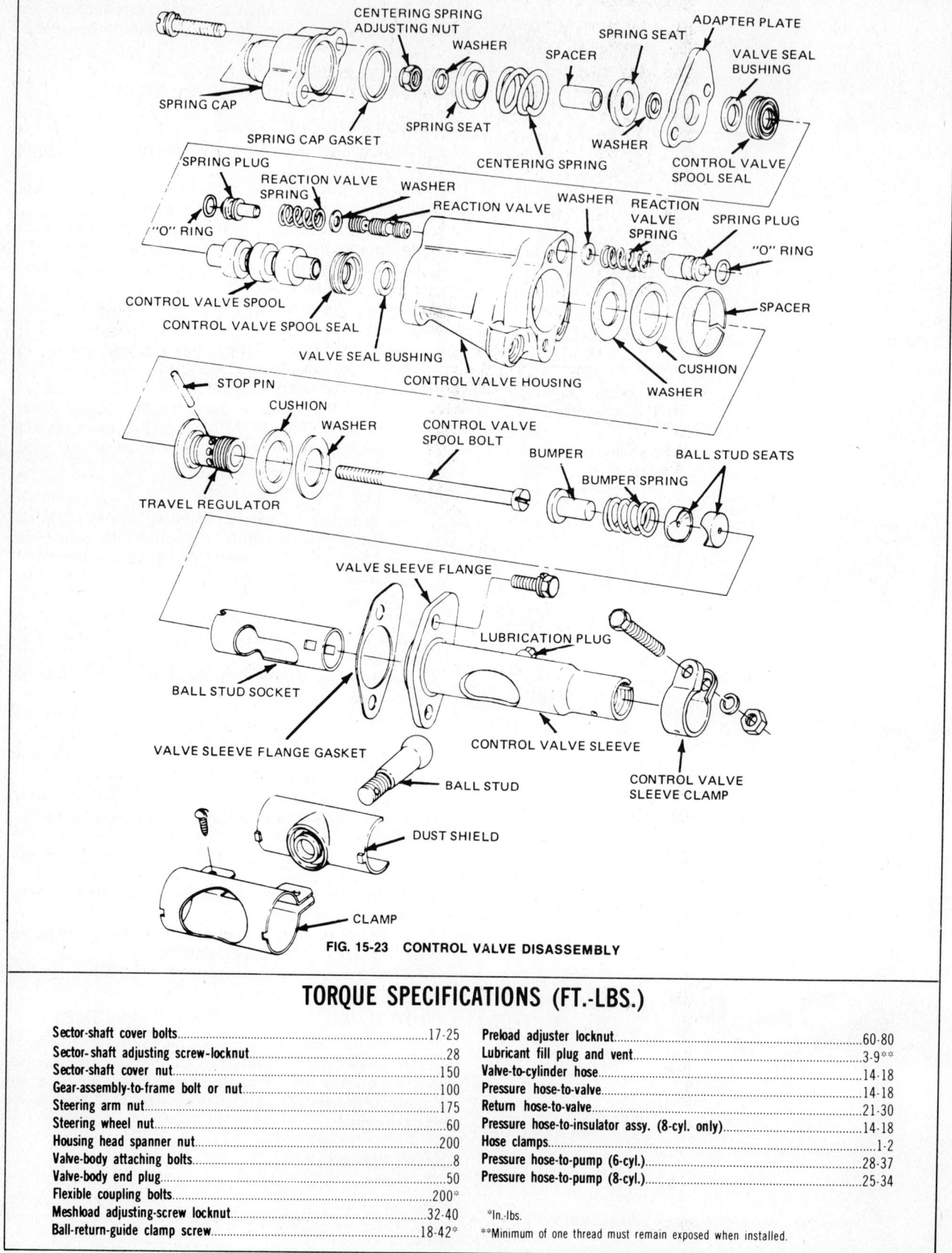

FIG. 15-23 CONTROL VALVE DISASSEMBLY

TORQUE SPECIFICATIONS (FT.-LBS.)

Sector-shaft cover bolts	17-25	
Sector-shaft adjusting screw-locknut	28	
Sector-shaft cover nut	150	
Gear-assembly-to-frame bolt or nut	100	
Steering arm nut	175	
Steering wheel nut	60	
Housing head spanner nut	200	
Valve-body attaching bolts	8	
Valve-body end plug	50	
Flexible coupling bolts	200*	
Meshload adjusting-screw locknut	32-40	
Ball-return-guide clamp screw	18-42*	
Preload adjuster locknut	60-80	
Lubricant fill plug and vent	3-9**	
Valve-to-cylinder hose	14-18	
Pressure hose-to-valve	14-18	
Return hose-to-valve	21-30	
Pressure hose-to-insulator assy. (8-cyl. only)	14-18	
Hose clamps	1-2	
Pressure hose-to-pump (6-cyl.)	28-37	
Pressure hose-to-pump (8-cyl.)	25-34	

*In.-lbs.
**Minimum of one thread must remain exposed when installed.

the travel regulator.

7. Rotate the travel regulator stop counterclockwise in the valve sleeve to remove the stop from the sleeve.

8. Remove the valve spool bolt, spacer and rubber washer from the regulator stop.

9. Remove the rubber boot and clamp from the valve sleeve.

10. Slide out the bumper, spring and ball stud seat from the valve sleeve, removing the ball stud socket from the sleeve.

11. Remove the return-port hose seat and relief valve.

12. Maverick/Comet Only—Remove the spring plug, O-ring and reaction-limiting valve.

TO ASSEMBLE

1. Coat all parts (except seals) with power steering fluid.

2. Maverick/Comet—Install the reaction valve, washers, springs and spring-plug/O-ring assemblies. Granada/Monarch—Install the plug and O-ring.

3. Install the return-port relief valve and hose seat.

4. Insert the flat end of the ball stud seat into the ball stud socket. Position the socket in the control valve sleeve to allow the threaded end of the ball stud to be pulled out through the slot in the sleeve.

5. Insert the other ball stud seat, spring and bumper in the socket, then install and tighten the travel regulator stop. Torque the travel regulator 5 to 10 ft.-lbs., then loosen and align the nearest hole in the stop with the slot in the ball stud socket.

6. Install the stop pin in the ball stud socket, travel regulator stop and valve spool bolt.

7. Insert the spool seal, seat bushing, washer, spacer and cushion in the housing sleeve end and carefully rotate the valve spool into the housing, with the large groove nearest the cap end **(Fig. 15-24)**.

8. Rotate the spool through the seal while pressing on the cushion at the sleeve end. With the spool barely protruding through the seal bushing, install the seal over the spool at the cap end.

9. Work the seal into the housing with a small, blunt screwdriver, taking care not to scratch the spool, seat or housing. Install the seal bushing, then slide the spool back and forth to check for free movement.

10. Install the body gasket on the sleeve and bolt it to the housing. Torque the bolts 140 to 225 in.-lbs. Ball stud should now move laterally for about 0.20-in.

11. Assemble the washer, spacer, adapter, spring seat, control-valve centering spring, the remaining spring seat and washer, and the control-valve-spool bolt nut. Torque the nut 90 to 110 in.-lbs., then loosen one-quarter turn beyond the point at which the spool bolt reaches its stop.

12. Move the ball stud back and forth to check free movement while holding adapter plate to the housing.

13. Replace the control-valve spring cap and gasket on adapter plate, tightening screws 72 to 100 in.-lbs.

14. Fit the boot and clamp over the stud. Boot garter spring must be attached. Thread the screws in loosely and move the stud sideways to determine center position. Hold there and position the clamp up against the grease fitting, tightening screws to secure clamp.

15. Remove the grease plug and grease with ⅓- to ½-oz. ESA-MIC75-A grease—*do not* exceed this amount.

PINTO/BOBCAT/MUSTANG/CAPRI/ MUSTANG II/FAIRMONT/ZEPHYR
Ford Integral Rack- and-Pinion Power Steering

STEERING GEAR DESCRIPTION

The Ford integral rack-and-pinion power-steering control valve **(Fig. 15-25)** uses relative rotational motion of an input shaft/valve sleeve to direct fluid flow. In operation, it is similar to the torsion-bar integral Ford design. Wheel resistance and car weight cause a torsion bar to deflect when the wheels are turned. This causes the valve spool and sleeve ports to change their positions, directing fluid under pressure to the proper end of the power cylinder **(Fig. 15-26)**. Pressure differences on the piston help move the rack to assist turning effort.

The piston is directly attached to the rack, with the housing tube functioning as the power cylinder. During a turning movement, oil in the opposite end of the power cylinder is forced to the control valve and back to the pump reservoir for recirculation. Stopping the application of steering effort causes the torsion bar to force the valve back to a centered position. This equalizes pressure on both sides of the piston, and the front wheels return to a straight-ahead position. The relative positions of the input shaft to the sleeve for right, left and straight-ahead or neutral maneuvers are shown in **Fig. 15-27**.

After 1977, some vehicles are fitted with TRW-built steering units which are essentially similar to the Ford, but have different features as listed below:

1. A new yoke and yoke adjuster plug.

2. No tube bracket as used in the Ford unit.

3. A combined tie rod/ball housing assembly. A special locking pin eliminates the drilled pin used in the Ford unit.

4. Gear/bearing lubrication by grease instead of oil.

5. A gear housing design change to accommodate a new lock ring which holds the rack bushing. This applies only to 1979 Mustang/Capri applications using the TRW rather than the Ford steering unit.

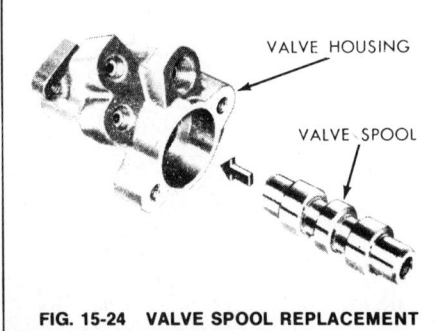
FIG. 15-24   VALVE SPOOL REPLACEMENT

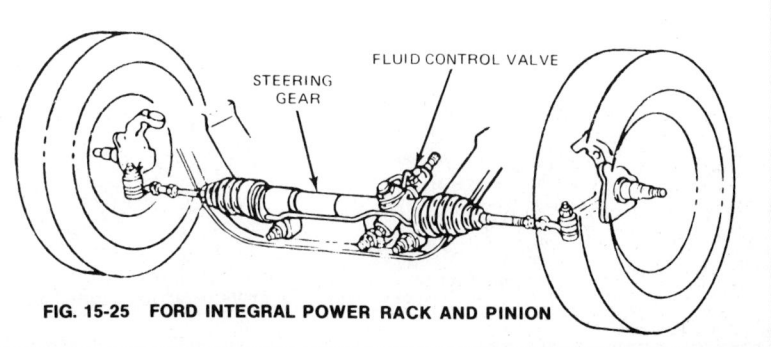
FIG. 15-25   FORD INTEGRAL POWER RACK AND PINION

STEERING GEAR ADJUSTMENT

Only one service adjustment can be made to the power rack-and-pinion steering gear, and the steering gear must be removed from the car to make it. A bench-mounted holding fixture, Ford tool T57L-500-B, is recommended for all steering gear work. Using a standard bench vise can damage the steering gear housing. See "Steering Gear Removal/Installation" for removal procedure.

TO ADJUST RACK YOKE-BEARING PRELOAD

1. Clean the steering gear exterior and attach it to the bench-mounted holding fixture.
2. Rotate the input shaft lock-to-lock twice to drain the power steering fluid.
3. Loosen the yoke plug locknut and attach an in.-lb. torque wrench to the yoke plug.
4. Set the rack at center of travel and tighten the yoke plug 45 to 50 in.-lbs.
5. Back off the yoke plug until the torque required to turn the input shaft is between 7 and 15 in.-lbs. Yoke plug should not be turned more than 45°.
6. Holding the yoke plug, torque locknut to specifications and recheck torque setting.

STEERING GEAR REMOVAL/INSTALLATION

TO REMOVE

1. Disconnect the flexible coupling to free the input shaft from the column shaft.

2. Remove the retaining cotter pins and nuts from the tie rod ends. Use a ball-joint separator tool to separate the studs from the spindle arms.
3. The number 2A crossmember must be removed on the Mustang to permit removal of the steering-gear attaching bolts.
4. Remove the steering-gear attaching bolts, rubber insulators, washers and nuts from number 2 crossmember **(Fig. 15-28)** and lower the gear sufficiently to allow access to the pump line fittings.
5. Remove the screw holding the power-steering hose bracket to the gear-mounted bracket.
6. Disconnect the pump lines from the steering-gear valve housing. Cap the ports and plug the lines.
7. Remove the steering gear assembly from the car.

TO INSTALL

1. Position and support the steering gear housing to permit reattachment of the pump lines to the valve housing ports. Torque the fittings to specifications.
2. Attach the hose bracket to the gear-mounted bracket, and torque screws to specifications.
3. Fit the input shaft into the flexible coupling and locate the steering gearbox to number 2 crossmember. Install bolts, washers and nuts **(Fig. 15-28).**
4. Torque the steering-gearbox attaching bolts to specifications in this sequence: right-hand nut first, outer left-hand nut next and center nut last. Incorrect tightening sequence can bend the gear housing.

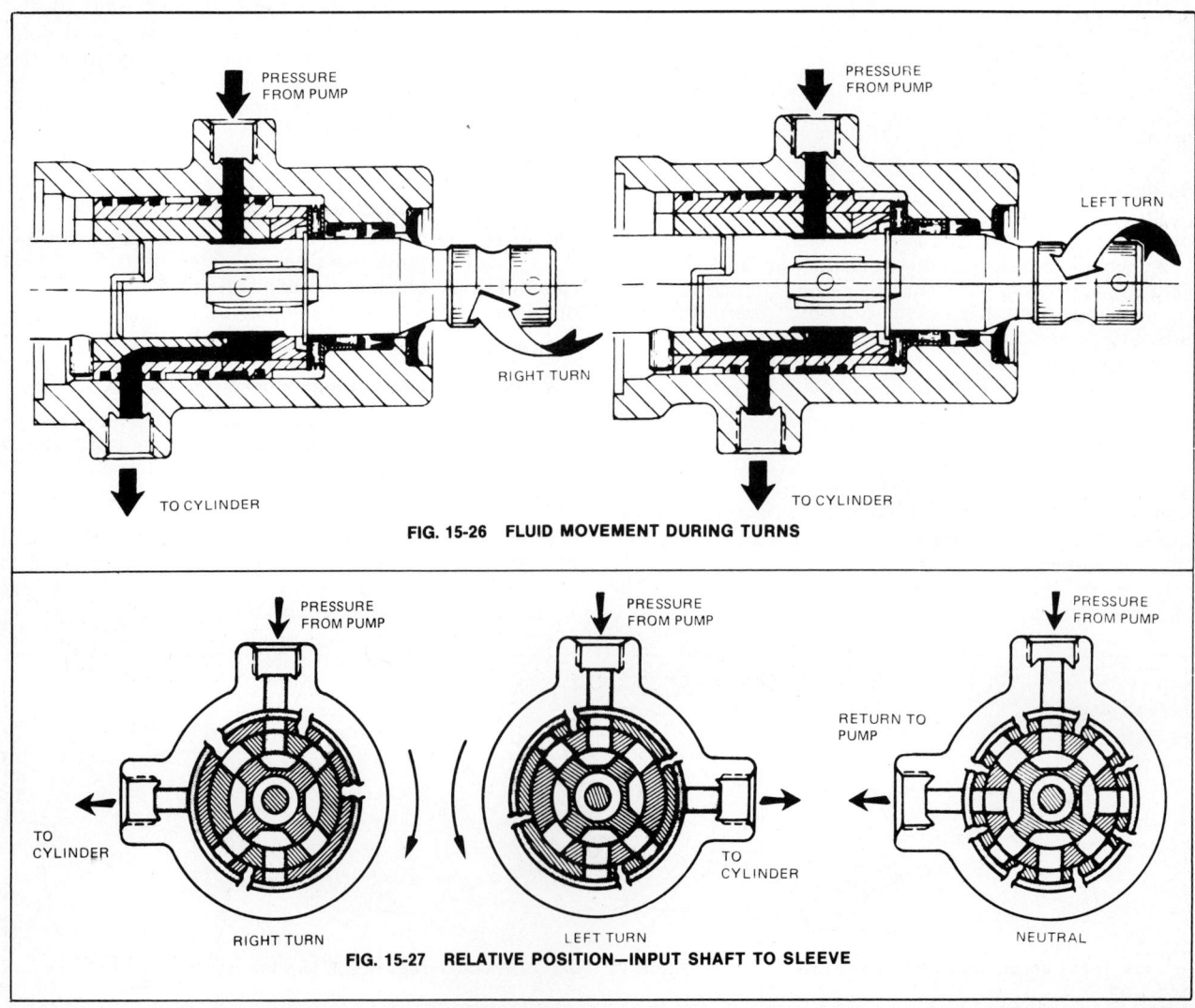

FIG. 15-26 FLUID MOVEMENT DURING TURNS

FIG. 15-27 RELATIVE POSITION—INPUT SHAFT TO SLEEVE

5. Reinstall number 2A crossmember if working on a Mustang.

6. Reconnect the tie rod ends to the spindle arms and replace the retaining nuts. Torque to specifications and install new cotter pins.

7. Install and torque the flexible coupling bolts to specifications.

8. Fill the power-steering pump reservoir, remove the coil wire and engage the starter. Cycle the steering wheel to distribute power steering fluid, then check fluid level and add more if necessary.

9. Replace the coil wire, start the engine and cycle the steering wheel again, checking for fluid leaks.

STEERING GEAR DISASSEMBLY/ASSEMBLY

Work on a clean bench with clean tools; *do not* use impact tools for the following procedures. Drain off excess fluid and clean the exterior of the steering gear thoroughly with solvent before beginning disassembly. Handle all interior parts carefully to prevent nicks, burrs and scratches. In order to properly overhaul this unit, the following special Ford tool is recommended: T57L-500-B (holding fixture).

TO DISASSEMBLE TIE ROD ENDS, BELLOWS AND TIE-ROD BALL-JOINT SOCKET

1. Loosen the jam nuts on the outer ends of the tie rods; remove the ends and nuts.

2. Remove and discard the four clamps which hold the bellows to the gear housing.

3. Drain and remove the bellows and breather tube.

4. Right and left tie rods and sockets are removed by drilling out the retaining pins.

5. Use a spanner wrench to remove the tie rod and ball socket.

6. Remove and discard locknut, inner thrust bearing and rack spring from the recess in the end of the rack.

TO ASSEMBLE

1. Install a new rack spring in the recess at the end of the rack.

2. Assemble the ball socket to the tie rod and install a new inner thrust bearing in the ball socket. Lubricate all parts.

3. Thread the new ball-joint locknut on the end of the rack, then thread the ball socket on the rack until it is tight.

4. Rotating the rod several times, adjust the ball socket until the tie rod end requires 4-6 lbs. effort to move. Measure, using a spring scale attached to the end of the tie rod.

5. Hold the ball socket in place and torque the locknut 25 to 35 ft.-lbs.

6. Drill a new hole to install the retaining pin. It should not enter locknut notches. Install and stake the retaining pin in place. Support the ball housing on a suitable surface when staking over the pin.

7. Fit the bellows and breather tube in position and install four new clamps. Fill each bellows with 2½ oz. lubricant.

8. Install the jam nuts and tie rod ends on the tie rods.

TO DISASSEMBLE INPUT SHAFT AND VALVE ASSEMBLY

1. Remove the fluid lines and flare gaskets from the ports.

2. Loosen the yoke plug locknut and yoke plug to relieve rack preload.

3. Remove the pinion bearing plug; hold the input shaft and remove the pinion bearing locknut. Discard the locknut.

4. Remove the valve housing from the gear housing and move the rack to the left stop (rack teeth exposed). Mark the position of the blocked tooth on the

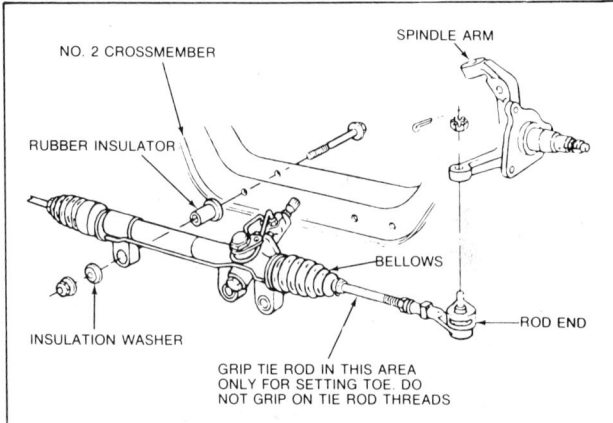

FIG. 15-28   POWER STEERING GEAR REMOVAL/INSTALLATION

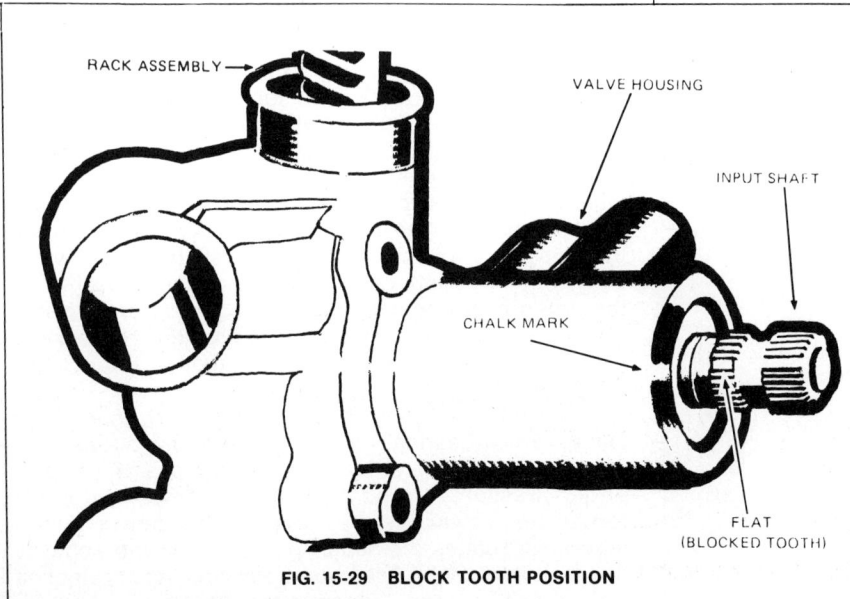

FIG. 15-29   BLOCK TOOTH POSITION

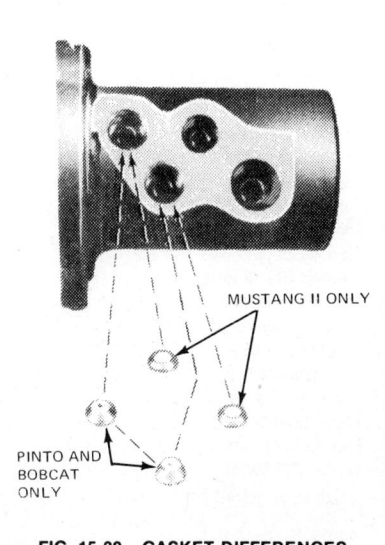

FIG. 15-30   GASKET DIFFERENCES

input shaft splines to the valve housing face with chalk or a file for ease in reassembly **(Fig. 15-29)**.

5. Work the input shaft and valve assembly out of the gear housing.

6. Use a slide hammer to remove the pinion bearing from the gear housing, then remove the two O-ring seals.

7. Remove and discard the pinion-shaft oil seal.

8. Slide the valve housing over the splined end of the input shaft and remove.

9. Remove the four Teflon O-rings from the input shaft and valve assembly.

10. If the input-shaft thrust needle bearing and two washers did not come out with the input shaft, remove them from the housing.

11. Remove the shaft support bearing, oil seal and dust seal, taking care not to damage valve housing surfaces.

TO ASSEMBLE

1. Install the input-shaft oil seal, with the lip facing the inside of the housing. To avoid contact with the support bearing, it must bottom in its bore.

2. Fill the dust seal bore with lubricant, and install the dust seal.

3. Lubricate and install the support bearing in the valve housing. It should not touch the oil seal.

4. Replace the Teflon O-rings in the valve assembly grooves.

5. Lubricate the thrust washers and needle bearing with power steering fluid. Position a washer on each side of the bearing, and install over the input shaft.

6. Lubricate the O-rings and valve with power steering fluid, then insert the assembly, splined end first, pushing it through until it bottoms and the full spline passes through the dust seal.

7. Install the O-ring on the flange protruding from the gear housing, then fit the oil seal, with the lip facing the input-shaft/valve assembly.

8. Install the pinion bearing through the plug bore in the lower gear housing, and position the O-ring around the bearing next to the gear housing.

9. Moving the rack to its left stop (teeth exposed), install the input-shaft/valve assembly in the gear housing bore. Line up the blocked teeth with the chalk mark made during disassembly **(Fig. 15-29)**.

10. Replace bolts and washers to attach the valve housing to gear housing and torque 12 to 15 ft.-lbs.

11. Fit the pinion bearing locknut on the pinion shaft.

Using an extra pinion bearing plug, drill a hole large enough to insert a 9/16-in. socket. Thread the plug into the bore and tighten to hold the bearing in place. Hold the input shaft, with the race away from the stop, and torque the locknut 44 to 66 ft.-lbs.

12. Install the unmodified bearing plug. Torque 60 to 100 ft.-lbs., and stake in place.

13. Install the flare gaskets in the gear- and valve-housing pressure line fittings **(Fig. 15-30)**. Replace the pressure lines, and torque the fittings to specifications.

14. Replace the tube bracket. Its tabs should engage in the gear housing slots.

15. Install the yoke plug locknut, adjust the bearing preload according to the procedure in "Steering Gear Adjustment," and torque the locknut 44 to 66 ft.-lbs.

POWER RACK AND PINION STEERING GEAR—TRW	
TORQUE	Ft-Lbs. (N.m)
Pump Pressure and Return Lines	10-15 (14-20)
(Mustang/Capri)	
(Pinto/Bobcat)	16-25 (22-39)
Gear-to-Crossmember Mounting Bolt Nut	80-100 (109-133)
Tie Rod End-to-Spindle Arm Nut	35-47 (48-63)[1]
Steering Flex Coupling Bolt	20-30 (28-40)
York Plug Locknut	44-66 (60-89)
Pressure Line Fittings at Valve Housing/Gear Housing	10-15 (14-20)
Valve Housing to Gear Housing Bolts	10-15 (14-20)
Pinion Bearing Locknut	23-34 (31-46)
Pinion Bearing Plug	40-60 (54-81)
Rack Bushing Locknut (Pinto/Bobcat)	80-120 (109-162)
Tie Rod End-to-Tie Rod Jam Nut	35-50 (48-68)
Tie Rod Ball Sockets-to-Rack	55-65 (75-88)

[1] Tighten to nearest cotter pin slot after torquing to specification.

ALL CHRYSLER CORPORATION CARS
Chrysler Constant-Control Power Steering
STEERING GEAR DESCRIPTION

The Chrysler constant-control power steering gearbox **(Fig. 15-31)** contains a sector shaft with sector gear and a power piston with gear teeth cut in its side. These teeth remain in constant mesh with the sector gear teeth. A wormshaft connects the steering wheel to the power piston by a coupling and is geared to the piston by recirculating ball contact. Steering gear fluid is supplied to the gearbox by an engine-driven pump through a pressure hose. Fluid is sent back to the pump reservoir from the gearbox, through a return line, for recirculation through the system.

A spool valve mounted on top of the steering gear directs the system fluid flow **(Figs. 15-31 & 32)**. Turn the steering wheel to the left, and the wormshaft will move out of the power piston a few thousandths of an inch, causing the center thrust bearing to move the same distance in the same direction. The bearing race then tips a pivot lever, which moves the spool valve downward. This lets gear fluid flow under pressure into the left-turn power chamber, forcing the power piston downward. This power piston movement rotates the sector shaft gear and transmits the motion through the steering linkage to the wheels.

Turning the steering wheel to the right causes the center thrust-bearing race to tip the pivot lever and move the spool valve upward, letting gear fluid flow, under pressure, to the right-turn chamber, where it forces the power piston upward. This power piston movement rotates the sector gear shaft in the opposite direction to that of a left turn, transmitting the motion through the steering linkage to the wheels.

TORQUE CHART—RACK AND PINION—FORD	
TORQUE	FT.-LBS.
Pressure Line Fitting (Pump-to-Gear ½ Hex)	16-25 [2]
Return Line Fitting	25-34 [2]
Hose Orientation Bracket-to-Gear Mounted Bracket Screw	7-12
Gear-to-Crossmember Mounting Bolt Nut	80-100
Tie-Rod-End-to-Spindle-Arm Nut	35-47 [1]
Tie-Rod-End-to-Tie-Rod Jam Nut	35-50
Steering Flex Coupling Bolt	20-30
Yoke Plug Locknut	44-66
Pressure Line Fittings at Valve	10-15 [3]
Pressure Line Fittings at Power Cylinder (Gear Housing)	10-15 [3]
Valve Housing to Gear Housing Bolts	12-15
Pinion Bearing Locknut	44-66 [4]
Pinion Bearing Plug	60-100 [5]
Rack Bushing Locknut	80-120 [6]
Tie-Rod Ball-Socket Locknut	25-35

[1] Tighten to nearest cotter pin slot after torquing to specification.
[2] 1978-79, 10-15 ft.-lbs.
[3] 1978-79, 14-20 ft.-lbs.
[4] 1978-79, 23-24 ft.-lbs.
[5] 1978-79, 40-60 ft.-lbs.
[6] 1978-79, 55-60 ft.-lbs.

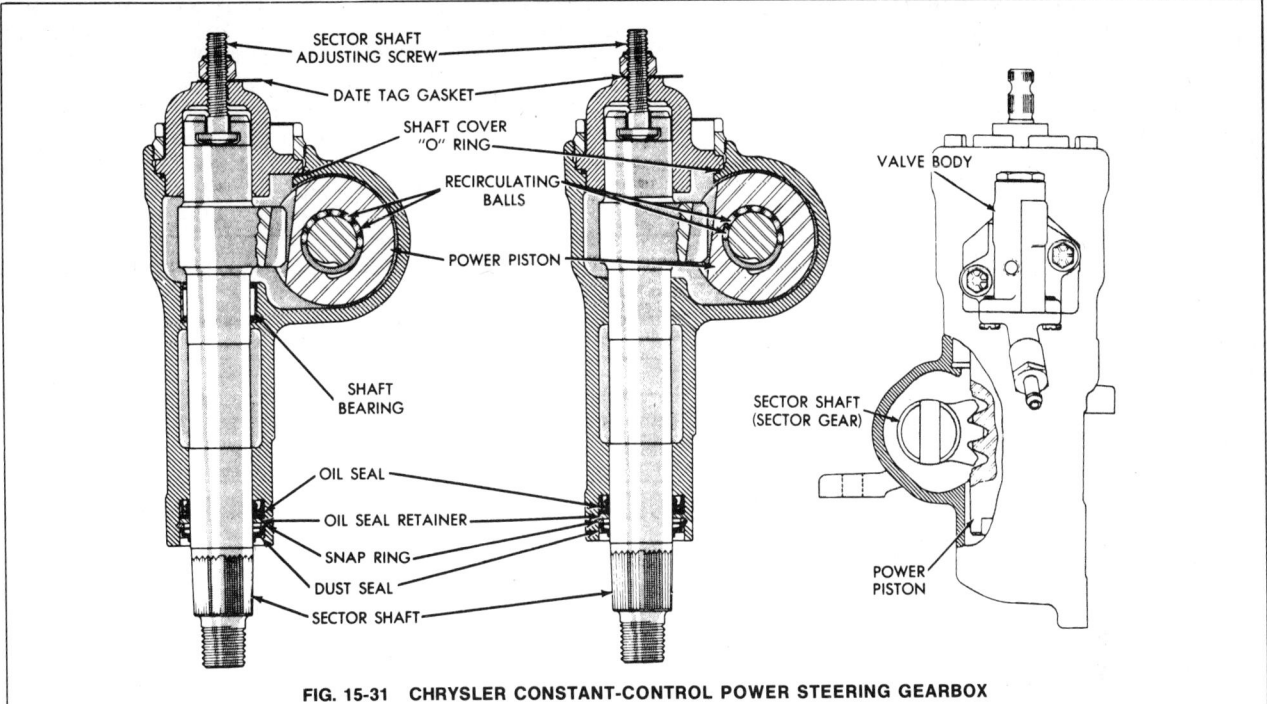

SECTOR SHAFT
ADJUSTING SCREW

DATE TAG GASKET

SHAFT COVER
"O" RING

RECIRCULATING
BALLS

POWER PISTON

SHAFT
BEARING

OIL SEAL

OIL SEAL RETAINER

SNAP RING

DUST SEAL

SECTOR SHAFT

VALVE BODY

SECTOR SHAFT
(SECTOR GEAR)

POWER
PISTON

FIG. 15-31   CHRYSLER CONSTANT-CONTROL POWER STEERING GEARBOX

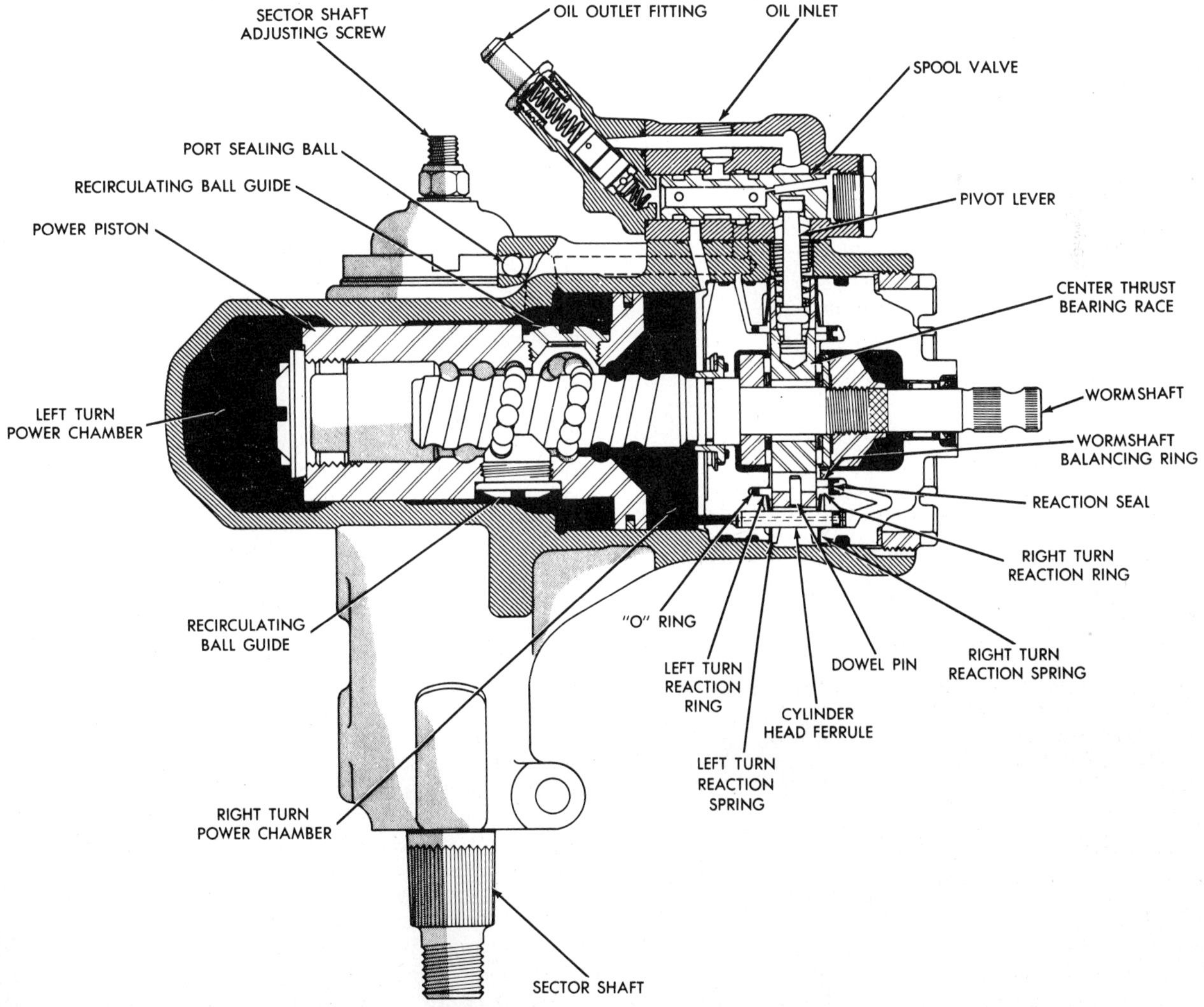

SECTOR SHAFT
ADJUSTING SCREW

OIL OUTLET FITTING

OIL INLET

SPOOL VALVE

PORT SEALING BALL

RECIRCULATING BALL GUIDE

POWER PISTON

PIVOT LEVER

CENTER THRUST
BEARING RACE

WORMSHAFT

WORMSHAFT
BALANCING RING

REACTION SEAL

RIGHT TURN
REACTION RING

RIGHT TURN
REACTION SPRING

LEFT TURN
POWER CHAMBER

RECIRCULATING
BALL GUIDE

"O" RING

LEFT TURN
REACTION
RING

DOWEL PIN

CYLINDER
HEAD FERRULE

LEFT TURN
REACTION
SPRING

RIGHT TURN
POWER CHAMBER

SECTOR SHAFT

FIG. 15-32   CHRYSLER CONSTANT-CONTROL CUTAWAY

STEERING GEAR ADJUSTMENT
TO ADJUST SECTOR SHAFT PRELOAD

1. Remove the retaining nut and lockwasher from the Pitman arm and use a puller to disconnect the arm from the steering-gearbox sector shaft.
2. Start the engine and let it run at idle.
3. Carefully turning the steering wheel, count the number of turns from lock-to-lock. Now turn the steering wheel back exactly one-half the number of turns to a center position.
4. Loosen the sector-shaft adjusting-screw locknut and turn the adjusting screw until backlash is felt in the steering gear arm **(Fig. 15-33)**. This is determined by holding the sector-shaft end lightly between thumb and forefinger.
5. Tighten the adjusting screw until backlash disappears, then tighten the adjusting screw three-eighths to one-half turn further. Torque the locknut to 28 ft.-lbs.
6. Reconnect the Pitman arm to the sector shaft, replace the washer and torque the retaining nut to 175 ft.-lbs.

STEERING GEAR REMOVAL/INSTALLATION

TO REMOVE

1. Disconnect the pressure and return lines from the power steering gearbox. Plug the hose ends to prevent fluid loss, and cap the gearbox fittings.
2. Disconnect the flexible coupling to free the steering gear shaft from the column shaft.
3. Remove the Pitman-arm retaining nut and lockwasher. Use a puller to remove the Pitman arm from the sector shaft.
4. Unbolt and remove the retaining bolts holding the gearbox to the frame. On some models, it may be necessary to:
   a) Disconnect the transmission-control-linkage torque-shaft bracket from the frame, and remove the starter.
   b) Loosen the left-front engine mount and raise the engine sufficiently to remove the steering gearbox.

FIG. 15-33 SECTOR SHAFT ADJUSTMENT

TO INSTALL

1. Position the gearbox on the frame and install the retaining bolts, lockwashers and nuts. Torque the nuts to 100 ft.-lbs.
2. If the starter and transmission-control-linkage torque-shaft bracket were removed, replace.
3. Rotate the wormshaft to center the sector shaft. Line up the master serrations on the sector shaft with the splines in the steering arm.
4. Install the lockwasher and retaining nut; torque nut to 175 ft.-lbs.
5. Reconnect the flexible coupling and torque the bolts to 200 in.-lbs.
6. Reconnect the pressure and return hoses to the gearbox valve-body fittings and torque to 230 in.-lbs.
7. Fill the power-steering-pump reservoir with power steering fluid, and start the engine. Gently turn the steering wheel lock-to-lock to bleed the system of air. Shut off the engine, check fluid level and add more, if necessary.

STEERING GEAR DISASSEMBLY/ASSEMBLY

Work on a clean bench with clean tools. Drain off excess fluid and clean the exterior of the gearbox thoroughly with solvent before beginning disassembly. Handle all interior parts **(Fig. 15-34)** carefully to prevent nicks, burrs and scratches. In order to properly overhaul this unit, the following special Chrysler tool is recommended: C-3786.

TO DISASSEMBLE

1. Clamp the steering gearbox in a vise and drain by slowly turning the wormshaft from stop to stop.
2. Removing the valve-body attaching screws, lift off the valve body and three O-rings **(Fig. 15-35)**.
3. Carefully remove the valve lever and spring by prying under its head with a screwdriver. If the slotted end of the valve lever is collapsed, bearing tolerances of the spherical head will be damaged, so use care in this step.
4. Loosen the sector-shaft adjusting-screw locknut and remove the sector-screw-cover spanner nut.
5. Turn the wormshaft to locate the sector shaft teeth at the center of piston travel, then loosen the steering powertrain retaining nut.
6. Set Chrysler tool C-3786 on the threaded end of the sector shaft, sliding it into the housing until the tool and shaft are both engaged with the bearings.
7. Rotate the wormshaft to its full left-turn position. This will compress the powertrain parts.
8. Remove the powertrain retaining nut. Holding the powertrain firmly compressed, use the gear shaft as a prying fulcrum and pry on the piston teeth with a screwdriver to remove the complete powertrain. Cylinder head, center race, spacer assembly and housing head must be maintained in close contact, or powertrain removal may damage center spacer or housing.
9. Secure the powertrain upright in a soft-jaw vise. Do not damage the piston assembly.
10. Remove the housing head from the wormshaft and the large O-ring from its groove in the housing head.
11. Direct air pressure into the ferrule chamber to remove the reaction seal from the groove in the housing head **(Fig. 15-36)**. Inspect the O-ring and seal grooves for burrs and passages for obstructions.
12. Remove the reaction spring, reaction ring, worm balancing ring and spacer.

13. Holding the wormshaft from turning, rotate the nut to release it from the knurled section, and remove. Cleaning the knurled sections with a wire brush, blow out the nut and wormshaft to remove contamination.

14. Remove the upper thrust-bearing race (thin) and bearing.

15. Remove the center bearing race.

16. Remove the lower thrust bearing and bearing race (thick).

17. Remove the cylinder head assembly and the two O-rings in the cylinder-head outer grooves.

18. Direct air pressure into the oil hole between the O-ring grooves to remove the reaction O-ring **(Fig. 15-37).**

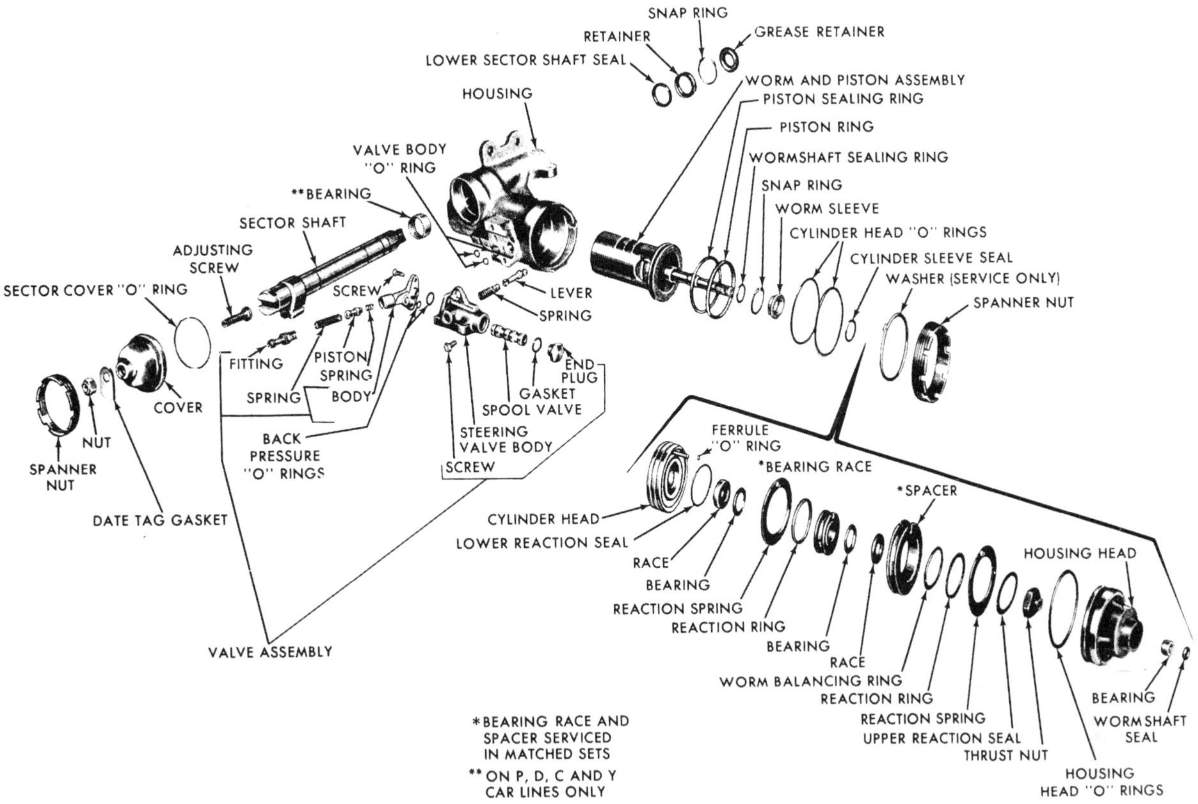

FIG. 15-34 CHRYSLER CONSTANT-CONTROL DISASSEMBLY

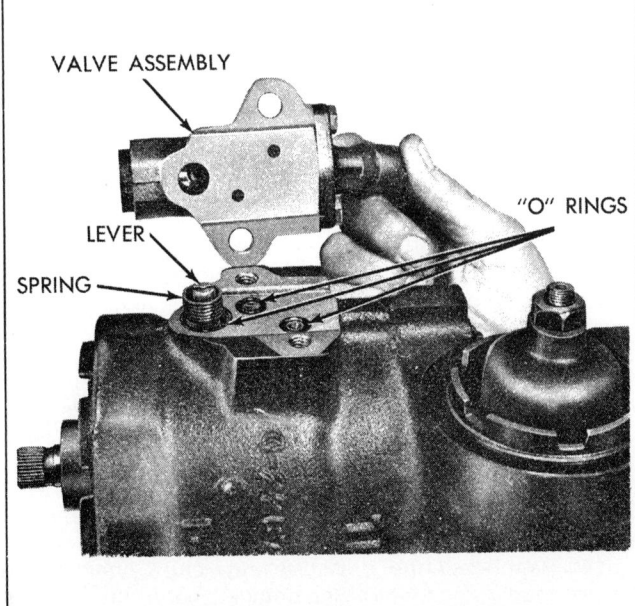

FIG. 15-35 REMOVING VALVE BODY ASSEMBLY

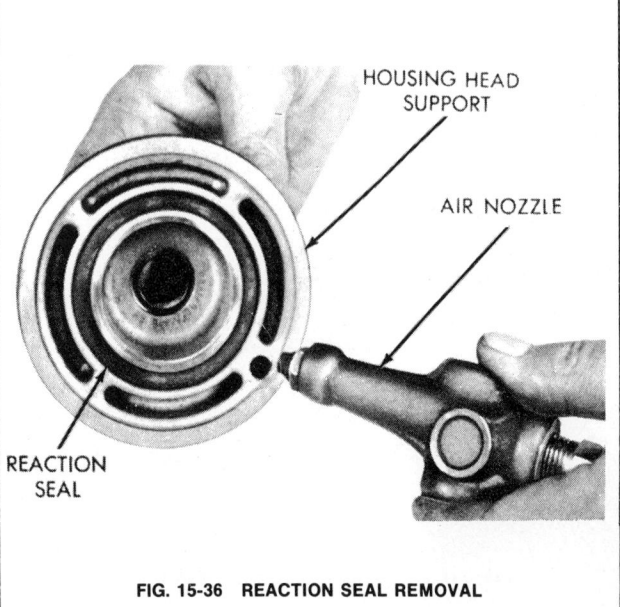

FIG. 15-36 REACTION SEAL REMOVAL

19. The snap ring, sleeve and rectangular oil-seal ring are removed from cylinder head counterbore.

20. Check wormshaft operation. The amount of torque necessary to rotate the shaft through its travel (in or out of the piston) should not exceed 1½ in.-lbs. Worm and piston are serviced as an assembly, and should not be disassembled.

21. Use a dial indicator to check side play, with the piston secured in a vise. The rack teeth must face up and the worm should be located in the approximate center of its travel. Measure vertical side play at a point 2 15/16 ins. from the piston flange; it should not exceed 0.008-in. when the end of the worm is lifted with a 1-lb. force.

TO ASSEMBLE

Assemble the components in the reverse order of disassembly, following the adjustments and preload requirements listed below:

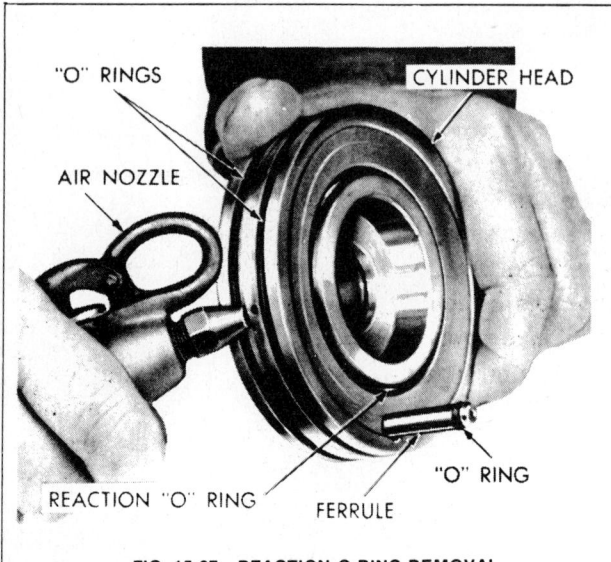

FIG. 15-37 REACTION O-RING REMOVAL

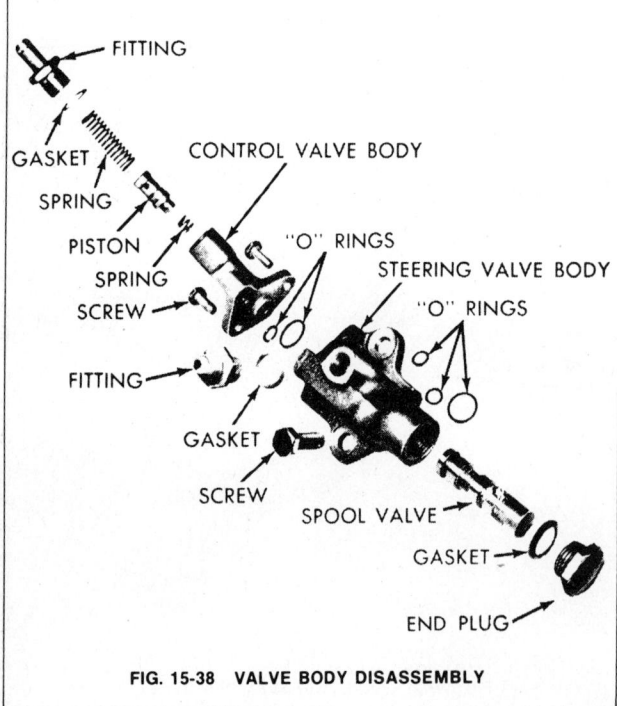

FIG. 15-38 VALVE BODY DISASSEMBLY

1. When installing the wormshaft, turn it clockwise one-half turn and hold it in this position with a socket wrench and splined nut. Tighten the adjusting nut to 50 ft.-lbs.

2. When reinstalling the powertrain to the housing, a tanged washer should be used under the powertrain-retaining spanner nut. Factory-assembled gearboxes do not include the tang washer, but one should be installed in the housing head to index with the housing groove when overhauling. Replace the spanner nut and torque 150 to 250 ft.-lbs.

3. Install the cover spanner nut and torque 110 to 200 ft.-lbs.

4. Replace the valve body on the housing; the valve lever must enter the hole in the spool valve. With O-ring seals in place, tighten the valve mounting screws to 7 ft.-lbs.

5. Adjust preload according to the procedure under "Steering Gear Adjustment."

VALVE BODY RECONDITIONING

The valve body consists of two subassemblies: a backpressure control valve and a steering valve body **(Fig. 15-38)**. The backpressure control valve can be serviced or replaced without steering valve removal or re-centering. Prepare the valve body for reconditioning as in Steps 1 and 2 of "Steering Gear Disassembly," then follow this procedure:

1. Remove the screws holding the control valve body to the steering valve body, and separate the two.

2. Remove the outlet fitting, spring, valve piston and cushion ring.

3. Shake out the spool valve carefully and check for nicks, burrs and scoring. The valve-body end plug should not be removed unless a gasket leak is evident.

4. The sharp edge of the valve is vital to its operation—if spool valve or valve body is burred, nicked or otherwise damaged, do not try to refurbish—*replace*.

5. Clean the valve bodies and piston with solvent. Blow out the passages with compressed air, then lubricate the pistons and bores with power steering fluid.

6. Align the spool valve in the valve body. The valve lever hole must line up with the lever opening in the valve body without sticking or binding.

7. If removed for gasket replacement, replace the end plug and tighten to 25 ft.-lbs.

8. Seat the piston cushion spring in the control-valve-body counterbore at the bottom of the housing. Lubricate the piston and insert the nose end into the body bore.

9. Be sure the cushion spring is not cocked, then install the spring on top of the piston. Replace the fittings and tighten to 20 ft.-lbs.

10. Fit two new O-rings on the control valve body and connect it to the steering valve body. Tighten the attaching screws to 95 in.-lbs.

11. Line up the lever hole in the spool valve with the valve-body lever opening.

12. Replace the valve body unit on the gearbox housing. The valve lever must enter the spool valve hole and the key section on the valve body bottom must nest with the housing keyway.

13. Replace the attaching screws and torque to 7 ft.-lbs. This will prevent leakage during valve centering operation.

14. Reconnect the pressure and return lines to the valve body, then start the engine. Turn the steering wheel gently from stop to stop to bleed air from the system, and add fluid to the reservoir as required.

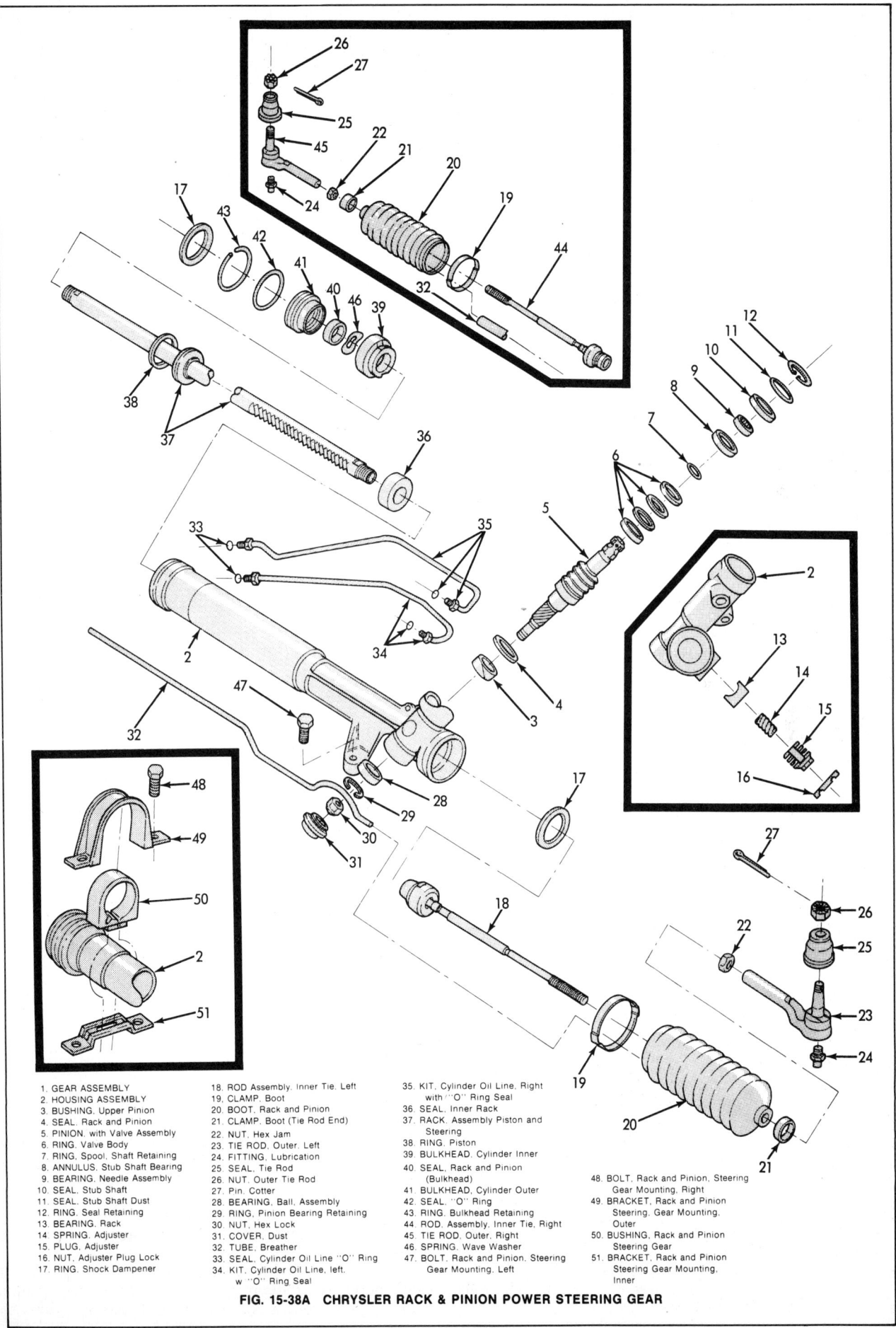

1. GEAR ASSEMBLY
2. HOUSING ASSEMBLY
3. BUSHING, Upper Pinion
4. SEAL, Rack and Pinion
5. PINION, with Valve Assembly
6. RING, Valve Body
7. RING, Spool, Shaft Retaining
8. ANNULUS, Stub Shaft Bearing
9. BEARING, Needle Assembly
10. SEAL, Stub Shaft
11. SEAL, Stub Shaft Dust
12. RING, Seal Retaining
13. BEARING, Rack
14. SPRING, Adjuster
15. PLUG, Adjuster
16. NUT, Adjuster Plug Lock
17. RING, Shock Dampener

18. ROD Assembly, Inner Tie, Left
19. CLAMP, Boot
20. BOOT, Rack and Pinion
21. CLAMP, Boot (Tie Rod End)
22. NUT, Hex Jam
23. TIE ROD, Outer, Left
24. FITTING, Lubrication
25. SEAL, Tie Rod
26. NUT, Outer Tie Rod
27. PIN, Cotter
28. BEARING, Ball, Assembly
29. RING, Pinion Bearing Retaining
30. NUT, Hex Lock
31. COVER, Dust
32. TUBE, Breather
33. SEAL, Cylinder Oil Line "O" Ring
34. KIT, Cylinder Oil Line, left,
    w "O" Ring Seal

35. KIT, Cylinder Oil Line, Right
    with "O" Ring Seal
36. SEAL, Inner Rack
37. RACK, Assembly Piston and
    Steering
38. RING, Piston
39. BULKHEAD, Cylinder Inner
40. SEAL, Rack and Pinion
    (Bulkhead)
41. BULKHEAD, Cylinder Outer
42. SEAL, "O" Ring
43. RING, Bulkhead Retaining
44. ROD, Assembly, Inner Tie, Right
45. TIE ROD, Outer, Right
46. SPRING, Wave Washer
47. BOLT, Rack and Pinion, Steering
    Gear Mounting, Left

48. BOLT, Rack and Pinion, Steering
    Gear Mounting, Right
49. BRACKET, Rack and Pinion
    Steering, Gear Mounting,
    Outer
50. BUSHING, Rack and Pinion
    Steering Gear
51. BRACKET, Rack and Pinion
    Steering Gear Mounting,
    Inner

FIG. 15-38A CHRYSLER RACK & PINION POWER STEERING GEAR

15. With the steering wheel in a straight-ahead position, stop and start the engine several times, tapping the valve body up or down until the steering wheel does not move when the engine is started or stopped. The valve body is now centered.

16. Tighten the valve-body-to-housing attachment screws to 200 in.-lbs.

ALL OMNI/HORIZON
Chrysler Rack & Pinion Power Steering
STEERING GEAR DESCRIPTION

The power steering gear used on Omni/Horizon models consists of a tubular housing which contains the toothed rack, a pinion, the rack slipper and slipper spring **(Fig.15-38A)**. An open center rotary-type control valve provides power assist by directing oil from the pump to either side of the rack piston. As the steering wheel is turned off-center, the torsion bar twists. This causes a rotary motion between the rotary valve body

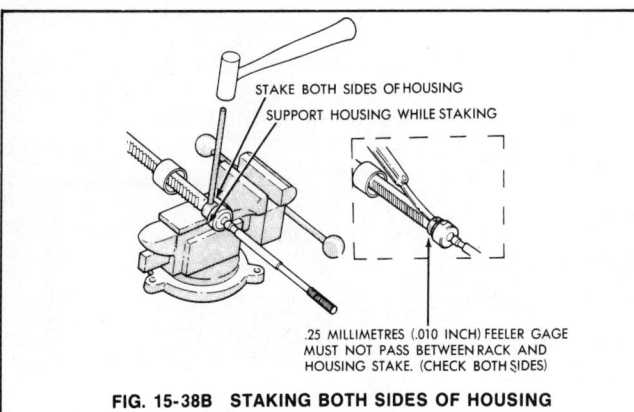

FIG. 15-38B STAKING BOTH SIDES OF HOUSING

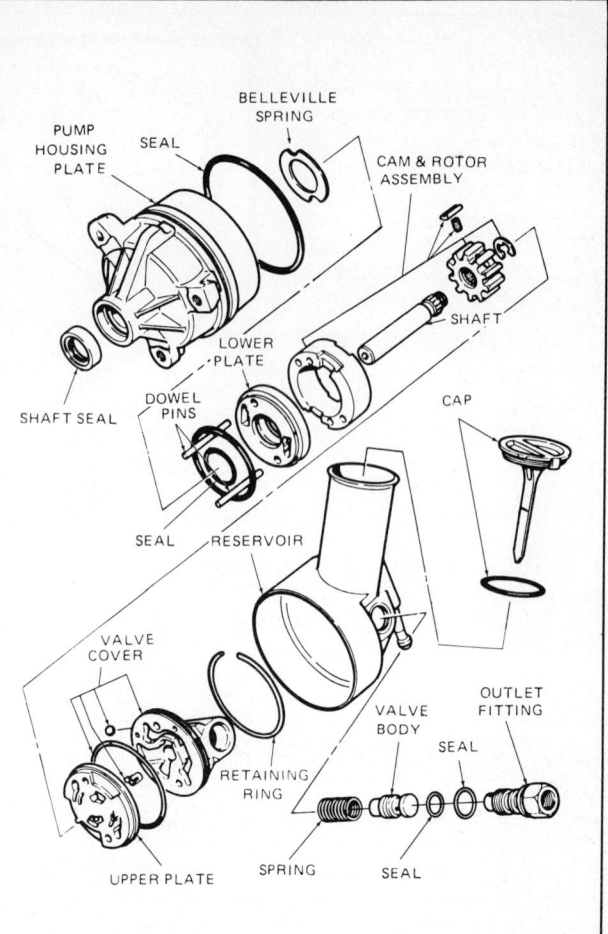

FIG. 15-39A FORD MODEL C II POWER STEERING PUMP

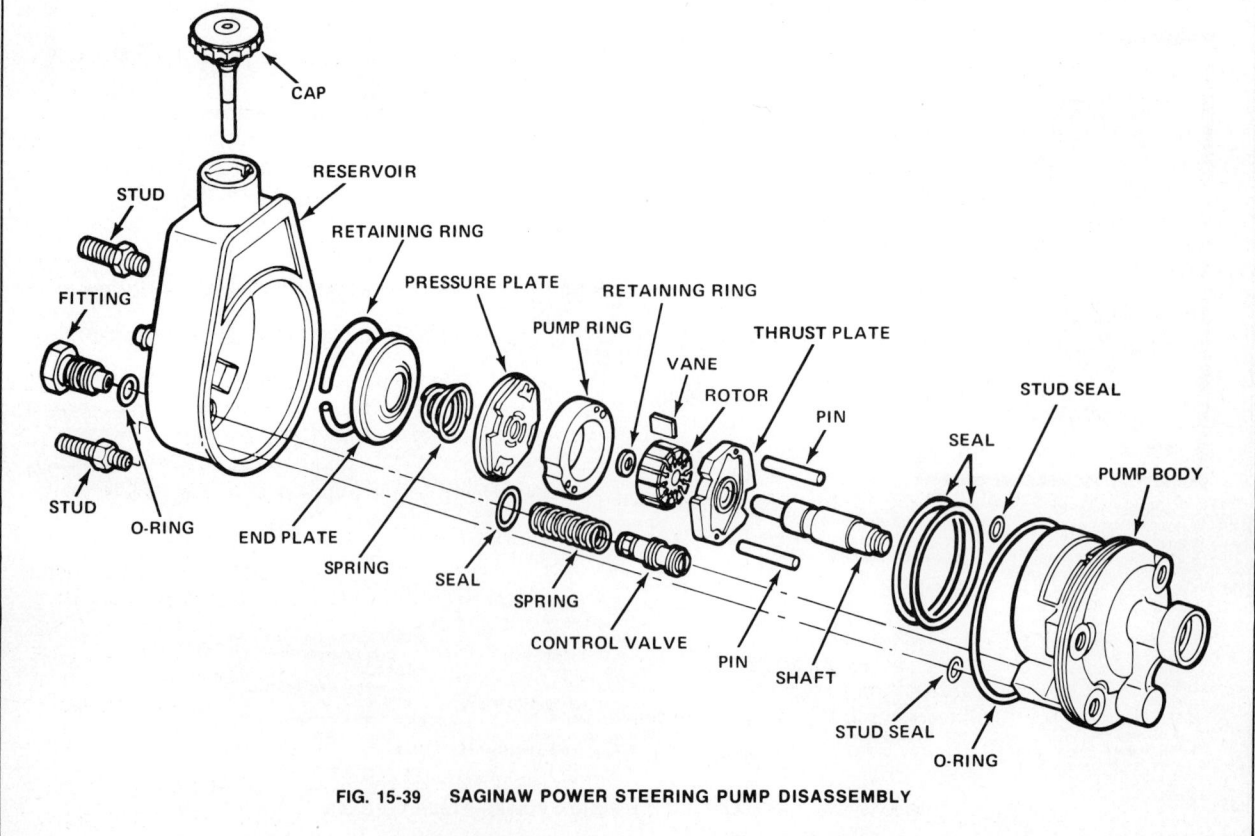

FIG. 15-39 SAGINAW POWER STEERING PUMP DISASSEMBLY

and valve spool which directs oil behind the integral rack piston to build up hydraulic pressure and thus assist in the turning effort. Drive tangs are provided on the pinion. These loosely engage a stub shaft to allow manual control in case the power steering pump drive belt breaks.

The rack piston is permanently attached to the rack. A piston ring seals the rack piston in the gear housing. The tie rods and gear housing are sealed by bellows-type oil seals or boots. Inner tie rod housings are threaded to the rack ends and staked in place.

STEERING GEAR REMOVAL/INSTALLATION

TO REMOVE

1. Use a puller to remove the tie rod ends.
2. Remove the splash shields and boot seal shields.
3. Remove the lower roll pin which holds the pinion shaft to the lower U-joint.
4. Disconnect the tubes leading to the power steering pump.
5. Remove the bolts holding the gear to the front suspension.
6. Loosen the crossmember from the frame and remove the steering gear.

TO INSTALL

1. Reverse the removal procedure sequence.
2. Torque the attaching bolts to 17-25 ft.-lbs. and inspect for oil leaks.

STEERING GEAR DISASSEMBLY/ASSEMBLY (FIG. 15-38A)

Work on a clean bench with clean tools; *do not* use impact tools for the following procedures. Drain off excess fluid and clean the exterior of the steering gear thoroughly with solvent before beginning disassembly. Handle all interior parts carefully to prevent nicks, burrs and scratches. The first two procedures can be done with the steering gear on the vehicle; the others require steering gear removal from the car.

Outer Tie Rod

TO DISASSEMBLE

1. Loosen the jam nut.
2. Remove the cotter pin and castle nut holding the outer tie rod to the steering knuckle.
3. Separate the outer tie rod from the steering knuckle and unthread the outer tie rod from the inner tie rod.

TO ASSEMBLE

1. Thread the new outer tie rod onto the inner tie rod.
2. Expand the outer boot clamp with pliers—leave it loose on the tie rod.
3. Turn the inner tie rod to make toe-in adjustment. Do not twist boot.
4. Torque the jam nut to 25-50 ft.-lbs. and install the outer boot clamp.

Boot Seal

TO DISASSEMBLE

1. Remove the outer tie rod and jam nut.
2. Expand and remove the outer boot clamp, then cut and discard the inner boot clamp.
3. Mark the location of the breather tube and remove the boot.

TO ASSEMBLE

1. Align the boot hole with the breather tube and slide the new boot over the housing lip.

2. Install a new inner boot clamp and follow the procedure for outer tie rod replacement.

Inner Tie Rod

TO DISASSEMBLE

1. Remove the outer tie rod and boot as outlined in the previous procedures.
2. Loosen the shock dampener ring from the inner tie rod housing and slide it back on the rack.
3. Place one wrench on the rack flat and another on the tie rod pivot housing flats. This will prevent rack damage when removing the tie rod.
4. Turn the housing counterclockwise until the tie rod assembly separates from the rack.

TO ASSEMBLE

1. Bottom the inner tie rod assembly on the rack, then torque the housing to 70 ft.-lbs. To prevent internal gear damage, hold the rack with a wrench while applying torque.
2. Support the rack and housing, then stake the tie rod housing on both sides to the rack flat **(Fig. 15-38B)**.
3. Use a 0.10-in. feeler gauge to check the stake. It must not pass between the rack and stake on either side.
4. Slide the shock dampener ring over the inner tie rod housing until it engages.
5. Replace boot and outer tie rod as outlined in the previous procedures.

Rack Bearing

TO DISASSEMBLE

1. Loosen the adjuster plug lock nut.
2. Turn the adjuster plug counterclockwise and separate from the housing.
3. Remove the spring and rack bearing from the housing assembly.

TO ASSEMBLE

1. Install the rack bearing, spring and adjuster plug. Coat the plug threads with lithium grease before installation.
2. Rotate the adjuster plug clockwise until it bottoms, then back off 40-60°. Check pinion torque to be sure it's within specifications before proceeding.
3. Thread the locknut in place, hold the adjuster plug stationary and torque the locknut to 50 ft.-lbs.

SAGINAW POWER STEERING PUMP

All General Motors and American Motors Cars Equipped With Saginaw Power Steering; All 1972-77 Ford/Mercury/Thunderbird; All 1972-79 Lincoln Continental, Mark IV & V; Chrysler Corporation Cars With .94 Pump

PUMP DESCRIPTION

The vane-type power steering pump is a constant-displacement pump. Although pump pressure varies somewhat among car applications, the pump housing, internal parts and operation are uniform. Because of this, pump overhaul is the same whether you are working on an AMC Pacer, Buick, Ford, Chevrolet, etc.

PUMP SERVICE

PULLEY AND SHAFT SEAL REPLACEMENT

On some cars, it may be necessary to remove the power steering pump to replace the shaft seal or pump

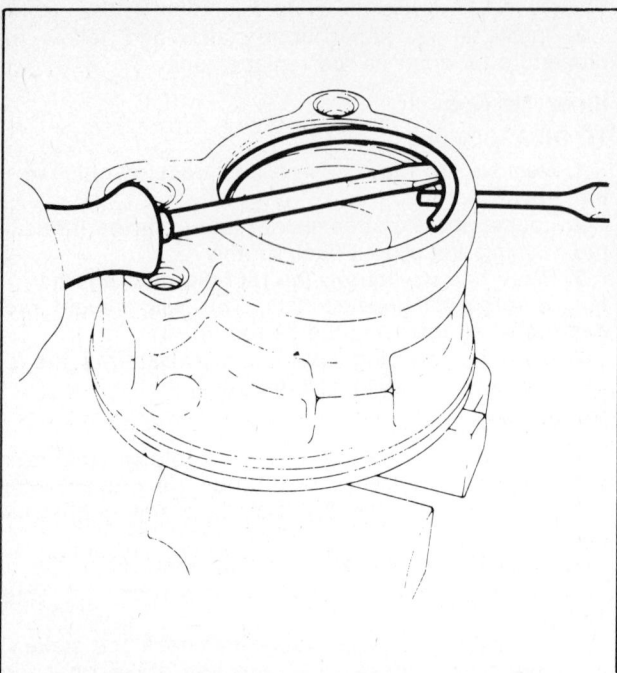

FIG. 15-40 RETAINING RING AND END PLATE REMOVAL

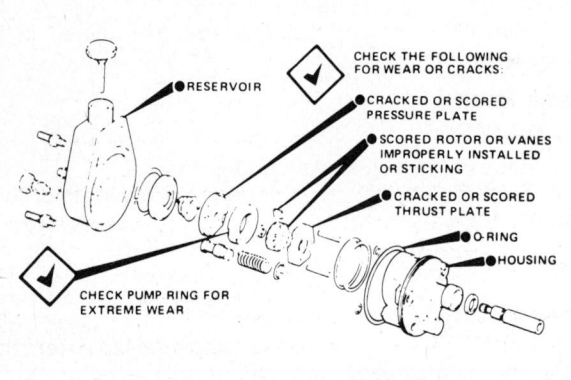

RESERVOIR

CHECK THE FOLLOWING FOR WEAR OR CRACKS:

CRACKED OR SCORED PRESSURE PLATE

SCORED ROTOR OR VANES IMPROPERLY INSTALLED OR STICKING

CRACKED OR SCORED THRUST PLATE

O-RING

HOUSING

CHECK PUMP RING FOR EXTREME WEAR

FIG. 15-41 CLEAN AND INSPECT PARTS

pulley. On other cars, such minor services can be performed without pump removal. The determining factor is pump location and the amount of working space available in the engine compartment. Follow the procedure outlined below:

1. Remove the pump if necessary.
2. Remove the pump pulley, using an appropriate puller.
3. Install a seal remover over the pump shaft, and thread into the shaft seal; then remove.
4. Lubricate a new seal with power steering fluid and install.
5. Install the pulley and replace the pump, if removed from the car.
6. Refill the pump reservoir with fluid, start the engine and check for leaks.

FLOW-CONTROL VALVE REPLACEMENT

1. Disconnect the pressure hose and plug it, then remove the fitting.
2. Insert a magnetic tool and withdraw the flow control valve and spring.
3. Fit a new valve in the valve spring and install the assembly in the housing bore.
4. Replace the fitting with a new seal and torque 30 to 35 ft.-lbs.
5. Reconnect hoses; torque fittings 30 to 35 ft.-lbs.
6. Refill the pump reservoir with fluid, start the engine and check for leaks.

PUMP DISASSEMBLY/ASSEMBLY

Work on a clean bench with clean tools. Handle all interior parts **(Fig. 15-39)** carefully to prevent nicks, burrs and scratches.

TO DISASSEMBLE

1. Remove the filler cap and drain the fluid from the reservoir.
2. Replace the cap and clean the entire pump assembly in solvent to prevent contamination of pump parts.
3. Remove the pulley with a puller and clamp the

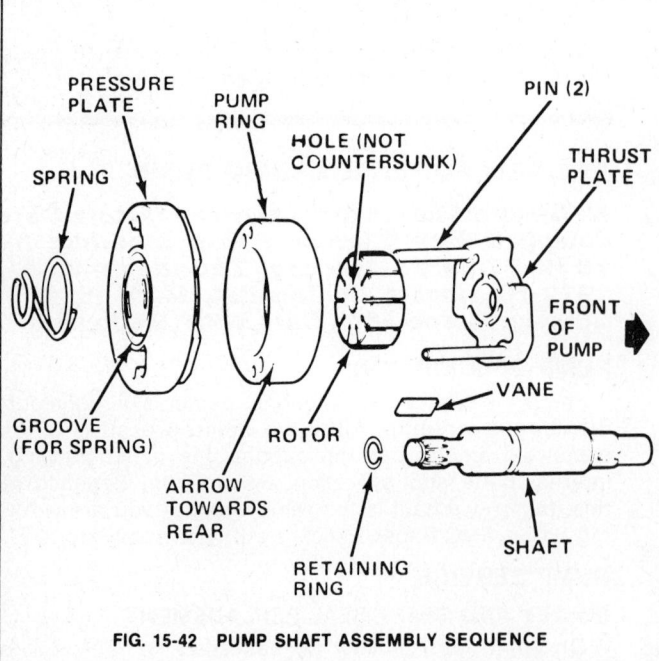

PRESSURE PLATE

PUMP RING

HOLE (NOT COUNTERSUNK)

PIN (2)

THRUST PLATE

SPRING

FRONT OF PUMP

GROOVE (FOR SPRING)

ROTOR

ARROW TOWARDS REAR

VANE

RETAINING RING

SHAFT

FIG. 15-42 PUMP SHAFT ASSEMBLY SEQUENCE

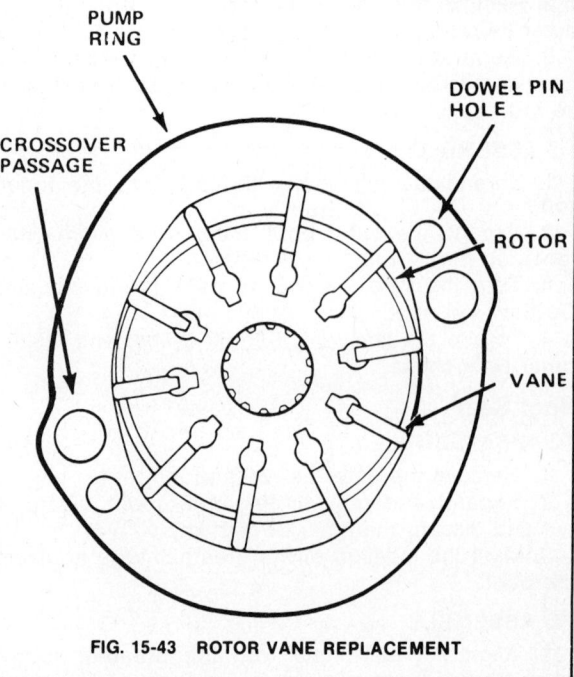

PUMP RING

DOWEL PIN HOLE

CROSSOVER PASSAGE

ROTOR

VANE

FIG. 15-43 ROTOR VANE REPLACEMENT

front hub in a vise, with the shaft pointing downward. *Do not* clamp too tightly, or bearing may distort.

4. Remove the fitting, mounting studs, and discard the seals and O-rings.

5. Rock the reservoir back and forth to unseat the O-ring; remove both from the pump body.

6. Remove and discard the mounting stud and fitting seals from the counter-bored spaces between the housing and reservoir.

7. Insert a small punch in the housing hole opposite the flow-control valve hole and remove the end-plate retaining ring **(Fig. 15-40).**

8. Invert the pump in a vise to free the flow control valve and spring.

9. Tap the shaft end with a soft hammer to remove the pressure plate, pump ring, rotor assembly and thrust plate.

10. Slide the rotor and thrust plate from the shaft after removing the snap ring. *Do not* drop the rotor blades.

11. Remove the end-plate O-rings and shaft seal.

12. Clean all parts in solvent, and inspect for wear or damage as shown in **Fig. 15-41.** Replace as necessary.

TO ASSEMBLE

1. Install a new shaft seal.

2. Replace the pressure plate and O-ring in the third groove from the rear of the housing.

3. Clamp the hub in a vise, with the shaft end facing downward. Insert both dowel pins.

4. Fit the shaft through the thrust plate and rotor, installing a new snap ring on the shaft. Rotor must move freely on the splines **(Fig. 15-42).**

5. Install the pump shaft assembly in the pump housing and position the pump ring on the dowel pins, with the arrow facing upward.

6. Place all 10 rotor vanes in the rotor slots, with their rounded ends facing outward as in **Fig. 15-43.**

7. Lubricate the outside and chamfered side of the pressure plate with petroleum jelly, and fit on the dowel, with the spring groove facing upward. Place a large socket on the plate and use it to seat the plate with hand pressure—the plate will move about 1/16-in.

8. Lubricate the new end-plate O-ring and fit it in the second groove from the rear of the housing.

9. Install the pressure plate spring in its center groove.

10. Lubricate the outside of the end plate with pe-

troleum jelly and set in the housing. Force the end plate into place and install the retaining ring.

11. Fit the flow control valve and spring into the bore, hex-head first.

12. Lubricate and fit the stud seals and fitting seal in their respective countersunk holes. Fit a new reservoir O-ring on the housing.

13. Lubricate the inside edge of the reservoir with petroleum jelly, and install it on the housing, pressing down gently until it seats in place.

14. Check alignment of the stud seals, and realign if necessary; then install the mounting studs and torque 30 to 35 ft.-lbs.

15. Install a new seal on the fitting and replace the fitting in the flow control valve. Torque 30 to 35 ft.-lbs.

16. Install the pulley and replace the pump on the pump bracket.

SAGINAW POWER STEERING PUMP TORQUE LIMITS (Ft.-Lbs.)		
	CORVETTE	ALL OTHERS
Pump and gear hose fitting	25	25
Return hose clamp screw	15	26
Pump mounting bolts	24	24-30
Pump mounting stud nut	25	25-30
Pump pulley nut	55	55-60
Power cylinder to relay rod nut	45	—
Power cylinder to frame bracket	23	—
Power cylinder frame bracket to frame nuts	17	—
Control valve to Pitman arm	45	—
Control valve clamp bolt	25	—

FORD-THOMPSON POWER STEERING PUMP

All Ford (Except 400 & 460-cu.-in. engines), Including Torino, Elite, Maverick, Granada, Mustang, Mustang II, Pinto; All Mercury (Except 400 & 460-cu.-in. engines), Including Montego, Cougar, Comet, Monarch, Bobcat; Chrysler Imperials With 1.2 Pump. Not Used After 1977.

PUMP DESCRIPTION

The Ford-Thompson **(Fig. 15-44)** is a belt-driven, slipper-type, constant-displacement pump. A service tag located behind the outlet-fitting nut indicates the basic model number and the suffix, which indicates exact application. These codes must always be used to obtain correct service parts, because there are slight differences in internal components according to model year and car application.

PUMP SERVICE

Shaft seal and pump pulley service require that the power steering pump be removed from its mounting bracket. Follow the procedure under "Pump Removal/Installation."

PULLEY AND SHAFT SEAL REPLACEMENT

1. Remove the pump and drain as much fluid through the filler pipe as possible, then secure the pump in a vise.

2. Fit a ⅜x16 capscrew in the pump shaft end to prevent damage to the shaft end.

3. Use an appropriate puller to remove the pulley by rotating it counterclockwise. *Do not* apply back-and-forth motion to the pump shaft, or internal thrust areas will be damaged.

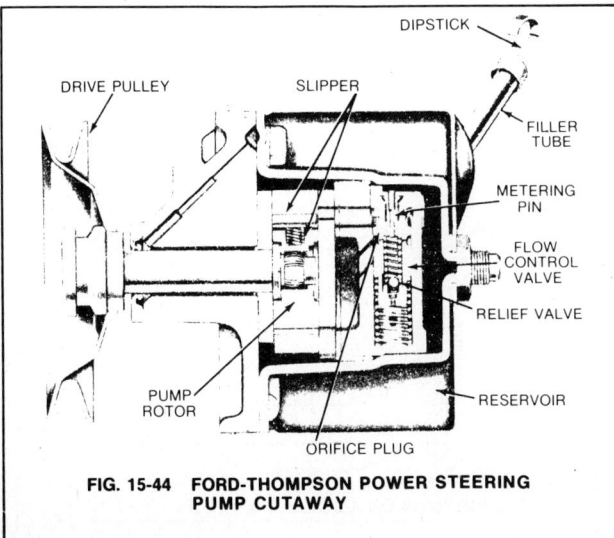

FIG. 15-44 FORD-THOMPSON POWER STEERING PUMP CUTAWAY

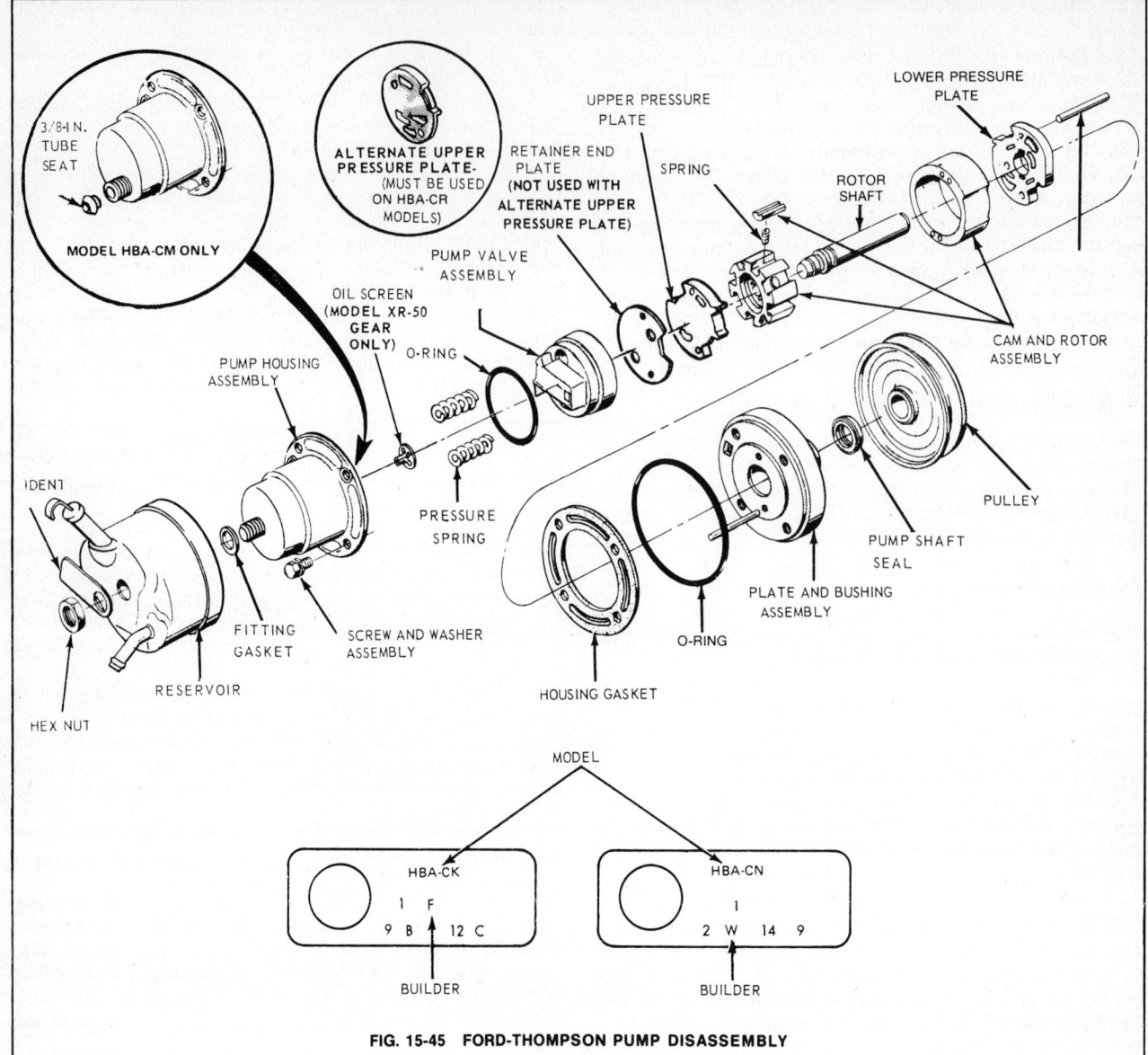

FIG. 15-45 FORD-THOMPSON PUMP DISASSEMBLY

SPECIFICATIONS
FORD-THOMPSON POWER STEERING PUMP TORQUE LIMITS (ft.-lbs.)

ENGINE APPLICATION (cu. ins.)	200	250	302	351	400	2.3L/2.8L
OPERATION						
Pressure Hose to Pump Nut		28-37	25-34	28-37		28-37
Pump Pivot Bolts		30-40	25-40		–	–
Belt Adjustment Nuts		–		30-40		–
Pump Bracket to Engine (Front Bolts)		–		45-65		–
Pump Bracket to Engine (Side)—6 cyl. only	19-25	30-45	–	–		30-45
Pump Bracket to Water Pump Housing	7-10	–	30-45	30-45		30-45
Pump to Bracket (Front Bolt)		30-45		30-45		30-45
Pump to Bracket (Rear Nut)	20-30	–	20-30	20-30		
Pressure Hose to Pump (Hose Clamp)		12-24 lb-in		12-24 lb-in		12-24
Pressure Hose to Gear (Nut)		14-18		16-25		16-25
Return Hose to Gear (Nut)		21-30		25-34		25-39
Belt Adjustment (Bolts)		30-45	25-40	–		–
Belt Adjustment (Nut)			Adjust for Proper Belt Tension			

4. Clean rust or dirt from the pulley end of the rotor shaft.

5. Wrap shim stock around the shaft and push it into the inside diameter of the seal until it reaches the bushing.

6. Pierce the metal-seal body face using a sheetmetal punch and pry out the old seal.

7. Remove shim stock from the shaft and place a new rotor shaft seal on the shaft seal installer. Tap the installer tool gently with a plastic or rubber hammer until the seal is flush with the end of the seal bore.

8. Place the pulley on the pump shaft and, using the remover tool, draw it onto the shaft until the pulley face is flush with the end of the shaft. Back-and-forth pressure on the shaft will damage the interior thrust areas.

PUMP REMOVAL/INSTALLATION

TO REMOVE

1. Disconnect the fluid return hose from the reservoir and drain the fluid into a container, then disconnect the pressure hose from the pump.

2. Remove the bolts attaching the pump to the mounting bracket, disconnect the V-belt from the pulley and remove the pump.

TO INSTALL

1. Fit the pump on the mounting bracket and install the bolts.

2. Place the V-belt on the pulley and adjust belt tension.

3. Connect the pressure hose to the pump fitting and the return hose to the pump.

4. Fill the pump reservoir with power steering fluid, and turn the steering wheel from lock-to-lock to bleed air from the system. Inspect for leaks and recheck fluid level.

PUMP DISASSEMBLY/ASSEMBLY

Work on a clean bench with clean tools. Plug the inlet and outlet openings with plugs or tape and clean the pump exterior thoroughly with solvent. *Do not* use solvent on the seals. Handle all interior parts **(Fig. 15-45)** carefully to prevent nicks, burrs and scratches.

TO DISASSEMBLE

1. Remove the pulley as outlined in Steps 1-3 of "Pulley and Shaft Seal Replacement."

2. Secure the pump in a holding fixture (Ford tool T69P-3A674-A is recommended), with the reservoir facing up.

3. Remove the outlet-fitting hex nut and service tag.

4. Reverse the pump, so the reservoir faces downward, and tap around the reservoir flange with a plastic or rubber hammer and a block of wood.

5. Reverse the pump again, loosen and remove the housing bolts and housing.

6. *Do not* remove the housing cover, O-ring seal, oil screen or pressure springs unless damaged—these parts normally remain in the pump housing.

7. Remove the pump cover gasket and the upper pressure plate.

8. Loose-fitting dowel pin is removed—*do not* bend the fixed dowel pin, which does not come out of the housing plate assembly.

9. Remove the rotor assembly. Do not dislodge the springs or slippers; do not disassemble further.

10. Invert the pump assembly and remove the shaft seal as outlined in Steps 4-6 of "Pulley and Shaft Seal Replacement."

11. Remove the pump rotor shaft and the lower pressure plate.

TO ASSEMBLE

1. Install the new shaft seal as in Step 7 of "Pulley and Shaft Seal Replacement."

2. Place the lower pressure plate on the anchor pin, with the wide chamfered slots at the center hole facing upward.

3. Lubricate the rotor shaft and insert it through the lower pressure plate and housing plate.

4. Install the cam/rotor assembly on the pump housing assembly. If the cam/rotor does not seat properly, turn rotor shaft slightly until spline teeth mesh.

5. Fit the loose dowel pin through the cam insert and the lower plate into the hole in the housing plate assembly. Both dowels will be of equal height when the loose dowel is properly installed.

6. Position the upper pressure plate, with the tapered notch against the cam insert. The fixed dowel passes through the round hole; the loose dowel passes through the elongated hole.

7. Install the pump-valve-assembly O-ring seal.

8. Position the pump valve assembly on the retainer end plate, with the large exhaust slot on the valve in line with the outer notches of the already-assembled parts. If the pump valve is correctly installed, the relief valve stem will line up with the lubrication return hole in the pump housing plate.

9. Line up the lubrication hole in the housing rim with the lubrication hole in the housing plate.

10. Install housing with even, downward pressure.

11. Replace the housing retaining bolts finger-tight and torque to specifications until the housing flange contacts the gasket.

12. Screw a ⅜x16 hex-head screw into the rotor shaft end finger-tight and use a torque wrench to check input torque. If it exceeds 15 in.-lbs., loosen the retaining bolts slightly. Rotate the rotor shaft; retorque the bolts and recheck the shaft torque.

13. Install the reservoir O-ring on the housing plate, using petroleum jelly instead of twisting it in place.

14. Align the reservoir flange notch with the pump-housing-plate/bushing-assembly notch, and tap the reservoir until it is fully seated on the housing plate.

15. Replace the service tag on the outlet valve fitting.

16. Install the outlet-valve fitting nut and torque 43 to 47 ft.-lbs.

17. Replace the pulley as outlined in Step 8 of "Pulley and Shaft Seal Replacement."

FORD MODEL CII POWER STEERING PUMP
All 1978 and Later Ford/Mercury Models

PUMP DESCRIPTION

This ten-slipper type aluminum pump contains an integral fiberglass nylon reservoir. The design incorporates a swivel pump pressure fitting which lets the pressure line move as necessary. Such movement is normal and does not indicate an undertorqued fitting.

PUMP SERVICE

Pulley and Shaft Seal Replacement

1. Remove the pump if necessary.

2. Remove the pump pulley, using an appropriate puller.

3. Clean the pulley end of the rotor shaft.

4. Wrap a piece of .005-in. shim stock around the rotor shaft. Push this shim stock into the ID of the seal until it touches the bushing. This will prevent scoring of the rotor shaft.

5. Pierce the metal face of the seal with an appropriate punch and pry the seal out.

6. Remove the shim stock. Apply Loctite 242 (271) or equivalent to the OD of a new seal. Apply Locquic NF or T to the housing seal bore.

7. Use a seal installer tool and a soft mallet to seat the seal flush with the end of the seal bore.

8. Install the pulley on the shaft until its face is flush within .010-in. of the pump shaft end.

PUMP DISASSEMBLY/ASSEMBLY

Work on a clean bench with clean tools. Handle all interior parts **(Fig. 15-39A)** carefully to prevent nicks, burrs and scratches.

TO DISASSEMBLE

1. Remove the pump pulley, using an appropriate puller.

2. Remove the outlet fitting, flow control valve and spring from the pump.

3. Remove the pump reservoir.

4. A special C-clamp (Ford tool T74P-3044-A1) must be used. Secure the clamp in a bench vise.

5. Install the lower support plate (included with the recommended C-clamp) over the pump rotor shaft.

6. Place the upper compressor plate into the upper part of the recommended C-clamp and hold in place.

7. Fit the pump assembly into the clamp with its rotor shaft pointing down.

8. Tighten the clamp until the valve cover bottoms slightly.

9. Insert a small drift through the hole in the side of the pump housing. Push inward on the valve cover retaining ring and hold the pressure while removing the retaining ring with a screwdriver.

10. Remove the pump assembly from the C-clamp.

11. Separate the pump valve cover from the body. Remove and discard the O-ring seal.

12. Remove the rotor shaft, upper plate, rotating group assembly and two dowel pins by pushing on the rotor shaft.

13. Tap the pump housing on the bench to dislodge the lower plate and Belleville spring. Remove and discard the O-ring seals.

14. Pry the rotor shaft seal out with a screwdriver.

TO ASSEMBLE

1. Reassemble the rotating group after cleaning and inspection. Place the rotor on its shaft splines with the triangle detent in the rotor counterbore facing up.

2. Fit the retaining ring in the groove at the end of the rotor shaft.

3. Position the insert cam over the rotor. Recessed notch on insert cam must face up.

4. The rotor should now extend halfway from the cam. Insert a spring into a rotor spring pocket.

5. Compress the spring with a slipper and install the slipper with its groove facing the cam profile. Repeat Steps 4 and 5 on the slipper cavity directly under the opposite inlet recess.

6. Hold the cam stationary. Index the rotor one space

and install another spring/slipper. Repeat until all 10 rotor cavities are filled.

7. Apply Loctite 242 (271) or equivalent to the OD of a new seal. Apply Locquic NF or T to the housing bore seal.

8. Use a seal installer tool and soft mallet to seat the seal flush with the end of the seal bore.

9. Set the pump housing plate on the bench with its pulley side down and insert the two dowel pins and Belleville spring in the housing. Dished surface of spring must face up.

10. Lubricate new inner and outer O-ring seals with power steering fluid and install on the lower pressure plate.

11. Fit the lower pressure plate with seals installed into the pump housing and over the dowel pins.

12. Place the assembly on the recommended C-clamp and insert a driver through the rotor shaft hole. Press on the lower plate until it bottoms in the housing. This seats the outer O-ring seal.

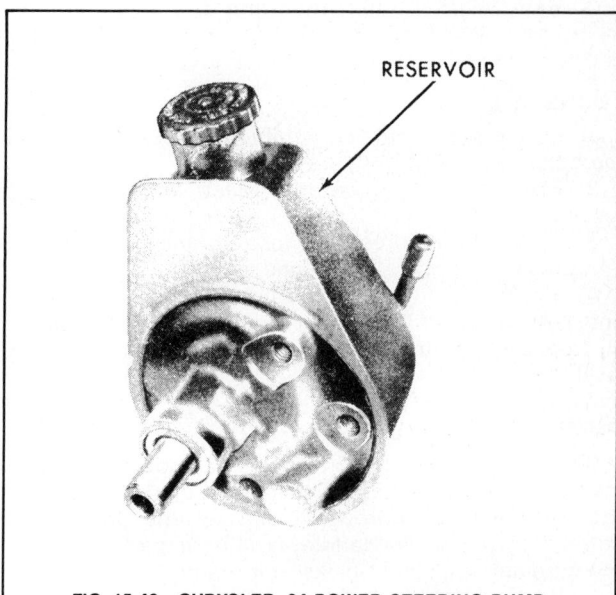

FIG. 15-46   CHRYSLER .94 POWER STEERING PUMP

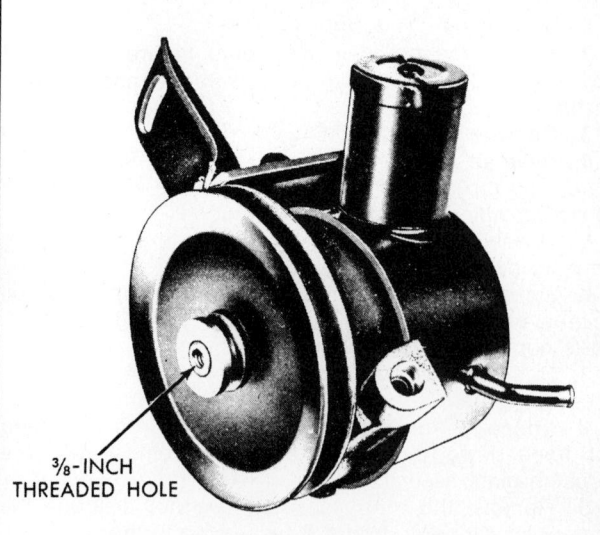

FIG. 15-47   CHRYSLER 1.06 POWER STEERING PUMP

13. Install the cam, rotor and slippers, and rotor shaft assembly in the housing over the dowel pins. Recessed notch in the cam insert should face the reservoir, approximately opposite the square mating lug on the housing.

14. Fit the upper pressure plate over the dowel pins. Its recess should align with that of the cam insert.

15. Install a new O-ring seal on the valve cover and lubricate with power steering fluid.

16. Check the plastic baffle in the valve cover for tightness. If loose, remove and coat with petroleum jelly, then reinstall.

17. Install the valve cover over the dowel pins. The outlet fitting hole in the valve cover must align with the square mating lug of the housing.

18. Replace the assembly in the C-clamp tool. Compress the valve cover into the pump housing and install the retaining ring with its ends near the housing access hole.

19. Remove the assembly from the C-clamp and position a new O-ring seal on the housing. Lubricate the seal with power steering fluid.

20. Replace the reservoir and install the flow control spring and valve.

21. Fit new O-ring seals on the outlet fitting. Lubricate the seals with power steering fluid.

22. Install the outlet fitting to the valve cover and torque to 25-34 ft.-lbs.

CHRYSLER POWER STEERING PUMP
Chrysler Corporation Cars

PUMP DESCRIPTION

Hydraulic pressure for the Chrysler power steering system is provided by one of three belt-driven pumps—the .94, 1.02 and 1.06 models. The .94 pump **(Fig. 15-46)** is a vane-type and identical to that used by Saginaw power steering systems; the 1.02 pump is a slipper-type identical to the Ford-TRW pump. For service procedures on these two models, see the Saginaw or Ford-Thompson sections.

The 1.06 pump used by Chrysler **(Fig. 15-47)** is a constant-displacement roller type, and can be visually identified by the pressure hose attachment on the pump face and the round reservoir. The same pump fitted with a longer reservoir neck is used on Chrysler Corporation cars equipped with the 400- or 440-cu.-in. engine. The 1.06 pump uses a two-stage flow control valve to provide high flow for better steering at low speeds. At high speeds, the flow is reduced to lower power-steering-system oil temperatures. **Use of this pump was discontinued after the 1976 model year.**

PUMP SERVICE

Chrysler recommends the use of the following special tools for all service sequences: C-4068 (puller), C-4062 (seal remover); SP-5323-A and SP-5399 (adapters).

OIL SEAL REPLACEMENT

1. Remove the pump from its mounting bracket according to the procedure outlined under the ''Pump Removal'' section.

2. Drain the reservoir of fluid and clean the pump exterior.

3. Use Chrysler drive pulley tool C-4068 to remove the pulley. Any attempt to remove or install the drive pulley without using this tool may result in serious internal damage to the pump.

4. Remove the shaft seal, using Chrysler tool C-4062 and adapter SP-5323-A.

5. Lubricate the new seal and install it with the lip facing toward the pump. Drive the seal in flush with the housing.

6. Replace the drive pulley and tighten the drive nut

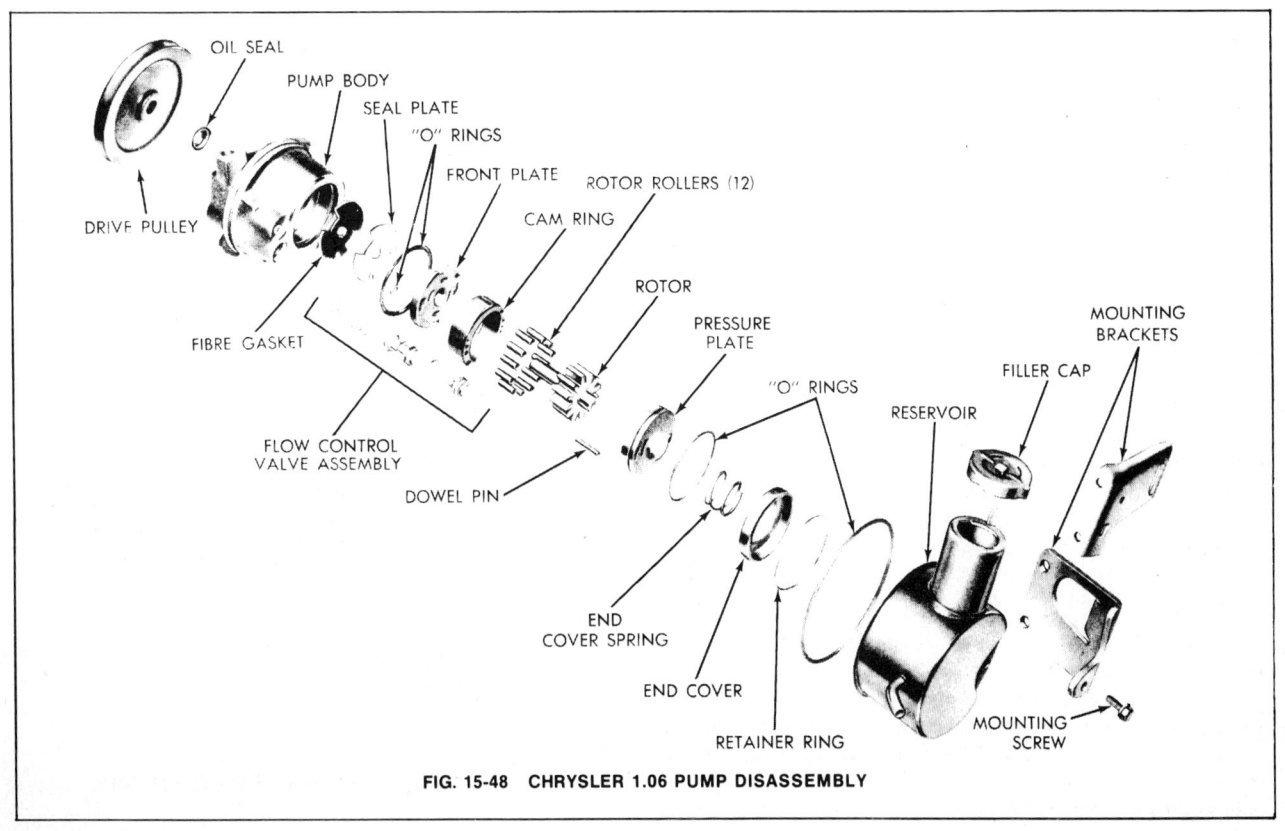

FIG. 15-48 CHRYSLER 1.06 PUMP DISASSEMBLY

against the thrust bearing. Some end play will exist when the pulley is installed flush with shaft end. This is normal and will be minimized in operation by the oil cushion between the end plates and rotor.

7. Reinstall the pump according to the steps outlined in the "Pump Installation" section.

PUMP REMOVAL/INSTALLATION

TO REMOVE

1. Loosen the mounting bolts and remove the drive belt.

2. Disconnect the high-pressure and return hoses at the pump.

3. Remove the bolts, and lift the pump and bracket from the engine.

TO INSTALL

1. Place the pump in position on the engine, and replace the bolts.

2. Fit the drive belt over the pulley and adjust, but *do not* pry on the pump neck. Torque the mounting bolts to 30 ft.-lbs.

3. Reconnect hoses, using a new pressure-hose O-ring. Torque the fittings to 30 ft.-lbs.

4. Fill the pump reservoir to the top of the filler neck with power steering fluid.

5. Start the engine and turn the steering wheel from lock-to-lock several times to bleed air from the system. Shut off the engine and recheck the fluid level, adding more if required.

PUMP DISASSEMBLY/ASSEMBLY

Work on a clean bench with clean tools. Clean the exterior of the pump thoroughly with solvent before beginning disassembly. Handle all interior parts **(Fig. 15-48)** carefully to prevent nicks, burrs and scratches. Use of the special Chrysler tools listed under the "Pump Service" section is recommended for overhaul of the 1.06 pump.

TO DISASSEMBLE

1. Secure the pump in a vise by the mounting bracket and remove the pulley, using Chrysler tool C-4068.

2. Remove the oil shaft seal as outlined under the "Pump Service" section.

3. Removing the pump from the vise, unbolt and remove the mounting bracket and reservoir.

4. Secure the pump in a soft-jaw vise, with the shaft down.

5. Tap the end-cover retaining ring with a punch and plastic hammer until one end of the ring is near the hole in the pump body. Disengage the ring from the pump-bore groove by inserting the punch in the hole.

6. Tap the end cover with a plastic hammer; the cover spring should push the cover up.

7. Invert the pump on a work bench, tap the drive shaft end to loosen the rotating group, and lift the pump body off.

8. Remove the brass seal plate and fiber gasket. Some pumps do not use a gasket; on others, it may be stuck to the housing floor.

9. Remove and discard the pressure-plate and end-cover O-rings.

10. Disengage the snap ring and remove the bore plug, flow control valve and spring from the housing. *Do not* disassemble the flow control valve unless necessary—see "Flow Control Valve" section for procedure, if required.

11. Using an Allen wrench, remove the clean-out plug

(Fig. 15-49), wash the pump body in solvent and blow all passages dry with compressed air.

TO ASSEMBLE

1. Install the clean-out plug and torque to 80 in.-lbs.

2. Lubricate and install a new shaft seal with its lip facing in toward the pump; drive the seal flush with the housing.

3. Fit a new end-cover O-ring in the pump bore groove and lubricate with power steering fluid.

4. Lubricate and fit a new reservoir-sealing O-ring in the pump body groove.

5. Install a new gasket and brass seal plate (in that order) to the housing floor bottom. The gasket must be used even if the pump was originally built without one. Align the gasket notch with the dowel pin hole in the housing—incorrect installation will cause immediate pump malfunctioning.

6. Align the index notch in the front plate with the dowel pin hole in the pump bore housing—install chamfered edge first.

7. Position the dowel pin in the cam ring and place the cam ring in the pump bore. The cam ring notch

CHRYSLER POWER STEERING PUMP TORQUE LIMITS (ft.-lbs.)	
High-pressure hose fitting, gear end (all models)	19
High-pressure hose fitting, pump end (all models)	30
Bracket bolts (.94 pump)	35
(1.06 pump)	18
Flow control valve plug (.94 pump)	4
(1.06 pump)	7
Bracket mounting bolts	30
Clean-out plug	7

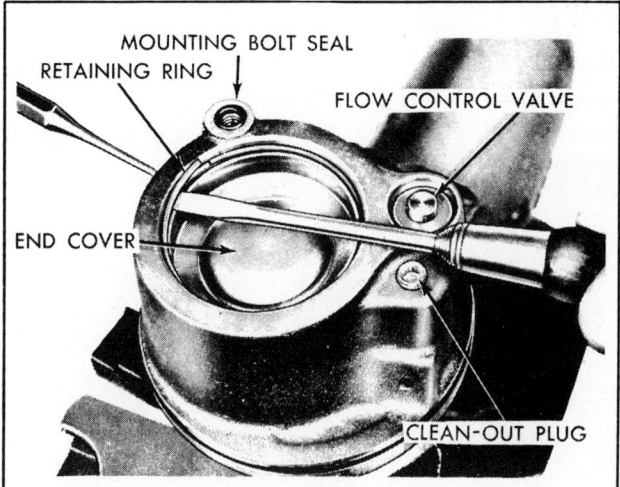

FIG. 15-49   RETAINING RING/CLEAN-OUT PLUG

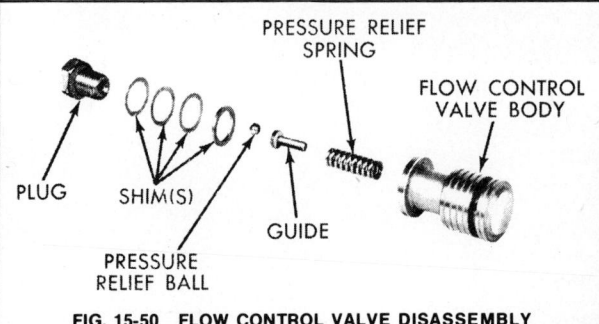

FIG. 15-50   FLOW CONTROL VALVE DISASSEMBLY

must face away from the pulley end of the pump; if the cam ring has two notches, the machined notch (sharp corners) faces up.

8. Check dowel pin position in the cam ring. If it is more than 3/16-in. above the cam ring, it is not properly seated in the housing index hole.

9. Fit the rotor and shaft in the cam ring and place the 12 steel rollers in the rotor cavities. Lubricate the rotor, rollers and inside of the cam with power steering fluid.

10. Rotate the shaft to make sure the rollers are seated parallel with the shaft, then fit the new O-ring to the pressure plate, align oil holes and install.

11. Fit the large coil spring over the raised section of the pressure plate and place the end cover over the spring, with the lip edge facing upward.

12. Press the end cover down below the retaining snap-ring groove and seat the snap ring in place.

13. Replace the reservoir mounting-bolt seal.

14. Lubricate and install the flow-control valve spring, then the valve (hex-plug-end first) and the O-ring on the bore plug. Replace the snap ring with its sharp edge facing upward.

15. Fit the reservoir to the pump body, align the mounting bolt hole and tap the reservoir in place with a plastic hammer.

16. Install and torque the mounting bolts to 18 ft.-lbs.

17. Replace the drive pulley and install the pump on the car according to the procedure in the "Pump Installation" section.

FLOW CONTROL VALVE

TO DISASSEMBLE

1. Secure the flow control valve **(Fig. 15-50)** by its land in a soft-jaw vise.

2. Remove the hex-head ball seat and shim(s). The same number and gauge of shims must be reinstalled.

3. Take the valve out of the vise and remove the pressure-relief ball, guide and spring.

4. Clean thoroughly, because dirt on the pressure-relief ball or ball seat will cause valve malfunction.

TO ASSEMBLE

1. Fit the spring, guide and pressure relief ball in the end of the flow control valve.

2. Replace the hex-head ball seat, using identical shimming to that removed, and torque to 50 in.-lbs.

3. Lubricate the valve and install the flow valve spring and valve in the bore.

4. Fit the new O-ring on the bore plug, lubricate with power steering fluid and carefully replace in the bore. The bore plug must not be depressed more than 1/16-in. beyond the retaining snap-ring groove.

5. Fit the snap ring into the groove and reinstall the flow control valve in the pump housing. 🎥

HOW TO: Saginaw Power Steering System Overhaul

1. Begin power steering system overhaul by unhooking fluid connecting hoses, prying off pump pulley and unbolting steering pump from its bracket.

2. Power steering pump can be damaged or distorted if too much pressure is applied against the reservoir during removal. Work slowly, don't force.

3. Plug hose fitting connectors and drain pump fluid over a container. *Do not* try to save fluid. It should not be reused—replace with fresh fluid.

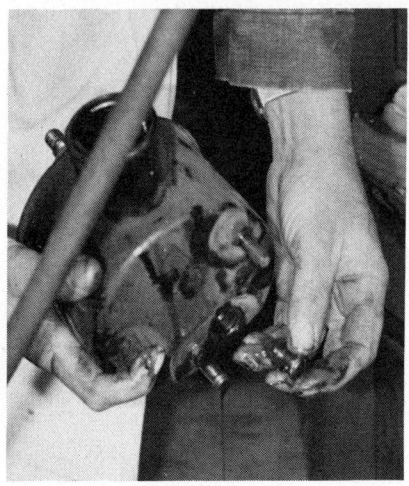

4. Now remove union and control valve by unscrewing hose fittings on the reservoir. Additional hydraulic fluid will drain out during this step.

5. Remove mounting studs and use mallet to tap around pump edge. This will free reservoir from pump housing for removal. Discard O-ring seal.

6. Using two screwdrivers, pry out the end-plate locking ring. The end plate is under spring tension at this point, so work carefully.

7. Once end plate is removed, the pump shaft assembly can be pulled out. Separate component parts and place them in a pan of clean solvent.

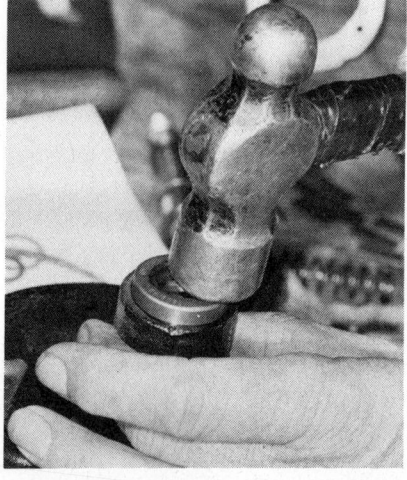

8. Pry old shaft seal from pump housing and discard. Clean housing thoroughly with solvent; install new seal, seating it flush with bore.

9. The two O-ring seals located inside pump housing should be removed and discarded. Insert new seals in respective grooves and seat properly.

10. Reinstall the pump shaft, then reassemble the rotor and vanes on the thrust plate. Cleanliness is very important at this point.

11. Once rotor/vane assembly has been inserted in the pump housing, the pump ring is installed. Make sure vanes do not slip out of position.

12. Install pressure plate and plate springs. Fit end plate over the springs and depress while installing end-plate locking ring in groove.

13. Insert control valve assembly and control valve spring into the pump housing. Make certain that the two seat properly with each other.

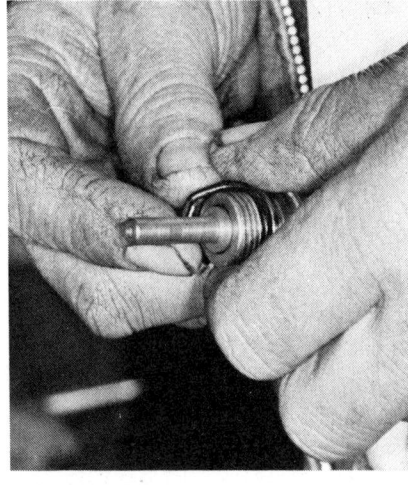

14. The union holds the control valve assembly in place. Be sure to replace the O-ring seal on the union before screwing it in position.

15. Remove the large O-ring on the pump housing and replace it with a new one. A damaged O-ring here is often the cause of a leaking pump.

16. With the replacement of the pump reservoir, this part of the overhaul is complete. Tap reservoir in place and install the studs.

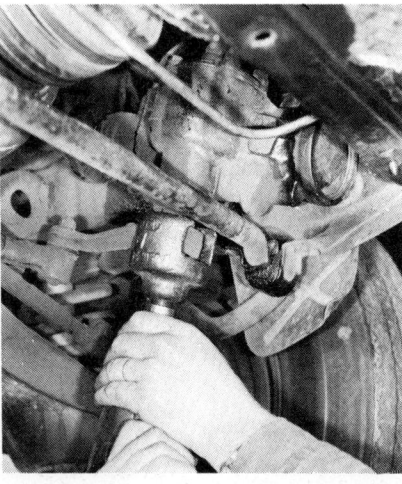

17. Disconnect the flexible coupling between input shaft and steering column shaft, then remove the Pitman-arm retaining nut with a puller.

18. You may need to pry Pitman arm from sector shaft in order to free gearbox. Remove gearbox mounting bolts; angle unit down and out of car.

HOW TO: Saginaw Power Steering System Overhaul

19. Unscrew two hose connector fittings from pressure and return ports. Note that pump end of hoses were plugged to avoid a mess from leaking fluid.

20. Pry end-cover retaining ring from the housing and remove end cover. Remove and discard the O-ring seal located immediately behind the end cover.

21. Unbolt the sector shaft cover and lift it up carefully to disengage sector teeth from ball nut teeth. Inspect teeth for wear or damage, clean shaft.

22. Remove adjuster plug locknut and unscrew adjuster plug with spanner wrench. Unless unit has been recently overhauled, no other tool will do the job.

23. Unscrew and remove adjuster plug, then rotate valve body and wormshaft to remove them from gearbox housing. Don't drop needle thrust bearing.

24. Ball-nut rack piston can be removed from other end of gearbox once valve body and wormshaft have been removed. Clean all parts in solvent.

25. Use a large screwdriver and pry out retaining ring, two back-up washers, two oil seals and needle bearing from the Pitman shaft exit.

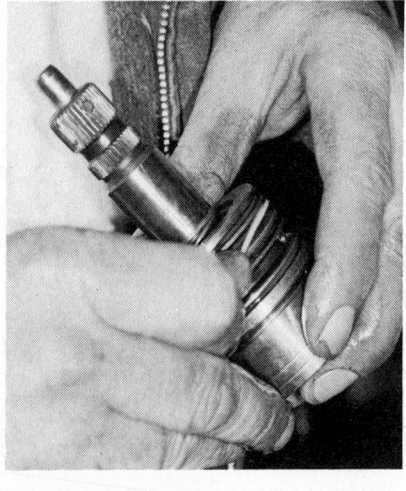

26. Inspect all parts carefully for wear. Replace O-rings located on valve body and shaft. Number of O-rings and valve body style may differ.

27. Clean all components with solvent and brush, then blow dry with compressed air. Reassembly of the gearbox begins with the rack piston.

28. Holding rack piston with one hand, insert valve body/wormshaft from opposite end. Rotate slightly as you push parts together to mesh.

29. Before replacing adjuster plug, disassemble it, and replace seal and needle bearing with new ones. Never reuse same seals or bearings.

30. Bearing installation tool is handy to seat new seal and needle bearing properly — pressure should only be applied against outer race.

31. Replace, tighten adjuster nut; slip new O-ring and gasket over Pitman shaft and position against side cover before replacing it on gearbox.

32. Work carefully when reinstalling sector shaft—teeth must mesh properly with those on ball nut, or gearbox will not work properly.

33. Once sector shaft fits into place, check seal and gasket for correct positioning before replacing sector cover bolts. Torque to 30 ft.-lbs.

34. Reinstall end cover, new O-ring seal. Hold in place and insert retaining snap ring in housing groove. Make sure snap ring is properly adjusted.

35. Torque the adjuster plug locknut after making worm-bearing preload adjustments, then replace flexible coupling on the end of the input shaft.

36. Some versions of Saginaw power steering gearbox do not use needle bearing here—this one does. Replace bearing and oil seals. Overhaul is done.

INDEX

SUSPENSION

Independent front suspensions on 1970-79 rear wheel drive American cars are either coil spring or torsion bar designs, and use individually suspended wheels. In the coil spring suspension, an unequal-length upper/lower control arm design is used. The coil spring can be either mounted on the lower arm (between the lower arm and the chassis as shown in **Fig. 16-1**) or on the upper arm (between the upper arm and chassis as shown in **Fig. 16-2**), and moves up and down to absorb road shock without transmitting it to the other wheel.

The torsion bar suspension uses a bar similar to a coiled spring but stretched until straight. This torsion bar is attached to the chassis at one end and to the upper or lower control arm at the other **(Fig. 16-3)**. When the control arm moves up or down, it twists the torsion bar, which in turn resists the twisting motion and returns the control arm to its usual position.

A stabilizer or anti-sway bar may also be used to help control body roll and suspension movement in the coil spring design. Attached to the lower control arm **(Figs. 16-1 & 16-2)**, it twists with body roll and, like a torsion bar, resists the twisting motion to keep the relationship between the suspension and body correct.

Except for the Corvette, all 1970-77 American cars use one of two rear suspension designs—longitudinal leaf springs with a solid axle or coil springs and a solid axle with appropriate locators.

The longitudinal leaf spring design consists of two leaf springs, usually stacks of progressively shorter leaves and a master leaf (occasionally one single broad leaf), solidly anchored toward the front of the car at the frame rail and fastened via a movable shackle at the rear **(Fig. 16-4)**. The shackle allows longitudinal movement. The axle housing rests on blocks placed slightly forward of the center of each spring, each end being attached solidly to and above the spring. In the case of a multiple spring, the leaves are held together by what

is called a center bolt, but which actually runs directly under the axle housing. Additional clips keep the longer secondary leaves in line.

A coil spring rear suspension system must be rigidly held in every direction, except that in which it is supposed to move—up and down. Two diagonal lower control arms, that also carry the springs, are used to prevent wrap-up and to locate the axle along the longitudinal line. Upper control arms run from the top of each side of the differential case forward and outward diagonally to the top of the rear crossmembers. These provide both lateral and additional longitudinal support, and further control axle twist **(Fig. 16-5)**. A rear sway

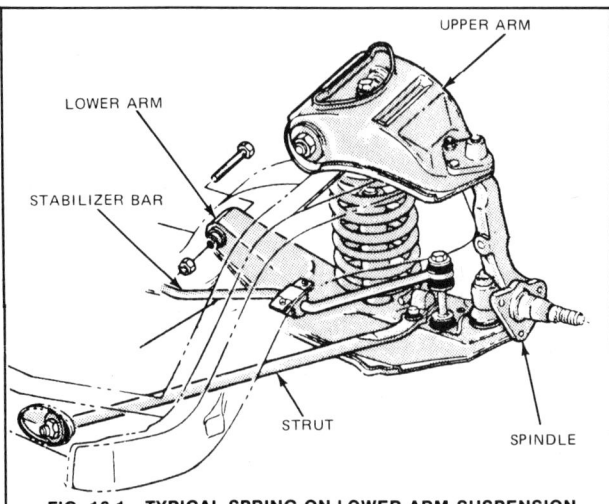

FIG. 16-1   TYPICAL SPRING-ON-LOWER-ARM SUSPENSION

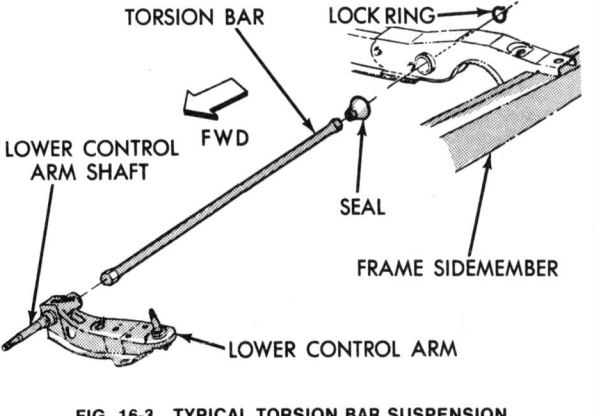

FIG. 16-3   TYPICAL TORSION BAR SUSPENSION

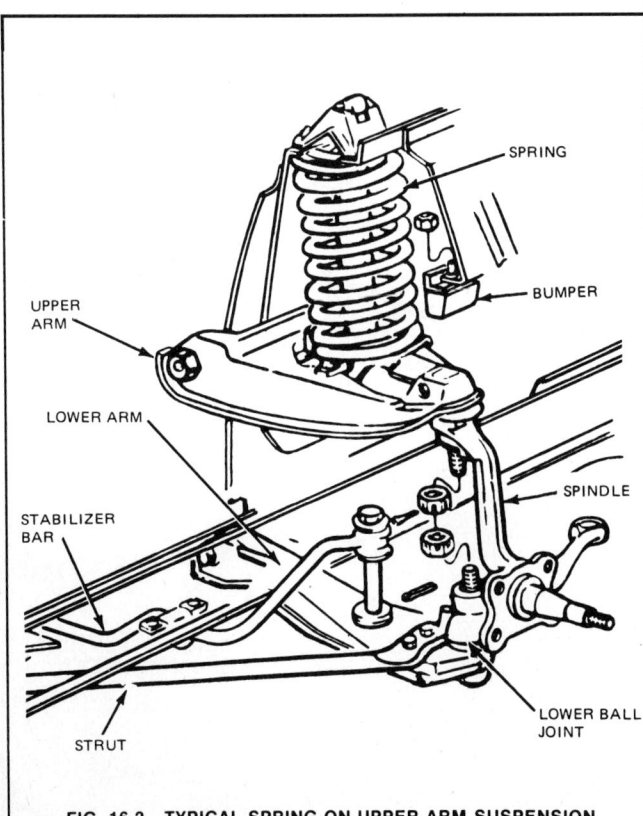

FIG. 16-2   TYPICAL SPRING-ON-UPPER-ARM SUSPENSION

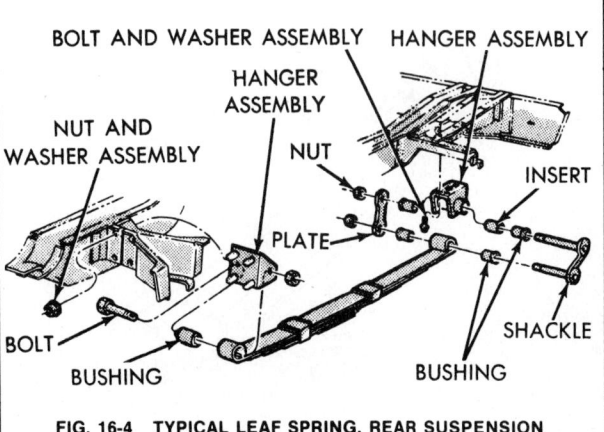

FIG. 16-4   TYPICAL LEAF SPRING, REAR SUSPENSION

bar may also be interconnected to the two lower control arms to torsionally resist individual motion of the suspension **(Fig. 16-6)**.

The Corvette uses a single transverse leaf spring, stack-mounted under the rear of the stationary center section, longitudinal torque arms, transverse strut rods and the axle halfshafts. This design is sometimes called a "three-link" suspension system. Unlike the longitudinal leaf and coil spring designs, this rear suspension is not self-aligning, and has definite camber and toe-in requirements for correct alignment **(Fig. 16-7)**.

STEERING LINKAGE

Two types of steering linkage are used with independent front suspension designs—parallelogram linkage and rack and pinion. In the parallelogram type, the steering gearbox shaft connects to a Pitman arm. This is attached to a relay rod, the other end of which connects to an idler arm mounted on the frame. The idler arm functions to support the relay rod and moves in concert with the Pitman arm. Two tie rods of equal length connect the relay rod to the front wheel steering knuckles to transmit changes in direction **(Fig. 16-8)**.

Rack and pinion linkage is less complex, consisting simply of two ties rods connecting the rack to the front wheels and transmitting the steering directional changes to the front wheels **(Fig. 16-9)**.

All steering linkage pivot points are a ball-joint bearing design—a tapered stud with a spherical end housed in a socket **(Fig. 16-10)**. The use of a ball joint permits the steering linkage to move up, down and/or pivot with the front suspension.

STEERING GEOMETRY

This describes the angular relationship between the steering linkage, suspension and tires **(Fig. 16-11)**, in relation to the road surface. Each of the following five angles involved has an interrelation with the others:

1. Caster.
2. Camber.
3. Toe-in.
4. Steering Axis Inclination (SAI).
5. Toe-out on turns (Turning Radius).

On torsion bar suspension designs, a sixth factor is introduced—suspension height. Angles 4 and 5 are fixed; angles 1, 2 and 3 can be adjusted mechanically on all domestic cars except the Ford Fairmont/Mercury Zephyr. On these cars, caster and camber is also fixed, with

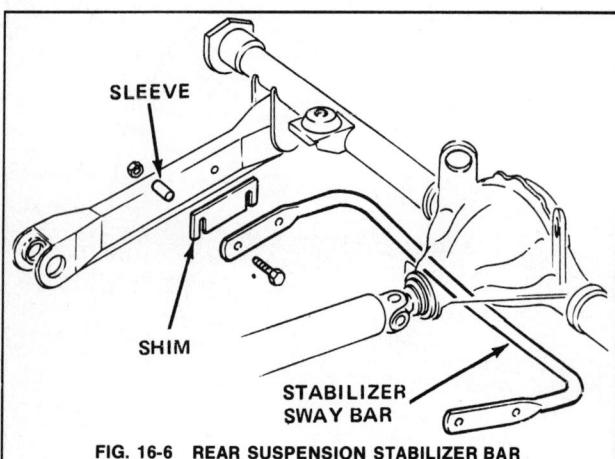

FIG. 16-6   REAR SUSPENSION STABILIZER BAR

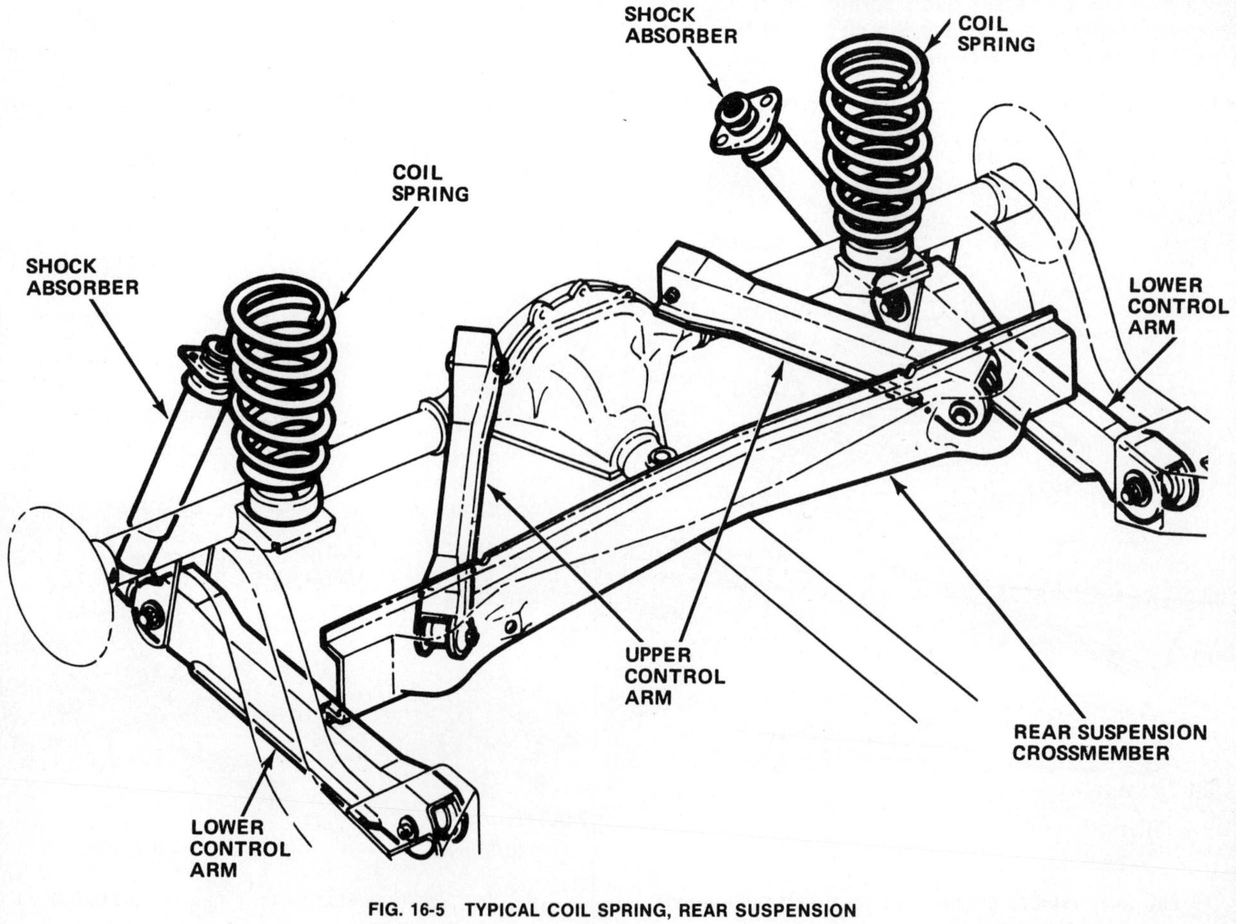

FIG. 16-5   TYPICAL COIL SPRING, REAR SUSPENSION

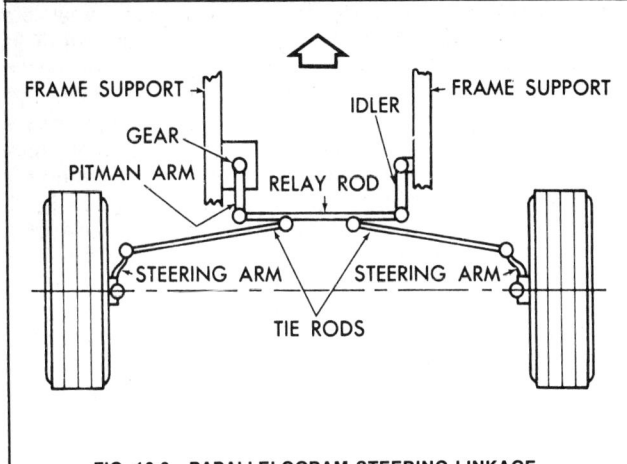

FIG. 16-8 PARALLELOGRAM STEERING LINKAGE

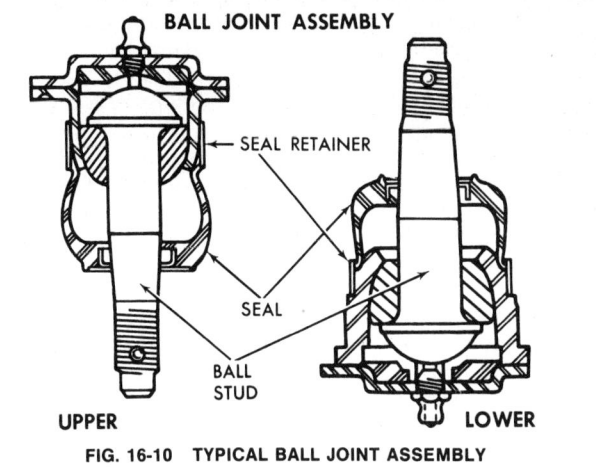

FIG. 16-10 TYPICAL BALL JOINT ASSEMBLY

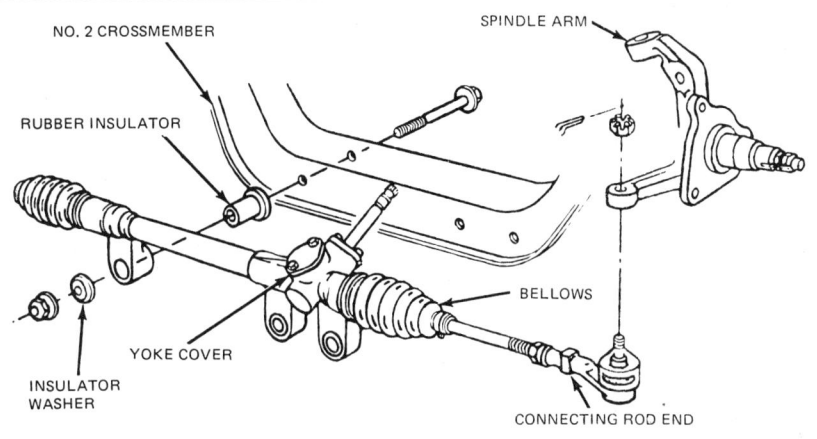

FIG. 16-9 RACK & PINION STEERING LINKAGE

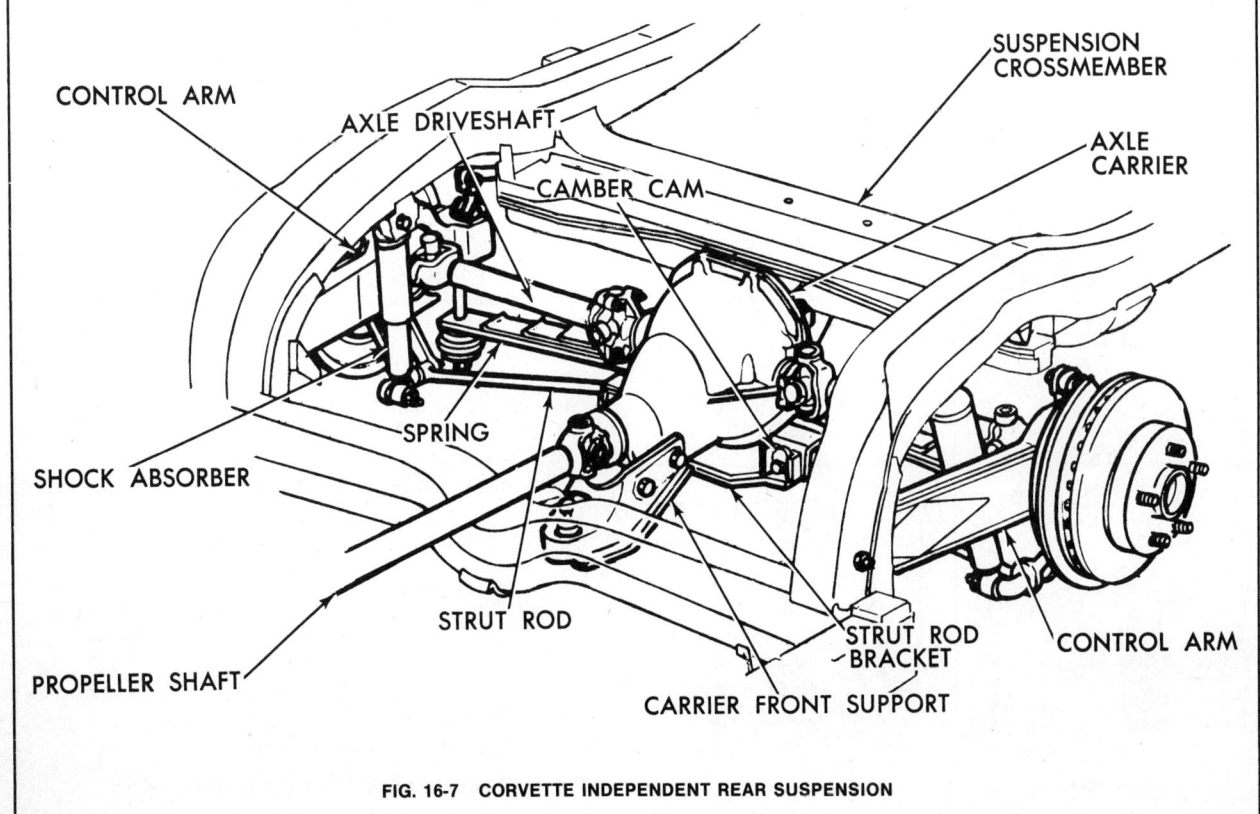

FIG. 16-7 CORVETTE INDEPENDENT REAR SUSPENSION

toe-in the only possible adjustment. Angles 4 and 5 can be used to determine if the suspension components are bent or damaged, and are especially useful when the caster/camber factors cannot be brought within the specifications recommended by the manufacturer.

Caster and camber settings should be done by an alignment shop equipped with front-end alignment racks and the necessary special tools and gauges, since it is impossible to accurately set these factors without the proper equipment. However, it is useful for the driver to understand what these factors are, and how the proper values are established with the various front end designs.

1. Caster—The forward (negative) or backward (positive) tilt of the spindle support arm at its top, expressed in degrees.

2. Camber—The inward (negative) or outward (positive) tilt of the top of the wheel from a true vertical position, expressed in degrees. A tire wear factor, excessive negative camber affects the inside of the tire tread, and excessive positive camber affects outside.

3. Toe-in—The difference in distance between the tires' leading edges and their trailing edges, expressed in inches. A serious factor in excessive tire wear, toe-in is the last adjustment angle to be set in front wheel alignment.

4. Steering Axis Inclination—The amount that the centerline of the spindle support is tilted from a true vertical, expressed in inches. A fixed relationship with camber, SAI changes only if components are bent or damaged.

5. Toe-out on Turns—The amount that one front wheel will turn more sharply than the other during a turning maneuver, expressed in degrees. A fixed relationship, turning radius changes only if components are bent or damaged.

6. Suspension Height—This factor is present and adjustable in torsion bar suspensions, and is expressed in inches. A ⅛-in. difference in suspension height from right to left is usually the allowable maximum.

SUSPENSION COMPONENT REPLACEMENT

SHOCK ABSORBERS

Three different types of shock absorber mountings account for the majority of installations: a bayonet stud, a mounting eye (with or without built-in retainers and bushings), and a combination of the mounting eye with bushings and a stud secured at right angles.

Shock absorber placement and method of attachment depends upon suspension design, but in every case, the suspension is jacked up and supported, and the shock unbolted at the bottom stud or hanger, then at the top, and removed. Installation is the reverse. Access to the top mounting nuts may be through an opening in the trunk floor or the engine compartment in some designs. Other mountings are located in the wheelwells, and require that the wheel be removed to provide sufficient working space.

Since shock absorbers limit the downward travel of the rear axle in most cases, coil-spring rear suspensions can be damaged if the wheels are not supported when the shocks are removed, dropping sufficiently to rupture the brake line(s). With such suspensions, safety stands should be placed under the rear axle housing to prevent the springs from an excessive drop that might cause suspension or brake line damage, and even a possible personal injury.

PRECAUTIONS

When new shock absorbers are installed, use the replacement bushings, washers and/or nuts that come with them. *Do not* grip the shock absorber barrel or piston rod with any tool during installation, or component damage may occur, resulting in leakage and improper operation. Follow special instructions, if provided with the replacement shock absorber unit, comparing it to the unit removed to avoid the possibility of installing the wrong shock. Prime the new shock to expel any air trapped in the cylinder by pulling the piston rod out full length and then compressing it several times. In many front shock installations, the shock is actually mounted inside the front coil spring. When replacing this type, it may be helpful to extend the shock to its full length before inserting it inside the spring. Then compress the shock only enough to attach the lower bolts or stud/nuts. The tension of the extended shock will hold the top of the shock in place while you attach the upper mounting bolts or stud/nuts.

COIL SPRINGS

Coil springs are under considerable tension, and their removal can cause severe personal damage if done incorrectly. Good judgment should be exercised and safety precautions observed at every step if spring removal/installation is undertaken.

FRONT SUSPENSION—SPRING ON LOWER ARM

1. With the car elevated to a working position, and

HEIGHT

TOE-IN

POSITIVE CASTER   NEGATIVE CASTER

FRONT OF CAR →

STEERING AXIS INCLINATION

PIVOT POINT

POSITIVE CAMBER   NEGATIVE CAMBER

0°   0°

TOE-OUT ON TURNS

WHEELS TURN ABOUT COMMON CENTER

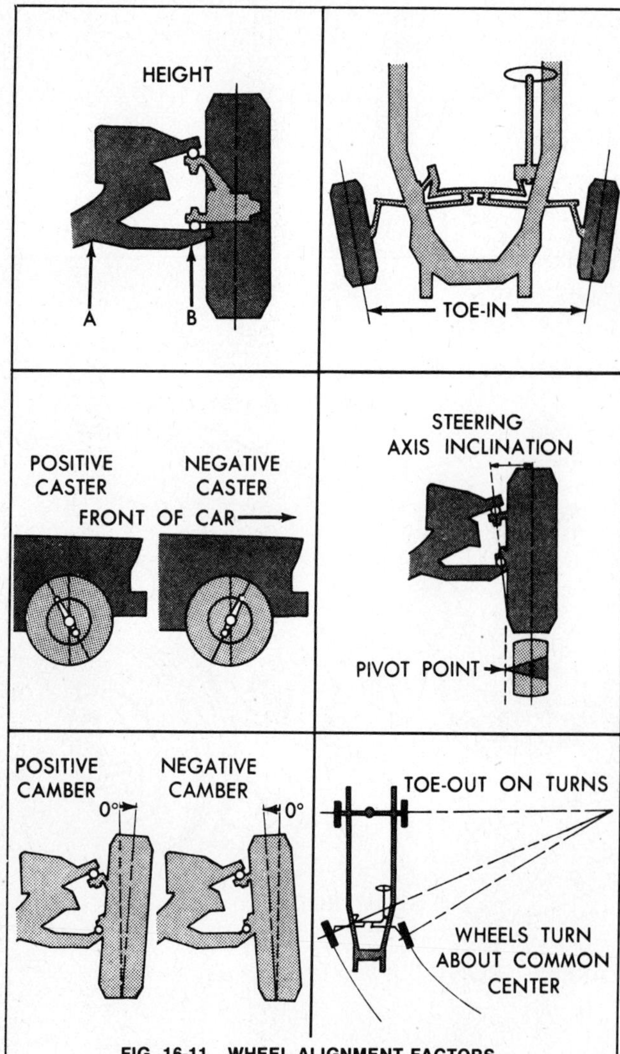

FIG. 16-11 WHEEL ALIGNMENT FACTORS

the front end supported by jackstands, remove the wheel/tire assembly.

2. Position a hydraulic jack under the lower control arm with a block of hard wood, as shown in **Fig. 16-12.**

3. Install a chain through the spring, and secure it around the control arm for safety.

4. Disconnect the shock absorber from the lower arm, and unfasten the strut or stabilizer bar, if used.

5. Disconnect the inner arm of two-attachment-point control arms, or remove the lower ball stud from the steering knuckle on three-attachment-point arms.

6. Disconnect the tie rod end from the steering knuckle, if necessary.

7. Carefully lower the hydraulic jack slowly to relieve the spring pressure on the lower arm.

8. Remove the spring.

FRONT SUSPENSION—SPRING ON UPPER ARM

1. With the car elevated to a working position, and the front end supported by jackstands, remove the wheel/tire assembly.

2. Install a spring compressor tool, as shown **in Fig. 16-13.**

3. Remove the upper-arm-to-spring-tower attaching nuts.

4. Swing the upper arm outward from the spring tower.

5. Carefully release the spring compressor tool, and remove it from the spring.

6. Remove the spring from the car.

REAR SUSPENSION—COIL SPRINGS

1. With the car elevated to a working position, and the rear axle supported by a hydraulic jack, disconnect the shock absorber from its lower mounting point.

2. Disconnect the rear-axle extension bracket or the upper control arm at the axle, and slowly lower the spring assembly until the suspension reaches the end

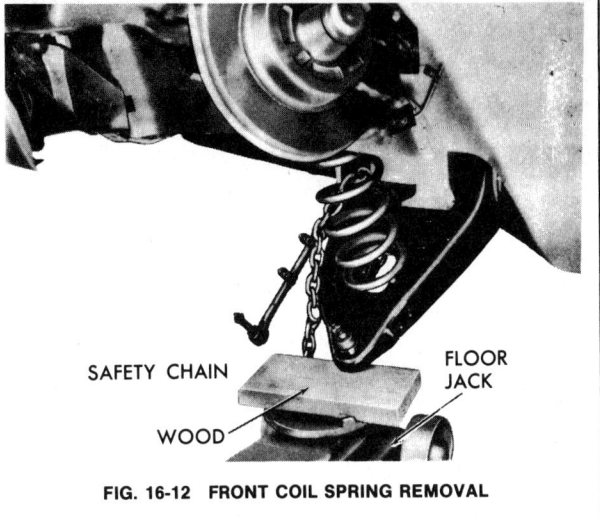

FIG. 16-12   **FRONT COIL SPRING REMOVAL**

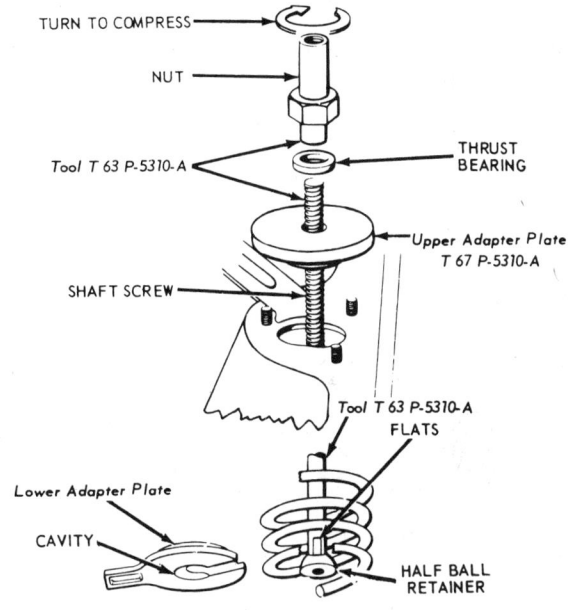

FIG. 16-13   **SPRING COMPRESSOR TOOL**

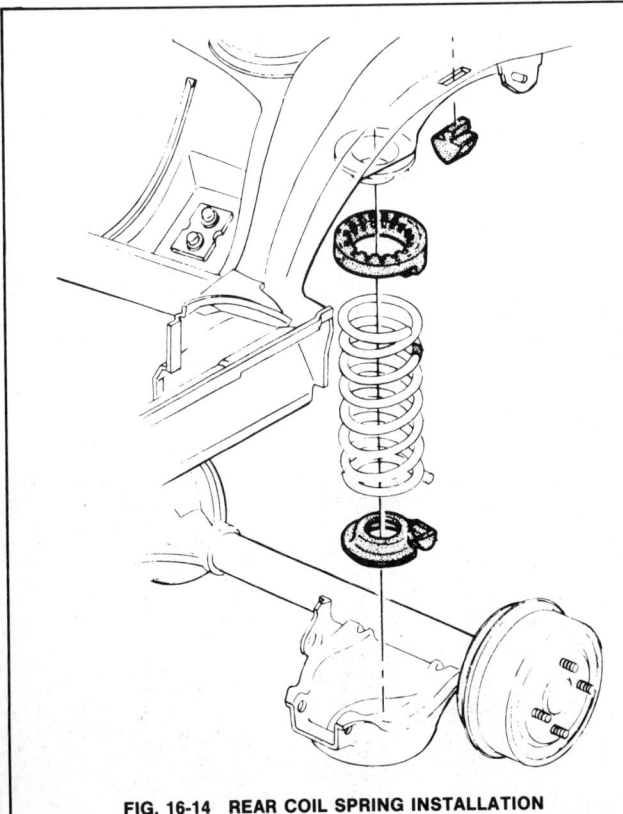

FIG. 16-14   **REAR COIL SPRING INSTALLATION**

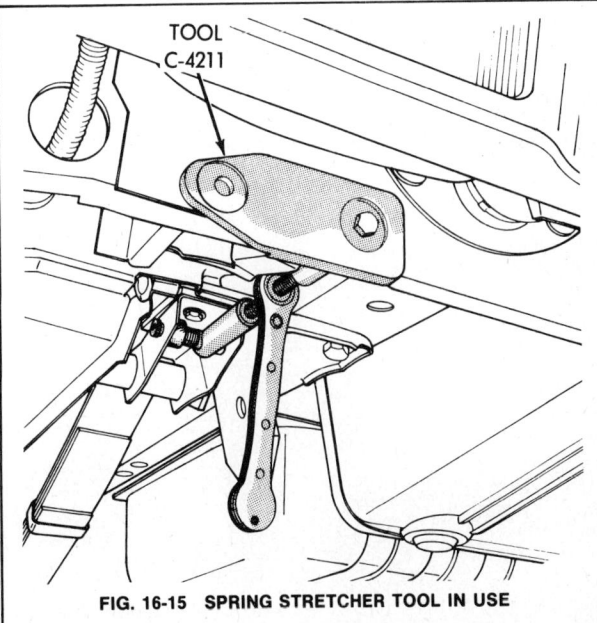

FIG. 16-15   **SPRING STRETCHER TOOL IN USE**

of its travel. If the brake hose is positioned in such a way as to interfere (it *must not* be stretched), disconnect it to provide slack in the line.

3. If the rear spring uses insulators or positioners between the spring and the spring seat, note their positions and remove (Fig. 16-14).

REAR SUSPENSION—LEAF SPRINGS

The rear springs on 1974-77 Chrysler, Imperial, Gran Fury and Monaco cars are preloaded, and should not be removed without the use of a spring stretcher, Chrysler tool C-4211 (Fig. 16-15).

1. With the car elevated to a working position, and the rear axle assembly supported by floor stands, position a hydraulic jack under the axle, and raise it until the weight is taken off the spring shackles.

2. Disconnect the shock absorber at its lower mounting stud.

3. Disconnect the rear sway-bar links, if so equipped.

4. Lower the hydraulic-jack/axle assembly until the springs hang free. Check the brake lines and, if necessary, disconnect to provide slack.

5. Loosen and remove the U-bolt nuts, bolts and spring plates.

6. a) On the Chrysler Corporation cars mentioned earlier, install the spring stretcher tool, as shown in **Fig. 16-15,** and apply tension to the spring, remove the rear hanger and bolts, and relieve spring tension, removing the tool. Loosen and remove the front hanger nut.

b) On all other cars, loosen and remove the front hanger nut, then the rear hanger bolts, letting the spring drop sufficiently to remove the front hanger and pivot bolts.

7. Loosen and remove the shackle nuts and shackle from the spring.

8. Reverse the procedure for installation.

BALL JOINT REPLACEMENT

Ball joints are used to connect the steering knuckle to the control arms. When properly installed, a rubber seal, nut and ball joint stud are the only visible parts of the ball joint assembly. The seal is provided to retain lubricant and prevent contamination from reaching the joint. If the seal is damaged, the entire ball joint assembly must be replaced. **Fig. 16-16** explains the four types of ball joint suspension and the inspections necessary to determine whether or not replacement is necessary. Ball joints used on many General Motors cars incorporate a wear indicator to assist in checking ball joint wear (Fig. 16-17).

Ford recommends that the upper and lower suspension arms on all Ford, Mercury and Lincoln cars be

All Ball Joint Suspensions fit into One of these FOUR Categories

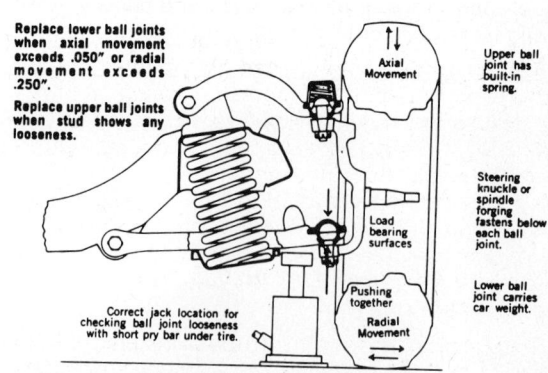

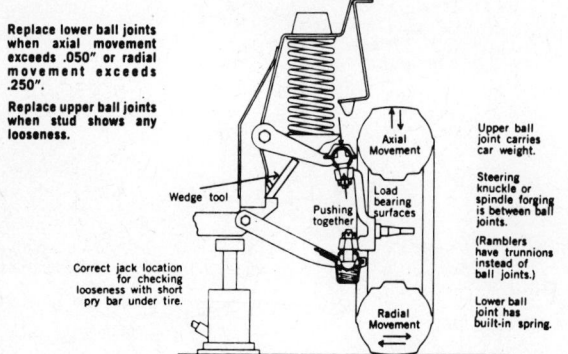

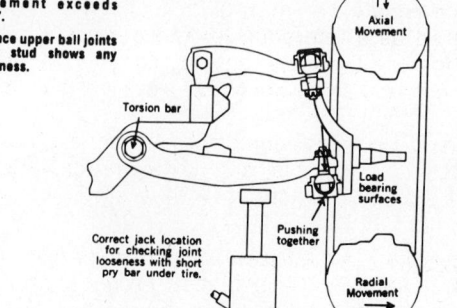

FIG. 16-16 BALL-JOINT SUSPENSION DESIGNS

serviced as a complete unit, and does not supply replacement ball joints or other suspension arm components individually. American Motors, Chrysler Corporation and General Motors cars use riveted, press-fit and threaded screw-in ball joints.

1. Riveted Ball Joint—When replacement is required, the rivets are chiseled off. If the rivets are drilled out, use caution not to enlarge the holes. Replacement ball joints for this type include special bolts to take the place of the rivets; ordinary bolts *must not* be used.

2. Press-Fit Ball Joint—Replacement of this type is best accomplished with the use of an arbor press and *removal* of the control arm, although a variety of costly special purpose tools are available for ball joint replacement *without removing* the control arm.

3. Threaded Screw-In Ball Joint—All Chrysler Corporation cars use this type. While special tools are available for ball joint replacement, it can be accomplished with a special ¾-in. drive socket, a 3-ft. handle and considerable effort.

Because of the safety factor involved in correctly removing/replacing such vital suspension components, we highly recommend that this area of automotive repair, like wheel alignment, be referred to the specialist shop that is properly equipped to do the job.

BUSHING REPLACEMENT

Sloppy front suspension bushings can become annoying and dangerous, causing abnormal tire wear and poor ride/control. If A-arm bushings are worn, it will be impossible to correctly align the front end. When stabilizer (or anti-sway bar) bushings are worn, the stabilizer will not function as effectively in limiting body lean on corners, and may cause rattles or squeaks when not cornering. Worn idler arm bushings will introduce slop into the steering linkage, with consequent lack of positive control and safety.

With the exception of A-arm bushings, all of these front suspension bushings can be replaced easily. Even if you have the spring-compressing equipment to actually remove the A-arms (which is necessary for bushing replacement), other special equipment is required to remove the old bushings and press in the new ones. This is another job best left up to a professional garage or front end shop which has the required tools.

STABILIZER BUSHINGS AND INSULATORS
(Fig. 16-18)

The stabilizer rides in two rubber insulators held onto the front of the frame with two U-shaped brackets. The outer ends of the stabilizer bar are retained to the lower A-arms by long bolts passing through washers, rubber bushings and usually tubular metal spacers (sleeves). It's best to replace all of the rubber bushings at the same time when one set is worn, but work on only one side of the car at a time, to keep the other side assembled as a reference for the correct order of installation for the washers and bushings. On some cars, you may have to remove the front splash shield for access.

1. Remove the bolts retaining the U-shaped brackets over the stabilizer insulators, and allow the stabilizer to drop. Cut off the old insulators with a sharp knife or razor.

2. Disassemble the stabilizer end bushings from one A-arm. The nut may be cotter-pinned in place, and will probably require penetrating oil to loosen the rust on the threads.

3. Lubricate one of the new rubber insulators with a silicone spray (make sure the lubricant you use is not

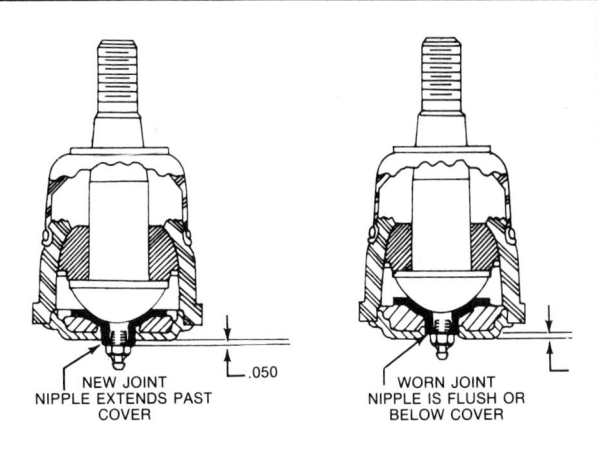

FIG. 16-17 BALL-JOINT WEAR INDICATOR

NEW JOINT NIPPLE EXTENDS PAST COVER — .050

WORN JOINT NIPPLE IS FLUSH OR BELOW COVER

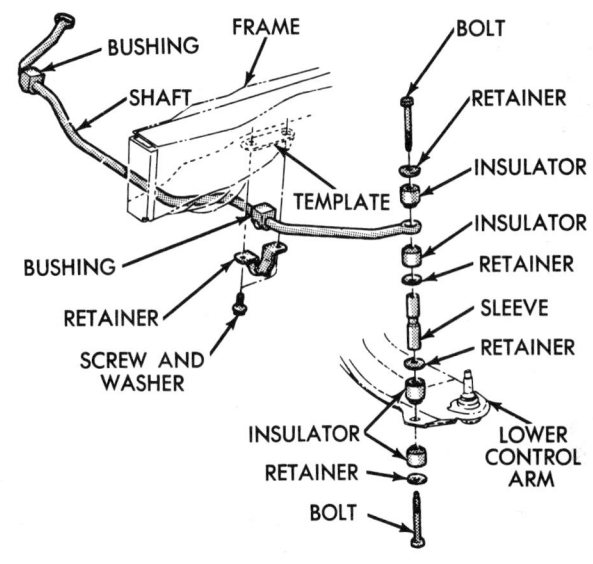

FIG. 16-18 STABILIZER INSULATORS AND BUSHINGS

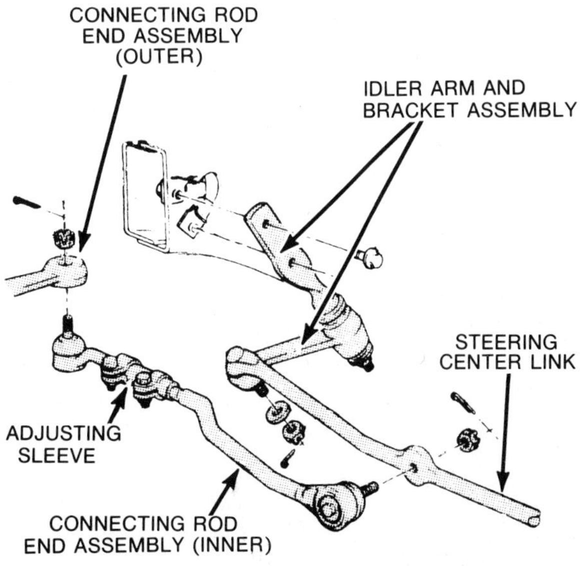

CONNECTING ROD END ASSEMBLY (OUTER)

IDLER ARM AND BRACKET ASSEMBLY

STEERING CENTER LINK

ADJUSTING SLEEVE

CONNECTING ROD END ASSEMBLY (INNER)

FIG. 16-19 IDLER ARM BUSHINGS

harmful to rubber parts) and slide it over the end of the stabilizer and into the position on the stabilizer where the old insulator went.

4. The new end-bushing kit will contain new bolts, washers and bushings. *Do not* use the old bolt and nut. Assemble one side, using the other side as a guide. Be sure the bolt goes through the assembly in the same direction as it did originally. If it used a cotter pin, install a new cotter pin.

5. Repeat operatons 2-4 on the other end of the stabilizer.

6. Reinstall the U-shaped brackets and bolts that retain the stabilizer insulators to the frame.

IDLER ARM/BUSHING

The idler arm and/or bushing **(Fig. 16-19)** should be replaced when any play can be felt when moving the idler arm up and down on its bracket. Rather than attempt to press a new bushing into the old idler arm, you can purchase a complete idler arm assembly, which will include the arm, installed bushing and the frame bracket. In fact, in some cases you may not be able to buy just the bushing, since some manufacturers feel that the idler arm is not a serviceable assembly. If you have manual steering and want to reduce the effort slightly, you can purchase a kit at an auto parts store to adapt ball bearings to the idler arm instead of the solid bushing. These work well, but they are equipped with grease fittings which you must remember to lube every time the chassis is lubed.

1. Place the front of the car on jackstands, with the rear wheels blocked.

2. Separate the idler arm from the relay rod by removing the cotter pin, nut and washer, and tapping a tie-rod wedge tool (sometimes called a tuning fork) between them. Without such a tool, you may hit one side of the idler arm with a hammer (around the attachment point to the relay rod) to loosen it, holding a heavier hammer on the opposite side as a backup.

3. Remove the bolts holding the idler arm bracket to the frame, and remove the idler arm assembly from the car.

4. When reinstalling the new parts, torque the nuts to specifications, and *do not* use substitute bolts. Use your old ones or the new ones, if included in the kit. Use cotter pins at the relay rod connection and the idler-arm-to-bracket connection.

STRUT ROD BUSHING

Except for Chrysler products that have torsion-bar front systems, the strut rod bushings can easily be replaced by the home mechanic. The Chrysler products are difficult even for a professional shop, so we won't discuss those here. But in every case where the bushings can be replaced at home, the front end will have to be realigned on professional equipment, since struts **(Figs. 16-1 & 16-2)** control caster setting.

1. Jack up the front of the car, but support the lower A-arms with jackstands. The easiest method is with a set of short drive-on ramps which raise the car but keep the suspension weighted. On Ford products with the spring mounted above the upper A-arm, a block of wood can be placed between the A-arm and the frame, while the weight of the car is still on the wheels. This will take the tension off the lower A-arm while you remove the strut rod.

2. Remove the cotter pin, front adjusting nut, washer and front bushing from the strut rod, and loosen the rear nut as far back as it will go. You may need a pry bar to separate the bushings from their inner sleeves.

3. Unbolt the rear of the strut rod from the lower A-arm. On some Cadillacs, you may have to disassemble one end of the stabilizer bar for working room. Pull back on strut rod to take it out of the frame bracket.

4. Install the new rear bushing and washer on the strut rod, insert the strut through the frame bracket and bolt the other end back onto the lower A-arm. New bushings from TRW and Moog have metal linings (often called high-performance replacements), and experts recommend these highly for replacing the stock soft-rubber bushings.

5. Install the new front bushing, washer and nut. Adjust the nuts to approximately the old positions, and reinstall the cotter pin. Have the front end realigned as soon as possible.